TH

EUR

YEARBOOK

2011
12

UEFA·com

THE EUROPEAN FOOTBALL YEARBOOK 2011/12

General Editor
Mike Hammond

The only authoritative annual on the European game

Further copies of The European Football Yearbook 2011/12 are available from:
www.carltonbooks.co.uk
hotline number +44 (0) 141 306 3100

The European Football Yearbook 2011/12

First published by Carlton Books Ltd, England in 2011
Printed by m press (sales) Ltd, England

ISBN 978-1-84732-847-2

UEFA – the Union of European Football Associations – is the governing body of football on the continent of Europe. UEFA's core mission is to promote, protect and develop European football at every level of the game, to promote the principles of unity and solidarity, and to deal with all questions relating to European football.

UEFA is an association of associations based on representative democracy, and is the governing body of European football.

UEFA
Route de Genève 46
Case postale
CH-1260 Nyon 2
Switzerland

Tel: +41 (0) 848 00 2727
Fax: +41 (0) 848 01 2727
Web: UEFA.com

Media Desk
Tel: +41 (0) 848 04 2727

All views expressed in the European Football Yearbook do not necessarily reflect those of UEFA. Every effort has been made to ensure the accuracy of the data in the European Football Yearbook, official and unofficial.

Front cover images (l to r): Adrián López (Spain Under-21), Lionel Messi (FC Barcelona), Radamel Falcao (FC Porto)

THE EUROPEAN FOOTBALL YEARBOOK 2011/12

General Editor
MIKE HAMMOND

Assistant Editor
Jesper Krogshede Sørensen

Nation-by-nation

Correspondents and Researchers
Mert Aydin (Turkey), Nikolai Belov (Russia), José Del Olmo (Spain), Sean DeLoughry (Republic of Ireland), Tamás Dénes (Hungary), Arno Funck (Luxembourg), Stoyan Georgiev (Bulgaria), Marshall Gillespie (Northern Ireland), Clas Glenning (Sweden), Miron Goihman (Moldova), Marcel Haisma (Netherlands), Michael Hansen (Denmark), Romeo Ionescu (Romania), Michel Jambonet (France), Valery Karpushkin (Latvia), Mikael Kirakosyan (Armenia), Jesper Krogshede Sørensen (Faroe Islands, Italy, Montenegro), Fuad & Feđa Krvavac (Bosnia & Herzegovina), Zdeněk Kučera (Czech Republic), Ambrosius Kutschera (Austria), Almantas Laužadis (Lithuania), Tarmo Lehiste (Estonia), Dag Lindholm (Norway), Ewan Macdonald (Scotland), Erlan Manashev (Kazakhstan), Goran Mancevski (FYROM), Rasim Mövsümov (Azerbaijan), Giovanni Nappi (Albania), Kazimerz Oleszek (Poland), Olexandr Pauk (Belarus, Ukraine), Humberto Pereira Silva (Portugal), Ivan Reić (Croatia), Mike Ritter & Silvia Schäfer (Germany), Revaz Shengelia (Georgia), Vídir Sigurdsson (Iceland), Dušan Stamenković (FYROM, Montenegro, Serbia), Andrej Stare (Slovenia), Edouard Stutz (Switzerland), Matej Széher (Slovakia), Mel Thomas (Wales), Vesa Tikander (Finland), Serge Van Hoof (Belgium), Victor Vassallo (Malta), Georgios J. Vassalos (Greece), Jacob Zelazo (Cyprus, Israel); additional assistance Emil Gasevski & Gabriel Mantz.

UEFA

Project management
David Farrelly, Rob Faulkner, Kadira Malkoč, Guillaume Sabran, Grégory Lepesqueux, Mary-Laure Bollini

Editorial
Coordination: Michael Harrold
Revision: Andrew Haslam, James Wirth
Contribution: Sam Adams, Richard Aikman, Kevin Ashby, John Atkin, Paul Bryan, Chris Burke, Mark Chaplin, Wayne Harrison, Patrick Hart, Simon Hart, Josh Hershman, Ian Holyman, Tom Kell, Mark Pettit, Paul Saffer, Matt Spiro

Data
Andy Lockwood, Dmitri Mamykin, Dominique Maurer, Jim Agnew

Production

Print
m press (sales) Ltd, England; Cliff Moulder

Distribution
Carlton Books Ltd; Martin Corteel, Jim Greenhough

Design
Nina Jensen, The Works

Artwork/Layout
Keith Jackson

Graphics
Mikhail Sipovich

Data Extraction
Delta3 (Davide Giulietti, Vincenzo Gianno, Paolo Calva, Antonio Bellissimo)

Photography
Getty Images, Sportsfile, Getty Images/AFP, Getty Images/Bongarts, Action Images

Foreword
Josep Guardiola

National three-letter codes

There are many instances throughout the European Football Yearbook where country names are abbreviated using three-letter codes. These codes are shown below, listed alphabetically by nation and divided into Europe and the Rest of the World.

Europe

ALB	Alb	Albania
AND	And	Andorra
ARM	Arm	Armenia
AUT	Aut	Austria
AZE	Aze	Azerbaijan
BLR	Blr	Belarus
BEL	Bel	Belgium
BIH	Bih	Bosnia & Herzegovina
BUL	Bul	Bulgaria
CRO	Cro	Croatia
CYP	Cyp	Cyprus
CZE	Cze	Czech Republic
DEN	Den	Denmark
ENG	Eng	England
EST	Est	Estonia
FRO	Fro	Faroe Islands
FIN	Fin	Finland
FRA	Fra	France
GEO	Geo	Georgia
GER	Ger	Germany
GRE	Gre	Greece
HUN	Hun	Hungary
ISL	Isl	Iceland
ISR	Isr	Israel
ITA	Ita	Italy
KAZ	Kaz	Kazakhstan
LVA	Lva	Latvia
LIE	Lie	Liechtenstein
LTU	Ltu	Lithuania
LUX	Lux	Luxembourg
MKD	Mkd	Former Yugoslav Republic of Macedonia (FYROM)
MLT	Mlt	Malta
MDA	Mda	Moldova
MNE	Mne	Montenegro
NED	Ned	Netherlands
NIR	Nir	Northern Ireland
NOR	Nor	Norway
POL	Pol	Poland
POR	Por	Portugal
IRL	Irl	Republic of Ireland
ROU	Rou	Romania
RUS	Rus	Russia
SMR	Smr	San Marino
SCO	Sco	Scotland
SRB	Srb	Serbia
SVK	Svk	Slovakia
SVN	Svn	Slovenia
ESP	Esp	Spain
SWE	Swe	Sweden
SUI	Sui	Switzerland
TUR	Tur	Turkey
UKR	Ukr	Ukraine
WAL	Wal	Wales

Rest of the World

AFG	Afg	Afghanistan
ALG	Alg	Algeria
ANG	Ang	Angola
ARG	Arg	Argentina
AUS	Aus	Australia
BHR	Bhr	Bahrain
BAN	Ban	Bangladesh
BRB	Brb	Barbados
BEN	Ben	Benin
BER	Ber	Bermuda
BOL	Bol	Bolivia
BOT	Bot	Botswana
BRA	Bra	Brazil
BFA	Bfa	Burkina Faso
BDI	Bdi	Burundi
CMR	Cmr	Cameroon
CAN	Can	Canada
CPV	Cpv	Cape Verde Islands
CAY	Cay	Cayman Islands
CTA	Cta	Central African Republic
CHA	Cha	Chad
CHI	Chi	Chile
CHN	Chn	China
COL	Col	Colombia
CGO	Cgo	Congo
COD	Cod	Congo DR
CRC	Crc	Costa Rica
CUB	Cub	Cuba
DJI	Dji	Djibouti
DOM	Dom	Dominican Republic
ECU	Ecu	Ecuador
EGY	Egy	Egypt
SLV	Slv	El Salvador
EQG	Eqg	Equatorial Guinea
ETH	Eth	Ethiopia
FIJ	Fij	Fiji
GAB	Gab	Gabon
GAM	Gam	Gambia
GHA	Gha	Ghana
GRN	Grn	Grenada
GUA	Gua	Guatemala
GUI	Gui	Guinea
GNB	Gnb	Guinea-Bissau
HAI	Hai	Haiti
HON	Hon	Honduras
HKG	Hkg	Hong Kong
IND	Ind	India
IDN	Idn	Indonesia
IRN	Irn	Iran
IRQ	Irq	Iraq
CIV	Civ	Ivory Coast
JAM	Jam	Jamaica
JPN	Jpn	Japan
JOR	Jor	Jordan
KEN	Ken	Kenya
KUW	Kuw	Kuwait
KGZ	Kgz	Kyrgyzstan
LIB	Lib	Lebanon
LBR	Lbr	Liberia
LBY	Lby	Libya
MAD	Mad	Madagascar
MWI	Mwi	Malawi
MLI	Mli	Mali
MTN	Mtn	Mauritania
MEX	Mex	Mexico
MAR	Mar	Morocco
MOZ	Moz	Mozambique
NAM	Nam	Namibia
ANT	Ant	Netherlands Antilles
NZL	Nzl	New Zealand
NIG	Nig	Niger
NGA	Nga	Nigeria
PRK	Prk	North Korea
OMA	Oma	Oman
PAK	Pak	Pakistan
PAN	Pan	Panama
PAR	Par	Paraguay
PER	Per	Peru
PHI	Phi	Philippines
QAT	Qat	Qatar
RWA	Rwa	Rwanda
KSA	Ksa	Saudi Arabia
SEN	Sen	Senegal
SLE	Sle	Sierra Leone
SIN	Sin	Singapore
SOL	Sol	Solomon Islands
SOM	Som	Somalia
RSA	Rsa	South Africa
KOR	Kor	South Korea
SKN	Skn	St Kitts & Nevis
VIN	Vin	St Vincent & Grenadines
SYR	Syr	Syria
TAH	Tah	Tahiti
TJK	Tjk	Tajikistan
TAN	Tan	Tanzania
THA	Tha	Thailand
TOG	Tog	Togo
TRI	Tri	Trinidad & Tobago
TUN	Tun	Tunisia
TKM	Tkm	Turkmenistan
UGA	Uga	Uganda
UAE	Uae	United Arab Emirates
USA	Usa	United States
URU	Uru	Uruguay
UZB	Uzb	Uzbekistan
VEN	Ven	Venezuela
VIE	Vie	Vietnam
ZAM	Zam	Zambia
ZIM	Zim	Zimbabwe

Contents

THE EUROPEAN FOOTBALL YEARBOOK 2011/12

Welcome

Foreword

The opportunity I have to be the first coach to provide the foreword for the European Football Yearbook for a second time not only reflects the continued achievements that we have had at FC Barcelona, but also the enduring effect that this publication has had over the past 20 years.

In 2010/11, we won Europe's premier club competition by defeating Manchester United FC at Wembley, and at the time I expressed how privileged I felt to be coaching this group of players, who have shown to a man that hard work has its rewards. This was obvious on and off the field.

On the field, we expressed ourselves with exciting football which has been praised in all circles. Off the field, the world saw our team spirit when Carles Puyol passed the captain's armband to Éric Abidal at Wembley, enabling him to lift the UEFA Champions League trophy. Whether you win or lose, there are human qualities, and Carles made a great gesture which is to his credit.

On the day, I know United were worthy opponents, especially as they cancelled out our opening goal and kept battling right to the end. These are qualities you expect from a team managed by Sir Alex Ferguson. I admired his achievements already, particularly with him having led United to three finals in four years. But more than that, to be at the top of this profession for so long takes immense qualities. My admiration for the way he has built a team and then reinvented new versions of that team over such a span of time is immense.

Of course, United and others will be chasing us during the coming months. For us, the task ahead will be to maintain the high standards we have set, in order to try to become the first side to retain the UEFA Champions League trophy. As holders, we know that every opponent will have the added incentive of knocking us off our perch, so we need to retain our composure and resolve and continue playing our brand of football.

In reading this book, you can see that many clubs, coaches and players have enjoyed success across Europe in the last 12 months, and the European Football Yearbook does a fantastic job of recognising all of these achievements – as well as all of the near misses. Congratulations to all those who achieved their goals, and to those who didn't, we await your renewed challenge in the 2011/12 season. Enjoy the adventure…

Josep Guardiola
Head coach
FC Barcelona
UEFA Champions League winners 2010/11

From the General Editor

Welcome to the 2011/12 edition of The European Football Yearbook.

I write this on the first day of August as one season of European football comes to an end, with the final of the UEFA European Under-19 Championship, while another prepares to get going in earnest with the start of the continent's major domestic leagues.

Football nowadays is a non-stop, round-the-year activity but, for the purposes of this publication, today is the day that we separate one season from another. So, what you now hold in your hands is a comprehensive review of everything important that has happened in European football over the past 12 months – and, in the case of some northern and eastern European countries and the two UEFA club competitions' early qualifying rounds, a bit more besides.

Those among you familiar with a publication that first appeared in 1988 will know what to expect from the thousand-plus pages that make up The European Football Yearbook. Our objective now, as back then, is to provide a work of reference that is not just authoritative and reliable but also attractive to look at and entertaining to read.

Fortunately, thanks to the invaluable assistance of UEFA, who have supported this project for the past five years, it is an objective that I believe the Yearbook continues to fulfil while expanding and improving edition by edition.

A few alterations have been made to the EFY's contents and layout this year. The major change is a re-working of the opening and closing pages of each chapter in the nation-by-nation section that makes up the bulk of the book. The opening page comprises member association directory details plus a summary of the country's domestic competitions, highlighted by the final league table. The closing page offers something new – addresses and contact details of all the current top-division clubs.

Our inclusion last year of birthdates for every top-division player was very well received, and readers' correspondence suggests that the club-by-club section containing league results/scorers and player appearances/goals data for every top-division team continues to be the most important statistical service that the Yearbook provides.

Another new addition this year comes in the form of the town and city insets that we have included on the country maps in the colour graphic guide section. The purpose of these is to indicate the different playing locations in towns and cities hosting more than one top-flight club.

As usual, the Yearbook leads with a colourful and comprehensive review of every UEFA competition, including an in-depth round-up of the qualifying campaign for UEFA EURO 2012 plus a final tournament schedule and venue location graphic for next summer's main event in Poland and Ukraine.

Let us hope that UEFA EURO 2012 lives up to its billing in the same manner as the 2011 UEFA Champions League final between FC Barcelona and Manchester United FC, a match that showcased all the very best in elite-class European football – even if it was a rather special footballer from Argentina who stole the show. Lionel Messi, of course, is included in our Top 100 Players of the Season selection – one of the Yearbook's most popular features and certainly its most provocative.

There have been many people involved in bringing this edition of The European Football Yearbook to fruition and I would like to thank every one of those contributors – their names are on page 5 – for their kind cooperation and assistance.

Special thanks, as always, go to three people – to my indispensable and trusty assistant, Jesper Krogshede Sørensen, whose attention to detail, resourcefulness and refusal to be beaten (who else could find the birthdate of that Albanian youngster who made just a one-minute substitute appearance?) make him the perfect team player; to Keith Jackson, for putting the book together with his customary efficiency and flair; and to David Farrelly, the man in Nyon without whose vision and dedication The European Football Yearbook would not be approaching its silver jubilee in such rude health.

My deepest gratitude of all, of course, goes to the patient and loving support of those closest to me – Sue, Rebecca and Charlie.

MIKE HAMMOND

1 August, 2011

THE EUROPEAN FOOTBALL YEARBOOK

TOP 100 PLAYERS

Turn to pages 317-368, where you will find pictorial, narrative and statistical profiles of the European Football Yearbook's Top 100 Players of the Season.

unicef
unicef
AON
AON
FINAL LONDON 2011
adidas
adidas

unicef

The 2010/11 season witnessed an extension of Spain's grip on European football silverware as their under-age teams continued to follow the example set by the senior side, the current holders of the UEFA European Championship and FIFA World Cup.

First of all, the UEFA European Under-21 Championship was captured in late June with a 2-0 victory over Switzerland in Denmark. The UEFA European Women's Under-17 Championship then followed as Spain retained the trophy thanks to a late goal in an entertaining final against France in Switzerland. Finally, and within a day of the women's U17 success, Spain completed a hat-trick of trophy successes as they captured the UEFA European Under-19 Championship in Romania.

Spain played second fiddle to England in the elite round stage of the UEFA European Under-17 Championship, thus failing to make the final tournament in Serbia, a competition that was won by the Netherlands, while Germany claimed the UEFA European Women's Under-19 Championship, running out 8-1 victors against Norway in the final. In other action, Braga's amateurs made home advantage count in the UEFA Regions' Cup as they defeated Ireland's Leinster & Munster selection 2-1 in the final. Eleven teams advanced from the UEFA European Futsal Championship qualifying rounds to join hosts Croatia in the final tournament, to be staged in February 2012.

At club level, it was a similar story to national team football, with Spanish sides taking the majority of silverware on offer in Europe. FC Barcelona defeated Manchester United FC 3-1 at Wembley in the UEFA Champions League final and Club Atlético de Madrid beat FC Internazionale Milano 2-0 in the UEFA Super Cup. The Iberian peninsula also provided the participants for the UEFA Europa League final in Dublin, with FC Porto winning 1-0 against Portuguese neighbours SC Braga.

UEFA Champions LEAGUE 2010/11

FC Barcelona confirmed their status as one of football's all-time great clubs by winning a fourth European Champion Clubs' Cup. As in 1992, when they captured their first continental crown, the venue for their triumph was Wembley Stadium. And as in 2009, in Rome, their victims in the final were Manchester United FC, defeated 3-1 on a night when Josep Guardiola's side took the breath away with a mesmerising performance. United had gone into the final full of confidence, having conceded only four goals en route – and with a record-breaking 19th English league title under their belts – but they were no match for the classy Catalans, who, domestic champions themselves for the third successive season, had already swept aside Arsenal FC, FC Shakhtar Donetsk and Real Madrid CF. Goals from Pedro, Lionel Messi and David Villa – the last two after Wayne Rooney had equalised for United – secured Barça's third UEFA Champions League success in six seasons. Man of the Match Messi also finished as the competition's top scorer for the third campaign running, matching Ruud van Nistelrooy's record 12-goal tally set in 2002/03.

UEFA
CHAMPIONS
LEAGUE

QUALIFYING PHASE

First and Second Qualifying Rounds

Barely a month after FC Internazionale Milano had triumphed in the 2009/10 UEFA Champions League the first participants in the 2010/11 competition set off on the long road to Wembley in the first qualifying round.

Early winners

Maltese champions Birkirkara FC and FK Rudar Pljevlja from Montenegro emerged triumphant from their respective ties, the former seeing off FC Santa Coloma 7-3 on aggregate having been awarded a 3-0 first-leg win after the game in Andorra was cancelled due to poor pitch conditions. Rudar were 7-1 victors over two legs against SP Tre Fiori from San Marino.

Neither team made it through the next stage, however. Birkirkara's 1-0 home win against MŠK Žilina was overturned by a 3-0 second-leg loss in Slovakia while Rudar went down 5-0 over two games against PFC Litex Lovech. Elsewhere in the second qualifying round there were big wins for Hapoel Tel-Aviv FC, who defeated FK Željezničar 6-0, FC BATE Borisov (6-1 against FH Hafnarfjördur), AC Omonia (5-0 against FK Renova) and AC Sparta Praha, who beat SK Liepājas Metalurgs 5-0 on aggregate.

Birkirkara skipper Michael Galea on the ball against FC Santa Coloma in the first qualifying round

Tight ties

It was a different story for Moldovan club FC Sheriff, who survived a 1-0 second-leg loss to eliminate FK Dinamo Tirana 3-2 on aggregate, and for AIK Solna, who edged out AS Jeunesse Esch 1-0 overall. HJK Helsinki needed extra time to see off the challenge of FK Ekranas, 2-0 in Finland and 2-1 overall, while a 3-2 win at home in Hungary gave Debreceni VSC a 4-3 aggregate success against FC Levadia Tallinn.

KKS Lech Poznań finally saw off İnter Bakı PİK on penalties, the Polish club coming through 9-8 in the shoot-out after each team had won their away leg 1-0. NK Dinamo Zagreb also endured a tense finale despite the cushion of a 5-1 first-leg advantage against FC Koper, hanging on to edge through despite a 3-0 loss in Slovenia.

First Qualifying Round Results

29/6/10, Estadi Comunal, Andorra la Vella
FC Santa Coloma 0-3 Birkirkara FC (w/o)
Referee: Buttimer (IRL)
6/7/10, Centenary, Ta' Qali
Birkirkara FC 4-3 FC Santa Coloma
Goal(s): 1-0 M. Galea 10, 1-1 N. Urbani 21, 2-1 M. Galea 31, 3-1 Cilia 35, 3-2 Jiménez 45, 4-2 Cilia 45+2, 4-3 M. Urbani 85
Referee: Madden (SCO)
Aggregate: 7-3; Birkirkara FC qualify.

30/6/10, Stadio Olimpico, Serravalle
SP Tre Fiori 0-3 FK Rudar Pljevlja
Goal(s): 0-1 Useni 31, 0-2 Vlahović 40, 0-3 I. Jovanović 90+5
Referee: Sant (MLT)
7/7/10, Stadion Podgorica, Podgorica
FK Rudar Pljevlja 4-1 SP Tre Fiori
Goal(s): 1-0 Ranđelović 7, 1-1 Vannoni 29, 2-1 Ranđelović 67, 3-1 Vlahović 83, 4-1 M. Jovanović 85
Referee: Sidenco (MDA)
Aggregate: 7-1; FK Rudar Pljevlja qualify.

Second Qualifying Round Results

13/7/10, Centenary, Ta' Qali
Birkirkara FC 1-0 MŠK Žilina
Goal(s): 1-0 Vukanac 1
Referee: Evans (WAL)
21/7/10, Štadión MŠK Žilina, Zilina
MŠK Žilina 3-0 Birkirkara FC
Goal(s): 1-0 Piaček 21, 2-0 Lietava 77, 3-0 Oravec 90+2
Referee: Szabó (HUN)
Aggregate: 3-1; MŠK Žilina qualify.

13/7/10, Stadion Salzburg, Salzburg
FC Salzburg 5-0 HB Tórshavn
Goal(s): 1-0 Zárate 21, 2-0 Jantscher 43, 3-0 Ulmer 46, 4-0 Wallner 64, 5-0 Hierländer 82
Referee: Satchi (MDA)
20/7/10, Gundadalur, Torshavn
HB Tórshavn 1-0 FC Salzburg
Goal(s): 1-0 Samuelsen 73
Referee: Asumaa (FIN)
Aggregate: 1-5; FC Salzburg qualify.

13/7/10, Daugava, Liepaja
SK Liepājas Metalurgs 0-3 AC Sparta Praha
Goal(s): 0-1 Kadlec 37, 0-2 Wilfried 51, 0-3 Wilfried 58
Referee: Eisner (AUT)
21/7/10, Stadion Letná, Prague
AC Sparta Praha 2-0 SK Liepājas Metalurgs
Goal(s): 1-0 Matějovský 12, 2-0 Zeman 43
Referee: Strahonja (CRO)
Aggregate: 5-0; AC Sparta Praha qualify.

13/7/10, Kadriorg, Tallinn
FC Levadia Tallinn 1-1 Debreceni VSC
Goal(s): 1-0 Neemelo 59, 1-1 Rezes 90
Referee: Kulbakov (BLR)
21/7/10, Stadion Oláh Gábor Út, Debrecen
Debreceni VSC 3-2 FC Levadia Tallinn
Goal(s): 0-1 Nahk 3, 1-1 Coulibaly 24, 2-1 Yannick 32, 2-2 Leitan 53, 3-2 Szakály 55
Referee: Hagen (NOR)
Aggregate: 4-3; Debreceni VSC qualify.

13/7/10, Råsundastadion, Solna
AIK Solna 1-0 AS Jeunesse Esch
Goal(s): 1-0 Engblom 57
Referee: Siejewicz (POL)
21/7/10, Stade de la Frontière, Esch-sur-Alzette
AS Jeunesse Esch 0-0 AIK Solna
Referee: Jones (WAL)
Aggregate: 0-1; AIK Solna qualify.

13/7/10, Dalymount Park, Dublin
Bohemian FC 1-0 The New Saints FC
Goal(s): 1-0 Brennan 66
Referee: Nijhuis (NED)
20/7/10, Park Hall, Shropshire
The New Saints FC 4-0 Bohemian FC
Goal(s): 1-0 Jones 6, 2-0 M. Williams 14, 3-0 Sharp 20, 4-0 M. Williams 73
Referee: Vad (HUN)
Aggregate: 4-1; The New Saints FC qualify.

13/7/10, Tofiq Bähramov-Republic stadium, Baku
İnter Bakı PİK 0-1 KKS Lech Poznań
Goal(s): 0-1 Wichniarek 47
Referee: Kever (SUI)
21/7/10, Miejski, Poznan
KKS Lech Poznań 0-1 İnter Bakı PİK (aet)
Goal(s): 0-1 Karlsons 84
Referee: Mažić (SRB)
Aggregate: 1-1; KKS Lech Poznań qualify after time 9-8 on penalties.

13/7/10, Lovech Stadion, Lovech
PFC Litex Lovech 1-0 FK Rudar Pljevlja
Goal(s): 1-0 I. Popov 8
Referee: Olsiak (SVK)
20/7/10, Stadion Podgorica, Podgorica
FK Rudar Pljevlja 0-4 PFC Litex Lovech
Goal(s): 0-1 Niflore 28, 0-2 Jelenković 39, 0-3 Bratu 74, 0-4 Bratu 90
Referee: Sukhina (RUS)
Aggregate: 0-5; PFC Litex Lovech qualify.

Mario Mandžukić struck twice for Dinamo Zagreb against Koper

13/7/10, GSP Stadium, Nicosia
AC Omonia 3-0 FK Renova
Goal(s): 1-0 Konstantinou 7(p), 2-0 Davidson 29, 3-0 Konstantinou 62
Referee: Kovařik (CZE)
20/7/10, National Arena Filip II Macedonian, Skopje
FK Renova 0-2 AC Omonia
Goal(s): 0-1 Aloneftis 15, 0-2 Leandro 24
Referee: Duarte Gomes (POR)
Aggregate: 0-5; AC Omonia qualify.

13/7/10, Stadion Maksimir, Zagreb
NK Dinamo Zagreb 5-1 FC Koper
Goal(s): 0-1 Bubanja 11, 1-1 Mandžukić 31, 2-1 Slepička 38, 3-1 Mandžukić 63, 4-1 Sammir 77, 5-1 Etto 81
Referee: Kinhöfer (GER)
20/7/10, Športni Park, Nova Gorica
FC Koper 3-0 NK Dinamo Zagreb
Goal(s): 1-0 Handanagič 11, 2-0 Guberac 54, 3-0 Brulc 78(p)
Referee: Banti (ITA)
Aggregate: 4-5; NK Dinamo Zagreb qualify.

13/7/10, Bloomfield Stadium, Tel-Aviv
Hapoel Tel-Aviv FC 5-0 FK Željezničar
Goal(s): 1-0 Al Lala 10, 2-0 Shivhon 12, 3-0 Bešlija 28(og), 4-0 Al Lala 31, 5-0 Al Lala 38
Referee: Clattenburg (ENG)
21/7/10, Asim Ferhatović Hase Stadion, Sarajevo
FK Željezničar 0-1 Hapoel Tel-Aviv FC
Goal(s): 0-1 Douglas 76
Referee: Clos Gomez (ESP)
Aggregate: 0-6; Hapoel Tel-Aviv FC qualify.

14/7/10, Gorodskoy Stadion, Borisov
FC BATE Borisov 5-1 FH Hafnarfjördur
Goal(s): 1-0 Nekhaichik 48, 2-0 Renan 58, 3-0 Nekhaichik 85, 4-0 Nekhaichik 88, 4-1 Björnsson 89, 5-1 Rodionov 90
Referee: Kakos (GRE)
21/7/10, Kaplakrikavöllur, Hafnarfjördur
FH Hafnarfjördur 0-1 FC BATE Borisov
Goal(s): 0-1 Rodionov 15
Referee: Kaasik (EST)
Aggregate: 1-6; FC BATE Borisov qualify.

14/7/10, Aukštaitija, Panevezys
FK Ekranas 1-0 HJK Helsinki
Goal(s): 1-0 Radavičius 3
Referee: Vollquartz (DEN)
21/7/10, Finnair Stadium, Helsinki
HJK Helsinki 2-0 FK Ekranas (aet)
Goal(s): 1-0 Ojala 77, 2-0 Šidlauskas 119(og)
Referee: McDonald (SCO)
Aggregate: 2-1; HJK Helsinki qualify after extra time.

14/7/10, Windsor Park, Belfast
Linfield FC 0-0 Rosenborg BK
Referee: Ennjimi (FRA)
21/7/10, Lerkendal Stadion, Trondheim
Rosenborg BK 2-0 Linfield FC
Goal(s): 1-0 Prica 32, 2-0 Henriksen 87
Referee: Schörgenhofer (AUT)
Aggregate: 2-0; Rosenborg BK qualify.

14/7/10, Stadionul Sheriff, Tiraspol
FC Sheriff 3-1 FK Dinamo Tirana
Goal(s): 1-0 Volkov 9, 1-1 Malacarne 12, 2-1 Nikolić 62, 3-1 Nádson 70
Referee: Stalhammar (SWE)
20/7/10, Stadiumi Kombëtar Qemal Stafa, Tirana
FK Dinamo Tirana 1-0 FC Sheriff
Goal(s): 1-0 Vila 18
Referee: Trattou (CYP)
Aggregate: 2-3; FC Sheriff qualify.

14/7/10, FK Partizan, Belgrade
FK Partizan 3-1 FC Pyunik
Goal(s): 1-0 Tomić 29, 1-1 Yedigaryan 30, 2-1 Moreira 45+1, 3-1 Cléo 59
Referee: Skjerven (NOR)
21/7/10, Yerevan Republican Stadium after Vazgen Sargsyan, Yerevan
FC Pyunik 0-1 FK Partizan
Goal(s): 0-1 Cléo 45+4
Referee: Borski (POL)
Aggregate: 1-4; FK Partizan qualify.

14/7/10, Tcentralny, Aktobe
FC Aktobe 2-0 FC Olimpi Rustavi
Goal(s): 1-0 Smakov 40(p), 2-0 Smakov 53
Referee: Yıldırım (TUR)
21/7/10, Poladi, Rustavi
FC Olimpi Rustavi 1-1 FC Aktobe
Goal(s): 1-0 Rekhviashvili 30, 1-1 Tleshev 90
Referee: Deaconu (ROU)
Aggregate: 1-3; FC Aktobe qualify.

Third Qualifying Round

There were mixed fortunes for some of Europe's biggest names in the third qualifying round, with Celtic FC and Fenerbahçe SK among the high-profile casualties. Other clubs, however, made light work of qualifying for the play-offs.

Big guns misfire

Celtic were always up against it from the moment they lost 3-0 at SC Braga, and a 2-1 second-leg victory in Glasgow was not enough to repair the damage. Fenerbahçe were undone by BSC Young Boys, drawing 2-2 in Switzerland only to go down 1-0 at home, and there were more Swiss celebrations as FC Basel 1893 ousted Debreceni VSC 5-1 over two legs. FC Unirea Urziceni, another recent group stage participant, lost out as Danny scored the only goal of their tie with FC Zenit St Petersburg.

Braga's Paulo César celebrates a tie-clinching away goal against Celtic

There were big victories for RSC Anderlecht, who knocked out The New Saints FC 6-1 over the two legs; FC Dynamo Kyiv – who beat KAA Gent by the same aggregate scoreline – and FK Partizan, who defeated HJK Helsinki 5-1. Rosenborg BK enjoyed the upper hand in their Scandinavian derby with AIK Solna, running out 4-0 winners, while FC Salzburg's 4-1 home win against AC Omonia completed a 5-2 aggregate success.

Ajax edge through

The going proved tougher for AFC Ajax, who needed a 3-3 second-leg draw in Greece to get the better of PAOK FC on away goals, while Moldova's FC Sheriff came through a penalty shoot-out to eliminate NK Dinamo Zagreb following two 1-1 draws.

AC Sparta Praha recorded a pair of 1-0 wins against KKS Lech Poznań, while Hapoel Tel-Aviv FC overturned a 1-0 loss at FC Aktobe with a 3-1 home triumph. FC København's bid for a first group stage appearance since 2006/07 got off to a positive start, the Danish champions building on a goalless draw at FC BATE Borisov with a 3-2 home triumph.

Third Qualifying Round Results

27/7/10, GSP Stadium, Nicosia
AC Omonia 1-1 FC Salzburg
Goal(s): 0-1 Zárate 8, 1-1 LuaLua 90+1(p)
Referee: Vad (HUN)
4/8/10, Stadion Salzburg, Salzburg
FC Salzburg 4-1 AC Omonia
Goal(s): 1-0 Švento 21, 2-0 Schiemer 37, 3-0 Schiemer 40, 4-0 Boghossian 58, 4-1 Rengifo 90
Referee: Johannesson (SWE)
Aggregate: 5-2; FC Salzburg qualify.

27/7/10, Racecourse Ground, Wrexham
The New Saints FC 1-3 RSC Anderlecht
Goal(s): 0-1 Kljestan 7, 0-2 Legear 18, 1-2 Jones 52, 1-3 Suárez 73
Referee: Čeferin (SVN)
3/8/10, Constant Vanden Stock Stadium, Brussels
RSC Anderlecht 3-0 The New Saints FC
Goal(s): 1-0 De Sutter 17, 2-0 Lukaku 69, 3-0 Lukaku 74
Referee: Balaj (ROU)
Aggregate: 6-1; RSC Anderlecht qualify.

27/7/10, Lovech Stadion, Lovech
PFC Litex Lovech 1-1 MŠK Žilina
Goal(s): 0-1 Majtán 65, 1-1 Wellington 78
Referee: Jakobsson (ISL)
4/8/10, Štadión MŠK Žilina, Zilina
MŠK Žilina 3-1 PFC Litex Lovech
Goal(s): 0-1 Sandrinho 50, 1-1 Rilke 52, 2-1 Oravec 70, 3-1 Ceesay 84
Referee: Einwaller (AUT)
Aggregate: 4-2; MŠK Žilina qualify.

27/7/10, Valeriy Lobanovskiy Stadium, Kyiv
FC Dynamo Kyiv 3-0 KAA Gent
Goal(s): 1-0 Yarmolenko 19, 2-0 Shevchenko 80, 3-0 Zozulya 90+2
Referee: Collum (SCO)
4/8/10, Jules Ottenstadion, Gent
KAA Gent 1-3 FC Dynamo Kyiv
Goal(s): 0-1 Harmash 32, 0-2 Milevskiy 55, 1-2 Coulibaly 85, 1-3 Gusev 89
Referee: Çakır (TUR)
Aggregate: 1-6; FC Dynamo Kyiv qualify.

27/7/10, Stadion Letná, Prague
AC Sparta Praha 1-0 KKS Lech Poznań
Goal(s): 1-0 Brabec 75
Referee: Tagliavento (ITA)
4/8/10, Miejski, Poznan
KKS Lech Poznań 0-1 AC Sparta Praha
Goal(s): 0-1 Kladrubský 50(p)
Referee: Fautrel (FRA)
Aggregate: 0-2; AC Sparta Praha qualify.

Anderlecht's teenage striker Romelu Lukaku strikes the first of his two goals at home to The New Saints

27/7/10, Stadionul Steaua, Bucharest
FC Unirea Urziceni 0-0 FC Zenit St Petersburg
Referee: Bruno Paixão (POR)
4/8/10, Petrovski Stadion, St Petersburg
FC Zenit St Petersburg 1-0 FC Unirea Urziceni
Goal(s): 1-0 Danny 33
Referee: Dean (ENG)
Aggregate: 1-0; FC Zenit St Petersburg qualify.

28/7/10, Gorodskoy Stadion, Borisov
FC BATE Borisov 0-0 FC København
Referee: Tudor (ROU)
4/8/10, Parken, Copenhagen
FC København 3-2 FC BATE Borisov
Goal(s): 1-0 César Santin 2, 2-0 W.K. Jørgensen 27, 2-1 Kontsevoi 40, 2-2 Nekhaichik 44, 3-2 N'Doye 59
Referee: Clattenburg (ENG)
Aggregate: 3-2; FC København qualify.

28/7/10, Stadionul Sheriff, Tiraspol
FC Sheriff 1-1 NK Dinamo Zagreb
Goal(s): 0-1 Sammir 3, 1-1 Erokhin 35
Referee: Kakos (GRE)
4/8/10, Stadion Maksimir, Zagreb
NK Dinamo Zagreb 1-1 FC Sheriff (aet)
Goal(s): 0-1 Volkov 16, 1-1 Sammir 55(p)
Referee: Braamhaar (NED)
Aggregate: 2-2; FC Sheriff qualify after time 6-5 on penalties.

28/7/10, Ferenc Szusza Stadion, Budapest
Debreceni VSC 0-2 FC Basel 1893
Goal(s): 0-1 Stocker 34, 0-2 Xhaka 90+2
Referee: Muñiz Fernández (ESP)
4/8/10, St Jakob-Park, Basel
FC Basel 1893 3-1 Debreceni VSC
Goal(s): 1-0 Çağdaş Atan 26, 2-0 Chipperfield 59, 3-0 Shaqiri 64, 3-1 Coulibaly 74
Referee: Bezborodov (RUS)
Aggregate: 5-1; FC Basel 1893 qualify.

28/7/10, Estádio Municipal de Braga, Braga
SC Braga 3-0 Celtic FC
Goal(s): 1-0 Alan 26(p), 2-0 Echiéjilé 76, 3-0 Matheus 88
Referee: Gumienny (BEL)
4/8/10, Celtic Park, Glasgow
Celtic FC 2-1 SC Braga
Goal(s): 0-1 Paulo César 20, 1-1 Hooper 52, 2-1 Juárez 79
Referee: Bebek (CRO)
Aggregate: 2-4; SC Braga qualify.

28/7/10, Stade de Suisse, Berne
BSC Young Boys 2-2 Fenerbahçe SK
Goal(s): 0-1 Emre Belözoğlu 5, 1-1 Dudar 18, 1-2 Stoch 42, 2-2 Costanzo 89(p)
Referee: Moen (NOR)
4/8/10, Şükrü Saracoğlu, Istanbul
Fenerbahçe SK 0-1 BSC Young Boys
Goal(s): 0-1 Bienvenu 40
Referee: Nikolaev (RUS)
Aggregate: 2-3; BSC Young Boys qualify.

Luis Suárez puts Ajax in front against PAOK in Amsterdam

28/7/10, Råsundastadion, Solna
AIK Solna 0-1 Rosenborg BK
Goal(s): 0-1 Henriksen 33
Referee: Kinhöfer (GER)
4/8/10, Lerkendal Stadion, Trondheim
Rosenborg BK 3-0 AIK Solna
Goal(s): 1-0 Prica 55, 2-0 Demidov 64, 3-0 Lustig 76
Referee: Iturralde González (ESP)
Aggregate: 4-0; Rosenborg BK qualify.

28/7/10, FK Partizan, Belgrade
FK Partizan 3-0 HJK Helsinki
Goal(s): 1-0 Iliev 8, 2-0 S. Ilić 42, 3-0 Cléo 90+2
Referee: Yefet (ISR)
4/8/10, Finnair Stadium, Helsinki
HJK Helsinki 1-2 FK Partizan
Goal(s): 0-1 Cléo 9, 1-1 Kamara 38, 1-2 Cléo 90+2
Referee: Kralovec (CZE)
Aggregate: 1-5; FK Partizan qualify.

28/7/10, Amsterdam ArenA, Amsterdam
AFC Ajax 1-1 PAOK FC
Goal(s): 1-0 Suárez 13, 1-1 Ivić 73
Referee: Chapron (FRA)
4/8/10, Toumbas Stadium, Salonika
PAOK FC 3-3 AFC Ajax
Goal(s): 1-0 Vieirinha 16, 1-1 Suárez 48, 1-2 De Jong 50, 1-3 Lindgren 55, 2-3 Salpingidis 56, 3-3 Ivić 90+1
Referee: Velasco Carballo (ESP)
Aggregate: 4-4; AFC Ajax qualify on away goals.

28/7/10, Tcentralny, Aktobe
FC Aktobe 1-0 Hapoel Tel-Aviv FC
Goal(s): 1-0 Smakov 67(p)
Referee: Kever (SUI)
3/8/10, Bloomfield Stadium, Tel-Aviv
Hapoel Tel-Aviv FC 3-1 FC Aktobe
Goal(s): 1-0 Zahavi 16, 2-0 Sahar 31, 3-0 Ba 35(og), 3-1 Tleshev 90
Referee: Schörgenhofer (AUT)
Aggregate: 3-2; Hapoel Tel-Aviv FC qualify.

Play-Offs

In their second season, the UEFA Champions League play-offs continued to provide plenty of excitement as 20 teams competed for the final ten places on offer in the competition's group stage.

Tottenham turnaround

The biggest turnaround came in the tie between BSC Young Boys and Tottenham Hotspur FC, the Swiss side racing into a three-goal lead within half an hour of kick-off in Berne thanks to goals from Senad Lulić, Henri Bienvenu and Xavier Hochstrasser. Tottenham were looking to reach the group stage for the first time and goals from Sébastien Bassong and Roman Pavlyuchenko revived their challenge, paving the way for a comfortable 4-0 second-leg success at White Hart Lane in which Peter Crouch scored a hat-trick.

Peter Crouch leaps to score the second goal of his hat-trick at home to Young Boys

The matches between SC Braga and Sevilla FC were equally gripping. The Portuguese side – also bidding for a group stage debut – won 1-0 at home thanks to Matheus's second-half header, then the same player struck a crucial goal 31 minutes into the return at the Estadio Ramón Sánchez Pizjuán. His team-mate Lima's hat-trick cemented Braga's place in the group stage with a 4-3 win on the night and 5-3 overall.

Group-stage returns

AJ Auxerre went down 1-0 in Russia against FC Zenit St Petersburg but surprisingly turned the tie on its head in France, Cédric Hengbart and Ireneusz Jeleń securing an aggregate triumph and the Ligue 1 side's first group stage participation since 2002/03. FC København also booked their return to the competition proper, holding off Rosenborg BK to win 1-0 at home in the second leg - with Icelandic defender Sölvi Ottesen on target - and progress on away goals after a 2-2 aggregate draw.

AFC Ajax were another team who had been absent from the group stage for several seasons, in their case since 2005/06, and they drew the first leg 1-1 at FC Dynamo Kyiv as they looked to seal a return. Luis Suárez and Mounir El Hamdaoui gave the Dutch side a two-goal cushion in Amsterdam and, although Andriy Shevchenko's late penalty left them hanging on, Martin Jol's team held firm.

Žilina debut

FC Basel 1893 seemingly enjoyed a more straightforward time of it, a 1-0 home win against FC Sheriff paving the way for a 4-0 aggregate triumph, although the tie was actually in the balance until Marco Streller's goal with 16 minutes remaining in Moldova. Alexander Frei added two more as the Swiss team ended a wait to appear at Europe's top table stretching back to 2002/03. MŠK Žilina made surprisingly light work of AC Sparta Praha, winning the first leg in the Czech Republic 2-0 before a 1-0 home triumph made them only the third Slovakian side to reach the group stage.

Basel's Alex Frei gets the better of Sheriff's Vladimir Branković

SV Werder Bremen and Hapoel Tel-Aviv FC both looked set fair for a comfortable passage to the group stage following their respective first legs. Clemens Fritz, Torsten Frings and Claudio Pizarro gave the former a 3-0 lead against UC Sampdoria, although Giampaolo Pazzini gave the Italian side hope with a 90th-minute response. Hapoel looked even more secure, a third-minute penalty from goalkeeper Vincent Enyeama setting them on the way to a 3-2 win away to FC Salzburg, with Ben Sahar and Itay Shechter securing the win.

Hapoel Tel-Aviv goalkeeper Vincent Enyeama points skywards after scoring a penalty against Salzburg

Second-leg scares

The Israeli champions were on the back foot when a Douglas da Silva own goal gave Salzburg a 42nd-minute lead in Tel-Aviv, and it was not until two minutes into added time, and Eran Zahavi's strike, that Hapoel could relax safe in the knowledge of becoming only the third Israeli side to qualify for the group stage. Bremen, meanwhile, had their first-leg lead wiped out within 13 minutes in Genoa, Pazzini scoring twice, and when Antonio Cassano made it 3-0 to Sampdoria with five minutes remaining, the German side looked doomed. Markus Rosenberg's added-time goal took the tie into an additional 30 minutes, however, where Pizarro's 100th-minute effort ensured it was Bremen who would progress at the end of an extraordinary tie.

FK Partizan and RSC Anderlecht shared a 2-2 draw in Belgrade, and Cléo – who had also been on target in the first leg – looked to have taken Partizan through when he added to his tally with a goal in each half in Brussels. The home side fought back, however, to earn a 2-2 draw, only to lose 3-2 on penalties. Partizan thus reached the group stage for the first time since 2003/04.

Play-Off Results

17/8/10, Petrovski Stadion, St Petersburg
FC Zenit St Petersburg 1-0 AJ Auxerre
Goal(s): 1-0 Kerzhakov 3
Referee: Kuipers (NED)
25/8/10, Stade Abbé-Deschamps, Auxerre
AJ Auxerre 2-0 FC Zenit St Petersburg
Goal(s): 1-0 Hengbart 9, 2-0 Jeleń 53
Referee: Skomina (SVN)
Aggregate: 2-1; AJ Auxerre qualify.

17/8/10, Lerkendal Stadion, Trondheim
Rosenborg BK 2-1 FC København
Goal(s): 1-0 Iversen 23, 2-0 Henriksen 57, 2-1 Grønkjær 84
Referee: Rocchi (ITA)
25/8/10, Parken, Copenhagen
FC København 1-0 Rosenborg BK
Goal(s): 1-0 Ottesen 33
Referee: Brych (GER)
Aggregate: 2-2; FC København qualify on away goal.

17/8/10, Stadion Letná, Prague
AC Sparta Praha 0-2 MŠK Žilina
Goal(s): 0-1 Ceesay 51, 0-2 Oravec 73
Referee: Atkinson (ENG)
25/8/10, Štadión MŠK Žilina, Zilina
MŠK Žilina 1-0 AC Sparta Praha
Goal(s): 1-0 Ceesay 18
Referee: Olegário Benquerença (POR)
Aggregate: 3-0; MŠK Žilina qualify.

17/8/10, Stade de Suisse, Berne
BSC Young Boys 3-2 Tottenham Hotspur FC
Goal(s): 1-0 Lulić 4, 2-0 Bienvenu 13, 3-0 Hochstrasser 28, 3-1 Bassong 42, 3-2 Pavlyuchenko 83
Referee: De Bleeckere (BEL)

Werder Bremen players celebrate after a decisive extra-time goal by Claudio Pizarro (centre) against Sampdoria in Genoa

25/8/10, White Hart Lane, London
Tottenham Hotspur FC 4-0 BSC Young Boys
Goal(s): 1-0 Crouch 5, 2-0 Defoe 32, 3-0 Crouch 61, 4-0 Crouch 78(p)
Referee: Duhamel (FRA)
Aggregate: 6-3; Tottenham Hotspur FC qualify.

17/8/10, Valeriy Lobanovskiy Stadium, Kyiv
FC Dynamo Kyiv 1-1 AFC Ajax
Goal(s): 0-1 Vertonghen 57, 1-1 Gusev 66
Referee: Busacca (SUI)
25/8/10, Amsterdam ArenA, Amsterdam
AFC Ajax 2-1 FC Dynamo Kyiv
Goal(s): 1-0 Suárez 43, 2-0 El Hamdaoui 75, 2-1 Shevchenko 84(p)
Referee: Undiano Mallenco (ESP)
Aggregate: 3-2; AFC Ajax qualify.

18/8/10, Estádio Municipal de Braga, Braga
SC Braga 1-0 Sevilla FC
Goal(s): 1-0 Matheus 62
Referee: Stark (GER)
24/8/10, Estadio Ramón Sánchez Pizjuán, Seville
Sevilla FC 3-4 SC Braga
Goal(s): 0-1 Matheus 31, 0-2 Lima 58, 1-2 Luís Fabiano 60, 2-2 Jesús Navas 84, 2-3 Lima 85, 2-4 Lima 90, 3-4 Kanouté 90+1
Referee: Rizzoli (ITA)
Aggregate: 3-5; SC Braga qualify.

18/8/10, Stadion Salzburg, Salzburg
FC Salzburg 2-3 Hapoel Tel-Aviv FC
Goal(s): 0-1 Enyeama 3(p), 1-1 Pokrivač 28, 1-2 Sahar 44, 1-3 Shechter 53, 2-3 Wallner 67(p)
Referee: Proença (POR)
24/8/10, Bloomfield Stadium, Tel-Aviv
Hapoel Tel-Aviv FC 1-1 FC Salzburg
Goal(s): 0-1 Douglas 42(og), 1-1 Zahavi 90+2
Referee: Vink (NED)
Aggregate: 4-3; Hapoel Tel-Aviv FC qualify.

18/8/10, St Jakob-Park, Basel
FC Basel 1893 1-0 FC Sheriff
Goal(s): 1-0 Stocker 54
Referee: Hauge (NOR)
24/8/10, Stadionul Sheriff, Tiraspol
FC Sheriff 0-3 FC Basel 1893
Goal(s): 0-1 Streller 74, 0-2 Frei 80, 0-3 Frei 87
Referee: Hansson (SWE)
Aggregate: 0-4; FC Basel 1893 qualify.

18/8/10, FK Partizan, Belgrade
FK Partizan 2-2 RSC Anderlecht
Goal(s): 0-1 Gillet 54, 1-1 Cléo 57, 2-1 Lecjaks 64(og), 2-2 Juhász 66
Referee: Larsen (DEN)
24/8/10, Constant Vanden Stock Stadium, Brussels
RSC Anderlecht 2-2 FK Partizan (aet)
Goal(s): 0-1 Cléo 15, 0-2 Cléo 53, 1-2 Lukaku 64, 2-2 Gillet 71
Referee: Thomson (SCO)
Aggregate: 4-4; FK Partizan qualify after extra time 3-2 on penalties.

18/8/10, Weserstadion, Bremen
SV Werder Bremen 3-1 UC Sampdoria
Goal(s): 1-0 Fritz 51, 2-0 Frings 67(p), 3-0 Pizarro 69, 3-1 Pazzini 90
Referee: Lannoy (FRA)
24/8/10, Stadio Luigi Ferraris, Genoa
UC Sampdoria 3-2 SV Werder Bremen (aet)
Goal(s): 1-0 Pazzini 8, 2-0 Pazzini 13, 3-0 Cassano 85, 3-1 Rosenberg 90+3, 3-2 Pizarro 100
Referee: Kassai (HUN)
Aggregate: 4-5; SV Werder Bremen qualify after extra time.

GROUP STAGE

GROUP A

Group A pitted defending champions FC Internazionale Milano against tournament regulars SV Werder Bremen and two UEFA Champions League newcomers, Tottenham Hotspur FC and FC Twente.

Opening draws

Twente were competing for the first time after a maiden Eredivisie title success in 2010, and they started with an encouraging home draw against Inter. In Rafael Benítez's first UEFA Champions League outing with the Nerazzurri, his team took the lead through Wesley Sneijder, conceded twice through Theo Janssen and Diego Milito's own goal but drew back level when Samuel Eto'o made it 2-2 before the break. There was an identical outcome at the Weserstadion in Bremen, where Tottenham offered early evidence of their attack-minded approach, going two up inside 18 minutes through Peter Crouch and a Petri Pasanen own goal, only for the home side to battle back as Hugo Almeida and Marko Marin struck either side of half-time.

White Hart Lane had not hosted Europe's elite competition since 1961/62 – when Tottenham were European Champion Clubs' Cup semi-finalists – but it staged a feast of entertainment when Twente visited on Matchday 2. It was an evening of mixed fortunes for Rafael van der Vaart, who missed a penalty, scored the opening goal and got sent off in his side's 4-1 victory. The home team had three spot-kicks in all – Roman Pavlyuchenko converted the second and third either side of Nacer Chadli's effort for Twente, before Gareth Bale completed the scoring.

Gareth Bale dazzled consistently for Tottenham in Group A

Eto'o excels

On the same night Inter put four unanswered goals past Bremen at San Siro, Eto'o scoring his second UEFA Champions League hat-trick. The Italian side looked set for an even bigger triumph when they went 4-0 up after 35 minutes of their next fixture, at home to Tottenham. It was a nightmare start for the visitors. Already trailing to Javier Zanetti's strike, they lost goalkeeper Heurelho Gomes to a red card in the eighth minute, then conceded the resultant Eto'o penalty and further goals by Dejan Stanković and Eto'o. However, Tottenham were to claw back some pride, with Bale's superb second-half hat-trick alerting Europe to the Welsman's prodigious talents.

The same evening Twente were denied a first win when, five minutes after Janssen's 75th-minute opener, Bremen's Marko Arnautovic equalised against his former club. Michel Preud'homme's men made amends in the return meeting in Germany, Chadli and Luuk de Jong securing a 2-0 success.

Bale to the fore

Tottenham had an even bigger boost on Matchday 4 as they swept Inter aside 3-1 on a pulsating evening in north London to climb top. Van der Vaart and Crouch put them in command, and although Eto'o reduced the arrears after 80 minutes, Pavlyuchenko's late third sealed a memorable success. The main talking point was the excellence, yet again, of 21-year-old Bale, who got the better of Maicon repeatedly down the left, setting up two goals. "Amazing," was the verdict of his manager, Harry Redknapp.

Tottenham then secured qualification with a 3-0 home defeat of Bremen, achieved through goals

Inter's Samuel Eto'o was the top scorer in the group stage with seven goals

by Younes Kaboul, Luka Modrić and Crouch. The result was no surprise given the Bundesliga club's struggles with an injury list stretching to double figures, which prompted coach Thomas Schaaf to give debuts to Dominik Schmidt and Felix Kroos, fast-tracked from Bremen's third-division reserve team.

Inter also secured progress with a game to spare thanks to Esteban Cambiasso's solitary 55th-minute strike against Twente, meaning the only question to answer on Matchday 6 was who would take first place. Inter crashed 3-0 at Bremen – Sebastian Prödl, Arnautovic and Claudio Pizarro bringing some consolation to the German side – so Tottenham did not even need a point at Twente. However, once more showing a taste for drama, they played out a 3-3 draw that ensured they finished as the group stage's joint top scorers, alongside arch-rivals Arsenal FC, with 18 goals.

Group A Results

14/9/10, FC Twente Stadion, Enschede
FC Twente 2-2 FC Internazionale Milano
Attendance: 23800
Goal(s): 0-1 Sneijder 13, 1-1 Janssen 20, 2-1 Milito 30(og), 2-2 Eto'o 41
Referee: Proença (POR)

14/9/10, Weserstadion, Bremen
SV Werder Bremen 2-2 Tottenham Hotspur FC
Attendance: 30344
Goal(s): 0-1 Pasanen 12(og), 0-2 Crouch 18, 1-2 Hugo Almeida 43, 2-2 Marin 47
Referee: Busacca (SUI)

29/9/10, White Hart Lane, London
Tottenham Hotspur FC 4-1 FC Twente
Attendance: 32518
Goal(s): 1-0 Van der Vaart 47, 2-0 Pavlyuchenko 50(p), 2-1 Chadli 56, 3-1 Pavlyuchenko 64(p), 4-1 Bale 85
Referee: Hauge (NOR)

29/9/10, Stadio Giuseppe Meazza, Milan
FC Internazionale Milano 4-0 SV Werder Bremen
Attendance: 48126
Goal(s): 1-0 Eto'o 21, 2-0 Eto'o 27, 3-0 Sneijder 34, 4-0 Eto'o 81
Referee: Undiano Mallenco (ESP)

20/10/10, Stadio Giuseppe Meazza, Milan
FC Internazionale Milano 4-3 Tottenham Hotspur FC
Attendance: 49551
Goal(s): 1-0 Zanetti 2, 2-0 Eto'o 11(p), 3-0 Stanković 14, 4-0 Eto'o 35, 4-1 Bale 52, 4-2 Bale 90, 4-3 Bale 90+1
Referee: Skomina (SVN)

20/10/10, FC Twente Stadion, Enschede
FC Twente 1-1 SV Werder Bremen
Attendance: 24000
Goal(s): 1-0 Janssen 75, 1-1 Arnautovic 80
Referee: Larsen (DEN)

2/11/10, White Hart Lane, London
Tottenham Hotspur FC 3-1 FC Internazionale Milano
Attendance: 34103
Goal(s): 1-0 Van der Vaart 18, 2-0 Crouch 61, 2-1 Eto'o 80, 3-1 Pavlyuchenko 89
Referee: Kassai (HUN)

2/11/10, Weserstadion, Bremen
SV Werder Bremen 0-2 FC Twente
Attendance: 29641
Goal(s): 0-1 Chadli 81, 0-2 De Jong 84
Referee: Hamer (LUX)

24/11/10, White Hart Lane, London
Tottenham Hotspur FC 3-0 SV Werder Bremen
Attendance: 33546
Goal(s): 1-0 Kaboul 6, 2-0 Modrić 45+1, 3-0 Crouch 79
Referee: Olegário Benquerença (POR)

24/11/10, Stadio Giuseppe Meazza, Milan
FC Internazionale Milano 1-0 FC Twente
Attendance: 29466
Goal(s): 1-0 Cambiasso 55
Referee: Lannoy (FRA)

7/12/10, FC Twente Stadion, Enschede
FC Twente 3-3 Tottenham Hotspur FC
Attendance: 24000
Goal(s): 0-1 Wisgerhof 12(og), 1-1 Landzaat 22(p), 1-2 Defoe 47, 2-2 Rosales 56, 2-3 Defoe 59, 3-3 Chadli 64
Referee: Velasco Carballo (ESP)

7/12/10, Weserstadion, Bremen
SV Werder Bremen 3-0 FC Internazionale Milano
Attendance: 30400
Goal(s): 1-0 Prödl 39, 2-0 Arnautovic 49, 3-0 Pizarro 88
Referee: Çakır (TUR)

Group A Table

	Pld	Home					Away					Total					Pts
		W	D	L	F	A	W	D	L	F	A	W	D	L	F	A	
1 Tottenham Hotspur FC	6	3	0	0	10	11	0	2	1	8	0	3	2	1	18	11	11
2 FC Internazionale Milano	6	3	0	0	9	11	0	1	2	3	0	3	1	2	12	11	10
3 FC Twente	6	0	3	0	6	11	1	0	2	3	0	1	3	2	9	11	6
4 SV Werder Bremen	6	1	1	1	5	12	0	1	2	1	0	1	2	3	6	12	5

GROUP B

Targeting a place in the last 16 for an eighth year running, Olympique Lyonnais initially lived up to their billing of Group B favourites, sweeping to the summit with wins against FC Schalke 04, Hapoel Tel-Aviv FC and SL Benfica. Yet the 2009/10 semi-finalists ultimately stuttered over the finishing line as the battle for qualification underwent a number of twists and turns.

Big-spending Schalke

Schalke were returning to the UEFA Champions League after a two-year absence but had acquired considerable experience in summer signings Raúl González and Klaas Jan Huntelaar. The former Real Madrid CF pair could do nothing to prevent an opening defeat at Lyon, though, with Michel Bastos scoring the only goal before Benedikt Höwedes' first-half dismissal for the Bundesliga runners-up. Israeli champions Hapoel succumbed on their group-stage debut, Luisão and Óscar Cardozo securing a home victory for Benfica despite the heroics of visiting goalkeeper Vincent Enyeama.

The Nigerian made history in unexpected fashion a fortnight later, becoming the first Hapoel player to score in the group stage - with a late penalty against Lyon. By then, however, Bastos had already registered twice, and Miralem Pjanić ensured the points returned to France with a third goal in added time. In what was looking increasingly like a three-horse race, Schalke's defeat of Benfica in Gelsenkirchen carried extra significance, Jefferson Farfán and Huntelaar scoring late on.

Raúl reminder

Normal service resumed for the evergreen Raúl on Matchday 3, the competition's all-time leading scorer opening his Schalke account with a double against Hapoel in Germany. José Manuel Jurado added an exquisite third before Itay Shechter's consolation. Although the Israeli team picked up their first point in the return fixture, holding Felix Magath's men to a goalless draw, it was not enough to keep their qualification hopes alive. Eli Gutman was neverthless proud of his players, saying: "It's a great honour for an Israeli side to be able to stand up to a club as big as Schalke."

A familiar feeling for the UEFA Champions League's all-time top scorer Raúl as he puts Schalke ahead against Hapoel Tel-Aviv

Another side teetering on the brink after three games were Benfica. The two-time European champions suffered a second consecutive loss at Lyon, for whom Jimmy Briand and Lisandro López were on target, before ressurecting their chances with a wonderful performance in the Lisbon return. Alan Kardec, Fábio Coentrão and Javi García gave the Eagles a three-goal lead at the interval. Left-back Coentrão capped a majestic individual display with his second before Lyon fought back to 4-3 thanks to Yoann Gourcuff, Bafétimbi Gomis and Dejan Lovren. "I was hoping the match would end quickly," said a relieved Jorge Jesus.

Benfica bow out

Sadly for the Benfica coach the next match started in identical fashion, his team conceding three unanswered goals to Hapoel at Bloomfield Stadium. The outstanding Eran Zahavi struck twice either side of a Douglas da Silva effort to clinch the first win for an Israeli club in the group stage since 2004. While their outstanding Matchday 5 performance kept Gutman's charges in contention for a UEFA Europa League berth, it ended

Benfica's hopes of a top-two finish after Schalke defeated Lyon in the night's other game.

The German club maintained their 100% home record with surprising ease, Farfán scoring one and Huntelaar two. The Ligue 1 outfit still clinched qualification with a game to spare, settling for runners-up spot despite a closing 2-2 draw against Hapoel. Lisandro struck first at Stade de Gerland only for Ben Sahar to level and Zahavi to put the visitors ahead with a stunning overhead kick. Hapoel were seconds away from a famous win when OL substitute Alexandre Lacazette shattered their dreams with an equalising goal that enabled Benfica to cling on to third place – and a switch to the UEFA Europa League – despite a closing 2-1 home defeat by Schalke.

Group B Results

14/9/10, Estádio do Sport Lisboa e Benfica, Lisbon
SL Benfica 2-0 Hapoel Tel-Aviv FC
Attendance: 31512
Goal(s): 1-0 Luisão 21, 2-0 Cardozo 68
Referee: Nikolaev (RUS)

14/9/10, Stade de Gerland, Lyon
Olympique Lyonnais 1-0 FC Schalke 04
Attendance: 35552
Goal(s): 1-0 Michel Bastos 21
Referee: Bebek (CRO)

29/9/10, Bloomfield Stadium, Tel-Aviv
Hapoel Tel-Aviv FC 1-3 Olympique Lyonnais
Attendance: 12226
Goal(s): 0-1 Michel Bastos 7(p), 0-2 Michel Bastos 36, 1-2 Enyeama 79(p), 1-3 Pjanić 90+4
Referee: Webb (ENG)

29/9/10, Arena AufSchalke, Gelsenkirchen
FC Schalke 04 2-0 SL Benfica
Attendance: 50436
Goal(s): 1-0 Farfán 73, 2-0 Huntelaar 85
Referee: Rocchi (ITA)

20/10/10, Arena AufSchalke, Gelsenkirchen
FC Schalke 04 3-1 Hapoel Tel-Aviv FC
Attendance: 50900
Goal(s): 1-0 Raúl 3, 2-0 Raúl 58, 3-0 Jurado 68, 3-1 Shechter 90+3
Referee: Collum (SCO)

20/10/10, Stade de Gerland, Lyon
Olympique Lyonnais 2-0 SL Benfica
Attendance: 36816
Goal(s): 1-0 Briand 21, 2-0 Lisandro López 51
Referee: Undiano Mallenco (ESP)

2/11/10, Estádio do Sport Lisboa e Benfica, Lisbon
SL Benfica 4-3 Olympique Lyonnais
Attendance: 37394
Goal(s): 1-0 Alan Kardec 20, 2-0 Fábio Coentrão 32, 3-0 Javi García 42, 4-0 Fábio Coentrão 67, 4-1 Gourcuff 74, 4-2 Gomis 85, 4-3 Lovren 90+5
Referee: Thomson (SCO)

2/11/10, Bloomfield Stadium, Tel-Aviv
Hapoel Tel-Aviv FC 0-0 FC Schalke 04
Attendance: 12132
Referee: De Bleeckere (BEL)

24/11/10, Arena AufSchalke, Gelsenkirchen
FC Schalke 04 3-0 Olympique Lyonnais
Attendance: 51132
Goal(s): 1-0 Farfán 13, 2-0 Huntelaar 20, 3-0 Huntelaar 89
Referee: Rizzoli (ITA)

24/11/10, Bloomfield Stadium, Tel-Aviv
Hapoel Tel-Aviv FC 3-0 SL Benfica
Attendance: 11668
Goal(s): 1-0 Zahavi 24, 2-0 Douglas 74, 3-0 Zahavi 90+2
Referee: Hamer (LUX)

7/12/10, Estádio do Sport Lisboa e Benfica, Lisbon
SL Benfica 1-2 FC Schalke 04
Attendance: 23348
Goal(s): 0-1 Jurado 19, 0-2 Höwedes 81, 1-2 Luisão 87
Referee: Webb (ENG)

7/12/10, Stade de Gerland, Lyon
Olympique Lyonnais 2-2 Hapoel Tel-Aviv FC
Attendance: 32245
Goal(s): 1-0 Lisandro López 62, 1-1 Sahar 63, 1-2 Zahavi 69, 2-2 Lacazette 88
Referee: Moen (NOR)

Group B Table

	Pld	Home					Away					Total					Pts
		W	D	L	F	A	W	D	L	F	A	W	D	L	F	A	
1 FC Schalke 04	6	3	0	0	8	3	1	1	1	2	0	4	1	1	10	3	13
2 Olympique Lyonnais	6	2	1	0	5	10	1	0	2	6	0	3	1	2	11	10	10
3 SL Benfica	6	2	0	1	7	12	0	0	3	0	0	2	0	4	7	12	6
4 Hapoel Tel-Aviv FC	6	1	1	1	4	10	0	1	2	3	0	1	2	3	7	10	5

Lisandro López scored for Lyon against Benfica and Hapoel Tel-Aviv

GROUP C

Manchester United FC and Valencia CF were most observers' favourites to progress from Group C at the outset, and they duly proved too strong for an obdurate Rangers FC side and Turkish newcomers Bursaspor.

Contrasting starts

United's opening game gave their manager, Sir Alex Ferguson, the opportunity to catch up again with Rangers counterpart Walter Smith, his one-time assistant both at Old Trafford and with the Scotland national team. It was Smith who was smiling, however, after a Manchester stalemate as Rangers' five-man defence held firm to earn a point. There was a baptism of fire for Bursaspor, first-time Turkish champions in 2010, who crashed 4-0 at home to Valencia. Bursaspor were competing in a major UEFA competition for the first time since 1986/87 and the Spanish team's experience told as Tino Costa, Aritz Aduriz, Pablo Hernández and Roberto Soldado all opened their goalscoring accounts in a commanding victory.

Bursapor lost again on Matchday 2 as Rangers continued their bright start thanks to Steven Naismith's first-half goal at Ibrox. There was only one goal in it at Mestalla too where substitute Javier Hernández hit his first in the competition late on for a Manchester United side setting a template of tight victories.

Narrow win

They produced another on Matchday 3, Nani's early long-range effort defeating Bursaspor on a night when Rangers' early momentum was checked by a 1-1 draw with Valencia. Rangers midfielder Maurice Edu raised home hopes by heading Smith's side in front after 34 minutes but deflated them moments after the restart by nodding into his own net. The result kept Rangers above Valencia but only for a fortnight more; when the teams reconvened at Mestalla, Unai Emery's men prevailed 3-0, Soldado scoring in each half before Tino Costa added gloss to the scoreline in added time. In response, Naismith twice struck the frame of the goal for Rangers.

With United winning 3-0 in Bursa on the same night – Darren Fletcher, Gabriel Obertan and Bébé got the goals – the expected top two were now firmly in place. Rangers did their best to change that when Ferguson returned to the club he once served as a player on Matchday 5 but Wayne Rooney's 87th-minute penalty consigned them to third place and secured United's passage to the last 16. It was Rooney's first goal since making his peace with United after a public contract dispute, and it extended the club's formidable UEFA Champions League away record to nine wins in ten.

Valencia win again

Over in Spain, Bursaspor finally scored their first UEFA Champions League goal – after 429 minutes of trying – through Pablo Batalla, only to concede six at the other end as Valencia secured qualification with their biggest victory in Europe for a decade, striker Soldado taking his group-stage tally to five with a double.

Valencia now needed to win at Old Trafford to qualify as group winners. They led at the break after Pablo Hernández's shot beat debutant Ben

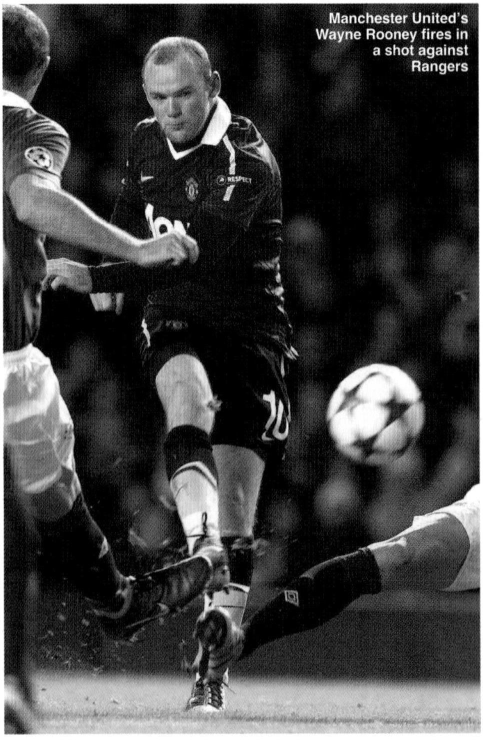

Manchester United's Wayne Rooney fires in a shot against Rangers

Amos in the United goal. Vicente Guaita, making his first start in the competition for Valencia, was in excellent form in the opposite goal but was finally beaten by a rare strike from Anderson in the 62nd minute, leaving honours even at 1-1. The Premier League team had topped their group for the fifth season running thanks largely to their defensive miserliness; none of the 15 other qualifiers had scored fewer than United's seven goals, but none had conceded just once either.

The final goal in the section arguably merited the biggest cheer – Sercan Yıldırım's 79th-minute effort for Bursaspor against Rangers, which earned Ertuğrul Sağlam's men their first UEFA Champions League point. Bursaspor fans also got a first glimpse of Kenny Miller, scorer of Rangers' spectacular first-half opener, who joined the Turkish side a month later.

Pablo Batalla (ball in hand) is congratulated by team-mate Turgay Bahadir after scoring Bursaspor's first goal in the UEFA Champions League

Group C Results

14/9/10, Old Trafford, Manchester
Manchester United FC 0-0 Rangers FC
Attendance: 74408
Referee: Olegário Benquerença (POR)

14/9/10, Bursa Atatürk, Bursa
Bursaspor 0-4 Valencia CF
Attendance: 22055
Goal(s): 0-1 Tino Costa 16, 0-2 Aduriz 41, 0-3 Pablo Hernández 68, 0-4 Soldado 76
Referee: Moen (NOR)

29/9/10, Ibrox Stadium, Glasgow
Rangers FC 1-0 Bursaspor
Attendance: 41905
Goal(s): 1-0 Naismith 18
Referee: Gumienny (BEL)

29/9/10, Estadi de Mestalla, Valencia
Valencia CF 0-1 Manchester United FC
Attendance: 34946
Goal(s): 0-1 Hernández 85
Referee: Kassai (HUN)

20/10/10, Ibrox Stadium, Glasgow
Rangers FC 1-1 Valencia CF
Attendance: 45153
Goal(s): 1-0 Edu 34, 1-1 Edu 46(og)
Referee: Rizzoli (ITA)

20/10/10, Old Trafford, Manchester
Manchester United FC 1-0 Bursaspor
Attendance: 72610
Goal(s): 1-0 Nani 7
Referee: Rocchi (ITA)

2/11/10, Estadi de Mestalla, Valencia
Valencia CF 3-0 Rangers FC
Attendance: 26821
Goal(s): 1-0 Soldado 33, 2-0 Soldado 71, 3-0 Tino Costa 90
Referee: Brych (GER)

2/11/10, Bursa Atatürk, Bursa
Bursaspor 0-3 Manchester United FC
Attendance: 19050
Goal(s): 0-1 Fletcher 48, 0-2 Obertan 73, 0-3 Bébé 77
Referee: Stark (GER)

24/11/10, Ibrox Stadium, Glasgow
Rangers FC 0-1 Manchester United FC
Attendance: 49764
Goal(s): 0-1 Rooney 87(p)
Referee: Busacca (SUI)

24/11/10, Estadi de Mestalla, Valencia
Valencia CF 6-1 Bursaspor
Attendance: 31225
Goal(s): 1-0 Mata 17(p), 2-0 Soldado 21, 3-0 Aduriz 30, 4-0 Joaquín 37, 5-0 Soldado 55, 5-1 Batalla 69, 6-1 Domínguez 78
Referee: Bruno Paixão (POR)

7/12/10, Old Trafford, Manchester
Manchester United FC 1-1 Valencia CF
Attendance: 74513
Goal(s): 0-1 Pablo Hernández 32, 1-1 Anderson 62
Referee: Proença (POR)

7/12/10, Bursa Atatürk, Bursa
Bursaspor 1-1 Rangers FC
Attendance: 9673
Goal(s): 0-1 Miller 19, 1-1 Sercan Yıldırım 79
Referee: Chapron (FRA)

Group C Table

		Home					Away					Total					
	Pld	W	D	L	F	A	W	D	L	F	A	W	D	L	F	A	Pts
1 Manchester United FC	6	1	2	0	2	1	3	0	0	5	0	4	2	0	7	1	14
2 Valencia CF	6	2	0	1	9	4	1	2	0	6	0	3	2	1	15	4	11
3 Rangers FC	6	1	1	1	2	6	0	2	1	1	0	1	3	2	3	6	6
4 Bursaspor	6	0	1	2	1	16	0	0	3	1	0	0	1	5	2	16	1

GROUP D

Acquaintances were renewed in Group D as FC Barcelona were paired with FC Rubin Kazan for the second year in succession. Having taken an impressive four points off the then holders in their debut campaign, the Russian champions hoped to build on that experience. Both teams, however, remained suitably wary of FC København – back for a second time after three seasons away – and Greek title holders Panathinaikos FC.

Joy for Rubin's Christian Noboa after he puts his team in front at home to Barcelona

Barcelona bonanza

The Greens were returning to the group stage following a year out and kicked off by taking the 20th-minute lead at Camp Nou through new recruit Sidney Govou. That only served to rouse Barcelona, and Lionel Messi equalised moments later before the hosts' own summer purchase David Villa put them ahead. The irrepressible Messi scored again just before half-time and he made light of Alexandros Tzorvas saving his 55th-minute penalty to play his part in further goals for Pedro Rodríguez and Dani Alves. Barça's 5-1 win represented a statement of intent, and FCK also laid down a Matchday 1 marker, Dame N'Doye's 87th-minute header fulfilling coach Ståle Solbakken's prediction of a 1-0 home victory against Rubin.

Kurban Berdyev's charges endeavoured to put that result behind them in their next outing and managed to frustrate Barcelona yet again, the visitors requiring a Villa penalty on the hour to salvage a 1-1 draw after Christian Noboa (30) had also converted from the spot. FCK maintained their momentum thanks to an impressive 2-0 success in Athens, N'Doye registering against his former employers and Martin Vingaard converting a free-kick before Gilberto Silva was dismissed for Nikos Nioplias's side shortly after the break.

More Messi magic

Barcelona took control of the section on Matchday 3 and, not for the first time, Messi proved their driving force. FCK travelled hoping to catch the Spanish champions on the break but they were rocked by a fantastic strike from the Argentinian maestro on 19 minutes. Although the Danish title holders threatened a leveller, Messi sealed a 2-0 triumph in added time. That presented Panathinaikos and Rubin with a superb opportunity to promote their respective causes, only for their game in Greece to finish goalless.

An identical scoreline in Russia two weeks later hardly proved more welcome for either side, and their rivals were able to nudge themselves closer to the last 16 via a 1-1 draw in Copenhagen. Messi's 31st-minute opener actually had the Blaugrana poised to progress with two games remaining, but the hosts answered back almost immediately through Brazilian midfielder Claudemir.

Barça through

Josep Guardiola's side did not spurn their next chance to cross the line, recording a 3-0 win in Athens, which came four days after ex-FC Porto coach Jesualdo Ferreira had replaced Nioplias at the Panathinaikos helm. Pedro struck in both halves and Messi posted his sixth group-stage goal as the Greek side were confirmed in fourth spot. In Kazan, a maiden home UEFA Champions League victory for Rubin at the sixth attempt prevented FCK from celebrating their own early qualification, Noboa claiming the only goal from the penalty spot in first-half added time.

If nerves might have been expected at Parken on Matchday 6, Solbakken's side ultimately cruised to the win they needed against Panathinaikos to finish second. Vingaard's cool finish pointed the way, and a spot-kick from Jesper Grønkjær plus Djibril Cissé's own goal settled matters in the second half, with Cédric Kanté's late consolation a mere footnote as FCK became the first Danish outfit to reach the round of 16. There was a first of sorts in Catalonia, too, as an experimental Barcelona XI finally overcame Rubin, Andreu Fontás and Víctor Vázquez opening their accounts for the club to down the UEFA Europa League-bound Russian side 2-0.

Group D Results

14/9/10, Camp Nou, Barcelona
FC Barcelona 5-1 Panathinaikos FC
Attendance: 69738
Goal(s): 0-1 Govou 20, 1-1 Messi 22, 2-1 David Villa 33, 3-1 Messi 45, 4-1 Pedro 78, 5-1 Dani Alves 90+3
Referee: Rizzoli (ITA)

14/9/10, Parken, Copenhagen
FC København 1-0 FC Rubin Kazan
Attendance: 29561
Goal(s): 1-0 N'Doye 87
Referee: Einwaller (AUT)

29/9/10, Centralni, Kazan
FC Rubin Kazan 1-1 FC Barcelona
Attendance: 23950
Goal(s): 1-0 Noboa 30(p), 1-1 David Villa 60(p)
Referee: Çakır (TUR)

29/9/10, OACA Spiros Louis Stadium, Athens
Panathinaikos FC 0-2 FC København
Attendance: 43607
Goal(s): 0-1 N'Doye 28, 0-2 Vingaard 37
Referee: Collum (SCO)

20/10/10, Camp Nou, Barcelona
FC Barcelona 2-0 FC København
Attendance: 75852
Goal(s): 1-0 Messi 19, 2-0 Messi 90+2
Referee: Lannoy (FRA)

20/10/10, OACA Spiros Louis Stadium, Athens
Panathinaikos FC 0-0 FC Rubin Kazan
Attendance: 36748
Referee: Gräfe (GER)

2/11/10, Centralni, Kazan
FC Rubin Kazan 0-0 Panathinaikos FC
Attendance: 16400
Referee: Chapron (FRA)

2/11/10, Parken, Copenhagen
FC København 1-1 FC Barcelona
Attendance: 37049
Goal(s): 0-1 Messi 31, 1-1 Claudemir 32
Referee: Balaj (ROU)

24/11/10, Centralni, Kazan
FC Rubin Kazan 1-0 FC København
Attendance: 18720
Goal(s): 1-0 Noboa 45+2(p)
Referee: Atkinson (ENG)

24/11/10, OACA Spiros Louis Stadium, Athens
Panathinaikos FC 0-3 FC Barcelona
Attendance: 58466
Goal(s): 0-1 Pedro 27, 0-2 Messi 62, 0-3 Pedro 69
Referee: Rocchi (ITA)

7/12/10, Camp Nou, Barcelona
FC Barcelona 2-0 FC Rubin Kazan
Attendance: 50436
Goal(s): 1-0 Fontás 51, 2-0 Víctor Vázquez 83
Referee: Eriksson (SWE)

7/12/10, Parken, Copenhagen
FC København 3-1 Panathinaikos FC
Attendance: 36797
Goal(s): 1-0 Vingaard 26, 2-0 Grønkjær 50(p), 3-0 Cissé 73(og), 3-1 Kanté 90+2
Referee: Meyer (GER)

Group D Table

		Home					Away					Total					
	Pld	W	D	L	F	A	W	D	L	F	A	W	D	L	F	A	Pts
1 FC Barcelona	6	3	0	0	9	3	1	2	0	5	0	4	2	0	14	3	14
2 FC København	6	2	1	0	5	5	1	0	2	2	0	3	1	2	7	5	10
3 FC Rubin Kazan	6	1	2	0	2	4	0	1	2	0	0	1	3	2	2	4	6
4 Panathinaikos FC	6	0	1	2	0	13	0	1	2	2	0	0	2	4	2	13	2

Barcelona's Javier Mascherano is challenged by FC København's Martin Vingaard

GROUP E

FC Bayern München and AS Roma were most people's favourites to qualify from UEFA Champions League Group E, and although they did ultimately make it through, FC Basel 1893 and CFR 1907 Cluj did enough to ensure that the top pair did not have it all their own way.

Winning beginnings

Bayern began the long process of exorcising the pain caused by their loss to FC Internazionale Milano in the 2010 final with a hard-earned 2-0 home win against Roma, Thomas Müller and substitute Miroslav Klose scoring in the final 11 minutes to crack the visitors' resolve. In the section's other opening-day fixture CFR relied on two early goals, from Ionuţ Rada and Lacina Traoré, to overcome Basel despite Valentin Stocker's reply in first-half added time.

Basel suffered another 2-1 defeat in the second set of matches despite taking an 18th-minute lead through the evergreen Alexander Frei. Bayern's Bastian Schweinsteiger levelled from the penalty spot 11 minutes into the second half after Müller had been felled by Benjamin Huggel, then, just as it looked like the match would end level, Schweinsteiger's close-range second in the 89th minute took the points to Munich. Basel ended the night bottom of the section as two Roma goals in three minutes midway through the second half, from Philippe Mexès and substitute Marco Borriello, got the Italian side up and running. Ionuţ Rada's 78th-minute response for CFR proved academic.

Bayern on top

Bayern cemented their place at the group's summit on Matchday 3, although they needed a helping hand from CFR in Munich. Cadú gave the visitors a surprise lead in the 28th minute, but his own goal brought Bayern level soon afterwards, and in the 37th minute another CFR player, Cristian Panin, also put through his own net. It was not until the 77th minute, and a Mario Gomez goal, that Bayern could relax, although Juan Culio's 86th-minute effort kept CFR in contention until the final whistle. It was a different story in the reverse fixture a fortnight later, however, Bayern running out comfortable 4-0 winners in Cluj-Napoca thanks to three goals from Gomez and one from Müller.

Roma's embryonic revival was brought to an abrupt halt by Basel, the Swiss side taking an 18th-minute lead at the Stadio Olimpico through Frei. Although Borriello swiftly equalised, Samuel Inkoom restored Basel's advantage a minute before half-time and the Swiss side completed their first group stage victory since 2003 thanks to a last-gasp third from replacement Cabral. That left three teams on three points heading into Matchday 4, but it was Roma who seized the initiative in the race for second place with a vital 3-2 win at Basel, achieved thanks to goals in the opening half-hour from Jérémy Ménez and Francesco Totti, which paved the way for Leandro Greco's 76th-minute clincher.

Rousing revival

Roma were also 3-2 winners in their penultimate fixture against Bayern, although that looked an unlikely outcome when the in-form Gomez scored twice in seven minutes shortly before half-time. Borriello and Daniele De Rossi subsequently drew Roma level before Francesco Totti's penalty sealed the points and kept the Italian side in second place. Basel kept alive their own qualification

Mario Gomez was on target six times for Bayern in Group E

hopes, with Federico Almerares scoring the only goal against a CFR side who ended with ten men following Felice Piccolo's late dismissal.

The Swiss side's lingering qualification aspirations were given short shrift by group winners Bayern in Munich on Matchday 6, Franck Ribéry finding the net twice either side of an Anatoliy Tymoshchuk effort. With Basel therefore finishing third, Roma and CFR played out a 1-1 draw in Romania, Traoré cancelling out Borriello's fourth goal of the group to earn the home team a point.

Roma captain Francesco Totti puts his team 2-0 up against Basel from the penalty spot

Group E Results

15/9/10, Fußball Arena München, Munich
FC Bayern München 2-0 AS Roma
Attendance: 66000
Goal(s): 1-0 Müller 79, 2-0 Klose 83
Referee: Lannoy (FRA)

15/9/10, Stadionul Dr Constantin Rădulescu, Cluj-Napoca
CFR 1907 Cluj 2-1 FC Basel 1893
Attendance: 9593
Goal(s): 1-0 Rada 9, 2-0 Traoré 12, 2-1 Stocker 45+2
Referee: Kelly (IRL)

28/9/10, St Jakob-Park, Basel
FC Basel 1893 1-2 FC Bayern München
Attendance: 37500
Goal(s): 1-0 Frei 18, 1-1 Schweinsteiger 56(p), 1-2 Schweinsteiger 89
Referee: Thomson (SCO)

28/9/10, Stadio Olimpico, Rome
AS Roma 2-1 CFR 1907 Cluj
Attendance: 30252
Goal(s): 1-0 Mexès 69, 2-0 Borriello 71, 2-1 Rada 78
Referee: Eriksson (SWE)

19/10/10, Stadio Olimpico, Rome
AS Roma 1-3 FC Basel 1893
Attendance: 22365
Goal(s): 0-1 Frei 12, 1-1 Borriello 21, 1-2 Inkoom 44, 1-3 Cabral 90+3
Referee: Nikolaev (RUS)

19/10/10, Fußball Arena München, Munich
FC Bayern München 3-2 CFR 1907 Cluj
Attendance: 64000
Goal(s): 0-1 Cadú 28, 1-1 Cadú 32(og), 2-1 Panin 37(og), 3-1 Gomez 77, 3-2 Culio 86
Referee: Atkinson (ENG)

3/11/10, St Jakob-Park, Basel
FC Basel 1893 2-3 AS Roma
Attendance: 36375
Goal(s): 0-1 Ménez 16, 0-2 Totti 26(p), 1-2 Frei 69, 1-3 Greco 76, 2-3 Shaqiri 83
Referee: Kuipers (NED)

3/11/10, Stadionul Dr Constantin Rădulescu, Cluj-Napoca
CFR 1907 Cluj 0-4 FC Bayern München
Attendance: 14097
Goal(s): 0-1 Gomez 12, 0-2 Gomez 24, 0-3 Gomez 71, 0-4 Müller 90
Referee: Gumienny (BEL)

23/11/10, Stadio Olimpico, Rome
AS Roma 3-2 FC Bayern München
Attendance: 42789
Goal(s): 0-1 Gomez 33, 0-2 Gomez 39, 1-2 Borriello 49, 2-2 De Rossi 81, 3-2 Totti 84(p)
Referee: Undiano Mallenco (ESP)

23/11/10, St Jakob-Park, Basel
FC Basel 1893 1-0 CFR 1907 Cluj
Attendance: 34239
Goal(s): 1-0 Almerares 15
Referee: Duhamel (FRA)

8/12/10, Fußball Arena München, Munich
FC Bayern München 3-0 FC Basel 1893
Attendance: 64000
Goal(s): 1-0 Ribéry 35, 2-0 Tymoshchuk 37, 3-0 Ribéry 50
Referee: Hansson (SWE)

8/12/10, Stadionul Dr Constantin Rădulescu, Cluj-Napoca
CFR 1907 Cluj 1-1 AS Roma
Attendance: 12800
Goal(s): 0-1 Borriello 21, 1-1 Traoré 88
Referee: Collum (SCO)

Group E Table

		Home					Away					Total					
	Pld	W	D	L	F	A	W	D	L	F	A	W	D	L	F	A	Pts
1 FC Bayern München	6	3	0	0	8	6	2	0	1	8	0	5	0	1	16	6	15
2 AS Roma	6	2	0	1	6	11	1	1	1	4	0	3	1	2	10	11	10
3 FC Basel 1893	6	1	0	2	4	11	1	0	2	4	0	2	0	4	8	11	6
4 CFR 1907 Cluj	6	1	1	1	3	12	0	0	3	3	0	1	1	4	6	12	4

GROUP F

UEFA Champions League newcomers MŠK Žilina were always likely to find the going tough alongside the powerful trio of Chelsea FC, Olympique de Marseille and FC Spartak Moskva in Group F – and so it proved as the Slovakian outsiders failed to pick up a single point.

Tough start

Pavel Hapal's team were given perhaps the hardest possible start with a home game against the English double-winners on Matchday 1. Semi-finalists in four of the previous six campaigns, Chelsea started their latest UEFA Champions League quest in clinical fashion, goals from Nicolas Anelka (twice), Michael Essien and Daniel Sturridge setting up an emphatic win before Tomáš Oravec's late consolation for the hosts.

In light of Chelsea's recent record, Marseille and Spartak knew they might be battling for second place, and it was Valeriy Karpin's side that seized the initiative by winning 1-0 at the Stade Vélodrome, the unfortunate César Azpilicueta marking his tournament debut by inadvertently giving the Russian outfit victory with a late own goal. OM found themselves six points off the pace when they lost again two weeks later, John Terry's effort and an Anelka penalty sealing another success for Chelsea at Stamford Bridge, while Spartak eased to a 3-0 success over Žilina thanks to Ari's double and another goal from his fellow Brazilian Ibson.

Chelsea's Daniel Sturridge blows a kiss to the crowd after scoring against Žilina

Marseille up and running

Didier Deschamps' side needed maximum points from their double confrontation with Žilina yet they were finding goals hard to come by. Finally, after almost four hours, Souleymane Diawara got Marseille's first of the campaign, heading in a second-half winner to deny the spirited visitors. That strike opened the floodgates as the 1993 winners ran amok in Slovakia, recording the biggest ever UEFA Champions League away win as André-Pierre Gignac's hat-trick, a Lucho González double and strikes from Gabriel Heinze and Loïc Rémy completed a stunning 7-0 triumph. "Goal difference could be important," noted Deschamps. "This gives us an edge."

Fans of the Mediterreanean club had been keeping a close eye on Spartak's results and by the end of Matchday 4 the two teams were level on six points. Karpin's charges simply could not live with Chelsea's powerful attacking play over the two meetings. Yuriy Zhirkov opened the scoring on his return to Russia before Anelka finished Spartak off prior to half-time. In the return fixture, the Frenchman scored for the fourth match running as the London club sealed qualification with two games to spare, Didier Drogba's penalty and two Branislav Ivanović goals ensuring another impressive result. Although Nikita Bazhenov scored a consolation, Karpin admitted: "Chelsea's players are just stronger individually. They were simply better than us."

Spartak swept aside

All was not lost, however. A draw at home to Marseille on Matchday 5 would have kept Spartak above the Ligue 1 champions courtesy of a superior head-to-head record, yet the visitors had other ideas. OM showed just how much they had improved, running out comfortable victors in Moscow courtesy of goals from Mathieu Valbuena, Rémy and Brandão. The outcome condemned

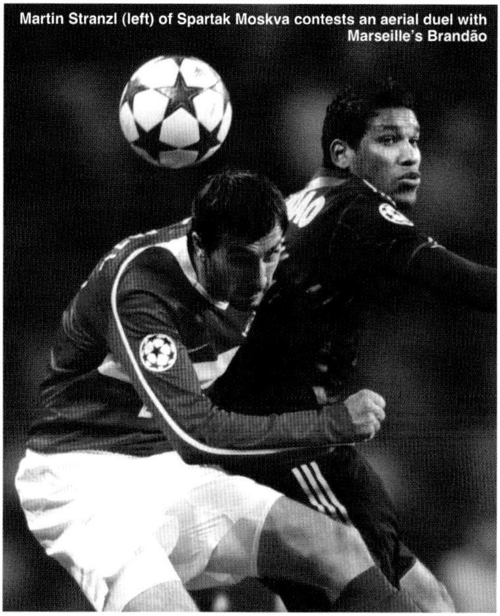

Martin Stranzl (left) of Spartak Moskva contests an aerial duel with Marseille's Brandão

Spartak to third spot and catapulted Marseille into the last 16 for the first time since 1999/2000.

If Chelsea had begun the group stage at breakneck pace, the momentum was with Marseille by the end. Brandão fired the French side to a fourth consecutive win on Matchday 6, preventing Carlo Ancelotti's team from becoming only the fifth team to win all six group games in the process. Žilina, meanwhile, were also showing signs of improvement, running Chelsea and Spartak close in their final games. Bello Babatounde gave the debutants a shock lead at Stamford Bridge before Sturridge's equaliser and a late winner from Florent Malouda, while Alex and Ibson broke Slovakian hearts again on Matchday 6 as Spartak recovered from Tomáš Majtán's opener.

Group F Results

15/9/10, Stade Vélodrome, Marseille
Olympique de Marseille 0-1 FC Spartak Moskva
Attendance: 45729
Goal(s): 0-1 Azpilicueta 81(og)
Referee: Meyer (GER)

15/9/10, Štadión MŠK Žilina, Zilina
MŠK Žilina 1-4 Chelsea FC
Attendance: 10829
Goal(s): 0-1 Essien 13, 0-2 Anelka 24, 0-3 Anelka 28, 0-4 Sturridge 48, 1-4 Oravec 55
Referee: Kuipers (NED)

28/9/10, Stamford Bridge, London
Chelsea FC 2-0 Olympique de Marseille
Attendance: 40675
Goal(s): 1-0 Terry 7, 2-0 Anelka 28(p)
Referee: De Bleeckere (BEL)

28/9/10, Luzhniki Stadion, Moscow
FC Spartak Moskva 3-0 MŠK Žilina
Attendance: 37000
Goal(s): 1-0 Ari 34, 2-0 Ari 61, 3-0 Ibson 89
Referee: Hansson (SWE)

19/10/10, Luzhniki Stadion, Moscow
FC Spartak Moskva 0-2 Chelsea FC
Attendance: 70012
Goal(s): 0-1 Zhirkov 23, 0-2 Anelka 43
Referee: Velasco Carballo (ESP)

19/10/10, Stade Vélodrome, Marseille
Olympique de Marseille 1-0 MŠK Žilina
Attendance: 49250
Goal(s): 1-0 Diawara 48
Referee: Vad (HUN)

3/11/10, Stamford Bridge, London
Chelsea FC 4-1 FC Spartak Moskva
Attendance: 40477
Goal(s): 1-0 Anelka 49, 2-0 Drogba 62(p), 3-0 Ivanović 66, 3-1 Bazhenov 86, 4-1 Ivanović 90+2
Referee: Çakır (TUR)

3/11/10, Štadión MŠK Žilina, Zilina
MŠK Žilina 0-7 Olympique de Marseille
Attendance: 9664
Goal(s): 0-1 Gignac 12, 0-2 Gignac 21, 0-3 Heinze 24, 0-4 Rémy 36, 0-5 Lucho González 52, 0-6 Gignac 54, 0-7 Lucho González 63
Referee: Johannesson (SWE)

23/11/10, Stamford Bridge, London
Chelsea FC 2-1 MŠK Žilina
Attendance: 40266
Goal(s): 0-1 Babatounde 19, 1-1 Sturridge 51, 2-1 Malouda 86
Referee: Schörgenhofer (AUT)

23/11/10, Luzhniki Stadion, Moscow
FC Spartak Moskva 0-3 Olympique de Marseille
Attendance: 43217
Goal(s): 0-1 Valbuena 18, 0-2 Rémy 54, 0-3 Brandão 68
Referee: Stark (GER)

8/12/10, Stade Vélodrome, Marseille
Olympique de Marseille 1-0 Chelsea FC
Attendance: 50604
Goal(s): 1-0 Brandão 81
Referee: Bezborodov (RUS)

8/12/10, Štadión MŠK Žilina, Zilina
MŠK Žilina 1-2 FC Spartak Moskva
Attendance: 7208
Goal(s): 1-0 Majtán 48, 1-1 Alex 54, 1-2 Ibson 61
Referee: Blom (NED)

Group F Table

		Home					Away					Total					
	Pld	W	D	L	F	A	W	D	L	F	A	W	D	L	F	A	Pts
1 Chelsea FC	6	3	0	0	8	4	2	0	1	6	0	5	0	1	14	4	15
2 Olympique de Marseille	6	2	0	1	2	3	2	0	1	10	0	4	0	2	12	3	12
3 FC Spartak Moskva	6	1	0	2	3	10	2	0	1	4	0	3	0	3	7	10	9
4 MŠK Žilina	6	0	0	3	2	19	0	0	3	1	0	0	0	6	3	19	0

GROUP G

With 20 European titles shared out between the four teams, Group G positively glowed with continental pedigree. AJ Auxerre were the odd team out in an illustrious array of previous winners, but question marks nonetheless surrounded their rivals, with AFC Ajax back after a five-year absence and both Real Madrid CF and AC Milan – drawn together for the second season running – operating under new management.

Real Madrid playmaker Mesut Özil is pursued by Milan's Gennaro Gattuso

Winning start

José Mourinho was the man now holding the Madrid reins and, fresh from guiding FC Internazionale Milano to the 2009/10 crown, he celebrated a winning start against Ajax at the Santiago Bernabéu. A 31st-minute own goal from the visitors' Vurnon Anita did little to enhance the sense of a dawning era, but Madrid's summer signings Mesut Özil and Ángel Di María were both involved as Gonzalo Higuaín completed a 2-0 victory 17 minutes from time. That was also the scoreline at San Siro as a quick-fire second-half double from new recruit Zlatan Ibrahimović got Massimiliano Allegri's Milan rolling against Auxerre.

The Burgundy club's daunting return to the competition for the first time since 2002/03 continued with a 1-0 home loss to Madrid, Di María's late strike sending the Merengues clear at the summit thanks to a 1-1 draw between Ajax and Milan in Amsterdam in what was a repeat of the 1969 and 1995 finals. Mounir El Hamdaoui fired Martin Jol's side into a 23rd-minute lead only for two former Ajax players to conjure a response, Clarence Seedorf teeing up Ibrahimović for an acrobatic finish.

Madrid in charge

The Rossoneri's chance to go top came on Matchday 3 as they sought to repeat their win in the Spanish capital from the previous season. It was not to be, however, as a 13th-minute Cristiano Ronaldo free-kick and an Özil strike almost immediately afterwards gave Madrid a five-point cushion. That allowed Ajax to revive their bid by defeating Auxerre 2-1, Demy de Zeeuw getting the seventh-minute opener and Luis Suárez adding a second before the break. Valter Birsa reduced the deficit from a free-kick after André Ooijer had been sent off, but Auxerre's comeback ended with Dennis Oliech's late dismissal.

Jean Fernandez's charges finally got off the mark in the return fixture, substitute Steeven Langil ensuring a 2-1 win six minutes from time - not long after Ajax centre-back Toby Alderweireld had cancelled out Frédéric Sammaritano's early breakthrough. Suddenly Auxerre were back in contention for the one qualification berth still on offer after Madrid sealed their progress the same night, Pedro León prompting animated celebrations from Mourinho with his last-gasp equaliser in a 2-2 draw at San Siro. The visitors had looked destined for defeat after Filippo Inzaghi had answered Higuaín's opener with a pair of typically predatory goals.

Milan qualify

Milan's frustration was acute, but they stamped their last-16 ticket at Auxerre on Matchday 5, Ibrahimović again breaking the French club's resistance on 64 minutes before Ronaldinho settled matters in added time. Madrid, meanwhile, made sure of top spot at Ajax, where late red cards for Xabi Alonso and Sergio Ramos removed little gloss from a 4-0 stroll, Karim Benzema and Álvaro Arbeloa finding the net in the first half and Cristiano Ronaldo registering twice in the last 20 minutes, his second a penalty.

The Portuguese superstar was on target again as Mourinho's troops signed off with another 4-0 success, though Benzema's hat-trick did most of the damage in Spain as Auxerre were consigned to the foot of the table. Third place and the UEFA Europa League berth thus belonged to Ajax, who returned from Milan savouring a 2-0 triumph in Frank de Boer's first outing as caretaker coach following Jol's resignation. De Zeeuw and Alderweireld secured the victory with memorable second-half strikes.

Group G Results

15/9/10, Estadio Santiago Bernabéu, Madrid
Real Madrid CF 2-0 AFC Ajax
Attendance: 69639
Goal(s): 1-0 Anita 31(og), 2-0 Higuaín 73
Referee: Skomina (SVN)

15/9/10, Stadio Giuseppe Meazza, Milan
AC Milan 2-0 AJ Auxerre
Attendance: 69317
Goal(s): 1-0 Ibrahimović 66, 2-0 Ibrahimović 69
Referee: Balaj (ROU)

Zlatan Ibrahimović scores one of his three goals against Auxerre

28/9/10, Stade Abbé-Deschamps, Auxerre
AJ Auxerre 0-1 Real Madrid CF
Attendance: 19525
Goal(s): 0-1 Di María 81
Referee: Larsen (DEN)

28/9/10, Amsterdam ArenA, Amsterdam
AFC Ajax 1-1 AC Milan
Attendance: 51276
Goal(s): 1-0 El Hamdaoui 23, 1-1 Ibrahimović 37
Referee: Brych (GER)

19/10/10, Amsterdam ArenA, Amsterdam
AFC Ajax 2-1 AJ Auxerre
Attendance: 51383
Goal(s): 1-0 De Zeeuw 7, 2-0 Suárez 41, 2-1 Birsa 56
Referee: Olegário Benquerença (POR)

19/10/10, Estadio Santiago Bernabéu, Madrid
Real Madrid CF 2-0 AC Milan
Attendance: 71657
Goal(s): 1-0 Cristiano Ronaldo 13, 2-0 Özil 14
Referee: Proença (POR)

3/11/10, Stade Abbé-Deschamps, Auxerre
AJ Auxerre 2-1 AFC Ajax
Attendance: 18727
Goal(s): 1-0 Sammaritano 9, 1-1 Alderweireld 79, 2-1 Langil 84
Referee: Clattenburg (ENG)

3/11/10, Stadio Giuseppe Meazza, Milan
AC Milan 2-2 Real Madrid CF
Attendance: 76357
Goal(s): 0-1 Higuaín 45, 1-1 Inzaghi 68, 2-1 Inzaghi 78, 2-2 Pedro León 90+4
Referee: Webb (ENG)

23/11/10, Amsterdam ArenA, Amsterdam
AFC Ajax 0-4 Real Madrid CF
Attendance: 48491
Goal(s): 0-1 Benzema 36, 0-2 Arbeloa 44, 0-3 Cristiano Ronaldo 70, 0-4 Cristiano Ronaldo 81(p)
Referee: Thomson (SCO)

23/11/10, Stade Abbé-Deschamps, Auxerre
AJ Auxerre 0-2 AC Milan
Attendance: 19244
Goal(s): 0-1 Ibrahimović 64, 0-2 Ronaldinho 90+1
Referee: Skomina (SVN)

8/12/10, Estadio Santiago Bernabéu, Madrid
Real Madrid CF 4-0 AJ Auxerre
Attendance: 54917
Goal(s): 1-0 Benzema 12, 2-0 Cristiano Ronaldo 49, 3-0 Benzema 72, 4-0 Benzema 88
Referee: Gumienny (BEL)

8/12/10, Stadio Giuseppe Meazza, Milan
AC Milan 0-2 AFC Ajax
Attendance: 72960
Goal(s): 0-1 De Zeeuw 57, 0-2 Alderweireld 66
Referee: Larsen (DEN)

Group G Table

		Home					Away					Total					
	Pld	W	D	L	F	A	W	D	L	F	A	W	D	L	F	A	Pts
1 Real Madrid CF	6	3	0	0	8	2	2	1	0	7	0	5	1	0	15	2	16
2 AC Milan	6	1	1	1	4	7	1	1	1	3	0	2	2	2	7	7	8
3 AFC Ajax	6	1	1	1	3	10	1	0	2	3	0	2	1	3	6	10	7
4 AJ Auxerre	6	1	0	2	2	12	0	0	3	1	0	1	0	5	3	12	3

GROUP H

UEFA Champions League Group H seemed to be a straightforward prospect for Arsenal FC – in the competition for the 13th consecutive season – but FC Shakhtar Donetsk further enhanced their burgeoning European reputation to leave the Gunners holding off SC Braga for second place.

Emphatic victory

Arsène Wenger's team initially gave the impression that they would make short shrift of the section, welcoming debutants Braga to the group stage with a 6-0 win in north London, Cesc Fàbregas and Carlos Vela each scoring twice and Andrey Arshavin and Marouane Chamakh once. The other Matchday 1 game was a considerably tighter affair, Darijo Srna scoring the only goal in the 71st minute in Ukraine as Shakhtar saw off an FK Partizan side competing in the group stage for the first time in seven years.

UEFA Cup winners in 2009, Shakhtar's bid to progress from a UEFA Champions League group at the sixth attempt gathered pace in their second game, Luiz Adriano scoring twice in the second period and Douglas Costa adding a late penalty in a 3-0 win at Braga. Arsenal also recorded another win although they were made to work hard in Belgrade in a match that featured three penalties, only one of which was converted. Arshavin gave the visitors the lead in the 15th minute before Cléo equalised from the spot just past the half-hour. Early in the second half Arshavin missed a penalty following a challenge that brought a red card for Marko Jovanović but Chamakh and Sébastien Squillaci spared the Russian's blushes with late goals in a 3-1 win.

Attacking Arsenal

The top two met in London on Matchday 3, and Arsenal continued their rich goalscoring form with a 5-1 win, Alex Song, Samir Nasri, Fàbregas, Jack Wilshere and Chamakh giving them a five-goal cushion before Eduardo marked his return to the club he had left in the summer with a late consolation. In Portugal, Braga got off the mark at the third attempt against a Partizan team whose 2-0 defeat left them still searching for their first ever group stage win after nine matches. Lima set Braga on their way with a sweetly struck first-half free-kick, and Matheus tapped in a clinching second in the final minute.

The 2009/10 Portuguese Liga runners-up made it two wins in a row a fortnight later, Moisés getting the only goal of their trip to Belgrade after 35 minutes. In Donetsk, Arsenal looked like their hitherto smooth progress to the knockout rounds would proceed apace when Theo Walcott raced clear to slide them into a tenth-minute lead at the Donbass Arena. Dmytro Chyhrynskiy levelled 18 minutes later, however, and Arsenal had no answer when Eduardo scored against his former employers again on the stroke of half-time.

Braga in contention

Arsenal's campaign unravelled further on Matchday 5 in Portugal, Matheus scoring twice in the final seven minutes to give Braga revenge for their opening-night defeat – and take them level with their opponents on nine points. Shakhtar took full advantage of Arsenal's latest setback with a 3-0 win away to Partizan, never looking back after Taras Stepanenko's 52nd-minute opener, with Jádson and Eduardo adding further goals.

Carlos Vela clips in the fifth of Arsenal's six goals at home to Braga

That meant Shakhtar needed a point in their final fixture against Braga to win the section while Arsenal had to beat Partizan at home to make certain of progress. When Cléo cancelled out Robin van Persie's 30th-minute penalty seven minutes after half-time, home nerves were jangling, but Arsenal avoided missing out on the last 16 for the first time since 1999/2000 thanks to goals from Walcott and Nasri in the final 20 minutes. Late strikes in Ukraine from Răzvan Raţ and Luiz Adriano, however, ensured that the Londoners would finish runners-up to Shakhtar.

Luiz Adriano was on target twice for Shakhtar in their 3-0 win at Braga

Group H Results

15/9/10, Arsenal Stadium, London
Arsenal FC 6-0 SC Braga
Attendance: 59333
Goal(s): 1-0 Fàbregas 9(p), 2-0 Arshavin 30, 3-0 Chamakh 34, 4-0 Fàbregas 53, 5-0 Vela 69, 6-0 Vela 84
Referee: Hamer (LUX)

15/9/10, Donbass Arena, Donetsk
FC Shakhtar Donetsk 1-0 FK Partizan
Attendance: 48512
Goal(s): 1-0 Srna 71
Referee: Velasco Carballo (ESP)

28/9/10, Estádio Municipal de Braga, Braga
SC Braga 0-3 FC Shakhtar Donetsk
Attendance: 12083
Goal(s): 0-1 Luiz Adriano 56, 0-2 Luiz Adriano 72, 0-3 Douglas Costa 90+2(p)
Referee: Blom (NED)

28/9/10, FK Partizan, Belgrade
FK Partizan 1-3 Arsenal FC
Attendance: 29348
Goal(s): 0-1 Arshavin 15, 1-1 Cléo 33(p), 1-2 Chamakh 71, 1-3 Squillaci 82
Referee: Stark (GER)

19/10/10, Estádio Municipal de Braga, Braga
SC Braga 2-0 FK Partizan
Attendance: 11454
Goal(s): 1-0 Lima 35, 2-0 Matheus 90
Referee: Duhamel (FRA)

19/10/10, Arsenal Stadium, London
Arsenal FC 5-1 FC Shakhtar Donetsk
Attendance: 60016
Goal(s): 1-0 Song 19, 2-0 Nasri 42, 3-0 Fàbregas 60(p), 4-0 Wilshere 66, 5-0 Chamakh 69, 5-1 Eduardo 82
Referee: Moen (NOR)

3/11/10, FK Partizan, Belgrade
FK Partizan 0-1 SC Braga
Attendance: 28295
Goal(s): 0-1 Moisés 35
Referee: Hansson (SWE)

3/11/10, Donbass Arena, Donetsk
FC Shakhtar Donetsk 2-1 Arsenal FC
Attendance: 51153
Goal(s): 0-1 Walcott 10, 1-1 Chyhrynskiy 28, 2-1 Eduardo 45
Referee: Busacca (SUI)

23/11/10, Estádio Municipal de Braga, Braga
SC Braga 2-0 Arsenal FC
Attendance: 14809
Goal(s): 1-0 Matheus 83, 2-0 Matheus 90+3
Referee: Kassai (HUN)

23/11/10, FK Partizan, Belgrade
FK Partizan 0-3 FC Shakhtar Donetsk
Attendance: 17473
Goal(s): 0-1 Stepanenko 52, 0-2 Jádson 59, 0-3 Eduardo 68
Referee: De Bleeckere (BEL)

8/12/10, Arsenal Stadium, London
Arsenal FC 3-1 FK Partizan
Attendance: 58845
Goal(s): 1-0 Van Persie 30(p), 1-1 Cléo 52, 2-1 Walcott 73, 3-1 Nasri 77
Referee: Tagliavento (ITA)

8/12/10, Donbass Arena, Donetsk
FC Shakhtar Donetsk 2-0 SC Braga
Attendance: 47627
Goal(s): 1-0 Raţ 78, 2-0 Luiz Adriano 83
Referee: Brych (GER)

Group H Table

			Home					Away					Total					
		Pld	W	D	L	F	A	W	D	L	F	A	W	D	L	F	A	Pts
1	FC Shakhtar Donetsk	6	3	0	0	5	6	2	0	1	7	0	5	0	1	12	6	15
2	Arsenal FC	6	3	0	0	14	7	1	0	2	4	0	4	0	2	18	7	12
3	SC Braga	6	2	0	1	4	11	1	0	2	1	0	3	0	3	5	11	9
4	FK Partizan	6	0	0	3	1	13	0	0	3	1	0	0	0	6	2	13	0

ROUND OF 16

The first knockout round provided its usual mixture of tension and excitement, showcasing European football at its finest. Holders FC Internazionale Milano made it through in dramatic fashion, while Real Madrid CF ended a seven-year wait for a quarter-final place and three English teams maintained their interest, with just Arsenal FC falling – at the expense of competition favourites FC Barcelona.

Holders stay alive

Leonardo had overseen a revival in Inter's Serie A fortunes since replacing Rafael Benítez in December 2010, although FC Bayern München, who had won on their two previous visits to Inter, presented arguably his sternest test yet in a repeat of the 2009/10 final. Inter's prospects were not helped by the absence for both games of Diego Milito, the holders' match-winner the season before in Madrid, who had succumbed to a thigh strain. Inter's worst fears were realised in the 90th minute at San Siro when Júlio César spilled Arjen Robben's shot into the path of Mario Gomez, who, with his marker Lúcio ball-watching, tucked in his seventh goal of the competition.

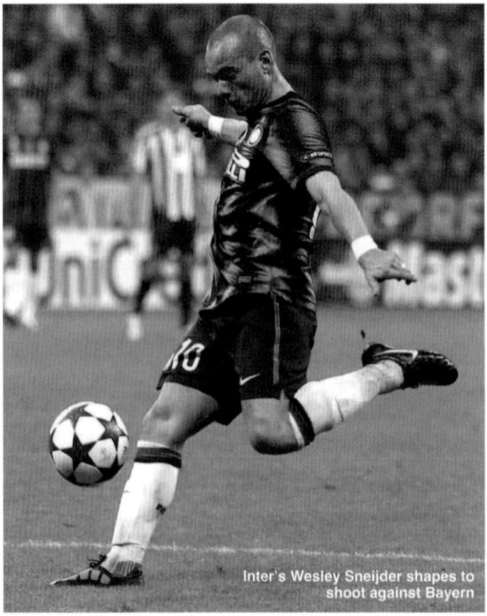
Inter's Wesley Sneijder shapes to shoot against Bayern

Inter therefore had to do what only one team had managed in the UEFA Champions League era – come back from losing a first leg at home – and they made a perfect start in Munich, Samuel Eto'o putting them in front in the fourth minute. However, Gomez brilliantly capitalised on another Júlio César fumble – again from a Robben shot - to restore Bayern's aggregate advantage, and when Thomas Müller gave Louis van Gaal's side a 31st-minute lead with a deft chip, the game looked to be up for the holders. Not so. Bayern wasted several chances to cement their advantage before Eto'o set up Wesley Sneijder to level the second leg three minutes past the hour and then, with just two minutes remaining, squared the ball for Goran Pandev to lash in a left-footed thunderbolt that crowned a famous fightback and took Inter through on away goals.

Engrossing contest

There were also several thrilling twists and turns to the Arsenal-Barcelona tie – a repeat of the 2009/10 quarter-final which the Spanish side, inspired by Lionel Messi, had won in memorable fashion. A repeat looked on the cards when David Villa gave the visitors a 26th-minute lead in London but the home team valiantly resisted their dominant opponents and levelled with 12 minutes remaining through Robin van Persie's shot from a tight angle. Five minutes later a lightning counterattack, instigated by Jack Wilshere and Cesc Fàbregas and carried into enemy territory by Samir Nasri, ended with Andrey Arshavin converting the Frenchman's pass to give Arsenal their first win against Barça at the sixth attempt.

Arsène Wenger's side lost Theo Walcott and Alex Song for the trip to Camp Nou, and although Fàbregas and Van Persie were passed fit to start, Arsenal's plans were further disrupted when Wojciech Szczęsny dislocated his finger and had to leave the field after 19 minutes. It was one-way traffic in the first half and just seconds before the interval Arsenal's densely packed defence was finally breached when Messi, with characteristic skill and composure, converted Andrés Iniesta's perfectly weighted pass after an unwise back-heel by Fàbregas. Although Sergio Busquets, deputising in central defence for the injured Carles Puyol and

Lionel Messi glides through the Arsenal defence in trademark fashion during Barcelona's 3-1 win at Camp Nou

suspended Gerard Piqué, headed into his own net eight minutes after half-time to put Arsenal back in the driving seat, the balance of the tie tipped decisively when Van Persie was dismissed for a second bookable offence three minutes later for kicking the ball away when flagged offside. Xavi put Barça back in front – and levelled the tie - in the 69th minute at the end of a mesmerising move; then, two minutes later, Messi rolled in the decisive third goal from the penalty spot after Laurent Koscielny had felled Pedro. Even then, Arsenal, who had not mustered a shot all evening and had relied largely on the sterling efforts of replacement 'keeper Manuel Almunia to keep the score down, might have stolen the tie but for a late gilt-edged chance squandered by Nicklas Bendtner's poor first touch.

Madrid end wait

The third 2009/10 encore paired Olympique Lyonnais with Real Madrid CF, the nine-time winners seeking to progress from the round of 16 for the first time since 2003/04 having lost 2-1 on aggregate to Claude Puel's team a year earlier. José Mourinho's side struck the first blow at the Stade de Gerland, Lyon old boy Karim Benzema coming off the bench in the 64th minute to open the scoring 43 seconds later. Bafétimbi Gomis replied for the home side with seven minutes remaining to preserve Lyon's unbeaten record against Madrid in their seventh meeting – but that record was shattered in the return at the Santiago Bernabéu. Madrid never looked back after Marcelo's exquisite 37th-minute opener, second-half goals from Benzema again – his sixth of the competition - and Ángel Di María completing a 4-1 aggregate win and ending the club's seven-year hoodoo.

Another team to make straightforward progress were Chelsea FC, aiming to get their hands on European club football's top prize having reached the semi-finals or better in five of the previous seven seasons. In contrast, their opponents FC København were in the knockout phase for the first time but went into the contest in good heart having collected a record 51 points in the first half of the Danish Superliga season. That counted for little against Chelsea's pedigree, however, Nicolas Anelka scoring in each half of the first leg at Parken to set the Blues serenely on the way to yet another quarter-final. Carlo Ancelotti's side were able to play out a goalless draw in a fairly uneventful return at Stamford Bridge.

Happy debutants

It was a happier story for the other two sides making their first appearances in the last 16. Tottenham Hotspur FC's only previous European Champion Clubs' Cup campaign, in 1961/62, had ended in the semi-finals, and Harry Redknapp's side picked up where they had left off in the group stage. Having won Group A ahead of Inter, the north London club were drawn against the other Milanese giants, AC Milan, and it was the newcomers who got the better of the seven-time champions in the first leg at San Siro, Heurelho Gomes providing a spectacular goalkeeping display and Peter Crouch scoring the only goal in the 80th minute after a dynamic burst forward by winger Aaron Lennon.

That marked Milan's third successive home defeat by Premier League opponents, and worse was to follow for Massimiliano Allegri's side, who lost captain Gennaro Gattuso for the second leg thanks to a booking – and to a further four-game ban following a post-match confrontation with Tottenham coach (and ex-Milan player) Joe Jordan. The Rossoneri's winless run against English clubs stretched from six games to seven at White Hart Lane. Although Milan had marginally the better of a tight, nervy contest, they were unable to fashion a breakthrough. Neither were Spurs, but they didn't need to, the 0-0 draw sending them gleefully through to the last eight.

Roma conquered

FC Shakhtar Donetsk's feat was perhaps even more impressive. Paired with AS Roma, the Ukrainian side travelled to Stadio Olimpico having not played a competitive match since Matchday 6. It mattered little, Mircea Lucescu's side recovering from Răzvan Raţ's 28th-minute own goal to take a 3-2 lead back to Ukraine. A minute after Raţ had been unable to prevent Simone Perrotta's header crossing the line Shakhtar levelled when Jádson's shot deflected in off Daniele De Rossi. Douglas Costa then cut in from the right to curl in Shakhtar's second in the 36th minute before taking advantage of a John Arne Riise slip to set up another Brazilian, Luiz Adriano, for a third five minutes later. Although Jérémy Ménez scored a stunning goal in the second half, Roma travelled to Donetsk in arrears and under pressure.

By the time of the second leg, Vincenzo Montella had replaced Claudio Ranieri as Roma coach, but the 36-year-old former striker was unable to inspire a turnaround. Instead Shakhtar recorded a fourth home win from as many games. Willian's low left-wing cross went straight in to give them the lead on the night in the 18th minute. The visitors then spurned a golden chance to draw level when Marco Borriello's penalty was saved by Andriy Pyatov before the dismissal of Philippe Mexès effectively ended Roma's hopes just before the break. Second-half goals from Willian and Eduardo completed an impressive win for Shakhtar, who thus reached the last eight for the first time.

United through again

Manchester United FC made progress to a fourth successive quarter-final – though not without the odd scare against French champions Olympique de Marseille. The teams shared a dull 0-0 draw in the first game at the Stade Vélodrome, but Marseille were undone by two well-worked United goals in the second leg at Old Trafford. Ryan Giggs and Wayne Rooney combined to play in Javier Hernández for the first, the Mexican ghosting in at

Shakhtar's Jádson in reflective mood after scoring against Roma in the Stadio Olimpico

the far post ahead of his marker in the fifth minute. Antonio Valencia's reverse pass gave Giggs the chance to set up Hernández for another simple finish in the 75th minute, and although Wes Brown headed Mathieu Valbuena's 82nd-minute corner into his own net to revive the visitors' hopes, Sir Alex Ferguson's side survived the closing stages to sneak through.

FC Schalke 04 also followed an away first-leg draw with a decisive home win. Real Madrid legend Raúl marked his return to Spain with a 64th-minute equaliser against Valencia CF – his record-extending 71st goal in Europe – to cancel out Roberto Soldado's opener. The German side – whose coach Felix Magath stepped down the week after the second leg – were without Lukas Schmitz for the return following the midfielder's added-time red card at Mestalla, and they again fell behind in the 17th minute in Gelsenkirchen, Ricardo Costa heading Valencia in front. This time, though, the Bundesliga outfit drew level five minutes before half-time, Peruvian striker Jefferson Farfán scoring with a superb curling free-kick, and seven minutes into the second period – after Valencia had spurned several chances – competition debutant Mario Gavranovic put Schalke in front for the first time in the tie with a shot that struck both posts before crossing the line. With Valencia committed to attack in search of a priceless away goal, Farfán galloped clear to clip in a clinching third goal deep into added time, confirming Schalke's fourth successive home win in the competition and their place in the quarter-finals for the first time since 2007/08.

Round of 16 Results

15/2/11, Stadio Giuseppe Meazza, Milan
AC Milan 0-1 Tottenham Hotspur FC
Attendance: 75652
Goal(s): 0-1 Crouch 80
Referee: Lannoy (FRA)
9/3/11, White Hart Lane, London
Tottenham Hotspur FC 0-0 AC Milan
Attendance: 34320
Referee: De Bleeckere (BEL)
Aggregate: 1-0; Tottenham Hotspur FC qualify.

15/2/11, Estadi de Mestalla, Valencia
Valencia CF 1-1 FC Schalke 04
Attendance: 42703
Goal(s): 1-0 Soldado 17, 1-1 Raúl 64
Referee: Nikolaev (RUS)
9/3/11, Arena AufSchalke, Gelsenkirchen
FC Schalke 04 3-1 Valencia CF
Attendance: 53517
Goal(s): 0-1 Ricardo Costa 17, 1-1 Farfán 40, 2-1 Gavranovic 52, 3-1 Farfán 90+4
Referee: Eriksson (SWE)
Aggregate: 4-2; FC Schalke 04 qualify.

Mario Gavranovic celebrates a crucial goal on his UEFA Champions League debut as Schalke overcome Valencia in Gelsenkirchen

16/2/11, Arsenal Stadium, London
Arsenal FC 2-1 FC Barcelona
Attendance: 59927
Goal(s): 0-1 David Villa 26, 1-1 Van Persie 78, 2-1 Arshavin 83
Referee: Rizzoli (ITA)
8/3/11, Camp Nou, Barcelona
FC Barcelona 3-1 Arsenal FC
Attendance: 95486
Goal(s): 1-0 Messi 45+3, 1-1 Busquets 53(og), 2-1 Xavi 69, 3-1 Messi 71(p)
Referee: Busacca (SUI)
Aggregate: 4-3; FC Barcelona qualify.

16/2/11, Stadio Olimpico, Rome
AS Roma 2-3 FC Shakhtar Donetsk
Attendance: 35873
Goal(s): 1-0 Raţ 28(og), 1-1 Jádson 29, 1-2 Douglas Costa 36, 1-3 Luiz Adriano 41, 2-3 Ménez 61
Referee: Olegário Benquerença (POR)
8/3/11, Donbass Arena, Donetsk
FC Shakhtar Donetsk 3-0 AS Roma
Attendance: 46543
Goal(s): 1-0 Willian 18, 2-0 Willian 58, 3-0 Eduardo 87
Referee: Webb (ENG)
Aggregate: 6-2; FC Shakhtar Donetsk qualify.

22/2/11, Parken, Copenhagen
FC København 0-2 Chelsea FC
Attendance: 36713
Goal(s): 0-1 Anelka 17, 0-2 Anelka 54
Referee: Kuipers (NED)
16/3/11, Stamford Bridge, London
Chelsea FC 0-0 FC København
Attendance: 36454
Referee: Moen (NOR)
Aggregate: 2-0; Chelsea FC qualify.

22/2/11, Stade de Gerland, Lyon
Olympique Lyonnais 1-1 Real Madrid CF
Attendance: 40299
Goal(s): 0-1 Benzema 65, 1-1 Gomis 83
Referee: Stark (GER)
16/3/11, Estadio Santiago Bernabéu, Madrid
Real Madrid CF 3-0 Olympique Lyonnais
Attendance: 70034
Goal(s): 1-0 Marcelo 37, 2-0 Benzema 66, 3-0 Di María 76
Referee: Skomina (SVN)
Aggregate: 4-1; Real Madrid CF qualify.

23/2/11, Stade Vélodrome, Marseille
Olympique de Marseille 0-0 Manchester United FC
Attendance: 57957
Referee: Brych (GER)
15/3/11, Old Trafford, Manchester
Manchester United FC 2-1 Olympique de Marseille
Attendance: 73996
Goal(s): 1-0 Hernández 5, 2-0 Hernández 75, 2-1 Brown 82(og)
Referee: Velasco Carballo (ESP)
Aggregate: 2-1; Manchester United FC qualify.

23/2/11, Stadio Giuseppe Meazza, Milan
FC Internazionale Milano 0-1 FC Bayern München
Attendance: 75925
Goal(s): 0-1 Gomez 90
Referee: Kassai (HUN)
15/3/11, Fußball Arena München, Munich
FC Bayern München 2-3 FC Internazionale Milano
Attendance: 66000
Goal(s): 0-1 Eto'o 4, 1-1 Gomez 21, 2-1 Müller 31, 2-2 Sneijder 63, 2-3 Pandev 88
Referee: Proença (POR)
Aggregate: 3-3; FC Internazionale Milano qualify on away goals.

QUARTER-FINALS

Although there was plenty of drama and intrigue in the UEFA Champions League quarter-finals – not to mention a string of notable landmarks – all four ties were effectively settled by the outcome of the first legs. Indeed, all four qualifiers would go on to reach the semi-finals with home and away wins.

Rangnick return

The biggest surprise came in Milan, where holders FC Internazionale Milano met FC Schalke 04 in a repeat of the 1997 UEFA Cup final that was won on penalties by the German club, who replaced Felix Magath with Ralf Rangnick barely a fortnight before the first leg. The former TSG 1899 Hoffenheim coach enjoyed a remarkable return as his new side recorded another memorable triumph at San Siro, although they could scarcely have made a worst start, Dejan Stanković volleying Inter in front after just 25 seconds with an extraordinary first-time effort from the centre circle. Joel Matip levelled in the 17th minute, only for Diego Milito to restore the home team's lead, but Inter, missing the suspended Lúcio in defence, had no response when Edu made it 2-2 five minutes before half-time. The second period belonged solely to Schalke. UEFA Champions League veteran Raúl put them in front for the first time eight minutes after the restart, and when Andrea Ranocchia's avoidable 57th-minute own goal was followed five minutes later by Cristian Chivu's second yellow card of the night, the Nerazzurri were on their knees. Edu completed their misery with his second goal – and Schalke's fifth – 15 minutes from time.

Schalke's Brazilian striker Edu scored twice in the German club's shock 5-2 win against Inter in Milan

While Inter had recovered from a home defeat to eliminate FC Bayern München in the previous round, they now needed to score four times to have any hope. That increased to five when Schalke struck first in the second leg, Raúl finding the net on the stroke of half-time for his second goal in the tie and 73rd in European competition. Thiago Motta made it 1-1 four minutes after half-time, but Inter never seriously threatened a comeback, and with nine minutes remaining Raúl's delightful chip sent central defender Benedikt Höwedes racing through to cement Schalke's semi-final spot in emphatic style.

Madrid in command

Tottenham Hotspur FC's first UEFA Champions League campaign had been full of memorable moments, yet their trip to the Santiago Bernabéu will stick in the mind for all the wrong reasons. The visitors, for whom Aaron Lennon fell ill shortly before kick-off, were already a goal down by the time Peter Crouch collected his second yellow card of the evening – for two needlessly over-zealous lunges – in the 15th minute, Emmanuel Adebayor – once of north London rivals Arsenal FC – having headed Madrid into an early lead. Despite their numerical disadvantage Tottenham made it to half-time without further alarm, but their defence was breached again 12 minutes after the break, Adebayor heading in his second goal – and tenth in ten games against Spurs – from another corner. Ángel Di María's fine curling shot made it three 18 minutes from time and when Heurelho

Gomes failed to keep out Cristiano Ronaldo's volley at his near post in the 87th minute, the tie was all but over.

That 4-0 drubbing left Spurs with only pride to play for at home, but they were denied even the consolation of a second-leg win. Madrid had become the first European visitors to win at White Hart Lane when eliminating Tottenham from the 1984/85 UEFA Cup quarter-finals, and they repeated the feat by the same 1-0 scoreline, another Gomes error allowing Cristiano Ronaldo's shot to squirm into the net five minutes into the second half for the only goal of the game – and the Portuguese superstar's 40th of the season – as Madrid reached the semi-finals for the first time since 2002/03.

Real Madrid's Ángel Di María tests Tottenham defenders Benoît Assou-Ekotto (left) and Michael Dawson

Shakhtar seen off

The tie between FC Barcelona and FC Shakhtar Donetsk promised to be a much closer contest, the Ukrainian side having won on their previous visit to Catalonia in December 2008 and also held Barça in check until the 115th minute of the 2009 UEFA Super Cup in Monaco. This time, though, there were no such problems for Josep Guardiola's side, who took the lead inside two minutes at Camp Nou through Andrés Iniesta. Dani Alves doubled the lead before half-time and Gerard Piqué made it three with a deflected effort eight minutes after the restart. Yaroslav Rakytskiy revived Shakhtar's dwindling hopes by deflecting in a free-kick, but within a minute Seydou Keita had restored Barcelona's three-goal cushion with a ferocious left-foot drive. Stand-in skipper Xavi then rounded off yet another devastating display of attacking football from the Blaugrana with a fifth goal four minutes from time.

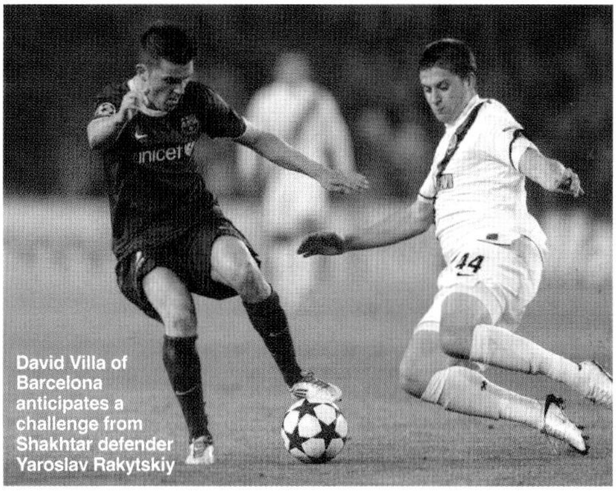
David Villa of Barcelona anticipates a challenge from Shakhtar defender Yaroslav Rakytskiy

Like Tottenham, Shakhtar sought the consolation of a second-leg win to ease the pain of elimination. Mircea Lucescu's side boasted a formidable 12-match unbeaten home run in Europe, but they had suffered a first reverse in 56 home matches four days before the game as FC Obolon Kyiv became the first visiting team to win at the Donbass Arena. Initially it looked as if they would be able to absorb that blow, with Douglas Costa and Jádson both being denied by Victor Valdés. But a second defeat in quick succession did follow, Lionel Messi doing the damage as he slotted in the only goal of the game - his ninth of the UEFA Champions League campaign - two minutes before half-time to set up a semi-final 'Clásico' against Real Madrid. It was the Argentinian's 48th goal of the season for Barcelona, surpassing the previous club record established by Ronaldo in 1996/97.

Final rematch

The remaining quarter-final was a repeat of the all-English 2008 final, won on penalties by Manchester United FC against Chelsea FC in Moscow. The London club had home advantage for the first game and every reason for confidence given that United had not won at Stamford Bridge for nine years and had gone down 2-1 there in a Premier League encounter just over a month earlier. That counted for nothing, however, 24 minutes in when Michael Carrick's superb crossfield pass was wonderfully collected by Ryan Giggs, who advanced to the byline before pulling the ball back for Wayne Rooney to angle his instep and steer in a precise shot. It was the fifth year running that the

England striker had scored in a UEFA Champions League quarter-final. Chelsea had their chances to equalise, coming closest when Didier Drogba's attempted cross towards Fernando Torres hit the post and Patrice Evra blocked Frank Lampard's follow-up effort on the line, but United, yet to concede on enemy territory in the competition and bolstered by the return from injury of the outstanding Rio Ferdinand, held firm – despite vehement home claims for a late penalty when Ramires went down under a challenge from Evra.

UEFA Champions League history may have been against Chelsea – only two teams had ever successfully recovered from a home first-leg defeat – but Carlo Ancelotti's team were not without hope for the trip to Old Trafford having been the last team to win there – in April 2010, 27 matches previously. Once more, however, they had to bow to the enduring brilliance of Giggs, the 37-year-old Welshman collecting Rooney's pass and playing a one-two with John O'Shea before squaring for Javier Hernández to open the scoring from close range two minutes before half-time. Ancelotti responded by replacing the ineffective Fernando Torres with Drogba at the break, and although the visitors went down to ten men following Ramires' second yellow card, it was the substitute who brought his team back into the contest with 13 minutes left, chesting down Michael Essien's through ball before shooting powerfully home. Chelsea's joy was short-lived, however, as United fashioned an immediate response, Giggs claiming his third assist of the tie as he played in Park Ji-Sung, whose left foot fired the ball low and true across Petr Čech to secure his team's fourth semi-final appearance in five years. Chelsea's quest for European football's holy grail, meanwhile, would have to be postponed for yet another year.

Ryan Giggs set up all three of Manchester United's goals against Chelsea

Quarter-Final Results

5/4/11, Estadio Santiago Bernabéu, Madrid
Real Madrid CF 4-0 Tottenham Hotspur FC
Attendance: 71657
Goal(s): 1-0 Adebayor 4, 2-0 Adebayor 57, 3-0 Di María 72, 4-0 Cristiano Ronaldo 87
Referee: Brych (GER)
13/4/11, White Hart Lane, London
Tottenham Hotspur FC 0-1 Real Madrid CF
Attendance: 34311
Goal(s): 0-1 Cristiano Ronaldo 50
Referee: Rizzoli (ITA)
Aggregate: 0-5; Real Madrid CF qualify.

5/4/11, Stadio Giuseppe Meazza, Milan
FC Internazionale Milano 2-5 FC Schalke 04
Attendance: 72770
Goal(s): 1-0 Stanković 1, 1-1 Matip 17, 2-1 Milito 34, 2-2 Edu 40, 2-3 Raúl 53, 2-4 Ranocchia 57(og), 2-5 Edu 75
Referee: Atkinson (ENG)
13/4/11, Arena AufSchalke, Gelsenkirchen
FC Schalke 04 2-1 FC Internazionale Milano
Attendance: 54142
Goal(s): 1-0 Raúl 45, 1-1 Thiago Motta 49, 2-1 Höwedes 81
Referee: Skomina (SVN)
Aggregate: 7-3; FC Schalke 04 qualify.

6/4/11, Stamford Bridge, London
Chelsea FC 0-1 Manchester United FC
Attendance: 37915
Goal(s): 0-1 Rooney 24
Referee: Undiano Mallenco (ESP)
12/4/11, Old Trafford, Manchester
Manchester United FC 2-1 Chelsea FC
Attendance: 74672
Goal(s): 1-0 Hernández 43, 1-1 Drogba 77, 2-1 Park 77
Referee: Olegário Benquerença (POR)
Aggregate: 3-1; Manchester United FC qualify.

6/4/11, Camp Nou, Barcelona
FC Barcelona 5-1 FC Shakhtar Donetsk
Attendance: 86518
Goal(s): 1-0 Iniesta 2, 2-0 Dani Alves 34, 3-0 Piqué 53, 3-1 Rakytskiy 60, 4-1 Keita 61, 5-1 Xavi 86
Referee: Thomson (SCO)
12/4/11, Donbass Arena, Donetsk
FC Shakhtar Donetsk 0-1 FC Barcelona
Attendance: 51759
Goal(s): 0-1 Messi 43
Referee: Meyer (GER)
Aggregate: 1-6; FC Barcelona qualify.

SEMI-FINALS

The UEFA Champions League semi-finals were steeped in European pedigree but, as in the previous round, the two ties were effectively settled by the first-leg outcomes and both FC Barcelona and Manchester United FC qualified for the Wembley final – a repeat of their 2009 meeting in Rome – with plenty to spare.

Decisive victory

United were paired with the competition's surprise package, FC Schalke 04, who were gracing the semi-finals for the first time. Surprise conquerors of holders FC Internazionale Milano in the quarter-finals, Ralf Rangnick's side had won all five of their previous home games in the competition, scoring 13 goals, but United had reason to be confident having not conceded a single goal in recording four wins and a draw on their travels. Against that, Sir Alex Ferguson's side had lost all four of their previous two-legged knockout ties against German opponents in the UEFA Champions League - semi-final reverses against Borussia Dortmund in 1996/97 and Bayer 04 Leverkusen in 2001/02, and quarter-final defeats by FC Bayern München in 2000/01 and 2009/10.

Of those pointers, however, it was United's formidable away record that would prove the most relevant in the first leg at the Arena AufSchalke. United were imperious, completely overrunning their inexperienced opponents with a vintage display. Only the brilliance of Manuel Neuer kept the scoresheet blank at the break, the giant Schalke goalkeeper making spectacular stops from Wayne Rooney, Javier Hernández and Ryan Giggs (twice) in the first period. The second half brought no respite. Within moments, Neuer had turned over a Michael Carrick header, then Giggs blazed wide after wrong-footing two defenders. Although José Manuel Jurado spurned a rare chance at the other end, Schalke showed only briefly as an attacking force and United eventually got the goals their overwhelming superiority deserved. The breakthrough arrived after 67 minutes when Rooney ran infield from the left and, holding off Peer Kluge, slipped a sublime pass through to Giggs, who put the ball through Neuer's legs to become, at 37 years and 148 days, the competition's oldest goalscorer. Two minutes later it was 2-0 as Rooney – back on the ground where he was sent off at the 2006 FIFA World Cup – collected a touch forward from Hernández and drove a first-time finish low to Neuer's right.

Emphatic win

Schalke had never won in England, and United had won all 14 ties in UEFA competition in which they had recorded a first-leg victory away from home. As against Chelsea FC in the previous round, that record would be maintained – despite Ferguson making nine changes to his first-leg line-up (to protect his first XI for a Premier League title-decider with Chelsea four days later). It was one of the two survivors, Antonio Valencia, who opened the scoring in the 26th minute. When a Schalke move broke down inside their half, Anderson fed the ball inside to Darron Gibson, whose wonderful, defence-splitting pass sent Valencia clear of Sergio Escudero to beat Neuer with a low finish.

Schalke goalkeeper Manuel Neuer climbs high to thwart Manchester United's Ryan Giggs

Schalke had put five goals past Inter at San Siro in the previous round but a repeat always appeared fanciful; United, after all, had never lost a European home tie by two goals. The visitors' plight worsened five minutes later when an error by Neuer brought United their second goal, the 'keeper reacting slowly to Gibson's powerful shot and the ball striking his arms before deflecting in off the post. Schalke's boisterous supporters did have a goal to celebrate in the 35th minute when Jurado swept a first-time shot past Edwin van der Sar after some uncertain United defending, but the home side came again in the second half, Anderson settling the outcome with two goals in rapid succession – and doubling his club tally in the process. His first came on 72 minutes when he drove in with his left after Valencia had set up the chance with a powerful surge down the right; his second was a simple tap-in after good approach play by Valencia and Dimitar Berbatov.

Manchester United midfielder Anderson (right) is congratulated after scoring the first of his two goals against Schalke at Old Trafford

Eventful encounter

The other semi-final was as fiercely contested as any Barcelona-Real Madrid CF tie, particularly as it marked a third and fourth meeting for the clubs in an 18-day period. Disappointingly, the first leg at the Santiago Bernabéu provided an undistinguished spectacle, featuring three red cards and five yellow as Madrid's hopes of recording a third European Cup semi-final success against their arch-rivals – following their wins in 1960 and 2002, both of which preceded a final victory – suffered a serious setback. The teams had drawn 1-1 in Madrid on 16 April, with José Mourinho's side then winning the Copa del Rey final four days later in Valencia, but Barça were to redress the balance when it mattered most.

Madrid, making a record 22nd semi-final appearance in the competition, were without the suspended Ricardo Carvalho, and they dropped back into pre-planned defensive mode from the off as they sought to absorb Barcelona pressure. With ten minutes on the clock, David Villa – who had ended an 11-game scoreless streak against CA Osasuna the previous weekend – came close to finding the net again after stealing in from the right to send a shot flying just past Iker Casillas's far post. Josep Guardiola's side fashioned another opening through the middle with half-time approaching, Lionel Messi escaping two markers before slipping a low pass through for Xavi, whose shot was parried by Casillas.

Messi magic

As the teams went off for the break, Barcelona's reserve goalkeeper José Pinto was sent off following an unsavoury melee involving a number of players and officials from both sides. Madrid started the second half more positively, but their momentum was checked in the 61st minute when Pepe was shown a red card for a high challenge on Dani Alves. An aggrieved Mourinho was subsequently sent to the stands for his protests and Barcelona quickly regained the upper hand, Villa bringing the best out of Casillas after cutting in from the left. A fractious, generally unpleasant encounter was then rescued by the genius of Messi, who silenced the Santiago Bernabéu with two memorable goals. His first owed much to Ibrahim Afellay, the substitute exploiting a Marcelo slip to advance into the penalty area and provide a cross that was steered in by the Barça No10 at the near post for his tenth goal of the European campaign. The Argentinian needed little help for his 11th three minutes from time, collecting a pass from Sergio Busquets just inside the Madrid half before racing past four defenders and slotting the ball across the exposed Casillas with his right foot. Unlike the match, it was a goal to treasure - an exceptional effort even by Messi's gloriously high standards.

With a 2-0 advantage, Barça were strong favourites to advance, particularly as Madrid – minus Mourinho, Pepe and Sergio Ramos for the trip to Camp Nou – had overturned a first-leg home defeat only once before in five UEFA competition ties. Barcelona, by contrast, had advanced on 30 of the 32 occasions in which they had won away first time round, and their prospects of doing so again were further enhanced 54 minutes into an evenly-matched encounter when Andrés Iniesta was afforded time and space to pick a perfectly-weighted pass through a sea of white shirts for Pedro to control and shoot beyond Casillas. Guardiola's side had already passed up a number of presentable openings, with Busquets, Villa and Messi all denied by the in-form Madrid goalkeeper, and although Ángel Di María set up Marcelo to equalise on the night after his shot had come back off the post, Barcelona held on in some comfort. To add to the crowd's jubilation, there was even time for an emotional late appearance from the bench by Éric Abidal just over a month after he had undergone an operation to have a tumour removed from his liver.

Semi-Final Results

26/4/11, Arena AufSchalke, Gelsenkirchen
FC Schalke 04 0-2 Manchester United FC
Attendance: 54142
Goal(s): 0-1 Giggs 67, 0-2 Rooney 69
Referee: Velasco Carballo (ESP)
4/5/11, Old Trafford, Manchester
Manchester United FC 4-1 FC Schalke 04
Attendance: 74687
Goal(s): 1-0 Valencia 26, 2-0 Gibson 31, 2-1 Jurado 35, 3-1 Anderson 72, 4-1 Anderson 76
Referee: Proença (POR)
Aggregate: 6-1; Manchester United FC qualify.

27/4/11, Estadio Santiago Bernabéu, Madrid
Real Madrid CF 0-2 FC Barcelona
Attendance: 71657
Goal(s): 0-1 Messi 76, 0-2 Messi 87
Referee: Stark (GER)
3/5/11, Camp Nou, Barcelona
FC Barcelona 1-1 Real Madrid CF
Attendance: 95701
Goal(s): 1-0 Pedro 54, 1-1 Marcelo 64
Referee: De Bleeckere (BEL)
Aggregate: 3-1; FC Barcelona qualify.

Lionel Messi gets in front of Sergio Ramos to give Barcelona the lead against Real Madrid at the Santiago Bernabéu

FINAL

Wembley Stadium in London provided the setting for a Catalan celebration as FC Barcelona turned on the style to beat Manchester United FC 3-1 and claim their fourth European crown.

The Catalan club were worthy winners, taking the lead midway through the first half thanks to a composed finish from Pedro. Although Wayne Rooney swiftly equalised with another well-worked goal, Barcelona responded with two superb second-half strikes from Lionel Messi and David Villa.

Dominant force

Barcelona's triumph against UC Sampdoria at the old Wembley in 1992 had secured the club's first European Champion Clubs' Cup following the disappointment of final defeats in 1961 and 1986, and this 2011 triumph cemented the Spanish champions' status as the continent's dominant force. A third UEFA Champions League in six seasons marked this Barcelona side out as one of the finest of their age, with two of those successes coming under Josep Guardiola – who had been a member of the Johan Cruyff-led 'Dream Team' that won the final European Champion Clubs' Cup in 1992.

For United, who had also tasted European Cup glory at Wembley, back in 1968, there would be no fourth victory in the world's most prestigious club competition. Instead Sir Alex Ferguson's team had to endure a repeat of their Rome defeat by Barcelona two years earlier.

Víctor Valdés foils Javier Hernández as Barcelona come under early pressure from United at Wembley

Manchester United goalkeeper Edwin van der Sar is beaten as Barcelona go 1-0 up through Pedro (not pictured)

Attacking formation

In the early stages of the contest it looked as if things might turn out differently for the English champions. Ferguson had selected an attacking formation, resisting the temptation to pack his midfield and instead fielding both Javier Hernández and Rooney in attack – although Dimitar Berbatov, United's top scorer in the Premier League with 20 goals, surprisingly did not even make the bench. United raced out of the starting blocks, pushing up and aiming to deny Barcelona the time and space in which to develop their celebrated pass-and-move possession game. For a while the ploy worked.

Barcelona looked edgy early on as first Hernández hustled a defender into losing the ball on the edge of his area, then former Liverpool FC midfielder Javier Mascherano, starting in central defence in place of injured captain Carles Puyol, failed to deal with Edwin van der Sar's long kick down the middle, forcing goalkeeper Víctor Valdés into emergency action as he raced off his line to punch the ball away to safety.

United pinned back

Before long, though, Barcelona clicked into gear, and it was they who fashioned the first clear opening, 15 minutes in, as Xavi drove in a low cross that Pedro, drifting free of Fábio, turned wide under pressure from Rio Ferdinand. Further opportunities ensued as Barcelona began to pin United back. David Villa flashed a shot narrowly wide from 20 metres out before forcing a low save from Van der Sar. Messi was then foiled twice in succession by superb challenges from Nemanja Vidić and Ferdinand, but in the 27th minute United's defence eventually cracked.

Xavi was the architect, advancing into United territory and picking out Pedro with a shrewd diagonal pass. The winger's movement had carried him clear of Vidić on the right side of the area and he applied a cool finish, wrong-footing Van der Sar with a neat side-foot shot into the near corner. It was only the fifth goal United had conceded in the competition all season.

Swift equaliser

The general pre-match consensus was that United would probably need to score first to have any hope of winning. Yet within seven minutes they were to draw level with a beautifully-fashioned goal of their own – which was also their first attempt on target. After Barcelona had surrendered possession following a throw-in, Rooney played a one-two with Michael Carrick, then slipped a pass to Ryan Giggs inside the area before meeting the Welshman's inviting return ball with an emphatic finish into the far corner.

Ferguson had predicted "the final of the decade", and a gripping first half almost produced another goal when Messi, who was dropping deep all the time in search of possession, scampered forward again. After feeding Villa on the right, the Argentinian was just a whisker away from meeting the return.

Messi strikes

United were somewhat fortunate and relieved to reach half-time on level terms, but there was no change to the general direction and flow of the play after the interval as Barça reasserted their control with a barrage of dangerous attacks. Van der Sar used his legs to save well from Dani Alves, who had crept unseen into the area on the right, but two

Wayne Rooney puts United on level terms with a sweet right-footed strike

David Villa seals Barça's 3-1 victory with a sumptuous curling shot from the edge of the penalty area

minutes later the Dutchman was beaten as Messi, afforded too much time and space just outside the area in a central position, drilled the ball low and true past him with his magic wand of a left foot. Messi's subsequent explosion of emotion showed just what the goal meant to him. It was his 53rd of the season and 12th in the UEFA Champions League campaign, yet his very first on English soil. More importantly, it had restored Barcelona's lead.

The little maestro began to take the game by the scruff of the neck, giving full rein to his prodigious and peerless talent. He could have scored twice more as Barcelona pressed hard for the third goal that would end United's resistance. Van der Sar denied him first with his legs before Fábio kept out his back-heeled effort with a goal-line block. It was all Barcelona, but United defended valiantly to keep their dream alive.

Exquisite finish

Forty-year-old Van der Sar, making the final appearance of his illustrious career, in his fifth UEFA Champions League final, offered a fitting reminder of his class with a full-length dive to foil Xavi, but he had no chance with Barcelona's third goal after 69 minutes. Although United halted Messi's dazzling surge into the danger zone from the right, the ball was cheaply surrendered to Sergio Busquets, who set up David Villa for an exquisite curling finish into the top corner from the edge of the penalty area.

There were still 18 minutes left to play, but despite the best efforts of Rooney, United's sole threat in attack, the Premier League champions could not concoct another chance of note, and Barcelona cruised through the closing stages without undue alarm. To raucous acclaim from the jubilant Barça fans, Guardiola was even able to send on skipper Puyol for the final few minutes so that he could share in the victory. The long-serving defender duly took the captain's armband from Xavi, but there was still a poignant moment to come at the victory presentation as both players deferred the honour of lifting the trophy to Éric Abidal, whose remarkable powers of recovery from cancer surgery earlier in the year had enabled him to complete the full 90 minutes.

Mesmerised

Barcelona celebrated joyously on the Wembley pitch. Their brilliant performance had illuminated one of the game's great theatres, and United's manager magnanimously led the chorus of approval for their outstanding display. "They mesmerise you with the passing, and we never really controlled Messi," Ferguson acknowledged. "When we got the lifeline from Wayne Rooney I expected us to do better in the second half but it wasn't to be. Great teams go in cycles and the cycle they're in at the moment is the best in Europe, there's no question about that. In my time as a manager, this is the best team we've faced – no one's given us a hiding like that. It's a great moment for them and they deserve it because they play the right way."

Meanwhile, Guardiola – who had become only the sixth man to win the European Cup as a coach and player in 2009 – was characteristically modest after getting his hands on the trophy for the third time. "I feel privileged to have these players. At the end of that [2009] final I said we'd played a good game, but when I looked at it again I wasn't that impressed. It's served its purpose because we played much better and created more chances than two years ago. The way we won is what I'm most proud of. This is how I want to play football."

Final Result

28/5/11, Wembley Stadium, London
FC Barcelona 3-1 Manchester United FC
Attendance: 87695
Barcelona: Víctor Valdés, Dani Alves (Puyol 88), Piqué, Xavi, David Villa (Keita 86), Iniesta, Messi, Mascherano, Busquets, Pedro (Afellay 90+2), Abidal. Coach: Josep Guardiola (ESP)
Man. United: Van der Sar, Evra, Ferdinand, Rooney, Giggs, Park, Hernández, Vidić, Carrick (Scholes 77), Fábio (Nani 69), Valencia. Coach: Sir Alex Ferguson (SCO)
Goal(s): 1-0 Pedro 27, 1-1 Rooney 34, 2-1 Messi 54, 3-1 David Villa 69
Yellow Card(s): Dani Alves 60 (Barcelona), Carrick 61 (Man. United), Valencia 79 (Man. United), Víctor Valdés 85 (Barcelona)
Referee: Kassai (HUN)

TOP GOALSCORERS

12	Lionel Messi (Barcelona)
8	Mario Gomez (Bayern)
	Samuel Eto'o (Internazionale)
7	Nicolas Anelka (Chelsea)
6	Karim Benzema (Real Madrid)
	Roberto Soldado (Valencia)
	Cristiano Ronaldo (Real Madrid)
5	Pedro (Barcelona)
	Raúl (Schalke)

Jubilant Barcelona players celebrate their UEFA Champions League success at Wembley

UEFA Europa LEAGUE 2010/11

Even by the standards set in the inaugural season of the UEFA Europa League, the 2010/11 edition yielded a catalogue of thrills, spills and very few nil-nils. Holders Club Atlético de Madrid, three-time UEFA Cup winners Juventus and a Borussia Dortmund side that would win the Bundesliga at a canter could not even negotiate the group stage. FC Porto, meanwhile, made serene progress, arriving at the final as unbeaten Portuguese champions on the back of a record-breaking 10-3 aggregate quarter-final victory over FC Spartak Moskva and a memorable semi-final triumph over Villarreal CF. Giant-killing neighbours SC Braga awaited them in Dublin, hoping that their defensive obduracy could claim another victim to add to a list that included Liverpool FC, FC Dynamo Kyiv and, in the semi-finals, Portuguese rivals SL Benfica. They would have no answer to Porto, however, nor to the prolific Radamel Falcao, the Colombian striker's record-extending 17th goal of the competition, headed home just before half-time, proving sufficient to seal the trophy for the Dragões and their highly talented young coach André Villas-Boas.

QUALIFYING PHASE

First Qualifying Round

Just 50 days after Club Atlético de Madrid won the inaugural UEFA Europa League in Hamburg, FC Flora Tallinn were celebrating after scoring the opening goal of the 2010/11 edition almost 3,000km away in Tbilisi.

Alo Dupikov was the man on target for the Estonian side, who nevertheless fell at the first hurdle after defeat by 1980/81 UEFA Cup Winners' Cup winners FC Dinamo Tbilisi. Anorthosis Famagusta FC, UEFA Champions League group stage contenders in 2008/09, were among the other notable names to progress thanks to a 4-0 aggregate triumph over FC Banants of Armenia.

Rabotnicki rout

The Former Yugoslav Republic of Macedonia's FK Rabotnicki racked up the round's biggest aggregate success, defeating FC Lusitans 11-0 with the help of Fábio's 21-minute second-leg hat-trick. Vladimir Yurchenko narrowly beat the Brazilian to the honour of scoring the first treble of the European season as FC Dnepr Mogilev followed up a 1-1 first-leg draw against Albania's KF Laçi with a 7-1 home win.

From Reykjavik to Ta' Qali and Belfast to Lankaran, 26 sides in all booked their second qualifying round berths. It was in Azerbaijan where the competition's first away-goals triumph occurred, Moldova's FC Olimpia Balti edging past Xäzär Länkäran FK.

First Qualifying Round Results

1/7/10, Niko Dovana, Durres
KF Laçi 1-1 FC Dnepr Mogilev
Goal(s): 1-0 Marashi 45+1, 1-1 Turlin 90+2
Referee: Pristovnik (CRO)
8/7/10, Spartak Stadion, Mogilev
FC Dnepr Mogilev 7-1 KF Laçi
Goal(s): 1-0 Bychenok 10, 2-0 Yurchenko 17(p), 3-0 Zenkovich 42, 4-0 Yurchenko 56, 4-1 Nimani 61, 5-1 Bychenok 80, 6-1 Yurchenko 81, 7-1 Chernykh 87
Referee: Minasyan (ARM)
Aggregate: 8-2; FC Dnepr Mogilev qualify.

1/7/10, National Arena Filip II, Skopje
FK Rabotnicki 5-0 FC Lusitans
Goal(s): 1-0 Zé Carlos 24, 2-0 Wandeir 35, 3-0 Fábio 55, 4-0 Fábio 57, 5-0 Muarem 60
Referee: Avram (ROU)
8/7/10, Estadi Comunal, Andorra la Vella
FC Lusitans 0-6 FK Rabotnicki
Goal(s): 0-1 Wandeir 25, 0-2 Fábio 33, 0-3 Fábio 42, 0-4 Fábio 54, 0-5 Wandeir 68, 0-6 Gligorov 71
Referee: Pisani (MLT)
Aggregate: 0-11; FK Rabotnicki qualify.

1/7/10, Stadiumi Kombëtar Qemal Stafa, Tirana
KF Tirana 0-0 Zalaegerszegi TE
Referee: Crangle (NIR)
8/7/10, ZTE, Zalaegerszeg
Zalaegerszegi TE 0-1 KF Tirana (aet)
Goal(s): 0-1 Karabeci 107
Referee: Spathas (GRE)
Aggregate: 0-1; KF Tirana qualify after extra time.

1/7/10, Gradski, Niksic
FK Zeta 1-1 FC Dacia Chisinau
Goal(s): 0-1 Orbu 39, 1-1 Peličić 77(p)
Referee: Aliyev (AZE)
8/7/10, Zimbru, Chisinau
FC Dacia Chisinau 0-0 FK Zeta
Referee: Kostadinov (BUL)
Aggregate: 1-1; FC Dacia Chisinau qualify on away goal.

1/7/10, Lilleküla Arena, Tallinn
JK Trans Narva 0-2 Myllykosken Pallo-47
Goal(s): 0-1 Votinov 47, 0-2 Gorškov 53(og)
Referee: Dabanović (MNE)

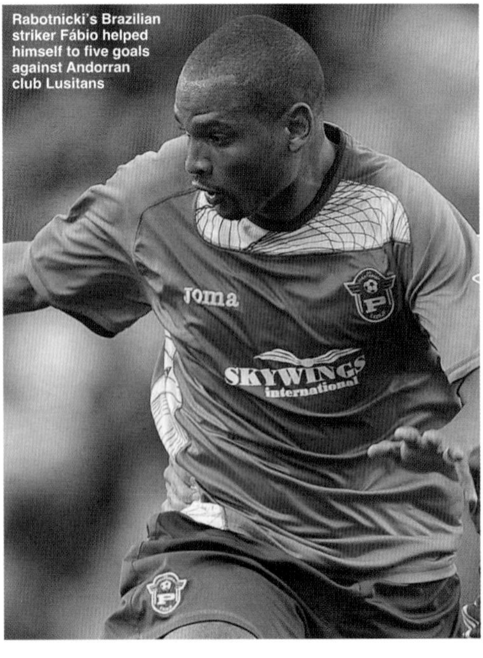

Rabotnicki's Brazilian striker Fábio helped himself to five goals against Andorran club Lusitans

8/7/10, Saviniemi Football Stadium, Myllykoski
Myllykosken Pallo-47 5-0 JK Trans Narva
Goal(s): 1-0 Ricketts 62, 2-0 Äijälä 67, 3-0 Äijälä 75, 4-0 Koljonen 77, 5-0 Felipe Benevides 80
Referee: Karasev (RUS)
Aggregate: 7-0; Myllykosken Pallo-47 qualify.

1/7/10, Boris Paichadze National Stadium, Tbilisi
FC Dinamo Tbilisi 2-1 FC Flora Tallinn
Goal(s): 0-1 Dupikov 9, 1-1 Kakhelishvili 22, 2-1 Khmaladze 64(p)
Referee: Hacmon (ISR)
8/7/10, Lilleküla Arena, Tallinn
FC Flora Tallinn 0-0 FC Dinamo Tbilisi
Referee: Moseychuk (UKR)
Aggregate: 1-2; FC Dinamo Tbilisi qualify.

1/7/10, FC Nitra, Nitra
FC Nitra 2-2 Győri ETO FC
Goal(s): 1-0 Tóth 14, 1-1 Kink 39, 1-2 Kink 58, 2-2 Sloboda 80
Referee: Stamatis (CYP)
8/7/10, ETO Park, Gyor
Győri ETO FC 3-1 FC Nitra
Goal(s): 0-1 Hodúr 10, 1-1 Aleksidze 22, 2-1 Nicorec 60, 3-1 Kink 90+2
Referee: Jug (SVN)
Aggregate: 5-3; Győri ETO FC qualify.

1/7/10, SC Hrvatskih vitezova, Dugopolje
HNK Šibenik 0-0 Sliema Wanderers FC
Referee: Strömbergsson (SWE)
8/7/10, Centenary, Ta' Qali
Sliema Wanderers FC 0-3 HNK Šibenik
Goal(s): 0-1 Medvid 64, 0-2 Jakoliš 73, 0-3 Bulat 89
Referee: Black (NIR)
Aggregate: 0-3; HNK Šibenik qualify.

1/7/10, Torpedo, Zhodino
FC Torpedo Zhodino 3-0 Fylkir
Goal(s): 1-0 Kryvobok 52, 2-0 Ogar 59, 3-0 Kontsevoi 66
Referee: Valašek (SVK)
8/7/10, Laugardalsvöllur, Reykjavik
Fylkir 1-3 FC Torpedo Zhodino
Goal(s): 1-0 Faye 32(p), 1-1 Ostroukh 41, 1-2 Kryvobok 86(p), 1-3 Kryvobok 88
Referee: Vinčič (SVN)
Aggregate: 1-6; FC Torpedo Zhodino qualify.

1/7/10, Shamrock Park, Portadown
Portadown FC 1-1 Skonto FC
Goal(s): 1-0 Lecky 38, 1-1 Laizāns 90+3
Referee: Vuckov (CRO)
8/7/10, Skonto Stadions, Riga
Skonto FC 0-1 Portadown FC
Goal(s): 0-1 Lecky 29
Referee: Vnuk (SVK)
Aggregate: 1-2; Portadown FC qualify.

1/7/10, Camp d'Esports del M.I. Consell General, Andorra la Vella
UE Santa Coloma 0-3 FK Mogren
Goal(s): 0-1 Grbić 14, 0-2 Ćulafić 83, 0-3 Ćetković 90+2
Referee: Anastasiou (CYP)
8/7/10, Gradski, Niksic
FK Mogren 2-0 UE Santa Coloma
Goal(s): 1-0 Ćulafić 18, 2-0 Gluščević 20
Referee: Kharitonashvili (GEO)
Aggregate: 5-0; FK Mogren qualify.

1/7/10, Zimbru, Chisinau
FC Olimpia Balti 0-0 Xäzär Länkäran FK
Referee: Direktorenko (LVA)

8/7/10, City Stadium, Lankaran
Xäzär Länkäran FK 1-1 FC Olimpia Balti
Goal(s): 0-1 Robens 14, 1-1 Lalín 78
Referee: Sevostyanik (BLR)
Aggregate: 1-1; FC Olimpia Balti qualify on away goal.

1/7/10, Hrazdan Central Stadium, Yerevan
Ulisses FC 0-0 Bnei Yehuda Tel-Aviv FC
Referee: Jemini (ALB)
8/7/10, Bloomfield Stadium, Tel-Aviv
Bnei Yehuda Tel-Aviv FC 1-0 Ulisses FC
Goal(s): 1-0 Menashe 45+1
Referee: Studer (SUI)
Aggregate: 1-0; Bnei Yehuda Tel-Aviv FC qualify.

1/7/10, Gundadalur, Torshavn
NSÍ Runavík 0-2 Gefle IF
Goal(s): 0-1 Gerndt 34, 0-2 Gerndt 60
Referee: Dunauskas (LTU)
8/7/10, Råsundastadion, Solna
Gefle IF 2-1 NSÍ Runavík
Goal(s): 1-0 Bernhardsson 22, 2-0 Berggren 63, 2-1 Potemkin 90+4
Referee: Nieminen (FIN)
Aggregate: 4-1; Gefle IF qualify.

1/7/10, Randers Stadium, Randers
Randers FC 6-1 F91 Dudelange
Goal(s): 1-0 Sane 16, 2-0 Movsisyan 17, 3-0 Olsen 33, 4-0 S. Pedersen 47(p), 4-1 Benzouien 49(p), 5-1 Brock-Madsen 88, 6-1 Movsisyan 90
Referee: Radovanović (MNE)
8/7/10, Jos Nosbaum, Dudelange
F91 Dudelange 2-1 Randers FC
Goal(s): 0-1 Lorentzen 17, 1-1 Caillet 37, 2-1 Gruszczyński 67
Referee: Hjaltalin (ISL)
Aggregate: 3-7; Randers FC qualify

1/7/10, Turku Stadium, Turku
TPS Turku 3-1 Port Talbot Town FC
Goal(s): 1-0 Ri. Riski 24, 2-0 Wusu 30, 3-0 Ri. Riski 35, 3-1 Rose 70
Referee: Szulc (POL)
8/7/10, GenQuip Stadium, Port Talbot
Port Talbot Town FC 0-4 TPS Turku
Goal(s): 0-1 Wusu 26, 0-2 Kolehmainen 32, 0-3 Ri. Riski 69, 0-4 Ro. Riski 90+1
Referee: Reinert (FRO)
Aggregate: 1-7; TPS Turku qualify.

1/7/10, Stebonheath Park, Llanelli
Llanelli AFC 2-2 FK Tauras
Goal(s): 0-1 Kižys 11, 1-1 D. Thomas 19, 1-2 Kižys 22, 2-2 S. Jones 47
Referee: Wouters (BEL)
8/7/10, Dariaus ir Girėno stadionas, Kaunas
FK Tauras 3-2 Llanelli AFC (aet)
Goal(s): 1-0 Irkha 17, 1-1 Llewellyn 19, 2-1 Irkha 31, 2-2 Bowen 36, 3-2 Regelskis 104
Referee: Spirkoski (MKD)
Aggregate: 5-4; FK Tauras qualify after extra time.

1/7/10, KR-völlur, Reykjavik
KR Reykjavík 3-0 Glentoran FC
Goal(s): 1-0 Gunnarsson 12, 2-0 Finnbogason 32, 3-0 Takefusa 63
Referee: Tsinkevich (BLR)
8/7/10, The Oval, Belfast
Glentoran FC 2-2 KR Reykjavík
Goal(s): 1-0 Callacher 22, 1-1 Finnbogason 45+1, 1-2 Black 54(og), 2-2 Hamilton 56(p)
Referee: Panayi (CYP)
Aggregate: 2-5; KR Reykjavík qualify.

1/7/10, Josy Barthel, Luxembourg
CS Grevenmacher 3-3 Dundalk FC
Goal(s): 0-1 Kuduzović 26, 0-2 Hatswell 51, 1-2 Heinz 63, 2-2 Gaspar 73, 3-2 Almeida 76, 3-3 Benichou 80(og)
Referee: Alecković (BIH)
8/7/10, Oriel Park, Dundalk
Dundalk FC 2-1 CS Grevenmacher
Goal(s): 1-0 Fenn 5(p), 2-0 Kuduzović 16, 2-1 Müller 90+1
Referee: Thórisson (ISL)
Aggregate: 5-4; Dundalk FC qualify.

1/7/10, Antonis Papadopoulos, Larnaca
Anorthosis Famagusta FC 3-0 FC Banants
Goal(s): 1-0 Katsavakis 24, 2-0 Okkas 31, 3-0 Cafú 64
Referee: McLean (SCO)
8/7/10, Yerevan Republican Stadium, Yerevan
FC Banants 0-1 Anorthosis Famagusta FC
Goal(s): 0-1 Laban 37
Referee: Virant (BEL)
Aggregate: 0-4; Anorthosis Famagusta FC qualify.

1/7/10, Tcentralny, Kostanay
FC Tobol Kostanay 1-2 HŠK Zrinjski
Goal(s): 1-0 Zhumaskaliyev 16, 1-1 Dragičević 52, 1-2 Dragičević 82
Referee: Piasecki (POL)
8/7/10, Gradski, Mostar
HŠK Zrinjski 2-1 FC Tobol Kostanay
Goal(s): 1-0 D. Džidić 10, 1-1 Zhumaskaliyev 57, 2-1 Pehar 72
Referee: Tritsonis (GRE)
Aggregate: 4-2; HŠK Zrinjski qualify.

1/7/10, David Abashidze, Zestafoni
FC Zestafoni 5-0 SC Faetano
Goal(s): 1-0 Gelashvili 21(p), 2-0 Dvali 22, 3-0 Gelashvili 23, 4-0 Dvali 64, 5-0 Gorgiashvili 90
Referee: Glođović (SRB)
8/7/10, Stadio Olimpico, Serravalle
SC Faetano 0-0 FC Zestafoni
Referee: Villamayor Rozados (AND)
Aggregate: 0-5; FC Zestafoni qualify.

1/7/10, Športni Park, Domzale
NK Olimpija Ljubljana 0-2 NK Široki Brijeg
Goal(s): 0-1 Wagner 45+1, 0-2 Cvijanovič 68(og)
Referee: Thual (FRA)
8/7/10, Pecara, Siroki Brijeg
NK Široki Brijeg 3-0 NK Olimpija Ljubljana
Goal(s): 1-0 Roskam 81, 2-0 Weitzer 83, 3-0 Mišić 90+3
Referee: Bezborodov (RUS)
Aggregate: 5-0; NK Široki Brijeg qualify.

1/7/10, Fredriksskans Idrottsplats, Kalmar
Kalmar FF 1-0 EB/Streymur
Goal(s): 1-0 Ricardo Santos 79
Referee: Podeschi (SMR)
8/7/10, Toftir, Toftir
EB/Streymur 0-3 Kalmar FF
Goal(s): 0-1 Israelsson 9, 0-2 Eriksson 46, 0-3 Ricardo Santos 50
Referee: Johnsen (NOR)
Aggregate: 0-4; Kalmar FF qualify.

1/7/10, Shakhter, Karagandy
FC Shakhter Karagandy 1-2 Ruch Chorzów
Goal(s): 1-0 Džidić 7, 1-1 Janoszka 45+1, 1-2 Grzyb 47(p)
Referee: Grobelnik (AUT)
8/7/10, Ruch, Chorzow
Ruch Chorzów 1-0 FC Shakhter Karagandy
Goal(s): 1-0 Sobiech 59
Referee: Mazeika (LTU)
Aggregate: 3-1; Ruch Chorzów qualify.

1/7/10, Tofiq Bähramov-Republic stadium, Baku
Qarabağ FK 4-1 FK Metalurg Skopje
Goal(s): 1-0 R.F. Sadiqov 26(p), 2-0 İsmayilov 45, 3-0 İmamaliyev 85, 4-0 Adamia 90+2, 4-1 Simonovski 90+4
Referee: Kovács (ROU)
8/7/10, National Arena Filip II, Skopje
FK Metalurg Skopje 1-1 Qarabağ FK
Goal(s): 0-1 İmamaliyev 69, 1-1 Krstev 78
Referee: Shandor (UKR)
Aggregate: 2-5; Qarabağ FK qualify.

Second Qualifying Round

From the more heralded names of Beşiktaş JK and Olympiacos FC to the lesser lights of Shamrock Rovers FC and OFK Beograd, the busiest nights on the UEFA club competition calendar threw up routine and romance aplenty.

With 40 games on each matchday, the two legs of the second qualifying round were always guaranteed to produce intrigue. They duly delivered too, though Beşiktaş and Olympiacos ensured at least part of the script followed familiar lines. Under the charge of new coaches Bernd Schuster and Ewald Lienen, respectively, the two clubs progressed via comfortable victories against Víkingur and KS Besa. The Athens giants' 11-1 aggregate success was the joint highest victory margin of the round, matched only by Mostar club HŠK Zrinjski's 13-3 triumph against SP Tre Penne of San Marino.

Paweł Brożek – one of Wisła Kraków's two goalscoring twins against Šiauliai

Heady rewards

It was not plain sailing for everyone, however, as Shamrock Rovers squeezed past Bnei Yehuda Tel-Aviv FC 2-1 and OFK edged FC Torpedo Zhodino 3-2. Their rewards were nonetheless bountiful, with Shamrock drawn against Juventus in the third qualifying round and OFK handed a meeting with Galatasaray AŞ. "It's something wonderful for our fans and players to play against them," said Shamrock manager Michael O'Neill.

FK Rabotnicki earned an equally lucrative tie after seeing off FC Mika to book a date with five-time European Cup winners Liverpool FC. Meanwhile, continental debutants FK Teteks made it a night to remember for the Former Yugoslav Republic of Macedonia, beating 2009/10 group stage entrants from Latvia, FK Ventspils, 3-1 on aggregate.

Anorthosis Famagusta FC recovered from a 2-0 first-leg deficit to conquer HNK Šibenik of Croatia. As for Wisła Kraków, they provided another notable plotline, defeating FC Šiauliai 7-0 overall with the help of a goal apiece in each leg from twin brothers Piotr and Paweł Brożek.

Second Qualifying Round Results

15/7/10, National Arena Filip II, Skopje
FK Rabotnicki 1-0 FC Mika
Goal(s): 1-0 Wandeir 87
Referee: Bognar (HUN)
22/7/10, MIKA Sport Complex, Yerevan
FC Mika 0-0 FK Rabotnicki
Referee: Příhoda (CZE)
Aggregate: 0-1; FK Rabotnicki qualify.

15/7/10, Centenary, Ta' Qali
Valletta FC 1-1 Ruch Chorzów
Goal(s): 0-1 Grzyb 18(p), 1-1 Scerri 75
Referee: Masiah (ISR)
22/7/10, Ruch, Chorzow
Ruch Chorzów 0-0 Valletta FC
Referee: De Marco (ITA)
Aggregate: 1-1; Ruch Chorzów qualify on away goal.

15/7/10, Omladinski, Belgrade
OFK Beograd 2-2 FC Torpedo Zhodino
Goal(s): 0-1 Kryvobok 14, 1-1 Žeravica 45+1, 1-2 Brusnikin 90+2, 2-2 Injac 90+4
Referee: Rubinos Pérez (ESP)
22/7/10, Gorodskoy Stadion, Borisov
FC Torpedo Zhodino 0-1 OFK Beograd
Goal(s): 0-1 Kecojević 67
Referee: Kari (FIN)
Aggregate: 2-3; OFK Beograd qualify.

15/7/10, Športni Park, Nova Gorica
ND Gorica 0-3 Randers FC
Goal(s): 0-1 Lorentzen 51, 0-2 Cramer 55, 0-3 Cramer 71
Referee: Özkahya (TUR)
22/7/10, Randers Stadium, Randers
Randers FC 1-1 ND Gorica
Goal(s): 1-0 Cramer 42, 1-1 Žigon 79
Referee: Muir (SCO)
Aggregate: 4-1; Randers FC qualify.

15/7/10, Borås Arena, Boras
IF Elfsborg 2-1 FC Iskra-Stal
Goal(s): 1-0 Keene 56, 2-0 Ericsson 79(p), 2-1 Tofan 87
Referee: Laperriere (SUI)
22/7/10, Stadionul Sheriff, Tiraspol
FC Iskra-Stal 0-1 IF Elfsborg
Goal(s): 0-1 Ishizaki 60
Referee: Göçek (TUR)
Aggregate: 1-3; IF Elfsborg qualify.

15/7/10, Franz Horr Stadion, Vienna
FK Austria Wien 2-2 NK Široki Brijeg
Goal(s): 0-1 Wagner 26, 1-1 Linz 50, 1-2 Topić 54, 2-2 Schumacher 57
Referee: Kuchin (KAZ)
22/7/10, Pecara, Siroki Brijeg
NK Široki Brijeg 0-1 FK Austria Wien
Goal(s): 0-1 Junuzovic 80
Referee: Muniz Fernández (ESP)
Aggregate: 2-3; FK Austria Wien qualify.

15/7/10, Dariaus ir Girėno stadionas, Kaunas
FK Tauras 0-3 APOEL FC
Goal(s): 0-1 Charalambides 50, 0-2 Hélio Pinto 80, 0-3 Manduca 83
Referee: Svendsen (DEN)
22/7/10, GSP Stadium, Nicosia
APOEL FC 3-1 FK Tauras
Goal(s): 1-0 Solari 18, 1-1 Irkha 48, 2-1 Trickovski 80, 3-1 Solari 86(p)
Referee: Gvardis (RUS)
Aggregate: 6-1; APOEL FC qualify.

15/7/10, Boris Paichadze National Stadium, Tbilisi
FC WIT Georgia 0-6 FC Baník Ostrava
Goal(s): 0-1 Fernando Neves 33, 0-2 Fernando Neves 56(p), 0-3 Pilík 61, 0-4 Fernando Neves 64(p), 0-5 Neuwirth 70, 0-6 Hušbauer 78
Referee: Rafati (GER)
22/7/10, Bazaly, Ostrava
FC Baník Ostrava 0-0 FC WIT Georgia
Referee: Jovanetić (SRB)
Aggregate: 6-0; FC Baník Ostrava qualify.

15/7/10, Ventspils Olimpiskais Centrs, Ventspils
FK Ventspils 0-0 FK Teteks
Referee: Malcolm (NIR)
22/7/10, National Arena Filip II Macedonian, Skopje
FK Teteks 3-1 FK Ventspils
Goal(s): 1-0 Postnikov 15(og), 2-0 Ristevski 34, 3-0 Gligorovski 54, 3-1 V. Bespalovs 80
Referee: Lechner (AUT)
Aggregate: 3-1; FK Teteks qualify.

15/7/10, Zimbru, Chisinau
FC Olimpia Balti 0-2 FC Dinamo Bucureşti
Goal(s): 0-1 Pulhac 41, 0-2 Ganea 83
Referee: Koukoulakis (GRE)
22/7/10, Dinamo, Bucharest
FC Dinamo Bucureşti 5-1 FC Olimpia Balti
Goal(s): 1-0 An. Cristea 3, 2-0 Ad. Cristea 32, 3-0 N'Doye 45, 4-0 Munteanu 59, 5-0 Torje 63(p), 5-1 Adaramola 90
Referee: Damato (ITA)
Aggregate: 7-1; FC Dinamo Bucureşti qualify.

15/7/10, Saviniemi Football Stadium, Myllykoski
Myllykosken Pallo-47 3-0 UE Sant Julià
Goal(s): 1-0 Ricketts 43, 2-0 Äijälä 56, 3-0 Äijälä 65(p)
Referee: Toussaint (LUX)
23/7/10, Estadi Comunal, Andorra la Vella
UE Sant Julià 0-5 Myllykosken Pallo-47
Goal(s): 0-1 Votinov 6, 0-2 Votinov 13, 0-3 Kurittu 49, 0-4 Okkonen 61, 0-5 Votinov 64
Referee: Whitby (WAL)
Aggregate: 5-1; Myllykosken Pallo-47 qualify.

15/7/10, Telenor Arena, Oslo
Stabæk Fotball 2-2 FC Dnepr Mogilev
Goal(s): 0-1 Turlin 14, 1-1 Skjelvik 22, 1-2 Kozlov 23, 2-2 Gunnarsson 53
Referee: Sipailo (LVA)
22/7/10, Spartak Stadion, Mogilev
FC Dnepr Mogilev 1-1 Stabæk Fotball
Goal(s): 0-1 Gunnarsson 37, 1-1 Yurchenko 85
Referee: Trutz (SVK)
Aggregate: 3-3; FC Dnepr Mogilev qualify on away goals.

15/7/10, Molde Stadion, Molde
Molde FK 1-0 FK Jelgava
Goal(s): 1-0 Fall 90+1
Referee: Munukka (FIN)
22/7/10, Sloka, Jurmala
FK Jelgava 2-1 Molde FK
Goal(s): 0-1 Fall 14, 1-1 Bormakovs 30, 2-1 Bogdaškins 45+1
Referee: Vejlgaard (DEN)
Aggregate: 2-2; Molde FK qualify on away goal.

15/7/10, ISS, Vantaa
FC Honka Espoo 1-1 Bangor City FC
Goal(s): 1-0 Savage 43, 1-1 C. Jones 58
Referee: Meckarovski (MKD)
22/7/10, The Racecourse Ground, Wrexham
Bangor City FC 2-1 FC Honka Espoo
Goal(s): 0-1 Koskinen 21, 1-1 Morley 85, 2-1 C. Jones 90+1
Referee: Amirkhanyan (ARM)
Aggregate: 3-2; Bangor City FC qualify.

15/7/10, Munaishi, Atyrau
FC Atyrau 0-3 Győri ETO FC (w/o) (original result 0-2)
Goal(s): 0-1 Pilibaitis 26, 0-2 Bouguerra 88
Referee: Verbist (BEL)
22/7/10, ETO Park, Gyor
Győri ETO FC 2-0 FC Atyrau
Goal(s): 1-0 Aleksidze 47, 2-0 Nicorec 52
Referee: Jareci (ALB)
Aggregate: 5-0; Győri ETO FC qualify.

15/7/10, Dinamo Stadion, Minsk
FC Dinamo Minsk 5-1 JK Sillamäe Kalev
Goal(s): 1-0 Sazankov 12, 2-0 Sazankov 33, 3-0 Putilo 60, 3-1 Kolyaev 79, 4-1 Rekish 87, 5-1 Chukhlei 90+2
Referee: Pamporidis (GRE)
22/7/10, Lilleküla Arena, Tallinn
JK Sillamäe Kalev 0-5 FC Dinamo Minsk
Goal(s): 0-1 Dragun 2, 0-2 Sazankov 17, 0-3 Chukhlei 19, 0-4 Rekish 46, 0-5 Chukhlei 65
Referee: Hategan (ROU)
Aggregate: 1-10; FC Dinamo Minsk qualify.

15/7/10, Råsundastadion, Solna
Gefle IF 1-2 FC Dinamo Tbilisi
Goal(s): 0-1 Vatsadze 11, 1-1 Berggren 51(p), 1-2 Khmaladze 87(p)
Referee: Batinić (CRO)
22/7/10, Boris Paichadze National Stadium, Tbilisi
FC Dinamo Tbilisi 2-1 Gefle IF
Goal(s): 1-0 Vatsadze 68, 2-0 Pirtskhalava 82, 2-1 Orlov 90+1
Referee: Yordanov (BUL)
Aggregate: 4-2; FC Dinamo Tbilisi qualify.

15/7/10, KR-völlur, Reykjavik
KR Reykjavík 0-3 FC Karpaty Lviv
Goal(s): 0-1 Guruli 46, 0-2 Tkachuk 51, 0-3 Batista 57
Referee: Lerjeus (SWE)
22/7/10, Ukrayina Stadion, Lviv
FC Karpaty Lviv 3-2 KR Reykjavík
Goal(s): 1-0 Zenjov 2, 2-0 Fedetskiy 25, 2-1 Finnbogason 61, 2-2 Finnbogason 65, 3-2 B. Baranets 69
Referee: Fabian (HUN)
Aggregate: 6-2; FC Karpaty Lviv qualify.

15/7/10, Olympique de la Pontaise, Lausanne
FC Lausanne-Sport 1-0 FK Borac Banja Luka
Goal(s): 1-0 Sílvio 19
Referee: Pettay (RUS)
22/7/10, Gradski Stadium Banja Luka, Banja Luka
FK Borac Banja Luka 1-1 FC Lausanne-Sport
Goal(s): 0-1 Roux 65, 1-1 Vukelja 69
Referee: Artur Soares Dias (POR)
Aggregate: 1-2; FC Lausanne-Sport qualify.

15/7/10, Fredriksskans Idrottsplats, Kalmar
Kalmar FF 0-0 FC Dacia Chisinau
Referee: Jilek (CZE)
22/7/10, Zimbru, Chisinau
FC Dacia Chisinau 0-2 Kalmar FF
Goal(s): 0-1 Israelsson 11, 0-2 Daniel Sobralense 88
Referee: Gil (POL)
Aggregate: 0-2; Kalmar FF qualify.

15/7/10, Josy Barthel, Luxembourg
FC Differdange 03 3-3 FK Spartak Zlatibor voda
Goal(s): 1-0 Veselinov 6(og), 2-0 Bettmer 11, 2-1 Ubiparip 14, 2-2 Torbica 28(p), 3-2 Piskor 73, 3-3 Siebenaler 89(og)
Referee: Rossi (SMR)
22/7/10, Vojvodina, Novi Sad
FK Spartak Zlatibor voda 2-0 FC Differdange 03
Goal(s): 1-0 Ubiparip 25, 2-0 Adamović 88
Referee: Richards (WAL)
Aggregate: 5-3; FK Spartak Zlatibor voda qualify.

15/7/10, Jules Ottenstadion, Gent
Cercle Brugge KSV 0-1 TPS Turku
Goal(s): 0-1 Ääritalo 32
Referee: Hermansen (DEN)
22/7/10, Turku Stadium, Turku
TPS Turku 1-2 Cercle Brugge KSV
Goal(s): 1-0 Johansson 39(p), 1-1 Reynaldo 51, 1-2 Van Eenoo 86
Referee: Grobelnik (AUT)
Aggregate: 2-2; Cercle Brugge KSV qualify on away goals.

15/7/10, Fir Park, Motherwell
Motherwell FC 1-0 Breidablik
Goal(s): 1-0 Forbes 63
Referee: Liesveld (NED)
22/7/10, Kópavogsvöllur, Kopavogur
Breidablik 0-1 Motherwell FC
Goal(s): 0-1 Murphy 42
Referee: Xistra (POR)
Aggregate: 0-2; Motherwell FC qualify.

15/7/10, Estádio da Madeira, Funchal
CS Marítimo 3-2 Sporting Fingal FC
Goal(s): 0-1 Crowe 33, 1-1 Ricardo Esteves 78, 2-1 Cherrad 85, 2-2 Fitzgerald 87, 3-2 Tchô 90+5
Referee: Wilmes (LUX)
22/7/10, Dalymount Park, Dublin
Sporting Fingal FC 2-3 CS Marítimo
Goal(s): 0-1 Alonso 20(p), 0-2 Marquinho 67, 1-2 Zayed 81, 1-3 Kanu 87, 2-3 Zayed 90
Referee: Borg (MLT)
Aggregate: 4-6; CS Marítimo qualify.

Dudu Cearense scored three times in Olympiacos's 11-1 aggregate win over Albanian side Besa

15/7/10, Windsor Park, Belfast
Cliftonville FC 1-0 HNK Cibalia
Goal(s): 1-0 Caldwell 82
Referee: Todorov (BUL)
22/7/10, Cibalia Vinkovci, Vinkovci
HNK Cibalia 0-0 Cliftonville FC
Referee: Turpin (FRA)
Aggregate: 0-1; Cliftonville FC qualify.

15/7/10, Shamrock Park, Portadown
Portadown FC 1-2 Qarabağ FK
Goal(s): 1-0 Lecky 29, 1-1 İsmayilov 67, 1-2 İsmayilov 86
Referee: Drachta (AUT)
22/7/10, Tofiq Bähramov-Republic stadium, Baku
Qarabağ FK 1-1 Portadown FC
Goal(s): 0-1 Braniff 71, 1-1 İsmayilov 83
Referee: Pristovnik (CRO)
Aggregate: 3-2; Qarabağ FK qualify.

15/7/10, Antonis Papadopoulos, Larnaca
Anorthosis Famagusta FC 0-2 HNK Šibenik
Goal(s): 0-1 Bloudek 10, 0-2 Bačelić-Grgić 61(p)
Referee: Marriner (ENG)
22/7/10, Stadion Poljud, Split
HNK Šibenik 0-3 Anorthosis Famagusta FC (aet)
Goal(s): 0-1 Laban 16, 0-2 Cristovão 25, 0-3 Okkas 96
Referee: Van Boekel (NED)
Aggregate: 2-3; Anorthosis Famagusta FC qualify after extra time.

15/7/10, Galgenwaard, Utrecht
FC Utrecht 4-0 KF Tirana
Goal(s): 1-0 Van Wolfswinkel 8, 2-0 Pashaj 27(og), 3-0 Asare 30, 4-0 Mertens 75
Referee: Trifonos (CYP)
22/7/10, Stadiumi Kombëtar Qemal Stafa, Tirana
KF Tirana 1-1 FC Utrecht
Goal(s): 0-1 Van Wolfswinkel 3, 1-1 Lila 11
Referee: Matejek (CZE)
Aggregate: 1-5; FC Utrecht qualify.

15/7/10, Brøndby, Brondby
Brøndby IF 3-0 FC Vaduz
Goal(s): 1-0 Nilsson 51, 2-0 Jallow 80, 3-0 Jallow 85
Referee: Tohver (EST)
22/7/10, Rheinpark, Vaduz
FC Vaduz 0-0 Brøndby IF
Referee: Vlk (SVK)
Aggregate: 0-3; Brøndby IF qualify.

15/7/10, Tallaght Stadium, Dublin
Shamrock Rovers FC 1-1 Bnei Yehuda Tel-Aviv FC
Goal(s): 0-1 Afek 26, 1-1 Bayly 90+1
Referee: Bergonzi (ITA)
22/7/10, Bloomfield Stadium, Tel-Aviv
Bnei Yehuda Tel-Aviv FC 0-1 Shamrock Rovers FC
Goal(s): 0-1 Stewart 70
Referee: Gautier (FRA)
Aggregate: 1-2; Shamrock Rovers FC qualify.

15/7/10, David Abashidze, Zestafoni
FC Zestafoni 3-0 Dukla Banská Bystrica
Goal(s): 1-0 Dvali 24, 2-0 Dzaria 48, 3-0 Dvali 65
Referee: Banari (MDA)
22/7/10, Štadión Štiavnicky, Banska Bystrica
Dukla Banská Bystrica 1-0 FC Zestafoni
Goal(s): 1-0 Ďuriš 28
Referee: Stanković (SRB)
Aggregate: 1-3; FC Zestafoni qualify.

15/7/10, Gradski, Mostar
HŠK Zrinjski 4-1 SP Tre Penne
Goal(s): 1-0 Ivanković 1, 2-0 Ivanković 20(p), 3-0 Sušić 32, 3-1 Džidić 35(og), 4-1 Zadro 37
Referee: Delferiere (BEL)
22/7/10, Stadio Olimpico, Serravalle
SP Tre Penne 2-9 HŠK Zrinjski
Goal(s): 0-1 Selimović 3, 0-2 Sušić 7, 0-3 Žižović 10, 0-4 Selimović 27, 1-4 Palazzi 28, 1-5 Zadro 52, 1-6 Žižović 55(p), 1-7 Zadro 65, 1-8 Pehar 69, 2-8 Palazzi 81, 2-9 Šunjić 87
Referee: McKeon (IRL)
Aggregate: 3-13; HŠK Zrinjski qualify.

15/7/10, ETO Park, Gyor
Videoton FC 1-1 NK Maribor
Goal(s): 0-1 Mezga 30, 1-1 Horváth 79
Referee: Shvetsov (UKR)
22/7/10, Stadion Ljudski vrt, Maribor
NK Maribor 2-0 Videoton FC
Goal(s): 1-0 Volaš 39, 2-0 Volaš 80
Referee: Mikulski (POL)
Aggregate: 3-1; NK Maribor qualify.

15/7/10, Stadiumi Kombëtar Qemal Stafa, Tirana
KS Besa 0-5 Olympiacos FC
Goal(s): 0-1 Óscar 19, 0-2 Óscar 30, 0-3 Dudu Cearense 46, 0-4 Diogo 70, 0-5 Diogo 84
Referee: Fernández Borbalán (ESP)
22/7/10, Georgios Karaiskakis Stadium, Piraeus
Olympiacos FC 6-1 KS Besa
Goal(s): 1-0 Dudu Cearense 46, 1-1 Lazarevski 48, 2-1 Derbyshire 53, 3-1 Maresca 75, 4-1 Dudu Cearense 79, 5-1 Fetfatzidis 88, 6-1 Maresca 90
Referee: Probert (ENG)
Aggregate: 11-1; Olympiacos FC qualify.

15/7/10, Georgi Asparuhov Stadion, Sofia
PFC Levski Sofia 6-0 Dundalk FC
Goal(s): 1-0 Yovov 12, 2-0 Mladenov 14, 3-0 Dembélé 42, 4-0 Mladenov 46, 5-0 Isa 86, 6-0 Isa 90+4
Referee: Orsato (ITA)
22/7/10, Oriel Park, Dundalk
Dundalk FC 0-2 PFC Levski Sofia
Goal(s): 0-1 Dembélé 4, 0-2 Dembélé 33
Referee: Aydınus (TUR)
Aggregate: 0-8; PFC Levski Sofia qualify.

15/7/10, Šiauliai central stadium, Siauliai
FC Šiauliai 0-2 Wisła Kraków
Goal(s): 0-1 Pa. Brożek 78, 0-2 Pi. Brożek 80
Referee: Levi (ISR)
22/7/10, Hutnik, Krakow
Wisła Kraków 5-0 FC Šiauliai
Goal(s): 1-0 Pi. Brożek 23, 2-0 Żurawski 48, 3-0 Díaz 62, 4-0 Pa. Brożek 66, 5-0 Boguski 90+1
Referee: João Ferreira (POR)
Aggregate: 7-0; Wisła Kraków qualify.

15/7/10, Bloomfield Stadium, Tel-Aviv
Maccabi Tel-Aviv FC 2-0 FK Mogren
Goal(s): 1-0 Ziv 49, 2-0 Medunjanin 52
Referee: Efong Nzolo (BEL)
22/7/10, Gradski, Niksic
FK Mogren 2-1 Maccabi Tel-Aviv FC
Goal(s): 0-1 Medunjanin 7, 1-1 Glušćević 58(p), 2-1 Glušćević 80
Referee: Velichko (BLR)
Aggregate: 2-3; Maccabi Tel-Aviv FC qualify.

15/7/10, BJK İnönü Stadyumu, Istanbul
Beşiktaş JK 3-0 Víkingur
Goal(s): 1-0 Nihat Kahveci 19, 2-0 Nihat Kahveci 65, 3-0 Mert Nobre 90
Referee: Egorov (RUS)
22/7/10, Toftir, Toftir
Víkingur 0-4 Beşiktaş JK
Goal(s): 0-1 Ekrem Dağ 3, 0-2 Nihat Kahveci 10, 0-3 Bobô 32, 0-4 Bobô 44
Referee: Gestranius (FIN)
Aggregate: 0-7; Beşiktaş JK qualify.

15/7/10, Tofiq Bähramov-Republic stadium, Baku
Bakı FK 0-3 FK Budućnost Podgorica
Match forfeit; original result 2-1
Goal(s): 0-1 Bećiraj 38, 1-1 Kajkut 77, 2-1 Jabá 90+3
Referee: Constantin (ROU)
22/7/10, Stadion Podgorica, Podgorica
FK Budućnost Podgorica 1-2 Bakı FK
Goal(s): 0-1 Šolić 28, 0-2 Jabá 42, 1-2 Brnović 64
Referee: Kalopoulos (GRE)
Aggregate: 4-2; FK Budućnost Podgorica qualify.

15/7/10, Marijampolė, Marijampole
FK Sūduva 0-2 SK Rapid Wien
Goal(s): 0-1 Hofmann 12, 0-2 Trimmel 81
Referee: Christoffersen (DEN)
22/7/10, Gerhard-Hanappi-Stadion, Vienna
SK Rapid Wien 4-2 FK Sūduva
Goal(s): 1-0 Jelavić 20, 1-1 Grigaitis 70, 1-2 Beniušis 85, 2-2 Gartler 86, 3-2 Gartler 89, 4-2 Jelavić 90
Referee: Vučemilović-Šimunović Jr. (CRO)
Aggregate: 6-2; SK Rapid Wien qualify.

Third Qualifying Round

Eleven weeks after leading Fulham FC to the UEFA Europa League final, Roy Hodgson made a successful return to the competition with Liverpool FC, whose seamless progress was not matched by some of the third qualifying round's other marquee clubs.

Hodgson began life on Merseyside with a 4-0 aggregate success against FK Rabotnicki, securing the Reds a play-off place alongside the likes of Juventus and Galatasaray AŞ. The Bianconeri, also featuring a new coach in Luigi Delneri, emerged 3-0 victors against Shamrock Rovers FC, while Galatasaray, held 2-2 at home in the opening instalment of their tie against OFK Beograd, eventually progressed as 7-3 winners.

Olympiacos upset

Other luminaries such as Sporting Clube de Portugal and Beşiktaş JK also kept their European campaigns alive – as did VfB Stuttgart despite a scare against Molde FK. Olympiacos FC had theirs brought to an abrupt halt, on the other hand, as opponents Maccabi Tel-Aviv FC recovered from a 2-1 loss in the first leg to win on away goals. Victorious coach Yossi Mizrahi called the result an "amazing achievement", while forward Barak Itzhaki said: "These are the moments players are born for."

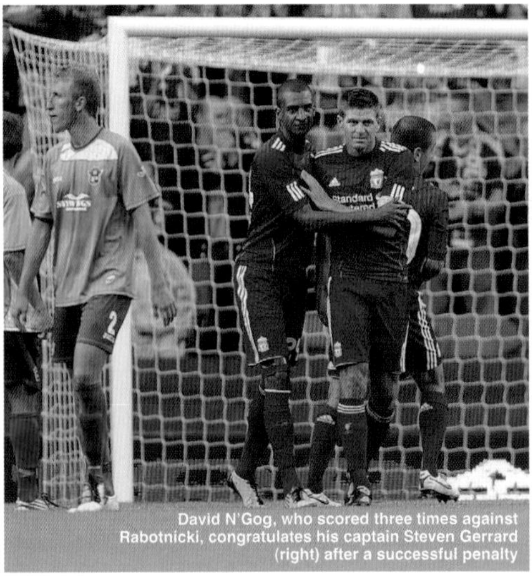

David N'Gog, who scored three times against Rabotnicki, congratulates his captain Steven Gerrard (right) after a successful penalty

CS Marítimo were the round's most emphatic winners, chalking up a club-record 8-2 victory at home to Bangor City FC en route to a 10-3 aggregate triumph. While that meant reason for cheer in Madeira, there was equal cause for celebration on the other side of the continent after European debutants FC Sibir Novosibirsk – the most easterly club ever to feature in UEFA competition – squeezed past Apollon Limassol FC of Cyprus. Hungary's Győri ETO FC were also surprise winners against Montpellier Hérault SC, holding the French side 1-1 on aggregate before prevailing in the only penalty shoot-out of the round.

Third Qualifying Round Results

27/7/10, Natsionalen Stadion Vasil Levski, Sofia
PFC CSKA Sofia 3-0 Cliftonville FC
Goal(s): 1-0 Vidanov 9, 2-0 Marquinhos 72, 3-0 Trifonov 74
Referee: Mazeika (LTU)
5/8/10, Windsor Park, Belfast
Cliftonville FC 1-2 PFC CSKA Sofia
Goal(s): 1-0 Boyce 42, 1-1 Kostadinov 85, 1-2 Marquinhos 88
Referee: Layushkin (RUS)
Aggregate: 1-5; PFC CSKA Sofia qualify.

29/7/10, Vojvodina, Novi Sad
FK Spartak Zlatibor voda 2-1 FC Dnipro Dnipropetrovsk
Goal(s): 1-0 Torbica 16(p), 1-1 Homenyuk 23, 2-1 Torbica 90(p)
Referee: Marriner (ENG)
5/8/10, Dnipro Arena, Dnipropetrovsk
FC Dnipro Dnipropetrovsk 2-0 FK Spartak Zlatibor voda
Goal(s): 1-0 Seleznev 45, 2-0 Holek 48
Referee: Studer (SUI)
Aggregate: 3-2; FC Dnipro Dnipropetrovsk qualify.

29/7/10, Ruch, Chorzow
Ruch Chorzów 1-3 FK Austria Wien
Goal(s): 1-0 Pulkowski 4, 1-1 Linz 7, 1-2 Hlinka 43, 1-3 Jun 73
Referee: Koukoulakis (GRE)
5/8/10, Franz Horr Stadion, Vienna
FK Austria Wien 3-0 Ruch Chorzów
Goal(s): 1-0 Klein 4(p), 2-0 Baumgartlinger 10, 3-0 Baumgartlinger 21
Referee: Van Boekel (NED)
Aggregate: 6-1; FK Austria Wien qualify.

29/7/10, Borås Arena, Boras
IF Elfsborg 5-0 FK Teteks
Goal(s): 1-0 Ishizaki 29, 2-0 Svensson 50, 3-0 Avdic 57, 4-0 Nordmark 66, 5-0 Keene 77
Referee: Todorov (BUL)
5/8/10, National Arena Filip II, Skopje
FK Teteks 1-2 IF Elfsborg
Goal(s): 1-0 Stojanovski 31, 1-1 Kurbegovic 42, 1-2 Jawo 56
Referee: Borg (MLT)
Aggregate: 1-7; IF Elfsborg qualify.

29/7/10, Molde Stadion, Molde
Molde FK 2-3 VfB Stuttgart
Goal(s): 0-1 Rudy 27, 1-1 Moström 65, 1-2 Kuzmanović 74, 2-2 Hoseth 76, 2-3 Harnik 82
Referee: Nijhuis (NED)
5/8/10, VfB Arena, Stuttgart
VfB Stuttgart 2-2 Molde FK
Goal(s): 0-1 Johansson 41, 0-2 Rindarøy 49, 1-2 Pogrebnyak 55, 2-2 Gebhart 90+3
Referee: Bergonzi (ITA)
Aggregate: 5-4; VfB Stuttgart qualify.

29/7/10, Galgenwaard, Utrecht
FC Utrecht 1-0 FC Luzern
Goal(s): 1-0 Mertens 35
Referee: Rasmussen (DEN)
5/8/10, Stadion Letzigrund, Zurich
FC Luzern 1-3 FC Utrecht
Goal(s): 0-1 Asare 13, 0-2 Van Wolfswinkel 22, 0-3 Silberbauer 28, 1-3 Pacar 53
Referee: Kulbakov (BLR)
Aggregate: 1-4; FC Utrecht qualify.

29/7/10, Spartak Stadion, Mogilev
FC Dnepr Mogilev 1-0 FC Baník Ostrava
Goal(s): 1-0 Zenkovich 63
Referee: Malek (POL)
5/8/10, Bazaly, Ostrava
FC Baník Ostrava 1-2 FC Dnepr Mogilev
Goal(s): 0-1 Yurchenko 24(p), 1-1 Řezník 26, 1-2 Zenkovich 70
Referee: Trattou (CYP)
Aggregate: 1-3; FC Dnepr Mogilev qualify.

29/7/10, Georgi Asparuhov Stadion, Sofia
PFC Beroe Stara Zagora 1-1 SK Rapid Wien
Goal(s): 0-1 Hofmann 45+1(p), 1-1 Zlatinov 85
Referee: Siejewicz (POL)
3/8/10, Gerhard-Hanappi-Stadion, Vienna
SK Rapid Wien 3-0 PFC Beroe Stara Zagora
Goal(s): 1-0 Jelavić 5, 2-0 Jelavić 60, 3-0 Katzer 71
Referee: Masiah (ISR)
Aggregate: 4-1; SK Rapid Wien qualify.

29/7/10, Saviniemi Football Stadium, Myllykoski
Myllykosken Pallo-47 1-2 FC Timişoara
Goal(s): 0-1 Tameş 34, 1-1 Ricketts 49, 1-2 Axente 74
Referee: McKeon (IRL)
5/8/10, Stadionul Dan Păltinişanu, Timisoara
FC Timişoara 3-3 Myllykosken Pallo-47
Goal(s): 0-1 Äijälä 18, 0-2 Ricketts 20, 0-3 Ricketts 25, 1-3 Axente 53, 2-3 Zicu 80, 3-3 Čišovský 90+2
Referee: Kuchin (KAZ)
Aggregate: 5-4; FC Timişoara qualify.

29/7/10, Turku Stadium, Turku
FC Inter Turku 1-5 KRC Genk
Goal(s): 0-1 De Bruyne 17, 0-2 Ogunjimi 44, 1-2 Grot 54, 1-3 Barda 61, 1-4 Vossen 77, 1-5 Vossen 85
Referee: Příhoda (CZE)
5/8/10, Cristal Arena, Genk
KRC Genk 3-2 FC Inter Turku
Goal(s): 1-0 Ogunjimi 24, 1-1 Antunez 35, 2-1 Tőzsér 80(p), 3-1 Huysegems 85, 3-2 Antunez 90
Referee: Aydınus (TUR)
Aggregate: 8-3; KRC Genk qualify.

29/7/10, Spartak Stadion, Novosibirsk
FC Sibir Novosibirsk 1-0 Apollon Limassol FC
Goal(s): 1-0 Medvedev 74
Referee: Kovařík (CZE)
5/8/10, Tsirion Stadium, Limassol
Apollon Limassol FC 2-1 FC Sibir Novosibirsk
Goal(s): 1-0 Semedo 12, 1-1 Shevchenko 63, 2-1 Núñez 71
Referee: Szabó (HUN)
Aggregate: 2-2; FC Sibir Novosibirsk qualify on away goal.

29/7/10, Randers Stadium, Randers
Randers FC 2-3 FC Lausanne-Sport
Goal(s): 1-0 Movsisyan 6, 1-1 Steuble 41, 1-2 Sílvio 62(p), 2-2 Movsisyan 81, 2-3 Sílvio 84
Referee: Hategan (ROU)
5/8/10, Olympique de la Pontaise, Lausanne
FC Lausanne-Sport 1-1 Randers FC
Goal(s): 0-1 Movsisyan 49, 1-1 Tosi 68
Referee: Black (NIR)
Aggregate: 4-3; FC Lausanne-Sport qualify.

29/7/10, Aalesund Stadion, Aalesund
Aalesunds FK 1-1 Motherwell FC
Goal(s): 0-1 Murphy 48, 1-1 Mathisen 90+3(p)
Referee: Toussaint (LUX)
5/8/10, Fir Park, Motherwell
Motherwell FC 3-0 Aalesunds FK
Goal(s): 1-0 Murphy 3, 2-0 Sutton 13, 3-0 Page 89
Referee: Trutz (SVK)
Aggregate: 4-1; Motherwell FC qualify.

29/7/10, Odense Stadion, Odense
Odense BK 5-3 HŠK Zrinjski
Goal(s): 0-1 Zadro 15, 1-1 Gíslason 16, 2-1 Absalonsen 23, 3-1 Utaka 31, 4-1 Andreasen 37, 5-1 Utaka 60, 5-2 Žižović 65(p), 5-3 Zadro 71
Referee: Norris (SCO)
5/8/10, Gradski, Mostar
HŠK Zrinjski 0-0 Odense BK
Referee: Jech (CZE)
Aggregate: 3-5; Odense BK qualify.

29/7/10, Ukrayina Stadion, Lviv
FC Karpaty Lviv 1-0 FC Zestafoni
Goal(s): 1-0 Khudobyak 6
Referee: Christoffersen (DEN)
5/8/10, David Abashidze, Zestafoni
FC Zestafoni 0-1 FC Karpaty Lviv
Goal(s): 0-1 Kozhanov 90+1
Referee: Skjerven (NOR)
Aggregate: 0-2; FC Karpaty Lviv qualify.

29/7/10, Fredriksskans Idrottsplats, Kalmar
Kalmar FF 1-1 PFC Levski Sofia
Goal(s): 0-1 Joãozinho 28, 1-1 Dauda 83
Referee: Jovanetić (SRB)
5/8/10, Georgi Asparuhov Stadion, Sofia
PFC Levski Sofia 5-2 Kalmar FF
Goal(s): 1-0 Dembélé 12, 2-0 Mladenov 33, 3-0 Dembélé 70, 3-1 Johansson 82, 3-2 Israelsson 84, 4-2 Isa 90+1, 5-2 Isa 90+2
Referee: Gautier (FRA)
Aggregate: 6-3; PFC Levski Sofia qualify.

29/7/10, Estádio da Madeira, Funchal
CS Marítimo 8-2 Bangor City FC
Goal(s): 1-0 Tchô 33, 2-0 Danilo Dias 38, 3-0 Baba Diawara 51, 3-1 Ward 73, 4-1 Danilo Dias 75, 5-1 Baba Diawara 78, 6-1 Tchô 79, 7-1 Kanu 80, 8-1 Fidelis 90+1, 8-2 Jebb 90+3
Referee: Drachta (AUT)
5/8/10, The Racecourse Ground, Wrexham
Bangor City FC 1-2 CS Marítimo
Goal(s): 1-0 Bull 9, 1-1 Adilson 48, 1-2 Marquinho 58
Referee: Fabian (HUN)
Aggregate: 3-10; CS Marítimo qualify.

29/7/10, Tallaght Stadium, Dublin
Shamrock Rovers FC 0-2 Juventus
Goal(s): 0-1 Amauri 3, 0-2 Amauri 75
Referee: Fernández Borbalán (ESP)
5/8/10, Alberto Braglia, Modena
Juventus 1-0 Shamrock Rovers FC
Goal(s): 1-0 Del Piero 74
Referee: Daloukas (GRE)
Aggregate: 3-0; Juventus qualify.

29/7/10, Hutnik, Krakow
Wisła Kraków 0-1 Qarabağ FK
Goal(s): 0-1 Nadirov 69
Referee: Hagen (NOR)
5/8/10, Tofiq Bähramov-Republic stadium, Baku
Qarabağ FK 3-2 Wisła Kraków
Goal(s): 1-0 İsmayilov 28, 2-0 Äliyev 33, 3-0 R.A. Sadiqov 35, 3-1 Pa. Brożek 56, 3-2 Boguski 88
Referee: Yıldırım (TUR)
Aggregate: 4-2; Qarabağ FK qualify.

29/7/10, Jan Breydelstadion, Bruges
Cercle Brugge KSV 1-0 Anorthosis Famagusta FC
Goal(s): 1-0 Foley 69
Referee: Shvetsov (UKR)
5/8/10, Antonis Papadopoulos, Larnaca
Anorthosis Famagusta FC 3-1 Cercle Brugge KSV
Goal(s): 1-0 Cafú 45+1, 2-0 Cafú 60, 2-1 Owusu 78, 3-1 Cafú 87
Referee: Jug (SVN)
Aggregate: 3-2; Anorthosis Famagusta FC qualify.

29/7/10, GSP Stadium, Nicosia
APOEL FC 1-0 FK Jablonec
Goal(s): 1-0 Solari 55
Referee: Evans (WAL)
5/8/10, Chance Arena, Jablonec nad Nisou
FK Jablonec 1-3 APOEL FC
Goal(s): 0-1 Paulo Jorge 24, 0-2 Charalambides 28, 1-2 Pavlík 33, 1-3 Solari 37
Referee: Asumaa (FIN)
Aggregate: 1-4; APOEL FC qualify.

29/7/10, Farum Park, Farum
FC Nordsjælland 0-1 Sporting Clube de Portugal
Goal(s): 0-1 Vukčević 24
Referee: Sukhina (RUS)
5/8/10, José Alvalade, Lisbon
Sporting Clube de Portugal 2-1 FC Nordsjælland
Goal(s): 1-0 Hélder Postiga 24, 1-1 Lawan 79, 2-1 Maniche 90+2
Referee: Strahonja (CRO)
Aggregate: 3-1; Sporting Clube de Portugal qualify.

29/7/10, Stadion Ljudski vrt, Maribor
NK Maribor 3-0 Hibernian FC
Goal(s): 1-0 Iličič 31, 2-0 Iličič 52, 3-0 Marcos Tavares 60
Referee: Ingvarsson (SWE)
5/8/10, Easter Road Stadium, Edinburgh
Hibernian FC 2-3 NK Maribor
Goal(s): 0-1 Marcos Tavares 20, 1-1 De Graaf 54, 1-2 Mezga 67(p), 1-3 Marcos Tavares 73, 2-3 De Graaf 89
Referee: Turpin (FRA)
Aggregate: 2-6; NK Maribor qualify.

29/7/10, Stadion FK Crvena zvezda, Belgrade
FK Crvena zvezda 1-2 ŠK Slovan Bratislava
Goal(s): 0-1 Ivana 43, 1-1 Trifunović 63, 1-2 Saláta 68
Referee: Neves Moreira De Sousa (POR)
5/8/10, Štadión Pasienky, Bratislava
ŠK Slovan Bratislava 1-1 FK Crvena zvezda
Goal(s): 1-0 Đorđević 2(og), 1-1 Kadu 73
Referee: Strömbergsson (SWE)
Aggregate: 3-2; ŠK Slovan Bratislava qualify.

29/7/10, Stadion Letná, Prague
FC Viktoria Plzeň 1-1 Beşiktaş JK
Goal(s): 1-0 Limberský 28, 1-1 Delgado 44(p)
Referee: Clos Gómez (ESP)
5/8/10, BJK İnönü Stadyumu, Istanbul
Beşiktaş JK 3-0 FC Viktoria Plzeň
Goal(s): 1-0 Ricardo Quaresma 38, 2-0 Delgado 57, 3-0 Hološko 71
Referee: Efong Nzolo (BEL)
Aggregate: 4-1; Beşiktaş JK qualify.

Robson of Marítimo takes on Bangor City's Chris Jones in a tie won 10-3 on aggregate by the Madeiran club

29/7/10, Stadion Graz Liebenau, Graz
SK Sturm Graz 2-0 FC Dinamo Tbilisi
Goal(s): 1-0 Feldhofer 48, 2-0 Kienast 59
Referee: Kaasik (EST)
5/8/10, Boris Paichadze National Stadium, Tbilisi
FC Dinamo Tbilisi 1-1 SK Sturm Graz
Goal(s): 1-0 Robertinho 11, 1-1 Muratović 40(p)
Referee: Mažić (SRB)
Aggregate: 1-3; SK Sturm Graz qualify.

29/7/10, ETO Park, Gyor
Győri ETO FC 0-1 Montpellier Hérault SC
Goal(s): 0-1 Giroud 32
Referee: Borski (POL)
5/8/10, La Mosson, Montpellier
Montpellier Hérault SC 0-1 Győri ETO FC (aet)
Goal(s): 0-1 Babić 40
Referee: Gestranius (FIN)
Aggregate: 1-1; Győri ETO FC qualify after extra time 4-3 on penalties.

29/7/10, Kiryat Eliazer, Haifa
Maccabi Haifa FC 1-0 FC Dinamo Minsk
Goal(s): 1-0 Dvalishvili 30
Referee: Orsato (ITA)
5/8/10, Dinamo Stadion, Minsk
FC Dinamo Minsk 3-1 Maccabi Haifa FC
Goal(s): 0-1 Dvalishvili 27, 1-1 Strakhanovich 35, 2-1 Putilo 55, 3-1 Putilo 90
Referee: Piccirillo (FRA)
Aggregate: 3-2; FC Dinamo Minsk qualify.

29/7/10, AZ Stadion, Alkmaar
AZ Alkmaar 2-0 IFK Göteborg
Goal(s): 1-0 Klavan 52, 2-0 Gudmundsson 56
Referee: Teixeira Vitienes (ESP)
5/8/10, Gamla Ullevi, Gothenburg
IFK Göteborg 1-0 AZ Alkmaar
Goal(s): 1-0 Selakovic 67
Referee: Circhetta (SUI)
Aggregate: 1-2; AZ Alkmaar qualify.

29/7/10, Miejski, Bialystok
Jagiellonia Białystok 1-2 Aris Thessaloniki FC
Goal(s): 0-1 Toni Calvo 4(p), 0-2 Toni Calvo 7, 1-2 Grzyb 24
Referee: Berntsen (NOR)
5/8/10, Kleanthis Vikelidis Stadium, Salonika
Aris Thessaloniki FC 2-2 Jagiellonia Białystok
Goal(s): 1-0 Cesarec 19, 1-1 Burkhardt 25, 1-2 Burkhardt 66, 2-2 Cesarec 75(p)
Referee: Deaconu (ROU)
Aggregate: 4-3; Aris Thessaloniki FC qualify.

29/7/10, National Arena Filip II, Skopje
FK Rabotnicki 0-2 Liverpool FC
Goal(s): 0-1 N'Gog 17, 0-2 N'Gog 58
Referee: Damato (ITA)
5/8/10, Anfield, Liverpool
Liverpool FC 2-0 FK Rabotnicki
Goal(s): 1-0 N'Gog 22, 2-0 Gerrard 40(p)
Referee: Sippel (GER)
Aggregate: 4-0; Liverpool FC qualify.

29/7/10, Stadion Podgorica, Podgorica
FK Budućnost Podgorica 1-2 Brøndby IF
Goal(s): 0-1 Adamović 73(og), 0-2 Jensen 87, 1-2 Bećiraj 90+3
Referee: Liesveld (NED)
5/8/10, Brøndby, Brondby
Brøndby IF 1-0 FK Budućnost Podgorica
Goal(s): 1-0 Jallow 11
Referee: Duarte Gomes (POR)
Aggregate: 3-1; Brøndby IF qualify.

29/7/10, Dinamo, Bucharest
FC Dinamo Bucureşti 3-1 HNK Hajduk Split
Goal(s): 1-0 An. Cristea 6(p), 2-0 Garat 40, 2-1 Tomasov 64, 3-1 Koné 70
Referee: Probert (ENG)
5/8/10, Stadion Poljud, Split
HNK Hajduk Split 3-0 FC Dinamo Bucureşti
Goal(s): 1-0 Vukušić 12, 2-0 Brkljača 23, 3-0 Tomasov 38
Referee: Xistra (POR)
Aggregate: 4-3; HNK Hajduk Split qualify.

29/7/10, Ali Sami Yen Stadyumu, Istanbul
Galatasaray AŞ 2-2 OFK Beograd
Goal(s): 1-0 Arda Turan 26, 2-0 Arda Turan 76, 2-1 Krstić 80, 2-2 Injac 86
Referee: Vollquartz (DEN)
5/8/10, Omladinski, Belgrade
OFK Beograd 1-5 Galatasaray AŞ
Goal(s): 0-1 Mustafa Sarp 12, 0-2 Kewell 22, 1-2 Nikolić 32, 1-3 Kewell 57(p), 1-4 Arda Turan 71, 1-5 Mehmet Batdal 81
Referee: Stalhammar (SWE)
Aggregate: 3-7; Galatasaray AŞ qualify.

29/7/10, Georgios Karaiskakis Stadium, Piraeus
Olympiacos FC 2-1 Maccabi Tel-Aviv FC
Goal(s): 0-1 Medunjanin 18(p), 1-1 Zairi 67, 2-1 Rommedahl 73
Referee: McDonald (SCO)
5/8/10, Bloomfield Stadium, Tel-Aviv
Maccabi Tel-Aviv FC 1-0 Olympiacos FC
Goal(s): 1-0 Colautti 42
Referee: Banti (ITA)
Aggregate: 2-2; Maccabi Tel-Aviv FC qualify on away goal.

Play-Offs

Former European Champion Clubs' Cup winners Celtic FC, Feyenoord and Aston Villa FC were among a bevy of big hitters to fall one step short of the group stage, while FC Lausanne-Sport of the Swiss second tier created another stir in a melting pot filled to the brim with upsets.

Celtic looked particularly unlikely to fall by the wayside when they took a 2-0 lead to FC Utrecht, but a Ricky van Wolfswinkel hat-trick earned the Dutch outfit a 4-0 home win and improbable progress. "It was not only the 11 men on the pitch who were superb, but everyone around the team was incredible," said Utrecht coach Ton du Chatinier. While Celtic were left aghast by such an unexpected exit, Villa found themselves in familiar territory as they were eliminated at this stage by SK Rapid Wien for the second season in succession. Villa, who missed a spot kick, enjoyed a 3-2 lead in the tie with 13 minutes remaining, only to succumb 4-3.

Lausanne surprise

Like Celtic, Feyenoord squandered a first-leg advantage – albeit a 1-0 one – on their way to defeat at the hands of KAA Gent. "I'm very proud of the squad and I think the fans are very satisfied with what we showed them," said Gent coach Francky Dury. Fellow Eredivisie outfit PSV Eindhoven performed a comeback of their own, meanwhile, recovering from FC Sibir Novosibirsk's late 1-0 win in Russia to triumph 5-1 on aggregate and end their rivals' inaugural European campaign.

Lausanne, play-off entrants as Swiss Cup runners-up, produced a shock to match any of those inflicted on the most illustrious names in this phase of the tournament. They shared a pair of 1-1 draws with FC Lokomotiv Moskva before triumphing 4-3 on penalties. "We're a small team from the Swiss second division, so getting into the Europa League is a big achievement for us," said coach Martin Rueda.

Turkish troubles

Four Turkish clubs harboured hopes of reaching the competition proper ahead of the final phase of qualifying, but only one plotted a successful path through. Istanbul giants Galatasaray AŞ and Fenerbahçe SK were the two most distinguished casualties, the former's departure proving particularly dramatic. FC Karpaty Lviv looked well placed after a 2-2 draw in Turkey but seemed destined for the exit door when Aydın Yılmaz put Frank Rijkaard's side in front 91 minutes into the return. Artem Fedetskiy struck back to give the Ukrainian side the away-goals advantage three minutes into added time, however, before being dismissed moments later.

PAOK FC eliminated Fenerbahçe in extra time, while Liverpool FC struck twice in the closing seven minutes to see off Trabzonspor AŞ. "It's a very good victory," said Reds manager Roy Hodgson. "They don't lose at home and we've beaten them." Only Beşiktaş JK were able to buck the trend and they did so in emphatic fashion, defeating HJK Helsinki 6-0 over two legs. Though not quite as serene, Manchester City FC and Juventus also advanced without any major concerns thanks to respective wins against FC Timişoara (3-0) and SK Sturm Graz (3-1).

Portuguese duo Sporting Clube de Portugal and FC Porto marched on in contrasting fashion, the Lisbon outfit's progress coming courtesy of a 3-0 win at Brøndby IF after a 2-0 home defeat in the opening leg. "We showed great spirit," said coach Paulo Sérgio. "It was a memorable night in the club's rich history, but we have higher goals now." Counterparts Porto enjoyed a far more tranquil time of it against KRC Genk, coming through 7-2 overall.

Play-Off Results

17/8/10, Kleanthis Vikelidis Stadium, Salonika
Aris Thessaloniki FC 1-0 FK Austria Wien
Goal(s): 1-0 Ruiz 90+3
Referee: Layushkin (RUS)
26/8/10, Franz Horr Stadion, Vienna
FK Austria Wien 1-1 Aris Thessaloniki FC
Goal(s): 0-1 Ruiz 42, 1-1 Linz 56
Referee: Stalhammar (SWE)
Aggregate: 1-2; Aris Thessaloniki FC qualify.

17/8/10, BJK İnönü Stadyumu, Istanbul
Beşiktaş JK 2-0 HJK Helsinki
Goal(s): 1-0 Hilbert 35, 2-0 Ricardo Quaresma 66
Referee: Hategan (ROU)
26/8/10, Finnair Stadium, Helsinki
HJK Helsinki 0-4 Beşiktaş JK
Goal(s): 0-1 Ricardo Quaresma 15, 0-2 Guti 67, 0-3 Necip Uysal 77, 0-4 Hološko 90+3
Referee: Rasmussen (DEN)
Aggregate: 0-6; Beşiktaş JK qualify.

Stuttgart's Timo Gebhart wheels away in delight after scoring a vital goal against Slovan Bratislava

19/8/10, Parc des Princes, Paris
Paris Saint-Germain FC 2-0 Maccabi Tel-Aviv FC
Goal(s): 1-0 Luyindula 3, 2-0 Hoarau 60
Referee: Blom (NED)
26/8/10, Bloomfield Stadium, Tel-Aviv
Maccabi Tel-Aviv FC 4-3 Paris Saint-Germain FC
Goal(s): 0-1 Hoarau 40(p), 1-1 Atar 48, 1-2 Giuly 64, 2-2 Avidor 68, 3-2 Medunjanin 83(p), 3-3 Nenê 90+3(p), 4-3 Atar 90+5
Referee: Dean (ENG)
Aggregate: 4-5; Paris Saint-Germain FC qualify.

19/8/10, BayArena, Leverkusen
Bayer 04 Leverkusen 3-0 SC Tavriya Simferopol
Goal(s): 1-0 Kadlec 1, 2-0 Kadlec 84, 3-0 Ballack 90+1(p)
Referee: Fautrel (FRA)
26/8/10, Lokomotiv Stadium, Simferopol
SC Tavriya Simferopol 1-3 Bayer 04 Leverkusen
Goal(s): 1-0 Idahor 5(p), 1-1 Vidal 50(p), 1-2 Holaido 75(og), 1-3 Castro 90+3
Referee: Tudor (ROU)
Aggregate: 1-6; Bayer 04 Leverkusen qualify.

19/8/10, Gerhard-Hanappi-Stadion, Vienna
SK Rapid Wien 1-1 Aston Villa FC
Goal(s): 0-1 Bannan 12, 1-1 Nuhiu 32
Referee: Hamer (LUX)
26/8/10, Villa Park, Birmingham
Aston Villa FC 2-3 SK Rapid Wien
Goal(s): 1-0 Agbonlahor 22, 1-1 Nuhiu 52, 2-1 Heskey 77, 2-2 Sonnleitner 78, 2-3 Gartler 81
Referee: Braamhaar (NED)
Aggregate: 3-4; SK Rapid Wien qualify.

19/8/10, Štadión Pasienky, Bratislava
ŠK Slovan Bratislava 0-1 VfB Stuttgart
Goal(s): 0-1 Harnik 88
Referee: Chapron (FRA)
26/8/10, VfB Arena, Stuttgart
VfB Stuttgart 2-2 ŠK Slovan Bratislava
Goal(s): 0-1 Dobrotka 9, 0-2 Sylvestr 53, 1-2 Gebhart 56, 2-2 Gentner 64
Referee: Nikolaev (RUS)
Aggregate: 3-2; VfB Stuttgart qualify.

19/8/10, Sóstói út, Nyiregyhaza
Debreceni VSC 2-0 PFC Litex Lovech
Goal(s): 1-0 Coulibaly 22, 2-0 Z. Laczkó 33
Referee: Trattou (CYP)
26/8/10, Lovech Stadion, Lovech
PFC Litex Lovech 1-2 Debreceni VSC
Goal(s): 0-1 Mbengono 53, 1-1 Niflore 68, 1-2 Czvitkovics 81
Referee: Malek (POL)
Aggregate: 1-4; Debreceni VSC qualify.

19/8/10, Råsundastadion, Solna
AIK Solna 0-0 PFC Levski Sofia
Referee: Kralovec (CZE)
26/8/10, Georgi Asparuhov Stadion, Sofia
PFC Levski Sofia 2-1 AIK Solna
Goal(s): 0-1 Bangura 11, 1-1 Mladenov 49, 2-1 Dembélé 51
Referee: Shvetsov (UKR)
Aggregate: 2-1; PFC Levski Sofia qualify.

19/8/10, Spartak Stadion, Novosibirsk
FC Sibir Novosibirsk 1-0 PSV Eindhoven
Goal(s): 1-0 Degtyarev 90+2
Referee: Skjerven (NOR)
26/8/10, PSV Stadion, Eindhoven
PSV Eindhoven 5-0 FC Sibir Novosibirsk
Goal(s): 1-0 Berg 38, 2-0 Engelaar 56, 3-0 Toivonen 64, 4-0 Dzsudzsák 73, 5-0 Dzsudzsák 90(p)
Referee: Johannesson (SWE)
Aggregate: 5-1; PSV Eindhoven qualify.

19/8/10, Gorodskoy Stadion, Borisov
FC BATE Borisov 3-0 CS Marítimo
Goal(s): 1-0 Olekhnovich 56, 2-0 Renan 60, 3-0 Pavlov 70
Referee: Jakobsson (ISL)
26/8/10, Estádio dos Barreiros, Funchal
CS Marítimo 1-2 FC BATE Borisov
Goal(s): 0-1 Pavlov 52, 1-1 Kanu 90, 1-2 Skavysh 90+2
Referee: Norris (SCO)
Aggregate: 1-5; FC BATE Borisov qualify.

19/8/10, Odense Stadion, Odense
Odense BK 2-1 Motherwell FC
Goal(s): 1-0 Sørensen 31, 2-0 Utaka 78, 2-1 Hateley 90+4
Referee: Szabó (HUN)
26/8/10, Fir Park, Motherwell
Motherwell FC 0-1 Odense BK
Goal(s): 0-1 Utaka 28
Referee: Koukoulakis (GRE)
Aggregate: 1-3; Odense BK qualify.

19/8/10, Feijenoord Stadion, Rotterdam
Feyenoord 1-0 KAA Gent
Goal(s): 1-0 Fer 78
Referee: Bruno Paixão (POR)
26/8/10, Jules Ottenstadion, Gent
KAA Gent 2-0 Feyenoord
Goal(s): 1-0 Soumahoro 34, 2-0 Coulibaly 61
Referee: Iturralde González (ESP)
Aggregate: 2-1; KAA Gent qualify.

19/8/10, Anfield, Liverpool
Liverpool FC 1-0 Trabzonspor AŞ
Goal(s): 1-0 Babel 45+1
Referee: Einwaller (AUT)
26/8/10, Hüseyin Avni Aker, Trabzon
Trabzonspor AŞ 1-2 Liverpool FC
Goal(s): 1-0 Gutiérrez 4, 1-1 Giray Kaçar 83(og), 1-2 Kuyt 88
Referee: Bebek (CRO)
Aggregate: 1-3; Liverpool FC qualify.

19/8/10, Celtic Park, Glasgow
Celtic FC 2-0 FC Utrecht
Goal(s): 1-0 Juárez 19, 2-0 Samaras 34
Referee: Moen (NOR)
26/8/10, Galgenwaard, Utrecht
FC Utrecht 4-0 Celtic FC
Goal(s): 1-0 Van Wolfswinkel 12(p), 2-0 Van Wolfswinkel 19(p), 3-0 Van Wolfswinkel 46, 4-0 Maguire 62
Referee: Velasco Carballo (ESP)
Aggregate: 4-2; FC Utrecht qualify.

19/8/10, GSP Stadium, Nicosia
AC Omonia 0-1 FC Metalist Kharkiv
Goal(s): 0-1 Dević 24
Referee: Vollquartz (DEN)
26/8/10, Metalist Stadion, Kharkiv
FC Metalist Kharkiv 2-2 AC Omonia
Goal(s): 0-1 Leandro 60, 0-2 Rengifo 64, 1-2 Dević 66, 2-2 Cleiton 71
Referee: Jug (SVN)
Aggregate: 3-2; FC Metalist Kharkiv qualify.

19/8/10, Stadionul Municipal, Vaslui
FC Vaslui 0-0 LOSC Lille Métropole
Referee: Yıldırım (TUR)
26/8/10, Lille Métropole, Villeneuve-d'Ascq
LOSC Lille Métropole 2-0 FC Vaslui
Goal(s): 1-0 Cabaye 69(p), 2-0 Chedjou 80
Referee: Hagen (NOR)
Aggregate: 2-0; LOSC Lille Métropole qualify.

19/8/10, Tannadice Park, Dundee
Dundee United FC 0-1 AEK Athens FC
Goal(s): 0-1 Djebbour 11
Referee: Strahonja (CRO)
26/8/10, Georgios Karaiskakis Stadium, Piraeus
AEK Athens FC 1-1 Dundee United FC
Goal(s): 1-0 Diop 23, 1-1 Daly 78
Referee: Kovařík (CZE)
Aggregate: 2-1; AEK Athens FC qualify.

19/8/10, Dnipro Arena, Dnipropetrovsk
FC Dnipro Dnipropetrovsk 0-1 KKS Lech Poznań
Goal(s): 0-1 Arboleda 5
Referee: Ingvarsson (SWE)
26/8/10, Miejski, Poznan
KKS Lech Poznań 0-0 FC Dnipro Dnipropetrovsk
Referee: Nijhuis (NED)
Aggregate: 1-0; KKS Lech Poznań qualify.

19/8/10, Arena Khimki, Moscow
PFC CSKA Moskva 4-0 Anorthosis Famagusta FC
Goal(s): 1-0 Doumbia 13, 2-0 Doumbia 20, 3-0 Tošić 48, 4-0 Tošić 74
Referee: Kever (SUI)
24/8/10, Antonis Papadopoulos, Larnaca
Anorthosis Famagusta FC 1-2 PFC CSKA Moskva
Goal(s): 1-0 Cafú 76, 1-1 Doumbia 85, 1-2 Mark González 89
Referee: Deaconu (ROU)
Aggregate: 1-6; PFC CSKA Moskva qualify.

19/8/10, Stadion Poljud, Split
HNK Hajduk Split 4-1 FC Unirea Urziceni
Goal(s): 0-1 Frunză 34, 1-1 Ibričić 39, 2-1 Ibričić 66, 3-1 Brkljača 78, 4-1 Čop 85
Referee: Damato (ITA)
26/8/10, Stadionul Steaua, Bucharest
FC Unirea Urziceni 1-1 HNK Hajduk Split
Goal(s): 1-0 Bilaşco 2, 1-1 Vukušić 88
Referee: Circhetta (SUI)
Aggregate: 2-5; HNK Hajduk Split qualify.

19/8/10, Cristal Arena, Genk
KRC Genk 0-3 FC Porto
Goal(s): 0-1 Falcao 29(p), 0-2 Souza 82, 0-3 Belluschi 90
Referee: Banti (ITA)
26/8/10, Estádio do Dragão, Porto
FC Porto 4-2 KRC Genk
Goal(s): 0-1 Vossen 22, 1-1 Hulk 36, 2-1 Fernando 53, 2-2 Vossen 56, 3-2 Hulk 59(p), 4-2 Hulk 63
Referee: Daloukas (GRE)
Aggregate: 7-2; FC Porto qualify.

19/8/10, Renzo Barbera, Palermo
US Città di Palermo 3-0 NK Maribor
Goal(s): 1-0 Maccarone 37(p), 2-0 Hernández 39, 3-0 Pastore 77
Referee: Mcdonald (SCO)
26/8/10, Stadion Ljudski vrt, Maribor
NK Maribor 3-2 US Città di Palermo
Goal(s): 1-0 Marcos Tavares 14, 2-0 Iličič 58, 2-1 Hernández 62, 2-2 Hernández 68, 3-2 Anđelković 89
Referee: Sukhina (RUS)
Aggregate: 3-5; US Città di Palermo qualify.

19/8/10, Jan Breydelstadion, Bruges
Club Brugge KV 2-1 FC Dinamo Minsk
Goal(s): 0-1 Dragun 6, 1-1 Hoefkens 71(p), 2-1 Blondel 84
Referee: Borski (POL)
26/8/10, Dinamo Stadion, Minsk
FC Dinamo Minsk 2-3 Club Brugge KV
Goal(s): 0-1 Hoefkens 5(p), 0-2 Dalmat 26, 0-3 Hoefkens 32(p), 1-3 Chukhlei 47, 2-3 Dragun 90
Referee: Duarte Gomes (POR)
Aggregate: 3-5; Club Brugge KV qualify.

19/8/10, José Alvalade, Lisbon
Sporting Clube de Portugal 0-2 Brøndby IF
Goal(s): 0-1 Kristiansen 43, 0-2 Jallow 52
Referee: Schörgenhofer (AUT)
26/8/10, Brøndby, Brondby
Brøndby IF 0-3 Sporting Clube de Portugal
Goal(s): 0-1 Evaldo 45, 0-2 Nuno Coelho 75, 0-3 Yannick Djaló 90+1
Referee: Jech (CZE)
Aggregate: 2-3; Sporting Clube de Portugal qualify.

19/8/10, Olympique de la Pontaise, Lausanne
FC Lausanne-Sport 1-1 FC Lokomotiv Moskva
Goal(s): 1-0 Traoré 28, 1-1 Sychev 65
Referee: Mazeika (LTU)
26/8/10, Lokomotiv Stadion, Moscow
FC Lokomotiv Moskva 1-1 FC Lausanne-Sport (aet)
Goal(s): 0-1 Sílvio 17, 1-1 Aliyev 85
Referee: Stavrev (MKD)
Aggregate: 2-2; FC Lausanne-Sport qualify after extra time 3-4 on penalties.

19/8/10, Stadionul Steaua, Bucharest
FC Steaua Bucureşti 1-0 Grasshopper-Club
Goal(s): 1-0 Stancu 71
Referee: Eriksson (SWE)
26/8/10, Stadion Letzigrund, Zurich
Grasshopper-Club 1-0 FC Steaua Bucureşti (aet)
Goal(s): 1-0 Salatic 77
Referee: Mažić (SRB)
Aggregate: 1-1; FC Steaua Bucureşti qualify after extra time 3-4 on penalties.

19/8/10, Ali Sami Yen Stadyumu, Istanbul
Galatasaray AŞ 2-2 FC Karpaty Lviv
Goal(s): 0-1 Kuznetsov 34, 0-2 Zenjov 41, 1-2 Baroš 59, 2-2 Baroš 86
Referee: Clattenburg (ENG)
26/8/10, Ukrayina Stadion, Lviv
FC Karpaty Lviv 1-1 Galatasaray AŞ
Goal(s): 0-1 Aydın Yılmaz 90+1, 1-1 Fedetskiy 90+3
Referee: Kinhöfer (GER)
Aggregate: 3-3; FC Karpaty Lviv qualify on away goals.

19/8/10, Stadio San Paolo, Naples
SSC Napoli 1-0 IF Elfsborg
Goal(s): 1-0 Lavezzi 45+1
Referee: Kakos (GRE)
26/8/10, Borås Arena, Boras
IF Elfsborg 0-2 SSC Napoli
Goal(s): 0-1 Cavani 29, 0-2 Cavani 38
Referee: Ennjimi (FRA)
Aggregate: 0-3; SSC Napoli qualify.

19/8/10, Coliseum Alfonso Pérez, Getafe
Getafe CF 1-0 APOEL FC
Goal(s): 1-0 Parejo 43
Referee: Čeferin (SVN)
26/8/10, GSP Stadium, Nicosia
APOEL FC 1-1 Getafe CF (aet)
Goal(s): 1-0 Aílton 41, 1-1 Cata Díaz 98
Referee: Kelly (IRL)
Aggregate: 1-2; Getafe CF qualify after extra time.

19/8/10, AZ Stadion, Alkmaar
AZ Alkmaar 2-0 FC Aktobe
Goal(s): 1-0 Holman 20, 2-0 Wernbloom 27
Referee: Yefet (ISR)
26/8/10, Tcentralny, Aktobe
FC Aktobe 2-1 AZ Alkmaar
Goal(s): 0-1 Wernbloom 10, 1-1 Tleshev 67, 2-1 Tleshev 89
Referee: Kulbakov (BLR)
Aggregate: 2-3; AZ Alkmaar qualify.

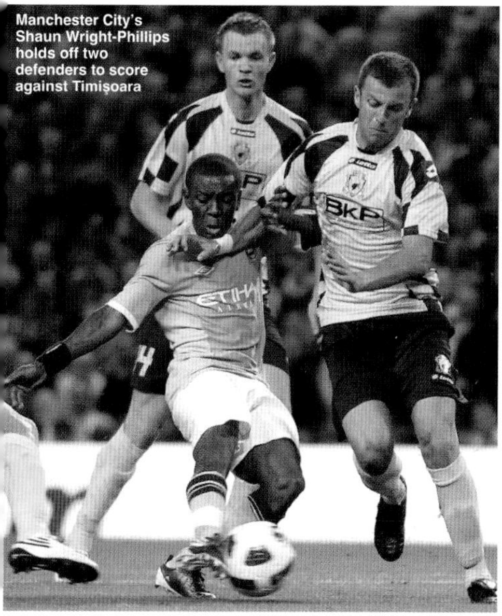
Manchester City's Shaun Wright-Phillips holds off two defenders to score against Timişoara

19/8/10, ETO Park, Gyor
Győri ETO FC 0-2 NK Dinamo Zagreb
Goal(s): 0-1 Rukavina 19, 0-2 Rukavina 28
Referee: Studer (SUI)
26/8/10, Stadion Maksimir, Zagreb
NK Dinamo Zagreb 2-1 Győri ETO FC
Goal(s): 0-1 Ceolin 17, 1-1 Sammir 45+2(p), 2-1 Sammir 84(p)
Referee: Marriner (ENG)
Aggregate: 4-1; NK Dinamo Zagreb qualify.

19/8/10, BVB Stadion Dortmund, Dortmund
Borussia Dortmund 4-0 Qarabağ FK
Goal(s): 1-0 Kagawa 13, 2-0 Barrios 21, 3-0 Barrios 29, 4-0 Kagawa 41
Referee: Balaj (ROU)
26/8/10, Tofiq Bähramov-Republic stadium, Baku
Qarabağ FK 0-1 Borussia Dortmund
Goal(s): 0-1 Barrios 90+1
Referee: Gumienny (BEL)
Aggregate: 0-5; Borussia Dortmund qualify.

19/8/10, Stadion Graz Liebenau, Graz
SK Sturm Graz 1-2 Juventus
Goal(s): 0-1 Bonucci 16, 1-1 Schildenfeld 82, 1-2 Amauri 90+1
Referee: Çakır (TUR)
26/8/10, Stadio Olimpico, Turin
Juventus 1-0 SK Sturm Graz
Goal(s): 1-0 Del Piero 53
Referee: Collum (SCO)
Aggregate: 3-1; Juventus qualify.

19/8/10, Natsionalen Stadion Vasil Levski, Sofia
PFC CSKA Sofia 3-0 The New Saints FC
Goal(s): 1-0 Aquaro 81, 2-0 Nelson 82, 3-0 Delev 90
Referee: Kaasik (EST)
26/8/10, The Racecourse Ground, Wrexham
The New Saints FC 2-2 PFC CSKA Sofia
Goal(s): 0-1 Aquaro 11, 1-1 M. Williams 14, 2-1 Evans 62, 2-2 Tiboni 80
Referee: Asumaa (FIN)
Aggregate: 2-5; PFC CSKA Sofia qualify.

19/8/10, Toumbas Stadium, Salonika
PAOK FC 1-0 Fenerbahçe SK
Goal(s): 1-0 Vieirinha 19
Referee: Gräfe (GER)
26/8/10, Şükrü Saracoğlu, Istanbul
Fenerbahçe SK 1-1 PAOK FC (aet)
Goal(s): 1-0 Emre Belözoğlu 50, 1-1 Muslimović 102
Referee: Tagliavento (ITA)
Aggregate: 1-2; PAOK FC qualify after extra time.

19/8/10, Estadio El Madrigal, Villarreal
Villarreal CF 5-0 FC Dnepr Mogilev
Goal(s): 1-0 Marchena 10, 2-0 Santi Cazorla 16, 3-0 Borja Valero 30, 4-0 Cani 44, 5-0 Nilmar 75
Referee: Evans (WAL)
26/8/10, Spartak Stadion, Mogilev
FC Dnepr Mogilev 1-2 Villarreal CF
Goal(s): 1-0 Yurchenko 19, 1-1 Nilmar 45+1, 1-2 Marco Ruben 90+1
Referee: Aydınus (TUR)
Aggregate: 1-7; Villarreal CF qualify.

19/8/10, Stadionul Dan Păltinişanu, Timisoara
FC Timişoara 0-1 Manchester City FC
Goal(s): 0-1 Balotelli 72
Referee: Meyer (GER)
26/8/10, City of Manchester Stadium, Manchester
Manchester City FC 2-0 FC Timişoara
Goal(s): 1-0 Wright-Phillips 43, 2-0 Boyata 59
Referee: Neves Moreira De Sousa (POR)
Aggregate: 3-0; Manchester City FC qualify.

GROUP STAGE

GROUP A

If ambitious Manchester City FC made expected progress at the head of the class, this was a section notable for the unhappy fate of three-time UEFA Cup winners Juventus, who failed to qualify despite not losing a single game.

The problem for Luigi Delneri's side was that they did not win one either, drawing all six of their fixtures and so finishing five points behind City and second-placed KKS Lech Poznań. Things might have been different for Juve had they held on to a 3-2 lead entering added time in their opening assignment against Lech. The Bianconeri had fought back from 2-0 down but were rocked by a magnificent 92nd-minute Artjoms Rudņevs strike that sealed a hat-trick for the young Latvian forward and set the tone for a frustrating campaign in Turin.

Lech Poznań striker Artjoms Rudņevs (left) scored a remarkable opening-night hat-trick against Juventus in Turin

Bakero impact

Although Juventus then drew at City, the Manchester outfit had already won at FC Salzburg and moved closer to the last 32 with a subsequent 3-1 home success against Lech on 21 October. By the time the sides reconvened in Poznan a fortnight later, the Polish title holders had a new coach, with José María Bakero having replaced Jacek Zieliński. The Spaniard promptly inspired them to a 3-1 victory against Roberto Mancini's men, secured by late goals from Manuel Arboleda and, spectacularly, Mateusz Możdżeń.

That was City's only defeat and, with Juventus and Salzburg playing out a second successive draw on the same night, it did not prove costly. Indeed, by the end of Matchday 5, the fate of all four teams was sealed. City qualified by downing Salzburg 3-0 at Eastlands – with Mario Balotelli scoring twice – and eliminating the Austrian champions at the same time.

Missed chance

For their part, Juventus travelled to snowy Poznan needing victory, only to fall behind when that man Rudņevs inflicted further punishment with an early header. Vincenzo Iaquinta equalised after 84 minutes, but when Juve substitute Alberto Libertazzi spurned a chance in the last minute, the Old Lady's fate was sealed.

Lech celebrated qualification by prevailing at winless Salzburg on Matchday 6 to climb level on points with City, although the Premier League club's superior goal difference – the head-to-head records were identical – ensured them top spot.

Group A Results

16/9/10, Stadion Salzburg, Salzburg
FC Salzburg 0-2 Manchester City FC
Attendance: 25150
Goal(s): 0-1 David Silva 8, 0-2 Jô 63
Referee: Dalooukas (GRE)

16/9/10, Stadio Olimpico, Turin
Juventus 3-3 KKS Lech Poznań
Attendance: 10837
Goal(s): 0-1 Rudņevs 14(p), 0-2 Rudņevs 30, 1-2 Chiellini 45+2, 2-2 Chiellini 50, 3-2 Del Piero 68, 3-3 Rudņevs 90+2
Referee: Bezborodov (RUS)

30/9/10, City of Manchester Stadium, Manchester
Manchester City FC 1-1 Juventus
Attendance: 35212
Goal(s): 0-1 Iaquinta 10, 1-1 A. Johnson 37
Referee: Iturralde González (ESP)

30/9/10, Miejski, Poznan
KKS Lech Poznań 2-0 FC Salzburg
Attendance: 42000
Goal(s): 1-0 Arboleda 47, 2-0 Peszko 80
Referee: Jakobsson (ISL)

21/10/10, City of Manchester Stadium, Manchester
Manchester City FC 3-1 KKS Lech Poznań
Attendance: 33388
Goal(s): 1-0 Adebayor 13, 2-0 Adebayor 25, 2-1 Tshibamba 50, 3-1 Adebayor 73
Referee: Tudor (ROU)

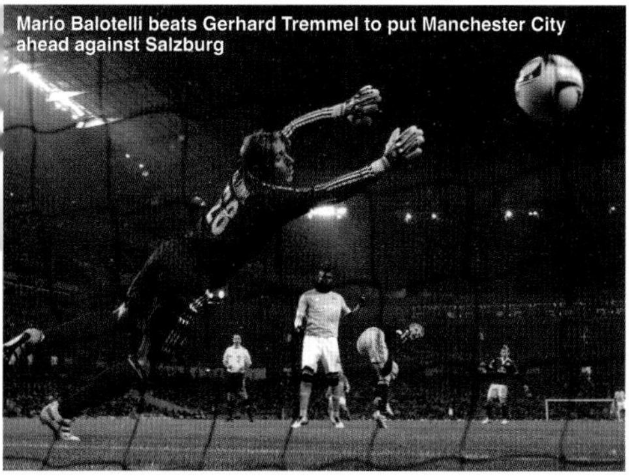

Mario Balotelli beats Gerhard Tremmel to put Manchester City ahead against Salzburg

21/10/10, Stadion Salzburg, Salzburg
FC Salzburg 1-1 Juventus
Attendance: 19200
Goal(s): 1-0 Švento 36, 1-1 Krasić 47
Referee: Szabó (HUN)

4/11/10, Miejski, Poznan
KKS Lech Poznań 3-1 Manchester City FC
Attendance: 42590
Goal(s): 1-0 Injac 31, 1-1 Adebayor 51, 2-1 Arboleda 86, 3-1 Możdżeń 90+1
Referee: Vink (NED)

4/11/10, Stadio Olimpico, Turin
Juventus 0-0 FC Salzburg
Attendance: 12162
Referee: Stalhammar (SWE)

1/12/10, City of Manchester Stadium, Manchester
Manchester City FC 3-0 FC Salzburg
Attendance: 37552
Goal(s): 1-0 Balotelli 18, 2-0 Balotelli 65, 3-0 A. Johnson 78
Referee: Kovařík (CZE)

1/12/10, Miejski, Poznan
KKS Lech Poznań 1-1 Juventus
Attendance: 42590
Goal(s): 1-0 Rudņevs 12, 1-1 Iaquinta 84
Referee: Teixeira Vitienes (ESP)

16/12/10, Stadion Salzburg, Salzburg
FC Salzburg 0-1 KKS Lech Poznań
Attendance: 5300
Goal(s): 0-1 Štilić 30
Referee: Layushkin (RUS)

16/12/10, Stadio Olimpico, Turin
Juventus 1-1 Manchester City FC
Attendance: 6992
Goal(s): 1-0 Giannetti 43, 1-1 Jô 77
Referee: Vad (HUN)

Group A Table

		Home					Away					Total					
	Pld	W	D	L	F	A	W	D	L	F	A	W	D	L	F	A	Pts
1 Manchester City FC	6	2	1	0	7	6	1	1	1	4	0	3	2	1	11	6	11
2 KKS Lech Poznań	6	2	1	0	6	8	1	1	1	5	0	3	2	1	11	8	11
3 Juventus	6	0	3	0	4	7	0	3	0	3	0	0	6	0	7	7	6
4 FC Salzburg	6	0	1	2	1	9	0	1	2	0	0	0	2	4	1	9	2

GROUP B

Seven months on from being crowned the inaugural UEFA Europa League champions in Hamburg, Club Atlético de Madrid were left licking their wounds after their trophy defence was surprisingly cut short by Bayer 04 Leverkusen and Aris Thessaloniki FC.

The reigning champions faced an uphill struggle right from the start, when a 1-0 defeat in Salonika dealt an immediate blow to their hopes of a top-two berth. The early portents appeared even more ominous for the holders given events in Germany, where Jupp Heynckes' Leverkusen announced their own intentions by seeing off Rosenborg BK 4-0. Patrick Helmes got the Bundesliga side up and running with just four minutes gone en route to one of three opening-night hat-tricks.

Rosenborg woe

Rosenborg quickly dusted themselves down to defeat Aris 2-1 in Trondheim on Matchday 2, but that was as good as it got for the Norwegian club, who failed to win another point and finished adrift in fourth spot.

Atlético thus found themselves involved in a three-way tussle for qualification and although they would ultimately become the team left by the wayside, Quique Sánchez Flores's charges looked to have rediscovered their verve on Matchdays 2, 3 and 4, drawing 1-1 with Leverkusen and beating Rosenborg twice.

Leverkusen's Patrick Helmes is challenged by Anthony Annan of Rosenborg

Decisive fixture

With Leverkusen collecting four points from their back-to-back games against Aris, they and Atlético were sitting pretty. Diego Forlán then increased the mood of optimism around the Liga side by registering at home against Aris on Matchday 5, the winner of the Golden Ball as best player at the 2010 FIFA World Cup finally opening his campaign account to level the scores at 1-1. It proved to be a false dawn for the Spanish club, however, as Aris went on to win 3-2, leaving Atlético captain Antonio López to admit: "Before kick-off, losing this match never crossed our minds."

The win left Aris with qualification in their own hands and they calmly sealed their progress by defeating Rosenborg 2-0. As it transpired, a draw would have sufficed as Atlético's survival hopes were extinguished for good in a 1-1 draw away to section winners Leverkusen, not far from Hamburg – the scene of their 2010 final triumph.

Ricardo Faty of Aris, who did the double over holders Atlético Madrid

Group B Results

16/9/10, BayArena, Leverkusen
Bayer 04 Leverkusen 4-0 Rosenborg BK
Attendance: 13065
Goal(s): 1-0 Helmes 4, 2-0 Reinartz 38, 3-0 Helmes 58, 4-0 Helmes 61
Referee: Vollquartz (DEN)

16/9/10, Kleanthis Vikelidis Stadium, Salonika
Aris Thessaloniki FC 1-0 Club Atlético de Madrid
Attendance: 16699
Goal(s): 1-0 Javito 59
Referee: Clattenburg (ENG)

30/9/10, Lerkendal Stadion, Trondheim
Rosenborg BK 2-1 Aris Thessaloniki FC
Attendance: 11016
Goal(s): 1-0 Moldskred 37, 1-1 Ruiz 43, 2-1 Prica 68
Referee: Braamhaar (NED)

30/9/10, Estadio Vicente Calderón, Madrid
Club Atlético de Madrid 1-1 Bayer 04 Leverkusen
Attendance: 28502
Goal(s): 0-1 Derdiyok 39, 1-1 Simão 51
Referee: Tagliavento (ITA)

21/10/10, Estadio Vicente Calderón, Madrid
Club Atlético de Madrid 3-0 Rosenborg BK
Attendance: 28472
Goal(s): 1-0 Godín 17, 2-0 Agüero 66, 3-0 Diego Costa 78
Referee: Zimmermann (SUI)

21/10/10, Kleanthis Vikelidis Stadium, Salonika
Aris Thessaloniki FC 0-0 Bayer 04 Leverkusen
Attendance: 16372
Referee: Ingvarsson (SWE)

4/11/10, Lerkendal Stadion, Trondheim
Rosenborg BK 1-2 Club Atlético de Madrid
Attendance: 14248
Goal(s): 0-1 Agüero 4, 1-1 Henriksen 52, 1-2 Tiago 84
Referee: Bezborodov (RUS)

4/11/10, BayArena, Leverkusen
Bayer 04 Leverkusen 1-0 Aris Thessaloniki FC
Attendance: 18265
Goal(s): 1-0 Vidal 90
Referee: Bruno Paixão (POR)

1/12/10, Estadio Vicente Calderón, Madrid
Club Atlético de Madrid 2-3 Aris Thessaloniki FC
Attendance: 21154
Goal(s): 0-1 Koke 2, 1-1 Forlán 11, 2-1 Agüero 16, 2-2 Koke 51(p), 2-3 Lazaridis 81
Referee: Bebek (CRO)

1/12/10, Lerkendal Stadion, Trondheim
Rosenborg BK 0-1 Bayer 04 Leverkusen
Attendance: 11096
Goal(s): 0-1 Sam 35
Referee: Kelly (IRL)

16/12/10, BayArena, Leverkusen
Bayer 04 Leverkusen 1-1 Club Atlético de Madrid
Attendance: 18903
Goal(s): 1-0 Helmes 69, 1-1 Fran Mérida 72
Referee: Tudor (ROU)

16/12/10, Kleanthis Vikelidis Stadium, Salonika
Aris Thessaloniki FC 2-0 Rosenborg BK
Attendance: 17283
Goal(s): 1-0 Cesarec 45+1, 2-0 Faty 90+2
Referee: Einwaller (AUT)

Group B Table

		Home					Away					Total					
	Pld	W	D	L	F	A	W	D	L	F	A	W	D	L	F	A	Pts
1 Bayer 04 Leverkusen	6	2	1	0	6	2	1	2	0	2	0	3	3	0	8	2	12
2 Aris Thessaloniki FC	6	2	1	0	3	5	1	0	2	4	0	3	1	2	7	5	10
3 Club Atlético de Madrid	6	1	1	1	6	7	1	1	1	3	0	2	2	2	9	7	8
4 Rosenborg BK	6	1	0	2	3	13	0	0	3	0	0	1	0	5	3	13	3

GROUP C

Sporting Clube de Portugal were in command of Group C from day one, making a winning start to their campaign by overcoming LOSC Lille Métropole 2-1. They subsequently laid down an even more substantial marker to the chasing pack with ten goals from their ensuing home encounters against PFC Levski Sofia and KAA Gent.

After putting five goals past Levski with no reply, the 5-1 defeat of Gent proved a particularly memorable occasion for Liedson, who celebrated his 300th Sporting appearance with two goals. Hélder Postiga also struck for the third time in as many games. However, when Francky Dury's side turned the tables on the Lisbon Lions with a 3-1 win on Matchday 4, the race for second place was thrown wide open.

Genk rally

If Sporting had been expected to clinch their fourth win in a row, no one told Gent. Despite having harvested just one point hitherto, the Belgians gave a spirited performance against the group leaders, taking the lead through a Tim Smolders penalty and scoring twice in the last 11 minutes though substitutes Ibrahima Conté and Shlomi Arbeitman following Abel's dismissal.

That victory narrowed the gap to a point from Lille, who required an 88th-minute Ivo Ivanov own goal to scrape a 2-2 draw in Bulgaria. Gent again seized the initiative on Matchday 5 after Lille lost 1-0 to Sporting, who sealed qualification as group winners with their 100th victory in UEFA competition thanks to Anderson Polga's volley.

Liedson scored twice against Gent on his 300th appearance for Sporting

Rousing finale

Gent triumphed by the same scoreline against Levski to leapfrog Lille and set up an exciting finale. "We now have to give everything to qualify," said Lille's Emerson ahead of a match from which his side had to emerge victorious to progress. Win they did, dominating a match that was played from start to finish in driving snow.

Les Dogues hit the woodwork three times but nevertheless emerged 3-0 victors thanks to goals from Ludovic Obraniak, Pierre-Alain Frau and Moussa Sow. Levski, meanwhile, signed off on a high note – a 1-0 success against Sporting – but their second group win came too late to prevent the Blues from finishing bottom.

Group C Results

16/9/10, Lille Métropole, Villeneuve-d'Ascq
LOSC Lille Métropole 1-2 Sporting Clube de Portugal
Attendance: 14457
Goal(s): 0-1 Vukčević 11, 0-2 Hélder Postiga 34, 1-2 Frau 57
Referee: Atkinson (ENG)

16/9/10, Georgi Asparuhov Stadion, Sofia
PFC Levski Sofia 3-2 KAA Gent
Attendance: 22240
Goal(s): 0-1 Azofeifa 23, 1-1 Joãozinho 42, 1-2 Šuler 48, 2-2 Dembélé 60, 3-2 Greene 84
Referee: Szabó (HUN)

30/9/10, José Alvalade, Lisbon
Sporting Clube de Portugal 5-0 PFC Levski Sofia
Attendance: 15081
Goal(s): 1-0 Daniel Carriço 30, 2-0 Maniche 43, 3-0 Diogo Salomão 53, 4-0 Hélder Postiga 61, 5-0 Matías Fernández 79
Referee: Kever (SUI)

30/9/10, Jules Ottenstadion, Gent
KAA Gent 1-1 LOSC Lille Métropole
Attendance: 7834
Goal(s): 1-0 De Smet 5, 1-1 Frau 21
Referee: Tudor (ROU)

21/10/10, José Alvalade, Lisbon
Sporting Clube de Portugal 5-1 KAA Gent
Attendance: 15008
Goal(s): 1-0 Diogo Salomão 7, 2-0 Liedson 13, 2-1 Wils 16, 3-1 Liedson 27, 4-1 Maniche 37, 5-1 Hélder Postiga 59
Referee: Kelly (IRL)

21/10/10, Lille Métropole, Villeneuve-d'Ascq
LOSC Lille Métropole 1-0 PFC Levski Sofia
Attendance: 14646
Goal(s): 1-0 Chedjou 49
Referee: Jakobsson (ISL)

4/11/10, Jules Ottenstadion, Gent
KAA Gent 3-1 Sporting Clube de Portugal
Attendance: 8795
Goal(s): 1-0 Smolders 7(p), 1-1 Carlos Saleiro 38, 2-1 Conté 79, 3-1 Arbeitman 82
Referee: Rasmussen (DEN)

4/11/10, Georgi Asparuhov Stadion, Sofia
PFC Levski Sofia 2-2 LOSC Lille Métropole
Attendance: 17440
Goal(s): 1-0 Dembélé 11, 1-1 Túlio de Melo 35, 2-1 Gadzhev 82, 2-2 Ivanov 88(og)
Referee: Mažić (SRB)

1/12/10, José Alvalade, Lisbon
Sporting Clube de Portugal 1-0 LOSC Lille Métropole
Attendance: 16569
Goal(s): 1-0 Anderson Polga 28
Referee: Nijhuis (NED)

1/12/10, Jules Ottenstadion, Gent
KAA Gent 1-0 PFC Levski Sofia
Attendance: 8662
Goal(s): 1-0 Wallace 77
Referee: Skjerven (NOR)

16/12/10, Lille Métropole, Villeneuve-d'Ascq
LOSC Lille Métropole 3-0 KAA Gent
Attendance: 15285
Goal(s): 1-0 Obraniak 30, 2-0 Frau 56, 3-0 Sow 89
Referee: Clos Gómez (ESP)

16/12/10, Georgi Asparuhov Stadion, Sofia
PFC Levski Sofia 1-0 Sporting Clube de Portugal
Attendance: 5000
Goal(s): 1-0 Mladenov 45
Referee: Kinhöfer (GER)

Group C Table

		Home					Away					Total					
	Pld	W	D	L	F	A	W	D	L	F	A	W	D	L	F	A	Pts
1 Sporting Clube de Portugal	6	3	0	0	11	6	1	0	2	3	0	4	0	2	14	6	12
2 LOSC Lille Métropole	6	2	0	1	5	6	0	2	1	3	0	2	2	2	8	6	8
3 KAA Gent	6	2	1	0	5	13	0	0	3	3	0	2	1	3	8	13	7
4 PFC Levski Sofia	6	2	1	0	6	11	0	0	3	0	0	2	1	3	6	11	7

Lille's Moussa Sow scored in the decisive Matchday 6 win against Levski

GROUP D

In a section that produced fewer goals than any other, it was little surprise that a solitary strike on Matchday 6 proved decisive in earning PAOK FC the runners-up berth behind table-topping Villarreal CF.

Although the Yellow Submarine finished a solitary point ahead of their Greek pursuers, they stamped their ticket with a game to spare. Such comfort looked unlikely after a 2-0 opening defeat at NK Dinamo Zagreb, on a night when PAOK drew 1-1 at Club Brugge KV, but if those results left Villarreal rooted to the foot of the table, they did not remain there for long.

Spoils shared

The Liga outfit got themselves back on track with a 2-1 victory against Club Brugge as Giuseppe Rossi and Gonzalo weighed in with goals. It was the quick response Juan Carlos Garrido's side needed, though PAOK now occupied first place following a 1-0 win against Dinamo.

Pavlos Dermitzakis was the man who had masterminded the Salonika club's rise to the summit but, come Matchday 3, he was gone. He blamed "bad results in the league" for his exit, leaving assistant Ioakim Chavos in charge. A 1-0 defeat away to Villarreal then changed the dynamic of the group almost as quickly as the same scoreline in PAOK's favour did after Matchday 4.

Big ambitions

As for Dinamo, they took four points from their double-header against Club Brugge to go second but were abruptly stopped in their tracks in early December. Rossi registered twice in a 3-0 win for Villarreal and immediately declared his team's desire "to win this tournament" as they checked into the round of 32 early.

Held by Club Brugge, PAOK knew a draw in Zagreb would send them through too. Having been breached just three times – only Bayer 04 Leverkusen boasted a tighter defence – the Greek club held firm again as Dimitris Salpingidis's solitary strike delivered a momentous win, the goalscorer later admitting his team-mates had been left "really exhausted" by a gruelling

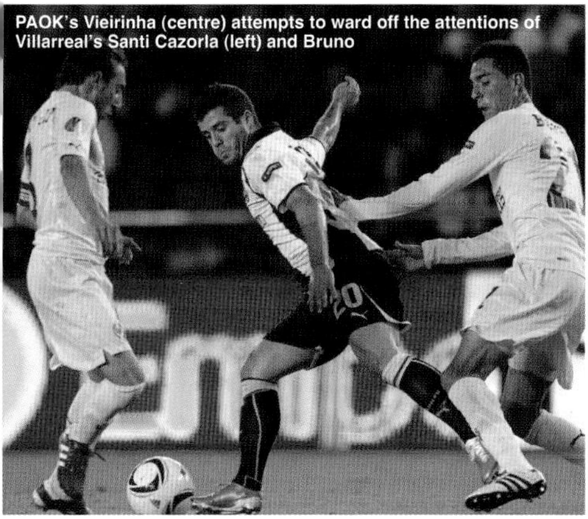
PAOK's Vieirinha (centre) attempts to ward off the attentions of Villarreal's Santi Cazorla (left) and Bruno

campaign. Over in Belgium, meanwhile, Rossi ended the group stage as joint second highest scorer on five goals after his double helped Villarreal seal a 2-1 success and top spot.

Group D Results

16/9/10, Stadion Maksimir, Zagreb
NK Dinamo Zagreb 2-0 Villarreal CF
Attendance: 17021
Goal(s): 1-0 Rukavina 18, 2-0 Sammir 80
Referee: Kralovec (CZE)

16/9/10, Jan Breydelstadion, Bruges
Club Brugge KV 1-1 PAOK FC
Attendance: 17525
Goal(s): 1-0 Kouemaha 61, 1-1 Malezas 78
Referee: Johannesson (SWE)

30/9/10, Estadio El Madrigal, Villarreal
Villarreal CF 2-1 Club Brugge KV
Attendance: 14900
Goal(s): 1-0 Rossi 41, 1-1 Donk 45+2, 2-1 Gonzalo 56
Referee: Layushkin (RUS)

30/9/10, Toumbas Stadium, Salonika
PAOK FC 1-0 NK Dinamo Zagreb
Attendance: 17297
Goal(s): 1-0 Ivić 56
Referee: Fautrel (FRA)

21/10/10, Estadio El Madrigal, Villarreal
Villarreal CF 1-0 PAOK FC
Attendance: 14760
Goal(s): 1-0 Marco Ruben 38
Referee: Borski (POL)

21/10/10, Stadion Maksimir, Zagreb
NK Dinamo Zagreb 0-0 Club Brugge KV
Attendance: 17270
Referee: Yefet (ISR)

4/11/10, Jan Breydelstadion, Bruges
Club Brugge KV 0-2 NK Dinamo Zagreb
Attendance: 18300
Goal(s): 0-1 Sammir 55, 0-2 Biščan 59
Referee: Einwaller (AUT)

4/11/10, Toumbas Stadium, Salonika
PAOK FC 1-0 Villarreal CF
Attendance: 22779
Goal(s): 1-0 Vieirinha 70
Referee: Braamhaar (NED)

2/12/10, Estadio El Madrigal, Villarreal
Villarreal CF 3-0 NK Dinamo Zagreb
Attendance: 11911
Goal(s): 1-0 Rossi 25(p), 2-0 Marco Ruben 62, 3-0 Rossi 80
Referee: Gräfe (GER)

2/12/10, Toumbas Stadium, Salonika
PAOK FC 1-1 Club Brugge KV
Attendance: 19424
Goal(s): 1-0 Vieirinha 25, 1-1 Šćepović 89
Referee: Courtney (NIR)

15/12/10, Stadion Maksimir, Zagreb
NK Dinamo Zagreb 0-1 PAOK FC
Attendance: 29226
Goal(s): 0-1 Salpingidis 60
Referee: Clattenburg (ENG)

15/12/10, Jan Breydelstadion, Bruges
Club Brugge KV 1-2 Villarreal CF
Attendance: 16265
Goal(s): 1-0 Kouemaha 28, 1-1 Rossi 30, 1-2 Rossi 34(p)
Referee: Mažić (SRB)

Giuseppe Rossi, of Group D winners Villarreal, jumps for joy

Group D Table

		Home					Away					Total					
	Pld	W	D	L	F	A	W	D	L	F	A	W	D	L	F	A	Pts
1 Villarreal CF	6	3	0	0	6	5	1	0	2	2	0	4	0	2	8	5	12
2 PAOK FC	6	2	1	0	3	3	1	1	1	2	0	3	2	1	5	3	11
3 NK Dinamo Zagreb	6	1	1	1	2	5	1	0	2	2	0	2	1	3	4	5	7
4 Club Brugge KV	6	0	1	2	2	8	0	2	1	2	0	0	3	3	4	8	3

GROUP E

Via Minsk and Tiraspol, an unexpected change of coach and the wintriest of weather, FC Dynamo Kyiv took a scenic, if ultimately untroubled, route through to the round of 32 alongside FC BATE Borisov.

The two eventual qualifiers were pitted against one another immediately, and a 2-2 draw in the Ukrainian capital suggested they were likely to be evenly matched throughout. Although that portent did ring true in the end, Matchday 1 was not a wholly accurate gauge of what was to come. AZ Alkmaar, after all, beat FC Sheriff 2-1 to move to the head of the section – the one and only time they would occupy a top-two berth.

Luzhny appointment

The Eredivisie outfit were brought back down to earth by a 4-1 reverse in Belarus, but it was events in Moldova on Matchday 2 that proved especially influential for the rest of the campaign. Sheriff beat Dynamo 2-0 to become the first Moldovan victors against Ukrainian opposition since independence and, with his defeated team bottom of the section on one point, coach Valeriy Gazzayev duly stepped down.

Oleh Luzhniy was handed the reins on a caretaker basis and the former Dynamo defender made an instant impact on the continent. His charges triumphed 2-1 in the Netherlands to consign AZ to just their second defeat in 40 European home games.

Freezing conditions

Winners again in the return encounter, Dynamo shot from bottom to second in the blink of an eye, but it was BATE who still led the way after posting two wins against Sheriff. Indeed, their 3-1 home triumph at the beginning of November sent them through to the last 32 for a first ever taste of springtime UEFA competition.

Despite that achievement, Viktor Goncharenko's side were emphatically put in their place on Matchday 5. Dynamo's 4-1 victory in freezing Minsk sent the visitors surging into top spot and prompted Luzhniy to suggest: "This is how we should always play." With their own progress now assured, Dynamo signed off with a 0-0 draw against Sheriff that guaranteed first place, BATE finding AZ's home ground a fortress again as they lost 3-0.

Sergei Sosnovskiy helped BATE reach the knockout phase with the only goal of the game away to Sheriff

Group E Results

16/9/10, AZ Stadion, Alkmaar
AZ Alkmaar 2-1 FC Sheriff
Attendance: 10624
Goal(s): 1-0 Gudmundsson 14, 1-1 Moreno 68(og), 2-1 Jaliens 83
Referee: Asumaa (FIN)

16/9/10, Valeriy Lobanovskiy Stadium, Kyiv
FC Dynamo Kyiv 2-2 FC BATE Borisov
Attendance: 12100
Goal(s): 0-1 Rodionov 3, 1-1 Milevskiy 34, 2-1 Eremenko 44, 2-2 Nekhaichik 54
Referee: Strömbergsson (SWE)

30/9/10, Dinamo Stadion, Minsk
FC BATE Borisov 4-1 AZ Alkmaar
Attendance: 12153
Goal(s): 1-0 Rodionov 5, 2-0 Kontsevoi 48, 3-0 Renan 77(p), 4-0 Olekhnovich 83, 4-1 Sigthórsson 89
Referee: Trattou (CYP)

30/9/10, Stadionul Sheriff, Tiraspol
FC Sheriff 2-0 FC Dynamo Kyiv
Attendance: 12600
Goal(s): 1-0 Erokhin 8, 2-0 Jymmy 37(p)
Referee: Jech (CZE)

21/10/10, AZ Stadion, Alkmaar
AZ Alkmaar 1-2 FC Dynamo Kyiv
Attendance: 12338
Goal(s): 0-1 Milevskiy 16, 1-1 Falkenburg 35, 1-2 Khacheridi 40
Referee: McDonald (SCO)

21/10/10, Stadionul Sheriff, Tiraspol
FC Sheriff 0-1 FC BATE Borisov
Attendance: 7000
Goal(s): 0-1 Sosnovskiy 8
Referee: Duarte Gomes (POR)

4/11/10, Dinamo Stadion, Minsk
FC BATE Borisov 3-1 FC Sheriff
Attendance: 11500
Goal(s): 1-0 Rodionov 15, 1-1 Erokhin 32, 2-1 Pavlov 70, 3-1 Renan 75
Referee: Malek (POL)

4/11/10, Valeriy Lobanovskiy Stadium, Kyiv
FC Dynamo Kyiv 2-0 AZ Alkmaar
Attendance: 15900
Goal(s): 1-0 Milevskiy 47, 2-0 Milevskiy 61
Referee: Berntsen (NOR)

2/12/10, Stadionul Sheriff, Tiraspol
FC Sheriff 1-1 AZ Alkmaar
Attendance: 3500
Goal(s): 0-1 Holman 17, 1-1 Rouamba 54
Referee: Zimmermann (SUI)

2/12/10, Dinamo Stadion, Minsk
FC BATE Borisov 1-4 FC Dynamo Kyiv
Attendance: 10620
Goal(s): 0-1 Vukojević 16, 0-2 Yarmolenko 43, 0-3 Gusev 50(p), 0-4 Milevskiy 68, 1-4 Nekhaichik 84
Referee: Muñiz Fernández (ESP)

15/12/10, AZ Stadion, Alkmaar
AZ Alkmaar 3-0 FC BATE Borisov
Attendance: 13852
Goal(s): 1-0 Sigthórsson 7, 2-0 Sigthórsson 84, 3-0 Maher 86
Referee: Deaconu (ROU)

15/12/10, Valeriy Lobanovskiy Stadium, Kyiv
FC Dynamo Kyiv 0-0 FC Sheriff
Attendance: 10800
Referee: Kircher (GER)

Group E Table

	Pld	Home					Away					Total					Pts
		W	D	L	F	A	W	D	L	F	A	W	D	L	F	A	
1 FC Dynamo Kyiv	6	1	2	0	4	6	2	0	1	6	0	3	2	1	10	6	11
2 FC BATE Borisov	6	2	0	1	8	11	1	1	1	3	0	3	1	2	11	11	10
3 AZ Alkmaar	6	2	0	1	6	10	0	1	2	2	0	2	1	3	8	10	7
4 FC Sheriff	6	1	1	1	3	7	0	1	2	2	0	1	2	3	5	7	5

Oleh Luzhniy took over the Dynamo Kyiv coaching reins in mid-competition and led the Ukrainian club to first place in Group E

GROUP F

The group stage's heaviest underdogs, its joint highest scorers and its leakiest defence made for a section with goals aplenty. 2005 UEFA Cup winners PFC CSKA Moskva might have stolen the show, but it was Swiss second-tier outfit FC Lausanne-Sport who put the whiff of romance in the air.

Tomáš Necid of CSKA Moskva shields the ball from Palermo's Nicola Rigoni

Domestic cup runners-up, Lausanne had already caused a stir by overcoming FC Lokomotiv Moskva in the play-offs, with coach Martin Rueda promising to "play free, attacking football" in the competition proper. Their shackles were possibly loosened too far, however, as Lokomotiv's city rivals CSKA inflicted a 3-0 opening defeat that set the tone for what was to come from both teams.

Prolific CSKA

Leonid Slutskiy's charges went from strength to strength thereafter, registering five consecutive victories to put their name in the hat with time to spare. Averaging three goals per game throughout made them more prolific than any of their peers bar FC Zenit St Petersburg, a boast in stark contrast to Lausanne's dubious honour of conceding an unparalleled 16 strikes.

Sandwiched between these two during the course of the campaign were AC Sparta Praha and US Città di Palermo. The Czech champions put their noses in front with a 3-2 home win against the Sicilians on Matchday 1 and still narrowly held sway at the midway point, despite handing Lausanne their one and only point by conceding a 95th-minute equaliser in a 3-3 thriller at the Letná.

Necid treble

Sparta exacted revenge by prevailing 3-1 in Switzerland to send themselves clear in second spot, Palermo having suffered back-to-back losses at the hands of CSKA. And so it came to the two rivals' Matchday 5 encounter, in which anything less than three points would be insufficient to keep the Serie A outfit's chances alive.

Twice Palermo led but twice they were pegged back in a 2-2 draw, meaning Sparta could breathe easily in their closing fixture against a CSKA side fresh from routing Lausanne 5-1, thanks largely to Czech striker Tomáš Necid's hat-trick. With both sides' work already done, a 1-1 stalemate ensued in the Czech capital to leave CSKA seven points clear at the summit.

Group F Results

16/9/10, Stadion Letná, Prague
AC Sparta Praha 3-2 US Città di Palermo
Attendance: 13766
Goal(s): 1-0 Wilfried 17, 1-1 Maccarone 38, 2-1 Kladrubský 68, 3-1 Kadlec 75, 3-2 Hernández 83
Referee: Kakos (GRE)

16/9/10, Olympique de la Pontaise, Lausanne
FC Lausanne-Sport 0-3 PFC CSKA Moskva
Attendance: 9531
Goal(s): 0-1 Vágner Love 22, 0-2 Ignashevich 68, 0-3 Vágner Love 80(p)
Referee: Evans (WAL)

30/9/10, Arena Khimki, Moscow
PFC CSKA Moskva 3-0 AC Sparta Praha
Attendance: 12900
Goal(s): 1-0 Doumbia 72, 2-0 Mark González 84(p), 3-0 Doumbia 86
Referee: Skjerven (NOR)

30/9/10, Renzo Barbera, Palermo
US Città di Palermo 1-0 FC Lausanne-Sport
Attendance: 9772
Goal(s): 1-0 Migliaccio 79
Referee: Kaasik (EST)

21/10/10, Renzo Barbera, Palermo
US Città di Palermo 0-3 PFC CSKA Moskva
Attendance: 17548
Goal(s): 0-1 Doumbia 34, 0-2 Doumbia 59, 0-3 Necid 82
Referee: Schörgenhofer (AUT)

21/10/10, Stadion Letná, Prague
AC Sparta Praha 3-3 FC Lausanne-Sport
Attendance: 12430
Goal(s): 0-1 Meoli 6, 1-1 Wilfried 10, 2-1 Kucka 21, 3-1 Wilfried 24, 3-2 Steuble 75, 3-3 Silvio 90+5
Referee: Asumaa (FIN)

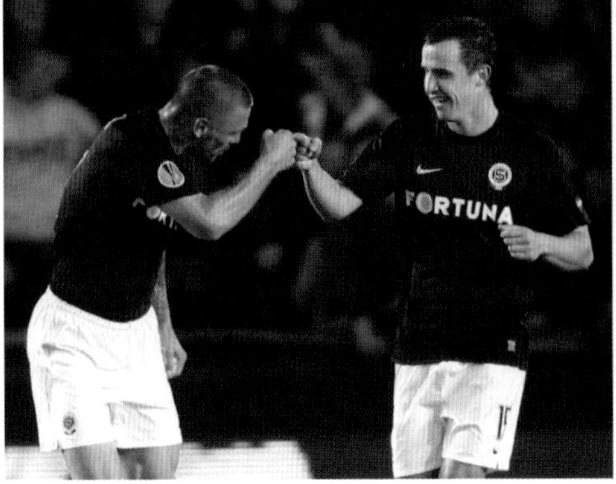
Jiří Kladrubský (right) celebrates a successful penalty kick for Sparta against Palermo with captain Tomáš Řepka

4/11/10, Olympique de la Pontaise, Lausanne
FC Lausanne-Sport 1-3 AC Sparta Praha
Attendance: 7200
Goal(s): 1-0 Katz 6, 1-1 Wilfried 45, 1-2 Kweuke 75, 1-3 Wilfried 90+6
Referee: Kulbakov (BLR)

4/11/10, Arena Khimki, Moscow
PFC CSKA Moskva 3-1 US Città di Palermo
Attendance: 11980
Goal(s): 0-1 Maccarone 10, 1-1 Honda 47, 2-1 Necid 50, 3-1 Necid 54
Referee: Neves Moreira de Sousa (POR)

2/12/10, Arena Khimki, Moscow
PFC CSKA Moskva 5-1 FC Lausanne-Sport
Attendance: 4500
Goal(s): 1-0 Necid 18, 2-0 Oliseh 22, 3-0 Tošić 40, 4-0 Dzagoev 71, 5-0 Necid 82, 5-1 Carrupt 90+2
Referee: Weiner (GER)

2/12/10, Renzo Barbera, Palermo
US Città di Palermo 2-2 AC Sparta Praha
Attendance: 8623
Goal(s): 1-0 Rigoni 23, 1-1 Kladrubský 51(p), 2-1 Pinilla 60(p), 2-2 Kucka 62
Referee: Strahonja (CRO)

15/12/10, Stadion Letná, Prague
AC Sparta Praha 1-1 PFC CSKA Moskva
Attendance: 12707
Goal(s): 0-1 Dzagoev 15, 1-1 Kadlec 44
Referee: Ingvarsson (SWE)

15/12/10, Olympique de la Pontaise, Lausanne
FC Lausanne-Sport 0-1 US Città di Palermo
Attendance: 7150
Goal(s): 0-1 Muñoz 84
Referee: Genov (BUL)

Group F Table

		Home					Away					Total					
	Pld	W	D	L	F	A	W	D	L	F	A	W	D	L	F	A	Pts
1 PFC CSKA Moskva	6	3	0	0	11	3	2	1	0	7	0	5	1	0	18	3	16
2 AC Sparta Praha	6	1	2	0	7	12	1	1	1	5	0	2	3	1	12	12	9
3 US Città di Palermo	6	1	1	1	3	11	1	0	2	4	0	2	1	3	7	11	7
4 FC Lausanne-Sport	6	0	0	3	1	16	0	1	2	4	0	0	1	5	5	16	1

GROUP G

FC Zenit St Petersburg left the chasing pack in their wake thanks to the group stage's only 100% record, ensuring that they finished a whopping 11 points ahead of their closest pursuers. The race for second was anything but as clear-cut.

Zenit sped out of the traps with 3-1 and 4-2 wins against RSC Anderlecht and AEK Athens FC respectively. While the latter had a 3-1 opening-day defeat of HNK Hajduk Split to fall back on, the Belgian side were still chasing their first point two fixtures in. Nevertheless, it was AEK who felt forced to take drastic action prior to Matchday 3, with ex-Sevilla FC boss Manuel Jiménez replacing Dušan Bajević at the helm.

Early blow

The Spaniard's first act was to preside over a 3-0 reverse in Brussels and although the home sequel – a 1-1 draw – did little to hint at a dramatic upturn in fortunes, seeds of recovery had been sown. Indeed, second spot still marginally belonged to AEK, prompting Anderlecht's Roland Juhász to admit he was "not as happy as I might have been".

Zenit, for their part, were blossoming, slotting a total of five goals past Hajduk over their two encounters. The Croatian outfit did at least put up a fight on Matchday 4, recovering from 3-0 down to make it 3-2, but Luciano Spalletti's team held firm to stride into the last 32 with a spring in their step.

Aleksandr Kerzhakov struck an opening-night hat-trick for Zenit at Anderlecht

Narrow escape

Having clinched the Russian Premier-Liga title in mid-November, Zenit were positively bouncing by the time Matchday 5 came around and promptly dispatched Anderlecht 3-1. With AEK prevailing by the same scoreline in Split, the runners-up berth was AEK's to lose heading into the group denouement.

And lose it they did. Three points clear, they required only a draw to progress, but Zenit were in no mood to surrender momentum and posted a 3-0 victory that left the door open for Anderlecht to waltz through. Over in Belgium, Ariël Jacobs' charges gladly grabbed their lifeline by downing Hajduk 2-0. "We've shown that we really were eager to qualify," said captain Mbark Boussoufa. "It was a narrow escape, but we still managed to get through."

Group G Results

16/9/10, Constant Vanden Stock Stadium, Brussels
RSC Anderlecht 1-3 FC Zenit St Petersburg
Attendance: 13336
Goal(s): 0-1 Kerzhakov 8, 0-2 Kerzhakov 33, 0-3 Kerzhakov 44, 1-3 Juhász 66
Referee: Gräfe (GER)

16/9/10, OACA Spiros Louis Stadium, Athens
AEK Athens FC 3-1 HNK Hajduk Split
Attendance: 16182
Goal(s): 1-0 Djebbour 12, 1-1 Ibričić 29(p), 2-1 Liberopoulos 65, 3-1 Scocco 89
Referee: Nijhuis (NED)

30/9/10, Stadion Poljud, Split
HNK Hajduk Split 1-0 RSC Anderlecht
Attendance: 33000
Goal(s): 1-0 Vukušić 90+5
Referee: Yıldırım (TUR)

30/9/10, Petrovskiy Stadion, St Petersburg
FC Zenit St Petersburg 4-2 AEK Athens FC
Attendance: 19000
Goal(s): 1-0 Hubočan 1, 2-0 Bruno Alves 13, 2-1 Liberopoulos 37, 3-1 Lazović 43(p), 4-1 Lazović 57, 4-2 Kafes 83(p)
Referee: Mažić (SRB)

21/10/10, Constant Vanden Stock Stadium, Brussels
RSC Anderlecht 3-0 AEK Athens FC
Attendance: 14508
Goal(s): 1-0 Boussoufa 31, 2-0 Lukaku 71, 3-0 Juhász 75
Referee: Kaasik (EST)

21/10/10, Petrovskiy Stadion, St Petersburg
FC Zenit St Petersburg 2-0 HNK Hajduk Split
Attendance: 19500
Goal(s): 1-0 Bukharov 25, 2-0 Danny 68
Referee: Kovařík (CZE)

4/11/10, Stadion Poljud, Split
HNK Hajduk Split 2-3 FC Zenit St Petersburg
Attendance: 28000
Goal(s): 0-1 Ionov 31, 0-2 Huszti 47(p), 0-3 Rosina 50, 1-3 M. Ljubičić 68, 2-3 Vukušić 82
Referee: Iturralde González (ESP)

Mbark Boussoufa skippered Anderlecht through to the knockout phase with a Matchday 6 win over Hajduk Split

4/11/10, OACA Spiros Louis Stadium, Athens
AEK Athens FC 1-1 RSC Anderlecht
Attendance: 11311
Goal(s): 1-0 Blanco 48(p), 1-1 Polák 55
Referee: Kever (SUI)

1/12/10, Stadion Poljud, Split
HNK Hajduk Split 1-3 AEK Athens FC
Attendance: 13726
Goal(s): 0-1 Scocco 50(p), 0-2 Manolas 61, 0-3 Blanco 84, 1-3 J. Buljat 90
Referee: Dean (ENG)

1/12/10, Petrovskiy Stadion, St Petersburg
FC Zenit St Petersburg 3-1 RSC Anderlecht
Attendance: 13900
Goal(s): 1-0 Ionov 12, 2-0 Bukharov 65, 2-1 Kanu 87, 3-1 Huszti 88
Referee: Borski (POL)

16/12/10, Constant Vanden Stock Stadium, Brussels
RSC Anderlecht 2-0 HNK Hajduk Split
Attendance: 14979
Goal(s): 1-0 De Sutter 12, 2-0 Suárez 41
Referee: Johannesson (SWE)

16/12/10, OACA Spiros Louis Stadium, Athens
AEK Athens FC 0-3 FC Zenit St Petersburg
Attendance: 13605
Goal(s): 0-1 Bukharov 43, 0-2 Rosina 67, 0-3 Denisov 88
Referee: Ennjimi (FRA)

Group G Table

		Home					Away					Total					
	Pld	W	D	L	F	A	W	D	L	F	A	W	D	L	F	A	Pts
1 FC Zenit St Petersburg	6	3	0	0	9	6	3	0	0	9	0	6	0	0	18	6	18
2 RSC Anderlecht	6	2	0	1	6	8	0	1	2	2	0	2	1	3	8	8	7
3 AEK Athens FC	6	1	1	1	4	13	1	0	2	5	0	2	1	3	9	13	7
4 HNK Hajduk Split	6	1	0	2	4	13	0	0	3	1	0	1	0	5	5	13	3

GROUP H

Despite struggling in the Bundesliga, VfB Stuttgart progressed serenely under the stewardship of three different coaches, finishing well clear of runners-up and section entertainers BSC Young Boys.

The Swiss outfit had at one stage looked poised to eliminate Tottenham Hotspur FC and reach the UEFA Champions League group stage, only to lose the second leg of their play-off 4-0. A 6-3 aggregate scoreline in that tie nonetheless hinted at what was to come from Vladimir Petković's side in this competition.

Away struggles

Beaten 3-0 by Stuttgart on Matchday 1, Young Boys were left propping up the standings, with the Bundesliga team, then coached by Christian Gross, heading straight to the summit. In Spain, meanwhile, Getafe CF made similar early gains by seeing off Odense BK 2-1.

OB also lost at home to Stuttgart on a night when Young Boys got off the mark courtesy of a 2-0 win against Getafe. “We were very aggressive and put Getafe under pressure – no team likes that,” explained goalkeeper/captain Marco Wölfli. A 4-2 victory against OB duly followed, before the Mr Hyde to Young Boys' Dr Jekyll reared his head in a 2-0 defeat in Odense.

Young Boys goalkeeper and captain Marco Wölfli

A moment of celebration for Stuttgart's Austrian international Martin Harnik as he strikes a late winner in Odense

Quick-fire goals

For their part, Stuttgart had dispensed with Gross following poor league form but continued to excel in continental combat by posting successive wins against Getafe. With qualification now in the bag, and Jens Keller in the dugout, they prepared to take on Young Boys determined, according to forward Martin Harnik, "to win every game in the group".

The Swabians looked a safe bet for victory when they took a 2-1 lead into the closing ten minutes in snowy Berne, but three goals in six minutes changed all that, giving Petković's charges a 4-2 triumph that earned them progress alongside their opponents. "We've shown we can beat anyone in our own stadium," said Scott Sutter, scorer of Young Boys' equaliser. Their goal achieved, the Swiss club signed off with a 1-0 loss in Spain, while new coach Bruno Labbadia helped Stuttgart bounce back emphatically with their fifth win of the section - 5-1 against OB.

Group H Results

16/9/10, VfB Arena, Stuttgart
VfB Stuttgart 3-0 BSC Young Boys
Attendance: 13800
Goal(s): 1-0 Cacau 23(p), 2-0 Gentner 59, 3-0 Taşçı 90+1
Referee: Banti (ITA)

16/9/10, Coliseum Alfonso Pérez, Getafe
Getafe CF 2-1 Odense BK
Attendance: 2420
Goal(s): 0-1 Andreasen 44, 1-1 Arizmendi 51, 2-1 Pedro Ríos 81
Referee: Courtney (NIR)

30/9/10, Odense Stadion, Odense
Odense BK 1-2 VfB Stuttgart
Attendance: 8854
Goal(s): 0-1 Kuzmanović 72, 1-1 Johansson 78, 1-2 Harnik 86
Referee: Deaconu (ROU)

30/9/10, Stade de Suisse, Berne
BSC Young Boys 2-0 Getafe CF
Attendance: 12830
Goal(s): 1-0 Degen 11, 2-0 Degen 64
Referee: Malek (POL)

21/10/10, Stade de Suisse, Berne
BSC Young Boys 4-2 Odense BK
Attendance: 12511
Goal(s): 1-0 Bienvenu 25, 2-0 Sutter 34, 2-1 Utaka 48, 3-1 D. Degen 61, 4-1 Lulić 74, 4-2 Sørensen 84(p)
Referee: Blom (NED)

21/10/10, VfB Arena, Stuttgart
VfB Stuttgart 1-0 Getafe CF
Attendance: 17400
Goal(s): 1-0 Marica 29
Referee: Kakos (GRE)

4/11/10, Odense Stadion, Odense
Odense BK 2-0 BSC Young Boys
Attendance: 5334
Goal(s): 1-0 Andreasen 12, 2-0 Andreasen 60
Referee: Stavrev (MKD)

4/11/10, Coliseum Alfonso Pérez, Getafe
Getafe CF 0-3 VfB Stuttgart
Attendance: 3459
Goal(s): 0-1 Marica 26, 0-2 Gebhart 64, 0-3 Harnik 76
Referee: Strahonja (CRO)

1/12/10, Stade de Suisse, Berne
BSC Young Boys 4-2 VfB Stuttgart
Attendance: 18627
Goal(s): 1-0 Degen 39, 1-1 Pogrebnyak 48, 1-2 Schipplock 68, 2-2 Sutter 81, 3-2 Mayuka 82, 4-2 Mayuka 87
Referee: Yefet (ISR)

1/12/10, Odense Stadion, Odense
Odense BK 1-1 Getafe CF
Attendance: 5599
Goal(s): 0-1 Pedro Ríos 17, 1-1 Andreasen 90+2
Referee: Kaasik (EST)

16/12/10, VfB Arena, Stuttgart
VfB Stuttgart 5-1 Odense BK
Attendance: 14000
Goal(s): 1-0 Gebhart 20, 2-0 Høegh 48(og), 3-0 Gentner 65, 4-0 Møller Christensen 70(og), 4-1 Utaka 72, 5-1 Marica 90+3
Referee: Hauge (NOR)

16/12/10, Coliseum Alfonso Pérez, Getafe
Getafe CF 1-0 BSC Young Boys
Attendance: 1631
Goal(s): 1-0 Adrián Sardinero 15
Referee: Vink (NED)

Group H Table

	Pld	Home					Away					Total					Pts
		W	D	L	F	A	W	D	L	F	A	W	D	L	F	A	
1 VfB Stuttgart	6	3	0	0	9	6	2	0	1	7	0	5	0	1	16	6	15
2 BSC Young Boys	6	3	0	0	10	10	0	0	3	0	0	3	0	3	10	10	9
3 Getafe CF	6	2	0	1	3	8	0	1	2	1	0	2	1	3	4	8	7
4 Odense BK	6	1	1	1	4	14	0	0	3	4	0	1	1	4	8	14	4

GROUP I

PSV Eindhoven marched confidently into the round of 32 with an unbeaten jaunt through Group I, but it was Ukraine's FC Metalist Kharkiv rather than 1989/90 UEFA Cup Winners' Cup winners UC Sampdoria who joined them in the next phase.

It took a late goal from Hungarian winger Balázs Dzsudzsák to earn PSV a 1-1 draw in their opener at home against Sampdoria, but despite that faltering start Fred Rutten's side soon regained their composure. A 2-0 win at Metalist on Matchday 2 was their first in a run of four straight victories, with their impressive 2-1 triumph in Genoa on Matchday 5 earning them progress at Sampdoria's expense.

Landmark result

PSV's series of wins included two against Debreceni VSC, who would go on to finish a distant fourth in the section. Debrecen old boy Dzsudzsák secured the decider as the Eredivisie hopefuls prevailed 2-1 in Hungary – ahead of a 3-0 home success – but he stayed true to his promise not to "run around the stadium with his shirt off" if he found the net against his old club.

PSV's Hungarian international Balázs Dzsudzsák scored against his old club Debrecen

Beaten in all six of their UEFA Champions League group stage outings the previous season, Debrecen did not find the going in the UEFA Europa League any easier, and their 5-0 home defeat by Metalist in their opening assignment was a landmark result for both clubs.

Early conclusion

Myron Markevych's Metalist succumbed to PSV in their subsequent fixture, but just as they did in the 2008/09 UEFA Cup round of 32, they got the better of Sampdoria over two fixtures to take a grip on second place. Cleiton hit the winner in a 2-1 home victory, which was followed by a goalless stalemate in Genoa. The Ukrainian outfit then confirmed their advance by edging Debrecen 2-1 in Kharkiv on Matchday 5.

That wrapped matters up going into the final day of fixtures, but Metalist still secured a third successive European clean sheet on their travels by drawing 0-0 at PSV. Elsewhere, a youthful Sampdoria lineup lost 2-0 at Debrecen as the Hungarian club at last celebrated their first win in 12 UEFA club competition group stage games.

Group I Results

16/9/10, Ferenc Puskás, Budapest
Debreceni VSC 0-5 FC Metalist Kharkiv
Attendance: 8000
Goal(s): 0-1 Edmar 24, 0-2 Cleiton 34, 0-3 Edmar 74, 0-4 Fininho 77, 0-5 Valyayev 89
Referee: Stavrev (MKD)

16/9/10, PSV Stadion, Eindhoven
PSV Eindhoven 1-1 UC Sampdoria
Attendance: 17500
Goal(s): 0-1 Cacciatore 25, 1-1 Dzsudzsák 90
Referee: Kircher (GER)

30/9/10, Stadio Luigi Ferraris, Genoa
UC Sampdoria 1-0 Debreceni VSC
Attendance: 12159
Goal(s): 1-0 Pazzini 18(p)
Referee: Kovařík (CZE)

30/9/10, Metalist Stadion, Kharkiv
FC Metalist Kharkiv 0-2 PSV Eindhoven
Attendance: 38100
Goal(s): 0-1 Dzsudzsák 27(p), 0-2 Engelaar 30
Referee: Chapron (FRA)

21/10/10, Ferenc Puskás, Budapest
Debreceni VSC 1-2 PSV Eindhoven
Attendance: 18000
Goal(s): 1-0 Mijadinoski 35, 1-1 Engelaar 40, 1-2 Dzsudzsák 66
Referee: Vollquartz (DEN)

Cleiton scored Metalist's winner at home to Sampdoria

21/10/10, Metalist Stadion, Kharkiv
FC Metalist Kharkiv 2-1 UC Sampdoria
Attendance: 34580
Goal(s): 0-1 Koman 32, 1-1 Taison 38, 2-1 Cleiton 73
Referee: Meyer (GER)

4/11/10, Stadio Luigi Ferraris, Genoa
UC Sampdoria 0-0 FC Metalist Kharkiv
Attendance: 13259
Referee: Teixeira Vitienes (ESP)

4/11/10, PSV Stadion, Eindhoven
PSV Eindhoven 3-0 Debreceni VSC
Attendance: 15000
Goal(s): 1-0 Afellay 22, 2-0 Reis 44, 3-0 S.Wuytens 88
Referee: Courtney (NIR)

1/12/10, Stadio Luigi Ferraris, Genoa
UC Sampdoria 1-2 PSV Eindhoven
Attendance: 12131
Goal(s): 1-0 Pazzini 45+3, 1-1 Toivonen 51, 1-2 Toivonen 90
Referee: Strömbergsson (SWE)

1/12/10, Metalist Stadion, Kharkiv
FC Metalist Kharkiv 2-1 Debreceni VSC
Attendance: 31200
Goal(s): 0-1 Czvitkovics 48, 1-1 Bódi 52(og), 2-1 Oliynyk 88
Referee: Stalhammar (SWE)

16/12/10, Ferenc Puskás, Budapest
Debreceni VSC 2-0 UC Sampdoria
Attendance: 5500
Goal(s): 1-0 Kabát 48, 2-0 Volta 86(og)
Referee: Sukhina (RUS)

16/12/10, PSV Stadion, Eindhoven
PSV Eindhoven 0-0 FC Metalist Kharkiv
Attendance: 15300
Referee: Kakos (GRE)

Group I Table

		Home					Away					Total					
	Pld	W	D	L	F	A	W	D	L	F	A	W	D	L	F	A	Pts
1 PSV Eindhoven	6	1	2	0	4	3	3	0	0	6	0	4	2	0	10	3	14
2 FC Metalist Kharkiv	6	2	0	1	4	4	1	2	0	5	0	3	2	1	9	4	11
3 UC Sampdoria	6	1	1	1	2	7	0	1	2	2	0	1	2	3	4	7	5
4 Debreceni VSC	6	1	0	2	3	13	0	0	3	1	0	1	0	5	4	13	3

GROUP J

Borussia Dortmund spent the autumn of 2010 sweeping aside their rivals in Germany but they found the UEFA Europa League another matter, with Paris Saint-Germain FC and two-time UEFA Cup winners Sevilla FC graduating from Group J.

Fellow contenders FC Karpaty Lviv of Ukraine overcame Galatasaray AŞ in the play-offs and they kicked off their campaign with a heroic effort at home against the Bundesliga club. Having trailed 2-0, goals from Oleh Holodyuk, Mykhaylo Kopolovets and Denys Kozhanov left them in a match-winning position with three minutes of normal time remaining, only for Lucas Barrios and Mario Götze to give Dortmund a thrilling 4-3 victory.

Dortmund draws

On the same night, PSG's one-time defender Antoine Kombouaré marshalled his side to a 1-0 win away against Sevilla, with summer signing Nenê scoring the only goal. "We knew our opponents' quality so we had to make sure we were switched on at all times," explained the Brazilian playmaker. "Then it was just a case of scoring when the opportunity came our way."

Sevilla atoned for that setback with a 1-0 success in Dortmund on Matchday 2, before engineering back-to-back wins against Karpaty. They thus went

Sevilla's Luca Cigarini celebrates his winning goal in Dortmund

PSG striker Guillaume Hoarau towers over a prostrate Nuri Şahin of Dortmund

into their 2 December rematch with PSG at the top of the standings, the Parisians having followed up a 2-0 home defeat of Karpaty with successive draws against Dortmund.

Nenê decisive

Nenê was to be the hero of the hour at the Parc des Princes. Frédéric Kanouté struck twice to level the scores after PSG had taken an early 2-0 lead, but – having prompted both his side's goals from corners – Nenê registered a stunning third just before the break. Guillaume Hoarau then made it 4-2 shortly after the interval as the French club confirmed their last-32 place.

Dortmund beat Karpaty to keep their chances alive ahead of the last-day reckoning but fell just short at the final hurdle, squandering a lead to draw 2-2 in Seville when a win would have sent them through at their hosts' expense. "We knew the game was of vital importance to our season," said Kanouté, who plundered Sevilla's second to clinch the runners-up spot behind PSG.

Group J Results

16/9/10, Estadio Ramón Sánchez Pizjuán, Seville
Sevilla FC 0-1 Paris Saint-Germain FC
Attendance: 24960
Goal(s): 0-1 Nenê 75
Referee: Schörgenhofer (AUT)

16/9/10, Ukrayina Stadion, Lviv
FC Karpaty Lviv 3-4 Borussia Dortmund
Attendance: 27700
Goal(s): 0-1 Nuri 12(p), 0-2 Götze 27, 1-2 Holodyuk 44, 2-2 Kopolovets 52, 3-2 Kozhanov 78, 3-3 Barrios 87, 3-4 Götze 90+2
Referee: Circhetta (SUI)

30/9/10, Parc des Princes, Paris
Paris Saint-Germain FC 2-0 FC Karpaty Lviv
Attendance: 9117
Goal(s): 1-0 Jallet 4, 2-0 Nenê 20
Referee: Strahonja (CRO)

30/9/10, BVB Stadion Dortmund, Dortmund
Borussia Dortmund 0-1 Sevilla FC
Attendance: 49100
Goal(s): 0-1 Cigarini 45+1
Referee: Dean (ENG)

21/10/10, BVB Stadion Dortmund, Dortmund
Borussia Dortmund 1-1 Paris Saint-Germain FC
Attendance: 50200
Goal(s): 1-0 Nuri 50(p), 1-1 Chantôme 87
Referee: Eriksson (SWE)

21/10/10, Ukrayina Stadion, Lviv
FC Karpaty Lviv 0-1 Sevilla FC
Attendance: 27925
Goal(s): 0-1 Kanouté 34
Referee: Nijhuis (NED)

4/11/10, Parc des Princes, Paris
Paris Saint-Germain FC 0-0 Borussia Dortmund
Attendance: 26204
Referee: Kralovec (CZE)

4/11/10, Estadio Ramón Sánchez Pizjuán, Seville
Sevilla FC 4-0 FC Karpaty Lviv
Attendance: 21394
Goal(s): 1-0 Alfaro 9, 2-0 Cigarini 31, 3-0 Alfaro 42, 4-0 Negredo 51
Referee: Yıldırım (TUR)

2/12/10, BVB Stadion Dortmund, Dortmund
Borussia Dortmund 3-0 FC Karpaty Lviv
Attendance: 40100
Goal(s): 1-0 Kagawa 5, 2-0 Hummels 49, 3-0 Lewandowski 89
Referee: Braamhaar (NED)

2/12/10, Parc des Princes, Paris
Paris Saint-Germain FC 4-2 Sevilla FC
Attendance: 18783
Goal(s): 1-0 Bodmer 17, 2-0 Hoarau 20, 2-1 Kanouté 32, 2-2 Kanouté 36, 3-2 Nenê 45, 4-2 Hoarau 47
Referee: Banti (ITA)

15/12/10, Estadio Ramón Sánchez Pizjuán, Seville
Sevilla FC 2-2 Borussia Dortmund
Attendance: 27062
Goal(s): 0-1 Kagawa 4, 1-1 Romaric 31, 2-1 Kanouté 35, 2-2 Subotić 49
Referee: Nikolaev (RUS)

15/12/10, Ukrayina Stadion, Lviv
FC Karpaty Lviv 1-1 Paris Saint-Germain FC
Attendance: 14000
Goal(s): 0-1 Luyindula 39, 1-1 Fedetskiy 45
Referee: Berntsen (NOR)

Group J Table

		Pld	Home					Away					Total					Pts
			W	D	L	F	A	W	D	L	F	A	W	D	L	F	A	
1	Paris Saint-Germain FC	6	2	1	0	6	4	1	2	0	3	0	3	3	0	9	4	12
2	Sevilla FC	6	1	1	1	6	7	2	0	1	4	0	3	1	2	10	7	10
3	Borussia Dortmund	6	1	1	1	4	7	1	2	0	6	0	2	3	1	10	7	9
4	FC Karpaty Lviv	6	0	1	2	4	15	0	0	3	0	0	0	1	5	4	15	1

GROUP K

At the halfway mark, Group K had produced just a solitary win, with Liverpool FC providing the exception courtesy of a 4-1 home defeat of FC Steaua Bucureşti. There was not a bore draw in sight, however – especially when SSC Napoli were in town.

Three times the Partenopei had looked to be dead and buried only for Edinson Cavani to orchestrate their resurrection on each occasion. The Uruguay striker scored a hat-trick as Walter Mazzarri's side came from 3-1 down to draw 3-3 at FC Utrecht in their penultimate outing, but Steaua were denied in even more dramatic fashion in Romania on Matchday 2.

Hollywood ending

Marius Lăcătuş's men raced into a 3-0 lead inside 16 minutes before having a player sent off and allowing Napoli to gradually recover, with Cavani completing the comeback when he made it 3-3 in the 98th minute. Amazingly, the summer signing from US Città di Palermo repeated the trick deep into added time on Matchday 6 as the Serie A high-fliers beat Steaua 1-0 to whip a last-32 spot from under their opponents' noses.

It was the sort of Hollywood ending that Napoli president and movie producer Aurelio De Laurentiis would have appreciated, but it was the stuff of nightmares for Steaua. The club's opening loss at Anfield had hastened the end of Ilie Dumitrescu's 40-day tenure, yet the Army Men quickly marched back into contention under Lăcătuş, with three draws and a 3-1 victory against Utrecht leaving them hopeful of progressing on the final night.

Liverpool's Steven Gerrard completes his hat-trick against Napoli at Anfield

Captain marvel

Liverpool had already sewn up first place by that stage, despite making their worst start to a league season in 57 years under new manager Roy Hodgson. Having guided Fulham FC to the 2009/10 final, Hodgson was on steadier ground in the UEFA Europa League, but his side still suffered a wobble as they trailed visitors Napoli 1-0 at half-time on Matchday 4.

On came captain Steven Gerrard for his only group stage appearance and 45 minutes later he took his bow with the match ball under his arm, a glorious hat-trick all but sealing his side's progress. Cavani was dethroned as the master of the Lazarus act – but not for long.

Group K Results

16/9/10, Anfield, Liverpool
Liverpool FC 4-1 FC Steaua Bucureşti
Attendance: 25605
Goal(s): 1-0 J. Cole 1, 1-1 Tănase 13, 2-1 N'Gog 55(p), 3-1 Lucas 81, 4-1 N'Gog 90+1
Referee: Muñiz Fernández (ESP)

16/9/10, Stadio San Paolo, Naples
SSC Napoli 0-0 FC Utrecht
Attendance: 25897
Referee: Vad (HUN)

30/9/10, Galgenwaard, Utrecht
FC Utrecht 0-0 Liverpool FC
Attendance: 23662
Referee: Duarte Gomes (POR)

30/9/10, Stadionul Steaua, Bucharest
FC Steaua Bucureşti 3-3 SSC Napoli
Attendance: 10203
Goal(s): 1-0 Cribari 2(og), 2-0 Tănase 11, 3-0 Kapetanos 16, 3-1 Vitale 44, 3-2 Hamšík 73, 3-3 Cavani 90+8
Referee: Borski (POL)

21/10/10, Galgenwaard, Utrecht
FC Utrecht 1-1 FC Steaua Bucureşti
Attendance: 24000
Goal(s): 1-0 Duplan 60, 1-1 Schut 75(og)
Referee: Ennjimi (FRA)

21/10/10, Stadio San Paolo, Naples
SSC Napoli 0-0 Liverpool FC
Attendance: 52910
Referee: Kinhöfer (GER)

Napoli striker Edinson Cavani – a last-gasp goalscorer in both games against Steaua

4/11/10, Anfield, Liverpool
Liverpool FC 3-1 SSC Napoli
Attendance: 33892
Goal(s): 0-1 Lavezzi 28, 1-1 Gerrard 76, 2-1 Gerrard 88(p), 3-1 Gerrard 89
Referee: Fautrel (FRA)

4/11/10, Stadionul Steaua, Bucharest
FC Steaua Bucureşti 3-1 FC Utrecht
Attendance: 8322
Goal(s): 1-0 Gardoş 29, 1-1 Mertens 33, 2-1 Stancu 52, 3-1 Stancu 53
Referee: Sukhina (RUS)

2/12/10, Galgenwaard, Utrecht
FC Utrecht 3-3 SSC Napoli
Attendance: 22500
Goal(s): 0-1 Cavani 5, 1-1 Van Wolfswinkel 6, 2-1 Van Wolfswinkel 28(p), 3-1 Demouge 35, 3-2 Cavani 42, 3-3 Cavani 70(p)
Referee: Iturralde González (ESP)

2/12/10, Stadionul Steaua, Bucharest
FC Steaua Bucureşti 1-1 Liverpool FC
Attendance: 13639
Goal(s): 0-1 Jovanović 19, 1-1 Éder Bonfim 61
Referee: Yıldırım (TUR)

15/12/10, Anfield, Liverpool
Liverpool FC 0-0 FC Utrecht
Attendance: 37800
Referee: Jakobsson (ISL)

15/12/10, Stadio San Paolo, Naples
SSC Napoli 1-0 FC Steaua Bucureşti
Attendance: 40631
Goal(s): 1-0 Cavani 90+3
Referee: Kralovec (CZE)

Group K Table

		Home					Away					Total					
	Pld	W	D	L	F	A	W	D	L	F	A	W	D	L	F	A	Pts
1 Liverpool FC	6	2	1	0	7	3	0	3	0	1	0	2	4	0	8	3	10
2 SSC Napoli	6	1	2	0	1	9	0	2	1	7	0	1	4	1	8	9	7
3 FC Steaua Bucureşti	6	1	2	0	7	11	0	1	2	2	0	1	3	2	9	11	6
4 FC Utrecht	6	0	3	0	4	7	0	2	1	1	0	0	5	1	5	7	5

GROUP L

FC Porto justified their billing as Group L favourites with a string of stylish performances that secured their qualification after four matches, maintained their unbeaten status throughout the group stage and advanced the reputation of André Villas-Boas as one of the most impressive young coaches in Europe.

Beşiktaş JK also qualified with room to spare but progress did not appear quite so assured on the evidence of their first three fixtures. The Turkish Süper Lig side were heading for a goalless stalemate against PFC CSKA Sofia on Matchday 1 when Fabian Ernst swooped with a last-gasp winner. The Black Eagles then had to come from behind to sink SK Rapid Wien courtesy of second-half strikes by Filip Hološko and Bobô.

Falcao prolific

Nine-man Porto, however, proved too strong for them on Matchday 3. With two goals already to his name, Colombian striker Radamel Falcao, who went on to lead the scoring charts at the group stage's conclusion, broke the deadlock at the BJK İnönü Stadyumu. Despite the first-half dismissal of Maicon, the visitors proved irrepressible thereafter, scoring twice more through Hulk.

"It was a fine night, both for me and for Porto," said the burly striker, whose goals were followed by Fernando's dismissal and Bobô's late consolation. By now Villas-Boas's side had one foot in the round of 32, and qualification was sealed in an

Fabian Ernst got Beşiktaş's campaign up and running with a late strike at home to CSKA Sofia

exciting rematch at the Estádio do Dragão, which produced another two red cards, and a goal for either side.

Sofia success

Nihat Kahveci cancelled out Falcao's first-half penalty with a spectacular strike after Cristian Rodríguez had been sent off before the hour. Beşiktaş's prospects of an away win diminished, though, when İbrahim Toraman saw red soon afterwards. Despite the 1-1 draw, Beşiktaş remained four points clear of their Austrian and Bulgarian rivals.

A place in the knockout phase was duly secured for Bernd Schuster's side with a 2-1 success in Sofia, where Tomáš Zápotočný and Hološko were on target. A 2-0 triumph against Rapid followed, while the Dragons posted successive 3-1 victories, Falcao plundering a hat-trick in Vienna on Matchday 5 to finish the group stage as the competition's leading marksman with seven goals to his name.

Porto's Radamel Falcao struck seven times in the group stage to become the competition's leading marksman

Group L Results

16/9/10, Estádio do Dragão, Porto
FC Porto 3-0 SK Rapid Wien
Attendance: 30014
Goal(s): 1-0 Rolando 26, 2-0 Falcao 65, 3-0 Rúben Micael 77
Referee: McDonald (SCO)

16/9/10, BJK İnönü Stadyumu, Istanbul
Beşiktaş JK 1-0 PFC CSKA Sofia
Attendance: 25035
Goal(s): 1-0 Ernst 90
Referee: Duhamel (FRA)

30/9/10, Ernst-Happel-Stadion, Vienna
SK Rapid Wien 1-2 Beşiktaş JK
Attendance: 50000
Goal(s): 1-0 Kavlak 51, 1-1 Hološko 55, 1-2 Bobô 64
Referee: Kulbakov (BLR)

30/9/10, Natsionalen Stadion Vasil Levski, Sofia
PFC CSKA Sofia 0-1 FC Porto
Attendance: 10600
Goal(s): 0-1 Falcao 16
Referee: Yefet (ISR)

21/10/10, Natsionalen Stadion Vasil Levski, Sofia
PFC CSKA Sofia 0-2 SK Rapid Wien
Attendance: 7996
Goal(s): 0-1 Vennegoor of Hesselink 28, 0-2 Hofmann 32
Referee: Trattou (CYP)

21/10/10, BJK İnönü Stadyumu, Istanbul
Beşiktaş JK 1-3 FC Porto
Attendance: 21722
Goal(s): 0-1 Falcao 26, 0-2 Hulk 59, 0-3 Hulk 78, 1-3 Bobô 90+2
Referee: Clos Gómez (ESP)

4/11/10, Estádio do Dragão, Porto
FC Porto 1-1 Beşiktaş JK
Attendance: 34139
Goal(s): 1-0 Falcao 36(p), 1-1 Nihat Kahveci 62
Referee: Tagliavento (ITA)

4/11/10, Ernst-Happel-Stadion, Vienna
SK Rapid Wien 1-2 PFC CSKA Sofia
Attendance: 48200
Goal(s): 0-1 Yanchev 50, 1-1 Salihi 56(p), 1-2 Marquinhos 64
Referee: Evans (WAL)

2/12/10, Ernst-Happel-Stadion, Vienna
SK Rapid Wien 1-3 FC Porto
Attendance: 47200
Goal(s): 1-0 Trimmel 39, 1-1 Falcao 42, 1-2 Falcao 86, 1-3 Falcao 88
Referee: Stavrev (MKD)

2/12/10, Natsionalen Stadion Vasil Levski, Sofia
PFC CSKA Sofia 1-2 Beşiktaş JK
Attendance: 9100
Goal(s): 0-1 Zápotočný 59, 0-2 Hološko 64, 1-2 Sheridan 79
Referee: Hagen (NOR)

15/12/10, Estádio do Dragão, Porto
FC Porto 3-1 PFC CSKA Sofia
Attendance: 22930
Goal(s): 1-0 Otamendi 22, 1-1 Delev 48, 2-1 Rúben Micael 54, 3-1 James Rodríguez 90+3
Referee: Circhetta (SUI)

15/12/10, BJK İnönü Stadyumu, Istanbul
Beşiktaş JK 2-0 SK Rapid Wien
Attendance: 16686
Goal(s): 1-0 Ricardo Quaresma 32, 2-0 Ernst 45
Referee: Rasmussen (DEN)

Group L Table

		Home					Away					Total					
	Pld	W	D	L	F	A	W	D	L	F	A	W	D	L	F	A	Pts
1 FC Porto	6	2	1	0	7	4	3	0	0	7	0	5	1	0	14	4	16
2 Beşiktaş JK	6	2	0	1	4	6	2	1	0	5	0	4	1	1	9	6	13
3 SK Rapid Wien	6	0	0	3	3	12	1	0	2	2	0	1	0	5	5	12	3
4 PFC CSKA Sofia	6	0	0	3	1	10	1	0	2	3	0	1	0	5	4	10	3

ROUND OF 32

After a group stage liberally seasoned with drama, the late goals and comebacks continued aplenty as the UEFA Europa League resumed following its winter hiatus with the round of 32.

The most telling last-gasp blow of all was landed by Rangers FC's Maurice Edu two minutes into added time of the second leg against Sporting Clube de Portugal. The Lisbon outfit returned from Glasgow with a 1-1 draw, courtesy of Matías Fernández's late header, and were leading 2-1 on the night when Edu turned in David Healy's low cross to send the Scottish champions through on away goals.

Comeback drama

Liverpool, giving Kenny Dalgish his first taste of European football as the club's manager, also left it late in a tight tie against AC Sparta Praha, which remained goalless for 176 minutes before Dirk Kuyt headed in Raul Meireles's corner at Anfield. Centre-back Sergei Ignashevich was PFC CSKA Moskva's saviour, following up Vágner Love's saved penalty ten minutes from time to stave off the prospect of extra time against a gallant PAOK FC side that fought hard in unfavourable conditions in an attempt to make good their first-leg deficit.

Matías Fernández heads in a late equaliser for Sporting against Rangers at Ibrox

FC Zenit St Petersburg matched CSKA's achievement at the expense of equally feisty, committed opposition in the shape of BSC Young Boys. Trailing 3-1 on aggregate to the Swiss side, the 2008 UEFA Cup winners scored the three unanswered goals they needed in temperatures nudging -10C and on a pitch shorn of green grass. FC Spartak Moskva also prevailed by the same 4-3 aggregate in the other Russia-Switzerland duel, against FC Basel 1893, despite trailing in both legs.

Napoli denied

Another Russian club, FC Rubin Kazan, fell short, however, as they attempted to come from behind against FC Twente. Trailing 2-0 after the home leg, Kurban Berdyev's side had recovered their deficit inside 24 minutes of the return with two spectacular strikes from their South American imports Cristian Ansaldi and Christian Noboa, only to be undone by a goal either side of half-time from their hosts.

SSC Napoli set the standard for dramatic fightbacks during a remarkable group-stage run, but their much-anticipated tie with Villarreal CF proved a bridge too far. After a goalless first leg, the lone Serie A survivors trailed 2-1 at half-time in Spain to a deflected goal from Italian striker Giuseppe Rossi before the introduction of Edinson Cavani set up a grandstand finish. The Uruguayan hit the post and Ezequiel Lavezzi was also denied by the woodwork as the Yellow Submarine somehow stayed afloat.

Portuguese trio

There was no happy ending for the other Spanish team, 2006 and 2007 UEFA Cup winners Sevilla FC, who, betrayed by wayward finishing, exited on away goals despite inflicting FC Porto's first continental loss of the season with a 1-0 second-leg victory in Portugal. SC Braga also sneaked through after overcoming a first-leg deficit against KKS Lech Poznań, while SL Benfica's first win in 19 games in Germany confirmed their superiority over Bundesliga strugglers VfB Stuttgart.

Bayer 04 Leverkusen and FC Dynamo Kyiv made light work of FC Metalist Kharkiv and Beşiktaş JK, respectively, thanks to some ruthless finishing, while AFC Ajax made mincemeat of RSC Anderlecht, going through 5-0 over the two legs. The Amsterdammers' domestic rivals PSV Eindhoven made less serene progress, trailing in each of their two matches against Ligue 1 table-toppers LOSC Lille Métropole before coming through 5-3 on aggregate.

The last 16 lineup was completed by Manchester City FC – 3-0 aggregate victors over Aris Thessaloniki FC, whose 43-year-old unbeaten home record in Europe nevertheless remained intact – and Paris Saint-Germain FC, who edged FC BATE Borisov on away goals after two draws.

Round of 32 Results

15/2/11, Kleanthis Vikelidis Stadium, Salonika
Aris Thessaloniki FC 0-0 Manchester City FC
Attendance: 18812
Referee: Undiano Mallenco (ESP)
24/2/11, City of Manchester Stadium, Manchester
Manchester City FC 3-0 Aris Thessaloniki FC
Attendance: 36748
Goal(s): 1-0 Džeko 7, 2-0 Džeko 12, 3-0 Y. Touré 75
Referee: Kralovec (CZE)
Aggregate: 3-0; Manchester City FC qualify.

17/2/11, Luzhniki Stadion, Moscow
FC Rubin Kazan 0-2 FC Twente
Attendance: 657
Goal(s): 0-1 De Jong 77, 0-2 Wisgerhof 88
Referee: Schörgenhofer (AUT)
24/2/11, FC Twente Stadion, Enschede
FC Twente 2-2 FC Rubin Kazan
Attendance: 23000
Goal(s): 0-1 Ansaldi 22, 0-2 Noboa 24, 1-2 Janssen 45+1, 2-2 Douglas 47
Referee: Borski (POL)
Aggregate: 4-2; FC Twente qualify.

17/2/11, Estádio do Sport Lisboa e Benfica, Lisbon
SL Benfica 2-1 VfB Stuttgart
Attendance: 44852
Goal(s): 0-1 Harnik 21, 1-1 Cardozo 70, 2-1 Jara 81
Referee: Braamhaar (NED)
24/2/11, VfB Arena, Stuttgart
VfB Stuttgart 0-2 SL Benfica
Attendance: 25800
Goal(s): 0-1 Salvio 31, 0-2 Cardozo 78
Referee: Dean (ENG)
Aggregate: 1-4; SL Benfica qualify.

17/2/11, Metalist Stadion, Kharkiv
FC Metalist Kharkiv 0-4 Bayer 04 Leverkusen
Attendance: 35150
Goal(s): 0-1 Derdiyok 23, 0-2 Castro 72, 0-3 Sam 90, 0-4 Sam 90+2
Referee: Gumienny (BEL)
24/2/11, BayArena, Leverkusen
Bayer 04 Leverkusen 2-0 FC Metalist Kharkiv
Attendance: 16212
Goal(s): 1-0 Rolfes 47, 2-0 Ballack 70
Referee: Collum (SCO)
Aggregate: 6-0; Bayer 04 Leverkusen qualify.

17/2/11, Stadio San Paolo, Naples
SSC Napoli 0-0 Villarreal CF
Attendance: 47529
Referee: Clattenburg (ENG)
24/2/11, Estadio El Madrigal, Villarreal
Villarreal CF 2-1 SSC Napoli
Attendance: 21061
Goal(s): 0-1 Hamšík 18, 1-1 Nilmar 42, 2-1 Rossi 45+1
Referee: Çakır (TUR)
Aggregate: 2-1; Villarreal CF qualify.

17/2/11, Stade Constant Vanden Stock, Brussels
RSC Anderlecht 0-3 AFC Ajax
Attendance: 21195
Goal(s): 0-1 Alderweireld 32, 0-2 Eriksen 59, 0-3 El Hamdaoui 67
Referee: Rocchi (ITA)
24/2/11, Amsterdam ArenA, Amsterdam
AFC Ajax 2-0 RSC Anderlecht
Attendance: 42591
Goal(s): 1-0 Sulejmani 11, 2-0 Sulejmani 17
Referee: Hansson (SWE)
Aggregate: 5-0; AFC Ajax qualify.

17/2/11, Miejski, Poznan
KKS Lech Poznań 1-0 SC Braga
Attendance: 29133
Goal(s): 1-0 Rudņevs 72
Referee: Bezborodov (RUS)
24/2/11, Estádio Municipal de Braga, Braga
SC Braga 2-0 KKS Lech Poznań
Attendance: 10007
Goal(s): 1-0 Alan 8, 2-0 Lima 36
Referee: Strömbergsson (SWE)
Aggregate: 2-1; SC Braga qualify.

17/2/11, BJK İnönü Stadyumu, Istanbul
Beşiktaş JK 1-4 FC Dynamo Kyiv
Attendance: 21809
Goal(s): 0-1 Vukojević 26, 1-1 Ricardo Quaresma 37, 1-2 Shevchenko 50, 1-3 Yussuf 56, 1-4 Gusev 90(p)
Referee: Proença (POR)
24/2/11, Valeriy Lobanovskiy Stadium, Kyiv
FC Dynamo Kyiv 4-0 Beşiktaş JK
Attendance: 15300
Goal(s): 1-0 Vukojević 3, 2-0 Yarmolenko 55, 3-0 Gusev 64, 4-0 Shevchenko 74
Referee: Chapron (FRA)
Aggregate: 8-1; FC Dynamo Kyiv qualify.

17/2/11, Dinamo Stadion, Minsk
FC BATE Borisov 2-2 Paris Saint-Germain FC
Attendance: 6080
Goal(s): 1-0 Renan 16, 1-1 Mevlüt 29, 2-1 Gordeichuk 80, 2-2 Luyindula 89
Referee: Yefet (ISR)
24/2/11, Parc des Princes, Paris
Paris Saint-Germain FC 0-0 FC BATE Borisov
Attendance: 17717
Referee: Blom (NED)
Aggregate: 2-2; Paris Saint-Germain FC qualify on away goals.

17/2/11, Ibrox Stadium, Glasgow
Rangers FC 1-1 Sporting Clube de Portugal
Attendance: 34095
Goal(s): 1-0 Whittaker 66, 1-1 Matias Fernández 89
Referee: Gräfe (GER)
24/2/11, José Alvalade, Lisbon
Sporting Clube de Portugal 2-2 Rangers FC
Attendance: 15375
Goal(s): 0-1 Diouf 19, 1-1 Pedro Mendes 42, 2-1 Yannick Djaló 83, 2-2 Edu 90+2
Referee: Tagliavento (ITA)
Aggregate: 3-3; Rangers FC qualify on away goals.

17/2/11, Stadion Letná, Prague
AC Sparta Praha 0-0 Liverpool FC
Attendance: 17569
Referee: Meyer (GER)
24/2/11, Anfield, Liverpool
Liverpool FC 1-0 AC Sparta Praha
Attendance: 42949
Goal(s): 1-0 Kuyt 86
Referee: Mažić (SRB)
Aggregate: 1-0; Liverpool FC qualify.

17/2/11, St. Jakob-Park, Basel
FC Basel 1893 2-3 FC Spartak Moskva
Attendance: 13073
Goal(s): 1-0 Frei 36, 2-0 Streller 41, 2-1 D. Kombarov 61, 2-2 Dzyuba 70, 2-3 Ananidze 90+2
Referee: Stavrev (MKD)
24/2/11, Luzhniki Stadion, Moscow
FC Spartak Moskva 1-1 FC Basel 1893
Attendance: 14977
Goal(s): 0-1 Chipperfield 15, 1-1 McGeady 90+1
Referee: Balaj (ROU)
Aggregate: 4-3; FC Spartak Moskva qualify.

17/2/11, Stade de Suisse, Berne
BSC Young Boys 2-1 FC Zenit St Petersburg
Attendance: 15026
Goal(s): 0-1 Lombaerts 20, 1-1 Lulić 46, 2-1 Mayuka 90+3
Referee: Kakos (GRE)
24/2/11, Petrovskiy Stadion, St Petersburg
FC Zenit St Petersburg 3-1 BSC Young Boys
Attendance: 15000
Goal(s): 0-1 Jemal 21, 1-1 Lazović 41, 2-1 Semak 52, 3-1 Shirokov 76
Referee: Jakobsson (ISL)
Aggregate: 4-3; FC Zenit St Petersburg qualify.

17/2/11, Estadio Ramón Sánchez Pizjuán, Seville
Sevilla FC 1-2 FC Porto
Attendance: 21555
Goal(s): 0-1 Rolando 58, 1-1 Kanouté 65, 1-2 Guarín 86
Referee: Thomson (SCO)
23/2/11, Estádio do Dragão, Porto
FC Porto 0-1 Sevilla FC
Attendance: 35609
Goal(s): 0-1 Luís Fabiano 71
Referee: Webb (ENG)
Aggregate: 2-2; FC Porto qualify on away goals.

17/2/11, Lille Métropole, Villeneuve-d'Ascq
LOSC Lille Métropole 2-2 PSV Eindhoven
Attendance: 16951
Goal(s): 1-0 Gueye 6, 2-0 Túlio de Melo 31, 2-1 Bouma 83, 2-2 Toivonen 84
Referee: Tudor (ROU)
24/2/11, PSV Stadion, Eindhoven
PSV Eindhoven 3-1 LOSC Lille Métropole
Attendance: 28000
Goal(s): 0-1 Frau 22, 1-1 Dzsudzsák 55, 2-1 Lens 67, 3-1 Marcelo 73
Referee: Iturralde González (ESP)
Aggregate: 5-3; PSV Eindhoven qualify.

17/2/11, Toumbas Stadium, Salonika
PAOK FC 0-1 PFC CSKA Moskva
Attendance: 22245
Goal(s): 0-1 Necid 29
Referee: Marriner (ENG)
22/2/11, Luzhniki Stadion, Moscow
PFC CSKA Moskva 1-1 PAOK FC
Attendance: 10500
Goal(s): 0-1 Muslimović 67, 1-1 Ignashevich 80
Referee: Duhamel (FRA)
Aggregate: 2-1; PFC CSKA Moskva qualify.

ROUND OF 16

AFC Ajax, Liverpool FC and Manchester City FC were high-profile casualties as the round of 16 threw up some intriguing contests involving teams from nine nations. First-leg advantage proved decisive, with just one of the opening fixtures ending all-square and no trailing teams managing to overcome their deficit a week later.

Portuguese prominence

SL Benfica established a 2-1 first-leg lead to take into the second encounter with Paris Saint-Germain FC thanks to goals from Maxi Pereira and Franco Jara. Nicolás Gaitán silenced a hostile French crowd in the Parc des Princes a week later to give Jorge Jesus's men a two-goal cushion, and although Mathieu Bodmer's sumptuous volley offered PSG a lifeline, the Eagles soared into the quarter-finals for the second year running. FC Porto's passage was more straightforward as they comfortably overcame PFC CSKA Moskva, winning both legs of the only tie involving two former UEFA Cup winners.

Having become synonymous with dramatic European comebacks in recent years, Liverpool's task of overturning Alan's first-leg penalty for SC Braga seemed far from insurmountable, especially at Anfield, yet they fell short. For all Dirk Kuyt's guile and the endeavour of Andy Carroll, making his first start for the Reds, Braga's defence stood firm to secure a famous triumph, a first European quarter-final berth, and a three-pronged Portuguese presence in the last eight.

Liverpool's new signing Andy Carroll shows his frustration as his team are eliminated at Anfield by Braga

Failed comebacks

FC Twente's Luuk de Jong opened and closed the scoring against FC Zenit St Petersburg with a brace of headers either side of Denny Landzaat's strike to give Michel Preud'homme's men a convincing first-leg lead in Enschede. The Dutch side almost squandered their advantage in Russia, though. First-half goals from Roman Shirokov and Aleksandr Kerzhakov ensured a frenetic finale, but with goalkeeper Nikolay Mihaylov excelling throughout, the Tukkers held their nerve to eliminate Russian opposition for the second round in succession.

It was a similar story for FC Dynamo Kyiv, who had veteran striker Andriy Shevchenko and in-form UEFA Europa League marksman Oleh Gusev to thank for their 2-0 win against Manchester City in the Ukrainian capital. When Mario Balotelli, who had squandered a simple early chance, was dismissed for an over-the-top challenge in the 36th minute of the second leg, the writing appeared to be on the wall for City. Aleksandar Kolarov's strike from a free-kick soon afterwards gave Roberto Mancini's charges hope but the reduced numbers aggravated their task and the second goal they required to take the tie into extra time never came.

Yellow Submarine cruise

One goal from Giuseppe Rossi and two from his Brazilian strike partner Nilmar, the second in added time, brought Villarreal CF a thrilling 3-2 first-leg victory at Bundesliga high-fliers Bayer 04 Leverkusen. Rossi, enjoying a productive run in the competition, was to have the final say in the tie a week later, scoring his team's second goal in a 2-1 win that preserved Spanish interest in the competition while eliminating the last surviving participants from Germany.

Ajax dominated against FC Spartak Moskva in Amsterdam but were left to rue a catalogue of missed chances – and brilliant saves from Ukrainian goalkeeper Andriy Dykan – when Alex's sucker punch earned the Russian club a surprise victory. The second-leg was a masterclass in counterattacking as Valeriy Karpin's side cruised into the quarter-finals with three unanswered goals. As Ajax went out, their domestic rivals PSV Eindhoven joined Twente in the last eight at the

Spartak Moskva goalkeeper Andriy Dykan – a busy man against Ajax in Amsterdam

expense of 2008 UEFA Cup runners-up Rangers FC, a 0-0 home draw preceding a 1-0 win in Glasgow, with Jeremain Lens scoring the only goal of the tie. The Scottish club's exit, allied to the elimination of both Liverpool and Manchester City, ended the prospect of a British club making the short trip across the Irish Sea to participate in the Dublin final.

Round of 16 Results

10/3/11, Estádio Municipal de Braga, Braga
SC Braga 1-0 Liverpool FC
Attendance: 12991
Goal(s): 1-0 Alan 18(p)
Referee: Gumienny (BEL)
17/3/11, Anfield, Liverpool
Liverpool FC 0-0 SC Braga
Attendance: 37494
Referee: Rocchi (ITA)
Aggregate: 0-1; SC Braga qualify.

10/3/11, PSV Stadion, Eindhoven
PSV Eindhoven 0-0 Rangers FC
Attendance: 26000
Referee: Hansson (SWE)
17/3/11, Ibrox Stadium, Glasgow
Rangers FC 0-1 PSV Eindhoven
Attendance: 35373
Goal(s): 0-1 Lens 14
Referee: Schörgenhofer (AUT)
Aggregate: 0-1; PSV Eindhoven qualify.

10/3/11, BayArena, Leverkusen
Bayer 04 Leverkusen 2-3 Villarreal CF
Attendance: 20126
Goal(s): 1-0 Kadlec 33, 1-1 Rossi 42, 1-2 Nilmar 70, 2-2 Castro 72, 2-3 Nilmar 90+4
Referee: Tagliavento (ITA)
17/3/11, Estadio El Madrigal, Villarreal
Villarreal CF 2-1 Bayer 04 Leverkusen
Attendance: 19779
Goal(s): 1-0 Santi Cazorla 33, 2-0 Rossi 61, 2-1 Derdiyok 82
Referee: Kuipers (NED)
Aggregate: 5-3; Villarreal CF qualify.

10/3/11, Estádio do Sport Lisboa e Benfica, Lisbon
SL Benfica 2-1 Paris Saint-Germain FC
Attendance: 33928
Goal(s): 0-1 Luyindula 14, 1-1 Maxi Pereira 42, 2-1 Jara 81
Referee: Kralovec (CZE)
17/3/11, Parc des Princes, Paris
Paris Saint-Germain FC 1-1 SL Benfica
Attendance: 40193
Goal(s): 0-1 Gaitán 27, 1-1 Bodmer 35
Referee: Collum (SCO)
Aggregate: 2-3; SL Benfica qualify.

10/3/11, Luzhniki Stadion, Moscow
PFC CSKA Moskva 0-1 FC Porto
Attendance: 20000
Goal(s): 0-1 Guarín 70
Referee: Schörgenhofer (AUT)
17/3/11, Estádio do Dragão, Porto
FC Porto 2-1 PFC CSKA Moskva
Attendance: 32712
Goal(s): 1-0 Hulk 1, 2-0 Guarín 24, 2-1 Tošić 29
Referee: Blom (NED)
Aggregate: 3-1; FC Porto qualify.

10/3/11, FC Twente Stadion, Enschede
FC Twente 3-0 FC Zenit St Petersburg
Attendance: 20750
Goal(s): 1-0 De Jong 25, 2-0 Landzaat 56, 3-0 De Jong 90+2
Referee: Clattenburg (ENG)
17/3/11, Petrovskiy Stadion, St Petersburg
FC Zenit St Petersburg 2-0 FC Twente
Attendance: 18000
Goal(s): 1-0 Shirokov 16, 2-0 Kerzhakov 38
Referee: Eriksson (SWE)
Aggregate: 2-3; FC Twente qualify.

10/3/11, Amsterdam ArenA, Amsterdam
AFC Ajax 0-1 FC Spartak Moskva
Attendance: 32841
Goal(s): 0-1 Alex 57
Referee: Gräfe (GER)
17/3/11, Luzhniki Stadion, Moscow
FC Spartak Moskva 3-0 AFC Ajax
Attendance: 33631
Goal(s): 1-0 D. Kombarov 21, 2-0 Welliton 30, 3-0 Alex 54
Referee: Atkinson (ENG)
Aggregate: 4-0; FC Spartak Moskva qualify.

10/3/11, Valeriy Lobanovskiy Stadium, Kyiv
FC Dynamo Kyiv 2-0 Manchester City FC
Attendance: 16315
Goal(s): 1-0 Shevchenko 25, 2-0 Gusev 77
Referee: Meyer (GER)
17/3/11, City of Manchester Stadium, Manchester
Manchester City FC 1-0 FC Dynamo Kyiv
Attendance: 27816
Goal(s): 1-0 Kolarov 39
Referee: Çakır (TUR)
Aggregate: 1-2; FC Dynamo Kyiv qualify.

QUARTER-FINALS

History was made as three Portuguese clubs reached the last four of a UEFA competition for the first time. Thirty-four goals were scored in the eight quarter-final matches, with three of the four ties virtually cut and dried after the opening legs.

Five-star Porto

Radamel Falcao's second European hat-trick of the campaign helped FC Porto to establish an emphatic 5-1 first-leg lead at home to FC Spartak Moskva. Porto were in scintillating form, cutting through the Spartak defence with ease to score four times in the last 20 minutes and effectively put the tie beyond their opponents' reach.

The newly-crowned Portuguese Liga champions did not let up in the return, either. Victorious in all of their previous six away games in the competition, André Villas-Boas's team ruthlessly put Spartak to the sword in the Luzhniki Stadium, scoring another five goals – against two for their opponents – to post the highest winning margin in a UEFA Cup or UEFA Europa League quarter-final and take their place in the last four as the competition's highest scorers.

Porto striker Radamel Falcao added to his copious haul of UEFA Europa League goals with four against Spartak Moskva

A moment of celebration for Villarreal's prolific striker Giuseppe Rossi, who scored in both legs against Twente

Rampant Rossi

There Porto would meet Villarreal CF, whose dominant first-leg performance at El Madrigal built up a similarly handsome lead over FC Twente. A superb display and exquisite goal by Giuseppe Rossi, combined with Nilmar's double and efforts from Carlos Marchena and Borja Valero, helped the Yellow Submarine cruise to a 5-1 victory. Marc Janko's added-time consolation served only to give the Tukkers a glimmer of hope for the return in Enschede.

Twente, one of four quarter-finalists who had crossed over mid-campaign from the UEFA Champions League, were further encouraged by Emir Bajrami's delightfully worked goal 32 minutes into the return leg, but Dwight Tiendalli's dismissal early in the second half and Rossi's tenth UEFA Europa League goal of the campaign – from the ensuing penalty – stopped the Dutch comeback in its tracks. Marco Ruben and Cani then added further goals for the Spanish side to wrap up a comprehensive 8-2 aggregate win.

Braga's bravery

Having knocked out three-time UEFA Cup winners Liverpool FC in the last 16, SC Braga might have been forgiven for resting on their laurels after a memorable European campaign. However, they further enhanced their credentials by prevailing in a closely contested tie against FC Dynamo Kyiv. Domingos Paciência's side had to do it the hard way after falling behind to Andriy Yarmolenko's goal six minutes into the away leg. Parity was soon restored when Oleh Gusev put through his own net, and when Andriy Shevchenko was dismissed just after the hour the tie looked Braga's for the taking. But victory eluded the in-form Portuguese side, and when they went down to ten men themselves 29 minutes into the return following Paulo César's sending off for a crude tackle on Yarmolenko, the balance appeared to have shifted towards Dynamo. Braga's ten men, though, defended with resolve and skill against a ponderous, unimaginative Shevchenko-less attack to claim a fifth successive home clean sheet in Europe and, as a result, qualify on the away-goals rule. Dynamo's misery was compounded late on when Goran Popov became the third player in the tie to see red.

Benfica impress

SL Benfica completed the last-four lineup, securing their first European semi-final berth for 17 years at the expense of PSV Eindhoven. Jorge Jesus's men were in charge from the off, taking a 3-0 lead inside 52 minutes in Lisbon. Substitute Zakaria Labyad pulled a goal back for the visitors, but Javier Saviola's goal deep into added time restored Benfica's advantage. Cheered on by specially invited members of their 1988 European Champion Clubs Cup-winning side (who defeated Benfica in the final), PSV flew out of the blocks in Eindhoven a week later. By 25 minutes a three-goal deficit was down to one thanks to goals from Balázs Dzsudzsák and Jeremain Lens. Yet, just as the pendulum appeared to be swinging their way, visiting captain Luisão spectacularly volleyed in off the crossbar on the stroke of half-time to put Benfica back in control. Like domestic title challengers Twente, PSV could not sustain their recovery after conceding, and midway through the second half Óscar Cardozo's penalty killed the tie, giving Benfica a 6-3 aggregate win and taking them through to an all-Portuguese semi-final against fellow UEFA Champions League exiles Braga.

Quarter-Final Results

7/4/11, Estádio do Dragão, Porto
FC Porto 5-1 FC Spartak Moskva
Attendance: 38209
Goal(s): 1-0 Falcao 37, 2-0 Varela 65, 3-0 D. Kombarov 70(og), 3-1 K. Kombarov 71, 4-1 Falcao 84, 5-1 Falcao 90+2
Referee: Gumienny (BEL)
14/4/11, Luzhniki Stadion, Moscow
FC Spartak Moskva 2-5 FC Porto
Attendance: 17088
Goal(s): 0-1 Hulk 28, 0-2 Rodríguez 45+2, 0-3 Guarín 47, 1-3 Dzyuba 52, 1-4 Falcao 54, 2-4 Ari 72, 2-5 Rúben Micael 89
Referee: Kassai (HUN)
Aggregate: 3-10; FC Porto qualify.

7/4/11, Estádio do Sport Lisboa e Benfica, Lisbon
SL Benfica 4-1 PSV Eindhoven
Attendance: 60026
Goal(s): 1-0 Aimar 37, 2-0 Salvio 45, 3-0 Salvio 52, 3-1 Labyad 80, 4-1 Saviola 90+4
Referee: Tagliavento (ITA)
14/4/11, PSV Stadion, Eindhoven
PSV Eindhoven 2-2 SL Benfica
Attendance: 29500
Goal(s): 1-0 Dzsudzsák 17, 2-0 Lens 25, 2-1 Luisão 45+2, 2-2 Cardozo 63(p)
Referee: Stark (GER)
Aggregate: 3-6; SL Benfica qualify.

7/4/11, Estadio El Madrigal, Villarreal
Villarreal CF 5-1 FC Twente
Attendance: 19094
Goal(s): 1-0 Marchena 23, 2-0 Borja Valero 43, 3-0 Nilmar 45+1, 4-0 Rossi 55, 5-0 Nilmar 81, 5-1 Janko 90+1
Referee: Nikolaev (RUS)
14/4/11, FC Twente Stadion, Enschede
FC Twente 1-3 Villarreal CF
Attendance: 23500
Goal(s): 1-0 Bajrami 32, 1-1 Rossi 60(p), 1-2 Marco Ruben 84(p), 1-3 Cani 90
Referee: Collum (SCO)
Aggregate: 2-8; Villarreal CF qualify.

7/4/11, Valeriy Lobanovskiy Stadium, Kyiv
FC Dynamo Kyiv 1-1 SC Braga
Attendance: 16115
Goal(s): 1-0 Yarmolenko 6, 1-1 Gusev 13(og)
Referee: Kuipers (NED)
14/4/11, Estádio Municipal de Braga, Braga
SC Braga 0-0 FC Dynamo Kyiv
Attendance: 14839
Referee: Eriksson (SWE)
Aggregate: 1-1; SC Braga qualify on away goal.

SEMI-FINALS

Villarreal CF were the only team that could prevent the 2010/11 UEFA Europa League final from becoming an all-Portuguese affair, but the Spanish side were to have no answer to an FC Porto team spearheaded by the record-breaking Radamel Falcao. SC Braga were less dominant against an SL Benfica outfit that had pipped them to the Liga title 12 months earlier, but their away-goals triumph was nevertheless an extraordinary feat for a small-town team that had never previously reached a European final.

Echoes of Mourinho

It was not the first time that one nation had supplied three of the four semi-finalists in a major European competition; West Germany had totally monopolised the 1978/79 UEFA Cup, providing all four teams. The one guarantee this time was that the inaugural UEFA Europa League winners, Club Atlético de Madrid, would be succeeded by a team from Iberia.

Villarreal's chances of keeping the trophy in Spain were buoyed by their impressive quarter-final win over FC Twente, but Porto, the newly-crowned Portuguese champions, went into the first leg on the back of a 12-game winning run. Echoes of José Mourinho's 2003 treble-winning side rang loud as they also had a Portuguese Cup final to look forward to. Villarreal, by contrast, had lost three of their previous six fixtures.

Cani gives Villarreal the lead in Porto

Radamel Falcao (front) completes his third hat-trick of the competition with a flying header

Falcao poker

Yet for 45 minutes in the Estádio do Dragão the Spanish outfit treated the form book with contempt. With Cani, Santi Cazorla and Borja Valero pulling the strings, they were all quick feet, feints and foraging, finally adding the final flourish to their dominance on the cusp of half-time when Cani's glancing header put them 1-0 up.

That fully merited half-time lead would be long forgotten by the end of the game, however. Falcao did most of the damage in a remarkable second-half comeback, bringing Porto level from the penalty spot then – after Fredy Guarín had put André Villas-Boas' side in front – grabbing centre stage with three further goals. He completed his third hat-trick of the campaign with a tap-in and diving header before making the final scoreline 5-1 with another brilliant headed effort in the last minute.

Record broken

It was the first four-goal haul of the Colombian international's career, taking his competition tally to 15 and equalling Jürgen Klinsmann's record set in the 1995/96 UEFA Cup. "I'm not done yet," he said after the game. And he would prove to be as good as his word in the return leg seven days later.

Again Cani broke the deadlock, on 17 minutes, and again the lead was merited as Villarreal set out full of verve and belief. Home hope was extinguished, however, just before half-time when Hulk's shot deflected in off Mateo Musacchio, and shortly after the restart Porto closed out the tie when Falcao, served from the left by Guarín, delivered his record 16th goal. Joan Capdevila's close-range volley restored local pride before Giuseppe Rossi's penalty ten minutes from time

Porto players celebrate going 2-1 up at home to Villarreal

made it 3-2 on the night, thus ending their visitors' perfect away record in the competition.

Braga pedigree

Nevertheless, it was Porto who were celebrating at the final whistle, a 7-4 aggregate win setting them up for a meeting with northern Portugal rivals Braga in Dublin. The Arsenalistas reached the final after adding Benfica to an impressive list of victims in two-legged ties during the 2010/11 campaign that already included Sevilla FC, Liverpool FC and FC Dynamo Kyiv.

Going into the tie the Eagles, twice European champions, had been firm favourites to eliminate a team sitting a place and 14 points behind them in their domestic league. They were also on a high having retained the Portuguese League Cup five days earlier.

Away goal

Second-half goals from Jardel and Óscar Cardozo preserved Benfica's record of having lost just once at home to Braga in their history. Yet it was the away goal from Braga that split those two home strikes, headed in by captain Vandinho, that would prove decisive in the final reckoning.

Óscar Cardozo struck the first-leg winner for Benfica from a trademark free-kick

Braga captain Vandinho scored a vital away goal in Lisbon but missed the second leg through suspension

The two teams reconvened a week later – minus Vandinho and Benfica's Pablo Aimar, both suspended – at the picturesque Estádio Municipal. There, a combination of Custódio's first-half header, gallant back-to-the-walls defending and a surprisingly insipid performance from the visitors carried Domingos Paciência's indefatigable side through to the first all-Portuguese UEFA final.

Semi-Final Results

28/4/11, Estádio do Sport Lisboa e Benfica, Lisbon
SL Benfica 2-1 SC Braga
Attendance: 57778
Goal(s): 1-0 Jardel 50, 1-1 Vandinho 53, 2-1 Cardozo 59
Referee: Thomson (SCO)
5/5/11, Estádio Municipal de Braga, Braga
SC Braga 1-0 SL Benfica
Attendance: 25384
Goal(s): 1-0 Custódio 19
Referee: Atkinson (ENG)
Aggregate: 2-2; SC Braga qualify on away goal.

28/4/11, Estádio do Dragão, Porto
FC Porto 5-1 Villarreal CF
Attendance: 44719
Goal(s): 0-1 Cani 45, 1-1 Falcao 49(p), 2-1 Guarín 61, 3-1 Falcao 67, 4-1 Falcao 75, 5-1 Falcao 90
Referee: Kuipers (NED)
5/5/11, Estadio El Madrigal, Villarreal
Villarreal CF 3-2 FC Porto
Attendance: 18523
Goal(s): 1-0 Cani 17, 1-1 Hulk 39, 1-2 Falcao 48, 2-2 Capdevila 75, 3-2 Rossi 80(p)
Referee: Rocchi (ITA)
Aggregate: 4-7; FC Porto qualify.

FINAL

Having captured their 25th domestic league title without losing a game, FC Porto were firm favourites to win the all-Portuguese UEFA Europa League final in Dublin. Northern Portuguese rivals SC Braga were not generally considered to be a major threat to André Villas-Boas's all-conquering side, yet they would prove as difficult to beat in the Dublin Arena as they had done in all of their previous matches. Although Porto duly prevailed, it was only by a single goal – scored, almost inevitably, by the tournament's record-breaking marksman, Radamel Falcao.

Braga had never previously advanced beyond the last 16 in European competition, but en route to the Dublin Arena they had defeated six clubs with European titles, Liverpool FC and SL Benfica among them. Although Porto were not expected to become a seventh, Villas-Boas was taking nothing for granted, pointing out that while he reluctantly accepted the favourites' tag being attached to his team, "Braga have beaten every favourite they've faced so far".

Familiar opponents

Although they had lost 92 of their previous 131 meetings with Porto, including both league games in 2010/11, Braga did not appear daunted by the unfavourable odds, quickly finding their shape both in attack and, particularly, defence. The Arsenalistas' march to the Republic of Ireland's first UEFA final had been marked by obduracy and dogged defending – and their 19th, and last, match of a marathon European season would prove to be no different.

Braga's approach did not make for a great spectacle on a chilly evening in the Irish capital. Although they created the first chance, on four minutes, when Custódio shot wide from the edge of the area, it was Porto, as expected, who made most of the running in attack. The lively Hulk created unease in the Braga defence when he cut in from the right and shot fractionally wide of the far post on seven minutes, but it was to be a rare moment of excitement in a drab, disjointed first period. Each time a Porto attack was repelled,

Radamel Falcao heads in Porto's winner against Braga in Dublin

Braga's 11-man defensive wall appeared to grow thicker and higher. While a mere 47km separated the two clubs – the shortest ever distance between UEFA club competition finalists – a yawning chasm divided them in their approach.

Costly lapse

Frustrations grew among the Porto faithful, but after 44 minutes of hammering in vain at the front door they went around the back and found it unlocked. Fredy Guarín intercepted Alberto Rodríguez's loose pass out of defence, advanced down the right and curved in a measured cross from deep that found Falcao with time, space and the freedom of the penalty area. The Colombia striker had already notched 16 goals in the campaign – a competition record - and he needed no second invitation to make it 17, directing a firm, accurate header beyond Artur into the far corner.

Domingos Paciência, the Braga coach, responded to this uncharacteristic defensive breach by ringing the changes at the interval, bringing on centre-back Kaká and adding Mossoró to the attack. Porto apparently failed to notice, because less than 60 seconds after the restart the latter dispossessed a defender and ran through unopposed towards goal, dribbling into the box with only Helton and his nerves to overcome. He failed to beat either, a tame low effort allowing the goalkeeper, on his 33rd birthday, to get his right leg in the way and boot the ball to safety.

Porto danger man Hulk is pursued by Braga's Custódio

Porto coach André Villas-Boas erupts with joy at the final whistle

Villas-Boas makes history

In his final game as Braga coach, Domingos looked on in anguish. A former long-time leader of the Porto attack in his playing days, he would surely have buried such a gilt-edged chance, especially with openings so scarce. It was a pivotal moment in the contest because although Alan ran himself into the ground to try and create further opportunities, Braga never really threatened again. Neither, in truth, did Porto who seemed sure in the knowledge that one goal would be enough. Despite a late long-ball blitz by Braga, their assumption proved to be correct and Villas-Boas, at 33, thus became the youngest coach to win a UEFA club competition. He was 95 days younger than Gianluca Vialli when the Italian had led Chelsea FC to the UEFA Cup Winners' Cup in 1998.

"The only thing we have to regret is that the spectacle wasn't of the Portuguese standard as we have played some amazing football this season," he said afterwards. "But that's nothing new in a European final and both teams had opportunities.

The most important thing is that Porto have this trophy in the cabinet again."

Falcao wrecking ball

It took just four days for the Dragons to add another piece of silverware to their collection, beating Vitória SC 6-2 in the Portuguese Cup final as Villas-Boas emulated José Mourinho's 2003 treble with the club. The coach, though, shared the plaudits, saying: "I am just a cog in a very effective club with super talents. Players are decisive in modern football. If you don't have the players you run into a wall."

For 44 minutes in Dublin they had done just that before unleashing their prolific Colombian centre-forward. Falcao was a fitting hero for a triumph that Porto fully deserved – if not for their relatively low-key final performance then certainly for the way in which their slick, ruthless attacking game had repeatedly blown holes in European defences all season. For a while Braga had looked like throwing a spanner in the works, but although Braga's gallant display enabled Domingos to get his wish and leave Dublin with his held high, the night belonged to Villas-Boas and Porto.

Final Result

18/5/11, Dublin Arena, Dublin
FC Porto 1-0 SC Braga
Attendance: 45391
Porto: Helton, Álvaro Pereira, Guarín (Belluschi 73), João Moutinho, Falcao, Hulk, Rolando, Varela (J. Rodríguez 79), Săpunaru, Fernando, Otamendi. Coach: André Villas-Boas (POR)
Braga: Artur, Rodríguez (Kaká 46), Paulão, Paulo César, Miguel Garcia, Lima (Meyong 66), Custódio, Sílvio, Alan, Hugo Viana (Mossoró 46), Vandinho. Coach: Domingos Paciência (POR)
Goal(s): 1-0 Falcao 44
Yellow Card(s): Hugo Viana 24 (Braga), Sílvio 30 (Braga), Săpunaru 49 (Porto), Miguel Garcia 55 (Braga), Mossoró 59 (Braga), Kaká 80 (Braga), Helton 90 (Porto), Rolando 90+3 (Porto)
Referee: Velasco Carballo (ESP)

TOP GOALSCORERS

17	Radamel Falcao (Porto)
11	Giuseppe Rossi (Villarreal)
6	Tomáš Necid (CSKA Moskva) Frédéric Kanouté (Sevilla) Bony Wilfried (Sparta Praha)
5	Nilmar (Villarreal) Artjoms Rudņevs (Lech Poznań) Edinson Cavani (Napoli) Fredy Guarín (Porto) Artem Milevskiy (Dynamo Kyiv) Balázs Dzsudzsák (PSV)

Captain and birthday boy Helton raises the trophy for 2010/11 UEFA Europa League winners FC Porto

IRELLI
KIA

UEFA SUPER CUP 2010

FC Internazionale Milano and Club Atlético de Madrid may have gone into their Monaco meeting on the back of European success, but neither club had ever contested a UEFA Super Cup, let alone picked up the trophy. Both clubs had overcome long waits for continental glory three months previously, with Inter ending their 45-year absence from the European Cup winners' circle by beating FC Bayern München 2-0 in Madrid, and Atlético picking up their first UEFA title since 1962 in the inaugural UEFA Europa League final in Hamburg. Inter, winners of an unprecedented treble in Italy under José Mourinho, had a new man at the helm in Rafael Benítez, and although he was determined to start his reign as his predecessor had finished, it was Atlético, under Quique Sánchez Flores, who ran out winners in the Stade Louis II.

Club Atlético de Madrid kicked off the new European club season as they ended the previous one by lifting a trophy - thanks to a 2-0 victory against FC Internazionale Milano in the UEFA Super Cup in Monaco.

It was the first time either team had taken part in the fixture and it was the UEFA Europa League holders who triumphed over the UEFA Champions League winners, José Antonio Reyes and Sergio Agüero making the difference with a couple of second-half strikes.

Last laugh

Rafael Benítez's Liverpool FC side had lost out to Atlético in the semi-finals of the UEFA Europa League the previous season, and although the Spaniard had moved on to take charge of Inter, it was his counterpart and compatriot Quique Sánchez Flores who again had the last laugh. Not even a late penalty for just-crowned UEFA Club Footballer of the Year Diego Milito could spoil a memorable night for the victors as David de Gea thwarted the Inter striker with a fine save. "Hopefully this prize will be the start of many," the young goalkeeper said afterwards. "Like in Hamburg, this is a dream for the whole club."

Benítez made one change to the side that had defeated FC Bayern München in the UEFA Champions League final under José Mourinho – when Inter claimed their first European Cup for 45 years – with Goran Pandev making way for Dejan Stanković. The Italian title holders started brightly, with Wesley Sneijder and Milito both having early efforts on goal.

Inter dangerman Diego Milito (right) is held off by Atlético defender Luis Perea

José Antonio Reyes strikes to put Atlético 1-0 up

Old boys

Summer signing Diego Godín was the only new addition to the Atlético team that had defeated Fulham FC in the UEFA Europa League final, but it was old boys Diego Forlán – scorer of both goals against Fulham and the winner of the summer's FIFA World Cup Golden Ball award – and Simão who soon caught the eye at the other end.

Patience, though, was the watchword for much of the first half as defences took control. Walter Samuel failed to convert Inter's best chance on 28 minutes when he headed Sneijder's cross over despite being unmarked, and that was followed by team-mate Samuel Eto'o driving wide.

Agüero denied

It was the Atlético fans, however, who ended the opening 45 minutes in louder voice, and their team should have gone into the break with a lead. With just over half an hour gone, Agüero shot wide after Reyes's clever pass had found him free in the area, and the Argentina striker then missed the target again four minutes before the interval after being teed up by Simão.

Atlético also fashioned the better chances after the restart and issued a warning on 59 minutes when Júlio César brilliantly tipped Reyes's shot round the post following a break instigated by the confident Forlán.

Reyes strikes

A goal was not long in coming, however, and just past the hour mark Reyes picked his spot perfectly, low to Júlio César's right, after bursting clear of Maicon. The goalkeeper got his hand to the ball but could not keep out the stinging shot, to the delight of the Atlético supporters who had made the trip to Monaco in impressive numbers.

Benítez's side, who had won the Italian Super Cup the week before, were struggling to make an impact, and Eto'o headed over 15 minutes from time with one of the few chances that came their way. The destination of the trophy was put beyond doubt with seven minutes remaining when Simão again broke free, surging forward down the left to square the ball for Agüero, who turned it low into the net to double the Spanish side's advantage.

Milito miss

Inter's misery was complete in the final minute when De Gea parried Milito's penalty high away to his left after Raúl García had brought down Pandev in the area, leaving Sánchez Flores to say: "We're extremely pleased to have won. We think we can feel very happy indeed and we want to share this with all our fans. We were fast and strong and each goal was clear-cut, so we played well. Inter work very well defensively and I imagined Maicon might cause problems going forward, but Simão and [full-back] Álvaro Domínguez negated him very well. We created dangerous opportunities; they played well, but quite frankly we deserved the victory."

Atlético's success meant that the challengers from UEFA's second club competition edged in front of their European champion counterparts in terms of overall victories in the UEFA Super Cup – 18-17. Agüero added: "We knew it would be a difficult game. We did really well to win it and it's a great start to the year." The Rojiblancos became the 23rd club to win the traditional curtain-raiser to the European season, and Agüero's fellow goalscorer Reyes was delighted to make the difference, saying: "It was a tremendous joy scoring in the final – every player dreams of that."

Result

27/8/10, Stade Louis II, Monaco
FC Internazionale Milano 0-2 Club Atlético de Madrid
Attendance: 17265
Internazionale: Júlio César, Zanetti, Stanković (Pandev 68), Lúcio, Eto'o, Sneijder (Coutinho 79), Maicon, Cambiasso, Milito, Samuel, Chivu. Coach: Rafael Benítez (ESP)
Atlético: De Gea, Forlán (Jurado 82), Raúl García, Agüero, Paulo Assunção, Godín, Ujfaluši, Álvaro Domínguez, Reyes (Mérida 69), Simão (Camacho 90+1), Perea. Coach: Quique Sánchez Flores (ESP)
Goal(s): 0-1 Reyes 62, 0-2 Agüero 83
Yellow Card(s): Simão 85 (Atlético), Raúl García 89 (Atlético), Samuel 90+2 (Internazionale)
Referee: Busacca (SUI)

Atlético celebrate their UEFA Super Cup triumph

UEFA Club Competition Statistics 2010/11

ALBANIA

FK DINAMO TIRANA

UEFA CHAMPIONS LEAGUE

Second Qualifying Round – FC Sheriff (MDA)
A 1-3 *Malacarne (12)*
Hidi, Pisha, Xhafa, Martinena, García (Sosa 79), Vila, Muzaka (Allmuça 72), Bakaj, Putinčanin, Malacarne, Diop. Coach: Luis Manuel Blanco (ARG)
Red Card(s): Bakaj 68
Yellow Card(s): Putinčanin 19, Diop 20, García 63
H 1-0 *Vila (18)*
Hidi, Pisha, Xhafa (Peqini 71), Martinena, Vila, Mallota (García 65), Muzaka (Daja 88), Putinčanin, Malacarne, Sosa, Sefa. Coach: Luis Manuel Blanco (ARG)
Yellow Card(s): Putinčanin 10, Vila 38, Sosa 77

KS BESA

UEFA EUROPA LEAGUE

Second Qualifying Round – Olympiacos FC (GRE)
H 0-5
Shehi, Aliju, Çikalleshi (Sem. Hadžibulić 65), M. Osmani (Shtini 81), Ferizović, Poçi, Marcos, Dhëmbi, Jakupi, Mihani (Hoxha 70), Lazarevski. Coach: Shpëtim Duro (ALB)
A 1-6 *Lazarevski (48)*
Bakaj, Aliju, Sem. Hadžibulić, Çikalleshi (Traga 84), M. Osmani, Ferizović, Poçi, Marcos, Dhëmbi (Shtini 72), Jakupi (Hoxha 76), Lazarevski. Coach: Shpëtim Duro (ALB)
Yellow Card(s): Aliju 33, Poçi 37, M. Osmani 42, Jakupi 45

KF TIRANA

UEFA EUROPA LEAGUE

First Qualifying Round – Zalaegerszegi TE (HUN)
H 0-0
I. Lika, Sina, Pashaj, Lila, Hajdari (Malindi 56), Plaku, Karabeci, Osmani, Pejić (Bicaj 85), Lilaj, Ahmataj. Coach: Sulejman Starova (ALB)
Yellow Card(s): Lila 53
A 1-0 *Karabeci (107)*
I. Lika, Sina, Pashaj, Lila, Hajdari (Malindi 61), Plaku (Sorra 119), Karabeci, Osmani, Pejić, Lilaj, Metani. Coach: Sulejman Starova (ALB)
Yellow Card(s): Plaku 119

Second Qualifying Round – FC Utrecht (NED)
A 0-4
I. Lika, Sina, Pashaj, Lila, Plaku, Hysa (Malindi 69), Karabeci (Nallbani 87), Osmani, Pejić, Lilaj, Ahmataj. Coach: Sulejman Starova (ALB)
Red Card(s): I. Lika 85
Yellow Card(s): I. Lika 9, Pashaj 36, I. Lika 85
H 1-1 *Lila (11)*
Nallbani, Sina, Pashaj (Metani 69), Lila, Plaku, Hysa (Malindi 63), Karabeci, Osmani, Pejić, Lilaj (Hajdari 83), Ahmataj. Coach: Sulejman Starova (ALB)
Yellow Card(s): Karabeci 86

KF LAÇI

UEFA EUROPA LEAGUE

First Qualifying Round – FC Dnepr Mogilev (BLR)
H 1-1 *Marashi (45+1)*
Llani, Brahja, Cela, Nina, Kaja, Kastrati, Vuçaj, Shazivari (Marashi 26), Nimani, Veliaj, Gega (Jushi 86). Coach: Stavri Nica (ALB)
Yellow Card(s): Kastrati 55
A 1-7 *Nimani (61)*
Llani, Brahja, Cela, Nina, Kaja (Shazivari 46), Kastrati, Vuçaj, Nimani, Veliaj, Gega (Marashi 30), Tafaj. Coach: Stavri Nica (ALB)
Red Card(s): Brahja 72
Yellow Card(s): Nina 16, Brahja 18, Gega 27, Brahja 72

ANDORRA

FC SANTA COLOMA

UEFA CHAMPIONS LEAGUE

First Qualifying Round – Birkirkara FC (MLT)
H 0-3 (w/o)
A 3-4 *N. Urbani (21), Jiménez (45), M. Urbani (85)*
Ricardo Fernández, Xavier Gil, Ayala, Sonejee (G. Sánchez 77), Genís García (Bodjo 54), N. Urbani, Jiménez, A. Sánchez, M. Urbani, Javi Sánchez, Ribolleda (Txema García 46). Coach: Xavier Roura Cuadros (ESP)
Yellow Card(s): Txema García 55, A. Sánchez 57, N. Urbani 83

UE SANT JULIÀ

UEFA EUROPA LEAGUE

Second Qualifying Round – Myllykosken Pallo-47 (FIN)
A 0-3
Burgos, Wagner, Ruiz, Yael, Matamala (Carballo 61), Xinos (Leites 84),

Vítor Pinto, Peppe, Salvat, Sebas Gómez (Iguacel 87), Varela. Coach: Daniel Tremonti (CHI)
Yellow Card(s): Matamala 38, Sebas Gómez 78
H 0-1 (match annulled)
Burgos, Wagner, Ruiz, Yael, Xinos, Peppe, Leites (Nastri 58), Salvat, Sebas Gómez, Carballo (Bernales 65), Moreno. Coach: Daniel Tremonti (CHI)
Yellow Card(s): Leites 41, Carballo 57, Moreno 67, Wagner 75
H 0-5
Goldswill, Ruiz, Yael, Xinos, Peppe, Leites (Nastri 62), Salvat, Sebas Gómez, Carballo (Vítor Pinto 55), Varela (Fernando Gonçalves 46), Moreno. Coach: Daniel Tremonti (CHI)
Yellow Card(s): Leites 34, Moreno 50

UE SANTA COLOMA

UEFA EUROPA LEAGUE

First Qualifying Round – FK Mogren (MNE)
H 0-3
Rivas, Nieto, Àlex Martínez, Sirvan, Gerard Aloy (Ribera 86), Antón (Orosa 71), Daniel Ballesteros, Prat, Bernat, Luis Miguel, Rubio. Coach: Lluis Miguel Aloy (AND)
Yellow Card(s): Nieto 3, Antón 54, Bernat 60
A 0-2
Rivas, Nieto (Prat 22), Orosa, Àlex Martínez, Sirvan, Gerard Aloy, Antón, Daniel Ballesteros (Àlex Blázquez 46), Bernat, Luis Miguel (Joel Huete 89), Rubio. Coach: Lluis Miguel Aloy (AND)
Yellow Card(s): Rubio 60, Sirvan 66, Àlex Blázquez 71

FC LUSITANS

UEFA EUROPA LEAGUE

First Qualifying Round – FK Rabotnicki (MKD)
A 0-5
Benitez, Hugo Veloso (Hernández 64), Luis Pinto, Pedro Reis (Raya 50), Luis Miguel, Felipe Barros, Bruno Silva, João Cunha, Franklin Soares, Abdian (Meza 53), Maciel. Coach: Vicens Marques (AND)
Yellow Card(s): João Cunha 23, Maciel 38, Luis Pinto 68
H 0-6
Benitez, Raya, Luis Pinto, Pedro Reis (Luis Miguel 46), Felipe Barros, Bruno Silva, Vítor Pereira, Laguna (Hugo Veloso 43), Hernández (Jorge Rebelo 83), Franklin Soares, Maciel. Coach: Vicens Marques (AND)
Yellow Card(s): Franklin Soares 44, Hernández 81

ARMENIA

FC PYUNIK

UEFA CHAMPIONS LEAGUE

Second Qualifying Round – FK Partizan (SRB)
A 1-3 *Yedigaryan (30)*
Lesko, S. Hovsepyan, Mkrtchyan, Marcos, Ghazaryan, Manoyan, Yusbashyan, Minasyan, Yedigaryan (Barseghyan 90+4), Adedeji, Goharyan (Manasyan 66). Coach: Vardan Minasyan (ARM)
Yellow Card(s): Minasyan 17
H 0-1
Lesko, Haroyan, S. Hovsepyan, Mkrtchyan, Marcos, Ghazaryan, Manoyan, Yusbashyan, Yedigaryan (E. Manucharyan 49), Adedeji, Goharyan (Malakyan 61). Coach: Vardan Minasyan (ARM)
Yellow Card(s): Haroyan 9, Yusbashyan 56, Goharyan 60, Ghazaryan 83

FC MIKA

UEFA EUROPA LEAGUE

Second Qualifying Round – FK Rabotnicki (MKD)
A 0-1
Klevinskas, Petrosyan, Mkoyan, Pedro López, A. Mkrtchyan, Montenegro (Voskanyan 26), Ednei, Tadevosyan, Edílson (Beglaryan 84), Demel (Grigalevičius 75), Alex. Coach: Armen Adamyan (ARM)
H 0-0
Klevinskas, Petrosyan (Hakobyan 64), Mkoyan, Pedro López, A. Mkrtchyan, Beglaryan (Grigalevičius 66), Tadevosyan, Edílson, Voskanyan (Ednei 75), Demel, Alex. Coach: Armen Adamyan (ARM)
Yellow Card(s): Alex 35, Pedro López 77

ULISSES FC

UEFA EUROPA LEAGUE

First Qualifying Round – Bnei Yehuda Tel-Aviv FC (ISR)
H 0-0
Malkov, Hakhnazaryan, N. Grigoryan, D. Grigoryan, Adamyan, V. Aleksanyan (Ugrekhelidze 32), Tbilashvili (Sahakyan 46), Andrikyan, Jikia (Ledenev 61), A. Grigoryan, Krasovski. Coach: Sevada Arzumanyan (ARM)
A 0-1
Malkov, Hakhnazaryan, N. Grigoryan, D. Grigoryan, Adamyan, Ugrekhelidze, Ledenev (Jikia 72), Tbilashvili (Sahakyan 67), Andrikyan (Davtyan 66), A. Grigoryan, Krasovski. Coach: Sevada Arzumanyan (ARM)
Yellow Card(s): A. Grigoryan 43

FC BANANTS

UEFA EUROPA LEAGUE

First Qualifying Round – Anorthosis Famagusta FC (CYP)
A 0-3
Ghazaryan, Daghbashyan, Nikolov, Arakelyan, Voskanyan (Balabekyan 74), Deniran, V. Poghosyan, Karapetyan, Hambartsumyan, Beto, Melkonyan (Kasule 40). Coach: Stevica Kuzmanoski (MKD)
Yellow Card(s): Kasule 62, Hambartsumyan 74, Karapetyan 78, Nikolov 85
H 0-1
Ghazaryan, Daghbashyan, Nikolov, Arakelyan, Deniran, Balabekyan (Avetisyan 90+2), Kasule, Karapetyan, Hambartsumyan, Beto (Voskanyan 84), Melkonyan (V. Poghosyan 46). Coach: Stevica Kuzmanoski (MKD)
Yellow Card(s): Melkonyan 26, Hambartsumyan 56

AUSTRIA

FC SALZBURG

UEFA CHAMPIONS LEAGUE

Second Qualifying Round – HB Tórshavn (FRO)
H 5-0 *Zárate (21), Jantscher (43), Ulmer (46), Wallner (64), Hierländer (82)*
Tremmel, Mendes da Silva (Pokrivač 60), Schwegler, Wallner (Hierländer 75), Zárate, Jantscher, Schiemer, Ulmer, Švento (Cziommer 60), Sekagya, Leitgeb. Coach: Huub Stevens (NED)
Yellow Card(s): Pokrivač 74
A 0-1
Walke, Dudić, Mendes da Silva (Pokrivač 34), Zárate, Jantscher (Ngwat-Mahop 71), Schiemer, Ulmer, Cziommer (Švento 46), Hierländer, Sekagya, Leitgeb. Coach: Huub Stevens (NED)
Yellow Card(s): Leitgeb 90+3

Third Qualifying Round – AC Omonia (CYP)
A 1-1 *Zárate (8)*
Tremmel, Mendes da Silva, Afolabi, Schwegler, Wallner (Tchoyi 71), Zárate, Schiemer (Dudić 86), Ulmer, Švento (Jantscher 81), Sekagya, Leitgeb. Coach: Huub Stevens (NED)
Yellow Card(s): Schiemer 45, Wallner 51, Schwegler 89, Mendes da Silva 90+1
H 4-1 *Švento (21), Schiemer (37, 40), Boghossian (58)*
Tremmel, Mendes da Silva (Hierländer 82), Afolabi, Schwegler, Zárate, Jantscher, Schiemer (Augustinussen 70), Švento, Sekagya, Leitgeb (Ngwat-Mahop 85), Boghossian. Coach: Huub Stevens (NED)
Yellow Card(s): Boghossian 26, Mendes da Silva 43, Jantscher 65

Play-Offs – Hapoel Tel-Aviv FC (ISR)
H 2-3 *Pokrivač (28), Wallner (67p)*
Tremmel, Afolabi, Schwegler, Pokrivač, Zárate (Ngwat-Mahop 78), Jantscher, Schiemer (Alan 67), Švento, Sekagya, Leitgeb, Boghossian (Wallner 59). Coach: Huub Stevens (NED)
Yellow Card(s): Schiemer 2, Jantscher 54
A 1-1 *Douglas (42og)*
Tremmel, Mendes da Silva, Afolabi, Schwegler, Wallner (Boghossian 74), Pokrivač, Zárate, Švento, Sekagya, Leitgeb, Ngwat-Mahop (Alan 65). Coach: Huub Stevens (NED)
Yellow Card(s): Ngwat-Mahop 36

UEFA EUROPA LEAGUE

Group A
Match 1 – Manchester City FC (ENG)
H 0-2
Tremmel, Mendes da Silva (Augustinussen 73), Afolabi, Schwegler, Pokrivač (Jantscher 55), Zárate, Schiemer, Švento, Sekagya, Leitgeb, Boghossian (Wallner 55). Coach: Huub Stevens (NED)
Yellow Card(s): Wallner 90
Match 2 – KKS Lech Poznań (POL)
A 0-2
Tremmel, Mendes da Silva, Afolabi, Schwegler, Zárate (Jantscher 57), Schiemer, Švento, Cziommer (Wallner 77), Sekagya, Leitgeb (Boghossian 77), Alan. Coach: Huub Stevens (NED)
Yellow Card(s): Cziommer 45+1
Match 3 – Juventus (ITA)
H 1-1 *Švento (36)*
Tremmel, Mendes da Silva (Leitgeb 52), Afolabi, Schwegler, Wallner, Pokrivač, Zárate (Jantscher 82), Schiemer, Švento, Sekagya, Hinteregger. Coach: Huub Stevens (NED)
Yellow Card(s): Zárate 63
Match 4 – Juventus (ITA)
A 0-0
Tremmel, Mendes da Silva (Augustinussen 80), Afolabi, Schwegler, Wallner (Alan 74), Pokrivač (Leitgeb 66), Zárate, Jantscher, Schiemer, Sekagya, Hinteregger. Coach: Huub Stevens (NED)
Yellow Card(s): Pokrivač 15, Sekagya 40, Jantscher 73
Match 5 – Manchester City FC (ENG)
A 0-3
Tremmel, Mendes da Silva (Augustinussen 67), Afolabi, Jantscher, Schiemer, Cziommer (Alan 56), Hierländer, Sekagya, Leitgeb, Hinteregger (Švento 46), Boghossian. Coach: Huub Stevens (NED)
Yellow Card(s): Afolabi 28, Boghossian 45, Sekagya 85
Match 6 – KKS Lech Poznań (POL)
H 0-1
Walke, Mendes da Silva, Afolabi, Zárate, Jantscher (Hierländer 68), Schiemer, Cziommer, Sekagya, Offenbacher (Alan 58), Hinteregger, Boghossian (Wallner 74). Coach: Huub Stevens (NED)
Yellow Card(s): Zárate 32, Alan 88, Cziommer 90

SK STURM GRAZ

UEFA EUROPA LEAGUE

Third Qualifying Round – FC Dinamo Tbilisi (GEO)
H 2-0 *Feldhofer (48), Kienast (59)*
Gratzei, Pürcher, Feldhofer, Weber, Hölzl (Ehrenreich 88), Bukva (Haas 81), Szabics, Standfest, Kienzl, Schildenfeld, Kienast (Muratović 77). Coach: Franco Foda (GER)
Yellow Card(s): Kienzl 90+1
A 1-1 *Muratović (40p)*
Gratzei, Pürcher, Feldhofer, Weber (Haas 66), Hölzl, Bukva, Muratović, Szabics (Kienast 78), Standfest, Kienzl (Foda 46), Schildenfeld. Coach: Franco Foda (GER)
Yellow Card(s): Weber 49, Schildenfeld 61

Play-Offs – Juventus (ITA)
H 1-2 *Schildenfeld (82)*
Gratzei, Pürcher, Feldhofer, Weber, Bukva, Szabics, Kainz (Klem 72), Standfest, Kienzl (Muratović 82), Schildenfeld, Kienast (Haas 75). Coach: Franco Foda (GER)
A 0-1
Gratzei, Pürcher, Weber, Bukva (Klem 71), Szabics (Haas 61), Burgstaller, Ehrenreich (Kainz 62), Standfest, Kienzl, Schildenfeld, Kienast. Coach: Franco Foda (GER)
Yellow Card(s): Ehrenreich 24

FK AUSTRIA WIEN

UEFA EUROPA LEAGUE

Second Qualifying Round – NK Široki Brijeg (BIH)
H 2-2 *Linz (50), Schumacher (57)*
Lindner, Dragovic, Klein (Margreitter 82), Linz, Ortlechner, Voříšek (Schumacher 46), Junuzovic, Liendl, Stankovic, Baumgartlinger (Hlinka 72), Suttner. Coach: Karl Daxbacher (AUT)
Yellow Card(s): Ortlechner 24, Liendl 27, Junuzovic 61, Dragovic 88
A 1-0 *Junuzovic (80)*
Lindner, Dragovic, Hlinka (Baumgartlinger 68), Klein, Linz, Jun, Ortlechner, Junuzovic, Liendl, Stankovic (Schumacher 61), Suttner (Leovac 74). Coach: Karl Daxbacher (AUT)
Red Card(s): Baumgartlinger 74

Third Qualifying Round – Ruch Chorzów (POL)
A 3-1 *Linz (7), Hlinka (43), Jun (73)*
Lindner, Dragovic, Hlinka, Klein, Linz (Schumacher 76), Jun (Salomon

36), Ortlechner, Voříšek, Junuzovic, Liendl (Leovac 80), Suttner. Coach: Karl Daxbacher (AUT)
Yellow Card(s): Junuzovic 50
H 3-0 *Klein (4p), Baumgartlinger (10, 21)*
Lindner, Dragovic (Margreitter 71), Hlinka, Klein, Linz, Jun (Tiffner 46), Ortlechner, Voříšek (Salomon 62), Liendl, Baumgartlinger, Suttner. Coach: Karl Daxbacher (AUT)

Play-Offs – Aris Thessaloniki FC (GRE)
A 0-1
Lindner, Margreitter, Dragovic, Hlinka, Klein, Linz (Schumacher 89), Jun (Stankovic 80), Voříšek, Liendl (Leovac 71), Baumgartlinger, Suttner. Coach: Karl Daxbacher (AUT)
Yellow Card(s): Klein 21, Baumgartlinger 63, Hlinka 86, Linz 89
H 1-1 *Linz (56)*
Lindner, Troyanski (Stankovic 62), Margreitter, Dragovic, Hlinka, Klein, Linz, Jun, Liendl (Schumacher 46), Baumgartlinger, Suttner (Leovac 74). Coach: Karl Daxbacher (AUT)

SK RAPID WIEN

UEFA EUROPA LEAGUE

Second Qualifying Round – FK Sūduva (LTU)
A 2-0 *Hofmann (12), Trimmel (81)*
Hedl, Patocka, Sonnleitner, Heikkinen, Salihi (Hinum 46), Hofmann, Katzer, Jelavić, Kavlak (Drazan 68), Kayhan, Trimmel (Dober 85). Coach: Peter Pacult (AUT)
Yellow Card(s): Drazan 88
H 4-2 *Jelavić (20, 90), Gartler (86, 89)*
Hedl, Patocka, Heikkinen, Katzer, Jelavić, Kavlak (Saurer 9), Eder, Drazan (Gartler 82), Kayhan, Trimmel, Pehlivan (Hinum 60). Coach: Peter Pacult (AUT)
Yellow Card(s): Pehlivan 27, Kayhan 66

Third Qualifying Round – PFC Beroe Stara Zagora (BUL)
A 1-1 *Hofmann (45+1p)*
Hedl, Patocka, Sonnleitner, Heikkinen, Hofmann, Katzer, Jelavić, Gartler (Salihi 65), Saurer (Trimmel 58), Dober, Hinum (Kulovits 90+2). Coach: Peter Pacult (AUT)
H 3-0 *Jelavić (5, 60), Katzer (71)*
Hedl, Patocka, Sonnleitner, Kulovits, Heikkinen, Salihi (Gartler 79), Hofmann, Katzer, Jelavić (Nuhiu 85), Saurer (Kavlak 62), Kayhan. Coach: Peter Pacult (AUT)

Play-Offs – Aston Villa FC (ENG)
H 1-1 *Nuhiu (32)*
Hedl, Sonnleitner, Heikkinen, Salihi (Gartler 73), Hofmann, Katzer, Nuhiu, Kavlak, Soma, Kayhan, Hinum (Drazan 86). Coach: Peter Pacult (AUT)
Yellow Card(s): Kayhan 11, Soma 18, Katzer 70
A 3-2 *Nuhiu (52), Sonnleitner (78), Gartler (81)*
Hedl, Sonnleitner, Heikkinen, Hofmann (Patocka 90+2), Katzer, Nuhiu, Kavlak, Saurer (Trimmel 73), Soma, Dober, Pehlivan (Gartler 78). Coach: Peter Pacult (AUT)
Yellow Card(s): Sonnleitner 72, Dober 83

Group L
Match 1 – FC Porto (POR)
A 0-3
Hedl, Sonnleitner, Kulovits, Hofmann (Trimmel 73), Nuhiu, Kavlak, Saurer (Drazan 62), Soma, Dober (Patocka 80), Kayhan, Hinum. Coach: Peter Pacult (AUT)
Yellow Card(s): Dober 18, Hinum 39
Match 2 – Beşiktaş JK (TUR)
H 1-2 *Kavlak (51)*
Hedl, Patocka, Sonnleitner, Kulovits, Hofmann, Nuhiu, Kavlak, Soma, Kayhan, Trimmel (Vennegoor of Hesselink 67), Pehlivan (Salihi 79). Coach: Peter Pacult (AUT)
Yellow Card(s): Pehlivan 60, Kulovits 75, Vennegoor of Hesselink 79
Match 3 – PFC CSKA Sofia (BUL)
A 2-0 *Vennegoor of Hesselink (28), Hofmann (32)*
Hedl, Sonnleitner, Heikkinen, Vennegoor of Hesselink (Nuhiu 77), Hofmann (Trimmel 84), Katzer, Kavlak, Saurer (Drazan 64), Soma, Kayhan, Pehlivan. Coach: Peter Pacult (AUT)
Yellow Card(s): Kavlak 13, Heikkinen 40
Match 4 – PFC CSKA Sofia (BUL)
H 1-2 *Salihi (56p)*
Hedl, Sonnleitner, Heikkinen, Salihi, Katzer (Trimmel 68), Nuhiu (Gartler 68), Kavlak, Drazan, Soma, Kayhan, Pehlivan (Dober 82). Coach: Peter Pacult (AUT)
Yellow Card(s): Drazan 67, Pehlivan 77
Match 5 – FC Porto (POR)
H 1-3 *Trimmel (39)*
Hedl, Patocka, Sonnleitner, Kulovits, Heikkinen, Drazan (Salihi 63), Gartler (Nuhiu 77), Saurer, Soma, Kayhan, Trimmel (Dober 83). Coach: Peter Pacult (AUT)
Yellow Card(s): Drazan 8, Patocka 80
Match 6 – Beşiktaş JK (TUR)
A 0-2
Payer, Sonnleitner, Kulovits (Saurer 46), Katzer, Kavlak, Drazan, Gartler, Soma, Kayhan (Patocka 67), Trimmel (Dober 46), Pehlivan. Coach: Peter Pacult (AUT)
Yellow Card(s): Kavlak 24, Pehlivan 81, Katzer 85

AZERBAIJAN

İNTER BAKI PİK

UEFA CHAMPIONS LEAGUE

Second Qualifying Round – KKS Lech Poznań (POL)
H 0-1
Lomaia, Zhelev, Kruglov (Karamli 52), Chertoganov, Červenka, Zlatinov, Levin, Kandelaki, Odikadze (Daçdämirov 81), Poškus (Karlsons 83), Mzhavanadze. Coach: Kakhaber Tskhadadze (GEO)
Yellow Card(s): Levin 39, Kruglov 51, Karamli 90+1
A 1-0 (aet; 8-9 on pens) *Karlsons (84)*
Lomaia, Accioly, Karamli (Kruglov 46), Chertoganov, Červenka, Zlatinov, Levin, Kandelaki, Odikadze, Poškus (Karlsons 84), Mzhavanadze (Daçdämirov 71). Coach: Kakhaber Tskhadadze (GEO)
Yellow Card(s): Červenka 27, Levin 53, Chertoganov 62, Karlsons 103, Lomaia 118, Zlatinov 122

BAKI FK

UEFA EUROPA LEAGUE

Second Qualifying Round – FK Budućnost Podgorica (MNE)
H 0-3 (w/o)
Original result 2-1 *Kajkut (77), Jabá (90+3)*
Sissokho, Kajkut, Boret, Nibombé, Skulić, Epalle, Fábio, Kargbo, Savinov, Šolić (Angulo 55), Jabá. Coach: Winfried Schafer (GER)
Yellow Card(s): Nibombé 65, Jabá 90+3
A 2-1 *Šolić (28), Jabá (42)*
Sissokho, Kajkut, Boret (Angulo 84), Nibombé, Skulić (Sofroni 75), Mähärrämov, Fábio (Qurbanov 62), Kargbo, Savinov, Šolić, Jabá. Coach: Winfried Schafer (GER)
Yellow Card(s): Boret 70

QARABAĞ FK

UEFA EUROPA LEAGUE

First Qualifying Round – FK Metalurg Skopje (MKD)
H 4-1 *R.F. Sadiqov (26p), İsmayilov (45), İmamäliyev (85), Adamia (90+2)*
Väliyev, Häşimov, R.A. Sadiqov, A. Kärimov (Yusifov 65), Mämmädov (S. Abasov 55), Äliyev, R.F. Sadiqov, İsmayilov (İmamäliyev 76), Teli, Agolli, Adamia. Coach: Qurban Qurbanov (AZE)
Red Card(s): Teli 51
Yellow Card(s): Teli 32, R.A. Sadiqov 74, Adamia 82
A 1-1 *İmamäliyev (69)*
Väliyev, Qarayev, Häşimov, Medvedev, R.A. Sadiqov, Yusifov (A. Kärimov 89), İmamäliyev, S. Abasov, R.F. Sadiqov, İsmayilov (Mämmädov 86), Adamia (Nadirov 83). Coach: Qurban Qurbanov (AZE)
Yellow Card(s): Qarayev 62

Second Qualifying Round – Portadown FC (NIR)
A 2-1 *İsmayilov (67, 86)*
Väliyev, Qarayev, Häşimov, Medvedev, R.A. Sadiqov, Mämmädov (A. Kärimov 76), İmamäliyev (Äliyev 46), S. Abasov, R.F. Sadiqov, Ismayilov, Adamia (Nadirov 82). Coach: Qurban Qurbanov (AZE)
H 1-1 *İsmayilov (83)*
Väliyev, Medvedev, R.A. Sadiqov, Mämmädov (Nadirov 62), Äliyev (A. Kärimov 76), S. Abasov, R.F. Sadiqov, Ismayilov, Teli, Agolli, Adamia. Coach: Qurban Qurbanov (AZE)

Third Qualifying Round – Wisła Kraków (POL)
A 1-0 *Nadirov (69)*
Väliyev, Medvedev, R.A. Sadiqov, Äliyev (Nadirov 69), S. Abasov, R.F. Sadiqov, Ismayilov, Teli, Agolli, Rubins (İmamäliyev 40), Adamia (A. Kärimov 90+3). Coach: Qurban Qurbanov (AZE)
H 3-2 *İsmayilov (28), Äliyev (33), R.A. Sadiqov (35)*
Väliyev, Medvedev, R.A. Sadiqov, Äliyev (Nadirov 61), S. Abasov, R.F. Sadiqov, Ismayilov, Teli, Agolli, Rubins (İmamäliyev 86), Adamia (A. Kärimov 81). Coach: Qurban Qurbanov (AZE)

Play-Offs – Borussia Dortmund (GER)
A 0-4
Väliyev, Medvedev, R.A. Sadiqov, İmamäliyev (Nadirov 46), Äliyev (Yusifov 46), S. Abasov, R.F. Sadiqov, Teli (Häşimov 70), Agolli, Rubins, Adamia. Coach: Qurban Qurbanov (AZE)
H 0-1
Väliyev, Medvedev, R.A. Sadiqov, Äliyev, S. Abasov (A. Kärimov 87), R.F. Sadiqov, Nadirov, Teli, Agolli, Rubins (Karimov 68), Adamia (Mämmädov 68). Coach: Qurban Qurbanov (AZE)
Yellow Card(s): Nadirov 8, Mämmädov 69

XÄZÄR LÄNKÄRAN FK

UEFA EUROPA LEAGUE

First Qualifying Round – FC Olimpia Balti (MDA)
A 0-0
Ağayev, Beqiri, Allahverdiyev, Lalín (X. Mämmädov 89), Ämirquliyev, Opara (Hüseynov 90+2), Qurbanov (Ramazanov 86), Todorov, Imedashvili, Souza, Devran. Coach: Ägasälim Mirçavadov (AZE)
Yellow Card(s): Imedashvili 33
H 1-1 *Lalín (78)*
Ağayev, Beqiri, Allahverdiyev, Ramazanov (Hüseynov 64), Lalín, Ämirquliyev, Opara (X. Mämmädov 68), Todorov, Imedashvili, Souza, Devran (Qurbanov 58). Coach: Ägasälim Mirçavadov (AZE)
Yellow Card(s): Hüseynov 80, Qurbanov 87, Ämirquliyev 90+1, Imedashvili 90+3, Allahverdiyev 90+5

BELARUS

FC BATE BORISOV

UEFA CHAMPIONS LEAGUE

Second Qualifying Round – FH Hafnarfjördur (ISL)
H 5-1 *Nekhaichik (48, 85, 88), Renan (58), Rodionov (90)*
Veremko, Likhtarovich (Olekhnovich 62), Shitov, Yurevich, Kontsevoi (Skavysh 78), Renan (Volodko 68), Nekhaichik, Radkov, Pavlov, Bordachev, Rodionov. Coach: Viktor Goncharenko (BLR)
Yellow Card(s): Radkov 23, Shitov 28, Kontsevoi 75
A 1-0 *Rodionov (15)*
Veremko, Likhtarovich, Sosnovskiy, Shitov, Volodko (Yurevich 77), Renan, Skavysh, Bordachev, Rodionov (Patotskiy 71), Olekhnovich (Pavlov 59), Baga. Coach: Viktor Goncharenko (BLR)
Yellow Card(s): Patotskiy 84, Veremko 90+1

Third Qualifying Round – FC København (DEN)
H 0-0
Veremko, Likhtarovich (Skavysh 77), Shitov, Yurevich, Kontsevoi (Renan 65), Nekhaichik, Radkov, Pavlov, Bordachev, Rodionov (Baga 85), Olekhnovich. Coach: Viktor Goncharenko (BLR)
Yellow Card(s): Shitov 87
A 2-3 *Kontsevoi (40), Nekhaichik (44)*
Veremko, Likhtarovich (Olekhnovich 61), Sosnovskiy, Yurevich, Kontsevoi, Renan, Nekhaichik, Radkov, Pavlov (Skavysh 69), Bordachev (Baga 82), Rodionov. Coach: Viktor Goncharenko (BLR)
Red Card(s): Sosnovskiy 90+2
Yellow Card(s): Pavlov 45+1, Nekhaichik 52, Sosnovskiy 85, Sosnovskiy 90+2

UEFA EUROPA LEAGUE

Play-Offs – CS Marítimo (POR)
H 3-0 *Olekhnovich (56), Renan (60), Pavlov (70)*
Veremko, Shitov, Yurevich, Kontsevoi (Patotskiy 90+2), Renan (Skavysh 85), Nekhaichik, Radkov, Pavlov (Baga 81), Bordachev, Rodionov, Olekhnovich. Coach: Viktor Goncharenko (BLR)
Yellow Card(s): Olekhnovich 47, Nekhaichik 51, Veremko 81, Rodionov 89
A 2-1 *Pavlov (52), Skavysh (90+2)*
Gutor, Likhtarovich (Skavysh 69), Shitov, Yurevich, Kontsevoi (Patotskiy 85), Renan (Baga 66), Radkov, Pavlov, Bordachev, Rodionov, Olekhnovich. Coach: Viktor Goncharenko (BLR)
Yellow Card(s): Likhtarovich 19, Kontsevoi 40, Yurevich 46

Group E
Match 1 – FC Dynamo Kyiv (UKR)
A 2-2 *Rodionov (3), Nekhaichik (54)*
Veremko, Likhtarovich (Baga 38), Shitov, Yurevich, Renan (Volodko 77), Nekhaichik, Radkov, Pavlov (Skavysh 64), Bordachev, Rodionov, Olekhnovich. Coach: Viktor Goncharenko (BLR)
Yellow Card(s): Bordachev 13, Shitov 29
Match 2 – AZ Alkmaar (NED)
H 4-1 *Rodionov (5), Kontsevoi (48), Renan (77p), Olekhnovich (83)*
Veremko, Sosnovskiy (Radkov 46), Shitov, Yurevich, Kontsevoi (Baga 77), Volodko, Renan (Skavysh 83), Nekhaichik, Bordachev, Rodionov, Olekhnovich. Coach: Viktor Goncharenko (BLR)
Yellow Card(s): Sosnovskiy 40, Radkov 57, Rodionov 90

Match 3 – FC Sheriff (MDA)
A 1-0 *Sosnovskiy (8)*
Veremko, Sosnovskiy, Shitov, Yurevich, Kontsevoi (Skavysh 83), Volodko, Renan (Baga 68), Nekhaichik, Bordachev, Rodionov, Olekhnovich (Likhtarovich 75). Coach: Viktor Goncharenko (BLR)
Yellow Card(s): Bordachev 62
Match 4 – FC Sheriff (MDA)
H 3-1 *Rodionov (15), Pavlov (70), Renan (75)*
Veremko, Likhtarovich (Skavysh 66), Sosnovskiy, Shitov, Yurevich, Renan (Radkov 82), Pavlov (Volodko 71), Bordachev, Rodionov, Olekhnovich, Baga. Coach: Viktor Goncharenko (BLR)
Yellow Card(s): Volodko 90+1
Match 5 – FC Dynamo Kyiv (UKR)
H 1-4 *Nekhaichik (84)*
Gutor, Likhtarovich, Sosnovskiy (Renan 46), Shitov, Yurevich, Volodko (Olekhnovich 78), Nekhaichik, Radkov, Bordachev, Rodionov, Baga (Skavysh 70). Coach: Viktor Goncharenko (BLR)
Yellow Card(s): Bordachev 8, Likhtarovich 26, Rodionov 39
Match 6 – AZ Alkmaar (NED)
A 0-3
Veremko, Likhtarovich (Volodko 85), Sosnovskiy (Olekhnovich 56), Shitov, Yurevich, Renan, Nekhaichik, Radkov, Pavlov (Skavysh 62), Rodionov, Baga. Coach: Viktor Goncharenko (BLR)
Yellow Card(s): Sosnovskiy 45+1, Likhtarovich 80

Round of 32 – Paris Saint-Germain FC (FRA)
H 2-2 *Renan (16), Gordeichuk (80)*
Gutor, Shitov, Yurevich, Volodko, Renan (Gordeichuk 75), Nekhaichik, Bordachev, Rodionov (Skavysh 83), Simić, Olekhnovich, Rudik (Likhtarovich 66). Coach: Viktor Goncharenko (BLR)
A 0-0
Gutor, Likhtarovich (Gordeichuk 61), Shitov, Yurevich, Volodko, Renan (Skavysh 77), Nekhaichik, Bordachev, Rodionov, Simić, Rudik (Olekhnovich 66). Coach: Viktor Goncharenko (BLR)
Yellow Card(s): Shitov 21, Nekhaichik 56

FC DINAMO MINSK

UEFA EUROPA LEAGUE

Second Qualifying Round – JK Sillamäe Kalev (EST)
H 5-1 *Sazankov (12, 33), Putilo (60), Rekish (87), Chukhlei (90+2)*
Gorbunov, Dragun, Strakhanovich (Kugan 81), Sazankov (Matveyenko 61), Kondratiyev, Putilo, Rekish, Veretilo, Martynovich, Buloichik (Chukhlei 46), Marakhovskiy. Coach: Vladimir Golmak (BLR)
Yellow Card(s): Kondratiyev 80
A 5-0 *Dragun (2), Sazankov (17), Chukhlei (19, 65), Rekish (46)*
Gorbunov, Dragun (Kugan 72), Strakhanovich, Chukhlei, Sazankov (Leonardo 46), Kondratiyev, Rekish, Montaroup, Veretilo, Buloichik, Marakhovskiy (Kruk 78). Coach: Vladimir Golmak (BLR)
Yellow Card(s): Dragun 56, Marakhovskiy 72

Third Qualifying Round – Maccabi Haifa FC (ISR)
A 0-1
Gorbunov, Dragun, Strakhanovich, Chukhlei (Leonardo 80), Sazankov (Shkabara 58), Kondratiyev, Putilo, Rekish (Buloichik 74), Montaroup, Veretilo, Marakhovskiy. Coach: Vladimir Golmak (BLR)
Yellow Card(s): Gorbunov 53
H 3-1 *Strakhanovich (35), Putilo (55, 90)*
Gorbunov, Dragun, Strakhanovich, Chukhlei (Shkabara 90+3), Kislyak (Buloichik 80), Sazankov (Rekish 70), Kondratiyev, Putilo, Montaroup, Veretilo, Marakhovskiy. Coach: Vladimir Golmak (BLR)
Yellow Card(s): Putilo 21, Strakhanovich 80, Chukhlei 90+1

Play-Offs – Club Brugge KV (BEL)
A 1-2 *Dragun (6)*
Gorbunov, Dragun, Strakhanovich, Chukhlei (Rekish 63), Kislyak (Shkabara 86), Sazankov (Leonardo 77), Kondratiyev, Putilo, Montaroup, Veretilo, Marakhovskiy. Coach: Vladimir Golmak (BLR)
Yellow Card(s): Montaroup 10, Sazankov 36, Strakhanovich 52, Marakhovskiy 70
H 2-3 *Chukhlei (47), Dragun (90)*
Gorbunov, Dragun, Vabha, Chukhlei, Kislyak (Buloichik 83), Sazankov (Bruno Furlan 68), Kondratiyev, Putilo, Rekish (Lucas 46), Montaroup, Veretilo. Coach: Vladimir Golmak (BLR)
Yellow Card(s): Kondratiyev 5, Putilo 24, Dragun 52, Kislyak 63

FC DNEPR MOGILEV

UEFA EUROPA LEAGUE

First Qualifying Round – KF Laçi (ALB)
A 1-1 *Turlin (90+2)*
Kopantsov, Kapov, Honchar, Shuneiko, Bychenok, Yurchenko, Tereshchenko (Lyasyuk 57), Poryvayev, Turlin, Tupchiy (Karpovich 86), Raspopov (Kozlov 46). Coach: Andrei Skorobogatko (BLR)
Yellow Card(s): Poryvayev 39
H 7-1 *Bychenok (10, 80), Yurchenko (17p, 56, 81), Zenkovich (42), Chernykh (87)*
Kopantsov, Kapov, Honchar, Obrazov, Shuneiko, Bychenok, Karpovich (Raspopov 61), Yurchenko, Poryvayev (Kozlov 46), Turlin, Zenkovich (Chernykh 67). Coach: Andrei Skorobogatko (BLR)
Yellow Card(s): Honchar 62, Shuneiko 78

Second Qualifying Round – Stabæk Fotball (NOR)
A 2-2 *Turlin (14), Kozlov (23)*
Kopantsov, Kapov, Honchar, Obrazov, Shuneiko, Bychenok, Karpovich, Tereshchenko (Chernykh 68), Turlin (Poryvayev 90), Kozlov (Raspopov 59), Zenkovich. Coach: Andrei Skorobogatko (BLR)
Yellow Card(s): Honchar 61
H 1-1 *Yurchenko (85)*
Kopantsov, Kapov, Obrazov, Zhevnerov, Shuneiko, Bychenok (Chernykh 73), Karpovich, Yurchenko, Tereshchenko, Turlin (Raspopov 89), Kozlov (Zenkovich 46). Coach: Andrei Skorobogatko (BLR)
Yellow Card(s): Shuneiko 64, Zhevnerov 84

Third Qualifying Round – FC Baník Ostrava (CZE)
H 1-0 *Zenkovich (63)*
Kopantsov, Kapov, Honchar, Obrazov, Zhevnerov, Bychenok (Raspopov 88), Karpovich, Yurchenko, Tereshchenko (Chernykh 78), Turlin (Kozlov 71), Zenkovich. Coach: Andrei Skorobogatko (BLR)
A 2-1 *Yurchenko (24p), Zenkovich (70)*
Kopantsov, Kapov, Honchar, Obrazov, Zhevnerov, Shuneiko (Raspopov 89), Bychenok (Turlin 81), Karpovich, Yurchenko, Tereshchenko (Chernykh 84), Zenkovich. Coach: Andrei Skorobogatko (BLR)
Yellow Card(s): Kapov 36, Yurchenko 45+2, Chernykh 90+1

Play-Offs – Villarreal CF (ESP)
A 0-5
Kopantsov, Kapov, Honchar (Raspopov 39), Obrazov, Zhevnerov, Shuneiko (Tupchiy 76), Karpovich, Yurchenko, Tereshchenko, Turlin, Zenkovich (Chernykh 63). Coach: Andrei Skorobogatko (BLR)
Yellow Card(s): Obrazov 45+1, Chernykh 67, Raspopov 82
H 1-2 *Yurchenko (19)*
Kopantsov, Kapov (Karpovich 90), Honchar, Obrazov, Zhevnerov, Shuneiko, Bychenok, Yurchenko, Tereshchenko, Turlin (Tupchiy 82), Zenkovich. Coach: Andrei Skorobogatko (BLR)
Yellow Card(s): Obrazov 30

FC TORPEDO ZHODINO

UEFA EUROPA LEAGUE

First Qualifying Round – Fylkir (ISL)
H 3-0 *Kryvobok (52), Ogar (59), Kontsevoi (66)*
Bushma, Ostroukh, Brusnikin (Solovei 65), Karolik (Aleksiyevich 73), Levitskiy, Kozlov, Karshakevich, Ogar, Kontsevoi, Kazarin, Kryvobok. Coach: Aleksandr Lisovskiy (BLR)
A 3-1 *Ostroukh (41), Kryvobok (86p, 88)*
Bushma, Ostroukh, Brusnikin (Solovei 74), Karolik (Aleksiyevich 67), Levitskiy, Kozlov, Martynets, Karshakevich, Kontsevoi, Kazarin (Gintov 82), Kryvobok. Coach: Aleksandr Lisovskiy (BLR)
Yellow Card(s): Kozlov 17, Brusnikin 43

Second Qualifying Round – OFK Beograd (SRB)
A 2-2 *Kryvobok (14), Brusnikin (90+2)*
Bushma, Ostroukh, Levitskiy, Kozlov, Aleksiyevich (Brusnikin 71), Martynets, Karshakevich, Kontsevoi, Kazarin, Papush (Solovei 57), Kryvobok (Karolik 45+2). Coach: Aleksandr Lisovskiy (BLR)
Yellow Card(s): Solovei 69, Ostroukh 84
H 0-1
Bushma, Ostroukh, Levitskiy, Kozlov (Gintov 62), Aleksiyevich, Martynets, Karshakevich, Kontsevoi, Kazarin (Brusnikin 58), Papush, Kryvobok (Karolik 72). Coach: Aleksandr Lisovskiy (BLR)
Yellow Card(s): Martynets 36, Gintov 68, Kontsevoi 90+2

BELGIUM

RSC ANDERLECHT

UEFA CHAMPIONS LEAGUE

Third Qualifying Round – The New Saints FC (WAL)
A 3-1 *Kljestan (7), Legear (18), Suárez (73)*
Proto, Mazuch (Lecjaks 83), Deschacht, Biglia, Suárez (De Sutter 76), Boussoufa, Legear, Kouyaté, Kljestan (Kanu 87), Juhász, Gillet. Coach: Ariël Jacobs (BEL)
Yellow Card(s): Boussoufa 64
H 3-0 *De Sutter (17), Lukaku (69, 74)*
Proto, Lecjaks, Suárez (Diandy 46), Chatelle, Mareček, Kljestan (Gillet 73), De Sutter (Lukaku 59), Juhász, Chavarría, Bernárdez, Rnić. Coach: Ariël Jacobs (BEL)

Play-Offs – FK Partizan (SRB)
A 2-2 *Gillet (54), Juhász (66)*
Proto, Mazuch, Deschacht, Lecjaks, Polák (Badibanga 90), Suárez, Boussoufa (Mareček 84), Lukaku (Kanu 61), Kouyaté, Juhász, Gillet. Coach: Ariël Jacobs (BEL)
Yellow Card(s): Gillet 73, Kouyaté 78
H 2-2 (aet; 2-3 on pens) *Lukaku (64), Gillet (71)*
Proto, Mazuch, Deschacht, Biglia, Polák, Suárez, Boussoufa, Lukaku, Kouyaté (Legear 60), Juhász, Gillet. Coach: Ariël Jacobs (BEL)
Yellow Card(s): Kouyaté 24, Lukaku 75, Deschacht 117

UEFA EUROPA LEAGUE

Group G
Match 1 – FC Zenit St Petersburg (RUS)
H 1-3 *Juhász (66)*
Proto, Deschacht, Biglia, Polák, Suárez, Boussoufa, Lukaku, Juhász, Bernárdez, Gillet, Rnić (Legear 46). Coach: Ariël Jacobs (BEL)
Yellow Card(s): Bernárdez 78
Match 2 – HNK Hajduk Split (CRO)
A 0-1
Proto, Mazuch, Deschacht, Biglia, Polák, Suárez (Lukaku 78), Boussoufa, Kouyaté, Mareček (Legear 66), Juhász, Gillet. Coach: Ariël Jacobs (BEL)
Match 3 – AEK Athens FC (GRE)
H 3-0 *Boussoufa (31), Lukaku (71), Juhász (75)*
Proto, Mazuch, Deschacht, Biglia, Polák, Kanu (Suárez 66), Boussoufa, Lukaku (Chavarría 79), Kljestan, Juhász, Gillet. Coach: Ariël Jacobs (BEL)
Yellow Card(s): Lukaku 48
Match 4 – AEK Athens FC (GRE)
A 1-1 *Polák (55)*
Proto, Mazuch, Lecjaks, Polák (Suárez 77), Boussoufa (Kanu 67), Legear (Badibanga 90), Lukaku, Kouyaté, Kljestan, Juhász, Gillet. Coach: Ariël Jacobs (BEL)
Yellow Card(s): Kanu 80, Legear 81
Match 5 – FC Zenit St Petersburg (RUS)
A 1-3 *Kanu (87)*
Proto, Mazuch, Lecjaks, Polák, Kanu, Legear (Suárez 46), Lukaku (De Sutter 77), Mareček (Badibanga 68), Kljestan, Juhász, Gillet. Coach: Ariël Jacobs (BEL)
Yellow Card(s): Kljestan 74
Match 6 – HNK Hajduk Split (CRO)
H 2-0 *De Sutter (12), Suárez (41)*
Proto, Mazuch, Lecjaks, Polák, Suárez, Boussoufa, Legear (Mareček 75), Kljestan, De Sutter (Lukaku 84), Juhász, Gillet. Coach: Ariël Jacobs (BEL)

Round of 32 – AFC Ajax (NED)
H 0-3
Proto, Mazuch, Biglia, Lecjaks, Suárez, Kanu, Boussoufa, Lukaku (De Sutter 68), Juhász, Wasilewski, Gillet (Kouyaté 81). Coach: Ariël Jacobs (BEL)
Yellow Card(s): Boussoufa 45, Juhász 68
A 0-2
Proto, Mazuch, Biglia, Lecjaks, Suárez, Kanu (Mareček 77), Lukaku, Kouyaté, Juhász, Wasilewski (De Sutter 72), Gillet. Coach: Ariël Jacobs (BEL)
Yellow Card(s): Kouyaté 22, Kanu 57

KAA GENT

UEFA CHAMPIONS LEAGUE

Third Qualifying Round – FC Dynamo Kyiv (UKR)
A 0-3
Jorgačević, Myrie (Smolders 73), Hanstveit, Wils, Thijs, Mboyo (Arbeitman 59), El Ghanassy, Adriano Duarte, De Smet (Coulibaly 83), Lepoint, Grondin. Coach: Francky Dury (BEL)
Yellow Card(s): De Smet 60, Adriano Duarte 89
H 1-3 *Coulibaly (85)*
Jorgačević, Šuler, Myrie, Thijs, El Ghanassy, Thompson, Adriano Duarte (Ljubijankič 46), Čustović (Arbeitman 46), Coulibaly, Lepoint (Smolders 69), Grondin. Coach: Francky Dury (BEL)
Yellow Card(s): Adriano Duarte 15, Grondin 27, Thompson 74

UEFA EUROPA LEAGUE

Play-Offs – Feyenoord (NED)
A 0-1
Jorgačević, Myrie, Hanstveit, Wils, Thijs, Azofeifa (De Smet 68), El Ghanassy (Smolders 83), Coulibaly, Škarabot, Soumahoro (Ljubijankič 69), Grondin. Coach: Francky Dury (BEL)
Yellow Card(s): Coulibaly 72, Myrie 85, De Smet 86
H 2-0 *Soumahoro (34), Coulibaly (61)*
Jorgačević, Myrie (Adriano Duarte 83), Hanstveit, Wils, Thijs (Ljubijankič 65), Azofeifa (Smolders 68), El Ghanassy, Thompson, Coulibaly, Soumahoro, Grondin. Coach: Francky Dury (BEL)
Yellow Card(s): Thompson 3, Soumahoro 83, Adriano Duarte 90

Group C
Match 1 – PFC Levski Sofia (BUL)
A 2-3 *Azofeifa (23), Šuler (48)*
Jorgačević, Šuler, Wils, Thijs, Azofeifa, Barić, De Smet (Arbeitman 68), Soumahoro (El Ghanassy 66), Wallace, Ljubijankič, Grondin (Smolders 78). Coach: Francky Dury (BEL)
Yellow Card(s): Grondin 13, Soumahoro 64, Thijs 90
Match 2 – LOSC Lille Métropole (FRA)
H 1-1 *De Smet (5)*
Jorgačević, Šuler, Wils, Smolders, Azofeifa, El Ghanassy, Barić, Coulibaly, De Smet (Arbeitman 84), Škarabot, Conté (Ljubijankič 65). Coach: Francky Dury (BEL)
Yellow Card(s): Azofeifa 39, De Smet 77
Match 3 – Sporting Clube de Portugal (POR)
A 1-5 *Wils (16)*
Jorgačević, Hanstveit, Wils, Smolders (Grondin 46), Thijs, Azofeifa, El Ghanassy (Soumahoro 67), Barić (Coulibaly 46), Škarabot, Conté, Ljubijankič. Coach: Francky Dury (BEL)
Yellow Card(s): Coulibaly 79
Match 4 – Sporting Clube de Portugal (POR)
H 3-1 *Smolders (7p), Conté (79), Arbeitman (82)*
Jorgačević, Šuler, Wils (Hanstveit 28), Smolders, Thijs, El Ghanassy, Barić, Coulibaly (Arbeitman 66), De Smet (Conté 73), Wallace, Ljubijankič. Coach: Francky Dury (BEL)
Yellow Card(s): Šuler 32, El Ghanassy 90
Match 5 – PFC Levski Sofia (BUL)
H 1-0 *Wallace (77)*
Jorgačević, Šuler, Wils, Smolders, Thijs, Azofeifa (Lepoint 90), El Ghanassy, Barić, Arbeitman, Wallace, Ljubijankič. Coach: Francky Dury (BEL)
Yellow Card(s): Wallace 81
Match 6 – LOSC Lille Métropole (FRA)
A 0-3
Jorgačević, Šuler, Wils, Smolders, Thijs, Azofeifa (Conté 46), El Ghanassy (Soumahoro 63), Coulibaly (Arbeitman 63), Wallace, Lepoint, Ljubijankič. Coach: Francky Dury (BEL)
Yellow Card(s): Wils 38, Coulibaly 40, Thijs 55, Wallace 65, Lepoint 87

CLUB BRUGGE KV

UEFA EUROPA LEAGUE

Play-Offs – FC Dinamo Minsk (BLR)
H 2-1 *Hoefkens (71p), Blondel (84)*
Stijnen, Van der Heyden, Hoefkens, Dalmat (Lestienne 79), Blondel, Marcos, Donk, Vargas (Dirar 46), Odjidja-Ofoe, Kouemaha (Akpala 66), Perišić. Coach: Adrie Koster (NED)
Yellow Card(s): Kouemaha 33, Perišić 66, Marcos 90+4
A 3-2 *Hoefkens (5p, 32p), Dalmat (26)*
Stijnen, Van der Heyden, Hoefkens, Dalmat (Geraerts 65), Dirar (Šćepović 73), Blondel, Akpala (Kouemaha 13), Marcos, Donk, Odjidja-Ofoe, Perišić. Coach: Adrie Koster (NED)
Yellow Card(s): Blondel 53, Marcos 67, Stijnen 85, Geraerts 90+2

Group D
Match 1 – PAOK FC (GRE)
H 1-1 *Kouemaha (61)*
Stijnen, Hoefkens, Dalmat (Vargas 80), Dirar, Donk, Vermeulen (Simaeys 24), Geraerts, Díaz, Odjidja-Ofoe, Kouemaha, Perišić. Coach: Adrie Koster (NED)
Yellow Card(s): Simaeys 32
Match 2 – Villarreal CF (ESP)
A 1-2 *Donk (45+2)*
De Vlieger (Coosemans 61), Hoefkens, Blondel (Van Gijseghem 86), Simaeys, Marcos, Donk, Vargas, Geraerts, Díaz, Odjidja-Ofoe (Dirar 77), Perišić. Coach: Adrie Koster (NED)
Red Card(s): Vargas 26
Yellow Card(s): Blondel 32, Donk 45+3
Match 3 – NK Dinamo Zagreb (CRO)
A 0-0
De Vlieger, Hoefkens, Dalmat, Dirar, Simaeys, Marcos, Geraerts, Díaz, Odjidja-Ofoe, Kouemaha, Perišić. Coach: Adrie Koster (NED)
Yellow Card(s): Dirar 5, Dalmat 42, De Vlieger 75
Match 4 – NK Dinamo Zagreb (CRO)
H 0-2
De Vlieger, Hoefkens, Dalmat (Lestienne 46), Blondel, Simaeys, Marcos (Šćepović 73), Donk, Geraerts, Díaz (Van der Heyden 53), Kouemaha, Perišić. Coach: Adrie Koster (NED)
Yellow Card(s): Geraerts 32, Marcos 59
Match 5 – PAOK FC (GRE)
A 1-1 *Šćepović (89)*
Stijnen, Van der Heyden, Šćepović, Blondel, Simaeys, Akpala (Dirar 62), Donk, Vermeulen (Odjidja-Ofoe 71), Geraerts, Van Gijseghem, Perišić (Dalmat 62). Coach: Adrie Koster (NED)
Yellow Card(s): Simaeys 43, Geraerts 55, Vermeulen 56, Odjidja-Ofoe 90+2
Match 6 – Villarreal CF (ESP)
H 1-2 *Kouemaha (28)*
De Vlieger, Dalmat, Blondel, Simaeys, Marcos, Donk, Vargas (Dirar 65), Van Gijseghem, Odjidja-Ofoe (Van der Heyden 73), Kouemaha, Perišić (Lestienne 65). Coach: Adrie Koster (NED)
Yellow Card(s): Donk 32, Dirar 85

KRC GENK

UEFA EUROPA LEAGUE

Third Qualifying Round – FC Inter Turku (FIN)
A 5-1 *De Bruyne (17), Ogunjimi (44), Barda (61), Vossen (77, 85)*
Courtois, Matoukou, Hubert, Tőzsér, De Bruyne (Camus 79), Ngcongca, Barda (Vossen 69), Buffel (Ndabashinze 83), Durwael, João Carlos, Ogunjimi. Coach: Frank Vercauteren (BEL)
H 3-2 *Ogunjimi (24), Tőzsér (80p), Huysegems (85)*
Courtois, Daeseleire, Joneleit, Hubert (Tőzsér 77), Camus, Ngcongca (Durwael 83), Huysegems, Ndabashinze, Yeboah, João Carlos, Ogunjimi (Koita 77). Coach: Frank Vercauteren (BEL)
Yellow Card(s): Koita 83, Joneleit 88

Play-Offs – FC Porto (POR)
H 0-3
Courtois, Joneleit, Matoukou, Hubert, Tőzsér, Vossen (Ogunjimi 46), De Bruyne (Camus 86), Ngcongca, Barda, Buffel (Ndabashinze 82), Pudil. Coach: Frank Vercauteren (BEL)
Red Card(s): Matoukou 66
Yellow Card(s): Tőzsér 28, Vossen 32, Pudil 90+2
A 2-4 *Vossen (22, 56)*
Koteles, Daeseleire, Camus, Tőzsér, Vossen (Ogunjimi 63), Ngcongca, Huysegems (De Bruyne 81), Ndabashinze, Yeboah (Aquino 69), Durwael, Pudil. Coach: Frank Vercauteren (BEL)
Yellow Card(s): Koteles 23, Tőzsér 30, Daeseleire 58, Ndabashinze 58, Pudil 90

CERCLE BRUGGE KSV

UEFA EUROPA LEAGUE

Second Qualifying Round – TPS Turku (FIN)
H 0-1
Verbist, Portier, Evens, Vidarsson (Serebrennikov 61), Viane, Cornelis, Boi, Foley (Wang 73), Reynaldo, Nyoni, Van Eenoo (Renato Neto 46). Coach: Bob Peeters (BEL)

A 2-1 *Reynaldo (51), Van Eenoo (86)*
Verbist, Evens, Vidarsson, Viane (Portier 46), Cornelis, Boi (D'Haene 78), Foley, Kelhar, Reynaldo (Nyoni 86), Renato Neto, Van Eenoo. Coach: Bob Peeters (BEL)
Yellow Card(s): Van Eenoo 35, Viane 38, Kelhar 53, Vidarsson 88

Third Qualifying Round – Anorthosis Famagusta FC (CYP)
H 1-0 *Foley (69)*
Verbist, Portier, Evens, Cornelis, Boi (Vidarsson 85), Serebrennikov, Foley, Kelhar, Renato Neto, Van Eenoo (Nyoni 74), D'Haene (Reynaldo 61). Coach: Bob Peeters (BEL)
A 1-3 *Owusu (78)*
Verbist, Portier (Viane 81), Evens, Vidarsson, Cornelis, Boi, Serebrennikov (Renato Neto 58), Kelhar, Reynaldo, D'Haene (Van Eenoo 62), Owusu. Coach: Bob Peeters (BEL)
Yellow Card(s): Serebrennikov 23

BOSNIA & HERZEGOVINA

FK ŽELJEZNIČAR

UEFA CHAMPIONS LEAGUE

Second Qualifying Round – Hapoel Tel-Aviv FC (ISR)
A 0-5
Šehić, Radovanovic, Bogičević, Savić, Zeba (Gancev 46), Stanić, Višća, Ćulum (Svraka 46), M. Bešlija, Mešić, Popović (Rovčanin 88). Coach: Amar Osim (BIH)
Yellow Card(s): Bogičević 73, Gancev 85
H 0-1
Šehić, Radovanovic, Gancev (Stanić 46), Bogičević, Savić (Ćulum 76), Rovčanin, Zeba, Višćca, M. Bešlija (Spahić 77), Svraka, Mešić. Coach: Amar Osim (BIH)
Yellow Card(s): Zeba 29, Rovčanin 44, Savić 50

FK BORAC BANJA LUKA

UEFA EUROPA LEAGUE

Second Qualifying Round – FC Lausanne-Sport (SUI)
A 0-1
Avdukić, Benović, Petrić, Stupar (Žarić 46), Nikolić (Sakan 58), Vukelja, Raspudić, Muminović, Mikić, Trivunović, Stanceski (Jandrić 85). Coach: Zoran Marić (SRB)
Yellow Card(s): Stupar 44, Muminović 72, Stanceski 79
H 1-1 *Vukelja (69)*
Avdukić, Benović, Vukelja, Raspudić, Muminović, Sakan (Srećo 74), Mikić, Jandrić (Nikolić 52), Žarić, Trivunović, Stanceski. Coach: Zoran Marić (SRB)
Yellow Card(s): Trivunović 8, Stanceski 43

NK ŠIROKI BRIJEG

UEFA EUROPA LEAGUE

First Qualifying Round – NK Olimpija Ljubljana (SVN)
A 2-0 *Wagner (45+1), Cvijanovič (68og)*
Bandović, Renato, Kožul (Markić 79), Barišić, Ljubić (Roskam 50), Topić, Šilić, Diogo (Ćorić 68), Varea, Wagner, Ivanković. Coach: Ivo Ištuk (BIH)
Yellow Card(s): Kožul 36, Roskam 69, Ćorić 80
H 3-0 *Roskam (81), Weitzer (83), Mišić (90+3)*
Bandović, Renato, Kožul (Weitzer 61), Barišić, Topić, Šilić, Diogo, Varea (Mišić 77), Wagner (Glavina 86), Ivanković, Roskam. Coach: Ivo Ištuk (BIH)
Yellow Card(s): Barišić 65, Varea 67, Weitzer 83, Mišić 90

Second Qualifying Round – FK Austria Wien (AUT)
A 2-2 *Wagner (26), Topić (54)*
Bandović, Renato, Kožul (Weitzer 70), Barišić, Topić, Šilić, Diogo, Varea (A. Pinjuh 61), Wagner (Brekalo 90+3), Ivanković, Roskam. Coach: Ivo Ištuk (BIH)
Yellow Card(s): Topić 33
H 0-1
Bandović, Renato, Kožul (Weitzer 82), Barišić, Ljubić (Mišić 32; A. Pinjuh 54), Topić, Šilić, Diogo, Varea, Ivanković, Roskam. Coach: Ivo Ištuk (BIH)
Yellow Card(s): Ivanković 59, Renato 90+1

HŠK ZRINJSKI

UEFA EUROPA LEAGUE

First Qualifying Round – FC Tobol Kostanay (KAZ)
A 2-1 *Dragičević (52, 82)*
Melher, Šunjić, Džidić, Stjepanović, Selimović (Zovko 90+3), Sušić, Ivanković, Žižović, Dragičević (Pehar 90), Zadro, Rizvanović. Coach: Dragan Jović (BIH)
Yellow Card(s): Selimović 80, Rizvanović 85, Sušić 90+4
H 2-1 *Džidić (10), Pehar (72)*
Melher, Šunjić, Džidić, Stjepanović, Selimović, Sušić (Pehar 69), Ivanković, Žižović, Dragičević, Zadro, Rizvanović. Coach: Dragan Jović (BIH)

Second Qualifying Round – SP Tre Penne (SMR)
H 4-1 *Ivanković (1, 20p), Sušić (32), Zadro (37)*
Melher, Šunjić, Džidić, Stjepanović, Selimović, Sušić (Pehar 87), Ivanković, Žižović, Dragičević, Zadro, Rizvanović. Coach: Dragan Jović (BIH)
A 9-2 *Selimović (3, 27), Sušić (7), Žižović (10, 55p), Zadro (52, 65), Pehar (69), Šunjić (87)*
Melher, Šunjić, J. Aničić, Stjepanović (Miličević 42), Selimović, Sušić, Ivanković (Bartulica 46), Žižović, Dragičević (Pehar 61), Zadro, Rizvanović. Coach: Dragan Jović (BIH)

Third Qualifying Round – Odense BK (DEN)
A 3-5 *Zadro (15, 71), Žižović (65p)*
Melher, Šunjić, J. Aničić, Stjepanović, Selimović, Sušić (Pehar 63), Žižović, Dragičević, Zadro, Rizvanović (Puljić 63), M. Aničić. Coach: Dragan Jović (BIH)
Yellow Card(s): Rizvanović 14, Stjepanović 70, Zadro 78
H 0-0
Melher, Šunjić, Džidić, Stjepanović, Selimović, Sušić (Pehar 82), Ivanković, Žižović, Dragičević, Zadro, M. Aničić. Coach: Dragan Jović (BIH)
Yellow Card(s): Stjepanović 87, M. Aničić 90

BULGARIA

PFC LITEX LOVECH

UEFA CHAMPIONS LEAGUE

Second Qualifying Round – FK Rudar Pljevlja (MNE)
H 1-0 *I. Popov (8)*
Galatto, Barthe, Zanev, Wellington (Bratu 69), Sandrinho, Doka Madureira (Tsvetanov 78), Niflore, Nikolov, Jelenković, Bodurov, I. Popov (Yanev 61). Coach: Angel Chervenkov (BUL)
A 4-0 *Niflore (28), Jelenković (39), Bratu (74, 90)*
Galatto, Barthe, Zanev, Petkov, Wellington, Sandrinho (Yanev 77), Niflore (Bratu 72), Nikolov, Jelenković, Bodurov, I. Popov (G. Milanov 63). Coach: Angel Chervenkov (BUL)
Yellow Card(s): Wellington 19, Bodurov 45

Third Qualifying Round – MŠK Žilina (SVK)
H 1-1 *Wellington (78)*
Galatto, Barthe, Zanev, Petkov, Wellington (G. Milanov 89), Sandrinho (Bratu 73), Niflore, Nikolov, Jelenković (Yanev 85), Bodurov, I. Popov. Coach: Angel Chervenkov (BUL)
Yellow Card(s): Barthe 71, Nikolov 87
A 1-3 *Sandrinho (50)*
Galatto, Zanev, Berberović, Yanev (Wellington 61), Sandrinho, G. Milanov, Niflore (Bratu 66), Nikolov, Jelenković, Bodurov, I. Popov. Coach: Angel Chervenkov (BUL)
Red Card(s): I. Popov 53
Yellow Card(s): Bodurov 22, I. Popov 25, I. Popov 53, Niflore 61, Jelenković 70, Berberović 73

UEFA EUROPA LEAGUE

Play-Offs – Debreceni VSC (HUN)
A 0-2
Golubović, Barthe, Berberović, Venkov, Petkov, Wellington (Tsvetanov 78), Sandrinho (Todorov 66), G. Milanov, Niflore (Yanev 71), Tsvetkov, Jelenković. Coach: Petko Petkov (BUL)
Red Card(s): Barthe 69
Yellow Card(s): Barthe 35, Barthe 69
H 1-2 *Niflore (68)*
Vinícius, Zanev, Petkov, Yanev, Wellington (Doka Madureira 61), Sandrinho, G. Milanov (Bratu 61), Niflore, Nikolov, Jelenković (Tsvetkov 83), Bodurov. Coach: Petko Petkov (BUL)

PFC BEROE STARA ZAGORA

UEFA EUROPA LEAGUE

Third Qualifying Round – SK Rapid Wien (AUT)
H 1-1 *Zlatinov (85)*
Ilchev, Iliev, Zhekov, Yordanov, Velev, Kostadinov (Zlatinov 70), Stankov (Hristov 57), Bachev, Penev, Kovachev, Dimitrov (Mladenov 78). Coach: Ilian Iliev (BUL)
Yellow Card(s): Stankov 45+1, Iliev 68
A 0-3
Ilchev, Iliev, Zhekov (Yordanov 62), Velev, Kostadinov (Genchev 58), Zlatinov, Hristov, Bachev, Penev, Kovachev (Tomash 32), Dimitrov. Coach: Ilian Iliev (BUL)
Yellow Card(s): Iliev 24, Dimitrov 32, Tomash 90

PFC CSKA SOFIA

UEFA EUROPA LEAGUE

Third Qualifying Round – Cliftonville FC (NIR)
H 3-0 *Vidanov (9), Marquinhos (72), Trifonov (74)*
Karadzhov, Vidanov, Stoyanov, Yanchev, Aquaro, Trifonov, Rui Miguel (Iliev 59), Galchev (Yanev 86), Tonev (Kostadinov 70), Minev, Marquinhos. Coach: Pavel Dochev (BUL)
Yellow Card(s): Galchev 39, Iliev 87
A 2-1 *Kostadinov (85), Marquinhos (88)*
Karadzhov, Vidanov, Yanchev (Galchev 67), Aquaro, Delev (Kostadinov 81), Trifonov, Iliev (Rui Miguel 58), Grandin, Popov, Yanev , Marquinhos. Coach: Pavel Dochev (BUL)
Yellow Card(s): Yanev 74

Play-Offs – The New Saints FC (WAL)
H 3-0 *Aquaro (81), Nelson (82), Delev (90)*
Karadzhov, Vidanov, Yanchev, Aquaro, Delev, Trifonov, Saidhodzha (Nelson 64), Iliev (Sheridan 54), Galchev, Tonev (Kostadinov 71), Marquinhos. Coach: Gjore Jovanovski (MKD)
Yellow Card(s): Galchev 36, Aquaro 45, Saidhodzha 61
A 2-2 *Aquaro (11), Tiboni (80)*
Karadzhov, Vidanov, Yanchev, Aquaro, Trifonov, Iliev (Marquinhos 59), Tiboni, Yanev , Tonev (Delev 78), Sheridan, Nelson (Kostadinov 86). Coach: Gjore Jovanovski (MKD)
Yellow Card(s): Karadzhov 65

Group L
Match 1 – Beşiktaş JK (TUR)
A 0-1
M'Bolhi, Vidanov, Stoyanov, Yanchev, Aquaro, Trifonov, Tiero (Galchev 46), Tonev (Trecarichi 59), Sheridan, Marquinhos, Nelson (Saidhodzha 79). Coach: Gjore Jovanovski (MKD)
Yellow Card(s): Stoyanov 57, Aquaro 90+3
Match 2 – FC Porto (POR)
H 0-1
M'Bolhi, Vidanov, Yanchev, Aquaro, Trifonov, Tiero (Trecarichi 58), Sheridan, Dechev, Marquinhos, Grillo (Delev 67), Michel (Galchev 79). Coach: Gjore Jovanovski (MKD)
Yellow Card(s): Aquaro 78
Match 3 – SK Rapid Wien (AUT)
H 0-2
M'Bolhi, Vidanov, Stoyanov (Dechev 72), Yanchev, Aquaro, Delev, Trifonov, Minev (Tiboni 46), Sheridan, Marquinhos, Nelson (Tonev 57). Coach: Gjore Jovanovski (MKD)
Yellow Card(s): Tiboni 47
Match 4 – SK Rapid Wien (AUT)
A 2-1 *Yanchev (50), Marquinhos (64)*
M'Bolhi, Stoyanov, Yanchev, Aquaro, Trifonov (Grillo 88), Galchev, Tonev (Yanev 90+3), Minev, Marquinhos, Nelson (Delev 82), Michel. Coach: Milen Radukanov (BUL)
Yellow Card(s): Nelson 39, Yanchev 51, Aquaro 59, Marquinhos 77, Stoyanov 90+1, Galchev 90+2
Match 5 – Beşiktaş JK (TUR)
H 1-2 *Sheridan (79)*
M'Bolhi, Vidanov, Stoyanov, Yanchev, Delev, Galchev (Yanev 74), Tonev (Sheridan 75), Minev, Marquinhos, Grillo, Michel. Coach: Milen Radukanov (BUL)
Yellow Card(s): Yanchev 58, Yanev 86
Match 6 – FC Porto (POR)
A 1-3 *Delev (48)*
M'Bolhi, Vidanov, Stoyanov, Yanchev (Galchev 88), Aquaro, Delev, Yanev , Tonev (Sheridan 77), Marquinhos, Grillo (Dechev 63), Michel. Coach: Milen Radukanov (BUL)
Yellow Card(s): Sheridan 81

PFC LEVSKI SOFIA

UEFA EUROPA LEAGUE

Second Qualifying Round – Dundalk FC (IRL)
H 6-0 *Yovov (12), Mladenov (14, 46), Dembélé (42), Isa (86, 90+4)*
Petkov, Stanchev, Ivanov, Yovov (Baltanov 52), Minev, Mladenov, Joãozinho, Tasevski (Alexandrov 64), Dembélé (Isa 77), Gadzhev, Miliev. Coach: Yasen Petrov (BUL)
A 2-0 *Dembélé (4, 33)*
Petkov, Mulder, Ivanov, Minev, Mladenov, Joãozinho (Kirov 71), Tasevski, Baltanov, Dembélé (Isa 56), Gadzhev (Ognyanov 61), Miliev. Coach: Yasen Petrov (BUL)

Third Qualifying Round – Kalmar FF (SWE)
A 1-1 *Joãozinho (28)*
Mitrev, Mulder, Ivanov, Yovov, Minev, Mladenov (Telkiyski 79), Joãozinho, Tasevski (Alexandrov 69), Dembélé, Gadzhev (Baltanov 86), Miliev. Coach: Yasen Petrov (BUL)
Yellow Card(s): Dembélé 45+1
H 5-2 *Dembélé (12, 70), Mladenov (33), Isa (90+1, 90+2)*
Petkov, Mulder, Ivanov, Yovov (Baltanov 24), Minev, Mladenov, Joãozinho, Tasevski (Ognyanov 69), Dembélé (Isa 73), Gadzhev, Miliev. Coach: Yasen Petrov (BUL)
Yellow Card(s): Ognyanov 83, Isa 90+3

Play-Offs – AIK Solna (SWE)
A 0-0
Mitrev, Mulder, Greene, Ivanov, Minev, Mladenov (Kirov 75), Joãozinho, Tasevski (Alexandrov 70), Dembélé, Gadzhev (Benzoukane 85), Miliev. Coach: Yasen Petrov (BUL)
Yellow Card(s): Ivanov 7, Greene 39, Mulder 58, Miliev 84
H 2-1 *Mladenov (49), Dembélé (51)*
Mitrev, Mulder, Ivanov, Yovov (Greene 76), Minev, Mladenov (Kirov 81), Joãozinho, Tasevski (Alexandrov 66), Dembélé, Gadzhev, Miliev. Coach: Yasen Petrov (BUL)
Yellow Card(s): Minev 45+1, Miliev 60, Tasevski 61, Gadzhev 90+3

Group C
Match 1 – KAA Gent (BEL)
H 3-2 *Joãozinho (42), Dembélé (60), Greene (84)*
Petkov, Mulder, Greene, Ivanov, Alexandrov (Ognyanov 76), Minev, Benzoukane, Mladenov (Kirov 90+2), Joãozinho, Tasevski (Isa 69), Dembélé. Coach: Yasen Petrov (BUL)
Yellow Card(s): Ivanov 52
Match 2 – Sporting Clube de Portugal (POR)
A 0-5
Petkov, Mulder, Greene, Ivanov, Yovov (Ognyanov 67), Minev, Mladenov (Slory 56), Joãozinho (Kirov 79), Tasevski, Dembélé, Miliev. Coach: Yasen Petrov (BUL)
Yellow Card(s): Dembélé 74, Mulder 75
Match 3 – LOSC Lille Métropole (FRA)
A 0-1
Mitrev, Mulder, Greene, Ivanov, Minev, Ognyanov (Isa 63), Mladenov (Slory 72), Joãozinho, Dembélé, Gadzhev, Miliev. Coach: Yasen Petrov (BUL)
Yellow Card(s): Mladenov 62
Match 4 – LOSC Lille Métropole (FRA)
H 2-2 *Dembélé (11), Gadzhev (82)*
Akalski, Mulder, Greene, Yovov (Ognyanov 60), Minev, Joãozinho, Tasevski (Ivanov 87), Slory (Mladenov 58), Dembélé, Gadzhev, Miliev. Coach: Yasen Petrov (BUL)
Yellow Card(s): Slory 26, Minev 64, Mitrev 84
Match 5 – KAA Gent (BEL)
A 0-1
Mitrev, Mulder (Stanchev 46), Greene, Yovov, Minev, Mladenov (Isa 77), Joãozinho, Baltanov (Ognyanov 53), Dembélé, Gadzhev, Miliev. Coach: Yasen Petrov (BUL)
Yellow Card(s): Dembélé 55, Miliev 78, Greene 85, Stanchev 90+3
Match 6 – Sporting Clube de Portugal (POR)
H 1-0 *Mladenov (45)*
Mitrev, Mulder, Greene, Ivanov, Mladenov (Kirov 89), Joãozinho, Tasevski (Ognyanov 77), Shtarkov, Dembélé, Gadzhev (Baltanov 90+3), Miliev. Coach: Yasen Petrov (BUL)
Yellow Card(s): Shtarkov 40, Gadzhev 90+3

CROATIA

NK DINAMO ZAGREB

UEFA CHAMPIONS LEAGUE

Second Qualifying Round – FC Koper (SVN)
H 5-1 *Mandžukić (31, 63), Slepička (38), Sammir (77), Etto (81)*
Butina, Ibáñez (Barbarić 85), Mesarić, Etto, Sammir, Chago, Badelj (Calello 76), Mandžukić, Slepička, Biščan, Morales (Sivonjić 60). Coach: Velimir Zajec (CRO)
Yellow Card(s): Mesarić 59, Mandžukić 64, Sivonjić 74, Sammir 77
A 0-3
Butina, Ibáñez (Mesarić 57), Calello, Etto, Sammir, Chago, Barbarić, Slepička (Morales 46), Biščan, Dodô, Sivonjić (Šimić 78). Coach: Sreten Čuk (CRO)
Red Card(s): Biščan 77
Yellow Card(s): Chago 24

Third Qualifying Round – FC Sheriff (MDA)
A 1-1 *Sammir (3)*
Butina, Ibáñez, Mesarić, Calello, Etto, Sammir (Sivonjić 85), Chago, Badelj (Dodô 69), Barbarić, Slepička (Šimić 63), Cufré. Coach: Velimir Zajec (CRO)
Red Card(s): Barbarić 61
Yellow Card(s): Barbarić 53, Barbarić 61, Calello 90+1
H 1-1 (aet; 5-6 on pens) *Sammir (55p)*
Lončarić, Mesarić (Ibáñez 46), Ademi (Calello 76), Etto, Sammir, Vrsaljko, Badelj, Slepička, Biščan, Cufré, Rukavina (Dodô 87). Coach: Velimir Zajec (CRO)
Yellow Card(s): Cufré 31, Badelj 83

UEFA EUROPA LEAGUE

Play-Offs – Győri ETO FC (HUN)
A 2-0 *Rukavina (19, 28)*
Lončarić, Ibáñez, Calello, Etto (Ademi 87), Sammir, Vrsaljko, Badelj, Biščan, Cufré, Rukavina (Sivonjić 76), Morales (Mesarić 56). Coach: Vahid Halilhodžić (BIH)
Yellow Card(s): Sivonjić 77
H 2-1 *Sammir (45+2p, 84p)*
Lončarić, Mesarić (Etto 33), Ademi, Kramarić (Chago 79), Sammir, Vrsaljko, Badelj, Biščan, Cufré, Rukavina, Morales (Dodô 66). Coach: Vahid Halilhodžić (BIH)
Yellow Card(s): Mesarić 20, Rukavina 73

Group D
Match 1 – Villarreal CF (ESP)
H 2-0 *Rukavina (18), Sammir (80)*
Kelava, Ademi, Sammir (Bećiraj 87), Tomečak, Vrsaljko, Badelj, Biščan, Cufré, Tonel, Rukavina (Ibáñez 72), Morales (Chago 56). Coach: Vahid Halilhodžić (BIH)
Yellow Card(s): Vrsaljko 20, Ademi 23, Kelava 79
Match 2 – PAOK FC (GRE)
A 0-1
Kelava, Ibáñez (Morales 77), Etto (Tomečak 71), Sammir, Vrsaljko, Chago, Badelj, Biščan, Cufré, Tonel, Rukavina (Bećiraj 83). Coach: Vahid Halilhodžić (BIH)
Yellow Card(s): Biščan 41, Tonel 73

Match 3 – Club Brugge KV (BEL)
H 0-0
Kelava, Ademi (Tomečak 69), Sammir, Vrsaljko, Chago, Badelj, Bišćan, Cufré, Tonel, Rukavina (Bećiraj 79), Morales (Ibáñez 87). Coach: Vahid Halilhodžić (BIH)
Yellow Card(s): Bećiraj 90+2
Match 4 – Club Brugge KV (BEL)
A 2-0 *Sammir (55), Bišćan (59)*
Kelava, Ibáñez, Calello (Barbarić 80), Sammir, Vrsaljko (Etto 72), Chago, Badelj, Bećiraj (Ademi 90), Bišćan, Cufré, Tonel. Coach: Vahid Halilhodžić (BIH)
Yellow Card(s): Cufré 12, Vrsaljko 46
Match 5 – Villarreal CF (ESP)
A 0-3
Kelava, Ibáñez, Calello, Ademi (Morales 79), Sammir (Rukavina 71), Vrsaljko, Badelj, Bećiraj (Barbarić 89), Bišćan, Cufré, Tonel. Coach: Vahid Halilhodžić (BIH)
Red Card(s): Bišćan 86
Yellow Card(s): Kelava 24
Match 6 – PAOK FC (GRE)
H 0-1
Kelava, Calello (Rukavina 59), Ademi (Slepička 67), Etto (Kramarić 75), Sammir, Tomečak, Badelj, Barbarić, Bećiraj, Cufré, Tonel. Coach: Vahid Halilhodžić (BIH)
Yellow Card(s): Badelj 53, Bećiraj 66

HNK HAJDUK SPLIT

UEFA EUROPA LEAGUE

Third Qualifying Round – FC Dinamo Bucureşti (ROU)
A 1-3 *Tomasov (64)*
Subašić, M. Ljubičić (Brkljača 44), J. Buljat, Vejić, Ibričić, Andrić, Strinić, Oremuš (Tomasov 46), Režić, Maloča, An. Sharbini. Coach: Stanko Poklepović (CRO)
Yellow Card(s): Subašić 5, Oremuš 29, J. Buljat 45+2, Vejić 55, Brkljača 87
H 3-0 *Vukušić (12), Brkljača (23), Tomasov (38)*
Subašić, J. Buljat, Ibričić, Andrić, Vukušić (Vejić 89), Tomasov (Režić 78), Strinić, Oremuš, Brkljača (Trebotić 70), Maloča, An. Sharbini. Coach: Stanko Poklepović (CRO)
Yellow Card(s): Ibričić 42, Subašić 82

Play-Offs – FC Unirea Urziceni (ROU)
H 4-1 *Ibričić (39, 66), Brkljača (78), Čop (85)*
Radošević, J. Buljat, Ibričić, Andrić, Vukušić (Čop 66), Tomasov, Strinić, Oremuš, Maloča (Vejić 87), Trebotić (Brkljača 74), An. Sharbini. Coach: Stanko Poklepović (CRO)
Yellow Card(s): Čop 85
A 1-1 *Vukušić (88)*
Subašić, J. Buljat, Ibričić, Andrić, Vukušić (Čop 89), Tomasov (Vejić 46), Jozinović, Oremuš, Brkljača, Maloča, An. Sharbini (Jonjić 76). Coach: Stanko Poklepović (CRO)
Red Card(s): Brkljača 66
Yellow Card(s): Brkljača 37, Subašić 45, Brkljača 66, Andrić 73, Vukušić 89

Group G
Match 1 – AEK Athens FC (GRE)
A 1-3 *Ibričić (29p)*
Subašić, M. Ljubičić, J. Buljat, Vejić, Ibričić, Vukušić, Tomasov (Oremuš 67), Strinić, Maloča, Bulku (Trebotić 81), An. Sharbini (Čop 61). Coach: Stanko Poklepović (CRO)
Yellow Card(s): Strinić 58
Match 2 – RSC Anderlecht (BEL)
H 1-0 *Vukušić (90+5)*
Subašić, M. Ljubičić, J. Buljat, Vejić, Ibričić, Vukušić, Tomasov (Bulku 52), Strinić, Brkljača (Trebotić 76), Maloča, An. Sharbini (Čop 63). Coach: Stanko Poklepović (CRO)
Yellow Card(s): Bulku 90, Maloča 90
Match 3 – FC Zenit St Petersburg (RUS)
A 0-2
Subašić, M. Ljubičić, J. Buljat, Ibričić, Vukušić, Strinić, Oremuš, Brkljača (Trebotić 87), Maloča, Bulku (Jozinović 80), An. Sharbini (Čop 46). Coach: Stanko Poklepović (CRO)
Yellow Card(s): Ibričić 26
Match 4 – FC Zenit St Petersburg (RUS)
H 2-3 *M. Ljubičić (68), Vukušić (82)*
Subašić, M. Ljubičić, J. Buljat, Vejić, Ibričić, Vukušić, Tomasov (Oremuš 61), Strinić, Maloča, Bulku, An. Sharbini. Coach: Goran Vučević (CRO)
Yellow Card(s): Vejić 67, Maloča 85, An. Sharbini 89
Match 5 – AEK Athens FC (GRE)
H 1-3 *J. Buljat (90)*
Radošević, M. Ljubičić (Andrić 53), J. Buljat, Ibričić, Vukušić, Tomasov (Čop 53), Jozinović, Strinić, Oremuš, Maloča, An. Sharbini. Coach: Goran Vučević (CRO)
Yellow Card(s): Maloča 11, J. Buljat 30, M. Ljubičić 36, Jozinović 53, Ibričić 88
Match 6 – RSC Anderlecht (BEL)
A 0-2
Radošević, J. Buljat, Vejić, Ibričić (Tomasov 60), Andrić, Vukušić, Jozinović (M. Ljubičić 60), Strinić, Oremuš, Jonjić, Trebotić (Andrijašević 78). Coach: Goran Vučević (CRO)
Yellow Card(s): Strinić 64, Vejić 73

HNK CIBALIA

UEFA EUROPA LEAGUE

Second Qualifying Round – Cliftonville FC (NIR)
A 0-1
Matković, Tomić, Kresinger, Grgić (Kvesić 89), Parmaković, Radotić (Prgomet 86), Božić, Jurić, Baraban (Šimunac 81), Mazalović, Lučić. Coach: Stanko Mršić (CRO)
Yellow Card(s): Matković 4, Jurić 14, Grgić 64
H 0-0
Matković, Tomić, Kresinger, Parmaković, Radotić, Božić (Čuljak 68), Jurić, Baraban, Mazalović (Prgomet 46), Lučić, Malčić (Grgić 46). Coach: Stanko Mršić (CRO)
Yellow Card(s): Tomić 24

HNK ŠIBENIK

UEFA EUROPA LEAGUE

First Qualifying Round – Sliema Wanderers FC (MLT)
H 0-0
Blažević, Cerić, Gusić, Alispahić, Husmani, Bačelić-Grgić (Elez 63), Jakoliš, Medvid, Fuštar, Spahija, Bloudek (Božić 63). Coach: Branko Karačić (CRO)
Yellow Card(s): Alispahić 45+1, Spahija 88
A 3-0 *Medvid (64), Jakoliš (73), Bulat (89)*
Blažević, Cerić, Jurčević, Alispahić, Husmani, Bačelić-Grgić (Elez 85), Jakoliš (Šubić 88), Medvid, Fuštar, Bulat, Bloudek (Baković 80). Coach: Branko Karačić (CRO)
Yellow Card(s): Alispahić 10, Bloudek 54, Blažević 57, Medvid 66, Bačelić-Grgić 75

Second Qualifying Round – Anorthosis Famagusta FC (CYP)
A 2-0 *Bloudek (10), Bačelić-Grgić (61p)*
Blažević, Cerić, Jurčević, Elez, Bačelić-Grgić, Jakoliš, Medvid, Fuštar (Baković 90+3), Božić (Jordan 76), Bulat, Bloudek (Gusić 83). Coach: Branko Karačić (CRO)
Yellow Card(s): Jurčević 24, Cerić 27, Bulat 77
H 0-3
Blažević, Cerić, Elez, Alispahić, Bačelić-Grgić, Jakoliš, Medvid, Fuštar (Baković 45), Božić, Bulat (Gusić 54), Bloudek (Maleš 99). Coach: Branko Karačić (CRO)
Yellow Card(s): Cerić 4, Alispahić 48, Medvid 57, Gusić 67, Bačelić-Grgić 90+4

CYPRUS

AC OMONIA

UEFA CHAMPIONS LEAGUE

Second Qualifying Round – FK Renova (MKD)
H 3-0 *Konstantinou (7p, 62), Davidson (29)*
Georgallides, Davidson, Wenzel, Karipidis, Makrides, Grammozis (Panagi 83), Kaseke, Konstantinou, Shpungin (Efrem 46), Leandro, Aloneftis (Víctor 81). Coach: Takis Lemonis (GRE)
Yellow Card(s): Konstantinou 64
A 2-0 *Aloneftis (15), Leandro (24)*
Georgallides, Davidson, Karipidis, Efrem, Makrides (Rengifo 46), Kaseke, Konstantinou (LuaLua 63), Iago Bouzón, Charalambous, Leandro, Aloneftis (Rueda 74). Coach: Takis Lemonis (GRE)

Third Qualifying Round – FC Salzburg (AUT)
H 1-1 *LuaLua (90+1p)*
Jevrić, Davidson, Karipidis, Efrem, Makrides, Kaseke (Avraam 64), Konstantinou (Rengifo 82), Iago Bouzón, Charalambous, Leandro, Aloneftis (LuaLua 46). Coach: Takis Lemonis (GRE)
Yellow Card(s): Kaseke 21
A 1-4 *Rengifo (90)*
Georgallides, Davidson, Karipidis, Makrides, Kaseke (Avraam 67), Konstantinou (Rengifo 72), Iago Bouzón, LuaLua (Efrem 59), Charalambous, Leandro, Aloneftis. Coach: Takis Lemonis (GRE)
Yellow Card(s): Charalambous 18, Avraam 88

UEFA EUROPA LEAGUE

Play-Offs – FC Metalist Kharkiv (UKR)
H 0-1
Georgallides, Davidson, Wenzel, Avraam (Rengifo 73), Makrides, Kaseke (Rueda 65), Konstantinou, Iago Bouzón, Charalambous, Leandro, Aloneftis (Efrem 55). Coach: Takis Lemonis (GRE)
Yellow Card(s): Iago Bouzón 29, Konstantinou 42, Leandro 65
A 2-2 *Leandro (60), Rengifo (64)*
Georgallides, Davidson, Wenzel, Efrem, Avraam, Makrides (Aloneftis 76), Kaseke (Rueda 80), Rengifo, Iago Bouzón, Charalambous (Víctor 86), Leandro. Coach: Takis Lemonis (GRE)
Yellow Card(s): Avraam 50, Iago Bouzón 62, Rengifo 74

APOLLON LIMASSOL FC

UEFA EUROPA LEAGUE

Third Qualifying Round – FC Sibir Novosibirsk (RUS)
A 0-1
Chvalovský, Oseni, Martorell, Mrdaković (Semedo 55), Bangura, Kosowski (Adorno 68), Morris, Núñez (Ogbuke 79), Kolář, Quinteros, González. Coach: Slobodan Krčmarević (SRB)
Yellow Card(s): Morris 10, Kosowski 12
H 2-1 *Semedo (12), Núñez (71)*
Chvalovský, Oseni (Bangura 85), Semedo (Toni 77), Kosowski, Adorno, Morris, Neva, Núñez (Ogbuke 81), Kolář, Quinteros, González. Coach: Slobodan Krčmarević (SRB)
Red Card(s): Kosowski 15
Yellow Card(s): Semedo 65, Quinteros 82

APOEL FC

UEFA EUROPA LEAGUE

Second Qualifying Round – FK Tauras (LTU)
A 3-0 *Charalambides (50), Hélio Pinto (80), Manduca (83)*
Chiotis, Paulo Jorge, Grncarov, Solari (Trickovski 69), Charalambides, Broerse, Manduca, Nuno Morais (Satsias 13), Solomou, Marcinho (Hélio Pinto 73), William. Coach: Ivan Jovanović (SRB)
Yellow Card(s): Charalambides 34
H 3-1 *Solari (18, 86p), Trickovski (80)*
Chiotis, Grncarov, Poursaitidis, Solari, Satsias (Michail 75), Hélio Pinto, Kontis, Alexandrou (Broerse 88), Solomou, Marcinho (Trickovski 64), William. Coach: Ivan Jovanović (SRB)

Third Qualifying Round – FK Jablonec (CZE)
H 1-0 *Solari (55)*
Chiotis, Paulo Jorge, Grncarov, Solari (Alexandrou 90+2), Charalambides (Trickovski 77), Broerse (Satsias 77), Manduca, Hélio Pinto, Solomou, Marcinho, William. Coach: Ivan Jovanović (SRB)
Yellow Card(s): Hélio Pinto 33
A 3-1 *Paulo Jorge (24), Charalambides (28), Solari (37)*
Chiotis, Paulo Jorge, Grncarov, Solari (Kontis 88), Charalambides, Broerse, Manduca (Michail 83), Hélio Pinto, Solomou, Marcinho (Almeida 66), William. Coach: Ivan Jovanović (SRB)
Yellow Card(s): Chiotis 30, Broerse 88

Play-Offs – Getafe CF (ESP)
A 0-1
Chiotis, Paulo Jorge, Grncarov, Solari (Trickovski 87), Charalambides (Poursaitidis 90+3), Manduca (Aílton 66), Hélio Pinto, Nuno Morais, Solomou, Marcinho, William. Coach: Ivan Jovanović (SRB)
Yellow Card(s): Paulo Jorge 76, Solari 78
H 1-1 (aet) *Aílton (41)*
Chiotis, Paulo Jorge, Grncarov, Solari (Broerse 74), Charalambides, Manduca (Trickovski 74), Hélio Pinto, Nuno Morais, Aílton, Solomou, William (Poursaitidis 90+1). Coach: Ivan Jovanović (SRB)
Red Card(s): Broerse 116
Yellow Card(s): Trickovski 104

ANORTHOSIS FAMAGUSTA FC

UEFA EUROPA LEAGUE

First Qualifying Round – FC Banants (ARM)
H 3-0 *Katsavakis (24), Okkas (31), Cafú (64)*
Kozáčík, Katsavakis, Marangos, Skopelitis, Okkas (Tofas 81),

Leiwakabessy (Vidović 74), Cristóvão (Miguel Pedro 71), Cafú, Laban, Janício, Georgiou. Coach: Guillermo Hoyos (ARG)
Yellow Card(s): Marangos 90+1
A 1-0 *Laban (37)*
Kozáčík, Katsavakis, Marangos (Papathanasiou 71), Skopelitis, Okkas, Leiwakabessy, Cristóvão (Konstantinou 77), Cafú, Laban (Mintikkis 62), Janício, Georgiou. Coach: Guillermo Hoyos (ARG)
Yellow Card(s): Kozáčík 42, Laban 60, Janício 84

Second Qualifying Round – HNK Šibenik (CRO)
H 0-2
Kozáčík, Katsavakis, Marangos (Miguel Pedro 64), Skopelitis, Okkas, Leiwakabessy, Cristóvão (Coto 51), Cafú, Laban (Papathanasiou 72), Janício, Konstantinou. Coach: Guillermo Hoyos (ARG)
Yellow Card(s): Konstantinou 8, Cristóvão 25, Kozáčík 60, Papathanasiou 90+1
A 3-0 (aet) *Laban (16), Cristóvão (25), Okkas (96)*
Argüello, Katsavakis, García (Konstantinou 90), Marangos (Vidović 102), Okkas, Leiwakabessy, Cristóvão (Coto 86), Cafú, Laban, Janício, Georgiou. Coach: Guillermo Hoyos (ARG)
Yellow Card(s): Georgiou 90+4

Third Qualifying Round – Cercle Brugge KSV (BEL)
A 0-1
Argüello, Katsavakis, Marangos (Coto 71), Skopelitis, Okkas, Leiwakabessy, Cristóvão (Papathanasiou 79), Cafú, Laban (Miguel Pedro 88), Janício, Georgiou. Coach: Guillermo Hoyos (ARG)
H 3-1 *Cafú (45+1, 60, 87)*
Argüello, Katsavakis, García, Skopelitis (Miguel Pedro 81), Okkas (Marangos 68), Leiwakabessy, Cristóvão (Fotheringham 74), Cafú, Laban, Janício, Georgiou. Coach: Guillermo Hoyos (ARG)
Yellow Card(s): Leiwakabessy 26, Georgiou 29

Play-Offs – PFC CSKA Moskva (RUS)
A 0-4
Argüello, Katsavakis, García, Marangos (Laborde 50), Okkas, Leiwakabessy, Cristóvão (Coto 60), Cafú (Kozáčík 78), Frontini, Laban, Janício. Coach: Guillermo Hoyos (ARG)
Red Card(s): Argüello 77
Yellow Card(s): Okkas 77, Laborde 82, Laban 83
H 1-2 *Cafú (76)*
Kozáčík, Brachi, García, Marangos, Okkas, Cristóvão (Chatzigeorgiou 68), Cafú, Frontini, Laborde (Consistre 20), Sielis (Vidović 61), Georgiou. Coach: Guillermo Hoyos (ARG)
Yellow Card(s): Marangos 36, Frontini 40, Georgiou 45, García 70, Brachi 84

CZECH REPUBLIC

AC SPARTA PRAHA

UEFA CHAMPIONS LEAGUE

Second Qualifying Round – SK Liepājas Metalurgs (LVA)
A 3-0 *Kadlec (37), Wilfried (51, 58)*
Blažek, Řepka, Hoheneder, Sionko, Matějovský, Wilfried (Lačný 83), Žofčák (Vacek 65), Kadlec, Kladrubský, Kucka (Jeslínek 78), Brabec. Coach: Jozef Chovanec (CZE)
H 2-0 *Matějovský (12), Zeman (43)*
Blažek, Řepka, Pamić, Lačný (Zeman 41), Matějovský (Žofčák 56), Kadlec, Kladrubský, Jeslínek, Kucka (Hoheneder 46), Brabec, Vacek. Coach: Jozef Chovanec (CZE)
Yellow Card(s): Vacek 27

Third Qualifying Round – KKS Lech Poznań (POL)
H 1-0 *Brabec (75)*
Blažek, Řepka, Pamić, Hoheneder, Sionko, Matějovský (Hejda 90+4), Wilfried (Třešňák 86), Kadlec (Jeslínek 72), Kladrubský, Kucka, Brabec. Coach: Jozef Chovanec (CZE)
Yellow Card(s): Wilfried 10, Kucka 37
A 1-0 *Kladrubský (50p)*
Blažek, Řepka, Pamić, Hoheneder, Sionko, Matějovský, Wilfried (Lačný 90+2), Kadlec (Žofčák 67), Kladrubský, Kucka (Hejda 75), Brabec. Coach: Jozef Chovanec (CZE)
Red Card(s): Matějovský 80, Sionko 85
Yellow Card(s): Wilfried 21, Brabec 32, Řepka 39

Play-Offs – MŠK Žilina (SVK)
H 0-2
Blažek, Řepka, Pamić, Hoheneder, Lačný (Třešňák 68), Kweuke, Žofčák (Zeman 77), Adiaba, Kucka, Brabec, Vachoušek (Jeslínek 90). Coach: Jozef Chovanec (CZE)
Yellow Card(s): Brabec 38, Řepka 66, Vachoušek 78
A 0-1
Blažek, Pamić (Třešňák 86), Hoheneder, Sionko (Kadeřábek 61), Wilfried, Kladrubský, Adiaba (Kweuke 46), Kucka, Krejčí, Vachoušek, Hejda. Coach: Jozef Chovanec (CZE)
Yellow Card(s): Kladrubský 37, Kucka 40, Vachoušek 52

UEFA EUROPA LEAGUE

Group F
Match 1 – US Città di Palermo (ITA)
H 3-2 *Wilfried (17), Kladrubský (68), Kadlec (75)*
Blažek, Řepka, Pamić, Hoheneder, Podaný, Sionko (Kadeřábek 90+1), Wilfried (Kweuke 90+2), Kadlec (Třešňák 83), Kladrubský, Adiaba, Brabec. Coach: Jozef Chovanec (CZE)
Yellow Card(s): Kladrubský 45+2, Řepka 65, Adiaba 66
Match 2 – PFC CSKA Moskva (RUS)
A 0-3
Blažek, Řepka, Pamić, Podaný (Zeman 82), Wilfried (Matějovský 90), Kadlec, Kladrubský (Kweuke 81), Adiaba, Kucka, Brabec, Vacek. Coach: Jozef Chovanec (CZE)
Yellow Card(s): Vacek 74, Řepka 83
Match 3 – FC Lausanne-Sport (SUI)
H 3-3 *Wilfried (10, 24), Kucka (21)*
Blažek, Řepka, Pamić, Podaný (Kladrubský 81), Sionko, Wilfried (Kweuke 76), Kušnír, Kadlec (Matějovský 90+3), Kucka, Brabec, Vacek. Coach: Jozef Chovanec (CZE)
Yellow Card(s): Sionko 79
Match 4 – FC Lausanne-Sport (SUI)
A 3-1 *Wilfried (45, 90+6), Kweuke (75)*
Blažek, Řepka, Pamić, Podaný, Kweuke, Wilfried, Kladrubský, Adiaba (Matějovský 69), Kucka, Brabec, Vacek (Hoheneder 90+3). Coach: Jozef Chovanec (CZE)
Yellow Card(s): Kucka 7, Wilfried 45+1, Kladrubský 67, Matějovský 74
Match 5 – US Città di Palermo (ITA)
A 2-2 Kladrubský (51p), Kucka (62)
Blažek, Řepka, Pamić, Podaný (Zeman 83), Kweuke (Hoheneder 90+3), Wilfried, Kušnír (Kadlec 70), Kladrubský, Kucka, Brabec, Vacek. Coach: Jozef Chovanec (CZE)
Yellow Card(s): Kušnír 18, Kweuke 54, Vacek 59, Brabec 59, Řepka 90
Match 6 – PFC CSKA Moskva (RUS)
H 1-1 Kadlec (44)
Zítka, Pamić, Podaný (Kweuke 68), Sionko (Zeman 77), Wilfried, Kadlec, Adiaba, Kucka (Matějovský 83), Brabec, Vacek, Hejda. Coach: Jozef Chovanec (CZE)

Round of 32 – Liverpool FC (ENG)
H 0-0
Blažek, Řepka, Pamić, Matějovský (Pekhart 90+2), Kweuke, Kušnír, Kadlec (Zeman 89), Brabec, Vacek, Abena, Kerić (Sionko 73). Coach: Jozef Chovanec (CZE)
Yellow Card(s): Řepka 39
A 0-1
Blažek, Řepka, Pamić (Kerić 90), Sionko (Podaný 74), Matějovský, Kweuke, Kušnír, Kadlec, Brabec, Vacek, Abena (Pekhart 78). Coach: Jozef Chovanec (CZE)
Yellow Card(s): Pamić 32, Matějovský 40, Kweuke 64

FC VIKTORIA PLZEŇ

UEFA EUROPA LEAGUE

Third Qualifying Round – Beşiktaş JK (TUR)
H 1-1 *Limberský (28)*
Krbeček, Rada, Limberský, Horváth, Petržela (Hájovský 90+1), Rezek, Bystroň, Jiráček (Hruška 86), Navrátil, Kolář (Střihavka 68), Rajtoral. Coach: Pavel Vrba (CZE)
Yellow Card(s): Rajtoral 44
A 0-3
Krbeček, Rada, Limberský, Horváth (Rýdel 83), Petržela (Hruška 75), Rezek, Bystroň, Jiráček, Navrátil, Kolář (Hájovský 75), Rajtoral. Coach: Pavel Vrba (CZE)
Red Card(s): Navrátil 31, Limberský 51
Yellow Card(s): Limberský 21, Rezek 45+1, Limberský 51

FK JABLONEC

UEFA EUROPA LEAGUE

Third Qualifying Round – APOEL FC (CYP)
A 0-1
Špit, Jablonský, Eliáš, Loučka, Kovařík (Piták 82), Vošahlík (Haurdić 65), Krajčík, Lafata, Jarolím, Pavlík, Drsek (Huber 47). Coach: František Komňacký (CZE)
Yellow Card(s): Eliáš 31, Loučka 34, Krajčík 87
H 1-3 *Pavlík (33)*
Špit, Zábojník, Pekhart, Eliáš (Piták 46), Loučka (Vošahlík 46), Kovařík, Krajčík, Lafata (Haurdić 81), Jarolím, Pavlík, Drsek. Coach: František Komňacký (CZE)
Yellow Card(s): Špit 80

FC BANÍK OSTRAVA

UEFA EUROPA LEAGUE

Second Qualifying Round – FC WIT Georgia (GEO)
A 6-0 *Fernando Neves (33, 56p, 64p), Pilík (61), Neuwirth (70), Hušbauer (78)*
Daněk, Fernando Neves, Řezník, Lukeš, Bolf, Šenkeřík (Frejlach 65), Greguš, Varadi, Marek (Hušbauer 68), Neuwirth, Pilík (Šmejkal 74). Coach: Miroslav Koubek (CZE)
H 0-0
Baránek, Fernando Neves, Řezník, Lukeš, Šenkeřík (Pilík 58), Greguš, Fantiš (Zeher 46), Frydrych, Vrt'o, Koukal, Wojnar (Hušbauer 72). Coach: Miroslav Koubek (CZE)
Yellow Card(s): Koukal 33, Frydrych 87, Lukeš 88

Third Qualifying Round – FC Dnepr Mogilev (BLR)
A 0-1
Daněk, Fernando Neves, Řezník, Lukeš, Bolf, Zeher (Šmejkal 69), Varadi, Marek, Frejlach (Hušbauer 74), Neuwirth, Pilík (Šenkeřík 46). Coach: Miroslav Koubek (CZE)
Yellow Card(s): Fernando Neves 44, Marek 72
H 1-2 *Řezník (26)*
Daněk, Fernando Neves, Řezník, Lukeš, Bolf (Greguš 83), Hušbauer (Pilík 68), Varadi, Marek, Frejlach, Šmejkal (Šenkeřík 57), Neuwirth. Coach: Miroslav Koubek (CZE)
Yellow Card(s): Varadi 7, Hušbauer 37, Bolf 79, Fernando Neves 87

DENMARK

FC KØBENHAVN

UEFA CHAMPIONS LEAGUE

Third Qualifying Round – FC BATE Borisov (BLR)
A 0-0
Wiland, Pospěch, Nørregaard, Ottesen, Claudemir, W.K. Jørgensen, César Santin (Grønkjær 82), N'Doye, Antonsson, Wendt, Vingaard. Coach: Ståle Solbakken (NOR)
Yellow Card(s): N'Doye 14
H 3-2 *César Santin (2), W.K. Jørgensen (27), N'Doye (59)*
Wiland, Pospěch, Nørregaard (Grønkjær 54), Ottesen, Claudemir ('Zanka' Jørgensen 88), W.K. Jørgensen, César Santin (Kristensen 80), N'Doye, Antonsson, Wendt, Vingaard. Coach: Ståle Solbakken (NOR)

Play-Offs – Rosenborg BK (NOR)
A 1-2 *Grønkjær (84)*
Wiland, Pospěch, Claudemir, W.K. Jørgensen, Grønkjær, N'Doye, Antonsson, Kristensen (Nørregaard 67), Wendt, Vingaard (Bergvold 67), 'Zanka' Jørgensen. Coach: Ståle Solbakken (NOR)
Yellow Card(s): Vingaard 6, W.K. Jørgensen 43
H 1-0 *Ottesen (33)*
Wiland, Pospěch, Ottesen, Claudemir, W.K. Jørgensen, Grønkjær (Larsson 90), César Santin (Nørregaard 67), N'Doye, Antonsson, Wendt, Vingaard ('Zanka' Jørgensen 90+1). Coach: Ståle Solbakken (NOR)

Group D
Match 1 – FC Rubin Kazan (RUS)
H 1-0 *N'Doye (87)*
Wiland, Pospěch, Ottesen, Claudemir (Nørregaard 90), W.K. Jørgensen, Grønkjær, César Santin (Bolaños 75), N'Doye, Antonsson, Wendt, Vingaard ('Zanka' Jørgensen 90). Coach: Ståle Solbakken (NOR)
Match 2 – Panathinaikos FC (GRE)
A 2-0 *N'Doye (28), Vingaard (37)*
Wiland, Pospěch, Claudemir (Delaney 79), W.K. Jørgensen, Grønkjær, N'Doye (César Santin 76), Antonsson, Wendt, Vingaard, 'Zanka' Jørgensen, Bolaños (Nørregaard 58). Coach: Ståle Solbakken (NOR)
Yellow Card(s): Claudemir 9, N'Doye 51
Match 3 – FC Barcelona (ESP)
A 0-2
Wiland, Pospěch, Claudemir, W.K. Jørgensen, Grønkjær, César Santin (Zohore 74), N'Doye, Antonsson, Wendt (Larsson 89), Vingaard (Bolaños 62), 'Zanka' Jørgensen. Coach: Ståle Solbakken (NOR)
Yellow Card(s): N'Doye 61, Pospěch 68
Match 4 – FC Barcelona (ESP)
H 1-1 *Claudemir (32)*
Wiland, Pospěch, Claudemir, W.K. Jørgensen, Grønkjær, N'Doye, Antonsson, Wendt, Vingaard, 'Zanka' Jørgensen, Bolaños. Coach: Ståle Solbakken (NOR)
Yellow Card(s): Pospěch 89
Match 5 – FC Rubin Kazan (RUS)
A 0-1
Wiland, Pospěch, Claudemir, W.K. Jørgensen, Grønkjær, N'Doye, Antonsson, Wendt, Vingaard (Zohore 73), 'Zanka' Jørgensen, Bolaños. Coach: Ståle Solbakken (NOR)
Yellow Card(s): Bolaños 10, Wendt 72

Match 6 – Panathinaikos FC (GRE)
H 3-1 *Vingaard (26), Grønkjær (50p), Cissé (73og)*
Wiland, Pospěch, Claudemir, W.K. Jørgensen, Grønkjær (Zohore 87), N'Doye (César Santin 80), Antonsson (Ottesen 77), Wendt, Vingaard, 'Zanka' Jørgensen, Bolaños. Coach: Ståle Solbakken (NOR)
Yellow Card(s): Grønkjær 52

Round of 16 – Chelsea FC (ENG)
H 0-2
Wiland, Pospěch, Claudemir, W.K. Jørgensen, Grønkjær (Zohore 87), César Santin (Vingaard 46), N'Doye, Antonsson, Wendt (Bengtsson 75), 'Zanka' Jørgensen, Bolaños. Coach: Ståle Solbakken (NOR)
Yellow Card(s): 'Zanka' Jørgensen 7, Pospěch 70
A 0-0
Wiland, Bengtsson (Zohore 61), Claudemir, W.K. Jørgensen, Grønkjær, N'Doye, Antonsson, Wendt, Vingaard (César Santin 74), 'Zanka' Jørgensen, Bolaños (Kristensen 90). Coach: Ståle Solbakken (NOR)
Yellow Card(s): Claudemir 67, Bolaños 81

No	Player	Nat	DoB	Aps	(s)	Gls
Goalkeepers						
21	Johan Wiland	SWE	24/1/81	8		
Defenders						
15	Mikael Antonsson	SWE	31/5/81	8		
12	Peter Larsson	SWE	30/4/84		(1)	
5	Sölvi Ottesen	ISL	18/2/84	1	(2)	
2	Zdeněk Pospěch	CZE	14/12/78	7		
17	Oscar Wendt	SWE	24/10/85	8		
25	Mathias 'Zanka' Jørgensen		23/4/90	7	(1)	
Midfielders						
30	Christian Bolaños	CRC	17/5/84	6	(2)	
6	Claudemir	BRA	27/3/88	8		1
27	Thomas Delaney		3/9/91		(2)	
16	Thomas Kristensen		17/4/83		(1)	
8	William Kvist Jørgensen		24/2/85	8		
4	Hjalte Nørregaard		8/4/81		(2)	
3	Pierre Bengtsson	SWE	18/6/88	1	(1)	
20	Martin Vingaard		20/3/85	7	(1)	2
Forwards						
10	Jesper Grønkjær		12/8/77	8		1
14	Dame N'Doye	SEN	21/2/85	8		2
11	César Santin	BRA	24/2/81	3	(3)	
18	Kenneth Zohore		31/1/94		(5)	

FC NORDSJÆLLAND

UEFA EUROPA LEAGUE

Third Qualifying Round – Sporting Clube de Portugal (POR)
H 0-1
Hansen, Kildentoft, Adu, Stokholm, N.B. Nielsen, Fetai (Mikkelsen 72), Parkhurst, M.L. Nielsen (Bernier 66), Laudrup (Granskov 84), Jensen, Bengtsson. Coach: Morten Wieghorst (DEN)
Yellow Card(s): Fetai 29, Bernier 80
A 1-2 *Lawan (79)*
Hansen, Kildentoft, Adu, Stokholm, Bernier (M.L. Nielsen 67), Mikkelsen (Granskov 84), N.B. Nielsen, Parkhurst, Laudrup (Lawan 63), Jensen, Bengtsson. Coach: Morten Wieghorst (DEN)
Yellow Card(s): Adu 16, Lawan 90+3

ODENSE BK

UEFA EUROPA LEAGUE

Third Qualifying Round – HŠK Zrinjski (BIH)
H 5-3 *Gíslason (16), Absalonsen (23), Utaka (31, 60), Andreasen (37)*
Carroll, Ruud, Håland (Helveg 46), Andreasen, Christensen, Utaka, Absalonsen, Toft, Sørensen, Traoré (Cacá 71), Gíslason (H. Hansen 46). Coach: Lars Olsen (DEN)
Yellow Card(s): Ruud 56, Traoré 65
A 0-0
Carroll, Ruud, Håland, Andreasen, Christensen, Helveg, Utaka (Demba-Nyrén 90), Sørensen, Traoré, Djemba-Djemba (H. Hansen 90+2), Gíslason. Coach: Lars Olsen (DEN)
Yellow Card(s): Gíslason 18, Traoré 50

Play-Offs – Motherwell FC (SCO)
H 2-1 *Sørensen (31), Utaka (78)*
Carroll, Ruud, Håland, Andreasen, Christensen, Utaka, Absalonsen, Sørensen, Cacá (H. Hansen 46), Djemba-Djemba, Gíslason (Johansson 74). Coach: Lars Olsen (DEN)
Yellow Card(s): Andreasen 90+3
A 1-0 *Utaka (28)*
Carroll, Ruud, Håland (Johansson 53), Andreasen, Christensen, Utaka (Kadrii 88), Toft (Demba-Nyrén 66), Sørensen, Traoré, Djemba-Djemba, Gíslason. Coach: Lars Olsen (DEN)
Red Card(s): Ruud 75, Christensen 85
Yellow Card(s): Ruud 21, Christensen 22, Djemba-Djemba 75, Ruud 75, Christensen 85

Group H
Match 1 – Getafe CF (ESP)
A 1-2 *Andreasen (44)*
Carroll, Håland, Andreasen, Helveg (Cacá 46), Utaka, Johansson (Toft 78), Troest, Sørensen, Traoré, Gíslason, Kadrii (Feldballe 88). Coach: Uffe Pedersen (DEN)
Yellow Card(s): Gíslason 67, Troest 81, Andreasen 86
Match 2 – VfB Stuttgart (GER)
H 1-2 *Johansson (78)*
Carroll, Ruud, Håland, Andreasen, Utaka, Johansson (Demba-Nyrén 80), Troest, Sørensen, Traoré (Feldballe 90), Djemba-Djemba, Gíslason (Kadrii 70). Coach: Uffe Pedersen (DEN)
Yellow Card(s): Traoré 15
Match 3 – BSC Young Boys (SUI)
A 2-4 *Utaka (48), Sørensen (84p)*
A.L. Hansen, Ruud, Håland, Christensen, Utaka (Demba-Nyrén 78), Johansson, Sørensen, Traoré, Djemba-Djemba, Gíslason (Helveg 72), Kadrii (Absalonsen 85). Coach: Uffe Pedersen (DEN)
Yellow Card(s): Ruud 15
Match 4 – BSC Young Boys (SUI)
H 2-0 *Andreasen (12, 60)*
Carroll, Ruud, Håland, Andreasen, Christensen, Utaka (Toft 88), Johansson, Absalonsen (Kadrii 82), Sørensen, Traoré (Gíslason 81), Djemba-Djemba. Coach: Uffe Pedersen (DEN)
Yellow Card(s): Ruud 35, Djemba-Djemba 66
Match 5 – Getafe CF (ESP)
H 1-1 *Andreasen (90+2)*
Carroll, Ruud, Håland, Andreasen, Christensen, Utaka, Toft, Sørensen, Traoré (Johansson 72), Djemba-Djemba, Kadrii (Feldballe 66). Coach: Henrik Clausen (DEN)
Yellow Card(s): Djemba-Djemba 70
Match 6 – VfB Stuttgart (GER)
A 1-5 *Utaka (72)*
Ousager, Ruud, Andreasen, Christensen, Helveg, Utaka (Falk 88), Toft (Johansson 76), Sørensen, Traoré (Feldballe 79), Djemba-Djemba, Høegh. Coach: Henrik Clausen (DEN)

BRØNDBY IF

UEFA EUROPA LEAGUE

Second Qualifying Round – FC Vaduz (LIE)
H 3-0 *Nilsson (51), Jallow (80, 85)*
Andersen, Von Schlebrügge (Van der Schaaf 43), Holmén, Nilsson, Bernburg (Larsen 66), Rasmussen, Jallow, Krohn-Dehli, Bischoff, Kristiansen (Madsen 77), Wass. Coach: Henrik Jensen (DEN)
Yellow Card(s): Bischoff 24
A 0-0
Andersen, Van der Schaaf, Nilsson, Farnerud, Rasmussen, Jallow (Madsen 72), Krohn-Dehli (Larsen 57), Bischoff, Jensen, Kristiansen (Bernburg 59), Wass. Coach: Henrik Jensen (DEN)
Yellow Card(s): Krohn-Dehli 43

Third Qualifying Round – FK Budućnost Podgorica (MNE)
A 2-1 *Adamović (73og), Jensen (87)*
Andersen, Van der Schaaf, Nilsson, Larsen, Rasmussen, Jallow (Bernburg 60), Krohn-Dehli (Madsen 85), Bischoff, Jensen, Kristiansen (Farnerud 60), Wass. Coach: Henrik Jensen (DEN)
Yellow Card(s): Nilsson 83
H 1-0 *Jallow (11)*
Andersen, Von Schlebrügge, Van der Schaaf, Frederiksen, Nilsson (Randrup 78), Farnerud (Madsen 80), Larsen, Jallow (Batata 64), Jensen, Kristiansen, Wass. Coach: Henrik Jensen (DEN)
Yellow Card(s): Van der Schaaf 43

Play-Offs – Sporting Clube de Portugal (POR)
A 2-0 *Kristiansen (43), Jallow (52)*
Andersen, Von Schlebrügge, Nilsson (Randrup 52), Larsen, Rasmussen, Jallow (Madsen 73), Krohn-Dehli, Bischoff, Jensen, Kristiansen (Farnerud 89), Wass. Coach: Henrik Jensen (DEN)
Yellow Card(s): Jensen 67
H 0-3
Andersen, Von Schlebrügge, Nilsson, Larsen, Rasmussen, Jallow (Batata 76), Krohn-Dehli, Bischoff, Jensen, Kristiansen, Wass. Coach: Henrik Jensen (DEN)
Yellow Card(s): Bischoff 45

RANDERS FC

UEFA EUROPA LEAGUE

First Qualifying Round – F91 Dudelange (LUX)
H 6-1 *Sane (16), Movsisyan (17, 90), Olsen (33), S. Pedersen (47p), Brock-Madsen (88)*
Ousted, Egholm, Karlsen, Lorentzen (Cramer 67), S. Pedersen, Movsisyan, Berg, Fenger, Sane (Brock-Madsen 87), Olsen (Sørensen 85), Fischer. Coach: Ove Christensen (DEN)
Yellow Card(s): Karlsen 10
A 1-2 *Lorentzen (17)*
Ousted, Ahmed (Fenger 58), Egholm, Lorentzen, S. Pedersen, Movsisyan (Karlsen 27), Berg, Olsen, Jensen (Hastrup 45+3), Fischer, Arzumanyan. Coach: Ove Christensen (DEN)
Red Card(s): Fenger 80
Yellow Card(s): S. Pedersen 53

Second Qualifying Round – ND Gorica (SVN)
A 3-0 *Lorentzen (51), Cramer (55, 71)*
Ousted, Ahmed, Egholm (Arzumanyan 81), Karlsen (Brock-Madsen 79), Lorentzen, S. Pedersen, Berg, Beckmann, Olsen (Fischer 72), Jensen, Cramer. Coach: Ove Christensen (DEN)
H 1-1 *Cramer (42)*
Ousted, Egholm, Karlsen (Sane 70), Lorentzen, S. Pedersen, Movsisyan (Brock-Madsen 66), Berg, Fenger, Olsen (Sørensen 58), Jensen, Cramer. Coach: Ove Christensen (DEN)
Yellow Card(s): S. Pedersen 41, Brock-Madsen 88

Third Qualifying Round – FC Lausanne-Sport (SUI)
H 2-3 *Movsisyan (6, 81)*
Ousted, Egholm (Ahmed 46), Karlsen, Lorentzen (Sane 90+2), Movsisyan, Berg, Beckmann, Fenger, Jensen, Fischer, Cramer (Olsen 75). Coach: Ove Christensen (DEN)
Yellow Card(s): Karlsen 53, Fenger 61, Beckmann 65, Fischer 90
A 1-1 *Movsisyan (49)*
Ousted, Egholm (Ahmed 82), Lorentzen, S. Pedersen, Movsisyan, Berg, Beckmann, Fenger, Sane (Olsen 75), Jensen, Cramer (Fischer 63). Coach: Ove Christensen (DEN)
Red Card(s): Fischer 90+5
Yellow Card(s): Beckmann 90+5

ENGLAND

CHELSEA FC

UEFA CHAMPIONS LEAGUE

Group F
Match 1 – MŠK Žilina (SVK)
A 4-1 *Essien (13), Anelka (24, 28), Sturridge (48)*
Čech, Ivanović, Essien, Benayoun (McEachran 79), Mikel, Malouda (Van Aanholt 88), Zhirkov, Sturridge (Kakuta 62), Terry, Alex, Anelka. Coach: Carlo Ancelotti (ITA)
Match 2 – Olympique de Marseille (FRA)
H 2-0 *Terry (7), Anelka (28p)*
Čech, Ivanović, Cole, Essien, Mikel (McEachran 88), Malouda, Zhirkov (Sturridge 73), Terry, Alex, Anelka, Kakuta (Ramires 62). Coach: Carlo Ancelotti (ITA)
Yellow Card(s): Mikel 82
Match 3 – FC Spartak Moskva (RUS)
A 2-0 *Zhirkov (23), Anelka (43)*
Čech, Ivanović, Cole (Van Aanholt 87), Essien, Mikel, Malouda (Kakuta 82), Zhirkov, Paulo Ferreira, Kalou (McEachran 74), Terry, Anelka. Coach: Carlo Ancelotti (ITA)
Yellow Card(s): Zhirkov 88
Match 4 – FC Spartak Moskva (RUS)
H 4-1 *Anelka (49), Drogba (62p), Ivanović (66, 90+2)*
Čech, Ivanović, Cole, Ramires, Drogba (Sturridge 76), Mikel (McEachran 69), Zhirkov, Paulo Ferreira, Kalou, Alex, Anelka (Kakuta 76). Coach: Carlo Ancelotti (ITA)
Yellow Card(s): Mikel 38
Match 5 – MŠK Žilina (SVK)
H 2-1 *Sturridge (51), Malouda (86)*
Turnbull, Ivanović, Ramires, Drogba, Malouda, Paulo Ferreira, Sturridge (Anelka 74), Van Aanholt, Bruma, Kakuta (Kalou 46), McEachran (Mellis 90+2). Coach: Carlo Ancelotti (ITA)
Yellow Card(s): Ramires 80
Match 6 – Olympique de Marseille (FRA)
A 0-1
Čech, Ivanović, Essien, Ramires, Drogba (Sturridge 62), Malouda, Bosingwa (Van Aanholt 79), Paulo Ferreira, Kalou, Terry (Bruma 72), McEachran. Coach: Carlo Ancelotti (ITA)

Round of 16 – FC København (DEN)
A 2-0 *Anelka (17, 54)*
Čech, Ivanović, Cole, Essien, Ramires, Lampard, Fernando Torres (Kalou 90+2), Malouda (Zhirkov 85), Bosingwa, Terry, Anelka (Drogba 73).
Coach: Carlo Ancelotti (ITA)
Yellow Card(s): Fernando Torres 35, Malouda 85, Terry 86
H 0-0
Čech, Ivanović, Cole, Ramires, Lampard, Drogba, Mikel (Essien 84), Bosingwa, Zhirkov (Malouda 75), Terry, Anelka (Fernando Torres 68).
Coach: Carlo Ancelotti (ITA)
Yellow Card(s): Drogba 54

Quarter-Finals – Manchester United FC (ENG)
H 0-1
Čech, Ivanović, Cole, Essien, Ramires, Lampard, Fernando Torres, Drogba (Anelka 70), Bosingwa (Mikel 79), Zhirkov (Malouda 70), Terry.
Coach: Carlo Ancelotti (ITA)
Yellow Card(s): Zhirkov 36, Ramires 60, Essien 66, Fernando Torres 90+3
A 1-2 *Drogba (77)*
Čech, Ivanović, Cole, Essien, Ramires, Lampard, Fernando Torres (Drogba 46), Malouda, Terry, Alex (Paulo Ferreira 82), Anelka (Kalou 61).
Coach: Carlo Ancelotti (ITA)
Red Card(s): Ramires 70
Yellow Card(s): Ramires 33, Malouda 37, Terry 41, Ramires 70

No	Player	Nat	DoB	Aps	(s)	Gls
Goalkeepers						
1	Petr Čech	CZE	20/5/82	9		
22	Ross Turnbull		4/1/85	1		
Defenders						
33	Alex	BRA	17/6/82	4		
3	Ashley Cole		20/12/80	7		
17	José Bosingwa	POR	24/8/82	4		
43	Jeffrey Bruma	NED	13/11/91	1	(1)	
2	Branislav Ivanović	SRB	22/2/84	10		2
19	Paulo Ferreira	POR	18/1/79	4	(1)	
26	John Terry		7/12/80	8		1
38	Patrick van Aanholt	NED	29/8/90	1	(3)	
Midfielders						
10	Yossi Benayoun	ISR	5/5/80	1		
5	Michael Essien	GHA	3/12/82	7	(1)	1
44	Gaël Kakuta	FRA	21/6/91	2	(3)	
8	Frank Lampard		20/6/78	4		
15	Florent Malouda	FRA	13/6/80	7	(2)	1
46	Josh McEachran		1/3/93	2	(4)	
52	Jacob Mellis		8/1/91		(1)	
12	John Obi Mikel	NGA	22/4/87	5	(1)	
7	Ramires	BRA	24/3/87	7	(1)	
18	Yuriy Zhirkov	RUS	20/8/83	6	(1)	1
Forwards						
39	Nicolas Anelka	FRA	14/3/79	7	(2)	7
11	Didier Drogba	CIV	11/3/78	5	(2)	2
9	Fernando Torres	ESP	20/3/84	3	(1)	
21	Salomon Kalou	CIV	5/8/85	3	(3)	
23	Daniel Sturridge		1/9/89	2	(3)	2

MANCHESTER UNITED FC

UEFA CHAMPIONS LEAGUE

Group C
Match 1 – Rangers FC (SCO)
H 0-0
Kuszczak, Ferdinand, Brown, Rooney, Smalling, Park (Owen 76), Hernández, Fábio (Evans 76), Fletcher, Valencia (Giggs 63), Gibson.
Coach: Sir Alex Ferguson (SCO)
Yellow Card(s): Giggs 90+5
Match 2 – Valencia CF (ESP)
A 1-0 *Hernández (85)*
Van der Sar, Evra, Ferdinand, Anderson (Hernández 77), Berbatov (Macheda 85), Park, Vidić, Carrick, Nani, Rafael (O'Shea 90+2), Fletcher.
Coach: Sir Alex Ferguson (SCO)
Match 3 – Bursaspor (TUR)
H 1-0 *Nani (7)*
Kuszczak, Evra, Anderson (Hernández 78), Smalling, Park (Obertan 71), Vidić, Carrick, Nani, Rafael, Fletcher, Macheda. Coach: Sir Alex Ferguson (SCO)
Yellow Card(s): Nani 40
Match 4 – Bursaspor (TUR)
A 3-0 *Fletcher (48), Obertan (73), Bébé (77)*
Van der Sar, Evra (Fábio 81), Berbatov, Smalling, Vidić, Carrick, Nani (Park 29), Scholes, Rafael, Fletcher (Bébé 63), Obertan. Coach: Sir Alex Ferguson (SCO)
Match 5 – Rangers FC (SCO)
A 1-0 *Rooney (87p)*
Van der Sar, Berbatov (Hernández 76), Rooney, Giggs, Smalling, Carrick, Nani (Obertan 77), Scholes (Anderson 67), Fábio, O'Shea, Evans. Coach: Sir Alex Ferguson (SCO)
Match 6 – Valencia CF (ESP)
H 1-1 *Anderson (62)*
Amos, Ferdinand (Smalling 50), Anderson (Fletcher 90), Berbatov, Rooney, Park, Vidić, Carrick, Nani (Giggs 81), Fábio, Rafael. Coach: Sir Alex Ferguson (SCO)
Yellow Card(s): Anderson 44

Round of 16 – Olympique de Marseille (FRA)
A 0-0
Van der Sar, Evra, Berbatov, Rooney, Smalling, Vidić, Carrick, Nani, O'Shea, Fletcher, Gibson (Scholes 73). Coach: Sir Alex Ferguson (SCO)
H 2-1 *Hernández (5, 75)*
Van der Sar, Evra, Brown, Rooney, Giggs, Smalling, Hernández, Carrick, Nani (Valencia 62), Scholes, O'Shea (Rafael 37; Fábio 70). Coach: Sir Alex Ferguson (SCO)
Yellow Card(s): Hernández 20

Quarter-Finals – Chelsea FC (ENG)
A 1-0 *Rooney (24)*
Van der Sar, Evra, Ferdinand, Rooney, Giggs, Park (Smalling 90+4), Hernández (Berbatov 78), Vidić, Carrick, Rafael (Nani 51), Valencia.
Coach: Sir Alex Ferguson (SCO)
Yellow Card(s): Vidić 74, Van der Sar 80
H 2-1 *Hernández (43), Park (77)*
Van der Sar, Evra, Ferdinand, Rooney, Giggs, Park, Hernández, Vidić, Carrick, Nani (Valencia 75), O'Shea. Coach: Sir Alex Ferguson (SCO)
Yellow Card(s): O'Shea 19, Evra 59

Semi-Finals – FC Schalke 04 (GER)
A 2-0 *Giggs (67), Rooney (69)*
Van der Sar, Evra, Ferdinand, Rooney (Nani 83), Giggs, Park (Scholes 73), Hernández (Anderson 73), Vidić, Carrick, Fábio, Valencia. Coach: Sir Alex Ferguson (SCO)
Yellow Card(s): Fábio 58
H 4-1 *Valencia (26), Gibson (31), Anderson (72, 76)*
Van der Sar, Anderson, Berbatov (Owen 77), Smalling, Nani, Scholes (Fletcher 73), Rafael (Evra 60), O'Shea, Evans, Valencia, Gibson. Coach: Sir Alex Ferguson (SCO)
Yellow Card(s): Gibson 37, Scholes 38, Anderson 42

Final – FC Barcelona (ESP)
N 1-3 *Rooney (34)*
Van der Sar, Evra, Ferdinand, Rooney, Giggs, Park, Hernández, Vidić, Carrick (Scholes 77), Fábio (Nani 69), Valencia. Coach: Sir Alex Ferguson (SCO)
Yellow Card(s): Carrick 61, Valencia 79

No	Player	Nat	DoB	Aps	(s)	Gls
Goalkeepers						
40	Ben Amos		10/4/90	1		
29	Tomasz Kuszczak	POL	20/3/82	2		
1	Edwin van der Sar	NED	29/10/70	10		
Defenders						
6	Wes Brown		13/10/79	2		
3	Patrice Evra	FRA	15/5/81	9	(1)	
20	Fábio	BRA	9/7/90	5	(2)	
5	Rio Ferdinand		7/11/78	7		
23	Jonny Evans	NIR	2/1/88	2	(1)	
22	John O'Shea	IRL	30/4/81	5	(1)	
21	Rafael	BRA	9/7/90	6	(1)	
12	Chris Smalling		22/11/89	7	(2)	
15	Nemanja Vidić	SRB	21/10/81	9		
Midfielders						
8	Anderson	BRA	13/4/88	4	(2)	3
16	Michael Carrick		28/7/81	11		
24	Darren Fletcher	SCO	1/2/84	5	(2)	1
28	Darron Gibson	IRL	25/10/87	3		1
11	Ryan Giggs	WAL	29/11/73	6	(2)	1
17	Nani	POR	17/11/86	9	(3)	1
13	Park Ji-sung	KOR	25/2/81	8	(1)	1
18	Paul Scholes		16/11/74	4	(3)	
25	Antonio Valencia	ECU	4/8/85	5	(2)	1
Forwards						
33	Bébé	POR	12/7/90		(1)	1
9	Dimitar Berbatov	BUL	30/1/81	6	(1)	
14	Javier Hernández	MEX	1/6/88	6	(3)	4
27	Federico Macheda	ITA	22/8/91	1	(1)	
26	Gabriel Obertan	FRA	26/2/89	1	(2)	1
7	Michael Owen		14/12/79		(2)	
10	Wayne Rooney		24/10/85	9		4

ARSENAL FC

UEFA CHAMPIONS LEAGUE

Group H
Match 1 – SC Braga (POR)
H 6-0 *Fàbregas (9p, 53), Arshavin (30), Chamakh (34), Vela (69, 84)*
Almunia, Sagna, Fàbregas, Koscielny, Nasri, Song (Denílson 63), Squillaci, Wilshere, Clichy, Arshavin (Eboué 69), Chamakh (Vela 63). Coach: Arsène Wenger (FRA)
Yellow Card(s): Sagna 64
Match 2 – FK Partizan (SRB)
A 3-1 *Arshavin (15), Chamakh (71), Squillaci (82)*
Fabiański, Sagna, Rosický, Denílson, Song, Squillaci, Wilshere (Nasri 74), Djourou, Arshavin (Clichy 83), Gibbs, Chamakh (Vela 75). Coach: Arsène Wenger (FRA)
Match 3 – FC Shakhtar Donetsk (UKR)
H 5-1 *Song (19), Nasri (42), Fàbregas (60p), Wilshere (66), Chamakh (69)*
Fabiański, Fàbregas (Denílson 64), Rosický, Nasri (Arshavin 72), Song, Squillaci, Wilshere, Djourou, Clichy, Eboué, Chamakh (Walcott 72). Coach: Arsène Wenger (FRA)
Match 4 – FC Shakhtar Donetsk (UKR)
A 1-2 *Walcott (10)*
Fabiański, Rosický, Nasri, Walcott (Emmanuel-Thomas 82), Squillaci, Wilshere, Djourou, Clichy, Eboué, Eastmond (Vela 59), Bendtner (Chamakh 73). Coach: Arsène Wenger (FRA)
Yellow Card(s): Eboué 27
Match 5 – SC Braga (POR)
A 0-2
Fabiański, Fàbregas (Nasri 69), Rosický, Walcott (Vela 77), Denílson, Squillaci, Wilshere, Djourou, Eboué, Gibbs, Bendtner (Chamakh 74). Coach: Arsène Wenger (FRA)
Yellow Card(s): Eboué 38, Denílson 70, Djourou 74, Vela 77, Rosický 84
Match 6 – FK Partizan (SRB)
H 3-1 *Van Persie (30p), Walcott (73), Nasri (77)*
Fabiański, Sagna, Koscielny, Nasri, Van Persie, Denílson, Song, Squillaci, Arshavin (Walcott 67), Gibbs (Eboué 24), Chamakh (Bendtner 76). Coach: Arsène Wenger (FRA)
Red Card(s): Sagna 85

Round of 16 – FC Barcelona (ESP)
H 2-1 *Van Persie (78), Arshavin (83)*
Szczęsny, Fàbregas, Koscielny, Nasri, Van Persie, Walcott (Bendtner 77), Song (Arshavin 68), Wilshere, Djourou, Clichy, Eboué. Coach: Arsène Wenger (FRA)
Yellow Card(s): Song 7, Nasri 28, Arshavin 83, Van Persie 86
A 1-3 *Busquets (53og)*
Szczęsny (Almunia 19), Diaby, Sagna, Fàbregas (Bendtner 78), Koscielny, Rosický (Arshavin 73), Nasri, Van Persie, Wilshere, Djourou, Clichy. Coach: Arsène Wenger (FRA)
Red Card(s): Van Persie 56
Yellow Card(s): Koscielny 16, Sagna 29, Wilshere 37, Van Persie 45+1, Van Persie 56

No	Player	Nat	DoB	Aps	(s)	Gls
Goalkeepers						
1	Manuel Almunia	ESP	19/5/77	1	(1)	
21	Łukasz Fabiański	POL	18/4/85	5		
53	Wojciech Szczęsny	POL	18/4/90	2		
Defenders						
22	Gaël Clichy	FRA	26/7/85	5	(1)	
20	Johan Djourou	SUI	18/1/87	6		
40	Craig Eastmond		9/12/90	1		
27	Emmanuel Eboué	CIV	4/6/83	4	(2)	
28	Kieran Gibbs		26/9/89	3		
6	Laurent Koscielny	FRA	10/9/85	4		
3	Bacary Sagna	FRA	14/2/83	4		
18	Sébastien Squillaci	FRA	11/8/80	6		1
Midfielders						
15	Denílson	BRA	16/2/88	3	(2)	
2	Abou Diaby	FRA	11/5/86	1		
41	Jay Emmanuel-Thomas		27/12/90		(1)	
4	Cesc Fàbregas	ESP	4/5/87	5		3
8	Samir Nasri	FRA	26/6/87	6	(2)	2
7	Tomáš Rosický	CZE	4/10/80	5		
17	Alex Song	CMR	9/9/87	5		1
19	Jack Wilshere		1/1/92	7		1
Forwards						
23	Andrey Arshavin	RUS	29/5/81	3	(3)	3
52	Nicklas Bendtner	DEN	16/1/88	2	(3)	
29	Marouane Chamakh	MAR	10/1/84	4	(2)	3
10	Robin van Persie	NED	6/8/83	3		2
11	Carlos Vela	MEX	1/3/89		(4)	2
14	Theo Walcott		16/3/89	3	(2)	2

TOTTENHAM HOTSPUR FC

UEFA CHAMPIONS LEAGUE

Play-Offs – BSC Young Boys (SUI)
A 2-3 *Bassong (42), Pavlyuchenko (83)*
Gomes, Bale, Pavlyuchenko, Palacios, Modrić (Kranjčar 46), Giovani, Defoe (Keane 66), Bassong, Dawson, Ćorluka, Assou-Ekotto

Huddlestone 36). Coach: Harry Redknapp (ENG)
Yellow Card(s): Assou-Ekotto 4, Bassong 68
H 4-0 *Crouch (5, 61, 78p), Defoe (32)*
Gomes (Cudicini 46), Bale (Kranjčar 82), Huddlestone, Lennon, Palacios, Crouch, Defoe (Pavlyuchenko 62), Dawson, Ćorluka, King, Assou-Ekotto. Coach: Harry Redknapp (ENG)
Yellow Card(s): Palacios 51, Pavlyuchenko 63

Group A
Match 1 – SV Werder Bremen (GER)
A 2-2 *Pasanen (12og), Crouch (18)*
Cudicini, Bale, Kaboul, Huddlestone, Lennon (Palacios 76), Jenas, Van der Vaart (Keane 49), Crouch, Ćorluka, King, Assou-Ekotto. Coach: Harry Redknapp (ENG)
Yellow Card(s): Huddlestone 52, Jenas 66
Match 2 – FC Twente (NED)
H 4-1 *Van der Vaart (47), Pavlyuchenko (50p, 64p), Bale (85)*
Gomes, Hutton, Bale, Huddlestone, Pavlyuchenko (Keane 89), Van der Vaart, Modrić (Lennon 82), Crouch (Jenas 66), Bassong, King, Assou-Ekotto. Coach: Harry Redknapp (ENG)
Red Card(s): Van der Vaart 61
Yellow Card(s): Van der Vaart 43, Van der Vaart 61
Match 3 – FC Internazionale Milano (ITA)
A 3-4 *Bale (52, 90, 90+1)*
Gomes, Hutton, Bale, Huddlestone (Palacios 80), Lennon, Jenas, Gallas, Modrić (Cudicini 11), Crouch (Keane 67), Bassong, Assou-Ekotto. Coach: Harry Redknapp (ENG)
Red Card(s): Gomes 8
Yellow Card(s): Palacios 89
Match 4 – FC Internazionale Milano (ITA)
H 3-1 *Van der Vaart (18), Crouch (61), Pavlyuchenko (89)*
Cudicini, Hutton, Bale, Kaboul, Huddlestone, Lennon (Palacios 85), Van der Vaart (Jenas 46), Gallas, Modrić, Crouch (Pavlyuchenko 76), Assou-Ekotto. Coach: Harry Redknapp (ENG)
Yellow Card(s): Hutton 39, Jenas 72, Modrić 90+2
Match 5 – SV Werder Bremen (GER)
H 3-0 *Kaboul (6), Modrić (45+1), Crouch (79)*
Gomes, Hutton, Bale, Kaboul, Lennon, Jenas (Palacios 20), Pavlyuchenko (Defoe 58), Gallas, Modrić, Crouch, Assou-Ekotto. Coach: Harry Redknapp (ENG)
Match 6 – FC Twente (NED)
A 3-3 *Wisgerhof (12og), Defoe (47, 59)*
Gomes, Bale, Jenas (Lennon 34), Pavlyuchenko (Keane 72), Palacios, Gallas, Defoe, Bassong, Kranjčar (Crouch 86), Ćorluka, Assou-Ekotto. Coach: Harry Redknapp (ENG)
Yellow Card(s): Jenas 32

Round of 16 – AC Milan (ITA)
A 1-0 *Crouch (80)*
Gomes, Lennon, Van der Vaart (Modrić 62), Palacios, Gallas, Crouch, Dawson, Ćorluka (Woodgate 59), Sandro, Assou-Ekotto, Pienaar (Kranjčar 76). Coach: Harry Redknapp (ENG)
H 0-0
Gomes, Lennon, Van der Vaart (Bale 66), Gallas, Modrić, Crouch (Pavlyuchenko 83), Dawson, Ćorluka, Sandro, Assou-Ekotto, Pienaar (Jenas 71). Coach: Harry Redknapp (ENG)

Quarter-Finals – Real Madrid CF (ESP)
A 0-4
Gomes, Bale, Jenas, Van der Vaart (Defoe 46), Gallas, Modrić, Crouch, Dawson, Ćorluka (Bassong 80), Sandro, Assou-Ekotto. Coach: Harry Redknapp (ENG)
Red Card(s): Crouch 15
Yellow Card(s): Crouch 8, Crouch 15, Van der Vaart 20, Defoe 74
H 0-1
Gomes, Bale, Huddlestone (Sandro 71), Lennon (Defoe 61), Pavlyuchenko, Van der Vaart, Gallas, Modrić (Kranjčar 83), Dawson, Ćorluka, Assou-Ekotto. Coach: Harry Redknapp (ENG)

No	Player	Nat	DoB	Aps	(s)	Gls
Goalkeepers						
23	Carlo Cudicini	ITA	6/9/73	2	(1)	
1	Heurelho Gomes	BRA	15/2/81	8		
Defenders						
32	Benoît Assou-Ekotto	CMR	24/3/84	10		
19	Sébastien Bassong	CMR	9/7/86	3	(1)	
22	Vedran Ćorluka	CRO	5/2/86	6		
20	Michael Dawson		18/11/83	4		
13	William Gallas	FRA	17/8/77	8		
2	Alan Hutton	SCO	30/11/84	4		
4	Younes Kaboul	FRA	4/1/86	3		1
26	Ledley King		12/10/80	2		
39	Jonathan Woodgate		22/1/80		(1)	
Midfielders						
3	Gareth Bale	WAL	16/7/89	8	(1)	4
6	Tom Huddlestone		28/12/86	5		
8	Jermaine Jenas		18/2/83	5	(3)	
21	Niko Kranjčar	CRO	13/8/84	1	(3)	
7	Aaron Lennon		16/4/87	7	(2)	
14	Luka Modrić	CRO	9/9/85	7	(1)	1
12	Wilson Palacios	HON	29/7/84	2	(4)	
40	Steven Pienaar	RSA	17/3/82	2		
30	Sandro	BRA	15/3/89	3	(1)	
11	Rafael van der Vaart	NED	11/2/83	7		2
Forwards						
15	Peter Crouch		30/1/81	8	(1)	4
18	Jermain Defoe		7/10/82	1	(3)	2
10	Robbie Keane	IRL	8/7/80		(4)	
9	Roman Pavlyuchenko	RUS	15/12/81	4	(2)	3

MANCHESTER CITY FC

UEFA EUROPA LEAGUE

Play-Offs – FC Timişoara (ROU)
A 1-0 *Balotelli (72)*
Hart, Zabaleta, Adebayor, Barry (Balotelli 57), Lescott, David Silva (A. Johnson 66), K. Touré, Tévez (Jô 77), Kompany, De Jong, Y. Touré. Coach: Roberto Mancini (ITA)
Yellow Card(s): Balotelli 74
H 2-0 *Wright-Phillips (43), Boyata (59)*
Hart, Richards, Kompany, Zabaleta, Wright-Phillips, Adebayor, David Silva, Vieira, Jô, De Jong (Cunningham 64), Boyata. Coach: Roberto Mancini (ITA)

Group A
Match 1 – FC Salzburg (AUT)
A 2-0 *David Silva (8), Jô (63)*
Hart, Bridge (Boyata 68), Kompany, Zabaleta, Barry, David Silva (Wright-Phillips 83), Jô, K. Touré, Tévez (Vieira 78), De Jong, Y. Touré. Coach: Roberto Mancini (ITA)
Yellow Card(s): K. Touré 47
Match 2 – Juventus (ITA)
H 1-1 *A. Johnson (37)*
Hart, Kompany, Zabaleta (Boyata 46), Adebayor (David Silva 73), A. Johnson, Boateng (Milner 84), Barry, Vieira, K. Touré, Tévez, Y. Touré. Coach: Roberto Mancini (ITA)
Yellow Card(s): Barry 63
Match 3 – KKS Lech Poznań (POL)
H 3-1 *Adebayor (13, 25, 73)*
Hart, Richards, Zabaleta (Bridge 85), Wright-Phillips (Jô 78), Adebayor, A. Johnson, Lescott, David Silva (Y. Touré 75), Vieira, De Jong, Boyata. Coach: Roberto Mancini (ITA)

Match 4 – KKS Lech Poznań (POL)
A 1-3 *Adebayor (51)*
Given, Richards, Bridge (Kolarov 70), Zabaleta, Milner (Kompany 78), Wright-Phillips (David Silva 46), Adebayor, A. Johnson, Lescott, Vieira, Boyata. Coach: Roberto Mancini (ITA)
Yellow Card(s): Richards 38, Bridge 40
Match 5 – FC Salzburg (AUT)
H 3-0 *Balotelli (18, 65), A. Johnson (78)*
Given, Zabaleta, Milner, Wright-Phillips, A. Johnson, Boateng, Lescott, Vieira, Jô, K. Touré (Richards 81), Balotelli (Adebayor 71). Coach: Roberto Mancini (ITA)
Match 6 – Juventus (ITA)
A 1-1 *Jô (77)*
Given, Richards, Bridge, Milner, Wright-Phillips (Chantler 90+2), A. Johnson, Boateng, Vieira, Jô, Boyata, Tchuimeni-Nimely (Zabaleta 61). Coach: Roberto Mancini (ITA)
Yellow Card(s): Zabaleta 74

Round of 32 – Aris Thessaloniki FC (GRE)
A 0-0
Hart, Richards, Wright-Phillips (Balotelli 77), Džeko (Zabaleta 84), Kolarov, Boateng, Barry, David Silva, K. Touré, Tévez, Y. Touré. Coach: Roberto Mancini (ITA)
Yellow Card(s): Džeko 77
H 3-0 *Džeko (7, 12), Y. Touré (75)*
Hart, Kompany (Zabaleta 35), Džeko, Kolarov, Boateng, Barry, Lescott, David Silva (Wright-Phillips 80), Tévez (Vieira 79), Y. Touré, Balotelli. Coach: Roberto Mancini (ITA)
Yellow Card(s): Kolarov 90+1

Round of 16 – FC Dynamo Kyiv (UKR)
A 0-2
Hart, Richards, Kompany, Zabaleta, Džeko, Kolarov (Wright-Phillips 82), Barry, Lescott, David Silva, Y. Touré, Balotelli (Tévez 57). Coach: Roberto Mancini (ITA)
Yellow Card(s): *Balotelli 53, Tévez 79*
H 1-0 *Kolarov (39)*
Hart, Richards, Kompany, Kolarov (Milner 88), Barry (A. Johnson 71), Lescott, David Silva (Džeko 76), Tévez, De Jong, Y. Touré, Balotelli. Coach: Roberto Mancini (ITA)
Red Card(s): Balotelli 36
Yellow Card(s): Tévez 45, Kompany 62, David Silva 72, De Jong 78, Y. Touré 90+6

ASTON VILLA FC

UEFA EUROPA LEAGUE

Play-Offs – SK Rapid Wien (AUT)
A 1-1 *Bannan (12)*
Guzan, Warnock, Downing, Albrighton (Weimann 80; Osbourne 86), Davies, Heskey, Reo-Coker, Beye, Lichaj, Bannan (Delfouneso 75), Hogg. Coach: Kevin MacDonald (SCO)
Yellow Card(s): Reo-Coker 34, Guzan 51
H 2-3 *Agbonlahor (22), Heskey (77)*
Guzan, Young, Ireland, Agbonlahor (Albrighton 40), Davies, Heskey, Petrov, Reo-Coker (Delfouneso 82), Beye, Cuéllar, Collins. Coach: Kevin MacDonald (SCO)
Yellow Card(s): Collins 86, Young 90

LIVERPOOL FC

UEFA EUROPA LEAGUE

Third Qualifying Round – FK Rabotnicki (MKD)
A 2-0 *N'Gog (17, 58)*
Cavalieri, Aquilani (Dalla Valle 83), Agger (Darby 72), Jovanović, Kyrgiakos, Lucas, N'Gog, Spearing, Kelly, Škrtel', Amoo (Eccleston 84). Coach: Roy Hodgson (ENG)
H 2-0 *N'Gog (22), Gerrard (40p)*
Cavalieri, Johnson, Gerrard (Aquilani 62), Cole, Jovanović (Maxi 67), Lucas (Spearing 73), Carragher, N'Gog, Kelly, Škrtel', Dani Pacheco. Coach: Roy Hodgson (ENG)

Play-Offs – Trabzonspor AŞ (TUR)
H 1-0 *Babel (45+1)*
Reina, Fábio Aurélio, Cole, Jovanović, Kyrgiakos, Maxi (N'Gog 73), Babel (Fernando Torres 46), Lucas, Carragher, Poulsen, Kelly. Coach: Roy Hodgson (ENG)
A 2-1 *Giray Kaçar (83og), Kuyt (88)*
Reina, Johnson, Fábio Aurélio (Dani Pacheco 77), Cole, Kyrgiakos, Kuyt, Lucas, Carragher, N'Gog (Babel 86), Poulsen (Škrtel' 90), Kelly. Coach: Roy Hodgson (ENG)

Group K
Match 1 – FC Steaua Bucureşti (ROU)
H 4-1 *Cole (1), N'Gog (55p, 90+1), Lucas (81)*
Reina, Konchesky, Raul Meireles, Agger, Cole (Eccleston 88), Kyrgiakos, Maxi (Dani Pacheco 85), Babel (Lucas 79), N'Gog, Spearing, Kelly. Coach: Roy Hodgson (ENG)
Yellow Card(s): Maxi 62
Match 2 – FC Utrecht (NED)
A 0-0
Reina, Johnson, Raul Meireles, Fernando Torres, Cole (Maxi 81), Kuyt, Lucas, Carragher, Poulsen, Kelly, Škrtel'. Coach: Roy Hodgson (ENG)
Yellow Card(s): Lucas 35, Raul Meireles 55, Kelly 61
Match 3 – SSC Napoli (ITA)
A 0-0
Reina, Konchesky (Fábio Aurélio 65), Jovanović, Babel (Cole 77), Carragher (Kyrgiakos 46), N'Gog, Spearing, Poulsen, Shelvey, Kelly, Škrtel'. Coach: Roy Hodgson (ENG)
Yellow Card(s): Škrtel' 28
Match 4 – SSC Napoli (ITA)
H 3-1 *Gerrard (76, 88p, 89)*
Reina, Johnson, Konchesky, Raul Meireles, Jovanović (Gerrard 46), Kyrgiakos, Carragher, N'Gog (Lucas 83), Spearing, Poulsen (Eccleston 65), Shelvey. Coach: Roy Hodgson (ENG)
Yellow Card(s): Johnson 25, Kyrgiakos 67
Match 5 – FC Steaua Bucureşti (ROU)
A 1-1 *Jovanović (19)*
Reina, Fábio Aurélio, Cole (N'Gog 75), Dani Pacheco (Lucas 90), Jovanović (Eccleston 79), Kyrgiakos, Babel, Wilson, Poulsen, Shelvey, Kelly. Coach: Roy Hodgson (ENG)
Match 6 – FC Utrecht (NED)
H 0-0
Jones, Fábio Aurélio, Cole, Jovanović (Kuyt 73), Babel, Wilson, Poulsen, Shelvey, Kelly, Škrtel' (Kyrgiakos 46), Eccleston (Dani Pacheco 56). Coach: Roy Hodgson (ENG)
Yellow Card(s): Eccleston 6

Round of 32 – AC Sparta Praha (CZE)
A 0-0
Reina, Johnson, Raul Meireles, Fábio Aurélio (Cole 37), Kyrgiakos, Maxi, Kuyt, Lucas, Wilson, Carragher, N'Gog (Škrtel' 83). Coach: Kenny Dalglish (SCO)
Yellow Card(s): N'Gog 39, Cole 81

1 1-0 *Kuyt (86)*
Reina, Raul Meireles, Agger (Škrteľ 85), Cole, Kyrgiakos, Kuyt, Lucas, Wilson, N'Gog, Poulsen (Spearing 65), Kelly (Carragher 46). Coach: Kenny Dalglish (SCO)
Yellow Card(s): Kelly 30, Poulsen 34, Carragher 59, Lucas 90+2

Round of 16 – SC Braga (POR)
A 0-1
Reina, Johnson, Raul Meireles, Cole, Kyrgiakos, Kuyt, Lucas, Carragher, Spearing, Poulsen (Carroll 57), Škrteľ. Coach: Kenny Dalglish (SCO)
Yellow Card(s): Poulsen 36
H 0-0
Reina, Johnson, Raul Meireles, Cole (N'Gog 75), Maxi (Spearing 75), Kuyt, Lucas, Wilson, Carragher, Carroll, Škrteľ. Coach: Kenny Dalglish (SCO)
Yellow Card(s): Carroll 52, Škrteľ 71, Raul Meireles 83

ESTONIA

FC LEVADIA TALLINN

UEFA CHAMPIONS LEAGUE

Second Qualifying Round – Debreceni VSC (HUN)
H 1-1 *Neemelo (59)*
Kaalma, Kalimullin, Morozov, Leitan, Nahk, Ivanov, Malov, Podholjuzin, Felipe Nunes, Neemelo (Dmitrijev 76), Teniste. Coach: Igor Prins (EST)
Yellow Card(s): Morozov 54
A 2-3 *Nahk (3), Leitan (53)*
Kaalma, Kalimullin, Morozov, Leitan, Nahk, Ivanov, Malov, Podholjuzin, Felipe Nunes (Subbotin 80), Neemelo, Teniste. Coach: Igor Prins (EST)
Red Card(s): Malov 74
Yellow Card(s): Malov 45+1, Morozov 47, Nahk 60, Kalimullin 67, Malov 74

JK SILLAMÄE KALEV

UEFA EUROPA LEAGUE

Second Qualifying Round – FC Dinamo Minsk (BLR)
A 1-5 *Kolyaev (79)*
Starodubtsev, Naumov, Kulik, Gorbunov, Tarassenkov, Kolyaev, Zubavičius (Dudarev 46), Aleksejev (Kabayev 71), Vihrov, Stankevičius (Gornev 69), Vasiliauskas. Coach: Vladimir Kazachyonok (RUS)
Yellow Card(s): Zubavičius 38, Vihrov 53
H 0-5
Starodubtsev, Naumov, Kulik, Gorbunov, Kolyaev, Kabayev (Nikulin 58), Zubavičius (Vihrov 81), Dubõkin, Aleksejev, Stankevičius, Jädal (Dudarev 24). Coach: Vladimir Kazachyonok (RUS)
Yellow Card(s): Naumov 68

JK TRANS NARVA

UEFA EUROPA LEAGUE

First Qualifying Round – Myllykosken Pallo-47 (FIN)
H 0-2
Stonys, Rimas, Gorškov, Kazakov (Lepik 38), Bezykornovas, Mitin, Felipe Lemos, Abramenko, Kitto, Starovoitov (Mandinho 63), Bazjukin (Saulėnas 70). Coach: Valeri Bondarenko (EST)
Yellow Card(s): Mitin 13, Starovoitov 35, Bezykornovas 60
A 0-5
Stonys, Rimas, Gorškov, Bezykornovas, Mitin, Felipe Lemos (Kazakov 46), Abramenko, Leontovitš (Mandinho 73), Lepik, Kitto, Bazjukin (Saulėnas 66). Coach: Valeri Bondarenko (EST)
Yellow Card(s): Mitin 59

FC FLORA TALLINN

UEFA EUROPA LEAGUE

First Qualifying Round – FC Dinamo Tbilisi (GEO)
A 1-2 *Dupikov (9)*
Pedõk, Kasimir, Minkenen, Konsa, Mošnikov (Post 82), Luts (Mašitšev 85), Dupikov (Alliku 73), Palatu, Jürgenson, Kams, Allas. Coach: Martin Reim (EST)
Yellow Card(s): Konsa 60, Allas 63, Minkenen 82
H 0-0
Meerits, Jahhimovitš, Kasimir, Minkenen (Alliku 74), Konsa, Luts, Dupikov (Post 46), Palatu, Jürgenson, Kams, Allas. Coach: Martin Reim (EST)
Yellow Card(s): Kasimir 21, Kams 28

FAROE ISLANDS

HB TÓRSHAVN

UEFA CHAMPIONS LEAGUE

Second Qualifying Round – FC Salzburg (AUT)
A 0-5
Dawid, Hreidarsson, Lag (Holm 77), Benjaminsen, Samuelsen, Fløtum (Akselsen 75), Rubeksen, Kuljić (Hanssen 59), Poulsen, Mortensen, Jørgensen. Coach: Kristján Gudmundsson (ISL)
H 1-0 *Samuelsen (73)*
Thomsen, Hreidarsson, Holm, Benjaminsen, Samuelsen, Fløtum (Mouritsen 89), Hanssen, Rubeksen, Poulsen, Mortensen, Jørgensen. Coach: Kristján Gudmundsson (ISL)
Yellow Card(s): Samuelsen 22, Mortensen 57, Fløtum 88

VÍKINGUR

UEFA EUROPA LEAGUE

Second Qualifying Round – Beşiktaş JK (TUR)
A 0-3
Túri, H. Jacobsen, Stanković, Vatnhamar (Á. Petersen 89), Klettskard (A. Olsen 75), E. Jacobsen, Sa. Jacobsen, Djurhuus (Bartalsstovu 46), Justinussen, B. Hansen, Niclassen. Coach: Jógvan Martin Olsen (FRO)
Yellow Card(s): Djurhuus 26, Vatnhamar 88

H 0-4
Túri, H. Jacobsen, Stanković, Vatnhamar (H. Hansen 87), Klettskard (Sv. Jacobsen 76), E. Jacobsen, Sa. Jacobsen, Djurhuus (Bartalsstovu 53), Justinussen, B. Hansen, Niclassen. Coach: Jógvan Martin Olsen (FRO)
Yellow Card(s): Djurhuus 33

EB/STREYMUR

UEFA EUROPA LEAGUE

First Qualifying Round – Kalmar FF (SWE)
A 0-1
Tórgard, G.Hansen, Davidsen, Jacobsen (B. Olsen 76), Jørgensen (Dam 65), Bø, Anghel, Djurhuus, Udsen, A.Hansen, Nielsen. Coach: Hedin Askham (FRO)
Yellow Card(s): Udsen 61
H 0-3
Tórgard, G.Hansen, Davidsen, Jacobsen, Jørgensen (Samuelsen 70), Bø, Anghel (Jacobsen 80), Djurhuus, Udsen, A.Hansen, Nielsen (Niclasen 61). Coach: Hedin Askham (FRO)
Yellow Card(s): Nielsen 23, Anghel 39, Dam Jacobsen 52

NSÍ RUNAVÍK

UEFA EUROPA LEAGUE

First Qualifying Round – Gefle IF (SWE)
H 0-2
Gángó, J. Joensen, Mortensen (D. Danielsen 79), J. Hansen, Davidsen, C. Jacobsen, Petersen, E. Hansen, Olsen (E. Danielsen 79), J. Fredriksberg, H. Lakjuni (Potemkin 62). Coach: Pauli Poulsen (FRO)
Yellow Card(s): Fredriksberg 56, C. Jacobsen 59
A 1-2 *Potemkin (90+4)*
Gángó, J. Joensen, Mortensen, J. Hansen, Davidsen, Petersen, E. Hansen (Potemkin 35), Olsen (D. Danielsen 71), E. Danielsen (Á. Frederiksberg 85), J. Fredriksberg, H. Lakjuni. Coach: Pauli Poulsen (FRO)
Yellow Card(s): Petersen 20, Joensen 54, E. Danielsen 78

FINLAND

HJK HELSINKI

UEFA CHAMPIONS LEAGUE

Second Qualifying Round – FK Ekranas (LTU)
A 0-1
Wallén, Kansikas, Kamara, Magnusson, Rafinha, Sorsa (Westö 83), Bah, Ojala, Riihilahti (Fowler 76), Hoesen, Zeneli (Parikka 62). Coach: Antti Muurinen (FIN)
Yellow Card(s): Ojala 51, Magnusson 54
H 2-0 (aet) *Ojala (77), Šidlauskas (119og)*
Wallén, Kansikas, Kamara, Rafinha, Sorsa, Mäkelä (Zeneli 72), Kärkkäinen, Parikka (Pelvas 63), Bah, Ojala, Riihilahti (Fowler 100). Coach: Antti Muurinen (FIN)
Red Card(s): Bah 55

Third Qualifying Round – FK Partizan (SRB)
A 0-3
Wallén, Kansikas, Kamara, Fowler (Parikka 46), Rafinha, Sorsa, Mäkelä (Pelvas 73), Kärkkäinen, Ojala, Riihilahti, Zeneli (Westö 27). Coach: Antti Muurinen (FIN)
Yellow Card(s): Kamara 90
H 1-2 *Kamara (38)*
Wallén, Kansikas, Kamara, Magnusson, Rafinha, Sorsa, Pelvas (Mäkelä 62), Parikka (Westö 75), Bah, Ojala, Riihilahti (Fowler 33). Coach: Antti Muurinen (FIN)
Yellow Card(s): Kamara 83

UEFA EUROPA LEAGUE

Play-Offs – Beşiktaş JK (TUR)
A 0-2
Wallén, Kansikas, Magnusson, Fowler, Rafinha, Sorsa, Westö (Parikka 69), Pelvas (Mäkelä 46), Bah, Ojala, Dema (Kärkkäinen 75). Coach: Antti Muurinen (FIN)
Yellow Card(s): Dema 7
H 0-4
Wallén, Magnusson, Fowler, Rafinha (Parikka 77), Mäkelä, Westö, Pelvas (Sorsa 46), Bah, Ojala, Sumusalo, Dema (Ring 71). Coach: Antti Muurinen (FIN)
Yellow Card(s): Fowler 38

FC INTER TURKU

UEFA EUROPA LEAGUE

Third Qualifying Round – KRC Genk (BEL)
H 1-5 *Grot (54)*
Reponen, Antunez, Nyman, Grot (Paajanen 80), Aho, Sanevuori, Nikkari, Kauko, Nwanganga (Osinachi 84), Mäkitalo (Furuholm 74), Lehtonen. Coach: Job Dragtsma (NED)
Yellow Card(s): Sanevuori 48, Mäkitalo 60, Nyman 74
A 2-3 *Antunez (35, 90)*
Monsalve, Davi Rancan, Antunez, Nyman, Osinachi (Kauppi 86), Aho, Paajanen, Ojala, Nikkari (Mäkitalo 68), Kauko, Lehtonen (Almeida 46). Coach: Job Dragtsma (NED)
Red Card(s): Davi Rancan 78

FC HONKA ESPOO

UEFA EUROPA LEAGUE

Second Qualifying Round – Bangor City FC (WAL)
H 1-1 *Savage (43)*
Peltonen, Koskinen, Aalto (Otaru 79), Vuorinen (Rasimus 70), Paatelainen (Vasara 65), Puustinen, Koskimaa, Savage, Heikkilä, Lepola, Schüller. Coach: Mika Lehkosuo (FIN)
Yellow Card(s): Aalto 31, Schüller 81
A 1-2 *Koskinen (21)*
Peltonen, Koskinen, Heilala, Paatelainen (Vasara 70), Vuorinen, Puustinen, Koskimaa, Savage, Otaru, Lepola, Schüller. Coach: Mika Lehkosuo (FIN)

TPS TURKU

UEFA EUROPA LEAGUE

First Qualifying Round – Port Talbot Town FC (WAL)
H 3-1 *Ri. Riski (24, 35), Wusu (30)*
Moisander, Jovanovic, Nyberg, Rähmönen, Manninen, Ri. Riski (Virtanen 75), Ääritalo (Ro. Riski 78), Kolehmainen, Johansson, Cleaver, Wusu. Coach: Marko Rajamäki (FIN)
Yellow Card(s): Rähmönen 88
A 4-0 *Wusu (26), Kolehmainen (32), Ri. Riski (69), Ro. Riski (90+1)*
Moisander, Nyberg, Rähmönen, Heinikangas (Jovanovic 63), Manninen (Milsom 46), Ri. Riski, Ääritalo, Kolehmainen, Johansson, Cleaver, Wusu (Ro. Riski 55). Coach: Marko Rajamäki (FIN)

Second Qualifying Round – Cercle Brugge KSV (BEL)
A 1-0 *Ääritalo (32)*
Moisander, Milsom, Nyberg, Rähmönen, Heinikangas, Manninen, Ri. Riski, Ääritalo (Ro. Riski 87), Kolehmainen, Johansson, Cleaver. Coach: Marko Rajamäki (FIN)
H 1-2 *Johansson (39p)*
Moisander, Milsom, Nyberg (Ferati 89), Rähmönen, Heinikangas, Manninen (Ro. Riski 80), Ri. Riski, Ääritalo (Jovanovic 66), Kolehmainen, Johansson, Cleaver. Coach: Marko Rajamäki (FIN)
Yellow Card(s): Milsom 4, Ri. Riski 55, Ro. Riski 88

MYLLYKOSKAN PALLO-47

UEFA EUROPA LEAGUE

First Qualifying Round – JK Trans Narva (EST)
A 2-0 *Votinov (47), Gorškov (53og)*
Kuismala, Hietanen, Timoska, Tuunainen (Uimaniemi 3), Okkonen, Votinov, Äijälä, Ricketts (Koljonen 90), Oksanen, Aho, Saxman (Felipe Benevides 76). Coach: Janne Lindberg (FIN)
Yellow Card(s): Timoska 70, Saxman 73
H 5-0 *Ricketts (62), Äijälä (67, 75), Koljonen (77), Felipe Benevides (80)*
Kuismala, Hietanen, Timoska, Uimaniemi, Okkonen (Felipe Benevides 70), Votinov, Äijälä, Ricketts (Koljonen 72), Oksanen, Aho, Saxman (Rautiainen 81). Coach: Janne Lindberg (FIN)
Yellow Card(s): Hietanen 61

Second Qualifying Round – UE Sant Julià (AND)
H 3-0 *Ricketts (43), Äijälä (56, 65p)*
Kuismala, Hietanen, Uimaniemi, Okkonen, Äijälä, Lindberg, Ricketts (Felipe Benevides 73), Oksanen (Alonen 85), Aho, Koljonen (Kurittu 65), Saxman. Coach: Janne Lindberg (FIN)
Yellow Card(s): Ricketts 53
A 1-0 *Votinov (30)* **(match annulled)**
Johansson, Hietanen, Timoska (Lindberg 70), Uimaniemi, Okkonen, Votinov, Äijälä, Ricketts (Alonen 61), Oksanen, Aho, Felipe Benevides. Coach: Janne Lindberg (FIN)
A 5-0 *Votinov (6, 13, 64), Kurittu (49), Okkonen (61)*
Johansson, Hietanen, Timoska (Rautiainen 69), Uimaniemi, Okkonen (Lindberg 65), Votinov, Äijälä, Oksanen, Kurittu (Koljonen 56), Aho, Saxman. Coach: Janne Lindberg (FIN)
Yellow Card(s): Kurittu 41, Aho 45+1

Third Qualifying Round – FC Timişoara (ROU)
H 1-2 *Ricketts (49)*
Kuismala, Hietanen, Timoska, Uimaniemi, Okkonen, Votinov (Kurittu 82), Äijälä, Lindberg, Ricketts (Koljonen 60), Oksanen (Felipe Benevides 87), Saxman. Coach: Janne Lindberg (FIN)
A 3-3 *Äijälä (18), Ricketts (20, 25)*
Kuismala, Hietanen, Timoska, Uimaniemi, Okkonen, Votinov, Äijälä, Ricketts (Kurittu 89), Oksanen (Felipe Benevides 73), Aho (Lindberg 57), Saxman. Coach: Janne Lindberg (FIN)
Yellow Card(s): Okkonen 62, Kuismala 88

FRANCE

OLYMPIQUE DE MARSEILLE

UEFA CHAMPIONS LEAGUE

Group F
Match 1 – FC Spartak Moskva (RUS)
H 0-1
Mandanda, Azpilicueta, Taiwo, Hilton, Cissé, Cheyrou, Lucho González (J. Ayew 83), Brandão (Gignac 62), Heinze, A. Ayew, Valbuena. Coach: Didier Deschamps (FRA)
Yellow Card(s): Brandão 61
Match 2 – Chelsea FC (ENG)
A 0-2
Mandanda, Cissé, Cheyrou (A. Ayew 59), Lucho González, Brandão, Gignac (Valbuena 59), Rémy, Kaboré, Mbia, Heinze, Diawara. Coach: Didier Deschamps (FRA)
Yellow Card(s): Mbia 27, Heinze 28
Match 3 – MŠK Žilina (SVK)
H 1-0 *Diawara (48)*
Mandanda, Azpilicueta, Taiwo, Lucho González (Abriel 75), Brandão (Rémy 66), Gignac (Cissé 83), Mbia, Heinze, A. Ayew, Diawara, Valbuena. Coach: Didier Deschamps (FRA)
Yellow Card(s): Valbuena 48, Taiwo 49, A. Ayew 52, Mbia 83
Match 4 – MŠK Žilina (SVK)
A 7-0 *Gignac (12, 21, 54), Heinze (24), Rémy (36), Lucho González (52, 63)*
Mandanda, Azpilicueta, Cheyrou, Lucho González, Gignac (Brandão 72), Rémy, Kaboré, Mbia, Heinze (Taiwo 62), Diawara, Valbuena (A. Ayew 62). Coach: Didier Deschamps (FRA)
Match 5 – FC Spartak Moskva (RUS)
A 3-0 *Valbuena (18), Rémy (54), Brandão (68)*
Mandanda, Azpilicueta, Cissé, Lucho González (Abriel 76), Brandão, Rémy (Kaboré 82), Mbia, Heinze, A. Ayew, Diawara, Valbuena (Cheyrou 69). Coach: Didier Deschamps (FRA)
Yellow Card(s): Mbia 13
Match 6 – Chelsea FC (ENG)
H 1-0 *Brandão (81)*
Mandanda, Taiwo, Cheyrou, Brandão, Rémy, Kaboré, N'Diaye (J. Ayew 86), Abriel (A. Ayew 63), Heinze, Diawara, Valbuena (Lucho González 63). Coach: Didier Deschamps (FRA)
Yellow Card(s): A. Ayew 82

Round of 16 – Manchester United FC (ENG)
H 0-0
Mandanda, Cissé (Cheyrou 70), Lucho González, Brandão, Rémy (Valbuena 79), Kaboré, Mbia, Heinze, A. Ayew, Diawara, Fanni. Coach: Didier Deschamps (FRA)
A 1-2 *Brown (82og)*
Mandanda, Taiwo, Cheyrou, Lucho González, Gignac (Valbuena 69), Rémy, Mbia (J. Ayew 80), Heinze, A. Ayew, Diawara, Fanni. Coach: Didier Deschamps (FRA)
Yellow Card(s): Valbuena 72, Rémy 90+3

No	Player	Nat	DoB	Aps	(s)	Gls
Goalkeepers						
30	Steve Mandanda		28/3/85	8		
Defenders						
2	César Azpilicueta	ESP	28/8/89	4		
21	Souleymane Diawara	SEN	24/12/78	7		1
24	Rod Fanni		6/12/81	2		
19	Gabriel Heinze	ARG	19/4/78	8		1
5	Hilton	BRA	13/9/77	1		
14	Leyti N'Diaye	SEN	19/8/85	1		
3	Taye Taiwo	NGA	16/4/85	4	(1)	
Midfielders						
18	Fabrice Abriel		6/7/79	1	(2)	
7	Benoît Cheyrou		3/5/81	5	(2)	
6	Édouard Cissé		30/3/78	4	(1)	
12	Charles Kaboré	BFA	9/2/88	4	(1)	
8	Lucho González	ARG	19/1/81	7	(1)	2
17	Stéphane Mbia	CMR	20/5/86	6		
28	Mathieu Valbuena		28/9/84	5	(3)	1
Forwards						
20	André Ayew	GHA	17/12/89	5	(3)	
15	Jordan Ayew	GHA	11/9/91		(3)	
9	Brandão	BRA	16/6/80	6	(1)	2
10	André-Pierre Gignac		5/12/85	4	(1)	3
11	Loïc Rémy		2/1/87	6	(1)	2

OLYMPIQUE LYONNAIS

UEFA CHAMPIONS LEAGUE

Group B
Match 1 – FC Schalke 04 (GER)
H 1-0 *Michel Bastos (21)*
Lloris, Diakhaté, Lovren, Briand (Källström 90+2), Pjanić, Lisandro López López, Michel Bastos (Pied 71), Kolodziejczak, Réveillère, Toulalan, Gourcuff (Makoun 86). Coach: Claude Puel (FRA)
Yellow Card(s): Michel Bastos 31, Kolodziejczak 40
Match 2 – Hapoel Tel-Aviv FC (ISR)
A 3-1 *Michel Bastos (7p, 36), Pjanić (90+4)*
Lloris, Diakhaté, Lovren, Källström, Briand, Michel Bastos (Gonalons 89), Réveillère, Gomis (Pied 63), Cissokho, Toulalan, Gourcuff (Pjanić 77). Coach: Claude Puel (FRA)
Yellow Card(s): Briand 29, Pied 66, Lovren 78
Match 3 – SL Benfica (POR)
H 2-0 *Briand (21), Lisandro López (51)*
Lloris, Cris, Diakhaté, Briand, Pjanić, Lisandro López (Gomis 82), Michel Bastos (Pied 64), Réveillère, Cissokho, Gonalons, Gourcuff (Källström 71). Coach: Claude Puel (FRA)
Yellow Card(s): Réveillère 41
Match 4 – SL Benfica (POR)
A 3-4 *Gourcuff (74), Gomis (85), Lovren (90+5)*
Lloris, Cris, Diakhaté (Gomis 59), Lovren, Briand, Pjanić (Makoun 71), Michel Bastos, Réveillère, Gonalons, Pied (Lacazette 71), Gourcuff. Coach: Claude Puel (FRA)
Yellow Card(s): Pjanić 22, Lovren 23
Match 5 – FC Schalke 04 (GER)
A 0-3
Lloris, Diakhaté, Lovren, Källström, Briand, Lisandro López (Pied 74), Michel Bastos, Réveillère, Cissokho (Gomis 46), Toulalan, Gourcuff (Pjanić 60). Coach: Claude Puel (FRA)
Yellow Card(s): Toulalan 80, Michel Bastos 88
Match 6 – Hapoel Tel-Aviv FC (ISR)
H 2-2 *Lisandro López (62), Lacazette (88)*
Lloris, Cris, Diakhaté, Briand, Pjanić (Lacazette 68), Lisandro López, Réveillère, Makoun, Gomis (Michel Bastos 59), Cissokho (Pied 78), Gonalons. Coach: Claude Puel (FRA)

Round of 16 – Real Madrid CF (ESP)
H 1-1 *Gomis (83)*
Lloris, Cris, Lovren, Källström (Pjanić 77), Michel Bastos (Briand 69), Réveillère, Gomis, Delgado (Pied 69), Cissokho, Toulalan, Gourcuff. Coach: Claude Puel (FRA)
Yellow Card(s): Michel Bastos 48, Cris 63, Pied 70
A 0-3
Lloris, Cris, Lovren, Källström, Briand (Gomis 46), Lisandro López, Réveillère, Delgado (Pjanić 80), Cissokho, Toulalan, Gourcuff (Pied 69). Coach: Claude Puel (FRA)
Yellow Card(s): Gourcuff 38, Cissokho 54

No	Player	Nat	DoB	Aps	(s)	Gls
Goalkeepers						
1	Hugo Lloris		26/12/86	8		
Defenders						
20	Aly Cissokho		15/9/87	6		
3	Cris	BRA	3/6/77	5		
4	Pape Diakhaté	SEN	21/6/84	6		
12	Thimothée Kolodziejczak		1/10/91	1		
5	Dejan Lovren	CRO	5/7/89	6		1
13	Anthony Réveillère		10/11/79	8		
Midfielders						
19	César Delgado	ARG	18/8/81	2		
21	Maxime Gonalons		10/3/89	3	(1)	
29	Yoann Gourcuff		11/7/86	7		1
6	Kim Källström	SWE	24/8/82	4	(2)	
38	Alexandre Lacazette		28/5/91		(2)	1
17	Jean II Makoun	CMR	29/5/83	1	(2)	
11	Michel Bastos	BRA	2/8/83	6	(1)	3
8	Miralem Pjanić	BIH	2/4/90	4	(4)	1
28	Jérémy Toulalan		10/9/83	5		
Forwards						
7	Jimmy Briand		2/8/85	7	(1)	1
18	Bafétimbi Gomis		6/8/85	3	(4)	2
9	Lisandro López	ARG	2/3/83	5		2
24	Jérémy Pied		23/2/89	1	(7)	

AJ AUXERRE

UEFA CHAMPIONS LEAGUE

Play-Offs – FC Zenit St Petersburg (RUS)
A 0-1
Sorin, Hengbart, Grichting, Coulibaly, Le Tallec, Birsa (Contout 70), Mignot, Oliech (Quercia 90), Pedretti, Jeleń, Ndinga. Coach: Jean Fernandez (FRA)
Yellow Card(s): Mignot 36, Le Tallec 82, Contout 87
H 2-0 *Hengbart (9), Jeleń (53)*
Sorin, Hengbart, Grichting, Coulibaly, Le Tallec (Birsa 64), Mignot, Oliech (Chafni 86), Pedretti, Contout, Jeleń, Ndinga. Coach: Jean Fernandez (FRA)
Yellow Card(s): Hengbart 21, Contout 79

Group G
Match 1 – AC Milan (ITA)
A 0-2
Sorin, Hengbart, Grichting, Coulibaly, Birsa (Le Tallec 73), Mignot, Oliech, Pedretti, Langil (Chafni 80), Jeleń, Ndinga. Coach: Jean Fernandez (FRA)
Yellow Card(s): Grichting 20
Match 2 – Real Madrid CF (ESP)
H 0-1
Sorin, Hengbart, Grichting, Dudka, Coulibaly, Chafni (Quercia 88), Oliech, Pedretti, Contout (Jeleń 46), Langil (Traoré 78), Ndinga. Coach: Jean Fernandez (FRA)
Yellow Card(s): Jeleń 75, Traoré 83

Match 3 – AFC Ajax (NED)
A 1-2 *Birsa (56)*
Sorin, Hengbart, Grichting, Dudka, Coulibaly, Chafni (Quercia 65), Birsa, Oliech, Pedretti, Contout (Bourgeois 79), Ndinga. Coach: Jean Fernandez (FRA)
Red Card(s): Oliech 85, Mignot 90
Yellow Card(s): Hengbart 20, Grichting 30, Chafni 62, Oliech 80, Oliech 85, Mignot 90
Match 4 – AFC Ajax (NED)
H 2-1 *Sammaritano (9), Langil (84)*
Sorin, Hengbart, Grichting, Dudka, Coulibaly, Birsa, Quercia (Langil 63), Sammaritano (Berthod 86), Pedretti, Contout (Chafni 80), Ndinga. Coach: Jean Fernandez (FRA)
Match 5 – AC Milan (ITA)
H 0-2
Sorin, Hengbart (Chafni 59), Grichting, Dudka, Coulibaly, Birsa, Oliech, Sammaritano (Quercia 65), Pedretti, Contout (Traoré 82), Ndinga. Coach: Jean Fernandez (FRA)
Match 6 – Real Madrid CF (ESP)
A 0-4
Sorin, Grichting, Dudka, Coulibaly, Chafni, Birsa (Langil 89), Mignot, Oliech, Pedretti (Sammaritano 62), Contout (Quercia 72), Traoré. Coach: Jean Fernandez (FRA)
Yellow Card(s): Mignot 34

No	Player	Nat	DoB	Aps	(s)	Gls
	Goalkeepers					
1	Olivier Sorin		16/4/81	6		
	Defenders					
23	Jérémy Berthod		24/4/84		(1)	
3	Adama Coulibaly	MLI	10/9/80	6		
4	Stéphane Grichting	SUI	30/3/79	6		
2	Cédric Hengbart		13/7/80	5		
12	Jean-Pascal Mignot		26/2/81	2		
	Midfielders					
7	Kamel Chafni	MAR	11/6/82	3	(3)	
5	Dariusz Dudka	POL	9/12/83	5		
21	Steeven Langil		4/3/88	2	(2)	1
29	Delvin Ndinga	CGO	14/3/88	5		
17	Benoît Pedretti		12/11/80	6		
15	Frédéric Sammaritano		23/3/86	2	(1)	1
27	Alain Traoré	BFA	1/1/88	1	(2)	
	Forwards					
9	Valter Birsa	SVN	7/8/86	5		1
25	Maxime Bourgeois		3/2/91		(1)	
18	Roy Contout		11/2/85	5		
22	Ireneusz Jeleń	POL	9/4/81	1	(1)	
8	Anthony Le Tallec		3/10/84		(1)	
14	Dennis Oliech	KEN	2/2/85	5		
11	Julien Quercia		17/8/86	1	(4)	

PARIS SAINT-GERMAIN FC

UEFA EUROPA LEAGUE

Play-Offs – Maccabi Tel-Aviv FC (ISR)
H 2-0 *Luyindula (3), Hoarau (60)*
Édel, Ceará, Sakho, Giuly, Luyindula, Hoarau (Mevlüt 74), Chantôme, Maurice (Sessegnon 83), Armand, Clément, Makonda (Jallet 76). Coach: Antoine Kombouaré (FRA)
A 3-4 *Hoarau (40p), Giuly (64), Nenê (90+3p)*
Édel, Sakho (Camara 78), Giuly, Luyindula, Hoarau (Maurice 67), Nenê, Chantôme, Armand, Clément, Makonda, Jallet. Coach: Antoine Kombouaré (FRA)
Yellow Card(s): Makonda 24

Group J
Match 1 – Sevilla FC (ESP)
A 1-0 *Nenê (75)*
Édel, Tiéné (Sakho 89), Camara, Luyindula, Mevlüt (Makelele 66), Nenê (Hoarau 76), Chantôme, Maurice, Armand, Clément, Jallet. Coach: Antoine Kombouaré (FRA)
Yellow Card(s): Tiéné 47
Match 2 – FC Karpaty Lviv (UKR)
H 2-0 *Jallet (4), Nenê (20)*
Édel, Sakho, Tiéné, Camara, Luyindula, Sessegnon (Makonda 90+1), Mevlüt (Kežman 69), Nenê (Hoarau 76), Chantôme, Clément, Jallet. Coach: Antoine Kombouaré (FRA)
Yellow Card(s): Sessegnon 34, Chantôme 49, Hoarau 77, Kežman 80
Match 3 – Borussia Dortmund (GER)
A 1-1 *Chantôme (87)*
Édel, Sakho, Makelele, Tiéné, Camara, Luyindula, Sessegnon, Mevlüt (Hoarau 72), Bodmer (Clément 68), Nenê (Chantôme 82), Jallet. Coach: Antoine Kombouaré (FRA)
Yellow Card(s): Tiéné 43
Match 4 – Borussia Dortmund (GER)
H 0-0
Édel, Ceará, Sakho, Tiéné, Camara, Luyindula, Sessegnon, Mevlüt (Chantôme 75), Bodmer (Hoarau 81), Nenê (Jallet 66), Clément. Coach: Antoine Kombouaré (FRA)
Yellow Card(s): Luyindula 22, Clément 43, Bodmer 58, Chantôme 84
Match 5 – Sevilla FC (ESP)
H 4-2 *Bodmer (17), Hoarau (20, 47), Nenê (45)*
Édel, Ceará, Sakho, Tiéné, Camara, Hoarau (Giuly 70), Sessegnon, Bodmer (Jallet 79), Nenê (Luyindula 66), Chantôme, Clément. Coach: Antoine Kombouaré (FRA)
Yellow Card(s): Chantôme 48, Jallet 90+1
Match 6 – FC Karpaty Lviv (UKR)
A 1-1 *Luyindula (39)*
Coupet, Ceará, Tiéné, Camara, Luyindula, Sessegnon, Mevlüt (Makhedjouf 90+1), Bodmer (Qasmi 78), Traoré, Clément, Makonda (Maurice 69). Coach: Gilles Bourges (FRA)
Yellow Card(s): Sessegnon 58, Tiéné 83

Round of 32 – FC BATE Borisov (BLR)
A 2-2 *Mevlüt (29), Luyindula (89)*
Édel, Ceará, Sakho, Camara, Giuly (Bodmer 68), Luyindula, Mevlüt (Makonda 83), Nenê (Maurice 63), Chantôme, Clément, Jallet. Coach: Yves Bertucci (FRA)
Yellow Card(s): Clément 36
H 0-0
Édel, Ceará, Tiéné, Camara, Luyindula, Mevlüt (Hoarau 67), Bodmer (Kebano 73), Chantôme, Maurice (Makonda 83), Armand, Clément. Coach: Antoine Kombouaré (FRA)
Yellow Card(s): Clément 14, Camara 75

Round of 16 – SL Benfica (POR)
A 1-2 *Luyindula (14)*
Édel, Ceará, Camara, Luyindula (Maurice 44), Mevlüt, Bodmer (Kebano 70), Traoré, Nenê, Chantôme, Armand, Makonda (Makhedjouf 75). Coach: Antoine Kombouaré (FRA)
Yellow Card(s): Armand 30, Ceará 39, Nenê 83, Camara 90+1
H 1-1 *Bodmer (35)*
Édel, Ceará (Maurice 78), Sakho, Makelele, Tiéné, Mevlüt (Hoarau 68), Bodmer (Giuly 68), Nenê, Chantôme, Armand, Jallet. Coach: Antoine Kombouaré (FRA)
Yellow Card(s): Chantôme 72, Armand 82

LOSC LILLE MÉTROPOLE

UEFA EUROPA LEAGUE

Play-Offs – FC Vaslui (ROU)
A 0-0
Landreau, Debuchy, Cabaye, Sow (Hazard 77), Obraniak (Túlio de Melo 35), Emerson, Frau (Gervinho 67), Béria, Chedjou, Mavuba, Dumont. Coach: Rudi Garcia (FRA)
H 2-0 *Cabaye (69p), Chedjou (80)*
Landreau, Debuchy, Balmont, Cabaye (Frau 85), Sow, Béria (Emerson 10), Chedjou, Rami, Mavuba, Hazard, Gervinho (Wade 89). Coach: Rudi Garcia (FRA)
Yellow Card(s): Mavuba 14, Balmont 53

Group C
Match 1 – Sporting Clube de Portugal (POR)
H 1-2 *Frau (57)*
Landreau, Debuchy, Vandam (Emerson 39), Balmont, Obraniak, Rozehnal, Frau, Rami, Mavuba (Cabaye 73), Gervinho, Dumont (Hazard 39). Coach: Rudi Garcia (FRA)
Yellow Card(s): Rami 8, Debuchy 75
Match 2 – KAA Gent (BEL)
A 1-1 *Frau (21)*
Landreau, Debuchy, Balmont, Gueye (Rami 78), Cabaye (Sow 84), Obraniak, Rozehnal, Emerson, Frau (Gervinho 69), Chedjou, Hazard. Coach: Rudi Garcia (FRA)
Yellow Card(s): Cabaye 31, Gueye 45
Match 3 – PFC Levski Sofia (BUL)
H 1-0 *Chedjou (49)*
Landreau, Vandam, Balmont (Mavuba 80), Gueye, Obraniak, Rozehnal, Frau (Sow 55), Béria, Chedjou, Hazard (Gervinho 71), Dumont. Coach: Rudi Garcia (FRA)
Yellow Card(s): Béria 78
Match 4 – PFC Levski Sofia (BUL)
A 2-2 *Túlio de Melo (35), Ivanov (88og)*
Landreau, Gueye, Souaré, Túlio de Melo (Hazard 76), Obraniak, Rozehnal, Béria, Chedjou, Mavuba (Cabaye 56), Gervinho (Sow 57), Dumont. Coach: Rudi Garcia (FRA)
Yellow Card(s): Mavuba 28, Sow 78
Match 5 – Sporting Clube de Portugal (POR)
A 0-1
Landreau, Balmont (Cabaye 78), Gueye (Frau 62), Túlio de Melo, Obraniak, Rozehnal, Emerson, Béria, Chedjou, Mavuba, Hazard (Sow 72). Coach: Rudi Garcia (FRA)
Yellow Card(s): Landreau 28, Túlio de Melo 28, Rozehnal 63, Chedjou 90+5
Match 6 – KAA Gent (BEL)
H 3-0 *Obraniak (30), Frau (56), Sow (89)*
Landreau, Debuchy, Balmont (Béria 85), Cabaye, Túlio de Melo, Obraniak, Rozehnal, Emerson, Frau (Mavuba 72), Rami, Hazard (Sow 61). Coach: Rudi Garcia (FRA)
Yellow Card(s): Rami 18, Túlio de Melo 62, Debuchy 87

Round of 32 – PSV Eindhoven (NED)
H 2-2 *Gueye (6), Túlio de Melo (31)*
Landreau, Debuchy (Béria 76), Vandam (Cabaye 70), Gueye, Túlio de Melo, Obraniak, Rozehnal, Emerson, Frau (Gervinho 83), Chedjou, Dumont. Coach: Rudi Garcia (FRA)
Yellow Card(s): Obraniak 13, Frau 51, Rozehnal 79, Chedjou 88
A 1-3 *Frau (22)*
Mouko, Vandam, Gueye, Túlio de Melo (Sow 69), Obraniak, Rozehnal, Emerson, Frau, Rami (Chedjou 77), Mavuba (Hazard 65), Dumont. Coach: Rudi Garcia (FRA)
Red Card(s): Frau 62
Yellow Card(s): Frau 55, Frau 62

MONTPELLIER HÉRAULT SC

UEFA EUROPA LEAGUE

Third Qualifying Round – Győri ETO FC (HUN)
A 1-0 *Giroud (32)*
Jourdren, Yanga M'Biwa, Spahić, Hasan (Aït-Fana 64), Estrada (Saihi 90), Pitau, Giroud, Camara, El-Kaoutari, Jeunechamp, Belhanda (Marveaux 71). Coach: René Girard (FRA)
Yellow Card(s): Jeunechamp 24, Estrada 90
H 0-1 (aet; 3-4 on pens)
Jourdren, Yanga M'Biwa, Spahić, Marveaux (Belhanda 63), Hasan (Camara 63), Estrada, Giroud, Aït-Fana, Stambouli, Saihi, Collin (Armand 94). Coach: René Girard (FRA)
Red Card(s): Pitau 90
Yellow Card(s): Collin 75, Spahić 114, Giroud 117, Saihi 118

GEORGIA

FC OLIMPI RUSTAVI

UEFA CHAMPIONS LEAGUE

Second Qualifying Round – FC Aktobe (KAZ)
A 0-2
Bediashvili, Gongadze, Kemoklidze, Kvakhadze, Rekhviashvili, Modebadze, Razmadze, Chelidze (Dolidze 85), Bolkvadze (Khidesheli 74) Chedia (Dobrovolski 55), Getsadze. Coach: Temur Makharadze (GEO)
Yellow Card(s): Gongadze 39
H 1-1 *Rekhviashvili (30)*
Bediashvili (Batiashvili 79), Gongadze, Kemoklidze, Kvakhadze, Rekhviashvili, Modebadze, Razmadze, Chelidze (Dolidze 68), Dobrovolski, Bolkvadze, Getsadze (Chedia 53). Coach: Temur Makharadze (GEO)
Yellow Card(s): Dobrovolski 61, Kemoklidze 75

FC WIT GEORGIA

UEFA EUROPA LEAGUE

Second Qualifying Round – FC Baník Ostrava (CZE)
H 0-6
Mikaberidze, Lomaia, Lipartia (Janelidze 71), Vasadze (Chimakadze 67), Gureshidze, Chakvetadze, Kvaratskhelia, Maisashvili (Kasradze 82), Klimiashvili, Bechvaia, Adamadze. Coach: Merab Kochlashvili (GEO)
Yellow Card(s): Maisashvili 56, Mikaberidze 64, Klimiashvili 70
A 0-0
Mikaberidze, Lomaia, Lipartia, Vasadze, Chakvetadze, Kvaratskhelia (Chimakadze 64), Maisashvili (Gureshidze 80), Klimiashvili, Bechvaia, Adamadze, Janelidze (Zakradze 75). Coach: Merab Kochlashvili (GEO)
Yellow Card(s): Chakvetadze 43, Mikaberidze 90

FC DINAMO TBILISI

UEFA EUROPA LEAGUE

irst Qualifying Round – FC Flora Tallinn (EST)
2-1 *Kakhelishvili (22), Khmaladze (64p)*
oria, Tomashvili, Chaduneli, Koshkadze, Khmaladze, Kakhelishvili, atsadze (Metreveli 85), Tekturmanidze (Pirtskhalava 76), Djousse ekvtadze 85), Ednilson, Kakubava. Coach: Kakha Kacharava (GEO)
ellow Card(s): Vatsadze 24, Tomashvili 25, Khmaladze 30, Djousse 82, irtskhalava 90+1
0-0
oria, Tomashvili, Koshkadze, Khmaladze, Kakhelishvili, Vatsadze Metreveli 72), Tekturmanidze (Gvelesiani 90+3), Djousse, Robertinho ekvtadze 85), Ednilson, Kakubava. Coach: Kakha Kacharava (GEO)

econd Qualifying Round – Gefle IF (SWE)
2-1 *Vatsadze (11), Khmaladze (87p)*
oria, Tomashvili, Koshkadze (Pirtskhalava 76), Khmaladze, Kakhelishvili, atsadze (Metreveli 82), Tekturmanidze, Djousse, Robertinho (Lekvtadze 4), Ednilson, Kakubava. Coach: Kakha Kacharava (GEO)
ellow Card(s): Tekturmanidze 47, Kakhelishvili 50
2-1 *Vatsadze (68), Pirtskhalava (82)*
oria, Tomashvili, Koshkadze, Khmaladze, Kakhelishvili, Vatsadze Metreveli 81), Tekturmanidze (Gvelesiani 85), Djousse, Robertinho Pirtskhalava 67), Ednilson, Kakubava. Coach: Kakha Kacharava (GEO)
ellow Card(s): Vatsadze 62

hird Qualifying Round – SK Sturm Graz (AUT)
0-2
oria, Tomashvili, Pirtskhalava (Robertinho 60), Koshkadze, Khmaladze, akhelishvili, Tekturmanidze, Djousse, Ednilson, Kakubava, Metreveli Sikharulidze 86). Coach: Kakha Kacharava (GEO)
ellow Card(s): Pirtskhalava 52
1-1 *Robertinho (11)*
oria, Tomashvili, Koshkadze, Khmaladze, Kakhelishvili, Vatsadze, ekturmanidze (Mamuchashvili 77), Djousse (Gvelesiani 69), Robertinho Gavashelishvili 83), Ednilson, Kakubava. Coach: Kakha Kacharava (GEO)
ed Card(s): Kakhelishvili 39, Khmaladze 61
ellow Card(s): Kakubava 52, Vatsadze 90+2

FC ZESTAFONI

UEFA EUROPA LEAGUE

First Qualifying Round – SC Faetano (SMR)
H 5-0 *Gelashvili (21p, 23), Dvali (22, 64), Gorgiashvili (90)*
Kvaskhvadze, Oniani (Kobakhidze 76), Benashvili, Daushvili, Gelashvili, Dzaria (Pipia 64), Dvali, Khidesheli, Grigalashvili, Eliava, Babunashvili (Gorgiashvili 56). Coach: Giorgi Geguchadze (GEO)
Yellow Card(s): Babunashvili 3, Grigalashvili 53, Daushvili 65
A 0-0
Mamaladze, Kobakhidze, Benashvili, Dzaria (Grigalashvili 70), Lomia (Gelashvili 63), Khidesheli, Gorgiashvili, Eliava, Mikaberidze (Dvali 63), Babunashvili, Pipia. Coach: Giorgi Geguchadze (GEO)
Yellow Card(s): Benashvili 64

Second Qualifying Round – Dukla Banská Bystrica (SVK)
H 3-0 *Dvali (24, 65), Dzaria (48)*
Kvaskhvadze, Oniani, Benashvili, Daushvili, Gelashvili, Dzaria, Dvali (Aladashvili 79), Khidesheli, Grigalashvili (Pipia 79), Eliava, Babunashvili (Aptsiauri 30). Coach: Giorgi Geguchadze (GEO)
Yellow Card(s): Gelashvili 60, Daushvili 90+2
A 0-1
Kvaskhvadze, Oniani, Benashvili (Aladashvili 57), Gelashvili, Dzaria, Dvali, Khidesheli, Gorgiashvili (Babunashvili 57), Aptsiauri (Pipia 83), Grigalashvili, Eliava. Coach: Giorgi Geguchadze (GEO)
Yellow Card(s): Eliava 79

Third Qualifying Round – FC Karpaty Lviv (UKR)
A 0-1
Kvaskhvadze, Oniani, Aladashvili, Daushvili, Gelashvili (Lomia 90+4), Dzaria (Pipia 80), Dvali, Khidesheli, Grigalashvili, Eliava, Babunashvili (Aptsiauri 58). Coach: Giorgi Geguchadze (GEO)
H 0-1
Kvaskhvadze, Oniani, Aladashvili, Daushvili (Benashvili 80), Gelashvili, Dzaria (Babunashvili 60), Dvali (Tsinamdzgvrishvili 67), Khidesheli, Aptsiauri, Grigalashvili, Eliava. Coach: Giorgi Geguchadze (GEO)
Yellow Card(s): Oniani 45

GERMANY

FC BAYERN MÜNCHEN

UEFA CHAMPIONS LEAGUE

Group E
Match 1 – AS Roma (ITA)
H 2-0 *Müller (79), Klose (83)*
Butt, Van Buyten, Hamit Altıntop (Klose 67), Olić (Gomez 67), Van Bommel, Lahm, Müller (Pranjić 82), Contento, Badstuber, Schweinsteiger, Kroos. Coach: Louis van Gaal (NED)
Yellow Card(s): Gomez 80
Match 2 – FC Basel 1893 (SUI)
A 2-1 *Schweinsteiger (56p, 89)*
Butt, Van Buyten, Hamit Altıntop (Gomez 46), Van Bommel, Klose (Tymoshchuk 77), Lahm, Pranjić, Müller, Badstuber, Schweinsteiger, Kroos (Olić 56). Coach: Louis van Gaal (NED)
Yellow Card(s): Badstuber 28, Kroos 35, Pranjić 57, Schweinsteiger 61
Match 3 – CFR 1907 Cluj (ROU)
H 3-2 *Cadú (32og), Panin (37og), Gomez (77)*
Butt, Hamit Altıntop, Ottl, Lahm, Pranjić, Müller, Badstuber, Schweinsteiger (Braafheid 80), Gomez, Kroos, Tymoshchuk. Coach: Louis van Gaal (NED)
Yellow Card(s): Schweinsteiger 70, Pranjić 83
Match 4 – CFR 1907 Cluj (ROU)
A 4-0 *Gomez (12, 24, 71), Müller (90)*
Butt, Van Buyten, Demichelis, Hamit Altıntop, Ottl, Lahm, Pranjić, Schweinsteiger (Müller 75), Gomez, Kroos, Tymoshchuk. Coach: Louis van Gaal (NED)
Yellow Card(s): Ottl 15, Schweinsteiger 25, Demichelis 60
Match 5 – AS Roma (ITA)
A 2-3 *Gomez (33, 39)*
Kraft, Van Buyten, Demichelis, Ribéry, Ottl, Lahm, Pranjić, Müller, Gomez, Kroos, Tymoshchuk. Coach: Louis van Gaal (NED)
Yellow Card(s): Kroos 19
Match 6 – FC Basel 1893 (SUI)
H 3-0 *Ribéry (35, 50), Tymoshchuk (37)*
Kraft, Breno, Ribéry, Van Bommel, Lahm, Müller, Contento, Schweinsteiger, Gomez, Kroos (Hamit Altıntop 68), Tymoshchuk. Coach: Louis van Gaal (NED)
Yellow Card(s): Gomez 83

Round of 16 – FC Internazionale Milano (ITA)
A 1-0 *Gomez (90)*
Kraft, Ribéry, Robben, Lahm, Pranjić (Breno 38), Müller, Badstuber, Luiz Gustavo, Schweinsteiger, Gomez, Tymoshchuk. Coach: Louis van Gaal (NED)
Yellow Card(s): Ribéry 34, Luiz Gustavo 87

H 2-3 *Gomez (21), Müller (31)*
Kraft, Breno (Kroos 90), Van Buyten (Badstuber 70), Ribéry, Robben (Hamit Altıntop 68), Lahm, Pranjić, Müller, Luiz Gustavo, Schweinsteiger, Gomez. Coach: Louis van Gaal (NED)
Yellow Card(s): Luiz Gustavo 38, Breno 57

No	Player	Nat	DoB	Aps	(s)	Gls
Goalkeepers						
1	Jörg Butt		28/5/74	4		
35	Thomas Kraft		22/7/88	4		
Defenders						
28	Holger Badstuber		13/3/89	4	(1)	
4	Edson Braafheid	NED	8/4/83		(1)	
2	Breno	BRA	13/10/89	2	(1)	
26	Diego Contento		1/5/90	2	(1)	
6	Martín Demichelis	ARG	20/12/80	2		
21	Philipp Lahm		11/11/83	8		
5	Daniel Van Buyten	BEL	7/2/78	5		
Midfielders						
8	Hamit Altıntop	TUR	8/12/82	4	(3)	
39	Toni Kroos		4/1/90	6	(1)	
30	Luiz Gustavo	BRA	23/7/87	2		
16	Andreas Ottl		1/3/85	3		
23	Danijel Pranjić	CRO	2/12/81	6	(1)	
7	Franck Ribéry	FRA	7/4/83	4		2
10	Arjen Robben	NED	23/1/84	2		
31	Bastian Schweinsteiger		1/8/84	7		2
44	Anatoliy Tymoshchuk	UKR	30/3/79	5	(1)	1
17	Mark van Bommel	NED	22/4/77	3		
Forwards						
33	Mario Gomez		10/7/85	6	(2)	8
18	Miroslav Klose		9/6/78	1	(1)	1
25	Thomas Müller		13/9/89	7	(1)	3
11	Ivica Olić	CRO	14/9/79	1	(1)	

FC SCHALKE 04

UEFA CHAMPIONS LEAGUE

Group B
Match 1 – Olympique Lyonnais (FRA)
A 0-1
Neuer, Sarpei (Schmitz 75), Höwedes, Plestan, Raúl, Rakitić, Farfán, Jones (Kluge 70), Huntelaar, Deac (Matip 45), Moritz. Coach: Felix Magath (GER)
Red Card(s): Höwedes 38
Match 2 – SL Benfica (POR)
H 2-0 *Farfán (73), Huntelaar (85)*
Neuer, Raúl, Rakitić (Jones 66), Schmitz, Papadopoulos, Farfán, Jurado (Kluge 78), Metzelder, Uchida (Sarpei 58), Huntelaar, Matip. Coach: Felix Magath (GER)
Yellow Card(s): Uchida 57, Farfán 62
Match 3 – Hapoel Tel-Aviv FC (ISR)
H 3-1 *Raúl (3, 58), Jurado (68)*
Neuer, Höwedes, Raúl, Schmitz, Farfán (Hao 67), Jurado, Metzelder, Uchida, Jones (Matip 75), Huntelaar, Moritz (Rakitić 53). Coach: Felix Magath (GER)
Yellow Card(s): Farfán 38
Match 4 – Hapoel Tel-Aviv FC (ISR)
A 0-0
Neuer, Escudero, Höwedes, Raúl, Rakitić (Edu 74), Kluge (Moritz 46), Farfán (Deac 81), Jurado, Metzelder, Uchida, Huntelaar. Coach: Felix Magath (GER)
Yellow Card(s): Rakitić 23, Jurado 30, Huntelaar 36, Höwedes 51
Match 5 – Olympique Lyonnais (FRA)
H 3-0 *Farfán (13), Huntelaar (20, 89)*
Neuer, Höwedes, Raúl, Kluge, Schmitz, Farfán (Edu 65), Jurado (Deac 85), Metzelder, Uchida, Jones (Matip 70), Huntelaar. Coach: Felix Magath (GER)
Yellow Card(s): Farfán 30, Jones 65
Match 6 – SL Benfica (POR)
A 2-1 *Jurado (19), Höwedes (81)*
Neuer, Höwedes, Raúl, Rakitić, Kluge (Matip 82), Schmitz, Papadopoulos, Jurado (Jendrišek 88), Metzelder, Uchida, Huntelaar (Edu 85). Coach: Felix Magath (GER)
Yellow Card(s): Huntelaar 63, Rakitić 78

Round of 16 – Valencia CF (ESP)
A 1-1 *Raúl (64)*
Neuer, Höwedes, Raúl, Kluge, Schmitz, Farfán (Draxler 78), Jurado (Edu 83), Metzelder, Uchida, Huntelaar (Hao 90), Matip. Coach: Felix Magath (GER)
Red Card(s): Schmitz 90+3
Yellow Card(s): Matip 16, Schmitz 65, Neuer 78, Jurado 80, Schmitz 90+3
H 3-1 *Farfán (40, 90+4), Gavranović (52)*
Neuer, Escudero, Höwedes, Raúl, Kluge (Sarpei 81), Farfán, Jurado (Draxler 76), Gavranović, Metzelder, Uchida, Matip (Papadopoulos 60). Coach: Felix Magath (GER)
Yellow Card(s): Kluge 27, Escudero 47, Farfán 74

Quarter-Finals – FC Internazionale Milano (ITA)
A 5-2 *Matip (17), Edu (40, 75), Raúl (53), Ranocchia (57og)*
Neuer, Sarpei, Höwedes, Raúl (Karimi 87), Edu, Baumjohann (Schmitz 76), Papadopoulos, Farfán, Jurado (Draxler 83), Uchida, Matip. Coach: Ralf Rangnick (GER)
Yellow Card(s): Farfán 45+3, Sarpei 60, Papadopoulos 67, Raúl 85
H 2-1 *Raúl (45), Höwedes (81)*
Neuer, Sarpei, Höwedes, Raúl, Edu (Charisteas 77), Baumjohann (Draxler 73), Papadopoulos, Jurado (Schmitz 87), Metzelder, Uchida, Matip. Coach: Ralf Rangnick (GER)
Yellow Card(s): Raúl 42, Papadopoulos 66, Schmitz 87

Semi-Finals – Manchester United FC (ENG)
H 0-2
Neuer, Sarpei (Escudero 73), Raúl, Edu, Baumjohann (Kluge 53), Papadopoulos, Farfán, Jurado (Draxler 83), Metzelder, Uchida, Matip. Coach: Ralf Rangnick (GER)
Yellow Card(s): Metzelder 34, Sarpei 71
A 1-4 *Jurado (35)*
Neuer, Escudero, Höwedes (Huntelaar 70), Raúl, Baumjohann (Edu 46), Papadopoulos, Farfán (Matip 75), Jurado, Metzelder, Uchida, Draxler. Coach: Ralf Rangnick (GER)
Yellow Card(s): Escudero 58

No	Player	Nat	DoB	Aps	(s)	Gls
Goalkeepers						
1	Manuel Neuer		27/3/86	12		
Defenders						
3	Sergio Escudero	ESP	2/9/89	3	(1)	
4	Benedikt Höwedes		29/2/88	10		2
21	Christoph Metzelder		5/11/80	10		
4	Kyriakos Papadopoulos	GRE	23/2/92	6	(1)	
5	Nicolas Plestan	FRA	2/6/81	1		
2	Hans Sarpei	GHA	28/6/76	4	(2)	
22	Atsuto Uchida	JPN	27/3/88	11		
Midfielders						
11	Alexander Baumjohann		23/1/87	4		
27	Ciprian Deac	ROU	16/2/86	1	(2)	
31	Julian Draxler		20/9/93	1	(5)	
19	Mario Gavranovic	SUI	24/11/89	1		1
8	Hao Junmin	CHN	24/3/87		(2)	
23	Jermaine Jones	USA	3/11/81	3	(1)	
18	José Manuel Jurado	ESP	29/6/86	11		3
16	Ali Karimi	IRN	8/11/78		(1)	
12	Peer Kluge		22/11/80	5	(3)	
32	Joel Matip	CMR	8/8/91	6	(5)	1

3	Christoph Moritz		27/1/90	2	(1)	
)	Ivan Rakitić	CRO	10/3/88	4	(1)	
3	Lukas Schmitz		13/10/88	5	(3)	
rwards						
5	Angelos Charisteas	GRE	9/2/80		(1)	
	Edu	BRA	30/11/81	3	(5)	2
7	Jefferson Farfán	PER	26/10/84	10		4
5	Klaas Jan Huntelaar	NED	12/8/83	7	(1)	3
3	Erik Jendrišek	SVK	26/10/86		(1)	
	Raúl González	ESP	27/6/77	12		5

SV WERDER BREMEN

UEFA CHAMPIONS LEAGUE

lay-Offs – UC Sampdoria (ITA)
3-1 *Fritz (51), Frings (67p), Pizarro (69)*
Viese, Pasanen (Boenisch 77), Borowski, Fritz, Hunt (Marin 85), Prödl, rings, Hugo Almeida (Arnautovic 89), Pizarro, Mertesacker, Bargfrede. oach: Thomas Schaaf (GER)
ellow Card(s): Fritz 53
2-3 *Rosenberg (90+3), Pizarro (100)*
Viese, Pasanen (Boenisch 79), Borowski (Arnautovic 63), Fritz, Marin, rödl, Wagner (Rosenberg 72), Frings, Pizarro, Mertesacker, Bargfrede. oach: Thomas Schaaf (GER)
ellow Card(s): Prödl 13, Arnautovic 79, Pizarro 93

roup A
latch 1 – Tottenham Hotspur FC (ENG)
2-2 *Hugo Almeida (43), Marin (47)*
Viese, Pasanen, Wesley (Borowski 67), Arnautovic, Fritz, Marin, Prödl, ilvestre, Frings, Hugo Almeida (Wagner 79), Bargfrede (Hunt 37). oach: Thomas Schaaf (GER)
ellow Card(s): Borowski 90+1
latch 2 – FC Internazionale Milano (ITA)
A 0-4
Viese, Wesley, Borowski (Pasanen 46), Arnautovic, Marin (Hunt 63), rödl, Silvestre, Jensen, Hugo Almeida (Wagner 78), Mertesacker, 3argfrede. Coach: Thomas Schaaf (GER)
Yellow Card(s): Jensen 44, Prödl 64
Match 3 – FC Twente (NED)
A 1-1 *Arnautovic (80)*
Wiese (Mielitz 37), Pasanen, Wesley, Fritz, Hunt, Prödl, Frings, Hugo Almeida (Arnautovic 59), Pizarro, Mertesacker, Bargfrede (Marin 77). Coach: Thomas Schaaf (GER)
Yellow Card(s): Fritz 18
Match 4 – FC Twente (NED)
H 0-2
Mielitz, Wesley, Marin, Hunt, Prödl, Jensen, Frings, Hugo Almeida, Pizarro, Mertesacker, Bargfrede (Arnautovic 59). Coach: Thomas Schaaf (GER)
Red Card(s): Frings 75
Match 5 – Tottenham Hotspur FC (ENG)
A 0-3
Wiese, Fritz, Marin, Hunt, Prödl, Kroos (Onur Ayık 55), Wagner, Jensen, Mertesacker, Schmidt, Bargfrede. Coach: Thomas Schaaf (GER)
Yellow Card(s): Fritz 42, Prödl 50, Wagner 53, Kroos 53
Match 6 – FC Internazionale Milano (ITA)
H 3-0 *Prödl (39), Arnautovic (49), Pizarro (88)*
Wiese, Pasanen (Silvestre 83), Arnautovic, Fritz, Marin, Hunt, Prödl, Frings (Bargfrede 78), Hugo Almeida (Pizarro 76), Mertesacker, Schmidt. Coach: Thomas Schaaf (GER)
Yellow Card(s): Pasanen 68

No	Player	Nat	DoB	Aps	(s)	Gls
Goalkeepers						
21	Sebastian Mielitz		18/7/89	1	(1)	
1	Tim Wiese		17/12/81	5		
Defenders						
8	Clemens Fritz		7/12/80	4		
29	Per Mertesacker		29/9/84	5		
3	Petri Pasanen	FIN	24/9/80	3	(2)	
15	Sebastian Prödl	AUT	21/6/87	6		1
41	Dominik Schmidt		1/7/87	2		
16	Mikaël Silvestre	FRA	9/8/77	2	(1)	
Midfielders						
44	Philipp Bargfrede		3/3/89	5	(1)	
6	Tim Borowski		2/5/80	1	(1)	
22	Torsten Frings		22/11/76	4		
14	Aaron Hunt		4/9/86	4	(2)	
20	Daniel Jensen	DEN	25/6/79	3		
10	Marko Marin		13/3/89	5	(1)	1
5	Wesley	BRA	24/6/87	4		
Forwards						
7	Marko Arnautovic	AUT	19/4/89	3	(2)	2
23	Hugo Almeida	POR	23/5/84	5		1
18	Felix Kroos		12/3/91	1		
46	Onur Ayık	TUR	28/1/90		(1)	
24	Claudio Pizarro	PER	3/10/78	2	(1)	1
36	Lennart Thy		25/2/92		(1)	
19	Sandro Wagner		29/11/87	1	(2)	

BAYER 04 LEVERKUSEN

UEFA EUROPA LEAGUE

Play-Offs – SC Tavriya Simferopol (UKR)
H 3-0 *Kadlec (1, 84), Ballack (90+1p)*
Adler, Schwaab, Reinartz, Friedrich, Bender (Ballack 46), Helmes (Derdiyok 66), Renato Augusto, Kiessling, Sam (Barnetta 46), Vidal, Kadlec. Coach: Jupp Heynckes (GER)
A 3-1 *Vidal (50p), Holaido (75og), Castro (90+3)*
Adler, Schwaab, Reinartz, Friedrich, Barnetta (Kadlec 77), Bender, Balitsch, Derdiyok (Jørgensen 80), Vidal, Castro, Burak Kaplan (Renato Augusto 46). Coach: Jupp Heynckes (GER)
Yellow Card(s): Derdiyok 5, Burak Kaplan 26, Balitsch 32, Castro 48, Barnetta 70, Vidal 85

Group B
Match 1 – Rosenborg BK (NOR)
H 4-0 *Helmes (4, 58, 61), Reinartz (38)*
Adler, Schwaab, Reinartz, Hyypiä, Friedrich, Bender (Balitsch 67), Helmes, Sam, Derdiyok (Barnetta 78), Castro (Vida 78), Jørgensen. Coach: Jupp Heynckes (GER)
Match 2 – Club Atlético de Madrid (ESP)
A 1-1 *Derdiyok (39)*
Adler, Schwaab, Reinartz, Hyypiä, Friedrich, Barnetta, Balitsch (Rolfes 61), Sam, Derdiyok (Helmes 68), Vidal (Bender 61), Kadlec. Coach: Jupp Heynckes (GER)
Yellow Card(s): Hyypiä 11, Sam 69, Barnetta 90
Match 3 – Aris Thessaloniki FC (GRE)
A 0-0
Adler, Reinartz, Friedrich, Rolfes (Derdiyok 76), Bender, Helmes, Balitsch (Vidal 61), Vida, Kadlec, Burak Kaplan, Jørgensen (Barnetta 60). Coach: Jupp Heynckes (GER)
Yellow Card(s): Kadlec 75
Match 4 – Aris Thessaloniki FC (GRE)
H 1-0 *Vidal (90)*
Adler, Reinartz, Friedrich, Bender (Rolfes 46), Helmes, Balitsch, Sam, Vidal, Kadlec, Burak Kaplan (Barnetta 62), Jørgensen (Derdiyok 46). Coach: Jupp Heynckes (GER)
Yellow Card(s): Vidal 90+1

Match 5 – Rosenborg BK (NOR)
A 1-0 *Sam (35)*
Giefer, Reinartz, Hyypiä, Friedrich, Bender, Helmes (Castro 85), Balitsch, Vida, Sam (Burak Kaplan 68), Kadlec, Jørgensen (Derdiyok 76). Coach: Jupp Heynckes (GER)
Match 6 – Club Atlético de Madrid (ESP)
H 1-1 *Helmes (69)*
Giefer, Schwaab, Hyypiä, Bender (Vidal 88), Helmes, Renato Augusto (Kiessling 46), Balitsch, Vida, Castro (Da Costa 46), Burak Kaplan, Jørgensen. Coach: Jupp Heynckes (GER)
Yellow Card(s): Vida 80

Round of 32 – FC Metalist Kharkiv (UKR)
A 4-0 *Derdiyok (23), Castro (72), Sam (90, 90+2)*
Adler, Reinartz, Friedrich, Bender, Renato Augusto (Rolfes 74), Balitsch (Castro 46), Vida, Sam, Derdiyok (Kiessling 79), Vidal, Kadlec. Coach: Jupp Heynckes (GER)
Yellow Card(s): Friedrich 29, Sam 45, Vidal 60, Castro 89
H 2-0 *Rolfes (47), Ballack (70)*
Adler, Schwaab, Friedrich, Rolfes (Kampl 64), Bender (Vidal 46), Renato Augusto (Da Costa 64), Kiessling, Ballack, Vida, Castro, Jørgensen. Coach: Jupp Heynckes (GER)
Yellow Card(s): Jørgensen 21

Round of 16 – Villarreal CF (ESP)
H 2-3 *Kadlec (33), Castro (72)*
Adler, Schwaab, Reinartz, Rolfes (Bender 89), Renato Augusto, Vida, Sam (Jørgensen 76), Derdiyok (Kiessling 46), Vidal, Kadlec, Castro. Coach: Jupp Heynckes (GER)
Yellow Card(s): Vidal 29
A 1-2 *Derdiyok (82)*
Adler, Reinartz, Hyypiä, Rolfes, Bender, Renato Augusto, Kiessling (Ballack 53), Vida (Schwaab 62), Derdiyok, Kadlec, Castro (Sam 42). Coach: Jupp Heynckes (GER)
Yellow Card(s): Reinartz 12, Kadlec 31, Schwaab 75, Bender 85

BORUSSIA DORTMUND

UEFA EUROPA LEAGUE

Play-Offs – Qarabağ FK (AZE)
H 4-0 *Kagawa (13, 41), Barrios (21, 29)*
Weidenfeller, Subotić, Kehl (Bender 66), Nuri, Hummels, Błaszczykowski (Götze 49), Barrios, Grosskreutz, Kagawa (Lewandowski 70), Piszczek, Schmelzer. Coach: Jürgen Klopp (GER)
Yellow Card(s): Hummels 55, Subotić 60, Bender 81
A 1-0 *Barrios (90+1)*
Weidenfeller, Subotić, Kehl, Nuri, Hummels, Barrios, Grosskreutz (Götze 61), Kagawa (Lewandowski 61), Owomoyela, Piszczek (Rangelov 76), Schmelzer. Coach: Jürgen Klopp (GER)
Yellow Card(s): Kagawa 10

Group J
Match 1 – FC Karpaty Lviv (UKR)
A 4-3 *Nuri (12p), Götze (27, 90+2), Barrios (87)*
Weidenfeller, Subotić, Nuri, Hummels, Barrios, Grosskreutz (Lewandowski 64), Bender (Antônio da Silva 80), Kagawa (Błaszczykowski 64), Owomoyela, Schmelzer, Götze. Coach: Jürgen Klopp (GER)
Yellow Card(s): Hummels 25, Lewandowski 68
Match 2 – Sevilla FC (ESP)
H 0-1
Weidenfeller, Subotić, Nuri, Hummels, Błaszczykowski (Lewandowski 76), Barrios, Grosskreutz (Antônio da Silva 86), Bender (Owomoyela 76), Kagawa, Piszczek, Schmelzer. Coach: Jürgen Klopp (GER)
Red Card(s): Schmelzer 49
Yellow Card(s): Schmelzer 45+1, Schmelzer 49, Grosskreutz 52, Hummels 70

Match 3 – Paris Saint-Germain FC (FRA)
H 1-1 *Nuri (50p)*
Weidenfeller, Subotić, Nuri, Hummels, Błaszczykowski (Feulner 82), Dedé, Barrios, Grosskreutz, Bender (Götze 46), Kagawa (Lewandowski 65), Piszczek. Coach: Jürgen Klopp (GER)
Match 4 – Paris Saint-Germain FC (FRA)
A 0-0
Weidenfeller, Subotić, Nuri, Hummels, Barrios (Lewandowski 68), Grosskreutz, Bender, Kagawa, Piszczek (Błaszczykowski 46), Schmelzer, Götze (Feulner 87). Coach: Jürgen Klopp (GER)
Yellow Card(s): Barrios 68
Match 5 – FC Karpaty Lviv (UKR)
H 3-0 *Kagawa (5), Hummels (49), Lewandowski (89)*
Weidenfeller, Subotić, Lewandowski, Nuri, Hummels, Błaszczykowski, Grosskreutz (Le Tallec 80), Bender (Antônio da Silva 67), Kagawa (Zidan 67), Piszczek, Schmelzer. Coach: Jürgen Klopp (GER)
Match 6 – Sevilla FC (ESP)
A 2-2 *Kagawa (4), Subotić (49)*
Weidenfeller, Subotić, Nuri, Hummels, Błaszczykowski (Lewandowski 67), Barrios, Bender (Antônio da Silva 78), Kagawa, Piszczek, Schmelzer (Le Tallec 88), Götze. Coach: Jürgen Klopp (GER)
Yellow Card(s): Schmelzer 36, Subotić 89, Weidenfeller 90

VFB STUTTGART

UEFA EUROPA LEAGUE

Third Qualifying Round – Molde FK (NOR)
A 3-2 *Rudy (27), Kuzmanović (74), Harnik (82)*
Ulreich, Molinaro, Niedermeier, Kuzmanović, Marica, Gebhart, Rudy (Didavi 72), Gentner, Celozzi, Pogrebnyak (Harnik 79), Träsch (Funk 79). Coach: Christian Gross (SUI)
Yellow Card(s): Träsch 29, Niedermeier 81, Gebhart 86
H 2-2 *Pogrebnyak (55), Gebhart (90+3)*
Ulreich, Molinaro, Niedermeier, Kuzmanović, Marica (Harnik 86), Gebhart, Funk (Boulahrouz 61), Rudy (Didavi 71), Gentner, Pogrebnyak, Träsch. Coach: Christian Gross (SUI)
Yellow Card(s): Kuzmanović 68

Play-Offs – ŠK Slovan Bratislava (SVK)
A 1-0 *Harnik (88)*
Ulreich, Degen, Molinaro, Niedermeier, Kuzmanović, Gebhart, Cacau (Marica 85), Gentner, Boulahrouz, Pogrebnyak (Harnik 67), Träsch (Audel 61). Coach: Christian Gross (SUI)
Yellow Card(s): Degen 45+1
H 2-2 *Gebhart (56), Gentner (64)*
Ulreich, Molinaro, Niedermeier, Kuzmanović, Marica (Harnik 46), Gebhart (Funk 89), Cacau, Gentner, Boulahrouz, Didavi (Audel 68), Träsch. Coach: Christian Gross (SUI)
Yellow Card(s): Gebhart 73, Cacau 90+3

Group H
Match 1 – BSC Young Boys (SUI)
H 3-0 *Cacau (23p), Gentner (59), Taşçı (90+1)*
Ulreich, Taşçı, Niedermeier, Kuzmanović, Boka, Cacau (Harnik 68), Camoranesi (Marica 80), Gentner, Didavi (Molinaro 84), Pogrebnyak, Träsch. Coach: Christian Gross (SUI)
Yellow Card(s): Pogrebnyak 55, Marica 87
Match 2 – Odense BK (DEN)
A 2-1 *Kuzmanović (72), Harnik (86)*
Ulreich, Molinaro (Boka 60), Taşçı, Kuzmanović, Marica, Delpierre, Cacau (Harnik 73), Camoranesi, Gentner, Celozzi, Bah. Coach: Christian Gross (SUI)
Yellow Card(s): Cacau 35, Boka 68, Gentner 74
Match 3 – Getafe CF (ESP)
H 1-0 *Marica (29)*
Ulreich, Niedermeier, Kuzmanović, Marica (Pogrebnyak 66), Boka, Cacau,

Camoranesi, Gentner, Boulahrouz (Bah 75), Celozzi, Träsch (Funk 65). Coach: Jens Keller (GER)
Yellow Card(s): Gentner 88
Match 4 – Getafe CF (ESP)
A 3-0 *Marica (26), Gebhart (64), Harnik (76)*
Ulreich, Molinaro, Taşçı (Gebhart 58), Harnik, Kuzmanović, Marica, Funk, Boka, Delpierre (Niedermeier 46), Camoranesi (Gentner 71), Bah. Coach: Jens Keller (GER)
Red Card(s): Marica 79
Yellow Card(s): Funk 49, Bah 75, Boka 86
Match 5 – BSC Young Boys (SUI)
A 2-4 *Pogrebnyak (48), Schipplock (68)*
Ziegler, Degen (Funk 69), Molinaro, Niedermeier, Harnik (Didavi 74), Kuzmanović, Camoranesi, Élson, Pogrebnyak (Schipplock 66), Bah, Bičakčić. Coach: Jens Keller (GER)
Yellow Card(s): Élson 32
Match 6 – Odense BK (DEN)
H 5-1 *Gebhart (20), Høegh (48og), Gentner (65), Møller Christensen (70og), Marica (90+3)*
Ulreich, Degen, Molinaro, Niedermeier, Kuzmanović, Marica, Gebhart (Camoranesi 59), Boka, Pogrebnyak (Cacau 71), Bah (Gentner 59), Bičakčić. Coach: Bruno Labbadia (GER)
Yellow Card(s): Gebhart 31, Kuzmanović 87

Round of 32 – SL Benfica (POR)
A 1-2 *Harnik (21)*
Ulreich, Molinaro, Taşçı, Harnik, Kuzmanović (Niedermeier 76), Delpierre, Cacau, Boulahrouz, Okazaki, Träsch, Hajnal (Élson 63). Coach: Bruno Labbadia (GER)
Yellow Card(s): Taşçı 14, Harnik 26, Delpierre 59
H 0-2
Ziegler (Ulreich 52), Molinaro, Niedermeier, Harnik, Kuzmanović, Delpierre, Boulahrouz (Gebhart 61), Okazaki, Träsch, Schipplock, Hajnal (Élson 78). Coach: Bruno Labbadia (GER)
Red Card(s): Kuzmanović 90+7
Yellow Card(s): Delpierre 46, Okazaki 77, Gebhart 81, Molinaro 90+1

GREECE

PANATHINAIKOS FC

UEFA CHAMPIONS LEAGUE

Group D
Match 1 – FC Barcelona (ESP)
A 1-5 *Govou (20)*
Tzorvas, Boumsong, Kanté, Cissé, Govou (Luis García 70), Leto (Ninis 80), Gilberto Silva, Marinos, Simão, Vyntra, Katsouranis (Karagounis 64). Coach: Nikos Nioplias (GRE)
Yellow Card(s): Karagounis 85
Match 2 – FC København (DEN)
H 0-2
Tzorvas, Sarriegi, Ninis (Plessis 58), Cissé, Leto, Luis García (Spiropoulos 46), Gilberto Silva, Marinos, Simão, Vyntra, Katsouranis (Karagounis 46). Coach: Nikos Nioplias (GRE)
Red Card(s): Gilberto Silva 48
Yellow Card(s): Gilberto Silva 36, Gilberto Silva 48, Karagounis 72
Match 3 – FC Rubin Kazan (RUS)
H 0-0
Tzorvas, Sarriegi, Boumsong, Cissé, Luis García, Marinos (Mavrias 78), Simão, Vyntra, Karagounis (Hristodoulopoulos 62), Katsouranis (Plessis 62), Spiropoulos. Coach: Nikos Nioplias (GRE)
Yellow Card(s): Simão 90+1
Match 4 – FC Rubin Kazan (RUS)
A 0-0
Tzorvas, Boumsong (Marinos 58), Kanté, Cissé, Luis García (Govou 69), Gilberto Silva, Simão, Vyntra, Karagounis (Hristodoulopoulos 81), Katsouranis, Spiropoulos. Coach: Nikos Nioplias (GRE)
Yellow Card(s): Vyntra 71, Karagounis 76, Marinos 85
Match 5 – FC Barcelona (ESP)
H 0-3
Tzorvas, Boumsong, Kanté, Cissé, Luis García (Petropoulos 63), Gilberto Silva, Hristodoulopoulos, Marinos (Dimoutsos 46), Vyntra, Katsouranis (Plessis 67), Spiropoulos. Coach: Jesualdo Ferreira (POR)
Yellow Card(s): Dimoutsos 66
Match 6 – FC København (DEN)
A 1-3 *Kanté (90+2)*
Tzorvas, Boumsong, Kanté, Cissé, Luis García (Petropoulos 74), Gilberto Silva (Ninis 46), Hristodoulopoulos (Leto 46), Marinos, Simão, Vyntra, Spiropoulos. Coach: Jesualdo Ferreira (POR)
Yellow Card(s): Simão 12, Marinos 44, Luis García 45+2, Leto 67

No	Player	Nat	DoB	Aps	(s)	Gls
	Goalkeepers					
30	Alexandros Tzorvas		12/8/82	6		
	Defenders					
4	Jean-Alain Boumsong	FRA	14/12/79	5		
5	Cédric Kanté	MLI	6/7/79	4		1
3	Josu Sarriegi	ESP	19/1/79	2		
31	Nikolaos Spiropoulos		10/10/83	4	(1)	
24	Loukas Vyntra		5/2/81	6		
	Midfielders					
21	Elini Dimoutsos		18/6/88		(1)	
15	Gilberto Silva	BRA	7/10/76	5		
26	Georgios Karagounis		6/3/77	2	(2)	
29	Konstantinos Katsouranis		21/6/79	5		
11	Sebastián Leto	ARG	30/8/86	2	(1)	
22	Stergos Marinos		17/9/87	5	(1)	
35	Haralambos Mavrias		21/2/94		(1)	
7	Sotirios Ninis		3/4/90	1	(2)	
19	Damien Plessis	FRA	5/3/88		(3)	
23	Simão	MOZ	23/7/88	5		
	Forwards					
9	Djibril Cissé	FRA	12/8/81	6		
10	Sidney Govou	FRA	27/7/79	1	(1)	1
20	Lazaros Hristodoulopoulos		19/12/86	2	(2)	
14	Luis García	ESP	24/6/78	5	(1)	
28	Antonios Petropoulos		28/1/86		(2)	

PAOK FC

UEFA CHAMPIONS LEAGUE

Third Qualifying Round – AFC Ajax (NED)
A 1-1 *Ivić (73)*
Chalkias (Krešić 15), Boussaïdi, Pablo García, Vitolo, Cirillo, Salpingidis (Papazoglou 90+2), Sorlin, Malezas, Vieirinha, Ivić (Fotakis 75), Sznaucner. Coach: Pavlos Dermitzakis (GRE)
Yellow Card(s): Boussaïdi 34, Vitolo 62
H 3-3 *Vieirinha (16), Salpingidis (56), Ivić (90+1)*
Krešić, Boussaïdi, Pablo García, Vitolo (Muslimović 64), Cirillo, Salpingidis, Sorlin, Contreras, Vieirinha, Ivić, Sznaucner (Filomeno 84). Coach: Pavlos Dermitzakis (GRE)
Yellow Card(s): Cirillo 61, Ivić 90+2

UEFA EUROPA LEAGUE

Play-Offs – Fenerbahçe SK (TUR)
H 1-0 *Vieirinha (19)*
Krešić, Boussaïdi, Pablo García, Vitolo, Salpingidis (Papazoglou 86), Muslimović (Sorlin 60), Malezas, Contreras, Lino, Vieirinha, Ivić (Filomeno 77). Coach: Pavlos Dermitzakis (GRE)
Red Card(s): Vitolo 57
Yellow Card(s): Vitolo 50, Vitolo 57, Ivić 73

A 1-1 (aet) *Muslimović (102)*
Krešić, Boussaïdi (Sznaucner 75), Pablo García, Salpingidis, Sorlin, Malezas, Contreras, Lino, Fotakis (Koutsianikoulis 91), Vieirinha, Filomeno (Muslimović 83). Coach: Pavlos Dermitzakis (GRE)
Yellow Card(s): Boussaïdi 6, Malezas 67, Pablo García 87, Muslimović 103

Group D
Match 1 – Club Brugge KV (BEL)
A 1-1 *Malezas (78)*
Krešić, Pablo García, Vitolo, Salpingidis (Filomeno 90+1), Malezas, Papazoglou (El Zhar 73), Contreras, Lino, Vieirinha, Ivić (Fotakis 89), Sznaucner. Coach: Pavlos Dermitzakis (GRE)
Yellow Card(s): Vitolo 10, Sznaucner 54
Match 2 – NK Dinamo Zagreb (CRO)
H 1-0 *Ivić (56)*
Krešić, Boussaïdi (Sakellariou 16), Pablo García, Vitolo, El Zhar (Salpingidis 80), Cirillo (Zuela 63), Muslimović, Contreras, Vieirinha, Ivić, Sznaucner. Coach: Pavlos Dermitzakis (GRE)
Yellow Card(s): Sakellariou 58, Sznaucner 81
Match 3 – Villarreal CF (ESP)
A 0-1
Krešić, Boussaïdi, Vitolo, El Zhar (Koutsianikoulis 85), Cirillo, Muslimović (Athanasiadis 80), Contreras, Fotakis, Vieirinha, Ivić, Sznaucner. Coach: Ioakim Havos (GRE)
Yellow Card(s): Cirillo 24, Contreras 57, Sznaucner 59, Boussaïdi 86
Match 4 – Villarreal CF (ESP)
H 1-0 *Vieirinha (70)*
Krešić, Boussaïdi, Pablo García, Vitolo, Cirillo, Salpingidis (Muslimović 65), Contreras, Fotakis (Filomeno 90+1), Vieirinha, Ivić (El Zhar 41), Sakellariou. Coach: Ioakim Havos (GRE)
Yellow Card(s): Contreras 13, Muslimović 87
Match 5 – Club Brugge KV (BEL)
H 1-1 *Vieirinha (25)*
Krešić, Pablo García, Vitolo, Cirillo, Salpingidis (Athanasiadis 82), Contreras, Fotakis, Vieirinha, Ivić (El Zhar 72), Sakellariou, Zuela. Coach: Ioakim Havos (GRE)
Yellow Card(s): Vitolo 33, Zuela 58, Cirillo 65
Match 6 – NK Dinamo Zagreb (CRO)
A 1-0 *Salpingidis (60)*
Chalkias, Boussaïdi, Pablo García, Vitolo, Cirillo, Salpingidis (El Zhar 68), Contreras, Fotakis (Balafas 90), Vieirinha, Sznaucner, Athanasiadis (Filomeno 82). Coach: Ioakim Havos (GRE)
Yellow Card(s): Pablo García 36, Salpingidis 60, Boussaïdi 82

Round of 32 – PFC CSKA Moskva (RUS)
H 0-1
Chalkias (Krešić 46), Pablo García, Vitolo (El Zhar 57), Cirillo, Salpingidis, Contreras, Lino, Vieirinha, Ivić (Athanasiadis 70), Sznaucner, Tsoukalas. Coach: Ioakim Havos (GRE)
Yellow Card(s): Vieirinha 90+1
A 1-1 *Muslimović (67)*
Krešić, Pablo García, Cirillo, Salpingidis, Muslimović, Contreras, Lino, Vieirinha, Ivić (Athanasiadis 87), Sznaucner, Tsoukalas. Coach: Ioakim Havos (GRE)
Yellow Card(s): Salpingidis 59, Krešić 79, Pablo García 90+2, Cirillo 90+7

OLYMPIACOS FC

UEFA EUROPA LEAGUE

Second Qualifying Round – KS Besa (ALB)
A 5-0 *Óscar (19, 30), Dudu Cearense (46), Diogo (70, 84)*
Nikopolidis, Modesto, Galitsios, Óscar (Mitroglou 67), Dudu Cearense (Katsikogiannis 84), Diogo, Zairi (Fetfatzidis 75), Mirallas, Raúl Bravo, Holebas, Maresca. Coach: Ewald Lienen (GER)
H 6-1 *Dudu Cearense (46, 79), Derbyshire (53), Maresca (75, 90), Fetfatzidis (88)*
Urko Pardo, Mellberg, Galitsios, Óscar (Mitroglou 46), Dudu Cearense, Diogo (Fetfatzidis 70), Zairi (Derbyshire 46), Mirallas, Raúl Bravo, Holebas, Maresca. Coach: Ewald Lienen (GER)

Third Qualifying Round – Maccabi Tel-Aviv FC (ISR)
H 2-1 *Zairi (67), Rommedahl (73)*
Nikopolidis, Modesto, Mellberg, Galitsios, Dudu Cearense, Derbyshire (Mitroglou 58), Diogo, Mirallas (Zairi 52), Holebas, Rommedahl (Ibagaza 82), Maresca. Coach: Ewald Lienen (GER)
Yellow Card(s): Holebas 17, Diogo 34
A 0-1
Nikopolidis, Modesto (Torosidis 46), Mellberg, Óscar, Dudu Cearense, Diogo, Zairi (Ibagaza 58), Holebas, A. Papadopoulos, Rommedahl, Maresca (Mitroglou 71). Coach: Ewald Lienen (GER)
Red Card(s): Diogo 90+1
Yellow Card(s): A. Papadopoulos 26, Zairi 32, Modesto 36

AEK ATHENS FC

UEFA EUROPA LEAGUE

Play-Offs – Dundee United FC (SCO)
A 1-0 *Djebbour (11)*
Saja, Kafes, Manolas, Jahić, Leonardo (Burns 71), Djebbour (Diop 81), Makos, Lagos, Scocco (Éder 89), Liberopoulos, Dellas. Coach: Dušan Bajević (SRB)
Yellow Card(s): Scocco 31, Liberopoulos 41, Makos 74, Dellas 84
H 1-1 *Diop (23)*
Saja, Kafes, Manolas, Jahić, Leonardo (Karabelas 89), Djebbour (Blanco 58), Makos, Lagos, Diop, Georgeas (Gentsoglou 46), Scocco. Coach: Dušan Bajević (SRB)
Yellow Card(s): Lagos 16, Jahić 26, Makos 90+1, Saja 90+2

Group G
Match 1 – HNK Hajduk Split (CRO)
H 3-1 *Djebbour (12), Liberopoulos (65), Scocco (89)*
Arabatzis, Kafes (Leonardo 74), Manolas, Jahić, Djebbour, Lagos, Diop, Burns (Patsatzoglou 70), Scocco, Liberopoulos (Blanco 90+2), Dellas. Coach: Dušan Bajević (SRB)
Yellow Card(s): Diop 28
Match 2 – FC Zenit St Petersburg (RUS)
A 2-4 *Liberopoulos (37), Kafes (83p)*
Arabatzis, Kafes, Patsatzoglou, Nasuti, Djebbour (Diop 58), Makos, Lagos, Scocco (Blanco 82), Liberopoulos (Jahić 46), Dellas, Gentsoglou. Coach: Bledar Kola (ALB)
Red Card(s): Nasuti 41
Yellow Card(s): Kafes 43, Makos 84
Match 3 – RSC Anderlecht (BEL)
A 0-3
Saja, Kafes, Makos (Djebbour 46), Argiriou, Blanco, Lagos, Éder (Leonardo 64), Diop, Scocco (Burns 22), Dellas, Gentsoglou. Coach: Manuel Jiménez (ESP)
Yellow Card(s): Makos 23, Argiriou 50, Lagos 83
Match 4 – RSC Anderlecht (BEL)
H 1-1 *Blanco (48p)*
Saja, Kafes, Patsatzoglou, Nasuti, Manolas, Leonardo (Éder 66), Djebbour, Dadomo, Blanco, Lagos (Froxylias 73), Gentsoglou (Makos 87). Coach: Manuel Jiménez (ESP)
Yellow Card(s): Gentsoglou 12, Leonardo 45+3
Match 5 – HNK Hajduk Split (CRO)
A 3-1 *Scocco (50p), Manolas (61), Blanco (84)*
Saja, Manolas, Jahić, Makos, Karabelas, Diop, Burns (Lagos 70), Scocco (Leonardo 77), Liberopoulos (Blanco 80), Dellas, Gentsoglou. Coach: Manuel Jiménez (ESP)
Yellow Card(s): Gentsoglou 31

Match 6 – FC Zenit St Petersburg (RUS)
H 0-3
Saja, Kafes, Manolas, Jahić, Makos (Leonardo 80), Karabelas, Blanco, Scocco, Liberopoulos, Dellas (Diop 74), Gentsoglou (Burns 55). Coach: Manuel Jiménez (ESP)
Yellow Card(s): Manolas 37, Makos 72

ARIS THESSALONIKI FC

UEFA EUROPA LEAGUE

Third Qualifying Round – Jagiellonia Białystok (POL)
A 2-1 *Toni Calvo (4p, 7)*
Sifakis, Neto, Ronaldo, Nafti (Prittas 79), Toni Calvo (Česnauskis 64), Toja, Cesarec, Koke (Kaznaferis 70), Michel, Javito, Lazaridis. Coach: Héctor Cúper (ARG)
Yellow Card(s): Cesarec 38, Toni Calvo 41, Neto 90+2
H 2-2 *Cesarec (19, 75p)*
Sifakis, Neto (Koulouheris 85), Ronaldo, Nafti (Prittas 77), Toni Calvo (Česnauskis 69), Toja, Cesarec, Koke, Michel, Javito, Lazaridis. Coach: Héctor Cúper (ARG)
Yellow Card(s): Toja 31, Nafti 59, Koulouheris 90, Sifakis 90+1

Play-Offs – FK Austria Wien (AUT)
H 1-0 *Ruiz (90+3)*
Sifakis, Neto, Oriol, Ronaldo, Nafti, Toja (Prittas 78), Cesarec (Ruiz 63), Koke, Michel, Javito, Česnauskis (Mendrinos 60). Coach: Héctor Cúper (ARG)
A 1-1 *Ruiz (42)*
Sifakis, Neto, Ronaldo, Nafti, Toni Calvo (Česnauskis 57), Toja (Prittas 55), Koke, Ruiz (Cesarec 74), Michel, Javito, Lazaridis. Coach: Héctor Cúper (ARG)
Yellow Card(s): Toja 33, Neto 57, Prittas 79, Ronaldo 85, Cesarec 86

Group B
Match 1 – Club Atlético de Madrid (ESP)
H 1-0 *Javito (59)*
Sifakis, Ronaldo, Koke, Ruiz (Kaznaferis 90+2), Faty, Michel, Mendrinos, Javito, Lazaridis, Vangjeli, Prittas. Coach: Héctor Cúper (ARG)
Yellow Card(s): Prittas 45, Ruiz 73, Vangjeli 90+2
Match 2 – Rosenborg BK (NOR)
A 1-2 *Ruiz (43)*
Sifakis, Ronaldo, Toni Calvo (Česnauskis 82), Koke, Ruiz (Cesarec 63), Faty (Toja 71), Michel, Javito, Lazaridis, Vangjeli, Prittas. Coach: Héctor Cúper (ARG)
Yellow Card(s): Vangjeli 21, Ronaldo 61
Match 3 – Bayer 04 Leverkusen (GER)
H 0-0
Sifakis, Ronaldo, Toni Calvo, Toja, Koke (Mendrinos 70), Ruiz, Faty, Michel, Javito, Lazaridis, Vangjeli. Coach: Héctor Cúper (ARG)
Yellow Card(s): Faty 60
Match 4 – Bayer 04 Leverkusen (GER)
A 0-1
Sifakis, Ronaldo, Toni Calvo (Kaznaferis 79), Toja, Koke (Prittas 90+1), Ruiz (Česnauskis 56), Faty, Michel, Javito, Lazaridis, Vangjeli. Coach: Héctor Cúper (ARG)
Match 5 – Club Atlético de Madrid (ESP)
A 3-2 *Koke (2, 51p), Lazaridis (81)*
Sifakis, Oriol, Toja, Cesarec (Ruiz 83), Koke (Prittas 77), Faty, Michel, Mendrinos (Kaznaferis 72), Javito, Lazaridis, Vangjeli. Coach: Héctor Cúper (ARG)
Yellow Card(s): Javito 59, Mendrinos 82, Sifakis 90+4
Match 6 – Rosenborg BK (NOR)
H 2-0 *Cesarec (45+1), Faty (90+2)*
Sifakis, Koulouheris, Toja, Cesarec (Ruiz 79), Koke (Faty 88), Michel, Mendrinos (Kaznaferis 83), Javito, Lazaridis, Vangjeli, Prittas. Coach: Héctor Cúper (ARG)

Round of 32 – Manchester City FC (ENG)
H 0-0
Sifakis, Neto (Castillo 88), Ronaldo, Toja, Faty, Michel, Bobadilla (Cesarec 72), Lazaridis, Vangjeli, Prittas, Sakata. Coach: Ioannis Mihalitsios (GRE)
A 0-3
Sifakis, Neto (Kaznaferis 80), Ronaldo, Toja, Faty, Michel, Bobadilla (Koke 61), Lazaridis, Vangjeli, Prittas, Sakata (Mendrinos 46). Coach: Ioannis Mihalitsios (GRE)
Yellow Card(s): Vangjeli 38, Neto 43, Prittas 72

HUNGARY

DEBRECENI VSC

UEFA CHAMPIONS LEAGUE

Second Qualifying Round – FC Levadia Tallinn (EST)
A 1-1 *Rezes (90)*
Malinauskas, Kabát (Rezes 69), Komlósi, Fodor, Mijadinoski, Bódi (Yannick 62), Nagy, Kiss (Dombi 78), Coulibaly, Szakály, Czvitkovics. Coach: András Herczeg (HUN)
Yellow Card(s): Komlósi 6, Nagy 30, Fodor 63
H 3-2 *Coulibaly (24), Yannick (32), Szakály (55)*
Malinauskas, Komlósi, Yannick (Dombi 85), Fodor, Mijadinoski, Nagy, Kiss, Coulibaly, Szakály (Varga 73), Kulcsár (Rezes 46), Czvitkovics. Coach: András Herczeg (HUN)
Yellow Card(s): Rezes 57

Third Qualifying Round – FC Basel 1893 (SUI)
H 0-2
Verpecz, Rezes (Farkas 54), Komlósi, Yannick (Dombi 74), Fodor, Bernáth, Mijadinoski, Kiss, Varga, Coulibaly, Czvitkovics. Coach: András Herczeg (HUN)
A 1-3 *Coulibaly (74)*
Verpecz, Komlósi, Yannick (Kabát 67), Bernáth, Mijadinoski, Kiss, Varga, Coulibaly, Kulcsár (Bódi 67), Czvitkovics (Farkas 81), Laczkó. Coach: András Herczeg (HUN)

UEFA EUROPA LEAGUE

Play-Offs – PFC Litex Lovech (BUL)
H 2-0 *Coulibaly (22), Laczkó (33)*
Malinauskas, Kabát (Farkas 81), Komlósi, Bernáth, Mijadinoski, Kiss, Varga, Coulibaly (Yannick 86), Szakály (Dombi 76), Czvitkovics, Laczkó. Coach: András Herczeg (HUN)
Yellow Card(s): Bernáth 76, Varga 90+1
A 2-1 *Yannick (53), Czvitkovics (81)*
Malinauskas, Kabát (Yannick 50), Komlósi, Bernáth, Mijadinoski, Kiss, Varga (Máté 90), Coulibaly, Szakály (Dombi 74), Czvitkovics, Laczkó. Coach: András Herczeg (HUN)
Yellow Card(s): Laczkó 24, Mijadinoski 58

Group I
Match 1 – FC Metalist Kharkiv (UKR)
H 0-5
Malinauskas, Kabát, Komlósi, Yannick (Coulibaly 46), Mijadinoski, Nagy, Kiss (Ramos 46), Varga, Szakály (Rezes 65), Czvitkovics, Laczkó. Coach: András Herczeg (HUN)
Red Card(s): Kabát 42
Yellow Card(s): Nagy 66
Match 2 – UC Sampdoria (ITA)
A 0-1
Malinauskas, Šimac, Yannick (Bódi 87), Mijadinoski, Nagy, Kiss, Varga, Coulibaly, Szakály (Kulcsár 46), Czvitkovics, Laczkó. Coach: András Herczeg (HUN)
Yellow Card(s): Laczkó 18, Mijadinoski 18, Kiss 62

Match 3 – PSV Eindhoven (NED)
H 1-2 *Mijadinoski (35)*
Malinauskas, Šimac, Yannick (Bódi 66), Fodor, Mijadinoski, Nagy, Kiss, Varga, Coulibaly, Szakály (Rezes 79), Czvitkovics. Coach: András Herczeg (HUN)
Match 4 – PSV Eindhoven (NED)
A 0-3
Malinauskas, Šimac, Mijadinoski, Bódi (Dombi 73), Nagy, Kiss, Varga, Coulibaly, Szakály, Czvitkovics, Laczkó. Coach: András Herczeg (HUN)
Yellow Card(s): Laczkó 64, Mijadinoski 90
Match 5 – FC Metalist Kharkiv (UKR)
A 1-2 *Czvitkovics (48)*
Malinauskas, Šimac, Kabát (Coulibaly 64), Bernáth, Mijadinoski, Bódi (Yannick 55), Kiss, Varga, Szakály (Ramos 81), Czvitkovics, Laczkó. Coach: András Herczeg (HUN)
Yellow Card(s): Šimac 22, Ramos 90+1
Match 6 – UC Sampdoria (ITA)
H 2-0 *Kabát (48), Volta (86og)*
Verpecz, Šimac, Kabát, Yannick (Kiss 66), Bernáth, Mijadinoski, Bódi (Dombi 89), Varga, Szakály (Fodor 90+2), Czvitkovics, Laczkó. Coach: András Herczeg (HUN)
Yellow Card(s): Bódi 78

VIDEOTON FC

UEFA EUROPA LEAGUE

Second Qualifying Round – NK Maribor (SVN)
H 1-1 *Horváth (79)*
Božović, Andić, Horváth, Lipták, Polonkai (Djordjić 46), Sándor, Farkas, Gosztonyi (Nikolić 83), Vujović (Lencse 46), André Alves, Elek. Coach: György Mezey (HUN)
Yellow Card(s): André Alves 73, Djordjić 77, Lipták 87
A 0-2
Božović, Horváth, Lipták, Polonkai (Djordjić 27), Sándor, Farkas, Gosztonyi, Lencse (Nikolić 62), Lázár, André Alves, Elek. Coach: György Mezey (HUN)
Yellow Card(s): Elek 19, Horváth 55

GYŐRI ETO FC

UEFA EUROPA LEAGUE

First Qualifying Round – FC Nitra (SVK)
A 2-2 *Kink (39, 58)*
Sánta, Stanišić, Fehér, Pilibaitis (Copa 31), Szabó (Völgyi 75), Aleksidze, Kink, Nicorec, Tokody, Đorđević, Koltai (Ćetković 63). Coach: Attila Pintér (HUN)
Yellow Card(s): Nicorec 87
H 3-1 *Aleksidze (22), Nicorec (60), Kink (90+2)*
Sánta, Fehér, Pilibaitis, Szabó, Aleksidze (Copa 75), Kiss (Babić 46), Kink, Nicorec, Tokody, Đorđević, Koltai (Ceolin 57). Coach: Attila Pintér (HUN)
Yellow Card(s): Nicorec 28, Kink 41, Tokody 53

Second Qualifying Round – FC Atyrau (KAZ)
A 3-0 *Pilibaitis (26), Bouguerra (88)*
Stevanović, Stanišić, Fehér, Pilibaitis, Szabó, Aleksidze (Trajković 46), Copa, Kink (Bouguerra 65), Babić, Đorđević, Koltai (Ceolin 46). Coach: Attila Pintér (HUN)
Yellow Card(s): Babić 19, Fehér 77, Bouguerra 79
H 2-0 *Aleksidze (47), Nicorec (52)*
Stevanović, Stanišić, Dinjar (Copa 59), Pilibaitis, Szabó, Aleksidze (Bouguerra 77), Kink, Nicorec, Babić, Đorđević, Koltai (Sharashenidze 67). Coach: Attila Pintér (HUN)

Third Qualifying Round – Montpellier Hérault SC (FRA)
H 0-1
Stevanović, Stanišić, Dinjar, Pilibaitis, Szabó, Aleksidze (Bouguerra 58), Ceolin, Nicorec (Copa 52), Babić, Đorđević, Koltai (Sharashenidze 66). Coach: Attila Pintér (HUN)
Yellow Card(s): Copa 82
A 1-0 *Babić (40)* **(aet; 4-3 on pens)**
Stevanović, Stanišić, Pilibaitis, Szabó, Aleksidze, Ceolin (Copa 66), Nicorec (Fehér 46), Babić, Tokody, Đorđević, Koltai (Ćetković 78). Coach: Attila Pintér (HUN)
Red Card(s): Stanišić 45
Yellow Card(s): Stanišić 6, Stanišić 45, Babić 89, Aleksidze 90+3

Play-Offs – NK Dinamo Zagreb (CRO)
H 0-2
Stevanović, Dinjar (Ji-Paraná 34), Fehér, Pilibaitis (Trajković 78), Szabó, Aleksidze, Ceolin, Copa (Bouguerra 53), Tokody, Đorđević, Koltai. Coach: Attila Pintér (HUN)
Yellow Card(s): Pilibaitis 21, Đorđević 52, Trajković 87, Szabó 90+1
A 1-2 *Ceolin (17)*
Stevanović, Stanišić (Szabó 33), Fehér, Pilibaitis, Aleksidze (Bouguerra 66), Ceolin, Völgyi, Babić, Tokody, Đorđević, Koltai (Dinjar 56). Coach: Attila Pintér (HUN)
Yellow Card(s): Szabó 45, Fehér 64, Stevanović 82, Babić 87, Völgyi 88

ZALAEGERSZEGI TE

UEFA EUROPA LEAGUE

First Qualifying Round – KF Tirana (ALB)
A 0-0
Vlaszák, Kocsárdi (Kovács 61), Bogunović, Pavićević, Illés (Horváth 78), Panikvar, Szalai, Máté (Magasföldi 46), Kamber, Miljatovič, Rajcomar. Coach: János Csank (HUN)
Yellow Card(s): Máté 43, Kamber 74
H 0-1 (aet)
Vlaszák, Kocsárdi, Bogunović, Pavićević (Rajcomar 106), Magasföldi (Balázs 46), Illés (Horváth 91), Panikvar, Rudņevs, Máté, Kamber, Miljatovič. Coach: János Csank (HUN)
Yellow Card(s): Panikvar 33, Illés 87, Miljatovič 90+2

ICELAND

FH HAFNARFJÖRDUR

UEFA CHAMPIONS LEAGUE

Second Qualifying Round – FC BATE Borisov (BLR)
A 1-5 *Björnsson (89)*
Gunnleifsson, Thrastarson (Bjarnason 59), Valgardsson, Nielsen (Motland 66), Snorrason, Vidarsson, Sverrisson, Vilhjálmsson, Gudnason, Sævarsson, Björnsson. Coach: Heimir Gudjónsson (ISL)
Yellow Card(s): Gunnleifsson 31
H 0-1
Gunnleifsson, Thrastarson, Valgardsson (Gunnlaugsson 43), Nielsen (Bjarnason 78), Snorrason, Vidarsson, Motland, Sverrisson, Vilhjálmsson, Jónsson, Björnsson (Gudnason 64). Coach: Heimir Gudjónsson (ISL)
Yellow Card(s): Vidarsson 75, Gunnlaugsson 82, Jónsson 90+3

BREIDABLIK

UEFA EUROPA LEAGUE

Second Qualifying Round – Motherwell FC (SCO)
A 0-1
Kale, Margeirsson, Helgason, Ársælsson, Steindórsson (Sigurgeirsson 73), Finnbogason, Kristjánsson, Elísabetarson, Jónsson, Adalsteinsson, Pétursson. Coach: Ólafur Helgi Kristjánsson (ISL)
H 0-1
Kale, Margeirsson (Baldvinsson 72), Helgason, Ársælsson, Steindórsson, Finnbogason, Kristjánsson, Elísabetarson, Jónsson (Gunnarsson 78), Adalsteinsson, Pétursson (Yeoman 61). Coach: Ólafur Helgi Kristjánsson (ISL)
Yellow Card(s): Pétursson 45+1

KR REYKJAVÍK

UEFA EUROPA LEAGUE

First Qualifying Round – Glentoran FC (NIR)
H 3-0 *Gunnarsson (12), Finnbogason (32), Takefusa (63)*
Moldskred, H. Sigurdsson, Gudjónsson, Finnbogason (G. Jónsson 88), Fridgeirsson, B. Sigurdsson, Hauksson (Kristjánsson 85), Takefusa (Baldvinsson 81), Arnarsson, Rutgers, Gunnarsson. Coach: Logi Ólafsson (ISL)
Yellow Card(s): Finnbogason 87
A 2-2 *Finnbogason (45+1), Black (54og)*
Moldskred, H. Sigurdsson, Gudjónsson, Finnbogason, Fridgeirsson, B. Sigurdsson, Hauksson, Takefusa (Diogo 66), Arnarsson (E. Einarsson 56), Rutgers, Gunnarsson (G. Jónsson 80). Coach: Logi Ólafsson (ISL)
Red Card(s): Fridgeirsson 55
Yellow Card(s): H. Sigurdsson 38, Gunnarsson 78

Second Qualifying Round – FC Karpaty Lviv (UKR)
H 0-3
Moldskred, H. Sigurdsson, Gudjónsson, Finnbogason, B. Sigurdsson, Hauksson, Takefusa (Kristjánsson 70), Arnarsson (Diogo 60), Rutgers, Gunnarsson (G. Jónsson 60), E. Einarsson. Coach: Logi Ólafsson (ISL)
A 2-3 *Finnbogason (61, 65)*
Moldskred, H. Sigurdsson, Gudjónsson, Fridgeirsson, B. Sigurdsson, Hauksson, Kristjánsson (Finnbogason 23), Rutgers, G. Jónsson (Arnarsson 60), Baldvinsson (Takefusa 69), Diogo. Coach: Rúnar Kristinsson (ISL)
Yellow Card(s): G. Jónsson 57, Hauksson 90+1

FYLKIR

UEFA EUROPA LEAGUE

First Qualifying Round – FC Torpedo Zhodino (BLR)
A 0-3
Thorgeirsson, Valdimarsson, Ásgeirsson, Gíslason, Stígsson (Faye 60), Hannesson, Óskarsson (Thorsteinsson 79), Jóhannesson, Breiddal, Ingason (Thráinsson 86), Pétursson. Coach: Ólafur Thórdarson (ISL)
Yellow Card(s): Hannesson 36
H 1-3 *Faye (32p)*
Bazi, Valdimarsson, Ásgeirsson, Hannesson, Jóhannesson, Thórhallsson, Faye, Breiddal (Thorsteinsson 70), Ingason (Thráinsson 70), Arnthórsson (Hermannsson 84), Jónsson. Coach: Ólafur Thórdarson (ISL)
Yellow Card(s): Thorsteinsson 90+3

ISRAEL

HAPOEL TEL-AVIV FC

UEFA CHAMPIONS LEAGUE

Second Qualifying Round – FK Željezničar (BIH)
H 5-0 *Al Lala (10, 31, 38), Shivhon (12), Bešlija (28og)*
Ben Senan, Douglas (Fransman 65), Shivhon (Maree 74), Shechter, Badir, Vermouth, Zahavi, Al Lala (Rocchi 56), Ben Dayan, Kenda, Yadin. Coach: Eli Gutman (ISR)
A 1-0 *Douglas (76)*
Ben Senan, Douglas, Shivhon (Maree 60), Shechter, Badir, Vermouth, Zahavi (Shish 71), Al Lala (Rocchi 46), Ben Dayan, Kenda, Yadin. Coach: Eli Gutman (ISR)
Yellow Card(s): Zahavi 11, Shish 90

Third Qualifying Round – FC Aktobe (KAZ)
A 0-1
Enyeama, Douglas, Shechter, Badir, Vermouth, Zahavi, Al Lala (Sahar 57), Ben Dayan, Kenda, Yadin, Rocchi (Shivhon 68). Coach: Eli Gutman (ISR)
Yellow Card(s): Al Lala 41, Douglas 66, Shivhon 90+2
H 3-1 *Zahavi (16), Sahar (31), Ba (35og)*
Enyeama, Douglas, Shivhon (Rocchi 64), Shechter, Badir, Sahar (Al Lala 54), Vermouth, Zahavi (Abutbul 70), Kenda, Shish, Yadin. Coach: Eli Gutman (ISR)
Yellow Card(s): Shish 28, Badir 45

Play-Offs – FC Salzburg (AUT)
A 3-2 *Enyeama (3p), Sahar (44), Shechter (53)*
Enyeama, Douglas, Shivhon (Rocchi 72), Shechter, Badir, Sahar (Maree 79), Vermouth (Fransman 90+1), Zahavi, Ben Dayan, Kenda, Yadin. Coach: Eli Gutman (ISR)
Yellow Card(s): Shivhon 37, Shechter 54, Kenda 66, Enyeama 75
H 1-1 *Zahavi (90+2)*
Enyeama, Douglas, Badir, Sahar (Shish 90+1), Maree (Fransman 65), Vermouth, Zahavi, Ben Dayan, Kenda, Yadin, Rocchi (Abutbul 74). Coach: Eli Gutman (ISR)

Group B
Match 1 – SL Benfica (POR)
A 0-2
Enyeama, Douglas, Bondarv, Fransman (Badir 74), Shechter, Sahar (Tamuz 58), Vermouth, Zahavi, Ben Dayan, Yadin, Rocchi (Shivhon 61). Coach: Eli Gutman (ISR)
Yellow Card(s): Shechter 22, Ben Dayan 60
Match 2 – Olympique Lyonnais (FRA)
H 1-3 *Enyeama (79p)*
Enyeama, Douglas, Bondarv, Shechter, Badir, Sahar (Tamuz 76), Vermouth, Zahavi (Abutbul 59), Ben Dayan, Yadin, Rocchi (Shivhon 59). Coach: Eli Gutman (ISR)
Yellow Card(s): Badir 7, Ben Dayan 45+1, Shechter 55, Abutbul 86
Match 3 – FC Schalke 04 (GER)
A 1-3 *Shechter (90+3)*
Enyeama, Douglas, Shechter, Badir, Vermouth, Zahavi, Abutbul (Toama 57), Kenda, Shish, Yadin (Fransman 73), Tamuz (Sahar 58). Coach: Eli Gutman (ISR)
Yellow Card(s): Vermouth 31

Match 4 – FC Schalke 04 (GER)
H 0-0
Enyeama, Douglas (Fransman 42), Bondarv, Badir, Sahar (Maree 70), Vermouth, Toama (Shivhon 61), Zahavi, Abutbul, Ben Dayan, Tamuz. Coach: Eli Gutman (ISR)
Yellow Card(s): Zahavi 5, Badir 39
Match 5 – SL Benfica (POR)
H 3-0 *Zahavi (24, 90+2), Douglas (74)*
Enyeama, Douglas, Bondarv, Fransman, Shechter (Shivhon 58), Vermouth, Zahavi, Abutbul (Badir 78), Ben Dayan, Yadin, Tamuz (Sahar 66). Coach: Eli Gutman (ISR)
Yellow Card(s): Ben Dayan 33, Yadin 43, Fransman 52
Match 6 – Olympique Lyonnais (FRA)
A 2-2 *Sahar (63), Zahavi (69)*
Enyeama, Douglas, Bondarv, Fransman, Shechter (Sahar 25), Vermouth, Zahavi, Abutbul (Badir 80), Shish, Yadin, Tamuz (Toama 62). Coach: Eli Gutman (ISR)
Yellow Card(s): Shish 8, Sahar 90+1

No	Player	Nat	DoB	Aps	(s)	Gls
Goalkeepers						
1	Vincent Enyeama	NGA	29/8/82	6		1
Defenders						
10	Walid Badir		12/3/74	3	(3)	
19	Dedi Ben Dayan		22/11/78	4		
4	Dani Bondarv		7/2/87	5		
3	Douglas da Silva	BRA	7/3/84	6		1
6	Bevan Fransman	RSA	31/10/83	3	(2)	
23	Omri Kenda		6/7/86	1		
25	Gal Shish		28/1/89	2		
Midfielders						
18	Shay Abutbul		16/1/83	4	(1)	
27	Romain Rocchi	FRA	2/10/81	2		
7	Yossi Shivhon		22/3/82		(4)	
15	Salim Toama		9/8/79	1	(2)	
14	Gil Vermouth		5/8/85	6		
26	Avihai Yadin		26/10/86	5		
Forwards						
12	Victor Maree		31/5/89		(1)	
11	Ben Sahar		10/8/89	3	(3)	1
9	Itay Shechter		22/2/87	5		1
99	Toto Tamuz		1/4/88	4	(2)	
16	Eran Zahavi		25/7/87	6		3

MACCABI HAIFA FC

UEFA EUROPA LEAGUE

Third Qualifying Round – FC Dinamo Minsk (BLR)
H 1-0 *Dvalishvili (30)*
Edree, Canuto, Maymon, Boccoli, Culma, Dvalishvili, Refaelov (Hemed 70), Ghadir (Golasa 55), Masilela, Osman, Katan (Adrien Silva 89). Coach: Elisha Levi (ISR)
Yellow Card(s): Canuto 40
A 1-3 *Dvalishvili (27)*
Edree, Canuto, Maymon, Boccoli, Culma, Dvalishvili (Hemed 74), Refaelov (Osman 54), Golasa (Adrien Silva 52), Masilela, Katan, Meshumar. Coach: Elisha Levi (ISR)
Yellow Card(s): Canuto 24, Culma 58

MACCABI TEL-AVIV FC

UEFA EUROPA LEAGUE

Second Qualifying Round – FK Mogren (MNE)
H 2-0 *Ziv (49), Medunjanin (52)*
Strauber, Saban, Baning, Nivaldo, Medunjanin (Sidibé 66), Itzhaki, Buzaglo (Malul 76), Ziv, Yeini (Avidor 46), Colautti, Strul. Coach: Avi Nimni (ISR)
Yellow Card(s): Avidor 74
A 1-2 *Medunjanin (7)*
Strauber, Saban, Baning, Nivaldo, Medunjanin, Itzhaki, Buzaglo (Avidor 61), Ziv, Yeini (Sidibé 61), Colautti (Cahalon 77), Strul. Coach: Avi Nimni (ISR)
Yellow Card(s): Strul 32, Nivaldo 57

Third Qualifying Round – Olympiacos FC (GRE)
A 1-2 *Medunjanin (18p)*
Strauber, Saban, Baning, Nivaldo, Medunjanin (Buzaglo 82), Itzhaki (Avidor 72), Ziv, Gafni, Sidibé, Colautti (Yeini 62), Strul. Coach: Avi Nimni (ISR)
Red Card(s): Baning 60
Yellow Card(s): Baning 10, Colautti 45+4, Baning 60, Ziv 68
H 1-0 *Colautti (42)*
Strauber, Saban, Nivaldo, Medunjanin, Itzhaki (Avidor 80), Ziv (Malul 86), Gafni, Sidibé, Yeini, Colautti (Buzaglo 69), Strul. Coach: Avi Nimni (ISR)
Yellow Card(s): Medunjanin 22, Gafni 66, Yeini 90+3

Play-Offs – Paris Saint-Germain FC (FRA)
A 0-2
Strauber, Saban, Baning (Yeini 73), Medunjanin, Itzhaki, Ziv, Atar (Avidor 65), Pavićević, Gafni (Buzaglo 64), Sidibé, Strul. Coach: Avi Nimni (ISR)
Yellow Card(s): Gafni 40, Baning 64
H 4-3 *Atar (48, 90+5), Avidor (68), Medunjanin (83p)*
Strauber, Saban, Medunjanin, Buzaglo (Cahalon 79), Ziv, Atar, Pavićević, Sidibé, Yeini (Malul 65), Colautti (Avidor 46), Strul. Coach: Avi Nimni (ISR)
Yellow Card(s): Yeini 12, Ziv 38, Saban 54, Pavićević 90+3, Medunjanin 90+4

BNEI YEHUDA TEL-AVIV FC

UEFA EUROPA LEAGUE

First Qualifying Round – Ulisses FC (ARM)
A 0-0
Aiyenugba, Mori, Linić, Rali, Zairi, Biton, Azoz, Hadad, Edri, Levi (Afek 46), Menashe (Baldut 65). Coach: Dror Kashtan (ISR)
Yellow Card(s): Rali 36
H 1-0 *Menashe (45+1)*
Aiyenugba, Mori (Garrido 46), Linić, Rali (Zairi 58), Baldut, Biton, Azoz, Afek (Levi 73), Hadad, Edri, Menashe. Coach: Dror Kashtan (ISR)
Yellow Card(s): Baldut 65, Levi 84

Second Qualifying Round – Shamrock Rovers FC (IRL)
A 1-1 *Afek (26)*
Aiyenugba, Linić, Garrido, Baldut, Zairi, Biton (Afek 19), Azoz, Yavruyan (Rali 57), Hadad, Edri, Menashe (Abu Zeid 73). Coach: Dror Kashtan (ISR)
Yellow Card(s): Azoz 51

H 0-1
Aiyenugba, Linić (Menashe 74), Garrido, Rali, Zairi, Abu Zeid (Levi 90+2), Azoz (Baldut 78), Afek, Yavruyan, Hadad, Edri. Coach: Dror Kashtan (ISR)
Yellow Card(s): Zairi 50

ITALY

FC INTERNAZIONALE MILANO

UEFA CHAMPIONS LEAGUE

Group A
Match 1 – FC Twente (NED)
A 2-2 *Sneijder (13), Eto'o (41)*
Júlio César, Zanetti, Lúcio, Eto'o, Sneijder, Maicon, Mariga, Cambiasso, Milito (Muntari 87), Samuel, Pandev (Coutinho 61). Coach: Rafael Benítez (ESP)
Yellow Card(s): Maicon 48
Match 2 – SV Werder Bremen (GER)
H 4-0 *Eto'o (21, 27, 81), Sneijder (34)*
Júlio César (Castellazzi 46), Córdoba, Stanković (Obi 80), Lúcio (Santon 62), Eto'o, Sneijder, Maicon, Cambiasso, Chivu, Coutinho, Biabiany. Coach: Rafael Benítez (ESP)
Match 3 – Tottenham Hotspur FC (ENG)
H 4-3 *Zanetti (2), Eto'o (11p, 35), Stanković (14)*
Júlio César, Zanetti, Stanković (Santon 50), Lúcio, Eto'o, Sneijder, Maicon, Samuel, Chivu (Pandev 61), Coutinho, Biabiany (Córdoba 75). Coach: Rafael Benítez (ESP)
Yellow Card(s): Chivu 17
Match 4 – Tottenham Hotspur FC (ENG)
A 1-3 *Eto'o (80)*
Castellazzi, Zanetti, Lúcio, Eto'o, Sneijder, Muntari (Obiora 53), Maicon, Samuel, Chivu, Pandev (Milito 71), Biabiany (Coutinho 64). Coach: Rafael Benítez (ESP)
Yellow Card(s): Samuel 36, Chivu 51, Lúcio 86
Match 5 – FC Twente (NED)
H 1-0 *Cambiasso (55)*
Castellazzi, Córdoba, Zanetti, Stanković, Lúcio, Eto'o, Sneijder (Obiora 87), Cambiasso, Materazzi, Pandev, Biabiany (Santon 80). Coach: Rafael Benítez (ESP)
Yellow Card(s): Córdoba 75
Match 6 – SV Werder Bremen (GER)
A 0-3
Orlandoni, Córdoba, Zanetti (Natalino 54), Thiago Motta (Mariga 76), Eto'o, Muntari, Cambiasso, Pandev, Biraghi, Santon (Biabiany 50), Obiora. Coach: Rafael Benítez (ESP)

Round of 16 – FC Bayern München (GER)
H 0-1
Júlio César, Zanetti, Stanković, Lúcio, Thiago Motta, Eto'o, Sneijder, Maicon, Ranocchia (Kharja 73), Cambiasso, Chivu. Coach: Leonardo (BRA)
Yellow Card(s): Zanetti 21, Sneijder 56, Thiago Motta 87
A 3-2 *Eto'o (4), Sneijder (63), Pandev (88)*
Júlio César, Stanković (Coutinho 51), Lúcio, Thiago Motta, Eto'o, Sneijder, Maicon, Ranocchia, Cambiasso, Chivu (Nagatomo 87), Pandev (Kharja 90). Coach: Leonardo (BRA)
Yellow Card(s): Lúcio 59, Pandev 89, Kharja 90+1, Thiago Motta 90+4

Quarter-Finals – FC Schalke 04 (GER)
H 2-5 *Stanković (1), Milito (34)*
Júlio César, Zanetti, Stanković (Kharja 24; Córdoba 63), Thiago Motta (Nagatomo 76), Eto'o, Sneijder, Maicon, Ranocchia, Cambiasso, Milito, Chivu. Coach: Leonardo (BRA)
Red Card(s): Chivu 62
Yellow Card(s): Stanković 13, Chivu 52, Chivu 62
A 1-2 *Thiago Motta (49)*
Júlio César, Zanetti, Stanković (Pandev 46), Lúcio, Thiago Motta, Eto'o, Sneijder (Coutinho 80), Maicon, Ranocchia, Milito, Nagatomo. Coach: Leonardo (BRA)
Yellow Card(s): Lúcio 30, Thiago Motta 58, Ranocchia 90

No	Player	Nat	DoB	Aps	(s)	Gls
Goalkeepers						
12	Luca Castellazzi		19/7/75	2	(1)	
1	Júlio César	BRA	3/9/79	7		
21	Paolo Orlandoni		12/8/72	1		
Defenders						
34	Cristiano Biraghi		1/9/92	1	(1)	
26	Cristian Chivu	ROU	26/10/80	6		
2	Iván Córdoba	COL	11/8/76	3	(2)	
6	Lúcio	BRA	8/5/78	8		
13	Maicon	BRA	26/7/81	8		
23	Marco Materazzi		19/8/73	1		
55	Yuto Nagatomo	JPN	12/9/86	1	(2)	
57	Felice Natalino		24/3/92		(1)	
15	Andrea Ranocchia		16/2/88	4		
25	Walter Samuel	ARG	23/3/78	3		
39	Davide Santon		2/1/91	1	(3)	
4	Javier Zanetti	ARG	10/8/73	8		1
Midfielders						
19	Esteban Cambiasso	ARG	18/8/80	7		1
29	Coutinho	BRA	12/6/92	2	(4)	
14	Houssine Kharja	MAR	9/11/82		(3)	
17	McDonald Mariga	KEN	4/4/87	1	(1)	
11	Sulley Muntari	GHA	27/8/84	2	(1)	
20	Joel Obi	NGA	22/5/91		(1)	
40	Nwankwo Obiora	NGA	12/7/91	1	(2)	
10	Wesley Sneijder	NED	9/6/84	9		3
5	Dejan Stanković	SRB	11/9/78	7		2
8	Thiago Motta		28/8/82	5		1
Forwards						
88	Jonathan Biabiany	FRA	28/4/88	4	(1)	
9	Samuel Eto'o	CMR	10/3/81	10		8
22	Diego Milito	ARG	12/6/79	3	(1)	1
27	Goran Pandev	MKD	27/7/83	5	(2)	1

AS ROMA

UEFA CHAMPIONS LEAGUE

Group E
Match 1 – FC Bayern München (GER)
A 0-2
Júlio Sérgio, Juan, Pizarro, Totti (Ménez 79), De Rossi, Perrotta, Borriello, N. Burdisso, Brighi, Cassetti, Rosi. Coach: Claudio Ranieri (ITA)
Match 2 – CFR 1907 Cluj (ROU)
H 2-1 *Mexès (69), Borriello (71)*
Lobonţ, Cicinho (Cassetti 64), Castellini, Mexès, Pizarro, Vučinić (Borriello 64), Totti, De Rossi, Perrotta, N. Burdisso, Ménez (Adriano 46). Coach: Claudio Ranieri (ITA)
Match 3 – FC Basel 1893 (SUI)
H 1-3 *Borriello (21)*
Lobonţ, Mexès, Pizarro, Totti, Taddei, Riise (Castellini 60), Perrotta (Júlio Baptista 74), Borriello, N. Burdisso, Brighi, Cassetti. Coach: Claudio Ranieri (ITA)
Yellow Card(s): Cassetti 53
Match 4 – FC Basel 1893 (SUI)
A 3-2 *Ménez (16), Totti (26p), Greco (76)*
Júlio Sérgio, Juan, Vučinić (Borriello 70), Totti, De Rossi, Riise, Perrotta, N. Burdisso (G. Burdisso 81), Fábio Simplício, Cassetti, Ménez (Greco 75). Coach: Claudio Ranieri (ITA)
Yellow Card(s): Cassetti 49, Perrotta 50, Ménez 75

Match 5 – FC Bayern München (GER)
H 3-2 *Borriello (49), De Rossi (81), Totti (84p)*
Júlio Sérgio, Mexès, Vučinić, De Rossi, Riise, Borriello, Greco (Fábio Simplício 46), N. Burdisso, Brighi, Cassetti, Ménez. Coach: Claudio Ranieri (ITA)
Yellow Card(s): Greco 13, Mexès 21
Match 6 – CFR 1907 Cluj (ROU)
A 1-1 *Borriello (21)*
Lobonţ, Castellini, Mexès, Totti, De Rossi, Borriello, N. Burdisso, Fábio Simplício, Brighi, Cassetti (Cicinho 64), Ménez (Greco 46). Coach: Claudio Ranieri (ITA)

Round of 16 – FC Shakhtar Donetsk (UKR)
H 2-3 *Raţ (28og), Ménez (61)*
Doni, Mexès, Vučinić (Borriello 68), Totti, Taddei, De Rossi, Riise (Castellini 46), Perrotta, N. Burdisso, Cassetti, Ménez. Coach: Claudio Ranieri (ITA)
Yellow Card(s): Cassetti 64, Ménez 75, Perrotta 77
A 0-3
Doni, Juan, Mexès, Pizarro, Vučinić (Brighi 65), Taddei (Rosi 46), De Rossi, Riise, Perrotta (Caprari 86), Borriello, N. Burdisso. Coach: Vincenzo Montella (ITA)
Red Card(s): Mexès 41
Yellow Card(s): Mexès 23, Mexès 41, Pizarro 57, Perrotta 65, Riise 82

No	Player	Nat	DoB	Aps	(s)	Gls
	Goalkeepers					
32	Doni	BRA	22/10/79	2		
27	Júlio Sérgio	BRA	8/11/78	3		
1	Bogdan Lobonţ	ROU	18/1/78	3		
	Defenders					
25	Guillermo Burdisso	ARG	26/9/88		(1)	
29	Nicolás Burdisso	ARG	12/4/81	8		
77	Marco Cassetti		29/5/77	6	(1)	
3	Paolo Castellini		25/3/79	2	(2)	
2	Cicinho	BRA	24/6/80	1	(1)	
4	Juan	BRA	1/2/79	3		
5	Philippe Mexès	FRA	30/3/82	6		1
17	John Arne Riise	NOR	24/9/80	5		
	Midfielders					
33	Matteo Brighi		14/2/81	4	(1)	
16	Daniele De Rossi		24/7/83	7		1
30	Fábio Simplício	BRA	23/9/79	2	(1)	
23	Leandro Greco		19/7/86	1	(2)	1
20	Simone Perrotta		17/9/77	6		
7	David Pizarro	CHI	11/9/79	4	(1)	
87	Aleandro Rosi		17/5/87	1	(1)	
11	Rodrigo Taddei	BRA	6/3/80	3		
	Forwards					
8	Adriano	BRA	17/2/82		(1)	
22	Marco Borriello		18/6/82	5	(3)	4
47	Gianluca Caprari		30/7/93		(1)	
19	Júlio Baptista	BRA	1/10/81		(1)	
94	Jérémy Ménez	FRA	7/5/87	5	(1)	2
10	Francesco Totti		27/9/76	6	(1)	2
9	Mirko Vučinić	MNE	1/10/83	5		

AC MILAN

UEFA CHAMPIONS LEAGUE

Group G
Match 1 – AJ Auxerre (FRA)
H 2-0 *Ibrahimović (66, 69)*
Abbiati, Pato (Robinho 55), Seedorf, Ibrahimović, Nesta, Zambrotta, Pirlo, Ambrosini (Boateng 15), Bonera, Antonini (Abate 71), Ronaldinho. Coach: Massimiliano Allegri (ITA)
Yellow Card(s): Seedorf 57, Zambrotta 83

Match 2 – AFC Ajax (NED)
A 1-1 *Ibrahimović (37)*
Abbiati, Gattuso, Seedorf (Abate 85), Ibrahimović, Nesta, Flamini (Boateng 52), Zambrotta, Pirlo, Thiago Silva, Robinho (Inzaghi 85), Antonini. Coach: Massimiliano Allegri (ITA)
Yellow Card(s): Robinho 39, Flamini 40, Zambrotta 59, Gattuso 65, Antonini 68
Match 3 – Real Madrid CF (ESP)
A 0-2
Amelia, Pato (Inzaghi 78), Gattuso (Boateng 59), Seedorf, Ibrahimović, Nesta, Zambrotta, Pirlo, Bonera, Antonini, Ronaldinho (Robinho 72). Coach: Massimiliano Allegri (ITA)
Yellow Card(s): Bonera 73, Boateng 76, Antonini 80
Match 4 – Real Madrid CF (ESP)
H 2-2 *Inzaghi (68, 78)*
Abbiati, Pato (Ambrosini 72), Gattuso (Seedorf 84), Ibrahimović, Nesta, Zambrotta, Abate, Pirlo, Boateng, Thiago Silva, Ronaldinho (Inzaghi 60). Coach: Massimiliano Allegri (ITA)
Yellow Card(s): Boateng 28, Abate 56, Ibrahimović 57, Gattuso 70
Match 5 – AJ Auxerre (FRA)
A 2-0 *Ibrahimović (64), Ronaldinho (90+1)*
Abbiati, Gattuso (Strasser 90+2), Seedorf (Boateng 76), Ibrahimović (Ronaldinho 85), Nesta, Flamini, Zambrotta, Abate, Ambrosini, Thiago Silva, Robinho. Coach: Massimiliano Allegri (ITA)
Yellow Card(s): Ambrosini 45+1, Nesta 86, Strasser 90+3
Match 6 – AFC Ajax (NED)
H 0-2
Amelia, Seedorf, Flamini (Boateng 26), Pirlo, Ambrosini (Ibrahimović 63), Bonera, Thiago Silva, Robinho (Merkel 76), Yepes, Antonini, Ronaldinho. Coach: Massimiliano Allegri (ITA)

Round of 16 – Tottenham Hotspur FC (ENG)
H 0-1
Abbiati (Amelia 18), Gattuso, Seedorf (Pato 46), Ibrahimović, Nesta, Flamini, Abate, Thiago Silva, Robinho, Yepes, Antonini. Coach: Massimiliano Allegri (ITA)
Yellow Card(s): Flamini 55, Yepes 61, Gattuso 76
A 0-0
Abbiati, Pato, Seedorf, Ibrahimović, Nesta, Flamini (Strasser 87), Jankulovski (Antonini 70), Abate, Boateng (Merkel 76), Thiago Silva, Robinho. Coach: Massimiliano Allegri (ITA)
Yellow Card(s): Jankulovski 48, Flamini 63, Pato 64

No	Player	Nat	DoB	Aps	(s)	Gls
	Goalkeepers					
32	Christian Abbiati		8/7/77	6		
1	Marco Amelia		2/4/82	2	(1)	
	Defenders					
77	Luca Antonini		4/8/82	5	(1)	
25	Daniele Bonera		31/5/81	3		
18	Marek Jankulovski	CZE	9/5/77	1		
13	Alessandro Nesta		19/3/76	7		
33	Thiago Silva	BRA	22/9/84	6		
76	Mario Yepes	COL	13/1/76	2		
19	Gianluca Zambrotta		19/2/77	5		
	Midfielders					
20	Ignazio Abate		12/11/86	4	(2)	
23	Massimo Ambrosini		29/5/77	3	(1)	
27	Kevin-Prince Boateng	GHA	6/3/87	2	(5)	
16	Mathieu Flamini	FRA	7/3/84	5		
8	Gennaro Gattuso		9/1/78	5		
52	Alexander Merkel	GER	22/2/92		(2)	
21	Andrea Pirlo		19/5/79	5		
10	Clarence Seedorf	NED	1/4/76	7	(1)	
14	Rodney Strasser	SLE	30/3/90		(2)	
	Forwards					
11	Zlatan Ibrahimović	SWE	3/10/81	7	(1)	4
9	Filippo Inzaghi		9/8/73		(3)	2
7	Pato	BRA	2/9/89	4	(1)	
70	Robinho	BRA	25/1/84	5	(2)	
80	Ronaldinho	BRA	21/3/80	4	(1)	1

UC SAMPDORIA

UEFA CHAMPIONS LEAGUE

Play-Offs – SV Werder Bremen (GER)
A 1-3 *Pazzini (90)*
Curci, Ziegler, Lucchini, Mannini (Guberti 65), Pazzini, Tissone (Poli 59), Palombo, Volta, Gastaldello, Semioli (Stankevičius 68), Cassano. Coach: Domenico Di Carlo (ITA)
Red Card(s): Lucchini 66
Yellow Card(s): Volta 18, Ziegler 52, Lucchini 61, Lucchini 66, Cassano 81
H 3-2 *Pazzini (8, 13), Cassano (85)*
Curci, Ziegler, Dessena, Guberti (Tissone 66; Mannini 73), Pazzini, Palombo, Stankevičius, Volta, Gastaldello, Semioli, Cassano (Pozzi 90). Coach: Domenico Di Carlo (ITA)
Yellow Card(s): Dessena 23, Gastaldello 77, Palombo 88

UEFA EUROPA LEAGUE

Group I
Match 1 – PSV Eindhoven (NED)
A 1-1 *Cacciatore (25)*
Curci, Ziegler, Mannini, Koman (Dessena 80), Palombo, Cacciatore, Volta, Gastaldello, Semioli (Padalino 68), Marilungo (Guberti 87), Cassano. Coach: Domenico Di Carlo (ITA)
Yellow Card(s): Semioli 12, Mannini 35, Koman 41, Cacciatore 63, Padalino 89
Match 2 – Debreceni VSC (HUN)
H 1-0 *Pazzini (18p)*
Curci, Dessena, Accardi, Lucchini, Mannini (Guberti 58), Pazzini, Koman (Marilungo 80), Palombo, Cacciatore (Zauri 73), Volta, Cassano. Coach: Domenico Di Carlo (ITA)
Yellow Card(s): Lucchini 58
Match 3 – FC Metalist Kharkiv (UKR)
A 1-2 *Koman (32)*
Curci, Ziegler, Dessena (Guberti 82), Pozzi, Koman (Tissone 74), Poli (Mannini 65), Cacciatore, Volta, Gastaldello, Marilungo, Cassano. Coach: Domenico Di Carlo (ITA)
Yellow Card(s): Cacciatore 26, Gastaldello 52, Volta 56
Match 4 – FC Metalist Kharkiv (UKR)
H 0-0
Júnior Costa, Ziegler, Dessena, Guberti (Koman 72), Pozzi, Poli (Mannini 63), Palombo, Cacciatore, Volta, Gastaldello, Marilungo (Pazzini 63). Coach: Domenico Di Carlo (ITA)
Yellow Card(s): Gastaldello 42
Match 5 – PSV Eindhoven (NED)
H 1-2 *Pazzini (45+3)*
Curci, Ziegler, Dessena, Lucchini (Volta 31), Pazzini, Koman (Guberti 69), Poli (Mannini 77), Palombo, Cacciatore, Gastaldello, Marilungo. Coach: Domenico Di Carlo (ITA)
Red Card(s): Marilungo 89
Yellow Card(s): Gastaldello 70, Poli 75, Marilungo 76, Marilungo 89, Dessena 90+3
Match 6 – Debreceni VSC (HUN)
A 0-2
Júnior Costa, Dessena, Koman, Pedro Obiang (Guberti 72), Poli (Mannini 80), Sammarco, Rossini, Volta, Grieco, Messina, Krstičić (Lamorte 88). Coach: Domenico Di Carlo (ITA)
Yellow Card(s): Rossini 81

US CITTÀ DI PALERMO

UEFA EUROPA LEAGUE

Play-Offs – NK Maribor (SVN)
H 3-0 *Maccarone (37p), Hernández (39), Pastore (77)*
Sirigu, Bovo, Migliaccio, Hernández (Kasami 78), Liverani, Cassani, Nocerino, Glik, Pastore, Maccarone (Pinilla 70), Balzaretti. Coach: Delio Rossi (ITA)
Yellow Card(s): Nocerino 9, Liverani 45+1, Bovo 52, Balzaretti 74, Pastore 75
A 2-3 *Hernández (62, 68)*
Sirigu, Bovo, Muñoz, Migliaccio, Hernández (Pinilla 76), Liverani (Rigoni 70), Cassani, Nocerino, Pastore, Maccarone (Kasami 57), Balzaretti. Coach: Delio Rossi (ITA)
Yellow Card(s): Maccarone 19, Nocerino 47, Muñoz 63

Group F
Match 1 – AC Sparta Praha (CZE)
A 2-3 *Maccarone (38), Hernández (83)*
Sirigu, Bovo, Migliaccio (Kasami 58), Hernández, Liverani, Rigoni (João Pedro 78), Glik, Pastore, Maccarone, Darmian, Balzaretti. Coach: Delio Rossi (ITA)
Yellow Card(s): Kasami 64
Match 2 – FC Lausanne-Sport (SUI)
H 1-0 *Migliaccio (79)*
Benussi, Kasami, Bovo, Muñoz, Migliaccio, Miccoli (Pinilla 43), Cassani, Nocerino, Pastore, García (Balzaretti 61), Maccarone (Darmian 86). Coach: Delio Rossi (ITA)
Match 3 – PFC CSKA Moskva (RUS)
H 0-3
Benussi, Goian, Bovo, Migliaccio, Hernández (João Pedro 76), Cassani, Nocerino, Pastore, Maccarone (Pinilla 64), Darmian (Kasami 56), Balzaretti. Coach: Delio Rossi (ITA)
Red Card(s): Pastore 74
Yellow Card(s): Benussi 22, Balzaretti 69, Pastore 74, Pastore 74, Pinilla 90+1
Match 4 – PFC CSKA Moskva (RUS)
A 1-3 *Maccarone (10)*
Benussi, Goian, Kasami, Bovo, Miccoli (Pinilla 61), Nocerino, Rigoni, Glik (Cassani 55), García (Balzaretti 65), Maccarone, Darmian. Coach: Delio Rossi (ITA)
Red Card(s): Nocerino 31
Yellow Card(s): Nocerino 17, Nocerino 31
Match 5 – AC Sparta Praha (CZE)
H 2-2 *Rigoni (23), Pinilla (60p)*
Benussi, Goian, Muñoz, Migliaccio, Liverani (Kasami 70), Cassani, Rigoni, Pastore, Maccarone (Bovo 52), Balzaretti, Pinilla (Miccoli 76). Coach: Delio Rossi (ITA)
Red Card(s): Goian 50, Pastore 90+3
Yellow Card(s): Migliaccio 12, Goian 44, Goian 50, Pastore 55, Pastore 90+3
Match 6 – FC Lausanne-Sport (SUI)
A 1-0 *Muñoz (84)*
Benussi, Kasami, João Pedro, Liverani, Cassani (Muñoz 57), Nocerino (Ardizzone 65), Rigoni, Glik, García, Maccarone (Zerbo 90), Prestia. Coach: Delio Rossi (ITA)
Yellow Card(s): García 74

SSC NAPOLI

UEFA EUROPA LEAGUE

Play-Offs – IF Elfsborg (SWE)
H 1-0 *Lavezzi (45+1)*
De Sanctis, Grava, Pazienza (Cavani 62), Aronica, Dossena (Zúñiga 83), Maggio, Hamšík (Blasi 77), Lavezzi, Gargano, Quagliarella, Cannavaro. Coach: Walter Mazzarri (ITA)
Yellow Card(s): Pazienza 37, Aronica 84
A 2-0 *Cavani (29, 38)*
De Sanctis, Grava, Pazienza, Aronica, Cavani, Dossena, Maggio (Zúñiga 55), Hamšík (Blasi 64), Lavezzi (Campagnaro 73), Gargano, Cannavaro. Coach: Walter Mazzarri (ITA)
Yellow Card(s): Cavani 41, Lavezzi 45+2

Group K
Match 1 – FC Utrecht (NED)
H 0-0
De Sanctis, Aronica, Cavani, Dossena (Maggio 69), Santacroce, Zúñiga, Yebda (Lucarelli 76), Lavezzi, Gargano, Cannavaro, Sosa (Hamšík 56). Coach: Walter Mazzarri (ITA)
Yellow Card(s): Yebda 54, Cavani 62, Gargano 80, Maggio 83, Santacroce 90+1
Match 2 – FC Steaua Bucureşti (ROU)
A 3-3 *Vitale (44), Hamšík (73), Cavani (90+8)*
De Sanctis, Grava, Vitale, Cavani, Maggio, Santacroce (Lavezzi 46), Zúñiga (Hamšík 58), Yebda (Dumitru 86), Gargano, Cribari, Sosa. Coach: Walter Mazzarri (ITA)
Yellow Card(s): Lavezzi 54, Gargano 90+1
Match 3 – Liverpool FC (ENG)
H 0-0
De Sanctis, Pazienza, Aronica, Cavani, Dossena, Maggio (Zúñiga 76), Campagnaro, Hamšík (Sosa 85), Lavezzi, Gargano (Yebda 83), Cannavaro. Coach: Walter Mazzarri (ITA)
Yellow Card(s): Pazienza 57
Match 4 – Liverpool FC (ENG)
A 1-3 *Lavezzi (28)*
De Sanctis, Pazienza, Aronica, Cavani, Dossena, Maggio, Campagnaro, Hamšík (Yebda 84), Lavezzi, Gargano, Cannavaro. Coach: Walter Mazzarri (ITA)
Yellow Card(s): Dossena 47, Campagnaro 67, De Sanctis 76, Cavani 90+3
Match 5 – FC Utrecht (NED)
A 3-3 *Cavani (5, 42, 70p)*
De Sanctis, Grava (Maggio 63), Vitale, Cavani, Campagnaro (Cannavaro 84), Hamšík, Zúñiga (Dumitru 87), Yebda, Lavezzi, Gargano, Cribari. Coach: Walter Mazzarri (ITA)
Yellow Card(s): Campagnaro 34, Hamšík 49, De Sanctis 78, Zúñiga 79, Gargano 83, Lavezzi 83, Yebda 83
Match 6 – FC Steaua Bucureşti (ROU)
H 1-0 *Cavani (90+3)*
De Sanctis, Vitale (Dossena 79), Pazienza, Aronica, Cavani, Maggio, Campagnaro (Sosa 52), Hamšík, Zúñiga, Yebda (Dumitru 68), Cannavaro. Coach: Nicolo Frustalupi (ITA)
Red Card(s): Cannavaro 90+6
Yellow Card(s): Maggio 73, Cannavaro 76, Zúñiga 90+4, Cannavaro 90+6

Round of 32 – Villarreal CF (ESP)
H 0-0
De Sanctis, Aronica, Cavani, Dossena, Mascara (Hamšík 61), Maggio, Campagnaro, Yebda (Pazienza 68), Lavezzi, Gargano (Sosa 78), Cribari. Coach: Walter Mazzarri (ITA)
Red Card(s): Aronica 90+5
Yellow Card(s): Dossena 47, Aronica 64, Cribari 90+2, Aronica 90+5
A 1-2 *Hamšík (18)*
De Sanctis, Víctor Ruiz, Dossena, Campagnaro, Hamšík, Zúñiga, Yebda (Pazienza 64), Lavezzi, Gargano, Cribari (Mascara 82), Sosa (Cavani 53). Coach: Walter Mazzarri (ITA)
Yellow Card(s): De Sanctis 45+2, Yebda 45+2, Víctor Ruiz 52, Campagnaro 61, Hamšík 76

JUVENTUS

UEFA EUROPA LEAGUE

Third Qualifying Round – Shamrock Rovers FC (IRL)
A 2-0 *Amauri (3, 75)*
Storari, Motta, Chiellini, Sissoko, Marchisio (Ekdal 89), Amauri, Bonucci, Lanzafame (Martínez 52), Pepe, Diego (Del Piero 82), De Ceglie. Coach: Luigi Delneri (ITA)
Yellow Card(s): Pepe 43, Marchisio 70
H 1-0 *Del Piero (74)*
Storari, Motta, Chiellini, Sissoko, Marchisio, Amauri (Trezeguet 81), Bonucci, Lanzafame, Pepe, Diego (Del Piero 46), De Ceglie. Coach: Luigi Delneri (ITA)
Yellow Card(s): Lanzafame 71

Play-Offs – SK Sturm Graz (AUT)
A 2-1 *Bonucci (16), Amauri (90+1)*
Storari, Motta, Chiellini, Sissoko, Marchisio (Felipe Melo 70), Amauri, Bonucci, Lanzafame (Martínez 55), Pepe, Diego (Del Piero 74), De Ceglie. Coach: Luigi Delneri (ITA)
Yellow Card(s): Marchisio 31, Chiellini 38
H 1-0 *Del Piero (53)*
Storari, Motta, Chiellini, Felipe Melo (Giandonato 85), Sissoko, Del Piero, Amauri (Lanzafame 43), Bonucci, Pepe, Martínez, De Ceglie. Coach: Luigi Delneri (ITA)
Yellow Card(s): Motta 81

Group A
Match 1 – KKS Lech Poznań (POL)
H 3-3 *Chiellini (45+2, 50), Del Piero (68)*
Manninger, Chiellini, Felipe Melo, Sissoko, Iaquinta (Marchisio 79), Del Piero, Lanzafame (Pepe 55), Grygera, Krasić, De Ceglie (Motta 45), Legrottaglie. Coach: Luigi Delneri (ITA)
Yellow Card(s): Felipe Melo 13, Sissoko 36
Match 2 – Manchester City FC (ENG)
A 1-1 *Iaquinta (10)*
Manninger, Chiellini, Sissoko, Marchisio, Iaquinta, Del Piero, Bonucci, Grygera, Martínez (Pepe 54), Krasić (Felipe Melo 75), De Ceglie (Motta 72). Coach: Luigi Delneri (ITA)
Yellow Card(s): Krasić 41, Grygera 73
Match 3 – FC Salzburg (AUT)
A 1-1 *Krasić (47)*
Manninger, Chiellini, Sissoko, Marchisio, Del Piero, Amauri, Bonucci, Grygera (Motta 80), Pepe (Krasić 46), Martínez (Felipe Melo 64), De Ceglie. Coach: Luigi Delneri (ITA)
Yellow Card(s): Martínez 57, Felipe Melo 81
Match 4 – FC Salzburg (AUT)
H 0-0
Storari, Motta, Sissoko, Marchisio, Del Piero, Amauri, Bonucci, Pepe (Giannetti 83), Krasić (Büchel 63), Legrottaglie, Giandonato (Liviero 51). Coach: Luigi Delneri (ITA)
Yellow Card(s): Sissoko 12, Marchisio 55
Match 5 – KKS Lech Poznań (POL)
A 1-1 *Iaquinta (84)*
Manninger, Chiellini, Sissoko (Felipe Melo 75), Marchisio, Iaquinta, Del Piero, Traoré (Libertazzi 80), Bonucci, Pepe (Lanzafame 67), Krasić, Camilleri. Coach: Luigi Delneri (ITA)

Match 6 – Manchester City FC (ENG)
H 1-1 *Giannetti (43)*
Manninger, Chiellini, Felipe Melo, Sissoko, Del Piero, Traoré (Boniperti 67), Grygera, Pepe, Krasić (Camilleri 57), Legrottaglie, Giannetti (Büchel 79). Coach: Luigi Delneri (ITA)
Yellow Card(s): Felipe Melo 78, Sissoko 87

KAZAKHSTAN

FC AKTOBE

UEFA CHAMPIONS LEAGUE

Second Qualifying Round – FC Olimpi Rustavi (GEO)
H 2-0 *Smakov (40p, 53)*
Sidelnikov, Ba, Bono, Badlo, Khairullin, Smakov, Golovskoy (Tleshev 71), Karpovich, Essomba, Averchenko (Darabayev 80), Perić (Khokhlov 87). Coach: Vladimir Mukhanov (RUS)
A 1-1 *Tleshev (90)*
Sidelnikov, Ba, Bono (Badlo 90+3), Khairullin, Smakov, Kenzhesariev, Golovskoy (Khokhlov 86), Karpovich, Essomba, Averchenko, Perić (Tleshev 46). Coach: Vladimir Mukhanov (RUS)
Yellow Card(s): Karpovich 45+1, Tleshev 61, Khairullin 62, Golovskoy 64, Ba 65, Bono 88

Third Qualifying Round – Hapoel Tel-Aviv FC (ISR)
H 1-0 *Smakov (67p)*
Sidelnikov, Ba, Bono, Badlo, Khairullin (Khokhlov 80), Smakov, Kenzhesariev, Karpovich, Essomba, Averchenko (Darabayev 55), Perić (Tleshev 45+1). Coach: Vladimir Mukhanov (RUS)
Yellow Card(s): Perić 16, Karpovich 38, Darabayev 87
A 1-3 *Tleshev (90)*
Sidelnikov, Ba, Bono, Badlo, Khairullin, Smakov, Kenzhesariev, Essomba, Khokhlov (Chichulin 56), Averchenko (Tleshev 46), Perić. Coach: Vladimir Mukhanov (RUS)
Yellow Card(s): Bono 44, Ba 45, Badlo 55, Perić 72, Tleshev 84, Khairullin 90+2

UEFA EUROPA LEAGUE

Play-Offs – AZ Alkmaar (NED)
A 0-2
Sidelnikov, Badlo, Chichulin, Smakov, Kenzhesariev, Darabayev, Karpovich, Essomba, Semenyov, Khokhlov, Averchenko (Lisenkov 86). Coach: Vladimir Mukhanov (RUS)
Yellow Card(s): Khokhlov 42, Karpovich 90
H 2-1 *Tleshev (67, 89)*
Sidelnikov, Ba, Bono, Chichulin, Khairullin (Perić 59), Smakov, Kenzhesariev, Tleshev, Karpovich, Essomba, Averchenko (Darabayev 70). Coach: Vladimir Mukhanov (RUS)
Yellow Card(s): Chichulin 19, Essomba 45, Karpovich 61, Bono 74

FC ATYRAU

UEFA EUROPA LEAGUE

Second Qualifying Round – Győri ETO FC (HUN)
H 0-3
Shabanov, Zhumabayev, Vorotnikov, Crnogorac, Shakin, Aliyev, Peikrishvili (Chureyev 84), Sakhalbayev (Larin 76), Kostrub, Frunza (Khizhnichenko 59), Mamonov. Coach: Viktor Pasulko (UKR)
Yellow Card(s): Aliyev 20, Frunza 44, Zhumabayev 86
A 0-2
Shabanov, Zhumabayev, Vorotnikov, Shakin (Khizhnichenko 62), Aliyev, Chureyev, Peikrishvili (Larin 70), Sakhalbayev (Mamonov 75), Kostrub, Frunza, Croitoru. Coach: Viktor Pasulko (UKR)
Yellow Card(s): Sahalbayev 45

FC SHAKHTER KARAGANDY

UEFA EUROPA LEAGUE

First Qualifying Round – Ruch Chorzów (POL)
H 1-2 *Džidić (7)*
Sarana, Đorđević, Vičius, Danaev, Kislitsyn, Borantayev (Borovskiy 72), Tarasov, Finonchenko, Bogdanov, Suchkov (Skorykh 61), Džidić. Coach: Vladimir Cheburin (KAZ)
Yellow Card(s): Suchkov 10, Sarana 46, Džidić 58
A 0-1
Sarana, Vičius, Danaev, Kislitsyn, Kozyulin, Skorykh, Tarasov, Finonchenko, Bogdanov, Suchkov (Borovskiy 70), Džidić. Coach: Vladimir Cheburin (KAZ)

FC TOBOL KOSTANAY

UEFA EUROPA LEAGUE

First Qualifying Round – HŠK Zrinjski (BIH)
H 1-2 *Zhumaskaliyev (16)*
Petukhov, Turtenwald, Abdulin, Nurgaliyev, Kharabara (Travin 81), Zhumaskaliyev, Bakayev, Sabirov (Suyumagambetov 58), Irismetov, Mukhanov, Yurin (Kuantayev 71). Coach: Ravil Sabitov (RUS)
Red Card(s): Travin 90+3
Yellow Card(s): Nurgaliyev 90+1
A 1-2 *Zhumaskaliyev (57)*
Petukhov, Turtenwald, Abdulin, Nurgaliyev (Malyshev 81), Zhumaskaliyev, Bakaev, Sabirov, Irismetov, Lotov, Kuantayev, Yurin. Coach: Ravil Sabitov (RUS)

LATVIA

SK LIEPĀJAS METALURGS

UEFA CHAMPIONS LEAGUE

Second Qualifying Round – AC Sparta Praha (CZE)
H 0-3
Spole, Kļava, Rafaļskis (Golovins 70), Tamošauskas, Rakeļs, Surņins, Kirhners (Aļeksejevs 54), Kalns, Grebis, Kavaliauskas, Puljiz. Coach: Rüdiger Abramczik (GER)
Yellow Card(s): Rafaļskis 45, Kļava 68
A 0-2
Spole (Šteinbors 46), Akahoshi, Kļava, Rafaļskis, Tamošauskas, Rakeļs, Surņins, Kalns, Jemeļins (Aļeksejevs 70), Kavaliauskas, Puljiz (Kirhners 64). Coach: Rüdiger Abramczik (GER)
Yellow Card(s): Tamošauskas 17, Surnins 58, Kļava 79, Aļeksejevs 89

FK JELGAVA

UEFA EUROPA LEAGUE

Second Qualifying Round – Molde FK (NOR)
A 0-1
Bogdanovs, V. Lapkovskis, Bormakovs (Petkevičs 87), Redjko, I. Lapkovskis, Kozlovs (Hohlovs 75), Lazdiņš, Savčenkovs, Bogdaškins, Gubins, Malašenoks (Medeckis 90+3). Coach: Dainis Kazakevičs (LVA)
Yellow Card(s): Savčenkovs 24, Gubins 49
H 2-1 *Bormakovs (30), Bogdaškins (45+1)*
Bogdanovs, Bormakovs (Petkevičs 70), Redjko, I. Lapkovskis (Hohlovs 74), Kozlovs, Lazdiņš, Savčenkovs, Bogdaškins, Kazura (V. Lapkovskis 46), Gubins, Malašenoks. Coach: Dainis Kazakevičs (LVA)
Yellow Card(s): Lapkovskis 79, Hohlovs 90+4

FK VENTSPILS

UEFA EUROPA LEAGUE

Second Qualifying Round – FK Teteks (MKD)
H 0-0
Koļinko, Krjauklis, Postnikov, E. Višņakovs (Žigajevs 49), A. Višņakovs, Dedov, Tukura, Zjuzins (Kosmačovs 73), V. Bespalovs, Gabovs (Shpakov 36), Solovjovs. Coach: Nunzio Zavettieri (ITA)
A 1-3 *V. Bespalovs (80)*
Koļinko, Postnikov, Kosmačovs, A. Višņakovs (E. Višņakovs 55), Dedov (Mishchenko 71), Chirkin, V. Bespalovs, Rugins (Žigajevs 52), Solovjovs, Kryuchkov, Shumilin. Coach: Nunzio Zavettieri (ITA)
Red Card(s): Chirkin 85
Yellow Card(s): Chirkin 38, Shumilin 45+2, Chirkin 85, Mishchenko 90+2

SKONTO FC

UEFA EUROPA LEAGUE

First Qualifying Round – Portadown FC (NIR)
A 1-1 *Laizāns (90+3)*
Ikstens (Māliņš 46), Smirnovs, Laizāns, Júnior, Dubra, Rode, Fertovs, Maksimenko, Tarasovs (Astafjevs 65), Karašausksas, Siņeļņikovs (Pētersons 16). Coach: Aleksandrs Starkovs (LVA)
H 0-1
Ikstens, Smirnovs, Laizāns, Júnior, Perepļotkins, Dubra, Rode, Fertovs, Maksimenko (Astafjevs 59), Tarasovs (Pētersons 33), Karašausksas (Turkovs 46). Coach: Aleksandrs Starkovs (LVA)

LIECHTENSTEIN

FC VADUZ

UEFA EUROPA LEAGUE

Second Qualifying Round – Brøndby IF (DEN)
A 0-3
Faivre, Bader, Schwegler, Denicolà, Sara, Bellon, Ciccone (Sabiá 79), Burgmeier (Christen 64), Sturm, Merenda, Arlan (Hasler 90+3). Coach: Eric Orie (NED)
Yellow Card(s): Bader 25, Bellon 28
H 0-0
Faivre, Bader, Schwegler, Denicolà (Rechsteiner 43), Sara, Bellon, Burgmeier, Oehri (Christen 58), Sturm, Merenda (Ciccone 78), Arlan. Coach: Eric Orie (NED)
Red Card(s): Bader 75
Yellow Card(s): Bader 28, Bellon 47, Bader 75, Ciccone 84

LITHUANIA

FK EKRANAS

UEFA CHAMPIONS LEAGUE

Second Qualifying Round – HJK Helsinki (FIN)
H 1-0 *Radavičius (3)*
Černiauskas, Gleveckas, Radavičius, Ademolu (Markevičius 90+3), Šidlauskas, Arlauskas, Rimkus, Kučys (Banys 85), Matović, Tomkevičius, Pogreban (Varnas 65). Coach: Valdas Urbonas (LTU)
Yellow Card(s): Šidlauskas 23, Radavičius 30, Gleveckas 61, Kučys 66, Banys 90
A 0-2 (aet)
Kauneckas, Gleveckas, Radavičius, Ademolu, Šidlauskas, Arlauskas (Skinderis 90), Rimkus (Varnas 68), Kučys, Matović, Tomkevičius, Galkevičius (Pogreban 58). Coach: Valdas Urbonas (LTU)
Red Card(s): Tomkevičius 87
Yellow Card(s): Tomkevičius 84, Skinderis 90+1, Kučys 90+4

FK SŪDUVA

UEFA EUROPA LEAGUE

Second Qualifying Round – SK Rapid Wien (AUT)
H 0-2
Valinčius, Valaitis, Skroblas, Kozyuberda, Chao (Urbšys 88), Leimonas, Grande, V. Slavickas, Esaú (Grigaitis 46), Gogberashvili, Beniušis (Lukšys 70). Coach: Donatas Vencevičius (LTU)
Yellow Card(s): Chao 23, V. Slavickas 27, Skroblas 39
A 2-4 *Grigaitis (70), Beniušis (85)*
Valinčius, Radžius, Valaitis, Skroblas, Kozyuberda, Leimonas, Urbšys (Lukšys 55), Grande, V. Slavickas (Chao 66), Grigaitis (Beniušis 73), Gogberashvili. Coach: Donatas Vencevičius (LTU)
Red Card(s): Skroblas 76
Yellow Card(s): Kozyuberda 3, Skroblas 50, Skroblas 76

FC ŠIAULIAI

UEFA EUROPA LEAGUE

Second Qualifying Round – Wisła Kraków (POL)
H 0-2
Kosov, Kančelskis, Jasaitis (Burkšaitis 83), Kuklys, Viktoravičius (Raskov 46), Kozlovs, Lunskis, Janušauskas (Lapeikis 61), Šilenas, Kolić, Pilypas. Coach: Rimas Viktoravičius (LTU)
Yellow Card(s): Jasaitis 2
A 0-5
Kosov, Kančelskis, Jasaitis, Kuklys, Kozlovs (Janušauskas 46; Pšelenskis 77), Lunskis, Šilenas, Lapeikis, Kolić, Raskov (Viktoravičius 67), Pilypas. Coach: Rimas Viktoravičius (LTU)
Red Card(s): Kančelskis 17
Yellow Card(s): Lunskis 74

FK TAURAS

UEFA EUROPA LEAGUE

First Qualifying Round – Llanelli AFC (WAL)
A 2-2 *Kižys (11, 22)*
Kilijonas, Lėkis, Regelskis, Jasaitis, Vaitkus, Mačiulis, Savastas (Gedgaudas 66), Mockus, Buitkus, Kižys, Daunoravičius (Vide 46). Coach: Gedeminas Jarmalavičius (LTU)
Yellow Card(s): Regelskis 28, Kižys 36
H 3-2 (aet) *Irkha (17, 31), Regelskis (104)*
Kilijonas, Lėkis, Regelskis, Jasaitis (Vide 69), Vaitkus, Mačiulis, Savastas, Mockus, Kižys, Irkha, Daunoravičius (Gedgaudas 38). Coach: Gedeminas Jarmalavičius (LTU)
Red Card(s): Lėkis 117
Yellow Card(s): Irkha 13, Regelskis 35, Lėkis 93, Kižys 104, Lėkis 117, Vide 121

Second Qualifying Round – APOEL FC (CYP)
H 0-3
Kilijonas, Kuzņecovs, Jasaitis (Bielskis 53), Vaitkus, Mačiulis, Vide (Auryla 71), Mockus, Buitkus, Irkha, Gedgaudas, Daunoravičius (Martišauskas 62). Coach: Gedeminas Jarmalavičius (LTU)
A 1-3 *Irkha (48)*
Kilijonas, Regelskis, Kuzņecovs, Jasaitis (Martišauskas 67), Vaitkus (Mockus 46), Mačiulis, Savastas, Buitkus, Irkha, Gedgaudas (Vide 61), Daunoravičius. Coach: Gedeminas Jarmalavičius (LTU)
Red Card(s): Kuzņecovs 84

LUXEMBOURG

AS JEUNESSE ESCH

UEFA CHAMPIONS LEAGUE

Second Qualifying Round – AIK Solna (SWE)
A 0-1
Oberweis, C. Leweck, Hoffmann, Portier, Servais, Peters, Collette, Piron (Pupovac 46), Rodriguez (Cantonnet 87), Fullenwarth (De Sousa 82), Martin. Coach: Jacques Muller (LUX)
Yellow Card(s): Moreira 87
H 0-0
Oberweis, C. Leweck, Hoffmann, Portier, Servais, Peters, Collette, Rodriguez (Gonçalves Fernandes 68), Pupovac (Piron 59), Fullenwarth (Cantonnet 21), Martin. Coach: Jacques Muller (LUX)
Yellow Card(s): Rodriguez 20, Hoffmann 62, Cantonnet 72, Collette 83

FC DIFFERDANGE 03

UEFA EUROPA LEAGUE

Second Qualifying Round – FK Spartak Zlatibor voda (SRB)
H 3-3 *Veselinov (6og), Bettmer (11), Piskor (73)*
Hym, Rodrigues, Siebenaler, Soraire (Kettenmeyer 70), Albanese, Bukvic, Bettmer, Jänisch (Franzoni 77), Lebresne (Diop 57), Piskor, Kintziger. Coach: Dan Theis (LUX)
Yellow Card(s): Siebenaler 36, Lebresne 51, Piskor 75, Kettenmeyer 80, Diop 86
A 0-2
Weber, Rodrigues, Siebenaler, Albanese (Franzoni 54), Bukvic, Kettenmeyer (Diop 46), Bettmer, Jänisch (Alunni 77), Lebresne, Piskor, Kintziger. Coach: Dan Theis (LUX)
Yellow Card(s): Jänisch 26

F91 DUDELANGE

UEFA EUROPA LEAGUE

First Qualifying Round – Randers FC (DEN)
A 1-6 *Benzouien (49p)*
Joubert, Abdullei (Gruszczyński 56), Mouny, Rentmeister, Caillet, Payal (Bensi 85), Da Mota, Benzouien, Remy, Wiggers, Melisse (Hareau 46). Coach: Marc Grosjean (BEL)
Yellow Card(s): Rentmeister 47, Hareau 51
H 2-1 *Caillet (37), Gruszczyński (67)*
Joubert, Rentmeister, Caillet, Bensi, Remy (Karaca 87), Wiggers, Olle-Nicolle, Guthleber, Gruszczyński, Melisse, Benzouien. Coach: Marc Grosjean (BEL)
Yellow Card(s): Olle-Nicolle 16

CS GREVENMACHER

UEFA EUROPA LEAGUE

First Qualifying Round – Dundalk FC (IRL)
H 3-3 *Heinz (63), Gaspar (73), Almeida (76)*
Pleimling, Benichou, Hartung, Baur (Stojadinovic 90+1), Louadj, Hoffmann, Gaspar, Müller (Braun 83), Mendes (Almeida 67), Furst, Heinz. Coach: Marc Thomé (LUX)
Yellow Card(s): Benichou 33, Hartung 77
A 1-2 *Müller (90+1)*
Pleimling, Benichou (Lorig 45), Hartung, Baur , Louadj, Hoffmann, Gaspar (Brzyski 72), Müller, Mendes (Almeida 61), Furst, Heinz. Coach: Marc Thomé (LUX)
Yellow Card(s): Hartung 14, Gaspar 51, Hoffmann 90+4

FORMER YUGOSLAV REPUBLIC OF MACEDONIA

FK RENOVA

UEFA CHAMPIONS LEAGUE

Second Qualifying Round – AC Omonia (CYP)
A 0-3
Elezi, Memedi, Bajrami (Fetai 67), Emini (Gafuri 81), Aliu (Jancevski 89), Nuhiu, M. Stepanovski, Statovci, Gashi, Ignjatovski, Stojanov. Coach: Nedzat Shabani (MKD)
Red Card(s): Ignjatovski 6
Yellow Card(s): Gashi 35, Memedi 69, Statovci 74, Aliu 87
H 0-2
Elezi, Memedi, Emini (Fetai 82), Aliu, Nuhiu, M. Stepanovski, Gafuri, Statovci (Bajrami 61), Gashi (Mickov 51), Jancevski, Stojanov. Coach: Nedzat Shabani (MKD)

FK TETEKS

UEFA EUROPA LEAGUE

Second Qualifying Round – FK Ventspils (LVA)
A 0-0
Ma. Jovanovski, D. Naumovski, D. Jovanovski, Ristov, Stojanovski, Ristevski (Radonjić 87), Peev (Belcev 90+2), Zaharievski, Miskovski, Gligorovski (Mi. Jovanovski 59), Hyseni. Coach: Toni Jakimovski (MKD)
Yellow Card(s): Gligorovski 41, Ristevski 50, Zaharievski 53, Ristov 84
H 3-1 *Postnikov (15og), Ristevski (34), Gligorovski (54)*
Ma. Jovanovski, D. Naumovski, D. Jovanovski, Ristov, Stojanovski, Ristevski, Peev (Mi. Jovanovski 71), Zaharievski, Miskovski (Belcev 48), Gligorovski, Hyseni (Radonjić 82). Coach: Toni Jakimovski (MKD)
Yellow Card(s): Gligorovski 42, Hyseni 42, D. Naumovski 46, Zaharievski 57, Ristov 59, D. Jovanovski 90+6

Third Qualifying Round – IF Elfsborg (SWE)
A 0-5
Ma. Jovanovski, D. Naumovski, D. Jovanovski, Mi. Jovanovski (Aliji 65), Urosevic (Simovski 49), Stojanovski, Ristevski, Belcev, Peev, Miskovski, Hyseni (Ristovski 80). Coach: Toni Jakimovski (MKD)
Yellow Card(s): Peev 43
H 1-2 *Stojanovski (31)*
Ma. Jovanovski, D. Naumovski, D. Jovanovski (Simovski 61), Ristov, Mi. Jovanovski, Stojanovski, Ristevski (Aliji 71), Belcev, Zaharievski, Gligorovski, Hyseni (Ristovski 46). Coach: Toni Jakimovski (MKD)
Yellow Card(s): Zaharievski 21, Mi. Jovanovski 64

FK RABOTNICKI

UEFA EUROPA LEAGUE

First Qualifying Round – FC Lusitans (AND)
H 5-0 *Zé Carlos (24), Wandeir (35), Fábio (55, 57), Muarem (60)*
Naumovski, Sekuloski, Bojovic, Dimovski, Fernando, Muarem, Zé Carlos (Petkovski 65), Fábio (Márcio 59), N. Gligorov, Tunevski, Wandeir (Sinković 73). Coach: Zoran Stratev (MKD)
A 6-0 *Wandeir (25, 68), Fábio (33, 42, 54), Gligorov (71)*
Bogatinov, Sekuloski (Adem 46), Bojović, Dimovski (G. Todorovski 59), Fernando, Muarem, Zé Carlos, Fábio (Petkovski 69), N. Gligorov, Tunevski, Wandeir. Coach: Zoran Stratev (MKD)
Yellow Card(s): Sekuloski 45+2, Fernando 85

Second Qualifying Round – FC Mika (ARM)
H 1-0 *Wandeir (87)*
Bogatinov, Sekuloski, Dimovski, Fernando, Muarem (Sinković 74), Zé Carlos (G. Todorovski 64), Adem, Fábio (Belica 41), N. Gligorov, Tunevski, Wandeir. Coach: Zoran Stratev (MKD)
Red Card(s): Fernando 38
Yellow Card(s): Wandeir 59, G. Todorovski 90+1
A 0-0
Bogatinov, Belica, Sekuloski, Dimovski, Muarem (Márcio 78), Zé Carlos (Fábio 64), G. Todorovski, Adem, N. Gligorov, Tunevski, Wandeir (Roberto Carlos 73). Coach: Zoran Stratev (MKD)
Yellow Card(s): Muarem 37, Márcio 84, Bogatinov 88

Third Qualifying Round – Liverpool FC (ENG)
H 0-2
Bogatinov, Belica, Sekuloski (Adem 44), Dimovski, Fernando, Zé Carlos (Mojsov 57), G. Todorovski, Fábio, N. Gligorov, Tunevski (Petkovski 78), Wandeir. Coach: Zoran Stratev (MKD)
A 0-2
Bogatinov, Belica, Dimovski, Fernando, Zé Carlos (Mojsov 62), G. Todorovski (Petkovski 88), Adem, Fábio (Márcio 81), N. Gligorov, Tunevski, Wandeir. Coach: Zoran Stratev (MKD)
Yellow Card(s): Zé Carlos 19, Mojsov 89

FK METALURG SKOPJE

UEFA EUROPA LEAGUE

First Qualifying Round – Qarabağ FK (AZE)
A 1-4 *Simonovski (90+4)*
Georgievski, Demiri, Kralevski, Ilievski (Bogdanovic 64), Kostovski, Đurić, Mihajlović (Kostencoski 70), Krstev, Petkovski (Simonovski 77), Tenekedziev, Vajs. Coach: Zikica Tasevski (MKD)
Yellow Card(s): Demiri 90
H 1-1 *Krstev (78)*
Nikov, Demiri, Kralevski, Kostencoski, Kostovski (Simonovski 72), Đurić (Mihajlović 84), Mitrev (Tenekedziev 46), Krstev, Petkovski, Dameski, Vajs. Coach: Zikica Tasevski (MKD)
Yellow Card(s): Đurić 17, Kralevski 82

MALTA

BIRKIRKARA FC

UEFA CHAMPIONS LEAGUE

First Qualifying Round – FC Santa Coloma (AND)
A 3-0 (w/o)
H 4-3 *M. Galea (10, 31), Cilia (35, 45+2)*
Lovizon, Paris, Nisević, Fenech, Cilia (Buhagiar 82), M. Galea, Decesare, Vukanac, Bajada (Tabone 75), Zerafa (Pulo 68), Muscat. Coach: Paul Zammit (MLT)
Yellow Card(s): Decesare 71, Vukanac 83

Second Qualifying Round – MŠK Žilina (SVK)
H 1-0 *Vukanac (1)*
Lovizon, Nisević, Fenech, M. Galea, Tabone, Decesare (Scicluna 85), Vukanac (Borg 72), Pulo (Scicluna 81), Bajada, Zerafa, Buhagiar. Coach: Paul Zammit (MLT)
Yellow Card(s): Decesare 15, Pulo 65, Lovizon 68, Buhagiar 69, Zerafa 77
A 0-3
Lovizon, Borg, Nisević (Scicluna 87), Fenech, M. Galea, Tabone (Pulo 67), Vukanac, Bajada, Zerafa, Buhagiar, Muscat (Paris 75). Coach: Paul Zammit (MLT)
Yellow Card(s): M. Galea 37, Buhagiar 81, Fenech 83

VALLETTA FC

UEFA EUROPA LEAGUE

Second Qualifying Round – Ruch Chorzów (POL)
H 1-1 *Scerri (75)*
Hogg, Caruana, Borg, Ramon, G. Agius, Zammit (Scerri 66), Briffa, Bezzina (Pace 80), Temile, Falzon (Sammut 56), Denni. Coach: Jesmond Zerafa (MLT)
A 0-0
Hogg, Caruana, Borg, Ramon (Bezzina 71), G. Agius, Briffa, Temile (Zammit 80), Pace, Denni, Sammut (Falzon 64), Scerri. Coach: Jesmond Zerafa (MLT)
Yellow Card(s): Denni 63

SLIEMA WANDERERS FC

UEFA EUROPA LEAGUE

First Qualifying Round – HNK Šibenik (CRO)
A 0-0
Szentpéteri, Portulez, Azzopardi, B. Muscat, Tidane, Scerri, Mifsud Triganza (Turner 90+2), Lattes, Gatt Baldacchino, Woods, Mintoff (Failla 57). Coach: Mark Marlow (MLT)
Yellow Card(s): Gatt Baldacchino 11, Azzopardi 42, Tidane 67, Mifsud Triganza 80, Szentpéteri 90+3
H 0-3
Szentpéteri, Azzopardi, B. Muscat, Tidane, Scerri, Mifsud Triganza (Mercieca 90), Lattes (Portulez 79), Gatt Baldacchino, Woods, Mintoff, Failla. Coach: Mark Marlow (MLT)
Red Card(s): Azzopardi 78
Yellow Card(s): Tidane 20, Scerri 26

MOLDOVA

FC SHERIFF

UEFA CHAMPIONS LEAGUE

Second Qualifying Round – KS Dinamo Tirana (ALB)
H 3-1 *Volkov (9), Nikolić (62), Nádson (70)*
Stoyanov, Volkov, Tarkhnishvili, Nikolić (Gheorghiev 75), Jymmy, Vranješ, Fred (Haceaturov 90+1), Bulat (Erokhin 46), Nádson, Branković, Adamović. Coach: Andrei Sosnitskiy (BLR)
Yellow Card(s): Volkov 14, Nikolić 63
A 0-1
Stoyanov, Volkov, Tarkhnishvili, Nikolić (Diedhiou 46), Jymmy, Erokhin, Vranješ, Bulat (Fred 57), Nádson, Branković, Adamović (Samardžić 80). Coach: Andrei Sosnitskiy (BLR)
Yellow Card(s): Branković 50, Fred 70, Tarkhnishvili 90+2

Third Qualifying Round – NK Dinamo Zagreb (CRO)
H 1-1 *Erokhin (35)*
Stoyanov, Volkov (Gheorghiev 88), Tarkhnishvili, Jymmy, Erokhin, Vranješ, Diedhiou (Nikolić 66), Samardžić, Nádson (Fred 32), Branković, Adamović. Coach: Andrei Sosnitskiy (BLR)
Yellow Card(s): Erokhin 29, Tarkhnishvili 77
A 1-1 (aet; 6-5 on pens) *Volkov (16)*
Stoyanov, Volkov, Jymmy, Erokhin, Vranješ, Diedhiou (Nikolić 72), Fred (Haceaturov 79), Samardžić, Nádson (Scripcenco 95), Branković, Adamović. Coach: Andrei Sosnitskiy (BLR)
Yellow Card(s): Fred 37, Samardžić 54, Nikolić 79, Adamović 113, Stoyanov 119

Play-Offs – FC Basel 1893 (SUI)
A 0-1
Stoyanov, Volkov (Gheorghiev 90+2), Erokhin, Balima, Vranješ, Rouamba, Diedhiou (Đurović 57), Samardžić, Nádson, Branković, Adamović (Haceaturov 79). Coach: Andrei Sosnitskiy (BLR)
Red Card(s): Erokhin 86
Yellow Card(s): Branković 17, Samardžić 53, Rouamba 58, Erokhin 76, Erokhin 85, Vranješ 85
H 0-3
Stoyanov, Volkov, Tarkhnishvili, Jymmy (Haceaturov 79), Balima, Vranješ, Rouamba, Diedhiou (Nikolić 66), Fred (Đurović 76), Nádson, Adamović. Coach: Andrei Sosnitskiy (BLR)
Red Card(s): Tarkhnishvili 76
Yellow Card(s): Tarkhnishvili 57, Volkov 71, Tarkhnishvili 76, Vranješ 85

UEFA EUROPA LEAGUE

Group E
Match 1 – AZ Alkmaar (NED)
A 1-2 *Moreno (68og)*
Stoyanov, Nikolić, Jymmy (Đurović 69), Erokhin (Fred 62), Balima, Rouamba, Diedhiou, Samardžić, Nádson, Branković, Adamović (Gauračs 88). Coach: Andrei Sosnitskiy (BLR)
Yellow Card(s): Adamović 42, Erokhin 57, Samardžić 62
Match 2 – FC Dynamo Kyiv (UKR)
H 2-0 *Erokhin (8), Jymmy (37p)*
Stoyanov, Volkov, Tarkhnishvili, Jymmy (Gauračs 62), Erokhin, Balima, Vranješ, Rouamba, Diedhiou (Branković 46), Nádson, Adamović (Samardžić 78). Coach: Andrei Sosnitskiy (BLR)
Yellow Card(s): Adamović 56
Match 3 – FC BATE Borisov (BLR)
H 0-1
Stoyanov, Tarkhnishvili, Erokhin, Gauračs (Jymmy 64), Balima (Gheorghiev 82), Vranješ, Rouamba, Diedhiou (Volkov 64), Nádson, Branković, Adamović. Coach: Andrei Sosnitskiy (BLR)
Yellow Card(s): Tarkhnishvili 19, Rouamba 48, Diedhiou 56
Match 4 – FC BATE Borisov (BLR)
A 1-3 *Erokhin (32)*
Stoyanov (Stajila 57), Volkov (Gauračs 71), Tarkhnishvili, Erokhin, Balima, Vranješ, Rouamba, Diedhiou, Nádson, Branković, Adamović (Haceaturov 74). Coach: Andrei Sosnitskiy (BLR)
Yellow Card(s): Vranješ 19, Rouamba 45, Tarkhnishvili 74
Match 5 – AZ Alkmaar (NED)
H 1-1 *Rouamba (54)*
Stajila, Volkov (Diedhiou 62), Jymmy, Erokhin, Balima (Gheorghiev 77), Vranješ, Rouamba, Samardžić, Nádson, Branković, Adamović (Fred 73). Coach: Andrei Sosnitskiy (BLR)
Yellow Card(s): Rouamba 32
Match 6 – FC Dynamo Kyiv (UKR)
A 0-0
Stajila, Volkov (Gauračs 90+3), Jymmy, Erokhin, Balima, Diedhiou (Nikolić 80), Fred (Gheorghiev 76), Samardžić, Nádson, Branković, Adamović. Coach: Andrei Sosnitskiy (BLR)
Yellow Card(s): Jymmy 49

FC ISKRA-STAL

UEFA EUROPA LEAGUE

Second Qualifying Round – IF Elfsborg (SWE)
A 1-2 *Tofan (87)*
Gaiduchevici, Gafina, Casian, Novicov, Popovici, Rudac, Mihaliov (Tofan 68), Kilikevych (Porfireanu 74), Feshchenko, Taranu (Chiriliuc 79), Burcovshi. Coach: Vlad Goian (MDA)
Yellow Card(s): Rudac 20, Feshchenko 40
H 0-1
Gaiduchevici, Gafina, Casian, Novicov, Porfireanu, Popovici, Rudac (Tofan 52), Mihaliov (Kilikevych 61), Feshchenko, Taranu (Gorodetschi 78), Burcovshi. Coach: Vlad Goian (MDA)
Yellow Card(s): Mihaliov 55, Novikov 62

FC OLIMPIA BALTI

UEFA EUROPA LEAGUE

First Qualifying Round – Xäzär Länkäran FK (AZE)
H 0-0
Pascenco, Ogada, Orlovschi, Ovseannicov, Robens, Tcaciuc, Cheltuiala (Kourouma 89), Valuta, Horolskiy (Pasecniuc 65), Camara, Adaramola (Somide 79). Coach: Nicolae Bunea (MDA)
Yellow Card(s): Cheltuiala 45+1
A 1-1 *Robens (14)*
Pascenco, Ogada, Orlovschi, Ovseannicov, Robens (Horolskiy 75), Tcaciuc (Kourouma 90+2), Cheltuiala, Pasecniuc, Valuta, Camara (Somide 86), Adaramola. Coach: Nicolae Bunea (MDA)
Yellow Card(s): Ogada 52, Pascenco 90+1

Second Qualifying Round – FC Dinamo Bucureşti (ROU)
H 0-2
Pascenco, Ogada, Orlovschi, Ovseannicov, Robens (Repinetschi 67), Tcaciuc (Somide 58), Cheltuiala, Pasecniuc (Horolskiy 81), Valuta, Camara, Adaramola. Coach: Nicolae Bunea (MDA)
Red Card(s): Cheltuiala 88
Yellow Card(s): Cheltuiala 41, Orlovschi 68, Cheltuiala 88
A 1-5 *Adaramola (90)*
Paius, Ogada, Verbetschi, Orlovschi, Ovseannicov, Robens (Somide 70), Tcaciuc, Pasecniuc (Horolskiy 46), Valuta (Gusacov 60), Camara, Adaramola. Coach: Nicolae Bunea (MDA)
Yellow Card(s): Adaramola 25, Paius 61, Ovseannicov 87

FC DACIA CHISINAU

UEFA EUROPA LEAGUE

First Qualifying Round – FK Zeta (MNE)
A 1-1 *Orbu (39)*
Matiughin, Popovici, Gorceac (Dragovozov 68), Orbu, Korgalidze, Bulat (Negrescu 78), Lomidze, Grosev, Gamezardashvili, Cojocari, Sischin (Bursuc 58). Coach: Vasilie Koselev (MDA)
Red Card(s): Gamezardashvili 76
Yellow Card(s): Gamezardashvili 1, Gamezardashvili 76
H 0-0
Matiughin, Popovici, Orbu (Guchashvili 90+1), Korgalidze (Gorceac 84), Bulat, Lomidze, Negrescu, Grosev, Bursuc, Cojocari, Sischin (Dragovozo 58). Coach: Igor Dobrovolskiy (MDA)
Red Card(s): Bulat 28
Yellow Card(s): Grosev 57, Bursuc 90+3

Second Qualifying Round – Kalmar FF (SWE)
A 0-0
Matiughin, Popovici, Korgalidze, Dragovozov, Lomidze, Grosev, Bursuc, Gamezardashvili, Cojocari, Guchashvili (Kum Dezire 57; Orbu 80), Sischin (Gorceac 50). Coach: Igor Dobrovolskiy (MDA)
Yellow Card(s): Popovici 39, Lomidze 56, Orbu 81
H 0-2
Matiughin, Orbu, Korgalidze, Dragovozov (Glega 63), Lomidze, Grosev (Sischin 70), Molla, Bursuc (Gorceac 78), Caraulan, Gamezardashvili, Cojocari. Coach: Igor Dobrovolskiy (MDA)
Yellow Card(s): Caraulan 58, Lomidze 71, Cojocari 90+3

MONTENEGRO

FK RUDAR PLJEVLJA

UEFA CHAMPIONS LEAGUE

First Qualifying Round – SP Tre Fiori (SMR)
A 3-0 *Useni (31), Vlahović (40), I. Jovanović (90+5)*
Radanović, Sekulić (Mićić 60), Ivanović, Igumanović, Bojović, Useni, Brnović (Minić 75), Tomić (I. Jovanović 68), Ranđelović, Vlahović, Bojić. Coach: Nebojša Vignjević (SRB)
Yellow Card(s): Tomić 25, Sekulić 53, Minić 80
H 4-1 *Ranđelović (7, 67), Vlahović (83), M. Jovanović (85)*
Radanović, Sekulić (Mićić 78), Ivanović, Igumanović, Bojović, Useni (I. Jovanović 61), Brnović, Tomić (M. Jovanović 46), Ranđelović, Vlahović, Bojić. Coach: Nebojša Vignjević (SRB)
Yellow Card(s): I. Jovanović 70

Second Qualifying Round – PFC Litex Lovech (BUL)
A 0-1
Radanović, Ivanović, Igumanović, Bojović, Mićić, Useni (Adžić 89), Brnović (Sekulić 79), M. Jovanović (I. Jovanović 56), Ranđelović, Vlahović, Bojić. Coach: Nebojša Vignjević (SRB)
Red Card(s): Bojović 85
Yellow Card(s): Useni 27, Ranđelović 33, Igumanović 40, Bojović 59, Bojović 85
H 0-4
Radanović, Ivanović, Igumanović, Adžić, Mićić (Sekulić 78), Useni, Brnović (M. Jovanović 58), I. Jovanović, Ranđelović, Vlahović (Idrizović 46), Bojić. Coach: Nebojša Vignjević (SRB)
Yellow Card(s): Adžić 18, Mićić 38, Useni 80

FK BUDUĆNOST PODGORICA

UEFA EUROPA LEAGUE

Second Qualifying Round – Bakı FK (AZE)
A 3-0 (w/o)
Original result 1-2 *Bećiraj (38)*
Dragojević, Đikanović, Ajković, Đokaj, Brnović, Mazić, Nikolić (P. Vukčević 83), Vuković, Bećiraj, Golubović (Bošković 81), Adamović. Coach: Nikola Rakojević (MNE)
Yellow Card(s): Nikolić 8, Đokaj 60

A 1-2 *Brnović (64)*
ragojević, Đikanović, Ajković, Đokaj, P. Vukčević, Mazić, Nikolić (Brnović 6), Kudemor, Vuković (Bošković 84), Bećiraj, Adamović. Coach: Nikola akojević (MNE)
ellow Card(s): Kudemor 12, Đikanović 31, Nikač 65, Brnović 75, jković 90+1

hird Qualifying Round – Brøndby IF (DEN)
1-2 *Bećiraj (90+3)*
ragojević, Đikanović, Ajković (Golubović 68), Brnović, P. Vukčević, azić, Bošković, Kudemor (Tiodorović 81), Vuković, Bećiraj, Adamović. oach: Nikola Rakojević (MNE)
ellow Card(s): Ajković 16, Bošković 57, P. Vukčević 84, olubović 90+4
0-1
ragojević, Đikanović, Brnović (S. Mugoša 84), P. Vukčević (Mi. adulović 46), Mazić, Bošković, Nikolić, Kudemor, Bećiraj, Golubović Nikač 61), Adamović. Coach: Nikola Rakojević (MNE)

FK MOGREN

UEFA EUROPA LEAGUE

irst Qualifying Round – UE Santa Coloma (AND)
3-0 *Grbić (14), Ćulafić (83), Ćetković (90+2)*
anjušević, Pejović, Simović, Janičić, Grbić (Ćulafić 76), Glušćević (B. ožović 46), Mirković, Jovanović, Nuhi (Nerić 62), Kapisoda, Ćetković. oach: Stevan Mojsilović (SRB)
ellow Card(s): Pejović 20, Grbić 36, Mirković 59, Simović 81, aničić 89
2-0 *Ćulafić (18), Glušćević (20)*
anjušević, Pejović, Simović, Janičić, Glušćević, Mirković, Jovanović Martinović 68), Ćulafić (Jovović 58), Kapisoda, B. Božović, Ćetković Marković 77). Coach: Stevan Mojsilović (SRB)
ellow Card(s): Kapisoda 87

econd Qualifying Round – Maccabi Tel-Aviv FC (ISR)
A 0-2
Janjušević, Pejović, Simović, Janičić, Grbić (Ćetković 65), Glušćević, Mirković, Jovanović, Nuhi, Kapisoda (Jovović 82), B. Božović (Ćulafić 60). Coach: Stevan Mojsilović (SRB)
Yellow Card(s): Jovanović 20, Janjušević 43
H 2-1 *Glušćević (58p, 80)*
Janjušević, Pejović, Simović, Janičić, Glušćević, Mirković (D. Božović 71), Jovanović, Ćulafić, Nuhi, Kapisoda (Grbić 46), Ćetković (B. Božović 46). Coach: Stevan Mojsilović (SRB)
Yellow Card(s): Mirković 3, Glušćević 80

FK ZETA

UEFA EUROPA LEAGUE

First Qualifying Round – FC Dacia Chisinau (MDA)
H 1-1 *Peličić (77p)*
Ivanović, Miloš M. Radulović, Boljević, Kaluđerović, Zlatičanin, Đuretić (Peličić 46), Kojašević, Petrović, Simović, Burzanović (Krkotić 46), Jugović (Lambulić 71). Coach: Dragoljub Đuretić (MNE)
Yellow Card(s): Radulović 50, Peličić 88
A 0-0
Ivanović, Miloš M. Radulović, Boljević, Kaluđerović, Zlatičanin, Krkotić (Lađić 61), Peličić, Kojašević, Petrović, Simović (Burzanović 76), Jugović (Lambulić 69). Coach: Dragoljub Đuretić (MNE)
Yellow Card(s): Radulović 28, Kojašević 67

NETHERLANDS

FC TWENTE

UEFA CHAMPIONS LEAGUE

Group A
Match 1 – FC Internazionale Milano (ITA)
H 2-2 *Janssen (20), Milito (30og)*
Mihaylov, Wisgerhof, Brama, Janssen, De Jong, Ruiz, Rosales, Douglas, Janko (Bajrami 78), Chadli (Landzaat 88), Tiendalli. Coach: Michel Preud'homme (BEL)
Yellow Card(s): Douglas 90+3
Match 2 – Tottenham Hotspur FC (ENG)
A 1-4 *Chadli (56)*
Mihaylov, Kuiper, Wisgerhof, Brama, Landzaat (De Jong 69), Janssen, Ruiz, Bajrami (Chadli 28), Rosales, Douglas, Janko. Coach: Michel Preud'homme (BEL)
Yellow Card(s): Mihaylov 40, Kuiper 54, Rosales 80
Match 3 – SV Werder Bremen (GER)
H 1-1 *Janssen (75)*
Mihaylov, Wisgerhof (Bengtsson 24), Brama, Landzaat (De Jong 86), Janssen, Ruiz, Rosales, Douglas, Janko, Chadli, Tiendalli. Coach: Michel Preud'homme (BEL)
Yellow Card(s): Brama 45+1, Tiendalli 61
Match 4 – SV Werder Bremen (GER)
A 2-0 *Chadli (81), De Jong (84)*
Mihaylov, Wisgerhof, Bengtsson (Schimpelsberger 76), Landzaat, De Jong (Stockentree 90+1), Ruiz, Rosales, Douglas, Janko, Chadli (Vujičević 86), Leugers. Coach: Michel Preud'homme (BEL)
Yellow Card(s): Douglas 41, Leugers 62, Bengtsson 68
Match 5 – FC Internazionale Milano (ITA)
A 0-1
Mihaylov, Wisgerhof, Brama, Janssen, De Jong, Ruiz, Rosales, Douglas, Janko (Landzaat 70), Chadli, Leugers (Buysse 80). Coach: Michel Preud'homme (BEL)
Yellow Card(s): Leugers 73
Match 6 – Tottenham Hotspur FC (ENG)
H 3-3 *Landzaat (22p), Rosales (56), Chadli (64)*
Boschker, Wisgerhof, Brama, Landzaat, Janssen, De Jong, Rosales, Douglas, Janko (Vujičević 72), Chadli, Tiendalli. Coach: Michel Preud'homme (BEL)

No	Player	Nat	DoB	Aps	(s)	Gls
Goalkeepers						
1	Sander Boschker		20/10/70	1		
13	Nikolay Mihaylov	BUL	28/6/88	5		
Defenders						
5	Rasmus Bengtsson	SWE	26/6/86	1	(1)	
23	Bart Buysse	BEL	16/10/86		(1)	
19	Douglas	BRA	12/1/88	6		
3	Nicky Kuiper		7/6/89	1		
34	Thilo Leugers	GER	9/1/91	2		
15	Roberto Rosales	VEN	20/11/88	6		1
36	Michael Schimpelsberger	AUT	12/2/91		(1)	
37	Mitch Stockentree		22/1/91		(1)	
33	Dwight Tiendalli		21/10/85	3		
4	Peter Wisgerhof		19/11/79	6		
Midfielders						
11	Emir Bajrami	SWE	7/3/88	1	(1)	
6	Wout Brama		21/8/86	5		
8	Theo Janssen		27/7/81	5		2
7	Denny Landzaat		6/5/76	4	(2)	1
27	Dario Vujičević	BIH	1/4/90		(2)	

Forwards						
22	Nacer Chadli	BEL	2/8/89	5	(1)	3
9	Luuk de Jong		27/8/90	4	(2)	1
21	Marc Janko	AUT	25/6/83	6		
10	Bryan Ruiz	CRC	18/8/85	5		

UEFA EUROPA LEAGUE

Round of 32 – FC Rubin Kazan (RUS)
A 2-0 *De Jong (77), Wisgerhof (88)*
Mihaylov, Onyewu, Wisgerhof, Brama, Landzaat, Janssen, De Jong, Ruiz (Bajrami 86), Rosales, Douglas, Chadli. Coach: Michel Preud'homme (BEL)
Yellow Card(s): Landzaat 25, Rosales 33, Janssen 34
H 2-2 *Janssen (45+1), Douglas (47)*
Mihaylov, Onyewu, Wisgerhof, Brama, Landzaat, Janssen, De Jong (Buysse 90+3), Ruiz (Bajrami 73), Rosales, Douglas, Chadli (Janko 87). Coach: Michel Preud'homme (BEL)
Yellow Card(s): Brama 62, Mihaylov 83

Round of 16 – FC Zenit St Petersburg (RUS)
H 3-0 *De Jong (25, 90+2), Landzaat (56)*
Mihaylov, Wisgerhof, Brama, Landzaat, Janssen, De Jong, Bajrami (John 76), Rosales, Douglas, Chadli, Buysse. Coach: Michel Preud'homme (BEL)
Yellow Card(s): Douglas 57, Buysse 70
A 0-2
Mihaylov, Onyewu, Wisgerhof, Brama, Landzaat, Janssen, De Jong, Bajrami (John 72), Rosales, Chadli, Buysse. Coach: Michel Preud'homme (BEL)

Quarter-Finals – Villarreal CF (ESP)
A 1-5 *Janko (90+1)*
Mihaylov, Onyewu, Wisgerhof, Brama (Landzaat 77), Janssen, De Jong (Janko 32), Ruiz (Chadli 60), Bajrami, Rosales, Douglas, Tiendalli. Coach: Michel Preud'homme (BEL)
Yellow Card(s): Rosales 58, Janko 70
H 1-3 *Bajrami (32)*
Boschker, Onyewu, Brama (Landzaat 61), Janssen, Ruiz (Bannink 78), Bajrami, Douglas, Janko (John 71), Buysse, Tiendalli, Leugers. Coach: Michel Preud'homme (BEL)
Red Card(s): Tiendalli 58
Yellow Card(s): Leugers 53

AFC AJAX

UEFA CHAMPIONS LEAGUE

Third Qualifying Round – PAOK FC (GRE)
H 1-1 *Suárez (13)*
Stekelenburg, Van der Wiel, Alderweireld, Vertonghen, Anita, Enoh, Sulejmani (Eriksen 67), De Jong, Emanuelson (Sarpong 79), Suárez, Lindgren (De Zeeuw 62). Coach: Martin Jol (NED)
Yellow Card(s): Emanuelson 11, Enoh 70, Vertonghen 78, Suárez 82
A 3-3 *Suárez (48), De Jong (50), Lindgren (55)*
Stekelenburg, Van der Wiel, Alderweireld, Vertonghen, Anita, Sulejmani (Eriksen 78), De Jong, Emanuelson, Suárez (Oleguer 90+3), Lindgren, De Zeeuw. Coach: Martin Jol (NED)
Yellow Card(s): Anita 76

Play-Offs – FC Dynamo Kyiv (UKR)
A 1-1 *Vertonghen (57)*
Stekelenburg, Van der Wiel, Vertonghen, Anita (Sulejmani 61), Enoh (Eriksen 69), El Hamdaoui, De Jong, Emanuelson, Suárez, De Zeeuw, Oleguer. Coach: Martin Jol (NED)
Yellow Card(s): Anita 42
H 2-1 *Suárez (43), El Hamdaoui (75)*
Stekelenburg, Van der Wiel, Alderweireld, Vertonghen, Enoh, Eriksen (Sulejmani 73), El Hamdaoui (Ooijer 85), De Jong, Emanuelson, Suárez, De Zeeuw. Coach: Martin Jol (NED)
Yellow Card(s): Suárez 46, Vertonghen 60, Alderweireld 90+3

Group G
Match 1 – Real Madrid CF (ESP)
A 0-2
Stekelenburg, Van der Wiel, Alderweireld, Anita, Enoh, Sulejmani (Eriksen 85), El Hamdaoui, De Jong, Emanuelson, Ooijer, De Zeeuw (Tainio 69). Coach: Martin Jol (NED)
Yellow Card(s): De Zeeuw 9
Match 2 – AC Milan (ITA)
H 1-1 *El Hamdaoui (23)*
Stekelenburg, Van der Wiel, Alderweireld, Vertonghen, Anita (Sulejmani 38), Enoh, El Hamdaoui, De Jong, Emanuelson, Suárez, De Zeeuw (Lindgren 79). Coach: Martin Jol (NED)
Yellow Card(s): Enoh 54
Match 3 – AJ Auxerre (FRA)
H 2-1 *De Zeeuw (7), Suárez (41)*
Stekelenburg, Van der Wiel, Vertonghen, Enoh, Sulejmani (Oleguer 60), El Hamdaoui, Emanuelson, Ooijer, Suárez, Lindgren, De Zeeuw. Coach: Martin Jol (NED)
Red Card(s): Ooijer 55
Yellow Card(s): Suárez 63
Match 4 – AJ Auxerre (FRA)
A 1-2 *Alderweireld (79)*
Stekelenburg, Van der Wiel, Alderweireld, Vertonghen, Anita (Sulejmani 58), Enoh (De Jong 46), El Hamdaoui, Emanuelson, Suárez, Lindgren, De Zeeuw (Eriksen 83). Coach: Martin Jol (NED)
Yellow Card(s): Van der Wiel 37, Suárez 84, Vertonghen 87
Match 5 – Real Madrid CF (ESP)
H 0-4
Stekelenburg, Van der Wiel, Alderweireld, Vertonghen, Anita, Enoh, Sulejmani (Eriksen 88), El Hamdaoui (De Zeeuw 46), De Jong (Lindgren 76), Emanuelson, Suárez. Coach: Martin Jol (NED)
Yellow Card(s): Enoh 35, De Zeeuw 60
Match 6 – AC Milan (ITA)
A 2-0 *De Zeeuw (57), Alderweireld (66)*
Stekelenburg, Van der Wiel, Alderweireld, Vertonghen, Enoh, Sulejmani, Eriksen, De Jong (El Hamdaoui 84), Emanuelson, Suárez (Tainio 90+2), De Zeeuw (Lindgren 82). Coach: Frank de Boer (NED)
Yellow Card(s): Suárez 35, Sulejmani 48

No	Player	Nat	DoB	Aps	(s)	Gls
Goalkeepers						
1	Maarten Stekelenburg		22/9/82	6		
Defenders						
3	Toby Alderweireld	BEL	2/3/89	5		2
5	Vurnon Anita		4/4/89	4		
23	Oleguer	ESP	2/2/80		(1)	
13	André Ooijer		11/7/74	2		
2	Gregory van der Wiel		3/2/88	6		
4	Jan Vertonghen	BEL	24/4/87	5		
Midfielders						
10	Siem de Jong		28/1/89	4	(1)	
20	Demy de Zeeuw		26/5/83	5	(1)	2
11	Urby Emanuelson		16/6/86	6		
6	Eyong Enoh	CMR	23/3/86	6		
8	Christian Eriksen	DEN	14/2/92	1	(3)	
18	Rasmus Lindgren	SWE	29/11/84	2	(3)	
19	Teemu Tainio	FIN	27/11/79		(2)	
Forwards						
9	Mounir El Hamdaoui	MAR	14/7/84	5	(1)	1
16	Luis Suárez	URU	24/1/87	5		1
7	Miralem Sulejmani	SRB	5/12/88	4	(2)	

UEFA EUROPA LEAGUE

Round of 32 – RSC Anderlecht (BEL)
A 3-0 *Alderweireld (32), Eriksen (59), El Hamdaoui (67)*
Stekelenburg, Van der Wiel, Alderweireld, Vertonghen, Enoh, Sulejmani (Özbiliz 81), Eriksen, El Hamdaoui, De Jong, Blind (Anita 77), Ebecilio. Coach: Frank de Boer (NED)
Yellow Card(s): Blind 35, Alderweireld 57
H 2-0 *Sulejmani (11, 17)*
Stekelenburg (Verhoeven 46), Van der Wiel, Alderweireld, Vertonghen,

noh (Lindgren 16), Sulejmani, Eriksen, El Hamdaoui, De Jong, Blind, becilio (De Zeeuw 71). Coach: Frank de Boer (NED)
ellow Card(s): Ebecilio 3

ound of 16 – FC Spartak Moskva (RUS)
0-1
tekelenburg, Van der Wiel, Alderweireld, Vertonghen, Anita, Sulejmani, riksen, De Jong, Blind, De Zeeuw (Enoh 74), Ebecilio (Özbiliz 85). oach: Frank de Boer (NED)
ellow Card(s): Vertonghen 52, Eriksen 78
0-3
erhoeven, Van der Wiel, Alderweireld, Vertonghen, Anita, Sulejmani zbiliz 46), Eriksen (Cvitanić 63), De Jong, Blind (Enoh 46), De Zeeuw, becilio. Coach: Frank de Boer (NED)
ellow Card(s): Enoh 77

PSV EINDHOVEN

UEFA EUROPA LEAGUE

lay-Offs – FC Sibir Novosibirsk (RUS)
0-1
saksson, Rodríguez, Vuković, Berg (Marcelo 63), Toivonen, Engelaar, ens, Amrabat, Hutchinson (Ojo 81), Pieters, Manolev. Coach: Fred utten (NED)
ed Card(s): Rodríguez 39
H 5-0 *Berg (38), Engelaar (56), Toivonen (64), Dzsudzsák (73, 90p)*
saksson, Marcelo, Vuković, Berg (Koevermans 71), Toivonen (Bakkal 0), Engelaar, Lens (Amrabat 86), Hutchinson, Pieters, Dzsudzsák, Manolev. Coach: Fred Rutten (NED)
Yellow Card(s): Pieters 58

Group I
Match 1 – UC Sampdoria (ITA)
H 1-1 *Dzsudzsák (90)*
Isaksson, Marcelo, Berg (Koevermans 75), Toivonen (Reis 84), Engelaar, Lens (Amrabat 80), Hutchinson, Pieters, Bouma, Afellay, Dzsudzsák. Coach: Fred Rutten (NED)
Yellow Card(s): Dzsudzsák 71
Match 2 – FC Metalist Kharkiv (UKR)
A 2-0 *Dzsudzsák (27p), Engelaar (30)*
Isaksson, Marcelo, Berg, Toivonen, Engelaar, Lens, Hutchinson, Pieters, Bouma (Rodríguez 65), Afellay (Bakkal 83), Dzsudzsák (Amrabat 75). Coach: Fred Rutten (NED)
Yellow Card(s): Bouma 42, Marcelo 78
Match 3 – Debreceni VSC (HUN)
A 2-1 *Engelaar (40), Dzsudzsák (66)*
Isaksson, Marcelo, Berg, Toivonen (Bakkal 84), Engelaar, Lens (Reis 46), Hutchinson, Pieters, Bouma, Afellay, Dzsudzsák. Coach: Fred Rutten (NED)
Yellow Card(s): Berg 34
Match 4 – Debreceni VSC (HUN)
H 3-0 *Afellay (22), Reis (44), Wuytens (88)*
Isaksson, Marcelo, Toivonen, Engelaar, Lens (Bakkal 64), Hutchinson, Pieters (Wuytens 77), Bouma (Rodríguez 46), Afellay, Dzsudzsák, Reis. Coach: Fred Rutten (NED)
Yellow Card(s): Bouma 38
Match 5 – UC Sampdoria (ITA)
A 2-1 *Toivonen (51, 90)*
Isaksson, Marcelo, Toivonen, Engelaar, Hutchinson, Pieters, Bouma, Afellay, Dzsudzsák, Manolev, Reis (Berg 84). Coach: Fred Rutten (NED)
Yellow Card(s): Toivonen 45+2, Marcelo 63, Pieters 76
Match 6 – FC Metalist Kharkiv (UKR)
H 0-0
Cássio, Marcelo, Rodríguez, Berg, Lens, Amrabat (Toivonen 68), Pieters (Vuković 46), Wuytens, Afellay (Dzsudzsák 90+1), Bakkal, Tamata. Coach: Fred Rutten (NED)

Round of 32 – LOSC Lille Métropole (FRA)
A 2-2 *Bouma (83), Toivonen (84)*
Isaksson, Rodríguez, Berg, Toivonen, Engelaar (Wuytens 67), Lens (Bakkal 67), Hutchinson, Pieters, Bouma (Marcelo 86), Dzsudzsák, Manolev. Coach: Fred Rutten (NED)
Yellow Card(s): Pieters 53, Engelaar 65, Bakkal 90+3
H 3-1 *Dzsudzsák (55), Lens (67), Marcelo (73)*
Isaksson, Marcelo, Berg, Toivonen, Engelaar (Wuytens 81), Lens, Hutchinson, Pieters, Bouma, Dzsudzsák (Bakkal 87), Manolev. Coach: Fred Rutten (NED)
Yellow Card(s): Dzsudzsák 59, Berg 68

Round of 16 – Rangers FC (SCO)
H 0-0
Isaksson, Marcelo, Berg (Koevermans 70), Toivonen (Bakkal 84), Engelaar, Lens, Hutchinson, Pieters, Bouma, Dzsudzsák, Manolev. Coach: Fred Rutten (NED)
A 1-0 *Lens (14)*
Isaksson, Marcelo, Berg (Bakkal 66), Toivonen, Engelaar, Lens, Hutchinson, Pieters, Bouma, Dzsudzsák, Tamata. Coach: Fred Rutten (NED)
Yellow Card(s): Engelaar 84

Quarter-Finals – SL Benfica (POR)
A 1-4 *Labyad (80)*
Isaksson, Marcelo, Berg (Labyad 78), Engelaar, Lens, Hutchinson, Pieters (Wuytens 72), Bouma, Dzsudzsák, Manolev, Bakkal. Coach: Fred Rutten (NED)
Yellow Card(s): Engelaar 54, Pieters 68
H 2-2 *Dzsudzsák (17), Lens (25)*
Isaksson, Marcelo (Berg 72), Rodríguez, Lens, Hutchinson, Wuytens, Dzsudzsák, Labyad, Manolev (Nijland 85), Bakkal, Tamata (Vuković 72). Coach: Fred Rutten (NED)
Yellow Card(s): Tamata 7, Dzsudzsák 27, Marcelo 35

FEYENOORD

UEFA EUROPA LEAGUE

Play-Offs – KAA Gent (BEL)
H 1-0 *Fer (78)*
Mulder, De Vrij, De Cler, El Ahmadi, Schaken, Fer, Bruins, Vlaar, Smolov (Castaignos 76), Wijnaldum, Martins Indi. Coach: Mario Been (NED)
Yellow Card(s): Wijnaldum 85
A 0-2
Mulder, De Vrij, De Cler (Cabral 81), Schaken (Castaignos 75), Fer, Bruins, Vlaar, Cissé (Smolov 59), Wijnaldum, Leerdam, Martins Indi. Coach: Mario Been (NED)
Yellow Card(s): Martins Indi 29, Fer 33

AZ ALKMAAR

UEFA EUROPA LEAGUE

Third Qualifying Round – IFK Göteborg (SWE)
H 2-0 *Klavan (52), Gudmundsson (56)*
Didulica, Jaliens, Marcellis (Swerts 65), Viergever (Ortíz 71), Falkenburg, Martens, Klavan, Wernbloom, Gudmundsson, Moisander, Benschop (Van der Velden 46). Coach: Gertjan Verbeek (NED)
Yellow Card(s): Wernbloom 44, Falkenburg 81
A 0-1
Didulica, Jaliens, Marcellis, Falkenburg (Sigthórsson 75), Martens, Klavan, Wernbloom, Gudmundsson, Van der Velden (Holman 65), Moisander, Ortíz. Coach: Gertjan Verbeek (NED)
Yellow Card(s): Didulica 72, Jaliens 90

Play-Offs – FC Aktobe (KAZ)
H 2-0 *Holman (20), Wernbloom (27)*
Didulica, Marcellis, Moreno, Falkenburg (Sigthórsson 71), Schaars, Martens (Ortíz 85), Klavan, Wernbloom, Gudmundsson, Moisander, Holman (Van der Velden 77). Coach: Gertjan Verbeek (NED)
Yellow Card(s): Marcellis 23, Moisander 79
A 1-2 *Wernbloom (10)*
Didulica, Marcellis, Moreno, Falkenburg (Jonathas 61), Schaars, Martens, Klavan, Wernbloom, Gudmundsson (Sigthórsson 68), Moisander, Holman (Ortíz 87). Coach: Gertjan Verbeek (NED)
Yellow Card(s): Moisander 15

Group E
Match 1 – FC Sheriff (MDA)
H 2-1 *Gudmundsson (14), Jaliens (83)*
Didulica, Jaliens, Marcellis, Moreno, Falkenburg (Jonathas 60), Schaars, Martens, Klavan (Poulsen 46), Wernbloom, Gudmundsson (Sigthórsson 77), Elm. Coach: Gertjan Verbeek (NED)
Match 2 – FC BATE Borisov (BLR)
A 1-4 *Sigthórsson (89)*
Romero, Marcellis, Moreno, Schaars, Jonathas, Klavan, Wernbloom (Van der Velden 77), Gudmundsson (Holman 67), Sigthórsson, Elm, Moisander (Jaliens 83). Coach: Gertjan Verbeek (NED)
Yellow Card(s): Romero 17
Match 3 – FC Dynamo Kyiv (UKR)
H 1-2 *Falkenburg (35)*
Romero, Marcellis, Moreno, Viergever, Falkenburg (Van der Velden 81), Schaars, Jonathas, Martens (Gudmundsson 77), Wernbloom, Moisander, Holman (Sigthórsson 68). Coach: Gertjan Verbeek (NED)
Red Card(s): Moisander 90+5
Yellow Card(s): Moisander 6, Wernbloom 22, Viergever 67, Schaars 67, Van der Velden 82, Moisander 90+5
Match 4 – FC Dynamo Kyiv (UKR)
A 0-2
Romero, Jaliens, Marcellis, Moreno, Schaars, Jonathas (Sigthórsson 73), Martens (Gudmundsson 73), Klavan, Wernbloom, Elm (Falkenburg 73), Holman. Coach: Gertjan Verbeek (NED)
Yellow Card(s): Sigthórsson 90+3
Match 5 – FC Sheriff (MDA)
A 1-1 *Holman (17)*
Romero, Marcellis, Moreno (Jaliens 71), Schaars, Martens (Ortíz 64), Klavan, Wernbloom, Sigthórsson, Elm (Falkenburg 75), Moisander, Holman. Coach: Gertjan Verbeek (NED)
Match 6 – FC BATE Borisov (BLR)
H 3-0 *Sigthórsson (7, 84), Maher (86)*
Romero, Jaliens, Moreno, Viergever (Poulsen 62), Falkenburg, Schaars, Martens (Gudmundsson 46), Wernbloom (Maher 71), Sigthórsson, Moisander, Holman. Coach: Gertjan Verbeek (NED)
Yellow Card(s): Viergever 25, Wernbloom 60, Schaars 76

FC UTRECHT

UEFA EUROPA LEAGUE

Second Qualifying Round – KF Tirana (ALB)
H 4-0 *Van Wolfswinkel (8), Pashaj (27og), Asare (30), Mertens (75)*
Sinouh, Cornelisse, Neşu, Van Wolfswinkel, Mertens (Oar 89), Asare, Schut (Van der Maarel 77), Maguire, Lensky, Mulenga (Loval 80), Wuytens. Coach: Ton du Chatinier (NED)
A 1-1 *Van Wolfswinkel (3)*
Sinouh, Cornelisse, Neşu, Van Wolfswinkel, Mertens (Sarota 70), Asare, Schut, Maguire, Lensky (Nijholt 79), Mulenga (Loval 60), Vorstermans. Coach: Ton du Chatinier (NED)

Third Qualifying Round – FC Luzern (SUI)
H 1-0 *Mertens (35)*
Sinouh, Cornelisse, Neşu, Silberbauer (Maguire 82), Van Wolfswinkel (Oar 68), Mertens, Asare, Schut, Lensky (Nijholt 73), Mulenga, Wuytens. Coach: Ton du Chatinier (NED)
Yellow Card(s): Asare 88
A 3-1 *Asare (13), Van Wolfswinkel (22), Silberbauer (28)*
Vorm, Cornelisse, Neşu, Silberbauer, Van Wolfswinkel (Loval 71), Mertens, Asare (Maguire 46), Schut, Lensky (Nijholt 77), Mulenga, Wuytens. Coach: Ton du Chatinier (NED)
Yellow Card(s): Cornelisse 4, Schut 61

Play-Offs – Celtic FC (SCO)
A 0-2
Vorm, Cornelisse, Neşu, Silberbauer, Van Wolfswinkel, Mertens, Asare, Schut, Lensky (Nijholt 82), Mulenga (Duplan 17), Wuytens. Coach: Ton d Chatinier (NED)
Yellow Card(s): Lensky 36, Nijholt 90+2
H 4-0 *Van Wolfswinkel (12p, 19p, 46), Maguire (62)*
Vorm, Cornelisse, Neşu, Duplan, Silberbauer, Van Wolfswinkel (Oar 90+1), Mertens (Nijholt 75), Asare (Maguire 53), Schut, Lensky, Wuytens Coach: Ton du Chatinier (NED)
Yellow Card(s): Mertens 39, Silberbauer 42, Neşu 89

Group K
Match 1 – SSC Napoli (ITA)
A 0-0
Vorm, Cornelisse, Neşu, Duplan (Maguire 83), Silberbauer, Van Wolfswinkel, Mertens (Danso 89), Demouge, Schut, Lensky, Wuytens. Coach: Ton du Chatinier (NED)
Yellow Card(s): Van Wolfswinkel 23, Demouge 37, Silberbauer 42
Match 2 – Liverpool FC (ENG)
H 0-0
Vorm, Cornelisse, Neşu, Duplan (Maguire 69), Silberbauer, Van Wolfswinkel, Mertens, Schut, Lensky (Nijholt 83), Mulenga, Wuytens. Coach: Ton du Chatinier (NED)
Match 3 – FC Steaua Bucureşti (ROU)
H 1-1 *Duplan (60)*
Vorm, Cornelisse, Neşu, Duplan, Silberbauer, Van Wolfswinkel, Mertens, Schut, Mulenga, Nijholt (Vorstermans 81), Wuytens. Coach: Ton du Chatinier (NED)
Yellow Card(s): Mertens 29, Wuytens 35
Match 4 – FC Steaua Bucureşti (ROU)
A 1-3 *Mertens (33)*
Vorm, Cornelisse, Neşu, Duplan (Danso 76), Silberbauer, Van Wolfswinkel, Mertens, Demouge (De Kogel 82), Schut, Lensky, Wuytens. Coach: Ton du Chatinier (NED)
Yellow Card(s): Neşu 22, Wuytens 90
Match 5 – SSC Napoli (ITA)
H 3-3 *Van Wolfswinkel (6, 28p), Demouge (35)*
Vorm, Cornelisse, Neşu, Duplan (De Kogel 84), Silberbauer (Nijholt 64), Van Wolfswinkel, Mertens, Demouge, Schut, Lensky (Maguire 53), Wuytens. Coach: Ton du Chatinier (NED)
Yellow Card(s): Van Wolfswinkel 75, Demouge 78, Nijholt 83
Match 6 – Liverpool FC (ENG)
A 0-0
Vorm, Cornelisse, Neşu, Duplan (Oar 71), Silberbauer, Van Wolfswinkel (De Kogel 45+1), Mertens, Maguire (Sarota 84), Keller, Nijholt, Wuytens. Coach: Ton du Chatinier (NED)

NORTHERN IRELAND

LINFIELD FC

UEFA CHAMPIONS LEAGUE

Second Qualifying Round – Rosenborg BK (NOR)
H 0-0
Blayney, Lindsay, Curran, Lowry (McAllister 70), Thompson, Bailie, B. Burns (Ervin 76), A. Burns, Garrett, Mulgrew, McCaul (Carvill 61). Coach: David Jeffrey (NIR)
Yellow Card(s): Garrett 67
A 0-2
Blayney, Lindsay, Curran, Lowry (Carvill 68), Thompson, Bailie, B. Burns, A. Burns (Munster 81), Garrett, Mulgrew, McCaul (Allen 63). Coach: David Jeffrey (NIR)
Yellow Card(s): Curran 37, Garrett 54

CLIFTONVILLE FC

UEFA EUROPA LEAGUE

Second Qualifying Round – HNK Cibalia (CRO)
H 1-0 *Caldwell (82)*
Connolly, R. Scannell, B. Holland, Donaghy, M. Holland, McMullan, C. Scannell (O'Connor 83), Garrett, Caldwell, Boyce (Patterson 90+2), Catney. Coach: Eddie Patterson (NIR)
Yellow Card(s): Donaghy 59
A 0-0
Connolly, R. Scannell, B. Holland, Donaghy, M. Holland (O'Hara 39), McMullan, C. Scannell (Patterson 79), Garrett, Caldwell (Smyth 85), Boyce, Catney. Coach: Eddie Patterson (NIR)
Yellow Card(s): McMullan 27, Connolly 64

Third Qualifying Round – PFC CSKA Sofia (BUL)
A 0-3
Connolly, R. Scannell, B. Holland, Donaghy, McMullan, C. Scannell (O'Connor 79), Garrett, Hutton, Caldwell, Boyce, Catney. Coach: Eddie Patterson (NIR)
Red Card(s): Garrett 84
Yellow Card(s): Garrett 19, Garrett 84, R. Scannell 90+3
H 1-2 *Boyce (42)*
Connolly, R. Scannell, B. Holland, Donaghy, McMullan, C. Scannell, Hutton, Caldwell, Boyce, Catney (Patterson 80), O'Connor (Smyth 75). Coach: Eddie Patterson (NIR)
Red Card(s): Donaghy 63
Yellow Card(s): C. Scannell 28, Donaghy 61, Donaghy 63, McMullan 64, Catney 74

GLENTORAN FC

UEFA EUROPA LEAGUE

First Qualifying Round – KR Reykjavík (ISL)
A 0-3
Morris, Clarke, McCabe (Gardiner 46), Ward, Waterworth (Southam 66), Hamilton, Gawley (Black 66), Jo. Taylor, McGovern, Hill, Fordyce. Coach: Scott Young (NIR)
H 2-2 *Callacher (22), Hamilton (56p)*
Morris, Nixon, Black, Clarke, Ward, Waterworth, Hamilton, Gawley, Callacher (Fordyce 75), McGovern, Gardiner (Martyn 56). Coach: Scott Young (NIR)
Yellow Card(s): Hamilton 45+2

PORTADOWN FC

UEFA EUROPA LEAGUE

First Qualifying Round – Skonto FC (LVA)
H 1-1 *Lecky (38)*
Armstrong, Redman, O'Hara, Ramsey, Kelly, Boyle, Clarke, Mouncey, Teggart (Haire 83), Lecky, McCafferty (Mackle 73). Coach: Ronnie McFall (NIR)
Red Card(s): Ramsey 88
Yellow Card(s): Mouncey 12, Ramsey 70, Ramsey 88, Haire 90+2
A 1-0 *Lecky (29)*
Miskelly, Mackle, Redman, O'Hara, Kelly, Boyle, Clarke (McCafferty 85), Braniff, Mouncey, Teggart (Haire 79), Lecky. Coach: Ronnie McFall (NIR)
Yellow Card(s): Clarke 33, Mackle 36

Second Qualifying Round – Qarabağ FK (AZE)
H 1-2 *Lecky (29)*
Miskelly, Redman, O'Hara, Ramsey, Kelly, Boyle, Braniff (Haire 80), Mouncey, Teggart, Lecky, McCafferty. Coach: Ronnie McFall (NIR)
Yellow Card(s): Lecky 30, McCafferty 80
A 1-1 *Braniff (71)*
Miskelly, Mackle (Christopher 90), Redman, O'Hara, Ramsey, Boyle, Clarke (McCullough 86), Braniff, Mouncey, Teggart (Haire 70), McCafferty. Coach: Ronnie McFall (NIR)
Yellow Card(s): Ramsey 37, O'Hara 90

NORWAY

ROSENBORG BK

UEFA CHAMPIONS LEAGUE

Second Qualifying Round – Linfield FC (NIR)
A 0-0
Örlund, Lustig, Dorsin, Annan, Winsnes, Moldskred (Olsen 87), Demidov, Stadsgaard, Iversen, Henriksen, Traoré (Strand 46). Coach: Nils Arne Eggen (NOR)
Yellow Card(s): Annan 65, Dorsin 87

H 2-0 *Prica (32), Henriksen (87)*
Örlund, Lustig, Dorsin, Annan, Moldskred (Olsen 74), Demidov, Stadsgaard, Iversen, Skjelbred (Strand 81), Henriksen, Prica (Winsnes 74). Coach: Nils Arne Eggen (NOR)

Third Qualifying Round – AIK Solna (SWE)
A 1-0 *Henriksen (33)*
Örlund, Lustig, Dorsin, Annan, Moldskred (Olsen 78), Demidov, Stadsgaard, Iversen, Skjelbred, Henriksen, Prica (Winsnes 72). Coach: Nils Arne Eggen (NOR)
H 3-0 *Prica (55), Demidov (64), Lustig (76)*
Örlund, Lustig, Dorsin, Annan, Moldskred (Olsen 55), Demidov, Stadsgaard, Iversen (Strand 74), Skjelbred, Henriksen, Prica (Bakenga 82). Coach: Nils Arne Eggen (NOR)

Play-Offs – FC København (DEN)
H 2-1 *Iversen (23), Henriksen (57)*
Örlund, Lustig, Dorsin, Annan, Olsen (Bakenga 65), Demidov, Stadsgaard, Iversen (Winsnes 85), Skjelbred, Henriksen, Prica. Coach: Nils Arne Eggen (NOR)
Yellow Card(s): Olsen 48, Annan 72
A 0-1
Örlund, Lustig, Dorsin, Olsen (Moldskred 77), Demidov, Stadsgaard, Iversen, Skjelbred (Winsnes 63), Wangberg (Strand 46), Henriksen, Prica. Coach: Nils Arne Eggen (NOR)
Yellow Card(s): Stadsgaard 45+1, Henriksen 83

UEFA EUROPA LEAGUE

Group B
Match 1 – Bayer 04 Leverkusen (GER)
A 0-4
Örlund, Lustig, Dorsin, Annan, Bjärsmyr, Strand (Saré 56), Demidov, Iversen (Olsen 79), Skjelbred, Henriksen (Jamtfall 72), Prica. Coach: Nils Arne Eggen (NOR)
Yellow Card(s): Prica 76
Match 2 – Aris Thessaloniki FC (GRE)
H 2-1 *Moldskred (37), Prica (68)*
Örlund, Lustig, Dorsin, Annan, Bjärsmyr, Moldskred (Olsen 90), Demidov, Iversen, Skjelbred, Henriksen, Prica (Jamtfall 86). Coach: Nils Arne Eggen (NOR)
Yellow Card(s): Prica 61, Dorsin 72
Match 3 – Club Atlético de Madrid (ESP)
A 0-3
Örlund, Lustig, Dorsin, Annan, Bjärsmyr, Moldskred, Demidov, Iversen (Jamtfall 82), Skjelbred (Saré 69), Henriksen, Prica. Coach: Nils Arne Eggen (NOR)
Yellow Card(s): Skjelbred 42
Match 4 – Club Atlético de Madrid (ESP)
H 1-2 *Henriksen (52)*
Örlund, Lustig, Dorsin, Annan (Saré 61), Bjärsmyr, Moldskred, Demidov, Iversen, Skjelbred, Henriksen, Prica. Coach: Nils Arne Eggen (NOR)
Yellow Card(s): Moldskred 28
Match 5 – Bayer 04 Leverkusen (GER)
H 0-1
Örlund, Lustig, Dorsin, Annan, Bjärsmyr, Moldskred, Demidov, Iversen, Skjelbred, Henriksen, Prica. Coach: Nils Arne Eggen (NOR)
Yellow Card(s): Annan 22
Match 6 – Aris Thessaloniki FC (GRE)
A 0-2
Örlund, Lustig, Dorsin, Annan, Bjärsmyr, Jamtfall (Iversen 65), Moldskred, Demidov, Skjelbred, Henriksen, Prica. Coach: Nils Arne Eggen (NOR)
Yellow Card(s): Prica 77

AALESUNDS FK

UEFA EUROPA LEAGUE

Third Qualifying Round – Motherwell FC (SCO)
H 1-1 *Mathisen (90+3p)*
Lindegaard, Jalasto, Sylling Olsen (Carlsen 70), Aarøy, Arneng, Herrera (Mathisen 57), Parr, Arnefjord, Jääger, Phillips, Larsen (Fredriksen 56). Coach: Kjetil Rekdal (NOR)
Yellow Card(s): Carlsen 88
A 0-3
Lindegaard, Tollås, Jalasto, Sylling Olsen, Fredriksen, Aarøy, Arneng, Herrera, Parr, Larsen (Carlsen 70), Mathisen (Fløtre 65). Coach: Kjetil Rekdal (NOR)
Yellow Card(s): Herrera 65

MOLDE FK

UEFA EUROPA LEAGUE

Second Qualifying Round – FK Jelgava (LVA)
H 1-0 *Fall (90+1)*
Lillebakk, Andreasson (Gjerde 84), Holm, Berg Hestad, Moström (Skjølsvik 79), Hoseth, Johansson (Thioune 60), Simonsen, Fall, Rindarøy, Forren. Coach: Kjell Jonevret (SWE)
Yellow Card(s): Fall 83
A 1-2 *Fall (14)*
Lillebakk, Holm (Thioune 55), Gjerde (Andreasson 66), Berg Hestad, Moström (Skjølsvik 77), Hoseth, Johansson, Simonsen, Fall, Rindarøy, Forren. Coach: Kjell Jonevret (SWE)

Third Qualifying Round – VfB Stuttgart (GER)
H 2-3 *Moström (65), Hoseth (76)*
Lillebakk, Andreasson, Holm, Berg Hestad (Skjølsvik 79), Thioune (Johansson 65), Moström (Runström 86), Hoseth, Simonsen, Fall, Rindarøy, Forren. Coach: Kjell Jonevret (SWE)
A 2-2 *Johansson (41), Rindarøy (49)*
Lillebakk, Andreasson, Berg Hestad, Thioune (Holm 79), Moström (Skjølsvik 89), Hoseth, Johansson (Diouf 86), Simonsen, Fall, Rindarøy, Forren. Coach: Kjell Jonevret (SWE)

STABÆK FOTBALL

UEFA EUROPA LEAGUE

Second Qualifying Round – FC Dnepr Mogilev (BLR)
H 2-2 *Skjelvik (22), Gunnarsson (53)*
Austbø, Eiríksson, Høiland, Onstad, Hauger, Hoff (Diogo 63), Gunnarsson, Diskerud, Hedenstad (Stenvoll 67), Skjelvik, Tømmernes (Hulsker 87). Coach: Jan Jönsson (SWE)
A 1-1 *Gunnarsson (37)*
Knudsen, Eiríksson, Høiland, Stenvoll (Farnerud 59), Hauger, Gunnarsson, Diogo, Diskerud (Pálmason 79), Hedenstad, Skjelvik, Tømmernes (Hulsker 87). Coach: Jan Jönsson (SWE)
Yellow Card(s): Diskerud 53, Høiland 88, Pálmason 90+3, Hulsker 90+4

POLAND

KKS LECH POZNAŃ

UEFA CHAMPIONS LEAGUE

Second Qualifying Round – İnter Bakı PİK (AZE)
H 1-0 *Wichniarek (47)*
Kotorowski, Gancarczyk, Bandrowski, Krivets, Štilić (Kiełb 63), Peszko (Wilk 90), Wichniarek (Mikołajczak 71), Bosacki, Injac, Wojtkowiak, Kikut. Coach: Jacek Zieliński (POL)
Yellow Card(s): Kikut 35, Gancarczyk 60
A 0-1 (aet; 9-8 on pens)
Kotorowski, Gancarczyk, Đurđević (Wilk 98), Arboleda, Krivets, Štilić, Peszko, Wichniarek (Kiełb 78), Bosacki, Injac, Wojtkowiak. Coach: Jacek Zieliński (POL)
Yellow Card(s): Štilić 101, Injac 114

Third Qualifying Round – AC Sparta Praha (CZE)
A 0-1
Kotorowski, Gancarczyk, Arboleda, Krivets (Mikołajczak 84), Štilić (Wilk 66), Drygas, Peszko, Wichniarek (Tshibamba 77), Bosacki, Injac, Wojtkowiak. Coach: Jacek Zieliński (POL)
Yellow Card(s): Drygas 24, Wojtkowiak 47, Peszko 55
H 0-1
Kotorowski, Gancarczyk, Arboleda, Wilk (Tshibamba 53), Krivets, Drygas (Štilić 57), Peszko, Wichniarek, Bosacki, Injac, Wojtkowiak (Kiełb 86). Coach: Jacek Zieliński (POL)
Red Card(s): Bosacki 80
Yellow Card(s): Wojtkowiak 32, Arboleda 77

UEFA EUROPA LEAGUE

Play-Offs – FC Dnipro Dnipropetrovsk (UKR)
A 1-0 *Arboleda (5)*
Burić, Đurđević, Arboleda, Bandrowski, Kiełb (Wilk 72), Krivets, Štilić (Możdżeń 89), Tshibamba (Zápotoka 86), Injac, Kikut, Henríquez. Coach: Jacek Zieliński (POL)
Yellow Card(s): Injac 27, Tshibamba 38
H 0-0
Burić, Đurđević, Arboleda, Bandrowski, Kiełb, Krivets (Zápotoka 90), Štilić (Drygas 84), Tshibamba (Wichniarek 68), Wojtkowiak, Kikut, Henríquez. Coach: Jacek Zieliński (POL)
Yellow Card(s): Bandrowski 3, Henríquez 64, Wichniarek 83

Group A
Match 1 – Juventus (ITA)
A 3-3 *Rudņevs (14p, 30, 90+2)*
Kotorowski, Đurđević, Arboleda, Krivets, Štilić (Tshibamba 80), Rudņevs, Peszko (Wichniarek 73), Injac, Wojtkowiak, Kikut (Wilk 80), Henríquez. Coach: Jacek Zieliński (POL)
Yellow Card(s): Arboleda 38, Peszko 66, Krivets 74, Wojtkowiak 78
Match 2 – FC Salzburg (AUT)
H 2-0 *Arboleda (47), Peszko (80)*
Burić, Arboleda, Krivets, Štilić, Rudņevs (Wichniarek 82), Peszko, Bosacki, Injac (Drygas 86), Wojtkowiak (Kiełb 53), Kikut, Henríquez. Coach: Jacek Zieliński (POL)
Yellow Card(s): Injac 43, Štilić 73, Peszko 89, Wichniarek 90+4
Match 3 – Manchester City FC (ENG)
A 1-3 *Tshibamba (50)*
Burić, Arboleda (Đurđević 70), Wilk (Štilić 55), Krivets, Drygas (Rudņevs 56), Peszko, Bosacki, Tshibamba, Injac, Kikut, Henríquez. Coach: Jacek Zieliński (POL)
Yellow Card(s): Bosacki 33
Match 4 – Manchester City FC (ENG)
H 3-1 *Injac (31), Arboleda (86), Możdżeń (90+1)*
Burić, Đurđević, Arboleda, Krivets, Štilić (Możdżeń 63), Rudņevs, Peszko (Wilk 73), Bosacki, Injac (Kiełb 52), Kikut, Henríquez. Coach: José María Bakero (ESP)
Yellow Card(s): Rudņevs 45+1, Đurđević 55, Możdżeń 90+3
Match 5 – Juventus (ITA)
H 1-1 *Rudņevs (12)*
Kotorowski, Đurđević, Arboleda, Krivets (Kikut 54), Štilić (Kamiński 83), Rudņevs (Możdżeń 61), Peszko, Bosacki, Injac, Wojtkowiak, Henríquez. Coach: José María Bakero (ESP)
Match 6 – FC Salzburg (AUT)
A 1-0 *Štilić (30)*
Kotorowski, Đurđević (Wojtkowiak 46), Arboleda, Krivets, Štilić (Bandrowski 77), Rudņevs, Peszko, Bosacki, Injac, Kikut, Henríquez (Wilk 36). Coach: José María Bakero (ESP)
Yellow Card(s): Henríquez 20, Wilk 88

Round of 32 – SC Braga (POR)
H 1-0 *Rudņevs (72)*
Kotorowski, Gancarczyk, Đurđević, Arboleda, Wilk (Kiełb 53), Krivets, Štilić, Rudņevs (Ubiparip 84), Bosacki, Kikut, Ślusarski (Możdżeń 46). Coach: José María Bakero (ESP)
Yellow Card(s): Wilk 20, Štilić 38
A 0-2
Kotorowski, Gancarczyk, Đurđević, Wołąkiewicz (Kiełb 61), Arboleda, Krivets, Štilić (Ubiparip 71), Rudņevs, Bosacki, Injac (Wilk 46), Kikut. Coach: José María Bakero (ESP)
Red Card(s): Kikut 87
Yellow Card(s): Gancarczyk 90+4

JAGIELLONIA BIAŁYSTOK

UEFA EUROPA LEAGUE

Third Qualifying Round – Aris Thessaloniki FC (GRE)
H 1-2 *Grzyb (24)*
Sandomierski, Kašćelan, Lewczuk (Hermes 23), Skerla, Kupisz, Grosicki, Lato (Burkhardt 60), Thiago Rangel, Norambuena, Frankowski (Makuszewski 82), Grzyb. Coach: Michał Probierz (POL)
A 2-2 *Burkhardt (25, 66)*
Sandomierski, Skerla, Kupisz, Grosicki, Hermes, Sidqy (Kašćelan 46), Norambuena, Makuszewski (Frankowski 50), Grzyb, Burkhardt (Lato 83), Kijanskas. Coach: Michał Probierz (POL)
Yellow Card(s): Sidqy 30

WISŁA KRAKÓW

UEFA EUROPA LEAGUE

Second Qualifying Round – FC Šiauliai (LTU)
A 2-0 *Pa. Brożek (78), Pi. Brożek (80)*
Jovanić, Sobolewski, Pi. Brożek, Boguski, Garguła (Jirsák 71), Díaz, Małecki (Żurawski 64), Čikoš, Pa. Brożek, Kowalski, Cléber. Coach: Henryk Kasperczak (POL)
H 5-0 *Pi. Brożek (23), Żurawski (48), Díaz (62), Pa. Brożek (66), Boguski (90+1)*
Jovanić, Sobolewski, Pi. Brożek (Kirm 77), Boguski, Garguła (Jirsák 63), Díaz, Čikoš, Pa. Brożek (Małecki 71), Kowalski, Cléber, Żurawski. Coach: Henryk Kasperczak (POL)

Third Qualifying Round – Qarabağ FK (AZE)
H 0-1
Jovanić, Bunoza, Sobolewski, Pi. Brożek, Boguski (Małecki 45), Paljic (Kirm 67), Jirsák, Čikoš, Pa. Brożek (Łobodziński 75), Kowalski, Żurawski. Coach: Henryk Kasperczak (POL)
Red Card(s): Bunoza 83
Yellow Card(s): Bunoza 51, Bunoza 83
A 2-3 *Pa. Brożek (56), Boguski (88)*
Jovanić, Sobolewski, Pi. Brożek, Boguski, Paljić (Pa. Brożek 46), Díaz, Jirsák (Wilk 46), Małecki (Łobodziński 79), Čikoš, Kowalski, Żurawski. Coach: Henryk Kasperczak (POL)
Yellow Card(s): Żurawski 65, Małecki 73

RUCH CHORZÓW

UEFA EUROPA LEAGUE

First Qualifying Round – FC Shakhter Karagandy (KAZ)
A 2-1 *Janoszka (45+1), Grzyb (47p)*
Pilarz, Stawarczyk, Grzyb, Nykiel (Malinowski 70), Olszar (Zając 52), Janoszka (Świerblewski 84), Grodzicki, Pulkowski, Sobiech, Straka, Jakubowski. Coach: Waldemar Fornalik (POL)
Yellow Card(s): Sobiech 85
H 1-0 *Sobiech (59)*
Pilarz, Grzyb, Nykiel, Zając (Malinowski 63), Janoszka, Grodzicki, Pulkowski (Piech 76), Sobiech (Stawarczyk 90+3), Sadlok, Straka, Jakubowski. Coach: Waldemar Fornalik (POL)
Yellow Card(s): Pilarz 40, Sobiech 55, Zając 63

Second Qualifying Round – Valletta FC (MLT)
A 1-1 *Grzyb (18p)*
Pilarz, Grzyb, Nykiel, Zając (Piech 59), Olszar (Flis 77), Janoszka, Grodzicki, Pulkowski, Sadlok, Straka (Malinowski 74), Jakubowski. Coach: Waldemar Fornalik (POL)
Yellow Card(s): Sadlok 41, Straka 55, Grzyb 78, Pilarz 86
H 0-0
Perdijić, Grzyb, Nykiel, Olszar (Piech 60), Janoszka (Bronowicki 78), Grodzicki, Pulkowski, Sobiech (Malinowski 89), Sadlok, Straka, Jakubowski. Coach: Waldemar Fornalik (POL)
Yellow Card(s): Straka 29

Third Qualifying Round – FK Austria Wien (AUT)
H 1-3 *Pulkowski (4)*
Pilarz, Grzyb, Nykiel, Olszar (Flis 69), Janoszka (Zając 46), Grodzicki, Pulkowski, Sobiech, Sadlok, Malinowski (Stawarczyk 79), Jakubowski. Coach: Waldemar Fornalik (POL)
Yellow Card(s): Sobiech 20, Olszar 58, Pulkowski 67, Grodzicki 85
A 0-3
Pilarz, Stawarczyk, Grzyb, Nykiel, Zając (Jankowski 80), Olszar (Bronowicki 62), Grodzicki, Pulkowski (Lisowski 69), Sadlok, Straka, Jakubowski. Coach: Waldemar Fornalik (POL)
Red Card(s): Grodzicki 4
Yellow Card(s): Pulkowski 2

PORTUGAL

SL BENFICA

UEFA CHAMPIONS LEAGUE

Group B
Match 1 – Hapoel Tel-Aviv FC (ISR)
H 2-0 *Luisão (21), Cardozo (68)*
Roberto, Luisão, Ruben Amorim, Javi García, Cardozo, Aimar (Airton 71) Carlos Martins, Fábio Coentrão, Gaitán (Maxi Pereira 57), David Luiz, Saviola (César Peixoto 87). Coach: Jorge Jesus (POR)
Match 2 – FC Schalke 04 (GER)
A 0-2
Roberto, Luisão, Javi García, Cardozo (Alan Kardec 71), Maxi Pereira, Carlos Martins, Fábio Coentrão, Gaitán (Salvio 46), David Luiz, César Peixoto, Saviola (Aimar 63). Coach: Jorge Jesus (POR)
Yellow Card(s): Gaitán 45+1, Salvio 49, Javi García 56
Match 3 – Olympique Lyonnais (FRA)
A 0-2
Roberto, Luisão, Javi García, Aimar (Jara 71), Maxi Pereira, Carlos Martins (Salvio 77), Fábio Coentrão, Gaitán, David Luiz, Saviola (César Peixoto 57), Alan Kardec. Coach: Jorge Jesus (POR)
Red Card(s): Gaitán 43
Yellow Card(s): Gaitán 34, Carlos Martins 37, Gaitán 43, Javi García 67
Match 4 – Olympique Lyonnais (FRA)
H 4-3 *Alan Kardec (20), Fábio Coentrão (32, 67), Javi García (42)*
Roberto, Luisão, Javi García, Salvio, Maxi Pereira, Carlos Martins (Felipe Menezes 74), Fábio Coentrão, David Luiz, César Peixoto, Saviola (Jara 70), Alan Kardec (Weldon 72). Coach: Jorge Jesus (POR)
Yellow Card(s): Luisão 23, Saviola 60, Roberto 90+1
Match 5 – Hapoel Tel-Aviv FC (ISR)
A 0-3
Roberto, Luisão, Javi García (Jara 79), Salvio (Carlos Martins 65), Aimar, Maxi Pereira, Fábio Coentrão, Gaitán, David Luiz, Saviola (Cardozo 46), Alan Kardec. Coach: Jorge Jesus (POR)
Yellow Card(s): Saviola 28
Match 6 – FC Schalke 04 (GER)
H 1-2 *Luisão (87)*
Roberto, Luisão, Ruben Amorim, Javi García, Cardozo, Maxi Pereira (Gaitán 46), Carlos Martins (Salvio 79), Fábio Coentrão, David Luiz, César Peixoto (Aimar 46), Saviola. Coach: Jorge Jesus (POR)
Yellow Card(s): David Luiz 68, Saviola 71, Aimar 77

No	Player	Nat	DoB	Aps	(s)	Gls
Goalkeepers						
12	Roberto	ESP	10/2/86	6		
Defenders						
25	César Peixoto		12/5/80	3	(2)	
23	David Luiz	BRA	22/4/87	6		
4	Luisão	BRA	13/2/81	6		2
14	Maxi Pereira	URU	8/6/84	5	(1)	
Midfielders						
10	Pablo Aimar	ARG	3/11/79	3	(2)	
2	Airton	BRA	21/2/90		(1)	
17	Carlos Martins		29/4/82	5	(1)	
18	Fábio Coentrão		11/3/88	6		2
16	Felipe Menezes	BRA	20/1/88		(1)	
6	Javi García	ESP	8/2/87	6		1
5	Ruben Amorim		27/1/85	2		

rwards

No	Player	Nat	DoB	Aps	(s)	Gls
	Alan Kardec	BRA	12/1/89	3	(1)	1
	Óscar Cardozo	PAR	20/5/83	3	(1)	1
	Nicolás Gaitán	ARG	23/2/88	4	(1)	
	Franco Jara	ARG	15/7/88		(3)	
	Eduardo Salvio	ARG	13/7/90	2	(3)	
	Javier Saviola	ARG	11/12/81	6		
	Weldon	BRA	6/8/80		(1)	

UEFA EUROPA LEAGUE

ound of 32 – VfB Stuttgart (GER)
2-1 *Cardozo (70), Jara (81)*
oberto, Luisão, Javi García, Cardozo, Salvio (Alan Kardec 75), Aimar arlos Martins 75), Jara (Felipe Menezes 87), Maxi Pereira, Fábio oentrão, Gaitán, Sidnei. Coach: Jorge Jesus (POR)
ellow Card(s): Fábio Coentrão 42, Javi García 88, Maxi Pereira 90+5
2-0 *Salvio (31), Cardozo (78)*
oberto, Airton, Luisão, Cardozo (Felipe Menezes 88), Salvio, Aimar arlos Martins 73), Jara (Alan Kardec 90+2), Maxi Pereira, Fábio oentrão, Gaitán, Sidnei. Coach: Jorge Jesus (POR)
ellow Card(s): Sidnei 44, Carlos Martins 81

ound of 16 – Paris Saint-Germain FC (FRA)
2-1 *Maxi Pereira (42), Jara (81)*
oberto, Luisão, Javi García, Cardozo, Salvio (Jara 66), Maxi Pereira, arlos Martins (César Peixoto 85), Fábio Coentrão, Gaitán (Aimar 71), idnei, Saviola. Coach: Jorge Jesus (POR)
ellow Card(s): Salvio 26
1-1 *Gaitán (27)*
oberto, Luisão, Javi García, Cardozo, Salvio, Aimar (César Peixoto 80), axi Pereira, Fábio Coentrão, Gaitán (Jardel 90), Sidnei, Saviola (Carlos artins 64). Coach: Jorge Jesus (POR)
ellow Card(s): Aimar 29, Maxi Pereira 78

uarter-Finals – PSV Eindhoven (NED)
4-1 *Aimar (37), Salvio (45, 52), Saviola (90+4)*
oberto, Luisão, Javi García, Cardozo (Felipe Menezes 90), Salvio, Aimar César Peixoto 78), Maxi Pereira, Fábio Coentrão, Gaitán (Jara 78), aviola, Jardel. Coach: Jorge Jesus (POR)
Yellow Card(s): Javi García 86
A 2-2 *Luisão (45+2), Cardozo (63p)*
Roberto, Luisão, Javi García, Cardozo, Salvio (Carlos Martins 20), Maxi Pereira, Fábio Coentrão, Gaitán (Airton 79), César Peixoto, Saviola Aimar 67), Jardel. Coach: Jorge Jesus (POR)

Semi-Finals – SC Braga (POR)
H 2-1 *Jardel (50), Cardozo (59)*
Roberto, Luisão, Javi García, Cardozo, Aimar, Maxi Pereira, Carlos Martins (Jara 65), Fábio Coentrão, César Peixoto (Gaitán 65), Saviola (Airton 86), Jardel. Coach: Jorge Jesus (POR)
Yellow Card(s): Aimar 53
A 0-1
Roberto, Luisão, Javi García, Cardozo, Maxi Pereira, Carlos Martins (Alan Kardec 81), Fábio Coentrão, Gaitán, César Peixoto (Jara 58), Saviola (Felipe Menezes 87), Jardel. Coach: Jorge Jesus (POR)
Yellow Card(s): César Peixoto 50, Maxi Pereira 59, Fábio Coentrão 75, Luisão 90+2

SC BRAGA

UEFA CHAMPIONS LEAGUE

Third Qualifying Round – Celtic FC (SCO)
H 3-0 *Alan (26p), Echiéjilé (76), Matheus (88)*
Mário Felgueiras, Rodríguez, Moisés, Paulo César, Miguel Garcia, Lima (Matheus 66), Echiéjilé, Andrés Madrid, Leandro Salino, Alan (Hélder Barbosa 90+1), Vandinho. Coach: Domingos Paciência (POR)
Yellow Card(s): Leandro Salino 90+1
A 1-2 *Paulo César (20)*
Mário Felgueiras, Rodríguez, Moisés, Paulo César, Miguel Garcia, Echiéjilé, Andrés Madrid (Paulão 86), Leandro Salino (Meyong 90+3), Alan, Vandinho, Matheus (Lima 67). Coach: Domingos Paciência (POR)
Yellow Card(s): Matheus 15, Miguel Garcia 23, Echiéjilé 56, Rodríguez 68

Play-Offs – Sevilla FC (ESP)
H 1-0 *Matheus (62)*
Felipe, Rodríguez, Moisés, Paulo César, Miguel Garcia (Sílvio 46), Echiéjilé, Aguiar (Lima 57), Leandro Salino, Alan, Vandinho, Matheus (Elton 75). Coach: Domingos Paciência (POR)
Yellow Card(s): Miguel Garcia 24, Paulo César 54
A 4-3 *Matheus (31), Lima (58, 85, 90)*
Felipe, Rodríguez, Moisés, Paulo César (Paulão 68), Echiéjilé, Aguiar (Lima 55), Leandro Salino, Sílvio, Alan, Vandinho, Matheus (Elton 80). Coach: Domingos Paciência (POR)
Yellow Card(s): Echiéjilé 15, Leandro Salino 18, Aguiar 43

Group H
Match 1 – Arsenal FC (ENG)
A 0-6
Felipe, Rodríguez, Moisés, Paulo César (Hélder Barbosa 70), Miguel Garcia, Aguiar, Sílvio, Alan, Hugo Viana (Mossoró 55), Vandinho, Matheus (Lima 60). Coach: Domingos Paciência (POR)
Yellow Card(s): Felipe 8, Rodríguez 20
Match 2 – FC Shakhtar Donetsk (UKR)
H 0-3
Felipe, Rodríguez (Paulão 36), Moisés, Paulo César, Miguel Garcia, Aguiar, Leandro Salino (Lima 55), Sílvio, Alan, Vandinho (Mossoró 74), Matheus. Coach: Domingos Paciência (POR)
Yellow Card(s): Matheus 87, Paulo César 90+1
Match 3 – FK Partizan (SRB)
H 2-0 *Lima (35), Matheus (90)*
Felipe, Paulão, Moisés, Paulo César (Leandro Salino 69), Lima (Mossoró 87), Echiéjilé, Andrés Madrid (Aguiar 73), Sílvio, Alan, Vandinho, Matheus. Coach: Domingos Paciência (POR)
Yellow Card(s): Andrés Madrid 54, Aguiar 86
Match 4 – FK Partizan (SRB)
A 1-0 *Moisés (35)*
Felipe, Rodríguez, Moisés, Mossoró (Leandro Salino 51), Paulo César, Echiéjilé, Aguiar, Sílvio, Alan (Andrés Madrid 68), Vandinho, Matheus (Lima 88). Coach: Domingos Paciência (POR)
Yellow Card(s): Moisés 50, Leandro Salino 82
Match 5 – Arsenal FC (ENG)
H 2-0 *Matheus (83, 90+3)*
Felipe, Rodríguez, Moisés, Miguel Garcia, Lima (Elton 81), Echiéjilé, Aguiar (Andrés Madrid 80), Leandro Salino, Alan, Vandinho (Hugo Viana 90), Matheus. Coach: Domingos Paciência (POR)
Yellow Card(s): Aguiar 55, Miguel Garcia 78
Match 6 – FC Shakhtar Donetsk (UKR)
A 0-2
Artur, Rodríguez, Paulo César, Miguel Garcia, Aguiar (Hugo Viana 72), Leandro Salino (Hélder Barbosa 81), Sílvio, Alan (Lima 69), Aníbal Capela, Vandinho, Matheus. Coach: Domingos Paciência (POR)
Yellow Card(s): Miguel Garcia 39

No	Player	Nat	DoB	Aps	(s)	Gls
Goalkeepers						
1	Artur	BRA	25/1/81	1		
84	Felipe	BRA	22/2/84	5		
Defenders						
48	Aníbal Capela		8/5/91	1		
20	Uwa Echiéjilé	NGA	20/1/88	3		
15	Miguel Garcia		4/2/83	4		
5	Moisés	BRA	25/7/79	5		1
3	Paulão	BRA	6/8/82	1	(1)	
2	Alberto Rodríguez	PER	31/3/84	5		
28	Sílvio		28/9/87	5		
Midfielders						
22	Luis Aguiar	URU	17/11/85	5	(1)	
30	Alan	BRA	19/9/79	6		
23	Andrés Madrid	ARG	29/7/81	1	(2)	
45	Hugo Viana		15/1/83	1	(2)	
25	Leandro Salino	BRA	22/4/85	3	(2)	
8	Mossoró	BRA	4/7/83	1	(3)	
88	Vandinho	BRA	15/1/78	6		

Forwards						
85	Elton	BRA	1/8/85		(1)	
10	Hélder Barbosa		25/5/87		(2)	
18	Lima	BRA	11/5/83	2	(4)	1
99	Matheus	BRA	15/1/83	6		3
9	Paulo César	BRA	5/1/80	5		

UEFA EUROPA LEAGUE

Round of 32 – KKS Lech Poznań (POL)
A 0-1
Artur, Rodríguez, Kaká, Hélder Barbosa (Alan 68), Miguel Garcia, Lima, Meyong (Mossoró 87), Leandro Salino, Custódio, Sílvio, Hugo Viana. Coach: Domingos Paciência (POR)
Yellow Card(s): Custódio 31, Hélder Barbosa 65
H 2-0 *Alan (8), Lima (36)*
Artur, Rodríguez, Kaká, Mossoró (Leandro Salino 69), Hélder Barbosa (Paulo César 68), Miguel Garcia, Lima, Custódio, Sílvio, Alan (Echiéjilé 82), Hugo Viana. Coach: Domingos Paciência (POR)
Yellow Card(s): Kaká 75, Artur 89

Round of 16 – Liverpool FC (ENG)
H 1-0 *Alan (18p)*
Artur, Rodríguez, Kaká, Mossoró (Paulão 69), Paulo César (Hélder Barbosa 90+4), Miguel Garcia, Lima (Meyong 78), Leandro Salino, Sílvio, Alan, Hugo Viana. Coach: Domingos Paciência (POR)
Yellow Card(s): Kaká 26
A 0-0
Artur, Rodríguez, Paulão, Paulo César, Miguel Garcia, Lima (Meyong 84), Leandro Salino (Mossoró 89), Sílvio, Alan, Hugo Viana, Vandinho (Kaká 74). Coach: Domingos Paciência (POR)
Yellow Card(s): Paulão 52, Vandinho 74

Quarter-Finals – FC Dynamo Kyiv (UKR)
A 1-1 *Gusev (13og)*
Artur, Paulão (Custódio 46), Kaká, Paulo César, Miguel Garcia, Lima (Meyong 83), Leandro Salino (Mossoró 74), Sílvio, Alan, Hugo Viana, Vandinho. Coach: Domingos Paciência (POR)
Yellow Card(s): Kaká 35, Miguel Garcia 50, Paulo César 52
H 0-0
Artur, Paulão, Paulo César, Lima (Hélder Barbosa 90+1), Meyong (Mossoró 70), Leandro Salino, Custódio, Sílvio, Alan, Hugo Viana, Vandinho. Coach: Domingos Paciência (POR)
Red Card(s): Paulo César 29
Yellow Card(s): Hugo Viana 29, Vandinho 41, Custódio 90+3

Semi-Finals – SL Benfica (POR)
A 1-2 *Vandinho (53)*
Artur, Rodríguez, Paulão, Miguel Garcia, Lima (Kaká 84), Meyong (Custódio 55), Leandro Salino, Sílvio, Alan, Hugo Viana (Mossoró 62), Vandinho. Coach: Domingos Paciência (POR)
Yellow Card(s): Rodríguez 6, Vandinho 39, Miguel Garcia 43
H 1-0 *Custódio (19)*
Artur, Rodríguez, Paulão, Mossoró (Kaká 80), Miguel Garcia, Lima (Leandro Salino 73), Meyong (Hélder Barbosa 87), Custódio, Sílvio, Alan, Hugo Viana. Coach: Domingos Paciência (POR)
Yellow Card(s): Sílvio 3, Paulão 60, Artur 90+5

Final – FC Porto (POR)
N 0-1
Artur, Rodríguez (Kaká 46), Paulão, Paulo César, Miguel Garcia, Lima (Meyong 66), Custódio, Sílvio, Alan, Hugo Viana (Mossoró 46), Vandinho. Coach: Domingos Paciência (POR)
Yellow Card(s): Hugo Viana 24, Sílvio 30, Săpunaru 49, Miguel Garcia 55, Mossoró 59, Kaká 80

No	Player	Nat	DoB	Aps	(s)	Gls
Goalkeepers						
1	Artur	BRA	25/1/81	9		
Defenders						
20	Uwa Echiéjilé	NGA	20/1/88		(1)	
4	Kaká	BRA	16/5/81	4	(4)	
15	Miguel Garcia		4/2/83	8		
3	Paulão	BRA	6/8/82	6	(1)	
2	Alberto Rodríguez	PER	31/3/84	7		
28	Sílvio		28/9/87	9		
Midfielders						
30	Alan	BRA	19/9/79	8	(1)	2
27	Custódio		24/5/83	5	(2)	1
45	Hugo Viana		15/1/83	9		
25	Leandro Salino	BRA	22/4/85	6	(2)	
8	Mossoró	BRA	4/7/83	3	(6)	
88	Vandinho	BRA	15/1/78	5		1
Forwards						
10	Hélder Barbosa		25/5/87	2	(3)	
18	Lima	BRA	11/5/83	9		1
19	Albert Meyong	CMR	19/10/80	4	(4)	
9	Paulo César	BRA	5/1/80	5	(1)	

FC PORTO

UEFA EUROPA LEAGUE

Play-Offs – KRC Genk (BEL)
A 3-0 *Falcao (29p), Souza (82), Belluschi (90)*
Helton, Maicon, Álvaro Pereira, Belluschi, João Moutinho, Falcao (Walter 82), Rolando, Varela (Souza 60), Săpunaru, Fernando, Ukra (Rúben Micael 74). Coach: André Villas-Boas (POR)
Yellow Card(s): Ukra 18, Maicon 32, Fernando 64, Helton 76, Álvaro Pereira 88
H 4-2 *Hulk (36, 59p, 63), Fernando (53)*
Beto, Maicon, Álvaro Pereira, João Moutinho (Belluschi 62), Falcao (Varela 56), Hulk, Rolando, Săpunaru, Souza, Fernando, Rúben Micael (Castro 69). Coach: André Villas-Boas (POR)
Yellow Card(s): Rolando 90

Group L
Match 1 – SK Rapid Wien (AUT)
H 3-0 *Rolando (26), Falcao (65), Rúben Micael (77)*
Helton, Maicon, Álvaro Pereira, João Moutinho, Falcao (Walter 78), C. Rodríguez, Hulk (Belluschi 68), Fucile, Rolando, Fernando, Rúben Micael (Castro 84). Coach: André Villas-Boas (POR)
Yellow Card(s): C. Rodríguez 61
Match 2 – PFC CSKA Sofia (BUL)
A 1-0 *Falcao (16)*
Helton, Maicon, Álvaro Pereira, Belluschi (Guarín 75), João Moutinho, Falcao (Walter 72), C. Rodríguez, Hulk (Varela 65), Săpunaru, Souza, Otamendi. Coach: André Villas-Boas (POR)
Yellow Card(s): Săpunaru 84
Match 3 – Beşiktaş JK (TUR)
A 3-1 *Falcao (26), Hulk (59, 78)*
Helton, Maicon, Álvaro Pereira, Belluschi, João Moutinho (Guarín 81), Falcao (Otamendi 46), C. Rodríguez (Varela 75), Hulk, Rolando, Săpunaru, Fernando. Coach: André Villas-Boas (POR)
Red Card(s): Maicon 43, Fernando 89
Yellow Card(s): Fernando 31, Fernando 89
Match 4 – Beşiktaş JK (TUR)
H 1-1 *Falcao (36p)*
Helton, Álvaro Pereira, Guarín, Belluschi (Souza 73), Falcao (Walter 79), C. Rodríguez, Hulk (João Moutinho 63), Fucile, Rolando, Rúben Micael, Otamendi. Coach: André Villas-Boas (POR)
Red Card(s): C. Rodríguez 59
Yellow Card(s): C. Rodríguez 39, C. Rodríguez 59
Match 5 – SK Rapid Wien (AUT)
A 3-1 *Falcao (42, 86, 88)*
Helton, João Moutinho, Falcao, Hulk, Fucile, Rolando, Varela (Ukra 46), Săpunaru, Fernando (Guarín 16), Rúben Micael (Belluschi 71), Otamendi. Coach: André Villas-Boas (POR)

Match 6 – PFC CSKA Sofia (BUL)
H 3-1 *Otamendi (22), Rúben Micael (54), J. Rodríguez (90+3)*
Helton, Maicon, Álvaro Pereira, Belluschi, Falcao (Hulk 60), Fucile, Walter, J. Rodríguez, Souza (Guarín 80), Rúben Micael (João Moutinho 71), Otamendi. Coach: André Villas-Boas (POR)

Round of 32 – Sevilla FC (ESP)
A 2-1 *Rolando (58), Guarín (86)*
Helton, Belluschi (Álvaro Pereira 86), João Moutinho, Hulk, Fucile, Rolando, Varela (Guarín 69), J. Rodríguez (C. Rodríguez 59), Săpunaru, Fernando, Otamendi. Coach: André Villas-Boas (POR)
Yellow Card(s): J. Rodríguez 25, João Moutinho 52, Guarín 87
H 0-1
Helton, Álvaro Pereira, Belluschi, João Moutinho (Săpunaru 74), Falcao (Guarín 74), Hulk, Fucile, Rolando, Varela (Maicon 86), Fernando, Otamendi. Coach: André Villas-Boas (POR)
Red Card(s): Álvaro Pereira 72
Yellow Card(s): Belluschi 50

Round of 16 – PFC CSKA Moskva (RUS)
A 1-0 *Guarín (70)*
Helton, Guarín (Souza 82), João Moutinho, Falcao, Hulk (C. Rodríguez 83), Fucile, Rolando, J. Rodríguez (Varela 57), Săpunaru, Fernando, Otamendi. Coach: André Villas-Boas (POR)
Yellow Card(s): Otamendi 63
H 2-1 *Hulk (1), Guarín (24)*
Helton, Guarín, João Moutinho, Falcao (Varela 77), Hulk (C. Rodríguez 87), Fucile, Rolando, J. Rodríguez (Belluschi 52), Săpunaru, Fernando, Otamendi. Coach: André Villas-Boas (POR)
Yellow Card(s): Fucile 37

Quarter-Finals – FC Spartak Moskva (RUS)
H 5-1 *Falcao (37, 84, 90+2), Varela (65), D. Kombarov (70og)*
Helton, Maicon, Álvaro Pereira, Guarín (Belluschi 69), João Moutinho, Falcao, Hulk (C. Rodríguez 80), Fucile, Rolando, Varela (J. Rodríguez 72), Fernando. Coach: André Villas-Boas (POR)
Yellow Card(s): João Moutinho 52
A 5-2 *Hulk (28), C. Rodríguez (45+2), Guarín (47), Falcao (54), Rúben Micael (89)*
Helton, Álvaro Pereira, Guarín, João Moutinho (Rúben Micael 46), Falcao (J. Rodríguez 72), C. Rodríguez, Hulk, Fucile (Săpunaru 28), Rolando, Fernando, Otamendi. Coach: André Villas-Boas (POR)

Semi-Finals – Villarreal CF (ESP)
H 5-1 *Falcao (49p, 67, 75, 90), Guarín (61)*
Helton, Álvaro Pereira, Guarín (Souza 79), João Moutinho, Falcao, C. Rodríguez (Varela 72), Hulk (J. Rodríguez 84), Rolando, Săpunaru, Fernando, Otamendi. Coach: André Villas-Boas (POR)
Yellow Card(s): Fernando 5, Hulk 26, Helton 83
A 2-3 *Hulk (39), Falcao (48)*
Helton, Álvaro Pereira, Guarín, João Moutinho (Souza 52), Falcao, C. Rodríguez (J. Rodríguez 32), Hulk, Rolando, Săpunaru, Fernando (Rúben Micael 61), Otamendi. Coach: André Villas-Boas (POR)
Yellow Card(s): Falcao 26, Săpunaru 60, Rúben Micael 74, Otamendi 79

Final – SC Braga (POR)
N 1-0 *Falcao (44)*
Helton, Álvaro Pereira, Guarín (Belluschi 73), João Moutinho, Falcao, Hulk, Rolando, Varela (J. Rodríguez 79), Săpunaru, Fernando, Otamendi. Coach: André Villas-Boas (POR)
Yellow Card(s): Săpunaru 49, Helton 90, Rolando 90+3

No	Player	at	DoB	Aps	(s)	Gls
Goalkeepers						
1	Helton	BRA	18/5/78	15		
Defenders						
5	Álvaro Pereira	URU	28/11/85	11	(1)	
13	Jorge Fucile	URU	19/11/84	10		
4	Maicon	BRA	14/9/88	5	(1)	
30	Nicolás Otamendi	ARG	12/2/88	12	(1)	1
14	Rolando		31/8/85	13		2
21	Cristian Săpunaru	ROU	5/4/84	9	(2)	
Midfielders						
26	André Castro		2/4/88		(1)	
7	Fernando Belluschi	ARG	10/9/83	6	(5)	
25	Fernando	BRA	25/7/87	12		
6	Fredy Guarín	COL	30/6/86	8	(6)	5
8	João Moutinho		8/9/86	13	(2)	
28	Rúben Micael		19/8/86	4	(2)	3
23	Souza	BRA	11/2/89	2	(4)	
Forwards						
9	Radamel Falcao	COL	10/2/86	14		17
12	Hulk	BRA	25/7/86	14	(1)	5
10	Cristian Rodríguez	URU	30/9/85	7	(4)	1
19	James Rodríguez	COL	12/7/91	4	(5)	1
27	Ukra		16/3/88		(1)	
17	Silvestre Varela		2/2/85	5	(5)	1
18	Walter	BRA	22/7/89	1	(3)	

SPORTING CLUBE DE PORTUGAL

UEFA EUROPA LEAGUE

Third Qualifying Round – FC Nordsjælland (DEN)
A 1-0 *Vukčević (24)*
Rui Patrício, Daniel Carriço, Anderson Polga, Evaldo, Pedro Mendes (Miguel Veloso 46), Maniche, Carlos Saleiro, Yannick Djaló (Liedson 81), Hélder Postiga, João Pereira, Vukčević (Valdés 71). Coach: Paulo Sérgio (POR)
H 2-1 *Hélder Postiga (24), Maniche (90+2)*
Rui Patrício, Daniel Carriço, Anderson Polga, Evaldo, Maniche, Valdés (Matías Fernández 71), Hélder Postiga (Sinama Pongolle 78), André Santos, Liedson, João Pereira, Vukčević (Yannick Djaló 62). Coach: Paulo Sérgio (POR)
Yellow Card(s): Liedson 53

Play-Offs – Brøndby IF (DEN)
H 0-2
Rui Patrício, Daniel Carriço, Evaldo, Maniche, Matías Fernández (Vukčević 56), Valdés (Carlos Saleiro 76), Hélder Postiga (Yannick Djaló 62), André Santos, Liedson, Nuno Coelho, João Pereira. Coach: Paulo Sérgio (POR)
Yellow Card(s): João Pereira 47, Daniel Carriço 90+3
A 3-0 *Evaldo (45), Nuno Coelho (75), Yannick Djaló (90+1)*
Rui Patrício, Daniel Carriço, Evaldo, Maniche, Yannick Djaló, Hélder Postiga (Matías Fernández 67), André Santos, Liedson (Carlos Saleiro 90+2), Nuno Coelho, Vukčević (Valdés 85), Abel. Coach: Paulo Sérgio (POR)
Yellow Card(s): Liedson 44

Group C
Match 1 – LOSC Lille Métropole (FRA)
A 2-1 *Vukčević (11), Hélder Postiga (34)*
Tiago, Torsiglieri, Daniel Carriço, Anderson Polga, Carlos Saleiro (Nuno Coelho 90+2), Zapater, Hélder Postiga, André Santos, Diogo Salomão (Evaldo 82), Vukčević (João Pereira 73), Abel. Coach: Paulo Sérgio (POR)
Yellow Card(s): Torsiglieri 10, Vukčević 45+1, Daniel Carriço 48, Anderson Polga 85
Match 2 – PFC Levski Sofia (BUL)
H 5-0 *Daniel Carriço (30), Maniche (43), Diogo Salomão (53), Hélder Postiga (61), Matías Fernández (79)*
Rui Patrício, Daniel Carriço, Anderson Polga, Evaldo, Maniche (André Santos 70), Matías Fernández, Zapater, Hélder Postiga (Carlos Saleiro 64), Diogo Salomão, João Pereira, Vukčević (Abel 77). Coach: Paulo Sérgio (POR)
Yellow Card(s): Daniel Carriço 84

Match 3 – KAA Gent (BEL)
H 5-1 *Diogo Salomão (7), Liedson (13, 27), Maniche (37), Hélder Postiga (59)*
Hildebrand, Daniel Carriço, Anderson Polga (Torsiglieri 44), Evaldo, Maniche (Zapater 63), Hélder Postiga, André Santos, Liedson (Vukčević 72), Diogo Salomão, João Pereira, Abel. Coach: Paulo Sérgio (POR)
Yellow Card(s): João Pereira 12, Hélder Postiga 19
Match 4 – KAA Gent (BEL)
A 1-3 *Carlos Saleiro (38)*
Hildebrand, Torsiglieri, Evaldo, Carlos Saleiro (Valdés 69), Yannick Djaló, Zapater, André Santos, Diogo Salomão (João Pereira 79), Cédric (Hélder Postiga 59), Nuno Coelho, Abel. Coach: Paulo Sérgio (POR)
Red Card(s): Abel 76
Yellow Card(s): Abel 7, André Santos 26, Abel 76
Match 5 – LOSC Lille Métropole (FRA)
H 1-0 *Anderson Polga (28)*
Rui Patrício, Daniel Carriço, Anderson Polga, Evaldo, Pedro Mendes, Maniche (Zapater 90+1), Yannick Djaló (Valdés 62), Hélder Postiga (Vukčević 80), André Santos, Liedson, João Pereira. Coach: Paulo Sérgio (POR)
Yellow Card(s): Hélder Postiga 25, Anderson Polga 41, João Pereira 42
Match 6 – PFC Levski Sofia (BUL)
A 0-1
Tiago, Torsiglieri, Evaldo, Maniche, Valdés (Carlos Saleiro 70), Yannick Djaló, Zapater (Diogo Salomão 46), Hélder Postiga, André Santos, Nuno Coelho (Cédric 76), Abel. Coach: Paulo Sérgio (POR)

Round of 32 – Rangers FC (SCO)
A 1-1 *Matías Fernández (89)*
Rui Patrício, Daniel Carriço, Anderson Polga, Evaldo, Pedro Mendes, Maniche (Matías Fernández 77), Yannick Djaló, Zapater, Hélder Postiga (Diogo Salomão 86), João Pereira, Cristiano (Carlos Saleiro 74). Coach: Paulo Sérgio (POR)
Yellow Card(s): Yannick Djaló 50, Daniel Carriço 62
H 2-2 *Pedro Mendes (42), Yannick Djaló (83)*
Rui Patrício, Torsiglieri, Anderson Polga, Evaldo, Pedro Mendes (Carlos Saleiro 81), Matías Fernández (Nuno Coelho 90+1), Yannick Djaló, Zapater, Hélder Postiga (André Santos 87), João Pereira, Abel. Coach: Paulo Sérgio (POR)
Yellow Card(s): Zapater 10

CS MARÍTIMO

UEFA EUROPA LEAGUE

Second Qualifying Round – Sporting Fingal FC (IRL)
H 3-2 *Ricardo Esteves (78), Cherrad (85), Tchô (90+5)*
Peçanha, Alonso, Robson, Ricardo Esteves, Marquinho (Danilo Dias 46), Roberto Sousa, Baba Diawara, Kanu (Cherrad 46), Djalma (Luciano Amaral 74), Tchô, João Guilherme. Coach: Mitchell van der Gaag (NED)
Yellow Card(s): Cherrad 46, Alonso 71
A 3-2 *Alonso (20p), Marquinho (67), Kanu (87)*
Peçanha, Alonso, Robson, Ricardo Esteves, Marquinho (Luciano Amaral 72), Roberto Sousa, Baba Diawara, Cherrad (Fidelis 90), Tchô (Kanu 81), Danilo Dias, João Guilherme. Coach: Mitchell van der Gaag (NED)
Yellow Card(s): Danilo Dias 45, Roberto Sousa 53, Ricardo Esteves 66

Third Qualifying Round – Bangor City FC (WAL)
H 8-2 *Tchô (33, 79), Danilo Dias (38, 75), Baba Diawara (51, 78), Kanu (80), Fidelis (90+1)*
Marcelo, Alonso, Robson, Ricardo Esteves, Marquinho (Kanu 64), Roberto Sousa, Baba Diawara, Cherrad (Rafael Miranda 70), Tchô (Fidelis 82), Danilo Dias, João Guilherme. Coach: Mitchell van der Gaag (NED)
A 2-1 *Adílson (48), Marquinho (58)*
Marcelo, Robson, Marquinho (Duventru 80), Baba Diawara, Adílson (Fidelis 72), Briguel, Tchô, Rafael Miranda, Luciano Amaral, Danilo Dias (Luís Olim 63), João Guilherme. Coach: Mitchell van der Gaag (NED)

Play-Offs – FC BATE Borisov (BLR)
A 0-3
Marcelo, Alonso, Robson, Ricardo Esteves, Marquinho (Cherrad 69), Robert Sousa, Baba Diawara, Tchô (Djalma 62), Rafael Miranda, Danilo Dias (Luciano Amaral 85), João Guilherme. Coach: Mitchell van der Gaag (NED)
Yellow Card(s): Ricardo Esteves 3, Djalma 77
H 1-2 *Kanu (90)*
Marcelo, Robson, Roberto Sousa, Baba Diawara, Djalma (Kanu 64), Briguel, Cherrad (Marquinho 46), Rafael Miranda (Adílson 60), Luciano Amaral, Danilo Dias, João Guilherme. Coach: Mitchell van der Gaag (NED
Yellow Card(s): Djalma 37, Robson 56

REPUBLIC OF IRELAND

BOHEMIAN FC

UEFA CHAMPIONS LEAGUE

Second Qualifying Round – The New Saints FC (WAL)
H 1-0 *Brennan (66)*
B. Murphy, Heary, Powell, Oman, Keegan, Cretaro (Byrne 75), Brennan, Madden, Shelley, Quigley, Higgins. Coach: Pat Fenlon (IRL)
Yellow Card(s): Shelley 37, Cretaro 58
A 0-4
B. Murphy, Heary, Powell (McGuinness 46), Oman, Keegan, Byrne (Greene 67), Brennan, Madden, Shelley, Quigley, Higgins (Cronin 46). Coach: Pat Fenlon (IRL)
Yellow Card(s): Powell 34, McGuinness 71, Keegan 82

SPORTING FINGAL FC

UEFA EUROPA LEAGUE

Second Qualifying Round – CS Marítimo (POR)
A 2-3 *Crowe (33), Fitzgerald (87)*
Clarke, O'Brien, Fitzgerald, Williams, Hawkins (Maher 73), Browne, Byrne (Cahill 88), Finn, Crowe (Zayed 64), Kirby, McFaul. Coach: Liam Buckley (IRL)
Yellow Card(s): Clarke 72, McFaul 82
H 2-3 *Zayed (81, 90)*
Clarke, O'Brien, Fitzgerald, Williams, Maher, Browne, Byrne, Finn, Crowe, Kirby, McFaul (Zayed 64). Coach: Liam Buckley (IRL)

SHAMROCK ROVERS FC

UEFA EUROPA LEAGUE

Second Qualifying Round – Bnei Yehuda Tel-Aviv FC (ISR)
H 1-1 *Bayly (90+1)*
Mannus, Stevens, Sives, Price (Dennehy 64), Rice, Chambers, Twigg, Kavanagh, Turner (Bayly 71), Stewart, D. Murray. Coach: Michael O'Neill (NIR)
Yellow Card(s): Dennehy 90+4

1-0 *Stewart (70)*
annus, Stevens, Sives, Price, Rice, Chambers (Dennehy 64), Twigg, ırner (Bradley 84), Stewart, D. Murray, Bayly (Kavanagh 58). Coach: ıchael O'Neill (NIR)
ellow Card(s): Rice 41, Twigg 83, Stewart 90+4

hird Qualifying Round – Juventus (ITA)
0-2
ıannus, Stevens, Sives, Price, Rice (Dennehy 66), Chambers (Kavanagh 3), Twigg, Turner, Stewart, D. Murray, Bayly (Bradley 90+3). Coach: ichael O'Neill (NIR)
ellow Card(s): Bayly 64
0-1
annus, Price, Rice (Bayly 59), Bradley, Chambers (Turner 46), Twigg, ynn, Kavanagh (Stewart 46), Murphy, Dennehy, D. Murray. Coach: ichael O'Neill (NIR)
ellow Card(s): Dennehy 42, Bradley 45, Flynn 58

DUNDALK FC

UEFA EUROPA LEAGUE

irst Qualifying Round – CS Grevenmacher (LUX)
3-3 *Kuduzović (26), Hatswell (51), Benichou (80og)*
regg, Kelly, Hatswell, Miller, G. Breen, Maher, Cawley, Kuduzović, Fenn, aynor (McGowan 79), Murphy (McGuigan 61). Coach: Ian Foster (ENG)
ellow Card(s): Hatswell 55, Kelly 62, Cawley 77, McGowan 81
2-1 *Fenn (5p), Kuduzović (16)*
regg, Kelly, Hatswell, Miller, G. Breen, Maher (McDonnell 77), Cawley, uduzović (J. Breen 90), Fenn, Gaynor, Mulvenna (McGowan 71). Coach: an Foster (ENG)
ellow Card(s): Maher 23

econd Qualifying Round – PFC Levski Sofia (BUL)
A 0-6
herrie, Kelly, Hatswell, Miller, G. Breen, Maher, Cawley, Kuduzović (McGowan 0), Fenn (Lennon 60), Gaynor, McGuigan. Coach: Ian Foster (ENG)
ellow Card(s): McGuigan 23
H 0-2
herrie, Hatswell, Miller, G. Breen, Maher, Kuduzović, Gaynor, Synnott, McGuigan, McDonnell, Lennon (Mulvenna 59). Coach: Ian Foster (ENG)

ROMANIA

CFR 1907 CLUJ

UEFA CHAMPIONS LEAGUE

Group E
Match 1 – FC Basel 1893 (SUI)
H 2-1 *Rada (9), Traoré (12)*
Nuno Claro, Panin, Mureşan, Dică, Traoré (Sforzini 79), Hugo Alcântara, Rafael Bastos (De Zerbi 54), Culio, Cadú, Hora (E. Koné 54), Rada. Coach: Sorin Cârţu (ROU)
Yellow Card(s): Panin 25, Rada 90+2
Match 2 – AS Roma (ITA)
A 1-2 *Rada (78)*
Nuno Claro, Panin, Dică, Kivuvu, Traoré (Bjelanović 82), Hugo Alcântara, Culio, Cadú, Hora (De Zerbi 76), Rada, Edimar (E. Koné 68). Coach: Sorin Cârţu (ROU)
Yellow Card(s): Dică 74
Match 3 – FC Bayern München (GER)
A 2-3 *Cadú (28), Culio (86)*
Stăncioiu, Panin, Dică, Kivuvu, Traoré (Bjelanović 76), De Zerbi, Piccolo, Rafael Bastos (Hora 56), Culio, Cadú, Rada. Coach: Sorin Cârţu (ROU)
Yellow Card(s): Dică 19, Panin 25
Match 4 – FC Bayern München (GER)
H 0-4
Stăncioiu, Panin, Dică (Edimar 46), Traoré, De Zerbi, Tomás Costa, Piccolo, Rafael Bastos (Hora 46), Culio, Cadú (Tony 78), Rada. Coach: Sorin Cârţu (ROU)
Yellow Card(s): Rafael Bastos 27, Traoré 76
Match 5 – FC Basel 1893 (SUI)
A 0-1
Nuno Claro, Tony, Kivuvu, Traoré (Bjelanović 46), Tomás Costa, Piccolo, Rafael Bastos, Culio (Sforzini 74), Cadú, Léo Veloso (E. Koné 58), Rada. Coach: Sorin Cârţu (ROU)
Red Card(s): Piccolo 88
Yellow Card(s): Léo Veloso 30, Cadú 62, Tomás Costa 80
Match 6 – AS Roma (ITA)
H 1-1 *Traoré (88)*
Stăncioiu, Panin, Dică (Léo Veloso 46), Kivuvu, Traoré, De Zerbi (Rafael Bastos 78), Culio, Cadú, Rada, E. Koné, Edimar (Bjelanović 63). Coach: Alin Minteuan (ROU)
Yellow Card(s): Culio 19, Traoré 88

No	Player	Nat	DoB	Aps	(s)	Gls
Goalkeepers						
1	Nuno Claro	POR	7/1/77	3		
44	Eduard Stăncioiu		3/3/81	3		
Defenders						
20	Cadú	POR	21/12/81	6		1
66	Edimar	BRA	21/5/86	2	(1)	
15	Hugo Alcântara	BRA	28/7/79	2		
23	Léo Veloso	BRA	29/5/87	1	(1)	
4	Cristian Panin		9/6/78	5		
13	Felice Piccolo	ITA	27/8/83	3		
24	Ionuţ Rada		6/7/82	6		2
2	Tony	POR	20/12/80	1	(1)	
Midfielders						
19	Juan Culio	ARG	30/8/83	6		1
7	Emil Dică		17/7/82	5		
22	Ioan Hora		21/8/88	2	(2)	
8	Dominique Kivuvu	ANG	16/9/87	4		
28	Emmanuel Koné	CIV	31/12/86	1	(3)	
6	Gabriel Mureşan		13/2/82	1		
16	Rafael Bastos	BRA	1/1/85	4	(1)	
11	Tomás Costa	ARG	30/1/85	2		
Forwards						
32	Saša Bjelanović	CRO	11/6/79		(4)	
10	Roberto De Zerbi	ITA	6/6/79	3	(2)	
99	Ferdinando Sforzini	ITA	4/12/84		(2)	
9	Lacina Traoré	CIV	20/8/90	6		2

FC UNIREA URZICENI

UEFA CHAMPIONS LEAGUE

Third Qualifying Round – FC Zenit St Petersburg (RUS)
H 0-0
Arlauskis, Galamaz, Bilaşco (Dalé 89), Paraschiv, Pădureţu, Marinescu, Bordeanu, Maftei, Neaga (Rusescu 86), Frunză (Onofraş 72), Marin. Coach: Roni Levi (ISR)
Red Card(s): Pădureţu 36
Yellow Card(s): Paraschiv 26, Galamaz 41
A 0-1
Arlauskis, Galamaz, Bilaşco, Rusescu (Neaga 58), Nicu, Brandán, Marinescu, Semedo (Dalé 53), Bordeanu, Maftei, Frunză (Onofraş 88). Coach: Roni Levi (ISR)

UEFA EUROPA LEAGUE

Play-Offs – HNK Hajduk Split (CRO)
A 1-4 *Frunză (34)*
Grigore, Galamaz, Bilaşco, Onofraş (Neaga 61), Rusescu (Dalé 74), Nicu, Brandán, Marinescu (Paraschiv 47), Bordeanu, Maftei, Frunză. Coach: Roni Levi (ISR)
Yellow Card(s): Paraschiv 51, Brandán 68
H 1-1 *Bilaşco (2)*
Grigore, Mehmedović, Galamaz, Bilaşco, Onofraş, Rusescu (Frunză 64), Nicu, Brandán, Bordeanu, Maftei, Neaga (Dalé 78). Coach: Eugen Nae (ROU)
Red Card(s): Maftei 82
Yellow Card(s): Rusescu 56, Bordeanu 59, Mehmedović 76

FC VASLUI

UEFA EUROPA LEAGUE

Play-Offs – LOSC Lille Métropole (FRA)
H 0-0
Kuciak, Papp, David Rivas, Pouga, Sânmărtean, Milanov, Pavlović, Hugo Luz, Costin (Bello 79), Wesley, Gladstone (Genchev 35). Coach: Juan Ramón López Caro (ESP)
Yellow Card(s): Luz 71, Papp 73
A 0-2
Kuciak, Papp, Genchev, Pouga, Sânmărtean, Milanov, Pavlović (Costin 52), Farkaš, Luz, Gheorghiu (Puia 69), Wesley (Pancu 81). Coach: Juan Ramón López Caro (ESP)
Red Card(s): Kuciak 68
Yellow Card(s): Genchev 18, Gheorghiu 25, Costin 65

FC STEAUA BUCUREŞTI

UEFA EUROPA LEAGUE

Play-Offs – Grasshopper-Club (SUI)
H 1-0 *Stancu (71)*
Tătăruşanu, Emeghara, Abrudan, Stoica, Kapetanos (Surdu 59), Tănase, Latovlevici, Nicoliţă (Răduţ 67), Geraldo Alves, Bicfalvi, Stancu (Angelov 85). Coach: Ilie Dumitrescu (ROU)
Yellow Card(s): Surdu 90+2
A 0-1 (aet; 4-3 on pens)
Tătăruşanu, Emeghara, Abrudan, Stoica (Angelov 55), Răduţ (Matei 83), Tănase, Latovlevici, Geraldo Alves, Surdu, Bicfalvi, Stancu. Coach: Ilie Dumitrescu (ROU)
Yellow Card(s): Abrudan 17, Geraldo Alves 30, Angelov 75, Emeghara 81, Latovlevici 92

Group K
Match 1 – Liverpool FC (ENG)
A 1-4 *Tănase (13)*
Tătăruşanu, Emeghara (Nicoliţă 20), Abrudan, Răduţ (Surdu 73), Kapetanos, Tănase, Latovlevici, Angelov (Éder Bonfim 52), Geraldo Alves, Bicfalvi, Stancu. Coach: Ilie Dumitrescu (ROU)
Yellow Card(s): Abrudan 44, Kapetanos 55, Éder Bonfim 90+1
Match 2 – SSC Napoli (ITA)
H 3-3 *Cribari (2og), Tănase (11), Kapetanos (16)*
Tătăruşanu, Gardoş, Kapetanos, Tănase (Răduţ 75), Latovlevici, Nicoliţă, Ricardo Vilano, Geraldo Alves, Stancu (Surdu 90+4), Éder Bonfim, Apostol (Angelov 79). Coach: Marius Lăcătuş (ROU)
Red Card(s): Kapetanos 31
Yellow Card(s): Tătăruşanu 63, Nicoliţă 90+8, Latovlevici 90+8
Match 3 – FC Utrecht (NED)
A 1-1 *Schut (75og)*
Tătăruşanu, Gardoş, Tănase, Latovlevici, Nicoliţă, Angelov (Răduţ 66), Ricardo Vilano, Geraldo Alves, Surdu (Szekely 77), Stancu, Éder Bonfim. Coach: Marius Lăcătuş (ROU)
Yellow Card(s): Geraldo Alves 74, Latovlevici 90+2
Match 4 – FC Utrecht (NED)
H 3-1 *Gardoş (29), Stancu (52, 53)*
Tătăruşanu, Gardoş, Tănase (Szekely 83), Latovlevici, Nicoliţă, Martinović, Ricardo Vilano, Geraldo Alves, Surdu (Angelov 87), Stancu, Apostol (Bicfalvi 46). Coach: Marius Lăcătuş (ROU)
Yellow Card(s): Ricardo Vilano 12, Nicoliţă 20, Martinović 38
Match 5 – Liverpool FC (ENG)
H 1-1 *Éder Bonfim (61)*
Tătăruşanu, Gardoş, Tănase, Latovlevici, Nicoliţă, Ricardo Vilano, Geraldo Alves, Surdu (Szekely 80), Bicfalvi (Angelov 46), Stancu, Éder Bonfim. Coach: Marius Lăcătuş (ROU)
Yellow Card(s): Surdu 20, Nicoliţă 63, Éder Bonfim 81
Match 6 – SSC Napoli (ITA)
A 0-1
Tătăruşanu, Gardoş (Bicfalvi 65), Szekely (Matei 90+4), Latovlevici, Martinović, Angelov (Răduţ 89), Ricardo Vilano, Geraldo Alves, Surdu, Stancu, Éder Bonfim. Coach: Marius Lăcătuş (ROU)
Yellow Card(s): Szekely 11, Éder Bonfim 66, Ricardo Vilano 76, Surdu 81, Martinović 90+6

FC TIMIŞOARA

UEFA EUROPA LEAGUE

Third Qualifying Round – Myllykosken Pallo-47 (FIN)
A 2-1 *Tameș (34), Axente (74)*
Pantilimon, Luchin, Alexa, Curtean (Axente 46), Tameș (Bourceanu 84), Scutaru, Mera, Chiacu (Contra 46), Magera, Goga, Čišovský. Coach: Vladimir Petrović (SRB)
Yellow Card(s): Magera 79
H 3-3 *Axente (53), Zicu (80), Čišovský (90+2)*
Taborda, Alexa, Sepsi, Axente, Tameș (Zicu 57), Mera, Magera (Mansour 72), Goga, Contra, Đukić (Bourceanu 46), Čišovský. Coach: Vladimir Petrović (SRB)
Yellow Card(s): Alexa 45, Contra 67, Čišovský 90+3, Zicu 90+3, Taborda 90+6, Mansour 90+6

Play-Offs – Manchester City FC (ENG)
H 0-1
Pantilimon, Luchin, Alexa, Curtean, Sepsi, Axente, Scutaru (Zicu 71), Magera (Goga 83), Contra (Mera 80), Čišovský, Bourceanu. Coach: Vladimir Petrović (SRB)
Yellow Card(s): Luchin 41
A 0-2
Pantilimon, Luchin, Alexa (Chiacu 82), Burcă, Curtean (Goga 57), Sepsi, Axente, Mera, Magera (Zicu 46), Contra, Bourceanu. Coach: Vladimir Petrović (SRB)

FC DINAMO BUCUREŞTI

UEFA EUROPA LEAGUE

Second Qualifying Round – FC Olimpia Balti (MDA)
A 2-0 *Pulhac (41), Ganea (83)*
Curcă, Pulhac, Moţi, Koné (Torje 65), Niculae, An. Cristea (Ganea 81), Ad. Cristea (Munteanu 65), Scarlatache, Mărgăritescu, Homei, N'Doye.

ach: Ioan Andone (ROU)
d Card(s): Niculae 58
llow Card(s): Moţi 71
5-1 *An. Cristea (3), Ad. Cristea (32), N'Doye (45), Munteanu (59), rje (63p)*
rcă, Pulhac, Moţi, Munteanu, An. Cristea, Ad. Cristea (Ganea 60), rje, Scarlatache (Garat 46), Mărgăritescu, Homei, N'Doye (Păun 69). ach: Ioan Andone (ROU)
llow Card(s): Moţi 46

ird Qualifying Round – HNK Hajduk Split (CRO)
3-1 *An. Cristea (6p), Garat (40), Koné (70)*
rcă, Pulhac, Koné, An. Cristea (Păun 77), Ganea, Ad. Cristea, Torje unteanu 54), Scarlatache, Homei, N'Doye, Garat. Coach: Ioan Andone OU)
llow Card(s): N'Doye 25, Torje 34, Pulhac 42, Koné 70
0-3
ırcă, Pulhac, Moţi, Koné, Niculae (An. Cristea 61), Ganea, Ad. Cristea, rje (Munteanu 70), Scarlatache, N'Doye, Garat (Homei 28). Coach: Ioan done (ROU)
llow Card(s): Ad. Cristea 34, N'Doye 74, Homei 86

RUSSIA

FC RUBIN KAZAN

UEFA CHAMPIONS LEAGUE

roup D
latch 1 – FC København (DEN)
0-1
yzhikov, Ansaldi, Salukvadze, Murawski, Noboa, Kaleshin, Orekhov, occhetti (Kuzmin 65), Martins (Kasaev 58), Carlos Eduardo (Gökdeniz 7), Kornilenko. Coach: Kurban Berdyev (RUS)
ellow Card(s): Orekhov 61, Kaleshin 84
latch 2 – FC Barcelona (ESP)
1-1 *Noboa (30p)*
yzhikov, Ansaldi, César Navas, Ryazantsev, Salukvadze, Murawski, oboa (Natcho 88), Kaleshin, Bocchetti, Gökdeniz (Martins 64), ornilenko (Sibaya 62). Coach: Kurban Berdyev (RUS)
ellow Card(s): Salukvadze 40, Ansaldi 74, Sibaya 80
latch 3 – Panathinaikos FC (GRE)
0-0
yzhikov, Ansaldi, César Navas, Ryazantsev, Kasaev (Bystrov 86), loboa, Kaleshin, Bocchetti, Gökdeniz (Martins 65), Natcho, Kornilenko Sibaya 90+6). Coach: Kurban Berdyev (RUS)
ellow Card(s): Gökdeniz 7, Noboa 78
latch 4 – Panathinaikos FC (GRE)
0-0
yzhikov, Ansaldi, César Navas, Ryazantsev, Kasaev (Gökdeniz 73), oboa, Kaleshin, Bocchetti, Natcho, Carlos Eduardo (Martins 73), ornilenko (Medvedev 85). Coach: Kurban Berdyev (RUS)
latch 5 – FC København (DEN)
1-0 *Noboa (45+2p)*
yzhikov, Ansaldi, César Navas, Ryazantsev, Kasaev (Bystrov 69), oboa, Kaleshin (Salukvadze 85), Bocchetti, Gökdeniz, Natcho, ornilenko (Medvedev 81). Coach: Kurban Berdyev (RUS)
ellow Card(s): Ryazantsev 42, Kaleshin 79
latch 6 – FC Barcelona (ESP)
A 0-2
yzhikov, Kuzmin, Ansaldi, César Navas, Ryazantsev (Kasaev 62), lurawski, Noboa, Kaleshin, Bocchetti, Martins (Medvedev 66), Gökdeniz Bystrov 75). Coach: Kurban Berdyev (RUS)
ellow Card(s): Ryzhikov 24

No	Player	Nat	DoB	Aps	(s)	Gls
Goalkeepers						
77	Sergei Ryzhikov		19/9/80	6		
Defenders						
3	Cristian Ansaldi	ARG	20/9/86	6		
27	Salvatore Bocchetti	ITA	30/11/86	6		
4	César Navas	ESP	14/2/80	5		
19	Vitaliy Kaleshin		3/10/80	6		
2	Oleg Kuzmin		9/5/81	1	(1)	
22	Aleksandr Orekhov		29/11/83	1		
9	Lasha Salukvadze	GEO	21/12/81	2	(1)	
Midfielders						
5	Pyotr Bystrov		15/7/79		(3)	
87	Carlos Eduardo	BRA	18/7/87	2		
61	Gökdeniz Karadeniz	TUR	11/1/80	4	(2)	
14	Alan Kasaev		8/4/86	3	(2)	
15	Rafał Murawski	POL	9/10/81	3		
66	Bibras Natcho	ISR	18/2/88	3	(1)	
16	Christian Noboa	ECU	9/4/85	6		2
8	Aleksandr Ryazantsev		5/9/86	5		
6	MacBeth Sibaya	RSA	25/11/77		(2)	
Forwards						
88	Sergei Kornilenko	BLR	14/6/83	5		
28	Obafemi Martins	NGA	28/10/84	2	(3)	
26	Aleksei Medvedev		5/1/77		(3)	

UEFA EUROPA LEAGUE

Round of 32 – FC Twente (NED)
H 0-2
Arlauskis, Kuzmin, Ansaldi, César Navas, Bystrov, Lebedenko (Medvedev 87), Noboa, Dyadyun, Bocchetti, Gökdeniz (Kasaev 73), Natcho. Coach: Kurban Berdyev (RUS)
Yellow Card(s): Ansaldi 70
A 2-2 *Ansaldi (22), Noboa (24)*
Ryzhikov, Ansaldi (Kuzmin 80), César Navas, Bystrov (Natcho 69), Ryazantsev, Lebedenko, Noboa, Kaleshin, Dyadyun, Bocchetti, Gökdeniz (Kasaev 75). Coach: Kurban Berdyev (RUS)
Yellow Card(s): César Navas 38, Noboa 53, Gökdeniz 59, Ryzhikov 62, Lebedenko 73

FC SPARTAK MOSKVA

UEFA CHAMPIONS LEAGUE

Group F
Match 1 – Olympique de Marseille (FRA)
A 1-0 *Azpilicueta (81og)*
Dykan, Sheshukov (Ari 88), Ibson, Welliton, Alex (Stranzl 90), Parshivlyuk, Makeev, Suchý, Pareja, McGeady (Sabitov 83), D. Kombarov. Coach: Valeriy Karpin (RUS)
Yellow Card(s): Alex 55
Match 2 – MŠK Žilina (SVK)
H 3-0 *Ari (34, 61), Ibson (89)*
Dykan, Sheshukov (Sabitov 90), Ari, Welliton (Ibson 67), Alex, Parshivlyuk, Makeev, Suchý, Pareja, McGeady, D. Kombarov (Maidana 84). Coach: Valeriy Karpin (RUS)
Match 3 – Chelsea FC (ENG)
H 0-2
Dykan, Sheshukov, Ibson, Ari (Ananidze 85), Welliton, Parshivlyuk, Makeev, Suchý, Pareja, McGeady, D. Kombarov. Coach: Valeriy Karpin (RUS)
Yellow Card(s): Suchý 56

Match 4 – Chelsea FC (ENG)
A 1-4 *Bazhenov (86)*
Dykan, Sheshukov (Drinčić 67), Ibson, Welliton, Alex (Kozlov 69), Makeev, Suchý, Ivanov, Pareja, McGeady (Bazhenov 80), D. Kombarov. Coach: Valeriy Karpin (RUS)
Yellow Card(s): D. Kombarov 43, Ivanov 66
Match 5 – Olympique de Marseille (FRA)
H 0-3
Dykan, Stranzl, Sheshukov (Drinčić 75), Ibson (Ananidze 76), Ari, Welliton, Makeev, Suchý, Pareja, McGeady, D. Kombarov. Coach: Valeriy Karpin (RUS)
Red Card(s): Welliton 64
Yellow Card(s): Sheshukov 31, Ibson 67
Match 6 – MŠK Žilina (SVK)
A 2-1 *Alex (54), Ibson (61)*
Dykan, Stranzl, Sheshukov, Ibson, Alex, Makeev (Ozobić 55), Suchý, Kozlov (Drinčić 46), McGeady, K. Kombarov (Ivanov 83), D. Kombarov. Coach: Valeriy Karpin (RUS)
Red Card(s): Ibson 77
Yellow Card(s): K. Kombarov 66

No	Player	Nat	DoB	Aps	(s)	Gls
Goalkeepers						
81	Andriy Dykan	UKR	16/7/77	6		
Defenders						
18	Andrei Ivanov		8/10/88	1	(1)	
16	Yevgeniy Makeev		24/7/89	6		
19	Nicolás Pareja	ARG	19/1/84	5		
15	Sergei Parshivlyuk		18/3/89	3		
5	Aleksandr Sheshukov		15/4/83	6		
3	Martin Stranzl	AUT	16/6/80	2	(1)	
17	Marek Suchý	CZE	29/3/88	6		
Midfielders						
12	Alex	BRA	25/3/82	4		1
27	Jano Ananidze	GEO	10/10/92		(2)	
8	Nikola Drinčić	MNE	7/9/84		(3)	
7	Ibson	BRA	7/11/83	5	(1)	2
99	Dmitriy Kombarov		22/1/87	6		
77	Kirill Kombarov		22/1/87	1		
2	Cristian Maidana	ARG	24/1/87		(1)	
64	Aiden McGeady	IRL	4/4/86	6		
48	Filip Ozobić	CRO	8/4/91		(1)	
6	Renat Sabitov		13/6/85		(2)	
Forwards						
9	Ari	BRA	11/12/85	3	(1)	2
21	Nikita Bazhenov		1/2/85		(1)	1
49	Aleksandr Kozlov		19/3/93	1	(1)	
11	Welliton	BRA	22/10/86	5		

UEFA EUROPA LEAGUE

Round of 32 – FC Basel 1893 (SUI)
A 3-2 *D. Kombarov (61), Dzyuba (70), Ananidze (90+2)*
Dykan, Sheshukov (Ananidze 46), Alex, Makeev (Yakovlev 85), Suchý, Rojo, Dzyuba, Rafael Carioca, McGeady, K. Kombarov, D. Kombarov. Coach: Valeriy Karpin (RUS)
Yellow Card(s): McGeady 34, Rafael Carioca 52, Alex 70, Dykan 82, Suchý 90
H 1-1 *McGeady (90+1)*
Dykan, Sheshukov, Alex, Makeev (Yakovlev 80), Suchý, Rojo, Dzyuba, Ananidze, McGeady, K. Kombarov, D. Kombarov. Coach: Valeriy Karpin (RUS)

Round of 16 – AFC Ajax (NED)
A 1-0 *Alex (57)*
Dykan, Ibson (Welliton 57), Alex, Makeev, Suchý, Rojo, Dzyuba, Rafael Carioca (Sheshukov 84), McGeady (Yakovlev 90+2), K. Kombarov, D. Kombarov. Coach: Valeriy Karpin (RUS)
Yellow Card(s): Suchý 38, Welliton 70, Rojo 77
H 3-0 *D. Kombarov (21), Welliton (30), Alex (54)*
Dykan, Sheshukov, Ibson, Welliton, Alex (Dzyuba 84), Makeev, Rojo, Rafael Carioca, McGeady (Ari 67), K. Kombarov, D. Kombarov. Coach: Valeriy Karpin (RUS)
Yellow Card(s): Rojo 78

Quarter-Finals – FC Porto (POR)
A 1-5 *K. Kombarov (71)*
Dykan, Ibson, Welliton, Alex, Makeev (Yakovlev 86), Suchý, Rojo, Rafael Carioca, McGeady (Dzyuba 68), K. Kombarov, D. Kombarov. Coach: Valeriy Karpin (RUS)
Yellow Card(s): D. Kombarov 16, Rojo 35, Ibson 60, Makeev 81, Suchý 8
H 2-5 *Dzyuba (52), Ari (72)*
Dykan, Sheshukov, Welliton (Ari 46), Alex, Makeev, Suchý, Dzyuba, Rafael Carioca (Ibson 69), Yakovlev, McGeady, K. Kombarov (D. Kombarov 46). Coach: Valeriy Karpin (RUS)
Yellow Card(s): Dzyuba 25

FC ZENIT ST PETERSBURG

UEFA CHAMPIONS LEAGUE

Third Qualifying Round – FC Unirea Urziceni (ROU)
A 0-0
Malafeev, Anyukov, Fernando Meira, Lombaerts, Danny, Kerzhakov, Hubočan, Shirokov (Fayzulin 70), Zyryanov (Rosina 59), Denisov, Bystrov (Kanunnikov 80). Coach: Luciano Spalletti (ITA)
Yellow Card(s): Denisov 14, Rosina 81
H 1-0 *Danny (33)*
Malafeev, Anyukov, Fernando Meira, Lombaerts, Danny, Kerzhakov (Kanunnikov 77), Hubočan, Shirokov (Fayzulin 64), Zyryanov, Denisov, Bystrov (Rosina 46). Coach: Luciano Spalletti (ITA)
Yellow Card(s): Hubočan 26, Shirokov 35, Malafeev 77, Anyukov 79

Play-Offs – AJ Auxerre (FRA)
H 1-0 *Kerzhakov (3)*
Malafeev, Anyukov, Bruno Alves, Lombaerts, Lazović (Huszti 60), Danny, Kerzhakov (Bukharov 78), Hubočan, Shirokov, Semak (Zyryanov 90), Denisov. Coach: Luciano Spalletti (ITA)
Yellow Card(s): Danny 33
A 0-2
Malafeev, Anyukov, Bruno Alves, Fernando Meira (Bukharov 79), Danny, Kerzhakov, Hubočan, Shirokov, Zyryanov (Lazović 55), Semak, Bystrov (Zhevnov 67). Coach: Luciano Spalletti (ITA)
Red Card(s): Malafeev 65, Hubočan 80
Yellow Card(s): Bystrov 56, Semak 57, Hubočan 77, Hubočan 80, Anyukov 81, Bruno Alves 85

UEFA EUROPA LEAGUE

Group G
Match 1 – RSC Anderlecht (BEL)
A 3-1 *Kerzhakov (8, 33, 44)*
Zhevnov, Bruno Alves, Lombaerts, Lazović, Danny (Križanac 90), Kerzhakov (Ionov 79), Shirokov (Fayzulin 36), Zyryanov, Luković, Semak, Denisov. Coach: Luciano Spalletti (ITA)
Yellow Card(s): Bruno Alves 19, Luković 30
Match 2 – AEK Athens FC (GRE)
H 4-2 *Hubočan (1), Bruno Alves (13), Lazović (43p, 57)*
Malafeev, Bruno Alves, Križanac, Lazović, Bukharov, Danny (Rosina 66), Hubočan, Zyryanov, Luković, Denisov (Shirokov 66), Bystrov (Kanunnikov 74). Coach: Luciano Spalletti (ITA)
Yellow Card(s): Malafeev 81
Match 3 – HNK Hajduk Split (CRO)
H 2-0 *Bukharov (25), Danny (68)*
Zhevnov, Anyukov, Križanac, Lombaerts, Lazović (Ionov 71), Bukharov, Danny (Kanunnikov 77), Fayzulin (Zyryanov 65), Luković, Semak, Denisov. Coach: Luciano Spalletti (ITA)
Yellow Card(s): Zyryanov 79
Match 4 – HNK Hajduk Split (CRO)
A 3-2 *Ionov (31), Huszti (47p), Rosina (50)*
Malafeev, Anyukov, Križanac (Kanunnikov 56), Fernando Meira, Bukharov,

Rosina (Lazović 72), Fayzulin, Huszti, Luković, Denisov (Semak 65), Ionov. Coach: Luciano Spalletti (ITA)
Yellow Card(s): Ionov 13
Match 5 – RSC Anderlecht (BEL)
H 3-1 *Ionov (12), Bukharov (65), Huszti (88)*
Malafeev, Križanac, Fernando Meira, Lombaerts, Bukharov (Kanunnikov 65), Danny, Shirokov, Rosina (Huszti 73), Zyryanov, Luković (Hubočan 80), Ionov. Coach: Luciano Spalletti (ITA)
Yellow Card(s): Shirokov 35, Luković 50, Lombaerts 75
Match 6 – AEK Athens FC (GRE)
A 3-0 *Bukharov (43), Rosina (67), Denisov (88)*
Malafeev, Bruno Alves, Lombaerts, Lazović (Huszti 74), Bukharov (Kanunnikov 83), Hubočan, Shirokov, Rosina, Zyryanov (Ionov 78), Luković, Denisov. Coach: Luciano Spalletti (ITA)
Yellow Card(s): Luković 39

Round of 32 – BSC Young Boys (SUI)
A 1-2 *Lombaerts (20)*
Malafeev, Anyukov, Bruno Alves, Lombaerts (Fernando Meira 54), Lazović (Bystrov 44), Danny, Kerzhakov, Hubočan, Shirokov (Semak 79), Denisov, Ionov. Coach: Luciano Spalletti (ITA)
Red Card(s): Bystrov 69
Yellow Card(s): Bystrov 45+1, Danny 53, Hubočan 65, Bystrov 69
H 3-1 *Lazović (41), Semak (52), Shirokov (76)*
Malafeev, Anyukov, Bruno Alves, Fernando Meira, Lazović (Fayzulin 90+2), Danny, Shirokov (Huszti 83), Zyryanov (Ionov 72), Luković, Semak, Denisov. Coach: Luciano Spalletti (ITA)
Yellow Card(s): Lazović 45+2, Semak 83, Fernando Meira 87

Round of 16 – FC Twente (NED)
A 0-3
Malafeev, Anyukov, Bruno Alves, Fernando Meira, Lazović, Danny, Shirokov (Fayzulin 69), Zyryanov (Huszti 69), Luković, Denisov, Ionov (Kerzhakov 86). Coach: Luciano Spalletti (ITA)
Yellow Card(s): Bruno Alves 38, Fernando Meira 55
H 2-0 *Shirokov (16), Kerzhakov (38)*
Zhevnov, Anyukov, Bruno Alves, Fernando Meira (Huszti 46), Lazović (Bukharov 64), Danny, Kerzhakov (Zyryanov 70), Shirokov, Luković, Denisov, Ionov. Coach: Luciano Spalletti (ITA)
Yellow Card(s): Danny 32, Bruno Alves 46, Anyukov 58

FC LOKOMOTIV MOSKVA

UEFA EUROPA LEAGUE

Play-Offs – FC Lausanne-Sport (SUI)
A 1-1 *Sychev (65)*
Guilherme, Rodolfo, Tarasov, Glushakov (Loskov 56), Sychev, Torbinskiy (Gatagov 70), Shishkin, Yanbayev, Aliyev, Maicon (Traoré 46), Burlak. Coach: Yuriy Semin (RUS)
Yellow Card(s): Tarasov 38
H 1-1 (aet; 3-4 on pens) *Aliyev (85)*
Guilherme, Rodolfo (Loskov 68), Sychev, Traoré, Torbinskiy (Maicon 77), Baša, Asatiani (Tarasov 46), Shishkin, Yanbayev, Gatagov, Aliyev. Coach: Yuriy Semin (RUS)
Yellow Card(s): Sychev 84

PFC CSKA MOSKVA

UEFA EUROPA LEAGUE

Play-Offs – Anorthosis Famagusta FC (CYP)
H 4-0 *Doumbia (13, 20), Tošić (48, 74)*
Akinfeev, Šemberas, Ignashevich, Doumbia (Dzagoev 69), Vágner Love (Necid 86), Mamayev, Nababkin, Tošić, V. Berezutskiy, Oliseh (Mark González 74), Schennikov. Coach: Leonid Slutskiy (RUS)
A 2-1 *Doumbia (85), Mark González (89)*
Akinfeev, Šemberas, Ignashevich, A. Berezutskiy, Doumbia, Dzagoev (Rahimić 80), Mamayev (Honda 63), Tošić (Mark González 68), V. Berezutskiy, Oliseh, Schennikov. Coach: Leonid Slutskiy (RUS)
Yellow Card(s): Mamayev 21, Honda 82

Group F
Match 1 – FC Lausanne-Sport (SUI)
A 3-0 *Vágner Love (22, 80p), Ignashevich (68)*
Akinfeev, Šemberas, Ignashevich, A. Berezutskiy, Vágner Love, Dzagoev (Honda 73), Mamayev, Mark González (Oliseh 64), Tošić (Necid 84), V. Berezutskiy, Schennikov. Coach: Leonid Slutskiy (RUS)
Yellow Card(s): Šemberas 32, Dzagoev 41, V. Berezutskiy 90+4
Match 2 – AC Sparta Praha (CZE)
H 3-0 *Doumbia (72, 86), Mark González (84p)*
Akinfeev, Šemberas, Ignashevich, A. Berezutskiy, Honda (Tošić 87), Doumbia (Necid 87), Vágner Love (Dzagoev 77), Mamayev, Mark González, Nababkin, V. Berezutskiy. Coach: Leonid Slutskiy (RUS)
Yellow Card(s): Ignashevich 89
Match 3 – US Città di Palermo (ITA)
A 3-0 *Doumbia (34, 59), Necid (82)*
Akinfeev, Ignashevich, Honda, Doumbia (Necid 59), Vágner Love (Dzagoev 76), Mamayev, Mark González (Tošić 65), Nababkin, V. Berezutskiy, Oliseh, Schennikov. Coach: Leonid Slutskiy (RUS)
Match 4 – US Città di Palermo (ITA)
H 3-1 *Honda (47), Necid (50, 54)*
Akinfeev, Šemberas, Honda (Dzagoev 71), Vágner Love, Mamayev (Aldonin 71), Mark González (Oliseh 68), Nababkin, Tošić, V. Berezutskiy, Schennikov, Necid. Coach: Leonid Slutskiy (RUS)
Match 5 – FC Lausanne-Sport (SUI)
H 5-1 *Necid (18, 82), Oliseh (22), Tošić (40), Dzagoev (71)*
Akinfeev, Šemberas, Ignashevich, Honda (Aldonin 61), Dzagoev, Tošić (Vasilyev 75), V. Berezutskiy, Rahimić, Oliseh (Mark González 61), Schennikov, Necid. Coach: Leonid Slutskiy (RUS)
Yellow Card(s): Ignashevich 90+2
Match 6 – AC Sparta Praha (CZE)
A 1-1 *Dzagoev (15)*
Chepchugov, Šemberas, A. Berezutskiy, Dzagoev, Tošić, Aldonin, Rahimić, Oliseh, Schennikov, Fedotov, Necid. Coach: Leonid Slutskiy (RUS)
Yellow Card(s): Dzagoev 33

Round of 32 – PAOK FC (GRE)
A 1-0 *Necid (29)*
Akinfeev, Šemberas, Ignashevich, Doumbia (Dzagoev 85), Mamayev, Nababkin, Cauņa (Aldonin 66), Tošić (A. Berezutskiy 90+2), V. Berezutskiy, Schennikov, Necid. Coach: Leonid Slutskiy (RUS)
Yellow Card(s): Nababkin 31, Mamayev 57
H 1-1 *Ignashevich (80)*
Akinfeev (Chepchugov 66), Šemberas, Ignashevich, Vágner Love (A. Berezutskiy 90+5), Mamayev, Nababkin, Cauņa (Aldonin 62), Tošić, V. Berezutskiy, Schennikov, Necid. Coach: Leonid Slutskiy (RUS)
Yellow Card(s): Necid 44

Round of 16 – FC Porto (POR)
H 0-1
Akinfeev, Šemberas, Ignashevich, Honda (Tošić 74), Doumbia (Necid 79), Vágner Love, Dzagoev, Mamayev, Nababkin, V. Berezutskiy, Schennikov. Coach: Leonid Slutskiy (RUS)
Yellow Card(s): Šemberas 19, Vágner Love 66

A 1-2 *Tošić (29)*
Akinfeev, Ignashevich, Honda, Doumbia (Necid 65), Vágner Love, Dzagoev (Mark González 73), Nababkin, Tošić (Oliseh 71), Aldonin, V. Berezutskiy, Schennikov. Coach: Leonid Slutskiy (RUS)
Yellow Card(s): Ignashevich 31, Tošić 45, Aldonin 48, Vágner Love 72, Honda 84

FC SIBIR NOVOSIBIRSK

UEFA EUROPA LEAGUE

Third Qualifying Round – Apollon Limassol FC (CYP)
H 1-0 *Medvedev (74)*
Kowalewski, Molosh, Vychodil, Makarenko (Belyayev 46), Antipenko (Shevchenko 41), Čížek (Aravin 64), Medvedev, Nagibin, Valentić, Filipenko, Astafyev. Coach: Igor Kriushenko (BLR)
Yellow Card(s): Molosh 8
A 1-2 *Shevchenko (63)*
Solosin, Vychodil, Čížek (Degtyarev 46), Medvedev, Nagibin, Bukhryakov, Shulenin (Makarenko 46), Valentić, Klimavičius, Astafyev, Shevchenko (Filipenko 87). Coach: Igor Kriushenko (BLR)
Yellow Card(s): Shulenin 21, Klimavičius 37, Valentić 62, Solosin 86

Play-Offs – PSV Eindhoven (NED)
H 1-0 *Degtyarev (90+2)*
Solosin, Vychodil, Joseph-Reinette, Bukhryakov, Sumulikoski, Aravin (Molosh 90+1), Cañas, Zinoviev (Degtyarev 64), Astafyev, Belyayev (Čížek 71), Shevchenko. Coach: Igor Kriushenko (BLR)
Red Card(s): Shevchenko 43
Yellow Card(s): Vychodil 20, Shevchenko 39, Shevchenko 43, Aravin 68
A 0-5
Solosin, Vychodil, Joseph-Reinette, Degtyarev, Bukhryakov, Sumulikoski (Klimavičius 71), Aravin, Cañas, Zinoviev (Čížek 76), Astafyev, Belyayev (Vasilyev 66). Coach: Igor Kriushenko (BLR)
Yellow Card(s): Zinovev 33, Aravin 35, Solosin 55, Astafyev 59

SAN MARINO

SP TRE FIORI

UEFA CHAMPIONS LEAGUE

First Qualifying Round – FK Rudar Pljevlja (MNE)
H 0-3
Micheletti, Nardone, Macerata, Canarezza, Benedettini, Tarini (F. Amici 73), Sossio (Grana 89), Martini, Lisi, Andreini, Vannoni (Menin 56). Coach: Floriano Sperindio (SMR)
Yellow Card(s): Canarezza 12, Lisi 32
A 1-4 *Vannoni (29)*
Micheletti, Nardone, Macerata, Canarezza, Benedettini, Tarini (Berardi 87), Lisi, Andreini, Vannoni, Menin (F. Amici 53), Macina (Manzari 80). Coach: Floriano Sperindio (SMR)
Yellow Card(s): Tarini 45, Canarezza 78, Benedettini 87

SP TRE PENNE

UEFA EUROPA LEAGUE

Second Qualifying Round – HŠK Zrinjski (BIH)
A 1-4 *Džidić (35og)*
F. Valentini, Zavoli, Franchini, Lisi (Francini 55), Valentini, Raggini, Cibelli Pignieri (Di Giuli 71), Protti (Rossi 62), Palazzi, Chiaruzzi. Coach: Stefano Ceci (ITA)
H 2-9 *Palazzi (28, 81)*
F. Valentini, Zavoli, Franchini, Raggini, Cibelli, Pignieri (Valli 80), Protti, Palazzi, Chiaruzzi (Rossi 39), Mikhaylovskiy, Simoncini (S. Valentini 55). Coach: Stefano Ceci (ITA)

SC FAETANO

UEFA EUROPA LEAGUE

First Qualifying Round – FC Zestafoni (GEO)
A 0-5
Dimetto, Valentini, Borroni, Viroli, Mi. Ricci (G. Rinaldi 74), A. Moroni, A. Della Valle, Pellegrino (Giardi 40), Raggini (Mariani 89), Bucci, M. Rinaldi. Coach: Sereno Uraldi (SMR)
Yellow Card(s): A. Della Valle 77, A. Moroni 83
H 0-0
Gozzi, Valentini, Borroni, Mi. Ricci (Viroli 67), A. Moroni, A. Della Valle, Pellegrino, Giardi, Raggini (Ugolini 90+1), Bucci, M. Rinaldi. Coach: Sereno Uraldi (SMR)
Yellow Card(s): Raggini 40, Mi. Ricci 57, M. Rinaldi 81

SCOTLAND

RANGERS FC

UEFA CHAMPIONS LEAGUE

Group C
Match 1 – Manchester United FC (ENG)
A 0-0
McGregor, Weir, Broadfoot, Papac, McCulloch, Edu, Davis, Miller (Lafferty 81), Naismith, Whittaker, Bougherra. Coach: Walter Smith (SCO)
Yellow Card(s): McGregor 45+1, McCulloch 90+6
Match 2 – Bursaspor (TUR)
H 1-0 *Naismith (18)*
McGregor, Weir, Broadfoot, Papac, McCulloch, Edu, Davis, Miller (Lafferty 87), Naismith, Whittaker, Bougherra. Coach: Walter Smith (SCO)
Yellow Card(s): Papac 80
Match 3 – Valencia CF (ESP)
H 1-1 *Edu (34)*
McGregor, Weir, Papac, Edu, Davis, Miller, Foster, Naismith, Whittaker, Weiss (Lafferty 88), Bougherra. Coach: Walter Smith (SCO)
Yellow Card(s): Bougherra 29, Edu 66, Weir 78

latch 4 – Valencia CF (ESP)
, 0-3
lcGregor, Weir, Broadfoot, Papac, McCulloch, Edu (Lafferty 84), Davis, liller, Naismith, Whittaker, Bougherra. Coach: Walter Smith (SCO)
latch 5 – Manchester United FC (ENG)
0-1
lcGregor, Weir, Broadfoot, McCulloch, Davis, Miller, Foster, Naismith, /hittaker, Weiss (Fleck 80), Hutton (Beattie 88). Coach: Walter Smith (SCO)
'ellow Card(s): Hutton 83, Naismith 86, Whittaker 90+3
latch 6 – Bursaspor (TUR)
1-1 *Miller (19)*
lcGregor, Weir, McCulloch, Davis, Miller (Beattie 63), Foster, Naismith Veiss 71), Whittaker, Bougherra, Hutton, Cole (McMillan 83). Coach: Valter Smith (SCO)
'ellow Card(s): Beattie 67

lo	Player	Nat	DoB	Aps	(s)	Gls
;oalkeepers						
	Allan McGregor		31/1/82	6		
)efenders						
!4	Madjid Bougherra	ALG	7/10/82	5		
	Kirk Broadfoot		8/8/84	4		
:5	Darren Cole		3/1/92	1		
!2	Richard Foster		31/7/85	3		
:3	Jordan McMillan		16/10/88		(1)	
;	Saša Papac	BIH	7/2/80	4		
}	David Weir		10/5/70	6		
16	Steven Whittaker		16/6/84	6		
Midfielders						
}	Steven Davis	NIR	1/1/85	6		
7	Maurice Edu	USA	18/4/86	4		1
10	John Fleck		24/8/91		(1)	
41	Kyle Hutton		5/2/91	2		
6	Lee McCulloch		14/5/78	5		
20	Vladimír Weiss	SVK	30/11/89	2	(1)	
Forwards						
19	James Beattie	ENG	27/2/78		(2)	
11	Kyle Lafferty	NIR	16/9/87		(4)	
9	Kenny Miller		23/12/79	6		1
14	Steven Naismith		14/9/86	6		1

UEFA EUROPA LEAGUE

Round of 32 – Sporting Clube de Portugal (POR)
H 1-1 *Whittaker (66)*
McGregor, Weir, Papac, Edu, Davis, Lafferty, Foster, Whittaker, Diouf, Weiss, Bougherra. Coach: Walter Smith (SCO)
Yellow Card(s): Bougherra 39, Diouf 45+1, Weiss 74, Lafferty 82
A 2-2 *Diouf (19), Edu (90+2)*
McGregor, Weir (Lafferty 70), Papac, Edu, Davis, Fleck (Weiss 71), Foster, Whittaker, Diouf (Healy 82), Bartley, Bougherra. Coach: Walter Smith (SCO)
Yellow Card(s): Edu 58

Round of 16 – PSV Eindhoven (NED)
A 0-0
Alexander, Weir, Edu, Davis, Lafferty (Wylde 80), Foster, Whittaker, Diouf (Weiss 64), Bartley, Bougherra, Hutton. Coach: Walter Smith (SCO)
Yellow Card(s): Lafferty 77
H 0-1
Alexander, Weir (Naismith 46), Papac, Edu, Davis, Lafferty (Diouf 66), Foster (Healy 85), Whittaker, Bartley, Bougherra, Wylde. Coach: Walter Smith (SCO)
Yellow Card(s): Bougherra 73

CELTIC FC

UEFA CHAMPIONS LEAGUE

Third Qualifying Round – SC Braga (POR)
A 0-3
Załuska, Juárez (Forrest 79), Hooiveld, Brown, Samaras, Cha, Maloney (Murphy 71), Ledley, Ki, Mulgrew, Loovens. Coach: Neil Lennon (NIR)
Yellow Card(s): Mulgrew 5, Ki 25, Hooiveld 42, Loovens 59
H 2-1 *Hooper (52), Juárez (79)*
Załuska, Juárez, Hooiveld, Brown (McCourt 88), Samaras, Cha, Maloney (Murphy 64), Ledley, Mulgrew (Fortuné 46), Loovens, Hooper. Coach: Neil Lennon (NIR)
Yellow Card(s): Hooiveld 32, Brown 58

UEFA EUROPA LEAGUE

Play-Offs – FC Utrecht (NED)
H 2-0 *Juárez (19), Samaras (34)*
Załuska, Juárez, Majstorovic, Brown, Samaras, Fortuné, Cha, Maloney, Ledley, Loovens, Kayal (Forrest 69). Coach: Neil Lennon (NIR)
Yellow Card(s): Samaras 56, Maloney 89
A 0-4
Załuska, Juárez (Ki 65), Majstorovic, Hooiveld, Brown (Maloney 51), Samaras (McCourt 72), Fortuné, Cha, Ledley, Kayal, Forrest. Coach: Neil Lennon (NIR)
Yellow Card(s): Załuska 18, Brown 39, Kayal 57

DUNDEE UNITED FC

UEFA EUROPA LEAGUE

Play-Offs – AEK Athens FC (GRE)
H 0-1
Perniš, Dillon, Dixon, Conway, S. Robertson (Cadamarteri 81), Daly, Buaben, Gomis, Kenneth, Watson, Goodwillie. Coach: Peter Houston (SCO)
Yellow Card(s): Conway 18, Buaben 50, Kenneth 90+2
A 1-1 *Daly (78)*
Perniš, Dillon, Dixon, Conway, S. Robertson, Cadamarteri (Goodwillie 49), D. Robertson (Swanson 59), Buaben, Gomis (Daly 63), Kenneth, Watson. Coach: Peter Houston (SCO)
Yellow Card(s): Dixon 52

HIBERNIAN FC

UEFA EUROPA LEAGUE

Third Qualifying Round – NK Maribor (SVN)
A 0-3
Stack, Hart, Hogg, Murray, De Graaf, Nish (Riordan 68), Rankin, McBride (Stokes 68), Hanlon, Wotherspoon (Galbraith 77), Miller. Coach: John Hughes (SCO)
Yellow Card(s): Rankin 50
H 2-3 *De Graaf (54, 89)*
Smith, Hart (Galbraith 70), Hogg, Murray (Wotherspoon 70), De Graaf, Nish, Riordan, McBride, Stokes, Bamba, Miller. Coach: John Hughes (SCO)
Yellow Card(s): Stokes 29, McBride 67

MOTHERWELL FC

UEFA EUROPA LEAGUE

Second Qualifying Round – Breidablik (ISL)
H 1-0 *Forbes (63)*
Randolph, Hammell, Reynolds, Craigan, Hateley, Humphrey (Smith 59), Jennings, Murphy, Sutton, Lasley, Forbes (Saunders 72). Coach: Craig Brown (SCO)
A 1-0 *Murphy (42)*
Randolph, Saunders, Hammell, Reynolds, Craigan, Hateley, Jennings, Murphy (McHugh 87), Sutton (Pollock 83), Lasley, Forbes (Humphrey 74). Coach: Craig Brown (SCO)
Yellow Card(s): Lasley 43, Craigan 45+1, Hammell 77

Third Qualifying Round – Aalesunds FK (NOR)
A 1-1 *Murphy (48)*
Randolph, Saunders, Hammell, Reynolds, Craigan, Hateley, Jennings, Murphy, Sutton (McHugh 46), Lasley, Forbes (Humphrey 46). Coach: Craig Brown (SCO)
H 3-0 *Murphy (3), Sutton (13), Page (89)*
Randolph, Saunders, Hammell, Reynolds, Craigan, Hateley, Humphrey, Jennings (Forbes 90), Murphy, Sutton (Page 86), Lasley (Fitzpatrick 74). Coach: Craig Brown (SCO)
Yellow Card(s): Fitzpatrick 80

Play-Offs – Odense BK (DEN)
A 1-2 *Hateley (90+4)*
Randolph, Saunders, Hammell, Reynolds, Craigan, Hateley, Humphrey, Jennings, Murphy (Blackman 73), Sutton (McHugh 85), Lasley (Forbes 72). Coach: Craig Brown (SCO)
Red Card(s): Jennings 88
Yellow Card(s): Reynolds 6, Jennings 50, Saunders 80, Jennings 88
H 0-1
Randolph, Saunders, Hammell, Reynolds, Craigan, Hateley, Humphrey, Murphy, Sutton, Lasley, Blackman. Coach: Craig Brown (SCO)
Yellow Card(s): Hateley 43, Saunders 51, Lasley 59

SERBIA

FK PARTIZAN

UEFA CHAMPIONS LEAGUE

Second Qualifying Round – FC Pyunik (ARM)
H 3-1 *Tomić (29), Moreira (45+1), Cléo (59)*
R. Ilić, Stevanović, Tomić, Petrović (B. Jovanović 85), Cléo, Moreira (Davidov 75), M. Jovanović, Lazevski, Krstajić, S. Ilić, Šćepović (Bogunović 55). Coach: Aleksandar Stanojević (SRB)
Yellow Card(s): Lazevski 73
A 1-0 *Cléo (45+4)*
R. Ilić, Stevanović, Tomić, Petrović (B. Jovanović 83), Cléo, Moreira, M. Jovanović, Krstajić (Stanković 36), S. Ilić, Kizito, Šćepović (Davidov 66). Coach: Aleksandar Stanojević (SRB)
Yellow Card(s): Stevanović 32, Tomić 42, Kizito 64

Third Qualifying Round – HJK Helsinki (FIN)
H 3-0 *Iliev (8), S. Ilić (42), Cléo (90+2)*
R. Ilić, Stevanović, Tomić, Petrović, Cléo, Moreira (Davidov 46), M. Jovanović, Lazevski, Krstajić (Stanković 73), S. Ilić (B. Jovanović 69), Iliev. Coach: Aleksandar Stanojević (SRB)
Yellow Card(s): B. Jovanović 81
A 2-1 *Cléo (9, 90+2)*
R. Ilić, Stevanović, Tomić, Petrović (B. Jovanović 70), Cléo, M. Jovanović, Lazevski, Krstajić (Stanković 82), S. Ilić, Iliev (Davidov 62), Smiljanić. Coach: Aleksandar Stanojević (SRB)
Yellow Card(s): M. Jovanović 41

Play-Offs – RSC Anderlecht (BEL)
H 2-2 *Cléo (57), Lecjaks (64og)*
R. Ilić, Stevanović, Tomić (Davidov 74), Petrović, Cléo, Moreira (Smiljanić 53), M. Jovanović, Lazevski, Krstajić, S. Ilić, Iliev (Bogunović 87). Coach: Aleksandar Stanojević (SRB)
A 2-2 (aet; 3-2 on pens) *Cléo (15, 53)*
R. Ilić, Stevanović, Tomić (Stanković 82), Petrović, Cléo, M. Jovanović, Lazevski, Krstajić, S. Ilić (Davidov 19), Iliev (Bogunović 101), Smiljanić. Coach: Aleksandar Stanojević (SRB)
Yellow Card(s): Petrović 6, Stevanović 45, M. Jovanović 48, Davidov 50, Krstajić 65, Cléo 107

Group H
Match 1 – FC Shakhtar Donetsk (UKR)
A 0-1
Stojković, Miljković, Kamara, Tomić, Cléo, Savić, Lazevski, Krstajić (Stanković 90+2), S. Ilić, Iliev (Boya 58), Smiljanić (Petrović 74). Coach: Aleksandar Stanojević (SRB)
Yellow Card(s): Boya 72, Petrović 88
Match 2 – Arsenal FC (ENG)
H 1-3 *Cléo (33p)*
Stojković, Stevanović, Kamara, Tomić (Savić 59), Petrović (Smiljanić 69), Cléo, Boya (Iliev 84), M. Jovanović, Lazevski, Krstajić, S. Ilić. Coach: Aleksandar Stanojević (SRB)
Red Card(s): M. Jovanović 56
Yellow Card(s): S. Ilić 59
Match 3 – SC Braga (POR)
A 0-2
Stojković, Miljković, Tomić (Babović 89), Cléo, Moreira (Kamara 46), Savić, Lazevski, Krstajić, S. Ilić, Šćepović (Boya 55), Smiljanić. Coach: Aleksandar Stanojević (SRB)
Yellow Card(s): Moreira 31
Match 4 – SC Braga (POR)
H 0-1
Stojković, Miljković, Petrović, Cléo, Moreira, Boya (Babović 59), M. Jovanović, Lazevski, Krstajić, S. Ilić, Iliev (Šćepović 78). Coach: Aleksandar Stanojević (SRB)
Yellow Card(s): Moreira 1, Petrović 55, Iliev 76
Match 5 – FC Shakhtar Donetsk (UKR)
H 0-3
Stojković, Stevanović, Petrović (Kamara 64), Cléo, Moreira (Davidov 73), M. Jovanović, Lazevski, Krstajić, S. Ilić (Iliev 84), Babović, Smiljanić. Coach: Aleksandar Stanojević (SRB)
Yellow Card(s): Smiljanić 39, Babović 40, S. Ilić 83
Match 6 – Arsenal FC (ENG)
A 1-3 *Cléo (52)*
Stojković, Kamara, Petrović, Cléo, Moreira (Brašanac 90+1), M. Jovanović, Savić, Lazevski, Krstajić, S. Ilić, Babović (Davidov 81). Coach: Aleksandar Stanojević (SRB)
Yellow Card(s): Krstajić 70

No	Player	Nat	DoB	Aps	(s)	Gls
Goalkeepers						
88	Vladimir Stojković		28/7/83	6		
Defenders						
20	Mladen Krstajić		4/3/74	6		
13	Marko Jovanović		26/3/88	4		
18	Aleksandar Lazevski	MKD	21/1/88	6		
2	Aleksandar Miljković		26/2/90	3		
15	Stefan Savić	MNE	8/1/91	3	(1)	
6	Vojislav Stanković		22/9/87		(1)	
3	Ivan Stevanović		24/6/83	2		
Midfielders						
25	Stefan Babović		7/1/87	2	(2)	
11	Pierre Boya	CMR	16/1/84	2	(2)	

4	Darko Brašanac		12/2/92		(1)	
3	Aleksandar Davidov		7/10/83		(2)	
2	Saša Ilić		30/12/77	6		
	Mohamed "Medo" Kamara	SLE	16/11/87	3	(2)	
0	Almani Moreira	GNB	16/6/78	4		
	Radosav Petrović		8/3/89	4	(1)	
9	Milan Smiljanić		19/11/86	3	(1)	
	Nemanja Tomić		21/1/88	3		
	orwards					
	Cléo	BRA	9/8/85	6		2
7	Ivica Iliev		27/10/79	2	(2)	
1	Marko Šćepović		23/5/91	1	(1)	

FK CRVENA ZVEZDA

UEFA EUROPA LEAGUE

Third Qualifying Round – ŠK Slovan Bratislava (SVK)
H 1-2 *Trifunović (63)*
Stamenković, Tošić, Koroman (Jeremić 82), Vilotić, Đorđević, Cadú, Jevtić (Trifunović 62), Perović, Ninkov, Bogdanović (Vesović 78), Milovanović. Coach: Ratko Dostanić (SRB)
Yellow Card(s): A. Jevtić 13, Djordjević 66
A 1-1 *Kadu (73)*
Stamenković, Tošić, Koroman (Jevtić 88), Trifunović, Vilotić, Đorđević, Cadú, Ninkov, Issah, Vesović (Jeremić 62), Milovanović (Subašić 81). Coach: Ratko Dostanić (SRB)
Red Card(s): Đorđević 57
Yellow Card(s): Milovanović 49, Issah 60

OFK BEOGRAD

UEFA EUROPA LEAGUE

Second Qualifying Round – FC Torpedo Zhodino (BLR)
H 2-2 *Žeravica (45+1), Injac (90+4)*
Šaranov, Mijatović, Trivunović, Nikolić, Žeravica (Beljić 65), Planić, Rodić, Krstić (Kecojević 46), Marković, Simić, Milić (Injac 55). Coach: Dejan Đurđević (SRB)
Red Card(s): Rodić 42
Yellow Card(s): Mijatović 34, Rodić 35, Rodić 42
A 1-0 *Kecojević (67)*
Šaranov, Mijatović, Kecojević, Trivunović, Nikolić, Žeravica, Planić (Petković 46), Injac (Aleksić 35), Simić, Milić, Milunović (Krstić 60). Coach: Dejan Đurđević (SRB)
Yellow Card(s): Kecojević 78

Third Qualifying Round – Galatasaray AŞ (TUR)
A 2-2 *Krstić (80), Injac (86)*
Šaranov, Mijatović (Filipović 46), Kecojević, Trivunović, Nikolić, Žeravica (Krstić 67), Rodić, Marković, Simić, Milić (Injac 78), Petković. Coach: Dejan Đurđević (SRB)
Yellow Card(s): Simić 51, Marković 61
H 1-5 *Nikolić (32)*
Šaranov, Kecojević, Trivunović, Nikolić, Žeravica (Filipović 74), Rodić, Krstić (Sinđić 59), Marković, Simić, Milić (Injac 75), Petković. Coach: Dejan Đurđević (SRB)
Red Card(s): Nikolić 57
Yellow Card(s): Trivunović 40, Nikolić 45+2, Sinđić 90+2

FK SPARTAK ZLATIBOR VODA

UEFA EUROPA LEAGUE

Second Qualifying Round – FC Differdange 03 (LUX)
A 3-3 *Ubiparip (14), Torbica (28p), Siebenaler (89og)*
Jorgić, Šarac, Simović, Milanković, Bratić, Torbica, Veselinov (Adamović 72), Ubiparip, Oletu (Nosković 85), Puškarić (Stevanović 61), Mirić. Coach: Dragan Miranović (SRB)
Yellow Card(s): Milanković 50, Stevanović 72
H 2-0 *Ubiparip (25), Adamović (88)*
Labus, Stevanović, Šarac, Simović, Milanković, Bratić, Torbica, Veselinov (Cheng 85), Ubiparip (Nosković 70), Antonić, Puškarić (Adamović 55). Coach: Dragan Miranović (SRB)
Yellow Card(s): Šarac 57, Stevanović 83, Adamović 88

Third Qualifying Round – FC Dnipro Dnipropetrovsk (UKR)
H 2-1 *Torbica (16p, 90p)*
Labus, Šarac, Simović, Milanković, Bratić, Adamović, Torbica, Veselinov (Mirić 46), Ubiparip (Nosković 76), Cheng (Puškarić 46), Antonić. Coach: Dragan Miranović (SRB)
Yellow Card(s): Bratić 12, Milanković 61, Torbica 90
A 0-2
Labus, Stevanović, Šarac, Simović, Bratić, Adamović, Torbica, Veselinov (Nosković 80), Ubiparip (Mirić 46), Antonić, Puškarić. Coach: Dragan Miranović (SRB)
Yellow Card(s): Stevanović 29, Veselinov 66, Bratić 86

SLOVAKIA

MŠK ŽILINA

UEFA CHAMPIONS LEAGUE

Second Qualifying Round – Birkirkara FC (MLT)
A 0-1
Dúbravka, Angelovič, Mráz, Rilke (Poliaček 60), Majtán (Fotyik 68), Jež, Oravec, Piaček, Šourek, Zošák (Leitner 80), Babatounde. Coach: Pavel Hapal (CZE)
Yellow Card(s): Piaček 33, Šourek 45+2, Mráz 56, Angelovič 90+4
H 3-0 *Piaček (21), Lietava (77), Oravec (90+2)*
Dúbravka, Angelovič, Mráz, Rilke (Poliaček 71), Majtán (Zošák 59), Jež, Oravec, Piaček, Šourek, Babatounde (Guldan 90+2), Lietava. Coach: Pavel Hapal (CZE)
Yellow Card(s): Lietava 45, Angelovič 73

Third Qualifying Round – PFC Litex Lovech (BUL)
A 1-1 *Majtán (65)*
Dúbravka, Guldan, Leitner, Rilke (Zošák 78), Majtán, Jež, Oravec (Chupáč 87), Piaček, Ceesay (Lietava 69), Šourek, Babatounde. Coach: Pavel Hapal (CZE)
Yellow Card(s): Oravec 52, Piaček 58
H 3-1 *Rilke (52), Oravec (70), Ceesay (84)*
Dúbravka, Pečalka, Guldan, Mráz, Rilke (Poliaček 81), Majtán (Zošák 63), Jež, Oravec, Ceesay (Fotyik 90+2), Šourek, Babatounde. Coach: Pavel Hapal (CZE)

Play-Offs – AC Sparta Praha (CZE)
A 2-0 *Ceesay (51), Oravec (73)*
Dúbravka, Pečalka, Guldan, Mráz, Rilke (Zošák 79), Majtán (Poliaček 87), Jež, Oravec, Piaček, Ceesay (Šourek 90+1), Babatounde. Coach: Pavel Hapal (CZE)
Yellow Card(s): Ceesay 36, Babatounde 68, Majtán 80
H 1-0 *Ceesay (18)*
Dúbravka, Pečalka, Guldan, Mráz, Rilke (Zošák 90+2), Majtán (Poliaček 74), Jež, Oravec, Piaček, Ceesay (Vittor 80), Babatounde. Coach: Pavel Hapal (CZE)
Yellow Card(s): Pečalka 54, Rilke 55

Group F
Match 1 – Chelsea FC (ENG)
H 1-4 *Oravec (55)*
Dúbravka, Pečalka, Guldan (Angelovič 79), Mráz, Rilke (Poliaček 57), Jež, Oravec, Piaček, Ceesay (Majtán 62), Babatounde, Vladavić. Coach: Pavel Hapal (CZE)
Match 2 – FC Spartak Moskva (RUS)
A 0-3
Dúbravka, Pečalka (Ceesay 46), Guldan, Mráz, Rilke (Vladavić 65), Majtán (Angelovič 82), Jež, Oravec, Piaček, Šourek, Vittor. Coach: Pavel Hapal (CZE)
Yellow Card(s): Guldan 17, Pečalka 41
Match 3 – Olympique de Marseille (FRA)
A 0-1
Dúbravka, Angelovič, Guldan, Leitner, Majtán (Oravec 68), Jež, Piaček, Ceesay, Šourek, Zošák (Vladavić 79), Gergel (Rilke 63). Coach: Pavel Hapal (CZE)
Yellow Card(s): Guldan 78
Match 4 – Olympique de Marseille (FRA)
H 0-7
Dúbravka, Angelovič, Pečalka, Leitner, Jež, Oravec, Ceesay (Majtán 78), Šourek, Babatounde, Vittor (Zošák 34), Vladavić (Gergel 60). Coach: Pavel Hapal (CZE)
Yellow Card(s): Pečalka 45
Match 5 – Chelsea FC (ENG)
A 1-2 *Babatounde (19)*
Dúbravka, Angelovič, Pečalka, Guldan, Majtán (Poliaček 85), Jež, Oravec (Ceesay 65), Piaček, Babatounde, Gergel, Vladavić (Rilke 90). Coach: Pavel Hapal (CZE)
Match 6 – FC Spartak Moskva (RUS)
H 1-2 *Majtán (48)*
Dúbravka, Angelovič, Pečalka, Guldan, Majtán (Mráz 85), Jež (Ceesay 69), Oravec, Piaček, Poliaček (Rilke 46), Babatounde, Gergel. Coach: Pavel Hapal (CZE)
Yellow Card(s): Guldan 25, Poliaček 45+1, Babatounde 45+1, Piaček 49, Pečalka 75

No	Player	Nat	DoB	Aps	(s)	Gls
Goalkeepers						
30	Martin Dúbravka		15/1/89	6		
Defenders						
2	Stanislav Angelovič		26/3/82	4	(2)	
5	Ľubomír Guldan		30/1/83	5		
7	Vladimír Leitner		28/6/74	2		
3	Mário Pečalka		28/12/80	5		
15	Jozef Piaček		20/6/83	5		
23	Ondřej Šourek	CZE	26/4/83	3		
Midfielders						
42	Roman Gergel		22/2/88	3	(1)	
12	Róbert Jež		10/7/81	6		
6	Patrik Mráz		1/2/87	2	(1)	
21	Pavol Poliaček		4/2/88	1	(2)	
9	Emil Rilke	CZE	19/11/83	2	(3)	
37	Sergio Vittor	ARG	9/6/89	2		
44	Admir Vladavić	BIH	29/6/82	3	(2)	
27	Štefan Zošák		3/4/84	1	(1)	
Forwards						
28	Bello Babatounde	BEN	6/10/89	4		1
18	Momodou Ceesay	GAM	24/12/88	3	(3)	
10	Tomáš Majtán		30/3/87	4	(2)	1
14	Tomáš Oravec		3/7/80	5	(1)	1

ŠK SLOVAN BRATISLAVA

UEFA EUROPA LEAGUE

Third Qualifying Round – FK Crvena zvezda (SRB)
A 2-1 *Ivana (43), Saláta (68)*
Putnocký, Saláta, Grendel (Kiss 82), Božić, Ivana, Sylvestr (Kuzma 75), Bagayoko (Kolčák 90+2), Guédé, Jánošík, Had, Dosoudil. Coach: Jozef Jankech (SVK)
Yellow Card(s): Saláta 13, Dosoudil 45, Božić 47
H 1-1 *Đorđević (2og)*
Putnocký, Saláta, Grendel (Kiss 68), Božić (Kolčák 89), Ivana (Kuzma 76), Sylvestr, Bagayoko, Guédé, Jánošík, Had, Dosoudil. Coach: Jozef Jankech (SVK)
Red Card(s): Dosoudil 57
Yellow Card(s): Grendel 19, Božić 21, Sylvestr 31, Had 51, Kiss 74

Play-Offs – VfB Stuttgart (GER)
H 0-1
Putnocký, Saláta, Dobrotka, Grendel (Kuzma 82), Ivana (Breznaník 61), Kiss, Sylvestr (Slovák 67), Bagayoko, Guédé, Jánošík, Had. Coach: Joze Jankech (SVK)
Yellow Card(s): Bagayoko 5, Had 85
A 2-2 *Dobrotka (9), Sylvestr (53)*
Putnocký, Saláta, Dobrotka, Grendel (Štepanovský 88), Božić, Ivana (Slovák 75), Breznaník, Sylvestr, Bagayoko, Guédé, Jánošík (Kiss 75). Coach: Jozef Jankech (SVK)
Red Card(s): Breznaník 55
Yellow Card(s): Breznaník 18, Sylvestr 34, Breznaník 55, Guédé 88, Štepanovský 90

DUKLA BANSKÁ BYSTRICA

UEFA EUROPA LEAGUE

Second Qualifying Round – FC Zestafoni (GEO)
A 0-3
Boroš, Hučko (Pich 66), Poljovka, Adámik, Pleva, Považanec, Pančík, Ďuriš, Gajdoš (Ďurica 77), Brašeň, Savič. Coach: Karol Marko (SVK)
Yellow Card(s): Savič 8, Brašeň 37, Ďuriš 60
H 1-0 *Ďuriš (28)*
Boroš, Hučko, Poljovka, Adámik, Seye, Pančík, Ďuriš, Gajdoš (Ďurica 75), Brašeň (Pich 64), Vajda (Pleva 68), Savič. Coach: Karol Marko (SVK)
Yellow Card(s): Vajda 49, Pich 71, Adámik 87

FC NITRA

UEFA EUROPA LEAGUE

First Qualifying Round – Győri ETO FC (HUN)
H 2-2 *Tóth (14), Sloboda (80)*
Hroššo, Kolmokov, Tóth, Štetina, Hodúr, Bališ (Sloboda 70), Kaspřák,

Glenda, Šimonek (Mikuš 46), Valenta (Kolár 56), Leško. Coach: Ivan Galád (SVK)
A 1-3 *Hodúr (10)*
Hroššo, Tóth, Štetina, Mikuš (Rák 51), Hodúr, Bališ (Kolár 46), Šimončič, Kaspřák, Glenda, Sloboda (Valenta 61), Leško. Coach: Ivan Galád (SVK)
Yellow Card(s): Sloboda 50, Leško 58, Kaspřák 89

SLOVENIA

FC KOPER

UEFA CHAMPIONS LEAGUE

Second Qualifying Round – NK Dinamo Zagreb (CRO)
A 1-5 *Bubanja (11)*
Hasič, Polovanec, Handanagič, Kovačevič, M. Pavlin (Guberac 85), Karič, Sesar, Marčeta, An. Struna (Al. Struna 56), Brulc (Jelenič 78), Bubanja. Coach: Nedžad Okčič (SVN)
Yellow Card(s): Karič 28, Marčeta 52
H 3-0 *Handanagič (11), Guberac (54), Brulc (78p)*
Hasič, Polovanec, Handanagič, Kovačevič (Guberac 46), Al. Struna, Karič (Marič 60), Sesar (Božičič 68), Marčeta, An. Struna, Brulc, Jelenič. Coach: Nedžad Okčič (SVN)
Yellow Card(s): Jelenič 14, Polovanec 20, Sesar 47, Božičič 79, Marič 88

NK MARIBOR

UEFA EUROPA LEAGUE

Second Qualifying Round – Videoton FC (HUN)
A 1-1 *Mezga (30)*
Pridigar, Mejač, Mezga (Iličič 71), Marcos Tavares, Volaš, Cvijanovič (Jelič 90+2), Bačinovič, Rajčevič, Viler, Anđelkovič (Džinič 80), Mertelj. Coach: Darko Milanič (SVN)
Yellow Card(s): *Mejač 45+2*
H 2-0 *Volaš (39, 80)*
Pridigar, Mejač, Mezga (Pavličić 89), Marcos Tavares, Volaš (Jelič 90+2), Bačinovič, Rajčevič, Iličič (Cvijanovič 78), Viler, Anđelkovič, Mertelj. Coach: Darko Milanič (SVN)
Yellow Card(s): Volaš 3, Bačinovič 78

Third Qualifying Round – Hibernian FC (SCO)
H 3-0 *Iličič (31, 52), Marcos Tavares (60)*
Pridigar, Mejač, Mezga (Cvijanović 71), Marcos Tavares, Volaš (Plut 90+2), Bačinovič, Rajčevič, Iličič (Pavličić 79), Viler, Anđelković, Mertelj. Coach: Darko Milanič (SVN)
A 3-2 *Marcos Tavares (20, 73), Mezga (67p)*
Pridigar, Mejač, Mezga (Cvijanović 90+1), Marcos Tavares, Volaš (Plut 90+3), Bačinovič, Rajčevič, Iličič, Viler, Anđelkovič, Mertelj. Coach: Darko Milanič (SVN)

Play-Offs – US Città di Palermo (ITA)
A 0-3
Pridigar, Mejač, Mezga (Radan 36), Marcos Tavares, Volaš (Cvijanović 46), Bačinovič (Dodlek 87), Rajčevič, Iličič, Viler, Anđelkovič, Mertelj. Coach: Darko Milanič (SVN)
Red Card(s): Pridigar 35
Yellow Card(s): Mejač 9, Viler 11

H 3-2 *Marcos Tavares (14), Iličič (58), Anđelkovič (89)*
Radan, Mezga, Marcos Tavares, Volaš (Berič 72), Cvijanovič (Plut 72), Bačinovič, Rajčevič, Iličič (Jelič 79), Viler, Anđelkovič, Mertelj. Coach: Darko Milanič (SVN)

ND GORICA

UEFA EUROPA LEAGUE

Second Qualifying Round – Randers FC (DEN)
H 0-3
Šimčič, Zarifovič, Balažič, Kršič, Velikonja (Volarič 90), M. Mevlja (Martinovič 60), Komel, Stojanovič (Arčon 75), Širok, Demirović, Rakuščček. Coach: David Peršič (SVN)
A 1-1 *Žigon (79)*
Šimčič, Zarifovič, Balažič, Kršič (Žigon 78), Velikonja, M. Mevlja, Komel, Stojanovič (Arčon 63), Demirović, Rakuščček, Gregorič (Širok 57). Coach: David Peršič (SVN)
Red Card(s): M. Mevlja 90+1
Yellow Card(s): M. Mevlja 83, Zarifovič 88, M. Mevlja 90+1

NK OLIMPIJA LJUBLJANA

UEFA EUROPA LEAGUE

First Qualifying Round – NK Široki Brijeg (BIH)
H 0-2
Botonjič, Kašnik, Vučkič, Gabriel (Jovič 62), Škerjanc, Cimerotič (Rakovič 46), Prašnikar (Rujovič 53), Cvijanovič, Lovrečič, Božič, Salkič. Coach: Safet Hadžič (SVN)
A 0-3
Botonjič, Kašnik, Jovič, Vučkič, Škerjanc, Rujovič (Prašnikar 88), Rakovič (Stojanovič 85), Cimerotič (Božič 84), Cvijanovič, Lovrečič, Salkič. Coach: Safet Hadžič (SVN)
Red Card(s): Jovič 68, Cvijanovič 79
Yellow Card(s): Cvijanovič 20, Jovič 49, Jovič 68, Vučkič 75, Cvijanovič 79, Lovrečič 80

SPAIN

FC BARCELONA

UEFA CHAMPIONS LEAGUE

Group D
Match 1 – Panathinaikos FC (GRE)
H 5-1 *Messi (22, 45), David Villa (33), Pedro (78), Dani Alves (90+3)*
Víctor Valdés, Dani Alves, Piqué (Milito 75), Puyol, Xavi (Mascherano 79), David Villa (Bojan 69), Iniesta, Messi, Busquets, Pedro, Abidal. Coach: Josep Guardiola (ESP)
Match 2 – FC Rubin Kazan (RUS)
A 1-1 *David Villa (60p)*
Víctor Valdés, Dani Alves, Piqué, Puyol, Xavi, David Villa (Bojan 86), Iniesta, Mascherano (Messi 60), Busquets, Pedro, Maxwell. Coach: Josep Guardiola (ESP)
Yellow Card(s): Puyol 52, Piqué 90+1
Match 3 – FC København (DEN)
H 2-0 *Messi (19, 90+2)*
Pinto, Dani Alves, Piqué, Puyol, David Villa (Xavi 73), Iniesta (Keita 89), Messi, Mascherano, Busquets, Maxwell (Pedro 73), Abidal. Coach: Josep Guardiola (ESP)
Yellow Card(s): Iniesta 81
Match 4 – FC København (DEN)
A 1-1 *Messi (31)*
Víctor Valdés, Dani Alves, Piqué, Puyol, Xavi, David Villa (Pedro 80), Iniesta, Messi, Keita, Busquets, Abidal. Coach: Josep Guardiola (ESP)
Yellow Card(s): Víctor Valdés 12, Busquets 50
Match 5 – Panathinaikos FC (GRE)
A 3-0 *Pedro (27, 69), Messi (62)*
Víctor Valdés, Dani Alves, Piqué (Abidal 72), Puyol, Xavi (Keita 71), David Villa, Iniesta, Messi, Mascherano, Pedro, Adriano (Maxwell 76). Coach: Josep Guardiola (ESP)
Yellow Card(s): Piqué 31
Match 6 – FC Rubin Kazan (RUS)
H 2-0 *Fontás (51), Víctor Vázquez (83)*
Pinto, Piqué, Bojan (Bartra 35), Jeffren (Víctor Vázquez 13), Mascherano, Busquets, Maxwell, Adriano, Fontás, Thiago, Jonathan (Messi 63). Coach: Josep Guardiola (ESP)

Round of 16 – Arsenal FC (ENG)
A 1-2 *David Villa (26)*
Víctor Valdés, Dani Alves, Piqué, Xavi, David Villa (Keita 68), Iniesta (Adriano 89), Messi, Busquets, Pedro, Maxwell, Abidal. Coach: Josep Guardiola (ESP)
Yellow Card(s): Iniesta 29, Piqué 58
H 3-1 *Messi (45+3, 71p), Xavi (69)*
Víctor Valdés, Dani Alves, Xavi, David Villa (Afellay 82), Iniesta, Messi, Mascherano (Keita 88), Busquets, Pedro, Adriano (Maxwell 90), Abidal. Coach: Josep Guardiola (ESP)

Quarter-Finals – FC Shakhtar Donetsk (UKR)
H 5-1 *Iniesta (2), Dani Alves (34), Piqué (53), Keita (61), Xavi (86)*
Víctor Valdés, Dani Alves, Piqué, Xavi, David Villa (Pedro 70), Iniesta (Afellay 90+1), Messi, Mascherano, Keita, Busquets, Adriano (Maxwell 77). Coach: Josep Guardiola (ESP)
Yellow Card(s): Iniesta 59
A 1-0 *Messi (43)*
Víctor Valdés, Dani Alves, Piqué (Milito 70), Xavi (Pedro 66), David Villa (Jeffren 75), Messi, Mascherano, Keita, Busquets, Afellay, Adriano. Coach: Josep Guardiola (ESP)
Yellow Card(s): Milito 71

Semi-Finals – Real Madrid CF (ESP)
A 2-0 *Messi (76, 87)*
Víctor Valdés, Dani Alves, Piqué, Puyol, Xavi, David Villa (Sergi Roberto 90+1), Messi, Mascherano, Keita, Busquets, Pedro (Afellay 71). Coach: Josep Guardiola (ESP)
Red Card(s): Pinto 45+2
Yellow Card(s): Dani Alves 44, Mascherano 57
H 1-1 *Pedro (54)*
Víctor Valdés, Dani Alves, Piqué, Puyol (Abidal 90), Xavi, David Villa (Keita 74), Iniesta, Messi, Mascherano, Busquets, Pedro (Afellay 90+2). Coach: Josep Guardiola (ESP)
Yellow Card(s): Pedro 82

Final – Manchester United FC (ENG)
N 3-1 *Pedro (27), Messi (54), David Villa (69)*
Víctor Valdés, Dani Alves (Puyol 88), Piqué, Xavi, David Villa (Keita 86), Iniesta, Messi, Mascherano, Busquets, Pedro (Afellay 90+2), Abidal. Coach: Josep Guardiola (ESP)
Yellow Card(s): Dani Alves 60, Víctor Valdés 85

No	Player	Nat	DoB	Aps	(s)	Gls
Goalkeepers						
13	José Pinto		8/11/75	2		
1	Víctor Valdés		14/1/82	11		
Defenders						
22	Éric Abidal	FRA	11/9/79	6	(2)	
32	Marc Bartra		15/1/91		(1)	
2	Dani Alves	BRA	6/5/83	12		2
26	Andreu Fontás		14/11/89	1		1
19	Maxwell	BRA	27/8/81	4	(3)	
18	Gabriel Milito	ARG	7/9/80		(2)	
3	Gerard Piqué		2/2/87	12		1
5	Carles Puyol		13/4/78	7	(1)	
Midfielders						
21	Adriano	BRA	26/10/84	5	(1)	
20	Ibrahim Afellay	NED	2/4/86	1	(5)	
16	Sergio Busquets		16/7/88	12		
8	Andrés Iniesta		11/5/84	10		1
34	Jonathan	MEX	26/4/90	1		
15	Seydou Keita	MLI	16/1/80	4	(5)	1
14	Javier Mascherano	ARG	8/6/84	10	(1)	
30	Thiago		11/4/91	1		
29	Víctor Vázquez		20/1/87		(1)	1
6	Xavi		25/1/80	11	(1)	2
Forwards						
9	Bojan Krkić		28/8/90	1	(2)	
7	David Villa		3/12/81	12		4
11	Jeffren		20/1/88	1	(1)	
10	Lionel Messi	ARG	24/6/87	11	(2)	12
17	Pedro		28/7/87	8	(4)	5
28	Sergi Roberto		7/2/92		(1)	

REAL MADRID CF

UEFA CHAMPIONS LEAGUE

Group G
Match 1 – AFC Ajax (NED)
H 2-0 *Anita (31og), Higuaín (73)*
Casillas, Ricardo Carvalho, Pepe, Cristiano Ronaldo, Marcelo, Xabi Alonso (L. Diarra 83), Arbeloa, Higuaín, Di María (Pedro León 80), Özil (Canales 88), Khedira. Coach: José Mourinho (POR)
Yellow Card(s): Xabi Alonso 28

Match 2 – AJ Auxerre (FRA)
A 1-0 *Di María (81)*
Casillas, Pepe, Sergio Ramos, Cristiano Ronaldo, Benzema (Özil 58), L. Diarra (Di María 74), Marcelo, Xabi Alonso, Arbeloa, Higuaín (M. Diarra 86), Khedira. Coach: José Mourinho (POR)
Yellow Card(s): Cristiano Ronaldo 39, Sergio Ramos 60, L. Diarra 67
Match 3 – AC Milan (ITA)
H 2-0 *Cristiano Ronaldo (13), Özil (14)*
Casillas, Ricardo Carvalho, Pepe, Cristiano Ronaldo, Marcelo, Xabi Alonso, Arbeloa, Higuaín (Benzema 89), Di María (Granero 87), Özil (L. Diarra 83), Khedira. Coach: José Mourinho (POR)
Yellow Card(s): Di María 81
Match 4 – AC Milan (ITA)
A 2-2 *Higuaín (45), Pedro León (90+4)*
Casillas, Ricardo Carvalho, Pepe (Pedro León 80), Sergio Ramos, Cristiano Ronaldo, Marcelo, Xabi Alonso, Higuaín (Benzema 74), Di María, Özil (Albiol 90+3), Khedira. Coach: José Mourinho (POR)
Yellow Card(s): Pepe 80, Ricardo Carvalho 90+1
Match 5 – AFC Ajax (NED)
A 4-0 *Benzema (36), Arbeloa (44), Cristiano Ronaldo (70, 81p)*
Casillas, Sergio Ramos, Cristiano Ronaldo, Benzema (Canales 82), L. Diarra (Mateos 81), Marcelo, Xabi Alonso, Arbeloa, Albiol, Pedro León (Di María 65), Özil. Coach: José Mourinho (POR)
Red Card(s): Xabi Alonso 87, Sergio Ramos 90+1
Yellow Card(s): Sergio Ramos 33, Cristiano Ronaldo 60, Xabi Alonso 68, Albiol 84, Xabi Alonso 87, Sergio Ramos 90+1
Match 6 – AJ Auxerre (FRA)
H 4-0 *Benzema (12, 72, 88), Cristiano Ronaldo (49)*
Dudek (Adán 45+4), Ricardo Carvalho, M. Diarra, Cristiano Ronaldo (Sarabia 72), Benzema, L. Diarra, Granero, Marcelo (Garay 76), Arbeloa, Albiol, Pedro León. Coach: Aitor Karanka (ESP)
Yellow Card(s): Albiol 26, M. Diarra 40

Round of 16 – Olympique Lyonnais (FRA)
A 1-1 *Benzema (65)*
Casillas, Ricardo Carvalho, Pepe, Sergio Ramos, Cristiano Ronaldo, Xabi Alonso, Arbeloa, Di María, Özil (Marcelo 75), Khedira (L. Diarra 68), Adebayor (Benzema 64). Coach: José Mourinho (POR)
Yellow Card(s): Sergio Ramos 10, Di María 45, Casillas 90+1
H 3-0 *Marcelo (37), Benzema (66), Di María (76)*
Casillas, Ricardo Carvalho, Pepe, Sergio Ramos, Cristiano Ronaldo (Adebayor 74), Benzema (L. Diarra 84), Marcelo, Xabi Alonso, Di María (Granero 78), Özil, Khedira. Coach: José Mourinho (POR)
Yellow Card(s): Pepe 9, Ricardo Carvalho 30

Quarter-Finals – Tottenham Hotspur FC (ENG)
H 4-0 *Adebayor (4, 57), Di María (72), Cristiano Ronaldo (87)*
Casillas, Ricardo Carvalho, Pepe, Sergio Ramos, Cristiano Ronaldo, Marcelo, Xabi Alonso, Di María (Kaká 77), Özil, Khedira (L. Diarra 61), Adebayor (Higuaín 75). Coach: José Mourinho (POR)
Yellow Card(s): Adebayor 12, Pepe 36
A 1-0 *Cristiano Ronaldo (50)*
Casillas, Ricardo Carvalho, Sergio Ramos (Granero 57), Cristiano Ronaldo (Kaká 65), Marcelo, Xabi Alonso (Benzema 75), Arbeloa, Albiol, Özil, Khedira, Adebayor. Coach: José Mourinho (POR)
Yellow Card(s): Ricardo Carvalho 39, Granero 79

Semi-Finals – FC Barcelona (ESP)
H 0-2
Casillas, Pepe, Sergio Ramos, Cristiano Ronaldo, L. Diarra, Marcelo, Xabi Alonso, Arbeloa, Albiol, Di María, Özil (Adebayor 46). Coach: José Mourinho (POR)
Red Card(s): Pepe 61
Yellow Card(s): Arbeloa 40, Sergio Ramos 53, Adebayor 83
A 1-1 *Marcelo (64)*
Casillas, Ricardo Carvalho, Cristiano Ronaldo, Kaká (Özil 60), L. Diarra, Marcelo, Xabi Alonso, Arbeloa, Albiol, Higuaín (Adebayor 55), Di María. Coach: Aitor Karanka (ESP)
Yellow Card(s): Ricardo Carvalho 13, L. Diarra 58, Xabi Alonso 69, Marcelo 75, Adebayor 85

No	Player	Nat	DoB	Aps	(s)	Gls
Goalkeepers						
13	Antonio Adán		13/5/87		(1)	
1	Iker Casillas		20/5/81	11		
25	Jerzy Dudek	POL	23/3/73	1		
Defenders						
18	Raúl Albiol		4/9/85	5	(1)	
17	Álvaro Arbeloa		17/1/83	9		1
19	Ezequiel Garay	ARG	10/10/86		(1)	
12	Marcelo	BRA	12/5/88	11	(1)	2
15	David Mateos		22/4/87		(1)	
3	Pepe	POR	26/2/83	8		
2	Ricardo Carvalho	POR	18/5/78	9		
4	Sergio Ramos		30/3/86	8		
Midfielders						
16	Sergio Canales		16/2/91		(2)	
22	Ángel Di María	ARG	14/2/88	8	(2)	3
10	Lassana Diarra	FRA	10/3/85	5	(5)	
6	Mahamadou Diarra	MLI	18/5/81	1	(1)	
11	Esteban Granero		2/7/87	1	(3)	
8	Kaká	BRA	22/4/82	1	(2)	
24	Sami Khedira	GER	4/4/87	8		
23	Mesut Özil	GER	15/10/88	9	(2)	1
21	Pedro León		24/11/86	2	(2)	1
33	Pablo Sarabia		11/5/92		(1)	
14	Xabi Alonso		25/11/81	11		
Forwards						
28	Emmanuel Adebayor	TGO	26/2/84	3	(3)	2
9	Karim Benzema	FRA	19/12/87	4	(4)	6
7	Cristiano Ronaldo	POR	5/2/85	12		6
20	Gonzalo Higuaín	ARG	10/12/87	5	(1)	2

VALENCIA CF

UEFA CHAMPIONS LEAGUE

Group C
Match 1 – Bursaspor (TUR)
A 4-0 *Tino Costa (16), Aduriz (41), Pablo Hernández (68), Soldado (76)*
César Sánchez, Bruno, David Navarro, Mehmet, Joaquín, Domínguez (Mata 77), Aduriz (Soldado 73), Pablo Hernández, Ricardo Costa, Mathieu, Tino Costa (Manuel Fernandes 81). Coach: Juan Carlos Carcedo (ESP)
Match 2 – Manchester United FC (ENG)
H 0-1
César Sánchez, Maduro, David Navarro, Albelda (Mehmet 86), Domínguez (Aduriz 59), Soldado, Mata, Pablo Hernández, Mathieu, Miguel, Tino Costa (Manuel Fernandes 75). Coach: Unai Emery (ESP)
Yellow Card(s): Aduriz 90+3
Match 3 – Rangers FC (SCO)
A 1-1 *Edu (46og)*
César Sánchez, Bruno, David Navarro, Mehmet, Domínguez (Soldado 46), Mata (Vicente 85), Aduriz, Pablo Hernández, Ricardo Costa, Mathieu, Tino Costa (Manuel Fernandes 76). Coach: Unai Emery (ESP)
Yellow Card(s): Aduriz 59, Mata 83
Match 4 – Rangers FC (SCO)
H 3-0 *Soldado (33, 71), Tino Costa (90)*
César Sánchez, David Navarro, Albelda, Joaquín (Pablo Hernández 85), Soldado (Manuel Fernandes 78), Mata, Aduriz, Ricardo Costa, Éver Banega (Tino Costa 70), Mathieu, Miguel. Coach: Unai Emery (ESP)
Yellow Card(s): Albelda 65
Match 5 – Bursaspor (TUR)
H 6-1 *Mata (17p), Soldado (21, 55), Aduriz (30), Joaquín (37), Domínguez (78)*
Moyá (Guaita 23), Bruno, Maduro, Albelda, Joaquín, Soldado (Isco 71), Mata, Aduriz (Domínguez 61), Ricardo Costa, Tino Costa, Jordi Alba. Coach: Unai Emery (ESP)
Yellow Card(s): Albelda 76, Jordi Alba 90+2

Match 6 – Manchester United FC (ENG)
A 1-1 *Pablo Hernández (32)*
Guaita, Albelda, Domínguez (Isco 54), Aduriz, Dealbert, Pablo Hernández (Feghouli 81), Ricardo Costa, Éver Banega, Mathieu, Miguel, Jordi Alba (Mata 68). Coach: Unai Emery (ESP)
Yellow Card(s): Albelda 60, Miguel 78

Round of 16 – FC Schalke 04 (GER)
H 1-1 *Soldado (17)*
Guaita, David Navarro, Mehmet, Domínguez (Joaquín 68), Soldado, Aduriz, Ricardo Costa, Éver Banega (Vicente 68), Mathieu (Jordi Alba 78), Miguel, Tino Costa. Coach: Unai Emery (ESP)
Yellow Card(s): Ricardo Costa 62
A 1-3 *Ricardo Costa (17)*
Guaita, Bruno, David Navarro, Mehmet, Joaquín, Mata, Aduriz (Jonas 75), Pablo Hernández (Soldado 64), Ricardo Costa, Éver Banega (Tino Costa 70), Mathieu. Coach: Unai Emery (ESP)
Yellow Card(s): Mathieu 83, Mata 90+3

No	Player	Nat	DoB	Aps	(s)	Gls
Goalkeepers						
1	César Sánchez		2/9/71	4		
13	Vicente Guaita		18/2/87	3	(1)	
25	Miguel Ángel Moyá		2/4/84	1		
Defenders						
2	Bruno		1/10/80	4		
4	David Navarro		25/5/80	6		
15	Ángel Dealbert		1/1/83	1		
22	Jérémy Mathieu	FRA	29/10/83	7		
23	Miguel	POR	4/1/80	4		
20	Ricardo Costa	POR	16/5/81	7		1
Midfielders						
6	David Albelda		1/9/77	4		
21	Éver Banega	ARG	29/6/88	4		
12	Sofiane Feghouli	FRA	26/12/89		(1)	
7	Joaquín		21/7/81	4	(1)	1
28	Jordi Alba		21/3/89	2	(1)	
3	Hedwiges Maduro	NED	13/2/85	2		
18	Manuel Fernandes	POR	5/2/86		(4)	
10	Juan Mata		28/4/88	5	(2)	1
5	Mehmet Topal	TUR	3/3/86	4	(1)	
19	Pablo Hernández		11/4/85	5	(1)	2
24	Tino Costa	ARG	9/1/85	5	(2)	2
14	Vicente		16/7/81		(2)	
Forwards						
11	Aritz Aduriz		11/2/81	7	(1)	2
8	Alejandro Domínguez	ARG	10/6/81	5	(1)	1
26	Isco		21/4/92		(2)	
16	Jonas	BRA	1/4/84		(1)	
9	Roberto Soldado		27/5/85	4	(3)	6

SEVILLA FC

UEFA CHAMPIONS LEAGUE

Play-Offs – SC Braga (POR)
A 0-1
Palop, Fazio, Fernando Navarro, Jesús Navas, Zokora, Luís Fabiano, Renato (Cigarini 83), Kanouté (Negredo 79), Escudé, Diego Capel (Perotti 70), Dabo. Coach: Antonio Álvarez (ESP)
Yellow Card(s): Diego Capel 60, Escudé 64, Fernando Navarro 67
H 3-4 *Luís Fabiano (60), Jesús Navas (84), Kanouté (90+1)*
Palop, Fazio, Jesús Navas, Zokora, Perotti, Luís Fabiano, Kanouté, Escudé, Cigarini (Renato 61), Dabo (Negredo 78), Konko (José Carlos 61). Coach: Antonio Álvarez (ESP)
Yellow Card(s): Zokora 43, Escudé 86, Perotti 87

UEFA EUROPA LEAGUE

Group J
Match 1 – Paris Saint-Germain FC (FRA)
H 0-1
Palop, Cáceres, Jesús Navas, Zokora, Luís Fabiano, Diego Capel (Perotti 61), Cigarini (Guarente 46), Dabo, Alexis, Konko, José Carlos (Kanouté 46). Coach: Antonio Álvarez (ESP)
Match 2 – Borussia Dortmund (GER)
A 1-0 *Cigarini (45+1)*
Palop, Cáceres, Fernando Navarro, Jesús Navas, Zokora, Perotti, Luís Fabiano (Negredo 82), Cigarini (Kanouté 53), Dabo (Escudé 66), Alexis, Guarente. Coach: Gregorio Manzano (ESP)
Yellow Card(s): Guarente 52, Kanouté 58, Fernando Navarro 66
Match 3 – FC Karpaty Lviv (UKR)
A 1-0 *Kanouté (34)*
Palop, Cáceres, Fernando Navarro, Zokora, Perotti, Kanouté (Romaric 68), Escudé, Negredo (Luís Fabiano 75), Dabo, Konko, Guarente (José Carlos 81). Coach: Gregorio Manzano (ESP)
Yellow Card(s): Guarente 9, Fernando Navarro 61, Escudé 90
Match 4 – FC Karpaty Lviv (UKR)
H 4-0 *Alfaro (9, 42), Cigarini (31), Negredo (51)*
Javi Varas, Cáceres, Fernando Navarro (Dabo 46), Zokora, Escudé, Alfaro, Diego Capel (Perotti 60), Negredo, Cigarini (Romaric 75), Konko, José Carlos. Coach: Gregorio Manzano (ESP)
Match 5 – Paris Saint-Germain FC (FRA)
A 2-4 *Kanouté (32, 36)*
Palop, Cáceres, Fernando Navarro, Romaric (Cigarini 78), Zokora (Negredo 46), Perotti, Renato, Kanouté, Escudé, Diego Capel (Alfaro 65), Dabo. Coach: Gregorio Manzano (ESP)
Yellow Card(s): Zokora 11, Fernando Navarro 33, Negredo 70, Perotti 90+1
Match 6 – Borussia Dortmund (GER)
H 2-2 *Romaric (31), Kanouté (35)*
Palop, Romaric (Fazio 86), Zokora, Perotti (Cáceres 61), Luís Fabiano, Kanouté (Renato 42), Escudé, Diego Capel, Dabo, Alexis, Konko. Coach: Gregorio Manzano (ESP)
Yellow Card(s): Romaric 24, Alexis 36, Zokora 83, Palop 90+4

Round of 32 – FC Porto (POR)
H 1-2 *Kanouté (65)*
Palop, Fazio, Cáceres, Fernando Navarro, Jesús Navas, Perotti (Diego Capel 86), Luís Fabiano (Negredo 73), Kanouté, Sergio Sánchez, Rakitić (Romaric 78), Medel. Coach: Gregorio Manzano (ESP)
Yellow Card(s): Cáceres 52, Perotti 52
A 1-0 *Luís Fabiano (71)*
Javi Varas, Fazio, Fernando Navarro, Jesús Navas, Zokora (Medel 46), Perotti (Rodri 86), Kanouté, Sergio Sánchez (Luís Fabiano 55), Negredo, Alexis, Rakitić. Coach: Gregorio Manzano (ESP)
Red Card(s): Alexis 77
Yellow Card(s): Fernando Navarro 14, Alexis 21, Alexis 77, Luís Fabiano 86

CLUB ATLÉTICO DE MADRID

UEFA EUROPA LEAGUE

Group B
Match 1 – Aris Thessaloniki FC (GRE)
A 0-1
De Gea, Valera, Antonio López, Tiago, Camacho (Mario Suárez 77), Forlán, Raúl García (Diego Costa 46), Fran Mérida (Reyes 60), Godín, Álvaro Domínguez, Simão. Coach: Quique Sánchez Flores (ESP)
Yellow Card(s): Fran Mérida 39, Raúl García 43, Antonio López 47, Simão 76
Match 2 – Bayer 04 Leverkusen (GER)
H 1-1 *Simão (51)*
De Gea, Forlán (Tiago 46), Raúl García (Fran Mérida 46), Paulo Assunção, Filipe Luís, Ujfaluši, Álvaro Domínguez, Reyes, Simão, Perea, Diego Costa. Coach: Quique Sánchez Flores (ESP)

Match 3 – Rosenborg BK (NOR)
H 3-0 *Godín (17), Agüero (66), Diego Costa (78)*
Joel, Valera (Perea 22), Tiago (Raúl García 71), Forlán (Agüero 65), Paulo Assunção, Filipe Luís, Godín, Ujfaluši, Reyes, Simão, Diego Costa. Coach: Quique Sánchez Flores (ESP)
Match 4 – Rosenborg BK (NOR)
A 2-1 *Agüero (4), Tiago (84)*
De Gea, Antonio López, Tiago, Raúl García, Agüero (Forlán 61), Paulo Assunção (Mario Suárez 71), Ujfaluši, Álvaro Domínguez, Simão, Perea, Diego Costa (Camacho 90+1). Coach: Quique Sánchez Flores (ESP)
Yellow Card(s): Agüero 53, De Gea 78
Match 5 – Aris Thessaloniki FC (GRE)
H 2-3 *Forlán (11), Agüero (16)*
De Gea, Antonio López (Fran Mérida 86), Mario Suárez, Tiago (Raúl García 86), Forlán, Agüero, Godín, Ujfaluši, Álvaro Domínguez, Reyes, Simão (Diego Costa 74). Coach: Quique Sánchez Flores (ESP)
Yellow Card(s): Tiago 32, Álvaro Domínguez 76, Raúl García 90
Match 6 – Bayer 04 Leverkusen (GER)
A 1-1 *Fran Mérida (72)*
De Gea, Valera, Mario Suárez (Tiago 84), Forlán (Diego Costa 67), Raúl García, Agüero, Paulo Assunção, Filipe Luís, Álvaro Domínguez, Simão (Fran Mérida 71), Perea. Coach: Quique Sánchez Flores (ESP)
Yellow Card(s): Mario Suárez 50

GETAFE CF

UEFA EUROPA LEAGUE

Play-Offs – APOEL FC (CYP)
H 1-0 *Parejo (43)*
Ustari, Cata Díaz, Mané, Borja (Albín 46), Gavilán, Adrián Colunga (Miku 67), Parejo, Rafa López, Boateng, Arizmendi (Manu del Moral 46), Torres. Coach: Míchel (ESP)
Yellow Card(s): Rafa López 49
A 1-1 (aet) *Cata Díaz (98)*
Ustari, Cata Díaz, Adrián Colunga (Miku 75), Albín (Mosquera 91), Parejo, Manu del Moral, Rafa López, Pedro Ríos (Arizmendi 46), Boateng, Marcano, Torres. Coach: Míchel (ESP)
Yellow Card(s): Torres 33, Parejo 37, Cata Díaz 47

Group H
Match 1 – Odense BK (DEN)
H 2-1 *Arizmendi (51), Pedro Ríos (81)*
Codina, Cata Díaz, Mané, Borja (Casquero 46), Gavilán (Miku 6), Adrián Colunga, Parejo (Pedro Ríos 73), Víctor Sánchez, Boateng, Arizmendi, Marcano. Coach: Míchel (ESP)
Yellow Card(s): Boateng 9, Casquero 52, Mané 61, Pedro Ríos 80
Match 2 – BSC Young Boys (SUI)
A 0-2
Ustari, Mané, Mario, Borja, Miku, Adrián Colunga (Pedro Ríos 74), Albín, Víctor Sánchez, Mosquera (Parejo 62), Marcano, Torres (Adrián Sardinero 69). Coach: Míchel (ESP)
Yellow Card(s): Torres 67, Víctor Sánchez 90+3
Match 3 – VfB Stuttgart (GER)
A 0-1
Ustari, Cata Díaz, Borja, Miku, Albín (Adrián Colunga 72), Manu del Moral, Rafa López, Víctor Sánchez (Casquero 46), Arizmendi (Gavilán 46), Pintos, Marcano. Coach: Míchel (ESP)
Yellow Card(s): Marcano 27
Match 4 – VfB Stuttgart (GER)
H 0-3
Ustari, Cata Díaz, Mané, İbrahim Kaş (Miku 65), Borja, Adrián Colunga, Albín, Víctor Sánchez, Boateng (Casquero 46), Arizmendi, Adrián Sardinero (Manu del Moral 58). Coach: Míchel (ESP)
Yellow Card(s): Mané 14, Casquero 46, Cata Díaz 46, Miku 78

Match 5 – Odense BK (DEN)
A 1-1 *Pedro Ríos (17)*
Ustari, Cata Díaz, Mané, Miku, Albín (Mosquera 86), Parejo (Borja 80), Manu del Moral (Víctor Sánchez 68), Pedro Ríos, Boateng, Marcano, Torres. Coach: Míchel (ESP)
Yellow Card(s): Torres 14, Mané 69, Parejo 80
Match 6 – BSC Young Boys (SUI)
H 1-0 *Adrián Sardinero (15)*
Ustari, Cata Díaz (Alex 41), İbrahim Kaş (Torres 72), Adrián Colunga, Albín, Arizmendi (Escassi 57), Pintos, Mosquera, Casquero, Adrián Sardinero, Adrián Cañas. Coach: Míchel (ESP)
Yellow Card(s): Adrián Colunga 20, İbrahim Kaş 34, Adrián Cañas 86, Pintos 90

VILLARREAL CF

UEFA EUROPA LEAGUE

Play-Offs – FC Dnepr Mogilev (BLR)
H 5-0 *Marchena (10), Santi Cazorla (16), Borja Valero (30), Cani (44), Nilmar (75)*
Diego López, Musacchio, Marchena, Ángel, Santi Cazorla (Montero 57), Cani, Capdevila, Senna, Borja Valero (Nilmar 46), Bruno, Rossi (Altidore 73). Coach: Juan Carlos Garrido (ESP)
Yellow Card(s): Senna 72
A 2-1 *Nilmar (45+1), Marco Ruben (90+1)*
Juan Carlos, Joan Oriol, Musacchio (Marchena 56), Nilmar (Marco Ruben 61), Altidore (Cani 72), Catalá, Matilla, Cristóbal, Montero, Kiko, Mario. Coach: Juan Carlos Garrido (ESP)
Red Card(s): Cristóbal 69
Yellow Card(s): Cristóbal 30, Cristóbal 69

Group D
Match 1 – NK Dinamo Zagreb (CRO)
A 0-2
Diego López, Gonzalo, Musacchio, Marco Ruben (Rossi 46), Cani (Santi Cazorla 63), Capdevila, Altidore, Senna, Bruno (Borja Valero 45+2), Montero, Mario. Coach: Juan Carlos Garrido (ESP)
Red Card(s): Senna 74
Yellow Card(s): Senna 35, Borja Valero 70, Senna 74
Match 2 – Club Brugge KV (BEL)
H 2-1 *Rossi (41), Gonzalo (56)*
Diego López, Gonzalo, Marchena, Ángel, Santi Cazorla, Cani (Montero 35), Capdevila, Altidore (Marco Ruben 86), Borja Valero, Bruno, Rossi (Matilla 76). Coach: Juan Carlos Garrido (ESP)
Yellow Card(s): Marchena 14, Cani 28, Santi Cazorla 90+2
Match 3 – PAOK FC (GRE)
H 1-0 *Marco Ruben (38)*
Diego López, Gonzalo, Musacchio, Ángel, Santi Cazorla (Montero 77), Marco Ruben (Altidore 82), Cani, Capdevila, Borja Valero, Bruno, Rossi (Nilmar 70). Coach: Juan Carlos Garrido (ESP)
Match 4 – PAOK FC (GRE)
A 0-1
Diego López, Gonzalo, Musacchio (Montero 72), Marchena, Ángel, Nilmar, Cani (Santi Cazorla 68), Capdevila, Altidore (Rossi 62), Borja Valero, Bruno. Coach: Juan Carlos Garrido (ESP)
Yellow Card(s): Nilmar 14, Ángel 28
Match 5 – NK Dinamo Zagreb (CRO)
H 3-0 *Rossi (25p, 80), Marco Ruben (62)*
Diego López, Musacchio, Marchena, Ángel, Santi Cazorla, Marco Ruben (Senna 63), Cani, Catalá, Borja Valero (Nilmar 79), Bruno, Rossi (Montero 82). Coach: Juan Carlos Garrido (ESP)
Yellow Card(s): Diego López 15, Rossi 26, Ángel 37, Marchena 89

Match 6 – Club Brugge KV (BEL)
A 2-1 *Rossi (30, 34p)*
Diego López, Gonzalo, Musacchio, Santi Cazorla (Ángel 81), Marco Ruben (Altidore 77), Cani (Borja Valero 59), Capdevila, Senna, Bruno, Rossi, Mario. Coach: Juan Carlos Garrido (ESP)
Yellow Card(s): Capdevila 72, Senna 80

Round of 32 – SSC Napoli (ITA)
A 0-0
Diego López, Gonzalo, Musacchio, Nilmar, Santi Cazorla (Catalá 87), Capdevila, Senna (Marchena 61), Borja Valero, Bruno, Rossi (Marco Ruben 77), Mario. Coach: Juan Carlos Garrido (ESP)
Yellow Card(s): Capdevila 29, Gonzalo 36, Marchena 89
H 2-1 *Nilmar (42), Rossi (45+1)*
Diego López, Gonzalo, Musacchio, Nilmar, Santi Cazorla (Catalá 78), Cani (Gullón 81), Capdevila, Borja Valero, Bruno, Rossi (Marco Ruben 89), Mario. Coach: Juan Carlos Garrido (ESP)
Yellow Card(s): Musacchio 41, Santi Cazorla 60, Capdevila 65, Nilmar 74

Round of 16 – Bayer 04 Leverkusen (GER)
A 3-2 *Rossi (42), Nilmar (70, 90+4)*
Diego López, Gonzalo, Musacchio, Marchena, Marco Ruben (Joan Oriol 84), Catalá, Borja Valero, Bruno, Rossi (Nilmar 69), Mario, Mubarak (Santi Cazorla 61). Coach: Juan Carlos Garrido (ESP)
Yellow Card(s): Musacchio 18, Mubarak 41, Catalá 57
H 2-1 *Santi Cazorla (33), Rossi (61)*
Diego López, Gonzalo, Musacchio, Marchena, Santi Cazorla (Cani 80), Marco Ruben, Catalá, Borja Valero (Capdevila 74), Bruno, Rossi (Nilmar 69), Mario. Coach: Juan Carlos Garrido (ESP)
Yellow Card(s): Gonzalo 70

Quarter-Finals – FC Twente (NED)
H 5-1 *Marchena (23), Borja Valero (43), Nilmar (45+1, 81), Rossi (55)*
Diego López, Gonzalo (Capdevila 71), Musacchio, Marchena, Nilmar, Santi Cazorla, Catalá (Kiko 82), Borja Valero (Cani 79), Bruno, Rossi, Mario. Coach: Juan Carlos Garrido (ESP)
Yellow Card(s): Santi Cazorla 84, Nilmar 88
A 3-1 *Rossi (60p), Marco Ruben (84p), Cani (90)*
Diego López, Musacchio, Marchena (Joan Oriol 76), Marco Ruben, Catalá, Matilla, Borja Valero (Cani 62), Bruno, Rossi (Peréz 73), Mario, Mubarak. Coach: Juan Carlos Garrido (ESP)
Yellow Card(s): Catalá 39

Semi-Finals – FC Porto (POR)
A 1-5 *Cani (45)*
Diego López, Musacchio, Marchena, Nilmar (Marco Ruben 72), Santi Cazorla, Cani (Matilla 71), Catalá, Borja Valero (Mubarak 67), Bruno, Rossi, Mario. Coach: Juan Carlos Garrido (ESP)
Yellow Card(s): Borja Valero 41, Diego López 48, Catalá 73
H 3-2 *Cani (17), Capdevila (75), Rossi (80p)*
Diego López, Musacchio, Nilmar (Senna 67), Santi Cazorla (Marchena 57), Marco Ruben, Cani, Capdevila, Matilla (Mubarak 57), Bruno, Rossi, Mario. Coach: Juan Carlos Garrido (ESP)
Yellow Card(s): Bruno 54, Mubarak 62

SWEDEN

AIK SOLNA

UEFA CHAMPIONS LEAGUE

Second Qualifying Round – AS Jeunesse Esch (LUX)
H 1-0 *Engblom (57)*
Turina, Karlsson, Johansson, Atta, Daníelsson, Tjernström, Ljubojević (Catovic 54), Antônio Flávio, Pavey, Engblom, Johnson (Gustafsson 85). Coach: Alex Miller (SCO)
A 0-0
Turina, Backman, Karlsson, Johansson, Atta, Daníelsson, Tjernström, Antônio Flávio (Lundberg 77), Pavey, Engblom (Ljubojević 69), Johnson. Coach: Alex Miller (SCO)

Third Qualifying Round – Rosenborg BK (NOR)
H 0-1
Turina, Backman, Karlsson, Johansson, Åhman Persson, Daníelsson (Lundberg 75), Tjernström, Ljubojević (Engblom 82), Pavey, Bangura, Johnson. Coach: Alex Miller (SCO)
Yellow Card(s): Åhman Persson 17, Turina 65, Bangura 77
A 0-3
Turina, Karlsson, Johansson, Åhman Persson (Lundberg 69), Atta, Daníelsson, Tjernström, Ljubojević (Antônio Flávio 59), Pavey, Bangura, Johnson. Coach: Alex Miller (SCO)
Yellow Card(s): Johansson 43

UEFA EUROPA LEAGUE

Play-Offs – PFC Levski Sofia (BUL)
H 0-0
Turina, Backman, Karlsson, Johansson, Åhman Persson, Daníelsson, Tjernström, Pavey, Lorentzson (Lundberg 70), Jagne (Antônio Flávio 60), Bangura. Coach: Alex Miller (SCO)
Yellow Card(s): Lorentzson 64
A 1-2 *Bangura (11)*
Turina, Backman, Karlsson, Johansson, Åhman Persson, Daníelsson (Ljubojević 86), Tjernström, Pavey, Bangura, Engblom (Antônio Flávio 46), Lundberg (Lorentzson 75). Coach: Alex Miller (SCO)
Yellow Card(s): Engblom 25, Lundberg 66, Johansson 73

IFK GÖTEBORG

UEFA EUROPA LEAGUE

Third Qualifying Round – AZ Alkmaar (NED)
A 0-2
Sandberg, A. Johansson, Hysén, Olsson (Bjarnason 60), Selakovic (Söder 78), Sigurdsson, G. Svensson, Jónsson, J. Johansson, Lund, Stiller (Ericsson 84). Coach: Stefan Rehn (SWE)
Yellow Card(s): Hysén 38, Lund 54, Bjarnason 90+2
H 1-0 *Selakovic (67)*
Sandberg, A. Johansson, Hysén, Selakovic, Sigurdsson, G. Svensson, Jónsson, J. Johansson (Söder 62), Lund (Bärkroth 82), Stiller, Bjarnason. Coach: Stefan Rehn (SWE)
Yellow Card(s): Selakovic 76

IF ELFSBORG

UEFA EUROPA LEAGUE

Second Qualifying Round – FC Iskra-Stal (MDA)
H 2-1 *Keene (56), Ericsson (79p)*
Christiansen, Florén, Karlsson, Andersson, Svensson, Ericsson, Mobaeck, Wikström, Nordmark (Hult 63), Keene (Jawo 81), Larsson (Ishizaki 71). Coach: Magnus Haglund (SWE)
Yellow Card(s): Larsson 43, Andersson 49
A 1-0 *Ishizaki (60)*
Covic, Florén, Andersson, Jönsson, Svensson, Mobaeck, Jawo, Keene, Klarström, Larsson (Nordmark 78), Ishizaki (Hult 82). Coach: Magnus Haglund (SWE)
Yellow Card(s): Jönsson 37

Third Qualifying Round – FK Teteks (MKD)
H 5-0 *Ishizaki (29), Svensson (50), Avdic (57), Nordmark (66), Keene (77)*
Covic, Florén, Andersson, Jönsson, Svensson, Avdic (Hult 81), Ericsson (Keene 62), Mobaeck, Klarström, Larsson, Ishizaki (Nordmark 65). Coach: Magnus Haglund (SWE)
Yellow Card(s): Svensson 39
A 2-1 *Kurbegovic (42), Jawo (56)*
Covic, Florén (Klarström 61), Karlsson, Mobaeck (Avdic 46), Jawo, Wikström, Lucic, Nordmark, Keene, Ishizaki (Ericsson 46), Kurbegovic. Coach: Magnus Haglund (SWE)

Play-Offs – SSC Napoli (ITA)
A 0-1
Christiansen, Florén, Jönsson, Svensson, Avdic, Mobaeck, Lucic, Keene (Karlsson 87), Klarström, Larsson (Jawo 70), Ishizaki (Ericsson 44). Coach: Magnus Haglund (SWE)
Yellow Card(s): Lucic 8, Jönsson 27, Florén 29
H 0-2
Covic, Florén, Andersson (Wikström 66), Svensson, Avdic, Ericsson, Mobaeck, Lucic, Keene (Jawo 76), Klarström (Karlsson 70), Larsson. Coach: Magnus Haglund (SWE)
Yellow Card(s): Larsson 67

KALMAR FF

UEFA EUROPA LEAGUE

First Qualifying Round – EB/Streymur (FRO)
H 1-0 *Ricardo Santos (79)*
Wastå, Lindberg, Carlsson (Åhlander 53), Rydström, Larsson, Dauda, Daniel Sobralense, Ricardo Santos, Israelsson (Marcel Sacramento 78), Johansson, Eriksson (Daniel Mendes 77). Coach: Nanne Bergstrand (SWE)
A 3-0 *Israelsson (9), Eriksson (46), Ricardo Santos (50)*
Wastå, Lindberg, Arajuuri, Rydström, Larsson, Daniel Sobralense (Johansson 88), Daniel Mendes (Bertilsson 70), Ricardo Santos (Marcel Sacramento 70), Israelsson, Eriksson, Nouri. Coach: Nanne Bergstrand (SWE)
Yellow Card(s): Lindberg 49

Second Qualifying Round – FC Dacia Chisinau (MDA)
H 0-0
Wastå, Carlsson, Rydström, Larsson, Daniel Sobralense (Marcel Sacramento 82), Daniel Mendes (Dauda 67), Ricardo Santos, Israelsson (Bertilsson 46), Johansson, Eriksson, Nouri. Coach: Nanne Bergstrand (SWE)
Yellow Card(s): Ricardo Santos 90
A 2-0 *Israelsson (11), Daniel Sobralense (88)*
Wastå, Carlsson, Rydström, Larsson, Daniel Sobralense, Daniel Mendes (Bertilsson 46), Ricardo Santos, Israelsson (Åhlander 89), Johansson (Augustsson 46), Eriksson, Nouri. Coach: Nanne Bergstrand (SWE)
Yellow Card(s): Israelsson 25

Third Qualifying Round – PFC Levski Sofia (BUL)
H 1-1 *Dauda (83)*
Wastå, Carlsson, Augustsson, Rydström, Larsson, Daniel Mendes (Bertilsson 78), Ricardo Santos, Israelsson (Marcel Sacramento 77), Johansson, Eriksson, Douglas (Dauda 77). Coach: Nanne Bergstrand (SWE)
Yellow Card(s): Douglas 44, Ricardo Santos 77
A 2-5 *Johansson (82), Israelsson (84)*
Wastå, Lantz (Bertilsson 46), Carlsson, Augustsson, Rydström, Larsson, Dauda (Daniel Mendes 46), Israelsson, Johansson, Eriksson, Douglas. Coach: Nanne Bergstrand (SWE)
Yellow Card(s): Daniel Mendes 84

GEFLE IF

UEFA EUROPA LEAGUE

First Qualifying Round – NSÍ Runavík (FRO)
A 2-0 *Gerndt (34, 60)*
Hugosson, Theorin, Senatore, Jawo (Frempong 82), Orlov, Bernhardsson, Portin, Dahlberg, Gerndt (Westlin 65), Lantto, Hansson. Coach: Per Olsson (SWE)
H 2-1 *Bernhardsson (22), Berggren (63)*
Hugosson, Theorin, Senatore, Jawo, Orlov (Berggren 59), Öhagen (Larsson 70), Bernhardsson, Gerndt, Lantto, Hansson (Dahlberg 53), Chibsah. Coach: Per Olsson (SWE)

Second Qualifying Round – FC Dinamo Tbilisi (GEO)
H 1-2 *Berggren (51p)*
Hugosson, Theorin, Senatore, Jawo, Orlov, Bernhardsson, Berggren, Dahlberg, Lantto, Hansson (Gerndt 46), Chibsah. Coach: Per Olsson (SWE)
A 1-2 *Orlov (90+1)*
Hugosson, Senatore, Orlov, Öhagen (Larsson 72), Bernhardsson, Portin, Dahlberg (Nyström 83), Lantto, Hansson, Westlin (Gram 55), Chibsah. Coach: Per Olsson (SWE)
Yellow Card(s): Chibsah 63, Gram 82

SWITZERLAND

FC BASEL 1893

UEFA CHAMPIONS LEAGUE

Third Qualifying Round – Debreceni VSC (HUN)
A 2-0 *Stocker (34), G. Xhaka (90+2)*
Costanzo, Çağdaş Atan, Huggel, Frei, Stocker (G. Xhaka 88), Shaqiri (Tembo 62), Abraham, Safari, Inkoom, Cabral, Zoua (Almerares 75). Coach: Thorsten Fink (GER)
Yellow Card(s): Cabral 49, Stocker 83
H 3-1 *Çağdaş Atan (26), Chipperfield (59), Shaqiri (64)*
Costanzo, Çağdaş Atan, Huggel (G. Xhaka 87), Yapi (Cabral 77), Chipperfield (Almerares 67), Shaqiri, Abraham, Safari, Inkoom, Tembo, Zoua. Coach: Thorsten Fink (GER)
Yellow Card(s): Inkoom 11

Play-Offs – FC Sheriff (MDA)
H 1-0 *Stocker (54)*
Costanzo, Çağdaş Atan, Huggel, Yapi, Frei (Chipperfield 88), Stocker, Shaqiri (Tembo 71), Abraham, Safari, Inkoom, Zoua (Almerares 80). Coach: Thorsten Fink (GER)
Yellow Card(s): Zoua 67
A 3-0 *Streller (74), Frei (80, 87)*
Costanzo, Çağdaş Atan, Huggel, Streller (Chipperfield 78), Yapi (Ferati 87), Frei, Stocker (Shaqiri 85), Abraham, Safari, Inkoom, Zoua. Coach: Thorsten Fink (GER)
Yellow Card(s): Frei 16, Çağdaş Atan 40

Group E
Match 1 – CFR 1907 Cluj (ROU)
A 1-2 *Stocker (45+2)*
Costanzo, Çağdaş Atan, Huggel, Streller, Yapi, Frei, Stocker (Chipperfield 73), Shaqiri, Abraham, Safari (Tembo 73), Inkoom. Coach: Thorsten Fink (GER)
Yellow Card(s): Streller 55

Match 2 – FC Bayern München (GER)
H 1-2 *Frei (18)*
Costanzo, Huggel (Cabral 87), Streller, Yapi (Almerares 90+1), Frei, Stocker, Shaqiri (Chipperfield 80), Abraham, Safari, Inkoom, Ferati. Coach: Thorsten Fink (GER)
Yellow Card(s): Streller 83
Match 3 – AS Roma (ITA)
A 3-1 *Frei (12), Inkoom (44), Cabral (90+3)*
Costanzo, Huggel, Streller (Cabral 81), Yapi, Frei (Almerares 90), Stocker (Chipperfield 70), Shaqiri, Abraham, Safari, Inkoom, Ferati. Coach: Thorsten Fink (GER)
Yellow Card(s): Inkoom 44, Chipperfield 73
Match 4 – AS Roma (ITA)
H 2-3 *Frei (69), Shaqiri (83)*
Costanzo, Huggel, Streller, Yapi, Frei, Stocker, Shaqiri, Abraham, Safari, Inkoom, Ferati (Chipperfield 88). Coach: Thorsten Fink (GER)
Red Card(s): Stocker 90+1
Yellow Card(s): Stocker 25, Streller 49, Stocker 90+1
Match 5 – CFR 1907 Cluj (ROU)
H 1-0 *Almerares (15)*
Costanzo, Yapi, Frei (Çağdaş Atan 90+2), Almerares, Shaqiri (G. Xhaka 87), Abraham, Safari, Inkoom, Cabral, Ferati, Tembo (Zanni 90). Coach: Thorsten Fink (GER)
Yellow Card(s): Almerares 14
Match 6 – FC Bayern München (GER)
A 0-3
Costanzo, Streller (G. Xhaka 46), Yapi, Frei, Stocker, Shaqiri (Tembo 76), Abraham, Safari, Inkoom, Cabral (Almerares 55), Ferati. Coach: Thorsten Fink (GER)
Yellow Card(s): Frei 73

No	Player	Nat	DoB	Aps	(s)	Gls
Goalkeepers						
1	Franco Costanzo	ARG	5/9/80	6		
Defenders						
19	David Abraham	ARG	15/7/86	6		
4	Çağdaş Atan	TUR	29/2/80	1	(1)	
28	Beg Ferati		10/11/86	5		
22	Samuel Inkoom	GHA	1/6/89	6		1
20	Behrang Safari	SWE	9/2/85	6		
32	Reto Zanni		9/2/80		(1)	
Midfielders						
24	Cabral		22/10/88	2	(2)	1
11	Scott Chipperfield	AUS	30/12/75		(4)	
8	Benjamin Huggel		7/7/77	4		
17	Xherdan Shaqiri		10/10/91	6		1
14	Valentin Stocker		12/4/89	5		1
34	Granit Xhaka		27/9/92		(2)	
10	Gilles Yapi	CIV	30/1/82	6		
Forwards						
15	Federico Almerares	ARG	2/5/85	1	(3)	1
13	Alexander Frei		15/7/79	6		3
9	Marco Streller		18/6/81	5		
30	Fwayo Tembo	ZAM	2/5/89	1	(2)	

UEFA EUROPA LEAGUE

Round of 32 – FC Spartak Moskva (RUS)
H 2-3 *Frei (36), Streller (41)*
Costanzo, Streller, Yapi (Cabral 87), Frei (Tembo 80), Stocker (Zoua 87), Shaqiri, Abraham, Safari, Kusunga, Steinhöfer, Xhaka. Coach: Thorsten Fink (GER)
Red Card(s): Shaqiri 78
Yellow Card(s): Stocker 34, Yapi 48, Kusunga 90+2
A 1-1 *Chipperfield (15)*
Costanzo, Chipperfield, Stocker, Abraham, Safari, Kusunga, Cabral, Steinhöfer, Tembo (Frei 67), Zoua, Xhaka (Yapi 76). Coach: Thorsten Fink (GER)
Yellow Card(s): Cabral 31, Zoua 74, Safari 86

BSC YOUNG BOYS

UEFA CHAMPIONS LEAGUE

Third Qualifying Round – Fenerbahçe SK (TUR)
H 2-2 *Dudar (18), Costanzo (89p)*
Bürki, Dudar, Sutter, Costanzo, T. Doubai (Mayuka 83), Bienvenu (M. Schneuwly 58), Spycher, Lulić (Regazzoni 65), Affolter, Degen, Jemal. Coach: Erminio Piserchia (ITA)
Yellow Card(s): Costanzo 74
A 1-0 *Bienvenu (40)*
Wölfli, Dudar, Sutter, Costanzo (Hochstrasser 62), T. Doubai (Raimondi 70), Bienvenu, Spycher, Lulić (C. Schneuwly 78), Affolter, Degen, Jemal. Coach: Vladimir Petković (SUI)
Yellow Card(s): Jemal 23, Affolter 57, Hochstrasser 72, Degen 86

Play-Offs – Tottenham Hotspur FC (ENG)
H 3-2 *Lulić (4), Bienvenu (13), Hochstrasser (28)*
Wölfli, Sutter, Costanzo (C. Schneuwly 65), T. Doubai, Bienvenu, Spycher, Lulić, Affolter, Degen (Raimondi 90), Hochstrasser, Jemal. Coach: Vladimir Petković (SUI)
Yellow Card(s): Bienvenu 72
A 0-4
Wölfli, Sutter (Regazzoni 61), Costanzo (M. Schneuwly 61), T. Doubai (C. Schneuwly 82), Bienvenu, Spycher, Lulić, Affolter, Degen, Hochstrasser, Jemal. Coach: Vladimir Petković (SUI)
Red Card(s): Lulić 77
Yellow Card(s): Lulić 37, Degen 68, Lulić 77

UEFA EUROPA LEAGUE

Group H
Match 1 – VfB Stuttgart (GER)
A 0-3
Wölfli, Nef, Sutter (Regazzoni 62), M. Schneuwly (C. Schneuwly 74), Costanzo, T. Doubai, Bienvenu, Spycher, Affolter, Hochstrasser (Mayuka 62), Jemal. Coach: Vladimir Petković (SUI)
Yellow Card(s): Nef 23, M. Schneuwly 39, Spycher 40, Jemal 87
Match 2 – Getafe CF (ESP)
H 2-0 *Degen (11, 64)*
Wölfli, Nef, Sutter, Costanzo (Hochstrasser 90), T. Doubai, Spycher, Lulić (Regazzoni 79), Affolter, Degen, Mayuka (Bienvenu 72), Jemal. Coach: Vladimir Petković (SUI)
Yellow Card(s): Lulić 67
Match 3 – Odense BK (DEN)
H 4-2 *Bienvenu (25), Sutter (34), Degen (61), Lulić (74)*
Wölfli, Nef, Sutter, Costanzo (Regazzoni 79), T. Doubai, Bienvenu (Raimondi 87), Spycher, Lulić, Affolter, Degen, Hochstrasser (Jemal 68). Coach: Vladimir Petković (SUI)
Yellow Card(s): Jemal 83
Match 4 – Odense BK (DEN)
A 0-2
Bürki, Nef, Sutter, Costanzo, T. Doubai (Hochstrasser 46), Bienvenu, Spycher, Lulić, Affolter, Regazzoni (Degen 67), Jemal (Mayuka 68). Coach: Vladimir Petković (SUI)
Match 5 – VfB Stuttgart (GER)
H 4-2 *Degen (39), Sutter (81), Mayuka (82, 87)*
Wölfli, Nef, Sutter, Costanzo (C. Schneuwly 56), T. Doubai (M. Schneuwly 67), Spycher, Lulić (Regazzoni 74), Affolter, Degen, Mayuka, Jemal. Coach: Vladimir Petković (SUI)
Yellow Card(s): Spycher 76, Regazzoni 86, Jemal 90
Match 6 – Getafe CF (ESP)
A 0-1
Wölfli, Nef, Sutter, Costanzo, T. Doubai, Spycher (Raimondi 57), Lulić, Affolter, Degen (M. Schneuwly 73), Hochstrasser (C. Schneuwly 57), Mayuka. Coach: Vladimir Petković (SUI)
Yellow Card(s): Spycher 42, Mayuka 73, Lulić 80, Nef 90+1

Round of 32 – FC Zenit St Petersburg (RUS)
H 2-1 *Lulić (46), Mayuka (90+3)*
Wölfli, Nef, Dudar (Raimondi 60), Sutter, Costanzo (Mayuka 83), T. Doubai, Bienvenu, Lulić, Affolter, Degen, Jemal. Coach: Vladimir Petković (SUI)
Yellow Card(s): Jemal 35, Dudar 55, Nef 63, Degen 72
A 1-3 *Jemal (21)*
Wölfli, Dudar, Sutter, T. Doubai, Bienvenu, Raimondi (C. Schneuwly 79), Spycher, Lulić (M. Schneuwly 85), Affolter, Degen (Mayuka 79), Jemal. Coach: Vladimir Petković (SUI)
Yellow Card(s): Dudar 65, Spycher 78

GRASSHOPPER-CLUB

UEFA EUROPA LEAGUE

Play-Offs – FC Steaua Bucureşti (ROU)
A 0-1
König, Voser, Paulinho, Vallori, Colina (Abrashi 46), Smiljanic, Lang (Emeghara 89), Rennella, Cabanas, Zuber (Adili 69), Salatic. Coach: Ciriaco Sforza (SUI)
Yellow Card(s): Salatic 90+2
H 1-0 (aet; 3-4 on pens) *Salatic (77)*
Benito, Voser, Paulinho, Vallori, Smiljanic, Emeghara, Lang (Hajrovic 46), Cabanas (Abrashi 82), Toko, Zuber (Adili 72), Salatic. Coach: Ciriaco Sforza (SUI)
Yellow Card(s): Emeghara 80, Paulinho 111

FC LUZERN

UEFA EUROPA LEAGUE

Third Qualifying Round – FC Utrecht (NED)
A 0-1
Zibung, Lukmon (Fanger 63), Kibebe, Renggli, Lustenberger, Yakin, Gygax (Prager 81), Ianu, Veškovac, Ferreira (Zverotić 58), Kukeli. Coach: Rolf Fringer (AUT)
Yellow Card(s): Ferreira 49
H 1-3 *Pacar (53)*
Zibung, Renggli, Lustenberger, Yakin (Prager 46), Gygax, Ianu (João Paiva 59), Veškovac, Zverotić, Ferreira, Kukeli (Pacar 46), Wiss. Coach: Rolf Fringer (AUT)
Yellow Card(s): Kukeli 15

FC LAUSANNE-SPORT

UEFA EUROPA LEAGUE

Second Qualifying Round – FK Borac Banja Luka (BIH)
H 1-0 *Sílvio (19)*
Favre, Katz, Sílvio, Roux (Hélin 74), Steuble (Stadelmann 90+4), Nelson, Meoli, Celestini, Carrupt (Mayila 90+2), Marazzi, Sonnerat. Coach: Martin Rueda (SUI)
Yellow Card(s): Marazzi 77
A 1-1 *Roux (65)*
Favre, Katz (Buntschu 74), Sílvio, Roux, Steuble, Nelson (Stadelmann 46), Meoli, Celestini, Carrupt (Avanzini 64), Marazzi, Sonnerat. Coach: Martin Rueda (SUI)
Yellow Card(s): Celestini 43, Stadelmann 60

Third Qualifying Round – Randers FC (DEN)
A 3-2 *Steuble (41), Sílvio (62p, 84)*
Favre, Katz, Sílvio, Roux (Tosi 64), Steuble, Nelson, Avanzini (Stadelmann 87), Meoli (Buntschu 46), Celestini, Marazzi, Sonnerat. Coach: Martin Rueda (SUI)
Yellow Card(s): Nelson 15, Steuble 38, Katz 76
H 1-1 *Tosi (68)*
Favre, Buntschu, Katz, Sílvio (Stadelmann 82), Roux (Tosi 57), Steuble, Avanzini (Carrupt 90+2), Meoli, Celestini, Marazzi, Sonnerat. Coach: Martin Rueda (SUI)
Red Card(s): Katz 80
Yellow Card(s): Sonnerat 45, Roux 51, Katz 75, Katz 80, Tosi 90+5

Play-Offs – FC Lokomotiv Moskva (RUS)
H 1-1 *Traoré (28)*
Favre, Buntschu, Munsy, Sílvio (Roux 72), Avanzini (Kilinc 85), Meoli, Celestini, Carrupt (Stadelmann 81), Marazzi, Sonnerat, Traoré. Coach: Martin Rueda (SUI)
A 1-1 (aet; 4-3 on pens) *Sílvio (17)*
Favre (Castejon 90+3), Katz, Munsy (Tosi 51), Sílvio, Avanzini (Kilinc 78), Meoli, Celestini, Carrupt, Marazzi, Sonnerat, Traoré. Coach: Martin Rueda (SUI)
Yellow Card(s): Avanzini 72

Group F
Match 1 – PFC CSKA Moskva (RUS)
H 0-3
Favre, Katz, Sílvio, Roux (Munsy 73), Avanzini (Carrupt 81), Gétaz, Celestini, Marazzi, Sonnerat, Traoré (Basha 64), Tosi. Coach: Martin Rueda (SUI)
Yellow Card(s): Marazzi 45+2, Katz 65, Avanzini 80
Match 2 – US Città di Palermo (ITA)
A 0-1
Favre, Rochat, Katz, Sílvio, Roux (Munsy 83), Avanzini (Pasche 82), Meoli, Celestini, Marazzi, Sonnerat, Tosi (Steuble 80). Coach: Martin Rueda (SUI)
Match 3 – AC Sparta Praha (CZE)
A 3-3 *Meoli (6), Steuble (75), Sílvio (90+5)*
Favre, Rochat, Katz (Roux 82), Munsy (Avanzini 74), Sílvio, Steuble, Pasche (Tosi 68), Meoli, Celestini, Marazzi, Sonnerat. Coach: Martin Rueda (SUI)
Yellow Card(s): Marazzi 22, Steuble 76, Meoli 88
Match 4 – AC Sparta Praha (CZE)
H 1-3 *Katz (6)*
Favre, Rochat, Katz (Roux 83), Sílvio, Steuble (Avanzini 62), Pasche, Meoli, Celestini, Marazzi, Sonnerat, Tosi (Munsy 70). Coach: Martin Rueda (SUI)
Yellow Card(s): Sonnerat 45, Katz 64
Match 5 – PFC CSKA Moskva (RUS)
A 1-5 *Carrupt (90+2)*
Castejon, Rochat, Katz, Sílvio (Carrupt 52), Steuble (Roux 77), Avanzini (Pasche 58), Meoli, Celestini, Marazzi, Sonnerat, Tosi. Coach: Martin Rueda (SUI)
Yellow Card(s): Marazzi 75, Carrupt 84
Match 6 – US Città di Palermo (ITA)
H 0-1
Favre, Rochat, Katz, Sílvio, Steuble, Avanzini (Pasche 77), Meoli, Celestini (Roux 87), Carrupt (Munsy 83), Sonnerat, Tosi. Coach: Martin Rueda (SUI)
Yellow Card(s): Sílvio 86, Tosi 90+2

TURKEY

BURSASPOR

UEFA CHAMPIONS LEAGUE

Group C
Match 1 – Valencia CF (ESP)
H 0-4
Ivankov, Gökçek Vederson, Ömer Erdoğan, Hüseyin Çimşir (Sercan Yıldırım 59), Insúa, Volkan Şen, Ozan İpek, Ali Tandoğan, Ergić (Svensson 77), Núñez (Turgay Bahadır 59), Stepanov. Coach: Ertuğrul Sağlam (TUR)
Match 2 – Rangers FC (SCO)
A 0-1
Ivankov, Gökçek Vederson, Ömer Erdoğan, Sercan Yıldırım (Turgay Bahadır 72), Volkan Şen, Svensson, Batalla (Núñez 72), Ozan İpek, Ali Tandoğan, Ergić (Insúa 39), Stepanov. Coach: Ertuğrul Sağlam (TUR)
Yellow Card(s): Ömer Erdoğan 42, Stepanov 85, Ali Tandoğan 88
Match 3 – Manchester United FC (ENG)
A 0-1
Ivankov, Gökçek Vederson, Ömer Erdoğan, Insúa, Sercan Yıldırım (Turgay Bahadır 46), Volkan Şen, Svensson, Ozan İpek, Ali Tandoğan (Mustafa Keçeli 71), Ergić, Stepanov (İbrahim Öztürk 46). Coach: Ertuğrul Sağlam (TUR)
Yellow Card(s): Ozan İpek 40, Ali Tandoğan 63
Match 4 – Manchester United FC (ENG)
H 0-3
Ivankov, Gökçek Vederson, Ömer Erdoğan, Insúa (Núñez 74), Sercan Yıldırım (Ozan İpek 74), Volkan Şen (İsmail Haktan Odabaşı 81), Svensson, Ali Tandoğan, Turgay Bahadır, Ergić, İbrahim Öztürk. Coach: Ertuğrul Sağlam (TUR)
Match 5 – Valencia CF (ESP)
A 1-6 *Batalla (69)*
Ivankov, Gökçek Vederson (Serdar Aziz 45), Ömer Erdoğan, Insúa, Sercan Yıldırım (İsmail Haktan Odabaşı 84), Volkan Şen, Svensson, Turgay Bahadır, Mustafa Keçeli, Ergić (Batalla 59), İbrahim Öztürk. Coach: Ertuğrul Sağlam (TUR)
Yellow Card(s): Ömer Erdoğan 16, Serdar Aziz 56
Match 6 – Rangers FC (SCO)
H 1-1 *Sercan Yıldırım (79)*
Yavuz Özkan, Serdar Aziz (Ömer Erdoğan 46), Gökçek Vederson, Hüseyin Çimşir (Batalla 46), Ozan Has, Insúa, Sercan Yıldırım, Ozan İpek, Mustafa Keçeli, Núñez (Turgay Bahadır 62), Stepanov. Coach: Ertuğrul Sağlam (TUR)
Yellow Card(s): Ozan İpek 65, Ozan Has 81

No	Player	Nat	DoB	Aps	(s)	Gls
Goalkeepers						
27	Dimitar Ivankov	BUL	30/10/75	5		
1	Yavuz Özkan		19/5/85	1		
Defenders						
21	Ali Tandoğan		25/12/77	4		
3	Gökçek Vederson	BRA	22/7/81	6		
38	İbrahim Öztürk		28/6/81	2	(1)	
23	Mustafa Keçeli		15/9/78	2	(1)	
4	Ömer Erdoğan		3/5/77	5	(1)	
2	Serdar Aziz		23/10/90	1	(1)	
55	Milan Stepanov	SRB	2/4/83	4		
Midfielders						
17	Pablo Batalla	ARG	16/1/84	1	(2)	1
25	Ivan Ergić	SRB	21/1/81	5		
5	Hüseyin Çimşir		26/5/79	2		
7	Federico Insúa	ARG	3/1/80	5	(1)	
35	İsmail Haktan Odabaşı		7/8/91		(2)	
6	Ozan Has		8/2/85	1		
20	Ozan İpek		10/10/86	4	(1)	
13	Gustav Svensson	SWE	9/2/87	4	(1)	
22	Turgay Bahadır		15/1/84	2	(4)	
10	Volkan Şen		7/7/87	5		
Forwards						
29	Leonel Núñez	ARG	13/10/84	2	(2)	
9	Sercan Yıldırım		5/4/90	5	(1)	1

FENERBAHÇE SK

UEFA CHAMPIONS LEAGUE

Third Qualifying Round – BSC Young Boys (SUI)
A 2-2 *Emre Belözoğlu (5), Stoch (42)*
Volkan Demirel, Bekir İrtegün, Emre Belözoğlu (Deivid 85), Kazım Kazım, Alex (Semih Şentürk 80), Stoch, Cristian, Önder Turacı, André Santos, Gökhan Ünal (Selçuk Şahin 72), Fábio Bilica. Coach: Aykut Kocaman (TUR)
Red Card(s): Kazım Kazım 43
Yellow Card(s): Bekir İrtegün 24, Kazım Kazım 25, Kazım Kazım 43, Önder Turacı 53, Alex 72, Fábio Bilica 87
H 0-1
Volkan Demirel, Bekir İrtegün (Gökhan Gönül 46), Emre Belözoğlu, İlhan Eker, Alex (Selçuk Şahin 46), Stoch, Cristian, André Santos, Gökhan Ünal, Fábio Bilica, Dia (Semih Şentürk 81). Coach: Aykut Kocaman (TUR)
Red Card(s): Stoch 53
Yellow Card(s): Bekir İrtegün 18, Stoch 37, Stoch 53, Fábio Bilica 77, Emre Belözoğlu 88

UEFA EUROPA LEAGUE

Play-Offs – PAOK FC (GRE)
A 0-1
Volkan Demirel, Lugano, İlhan Eker, Alex, Cristian, Selçuk Şahin (Gökhan Ünal 80), Semih Şentürk (Niang 46), André Santos, Mehmet Topuz, Gökhan Gönül, Caner Erkin (Özer Hurmacı 70). Coach: Aykut Kocaman (TUR)
Yellow Card(s): Caner Erkin 5, Semih Şentürk 27, Lugano 44, André Santos 74
H 1-1 *Emre Belözoğlu (50)*
Volkan Demirel, Lugano, Emre Belözoğlu (Selçuk Şahin 75), Niang, Alex, Stoch, Cristian (Gökhan Ünal 106), André Santos, Mehmet Topuz (Özer Hurmacı 91), Fábio Bilica, Gökhan Gönül. Coach: Aykut Kocaman (TUR)
Yellow Card(s): Mehmet Topuz 55, Lugano 113

TRABZONSPOR AŞ

UEFA EUROPA LEAGUE

Play-Offs – Liverpool FC (ENG)
A 0-1
Onur Kıvrak, Čale, Głowacki, Ceyhun Gülselam, Selçuk İnan, Gutiérrez, Umut Bulut (Yattara 86), Egemen Korkmaz, Burak Yılmaz (Alanzinho 56), Colman (Giray Kaçar 77), Serkan Balcı. Coach: Şenol Güneş (TUR)
Yellow Card(s): Serkan Balcı 52, Ceyhun Gülselam 55, Egemen Korkmaz 79, Čale 86

1-2 *Gutiérrez (4)*
nur Kıvrak, Čale (Jajá 87), Ceyhun Gülselam (Barış Ataş 65), Selçuk an, Gutiérrez, Egemen Korkmaz, Burak Yılmaz, Colman, Giray Kaçar, erkan Balcı, Yattara (Alanzinho 46). Coach: Şenol Güneş (TUR)
ellow Card(s): Ceyhun Gülselam 39, Burak Yılmaz 41, Egemen orkmaz 73

GALATASARAY AŞ

UEFA EUROPA LEAGUE

hird Qualifying Round – OFK Beograd (SRB)
2-2 *Arda Turan (26, 76)*
ykut Erçetin, Neill, Barış Özbek (Cana 83), Arda Turan, Mehmet Batdal Kewell 68), Mustafa Sarp, Ayhan Akman, Hakan Balta, Sabri Sarıoğlu, ervet Çetin, Serdar Özkan (Pino 59). Coach: Frank Rijkaard (NED)
ellow Card(s): Neill 89
5-1 *Mustafa Sarp (12), Kewell (22, 57p), Arda Turan (71), Mehmet atdal (81)*
ykut Erçetin, Neill, Arda Turan (Ali Turan 82), Mustafa Sarp, Ayhan kman, Cana, Hakan Balta, Sabri Sarıoğlu, Servet Çetin, Serdar Özkan Pino 61), Kewell (Mehmet Batdal 72). Coach: Frank Rijkaard (NED)
ellow Card(s): Ayhan Akman 36, Mustafa Sarp 40, Kewell 67

lay-Offs – FC Karpaty Lviv (UKR)
2-2 *Baroš (59, 86)*
ykut Erçetin, Neill, Ali Turan, Arda Turan, Mehmet Batdal (Baroš 36), lustafa Sarp, Ayhan Akman, Hakan Balta (Serkan Kurtuluş 79), Servet etin, Serdar Özkan (Barış Özbek 54), Kewell. Coach: Frank Rijkaard (NED)
ellow Card(s): Ali Turan 28, Barış Özbek 56
1-1 *Aydın Yılmaz (90+1)*
Jfuk Ceylan, Neill, Ali Turan (Emre Çolak 81), Barış Özbek, Arda Turan, aroš, Mustafa Sarp (Aydın Yılmaz 74), Ayhan Akman, Hakan Balta, ervet Çetin, Serdar Özkan (Cana 49). Coach: Frank Rijkaard (NED)
ellow Card(s): Hakan Balta 38, Arda Turan 41, Servet Çetin 74, Ali uran 75

BEŞİKTAŞ JK

UEFA EUROPA LEAGUE

Second Qualifying Round – Víkingur (FRO)
H 3-0 *Nihat Kahveci (19, 65), Mert Nobre (90)*
Hakan Arıkan, Sivok, Ricardo Quaresma, Nihat Kahveci (Mert Nobre 83), Delgado (Necip Uysal 83), Bobô, Rodrigo Tabata, İbrahim Üzülmez, brahim Toraman, Ernst, Erhan Güven (Ekrem Dağ 73). Coach: Bernd Schuster (GER)
Yellow Card(s): İbrahim Toraman 90+2
A 4-0 *Ekrem Dağ (3), Nihat Kahveci (10), Bobô (32, 44)*
Hakan Arıkan, İsmail Köybaşı, Sivok (Ferrari 46), Ricardo Quaresma, Nihat Kahveci, Delgado, Bobô, Ekrem Dağ (Onur Bayramoğlu 57), Ernst (Uğur nceman 46), Zápotočný, Erhan Güven. Coach: Bernd Schuster (GER)
Yellow Card(s): Uğur İnceman 81, Ferrari 90+1

Third Qualifying Round – FC Viktoria Plzeň (CZE)
A 1-1 *Delgado (44p)*
Hakan Arıkan, Sivok, Ricardo Quaresma, Nihat Kahveci (Necip Uysal 46), Hilbert (Rodrigo Tabata 67), Delgado, Mert Nobre (Bobô 77), İbrahim Üzülmez, brahim Toraman, Ernst, Erhan Güven. Coach: Bernd Schuster (GER)
Yellow Card(s): Sivok 15, Delgado 76, Necip Uysal 79
H 3-0 *Ricardo Quaresma (38), Delgado (57), Hološko (71)*
Hakan Arıkan, Ricardo Quaresma, Delgado (Rodrigo Tabata 59), Bobô (Nihat Kahveci 67), Necip Uysal, İbrahim Üzülmez, İbrahim Toraman (Ferrari 46), Hološko, Ernst, Zápotočný, Erhan Güven. Coach: Bernd Schuster (GER)
Yellow Card(s): Delgado 30

Play-Offs – HJK Helsinki (FIN)
H 2-0 *Hilbert (35), Ricardo Quaresma (66)*
Cenk Gönen, İsmail Köybaşı, Ricardo Quaresma (Nihat Kahveci 88), Hilbert, Bobô (Hološko 83), Guti, Rodrigo Tabata (Necip Uysal 70), Ekrem Dağ, Ferrari, Ernst, Zápotočný. Coach: Bernd Schuster (GER)
Yellow Card(s): Zápotočný 63
A 4-0 *Ricardo Quaresma (15), Guti (67), Necip Uysal (77), Hološko (90+3)*
Cenk Gönen, İsmail Köybaşı, Ricardo Quaresma (Hološko 68), Hilbert, Bobô (Mert Nobre 81), Guti (Nihat Kahveci 74), Ekrem Dağ, Necip Uysal, Ferrari, Ernst, Zápotočný. Coach: Bernd Schuster (GER)

Group L
Match 1 – PFC CSKA Sofia (BUL)
H 1-0 *Ernst (90)*
Hakan Arıkan, Hilbert, Mert Nobre, Guti, Rodrigo Tabata (Bobô 72), Ekrem Dağ, İbrahim Üzülmez, Hološko (Ricardo Quaresma 59), Ferrari (İbrahim Toraman 37), Ernst, Zápotočný. Coach: Bernd Schuster (GER)
Match 2 – SK Rapid Wien (AUT)
A 2-1 *Hološko (55), Bobô (64)*
Hakan Arıkan, Ricardo Quaresma (Hološko 32), Hilbert, Bobô (Mert Nobre 75), Guti (Necip Uysal 86), Rodrigo Tabata, İbrahim Üzülmez, İbrahim Toraman, Ferrari, Ernst, Mehmet Aurélio. Coach: Bernd Schuster (GER)
Yellow Card(s): İbrahim Toraman 45+2, Hakan Arıkan 90+1
Match 3 – FC Porto (POR)
H 1-3 *Bobô (90+2)*
Hakan Arıkan, Nihat Kahveci, Hilbert, Mert Nobre (Ersan Gülüm 83), Bobô, Rodrigo Tabata, Necip Uysal, İbrahim Üzülmez (İsmail Köybaşı 78), İbrahim Toraman, Ernst, Zápotočný (Ali Küçik 71). Coach: Bernd Schuster (GER)
Yellow Card(s): Nihat Kahveci 31, İbrahim Üzülmez 69
Match 4 – FC Porto (POR)
A 1-1 *Nihat Kahveci (62)*
Hakan Arıkan, Nihat Kahveci (Erhan Güven 90+2), Hilbert, Bobô (Necip Uysal 84), Guti, Rodrigo Tabata (Hološko 46), İbrahim Üzülmez, İbrahim Toraman, Ersan Gülüm, Ernst, Mehmet Aurélio. Coach: Bernd Schuster (GER)
Red Card(s): İbrahim Toraman 67
Yellow Card(s): İbrahim Toraman 29, Hilbert 44, İbrahim Üzülmez 59, İbrahim Toraman 67, Ersan Gülüm 87
Match 5 – PFC CSKA Sofia (BUL)
A 2-1 *Zápotočný (59), Hološko (64)*
Cenk Gönen (Hakan Arıkan 46), İsmail Köybaşı, Hilbert, Mert Nobre (Ali Küçik 46), Guti, Rodrigo Tabata (Necip Uysal 76), Ersan Gülüm, Hološko, Ernst, Zápotočný, Mehmet Aurélio. Coach: Bernd Schuster (GER)
Yellow Card(s): İsmail Köybaşı 27, Hilbert 84
Match 6 – SK Rapid Wien (AUT)
H 2-0 *Ricardo Quaresma (32), Ernst (45)*
Cenk Gönen, İsmail Köybaşı, Ricardo Quaresma (Mert Nobre 68), Hilbert (Erhan Güven 82), Guti, Rodrigo Tabata, Ferrari, Ernst, Zápotočný (Ersan Gülüm 23), Ali Küçik, Mehmet Aurélio. Coach: Bernd Schuster (GER)
Yellow Card(s): Ersan Gülüm 89

Round of 32 – FC Dynamo Kyiv (UKR)
H 1-4 *Ricardo Quaresma (37)*
Hakan Arıkan, İsmail Köybaşı, Sivok, Ricardo Quaresma, Hilbert, Mert Nobre (Hugo Almeida 69), Bobô, Guti, Ferrari, Ernst (Erhan Güven 56), Mehmet Aurélio (Necip Uysal 80). Coach: Bernd Schuster (GER)
Red Card(s): Ricardo Quaresma 90+3
Yellow Card(s): Sivok 60, Ricardo Quaresma 87, Hakan Arıkan 89
A 0-4
Rüştü Reçber, İsmail Köybaşı, Sivok, Hilbert, Bobô, Guti (Onur Bayramoğlu 72), Necip Uysal, Ferrari (İbrahim Toraman 59), Ernst, Hugo Almeida (Mert Nobre 58), Mehmet Aurélio. Coach: Bernd Schuster (GER)
Yellow Card(s): Ferrari 30, Mehmet Aurélio 53, Hugo Almeida 57

UKRAINE

FC SHAKHTAR DONETSK

UEFA CHAMPIONS LEAGUE

Group H
Match 1 – FK Partizan (SRB)
H 1-0 *Srna (71)*
Pyatov, Hübschman, Kucher, Jádson (Alex Teixeira 58), Luiz Adriano (Vitsenets 83), Willian, Hai, Douglas Costa, Raţ, Srna, Rakytskiy. Coach: Mircea Lucescu (ROU)
Yellow Card(s): Srna 67
Match 2 – SC Braga (POR)
A 3-0 *Luiz Adriano (56, 72), Douglas Costa (90+2p)*
Pyatov, Hübschman (Vitsenets 79), Kucher, Luiz Adriano (Eduardo 75), Willian, Hai (Jádson 66), Douglas Costa, Mkhitaryan, Raţ, Srna, Rakytskiy. Coach: Mircea Lucescu (ROU)
Yellow Card(s): Raţ 40, Hübschman 51, Mkhitaryan 61, Douglas Costa 89
Match 3 – Arsenal FC (ENG)
A 1-5 *Eduardo (82)*
Pyatov, Hübschman, Kucher, Luiz Adriano (Eduardo 64), Willian (Douglas Costa 46), Hai (Jádson 68), Mkhitaryan, Raţ, Alex Teixeira, Srna, Rakytskiy. Coach: Mircea Lucescu (ROU)
Yellow Card(s): Hübschman 58, Luiz Adriano 59
Match 4 – Arsenal FC (ENG)
H 2-1 *Chyhrynskiy (28), Eduardo (45)*
Pyatov, Hübschman, Jádson (Douglas Costa 73), Luiz Adriano (Marcelo Moreno 88), Willian, Eduardo, Hai (Alex Teixeira 62), Raţ, Chyhrynskiy, Srna, Rakytskiy. Coach: Mircea Lucescu (ROU)
Yellow Card(s): Hübschman 27, Hai 47, Raţ 83
Match 5 – FK Partizan (SRB)
A 3-0 *Stepanenko (52), Jádson (59), Eduardo (68)*
Pyatov, Jádson (Alex Teixeira 75), Luiz Adriano, Willian, Stepanenko, Hai (Vitsenets 74), Douglas Costa (Eduardo 62), Raţ, Chyhrynskiy, Srna, Rakytskiy. Coach: Mircea Lucescu (ROU)
Yellow Card(s): Hai 32, Stepanenko 48, Chyhrynskiy 67
Match 6 – SC Braga (POR)
H 2-0 *Raţ (78), Luiz Adriano (83)*
Pyatov, Jádson (Mkhitaryan 73), Luiz Adriano, Willian, Stepanenko, Hai (Kobin 84), Douglas Costa (Alex Teixeira 62), Raţ, Chyhrynskiy, Srna, Rakytskiy. Coach: Mircea Lucescu (ROU)

Round of 16 – AS Roma (ITA)
A 3-2 *Jádson (29), Douglas Costa (36), Luiz Adriano (41)*
Pyatov, Hübschman, Jádson (Alex Teixeira 85), Luiz Adriano, Willian, Douglas Costa (Eduardo 66), Mkhitaryan (Vitsenets 78), Raţ, Chyhrynskiy, Srna, Rakytskiy. Coach: Mircea Lucescu (ROU)
Yellow Card(s): Chyhrynskiy 34, Luiz Adriano 61, Rakytskiy 85, Pyatov 88
H 3-0 *Willian (18, 58), Eduardo (87)*
Pyatov, Hübschman, Jádson, Luiz Adriano (Marcelo Moreno 75), Willian, Douglas Costa (Eduardo 60), Mkhitaryan (Alex Teixeira 67), Raţ, Chyhrynskiy, Srna, Rakytskiy. Coach: Mircea Lucescu (ROU)
Yellow Card(s): Mkhitaryan 28, Srna 45+4

Quarter-Finals – FC Barcelona (ESP)
A 1-5 *Rakytskiy (60)*
Pyatov, Hübschman (Eduardo 82), Jádson (Fernandinho 70), Luiz Adriano, Willian (Alex Teixeira 75), Douglas Costa, Mkhitaryan, Raţ, Ishchenko, Srna, Rakytskiy. Coach: Mircea Lucescu (ROU)
Yellow Card(s): Raţ 51, Rakytskiy 66, Fernandinho 77
H 0-1
Pyatov, Hübschman (Fernandinho 75), Jádson, Luiz Adriano (Marcelo Moreno 66), Willian, Shevchuk, Kobin, Douglas Costa (Eduardo 58), Mkhitaryan, Ishchenko, Rakytskiy. Coach: Mircea Lucescu (ROU)
Yellow Card(s): Mkhitaryan 56, Ishchenko 60

No	Player	Nat	DoB	Aps	(s)	Gls
Goalkeepers						
30	Andriy Pyatov		28/6/84	10		
Defenders						
27	Dmytro Chyhrynskiy		7/11/86	5		1
32	Mykola Ishchenko		9/3/83	2		
5	Olexandr Kucher		22/10/82	3		
44	Yaroslav Rakytskiy		3/8/89	10		1
26	Răzvan Raţ	ROU	26/5/81	9		1
13	Vyacheslav Shevchuk		13/5/79	1		
Midfielders						
29	Alex Teixeira	BRA	6/1/90	1	(7)	
20	Douglas Costa	BRA	14/9/90	8	(2)	2
7	Fernandinho	BRA	4/5/85		(2)	
19	Olexiy Hai		6/11/82	6		
3	Tomáš Hübschman	CZE	4/9/81	8		
8	Jádson	BRA	5/10/83	8	(2)	2
14	Vasyl Kobin		24/5/85	1	(1)	
33	Darijo Srna	CRO	1/5/82	9		1
15	Taras Stepanenko		8/8/89	2		1
90	Vitaliy Vitsenets		3/8/90		(4)	
10	Willian	BRA	9/8/88	10		2
Forwards						
11	Eduardo	CRO	25/2/83	1	(7)	4
9	Luiz Adriano	BRA	12/4/87	10		4
99	Marcelo Moreno	BOL	18/6/87		(3)	
22	Henrik Mkhitaryan	ARM	21/1/89	6	(1)	

FC DYNAMO KYIV

UEFA CHAMPIONS LEAGUE

Third Qualifying Round – KAA Gent (BEL)
H 3-0 *Yarmolenko (19), Shevchenko (80), Zozulya (90+2)*
Boiko, Danilo Silva, Betão, Vukojević, Shevchenko, Yarmolenko, Milevskiy (Bertoglio 50; Leandro Almeida 90), Mykhalyk, Harmash, Magrão, Eremenko (Zozulya 76). Coach: Valeriy Gazzayev (RUS)
Yellow Card(s): Betão 58
A 3-1 *Harmash (32), Milevskiy (55), Gusev (89)*
Boiko, Danilo Silva, Betão, Vukojević, Shevchenko, Yarmolenko (Gusev 77), Milevskiy, Mykhalyk, Harmash, Magrão (El Kaddouri 43), Eremenko (Zozulya 68). Coach: Valeriy Gazzayev (RUS)
Yellow Card(s): Danilo Silva 16, El Kaddouri 85, Milevskiy 87

Play-Offs – AFC Ajax (NED)
H 1-1 *Gusev (66)*
Koval, Betão, Vukojević, Popov, Shevchenko (El Kaddouri 77), Yarmolenko (André 70), Mykhalyk, Harmash, Gusev (Danilo Silva 82), Eremenko, Leandro Almeida. Coach: Valeriy Gazzayev (RUS)
Red Card(s): Harmash 56
Yellow Card(s): Harmash 30, Harmash 56, Vukojević 60
A 1-2 *Shevchenko (84p)*
Koval, Danilo Silva, Vukojević (André 88), Popov, Shevchenko, Yarmolenko, Milevskiy (Guilherme 86), Mykhalyk, Gusev (Ninković 76), Eremenko, Khacheridi. Coach: Valeriy Gazzayev (RUS)
Yellow Card(s): Vukojević 13, Danilo Silva 18, Gusev 53, Shevchenko 54, Eremenko 57

UEFA EUROPA LEAGUE

Group E
Match 1 – FC BATE Borisov (BLR)
H 2-2 *Milevskiy (34), Eremenko (44)*
Koval, Betão, Yarmolenko, Milevskiy, Mykhalyk, Gusev (Harmash 57), Magrão (El Kaddouri 79), Eremenko, Khacheridi, Ninković, Leandro Almeida (André 74). Coach: Valeriy Gazzayev (RUS)
Yellow Card(s): Eremenko 60, Mykhalyk 64, Khacheridi 75

Match 2 – FC Sheriff (MDA)
0-2
Boiko, Vukojević, Shevchenko, Yarmolenko, Milevskiy, Gusev, Eremenko, El Kaddouri (Popov 46), Khacheridi, Ninković (Harmash 71), Yussuf. Coach: Valeriy Gazzayev (RUS)
Yellow Card(s): Khacheridi 36, Shevchenko 61, Milevskiy 81
Match 3 – AZ Alkmaar (NED)
A 2-1 *Milevskiy (16), Khacheridi (40)*
Koval, Betão, Vukojević, Shevchenko (Danilo Silva 58), Milevskiy (Zozulya 90), Mykhalyk, Gusev (Yarmolenko 76), Eremenko, El Kaddouri, Khacheridi, Leandro Almeida. Coach: Oleh Luzhniy (UKR)
Yellow Card(s): Eremenko 87
Match 4 – AZ Alkmaar (NED)
H 2-0 *Milevskiy (47, 61)*
Koval, Betão, Vukojević, Yarmolenko (Ninković 59), Milevskiy (Zozulya 90+1), Mykhalyk (Yussuf 52), Gusev, Eremenko, El Kaddouri, Khacheridi, Leandro Almeida. Coach: Oleh Luzhniy (UKR)
Yellow Card(s): Zozulya 90+3, Khacheridi 90+3
Match 5 – FC BATE Borisov (BLR)
A 4-1 *Vukojević (16), Yarmolenko (43), Gusev (50p), Milevskiy (68)*
Shovkovskiy, Betão, Vukojević, Popov, Yarmolenko, Milevskiy (Kravets 90+1), Mykhalyk, Gusev, Eremenko (Zozulya 79), El Kaddouri (Harmash 84), Leandro Almeida. Coach: Oleh Luzhniy (UKR)
Yellow Card(s): Leandro Almeida 20, Mykhalyk 26
Match 6 – FC Sheriff (MDA)
H 0-0
Shovkovskiy, Betão (Nesmachniy 57), Vukojević, Popov, Shevchenko, Yarmolenko, Milevskiy (Zozulya 88), Mykhalyk, Eremenko, Khacheridi, Leandro Almeida. Coach: Oleh Luzhniy (UKR)
Yellow Card(s): Khacheridi 22, Milevskiy 48

Round of 32 – Beşiktaş JK (TUR)
A 4-1 *Vukojević (26), Shevchenko (50), Yussuf (56), Gusev (90p)*
Shovkovskiy, Danilo Silva, Vukojević, Shevchenko (Kravets 84), Yarmolenko (Harmash 89), Milevskiy, Mykhalyk (Popov 73), Gusev, Eremenko, Yussuf, Leandro Almeida. Coach: Yuriy Semin (RUS)
Yellow Card(s): Shevchenko 70
H 4-0 *Vukojević (3), Yarmolenko (55), Gusev (64), Shevchenko (74)*
Shovkovskiy, Danilo Silva, Vukojević, Popov, Shevchenko (Zozulya 77), Yarmolenko (Ninković 63), Milevskiy (Kravets 69), Gusev, Eremenko, Yussuf, Leandro Almeida. Coach: Yuriy Semin (RUS)
Yellow Card(s): Zozulya 83

Round of 16 – Manchester City FC (ENG)
H 2-0 *Shevchenko (25), Gusev (77)*
Shovkovskiy, Danilo Silva, Vukojević, Popov, Shevchenko (Ninković 88), Yarmolenko, Milevskiy, Gusev, Eremenko, Khacheridi, Yussuf. Coach: Yuriy Semin (RUS)
Yellow Card(s): Yussuf 82
A 0-1
Shovkovskiy, Danilo Silva, Vukojević, Popov, Shevchenko (Harmash 62), Yarmolenko (Betão 90+2), Gusev, Eremenko, Ninković (Zozulya 46), Yussuf, Leandro Almeida. Coach: Yuriy Semin (RUS)
Yellow Card(s): Yussuf 39, Ninković 44, Leandro Almeida 50

Quarter-Finals – SC Braga (POR)
H 1-1 *Yarmolenko (6)*
Shovkovskiy, Danilo Silva, Vukojević, Popov, Yarmolenko, Milevskiy, Gusev, Kravets (Shevchenko 46), Eremenko, Khacheridi, Yussuf. Coach: Yuriy Semin (RUS)
Red Card(s): Shevchenko 62
Yellow Card(s): Yarmolenko 50, Shevchenko 53, Shevchenko 62, Popov 69
A 0-0
Shovkovskiy, Danilo Silva, Vukojević, Popov, Yarmolenko, Milevskiy, Gusev, Kravets (Harmash 65), Eremenko, Khacheridi (Leandro Almeida 46), Yussuf. Coach: Yuriy Semin (RUS)
Red Card(s): Popov 87
Yellow Card(s): Kravets 15, Khacheridi 29, Gusev 52, Popov 72, Popov 87

SC TAVRIYA SIMFEROPOL

UEFA EUROPA LEAGUE

Play-Offs – Bayer 04 Leverkusen (GER)
A 0-3
Postranskiy, Leandro, Marković, Kovpak, Idahor (Gigiadze 82), Monakhov, Shinder (Holaido 46), Matyazh (Lutsenko 71), Galyuza, Ljubenović, Humenyuk. Coach: Serhiy Puchkov (UKR)
Yellow Card(s): Leandro 64, Holaido 75
H 1-3 *Idahor (5p)*
Postranskiy, Marković, Mukhovikov (Leandro 34), Kornev, Kovpak, Idahor (Feshchuk 81), Monakhov, Lutsenko (Platon 57), Galyuza, Ljubenović, Holaido. Coach: Serhiy Puchkov (UKR)
Yellow Card(s): Monakhov 9, Holaido 30, Lutsenko 32

FC METALIST KHARKIV

UEFA EUROPA LEAGUE

Play-Offs – AC Omonia (CYP)
A 1-0 *Dević (24)*
Startsev, Romanchuk, Villagra, Berezovchuk, Shelayev, Valyayev (Gueye 85), Edmar, Cleiton (Bordian 71), Fininho, Obradović, Dević (Vorobei 80). Coach: Myron Markevych (UKR)
Yellow Card(s): Shelayev 45+2, Fininho 62
H 2-2 *Dević (66), Cleiton (71)*
Startsev, Romanchuk, Villagra, Berezovchuk (Bordian 87), Shelayev (Oliynyk 67), Valyayev, Edmar, Cleiton (Pshenychnykh 89), Fininho, Obradović, Dević. Coach: Myron Markevych (UKR)
Yellow Card(s): Obradović 69

Group I
Match 1 – Debreceni VSC (HUN)
A 5-0 *Edmar (24, 74), Cleiton (34), Fininho (77), Valyayev (89)*
Dišljenković, Villagra, Valyayev, Edmar, Vorobei (Oliynyk 55), Cleiton, Fininho, Pshenychnykh, Obradović, Gueye (Bordian 80), Taison (Kaita 77). Coach: Myron Markevych (UKR)
Yellow Card(s): Villagra 41, Fininho 45+1
Match 2 – PSV Eindhoven (NED)
H 0-2
Dišljenković, Romanchuk, Villagra, Shelayev, Valyayev (Kaita 46), Edmar, Vorobei (Oliynyk 31; Postupalenko 82), Fininho, Obradović, Gueye, Taison. Coach: Myron Markevych (UKR)
Red Card(s): Villagra 26
Yellow Card(s): Taison 36
Match 3 – UC Sampdoria (ITA)
H 2-1 *Taison (38), Cleiton (73)*
Dišljenković, Valyayev, Edmar, Cleiton (Vorobei 87), Fininho (Oliynyk 63), Pshenychnykh, Obradović, Gueye, Dević (Shelayev 84), Bordian, Taison. Coach: Myron Markevych (UKR)
Red Card(s): Taison 56
Yellow Card(s): Dević 46, Fininho 50
Match 4 – UC Sampdoria (ITA)
A 0-0
Dišljenković, Villagra (Shelayev 74), Valyayev, Edmar, Cleiton, Oliynyk (Vorobei 87), Fininho, Obradović, Gueye, Dević (Romanchuk 63), Bordian. Coach: Myron Markevych (UKR)
Yellow Card(s): Gueye 45, Dišljenković 89

Match 5 – Debreceni VSC (HUN)
H 2-1 *Bódi (52og), Oliynyk (88)*
Startsev, Villagra, Valyayev, Edmar, Cleiton, Oliynyk, Pshenychnykh, Obradović, Gueye, Dević (Vorobei 73), Bordian (Lysenko 46; Shelayev 90+4). Coach: Myron Markevych (UKR)
Yellow Card(s): Edmar 57, Obradović 90+1
Match 6 – PSV Eindhoven (NED)
A 0-0
Startsev, Villagra, Shelayev, Edmar (Lysenko 81), Cleiton, Oliynyk, Pshenychnykh, Obradović, Gueye, Bordian (Vorobei 61), Taison. Coach: Myron Markevych (UKR)
Yellow Card(s): Cleiton 41, Villagra 59

Round of 32 – Bayer 04 Leverkusen (GER)
H 0-4
Dišljenković, Villagra, Valyayev, Cleiton, Oliynyk, Fininho, Pshenychnykh (Berezovchuk 15), Cristaldo (Lysenko 68), Obradović, Blanco, Taison. Coach: Myron Markevych (UKR)
Yellow Card(s): Villagra 23, Taison 47
A 0-2
Dišljenković, Romanchuk, Shelayev, Cleiton (Vorobei 76), Oliynyk, Fininho, Obradović, Blanco, Gueye, Dević (Cristaldo 57), Taison (Valyayev 57). Coach: Myron Markevych (UKR)
Yellow Card(s): Shelayev 29

FC DNIPRO DNIPROPETROVSK

UEFA EUROPA LEAGUE

Third Qualifying Round – FK Spartak Zlatibor voda (SRB)
A 1-2 *Homenyuk (23)*
Kanibolotskiy, Kravchenko, Homenyuk, Konoplyanka, Seleznev (Nazarenko 59), Cheberyachko, Rusol, Ferreyra, Denisov, Pashayev, Kalynychenko (Fedorchuk 59). Coach: Volodymyr Bessonov (UKR)
Yellow Card(s): Cheberyachko 20, Konoplyanka 35, Denisov 47
H 2-0 *Seleznev (45), Holek (48)*
Kanibolotskiy, Lobjanidze, Kravchenko (Rotan 29), Konoplyanka, Seleznev (Homenyuk 71), Cheberyachko, Rusol, Ferreyra, Denisov, Holek, Kalynychenko (Nazarenko 75). Coach: Volodymyr Bessonov (UKR)
Yellow Card(s): Konoplyanka 62

Play-Offs – KKS Lech Poznań (POL)
H 0-1
Kanibolotskiy, Lobjanidze, Seleznev, Cheberyachko, Rusol, Ferreyra (Kravchenko 46), Denisov, Hladkiy (Shakhov 66), Pashayev (Homenyuk 58), Holek, Kalynychenko. Coach: Volodymyr Bessonov (UKR)
A 0-0
Kanibolotskiy, Kravchenko, Mandzyuk, Konoplyanka, Seleznev (Hladkiy 61), Cheberyachko, Rusol, Denisov, Holek, Kalynychenko (Homenyuk 55), Rotan. Coach: Volodymyr Bessonov (UKR)
Yellow Card(s): Kravchenko 19, Cheberyachko 25, Rusol 27

FC KARPATY LVIV

UEFA EUROPA LEAGUE

Second Qualifying Round – KR Reykjavík (ISL)
A 3-0 *Guruli (46), Tkachuk (51), Batista (57)*
Tlumak, Milošević, Tubić, Godwin (Habovda 80), Kozhanov (Zenjov 61), Guruli, Petrivskiy, Khudobyak, Tkachuk, Batista (Nenu 65), Danilo Avelar. Coach: Oleg Kononov (BLR)
Yellow Card(s): Godwin 33, Tubić 73
H 3-2 *Zenjov (2), Fedetskiy (25), B. Baranets (69)*
Rudenko, Milošević, Oshchypko (Martynyuk 67), Zenjov (Habovda 46), Kopolovets, H. Baranets (Tkachuk 81), B. Baranets, Tarasenko, Fedetskiy, Nenu, Danilo Avelar. Coach: Oleg Kononov (BLR)

Third Qualifying Round – FC Zestafoni (GEO)
H 1-0 *Khudobyak (6)*
Tlumak, Milošević, Tubić, Godwin (H. Baranets 76), Oshchypko, Kozhanov (B. Baranets 85), Zenjov (Guruli 53), Khudobyak, Tkachuk, Fedetskiy, Batista. Coach: Oleg Kononov (BLR)
Yellow Card(s): Kozhanov 30, Milošević 86
A 1-0 *Kozhanov (90+1)*
Tlumak, Milošević, Tubić, Godwin, Oshchypko (Danilo Avelar 32), Kozhanov (H. Baranets 90+4), Zenjov (Guruli 45+3), Khudobyak, Tkachuk, Fedetskiy, Batista. Coach: Oleg Kononov (BLR)
Yellow Card(s): Batista 66, Tubić 70

Play-Offs – Galatasaray AŞ (TUR)
A 2-2 *Kuznetsov (34), Zenjov (41)*
Tlumak, Milošević, Godwin, Kozhanov (Hudyma 65), Zenjov (Kopolovets 85), Khudobyak, Holodyuk, Fedetskiy, Checher, Kuznetsov (Batista 72), Danilo Avelar. Coach: Oleg Kononov (BLR)
Yellow Card(s): Khudobyak 64, Godwin 90
H 1-1 *Fedetskiy (90+3)*
Tlumak, Milošević, Tubić, Kozhanov (Kopolovets 79), Zenjov (Batista 89), Khudobyak, Holodyuk (Guruli 41), Tkachuk, Fedetskiy, Kuznetsov, Danilo Avelar. Coach: Oleg Kononov (BLR)
Red Card(s): Kuznetsov 71, Fedetskiy 90+4
Yellow Card(s): Fedetskiy 4, Tlumak 89, Fedetskiy 90+4

Group J
Match 1 – Borussia Dortmund (GER)
H 3-4 *Holodyuk (44), Kopolovets (52), Kozhanov (78)*
Tlumak, Milošević, Tubić, Godwin, Kozhanov (Checher 90+2), Zenjov, Petrivskiy, Khudobyak, Holodyuk, Batista (Kopolovets 13), Danilo Avelar. Coach: Oleg Kononov (BLR)
Yellow Card(s): Tlumak 12, Godwin 45+2, Kopolovets 85, Petrivskiy 90
Match 2 – Paris Saint-Germain FC (FRA)
A 0-2
Tlumak, Tubić, Godwin, Kozhanov (Hudyma 71), Guruli (Holodyuk 57), Zenjov (Kopolovets 57), Khudobyak, Fedetskiy, Checher, Kuznetsov, Danilo Avelar. Coach: Oleg Kononov (BLR)
Yellow Card(s): Godwin 55
Match 3 – Sevilla FC (ESP)
H 0-1
Rudenko, Tubić, Kozhanov (Hudyma 75), Zenjov (Kuznetsov 46), Khudobyak, Holodyuk, Kopolovets (Habovda 57), Tkachuk, Fedetskiy, Checher, Danilo Avelar. Coach: Oleg Kononov (BLR)
Red Card(s): Checher 88
Yellow Card(s): Checher 71, Holodyuk 79, Checher 88
Match 4 – Sevilla FC (ESP)
A 0-4
Tlumak, Milošević, Tubić, Godwin, Kozhanov (Kopolovets 69), Guruli (Tkachuk 40), Khudobyak, Holodyuk, Fedetskiy, Kuznetsov (Zenjov 62), Danilo Avelar. Coach: Oleg Kononov (BLR)
Yellow Card(s): Fedetskiy 26
Match 5 – Borussia Dortmund (GER)
A 0-3
Rudenko, Tubić, Godwin (H. Baranets 77), Kozhanov (B. Baranets 86), Khudobyak, Kopolovets (Guruli 63), Tkachuk, Fedetskiy, Checher, Kuznetsov, Danilo Avelar. Coach: Oleg Kononov (BLR)
Yellow Card(s): Godwin 25, Kopolovets 48
Match 6 – Paris Saint-Germain FC (FRA)
H 1-1 *Fedetskiy (45)*
Tlumak, Milošević, Tubić, Kozhanov (Guruli 68), Khudobyak, Martynyuk, Tkachuk, H. Baranets (Habovda 62), Fedetskiy, Kuznetsov (Hudyma 81), Danilo Avelar. Coach: Oleg Kononov (BLR)
Yellow Card(s): Fedetskiy 87

WALES

THE NEW SAINTS FC

UEFA CHAMPIONS LEAGUE

Second Qualifying Round – Bohemian FC (IRL)
A 0-1
Harrison, D. Holmes, Marriott, Baker, Evans, Ruscoe, Hogan, Sharp, M. Williams (Darlington 83), Jones, Berkeley (Wood 77). Coach: Mike Davies (WAL)
Yellow Card(s): Jones 51
H 4-0 *Jones (6), M. Williams (14, 73), Sharp (20)*
Harrison, D. Holmes, Marriott, Baker, Evans, Ruscoe, Hogan, Sharp (Darlington 90+1), M. Williams, Jones, Berkeley (Wood 89). Coach: Mike Davies (WAL)
Yellow Card(s): Sharp 34

Third Qualifying Round – RSC Anderlecht (BEL)
H 1-3 *Jones (52)*
Harrison, D. Holmes, Marriott (T. Holmes 21), Baker, Evans, Ruscoe, Hogan, Sharp (Darlington 84), M. Williams, Jones, Berkeley (Seargeant 78). Coach: Mike Davies (WAL)
A 0-3
Harrison, D. Holmes, Baker, Evans (Edwards 73), T. Holmes, Ruscoe, Hogan, Sharp (Darlington 83), M. Williams, Jones, Wood (Seargeant 87). Coach: Mike Davies (WAL)
Yellow Card(s): T. Holmes 57

UEFA EUROPA LEAGUE

Play-Offs – PFC CSKA Sofia (BUL)
A 0-3
Harrison, D. Holmes, Baker, Evans, T. Holmes, Ruscoe, Hogan, Sharp (Berkeley 76), M. Williams (Darlington 87), Seargeant, Jones (Wood 79). Coach: Mike Davies (WAL)
Yellow Card(s): Hogan 18
H 2-2 *M. Williams (14), Evans (62)*
Harrison, D. Holmes, Baker, Evans, T. Holmes, Ruscoe, Hogan, Sharp (Berkeley 86), M. Williams, Seargeant, Jones (Wood 83). Coach: Mike Davies (WAL)
Red Card(s): M. Williams 66
Yellow Card(s): Baker 25, M. Williams 37, M. Williams 66

BANGOR CITY FC

UEFA EUROPA LEAGUE

Second Qualifying Round – FC Honka Espoo (FIN)
A 1-1 *C. Jones (58)*
Smith, Hoy, Roberts, Morley, Brewerton (Edwards 52), Johnston, Jebb (Bull 61), Garside, Davies (Williams 78), Ward, C. Jones. Coach: Nev Powell (WAL)
Yellow Card(s): Johnston 35, Smith 57, C. Jones 64, Morley 90
H 2-1 *Morley (85), C. Jones (90+1)*
Smith, Hoy, Roberts, Morley, Brewerton, Johnston, Jebb (Bull 62), Davies, Ward, Edwards, Jones. Coach: Nev Powell (WAL)
Yellow Card(s): Ward 79

Third Qualifying Round – CS Marítimo (POR)
A 2-8 *Ward (73), Jebb (90+3)*
Smith, Hoy, Roberts, Morley, Brewerton, Johnston, Davies (Ward 46), Edwards, C. Jones (Hurdman 81), Bull, Williams (Jebb 66). Coach: Nev Powell (WAL)
Red Card(s): Brewerton 45+2
Yellow Card(s): Brewerton 7, Hoy 35, Brewerton 45+2, Hurdman 82
H 1-2 *Bull (9)*
Smith, Hoy, Roberts, Morley, Johnston, Jebb (Davies 66), Garside (Hurdman 67), Ward, Edwards (Williams 77), C. Jones, Bull. Coach: Nev Powell (WAL)
Yellow Card(s): Edwards 47, Garside 51

LLANELLI AFC

UEFA EUROPA LEAGUE

First Qualifying Round – FK Tauras (LTU)
H 2-2 *D. Thomas (19), S. Jones (47)*
Morris, C. Thomas, Giles, Venables, S. Jones, D. Thomas, Corbisiero, Holloway, Llewellyn (Legg 75), Moses, Follows (Griffiths 61). Coach: Andy Legg (WAL)
Red Card(s): Holloway 88
Yellow Card(s): Moses 59, Venables 65
A 2-3 (aet) *Llewellyn (19), Bowen (36)*
Morris, C. Thomas, Giles, Venables, S. Jones (Follows 112), D. Thomas, Bowen, Corbisiero, Griffiths, Llewellyn (Legg 106), Moses. Coach: Gary Lloyd (WAL)
Red Card(s): Griffiths 54, Moses 112
Yellow Card(s): C. Thomas 13, Griffiths 39, Griffiths 54, Llewellyn 62, Morris 89, Venables 118, Legg 120+1, Corbisiero 120+2

PORT TALBOT TOWN FC

UEFA EUROPA LEAGUE

First Qualifying Round – TPS Turku (FIN)
A 1-3 *Rose (70)*
Kendall, De Vulgt (Holland 46), Grist, Lewis, Rees, Surman, Rose (L. Bowen 87), McCreesh, Barrow, John (Fahiya 87), Phillips. Coach: Mark Jones (WAL)
Yellow Card(s): Phillips 21, Surman 84, Lewis 90+3
H 0-4
Kendall, Grist, Lewis, Rees, Surman, Rose, McCreesh (L. Bowen 76), Barrow, John, Holland (Brooks 45+2), Palmer (Thomas 67). Coach: Mark Jones (WAL)
Yellow Card(s): Barrow 28, Lewis 33, Brooks 54

UEFA EURO 2012

Europe's most successful nations from the 2010 FIFA World Cup – Spain, the Netherlands and Germany – carried their form over from South Africa to dominate their UEFA EURO 2012 qualifying groups. But while those three teams boasted perfect records during the 2010/11 season, other traditional giants found the going much tougher. France were humbled at home by Belarus in Laurent Blanc's first competitive game, while Portugal, the Czech Republic and Russia endured shock defeats at the hands of Norway, Lithuania and Slovakia, respectively, as the battle to qualify for the finals in Poland and Ukraine intensified. Les Bleus at least steadied the ship, climbing to the top of their section, while another major power to suffer World Cup woe in 2010, Italy, enjoyed a smooth revival under Cesare Prandelli. Outsiders Hungary and Israel, meanwhile, remained in contention to qualify, although it was the concerted challenge of competition debutants Montenegro in Group G, where they remained unbeaten and level on points with England, that provided the biggest story of all.

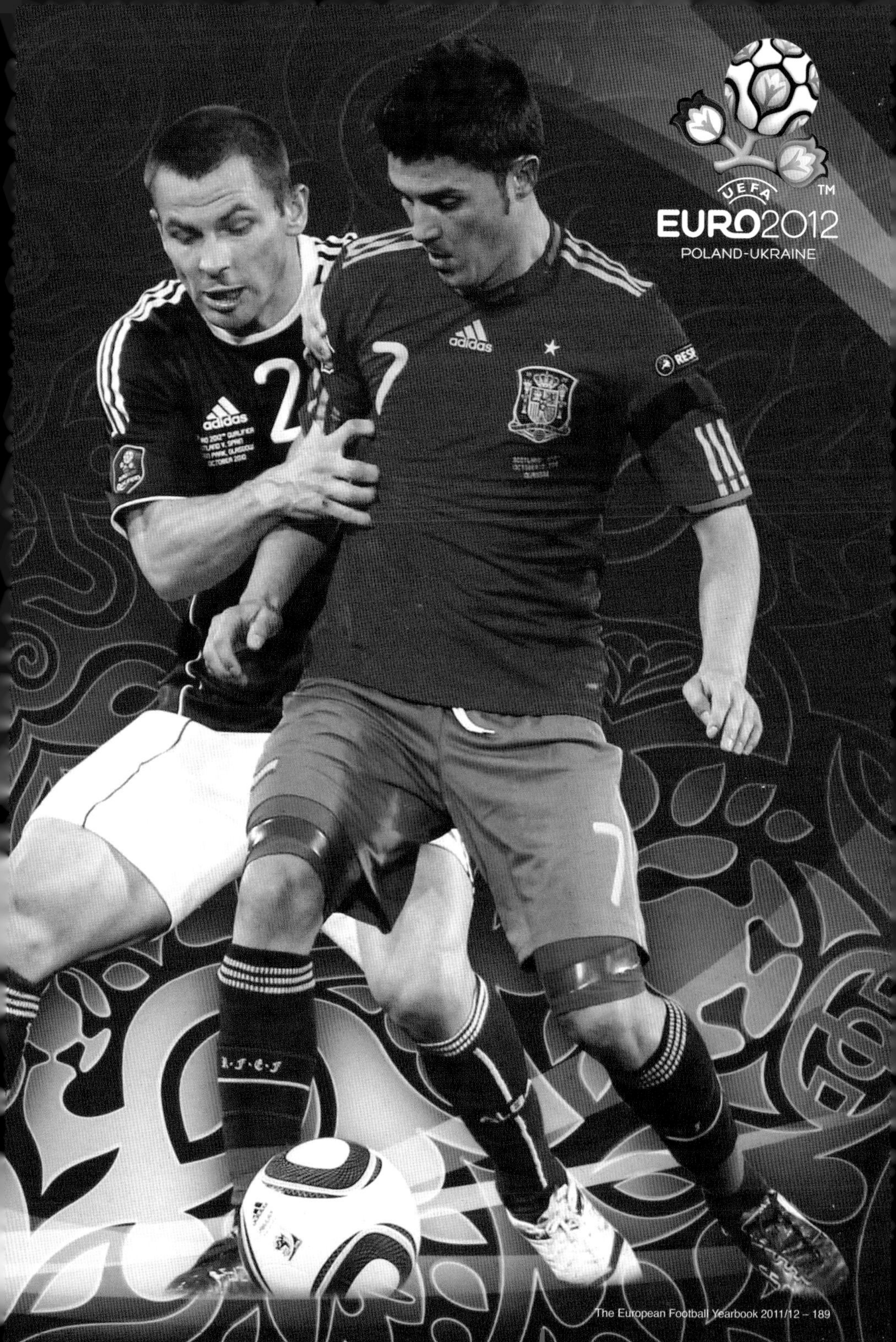
UEFA
EURO2012
POLAND-UKRAINE

	CITY	MATCH DAY 1				MATCH DAY 2				MATCH DAY 3			
		FRI 08 JUNE	SAT 09 JUNE	SUN 10 JUNE	MON 11 JUNE	TUE 12 JUNE	WED 13 JUNE	THU 14 JUNE	FRI 15 JUNE	SAT 16 JUNE	SUN 17 JUNE	MON 18 JUNE	TUE 19 JUNE
POLAND	WARSAW	Match 1 POL - A2 18:00				Match 10 POL - A3 20:45				Match 18 A2 - A3 20:45			
POLAND	WROCLAW	Match 2 A3 - A4 20:45				Match 9 A2 - A4 18:00				Match 17 A4 - POL 20:45			
POLAND	GDANSK			Match 5 C1 - C2 18:00				Match 14 C1 - C3 20:45				Match 21 C4 - C1 20:45	
POLAND	POZNAN			Match 6 C3 - C4 20:45				Match 13 C2 - C4 18:00				Match 22 C2 - C3 20:45	
UKRAINE	KYIV				Match 8 UKR - D2 20:45				Match 15 D2 - D4 18:00				Match 24 D2 - D3 20:45
UKRAINE	DONETSK				Match 7 D3 - D4 18:00				Match 16 UKR - D3 20:45				Match 23 D4 - UKR 20:45
UKRAINE	KHARKIV		Match 3 B1 - B2 18:00				Match 12 B1 - B3 20:45				Match 19 B4 - B1 20:45		
UKRAINE	LVIV		Match 4 B3 - B4 20:45				Match 11 B2 - B4 18:00				Match 20 B2 - B3 20:45		

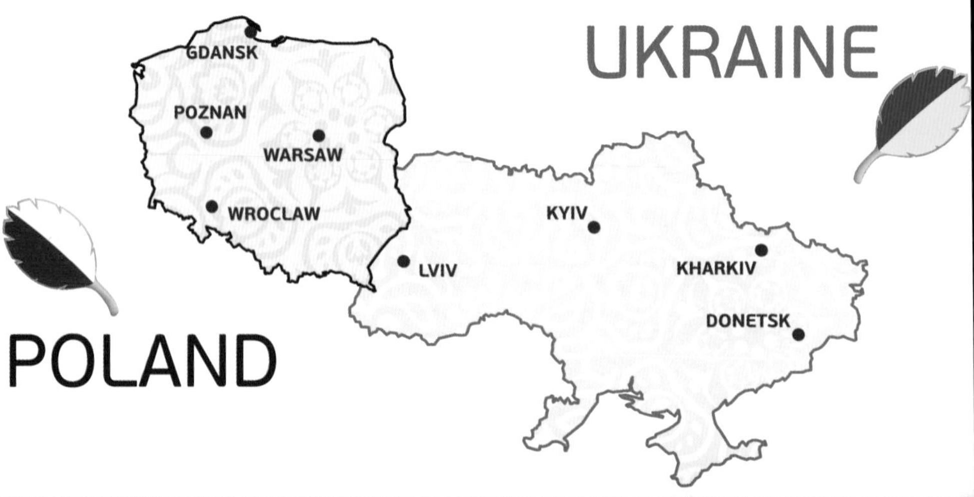

MATCH SCHEDULE

ll kick-off times are CET / local kick-off times in Ukraine are 19:00 and 21:45. UEFA will publish the final match schedule after the final draw on 2 December 2011.

REST DAY	QUARTER-FINALS				REST DAYS		SEMI-FINALS		REST DAYS		FINAL
WED 20 JUNE	THU 21 JUNE	FRI 22 JUNE	SAT 23 JUNE	SUN 24 JUNE	MON 25 JUNE	TUE 26 JUNE	WED 27 JUNE	THU 28 JUNE	FRI 29 JUNE	SAT 30 JUNE	SUN 01 JULY
	Match 25 WA - RB 20:45	Match 26 WB - RA 20:45	Match 27 WC - RD 20:45	Match 28 WD - RC 20:45			Match 29 W25 - W27 20:45	Match 30 W26 - W28 20:45			Match 31 W29 - W30 20:45

VENUES

POLAND	MATCHES
National Stadium, Warsaw (50,000)	5
Municipal Stadium, Wroclaw (40,000)	3
Municipal Stadium, Gdansk (40,000)	4
Municipal Stadium, Poznan (40,000)	3

UKRAINE	MATCHES
Olympic Stadium, Kyiv (60,000)	5
Donbass Arena, Donetsk (50,000)	5
Metalist Stadium, Kharkiv (30,000)	3
New Lviv Stadium, Lviv (30,000)	3

UEFA EUROPEAN CHAMPIONSHIP PREVIOUS TOURNAMENTS

YEAR	HOST NATION	WINNERS
1960	France	USSR
1964	Spain	Spain
1968	Italy	Italy
1972	Belgium	West Germany
1976	Yugoslavia	Czechoslovakia
1980	Italy	West Germany
1984	France	France
1988	West Germany	Netherlands
1992	Sweden	Denmark
1996	England	Germany
2000	Belgium/Netherlands	France
2004	Portugal	Greece
2008	Austria/Switzerland	Spain

QUALIFYING COMPETITION

GROUP A

Three-time European champions Germany looked certain to top Group A as they went into the summer break with maximum points, but the race for the runners-up spot promised to go to the wire as Turkey, Belgium and Austria fought to keep their qualification hopes alive.

Contract extension

The German Football Association (DFB) played the continuity card by extending Joachim Löw's contract until 2012 in the aftermath of the team's run to the last four of the 2010 FIFA World Cup, and he was rewarded with a further two-year extension after his side's swashbuckling start to their qualifying campaign. Löw's charges were close to flawless as they advanced towards Poland/Ukraine, winning their first seven matches, scoring 22 goals and conceding just three.

While Löw introduced some fresh blood, the familiar names did the damage early on, Miroslav Klose scoring the only goal away to Belgium before helping himself to two more in the 6-1 mauling of Azerbaijan. Local lad Lukas Podolski also found the target in Cologne, ensuring a miserable return to his homeland for Azeri coach Berti Vogts.

Gomez late show

Azerbaijan were not the only team to succumb to the might of the three-time world champions and their irrepressible No11. Klose registered another double against Turkey before lifting his tally to eight goals in five games by slotting three past Kazakhstan over the course of two comfortable victories. There was almost a minor slip in Austria on 3 June, but Mario Gomez headed home skipper Philipp Lahm's superbly-flighted cross in the 90th minute to complete his brace and seal a 2-1 triumph. Normal service resumed in Azerbaijan four days later, with Gomez, the German Bundesliga's top scorer in 2010/11, notching his fourth goal of the campaign in a 3-1 triumph.

Germany's victims could console themselves in the knowledge that no other team was picking up points against the runaway leaders. With Azerbaijan and Kazakhstan predictably struggling, the meetings between the three principal contenders for second place gained extra importance.

Turkish triumph

Belgium renewed acquaintance with Turkey just four days after their opening loss at home to Germany, and life did not get any easier for their new boss Georges Leekens in Istanbul. The Red Devils had taken four points off Turkey in 2010 FIFA World Cup qualifying but they were edged out 3-2 in a captivating contest after losing Vincent Kompany to a red card. Although Daniel Van Buyten scored twice, Hamit Altıntop, Semih Şentürk and Arda Turan all struck for a team now led by experienced Dutchman Guud Hiddink.

It was Turkey's second win following a 3-0 opening-day success in Kazakhstan, yet trouble was just around the corner. A confidence-puncturing 3-0 reverse in Berlin was followed by a far more worrying loss in Azerbaijan later that week. Azeri captain Räşad F. Sadıqov scored the only goal, prompting euphoric scenes in Baku. "I'm asking the press not to lavish too many compliments on our players," Vogts said. "This time luck was on our side." The former Germany coach was not wrong to urge caution because Azerbaijan were to lose their next three fixtures, including a 2-1 setback in Kazakhstan, and they ended the season joint bottom alongside their eastern European neighbours with three points.

Eight-goal thriller

Both Belgium and Austria took advantage of Turkey's poor form. Leekens' side recovered from their early wobbles by stringing together five matches without defeat, beginning with a 2-0 success over Kazakhstan. Austria, meanwhile, helped themselves to maximum points from their first two games, against Azerbaijan and Kazakhstan, before travelling to Brussels for another of the section's key meetings. Leading 3-2 with three minutes remaining, the UEFA EURO 2008 co-hosts looked poised to clinch a memorable victory despite being down to ten men following the sending-off of Paul Scharner. Belgium

Mario Gomez struck twice as Germany overcame Austria 2-1 in Vienna

reacted, however, scoring two quick-fire goals through Marvin Ogunjimi and Nicolas Lombaerts to spark wild celebrations in the Stade Roi Baudouin. But there was to be yet another twist as Austria's Martin Harnik made it 4-4 deep into added time.

In comparison, the return in Vienna proved something of an anti-climax, Axel Witsel scoring early in each half to inflict a first defeat on Dietmar Constantini's men and secure Belgium's second victory. That result seemed to knock the stuffing out of Austria, who faded thereafter, suffering a 2-0 defeat in Turkey, for whom Arda and Gökhan Gönül scored, and agonisingly succumbing to Gomez's last-gasp effort in front of a packed house in Vienna.

Missed penalty

Those three successive defeats left Austria with much ground to make up, although their cause was helped by Belgium and Turkey cancelling each other out in Brussels. Belgium entered the 3 June fixture in confident mood having moved a point clear in second thanks to their 4-1 success over Azerbaijan in March – Jan Vertonghen, Timmy Simons, Nacer Chadli and Jelle Vossen supplying the goals – and they looked on course for another victory when Ogunjimi netted from close range on four minutes. Burak Yılmaz then pulled Hiddink's team level before Witsel squandered a glorious chance for the hosts, firing a penalty over the bar 15 minutes from time. Although Belgium remained in second place, Turkey trailed them by just one point with a game in hand and what appeared to be an easier run-in.

Group A Results

3/9/10, Roi Baudouin, Brussels
Belgium 0-1 Germany
Attendance: 41126
Belgium: Bailly, Alderweireld, Van Buyten, Kompany, Vermaelen, Simons (Vossen 83), Hazard (Defour 73), Vertonghen, Lukaku (Benteke 73), Fellaini, Dembélé. Coach: Georges Leekens (BEL)
Germany: Neuer, Jansen (Westermann 46), Khedira, Schweinsteiger, Özil (Cacau 88), Podolski (Kroos 70), Klose, Müller, Badstuber, Lahm, Mertesacker. Coach: Joachim Löw (GER)
Goal(s): 0-1 Klose 51
Yellow Card(s): Kompany 12 (Belgium), Schweinsteiger 45+1 (Germany), Cacau 90+1 (Germany)
Referee: Hauge (NOR)

3/9/10, Astana Arena, Astana
Kazakhstan 0-3 Turkey
Attendance: 15800
Kazakhstan: Sidelnikov, Kirov, Abdulin, Kislitsyn (Rozhkov 85), Karpovich (Rodionov 64), Ostapenko (Maltsev 72), Zhumaskaliyev, Nurgaliyev, Schmidtgal, Popov, Azovski. Coach: Bernd Storck (GER)
Turkey: Onur Kıvrak, Servet Çetin, Hakan Balta, Emre Belözoğlu, Hamit Altıntop, Nihat Kahveci (Selçuk İnan 82), Tuncay Şanlı (Halil Altıntop 80), Arda Turan, Mehmet Aurélio (Kazım Kazım 89), Ömer Erdoğan, Sabri Sarıoğlu. Coach: Guus Hiddink (NED)
Goal(s): 0-1 Arda Turan 24, 0-2 Hamit Altıntop 26, 0-3 Nihat Kahveci 76
Yellow Card(s): Karpovich 58 (Kazakhstan), Zhumaskaliyev 62 (Kazakhstan)
Referee: Vad (HUN)

7/9/10, Stadion Salzburg, Salzburg
Austria 2-0 Kazakhstan
Attendance: 22500
Austria: Macho, Schiemer, Pogatetz, Fuchs, Jantscher (Alaba 66), Kavlak, Prödl, Dag, Harnik (Hoffer 66), Linz, Janko (Maierhofer 78). Coach: Dietmar Constantini (AUT)
Kazakhstan: Sidelnikov, Geteriyev, Kirov, Abdulin, Kislitsyn (Rozhkov 75), Karpovich, Averchenko, Maltsev (Khizhnichenko 46), Zhumaskaliyev, Nurgaliyev (Azovski 59), Popov. Coach: Bernd Storck (GER)
Goal(s): 1-0 Linz 90+1, 2-0 Hoffer 90+2
Yellow Card(s): Nurgaliyev 45+1 (Kazakhstan), Kislitsyn 53 (Kazakhstan), Jantscher 60 (Austria), Rozhkov 80 (Kazakhstan)
Referee: Strahonja (CRO)

7/9/10, Müngersdorfer Stadion, Cologne
Germany 6-1 Azerbaijan
Attendance: 43751
Germany: Neuer, Riether, Khedira, Schweinsteiger (Cacau 78), Özil, Podolski, Klose, Müller (Marin 61), Badstuber, Lahm, Mertesacker (Westermann 11). Coach: Joachim Löw (GER)
Azerbaijan: K. Ağayev, Mälikov, Yunisoğlu (V. Hüseynov 56), Şükürov, Allahverdiyev, Cavadov, Chertoganov (Räşad A. Sadiqov 64), Abbasov, Räşad F. Sadıqov, Nadirov (Abdullayev 85), Medvedev. Coach: Berti Vogts (GER)
Goal(s): 1-0 Westermann 28, 2-0 Podolski 45+1, 3-0 Klose 45+2, 4-0 Räşad F. Sadıqov 53 (og), 4-1 Cavadov 57, 5-1 Badstuber 86, 6-1 Klose 90+2
Referee: Strömbergsson (SWE)

7/9/10, Şükrü Saracoğlu, Istanbul
Turkey 3-2 Belgium
Attendance: 43538
Turkey: Onur Kıvrak, Servet Çetin, İsmail Köybaşı, Emre Belözoğlu, Hamit Altıntop, Tuncay Şanlı (Selçuk Şahin 82), Arda Turan, Mehmet Aurélio, Ömer Erdoğan, Selçuk İnan (Semih Şentürk 46), Sabri Sarıoğlu (Gökhan Gönül 73). Coach: Guus Hiddink (NED)
Belgium: Bailly, Alderweireld, Van Buyten, Kompany, Vermaelen, Simons, G. Gillet (Hazard 82), Vertonghen, Lukaku (Witsel 76), Fellaini, Dembélé (Mirallas 64). Coach: Georges Leekens (BEL)
Goal(s): 0-1 Van Buyten 28, 1-1 Hamit Altıntop 48, 2-1 Semih Şentürk 66, 2-2 Van Buyten 69, 3-2 Arda Turan 78
Red Card(s): Kompany 64 (Belgium)
Yellow Card(s): Emre Belözoğlu 32 (Turkey), Kompany 40 (Belgium), Van Buyten 45+2 (Belgium), Kompany 64 (Belgium), Selçuk Şahin 90+1 (Turkey), Alderweireld 90+3 (Belgium)
Referee: Skomina (SVN)

8/10/10, Ernst-Happel-Stadion, Vienna
Austria 3-0 Azerbaijan
Attendance: 26500
Austria: Macho, Schiemer, Fuchs, Junuzovic (Baumgartlinger 78), Arnautovic, Prödl, Scharner, Klein, Harnik (Kavlak 55), Linz (Hoffer 59), Maierhofer. Coach: Dietmar Constantini (AUT)
Azerbaijan: K. Ağayev, Mälikov, Yunisoğlu, Şükürov, Allahverdiyev, Cavadov (Räşad A. Sadiqov 74), Abbasov, Mämmädov (Nadirov 59), Äliyev, Räşad F. Sadıqov, Ämirquliyev. Coach: Berti Vogts (GER)
Goal(s): 1-0 Prödl 3, 2-0 Arnautović 53, 3-0 Arnautović 90+2
Yellow Card(s): Allahverdiyev 7 (Azerbaijan), Prödl 10 (Austria), Yunisoğlu 36 (Azerbaijan), Äliyev 73 (Azerbaijan)
Referee: Vollquartz (DEN)

8/10/10, Olympiastadion, Berlin
Germany 3-0 Turkey
Attendance: 74244
Germany: Neuer, Westermann, Khedira, Özil (Marin 90), Podolski (Träsch 86), Klose (Cacau 90), Müller, Badstuber, Lahm, Mertesacker, Kroos. Coach: Joachim Löw (GER)
Turkey: Volkan Demirel, Servet Çetin, Ömer Erdoğan, Emre Belözoğlu, Hamit Altıntop, Gökhan Gönül, Özer Hurmacı, Mehmet Aurélio (Tuncay Şanlı 24), Nuri Şahin (Sercan Yıldırım 78), Halil Altıntop (Semih Şentürk 63), Sabri Sarıoğlu. Coach: Guus Hiddink (NED)
Goal(s): 1-0 Klose 42, 2-0 Özil 79, 3-0 Klose 87
Yellow Card(s): Servet Çetin 45+5 (Turkey)
Referee: Webb (ENG)

8/10/10, Astana Arena, Astana
Kazakhstan 0-2 Belgium
Attendance: 8500
Kazakhstan: Sidelnikov, Geteriyev, Kirov, Abdulin, Kislitsyn, Karpovich, Zhumaskaliyev (Averchenko 87), Khizhnichenko, Nurgaliyev (Rozhkov 74), Schmidtgal, Popov. Coach: Bernd Storck (GER)
Belgium: Bailly, Alderweireld, Van Buyten, Lombaerts, Deschacht, Simons, Witsel, Fellaini, Lukaku (Ogunjimi 46), Vossen, Van Damme (Legear 79). Coach: Georges Leekens (BEL)

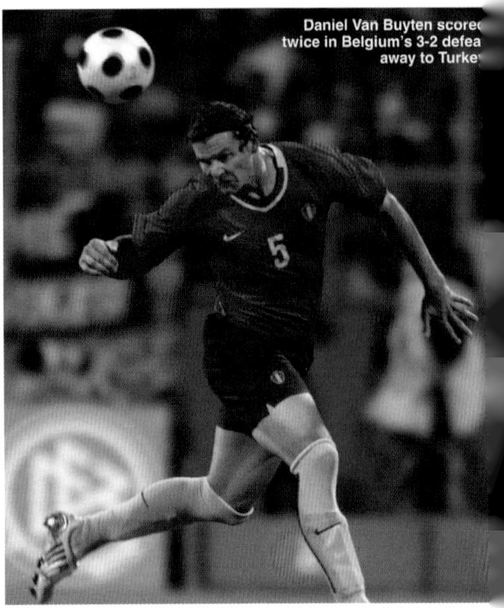
Daniel Van Buyten scored twice in Belgium's 3-2 defeat away to Turkey

Goal(s): 0-1 Ogunjimi 52, 0-2 Ogunjimi 70
Red Card(s): Kislitsyn 68 (Kazakhstan)
Yellow Card(s): Vossen 19 (Belgium), Fellaini 26 (Belgium), Kislitsyn 51 (Kazakhstan), Karpovich 55 (Kazakhstan), Kislitsyn 68 (Kazakhstan)
Referee: Borski (POL)

12/10/10, Tofiq Bähramov-Republic stadium, Baku
Azerbaijan 1-0 Turkey
Attendance: 29500
Azerbaijan: K. Ağayev, Mälikov (Chertoganov 45+2), Yunisoğlu, Şükürov, Allahverdiyev, Cavadov (V. Hüseynov 85), Räşad F. Sadıqov, Abişov, Nadirov, Ämirquliyev, F. Quliyev (Äliyev 71). Coach: Berti Vogts (GER)
Turkey: Volkan Demirel, Servet Çetin, Hakan Balta, Emre Belözoğlu, Hamit Altıntop, Gökhan Gönül, Semih Şentürk, Tuncay Şanlı (Sercan Yıldırım 62), Özer Hurmacı (Nihat Kahveci 46), Selçuk İnan (Halil Altıntop 82), İbrahim Toraman. Coach: Guus Hiddink (NED)
Goal(s): 1-0 Räşad F. Sadıqov 38
Yellow Card(s): Hakan Balta 58 (Turkey), Şükürov 58 (Azerbaijan), Ämirquliyev 60 (Azerbaijan), K. Ağayev 80 (Azerbaijan), Chertoganov 87 (Azerbaijan)
Referee: Deaconu (ROU)

12/10/10, Roi Baudouin, Brussels
Belgium 4-4 Austria
Attendance: 24231
Belgium: Bailly, Alderweireld (Boyata 46), Kompany, Vertonghen, Simons (Lukaku 73), Witsel, Fellaini (Hazard 81), Ogunjimi, Vossen, Legear, Lombaerts. Coach: Georges Leekens (BEL)
Austria: Macho, Schiemer, Fuchs, Junuzovic (Pehlivan 72), Arnautovic (Harnik 88), Kavlak (Hoffer 56), Baumgartlinger, Prödl, Scharner, Klein, Maierhofer. Coach: Dietmar Constantini (AUT)
Goal(s): 1-0 Vossen 11, 1-1 Schiemer 14, 1-2 Arnautovic 29, 2-2 Fellaini 47, 2-3 Schiemer 62, 3-3 Ogunjimi 87, 4-3 Lombaerts 90, 4-4 Harnik 90+3
Red Card(s): Scharner 68 (Austria)
Yellow Card(s): Maierhofer 28 (Austria), Schiemer 36 (Austria), Lombaerts 45+1 (Belgium), Simons 64 (Belgium), Klein 83 (Austria)
Referee: Dean (ENG)

12/10/10, Astana Arena, Astana
Kazakhstan 0-3 Germany
Attendance: 18000
Kazakhstan: Sidelnikov, Geteriyev, Kirov, Abdulin, Zhumaskaliyev, Khizhnichenko (Finonchenko 79), Nurgaliyev (Averchenko 63), Schmidtgal, Popov, Azovski, Irismetov (Rozhkov 68). Coach: Bernd Storck (GER)
Germany: Neuer, Westermann, Khedira, Özil (Cacau 79), Podolski, Klose (Gomez 55), Müller (Marin 71), Badstuber, Lahm, Mertesacker, Kroos. Coach: Joachim Löw (GER)
Goal(s): 0-1 Klose 48, 0-2 Gomez 76, 0-3 Podolski 85
Yellow Card(s): Abdulin 37 (Kazakhstan), Irismetov 60 (Kazakhstan)
Referee: Tudor (ROU)

25/3/11, Ernst-Happel-Stadion, Vienna
Austria 0-2 Belgium
Attendance: 45000
Austria: Macho, Dragovic, Pogatetz, Fuchs, Alaba (Pehlivan 54), Junuzovic (Korkmaz 69), Arnautovic, Dag, Baumgartlinger, Harnik, Janko (Maierhofer 54). Coach: Dietmar Constantini (AUT)
Belgium: Mignolet, Ciman, Van Buyten, Kompany, Vertonghen, Simons, Chadli, Defour, Ogunjimi (Mirallas 80), Witsel, Dembélé. Coach: Georges Leekens (BEL)
Goal(s): 0-1 Witsel 6, 0-2 Witsel 50
Yellow Card(s): Kompany 41 (Belgium)
Referee: Bezborodov (RUS)

26/3/11, Fritz-Walter-Stadion, Kaiserslautern
Germany 4-0 Kazakhstan
Attendance: 47849
Germany: Neuer, Aogo, Khedira, Schweinsteiger (Kroos 77), Özil, Podolski (Gomez 65), Klose, Müller (Götze 78), Badstuber, Lahm, Mertesacker. Coach: Joachim Löw (GER)
Kazakhstan: Loria, Chernyshev, Abdulin, Chichulin, Irismetov, Khizhnichenko, Zhumaskaliyev (Bayzhanov 46), Konysbayev, Nurgaliyev (Kukeev 60), Nurdauletov, Geteriyev (Ostapenko 81). Coach: Miroslav Beránek (CZE)
Goal(s): 1-0 Klose 3, 2-0 Müller 25, 3-0 Müller 43, 4-0 Klose 88
Yellow Card(s): Irismetov 25 (Kazakhstan)
Referee: Stavrev (MKD)

29/3/11, Şükrü Saracoğlu, Istanbul
Turkey 2-0 Austria
Attendance: 40420
Turkey: Volkan Demirel, Servet Çetin, Hakan Balta, Serdar Kesimal, Hamit Altıntop, Gökhan Gönül, Selçuk İnan, Mehmet Ekici (Mehmet Topuz 63), Arda Turan (Mehmet Topal 89), Burak Yılmaz (Semih Şentürk 72), Nuri Şahin. Coach: Guus Hiddink (NED)
Austria: Macho, Dragovic, Pogatetz, Fuchs, Pehlivan (Korkmaz 57), Alaba, Dag, Baumgartlinger (Hoffer 46), Scharner, Harnik (Arnautović 69), Maierhofer. Coach: Dietmar Constantini (AUT)
Goal(s): 1-0 Arda Turan 28, 2-0 Gökhan Gönül 78
Yellow Card(s): Pogatetz 13 (Austria), Fuchs 73 (Austria), Mehmet Topuz 83 (Turkey), Scharner 90+2 (Austria)
Referee: Kralovec (CZE)

29/3/11, Roi Baudouin, Brussels
Belgium 4-1 Azerbaijan
Attendance: 34985
Belgium: Mignolet, Ciman, Van Buyten (Van Damme 80), Lombaerts, Vertonghen, Simons, Chadli, Defour (Odjidja-Ofoe 90), Vossen, Witsel, Dembélé (Hazard 64). Coach: Georges Leekens (BEL)
Azerbaijan: K. Ağayev, Mälikov, Şükürov, Cavadov (Nadirov 76), Chertoganov, Mämmädov (C. Hüseynov 78), Äliyev, Räşad F. Sadıqov, Abişov, Ämirquliyev, Levin. Coach: Berti Vogts (GER)
Goal(s): 1-0 Vertonghen 12, 1-1 Abişov 16, 2-1 Simons 32 (p), 3-1 Chadli 45+1, 4-1 Vossen 74
Yellow Card(s): Mälikov 30 (Azerbaijan)
Referee: Stalhammar (SWE)

3/6/11, Ernst-Happel-Stadion, Vienna
Austria 1-2 Germany
Attendance: 47500
Austria: Gratzei, Pogatetz, Fuchs, Kulovits, Alaba, Hoffer (Janko 88), Dag (Junuzović 66), Baumgartlinger, Scharner, Klein, Harnik (Royer 81). Coach: Dietmar Constantini (AUT)
Germany: Neuer, Schmelzer, Friedrich, Hummels, Khedira (Badstuber 69), Özil, Podolski (Schürrle 67), Müller, Lahm, Kroos (Aogo 90+3), Gomez. Coach: Joachim Löw (GER)
Goal(s): 0-1 Gomez 44, 1-1 Friedrich 50 (og), 1-2 Gomez 90
Yellow Card(s): Baumgartlinger 29 (Austria), Scharner 80 (Austria), Özil 86 (Germany), Gomez 90+1 (Germany)
Referee: Busacca (SUI)

3/6/11, Roi Baudouin, Brussels
Belgium 1-1 Turkey
Attendance: 44185
Belgium: Mignolet, Alderweireld, Kompany, Lombaerts, Vertonghen (Vermaelen 46), Simons, Chadli, Defour (Vossen 88), Ogunjimi, Witsel, Hazard (Mertens 60). Coach: Georges Leekens (BEL)
Turkey: Volkan Demirel, Servet Çetin, Serdar Kesimal, Emre Belözoğlu, Selçuk İnan (Mehmet Topal 78), Çağlar Birinci, Arda Turan (Semih Şentürk 85), Burak Yılmaz (Mehmet Ekici 76), Kazım Kazım, Selçuk Şahin, Sabri Sarıoğlu. Coach: Guus Hiddink (NED)
Goal(s): 1-0 Ogunjimi 4, 1-1 Burak Yılmaz 22
Yellow Card(s): Defour 37 (Belgium), Kazım Kazım 37 (Turkey)
Referee: Rizzoli (ITA)

3/6/11, Astana Arena, Astana
Kazakhstan 2-1 Azerbaijan
Attendance: 10000
Kazakhstan: Nesterenko, Logvinenko (Rozhkov 65), Mukhtarov, Nurdauletov, Geteriyev, Smakov, Schmidtgal, Khairullin (Kirov 82), Konysbayev, Gridin, Ostapenko (Khizhnichenko 79). Coach: Miroslav Beránek (CZE)
Azerbaijan: K. Ağayev, Mälikov, Räşad A. Sadiqov, Cavadov, Äliyev (M. Hüseynov 79), Räşad F. Sadıqov, Abişov, C. Hüseynov (Nadirov 61), Medvedev, Levin, İsmayilov. Coach: Berti Vogts (GER)
Goal(s): 1-0 Gridin 57, 1-1 Nadirov 63, 2-1 Gridin 68
Yellow Card(s): Schmidtgal 77 (Kazakhstan)
Referee: Norris (SCO)

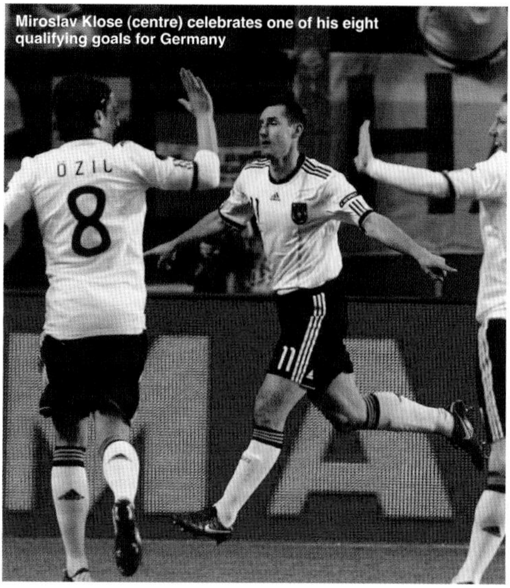

Miroslav Klose (centre) celebrates one of his eight qualifying goals for Germany

7/6/11, Tofiq Bähramov-Republic stadium, Baku
Azerbaijan 1-3 Germany
Attendance: 30000
Azerbaijan: K. Ağayev, Mälikov, Allahverdiyev, Cavadov (M. Hüseynov 71), Chertoganov (Räşad A. Sadiqov 86), V. Hüseynov, Räşad F. Sadıqov, Abişov, Nadirov, Ämirquliyev, İsmayilov (İsayev 57). Coach: Berti Vogts (GER)
Germany: Neuer, Aogo, Hummels, Özil (Götze 81), Podolski (Schürrle 75), Müller (Holtby 88), Badstuber, Lahm, Kroos, Höwedes, Gomez. Coach: Joachim Löw (GER)
Goal(s): 0-1 Özil 29, 0-2 Gomez 40, 1-2 M. Hüseynov 89, 1-3 Schürrle 90+3
Yellow Card(s): Höwedes 22 (Germany), Nadirov 64 (Azerbaijan)
Referee: Koukoulakis (GRE)

Group A Table

		Home					Away					Total					
	Pld	W	D	L	F	A	W	D	L	F	A	W	D	L	F	A	Pts
1 Germany	7	3	0	0	13	3	4	0	0	9	0	7	0	0	22	3	21
2 Belgium	7	1	2	1	9	10	2	0	1	6	0	3	2	2	15	10	11
3 Turkey	6	2	0	0	5	7	1	1	2	4	0	3	1	2	9	7	10
4 Austria	6	2	0	2	6	10	0	1	1	4	0	2	1	3	10	10	7
5 Azerbaijan	6	1	0	1	2	18	0	0	4	3	0	1	0	5	5	18	3
6 Kazakhstan	6	1	0	3	2	15	0	0	2	0	0	1	0	5	2	15	3

Remaining Fixtures

2/9/11
Azerbaijan – Belgium
Germany – Austria
Turkey – Kazakhstan

6/9/11
Azerbaijan – Kazakhstan
Austria – Turkey

7/10/11
Azerbaijan – Austria
Belgium – Kazakhstan
Turkey – Germany

11/10/11
Germany – Belgium
Kazakhstan – Austria
Turkey – Azerbaijan

Turkey coach Guus Hiddink (right) talks tactics with midfielder Hamit Altıntop

GROUP B

Russia and the Republic of Ireland were both looking to put the disappointment of FIFA World Cup play-off defeats behind them, but they faced stiff competition in Group B from an emerging Slovakia team buoyed by their exploits in South Africa, where they reached the last 16.

Stoch strikes

Semi-finalists at UEFA EURO 2008, Russia began their 2012 campaign with a routine 2-0 win away to Andorra, Pavel Pogrebnyak's double extending the tiny principality's winless run to 32 competitive matches, but new coach Dick Advocaat would taste defeat in only his second official outing. Slovakia had demonstrated their giant-killing potential by eliminating Italy from the World Cup, and Vladimír Weiss's men rose to the occasion once again in Moscow, defending brilliantly throughout and claiming the points courtesy of Miroslav Stoch's stunning goal on 27 minutes. "It was a great goal and a great result," Stoch enthused. "It's not every day you score against Russia and it's not every day you win in Russia either."

That result might have raised eyebrows, but it was merely a sign of things to come in an unpredictable, topsy-turvy section. No sooner had one team strung together a couple of wins than they were brought crudely down to earth. Ireland, for example, were setting the early pace having triumphed 1-0 in Armenia and beaten Andorra 3-1 in Dublin, yet any hopes they harboured of breaking clear were stalled by a sobering reverse at home to Russia. Giovanni Trapattoni's side found themselves three goals down inside 50 minutes at their new Dublin home, with Aleksandr Kerzhakov, Alan Dzagoev and Roman Shirokov all scoring to stun the locals into stony silence, before Robbie Keane's penalty and a Shane Long effort gave the final scoreline some respectability.

Slip-up

Meanwhile, Slovakia, who had edged past the Former Yugoslav Republic of Macedonia 1-0 in their opening game, also slipped up in their third match, crashing unexpectedly to a 3-1 loss in Armenia, for whom Yura Movsisyan, Gevorg Ghazaryan and Henrikh Mkhitaryan were all on target.

Russia's players celebrate at the final whistle after their 3-2 victory over the Republic of Ireland in Dublin

Despite the hiccups, Russia, Ireland and Slovakia had unsurprisingly emerged as frontrunners, all three sharing top spot with six points from three games. Armenia were proving they could not be taken lightly, however. Indeed, Vardan Minasyan's underdogs briefly moved to the group summit when they put four unanswered goals past Andorra just days after their victory over Slovakia, with Movsisyan, Mkhitaryan and Ghazaryan all finding the net for the second time within a week. Their unbeaten run was stretched to four games following a hard-fought goalless draw with Russia in Yerevan, but Roman Pavlyuchenko finally broke Armenian resistance in the return fixture, plundering a hat-trick as Russia came from behind to win 3-1 in St Petersburg.

Even if their own chances of qualification were dented by that result, Armenia's ability to take points off the leaders seemed set to have a major bearing on the final outcome – particularly with the three favourites threatening to cancel one another out. That is exactly what happened at the Štadión MŠK Žilina in October when Slovakia and Ireland played out a 1-1 stalemate. Ján Ďurica and Sean St Ledger scored the goals, but it was Slovakia goalkeeper Ján Mucha – a mere bench-warmer at English Premier League club Everton FC – who emerged as the hosts' hero when he saved Keane's penalty.

Centurion Karhan

It had also been a special occasion for 1. FSV Mainz 05 midfielder Miroslav Karhan, described by his coach as Slovakia's best player as he won his 100th international cap. Karhan, who had missed Slovakia's World Cup adventure through injury, returned the compliment, saying: "If I should add one thing, it is a thank you to the coach Vladimír Weiss who believed in me when others said I was too old and not right for the national team."

Keane, who was also eyeing fresh landmarks, soon put that penalty miss behind him. Ireland's record scorer had taken his international tally to 46 with strikes against Andorra, Russia and FYROM before adding three further goals in the Nations Cup in May. His 50th and 51st goals arrived on 4 June as he registered twice in Ireland's 2-0 triumph in Skopje. "It's not about me, it's about the team qualifying for Poland and Ukraine," insisted Keane when asked to comment on his achievement. Instead it was left to team-mate Shay Given to lead the tributes to the half-centurion: "Robbie has a phenomenal record and he deserves all the headlines and all the credit," the goalkeeper said. "Not just for his goals but for his leadership and the way he has worked."

Ireland poised

Thanks to the exploits of their talismanic striker, Ireland were handily poised to reach their first major finals for a decade. Like Russia and Slovakia, Trapattoni's team had 13 points from six matches but topped the pool having scored more goals than the Russians. Armenia sat five points adrift, while FYROM looked stranded on four points, with rock-bottom Andorra bidding merely to end their run of six straight defeats when the action resumed in 2011/12.

Group B Results

3/9/10, Estadi Comunal, Andorra la Vella
Andorra 0-2 Russia
Attendance: 1100
Andorra: Gómes, Rubio (Lorenzo 57), Bernaus, Silva, Lima, Pujol (Mejías 88), Vieira, Gómez, Moreno (Jiménez 76), C. Martínez, Ayala. Coach: Koldo Álvarez (AND)
Russia: Akinfeev, Anyukov, V. Berezutskiy, Ignashevich, Bilyaletdinov, Semshov, Shirokov, Zyryanov, Pogrebnyak (Pavlyuchenko 85), Arshavin, Bystrov (Dzagoev 60). Coach: Dick Advocaat (NED)
Goal(s): 0-1 Pogrebnyak 14, 0-2 Pogrebnyak 64 (p)
Yellow Card(s): Ayala 20 (Andorra), Lima 26 (Andorra), Pujol 28 (Andorra), C. Martínez 66 (Andorra), Bilyaletdinov 75 (Russia)
Referee: Borg (MLT)

3/9/10, Yerevan Republican Stadium, Yerevan
Armenia 0-1 Republic of Ireland
Attendance: 8600
Armenia: Berezovski, K. Mkrtchyan, Hovsepyan, Arzumanyan, Arakelyan, Artur Yedigaryan (Manoyan 68), Malakyan (Manucharyan 79), Movsisyan, Pachajyan, Artak Yedigaryan (Hambartsumyan 71), Mkhitaryan. Coach: Vardan Minasyan (ARM)
Republic of Ireland: Given, St Ledger, Kilbane, O'Shea, Dunne, Whelan, Lawrence, Green, Doyle, Keane (Keogh 85), McGeady (Fahey 68). Coach: Giovanni Trapattoni (ITA)
Goal(s): 0-1 Fahey 76
Yellow Card(s): Artak Yedigaryan 62 (Armenia), Whelan 88 (Republic of Ireland)
Referee: Szabó (HUN)

3/9/10, Štadión Pasienky, Bratislava
Slovakia 1-0 FYROM
Attendance: 5980
Slovakia: Mucha, Pekarík (Sylvestr 90), Škrteľ, Weiss (Jendrišek 61), Štrba, Stoch, Sapara, Hološko, Hubočan, Saláta (Kucka 76), Hamšík. Coach: Vladimír Weiss (SVK)
FYROM: Nuredinoski, Sikov, G. Popov, Noveski, Mitreski, Georgievski, Trickovski (Grncarov 80), Sumulikoski, Pandev, Naumoski (Ristic 61), Despotovski (Lazevski 73). Coach: Mirsad Jonuz (MKD)
Goal(s): 1-0 Hološko 90+1
Red Card(s): Sikov 85 (FYROM)
Yellow Card(s): Despotovski 54 (FYROM), Sikov 66 (FYROM), Nuredinoski 77 (FYROM), Škrteľ 81 (Slovakia), Sikov 85 (FYROM), Pandev 86 (FYROM), Stoch 86 (Slovakia)
Referee: Circhetta (SUI)

7/9/10, National Arena Filip II, Skopje
FYROM 2-2 Armenia
Attendance: 9000
FYROM: Nuredinoski, Todorovski, G. Popov, Noveski, Mitreski, Georgievski (Despotovski 67), Trickovski, Sumulikoski, Ristic (Naumoski 62), Pandev, Gjurovski (Ilijoski 75). Coach: Vlatko Kostov (MKD)
Armenia: Berezovski, K. Mkrtchyan (Mkoyan 90+2), Hovsepyan, Arzumanyan, Arakelyan, Manoyan, Malakyan (Manucharyan 60), Movsisyan, Pachajyan (Artur Yedigaryan 70), Artak Yedigaryan, Mkhitaryan. Coach: Vardan Minasyan (ARM)
Goal(s): 0-1 Movsisyan 41, 1-1 Gjurovski 42, 1-2 Manucharyan 90+1, 2-2 Naumoski 90+6 (p)
Yellow Card(s): Gjurovski 42 (FYROM), K. Mkrtchyan 63 (Armenia), Arakelyan 67 (Armenia), Naumoski 67 (FYROM), Movsisyan 77 (Armenia)
Referee: Berntsen (NOR)

7/9/10, Dublin Arena, Dublin
Republic of Ireland 3-1 Andorra
Attendance: 40283
Republic of Ireland: Given, St Ledger, Kilbane, O'Shea (Kelly 75), Dunne, Whelan (Gibson 61), Lawrence, Green, Doyle (Keogh 82), Keane, McGeady. Coach: Giovanni Trapattoni (ITA)
Andorra: Gómes, Bernaus, Silva, Lima, Pujol (Sonejee 86), Vieira, Gómez, Moreno (Jiménez 59), C. Martínez, Ayala (Andorrà 71), Escura. Coach: Koldo Álvarez (AND)
Goal(s): 1-0 Kilbane 15, 2-0 Doyle 41, 2-1 C. Martínez 45, 3-1 Keane 54
Yellow Card(s): Silva 31 (Andorra), Lima 34 (Andorra), Moreno 58 (Andorra), Dunne 62 (Republic of Ireland)
Referee: Trattou (CYP)

7/9/10, Lokomotiv Stadion, Moscow
Russia 0-1 Slovakia
Attendance: 27052
Russia: Akinfeev, Anyukov, V. Berezutskiy, Ignashevich (Bilyaletdinov 81), Zhirkov, Semshov (Bystrov 61), Shirokov, Zyryanov, Pogrebnyak (Pavlyuchenko 71), Arshavin, Dzagoev. Coach: Dick Advocaat (NED)
Slovakia: Mucha, Škrteľ, Zabavník, Karhan (Sapara 73), Štrba, Stoch (Pečalka 90+2), Hološko, Hubočan, Saláta, Hamšík, Kucka (Jendrišek 58). Coach: Vladimír Weiss (SVK)
Goal(s): 0-1 Stoch 27
Yellow Card(s): Zhirkov 33 (Russia), Kucka 38 (Slovakia)
Referee: De Bleeckere (BEL)

8/10/10, Estadi Comunal, Andorra la Vella
Andorra 0-2 FYROM
Attendance: 550
Andorra: Gómes, Bernaus, Silva, C. Martínez (Jiménez 74), Vieira, Gómez, Moreno, Mejías (Lorenzo 62), Ayala (Bousenine 86), Escura, Vales. Coach: Koldo Álvarez (AND)
FYROM: Nuredinoski, Sikov, Noveski, Mitreski, Georgievski (Gjurovski 34), Trickovski, Sumulikoski (Grncarov 83), Ristic, Naumoski (A. Ibraimi 73), Despotovski, Lazarevski. Coach: Mirsad Jonuz (MKD)
Goal(s): 0-1 Naumoski 42, 0-2 Sikov 60
Yellow Card(s): Escura 44 (Andorra)
Referee: Mazeika (LTU)

8/10/10, Yerevan Republican Stadium, Yerevan
Armenia 3-1 Slovakia
Attendance: 8500
Armenia: Berezovski, K. Mkrtchyan, Hovsepyan, Arzumanyan (Arakelyan 79), Marcos (Artur Yedigaryan 72), G. Ghazaryan, Movsisyan, Mkoyan, Pachajyan (Manucharyan 46), Artak Yedigaryan, Mkhitaryan. Coach: Vardan Minasyan (ARM)
Slovakia: Mucha, Pekarík, Škrteľ, Zabavník (Šebo 81), Karhan, Weiss, Šesták, Stoch (Hološko 57), Kopúnek (Kucka 57), Saláta, Hamšík. Coach: Vladimír Weiss (SVK)
Goal(s): 1-0 Movsisyan 23, 1-1 Weiss 37, 2-1 G. Ghazaryan 50, 3-1 Mkhitaryan 89

Yellow Card(s): Škrteľ 18 (Slovakia), K. Mkrtchyan 19 (Armenia), Kopúnek 48 (Slovakia), Zabavník 68 (Slovakia)
Referee: Orsato (ITA)

8/10/10, Dublin Arena, Dublin
Republic of Ireland 2-3 Russia
Attendance: 50411
Republic of Ireland: Given, St Ledger, Kilbane, O'Shea, Dunne, Whelan (Gibson 66), Lawrence (Long 62), Green, Doyle (Fahey 71), Keane, McGeady. Coach: Giovanni Trapattoni (ITA)
Russia: Akinfeev, Anyukov, V. Berezutskiy, Ignashevich, Zhirkov, Shirokov, Denisov, Zyryanov (Semshov 68), Kerzhakov (Pogrebnyak 80), Arshavin, Dzagoev (A. Berezutskiy 85). Coach: Dick Advocaat (NED)
Goal(s): 0-1 Kerzhakov 11, 0-2 Dzagoev 29, 0-3 Shirokov 50, 1-3 Keane 72 (p), 2-3 Long 78
Yellow Card(s): Denisov 27 (Russia), St Ledger 32 (Republic of Ireland), Doyle 57 (Republic of Ireland), Anyukov 60 (Russia), A. Berezutskiy 89 (Russia)
Referee: Blom (NED)

12/10/10, Yerevan Republican Stadium, Yerevan
Armenia 4-0 Andorra
Attendance: 12000
Armenia: Berezovski, Hovsepyan, Arzumanyan, Artur Yedigaryan, Marcos (Yusbashyan 83), G. Ghazaryan (Malakyan 67), Manucharyan, Movsisyan (Goharyan 53), Mkoyan, Artak Yedigaryan, Mkhitaryan. Coach: Vardan Minasyan (ARM)
Andorra: Gómes, Bernaus, Silva, Lima, C. Martínez (Rubio 87), Vieira, Gómez, Moreno (Jiménez 51), Vales (Andorrà 64), Ayala, Escura. Coach: Koldo Álvarez (AND)
Goal(s): 1-0 G. Ghazaryan 4, 2-0 Mkhitaryan 16, 3-0 Movsisyan 33, 4-0 Marcos 52
Yellow Card(s): Silva 58 (Andorra), Lima 61 (Andorra), Vieira 68 (Andorra), Andorrà 74 (Andorra)
Referee: Mikulski (POL)

Ireland defender Richard Dunne outjumps his Slovakian counterpart Kornel Saláta during the 1-1 draw in Zilina

12/10/10, National Arena Filip II, Skopje
FYROM 0-1 Russia
Attendance: 10500
FYROM: Nuredinoski, Sikov, Noveski, Mitreski, Trickovski, Sumulikoski, Gjurovski (Alimi 79), Naumoski, Despotovski (Georgievski 78), Lazevski, A. Ibraimi (Ristic 49). Coach: Mirsad Jonuz (MKD)
Russia: Akinfeev, Anyukov, V. Berezutskiy, Ignashevich, Zhirkov, Shirokov, Denisov, Zyryanov, Kerzhakov (Pogrebnyak 79), Arshavin (Bystrov 81), Dzagoev (A. Berezutskiy 61). Coach: Dick Advocaat (NED)
Goal(s): 0-1 Kerzhakov 8
Yellow Card(s): Noveski 22 (FYROM), Sikov 36 (FYROM), Zyryanov 50 (Russia), Anyukov 57 (Russia), Ignashevich 72 (Russia)
Referee: Johannesson (SWE)

12/10/10, Štadión MŠK Žilina, Zilina
Slovakia 1-1 Republic of Ireland
Attendance: 10892
Slovakia: Mucha, Ďurica, Zabavník, Karhan, Weiss (Stoch 70), Šesták (Hološko 70), Hubočan, Saláta, Hamšík, Jendrišek (Oravec 84), Kucka. Coach: Vladimír Weiss (SVK)
Republic of Ireland: Given, St Ledger, Kilbane, O'Shea, Dunne, Whelan, Fahey (Keogh 71), Green (Gibson 42), Long, Keane, McGeady. Coach: Giovanni Trapattoni (ITA)
Goal(s): 0-1 St Ledger 16, 1-1 Ďurica 36
Yellow Card(s): Hubočan 18 (Slovakia), Šesták 32 (Slovakia), Mucha 45+1 (Slovakia), Karhan 90+1 (Slovakia)
Referee: Undiano Mallenco (ESP)

26/3/11, Estadi Comunal, Andorra la Vella
Andorra 0-1 Slovakia
Attendance: 850
Andorra: Gómes, Rubio, Bernaus, E. García, Lima, C. Martínez, Gómez (Vieira 72), Jiménez (Sonejee 87), Moreno, Vales, Ayala (Juli Sánchez 81). Coach: Koldo Álvarez (AND)
Slovakia: Mucha, Pekarík, Škrteľ, Ďurica, Vittek (Piroska 78), Stoch (Saláta 90), Hamšík, Jendrišek (Hološko 87), Lukšík, Kóňa, Šebo. Coach: Vladimír Weiss (SVK)
Goal(s): 0-1 Šebo 21
Yellow Card(s): Moreno 35 (Andorra), Stoch 54 (Slovakia), Jiménez 58 (Andorra), Mucha 65 (Slovakia)
Referee: Masiah (ISR)

26/3/11, Yerevan Republican Stadium, Yerevan
Armenia 0-0 Russia
Attendance: 14800
Armenia: Berezovski, Hayrapetyan (Artak Yedigaryan 67), Hovsepyan, Arzumanyan, K. Mkrtchyan, Marcos (Artur Yedigaryan 57), Malakyan (Manucharyan 49), G. Ghazaryan, Movsisyan, Mkoyan, Mkhitaryan. Coach: Vardan Minasyan (ARM)
Russia: Akinfeev, Shishkin, V. Berezutskiy, Ignashevich, Zhirkov, Shirokov, Denisov, Zyryanov, Kerzhakov (Pogrebnyak 78), Arshavin (Bilyaletdinov 90), Dzagoev. Coach: Dick Advocaat (NED)
Yellow Card(s): Hayrapetyan 33 (Armenia), Shishkin 63 (Russia), Manucharyan 87 (Armenia)
Referee: Thomson (SCO)

26/3/11, Dublin Arena, Dublin
Republic of Ireland 2-1 FYROM
Attendance: 33200
Republic of Ireland: Westwood, Foley, Kilbane, O'Dea, Dunne, Whelan, McGeady, Gibson (Fahey 77), Doyle (Long 20), Keane (McCarthy 87), Duff. Coach: Giovanni Trapattoni (ITA)
FYROM: Nuredinovski, Sikov, G. Popov, Noveski, Trickovski, Sumulikoski, Pandev, Naumoski (Ristic 68), Grncarov, Tasevski (Gjurovski 61), Demiri (Georgievski 84). Coach: Mirsad Jonuz (MKD)
Goal(s): 1-0 McGeady 2, 2-0 Keane 21, 2-1 Trickovski 45
Yellow Card(s): Westwood 48 (Republic of Ireland), Grncarov 50 (FYROM), G. Popov 57 (FYROM), Dunne 67 (Republic of Ireland), Gibson 70 (Republic of Ireland), Demiri 80 (FYROM)
Referee: Vad (HUN)

4/6/11, National Arena Filip II, Skopje
FYROM 0-2 Republic of Ireland
Attendance: 29500
FYROM: Bogatinov, Grncarov, G. Popov, Noveski, Sikov, Trickovski, Sumulikoski, Demiri (Savic 72), Pandev, Naumoski (Hasani 10), Despotovski (Gjurovski 57). Coach: Mirsad Jonuz (MKD)
Republic of Ireland: Given, Kelly, Kilbane, O'Shea, O'Dea, Whelan, McGeady, Andrews, Cox (Long 65), Keane, Hunt. Coach: Giovanni Trapattoni (ITA)
Goal(s): 0-1 Keane 8, 0-2 Keane 37
Yellow Card(s): Cox 16 (Republic of Ireland)
Referee: Meyer (GER)

4/6/11, Petrovskiy Stadion, St Petersburg
Russia 3-1 Armenia
Attendance: 18000
Russia: Akinfeev, Anyukov (Yanbaev 75), V. Berezutskiy, Ignashevich, Zhirkov, Semshov (Glushakov 69), Denisov, Zyryanov (Dzagoev 82), Pavlyuchenko, Arshavin, Torbinskiy. Coach: Dick Advocaat (NED)
Armenia: Berezovski, Hayrapetyan, Hovsepyan, Arzumanyan, K. Mkrtchyan (Artak Yedigaryan 90), Marcos (Artur Yedigaryan 67), G. Ghazaryan, Movsisyan, Mkoyan, Mkhitaryan, Pachajyan (Manucharyan 57). Coach: Vardan Minasyan (ARM)
Goal(s): 0-1 Marcos 25, 1-1 Pavlyuchenko 26, 2-1 Pavlyuchenko 59, 3-1 Pavlyuchenko 73 (p)
Yellow Card(s): Movsisyan 21 (Armenia), Ignashevich 37 (Russia), Pachajyan 55 (Armenia), Artur Yedigaryan 71 (Armenia), Arzumanyan 76 (Armenia), Mkoyan 87 (Armenia), V. Berezutskiy 90+3 (Russia)
Referee: Lannoy (FRA)

Ireland's evergreen captain Robbie Keane finds the net at home to FYROM

4/6/11, Štadión Pasienky, Bratislava
Slovakia 1-0 Andorra
Attendance: 4300
Slovakia: Kello, Ďurica, Čech (Saláta 83), Karhan, Jež, Vittek, Hološko (Žofčák 74), Hubočan, Hamšík, Kucka (Šesták 46), Šebo. Coach: Vladimír Weiss (SVK)
Andorra: Gómes, Rubio, Bernaus, E. García, Lima, Vieira, Jiménez (Salvat 86), Silva (Gómez 63), C. Martínez, Vales, Ayala (Andorrà 16). Coach: Koldo Álvarez (AND)
Goal(s): 1-0 Karhan 63
Yellow Card(s): Jež 13 (Slovakia), Vales 32 (Andorra), Andorrà 76 (Andorra)
Referee: Jemini (ALB)

Group B Table

	Pld	Home					Away					Total					Pts
		W	D	L	F	A	W	D	L	F	A	W	D	L	F	A	
1 Republic of Ireland	6	2	0	1	7	6	2	1	0	4	0	4	1	1	11	6	13
2 Russia	6	1	0	1	3	4	3	1	0	6	0	4	1	1	9	4	13
3 Slovakia	6	2	1	0	3	4	2	0	1	3	0	4	1	1	6	4	13
4 Armenia	6	2	1	1	7	7	0	1	1	3	0	2	2	2	10	7	8
5 FYROM	6	0	1	2	2	8	1	0	2	3	0	1	1	4	5	8	4
6 Andorra	6	0	0	3	0	13	0	0	3	1	0	0	0	6	1	13	0

Remaining Fixtures

2/9/11
Andorra – Armenia
Republic of Ireland – Slovakia
Russia – FYROM

6/9/11
FYROM – Andorra
Russia – Republic of Ireland
Slovakia – Armenia

7/10/11
Andorra – Republic of Ireland
Armenia – FYROM
Slovakia – Russia

11/10/11
FYROM – Slovakia
Russia – Andorra
Republic of Ireland – Armenia

GROUP C

The disappointment of exiting the 2010 FIFA World Cup at the group stage prompted a changing of the guard for the Italian national team, with Cesare Prandelli replacing Marcello Lippi as coach and bringing with him a host of young players and fresh ideas.

New-look Italy

The former ACF Fiorentina boss was selected partly for his proven ability to work with younger players, and he signalled his intent by naming five uncapped starlets in his squad for the opening qualifier away to Estonia. "It's easier to blood youngsters at club level as there you have the possibility of working with them week in, week out," explained the one-time Juventus midfielder.

Initially the 2006 world champions struggled. Prandelli's debut ended with a friendly defeat by Ivory Coast, and a disjointed first-half performance in Tallinn suggested his new-look team – shorn of the retired Fabio Cannavaro – would need time to

Italy's new head coach Cesare Prandelli passes on instructions

find its feet. Indeed, a major upset was on the cards when Sergei Zenjov pounced on a mistake from goalkeeper Salvatore Sirigu to give Estonia the lead, only for a couple of Andrea Pirlo corners to save Azzurri blushes, with Antonio Cassano and Leonardo Bonucci providing the finishes to clinch a 2-1 win.

Bridge-building win

Cassano, who had been snubbed for South Africa, was enjoying an exciting renaissance under Prandelli and he turned in another match-winning display in the coach's first competitive home match, against the Faroe Islands, scoring one goal and setting up another during a 5-0 romp in Florence. Alberto Gilardino, Daniele De Rossi, Fabio Quagliarella and Pirlo were also on the scoresheet as the Azzurri went some way towards repairing the damaged relationship with their fans. "It was a wonderful evening because we managed to involve the people in the stadium and achieved our goal of creating a special atmosphere," Prandelli enthused.

Although Italy were subsequently held to a goalless draw in Belfast, they improved thereafter and by the end of the season appeared to have recovered the swagger of old. They were awarded a 3-0 win against Serbia in October after the Genoa encounter was abandoned due to crowd disturbances and flares thrown by away fans, and they followed that up by securing two more wins in more orthodox fashion. Newly-naturalised Brazilian-born midfielder Thiago Motta scored the only goal away to Slovenia, while Rossi, Cassano and Giampaolo Pazzini accounted for Estonia in Modena, taking the Italians' end-of-season tally to a healthy 16 points from six games, five more than closest pursuers Slovenia who had played a game more.

Precarious position

Slovenia's position looked slightly precarious given that two of their three wins had come against the Faroese. Matjaž Kek's team made an uncertain start in September, losing out to Corry Evans' 70th-minute strike for Northern Ireland in Maribor, before letting a lead slip late on away to fellow 2010 World Cup first-round fallers Serbia. Milivoje Novakovič had handed the visitors the lead on 63 minutes, only for Nikola Žigić to level four minutes from time.

Bidding to reach the finals for the second time, Slovenia sparked into life in October, picking up six points in four days. FC Groningen youngster Tim Matavž announced his arrival by scoring a hat-trick in the 5-1 win over the Faroe Islands, while an own goal from Andrei Sidorenkov handed Slovenia the points in Estonia. Goals were proving hard to come by, however, and after the 1-0 home defeat by Italy and a scoreless draw in Northern Ireland, Matavž became the first Slovenian scorer in 305 minutes when he netted again in the return fixture against the Faroese. Rógvi Baldvinsson also beat his own goalkeeper in Toftir as the visitors claimed a 2-0 triumph.

Shock home defeat

Serbia and Northern Ireland went into the summer having completed two games fewer than Slovenia, although the Serbs – three points adrift in third place – possessed only one game in hand having being forced to forfeit the encounter in Italy. While Vladimir Petrović's charges had good reason to regret the unruly behaviour of their supporters, their poor performance in Belgrade against Estonia four days earlier threatened to be equally costly. A routine win looked likely after Žigić scored, but the visitors turned the contest on its head with strikes from Tarmo Kink and Konstantin Vassiljev before a stoppage-time Aleksandar Luković own goal settled the outcome. Jubilant in victory, Estonia then undid most of their good work by taking just one point from their next four games – also at Serbia's expense, in a 1-1 home draw – and becoming the Faroe Islands' first victims in a EURO qualifier for 16 years, Fródi Benjaminsen and Arnbjørn Hansen striking to seal a memorable 2-0 win in early June.

The inconsistency of Italy's pursuers meant that any team down to Northern Ireland in fifth place was still capable of taking the runners-up berth with a strong finish to the campaign. Nigel Worthington's side were beaten only once in their first five games, going down 2-1 away to Serbia, for whom Marko Pantelić and Zoran Tošić scored. But after winning their opener in Slovenia and drawing at home to Italy, Northern Ireland's ambitions of reaching a first major tournament for over a quarter of a century were checked by disappointing draws away to the Faroe Islands (1-1) and at home to Slovenia (0-0).

Sergei Zenjov (No10) is congratulated after opening the scoring for Estonia against Italy in Tallinn

Group C Results

11/8/10, Lilleküla Arena, Tallinn
Estonia 2-1 Faroe Islands
Attendance: 5470
Estonia: Pareiko, Piiroja, Kruglov (Post 70), Dmitrijev, S. Puri (Purje 76), Oper (Saag 62), Kink, Vassiljev, Klavan, Jääger, Bärengrub. Coach: Tarmo Rüütli (EST)
Faroe Islands: Nielsen, Næs, Davidsen, Gregersen, Rubeksen, Petersen (Løkin 85), Benjaminsen, Samuelsen (J. Hansen 74), Borg (Poulsen 67), Holst, Edmundsson. Coach: Brian Kerr (IRL)
Goal(s): 0-1 Edmundsson 28, 1-1 Saag 90+1, 2-1 Piiroja 90+3
Yellow Card(s): Holst 21 (Faroe Islands), Edmundsson 36 (Faroe Islands), Nielsen 40 (Faroe Islands), Borg 52 (Faroe Islands)
Referee: Vučemilović-Šimunović Jr. (CRO)

3/9/10, Lilleküla Arena, Tallinn
Estonia 1-2 Italy
Attendance: 8600
Estonia: Pareiko, Rähn, Piiroja, Kruglov (Kink 82), Dmitrijev, S. Puri (Purje 77), Zenjov (Saag 63), Vunk, Vassiljev, Klavan, Jääger. Coach: Tarmo Rüütli (EST)
Italy: Sirigu, Molinaro, Chiellini, De Rossi, Pepe (Quagliarella 60), Pazzini, Cassano (Antonelli 80), Cassani, Montolivo (Palombo 75), Bonucci, Pirlo. Coach: Cesare Prandelli (ITA)
Goal(s): 1-0 Zenjov 31, 1-1 Cassano 60, 1-2 Bonucci 63
Yellow Card(s): Vunk 56 (Estonia), Klavan 85 (Estonia), Piiroja 90+7 (Estonia)
Referee: Velasco Carballo (ESP)

3/9/10, Tórsvøllur, Torshavn
Faroe Islands 0-3 Serbia
Attendance: 1847
Faroe Islands: Nielsen, Udsen (Mouritsen 46), Rubeksen, Davidsen, Gregersen, Næs, Benjaminsen, Petersen (J. Hansen 73), Samuelsen, Holst (A. Hansen 79), Edmundsson. Coach: Brian Kerr (IRL)
Serbia: Đuričić, Rukavina, Vidić, Lazović (Ninković 83), Stanković (Petrović 58), M. Jovanović, Obradović (Luković 46), Krasić, Žigić, Subotić, Kuzmanović. Coach: Rešad Kunovac (SRB)
Goal(s): 0-1 Lazović 14, 0-2 Stanković 18, 0-3 Žigić 90+1
Yellow Card(s): Obradović 32 (Serbia), Rukavina 86 (Serbia)
Referee: Toussaint (LUX)

3/9/10, Stadion Ljudski vrt, Maribor
Slovenia 0-1 Northern Ireland
Attendance: 12000
Slovenia: S. Handanovič, Brečko, Cesar, Koren, Ljubijankič (Matavž 88), Birsa, Novakovič (Dedič 74), Jokič, Kirm (Iličič 74), Radosavljevič, Mavrič. Coach: Matjaž Kek (SVN)
Northern Ireland: Taylor, McAuley, Cathcart, Craigan, Baird, Davis, McCann (C. Evans 67), Healy (Lafferty 67), Feeney, Brunt (Gorman 89), Hughes. Coach: Nigel Worthington (NIR)
Goal(s): 0-1 C. Evans 70
Yellow Card(s): Healy 26 (Northern Ireland), Brunt 47 (Northern Ireland), Lafferty 83 (Northern Ireland)
Referee: Balaj (ROU)

7/9/10, Stadio Artemio Franchi, Florence
Italy 5-0 Faroe Islands
Attendance: 19266
Italy: Viviano, De Silvestri, Chiellini, De Rossi (Palombo 76), Cassano, Gilardino (Pazzini 59), Antonelli, Montolivo, Bonucci, Pirlo, Rossi (Quagliarella 59). Coach: Cesare Prandelli (ITA)
Faroe Islands: Nielsen, Løkin (Næs 74), Rubeksen, Gregersen, Bø, Davidsen, Benjaminsen, Petersen, Mouritsen (Holst 74), Samuelsen, Edmundsson (Udsen 89). Coach: Brian Kerr (IRL)
Goal(s): 1-0 Gilardino 11, 2-0 De Rossi 22, 3-0 Cassano 27, 4-0 Quagliarella 81, 5-0 Pirlo 90
Yellow Card(s): Davidsen 7 (Faroe Islands)
Referee: Kulbakov (BLR)

7/9/10, Stadion FK Crvena zvezda, Belgrade
Serbia 1-1 Slovenia
Attendance: 24028
Serbia: Đuričić, Rukavina, Vidić, Tošić (Krasić 46), Lazović, Stanković (Kačar 71), Luković, M. Jovanović (Ninković 64), Žigić, Subotić, Kuzmanović. Coach: Rešad Kunovac (SRB)

Slovenia: S. Handanovič, Brečko, Cesar, Koren, Birsa (Iličič 78), Novakovič, Jokič, Dedič (Ljubijankič 77), Kirm (Stevanovič 89), Radosavljevič, Mavrič. Coach: Matjaž Kek (SVN)
Goal(s): 0-1 Novakovič 63, 1-1 Žigić 86
Yellow Card(s): Stanković 14 (Serbia), Radosavljevič 14 (Slovenia), S. Handanovič 16 (Slovenia), Kirm 32 (Slovenia), M. Jovanović 37 (Serbia), Žigić 42 (Serbia), Luković 58 (Serbia), Vidić 88 (Serbia), Mavrič 90+2 (Slovenia), Kuzmanović 90+4 (Serbia)
Referee: Olegário Benquerença (POR)

8/10/10, Windsor Park, Belfast
Northern Ireland 0-0 Italy
Attendance: 15200
Northern Ireland: Taylor, McAuley, J. Evans, Craigan, Baird, Davis, McCann (C. Evans 80), Healy (Lafferty 66), Feeney, Brunt (McGinn 71), Hughes. Coach: Nigel Worthington (NIR)
Italy: Viviano, Criscito, Chiellini, De Rossi, Mauri (Marchisio 79), Pepe (Rossi 84), Cassano, Borriello (Pazzini 74), Cassani, Pirlo, Bonucci. Coach: Cesare Prandelli (ITA)
Referee: Chapron (FRA)

8/10/10, FK Partizan, Belgrade
Serbia 1-3 Estonia
Attendance: 12000
Serbia: Stojković, Lomić, Kačar (Ninković 46), Vidić, Ivanović, Stanković, Luković, M. Jovanović (Tošić 46), Krasić, Žigić, Kuzmanović (Lazović 79). Coach: Vladimir Petrović (SRB)
Estonia: Pareiko, Rähn, Piiroja, Kruglov, Dmitrijev, S. Puri (Purje 70), Kink (Saag 64), Zenjov (Vunk 87), Vassiljev, Klavan, Jääger. Coach: Tarmo Rüütli (EST)
Goal(s): 1-0 Žigić 60, 1-1 Kink 63, 1-2 Vassiljev 73, 1-3 Luković 90+1 (og)
Yellow Card(s): Piiroja 10 (Estonia), Dmitrijev 53 (Estonia), Vassiljev 80 (Estonia), Krasić 80 (Serbia), Vidić 87 (Serbia), Lazović 90 (Serbia)
Referee: Layushkin (RUS)

A chance goes begging for Northern Ireland striker Kyle Lafferty against Serbia in Belgrade

8/10/10, ŠRC Stožice, Ljubljana
Slovenia 5-1 Faroe Islands
Attendance: 15750
Slovenia: S. Handanovič, Brečko, Šuler, Cesar, Koren, Birsa (Kirm 51), Novakovič (Dedič 73), Jokič, Radosavljevič (Bačinovič 59), Iličič, Matavž. Coach: Matjaž Kek (SVN)
Faroe Islands: Mikkelsen, Rubeksen, Næs, Gregersen, Bø, J. Hansen, Benjaminsen, Løkin (Elttør 41), Udsen (Petersen 81), Holst (Mouritsen 81), Edmundsson. Coach: Brian Kerr (IRL)
Goal(s): 1-0 Matavž 25, 2-0 Matavž 36, 3-0 Matavž 65, 4-0 Novakovič 72 (p), 5-0 Dedič 84, 5-1 Mouritsen 90+3
Yellow Card(s): J. Hansen 17 (Faroe Islands), Gregersen 26 (Faroe Islands), Cesar 29 (Slovenia), Benjaminsen 52 (Faroe Islands), Rubeksen 70 (Faroe Islands)
Referee: Todorov (BUL)

12/10/10, Lilleküla Arena, Tallinn
Estonia 0-1 Slovenia
Attendance: 5722
Estonia: Pareiko, Rähn (Palatu 55), Kruglov, Dmitrijev, S. Puri (Purje 69), Kink (Zenjov 59), Vassiljev, Klavan, Jääger, Saag, Sidorenkov. Coach: Tarmo Rüütli (EST)
Slovenia: S. Handanovič, Brečko, Šuler, Cesar, Koren, Birsa (Ljubijankič 90+1), Novakovič, Jokič, Radosavljevič, Iličič (Kirm 67), Matavž (Dedič 53). Coach: Matjaž Kek (SVN)
Goal(s): 0-1 Sidorenkov 67 (og)
Yellow Card(s): Kruglov 34 (Estonia), Birsa 83 (Slovenia)
Referee: Skjerven (NOR)

12/10/10, Svangaskard Stadion, Toftir
Faroe Islands 1-1 Northern Ireland
Attendance: 1921
Faroe Islands: Mikkelsen, Næs, E. Jacobsen, Davidsen, Gregersen, Udsen (Petersen 68), Benjaminsen, Samuelsen (A. Hansen 78), Holst (J. Hansen 85), Edmundsson, Elttør. Coach: Brian Kerr (IRL)
Northern Ireland: Taylor, McAuley, J. Evans, Craigan, Baird, Davis, McGinn (C. Evans 83), Lafferty, Feeney (Healy 50), Brunt, Hughes. Coach: Nigel Worthington (NIR)
Goal(s): 1-0 Holst 60, 1-1 Lafferty 76
Yellow Card(s): Næs 38 (Faroe Islands), Gregersen 72 (Faroe Islands), A. Hansen 84 (Faroe Islands), Davis 87 (Northern Ireland)
Referee: Zimmermann (SUI)

12/10/10, Stadio Luigi Ferraris, Genoa
Italy 3-0 Serbia (w/o; match abandoned after 6 mins)
Attendance: 28000
Italy: Viviano, Criscito, Chiellini, Mauri, Marchisio, Cassano, Palombo, Zambrotta, Pazzini, Pirlo, Bonucci. Coach: Cesare Prandelli (ITA)
Serbia: Brkić, Kačar, Ivanović, Tošić, Mrđa, Stanković, Luković, Krasić, Subotić, Rajković, Kuzmanović. Coach: Vladimir Petrović (SRB)
Yellow Card(s): Rajković 3 (Serbia)
Referee: Thomson (SCO)

25/3/11, Stadion FK Crvena zvezda, Belgrade
Serbia 2-1 Northern Ireland
Attendance: 350
Serbia: Brkić, Kolarov, Biševac, Ivanović, Tošić, Ljajić (M. Jovanović 46), Pantelić, Stanković, Milijaš (Ninković 46), Krasić (Petrović 86), Subotić. Coach: Vladimir Petrović (SRB)
Northern Ireland: Camp, Cathcart, J. Evans (McCourt 86), McAuley, Baird, C. Evans, Clingan, Gorman (Feeney 78), Lafferty (Healy 46), Brunt, Hughes. Coach: Nigel Worthington (NIR)
Goal(s): 0-1 McAuley 40, 1-1 Pantelić 65, 2-1 Tošić 74
Yellow Card(s): J. Evans 27 (Northern Ireland), Stanković 37 (Serbia), Pantelić 45+2 (Serbia), Krasić 55 (Serbia), Healy 62 (Northern Ireland)
Referee: Gumienny (BEL)

25/3/11, ŠRC Stožice, Ljubljana
Slovenia 0-1 Italy
Attendance: 15790
Slovenia: S. Handanovič, Brečko (Andjelković 70), Šuler, Cesar, Koren, Birsa (Iličič 74), Novakovič, Jokič, Dedič (Ljubijankič 56), Kirm, Radosavljevič. Coach: Matjaž Kek (SVN)
Italy: Buffon, Maggio, Chiellini, Thiago Motta, Mauri (Nocerino 63), Pazzini, Cassano (Rossi 74), Aquilani, Balzaretti, Montolivo (Marchisio 87), Bonucci. Coach: Cesare Prandelli (ITA)
Goal(s): 0-1 Thiago Motta 73
Yellow Card(s): Montolivo 55 (Italy), Cesar 80 (Slovenia), Thiago Motta 90+1 (Italy)
Referee: Brych (GER)

29/3/11, Lilleküla Arena, Tallinn
Estonia 1-1 Serbia
Attendance: 5185
Estonia: Pareiko, Rähn, Piiroja, Kruglov, Dmitrijev, S. Puri (Purje 29), Vassiljev, Klavan, Jääger, Ahjupera (Oper 55), Saag (Kink 66). Coach: Tarmo Rüütli (EST)
Serbia: Brkić, Kolarov, Biševac, Vidić, Ivanović, Tošić, Pantelić, Milijaš, M. Jovanović (Žigić 74), Petrović, Ninković (Trivunović 14). Coach: Vladimir Petrović (SRB)
Goal(s): 0-1 Pantelić 38, 1-1 Vassiljev 84
Yellow Card(s): Piiroja 16 (Estonia), Vassiljev 46 (Estonia), Purje 52 (Estonia), Milijaš 66 (Serbia), Biševac 83 (Serbia), Rähn 90+1 (Estonia)
Referee: Nijhuis (NED)

29/3/11, Windsor Park, Belfast
Northern Ireland 0-0 Slovenia
Attendance: 14200
Northern Ireland: Camp, Cathcart, J. Evans, McAuley, Craigan, Baird, C. Evans (Boyce 90+1), Clingan, Feeney (McCourt 82), Brunt, McCann (McQuoid 72). Coach: Nigel Worthington (NIR)
Slovenia: S. Handanovič, Brečko, Šuler, Koren, Birsa, Novakovič (Dedič 84), Jokič, Bačinovič (Šukalo 90), Kirm, Iličič (Ljubijankič 29), M. Mavrič. Coach: Matjaž Kek (SVN)
Yellow Card(s): Koren 34 (Slovenia), Bačinovič 38 (Slovenia), Baird 43 (Northern Ireland), C. Evans 53 (Northern Ireland), Brunt 89 (Northern Ireland)
Referee: Kuipers (NED)

3/6/11, Svangaskard Stadion, Toftir
Faroe Islands 0-2 Slovenia
Attendance: 974
Faroe Islands: Mikkelsen, Næs (S. Olsen 81), E. Hansen, Davidsen, Baldvinsson, Udsen (Danielsen 45+2), Benjaminsen, Justinussen, Elttør, Edmundsson, Holst (Mouritsen 75). Coach: Brian Kerr (IRL)
Slovenia: S. Handanovič, Brečko, Šuler, Cesar, Koren, Birsa (Mavrič 47), Novakovič (Ljubijankič 55), Jokič, Iličič, Bačinovič, Matavž (Kirm 76). Coach: Matjaž Kek (SVN)
Goal(s): 0-1 Matavž 29, 0-2 Baldvinsson 47 (og)
Red Card(s): Šuler 25 (Slovenia)
Yellow Card(s): Edmundsson 39 (Faroe Islands), Davidsen 62 (Faroe Islands)
Referee: Drachta (AUT)

3/6/11, Stadio Alberto Braglia, Modena
Italy 3-0 Estonia
Attendance: 19434
Italy: Buffon, Maggio, Chiellini, Balzaretti, Marchisio, Cassano (Pazzini 65), Aquilani (Nocerino 24), Ranocchia, Montolivo, Pirlo, Rossi (Giovinco 79). Coach: Cesare Prandelli (ITA)
Estonia: Pareiko, Teniste (Saag 58), Rähn, Piiroja, Kruglov, S. Puri, Kink (Kams 79), Zenjov (Ahjupera 58), Vunk, Klavan, Jääger. Coach: Tarmo Rüütli (EST)
Goal(s): 1-0 Rossi 21, 2-0 Cassano 39, 3-0 Pazzini 68
Yellow Card(s): Aquilani 8 (Italy), Klavan 42 (Estonia), Vunk 54 (Estonia)
Referee: Tudor (ROU)

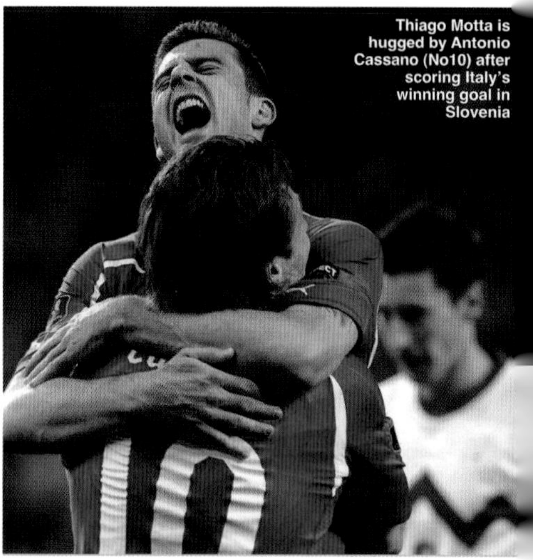
Thiago Motta is hugged by Antonio Cassano (No10) after scoring Italy's winning goal in Slovenia

7/6/11, Svangaskard Stadion, Toftir
Faroe Islands 2-0 Estonia
Attendance: 1715
Faroe Islands: Mikkelsen, Næs, E. Hansen, Gregersen, Baldvinsson, Danielsen, Benjaminsen, Elttør (S. Olsen 90+1), Justinussen, A. Hansen (Samuelsen 69), Holst (Mouritsen 85). Coach: Brian Kerr (IRL)
Estonia: Pareiko, Rähn, Piiroja, Kruglov, S. Puri, Kink, Zenjov, Vassiljev, Jääger, Ahjupera (Kams 66), Saag (Mošnikov 82). Coach: Tarmo Rüütli (EST)
Goal(s): 1-0 Benjaminsen 43 (p), 2-0 A.Hansen 47
Red Card(s): S. Puri 57 (Estonia), Justinussen 89 (Faroe Islands)
Yellow Card(s): S. Puri 42 (Estonia), Zenjov 46 (Estonia), S. Puri 57 (Estonia), Pareiko 75 (Estonia), Justinusen 75 (Faroe Islands), Justinussen 89 (Faroe Islands)
Referee: Munukka (FIN)

Group C Table

		Home					Away					Total					
	Pld	W	D	L	F	A	W	D	L	F	A	W	D	L	F	A	Pts
1 Italy	6	3	0	0	11	1	2	1	0	3	0	5	1	0	14	1	16
2 Slovenia	7	1	0	2	5	4	2	2	0	4	0	3	2	2	9	4	11
3 Serbia	6	1	1	1	4	9	1	1	1	4	0	2	2	2	8	9	8
4 Estonia	7	1	1	2	4	11	1	0	2	3	0	2	1	4	7	11	7
5 Northern Ireland	5	0	2	0	0	3	1	1	1	3	0	1	3	1	3	3	6
6 Faroe Islands	7	1	1	2	3	18	0	0	3	2	0	1	1	5	5	18	4

Remaining Fixtures

10/8/11
Northern Ireland – Faroe Islands

2/9/11
Faroe Islands – Italy
Northern Ireland – Serbia
Slovenia – Estonia

6/9/11
Estonia – Northern Ireland
Italy – Slovenia
Serbia – Faroe Islands

7/10/11
Northern Ireland – Estonia
Serbia – Italy

11/10/11
Italy – Northern Ireland
Slovenia – Serbia

GROUP D

France were one of several major European teams looking to bounce back from a poor 2010 FIFA World Cup, and a wave of optimism swept the nation following the appointment of the talismanic Laurent Blanc, a world champion in 1998, as the successor to the unloved Raymond Domenech as national coach. It was not long, however, before Les Bleus received a harsh reality check.

Kislyak stunner

Blanc was afforded a warm reception by the Stade de France public prior to the opening qualifier against Belarus, yet excitement soon turned to anxiety as the youthful home team – which included only five survivors from South Africa – struggled to break down a well-organised visiting unit. With France growing frustrated, Bernd Stange's men stunned the two-time European champions with a clinical breakaway goal on 86 minutes, substitute Sergei Kislyak sweeping home after fine work from Vyacheslav Hleb.

As the home fans booed and Blanc contemplated the size of the task that lay ahead of him, Belarus celebrated a victory that goalkeeper Yuriy Zhevnov called "one of the biggest in our history". Zhevnov added: "It's going to take a bit of time before we realise what we've done." Disappointingly, the win was backed up by a pair of goalless draws against Romania and Luxembourg, but Belarus remained reasonably well placed at the end of the autumn phase after beating Albania with goals from Vitaliy Rodionov and Sergei Krivets.

France's new head coach Laurent Blanc turned things around after a poor start for Les Bleus in Group D

Timely triumph

France, meanwhile, arrived in Sarajevo for their second game under intense pressure. Bosnia & Herzegovina had already seen off Luxembourg 3-0 with efforts from Senijad Ibričić, Miralem Pjanić and Edin Džeko, giving them the opportunity to put six points between themselves and the section favourites with another win. The visitors delivered a much-improved display, however, controlling the midfield throughout and sealing a deserved 2-0 triumph with late goals from Karim Benzema and Florent Malouda.

Blanc's first victory would prove a turning point. The 2000 European champions showed impressive patience again in their next outing, at home to Romania, scoring twice in the last seven minutes through substitutes Loïc Rémy and Yoann Gourcuff and thus giving the supporters in Saint-Denis something to shout about at last. "It was tense because for as long as it stayed goalless there was always the chance of losing," defender Gaël Clichy pointed out. "But the fans kept encouraging us and we turned in a strong performance." With confidence flooding back, France's sequence of 2-0 wins was extended to four as they clinched back-to-back victories over Luxembourg and surged to the top of the standings. Although the 2010/11 season ended with a 1-1 draw in Minsk, Les Bleus remained in command of the section, a point clear of Belarus with a game in hand.

Lucescu resigns

No other side managed to get any sort of run going, which left the group bunched up with just four points separating Belarus in second from Albania in fifth. Bosnia & Herzegovina, in particular, proved highly inconsistent, recovering from the home defeat against France by drawing 1-1 in Albania and defeating Romania 2-1, only to lose their next outing 3-0 in Bucharest. Adrian Mutu opened the scoring before two Ciprian Marica goals sealed a fine win for a Romanian team that had failed to live up to expectations until then. Indeed, after witnessing his team take just two points from their first four fixtures, Răzvan

Lucescu was coming under increasing pressure. Despite overseeing successive wins over Luxembourg and Bosnia & Herzegovina, the coach announced his resignation in June after two years at the helm.

The timing of Lucescu's departure seemed odd because Romania's situation was far from desperate. They had actually leapfrogged Bosnia & Herzegovina following the Bucharest triumph – before Safet Sušić's charges moved back up to third courtesy of a 2-0 victory over Albania in Zenica four days later. Haris Medunjanin set the ball rolling on 67 minutes and after Andi Lila had been sent off for the visitors, Darko Maletić made sure of the points in added time.

Albania aspire

Belarus, Bosnia & Herzegovina and Romania ended the 2010/11 campaign one, three and five points, respectively, behind France, and while it was no great surprise to see those three nations competing for qualification, Albania's emergence, with eight points from six games, added some unexpected intrigue. Although yet to face France, Josip Kuže's side took points off every opponent they encountered. Gjergji Muzaka's strike three minutes from time secured a creditable 1-1 draw in Romania first time out, before Hamdi Salihi's solitary goal clinched victory over Luxembourg on 7 September, taking Albania briefly to the group summit. Klodian Duro's free-kick then cancelled out Vedad Ibišević's strike as honours were shared with Bosnia & Herzegovina in Tirana, and although Albania's unbeaten record ended with a pair of 2-0 defeats on trips to Minsk and Zenica, they remained in contention for second spot thanks to their slender home win over Belarus in March, when Salihi, a prolific marksman in Austrian football, again scored the all-important goal.

Group D Results

3/9/10, Stade de France, Paris
France 0-1 Belarus
Attendance: 76395
France: Lloris, Sagna, Rami, Mexès, Rémy (Valbuena 34), Ménez (Saha 69) (Gameiro 80), Hoarau, Malouda, M'Vila, Diaby, Clichy. Coach: Laurent Blanc (FRA)
Belarus: Zhevnov, Kulchiy, Martynovich, Yurevich, Tigorev, Omelyanchuk, V. Hleb (Putilo 89), A. Hleb, Rodionov (Kornilenko 85), Kutuzov (Kislyak 75), Shitov. Coach: Bernd Stange (GER)
Goal(s): 0-1 Kislyak 86
Yellow Card(s): Tigorev 14 (Belarus), Rodionov 49 (Belarus)
Referee: Collum (SCO)

3/9/10, Josy Barthel, Luxembourg
Luxembourg 0-3 Bosnia & Herzegovina
Attendance: 7327
Luxembourg: Joubert, Kintziger, Jänisch, Hoffmann, Schnell, Peters, Bensi (Kitenge 46), Bettmer (Laterza 86), Collette (Da Mota 76), Mutsch, Gerson. Coach: Michel Ney (LUX)
Bosnia & Herzegovina: Hasagić, Spahić, Rahimić (Jahić 68), Pjanić (Zec 78), Misimović, Džeko, Nadarević, Ibišević, Lulić, Ibričić (Medunjanin 73), Mujdža. Coach: Safet Sušić (BIH)
Goal(s): 0-1 Ibričić 6, 0-2 Pjanić 12, 0-3 Džeko 16
Yellow Card(s): Hoffmann 11 (Luxembourg), Bensi 38 (Luxembourg)
Referee: Banari (MDA)

3/9/10, Stadionul Ceahlăul, Piatra Neamt
Romania 1-1 Albania
Attendance: 13400
Romania: Lobonţ, Contra (Mureşan 56), Raţ , Tamaş, Rădoi, Torje, Deac, Marica, Florescu, Cociş (Herea 77), D. Niculae (Stancu 64). Coach: Răzvan Lucescu (ROU)
Albania: Beqaj, Lila, Vangjeli, Dallku, Cana, Curri, Agolli, Bulku, Duro (Muzaka 81), Skela (Lika 79), Bogdani (Salihi 57). Coach: Josip Kuže (CRO)
Goal(s): 1-0 Stancu 80, 1-1 Muzaka 87
Yellow Card(s): Raţ 40 (Romania), Vangjeli 50 (Albania), Herea 87 (Romania)
Referee: Schörgenhofer (AUT)

7/9/10, Stadiumi Kombëtar Qemal Stafa, Tirana
Albania 1-0 Luxembourg
Attendance: 10000
Albania: Beqaj, Dallku, Cana, Curri, Agolli, Bulku, Duro (Lila 90+1), Skela, Salihi, Muzaka (Hyka 80), Bogdani. Coach: Josip Kuže (CRO)
Luxembourg: Joubert, Kintziger, Blaise, Hoffmann, Schnell, Peters, Laterza (Martino 81), Bettmer (Collette 90+1), Da Mota, Payal, Mutsch. Coach: Luc Holtz (LUX)
Goal(s): 1-0 Salihi 37
Red Card(s): Mutsch 58 (Luxembourg)
Yellow Card(s): Mutsch 23 (Luxembourg), Peters 28 (Luxembourg), Mutsch 58 (Luxembourg), Bogdani 85 (Albania), Bulku 86 (Albania)
Referee: Trutz (SVK)

Romania striker Ciprian Marica – a double goalscorer in the 3-0 home win over Bosnia & Herzegovina

7/9/10, Dinamo Stadion, Minsk
Belarus 0-0 Romania
Attendance: 26354
Belarus: Zhevnov, Kulchiy, Martynovich, Yurevich, Omelyanchuk, Kornilenko (Rodionov 76), V. Hleb, A. Hleb (Putilo 73), Kutuzov (Krivets 87), Kislyak, Shitov. Coach: Bernd Stange (GER)
Romania: Pantilimon, Raţ , Tamaş, Chivu, Rădoi, Torje (Cociş 46), Deac (Marica 83), Florescu, Maftei, Bilaşco, Stancu (D. Niculae 73). Coach: Răzvan Lucescu (ROU)
Yellow Card(s): Deac 72 (Romania), Rădoi 88 (Romania), Maftei 90+1 (Romania)
Referee: Kralovec (CZE)

7/9/10, Asim Ferhatović Hase Stadion, Sarajevo
Bosnia & Herzegovina 0-2 France
Attendance: 28000
Bosnia & Herzegovina: Hasagić, Spahić, Rahimić (Zec 74), Pjanić, Misimović, Džeko, Nadarević, Ibišević (Jahić 74), Lulić, Ibričić, Mujdža. Coach: Safet Sušić (BIH)
France: Lloris, Sagna, Rami, Mexès, Benzema, Malouda (Matuidi 80), M'Vila, A. Diarra, Diaby, Valbuena, Clichy. Coach: Laurent Blanc (FRA)
Goal(s): 0-1 Benzema 72, 0-2 Malouda 78
Yellow Card(s): Valbuena 40 (France), Pjanić 45 (Bosnia & Herzegovina), Ibričić 71 (Bosnia & Herzegovina)
Referee: Brych (GER)

8/10/10, Stadiumi Kombëtar Qemal Stafa, Tirana
Albania 1-1 Bosnia & Herzegovina
Attendance: 14220
Albania: Beqaj, Lila, Vangjeli, Dallku, Cana, Agolli, Bulku, Duro, Salihi (Hyka 85), Muzaka (Lika 65), Bogdani (Skela 46). Coach: Džemal Mustedanagić (BIH)
Bosnia & Herzegovina: Hasagić (Begović 46), Spahić, Mravac (Pandža 46), Rahimić, Pjanić, Misimović, Džeko (Ibričić 89), Ibišević, Medunjanin, Lulić, Mujdža. Coach: Safet Sušić (BIH)
Goal(s): 0-1 Ibišević 21, 1-1 Duro 45+2
Yellow Card(s): Bogdani 9 (Albania), Dallku 38 (Albania), Lulić 39 (Bosnia & Herzegovina), Mravac 45 (Bosnia & Herzegovina), Spahić 53 (Bosnia & Herzegovina)
Referee: Jakobsson (ISL)

8/10/10, Josy Barthel, Luxembourg
Luxembourg 0-0 Belarus
Attendance: 1857
Luxembourg: Joubert, Kintziger, Blaise, Hoffmann, Schnell, Peters, Laterza, Bettmer (Gerson 62), Payal (Kettenmeyer 77), C. Leweck, Joachim (Da Mota 66). Coach: Luc Holtz (LUX)
Belarus: Zhevnov, Kulchiy, Martynovich, Kalachev, Yurevich (Molosh 87), Tigorev (Putilo 67), Omelyanchuk, Kornilenko, V. Hleb (Rodionov 67), Kislyak, Shitov. Coach: Bernd Stange (GER)
Red Card(s): Kornilenko 69 (Belarus)
Yellow Card(s): Kulchiy 59 (Belarus), Kalachev 74 (Belarus), Kintziger 74 (Luxembourg)
Referee: Stavrev (MKD)

9/10/10, Stade de France, Paris
France 2-0 Romania
Attendance: 79299
France: Lloris, Réveillère, Rami, Mexès, Benzema (Payet 86), Nasri (Gourcuff 74), Malouda, M'Vila, A. Diarra, Valbuena (Rémy 68), Clichy. Coach: Laurent Blanc (FRA)
Romania: Pantilimon, Săpunaru, Raţ , Tamaş, Chivu, Rădoi, Florescu, Cociş (Roman 87), Stancu, Zicu (Deac 46), D. Niculae (Marica 63). Coach: Răzvan Lucescu (ROU)
Goal(s): 1-0 Rémy 83, 2-0 Gourcuff 90+3
Yellow Card(s): Săpunaru 30 (Romania), A. Diarra 45 (France), Mexès 82 (France), Florescu 86 (Romania)
Referee: Proença (POR)

12/10/10, Dinamo Stadion, Minsk
Belarus 2-0 Albania
Attendance: 7000
Belarus: Zhevnov, Kulchiy (Krivets 75), Martynovich, Kalachev, Tigorev, Omelyanchuk, Putilo (V. Hleb 83), Kislyak, Shitov, Rodionov, Molosh (Yurevich 87). Coach: Bernd Stange (GER)
Albania: Beqaj, Lila, Vangjeli, Dallku, Agolli, Bulku (Muzaka 59), Duro, Skela (Kapllani 81), Teli, Lika (Bakaj 76), Salihi. Coach: Džemal Mustedanagić (BIH)
Goal(s): 1-0 Rodionov 10, 2-0 Krivets 77
Red Card(s): Dallku 90 (Albania)
Yellow Card(s): Dallku 10 (Albania), Lika 28 (Albania), Skela 42 (Albania), Molosh 47 (Belarus), Kalachev 52 (Belarus), Putilo 79 (Belarus), Dallku 90 (Albania)
Referee: Rasmussen (DEN)

12/10/10, Stade Municipal Saint-Symphorien, Metz
France 2-0 Luxembourg
Attendance: 24710
France: Lloris, Réveillère, Rami, Mexès, Gourcuff, Hoarau (Rémy 73), Benzema (Payet 63), Malouda (Nasri 63), A. Diarra, Diaby, Clichy. Coach: Laurent Blanc (FRA)
Luxembourg: Joubert, Blaise, Hoffmann, Schnell, Peters, Bettmer (Da Mota 84), Payal, C. Leweck, Joachim (Kitenge 53), Laterza (Strasser 69), Mutsch. Coach: Luc Holtz (LUX)
Goal(s): 1-0 Benzema 22, 2-0 Gourcuff 76
Red Card(s): Peters 54 (Luxembourg)
Yellow Card(s): Peters 30 (Luxembourg), Rami 42 (France), Peters 54 (Luxembourg)
Referee: Jug (SVN)

25/3/11, Josy Barthel, Luxembourg
Luxembourg 0-2 France
Attendance: 8052
Luxembourg: Joubert, Blaise, Hoffmann, Schnell, C. Leweck (Plein 90), Bettmer, Payal, Joachim, Laterza (Martino 54), Mutsch, Gerson (Da Mota 71). Coach: Luc Holtz (LUX)
France: Lloris, Sagna, Evra, Rami, Mexès, Ribéry, Gourcuff, Benzema, Nasri, Malouda, M'Vila. Coach: Laurent Blanc (FRA)
Goal(s): 0-1 Mexès 28, 0-2 Gourcuff 72
Yellow Card(s): Mutsch 83 (Luxembourg)
Referee: Hagen (NOR)

26/3/11, Stadiumi Kombëtar Qemal Stafa, Tirana
Albania 1-0 Belarus
Attendance: 13826
Albania: Ujkani, Lila, Vangjeli, Cana, Agolli, Bulku, Skela (Duro 81), Lala, Teli, Salihi (Muzaka 90+3), Bogdani (Bakaj 75). Coach: Josip Kuže (CRO)
Belarus: Veremko, Kulchiy (Bychenok 62), Martynovich, Shitov, Molosh, Tigorev, Omelyanchuk, V. Hleb, Krivets (Kovel 46), Putilo (Sitko 82), Kislyak. Coach: Bernd Stange (GER)
Goal(s): 1-0 Salihi 62
Yellow Card(s): Salihi 17 (Albania), Lala 18 (Albania), Kulchiy 21 (Belarus), Shitov 32 (Belarus), Cana 38 (Albania), V. Hleb 49 (Belarus), Molosh 53 (Belarus)
Referee: Strömbergsson (SWE)

26/3/11, Bilino Polje, Zenica
Bosnia & Herzegovina 2-1 Romania
Attendance: 13000
Bosnia & Herzegovina: Hasagić, Spahić, Mravac, Rahimić, Pjanić, Misimović (Ibričić 81), Džeko, Mujdža, Ibišević (Muslimović 76), Lulić, Medunjanin (Maletić 70). Coach: Safet Sušić (BIH)
Romania: Pantilimon, Raţ , Tamaş, Alexa, Marica, Mutu, Torje (Cociş 70), Râpă, Goian, Florescu (Ropotan 76), Deac (Zicu 85). Coach: Răzvan Lucescu (ROU)
Goal(s): 0-1 Marica 29, 1-1 Ibišević 63, 2-1 Džeko 83
Yellow Card(s): Ibišević 54 (Bosnia & Herzegovina), Rahimić 78 (Bosnia & Herzegovina)
Referee: Teixeira Vitienes (ESP)

29/3/11, Stadionul Ceahlăul, Piatra Neamt
Romania 3-1 Luxembourg
Attendance: 13500
Romania: Tătăruşanu, Săpunaru, Raţ , Tamaş (Goian 65), Zicu, Ropotan, Marica, Mutu (Alexe 84), Stancu (Torje 46), Gardoş, Mureşan. Coach: Răzvan Lucescu (ROU)
Luxembourg: Joubert, Blaise, Hoffmann, Schnell (Martino 90), Peters, C. Leweck, Bettmer (Laterza 81), Payal, Joachim, Mutsch, Gerson (Da Mota 58). Coach: Luc Holtz (LUX)
Goal(s): 0-1 Gerson 22, 1-1 Mutu 24, 2-1 Mutu 68, 3-1 Zicu 78
Yellow Card(s): Blaise 18 (Luxembourg), Tamaş 36 (Romania), Mutsch 82 (Luxembourg), Ropotan 87 (Romania)
Referee: Göçek (TUR)

3/6/11, Dinamo Stadion, Minsk
Belarus 1-1 France
Attendance: 26500
Belarus: Veremko, Martynovich, Kalachev (V. Hleb 90), Trubilo, Tigorev, Omelyanchuk, Voronkov, Putilo (Kislyak 86), Bordachev, Verkhovtsov, Shitov. Coach: Bernd Stange (GER)
France: Lloris, Sagna, Rami, Ribéry, Benzema, Nasri, Sakho, Malouda, A. Diarra, Diaby (Rémy 73), Abidal. Coach: Laurent Blanc (FRA)
Goal(s): 1-0 Abidal 20 (og), 1-1 Malouda 22
Yellow Card(s): Rami 19 (France), Sagna 25 (France), Kalachev 33 (Belarus), Veremko 86 (Belarus)
Referee: Fernández Borbalán (ESP)

3/6/11, Giuleşti-Valentin Stănescu, Bucharest
Romania 3-0 Bosnia & Herzegovina
Attendance: 8200
Romania: Tătăruşanu, Raţ, Tamaş, Mureşan, Marica (Alexe 87), Mutu (Surdu 83), Torje, Papp, Bourceanu, Sânmărtean (Tănase 63), Săpunaru. Coach: Răzvan Lucescu (ROU)
Bosnia & Herzegovina: Hasagić, Spahić, Mravac, Rahimić, Pjanić, Misimović, Džeko (Muslimović 64), Mujdža, Lulić, Ibričić (Štilić 64), Medunjanin (Ibišević 46). Coach: Safet Sušić (BIH)
Goal(s): 1-0 Mutu 37, 2-0 Marica 41, 3-0 Marica 55
Yellow Card(s): Torje 68 (Romania), Săpunaru 72 (Romania), Štilić 77 (Bosnia & Herzegovina), Surdu 90+1 (Romania)
Referee: Eriksson (SWE)

7/6/11, Dinamo Stadion, Minsk
Belarus 2-0 Luxembourg
Attendance: 9500
Belarus: Zhevnov, Kulchiy (Kislyak 87), Kalachev, Trubilo (V. Hleb 62), Tigorev, Omelyanchuk, Voronkov (Kornilenko 46), Putilo, Bordachev, Verkhovtsov, Shitov. Coach: Bernd Stange (GER)
Luxembourg: Joubert, Martino, Blaise, Hoffmann, Schnell, Peters, C. Leweck (Collette 84), Da Mota (Laterza 77), Payal, Malget (Kitenge 60), Gerson. Coach: Luc Holtz (LUX)
Goal(s): 1-0 Kornilenko 48 (p), 2-0 Putilo 73
Yellow Card(s): Voronkov 38 (Belarus), Payal 46 (Luxembourg)
Referee: Salmanov (AZE)

7/6/11, Bilino Polje, Zenica
Bosnia & Herzegovina 2-0 Albania
Attendance: 9000
Bosnia & Herzegovina: Hasagić, Pandža, Spahić, Rahimić, Pjanić (Bešić 77), Misimović, Džeko, Mujdža (Maletić 73), Ibišević (Muslimović 61), Lulić, Medunjanin. Coach: Safet Sušić (BIH)
Albania: Ujkani, Vangjeli, Dallku, Cana, Curri, Agolli (Lila 60), Bulku, Skela, Lala (Muzaka 73), Salihi, Bogdani (Duro 46). Coach: Josip Kuže (CRO)
Goal(s): 1-0 Medunjanin 67, 2-0 Maletić 90+1
Red Card(s): Lila 87 (Albania)
Yellow Card(s): Maletić 77 (Bosnia & Herzegovina), Duro 78 (Albania)
Referee: Blom (NED)

Group D Table

		Home					Away					Total					
	Pld	W	D	L	F	A	W	D	L	F	A	W	D	L	F	A	Pts
1 France	6	2	0	1	4	2	2	1	0	5	0	4	1	1	9	2	13
2 Belarus	7	2	2	0	5	2	1	1	1	1	0	3	3	1	6	2	12
3 Bosnia & Herzegovina	6	2	0	1	4	7	1	1	1	4	0	3	1	2	8	7	10
4 Romania	6	2	1	0	7	6	0	1	2	1	0	2	2	2	8	6	8
5 Albania	6	2	1	0	3	6	0	1	2	1	0	2	2	2	4	6	8
6 Luxembourg	7	0	1	2	0	13	0	0	4	1	0	0	1	6	1	13	1

Remaining Fixtures

2/9/11
Albania – France
Belarus – Bosnia & Herzegovina
Luxembourg – Romania

6/9/11
Bosnia & Herzegovina – Belarus
Luxembourg – Albania
Romania – France

7/10/11
Bosnia & Herzegovina – Luxembourg
France – Albania
Romania – Belarus

11/10/11
Albania – Romania
France – Bosnia & Herzegovina

GROUP E

The Netherlands, inspired by ace striker Klaas Jan Huntelaar, led the way in the most prolific of the nine UEFA EURO 2012 qualifying groups, maintaining the remarkably consistent run of form under Bert van Marwijk that had enabled them to finish runners-up at the 2010 FIFA World Cup finals in South Africa.

Goals galore

No fewer than 77 goals were scored in the first 19 Group E matches – an average of more than four a game and easily the highest of the nine pools. Although the Dutch outgunned their rivals – thanks in no small part to Huntelaar's contribution of eight goals, which made him the competition's joint-leading marksman – Sweden also showed fine form, finding the net 20 times, while Hungary weighed in with 18 goals. Only San Marino fired blanks, failing to score in their first seven outings and conceding 33 times.

The Netherlands were the first team to put San Marino to the sword, Van Marwijk's tyros signalling their intent with five unanswered goals in Serravalle. Huntelaar, a World Cup substitute, seized the opportunity to strengthen his claim on the centre-forward berth by scoring a hat-trick while Ruud van Nistelrooy also found the net on his return after two years in the wilderness. Huntelaar had been forced to settle for cameos in South

Klaas Jan Huntelaar powered the Netherlands to the top of the Group E table with eight goals in their first four fixtures

Africa but the FC Schalke 04 forward was now thriving as a starter, grabbing two more goals in a 2-1 win over Finland in Rotterdam four days later. "It has been an excellent week," said the ex-AC Milan and Real Madrid CF forward, adding: "It is good to be a striker for the Dutch team. The way the Oranje play suits me best."

Six in three

The 1988 European champions found Moldova a tougher nut to crack a month later, but Huntelaar's sixth strike in three games proved enough for victory in Chisinau, and the floodgates re-opened with 13 goals in the Netherlands' next three fixtures.

Sweden arrived in Amsterdam on 12 October in confident mood having eased to victories in their opening two games, Pontus Wernbloom's double accounting for Hungary before Zlatan Ibrahimović turned on the style against San Marino in front of a sell-out crowd in Malmo. The Milan forward, playing in his home town for the first time in nine years, thrilled an adoring public by scoring twice, while a pair of own goals and strikes from Andreas Granqvist and Marcus Berg completed a 6-0 rout. "It's difficult to describe the feeling," Ibrahimović said. "It felt fantastic – from the warm-up to the final whistle. When we were down to ten men [after Olof Mellberg's dismissal], the fans became our 11th man."

Huntelaar strikes again

Erik Hamrén's men were soon brought down to earth in the Dutch capital, however, Huntelaar maintaining his extraordinary average of two goals a game while Ibrahim Afellay – another World Cup bit-part player – also recorded a double in a convincing 4-1 triumph. Huntelaar's latest salvo took his international tally to 24 goals, equalling the legendary Marco van Basten's total despite having played 18 games fewer.

Sweden were not derailed by the heavy loss, winning their next three games. Mikael Lustig and Sebastian Larsson scored in Solna to seal a 2-1 victory over Moldova, who were then dispatched 4-1 in Chisinau following Johan Elmander's brace and further efforts from Ola Toivonen and Alexander Gerndt. Hamrén felt confident enough to leave Ibrahimović on the bench for the visit of Finland four days later, but the striker, who was working his way back to full fitness, entered the fray earlier than planned when Toivonen left the field injured after 25 minutes. The substitute duly helped himself to a hat-trick, inspiring a resounding 5-0 triumph that was book-ended by strikes from Kim Källström and Emir Bajrami. "It was probably the best substitution I've ever made," Hamrén joked.

Dutch double

Despite winning five of their six matches, Sweden remained three points adrift of the seemingly unstoppable Oranje who had wrapped up their 2010/11 campaign in March with back-to-back wins over Hungary. Sándor Egervári's team had warmed up for the double Dutch showdown by securing three successive wins. Moldova were defeated 2-1 in Budapest thanks to goals from Gergely Rudolf and Vladimir Koman, Ádám Szalai hit a hat-trick in the 8-0 demolition of San Marino, and Balász Dzsudzsák's late winner sealed an impressive 2-1 success in Finland.

Yet again, however, the Netherlands proved a class apart, running out resounding 4-0 victors in the Hungarian capital through Rafael van der Vaart, Afellay, Dirk Kuyt and Robin van Persie, then prevailing 5-3 in a thrilling contest at the Amsterdam ArenA. The visitors had Van Marwijk's team worried when Zoltán Gera scored his second goal of the evening to make it 3-3 with 15 minutes remaining, but two quick goals from Kuyt secured the team's perfect qualifying record under Van Marwijk with their 14th win in 14 matches.

No way back

A solid 3-0 triumph in San Marino in June provided solace for Hungary as goals from Zoltán Lipták, Imre Szabics and Vladimir Koman kept alive their faint qualification hopes. There appeared to be no way back for Finland, though, the Scandinavians having collected just six points – all at the expense of San Marino – from their six matches, the same number as Moldova. Named as Stuart Baxter's replacement in March, new Finland coach Mixu Paatelained clearly had much work to do ahead of the team's final four fixtures, three of which were at home. Both the Netherlands and Sweden were scheduled to play in Helsinki before their last-day showdown in the Råsundastadion on 11 October.

Zoltán Gera scored twice in vain as Hungary lost 5-3 to the Netherlands in Amsterdam

Group E Results

3/9/10, Zimbru, Chisinau
Moldova 2-0 Finland
Attendance: 10300
Moldova: St. Namasco, Savinov, Boret, Epureanu, Tigirlas (Bugaiov 68), Cebotari, Frunza, Josan (Suvorov 58), Bulgaru, Bordian, Doros (V. Andronic 75). Coach: Gavril Balint (ROU)
Finland: Fredrikson, Pasanen, Moisander, Hyypiä, R. Eremenko, Litmanen (Hämäläinen 46), Sparv, Johansson, Porokara (Väyrynen 75), A. Eremenko Jr. (Forssell 81), Heikkinen. Coach: Stuart Baxter (ENG)
Goal(s): 1-0 Suvorov 69, 2-0 Doroş 74
Red Card(s): Hyypiä 36 (Finland)
Yellow Card(s): Tigirlas 68 (Moldova), V. Andronic 87 (Moldova)
Referee: Malek (POL)

3/9/10, Stadio Olimpico, Serravalle
San Marino 0-5 Netherlands
Attendance: 4127
San Marino: A. Simoncini, F. Vitaioli, Vannucci, Berretti, D. Simoncini (Bacciocchi 61), Ales. Della Valle, Valentini, Mazza, Man. Marani (Gasperoni 76), Selva, M. Vitaioli (Ciacci 82). Coach: Giampaolo Mazza (SMR)
Netherlands: Stekelenburg, Van der Wiel, Maduro, Mathijsen, Pieters, Van Bommel, Kuyt (Van Nistelrooy 67), N. De Jong (Van Der Vaart 46), Huntelaar, Sneijder, Elia (Afellay 59). Coach: Bert van Marwijk (NED)
Goal(s): 0-1 Kuyt 16 (p), 0-2 Huntelaar 38, 0-3 Huntelaar 48, 0-4 Huntelaar 66, 0-5 Van Nistelrooy 90
Yellow Card(s): D. Simoncini 15 (San Marino), Maduro 35 (Netherlands), Ales. Della Valle 45 (San Marino), Berretti 45+1 (San Marino), Bacciocchi 64 (San Marino)
Referee: Evans (WAL)

3/9/10, Råsundastadion, Solna
Sweden 2-0 Hungary
Attendance: 32304
Sweden: Isaksson (Wiland 46), Lustig, Mellberg, Majstorovic, Safari, Toivonen, Svensson (Källström 33), Ibrahimović, Elmander (S. Larsson 49), Wernbloom, Bajrami. Coach: Erik Hamrén (SWE)
Hungary: Király, Lipták, Lázár, Juhász, Laczkó, Vadócz, Dzsudzsák (Huszti 46), Rudolf (Hajnal 82), Koman, Gera, Elek (Priskin 59). Coach: Sándor Egervári (HUN)
Goal(s): 1-0 Wernbloom 51, 2-0 Wernbloom 73
Yellow Card(s): Lipták 66 (Hungary), Toivonen 75 (Sweden), Király 86 (Hungary), Laczkó 90+1 (Hungary), Lázár 90+3 (Hungary)
Referee: Atkinson (ENG)

7/9/10, Ferenc Szusza, Budapest
Hungary 2-1 Moldova
Attendance: 9209
Hungary: Király, Lipták, Lázár, Juhász, Laczkó, Czvitkovics (Szalai 46), Dzsudzsák, Rudolf (Vanczák 64), Koman (Vadócz 88), Gera, Elek. Coach: Sándor Egervári (HUN)
Moldova: St. Namasco, Epureanu, Racu, Tigirlas, Cebotari (Cojocari 71), Frunza (Bugaiov 84), Josan (Doros 59), Bulgaru, Bordian, Suvorov, Bolohan. Coach: Gavril Balint (ROU)
Goal(s): 1-0 Rudolf 50, 2-0 Koman 66, 2-1 Suvorov 79
Yellow Card(s): Lipták 11 (Hungary), Frunza 28 (Moldova), Lázár 33 (Hungary)
Referee: Kovařík (CZE)

7/9/10, Feijenoord Stadion, Rotterdam
Netherlands 2-1 Finland
Attendance: 25000
Netherlands: Stekelenburg, Van der Wiel, Heitinga, Mathijsen, Anita, Van Bommel, Afellay (Lens 74), N. De Jong, Huntelaar (Van Nistelrooy 82), Sneijder, Van Der Vaart (Elia 64). Coach: Bert van Marwijk (NED)

Finland: Fredrikson, Pasanen, Moisander, Lampi, Väyrynen, R. Eremenko, Forssell (A. Eremenko Jr. 80), Sparv, Sjölund (Johansson 68), Hämäläinen (Porokara 46), Heikkinen. Coach: Stuart Baxter (ENG)
Goal(s): 1-0 Huntelaar 7, 2-0 Huntelaar 16 (p), 2-1 Forssell 18
Yellow Card(s): Heikkinen 16 (Finland), R. Eremenko 33 (Finland), Sparv 60 (Finland)
Referee: Nikolaev (RUS)

7/9/10, Swedbank Stadium, Malmo
Sweden 6-0 San Marino
Attendance: 21083
Sweden: Wiland, Lustig, Mellberg, Majstorovic, Safari, Toivonen (Granqvist 46), S. Larsson, Källström, Ibrahimović (Berg 82), Wernbloom (Elmander 69), Bajrami. Coach: Erik Hamrén (SWE)
San Marino: A. Simoncini, F. Vitaioli, Vannucci, Bacciocchi (Valentini 79), D. Simoncini, Ales. Della Valle, M. Vitaioli, Mazza, Man. Marani (Berretti 56), Selva, Chiaruzzi (Gasperoni 72). Coach: Giampaolo Mazza (SMR)
Goal(s): 1-0 Ibrahimović 7, 2-0 D. Simoncini 11 (og), 3-0 A. Simoncini 26 (og), 4-0 Granqvist 51, 5-0 Ibrahimović 77, 6-0 Berg 90+2
Red Card(s): Mellberg 33 (Sweden)
Yellow Card(s): Man. Marani 26 (San Marino), F. Vitaioli 59 (San Marino)
Referee: McKeon (IRL)

8/10/10, Ferenc Puskás, Budapest
Hungary 8-0 San Marino
Attendance: 10596
Hungary: Király, Vermes, Vanczák, Juhász, Laczkó, Elek (Vadócz 64), Dzsudzsák, Rudolf, Szalai (Priskin 64), Gera, Koman (Czvitkovics 79). Coach: Sándor Egervári (HUN)
San Marino: A. Simoncini, Valentini, Vannucci, Bacciocchi (Albani 52), Ales. Della Valle, F. Vitaioli, Berretti, Bollini (Cervellini 84), Montagna, Man. Marani, M. Vitaioli (Bugli 77). Coach: Giampaolo Mazza (SMR)
Goal(s): 1-0 Rudolf 11, 2-0 Szalai 18, 3-0 Rudolf 25, 4-0 Szalai 27, 5-0 Szalai 48, 6-0 Koman 60, 7-0 Dzsudzsák 89, 8-0 Gera 90+3 (p)
Red Card(s): Valentini 90+2 (San Marino)
Yellow Card(s): Valentini 38 (San Marino), Ales. Della Valle 43 (San Marino), Valentini 90+2 (San Marino)
Referee: Kaasik (EST)

8/10/10, Zimbru, Chisinau
Moldova 0-1 Netherlands
Attendance: 10500
Moldova: St. Namasco, Golovatenco, Epureanu, Racu, Cebotari (V. Andronic 69), Frunza (Bugaiov 46), Bulgaru, Bordian, Doros (Josan 78), Suvorov, Bolohan. Coach: Gavril Balint (ROU)
Netherlands: Stekelenburg, Van der Wiel, Heitinga, Mathijsen, Pieters, Van Bommel, Kuyt, Van Der Vaart, Huntelaar, Sneijder, Afellay (Emanuelson 90). Coach: Bert van Marwijk (NED)
Goal(s): 0-1 Huntelaar 37
Referee: Meyer (GER)

12/10/10, Olympic Stadium, Helsinki
Finland 1-2 Hungary
Attendance: 18532
Finland: Jääskeläinen, Pasanen, Moisander, Hyypiä, Väyrynen, R. Eremenko, Forssell, Sparv (Litmanen 72), Sjölund (Kuqi 81), Porokara (A. Eremenko Jr 71), Heikkinen. Coach: Stuart Baxter (ENG)
Hungary: Király, Vermes, Lipták, Juhász, Laczkó (Vanczák 86), Elek, Dzsudzsák, Rudolf (Koman 46), Szalai, Gera, Vadócz (Pintér 75). Coach: Sándor Egervári (HUN)
Goal(s): 0-1 Szalai 50, 1-1 Forssell 86, 1-2 Dzsudzsák 90+4
Yellow Card(s): Lipták 37 (Hungary), Väyrynen 41 (Finland), Elek 88 (Hungary)
Referee: Kelly (IRL)

Zlatan Ibrahimović came off the bench to score a hat-trick in Sweden's final qualifier of the season, a 5-0 win at home to Finland

12/10/10, Amsterdam ArenA, Amsterdam
Netherlands 4-1 Sweden
Attendance: 46000
Netherlands: Stekelenburg, Van der Wiel, Heitinga, Mathijsen, Pieters, Van Bommel (Brama 72), Kuyt (Lens 29), Van Der Vaart, Huntelaar (Van Nistelrooy 84), Sneijder, Afellay. Coach: Bert van Marwijk (NED)
Sweden: Isaksson, Lustig, Majstorovic, Safari (Wendt 46), Toivonen (Berg 79), S. Larsson, Svensson, Ibrahimović, Elmander, Granqvist, Wernbloom (Källström 54). Coach: Erik Hamrén (SWE)
Goal(s): 1-0 Huntelaar 4, 2-0 Afellay 37, 3-0 Huntelaar 55, 4-0 Afellay 59, 4-1 Granqvist 69
Yellow Card(s): S. Larsson 49 (Sweden), Toivonen 66 (Sweden)
Referee: Lannoy (FRA)

12/10/10, Stadio Olimpico, Serravalle
San Marino 0-2 Moldova
Attendance: 714
San Marino: A. Simoncini, F. Vitaioli, Vannucci, Mazza, D. Simoncini, Bacciocchi, Cervellini (Berretti 60), Bollini (Ciacci 67), Montagna (Coppini 81), Man. Marani, M. Vitaioli. Coach: Giampaolo Mazza (SMR)
Moldova: St. Namasco, Golovatenco, Boret, Epureanu, Cojocari (Savinov 81), V. Andronic, Frunza, Josan (Zmeu 69), Bordian, Suvorov, Bugaiov (Doros 62). Coach: Gavril Balint (ROU)
Goal(s): 0-1 Josan 20, 0-2 Doros 86 (p)
Yellow Card(s): M. Vitaioli 27 (San Marino), Cojocari 42 (Moldova), Bacciocchi 86 (San Marino), Ciacci 90+3 (San Marino)
Referee: Courtney (NIR)

17/11/10, Olympic Stadium, Helsinki
Finland 8-0 San Marino
Attendance: 8192
Finland: Fredrikson, Pasanen, Moisander, Lampi, Väyrynen, R. Eremenko, Forssell, Sjölund (Litmanen 46), A. Eremenko Jr (Kuqi 80), Hämäläinen (Porokara 70), Heikkinen. Coach: Olli Huttunen (FIN)
San Marino: A. Simoncini, Bugli, Cervellini, Albani, Ales. Della Valle, F. Vitaioli (Vannucci 72), Berretti (Alex Della Valle 67), Coppini, M. Vitaioli, Selva, Montagna (Man. Marani 79). Coach: Giampaolo Mazza (SMR)
Goal(s): 1-0 Väyrynen 39, 2-0 Hämäläinen 49, 3-0 Forssell 51, 4-0 Forssell 59, 5-0 Hämäläinen 67, 6-0 Litmanen 71 (p), 7-0 Porokara 73, 8-0 Forssell 78
Yellow Card(s): Albani 70 (San Marino), Selva 83 (San Marino), R. Eremenko 89 (Finland)
Referee: Matejek (CZE)

25/3/11, Ferenc Puskás, Budapest
Hungary 0-4 Netherlands
Attendance: 23817
Hungary: Király, Lipták, Vanczák, Juhász, Laczkó, Elek (Priskin 79), Dzsudzsák, Rudolf, Varga (Vadócz 46), Gera, Koman (Czvitkovics 46). Coach: Sándor Egervári (HUN)
Netherlands: Vorm, Van der Wiel, Heitinga, Mathijsen, Pieters, N. De Jong, Kuyt (Van Nistelrooy 82), Van der Vaart (Strootman 82), Van Persie, Sneijder, Afellay (Elia 63). Coach: Bert van Marwijk (NED)
Goal(s): 0-1 Van der Vaart 8, 0-2 Afellay 45, 0-3 Kuyt 54, 0-4 Van Persie 62
Yellow Card(s): Van Persie 18 (Netherlands), Koman 44 (Hungary), Elek 59 (Hungary), Vanczák 61 (Hungary), Lipták 67 (Hungary)
Referee: Velasco Carballo (ESP)

29/3/11, Amsterdam ArenA, Amsterdam
Netherlands 5-3 Hungary
Attendance: 51700
Netherlands: Vorm, Van der Wiel, Heitinga, Mathijsen, Pieters (Emanuelson 64), N. De Jong, Kuyt (Elia 90), Van der Vaart, Van Persie (Van Nistelrooy 46), Sneijder, Afellay. Coach: Bert van Marwijk (NED)
Hungary: Fülöp, Lázár, Vanczák, Juhász, Laczkó, Vadócz (Czvitkovics 90), Dzsudzsák, Rudolf, Priskin (Tőköli 73), Gera, Pintér (Koman 46). Coach: Sándor Egervári (HUN)
Goal(s): 1-0 Van Persie 13, 1-1 Rudolf 46, 1-2 Gera 50, 2-2 Sneijder 61, 3-2 Van Nistelrooy 73, 3-3 Gera 75, 4-3 Kuyt 78, 5-3 Kuyt 81
Yellow Card(s): Lázár 23 (Hungary), Pintér 39 (Hungary), Juhász 59 (Hungary)
Referee: Moen (NOR)

29/3/11, Råsundastadion, Solna
Sweden 2-1 Moldova
Attendance: 25544
Sweden: Isaksson, Lustig, Granqvist, Antonsson, Wendt, Wernbloom (R. Elm 65), S. Larsson, Bajrami (M. Olsson 73), Källström, Ibrahimović, Elmander (Gerndt 89). Coach: Erik Hamrén (SWE)
Moldova: St. Namasco, Armas, Golovatenco, Bolohan, Boret, Racu, Gatcan (V. Andronic 83), Cebotaru, Frunza (Bugaiov 46), Doros (Cheptine 72), Suvorov. Coach: Gavril Balint (ROU)
Goal(s): 1-0 Lustig 30, 2-0 S. Larsson 82, 2-1 Suvorov 90+2
Yellow Card(s): Wernbloom 17 (Sweden), Källström 88 (Sweden)
Referee: Kircher (GER)

3/6/11, Zimbru, Chisinau
Moldova 1-4 Sweden
Attendance: 10500
Moldova: St. Namasco, Armas, Golovatenco, Bolohan, Gatcan (Tigirlas 46), Racu, Cebotari (Patras 78), Bugaiov, Doros (Boghiu 63), Suvorov, Ivanov. Coach: Gavril Balint (ROU)
Sweden: Isaksson, Lustig, Mellberg, Majstorovic, S. Larsson, Svensson, Källström, Elmander (Gerndt 76), Hysén (Bajrami 41), Wendt, Toivonen (Wernbloom 69). Coach: Erik Hamrén (SWE)
Goal(s): 0-1 Toivonen 11, 0-2 Elmander 30, 0-3 Elmander 58, 1-3 Bugaiov 61, 1-4 Gerndt 88
Referee: Marriner (ENG)

3/6/11, Stadio Olimpico, Serravalle
San Marino 0-1 Finland
Attendance: 1218
San Marino: A. Simoncini, F. Vitaioli (Bacciocchi 88), Vannucci, Cervellini, D. Simoncini, Ales. Della Valle, Bollini, Mazza (Berretti 77), Ma. Marani, Selva, M. Vitaioli (Montagna 81). Coach: Giampaolo Mazza (SMR)
Finland: Hradecky, Pasanen, Moisander, Lampi, Väyrynen, Hetemaj (Sjölund 84), Forssell (Sadik 90), Heikkinen, A. Eremenko Jr (Riski 68), Hämäläinen, Raitala. Coach: Mixu Paatelainen (FIN)
Goal(s): 0-1 Forssell 41
Yellow Card(s): Ales. Della Valle 49 (San Marino), D. Simoncini 80 (San Marino)
Referee: Sipailo (LVA)

7/6/11, Stadio Olimpico, Serravalle
San Marino 0-3 Hungary
Attendance: 1915
San Marino: A. Simoncini, F. Vitaioli (Alex Della Valle 46), Vannucci, Cervellini, Benedettini, Ales. Della Valle, M. Vitaioli, Bollini (Bacciocchi 79), Ma. Marani (Berretti 64), Selva, Mazza. Coach: Giampaolo Mazza (SMR)
Hungary: Király, Lipták (Pintér 87), Vanczák, Juhász, Laczkó, Elek, Dzsudzsák, Szabics (Koltai 83), Németh, Hajnal (Czvitkovics 71), Koman. Coach: Sándor Egervári (HUN)
Goal(s): 0-1 Lipták 40, 0-2 Szabics 49, 0-3 Koman 83
Yellow Card(s): Juhász 17 (Hungary), Cervellini 29 (San Marino), A. Simoncini 41 (San Marino), Vanczák 64 (Hungary), Ales. Della Valle 73 (San Marino), Berretti 75 (San Marino)
Referee: Radovanović (MNE)

7/6/11, Råsundastadion, Solna
Sweden 5-0 Finland
Attendance: 32128
Sweden: Isaksson, Lustig, Mellberg, Majstorovic, Bajrami, S. Larsson (Wilhelmsson 89), Svensson, Källström, Elmander (Wernbloom 81), Wendt, Toivonen (Ibrahimović 25). Coach: Erik Hamrén (SWE)
Finland: Jaakkola, Pasanen, Moisander, Toivio, Väyrynen, R. Eremenko, Hetemaj, Forssell, Heikkinen (Halsti 46), A. Eremenko Jr (Ring 80), Hämäläinen (Ääritalo 46). Coach: Mixu Paatelainen (FIN)
Goal(s): 1-0 Källström 11, 2-0 Ibrahimović 31, 3-0 Ibrahimović 35, 4-0 Ibrahimović 53, 5-0 Bajrami 83
Yellow Card(s): A. Eremenko Jr 10 (Finland)
Referee: Gautier (FRA)

Group E Table

		Pld	Home					Away					Total					Pts
			W	D	L	F	A	W	D	L	F	A	W	D	L	F	A	
1	Netherlands	6	3	0	0	11	5	3	0	0	10	0	6	0	0	21	5	18
2	Sweden	6	4	0	0	15	6	1	0	1	5	0	5	0	1	20	6	15
3	Hungary	7	2	0	1	10	13	2	0	2	8	0	4	0	3	18	13	12
4	Finland	6	1	0	1	9	11	1	0	3	2	0	2	0	4	11	11	6
5	Moldova	6	1	0	2	3	9	1	0	2	4	0	2	0	4	7	9	6
6	San Marino	7	0	0	4	0	33	0	0	3	0	0	0	0	7	0	33	0

Remaining Fixtures

2/9/11
Finland – Moldova
Hungary – Sweden
Netherlands – San Marino

6/9/11
Finland – Netherlands
Moldova – Hungary
San Marino – Sweden

7/10/11
Finland – Sweden
Netherlands – Moldova

11/10/11
Hungary – Finland
Moldova – San Marino
Sweden – Netherlands

GROUP F

A new dawn beckoned for 2004 European champions Greece with the announcement that coach Otto Rehhagel was standing down after nine years at the helm. Following in the footsteps of the revered German was never going to be an easy task, but Rehhagael's successor Fernando Santos made an admirable start as he guided the rejuvenated team to the top of Group F after six matches with a one-point lead over Croatia.

Greece coach Fernando Santos barks orders from the touchline

Young blood

The native Portuguese, who cut his managerial teeth during spells at Panathinaikos FC, AEK Athens FC and PAOK FC, conceded on taking over that Greece were entering "a transitional phase" and made plain his desire to introduce fresh young players. "There is talent in Greece," he said, "young players who in the past couple of years have made good progress. Now we have to support them and bed them in alongside players who were involved in those previous campaigns to build a team that can compete at the highest level."

The revolution got off to an inauspicious start. Greece's campaign was just three minutes old when Aleksandre Iashvili handed Georgia a shock lead in Piraeus, and only a late equaliser from defender Nikolaos Spiropoulos spared the hosts' blushes. Another stalemate followed, but a goalless draw away to group seeds Croatia was considered a point gained rather than two lost and Santos continued to blood youngsters such as Olympiacos FC's teenage playmaker Ioannis Fetfatzidis, who made his international bow in the third game against Latvia. His perseverance paid off as a solitary strike from Vassilis Torosidis clinched Greece's first win and sparked a run of four straight successes.

Karagounis landmark

The Latvia match represented a landmark moment for Georgios Karagounis, the veteran captain becoming only the third Greece player to earn 100 caps. "I don't know how many more matches I'll play," the Panathinaikos midfielder said, "but my aim is to help the squad play in the EURO finals for the third consecutive time." Karagounis followed up his words with actions, scoring the winner from the spot against Israel, before another Torosidis strike – this time in added time – spared the team's blushes with a 1-0 win over Malta in Ta' Qali. Greece's youngsters then took centre stage in June, propelling the team to the top of the table with another win over Malta, 3-1 in Piraeus. Nineteen-year-old FC Schalke 04 defender Kyriakos Papadopoulos marked his debut with a goal, while Fetfatzidis registered his first two competitive strikes.

Greece's surge enabled them to overtake early pacesetters Croatia. Quarter-finalists in 1996 and 2008, Slaven Bilić's men made a decent start, chalking up a 3-0 win in Latvia thanks to goals from Mladen Petrić, Ivica Olić and Darijo Srna. Although Croatia were subsequently held on home soil by Greece, Niko Kranjčar, out of favour at his club Tottenham Hotspur FC, struck back-to-back doubles to inspire further wins over Israel (2-1) and Malta (3-0). There was a shock to the sytem in Tbilisi, however, when Levan Kobiashvili's 90th-minute goal inflicted Croatia's first defeat and simultaneously pulled Georgia into contention for qualification.

Heady times

The eastern European nation had drawn three of their opening four qualifiers, claiming their first victory against Malta, yet they were undefeated in ten outings under Temur Ketsbaia and, with that last-gasp win, had clambered to within a point of Croatia. These were heady times for a team that had so often flattered to deceive, but no sooner had Georgia's hopes been raised than they were dashed. Four days later Kestbaia suffered his first defeat – 0-1 in Israel – before, in June, Croatia gained revenge in Split by coming from a goal down to win 2-1 with two goals in three minutes from Mario Mandžukić and Nikola Kalinić.

Like Greece and Croatia, Israel carried genuine hope of qualification into the latter stages having taken nine points from nine in the first half of 2011 thanks to two victories over Latvia either side of that defeat of Georgia. Biram Kayal's 81st-minute header sealed a 2-1 home success over Aleksandrs Starkovs' side before Yossi Benayoun and Tal Ben Haim hit the target to ensure the same scoreline in Riga, thus earning a first away win for the side under French coach Luis Fernandez. Seeking to reach their first EURO finals, Israel sat level with Croatia and just a point behind leaders Greece having played one game more than both of their rivals.

Nikola Kalinić scored Croatia's crucial winner against Georgia to seal his country's first victory at the Poljud Stadium in Split for 16 years

Added-time agony

At the bottom of the standings Latvia, shock qualifiers in 2004, had just four points and were all but eliminated after the back-to-back defeats by Israel. Yet they were four points better off than basement team Malta, who lost every one of their first six games but twice came within seconds of claiming their first point only to concede agonisingly in added time against both Georgia and Greece.

Group F Results

2/9/10, Ramat Gan Stadium, Ramat Gan
Israel 3-1 Malta
Attendance: 17365
Israel: Awat, Ben Haim (I), Bondarv, Kayal (Golasa 86), A. Cohen, Refaelov, Benayoun, Zahavi (Vermouth 51), Sahar (Arbeitman 73), Ben Dayan, T. Cohen. Coach: Luis Fernandez (FRA)
Malta: Hogg, Caruana, Mamo, Sciberras, Agius, Bogdanovic (Cohen 57), Briffa (Failla 82), Mifsud, S. Bajada, Herrera (Muscat 80), Pace. Coach: John Buttigieg (MLT)
Goal(s): 1-0 Benayoun 7, 1-1 Pace 38, 2-1 Benayoun 64 (p), 3-1 Benayoun 75
Yellow Card(s): Bogdanovic 34 (Malta), Benayoun 40 (Israel), Cohen 61 (Malta), Pace 90 (Malta)
Referee: Ennjimi (FRA)

3/9/10, Georgios Karaiskakis Stadium, Piraeus
Greece 1-1 Georgia
Attendance: 14794
Greece: Sifakis, Seitaridis (Mitroglou 71), Spiropoulos, Samaras (Ninis 59), A. Papadopoulos, Karagounis, Salpingidis, Torosidis, Gekas, Papastathopoulos, Katsouranis. Coach: Fernando Santos (POR)
Georgia: Revishvili, Lobjanidze, Asatiani, Kaladze, Amisulashvili, Khizanishvili, Gogua (Merebashvili 87), Kvirkvelia, Iashvili (Ananidze 54), Kobiashvili, Dvalishvili (Gelashvili 60). Coach: Temuri Ketsbaia (GEO)
Goal(s): 0-1 Iashvili 3, 1-1 Spiropoulos 72
Yellow Card(s): Samaras 37 (Greece), Lobjanidze 44 (Georgia), Katsouranis 74 (Greece), Khizanishvili 81 (Georgia), A. Papadopoulos 83 (Greece)
Referee: Clos Gomez (ESP)

3/9/10, Skonto Stadions, Riga
Latvia 0-3 Croatia
Attendance: 7600
Latvia: Vaņins, Kļava, Laizāns (Astafjevs 87), Ivanovs, Mihadjuks, Cauņa, Verpakovskis, Rubins (Žigajevs 85), Karlsons (Rudņevs 63), Gorkšs, Rafaļskis. Coach: Aleksandrs Starkovs (LVA)
Croatia: Runje, Strinić, Šimunić, Ćorluka, Rakitić, Vukojević (Pranjić 70), Eduardo (Jelavić 62), Srna, Olić, Kranjčar, Petrić (Mandžukić 84). Coach: Slaven Bilić (CRO)
Goal(s): 0-1 Petrić 43, 0-2 Olić 51, 0-3 Srna 82
Yellow Card(s): Vukojević 37 (Croatia), Mihadjuks 76 (Latvia), Verpakovskis 76 (Latvia), Srna 90 (Croatia)
Referee: Kuipers (NED)

7/9/10, Stadion Maksimir, Zagreb
Croatia 0-0 Greece
Attendance: 24399
Croatia: Runje, Strinić, Šimunić, Ćorluka, Pranjić, Vukojević (Rakitić 57), Modrić, Srna, Olić (Eduardo 73), Kranjčar, Petrić (Jelavić 46). Coach: Slaven Bilić (CRO)
Greece: Sifakis, Tzavelas, Tziolis, Samaras, A. Papadopoulos, Karagounis (Ninis 70), Vyntra, Salpingidis (Gekas 59), Torosidis (Seitaridis 90+2), Papastathopoulos, Katsouranis. Coach: Fernando Santos (POR)
Yellow Card(s): Torosidis 16 (Greece), Tzavelas 46 (Greece), Rakitić 62 (Croatia), Srna 68 (Croatia), Papastathopoulos 79 (Greece)
Referee: Larsen (DEN)

7/9/10, Boris Paichadze National Stadium, Tbilisi
Georgia 0-0 Israel
Attendance: 45000
Georgia: Revishvili, Lobjanidze, Asatiani, Kaladze, Amisulashvili, Khizanishvili, Gogua (Aptsiauri 75), Ananidze, Iashvili (Siradze 46), Kobiashvili, Dvalishvili (Merebashvili 63). Coach: Temuri Ketsbaia (GEO)
Israel: Awat, Ben Haim (I), Bondarv, Kayal, A. Cohen, Refaelov (Vermouth 75), Keinan, Benayoun, Sahar (Arbeitman 53), Ben Dayan, T. Cohen (Zahavi 61). Coach: Luis Fernandez (FRA)
Yellow Card(s): Ben Haim (I) 21 (Israel), Lobjanidze 29 (Georgia), Kobiashvili 42 (Georgia), Bondarv 69 (Israel)
Referee: Kever (SUI)

7/9/10, Ta' Qali National Stadium, Ta' Qali
Malta 0-2 Latvia
Attendance: 6255
Malta: Hogg, Caruana, Mamo (R. Fenech 77), Sciberras (Failla 77), Agius, S. Bajada, Briffa, Mifsud, Cohen, Muscat (Bogdanovic 59), Pace. Coach: John Buttigieg (MLT)
Latvia: Vaņins, Kļava, Laizāns, Ivanovs, Mihadjuks, Cauņa, Verpakovskis (Perepļotkins 90+2), Rubins, Gorkšs, Rafaļskis (Astafjevs 82), Rudņevs (Karlsons 70). Coach: Aleksandrs Starkovs (LVA)
Goal(s): 0-1 Gorkšs 43, 0-2 Verpakovskis 85
Yellow Card(s): Kļava 34 (Latvia), Agius 39 (Malta), Mifsud 58 (Malta), Rafaļskis 61 (Latvia), Bogdanovic 65 (Malta)
Referee: Asumaa (FIN)

8/10/10, Boris Paichadze National Stadium, Tbilisi
Georgia 1-0 Malta
Attendance: 38000
Georgia: Revishvili, Salukvadze, Asatiani, Kaladze, Amisulashvili, Khizanishvili, Gogua, Ananidze (Daushvili 73), Merebashvili (Iashvili 46), Kobiashvili, Dvalishvili (Siradze 46). Coach: Temuri Ketsbaia (GEO)
Malta: Haber, Caruana, Mamo, Sciberras (R. Fenech 69), Agius, Briffa, Mifsud, Cohen (Grima 90), S. Bajada, Schembri (P. Fenech 80), Pace. Coach: John Buttigieg (MLT)
Goal(s): 1-0 Siradze 90+1
Yellow Card(s): Khizanishvili 31 (Georgia), Cohen 56 (Malta), Schembri 59 (Malta), Agius 65 (Malta)
Referee: Black (NIR)

8/10/10, Georgios Karaiskakis Stadium, Piraeus
Greece 1-0 Latvia
Attendance: 13520
Greece: Sifakis, Tzavelas, Tziolis, Samaras, A. Papadopoulos, Mitroglou (Salpingidis 77), Karagounis (Kafes 90), Torosidis, Ninis (Fetfatzidis 82), Papastathopoulos, Katsouranis. Coach: Fernando Santos (POR)
Latvia: Vaņins, Kļava, Astafjevs, Laizāns (Perepļotkins 82), Ivanovs, Cauņa, Verpakovskis, Rubins (Žigajevs 65), Gorkšs, Zirnis, Rudņevs (Karlsons 73). Coach: Aleksandrs Starkovs (LVA)
Goal(s): 1-0 Torosidis 58
Yellow Card(s): Torosidis 27 (Greece), Verpakovskis 45 (Latvia), Žigajevs 75 (Latvia), Zirnis 82 (Latvia), Tziolis 90 (Greece)
Referee: Damato (ITA)

9/10/10, Ramat Gan Stadium, Ramat Gan
Israel 1-2 Croatia
Attendance: 33421
Israel: Awat, Ben Haim (I), Natcho, Vermouth, A. Cohen, Barda (Refaelov 56), Shechter, Keinan, Ziv, E. Cohen (Golasa 69), T. Cohen (Colautti 51). Coach: Luis Fernandez (FRA)
Croatia: Runje, Strinić, Šimunić, Ćorluka, Pranjić, Rakitić (Vukojević 77), Eduardo (Mandžukić 57), Modrić, Schildenfeld, Olić (Bilić 72), Kranjčar. Coach: Slaven Bilić (CRO)
Goal(s): 0-1 Kranjčar 36 (p), 0-2 Kranjčar 41, 1-2 Shechter 81
Yellow Card(s): Keinan 35 (Israel), Shechter 36 (Israel), Kranjčar 59 (Croatia), Ben Haim (I) 65 (Israel), Golasa 88 (Israel), Vukojević 90+3 (Croatia)
Referee: Stark (GER)

12/10/10, Georgios Karaiskakis Stadium, Piraeus
Greece 2-1 Israel
Attendance: 16935
Greece: Sifakis, Spiropoulos, Samaras (Mitroglou 81), A. Papadopoulos, Karagounis, Vyntra, Salpingidis (Maniatis 87), Kafes, Ninis (Fetfatzidis 15), Papastathopoulos, Katsouranis. Coach: Fernando Santos (POR)
Israel: Awat, Bondarv, Gershon, Natcho (Vermouth 63), A. Cohen, Colautti (Barda 75), Shechter, Keinan, Refaelov, T. Cohen (E. Cohen 69), Golasa. Coach: Luis Fernandez (FRA)
Goal(s): 1-0 Salpingidis 22, 1-1 Spiropoulos 59 (og), 2-1 Karagounis 63 (p)
Yellow Card(s): Shechter 45+1 (Israel), E. Cohen 75 (Israel), Fetfatzidis 85 (Greece)
Referee: Hansson (SWE)

12/10/10, Skonto Stadions, Riga
Latvia 1-1 Georgia
Attendance: 4330
Latvia: Vaņins, Kļava, Astafjevs, Laizāns (Grebis 82), Ivanovs, Cauņa, Rubins, Gorkšs, Zirnis, Rudņevs, Žigajevs (Perepļotkins 86). Coach: Aleksandrs Starkovs (LVA)
Georgia: Revishvili, Lobjanidze, Asatiani, Kaladze, Amisulashvili, Daushvili, Ananidze (Salukvadze 79), Kvirkvelia (Gogua 69), Iashvili (Koshkadze 88), Kobiashvili, Siradze. Coach: Temuri Ketsbaia (GEO)
Goal(s): 0-1 Siradze 74, 1-1 Cauņa 90+1
Yellow Card(s): Kļava 48 (Latvia), Gorkšs 64 (Latvia), Siradze 75 (Georgia), Gogua 82 (Georgia), Revishvili 88 (Georgia)
Referee: Neves Moreira De Sousa (POR)

17/11/10, Stadion Maksimir, Zagreb
Croatia 3-0 Malta
Attendance: 9000
Croatia: Runje, Ćorluka, Pranjić, Rakitić (Iličević 69), Eduardo (Mandžukić 78), Modrić, Srna, Schildenfeld, Dujmović, Kranjčar, Petrić (Kalinić 61). Coach: Slaven Bilić (CRO)
Malta: Hogg, Caruana, S. Bajada, Sciberras (P. Fenech 88), Hutchinson, Grima, Briffa, Mifsud, Bogdanovic (Sammut 82), Schembri (R. Fenech 70), Pace. Coach: John Buttigieg (MLT)
Goal(s): 1-0 Kranjčar 18, 2-0 Kranjčar 42, 3-0 Kalinić 81
Yellow Card(s): Srna 74 (Croatia), Grima 84 (Malta)
Referee: Duarte Gomes (POR)

26/3/11, Boris Paichadze National Stadium, Tbilisi
Georgia 1-0 Croatia
Attendance: 55000
Georgia: Revishvili, Salukvadze, Khubutia, Kaladze, Amisulashvili, Khizanishvili, Kankava, Daushvili (Gogua 73), Iashvili (Martsvaladze 62), Kobiashvili, Dvalishvili (Siradze 46). Coach: Temuri Ketsbaia (GEO)
Croatia: Runje, Strinić, Lovren, Ćorluka, Rakitić (Perišić 61), Modrić, Srna, Kalinić, Dujmović, Kranjčar (Jelavić 70), Petrić (Pranjić 84). Coach: Slaven Bilić (CRO)
Goal(s): 1-0 Kobiashvili 90
Yellow Card(s): Dujmović 52 (Croatia), Kranjčar 66 (Croatia), Martsvaladze 71 (Georgia)
Referee: Tagliavento (ITA)

26/3/11, Bloomfield Stadium, Tel-Aviv
Israel 2-1 Latvia
Attendance: 10801
Israel: Awat, Ben Haim (I), Gershon, Natcho, Kayal, Refaelov (Vermouth 84), Barda (Buzaglo 69), Tawatha, Ziv (Sahar 66), I. Cohen, Damari. Coach: Luis Fernandez (FRA)
Latvia: Vaņins, Kačanovs, Krjauklis, Ivanovs, Verpakovskis (Turkovs 73), Rubins (Perepļotkins 57), Lukjanovs, Gorkšs, Rafaļskis (Žigajevs 58), Lazdiņš, Rudņevs. Coach: Aleksandrs Starkovs (LVA)
Goal(s): 1-0 Barda 16, 1-1 Gorkšs 62, 2-1 Kayal 81
Yellow Card(s): Kačanovs 54 (Latvia), Natcho 85 (Israel), Tawatha 90 (Israel)
Referee: Mažić (SRB)

26/3/11, Ta' Qali National Stadium, Ta' Qali
Malta 0-1 Greece
Attendance: 10605
Malta: Haber, Caruana (Pace 46), Mamo, Sciberras, Agius, Hutchinson, Bogdanovic, Briffa, Mifsud, S. Bajada (R. Fenech 78), Schembri (Cohen 90+1). Coach: John Buttigieg (MLT)
Greece: Tzorvas, Tzavelas, Samaras, A. Papadopoulos, Karagounis, Salpingidis (Fetfatzidis 61), Torosidis, Ninis (Kone 81), Papastathopoulos, Katsouranis, Liberopoulos (Mitroglou 70). Coach: Fernando Santos (POR)
Goal(s): 0-1 Torosidis 90+2
Red Card(s): Papastathopoulos 84 (Greece)
Yellow Card(s): Tzavelas 57 (Greece), Torosidis 88 (Greece), Cohen 90+2 (Malta)
Referee: Weiner (GER)

29/3/11, Bloomfield Stadium, Tel-Aviv
Israel 1-0 Georgia
Attendance: 13716
Israel: Awat, Bondarv, Ben Haim (I), Gershon, Natcho (Ben Haim (II) 52), Kayal, A. Cohen, Refaelov (Vermouth 63), Barda (Benayoun 71), Buzaglo, Keinan. Coach: Luis Fernandez (FRA)
Georgia: Revishvili, Salukvadze, Khubutia, Kaladze, Amisulashvili, Khizanishvili, Kankava, Daushvili (Kvirkvelia 46), Iashvili (Dvalishvili 63), Kobiashvili, Martsvaladze (Siradze 73). Coach: Temuri Ketsbaia (GEO)
Goal(s): 1-0 Ben Haim (II) 59
Yellow Card(s): Amisulashvili 44 (Georgia), Martsvaladze 45 (Georgia), A. Cohen 62 (Israel), Bondarv 76 (Israel), Kobiashvili 89 (Georgia)
Referee: Fautrel (FRA)

3/6/11, Stadion Poljud, Split
Croatia 2-1 Georgia
Attendance: 28000
Croatia: Runje, Šimunić, Ćorluka, Pranjić, Vukojević (Dujmović 71), Eduardo, Modrić, Srna, Mandžukić, Perišić (Klasnić 71), Jelavić (Kalinić 46). Coach: Slaven Bilić (CRO)
Georgia: Loria, Salukvadze, Khubutia, Kaladze, Grigalava, Kashia (Ananidze 80), Kankava, Kvirkvelia, Iashvili (Daushvili 62), Khizanishvili, Siradze (Dvalishvili 56). Coach: Temuri Ketsbaia (GEO)
Goal(s): 0-1 Kankava 17, 1-1 Mandžukić 76, 2-1 Kalinić 78
Yellow Card(s): Iashvili 26 (Georgia), Khubutia 75 (Georgia), Kalinić 78 (Croatia)
Referee: Johannesson (SWE)

4/6/11, Georgios Karaiskakis Stadium, Piraeus
Greece 3-1 Malta
Attendance: 14746
Greece: Konstantopoulos, Spiropoulos, Moras, Tziolis, Karagounis (Kafes 70), Salpingidis (Mitroglou 89), Torosidis, Ninis (Hristodoulopoulos 80), Katsouranis, K. Papadopoulos, Fetfatzidis. Coach: Fernando Santos (POR)
Malta: Hogg, Caruana, Sciberras, Agius, R. Fenech, Bogdanovic (Cohen 60), Briffa, Mifsud, Hutchinson (P. Fenech 87), Schembri, S. Bajada (Failla 80). Coach: John Buttigieg (MLT)
Goal(s): 1-0 Fetfatzidis 7, 2-0 K. Papadopoulos 26, 2-1 Mifsud 54, 3-1 Fetfatzidis 63
Yellow Card(s): K. Papadopoulos 15 (Greece)
Referee: Gil (POL)

Yossi Benayoun returned from injury to score in Israel's 2-1 victory over Latvia in Riga

4/6/11, Skonto Stadions, Riga
Latvia 1-2 Israel
Attendance: 6147
Latvia: Vaņins, Kļava, Krjauklis, Ivanovs, Lazdiņš, Cauņa, Rafaļskis (Žigajevs 28), Višņakovs (Rugins 71), Rudņevs, Gorkšs, Perepļotkins (Gauračs 60). Coach: Aleksandrs Starkovs (LVA)
Israel: Awat, Shpungin, Ben Haim (I), Gershon, A. Cohen, Refaelov (Ben Haim (II) 79), Hemed, Buzaglo (Natcho 69), Keinan, Benayoun, Zahavi (Golasa 89). Coach: Luis Fernandez (FRA)
Goal(s): 0-1 Benayoun 19, 0-2 Ben Haim (I) 43 (p), 1-2 Cauņa 62 (p)
Yellow Card(s): Ivanovs 45+1 (Latvia), Žigajevs 76 (Latvia), Kļava 82 (Latvia), Ben Haim (II) 90+1 (Israel)
Referee: Kelly (IRL)

Group F Table

		Home					Away					Total					
	Pld	W	D	L	F	A	W	D	L	F	A	W	D	L	F	A	Pts
1 Greece	6	3	1	0	7	3	1	1	0	1	0	4	2	0	8	3	14
2 Croatia	6	2	1	0	5	3	2	0	1	5	0	4	1	1	10	3	13
3 Israel	7	3	0	1	7	7	1	1	1	3	0	4	1	2	10	7	13
4 Georgia	7	2	1	0	2	5	0	2	2	3	0	2	3	2	5	5	9
5 Latvia	6	0	1	2	2	9	1	0	2	3	0	1	1	4	5	9	4
6 Malta	6	0	0	2	0	13	0	0	4	2	0	0	0	6	2	13	0

Remaining Fixtures

2/9/11
Georgia – Latvia
Israel – Greece
Malta – Croatia

6/9/11
Croatia – Israel
Latvia – Greece
Malta – Georgia

7/10/11
Greece – Croatia
Latvia – Malta

11/10/11
Croatia – Latvia
Georgia – Greece
Malta – Israel

GROUP G

With three matches to go, Group G favourites England and underdogs Montenegro stood level on 13 points at the top of the table, with automatic qualification set to be decided by the outcome of the summit showdown in Podgorica on 7 October. Switzerland and Bulgaria, both six points adrift, appeared to be out of contention while Wales were left stranded at the foot of the table without a point.

Surprise challenge

That Montenegro should emerge as genuine contenders to reach the finals at the first time of asking constituted one of the most remarkable stories of the whole UEFA EURO 2012 qualifying campaign. The young nation endured a torrid time in their initial attempt to reach a major finals following the split from Serbia, winning only one of their ten 2010 FIFA World Cup qualifiers. Yet the improvement was as sudden as it was unexpected – even if skipper Mirko Vučinić did not quite see it that way. "We were new to international football and had no experience," the striker said of the flawed World Cup tilt. "We were building a team while playing big games. Now, you can see we are a completed team – not one in construction."

Vučinić's importance was heightened by the prolonged absence of his injured strike partner Stevan Jovetić, but the talismanic hitman backed up his words by striking the only goal of Montenegro's opener against Wales in Podgorica. Four days later, in Sofia, Zlatko Kranjčar's team bagged another 1-0 victory. Once again a defence expertly marshalled by Marko Baša coupled with a fine goalkeeping display from Mladen Božović kept the opposition at bay, meaning Elsad Zverotić's long-range strike condemned Stanimir Stoilov's hosts to a surprise defeat. "No one believed we could beat Wales and Bulgaria without Jovetić," said an elated Božović. "But we played with confidence and we deserved both victories."

Matthäus takes over

Amid the euphoria of the Sofia triumph, Kranjčar probably spared a sympathetic thought for his opposite number. Stoilov decided to resign in the aftermath of the defeat, which had come hot on the

Mirko Vučinić (No9) forces a save from Wales goalkeeper Wayne Hennessey during Montenegro's opening 1-0 win in Podgorica

heels of a 4-0 hammering by England at Wembley. It was subsequently left to Lothar Matthäus to reignite Bulgaria's flagging campaign, and the German legend made a decent fist of a tough task, going unbeaten in his first three qualifiers. Ivelin Popov scored in Wales' Millennium Stadium to give Matthäus a winning start before Switzerland secured a goalless draw in the Bulgarian capital. Yet probably the most accurate gauge of the team's improvement was the assured performance in drawing 1-1 away to Montenegro in June, Popov again finding the net – with the first EURO goal ever scored against Montenegro – to cancel out Radomir Đalović's opener.

Given the fast pace set at the top of the table, Bulgaria's improvement seemed forlorn. Incredibly, Kranjčar's first-timers extended their 100% record to three matches at home to Switzerland, clinching their third successive 1-0 win thanks to another Vučinić goal. The stage was now set for a top-of-the-table showdown at Wembley on 12 October. Like Montenegro, England also boasted a faultless record to that point, and while they had only played two matches, Fabio Capello's charges appeared to have recovered their verve after a lamentable FIFA World Cup campaign in South Africa. Jermain Defoe's smart left-footed hat-trick and a further strike from Adam Johnson ensured that Bulgaria were brushed aside on home soil in their opening qualifier, then four days later an outstanding display in Basel brought a fine 3-1 triumph over Switzerland courtesy of goals from Wayne Rooney, Darren Bent and a second in a week from the impressive Johnson.

Summit stalemate

A month later, however, England were to meet their match against a well-drilled Montenegro. To the audible frustration of a capacity Wembley crowd, the hosts were short of ideas, struggled to create clear chances and might even have lost had Milan Jovanović's late effort gone in rather than bounce off the crossbar. They did have a strong claim for a penalty when Ashley Cole was upended by Đalović, but over the 90 minutes the draw was a fair outcome.

England were to drop further points at home before the season was out. Wales, missing injured talisman Gareth Bale, had been swept aside with two goals inside the first 15 minutes during a dominant display in Cardiff in March, but Switzerland proved far tougher opponents at Wembley in June. Indeed, after Tranquillo Barnetta had twice embarrassed the England defence with free-kicks in the first half, the home team, minus the injured Steven Gerrard and suspended Rooney, had to fight back to preserve their unbeaten record, earning a share of the spoils through a Frank Lampard spot kick – his second in successive qualifiers – and substitute Ashley Young's well struck equaliser. Bent should have won the game with an easy chance that he skied over an open goal 19 minutes from time, but England visibly tired towards the end, and when Montenegro were held at home by Bulgaria later that evening, enabling England to remain top of the table on goal difference, the 2-2 draw did not seem quite so costly.

Solitary success

Switzerland's bright performance at Wembley – their second away draw in succession – confirmed their recovery from a poor start but, with just one win from five games, Ottmar Hitzfeld's team were practically out of the running. Their solitary triumph came in October at home to Wales, Valentin Stocker helping himself to two goals, Marco Streller also scoring and Gökhan Inler converting a late penalty to seal a reinvigorating 4-1 success in Basel.

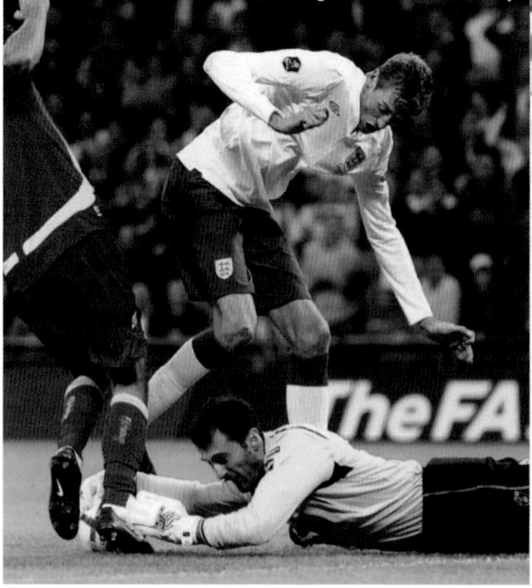

England's Peter Crouch is foiled by Montenegro goalkeeper Mladen Božović during the 0-0 draw at Wembley

Group G Results

3/9/10, Wembley Stadium, London
England 4-0 Bulgaria
Attendance: 73426
England: Hart, G. Johnson, A. Cole, Gerrard, Dawson (Cahill 57), Jagielka, Walcott (A. Johnson 74), Barry, Defoe (Young 87), Rooney, Milner. Coach: Fabio Capello (ITA)
Bulgaria: Mihaylov, Manolev (Minev 65), I. Stoyanov, Angelov, Popov (Peev 79), Yankov, Bojinov (Rangelov 63), Ivan Ivanov, Milanov, M. Petrov, S. Petrov. Coach: Stanimir Stoilov (BUL)
Goal(s): 1-0 Defoe 3, 2-0 Defoe 61, 3-0 A. Johnson 83, 4-0 Defoe 86
Yellow Card(s): Popov 62 (Bulgaria), Milner 90 (England)
Referee: Kassai (HUN)

3/9/10, Stadion Podgorica, Podgorica
Montenegro 1-0 Wales
Attendance: 7442
Montenegro: M. Božović, Pavićević, Baša, Jovanović, Vukčević (Bećiraj 87), Vučinić, Đalović (Novaković 83), Bošković (V. Božović 74), Peković, Zverotić, Džudović. Coach: Zlatko Kranjčar (CRO)
Wales: Hennessey, Ricketts, Gunter, Edwards (Earnshaw 68), J. Collins (Morgan 75), Williams, Vaughan, Bellamy, Morison (Church 78), Ledley, Bale. Coach: John Toshack (WAL)
Goal(s): 1-0 Vučinić 30
Yellow Card(s): Pavićević 8 (Montenegro), Morison 45 (Wales), Ricketts 49 (Wales), Džudović 53 (Montenegro), Bale 57 (Wales), Peković 70 (Montenegro)
Referee: Kakos (GRE)

7/9/10, Natsionalen Stadion Vasil Levski, Sofia
Bulgaria 0-1 Montenegro
Attendance: 9470
Bulgaria: Mihaylov, I. Stoyanov, Minev, Angelov, Popov, Rangelov (Bojinov 46), Peev (Domovchiyski 66), Ivan Ivanov, Milanov (Genchev 46), M. Petrov, S. Petrov. Coach: Stanimir Stoilov (BUL)
Montenegro: M. Božović, Pavićević, Baša, Jovanović, Vukčević, Vučinić, Đalović (Kašćelan 77), Bošković (V. Božović 64), Peković, Zverotić (Novaković 68), Džudović. Coach: Zlatko Kranjčar (CRO)
Goal(s): 0-1 Zverotić 36
Yellow Card(s): Peković 45 (Montenegro), S. Petrov 52 (Bulgaria), Bošković 55 (Montenegro), Angelov 63 (Bulgaria), M. Petrov 79 (Bulgaria)
Referee: Bezborodov (RUS)

7/9/10, St Jakob-Park, Basel
Switzerland 1-3 England
Attendance: 37500
Switzerland: Benaglio, Lichtsteiner, Ziegler, Von Bergen, Schwegler (Costanzo 83), Inler, Frei, Grichting, D. Degen (Streller 64), Derdiyok, Margairaz (Shaqiri 46). Coach: Ottmar Hitzfeld (GER)
England: Hart, G. Johnson, A. Cole, Gerrard, Lescott, Jagielka, Walcott (A. Johnson 13), Barry, Defoe (Bent 71), Rooney (Wright-Phillips 79), Milner. Coach: Fabio Capello (ITA)
Goal(s): 0-1 Rooney 10, 0-2 A. Johnson 69, 1-2 Shaqiri 71, 1-3 Bent 88
Red Card(s): Lichtsteiner 65 (Switzerland)
Yellow Card(s): Lichtsteiner 57 (Switzerland), Milner 60 (England), Lichtsteiner 65 (Switzerland), A. Cole 76 (England), Grichting 81 (Switzerland)
Referee: Rizzoli (ITA)

8/10/10, Stadion Podgorica, Podgorica
Montenegro 1-0 Switzerland
Attendance: 10750
Montenegro: M. Božović, Baša, Jovanović, Vukčević (Bećiraj 84), Vučinić, Đalović (Batak 90+2), Bošković (Kašćelan 46), Novaković, Zverotić, Džudović, Savić. Coach: Zlatko Kranjčar (CRO)
Switzerland: Wölfli, Ziegler, Von Bergen, Schwegler, Inler, Frei, Streller (Derdiyok 67), Grichting, Stocker (Yakin 76), Sutter, Shaqiri (Barnetta 67). Coach: Ottmar Hitzfeld (GER)
Goal(s): 1-0 Vučinić 68
Yellow Card(s): Vukčević 65 (Montenegro), Vučinić 68 (Montenegro)
Referee: Iturralde González (ESP)

8/10/10, Cardiff City Stadium, Cardiff
Wales 0-1 Bulgaria
Attendance: 14061
Wales: Hennessey, Gunter, D. Collins, Williams, J. Collins, Ricketts, Edwards (Church 69), Vaughan, Morison (Robson-Kanu 82), Ledley (King 59), Bale. Coach: Brian Flynn (WAL)
Bulgaria: Mihaylov, Iliev (Vidanov 37), Zanev, Georgiev, Popov, Makriev (Yankov 87), Peev (Rangelov 72), Ivan Ivanov, M. Petrov, S. Petrov, Bodurov. Coach: Lothar Matthäus (GER)
Goal(s): 0-1 Popov 48
Red Card(s): Gunter 90+3 (Wales)
Yellow Card(s): Ricketts 42 (Wales), Georgiev 50 (Bulgaria), Bodurov 80 (Bulgaria), M. Petrov 90+1 (Bulgaria), Zanev 90+3 (Bulgaria)
Referee: Eriksson (SWE)

12/10/10, Wembley Stadium, London
England 0-0 Montenegro
Attendance: 73451
England: Hart, G. Johnson, A. Cole, Gerrard, Ferdinand, Lescott, Young (Wright-Phillips 74), Barry, Crouch (Davies 70), Rooney, A. Johnson. Coach: Fabio Capello (ITA)
Montenegro: M. Božović, Baša, Jovanović, Vukčević, Đalović (Delibašić 77), Bošković (Bećiraj 83), Novaković (Kašćelan 62), Peković, Zverotić, Džudović, Savić. Coach: Zlatko Kranjčar (CRO)
Yellow Card(s): Džudović 25 (Montenegro), Savić 52 (Montenegro), Rooney 53 (England), Baša 57 (Montenegro), Young 60 (England), Barry 63 (England), Kašćelan 64 (Montenegro), Davies 86 (England), Vukčević 90+4 (Montenegro)
Referee: Gräfe (GER)

12/10/10, St Jakob-Park, Basel
Switzerland 4-1 Wales
Attendance: 26000
Switzerland: Benaglio (Wölfli 8), Lichtsteiner, Ziegler, Von Bergen, Schwegler (Fernandes 90+1), Barnetta, Inler, Frei (Derdiyok 79), Streller, Grichting, Stocker. Coach: Ottmar Hitzfeld (GER)
Wales: Hennessey, Blake (Ribeiro 54), D. Collins, J. Collins, Crofts, Williams, Edwards (Morison 77), King, Church, Vaughan (MacDonald 89), Bale. Coach: Brian Flynn (WAL)
Goal(s): 1-0 Stocker 8, 1-1 Bale 13, 2-1 Streller 21, 3-1 Inler 82 (p), 4-1 Stocker 89
Yellow Card(s): King 7 (Wales), Lichtsteiner 18 (Switzerland), Barnetta 35 (Switzerland), J. Collins 70 (Wales)
Referee: Hamer (LUX)

26/3/11, Natsionalen Stadion Vasil Levski, Sofia
Bulgaria 0-0 Switzerland
Attendance: 9600
Bulgaria: Mihaylov, Manolev, Bandalovski, Zanev, Georgiev, Delev (Lazarov 81), Popov (Angelov 85), Makriev (Genkov 52), Ivan Ivanov, S. Petrov, K. Stoyanov. Coach: Lothar Matthäus (GER)
Switzerland: Wölfli, Lichtsteiner, Ziegler, Von Bergen, Behrami (Fernandes 17), Inler, Frei, Streller (Gavranovic 77), Grichting, Stocker (Derdiyok 67), Dzemaili. Coach: Ottmar Hitzfeld (GER)
Yellow Card(s): Behrami 14 (Switzerland), K. Stoyanov 16 (Bulgaria), Georgiev 68 (Bulgaria), Derdiyok 76 (Switzerland), Manolev 87 (Bulgaria)
Referee: Collum (SCO)

26/3/11, Millennium Stadium, Cardiff
Wales 0-2 England
Attendance: 68959
Wales: Hennessey, Gunter, D. Collins, Crofts, J. Collins, Williams, Ledley, Bellamy, Morison (Evans 65), Ramsey, King (Vaughan 65). Coach: Gary Speed (WAL)
England: Hart, G. Johnson, A. Cole, Parker (Jagielka 89), Dawson, Terry, Lampard, Wilshere (Downing 82), Bent, Rooney (Milner 70), Young. Coach: Fabio Capello (ITA)
Goal(s): 0-1 Lampard 7 (p), 0-2 Bent 15
Yellow Card(s): Rooney 37 (England), Crofts 56 (Wales), Ledley 70 (Wales), Vaughan 82 (Wales), Bellamy 83 (Wales), G. Johnson 84 (England), J. Collins 87 (Wales)
Referee: Olegário Benquerença (POR)

4/6/11, Wembley Stadium, London
England 2-2 Switzerland
Attendance: 84459
England: Hart, G. Johnson, A. Cole (Baines 31), Parker, Ferdinand, Terry, Walcott (Downing 78), Lampard (Young 46), Bent, Wilshere, Milner. Coach: Fabio Capello (ITA)
Switzerland: Benaglio, Lichtsteiner, Ziegler, Senderos, Barnetta (Emeghara 90), Inler, Derdiyok (Mehmedi 75), Behrami (Dzemaili 59), Xhaka, Djourou, Shaqiri. Coach: Ottmar Hitzfeld (GER)
Goal(s): 0-1 Barnetta 32, 0-2 Barnetta 35, 1-2 Lampard 37 (p), 2-2 Young 51
Yellow Card(s): Djourou 36 (Switzerland), Behrami 45 (Switzerland), Wilshere 64 (England), Ferdinand 88 (England)
Referee: Skomina (SVN)

4/6/11, Stadion Podgorica, Podgorica
Montenegro 1-1 Bulgaria
Attendance: 11500
Montenegro: M. Božović, Pavićević (Kašćelan 82), Baša, Vučinić, Đalović, Peković, Pejović, Zverotić (Jovetić 72), Drinčić, V. Božović (Fatić 76), Savić. Coach: Zlatko Kranjčar (CRO)
Bulgaria: Mihaylov, Manolev, Bandalovski, Zanev, Bodurov, Yanev (Genkov 84), Popov, Ivan Ivanov, Marquinhos, M. Petrov (Delev 88), S. Petrov (Yankov 46). Coach: Lothar Matthäus (GER)
Goal(s): 1-0 Đalović 53, 1-1 Popov 66
Yellow Card(s): V. Božović 54 (Montenegro), Marquinhos 54 (Bulgaria), Pavićević 71 (Montenegro), Peković 78 (Montenegro)
Referee: Yefet (ISR)

Switzerland's Tranquillo Barnetta celebrates the first of his two free-kick goals against England at Wembley

Group G Table

		Home					Away					Total					
	Pld	W	D	L	F	A	W	D	L	F	A	W	D	L	F	A	Pts
1 England	5	1	2	0	6	3	2	0	0	5	0	3	2	0	11	3	11
2 Montenegro	5	2	1	0	3	1	1	1	0	1	0	3	2	0	4	1	11
3 Switzerland	5	1	0	1	5	7	0	2	1	2	0	1	2	2	7	7	5
4 Bulgaria	5	0	1	1	0	6	1	1	1	2	0	1	2	2	2	6	5
5 Wales	4	0	0	2	0	8	0	0	2	1	0	0	0	4	1	8	0

Remaining Fixtures

2/9/11
Bulgaria – England
Wales – Montenegro

6/9/11
England – Wales
Switzerland – Bulgaria

7/10/11
Montenegro – England
Wales – Switzerland

11/10/11
Bulgaria – Wales
Switzerland – Montenegro

GROUP H

Portugal have been quarter-finalists at least at each of the last four UEFA European Championships and they set out as clear favourites to win Group H – despite the amount of travelling that would be required in making three visits to Scandinavia and one to Cyprus. It soon became apparent, however, that Cristiano Ronaldo and company would not have everything their own way.

Impressive run

Portugal had been beaten only once in 20 matches under coach Carlos Queiroz leading up to the qualifying campaign, and even then the 1-0 defeat by Spain in the last 16 of the 2010 FIFA World Cup hardly constituted a blemish. They also possessed a flawless record against their opening-day opponents Cyprus, having won all eight of the countries' previous encounters. Although coach Queiroz was suspended, a routine win in Guimaraes appeared to be the safest of bets.

Cyprus, however, had not read the script. Twice they went ahead inside the first 11 minutes, Efstathios Aloneftis and Michalis Konstantinou scoring either side of a Hugo Almeida equaliser and thus setting the tone for what would be a rollercoaster of a contest. Raul Meireles levelled before half-time and Danny gave the hosts the advantage for the first time on 50 minutes, only for substitute Yiannis Okkas to restore parity again with his first touch. And there was more to come. Manuel Fernandes thought he had seen the islanders off on the hour with his long-range thunderbolt, but

Portugal's Raul Meireles attemps to hurdle a prostrate Bjorn Helge Riise of Norway

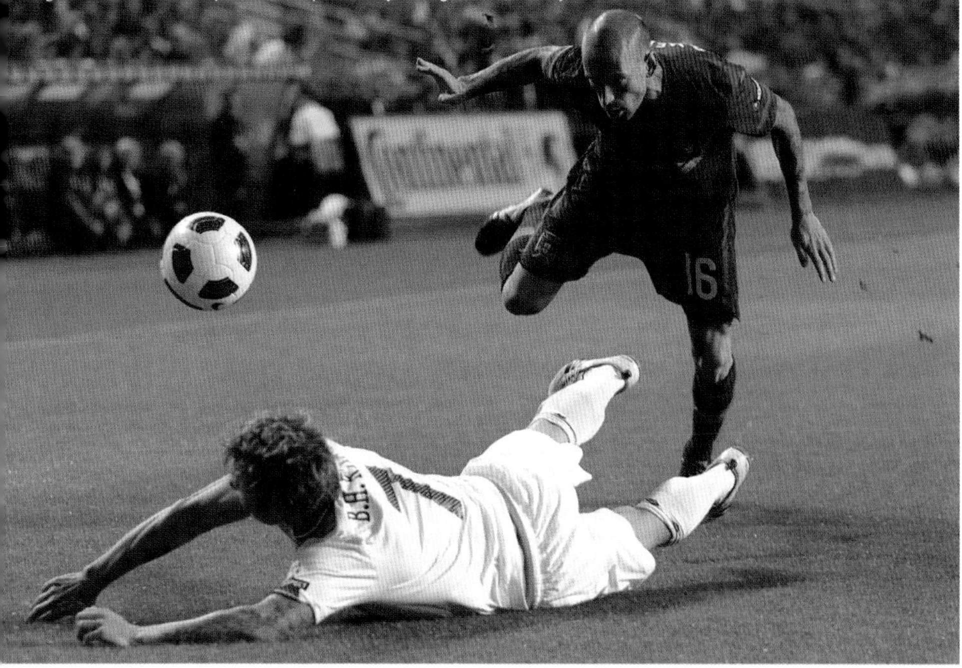

Andreas Avraam's last-minute effort made it 4-4, sealing one of Cyprus' best-ever results.

Shell-shocked skipper

"It's hard to say what happened," sighed Portugal's shell-shocked captain Ricardo Carvalho. "They scored every time we made a mistake." For Cyprus defender Ilias Charalambous, the result was reward for their audacious tactics. "We play to win all games," he said. "That's the strategy of our coach [Angelos Anastasiadis], and that's what makes us better year by year."

A trip to Oslo to take on a physical Norway team was hardly the ideal antidote for the shaken Portuguese and, with Queiroz still serving his ban and assistant Agostinho Oliveira again sitting in, they duly succumbed to a damaging defeat, Erik Huseklepp registering the only goal after John Carew had blocked goalkeeper Eduardo's clearance. Targeting their first finals appearance for 12 years, the Scandinavian team had already won their opening fixture in Iceland thanks to strikes from Brede Hangeland and Mohammed Abdellaoue, and they would go on to make it three wins in a row with a 2-1 triumph in Cyprus the following month.

Career high

Egil Olsen, who had guided Norway to two FIFA World Cups in the 1990s, seemed to be working his magic again. "I'm the first to admit our attacking play leaves a lot to be desired, but defensively we're world class," he enthused. Skipper Hangeland, meanwhile, described the Portugal win as "one of the high points of my career", adding: "All the lads gave their all, and the aggression we showed in defence has to be admired. I'm proud to captain this team."

The Portuguese Football Federation took drastic action, replacing Queiroz with Paulo Bento ahead of the crucial third game against Denmark. Thomas Kahlenberg's last-gasp strike had given the Danes a winning, if unconvincing, start against Iceland in Copenhagen, but Morten Olsen's men could not live with a revitalised Portugal in Porto. An electric performance from Nani ensured a perfect start for the new coach, the Manchester United FC winger hitting a first-half brace before Ronaldo added the gloss to a 3-1 triumph in the closing stages.

Back in contention

The relief was palpable, and five days later Portugal were right back in contention after recording another 3-1 win, away to Iceland. Although Heidar Helguson cancelled out Ronaldo's third-minute free-kick, the momentum was always with the visitors, who condemned Iceland to a third straight loss with strikes from Raul Meireles and Hélder Postiga.

Portugal's plight was also aided by their rivals' capacity for taking points off one another. Having seen off Cyprus with first international goals from Morten Rasmussen and Kasper Lorentzen, Denmark became the first side to deny Norway victory in March, securing a deserved 1-1 draw at the Ullevaal Stadion. It might have been even better for the visitors, who opened the scoring through long-serving winger Dennis Rommedahl, but Huseklepp struck another vital goal nine minutes from time.

Vital win

That slip-up offered Portugal an opportunity to go top on goal difference by gaining revenge on Norway in June. They duly delivered, Postiga grabbing his second goal in as many games to seal a vital, and deserved, 1-0 win in Lisbon. "Going top is important," stressed the match winner. "We played against a very good team, who arrived here as group leaders. It was difficult but we showed we knew how to close it out."

Denmark ensured a three-way tie at the top after five matches, moving second, above Norway, after strikes from Lasse Schøne and Christian Eriksen – also with his first for his country – clinched a 2-0 success away to bottom-of-the-table Iceland. For Ólafur Jóhannesson's side, a third successive home defeat signalled the end of their faint hopes. Iceland's only point in the opening five rounds had arrived courtesy of a goalless draw away to Cyrpus, who, despite the promise of their opening performance in Portugal, added only one further point to their total, a disappointment that resulted in the departure of coach Anastasiadis and his replacement, for the second half of the qualifying campaign, by fellow Greek Nikos Nioplias.

Christian Eriksen scored his first senior international goal in Denmark's 2-0 win over Iceland in Reykjavik

Group H Results

3/9/10, Laugardalsvöllur, Reykjavik
Iceland 1-2 Norway
Attendance: 6137
Iceland: Gunnleifsson, Ottesen, K. Sigurdsson, I. Sigurdsson, Steinsson (B. Bjarnason 76), Gudmundsson (Gíslason 87), V. Gunnarsson (Adalsteinsson 76), Helguson, E. Jónsson, A. Gunnarsson, G. Sigurdsson. Coach: Ólafur Jóhannesson (ISL)
Norway: Knudsen, Høgli, Wæhler, Hangeland, J.A. Riise, B.H. Riise (Iversen 57), Hauger, Abdellaoue (Solli 88), Gamst Pedersen, Grindheim, Huseklepp (Ruud 76). Coach: Egil Olsen (NOR)
Goal(s): 1-0 Helguson 38, 1-1 Hangeland 58, 1-2 Abdellaoue 75
Yellow Card(s): A. Gunnarsson 32 (Iceland), Hangeland 83 (Norway)
Referee: Banti (ITA)

3/9/10, Estádio D. Afonso Henriques, Guimaraes
Portugal 4-4 Cyprus
Attendance: 9100
Portugal: Eduardo, Bruno Alves, Ricardo Carvalho, Ricardo Quaresma, Danny (Liedson 61), Miguel, Manuel Fernandes (João Moutinho 79), Raul Meireles, Nani, Hugo Almeida (Yannick Djaló 84), Fábio Coentrão. Coach: Agostinho Oliveira (POR)
Cyprus: Georgallides, Charalambous, Merkis, Aloneftis (Okkas 56), Elia (Poursaitides 66), Charalambides (Nicolaou 76), Konstantinou, Makridis, Satsias, Dobrašinović, Avraam. Coach: Angelos Anastasiadis (GRE)
Goal(s): 0-1 Aloneftis 3, 1-1 Hugo Almeida 8, 1-2 Konstantinou 11, 2-2 Raul Meireles 29, 3-2 Danny 50, 3-3 Okkas 57, 4-3 Manuel Fernandes 60, 4-4 Avraam 89
Yellow Card(s): Charalambous 67 (Cyprus)
Referee: Clattenburg (ENG)

7/9/10, Parken, Copenhagen
Denmark 1-0 Iceland
Attendance: 18908
Denmark: Lindegaard, C. Poulsen, Kjær, Agger, Jessen, Jacobsen, Eriksen (Junker 56), Kahlenberg, Pedersen (Skoubo 71), Rommedahl, Krohn-Dehli (Vingaard 76). Coach: Morten Olsen (DEN)
Iceland: Gunnleifsson, Ottesen, K. Sigurdsson, I. Sigurdsson, B. Sævarsson, Gudmundsson (B. Bjarnason 90+2), Helguson (Sigthórsson 77), E. Jónsson, A. Gunnarsson, G. Sigurdsson, Gíslason. Coach: Ólafur Jóhannesson (ISL)
Goal(s): 1-0 Kahlenberg 90+1
Yellow Card(s): E. Jónsson 57 (Iceland), G. Sigurdsson 61 (Iceland), Gíslason 82 (Iceland), Skoubo 89 (Denmark)
Referee: McDonald (SCO)

7/9/10, Ullevaal Stadion, Oslo
Norway 1-0 Portugal
Attendance: 24535
Norway: Knudsen, Høgli, Wæhler (Demidov 28), Hangeland, B.H. Riise, Hauger, Carew (Abdellaoue 38), Gamst Pedersen, Ruud, Grindheim (Yttergård Jenssen 86), Huseklepp. Coach: Egil Olsen (NOR)
Portugal: Eduardo, Bruno Alves, Sílvio, Ricardo Carvalho, Ricardo Quaresma (Liedson 84), Miguel Veloso, Manuel Fernandes, Raul Meireles, Nani, Hugo Almeida, Tiago (Danny 72). Coach: Agostinho Oliveira (POR)
Goal(s): 1-0 Huseklepp 21
Yellow Card(s): Raul Meireles 62 (Portugal), B.H. Riise 65 (Norway), Hugo Almeida 90+1 (Portugal)
Referee: Duhamel (FRA)

8/10/10, Antonis Papadopoulos, Larnaca
Cyprus 1-2 Norway
Attendance: 7648
Cyprus: Georgallides, Charalambous (Efrem 86), Merkis (Christofi 81), Aloneftis, Okkas, Charalambides (Satsias 46), Konstantinou, Makridis, Dobrašinović, Avraam, Poursaitides. Coach: Angelos Anastasiadis (GRE)
Norway: Knudsen, Høgli, Wæhler, Hangeland, J.A. Riise, B.H. Riise (Vaagan Moen 74), Hauger, Carew (Abdellaoue 83), Gamst Pedersen, Grindheim, Huseklepp (Ruud 80). Coach: Egil Olsen (NOR)
Goal(s): 0-1 J.A. Riise 2, 0-2 Carew 42, 1-2 Okkas 58
Yellow Card(s): Poursaitides 6 (Cyprus), J.A. Riise 13 (Norway), Carew 71 (Norway), Satsias 76 (Cyprus)
Referee: Gumienny (BEL)

8/10/10, Estádio do Dragão, Porto
Portugal 3-1 Denmark
Attendance: 27117
Portugal: Eduardo, Pepe, João Pereira, Fábio Coentrão, Ricardo Carvalho, Cristiano Ronaldo, João Moutinho, Raul Meireles, Nani (Varela 88), Hugo Almeida (Hélder Postiga 69), Carlos Martins (Tiago 75). Coach: Paulo Bento (POR)
Denmark: Sørensen (Lindegaard 32), C. Poulsen, Kjær, Krøldrup, Silberbauer, Jacobsen, Jensen (Eriksen 58), W.K. Jørgensen (Løvenkrands 72), Pedersen, Rommedahl, Vingaard. Coach: Morten Olsen (DEN)
Goal(s): 1-0 Nani 29, 2-0 Nani 30, 2-1 Ricardo Carvalho 79 (og), 3-1 Cristiano Ronaldo 85
Yellow Card(s): Silberbauer 2 (Denmark)
Referee: Braamhaar (NED)

12/10/10, Parken, Copenhagen
Denmark 2-0 Cyprus
Attendance: 15544
Denmark: Lindegaard, C. Poulsen, Kjær, Agger (Krøldrup 39), Jessen, Jacobsen, Krohn-Dehli (Eriksen 65), Lorentzen, Pedersen, Rommedahl, Junker (Rasmussen 46). Coach: Morten Olsen (DEN)
Cyprus: Georgallides, Charalambous (Christou 28), Merkis, Aloneftis (Charalambides 55), Okkas, Konstantinou, Makridis, Satsias, Dobrašinović, Avraam (Garpozis 63), Poursaitides. Coach: Angelos Anastasiadis (GRE)
Goal(s): 1-0 Rasmussen 48, 2-0 Lorentzen 81
Yellow Card(s): Satsias 77 (Cyprus), Pedersen 88 (Denmark)
Referee: Muniz Fernandez (ESP)

12/10/10, Laugardalsvöllur, Reykjavik
Iceland 1-3 Portugal
Attendance: 9767
Iceland: Gunnleifsson, R. Sigurdsson, B. Sævarsson (V. Gunnarsson 85), K. Sigurdsson, I. Sigurdsson (Adalsteinsson 85), Steinsson, Skúlason, Gudjohnsen, Helguson, Daníelsson, T. Bjarnason (Thorvaldsson 68). Coach: Ólafur Jóhannesson (ISL)
Portugal: Eduardo, Pepe, João Pereira, Fábio Coentrão, Ricardo Carvalho, Cristiano Ronaldo, João Moutinho, Raul Meireles, Nani (Danny 87), Hugo Almeida (Hélder Postiga 65), Carlos Martins (Tiago 77). Coach: Paulo Bento (POR)
Goal(s): 0-1 Cristiano Ronaldo 3, 1-1 Helguson 17, 1-2 Raul Meireles 27, 1-3 Hélder Postiga 72
Yellow Card(s): Skúlason 36 (Iceland), Eduardo 17 (Portugal), Tiago 79 (Portugal), Gudjohnsen 79 (Iceland)
Referee: Einwaller (AUT)

26/3/11, GSP Stadium, Nicosia
Cyprus 0-0 Iceland
Attendance: 2088
Cyprus: Giorgallides, Sielis (Demetriou 46), Merkis, Aloneftis, Christofi (Alexandrou 73), Charalambides, Makridis, Michail, Dobrašinović, Avraam, Poursaitides (Elia 61). Coach: Angelos Anastasiadis (GRE)
Iceland: Magnússon, B. Sævarsson, K. Sigurdsson, I. Sigurdsson, Sigurdsson (B. Bjarnason 90+1), Hreidarsson, Gíslason (Finnbogason 63), Gudmundsson (Smárason 59), H. Helguson, E. Jónsson, A. Gunnarsson. Coach: Ólafur Jóhannesson (ISL)
Yellow Card(s): K. Sigurdsson 21 (Iceland), Merkis 42 (Cyprus), E. Jónsson 72 (Iceland), Magnússon 88 (Iceland)
Referee: Čeferin (SVN)

Cyprus coach Angelos Anastasiadis was relieved of his duties halfway through the qualifying campaign

26/3/11, Ullevaal Stadion, Oslo
Norway 1-1 Denmark
Attendance: 24828
Norway: Jarstein, Wæhler, Hangeland, J.A. Riise, B.H. Riise, Hauger, Abdellaoue, Gamst Pedersen, Ruud (Braaten 78), Grindheim, Huseklepp (Iversen 89). Coach: Egil Olsen (NOR)
Denmark: Sørensen, C. Poulsen (J. Poulsen 70), M. Jørgensen, Agger, Silberbauer, Jacobsen, W.K. Jørgensen, Eriksen, Krohn-Dehli (Enevoldsen 82), Rommedahl (Wass 90+3), Bendtner. Coach: Morten Olsen (DEN)
Goal(s): 0-1 Rommedahl 27, 1-1 Huseklepp 81
Yellow Card(s): Jacobsen 34 (Denmark), Wæhler 37 (Norway)
Referee: Rocchi (ITA)

4/6/11, Laugardalsvöllur, Reykjavik
Iceland 0-2 Denmark
Attendance: 7629
Iceland: Magnússon, B. Sævarsson, K. Sigurdsson, Hreidarsson, Skúlason (Finnbogason 66), Gudjohnsen, G. Sigurdsson, Helguson (Gudmundsson 77), Eiríksson, A. Gunnarsson, Sigthórsson. Coach: Ólafur Jóhannesson (ISL)
Denmark: Sørensen, Zimling, Kjær, Svensson, S. Poulsen, Jacobsen, W.K. Jørgensen (C. Poulsen 60), Eriksen, Krohn-Dehli (Schøne 46), Rommedahl, Bendtner. Coach: Morten Olsen (DEN)
Goal(s): 0-1 Schøne 60, 0-2 Eriksen 75
Yellow Card(s): K. Sigurdsson 22 (Iceland), Skúlason 66 (Iceland)
Referee: Aydınus (TUR)

Hélder Postiga (right) jumps for joy, with team-mate Carlos Martins in attendance, after scoring Portugal's winning goal at home to Norway

4/6/11, Estádio do Sport Lisboa e Benfica, Lisbon
Portugal 1-0 Norway
Attendance: 47829
Portugal: Eduardo, Bruno Alves, Pepe, Fábio Coentrão, Cristiano Ronaldo, João Moutinho, Raul Meireles, Nani (Varela 86), Carlos Martins (Rúben Micael 69), João Pereira (Sílvio 73), Hélder Postiga. Coach: Paulo Bento (POR)
Norway: Jarstein, Høgli, Demidov, Hangeland, J.A. Riise, B.H. Riise, Hauger, Carew (Abdellaoue 60), Gamst Pedersen, Grindheim (Henriksen 83), Huseklepp (Braaten 75). Coach: Egil Olsen (NOR)
Goal(s): 1-0 Hélder Postiga 53
Referee: Çakır (TUR)

Group H Table

	Pld	Home W	D	L	F	A	Away W	D	L	F	A	Total W	D	L	F	A	Pts
1 Portugal	5	2	1	0	8	7	1	0	1	3	0	3	1	1	11	7	10
2 Denmark	5	2	0	0	3	4	1	1	1	4	0	3	1	1	7	4	10
3 Norway	5	1	1	0	2	4	2	0	1	4	0	3	1	1	6	4	10
4 Cyprus	4	0	1	1	1	8	0	1	1	4	0	0	2	2	5	8	2
5 Iceland	5	0	0	3	2	8	0	1	1	0	0	0	1	4	2	8	1

Remaining Fixtures

2/9/11
Cyprus – Portugal
Norway – Iceland

6/9/11
Denmark – Norway
Iceland – Cyprus

7/10/11
Cyprus – Denmark
Portugal – Iceland

11/10/11
Denmark – Portugal
Norway – Cyprus

GROUP I

To the surprise of absolutely no one, defending European champions and 2010 FIFA World Cup winners Spain took complete charge of Group I with victories in each of their opening five matches. Second place was still up for grabs, but the Czech Republic, qualifiers for each of the previous four UEFA European Championship final tournaments, looked firm favourites for a play-off place in their tussle with Scotland.

Professional job

From the euphoria of Johannesburg to the nitty-gritty of a qualifying game in Vaduz, Vicente Del Bosque's World Cup-winning stars might have been excused for struggling to lift themselves for the opening game, yet their professional attitude in Liechtenstein was hugely impressive. Two Fernando Torres goals and further strikes from David Villa and David Silva secured a comprehensive victory as Spain picked up where they had left off in South Africa. "We tried to apply the same style and intensity as during the World Cup," midfielder Xabi Alonso explained. "There's no question this was the approach we required."

Spain's David Villa is pursued by the Czech Republic's Tomáš Hübschman

As long as the Spaniards managed to maintain that intensity, they were always going to take some stopping. Lithuania were their next victims, surrendering a three-game unbeaten record after Fernando Llorente's double and another Silva goal set up a 3-1 triumph in Salamanca. Raimondas Žutautas's side would lose by the same score in Kaunas several months later, Marius Stankevičius cancelling out Xavi's opener, only for Tadas Kijanskas to put Spain back in front with an own goal and Juan Mata to add a third.

Surprise win

Lithuania had nevertheless emerged as dark horses having held Scotland to a goalless draw in Kaunas in their opening fixture before claiming an unexpected 1-0 win away to the Czech Republic courtesy of Darvydas Šernas's 27th-minute strike. Goalkeeper Žydrūnas Karčemarskas was one of Lithuania's heroes in Olomouc, pulling off a series of superb saves including one from a Milan Baroš penalty, although neither he nor the goalscorer were claiming credit for the triumph. "The whole team played well," stressed Šernas.

Another victory on 3 June in Liechtenstein would have been the perfect way to sign off an encouraging year, but Lithuania were in for a shock as the hosts – despite missing several key players – claimed their first competitive victory in four years. Philippe Erne, who was replacing the suspended record scorer Mario Frick, recorded his first international goal before Michele Polverino sealed a remarkable 2-0 success for Hans-Peter Zaugg's minnows. "What we've achieved is unbelievable," enthused goalkeeper Benjamin Büchel who had capably filled in for regular custodian Peter Jehle.

Ultra-defensive Scots

While Liechtenstein were delighted to get off the mark, Lithuania's defeat meant that Scotland, inactive in the first half of 2011, were left as the only realistic challengers to the Czech Republic for second place. Runners-up in 1996 and beaten semi-finalists eight years later, the Czechs were under pressure ahead of the visit of Craig Levein's side in October having already lost once on home soil to Lithuania. Scotland set themselves up to secure a point with an ultra-defensive formation shorn of strikers, but crucially Roman Hubník's headed goal 21 minutes before the end swung the contest in favour of Michal Bílek's charges.

Scotland's early efforts conformed to type – resilient against the strong teams but lacklustre against the supposedly weaker ones. Having been held in Lithuania, they only just scraped a win at home to Liechtenstein at Hampden Park, Stephen McManus heading home deep into added time after Kenny Miller had cancelled out Frick's opener. Conversely, they pushed Spain extremely hard a month later in the same stadium. The visitors looked to be strolling when David Villa's spot kick was followed by an Andrés Iniesta goal, but Steven Naismith, with his first international goal, halved the deficit before Gerard Piqué induced a mighty roar from the Hampden crowd by turning a James Morrison cross into his own net eight minutes later. However, just as the Tartan Army prepared to celebrate a tremendous point, Llorente, who had been dropped despite his two goals against Lithuania four days earlier, came off the bench to volley in Joan Capdevila's inviting cross from the left and seal a dramatic 3-2 victory.

Historic night

Llorente said he had understood Del Bosque's decision to leave him out, and David Villa's prolific form continued to justify the coach's preference. The striker, enjoying life at his new club FC Barcelona, ensured the continuation of Spain's perfect run in March by scoring both goals in a 2-1 triumph over the Czech Republic, who had taken a shock lead through Jaroslav Plašil in Granada. On an historic night, Xavi collected his 100th cap while Villa became Spain's all-time leading scorer, easing clear of Raúl with his 45th and 46th international goals. Despite that defeat, the Czechs secured a five-point cushion over Scotland and Lithuania four days later thanks to a second 2-0 win over Liechtenstein. Tomáš Necid and Václav Kadlec had scored the goals in Vaduz in October, and it was Baroš and Michal Kadlec who ensured a repetition of the scoreline five and a half months later in Ceske Budejovice.

Michele Polverino sealed an unlikely 2-0 win for Liechtenstein at home to Lithuania

Group I Results

3/9/10, Rheinpark, Vaduz
Liechtenstein 0-4 Spain
Attendance: 6100
Liechtenstein: Jehle, L. Eberle (Rechsteiner 45), Mi. Stocklasa, Oehri (Vogt 46), Ma. Stocklasa, Frick, Burgmeier, D. Hasler, Erne, Wieser (R. Büchel 82), Polverino. Coach: Hans-Peter Zaugg (SUI)
Spain: Casillas, Piqué, Marchena, Iniesta (Pedro 65), David Villa, Xavi (Fàbregas 46), Fernando Torres (David Silva 57), Capdevila, Xabi Alonso, Sergio Ramos, Busquets. Coach: Vicente del Bosque (ESP)
Goal(s): 0-1 Fernando Torres 18, 0-2 David Villa 26, 0-3 Fernando Torres 54, 0-4 David Silva 62
Yellow Card(s): D. Hasler 40 (Liechtenstein)
Referee: Yıldırım (TUR)

3/9/10, Dariaus ir Girėno stadionas, Kaunas
Lithuania 0-0 Scotland
Attendance: 5248
Lithuania: Karčemarskas, Šemberas, Radavičius, Kijanskas, Skerla, Panka, E. Česnauskis, Danilevičius (Ivaškevičius 90), Šernas (Lukša 80), Mikoliūnas (Poškus 71), Stankevičius. Coach: Raimondas Žutautas (LTU)
Scotland: McGregor, Hutton, Whittaker (Berra 90), McManus, Weir, McCulloch, D. Fletcher, Robson (McFadden 69), Miller, Brown (Morrison 76), Naismith. Coach: Craig Levein (SCO)
Yellow Card(s): Kijanskas 15 (Lithuania), Radavičius 18 (Lithuania), Brown 42 (Scotland), Skerla 67 (Lithuania), McCulloch 72 (Scotland), Ivaškevičius 90+3 (Lithuania)
Referee: Çakır (TUR)

7/9/10, Andruv Stadión, Olomouc
Czech Republic 0-1 Lithuania
Attendance: 12038
Czech Republic: Čech, M. Kadlec, R. Hubník, Polák (Štajner 69), Fenin (Necid 59), Rosický, Pudil (Bednář 84), Pospěch, Plašil, Baroš, Hübschman. Coach: Michal Bílek (CZE)
Lithuania: Karčemarskas, Šemberas, Radavičius, Kijanskas, Skerla, Panka, E. Česnauskis, Danilevičius (Ivaškevičius 90), Šernas (Poškus 61), Mikoliūnas (Lukša 79), Stankevičius. Coach: Raimondas Žutautas (LTU)
Goal(s): 0-1 Šernas 27
Yellow Card(s): Šernas 19 (Lithuania), E. Česnauskis 42 (Lithuania), Šemberas 74 (Lithuania), R. Hubník 90+2 (Czech Republic)
Referee: Yefet (ISR)

7/9/10, Hampden Park, Glasgow
Scotland 2-1 Liechtenstein
Attendance: 37050
Scotland: McGregor, Hutton, L. Wallace (Robson 54), McManus, Weir, McCulloch, D. Fletcher, Brown, Miller, Boyd (Naismith 66), McFadden (Morrison 46). Coach: Craig Levein (SCO)
Liechtenstein: Jehle, Mi. Stocklasa, Rechsteiner, Oehri, Ma. Stocklasa, Frick (D'Elia 79), Burgmeier, D. Hasler (N. Hasler 90+2), Erne, Wieser (R. Büchel 71), Polverino. Coach: Hans-Peter Zaugg (SUI)
Goal(s): 0-1 Frick 47, 1-1 Miller 63, 2-1 McManus 90+7
Yellow Card(s): Burgmeier 9 (Liechtenstein), Wieser 31 (Liechtenstein), Ma. Stocklasa 51 (Liechtenstein), Robson 57 (Scotland), Frick 67 (Liechtenstein), Rechsteiner 68 (Liechtenstein), McCulloch 86 (Scotland), McGregor 88 (Scotland), D'Elia 90+1 (Liechtenstein), P
Referee: Shvetsov (UKR)

8/10/10, Eden, Prague
Czech Republic 1-0 Scotland
Attendance: 14922
Czech Republic: Čech, Suchý, M. Kadlec, R. Hubník, Necid (Holek 84), Polák, Magera (Bednář 59), Rosický, Pospěch, Plašil (Rajnoch 90+4), Hübschman. Coach: Michal Bílek (CZE)
Scotland: McGregor, Hutton, Whittaker, McManus, Weir, G. Caldwell (Miller 76), D. Fletcher, Mackie (Iwelumo 76), Naismith, Morrison (Robson 84), Dorrans. Coach: Craig Levein (SCO)
Goal(s): 1-0 R. Hubník 69
Yellow Card(s): Whittaker 13 (Scotland), Necid 15 (Czech Republic), Hübschman 33 (Czech Republic), Weir 83 (Scotland), Robson 86 (Scotland)
Referee: Bebek (CRO)

8/10/10, Helmántico, Salamanca
Spain 3-1 Lithuania
Attendance: 16800
Spain: Casillas, Piqué, Puyol, Iniesta, David Villa (Pablo Hernández 76), Capdevila, Sergio Ramos (Arbeloa 82), Busquets, Llorente (Aduriz 77), Santi Cazorla, David Silva. Coach: Vicente del Bosque (ESP)

Lithuania: Karčemarskas, Šemberas, Radavičius, Kijanskas, Skerla, Panka, E. Česnauskis (Poškus 85), Danilevičius (Ivaškevičius 82), Šernas, Mikoliūnas (D. Česnauskis 59), Stankevičius. Coach: Raimondas Žutautas (LTU)
Goal(s): 1-0 Llorente 47, 1-1 Šernas 54, 2-1 Llorente 56, 3-1 David Silva 79
Referee: Rocchi (ITA)

12/10/10, Rheinpark, Vaduz
Liechtenstein 0-2 Czech Republic
Attendance: 2555
Liechtenstein: Jehle, Mi. Stocklasa, Rechsteiner, Oehri, Ma. Stocklasa, T. Beck (N. Hasler 66), Frick, Burgmeier, Erne (Hanselmann 78), Wieser (R. Büchel 84), Polverino. Coach: Hans-Peter Zaugg (SUI)
Czech Republic: Čech, Suchý, M. Kadlec, R. Hubník, Necid (Petržela 89), Polák (Štajner 59), Rosický, Pospěch, Plašil, V. Kadlec (Bednář 64), Hübschman. Coach: Michal Bílek (CZE)
Goal(s): 0-1 Necid 12, 0-2 V. Kadlec 29
Yellow Card(s): Polverino 47 (Liechtenstein), Wieser 57 (Liechtenstein), Mi. Stocklasa 65 (Liechtenstein), Štajner 72 (Czech Republic)
Referee: Sukhina (RUS)

12/10/10, Hampden Park, Glasgow
Scotland 2-3 Spain
Attendance: 51322
Scotland: McGregor, Bardsley, Whittaker, McManus, Weir, McCulloch (Adam 46), D. Fletcher, Morrison (Maloney 88), Miller, Naismith, Dorrans (Mackie 80). Coach: Craig Levein (SCO)
Spain: Casillas, Piqué, Puyol, Iniesta, David Villa, Capdevila, Xabi Alonso, Sergio Ramos, Busquets (Marchena 90), Santi Cazorla (Pablo Hernández 70), David Silva (Llorente 76). Coach: Vicente del Bosque (ESP)
Goal(s): 0-1 David Villa 44 (p), 0-2 Iniesta 55, 1-2 Naismith 58, 2-2 Piqué 66 (og), 2-3 Llorente 79
Red Card(s): Whittaker 89 (Scotland)
Yellow Card(s): Whittaker 44 (Scotland), Miller 73 (Scotland), Whittaker 89 (Scotland)
Referee: Busacca (SUI)

25/3/11, Los Cármenes, Granada
Spain 2-1 Czech Republic
Attendance: 16301
Spain: Casillas, Piqué, Iniesta, David Villa, Xavi, Capdevila (Santi Cazorla 58), Xabi Alonso (Fernando Torres 46), Sergio Ramos, Busquets, Arbeloa, Jesús Navas (Marchena 86). Coach: Vicente del Bosque (ESP)
Czech Republic: Čech, M. Kadlec, R. Hubník, Sivok, Rezek (Necid 84), Rosický, Pudil (Hloušek 78), Pospěch, Plašil, Baroš, Hübschman. Coach: Michal Bílek (CZE)
Goal(s): 0-1 Plašil 29, 1-1 David Villa 69, 2-1 David Villa 72 (p)
Yellow Card(s): Xabi Alonso 39 (Spain), Pospěch 46 (Czech Republic), Rezek 60 (Czech Republic), Arbeloa 84 (Spain)
Referee: Kassai (HUN)

29/3/11, Strelecky Ostrov, Ceske Budejovice
Czech Republic 2-0 Liechtenstein
Attendance: 6600
Czech Republic: Čech, M. Kadlec, R. Hubník, Sivok, Rosický (Polák 84), Pospěch, Plašil, Baroš, Hübschman, Lafata (Necid 59), Morávek (Hloušek 56). Coach: Michal Bílek (CZE)
Liechtenstein: Jehle, Mi. Stocklasa, Rechsteiner, Ma. Stocklasa, T. Beck, Frick, Burgmeier, M. Büchel (Kieber 10) (A. Christen 81), D. Hasler, Erne, N. Hasler. Coach: Hans-Peter Zaugg (SUI)
Goal(s): 1-0 Baroš 3, 2-0 M. Kadlec 70
Yellow Card(s): Mi. Stocklasa 38 (Liechtenstein), Rechsteiner 56 (Liechtenstein), M. Frick 58 (Liechtenstein), T. Beck 70 (Liechtenstein), Plašil 81 (Czech Republic)
Referee: Hategan (ROU)

29/3/11, Dariaus ir Girėno stadionas, Kaunas
Lithuania 1-3 Spain
Attendance: 9180
Lithuania: Karčemarskas, Šemberas, Kijanskas, Skerla, Žaliukas, Panka, E. Česnauskis, Danilevičius (Galkevičius 85), Šernas (Labukas 74), Mikoliūnas (Radavičius 71), Stankevičius. Coach: Raimondas Žutautas (LTU)
Spain: Casillas, Albiol, Piqué (Sergio Ramos 90), Iraola, David Villa (David Silva 54), Xavi, Xabi Alonso, Arbeloa, Javi Martínez, Llorente, Santi Cazorla (Mata 67). Coach: Vicente del Bosque (ESP)
Goal(s): 0-1 Xavi Hernández 19, 1-1 Stankevičius 57, 1-2 Kijanskas 70 (og), 1-3 Mata 83
Referee: Duhamel (FRA)

3/6/11, Rheinpark, Vaduz
Liechtenstein 2-0 Lithuania
Attendance: 1886
Liechtenstein: B. Büchel, Ma. Stocklasa, Fischer (M. Christen 72), T. Beck (A. Christen 84), Burgmeier, M. Büchel, Erne (Hanselmann 87), N. Hasler, Ritzberger, Kaufmann, Polverino. Coach: Hans-Peter Zaugg (SUI)
Lithuania: Šetkus, Šemberas, Radavičius, Kijanskas, Skerla, Panka, E. Česnauskis (Savenas 68), Danilevičius (Labukas 46), Šernas, Mikoliūnas, Stankevičius (D. Česnauskis 46). Coach: Raimondas Žutautas (LTU)
Goal(s): 1-0 Erne 7, 2-0 Polverino 36
Yellow Card(s): Šernas 8 (Lithuania), Danilevičius 14 (Lithuania), Radavičius 77 (Lithuania), T. Beck 78 (Liechtenstein), Kaufmann 81 (Liechtenstein)
Referee: Kuchin (KAZ)

Group I Table

		Home					Away					Total					
	Pld	W	D	L	F	A	W	D	L	F	A	W	D	L	F	A	Pts
1 Spain	5	2	0	0	5	5	3	0	0	10	0	5	0	0	15	5	15
2 Czech Republic	5	2	0	1	3	3	1	0	1	3	0	3	0	2	6	3	9
3 Scotland	4	1	0	1	4	5	0	1	1	0	0	1	1	2	4	5	4
4 Lithuania	5	0	1	1	1	8	1	0	2	2	0	1	1	3	3	8	4
5 Liechtenstein	5	1	0	2	2	10	0	0	2	1	0	1	0	4	3	10	3

Remaining Fixtures

2/9/11
Lithuania – Liechtenstein

3/9/11
Scotland – Czech Republic

6/9/11
Scotland – Lithuania
Spain – Liechtenstein

7/10/11
Czech Republic – Spain

8/10/11
Liechtenstein – Scotland

11/10/11
Lithuania – Czech Republic
Spain – Scotland

TOP GOALSCORERS
(All groups)

8	Klaas Jan HUNTELAAR (Netherlands)
	Miroslav KLOSE (Germany)
6	Mikael FORSSELL (Finland)
5	Zlatan IBRAHIMOVIĆ (Sweden)
	Robbie KEANE (Republic of Ireland)
4	Ádám SZALAI (Hungary)
	Tim MATAVŽ (Slovenia)
	Mario GOMEZ (Germany)
	Yossi BENAYOUN (Israel)
	Marvin OGUNJIMI (Belgium)
	Dirk KUYT (Netherlands)
	DAVID VILLA (Spain)
	Niko KRANJČAR (Croatia)
	Gergely RUDOLF (Hungary)

UEFA U21 Championship 2011

The northern Danish peninsula of Jutland was the setting for the 2011 UEFA European Under-21 Championship finals, which offered a Nordic flavour but ended with a Spanish celebration. The eight-team tournament comprised 16 matches over 15 days in the four venues of Aarhus, Aalborg, Herning and Viborg. Switzerland played the role of party-poopers at the official opening game in Aalborg on 11 June by beating Denmark 1-0 and were still there two weeks later for the final, only to see their hopes founder against a Spain side whose 2-0 victory secured their third U21 title. In between, a championship played out on long summer evenings offered a showcase of young talent and no little drama – not least on a topsy-turvy final day of group action that brought heartache for England, Iceland and the hosts. It also produced a surprise Olympic qualifier as Belarus won a ticket to the London Games by defeating the Czech Republic in a third-place play-off.

UEFA
UNDER21
CHAMPIONSHIP

QUALIFYING ROUND

GROUP 1

Romania and Russia resumed their campaigns locked on 18 points and, with their nearest challengers Moldova a distant third, all was set to be decided in the final two matches between the leaders.

Romania took command with a 3-0 win against Russia in Botosani on 3 September thanks to goals from Eric Bicfalvi, Sabrin Sburlea and Ioan Hora and their position as group winners was confirmed four days later in St Petersburg following a goalless draw. Russia's surprise defeat by the Faroe Islands in only their second game ultimately cost them a play-off berth as one of the four best runners-up.

Group 1 Results

28/3/09
Romania 2-0 Andorra

1/4/09
Russia 4-0 Andorra

6/6/09
Latvia 4-0 Andorra
Faroe Islands 0-4 Romania

9/6/09
Faroe Islands 1-0 Russia

12/8/09
Andorra 0-2 Romania
Moldova 1-0 Latvia

5/9/09
Faroe Islands 1-1 Moldova
Latvia 0-4 Russia

8/9/09
Andorra 0-4 Russia
Romania 3-0 Moldova

9/9/09
Faroe Islands 1-3 Latvia

9/10/09
Latvia 5-1 Romania

10/10/09
Russia 2-0 Faroe Islands
Moldova 1-0 Andorra

13/10/09
Romania 3-0 Faroe Islands

14/10/09
Russia 3-1 Moldova

14/11/09
Romania 4-1 Latvia
Moldova 0-3 Russia

18/11/09
Latvia 0-1 Faroe Islands

21/11/09
Andorra 1-1 Faroe Islands

3/3/10
Andorra 1-3 Moldova

11/8/10, Petrovskiy, St Petersburg
Russia 2-1 Latvia
Goal(s): 1-0 Dzyuba 18, 1-1 Turkovs 55(p), 2-1 Dzyuba 65

11/8/10, Zimbru 2, Chisinau
Moldova 0-1 Romania
Goal(s): 0-1 Ganea 23(p)

11/8/10, Gundadalur, Torshavn
Faroe Islands 3-1 Andorra
Goal(s): 0-1 Blanco 32, 1-1 Kamban 51, 2-1 Baldvinsson 74, 3-1 K. Jacobsen 89

3/9/10, Municipal, Botosani
Romania 3-0 Russia
Goal(s): 1-0 Bicfalvi 27, 2-0 Sburlea 37, 3-0 Hora 86

4/9/10, Estadi Comunal, Andorra la Vella
Andorra 0-1 Latvia
Goal(s): 0-1 Dubra 14

4/9/10, Zimbru 2, Chisinau
Moldova 1-0 Faroe Islands
Goal(s): 1-0 Ioniţa 80

7/9/10, Sloka, Jurmala
Latvia 1-1 Moldova
Goal(s): 0-1 Vornişel 35, 1-1 Carauş 80(og)

7/9/10, Petrovskiy, St Petersburg
Russia 0-0 Romania

Group 1 Table

	Pld	Home					Away					Total					
		W	D	L	F	A	W	D	L	F	A	W	D	L	F	A	Pts
1 Romania	10	5	0	0	15	6	3	1	1	8	0	8	1	1	23	6	25
2 Russia	10	4	1	0	11	6	3	0	2	11	0	7	1	2	22	6	22
3 Moldova	10	3	0	2	3	13	1	2	2	6	0	4	2	4	9	13	14
4 Latvia	10	2	1	2	10	15	2	0	3	6	0	4	1	5	16	15	13
5 Faroe Islands	10	2	1	2	6	16	1	1	3	2	0	3	2	5	8	16	11
6 Andorra	10	0	1	4	2	25	0	0	5	1	0	0	1	9	3	25	1

Fabian Frei scored the goal that secured Switzerland top spot in Group 2

GROUP 2

After spurning two chances to win the section prior to the recess, Switzerland completed the job at the third time of asking with a 1-0 victory against the Republic of Ireland in Lugano.

Fabian Frei scored the only goal of the game, his third in the group phase, three minutes into the second half as Pierluigi Tami's side belatedly saw off the challenge of Turkey. Turkey finished second, four points off the pace, after concluding their campaign with a 1-0 defeat at home to Georgia and victory against Ireland by the same score.

Group 2 Results

31/3/09
Republic of Ireland 0-3 Turkey

5/6/09
Switzerland 2-1 Armenia

9/6/09
Armenia 2-5 Turkey

12/8/09
Switzerland 0-1 Estonia

4/9/09
Armenia 1-3 Switzerland

5/9/09
Estonia 2-0 Georgia

9/9/09
Georgia 4-0 Turkey
Estonia 1-1 Republic of Ireland

9/10/09
Estonia 1-4 Switzerland
Republic of Ireland 1-1 Georgia

13/10/09
Turkey 1-0 Armenia
Republic of Ireland 1-1 Switzerland

14/11/09
Georgia 1-1 Republic of Ireland
Armenia 1-1 Estonia
Turkey 1-3 Switzerland

17/11/09
Armenia 4-1 Republic of Ireland

18/11/09
Turkey 0-0 Estonia
Switzerland 1-0 Georgia

3/3/10
Georgia 2-0 Estonia
Republic of Ireland 1-2 Armenia

20/5/10
Estonia 2-3 Armenia

23/5/10
Estonia 1-0 Turkey

26/5/10
Switzerland 0-2 Turkey

30/5/10
Georgia 0-0 Switzerland

10/8/10, Tallaght Stadium, Dublin
Republic of Ireland 5-0 Estonia
Goal(s): 1-0 Stokes 15, 2-0 Stokes 30(p), 3-0 McCarthy 62, 4-0 Coleman 87, 5-0 Garvan 90+1

11/8/10, Yerevan Republican, Yerevan
Armenia 2-3 Georgia
Goal(s): 0-1 Ananidze 36(p), 0-2 Vatsadze 50, 1-2 Mkhitaryan 78(p), 1-3 Kvekveskiri 81, 2-3 V. Poghosyan 88

3/9/10, Cornaredo, Lugano
Switzerland 1-0 Republic of Ireland
Goal(s): 1-0 F. Frei 48

4/9/10, Sakarya Atatürk, Sakarya
Turkey 0-1 Georgia
Goal(s): 0-1 Hasan Ali Kaldırım 50(og)

7/9/10, Ismetpasa, Kocaeli
Turkey 1-0 Republic of Ireland
Goal(s): 1-0 Tevfik Köse 81

7/9/10, Mikheil Meskhi, Tbilisi
Georgia 0-2 Armenia
Goal(s): 0-1 Dashyan 90+2, 0-2 V. Poghosyan 90+3

Group 2 Table

		Home					Away					Total					
	Pld	W	D	L	F	A	W	D	L	F	A	W	D	L	F	A	Pts
1 Switzerland	10	3	0	2	4	8	3	2	0	11	0	6	2	2	15	8	20
2 Turkey	10	2	1	2	3	11	3	0	2	10	0	5	1	4	13	11	16
3 Georgia	10	2	2	1	7	9	2	1	2	5	0	4	3	3	12	9	15
4 Armenia	10	1	1	3	10	19	3	0	2	8	0	4	1	5	18	19	13
5 Estonia	10	2	1	2	7	16	1	2	2	2	0	3	3	4	9	16	12
6 Republic of Ireland	10	1	2	2	8	15	0	2	3	3	0	1	4	5	11	15	7

GROUP 3

After trailing all campaign, Italy sealed top spot with a 1-0 victory on the final day against Wales.

Brian Flynn's side entered the closing straight three points clear of the Azzurrini with two games to play and both sides won their penultimate fixtures, Wales 1-0 in Hungary to end the latter's challenge and set up the decider with Italy in Pescara. Needing only a draw, Wales were undone by Mattia Mustacchio's 14th-minute strike, which meant that despite finishing level on points, Italy were top courtesy of a better head-to-head record on away goals. The five-times champions were through by the slenderest of margins.

Mattia Mustacchio turns in celebration after scoring Italy's all-important winner against Wales in Pescara

Group 3 Results

27/3/09
Luxembourg 0-0 Wales

31/3/09
Wales 5-1 Luxembourg

6/6/09
Hungary 3-0 Luxembourg

10/6/09
Luxembourg 0-1 Hungary

12/8/09
Wales 4-1 Hungary

4/9/09
Bosnia & Herzegovina 0-1 Luxembourg
Wales 2-1 Italy

8/9/09
Italy 2-0 Luxembourg

10/10/09
Wales 2-0 Bosnia & Herzegovina

13/10/09
Italy 1-1 Bosnia & Herzegovina

13/11/09
Hungary 2-0 Italy

17/11/09
Luxembourg 0-4 Italy

18/11/09
Bosnia & Herzegovina 2-1 Wales

2/3/10
Luxembourg 0-1 Bosnia & Herzegovina

3/3/10
Italy 2-0 Hungary

11/8/10, Bilino Polje, Zenica
Bosnia & Herzegovina 0-2 Hungary
Goal(s): 0-1 Németh 79, 0-2 Gosztonyi 82

3/9/10, Grbavica, Sarajevo
Bosnia & Herzegovina 0-1 Italy
Goal(s): 0-1 Soriano 75

4/9/10, Sóstói, Szekesfehervar
Hungary 0-1 Wales
Goal(s): 0-1 Robson-Kanu 68

7/9/10, Adriatico, Pescara
Italy 1-0 Wales
Goal(s): 1-0 Mustacchio 14

7/9/10, Albert Flórián Stadium, Budapest
Hungary 0-0 Bosnia & Herzegovina

Group 3 Table

		Home					Away					Total					
	Pld	W	D	L	F	A	W	D	L	F	A	W	D	L	F	A	Pts
1 Italy	8	3	1	0	6	5	2	0	2	6	0	5	1	2	12	5	16
2 Wales	8	4	0	0	13	6	1	1	2	2	0	5	1	2	15	6	16
3 Hungary	8	2	1	1	5	7	2	0	2	4	0	4	1	3	9	7	13
4 Bosnia & Herzegovina	8	1	0	3	2	8	1	2	1	2	0	2	2	4	4	8	8
5 Luxembourg	8	0	1	3	0	16	1	0	3	2	0	1	1	6	2	16	4

GROUP 4

The Netherlands confirmed top spot in Group 4 with a game to spare, dropping points only in their final match against Spain, who joined them in the play-offs as one of the four best runners-up.

A 3-0 win in Liechtenstein, their seventh in succession, wrapped up the section for Cor Pot's side, but Spain still had plenty to play for. Luis Milla's team passed their biggest test with a 2-1 victory over the Jong Oranje on 2 September, Sergio Canales and Diego Capel scoring, before Canales struck again five minutes from time in Poland to secure a 1-0 win and Spain's play-off place.

Group 4 Results

9/6/09
Poland 2-0 Liechtenstein

4/9/09
Spain 2-0 Poland
Netherlands 2-0 Finland

7/9/09
Liechtenstein 0-4 Spain

8/9/09
Poland 2-1 Finland

9/10/09
Liechtenstein 0-5 Poland
Finland 0-1 Netherlands

13/10/09
Poland 0-4 Netherlands
Liechtenstein 0-4 Finland

13/11/09
Spain 1-0 Finland
Netherlands 3-0 Liechtenstein

17/11/09
Netherlands 2-1 Spain

2/3/10
Spain 3-1 Liechtenstein

3/3/10
Netherlands 3-2 Poland

11/8/10, Rheinpark, Vaduz
Liechtenstein 0-3 Netherlands
Goal(s): 0-1 Falkenburg 42, 0-2 Toornstra 55, 0-3 Dost 78

11/8/10, Arto Tolsa Areena, Kotka
Finland 1-1 Spain
Goal(s): 1-0 Kauko 8, 1-1 Bojan 31(p)

2/9/10, El Collao, Alcoy
Spain 2-1 Netherlands
Goal(s): 1-0 Canales 26, 1-1 Dost 31, 2-1 Diego Capel 54

3/9/10, Porin, Pori
Finland 2-0 Poland
Goal(s): 1-0 Hjelm 26(p), 2-0 Mannström 73

7/9/10, Groclin Dyskobolia, Grodzisk Wielkopolski
Poland 0-1 Spain
Goal(s): 0-1 Canales 85

7/9/10, Finnair Stadium, Helsinki
Finland 3-0 Liechtenstein
Goal(s): 1-0 Pelvas 21, 2-0 Pukki 37, 3-0 Riski 61

Group 4 Table

		Home					Away					Total					
	Pld	W	D	L	F	A	W	D	L	F	A	W	D	L	F	A	Pts
1 Netherlands	8	4	0	0	10	5	3	0	1	9	0	7	0	1	19	5	21
2 Spain	8	4	0	0	8	5	2	1	1	7	0	6	1	1	15	5	19
3 Finland	8	2	1	1	6	7	1	0	3	5	0	3	1	4	11	7	10
4 Poland	8	2	0	2	4	13	1	0	3	7	0	3	0	5	11	13	9
5 Liechtenstein	8	0	0	4	0	27	0	0	4	1	0	0	0	8	1	27	0

GROUP 5

The Czech Republic advanced with the best record in the group stage and as one of only two undefeated sides, but they still had to wait until their final match to seal first place.

After returning with a 5-0 rout of San Marino, they dropped their first points in a 1-1 draw with Germany, whose hopes of a successful trophy defence had already been dashed in a thumping 4-1 defeat by surprise package Iceland the previous month. Eyjólfur Sverrisson's side went into their final game needing to beat the Czech Republic to win the group. Despite going down 3-1, they deservedly reached the play-offs on goal difference.

Group 5 Results

9/6/09
San Marino 0-8 Czech Republic

12/8/09
Iceland 0-2 Czech Republic

4/9/09
Germany 6-0 San Marino
Czech Republic 2-0 Northern Ireland

8/9/09
Northern Ireland 2-6 Iceland
Germany 1-2 Czech Republic

9/10/09
Iceland 8-0 San Marino

13/10/09
Iceland 2-1 Northern Ireland

13/11/09
Northern Ireland 1-1 Germany
San Marino 0-6 Iceland

17/11/09
Northern Ireland 1-2 Czech Republic
San Marino 0-11 Germany

2/3/10
Germany 2-2 Iceland
San Marino 0-3 Northern Ireland

11/8/10, Kaplakrikavöllur, Hafnarfjordur
Iceland 4-1 Germany
Goal(s): 1-0 Bjarnason 5, 1-1 Grosskreutz 49, 2-1 Sigurdsson 53, 3-1 Sigthórsson 54, 4-1 Finnbogason 84

11/8/10, Na Julisce, Prague
Czech Republic 5-0 San Marino
Goal(s): 1-0 Pekhart 3, 2-0 Pekhart 14, 3-0 Kovařík 22, 4-0 Pekhart 40, 5-0 Chramosta 47(p)

3/9/10, Mestský, Mlada Boleslav
Czech Republic 1-1 Germany
Goal(s): 1-0 Mareček 38, 1-1 Kirchhoff 71

3/9/10, The Showgrounds, Coleraine
Northern Ireland 4-0 San Marino
Goal(s): 1-0 Little 4, 2-0 McGivern 15(p), 3-0 Little 85(p), 4-0 Grigg 90+2

7/9/10, Sportpark, Ingolstadt
Germany 3-0 Northern Ireland
Goal(s): 1-0 Holtby 42, 2-0 Holtby 60, 3-0 Herrmann 67

7/9/10, Chance Arena, Jablonec nad Nisou
Czech Republic 3-1 Iceland
Goal(s): 1-0 Vácha 20, 2-0 Pekhart 65, 3-0 Kovařík 67, 3-1 Finnbogason 80

Group 5 Table

		Home					Away					Total					
	Pld	W	D	L	F	A	W	D	L	F	A	W	D	L	F	A	Pts
1 Czech Republic	8	3	1	0	11	4	4	0	0	14	0	7	1	0	25	4	22
2 Iceland	8	3	0	1	14	11	2	1	1	15	0	5	1	2	29	11	16
3 Germany	8	2	1	1	12	10	1	2	1	14	0	3	3	2	26	10	12
4 Northern Ireland	8	1	1	2	8	16	1	0	3	4	0	2	1	5	12	16	7
5 San Marino	8	0	0	4	0	51	0	0	4	0	0	0	0	8	0	51	0

GROUP 6

Sweden held off a late challenge from Israel to win Group 6, advancing despite a surprise home defeat by their rivals in their penultimate game.

Sweden's progress looked a formality after winning five of their first six games and drawing the other, but goals from Bebars Natcho and Idan Vered in Gothenburg on 3 September gave Israel a 2-1 win and hope going into their final match. Trailing Sweden by three points, Guy Luzon's side kept the pressure on by beating Montenegro 5-0, but Sweden held their nerve against Bulgaria in Lovech, Jiloan Hamad's 90th-minute strike earning a 1-0 victory and top spot.

Group 6 Results

29/3/09
Israel 1-1 Kazakhstan

2/4/09
Kazakhstan 2-0 Bulgaria

7/6/09
Kazakhstan 0-2 Montenegro

10/6/09
Bulgaria 3-4 Israel

4/9/09
Bulgaria 3-0 Kazakhstan
Montenegro 0-2 Sweden

9/9/09
Kazakhstan 1-2 Israel
Sweden 2-1 Bulgaria

10/10/09
Bulgaria 1-1 Montenegro

11/10/09
Kazakhstan 1-1 Sweden

14/10/09
Montenegro 3-1 Kazakhstan

14/11/09
Montenegro 1-0 Israel

15/11/09
Sweden 5-1 Kazakhstan

18/11/09
Israel 4-0 Bulgaria

3/3/10
Montenegro 2-0 Bulgaria

4/6/10
Israel 0-1 Sweden

8/6/10
Sweden 2-0 Montenegro

3/9/10, Gamla Ullevi, Gothenburg
Sweden 1-2 Israel
Goal(s): 0-1 Natcho 38, 0-2 Vered 64, 1-2 Mehmeti 77

7/9/10, Lovech Stadion, Lovech
Bulgaria 0-1 Sweden
Goal(s): 0-1 Hamad 90

7/9/10, Haberfeld Stadium, Rishon Le Zion
Israel 5-0 Montenegro
Goal(s): 1-0 Natcho 2, 2-0 Bar Buzaglo 27(p), 3-0 Bar Buzaglo 57, 4-0 Natcho 77, 5-0 Chekol 86

Group 6 Table

		Home					Away					Total					
	Pld	W	D	L	F	A	W	D	L	F	A	W	D	L	F	A	Pts
1 Sweden	8	3	0	1	10	5	3	1	0	5	0	6	1	1	15	5	19
2 Israel	8	2	1	1	10	8	3	0	1	8	0	5	1	2	18	8	16
3 Montenegro	8	3	0	1	6	11	1	1	2	3	0	4	1	3	9	11	13
4 Kazakhstan	8	1	1	2	4	17	0	1	3	3	0	1	2	5	7	17	5
5 Bulgaria	8	1	1	2	7	16	0	0	4	1	0	1	1	6	8	16	4

GROUP 7

Group 7 resumed with Croatia two points clear of Slovakia and with Serbia also still in contention, but it soon became a two-horse race.

Slovakia beat Serbia 2-1 in Novi Sad while Croatia's 4-1 victory against Norway put them in pole position going into the final set of games. With Dražen Ladić's side boasting a better head-to-head record against Slovakia, a draw in Serbia would guarantee them top spot and they obtained the result they required thanks to two Ivan Perišić goals. Slovakia missed out on a play-off place after slumping to a 4-1 defeat at home to Norway.

Alfred Finnbogason completes the scoring as Iceland defeat holders Germany 4-1 in a pivotal Group 5 clash

Group 7 Results

7/6/09
Croatia 0-2 Cyprus

10/6/09
Norway 2-2 Slovakia

12/8/09
Cyprus 1-3 Norway

5/9/09
Serbia 1-2 Slovakia
Norway 1-3 Croatia

9/9/09
Slovakia 1-0 Cyprus
Norway 0-1 Serbia

9/10/09
Serbia 2-0 Cyprus

13/10/09
Croatia 3-1 Serbia

14/10/09
Cyprus 0-1 Slovakia

14/11/09
Cyprus 1-2 Croatia

15/11/09
Serbia 3-2 Norway

18/11/09
Slovakia 1-2 Croatia

19/5/10
Croatia 1-1 Slovakia

11/8/10, FC ViOn, Zlate Moravce
Slovakia 2-1 Serbia
Goal(s): 1-0 Sylvestr 14, 2-0 Sylvestr 60, 2-1 Đuričić 69

11/8/10, NK Varaždin, Varazdin
Croatia 4-1 Norway
Goal(s): 1-0 Lovren 3, 2-0 Jajalo 25, 2-1 Henriksen 52, 3-1 Lovren 82, 4-1 Kreilach 90

3/9/10, Aalesund Stadion, Aalesund
Norway 1-3 Cyprus
Goal(s): 0-1 Sielis 51, 0-2 Pittaras 59, 0-3 Pittaras 65, 1-3 Fellah 78

4/9/10, Cika Daca, Kragujevac
Serbia 2-2 Croatia
Goal(s): 1-0 Šćepović 3, 1-1 Perišić 12, 1-2 Perišić 31, 2-2 Đuričić 82

7/9/10, FC ViOn, Zlate Moravce
Slovakia 1-4 Norway
Goal(s): 0-1 Fellah 20, 0-2 Fellah 55, 1-2 Sylvestr 76, 1-3 Elyounoussi 83, 1-4 Elyounoussi 84

7/9/10, Dasaki Achnas, Famagusta
Cyprus 1-3 Serbia
Goal(s): 0-1 Šćepović 36, 1-1 Efrem 50(p), 1-2 Marković 54, 1-3 Savić 78

Group 7 Table

	Pld	Home					Away					Total					Pts
		W	D	L	F	A	W	D	L	F	A	W	D	L	F	A	
1 Croatia	8	2	1	1	8	10	3	1	0	9	0	5	2	1	17	10	17
2 Slovakia	8	2	0	2	5	11	2	2	0	6	0	4	2	2	11	11	14
3 Serbia	8	2	1	1	8	12	2	0	2	6	0	4	1	3	14	12	13
4 Norway	8	0	1	3	4	18	2	0	2	10	0	2	1	5	14	8	7
5 Cyprus	8	0	0	4	3	13	2	0	2	5	0	2	0	6	8	13	6

GROUP 8

Ukraine finished undefeated as Group 8 leaders following a 0-0 draw against Slovenia but with the joint lowest points total of any of the sides to reach the play-offs after winning four and drawing four of their eight matches.

Fittingly they qualified after a draw, 2-2 at home to France, with a game to go, but not without a scare. France needed to win to remain in contention and they battled back to pull level in Kyiv after falling two goals behind. France's chances had faded with defeat the previous month by Belgium, who too faltered with the finishing line in sight, drawing 2-2 in Slovenia.

Group 8 Results

31/3/09
Malta 0-2 Slovenia

9/6/09
Ukraine 1-0 Malta

4/9/09
Malta 0-1 Belgium

5/9/09
Slovenia 1-3 France

8/9/09
Belgium 2-0 Slovenia
France 2-2 Ukraine

9/10/09
Ukraine 1-1 Belgium
Malta 0-2 France

13/10/09
Belgium 0-0 France

14/10/09
Slovenia 0-2 Ukraine

13/11/09
Slovenia 1-0 Malta
Belgium 0-2 Ukraine

17/11/09
France 1-0 Slovenia

3/3/10
Belgium 1-0 Malta

29/5/10
Malta 0-3 Ukraine

11/8/10, Rabine, Vannes
France 0-1 Belgium
Goal(s): 0-1 Mokulu Tembe 8

3/9/10, Ob Jezeru, Velenje
Slovenia 2-2 Belgium
Goal(s): 0-1 Mununga 44, 0-2 Dequevy 60, 1-2 Mihelič 63(p), 2-2 H. Vučkič 81

3/9/10, Obolon, Kyiv
Ukraine 2-2 France
Goal(s): 1-0 Butko 54, 2-0 Rakytskiy 58(p), 2-1 Bakar 62, 2-2 Rivière 74

7/9/10, La Licorne, Amiens
France 2-0 Malta
Goal(s): 1-0 Kitambala 58, 2-0 Yanga-Mbiwa 66

7/9/10, Obolon, Kyiv
Ukraine 0-0 Slovenia

Group 8 Table

	Pld	Home					Away					Total					Pts
		W	D	L	F	A	W	D	L	F	A	W	D	L	F	A	
1 Ukraine	8	1	3	0	4	5	3	1	0	9	0	4	4	0	13	5	16
2 Belgium	8	2	1	1	3	5	2	2	0	5	0	4	3	1	8	5	15
3 France	8	2	1	1	5	6	2	2	0	7	0	4	3	1	12	6	15
4 Slovenia	8	1	1	2	4	10	1	1	2	2	0	2	2	4	6	10	8
5 Malta	8	0	0	4	0	13	0	0	4	0	0	0	0	8	0	13	0

GROUP 9

Greece got the better of 2009 runners-up England to claim top spot in Group 9, but Stuart Pearce's side finished strongly to earn a play-off place.

Key to their progress was a 1-0 win in Portugal on 3 September which ended their hosts' challenge, Chelsea FC striker Daniel Sturridge getting the goal that briefly took England to within a point of the leaders. Greece quickly quashed those hopes with a 2-1 victory in the Former Yugoslav Republic of Macedonia the following day, though England joined them in the play-offs after completing their campaign with a 3-0 home win over Lithuania.

Group 9 Results

28/3/09
Greece 3-1 FYROM

6/6/09
Lithuania 0-1 Greece

4/9/09
FYROM 1-2 England
Portugal 4-1 Lithuania

8/9/09
Greece 1-1 England

9/9/09
FYROM 1-1 Lithuania

9/10/09
Greece 2-1 Portugal
England 6-3 FYROM

13/10/09
FYROM 1-1 Portugal
Greece 1-0 Lithuania

13/11/09
Lithuania 1-0 FYROM

14/11/09
England 1-0 Portugal

17/11/09
Lithuania 0-0 England
Portugal 2-1 Greece

3/3/10
England 1-2 Greece

11/8/10, Marijampole, Marijampole
Lithuania 0-1 Portugal
Goal(s): 0-1 Ukra 16

3/9/10, Cidade de Barcelos, Barcelos
Portugal 0-1 England
Goal(s): 0-1 Sturridge 32

4/9/10, Mladost, Strumica
FYROM 1-2 Greece
Goal(s): 0-1 Siovas 39, 1-1 Georgievski 64, 1-2 Papazoglou 80

7/9/10, Community, Colchester
England 3-0 Lithuania
Goal(s): 1-0 Welbeck 62, 2-0 Albrighton 79, 3-0 Welbeck 90+1

7/9/10, Dr. Jorge Sampaio, Vila Nova de Gaia (Porto)
Portugal 3-1 FYROM
Goal(s): 1-0 Bébé 23, 2-0 Bura 87, 3-0 João Silva 90+2, 3-1 Altiparmakovski 90+4

Group 9 Table

		Home					Away					Total					
	Pld	W	D	L	F	A	W	D	L	F	A	W	D	L	F	A	Pts
1 Greece	8	3	1	0	7	7	3	0	1	6	0	6	1	1	13	7	19
2 England	8	3	0	1	11	7	2	2	0	4	0	5	2	1	15	7	17
3 Portugal	8	3	0	1	9	8	1	1	2	3	0	4	1	3	12	8	13
4 Lithuania	8	1	1	2	1	11	0	1	3	2	0	1	2	5	3	11	5
5 FYROM	8	0	2	2	4	19	0	0	4	5	0	0	2	6	9	19	2

Daniel Sturridge – England's match-winner in Portugal

GROUP 10

In a thrilling finale, Scotland won Group 10 with virtually the last kick of the campaign, Chris Maguire's 89th-minute strike earning Billy Stark's side a 2-1 victory against Austria in Aberdeen.

Scotland, Austria and Belarus all started the final day locked on 14 points, and the latter seemed on course to win the section after beating Azerbaijan 1-0. Scotland's chances decreased after Marko Arnautovic fired Austria ahead after ten minutes at Pittodrie, but Barry Bannan equalised 19 minutes later. Maguire's dramatic intervention changed everything, putting Scotland top, knocking Austria out and leaving Belarus to advance to the play-offs as one of the four best runners-up.

Group 10 Results

28/3/09
Albania 0-1 Scotland

1/4/09
Scotland 5-2 Albania

12/8/09
Belarus 2-1 Austria

5/9/09
Albania 1-0 Azerbaijan
Austria 1-0 Scotland

9/9/09
Austria 3-1 Albania
Azerbaijan 2-3 Belarus

10/10/09
Scotland 1-0 Belarus
Azerbaijan 1-2 Austria

14/10/09
Belarus 4-2 Albania

13/11/09
Albania 2-2 Austria

14/11/09
Azerbaijan 0-4 Scotland

17/11/09
Albania 1-2 Belarus

18/11/09
Austria 4-0 Azerbaijan

2/3/10
Scotland 2-2 Azerbaijan

11/8/10, Waldstadion, Pasching
Austria 3-3 Belarus
Goal(s): 1-0 Nuhiu 29, 1-1 Sivakov 31, 2-1 Arnautovic 35(p), 3-1 Grünwald 44, 3-2 Rekish 75, 3-3 Rekish 90

3/9/10, Gorodskoy Stadion, Borisov
Belarus 1-1 Scotland
Goal(s): 1-0 Nekhaichik 36, 1-1 Maguire 64(p)

4/9/10, Tofiq Bähramov-Republic stadium, Baku
Azerbaijan 3-2 Albania
Goal(s): 1-0 Soltanov 17, 2-0 Seyidov 37, 3-0 Gurbanov 43, 3-1 Cikalleshi 45, 3-2 Bala 87

7/9/10, Pittodrie, Aberdeen
Scotland 2-1 Austria
Goal(s): 0-1 Arnautovic 10, 1-1 Bannan 29, 2-1 Maguire 89

7/9/10, Gorodskoy Stadion, Borisov
Belarus 1-0 Azerbaijan
Goal(s): 1-0 Nekhaichik 76

Group 10 Table

		Home					Away					Total					
	Pld	W	D	L	F	A	W	D	L	F	A	W	D	L	F	A	Pts
1 Scotland	8	3	1	0	10	7	2	1	1	6	0	5	2	1	16	7	17
2 Belarus	8	3	1	0	8	11	2	1	1	8	0	5	2	1	16	11	17
3 Austria	8	3	1	0	11	11	1	1	2	6	0	4	2	2	17	11	14
4 Albania	8	1	1	2	4	20	0	0	4	7	0	1	1	6	11	20	4
5 Azerbaijan	8	1	0	3	6	19	0	1	3	2	0	1	1	6	8	19	4

PLAY-OFFS

Iceland reached the finals for the first time following an extraordinary qualifying campaign in which they finished as the competition's top scorers with 34 goals.

Six senior internationals featured for Iceland in the first leg of the play-offs against Scotland, and despite falling behind to Jamie Murphy's 19th-minute strike Eyjölfur Sverrisson's side recovered with goals from Johann Gudmundsson and Almarr Ormarsson to take a slender 2-1 lead to Edinburgh. There, Gylfi Thor Sigurdsson's thumping 74th-minute strike looked to have made the tie safe but Jamie Murphy's spectacular equaliser straight from the kick-off threw the tie back in the balance. Sigurdsson set the Icelandic celebrations in motion with his second goal ten minutes from time.

Switzerland took a giant step towards their first finals appearances since 2004 with a commanding 4-1 first-leg victory over Sweden in Sion. Goals from Fabien Frei and Xavier Hochstrasser put the hosts 2-0 up within 18 minutes, and although Guillermo Molins pulled one back for the 2009 semi-finalists Admir Mehmedi quickly restored Switzerland's two-goal advantage. Sweden's hopes were further hit when Yann Sommer saved Denni Avdic's 73rd-minute penalty, and their problems worsened when Pajtim Kasami added a fourth late on. Pierre Bengtsson gave Sweden a lifeline early on in the return in Malmo, but Nassim Ben Khalifa's equaliser two minutes after half-time duly confirmed Switzerland's place in Denmark.

Iceland's Gylfi Sigurdsson – a two-goal hero against Scotland

The Czech Republic dropped just two points during the qualifying group stage and they picked up where they left off in the play-offs against Greece, who, despite pipping England to top spot in Group 9, were no match for Jakub Dovalil's side. Playing on his home ground, FK Jablonec's Jan Vošahlík put the Czech Republic ahead two minutes in. His club colleague Tomáš Pekhart scored a penalty after 19 minutes before another Jablonec player, Libor Kozák, completed the scoring. There was no let-up in the return, with Pekhart scoring his competition-leading ninth goal and Kozák again finding the target in a 2-0 win.

England held their nerve to reach their third finals n succession, at Romania's expense, with all the goals coming in a 20-minute second-half spell at the end of the first leg. Romania had looked the more likely scorers in the first half in Norwich, but Stuart Pearce's side struck first when Jordan Henderson broke the deadlock with a 71st-minute volley. Romania were not behind for long, Ryan Bertrand deflecting Ioan Hora's cross beyond Frank Fielding, but Chris Smalling turned in a corner with seven minutes left to give the 2009 runners-up a lead to defend in Botosani. Two smart Fielding saves from Gabriel Torje ensured they accomplished their mission in a goalless draw.

Goals from Adrián and Mikel San José gave Spain a narrow advantage in the first leg before Croatia were swept aside in the second. Thiago Alcántara again shone for La Roja, and his sublime through ball allowed Adrián to open the scoring on 21 minutes. Although Dejan Školnik quickly equalised, San José's 42nd-minute header gave Spain the edge. Croatia's problems deepened in Varazdin where captain Ivan Rakitić was injured after 14 minutes, and when Álvaro Domínguez fired Spain in front on 67 minutes the tie was all but over. Dejan Lovren was dismissed soon afterwards and Spain took advantage with late goals from Adrián López and Jeffren.

Belarus pulled off arguably the biggest surprise of the qualifying campaign when they recovered from

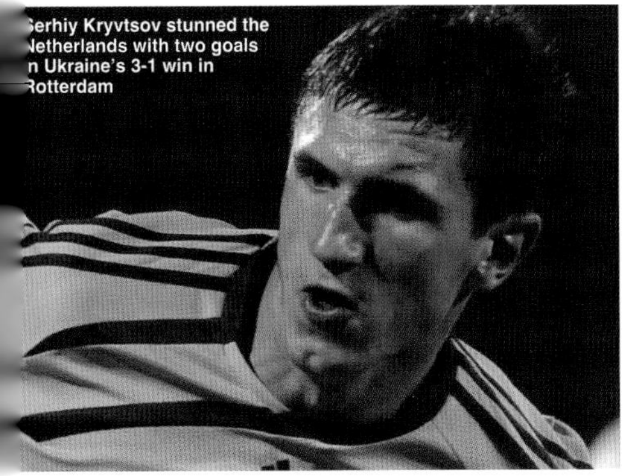

Serhiy Kryvtsov stunned the Netherlands with two goals in Ukraine's 3-1 win in Rotterdam

a two-goal deficit to knock out Italy. Mattia Destro and Stefano Okaka Chuka scored in each half in Rieti to put Pierluigi's Casiraghi side in control of the tie, but that advantage was quickly wiped out in the return. With captain Lorenzo De Silvestri and Ezequiel Schelotto suspended, Italy were caught flat-footed as Belarus flew at them from the start. Vladimir Yurchenko scored twice in the first five minutes to pull the tie level and an incredible turnaround was complete when Oleg Veretilo struck the winner in the sixth minute of extra time.

Ukraine had lost to the Netherlands in the 2006 final, and they made the most of their opportunity for revenge. Two goals in the first seven minutes from Serhiy Kryvtsov, supplemented by Yevhen Konoplyanka's second-half penalty, put them 3-0 ahead in Rotterdam. Luuk de Jong replied for the Jong Oranje but their miserable night was summed up by Donny Gorter's dismissal. The return looked a formality until Bas Dost pulled a goal back shortly before half-time. When John Goossens scored a second with 33 minutes to play, the pressure was on. Ukraine, however, hung on to secure their place in the finals on the away-goals rule.

Play-Off Results

7/10/10, Laugardalsvöllur, Reykjavik
Iceland 2-1 Scotland
Goal(s): 0-1 Murphy 19, 1-1 Gudmundsson 34, 2-1 Ormarsson 78
Referee: Nijhuis (NED)
11/10/10, Easter Road Stadium, Edinburgh
Scotland 1-2 Iceland
Goal(s): 0-1 Sigurdsson 74, 1-1 Maguire 75, 1-2 Sigurdsson 80
Referee: Strömbergsson (SWE)
Aggregate: Iceland qualify 4-2.

7/10/10, Tourbillon, Sion
Switzerland 4-1 Sweden
Goal(s): 1-0 F. Frei 2, 2-0 Hochstrasser 20, 2-1 Molins 50, 3-1 Mehmedi 52, 4-1 Kasami 83
Referee: Bezborodov (RUS)
11/10/10, Swedbank Stadium, Malmo
Sweden 1-1 Switzerland
Goal(s): 1-0 P.Bengtsson 15, 1-1 Ben Khalifa 47
Referee: Strahonja (CRO)
Aggregate: Switzerland qualify 5-2.

8/10/10, Chance Arena, Jablonec nad Nisou
Czech Republic 3-0 Greece
Goal(s): 1-0 Vošahlík 2, 2-0 Pekhart 19(p), 3-0 Kozák 77
Referee: Studer (SUI)
12/10/10, Asteras Tripolis, Tripoli Arkadia
Greece 0-2 Czech Republic
Goal(s): 0-1 Pekhart 19, 0-2 Kozák 79
Referee: Moen (NOR)
Aggregate: Czech Republic qualify 5-0.

8/10/10, Centro d'Italia, Rieti
Italy 2-0 Belarus
Goal(s): 1-0 Destro 30, 2-0 Okaka Chuka 61
Referee: Koukoulakis (GRE)
12/10/10, Gorodskoy Stadion, Borisov
Belarus 3-0 Italy (aet)
Goal(s): 1-0 Yurchenko 4, 2-0 Yurchenko 5, 3-0 Veretilo 96
Referee: Çakır (TUR)
Aggregate: Belarus qualify 3-2 after extra time.

8/10/10, Carrow Road, Norwich
England 2-1 Romania
Goal(s): 1-0 Henderson 63, 1-1 Hora 71, 2-1 Smalling 83
Referee: Tagliavento (ITA)
12/10/10, Municipal, Botosani
Romania 0-0 England
Referee: Fautrel (FRA)
Aggregate: England qualify 2-1.

9/10/10, Sparta Stadium, Rotterdam
Netherlands 1-3 Ukraine
Goal(s): 0-1 Kryvtsov 2, 0-2 Kryvtsov 7, 0-3 Konoplyanka 73(p), 1-3 De Jong 79
Referee: Clattenburg (ENG)
12/10/10, Valeriy Lobanovskiy Stadium, Kyiv
Ukraine 0-2 Netherlands
Goal(s): 0-1 Dost 45, 0-2 Goossens 57
Referee: Schörgenhofer (AUT)
Aggregate: 3-3; Ukraine qualify on away goals.

9/10/10, Municipal El Plantío, Burgos
Spain 2-1 Croatia
Goal(s): 1-0 Adrián 21, 1-1 Školnik 22, 2-1 San José 42
Referee: Vad (HUN)
12/10/10, NK Varaždin, Varazdin
Croatia 0-3 Spain
Goal(s): 0-1 Álvaro Domínguez 67, 0-2 Adrián 89, 0-3 Jeffren 90+1
Referee: Collum (SCO)
Aggregate: Spain qualify 5-1.

TOP GOALSCORERS
(Qualifying)

9	Tomáš Pekhart (Czech Republic)
7	Edgars Gauračs (Latvia)
6	Henrik Mkhitaryan (Armenia) Atdhe Nuhiu (Austria) Johann Gudmundsson (Iceland) Chris Maguire (Scotland) Jakub Sylvestr (Slovakia)
5	Mats Hummels (Germany) Alfred Finnbogason (Iceland) Gylfi Sigurdsson (Iceland) Gabriel Torje (Romania) Jamie Murphy (Scotland)

FINAL TOURNAMENT

GROUP A

Switzerland were to emerge as the dominant force in Group A as they won all three of their matches to leave the other three teams scrapping for second place. It was Belarus who qualified alongside them as runners-up by the narrowest of margins to leave Denmark and Iceland contemplating what might have been.

This section might have looked less formidable than Group B on paper, but Denmark coach Keld Bordinggaard admitted before the hosts' opening match that this was no guarantee of a straightforward passage. "Many people say we were very lucky with the draw. I tend to agree, but a lucky draw is not the same as an easy draw. There are no easy games," said Bordinggaard. And so it proved.

Shaqiri strikes

Switzerland were Denmark's first opponents, and their Aalborg meeting set the tone for a frustrating campaign as despite ten attempts on target the hosts failed to get the ball past an inspired Yann Sommer. Xherdan Shaqiri capped an eye-catching display with a brilliant solo goal that won the game.

Belarus were the other opening-day winners against an Iceland side whose Under-21 finals debut did not go to plan. Eyjólfur Sverrisson's much-fancied youngsters spurned several good chances before their fortunes plummeted with Aron Gunnarsson's penalty-area foul on Stanislav Dragun 14 minutes from time. Gunnarsson was sent off and Andrei Voronkov converted the spot kick before Maksim Skavysh added a late second to boost a Belarusian side that had entered the tournament missing key striker Vladimir Yurchenko.

With Gunnarsson banned and Johann Gudmundsson injured, Iceland then conceded a minute into their second outing against Switzerland. Fabian Frei scored that goal, and Innocent Emeghara went on to double the lead for a Swiss side now with a firm grip on the group. Their success was perhaps no surprise given their accumulated international experience, with six senior internationals, four players from their 2009 FIFA U-17 World Cup triumph and, in impressive midfielder Granit Xhaka, a player who belonged to both categories.

Hopes revived

Denmark revived their hopes by coming from behind to defeat Belarus. Although Dmitriy Baga struck first, the Danes were gifted the lifeline of a penalty two minutes later, Christian Eriksen tapping in the rebound after Aleksandr Gutor had stopped his first attempt. Eriksen was the Danes' great hope, the AFC Ajax playmaker having stepped down from the seniors to provide a creative edge, but it was a spectacular first U21 goal from Nicolai Jørgensen, a curling right-foot shot from the left, that sealed victory.

Denmark now lay second entering their final match, yet they ended up bottom, their hopes in tatters, after a 3-1 loss to Iceland – the first defeat by their fellow Scandinavians at U21 level. "Once again we created many chances but didn't score more," sighed coach Bordinggaard after his side scored just once from over 20 goal attempts. By the time Bashkim Kadrii finally headed in for the hosts nine minutes from time they were trailing to strikes from Kolbeinn Sigthórsson and Birkir Bjarnason. With

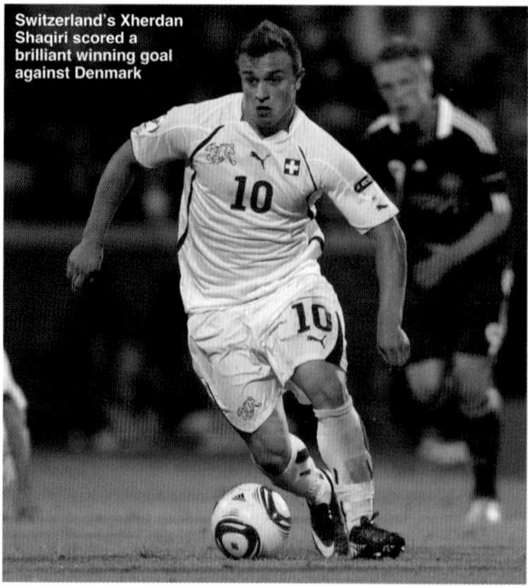
Switzerland's Xherdan Shaqiri scored a brilliant winning goal against Denmark

Switzerland beating Belarus in Aarhus, a frantic finish ensued as the Danes chased the equaliser they needed. Instead Iceland got a third through Hjörtur Valgardsson and both sides were left empty-handed. Belarus, a man short after Sergei Matveychik's dismissal, had fallen 3-0 to the Swiss – Admir Mehmedi (twice) and Frank Feltscher scoring – yet it was Georgiy Kondratyev's side who progressed into the last four.

Head-to-head advantage

With Switzerland on nine points, the remaining trio all had three points apiece and an identical goal difference of 3-5. However, in a three-way head-to-head, with the results against Switzerland removed, the Belarusians were a single goal better off than Iceland. While Kondratyev thanked Iceland for a "great present", Sverisson's pride in his first-timers was mixed with sadness. "We only needed one more goal to succeed and there's obviously disappointment," he said.

As for Switzerland, only the second team to negotiate the group stage at an U21 finals without conceding, their success had Pierluigi Tami realigning his targets. "Everything is possible now," he declared.

Group A Results

11/6/11, Aarhus Stadion, Aarhus
Belarus 2-0 Iceland
Attendance: 2817
Belarus: Gutor, Dragun, Politevich, Baga (Rekish 75), Sivakov, Bukatkin, Perepechko (Kvaschinskiy 90+1), Voronkov (Skavysh 78), Polyakov, Veretilo, Filipenko. Coach: Georgiy Kondratyev (BLR)
Iceland: Björnsson, Eyjólfsson, Jónsson, Valgardsson, Gudmundsson (Finnbogason 32), Vidarsson (Bjarnason 83), Sigurdsson, Smárason (Gíslason 61), Gunnarsson, Sigthórsson, Fjóluson. Coach: Eyjólfur Sverrisson (ISL)
Goal(s): 1-0 Voronkov 77(p), 2-0 Skavysh 87
Red Card(s): Gunnarsson 76 (Iceland)
Yellow Card(s): Bukatkin 26 (Belarus), Politevich 65 (Belarus), Gíslason 79 (Iceland)
Referee: Stavrev (MKD)

11/6/11, Aalborg Stadion, Aalborg
Denmark 0-1 Switzerland
Attendance: 9678
Denmark: Andersen, M. Jørgensen, Bjelland, Boilesen (Juelsgård 82), Wass (Dalsgaard 82), Jensen, Eriksen, Fenger, N. B. Nielsen, Povlsen, Kadrii (N. Jørgensen 57). Coach: Keld Bordinggaard (DEN)
Switzerland: Sommer, Koch, Rossini, Lustenberger, Emeghara, Frei (Hochstrasser 70), Shaqiri (Klose 90+3), Mehmedi (Kasami 85), Xhaka, Affolter, Berardi. Coach: Pierluigi Tami (SUI)
Goal(s): 0-1 Shaqiri 48
Yellow Card(s): Berardi 62 (Switzerland), N. B. Nielsen 90+4 (Denmark)
Referee: Schörgenhofer (AUT)

14/6/11, Aalborg Stadion, Aalborg
Switzerland 2-0 Iceland
Attendance: 1903
Switzerland: Sommer, Koch, Rossini, Lustenberger, Emeghara, Frei (Costanzo 66), Shaqiri, Xhaka (Abrashi 68), Klose, Gavranović (Ben Khalifa 84), Berardi. Coach: Pierluigi Tami (SUI)
Iceland: Björnsson, Eyjólfsson, Jónsson, Valgardsson, Vidarsson (Bjarnason 60), Gíslason, Sigurdsson, Kristjánsson, Sigthórsson, Finnbogason (Sigurdarson 46), Fjóluson. Coach: Eyjólfur Sverrisson (ISL)
Goal(s): 1-0 Frei 1, 2-0 Emeghara 40
Yellow Card(s): Vidarsson 12 (Iceland), Xhaka 38 (Switzerland), Sigurdsson 44 (Iceland), Ben Khalifa 89 (Switzerland), Eyjólfsson 90+3 (Iceland)
Referee: Strahonja (CRO)

14/6/11, Aarhus Stadion, Aarhus
Denmark 2-1 Belarus
Attendance: 18152
Denmark: Andersen, M. Jørgensen, Bjelland, Boilesen, Albæk, Wass, Jensen (Povlsen 77), N. Jørgensen (Fenger 81), Eriksen, N. B. Nielsen, Dalsgaard (Kadrii 62). Coach: Keld Bordinggaard (DEN)
Belarus: Gutor, Dragun, Politevich, Baga, Sivakov, Bukatkin (Rekish 46), Perepechko (Nekhaichik 76), Voronkov (Skavysh 58), Polyakov, Veretilo, Filipenko. Coach: Georgiy Kondratyev (BLR)
Goal(s): 0-1 Baga 20, 1-1 Eriksen 22, 2-1 N. Jørgensen 71
Yellow Card(s): Bukatkin 32 (Belarus), Albæk 64 (Denmark), Politevich 88 (Belarus)
Referee: Tagliavento (ITA)

18/6/11, Aalborg Stadion, Aalborg
Iceland 3-1 Denmark
Attendance: 9308
Iceland: Björnsson, Eyjólfsson, Jónsson, Valgardsson, Bjarnason (Smárason 79), Gudmundsson, Gíslason (Sigurdarson 68), Sigurdsson, Gunnarsson, Sigthórsson, Fjóluson. Coach: Eyjólfur Sverrisson (ISL)
Denmark: Andersen, M. Jørgensen, Bjelland, Boilesen, Wass (Fenger 78), Jensen (Agger 88), N. Jørgensen, Eriksen, N. B. Nielsen (Dalsgaard 62), Povlsen, Kadrii. Coach: Keld Bordinggaard (DEN)
Goal(s): 1-0 Sigthórsson 58, 2-0 Bjarnason 60, 2-1 Kadrii 81, 3-1 Valgardsson 90+2
Yellow Card(s): Sigurdsson 23 (Iceland), Gunnarsson 45+1 (Iceland), Gíslason 57 (Iceland), Jensen 83 (Denmark), N. Jørgensen 90+3 (Denmark)
Referee: Mažić (SRB)

18/6/11, Aarhus Stadion, Aarhus
Switzerland 3-0 Belarus
Attendance: 1604
Switzerland: Sommer, Koch, Rossini, Lustenberger, Emeghara (F. Feltscher 65), Frei, Shaqiri, Mehmedi, Xhaka (Abrashi 52), Klose, Berardi (Daprelà 75). Coach: Pierluigi Tami (SUI)
Belarus: Gutor, Dragun, Matveychik, Baga, Sivakov, Skavysh (Voronkov 54), Perepechko (Kvaschinskiy 46) (Gaiduchik 70), Nekhaichik, Polyakov, Veretilo, Filipenko. Coach: Georgiy Kondratyev (BLR)
Goal(s): 1-0 Mehmedi 6(p), 2-0 Mehmedi 43, 3-0 F. Feltscher 90+3
Red Card(s): Matveychik 68 (Belarus)
Yellow Card(s): Veretilo 5 (Belarus), Xhaka 27 (Switzerland), Nekhaichik 29 (Belarus), Matveychik 41 (Belarus), Kvaschinskiy 65 (Belarus), Matveychik 68 (Belarus), Mehmedi 83 (Switzerland)
Referee: Strömbergsson (SWE)

Group A Table

	Pld	W	D	L	F	A	Pts
1 Switzerland	3	3	0	0	6	0	9
2 Belarus	3	1	0	2	3	5	3
3 Iceland	3	1	0	2	3	5	3
4 Denmark	3	1	0	2	3	5	3

GROUP B

However impressive they might have been in qualifying, it was the misfortune of the Czech Republic, England and Ukraine to encounter a force majeure in Group B – namely, Luis Milla's Spain.

Yet while each of the quartet could still qualify for the semi-finals as they went into their third game, Spain's case for progress was already stronger than the rest. Milla's men, with FIFA World Cup winners Javi Martínez and Juan Mata heading a talented troupe, took on the mantle of their senior national team counterparts – the reigning world and European champions – and wore it with pride and distinction.

Ander Herrera, Spain's goalscorer, in Group B action against England

Points shared

Nevertheless, when confronted by a fellow two-time winner of this event in their opening fixture a dominant Spain were unable to see off an England side who had travelled with high hopes to Denmark despite several key absentees, among them senior internationals Jack Wilshere, Andy Carroll, Micah Richards and Kieran Gibbs. Leading through Ander Herrera's header, which television replays suggested had involved the illegal use of a forearm, Spain became bogged down in their search for a second goal against Stuart Pearce's squad, and they were undone at the death by Danny Welbeck's sharply-taken equaliser, which might also have been disallowed for offside.

The Czech Republic, meanwhile, consolidated their reputation as the only unbeaten team in qualifying when they dispatched a Ukraine outfit boasting UEFA Champions League and senior international experience. Bořek Dočkal played a captain's role with two fine goals before Maxym Biliy grabbed a late consolation.

Standard set

The Czechs' 11-match unbeaten sequence was to end in their next game, however, with a 2-0 defeat to Spain, who thus leapfrogged them to the top of the table. Adrián López, a striker who had just endured relegation with RC Deportivo La Coruña, raised his morale by scoring both Spanish goals from Mata passes. The standard having been set by the Spanish, Ukraine and England subsequently laboured to meet it – although English forward Daniel Sturridge rattled the woodwork during the sides' soporific goalless draw. Pearce's attempt to make it third time lucky, after semi-final and final defeats in 2007 and 2009, was proving slow to materialise.

All four teams remained in contention to reach the semi-finals when Group B concluded, seven days after it had started, on 19 June. Three points separated leaders Spain and bottom-placed Ukraine, but the congestion began to clear from the moment Mata took advantage of a Ukrainian defensive slip to put Spain ahead in Herning. When Adrián poached his third goal of the tournament after 27 minutes, the chances of Pavlo Yakovenko's charges booking their first semi-final since 2006 were practically irretrievable, and Mata's second-half penalty duly confirmed the inevitable. Next stop for a number of the Ukrainian players would be UEFA EURO 2012.

Late turnaround

Meanwhile, the Czechs, needing a point to advance, suddenly found themselves in arrears 14 minutes from the end of a tight, tense contest in Viborg when Welbeck nodded England in front. But the Young Lions were unable to preserve their lead and Czech substitutes Jan Chramosta and Tomáš Pekhart proceeded to swing the pendulum in the other direction. First Chramosta scrambled in the all-important equaliser with one minute of normal time left; then Pekhart, dropped after failing to replicate his top-scoring exploits of the qualifying competition, completed the turnaround on the break with the last kick of the game.

Czech coach Jakub Dovalil, who in 2006 had lost the final of the UEFA European U17 Championship with the same generation of players – including Jutland campaigners Pekhart, Marek Štěch, Radim Řezník, Ondřej Mazuch and Lukáš Vácha – would now get a shot at redemption, while Pearce's England bowed out with several reputations battered and bruised. As for Milla's marvels, they were already being widely tipped to take home the crown.

Group B Results

12/6/11, Viborg Stadion, Viborg
Czech Republic 2-1 Ukraine
Attendance: 4251
Czech Republic: Vaclík, Lecjaks, Mazuch, Čelůstka, Vácha (Mareček 90+2), Hořava (Morávek 46), Dočkal, Pekhart, Kovařík (Hloušek 75), Gecov, Suchý. Coach: Jakub Dovalil (CZE)
Ukraine: Kanibolotskiy, Butko, Rakytskiy, Putivtsev, Konoplyanka, Stepanenko (Partsvaniya 54), Morozyuk (Biliy 64), Zozulya, Yarmolenko (Kravets 87), Krivtsov, Chesnakov. Coach: Pavlo Yakovenko (UKR)
Goal(s): 1-0 Dočkal 49, 2-0 Dočkal 56, 2-1 Biliy 87
Yellow Card(s): Pekhart 28 (Czech Republic), Zozulya 44 (Ukraine), Gecov 46 (Czech Republic), Morávek 54 (Czech Republic), Vácha 90 (Czech Republic)
Referee: Mažić (SRB)

12/6/11, Herning Stadion, Herning
Spain 1-1 England
Attendance: 8046
Spain: De Gea, Álvaro Domínguez, Javi Martínez, Jeffren (Bojan 80), Adrián López (Parejo 72), Mata, Montoya, Dídac, Ander Herrera (Diego Capel 86), Thiago, Botía. Coach: Luis Milla (ESP)
England: Fielding, Mancienne (Rodwell 67), Bertrand, Smalling, Jones, Henderson, Welbeck, Sturridge, Walker, Cleverley (Sinclair 81), Rose (Lansbury 67). Coach: Stuart Pearce (ENG)
Goal(s): 1-0 Ander Herrera 14, 1-1 Welbeck 88
Yellow Card(s): Thiago 24 (Spain), Welbeck 35 (England), Ander Herrera 70 (Spain)
Referee: Strömbergsson (SWE)

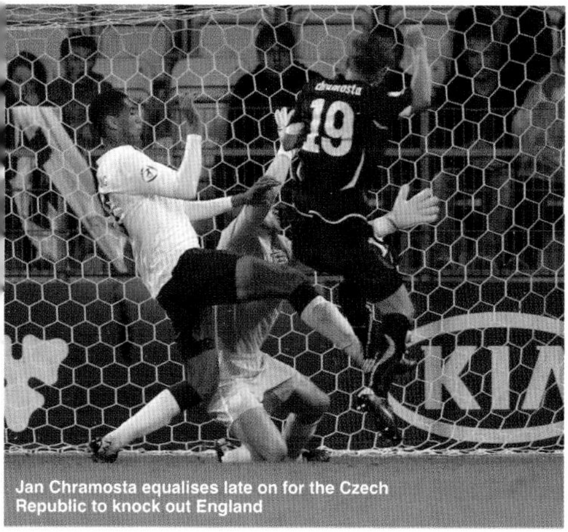
Jan Chramosta equalises late on for the Czech Republic to knock out England

15/6/11, Viborg Stadion, Viborg
Czech Republic 0-2 Spain
Attendance: 4662
Czech Republic: Vaclík, Lecjaks, Mazuch, Čelůstka, Vácha, Dočkal, Morávek (Kadlec 63), Pekhart (Kozák 46), Gecov, Suchý, Hloušek (Černý 77). Coach: Jakub Dovalil (CZE)
Spain: De Gea, Álvaro Domínguez, Javi Martínez, Adrián López (Parejo 74), Mata (Nsue 89), Montoya, Dídac, Ander Herrera, Thiago, Botía, Muniain (Diego Capel 83). Coach: Luis Milla (ESP)
Goal(s): 0-1 Adrián López 27, 0-2 Adrián López 47
Yellow Card(s): Javi Martínez 25 (Spain), Mata 25 (Spain), Vácha 33 (Czech Republic), Adrián López 47 (Spain), Botía 53 (Spain), Kozák 62 (Czech Republic), Mazuch 80 (Czech Republic)
Referee: Schörgenhofer (AUT)

15/6/11, Herning Stadion, Herning
Ukraine 0-0 England
Attendance: 3495
Ukraine: Kanibolotskiy, Butko, Selin, Rakytskiy, Konoplyanka (Yarmolenko 65), Holodyuk, Krivtsov, Biliy, Chesnakov, Harmash, Kravets (Zozulya 70). Coach: Pavlo Yakovenko (UKR)
England: Fielding, Mancienne (Muamba 89), Bertrand, Smalling, Jones, Henderson, Welbeck, Sturridge, Walker, Rodwell (Lansbury 57), Rose (Sinclair 57). Coach: Stuart Pearce (ENG)
Yellow Card(s): Konoplyanka 24 (Ukraine), Holodyuk 31 (Ukraine), Biliy 35 (Ukraine), Rodwell 38 (England), Sinclair 61 (England), Rakytskiy 62 (Ukraine), Muamba 90+1 (England), Jones 90+3 (England)
Referee: Stavrev (MKD)

19/6/11, Viborg Stadion, Viborg
England 1-2 Czech Republic
Attendance: 5262
England: Fielding, Bertrand, Muamba, Smalling, Jones, Henderson (Lansbury 64), Welbeck, Sturridge, Sinclair (Rose 87), Walker, Cleverley (Albrighton 76). Coach: Stuart Pearce (ENG)
Czech Republic: Vaclík, Lecjaks, Mazuch, Čelůstka, Dočkal, Kozák (Pekhart 83), Morávek (Chramosta 83), Kovařík (Černý 68), Gecov, Suchý, Mareček. Coach: Jakub Dovalil (CZE)
Goal(s): 1-0 Welbeck 76, 1-1 Chramosta 89, 1-2 Pekhart 90+4
Yellow Card(s): Walker 69 (England), Suchý 80 (Czech Republic), Chramosta 90 (Czech Republic)
Referee: Tagliavento (ITA)

19/6/11, Herning Stadion, Herning
Ukraine 0-3 Spain
Attendance: 3302
Ukraine: Kanibolotskiy, Butko, Selin, Rakytskiy, Konoplyanka, Zozulya, Yarmolenko (Vitsenets 81), Krivtsov, Biliy (Holodyuk 39), Chesnakov, Harmash. Coach: Pavlo Yakovenko (UKR)
Spain: De Gea, Álvaro Domínguez, Javi Martínez (Parejo 76), Adrián López (Bojan 80), Mata, Montoya (Azpilicueta 82), Dídac, Ander Herrera, Thiago, Botía, Muniain. Coach: Luis Milla (ESP)
Goal(s): 0-1 Mata 10, 0-2 Adrián López 27, 0-3 Mata 72(p)
Red Card(s): Harmash 71 (Ukraine)
Yellow Card(s): Kanibolotskiy 27 (Ukraine), Yarmolenko 45 (Ukraine), Harmash 66 (Ukraine), Montoya 70 (Spain), Konoplyanka 73 (Ukraine), De Gea 74 (Spain)
Referee: Strahonja (CRO)

Group B Table

	Pld	W	D	L	F	A	Pts
1 Spain	3	2	1	0	6	1	7
2 Czech Republic	3	2	0	1	4	4	6
3 England	3	0	2	1	2	3	2
4 Ukraine	3	0	1	2	1	5	1

SEMI-FINALS

Group winners and favourites Spain and Switzerland made it through to the final, but neither team had it easy in semi-final contests that both went to extra time.

Luis Milla's Spain were widely expected to beat first-time semi-finalists Belarus comfortably but the eastern Europeans came very close to producing the tournament's biggest upset in Viborg. Georgiy Kondratyev's men had scraped into the semi-finals with two defeats, yet now they produced their best display, frustrating their opponents with a superb defensive effort and taking the lead through Andrei Voronkov seven minutes before the interval.

Overhead strike

The goal followed Aleksandr Perepechko's long throw into the box. Mikhail Sivakov flicked the ball on and Voronkov conjured an improvised overhead finish, the ball crossing the line almost in slow motion with goalkeeper David de Gea rooted to the spot. It was Belarus's only shot on target, yet it was almost enough. While Spain had 73% of possession, an elusive equaliser would not come – Ander Herrera and Juan Mata threatened with headers, Adrián López struck the outside of the post and was then twice denied by Aleksandr Gutor.

Adrián López celebrates putting Spain 2-1 up in their semi-final against Belarus

Milla threw on Diego Capel and Jeffren in the hope of getting better penetration out wide, and the ploy paid off. With 89 minutes on the clock, Spain finally shattered the Belarusian resistance as a typically patient passing move ended with Jeffren crossing from the right and the in-form Adrián flashing in a volley at Gutor's near post. Kondratyev lamented the late lapse of concentration – "the plan worked fine for us for 89 minutes" – but from that moment on there was only going to be one winner. In the last minute of the first period of extra time, Adrián nodded in his fifth goal of the championship from Capel's enticing cross before Jeffren made sure by smashing home a spectacular third goal from 25 metres.

Long evening

It was also a long evening in Herning, where it took Switzerland 114 minutes to break down the stubborn ranks of the Czech Republic. Admir Mehmedi was the man who ended the stalemate, cutting across Jan Chramosta and arrowing in a shot from 25 metres that bounced over the outstretched hand of Tomáš Vaclík and landed in the bottom corner. It brought Switzerland their fourth consecutive victory.

The Swiss had come closest to winning the match in normal time when Xherdan Shaqiri was denied by the far post after beating Vaclík with a fierce low strike from distance in the 89th minute. Prior to that, it had been a disappointingly drab game of few chances dominated by the two defences, with neither goalkeeper being required to make a save before half-time.

Czech coach Jakub Dovalil had stuck with Libor Kozák as his lone front man, ignoring the claims of his scoring substitutes against England, Chramosta and Tomáš Pekhart, but Kozák cut an isolated figure and sliced wide his only opportunity soon after the interval. The Czechs, by their coach's admission, "performed really badly", despite the introduction of Chramosta and Pekhart as the clock ticked down.

First final

Instead it was Switzerland coach Pierluigi Tami, having sent on Mario Gavranovic to join Mehmedi in attack, who got his reward. Mehmedi's third strike of the tournament – which would secure him the Silver Boot as second-highest scorer – carried

Switzerland's match winner Admir Mehmedi on the ball against the Czech Republic

the Swiss into their first final and also ensured their first Olympic Games appearance since 1928.

"It's 83 years since Switzerland were in the Olympics, so it's something very special," said Tami. "We took few risks but still tried to score goals and take the game to them. In the end it was a deserved victory."

Semi-Final Results

22/6/11, Viborg Stadion, Viborg
Spain 3-1 Belarus (aet)
Attendance: 7529
Spain: De Gea, Álvaro Domínguez (Bojan 77), Javi Martínez, Adrián López, Mata, Montoya, Dídac, Ander Herrera (Diego Capel 58), Thiago, Botía, Muniain (Jeffren 70). Coach: Luis Milla (ESP)
Belarus: Gutor, Dragun, Politevich, Sivakov, Skavysh (Rekish 84), Perepechko (Baga 61), Voronkov (Bukatkin 69), Nekhaichik, Polyakov, Veretilo, Filipenko. Coach: Georgiy Kondratyev (BLR)
Goal(s): 0-1 Voronkov 38, 1-1 Adrián López 89, 2-1 Adrián López 105, 3-1 Jeffren 113
Yellow Card(s): Nekhaichik 17 (Belarus), Adrián López 36 (Spain), Skavysh 37 (Belarus), Sivakov 67 (Belarus), Botía 80 (Spain), Veretilo 90+4 (Belarus), Javi Martínez 115 (Spain)
Referee: Strömbergsson (SWE)

22/6/11, Herning Stadion, Herning
Switzerland 1-0 Czech Republic (aet)
Attendance: 5038
Switzerland: Sommer, Koch, Rossini, Lustenberger, Emeghara (Costanzo 111), Frei (Gavranović 78), Shaqiri, Mehmedi, Klose, Hochstrasser (Abrashi 71), Berardi. Coach: Pierluigi Tami (SUI)
Czech Republic: Vaclík, Mazuch, Čelůstka, Vácha, Dočkal, Kozák (Pekhart 63), Morávek (Chramosta 83), Gecov, Černý (Kadlec 112), Suchý, Mareček. Coach: Jakub Dovalil (CZE)
Goal(s): 1-0 Mehmedi 114
Yellow Card(s): Mazuch 23 (Czech Republic), Frei 45 (Switzerland), Černý 65 (Czech Republic), Mehmedi 115 (Switzerland), Vácha 117 (Czech Republic)
Referee: Schörgenhofer (AUT)

2012 OLYMPIC GAMES QUALIFICATION PLAY-OFF

Belarus, so close to eliminating Spain in the semi-finals, claimed the much coveted consolation prize of a place in the 2012 London Olympics by defeating the Czech Republic in a specially arranged third-place play-off in Aalborg.

A tight contest in a virtually empty stadium was settled late on when defender Yegor Filipenko swept home a cross from the right in a crowded penalty area to spark intense celebrations that would not have been out of place at the final later the same day in Aarhus.

Play-Off Result

25/6/11, Aalborg Stadion, Aalborg
Czech Republic 0-1 Belarus
Attendance: 870
Czech Republic: Vaclík, Lecjaks (Kovařík 13), Mazuch, Čelůstka, Vácha, Hořava, Dočkal, Gecov, Suchý, Chramosta (Kadlec 83), Hloušek (Kozák 46). Coach: Jakub Dovalil (CZE)
Belarus: Gutor, Dragun, Matveychik (Polyakov 76), Politevich, Sivakov, Skavysh (Rekish 83), Perepechko (Baga 34), Voronkov, Nekhaichik, Veretilo, Filipenko. Coach: Georgiy Kondratyev (BLR)
Goal(s): 0-1 Filipenko 88
Red Card(s): Vácha 75 (Czech Republic)
Yellow Card(s): Veretilo 26 (Belarus), Vácha 31 (Czech Republic), Voronkov 44 (Belarus), Skavysh 60 (Belarus), Vácha 75 (Czech Republic), Kozák 78 (Czech Republic), Gecov 82 (Czech Republic), Gutor 90+1 (Belarus)
Referee: Mažić (SRB)

Yegor Filipenko points skywards after scoring Belarus's late winning goal in the Olympic Games qualifying play-off
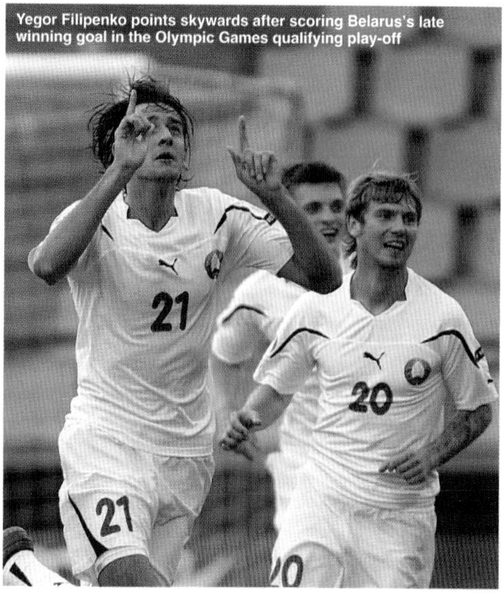

FINAL

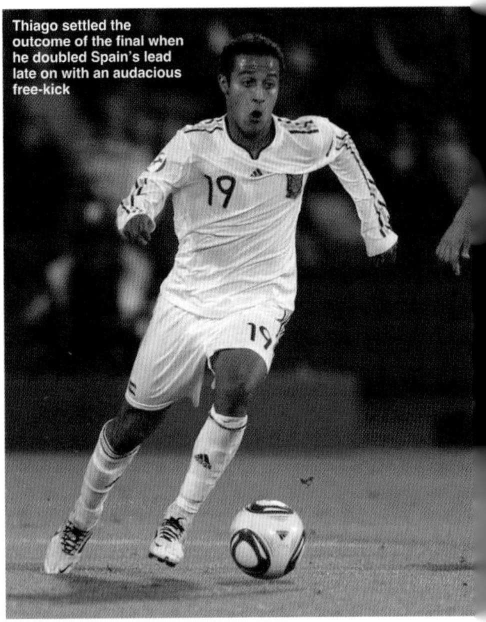
Thiago settled the outcome of the final when he doubled Spain's lead late on with an audacious free-kick

Spain secured their first European Under-21 crown since 1998, and third overall, as Luis Milla's youngsters maintained the trend of football's major prizes falling into Spanish hands.

They were deserved winners of the Aarhus final despite the best efforts of a Swiss side seeking their first success at this level. Switzerland coach Pierluigi Tami had billed the match as "the best final" between the tournament's two best teams – and two group winners – and his side did a better job than any other of denying Spain possession, limiting them to 56% – less of the ball than they had enjoyed in any previous game. Yet it was still not enough as Ander Herrera's 41st-minute header and an extravagant Thiago free-kick nine minutes from time enabled Milla's squad to follow their FIFA World Cup and UEFA European Championship-winning seniors on to the victory podium.

Slow start

A mocked-up Viking longboat appeared on the Aarhus Stadion pitch for the pre-match closing ceremony, but once the match got under way there was little raiding to report in a slow, uneventful opening phase. Adrián López, who ended the night holding the Golden Shoe, dragged an early shot across the face of goal for a Spain team that was unchanged for the fourth game running.

Switzerland's Tami had reintroduced Granit Xhaka to his midfield after a semi-final suspension, but it was the left foot of his playmaker, Xherdan Shaqiri, that delivered the first shot in anger on the half-hour. Sneaking between a defender and a wayward bouncing ball, Shaqiri applied true direction on the half-volley with his less favoured right foot only to strike it straight at David de Gea, who made the save.

Fabian Lustenberger of Switzerland stretches to dispossess Spain's Ander Herrera

The first-half stalemate persisted until four minutes from the interval when a delicious curling centre from left back Dídac was met firmly by the head of midfielder Herrera. It was the Athletic Club midfielder's second goal of the finals and the first the Swiss had conceded in 431 minutes in Denmark. "They had their chance with Xherdan Shaqiri in the first half but we took ours soon after and that gave us confidence," Spain coach Milla said afterwards.

Spain on top

Switzerland needed a response but they struggled to open Spain up, despite one half-chance that Innocent Emeghara slid straight at De Gea. Tami reacted by introducing a second striker in Mario Gavranovic – as he had in the semi-final – as well as midfielders Amir Abrashi and Pajtim Kasami, but it was Spain who continued to create the better opportunities.

Iker Muniain flashed one attempt against Yann Sommer's hands, Javi Martínez blazed over, then Alberto Botía powered a free header wastefully over from a Juan Mata corner. Finally, with less than 15 minutes remaining, Switzerland created two chances in quick succession from Shaqiri free-kicks, but neither Kasami nor Timm Klose was able to get his header on target, the latter's effort flying narrowly wide of the far post.

"We had two great chances at 1-0 down from set pieces," Tami reflected. "That lifted us but you have to take these opportunities, and straight afterwards Spain went and scored a super goal which finished the game."

Spectacular strike

That goal, by man of the match Thiago, had the 16,110 crowd on their feet as he caught Sommer off guard with an audacious 40-metre free-kick, sealing Spain's success in eye-catching fashion. The FC Barcelona midfielder said it was pure instinct. "I saw the goalkeeper and I took the decision without thinking. Luckily, it went in."

It was a stamp of quality from Milla's masters of possession and ensured that captain Javi Martínez, like team-mate Mata a world champion 12 months earlier in South Africa, would soon be lifting another trophy and sparking yet more Spanish celebrations.

Final Result

25/6/11, Aarhus Stadion, Aarhus
Switzerland 0-2 Spain
Attendance: 16110
Switzerland: Sommer, Koch, Rossini, Lustenberger, Emeghara (Gavranović 53), Frei (Abrashi 54), Shaqiri, Mehmedi, Xhaka (Kasami 67), Klose, Berardi. Coach: Pierluigi Tami (SUI)
Spain: De Gea, Álvaro Domínguez, Javi Martínez, Adrián López (Jeffren 80), Mata, Montoya, Dídac, Ander Herrera (Diego Capel 90), Thiago, Botía, Muniain (Parejo 85). Coach: Luis Milla (ESP)
Goal(s): 0-1 Ander Herrera 41, 0-2 Thiago 81
Yellow Card(s): Lustenberger 16 (Switzerland), Berardi 61 (Switzerland), Javi Martínez 77 (Spain), De Gea 90+4 (Spain)
Referee: Tagliavento (ITA)

TOP GOALSCORERS
Final Tournament

5	Adrián López (Spain)
3	Admir Mehmedi (Switzerland)
2	Danny Welbeck (England)
	Andrei Voronkov (Belarus)
	Ander Herrera (Spain)
	Juan Mata (Spain)
	Bořek Dočkal (Czech Republic)

Jubilation for Spain as captain Javi Martínez lifts the UEFA European Under-21 Championship trophy

FINAL TOURNAMENT SQUADS / APPEARANCES / GOALS

BELARUS

No	Player	DoB	Aps	(s)	Gls	Club
Goalkeepers						
12	Artem Gomelko	8/12/89				Lokomotiv Moskva (RUS)
22	Dmitriy Gushchenko	12/5/88				Vitebsk
1	Aleksandr Gutor	18/4/89	5			BATE
Defenders						
21	Yegor Filipenko	10/4/88	5		1	BATE
17	Vitaliy Gaiduchik	12/7/89		(1)		Dinamo Brest
3	Sergei Matveychik	5/6/88	2			Gomel
6	Yuri Ostroukh	21/1/88				Vedrich-97
4	Sergei Politevich	9/4/90	4			Dinamo Minsk
18	Denis Polyakov	17/4/91	4	(1)		Shakhtyor
14	Yuriy Ryzhko	10/10/89				Zhodino
20	Oleg Veretilo	10/7/88	5			Dinamo Minsk
Midfielders						
5	Dmitriy Baga	4/1/90	3	(2)	1	BATE
8	Nikita Bukatkin	7/3/88	2	(1)		Naftan
2	Stanislav Dragun	4/6/88	5			Dinamo Minsk
16	Mikhail Gordeichuk	23/10/89				BATE
13	Pavel Nekhaichik	15/7/88	3	(1)		BATE
10	Aleksandr Perepechko	7/4/89	5			Dinamo Minsk
15	Dmitriy Rekish	14/9/88		(4)		Dinamo Minsk
19	Yevgeniy Savostyanov	30/1/88				Neman
7	Mikhail Sivakov	16/1/88	5			Cagliari (ITA)
Forwards						
23	Vladimir Khvashchinskiy	10/5/90		(2)		Dinamo Brest
9	Maksim Skavysh	13/11/89	3	(2)	1	BATE
11	Andrei Voronkov	8/2/89	4	(1)	2	Kryvbas (UKR)

DENMARK

No	Player	DoB	Aps	(s)	Gls	Club
Goalkeepers						
16	Mikkel Andersen	17/12/88	3			Reading (ENG)
23	Nicklas Højlund	6/3/90				Lyngby
1	Jonas Lössl	1/2/89				Midtjylland
Defenders						
4	Andreas Bjelland	11/7/88	3			Nordsjælland
5	Nicolai Boilesen	16/2/92	3			Ajax (NED)
3	Mathias "Zanka" Jørgensen	23/4/90	3			København
15	Jesper Juelsgård Kristensen	26/1/89		(1)		Midtjylland
13	Lasse Nielsen	8/1/88				AaB
2	Anders Randrup	16/7/88				Brøndby
19	Frederik Sørensen	14/4/92				Juventus (ITA)
7	Daniel Wass	31/5/89	3			Brøndby
Midfielders						
6	Mads Albæk	14/1/90	1			Midtjylland
17	Thomas Delaney	3/9/91				København
10	Christian Eriksen	14/2/92	3		1	Ajax (NED)
12	Mads Fenger	10/9/90	1	(2)		Randers
8	Mike Jensen	19/2/88	3			Brøndby
22	Bashkim Kadrii	9/7/91	2	(1)	1	OB
20	Matti Lund Nielsen	8/5/88				Nordsjælland
18	Kasper Povlsen	26/9/89	2	(1)		AGF
Forwards						
11	Nicolaj Agger	23/10/88		(1)		Brøndby
21	Henrik Dalsgaard	27/7/89	1	(2)		AaB
14	Nicki Bille Nielsen	7/2/88	3			Villarreal (ESP)
9	Nicolai Jørgensen	15/1/91	2	(1)	1	Leverkusen (GER)

CZECH REPUBLIC

No	Player	DoB	Aps	(s)	Gls	Club
Goalkeepers						
23	Jan Hanuš	28/4/88				Slavia Praha
16	Marek Štěch	28/1/90				West Ham (ENG)
1	Tomáš Vaclík	29/3/89	5			Žižkov
Defenders						
5	Ondřej Čelůstka	18/6/89	5			Slavia Praha
21	Jan Hošek	1/4/89				Teplice
2	Jan Lecjaks	9/8/90	4			Anderlecht (BEL)
4	Ondřej Mazuch	15/3/89	5			Anderlecht (BEL)
3	Radim Řezník	20/1/89				Baník
17	Marek Suchý	29/3/88	5			Spartak Moskva (RUS)
Midfielders						
8	Bořek Dočkal	30/9/88	5		2	Liberec
13	Marcel Gecov	1/1/88	5			Liberec
22	Adam Hloušek	20/12/88	2	(1)		Slavia Praha
77	Tomáš Hořava	29/5/88	2			Sigma
12	Jan Kovařík	19/6/88	2	(1)		Jablonec
15	Milan Černý	16/3/88	1	(2)		Slavia Praha
18	Lukáš Mareček	17/4/90	2	(1)		Anderlecht (BEL)
10	Jan Morávek	1/11/89	3	(1)		Schalke (GER)
6	Lukáš Vácha	13/5/89	4			Liberec
Forwards						
19	Jan Chramosta	12/10/90	1	(2)	1	Mladá Boleslav
14	Václav Kadlec	20/5/92		(3)		Sparta Praha
9	Libor Kozák	30/5/89	2	(2)		Lazio (ITA)
11	Tomáš Pekhart	26/5/89	2	(2)	1	Jablonec
20	Michael Rabušic	17/9/89				Brno

ENGLAND

No	Player	DoB	Aps	(s)	Gls	Club
Goalkeepers						
1	Frank Fielding	4/4/88	3			Derby
13	Alex McCarthy	3/12/89				Reading
23	Jason Steele	18/8/90				Middlesbrough
Defenders						
3	Ryan Bertrand	5/8/89	3			Chelsea
16	Jack Cork	25/6/89				Chelsea
6	Phil Jones	21/2/92	3			Blackburn
5	Chris Smalling	22/11/89	3			Man. United
15	James Tomkins	29/3/89				West Ham
14	Kyle Walker	28/5/90	3			Tottenham
Midfielders						
7	Marc Albrighton	18/11/89		(1)		Aston Villa
17	Thomas Cleverley	12/8/89	2			Man. United
8	Jordan Henderson	17/6/90	3			Sunderland
18	Henri Lansbury	12/10/90		(3)		Arsenal
2	Michael Mancienne	8/1/88	2			Chelsea
4	Fabrice Muamba	6/4/88	1	(1)		Bolton
19	Jack Rodwell	11/3/91	1	(1)		Everton
20	Danny Rose	2/7/90	2	(1)		Tottenham
Forwards						
21	Nathan Delfouneso	2/2/91				Aston Villa
11	Scott Sinclair	25/3/89	1	(2)		Swansea (WAL)
10	Daniel Sturridge	1/9/89	3			Chelsea
9	Danny Welbeck	26/11/90	3		2	Man. United
22	Connor Wickham	31/3/93				Ipswich

UEFA European Under-21 Championship

ICELAND

No	Player	DoB	Aps	(s)	Gls	Club
	oalkeepers					
	Haraldur Björnsson	11/1/89	3			Valur
0	Arnar Darri Pétursson	16/3/91				SønderjyskE (DEN)
2	Óskar Pétursson	26/1/89				Grindavík
	efenders					
	Hólmar Örn Eyjólfsson	6/8/90	3			West Ham (ENG)
3	Jón Gudni Fjóluson	10/4/89	3			Fram
	Skúli Jón Fridgeirsson	30/7/88				KR
3	Elfar Freyr Helgason	27/7/89				Breidablik
8	Andrés Már Jóhannesson	21/12/88				Fylkir
	Eggert Gunnthór Jónsson	18/8/88	3			Hearts (SCO)
4	Thórarinn Ingi Valdimarsson	23/4/90				ÍBV
	Hjörtur Logi Valgardsson	27/9/88	3		1	Göteborg (SWE)
	idfielders					
	Birkir Bjarnason	27/5/88	1	(2)	1	Viking (NOR)
	Johann Berg Gudmundsson	27/10/90	2			AZ (NED)
7	Aron Einar Gunnarsson	22/4/89	2			Coventry (ENG)
6	Gudmundur Kristjánsson	1/3/89	1			Breidablik
5	Almarr Ormarsson	25/2/88				Fram
0	Gylfi Thór Sigurdsson	8/9/89	3			Hoffenheim (GER)
1	Arnór Smárason	7/9/88	1	(1)		Esbjerg (DEN)
	Bjarni Thór Vidarsson	5/3/88	2			Mechelen (BEL)
	orwards					
1	Alfred Finnbogason	1/2/89	1	(1)		Lokeren (BEL)
	Rúrik Gíslason	25/2/88	2	(1)		OB (DEN)
9	Kolbeinn Sigthórsson	14/3/90	3		1	AZ (NED)
2	Björn Bergmann Sigurdarson	26/2/91		(2)		Lillestrøm (NOR)

SWITZERLAND

No	Player	DoB	Aps	(s)	Gls	Club
	Goalkeepers					
12	Kevin Fickentscher	6/7/88				Sion
21	Benjamin Siegrist	31/1/92				Aston Villa (ENG)
1	Yann Sommer	17/12/88	5			Basel
	Defenders					
16	François Affolter	13/3/91	1			Young Boys
23	Gaetano Berardi	21/8/88	5			Brescia (ITA)
3	Fabio Daprelà	19/2/91		(1)		Brescia (ITA)
15	Timm Klose	9/5/88	4	(1)		Thun
2	Philippe Koch	8/2/91	5			Zürich
20	Daniel Pavlovic	22/4/88				Grasshoppers
5	Jonathan Rossini	5/4/89	5			Sampdoria (ITA)
	Midfielders					
18	Amir Abrashi	27/3/90		(4)		Grasshoppers
8	Moreno Costanzo	20/2/88		(2)		Young Boys
17	Frank Feltscher	17/5/88		(1)	1	Bellinzona
22	Xavier Hochstrasser	1/7/88	1	(1)		Young Boys
4	Pajtim Kasami	2/6/92		(2)		Palermo (ITA)
6	Fabian Lustenberger	2/5/88	5			Hertha (GER)
10	Xherdan Shaqiri	10/10/91	5		1	Basel
14	Granit Xhaka	27/9/92	4			Basel
	Forwards					
13	Nassim Ben Khalifa	13/1/92		(1)		Wolfsburg (GER)
7	Innocent Emeghara	27/5/89	5		1	Grasshoppers
9	Fabian Frei	8/1/89	5		1	St Gallen
19	Mario Gavranovic	24/11/89	1	(2)		Schalke (GER)
11	Admir Mehmedi	16/3/91	4		3	Zürich

SPAIN

No	Player	DoB	Aps	(s)	Gls	Club
	oalkeepers					
3	David de Gea	7/11/90	5			Atlético
3	Diego Mariño	9/5/90				Villarreal
	Rubén Miño	18/1/89				Barcelona
	efenders					
	Álvaro Domínguez	15/5/89	5			Atlético
	César Azpilicueta	28/8/89		(1)		Marseille (FRA)
0	Alberto Botía	27/1/89	5			Sporting Gijón
7	Dídac Vila	9/6/89	5			Milan (ITA)
5	José Angel Valdés	5/9/89				Sporting Gijón
2	Martín Montoya	14/4/91	5			Barcelona
6	Victor Ruiz	25/1/89				Napoli (ITA)
	Mikel San José	30/5/89				Athletic
	idfielders					
1	Diego Capel	16/2/88		(4)		Sevilla
8	Ander Herrera	14/8/89	5		2	Zaragoza
	Javi Martínez	2/9/88	5			Athletic
0	Juan Mata	28/4/88	5		2	Valencia
	Daniel Parejo	16/4/89		(4)		Getafe
1	Rubén Pérez	26/4/89				Deportivo
9	Thiago Alcántara	11/4/91	5		1	Barcelona
	orwards					
	Adrián López	8/1/88	5		5	Deportivo
	Bojan Krkić	28/8/90		(3)		Barcelona
	Jeffren Suárez	20/1/88	1	(2)	1	Barcelona
22	Iker Muniain	19/12/92	4			Athletic
4	Emilio Nsue	30/9/89		(1)		Mallorca

UKRAINE

No	Player	DoB	Aps	(s)	Gls	Club
	Goalkeepers					
12	Denys Boiko	29/1/88				Dynamo Kyiv
1	Anton Kanibolotskiy	16/5/88	3			Dnipro
23	Dmytro Nepogodov	17/2/88				Metalurh Donetsk
	Defenders					
2	Bohdan Butko	13/1/91	3			Volyn
15	Serhiy Krivtsov	15/3/91	3			Shakhtar
18	Oleksiy Kurilov	24/4/88				Vorskla
20	Olexandr Matveyev	11/2/89				Vorskla
13	Temur Partsvaniya	6/7/91		(1)		Dynamo Kyiv
5	Artem Putivtsev	29/8/88	1			Illychivets
4	Yaroslav Rakytskiy	3/8/89	3			Shakhtar
3	Yevhen Selin	9/5/88	2			Vorskla
	Midfielders					
16	Maxym Biliy	27/4/89	2	(1)	1	Zorya
17	Volodymyr Chesnakov	12/2/88	3			Vorskla
21	Valeriy Fedorchuk	5/10/88				Kryvbas
19	Denys Harmash	19/4/90	2			Dynamo Kyiv
14	Oleh Holodyuk	2/1/88	1	(1)		Karpaty
7	Yevhen Konoplyanka	29/9/89	3			Dnipro
9	Mykola Morozyuk	17/1/88	1			Metalurh Donetsk
8	Taras Stepanenko	8/8/89	1			Shakhtar
6	Vitaliy Vitsenets	3/8/90		(1)		Shakhtar
	Forwards					
22	Artem Kravets	3/6/89	1	(1)		Dynamo Kyiv
11	Andriy Yarmolenko	23/10/89	2	(1)		Dynamo Kyiv
10	Roman Zozulya	17/11/89	2	(1)		Dynamo Kyiv

UEFA U19 Championship 2010/11

The tenth UEFA European Under-19 Championship, staged in Romania, ended the same way as four of its nine predecessors – with Spain lifting the trophy. Ginés Meléndez's side were worthy champions, but they were made to work hard for their triumph in the final, in Chajna, twice falling behind to a resilient Czech Republic side before Valencia CF striker Paco Alcácer came off the bench to win the match with two smartly taken goals in the last 12 minutes of extra time. The victory followed Spain's successes in 2002, 2004, 2006 and 2007 – with Meléndez playing a part in all but the first – and ensured that the Iberian side would keep the trophy. Prior to overcoming the Czechs, who had won all four of their previous games, Spain overwhelmed the Republic of Ireland in the semi-finals and scored eight goals in winning their first two Group B matches. The only blot on their copybook was an inconsequential 3-0 defeat by Turkey in their final group fixture.

UEFA
UNDER19
CHAMPIONSHIP

QUALIFYING / ELITE ROUNDS

While most of the big names made it through the UEFA European Under-19 Championship qualifying round, Scotland, Slovenia and Austria – all semi-finalists or better in recent years – were not so fortunate. The elite round would also produce its fair share of shocks and surprises.

Serbia, semi-finalists in 2009, were the first team to book their place in Romania, edging out Wales and Norway in a three-way tie in Group 6. The Czech Republic then held off Russia, the Netherlands and Israel to win Group 5 and reach the finals for the first time since hosting the tournament in 2008. Group 3 provided the first surprise, with Greece ousting holders France after Konstantinos Rougalas had struck to secure a decisive 2-1 win in the second set of matches. Portugal and Croatia had met in the 2010 finals and were paired again in Group 1 but both had their thunder stolen by Belgium, who qualified for the first time since 2006.

Also ending a long wait to play in the finals were the Republic of Ireland, who had not featured since 2002 yet overwhelmed Italy 3-0 to finish on top of the pile in Group 4. The last two sections to be completed each had dramatic conclusions. Both Germany and Turkey won their first two Group 7 matches, and it was the latter who went through thanks to Muhammet Demir's first-half goal in the decider. There was a similar scenario in Group 2 as England and Spain met in their final qualifier – as they had done in the 2010 semi-finals - having each picked up two victories. Spain, four-time winners, were to emerge triumphant again, a 1-1 draw taking them through to the finals on goal difference.

Qualifying Round Results

Group 1

20-25/10/10 Carmarthen, Llanelli, Bridgend
Turkey 3-3 Wales, Iceland 4-0 Kazakhstan, Turkey 5-1 Kazakhstan, Wales 2-1 Iceland, Iceland 1-2 Turkey, Kazakhstan 1-1 Wales

Group 1 Table

	Pld	W	D	L	F	A	Pts
1 Turkey	3	2	1	0	10	5	7
2 Wales	3	1	2	0	6	5	5
3 Iceland	3	1	0	2	6	4	3
4 Kazakhstan	3	0	1	2	2	10	1

Group 2

28/9-3/10/10 Rakvere, Tallinn
Scotland 7-0 Liechtenstein, Norway 0-2 Estonia, Liechtenstein 0-5 Norway, Scotland 2-1 Estonia, Norway 4-2 Scotland, Estonia 3-0 Liechtenstein

Group 2 Table

	Pld	W	D	L	F	A	Pts
1 Estonia	3	2	0	1	6	2	6
2 Norway	3	2	0	1	9	4	6
3 Scotland	3	2	0	1	11	5	6
4 Liechtenstein	3	0	0	3	0	15	0

Group 3

11-16/10/10 Ferreira, Parchal, Lagos, Faro-Loule
Greece 0-1 Georgia, Portugal 2-2 Azerbaijan, Greece 1-0 Azerbaijan, Georgia 0-3 Portugal, Portugal 1-1 Greece, Azerbaijan 3-0 Georgia

Group 3 Table

	Pld	W	D	L	F	A	Pts
1 Portugal	3	1	2	0	6	3	5
2 Greece	3	1	1	1	2	2	4
3 Azerbaijan	3	1	1	1	5	3	4
4 Georgia	3	1	0	2	1	6	3

Group 4

7-12/10/10 Angelholm, Helsingborg, Laholm
Russia 4-2 Sweden, Ukraine 2-0 Denmark, Sweden 0-1 Ukraine, Russia 1-2 Denmark, Ukraine 1-2 Russia, Denmark 3-0 Sweden

Group 4 Table

	Pld	W	D	L	F	A	Pts
1 Ukraine	3	2	0	1	4	2	6
2 Russia	3	2	0	1	7	5	6
3 Denmark	3	2	0	1	5	3	6
4 Sweden	3	0	0	3	2	8	0

Group 5

1-6/10/10 Sarajevo
Belarus 2-1 Bosnia & Herzegovina, Czech Republic 0-1 FYROM, Belarus 3-0 FYROM, Bosnia & Herzegovina 0-0 Czech Republic, Czech Republic 3-0 Belarus, FYROM 1-1 Bosnia & Herzegovina

Group 5 Table

	Pld	W	D	L	F	A	Pts
1 Belarus	3	2	0	1	5	4	6
2 FYROM	3	1	1	1	2	4	4
3 Czech Republic	3	1	1	1	3	1	4
4 Bosnia & Herzegovina	3	0	2	1	2	3	2

Group 6

25-30/10/10 Tatabanya, Telki
Hungary 0-1 Moldova, Poland 2-0 Finland, Hungary 1-0 Finland, Moldova 0-0 Poland, Poland 0-2 Hungary, Finland 6-2 Moldova

Group 6 Table

	Pld	W	D	L	F	A	Pts
1 Hungary	3	2	0	1	3	1	6
2 Poland	3	1	1	1	2	2	4
3 Moldova	3	1	1	1	3	6	4
4 Finland	3	1	0	2	6	5	3

Group 7

7/-12/10/10 Jurmala, Rig
Croatia 2-2 Faroe Islands, Italy 2-1 Latvia, Italy 3-0 Faroe Islands, Latvia 1-2 Croatia, Croatia 1-3 Italy, Faroe Islands 1-2 Latvia

Group 7 Table

	Pld	W	D	L	F	A	Pts
1 Italy	3	3	0	0	8	2	9
2 Croatia	3	1	1	1	5	6	4
3 Latvia	3	1	0	2	4	5	3
4 Faroe Islands	3	0	1	2	3	7	1

Group 8

8-13/10/10 Vise, Malmedy, Verviers
England 6-1 Albania, Belgium 4-1 Cyprus, Cyprus 0-4 England, Belgium 2-0 Albania, England 1-2 Belgium, Albania 0-0 Cyprus

Group 8 Table

	Pld	W	D	L	F	A	Pts
1 Belgium	3	3	0	0	8	2	9
2 England	3	2	0	1	11	3	6
3 Cyprus	3	0	1	2	1	8	1
3 Albania	3	0	1	2	1	8	1

Group 9

7-12/10/10 Murska Sobota, Lendava
Slovakia 4-0 Malta, Netherlands 2-0 Slovenia, Netherlands 3-0 Malta, Slovenia 0-1 Slovakia, Slovakia 0-2 Netherlands, Malta 0-4 Slovenia

Group 9 Table

	Pld	W	D	L	F	A	Pts
1 Netherlands	3	3	0	0	7	0	9
2 Slovakia	3	2	0	1	5	2	6
3 Slovenia	3	1	0	2	4	3	3
4 Malta	3	0	0	3	0	11	0

Group 10

7-12/10/10 Teteven, Mezdra

Republic of Ireland 5-0 Luxembourg, Serbia 3-0 Bulgaria, Republic of Ireland 2-1 Bulgaria, Luxembourg 0-3 Serbia, Serbia 1-0 Republic of Ireland, Bulgaria 3-0 Luxembourg

Group 10 Table

	Pld	W	D	L	F	A	Pts
1 Serbia	3	3	0	0	7	0	9
2 Republic of Ireland	3	2	0	1	7	2	6
3 Bulgaria	3	1	0	2	4	5	3
4 Luxembourg	3	0	0	3	0	11	0

Group 11

19-24/10/10 Marijampole

Israel 3-0 Armenia, Spain 6-0 Lithuania, Spain 3-0 Armenia, Lithuania 0-1 Israel, Israel 0-3 Spain, Armenia 1-0 Lithuania

Group 11 Table

	Pld	W	D	L	F	A	Pts
1 Spain	3	3	0	0	12	0	9
2 Israel	3	2	0	1	4	3	6
3 Armenia	3	1	0	2	1	6	3
4 Lithuania	3	0	0	3	0	8	0

Group 12

8/-13/10/10 Seekirchen, Grodig

France 3-0 San Marino, Austria 1-1 Montenegro, France 2-0 Montenegro, San Marino 0-4 Austria, Austria 0-1 France, Montenegro 5-0 San Marino

Group 12 Table

	Pld	W	D	L	F	A	Pts
1 France	3	3	0	0	6	0	9
2 Montenegro	3	1	1	1	6	3	4
3 Austria	3	1	1	1	5	2	4
4 San Marino	3	0	0	3	0	12	0

Group 13

8-13/10/10 Sandhausen, Heidelberg, Hoffenheim, Forst, Mannheim

Germany 10-0 Andorra, Switzerland 0-0 Northern Ireland, Germany 2-1 Northern Ireland, Andorra 0-6 Switzerland, Switzerland 2-2 Germany, Northern Ireland 2-1 Andorra

Group 13 Table

	Pld	W	D	L	F	A	Pts
1 Germany	3	2	1	0	14	3	7
2 Switzerland	3	1	2	0	8	2	5
3 Northern Ireland	3	1	1	1	3	3	4
4 Andorra	3	0	0	3	1	18	0

Elite Round Results

Group 1

24-29/5/11 Porec, Rovinj, Novigrad, Umag

Belgium 1-0 Portugal, Estonia 0-1 Croatia, Belgium 3-2 Croatia, Portugal 3-0 Estonia, Estonia 0-0 Belgium, Croatia 0-1 Portugal

Group 1 Table

	Pld	W	D	L	F	A	Pts
1 Belgium	3	2	1	0	4	2	7
2 Portugal	3	2	0	1	4	1	6
3 Croatia	3	1	0	2	3	4	3
4 Estonia	3	0	1	2	0	4	1

Group 2

31/5-5/6/11 Lausanne, Yverdon, Nyon

Spain 2-1 Switzerland, England 1-0 Montenegro, Spain 3-0 Montenegro, Switzerland 2-3 England, England 1-1 Spain, Montenegro 2-3 Switzerland

Group 2 Table

	Pld	W	D	L	F	A	Pts
1 Spain	3	2	1	0	6	2	7
2 England	3	2	1	0	5	3	7
3 Switzerland	3	1	0	2	6	7	3
4 Montenegro	3	0	0	3	2	7	0

Group 3

20-25/5/11 Senec, Velky Biel, Nitra

Slovakia 1-2 Greece, France 2-0 Belarus, Belarus 0-5 Slovakia, France 1-2 Greece, Slovakia 0-2 France, Greece 1-0 Belarus

Group 3 Table

	Pld	W	D	L	F	A	Pts
1 Greece	3	3	0	0	5	2	9
2 France	3	2	0	1	5	2	6
3 Slovakia	3	1	0	2	6	4	3
4 Belarus	3	0	0	3	0	8	0

Group 4

24-29/5/11 Szczecinek, Koszalin, Kolobrzeg

Italy 1-0 Ukraine, Republic of Ireland 1-0 Poland, Ukraine 0-0 Republic of Ireland, Italy 3-1 Poland, Republic of Ireland 3-0 Italy, Poland 1-1 Ukraine

Group 4 Table

	Pld	W	D	L	F	A	Pts
1 Republic of Ireland	3	2	1	0	4	0	7
2 Italy	3	2	0	1	4	4	6
3 Ukraine	3	0	2	1	1	2	2
4 Poland	3	0	1	2	2	5	1

Group 5

19-24/5/11 Breclav, Kyjov, Lanzhot

Netherlands 1-1 Israel, Russia 0-0 Czech Republic, Netherlands 0-1 Czech Republic, Israel 1-3 Russia, Russia 1-1 Netherlands, Czech Republic 2-1 Israel

Group 5 Table

	Pld	W	D	L	F	A	Pts
1 Czech Republic	3	2	1	0	3	1	7
2 Russia	3	1	2	0	4	2	5
3 Netherlands	3	0	2	1	2	3	2
4 Israel	3	0	1	2	3	6	1

Group 6

28/4-3/5/11 Sarpsborg, Moss

Serbia 2-3 Wales, Norway 4-0 Moldova, Serbia 5-0 Moldova, Wales 1-3 Norway, Norway 0-3 Serbia, Moldova 0-2 Wales

Group 6 Table

	Pld	W	D	L	F	A	Pts
1 Serbia	3	2	0	1	10	3	6
2 Wales	3	2	0	1	6	5	6
3 Norway	3	2	0	1	7	4	6
4 Moldova	3	0	0	3	0	11	0

Group 7

31/5-5/6/11 Antalya

Germany 3-0 Hungary, Turkey 3-1 FYROM, Germany 5-0 FYROM, Hungary 1-6 Turkey, Turkey 1-0 Germany, FYROM 2-4 Hungary

Group 7 Table

	Pld	W	D	L	F	A	Pts
1 Turkey	3	3	0	0	10	2	9
2 Germany	3	2	0	1	8	1	6
3 Hungary	3	1	0	2	5	11	3
4 FYROM	3	0	0	3	3	12	0

TOP GOALSCORERS

(Qualifying & Elite rounds)

8 Muhammet Demir (Turkey)

7 Moritz Leitner (Germany)

6 Nenad Lukić (Serbia)
Isco (Spain)
Mushaga Bakenga (Norway)

FINAL TOURNAMENT

GROUP A

The Czech Republic were the dominant side in UEFA European Under-19 Championship Group A, recording three victories from as many games to win the section by five points from the Republic of Ireland, who held off the challenge of Greece and Romania to reach the last four.

Breathless start

The start to the section could scarcely have been more exciting as Ireland, appearing in the finals for the first time since 2002, returned with a bang, taking a second-minute lead through Anthony O'Connor. Although Giorgos Katidis brought Greece level within three minutes, Paul Doolin's side secured a winning start when O'Connor restored their advantage six minutes into the second period.

To the delight of a crowd of more than 3,500 in Chiajna, Lucian Burchel's Romania also began brightly, taking the lead against the Czech Republic on the half-hour when Nicolae Stanciu's cross caught out Tomáš Koubek. The Czech goalkeeper's blushes were spared just before the interval when Tomáš Přikryl levelled, and Jaroslav Hřebík's side moved in front a minute past the hour as Tomáš Jeleček held his nerve to convert a penalty. Victory was assured when Vojtěch Hadaščok added a late third.

Czechs in command

The Czech Republic again fell behind on Matchday 2 as John O'Sullivan deflected in a long-range Derrick Williams effort to put Ireland in front in the tenth minute, but once more they rallied strongly. This time the turnaround was even more dramatic, Jakub Brabec levelling with a 69th-minute header before Patrik Lácha clinched the points with a stunning long-range shot two minutes later as the Czechs closed in on the semi-finals.

Greece got their own aspirations of progressing back on course by inflicting a second defeat on the hosts in Berceni. Kostas Fortounis scored the only goal of a tense contest eight minutes before half-time, running on to Dimitris Kolovos's defence-splitting pass before clipping a shot over Laurenţiu Brănescu. The Romania goalkeeper did prevent the same player adding a late second when clean through, however, making a fine block.

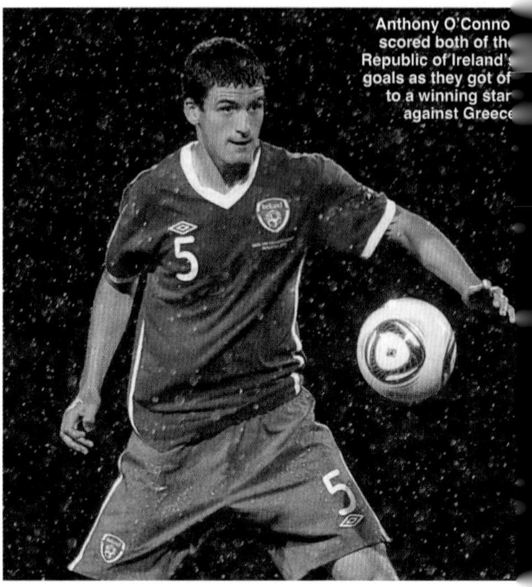

Anthony O'Conno scored both of th Republic of Ireland' goals as they got of to a winning star against Greece

Worthy winner

The Czechs thus needed a point in their final match against Greece in Mogosaia to guarantee qualification for the last four as section winners. Alhough Hřebík's charges initially looked uncertain whether to stick or twist, they were roused by a fine Koubek save from Fortounis midway through the opening period. Patrik Lácha and Tomáš Jeleček stretched Greece No1 Stefanos Kapino before the only goal finally arrived 20 minutes from time. Přikryl exchanged passes with Lácha to breach the defence yet looked to have overrun the ball, only to reach it ahead of Kapino, cleverly take it around the 'keeper and roll it into the net from a narrow angle with his other foot as he fell to the ground.

That took the Czechs into the U19 semi-finals for the fourth time, and they were joined there by Ireland despite the hosts collecting their first point in Berceni. It was Romania who looked the likelier to force a breakthrough, Stanciu hitting the crossbar, Sebastian Remeş's effort being headed off the line and Romario Benzar forcing a good save from Aaron McCarey, but Doolin's team held firm for the draw they needed to progress.

Group A Results

20/7/11, Concordia, Chiajna
Romania 1-3 Czech Republic
Romania: Brănescu, Peteleu (Ilie 5) (Gugu 77), Murgoci, Remeş, Avrămia, Benzar, Năstăsie, Cârstocea (Walleth 67), Roman, Stanciu, Serediuc. Coach: Lucian Burchel (ROU)
Czech Republic: Koubek, Brabec, Jánoš (Kraus 90+2), Kalas, Kadeřábek, Sladký, Skalák (Hadaščok 69), Jeleček, Krejčí, Přikryl (Fantiš 89), Hála. Coach: Jaroslav Hřebík (CZE)
Goal(s): 1-0 Stanciu 29, 1-1 Přikryl 44, 1-2 Jeleček 61(p), 1-3 Hadaščok 85
Yellow Card(s): Serediuc 12 (Romania), Sladký 18 (Czech Republic), Cârstocea 41 (Romania), Remeş 60 (Romania), Krejčí 72 (Czech Republic)
Referee: Turpin (FRA)

20/7/11, Football Centre FRF, Buftea
Greece 1-2 Republic of Ireland
Greece: Kapino, Stafylidis, Lagos, Potouridis, Mavrias, Fortounis, Karelis (Bakasetas 55), Marinakis (Kolovos 72), Rougalas, Diamantakos (Kotsaridis 46), Katidis. Coach: Leonidas Vokolos (GRE)
Republic of Ireland: McCarey, Doherty, Williams (Shaughnessy 80), Egan, O'Connor, Hendrick, Carruthers, O'Sullivan (Ferdinand 85), Murphy (Smith 79), Forde, Murray . Coach: Paul Doolin (IRL)
Goal(s): 0-1 O'Connor 2, 1-1 Katidis 5, 1-2 O'Connor 51
Yellow Card(s): Carruthers 30 (Republic of Ireland), Hendrick 33 (Republic of Ireland), Lagos 41 (Greece), Doherty 57 (Republic of Ireland), Fortounis 69 (Greece), Rougalas 89 (Greece)
Referee: Gil (POL)

23/7/11, Football Centre FRF, Mogosoaia
Czech Republic 2-1 Republic of Ireland
Czech Republic: Koubek, Brabec, Jánoš (Polom 77), Kalas, Kadeřábek, Sladký (Kraus 55), Skalák (Lácha 46), Jeleček, Krejčí, Přikryl, Hála. Coach: Jaroslav Hřebík (CZE)
Republic of Ireland: McCarey, Doherty, Williams, Egan, O'Connor, Hendrick, Carruthers, O'Sullivan (Ferdinand 57), Forde, Murray (Knight 77), Smith (Murphy 64). Coach: Paul Doolin (IRL)
Goal(s): 0-1 O'Sullivan 10, 1-1 Brabec 69, 2-1 Lácha 71
Yellow Card(s): Sladký 23 (Czech Republic), Hála 36 (Czech Republic), Ferdinand 59 (Republic of Ireland), Williams 69 (Republic of Ireland)
Referee: Bognar (HUN)

23/7/11, City Stadium, Berceni
Romania 0-1 Greece
Romania: Brănescu, Murgoci, Remeş, Benzar, Năstăsie (Chitoşcă 62), Cârstocea, Stanciu, Serediuc, Walleth (Amet 70), Gugu, Gavra (Roman 46). Coach: Lucian Burchel (ROU)
Greece: Kapino, Stafylidis, Potouridis, Mavrias (Bouzas 79), Kotsaridis (Stamogiannos 73), Bakasetas (Karelis 69), Fortounis, Marinakis, Rougalas, Katidis, Kolovos. Coach: Leonidas Vokolos (GRE)
Goal(s): 0-1 Fortounis 37
Yellow Card(s): Stanciu 14 (Romania), Stafylidis 23 (Greece), Murgoci 36 (Romania), Năstăsie 45+2 (Romania), Benzar 55 (Romania), Serediuc 75 (Romania), Mavrias 77 (Greece), Cârstocea 82 (Romania)
Referee: Attwell (ENG)

26/7/11, City Stadium, Berceni
Republic of Ireland 0-0 Romania
Republic of Ireland: McCarey, Doherty, Egan, O'Connor, Hendrick, Carruthers (Wearen 74), O'Sullivan, Murphy (Smith 64), Forde, Murray (Knight 56), Shaughnessy. Coach: Paul Doolin (IRL)
Romania: Brănescu, Murgoci, Remeş, Avrămia, Benzar, Năstăsie, Roman (Gavra 62), Stanciu, Gugu (Ilie 46), Amet, Chitoşcă (Walleth 90+2). Coach: Lucian Burchel (ROU)
Yellow Card(s): Amet 30 (Romania), Gugu 33 (Romania), Murgoci 52 (Romania), Doherty 69 (Republic of Ireland), O'Connor 84 (Republic of Ireland)
Referee: Kuchin (KAZ)

26/7/11, Football Centre FRF, Mogosoaia
Czech Republic 1-0 Greece
Czech Republic: Koubek, Brabec, Jánoš (Fantiš 90+3), Kalas, Kadeřábek, Lácha (Jugas 90+5), Jeleček, Krejčí, Přikryl (Skalák 90+6), Hála, Polom. Coach: Jaroslav Hřebík (CZE)
Greece: Kapino, Stafylidis, Lagos (Kotsaridis 67), Potouridis, Mavrias (Diamantakos 75), Bakasetas, Fortounis, Marinakis, Rougalas (Karelis 84), Katidis, Kolovos. Coach: Leonidas Vokolos (GRE)
Goal(s): 1-0 Přikryl 70
Yellow Card(s): Lagos 46 (Greece), Stafylidis 76 (Greece), Bakasetas 80 (Greece), Kotsaridis 85 (Greece), Fortounis 90+2 (Greece)
Referee: Hagen (NOR)

Group A Table

	Pld	W	D	L	F	A	Pts
1 Czech Republic	3	3	0	0	6	2	9
2 Republic of Ireland	3	1	1	1	3	3	4
3 Greece	3	1	0	2	2	3	3
4 Romania	3	0	1	2	1	4	1

GROUP B

Although Spain set the pace in Group B, winning the section with a game to spare and scoring eight goals, the four-time winners suffered a torrid time in their final encounter against a Turkey team chasing a semi-final spot. That place would eventually go to Serbia, however, after they edged out Kemal Özdeş's side, leaving Belgium bottom.

Decisive victory

Serbia and Turkey were both without three key players through suspension for their opening encounter in Berceni, and initially it was Özdeş's Turkey who had fewer problems overcoming the handicap. The game turned, however, when Ömer Ali Şahiner prodded wide with only the goalkeeper to beat midway through the first half. Miloš Jojić made him pay when he scored a thunderous opener in the 57th minute before substitute Nikola Trujić raced clear to finish coolly and give Serbia a 2-0 win.

Spain also began positively against Belgium in Mogosaia, taking the lead through Álvaro Morata, but the game was then abandoned after 15 minutes due to adverse weather conditions. The teams reconvened the following day, and Belgium were up against it from the moment goalkeeper Koen Casteels was sent off in the 13th minute for fouling Morata, especially as Pablo Sarabia put Spain in front with the ensuing spot kick. The ten men of Belgium levelled less than 60 seconds after half-time thanks to Florent Cuvelier's powerful low strike, but substitute Paco Alcácer came off the bench to restore Spain's advantage before Juan Muñiz Gallego and Morata added added gloss to the win in added time.

Spain surge

Spain carried on where they had left off as the two first-game victors met in Chiajna, scoring three times against Serbia in the opening 22 minutes. Morata scored either side of Juanmi's 15th-minute effort, and the Real Madrid CF striker completed his hat-trick 15 minutes from time to take the four-time champions into the last four as group winners with a match to spare.

In Buftea, Belgium found themselves reduced to ten men for the second game running when Igor Vetokele was sent off three minutes before half-time following a collision with Turkey's Ömer Ali Şahiner. Despite another brave rearguard display, Belgium looked doomed when Ali Dere tapped in the rebound after Ömer Ali's effort had been saved 13 minutes from time, yet Turkish delight was short-lived as Jonas Vervaeke beat Ömer Kahveci to Tom Pietermaat's long free-kick and headed a 90th-minute equaliser into an empty net.

With Spain already through, the other three teams all had the opportunity to join them in the final round of games. In a repeat of the 2004 final, Turkey's hopes were boosted when Spain's Jonás Ramalho headed into his own net in the 31st minute. It got even better for Özdeş's side after the restart with Kamil Çörekçi tapping in a second, and Spain's misfortune was complete when Sergi Gómez made it 3-0 with another own goal.

Serbia's Andrej Mrkela goes past the challenge of Franco Zennaro before opening the scoring against Belgium

That result proved academic, however, as Serbia sealed their progress thanks to a 1-1 draw with Belgium in Buftea. Needing just a point, Dejan Govedarica's men took charge with Andrej Mrkela's fine shot in the sixth minute, and although Marnick Vermijl levelled after the break to set up a tense finale, Serbia held on to advance ahead of Turkey on the head-to-head rule.

Group B Results

20/7/11, City Stadium, Berceni
Serbia 2-0 Turkey
Serbia: Perić, Petković, Malbašić (Trujić 64), Jojić, Mrkela (Krneta 90+3), Čaušić, Pantić, Vitas, Pešić (Despotović 76), Rogač, Kuzmanović. Coach: Dejan Govedarica (SRB)
Turkey: Ömer Kahveci, Okan Alkan (Hasan Ahmet Sari 71), Kamil Çörekçi, Sezer Özmen, Orhan Gülle, Ömer Ali Şahiner, Gökay Iravul, Engin Bekdemir (Berkay Öztuvan 58), Sefa Başıbüyük, Atınç Nukan, Ali Dere. Coach: Kemal Özdeş (TUR)
Goal(s): 1-0 Jojić 57, 2-0 Trujić 90
Yellow Card(s): Jojić 25 (Serbia), Okan Alkan 51 (Turkey), Trujić 90+1 (Serbia)
Referee: Kuchin (KAZ)

20/7/11, Football Centre FRF, Mogosoaia
Spain – Belgium (match abandoned after 15 mins)
Spain: Badia, Sergi Gómez, Miquel, Aurtenetxe, Rubén Pardo, Morata, Álex, Sarabia, Albert Blázquez, Juanmi, Deulofeu. Coach: Ginés Meléndez (ESP)
Belgium: Casteels, Ngawa, Arslanagic, De Bock, Vansteenkiste, Pietermaat, Trompet, Lestienne, Hazard, Van der Bruggen, Cuvelier. Coach: Marc Van Geersom (BEL)
Goal(s): 1-0 Morata 12
Referee: Attwell (ENG)

21/7/11, Football Centre FRF, Mogosoaia
Spain 4-1 Belgium
Spain: Badia, Sergi Gómez, Miquel, Aurtenetxe, Rubén Pardo, Morata, Álex, Sarabia, Albert Blázquez (Carvajal 64), Juanmi (Paco Alcácer 50), Deulofeu (Muñiz Gallego 61). Coach: Ginés Meléndez (ESP)
Belgium: Casteels, Ngawa, Arslanagic (Kaminski 14), De Bock, Vansteenkiste, Pietermaat, Trompet, Lestienne (Vetokele 77), Hazard (Cerigioni 66), Van der Bruggen, Cuvelier. Coach: Marc Van Geersom (BEL)
Goal(s): 1-0 Sarabia 15(p), 1-1 Cuvelier 46, 2-1 Paco Alcácer 65, 3-1 Muñiz Gallego 90+1, 4-1 Morata 90+3
Red Card(s): Casteels 13 (Belgium)
Yellow Card(s): Hazard 22 (Belgium), Juanmi 34 (Spain), Trompet 35 (Belgium)
Referee: Attwell (ENG)

23/7/11, Football Centre FRF, Buftea
Turkey 1-1 Belgium
Turkey: Ömer Kahveci, Okan Alkan (Ali Dere 46), Kamil Çörekçi, Furkan Şeker, Sezer Özmen, Orhan Gülle, Ömer Ali Şahiner, Gökay Iravul (Hasan Ahmet Sari 76), Nadir Çiftçi, Sefa Başıbüyük, Şervan Taştan (Engin Bekdemir 50). Coach: Kemal Özdeş (TUR)
Belgium: Kaminski, Ngawa, De Bock, Pietermaat, Vermijl, Trompet (Van der Bruggen 83), Lestienne (Cerigioni 67), Mpoku (Zennaro 83), Vervaeke, Cuvelier, Vetokele. Coach: Marc Van Geersom (BEL)
Goal(s): 1-0 Ali Dere 77, 1-1 Vervaeke 90
Red Card(s): Vetokele 42 (Belgium)
Yellow Card(s): Okan Alkan 45 (Turkey), De Bock 62 (Belgium), Lestienne 65 (Belgium), Gökay Iravul 67 (Turkey), Ali Dere 87 (Turkey)
Referee: Hagen (NOR)

23/7/11, Concordia, Chiajna
Serbia 0-4 Spain
Serbia: Perić, Petković, Čosić, Jojić, Brašanac (Mrkela 46), Čaušić, Lukić, Vitas, Pešić (Despotović 66), Rogač (Trujić 46), Kuzmanović. Coach: Dejan Govedarica (SRB)
Spain: Badia, Carvajal, Sergi Gómez, Miquel, Aurtenetxe, Rubén Pardo, Morata, Sarabia (Muñiz Gallego 81), Juanmi (Álex 58), Campaña, Deulofeu (Borja González 74). Coach: Ginés Meléndez (ESP)
Goal(s): 0-1 Morata 13, 0-2 Juanmi 15, 0-3 Morata 22, 0-4 Morata 75
Yellow Card(s): Kuzmanović 37 (Serbia), Aurtenetxe 56 (Spain), Jojić 68 (Serbia), Morata 72 (Spain)
Referee: Gil (POL)

26/7/11, Football Centre FRF, Buftea
Belgium 1-1 Serbia
Belgium: Kaminski, Ngawa, De Bock, Vansteenkiste, Pietermaat, Vermijl, Lestienne, Hazard (Cerigioni 62), Vervaeke, Zennaro (Trompet 82), Van der Bruggen (Mpoku 65). Coach: Marc Van Geersom (BEL)
Serbia: Perić, Petković (Krneta 59), Čosić, Mrkela (Malbašić 78), Brašanac, Despotović, Čaušić, Lukić, Pantić, Trujić (Rogač 90+3), Vitas. Coach: Dejan Govedarica (SRB)
Goal(s): 0-1 Mrkela 6, 1-1 Vermijl 73
Yellow Card(s): Čaušić 25 (Serbia), Petković 56 (Serbia), Brašanac 70 (Serbia), Mpoku 81 (Belgium), Despotović 86 (Serbia), Lestienne 90+1 (Belgium)
Referee: Turpin (FRA)

26/7/11, Concordia, Chiajna
Turkey 3-0 Spain
Turkey: Ömer Kahveci, Kamil Çörekçi, Furkan Şeker, Sezer Özmen, Orhan Gülle, Ömer Ali Şahiner (Nadir Çiftçi 78), Gökay Iravul (Şervan Taştan 71), Muhammet Demir (Berkay Öztuvan 83), Engin Bekdemir, Sefa Başıbüyük, Ali Dere. Coach: Kemal Özdeş (TUR)
Spain: Ortolá, Sergi Gómez, Miquel, Álex (Rubén Pardo 71), Borja González, Paco Alcácer (Deulofeu 46), Albert Blázquez, Ramalho, Juanmi (Sarabia 46), Campaña, Muñiz Gallego. Coach: Ginés Meléndez (ESP)
Goal(s): 1-0 Ramalho 31(og), 2-0 Kamil Çörekçi 51, 3-0 Sergi Gómez 56(og)
Yellow Card(s): Furkan Şeker 38 (Turkey), Engin Bekdemir 84 (Turkey), Sarabia 90+2 (Spain)
Referee: Bognar (HUN)

Group B Table

	Pld	W	D	L	F	A	Pts
1 Spain	3	2	0	1	8	4	6
2 Serbia	3	1	1	1	3	5	4
3 Turkey	3	1	1	1	4	3	4
4 Belgium	3	0	2	1	3	6	2

SEMI-FINALS

Group winners Spain and the Czech Republic made it through to the final in contrasting fashion, the former producing a scintillating display of attacking football to sweep aside the Republic of Ireland while the latter had to withstand a spirited fightback from Serbia.

The first semi-final was held in Mogosaia, a happy hunting ground for the Czechs, who had won their last two games there, and before 20 minutes had elapsed Jaroslav Hřebík's team were three goals to the good.

Jiří Skalák celebrates scoring the Czech Republic's fourth goal in the semi-final victory over Serbia

Tomáš Přikryl opened the scoring in the sixth minute, exchanging passes with Patrik Lácha and outstripping the Serbia defence to calmly slot past goalkeeper Nikola Perić. Ten minutes later Serbia left Jakub Brabec unmarked to meet Adam Jánoš's left-wing cross, and although Perić saved his header, Tomáš Kalas reacted fastest to slam in the rebound. The goalkeeper was forced to pick the ball out of his net for a third time in the 19th minute after Přikryl was felled by Darko Brašanac and Tomáš Jelеček calmly placed the penalty just inside the right-hand post.

Despotović double

If the Czechs thought they had the game won, however, they were in for a rude awakening, and by the 28th minute the Serbian deficit was down to just one goal. Đorđe Despotović was the instigator, racing on to a quick free-kick to thump the ball high into the net before supplying an equally emphatic finish to Filip Malbašić's low left-wing cross.

Hřebík later praised the mental strength his side showed at that point as they gradually regained control of the contest. After passing up a number of further opportunities, it was left to Jiří Skalák to clinch the win in added time at the end of the game, the substitute slotting in Přikryl's cross to confirm his side's progress to a first U19 final.

Record-equalling win

Spain reached their sixth final with a 5-0 win in Chiajna, equalling their own record margin for a U19 semi-final victory achieved against Austria in 2006. Ginés Meléndez's side were two goals to the good at half-time thanks to fine strikes from Gerard Deulofeu and Pablo Sarabia, the former opening the scoring with a curling shot in the 27th minute before captain Sarabia swivelled sharply to fire in a second.

Seconds after half-time Deulofeu's pass picked out Juanmi, who finished off the underside of the crossbar, yet despite their handsome lead Spain continued to pour forward. A fourth goal arrived 11 minutes from time when Álvaro Morata rounded Aaron McCarey and slotted in Juanmi's through pass, and the Real Madrid CF striker took his tournament tally to six goals in added time, making no mistake from the penalty spot after Jeffrey Hendrick had handled Ignasi Miquel's chipped pass.

Semi-Final Results

29/7/11, Football Centre FRF, Mogosoaia
Czech Republic 4-2 Serbia
Czech Republic: Koubek, Brabec, Jánoš, Kalas, Kadeřábek (Fantiš 90+3), Lácha (Skalák 49), Jeleček, Krejčí, Přikryl (Jugas 90+4), Hála, Polom. Coach: Jaroslav Hřebík (CZE)
Serbia: Perić, Petković, Malbašić (Pešić 80), Ćosić, Mrkela (Trujić 76), Brašanac, Despotović, Čaušić, Lukić (Jojić 73), Pantić, Vitas. Coach: Dejan Govedarica (SRB)
Goal(s): 1-0 Přikryl 6, 2-0 Kalas 16, 3-0 Jeleček 19(p), 3-1 Despotović 23, 3-2 Despotović 28, 4-2 Skalák 90+1
Yellow Card(s): Malbašić 22 (Serbia), Lácha 42 (Czech Republic), Ćosić 80 (Serbia), Skalák 90+1 (Czech Republic)
Referee: Kuchin (KAZ)

29/7/11, Concordia, Chiajna
Spain 5-0 Republic of Ireland
Spain: Badia, Carvajal (Albert Blázquez 82), Sergi Gómez, Miquel, Aurtenetxe, Rubén Pardo, Morata, Álex, Sarabia (Muñiz Gallego 66), Juanmi, Deulofeu (Paco Alcácer 80). Coach: Ginés Meléndez (ESP)
Republic of Ireland: McCarey, Williams, Egan, O'Connor, Hendrick, Carruthers (Wearen 62), O'Sullivan, Murphy (Smith 46), Forde, Murray (Knight 71), Shaughnessy. Coach: Paul Doolin (IRL)
Goal(s): 1-0 Deulofeu 27, 2-0 Sarabia 40, 3-0 Juanmi 46, 4-0 Morata 79, 5-0 Morata 90+1(p)
Yellow Card(s): Hendrick 38 (Republic of Ireland), Murray 54 (Republic of Ireland), McCarey 58 (Republic of Ireland), Carvajal 77 (Spain)
Referee: Turpin (FRA)

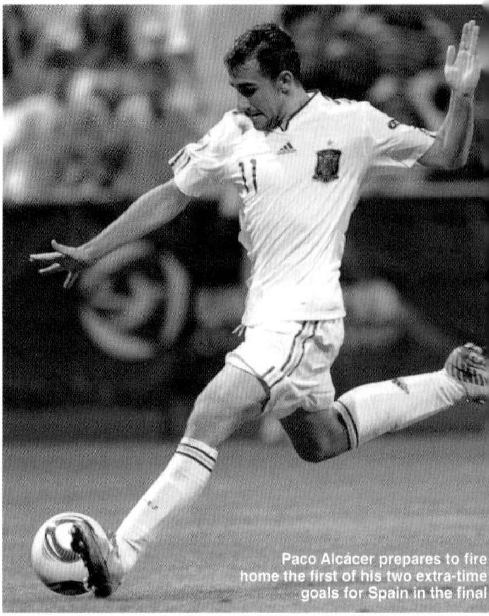
Paco Alcácer prepares to fire home the first of his two extra-time goals for Spain in the final

FINAL

Substitute Paco Alcácer scored twice in the second half of extra time as Spain twice came from behind in an engrossing final to defeat the Czech Republic and claim a fifth UEFA European Under-19 Championship title

After an even first half in Chiajna, the Czechs struck first seven minutes after half-time thanks to Ladislav Krejčí's fierce low shot. Spain, beaten in the 2010 final and seeking a fifth triumph in the competition that would enable them to keep the trophy, pressed hard and got their reward in the 85th minute thanks to Jon Aurtenetxe's opportunistic strike. Substitute Patrik Lácha restored the Czech lead with a beautifully worked goal in the 97th minute, but Paco Alcácer replied 11 minutes later and then decided a gripping contest in Spain's favour in the 115th minute.

Czech breakthrough

The Czechs were first to threaten, a slick move down the left ending with Krejčí flashing a cross-shot past the far post. Spain produced some typically slick first-half interchanges, with Pablo Sarabia a regular threat down the right while Álvaro Morata and Rubén Pardo also bristled with attacking menace.

The Czechs, however, regularly posed problems from set pieces, Jakub Brabec going close from a corner early in the second period. Their 51st-minute breakthrough, however, came from open play. Substitute Martin Sladký started the move, winning possession just inside the Spain half, but the rest was all Krejčí's own work, the classy midfielder holding off three defenders to drill a firm and accurate left-foot shot across Edgar Badia and into the far corner.

Spain coach Ginés Meléndez promptly brought on Alcácer, the top scorer at the 2010 U17 finals, and the replacement nearly made an immediate impact, Tomáš Koubek being forced to parry a fierce shot at his near post. The No11 then steered Sarabia's delightful left-wing cross wide before Koubek denied him again with another block, but Spain kept coming and finally levelled with five minutes remaining, left-back Aurtenetxe diverting in Pardo's speculative volley into a crowded penalty area from close range.

Alcácer strikes

Meléndez's side had enough opportunities over the 90 minutes to win the game without the need for extra time, but instead their failure to cope with Krejčí led to the concession of a second goal seven minutes into the first additional period. The Czech No13 burst into the area on the left and pulled the ball back brilliantly for Lácha to stretch and slide it low beyond Badia.

Again Spain would not admit defeat, however, and Morata – the tournament's top scorer with six goals – showed another dimension to his game when he headed on for Alcácer to equalise with a sweet right-foot shot. Seven minutes later the Valencia CF forward finally settled the contest, another composed finish beating Koubek and giving Spain the victory that enabled them to keep the U19 trophy for good.

Final Result

1/8/11, Concordia, Chiajna
Czech Republic 2-3 Spain (aet)
Attendance: 4300
Czech Republic: Koubek, Brabec, Jánoš, Kalas, Kadeřábek, Skalák (Lácha 79), Jeleček, Krejčí, Přikryl (Fantiš 102), Hála, Polom (Sladký 36). Coach: Jaroslav Hřebík (CZE)
Spain: Badia, Sergi Gómez, Miquel, Aurtenetxe, Pardo, Morata, Álex (Campaña 55), Sarabia (Muñiz Gallego 78), Albert Blázquez, Juanmi (Paco Alcácer 54), Deulofeu. Coach: Ginés Meléndez (ESP)
Goal(s): 1-0 Krejčí 52, 1-1 Aurtenetxe 85, 2-1 Lácha 97, 2-2 Paco Alcácer 108, 2-3 Paco Alcácer 115
Yellow Card(s): Álex 47 (Spain), Skalák 66 (Czech Republic), Brabec 69 (Czech Republic), Fantiš 107 (Czech Republic), Campaña 119 (Spain)
Referee: Attwell (ENG)

TOP GOALSCORERS
(Final Tournament)

6	Álvaro Morata (Spain)
3	Paco Alcácer (Spain) Tomáš Přikryl (Czech Republic)
2	Patrik Lácha (Czech Republic) Đorđe Despotović (Serbia) Anthony O'Connor (Republic of Ireland) Juanmi (Spain) Pablo Sarabia (Spain) Tomáš Jeleček (Czech Republic)

Jubilant Spain players celebrate with the UEFA European Under-19 Championship trophy

FINAL TOURNAMENT SQUADS / APPEARANCES / GOALS

BELGIUM

No	Player	DoB	Aps	(s)	Gls
Goalkeepers					
1	Koen Casteels	25/6/92	1		
12	Thomas Kaminski	23/10/92	2	(1)	
21	Matz Sels	28/2/92			
Defenders					
3	Dino Arslanagic	24/4/93	1		
4	Laurens De Bock	7/11/92	3		
2	Pierre-Yves Ngawa	9/2/92	3		
6	Tom Pietermaat	6/9/92	3		
5	Jannes Vansteenkiste	17/2/93	2		
7	Marnick Vermijl	13/1/92	2		1
13	Jonas Vervaeke	10/1/92	2		1
14	Franco Zennaro	1/4/93	1	(1)	
Midfielders					
16	Florent Cuvelier	12/9/92	2		1
8	Jore Trompet	30/7/92	2	(1)	
15	Hannes Van der Bruggen	1/4/93	2	(1)	
Forwards					
18	Alessandro Cerigioni	30/9/92		(3)	
10	Thorgan Hazard	29/3/93	2		
9	Maxime Lestienne	17/6/92	3		
11	Paul-José Mpoku	19/4/92	1	(1)	
17	Igor Vetokele	23/3/92	1	(1)	

GREECE

No	Player	DoB	Aps	(s)	Gls
Goalkeepers					
12	Kostas Kaldelis	22/3/92			
1	Stefanos Kapino	18/3/94	3		
Defenders					
14	Nikos Marinakis	12/9/93	3		
5	Giannis Potouridis	27/2/92	3		
2	Nikos Skondras	16/11/92			
3	Kostas Stafylidis	2/12/93	3		
6	Panagiotis Stamogiannos	30/1/92		(1)	
Midfielders					
13	Vasilis Bouzas	30/6/93		(1)	
10	Kostas Fortounis	16/10/92	3		1
17	Giorgos Katidis	12/2/93	3		1
18	Dimitris Kolovos	27/4/93	2	(1)	
8	Kostas Kotsaridis	12/6/92	1	(2)	
4	Tasos Lagos	12/4/92	2		
7	Charis Mavrias	21/2/94	3		
15	Kostas Rougalas	13/10/93	3		
Forwards					
9	Anastasios Bakasetas	28/6/93	2	(1)	
16	Dimitris Diamantakos	5/3/93	1	(1)	
11	Nikos Karelis	24/2/92	1	(2)	

CZECH REPUBLIC

No	Player	DoB	Aps	(s)	Gls
Goalkeepers					
1	Tomáš Koubek	26/8/92	5		
16	Jakub Zapletal	30/3/92			
Defenders					
2	Jakub Brabec	6/8/92	5		1
4	Adam Jánoš	20/7/92	5		
12	Tomáš Jeleček	25/2/92	5		2
3	Jakub Jugas	5/5/92		(2)	
6	Pavel Kadeřábek	25/4/92	5		
5	Tomáš Kalas	15/5/93	5		1
11	Patrik Lácha	20/1/92	2	(2)	2
18	Roman Polom	11/1/92	3	(1)	
Midfielders					
17	Martin Hála	24/3/92	5		
7	Martin Kraus	30/5/92		(2)	
13	Ladislav Krejčí	5/7/92	5		1
8	Martin Sladký	1/3/92	2	(1)	
Forwards					
10	Antonín Fantiš	15/4/92		(4)	
15	Vojtěch Hadaščok	8/1/92		(1)	1
14	Tomáš Přikryl	4/7/92	5		3
9	Jiří Skalák	12/3/92	3	(2)	1

REPUBLIC OF IRELAND

No	Player	DoB	Aps	(s)	Gls
Goalkeepers					
1	Aaron McCarey	14/1/92	4		
16	Sean McDermott	30/5/93			
Defenders					
2	Matthew Doherty	16/1/92	3		
4	John Egan	20/10/92	4		
5	Anthony O'Connor	25/10/92	4		2
18	Joseph Shaughnessy	6/7/92	2	(1)	
17	Declan Walker	1/3/92			
3	Derrick Williams	17/1/93	3		
Midfielders					
7	Samir Carruthers	4/4/93	4		
12	Kane Ferdinand	7/10/92		(2)	
11	Anthony Forde	16/11/93	4		
6	Jeffrey Hendrick	31/1/92	4		
9	Kevin Knight	13/2/93		(3)	
15	Sean Murray	11/10/93	4		
14	Eoin Wearen	2/10/92		(2)	
Forwards					
10	Conor Murphy	11/11/92	3	(1)	
8	John O'Sullivan	18/9/93	4		1
19	Connor Smith	18/2/93	1	(3)	

ROMANIA

No	Player	DoB	Aps	(s)	Gls
Goalkeepers					
1	Laurenţiu Brănescu	30/3/94	3		
12	Radu Chiriţă	8/5/92			
Defenders					
5	Adrian Avrămia	31/1/92	2		
14	Ionuţ Gugu	20/5/92	2	(1)	
3	Lucian Murgoci	25/3/92	3		
2	Ionuţ Peteleu	20/8/92	1		
4	Sebastian Remeş	19/1/92	3		
Midfielders					
15	Enghin Amet	19/7/92	1	(1)	
6	Romario Benzar	26/3/92	3		
8	Alin Cârstocea	16/1/92	2		
10	Nicolae Stanciu	7/5/93	3		1
13	Patrick Walleth	27/1/92	1	(2)	
Forwards					
17	Sebastian Chitoşcă	2/10/92	1	(1)	
18	Cristian Gavra	3/4/93	1	(1)	
16	Florin Ilie	18/6/92		(2)	
7	Ionuţ Năstăsie	7/1/92	3		
9	Mihai Roman	31/5/92	2	(1)	
11	Tiberiu Serediuc	2/7/92	2		

SPAIN

No	Player	DoB	Aps	(s)	Gls
Goalkeepers					
1	Edgar Badia	12/2/92	4		
13	Adrián Ortolá	20/8/93	1		
Defenders					
12	Albert Blázquez	21/1/92	3	(1)	
5	Jon Aurtenetxe	3/1/92	4		1
2	Daniel Carvajal	11/1/92	2	(1)	
4	Ignasi Miquel	28/9/92	5		
14	Jonás Ramalho	10/6/93	1		
3	Sergi Gómez	28/3/92	5		
Midfielders					
8	Álex	15/10/92	4	(1)	
16	José Campaña	31/5/93	2	(1)	
15	Juanmi	20/5/93	5		2
18	Juan Muñiz Gallego	14/3/92	1	(4)	1
6	Rubén Pardo	22/10/92	4	(1)	
10	Pablo Sarabia	11/5/92	4	(1)	2
Forwards					
9	Borja González	25/8/92	1	(1)	
17	Gerard Deulofeu	13/3/94	4	(1)	1
7	Álvaro Morata	23/10/92	4		6
11	Paco Alcácer	30/8/93	1	(3)	3

SERBIA

No	Player	DoB	Aps	(s)	Gls
Goalkeepers					
1	Nikola Perić	4/2/92	4		
12	Spasoje Stefanović	12/10/92			
Defenders					
5	Uroš Ćosić	24/10/92	3		
2	Jovan Krneta	4/5/92		(2)	
18	Danilo Kuzmanović	4/1/92	2		
13	Aleksandar Pantić	11/4/92	3		
3	Marko Petković	3/9/92	4		
15	Uroš Vitas	6/7/92	4		
Midfielders					
8	Darko Brašanac	12/2/92	3		
10	Goran Čaušić	5/5/92	4		
6	Miloš Jojić	19/3/92	2	(1)	1
11	Nenad Lukić	2/9/92	3		
4	Filip Malbašić	18/11/92	2	(1)	
7	Andrej Mrkela	9/4/92	3	(1)	1
17	Ivan Rogač	18/6/92	2	(1)	
Forwards					
9	Djordje Despotović	4/3/92	2	(2)	2
16	Aleksandar Pešić	21/5/92	2	(1)	
14	Nikola Trujić	14/4/92	1	(3)	1

TURKEY

No	Player	DoB	Aps	(s)	Gls
Goalkeepers					
12	Aykut Özer	1/1/93			
1	Ömer Kahveci	15/2/92	3		
Defenders					
15	Atınç Nukan	20/7/93	1		
14	Berkay Öztuvan	5/2/92		(2)	
4	Furkan Şeker	17/3/92	2		
3	Kamil Çörekçi	1/2/92	3		1
2	Okan Alkan	1/10/92	2		
13	Sefa Başıbüyük	18/10/93	3		
5	Sezer Özmen	7/7/92	3		
Midfielders					
10	Engin Bekdemir	7/2/92	2	(1)	
8	Gökay Iravul	18/10/92	3		
11	Nadir Çiftçi	12/2/92	1	(1)	
7	Ömer Ali Şahiner	2/1/92	3		
6	Orhan Gülle	15/1/92	3		
16	Şervan Taştan	20/5/93	1	(1)	
Forwards					
17	Ali Dere	29/9/92	2	(1)	1
18	Hasan Ahmet Sari	21/1/92		(2)	
9	Muhammet Demir	10/1/92	1		

UEFA U17 Championship 2010/11

The highest-scoring UEFA men's youth final on record put the gloss on a gripping European Under-17 Championship in Serbia. The Netherlands were the overall victors, having taken impressive charge of Group B to finish top on seven points. Denmark were even more emphatic in progressing from the other section – with three wins from three – but were eliminated in the semi-finals by Germany, who had come back from the brink of elimination after two matches to reach the final. They were joined there by the Dutch, 1-0 winners against holders England in the last four, for a repeat of both teams' opening fixture of the tournament. The Netherlands had prevailed 2-0 in that game and were triumphant once more in the final, winning 5-2 – despite trailing twice in the first half – to clinch a first ever U17 title. Having been defeated by the same opponents in the 2009 final, it was fitting revenge for Albert Stuivenberg and his team.

UEFA
UNDER17™
CHAMPIONSHIP

QUALIFYING / ELITE ROUNDS

Perhaps the most momentous game in qualifying for the 2011 UEFA European Under-17 Championship was the very last elite round fixture, when holders England needed to repeat their 2010 final victory against Spain to make it to Serbia and duly did, 2-1. Other than in 2005, it was Spain's only non-qualification since the 1980s at this level.

France, defeated by England in the 2010 semi-finals, qualified in extraordinary style. Trailing Norway by two on goal difference ahead of the last games, they thrashed Belarus by an elite-round record 9-0 while their rivals were restricted to 5-0 by Georgia. Making a total of three past champions in the finals, Germany were the only side to win all six qualifiers, including a trio of 2-0 elite round successes. The side they overcame in the 2009 final, the Netherlands, also qualified, like Germany and France, as group hosts.

The 2006 runners-up, the Czech Republic, lost their last qualifying round game 6-1 to Turkey but went through the opening stage as one of the two best third-placed teams and became the first team to do so and then top an elite round group thanks to a 1-1 draw that denied unbeaten Scotland. Romania had never before reached a U17 final tournament but became the 31st nation to do so. In the qualifying round against Liechtenstein, Romania's Fabian Himcinschi had equalled the competition record of five goals – just as Denmark's Viktor Fischer did against Lithuania. Fischer's team also made it through to Serbia with a stoppage-time goal against Greece that lifted them above a deflated Republic of Ireland.

Qualifying Round Results

Group 1

27/9-2/10/10 Krk, Crikvenica, Kostrena, Cavle
Greece 1-0 Bulgaria, Croatia 2-2 Israel, Greece 4-1 Israel, Bulgaria 1-2 Croatia, Croatia 0-0 Greece, Israel 1-0 Bulgaria

Group 1 Table

	Pld	W	D	L	F	A	Pts
1 Greece	3	2	1	0	5	1	7
2 Croatia	3	1	2	0	4	3	5
3 Israel	3	1	1	1	4	6	4
4 Bulgaria	3	0	0	3	1	4	0

Group 2

15-20/10/10 Kuusalu, Tallinn
Austria 3-0 Bosnia & Herzegovina, Germany 5-0 Estonia, Bosnia & Herzegovina 1-6 Germany, Austria 1-1 Estonia, Germany 2-1 Austria, Estonia 1-4 Bosnia & Herzegovina

Group 2 Table

	Pld	W	D	L	F	A	Pts
1 Germany	3	3	0	0	13	2	9
2 Austria	3	1	1	1	5	3	4
3 Bosnia & Herzegovina	3	1	0	2	5	1	3
4 Estonia	3	0	1	2	2	10	1

Group 3

18-23/10/10 Tbilisi
Poland 1-2 Georgia, England 3-0 Sweden, Poland 0-0 Sweden, Georgia 1-1 England, England 1-0 Poland, Sweden 0-1 Georgia

Group 3 Table

	Pld	W	D	L	F	A	Pts
1 England	3	2	1	0	5	1	7
2 Georgia	3	2	1	0	4	2	7
3 Poland	3	0	1	2	1	3	1
4 Sweden	3	0	1	2	0	4	1

Group 4

25-30/9/10 Ta' Qali
Republic of Ireland 3-1 Malta, Norway 2-0 Albania, Albania 0-2 Republic of Ireland, Norway 3-0 Malta, Republic of Ireland 0-1 Norway, Malta 1-1 Albania

Group 4 Table

	Pld	W	D	L	F	A	Pts
1 Norway	3	3	0	0	6	0	9
2 Republic of Ireland	3	2	0	1	5	2	6
3 Albania	3	0	1	2	1	5	1
4 Malta	3	0	1	2	2	7	1

Group 5

22-27/10/10 Fao, Povoa do Varzim, Maia, Barcelos
Portugal 2-0 Azerbaijan, Northern Ireland 0-0 Montenegro, Portugal 3-0 Montenegro, Azerbaijan 0-6 Northern Ireland, Northern Ireland 1-3 Portugal, Montenegro 2-1 Azerbaijan

Group 5 Table

	Pld	W	D	L	F	A	Pts
1 Portugal	3	3	0	0	8	1	9
2 Northern Ireland	3	1	1	1	7	3	4
3 Montenegro	3	1	1	1	2	4	4
4 Azerbaijan	3	0	0	3	1	10	0

Group 6

21-26/9/10 Molodechno, Zhodino, Minsk
Romania 1-0 Kazakhstan, Belarus 12-0 Liechtenstein, Romania 9-0 Liechtenstein, Kazakhstan 2-6 Belarus, Belarus 0-2 Romania, Liechtenstein 0-2 Kazakhstan

Group 6 Table

	Pld	W	D	L	F	A	Pts
1 Romania	3	3	0	0	12	0	9
2 Belarus	3	2	0	1	18	4	6
3 Kazakhstan	3	1	0	2	4	7	3
4 Liechtenstein	3	0	0	3	0	23	0

Group 7

22-27/9/10 Reykjavik, Akranes, Grindavik, Keflavik
Turkey 3-0 Armenia, Czech Republic 4-2 Iceland, Czech Republic 1-1 Armenia, Iceland 2-0 Turkey, Turkey 6-1 Czech Republic, Armenia 1-2 Iceland

Group 7 Table

	Pld	W	D	L	F	A	Pts
1 Iceland	3	2	0	1	6	5	6
2 Turkey	3	2	0	1	9	3	6
3 Czech Republic	3	1	1	1	6	9	4
4 Armenia	3	0	1	2	2	6	1

Group 8

22-27/9/10 Marijampole, Kaunas
Wales 0-1 Denmark, Belgium 5-2 Lithuania, Belgium 0-2 Denmark, Lithuania 1-0 Wales, Wales 0-4 Belgium, Denmark 7-0 Lithuania

Group 8 Table

	Pld	W	D	L	F	A	Pts
1 Denmark	3	3	0	0	10	0	9
2 Belgium	3	2	0	1	9	4	6
3 Lithuania	3	1	0	2	3	12	3
4 Wales	3	0	0	3	0	6	0

Group 9

27/10-1/11/10 Paphos
France 1-0 Slovenia, Italy 1-0 Cyprus, France 1-1 Cyprus, Slovenia 2-3 Italy, Italy 2-1 France, Cyprus 0-2 Slovenia

Group 9 Table

	Pld	W	D	L	F	A	Pts
1 Italy	3	3	0	0	6	3	9
2 France	3	1	1	1	3	3	4
3 Slovenia	3	1	0	2	4	4	3
4 Cyprus	3	0	1	2	1	4	1

Group 10

20-25/9/10 Buk, Szombathely

Slovakia 3-0 Faroe Islands, Hungary 5-0 Andorra, Slovakia 5-0 Andorra, Faroe Islands 0-2 Hungary, Hungary 1-1 Slovakia, Andorra 0-0 Faroe Islands

Group 10 Table

	Pld	W	D	L	F	A	Pts
1 Slovakia	3	2	1	0	9	1	7
2 Hungary	3	2	1	0	8	1	7
3 Faroe Islands	3	0	1	2	0	5	1
4 Andorra	3	0	1	2	0	10	1

Group 11

21-26/10/10 San Marino, Serravalle

Ukraine 1-0 San Marino, Netherlands 1-0 Latvia, Ukraine 0-0 Latvia, San Marino 0-6 Netherlands, Netherlands 1-1 Ukraine, Latvia 2-0 San Marino

Group 11 Table

	Pld	W	D	L	F	A	Pts
1 Netherlands	3	2	1	0	8	1	7
2 Ukraine	3	1	2	0	2	1	5
3 Latvia	3	1	1	1	2	1	4
4 San Marino	3	0	0	3	0	9	0

Group 12

17-22/9/10 Beggen, Junglinster, Bettembourg

Scotland 1-0 FYROM, Switzerland 1-0 Luxembourg, Switzerland 3-1 FYROM, Luxembourg 1-2 Scotland, Scotland 0-0 Switzerland, FYROM 0-3 Luxembourg

Group 12 Table

	Pld	W	D	L	F	A	Pts
1 Switzerland	3	2	1	0	4	1	7
2 Scotland	3	2	1	0	3	1	7
3 Luxembourg	3	1	0	2	4	3	3
4 FYROM	3	0	0	3	1	7	0

Group 13

16-21/10/10 Benidorm, La Nucía

Russia 1-1 Finland, Spain 4-1 Moldova, Russia 5-1 Moldova, Finland 0-3 Spain, Spain 2-1 Russia, Moldova 0-2 Finland

Group 13 Table

	Pld	W	D	L	F	A	Pts
1 Spain	3	3	0	0	9	2	9
2 Russia	3	1	1	1	7	4	4
3 Finland	3	1	1	1	3	4	4
4 Moldova	3	0	0	3	2	11	0

Elite Round Results

Group 1

9-14/3/11 Nardo, Lecce

Italy 0-0 Scotland, Slovakia 0-1 Czech Republic, Italy 1-2 Czech Republic, Scotland 2-0 Slovakia, Slovakia 1-1 Italy, Czech Republic 1-1 Scotland

Group 1 Table

	Pld	W	D	L	F	A	Pts
1 Czech Republic	3	2	1	0	4	2	7
2 Scotland	3	1	2	0	3	1	5
3 Italy	3	0	2	1	2	3	2
4 Slovakia	3	0	1	2	1	4	1

Group 2

24-29/3/11 Rotterdam, Barendrecht

Portugal 0-0 Croatia, Netherlands 2-1 Austria, Portugal 0-2 Austria, Croatia 0-0 Netherlands, Netherlands 1-0 Portugal, Austria 0-2 Croatia

Group 2 Table

	Pld	W	D	L	F	A	Pts
1 Netherlands	3	2	1	0	3	1	7
2 Croatia	3	1	2	0	2	0	5
3 Austria	3	1	0	2	3	4	3
4 Portugal	3	0	1	2	0	3	1

Group 3

23-28/3/11 Komotini, Agii-Theodori

Greece 2-0 Latvia, Denmark 2-2 Republic of Ireland, Republic of Ireland 1-1 Greece, Denmark 1-0 Latvia, Greece 0-1 Denmark, Latvia 1-4 Republic of Ireland

Group 3 Table

	Pld	W	D	L	F	A	Pts
1 Denmark	3	2	1	0	4	2	7
2 Republic of Ireland	3	1	2	0	7	4	5
3 Greece	3	1	1	1	3	2	4
4 Latvia	3	0	0	3	1	7	0

Group 4

24-29/3/11 Krefeld, Ratingen, Buderich, Dusseldorf

Germany 2-0 Turkey, Switzerland 1-0 Ukraine, Turkey 2-1 Switzerland, Germany 2-0 Ukraine, Switzerland 0-2 Germany, Ukraine 2-2 Turkey

Group 4 Table

	Pld	W	D	L	F	A	Pts
1 Germany	3	3	0	0	6	0	9
2 Turkey	3	1	1	1	4	5	4
3 Switzerland	3	1	0	2	2	4	3
4 Ukraine	3	0	1	2	2	5	1

Fabian Himcinschi scored eight goals for Romania during the qualifying phase

Group 5

26-31/3/11 Geel, Mol, Tielen

England 3-2 Northern Ireland, Spain 3-1 Belgium, Spain 5-1 Northern Ireland, Belgium 1-2 England, England 2-1 Spain, Northern Ireland 2-1 Belgium

Group 5 Table

	Pld	W	D	L	F	A	Pts
1 England	3	3	0	0	7	4	9
2 Spain	3	2	0	1	9	4	6
3 Northern Ireland	3	1	0	2	5	9	3
4 Belgium	3	0	0	3	3	7	0

Group 6

25-30/3/11 Saint Herblain, Nantes, Vigneux de Bretagne, Carquefou

Norway 5-1 Belarus, Georgia 0-2 France, Belarus 1-0 Georgia, Norway 2-2 France, Georgia 0-5 Norway, France 9-0 Belarus

Group 6 Table

	Pld	W	D	L	F	A	Pts
1 France	3	2	1	0	13	2	7
2 Norway	3	2	1	0	12	3	7
3 Belarus	3	1	0	2	2	14	3
4 Georgia	3	0	0	3	0	8	0

Group 7

24-29/3/11 Buk, Szombathely

Romania 0-0 Iceland, Hungary 1-2 Russia, Romania 2-1 Russia, Iceland 0-2 Hungary, Hungary 1-2 Romania, Russia 2-0 Iceland

Group 7 Table

	Pld	W	D	L	F	A	Pts
1 Romania	3	2	1	0	4	2	7
2 Russia	3	2	0	1	5	3	6
3 Hungary	3	1	0	2	4	4	3
4 Iceland	3	0	1	2	0	4	1

TOP GOALSCORERS
(Qualifying & Elite rounds)

10	Pavel Savitskiy (Belarus)
8	Fabian Himcinschi (Romania) Samed Yesil (Germany) Abdallah Yaisien (France)
7	Serder Serderov (Russia) Viktor Fischer (Denmark)
5	Martin Rønning (Norway)

FINAL TOURNAMENT

GROUP A

Connor Wickham struck the last goal of the 2010 UEFA European Under-17 Championship finals to secure the trophy for England in Liechtenstein, and the holders were quickest out of the blocks as they sought to defend their title in Serbia.

Hallam Hope scored the first of his three group-stage goals after just eight minutes of their opening Group A encounter against France, suggesting that John Peacock's team were unlikely to relinquish their crown without a fight. Pegged back soon afterwards, they led once more before being forced to settle for a 2-2 draw against Les Mini-Bleus. Denmark's meeting with hosts Serbia looked set to end with the same scoreline before AFC Ajax's Viktor Fischer hooked a late winner to put Thomas Frank's self-confessed "dark horses" top. Unexpected pacesetters they may have been, but Frank promised more: "The biggest surprise will be when we get to the semi-finals, and we will," he said.

Fearsome Fischer

The validity of those assertive words was set to be tested in Denmark's second fixture, against England. With Fischer high on confidence, though, the defending champions scarcely stood a chance. Denmark's No10 struck a fearsome first goal, Kenneth Zohore added a swift second and, despite England's second-half fightback, Peacock oversaw his first competitive defeat since the last group game of the 2009 finals. Concurrently, over in Indjija, Serbia appeared to have shaken off their opening-night nerves to take the lead against France in front of an expectant home crowd, but the scores were soon level and the spoils eventually shared, meaning Denmark were confirmed as section winners with a game to spare.

Frank therefore made seven changes for the final fixture of the group stage. France coach Patrick Gonfalone, whose side went into the game knowing victory would see them through, hoped to catch his Danish counterpart cold. Unable to control events in Novi Sad, England and Serbia could only win and hope for a France slip-up to qualify at their expense. Peacock's charges duly came flying out of the blocks to take a 3-0 lead inside 18 minutes – with Hope twice on the mark – and effectively ensure their win. The final hour was spent with their fingers crossed hoping for Denmark to do them a favour in the other match.

Solo strike

With his team on the back foot for much of the game, Frank slowly begun to introduce his key players against a France side who were dominant but unable to find the breakthrough they needed. One such substitute, Christian Nørgaard, was to have the final say. His splendid solo goal with 15 minutes remaining not only extinguished France's fading hopes but also assured England of progress and kept Denmark's 100% record intact. "We've had the ups and downs of youth football in the last three days," said a relieved Peacock, with Serbia coach Milovan Ðorić – whose charges finished bottom and therefore missed out to France on a FIFA U-17 World Cup berth – gallantly adding: "I am guilty for everything; don't say anything bad about my players".

Denmark hotshot Viktor Fischer sets off on a celebratory run after scoring against England

Group A Results

3/5/11, Karađorđe, Novi Sad
Serbia 2-3 Denmark
Serbia: Stošić, Jakšić, Nastić (Kostić 47), Radaković, Savić, Marinković, Marković, Meleg, Ješić, Popadić (Filipović 62), Stojanović (Ožegović 41). Coach: Milovan Đorić (SRB)
Denmark: Korch, Aaquist, Holst, Johannesen, Durmisi, Olsen, Nørgaard, Christensen (Højbjerg 41), Zohore, Fischer (Poulsen 78), Andersen (Amankwaa 17). Coach: Thomas Frank (DEN)
Goal(s): 1-0 Ješić 31, 1-1 Johannesen 33, 1-2 Nastić 39(og), 2-2 Ožegović 54, 2-3 Fischer 76
Yellow Card(s): Nastić 45 (Serbia), Nørgaard 48 (Denmark), Holst 56 (Denmark), Johannesen 67 (Denmark), Aaquist 80+4 (Denmark)
Referee: McLean (SCO)

3/5/11, Gradski Stadion, Indjija
France 2-2 England
France: Beunardeau, Ikoko, Mendy, Calvet, Zouma, Tameze Aoutsa, Meite, Nangis (Laborde 56), Yaisien, Haller, Madianga (Vercleyen 56). Coach: Patrick Gonfalone (FRA)
England: Pickford, Cousins, Smith, Lundstram, Jackson, Powell (Clayton 71), Hope, Magri, Henshall (Morgan 71), Redmond, Turgott. Coach: John Peacock (ENG)
Goal(s): 0-1 Hope 8, 1-1 Haller 15, 1-2 Powell 28, 2-2 Haller 65
Yellow Card(s): Mendy 46 (France), Turgott 80 (England)
Referee: Liany (ISR)

6/5/11, Gradski Stadion, Indjija
Serbia 1-1 France
Serbia: Latinović, Jakšić, Nastić, Radaković, Marinković, Meleg, Popadić, Todorić (Stojanović 63), Filipović, Ninković (Ožegović 41), Mandić (Marković 67). Coach: Milovan Đorić (SRB)
France: Mpasi Nzau, Mendy, Calvet, Tameze Aoutsa, Meite, Yaisien, Haller (Nkusu 68), Conte, Laporte, Toure (Nangis 44), Vercleyen (Laborde 56). Coach: Patrick Gonfalone (FRA)
Goal(s): 1-0 Mandić 39, 1-1 Meite 40+1
Yellow Card(s): Meleg 35 (Serbia), Popadić 46 (Serbia), Meite 60 (France), Calvet 76 (France), Laporte 80 (France)
Referee: Tritsonis (GRE)

6/5/11, Karađorđe, Novi Sad
Denmark 2-0 England
Denmark: Korch, Aaquist, Holst, Johannesen, Durmisi, Olsen (Højbjerg 80), Nørgaard, Christensen, Zohore (Poulsen 70), Fischer (Sørensen 70), Amankwaa. Coach: Thomas Frank (DEN)
England: Pickford, Cousins, Smith, Lundstram, Chalobah, Sterling (Clayton 38), Powell, Hope (Morgan 66), Magri, Redmond (Henshall 55), Turgott. Coach: John Peacock (ENG)
Goal(s): 1-0 Fischer 13, 2-0 Zohore 21
Yellow Card(s): Olsen 34 (Denmark), Durmisi 80+4 (Denmark)
Referee: Delferiere (BEL)

9/5/11, Gradski Stadion, Indjija
England 3-0 Serbia
England: Pickford, Cousins, Smith, Lundstram, Chalobah, Powell (Clayton 40+3), Hope (Morgan 65), Caskey, Magri, Henshall, Turgott (Redmond 74). Coach: John Peacock (ENG)
Serbia: Latinović, Jakšić, Nastić, Radaković, Savić (Mandić 34), Marinković, Marković, Meleg, Ješić (Ninković 41), Stojanović, Filipović. Coach: Milovan Đorić (SRB)
Goal(s): 1-0 Smith 7, 2-0 Hope 9, 3-0 Hope 18
Yellow Card(s): Ninković 50 (Serbia), Mandić 52 (Serbia), Smith 63 (England), Caskey 79 (England), Marković 80+2 (Serbia)
Referee: Tohver (EST)

9/5/11, Karađorđe, Novi Sad
Denmark 1-0 France
Denmark: Schultz, Aaquist, Johannesen, Durmisi (Fischer 41), Christensen (Nørgaard 57), Jensen, Højbjerg, Nissen, Sørensen (Zohore 67), Poulsen, Andersen. Coach: Thomas Frank (DEN)
France: Mpasi Nzau, Ikoko, Mendy, Calvet, Zouma, Tameze Aoutsa, Meite, Nangis (Laporte 70), Yaisien, Haller (Nkusu 58), Laborde (Vercleyen 46). Coach: Patrick Gonfalone (FRA)
Goal(s): 1-0 Nørgaard 65
Yellow Card(s): Aaquist 26 (Denmark), Nissen 70 (Denmark)
Referee: Artur Soares (POR)

Group A Table

	Pld	W	D	L	F	A	Pts
1 Denmark	3	3	0	0	6	2	9
2 England	3	1	1	1	5	4	4
3 France	3	0	2	1	3	4	2
4 Serbia	3	0	1	2	3	7	1

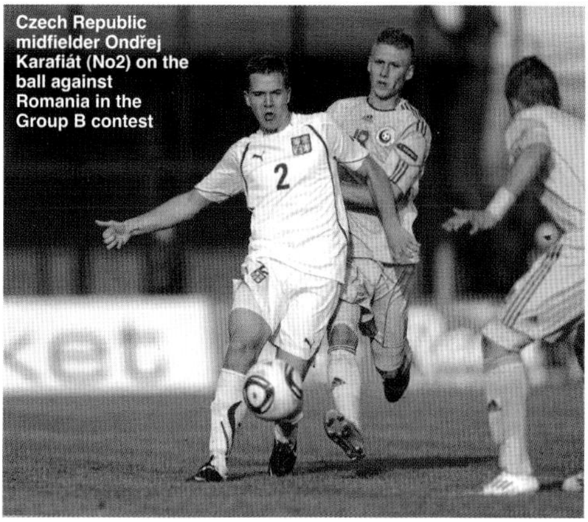
Czech Republic midfielder Ondřej Karafiát (No2) on the ball against Romania in the Group B contest

GROUP B

The two pre-tournament favourites, Germany and the Netherlands, met in the opening Group B encounter in Smederevo, and it was the Dutch who deservedly came out on top, 2-0. The first half was tight but defender Karim Rekik stole in to head the Netherlands in front on 50 minutes from Tonny Trindade de Vilhena's corner. Rekik and fellow Feyenoord centre-back Terence Kongolo kept Germany quiet before Arsenal FC midfielder Kyle Ebecilio – suspended for the elite round – doubled the lead late on.

Late equaliser

Over in Belgrade, finals debutants Romania took a 52nd-minute lead against the Czech Republic with a tremendous solo goal from Fabian Himcinschi, but their attempts to cling on for victory were thwarted three minutes from time. Nikolas Salašovič did the damage, his long-range strike finally beating impressive Juventus goalkeeper Constantin Brănescu.

Consequently, victory for the Netherlands against Romania in Belgrade would take them into their third semi-final in four years – all under coach Albert Stuivenberg. They made the perfect start when Trindade de Vilhena converted a Nick de Bondt cross touched on by Anass Achahbar, who had also set up Ebecilio's goal against Germany. Romania never looked like equalising, and that win secured first place for the Netherlands as Germany drew 1-1 with the Czech Republic in Smederevo.

Penalty saves

Lukáš Juliš scored a memorable goal for the Czechs on 12 minutes, and impressive goalkeeper Lukáš Zima made a string of fine saves, not least in keeping out second-half penalties from Emre Can – who had hit the woodwork just before – and Samed Yesil, with Jan Štěrba being sent off for conceding the latter six minutes from time. In the last minute, though, Yesil, Germany's top scorer in qualifying who had been suspended for the opening fixture, did finally beat Zima to prevent an early elimination for the 2009 champions.

Nevertheless, Germany remained bottom of the group, and to make it through to the semi-finals they had to beat Romania in Smederevo and hope the Czech Republic failed to defeat the Netherlands – who rested seven regulars – in Belgrade. Romania coach Adrian Văsâi had stated before the tournament that third place and a FIFA U-17 World Cup berth was his team's aim. They duly sat back, allowing Germany, who had to withdraw injured playmaker Levent Aycicek just before kick-off, few openings in the first half.

Yesil strikes again

Two minutes after the interval, however, Yesil headed in an Okan Aydin corner to score for the seventh consecutive competitive game. Now Romania had to press, but they could not break through, and further good news for Germany came with the confirmation that the Czech Republic had drawn 0-0 with the Netherlands.

However, Germany paid a heavy price for defending their lead, bookings for full-back Mitchell Weiser, central defender Nico Perrey, winger Fabian Schnellhardt and – most crucially – Yesil ruling all four players out of the semi-final. Furthermore, it was revealed that Aycicek had sustained a tournament-ending injury when he was fouled for the second penalty against the Czech Republic. After three draws, the Czechs were eliminated but, unlike Romania, at least had the consolation of a World Cup trip to Mexico.

Samed Yesil of Germany takes on the Romania defence

Group B Results

3/5/11, FK Smederevo, Smederevo
Germany 0-2 Netherlands
Germany: Vlachodimos, Weiser, Röcker, Perrey, Yalcin, Can, Aycicek, Weihrauch, Ayhan, Quaschner (Schnellhardt 62), Aydin (Berko 66). Coach: Steffen Freund (GER)
Netherlands: De Jong, Disveld, Kongolo, Rekik, Willems, Ebecilio, Ayoub, Achahbar, Trindade de Vilhena, Depay (Gravenberch 75), De Bondt (Ake 62). Coach: Albert Stuivenberg (NED)
Goal(s): 0-1 Rekik 50, 0-2 Ebecilio 76
Yellow Card(s): Berko 67 (Germany)
Referee: Artur Soares (POR)

3/5/11, FK Obilić, Belgrade
Czech Republic 1-1 Romania
Czech Republic: Zima, Karafiát, Adamec, Lüftner, Salašovič, Svoboda, Linhart (Juliš 46), Kundrátek (Stratil 62), Holub (Nerad 54), Štěrba, Mašek. Coach: Josef Csaplár (CZE)
Romania: Brănescu, Mişu (Birău 69), Schuller, Mitache, Puţanu, Vaştag, Ţiru, Himcinschi (Buia 71), Bumba, Petresc (Paius 51), Roşu. Coach: Adrian Văsâi (ROU)
Goal(s): 0-1 Himcinschi 52, 1-1 Salašovič 77
Yellow Card(s): Kundrátek 22 (Czech Republic), Mitache 33 (Romania), Himcinschi 52 (Romania), Mişu 57 (Romania), Adamec 64 (Czech Republic), Vaştag 65 (Romania), Stratil 68 (Czech Republic), Karafiát 73 (Czech Republic)
Referee: Tohver (EST)

6/5/11, FK Smederevo, Smederevo
Germany 1-1 Czech Republic
Germany: Vlachodimos, Weiser, Röcker, Günter, Perrey, Yalcin, Can, Yesil, Aycicek (Weihrauch 78), Aydin, Schnellhardt. Coach: Steffen Freund (GER)
Czech Republic: Zima, Karafiát, Nerad (Filip 56), Adamec, Lüftner, Čermák, Salašovič, Juliš (Linhart 78), Kundrátek, Štěrba, Mašek (Svoboda 47). Coach: Josef Csaplár (CZE)
Goal(s): 0-1 Juliš 12, 1-1 Yesil 80
Red Card(s): Štěrba 74 (Czech Republic)
Yellow Card(s): Weiser 48 (Germany), Yesil 58 (Germany), Zima 75 (Czech Republic), Perrey 79 (Germany), Schnellhardt 80+3 (Germany)
Referee: McLean (SCO)

6/5/11, FK Obilić, Belgrade
Netherlands 1-0 Romania
Netherlands: De Jong, Disveld, Kongolo, Rekik, Willems, Ebecilio, Ayoub, Achahbar, Trindade de Vilhena, Depay, De Bondt. Coach: Albert Stuivenberg (NED)
Romania: Brănescu, Schuller, Mitache, Puţanu, Vaştag (Paius 76), Filip, Ţîru, Himcinschi (Buia 62), Bumba, Petresc, Roşu. Coach: Adrian Văsâi (ROU)
Goal(s): 1-0 Trindade de Vilhena 8
Yellow Card(s): Petresc 68 (Romania), Buia 75 (Romania)
Referee: Liany (ISR)

9/5/11, FK Smederevo, Smederevo
Romania 0-1 Germany
Romania: Brănescu, Mişu, Schuller, Mitache, Puţanu, Filip, Ţîru, Himcinschi, Bumba (Roman 56), Petresc (Buia 47), Roşu (Paius 67). Coach: Adrian Văsâi (ROU)
Germany: Vlachodimos, Weiser, Röcker, Günter, Perrey, Yalcin, Can, Yesil, Aydin (Berko 72), Mende, Schnellhardt (Ayhan 80+1). Coach: Steffen Freund (GER)
Goal(s): 0-1 Yesil 42
Yellow Card(s): Ţîru 22 (Romania), Weiser 41 (Germany), Perrey 62 (Germany), Schnellhardt 65 (Germany), Brănescu 74 (Romania), Yesil 74 (Germany), Can 78 (Germany), Schuller 80+5 (Romania)
Referee: Tritsonis (GRE)

9/5/11, FK Obilić, Belgrade
Netherlands 0-0 Czech Republic
Netherlands: Leeuwenburgh, Disveld, Rekik, Chacon, Ayoub (Willems 49), Depay (De Bondt 41), Gravenberch, Haye, Van Overeem (Ebecilio 75), Ake, Koch. Coach: Albert Stuivenberg (NED)
Czech Republic: Zima, Karafiát, Filip, Adamec, Lüftner, Čermák, Kadula, Salašovič, Juliš (Linhart 53), Svoboda (Stratil 46), Mašek. Coach: Josef Csaplár (CZE)
Referee: Delferiere (BEL)

Group B Table

	Pld	W	D	L	F	A	Pts
1 Netherlands	3	2	1	0	3	0	7
2 Germany	3	1	1	1	2	3	4
3 Czech Republic	3	0	3	0	2	2	3
4 Romania	3	0	1	2	1	3	1

SEMI-FINALS

Clear winners of their respective groups, the Netherlands and Denmark bounded into the last four as firm favourites to reach the final. But while one semi-final would go to form, the other turned out to be an impressive show of defiance against the odds.

Unbreachable defence

The Netherlands had topped Group B at a relative canter, defeating Germany 2-0 and Romania 1-0 before resting seven players for their goalless draw against the Czech Republic. Proving remarkably tricky to breach having not conceded for five successive fixtures, Albert Stuivenberg's side once again displayed impressive compactness to see off England.

The holders found themselves on the back foot in next to no time, showing little prospect of building on the momentum gained from the clinical 3-0 victory against Serbia with which they had secured qualification. Indeed, Anass Achahbar had twice gone close by the time Arsenal FC midfielder Kyle Ebicilio – a constant thorn in England's side – surged through the heart of the defence before finishing past Jordan Pickford in a virtual repeat of his strike against Germany.

Holders eliminated

John Peacock sent on Adam Morgan in an attempt to provide the tireless Hallam Hope with more support, and the Liverpool FC forward threatened a second-half equaliser when his free-kick narrowly veered off target. Nathan Redmond was equally close with his effort from the right but, in truth, a consummate Dutch defence was seldom stretched. Ebecilio could even have added a second had he not rolled his shot narrowly wide, but it mattered not – the Netherlands had done enough.

Germany faced a mountainous task to set up a repeat of not only their Group B meeting with the Dutch the previous week, but also of the 2009 final in Magdeburg. Denied the suspended right-back Mitchell Weiser, centre-half Nico Perrey, winger Fabian Schnellhardt and top scorer Samed Yesil, as well as the injured Levent Aycicek, Steffen Freund somehow engineered his team's progress.

Kyle Ebecilio scores the Netherlands' winner against holders England

Lucky deflection

He did so with more than a slice of fortune, however, Kaan Ayhan's free-kick taking a decisive deflection to put Germany in front on 58 minutes. Thomas Frank's side, perfect in the group stage, responded admirably but were not rewarded for their patience.

Germany remained compact and duly snatched a second with ten minutes remaining when Nils Quaschner unwittingly turned in Cimo Röcker's free-kick from the right. Although Denmark still refused to lie down, Germany once again carved out the best opportunity of the closing stages as Emre Can's effort rattled the crossbar.

Semi-Final Results

12/5/11, Karađorđe, Novi Sad
Netherlands 1-0 England
Netherlands: De Jong, Disveld, Kongolo, Rekik, Willems, Ebecilio, Ayoub, Achahbar (Haye 77), Trindade de Vilhena, Depay (Gravenberch 41), De Bondt (Ake 68). Coach: Albert Stuivenberg (NED)
England: Pickford, Cousins, Smith, Lundstram, Jackson (Morgan 50), Chalobah, Hope, Caskey (Clayton 66), Magri, Henshall (Redmond 50), Turgott. Coach: John Peacock (ENG)
Goal(s): 1-0 Ebecilio 26
Yellow Card(s): Rekik 56 (Netherlands), Disveld 78 (Netherlands)
Referee: Artur Soares (POR)

12/5/11, Karadjordje, Novi Sad
Denmark 0-2 Germany
Denmark: Korch, Holst, Johannesen, Durmisi, Olsen, Nørgaard, Christensen (Andersen 60), Zohore, Fischer, Amankwaa (Poulsen 69), Nissen (Jensen 69). Coach: Thomas Frank (DEN)
Germany: Vlachodimos, Röcker, Günter, Yalcin, Can, Ayhan, Quaschner (Weihrauch 80+4), Aydin, Mende, Berko (Toljan 72), Kacinoglu. Coach: Steffen Freund (GER)
Goal(s): 0-1 Ayhan 58, 0-2 Quaschner 70
Yellow Card(s): Can 25 (Germany), Durmisi 48 (Denmark), Berko 67 (Germany), Günter 80+2 (Germany)
Referee: McLean (SCO)

Nils Quaschner (No14) turns in a free-kick to put Germany 2-0 up in their semi-final against Denmark

FINAL

The Netherlands won the UEFA European Under-17 Championship for the first time thanks to a record-breaking 5-2 victory against Germany.

Defeated by the same opponents in the 2009 final, Albert Stuivenberg's side had overcome Germany 2-0 in their tournament opener, but initially they looked unlikely to repeat the feat. Samed Yesil and Okan Aydin twice gave Germany the lead, only for Tonny Trindade de Vilhena to equalise on both occasions. Then came a scintillating second-half performance that blew Germany away, Memphis Depay and Terence Kongolo scoring in quick succession before Kyle Ebecilio's late fifth. No team had ever struck five goals in a UEFA men's youth final, and this was also the overall highest-scoring final at this level.

Early opener

Having not conceded in six successive matches prior to the final, it took a sizeable slice of fortune after just eight minutes for the Netherlands defence to be beaten. Yesil bucked the tournament's trend of slow-paced starts when he accelerated into the penalty area and beat Boy de Jong via the aid of a deflection off Kongolo.

It did not take the Netherlands long to respond, Trindade de Vilhena drawing them level on 23 minutes with a carbon-copy of Ebecilio's effort against England. Anass Achahbar was again the pivot, receiving the No10's pass before flicking the ball back into his path for a toe-poked finish.

Quick response

There was nothing quite so intricate about Germany's second, Aydin letting fly with a fierce right-footed shot that whistled past De Jong from 25 metres. Germany No1 Odisseas Vlachodimos was also beaten just two minutes later, spilling Depay's cross to allow Trindade de Vilhena to gobble up the rebound.

The 4,261-strong crowd had scarcely had the chance to catch their breath after an engaging first half when the Netherlands went in front for the first time. On this occasion Depay was the scorer, controlling exquisitely before setting off on a mazy run that was concluded with a clinical finish.

Dominant Dutch

Brimming with confidence, the Netherlands sensed their opportunity to turn the screw, Achahbar attempting an ambitious lob and Depay unleashing a vicious free-kick that was well saved. The resulting corner proved decisive, with Ebecilio heading back across goal for Kongolo to apply the finish.

By now Germany were a beaten side. The Netherlands knew their work was done but ruthlessly pressed home their advantage, Ebecilio adding a fifth goal with three minutes remaining. The Arsenal FC midfielder stole into the penalty area in combination with former Feyenoord colleague Achahbar before sweeping the return decisively past Vlachodimos.

Winning coach Stuivenberg savoured the triumph, saying: "In the end we are very happy with the result and the way we played the second half. We deserved this title this time, we were very close two years ago and this is our revenge." His Germany counterpart Steffen Freund reflected on the tournament with pride, adding: "Winning and losing is part of football. These five games have been a fantastic experience for my team."

High-fives for Dutch duo Memphis Depay (No11) and Tonny Trinidade de Vilhena as they help their team to a 5-2 win over

Final Result

15/5/11, Karađorđe, Novi Sad
Germany 2-5 Netherlands
Attendance: 4261
Germany: Vlachodimos, Weiser, Röcker (Toljan 65), Günter, Perrey (Weihrauch 73), Yalcin, Can, Yesil, Aydin, Mende (Berko 57), Schnellhardt. Coach: Steffen Freund (GER)
Netherlands: De Jong, Disveld, Kongolo, Rekik, Willems, Ebecilio, Ayoub, Achahbar, Trindade de Vilhena, Depay (Gravenberch 71), De Bondt (Ake 64). Coach: Albert Stuivenberg (NED)
Goal(s): 1-0 Yesil 8, 1-1 Trindade de Vilhena 23, 2-1 Aydin 32, 2-2 Trindade de Vilhena 34, 2-3 Depay 43, 2-4 Kongolo 53, 2-5 Ebecilio 77
Yellow Card(s): Aydin 33 (Germany), Willems 36 (Netherlands)
Referee: Tohver (EST)

Joy for the Netherlands as they lift the UEFA European Under-17 Championship trophy for the first time

FINAL TOURNAMENT SQUADS / APPEARANCES / GOALS

CZECH REPUBLIC

No	Player	DoB	Aps	(s)	Gls
Goalkeepers					
1	Patrik Macej	11/6/94			
16	Lukáš Zima	9/1/94	3		
Defenders					
5	Luboš Adamec	27/4/94	3		
3	Jan Filip	6/3/94	1	(1)	
6	Michael Lüftner	14/3/94	3		
15	Jan Štěrba	8/7/94	2		
Midfielders					
7	Aleš Čermák	1/10/94	2		
8	Jindřich Kadula	10/6/94	1		
2	Ondřej Karafiát	1/12/94	3		
13	Patrik Kundrátek	15/2/94	2		
4	Petr Nerad	6/2/94	1	(1)	
9	Nikolas Salašovič	20/9/94	3		1
Forwards					
14	Michal Holub	6/3/94	1		
10	Lukáš Juliš	2/12/94	2	(1)	1
12	Zdeněk Linhart	5/3/94	1	(2)	
17	Dominik Mašek	10/7/95	3		
18	Lukáš Stratil	29/1/94		(2)	
11	Patrik Svoboda	13/4/94	2	(1)	

ENGLAND

No	Player	DoB	Aps	(s)	Gls
Goalkeepers					
13	Ben Garratt	25/4/94			
1	Jordan Pickford	7/3/94	4		
Defenders					
6	Nathaniel Chalobah	12/12/94	3		
2	Jordan Cousins	6/3/94	4		
5	Adam Jackson	18/5/94	2		
15	Samuel Magri	30/3/94	4		
12	Courtney Meppen Walters	2/8/94			
3	Bradley Smith	9/4/94	4		1
Midfielders					
11	Jake Caskey	25/4/94	2		
19	Jack Dunn*	19/11/94			
4	John Lundstram	18/2/94	4		
8	Nick Powell	23/3/94	3		1
17	Nathan Redmond	6/3/94	2	(2)	
18	Blair Turgott	22/5/94	4		
Forwards					
10	Max Clayton	9/8/94		(4)	
16	Alex Henshall	15/2/94	3	(1)	
9	Hallam Hope	17/3/94	4		3
14	Adam Morgan	21/4/94		(4)	
7	Raheem Sterling	8/12/94	1		

** supplementary player*

DENMARK

No	Player	DoB	Aps	(s)	Gls
Goalkeepers					
1	Oliver Korch	18/6/94	3		
16	Christian Schultz	13/5/94	1		
Defenders					
2	Mads Aaquist	31/12/94	3		
5	Riza Durmisi	8/1/94	4		
3	Frederik Holst	24/9/94	3		
12	Patrick Jensen	4/4/94	1	(1)	
4	Nicolai Johannesen	22/5/94	4		1
14	Derrick Nissen	29/3/94	2		
Midfielders					
18	Lucas Andersen	13/9/94	2	(1)	
8	Lasse Christensen	15/8/94	4		
13	Pierre Højbjerg	5/8/95	1	(2)	
7	Christian Nørgaard	10/3/94	3	(1)	1
6	Patrick Olsen	23/4/94	3		
Forwards					
11	Danny Amankwaa	30/1/94	2	(1)	
10	Viktor Fischer	9/6/94	3	(1)	2
17	Yussuf Poulsen	15/6/94	1	(3)	
15	Lee Sørensen	30/4/94	1	(1)	
9	Kenneth Zohore	31/1/94	3	(1)	1

FRANCE

No	Player	DoB	Aps	(s)	Gls
Goalkeepers					
1	Quentin Beunardeau	27/2/94	1		
16	Lionel Mpasi Nzau	1/8/94	2		
Defenders					
4	Raphaël Calvet	7/2/94	3		
12	Antoine Conte	29/1/94	1		
2	Jordan Ikoko	3/2/94	2		
13	Aymeric Laporte	27/5/94	1	(1)	
3	Benjamin Mendy	17/7/94	3		
5	Kurt Zouma	27/10/94	2		
Midfielders					
14	Karl Madianga	30/1/94	1		
8	Soualiho Meite	17/3/94	3		1
7	Adam Nkusu	29/1/94		(2)	
6	Adrien Tameze Aoutsa	4/2/94	3		
15	Abdoulaye Toure	3/3/94	1		
17	Jordan Vercleyen	7/2/94	1	(2)	
10	Abdallah Yaisien	23/4/94	3		
Forwards					
11	Sébastien Haller	22/6/94	3		2
18	Gaëtan Laborde	3/5/94	1	(2)	
9	Lenny Nangis	24/3/94	2	(1)	

GERMANY

No	Player	DoB	Aps	(s)	Gls
Goalkeepers					
1	Odisseas Vlachodimos	26/4/94	5		
7	Cedric Wilmes	13/1/94			
Defenders					
13	Kaan Ayhan	10/11/94	2	(1)	1
4	Koray Günter	16/8/94	4		
22	Koray Kacinoglu	20/7/94	1		
5	Nico Perrey	2/2/94	4		
3	Cimo Röcker	21/1/94	5		
17	Jeremy Toljan*	8/8/94		(2)	
Midfielders					
10	Levent Aycicek	14/2/94	2		
8	Emre Can	12/1/94	5		
16	Sven Mende	18/1/94	3		
18	Fabian Schnellhardt	12/1/94	3	(1)	
2	Mitchell Weiser	21/4/94	4		
6	Robin Yalcin	25/1/94	5		
Forwards					
15	Okan Aydin	8/5/94	5		1
21	Erich Berko	6/9/94	1	(3)	
14	Nils Quaschner	22/4/94	2		1
11	Patrick Weihrauch	3/3/94	1	(3)	
9	Samed Yesil	25/5/94	3		3

** supplementary player*

ROMANIA

No	Player	DoB	Aps	(s)	Gls
Goalkeepers					
1	Constantin Brănescu	30/3/94	3		
12	George Şerban	31/1/94			
Defenders					
2	Ionuţ Mişu	19/9/94	2		
4	Bogdan Mitache	1/1/94	3		
7	Ioan Petresc	27/4/94	3		
5	Adrian Puţanu	9/1/94	3		
3	Eduard Schuller	19/3/94	3		
Midfielders					
14	Daniel Birău	21/3/94		(1)	
10	Claudiu Bumba	5/1/94	3		
7	Steliano Filip	15/5/94	2		
8	Bogdan Ţîru	15/3/94	3		
16	Alin Roman	27/1/94		(1)	
18	Iulian Roşu	30/5/94	3		
6	Andrei Vaştag	21/3/94	2		
Forwards					
11	Darius-Grazian Buia	30/4/94		(3)	
9	Fabian Himcinschi	12/5/94	3		1
15	Daniel Paius	24/9/94		(3)	

NETHERLANDS

No	Player	DoB	Aps	(s)	Gls
Goalkeepers					
1	Boy de Jong	10/4/94	4		
16	Peter Leeuwenburgh	23/3/94	1		
Defenders					
15	Nathan Ake	18/2/95	1	(3)	
2	Daan Disveld	20/1/94	5		
13	Thom Haye	9/2/95	1	(1)	
17	Menno Koch	2/7/94	1		
3	Terence Kongolo	14/2/94	4		1
4	Karim Rekik	2/12/94	5		1
5	Jetro Willems	30/3/94	4	(1)	
Midfielders					
8	Yassine Ayoub	6/3/94	5		
11	Memphis Depay	13/2/94	5		1
6	Kyle Ebecilio	17/2/94	4	(1)	3
10	Tonny Trindade de Vilhena	3/1/95	4		3
14	Joris van Overeem	1/6/94	1		
Forwards					
9	Anass Achahbar	13/1/94	4		
7	Michael Chacon	11/4/94	1		
18	Nick de Bondt	21/4/94	4	(1)	
12	Danzell Gravenberch	13/1/94	1	(3)	

SERBIA

No	Player	DoB	Aps	(s)	Gls
Goalkeepers					
12	Nemanja Latinović	21/2/94	2		
1	Nikola Stošić	15/3/94	1		
Defenders					
2	Nemanja Jakšić	11/7/95	3		
14	Dobrosav Kostić	4/9/94		(1)	
6	Marko Marinković	6/1/94	3		
3	Bojan Nastić	6/7/94	3		
11	Ognjen Popadić	10/2/94	2		
5	Milan Savić	4/4/94	2		
15	Nikola Todorić	11/5/94	1		
Midfielders					
17	Aleksandar Filipović	20/12/94	2	(1)	
7	Lazar Marković	2/3/94	2	(1)	
8	Dejan Meleg	1/10/94	3		
18	Nikola Ninković	19/12/94	1	(1)	
4	Uroš Radaković	31/3/94	3		
16	Luka Stojanović	4/1/94	2	(1)	
Forwards					
9	Vojno Ješić	4/3/94	2		1
19	Nikola Mandić	15/1/94	1	(1)	1
20	Ognjen Ožegović	9/6/94		(2)	1

TOP GOALSCORERS (Final Tournament)

3 Samed Yesil (Germany)
Hallam Hope (England)
Tonny Trinidade de Vilhena (Netherlands)
Kyle Ebecilio (Netherlands)

2 Sébastien Haller (France)
Viktor Fischer (Denmark)

Samed Yesil

Hallam Hope

Tonny Trinidade de Vilhena

Kyle Ebecilio

RESPECT

UEFA REGIONS' CUP 2010/11

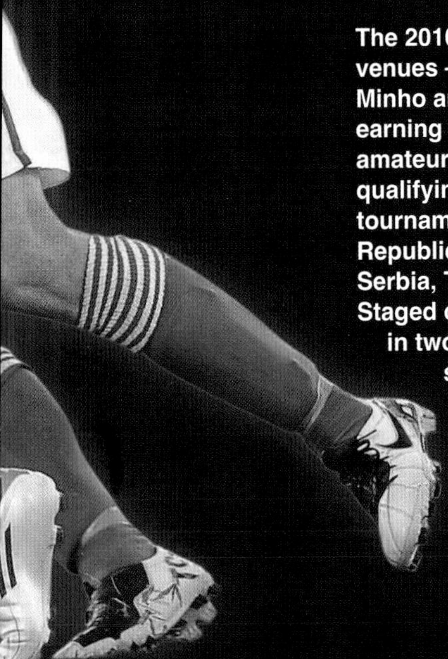

The 2010/11 UEFA Regions' Cup took place in four venues – Vila Verde, Fao, Braga and Barcelos – in the Minho area of northern Portugal, with eight sides earning the right to challenge for the top prize in amateur football by progressing through the qualifying phase. The seventh edition of the biennial tournament comprised sides from the Czech Republic, Germany, the Republic of Ireland, Russia, Serbia, Turkey, Ukraine and, of course, Portugal. Staged over a week in late June, the teams competed in two groups of four, with the winner of each section progressing to the final in Barcelos – home of Portuguese top-flight club Gil Vicente FC. Ten years after losing in the final, Braga prevailed 2-1 against Leinster & Munster. The victory maintained their flawless record in the competition, giving them seven wins out of seven.

QUALIFYING ROUNDS

The UEFA Youth and Amateur Football Committee's first vice-chairman Jim Boyce has long been an advocate of perhaps the least known of UEFA's competitions, saying: "The Regions' Cup has been a tremendous innovation by UEFA. It is for players who never dreamt they would have the opportunity of playing in a European competition – it's like their World Cup."

A total of 39 associations put forward teams to compete in the qualifying phase of the seventh UEFA Regions' Cup, which features only amateur players, with Portuguese side Braga – runners-up in 2001 – chosen to host the finals after they had come through the intermediary round. Ankara were the only side to battle through from the preliminary round to the final tournament, making Turkey the 25th nation to be represented at the finals.

Elsewhere, Germany's Württembergischer FV secured a mighty 14-1 win against Fthiotida of Greece, which included an eight-minute Julian Schwarz hat-trick, while Belgrade won their qualifying group by the drawing of lots after they finished Group 5 with exactly the same record as hosts South-West Bulgaria.

Six goals made South Region Russia's Sergei Lednev the top scorer in qualifying while Ukrainian team Yednyst Plysky averaged five goals a game in the intermediary round and did not concede, giving them the best goal difference in the competition – an impressive +15.

Ankara players celebrate a goal en route to the final tournament in Portugal

Preliminary Round Results

Group A

24-28/9/10 Split, Dugopolje, Imotski, Klis, Solin, Sinj
Ankara 4-1 Gwent County FA, Dalmacija 1 1-1 Guernsey, Ankara 0-0 Dalmacija, Guernsey 3-0 Gwent County FA, Guernsey 0-3 Ankara, Gwent County FA 3-6 Dalmacija

Group A Table

	Pld	W	D	L	F	A	Pts
1 Ankara	3	2	1	0	7	1	7
2 Dalmacija	3	1	2	0	7	4	5
3 Guernsey	3	1	1	1	4	4	4
4 Gwent County FA	3	0	0	3	4	13	0

Group B

31/8-4/9/10 Buk, Sopron
Malatia 0-5 FC Carmiel Safed, West Hungary 4-1 Prahova Muntenia, Malatia 1-2 West Hungary, Prahova Muntenia 0-2 FC Carmiel Safed, Prahova Muntenia 3-1 Malatia, FC Carmiel Safed 1-0 West Hungary

Group B Table

	Pld	W	D	L	F	A	Pts
1 FC Carmiel Safed	3	3	0	0	8	0	9
2 West Hungary	3	2	0	1	6	3	6
3 Prahova Muntenia	3	1	0	2	4	7	3
4 Malatia	3	0	0	3	2	10	0

Group C

25-29/9/10 Strumic
South East FYROM 3-1 Sandarna BK, Eastern Region Northern Ireland 4-0 FC Tartu, South East FYROM 1-1 Eastern Region Northern Ireland, FC Tartu 0-1 Sandarna BK FC Tartu 0-8 South East FYROM, Sandarna BK 0-1 Eastern Region Northern Ireland

Group C Table

	Pld	W	D	L	F	A	Pts
1 South East FYROM	3	2	1	0	12	2	7
2 Eastern Region Northern Ireland	3	2	1	0	6	1	7
3 Sandarna BK	3	1	0	2	2	4	3
4 FC Tartu	3	0	0	3	0	13	0

Intermediary Round Results

Group 1

7-11/12/10 Ta' Qali
Fthiotida 1-3 Federación Gallega, Malta 0-1 Württembergischer FV, Federación Gallega 1-1 Württembergischer FV, Malta 0-0 Fthiotida, Federación Gallega 6-0 Malta, Württembergischer FV 14-1 Fthiotida

Group 1 Table

	Pld	W	D	L	F	A	Pts
1 Württembergischer FV	3	2	1	0	16	2	7
2 Federación Gallega	3	2	1	0	10	2	7
3 Malta	3	0	1	2	0	7	1
4 Fthiotida	3	0	1	2	2	17	1

Action from Württemberg's remarkable 14-1 victory over Fthiotida in the intermediary round

Group 2

1-5/12/10 Esposende, Barcelos, Fao

Ticino 2-3 Team Centre, East, West and Central Scotland 1-3 Braga, East, West and Central Scotland 1-2 Ticino, Team Centre 0-2 Braga, Team Centre 2-3 East, West and Central Scotland, Braga 4-0 Ticino

Group 2 Table

	Pld	W	D	L	F	A	Pts
1 Braga	3	3	0	0	9	1	9
2 Team Centre	3	1	0	2	5	7	3
3 East, West and Central Scotland	3	1	0	2	5	7	3
4 Ticino	3	1	0	2	4	8	3

Group 3

23-27/10/10 Dublin

Leinster & Munster 0-0 Abruzzo, San Marino 0-6 Ligue de Normandie, Leinster & Munster 2-0 San Marino, Ligue de Normandie 1-1 Abruzzo, Ligue de Normandie 0-3 Leinster & Munster, Abruzzo 1-0 San Marino

Group 3 Table

	Pld	W	D	L	F	A	Pts
1 Leinster & Munster	3	2	1	0	5	0	7
2 Abruzzo	3	1	2	0	2	1	5
3 Ligue de Normandie	3	1	1	1	7	4	4
4 San Marino	3	0	0	3	0	9	0

Group 4

5/-9/4/11 Krizevci, Verzej

FC Carmiel Safed 0-1 Ankara, MNZ Murska Sobota 1-1 South East FYROM, MNZ Murska Sobota 3-1 FC Carmiel Safed, Ankara 3-0 South East FYROM, Ankara 3-1 MNZ Murska Sobota, South East FYROM 2-0 FC Carmiel Safed

Group 4 Table

	Pld	W	D	L	F	A	Pts
1 Ankara	3	3	0	0	7	1	9
2 MNZ Murska Sobota	3	1	1	1	5	5	4
3 South East FYROM	3	1	1	1	3	4	4
4 FC Carmiel Safed	3	0	0	3	1	6	0

Group 5

16-20/4/11 Teteven, Mezdra

South-West Bulgaria 0-0 Slovak Western Region, Belgrade 2-0 Eastern Region Northern Ireland, South-West Bulgaria 0-0 Belgrade, Eastern Region Northern Ireland 0-1 Slovak Western Region, Eastern Region Northern Ireland 0-2 South-West Bulgaria, Slovak Western Region 0-0 Belgrade

Group 5 Table

	Pld	W	D	L	F	A	Pts
1 Belgrade	3	1	2	0	2	0	5
1 South-West Bulgaria	3	1	2	0	2	0	5
3 Slovak Western Region	3	1	2	0	1	0	5
4 Eastern Region Northern Ireland	3	0	0	3	0	5	0

NB Belgrade qualify by drawing of lots.

Group 6

23-27/4/11 Stare Mesto, Morkovice, Spytihněv, Kromeriz

Dalmacija 0-3 FK Alytis, Zlín Region 0-0 West Hungary, FK Alytis 3-3 West Hungary, Zlín Region 4-1 Dalmacija, FK Alytis 0-1 Zlín Region, West Hungary 3-0 Dalmacija

Group 6 Table

	Pld	W	D	L	F	A	Pts
1 Zlín Region	3	2	1	0	5	1	7
2 West Hungary	3	1	2	0	6	3	5
3 FK Alytis	3	1	1	1	6	4	4
4 Dalmacija	3	0	0	3	1	10	0

Group 7

3-7/8/10 Libiaz, Wolbrom, Myslenice

Małopolska 1-1 South Region Russia, Helsinki 3-2 FC Azot, Małopolska 4-1 Helsinki, FC Azot 0-5 South Region Russia, FC Azot 1-3 Małopolska, South Region Russia 5-0 Helsinki

Group 7 Table

	Pld	W	D	L	F	A	Pts
1 South Region Russia	3	2	1	0	11	1	7
2 Małopolska	3	2	1	0	8	3	7
3 Helsinki	3	1	0	2	4	11	3
4 FC Azot	3	0	0	3	3	11	0

Group 8

28/8-1/9/10 Chernigov, Plysky

FK Flaminko/RFS 0-1 ARF Ialoveni, Yednyst Plysky 5-0 Chevik, Yednyst Plysky 8-0 FK Flaminko/RFS, ARF Ialoveni 2-0 Chevik, ARF Ialoveni 0-2 Yednyst Plysky, Chevik 1-4 FK Flaminko/RFS

Group 8 Table

	Pld	W	D	L	F	A	Pts
1 Yednyst Plysky	3	3	0	0	15	0	9
2 ARF Ialoveni	3	2	0	1	3	2	6
3 FK Flaminko/RFS	3	1	0	2	4	10	3
4 Chevik	3	0	0	3	1	11	0

TOP GOALSCORERS
QUALIFYING ROUNDS

6	Sergei Lednev (South Region Russia)
5	Vadim Tarykin (Yednyst Plysky)
	Fatih Deniz (Ankara)
4	Emmanuel Affagard (Ligue de Normandie)

FINAL TOURNAMENT

GROUP A

Coached by former Portugal defender Dito, hosts Braga were strongly fancied to top a section that also contained Czech outfit Zlín Region, German side Württembergischer FV and Ukraine's Yednyst Plysky. Dito's men served notice of their potential with an opening-day 3-1 victory against Zlín at the Estádio 1° Maio, the former base of SC Braga. Powerful Württemberg proved too strong for Yednyst on the same day, although Wolfgang Kopp's charges did require a second-half penalty save from 'keeper Julian Hauser to preserve their 2-0 lead.

Braga made it two wins from two with a 2-1 defeat of Yednyst, a match that hinged on Simão Barbosa saving Volodymyr Matsuta's spot kick with the score at 1-1. Zlín's 1-0 triumph against Württemberg in the other game meant that Braga only required a point against the latter to reach the final. They did even better, claiming a 3-1 success that preserved their 100% record since qualifying began. Zlín took second place and a bronze medal thanks to a 2-1 victory over Yednyst.

Group A Results

21/6/11, Primeiro de Maio, Braga
Braga 3-1 Zlín Region
Goal(s): 1-0 Hugo Veiga 45(p), 2-0 Diogo Leite 54, 3-0 João Silva 65, 3-1 Daněk 68(p)
Referee: Lechner (AUT)

21/6/11, Municipal, Vila Verde
Yednyst Plysky 0-2 Württembergischer FV
Goal(s): 0-1 Faber 10, 0-2 Kleinschrodt 30
Referee: Valášek (SVK)

23/6/11, Cidade de Barcelos, Barcelos
Braga 2-1 Yednyst Plysky
Goal(s): 0-1 Babor 10, 1-1 José Ferreira 22(p), 2-1 Daniel Simões 59
Referee: Jemini (ALB)

23/6/11, Sports Center CF Fão, Fao
Zlín Region 1-0 Württembergischer FV
Goal(s): 1-0 Stojaspal 78
Referee: Pristovnik (CRO)

26/6/11, Municipal, Vila Verde
Württembergischer FV 1-3 Braga
Goal(s): 0-1 José Ferreira 37, 0-2 Pedro Nobre 45+3, 1-2 Kleinschrodt 67, 1-3 José Ferreira 88
Referee: Johnsen (NOR)

26/6/11, Primeiro de Maio, Braga
Zlín Region 2-1 Yednyst Plysky
Goal(s): 0-1 Babor 34, 1-1 Školník 68(p), 2-1 Valko 70(og)
Referee: Anastasiou (CYP)

Group A Table

	Pld	W	D	L	F	A	Pts
1 Braga	3	3	0	0	8	3	9
2 Zlín Region	3	2	0	1	4	4	6
3 Württembergischer FV	3	1	0	2	3	4	3
4 Yednyst Plysky	3	0	0	3	2	6	0

GROUP B

Serbian representatives Belgrade were in the driving seat in Group B after the opening games following a thrilling 3-2 success against South Region Russia and a goalless draw between Ireland's Leinster & Munster and Turkish side Ankara. That situation changed, however, when Ray Whelehan scored the only goal a few days later as Leinster & Munster prevailed against Jovica Milikić's side. Ankara joined the Irish team on four points thanks to a 2-1 defeat of ten-man South Region, in which Rodion Chalov squandered the Russians' second penalty of the match.

That meant Ankara, who led Leinster & Munster on goal difference, would reach the final with three points against Belgrade – barring a sizeable victory for their Irish rivals. Things started well for Hameş Şentürk's men when Leinster & Munster trailed to South Region, but their situation soon deteriorated as they fell behind and had two players sent off. Ankara's disappointment was complete when Ognjen Gostiljac rounded off a 2-0 win for Belgrade, but the Serbians' celebrations were cut short by the news from Barcelos that Leinster & Munster had come back to win 2-1 and claim their place in the final.

Belgrade's Marko Gudović scores against South Russia Region

Regions' Cup winners Braga show off their medals

Group B Results

21/6/11, Cidade de Barcelos, Barcelos
Ankara 0-0 Leinster & Munster
Referee: Pristovnik (CRO)

21/6/11, Sports Center CF Fão, Fao
South Region Russia 2-3 Belgrade
Goal(s): 0-1 Živković 4, 0-2 Blagojević 35, 1-2 Valiulin 37, 1-3 Gudović 73, 2-3 Avanyan 80
Referee: Anastasiou (CYP)

23/6/11, Municipal, Vila Verde
South Region Russia 1-2 Ankara
Goal(s): 0-1 Fatih Deniz 13, 1-1 Tyukalkin 44(p), 1-2 Muhittin Çetinkaya 79
Referee: Lechner (AUT)

23/6/11, Municipal, Vila Verde
Belgrade 0-1 Leinster & Munster
Goal(s): 0-1 Whelehan 52
Referee: Johnsen (NOR)

26/6/11, Cidade de Barcelos, Barcelos
Leinster & Munster 2-1 South Region Russia
Goal(s): 0-1 Ushakov 13, 1-1 Barbour 64, 2-1 O'Sullivan 68
Referee: Jemini (ALB)

26/6/11, Sports Center CF Fão, Fao
Belgrade 2-0 Ankara
Goal(s): 1-0 Živković 41(p), 2-0 Gostiljac 81
Referee: Valášek (SVK)

Group B Table

	Pld	W	D	L	F	A	Pts
1 Leinster & Munster	3	2	1	0	3	1	7
2 Belgrade	3	2	0	1	5	3	6
3 Ankara	3	1	1	1	2	3	4
4 South Region Russia	3	0	0	3	4	7	0

FINAL

Braga had early problems against a wily, powerful Leinster & Munster side in the Barcelos final, although they, like their Irish guests, struck the crossbar in the first half. But the tide had begun to turn in the nimble hosts' favour by the time the classy Pedro Nobre arrowed in their opener just after the hour.

Gerard Smith's team struck back quickly when David O'Sullivan rifled home after Rui Vieira spilled Ray Whelehan's free-kick, but the decisive blow was struck on 84 minutes when Braga right-back José Fortunato chipped goalkeeper Brendan O'Donnell from out on the flank. "There is tons of quality in the lower divisions where these guys play and the people in charge of bigger clubs should really take the time to find out just how good they are," said winning coach Dito afterwards.

Final Result

28/6/11, Cidade de Barcelos, Barcelos
Braga 2-1 Leinster & Munster
Attendance: 1036
Braga: Rui Vieira, José Fortunato, Costa, Daniel Simões, João Silva, Manuel Gonçalves (José Costa 63), José Ferreira (Diogo Gomes 73), Pedro Nobre, Hugo Veiga, Diogo Leite, Luís Ribeiro (Renato Reis 60). Coach: Dito (POR)
Leinster & Munster: O'Connell, Hoey, Carrig, Walsh, Barbour (Keddy 80), Dunne, O'Sullivan, Lacey, Whelehan, Higgins (Breen 88), Kavanagh (Loughran 46). Coach: Gerard Smith (IRL)
Goal(s): 1-0 Pedro Nobre 62, 1-1 O'Sullivan 68, 2-1 José Fortunato 84
Yellow Card(s): Manuel Gonçalves 39 (Braga), Loughran 49 (Leinster & Munster), José Ferreira 70 (Braga), Hoey 75 (Leinster & Munster), Renato Reis 90+4 (Braga)
Referee: Johnsen (NOR)

TOP GOALSCORERS
FINAL TOURNAMENT

3	José Ferreira (Braga)
2	Olexandr Babor (Yednyst Plysky)
	Martin Kleinschrodt (Württemberg)
	Pedro Nobre (Braga)
	Stefan Živković (Belgrade)
	David O'Sullivan (Leinster & Munster)

UEFA Women's Champions League 2010/11

There was a familiar lineup to the second UEFA Women's Champions League final as Olympique Lyonnais and 1. FFC Turbine Potsdam came face to face for the second successive year. The outcome, however, was different. Whereas in 2010 Potsdam had maintained Germany's dominance of the European scene with a penalty shoot-out success in Getafe, this time Lyon took France's first female continental club title by securing a deserved 2-0 win at Craven Cottage in London. It was a fitting reward for years of investment by Lyon president Jean-Michel Aulas, who since the 2010 final had made ambitious alterations, appointing a new coach, Patrice Lair, and recruiting French internationals Camille Abily, Sonia Bompastor and Eugénie Le Sommer to give the team a strength in depth that was illustrated by their world-class substitutes' bench in the final. Lyon, who won all 22 of their French league fixtures in 2010/11, thus became only the third non-German club – after Umeå IK and Arsenal LFC – to be crowned European champions.

UEFA
WOMEN'S
CHAMPIONS
LEAGUE
UEFA
WOMEN'S CHAMPIONS LEAGUE
UEFA
WOMEN'S CHAMPIONS LEAGUE

QUALIFYING ROUND

Group 1

5-10/8/10 Brondby

FC NSA Sofia 7-0 Gazi Üniversitesispor, Brøndby IF 6-0 FC Roma Calfa, Brøndby IF 12-0 Gazi Üniversitesispor, FC Roma Calfa 0-4 FC NSA Sofia, FC NSA Sofia 0-3 Brøndby IF, Gazi Üniversitesispor 3-3 FC Roma Calfa

Group 1 Table

	Pld	W	D	L	F	A	Pts
1 Brøndby IF	3	3	0	0	21	0	9
2 FC NSA Sofia	3	2	0	1	11	3	6
3 FC Roma Calfa	3	0	1	2	3	13	1
4 Gazi Üniversitesispor	3	0	1	2	3	22	1

Group 2

5-10/8/10 Siauliai, Pakruojis

Everton 6-0 KÍ Klaksvík, FK Gintra Universitetas 4-0 ZFK Borec, Everton 10-0 ZFK Borec, KÍ Klaksvík 0-0 FK Gintra Universitetas, FK Gintra Universitetas 0-7 Everton, ZFK Borec 0-2 KÍ Klaksvík

Group 2 Table

	Pld	W	D	L	F	A	Pts
1 Everton	3	3	0	0	23	0	9
2 FK Gintra Universitetas	3	1	1	1	4	7	4
3 KÍ Klaksvík	3	1	1	1	2	6	4
4 ZFK Borec	3	0	0	3	0	16	0

Group 3

5-10/8/10 Larnaca, Limassol

Umeå IK 3-0 ASA Tel-Aviv FC, WFC SFK 2000 Sarajevo 1-6 Apollon Limassol LFC, Umeå IK 1-4 Apollon Limassol LFC, ASA Tel-Aviv FC 3-1 WFC SFK 2000 Sarajevo, WFC SFK 2000 Sarajevo 0-1 Umeå IK, Apollon Limassol LFC 3-0 ASA Tel-Aviv FC

Group 3 Table

	Pld	W	D	L	F	A	Pts
1 Apollon Limassol LFC	3	3	0	0	13	2	9
2 Umeå IK	3	2	0	1	5	4	6
3 ASA Tel-Aviv FC	3	1	0	2	3	7	3
4 WFC SFK 2000 Sarajevo	3	0	0	3	2	10	0

Group 4

5-10/8/10 Kopavogur, Reykjavik

FCF Juvisy Essonne 5-1 FCM Târgu Mureş, Breidablik 8-1 FC Levadia Tallinn, FCF Juvisy Essonne 12-0 FC Levadia Tallinn, FCM Târgu Mureş 0-7 Breidablik, Breidablik 3-3 FCF Juvisy Essonne, FC Levadia Tallinn 1-2 FCM Târgu Mureş

Group 4 Table

	Pld	W	D	L	F	A	Pts
1 FCF Juvisy Essonne	3	2	1	0	20	4	7
2 Breidablik	3	2	1	0	18	4	7
3 FCM Târgu Mureş	3	1	0	2	3	13	3
4 FC Levadia Tallinn	3	0	0	3	2	22	0

Group 5

5-10/8/10 Krsko, Ivančna Gorica

ASD CF Bardolino Verona 7-0 Swansea City Ladies FC, ASD CF Bardolino Verona 3-0 FC Baia Zugdidi, Swansea City Ladies FC 0-4 ŽNK Krka, ŽNK Krka 4-0 FC Baia Zugdidi, ŽNK Krka 1-4 ASD CF Bardolino Verona, FC Baia Zugdidi 1-2 Swansea City Ladies FC

Group 5 Table

	Pld	W	D	L	F	A	Pts
1 ASD CF Bardolino Verona	3	3	0	0	14	1	9
2 ŽNK Krka	3	2	0	1	9	4	6
3 Swansea City Ladies FC	3	1	0	2	2	12	3
4 FC Baia Zugdidi	3	0	0	3	1	9	0

Group 6

5-10/8/10 Osijek, Vinkovci

FC Rossiyanka 5-0 WFC Osijek, SU 1° Dezembro 1-4 St Francis FC, FC Rossiyanka 9-0 St Francis FC, WFC Osijek 1-4 SU 1° Dezembro, SU 1° Dezembro 1-4 FC Rossiyanka, St Francis FC 5-3 WFC Osijek

Group 6 Table

	Pld	W	D	L	F	A	Pts
1 FC Rossiyanka	3	3	0	0	18	1	9
2 St Francis FC	3	2	0	1	9	13	6
3 SU 1° Dezembro	3	1	0	2	6	9	3
4 WFC Osijek	3	0	0	3	4	14	0

Group 7

5-10/8/10 Castledawson, Ballymena, Dungannon

FCR 2001 Duisburg 3-0 ŠK Slovan Bratislava, Glasgow City LFC 8-0 Newtownabbey Strikers WFC, ŠK Slovan Bratislava 0-4 Glasgow City LFC, FCR 2001 Duisburg 6-1 Newtownabbey Strikers WFC, Glasgow City LFC 0-4 FCR 2001 Duisburg, Newtownabbey Strikers WFC 0-1 ŠK Slovan Bratislava

Group 7 Table

	Pld	W	D	L	F	A	Pts
1 FCR 2001 Duisburg	3	3	0	0	13	1	9
2 Glasgow City LFC	3	2	0	1	12	4	6
3 ŠK Slovan Bratislava	3	1	0	2	1	7	3
4 Newtownabbey Strikers WFC	3	0	0	3	1	15	0

Sonja Fuss helped Duisburg to top their qualifying round group

ROUND OF 32

22/9/10, Delijski Vis, Nis
ŽFK Mašinac PZP 1-3 Arsenal Ladies FC
Goal(s): 0-1 Yankey 12, 1-1 Radojičić 62, 1-2 Flaherty 86, 1-3 Carter 88
14/10/10, Meadow Park, Borehamwood
Arsenal Ladies FC 9-0 ŽFK Mašinac PZP
Goal(s): 1-0 Yankey 19, 2-0 White 23, 3-0 Little 26, 4-0 Little 42, 5-0 Davison 52, 6-0 Nobbs 55, 7-0 Sampanidis 79(og), 8-0 Carter 85, 9-0 Ludlow 90+2
Aggregate: 12-1; Arsenal Ladies FC qualify.

22/9/10, Dinamo-Juni, Minsk
Zorka-BDU 1-2 Røa IL
Goal(s): 0-1 Thorsnes 13, 1-1 Barkovskaya 45+1, 1-2 Stange 78
13/10/10, RöA Stadium, Oslo
Røa IL 0-0 Zorka-BDU
Aggregate: 2-1; Zorka-BDU qualify.

22/9/10, OSiR, Racibórz
RTP Unia Racibórz 1-2 Brøndby IF
Goal(s): 1-0 Winczo 37, 1-1 S. Andersen 54, 1-2 Kur Larsen 67
13/10/10, Brøndby, Brondby
Brøndby IF 0-1 RTP Unia Racibórz
Goal(s): 0-1 Stobba 7
Aggregate: 2-2; RTP Unia Racibórz qualify on away goal(s).

22/9/10, Tsirion Stadium, Limassol
Apollon Limassol LFC 1-2 WFC Zvezda 2005 Perm
Goal(s): 1-0 Rus 27, 1-1 Ruiz 48, 1-2 Leyva Moran 76(p)
13/10/10, Zvezda, Perm
WFC Zvezda 2005 Perm 2-1 Apollon Limassol LFC
Goal(s): 1-0 Kurochkina 53, 2-0 Dyatel 60, 2-1 Kostova 71
Aggregate: 4-2; WFC Zvezda 2005 Perm qualify.

22/9/10, Matija Gubec, Krsko
ŽNK Krka 0-7 Linköpings FC
Goal(s): 0-1 Sällström 6, 0-2 Asllani 10, 0-3 Fors 22(p), 0-4 Ikidi 33, 0-5 Asllani 35, 0-6 M. Karlsson 68, 0-7 M. J. Karlsson 73
14/10/10, Folkungavallen, Linkoping
Linköpings FC 5-0 ŽNK Krka
Goal(s): 1-0 Sällström 13, 2-0 Brännström 60, 3-0 M. J. Karlsson 70, 4-0 Fors 84, 5-0 Fors 90+4
Aggregate: 12-0; Linköpings FC qualify.

22/9/10, State Olympic educational sport Centre "Chernigiv", Chernigov
FC Legenda Chernigiv 1-3 FC Rossiyanka
Goal(s): 1-0 Melkonyants 32, 1-1 Petrova 49, 1-2 Petrova 80, 1-3 Skotnikova 81
14/10/10, Krasnoarmeysk, Krasnoarmeysk
FC Rossiyanka 4-0 FC Legenda Chernigiv
Goal(s): 1-0 Nyandeni 4, 2-0 Nyandeni 33, 3-0 Mokshanova 38, 4-0 Slonova 80
Aggregate: 7-1; FC Rossiyanka qualify.

22/9/10, Toumbas Stadium, Salonika
FC PAOK Thessaloniki 1-0 SV Neulengbach
Goal(s): 1-0 Panteliadou 27
13/10/10, Wienerwaldstadion, Neulengbach
SV Neulengbach 3-0 FC PAOK Thessaloniki
Goal(s): 1-0 Burger 11, 2-0 Burger 19, 3-0 Burger 43
Aggregate: 3-1; SV Neulengbach qualify.

22/9/10, Wiklöf Holding Arena, Maarianhamina
Åland United 0-9 1. FFC Turbine Potsdam
Goal(s): 0-1 Bajramaj 5, 0-2 Mittag 17, 0-3 Schmidt 34, 0-4 Nagasato 35, 0-5 Kemme 58, 0-6 Peter 70, 0-7 Mittag 72, 0-8 Demann 79, 0-9 Mittag 90+3
13/10/10, Karl Liebknecht, Potsdam
1. FFC Turbine Potsdam 6-0 Åland United
Goal(s): 1-0 Bajramaj 1, 2-0 Wesely 4, 3-0 Kessler 30, 4-0 Mittag 40, 5-0 Schmidt 59, 6-0 Peter 68
Aggregate: 15-0; 1. FFC Turbine Potsdam qualify.

22/9/10, AZ Stadion, Alkmaar
AZ Alkmaar 1-2 Olympique Lyonnais
Goal(s): 0-1 Le Sommer 53, 0-2 Renard 67, 1-2 Van den Heiligenberg 72
14/10/10, Stade de Gerland, Lyon
Olympique Lyonnais 8-0 AZ Alkmaar
Goal(s): 1-0 Schelin 10, 2-0 Schelin 23, 3-0 Renard 27, 4-0 Schelin 33, 5-0 Thomis 40, 6-0 Dickenmann 65, 7-0 Cruz Trana 69, 8-0 Le Sommer 90+1(p)
Aggregate: 10-1; Olympique Lyonnais qualify.

22/9/10, Hjørring Stadion, Hjorring
Fortuna Hjørring 8-0 ASD CF Bardolino Verona
Goal(s): 1-0 Bukh 4, 2-0 Paaske-Sørensen 7, 3-0 J. Jensen 39, 4-0 Paaske-Sørensen 64, 5-0 Mogensen 67, 6-0 Paaske-Sørensen 69, 7-0 Paaske-Sørensen 88, 8-0 Paaske-Sørensen 90+2
13/10/10, Marc'Antonio Bentegodi, Verona
ASD CF Bardolino Verona 1-6 Fortuna Hjørring
Goal(s): 0-1 Igbo 4, 1-1 Girelli 17, 1-2 Paaske-Sørensen 18, 1-3 Mogensen 52, 1-4 Munk 72, 1-5 Paaske-Sørensen 76, 1-6 Munk 90+3
Aggregate: 1-14; Fortuna Hjørring qualify.

22/9/10, Schützenwiese, Winterthur
FC Zürich 2-3 ASD Torres CF
Goal(s): 1-0 Kiwic 2(p), 1-1 Camporese 24, 2-1 Zumbühl 36, 2-2 Fuselli 38, 2-3 Camporese 51
13/10/10, Vanni Sanna, Sassari
ASD Torres CF 4-1 FC Zürich
Goal(s): 1-0 Fuselli 16, 2-0 Camporese 26, 3-0 Camporese 29, 4-0 Domenichetti 55, 4-1 Brandenberger 84
Aggregate: 7-3; ASD Torres CF qualify.

23/9/10, Kópavogsvöllur, Kopavogur
Breidablik 0-3 FCF Juvisy Essonne
Goal(s): 0-1 Soubeyrand 7, 0-2 Thiney 72, 0-3 Tonazzi 78
14/10/10, Robert Bobin, Evry
FCF Juvisy Essonne 6-0 Breidablik
Goal(s): 1-0 Coquet 33, 2-0 Coquet 56, 3-0 Machart 59, 4-0 Thiney 61, 5-0 Machart 73, 6-0 Machart 86
Aggregate: 9-0; FCF Juvisy Essonne qualify.

23/9/10, Municipal State Enterprise "Shakhter" Stadium, Karaganda
CSHVSM 0-5 FCR 2001 Duisburg
Goal(s): 0-1 Grings 19, 0-2 Grings 28, 0-3 Laudehr 34, 0-4 Grings 48, 0-5 Grings 88
13/10/10, PCC Stadion, Duisburg
FCR 2001 Duisburg 6-0 CSHVSM
Goal(s): 1-0 Grings 45+1, 2-0 Müller 50, 3-0 Grings 71, 4-0 Grings 75, 5-0 Grings 78, 6-0 Laudehr 86
Aggregate: 11-0; FCR 2001 Duisburg qualify.

23/9/10, Hidegkúti Nándor, Budapest
MTK Hungária FC 0-0 Everton
14/10/10, Stobart Halton, Widnes
Everton 7-1 MTK Hungária FC
Goal(s): 1-0 Dowie 9, 2-0 Chaplen 11, 3-0 Duggan 21, 4-0 Gál 45+1(og), 4-1 D. Papp 66, 5-1 Duggan 67, 6-1 Chaplen 73, 7-1 Chaplen 90+1
Aggregate: 7-1; Everton qualify.

23/9/10, Teresa Rivero, Madrid
Rayo Vallecano de Madrid 3-0 Valur Reykjavík
Goal(s): 1-0 Natalia 4, 2-0 Adriana 36, 3-0 Hermoso 59
13/10/10, Hlídarendi, Reykjavik
Valur Reykjavík 1-1 Rayo Vallecano de Madrid
Goal(s): 0-1 Adriana 57, 1-1 Galán 88(og)
Aggregate: 1-4; Rayo Vallecano de Madrid qualify.

29/9/10, Stayen, Sint-Truiden
K. Sint-Truidense VV 0-3 AC Sparta Praha
Goal(s): 0-1 L. Martínková 5, 0-2 Kožárová 67, 0-3 Čulová 85
14/10/10, TJ Lokomotiva Praha, Prague
AC Sparta Praha 7-0 K. Sint-Truidense VV
Goal(s): 1-0 L. Martínková 27, 2-0 Pivoňková 36, 3-0 L. Martínková 38, 4-0 Ondrušová 52, 5-0 Došková 70, 6-0 I. Martínková 76, 7-0 Ondrušová 85
Aggregate: 10-0; AC Sparta Praha qualify.

ROUND OF 16

3/11/10, Folkungavallen, Linkoping
Linköpings FC 2-0 AC Sparta Praha
Goal(s): 1-0 Rohlin 54, 2-0 Samuelsson 81
10/11/10, TJ Lokomotiva Praha, Prague
AC Sparta Praha 0-1 Linköpings FC
Goal(s): 0-1 Asllani 62
Aggregate: 0-3; Linköpings FC qualify.

Yuki Nagasoto scored a hat-trick for Potsdam in their 9-0 away win at Neulengbach

3/11/10, Karl Liebknecht, Potsdam
1. FFC Turbine Potsdam 7-0 SV Neulengbach
Goal(s): 1-0 Kessler 7, 2-0 Mittag 28, 3-0 Zietz 58, 4-0 Odebrecht 63, 5-0 Nagasato 65, 6-0 Mittag 77, 7-0 Zietz 90+2
10/11/10, Wienerwaldstadion, Neulengbach
SV Neulengbach 0-9 1. FFC Turbine Potsdam
Goal(s): 0-1 Wesely 13, 0-2 Bajramaj 22, 0-3 Bajramaj 25, 0-4 Zietz 45+2(p), 0-5 Nagasato 53, 0-6 Nagasato 71, 0-7 Mittag 75, 0-8 Nagasato 82, 0-9 Bagehorn 87
Aggregate: 0-16; 1. FFC Turbine Potsdam qualify.

3/11/10, PCC Stadion, Duisburg
FCR 2001 Duisburg 4-2 Fortuna Hjørring
Goal(s): 0-1 J. Jensen 16, 1-1 Knaak 45, 2-1 Wensing 45+2, 2-2 Petersen 54, 3-2 Grings 56, 4-2 Islacker 82
10/11/10, Hjørring Stadion, Hjorring
Fortuna Hjørring 0-3 FCR 2001 Duisburg
Goal(s): 0-1 Weichelt 32, 0-2 Weichelt 47, 0-3 Islacker 89
Aggregate: 2-7; FCR 2001 Duisburg qualify.

3/11/10, RöA Stadium, Oslo
Røa IL 1-1 WFC Zvezda 2005 Perm
Goal(s): 1-0 Thorsnes 87, 1-1 Khodyreva 90+4
10/11/10, Zvezda, Perm
WFC Zvezda 2005 Perm 4-0 Røa IL
Goal(s): 1-0 Dyatel 24, 2-0 Ruiz 70, 3-0 Apanaschenko 82, 4-0 Dyachkova 90+1
Aggregate: 5-1; WFC Zvezda 2005 Perm qualify.

3/11/10, Brøndby, Brondby
Brøndby IF 1-4 Everton
Goal(s): 1-0 Kur Larsen 3, 1-1 Williams 56(p), 1-2 Duggan 79, 1-3 Chaplen 81, 1-4 Chaplen 86
11/11/10, Stobart Halton, Widnes
Everton 1-1 Brøndby IF
Goal(s): 0-1 Troelsgaard 11, 1-1 Scott 71
Aggregate: 5-2; Everton qualify.

4/11/10, Vanni Sanna, Sassari
ASD Torres CF 1-2 FCF Juvisy Essonne
Goal(s): 0-1 Tonazzi 45, 0-2 Coquet 73, 1-2 Pintus 74
10/11/10, Robert Bobin, Evry
FCF Juvisy Essonne 2-2 ASD Torres CF (aet)
Goal(s): 1-0 Tonazzi 12, 1-1 Iannella 60, 1-2 Fuselli 80, 2-2 Tonazzi 92
Aggregate: 4-3; FCF Juvisy Essonne qualify after extra time.

4/11/10, Krasnoarmeysk, Krasnoarmeysk
FC Rossiyanka 1-6 Olympique Lyonnais
Goal(s): 0-1 Schelin 11, 0-2 Abily 18, 0-3 Schelin 30, 1-3 Oghiabeva 53, 1-4 Schelin 72, 1-5 Schelin 79, 1-6 Nécib 81
10/11/10, Stade de Gerland, Lyon
Olympique Lyonnais 5-0 FC Rossiyanka
Goal(s): 1-0 Le Sommer 22(p), 2-0 Kozhnikova 50(og), 3-0 Bompastor 53, 4-0 Dickenmann 67, 5-0 Brétigny 89
Aggregate: 11-1; Olympique Lyonnais qualify.

4/11/10, Teresa Rivero, Madrid
Rayo Vallecano de Madrid 2-0 Arsenal Ladies FC
Goal(s): 1-0 Natalia 1, 2-0 Sonia 74
11/11/10, Meadow Park, Borehamwood
Arsenal Ladies FC 4-1 Rayo Vallecano de Madrid
Goal(s): 1-0 Yankey 11, 2-0 Fleeting 61, 3-0 Grant 68, 3-1 Adriana 78, 4-1 Beattie 90+1
Aggregate: 4-3; Arsenal Ladies FC qualify.

QUARTER-FINALS

The draw for the quarter-finals of the 2010/11 UEFA Women's Champions League set up a possible semi-final rematch between 1. FFC Turbine Potsdam and their predecessors as holders, FCR 2001 Duisburg, and it duly came to pass.

Potsdam came away from their first leg at France's FCF Juvisy Essonne 3-0 up, and it was 6-2 in the return as Isabel Kerschowski and Yuki Nagasato both scored twice. Duisburg also met first-time quarter-finalists in Everton. In the opener in Widnes, Duisburg were without key players Inka Grings and Linda Bresonik, but Kozue Ando broke the deadlock on 52 minutes and Alexandra Popp swiftly added two more either side of a Natasha Dowie goal. Grings was back for the return and found the net in a 2-1 win that sealed a 5-2 aggregate triumph.

Olympique Lyonnais, having put 11 goals past WFC Rossiyanka in the round of 16, faced another Russian side, 2009 runners-up Zvezda-2005. In Perm the visitors tore into Zvezda but were held 0-0, ending Lyon's perfect run of 22 competitive wins in 2010/11. It was a similar story at Stade de Gerland until, on the hour, substitute Lara Dickenmann struck from distance for a 1-0 home win. The aggregate shot count over the tie was 38-4 in Lyon's favour.

Katie Chapman struck late to take Arsenal through on away goals against Linköping

It was the classic game of two halves at Borehamwood when Arsenal LFC welcomed Linköpings FC. The Swedish visitors dominated before the break but only had a Linda Sällström individual effort to show for it. In the second period the Gunners switched to 4-3-3 and, having levelled through Ellen White, could even have taken the lead. Still, at 1-1, Linköping appeared favourites to progress and they twice led the second leg, only for Sällström's opener to be cancelled out by Rachel Yankey and Kosovare Asllani's effort to be equalised with ten minutes left by a decisive away goal from Katie Chapman. Arsenal thus progressed narrowly for the second tie in a row after their stoppage-time round of 16 victory over Rayo Vallecano de Madrid.

Quarter-Final Results

16/3/11, Robert Bobin, Evry
FCF Juvisy Essonne 0-3 1. FFC Turbine Potsdam
Juvisy Essonne: Malet, Guilbert, Butel, Coquet, Soubeyrand, Trimoreau, Mendes, Tonazzi, Butel, Machart (Fernandes 24), Thiney. Coach: Sandrine Mathivet (FRA)
Potsdam: Sarholz, Peter, Henning, Bajramaj, Zietz, Wesely, Odebrecht, Nagasato (I. Kerschowski 75), Schmidt, Kemme, Mittag. Coach: Bernd Schröder (GER)
Goal(s): 0-1 Schmidt 8, 0-2 Bajramaj 28, 0-3 Soubeyrand 65(og)
Yellow Card(s): Schmidt 17 (Potsdam), Zietz 25 (Potsdam), Mittag 79 (Potsdam)
Referee: Monzul (UKR)
23/3/11, Karl Liebknecht, Potsdam
1. FFC Turbine Potsdam 6-2 FCF Juvisy Essonne
Potsdam: Schumann, Peter, I. Kerschowski, Henning, Zietz (Demann 67), Wesely, Odebrecht, Nagasato, Schmidt (Kerschowski 46), Kemme (Schröder 69), Mittag. Coach: Bernd Schröder (GER)
Juvisy Essonne: Malet, Guilbert, Butel (Levasseur 84), Coquet, Soubeyrand, Trimoreau, Mendes (Fernandes 56), Tonazzi, Butel, Machart (Benmokhtar 79), Thiney. Coach: Sandrine Mathivet (FRA)
Goal(s): 1-0 I. Kerschowski 18, 2-0 Nagasato 31, 3-0 Nagasato 33, 3-1 Tonazzi 37, 4-1 Schmidt 45+1, 4-2 Thiney 52, 5-2 Mittag 62, 6-2 I. Kerschowski 75
Red Card(s): Guilbert 63 (Juvisy Essonne)
Yellow Card(s): Guilbert 35 (Juvisy Essonne), Guilbert 63 (Juvisy Essonne), Trimoreau 68 (Juvisy Essonne)
Referee: Ihringova (ENG)
Aggregate: 9-2; 1. FFC Turbine Potsdam qualify.

Duisburg players pile in to celebrate scoring against Everton

17/3/11, Meadow Park, Borehamwood
Arsenal Ladies FC 1-1 Linköpings FC
Arsenal: Byrne, Houghton, F. White, Grant (Carter 54), Nobbs, E. White, Yankey (Fleeting 85), Beattie, Little, Chapman, Fahey. Coach: Laura Harvey (ENG)
Linköping: Lundgren, Rohlin, Fors (J. Andersson 70), Holstad-Berge, P. Larsson, Heimersson, Samuelsson, Sällström, Schjelderup (Klinga 88), Krantz, Gill. Coach: Jörgen Petersson (SWE)
Goal(s): 0-1 Sällström 16, 1-1 E. White 66
Yellow Card(s): Fors 53 (Linköping), P. Larsson 75 (Linköping), F. White 77 (Arsenal)
Referee: Dorcioman (ROU)
23/3/11, Kopparvallen, Atvidaberg
Linköpings FC 2-2 Arsenal Ladies FC
Linköping: Lundgren, Rohlin, Fors (Asllani 46), Holstad-Berge, P. Larsson, Heimersson, Samuelsson, Sällström, Schjelderup, Krantz (J. Andersson 87), Gill. Coach: Jörgen Petersson (SWE)
Arsenal: Byrne, Houghton, F. White, Nobbs (Grant 80), E. White (Coombs 90+2), Yankey, Beattie, Carter (Fleeting 65), Little, Chapman, Fahey. Coach: Laura Harvey (ENG)
Goal(s): 1-0 Sällström 17, 1-1 Yankey 40, 2-1 Asllani 57, 2-2 Chapman 80
Yellow Card(s): Fahey 62 (Arsenal), Yankey 67 (Arsenal)
Referee: Staubli (SUI)
Aggregate: 3-3; Arsenal Ladies FC qualify on away goals.

17/3/11, Zvezda, Perm
WFC Zvezda 2005 Perm 0-0 Olympique Lyonnais
Zvezda 2005 Perm: Baranova, Suslova, Dyatel, Kurochkina (Leyva 89), Apanaschenko, Tsybutovich, Ruiz, Polyakova, Khodyreva, Boychenko (Ndimeni 80), Pekur. Coach: Natalia Zinchenko (RUS)
Lyon: Bouhaddi, Renard, Henry (Cruz Trana 46), Schelin, Le Sommer (Thomis 55), Nécib, Kaci, Bompastor, Viguier, Dickenmann (Brétigny 81), Abily. Coach: Patrice Lair (FRA)
Yellow Card(s): Suslova 56 (Zvezda 2005 Perm), Bompastor 80 (Lyon)
Referee: Spinelli (ITA)

23/3/11, Stade de Gerland, Lyon
Olympique Lyonnais 1-0 WFC Zvezda 2005 Perm
Lyon: Bouhaddi, Renard, Georges, Henry, Schelin (Le Sommer 71), Nécib, Cruz Trana (Brétigny 90), Thomis (Dickenmann 51), Bompastor, Viguier, Abily. Coach: Patrice Lair (FRA)
Zvezda 2005 Perm: Baranova, Suslova (Kutusheva 75), Dyatel (Leyva 82), Kurochkina, Apanaschenko, Tsybutovich, Ruiz (Ndimeni 63), Polyakova, Khodyreva, Boychenko, Pekur. Coach: Natalia Zinchenko (RUS)
Goal(s): 1-0 Dickenmann 60
Red Card(s): Pekur 77 (Zvezda 2005 Perm)
Yellow Card(s): Bompastor 9 (Lyon), Pekur 13 (Zvezda 2005 Perm), Kurochkina 38 (Zvezda 2005 Perm), Tsybutovich 40 (Zvezda 2005 Perm), Pekur 77 (Zvezda 2005 Perm)
Referee: Steinhaus (GER)
Aggregate: 1-0; Olympique Lyonnais qualify.

17/3/11, Stobart Halton, Widnes
Everton 1-3 FCR 2001 Duisburg
Everton: Brown, Easton (Bronze 62), Unitt, Williams, Whelan, Johnson, Handley, Scott, Dowie, Duggan (Harries 83), Chaplen. Coach: Maureen Marley (ENG)
Duisburg: Bellinghoven, Wensing, Oster (Van Bonn 88), Kiesel-Griffioen, Laudehr, Maes, Fuss, Islacker (Weichelt 79), Himmighofen, Popp, Ando (Knaak 67). Coach: Marco Ketelaer (GER)
Goal(s): 0-1 Ando 52, 0-2 Popp 59, 1-2 Dowie 60, 1-3 Popp 65
Yellow Card(s): Popp 33 (Duisburg)
Referee: Damkova (CZE)
23/3/11, PCC Stadion, Duisburg
FCR 2001 Duisburg 2-1 Everton
Duisburg: Bellinghoven, Van Bonn (Bresonik 73), Oster, Kiesel-Griffioen, Grings, Laudehr, Maes, Fuss (Krahn 59), Islacker, Himmighofen, Ando (Knaak 55). Coach: Marco Ketelaer (GER)
Everton: Brown, Unitt, Williams, Whelan, Johnson, Handley (Chaplen 66), Scott, Dowie, Duggan (Parris 84), Harries, Bronze. Coach: Maureen Marley (ENG)
Goal(s): 1-0 Laudehr 22, 2-0 Grings 79(p), 2-1 Harries 90+3
Yellow Card(s): Duggan 75 (Everton), Grings 85 (Duisburg), Laudehr 87 (Duisburg), Islacker 89 (Duisburg)
Referee: Palmqvist (SWE)
Aggregate: 5-2; FCR 2001 Duisburg qualify.

SEMI-FINALS

1. FFC Turbine Potsdam went into their all-German semi-final with FCR 2001 Duisburg as marginal favourites having finished top of the Frauen-Bundesliga, two places in front of their rivals. Furthermore, in the two league encounters Turbine had drawn away and won at home. In the previous season's European semi-final tie both legs had been 1-0 home wins before Potsdam prevailed on penalties; this time the opener in Duisburg ended 2-2, the visitors twice having leads cancelled out, with Inka Grings striking her 13th goal of the competition – just one off the record. She would not match it in the return leg, however, as the only goal came from Potsdam's Yuki Nagasato.

That result ensured a re-run of the 2010 final. A crowd of 20,123 – a record for a women's game in France and the highest for this competition outside of a final – witnessed Olympique Lyonnais's first leg against Arsenal LFC, and with 11 minutes elapsed Lotta Schelin had scored twice to give Lyon a commanding lead for the return. Although Lyon winger Élodie Thomis was injured before the second leg, Eugénie Le Sommer proved a more than adequate replacement, scoring twice before half-time and making another goal for Lara Dickenmann. Two replies from Arsenal after the break were of little consequence as Lyon progressed with a healthy 5-2 aggregate.

Semi-Final Results

9/4/11, PCC Stadion, Duisburg
FCR 2001 Duisburg 2-2 1. FFC Turbine Potsdam
Duisburg: Bellinghoven, Wensing, Oster, Kiesel-Griffioen, Grings, Bresonik, Maes, Fuss, Islacker (Knaak 78), Himmighofen (Krahn 71), Popp. Coach: Marco Ketelaer (GER)
Potsdam: Sarholz, Peter, I. Kerschowski, Henning (M. Kerschowski 70), Bajramaj, Zietz, Odebrecht, Nagasato, Schmidt, Kemme, Mittag. Coach: Bernd Schröder (GER)
Goal(s): 0-1 I. Kerschowski 16, 1-1 Grings 32, 1-2 Nagasato 35, 2-2 Oster 42
Yellow Card(s): Schmidt 65 (Potsdam)
Referee: Dorcioman (ROU)
17/4/11, Karl Liebknecht, Potsdam
1. FFC Turbine Potsdam 1-0 FCR 2001 Duisburg
Potsdam: Sarholz, Peter, I. Kerschowski, Bajramaj, Zietz, Wesely, Odebrecht, Nagasato, Schröder (M. Kerschowski 46), Kemme, Mittag. Coach: Bernd Schröder (GER)
Duisburg: Bellinghoven, Wensing, Oster (Weichelt 70), Kiesel-Griffioen, Grings, Bresonik, Laudehr, Maes (Knaak 59), Fuss, Popp, Ando. Coach: Marco Ketelaer (GER)
Goal(s): 1-0 Nagasato 40
Yellow Card(s): Odebrecht 25 (Potsdam), Bajramaj 43 (Potsdam), Popp 78 (Duisburg)
Referee: Heikkinen (FIN)
Aggregate: 3-2; 1. FFC Turbine Potsdam qualify.

9/4/11, Stade de Gerland, Lyon
Olympique Lyonnais 2-0 Arsenal Ladies FC
Lyon: Bouhaddi, Renard, Georges, Henry, Schelin, Necib (Kaci 65), Cruz Trana, Thomis (Bretigny 75), Viguier, Dickenmann (Le Sommer 58), Abily. Coach: Patrice Lair (FRA)
Arsenal: Byrne, Houghton, F. White, Grant, Nobbs, E. White, Yankey, Beattie, Carter (Coombs 87), Little, Chapman. Coach: Laura Harvey (ENG)
Goal(s): 1-0 Schelin 2, 2-0 Schelin 11
Yellow Card(s): E. White 52 (Arsenal), Georges 79 (Lyon)
Referee: Gaál (HUN)
16/4/11, Meadow Park, Borehamwood
Arsenal Ladies FC 2-3 Olympique Lyonnais
Arsenal: Byrne, Houghton, Flaherty (Tracy 84), F. White (Beattie 74), Grant, Nobbs, E. White, Yankey, Carter (Fleeting 52), Chapman, Fahey. Coach: Laura Harvey (ENG)
Lyon: Bouhaddi, Renard (Kaci 51), Georges, Henry, Schelin, Le Sommer (Bretigny 72), Cruz Trana (Necib 48), Bompastor, Viguier, Dickenmann, Abily. Coach: Patrice Lair (FRA)
Goal(s): 0-1 Le Sommer 16, 0-2 Le Sommer 34, 0-3 Dickenmann 45+1, 1-3 Fleeting 68, 2-3 E. White 85
Yellow Card(s): Renard 31 (Lyon), Necib 87 (Lyon)
Referee: Pedersen (NOR)
Aggregate: 2-5; Olympique Lyonnais qualify.

Lotte Schelin scored both goals in Lyon's 2-0 home win over Arsenal

FINAL

The 2011 UEFA Women's Champions League final, staged at Fulham FC's Craven Cottage home in west London, brought together the same two teams that had contested the 2010 showpiece in the outskirts of Madrid.

Renard pounces

Defending champions Potsdam were missing the influential Yuki Nagasato through a knee injury, but they had the better of the opening exchanges before Lyon gradually wrested control and took the lead in the 27th minute. Having been dominant down their right, it was a Lyon corner from that flank that produced the goal. Sonia Bompastor's cross was knocked back by Amandine Henry to Lotte Schelin, and although the Sweden striker's effort was blocked by 2010 final hero Anna Felicitas Sarholz in the Potsdam goal, right-back Wendie Renard was there to poke in the rebound.

Wendie Renard – scorer of Lyon's opening goal in the final against Potsdam

France international Eugénie Le Sommer came off the bench to set up Lyon's decisive second goal

The German champions, bidding to equal compatriots 1. FFC Frankfurt's record of three European titles, struggled to trouble Lyon's outstanding goalkeeper Sarah Bouhaddi for the rest of the first half, but they enjoyed their best spell of the match early in the second period. Three times they looked set to equalise, only for Inka Wesley to head off target and Bouhaddi to save from Isabel Kerschowski, whose cross then just eluded the control of Anja Mittag in front of the Lyon goal.

Super subs seal it

After that triple scare Lyon began to deal more comfortably with the Potsdam pressure – despite some surging runs by Fatmire Bajramaj, playing her last game for the club before departing for Frankfurt. The strength in depth of Lyon's squad soon bore fruit. While veteran Potsdam coach

Lyon's Elodie Thomis (left) tussles with Potsdam's Isabel Kerschowski

Bernd Schröder made no substitutions, Lair introduced Lara Dickenmann and Eugénie Le Sommer, two players who had provided crucial contributions in the previous two rounds. With five minutes to go Le Sommer broke down the right and sent a ball into the box for Dickenmann to seal victory with an emphatic finish.

"In the first half we were better than them, then it got a bit more difficult physically, but we defended well and did not concede," said Camille Abily, named Player of the Match by UEFA's Technical Team for her staunch performance in midfield.

Final Result

26/5/11, Craven Cottage, London
Olympique Lyonnais 2-0 1. FFC Turbine Potsdam
Attendance: 14303
Lyon: Bouhaddi, Renard, Georges, Henry, Schelin, Necib (Dickenmann 55), Cruz Trana, Thomis (Le Sommer 73), Bompastor, Viguier, Abily. Coach: Patrice Lair (FRA)
Potsdam: Sarholz, Peter, I. Kerschowski, Henning, Bajramaj, Zietz, Wesely, Odebrecht, Schmidt, Kemme, Mittag. Coach: Bernd Schröder (GER)
Goal(s): 1-0 Renard 27, 2-0 Dickenmann 85
Yellow Card(s): Abily 60 (Lyon)
Referee: Damkova (CZE)

TOP GOALSCORERS

11	Inka Grings (Duisburg)
9	Yuki Nagasato (Potsdam) Lotta Schelin (Lyon)
8	Anja Mittag (Potsdam)
7	Cathrine Paaske-Sørensen (Fortuna Hjørring)
5	Eugénie Le Sommer (Lyon) Brooke Chaplen (Everton) Laëtitia Tonazzi (Juvisy Essonne) Lara Dickenmann (Lyon) Fatmire Bajramaj (Potsdam)

Lyon celebrate their UEFA Women's Champions League triumph

UEFA Women's U19 Championship 2010/11

Norway and hosts Italy enjoyed spells in the limelight at the 2011 UEFA European Women's Under-19 Championship, but it was Germany who shone brightest throughout before dazzling Norway into submission in the final. If a familiar name prevailed in the end, there were surprises along the way, with neither France nor England, winners the previous two seasons, making it to the final tournament in Emilia-Romagna. The Netherlands and Norway, respectively, saw them off in qualifying, taking their places in Group B alongside Spain and Germany – a section that always looked like producing the champions despite an impressive showing on home soil from Group A frontrunners Italy. Spearheaded by Melissa Bjånesøy, Norway made it through to the final, and against Germany in Imola the striker maintained her record of scoring in every game with her seventh goal of the tournament. It had little value, however, as Germany racked up eight goals at the other end to seal a remarkable, record-breaking victory.

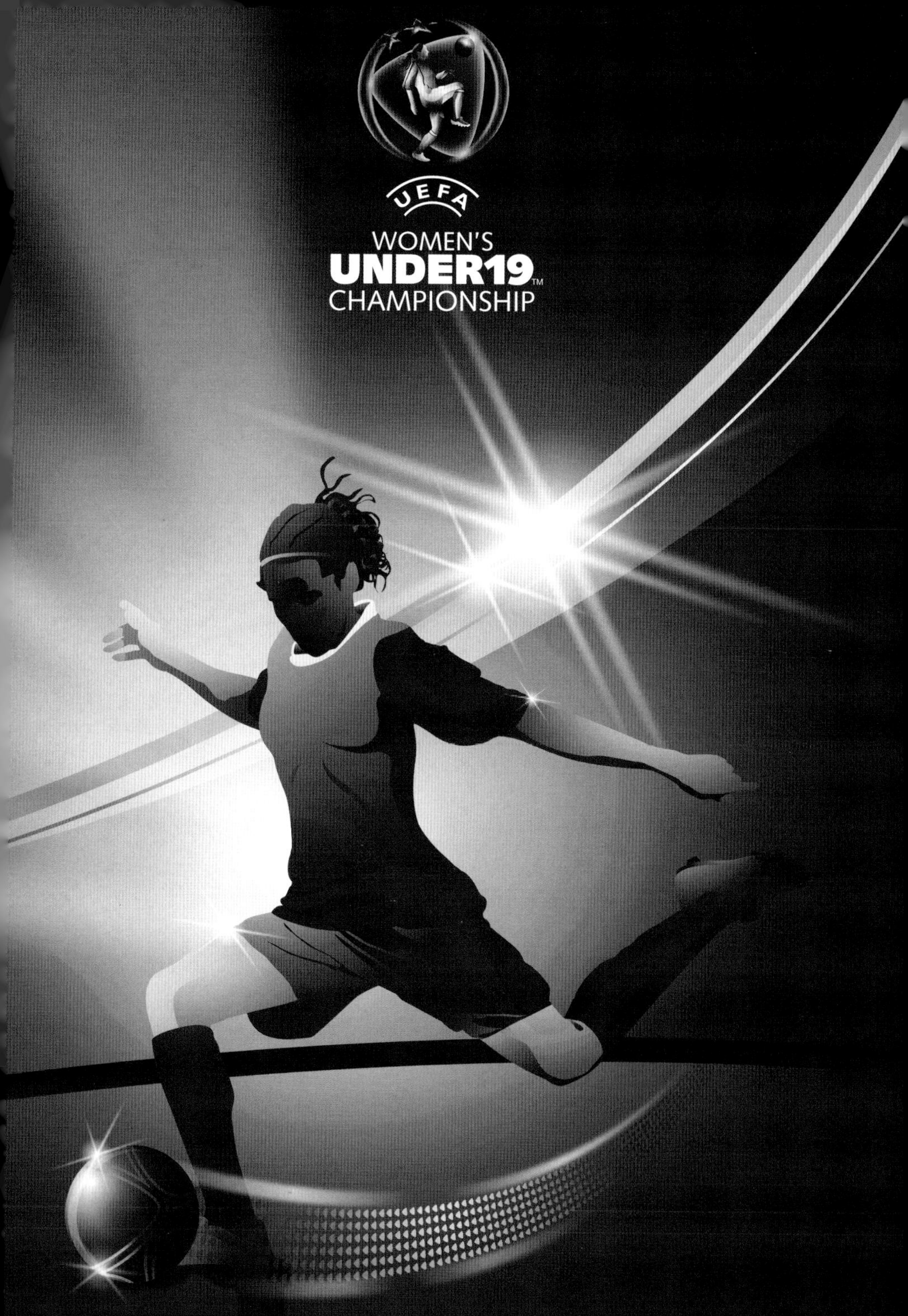
UEFA
WOMEN'S
UNDER19™
CHAMPIONSHIP

QUALIFYING ROUNDS

The road to a final tournament can often be fraught with danger, especially when the favoured teams are handed a difficult draw. Even so, few imagined that France and England, winners of the UEFA Women's Under-19 Championship for the previous two seasons, and finalists in 2010, would both fail to make it through to the 2011 tournament in Italy.

Les Bleuettes' second qualifying round campaign was over almost as soon as it had begun, a 3-0 defeat by Denmark delivering a blow from which they never really recovered. It was an emerging Netherlands team that won Group 1, a record 11-0 victory over Lithuania and 3-0 win against Denmark rendering a 1-0 loss to France academic. England, meanwhile, succumbed to Norway on the final day in Group 4, Jordan Nobbs missing a penalty in a 1-0 defeat when a draw would have seen them progress.

Lieke Martens scored eight qualifying goals for the Netherlands

After surprisingly being held 0-0 by Wales, Germany made serene progress along with Spain, Switzerland and Russia. Indeed, Russia advanced with a game to spare, and a weakened side lost 1-0 to Belgium in their final outing, enabling their victorious opponents to progress to the finals as best runners-up.

First Qualifying Round Results

Group 1

11-16/9/10 Chisinau, Orhei

England 4-0 Moldova, Finland 5-0 Armenia, England 9-0 Armenia, Moldova 0-4 Finland, Finland 0-2 England, Armenia 0-2 Moldova

Group 1 Table

	Pld	W	D	L	F	A	Pts
1 England	3	3	0	0	15	0	9
2 Finland	3	2	0	1	9	2	6
3 Moldova	3	1	0	2	2	8	3
4 Armenia	3	0	0	3	0	16	0

Group 2

11-16/9/10 Marijampole, Vinograd

Belgium 4-0 Lithuania, Estonia - Azerbaijan (cancelled), Belgium - Azerbaijan (cancelled), Lithuania 1-0 Estonia, Estonia 0-6 Belgium, Azerbaijan - Lithuania (cancelled)

Group 2 Table

	Pld	W	D	L	F	A	Pts
1 Belgium	2	2	0	0	10	0	6
2 Lithuania	2	1	0	1	1	4	3
3 Estonia	2	0	0	2	0	7	0

NB Azerbaijan withdrew without playing a game.

Group 3

11-16/9/10 Sarajevo

Denmark 4-0 Greece, Spain 4-0 Bosnia & Herzegovina, Denmark 2-0 Bosnia & Herzegovina, Greece 0-6 Spain, Spain 1-1 Denmark, Bosnia & Herzegovina 0-3 Greece

Group 3 Table

	Pld	W	D	L	F	A	Pts
1 Spain	3	2	1	0	11	1	7
2 Denmark	3	2	1	0	7	1	7
3 Greece	3	1	0	2	3	10	3
4 Bosnia & Herzegovina	3	0	0	3	0	9	0

Group 4

11-16/9/10 Tatabanya, Telki

Austria 4-0 Portugal, Hungary 7-0 Latvia, Austria 10-0 Latvia, Portugal 3-0 Hungary, Hungary 0-7 Austria, Latvia 0-5 Portugal

Group 4 Table

	Pld	W	D	L	F	A	Pts
1 Austria	3	3	0	0	21	0	9
2 Portugal	3	2	0	1	8	4	6
3 Hungary	3	1	0	2	7	10	3
4 Latvia	3	0	0	3	0	22	0

Group 5

11-16/9/10 Strumica

Switzerland 3-2 FYROM, Poland 5-0 Kazakhstan, Switzerland 4-0 Kazakhstan, FYROM 1-3 Poland, Poland 0-4 Switzerland, Kazakhstan 1-2 FYROM

Group 5 Table

	Pld	W	D	L	F	A	Pts
1 Switzerland	3	3	0	0	11	2	9
2 Poland	3	2	0	1	8	5	6
3 FYROM	3	1	0	2	5	7	3
4 Kazakhstan	3	0	0	3	1	11	0

Group 6

11-16/9/10 Stojnci, Velenje, Smartno ob Paki
Wales 21-0 Georgia, France 1-0 Slovenia, Wales 4-2 Slovenia, Georgia 0-11 France, France 5-1 Wales, Slovenia 15-0 Georgia

Group 6 Table

	Pld	W	D	L	F	A	Pts
1 France	3	3	0	0	17	1	9
2 Wales	3	2	0	1	26	7	6
3 Slovenia	3	1	0	2	17	5	3
4 Georgia	3	0	0	3	0	47	0

Group 7

11-16/9/10 Sarpsborg, Moss, Fredrikstad
Netherlands 9-1 Faroe Islands, Norway 8-0 Belarus, Belarus 0-9 Netherlands, Norway 4-0 Faroe Islands, Netherlands 1-1 Norway, Faroe Islands 0-0 Belarus

Group 7 Table

	Pld	W	D	L	F	A	Pts
1 Netherlands	3	2	1	0	19	2	7
2 Norway	3	2	1	0	13	1	7
3 Faroe Islands	3	0	1	2	1	13	1
4 Belarus	3	0	1	2	0	17	1

Group 8

11-16/9/10 Skovde, Lidkoping, Tidaholm
Scotland 3-3 Serbia, Sweden 4-0 Slovakia, Scotland 4-0 Slovakia, Serbia 0-2 Sweden, Sweden 0-1 Scotland, Slovakia 3-4 Serbia

Group 8 Table

	Pld	W	D	L	F	A	Pts
1 Scotland	3	2	1	0	8	3	7
2 Sweden	3	2	0	1	6	1	6
3 Serbia	3	1	1	1	7	8	4
4 Slovakia	3	0	0	3	3	12	0

Group 9

11-16/9/10 Slany, Prague
Romania 3-2 Turkey, Czech Republic 4-2 Northern Ireland, Romania 1-2 Northern Ireland, Turkey 1-1 Czech Republic, Czech Republic 4-0 Romania, Northern Ireland 0-1 Turkey

Group 9 Table

	Pld	W	D	L	F	A	Pts
1 Czech Republic	3	2	1	0	9	3	7
2 Turkey	3	1	1	1	4	4	4
3 Northern Ireland	3	1	0	2	4	6	3
4 Romania	3	1	0	2	4	8	3

Group 10

11-16/9/10 Teteven, Mezdra
Iceland 2-0 Bulgaria, Ukraine 2-1 Israel, Iceland 2-0 Israel, Bulgaria 0-1 Ukraine, Ukraine 0-4 Iceland, Israel 4-1 Bulgaria

Group 10 Table

	Pld	W	D	L	F	A	Pts
1 Iceland	3	3	0	0	8	0	9
2 Ukraine	3	2	0	1	3	5	6
3 Israel	3	1	0	2	5	5	3
4 Bulgaria	3	0	0	3	1	7	0

Group 11

11-16/9/10 Osijek
Republic of Ireland 5-0 Cyprus, Russia 1-0 Croatia, Republic of Ireland 0-1 Croatia, Cyprus 0-7 Russia, Russia 3-0 Republic of Ireland, Croatia 8-0 Cyprus

Group 11 Table

	Pld	W	D	L	F	A	Pts
1 Russia	3	3	0	0	11	0	9
2 Croatia	3	2	0	1	9	1	6
3 Republic of Ireland	3	1	0	2	5	4	3
4 Cyprus	3	0	0	3	0	20	0

Second Qualifying Round Results

Group 1

31/3-5/4/11 Odense, Haderslev, Vejle
Netherlands 11-0 Lithuania, France 0-3 Denmark, France 7-0 Lithuania, Denmark 0-3 Netherlands, Netherlands 0-1 France, Lithuania 0-9 Denmark

Group 1 Table

	Pld	W	D	L	F	A	Pts
1 Netherlands	3	2	0	1	14	1	6
2 Denmark	3	2	0	1	12	3	6
3 France	3	2	0	1	8	3	6
4 Lithuania	3	0	0	3	0	27	0

Group 2

31/3-5/4/11 Sochi
Russia 1-0 Finland, Belgium 2-2 Serbia, Russia 2-1 Serbia, Finland 3-3 Belgium, Belgium 1-0 Russia, Serbia 4-6 Finland

Group 2 Table

	Pld	W	D	L	F	A	Pts
1 Russia	3	2	0	1	3	2	6
2 Belgium	3	1	2	0	6	5	5
3 Finland	3	1	1	1	9	8	4
4 Serbia	3	0	1	2	7	10	1

Group 3

31/3-5/4/11 Llanelli, Carmarthen
Iceland 1-3 Turkey, Germany 1-1 Wales, Germany 2-0 Turkey, Wales 0-2 Iceland, Iceland 0-3 Germany, Turkey 0-1 Wales

Group 3 Table

	Pld	W	D	L	F	A	Pts
1 Germany	3	2	1	0	6	1	7
2 Wales	3	1	1	1	2	3	4
3 Turkey	3	1	0	2	3	4	3
4 Iceland	3	1	0	2	3	6	3

Group 4

31/3-5/4/11 Novigrad, Umag
England 3-0 Croatia, Norway 2-0 Portugal, England 3-0 Portugal, Croatia 0-2 Norway, Portugal 2-1 Croatia, Norway 1-0 England

Group 4 Table

	Pld	W	D	L	F	A	Pts
1 Norway	3	3	0	0	5	0	9
2 England	3	2	0	1	6	1	6
3 Portugal	3	1	0	2	2	6	3
4 Croatia	3	0	0	3	1	7	0

Group 5

31/3-5/4/11 Simferopol
Switzerland 1-1 Sweden, Czech Republic 4-1 Ukraine, Sweden 0-0 Czech Republic, Switzerland 1-0 Ukraine, Czech Republic 1-4 Switzerland, Ukraine 1-7 Sweden

Group 5 Table

	Pld	W	D	L	F	A	Pts
1 Switzerland	3	2	1	0	6	2	7
2 Sweden	3	1	2	0	8	2	5
3 Czech Republic	3	1	1	1	5	5	4
4 Ukraine	3	0	0	3	2	12	0

Group 6

31/3-5/4/11 Graz, Anger
Spain 3-0 Poland, Austria 3-3 Scotland, Scotland 1-2 Spain, Austria 5-0 Poland, Spain 4-0 Austria, Poland 2-2 Scotland

Group 4 Table

	Pld	W	D	L	F	A	Pts
1 Spain	3	3	0	0	9	1	9
2 Austria	3	1	1	1	8	7	4
3 Scotland	3	0	2	1	6	7	2
4 Poland	3	0	1	2	2	10	1

TOP GOALSCORERS
(Qualifying Rounds)

10	Lisa Makas (Austria)
8	Lieke Martens (Netherlands) Elin Rubensson (Sweden)
7	Sarah Puntigam (Austria) Ellen Jansen (Netherlands) Melissa Bjånesøy (Norway) Leyla Güngör (Turkey)
6	Cora Canetta (Switzerland) Linda Norrena (Finland) Lucie Voňková (Czech Republic)

FINAL TOURNAMENT

GROUP A

Quite whether Corrado Corradini, the coach of tournament hosts Italy, was bluffing when he played down his side's chances of progressing to the semi-finals, only he knows, but his comments on the eve of the tournament betrayed a man concerned about mental fortitude.

Corradini claimed his team felt "an incredible amount of pressure and responsibility" as they set about qualifying from a group comprising Russia, Belgium and Switzerland. "Many people have worked hard to make this tournament happen and we don't want to let anyone down," he added. His fears proved unfounded. Three wins later and Italy were in the semi-finals.

Indeed the Azzurrine needed only two bites of the cherry to secure top spot and, with it, a FIFA U-20 Women's World Cup berth. Their campaign began with a 2-1 victory over Russia, with Lisa Alborghetti scoring the winner on 56 minutes after Nadezhda Koltakova had cancelled out Katia Coppola's early strike. Their second match was an even tighter affair, one goal proving enough as Coppola broke the deadlock against Switzerland six minutes from time.

Lisa Alborghetti was on target for Italy against Russia and Belgium

Belgium punished

Italy's third group match was academic, but the 2008 winners triumphed again, three goals in five second-half minutes overturning a 1-0 deficit to inflict a third successive defeat on already-eliminated Belgium. Cecilia Salvai, defender-turned-striker Roberta Filippozzi and substitute Alborghetti were on target against opponents whose attractive playing style was undermined by naive defending throughout the tournament.

The battle for second place and qualification for the semi-finals therefore came down to a final-day decider between Switzerland and Russia. The latter had also inflicted a 3-1 defeat on Belgium – thanks to Anna Cholovyaga's double and a goal from captain Tatiana Ananyeva – but Switzerland managed one more in their meeting with the Red Devils, Eseosa Aigbogun, Corina Saner, Michelle Probst and Nadine Fässler all finding the net in a 4-1 win.

Küffer to the rescue

That result gave Yannick Schwery's side a marginally better goal difference, which meant they required only a draw to qualify. Russia did not make it easy for them. Indeed, a murky evening at Cervia's Stadio Dei Pini was illuminated by a dazzling display of goalkeeping from Switzerland's Pascale Küffer. The 18-year-old withstood a late barrage to secure a goalless draw and her side's passage to the last four for the second time in three years. "She saved us," acknowledged Schwery, a former goalkeeper himself. Küffer's reward, if it could be labelled as such, was a daunting semi-final against the attacking power of Group B winners Germany.

Group A Results

30/5/11, Romeo Galli, Imola
Italy 2-1 Russia
Italy: Giuliani, Salvai, Ledri, Franco, Linari, Filippozzi, Mason (Lecce 46), Mauri, Alborghetti (Pederzoli 90+3), Rosucci, Coppola. Coach: Corrado Corradini (ITA)
Russia: Shirokova, Ananyeva, Veselukha, Kutusheva (Pozdeeva 46), Kobeleva, Cholovyaga, Orlova, Mashkova, Vlasenko (Korneychenko 71), Makarenko, Koltakova (Blynskaya 62). Coach: Aleksandr Shagov (RUS)
Goal(s): 1-0 Coppola 3, 1-1 Koltakova 13, 2-1 Alborghetti 56
Yellow Card(s): Pozdeeva 63 (Russia), Makarenko 77 (Russia)
Referee: Braz Bastos (POR)

:seosa Aigbogun
ɔpened the scoring
ɔr Switzerland in their
-1 win over Belgium

30/5/11, Enrico Nanni, Bellaria
Switzerland 4-1 Belgium
Switzerland: Küffer, Gerber, Jörg (Fässler 72), Probst, Fimian, Canetta (Hinnen 87), Wälti, Aigbogun, Herzog (Baker 62), Saner, Gensetter. Coach: Yannick Schwery (SUI)
Belgium: D'Haeseleir, Van Kerkhoven, Verbist, Renier, Vindevoghel (Daniels 57), Vanhaevermaet, Coryn, Wullaert, Charlier (Aga 46), Mignon (Ninclaus 75), Verdonck. Coach: Jean-Marie Greven (BEL)
Goal(s): 1-0 Aigbogun 23, 2-0 Saner 35, 2-1 Aga 58, 3-1 Probst 89, 4-1 Fässler 90+3
Yellow Card(s): Verbist 45+2 (Belgium), Verdonck 89 (Belgium)
Referee: Larsson (SWE)

2/6/11, Dei Pini, Cervia
Italy 1-0 Switzerland
Italy: Giuliani, Ledri, Franco, Linari, Filippozzi, Mauri, Alborghetti, Rosucci, Coppola (Pederzoli 86), Pedretti (De Angelis 81), Lecce (Mason 64). Coach: Corrado Corradini (ITA)
Switzerland: Küffer, Gerber, Jörg (Fässler 73), Probst, Fimian (Hinnen 85), Canetta, Wälti, Aigbogun, Herzog (Schweer 46), Saner, Gensetter. Coach: Yannick Schwery (SUI)
Goal(s): 1-0 Coppola 84
Yellow Card(s): Wälti 49 (Switzerland), Linari 54 (Italy), Mason 67 (Italy), Franco 80 (Italy), Rosucci 90+4 (Italy)
Referee: Asulin (ISR)

2/6/11, Tullo Morgagni, Forli
Russia 3-1 Belgium
Russia: Shirokova, Ananyeva, Veselukha, Pozdeeva (Kiskonen 65), Kobeleva, Cholovyaga, Orlova (Kutusheva 39), Mashkova, Vlasenko (Blynskaya 48), Makarenko, Koltakova. Coach: Aleksandr Shagov (RUS)
Belgium: D'Haeseleir, Ninclaus (Demeyere 77), Van Kerkhoven, Verbist (Charlier 82), Renier, Vanhaevermaet, Aga, Coryn, Wullaert, Daniels (Mignon 66), Sneyers. Coach: Jean-Marie Greven (BEL)
Goal(s): 1-0 Cholovyaga 22, 1-1 Vanhaevermaet 36, 2-1 Cholovyaga 62, 3-1 Ananyeva 64
Referee: Zinck (FRA)

5/6/11, Enrico Nanni, Bellaria
Belgium 1-3 Italy
Belgium: Langeraert, Van Kerkhoven, Renier, Vindevoghel (Verbist 74), Vanhaevermaet, Aga, Wullaert, Daniels, Demeyere (Ninclaus 35), Mignon, Verdonck (Charlier 46). Coach: Jean-Marie Greven (BEL)
Italy: Casaroli, Salvai, Ledri, Filippozzi, Mauri, Coppola (Mason 85), De Angelis, Vitale, Venturini, Pederzoli (Alborghetti 56), Lecce. Coach: Corrado Corradini (ITA)
Goal(s): 1-0 Aga 30, 1-1 Salvai 64, 1-2 Filippozzi 67, 1-3 Alborghetti 69
Yellow Card(s): Verdonck 42 (Belgium), Filippozzi 54 (Italy), Daniels 78 (Belgium)
Referee: Lehtovaara (FIN)

5/6/11, Dei Pini, Cervia
Russia 0-0 Switzerland
Russia: Shirokova, Ananyeva (Kiskonen 45+2), Kutusheva, Pozdeeva (Blynskaya 42), Kobeleva, Cholovyaga, Orlova, Mashkova, Vlasenko (Veselukha 67), Makarenko, Koltakova. Coach: Aleksandr Shagov (RUS)
Switzerland: Küffer, Mallaun, Gerber, Jörg (Hinnen 73), Probst, Fimian (Fässler 14), Canetta, Wälti, Aigbogun (Baker 84), Saner, Gensetter. Coach: Yannick Schwery (SUI)
Yellow Card(s): Blynskaya 54 (Russia), Canetta 55 (Switzerland), Kiskonen 61 (Russia), Koltakova 77 (Russia)
Referee: Larsson (SWE)

Group A Table

	Pld	W	D	L	F	A	Pts
1 Italy	3	3	0	0	6	2	9
2 Switzerland	3	1	1	1	4	2	4
3 Russia	3	1	1	1	4	3	4
4 Belgium	3	0	0	3	3	10	0

GROUP B

It is almost a prerequisite for final tournament draws to conjure up a so-called 'group of death'. It may have become a hackneyed term over the years, but on the eve of the finals in Italy the coaches of the four Group B contenders – Germany, Spain, Norway and the Netherlands – were all buying into the cliché. "I wasn't here for the draw," said Norway boss Jarl Torske, "so when I saw the result I said 'Oh my God'. I reckon these are the best teams here."

It was Germany, however, who quickly emerged as the pick of the bunch, goals from Isabella Schmid, Lena Lotzen and Anja Hegenauer securing a 3-1 opening-day victory over Torske's charges in Cervia. Although Germany were forced to work harder for the points three days later against Spain, the three-time champions were on the front foot for much of the game and deservedly sealed a 1-0 win 12 minutes into the second half when Eunice Beckmann, guilty of an earlier miss, finished off a rapid counterattack.

Germany through

Those two victories took Germany through to the semi-finals as Group B winners with a game to spare, providing an early reward for coach Maren Meinert, who had cut short her maternity leave to take her place in the dugout. For Spain, however, it was another case of what might have been, their opening encounter against the Netherlands having resulted in a 1-1 draw.

The Oranje had been semi-finalists 12 months earlier, going home unbeaten after a penalty shoot-out defeat by England, but they never scaled those heights in Italy. Their campaign was over almost as soon as it had begun when they went down 3-0 to Norway on their second outing, Melissa Bjånesøy scoring either side of Kristine Hegland's 39th-minute effort.

Spirited display

That defeat left the Netherlands needing to beat Germany 3-0 to stand any chance of clinching second place. It was an unlikely outcome, and although Johan van Heertum's charges put up a spirited performance, they were to bow out with another defeat, Ivana Rudelic striking an added-time winner as Germany came from behind to win 2-1 and preserve their 100% record.

Second place was thus decided in Forli, where Norway met Spain to the backdrop of rolling thunder. It was the Scandinavian side who whipped up a storm on the field, never looking back after Bjånesøy's seventh-minute opener. Andrine Hegerberg, Hegland and substitute Guro Reiten were also on target before Bjånesøy's fifth goal of the finals – she had scored the consolation against Germany – sealed a 5-1 win that sent Norway through and provided coach Torske with the perfect 62nd birthday present.

Group B Results

30/5/11, Dei Pini, Cervia
Germany 3-1 Norway
Germany: Schmitz, Maier, Simon, Elsig, Wensing, Hendrich, Beckmann (Rudelic 73), Schmid, Rolser (Hegenauer 66), Petzelberger, Lotzen (Cramer 83). Coach: Maren Meinert (GER)
Norway: Fimreite, Sønstevold, Søndenå, Knudsen, Tengesdal, Thorisdottir, An. Hegerberg (Ada Hegerberg 73), Skaug (Dekkerhus 46), Hansen (Reiten 85), Bjånesøy, Hegland. Coach: Jarl Torske (NOR)
Goal(s): 1-0 Schmid 26, 1-1 Bjånesøy 35, 2-1 Lotzen 45+1, 3-1 Hegenauer 90+3
Yellow Card(s): Thorisdottir 39 (Norway), Hegenauer 87 (Germany)
Referee: Zinck (FRA)

30/5/11, Tullo Morgagni, Forli
Spain 1-1 Netherlands
Spain: Paños, Merino, Pereira, Putellas, Buceta (Laura 56), Beristain, García (Lázaro 84), Pérez de Heredia, Ouahabi, Calderón (Leire 61), Agoues. Coach: Ángel Vilda (ESP)
Netherlands: Du Ry, Compier, Van Lunteren (De Boer 75), Worm, K. Bakker, Van Dongen, Coolen (Van de Wetering 82), Middag, Martens, Jansen, Rijsdijk (Van de Sanden 64). Coach: Johan van Heertum (NED)
Goal(s): 1-0 Beristain 11, 1-1 Rijsdijk 49
Yellow Card(s): Ouahabi 67 (Spain)
Referee: Lehtovaara (FIN)

2/6/11, Enrico Nanni, Bellaria
Germany 1-0 Spain
Germany: Schmitz, Maier, Simon (Hegenauer 64), Elsig, Wensing, Hendrich, Beckmann (Rudelic 81), Schmid, Rolser (Cramer 31), Petzelberger, Lotzen. Coach: Maren Meinert (GER)
Spain: Paños, Merino, Laura, Pereira, Putellas, Buceta, Beristain, Altonaga (García 68), Ouahabi (Leire 46), Calderón, Agoues (Luna 58). Coach: Ángel Vilda (ESP)
Goal(s): 1-0 Beckmann 57
Yellow Card(s): Maier 90 (Germany)
Referee: Braz Bastos (POR)

2/6/11, Romeo Galli, Imola
Norway 3-0 Netherlands
Norway: Fimreite, Sønstevold, Søndenå, Knudsen, Thorisdottir, An. Hegerberg, Bjånesøy (Hansen 75), Hegland, Dekkerhus (Vassbø 89), Ada Hegerberg, Aardalen (Skaug 46). Coach: Jarl Torske (NOR)
Netherlands: Du Ry, Compier, Van Lunteren, Worm, K. Bakker (Rijsdijk 46), Van Dongen, Coolen, Middag, Martens, Jansen (L. Bakker 65), Van de Sanden. Coach: Johan van Heertum (NED)
Goal(s): 1-0 Bjånesøy 6(p), 2-0 Hegland 39, 3-0 Bjånesøy 57
Referee: Pirie (SCO)

Norway's Melissa Bjånesøy (left) challenges Germany's Luisa Wensing

5/6/11, Romeo Galli, Imola
Netherlands 1-2 Germany
Netherlands: Du Ry, Compier, Van Lunteren, Worm, K. Bakker (De Boer 56), Van Dongen, Coolen, Middag (Van de Wetering 79), Martens, Van de Sanden, Rijsdijk. Coach: Johan van Heertum (NED)
Germany: Abt, Elsig, Wensing, Hendrich (Schmid 46), Petzelberger, Nati (Maier 46), Demann, Rudelic, Cramer, Pyko, Hegenauer (Lotzen 66). Coach: Maren Meinert (GER)
Goal(s): 1-0 Van de Sanden 58, 1-1 Lotzen 67, 1-2 Rudelic 90+1
Yellow Card(s): Van de Wetering 84 (Netherlands)
Referee: Asulin (ISR)

5/6/11, Tullo Morgagni, Forli
Norway 5-1 Spain
Norway: Fimreite, Sønstevold, Søndenå, Knudsen, Thorisdottir (Vassbø 87), An. Hegerberg (Reiten 79), Skaug, Bjånesøy, Hegland, Dekkerhus (Hansen 46), Ada Hegerberg. Coach: Jarl Torske (NOR)
Spain: Paños, Merino, Laura, Luna (Agoues 46), Pereira, Leire, Buceta, Lázaro, Beristain, García, Calderón. Coach: Ángel Vilda (ESP)
Goal(s): 1-0 Bjånesøy 7, 2-0 An. Hegerberg 33, 3-0 Hegland 45+1, 3-1 Knudsen 61(og), 4-1 Reiten 85, 5-1 Bjånesøy 90
Yellow Card(s): Leire 64 (Spain)
Referee: Pirie (SCO)

Group B Table

	Pld	W	D	L	F	A	Pts
1 Germany	3	3	0	0	6	2	9
2 Norway	3	2	0	1	9	4	6
3 Netherlands	3	0	1	2	2	6	1
4 Spain	3	0	1	2	2	7	1

Katia Coppola of Italy on the ball in the semi-final against Norway

SEMI-FINALS

There was plenty of interest in both semi-final ties, with Switzerland taking on dominant neighbours Germany and, first of all, hosts Italy entertaining Norway in a mouth-watering repeat of the 2008 final.

The Azzurrine's hopes of a home victory were to end in a five-goal thriller in Bellaria. The 2008 final had been tense and tight, with Corrado Corradini's side prevailing 1-0, but the re-match three years on was to be a more open affair, and the game was only 12 minutes old when the irrepressible Melissa Bjånesøy broke the deadlock with her sixth goal of the finals.

Swift response

Italy hit back swiftly through Elisa Lecce following a sumptuous Martina Rosucci through ball, and shortly after half-time they repeated the trick, equalising again within a minute of Ada Hegerberg restoring the visitors' advantage. Katia Coppola's third goal of the tournament sparked a promising second-half spell for Italy, only for 16-year-old Caroline Hansen to come off the bench and put Norway in front again with a goal scored directly from a corner.

The only real surprise thereafter came when Bjånesøy was denied another goal by Laura Giuliani as Italy's goalkeeper endeavoured to make amends for Hansen's strike, but Norway – and Bjånesøy – had done enough and they held on to reach the final for the third time. Three hours later they discovered that their opponents would be the only side to have defeated them in Emilia-Romagna – Germany.

Worthy winners

Maren Meinert's side were worthy winners in Imola as Switzerland failed to cope with the intensity of their pressing and the frequency of their attacks. Germany might conceivably have been three goals to the good before Romana Petzelberger finished coolly midway through the first half, finally getting the better of Swiss goalkeeper Pascale Küffer, who had repeatedly denied Eunice Beckmannn hitherto.

Surprisingly Switzerland hauled themselves level with a goal from their only shot of the half, a 25-

Cora Canetta scored a spectacular equaliser for Switzerland against Germany

metre thunderbolt from Cora Canetta, but there was no respite from Germany's midfield dominance in the second period. Beckmann finally got her goal nine minutes after half-time, reacting first to Petzelberger's clever free-kick, before Lena Lotzen ended the match as a contest six minutes from time. Coach Meinart's satisfaction in taking Germany through to the final for the first time in four years was tempered by the team's disappointing conversion rate. "I'm not sure we'll win many more matches after wasting so many chances," she warned.

Semi-Final Results

8/6/11, Enrico Nanni, Bellaria
Italy 2-3 Norway
Italy: Giuliani, Salvai, Ledri, Franco, Linari, Filippozzi (Vitale 82), Mauri, Alborghetti, Rosucci, Coppola, Lecce (Mason 71). Coach: Corrado Corradini (ITA)
Norway: Fimreite, Sønstevold, Søndenå, Knudsen, Thorisdottir, An. Hegerberg, Skaug, Bjånesøy, Hegland, Dekkerhus (Reiten 71), Ada Hegerberg (Hansen 61). Coach: Jarl Torske (NOR)
Goal(s): 0-1 Bjånesøy 12, 1-1 Lecce 22, 1-2 Ada Hegerberg 48, 2-2 Coppola 49, 2-3 Hansen 65
Yellow Card(s): Ledri 73 (Italy), Hansen 83 (Norway)
Referee: Zinck (FRA)

8/6/11, Romeo Galli, Imola
Germany 3-1 Switzerland
Germany: Schmitz, Maier (Hegenauer 33), Simon (Cramer 89), Elsig, Wensing, Hendrich, Beckmann (Rudelic 67), Schmid, Petzelberger, Lotzen, Demann. Coach: Maren Meinert (GER)
Switzerland: Küffer, Mallaun, Gerber, Jörg (Hinnen 83), Probst, Canetta, Wälti, Aigbogun, Fässler (Fai 62), Saner (Schweer 82), Gensetter. Coach: Yannick Schwery (SUI)
Goal(s): 1-0 Petzelberger 21, 1-1 Canetta 38, 2-1 Beckmann 54, 3-1 Lotzen 84
Yellow Card(s): Simon 88 (Germany)
Referee: Pirie (SCO)

FINAL

Three-time champions Germany went into the final against twice runners-up Norway as overwhelming favourites but with coach Maren Meinert still voicing concerns about her team's inability to turn their superiority into goals. It was a fear that would prove unfounded as Germany ran riot in Imola.

For the first half of the contest, however, Meinert appeared to have a point as all Germany had to show for an impressive display of overwhelming dominance – in which they suffocated Norway's attacking ambitions before passing them into submission – was Luisa Wensing's diving header from a Ramona Petzelberger corner. It had been the same story when the two sides met 13 days earlier in Cervia, with Germany squandering chances while the free-scoring Melissa Bjånesøy lurked menacingly at the other end – and victory not being cemented until the last minute.

Deluge of goals

There would be no repeat in Imola. Germany's lead was doubled shortly after half-time when a wonderful move involving Carolin Simon and Lena Lotzen culminated in Isabella Schmid beating Ane Fimreite from distance. The floodgates were being

Luisa Wensing celebrates Germany's opening goal in the final against Norway

prised open and Germany's third goal was born of another clever interchange, this time between Schmid and Eunice Beckmann, whose neat pass was dispatched by Lotzen.

Norway had no answer to the onslaught and on 58 minutes found themselves 4-0 down as Lotzen's cushioned header was lashed emphatically into the roof of the net by captain Petzelberger. Moments later Lotzen rose highest to head in Jennifer Cramer's cross, and soon afterwards the downcast Norwegians were caught on the break, Ivana Rudelic burying a cross from fellow substitute Anja Hegenauer to make it 6-0.

Record defeat

Bjånesøy at least got Norway on the scoreboard with her tournament-topping seventh goal of the finals when she turned in Caroline Hansen's corner, but Germany were not yet done. Schmid compounded Norway's misery with another long shot before Hegenauer completed the scoring – and a remarkable 8-1 victory – with a 20-metre strike two minutes from time.

It was a record scoreline for the UEFA Women's European U19 Championship final, obliterating the previous-best three-goal margin, and it left Norway coach Jarl Torske "embarrassed and humiliated". Yet there was no shame in his side, the youngest of the tournament, being overrun by a team in such supreme form. Germany had saved their very best until last and, after a four-year wait, had conquered Europe again for the fourth time.

Germany's top scorer Lena Lotzen strikes for goal

Final Result

11/6/11, Romeo Galli, Imola
Norway 1-8 Germany
Attendance: 1300
Norway: Fimreite, Sønstevold (Aardalen 74), Søndenå, Knudsen, Thorisdottir, An. Hegerberg, Skaug, Bjånesøy, Hegland, Dekkerhus (Reiten 70), Ada Hegerberg (Hansen 46). Coach: Jarl Torske (NOR)
Germany: Schmitz, Maier, Simon (Pyko 58), Elsig, Wensing, Hendrich (Hegenauer 64), Beckmann (Rudelic 63), Schmid, Petzelberger, Lotzen, Cramer. Coach: Maren Meinert (GER)
Goal(s): 0-1 Wensing 29, 0-2 Schmid 50, 0-3 Lotzen 55, 0-4 Petzelberger 58, 0-5 Lotzen 60, 0-6 Rudelic 70, 1-6 Bjånesøy 72, 1-7 Schmid 79, 1-8 Hegenauer 88
Referee: Braz Bastos (POR)

TOP GOALSCORERS
(Final Tournament)

7	Melissa Bjånesøy (Norway)
5	Lena Lotzen (Germany)
3	Katia Coppola (Italy) Isabella Schmid (Germany)

Germany celebrate with the trophy after their comprehensive 8-1 victory over Norway in Imola

UEFA Women's U17 Championship 2010/11

Three old adversaries and a promising newcomer graced the final round of the UEFA European Women's Under-17 Championship in Nyon, Switzerland in late July 2011. Twice-winners Germany were back on the big stage; Spain were looking to pick up their second successive European crown at this level; France – finalists in 2008 and semi-finalists in 2009 - were eager to conquer a first U17 trophy; while Iceland came to the final tournament as first-timers following a splendid qualifying competition. The championship, however, is as much about player development as it is about winning silverware. The job of all four coaches at the tournament - Francisco Rubio (France), Ralf Peter (Germany), Thorlákur Árnason (Iceland) and Jorge Vilda (Spain) - was also to prepare players for future assignments at older age-group and, eventually, senior levels in the years to come. The 2011 tournament duly lived up to its billing as a shop window for some of the most talented youngsters in Europe.

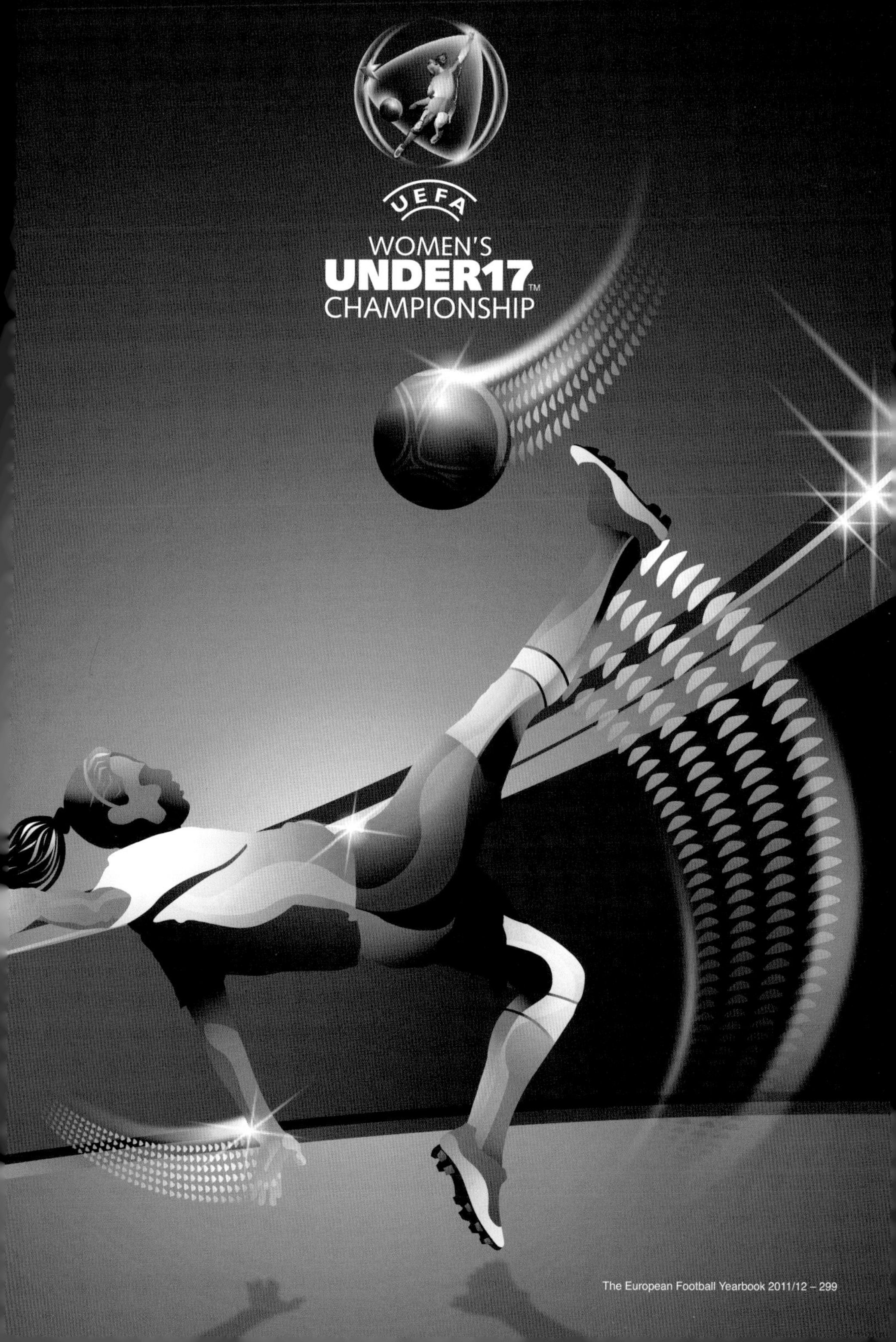
UEFA
WOMEN'S
UNDER17
CHAMPIONSHIP

QUALIFYING ROUNDS

Surprise casualties in the first qualifying round of the 2011 UEFA European Women's Under-17 Championship included 2010 runners-up the Republic of Ireland and semi-finalists the Netherlands, the latter being eliminated in the first qualifying round by holders Spain. Like France and Iceland, Spain then progressed from the second qualifying round with a game to spare. They opened Group 2 with a 2-0 defeat of Belgium and saw off Italy 6-1, rendering a 3-1 loss to the Czech Republic insignificant.

Runners-up in 2008 and third a year later, France returned to the finals from Group 4. Having sneaked through as the fifth-best first qualifying round runners-up, they defeated Scotland 4-1 and home side Switzerland 2-0 to ensure qualification before a 2-0 win against Wales.

Iceland earned a finals debut with six qualifying wins, beating England and Group 1 hosts Poland 2-0 in the second stage before, with the pressure off, they overcame Sweden 4-1. Their star was Aldís Kara Lúdvíksdóttir, who struck a record 11 qualifying goals.

Group 3 proved closer as Germany, awarded a first-round bye, and hosts Denmark both won their opening two games. But Germany, winners in 2008 and 2009 and semi-finalists in 2010, maintained their perfect qualification record with a 3-0 victory in the decider. Germany's earlier 9-0 defeat of Russia was a record scoreline for the second qualifying round.

First Qualifying Round Results

Group 1

25-30/9/10 Jyvaskyla, Vaajakoski
Finland 8-0 Kazakhstan, Norway 3-3 Serbia, Finland 1-0 Serbia, Kazakhstan 0-8 Norway, Norway 0-0 Finland, Serbia 1-1 Kazakhstan

Group 1 Table

	Pld	W	D	L	F	A	Pts
1 Finland	3	2	1	0	9	0	7
2 Norway	3	1	2	0	11	3	5
3 Serbia	3	0	2	1	4	5	2
4 Kazakhstan	3	0	1	2	1	17	1

Group 2

16-21/10/10 Dungannon, Portadown, Belfast, Lurgan
Czech Republic 8-0 FYROM, Republic of Ireland 1-0 Northern Ireland, Czech Republic 3-0 Northern Ireland, FYROM 0-4 Republic of Ireland, Republic of Ireland 0-2 Czech Republic, Northern Ireland 4-0 FYROM

Group 2 Table

	Pld	W	D	L	F	A	Pts
1 Czech Republic	3	3	0	0	13	0	9
2 Republic of Ireland	3	2	0	1	5	2	6
3 Northern Ireland	3	1	0	2	4	4	3
4 FYROM	3	0	0	3	0	16	0

Gudmunda Brynja Oladóttir was on target nine times for first-time qualifiers Iceland

Claire Lavogez scored nine goals to help France reach the finals

Group 3

15-20/10/10 Budapest, Telki
Denmark 6-0 Moldova, Hungary 1-2 Slovenia, Denmark 3-0 Slovenia, Moldova 1-6 Hungary, Hungary 1-2 Denmark, Slovenia 1-0 Moldova

Group 3 Table

	Pld	W	D	L	F	A	Pts
1 Denmark	3	3	0	0	11	1	9
2 Slovenia	3	2	0	1	3	4	6
3 Hungary	3	1	0	2	8	5	3
4 Moldova	3	0	0	3	1	13	0

Group 4

3-8/10/10 Poortugaal
Netherlands 3-0 Belarus, Spain 13-0 Georgia, Spain 2-0 Belarus, Georgia 0-14 Netherlands, Belarus 2-0 Georgia, Netherlands 0-1 Spain

Group 4 Table

	Pld	W	D	L	F	A	Pts
1 Spain	3	3	0	0	16	0	9
2 Netherlands	3	2	0	1	17	1	6
3 Belarus	3	1	0	2	2	5	3
4 Georgia	3	0	0	3	0	29	0

Group 5

20-25/9/10 Teteven, Pravets
Italy 4-0 Bulgaria, Iceland 14-0 Lithuania, Italy 7-0 Lithuania, Bulgaria 0-10 Iceland, Iceland 5-1 Italy, Lithuania 1-0 Bulgaria

Group 5 Table

	Pld	W	D	L	F	A	Pts
1 Iceland	3	3	0	0	29	1	9
2 Italy	3	2	0	1	12	5	6
3 Lithuania	3	1	0	2	1	21	3
4 Bulgaria	3	0	0	3	0	15	0

Group 6

3-8/10/10 Deinze, Aalst, Wetteren

Belgium 7-0 Armenia, England 2-0 Turkey, Armenia 0-7 England, Belgium 3-0 Turkey, Turkey 7-0 Armenia, England 0-0 Belgium

Group 6 Table

	Pld	W	D	L	F	A	Pts
1 Belgium	3	2	1	0	10	0	7
2 England	3	2	1	0	9	0	7
3 Turkey	3	1	0	2	7	5	3
4 Armenia	3	0	0	3	0	21	0

Group 7

6-11/10/10 Lindabrunn, Neulengbach

Scotland 1-0 Romania, Ukraine 0-1 Austria, Romania 2-0 Ukraine, Scotland 3-1 Austria, Ukraine 0-2 Scotland, Austria 0-0 Romania

Group 7 Table

	Pld	W	D	L	F	A	Pts
1 Scotland	3	3	0	0	6	1	9
2 Romania	3	1	1	1	2	1	4
3 Austria	3	1	1	1	2	3	4
4 Ukraine	3	0	0	3	0	5	0

Group 8

5-10/10/10 St-Paul lès Dax, Capbreton

Sweden 3-0 Croatia, France 9-0 Israel, Sweden 2-0 Israel, Croatia 0-4 France, France 2-3 Sweden, Israel 2-2 Croatia

Group 8 Table

	Pld	W	D	L	F	A	Pts
1 Sweden	3	3	0	0	8	2	9
2 France	3	2	0	1	15	3	6
3 Croatia	3	0	1	2	2	9	1
4 Israel	3	0	1	2	2	13	1

Group 9

14-19/10/10 Salaspils, Ogre

Poland 9-0 Estonia, Switzerland 6-0 Latvia, Switzerland 6-0 Estonia, Latvia 0-11 Poland, Poland 0-1 Switzerland, Estonia 5-1 Latvia

Group 9 Table

	Pld	W	D	L	F	A	Pts
1 Switzerland	3	3	0	0	13	0	9
2 Poland	3	2	0	1	20	1	6
3 Estonia	3	1	0	2	5	16	3
4 Latvia	3	0	0	3	1	22	0

Group 10

26/9-1/10/10 Sochi

Wales 4-0 Faroe Islands, Russia 3-2 Greece, Wales 4-1 Greece, Faroe Islands 0-2 Russia, Russia 2-2 Wales, Greece 5-1 Faroe Islands

Group 10 Table

	Pld	W	D	L	F	A	Pts
1 Wales	3	2	1	0	10	3	7
2 Russia	3	2	1	0	7	4	7
3 Greece	3	1	0	2	8	8	3
4 Faroe Islands	3	0	0	3	1	11	0

Second Qualifying Round Results

Group 1

9-14/4/11 Sosnowiec, Jaworzno

Sweden 1-3 Poland, Iceland 2-0 England, Iceland 2-0 Poland, England 1-0 Sweden, Sweden 1-4 Iceland, Poland 2-1 England

Group 1 Table

	Pld	W	D	L	F	A	Pts
1 Iceland	3	3	0	0	8	1	9
2 Poland	3	2	0	1	5	4	6
3 England	3	1	0	2	2	4	3
4 Sweden	3	0	0	3	2	8	0

Group 2

9-14/4/11 Rokycany, Zruč-Senec

Spain 2-0 Belgium, Czech Republic 1-1 Italy, Spain 6-1 Italy, Belgium 1-0 Czech Republic, Czech Republic 3-1 Spain, Italy 0-1 Belgium

Group 2 Table

	Pld	W	D	L	F	A	Pts
1 Spain	3	2	0	1	9	4	6
2 Belgium	3	2	0	1	2	2	6
3 Czech Republic	3	1	1	1	4	3	4
4 Italy	3	0	1	2	2	8	1

Group 3

21-26/4/11 Esbjerg, Varde

Germany 5-0 Finland, Denmark 5-0 Russia, Germany 9-0 Russia, Finland 1-3 Denmark, Denmark 0-3 Germany, Russia 0-2 Finland

Group 3 Table

	Pld	W	D	L	F	A	Pts
1 Germany	3	3	0	0	17	0	9
2 Denmark	3	2	0	1	8	4	6
3 Finland	3	1	0	2	3	8	3
4 Russia	3	0	0	3	0	16	0

Fabienne Dongus was Germany's top scorer in qualifying with seven goals

Group 4

9-14/4/11 Kussnacht, Freienbach, Rapperswil-Jona

Switzerland 1-1 Wales, Scotland 1-4 France, Switzerland 0-2 France, Wales 1-1 Scotland, Scotland 3-0 Switzerland, France 2-0 Wales

Group 4 Table

	Pld	W	D	L	F	A	Pts
1 France	3	3	0	0	8	1	9
2 Scotland	3	1	1	1	5	5	4
3 Wales	3	0	2	1	2	4	2
4 Switzerland	3	0	1	2	1	6	1

TOP GOALSCORERS

(Qualifying Rounds)

11	Aldís Kara Lúdvíksdóttir (Iceland)
10	Hannah Keryakoplis (Wales)
9	Gudmunda Brynja Oladóttir (Iceland) Claire Lavogez (France)
7	Fabienne Dongus (Germany)
6	Lorena Valderas (Spain) Camilla Andersen (Denmark) Eliska Šturmová (Czech Republic) Valentina Giacinti (Italy) Madeleine Stegius (Sweden) Caroline Weir (Scotland)

FINAL TOURNAMENT

SEMI-FINALS

Spain and France emerged victorious from their semi-final encounters at Nyon's Colovray stadium – situated just across the road from UEFA headquarters.

Spain were comfortable 4-0 winners against Iceland. They were never in serious trouble, and the hopeful young Icelanders, in their U17 final-round debut, were unable to carry their free-scoring exploits through to the final stages. Spain, playing their patient possession football and posing a constant threat, dominated from the opening whistle and were ahead on 12 minutes through Marina García. Alexia Putellas swiftly added two more goals before the half-time interval. La Rojita's superiority was underlined in the second half when a Glódís Perla Viggosdóttir own goal made it 4-0.

Cliffhanger

The second semi-final turned out to be a cliffhanger, as old rivals Germany and France battled their way to a 2-2 draw at the end of normal time. Lina Magull fired Germany into an early lead, but goals from Claire Lavogez and Lydia Belkacemi tipped the balance in France's favour after the break. German substitute Annabel Jäger levelled with 12 minutes to go, however, to set up a tense penalty shoot-out. In what was evidently a stressful experience for such young players France held their nerve just a little better, and as the shoot-out score swung to and fro, they finally triumphed 6-5 to reach the final and end Germany's hopes of a third European women's U17 title in four years. It was France's first victory over Germany in the competition in four attempts.

Semi-Final Results

28/7/11, Colovray, Nyon
Iceland 0-4 Spain
Iceland: Ar. Kristinsdóttir, Arnardóttir, Aradóttir, Viggosdóttir, Pedersen, Thrastadróttir, Gardarsdóttir, Lúdvíksdóttir (Jessen 58), Óladóttir (Ellertsdottir 41), Antonsdóttir, Baldursdóttir (Abrahamsdóttir 62). Coach: Thorlákur Árnason (ISL)
Spain: Gil, Ivana (Paula López 72), Laura, Gema (Maestro 66), García, Pinel (Pereira 56), Barea, Putellas, Pomares, Carreño, Mendoza. Coach: Jorge Vilda (ESP)
Goal(s): 0-1 García 12, 0-2 Putellas 34, 0-3 Putellas 36, 0-4 Viggosdóttir 67(og)
Yellow Card(s): Putellas 72 (Spain)
Referee: Ghisletta (SUI)

Spain's Alexia Putellas (left) is pursued by Iceland's Thórbjorg Aradóttir

28/7/11, Colovray, Nyon
Germany 2-2 France
Germany: Abt, Romert , Seifert, Leiding, Bröckl, Magull, Dallmann, Leupolz, Petermann, Däbritz, F. Dongus (Jäger 63). Coach: Ralf Peter (GER)
France: Durand, Huchet, Lorgere (Adram 41), Kerrache, Mbock Bathy Nka, Belkacemi, Declercq, Toletti (Wenger 41), Lavogez, Vaysse, Diani. Coach: Francisco Rubio (FRA)
Goal(s): 1-0 Magull 8, 1-1 Lavogez 49, 1-2 Belkacemi 60, 2-2 Jäger 68
Yellow Card(s): Jäger 76 (Germany)
Referee: Mpoumpouri (GRE)

FINAL/THIRD PLACE PLAY-OFF

Germany were bitterly disappointed to lose their semi-final but coach Ralf Peter set his players a new target of third place and they achieved their objective in some style with a fine display of attacking football that saw Iceland swept aside 8-2.

Hat-tricks from Lina Magull and Annabel Jäger, plus a strike from Sara Däbritz and a Melanie Leupolz free-kick, ensured that Germany maintained their impressive competitive record at this level, having won 26 of their 29 games and lost just two. Replies from Telma Thrastadróttir and substitute Aldís Kara Lúdvíksdóttir gave Iceland some consolation on a difficult afternoon for the final-tournament debutants.

Defences on top

The final promised plenty of riches, with Spain and France vowing to take the game to each other. Both teams remained true to their word, but two stern defences ensured a stalemate for most of the match. Chances were at a premium in the first half, although Spain did the lion's share of the attacking and had the majority of possession.

The pattern of play did not alter much in the second half. Spain had most of the ball, but France held them at bay and counter-attacked strongly. The exchanges were tight and closely-fought, and it seemed inevitable that the match would go to a penalty shoot-out as goalscoring opportunities became increasingly rare. But in added time, with Swiss referee Simona Ghisletta looking at her watch, Spain winger Alba Pomares found herself free in the penalty area. She looked up, let fly, and her dipping shot evaded goalkeeper Solène Durand, struck the crossbar and bounced down into the net to give Spain victory right at the death and their second successive women's U17 crown.

Third Place Play-off Result

31/7/11, Colovray, Nyon
Iceland 2-8 Germany
Iceland: Omarsdottir, Jessen (Gardarsdóttir 46), Arnardóttir (Baldursdóttir 41), Aradóttir, Viggosdóttir, Pedersen, Thrastadróttir, Óladóttir, Antonsdóttir, Ólafsdóttir, Abrahamsdóttir (Lúdvíksdóttir 56). Coach: Thorlákur Árnason (ISL)
Germany: Abt (Kämper 41), Seifert, Leiding (Schedel 57), Bröckl, Magull, Dallmann, Leupolz, Petermann, Däbritz (Barth 57), F. Dongus, Jäger. Coach: Ralf Peter (GER)
Goal(s): 0-1 Däbritz 12, 0-2 Magull 14, 0-3 Jäger 26, 0-4 Jäger 38, 0-5 Magull 40+1, 0-6 Magull 47(p), 1-6 Thrastadróttir 48, 1-7 Jäger 67, 1-8 Leupolz 68, 2-8 Lúdvíksdóttir 80
Yellow Card(s): Leupolz 46 (Germany), Petermann 57 (Germany), Magull 80+4 (Germany)
Referee: Mpoumpouri (GRE)

Final Result

31/7/11, Colovray, Nyon
Spain 1-0 France
Attendance: 1500
Spain: Gil, Ivana, Laura, Gema, García, Pinel (Pereira 76), Barea (Ortiz 56), Putellas, Pomares, Carreño (Jiménez 40+1), Mendoza. Coach: Jorge Vilda (ESP)
France: Durand, Huchet, Kerrache, Mbock Bathy Nka, Belkacemi, Declercq, Toletti, Wenger (Le Bihan 79), Lavogez, Vaysse, Diani (Hurez 36; Lorgere 55). Coach: Francisco Rubio (FRA)
Goal(s): 1-0 Pomares 80+2
Referee: Ghisletta (SUI)

TOP GOALSCORERS
(Final Tournament)

4	Annabel Jäger (Germany)
	Lina Magull (Germany)
2	Alexia Putellas (Spain)

Annabel Jäger

Lina Magull

Spain's triumphant players pose with the UEFA Women's Under-17 Championship trophy

13

UEFA Futsal EURO 2012

While holders Spain, former champions Italy and Russia, and past runners-up Portugal and Ukraine all successfully negotiated UEFA Futsal EURO 2012 qualifying, Turkey sprang a surprise by progressing from the preliminary round all the way through to the final tournament in Croatia. They only just made it over the first hurdle, having lost their second preliminary-round fixture to newcomers Switzerland, but they eventually progressed to the next stage alongside Latvia, the Former Yugoslav Republic of Macedonia (FYROM), France, Finland and debutants Norway. Of these, however, only Turkey went on to reach the finals – as one of the five best qualifying round runners-up that accompanied the six group winners. For the draw in Zagreb, on 9 September 2011, hosts Croatia are joined in Pot 1 by Spain, Portugal and Italy. Russia, the Czech Republic, Ukraine and Serbia make up Pot 2, while Turkey are grouped with Azerbaijan, Romania and Slovenia in Pot 3. There will be four groups of three, from which the top two teams enter the knockout phase.

PRELIMINARY ROUND

GROUP A

21-24/1/11 Izmir

Moldova 4-3 Switzerland
Turkey 5-1 Montenegro
Montenegro 3-2 Moldova
Turkey 2-3 Switzerland
Switzerland 2-5 Montenegro
Moldova 2-4 Turkey

Group A Table

	Pld	W	D	L	F	A	Pts
1 Turkey	3	2	0	1	11	6	6
2 Montenegro	3	2	0	1	9	9	6
3 Moldova	3	1	0	2	8	10	3
4 Switzerland	3	1	0	2	8	11	3

GROUP C

21-24/1/11 Skopje

Georgia 8-0 Estonia
FYROM 3-1 England
England 0-4 Georgia
FYROM 6-2 Estonia
Estonia 2-3 England
Georgia 1-2 FYROM

Group C Table

	Pld	W	D	L	F	A	Pts
1 FYROM	3	3	0	0	11	4	9
2 Georgia	3	2	0	1	13	2	6
3 England	3	1	0	2	4	9	3
4 Estonia	3	0	0	3	4	17	0

GROUP E

20-23/1/11 Tampere

Cyprus 5-2 San Marino
Finland 9-0 Albania
Finland 7-0 San Marino
Albania 7-6 Cyprus
San Marino 2-4 Albania
Cyprus 2-2 Finland

Group E Table

	Pld	W	D	L	F	A	Pts
1 Finland	3	2	1	0	18	2	7
2 Albania	3	2	0	1	11	17	6
3 Cyprus	3	1	1	1	13	11	4
4 San Marino	3	0	0	3	4	16	0

GROUP B

21-24/1/11 Hafnarfjördur

Greece 2-2 Armenia
Iceland 4-5 Latvia
Latvia 4-0 Greece
Iceland 6-1 Armenia
Armenia 1-2 Latvia
Greece 4-5 Iceland

Group B Table

	Pld	W	D	L	F	A	Pts
1 Latvia	3	3	0	0	11	5	9
2 Iceland	3	2	0	1	15	10	6
3 Greece	3	0	1	2	6	11	1
4 Armenia	3	0	1	2	4	10	1

GROUP D

21-24/1/11 Cospicua

Lithuania 3-6 Bulgaria
Malta 1-6 France
France 3-1 Lithuania
Malta 0-7 Bulgaria
Bulgaria 1-2 France
Lithuania 5-1 Malta

Group D Table

	Pld	W	D	L	F	A	Pts
1 France	3	3	0	0	11	3	9
2 Bulgaria	3	2	0	1	14	5	6
3 Lithuania	3	1	0	2	9	10	3
4 Malta	3	0	0	3	2	18	0

GROUP F

20-23/1/11 Dublin

Israel 3-7 Norway
Republic of Ireland 1-2 Andorra
Andorra 4-1 Israel
Republic of Ireland 0-5 Norway
Norway 7-3 Andorra
Israel 3-0 Republic of Ireland

Group F Table

	Pld	W	D	L	F	A	Pts
1 Norway	3	3	0	0	19	6	9
2 Andorra	3	2	0	1	9	9	6
3 Israel	3	1	0	2	7	11	3
4 Republic of Ireland	3	0	0	3	1	10	0

QUALIFYING ROUND

GROUP 1

Kazakhstan and France faced a tough draw against Spain – bidding to win a fourth straight European title – and hosts Azerbaijan, who reached the semis on their 2010 finals debut.

In the circumstances their opening results were respectable, France losing 4-0 to Spain and Kazakhstan going down 6-3 to Azerbaijan, for whom Serjão, Felipe and Biro Jade reprised their form of the 2010 tournament, contributing two goals apiece.

Azerbaijan's Serjão – the leading scorer in the qualifying round with five goals

A day later matters were settled. Spain raced to a 5-0 win against Kazakhstan, and Azerbaijan defeated France 4-2. Results elsewhere meant that whatever happened in the group decider, either Spain or Azerbaijan would at least progress as a best runner-up. Second place is anathema to Spain, though, and they hammered Azerbaijan 8-3 to complete an impressive campaign without the injured Kike or retired duo, Javi Rodríguez and Daniel. Serjão's two consolation goals for Azerbaijan took his tally to five – the best of the round.

Pula celebrates a goal for Group 2 winners Russia

24-27/2/11 Baku
Spain 4-0 France
Azerbaijan 6-3 Kazakhstan
Kazakhstan 0-5 Spain
Azerbaijan 4-2 France
France 0-2 Kazakhstan
Spain 8-3 Azerbaijan

Group 1 Table

	Pld	W	D	L	F	A	Pts
1 Spain	3	3	0	0	17	3	9
2 Azerbaijan	3	2	0	1	13	13	6
3 Kazakhstan	3	1	0	2	5	11	3
4 France	3	0	0	3	2	10	0

GROUP 2

The Netherlands had high hopes of qualifying for the first time since 2005 on home territory in Rotterdam.

With Russia favourites, the opener between the Oranje and Serbia had a decisive look. Russia duly began with a comfortable 5-1 victory over Finland while the other game more than lived up to expectations. Zaid El Morabiti scored for the Netherlands after 22 seconds and it was soon 2-0, but Serbia pulled one back before the break and equalised on 34 minutes. Vladan Cvetanović then missed a Serbia penalty and just 34 seconds remained when Mohammed Attaibi put the Dutch back ahead – only for Cvetanović to atone for his earlier faux pas and make it 3-3 immediately afterwards.

A 5-2 win against Finland put the Netherlands second as Russia beat Serbia 3-0 to qualify. On the final day Serbia defeated Finland 6-0, which left the Dutch having to deny Russia a third win. However, they lost, 2-0, and Serbia were through to their third straight finals.

24-27/2/11 Rotterdam
Russia 5-1 Finland
Netherlands 3-3 Serbia
Serbia 0-3 Russia
Netherlands 5-2 Finland
Finland 0-6 Serbia
Russia 2-0 Netherlands

Group 2 Table

	Pld	W	D	L	F	A	Pts
1 Russia	3	3	0	0	10	1	9
2 Serbia	3	1	1	1	9	6	4
3 Netherlands	3	1	1	1	8	7	4
4 Finland	3	0	0	3	3	16	0

GROUP 3

Portugal reached the final for the first time in 2010 to cap Orlando Duarte's decade in charge.

But new coach Jorge Braz's debut was a difficult one as his team struggled to defeat FYROM 3-1. Hosts Poland scored twice in the last three minutes to draw 2-2 with a Belarus side aiming to emulate their maiden qualification the previous year.

In those finals, Belarus had played out a thrilling 5-5 draw with Portugal. However, this time their opponents won easily, 5-1. Poland then got a taste of their own medicine, racing two up against FYROM only to be pegged back to 2-2 with 89 seconds left. Belarus secured a 2-1 win against FYROM on the final day and were then

Cardinal sends Portugal on the way to a 5-1 win over Belarus

confirmed in second place as Portugal routed Poland 6-0 to finish five points clear. Results in the other groups, however, meant that Belarus were the sole runners-up to miss out on the finals – by virtue of an inferior goal difference to that of Serbia.

24-27/2/11 Bielsko Biala
Portugal 3-1 FYROM
Poland 2-2 Belarus
Belarus 1-5 Portugal
Poland 2-2 FYROM
FYROM 1-2 Belarus
Portugal 6-0 Poland

Group 3 Table

	Pld	W	D	L	F	A	Pts
1 Portugal	3	3	0	0	14	2	9
2 Belarus	3	1	1	1	5	8	4
3 Poland	3	0	2	1	4	10	2
4 FYROM	3	0	1	2	4	7	1

David Fric helped the Czech Republic to qualify from Group 4

GROUP 4

Group 4 looked to be the most competitive section, and so it proved.

Norway may have lacked the experience of their opponents but their dashing style under journalist-turned-coach Esten Sæther had impressed in the preliminary round, and they scored first against 2010 bronze medalists the Czech Republic before falling to a narrow 4-3 defeat. The second game was even more thrilling, hosts Romania staging a remarkable recovery from 5-1 down at the break to draw level against Slovakia, who then snatched a win with Anton Brunovský's face-saving 39th-minute goal.

The next day the Czech Republic beat Slovakia 5-3, while Romania defeated Norway 3-1. That set up an enthralling final day and in the early game Slovakia gave themselves hope of a first qualification by overcoming Norway 4-0. However, when Romania took a 27th-minute lead against the Czech Republic through Cosmin Gherman, both teams knew the scoreline would guarantee their joint qualification at Slovakia's expense – and that was how it ended.

24-27/2/11 Targu-Mures
Czech Republic 4-3 Norway
Romania 5-6 Slovakia
Slovakia 3-5 Czech Republic
Romania 3-1 Norway
Norway 0-4 Slovakia
Czech Republic 0-1 Romania

Group 4 Table

	Pld	W	D	L	F	A	Pts
1 Czech Republic	3	2	0	1	9	7	6
2 Romania	3	2	0	1	9	7	6
3 Slovakia	3	2	0	1	13	10	6
4 Norway	3	0	0	3	4	11	0

Serhiy Cheporniuk of Group 5 winners Ukraine

GROUP 5

This section contained three 2010 finalists – Ukraine, Hungary and Belgium – but, surprisingly, only one would make it through to the 2012 edition.

Coached by former Fenerbahçe SK striker Ömer Kaner, Turkey managed just one preliminary round point in the previous tournament, yet this time they not only made it through that stage but opened the qualifying round by surprising 2010 finals hosts Hungary 3-2, having trailed 2-0 at half-time.

The opening fixture in Kharkiv was also close, Ukraine leading Belgium by four goals at the break before holding on to win 4-3. That proved an unlucky scoreline for Belgium, who lost by the same margin against Hungary, Tamás Nagy scoring the winner with two seconds left. Ukraine, meanwhile, romped to a 12-2 win against Turkey – the biggest victory margin of the entire competition. To their credit, though, Turkey recovered to beat Belgium 3-2, twice conceding equalisers, one in the last minute, before Cihan Özcan completed a momentous hat-trick ten seconds from time. Now Turkey needed Ukraine to avoid defeat against Hungary; they duly won 4-1.

24-27/2/11 Kharkiv
Ukraine 4-3 Belgium
Hungary 2-3 Turkey
Belgium 3-4 Hungary
Ukraine 12-2 Turkey
Turkey 3-2 Belgium
Hungary 1-4 Ukraine
Spain 8-3 Azerbaijan

Group 5 Table

	Pld	W	D	L	F	A	Pts
1 Ukraine	3	3	0	0	20	6	9
2 Turkey	3	2	0	1	8	16	6
3 Hungary	3	1	0	2	7	10	3
4 Belgium	3	0	0	3	8	11	0

GROUP 6

The tight drama of the other pools was generally absent from Group 6.

Italy saw off Latvia 6-1 in their opening fixture, while hosts Slovenia defeated Bosnia & Herzegovina 5-1. A day later Italy scored four without reply against Bosnia & Herzegovina, which meant that a Slovenia victory against Latvia would ensure qualification for the top two with a game to spare.

Benjamin Melink sealed Slovenia's qualification with the winning goal against Latvia

In the first five minutes, though, Slovenia had conceded two own goals, either side of a Rok Mordej strike that had briefly levelled matters. Maksims Seņs then made it 3-1 to Latvia but Damir Pertič, the man responsible for the second own goal, pulled one back before the break, and in the second half Gašper Vrhovec and Benjamin Melink were on target within a minute of each other to give Slovenia a 4-3 win and a second straight qualification. Italy, quarter-finalists in 2010, took first place ahead of Slovenia by winning the group decider 2-0.

24-27/2/11 Lasko
Italy 6-1 Latvia
Slovenia 5-1 Bosnia & Herzegovina
Bosnia & Herzegovina 0-4 Italy
Slovenia 4-3 Latvia
Latvia 2-3 Bosnia & Herzegovina
Italy 2-0 Slovenia

Group 6 Table

	Pld	W	D	L	F	A	Pts
1 Italy	3	3	0	0	12	1	9
2 Slovenia	3	2	0	1	9	6	6
3 Bosnia & Herzegovina	3	1	0	2	4	11	3
4 Latvia	3	0	0	3	6	13	0

UEFA Futsal Cup 2010/11

ASD Città di Montesilvano C/5 proved themselves a novelty act of stellar dimensions at the 2010/11 UEFA Futsal Cup finals in Kazakhstan. Not content with marking their debut season in the competition by securing a place among Europe's top four clubs, the Italian title holders went on to become European champions. The team from the Adriatic coast saw off holders SL Benfica with surprising comfort in the semi-finals before repeating that ultra-efficient show against the outgoing champions' Lisbon neighbours Sporting Clube de Portugal in the title decider. For Benfica, there was not even a bronze medal to take home with them as they succumbed to tournament hosts Kairat Almaty in the third-place play-off. Playing at the 5,000-capacity Baluan Sholak Sport Palace in Almaty, Kairat seemed to specialise in thrillers. Having lost a close semi-final to Sporting, they rallied to defeat Benfica on penalties in a riveting consolation match.

UEFA
FUTSAL
CUP®
Città di Montesilvano
Calcio a 5
1984
SCP
SPORTING
PORTUGAL
KAIRAT
AFC
Alma-Ata Futsal Club 1995
SLB

QUALIFYING

Only one team made it through the elite round of the 2010/11 UEFA Futsal Cup without dropping a point – holders SL Benfica. They edged out Croatia's MNK Nacional Zagreb 1-0 and Ukraine's FC Time Lviv 2-1 – with Pedro Costa scoring the winner three seconds from the end – before overcoming Serbian Group 1 hosts KMF Ekonomac Kragujevac 5-2.

As one of the top four seeds Benfica were excused the main round, but of the other three only Kairat Almaty accompanied them through. Staging Group 3, they opened with a 5-0 defeat of Poland's Akademia FC Pniewy before seeing off Slov-Matic Bratislava 3-1. However, they still needed a point against the sole competition ever-presents, Iberia Star Tbilisi, who led at half-time after Betinho and Roninho had scored to eclipse Dinmukhambet Suleimenov's opener. On 29 minutes, however, Leo's penalty earned Kairat a 2-2 draw.

Preliminary round Group B action between ZC Excess Futsal and KF Tirana in Malta

For the first time, Spain were not represented in the finals. Murcia FS led Group D in Lisbon after two wins, which left them needing a draw against hosts Sporting Clube de Portugal. It turned out to be a thriller, with Murcia leading early on, falling behind and equalising twice before Alex scored with 44 seconds left to seal Sporting's 5-3 victory.

Group B also produced drama as 2009 champions MFK Sinara Ekaterinburg welcomed to Russia 2010 bronze-medallists Araz Naxçivan, Italian debutants ASD Città Di Montesilvano C/5 and sole preliminary round survivors AGBU Ararat Nicosia FC. Montesilvano's opening 2-1 defeat of Ekaterinburg proved decisive as they then held Araz 2-2 and beat AGBU Ararat 10-0 to finish a point clear of the Russian side, whose two subsequent victories counted for nought.

Preliminary Round Results

Group A

16-18/8/10 Kaunas

FK Nautara Kaunas 3-5 Sporting Fingal SC, Sporting Fingal SC 7-3 FC Kaghsi Yerevan, FC Kaghsi Yerevan 2-1 FK Nautara Kaunas

Group A Table

	Pld	W	D	L	F	A	Pts
1 Sporting Fingal SC	2	2	0	0	12	6	6
2 FC Kaghsi Yerevan	2	1	0	1	5	8	3
3 FK Nautara Kaunas	2	0	0	2	4	7	0

Group B

16-19/8/10 Cospicua

FS Ilves Tampere 3-1 KF Tirana, ZC Excess Futsal 2-5 BGA Futsal, BGA Futsal 1-2 FS Ilves Tampere, ZC Excess Futsal 4-2 KF Tirana, KF Tirana 4-5 BGA Futsal, FS Ilves Tampere 5-5 ZC Excess Futsal

Group B Table

	Pld	W	D	L	F	A	Pts
1 FS Ilves Tampere	3	2	1	0	10	7	7
2 BGA Futsal	3	2	0	1	11	8	6
3 ZC Excess Futsal	3	1	1	1	11	12	4
4 KF Tirana	3	0	0	3	7	12	0

Group C

14-17/8/10 Vienna

SC Tornado Chisinau 5-0 Perth Saltires, Stella Rossa Wien 3-8 MNK Orlić Sarajevo, MNK Orlić Sarajevo 7-4 SC Tornado Chisinau, Stella Rossa Wien 2-2 Perth Saltires, Perth Saltires 1-11 MNK Orlić Sarajevo, SC Tornado Chisinau 7-6 Stella Rossa Wien

Group C Table

	Pld	W	D	L	F	A	Pts
1 MNK Orlić Sarajevo	3	3	0	0	26	8	9
2 SC Tornado Chisinau	3	2	0	1	16	13	6
3 Stella Rossa Wien	3	0	1	2	11	17	1
4 Perth Saltires	3	0	1	2	3	18	1

Group D

18-21/8/10 Nicosia

FC Levski Sofia West 3-3 FC Anzhi Tallinn, AGBU Ararat Nicosia FC 3-1 SD Croatia Berlin, SD Croatia Berlin 6-4 FC Levski Sofia West, AGBU Ararat Nicosia FC 6-2 FC Anzhi Tallinn, FC Anzhi Tallinn 3-7 SD Croatia Berlin, FC Levski Sofia West 4-0 AGBU Ararat Nicosia FC

Group D Table

	Pld	W	D	L	F	A	Pts
1 AGBU Ararat Nicosia FC	3	2	0	1	9	7	6
2 SD Croatia Berlin	3	2	0	1	14	10	6
3 FC Levski Sofia West	3	1	1	1	11	9	4
4 FC Anzhi Tallinn	3	0	1	2	8	16	1

Group E

19-22/8/10 Skopje

KMF Danilovgrad 3-7 KFUM Futsal Oslo, KMF Zelezarec Skopje 13-5 Istanbul Üniversitesi SK, Istanbul Üniversitesi SK 3-8 KMF Danilovgrad, KMF Zelezarec Skopje 1-1 KFUM Futsal Oslo, KFUM Futsal Oslo 7-3 Istanbul Üniversitesi SK, KMF Danilovgrad 1-3 KMF Zelezarec Skopje

Group E Table

	Pld	W	D	L	F	A	Pts
1 KMF Zelezarec Skopje	3	2	1	0	17	7	7
2 KFUM Futsal Oslo	3	2	1	0	15	7	7
3 KMF Danilovgrad	3	1	0	2	12	13	3
4 Istanbul Üniversitesi SK	3	0	0	3	11	28	0

Group F

16-19/8/10 Gyor

Helvécia Futsal London 4-2 FC Encamp, Győri ETO FC 6-3 MNK Croatia 97 Appenzell, MNK Croatia 97 Appenzell 2-3 Helvécia Futsal London, Győri ETO FC 10-0 FC Encamp, FC Encamp 4-12 MNK Croatia 97 Appenzell, Helvécia Futsal London 2-7 Győri ETO FC

Group F Table

	Pld	W	D	L	F	A	Pts
1 Győri ETO FC	3	3	0	0	23	5	9
2 Helvécia Futsal London	3	2	0	1	9	11	6
3 MNK Croatia 97 Appenzell	3	1	0	2	17	13	3
4 FC Encamp	3	0	0	3	6	26	0

Group G

14-17/8/10 Hafnarfjordur

Club Futsal Eindhoven 3-3 Kremlin Bicêtre United, FC Keflavík 10-6 Vimmerby IF, Vimmerby IF 1-12 Club Futsal Eindhoven, FC Keflavík 5-17 Kremlin Bicêtre United, Kremlin Bicêtre United 18-2 Vimmerby IF, Club Futsal Eindhoven 16-5 FC Keflavík

Group G Table

	Pld	W	D	L	F	A	Pts
1 Kremlin Bicêtre United	3	2	1	0	38	10	7
2 Club Futsal Eindhoven	3	2	1	0	31	9	7
3 FC Keflavík	3	1	0	2	20	39	3
4 Vimmerby IF	3	0	0	3	9	40	0

Main Round Results

Group 1

27-30/9/10 Bratislava

Sporting Clube de Portugal 5-1 KMF Zelezarec Skopje, Slov-Matic Bratislava 2-1 FC Kobarid, FC Kobarid 1-2 Sporting Clube de Portugal, Slov-Matic Bratislava 4-1 KMF Zelezarec Skopje, Sporting Clube de Portugal 2-1 Slov-Matic Bratislava, KMF Zelezarec Skopje 3-5 FC Kobarid

Group 1 Table

	Pld	W	D	L	F	A	Pts
1 Sporting Clube de Portugal	3	3	0	0	9	3	9
2 Slov-Matic Bratislava	3	2	0	1	7	4	6
3 FC Kobarid	3	1	0	2	7	7	3
4 KMF Zelezarec Skopje	3	0	0	3	5	14	0

BGA Futsal take on Ilves Tampere in the preliminary round

Group 2

30/9-3/10/10 Lviv

Athina '90 Athens 3-4 MNK Orlić Sarajevo, FC Time Lviv 5-1 AGBU Ararat Nicosia FC, AGBU Ararat Nicosia FC 2-2 Athina '90 Athens, FC Time Lviv 2-1 MNK Orlić Sarajevo, MNK Orlić Sarajevo 2-4 AGBU Ararat Nicosia FC, Athina '90 Athens 3-9 FC Time Lviv

Group 2 Table

	Pld	W	D	L	F	A	Pts
1 FC Time Lviv	3	3	0	0	16	5	9
2 AGBU Ararat Nicosia FC	3	1	1	1	7	9	4
3 MNK Orlić Sarajevo	3	1	0	2	7	9	3
4 Athina '90 Athens	3	0	1	2	8	15	1

Group 3

28/9-1/10/10 Tirgu Mures

Araz Naxçivan 7-4 Sporting Fingal SC, City'US Târgu Mureş 7-1 FK Nikars Riga, FK Nikars Riga 2-7 Araz Naxçivan, City'US Târgu Mureş 8-2 Sporting Fingal SC, Sporting Fingal SC 1-4 FK Nikars Riga, Araz Naxçivan 3-1 City'US Târgu Mureş

Group 3 Table

	Pld	W	D	L	F	A	Pts
1 Araz Naxçivan	3	3	0	0	17	7	9
2 City'US Târgu Mureş	3	2	0	1	16	6	6
3 FK Nikars Riga	3	1	0	2	7	15	3
4 Sporting Fingal SC	3	0	0	3	7	19	0

Group 4

27-30/9/10 Chrudim

Iberia Star Tbilisi 5-5 Győri ETO FC, FK EP Chrudim 6-2 FC Mapid Minsk, FC Mapid Minsk 4-6 Iberia Star Tbilisi, FK EP Chrudim 5-3 Győri ETO FC, Győri ETO FC 1-3 FC Mapid Minsk, Iberia Star Tbilisi 5-0 FK EP Chrudim

Group 4 Table

	Pld	W	D	L	F	A	Pts
1 Iberia Star Tbilisi	3	2	1	0	16	9	7
2 FK EP Chrudim	3	2	0	1	11	10	6
3 FC Mapid Minsk	3	1	0	2	9	13	3
4 Győri ETO FC	3	0	1	2	9	13	1

Group 5

29/9-2/10/10 Montesilvano

MNK Nacional Zagreb 7-1 FS Ilves Tampere, ASD Città Di Montesilvano C/5 6-1 ASA Tel Aviv, ASA Tel Aviv 2-2 MNK Nacional Zagreb, ASD Città Di Montesilvano C/5 6-1 FS Ilves Tampere, FS Ilves Tampere 3-7 ASA Tel Aviv, MNK Nacional Zagreb 1-2 ASD Città Di Montesilvano C/5

Group 5 Table

	Pld	W	D	L	F	A	Pts
1 ASD Città Di Montesilvano C/5	3	3	0	0	14	3	9
2 MNK Nacional Zagreb	3	1	1	1	10	5	4
3 ASA Tel Aviv	3	1	1	1	10	11	4
4 FS Ilves Tampere	3	0	0	3	5	20	0

Group 6

28/9-1/10/10 Kragujevac

KMF Ekonomac Kragujevac 3-1 Akademia FC Pniewy, Action 21 Charleroi 9-0 Kremlin Bicêtre United, Akademia FC Pniewy 6-2 Action 21 Charleroi, KMF Ekonomac Kragujevac 7-1 Kremlin Bicêtre United, Kremlin Bicêtre United 0-4 Akademia FC Pniewy, Action 21 Charleroi 2-3 KMF Ekonomac Kragujevac

Group 6 Table

	Pld	W	D	L	F	A	Pts
1 KMF Ekonomac Kragujevac	3	3	0	0	13	4	9
2 Akademia FC Pniewy	3	2	0	1	11	5	6
3 Action 21 Charleroi	3	1	0	2	13	9	3
4 Kremlin Bicêtre United	3	0	0	3	1	20	0

Elite Round Results

Group A

25-28/11/10 Kragujevac
KMF Ekonomac Kragujevac 7-1 FC Time Lviv, SL Benfica 1-0 MNK Nacional Zagreb, KMF Ekonomac Kragujevac 4-1 MNK Nacional Zagreb, FC Time Lviv 1-2 SL Benfica, MNK Nacional Zagreb 1-4 FC Time Lviv, SL Benfica 5-2 KMF Ekonomac Kragujevac

Group A Table

	Pld	W	D	L	F	A	Pts
1 SL Benfica	3	3	0	0	8	3	9
2 KMF Ekonomac Kragujevac	3	2	0	1	13	7	6
3 FC Time Lviv	3	1	0	2	6	10	3
4 MNK Nacional Zagreb	3	0	0	3	2	9	0

Group B

22-25/11/10 Ekaterinburg
Araz Naxçivan 2-1 AGBU Ararat Nicosia FC, MFK Sinara Ekaterinburg 1-2 ASD Città Di Montesilvano C/5, ASD Città Di Montesilvano C/5 2-2 Araz Naxçivan, MFK Sinara Ekaterinburg 12-1 AGBU Ararat Nicosia FC, AGBU Ararat Nicosia FC 0-10 ASD Città Di Montesilvano C/5, Araz Naxçivan 2-3 MFK Sinara Ekaterinburg

Group B Table

	Pld	W	D	L	F	A	Pts
1 ASD Città Di Montesilvano C/5	3	2	1	0	14	3	7
2 MFK Sinara Ekaterinburg	3	2	0	1	16	5	6
3 Araz Naxçivan	3	1	1	1	6	6	4
4 AGBU Ararat Nicosia FC	3	0	0	3	2	24	0

Group C

20-23/11/10 Almaty
Iberia Star Tbilisi 3-1 Slov-Matic Bratislava, Kairat Almaty 5-0 Akademia FC Pniewy, Akademia FC Pniewy 5-0 Iberia Star Tbilisi, Kairat Almaty 3-1 Slov-Matic Bratislava, Slov-Matic Bratislava 3-0 Akademia FC Pniewy, Iberia Star Tbilisi 2-2 Kairat Almaty

Group C Table

	Pld	W	D	L	F	A	Pts
1 Kairat Almaty	3	2	1	0	10	3	7
2 Iberia Star Tbilisi	3	1	1	1	5	8	4
3 Slov-Matic Bratislava	3	1	0	2	5	6	3
4 Akademia FC Pniewy	3	1	0	2	5	8	3

Group D

25-28/11/10 Odivelas
Murcia FS 6-0 City'US Târgu Mureş, Sporting Clube de Portugal 4-4 FK EP Chrudim, FK EP Chrudim 1-3 Murcia FS, Sporting Clube de Portugal 4-1 City'US Târgu Mureş, Murcia FS 3-5 Sporting Clube de Portugal, City'US Târgu Mureş 5-7 FK EP Chrudim

Group D Table

	Pld	W	D	L	F	A	Pts
1 Sporting Clube de Portugal	3	2	1	0	13	8	7
2 Murcia FS	3	2	0	1	12	6	6
3 FK EP Chrudim	3	1	1	1	12	12	4
4 City'US Târgu Mureş	3	0	0	3	6	17	0

SEMI-FINALS

The Alatau mountain range that provides an imposing backdrop to Almaty was not the only impressive spectacle to take in from Kazakhstan's largest city in the spring of 2011. Not with the UEFA Futsal Cup in town.

Sporting's Caio Japa scored twice in the 3-2 semi-final win over tournament hosts Kairat Almaty

Elite quartet

A field of 48 clubs had been reduced, over three rounds of qualifying competition (preliminary, main and elite), to a select band of four. This quartet jostled for position at the Baluan Sholak Sport Palace during the semi-finals on Friday 29 April and the final and third-place match on Sunday 1 May.

The action began with an exciting encounter between tournament hosts Kairat Almaty and Sporting Clube de Portugal, both of whom were attempting to better previous competition bests of third place. The Portuguese team won 3-2 with second-half strikes from Divanei and Caio Japa (two) after a tight contest developed into an epic one. Orlando Duarte's Sporting survived a brave Kairat comeback from two goals down to reach their first final, but frustratingly for João Carlos Barbosa's Kazakh champions – who had restored hope with Leo Santana's late double – this was a fourth semi-final defeat.

New horizons

Next up were holders SL Benfica against ASD Città di Montesilvano C/5. Benfica had stolen the limelight in Lisbon 12 months before, but for Italy's UEFA Futsal Cup debutants Montesilvano, a new horizon beckoned in this most eastern of UEFA tournaments. Fulvio Colini's men underlined their status as the surprise package of the campaign by ending the European champions' reign. Leandro Cuzzolino's goal gave the Italian champions a precious lead that they refused to surrender in the face of sustained pressure. Cristian Borruto and goalkeeper Stefano Mammarella rubber-stamped the 3-0 victory late on as Paulo Fernandes's Benfica were denied an all-Portuguese final against neighbours Sporting.

Arnaldo Pereira of outgoing champions Benfica

Semi-Final Results

29/4/11, Baluan Sholak Sport Palace, Almaty
Sporting Clube de Portugal 3-2 Kairat Almaty
Sporting: João Benedito, Cristiano, Leitão, Pedro Cary, João Matos, Déo, Marcelo Silva, Jorge Fernandes, Divanei, Caio Japa, Alex, Mário Freitas. Coach: Orlando Duarte (POR)
Kairat: Khalyavin, Jeronimo, Anderson, Giva, Kelson, Katata, Leo Santana, Zhamankulov, Suleimenov, Leo, Felipe, Silva. Coach: João Carlos Barbosa (BRA)
Goal(s): 1-0 Divanei 24, 2-0 Caio Japa 27, 2-1 Leo Santana 34, 2-2 Leo Santana 36, 3-2 Caio Japa 36

29/4/11, Baluan Sholak Sport Palace, Almaty
SL Benfica 0-3 ASD Città di Montesilvano C/5
Benfica: Bébé, Vítor Hugo, Joel Queirós, Arnaldo Pereira, Gonçalo, Davi, Pedro Costa, Diece, Marinho, Anilton, César Paulo, Sol. Coach: Paulo Fernandes (POR)
Montesilvano: Mammarella, Dell'Oso, Forte, Ghiotti, Da Silva, Cuzzolino, Caputo, Baptistella, Garcias, Borruto, Calderolli, Foglia. Coach: Fulvio Colini (ITA)
Goal(s): 0-1 Cuzzolino 22, 0-2 Borruto 34, 0-3 Mammarella 35
Yellow Card(s): Da Silva 1 (Montesilvano), Cuzzolino 16 (Montesilvano), César Paulo 25 (Benfica), Diece 35 (Benfica)

FINAL

Leandro Cuzzolino puts Montesilvano 5-0 up against Sporting in the final

Now a city of roughly two million people, Almaty had developed as a trading post on the Silk Road to and from China, and the prize commodity available in the Sunday final was a trophy enjoying its tenth anniversary. To some surprise, ASD Città di Montesilvano C/5 became the new name on the UEFA Futsal Cup after seeing off fellow first-time finalists Sporting Clube de Portugal 5-2.

Ruthless display

Fulvio Colini's men turned their weapons of dogged defending and clinical finishing on to a second Lisbon outfit in three days. The team in red delivered a lethal dose to the opposition in a ruthless first-half display capped by goals from Hernan Garcias, Adriano Foglia (two) and Fabricio Calderolli. When Leandro Cuzzolino slotted a fifth midway through the second 20-minute period, the contest was over, leaving Leitão's late double for Sporting with only damage-limitation value.

Montesilvano thus became the sixth club to lift the trophy in what was the competition's tenth final – and in the process put Italian futsal in the company of previous winning nations Spain, Belgium, Russia and Portugal. Not untypically, coach Colini downplayed the tactical achievement of outwitting first Benfica and then Sporting, merely attributing Italy's first UEFA Futsal Cup triumph to his side's "great strength in our heads, heart and legs". He added: "Winning a championship by three goals, arguably against the favourites, is a great achievement."

Kairat consolation

Nor was the bronze medal to be undervalued in the third-place play-off. Kairat Almaty claimed the consolation prize with a 5-3 penalty shoot-out win after a pulsating 3-3 draw with SL Benfica. The home side were pushed all the way, however, after the first-half advantage given to them by Leo Santana and Sidnei Silva was overturned by strikes from Benfica's Joel Queirós, Gonçalo and César Paulo. Kairat equalised late on through Felipe then prevailed on spot kicks thanks to Anderson's penalty after Marinho had missed for the outgoing champions.

João Carlos Barbosa's valiant team duly matched their third-place finish of 2009. A second accolade followed as Kairat's dynamic Brazilian No4 Leo Santana was confirmed as the final tournament's three-goal leading marksman. Although disappointed not to see their home team lift the trophy, the spectators at the Baluan Sholak had witnessed top-class futsal during the competition's fifth four-team finals. If there were summits to scale at the foot of the Alatau mountains, the players and coaches were certainly not found wanting.

Third-Place Play-Off Result

1/5/11, Baluan Sholak Sport Palace, Almaty
Kairat Almaty 3-3 SL Benfica (5-3 on pens)
Kairat: Khalyavin, Jeronimo, Giva, Kelson, Suleimenov, Katata, Anderson, Leo Santana, Zhamankulov, Leo, Felipe, Silva. Coach: João Carlos Barbosa (BRA)
Benfica: Bébé, Vítor Hugo, Joel Queirós, Gonçalo, Davi, César Paulo, Pedro Costa, Arnaldo Pereira, Marinho, Teka, Anilton, Sol. Coach: Paulo Fernandes (POR)
Goal(s): 1-0 Leo Santana 6, 2-0 Silva 11, 2-1 Joel Queirós (pp), 2-2 Gonçalo 23, 2-3 César Paulo 30, 3-3 Felipe 36
Red Card(s): Davi 27 (Benfica), Kelson 30 (Kairat)
Yellow Card(s): Giva 3 (Kairat), Katata 4 (Kairat), Kelson 12 (Kairat), Bébé 14 (Benfica), Kelson 30 (Kairat)

Final Result

1/5/11, Baluan Sholak Sport Palace, Almaty
Sporting Clube de Portugal 2-5 ASD Città di Montesilvano C/5
Sporting: João Benedito, Cristiano, Leitão, Pedro Cary, João Matos, Déo, Marcelo Silva, Divanei, Caio Japa, Alex, Cardinal, Mário Freitas. Coach: Orlando Duarte (POR)
Montesilvano: Mammarella, Dell'Oso, Forte, Ghiotti, Garcias, Foglia, Fragassi, Caputo, Baptistella, Borruto, Calderolli, Cuzzolino. Coach: Fulvio Colini (ITA)
Goal(s): 0-1 Garcias 0, 0-2 Foglia 7, 0-3 Foglia 11, 0-4 Calderolli 19, 0-5 Cuzzolino 29(p), 1-5 Leitão 31, 2-5 Leitão 38
Yellow Card(s): Cardinal 9 (Sporting), Marcelo Silva 29 (Sporting), Alex 29 (Sporting), Calderolli 35 (Montesilvano), Fragassi 39 (Montesilvano)

First-time winners Montesilvano celebrate their UEFA Futsal Cup triumph in Kazakhstan

THE EUROPEAN FOOTBALL YEARBOOK

TOP 100 PLAYERS

Welcome to the Top 100 Players of the Season chapter – one of the European Football Yearbook's most popular features.

Overleaf is an alphabetical list of the 100 footballers who, thanks to their outstanding efforts and deeds during the 2010/11 season for club, country or – in many cases – both, have been voted by the EFY's editorial committee into this year's selection.

As always, the choice has not been easy. While many players were obvious picks, there are some who missed out by a hair's breadth and others who only just made the cut. Rest assured, however, that the final 100 was only determined after much careful thought and deliberation.

The written profiles of the chosen players, which appear on pages 319-368, should help to explain the reasons for their inclusion. The text is accompanied by an action photo and some basic background and career statistics, which we trust you will also find useful.

Please note that all statistical information is up to date as of 31 July 2011.

Enjoy the read.

MIKE HAMMOND
General Editor

TOP 100 PLAYERS

Mohammed ABDELLAOUE (Vålerenga Fotball/ Hannover 96, Norway)
Éric ABIDAL (FC Barcelona, France)
Charlie ADAM (Blackpool FC, Scotland)
ALEX (Fenerbahçe SK, Brazil)
Gareth BALE (Tottenham Hotspur FC, Wales)
Lucas BARRIOS (Borussia Dortmund, Paraguay)
Karim BENZEMA (Real Madrid CF, France)
BORJA VALERO (Villarreal CF, Spain)
Mladen BOŽOVIĆ (Videoton FC, Montenegro)
BURAK Yılmaz (Trabzonspor AŞ, Turkey)
Iker CASILLAS (Real Madrid CF, Spain)
Edinson CAVANI (SSC Napoli, Uruguay)
Petr ČECH (Chelsea FC, Czech Republic)
Nacer CHADLI (FC Twente, Belgium)
Papiss Demba CISSÉ (SC Freiburg, Senegal)
CRISTIANO RONALDO (Real Madrid CF, Portugal)
DANI ALVES (FC Barcelona, Brazil)
DANNY (FC Zenit St Petersburg, Portugal)
DAVID LUIZ (SL Benfica/Chelsea FC, Brazil)
DAVID VILLA (FC Barcelona, Spain)
Ángel DI MARÍA (Real Madrid CF, Argentina)
Antonio DI NATALE (Udinese Calcio, Italy)
Balázs DZSUDZSÁK (PSV Eindhoven, Hungary)
Christian ERIKSEN (AFC Ajax, Denmark)
Samuel ETO'O (FC Internazionale Milano, Cameroon)
Radamel FALCAO (FC Porto, Colombia)
Alexander FREI (FC Basel 1893, Switzerland)
Kevin GAMEIRO (FC Lorient, France)
GERVINHO (LOSC Lille Métropole, Ivory Coast)
Ryan GIGGS (Manchester United FC, Wales)
Mario GOMEZ (FC Bayern München, Germany)
Mario GÖTZE (Borussia Dortmund, Germany)
Kevin GROSSKREUTZ (Borussia Dortmund, Germany)
Marek HAMŠÍK (SSC Napoli, Slovakia)
Joe HART (Manchester City FC, England)
Eden HAZARD (LOSC Lille Métropole, Belgium)
Javier HERNÁNDEZ (Manchester United FC, Mexico)
HULK (FC Porto, Brazil)
Mats HUMMELS (Borussia Dortmund, Germany)
Klaas Jan HUNTELAAR (FC Schalke 04, Netherlands)
Zlatan IBRAHIMOVIĆ (AC Milan, Sweden)
Andrés INIESTA (FC Barcelona, Spain)
Emilio IZAGUIRRE (Celtic FC, Honduras)
Theo JANSSEN (FC Twente, Netherlands)
JOÃO MOUTINHO (FC Porto, Portugal)
William Kvist JØRGENSEN (FC København, Denmark)
Shinji KAGAWA (Borussia Dortmund, Japan)
Aleksandr KERZHAKOV (FC Zenit St Petersburg, Russia)
Sami KHEDIRA (Real Madrid CF, Germany)
Vincent KOMPANY (Manchester City FC, Belgium)
Dirk KUYT (Liverpool FC, Netherlands)
Fernando LLORENTE (Athletic Club, Spain)
Yann M'VILA (Stade Rennais FC, France)
MARCELO (Real Madrid CF, Brazil)
Juan MATA (Valencia CF, Spain)
Lionel MESSI (FC Barcelona, Argentina)
Kenny MILLER (Rangers FC/Bursaspor, Scotland)
Kevin MIRALLAS (Olympiacos FC, Belgium)
Luka MODRIĆ (Tottenham Hotspur FC, Croatia)
NANI (Manchester United FC, Portugal)
Samir NASRI (Arsenal FC, France)
NENÊ (Paris Saint-Germain FC, Brazil)
Manuel NEUER (FC Schalke 04, Germany)
NURİ Şahin (Borussia Dortmund, Turkey)
Peter ODEMWINGIE (FC Lokomotiv Moskva/West Bromwich Albion FC/Nigeria)
Mesut ÖZIL (Real Madrid CF, Germany)
PATO (AC Milan, Brazil)
PEDRO Rodríguez (FC Barcelona, Spain)
Ivan PERIŠIĆ (Club Brugge KV, Croatia)
Radosav PETROVIĆ (FK Partizan, Serbia)
Gerard PIQUÉ (FC Barcelona, Spain)
Carles PUYOL (FC Barcelona, Spain)
Yaroslav RAKYTSKIY (FC Shakhtar Donetsk, Ukraine)
Adil RAMI (LOSC Lille Métropole, France)
RAÚL González (FC Schalke 04, Spain)
Wayne ROONEY (Manchester United FC, England)
Giuseppe ROSSI (Villarreal CF, Italy)
Alexis SÁNCHEZ (Udinese Calcio, Chile)
SANTI CAZORLA (Villarreal CF, Spain)
André SCHÜRRLE (1. FSV Mainz 05, Germany)
Xherdan SHAQIRI (FC Basel 1893, Switzerland)
Gylfi SIGURDSSON (TSG 1899 Hoffenheim, Iceland)
Wesley SNEIJDER (FC Internazionale Milano, Netherlands)
Roberto SOLDADO (Valencia CF, Spain)
Moussa SOW (LOSC Lille Métropole, Senegal)
Carlos TÉVEZ (Manchester City FC, Argentina)
THIAGO SILVA (AC Milan, Brazil)
Yaya TOURÉ (Manchester City FC, Ivory Coast)
Edwin VAN DER SAR (Manchester United FC, Netherlands)
Rafael VAN DER VAART (Tottenham Hotspur FC, Netherlands)
Robin VAN PERSIE (Arsenal FC, Netherlands)
Jan VERTONGHEN (AFC Ajax, Belgium)
VÍCTOR VALDÉS (FC Barcelona, Spain)
Arturo VIDAL (Bayer 04 Leverkusen, Chile)
Nemanja VIDIĆ (Manchester United FC, Serbia)
WELLITON (FC Spartak Moskva, Brazil)
Jack WILSHERE (Arsenal FC, England)
XABI ALONSO (Real Madrid CF, Spain)
XAVI Hernández (FC Barcelona, Spain)
Andriy YARMOLENKO (FC Dynamo Kyiv, Ukraine)

NB Clubs indicated are those the players belonged to in the 2010/11 season.

Key to competitions: WCF = FIFA World Cup final tournament; WCQ = FIFA World Cup qualifying round; ECF = UEFA EURO final tournament; ECQ = UEFA EURO qualifying round; CC = FIFA Confederations Cup; CA = Copa América; ANF = Africa Cup of Nations final tournament; ANQ = Africa Cup of Nations qualifying round; CGC = CONCACAF Gold Cup

When Mohammed 'Moa' Abdellaoue left Vålerenga Fotball for Hannover 96 in August 2010, he was leading the Norwegian Tippeligaen top-scorer standings with 15 goals – the precise number he had registered in his two previous top-flight campaigns combined. His departure to Germany was a bitter blow to the Oslo club's title ambitions, but Vålerenga's pain was Hannover's gain as the 25-year-old striker hit the ground running in the Bundesliga, scoring four goals in his first six matches. He went on to reach double figures, combining superbly with Ivory Coast striker Didier Konan Ya – another ex-Tippeligaen star (with Rosenborg BK) – as the Lower Saxony side challenged hard for a place in the UEFA Champions League, eventually finishing in fourth position, 11 places higher than in 2009/10. Less than a week after scoring his first Bundesliga goal, in a 2-1 victory at FC Schalke 04, Abdellaoue grabbed his first for Norway, a crucial strike against Iceland in Reykjavik that got his country's UEFA EURO 2012 qualifying campaign off to the perfect start with a 2-1 win.

INTERNATIONAL CAREER

NORWAY
Debut – 20/8/08 v Republic of Ireland (h, Oslo, friendly), drew 1-1
First Goal – 3/9/10 v Iceland (a, Reykjavik, ECQ), won 2-1
Caps 14; **Goals** 2

CLUB CAREER

Major Honours – Norwegian Cup (2008)
Clubs: 03-07 Skeid Fotball; 08-10 Vålerenga Fotball; 10- Hannover 96 (GER)

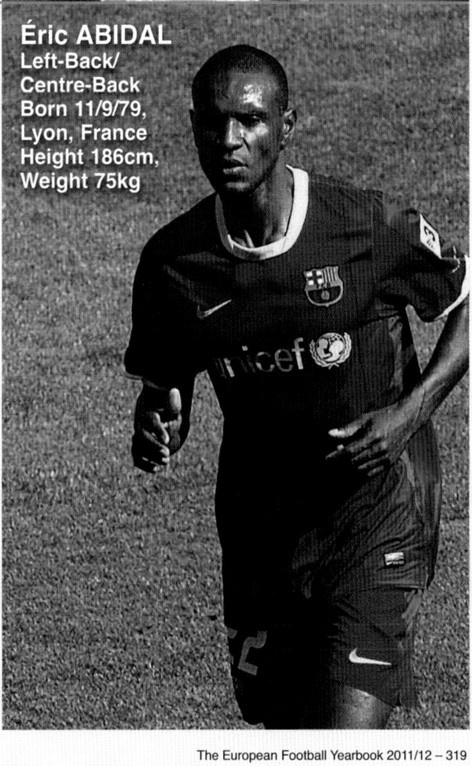

On 17 March 2011 Éric Abidal underwent emergency surgery to have a tumour removed from his liver. Less than two months later, the French international defender was back on the field of play for FC Barcelona, making a late appearance – to a tumultuous ovation from the Camp Nou crowd – in the second leg of their UEFA Champions League semi-final against Real Madrid CF. Even more astonishing was the Frenchman's inclusion in the Barça starting XI for the final at Wembley against Manchester United FC a few weeks later. Furthermore, his remarkable powers of recovery enabled him to last the full 90 minutes of the 3-1 victory, and in a noble gesture from his team-mates, he was handed the captain's armband and sent forward to lift the trophy. Abidal's second UEFA Champions League win was accompanied by his sixth national domestic title in seven seasons and also his first goal for Barça – a decisive strike in a Copa del Rey fifth-round tie against Athletic Club in Bilbao.

INTERNATIONAL CAREER

FRANCE
Debut – 18/8/04 v Bosnia & Herzegovina (h, Rennes, friendly) drew 1-1
Caps 55; **Goals** 0
Major Tournaments – FIFA World Cup 2006; UEFA EURO 2008; FIFA World Cup 2010

CLUB CAREER

Major Honours – UEFA Champions League (2009, 2011); UEFA Super Cup (2009); FIFA Club World Cup (2009); French Championship (2005, 2006, 2007); Spanish Championship (2009, 2010, 2011); Spanish Cup (2009)
Clubs: 00-02 AS Monaco FC; 02-04 LOSC Lille Métropole; 04-07 Olympique Lyonnais; 07- FC Barcelona (ESP)

Charlie ADAM
Midfielder
Born 10/12/85, Dundee, Scotland
Height 185cm, Weight 83kg

Blackpool FC lost their battle against relegation from the English Premier League, but the newly-promoted club from the northern seaside town fought gallantly against the odds to the end, their fate sealed only with a final-day 4-2 defeat at just-crowned champions Manchester United FC. Widespread pre-season forecasts that Blackpool would be down by Christmas had overlooked the excellence of the club's Scottish playmaker Charlie Adam. Formerly of Rangers FC, the 25-year-old left-footer advanced his career with a brilliant debut campaign in England's top flight, scoring a dozen goals – including one in each of the last three games, when they were needed most – and repeatedly catching the eye with his clever passing and precise delivery from set pieces. Liverpool FC were keen to sign him in January but had to wait another six months before they could secure his signature. In the meantime Adam re-established himself as a regular in the Scottish national side, starting five successive friendlies as Craig Levein's side prepared for the resumption of UEFA EURO 2012 hostilities in the early autumn.

INTERNATIONAL CAREER

SCOTLAND
Debut – 30/5/07 v Austria (a, Vienna, friendly), won 1-0
Caps 11; **Goals** 0

CLUB CAREER

Clubs: 03-09 Rangers FC; 04-05 Ross County FC (loan); 05-06 Saint Mirren FC (loan); 09-11 Blackpool FC (ENG); 11- Liverpool FC (ENG)

Alexsandro de Souza "ALEX"
Attacking Midfielder
Born 14/9/77, Curitiba, Brazil
Height 174cm, Weight 70kg

If he wasn't already a Fenerbahçe SK legend before the 2010/11 season, Alex, the Istanbul club's long-serving Brazilian, certainly warranted the distinction by the end of it. At the age of 33, the skilful left-footer's seventh season at the club turned out to be his finest yet, not just in terms of the 28 goals he struck to claim the Süper Lig's Golden Boot, but also with his overall contribution to Fenerbahçe's record-breaking 18th domestic title. Also credited with 14 assists, he proved to be an inspirational captain, his early-season spat with the club's new coach Aykut Kocaman consigned to ancient history as the team powered to the title with a remarkable run of 17 wins in their last 18 matches. Among Alex's highlights were a hat-trick away to Beşiktaş JK, the winner at Galatasaray AŞ and five goals, including three penalties, in the last home game of the season, against MKE Ankaragücü. A new contract extension signed in February ensured that Fener fans would be able to savour the Brazilian's talents for another two years.

INTERNATIONAL CAREER

BRAZIL
Major Honours – Copa América (1999, 2004)
Debut – 23/9/98 v Yugoslavia (h, Sao Luis, friendly), drew 1-1
First Goal – 26/6/99 v Latvia (h, Curitiba, friendly), won 3-0
Caps 48; **Goals** 12
Major Tournaments – Copa América 1999; FIFA Confederations Cup 1999; Copa América 2001; FIFA Confederations Cup 2003; Copa América 2004

CLUB CAREER

Major Honours – Brazilian Championship (2003); Turkish Championship (2005, 2007, 2011); Brazilian Cup (1998, 2003)
Clubs: 96 Coritiba FBC; 97-99 SE Palmeiras; 00 CR Flamengo (loan); 01 Parma FC (ITA); 01-04 Cruzeiro EC; 04- Fenerbahçe SK (TUR)

Two majestic individual performances for Tottenham Hotspur FC against FC Internazionale Milano in the group stage of the UEFA Champions League served notice to Europe and beyond that Gareth Bale was a footballer of very special talents. His hat-trick at San Siro – in a 4-3 defeat – was followed by an even more dazzling display at White Hart Lane, where he ran Inter's Brazilian right-back Maicon ragged and brilliantly set up two second-half goals in a famous 3-1 win. Although those two performances stood out, they were by no means isolated. Indeed, the young Welshman, who had endured many woes and misfortunes during his early years at Spurs, raised his game to such an exalted and consistent level in 2010/11 that he was voted England's Player of the Year by his fellow professionals. Fast, skilful and an excellent crosser of the ball on the run, he is now firmly established as a left-sided midfielder, having been successfully converted from left-back by Spurs manager Harry Redknapp. Already Wales' youngest senior international and goalscorer, the multi-talented 22-year-old seems sure to achieve many more milestones in the years to come.

INTERNATIONAL CAREER

WALES
Debut – 27/5/06 v Trinidad & Tobago (n, Graz, friendly), won 2-1
First Goal – 7/10/06 v Slovakia (h, Cardiff, ECQ), lost 1-5
Caps 27; **Goals** 3

CLUB CAREER

Clubs: 06-07 Southampton FC (ENG); 07- Tottenham Hotspur FC (ENG)

Gareth BALE
Left-Back/Left Midfielder
Born 16/7/89, Cardiff, Wales
Height 183cm, Weight 74kg

The attacking spearhead of Borussia Dortmund's German Bundesliga triumph, Lucas Barrios was also the team's leading marksman, scoring 16 goals. That was three fewer than the Argentina-born Paraguay international striker had registered in his debut Bundesliga campaign the previous season, but it was also twice as many as any other Dortmund player managed. An assured penalty-box predator, the 26-year-old improved his application and work-rate in 2010/11 and successfully held off the threat to his position from new Polish recruit Robert Lewandowski. Furthermore, he found his best form on the big occasions, opening the scoring home and away to FC Bayern München and firing Dortmund in front in the title-clinching victory against 1. FC Nürnberg. Called to international duty at the 2011 Copa América in his native Argentina, he helped Paraguay reach the final, scoring one goal – in the group game against Venezuela. Dortmund fans, among others, would have been surprised to see him dropped for the final, his second-half introduction coming too late to rescue Paraguay from a 3-0 defeat by Uruguay.

INTERNATIONAL CAREER

PARAGUAY
Debut – 26/5/10 v Republic of Ireland (a, Dublin, friendly), lost 1-2
First Goal – 26/5/10 v Republic of Ireland (a, Dublin, friendly), lost 1-2
Caps 21; **Goals** 6
Major Tournaments – FIFA World Cup 2010; Copa América 2011

CLUB CAREER

Major Honours – Chilean Championship (clausura 2008); German Championship (2011)
Clubs: 03-04 Argentinos Juniors (ARG); 04 CA Tigre (ARG) (loan); 05 CD Temuco (CHI); 06 CA Tiro Federal (ARG); 06-07 CD Cobreloa (CHI); 07 Club Atlas (MEX); 08-09 Colo-Colo (CHI); 09- Borussia Dortmund (GER)

Lucas BARRIOS
Striker
Born 13/11/84, San Fernando, Argentina
Height 187cm, Weight 83kg

Karim BENZEMA
Striker
Born 17/12/87, Lyon, France
Height 183cm, Weight 74kg

Dropped from France's 2010 FIFA World Cup squad and despatched to the substitutes' bench by Real Madrid CF's new coach José Mourinho, Karim Benzema's fledgling career appeared to be at its lowest ebb as the 2010/11 season got underway. However, the young striker responded positively to the double challenge and was rewarded with a timely renaissance that brought him several important goals at both club and international level. Recalled to lead France's attack for their second UEFA EURO 2012 qualifier, away to Bosnia & Herzegovina, he opened the scoring in a crucial 2-0 win and thereafter re-established himself as the No1 striker in Laurent Blanc's new-look side with three goals in as many games, the last of them bringing France a prestigious 1-0 win at home to Brazil. Benzema also made the most of a long-term injury to Madrid's first-choice centre-forward Gonzalo Higuaín, scoring six goals in the UEFA Champions League and 15 in La Liga. His European tally included a hat-trick against AJ Auxerre and one in each leg of the round of 16 tie against his former club Olympique Lyonnais. Indeed, Benzema found the net at the Stade de Gerland within a minute of entering as a substitute to help Madrid end a jinx that had seen them eliminated from that round in each of the previous six seasons.

INTERNATIONAL CAREER

FRANCE
Debut – 28/3/07 v Austria (h, Saint-Denis, friendly), won 1-0
First Goal – 28/3/07 v Austria (h, Saint-Denis, friendly), won 1-0
Caps 37; **Goals** 12
Major Tournaments – UEFA EURO 2008

CLUB CAREER

Major Honours – French Championship (2005, 2006, 2007, 2008); French Cup (2008); Spanish Cup (2011)
Clubs: 04-09 Olympique Lyonnais; 09- Real Madrid CF (ESP)

BORJA VALERO Iglesias
Midfielder
Born 12/1/85, Madrid, Spain
Height 175cm, Weight 73kg

It takes some doing to break into a national side that is on the crest of a wave after winning both the UEFA European Championship and the FIFA World Cup, but Borja Valero's first international cap for Spain, in an end-of-season friendly against the United States in Boston, was considered by many to be long overdue. The do-it-all midfielder enjoyed an excellent season on loan at his former club RCD Mallorca in 2009/10, but he topped that with an even better 2010/11 campaign at Villarreal CF. Again, he was only on loan from his English parent club West Bromwich Albion FC, but his terrific consistency for Villarreal in the Spanish championship – where they finished fourth – and the UEFA Europa League – where they reached the semi-finals – led to his becoming a permanent crew member of the Yellow Submarine at the end of the season. Whether he becomes a regular for his country remains to be seen, but if he maintains his level of performance for Villarreal in 2011/12, a place in the squad should be his at the UEFA EURO 2012 finals in Poland/Ukraine.

INTERNATIONAL CAREER

SPAIN
Debut – 4/6/11 v United States (a, Boston, friendly), won 4-0
Caps 1; **Goals** 0

CLUB CAREER

Clubs: 05-07 Real Madrid CF B; 07-08 RCD Mallorca; 08-11 West Bromwich Albion FC (ENG); 09-10 RCD Mallorca (loan); 10-11 Villarreal CF (loan); 11- Villarreal CF

With Montenegro's first-choice goalkeeper Vukašin Poleksić serving a two-year suspension for alleged match-fixing, his understudy Mladen Božović had the opportunity to make a name for himself in the team's UEFA EURO 2012 qualifying campaign. He seized it with both hands, keeping clean sheets in each of the team's first four qualifiers – plus three friendly internationals besides – to become the principal figure in the competition's most unlikely success story. Although Božović finally conceded in the last qualifier of the season, 1-1 at home to Bulgaria, a result which which meant that Montenegro failed to leapfrog England into first place in Group G, it was a rare blip in a season that also brought him his fifth domestic championship winner's medal in four seasons. After contributing towards title wins in both Montenegro and Serbia in 2007/08, then claiming two more Serbian crowns with FK Partizan, he left Belgrade for the Hungarian town of Szekesfehervar in the summer of 2010 and went on to lift the NB I title, starting 25 of the 30 matches for Videoton FC, who replaced Poleksić's club, Debreceni VSC, as the new champions of Hungary.

INTERNATIONAL CAREER

MONTENEGRO
Debut – 3/6/07 v Colombia (n, Matsumoto, Kirin Cup), lost 0-1
Caps 16; **Goals** 0

CLUB CAREER

Major Honours – Montenegrin Championship (2008); Serbian Championship (2008, 2009, 2010); Hungarian Championship (2011); Serbian Cup (2008, 2009)
Clubs: 01-03 FK Zabjelo; 03-08 FK Budućnost Podgorica; 04-05 FK Mladost Podgorica (loan); 05-06 FK Kom (loan); 08-10 FK Partizan (SRB); 10- Videoton FC (HUN)

Mladen BOŽOVIĆ

Goalkeeper
Born 1/8/84, Podgorica, Montenegro
Height 196cm, Weight 92kg

Trabzonspor AŞ came within a whisker of winning their first Turkish championship title for 27 years in 2010/11, finishing runners-up to Fenerbahçe SK only by virtue of an inferior record in the matches between the two teams. The man who fronted the Black Sea club's challenge was a striker who had been offloaded to them from Fener midway through the previous season following a six-month loan at Eskişehirspor. Branded a flop at the Istanbul club, Burak Yılmaz resurrected his career with 19 goals in 2010/11 – the second-highest total in the Süper Lig. Eleven of them were scored outside Trabzon, including the winner at Galatasaray AŞ, but Burak's most important goal of the season came outside Turkey – in the Belgian capital of Brussels, where his first international goal, coolly converted at close range from Arda Turan's pass, gave the Turkish national side a potentially priceless 1-1 draw in a pivotal UEFA EURO 2012 encounter.

INTERNATIONAL CAREER

TURKEY
Debut – 12/4/06 v Azerbaijan (a, Baku, friendly), drew 1-1
First Goal – 3/6/11 v Belgium (a, Brussels, ECQ), drew 1-1
Caps 8; **Goals** 1

CLUB CAREER

Major Honours – Turkish Cup (2007, 2010)
Clubs: 02-06 Antalyaspor; 06-08 Beşiktaş JK; 08 Manisaspor; 08-10 Fenerbahçe SK; 09-10 Eskişehirspor (loan); 10- Trabzonspor AŞ

BURAK Yılmaz

Striker
Born 15/7/85, Antalya, Turkey
Height 186cm, Weight 75kg

Iker CASILLAS Fernández

Goalkeeper
Born 20/5/81, Madrid, Spain
Height 185cm, Weight 79kg

After fulfilling the dream of every footballer by captaining his country to victory at the FIFA World Cup, Iker Casillas was entitled to have a season out of the limelight in 2010/11. In truth, he was not at his best for Spain, letting in four goals in a Lisbon friendly against Portugal and keeping just one clean sheet in five UEFA EURO 2012 qualifiers, but he did close to within five caps of Andoni Zubizarreta's long-standing appearance record. For Real Madrid CF he was as defiant and resolute as ever, recovering brilliantly from the 5-0 mauling his team received from FC Barcelona in November – for which he was exempt from blame – with four outstanding displays against the Catalans in the spring, the second of which brought victory in the final of the Copa del Rey, enabling Casillas to get his hands on the last important winner's medal missing from his extraordinary collection. In all, he conceded just 40 goals in 54 club appearances in 2010/11 – the best goal-per-game average in any of his 12 seasons at Madrid.

INTERNATIONAL CAREER

SPAIN
Major Honours – FIFA World Cup (2010); UEFA European Championship (2008)
Debut – 3/6/00 v Sweden (a, Gothenburg, friendly), drew 1-1
Caps 121; **Goals** 0
Major Tournaments – UEFA EURO 2000; FIFA World Cup 2002; UEFA EURO 2004; FIFA World Cup 2006; UEFA EURO 2008; FIFA Confederations Cup 2009; FIFA World Cup 2010

CLUB CAREER

Major Honours – UEFA Champions League (2000, 2002); UEFA Super Cup (2002); World Club Cup (2002); Spanish Championship (2001, 2003, 2007, 2008); Spanish Cup (2011)
Clubs: 99- Real Madrid CF

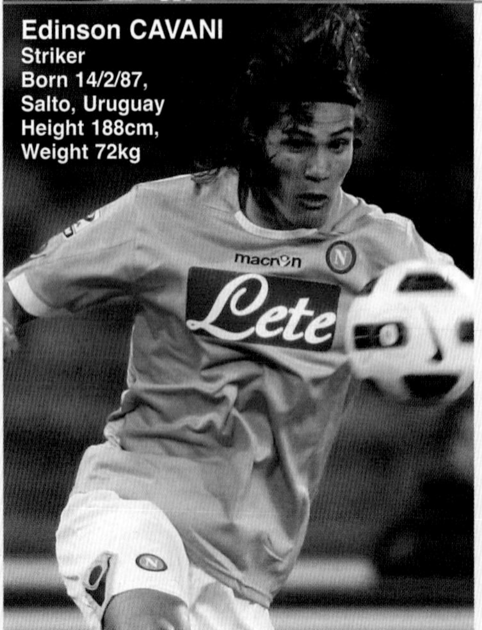

Edinson CAVANI

Striker
Born 14/2/87, Salto, Uruguay
Height 188cm, Weight 72kg

Prior to the 2010/11 season Edinson Cavani had never scored a senior hat-trick. By the end of it the powerful Uruguayan striker had notched one for his country – in a friendly against Indonesia – and no fewer than four for SSC Napoli – three in Serie A (against Juventus, UC Sampdoria and S.S. Lazio) en route to a club-record tally of 26 goals, and another against FC Utrecht in the UEFA Europa League, where he struck seven times in all, including two vital stoppage-time strikes against FC Steaua Bucureşti. It was a phenomenal first season for the new signing from US Città di Palermo, and with Napoli safely qualified for the UEFA Champions League, it was little wonder that the man who had done most to take them there was rewarded with a lucrative new long-term contract. Cavani's season of joy continued into the summer, when he helped Uruguay win the Copa América – albeit in a peripheral role as understudy to the team's established forward pairing of Luis Suárez and Diego Forlán.

INTERNATIONAL CAREER

URUGUAY
Major Honours – Copa América (2011)
Debut – 6/2/08 v Colombia (h, Montevideo, friendly), drew 2-2
First Goal – 6/2/08 v Colombia (h, Montevideo, friendly), drew 2-2
Caps 31; **Goals** 9
Major Tournaments – FIFA World Cup 2010; Copa América 2011

CLUB CAREER

Major Honours – Uruguayan Championship (2006 apertura)
Clubs: 06-07 Danubio FC; 07-10 US Città di Palermo (ITA); 10- SSC Napoli (ITA)

Chelsea FC won no silverware in 2010/11, but there was a prize for their goalkeeper as Petr Čech scooped the supporters' player of the year trophy for the first time in his seven seasons at the club. The giant Czech international missed the pre-season FA Community Shield, which Chelsea lost 3-1 to Manchester United FC, but returned for the opening game of the Premier League campaign and went on to start all 38 matches, conceding just 33 goals and keeping 15 clean sheets. Always dependable, occasionally spectacular, he was just as efficient in the UEFA Champions League, conceding just six times in nine matches. Where Chelsea fans recognised his efforts at the end of the season, Čech received double acclaim back in his homeland at Christmas as he was voted the Czech Republic Footballer of the Year for 2010 in two official polls. With over 300 appearances for Chelsea and 83 international caps, Čech's status as one of the outstanding goalkeepers of his generation is already assured. At just 29, however, his best years may be yet to come.

INTERNATIONAL CAREER

CZECH REPUBLIC
Debut – 12/2/02 v Hungary (n, Larnaca, friendly), won 2-0
Caps 83; **Goals** 0
Major Tournaments – UEFA EURO 2004; FIFA World Cup 2006; UEFA EURO 2008

CLUB CAREER

Major Honours – English Premier League (2005, 2006, 2010); English FA Cup (2007, 2009, 2010); English League Cup (2005, 2007)
Clubs: 99-01 FK Chmel Blšany; 01-02 AC Sparta Praha; 02-04 Stade Rennais FC (FRA); 04- Chelsea FC (ENG)

A dual citizen of Morocco and Belgium, Nacer Chadli had a tough decision to make when approached by the national teams of both countries in the autumn of 2010. Unsolicited by either while playing inconspicuously in the Dutch second tier for AGOVV Apeldoorn, the young winger suddenly became hot property following his transfer to Dutch champions FC Twente and a string of stunning performances in his early weeks at the Enschede club. Eventually he chose Belgium, the land of his birth, but not before he had donned the shirt of Morocco in a friendly against Northern Ireland. He made his debut for Belgium 12 weeks later and cemented his affiliation the following month with a first competitive appearance in a UEFA EURO 2012 qualifier against Austria. Four days after that he scored his first international goal, in a 4-1 win against Azerbaijan. Fast and penetrative, Chadli is also a fine finisher – as he demonstrated by scoring three goals in the UEFA Champions League and another seven in the Eredivisie, the first of them a crucial winning strike at PSV Eindhoven. He also found the net three times in the Dutch Cup, which Twente won with a 3-2 victory over AFC Ajax in the final.

INTERNATIONAL CAREER

BELGIUM
Debut – 9/2/11 v Finland (h, Ghent, friendly), drew 1-1
First Goal – 29/3/11 v Azerbaijan (h, Brussels, ECQ), won 4-1
Caps 4; **Goals** 1
MOROCCO
Debut – 17/11/10 v Northern Ireland (a, Belfast, friendly), drew 1-1
Caps 1; **Goals** 0

CLUB CAREER

Major Honours – Dutch Cup (2011)
Clubs: 07-10 AGOVV Apeldoorn (NED); 10- FC Twente (NED)

Papiss Demba CISSÉ
Striker
Born 3/6/85, Dakar, Senegal
Height 183cm, Weight 73kg

When Papiss Demba Cissé joined SC Freiburg from FC Metz in December 2009 for a club-record €1.5m fee, his arrival was not generally greeted with enthusiasm. After all, he was a largely unknown striker from Senegal operating in the French second division. But after a promising first half-season, which he concluded with two goals against Borussia Dortmund, the powerful young striker made a sensational start to his first full Bundesliga campaign, scoring seven goals in his first seven matches and reaching double figures by mid-November. He went on to score 22 times in 32 starts, providing mid-table security for a club widely tipped for relegation. His tally placed him second only to FC Bayern München's Mario Gomez in the goal charts and was the highest number ever recorded in a single Bundesliga campaign by an African player, beating the 20-goal mark set by Eintracht Frankfurt's Ghanaian striker Tony Yeboah 18 years earlier. Cissé impressed for his country, too, scoring five international goals during the season, including a hat-trick in an Africa Cup of Nations qualifier against Mauritius.

INTERNATIONAL CAREER

SENEGAL
Debut – 12/8/09 v Congo DR (a, Kinshasha, friendly), won 2-1
First Goal – 12/8/09 v Congo DR (a, Kinshasha, friendly), won 2-1
Caps 10; **Goals** 7

CLUB CAREER

Clubs: 05-09 FC Metz (FRA); 05-06 AS Cherbourg (FRA) (loan); 08 LB Châteauroux (FRA) (loan); 09- SC Freiburg (GER)

CRISTIANO RONALDO Santos Aveiro
Winger/Striker
Born 5/2/85, Funchal, Madeira, Portugal
Height 184cm, Weight 78kg

The arrival of his fellow countryman José Mourinho at the Santiago Bernabéu was always likely to bring out the best in Cristiano Ronaldo, but nobody could possibly have foreseen that the Portuguese superstar would end the season by setting a new individual goalscoring record for La Liga. A late burst of 11 goals in the final four games elevated his aggregate haul to a staggering 40 – two more than the previous record tally jointly held by Athletic Club's Telmo Zarra and Real Madrid CF's Hugo Sánchez. Ronaldo's stockpile, which included eight penalties but just four of his trademark free-kicks, earned him the Pichichi and the ESM Golden Shoe – with FC Barcelona's Lionel Messi a distant second in both listings – but it did not bring Madrid the Spanish title. Nor did his six strikes in Europe help to deliver the UEFA Champions League. The last of his seven goals in the Copa del Rey, however, did strike gold as his superb extra-time header in the final against Barcelona enabled Madrid to recapture Spain's domestic cup for the first time in 18 years.

INTERNATIONAL CAREER

PORTUGAL
Debut – 20/8/03 v Kazakhstan (h, Chaves, friendly), won 1-0
First Goal – 12/6/04 v Greece (h, Porto, ECF), lost 1-2
Caps 81; **Goals** 26
Major Tournaments – UEFA EURO 2004; FIFA World Cup 2006; UEFA EURO 2008; FIFA World Cup 2010

CLUB CAREER

Major Honours – UEFA Champions League (2008); FIFA Club World Cup (2008); English Premier League (2007, 2008, 2009); English FA Cup (2004); Spanish Cup (2011); English League Cup (2006, 2009)
Clubs: 02-03 Sporting Clube de Portugal; 03-09 Manchester United FC (ENG); 09- Real Madrid CF (ESP)

Left-back has been a contentious position during Josep Guardiola's time in charge of FC Barcelona, but there has never been an issue over on the other flank. Since his arrival from Sevilla FC in 2008, Dani Alves has been the team's right-back of choice on a permanent basis. The Brazilian international completed a hat-trick of Spanish Liga titles for the Catalans in 2010/11 and enjoyed arguably his best season yet, setting up 14 goals and scoring a couple himself. His dynamic forward raids were also a feature of Barça's UEFA Champions League triumph. Unlike in 2009, he got to play in the final and enjoy the fruits of a season's labour in which he started all bar one of the team's European fixtures. His popularity outside Camp Nou would be greater, however, were it not for his reputation for playacting. He certainly did himself no favours with his persistently unsporting behaviour in the first leg of the UEFA Champions League semi-final against Real Madrid CF.

INTERNATIONAL CAREER

BRAZIL

Major Honours – Copa América (2007); FIFA Confederations Cup (2009)
Debut – 10/10/06 v Ecuador (n, Solna, friendly), won 2-1
First Goal – 15/7/07 v Argentina (n, Maracaibo, CA), won 3-0
Caps 49; **Goals** 5
Major Tournaments – Copa América 2007; FIFA Confederations Cup 2009; FIFA World Cup 2010; Copa América 2011

CLUB CAREER

Major Honours – UEFA Champions League (2009, 2011); UEFA Cup (2006, 2007); UEFA Super Cup (2006, 2009); FIFA Club World Cup (2009); Spanish Championship (2009, 2010, 2011); Spanish Cup (2007, 2009)
Clubs: 01-02 EC Bahia; 02-08 Sevilla FC (ESP); 08- FC Barcelona (ESP)

Although his 2010 season was interrupted by a disappointing FIFA World Cup with Portugal, Danny ended it with the title of Russian Premier-Liga Player of the Year. It was a tremendous feat given that he had missed most of the previous season with a career-threatening knee injury. The creative hub of an FC Zenit St Petersburg side that won both major domestic trophies, he was especially inspirational in the league, starting 27 matches – more than any other Zenit player – and scoring ten goals – which matched his previous best tally of 2008, the year in which he switched to Zenit in mid-campaign from FC Dinamo Moskva for a Russian record fee of €30m. While Danny has struggled to make an impact at international level, the 28-year-old enjoys superstar status in Russia, and the new long-term contract he signed for Zenit in June 2011 suggests that he is more than happy to keep it that way.

INTERNATIONAL CAREER

PORTUGAL

Debut – 20/8/08 v Faroe Islands (h, Aveiro, friendly), won 5-0
First Goal – 19/11/08 v Brazil (a, Gama, friendly), lost 2-6
Caps 21; **Goals** 3
Major Tournaments – FIFA World Cup 2010

CLUB CAREER

Major Honours – UEFA Super Cup (2008); Russian Championship (2010); Russian Cup (2010)
Clubs: 01-02 CS Marítimo; 02-05 Sporting Clube de Portugal; 03-04 CS Marítimo (loan); 05-08 FC Dinamo Moskva (RUS); 08- FC Zenit St Petersburg (RUS)

DAVID LUIZ Moreira Marinho

Centre-Back
Born 22/4/87, Diadema, Brazil
Height 188cm, Weight 84kg

Brazilian defender David Luiz's move from SL Benfica to Chelsea FC during the January 2011 transfer window was rather overshadowed by the west London club's simultaneous signing of Fernando Torres from Liverpool FC for an English record fee of £50m. But while the out-of-form Spanish international striker endured a torrid settling-in period at Stamford Bridge, the tousle-haired centre-back, who cost half as much, slotted in alongside captain John Terry without fuss or fanfare and quickly became a favourite of the Chelsea faithful. A prominent member of Benfica's 2009/10 Portuguese Liga title-winning side and – after winning his first international cap for Brazil – a UEFA Champions League ever-present in the 2010/11 group stage, he was ineligible for Chelsea in Europe but made an immediate impact on the domestic scene, winning the official Premier League Player of the Month award for March, during which he not only demonstrated his class in defence but also scored his first two goals for the club – in crucial home wins against Manchester United FC and Manchester City FC.

INTERNATIONAL CAREER

BRAZIL
Debut – 10/8/10 v United States (a, East Rutherford, friendly), won 2-0
Caps 6; **Goals** 0
Major Tournaments – Copa América 2011

CLUB CAREER

Major Honours – Portuguese Championship (2010)
Clubs: 06-07 EC Vitória; 07-11 SL Benfica (POR); 11- Chelsea FC (ENG)

DAVID VILLA Sánchez

Striker
Born 3/12/81, Langreo, Spain
Height 175cm, Weight 69kg

After five years at Valencia CF where he was the team's major star, David Villa became one of many at FC Barcelona. Procured at a cost of €40m, there was considerable pressure on the striker to maintain the prolific form that had brought him 129 goals in 212 games for Valencia. He did not disappoint. Despite being regularly deployed on the left wing to accommodate Lionel Messi in the centre, he scored 23 goals in 50 matches for the Catalans, including one on each of his Liga and UEFA Champions League debuts, a double in the epic 5-0 win at home to Real Madrid CF and an exquisite strike to seal victory over Manchester United FC at Wembley. Spain's leading scorer at both UEFA EURO 2008 and the 2010 FIFA World Cup also became his country's all-time record marksman, supplanting Raúl with the first of his two goals in a 2-1 win over the Czech Republic in Granada that enabled Spain to maintain their 100% record in the UEFA EURO 2012 qualifying campaign.

INTERNATIONAL CAREER

SPAIN
Major Honours – FIFA World Cup (2010); UEFA European Championship (2008)
Debut – 9/2/05 v San Marino (h, Almeria, WCQ), won 5-0
First Goal – 16/11/05 v Slovakia (a, Bratislava, WCQ) drew 1-1
Caps 75; **Goals** 47
Major Tournaments – FIFA World Cup 2006; UEFA EURO 2008; FIFA Confederations Cup 2009; FIFA World Cup 2010

CLUB CAREER

Major Honours – UEFA Champions League (2011); Spanish Championship (2011); Spanish Cup (2004, 2008)
Clubs: 00-03 Real Sporting de Gijón; 03-05 Real Zaragoza; 05-10 Valencia CF; 10- FC Barcelona

Ángel Fabián DI MARÍA
Midfielder/Winger
Born 14/2/88, Rosario, Argentina
Height 180cm, Weight 65kg

A sumptuous 2009/10 season in Portugal with SL Benfica earned Ángel Di María a lucrative five-year contract with Real Madrid CF, and the lithe left-footer proved just as entertaining and effective in the capital of Spain as he had in the Portuguese equivalent. He arrived in Madrid after a disappointing FIFA World Cup for Argentina, but a spectacular winning strike for his country in a friendly against the Republic of Ireland – the first international goal scored at the new Dublin Arena – enabled him to kick off his Madrid career with a spring in his step. A late winner at AJ Auxerre in the UEFA Champions League was an early highlight, but there was an even better goal to come from him in the quarter-final of the competition – a beautiful curling shot into the top corner against Tottenham Hotspur FC. Madrid's victory in the Copa del Rey final against FC Barcelona was a bittersweet experience for the 23-year-old, for although he set up Cristiano Ronaldo's goal with a fabulous cross from the left, his evening was spoiled when he received a red card in the last minute of extra time.

INTERNATIONAL CAREER

ARGENTINA
Debut – 6/9/08 v Paraguay (h, Buenos Aires, WCQ), drew 1-1
First Goal – 24/5/10 v Canada (h, Buenos Aires, friendly), won 5-0
Caps 23; **Goals** 4
Major Tournaments – FIFA World Cup 2010; Copa América 2011

CLUB CAREER

Major Honours – Portuguese Championship (2010); Spanish Cup (2011)
Clubs: 05-07 CA Rosario Central; 07-10 SL Benfica (POR); 10- Real Madrid CF (ESP)

Antonio DI NATALE
Striker
Born 13/10/77, Naples, Italy
Height 177cm, Weight 70kg

Serie A's top marksman in 2009/10, Antonio Di Natale provided an encore in 2010/11, scoring 28 goals to help Udinese Calcio qualify for the play-offs of the UEFA Champions League. The first player to successfully defend the capocannoniere crown since Giuseppe Signori in 1993/94, Di Natale's final tally – which contained three hat-tricks, including one against his hometown club SSC Napoli – was one down on the previous season. He would have matched it had he not missed a penalty in the final game of the season – a goalless draw at home to newly crowned champions AC Milan that secured Udinese's fourth-place finish. Di Natale had taken part in the 2005/06 UEFA Champions League campaign, scoring three goals, and, despite interest from other clubs and the departure of his chief attacking accomplice Alexis Sánchez to FC Barcelona, the 33-year-old was happy to stick around and spearhead another European challenge in 2011/12.

INTERNATIONAL CAREER

ITALY
Debut – 20/11/02 v Turkey (h, Pescara, friendly), drew 1-1
First Goal – 18/2/04 v Czech Republic (h, Palermo, friendly), drew 2-2
Caps 36; **Goals** 10
Major Tournaments – UEFA EURO 2008; FIFA World Cup 2010

CLUB CAREER

Clubs: 96-04 Empoli FC; 97-98 Iperzola Ponteroncariale (loan); 98 AS Varese 1910 (loan); 98-99 FCE Viareggio (loan); 04- Udinese Calcio

Balázs DZSUDZSÁK
Left Midfielder/Winger
Born 23/12/86, Nyirlugos, Hungary
Height 179cm, Weight 72kg

The leading Hungarian footballer of his generation, Balázs Dzsudzsák caused much consternation in his homeland when he left PSV Eindhoven in the summer for a lucrative transfer to little-known Russian Premier-Liga club FC Anzhi Makhachkala. It had been widely anticipated by Dzsudzsák's legion of fans in Hungary that he would move to one of Europe's elite clubs in Germany, England or Italy, but the financial rewards at ambitious Anzhi were too much for the talented 24-year-old to resist. Although he won no silverware with PSV in 2010/11, his final season in Eindhoven was unquestionably his best. He scored 24 goals in 49 games and was the club's leading marksman in both the Eredivisie (with 16) and the UEFA Europa League (with seven). Pacy and penetrative, the flying winger's powerful left-foot shot was responsible for several spectacular goals, the best of all perhaps an outrageous free-kick against LOSC Lille Métropole. He was also on target with a crucial goal for Hungary, supplying the late winner in a UEFA EURO 2012 qualifier against Finland in Helsinki.

INTERNATIONAL CAREER

HUNGARY
Debut – 2/6/07 v Greece (a, Heraklion, ECQ), lost 0-2
First Goal – 24/5/08 v Greece (h, Budapest, friendly), won 3-2
Caps 37; **Goals** 5

CLUB CAREER

Major Honours – Hungarian Championship (2005, 2006, 2007); Dutch Championship (2008)
Clubs: 04-08 Debreceni VSC; 08-11 PSV Eindhoven (NED); 11- FC Anzhi Makhachkala (RUS)

Christian ERIKSEN
Midfielder
Born 14/2/92, Middelfart, Denmark
Height 180cm, Weight 65kg

The high promise that persuaded Denmark coach Morten Olsen to include Christian Eriksen in his squad for the 2010 FIFA World Cup – where he was the tournament's youngest participant – was fulfilled in 2010/11 as the gifted young playmaker developed into a star turn not just for his country but also at club level for AFC Ajax. A graduate of the Amsterdam club's celebrated youth academy, which he joined at the age of 16, Eriksen took only a couple of years to establish himself as a fully-fledged first-teamer. He was particularly prominent during the second half of the 2010/11 campaign as Ajax overtook PSV Eindhoven and – on the final day – FC Twente to win their first Eredivisie title for seven years. For his considerable contributions Eriksen was voted the Eredivisie's young player of the year. A fine athlete with two good feet and an eye for the killer pass, the 19-year-old is already being revered as the most talented Danish footballer to have emerged for years. He gave a man-of-the-match display for the national team in a February friendly against England in Copenhagen and, in June, scored his first senior international goal in a UEFA EURO 2012 qualifying win in Iceland – just before he returned home to play a starring role for the host nation at the finals of the UEFA European Under-21 Championship.

INTERNATIONAL CAREER

DENMARK
Debut – 3/3/10 v Austria (a, Vienna, friendly), lost 1-2
First Goal – 4/6/11 v Iceland (a, Reykjavik, ECQ), won 2-0
Caps 14; **Goals** 1
Major Tournaments – FIFA World Cup 2010

CLUB CAREER

Major Honours – Dutch Championship (2011); Dutch Cup (2010)
Clubs: 10- AFC Ajax (NED)

Samuel Eto'o added only a second Coppa Italia to his vast collection of major honours in 2010/11 but while the previous season, his first at FC Internazionale Milano, had delivered a historic treble, the Cameroonian striker seemed much more at ease back in his familiar centre-forward role following the departure of coach José Mourinho. Leading Inter's line brilliantly all season, he scored 37 goals in all competitions – a career-best tally secured with a double in the Coppa Italia final against US Città di Palermo. Eto'o started the campaign as he finished it with two goals in the Italian Super Cup against AS Roma and registered his first Inter hat-trick a few weeks later, against SV Werder Bremen. Arguably his best overall performance came against another German club when he scored one goal and set up two others as Inter memorably came from behind to beat FC Bayern München 3-2 in Munich and reach the UEFA Champions League quarter-finals.

INTERNATIONAL CAREER

CAMEROON
Major Honours – Africa Cup of Nations (2000, 2002)
Debut – 9/3/97 v Costa Rica (a, San Jose, friendly), lost 0-5
First Goal – 28/1/00 v Ivory Coast (n, Accra, ANF), won 3-0
Caps 105; **Goals** 50
Major Tournaments – FIFA World Cup 1998; Africa Cup of Nations 2000; FIFA Confederations Cup 2001; Africa Cup of Nations 2002; FIFA World Cup 2002; FIFA Confederations Cup 2003; Africa Cup of Nations 2004; Africa Cup of Nations 2006; Africa Cup of Nations 2008; Africa Cup of Nations 2010; FIFA World Cup 2010

CLUB CAREER

Major Honours – UEFA Champions League (2006, 2009, 2010); Spanish Championship (2005, 2006, 2009); FIFA Club World Cup (2010); Italian Championship (2010); Spanish Cup (2003, 2009); Italian Cup (2010, 2011)
Clubs: 97-00 Real Madrid CF (ESP); 97-98 CD Leganés (ESP) (loan); 99 RCD Espanyol (loan); 00-04 RCD Mallorca (ESP); 04-09 FC Barcelona (ESP); 09- FC Internazionale Milano (ITA)

Samuel ETO'O Fils
Striker
Born 10/3/81, Nkon, Cameroon
Height 180cm, Weight 75kg

Radamel Falcao scored 16 goals in 22 games to help FC Porto win the 2010/11 Portuguese Liga title, but it was his record-breaking proficiency in the club's UEFA Europa League triumph that made 2010/11 an extra special season for the 25-year-old Colombian striker. His insatiable hunger for goals brought him no fewer than 18 in the European campaign – one in the play-offs (which is discounted in the official records), seven in the group stage and a remarkable ten from the quarter-finals onwards, with FC Spartak Moskva conceding four, Villarreal CF five and even SC Braga's notoriously rock-solid defence surrendering to Falcao's predatory powers in Dublin, where, fittingly, his superb header just before the interval decided the outcome of the final. Even before that strike Falcao was assured of a place in the record books, having already surpassed Jürgen Klinsmann's previous milestone of 15 UEFA Cup goals in one season.

INTERNATIONAL CAREER

COLOMBIA
Debut – 7/2/07 v Uruguay (h, Cucuta, friendly), lost 1-3
First Goal – 3/6/07 v Montenegro (n, Matsumoto, Kirin Cup), won 1-0
Caps 33; **Goals** 9
Major Tournaments – Copa América 2011

CLUB CAREER

Major Honours – UEFA Europa League (2011); Argentinian Championship (clausura 2008); Portuguese Championship (2011); Portuguese Cup (2010, 2011)
Clubs: 05-09 CA River Plate (ARG); 09- FC Porto (POR)

Radamel FALCAO García Zárate
Striker
Born 10/2/86, Magdalena, Colombia
Height 175cm, Weight 78kg

Alexander FREI
Striker
Born 15/7/79, Basel, Switzerland
Height 179cm, Weight 74kg

Switzerland's captain and all-time top goalscorer Alexander Frei ended his international career almost a decade to the day after it began when he responded to criticism of his performance in a goalless draw against Bulgaria in Sofia by retiring from the team with immediate effect. Having scored a goal every other game for his country during ten years of outstanding service, the 31-year-old striker deserved a more fitting farewell, but at least he bowed out while still at the top of his game. Frei scored 27 goals in the 2010/11 Swiss Super League to propel FC Basel 1893 to a successful title defence. It was the first time he had won the Golden Boot in his homeland – though he had claimed the equivalent prize in France, with Stade Rennais FC, six years earlier. His form was especially strong in the spring, when he struck 17 times in 18 games. Furthermore, he scored at least one goal against every other team in the division, including six against the side that Basel beat to the title by a single point – FC Zürich.

INTERNATIONAL CAREER

SWITZERLAND
Debut – 24/3/01 v Yugoslavia (a, Belgrade, WCQ), drew 1-1
First Goal – 28/3/01 v Luxembourg (h, Zurich, WCQ), won 5-0
Caps 84; **Goals** 42
Major Tournaments – UEFA EURO 2004; FIFA World Cup 2006; UEFA EURO 2008; FIFA World Cup 2010

CLUB CAREER

Major Honours – Swiss Championship (2010, 2011); Swiss Cup (2001, 2010)
Clubs: 97-98 FC Basel 1893; 98-99 FC Thun; 99-00 FC Luzern; 01-02 Servette FC; 03-06 Stade Rennais FC (FRA); 06-09 Borussia Dortmund (GER); 09- FC Basel 1893

Kevin GAMEIRO
Striker
Born 9/5/87, Senlis, France
Height 172cm, Weight 62kg

By scoring 22 Ligue 1 goals for FC Lorient in 2010/11, Kevin Gameiro prolonged an impressive sequence that had seen him increase his tally every season since he scored one goal for RC Strasbourg in his debut campaign in 2005/06. It was a tough ask for the young striker to improve on his 2009/10 total of 17, but after a proposed mid-season transfer to Valencia CF failed to materialise, he hit a purple patch, scoring seven goals in four games including a hat-trick – his first for Lorient – in a 5-1 win against another club keen to recruit him, FC Girondins de Bordeaux. His 18th goal of the season came in a 1-1 draw against champions-to-be LOSC Lille Métropole and he closed his account on the final day with his 22nd of the season and 50th in all for the Brittany club in France's top division. That would remain his final tally because in the summer – after scoring his first international goal for France, in a friendly against Ukraine – the sharpshooting 24-year-old got his wish to move to a bigger club when Paris Saint-Germain FC signed him up for €11m on a four-year contract.

INTERNATIONAL CAREER

FRANCE
Debut – 3/9/10 v Belarus (h, Saint-Denis, ECQ), lost 0-1
First Goal – 6/6/11 v Ukraine (a, Donetsk, friendly), won 4-1
Caps 5; **Goals** 1

CLUB CAREER

Clubs: 05-08 RC Strasbourg; 08-11 FC Lorient; 11- Paris Saint-Germain FC

Gervais Yao Kouassi "GERVINHO"
Winger/Striker
Born 27/5/87, Anyama, Ivory Coast
Height 179cm, Weight 68kg

A versatile forward of pace and guile, Gervinho played a leading role in helping LOSC Lille Métropole to an unlikely French double in 2010/11. The Ivory Coast international registered 15 goals and ten assists in the club's Ligue 1 triumph and also contributed three goals in the Coupe de France, including a decisive strike in the semi-final away to OGC Nice. Having already formed a strong understanding with Belgian youngster Eden Hazard in his first season at Lille, Gervinho struck up another productive partnership with the team's new centre-forward Moussa Sow, the Ivorian's clever movement and shrewd interplay allowing the Senegalese striker to flourish up front like never before. Gervinho's most important goal of the season was the winner at home to FC Sochaux-Montbéliard that took Lille to the brink of the title, which they wrapped up three days later in Paris. It was to be his final goal for Lille as in July he crossed the English Channel to join Arsenal FC.

INTERNATIONAL CAREER

IVORY COAST
Debut – 21/11/07 v Qatar (a, Doha, friendly), won 6-1
First Goal – 14/11/09 v Guinea (h, Abidjan, WCQ), won 3-0
Caps 24; **Goals** 6
Major Tournaments – Africa Cup of Nations 2008; Africa Cup of Nations 2010; FIFA World Cup 2010

CLUB CAREER

Major Honours – French Championship (2011); French Cup (2011)
Clubs: 05-07 KSK Beveren (BEL); 07-09 Le Mans UC 72 (FRA); 09-11 LOSC Lille Métropole (FRA); 11- Arsenal FC (ENG)

Ryan GIGGS
Midfielder
Born 29/11/73, Cardiff, Wales
Height 179cm, Weight 72kg

At 37 years of age, the records continue to tumble for Ryan Giggs. He added a few more in 2010/11, notably winning a record 12th Premier League title with Manchester United FC while eclipsing Bobby Charlton's club league appearance record of 606 matches. His unique feat of scoring in every Premier League season was preserved on the opening day with a goal against Newcastle United FC. He added just three more in all competitions over the following nine months, the most important being the opener in United's UEFA Champions League semi-final first leg at FC Schalke 04, which also made him the oldest goalscorer in the competition's history. In the previous round, against Chelsea FC, he provided the assists for all three of United's goals, and he was at it again in the final, setting up Wayne Rooney for the equaliser against FC Barcelona at Wembley. With so much still to offer, it was no surprise that the yoga-practising veteran agreed to extend his United contract for another season – even if he was to continue without his two contemporaries, Gary Neville and Paul Scholes, who both decided to retire.

INTERNATIONAL CAREER

WALES
Debut – 16/10/91 v Germany (a, Nuremberg, ECQ), lost 1-4
First Goal – 31/3/93 v Belgium (h, Cardiff, WCQ), won 2-0
Caps 64; **Goals** 12

CLUB CAREER

Major Honours – UEFA Champions League (1999, 2008); UEFA Super Cup (1991); World Club Cup (1999); FIFA Club World Cup (2008); English Premier League (1993, 1994, 1996, 1997, 1999, 2000, 2001, 2003, 2007, 2008, 2009, 2011); English FA Cup (1994, 1996, 1999, 2004); English League Cup (1992, 2006, 2009, 2010)
Clubs: 90- Manchester United FC (ENG)

Mario GOMEZ
Striker
Born 10/7/85, Riedlingen, Germany
Height 189cm, Weight 86kg

Ostracised for much of FC Bayern München's 2009/10 German double-winning campaign and only a late substitute in the UEFA Champions League final against FC Internazionale Milano, Mario Gomez bounced back in grand style in 2010/11, belatedly justifying the Bundesliga-record fee that had brought him to the club from VfB Stuttgart by scoring 39 goals in all competitions, including 28 in the Bundesliga – the highest tally in the division – and eight in the UEFA Champions League. Unfortunately, the recovery of his best form was not enough to win his team any trophies – nor even to gain revenge on Inter as his two goals against the Italians in the first knockout round ultimately went to waste. However, the powerful, two-footed striker's sustained run of form – which included five Bundeslga hat-tricks, including one away to former club Stuttgart – was enough to convince Joachim Löw to reinstate him in the German national side, and Gomez repaid the Bundestrainer's trust by scoring five goals in four matches, including a smartly taken double against Austria in Vienna that maintained the team's perfect record in their UEFA EURO 2012 qualifying group.

INTERNATIONAL CAREER

GERMANY
Debut – 7/2/07 v Switzerland (h, Dusseldorf, friendly), won 3-1
First Goal – 7/2/07 v Switzerland (h, Dusseldorf, friendly), won 3-1
Caps 46; **Goals** 19
Major Tournaments – UEFA EURO 2008; FIFA World Cup 2010

CLUB CAREER

Major Honours – German Championship (2007, 2010); German Cup (2010)
Clubs: 03-09 VfB Stuttgart; 09- FC Bayern München

Mario GÖTZE
Attacking Midfielder
Born 3/6/92, Memmingen, Germany
Height 176cm, Weight 64kg

As if Germany did not have enough highly gifted youngsters on show at the 2010 FIFA World Cup, another one entered the fray in 2010/11. Mario Götze, just 18 at the start of the season and still 18 at the end of it, became the second youngest player to represent Germany at senior level – after the great Uwe Seeler – when he made his debut in a friendly against Sweden in November 2010. He earned his elevation with a string of dazzling displays in the Bundesliga for Borussia Dortmund. Handed a regular first-team berth by coach Jürgen Klopp following a memorable first start in Europe, which he marked with two goals in a 4-3 away win at FC Karpaty Lviv, he held his place all season, missing only one league game and making a major contribution to Dortmund's title triumph with six goals and 16 assists. Small and slippery, with excellent footwork and a sudden burst of pace, Götze has inevitably been branded as the 'German Lionel Messi'. Whether that tag proves to be an inspiration or a burden remains to be seen, but there is no doubt that the youngster possesses a rare talent that could carry him to the very peak of his profession.

INTERNATIONAL CAREER

GERMANY
Debut – 17/11/10 v Sweden (a, Gothenburg, friendly), drew 0-0
Caps 6; **Goals** 0

CLUB CAREER

Major Honours – German Championship (2011)
Clubs: 09- Borussia Dortmund

As a long-time Borussia Dortmund supporter and hometown boy, Kevin Grosskreutz probably savoured the club's 2010/11 German Bundesliga triumph more than most. He certainly made an important contribution to it, appearing in all 34 matches (32 from the start) and scoring eight goals, including two in the 3-1 win at closest pursuers Bayer 04 Leverkusen just after the winter break that opened the gates to Dortmund's first national title for nine years. Handed his international debut just before the 2010 FIFA World Cup, Grosskreutz did not travel to South Africa but he was one of five Dortmund youngsters called up by Germany coach Joachim Löw during the 2010/11 season. Indeed, he made his first international start in a November 2010 friendly against Sweden alongside club colleagues Mats Hummels and Marcel Schmelzer – before making way for a fourth Dortmund player, Mario Götze, 12 minutes from time. A tireless runner who has discovered his natural habitat on the left-hand side of midfield, the 23-year-old improved both his temperament and technique in 2010/11 and, having signed a new long-term contract, should be a major asset to Dortmund for many years to come.

INTERNATIONAL CAREER

GERMANY
Debut – 13/5/10 v Malta (h, Aachen, friendly), won 3-0
Caps 3; **Goals** 0

CLUB CAREER

Major Honours – German Championship (2011)
Clubs: 07-09 Rot Weiss Ahlen; 09- Borussia Dortmund

Kevin GROSSKREUTZ
Winger/Attacking Midfielder
Born 19/7/88, Dortmund, Germany
Height 186cm, Weight 72kg

A perennially consistent performer for SSC Napoli since his arrival from another Italian club, Brescia Calcio, in 2007, Marek Hamšík finally gained reward for his efforts in 2010/11 – not with a first career trophy but with qualification for the group stage of the 2011/12 UEFA Champions League and the opportunity to test his considerable talents on the club game's biggest stage. While new signing Edinson Cavani, with his 26 Serie A goals, was universally acknowledged as the man who made the difference for Napoli, Hamšík also played a major role in transforming the team from also-rans into genuine title contenders. All but one of his 11 league goals contributed to victories, and Cavani would not have been nearly so prolific without the elegant Slovakian international playmaker's probing runs and perfectly weighted through balls. The captain of the Slovakia team that knocked Italy out of the 2010 FIFA World Cup, Hamšík did not add to his tally of eight international goals during the 2010/11 season but he was on the field for every minute of Slovakia's UEFA EURO 2012 qualifying campaign, the highlight of which was a precious 1-0 victory over Russia in Moscow.

INTERNATIONAL CAREER

SLOVAKIA
Debut – 7/2/07 v Poland (n, Jerez, friendly), drew 2-2
First Goal – 13/10/07 v San Marino (h, Dubnica, ECQ), won 7-0
Caps 46; **Goals** 8
Major Tournaments – FIFA World Cup 2010

CLUB CAREER

Clubs: 04 ŠK Slovan Bratislava; 04-07 Brescia Calcio (ITA); 07- SSC Napoli (ITA)

Marek HAMŠÍK
Midfielder
Born 27/7/87, Banska Bystrica, Slovakia
Height 180cm, Weight 73kg

Joe HART
Goalkeeper
Born 19/4/87, Shrewsbury, England
Height 191cm, Weight 80kg

A frustrated onlooker at the 2010 FIFA World Cup, Joe Hart was belatedly promoted to the position of England's No1 goalkeeper by Fabio Capello after the tournament. He went on to establish himself in the role, starting all but one of his country's nine internationals in 2010/11 – the only one he missed was the only one they lost, a friendly against France – and performing with sufficient skill and confidence to claim the position as his own for the foreseeable future. It was also a breakthrough season for the 24-year-old at club level. Back at Manchester City FC after an impressive season on loan at Birmingham City FC, the big blond 'keeper found favour with another Italian coach, Roberto Mancini, who selected him ahead of veteran Shay Given and was rewarded with an inspired opening-day display in a 0-0 draw at Tottenham Hotspur FC. By the end of the season Hart had not only started every Premier League game but was recognised with the Golden Glove as the division's top goalkeeper, keeping 18 clean sheets. Furthermore, he brilliantly kept his goal intact in both the semi-final and final of the FA Cup, which City won to end a trophy drought stretching back to 1976.

INTERNATIONAL CAREER

ENGLAND
Debut – 1/6/08 v Trinidad & Tobago (a, Port of Spain, friendly), won 3-0
Caps 11; **Goals** 0
Major Tournaments – FIFA World Cup 2010

CLUB CAREER

Major Honours – English FA Cup (2011)
Clubs: 03-06 Shrewsbury Town FC; 06- Manchester City FC; 07 Tranmere Rovers FC (loan); 07 Blackpool FC (loan); 09-10 Birmingham City FC (loan)

Eden HAZARD
Attacking Midfielder
Born 7/1/91, La Louviere, Belgium
Height 170cm, Weight 69kg

Eden Hazard's third full season with LOSC Lille Métropole did not start as he would have wanted. Out of sorts and omitted from the Belgian national side, the multi-talented youngster faced the first major challenge of his fledgling career. But those who openly questioned his mental strength were made to eat their words as the youngster got to grips with the situation, recovered his form and went on to inspire Lille to a remarkable Ligue 1/Coupe de France double. Hazard's contribution to the title win was more than the black-and-white statistics of seven goals and ten assists. He was everything Lille boss Rudi Garcia wanted from him and much more besides, crafting and shaping the team's adventurous attacking play with his imaginative passes and penetrative dribbles. Having been voted Ligue 1's Young Player of the Year by his fellow professionals in each of the previous two seasons, Hazard scooped the senior prize in 2010/11, becoming, at 20, the youngest ever winner of a prestigious award that included in its roll of honour such illustrious names as David Ginola, Zinédine Zidane and Didier Drogba.

INTERNATIONAL CAREER

BELGIUM
Debut – 19/11/08 v Luxembourg (a, Luxembourg, friendly), drew 1-1
Caps 20; **Goals** 0

CLUB CAREER

Major Honours – French Championship (2011); French Cup (2011)
Clubs: 07- LOSC Lille Métropole (FRA)

Although few were aware of it at the time, Manchester United FC pulled off a major coup when they signed Javier Hernández from CD Guadalajara just before the 2010 FIFA World Cup. There were glimpses of the young Mexican striker's goalscoring prowess in South Africa, but not even the scouts who persuaded the powers-that-be at Old Trafford to sign him could have imagined that he would have such a profound impact on his first season in English football. Announcing himself as 'Chicharito' ('Little Pea'), Hernández drew inevitable comparisons with another former 'unknown' United newcomer, Ole Gunnar Solskjær, as he outscored Wayne Rooney and usurped Dimitar Berbatov at the focal point of the United attack. He registered 20 goals in total, 13 of them contributing towards United's Premier League title triumph and another four – all crucial – helping the team reach the UEFA Champions League final. He looked slightly overawed against FC Barcelona at Wembley, but the confidence was fully restored a few weeks later as he inspired Mexico to victory at the CONCACAF Gold Cup, winning dual recognition as the tournament's top goalscorer and most valuable player.

INTERNATIONAL CAREER

MEXICO
Major Honours – CONCACAF Gold Cup (2011)
Debut – 30/9/09 v Colombia (n, Dallas, friendly), lost 1-2
First Goal – 24/2/10 v Bolivia (n, San Francisco, friendly), won 5-0
Caps 29; **Goals** 19
Major Tournaments – FIFA World Cup 2010; CONCACAF Gold Cup 2011

CLUB CAREER

Major Honours – Mexican Championship (apertura 2006); English Premier League (2011)
Clubs: 06-10 CD Guadalajara; 10- Manchester United FC (ENG)

Javier HERNÁNDEZ Balcazar
Striker
Born 1/6/88, Guadalajara, Mexico
Height 175cm, Weight 71kg

An enigmatic figure during his first two seasons at FC Porto, Hulk gave full rein to his talents in 2010/11. The barrel-chested Brazilian with the mazy dribble and the explosive left foot repeatedly tore defences apart – both in Portugal and in Europe – as André Villas-Boas's all-conquering team captured a glorious treble of Portuguese League, Portuguese Cup and UEFA Europa League. Hulk left the bulk of the goalscoring in Europe to his Colombian strike partner Radamel Falcao, but on the domestic front he was the club's main marksman, topping the Liga scoring charts with 23 goals. It was not just the run-of-the-mill Portuguese defences that failed to cope with his potent cocktail of strength, speed and skill. Defending champions SL Benfica conceded three times to him in the league – albeit twice from the penalty spot – and once more in the semi-finals of the Taça de Portugal. His all-competition end-of-season statistics made mightily impressive reading – 36 goals and 21 assists. No wonder Porto re-negotiated his contract and warded off would-be purchasers by inserting in it a €100m buy-out clause.

INTERNATIONAL CAREER

BRAZIL
Debut – 14/11/09 v England (n, Doha, friendly), won 1-0
Caps 3; **Goals** 0

CLUB CAREER

Major Honours – UEFA Europa League (2011); Portuguese Championship (2009, 2011); Portuguese Cup (2009, 2010, 2011)
Clubs: 04 SC Vitória; 05-08 Kawasaki Frontale (JPN); 06 Consadole Sapporo (JPN) (loan); 07 Tokyo Verdy (JPN) (loan); 08 Tokyo Verdy (JPN); 08- FC Porto (POR)

Givanildo Vieira da Souza "HULK"
Winger/Striker
Born 25/7/86, Campina Grande, Brazil
Height 180cm, Weight 75kg

Mats HUMMELS
Centre-Back
Born 16/12/88, Bergisch Gladbach, Germany
Height 192cm, Weight 90kg

Considered surplus to requirements at FC Bayern München, the club that developed him as a youth, Mats Hummels has developed into an outstanding central defender – and occasional defensive midfielder – at Borussia Dortmund. As intelligent and stylish off the field as he is on it, the 22-year-old enjoyed a wonderful 2010/11 season, brilliantly marshalling a Dortmund defence that conceded only 22 goals en route to a runaway Bundesliga title success. His partnership with Serbian centre-back Neven Subotić was far and away the most effective in the league, conceding more than one goal in just two games. In addition to his defensive duties, Hummels also found time to contribute five goals, the most memorable of them a towering header that completed a 3-1 win over ex-club Bayern in Munich. A member of Germany's UEFA European Under-21 Championship-winning squad in 2009, he seems likely to be involved with the senior Nationalmannschaft at UEFA EURO 2012, having started each of Germany's last four internationals in 2010/11, including the two June qualifiers against Austria and Azerbaijan.

INTERNATIONAL CAREER

GERMANY
Debut – 13/5/10 v Malta (h, Aachen, friendly), won 3-0
Caps 7; **Goals** 0

CLUB CAREER

Major Honours – German Championship (2011)
Clubs: 07-09 FC Bayern München; 08-09 Borussia Dortmund (loan); 09- Borussia Dortmund

Klaas Jan HUNTELAAR
Striker
Born 12/8/83, Drempt, Netherlands
Height 186cm, Weight 80kg

Used only as a substitute by the Netherlands at the 2010 FIFA World Cup, and not all in the final, Klaas Jan Huntelaar returned to the Oranje attack at the start of the UEFA EURO 2012 qualifying campaign and showed coach Bert van Marwijk what might have been had he brought him on against Spain in Johannesburg by scoring eight goals in the first four qualifiers. He subsequently scored in each of the team's next two friendlies to move past Marco van Basten in the Netherlands' all-time goalscoring list. The irony was that Huntelaar would probably still have been on the bench had first-choice central striker Robin van Persie not been laid low with injury. At club level, Huntelaar left AC Milan for FC Schalke 04 and made a good start for the Gelsenkirchen side, scoring in five successive Bundesliga games and adding three goals in the UEFA Champions League group stage, but a knee injury put him out of action for a couple of months in the spring. He did, however, return in time for the German Cup final in Berlin and marked the occasion by scoring two goals in a 5-0 rout of second-tier MSV Duisburg to win his first major trophy in four years and his first outside the Netherlands.

INTERNATIONAL CAREER

NETHERLANDS
Debut – 16/8/06 v Republic of Ireland (a, Dublin, friendly), won 4-0
First Goal – 16/8/06 v Republic of Ireland (a, Dublin, friendly), won 4-0
Caps 44, **Goals** 26
Major Tournaments – UEFA EURO 2008; FIFA World Cup 2010

CLUB CAREER

Major Honours – Dutch Cup (2006, 2007); German Cup (2011)
Clubs: 02-04 PSV Eindhoven; 03 De Graafschap (loan); 03/04 AGOVV Apeldoorn (loan); 04-06 sc Heerenveen; 06-09 AFC Ajax; 09 Real Madrid CF (ESP); 09-10 AC Milan (ITA); 10- FC Schalke 04 (GER)

Zlatan IBRAHIMOVIĆ

Striker
Born 3/10/81, Malmo, Sweden
Height 192cm, Weight 84kg

But for the two Italian Serie A titles stripped from Juventus in 2004/05 and 2005/06, Zlatan Ibrahimović would be on a sensational streak of eight successive domestic championship wins – for five different clubs in three different countries. The big Swedish striker's talismanic qualities were evident once again in 2010/11 as he joined AC Milan on a one-year loan from FC Barcelona and, as in his three seasons at rivals FC Internazionale Milano, inspired the club to the scudetto. He scored 14 goals in Serie A – all in singles, including a winning penalty against Inter – and another four in Europe. If the autumn and winter were hugely uplifting, the spring, however, was something of a letdown as Ibrahimović once again failed to do himself justice against an English club – Milan were eliminated from the UEFA Champions League by Tottenham Hotspur FC – then missed the final weeks of the season through suspension and injury. The new Sweden captain did, however, return to international duty with a bang in June, coming off the bench to fire a tremendous hat-trick against Finland.

INTERNATIONAL CAREER

SWEDEN
Debut – 31/1/01 v Faroe Islands (h, Vaxjo, friendly), drew 0-0
First Goal – 7/10/01 v Azerbaijan (h, Solna, WCQ), won 3-0
Caps 69; **Goals** 28
Major Tournaments – FIFA World Cup 2002; UEFA EURO 2004; FIFA World Cup 2006; UEFA EURO 2008

CLUB CAREER

Major Honours – UEFA Super Cup (2009); FIFA Club World Cup (2009); Dutch Championship (2002, 2004); Italian Championship (2007, 2008, 2009, 2011); Spanish Championship (2010); Dutch Cup (2002)
Clubs: 99-01 Malmö FF; 01-04 AFC Ajax (NED); 04-06 Juventus (ITA); 06-09 FC Internazionale Milano (ITA); 09-11 FC Barcelona (ESP); 10-11 AC Milan (ITA) (loan); 11- AC Milan (ITA)

Andrés INIESTA Luján

Attacking Midfielder
Born 11/5/84, Fuentealbilla, Spain
Height 170cm, Weight 65kg

As he proved with his winning goal for Spain in the 2010 FIFA World Cup final, Andrés Iniesta is a man for the big occasion. Injured and absent from the first leg of the UEFA Champions League semi-final against Real Madrid CF, he returned for the second encounter at Camp Nou and set up Pedro's tie-clinching goal with an exquisite defence-splitting pass. He was also exceptional in the final, repeatedly stretching the Manchester United FC rearguard with his perpetual movement and probing passes. The runner-up to Lionel Messi in the 2010 FIFA Ballon d'Or vote, Iniesta scored more league goals for Barça in 2010/11 than in any previous season, his eight Liga strikes supplementing one against FC Shakhtar Donetsk in Europe. A goal at Wembley would have taken him to double figures for the first time, but on three occasions he was denied by fine saves from United 'keeper Edwin van der Sar.

INTERNATIONAL CAREER

SPAIN
Major Honours – FIFA World Cup (2010); UEFA European Championship (2008)
Debut – 27/5/06 v Russia (h, Albacete, friendly), drew 0-0
First Goal – 7/2/07 v England (a, Manchester, friendly), won 1-0
Caps 58; **Goals** 8
Major Tournaments – FIFA World Cup 2006; UEFA EURO 2008; FIFA World Cup 2010

CLUB CAREER

Major Honours – UEFA Champions League (2006, 2009, 2011); UEFA Super Cup (2009); FIFA Club World Cup (2009); Spanish Championship (2005, 2006, 2009, 2010, 2011); Spanish Cup (2009)
Clubs: 00- FC Barcelona

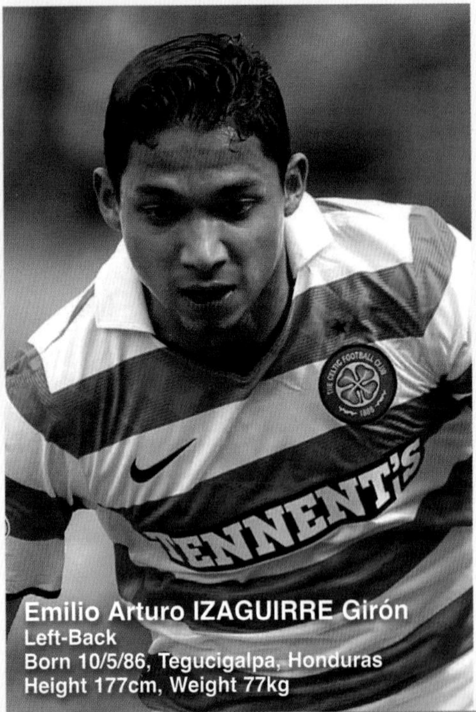

Emilio Arturo IZAGUIRRE Girón
Left-Back
Born 10/5/86, Tegucigalpa, Honduras
Height 177cm, Weight 77kg

Celtic FC signed 15 new players in the summer of 2010 as new manager Neil Lennon looked to construct a multi-cultural squad that would take Scotland by storm. Of those for whom a fee was paid, Honduran international Emilio Izaguirre was among the cheapest, but he would prove to be the best of the bunch by some distance, eclipsing the likes of Joe Ledley, Efrain Juárez, Biram Kayal and even top goalscorer Gary Hooper. The diminutive left-back, a member of Honduras's 2010 FIFA World Cup squad, turned out to be the revelation of the Scottish Premier League, collecting both main player of the season awards – from the country's journalists as well as his fellow players - as the Hoops won the Scottish Cup and narrowly missed out on the SPL title. A key influence both in defence and going forward, Izaguirre conjured up a steady supply of assists for his team-mates. The only problem for Celtic was that his performances were so impressive that he inevitably attracted the attention of scouts from bigger clubs in England and overseas.

INTERNATIONAL CAREER

HONDURAS
Debut – 27/1/07 v Denmark "B" (h, Tegucigalpa, friendly), drew 1-1
First Goal – 2/6/07 v Trinidad & Tobago (h, San Pedro Sula, friendly), won 3-1
Caps 45; **Goals** 1
Major Tournaments – CONCACAF Gold Cup 2007; FIFA World Cup 2010; CONCACAF Gold Cup 2011

CLUB CAREER

Major Honours – Honduran Championship (2007); Scottish Cup (2011)
Clubs: 04-10 CD Motagua; 10- Celtic FC (SCO)

Theo JANSSEN
Midfielder
Born 27/7/81, Arnhem, Netherlands
Height 180cm, Weight 80kg

There could be only one winner in 2010/11 of the Gouden Schoen – the trophy presented to the Dutch Eredivisie player of the year. FC Twente midfielder Theo Janssen enjoyed the season of his life, scoring 20 goals in all competitions – he had never previously reached double figures and managed just two in 2009/10 – and inspiring the Enschede club to victory in the Dutch Cup and a hard-fought runners-up spot in their defence of the Eredivisie title. It was no surprise when AFC Ajax, the team that snatched the league crown from Twente on the final day, announced that they had signed the midfielder a few days later. Four of Janssen's goals had been scored against the Amsterdam club – three in the league and one in the cup final, where he also supplied the immaculate in-swinging cross that Marc Janko headed home to give Twente an extra-time winner. Janssen also scored three times against PSV Eindhoven, including one terrific effort when he ran from the halfway line before lifting the ball deftly over the goalkeeper. His left foot was a deadly weapon all season long, and although he turned 30 during the summer, Ajax fans will be hoping that the maverick midfielder can turn on the style again in 2011/12.

INTERNATIONAL CAREER

NETHERLANDS
Debut – 16/8/06 v Republic of Ireland (a, Dublin, friendly), won 4-0
Caps 5; **Goals** 0

CLUB CAREER

Major Honours – Dutch Championship (2010); Dutch Cup (2011)
Clubs: 98-08 Vitesse; 03-04 KRC Genk (BEL) (loan); 08-11 FC Twente; 11- AFC Ajax

When João Moutinho left Sporting Clube de Portugal for FC Porto in the summer of 2010, it did not go down well with the Lisbon club, whose president at the time, José Bettencourt, had some choice words to say about the player's sudden switch of allegiance. The gifted young midfielder had given Sporting six years of valuable service, shunning offers before, so the criticism seemed rather harsh. But if there was anger and frustration at Sporting as the player departed, those feelings can only have intensified over the following 12 months as the 24-year-old schemer played a pivotal role in helping Porto to a magnificent treble of Portuguese Liga, Taça de Portugal and UEFA Europa League. As had always been the case during his time at Sporting, Moutinho avoided injury and barely missed a game. He clocked up exactly 50 appearances in all competitions over the season, and while Porto boss André Villas-Boas repeatedly sang his praises, his former Sporting coach, Paulo Bento, also made him a key figure in the Portuguese national team – a major boost for the player following his surprise exclusion from the 2010 FIFA World Cup squad by previous coach Carlos Queiroz.

INTERNATIONAL CAREER

PORTUGAL
Debut – 17/8/05 v Egypt (h, Ponta Delgada, friendly), won 2-0
First Goal – 31/5/08 v Georgia (h, Viseu, friendly), won 2-0
Caps 34; **Goals** 1
Major Tournaments – UEFA EURO 2008

CLUB CAREER

Major Honours – UEFA Europa League (2011); Portuguese Championship (2011); Portuguese Cup (2007, 2008, 2011)
Clubs: 04-10 Sporting Clube de Portugal; 10- FC Porto

Although William Kvist Jørgensen had already won four Danish Superliga titles with FC København prior to the 2010/11 season, his fifth meant much more to him than any of the others. It was the first one in which he operated in central midfield. Previously he had been used on the fringes of the side at either right-back or on the right-hand side of midfield. In 2010/11, coach Ståle Solbakken converted him into the team's central cog, and he responded brilliantly, orchestrating FCK's play with such poise and control that it seemed he had been doing it for years. Jørgensen was voted Danish Footballer of the Year at the end of 2010 – at a time when FCK held a 19-point lead at the top of the Superliga table and had just become the first Danish team to reach the knockout phase of the UEFA Champions League – and there was further recognition at the end of the campaign when he won the Superliga Player of the Year award. The 26-year-old was an unused member of Denmark's 2010 FIFA World Cup squad, but his coming of age in 2010/11 ensured him a regular berth in Morten Olsen's side for the UEFA EURO 2012 qualifying campaign. It also earned him a summer move to German Bundesliga club VfB Stuttgart, with whom he signed a four-year contract.

INTERNATIONAL CAREER

DENMARK
Debut – 22/8/07 v Republic of Ireland (h, Aarhus, friendly), lost 0-4
Caps 20; **Goals** 0
Major Tournaments – FIFA World Cup 2010

CLUB CAREER

Major Honours – Danish Championship (2006, 2007, 2009, 2010, 2011); Danish Cup (2009)
Clubs: 04-11 FC København; 11- VfB Stuttgart (GER)

When Shinji Kagawa arrived in Germany, the supporters of Borussia Dortmund knew very little of him. Less than a month into the season, however, the feisty youngster from Japan was already being fêted as a cult hero. A brace of goals on his European debut was a useful start, but that paled into insignificance compared to his brilliant two-goal, man-of-the-match display in a 3-1 win over arch-rivals FC Schalke 04. A key member of Jürgen Klopp's team from day one, Kagawa became the revelation of the autumn campaign, scoring eight goals in 17 Bundesliga appearances plus another four in Europe. Just as Dortmund fans were licking their lips at what might come in the spring, however, Kagawa fractured his foot in January while competing at the AFC Asian Cup. The injury, which would put him out of action for four months, was sustained in the semi-final against South Korea after he had struck twice in the quarter-final victory over hosts Qatar. Japan went on to win the final against Australia without him, and it was a similar story for Dortmund in the Bundesliga.

INTERNATIONAL CAREER

JAPAN
Major Honours – AFC Asian Cup (2011)
Debut – 24/5/08 v Ivory Coast (h, Toyota, Kirin Cup), won 1-0
First Goal – 9/10/08 v United Arab Emirates (h, Niigata, friendly), drew 1-1
Caps 22; **Goals** 5
Major Tournaments – AFC Asian Cup 2011

CLUB CAREER

Major Honours – German Championship (2011)
Clubs: 06-10 Cerezo Osaka; 10- Borussia Dortmund (GER)

A prolific goalscorer during his first spell at FC Zenit St Petersburg, from 2001-06, Aleksandr Kerzhakov made a triumphant return to the club in 2010, winning the Russian Cup and top-scoring with 13 goals as Zenit reclaimed the Premier-Liga title. He also rediscovered his scoring touch with the Russian national side, making peace with his former Zenit coach Dick Advocaat, with whom he had fallen out four years earlier, and registering two important goals in the UEFA EURO 2012 qualifying competition away to the Republic of Ireland and the Former Yugoslav Republic of Macedonia. During his first spell at Zenit, Kerzhakov had developed a highly effective forward partnership with fellow Russian international Andrey Arshavin; in 2010 he found an equally effective foil in Portuguese playmaker Danny. The only disappointment in a fabulous year for Zenit was their failure to qualify for the UEFA Champions League – despite Kerzhakov's winner in the first leg of the play-off against AJ Auxerre – but the striker made a grand entrance into the UEFA Europa League with a match-winning hat-trick of stunning quality against RSC Anderlecht in Brussels.

INTERNATIONAL CAREER

RUSSIA
Debut – 27/3/02 v Estonia (a, Tallinn, friendly), lost 1-2
First Goal – 21/8/02 v Sweden (h, Moscow, friendly), drew 1-1
Caps 54; **Goals** 17
Major Tournaments – FIFA World Cup 2002; UEFA EURO 2004

CLUB CAREER

Major Honours – UEFA Cup (2007); Russian Championship (2010); Spanish Cup (2007); Russian Cup (2010)
Clubs: 00 FC Svetogorets Svetogorsk; 01-06 FC Zenit St Petersburg; 07-08 Sevilla FC (ESP); 08-09 FC Dinamo Moskva; 10- FC Zenit St Petersburg

There was an enormous amount of pressure on Sami Khedira when he joined Real Madrid CF from VfB Stuttgart on a five-year contract in the summer of 2010. The midfielder's reputation had soared during the FIFA World Cup in South Africa, where he proved a more than capable deputy for injured Germany skipper Michael Ballack, but some of the cogniscenti at the Santiago Bernabéu questioned whether he might be a one-tournament wonder ill-equipped to handle the unrelenting pressure of playing week in, week out for Real Madrid. The club's new coach José Mourinho had plenty of faith in the young German, however, and installed him alongside Xabi Alonso in Madrid's midfield engine room. Khedira repaid him with a succession of strong, resolute performances that not only sealed his place in the first XI but also won over the local sceptics. Khedira was especially prominent in Madrid's UEFA Champions League campaign, so it was a major blow to both him and the team when he was forced to miss both legs of the semi-final against FC Barcelona through injury.

INTERNATIONAL CAREER

GERMANY
Debut – 5/9/09 v South Africa (h, Leverkusen, friendly), won 2-0
First Goal – 10/7/10 v Uruguay (n, Port Elizabeth, WCF), won 3-2
Caps 20; **Goals** 1
Major Tournaments – FIFA World Cup 2010

CLUB CAREER

Major Honours – German Championship (2007); Spanish Cup (2011)
Clubs: 06-10 VfB Stuttgart; 10- Real Madrid CF (ESP)

Highly acclaimed during the early years of his career with RSC Anderlecht, Vincent Kompany fulfilled his potential as a top-class defender during his third season at Manchester City FC. The Belgian international had been predominantly used as a holding midfielder during his first 18 months at City by manager Mark Hughes, but the Welshman's successor, Roberto Mancini, restored him to his more familiar domain and Kompany's outstanding efforts in central defence during the 2010/11 campaign, in which he racked up 50 appearances, proved the Italian right. Whether partnered by Kolo Touré or – following the Ivorian's suspension – Joleon Lescott, Kompany was a model of composure and dependability. In the absence of the injured Carlos Tévez, he captained City to their FA Cup semi-final victory over Manchester United FC at Wembley and returned to the national stadium four weeks later to help the club lift the trophy after a 1-0 win over Stoke City FC. Kompany's season ended on a disappointing note, however, when Belgium could only draw 1-1 at home to Turkey in a crucial UEFA EURO 2012 qualifier – a result that seemed likely to delay his ambition of representing his country in a major international tournament.

INTERNATIONAL CAREER

BELGIUM
Debut – 18/2/04 v France (h, Brussels, friendly), lost 0-2
First Goal – 19/5/10 v Bulgaria (h, Brussels, friendly), won 2-1
Caps 39; **Goals** 1

CLUB CAREER

Major Honours – Belgian Championship (2004, 2006); English FA Cup (2011)
Clubs: 03-06 RSC Anderlecht; 06-08 Hamburger SV (GER); 08- Manchester City FC (ENG)

Dirk KUYT
Striker/Right Midfielder
Born 22/7/80, Katwijk aan Zee, Netherlands
Height 184cm, Weight 84kg

Liverpool FC underwent a season of transition in 2010/11, with not one but two new managers and an abundance of activity on the transfer front. The upheaval did not affect Dirk Kuyt, though. The indefatigable, ultra-reliable Dutchman just went about his business in the usual way, without fuss or fanfare, and ended the season as the Reds' top scorer with a personal-best Premier League haul of 13 goals. Already a Kop favourite, Kuyt enhanced his popularity by scoring his first Liverpool hat-trick against arch-rivals Manchester United FC, in a 3-1 win at Anfield. That prompted an impressive burst of goalscoring in the closing weeks of the campaign, the highlight of which was probably a penalty he scored in the 12th minute of added time to earn an improbable 1-1 draw at Arsenal FC – after his compatriot Robin van Persie had put the home side ahead, also from the spot, moments earlier. Kuyt also enjoyed a productive season for the Netherlands, three of his six goals coming in a UEFA EURO 2012 qualifying double-header against Hungary at the end of March.

INTERNATIONAL CAREER

NETHERLANDS
Debut – 3/9/04 v Liechtenstein (h, Utrecht, friendly), won 3-0
First Goal – 9/10/04 v FYROM (a, Skopje, WCQ), drew 2-2
Caps 78; **Goals** 22
Major Tournaments – FIFA World Cup 2006; UEFA EURO 2008; FIFA World Cup 2010

CLUB CAREER

Major Honours – Dutch Cup (2003)
Clubs: 98 Quick Boys; 98-03 FC Utrecht; 03-06 Feyenoord; 06- Liverpool FC (ENG)

Fernando LLORENTE Torres
Striker
Born 26/2/85, Pamplona, Spain
Height 193cm, Weight 88kg

Tall, strong and powerful in the air, Fernando Llorente has all the characteristics of the classic centre-forward. He is also excellent at shielding the ball and bringing others into play. As with all of the best strikers, though, his chief asset is his ability to put the ball in the net, and in 2010/11 he enjoyed his most productive season yet in the Spanish Liga for Athletic Club, scoring 18 goals to help the Bilbao outfit reach sixth place and qualify for the UEFA Europa League. Fit and firing on all cylinders throughout the campaign, Llorente was a persistent menace to Primera Divisíón defences. Only five of the 20 teams stopped him from scoring against them, and although his goal away to Real Madrid CF was a mere consolation in a 5-1 defeat, persistent rumours circulated thereafter that the Estádio Santiago Bernabéu would soon become his new home. 2010/11 was also a breakthrough season for the Basque striker at international level as he stood in regularly for the out-of-sorts Fernando Torres and scored three goals in two UEFA EURO 2012 qualifiers, including the winner – three minutes after coming off the bench – in a 3-2 victory over Scotland at Hampden Park.

INTERNATIONAL CAREER

SPAIN
Major Honours – FIFA World Cup (2010)
Debut – 19/11/08 v Chile (h, Villarreal, friendly), won 3-0
First Goal – 11/2/09 v England (h, Seville, friendly), won 2-0
Caps 16; **Goals** 7
Major Tournaments – FIFA World Cup 2010

CLUB CAREER

Clubs: 03-04 CD Baskonia; 04-05 Athletic Club B; 05- Athletic Club

Yann M'VILA
Midfielder
Born 29/6/90, Amiens, France
Height 183cm, Weight 78kg

A vastly experienced French youth international, Yann M'Vila made his senior debut for Les Bleus in the first match of new coach Laurent Blanc's reign – a friendly away to Norway from which all members of the country's 2010 FIFA World Cup squad were excluded as a punishment for their misbehaviour in South Africa. For several participants in Oslo there would be no subsequent call-ups, but M'Vila performed so impressively in his midfield holding role that Blanc not only retained him for the UEFA EURO 2012 qualifying campaign but proceeded to make him one of the cornerstones of his new-look team. For a 20-year-old with just one full season of top-flight football behind him, it was a meteoric rise, but nobody could claim that M'Vila did not deserve the recognition. An excellent second Ligue 1 campaign, with Stade Rennais FC, merely enhanced his international claims. Surprise title contenders for the first two thirds of the season, the Bretons fell off the pace in the spring but M'Vila held his own game together and was rewarded for his season-long consistency with a place in the official Ligue 1 Team of the Year. Despite growing interest from elsewhere, M'Vila decided to stay on at Rennes, extending his contract to 2015.

INTERNATIONAL CAREER

FRANCE
Debut – 11/8/10 v Norway (a, Oslo, friendly), lost 1-2
Caps 10; **Goals** 0

CLUB CAREER

Clubs: 09- Stade Rennais FC

MARCELO Vieira da Silva Júnior
Left-Back
Born 12/5/88, Rio de Janeiro, Brazil
Height 174cm, Weight 73kg

A Real Madrid CF player since January 2007, when he was recruited from Fluminense FC as the prospective replacement at left-back for his illustrious compatriot Roberto Carlos, Marcelo was later moved forward into a wide midfield role by coach Juande Ramos and retained in that position by Manuel Pellegrini. In 2010/11, however, new Madrid boss José Mourinho declared that in his favoured 4-2-3-1 system the only way he could incorporate the Brazilian was to restore him to his former position at left-back. The problem was that while Mourinho was well aware of Marcelo's skill and adventure going forward, he had reservations about both his defensive aptitude and his lack of discipline. Those doubts soon disappeared, though, as the youngster added steel to the silk and became one of the team's most consistent performers. The UEFA Champions League brought out the best – and occasionally the worst – in him. His outstanding technique was showcased by a brilliant solo goal in the first knockout round at home to Olympique Lyonnais, and although he also scored in the semi-final against FC Barcelona, by then Madrid were already 3-0 down and on their way out of the competition.

INTERNATIONAL CAREER

BRAZIL
Debut – 5/9/06 v Wales (n, London, friendly), won 2-0
First Goal – 5/9/06 v Wales (n, London, friendly), won 2-0
Caps 6; **Goals** 1

CLUB CAREER

Major Honours – Spanish Championship (2007, 2008); Spanish Cup (2011)
Clubs: 05-06 Fluminense FC; 07- Real Madrid CF (ESP)

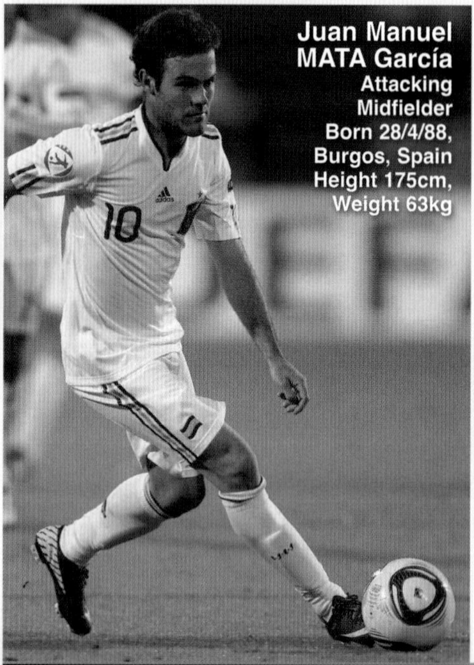

A FIFA World Cup winner with Spain in 2010, Juan Mata added another international title to his CV with victory at the 2011 UEFA European Under-21 Championship in Denmark. The most experienced member of Luis Milla's victorious squad, Mata wore the No10 shirt with distinction, starting all five matches, scoring two goals and excelling with his skill and industry throughout. He travelled north having enjoyed an excellent domestic season with his club Valencia CF. Although they were eliminated from the UEFA Champions League in the last 16 by FC Schalke 04, they did ensure an immediate return to the competition by taking third place in La Liga. With Spanish internationals David Villa and David Silva having flown the Mestalla nest, Mata had a more influential role in the team, and he bore the extra responsibility well, two of his eight league goals coming in a thumping 5-0 win over local rivals Villarreal CF in April that provided the highlight of the season for both him and his club.

INTERNATIONAL CAREER

SPAIN

Major Honours – FIFA World Cup (2010)
Debut – 28/3/09 v Turkey (h, Madrid, WCQ), won 1-0
First Goal – 9/9/09 v Estonia (h, Merida, WCQ), won 3-0
Caps 11; **Goals** 4
Major Tournaments – FIFA Confederations Cup 2009; FIFA World Cup 2010

CLUB CAREER

Major Honours – Spanish Cup (2008)
Clubs: 06-07 Real Madrid Castilla; 07- Valencia CF

Unquestionably the finest player of his generation, Lionel Messi can now be classified without reservation as one of the greatest footballers ever to have played the game. Not only is he a genius but, unlike the man to whom he has always been – and probably forever will be – compared, Diego Maradona, his genius seemingly comes without flaws. Questions remain about his inability to shine in the international arena following another summer of disappointment for Argentina – this time on home soil in the Copa América – but for FC Barcelona, the little maestro never ceases to impress and amaze. In fact, hard though it is to fathom, Messi just gets better every year. In 2010/11 he claimed a club record by scoring 53 goals in all competitions, eclipsing his own figure of 47 from the previous season. He became the inaugural winner of the unified FIFA Ballon d'Or, effectively retaining both prizes, and claimed the UEFA Champions League's top-scorer crown for the third successive year, completing his 12-goal haul against Manchester United FC in the final and gracing the most important club fixture in the game with one of its all-time great individual performances.

INTERNATIONAL CAREER

ARGENTINA

Debut – 17/8/05 v Hungary (a, Budapest, friendly), won 2-1
First Goal – 1/3/06 v Croatia (n, Basel, friendly), lost 2-3
Caps 61; **Goals** 17
Major Tournaments – FIFA World Cup 2006; Copa América 2007; FIFA World Cup 2010; Copa América 2011

CLUB CAREER

Major Honours – UEFA Champions League (2006, 2009, 2011); UEFA Super Cup (2009); FIFA Club World Cup (2009); Spanish Championship (2005, 2006, 2009, 2010, 2011); Spanish Cup (2009)
Clubs: 04- FC Barcelona (ESP)

Kenny Miller played only half a season for Rangers FC in 2010/11 but still ended up as the Scottish Premier League's top scorer. Inspired by the No9 shirt that he had acquired from the departed Kris Boyd, he struck ten goals in the opening six SPL games – all victories – before adding a couple against Celtic FC in the first Old Firm encounter of the season, which the defending champions won 3-1 at Parkhead. The spree did not stop there, and by the turn of the year he had amassed 21 league goals. It seemed illogical for Rangers to sell him at that point, but Bursaspor, against whom Miller had also scored in the UEFA Champions League, came in with an offer that the Ibrox board accepted, so off he trooped to Turkey. Six months later he was back in the United Kingdom, joining English Championship side Cardiff City FC. While in Turkey he was handed the captaincy of the Scottish national team and he celebrated the honour by scoring a couple of goals in the Nations Cup against Northern Ireland and Wales.

INTERNATIONAL CAREER

SCOTLAND
Debut – 25/4/01 v Poland (a, Bydgoszcz, friendly), drew 1-1
First Goal – 29/3/03 v Iceland (h, Glasgow, ECQ), won 2-1
Caps 55; **Goals** 14

CLUB CAREER

Major Honours – Scottish Championship (2007, 2009, 2010, 2011); Scottish Cup (2007, 2009); Scottish League Cup (2010)
Clubs: 96-00 Hibernian FC; 98-99 Stenhousemuir FC (loan); 00-01 Rangers FC; 01-06 Wolverhampton Wanderers FC (ENG); 06-07 Celtic FC; 07-08 Derby County FC (ENG); 08-11 Rangers FC; 11 Bursaspor (TUR); 11- Cardiff City FC (WAL)

A loan transfer from AS Saint-Étienne to Olympiacos FC turned out to be an inspired career move for young Belgian striker Kevin Mirallas. He proved so effective in the first half of the Greek Super League season that Olympiacos signed him up permanently on a four-year contract in January. Although his excellent club form was not reflected by increased involvement with the Belgian national team – he made just two substitute appearances for Georges Leekens' side in 2010/11 – it made him a very popular person in Piraeus. Having surrendered the Greek Super League title to arch-rivals Panathinaikos FC in 2009/10, Olympiacos were eager to wrest it back. They did so in emphatic style, and Mirallas was one of the main reasons why. Not only was he the team's top scorer, with 14 goals, but his versatility enabled him to operate in a variety of positions, from central striker to right winger to attacking midfielder. Some of his goals were especially memorable, including a couple against Panathinaikos and another against AEK Athens FC in the 6-0 win at the Georgios Karaiskakis Stadium that sealed the Super League title.

INTERNATIONAL CAREER

BELGIUM
Debut – 22/8/07 v Serbia (h, Brussels, ECQ), won 3-2
First Goal – 22/8/07 v Serbia (h, Brussels, ECQ), won 3-2
Caps 22; **Goals** 4

CLUB CAREER

Major Honours – Greek Championship (2011)
Clubs: 04-08 LOSC Lille Métropole (FRA); 08-10 AS Saint-Étienne (FRA); 10- Olympiacos FC (GRE)

Luka MODRIĆ
Midfielder
Born 9/9/85, Zadar, Croatia
Height 174cm, Weight 65kg

Luka Modrić's third season at Tottenham Hotspur FC saw the Croatian midfield strategist up his game to a new level. Playing in the UEFA Champions League brought out the best in him, and he was an inspirational figure throughout the north London club's run to the quarter-finals, giving a world-class display in the group game at home to holders FC Internazionale Milano, which Spurs won 3-1. With his appetite for elite European club football duly whetted, it was hardly surprising that Modrić professed a desire to make a quick return to the UEFA Champions League. With Spurs having failed to qualify for the 2011/12 competition, strong interest in the player inevitably emerged from Premier League rivals Chelsea FC and Manchester United FC. A clever, inventive playmaker of the old school, Modrić has been a virtually immovable presence in the Croatian national team since he made his debut in 2006, and although his club colleague Niko Kranjčar – largely redundant at Spurs – outshone him on the international stage in 2010/11, Modrić did his fair share to keep Slaven Bilić's team on track for their third successive UEFA European Championship finals.

INTERNATIONAL CAREER

CROATIA
Debut – 1/3/06 v Argentina (n, Basel, friendly), won 3-2
First Goal – 16/8/06 v Italy (a, Livorno, friendly), won 2-0
Caps 47; **Goals** 7
Major Tournaments – FIFA World Cup 2006; UEFA EURO 2008

CLUB CAREER

Major Honours – Croatian Championship (2006, 2007, 2008); Croatian Cup (2007, 2008)
Clubs: 02-08 NK Dinamo Zagreb; 03/04 HŠK Zrinjski (BIH) (loan); 04/05 NK Inter Zaprešić (loan); 08- Tottenham Hotspur FC (ENG)

Luís Carlos Almeida da Cunha "NANI"
Winger
Born 17/11/86, Praia, Cape Verde
Height 177cm, Weight 70kg

Considered by some to be a poor man's Cristiano Ronaldo during his first couple of seasons at Manchester United FC, Nani finally emerged from his compatriot's giant shadow in 2010/11, playing a leading role in the club's Premier League triumph. A consistently resourceful and skilful presence on the wing for Sir Alex Ferguson's team, he scored nine league goals, supplied an abundance of assists and was rewarded both with a place in the PFA Premier League Team of the Year and a nomination for PFA Young Player of the Year. He also won the vote from his team-mates as United's player of the year, although there was disappointment for the 24-year-old when he was only selected on the bench for the UEFA Champions League final against FC Barcelona. A Portuguese international since 2006, he missed the 2010 FIFA World Cup through injury but was back as a leading light in 2010/11, starting all five of the team's UEFA EURO 2012 qualifiers and scoring twice in a crucial 3-1 win at home to Denmark.

INTERNATIONAL CAREER

PORTUGAL
Debut – 1/9/06 v Denmark (h, Copenhagen, friendly), lost 2-4
First Goal – 1/9/06 v Denmark (h, Copenhagen, friendly), lost 2-4
Caps 45; **Goals** 9
Major Tournaments – UEFA EURO 2008

CLUB CAREER

Major Honours – UEFA Champions League (2008); FIFA Club World Cup (2008); English Premier League (2008, 2009, 2011); Portuguese Cup (2007); English League Cup (2009, 2010)
Clubs: 05-07 Sporting Clube de Portugal; 07- Manchester United FC (ENG)

After a modest 2009/10 season that ended with the disappointment of omission from France's FIFA World Cup squad, Samir Nasri pulled his socks up and performed brilliantly for Arsenal FC in 2010/11. During the autumn he was arguably the leading attraction in the Premier League, displaying the kind of form that had earned him the 'new Zidane' tag in his early days at Olympique de Marseille. The jurors at France Football magazine were sufficiently impressed to elect him as the 2010 French Footballer of the Year. To his spellbinding footwork and exquisite balance he added a sharp eye for goal, scoring eight times in the Premier League and twice in the UEFA Champions League before the turn of the year. The flow of goals later dried up as Arsenal's hopes of collecting a first major trophy in six years gradually faded and died, but Nasri still made it into the PFA Premier League Team of the Year. He was also back as a regular for his country, Laurent Blanc selecting him from the start in six of his first ten matches in charge of Les Bleus. Throughout the summer rumours abounded that Nasri would be leaving Arsenal for pastures new, with Premier League champions Manchester United FC reportedly leading the race for his signature.

INTERNATIONAL CAREER

FRANCE
Debut – 28/3/07 v Austria (h, Saint-Denis, friendly), won 1-0
First Goal – 6/6/07 v Georgia (h, Auxerre, ECQ), won 1-0
Caps 22; **Goals** 2
Major Tournaments – UEFA EURO 2008

CLUB CAREER

Clubs: 04-08 Olympique de Marseille; 08- Arsenal FC (ENG)

Paris Saint-Germain FC's season ended in double disappointment as they lost the final of the Coupe de France to LOSC Lille Métropole and just missed out on qualification for the UEFA Champions League by finishing fourth in Ligue 1. One consolation for PSG fans, however, was the pleasure that had been given to them by their new Brazilian recruit from AS Monaco FC, Nenê. With his magic wand of a left foot, the 29-year-old bewitched and bedazzled spectators and opponents alike, and, as at Monaco the previous season, he finished up as the team's top scorer in Ligue 1 with 14 goals. All but one of those came in the first half of the season, when he was in irrepressible form, adding another four strikes in Europe, including the winner away to Sevilla FC, as PSG topped a tough UEFA Europa League group that also contained German Bundesliga high-fliers Borussia Dortmund. In January, he swapped his shirt number from 19 to 10 following Stephane Sessegnon's loan move to Sunderland AFC and, rather spookily, his goal touch suddenly deserted him. He still managed six assists in the spring, but there was just one more goal in the league plus another, against Angers SCO, in the semi-final of the French Cup.

INTERNATIONAL CAREER

BRAZIL
uncapped

CLUB CAREER

Clubs: 99-01 Paulista FC; 01-02 SE Palmeiras; 02-03 Santos FC; 03-04 RCD Mallorca (ESP); 04-06 Deportivo Alavés (ESP); 06-07 RC Celta de Vigo (ESP); 07-10 AS Monaco FC (FRA); 08/09 RCD Espanyol (ESP) (loan); 10- Paris Saint-Germain FC (FRA)

Manuel NEUER

Goalkeeper
Born 27/3/86, Gelsenkirchen, Germany
Height 193cm, Weight 90kg

Appointed club captain of FC Schalke 04 at the start of the 2010/11 season, Manuel Neuer departed his hometown club at the end of it, joining FC Bayern München on a five-year contract in an €18m move that makes him the third most expensive goalkeeper of all time. The 25-year-old, who retained his place as the German national team's No1'keeper ahead of René Adler for the UEFA EURO 2012 qualifying campaign, saw his value increase considerably during his final season at Schalke, notably by helping the Gelsenkirchen club to defy the odds and reach the last four of the UEFA Champions League. His remarkable performance in the first leg of the semi-final against Manchester United FC, when he kept his team in the tie with a succession of brilliant saves, led many to believe that Old Trafford would be his next port of call – particularly as United boss Sir Alex Ferguson sought him out to shake hands at the final whistle – but negotiations with Bayern were already underway and it was the Munich giants who eventually got their man. Neuer did leave Schalke on a high, however, winning his first major trophy with a 5-0 victory over MSV Duisburg in the final of the German Cup.

INTERNATIONAL CAREER

GERMANY
Debut – 2/6/09 v United Arab Emirates (a, Dubai, friendly), won 7-2
Caps 20; **Goals** 0
Major Tournaments – FIFA World Cup 2010

CLUB CAREER

Major Honours – German Cup (2011)
Clubs: 05-11 FC Schalke 04; 11- FC Bayern München

NURİ Şahin

Midfielder
Born 5/9/88, Ludenscheid, Germany
Height 180cm, Weight 72kg

There was a sting in the tail to Borussia Dortmund's 2010/11 Bundesliga title celebrations when it was revealed that the team's midfield conductor-in-chief, Nuri Şahin, was leaving the club to join Spanish giants Real Madrid CF on a six-year contract. The young Turkish international – referred to as 'Nuri' by Turks and 'Şahin' by Germans – was voted Bundesliga Player of the Season by a landslide margin in a post-season poll conducted by kicker magazine. A headline-grabber in the early weeks of the campaign when he struck important goals against VfL Wolfsburg, FC Bayern München and 1. FC Köln, the 22-year-old schemer had a huge influence on Jürgen Klopp's side throughout the season, his outstanding vision and distribution being supplemented by a first-class delivery at set pieces with his magical left foot. He scored against Bayern again in the spring with a beautiful long-range strike in Munich and ended the campaign with six goals and a dozen assists. He will be badly missed by the German club, but at a cost of just €10m Madrid will surely feel they have grabbed themselves a bargain.

INTERNATIONAL CAREER

TURKEY
Debut – 8/10/05 v Germany (h, Istanbul, friendly), won 2-1
First Goal – 8/10/05 v Germany (h, Istanbul, friendly), won 2-1
Caps 26; **Goals** 1

CLUB CAREER

Major Honours – German Championship (2011); Dutch Cup (2008)
Clubs: 05-11 Borussia Dortmund (GER); 07-08 Feyenoord (NED) (loan); 11- Real Madrid CF (ESP)

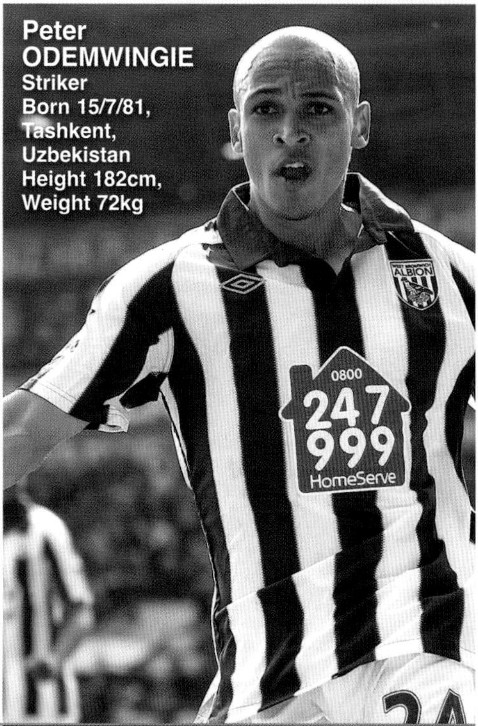

Peter ODEMWINGIE

Striker
Born 15/7/81, Tashkent, Uzbekistan
Height 182cm, Weight 72kg

A fabulous first season in English football brought Peter Odemwingie two player of the month awards and 15 Premier League goals. It was a record tally in the competition for a West Bromwich Albion FC player and earned the Nigerian international striker cult status at the West Midlands club. The newly-promoted team from the Birmingham suburbs signed Odemwingie for an undisclosed fee from Russian Premier-Liga side FC Lokomotiv Moskva on 20 August 2010. The following day he made his debut and scored the only goal in a 1-0 victory at home to Sunderland AFC. It was the perfect start, and he consolidated it with further vital goals against Birmingham City FC and Arsenal FC. The Baggies changed managers in mid-season when Roberto Di Matteo was fired and Roy Hodgson hired, but Odemwingie's lust for goals continued. Indeed, he became even more prolific in the closing weeks, rattling off five in as many games to become the fifth best marksman in the division, with only Carlos Tévez, Dimitar Berbatov, Robin van Persie and Darren Bent scoring more.

INTERNATIONAL CAREER

NIGERIA
Debut – 4/5/02 v Kenya (h, Lagos, friendly), won 3-0
First Goal – 21/6/03 v Angola (h, Benin City, ANQ), drew 2-2
Caps 53; **Goals** 9
Major Tournaments – Africa Cup of Nations 2004; Africa Cup of Nations 2006; Africa Cup of Nations 2008; Africa Cup of Nations 2010; FIFA World Cup 2010

CLUB CAREER

Clubs: 00-02 Bendel Insurance FC; 02-05 RAA La Louvière (BEL); 05-07 LOSC Lille Métropole (FRA); 07-10 FC Lokomotiv Moskva (RUS); 10- West Bromwich Albion FC (ENG)

Mesut ÖZIL

Attacking Midfielder
Born 15/10/88, Gelsenkirchen, Germany
Height 182cm, Weight 73kg

After a wonderful FIFA World Cup with Germany in South Africa, Mesut Özil reinforced his reputation as one of European football's finest young talents with an outstanding debut season for Real Madrid CF. The left-footed schemer was an immediate hit with the Madrid public, his elegant, gliding running style and crafty playmaking skills fitting in very much with the locals' idea of what a €15m midfielder should look and play like. The former SV Werder Bremen star scored in four successive matches at the Santiago Bernabéu in the autumn – three in La Liga and one in the UEFA Champions League, against AC Milan – but, unlike the FC Barcelona player to whom he was often compared, Lionel Messi, it was his consistent ability to create chances for others, rather than score them himself, that defined his season. He was officially credited with 25 assists, including 17 in the domestic league and six in Europe. Although both major prizes eluded Madrid, he did claim his second domestic cup in three seasons, adding the Copa del Rey to the DFB-Pokal that he won with Bremen in 2009.

INTERNATIONAL CAREER

GERMANY
Debut – 11/2/09 v Norway (h, Dusseldorf, friendly), lost 0-1
First Goal – 5/9/09 v South Africa (h, Leverkusen, friendly), won 2-0
Caps 26; **Goals** 4
Major Tournaments – FIFA World Cup 2010

CLUB CAREER

Major Honours – German Cup (2009); Spanish Cup (2011)
Clubs: 06-08 FC Schalke 04; 08-10 SV Werder Bremen; 10- Real Madrid CF (ESP)

Alexandre Rodrigues da Silva "PATO"

Striker
Born 2/9/89, Pato Branco, Brazil
Height 179cm, Weight 71kg

A consistent scorer for AC Milan ever since he burst on to the Serie A scene as an 18-year-old, Pato lifted his aggregate tally of league goals in Italy to 50 (in just 102 matches) during a 2010/11 season that brought the Rossoneri their first scudetto for seven years. The young Brazilian striker matched his attacking accomplices Zlatan Ibrahimović and Robinho by contributing 14 goals to the title triumph. It was an impressive figure given that he missed much of the season through injury and started only half of the 38 matches. With Ibrahimović absent, Pato was the star of the show when Milan beat FC Internazionale Milano 3-0 in the big derby game at the beginning of April, scoring twice, and his winning goal at ACF Fiorentina the following weekend was just as important in maintaining the team's title charge. A surprise absentee from Brazil's 2010 FIFA World Cup squad, Pato returned to the Seleção and became the regular No9 under new coach Mano Menezes, scoring three goals in friendlies and a double at the Copa América against Ecuador.

INTERNATIONAL CAREER

BRAZIL
Major Honours – FIFA Confederations Cup (2009)
Debut – 26/3/08 v Sweden (n, London, friendly), won 1-0
First Goal – 26/3/08 v Sweden (n, London, friendly), won 1-0
Caps 16; **Goals** 6
Major Tournaments – FIFA Confederations Cup 2009; Copa América 2011

CLUB CAREER

Major Honours – FIFA Club World Cup (2006); South American Super Cup (2007); Italian Championship (2011)
Clubs: 06-08 SC Internacional; 08- AC Milan (ITA)

PEDRO Rodríguez Ledesma

Winger/Striker
Born 28/7/87, Santa Cruz, Tenerife, Spain
Height 169cm, Weight 64kg

With so many stellar performers surrounding him at FC Barcelona, it is not easy for Pedro to grab the limelight, but having broken through into Josep Guardiola's side in 2009/10, the young Canary Islander continued his steady progress in 2010/11 to become one of the team's most valuable and consistent performers. He even enjoyed the odd moment of personal glory, not least on his last outing of the season when he opened the scoring against Manchester United FC in the UEFA Champions League final. His Wembley strike – a calm, measured shot that wrong-footed Edwin van der Sar – followed hot on the heels of another high-profile strike in the second leg of the semi-final at home to Real Madrid CF. It was during the colder months that the two-footed winger enjoyed his most productive period on the domestic front, scoring all 13 of his Liga goals in November, December, January and February to help Barça compile a club-record run of 16 successive victories that provided the platform for their third successive Spanish championship crown.

INTERNATIONAL CAREER

SPAIN
Major Honours – FIFA World Cup (2010)
Debut – 29/5/10 v Saudi Arabia (n, Innsbruck, friendly), won 3-2
First Goal – 8/6/10 v Poland (h, Murcia, friendly), won 6-0
Caps 13; **Goals** 2
Major Tournaments – FIFA World Cup 2010

CLUB CAREER

Major Honours – UEFA Champions League (2009, 2011); UEFA Super Cup (2009); FIFA Club World Cup (2009); Spanish Championship (2009, 2010, 2011); Spanish Cup (2009)
Clubs: 07- FC Barcelona

Tipped for the top while playing youth football for his hometown club HNK Hajduk Split, Ivan Perišić now has the opportunity to prove those soothsayers right. A magnificent 2010/11 season with Club Brugge KV in Belgium earned the 22-year-old Croatian a summer transfer to German champions Borussia Dortmund and the chance to make a name for himself in the UEFA Champions League. Perišić journeyed to Germany bursting with confidence after a second season in Bruges that brought him 22 goals and the twin distinction of being the Eerste Klasse's top scorer and player of the year. He claimed the latter prize – ahead of R. Standard de Liège midfielder Axel Witsel and KRC Genk striker Jelle Vossen – despite performing in a Club Brugge side that never challenged for the league title. In fact, without the goals and the canny creativity of their young Croatian star, Adrie Koster's team might not even have reached the championship play-offs. Another reward for Perišić was a first cap for the Croatian national team. With his profile now raised at Dortmund, many more international appearances are expected to follow.

INTERNATIONAL CAREER

CROATIA
Debut – 26/3/11 v Georgia (a, Tbilisi, ECQ), lost 0-1
Caps 3; **Goals** 0

CLUB CAREER

Clubs: 07-09 FC Sochaux-Montbéliard (FRA); 09 KSV Roeselare (BEL) (loan); 09-11 Club Brugge KV (BEL); 11- Borussia Dortmund (GER)

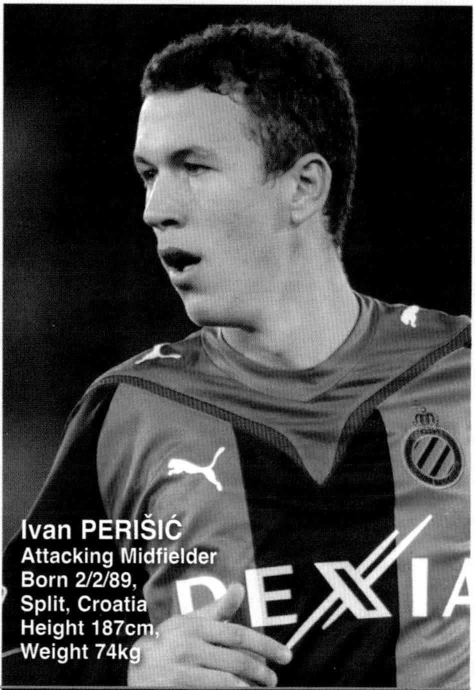

Ivan PERIŠIĆ
Attacking Midfielder
Born 2/2/89, Split, Croatia
Height 187cm, Weight 74kg

When Radosav Petrović joined FK Partizan in May 2008 from little-known FK Radnički Obrenovac, no one could have imagined that three years later the tall defensive midfielder would become the key player for the Belgrade giants, a three-time national champion and also one of the most important members of the Serbian national team. Although originally from FK Jedinstvo Ub, traditionally a feeder club for arch-rivals FK Crvena zvezda, Petrović did not take long to become a firm favourite of the Partizan fans, his no-nonsense tackling, accurate passing, strength, stamina and cool temperament all combining to make him the team's controlling midfield pivot. In 2010/11 he added a new attacking string to his bow, scoring nine goals for Partizan in the SuperLiga and a memorable first international strike for Serbia in an end-of-season friendly against South Korea. A move to Dutch club Vitesse looked on the cards in the early summer, but when that broke down Petrović entered negotiations with Blackburn Rovers FC for a high-profile move to the English Premier League.

INTERNATIONAL CAREER

SERBIA
Debut – 12/8/09 v South Africa (a, Atteridgeville, friendly), won 3-1
First Goal – 3/6/11 v South Korea (a, Seoul, friendly), lost 1-2
Caps 18; **Goals** 1
Major Tournaments – FIFA World Cup 2010

CLUB CAREER

Major Honours – Serbian Championship (2009, 2010, 2011); Serbian Cup (2009, 2011)
Clubs: 06-07 FK Jedinstvo Ub; 07-08 FK Radnički Obrenovac; 08- FK Partizan

Radosav PETROVIĆ
Midfielder
Born 8/3/89, Ub, Serbia
Height 194cm, Weight 83kg

TOP 100 PLAYERS

Gerard PIQUÉ Bernabéu
Centre-Back
Born 2/2/87, Barcelona, Spain
Height 190cm, Weight 84kg

The inexorable rise of Gerard Piqué continued apace in 2010/11 as the young FC Barcelona defender added more illustrious entries to his personal roll of honour. Outstanding once again in the Catalan club's UEFA Champions League triumph, and no less influential in their retention of the Liga title, the 24-year-old Spanish international was the rock at the heart of a defence that was destabilised by Carles Puyol's extended absence through injury. Powerful in the air, strong in the tackle, quick to spot danger and even quicker to snuff it out, Piqué is now widely recognised as one of the most accomplished centre-backs in the game. He has certainly come a long way in a short time since he left Manchester United FC for Barça in 2008. It is an irony not lost on his former employers that his two UEFA Champions League final wins have both come against the club that groomed him for greatness.

INTERNATIONAL CAREER

SPAIN
Major Honours – FIFA World Cup (2010)
Debut – 11/2/09 v England (h, Seville, friendly), won 2-0
First Goal – 28/3/09 v Turkey (h, Madrid, WCQ), won 1-0
Caps 33; **Goals** 4
Major Tournaments – FIFA Confederations Cup 2009; FIFA World Cup 2010

CLUB CAREER

Major Honours – UEFA Champions League (2008, 2009, 2011); UEFA Super Cup (2009); FIFA Club World Cup (2009); English Premier League (2008); Spanish Championship (2009, 2010, 2011); Spanish Cup (2009); English League Cup (2006)
Clubs: 04-08 Manchester United FC (ENG); 06-07 Real Zaragoza (loan); 08- FC Barcelona

Carles PUYOL i Saforcada
Centre-Back
Born 13/4/78, Pobla de Segur, Spain
Height 180cm, Weight 79kg

FC Barcelona did not lose many matches during a season in which they won the UEFA Champions League, retained the Spanish title and reached the final of the Copa del Rey, but when they did, significantly their captain was not playing. The only defeat Carles Puyol suffered in 2010/11 was for Spain in a friendly against Portugal. His 28 club appearances predominantly brought wins, so it was a relief for the Catalan fans that he became available again after a three-month injury lay-off to face Real Madrid CF in the UEFA Champions League semi-final – even if he had to fill in as an emergency left-back. Madrid were duly conquered, but the Barça skipper was not fit for the final, against Manchester United FC. The team survived without him, though, and he came on late in the game to share in the joy of victory – if not to lift the trophy, an honour he generously passed on to the man he had substituted, Éric Abidal.

INTERNATIONAL CAREER

SPAIN
Major Honours – FIFA World Cup (2010); UEFA European Championship (2008)
Debut – 15/11/00 v Netherlands (h, Seville, friendly), lost 1-2
First Goal – 17/4/02 v Northern Ireland (a, Belfast, friendly), won 5-0
Caps 94; **Goals** 3
Major Tournaments – FIFA World Cup 2002; UEFA EURO 2004; FIFA World Cup 2006; UEFA EURO 2008; FIFA Confederations Cup 2009; FIFA World Cup 2010

CLUB CAREER

Major Honours – UEFA Champions League (2006, 2009, 2011); UEFA Super Cup (2009); FIFA Club World Cup (2009); Spanish Championship (2005, 2006, 2009, 2010, 2011); Spanish Cup (2009)
Clubs: 99- FC Barcelona

An ever-present member of the FC Shakhtar Donetsk side that reached the 2010/11 UEFA Champions League quarter-finals, Yaroslav Rakytskiy also left his mark on the competition by scoring against FC Barcelona in Camp Nou. Unfortunately for his team, they lost the game 5-1 and eventually went out to the eventual champions 6-1 on aggregate, but the pacy, powerful 21-year-old had every reason to look back on the campaign with pride, helping Shakhtar keep clean sheets in five of their ten games and claim famous wins over Arsenal FC and AS Roma. Mircea Lucescu's team may have found Barcelona too hot to handle, but they were imperious back home in Ukraine, winning the domestic double, with Rakytskiy again the most dependable and assiduous figure in the team's back four. His rapid development has earned him a regular place in the Ukrainian national side, and although he missed the first two games under new coach Oleh Blokhin in June, that was because he was preparing to play for his country at the UEFA European Under-21 Championship in Denmark. Despite Ukraine's group-stage exit, Rakytskiy performed well and will surely benefit from the tournament experience when he represents the seniors at UEFA EURO 2012.

INTERNATIONAL CAREER

UKRAINE
Debut – 10/10/09 v England (h, Dnipropetrovsk, WCQ), won 1-0
First Goal – 14/10/09 v Andorra (a, Andorra la Vella, WCQ), won 6-0
Caps 10; **Goals** 3

CLUB CAREER

Major Honours – Ukrainian Championship (2010, 2011); Ukrainian Cup (2011)
Clubs: 09- FC Shakhtar Donetsk

Adil Rami's brilliant season for club and country was only partially interrupted in January when he agreed a transfer from LOSC Lille Métropole to Valencia CF. Fortunately, the Spanish club allowed him to return on loan to Lille for the remainder of the campaign so he was able to pick up where he had left off and help the northern French club to a historic Ligue 1/Coupe de France double. The 25-year-old Corsican was the cornerstone of a Lille defence that played second fiddle to the team's exciting attacking unit but still held its own, conceding at an average of less than a goal a game. Rami started 36 of the team's Ligue 1 fixtures and was a tower of strength also in the French Cup, helping Lille record clean sheets in every game from the quarter-final onwards. His consistent club form was carried over into the French national team where, having earned his first cap in Laurent Blanc's first game as coach, he remained in situ for the next nine, forming an impressive new central defensive partnership with AS Roma's Philippe Mexès that should, barring mishaps, be a keystone of the French challenge at UEFA EURO 2012.

INTERNATIONAL CAREER

FRANCE
Debut – 11/8/10 v Norway (a, Oslo, friendly), lost 1-2
Caps 11; **Goals** 0

CLUB CAREER

Major Honours – French Championship (2011); French Cup (2011)
Clubs: 03-06 EFC Fréjus; 07-11 LOSC Lille Métropole; 11- Valencia CF (ESP)

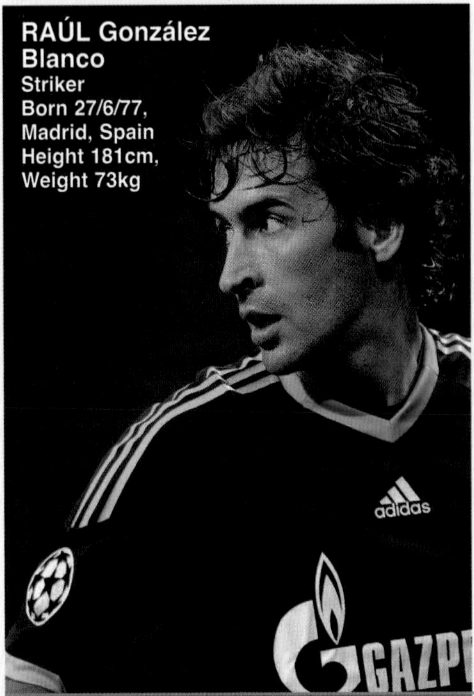

RAÚL González Blanco

Striker
Born 27/6/77, Madrid, Spain
Height 181cm, Weight 73kg

After 18 years at Real Madrid CF, for whom he scored 323 goals in 741 senior appearances, Rául decided to try something new, signing a two-year contract with FC Schalke 04. Having vowed never to play for another Spanish club, and with his time clearly up at the Santiago Bernabéu, it was a sound move – both for the player and his new German club. Raúl's vast experience of the UEFA Champions League proved more than helpful as the Gelsenkirchen outfit upset the form book to reach the semi-finals. His five goals, including one in each leg of the quarter-final victory over holders FC Internazionale Milano, enabled him not only to increase his cumulative record tally in the competition to 71 but also to become the all-time leading marksman in all UEFA club competitions, with 73. He also managed a respectable return of 13 goals in the Bundesliga and was clearly overjoyed at the end of the season when he won the first domestic cup of his career as Schalke defeated MSV Duisburg 5-0 in Berlin to lift the DFB-Pokal.

INTERNATIONAL CAREER

SPAIN
Debut – 9/10/96 v Czech Republic (a, Prague, WCQ), drew 0-0
First Goal – 14/12/96 v Yugoslavia (h, Valencia, WCQ), won 2-0
Caps 102; **Goals** 44
Major Tournaments – FIFA World Cup 1998; UEFA EURO 2000; FIFA World Cup 2002; UEFA EURO 2004; FIFA World Cup 2006

CLUB CAREER

Major Honours – UEFA Champions League (1998, 2000, 2002); UEFA Super Cup (2002); World Club Cup (1998, 2002); Spanish Championship (1995, 1997, 2001, 2003, 2007, 2008); German Cup (2011)
Clubs: 94-10 Real Madrid CF; 10- FC Schalke 04 (GER)

Wayne ROONEY

Striker
Born 24/10/85, Liverpool, England
Height 178cm, Weight 82kg

It took Wayne Rooney several months to get over his disastrous performance at the 2010 FIFA World Cup. He may not have found redemption with England fans, continuing to play carelessly for his country, scoring just one goal, and incurring a silly suspension that made him unavailable for the final UEFA EURO 2012 qualifier of the season at home to Switzerland. But for Manchester United FC, he finally rediscovered his form and fitness in the second half of the season and was truly outstanding at the business end of the UEFA Champions League, scoring important away goals at Chelsea FC and FC Schalke 04 and supplementing a fine equaliser in the Wembley final against FC Barcelona with a superb all-round performance. He certainly needed to appease the United faithful after openly criticising the club's ambition during an unsavoury contract stand-off in the autumn, but with ten Premier League goals after Christmas, including a wonderful acrobatic winner in the derby against Manchester City FC at Old Trafford, he eventually played a major part in the club's record-breaking 19th English title success.

INTERNATIONAL CAREER

ENGLAND
Debut – 2/2/03 v Australia (h, London, friendly), lost 1-3
First Goal – 6/9/03 v FYROM (a, Skopje, ECQ), won 2-1
Caps 70; **Goals** 26
Major Tournaments – UEFA EURO 2004; FIFA World Cup 2006; FIFA World Cup 2010

CLUB CAREER

Major Honours – UEFA Champions League (2008); FIFA Club World Cup (2008); English Premier League (2007, 2008, 2009, 2011); English League Cup (2006, 2009, 2010)
Clubs: 02-04 Everton FC; 04- Manchester United FC

Giuseppe ROSSI
Striker
Born 1/2/87, Teaneck, New Jersey, USA
Height 175cm, Weight 73kg

Giuseppe Rossi struck a rich vein of form in 2010/11 that was to last from the beginning of the season right through to the end, bringing the young American-Italian striker 18 goals in La Liga and 11 in the UEFA Europa League for his club, Villarreal CF, plus another three at international level for Italy. Having controversially failed to make the cut for Marcello Lippi's 2010 FIFA World Cup squad, Rossi made the most of his opportunity to impress new Azzurri boss Cesare Prandelli, doubling his international goal tally with fine strikes against Germany, Ukraine and – in a UEFA EURO 2012 qualifier – Estonia. Prandelli could hardly have ignored the 24-year-old's claims, for he was consistently at the top of his game for Villarreal, giving defences the run-around time and again with his scampering surges, deft ball control and lethal finishing. As the Yellow Submarine sailed into fourth place in the Primera Divisíón and the semi-finals of the UEFA Europa League, the good news for the club's followers was that, despite strong interest from FC Barcelona, Rossi seemed set to remain aboard for the foreseeable future having signed a long-term contract extension midway through the season.

INTERNATIONAL CAREER

ITALY
Debut – 11/10/08 v Bulgaria (a, Sofia, WCQ), drew 0-0
First Goal – 6/6/09 v Northern Ireland (h, Pisa, friendly), won 3-0
Caps 23; **Goals** 6
Major Tournaments – FIFA Confederations Cup 2009

CLUB CAREER

Clubs: 05-07 Manchester United FC (ENG); 06 Newcastle United FC (ENG) (loan); 07 Parma FC (loan); 07- Villarreal CF (ESP)

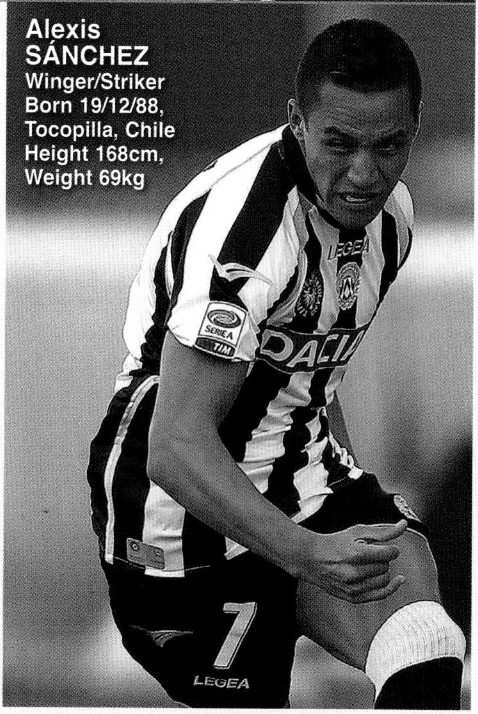

Alexis SÁNCHEZ
Winger/Striker
Born 19/12/88, Tocopilla, Chile
Height 168cm, Weight 69kg

Having advertised his talents to a global audience while playing for Chile at the 2010 FIFA World Cup, Alexis Sánchez treated the Italian public to a season-long masterclass with Udinese Calcio. The reward for his brilliant Serie A campaign, which ended with Udinese celebrating an unlikely fourth-place finish and access to the UEFA Champions League, was a dream transfer to European champions FC Barcelona. Time will tell how and where the multi-talented 22-year-old fits into Josep Guardiola's all-conquering team, but he is sure to be an asset. Naturally skilful, with the ability and the willingness to take players on, Sánchez is difficult to categorise. He has the versatility to operate in any attacking role – out wide, up top or, perhaps most effectively, from a deep-lying position in the 'hole' behind the main striker. He dovetailed brilliantly with Serie A's top marksman Antonio Di Natale in 2010/11 and also scored 12 goals himself, including four on one unforgettable February afternoon in Sicily when Udinese thrashed US Città di Palermo 7-0.

INTERNATIONAL CAREER

CHILE
Debut – 27/4/06 v New Zealand (h, La Calera, friendly), won 1-0
First Goal – 7/9/07 v Switzerland (n, Vienna, friendly), lost 1-2
Caps 41; **Goals** 14
Major Tournaments – FIFA World Cup 2010; Copa América 2011

CLUB CAREER

Major Honours – Chilean Championship (clausura 2006, apertura 2007); Argentinian Championship (clausura 2008)
Clubs: 05-06 CD Cobreloa; 06-11 Udinese Calcio (ITA); 06-07 Colo-Colo (loan); 07-08 CA River Plate (ARG) (loan); 11- FC Barcelona (ESP)

A frustrating 2009/10 campaign in which he was frequently inhibited by injury – and therefore missed out on Spain's FIFA World Cup triumph – was swiftly forgotten in 2010/11 as a fit, refreshed Santi Cazorla returned to his very best form. His club, Villarreal CF, were the principal beneficiaries as his speed, creativity and tireless effort helped the team reach the semi-finals of the UEFA Europa League and claim a top-four berth in La Liga. The 26-year-old missed just one domestic league game and also featured strongly in the European run, scoring a lovely goal in the last-16 tie against Bayer 04 Leverkusen. Restored by Vicente del Bosque to the national side, Cazorla started three of Spain's five UEFA EURO 2012 qualifiers and ended the season by scoring twice in the world champions' 4-0 victory over the United States in Boston. In July, with his reputation at an all-time high, he was bought for €22m by Málaga CF, rejoining his former Villarreal coach Manuel Pellegrini at the big-spending club from the Costa del Sol.

INTERNATIONAL CAREER

SPAIN

Major Honours – UEFA European Championship (2008)

Debut – 31/5/08 v Peru (h, Huelva, friendly), won 2-1

First Goal – 19/11/08 v Chile (h, Villarreal, friendly), won 3-0

Caps 34; **Goals** 4

Major Tournaments – UEFA EURO 2008; FIFA Confederations Cup 2009

CLUB CAREER

Clubs: 03-06 Villarreal CF; 06-07 RC Recreativo de Huelva; 07-11 Villarreal CF; 11- Málaga CF

The 2010/11 season was only a few weeks old when it was announced that 1. FSV Mainz 05 striker André Schürrle would be leaving the club at the end of the campaign to join Bayer 04 Leverkusen – the team against whom he had made his Bundesliga debut only a year or so earlier. With his future settled, the gifted youngster might have been tempted to take it easy in his final season as a Mainz player. On the contrary, he proved inspirational, scoring a club-record tally of 15 Bundesliga goals to help Thomas Tuchel's unsung team finish fifth and qualify for the UEFA Europa League. At the time Schürrle put pen to paper on his new contract with Leverkusen, Mainz were actually leading the Bundesliga, their first seven matches all resulting in victory. Although they eventually slipped off the pace, Schürrle's unwaveringly consistent form helped to ensure that they remained comfortably in the European qualification bracket for the duration of the season. The 20-year-old ended his time at Mainz with goals in each of his last two games, and he also signed off his first season as a German international with a stoppage-time strike in the June UEFA EURO 2012 qualifier in Azerbaijan, having already opened his account for the Nationalmannschaft nine days earlier with the winning goal in a friendly against Uruguay.

INTERNATIONAL CAREER

GERMANY

Debut – 17/11/10 v Sweden (a, Gothenburg, friendly), drew 0-0

First Goal – 29/5/11 v Uruguay (h, Sinsheim, friendly), won 2-1

Caps 5; **Goals** 2

CLUB CAREER

Clubs: 09-11 1. FSV Mainz 05; 11- Bayer 04 Leverkusen

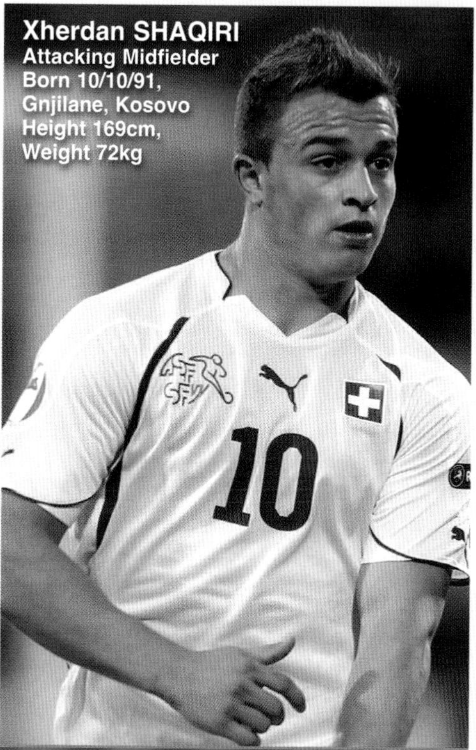

A new rising star of European football emerged in 2010/11 as 19-year-old Xherdan Shaqiri blossomed both at club level, with FC Basel 1893, and in the national colours of Switzerland. Already a full Swiss international in 2009/10, and indeed a fringe member of Ottmar Hitzfeld's squad at the FIFA World Cup in South Africa, the young Kosovo-born left-footer was given the opportunity to parade his skills on a more regular basis with the national side and opened his international goal account with a majestic long-range strike in the team's opening UEFA EURO 2012 qualifier at home to England. A full 90-minute workout in the return fixture at Wembley in June preceded an outstanding performance from the stocky playmaker at the UEFA European Under-21 Championship in Denmark. Arguably the most technically gifted player on show at the finals, he scored a superb goal in the opening game against the hosts and drove his team all the way to the final against Spain. It was a fitting culmination to a season in which Shaqiri also played a prominent role in helping Basel reach the group stage of the UEFA Champions League and successfully defend their Swiss Super League title.

INTERNATIONAL CAREER

SWITZERLAND
Debut – 3/3/10 v Uruguay (h, St Gallen, friendly), lost 1-3
First Goal – 7/9/10 v England (h, Basel, ECQ), lost 1-3
Caps 11; **Goals** 1
Major Tournaments – FIFA World Cup 2010

CLUB CAREER

Major Honours – Swiss Championship (2010, 2011); Swiss Cup (2010)
Clubs: 09- FC Basel 1893

2010/11 was a hugely disappointing season for the Icelandic national side as they collected just one point from their first five UEFA EURO 2012 qualifying ties, but a great deal of pride was restored by the country's Under-21 team, who reached the European finals in Denmark thanks to an astonishing 4-1 win over Germany and a play-off victory against Scotland in which the team's playmaker, Gylfi Sigurdsson, sealed qualification with two magnificent long-range goals. Unfortunately, Eyjólfur Sverrisson's side failed to get beyond the group stage at the finals but Sigurdsson and his team-mates certainly went out with a fight as they defeated Denmark 3-1 in their last game. There was a lot of focus on Sigurdsson at the tournament because in addition to those two memorable goals in Edinburgh he had made quite a name for himself in Germany with TSG 1899 Hoffenheim. Despite being deployed more often than not as a substitute, the former Reading FC midfielder ended his debut Bundesliga campaign as both the team's top scorer, with nine goals, and the Hoffenheim fans' player of the

INTERNATIONAL CAREER

ICELAND
Debut – 29/5/10 v Andorra (h, Reykjavik, friendly), won 4-0
Caps 5; **Goals** 0

CLUB CAREER

Clubs: 08-10 Reading FC (ENG); 08 Shrewsbury Town FC (ENG) (loan); 09 Crewe Alexandra FC (ENG) (loan); 10- TSG 1899 Hoffenheim (GER)

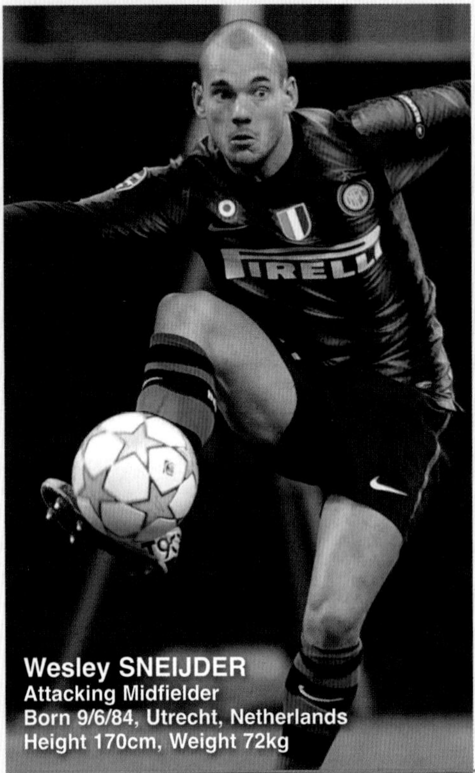

Wesley SNEIJDER
Attacking Midfielder
Born 9/6/84, Utrecht, Netherlands
Height 170cm, Weight 72kg

It would have been difficult, if not impossible, for Wesley Sneijder to match his great feats of 2009/10, when he won the treble with FC Internazionale Milano and inspired the Netherlands to the FIFA World Cup final, but he was once again a hugely influential figure for both club and country in 2010/11. Samuel Eto'o would certainly not have enjoyed himself quite so much at the apex of the Inter attack without Sneijder's creative midfield promptings, and although the Dutchman managed just seven goals himself, he tended to choose special occasions on which to score, his superb strike against FC Bayern München that turned the UEFA Champions League last-16 tie in Inter's favour a shining example. Sneijder started and finished all of the Netherlands' first six UEFA EURO 2012 qualifiers, though he saved his best moment for a friendly against Austria, a wonderful volley bringing him a 20th international goal. Although he signed a new long-term deal with Inter in October 2010, the 27-year-old was repeatedly linked in the summer with a move to Manchester United FC.

INTERNATIONAL CAREER

NETHERLANDS
Debut – 30/4/03 v Portugal (h, Eindhoven, friendly), drew 1-1
First Goal – 11/10/03 v Moldova (h, Eindhoven, ECQ), won 5-0
Caps 76; **Goals** 21
Major Tournaments – UEFA EURO 2004; FIFA World Cup 2006; UEFA EURO 2008; FIFA World Cup 2010

CLUB CAREER

Major Honours – UEFA Champions League (2010); FIFA Club World Cup (2010); Dutch Championship (2004); Spanish Championship (2008); Italian Championship (2010); Dutch Cup (2006, 2007); Italian Cup (2010, 2011)
Clubs: 02-07 AFC Ajax; 07-09 Real Madrid CF (ESP); 09- FC Internazionale Milano (ITA)

Roberto SOLDADO Rillo
Striker
Born 27/5/85, Valencia, Spain
Height 179cm, Weight 72kg

With 29 Liga goals in his two seasons at Getafe CF, Roberto Soldado was seen as the ideal replacement for the departed David Villa at Valencia CF. Rejected earlier in his career by Real Madrid CF, Soldado was eager to prove his worth at a big club, and a return to the city of his birth proved to be a smart move as he enjoyed the most prolific season of his senior career. Strikers are judged by the number of goals they score, and Soldado certainly delivered on that count. He was on target 18 times in La Liga and six in the UEFA Champions League. A third-place finish in the domestic league ensured a return to Europe's top table for Valencia, and Soldado was the man who propelled them there with 12 goals in the last two months of the campaign, his purple patch instigated by a memorable four-goal salvo back at former club Getafe. Although a return to the Spanish national team – after a four-year absence – was mooted, unlike team-mates Juan Mata, Pablo Hernández and Aritz Aduriz, he did not receive a call-up.

INTERNATIONAL CAREER

SPAIN
Debut – 2/6/07 v Latvia (a, Riga, ECQ), won 2-0
Caps 2; **Goals** 0

CLUB CAREER

Major Honours – Spanish Championship (2008)
Clubs: 02-08 Real Madrid CF; 06-07 CA Osasuna (loan); 08-10 Getafe CF; 10- Valencia CF

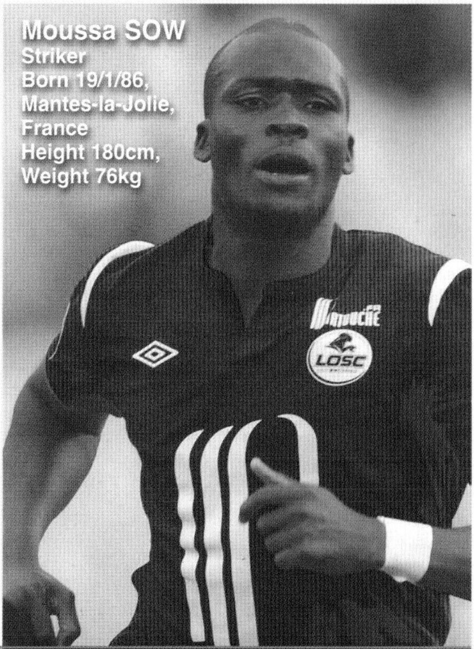

Offloaded by Stade Rennais FC in the summer of 2010, French-born Senegalese international striker Moussa Sow was at the crossroads of his career. Fortunately he followed the signpost pointing north and went on to become the goalscoring sensation of the 2010/11 French season, finding the net 25 times to win the Ligue 1 Golden Boot and help his new club LOSC Lille Métropole to an astonishing domestic double. The season could hardly have ended more sweetly for the powerful striker as he marked the club's trophy-winning celebrations with a hat-trick in a 3-2 last-day win at home to the club that had released him 12 months earlier. Sharp and alert in the penalty box, where he feasted all season on the chances created for him by the skills of Eden Hazard and Gervinho, Sow also offered power, skill and athleticism. Although the majority of his goals were poached from close range, there were a few spectacular strikes in there as well, notably a brilliant scissors kick against Olympique Lyonnais.

INTERNATIONAL CAREER

SENEGAL
Debut – 12/8/09 v DR Congo (n, Blois, friendly), won 2-1
First Goal – 5/9/10 v DR Congo (a, Lubumbashi, ANQ), won 4-2
Caps 11; **Goals** 3

CLUB CAREER

Major Honours – French Championship (2011); French Cup (2011)
Clubs: 06-10 Stade Rennais FC (FRA); 07-08 CS Sedan Ardennes (FRA) (loan); 10- LOSC Lille Métropole (FRA)

Carlos Tévez ended his first season as captain of Manchester City FC by becoming the first player to lift a major trophy for the club in 35 years. Although it was an open secret that the Argentinian striker was unhappy living in Manchester – he filed a transfer request in mid-season – his commitment to the City cause was never in doubt. Absent for the FA Cup semi-final win against former club Manchester United FC with a hamstring injury, he returned to skipper the team to victory against Stoke City FC in the final. He did not score at Wembley but three days later, against the same opposition, he supplied two sumptuous goals – one of them an incredible bending free-kick – to join United's Dimitar Berbatov as the Premier League's top marksman on 20. That double was vital in helping City secure guaranteed qualification for the UEFA Champions League. The big question, however, was whether the team's biggest star, still anxious to leave, would be around to enjoy the benefits in 2011/12.

INTERNATIONAL CAREER

ARGENTINA
Debut – 30/3/04 v Ecuador (h, Buenos Aires, WCQ), won 1-0
First Goal – 17/7/04 v Peru (a, Chiclayo, CA), won 1-0
Caps 64; **Goals** 13
Major Tournaments – Copa América 2004; FIFA Confederations Cup 2005; FIFA World Cup 2006; Copa América 2007; FIFA World Cup 2010; Copa América 2011

CLUB CAREER

Major Honours – UEFA Champions League (2008); Copa Libertadores (2003); World Club Cup (2003); Argentinian Championship (apertura 2003); Brazilian Championship (2005); English Premier League (2008); English FA Cup (2011)
Clubs: 01-04 CA Boca Juniors; 05-06 SC Corinthians (BRA); 06-07 West Ham United FC (ENG); 07-09 Manchester United FC (ENG); 09- Manchester City FC (ENG)

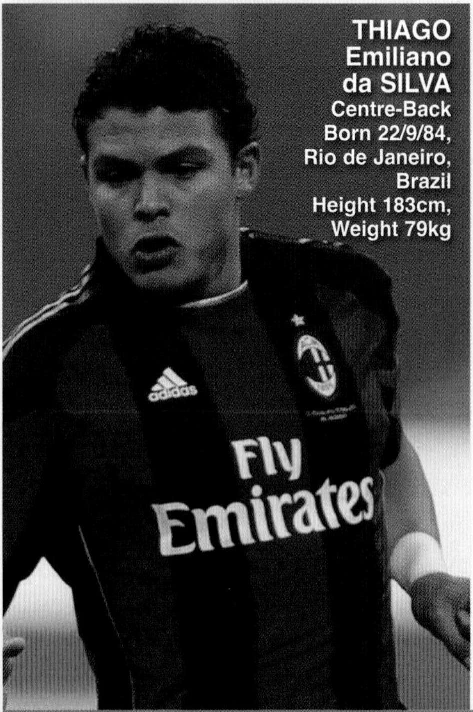

THIAGO Emiliano da SILVA

Centre-Back
Born 22/9/84, Rio de Janeiro, Brazil
Height 183cm, Weight 79kg

AC Milan's first Serie A title triumph in seven seasons was founded on an outstanding defence, and the linchpin of that sturdiest of back lines was Thiago Silva. The Brazilian international began the campaign by scoring a goal in the opening-day 4-0 win at home to US Lecce, but thereafter it was all about keeping things tight at the back and, with the exception of one off-day in early January, when Udinese Calcio came to San Siro and matched Milan in a crazy 4-4 draw, the elegant Brazilian, ably supported by the experienced Alessandro Nesta, did a masterful job. Massimiliano Allegri's side conceded just 24 league goals, a mere seven of that number in the second half of the campaign, and when they went out of the UEFA Champions League, to Tottenham Hotspur FC, it was chiefly the fault of the team's misfiring strikers. After winning the scudetto, Thiago Silva declared it his ambition to emulate Paolo Maldini and keep on playing for Milan to the age of 40. A new five-year contract, signed in May, will take the 26-year-old part of the way there.

INTERNATIONAL CAREER

BRAZIL
Debut – 12/10/08 v Venezuela (a, San Cristobal, WCQ), won 4-0
Caps 18; **Goals** 0
Major Tournaments – FIFA World Cup 2010; Copa América 2011

CLUB CAREER

Major Honours – Italian Championship (2011); Brazilian Cup (2007)
Clubs: 01-03 RS Futebol Clube; 04 EC Juventude; 04 FC Porto (POR); 05 FC Dinamo Moskva (RUS); 06-09 Fluminense FC; 09- AC Milan (ITA)

Yaya TOURÉ

Midfielder
Born 13/5/83, Bouake, Ivory Coast
Height 187cm, Weight 78kg

There were mixed emotions in the Touré family in 2010/11. As defender Kolo lost the Manchester City FC club captaincy, then incurred a lengthy suspension after failing a drug test, his younger brother Yaya, who joined him at the Premier League club in July 2010 following a big-money move from FC Barcelona, went on to become City's goalscoring hero in both the semi-final and the final of the FA Cup. His two goals at Wembley, against Manchester United FC and Stoke City FC, entered club folklore as the blue half of Manchester finally experienced the joy of winning a major trophy after three and a half decades of hurt and frustration. The powerful Ivorian also brought his influence to bear in the Premier League, scoring eight goals in 35 starts as City finished third to qualify for the UEFA Champions League – a competition Touré won with Barcelona in 2009.

INTERNATIONAL CAREER

IVORY COAST
Debut – 20/6/04 v Egypt (a, Alexandria, WCQ), won 2-1
First Goal – 24/1/06 v Madagascar (n, Cairo, ANF), won 2-1
Caps 57; **Goals** 7
Major Tournaments – Africa Cup of Nations 2006; FIFA World Cup 2006; Africa Cup of Nations 2008; Africa Cup of Nations 2010; FIFA World Cup 2010

CLUB CAREER

Major Honours – UEFA Champions League (2009); UEFA Super Cup (2009); FIFA Club World Cup (2009); Greek Championship (2006); Spanish Championship (2009, 2010); Greek Cup (2006); Spanish Cup (2009); English FA Cup (2011)
Clubs: 01-03 KSK Beveren (BEL); 03-05 FC Metalurh Donetsk (UKR); 05-06 Olympiacos FC (GRE); 06-07 AS Monaco FC (FRA); 07-10 FC Barcelona (ESP); 10- Manchester City FC (ENG)

Edwin van der Sar did not quite save his best till last. That would only have been true if, like another great Manchester United FC goalkeeper, Peter Schmeichel, his final game for the club had concluded with victory in the UEFA Champions League final. Performing under the Wembley arch in the year's biggest club game was nevertheless a fitting stage on which to end his professional career. The 40-year-old Dutchman's sixth season at United was just as impressive as those that preceded it. His one serious error – a fumble against West Bromwich Albion FC at Old Trafford that denied United a perfect home record in the Premier League – was only memorable because of its rarity. Otherwise the big 'keeper was virtually flawless. He won United many Premier League points with terrific saves, and in Europe he conceded just three goals before the final, none at all in his six matches away from Old Trafford. David de Gea, United's new goalkeeper, is half Van der Sar's age. He has a very hard act to follow.

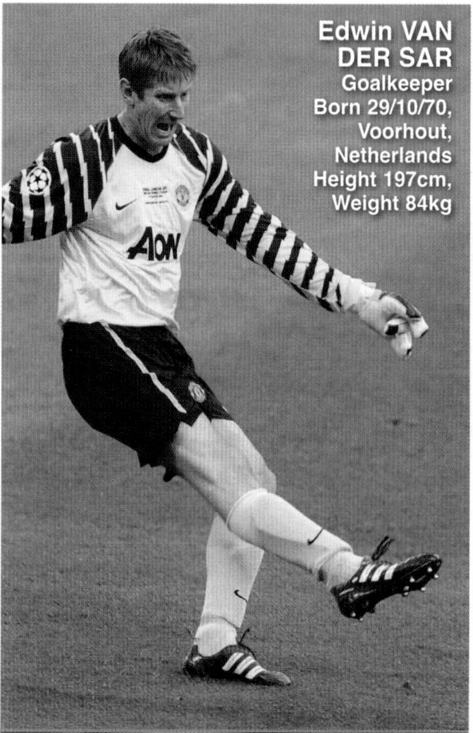

INTERNATIONAL CAREER

NETHERLANDS
Debut – 7/6/95 v Belarus (a, Minsk, ECQ), lost 0-1
Caps 130; **Goals** 0
Major Tournaments – FIFA World Cup 1994; UEFA EURO '96; FIFA World Cup 1998; UEFA EURO 2000; UEFA EURO 2004; FIFA World Cup 2006; UEFA EURO 2008

CLUB CAREER

Major Honours – UEFA Champions League (1995, 2008); UEFA Super Cup (1996); World Club Cup (1995); FIFA Club World Cup (2008); Dutch Championship (1994, 1995, 1996, 1998); English Premier League (2007, 2008, 2009, 2011); Dutch Cup (1993, 1998, 1999); English League Cup (2006, 2009, 2010)
Clubs: 90-99 AFC Ajax; 99-01 Juventus (ITA); 01-05 Fulham FC (ENG); 05-11 Manchester United FC (ENG)

Recruited by Tottenham Hotspur FC from Real Madrid CF for a cut-price fee in the final seconds of the 2010 summer transfer window, Rafael van der Vaart became an immediate hit in north London, scoring in his first four Premier League outings at White Hart Lane and his first two in the UEFA Champions League, the second of them a rousing 3-1 victory against FC Internazionale Milano. The Dutchman's two seasons in Spain had not gone to plan, but in England the technically gifted left-footer returned to the kind of form that had made him a serial match winner at both AFC Ajax and Hamburger SV. Nominated for the PFA Player of the Year award, he did fade in the spring – and was notably underpowered in the two European quarter-final ties against former club Madrid – but, with 13 league goals, he was the only Tottenham player to reach double figures. He also re-established himself as a regular starter for the Netherlands, reaching 90 caps in the UEFA EURO 2012 double-header against Hungary in March.

INTERNATIONAL CAREER

NETHERLANDS
Debut – 6/10/01 v Andorra (h, Arnhem, WCQ), won 4-0
First Goal – 6/9/03 v Austria (h, Rotterdam, ECQ), won 3-1
Caps 90; **Goals** 17
Major Tournaments – UEFA EURO 2004; FIFA World Cup 2006; UEFA EURO 2008; FIFA World Cup 2010

CLUB CAREER

Major Honours – Dutch Championship (2002, 2004); Dutch Cup (2002)
Clubs: 00-05 AFC Ajax; 05-08 Hamburger SV (GER); 08-10 Real Madrid CF (ESP); 10- Tottenham Hotspur FC (ENG)

Robin VAN PERSIE
Striker
Born 6/8/83, Rotterdam, Netherlands
Height 188cm, Weight 78kg

Out of action for the first half of the 2010/11 season with an ankle injury, Robin van Persie returned with a bang in the New Year, scoring 18 Premier League goals for Arsenal FC in 17 starts – including at least one in each of the team's nine away fixtures – and another in the UEFA Champions League last-16 tie at home to FC Barcelona. Arsenal won that first leg 2-1 but lost 3-1 at Camp Nou after Van Persie was sent off, his second yellow card, for shooting at goal after he had been flagged offside, bringing a furious reaction from both the player and his manager. Had the Dutchman remained on the field, Arsenal's season might have turned out differently. As it transpired, their four-pronged trophy assault came to nought – and this with their best striker in the form of his life. Van Persie also scored in the final of the League Cup, a match in which he captained the side in the absence of regular skipper Cesc Fàbregas, but Birmingham City FC scored a late winner and the Gunners' long wait for a trophy continued. A return to the Dutch national side in the spring also brought a goal in each of Van Persie's first two outings in the UEFA EURO 2012 qualifying campaign, both against Hungary, the first in Budapest, the second in Amsterdam.

INTERNATIONAL CAREER

NETHERLANDS
Debut – 4/6/05 v Romania (h, Rotterdam, WCQ), won 2-0
First Goal – 8/6/05 v Finland (a, Helsinki, WCQ), won 4-0
Caps 56; **Goals** 21
Major Tournaments – FIFA World Cup 2006; UEFA EURO 2008; FIFA World Cup 2010

CLUB CAREER

Major Honours – UEFA Cup (2002); FA Cup (2005)
Clubs: 01-04 Feyenoord; 04- Arsenal FC (ENG)

Jan VERTONGHEN
Defender/Midfielder
Born 24/4/87,
Sint-Niklaas, Belgium
Height 189cm,
Weight 79kg

An AFC Ajax player since he joined the club's famous youth academy in 2003, Jan Vertonghen had the honour of captaining the team to the last-day 3-1 victory over FC Twente in the Amsterdam ArenA that brought the club a first Dutch title since 2004. With regular skipper Maarten Stekelenburg unavailable in the last weeks of the campaign because of a broken thumb, the Belgian defender proved to be a redoubtable leader, inspiring the team to victories in each of their last six league games. Over the Eredivisie season as a whole Vertonghen was arguably Ajax's stand-out performer. He missed only two matches and scored half a dozen goals. Extremely versatile, his ability to play at centre-back, left-back or even in midfield served Ajax well, and he was also a prominent figure during the season for the Belgian national side, starting all but one of their ten matches and scoring his first competitive international goal in a UEFA EURO 2012 qualifier against Azerbaijan.

INTERNATIONAL CAREER

BELGIUM
Debut – 2/6/07 v Portugal (h, Brussels, ECQ), lost 1-2
First Goal – 12/8/09 v Czech Republic (a, Teplice, friendly), lost 1-3
Caps 31; **Goals** 2

CLUB CAREER

Major Honours – Dutch Championship (2011); Dutch Cup (2010)
Clubs: 06- AFC Ajax (NED); 06-07 RKC Waalwijk (loan)

It was once frequently said of Víctor Valdés that he was FC Barcelona's weak link. No one would dare to venture such a rash opinion now that he has spent eight seasons as the team's undisputed first-choice goalkeeper and, as a consequence, become the most successful 'number one' in the Catalan club's history. The underrated 29-year-old claimed his third UEFA Champions League winner's medal and his fifth Spanish championship crown in 2010/11, and played a big hand in both. For the third season running – and the fourth time in all – he won the prestigious Zamora trophy for the 'keeper in La Liga with the best ratio of goals-per-game conceded. Valdés's figure of just 16 against in his 32 appearances constituted the best percentage rate in the Primera División for 17 years – and the second best of all time since the man after whom the trophy was named, Ricardo Zamora, became its inaugural winner back in 1928/29.

INTERNATIONAL CAREER

SPAIN
Major Honours – FIFA World Cup (2010)
Debut – 3/6/10 v South Korea (n, Innsbruck, friendly), won 1-0
Caps 4; **Goals** 0
Major Tournaments – FIFA World Cup 2010

CLUB CAREER

Major Honours – UEFA Champions League (2006, 2009, 2011); UEFA Super Cup (2009); FIFA Club World Cup (2009); Spanish Championship (2005, 2006, 2009, 2010, 2011); Spanish Cup (2009)
Clubs: 02- FC Barcelona

VÍCTOR VALDÉS i Arribas
Goalkeeper
Born 14/1/82, L'Hospitalet de Llobregat, Spain
Height 186cm, Weight 76kg

Deployed predominantly as a defensive midfielder during his first three seasons at Bayer 04 Leverkusen, Chilean international Arturo Vidal was moved forward into a more attacking role by coach Jupp Heynckes in 2010/11 and he proved such a success there the Leverkusen fans barely missed their returning hero Michael Ballack, whose first season back at the club after eight years away was decimated by injury. Vidal, who started all four matches for his country at the 2010 FIFA World Cup, was especially impressive while Ballack was out of action during the autumn. He ended the season as Leverkusen's top scorer, although six of his ten goals came from penalty kicks, all of them scored before Christmas. His set-piece play and crossing were among the best in the Bundesliga, and his consistency of performance was central to the club's achievement of taking second place behind champions Borussia Dortmund. Vidal would not be able to enjoy the fruits of his labour in the UEFA Champions League, however, as he was sold in July to a team that had not qualified at all for Europe, albeit a rather illustrious one - Italian record champions Juventus.

INTERNATIONAL CAREER

CHILE
Debut – 7/2/07 v Venezuela (a, Maracaibo, friendly), won 1-0
First Goal – 5/9/09 v Venezuela (h, Santiago, WCQ), drew 2-2
Caps 34; **Goals** 3
Major Tournaments – FIFA World Cup 2010; Copa América 2011

CLUB CAREER

Major Honours – Chilean Championship (apertura 2006; clausura 2006; apertura 2007)
Clubs: 05-07 Colo-Colo; 07-11 Bayer 04 Leverkusen (GER); 11- Juventus (ITA)

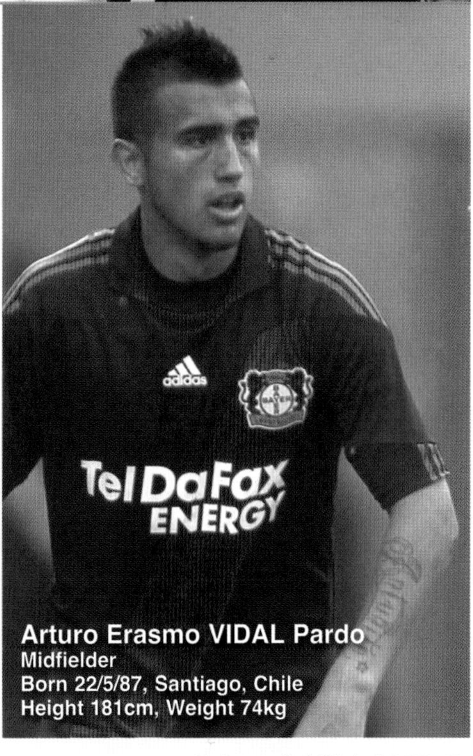

Arturo Erasmo VIDAL Pardo
Midfielder
Born 22/5/87, Santiago, Chile
Height 181cm, Weight 74kg

Nemanja VIDIĆ

Centre-Back
Born 21/10/81, Titovo Uzice, Serbia
Height 188cm, Weight 84kg

Resolute and resilient, Nemanja Vidić typified the never-say-die attitude that enabled Manchester United FC to regain the Premier League title and reach their third UEFA Champions League final in four years. Handed the captaincy – and a new four-year contract – in August, the Serbian international centre-back appeared to thrive on the extra responsibility. With his predecessor, and regular central defensive partner, Rio Ferdinand frequently absent through injury, Vidić had to form new alliances in the heart of the United back four, but his application and dependability never fluctuated. It was February before United lost a league game, and although they had often looked vulnerable to defeat away from Old Trafford before then, Vidić consistently inspired the team to come back and win or draw. A notable example came at Aston Villa FC in mid-November, when United were 2-0 down with less than ten minutes remaining before Vidić rescued them with a late equaliser. He also scored the winning goal against Chelsea FC in the Old Trafford title decider in early May. A prime candidate for Footballer of the Year, he must have considered himself unfortunate when the prestigious award went to a player from a team at the bottom of the Premier League table, Scott Parker of West Ham United FC.

INTERNATIONAL CAREER

SERBIA
Debut – 12/10/02 v Italy (a, Naples, ECQ), drew 1-1
First Goal – 15/8/05 v Poland (n, Kyiv, friendly), lost 2-3
Caps 54; **Goals** 2
Major Tournaments – FIFA World Cup 2006; FIFA World Cup 2010

CLUB CAREER

Major Honours – UEFA Champions League (2008); FIFA Club World Cup (2008); Serbo-Montenegrin Championship (2004); English Premier League (2007, 2008, 2009, 2011); Yugoslav Cup (2002); Serbo-Montenegrin Cup (2004); English League Cup (2006, 2009, 2010)
Clubs: 00-04 FK Crvena zvezda; 00-01 FK Spartak Subotica (loan); 04-06 FK Spartak Moskva (RUS); 06- Manchester United FC (ENG)

WELLITON Soares de Morais

Striker
Born 22/10/86, Conceicao do Araguaia, Brazil
Height 175cm, Weight 76kg

FC Spartak Moskva's Brazilian striker Welliton completed a rare feat in 2010 by retaining the Russian Premier-Liga Golden Boot. He thus became the first player to win the award outright two seasons running since FC Rotor Volgograd's Oleg Veretennikov in 1998. The diminutive, fleet-footed Brazilian forward scored 21 goals in 2009 and 19 in 2010 – both highly respectable winning totals. His 2010 haul was five more than anyone else managed, and although it could only take Spartak to fourth place in the league, a long way distant of champions FC Zenit St Petersburg, his consistent scoring did raise the possibility of the 24-year-old switching his international allegiance from Brazil to Russia. As in 2009, August proved to be the striker's favourite month. The previous year he had scored seven goals in four games; in 2010 he grabbed back-to-back hat-tricks, away to FC Lokomotiv Moskva and at home to FC Tom Tomsk, the second of them arriving in just six minutes – the fastest in Spartak's history.

INTERNATIONAL CAREER

BRAZIL
uncapped

CLUB CAREER

Clubs: 05-07 Goiás EC; 06 Ituano FC (loan); 07- FC Spartak Moskva (RUS)

Jack WILSHERE

Midfielder
Born 1/1/92, Stevenage, England
Height 170cm, Weight 65kg

Englishmen who break into Arsène Wenger's Arsenal FC team are generally required to have a special talent. Nineteen-year-old Jack Wilshere certainly fits that description. The young left-footed schemer returned to the north London club after an impressive loan spell at Bolton Wanderers FC and not only became a fixture in the Gunners midfield but played so often and so well that by the end of the campaign he was voted by Arsenal supporters as the club's player of the season. He was also crowned PFA Young Player of the Year and fast-tracked into Fabio Capello's England side, where he looked totally at ease, his confidence on the ball and technical expertise suggesting that his country had finally found a midfielder with the ability to dictate the tempo of a game at international level. Time will tell whether Wilshere fully develops his vast potential, but there was considerable disappointment for England supporters when he was denied the opportunity to represent his country at the UEFA European Under-21 Championship in June after Arsenal convinced the FA that he was too exhausted to compete.

INTERNATIONAL CAREER

ENGLAND
Debut – 11/8/10 v Hungary (h, Wembley, friendly), won 2-1
Caps 5; **Goals** 0

CLUB CAREER

Clubs: 08- Arsenal FC; 10 Bolton Wanderers FC (loan)

XABIer ALONSO Olano

Midfielder
Born 25/11/81, Tolosa, Spain
Height 183cm, Weight 77kg

Xabi Alonso's second season at Real Madrid CF, under José Mourinho, was every bit as impressive as his first, under Manuel Pellegrini. Madrid's answer to FC Barcelona's Xavi in the way that he sets the rhythm of the play from his base camp in and around the centre circle, Xabi Alonso's distribution of the ball is second to none, be it with quick, sharp one-twos over a few metres or long, searching diagonals to the flanks. Hard-working too, he played 50 matches for Madrid in 2010/11 and rarely skipped a beat, claiming his first trophy for the club with victory over Barcelona in the final of the Copa del Rey. His only goal of the campaign came in that competition – in an early round against Real Murcia – but he did manage another for the Spanish national team, for whom he was again a regular performer, in a June friendly away to Venezuela. It was his tenth goal for Spain in 86 international appearances. Still in his prime at 29, Xabi Alonso should remain a pivotal figure for La Roja both in Poland/Ukraine next summer and for the defence of their world crown in Brazil in 2014.

INTERNATIONAL CAREER

SPAIN
Major Honours – FIFA World Cup (2010); UEFA European Championship (2008)
Debut – 30/4/03 v Ecuador (h, Madrid, friendly), won 4-0
First Goal – 14/6/06 v Ukraine (n, Leipzig, WCF), won 4-0
Caps 86; **Goals** 10
Major Tournaments – UEFA EURO 2004; FIFA World Cup 2006; UEFA EURO 2008; FIFA Confederations Cup 2009; FIFA World Cup 2010

CLUB CAREER

Major Honours – UEFA Champions League (2005); UEFA Super Cup (2005); English FA Cup (2006); Spanish Cup (2011)
Clubs: 99-04 Real Sociedad de Fútbol; 00 SD Éibar (loan); 04-09 Liverpool FC (ENG); 09- Real Madrid CF

If great footballers are defined by those who play their best when it matters most – in the biggest tournaments and the biggest games – then Xavi qualifies as one without reservation. As the midfield string-puller for both FC Barcelona and Spain, he has had plenty of opportunities to prove himself on the grandest of stages, and almost unfailingly he has delivered. He did so again in the 2011 UEFA Champions League final against Manchester United FC. For the first few minutes it looked as if United might have the measure of him, but the Catalans' captain for the day soon found his rhythm and before long he was in total control, setting up Barça's first goal and keeping his team on the front foot until the trophy was safely won for the third time in six years. The 31-year-old gave other masterful performances at home to Arsenal FC and FC Shakhtar Donetsk, and although Real Madrid CF partially succeeded in curbing his influence when the two Spanish giants met four times in 17 days in the spring, Madrid coach José Mourinho's wholesale change of strategy against the Catalans was the consequence of another epic Xavi display in November when Barça tore Madrid to shreds at Camp Nou in a never-to-be-forgotten 5-0 victory.

INTERNATIONAL CAREER

SPAIN
Major Honours – FIFA World Cup (2010); UEFA European Championship (2008)
Debut – 15/11/00 v Netherlands (h, Seville, friendly), lost 1-2
First Goal – 26/3/05 v China (h, Salamanca, friendly), won 3-0
Caps 101; **Goals** 10
Major Tournaments – FIFA World Cup 2002; UEFA EURO 2004; FIFA World Cup 2006; UEFA EURO 2008; FIFA Confederations Cup 2009; FIFA World Cup 2010

CLUB CAREER

Major Honours – UEFA Champions League (2006, 2009, 2011); UEFA Super Cup (2009); FIFA Club World Cup (2009); Spanish Championship (1999, 2005, 2006, 2009, 2010, 2011); Spanish Cup (2009)
Clubs: 97- FC Barcelona

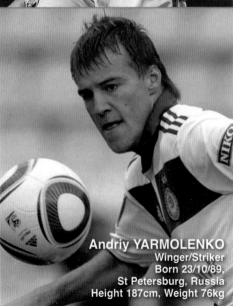

UEFA EURO 2012 co-hosts Ukraine will be looking for a hero next summer, and FC Dynamo Kyiv starlet Andriy Yarmolenko could be the man to oblige. The young Russian-born forward had a foretaste of the main event when he represented Ukraine at the 2011 UEFA European Under-21 Championship finals in Denmark, but above all it was the excellent form he displayed for Dynamo in the preceding months that will have encouraged new Ukraine coach Oleh Blokhin to believe that Yarmolenko might be the man for the big occasion. Often outperforming Andriy Shevchenko in the Dynamo attack, the crafty, pacy 21-year-old scored 11 goals in the Ukrainian Premier-Liha and another four in a marathon European campaign that began in the third qualifying round of the UEFA Champions League and ended in the quarter-finals of the UEFA Europa League. Yarmolenko opened the scoring in the latter tie, against SC Braga, but could not prevent Dynamo's elimination on the away-goals rule.

INTERNATIONAL CAREER

UKRAINE
Debut – 5/9/09 v Andorra (h, Kyiv, WCQ), won 5-0
First Goal – 5/9/09 v Andorra (h, Kyiv, WCQ), won 5-0
Caps 11; **Goals** 2

CLUB CAREER

Major Honours – Ukrainian Championship (2009)
Clubs: 06 FC Desna Chernihiv; 07-08 FC Dynamo-2 Kyiv; 08- FC Dynamo Kyiv

Nation-by-nation

Welcome to the Nation-by-nation section of the European Football Yearbook.

Here you will find separate chapters, alphabetically arranged, on each of the 53 UEFA member associations.

Nation-by-nation explained

Included for each UEFA member association is a narrative and pictorial review of the season accompanied by the following statistics:

COMMUNICATION

The member association's official logo, name, address, contact details and senior officials as of 31 July 2011.

DOMESTIC COMPETITION SUMMARY

Final Table

The final standings of the member association's top division including home, away and total records.

Key: Pld = matches played, W = matches won, D = matches drawn, L = matches lost, F = goals for (scored), A = goals against (conceded), Pts = points; Comp = UEFA club competition qualified for (UCL = UEFA Champions League; UEL = UEFA Europa League)

.... = play-off line
- - - - - - - - = relegation line

Any peculiarities, such as the deduction of points or clubs withdrawn, are indicated as NB at the foot of the table.

The league's top scorer(s), promoted club(s) and the result of the domestic cup final are also indicated.

National Team

International honours, major international tournament appearances and the member association's top five international cap-holders and goalscorers are included in this panel.

National Team Results

Details on all international matches played between August 2010 and June 2011 with date, opponent, venue, result and scorer details.

Key: H = home, A = away, N = neutral.
og = own goal, p = penalty, (aet) = after extra time, (ECQ) = UEFA EURO 2012 qualification round match.

National Team Appearances

Details on all participants in the aforementioned matches (coaches and players), including name, date of birth and, for each player, club, match-by-match appearances, minutes played and all-time international caps and goals scored.

Opponents are ranged across the top and abbreviated with the appropriate three-letter country codes – capital letters identify a UEFA EURO 2012 qualification round match.

Changes of national team coach are indicated with the appropriate date; temporary coaches are indicated in brackets.

Non-native clubs are indicated with the appropriate three-letter country code.

*Key: G = goalkeeper, D = defender, M = midfielder, A = attacker, s = substitute, * = sending-off.*

The number appearing after the letter indicates the time a substitution took place. The number preceding an asterisk indicates the time a sending-off took place.

CLUB-BY-CLUB

Information on each top-division club is provided in four parts:

1) Club name followed by the coach(es)/manager(s) used during the season and, in the case of new appointments, the dates on which they took place.
2) The year the club was founded and the club's home stadium (with capacity), followed, where applicable, by major honours, including European, international and domestic competitions. National 'super cups', secondary leagues and minor or age-restricted knockout competitions are not included.
3) League fixtures, including dates, opponents, results and scorers.

Key: h = home, a = away, og = own goal, (p) = penalty, (w/o) = walkover/forfeit

4) A list of all players used in the league campaign, including name, nationality, date of birth, playing position, appearances and goals. Where applicable, and known, squad numbers are also included.

Key: No = squad (jersey) number, Name = full name (listed alphabetically with family name or football nickname in capitals), Nat = nationality (native unless listed with three-letter country code), DoB = date of birth,

Pos = playing position, Aps = number of appearances in the starting lineup, (s) = number of appearances as a substitute, Gls = number of goals scored, G = goalkeeper, D = defender, M = midfielder; A = attacker.

Top Goalscorers

A list of the top ten goalscorers (with clubs) in the member association's top division (league goals only).

Promoted Club(s)

Information on each promoted club is provided in two parts:

1) Club name followed by the coach(es)/manager(s) used during the season and, in the case of new appointments, the dates on which they took place.
2) The year the club was founded and the club's home stadium (with capacity), followed, where applicable, by major honours, including European, international and domestic competitions. National 'super cups', secondary leagues and minor or age-restricted knockout competitions are not included.

Second Level Final Table

The final classification of the member association's second level (i.e. feeder league to the top division) table(s). Play-off details, where applicable, are also indicated.

Key: Pld = matches played, W = matches won, D = matches drawn, L = matches lost, F = goals for (scored), A = goals against (conceded), Pts = points.

- - - - - - - = promotion line (at the top)
.... = play-off line
- - - - - - - = relegation line (at the bottom)

Any peculiarities, such as the deduction of points or clubs withdrawn, are indicated as NB at the foot of the final league table.

Domestic Cup(s)

Results from the member association's main domestic knockout competition, beginning at the round in which the top-division clubs (or some of them) enter. Goalscorers and times of goals are indicated from the quarter-final stage with complete lineups for the final. Details of the latter stages of significant secondary knockout competitions are also included for some member associations.

Key: (aet) = after extra time

CLUB COMMUNICATION

Address, contact details and media officers for the member association's top-division clubs as of 31 July 2011.

NB A complete key to all three-letter country codes can be found on page 6.

INDEX

ALBANIA

Albanie I Albanien

Federata Shqiptarë e Futbollit (FShF)

COMMUNICATION

Address Rruga e Elbasanit
AL-Tiranë
Tel +355 42 346 605
Fax +355 42 346 609
E-mail fshf@fshf.org.al
Website fshf.org

President Armand Duka
General Secretary Eduard Prodani
Media Officer Tritan Kokona

Year of Formation 1930

National Stadium Qemal Stafa, Tirana (16,230)

DOMESTIC COMPETITION SUMMARY 2010/11

KATEGORIA SUPERIORE FINAL TABLE

			Home					Away					Total						
		Pld	W	D	L	F	A	W	D	L	F	A	W	D	L	F	A	Pts	Comp
1	KS Skënderbeu	33	17	0	0	37	6	6	4	6	15	17	23	4	6	52	23	73	UCL
2	KS Flamurtari	33	17	0	0	47	7	5	3	8	15	19	22	3	8	62	26	66	UEL
3	KF Vllaznia	33	11	4	2	26	15	6	4	6	14	12	17	8	8	40	27	59	UEL
4	KF Laçi	33	10	3	4	23	13	4	2	10	21	31	14	5	14	44	44	47	
5	KF Tirana	33	9	4	4	28	12	2	7	7	14	19	11	11	11	42	31	44	UEL
6	KS Bylis	33	11	3	2	25	10	2	1	14	19	38	13	4	16	44	48	43	
7	KS Kastrioti	33	10	3	3	28	16	1	6	10	12	31	11	9	13	40	47	42	
8	KS Teuta	33	8	5	3	27	16	3	4	10	11	24	11	9	13	38	40	42	
9	KS Shkumbini	33	10	4	2	32	24	2	2	13	11	30	12	6	15	43	54	42	
10	FK Dinamo Tirana	33	6	6	5	23	20	4	3	9	23	30	10	9	14	46	50	39	
11	KS Besa	33	8	5	3	19	14	2	4	11	16	33	10	9	14	35	47	39	*Relegated*
12	KF Elbasani	33	3	3	10	18	30	1	0	16	12	49	4	3	26	30	79	12	*Relegated*

NB KS Flamurtari and KF Elbasani – 3 pts deducted.

Top Scorer Daniel Xhafa (Flamurtari), 19 goals

Promoted Clubs KS Pogradeci
FK Tomori
KS Kamza
KF Apolonia

Cup Final KF Tirana 1, FK Dinamo Tirana 1 (aet; 4-3 on pens)

Long wait over for Skënderbeu

There was an unfamiliar look to Albania's Kategoria Superiore in 2010/11. An off-season for the two clubs from the capital, KF Tirana and FK Dinamo Tirana, was seized upon by the provincials, foremost among them KS Skënderbeu, from the eastern town of Korca, and KS Flamurtari, from the southern port of Vlora.

Neither club had challenged in 2009/10, when Dinamo took the title. Indeed Skënderbeu had only retained their top-flight status after surviving a promotion/relegation play-off. Now, curiously, the roles were reversed as Dinamo swapped first place for tenth and avoided relegation in a play-off while Skënderbeu climbed the equivalent ladder to Dinamo's snake and leapt nine places to finish first, claiming their first national title for 78 years.

Heavy investment

Although Skënderbeu's wait was long, their success was not wholly unsurprising given the pre-season investment made by wealthy club president Agim Zeqo. In addition to overhauling the playing squad, he brought in Dinamo's title-winning boss Shkëlqim Muça as coach. Muça would do a decent job, taking Skënderbeu to second place, three points behind Gurgash Magani's Flamurtari, at the winter break. But although the team had a perfect record at home, their away results were a problem, so in February, with Albanian international Gjergji Muzaka having already arrived from Dinamo, the president fired Muça and hired Shpëtim Duro, who had led KS Besa to an Albanian Cup triumph and league runners-up spot in 2009/10, to replace him.

With Duro in charge and Muzaka offering impressive support in attack to top-scoring Argentinian striker Rafael Sosa, Skënderbeu made a powerful charge to the title. Flamurtari, chasing a first championship win for 20 years, were defeated 1-0 at home in Duro's first game, and thereafter Skënderbeu dropped only two points – ironically away to the coach's ex-club Besa, who were heading for a shock relegation – en route to sealing the title in the penultimate round with a 1-0 home win over the other automatically relegated club, KF Elbasani.

While Skënderbeu were claiming their 17th win out of 17 at home, Flamurtari, who had lost ground by dropping ten further points since their defeat in Korca, conceded the crown in regrettable circumstances away to third-placed KF Vllaznia. Leading 1-0 through striker Daniel Xhafa's 19th-goal of the season (which gave the 34-year-old the Golden Boot for the second year running, with one goal more than his winning haul for Besa in 2009/10), Flamurtari's players walked off the pitch in protest at the awarding of a late penalty to the home side. Their action not only led to the match being awarded 2-0 to Vllaznia but also to a further three-point deduction. On the final day Flamurtari defeated Skënderbeu 1-0 in Vlora, thus completing their own flawless home record, but it was a hollow victory tainted by provocative and aggressive behaviour from the home fans, which left the Skënderbeu players and staff requiring police protection and an escort out of town.

Altin Lala – Albania's new record cap-holder

ALBANIA

Cup salvation

A seven-point gap between champions and runners-up was matched by the same distance between second place and third. Below Vllaznia, strong finishers under coach Mirel Josa, who had returned to his former club in October, there was a 12-point gap to KF Laçi, who finished an impressive fourth for the second season running under Stavri Nica. Every club beneath Laç endured a season of struggle, including Tirana, who, beset by internal strife, could only win as many matches as they lost (and drew). Their season was salvaged only by victory in the Albanian Cup, which arrived in dramatic circumstances after a penalty shoot-out win in the final against Dinamo.

Tirana's triumph enabled them to move ahead of Dinamo in the competition's all-time roll of honour, 14 to 13, with only FK Partizani, another Tirana club, ahead of them on 15. The hero of the final was Tirana's ex-Dinamo goalkeeper Ilion Lika, who saved three spot-kicks after the match had ended 1-1, with Tirana's top-scoring Croatian import Pero Pejić having cancelled out an early goal scored by Dinamo's Serbian striker Mladen Brkić, who had started the season with Skënderbeu. That the match should end without a conventional winner was hardly surprising given that Tirana had failed to win any of their last five league games and Dinamo their last nine.

At least Dinamo recovered to win their promotion/relegation play-off, 4-1 in Kavaje to KS Besëlidhja Lezhë, four days later. With the Kategoria Superiore increasing in number to 14 teams (and reducing the amount of games from 33 to 26) in 2011/12, it was possible for as many as six teams to gain promotion, but with KF Mamurasi losing the other play-off to KS Shkumbini, only the top four went up. They included KS Kamza, a team from the Tirana suburbs once known as KS Dajti, who were controversially denied promotion back in 1973. The other end of the table saw the sad and shocking relegation to Albania's third tier of once-great Partizani.

National Team

Top Five All-time Caps – Altin Lala (74); Klodian Duro, Ervin Skela & Foto Strakosha (73); Igli Tare (68)

Top Five All-time Goals – Alban Bushi (14); Ervin Skela (13); Erjon Bogdani (12); Altin Rraklli (11); Sokol Kushta & Igli Tare (10)

Highest ranking

It was a pleasing season for the Albanian national team, with eight points garnered from six UEFA EURO 2012 qualifiers and, consequently, a rise to 50th place in the April 2011 FIFA world rankings – the country's highest position to date. The team's Croatian coach Josip Kuže suffered a stroke in October and had to be replaced on the bench for that month's qualifiers against Bosnia & Herzegovina in Tirana and Belarus in Minsk, which yielded just one point under his assistant, Džemal Mustedanagić, but Kuže was back to steer the team to a home win over Belarus in March, the winning goal coming from Hamdi Salihi, who enjoyed another fine season in Austria with SK Rapid Wien.

An intriguing sideshow developed during the season between midfield trio Klodian Duro, Ervin Skela and Altin Lala to become Albania's most-capped international, with 35-year-old Lala, of German club Hannover 96, becoming the first to overtake previous record-holder Foto Strakosha when he made his 74th appearance away to Bosnia & Herzegovina in June.

NATIONAL TEAM RESULTS 2010/11

11/8/10	Uzbekistan	H	Durres	1-0	*Salihi (14)*
3/9/10	Romania (ECQ)	A	Piatra Neamt	1-1	*Muzaka (87)*
7/9/10	Luxembourg (ECQ)	H	Tirana	1-0	*Salihi (37)*
8/10/10	Bosnia & Herzegovina (ECQ)	H	Tirana	1-1	*Duro (45+2)*
12/10/10	Belarus (ECQ)	A	Minsk	0-2	
17/11/10	FYROM	H	Korce	0-0	
9/2/11	Slovenia	H	Tirana	1-2	*Bulku (62)*
26/3/11	Belarus (ECQ)	H	Tirana	1-0	*Salihi (62)*
7/6/11	Bosnia & Herzegovina (ECQ)	A	Zenica	0-2	
20/6/11	Argentina	A	Buenos Aires	0-4	

NATIONAL TEAM APPEARANCES 2010/11

oach – Josip KUŽE (CRO)	13/11/52													
/10/10) (Džemal MUSTEDANAGIĆ (BIH))	8/6/55		Uzb	ROU	LUX	BIH	BLR	Mkd	Svn	BLR	BIH	Arg	Caps	Goals
'jan BEQAJ	25/8/75	Olympiakos (CYP)	G	G	G	G	G							
		/Ermis (CYP)							s46			G73	43	
ebatik CURRI	28/12/83	Gençlerbirliği (TUR)	D	D	D						D		35	1
rmend DALLKU	16/6/83	Vorskla (UKR)	D	D	D	D	D	D	D		D		46	1
							90*							
orik CANA	27/7/83	Galatasaray (TUR)	D	M	D	D			D	D	D		50	1
isti VANGJELI	5/9/85	Aris (GRE)	D75	D		D	D	D55	D73	D	D	D	30	-
nsi AGOLLI	11/10/82	Qarabağ (AZE)	M	M	M	M	M	M65	M	M	M60		26	2
vin BULKU	3/3/81	unattached	M75											
		/Hajduk (CRO)		M	M	M	M59	M74	s56	M	M	M	36	1
odian DURO	21/12/77	unattached	M75											
		/LASK (AUT)		M81	M91	M	M	M63	M56	s81	s46		73	5
jergji MUZAKA	26/9/84	Dinamo Tirana	M81	s81	M80	M65	s59	M57						
		/Skënderbeu							s56	s93	s73	M	15	1
rjon BOGDANI	14/4/77	Cesena (ITA)	A55	A57	A	A46			A64	A75	A46		62	12
amdi SALIHI	19/1/84	Rapid Wien (AUT)	A75	s57	A	A85	A	A73	A81	A93	A		30	7
lis BAKAJ	25/6/87	Dinamo Tirana	s55				s76	s55						
		/Dinamo Bucureşti (ROU)							s64	s75		A66	14	-
ahmir HYKA	8/3/88	Mainz (GER)	s75											
		/Panionios (GRE)			s80	s85		s57						
		/Tirana										s46	22	1
dmond KAPLLANI	31/7/82	Augsburg (GER)	s75									A67	32	6
		/Paderborn (GER)					s81							
ndi LILA	12/2/86	Tirana	s75	D	s91	D	D	D	D	D	s60	D	20	-
											87*			
orian BYLYKBASHI	8/8/80	unattached	s75										6	-
miljano VILA	12/3/88	Dinamo Tirana	s81					s74				M46	9	1
rvin SKELA	17/11/76	unattached		M79	M	s46	M81							
		/Arka (POL)								M81	M		73	13
ilman LIKA	13/1/87	Diyarbakırspor (TUR)		s79		s65	M76							
		/Tirana							s73			s57	15	-
Admir TELI	2/6/81	Qarabağ (AZE)					D	D	D	D			9	-
Samir UJKANI	5/7/88	Novara (ITA)						G	G46	G	G		8	-
Altin LALA	18/11/75	Hannover (GER)						M	M56	M	M73		74	3
Ledian MEMUSHAJ	7/12/86	Chievo (ITA)						s63						
		/Portosummaga (ITA)							s81				2	-
Endrit VRAPI	23/5/82	Skënderbeu						s65				D80	10	-
Ahmed JANUZI	8/7/88	Vorskla (UKR)						s73					1	-
Franc VELIU	11/11/88	Flamurtari										D	1	-
gli ALLMUÇA	25/10/80	Dinamo Tirana										M57	1	-
Armando VAJUSHI	3/12/91	Vllaznia										s66	1	-
Agonit SALLAJ	14/2/92	Xamax (SUI)										s67	1	-
sli HIDI	15/10/80	Olympiakos (CYP)										s73	15	-
Renato ARAPI	28/8/86	Skënderbeu										s80	1	-

CLUB-BY-CLUB

KS BESA

Coach – Shpëtim Duro; (20/9/10) Përparim Daiu; (3/11/10) Gjert Haxhiu
Founded – 1922
Stadium – Besa (7,000)
MAJOR HONOURS: Albanian Cup – (2) 2007, 2010.

2010				
23/8	Skënderbeu	h	0-2	*(w/o; match abandoned after 88 mins at 0-1)*
28/8	Dinamo	a	1-2	*Çikalleshi*
11/9	Flamurtari	h	0-0	
19/9	Teuta	h	0-0	
27/9	Shkumbini	a	2-2	*Mihani, Çikalleshi*
2/10	Vllaznia	h	0-1	
16/10	Elbasan	a	1-1	*Mihani (p)*
25/10	Tirana	h	2-1	*Mihani, Çikalleshi*
30/10	Bylis	a	1-3	*Çikalleshi (p)*
6/11	Kastrioti	h	0-0	
12/11	Laç	a	0-1	
20/11	Skënderbeu	a	0-4	
30/11	Dinamo	h	1-1	*Mihani*
13/12	Flamurtari	a	0-1	
18/12	Teuta	a	2-1	*Velija, Çikalleshi (p)*
24/12	Shkumbini	h	2-1	*Marcos, Çikalleshi*
2011				
22/1	Vllaznia	a	1-2	*Sefa*
30/1	Elbasan	h	2-0	*Mihani, Nora*
6/2	Tirana	a	0-0	
12/2	Bylis	h	2-1	*Mihani (p), Shtini*
19/2	Kastrioti	a	1-2	*Shtini*
25/2	Laç	h	1-2	*Djarmati (p)*
6/3	Vllaznia	a	0-2	
12/3	Skënderbeu	h	0-0	
20/3	Flamurtari	a	0-3	
1/4	Bylis	h	2-1	*Shtini, Marcos*
10/4	Elbasan	a	1-0	*Shameti*
16/4	Teuta	a	2-4	*Sefa, Nora*
20/4	Kastrioti	h	3-2	*Marcos, Mançaku, Poçi (p)*
24/4	Shkumbini	a	2-2	*Sefa, Nora (p)*
30/4	Dinamo	h	1-0	*Nora*
4/5	Laç	a	2-3	*Dhëmbi, Lazarevski*
16/5	Tirana	h	3-2	*Shtini, Nora (p), Sefa*

No	Name	Nat	DoB	Pos	Aps	(s)	Gls
4	Betim ALIJU	MKD	17/3/89	D	3	(6)	
10	Darlien BAJAZITI		7/7/94	A	1		
12	Edvan BAKAJ		9/7/87	G	15		
	Saimir ÇELHAKA		21/11/90	D		(1)	
7	Sokol ÇIKALLESHI		27/7/90	A	14	(1)	6
18	Eglajd DEDEJ		2/3/90	M	1	(4)	
20	Paulin DHËMBI		9/8/79	M	23	(1)	1
25	Matko DJARMATI	CRO	24/2/82	D	15	(1)	1
8	Mirel DUKA		9/1/91	M	10	(9)	
	Aldo DURO		23/2/91	M		(1)	
6	Edin FERIZOVIĆ	SRB	12/10/77	D	14		
12	Taulant GUMA		27/3/86	G		(1)	
10	Sead HADŽIBULIĆ	SRB	30/1/83	A	10		
22	Semir HADŽIBULIĆ	SRB	16/8/86	A	11	(2)	
19	Mateo HASA		25/3/93	M	2	(8)	
13	Erand HOXHA		25/4/85	M	5	(2)	
17	Besmir HYLVIU		11/1/92	A	1		
24	Akil JAKUPI		1/8/82	D	28		
8	Besmir KOLLÇAKU		4/11/92	A		(1)	
22	Elvis KOTORRI		30/4/70	G	17		
5	Gëzim KRASNIQI		5/1/90	D	7	(9)	
29	Dimitrija LAZAREVSKI	MKD	23/9/82	M	29		1
21	Bledar MANÇAKU		19/2/82	M	12		1
17	MARCOS dos Santos	BRA	18/5/81	A	27	(5)	3
23	Meglid MIHANI		1/9/83	M	19		6
30	Marius NGJELA		22/1/83	A	8	(5)	
30	Arlind NORA		4/7/80	A	11	(2)	5
12	Alfred OSMANI		20/2/83	G	1		
8	Minas OSMANI	MKD	22/5/85	D	5	(4)	
29	Skerdian PERJA		3/3/92	A		(1)	
13	Artion POÇI		23/7/77	D	27		1
9	Fatjon SEFA		27/4/84	A	13	(2)	4
6	Ylli SHAMETI		7/6/84	D	14		1
9	Arjel SHTINI		7/2/92	D	9	14	4
16	Bazjon TRAGA		16/8/88	D	3	(5)	
25	Bilal VELIJA	MKD	22/10/82	D	8		1

KS BYLIS

Coach – Ilir Spahiu; (13/9/10) (Agim Meta); (20/9/10) Nikola Ilievski (MKD); (7/3/11) (Elidon Demiri); (17/3/11) Agim Canaj
Founded – 1972
Stadium – Adush Muça (5,000)

2010				
22/8	Vllaznia	a	2-3	*Dimo, Popović*
28/8	Elbasan	h	1-2	*Dimo*
12/9	Tirana	a	1-2	*Gega*
19/9	Flamurtari	a	0-1	
25/9	Kastrioti	h	1-0	*Dimo*
30/9	Laç	a	1-3	*Dimo*
16/10	Skënderbeu	h	1-1	*Egbo (p)*
24/10	Dinamo	a	1-2	*Dimo*
30/10	Besa	h	3-1	*Madjo, Dimo, Xhafa*
8/11	Teuta	a	0-6	
13/11	Shkumbini	h	3-2	*Xhafa 2, Madjo*
19/11	Vllaznia	h	0-0	
27/11	Elbasan	a	2-3	*Xhafa, Begaj*
11/12	Tirana	h	1-1	*Popović*
18/12	Flamurtari	h	1-0	*Begaj*
24/12	Kastrioti	a	1-2	*Kule*
2011				
22/1	Laç	h	1-2	*Washington*
29/1	Skënderbeu	a	0-2	
5/2	Dinamo	h	3-1	*Washington 2, Xhafa*
12/2	Besa	a	1-2	*Dimo*
21/2	Teuta	h	3-0	*Xhafa 2, Dimo*
26/2	Shkumbini	a	2-4	*Shoshi, Arbëri*
7/3	Skënderbeu	a	1-3	*Dimo (p)*
13/3	Flamurtari	h	1-0	*Xhafa*
19/3	Elbasan	a	2-0	*Gega, Abazaj*
1/4	Besa	a	1-2	*Abazaj*
10/4	Teuta	h	1-0	*Xhafa*
16/4	Kastrioti	a	1-2	*Abazaj*
20/4	Shkumbini	h	2-0	*Dimo, Arbëri*
24/4	Dinamo	a	1-1	*Abazaj*
29/4	Laç	h	1-0	*Shoshi*
4/5	Tirana	a	2-0	*Gega, Xhafa*
16/5	Vllaznia	h	2-0	*Shoshi, Genivaldo*

No	Name	Nat	DoB	Pos	Aps	(s)	Gls
14	Orjand ABAZAJ		17/1/85	A	13	(2)	4
7	Polizoi ARBËRI		9/9/88	D	25	(2)	2
5	Mirjan BEGAJ		19/2/86	M	16	(2)	2
20	Almir BEKTOVIĆ	SRB	18/6/82	M	7	(2)	
13	Gentian BESHA		11/8/84	D	5	(2)	
8	Romans BEZZUBOVS	LVA	15/5/79	D	5	(2)	
	Darijo BIŠČAN	SVN	26/8/85	A	2	(4)	
	DENIS Viana da Silva	BRA	3/9/86	D	4		
2	Amarildo DIMO		25/8/82	A	27	(1)	10
	EDMAR Flavio de Almeida Menezes	BRA	4/7/87	M	1	(2)	
1	Emmanuel EGBO	NGA	27/5/83	G	9	(2)	1
12	Stivi FRASHËRI		29/8/90	G	21	(1)	
21	Armand GEGA		21/1/87	M	21	(4)	3
	GENIVALDO Sousa	BRA	24/7/82	D	12	(1)	1
	Klaudio GOXHAJ		18/3/88	M	1	(3)	
10	Romeo HAMZA		1/6/83	A	1	(5)	
18	Hektor IDRIZI		15/4/89	D	6	(14)	
	Marko JOVANOVIĆ	SRB	21/11/78	A	3	(6)	
	Shkëlzen KELMENDI		14/1/85	D	10	(3)	
4	Bruno KEPI		4/10/89	D	11	(7)	
14	Erlind KORESHI		9/2/87	M	21	(4)	
22	Marenglen KULE		12/3/83	M	15		1
11	Luciano LINO da Silva	BRA	10/3/89	M	1	(2)	
	LUIZ EDUARDO da Silva Lobato	BRA	2/12/86	D	13	(1)	

Guy Bertrand MADJO	CMR	1/6/84	A	12	(2)	2
Marjol MIHO		14/5/83	A	3	(1)	
Jamie PHOENIX	ENG	15/1/85	A	1		
Dusan POPOVIĆ	SRB	20/4/81	A	15		2
Kire RISTEVSKI	MKD	22/10/90	D	13		
Klevis ROSHI		11/7/84	M	1		
Marenglen SHOSHI		29/1/87	D	29		3
Goran SIMOV	SRB	31/3/75	G	3		
Gentian STOJKU		24/7/74	D	5		
Klodian SULOLLARI		27/7/90	M	1	(6)	
WASHINGTON Luis Batista	BRA	8/9/83	A	6	(5)	3
Fjodor XHAFA		8/3/77	A	24	(4)	10

FK DINAMO TIRANA

Coach – Luis Manuel Blanco (ARG); (1/1/11) Ilir Daja; (7/2/11) Artan Mërgjyshi

Founded – 1950

Stadium – Qemal Stafa (16,230)

MAJOR HONOURS: Albanian League – (18) 1950, 1951, 1952, 953, 1955, 1956, 1960, 1967, 1973, 1975, 1976, 1977, 1980, 1986, 1990, 2002, 2008, 2010; Albanian Cup – (13) 1950, 1951, 1952, 1953, 1954, 1960, 1971, 1974, 1978, 1982, 1989, 1990, 2003.

010				
1/8	Flamurtari	h	0-1	
3/8	Besa	h	2-1	*Vila 2*
3/9	Teuta	a	2-1	*Bakaj El., Martinena*
8/9	Shkumbini	h	1-0	*Bakaj El.*
5/9	Vllaznia	a	4-0	*Martinena 3, Bakaj El.*
/10	Elbasan	h	2-1	*Bakaj El. 2*
8/10	Tirana	a	1-1	*Martinena*
4/10	Bylis	h	2-1	*Malacarne, Vila*
/11	Kastrioti	a	2-1	*Vila, Allmuça*
/11	Laç	h	3-3	*Vila, Bakaj El., Sefa*
3/11	Skënderbeu	a	2-3	*Muzaka, Bakaj El.*
1/11	Flamurtari	a	1-3	*Bakaj El.*
0/11	Besa	a	1-1	*Vila*
2/12	Teuta	h	1-2	*Vila (p)*
0/12	Shkumbini	a	0-1	
3/12	Vllaznia	h	0-0	
011				
6/1	Elbasan	a	3-1	*Bakaj El. 2 (1p), Vila*
1/1	Tirana	h	1-2	*Bakaj El.*
/2	Bylis	a	1-3	*Vila*
2/2	Kastrioti	h	0-0	
9/2	Laç	a	0-0	
5/2	Skënderbeu	h	1-3	*Allmuça*
/3	Shkumbini	h	4-1	*Vila 2, Opoku, Allmuça*
2/3	Elbasan	h	3-1	*Ferraj, Brkić, Martinena*
0/3	Laç	a	0-1	
/4	Tirana	h	0-0	
1/4	Vllaznia	a	1-3	*Vila (p)*
5/4	Skënderbeu	h	2-3	*Brkić 2*
20/4	Flamurtari	a	2-6	*Allmuça, Lala*
24/4	Bylis	h	1-1	*Vila*
30/4	Besa	a	0-1	
4/5	Teuta	h	0-0	
16/5	Kastrioti	a	3-4	*Orelesi, Allmuça, Ferraj (p)*

No	Name	Nat	DoB	Pos	Aps	(s)	Gls
14	Igli ALLMUÇA		25/10/80	M	29		5
22	George AMBOUROUET	GAB	1/5/86	M	23		
31	Edvan BAKAJ		20/7/87	G	1	(1)	
19	Elis BAKAJ		25/6/87	A	16		11
10	Mladen BRKIĆ	SRB	30/10/80	A	11	(3)	3
4	Asjon DAJA		14/3/90	M	2	(5)	
	Gers DELIA		2/6/92	M		(1)	
	Nertil FERRAJ		11/9/87	M	7	(4)	2
10	Esteban Jesús GARCÍA	ARG	20/4/84	A		(8)	
	Sajmir GJOKEJA		31/3/85	M		(3)	
24	Bledion GUGA		20/2/86	D	1	(2)	
12	Isli HIDI		15/10/80	G	7		
1	Alban HOXHA		23/5/87	G	25		
	Eni IMAMI		19/12/92	D		(3)	
19	Endri LALA		23/2/92	M	2	(7)	1
2	Lucas Damián MALACARNE	ARG	25/11/88	D	29	(1)	1
13	Renato MALLOTA		24/6/86	M	6	(7)	
	Antonio MARKU		24/3/92	M		(1)	
9	Néstor Gabriel MARTINENA	ARG	22/1/87	D	24	(2)	6
17	Milovan MILOVIĆ	SRB	24/10/80	D	15		
	Leutrim MULGECI		8/1/91	M		(1)	
17	Gjergji MUZAKA		26/9/84	A	14	(1)	1
25	Jordan OPOKU	GHA	8/10/83	M	14	(1)	1
18	Nurudeen ORELESI	NGA	10/4/89	M	25	(1)	1
15	Roland PEQINI		25/11/90	M	4	(8)	
5	Arjan PISHA		18/1/77	D	25		
21	Marko PUTINČANIN	SRB	16/12/87	D	20	(3)	
29	Fatjon SEFA		27/4/84	A	7	(7)	1
20	Isidor SEKSERI		19/11/86	M	10	(10)	
11	Emiljano VILA		12/3/88	A	29	(1)	13
6	Erjon XHAFA		31/5/82	D	17	(2)	
	Hegi ZIJAI		10/4/92	M		(1)	

KF ELBASANI

Coach – Krenar Alimehmeti; (1/1/11) Esad Karišik (SRB); (28/2/11) Ilirjan Filja

Founded – 1923

Stadium – Ruzhdi Bizhuta (7,500)

MAJOR HONOURS: Albanian League – (2) 1984, 2006; Albanian Cup – (2) 1975, 1992.

2010				
22/8	Tirana	h	1-1	*Ristevski*
28/8	Bylis	a	2-1	*Gava, Sadiku*
11/9	Kastrioti	h	1-1	*Sadiku*
18/9	Laç	a	0-1	
26/9	Skënderbeu	h	1-0	*Merxha*
1/10	Dinamo	a	1-2	*Dalipi*
16/10	Besa	h	1-1	*Sadiku*
23/10	Teuta	a	1-2	*Lloga*
31/10	Shkumbini	h	1-2	*Dalipi*
7/11	Vllaznia	a	0-3	
14/11	Flamurtari	h	1-2	*og (Sakaj)*
20/11	Tirana	a	1-3	*Dalipi*
27/11	Bylis	h	3-2	*Dalipi, Sadiku, Radović*
11/12	Kastrioti	a	1-3	*Dalipi*
19/12	Laç	h	2-3	*Sadiku, Dalipi*
23/12	Skënderbeu	a	0-1	
2011				
26/1	Dinamo	h	1-3	*Bakiu*
30/1	Besa	a	0-2	
6/2	Teuta	h	2-0	*Kaçi, Merxha*
11/2	Shkumbini	a	2-3	*Merxha, Bakiu*
20/2	Vllaznia	h	0-4	
27/2	Flamurtari	a	0-4	
5/3	Flamurtari	a	0-8	
12/3	Dinamo	a	1-3	*Kasollja*
19/3	Bylis	h	0-2	
1/4	Laç	a	1-3	*Dosti*
10/4	Besa	h	0-1	
15/4	Tirana	a	1-6	*Bakiu (p)*
20/4	Teuta	h	2-4	*Bakiu, Dalipi*
25/4	Vllaznia	a	1-3	*og (Rajović)*
29/4	Kastrioti	h	1-2	*Bakiu*
4/5	Skënderbeu	a	0-1	
16/5	Shkumbini	h	1-2	*Tafani*

No	Name	Nat	DoB	Pos	Aps	(s)	Gls
20	Endri BAKIU		6/1/87	A	11	(9)	5
	Erald BEGOLLI		12/2/84	D		(1)	
23	Aldo BELLO		23/9/86	D	9	(4)	
10	Dorjan BYLYKBASHI		8/8/80	M	3		
21	Heltlem ÇAPJA		3/2/83	D	20	(3)	
	Albi ÇELIKU		1/1/90	D		(1)	
10	Endri DALIPI		2/5/83	M	25	(5)	7
	Dejan DOSTI		15/2/91	M	1	(2)	1
12	Albano DUSHKU		28/11/87	G	5	(3)	
8	Orgest GAVA		29/3/90	D	25	(5)	1
19	Endri HALILAJ		8/8/90	M	1	(3)	
	Ardit HILA		6/1/93	D	1		
15	Erand HOXHA		25/4/85	M		(1)	
7	Renato HYSHMERI		4/3/89	M	25	(2)	
	Domeniko IBRAHIMI		21/9/90	M	1	(4)	
18	Mensur IDRIZI	MKD	3/8/83	M	15		
5	Đuro JANDRIĆ	SRB	30/10/83	D	10		
11	Albert KAÇI		11/6/81	A	5		1

No	Name	Nat	DoB	Pos	Aps	(s)	Gls
20	Ganjol KAÇULI		22/9/89	M	9	(1)	
	Ervis KAPJA		30/8/83	D	1		
	Merdian KASOLLJA		29/5/83	M	5	(1)	1
	Theodhori KREKASI		22/9/92	M	1		
13	Engert KUÇI		27/9/85	M	8	(5)	
1	Ervin LLANI		24/4/83	G	27	(1)	
	Jurgen LLESHI		5/4/94	M		(1)	
22	Altin LLOGA	MKD	10/11/89	A	4	(11)	1
6	Armando MEHMETAJ		23/4/83	M	23	(1)	
17	Erjol MERXHA		24/1/79	M	25	(1)	3
20	Emiljano MUSTA		31/1/92	D	4	(1)	
9	Serxhio PIKU		8/2/90	A		(1)	
24	Aleksandar RADOVIĆ	MNE	30/3/87	M	6	(3)	1
5	Daniel RAMAZANI		14/1/87	D	13		
9	Miroslav RIKANOVIĆ	SRB	20/1/83	D	4		
13	Kire RISTEVSKI	MKD	22/10/90	D	10	(2)	1
11	Jasmin RRABOSHTA		30/4/90	A	10	(4)	
1	Shkëlzen RUÇI		1/7/92	G	1	(2)	
9	Armando SADIKU		27/5/85	A	14		5
4	Almir SULEJMANOVIČ	SVN	26/1/78	D	28	(1)	
	Ornald TAFANI		7/1/93	A	1	(2)	1
16	Mateos TOÇI		16/5/93	M	8	(1)	
7	Nikola VASILIĆ	SRB	20/1/89	M	3	(2)	
	Renald ZENELI		30/6/91	M	1	(1	

KS FLAMURTARI

Coach – Gugash Magani

Founded – 1923

Stadium – Flamurtari (9,000)

MAJOR HONOURS: Albanian League – (1) 1991; Albanian Cup – (3) 1985, 1988, 2009.

2010				
21/8	Dinamo	a	1-0	*Xhafa*
27/8	Tirana	h	2-1	*Roshi, Xhafa*
11/9	Besa	a	0-0	
19/9	Bylis	h	1-0	*Ahmataj*
25/9	Teuta	a	1-2	*Progri*
1/10	Kastrioti	h	3-0	*Lena, Shehaj, Xhafa*
17/10	Shkumbini	a	1-3	*Xhafa*
24/10	Laç	h	1-0	*Ahmataj*
30/10	Vllaznia	a	3-1	*Sakaj (p), Liçaj, Xhafa*
7/11	Skënderbeu	h	4-0	*Xhafa, Sakaj (p), Progri, Bajevski*
14/11	Elbasan	a	2-1	*Xhafa, Ahmataj*
21/11	Dinamo	h	3-1	*Bajevski, Xhafa 2*
28/11	Tirana	a	1-2	*Xhafa*
13/12	Besa	h	1-0	*Devolli*
18/12	Bylis	a	0-1	
23/12	Teuta	h	1-0	*Ahmataj*
2011				
21/1	Kastrioti	a	2-1	*Xhafa, Lena*
30/1	Shkumbini	h	4-2	*Roshi 2, Plaku, Xhafa*
4/2	Laç	a	1-0	*Xhafa*
13/2	Vllaznia	h	2-0	*Plaku, Ahmataj*
21/2	Skënderbeu	a	0-1	
27/2	Elbasan	h	4-0	*Plaku 2, Xhafa, Sakaj (p)*
5/3	Elbasan	h	8-0	*Progri, Xhafa, Grami 2, Roshi, Plaku 2 (1p), Shehaj*
13/3	Bylis	a	0-1	
20/3	Besa	h	3-0	*og (Jakupi), Progri 2*
2/4	Teuta	a	1-1	*Ahmataj*
9/4	Kastrioti	h	1-0	*Plaku*
15/4	Shkumbini	a	1-2	*Veliu*
20/4	Dinamo	h	6-2	*Xhafa 2, Roshi, Lena, Progri, Moçka (p)*
25/4	Laç	a	1-1	*Ahmataj*
30/4	Tirana	h	2-1	*Plaku, Xhafa*
4/5	Vllaznia	a	0-2	*(w/o; match abandoned after 89 mins at 1-0 Xhafa)*
16/5	Skënderbeu	h	1-0	*Begaj*

No	Name	Nat	DoB	Pos	Aps	(s)	Gls
23	Julian AHMATAJ		24/5/79	M	29		7
18	Aleksander BAJEVSKI	MKD	8/12/79	A	11	(5)	2
6	Halim BEGAJ		29/11/85	D	7	(13)	1
5	Julian BRAHJA		6/12/80	D	27		
14	Bledar DEVOLLI		15/1/78	M	22	(3)	1
4	Elton GRAMI		6/6/84	M	11	(12)	2
20	Taulant KUQI		11/11/85	D	3	(18)	
17	Nijaz LENA	MKD	25/6/86	A	27	(3)	3
8	Ledio LIÇAJ		19/1/87	M	4	(9)	1
1	Shpëtim MOÇKA		20/10/89	G	21		1
10	Sebino PLAKU		20/5/85	A	16		8
7	Gerard PROGRI		6/11/86	D	28	(2)	6
25	Zekirija RAMADAN	MKD	21/8/78	D	12	(2)	
9	Odhise ROSHI		22/5/91	A	19	(3)	5
28	Artan SAKAJ		8/12/80	D	27		3
10	Ardit SHEHAJ		23/9/90	A	2	(19)	2
12	Mikel SPAHO		30/8/82	G	12	(2)	
11	Franc VELIU		11/11/88	D	30		
22	Daniel XHAFA		1/5/77	A	30	(1)	19
19	Hajr ZEQIRI		11/10/88	M	25	(1)	

KS KASTRIOTI

Coach – Ramazan Ndreu

Founded – 1946

Stadium – Kastrioti (5,500)

2010				
22/8	Shkumbini	a	2-2	*Djarmati, Jushi*
28/8	Vllaznia	h	0-0	
11/9	Elbasan	a	1-1	*Babić*
20/9	Tirana	h	0-0	
25/9	Bylis	a	0-1	
1/10	Flamurtari	a	0-3	
15/10	Laç	h	3-1	*Tepshi, Babić, Muçollari*
24/10	Skënderbeu	a	1-5	*Alikaj*
1/11	Dinamo	h	1-2	*Babić*
6/11	Besa	a	0-0	
15/11	Teuta	h	3-1	*Leçi, Alviž, Babić*
22/11	Shkumbini	h	2-0	*Shameti, Turdiu (p)*
28/11	Vllaznia	a	0-1	
11/12	Elbasan	h	3-1	*Alikaj, Alviž, Babić*
17/12	Tirana	a	0-4	
24/12	Bylis	h	2-1	*Alikaj 2*
2011				
21/1	Flamurtari	h	1-2	*Xhafa*
28/1	Laç	a	0-2	
6/2	Skënderbeu	h	0-0	
12/2	Dinamo	a	0-0	
19/2	Besa	h	2-1	*Alviž, Kalari*
27/2	Teuta	a	1-1	*Alviž (p)*
6/3	Laç	a	1-3	*Piškor (p)*
12/3	Tirana	h	2-0	*Alviž, Inkango*
20/3	Vllaznia	a	1-1	*Muçollari*
2/4	Skënderbeu	h	0-2	
9/4	Flamurtari	a	0-1	
16/4	Bylis	h	2-1	*Inkango, Hoxha*
20/4	Besa	a	2-3	*Inkango, Babić*
25/4	Teuta	h	3-1	*Alikaj, Inkango, Babić*
29/4	Elbasan	a	2-1	*Muçollari 2*
4/5	Shkumbini	a	1-2	*Inkango*
16/5	Dinamo	h	4-3	*Inkango 2, Alikaj, Ragipović*

No	Name	Nat	DoB	Pos	Aps	(s)	Gls
10	Enkeleid ALIKAJ		27/12/81	M	27	(5)	6
16	Robert ALVIŽ	CRO	6/9/84	D	29	(1)	5
7	Ivan BABIĆ	CRO	29/4/84	A	25	(3)	7
9	Boris BAKOVIĆ	CRO	31/7/84	M	1	(3)	
	Marko BAŠIĆ	CRO	13/9/84	M	7	(5)	
2	Fatmir CACA		28/5/85	D	31		
20	Matko DJARMATI	CRO	24/2/82	D	12	(2)	1
	Genti GJONDEDA		23/6/84	M	1	(6)	
19	Anton GRISHI		9/1/91	M	1	(7)	
1	Argjent HALILI		16/11/82	G	31		
3	Rigers HOXHA		3/9/85	D	17	(7)	1
27	Bruce INKANGO	FRA	18/5/84	D	11	(2)	7
11	Kelvin JUSHI		18/4/89	M		(3)	1
	Renaldo KALARI		25/6/84	A	18	(4)	1
5	Liridon LEÇI		11/2/85	D	13		1
18	Arbër MALAJ		11/4/89	D	2	(10)	
	Migen METANI		5/5/89	M		(1)	
21	Elton MUÇOLLARI		14/9/80	M	31		4
	Davor PIŠKOR	CRO	23/4/82	D	4	(11)	1
22	Kenan RAGIPOVIĆ	SRB	16/9/82	M	27		1
13	Ylli SHAMETI		7/6/84	D	9		1
	Filip STOJANOVIĆ	SRB	21/1/88	M	4	(5)	

No	Name	Nat	DoB	Pos	Aps	(s)	Gls
	Gledis TAFAJ		29/6/85	G	2		
	Guido TEPSHI		8/4/91	A	5	(9)	1
	Erald TURDIU		15/7/84	A	10		1
	Erjon XHAFA		29/6/86	D	29	(2)	1
	Ante ZORE	CRO	5/9/85	M	16	(5)	

KF LAÇI

Coach – Stavri Nica

Founded – 1965

Stadium – Laçi (3,500)

010				
1/8	Teuta	a	0-0	
0/8	Shkumbini	h	2-0	*Cavrić, Hysa*
2/9	Vllaznia	a	1-2	*Selimi*
3/9	Elbasan	h	1-0	*Mile*
5/9	Tirana	a	0-2	
/9	Bylis	h	3-1	*Selimi 2 (1p), Mile*
5/10	Kastrioti	a	1-3	*Selimi (p)*
4/10	Flamurtari	a	0-1	
0/10	Skënderbeu	h	0-1	
11	Dinamo	a	3-3	*Mile, Vuçaj, Kaja*
2/11	Besa	h	1-0	*Shazivari*
/11	Teuta	h	1-0	*Marashi*
8/11	Shkumbini	a	1-2	*Mile*
/12	Vllaznia	h	0-1	
9/12	Elbasan	a	3-2	*Marashi, Buljan, Hysa*
4/12	Tirana	h	1-1	*Mile (p)*
011				
2/1	Bylis	a	2-1	*Shazivari, Hysa*
8/1	Kastrioti	h	2-0	*Buljan, Dragičević*
/2	Flamurtari	h	0-1	
2/2	Skënderbeu	a	1-2	*Hysa*
9/2	Dinamo	h	0-0	
5/2	Besa	a	2-1	*Hysa, Selimi*
/3	Kastrioti	h	3-1	*Selimi, Dragičević, Hysa*
1/3	Shkumbini	a	5-2	*Dragičević 3, Selimi, Hysa*
0/3	Dinamo	h	1-0	*Buljan*
/4	Elbasan	h	3-1	*Hysa 2, Kaja*
1/4	Tirana	a	0-4	
6/4	Vllaznia	h	1-3	*Hysa*
0/4	Skënderbeu	a	0-2	
5/4	Flamurtari	h	1-1	*Hysa*
9/4	Bylis	a	0-1	
/5	Besa	h	3-2	*Dragičević, Buljan, Hysa*
6/5	Teuta	a	2-3	*Hysa 2*

No	Name	Nat	DoB	Pos	Aps	(s)	Gls
2	Olti BISHANI		11/1/88	G	1		
	Stipe BULJAN	CRO	21/9/83	D	27		4
21	Besnik BURAKU		30/11/88	D	1	(1)	
	Roland BUSHI		26/2/91	M	1		
25	Silvio CAVRIĆ	CRO	10/7/85	M	14	(2)	1
2	Elton DOKU		1/10/86	D	26		
	Mate DRAGIČEVIĆ	CRO	19/11/79	M	8	(3)	6
3	Ardian GEGA		4/6/86	D	1	(6)	
19	Arbër HALITI		25/1/82	M	1	(2)	
20	Flogert HIMA		29/1/89	M		(1)	
15	Vilfor HYSA		9/9/89	A	30	(1)	14
5	Ervis KAJA		29/7/87	D	28	(2)	2
14	Miodrag KARADŽIĆ	MNE	20/7/87	M	6	(11)	
6	Sajmir KASTRATI		7/3/87	M	21	(2)	
	Kleo LASKA		15/9/92	D		(2)	
	Bledar MALAJ		13/6/88	G	3		
7	Julian MALO		2/2/85	A	1		
11	Bledar MARASHI		3/10/90	M	10	(14)	2
9	Vangjëll MILE		1/7/86	A	23	(7)	5
	Borko MILENKOVIĆ	SRB	7/10/84	M	16		
17	Denis MUSTAFARAJ		2/4/85	M	15	(4)	
16	Armand PASHA		17/1/91	D	1	(1)	
3	Ervin REXHA		1/11/91	D	12	(6)	
13	Nezbedin SELIMI	SUI	6/11/84	A	25	(3)	7
17	Elio SHAZIVARI		14/4/85	M	23	(5)	2
1	Bledar VASHAKU		8/11/81	G	29		
	Stanislav VIDAKOVIĆ	CRO	14/10/85	M	9	(2)	
10	Erjon VUÇAJ		25/12/90	A	27	(2)	1
22	Alfred ZEFI		20/8/91	D	4	(4)	

KS SHKUMBINI

Coach – Mirel Josa; (1/9/10) Agim Canaj; (3/12/10) Përparim Daiu; (13/3/11) Kristaq Mile

Founded – 1924

Stadium – Fusha Sportive (6,000)

2010				
22/8	Kastrioti	h	2-2	*Nora, Kuli (p)*
30/8	Laç	a	0-2	
12/9	Skënderbeu	h	3-1	*Kuli 3*
18/9	Dinamo	a	0-1	
27/9	Besa	h	2-2	*Dervishi, Veliaj*
2/10	Teuta	a	0-1	
17/10	Flamurtari	h	3-1	*Shenaj, Grizha 2*
23/10	Vllaznia	h	1-0	*Grbović*
31/10	Elbasan	a	2-1	*Veliaj, Grbović*
6/11	Tirana	h	1-3	*Grizha*
13/11	Bylis	a	2-3	*Kuli, Nora*
22/11	Kastrioti	a	0-2	
28/11	Laç	h	2-1	*Kuli, Grbović*
12/12	Skënderbeu	a	0-1	
20/12	Dinamo	h	1-0	*Mujdragić*
24/12	Besa	a	1-2	*Nora*
2011				
26/1	Teuta	h	1-1	*Kuli*
30/1	Flamurtari	a	2-4	*Shenaj, Grbović*
5/2	Vllaznia	a	0-0	
11/2	Elbasan	h	3-2	*Grbović 2, Dervishi*
20/2	Tirana	a	0-0	
26/2	Bylis	h	4-2	*Grbović, Gjyla, Mustafaj 2*
6/3	Dinamo	a	1-4	*Belcev*
11/3	Laç	h	2-5	*Kuli (p), Grbović*
20/3	Tirana	a	0-1	
1/4	Vllaznia	h	1-0	*Shenaj*
9/4	Skënderbeu	a	0-2	
15/4	Flamurtari	h	2-1	*Mustafaj 2*
20/4	Bylis	a	0-2	
24/4	Besa	h	2-2	*Grbović, Mustafaj*
30/4	Teuta	a	1-3	*Gjata*
4/5	Kastrioti	h	2-1	*Kuli (p), Mustafaj*
16/5	Elbasan	a	2-1	*Mustafaj, Gjyla*

No	Name	Nat	DoB	Pos	Aps	(s)	Gls
	Liridon AHMETI		16/7/83	D	1	(4)	
3	Renato ARAPI		28/8/86	D	16		
1	Ibrahim BEJTJA		15/9/89	G	15		
14	Marjan BELCEV	MKD	22/10/82	M	9	(5)	1
8	Gentian ÇELA		9/2/81	M	2	(7)	
22	Roland DERVISHI		16/2/82	A	15	(10)	2
19	Arvis GJATA		23/6/87	D	2	(5)	1
20	Genti GJONDEDA		23/6/84	M	2	(8)	
11	Viktor GJYLA		11/5/82	M	27	(2)	2
17	Altin GRBOVIĆ	SRB	13/3/86	A	9	(13)	9
66	Robert GRIZHA		10/3/82	D	8		3
4	Aldin GURDIJELJAĆ	SRB	7/1/78	M	10	(1)	
19	Bledar HODO		21/6/85	D	5	(3)	
	Albano Astrit ISAJ		19/4/91	M		(2)	
	Endri KARAJ		1/12/91	D		(1)	
1	Elvis KOTORRI		30/4/70	G	16		
14	Driton KRASNIQI		15/8/84	M	18	(1)	
4	Aleksander KRSTEVSKI	MKD	3/9/83	M	5	(1)	
10	Bekim KULI		1/9/82	A	27		9
	Amarildo LUNDRAXHIU		27/12/92	M	1		
	Emiljano LUNDRAXHIU		9/5/94	D	1	(1)	
	Artur MAGANI		8/7/94	A		(1)	
21	Bledar MANÇAKU		19/2/82	M	7	(3)	
	Alban MERSINI		30/6/90	M	1		
5	Ahmed MUJDRAGIĆ	SRB	13/3/86	D	30		1
9	Erjon MUSTAFAJ		29/1/89	M	24	(3)	7
	Jurgen NEXHA		30/8/93	D	1		
18	Arlind NORA		4/7/80	A	11	(3)	3
7	Lorenc PASHA		24/1/85	M	17	(7)	
3	Vladimir SEKULOVSKI	MKD	10/7/80	D	13		
	Elidon SELAÇI		3/5/90	G	2		
13	Fejzo SHENAJ		24/11/84	D	29		3
28	Emiljano VELIAJ		9/2/85	M	29	(1)	2
	Jurgen VOGLI		12/6/93	M	1	(1)	
15	Klement XHYRA		5/5/84	D	9	(6)	

KS SKËNDERBEU

Coach – Shkëlqim Muça; (17/2/11) Shpëtim Duro
Founded – 1923
Stadium – Skënderbeu (7,000)
MAJOR HONOURS: Albanian League – (2) 1933, 2011.

2010				
23/8	Besa	a	2-0	*(w/o; match abandoned after 88 mins at 1-0 Marković)*
29/8	Teuta	h	2-0	*Sosa, Shkëmbi (p)*
12/9	Shkumbini	a	1-3	*Shkëmbi*
19/9	Vllaznia	h	2-0	*Jolić 2*
26/9	Elbasan	a	0-1	
3/10	Tirana	h	2-1	*Biskup, Sosa*
16/10	Bylis	a	1-1	*Sosa*
24/10	Kastrioti	h	5-1	*Jolić, Sosa, Brkić 3 (1p)*
30/10	Laç	a	1-0	*Vishaj*
7/11	Flamurtari	a	0-4	
13/11	Dinamo	h	3-2	*Jolić, Biskup, Brkić*
20/11	Besa	h	4-0	*og (Jakupi), Brkić 2, Jolić*
29/11	Teuta	a	0-2	
12/12	Shkumbini	h	1-0	*Brkić*
19/12	Vllaznia	a	1-2	*Sosa*
23/12	Elbasan	h	1-0	*Shkëmbi*
2011				
29/1	Bylis	h	2-0	*Shkëmbi (p), Muzaka*
3/2	Tirana	a	0-0	
6/2	Kastrioti	a	0-0	
12/2	Laç	h	2-1	*Sefa, Muzaka*
21/2	Flamurtari	h	1-0	*Shkëmbi (p)*
25/2	Dinamo	a	3-1	*Shkëmbi (p), Sosa 2*
7/3	Bylis	h	3-1	*Muzaka 2, Sosa*
12/3	Besa	a	0-0	
20/3	Teuta	h	1-0	*Vishaj*
2/4	Kastrioti	a	2-0	*Bratić, Sosa*
9/4	Shkumbini	h	2-0	*Sosa, Bratić*
15/4	Dinamo	a	3-2	*Muzaka 2, Sosa*
20/4	Laç	h	2-0	*Shkëmbi (p), Sosa*
25/4	Tirana	a	1-0	*Shkëmbi (p)*
30/4	Vllaznia	h	3-0	*Muzaka, Sosa, Bratić*
4/5	Elbasan	h	1-0	*Muzaka*
16/5	Flamurtari	a	0-1	

No	Name	Nat	DoB	Pos	Aps	(s)	Gls
	Eftimiov AKSENTIEV	MKD	17/8/85	A	1	(3)	
4	Renato ARAPI		28/8/86	D	15		
33	Klodian ASLLANI		20/8/76	A	2	(6)	
6	Ditmar BICI		26/2/89	D	22	(1)	
16	Luko BISKUP	CRO	14/6/81	D	22	(5)	2
23	Davor BRATIĆ	CRO	25/5/87	M	29	(1)	3
9	Mladen BRKIĆ	SRB	30/10/80	A	13	(3)	7
	Sokol ÇIKALLESHI		27/7/90	A	4		
5	Alban DRAGUSHA		11/12/81	D	13		
7	Erbim FAGU		15/4/87	D	30	(1)	
24	Dejan GRABIĆ	SVN	21/9/80	D	2	(3)	
26	Mensur IDRIZI	MKD	3/8/83	D	2	(12)	
31	Ivan JOLIĆ	BIH	18/5/80	A	15	(9)	5
18	Stavrion LAKO		24/3/80	D	6	(7)	
3	Vlado MARKOVIĆ	BIH	26/8/85	M	23	(5)	1
11	Gjergji MUZAKA		26/9/84	A	15	(1)	8
2	Borce RISTOVSKI	MKD	12/11/84	M	6	(4)	
8	Jetmir SEFA		30/1/87	A	17		1
26	Orges SHEHI		20/9/77	G	33		
10	Bledi SHKËMBI		13/8/79	M	30		8
17	Rafael SOSA	ARG	7/5/88	A	28	(1)	13
	Grigor TOPALLI		1/11/92	M		(7)	
19	Butrint VISHAJ		9/7/87	M	7	(17)	2
4	Endrit VRAPI		23/5/82	D	28		

KS TEUTA

Coach – Edi Martini
Founded – 1925
Stadium – Niko Dovana (8,000)
MAJOR HONOURS: Albanian League – (1) 1994; Albanian Cup – (3) 1995, 2000, 2005.

2010				
21/8	Laç	h	0-0	
29/8	Skënderbeu	a	0-2	
13/9	Dinamo	h	1-2	*Frashëri*
19/9	Besa	a	0-0	
25/9	Flamurtari	h	2-1	*Çota 2*
2/10	Shkumbini	h	1-0	*Çota*
15/10	Vllaznia	a	0-0	
23/10	Elbasan	h	2-1	*Çota, Pepa*
31/10	Tirana	a	0-2	
8/11	Bylis	h	6-0	*Pepa 2, og (Shoshi), Sheta, Çota 2*
15/11	Kastrioti	a	1-3	*Pepa*
21/11	Laç	a	0-1	
29/11	Skënderbeu	h	2-0	*Çota, og (Lako)*
12/12	Dinamo	a	2-1	*Pepa, Frashëri*
18/12	Besa	h	1-2	*Dosti*
23/12	Flamurtari	a	0-1	
2011				
26/1	Shkumbini	a	1-1	*Çota*
30/1	Vllaznia	h	0-3	
6/2	Elbasan	a	0-2	
13/2	Tirana	h	0-0	
21/2	Bylis	a	0-3	
27/2	Kastrioti	h	1-1	*Tafili*
7/3	Tirana	a	2-1	*Pepa 2*
12/3	Vllaznia	h	0-0	
20/3	Skënderbeu	a	0-1	
2/4	Flamurtari	h	1-1	*Frashëri*
10/4	Bylis	a	0-1	
16/4	Besa	h	4-2	*Pepa 3 (1p), Frashëri*
20/4	Elbasan	a	4-2	*Frashëri 2, Pepa, Xhemali*
25/4	Kastrioti	a	1-3	*Pepa*
30/4	Shkumbini	h	3-1	*Rugova, Frashëri, Pepa*
4/5	Dinamo	a	0-0	
16/5	Laç	h	3-2	*Tahiri 2, Hoxha A.*

No	Name	Nat	DoB	Pos	Aps	(s)	Gls
22	Andi BAKIASI		23/4/87	D	8	(8)	
	Granit CANA		23/7/91	M		(2)	
	Albano ÇAUSHAJ		26/3/90	M	2	(7)	
9	Mirel ÇOTA		14/5/88	A	17	(3)	8
3	Edmond DOÇI		1/3/81	D	8	(3)	
20	Albi DOSTI		13/9/91	A	7	(5)	1
19	Erlis FRASHËRI		19/5/88	A	26	(5)	7
21	Erjon HOTI		8/5/83	M	28		
14	Altin HOXHA		21/10/90	D	26		1
5	Rustem HOXHA		4/7/91	D	16		
23	Xhavit KALOTI		11/2/89	M	9	(3)	
	Ervis KRAJA		26/6/77	D	13	(2)	
	Ergys MERSINI		30/9/89	M		(1)	
	Eni NAÇO		23/8/90	G	1		
	Ansi NIKA		22/8/90	D	3	(5)	
4	Jetmir NINA		21/5/86	M	18	(5)	
13	Brunild PEPA		22/11/90	A	27	(3)	13
1	Bledian RIZVANI		2/7/85	G	32		
	Dardan RUGOVA		8/9/90	M	10	(2)	1
6	Taulant SEFGJINI		21/7/86	M	11	(9)	
2	Arjan SHETA		13/2/81	D	28		1
19	Shaqir STAFA		23/4/87	D	21	(3)	
17	Alsid TAFILI		20/8/87	A	23	(6)	1
8	Flamur TAHIRI	MKD	24/11/90	D	25	(2)	2
15	Jozef THANA		14/12/88	M		(2)	
7	Orjan XHEMALI		7/6/89	D	4	(18)	1

KF TIRANA

Coach – Sulejman Starova; (6/10/10) Nevil Dede; (7/2/11) Miša Krističević (CRO)
Founded – 1920
Stadium – Selman Stërmasi (8,000) & Qemal Stafa (16,230)
MAJOR HONOURS: Albanian League – (25) 1930, 1931, 1932, 1933, 1934, 1936, 1937, 1965, 1966, 1968, 1970, 1982, 1985, 1988, 1989, 1995, 1996, 1997, 1999, 2000, 2003, 2004, 2005, 2007, 2009; Albanian Cup – (14) 1939, 1963, 1976, 1977, 1983, 1984, 1986, 1994, 1996, 1999, 2001, 2002, 2006, 2011.

010

2/8	Elbasan	a	1-1	*Lila (p)*
7/8	Flamurtari	a	1-2	*Plaku*
2/9	Bylis	h	2-1	*Pejić 2*
0/9	Kastrioti	a	0-0	
6/9	Laç	h	2-0	*Pejić, Malindi*
/10	Skënderbeu	a	1-2	*Muka*
8/10	Dinamo	h	1-1	*Osmani*
5/10	Besa	a	1-2	*Lila*
1/10	Teuta	h	2-0	*Pejić 2*
/11	Shkumbini	a	3-1	*Pejić, Žižović, Tusha*
4/11	Vllaznia	h	0-2	
0/11	Elbasan	h	3-1	*Pejić 2, Morina*
7/11	Flamurtari	h	2-1	*Pejić, Plaku*
1/12	Bylis	a	1-1	*Lilaj*
7/12	Kastrioti	h	4-0	*Pejić 2, Plaku, Lila*
4/12	Laç	a	1-1	*Pejić (p)*

011

1/1	Dinamo	a	2-1	*Morina, Lila (p)*
/2	Skënderbeu	h	0-0	
/2	Besa	h	0-0	
3/2	Teuta	a	0-0	
0/2	Shkumbini	h	0-0	
6/2	Vllaznia	a	0-0	
/3	Teuta	h	1-2	*og (Sheta)*
2/3	Kastrioti	a	0-2	
0/3	Shkumbini	h	1-0	*Hyka*
/4	Dinamo	a	0-0	
1/4	Laç	h	4-0	*Hyka 2, Lika G., Lila (p)*
5/4	Elbasan	h	6-1	*Hyka, Bala, Lila (p), Gvozdenović, Hajdari, Morina*
0/4	Vllaznia	a	0-1	
5/4	Skënderbeu	h	0-1	
0/4	Flamurtari	a	1-2	*Pejić*
/5	Bylis	h	0-2	
6/5	Besa	a	2-3	*Pejić, Bala*

No	Name	Nat	DoB	Pos	Aps	(s)	Gls
4	Orjand ABAZAJ		17/1/85	A	4	(5)	
21	Shpëtim BABAJ		9/12/81	D	4	(3)	
	Bekim BALA		11/1/91	A	10	(3)	2
	Alban BUSHI		20/3/73	A	3	(2)	
	Rezart DABULLA		24/10/79	D	5	(2)	
16	Erjon DUSHKU		25/2/85	D	26	(1)	
4	Ivan GVOZDENOVIĆ	SRB	19/8/78	M	28		1
7	Blerti HAJDARI		1/9/90	A	2	(9)	1
18	Rahman HALLAÇI		12/11/83	D	2	(2)	
	Jahmir HYKA		8/3/88	M	9	(2)	4
13	Erando KARABECI		6/9/88	M	27	(3)	
	Gilman LIKA		13/1/87	M	12	(1)	1
12	Ilion LIKA		17/5/80	G	30		
6	Andi LILA		12/2/86	D	25	(1)	6
8	Sabien LILAJ		10/2/89	M	24	(1)	1
17	Enco MALINDI		15/1/89	A	1	(3)	1
	Migen METANI		29/6/86	M		(2)	
	Mario MORINA		16/10/92	M	6	(11)	3
	Gentian MUÇA		13/5/87	M	8	(6)	
10	Devi MUKA		21/12/76	M	8		1
1	Blendi NALLBANI		30/5/71	G	3		
	Marvin NALLBANI		30/9/92	M		(1)	
19	Tefik OSMANI		8/6/85	D	28		1
	Entonio PASHAJ		11/11/84	M	11	(3)	
22	Pero PEJIĆ	CRO	3/7/82	A	26	(1)	14
9	Sebino PLAKU		20/5/85	A	13	(2)	3
23	Artūras SILIGALIS	LVA	3/5/85	D	3	(3)	
2	Elvis SINA		14/11/78	D	25	(4)	
11	Ergys SORRA		23/7/89	M	1	(6)	
	Afrim TAKU		4/8/89	M	2	(3)	
	Gerard TUSHA		2/5/91	D	3	(9)	1
28	Mladen ŽIŽOVIĆ	BIH	27/12/80	M	14	(3)	1

KF VLLAZNIA

Coach – Mojas Radonjić (MNE); (26/10/10) Mirel Josa

Founded – 1919

Stadium – Loro Boriçi (16,000)

MAJOR HONOURS: Albanian League – (9) 1945, 1946, 1972, 1974, 1978, 1983, 1992, 1998, 2001; Albanian Cup – (6) 1965, 1972, 1979, 1981, 1987, 2008.

2010

22/8	Bylis	h	3-2	*Rajović, Sinani, Jovanović*
28/8	Kastrioti	a	0-0	
12/9	Laç	h	2-1	*Sinani, Shtupina*
19/9	Skënderbeu	a	0-2	
25/9	Dinamo	h	0-4	
2/10	Besa	a	1-0	*Sinani*
15/10	Teuta	h	0-0	
23/10	Shkumbini	a	0-1	
30/10	Flamurtari	h	1-3	*Jovanović*
7/11	Elbasan	h	3-0	*Nallbani, Sinani 2*
14/11	Tirana	a	2-0	*Vajushi, Sinani*
19/11	Bylis	a	0-0	
28/11	Kastrioti	h	1-0	*Vajushi*
11/12	Laç	a	1-0	*Gocaj*
19/12	Skënderbeu	h	2-1	*Nallbani, og (Fagu)*
23/12	Dinamo	a	0-0	

2011

22/1	Besa	h	2-1	*og (Djarmati), Shtupina*
30/1	Teuta	a	3-0	*Sinani 3*
5/2	Shkumbini	h	0-0	
13/2	Flamurtari	a	0-2	
20/2	Elbasan	a	4-0	*Sukaj 2, Shtupina, Hodo*
26/2	Tirana	h	0-0	
6/3	Besa	h	2-0	*Shtupina, Sukaj*
12/3	Teuta	a	0-0	
20/3	Kastrioti	h	1-1	*Sukaj*
1/4	Shkumbini	a	0-1	
11/4	Dinamo	h	3-1	*Sukaj 2, Shtupina*
16/4	Laç	a	3-1	*Sinani, Gocaj, Hasani*
20/4	Tirana	h	1-0	*Rajović (p)*
25/4	Elbasan	h	3-1	*Nallbani, Vajushi, Sinani*
30/4	Skënderbeu	a	0-3	
4/5	Flamurtari	h	2-0	*(w/o; match abandoned after 89 mins at 0-1)*
16/5	Bylis	a	0-2	

No	Name	Nat	DoB	Pos	Aps	(s)	Gls
21	Abraham ALECHENWU	NGA	16/3/86	D	10	(4)	
8	Amarildo BELISHA		11/7/81	M	24	(4)	
13	Sadush DANI		6/11/82	D	3	(3)	
11	Ari DJEPAXHIA		4/10/92	A	7		
	Bekim ERKOÇEVIÇ		23/4/92	A		(1)	
22	Olsi GOCAJ		30/9/89	D	25	(1)	2
1	Armir GRIMA		16/6/74	G	5		
5	Edom HASANI		9/1/92	M	13	(14)	1
	Bledar HODO		21/6/85	D	1	(6)	1
3	Vladimir JAŠIĆ	SRB	4/1/84	M	25	(1)	
17	Marko JOVANOVIĆ	SRB	21/10/78	A	4	(8)	2
23	Daniel JUMIĆ	SRB	27/6/86	D	3		
16	Albert KAÇI		11/6/81	A	7	(7)	
	Ervis KRAJA		26/6/77	D	2		
6	Liridon KUKAJ		22/6/83	D	20	(1)	
20	Ilir NALLBANI		11/7/82	M	21	(4)	3
19	Valdano NIMANI		5/3/87	A	8	(12)	
18	Blažo RAJOVIĆ	BIH	26/3/86	D	27	(1)	2
	Fabiol REXHEPI		18/12/91	G	1		
	Holkid SELMANI		17/8/91	A		(1)	
	Klodian SEMINA		19/1/89	M	2	(3)	
	Stivi SHABA		19/12/92	M		(1)	
7	Ndriçim SHTUPINA		18/3/87	A	17	(11)	5
9	Vioresin SINANI		4/11/77	A	24	(5)	11
2	Dritan SMAJLI		12/2/85	D	28		
10	Xhevair SUKAJ		5/10/87	A	8	(3)	6
15	Arsen SYKAJ		11/4/90	M	20	(2)	
14	Armando VAJUSHI		3/12/91	A	31		3
24	Miroslav VUJADINOVIĆ	MNE	22/4/83	G	27		

TOP GOALSCORERS 2010/11

19 Daniel XHAFA (Flamurtari)

14 Vilfor HYSA (Laç)
Pero PEJIĆ (Tirana)

13 Emiljano VILA (Dinamo)
Rafael SOSA (Skënderbeu)
Brunild PEPA (Teuta)

11 Elis BAKAJ (Dinamo)
Sebino PLAKU (Tirana/Flamurtari)
Vioresin SINANI (Vllaznia)

10 Amarildo DIMO (Bylis)
Fjodor XHAFA (Bylis)
Mladen BRKIĆ (Skënderbeu/Dinamo)

PROMOTED CLUBS

KS POGRADECI
Coach – Ylli Çekiçi
Founded – 1932
Stadium – Gjoli Kyqyku (5,000)

FK TOMORI
Coach – Eqerem Memushi; (22/1/11) Artan Bano
Founded – 1923
Stadium – Tomori (12,500)

KS KAMZA
Coach – Eduart Zhupa; (22/11/10) (Bashkim Doku); (30/11/10) Skerdi Bejzade
Founded – 1936
Stadium – Kamza (3,500)

KF APOLONIA
Coach – Ernest Gjoka; (16/2/11) (Edmond Mustafaraj); (22/2/11) Eqerem Memushi
Founded – 1925
Stadium – Loni Papuçiu (7,500)
MAJOR HONOURS: Albanian Cup – (1) 1998.

SECOND LEVEL FINAL TABLE 2010/11

		Pld	W	D	L	F	A	Pts
1	KS Pogradeci	30	22	2	6	56	27	68
2	FK Tomori	30	20	3	7	50	24	63
3	KS Kamza	30	17	9	4	42	20	60
4	KF Apolonia	30	18	6	6	50	31	60
5	KS Besëlidhja Lezhë	30	16	9	5	40	17	57
6	KF Mamurrasi	30	13	4	13	29	29	43
7	KS Lushnja	30	12	3	15	35	25	39
8	KS Gramozi	30	12	3	15	34	45	39
9	KS Ada Velipojë	30	11	4	15	40	41	37
10	KS Luftëtari Gjirokastër	30	10	7	13	22	34	37
11	KS Burreli	30	10	6	14	29	37	36
12	KF Vlora	30	10	4	16	36	47	34
13	KF Gramshi	30	8	7	15	24	33	31
14	KS Tërbuni	30	8	7	15	27	42	31
15	KF Bilisht Sport	30	8	3	19	30	64	27
16	FK Partizani	30	4	5	21	16	44	17

PROMOTION/RELEGATION PLAY-OFFS

(25/5/11)
Shkumbini 1, Mamurrasi 0 (aet)
(26/5/11)
Dinamo Tirana 4, Besëlidhja 1

DOMESTIC CUP 2010/11

KUPA E SHQIPËRISË

FIRST ROUND

(20/10/10 & 4/11/10)
Ada v Apolonia 2-1; 0-0 *(2-1)*
Besëlidhja v Bylis 1-3; 0-4 *(1-7)*
Burreli v Skënderbeu 2-2; 1-2 *(3-4)*
Gramshi v Elbasan 0-0; 1-2 *(1-2)*
Luftëtari v Gramozi 0-0; 1-2 *(1-2)*
Luzi 2008 v Dinamo Tirana 0-3; 2-7 *(2-10)*
Mamurrasi v Teuta 2-3; 1-1 *(3-4)*
Memaliaj v Laç 1-1; 2-3 *(3-4)*
Partizani v Kamza 0-1; 0-0 *(0-1)*
Pogradeci v Lushnja 1-0; 1-4 *(2-4)*
Skrapari v Tirana 0-1; 0-4 *(0-5)*
Sopoti v Besa 0-3; 2-7 *(2-10)*
Tërbuni v Vllaznia 1-1; 0-5 *(1-6)*
Tomori v Flamurtari 0-0; 2-4 *(2-4)*
Vlora v Shkumbini 0-3 (w/o); 1-4 *(1-7)*

(26/10/10 & 4/11/10)
Bilisht Sport v Kastrioti 2-2; 0-2 *(2-4)*

SECOND ROUND

(24/11/10 & 8/12/10)
Ada v Tirana 0-3; 2-2 *(2-5)*
Bylis v Flamurtari 0-0; 1-0 *(1-0)*
Elbasan v Vllaznia 0-1; 0-4 *(0-5)*
Gramozi v Laç 2-2; 0-4 *(2-6)*
Kamza v Dinamo Tirana 2-3; 0-2 *(2-5)*
Lushnja v Besa 0-0; 0-1 *(0-1)*

(25/11/10 & 8/12/10)
Kastrioti v Shkumbini 1-3; 2-2 *(3-5)*
Skënderbeu v Teuta 0-0; 2-0 *(2-0)*

QUARTER-FINALS

(16/2/11 & 2/3/11)
Bylis 2 *(Abazaj 11, Dimo 75p)*, Tirana 1 *(Lilaj 65)*
Tirana 5 *(Dushku 15, Pejić 35, Gvozdenović 66, Hyka 68, Lila 73)*, Bylis 1 *(Dimo 90+1p)*
(Tirana 6-3)

Shkumbini 2 *(Dervishi 36, Grbović 66)*, Dinamo Tirana 1 *(Allmuça 17)*
Dinamo Tirana 2 *(Orelesi 62, Sekseri 90)*, Shkumbini 1 *(Grbović 15) (aet)*
(3-3; Dinamo Tirana 9-8 on pens)

Skënderbeu 1 *(Muzaka 14)*, Besa 3 *(Marcos 8, Mihani 57p, Nora 70)*
Besa 2 *(Shameti 2, Marcos 58)*, Skënderbeu 2 *(Shkëmbi 38p, Muzaka 67)*
(Besa 5-3)

Vllaznia 2 *(Shtupina 62, Sukaj 73)*, Laç 0
Laç 2 *(Dragičević 17, Mile 55p)*, Vllaznia 4 *(Shtupina 30, Sukaj 36, 90+3p, Vajushi 49)*
(Vllaznia 6-2)

SEMIFINALS

(16/3/11 & 6/4/11)
Tirana 1 *(Mançaku 21og)*, Besa 0
Besa 1 *(Marcos 23)*, Tirana 1 *(Bala 71)*
(Tirana 2-1)

Vllaznia 2 *(Nallbani 45, Sukaj 58)*, Dinamo Tirana 1 *(Martinena 87)*
Dinamo Tirana 1 *(Brkić 20)*, Vllaznia 0
(2-2; Dinamo Tirana on away goal)

FINAL

(22/5/11)
Niko Dovana, Durres
KF TIRANA 1 *(Pejić 51)*
FK DINAMO TIRANA 1 *(Brkić 18)*
(aet; 4-3 on pens)
Referee – *Jemini*
TIRANA – *Lika I., Lila, Gvozdenović, Dushku, Osmani, Karabeci (Muça 46), Lilaj, Hyka, Lika G. (Bala 52), Žižović (Sina 92), Pejić.*
Sent off: *Osmani (105).*
DINAMO TIRANA – *Hoxha, Malacarne, Milović, Mallota (Daja 90), Ferraj, Vila, Orelesi, Opoku, Martinena, Brkić (Peqini 90), Allmuça.*
Sent off: *Peqini (118)*

CLUB COMMUNICATION 2011/12

KF Apolonia
Rr. 16 Prilli, Rr. R. Aranitasi
AL-Fier

Tel +355 42 251 311
Fax +355 42 251 312
Web kfapoloniafier.wordpress.com
Email info@kfapollonia.com.al
Media Officer Maksim Tashi

KS Bylis
City Comunal Stadium
AL-Ballsh

Tel +355 68 228 6071
Fax +355 68 228 6071
Web
Email
Media Officer

FK Dinamo Tirana
Grigor Heba str 1, Kompleksi Sportiv Dinamo
AL-Tiranë

Tel +355 42 303 36
Fax +355 42 223 92
Web dinamo.al
Email info@fcdinamotirana.eu
Media Officer Andi Matraxhiu

KS Flamurtari
Lagja Pavaresisë Rruga Skele-Vlore
Stadiumi Flamurtari, AL-Vlorë

Tel +355 33 222 762
Fax +355 33 224 275
Web skflamurtari.com
Email futbolli@bashkiavlore.org
Media Officer Moisi Dalipi

KS Kamza
c/o Stadiumi Kamëz
AL-Kamëz

Tel +355 47 200 177
Fax +355 47 200 177
Web
Email bashkiakamez@gmail.com
Media Officer

KS Kastrioti
Lagja nr 2 Krujë, Kastrioti
AL-Krujë

Tel +355 824 21 86
Fax +355 824 21 86
Web
Email
Media Officer

KF Laçi
Lagjia 4, Stadiumi i Lacit
AL-Laç

Tel +355 222 190
Fax +355 222 190
Web
Email
Media Officer Isuf Myrtja

KS Pogradeci
c/o Stadiumi Gjorgji KyÁyku
AL-Pogradec

Tel
Fax
Web
Email
Media Officer

KS Shkumbini
Bulevardi Mustafa Gjinishi
AL-Peqin

Tel +355 5 123 200
Fax +355 5 123 200
Web ksshkumbini.com
Email ksshkumbini@yahoo.com
Media Officer Gazmend Vogli

KS Skënderbeu
Stadiumi Skënderbeu, Zona Sportive Korçë
AL-Korcë

Tel +355 824 2186
Fax +355 824 2186
Web skenderbeukorce.webs.com
Email kfskenderbeu@gmail.com
Media Officer Tonin Frroku

KS Teuta
Stadiumi Niko Dovana L.18, Rr. A. Goga
AL-Durrës

Tel +355 52 217 98
Fax +355 52 217 95
Web kfteuta.com
Email kfteuta@yahoo.com
Media Officer Bleda Kadiu

KF Tirana
Stadiumi Selman Stërmasi, Rr. Muhamet Gjollesha, AL-Tiranë

Tel +355 42 568 99
Fax +355 42 568 99
Web sktirana.com
Email kftirana@albmail.com
Media Officer Dritan Lundra

FK Tomori
Stadiumi Tomorri, Lagja 30 Vjetori
AL-Berat

Tel +355 62 34 627
Fax
Web fktomori.com
Email
Media Officer

KF Vllaznia
Stadiumi Loro Boriçi, Musa Luli 1
AL-Shkodër

Tel +355 222 42305
Fax +355 222 47513
Web vllaznia.eu
Email info@vllaznia.eu
Media Officer Gjergj Kola

ANDORRA

Andorre I Andorra

Federació Andorrana de Futbol (FAF)

COMMUNICATION

Address Avinguda Carlemany
67 3° pis
Apartado postal 65
AD-Escaldes-Engordany

Tel +376 805 830

Fax +376 862 006

E-mail administracio@fedandfut.com

Website fedandfut.com

President Antoni Giribet Fiter

General Secretary Tomás Gea

Media Officer Andrea Vidal

Year of Formation 1994

National Stadium Comunal, Andorra la Vella (1,249)

DOMESTIC COMPETITION SUMMARY 2010/11

PRIMERA DIVISIÓ FINAL TABLE

PLAY-OFFS
Championship Group

		Home					Away					Total						
	Pld	W	D	L	F	A	W	D	L	F	A	W	D	L	F	A	Pts	Comp
1 FC Santa Coloma	20	9	1	0	34	4	5	4	1	37	7	14	5	1	71	11	47	UCL
2 UE Sant Julià	20	6	4	0	24	4	6	3	1	23	5	12	7	1	47	9	43	UEL
3 FC Lusitans	20	7	3	0	22	6	4	2	4	21	14	11	5	4	43	20	38	UEL
4 UE Santa Coloma	20	6	0	4	25	12	4	0	6	29	15	10	0	10	54	27	30	UEL

PLAY-OFFS
Championship Group

		Home					Away					Total						
	Pld	W	D	L	F	A	W	D	L	F	A	W	D	L	F	A	Pts	Comp
5 CE Principat	20	5	2	3	30	16	3	2	5	19	18	8	4	8	49	34	28	
6 Inter Club d'Escaldes	20	2	2	6	8	29	4	1	5	20	25	6	3	11	28	54	21	
7 FC Encamp	20	2	1	7	14	39	2	0	8	10	40	4	1	15	24	79	13	*Relegated*
8 FC Casa del Benfica	20	1	1	8	9	55	0	2	8	6	42	1	3	16	15	97	6	*Relegated*

NB League splits into two groups of four after 14 matches.

Top Scorer Victor Bernat (UE Santa Coloma), 16 goals

Promoted Clubs FC Rànger's
UE Engordany

Cup Final UE Sant Julià 3, UE Santa Coloma 1 (aet)

Rivals retain their trophies

A season that began with Andorra sending four clubs, rather than the usual two, into European competition ended with the two major domestic trophies being retained as FC Santa Coloma claimed their sixth league title in 11 years before Primera Divisió runners-up UE Sant Julià defeated the champions 3-1 after extra time, with ten men, to win the final of the Copa Constitució.

Andorra players celebrate a rare international goal – against the Republic of Ireland in Dublin

The country's top two clubs both fell at the first hurdle in Europe but not in the manner anticipated, Santa Coloma having to forfeit their opening tie in the UEFA Champions League against Birkirkara FC because of unplayable pitch conditions and Sant Julià's UEFA Europa League home leg against Myllykosken Pallo-47 having to be abandoned and replayed because of adverse weather.

Play-off power

A return to the UEFA Champions League was secured by FC Santa Coloma with a game to spare in early March when they clinched the league title with a 1-0 win over UE Santa Coloma. At the end of the first phase of the championship, FC Santa Coloma had trailed Sant Julià by a point, with FC Lusitans also challenging, a point further back. But the defending champions powered to the front in the play-offs, winning four and drawing two of their six fixtures.

A key man for the champions was midfielder Óscar Sonejee, who also found time during the season to increase his record number of caps for Andorra to 87. He was given little competitive action for his country, however, as Andorra, led into the UEFA EURO 2012 qualifying campaign by their second most-capped individual, goalkeeper-turned-coach Koldo, stretched their sorry sequence of competitive defeats to 30 while maintaining their unenviable record of never having obtained a single UEFA European Championship qualifying point. Nevertheless, there was ample consolation in restricting their opponents to just 16 goals in six matches and scoring a belter themselves through young midfielder Cristian Martínez against the Republic of Ireland in Dublin.

National Team

Top Five All-time Caps – Óscar Sonejee (87); Jesús Álvarez "Koldo" (78); Manolo Jiménez (77); José Manuel García "Txema" (72); Ildefons Lima (68)

Top Five All-time Goals – Ildefons Lima (7); Jesús Julián Lucendo (3); Emiliano González, Marc Pujol, Justo Ruiz, Juli Sánchez, Óscar Sonejee & Fernando Silva (2)

NATIONAL TEAM RESULTS 2010/11

11/8/10	Cyprus	A	Larnaca	0-1	
3/9/10	Russia (ECQ)	H	Andorra la Vella	0-2	
7/9/10	Republic of Ireland (ECQ)	A	Dublin	1-3	*Martínez C. (45)*
8/10/10	FYROM (ECQ)	H	Andorra la Vella	0-2	
12/10/10	Armenia (ECQ)	A	Yerevan	0-4	
9/2/11	Moldova	N	Lagos (POR)	1-2	*Ayala (52)*
26/3/11	Slovakia (ECQ)	H	Andorra la Vella	0-1	
4/6/11	Slovakia (ECQ)	A	Bratislava	0-1	

NATIONAL TEAM APPEARANCES 2010/11

Coach – Jesús Álvarez "KOLDO"	4/9/70		Cyp	RUS	IRL	MKD	ARM	Mda	SVK	SVK	Caps	Goals
José Antonio GÓMES	3/12/86	Ciudad de Vícar (ESP) /San Rafael (ESP)	G	G	G	G	G	G	G	G	19	-
Jordi RUBIO	1/11/87	UE Santa Coloma	D	D57			s87	D70	D	D	13	-
Fernando SILVA	16/5/77	Imperio de Mérida (ESP) /Guadiana (ESP)	D	D	D	D	D	s75		A63	40	2
Ildefons LIMA	10/12/79	Bellinzona (SUI)	D50	D	D		D	D 37*	D	D	68	7
Jordi ESCURA	19/4/80	Alcarrás (ESP)	D		D	D	D	s70			66	-
Marcio VIEIRA	10/10/84	Atlético Monzon (ESP)	M69	M	M	M	M		s72	M	35	-
Cristian MARTÍNEZ	16/10/89	FC Andorra (ESP)	M85	M	M	M74	M87	M85	M	M	11	1
Xavier ANDORRÀ	7/6/85	FC Andorra (ESP)	M53		s71		s64	s90		s16	24	-
Marc PUJOL	21/8/82	FC Andorra (ESP)	M85	M88	M86						48	2
Sergi MORENO	25/11/87	Hellín Deportivo (ESP)	M60	M76	M59	M	M51	s49	M		34	-
Sebastià GÓMEZ	1/11/83	Sant Julià	A	A	A	A	A	A75	A72	s63	10	-
Óscar SONEJEE	26/3/76	FC Santa Coloma	s50		s86			D	s87		87	2
José Manuel AYALA	8/4/80	FC Andorra (ESP)	s53	M	M71	M86	M	M	M81	M16	56	1
Manolo JIMÉNEZ	12/8/76	FC Santa Coloma	s60	s76	s59	s74	s51	M49	M87	M86	77	1
Daniel MEJÍAS	26/7/82	FC Andorra (ESP)	s69	s88		M62					4	-
Àlexandre MARTÍNEZ	4/3/87	UE Santa Coloma	s85								2	-
Samir BOUSENINE	7/2/91	FC Andorra (ESP)	s85			s86					4	-
Marc BERNAUS	2/2/77	Girona (ESP)		D	D	D	D	D	D	D	25	1
Ivan LORENZO	15/4/86	Alcampell (ESP)		s57		s62					4	-
Marc VALES	4/4/90	Atlético Monzon (ESP)				D	M64	M90	M	M	18	-
Juli SÁNCHEZ	20/6/78	FC Santa Coloma						M49	s81		63	2
Emili GARCÍA	11/1/89	FC Andorra (ESP)						s49	D	D	6	-
David MANEIRO	16/2/89	FC Andorra (ESP)						s85			2	-
Joaquim SALVAT	18/12/80	Sant Julià								s86	1	-

SECOND LEVEL FINAL TABLES 2010/11

FIRST PHASE

		Pld	W	D	L	F	A	Pts
1	FC Rànger's	18	14	2	2	63	16	44
2	FC Lusitans B	18	14	1	3	69	19	43
3	UE Engordany	18	13	1	4	47	25	40
4	UE Extremenya	18	11	2	5	63	24	35
5	FC Santa Coloma B	18	11	1	6	42	40	34
6	Atlètic Club d'Escaldes	18	5	2	11	32	54	17
7	Penya Encarnada	18	4	1	13	27	50	13
8	La Massana	18	3	4	11	25	55	13
9	CE Principat B	18	4	1	13	24	66	13
10	CE Jenlai	18	3	1	14	25	68	10

SECOND PHASE

	Promotion Pool	Pld	W	D	L	F	A	Pts
1	FC Lusitans B	24	19	2	3	80	22	59
2	FC Rànger's	24	18	2	4	74	24	56
3	UE Engordany	24	14	2	8	58	37	44
4	UE Extremenya	24	12	2	10	72	43	38

NB FC Lusitans B ineligible for promotion; FC Rànger's promoted directly; UE Engordany entered play-offs.

PROMOTION/RELEGATION PLAY-OFFS

(17/4/11)
FC Encamp 1, UE Engordany 3
(1/5/11)
UE Engordany 2, FC Encamp 0
(UE Engordany 5-1)

TOP GOALSCORERS 2010/11

16 Victor BERNAT (UE Santa Coloma)

15 Norberto URBANI (FC Santa Coloma)

13 Juan RAYA (Lusitans)

12 Alejandro ROMERO (FC Santa Coloma)

11 Marc FILLOLA (Principat)

10 Boris ANTÓN (UE Santa Coloma)
Marcelo IGUACEL (Sant Julià)
Mariano URBANI (FC Santa Coloma)

9 PEDRO REIS (Lusitans)
Alejandro IZQUIERDO (Encamp)
Paulo VIEGAS (Principat)

DOMESTIC CUP 2010/11

COPA CONSTITUCIÓ

SECOND ROUND

(23/1/11)
Extremenya 1, Casa del Benfica 2
Atlètic Escaldes 1, Inter Escaldes 6
Engordany 1, Encamp 6
Rànger's 3, Principat 1

Byes – Lusitans, FC Santa Coloma, UE Santa Coloma, Sant Julià

QUARTER-FINALS

(30/3/11 & 6/4/11)
Rànger's v Sant Julià 0-3; 1-8 *(1-11)*

(3/4/11 & 10/4/11)
Encamp v FC Santa Coloma 0-9; 0-10 *(w/o) (0-19)*
Inter Escaldes v Lusitans 0-6; 1-2 *(1-8)*
Casa del Benfica v UE Santa Coloma 0-7 *(w/o)*; 0-4 *(w/o) (0-11)*

SEMI-FINALS

(17/4/11 & 1/5/11)
FC Santa Coloma 2 *(Jiménez 12p, Bousenine 90+4)*, Sant Julià 3 *(Riera 39, Varela 62, Iguacel 90+3)*
Sant Julià 2 *(Riera 17, Hugo 87)*, FC Santa Coloma 3 *(Bousenine 1, 46, Juli Sánchez 67) (aet)*
(5-5; Sant Julià 4-1 on pens)

UE Santa Coloma 2 *(Antón 21, Rodríguez 64)*, Lusitans 1 *(Raya 4)*
Lusitans 1 *(Maciel 15)*, UE Santa Coloma 2 *(Rodríguez 1, Bernat 58)*
(UE Santa Coloma 4-2)

FINAL

(22/5/11)
Aixovall stadium, Andorra la Vella
UE SANT JULIÀ 3 *(Varela 49, Salvat 94, Iguacel 102)*
UE SANTA COLOMA 1 *(Antón 51)*
(aet)
Referee – *Rui Maciel*
SANT JULIÀ – *Perianes, Wagner, Ruiz, Varela, Peppe, Edjang (Matamala 106), Jacques, Muñoz, Riera (Iguacel 46), Salvat, Sebas Gómez (Trejo 80).*
Sent off: *Varela (80).*
UE SANTA COLOMA – *Rivas, Rubio, Nieto (Rui Gonçalves 105), Àlex Martínez, Roca (Vall 110), Aloy (Guida 73), Antón, Rodríguez, Alves, López, Bernat.*

CLUB COMMUNICATION 2011/12

UE Engordany

Av. Fiter i Rossell nº89 Esc. B 1° 1ª
AD-700 Escaldes-Engordany

Tel +376 826421
Fax +376 826421
Web ueengordany.es.tl
Email ueengordany@andorra.ad
Media Officer Jose Luis Donsion

Inter Club d'Escaldes

C/ Terravella nº9 6° 1ª
AD-500 Andorra la Vella

Tel +376 821 753
Fax +376 830 048
Web
Email elderbarroso@hotmail.com
Media Officer Cristiana Barroso

FC Lusitans

Av. Dr. Mitjavila, nº8 baixos
AD-500 Andorra la Vella

Tel +376 332 941
Fax +376 860 070
Web futbolclub-lusitanos.com
Email fclusitanos@andorra.ad
Media Officer Jose Luis Carvalho

CE Principat

Av. Salou s/n
AD-500 Andorra la Vella

Tel +376 806 410
Fax +376 806 414
Web ceprincipat.com
Email gestionsj.r@andorra.ad
Media Officer Victor Duaso

Ranger's FC

C/ Prada Motxilla nº6 Ed. L'Ametller 5° B
AD-500 Andorra la Vella

Tel +376 321 059 / +376 341 987
Fax +376 722 669
Web
Email rangersfc@andorra.ad
Media Officer Josep Cerezo

UE Sant Julià

Av. Rocafort s/n nº20 Baixos
AD-600 Sant Julià de Lória

Tel +376 842 668
Fax +376 842 668
Web
Email uesantjulia@gmail.com
Media Officer Francesc Fernandez

FC Santa Coloma

Av. Meritxell nº9 4° 2ª
AD-500 Andorra la Vella

Tel +376 813 617
Fax +376 865 617
Web fclubsantacoloma.com
Email info@fclubsantacoloma.com
Media Officer Silvia Casals

UE Santa Coloma

Av. Santa Coloma nº65 2° 1ª
AD-500 Andorra la Vella

Tel +376 823 698
Fax +376 823 698
Web uesantacoloma.com
Email info@uesantacoloma.com
Media Officer Marc Ransanz

ARMENIA

Arménie I Armenien

Hayastani Futboli Federacia (HFF)

COMMUNICATION

Address Khanjyan Street 27
AM-0010 Yerevan
Tel +374 10 568883
Fax +374 10 547173
E-mail media@ffa.am
Website ffa.am

President Ruben Hayrapetyan
Vice-President Armen Minasyan
Media Officer Tigran Israelyan

Year of Formation 1992

National Stadium Hanrapetakan, Yerevan (14,403)

DOMESTIC COMPETITION SUMMARY 2010/11

PREMIER LEAGUE FINAL TABLE

			Home					Away					Total						
		Pld	W	D	L	F	A	W	D	L	F	A	W	D	L	F	A	Pts	Comp
1	FC Pyunik	28	11	1	2	42	13	9	4	1	31	9	20	5	3	73	22	65	UCL
2	FC Banants	28	10	3	1	37	11	10	1	3	21	13	20	4	4	58	24	64	UEL
3	Ulisses FC	28	7	4	3	20	10	10	0	4	24	13	17	4	7	44	23	55	UEL
4	FC Mika	28	9	0	5	30	13	5	4	5	17	18	14	4	10	47	31	46	UEL
5	FC Impuls	28	5	5	4	15	17	5	2	7	14	26	10	7	11	29	43	37	
6	FC Gandzasar	28	4	2	8	15	23	4	1	9	9	22	8	3	17	24	45	27	
7	FC Kilikia	28	3	2	9	12	26	1	1	12	7	34	4	3	21	19	60	15	
8	FC Shirak	28	2	0	12	8	24	0	4	10	14	44	2	4	22	22	68	10	

NB No relegation; FC Kilikia withdrew from 2011 Premier League.

Top Scorer Gevorg Ghazaryan (FC Pyunik) & Marcos (FC Pyunik), 16 goals

Promoted Club FC Ararat

Cup Final FC Mika 4, FC Shirak 1

Persistent Pyunik make it ten in a row

FC Pyunik's grip on the Armenian Premier League title extended to a tenth successive season, but it was very nearly prised free by FC Banants, who challenged their Yerevan rivals from first kick to last and were left to lament the concession of a stoppage-time goal to their rivals in a title-deciding, top-of-the-table clash two rounds from the end.

Pyunik ultimately prevailed by winning their final match 1-0 at FC Kilikia – thanks to a penalty from their Brazilian-born Armenian international Marcos Pizelli that enabled him to join team-mate Gevorg Ghazaryan at the head of the division's top-scorer charts – but it was the 1-0 win a fortnight earlier at home to Banants that effectively secured Pyunik's remarkable ten-in-a-row feat.

Crucial strike

Midfielder Karlen Mkrtchyan's crucial added-time strike not only enabled Pyunik to win the game but also to leapfrog a Banants side that had led the standings for the previous four months and appeared destined for a first ever Premier League title. Although Banants had been beaten 4-0 by Pyunik in the 2010 Cup final, the year's previous three league encounters had brought them five points (against two for their rivals), including a 3-2 away win in June – a month in which, extraordinarily, Pyunik surrendered their position at the top of the table, and their unbeaten record, with three successive defeats.

Coach Vardan Minasyan and his young players showed their mettle, however, by dropping just six more points – all from draws – in their remaining 15 matches and thus ending the campaign with precisely the same number of wins (20), draws (5) and defeats (3) – and therefore points (65) – as in 2009. Whereas that record had given them a seven-point victory margin the previous season, this time they edged home by just one point. Mkrtchyan and Minasyan were bestowed with the end-of-season individual prizes for Player and Coach of the Year, respectively, with another Pyunik player, Ghazaryan, taking the runners-up spot behind Mkrtchyan. Other notables in the title-winning line-up were attacking midfielder Marcos and indefatigable veteran defender Sargis Hovsepyan, at 38 some 15-20 years older than most of his team-mates.

Brazilian trio

Whereas Pyunik's regular first XI featured just one non-Armenian – Belarusian goalkeeper Artur Lesko – it was a different story at Banants, who, led by a Macedonian coach in Stevica Kuzmanovski, relied heavily on their foreign legion, notably Brazilian trio Beto, José Júnior and – during the first half of the season – goal-a-game striker Santos du Bala.

Third place in the Premier League went for the second straight year to Ulisses FC, while FC Mika traded places with Banants as they dropped from second to fourth. Mika's UEFA Europa League qualification was sealed in May 2011 when they maintained their 100 per cent success rate in the Armenian Cup final by lifting the trophy for the sixth time in 12 years. Their victims were FC Shirak, who, having finished bottom of the 2010 Premier League but been granted special dispensation by the Football Federation of Armenia to retain their top-flight status, began the new year by eliminating both Pyunik and

Vardan Minasyan enjoyed success with both Pyunik and the Armenian national team

Ulisses from the Cup before they succumbed 4-1 to Mika in the final.

Mika's win ensured that Armenia would be represented in 2011/12 UEFA club competition by the same quartet that had been collectively demolished in 2010/11, all four having fallen at the first hurdle while mustering just a single goal between them. Much more successful in their international engagements were the Armenian national side, led concurrently by Pyunik boss Minasyan, who collected eight points from their first six UEFA EURO 2012 qualifiers.

Memorable October

Although defeated at home by the Republic of Ireland in their Group B opener, Armenia recovered well, snatching a late equaliser in Skopje before overpowering both Slovakia (3-1) and Andorra (4-0) in Yerevan over the course of four memorable October days. In the spring they also made a nuisance of themselves against Russia, drawing 0-0 at home before taking the lead during a 3-1 defeat in St Petersburg. All in all, it was a considerable improvement on the 2010 FIFA World Cup qualifying campaign and further evidence of Minasyan's coaching and motivational skills.

Even more noteworthy perhaps was the astonishing durability of skipper and record cap-holder Hovsepyan, who for the third season in a row started and finished every one of Armenia's international fixtures. Other key contributors to the team's improved fortunes were striker Yura Movsisyan, who scored in three consecutive qualifiers, and gifted young attacking midfielder Henrikh Mkhitaryan, who also made his mark at club level with FC Shakhtar Donetsk – both in the UEFA Champions League and in domestic competition, where he won the Ukrainian league and cup double.

National Team

Top Five All-time Caps – Sargis Hovsepyan (119); Artur Petrosyan (69); Roman Berezovski (65); Harutyun Vardanyan (63); Hamlet Mkhitaryan (56)

Top Five All-time Goals – Artur Petrosyan (11); Ara Hakobyan (7); Edgar Manucharyan & Armen Shahgeldyan (6); Arman Karamyan (5)

NATIONAL TEAM RESULTS 2010/11

11/8/10	Iran	H	Yerevan	1-3	*Mkrtchyan A. (37)*
3/9/10	Republic of Ireland (ECQ)	H	Yerevan	0-1	
7/9/10	FYROM (ECQ)	A	Skopje	2-2	*Movsisyan (41), Manucharyan (90+1)*
8/10/10	Slovakia (ECQ)	H	Yerevan	3-1	*Movsisyan (23), Ghazaryan G. (50), Mkhitaryan (89)*
12/10/10	Andorra (ECQ)	H	Yerevan	4-0	*Ghazaryan G. (4), Mkhitaryan (16), Movsisyan (33), Marcos (52)*
9/2/11	Georgia	N	Limassol (CYP)	1-2	*Manucharyan (63p)*
26/3/11	Russia (ECQ)	H	Yerevan	0-0	
4/6/11	Russia (ECQ)	A	St Petersburg	1-3	*Marcos (25)*

NATIONAL TEAM APPEARANCES 2010/11

Coach – Vardan MINASYAN	**5/1/74**		Irn	IRL	MKD	SVK	AND	Geo	RUS	RUS	Caps	Goals
Stepan GHAZARYAN	11/1/85	Banants	G								2	-
Sargis HOVSEPYAN	2/11/72	Pyunik	D	D	D	D	D	D	D	D	119	2
Ararat ARAKELYAN	1/2/84	Banants	D	D	D	s79		D46			33	2
Robert ARZUMANYAN	24/7/85	Randers (DEN) /Jagiellonia (POL)	D	D	D	D79	D		D	D	49	4
Aghvan MKRTCHYAN	27/2/81	Mika	D74								45	1
Artur YEDIGARYAN	26/6/87	PAS Hamedan (IRN)	M88	M68	s70	s72	M		s57	s67	18	-
David MANOYAN	5/7/90	Pyunik	M90	s68	M						6	-
Levon PACHAJYAN	20/9/83	Sanat Naft (IRN)	M	M	M70	M46				M57	38	2
MARCOS Pizelli Pinheiro	3/10/84	Pyunik	M74			M72	M83	M	M57	M67	13	3
Samvel MELKONYAN	15/3/84	Banants	M								29	-
Yura MOVSISYAN	2/8/87	Randers (DEN) /Krasnodar (RUS)	A16	A	A	A	A53		A	A	7	3
Edgar MANUCHARYAN	19/1/87	Pyunik	s16	s79	s60	s46	A	A85	s49	s57	30	6

NATIONAL TEAM APPEARANCES 2010/11 (contd.)

			Irn	IRL	MKD	SVK	AND	Geo	RUS	RUS	Caps	Goals
Artak DASHYAN	20/11/89	Metalurh Donetsk (UKR)	s74								3	-
Hovhannes HAMBARTSUMYAN	4/10/90	Banants	s74	s71							2	-
Artak GRIGORYAN	19/10/87	Ulisses	s88								1	-
Artur VOSKANYAN	13/8/76	Banants	s90								53	1
Roman BEREZOVSKI	5/8/74	Khimki (RUS)		G	G	G	G		G	G	65	-
Artak YEDIGARYAN	18/3/90	Pyunik		D71	D	D	D	M	s67	s90	8	-
Henrikh MKHITARYAN	21/1/89	Shakhtar (UKR)		M	M	M	M	M	M	M	22	4
Karlen MKRTCHYAN	25/11/88	Pyunik		M	M92	M			M			
		/Metalurh Donetsk (UKR)								M90	14	-
Edgar MALAKYAN	22/9/90	Pyunik		M79	M60		s67	M	M49		7	-
Hrayr MKOYAN	2/9/86	Mika			s92	D	D	D	D	D	10	-
Gevorg GHAZARYAN	5/4/88	Pyunik				M	M67	M	M	M	17	3
Hovhannes GOHARYAN	18/3/88	Pyunik					s53				6	1
Artur YUSBASHYAN	7/9/89	Pyunik					s83	s46			3	-
Gevorg KASPAROV	25/7/80	Mika						G			18	-
Levon HAYRAPETYAN	17/4/89	Lechia Gdańsk (POL)						D	D67	D	3	-
Artak ALEKSANYAN	10/3/91	Pyunik						s85			2	-

CLUB-BY-CLUB

FC BANANTS

Coach – Stevica Kuzmanovski (MKD)
Founded – 1992
Stadium – Hanrapetakan (14,403)
MAJOR HONOURS: Armenian Cup – (2) 1992, 2007.

2010				
28/3	Mika	a	0-4	
3/4	Impuls	h	5-2	*og (Cherevko), Melkonyan 3 (2p), Santos Du Bala*
10/4	Ulisses	a	2-2	*Santos Du Bala 2*
17/4	Gandzasar	a	2-1	*Melkonyan (p), Balabekyan*
25/4	Pyunik	h	1-1	*Gyozalyan No.*
1/5	Kilikia	a	3-0	*Arakelyan, Santos Du Bala, Gyozalyan No.*
5/5	Shirak	h	5-1	*Karapetyan, Santos Du Bala, Poghosyan V., Melkonyan, Gyozalyan No.*
15/5	Mika	h	2-0	*Santos Du Bala 2*
30/5	Impuls	a	1-0	*Beto*
6/6	Ulisses	h	2-0	*Beto, Santos Du Bala*
12/6	Gandzasar	h	3-0	*Santos Du Bala 2, Deniran*
20/6	Pyunik	a	3-2	*Santos Du Bala, Arakelyan, Deniran*
27/6	Kilikia	h	2-0	*Deniran, Melkonyan*
25/7	Shirak	a	3-0	*Kasule, Balabekyan, Beto*
1/8	Mika	a	1-0	*Machado*
6/8	Impuls	h	6-1	*Melkonyan, Deniran, Machado, Balabekyan, Hambartsumyan, Poghosyan V.*
15/8	Ulisses	a	0-1	
22/8	Gandzasar	a	1-0	*Balabekyan*
28/8	Pyunik	h	2-2	*Beto, Deniran*
11/9	Kilikia	a	2-1	*José Júnior, Voskanyan*
19/9	Shirak	h	1-1	*José Júnior*
28/9	Mika	h	2-1	*Deniran, Voskanyan (p)*
2/10	Impuls	a	1-0	*Melkonyan*
16/10	Ulisses	h	0-2	
23/10	Gandzasar	h	5-0	*Beto 2, Deniran, Melkonyan, José Júnior*
31/10	Pyunik	a	0-1	
6/11	Kilikia	h	1-0	*Balabekyan*
14/11	Shirak	a	2-1	*Avetisyan, Nikolov*

No	Name	Nat	DoB	Pos	Aps	(s)	Gls
6	Ararat ARAKELYAN		1/2/84	M	24	(2)	2
12	Khachatur AVETISYAN		6/5/93	A	2	(7)	1
11	Arsen BALABEKYAN		24/11/86	A	9	(14)	5
7	Aram BAREGHAMYAN		1/6/88	M	2	(10)	
24	Tigran BARSEGHYAN		22/9/93	D		(1)	
20	Webert da Silva Miguel "BETO"	BRA	15/11/86	M	24		6
3	Gagik DAGHBASHYAN		19/10/90	D	25		
10	Ortega DENIRAN	NGA	28/5/86	A	19	(1)	7
22	Stepan GHAZARYAN		11/1/85	G	26		
14	Narek GYOZALYAN		10/7/92	M		(2)	
18	Norayr GYOZALYAN		15/3/90	A		(9)	3
9	JOSÉ Carlos Nogueira JÚNIOR	BRA	18/7/85	A	7	(3)	3
5	Artur HAKOBYAN		13/9/88	A		(3)	
19	Hovhannes HAMBARTSUMYAN		4/10/90	D	23	(2)	1
20	Benik HOVHANNISYAN		12/10/90	M	1		
15	Edvard KAKOSYAN		4/6/86	D	7	(1)	
17	Sargis KARAPETYAN		24/4/90	M	18	(7)	1
13	Noah Babadi KASULE	UGA	5/5/85	M	17	(8)	1
15	Grisha KHACHATRYAN		1/3/92	D	2		
2	Darko LOVRIĆ	SRB	24/11/80	D	7		
31	Alexandre Júnior MACHADO Souza	BRA	12/11/85	A	5	(3)	2
21	Samvel MELKONYAN		15/3/84	M	26	(1)	9
4	Nikolay NIKOLOV	BUL	25/8/81	D	25	(1)	1
25	Ararat POGHOSYAN		11/9/93	M		(2)	
16	Valter POGHOSYAN		16/5/92	M	10	(11)	2
9	Eduardo Roberto dos Santos "SANTOS DU BALA"	BRA	2/2/81	A	11		11
26	Davit SUJYAN		3/1/92	M		(2)	
8	Artur VOSKANYAN		13/8/76	M	16	(4)	2
1	Tsvetomir TSANKOV	BUL	6/6/84	G	2		
6	Vachik YEGHIAZARYAN		8/11/92	D		(1)	
18	Armen ZAKARYAN		7/5/92	D		(2)	

FC GANDZASAR

Coach – Slava Gabrielyan; (10/5/10) (Albert Sargsyan)
Founded – 2004
Stadium – Lernagorts (3,500)

2010				
28/3	Kilikia	a	1-3	*Avetisyan*
2/4	Ulisses	h	0-1	
11/4	Shirak	a	1-0	*Avetisyan*
17/4	Banants	h	1-2	*Avetisyan*
25/4	Mika	a	0-2	
1/5	Pyunik	h	1-6	*Kocharyan*
7/5	Impuls	a	0-1	
16/5	Kilikia	h	3-0	*Oseyan, Erzrumyan, Avetisyan (p)*
29/5	Ulisses	a	0-1	
5/6	Shirak	h	1-0	*Tatintsyan (p)*
12/6	Banants	a	0-3	
19/6	Mika	h	1-1	*Erzrumyan*
26/6	Pyunik	a	1-0	*Kocharyan*
3/7	Impuls	h	1-2	*Kocharyan*
31/7	Kilikia	a	2-0	*Nasibyan, Kocharyan*
7/8	Ulisses	h	0-3	
14/8	Shirak	a	2-0	*Khanishvili, Kocharyan*
22/8	Banants	h	0-1	
28/8	Mika	a	0-1	
14/9	Pyunik	h	0-3	
18/9	Impuls	a	1-1	*Nasibyan*
26/9	Kilikia	h	3-0	*(w/o)*
3/10	Ulisses	a	1-2	*Oseyan*
17/10	Shirak	h	3-3	*Kocharyan 2, Khachatryan (p)*
23/10	Banants	a	0-5	
31/10	Mika	h	0-1	
7/11	Pyunik	a	0-3	
14/11	Impuls	h	1-0	*Kocharyan (p)*

No	Name	Nat	DoB	Pos	Aps	(s)	Gls
18	Hayrapet AVAGYAN		8/5/89	A	2	(3)	
8	Arsen AVETISYAN		8/10/73	A	12	(5)	4
77	Levan BUBUTEISHVILI	GEO	14/7/83	G	10		
14	Serge Charles COUDIE MALAN	CGO	1/8/90	M	4	(1)	
4	Hayk CHILINGARYAN		1/2/89	D	5	(6)	
11	Vahe DAVTYAN		17/8/83	M	8	(10)	
22	Sergei ERZRUMYAN		22/11/80	M	12	(2)	2
20	Hovhannes GRIGORYAN		9/3/85	D	23	(1)	
19	Vruyr GRIGORYAN		6/7/92	M		(1)	
14	Martun HAKOBYAN		26/11/90	A		(5)	
16	Alen HAMBARTSUMYAN		1/3/92	A	4	(4)	
29	Lasha JANGIDZE	GEO	11/5/83	M	7	(1)	
23	Ara KHACHATRYAN		21/10/81	M	18	(1)	1
24	David KHANISHVILI	GEO	27/4/82	M	20	(2)	1
10	Artur KOCHARYAN		14/9/74	A	25		8
19	Claudio LUK	URU	25/12/91	M	3		
3	Beniamin MANUCHARYAN		2/1/81	M	4	(12)	
16	Vache MARTIROSYAN		6/9/92	M		(2)	
8	Sargis NASIBYAN		7/7/90	A	15	(7)	2
29	Argin NAZARYAN	USA	14/7/87	M	5	(2)	
7	Artak OSEYAN		16/2/87	M	24		2
6	Andranik SARGSYAN		7/3/85	M	20	(3)	
33	Nikolay SARGSYAN		9/5/81	G	17		
17	Karen STEPANYAN		1/12/85	D	3	(1)	
13	Armen TATINTSYAN		4/10/81	D	23		1
30	Artashes ZAKARYAN		29/11/87	D	11	(1)	
26	Karen ZAKARYAN		28/1/78	D	22	(2)	

FC IMPULS

Coach – Varuzhan Sukiasyan; (10/6/10) Armen Gyulbudaghyants
Founded – 2008
Stadium – Dilijan City (2,300)

2010				
27/3	Ulisses	h	0-3	
3/4	Banants	a	2-5	*Badoyan, Ayvazyan*
10/4	Pyunik	h	0-0	
17/4	Kilikia	a	1-0	*Jenebyan*
25/4	Shirak	h	2-1	*Minasyan, Voskanyan*
2/5	Mika	a	0-1	
7/5	Gandzasar	h	1-0	*Nranyan*
15/5	Ulisses	a	0-2	
30/5	Banants	h	0-1	
5/6	Pyunik	a	0-3	
13/6	Kilikia	h	0-3	*(w/o; original result 2-3 Hovakimyan (p), Minasyan)*
20/6	Shirak	a	1-0	*Giménez*
26/6	Mika	h	2-2	*Giménez (p), Elton*
3/7	Gandzasar	a	2-1	*Hovakimyan, Minasyan*
1/8	Ulisses	h	2-1	*Elton 2*
5/8	Banants	a	1-6	*Petrosyan A.*
15/8	Pyunik	h	1-1	*Elton*
21/8	Kilikia	a	0-0	
28/8	Shirak	h	2-2	*Elton, Voskanyan*
11/9	Mika	a	0-2	
18/9	Gandzasar	h	1-1	*Muradyan*
26/9	Ulisses	a	2-1	*Voskanyan 2*
2/10	Banants	h	0-1	
17/10	Pyunik	a	3-3	*Badoyan, Hovakimyan, Nranyan*
23/10	Kilikia	h	2-0	*Elton, Badoyan*
31/10	Shirak	a	2-1	*Petrosyan A., Badoyan*
6/11	Mika	h	2-1	*Hovakimyan, Voskanyan*
14/11	Gandzasar	a	0-1	

No	Name	Nat	DoB	Pos	Aps	(s)	Gls
12	Mayis AZIZYAN		1/5/78	G	16		
8	Vahagn AYVAZYAN		16/4/92	M	4	(13)	1
17	Zaven BADOYAN		4/3/87	M	27		4
15	Valodya BAGHDASARYAN		18/8/92	M		(4)	
24	Andriy CHEREVKO	UKR	30/7/85	D	8		
23	ELTON Luis Santos Cardoso	BRA	30/9/90	A	16		6
21	GERALDO José Leal de Souza	BRA	22/6/81	M		(2)	
5	Juliano GIMÉNEZ	BRA	4/12/84	D	20		2
3	Aghvan HAYRAPETYAN		19/1/87	M	3	(3)	
16	Albert HOVAKIMYAN		15/9/91	A	12	(4)	4
14	Artak HOVHANNISYAN		8/9/88	M		(2)	
31	Rumyan HOVSEPYAN		13/11/91	M		(1)	
27	Romeo JENEBYAN		10/9/79	M	4	(2)	1
14	Karen V. KHACHATRYAN		22/4/88	D	7	(9)	
21	Avetik KIRAKOSYAN		21/6/83	M	24	(3)	
4	LEONARDO dos Santos Fereira	BRA	2/12/86	A		(2)	
17	Sylvain Nduman MOUKASSA	CGO	20/10/91	A	4	(2)	
1	Grigor MELIKSETYAN		18/8/86	G	7		
11	Hrachya MIKAYELYAN		9/1/75	D	22	(3)	
20	Arman MINASYAN		6/1/84	M	13	(4)	3
6	Vahe MIRAKYAN		6/6/93	M		(12)	
10	Karen MURADYAN		11/8/81	A	18	(4)	1
9	Gevorg NRANYAN		9/3/86	A	11	(6)	2
18	Artur PETROSYAN		15/6/83	M	27		2
10	Vardan A. PETROSYAN		27/2/82	A	3	(1)	
1	Gevorg PRAZYAN		24/7/89	G	5		
11	Sergey RAVINA	BLR	13/3/85	M	4	(5)	
13	Mikhe SIMONYAN	GEO	29/7/87	D	25		
22	Zhora STEPANYAN		31/1/91	M	1	(11)	
8	Andranik TADEVOSYAN		2/3/85	D		(1)	
3	Yeghishe VARDANYAN		19/8/92	M	4	(1)	
7	Tigran VOSKANYAN		21/1/89	M	23	(3)	5
26	Revik YEGHIAZARYAN		1/6/91	D		(1)	

FC KILIKIA

Coach – Abraham Khashmanyan;
(23/4/10) (Samvel Darbinyan)
Founded – 1992
Stadium – Hrazdan (45,000)

2010				
27/3	Gandzasar	h	3-1	*Movsisyan, Gharabaghtsyan, Mnatsakanyan*
3/4	Shirak	h	3-1	*Khachatryan K., Movsisyan, Mkrtchyan*
11/4	Mika	a	0-2	
17/4	Impuls	h	0-1	
25/4	Ulisses	a	0-2	
1/5	Banants	h	0-3	
6/5	Pyunik	h	0-3	
16/5	Gandzasar	a	0-3	
30/5	Shirak	a	1-4	*Khachatryan K.*
6/6	Mika	h	1-1	*Grigoryan T.*
13/6	Impuls	a	3-0	*(w/o; original result 3-2 Gharabaghtsyan, Khachatryan K., Movsisyan)*
19/6	Ulisses	h	1-3	*Gharabaghtsyan*
27/6	Banants	a	0-2	
3/7	Pyunik	a	2-4	*Khachatryan K. 2*
31/7	Gandzasar	h	0-2	
8/8	Shirak	h	2-1	*Khachatryan K., Grigoryan M.*
14/8	Mika	a	1-4	*Petrosyan*
21/8	Impuls	h	0-0	
28/8	Ulisses	a	0-0	
11/9	Banants	h	1-2	*Grigoryan M. (p)*
18/9	Pyunik	a	0-5	
26/9	Gandzasar	a	0-3	*(w/o)*
3/10	Shirak	a	0-2	
16/10	Mika	h	1-4	*Mnatsakanyan*
23/10	Impuls	a	0-2	
31/10	Ulisses	h	0-3	
6/11	Banants	a	0-1	
14/11	Pyunik	h	0-1	

No	Name	Nat	DoB	Pos	Aps	(s)	Gls
22	Artashes ARAKELYAN		11/2/85	D	23		
20	Artyom ARAKELYAN		11/2/85	M	12	(2)	
9	Artur A. AVAGYAN		4/7/87	M	14		
21	Aghvan AYVAZYAN		14/2/86	D	9	(1)	
5	Armen BABAYAN		21/6/83	A	16	(2)	
7	Arkadi CHILINGARYAN		9/5/79	M	20		
2	Vahagn GEVORGYAN		4/8/88	D	1	(1)	
24	Tigran GHARABAGHTSYAN		6/6/84	A	10		3
8	Grigor GRIGORYAN		28/10/80	M	9	(1)	
13	Mkhitar GRIGORYAN		20/2/86	M	18		2
19	Tigran GRIGORYAN		22/3/91	M	1	(20)	1
24	Vladimir GSPEYAN		16/12/89	M	3	(1)	
25	Erik HARUTYUNYAN		24/4/86	M		(2)	
15	Rafayel HARUTYUNYAN		8/6/92	A		(1)	
5	Narek KARAMYAN		20/6/92	M	11	(1)	
1	Armen KHACHATRYAN		25/4/84	G	13		
3	Ashot KHACHATRYAN		22/1/87	D	5	(2)	
17	Karen N. KHACHATRYAN		10/6/85	A	14		6
23	Garegin MASHUMYAN		1/9/89	M	4	(7)	
2	Artur MESROPYAN		15/1/85	A	6	(1)	
18	Artur S. MINASYAN		9/8/78	M	14	(5)	
10	Hayk MKRTCHYAN		5/11/89	A	17		1
1	Martik MKRTUMYAN		4/3/85	G	14	(1)	
11	Hovhannes MNATSAKANYAN		23/10/85	A	19		2
7	Sargis MOVSISYAN		10/7/84	A	13		3
16	Vladimir STEPANYAN		7/8/84	M	8	(2)	
6	Samvel PETROSYAN		15/4/83	A	6	(4)	1
16	Arkadi YEPREMYAN		10/9/80	D	17		

FC MIKA

Coach – Armen Adamyan; (10/8/10) Armen Shahgeldyan
Founded – 1997
Stadium – Mika (7,140)
MAJOR HONOURS: Armenian Cup – (6) 2000, 2001, 2003, 2005, 2006, 2011.

2010				
28/3	Banants	h	4-0	*Beglaryan, Alex, Ednei, Grigalevičius*
2/4	Pyunik	a	2-4	*Montenegro (p), Grigalevičius*
11/4	Kilikia	h	2-0	*Montenegro, Edílson*
17/4	Shirak	a	1-0	*Hambartsumyan*
25/4	Gandzasar	h	2-0	*Hakobyan, Beglaryan*
2/5	Impuls	h	1-0	*Mkoyan*
8/5	Ulisses	a	0-0	
15/5	Banants	a	0-2	
30/5	Pyunik	h	0-2	
6/6	Kilikia	a	1-1	*Ednei*
12/6	Shirak	h	6-1	*Ednei 2 (1p), Petrosyan, Edílson 2, Demel*
19/6	Gandzasar	a	1-1	*Demel*
26/6	Impuls	a	2-2	*Demel, Montenegro (p)*
27/7	Ulisses	h	0-1	
1/8	Banants	h	0-1	
5/8	Pyunik	a	0-2	
14/8	Kilikia	h	4-1	*Edílson, Ednei, Demel, Tadevosyan*
21/8	Shirak	a	1-0	*Ednei (p)*
28/8	Gandzasar	h	1-0	*Ednei (p)*
11/9	Impuls	h	2-0	*Ednei, Movsisyan*
19/9	Ulisses	a	2-1	*Edílson, Tadevosyan*
28/9	Banants	a	1-2	*Beglaryan*
2/10	Pyunik	h	1-3	*Demel*
16/10	Kilikia	a	4-1	*Alex 2, Beglaryan, Ednei (p)*
23/10	Shirak	h	5-1	*Demel 2, Ednei (p), Tadevosyan, Edílson*
31/10	Gandzasar	a	1-0	*Beglaryan*
6/11	Impuls	a	1-2	*Demel*
14/11	Ulisses	h	2-3	*Beglaryan (p), Mkrtchyan A.*

No	Name	Nat	DoB	Pos	Aps	(s)	Gls
22	ALEX Henrique da Silva	BRA	6/1/82	D	27		3
25	Armen AVAGYAN		5/2/90	A		(4)	
10	Narek BEGLARYAN		1/9/85	A	21	(5)	6
9	Boti DEMEL	CIV	3/3/89	A	19		8
9	EDÍLSON Abdala Júnior	BRA	25/1/87	M	7	(8)	6
15	EDNEI Fereira de Oliviera	BRA	30/11/85	M	21	(6)	10
4	Stepan GEVORGYAN	RUS	14/6/88	A	3	(3)	
23	Rafayel GHAZARYAN		17/5/90	M	3	(7)	
10	Mindaugas GRIGALEVIČIUS	LTU	3/12/81	A	15	(4)	2
18	Artur GRIGORYAN		2/10/89	M		(1)	
1	Soso GRISHIKASHVILI	GEO	25/12/73	G	3		
3	Stepan HAKOBYAN		21/1/85	D	6	(7)	1
14	Vigen HAMBARTSUMYAN		14/1/87	M	2	(3)	1
12	Artur HARUTYUNYAN		8/12/85	G	3		
4	Hayk ISHKHANYAN		24/6/89	D	5	(5)	
1	Gevorg KASPAROV		25/7/80	G	11		
1	Saulius KLEVINSKAS	LTU	2/4/84	G	11		
11	Avag MARGARYAN		13/1/89	D		(2)	
5	Hrayr MKOYAN		2/9/86	D	23	(1)	1
17	Aghvan MKRTCHYAN		27/2/81	D	18	(2)	1
16	Grigor MKRTCHYAN		26/1/88	M		(8)	
8	Ulisses Kano MONTENEGRO	ESP	5/5/83	M	9	(3)	3
24	Sargis MOVSISYAN		10/7/84	A	4	(5)	1
6	PEDRO Jesús LÓPEZ Pérez de Tudela	ESP	25/8/83	M	16	(7)	
2	Armen S. PETROSYAN		26/9/85	M	25	(1)	1
13	Gevorg POGHOSYAN		26/8/86	D	23	(2)	
7	Andranik SHAHGELDYAN		10/11/94	A	6	(9)	
18	Alexander TADEVOSYAN		9/8/90	D	24		3
20	Aram VOSKANYAN		28/8/75	A		(6)	

FC PYUNIK

Coach – Vardan Minasyan
Founded – 1992
Stadium – Hanrapetakan (14,403)
MAJOR HONOURS: Armenian League – (13) 1992 (shared), 1996, 1997, 2001, 2002, 2003, 2004, 2005, 2006, 2007, 2008, 2009, 2010; Armenian Cup – (5) 1996, 2002, 2004, 2009, 2010.

2010

27/3	Shirak	a	3-0	*Tadevosyan, Marcos, Minasyan*
2/4	Mika	h	4-2	*Ghazaryan, Hovsepyan S. (p), Mkrtchyan, Tadevosyan*
10/4	Impuls	a	0-0	
17/4	Ulisses	h	1-0	*Marcos*
25/4	Banants	a	1-1	*Marcos*
1/5	Gandzasar	a	6-1	*Tadevosyan 2, Yedigaryan, Ghazaryan 3*
5/5	Kilikia	a	3-0	*Marcos, Mkrtchyan, Minasyan*
14/5	Shirak	h	4-1	*Yedigaryan, Ghazaryan 3*
30/5	Mika	a	2-0	*Minasyan, og (Mkoyan)*
5/6	Impuls	h	3-0	*Yusbashyan, Malakyan, Ghazaryan*
13/6	Ulisses	a	1-3	*Marcos (p)*
20/6	Banants	h	2-3	*Manasyan, Marcos*
26/6	Gandzasar	h	0-1	
3/7	Kilikia	h	4-2	*Marcos 2, Goharyan, Yedigaryan*
31/7	Shirak	a	4-0	*Marcos (p), Manucharyan E., Ghazaryan, Goharyan*
5/8	Mika	h	2-0	*Malakyan, Ghazaryan*
15/8	Impuls	a	1-1	*Barseghyan*
22/8	Ulisses	h	5-1	*Manucharyan E., Ghazaryan, Malakyan 2, Goharyan*
28/8	Banants	a	2-2	*Mkrtchyan, Manucharyan E.*
14/9	Gandzasar	a	3-0	*Manucharyan E., Marcos, Goharyan*
18/9	Kilikia	h	5-0	*Ghazaryan, Marcos (p), Goharyan 2, Manoyan*
27/9	Shirak	h	5-0	*Ghazaryan 3, Marcos, Yedigaryan*
2/10	Mika	a	3-1	*Marcos 2, Manucharyan E. (p)*
17/10	Impuls	h	3-3	*Yedigaryan, Minasyan, Goharyan*
23/10	Ulisses	a	1-0	*Yedigaryan*
31/10	Banants	h	1-0	*Mkrtchyan*
7/11	Gandzasar	h	3-0	*Malakyan, Ghazaryan, Marcos*
14/11	Kilikia	a	1-0	*Marcos (p)*

No	Name	Nat	DoB	Pos	Aps	(s)	Gls
23	Yinka ADEDEJI	NGA	26/3/85	D	11		
24	Davit AZIN	GER	11/1/90	M		(4)	
77	Artur BARSEGHYAN		16/11/86	M		(9)	1
20	Michael Uremu EGBETA	NGA	15/11/91	M	2	(3)	
10	Gevorg GHAZARYAN		5/4/88	M	22	(2)	16
88	Hovhannes GOHARYAN		18/3/88	A	7	(7)	7
91	Levon HAYRAPETYAN		17/4/89	M	4		
3	Varazdat HAROYAN		24/8/92	D	14	(3)	
26	Grigor HOVHANNISYAN		8/12/93	D	2	(1)	
99	Edvard HOVHANNISYAN		28/2/90	G	3		
32	Hovhannes HOVHANNISYAN		15/10/93	M		(2)	
29	Kamo HOVHANNISYAN		5/10/92	M	1	(15)	
81	Aram HOVSEPYAN		6/6/91	A	2	(8)	
4	Sargis HOVSEPYAN		2/11/72	D	26		1
3	Gevorg KHACHATRYAN		26/6/91	D	2	(1)	
1	Artur LESKO	BLR	25/4/84	G	25		
9	Edgar MALAKYAN		22/9/90	M	22		5
27	Mihran MANASYAN		13/1/89	A	1	(4)	1
11	David MANOYAN		5/7/90	A	25	(1)	1
13	Edgar MANUCHARYAN		19/1/87	A	12		5
22	Khoren MANUCHARYAN		7/9/92	A	1	(9)	
8	MARCOS Pizelli Pinheiro		3/10/84	M	26		16
16	Vahagn MINASYAN		25/4/85	D	19	(1)	4
6	Karlen MKRTCHYAN		25/11/88	M	26		4
18	Argin NAZARYAN	USA	14/7/87	M		(1)	
28	Gagik POGHOSYAN		4/5/93	M		(1)	
19	Albert TADEVOSYAN		13/9/90	A	7	(1)	4
17	Artak YEDIGARYAN		18/3/90	D	20	(7)	6
15	Artur YUSBASHYAN		7/9/79	M	28		1

FC SHIRAK

Coach – Vardan Bichakhchyan
Founded – 1958
Stadium – Gyumri City (3,020) & Arnar, Ijevan (3,000)
MAJOR HONOURS: Armenian League – (3) 1992 (shared), 1994, 1999.

2010

27/3	Pyunik	h	0-3	
3/4	Kilikia	a	1-3	*Barikyan*
11/4	Gandzasar	h	0-1	
17/4	Mika	h	0-1	
25/4	Impuls	a	1-2	*Hovhannisyan G.*
2/5	Ulisses	h	0-2	
5/5	Banants	a	1-5	*Nalbandyan*
14/5	Pyunik	a	1-4	*Barikyan (p)*
30/5	Kilikia	h	4-1	*Barikyan, Nalbandyan, Harutyunyan, Gasparyan*
5/6	Gandzasar	a	0-1	
12/6	Mika	a	1-6	*Nalbandyan*
20/6	Impuls	h	0-1	
27/6	Ulisses	a	0-4	
25/7	Banants	h	0-3	
31/7	Pyunik	h	0-4	
8/8	Kilikia	a	1-2	*Sargsyan*
14/8	Gandzasar	h	0-2	
21/8	Mika	h	0-1	
28/8	Impuls	a	2-2	*Nalbandyan, Barikyan (p)*
11/9	Ulisses	h	0-1	
19/9	Banants	a	1-1	*Barikyan*
27/9	Pyunik	a	0-5	
3/10	Kilikia	h	2-0	*Nalbandyan, Sargsyan*
17/10	Gandzasar	a	3-3	*Mkrtchyan 2, Barikyan*
23/10	Mika	a	1-5	*Nalbandyan*
31/10	Impuls	h	1-2	*Nalbandyan*
6/11	Ulisses	a	1-1	*Nalbandyan*
14/11	Banants	h	1-2	*Nalbandyan*

No	Name	Nat	DoB	Pos	Aps	(s)	Gls
22	Norayr ABRAHAMYAN		30/10/85	G	22	(1)	
12	Andranik BARIKYAN		11/9/80	A	19	(2)	6
24	Aghvan DAVOYAN		21/3/90	M	7	(5)	
25	Artur DAVTYAN		13/5/90	M	1	(1)	
5	Tigran L. DAVTYAN		10/6/78	A	20		
1	Gela DZAMUNASHVILI	GEO	31/3/83	G	6	(1)	
12	Rafayel GAREGINYAN		8/11/82	D	1		
8	Vladimir GASPARYAN		31/8/80	A	6	(15)	1
6	Armen GHAZARYAN		30/1/88	D	12	(1)	
13	Davit HAKOBYAN		21/3/93	M	2	(22)	
15	Ararat HARUTYUNYAN		24/8/75	M	14	(3)	1
21	Gevorg HOVHANNISYAN		16/6/83	D	22		1
3	Arsen HOVHANNISYAN		21/5/89	M	1	(1)	
14	Karen KARAPETYAN		4/6/87	M		(2)	
7	Karen G. KHACHATRYAN		8/5/81	M	18		
31	Arman MARGARYAN		8/3/89	M	1	(6)	
2	Artyom MIKAYELYAN		12/7/91	D	5	(3)	
18	Ara MKRTCHYAN		3/11/84	A	22	(5)	2
10	Hrachya MNATSAKANYAN		16/12/85	M	21		
17	Mikheil MURMANISHVILI	GEO	21/8/89	M		(8)	
16	Mkrtich NALBANDYAN		5/2/89	A	22	(3)	9
20	Rafayel PALTAJYAN		2/2/84	M	21		
16	Edvard PANOSYAN		4/2/86	M	13	(4)	
17	Garnik SARGSYAN		11/3/83	A	23	(2)	2
4	Hovhannes TAHMAZYAN		11/1/70	D	20		
11	Edvard VARDANYAN		20/6/82	M	9	(12)	

ULISSES FC

Coach – Sevada Arzumanyan
Founded – 2006
Stadium – Hrazdan (45,000)

2010

27/3	Impuls	a	3-0	*Adamyan, Tbilashvili 2*
2/4	Gandzasar	a	1-0	*Aleksanyan V.*
10/4	Banants	h	2-2	*Petrosyan, Hakobyan*

7/4	Pyunik	a	0-1	
5/4	Kilikia	h	2-0	*Grigoryan A. 2*
/5	Shirak	a	2-0	*Aleksanyan V., Sahakyan*
/5	Mika	h	0-0	
5/5	Impuls	h	2-0	*Aleksanyan V., Adamyan*
9/5	Gandzasar	h	1-0	*Hakobyan*
/6	Banants	a	0-2	
3/6	Pyunik	h	3-1	*Grigoryan A., Grigoryan D., Sahakyan*
9/6	Kilikia	a	3-1	*Sahakyan, Krasovski, Jikia*
7/6	Shirak	h	4-0	*Adamyan, Aleksanyan V., Jikia, Grigoryan A.*
7/7	Mika	a	1-0	*Grigoryan N.*
/8	Impuls	a	1-2	*Petrosyan*
/8	Gandzasar	a	3-0	*Grigoryan D., Jikia, og (Zakaryan A.)*
15/8	Banants	h	1-0	*Sahakyan*
22/8	Pyunik	a	1-5	*Davtyan*
28/8	Kilikia	h	0-0	
11/9	Shirak	a	1-0	*Grigoryan N.*
19/9	Mika	h	1-2	*Jikia*
26/9	Impuls	h	1-2	*Krasovski*
3/10	Gandzasar	h	2-1	*Krasovski. Jikia*
16/10	Banants	a	2-0	*Adamyan, Krasovski*
23/10	Pyunik	h	0-1	
31/10	Kilikia	a	3-0	*Aleksanyan V. 2 (1p), Andrikyan*
6/11	Shirak	h	1-1	*Jikia*
14/11	Mika	a	3-2	*Davtyan, Tbilashvili, Ngavouka-Tseke*

No	Name	Nat	DoB	Pos	Aps	(s)	Gls
10	Artyom ADAMYAN		2/9/80	A	20	(5)	4
88	Manvel AFRIKYAN		8/8/85	G	2		
3	Karen ALEKSANYAN		17/6/80	M	11	(6)	
20	Valeri ALEKSANYAN		4/9/84	D	22	(2)	6
4	Artak ANDRIKYAN		24/1/88	D	14	(4)	1
23	Arayik AVETISYAN		17/9/92	D	2		
7	Artur BARSEGHYAN		16/11/86	M	2		
14	Narek DAVTYAN		24/8/88	M	8	(9)	2
33	Artak G. GRIGORYAN		19/10/87	A	21	(2)	4
8	David Zh. GRIGORYAN		28/12/82	M	19	(5)	2
5	Norayr GRIGORYAN		7/1/83	M	28		2
30	Shota JIKIA	GEO	30/12/84	A	13	(6)	6
3	Tigran HAKHNAZARYAN		18/4/87	D	21	(1)	
9	Ara HAKOBYAN		4/11/80	A	1	(5)	2
77	Georgi KRASOVSKI	GEO	20/12/79	M	22		4
1	Vladimir MALKOV	RUS	15/1/80	G	26		
21	Yeghishe MELIKYAN		13/8/79	M	11	(1)	
18	Rafayel MKRTCHYAN		4/1/85	A	4		
11	Karen NAVOYAN		10/8/79	M	3		
91	Lie Pato NGAVOUKA-TSEKE	CGO	15/1/91	M	1	(4)	1
9	Alexander PETROSYAN		28/5/86	A	5	(9)	2
87	Norayr SAHAKYAN		9/7/87	M	12	(8)	4
22	Gaga TBILASHVILI	GEO	1/10/84	A	12	(6)	3
6	Armen TIGRANYAN		16/8/85	M	10	(1)	
2	Arman TUTYAN		20/12/92	M	6		
17	Tengiz UGREKHELIDZE	GEO	29/7/81	D	12	(1)	

TOP GOALSCORERS 2010

16	Gevorg GHAZARYAN (Pyunik) MARCOS (Pyunik)
11	SANTOS DU BALA (Banants)
10	EDNEI (Mika)
9	Samvel MELKONYAN (Banants) Mkrtich NALBANDYAN (Shirak)
8	Artur KOCHARYAN (Gandzasar) Boti DEMEL (Mika)
7	Ortega DENIRAN (Banants) Hovhannes GOHARYAN (Pyunik)

PROMOTED CLUB

FC ARARAT

Coach – Tigran Yesayan

Founded – 1935

Stadium – City, Abovyan (5,500)

MAJOR HONOURS: USSR League – (1) 1973; Armenian League – (1) 1993; USSR Cup – (2) 1973, 1975; Armenian Cup – (5) 1993, 1994, 1995, 1997, 2008.

SECOND LEVEL FINAL TABLE 2010

		Pld	W	D	L	F	A	Pts
1	FC Ararat	24	17	4	3	50	19	55
2	FC Banants-2	24	16	2	6	59	35	50
3	FC Pyunik-2	24	16	2	6	52	20	50
4	FC Gandzasar-2	24	13	5	6	37	20	44
5	FC Shengavit	24	8	7	9	42	41	31
6	FC Mika-2	24	7	5	12	28	44	26
7	FC Impuls-2	24	5	4	15	22	41	19
8	FC Pyunik-3	24	5	3	16	22	53	18
9	FC Shirak-2	24	4	2	18	18	57	14

NB No relegation.

DOMESTIC CUP 2011

ARMENIAN INDEPENDENCE CUP

QUARTER-FINALS

(10/3/11 & 14/3/11)
Banants 3 *(Avetisyan 6, Gyozalyan No. 76, Beto 78)*, Gandzasar 0
Gandzasar 1 *(Avetisyan 84)*, Banants 0
(Banants 3-1)

Shirak 1 *(Barikyan 34)*, Pyunik 1 *(Hovsepyan S. 87)*
Pyunik 0, Shirak 1 *(Tiago 37)*
(Shirak 2-1)

Ulisses 1 *(Adamyan 77)*, Ararat 0
Ararat 0, Ulisses 1 *(Manasyan 30)*
(Ulisses 2-0)

(11/3/11 &15/3/11)
Mika 3 (Beglaryan 18, Pedro López 50, Ednei 62), Impuls 0
Impuls 2 (Hovhannisyan 66, Kakosyan 75), Mika 2 (Beglaryan 24, Mkrtchyan A. 30)
(Mika 5-2)

SEMI-FINALS

(30/3/11 & 20/4/11)
Mika 3 *(Beglaryan 33, 90, Dong 52)*, Banants 3 *(Bruno Correa 17, Poghosyan V. 26, Arakelyan Ara. 45)*
Banants 0, Mika 1 *(Mkrtchyan A. 62)*
(Mika 4-3)

(6/4/11 & 27/4/11)
Shirak 0, Ulisses 1 *(Nranyan 90)*
Ulisses 0, Shirak 2 *(Grigoryan H. 30, Nalbandyan 99) (aet)*
(Shirak 2-1)

FINAL

(11/5/11)
Hanrapetakan stadium, Yerevan
FC MIKA 4 *(Alex 16, Beglaryan 35, 68, Dong 90+1)*
FC SHIRAK 1 *(Barikyan 42)*
Referee – *Fernández Borbolan (ESP)*
MIKA – *Kasparov, Alex, Mkoyan, Poghosyan (Dong 65), Tadevosyan, Ednei, Mkrtchyan A., Pedro López (Shahgeldyan 82), Voskanyan An. (Petrosyan 67), Beglaryan, Voskanyan Ar. (Mandricenco 46).*
SHIRAK – *Logvinov, Ghazaryan (Khachatryan K.N. 46), Hovhannisyan G., Tiago (Grigoryan H. 22), Aleksanyan, Davtyan T., Hakobyan, Oseyan (Mnatsakanyan 85), Tigranyan, Barikyan, Nalbandyan.*

CLUB COMMUNICATION 2011

FC Ararat
2 Agathangeghos Street
AM-0010 Yerevan

Tel	+374 10 54 43 40
Fax	+374 10 54 43 20
Web	fcararat.com
Email	araratfc@mail.ru
Media Officer	Ara Hakobyan

FC Banants
Jivani, str.2
AM-Yerevan

Tel	+374 10 74 78 68
Fax	+374 10 74 77 45
Web	fcbanants.com
Email	info@fcbanants.com
Media Officer	Khachik Chakhoyan

FC Gandzasar
1 Shinararner Street, Syunik Marz
AM-3304 Kapan

Tel	+374 28 52 28 11
Fax	+374 28 52 28 11
Web	
Email	gandzasar@list.ru
Media Officer	Ashot Asatryan

FC Impuls
138 Artsakhi str.
AM-Yerevan

Tel	+374 10 36 21 60
Fax	+374 10 45 53 88
Web	fcimpulse.com
Email	erebunidilijan@mail.ru
Media Officer	Hayk Ugujyan

FC Mika
41 Manandyan str.
AM-0106 Yerevan

Tel	+374 10 42 92 71
Fax	+374 10 42 92 74
Web	fcmika.am
Email	ashotmart@mail.ru
Media Officer	Ashot Martirosyan

FC Pyunik
7 Masis str., Kilikia Sport Town
AM-0082 Yerevan

Tel	+374 10 54 59 73
Fax	+374 10 54 59 76
Web	fcpyunik.am
Email	fcpyunik@mail.ru
Media Officer	Vahan Danielyan

FC Shirak
Ozanyan Street 6
AM-0500 Gyumri

Tel	+374 31 23 54 05
Fax	+374 31 23 14 05
Web	fcshirak.am
Email	info@fcshirak.am
Media Officer	Artur Nazaryan

Ulisses FC
39 N. Charbakh str., 13 Soghomon
Tarontsi str., AM-86 Yerevan

Tel	+374 10 55 45 87
Fax	+374 10 55 45 87
Web	fculisses.am
Email	fculysses@gmail.com
Media Officer	Karen Giloyan

AUSTRIA

Autriche | Österreich

Österreichischer Fussball-Bund (ÖFB)

COMMUNICATION

Address Ernst-Happel-Stadion
Sektor A/F
Meiereistrasse 7
AT-1020 Wien

Tel +43 1 727 180

Fax +43 1 728 1632

E-mail office@oefb.at

Website oefb.at

President Leo Windtner

General Secretary Alfred Ludwig

Media Officer Peter Klinglmüller

Year of Formation 1904

National Stadium Ernst-Happel-Stadion, Vienna (50,000)

DOMESTIC COMPETITION SUMMARY 2010/11

BUNDESLIGA FINAL TABLE

			Home					Away					Total						
		Pld	W	D	L	F	A	W	D	L	F	A	W	D	L	F	A	Pts	Comp
1	SK Sturm Graz	36	10	4	4	30	16	9	5	4	36	17	19	9	8	66	33	66	UCL
2	FC Salzburg	36	9	6	3	32	17	8	6	4	21	14	17	12	7	53	31	63	UEL
3	FK Austria Wien	36	8	3	7	31	19	9	7	2	34	18	17	10	9	65	37	61	UEL
4	SV Ried	36	10	5	3	25	17	6	5	7	26	21	16	10	10	51	38	58	UEL
5	SK Rapid Wien	36	9	4	5	32	19	5	7	6	20	23	14	11	11	52	42	53	
6	FC Wacker Innsbruck	36	8	5	5	20	17	5	6	7	23	25	13	11	12	43	42	50	
7	SC Wiener Neustadt	36	9	5	4	25	19	5	3	10	19	33	14	8	14	44	52	50	
8	Kapfenberger SV	36	4	8	6	24	31	5	3	10	18	30	9	11	16	42	61	38	
9	SV Mattersburg	36	3	8	7	18	29	4	2	12	11	27	7	10	19	29	56	31	
10	LASK Linz	36	2	3	13	12	34	1	7	10	10	41	3	10	23	22	75	19	*Relegated*

Top Scorer Roland Linz (Austria Wien), 21 goals

Promoted Club FC Admira/Wacker Mödling

Cup Final SV Ried 2, SC Austria Lustenau 0

Big guns spiked by Sturm

There was a surprise outcome to a thrilling battle for the 2010/11 Austrian Bundesliga as SK Sturm Graz held off the dual challenge of FK Austria Wien and defending champions FC Salzburg to win the title for only the third time. With SV Ried, who led the Bundesliga at the winter break, succeeding Sturm as Austrian Cup winners, it was a memorable season for the underdogs.

For every winner there is a loser, however, and for Salzburg and the two capital powerhouses, Austria Wien and SK Rapid Wien, the campaign was one of general disillusionment – not just domestically but on the European front as well. Salzburg failed once again to reach the UEFA Champions League group stage, falling unexpectedly to Israeli opposition in the play-offs for the second year running, and unlike the previous season when they had the consolation of winning all six UEFA Europa League group games, this time they failed to win any. Likewise Rapid, who, having staged an impressive encore to overcome Aston Villa FC in the UEFA Europa League play-offs, lost five of their six group games. Austria Wien were eliminated at the play-off stage of the same competition, by Aris Thessaloniki FC – and the same fate befell Sturm, albeit in a nothing-to-lose tie against Juventus.

Paced to perfection

In retrospect, Sturm's early European exit aided their domestic ambitions. Cleverly commanded by long-serving German coach Franco Foda, whose connection to the club went all the way back to 1997 and included back-to-back Austrian titles as a player, Sturm paced their title challenge to perfection. Always in contention, they never went more than two games without a win. They also saved their best till last by winning their final three fixtures to end up with a three-point victory margin over fast-finishing Salzburg.

Although Sturm's points haul of 66 was the lowest for a Bundesliga champion since the introduction of three points for a win, it proved sufficient for their first title in 12 years. They also scored 66 goals – the best in the division – and although Sturm's top marksman, 19-goal Roman Kienast, missed out on the Golden Boot to Austria Wien's evergreen striker Roland Linz (21 goals), his strike partnership with Hungarian international Imre Szabics was the most potent around, with Bosnian No10 Samir Muratović proving a more than useful deputy, not least with goals in each of those last three victories. Andreas Hölzl was Sturm's midfield linchpin, with goalkeeper Christian Gratzei and Croatian Gordon Schildenfeld the key figures at the back.

Salzburg, who never topped the table all season, sacked coach Huub Stevens in early April and won five of their last six games under his compatriot replacement Ricardo Moniz, including a final-day 4-2 triumph at Austria Wien, to finish as runners-up. Rapid coach Peter Pacult lasted three days longer than Stevens before he, too, was jettisoned – although with the exception of 18-goal Albanian striker Hamdi Salihi, Rapid's players were as much to blame as their coach for a season of major underachievement. Their fans did themselves no favours either when they invaded the pitch during the Vienna derby at home to Austria in the

Roman Kienast was Sturm's top scorer in their Bundesliga triumph

National Team

International Tournament Appearances –
FIFA World Cup Finals – (7) 1934 (4th), 1954 (3rd), 1958, 1978 (2nd phase), 1982 (2nd phase), 1990, 1998.
UEFA European Championship – (1) 2008.

Top Five All-time Caps – Andreas Herzog (103); Anton Polster (95); Gerhard Hanappi (93); Karl Koller (86); Friedl Koncilia & Bruno Pezzey (84)

Top Five All-time Goals – Anton Polster (44); Hans Krankl (34); Johann Horvath (29); Erich Hof (28); Anton Schall (27)

penultimate round, forcing a first-half abandonment and the concession of a 3-0 win to their rivals, who were 2-0 up at the time. The title hopes of Karl Daxbacher's Violetten had effectively crumbled the previous month when they surrendered top spot after collecting just two points from a nightmarish four-game spell.

Ried held a four-point lead in the Bundesliga at Christmas but although a final placing of fourth was a disappointment, Paul Gludovatz's side proved to be a redoutable force in the ÖFB-Cup, eliminating holders Sturm in the quarter-final and Rapid in the semis before overcoming second-tier SC Austria Lustenau 2-0 in the final, with striker Markus Hammerer scoring both goals, to record their first victory in the competition since 1998.

Spring defeats

Discounting the 2008 finals that they co-hosted, Austria have never qualified for a UEFA European Championship, and that trend looked certain to continue when Dietmar Constantini's young side lost three successive qualifiers in the spring – the last of them, somewhat unluckily, 2-1 at home to Germany. It was a season in which no Austrian international really excelled, although Martin Harnik made good progress at VfB Stuttgart and Marc Janko enjoyed a fine first season abroad, at FC Twente, which he crowned by heading his team's extra-time winner against AFC Ajax in the Dutch Cup final.

NATIONAL TEAM RESULTS 2010/11

11/8/10	Switzerland	H	Klagenfurt	0-1	
7/9/10	Kazakhstan (ECQ)	H	Salzburg	2-0	*Linz (90+1), Hoffer (90+2)*
8/10/10	Azerbaijan (ECQ)	H	Vienna	3-0	*Prödl (3), Arnautovic (53, 90+2)*
12/10/10	Belgium (ECQ)	A	Brussels	4-4	*Schiemer (14, 62), Arnautovic (29), Harnik (90+3)*
17/11/10	Greece	H	Vienna	1-2	*Fuchs (67)*
9/2/11	Netherlands	A	Eindhoven	1-3	*Arnautovic (84p)*
25/3/11	Belgium (ECQ)	H	Vienna	0-2	
29/3/11	Turkey (ECQ)	A	Istanbul	0-2	
3/6/11	Germany (ECQ)	H	Vienna	1-2	*Friedrich (50og)*
7/6/11	Latvia	H	Graz	3-1	*Dibon (75), Harnik (81, 90+6p)*

NATIONAL TEAM APPEARANCES 2010/11

Coach – Dietmar CONSTANTINI	**30/5/55**		**Sui**	**KAZ**	**AZE**	**BEL**	**Gre**	**Ned**	**BEL**	**TUR**	**GER**	**Lva**	**Caps**	**Goals**
Christian GRATZEI	19/9/81	Sturm	G				s46				G	G	7	-
Ekrem DAG	5/12/80	Beşiktaş (TUR)	D46	D					D	D	D66		6	-
Sebastian PRÖDL	21/6/87	Werder GER)	D	D	D	D	D	D					29	3
Emanuel POGATETZ	16/1/83	Hannover (GER)	D	D				D	D	D	D		43	2
Christian FUCHS	7/4/86	Mainz (GER)	D	D	D	D	D	D	D	D	D	D97	41	1
Franz SCHIEMER	21/3/86	Salzburg	M	M	D	D	D	M					19	4
Julian BAUMGARTLINGER	2/1/88	Austria Wien	M		s78	M		M	M	M46	M	M62	13	-
Patrick WOLF	4/5/81	Wiener Neustadt	M46										2	-
Zlatko JUNUZOVIC	26/9/87	Austria Wien	M79		M78	M72	M	M62	M69		s66	M91	13	-
Jakob JANTSCHER	8/1/89	Salzburg	M79	M66			s88						9	1
Erwin HOFFER	14/4/87	Kaiserslautern (GER)	A46	s66	s59	s56		s62		s46	A88	s62	24	3
Florian KLEIN	17/11/86	Austria Wien	s46		D	D	D	D72			D	D	8	-
Ümit KORKMAZ	17/9/85	Eintracht (GER)	s46											
		/Bochum (GER)							s69	s57			10	-
Martin HARNIK	10/6/87	Stuttgart (GER)	s46	M66	M55	s88			M	M69	M81	M	24	5

NATIONAL TEAM APPEARANCES 2010/11 (contd.)

			Sui	KAZ	AZE	BEL	Gre	Ned	BEL	TUR	GER	Lva	Caps	Goal
Andreas HÖLZL	16/3/85	Sturm	s79										10	2
Roland LINZ	9/8/81	Austria Wien	s79	A	A59		s69						39	8
Jürgen MACHO	24/8/77	Panionios (GRE)		G	G	G	G46	G	G	G			26	-
Veli KAVLAK	3/11/88	Rapid Wien		M	s55	M56	M58	s85					13	-
Marc JANKO	25/6/83	Twente (NED)		A78			s58		A54		s88		20	7
David ALABA	24/6/92	Bayern (GER)		s66			M				M	M94	10	-
		/Hoffenheim (GER)						M85	M54	M				
Stefan MAIERHOFER	16/8/82	Duisburg (GER)		s78	A	A	A69	A	s54	A			17	1
Marko ARNAUTOVIC	19/4/89	Werder (GER)			M	M88	M88	M	M	s69			11	4
Paul SCHARNER	11/3/80	West Brom (ENG)			M	M	s69			M	M		35	-
						68*								
Yasin PEHLIVAN	5/1/89	Rapid Wien				s72	M69	s72	s54	M57			13	-
Aleksandar DRAGOVIC	6/3/91	Basel (SUI)							D	D			11	-
Stefan KULOVITS	19/4/83	Rapid Wien									M	M	3	-
Daniel ROYER	22/5/90	Ried									s81	s62	2	-
Christopher DIBON	2/11/90	Admira/Wacker										D	1	1
Manuel ORTLECHNER	4/3/80	Austria Wien										D	7	-
Roman KIENAST	29/3/84	Sturm										A62	11	1
Manuel WEBER	28/8/85	Sturm										s91	1	-
Christopher DRAZAN	2/10/90	Rapid Wien										s94	3	-
Thomas SCHRAMMEL	5/9/87	Ried										s97	1	-

CLUB-BY-CLUB

FK AUSTRIA WIEN

Coach – Karl Daxbacher

Founded – 1911

Stadium – Franz Horrstadion (13,400)

MAJOR HONOURS: Austrian League – (23) 1924, 1926, 1949, 1950, 1953, 1961, 1962, 1963, 1969, 1970, 1976, 1978, 1979, 1980, 1981, 1984, 1985, 1986, 1991, 1992, 1993, 2003, 2006; Austrian Cup – (27) 1921, 1924, 1925, 1926, 1933, 1935, 1936, 1948, 1949, 1960, 1962, 1963, 1967, 1971, 1974, 1977, 1980, 1982, 1986, 1990, 1992, 1994, 2003, 2005, 2006, 2007, 2009.

2010				
18/7	Mattersburg	h	2-0	*Liendl, Linz*
25/7	LASK	a	4-3	*Linz 2, Klein, Ortlechner*
1/8	Wiener Neustadt	a	0-0	
8/8	Ried	h	0-1	
21/8	Kapfenberg	a	1-1	*Linz*
29/8	Wacker	h	0-3	
12/9	Rapid	a	1-0	*Linz*
22/9	Salzburg	h	0-0	
26/9	Sturm	a	2-0	*Junuzovic 2*
2/10	Sturm	h	2-3	*Hlinka, Linz*
17/10	Mattersburg	a	3-0	*Stankovic 2, Junuzovic*
23/10	LASK	h	4-1	*Hlinka, Tadic 2, Stankovic*
30/10	Wiener Neustadt	h	1-1	*Linz*
6/11	Ried	a	1-2	*Linz*
13/11	Kapfenberg	h	5-1	*og (Fukal), Linz, Junuzovic, Baumgartlinger, Suttner*
21/11	Wacker	a	1-0	*Junuzovic*
28/11	Rapid	h	0-1	
4/12	Salzburg	a	1-1	*Dragovic*
11/12	Mattersburg	a	2-1	*Tadic, Stankovic*
2011				
12/2	Ried	h	1-0	*Margreitter*
19/2	Wiener Neustadt	h	4-0	*Linz 2, Suttner, Barazite*
26/2	LASK	a	4-0	*Liendl, Barazite, Junuzovic, Linz*
2/3	Sturm	h	2-2	*Klein (p), Ortlechner*
5/3	Wacker	a	3-0	*Jun, Linz, Junuzovic*
13/3	Rapid	h	0-1	
20/3	Salzburg	a	1-1	*Junuzovic*
2/4	Kapfenberg	h	2-0	*Jun 2*
10/4	Kapfenberg	a	3-3	*Linz 2, Stankovic*
16/4	SV Mattersburg	h	0-1	
24/4	Ried	a	1-1	*Linz*
30/4	Wiener Neustadt	a	2-4	*Stankovic, Tadic*
7/5	LASK	h	5-0	*Liendl, Linz 2, Tadic, Barazite*
11/5	Sturm	a	1-1	*Linz*
14/5	Wacker	h	1-0	*Jun*
22/5	Rapid	a	3-0	*(w/o; match abandoned after 26 mins at 2-0 Linz, Junuzovic)*
25/5	Salzburg	h	2-4	*Linz, Barazite*

No	Name	Nat	DoB	Pos	Aps	(s)	Gls
21	Robert ALMER		20/3/84	G	10		
39	Nacer BARAZITE	NED	27/5/90	A	14	(2)	4
26	Julian BAUMGARTLINGER		2/1/88	M	28	(3)	1
27	Emir DILAVER		7/5/91	D	2	(1)	
4	Aleksandar DRAGOVIC		6/3/91	D	18		1
20	Alexander GORGON		28/10/88	M	1	(2)	
6	Peter HLINKA	SVK	5/12/78	M	21	(4)	2
4	Niklas HOHENEDER		17/8/85	D		(6)	
11	Tomáš JUN	CZE	17/1/83	A	17	(9)	4

No	Name	Nat	DoB	Pos	Aps	(s)	Gls
6	Zlatko JUNUZOVIC		26/9/87	M	33		9
	Florian KLEIN		17/11/86	M	36		2
0	Fabian KOCH		24/6/89	M	6	(4)	
2	Marin LEOVAC	CRO	7/1/88	D	14	(4)	
8	Michael LIENDL		25/10/85	M	22	(8)	3
3	Heinz LINDNER		17/7/90	G	23	(1)	
	Roland LINZ		9/8/81	A	36		21
	Georg MARGREITTER		7/11/88	D	26	(1)	1
4	Manuel ORTLECHNER		4/3/80	D	27	(2)	2
	Szabolcs SÁFÁR	HUN	20/8/74	G	3		
	Patrick SALOMON		10/6/88	M		(7)	
0	Thiago Maier dos Santos "SCHUMACHER"	BRA	31/3/86	A	1	(10)	
9	Marko STANKOVIC		17/2/86	A	24	(5)	6
9	Markus SUTTNER		16/4/87	D	22	(5)	2
8	Dario TADIC		11/5/90	A	6	(10)	5
7	Andreas TIFFNER		10/2/91	A		(1)	
	Fernando TROYANSKI	ARG	24/11/77	D	1	(1)	
5	Petr VOŘÍŠEK	CZE	19/3/79	M	4	(3)	
	Manuel WALLNER		25/10/88	D	1		

KAPFENBERGER SV

Coach – Werner Gregoritsch

Founded – 1919

Stadium – Franz Fekete Stadion (10,000)

2010				
17/7	Salzburg	h	0-0	
24/7	Sturm	a	0-2	
31/7	Mattersburg	h	3-1	*Alar, Sencar, Felfernig*
7/8	LASK	a	1-0	*Alar*
21/8	Austria Wien	h	1-1	*Alar*
28/8	Ried	a	0-1	
11/9	Wiener Neustadt	a	0-3	
22/9	Wacker	h	2-4	*Taboga, Kröpfl*
25/9	Rapid	a	2-3	*Felfernig, Sencar*
3/10	Rapid	h	0-0	
16/10	Salzburg	a	2-0	*Koçin, Tieber*
23/10	Sturm	h	0-4	
30/10	Mattersburg	a	1-0	*Spirk*
6/11	LASK	h	4-1	*Spirk 2, Alar, Hüttenbrenner*
13/11	Austria Wien	a	1-5	*Alar*
20/11	Ried	h	3-3	*Hüttenbrenner, Alar 2*
27/11	Wiener Neustadt	h	1-2	*Alar*
4/12	Wacker	a	3-1	*Elsneg, Alar, Erkinger*
11/12	LASK	h	2-2	*Gregoritsch, Alar*
2011				
12/2	Sturm	a	0-2	
26/2	Rapid	a	0-2	
2/3	Salzburg	h	0-1	
5/3	Wiener Neustadt	a	1-1	*Elsneg*
9/3	Wacker	h	0-0	
12/3	SV Mattersburg	a	1-1	*Gregoritsch*
19/3	Ried	h	2-1	*Alar 2*
2/4	Austria Wien	a	0-2	
10/4	Austria Wien	h	3-3	*Alar, Mavrič (p), Felfernig*
16/4	LASK	a	3-0	*Alar, Mavrič, Hüttenbrenner*
23/4	Sturm	h	0-5	
30/4	Wacker	a	1-1	*Sencar*
7/5	Rapid	h	1-1	*Mavrič (p)*
10/5	Salzburg	a	2-4	*Mavrič (p), Elsneg*
14/5	Wiener Neustadt	h	0-1	
22/5	SV Mattersburg	h	2-1	*Sencar, Elsneg*
25/5	Ried	a	0-2	

No	Name	Nat	DoB	Pos	Aps	(s)	Gls
19	Deni ALAR		18/1/90	A	25	(7)	14
11	Dieter ELSNEG		4/2/90	A	27	(8)	4
13	Stefan ERKINGER		1/9/81	M	22	(2)	1
14	Markus FELFERNIG		18/6/83	M	17	(12)	3
5	Milan FUKAL	CZE	16/5/75	D	28	(2)	
37	Manfred GOLLNER		22/12/90	D	2	(1)	
34	Michael GREGORITSCH		14/4/94	M	8	(16)	2
38	Mario GRGIC		10/9/91	M	3		
42	Robert GUCHER		20/2/91	M	6	(5)	
44	Thomas HIRSCHHOFER		30/1/92	A		(1)	
20	Boris HÜTTENBRENNER		23/9/85	M	27	(5)	3
33	Umut KOÇIN	GER	2/6/88	M	22		1
26	Patrick KOSTNER		28/2/88	G	2		
8	Christoph KRÖPFL		4/5/90	M	15	(4)	1
43	Steven LEWERENZ	GER	18/5/91	A	2	(4)	
24	Matej MAVRIČ	SVN	29/1/79	D	30	(2)	4
9	Srđan PAVLOV	SRB	28/1/84	A	1	(2)	
2	René PITTER		8/7/89	M	4	(2)	
22	Andreas RAUSCHER		25/1/78	D	3		
23	Manuel SCHMID		23/8/81	M	12	(3)	
6	Thomas SCHÖNBERGER		14/10/86	D	12	(2)	
10	David SENCAR		29/1/84	M	22	(2)	4
31	Makhmednaim SHARIFI	RUS	3/6/92	D	10	(2)	
30	Ralph SPIRK		26/10/86	M	10	(6)	3
17	Lukas STADLER		28/10/90	A	4	(4)	
4	Dominique TABOGA		6/11/82	D	30	(1)	1
21	Michael TIEBER		4/9/88	A	2	(14)	1
41	Tomasz WELNICKI	POL	18/3/90	D	16		
1	Raphael WOLF	GER	6/6/88	G	34		

LASK LINZ

Coach – Helmut Kraft; (13/11/10) Georg Zellhofer; (2/3/11) Walter Schachner

Founded – 1908

Stadium – Stadion der Stadt Linz Gugl (18,400)

MAJOR HONOURS: Austrian League – (1) 1965; Austrian Cup – (1) 1965.

2010				
17/7	Wiener Neustadt	a	0-5	
25/7	Austria Wien	h	3-4	*Aufhauser 2, Mayrleb*
31/7	Ried	a	0-1	
7/8	Kapfenberg	h	0-1	
21/8	Wacker	a	0-2	
29/8	Rapid	h	1-0	*Aufhauser*
11/9	Salzburg	a	0-0	
21/9	Sturm	h	0-4	
25/9	Mattersburg	a	3-3	*Duro (p), Zickler, Kogler*
2/10	Mattersburg	h	0-1	
16/10	Wiener Neustadt	h	2-1	*Sobkova, og (Ramsebner)*
23/10	Austria Wien	a	1-4	*Piermayr*
30/10	Ried	h	0-3	
6/11	Kapfenberg	a	1-4	*Duro (p)*
13/11	Wacker	h	0-0	
20/11	Rapid	a	0-5	
27/11	Salzburg	h	1-2	*Aufhauser*
4/12	Sturm	a	0-5	
11/12	Kapfenberg	a	2-2	*Mayrleb, Chinchilla*
2011				
12/2	SV Mattersburg	h	0-1	
19/2	Ried	a	0-2	
26/2	Austria Wien	h	0-4	
2/3	Wiener Neustadt	h	2-3	*Aufhauser 2 (1p)*
5/3	Sturm	a	1-1	*Marrero*
12/3	Wacker	h	0-1	
19/3	Rapid	a	0-0	
3/4	Salzburg	h	1-1	*Kaufmann*
9/4	Salzburg	a	1-0	*Kragl*
16/4	Kapfenberg	h	0-3	
23/4	SV Mattersburg	a	1-1	*Kogler*
30/4	Ried	h	1-1	*Piermayr*
7/5	Austria Wien	a	0-5	
11/5	Wiener Neustadt	a	0-0	
14/5	Sturm	h	0-2	
22/5	Wacker	a	0-1	
25/5	Rapid	h	1-2	*Kaufmann*

No	Name	Nat	DoB	Pos	Aps	(s)	Gls
33	Cem ATAN		30/6/85	M	2	(6)	
6	René AUFHAUSER		21/6/76	M	32		6
24	Shawn Maurice BARRY	USA	23/4/90	D	1	(1)	
21	Wolfgang BUBENIK		31/3/81	M	28	(1)	
55	Haris BUKVA		15/3/88	M	14	(1)	
4	Pablo CHINCHILLA Vega	CRC	21/12/78	D	14	(1)	1
18	Patrick DERDAK		16/2/90	A		(4)	
10	Klodian DURO	ALB	21/12/77	M	13	(5)	2
12	Florian HART		11/5/90	D	19	(4)	
13	Thomas HÖLTSCHL		30/4/90	M	1	(3)	
34	JUAN Ramón RUANO Santana	ESP	29/11/83	M	2	(9)	
11	Leonhard KAUFMANN		12/1/89	M	15	(13)	2
23	Daniel KOGLER		16/8/88	A	14	(11)	2
17	Lukas KRAGL		12/1/90	A	22	(3)	1
14	Thomas KRAMMER		18/2/83	M	11	(5)	
29	Petr LUKÁŠ	CZE	24/4/78	D	13		
28	Justice MAJABVI	ZIM	26/3/84	M	30	(1)	
1	Thomas MANDL		7/2/79	G	34		
40	Aridane Tenesor MARRERO Hernández	ESP	1/10/83	A	9		1
9	Christian MAYRLEB		8/6/72	A	12	(5)	2
5	Florian METZ		18/9/85	D	12	(3)	
20	Pavao PERVAN		13/11/87	G	2		
19	Thomas PIERMAYR		2/8/89	D	22	(1)	2
31	RUBÉN López GARCÍA	ESP	9/7/79	D	6		
16	Robert SCHELLANDER		31/1/83	M	23	(1)	
15	Emanuel SCHREINER		2/2/89	D	4	(1)	
30	Daniel SOBKOVA		17/7/85	M	7	(5)	1
27	Emin SULIMANI		4/8/86	M	7	(2)	
8	Gernot TRAUNER		25/3/92	M	6	(7)	
2	Ulrich WINKLER		6/3/85	D	12	(1)	
7	Alexander ZICKLER	GER	28/2/74	A	9	(6)	1

SV MATTERSBURG

Coach – Franz Lederer

Founded – 1922

Stadium – Pappelstadion (15,700)

2010				
18/7	Austria Wien	a	0-2	
24/7	Ried	h	1-4	*Bürger*
31/7	Kapfenberg	a	1-3	*Bürger*
7/8	Wacker	h	0-2	
22/8	Rapid	a	0-2	
28/8	Salzburg	h	1-0	*Seidl*
11/9	Sturm	a	0-2	
22/9	Wiener Neustadt	h	0-3	
25/9	LASK	h	3-3	*Salamon, Bürger, Waltner*
2/10	LASK	a	1-0	*Bürger*
17/10	Austria Wien	h	0-3	
23/10	Ried	a	3-1	*Bürger 2, Spuller*
30/10	Kapfenberg	h	0-1	
6/11	Wacker	a	1-2	*Salamon*
13/11	Rapid	h	2-2	*Bürger 2*
20/11	Salzburg	a	0-1	
27/11	Sturm	h	1-1	*Doleschal*
4/12	Wiener Neustadt	a	0-1	
11/12	Austria Wien	h	1-2	*Pöllhuber*
2011				
12/2	LASK	a	1-0	*Waltner*
19/2	Sturm	h	1-1	*Waltner*
26/2	Wacker	a	0-2	
1/3	Rapid	h	1-0	*Pöllhuber*
5/3	Salzburg	a	0-2	
12/3	Kapfenberg	h	1-1	*Bürger*
19/3	Wiener Neustadt	a	1-2	*Gartner*
2/4	Ried	a	1-1	*Höller*
9/4	Ried	h	2-2	*Bürger, Naumoski*
16/4	Austria Wien	a	1-0	*Waltner*
23/4	LASK	h	1-1	*Bürger*
30/4	Sturm	a	0-4	
7/5	Wacker	h	2-1	*Spuller, Bürger*
11/5	Rapid	a	0-0	
15/5	Salzburg	h	0-1	
22/5	Kapfenberg	a	1-2	*Bürger*
25/5	Wiener Neustadt	h	1-1	*Bürger*

No	Name	Nat	DoB	Pos	Aps	(s)	Gls
21	Stefan BLIEM		5/5/83	G	5		
1	Thomas BORENITSCH		19/12/80	G	28	(1)	
33	Patrick BÜRGER		27/6/87	A	31	(3)	14
26	Peter CHRAPPAN		21/12/84	D	20	(1)	
7	Dominik DOLESCHAL		9/5/89	A	16	(1)	1
17	Patrick FARKAS		9/9/92	M	30		
15	Christian GARTNER		3/4/94	M	5	(1)	1
31	Dominik HÖFEL		22/1/87	M		(1)	
9	Alois HÖLLER		15/3/89	M	31	(1)	1
13	Stefan ILSANKER		18/5/89	M	22	(4)	
11	Matthias LINDNER		7/9/88	A		(1)	
4	Nedeljko MALIĆ	BIH	15/5/88	D	34		
5	Michael MÖRZ		2/4/80	M	26	(2)	
24	Ilco NAUMOSKI	MKD	29/7/83	A	23	(2)	1
25	Ivan PARLOV	CRO	3/4/84	M	10	(4)	
6	Anton PAUSCHENWEIN		24/1/81	D	5	(11)	
2	Alexander PÖLLHUBER		30/4/85	D	22	(1)	2
16	Marvin POTZMANN		7/12/83	M		(1)	
18	Lukas RATH		18/1/92	D	6	(3)	
27	Thorsten RÖCHER		11/6/91	A		(5)	
20	Thomas SALAMON		18/1/89	M	8	(12)	2
30	David SCHARTNER		7/9/88	G	3	(1)	
19	Markus SCHMIDT		12/10/77	M	16	(2)	
3	Goce SEDLOSKI	MKD	10/4/74	D		(1)	
12	Manuel SEIDL		26/10/88	D	28	(4)	1
28	Ronald SPULLER		22/6/81	M	17	(11)	2
23	Philipp STEINER		20/12/86	D		(1)	
29	Róbert WALTNER	HUN	20/9/77	A	10	(14)	4

SK RAPID WIEN

Coach – Peter Pacult; (11/4/11) Zoran Barisic

Founded – 1899

Stadium – Gerhard Hanappi Stadion (17,500)

MAJOR HONOURS: Austrian League – (32) 1912, 1913, 1916, 1917, 1919, 1920, 1921, 1923, 1929, 1930, 1935, 1938, 1940, 1941, 1946, 1948, 1951, 1952, 1954, 1956, 1957, 1960, 1964, 1967, 1968, 1982, 1983, 1987, 1988, 1996, 2005, 2008; German League – (1) 1941; Austrian Cup – (14) 1919, 1920, 1927, 1946, 1961, 1968, 1969, 1972, 1976, 1983, 1984, 1985, 1987, 1995; German Cup – (1) 1938.

2010				
18/7	Wacker	a	0-4	
25/7	Wiener Neustadt	h	1-2	*Jelavić*
1/8	Salzburg	h	2-1	*Saurer, Hofmann*
8/8	Sturm	a	2-0	*Patocka, Jelavić*
22/8	Mattersburg	h	2-0	*Sonnleitner, Salihi*
29/8	LASK	a	0-1	
12/9	Austria Wien	h	0-1	
22/9	Ried	a	1-3	*Vennegoor of Hesselink*
25/9	Kapfenberg	h	3-2	*Salihi 2, Vennegoor of Hesselink*
3/10	Kapfenberg	a	0-0	
16/10	Wacker	h	1-1	*Hofmann*
24/10	Wiener Neustadt	a	1-1	*Katzer*
31/10	Salzburg	a	1-1	*Heikkinen*
7/11	Sturm	h	3-1	*Sonnleitner, Gartler 2*
13/11	Mattersburg	a	2-2	*Pehlivan, Nuhiu*
20/11	LASK	h	5-0	*Salihi 4, Gartler*
28/11	Austria Wien	a	1-0	*Salihi*
5/12	Ried	h	3-0	*Patocka, Sonnleitner, Nuhiu*
11/12	Wacker	h	3-3	*Salihi 2, Gartler*
2011				
12/2	Wiener Neustadt	a	0-2	
20/2	Salzburg	a	1-1	*Soma*
26/2	Kapfenberg	h	2-0	*Nuhiu, Trimmel*
1/3	SV Mattersburg	a	0-1	
6/3	Ried	h	2-0	*Salihi 2*
13/3	Austria Wien	a	1-0	*Salihi*

9/3	LASK	h	0-0	
/4	Sturm	a	3-3	*Prokopic, Salihi (p), Hofmann*
/4	Sturm	h	0-2	
6/4	Wacker	a	3-0	*Salihi (p), Drazan, Hofmann*
3/4	Wiener Neustadt	h	4-1	*Salihi 2 (1p), Hofmann, Saurer*
/5	Salzburg	h	1-2	*Nuhiu*
/5	Kapfenberg	a	1-1	*Kulovits*
1/5	SV Mattersburg	h	0-0	
4/5	Ried	a	1-2	*Nuhiu*
2/5	Austria Wien	h	0-3	*(w/o; match abandoned after 26 mins at 0-2)*
5/5	LASK	a	2-1	*Heikkinen, Salihi*

lo	Name	Nat	DoB	Pos	Aps	(s)	Gls
3	Andreas DOBER		31/3/86	D	3	(6)	
9	Christopher DRAZAN		2/10/90	M	16	(7)	1
8	Hannes EDER		5/9/83	D	1	(2)	
0	Rene GARTLER		21/10/85	A	10	(6)	4
	Raimund HEDL		31/8/74	G	21		
	Markus HEIKKINEN	FIN	13/10/78	M	30		2
6	Thomas HINUM		24/7/87	M	6	(5)	
1	Steffen HOFMANN	GER	9/9/80	M	23	(2)	5
6	Nikica JELAVIĆ	CRO	27/8/85	A	4		2
4	Markus KATZER		11/12/79	D	31	(1)	1
7	Veli KAVLAK		3/11/88	M	20	(1)	
5	Tanju KAYHAN		22/7/89	D	30		
7	Vasil KULESKI		21/3/93	M		(2)	
7	Stefan KULOVITS		19/4/83	M	15	(2)	1
5	Atdhe NUHIU		29/7/89	A	10	(18)	5
3	Jürgen PATOCKA		30/7/77	D	12	(4)	2
24	Helge PAYER		9/8/79	G	15		
35	Yasin PEHLIVAN		5/1/89	M	19	(1)	1
16	Boris PROKOPIC		29/3/88	M	11	(1)	1
9	Hamdi SALIHI	ALB	19/1/84	A	26	(6)	18
21	Christoph SAURER		22/1/86	M	13	(9)	2
36	Michael SCHIMPELSBERGER		12/2/91	D	4	(2)	
22	Ragnvald SOMA	NOR	10/11/79	D	32		1
5	Mario SONNLEITNER		8/10/86	D	30		3
28	Christopher TRIMMEL		24/2/87	A	5	(23)	1
10	Jan VENNEGOOR OF HESSELINK	NED	7/11/78	A	9	(1)	2

SV RIED

Coach – Paul Gludovatz

Founded – 1912

Stadium – Keine Sorgen Arena (7,680)

MAJOR HONOURS: Austrian Cup – (2) 1998, 2011.

2010				
17/7	Sturm	h	0-3	
24/7	Mattersburg	a	4-1	*Nacho, Riegler, Hadžić, Lexa*
31/7	LASK	h	1-0	*Brenner*
8/8	Austria Wien	a	1-0	*Hackmair*
21/8	Wiener Neustadt	a	5-0	*Guillem Martí 3 (1p), Iván Carril, Schrammel*
28/8	Kapfenberg	h	1-0	*Guillem Martí*
11/9	Wacker	a	0-1	
22/9	Rapid	h	3-1	*Iván Carril, Nacho, Hadžić*
25/9	Salzburg	a	0-1	
3/10	Salzburg	h	1-2	*Hadžić*
16/10	Sturm	a	1-0	*Guillem Martí*
23/10	Mattersburg	h	1-3	*Hadžić*
30/10	LASK	a	3-0	*Guillem Martí, Stocklasa, Royer*
6/11	Austria Wien	h	2-1	*Mader, Royer*
13/11	Wiener Neustadt	h	2-0	*Schrammel, Guillem Martí*
20/11	Kapfenberg	a	3-3	*Riegler, Iván Carril 2*
27/11	Wacker	h	1-0	*Guillem Martí*
5/12	Rapid	a	0-3	
11/12	Wiener Neustadt	h	1-0	*Nacho*
2011				
12/2	Austria Wien	a	0-1	
19/2	LASK	h	2-0	*Hadžić, Royer*
27/2	Sturm	a	0-1	
2/3	Wacker	h	2-2	*Guillem Martí, Glasner*
6/3	Rapid	a	0-2	
12/3	Salzburg	h	2-2	*Glasner, Hammerer*
19/3	Kapfenberg	a	1-2	*Royer*
2/4	SV Mattersburg	h	1-1	*Brenner*
9/4	SV Mattersburg	a	2-2	*Stocklasa, Glasner*
17/4	Wiener Neustadt	a	2-0	*Brenner, Hammerer*
24/4	Austria Wien	h	1-1	*Hammerer*
30/4	LASK	a	1-1	*Stocklasa*
8/5	Sturm	h	0-0	
11/5	Wacker	a	1-1	*Riegler*
14/5	Rapid	h	2-1	*Iván Carril, Lexa*
22/5	Salzburg	a	2-2	*Reifeltshammer, og (Afolabi)*
25/5	Kapfenberg	h	2-0	*Lexa, Reifeltshammer*

No	Name	Nat	DoB	Pos	Aps	(s)	Gls
33	Hubert AUER		19/12/81	G	1	(1)	
18	Ewald BRENNER		26/6/75	M	32	(2)	3
1	Thomas GEBAUER	GER	30/6/82	G	16		
5	Oliver GLASNER		28/8/74	D	27		3
9	GUILLEM MARTÍ Misut	ESP	5/9/85	A	26	(8)	9
19	Peter HACKMAIR		26/6/87	M		(4)	1
20	Anel HADŽIĆ	BIH	16/8/89	M	28	(5)	5
21	Markus HAMMERER		31/8/89	A	10	(23)	3
30	Wolfgang HESL	GER	13/1/86	G	19	(1)	
25	Philipp HUSPEK		5/2/91	M	1	(4)	
13	IVÁN CARRIL Regueiro	ESP	13/2/84	M	28	(2)	5
8	Stefan LEXA		1/11/76	M	22	(2)	3
10	Florian MADER		14/9/82	A	31	(1)	1
11	Ignacio "NACHO" Rodriguez Ortiz	ESP	6/11/82	A	16	(11)	3
6	Mark PRETTENTHALER		11/4/83	D	18	(5)	
28	Thomas REIFELTSHAMMER		3/7/87	D	6	(6)	2
14	Jan Marc RIEGLER		18/4/88	D	20	(5)	3
7	Daniel ROYER		22/5/90	M	29	(6)	4
23	Michael SAMMER		23/8/91	M		(4)	
3	Thomas SCHRAMMEL		5/9/87	M	34		2
2	Martin STOCKLASA	LIE	29/5/79	D	31		3
29	Marcel ZIEGL		20/12/92	D		(6)	
22	Robert ZULJ		5/12/92	A	1	(11)	

FC SALZBURG

Coach – Huub Stevens (NED); (8/4/11) Ricardo Moniz (NED)

Founded – 1933

Stadium – Bullen Arena Wals-Siezenheim (30,900)

MAJOR HONOURS: Austrian League – (6) 1994, 1995, 1997, 2007, 2009, 2010.

2010				
17/7	Kapfenberg	a	0-0	
1/8	Rapid	a	1-2	*Jantscher*
7/8	Wiener Neustadt	h	4-2	*Jantscher 2, Zárate, Boghossian*
28/8	Mattersburg	a	0-1	
11/9	LASK	h	0-0	
22/9	Austria Wien	a	0-0	
25/9	Ried	h	1-0	*Wallner*
3/10	Ried	a	2-1	*Mendes da Silva, Hierländer*
16/10	Kapfenberg	h	0-2	
24/10	Wacker	a	1-0	*Zárate*
27/10	Wacker	h	4-0	*Zárate, Wallner 2, Jantscher*
31/10	Rapid	h	1-1	*Wallner*
7/11	Wiener Neustadt	a	0-1	
14/11	Sturm	a	0-0	
20/11	Mattersburg	h	1-0	*Wallner (p)*
24/11	Sturm	h	2-0	*Wallner 2*
27/11	LASK	a	2-1	*Wallner, Mendes da Silva*
4/12	Austria Wien	h	1-1	*Mendes da Silva*
12/12	Sturm	h	2-1	*Wallner, Alan*
2011				
13/2	Wacker	a	1-1	*Cziommer*
20/2	Rapid	h	1-1	*Wallner*
26/2	Wiener Neustadt	a	0-1	
2/3	Kapfenberg	a	1-0	*Wallner (p)*
5/3	SV Mattersburg	h	2-0	*Cziommer, Švento*
12/3	Ried	a	2-2	*Cziommer, Wallner (p)*

20/3	Austria Wien	h	1-1	*Dudić*
3/4	LASK	a	1-1	*Wallner*
9/4	LASK	h	0-1	
16/4	Sturm	a	3-0	*Alan 3*
23/4	Wacker	h	2-3	*Dudić, Zárate*
1/5	Rapid	a	2-1	*Zárate, Alan*
7/5	Wiener Neustadt	h	4-0	*Cziommer (p), Alan 2, Wallner*
10/5	Kapfenberg	h	4-2	*Cziommer, Wallner 2, Švento*
15/5	SV Mattersburg	a	1-0	*Wallner (p)*
22/5	Ried	h	2-2	*Leitgeb, Alan*
25/5	Austria Wien	a	4-2	*Jantscher, Alan 2, Wallner*

No	Name	Nat	DoB	Pos	Aps	(s)	Gls
5	Rabiu AFOLABI	NGA	18/4/80	D	33		
27	ALAN Douglas Borges de Carvalho	BRA	10/7/89	A	11	(13)	10
8	Thomas AUGUSTINUSSEN	DEN	20/3/81	M		(9)	
2	László BODNÁR	HUN	25/2/79	D	6	(2)	
43	Joaquín BOGHOSSIAN	URU	19/6/87	A	5	(13)	1
19	Simon CZIOMMER	GER	6/11/80	M	24	(2)	5
3	Milan DUDIĆ	SRB	1/11/79	D	9	(5)	2
1	Eddie GUSTAFSSON	SWE	31/3/77	G	8		
22	Stefan HIERLÄNDER		3/2/91	M	8	(13)	1
36	Martin HINTEREGGER		7/9/92	D	20	(2)	
14	Jakob JANTSCHER		8/1/89	M	21	(7)	5
24	Christoph LEITGEB		14/4/85	M	34	(2)	1
4	David MENDES DA SILVA	NED	4/8/82	M	21		3
29	Louis Clement NGWAT-MAHOP	CMR	16/9/87	A		(3)	
35	Daniel OFFENBACHER		18/2/92	M		(4)	
10	Nikola POKRIVAČ	CRO	26/11/85	M	6	(2)	
15	Franz SCHIEMER		21/3/86	D	26		
6	Christian SCHWEGLER	SUI	6/6/84	D	14		
23	Ibrahim SEKAGYA	UGA	19/12/80	D	25	(5)	
18	Dušan ŠVENTO	SVK	1/8/85	A	30		2
39	Georg TEIGL		9/2/91	M	1	(7)	
28	Gerhard TREMMEL	GER	16/11/78	G	28		
17	Andreas ULMER		30/10/85	D	9		
38	Johan VONLANTHEN	SUI	1/2/86	M		(1)	
7	Roman WALLNER		4/2/82	A	25	(7)	18
11	Gonzalo Eulogio ZÁRATE	ARG	6/8/84	A	32	(3)	5

SK STURM GRAZ

Coach – Franco Foda (GER)
Founded – 1909
Stadium – UPC-Arena (15,400)
MAJOR HONOURS: Austrian League – (3) 1998, 1999, 2011; Austrian Cup – (4) 1996, 1997, 1999, 2010.

2010

17/7	Ried	a	3-0	*Szabics 2, Standfest*
24/7	Kapfenberg	h	2-0	*Kienast 2*
1/8	Wacker	a	2-2	*Bukva 2*
8/8	Rapid	h	0-2	
29/8	Wiener Neustadt	h	4-2	*Feldhofer, Kienast 2, Schildenfeld*
11/9	Mattersburg	h	2-0	*Haas, Bukva*
21/9	LASK	a	4-0	*Kienast 2, Szabics, Hölzl*
26/9	Austria Wien	h	0-2	
2/10	Austria Wien	a	3-2	*Hölzl, Szabics, Kienast*
16/10	Ried	h	0-1	
23/10	Kapfenberg	a	4-0	*og (Fukal), Kienast 2, Burgstaller*
30/10	Wacker	h	2-0	*Szabics, Kienast*
7/11	Rapid	a	1-3	*Schildenfeld*
14/11	Salzburg	h	0-0	
20/11	Wiener Neustadt	a	3-0	*Hölzl, Muratović, Haas*
24/11	Salzburg	a	0-2	
27/11	Mattersburg	a	1-1	*Muratović*
4/12	LASK	h	5-0	*Weber, Kienast 2 (1p), Salmutter (p), og (Chinchilla)*
12/12	Salzburg	a	1-2	*Kienast*

2011

12/2	Kapfenberg	h	2-0	*Kienast, Weinberger*
19/2	SV Mattersburg	a	1-1	*Muratović*
27/2	Ried	h	1-0	*Haas*
2/3	Austria Wien	a	2-2	*Muratović, Weinberger*
5/3	LASK	h	1-1	*Haas (p)*
12/3	Wiener Neustadt	h	1-0	*Haas*
19/3	Wacker	a	0-1	
2/4	Rapid	h	3-3	*Wolf, Szabics, Kienast*
9/4	Rapid	a	2-0	*Kienast, Szabics*
16/4	Salzburg	h	0-3	
23/4	Kapfenberg	a	5-0	*Kainz, Muratović 2, Hölzl, Szabics*
30/4	SV Mattersburg	h	4-0	*Kienast (p), Weber, Szabics, Salmutter*
8/5	Ried	a	0-0	
11/5	Austria Wien	h	1-1	*Kienast*
14/5	LASK	a	2-0	*Muratović, Kienast*
22/5	Wiener Neustadt	a	2-1	*Kainz, Muratović (p)*
25/5	Wacker	h	2-1	*Hölzl, Muratović*

No	Name	Nat	DoB	Pos	Aps	(s)	Gls
9	Haris BUKVA		15/3/88	M	10		3
13	Thomas BURGSTALLER		9/1/80	D	17	(3)	1
22	Silvije ČAVLINA	CRO	22/4/77	G	10		
17	Martin EHRENREICH		10/5/83	D	5	(12)	
5	Ferdinand FELDHOFER		23/10/79	D	18		1
29	Sandro FODA	GER	28/12/89	M	1	(4)	
1	Christian GRATZEI		19/9/81	G	26		
7	Mario HAAS		16/9/74	A	1	(30)	5
12	Dominic HASSLER		30/3/81	A		(1)	
8	Andreas HÖLZL		16/3/85	M	32	(1)	5
14	Florian KAINZ		24/10/92	M	9	(4)	2
24	Roman KIENAST		29/3/84	A	30	1	19
19	Mario KIENZL		19/12/83	M	26	(1)	
27	Christian KLEM		21/4/91	M	6	(12)	
15	Patrick MEVOUNGOU	CMR	15/2/86	M	7	(5)	
10	Samir MURATOVIĆ	BIH	25/2/76	M	6	(17)	9
2	Timo PERTHEL	GER	11/2/89	M	20		
4	Dominic PÜRCHER		24/6/88	D	15	(4)	
21	Klaus SALMUTTER		3/1/84	M	10	(5)	2
23	Gordon SCHILDENFELD	CRO	18/3/85	D	36		2
18	Joachim STANDFEST		30/5/80	D	32		1
11	Imre SZABICS	HUN	22/3/81	A	32	(1)	9
6	Manuel WEBER		28/8/85	M	34		2
26	Marvin WEINBERGER		4/4/89	A	4	(2)	2
33	Patrick WOLF		4/5/81	M	9		1

FC WACKER INNSBRUCK

Coach – Walter Kogler
Founded – 1915
Stadium – Tivoli (17,400)
MAJOR HONOURS: Austrian League – (10) 1971, 1972, 1973, 1975, 1977, 1989, 1990, 2000, 2001, 2002; Austrian Cup – (7) 1970, 1973, 1975, 1978, 1979, 1989, 1993.

2010

18/7	Rapid	h	4-0	*Schreter 2, Koch, Löffler*
1/8	Sturm	h	2-2	*Schreter 2 (1p)*
7/8	Mattersburg	a	2-0	*Bammer, Perstaller*
21/8	LASK	h	2-0	*Burgič, Prokopic*
29/8	Austria Wien	a	3-0	*Schreter, Perstaller, Prokopic*
11/9	Ried	h	1-0	*Prokopic*
22/9	Kapfenberg	a	4-2	*Schreter, og (Taboga), Bea, Abrahám*
25/9	Wiener Neustadt	h	0-0	
2/10	Wiener Neustadt	a	0-1	
16/10	Rapid	a	1-1	*Öbster*
24/10	Salzburg	h	0-1	
27/10	Salzburg	a	0-4	
30/10	Sturm	a	0-2	
6/11	Mattersburg	h	2-1	*Schreter (p), Perstaller*
13/11	LASK	a	0-0	
21/11	Austria Wien	h	0-1	
27/11	Ried	a	0-1	
4/12	Kapfenberg	h	1-3	*Bammer*
11/12	Rapid	a	3-3	*Burgič 2, Schreter (p)*

011

3/2	Salzburg	h	1-1	*Schreter*
6/2	SV Mattersburg	h	2-0	*Öbster, Burgič*
'3	Ried	a	2-2	*Schreter (p), Carlos Merino*
'3	Austria Wien	h	0-3	
3	Kapfenberg	a	0-0	
2/3	LASK	a	1-0	*Burgič*
9/3	Sturm	h	1-0	*og (Schildenfeld)*
'4	Wiener Neustadt	a	2-2	*Perstaller 2*
'4	Wiener Neustadt	h	1-0	*Burgič*
6/4	Rapid	h	0-3	
3/4	Salzburg	a	3-2	*Perstaller 2, Carlos Merino*
0/4	Kapfenberg	h	1-1	*Perstaller*
/5	SV Mattersburg	a	1-2	*Carlos Merino*
1/5	Ried	h	1-1	*Köfler*
4/5	Austria Wien	a	0-1	
2/5	LASK	h	1-0	*Öbster*
5/5	Sturm	a	1-2	*Hauser*

lo	Name	Nat	DoB	Pos	Aps	(s)	Gls
	Tomáš ABRAHÁM	CZE	18/4/79	M	36		1
3	Andreas BAMMER		18/7/84	A	3	(19)	2
	Iñaki BEA Jáuregi	ESP	27/6/78	D	34	(1)	1
4	Thomas BERGMANN		20/9/89	D	9	(5)	
	Bülent Kaan BILGEN		5/4/77	D	12	(8)	
	Miran BURGIČ	SVN	25/9/84	A	33	(1)	6
1	CARLOS MERINO González	ESP	15/3/80	M	9	(5)	3
	Dario DAKOVIC		24/4/87	D	12	(3)	
9	Alexander FRÖSCHL		15/7/92	A		(2)	
	Pascal GRÜNWALD		13/11/82	G	28		
	Georg HARDING		30/8/81	M	25	(4)	
	Alexander HAUSER		23/6/84	M	24		1
6	Lukas HINTERSEER		28/3/91	A	1	(2)	
9	Muhammed ILDIZ		14/5/91	M	5	(9)	
1	Fabian KOCH		24/6/89	D	16	(2)	1
3	Marco KOFLER		8/5/89	D	1		
5	Marco KÖFLER		14/11/90	M	2	(2)	1
25	Thomas LÖFFLER		1/5/89	M	6	(7)	1
0	Ernst ÖBSTER		17/3/84	A	18	(8)	3
22	Julius PERSTALLER		8/4/89	A	19	(17)	8
17	Harald PICHLER		18/6/87	M	31	(1)	
30	Harald PLANER		24/12/78	G	5		
26	Benjamin PRANTER		22/9/89	A		(1)	
24	Boris PROKOPIC		29/3/88	M	19		3
13	Marcel SCHRETER		29/9/81	A	28	(4)	10
20	Fabian SCHUMACHER		16/3/87	G	3		
3	Martin ŠVEJNOHA	CZE	25/11/77	D	17	(4)	
24	Christopher WERNITZNIG		24/2/90	M		(1)	

SC WIENER NEUSTADT

Coach – Peter Schöttel

Founded – 2008

Stadium – Stadion Wiener Neustadt (7,500)

2010

17/7	LASK	h	5-0	*Simkovic, Sadović, Aigner 2 (2p), Grünwald (p)*
25/7	Rapid	a	2-1	*Aigner, Burgstaller*
1/8	Austria Wien	h	0-0	
7/8	Salzburg	a	2-4	*Burgstaller, Aigner*
21/8	Ried	h	0-5	
29/8	Sturm	a	2-4	*Burgstaller, Aigner*
11/9	Kapfenberg	h	3-0	*Simkovic, Wolf, Grünwald*
22/9	Mattersburg	a	3-0	*Aigner, Wolf, Simkovic*
25/9	Wacker	a	0-0	
2/10	Wacker	h	1-0	*Aigner (p)*
16/10	LASK	a	1-2	*Sadović*
24/10	Rapid	h	1-1	*Aigner (p)*
30/10	Austria Wien	a	1-1	*Koštál*
7/11	Salzburg	h	1-0	*Wolf*
13/11	Ried	a	0-2	
20/11	Sturm	h	0-3	
27/11	Kapfenberg	a	2-1	*Wolf, Simkovic*
4/12	Mattersburg	h	1-0	*Thonhofer*
11/12	Ried	a	0-1	

2011

12/2	Rapid	h	2-0	*Sadović, Burgstaller*
19/2	Austria Wien	a	0-4	
26/2	Salzburg	h	1-0	*Koštál*
2/3	LASK	a	3-2	*Sadović 2, Grünwald*
5/3	Kapfenberg	h	1-1	*Sadović*
12/3	Sturm	a	0-1	
19/3	SV Mattersburg	h	2-1	*Koštál, Grünwald*
2/4	Wacker	h	2-2	*Burgstaller, Sadović*
9/4	Wacker	a	0-1	
17/4	Ried	h	0-2	
23/4	Rapid	a	1-4	*Aigner*
30/4	Austria Wien	h	4-2	*Aigner 2, Simkovic, Grünwald*
7/5	Salzburg	a	0-4	
11/5	LASK	h	0-0	
14/5	Kapfenberg	a	1-0	*Helly*
22/5	Sturm	h	1-2	*Grünwald*
25/5	SV Mattersburg	a	1-1	*Simkovic*

No	Name	Nat	DoB	Pos	Aps	(s)	Gls
20	Hannes AIGNER		16/3/81	A	30		11
28	Bernd BESENLEHNER		24/11/86	M	1	(1)	
30	Guido BURGSTALLER		24/4/89	M	20	(5)	5
18	DIEGO VIANA	BRA	5/5/83	A	2	(9)	
7	Rene FELIX		23/6/90	M	1	(6)	
32	Sašo FORNEZZI	SVN	11/11/82	G	32		
10	Alexander GRÜNWALD		1/5/89	M	31	(2)	6
22	Christian HASELBERGER		2/6/89	D	1	(9)	
17	Thomas HELLY		20/10/90	A	6	(8)	1
13	Wolfgang KLAPF		14/12/78	D	8	(7)	
21	Václav KOLOUŠEK	CZE	13/4/76	M	9	(7)	
2	Pavel KOŠTÁL	CZE	17/9/80	D	29		3
3	Thomas KRAL		8/1/90	D	9		
31	Matthias MAAK		12/5/92	M	1	(6)	
15	Michael MADL		21/3/88	D	21	(2)	
24	Ihsan POYRAZ		5/3/88	G	1		
25	Christian RAMSEBNER		26/3/89	D	24	(3)	
1	Manfred RAZENBÖCK		4/7/78	G	2		
23	Mario REITER		23/10/86	M	17	(6)	
9	Mirnel SADOVIĆ	BIH	25/5/84	A	18	(8)	7
18	Edin SALKIC		16/6/89	A	2	(7)	
16	Andreas SCHICKER		6/7/86	D	33	(1)	
27	Jörg SIEBENHANDL		18/1/90	G	1		
8	Tomas SIMKOVIC		16/4/87	M	30		6
6	Michael STANISLAW		5/6/87	M	14	(13)	
26	Christian THONHOFER		26/5/85	D	35		1
11	Christopher TVRDY		20/2/92	M		(1)	
33	Patrick WOLF		4/5/81	M	18		4

TOP GOALSCORERS 2010/11

21	Roland LINZ (Austria Wien)
19	Roman KIENAST (Sturm)
18	Hamdi SALIHI (Rapid)
	Roman WALLNER (Salzburg)
14	Deni ALAR (Kapfenberg)
	Patrick BÜRGER (Mattersburg)
11	Hannes AIGNER (Wiener Neustadt)
10	ALAN (Salzburg)
	Marcel SCHRETER (Wacker)
9	Zlatko JUNUZOVIC (Austria Wien)
	GUILLEM MARTÍ (Ried)
	Samir MURATOVIĆ (Sturm)
	Imre SZABICS (Sturm)

PROMOTED CLUB

FC ADMIRA/WACKER MÖDLING

Coach - Dietmar Kühbauer
Founded - 1905
Stadium - Trenkwalder Arena (12,000)
MAJOR HONOURS: Austrian League – (8) 1927, 1928, 1932, 1934, 1936, 1937, 1939, 1966; Austrian Cup – (5) 1928, 1932, 1934, 1964, 1966

SECOND LEVEL FINAL TABLE 2010/11

		Pld	W	D	L	F	A	Pts
1	FC Admira/Wacker Mödling	36	23	6	7	85	45	75
2	SCR Altach	36	22	8	6	76	37	74
3	SC Austria Lustenau	36	16	6	14	55	51	54
4	Wolfsberger AC/St Andrä	36	15	7	14	56	50	52
5	SKN St Pölten	36	13	12	11	55	55	51
6	SV Grödig	36	12	10	14	51	60	46
7	FC Lustenau 07	36	11	9	16	51	60	42
8	TSV Hartberg	36	10	9	17	44	60	39
9	First Vienna FC	36	9	7	20	47	67	34
10	FC Gratkorn	36	9	6	21	47	82	33

DOMESTIC CUP 2010/11

ÖFB-CUP

FIRST ROUND

(12/8/10)
Mattersburg Amateure 0, Austria Wien Amateure 1

(13/8/10)
Amstetten 2, Admira/Wacker Mödling 1
Bregenz 1, Lustenau 07 2
Floridsdorfer AC Team für Wien 1, Kapfenberg 2
Horn 1, Sturm 2
Kufstein 4, Anif 4 *(aet; 5-4 on pens)*
Parndorf 4, Feldkirchen 0
Seekirchen 3, Post SV 2
Sierning 1, Hartberg 3
Sollenau 4, Favoritner AC 2
St Pölten Amateure 1, Salzburg 4
Wacker Innsbruck Amateure 3, Grödig 5
Wattens 1, Vienna 2

(14/8/10)
Austria Klagenfurt/St Stefan 1, LASK 2
Austria Salzburg 0, Austria Lustenau 3
Austria/Kapfenberg Amateure 3, LASK Juniors 1
Dornbirn 1, Wiener Neustadt 0
Gaflenz 2, Illmitz 1
Gleinstätten 5, Villacher SV 3
Höchst 1, Salzburg Juniors 1 *(aet; 4-3 on pens)*
Neuhofen/Ried Amateure 0, Austria Wien 3
Paldau 1, Waidhofen/Ybbs 4
Rapid Wien Amateure 2, Rapid Wien 5
Reichenau 0, Altach 8
Retz 2, Gratkorn 2 *(aet; 2-4 on pens)*
SAK Klagenfurt 2, Wolfsberger AC/St Andrä 2 *(aet; 2-4 on pens)*
Vöcklamarkt 0, Wacker Innsbruck 3
Voitsberg 7, Wallern 1
Vorwärts Steyr 1, St Pölten 0

(15/8/10)
Sturm Amateure 0, Ried 5

(17/8/10)
Allerheiligen 2, Blau-Weiss Linz 3
Stegersbach 1, Mattersburg 5

SECOND ROUND

(16/9/10)
Amstetten 0, Altach 2

(17/9/10)
Dornbirn 1, Mattersburg 2
Kapfenberg 3, Gratkorn 1
Kufstein 0, Grödig 3
Seekirchen 2, Hartberg 6
Sollenau 2, LASK 4
Vorwärts Steyr 3, Wolfsberger AC/St Andrä 2
Waidhofen/Ybbs 0, Ried 4

(18/9/10)
Austria/Kapfenberg Amateure 0, Austria Wien 3
Gaflenz 1, Wacker Innsbruck 5
Höchst 0, Austria Lustenau 3
Parndorf 1, Sturm 2
Voitsberg 0, Vienna 1

(19/9/10)
Austria Wien Amateure 1, Rapid Wien 1 *(aet; 3-4 on pens)*
Blau-Weiss Linz 3, Salzburg 1

(20/9/10)
Gleinstätten 2, Lustenau 07 4

THIRD ROUND

(9/11/10)
Austria Lustenau 0, Grödig 0 *(aet; 5-4 on pens)*
Kapfenberg 2, Lustenau 07 0 *(aet)*
LASK 0, Ried 1
Vienna 2, Altach 1 *(aet)*

(10/11/10)
Austria Wien 2, Wacker Innsbruck 1 *(aet)*
Blau-Weiss Linz 0, Mattersburg 1
Rapid Wien 3, Hartberg 0
Vorwärts Steyr 0, Sturm 1 *(aet)*

QUARTER-FINALS

(19/4/11)
Austria Wien 0, Austria Lustenau 4 *(Roth 21, 36, Pöllhuber 49, Karatay 65)*
Vienna 0, Kapfenberg 2 *(Pavlov 68, Wendler 90)*

(20/4/11)
Rapid Wien 2 *(Vennegoor of Hesselink 10, Katzer 69)*, Mattersburg 0
Ried 2 *(Royer 17, Hadžić 90+4)*, Sturm 1 *(Prettenthaler 90+5og)*

SEMI-FINALS

(3/5/11)
Kapfenberg 1 *(Schönberger 38)*, Austria Lustenau 2 *(Roth 15, Boller 35)*

(4/5/11)
Ried 2 *(Hammerer 72, Lexa 83)*, Rapid Wien 1 *(Salihi 36)*

FINAL

(29/5/11)
Ernst-Happel-Stadion, Vienna
SV RIED 2 *(Hammerer 41, 67)*
SC AUSTRIA LUSTENAU 0
Referee – *Krassnitzer*
RIED – *Gebauer, Stocklasa, Glasner, Riegler (Prettenthaler 63), Brenner, Mader, Schrammel, Lexa, Iván Carril (Hadžić 81), Royer, Hammerer (Nacho 86).*
AUSTRIA LUSTENAU – *Kofler, Zech, Stückler, Kampel, Danilo Soares, Dürr, Leitgeb (Rotter 70), Micic, Roth, Boller (Honeck 88), Karatay (Krajic 71).*

CLUB COMMUNICATION 2011/12

FC Admira/Wacker Mödling

Johann Steinböckstrasse 5b
AT-Maria Enzersdorf

Tel	+43 2236 48710
Fax	+43 2236 48710 35
Web	trenkwalder-admira.com
Email	office@ trenkwalder-admira.com
Media Officer	Christoph Lichtnegger

FK Austria Wien

Fischhofgasse 12
AT-Wien

Tel	+43 1 6880150
Fax	+43 1 6880150 390
Web	fk-austria.at
Email	fak@fk-austria.at
Media Officer	Christoph Pflug

Kapfenberger SV

J.-Brandl-Gasse 25
AT-Kapfenberg

Tel	+43 (0) 3862 220 70
Fax	+43 (0) 3862 281 75
Web	ksv-fussball.at
Email	info@ksv-fussball.at
Media Officer	Markus Kubesch

SV Mattersburg

Michael Koch Str 50
AT-Mattersburg

Tel	+43 2626 625 10
Fax	+43 2626 627 21
Web	svm.at
Email	office@svm.at
Media Officer	Martin Pucher

SK Rapid Wien

Keisslergasse 3
AT-Wien

Tel	+43 1 727 43 0
Fax	+43 1 727 43 25
Web	skrapid.at
Email	info@skrapid.com
Media Officer	Sharif Shoukry

SV Ried

Volksfestplatz 2
AT-Ried im Innkreis

Tel	+43 7752 811 00
Fax	+43 7752 811 00 33
Web	svried.at
Email	office@svried.at
Media Officer	Christian Huber

FC Salzburg

Stadionstrasse 2/3
AT-Wals-Siezenheim

Tel	+43 662 433 332 0
Fax	+43 662 433 332 44 81
Web	redbulls.com
Email	soccerrbs.office@ redbulls.com
Media Officer	Thomas Blazek

SK Sturm Graz

Sternäckerweg 118
AT-Graz

Tel	+43 316 771 771 0
Fax	+43 316 771 771 77
Web	sksturm.at
Email	office@sksturm.at
Media Officer	Markus Hatzl

FC Wacker Innsbruck

Stadionstrasse 1b
AT-Innsbruck

Tel	+43 512 5888770
Fax	+43 512 588877 30
Web	fc-wacker-innsbruck.at
Email	office@wackerinnsbruck.at
Media Officer	Florian Sitz

SC Wiener Neustadt

Giltschwertgasse 81
AT-Wiener Neustadt

Tel	+43 2622 29 880
Fax	+43 2622 29 880 33
Web	scwn.at
Email	office@scwn.at
Media Officer	Christoph Ungerböck

AZERBAIJAN

Azerbaïdjan I Aserbeidschan

Azärbaycan Futbol Federasiyaları Assosiasiyası (AFFA)

AFFA

COMMUNICATION

Address	Nobel Prospekti 2208 AZ-1025 Bakı	**President**	Rövnaq Abdullayev
Tel	+994 12 490 8721	**General Secretary**	Elkhan Mämmädov
Fax	+994 12 490 8722	**Media Officer**	Mikayıl Quliyev
E-mail	info@affa.az	**Year of Formation**	1992
Website	affa.az	**National Stadium**	Tofiq Bähramov adına Respublika, Baku (29,850)

DOMESTIC COMPETITION SUMMARY 2010/11

PREMYER LİQA FINAL TABLE

SECOND PHASE

Championship Pool		Pld	Home W	D	L	F	A	Away W	D	L	F	A	Total W	D	L	F	A	Pts	Comp
1	Neftçi PFK	32	9	6	1	24	8	10	4	2	29	9	19	10	3	53	17	67	UCL
2	Xäzär Länkäran FK	32	10	5	1	23	7	6	7	3	15	11	16	12	4	38	18	60	UEL
3	Qarabağ FK	32	11	3	2	29	7	6	4	6	12	15	17	7	8	41	22	58	UEL
4	Olimpik-Şüvälan PFK	32	10	4	2	23	8	3	6	7	13	20	13	10	9	36	28	49	UEL
5	İnter Bakı PİK	32	7	6	3	15	11	6	4	6	14	13	13	10	9	29	24	49	
6	Bakı FK	32	5	5	6	17	17	5	5	6	16	15	10	10	12	33	32	40	

Relegation Pool		Pld	Home W	D	L	F	A	Away W	D	L	F	A	Total W	D	L	F	A	Pts	Comp
7	Qäbälä FK	32	8	5	3	17	7	5	7	4	14	11	13	12	7	31	18	51	
8	Muğan Salyan PFK	32	10	4	2	18	9	3	4	9	11	22	13	8	11	29	31	47	
9	Gäncä PFK	32	6	6	4	16	14	2	6	8	17	23	8	12	12	33	37	36	
10	Turan PFK	32	5	3	8	14	19	2	3	11	10	28	7	6	19	24	47	27	
11	Simurq Zaqatala PFK	32	1	5	10	10	24	3	2	11	10	28	4	7	21	20	52	19	
12	MOİK Bakı PFK	32	3	3	10	10	34	1	3	12	4	21	4	6	22	14	55	18	*Relegated*

NB League split into two halves after 22 matches, with each club playing ten further matches exclusively against clubs from its half of the table. Muğan Salyan PFK withdrew from 2011/12 Premyer Liqa, enabling Simurq Zaqatala PFK to avoid relegation.

Top Scorer Giorgi Adamia (Qarabağ), 18 goals

Promoted Clubs Rävan Bakı FK
Sumqayıt Şähär PFK

Cup Final Xäzär Länkäran FK 1, İnter Bakı PİK 1 (aet; 4-2 on pens)

Foreign aid benefits Neftçi

Azerbaijan's most decorated club, Neftçi PFK, became national champions again in 2010/11 after a six-year wait. Led by rookie coach Arif Äsädov, a former defender and FIFA U-17 World Cup winner with the Soviet Union, Neftçi were largely indebted to the contributions of their imported stars such as ex-Belgium striker Émile Mpenza, Macedonian defender Igor Mitreski, top-scoring Uzbekistani striker Bakhodir Nasimov and Brazilian trio Flavinho, Dênis and – following his mid-season move from Santos FC – Rodriguinho.

Neftçi were undoubtedly the strongest team in the Premyer Liqa, picking up points consistently both at home in Baku and on their travels. They led the title race virtually from start to finish and the only time they went more than two games without a win was at the very end of the campaign after the title was safely in their possession. Just one point ahead at the 22-match split, they left their rivals standing with a powerful surge in the second phase, and the club's sixth championship was duly secured in a 3-1 victory at Olimpik-Şüvälan PFK on May Day.

Cup success

The only blot on Neftçi's record was their inability to beat runners-up Xäzär Länkaran FK, losing one and drawing three of their four league encounters. Furthermore, they failed to win either of the two legs in their domestic cup quarter-final against the same opponents, who took the tie 5-4 on aggregate, then defeated holders Bakı FK on the away-goals rule in the semis, before claiming the trophy for the third time in five years with a penalty shoot-out win in the final against 2009/10 champions İnter Bakı PİK.

Xäzär Länkaran were coached by former Romanian international defender Mircea Rednic, and there was another famous international figure in charge at Qäbälä FK – namely, ex-Arsenal FC and England captain Tony Adams. It was a homegrown coach, however, who, for the second season running, did most to put Azerbaijani club football on the European map, the country's all-time top goalscorer Qurban Qurbanov leading Qarabağ FK through three qualifying rounds of the UEFA Europa League, the last of them at the expense of Polish heavyweights Wisła Kraków, before they fell to future German champions Borussia Dortmund.

Qurban Qurbanov – the coach of impressive European campaigners Qarabağ

Star skipper

Qurbanov has already been touted as a future coach of the Azerbaijan national side – a role performed in the UEFA EURO 2012 qualifying campaign by German veteran Berti Vogts, whose team lost five of their opening six matches. As four of those defeats were away and the other at home to Germany, arguably the only surprise of Azerbaijan's campaign was their 1-0 win in Baku over Turkey – a victory secured by a goal from captain Räşad F. Sadıgov, who was then playing his club football in Turkey with Eskişehirspor. One of only two foreign-based players used by Vogts in the campaign, Sadıqov was subsequently voted as Azerbaijan's 2010 Footballer of the Year – before returning home in the winter break to rejoin former club Qarabağ.

National Team

Top Five All-time Caps – Aslan Kärimov (79); Tärlan Ähmädov (73); Mahmud Qurbanov (72); Qurban Qurbanov & Räşad F. Sadıqov (68)

Top Five All-time Goals – Qurban Qurbanov (12); Elvin Mämmädov (7), Vaqif Cavadov, Branimir Subašić & Zaur Tağızadä (6)

AZERBAIJAN

AFFA

NATIONAL TEAM RESULTS 2010/11

11/8/10	Kuwait	H	Baku	1-1	*Mämmädov (42)*
7/9/10	Germany (ECQ)	A	Cologne	1-6	*Cavadov (57)*
8/10/10	Austria (ECQ)	A	Vienna	0-3	
12/10/10	Turkey (ECQ)	H	Baku	1-0	*Sadıqov R.F. (38)*
17/11/10	Montenegro	A	Podgorica	0-2	
9/2/11	Hungary	N	Dubai (UAE)	0-2	
29/3/11	Belgium (ECQ)	A	Brussels	1-4	*Abışov (16)*
3/6/11	Kazakhstan (ECQ)	A	Astana	1-2	*Nadirov (63)*
7/6/11	Germany (ECQ)	H	Baku	1-3	*Hüseynov M. (89)*

NATIONAL TEAM APPEARANCES 2010/11

Coach – Berti VOGTS (GER)	**30/12/46**		**Kuw**	**GER**	**AUT**	**TUR**	**Mne**	**Hun**	**BEL**	**KAZ**	**GER**	**Caps**	**Goals**
Kamran AĞAYEV	9/2/86	Xäzär Länkäran	G	G	G	G	G	G	G	G	G	24	-
Ruslan ÄMİRCANOV	1/2/85	Neftçi	D86									3	-
Volodimir LEVIN	23/1/84	İnter Bakı	D				D74		D	D		17	-
Räşad F. SADIQOV	16/6/82	Qarabağ /Eskişehirspor (TUR)	D46	D	D	D		D	D	D	D	68	4
Maksim MEDVEDEV	29/9/89	Qarabağ	D46	D						D		11	-
Elnur ALLAHVERDİYEV	2/11/83	Xäzär Länkäran	M	M	D	D	D	D			D	18	-
Mahir ŞÜKÜROV	12/12/82	Anzhi (RUS)	M	M	M	M	D	M	D			51	-
Räşad Ä. SADİQOV	8/10/83	Qarabağ	M66	s64	s74					M	s86	15	-
Elvin MÄMMÄDOV	18/7/88	Qarabağ	M78		M59		M46		M78			25	7
Vaqif CAVADOV	25/5/89	Twente (NED) /Bakı	M	A	M74	A85	s66	M	A76	M	A71	37	6
Färid QULİYEV	6/1/86	Neftçi	A46			M71	s46					7	1
Ruslan ABIŞOV	10/10/87	Neftçi	s46			M	M	M	M	M	M	16	2
Rauf ÄLİYEV	12/2/89	Qarabağ	s46		A	s71	A66	s46	M	A79		12	-
Rail MÄLİKOV	18/12/85	Neftçi	s46	D	D	D45		D83	D	D	D	38	-
Samir ABASOV	1/2/78	Qarabağ	s66	M	M							46	-
Rahid ÄMİRQULİYEV	1/9/89	Xäzär Länkäran	s78		M	M	M84	M	M		M	13	-
Cavid HÜSEYNOV	9/3/88	Neftçi	s86				s66	s83	s78	M61		24	-
Saşa YUNİSOĞLU	18/12/85	Qäbälä		D56	D	D	D					27	-
Aleksandr CHERTOGANOV	8/2/80	İnter Bakı		M64		s45	M66	M70	M		M86	41	-
Vüqar NADİROV	15/6/87	Qarabağ		M85	s59	M	M		s76	s61	M	37	2
Vurğun HÜSEYNOV	25/4/88	Turan		s56		s85	s74	D			D	7	-
Araz ABDULLAYEV	18/4/92	Neftçi		s85								3	-
Amit QULUZADÄ	20/11/92	Neftçi					s84					3	-
Murad HÜSEYNOV	25/1/89	Qäbälä						A46		s79	s71	3	1
Arif İSAYEV	28/7/85	Qäbälä						s70			s57	2	-
Äfran İSMAYILOV	8/10/88	Qarabağ								M	M57	3	1

CLUB-BY-CLUB

BAKI FK

Coach – Winfried Schäfer (GER); (15/1/11) Aleksandrs Starkovs (LVA)

Founded – 1997

Stadium – Tofiq Bähramov adına Respublika stadionu (29,850)

MAJOR HONOURS: Azerbaijan League – (2) 2006, 2009; Azerbaijan Cup – (2) 2005, 2010.

2010				
7/8	Olimpik-Şüvälan	h	2-3	*Jabá 2*
15/8	Muğan	a	0-1	
22/8	Qäbälä	h	2-1	*Fábio, Jabá (p)*
12/9	Gäncä	h	1-1	*Nibombé*
19/9	Simurq	a	1-1	*Sofroni*
27/9	Turan	h	3-1	*Borbiconi, Cavadov, Skulić*
2/10	Xäzär Länkäran	a	1-1	*Cavadov*
16/10	MOİK	h	2-1	*Juninho, Cavadov*
20/10	Qarabağ	a	0-2	
24/10	İnter	a	0-1	
31/10	Neftçi	h	0-2	
6/11	Gäncä	a	3-1	*Barakat, Leo Rocha 2*
13/11	Qarabağ	h	2-0	*Borbiconi, Leo Rocha*
20/11	MOİK	a	4-0	*Skulić 2, Epalle, Kajkut*
27/11	Xäzär Länkäran	h	1-1	*Cäfärquliyev*
5/12	Simurq	h	0-1	
11/12	Neftçi	a	2-0	*og (Dênis), Jabá*
18/12	İnter	h	1-2	*Borbiconi*
23/12	Qäbälä	a	1-0	*Jabá*
2011				
12/2	Muğan	h	1-1	*Quliyev*

9/2	Turan	a	1-0	*Jabá*
5/2	Olimpik-Şüvälan	a	0-0	
3/3	Neftçi	h	0-1	
8/3	İnter	a	1-1	*Jabá*
/4	Xäzär Länkäran	h	0-0	
0/4	Olimpik-Şüvälan	a	0-1	
6/4	Qarabağ	h	0-0	
3/4	Neftçi	a	0-2	
/5	Qarabağ	a	2-2	*og (Häşimov), Cavadov*
/5	Olimpik-Şüvälan	h	2-1	*Šolić, Sofroni*
3/5	Xäzär Länkäran	a	0-2	
8/5	İnter	h	0-1	

No	Name	Nat	DoB	Pos	Aps	(s)	Gls
4	Nicat ABDULLAYEV		22/4/92	A		(2)	
5	Jefferson ANGULO Murillo	COL	26/12/86	M	2	(5)	
	Rafael ÄMİRBÄYOV		23/2/76	D	2	(1)	
1	Adnan BARAKAT	NED	3/9/82	D	16	(5)	1
3	Stevan BATES	SRB	29/11/81	D	12		
	Stéphane BORBICONI	FRA	22/3/79	D	20		3
	Vadim BORET	MDA	5/9/76	D	12	(1)	
21	Emin CÄFÄRQULİYEV		17/6/90	D	3	(1)	1
	Vaqif CAVADOV		25/5/89	A	19	(4)	4
0	Joël Dieudonné Martin EPALLE Newaka	CMR	20/2/78	M	5	(5)	1
20	FÁBIO Luis Ramin		10/4/81	M	18	(6)	1
17	Rähman HACIYEV		25/7/93	M		(1)	
22	Säbuhi HÄSÄNOV		8/7/87	D	1		
35	Silvino João de Carvalho "JABÁ"	BRA	20/5/81	A	25		7
55	Osvaldo José Martins Júnior "JUNINHO"	BRA	7/7/82	M	10	(4)	1
2	Saša KAJKUT	BIH	7/7/84	A	2	(7)	1
30	Ibrahim KARGBO	SLE	10/4/82	M	21	(4)	
99	LEOnardo da Silva ROCHA	BRA	7/3/85	M	9	(6)	3
39	Ruslan LEVIHA	UKR	31/1/83	A	8	(5)	
15	Cämşid MÄHÄRRÄMOV		3/10/83	D	30		
13	Aqil MÄMMÄDOV		1/5/89	G	2		
6	Daré NIBOMBÉ	TOG	16/6/80	D	10	(1)	1
29	Äziz QULİYEV		2/5/87	M	17	(3)	1
7	Mahmud QURBANOV		10/5/73	M	5	(9)	
32	Alexei SAVINOV	MDA	19/4/79	D	14	(2)	
23	Khalidou SISSOKHO	SEN	28/8/78	G	4		
8	Ernad SKULIĆ	CRO	2/5/80	M	15	(1)	3
12	Veaceslav SOFRONI	MDA	30/4/84	A	7	(7)	2
27	Bäxtiyar SOLTANOV		21/6/89	A	6	(7)	
1	Marko ŠARLIJA	CRO	31/1/82	G	26		
77	Aleksandar ŠOLIĆ	BIH	29/1/81	M	24	(3)	1
18	Radomir TODOROV	BUL	11/8/80	D	7		

GÄNCÄ PFK

Coach – Fuad İsmayılov; (19/3/11) Mehman Allahverdiyev

Founded – 1959

Stadium – Gäncä şähär stadionu (25,000)

MAJOR HONOURS: Azerbaijan League – (3) 1995, 1998, 1999; Azerbaijan Cup – (4) 1994, 1997, 1998, 2000.

2010				
7/8	Simurq	h	1-1	*Allahquliyev*
21/8	Olimpik-Şüvälan	h	1-1	*Junivan*
28/8	Muğan	a	1-1	*Zärgärov*
12/9	Bakı	a	1-1	*Junivan*
18/9	Turan	h	1-1	*Hüseynov İ.*
22/9	Qarabağ	a	0-3	
26/9	İnter	h	1-0	*Zärgärov*
2/10	MOİK	a	5-0	*Junivan 2, Zärgärov, Sultanov C. (p), Feutchine*
17/10	Xäzär Länkäran	h	4-1	*Junivan, Zärgärov, Allahquliyev 2*
23/10	Neftçi	a	2-6	*Allahquliyev, Junivan*
31/10	Qäbälä	h	0-0	
6/11	Bakı	h	1-3	*Sultanov C. (p)*
12/11	Turan	a	1-2	*Junivan*
20/11	Simurq	a	0-0	
27/11	MOİK	h	1-0	*Junivan*
5/12	Muğan	h	3-0	*Allahquliyev, Kärimov Ş., Junivan*
11/12	Xäzär Länkäran	a	0-1	
18/12	Neftçi	h	0-4	
23/12	İnter	a	0-1	
2011				
12/2	Olimpik-Şüvälan	a	0-0	
20/2	Qarabağ	h	0-1	
27/2	Qäbälä	a	0-0	
13/3	Turan	a	0-1	
18/3	Simurq	h	0-1	
2/4	Qäbälä	a	1-1	*Junivan*
10/4	Muğan	h	1-1	*Allahquliyev*
17/4	MOİK	a	2-0	*Feutchine, Allahquliyev*
24/4	Turan	h	1-0	*Allahquliyev*
30/4	MOİK	h	1-0	*Allahquliyev*
8/5	Muğan	a	1-2	*og (Hodžić)*
12/5	Qäbälä	h	0-0	
19/5	Simurq	a	3-4	*Abdulov, Seyidov, Äzizov*

No	Name	Nat	DoB	Pos	Aps	(s)	Gls
27	Ramazan ABBASOV		22/9/83	M	3	(1)	
21	Samir ABDULOV		8/5/87	M	1	(6)	1
11	Sabir ALLAHQULİYEV		12/5/88	A	21	(7)	9
14	Rafael ÄMİRBÄYOV		23/2/76	D	7	(1)	
23	Elxan ÄZİZOV		30/9/89	M	1		1
13	Zurab DZAMASHVILI	GEO	13/10/81	M	24	(1)	
8	Guy Armand FEUTCHINE	CMR	18/11/76	A	24	(4)	2
25	Kristaps GREBIS	LVA	13/12/80	A	4	(1)	
3	Vasif HAQVERDİYEV		15/10/78	D	6	(2)	
27	Täbriz HÜSEYNLİ		24/10/91	A	1		
16	Habil HÜSEYNOV		12/5/89	G	1		
18	İbrahim HÜSEYNOV		16/8/77	M		(6)	1
8	Mähärräm HÜSEYNOV		5/7/92	D	1		
7	Ramal HÜSEYNOV		16/12/84	M	23	(1)	
20	Vüsal HÜSEYNOV		9/8/82	M	6	(4)	
10	Vüsal İBRAHİMOV		23/8/91	M	1		
23	JUNIVAN Soares de Melo	BRA	20/11/77	A	26	(3)	10
10	Känan KÄRİMOV		5/8/76	A	1		
15	Şahin KÄRİMOV		12/1/85	D	28	(2)	1
20	Volodymy KOZLENKO	UKR	22/3/79	D	2	(3)	
1	Edis KURTANOVIĆ	BIH	25/11/81	G	26		
22	Ruslan MÄCİDOV		22/8/85	G	3		
4	Azär MÄMMÄDOV		7/2/76	D	30		
5	Mätläb MÄMMÄDOV		14/8/81	D	15	(5)	
3	Nicat MÄMMÄDOV		1/5/89	D	1		
17	Orxan MÄMMÄDOV		21/7/87	D		(1)	
24	Levan MDIVNISHVILI	GEO	3/10/82	M	1	(5)	
2	Xäyal MUSTAFAYEV		27/12/80	D	22	(1)	
28	Patrice NOUKEU	CMR	22/11/82	M	2	(6)	
14	Asäf QÄDİRİ		7/8/84	M	2	(2)	
8	Giorgi SETURIDZE	GEO	1/4/85	M	6	(12)	
6	Elçin SEYİDOV		31/8/88	M	1		1
9	Ceyhun SULTANOV		12/6/79	M	27		2
17	Renat SULTANOV		23/3/83	D	5		
6	Samir ZÄRGÄROV		29/8/86	M	21	(4)	4
24	Vladimir ZELENBABA	SRB	6/2/82	D	7	(3)	
16	Xäyal ZEYNALOV		13/5/82	G	2		

İNTER BAKI PİK

Coach – Kakhaber Tskhadadze (GEO)

Founded – 2004

Stadium – Şäfa (7,852)

MAJOR HONOURS: Azerbaijan League – (2) 2008, 2010.

2010				
8/8	Turan	a	3-0	*Poškus, Souza, Kruglov*
15/8	MOİK	h	1-0	*Souza (p)*
21/8	Xäzär Länkäran	a	0-0	
28/8	Neftçi	h	0-2	
11/9	Qarabağ	h	1-0	*Chertoganov*
19/9	Qäbälä	a	1-0	*Ämiraslanov*
26/9	Gäncä	a	0-1	
1/10	Muğan	h	1-0	*Karlsons (p)*
16/10	Olimpik-Şüvälan	a	0-5	
24/10	Bakı	h	1-0	*Accioly*
31/10	Simurq	a	1-0	*Despotovski*

6/11	Neftçi	a	1-1	*Zlatinov*
13/11	Qäbälä	h	0-0	
20/11	Turan	h	3-0	*Odikadze, Souza, Poškus*
28/11	Muğan	a	0-1	
4/12	Qarabağ	a	0-1	
11/12	Olimpik-Şüvälan	h	1-1	*Zlatinov*
18/12	Bakı	a	2-1	*og (Borbiconi), Červenka*
23/12	Gäncä	h	1-0	*Poškus*
2011				
13/2	Simurq	h	2-0	*Ämiraslanov, Accioly*
19/2	MOİK	a	4-0	*Kruglov, Odikadze, Kandelaki, Levin*
27/2	Xäzär Länkäran	h	1-3	*Karlsons (p)*
12/3	Qarabağ	h	0-2	
18/3	Bakı	h	1-1	*Poškus*
3/4	Olimpik-Şüvälan	a	0-1	
9/4	Neftçi	h	1-1	*Poškus*
16/4	Xäzär Länkäran	a	1-1	*Odikadze*
24/4	Qarabağ	a	0-1	
30/4	Xäzär Länkäran	h	1-1	*Mämmädov A.*
8/5	Neftçi	a	0-0	
13/5	Olimpik-Şüvälan	h	0-0	
18/5	Bakı	a	1-0	*Ämiraslanov*

No	Name	Nat	DoB	Pos	Aps	(s)	Gls
16	Elnur ABDULOV		18/9/92	A		(1)	
44	Valeri ABRAMIDZE	GEO	17/1/80	D	21		
4	Danildo José ACCIOLY Filho	BRA	30/3/81	D	22	(2)	2
9	Rövşän ÄMİRASLANOV		18/3/86	M	14	(5)	3
8	Aleksandr CHERTOGANOV		8/2/80	M	29	(1)	1
13	Branislav ČERVENKA	CZE	27/9/75	M	25	(4)	1
21	Arif DAŞDÄMİROV		10/2/87	D	25	(5)	
12	Filip DESPOTOVSKI	MKD	18/11/82	D	11	(1)	1
84	FILIPE José MACHADO	BRA	13/3/84	M	4	(3)	
77	Daniel GENOV	BUL	19/5/89	M		(6)	
7	Nizami HACIYEV		18/2/88	M		(1)	
18	Ilia KANDELAKI	GEO	26/12/81	D	23	(1)	1
20	Ģirts KARLSONS	LVA	7/6/81	A	15	(14)	2
72	Dmitri KRAMARENKO		12/9/74	G	10		
6	Dmitri KRUGLOV	EST	24/5/84	D	24	(8)	2
15	Volodimir LEVIN		23/1/84	D	21	(2)	1
1	Giorgi LOMAIA	GEO	8/8/79	G	22		
11	Asif MÄMMÄDOV		5/8/86	M	4	(5)	1
10	Camal MÄMMÄDOV		26/12/83	M		(1)	
88	Kakhaber MZHAVANADZE	GEO	2/10/78	D	8	(7)	
19	David ODIKADZE	GEO	14/4/81	M	26	(2)	3
32	Robertas POŠKUS	LTU	5/5/79	A	17	(9)	5
23	Şähriyar RÄHİMOV		6/4/88	M	4	(7)	
35	Mário Sérgio Aumarante Santana SOUZA	BRA	30/12/77	M	7	(3)	3
28	Bachana TSKHADADZE	GEO	23/10/87	A		(1)	
5	Zhivko ZHELEV	BUL	23/7/79	D	1		
14	Petar ZLATINOV	BUL	13/3/81	M	19	(5)	2

MOİK BAKI PFK

Coach – Ramil Äliyev

Founded – 1960

Stadium – Tofiq İsmayılov adına Suraxanı qäsäbä stadionu (2,800); Tofiq Bähramov adına Respublika stadionu (29,850); Şäfa (7,852); İsmät Qayıbov adına Bakıxanov qäsäbä stadionu (2,000); Bakı FK training center (500)

2010				
8/8	Muğan	h	3-2	*Qurbanov, Qasımov 2*
15/8	İnter	a	0-1	
22/8	Qarabağ	h	0-1	
29/8	Qäbälä	a	0-0	
12/9	Xäzär Länkäran	a	0-3	
18/9	Neftçi	h	0-4	
26/9	Olimpik-Şüvälan	a	0-2	
2/10	Gäncä	h	0-5	
16/10	Bakı	a	1-2	*og (Nibombé)*
24/10	Simurq	h	0-2	
30/10	Turan	a	0-2	
5/11	Qarabağ	a	0-3	
12/11	Olimpik-Şüvälan	h	1-1	*Qurbanov (p)*
20/11	Bakı	h	0-4	
27/11	Gäncä	a	0-1	
4/12	Qäbälä	h	0-3	
11/12	Muğan	a	0-1	
18/12	Xäzär Länkäran	h	0-2	
23/12	Simurq	a	1-1	*Babayev O.*
2011				
12/2	Turan	h	0-2	
19/2	İnter	h	0-4	
25/2	Neftçi	a	0-1	
13/3	Qäbälä	h	1-1	*Cäfärquliyev*
18/3	Turan	a	0-1	
2/4	Muğan	h	0-0	
9/4	Simurq	a	2-1	*Häşimov A., İsgändärov*
17/4	Gäncä	h	0-2	
24/4	Qäbälä	a	0-0	
30/4	Gäncä	a	0-1	
7/5	Simurq	h	1-0	*Usubov*
12/5	Muğan	a	0-1	
19/5	Turan	h	4-1	*Babayev O. 2, Baxşäliyev, Äkbärov*

No	Name	Nat	DoB	Pos	Aps	(s)	Gls
7	Namiq ADİLOV		15/5/82	M	1	(5)	
5	Ceyhun ADIŞİRİNOV		30/6/86	D	4	(3)	
25	Cavidan AĞAYEV		2/3/90	M	7	(1)	
12	Sälahät AĞAYEV		4/11/91	G	8		
25	Natiq ÄKBÄROV		24/5/85	D	18	(2)	1
24	Ramil ÄLİYEV		5/2/86	D	24	(1)	
4	Vüqar ÄSGÄROV		26/6/86	M	20	(5)	
16	Näriman ÄZİMOV		29/9/86	A	1	(5)	
10	Orxan BABAYEV		3/11/87	M	6	(9)	3
20	Samir BABAYEV		10/8/87	D	9		
20	Araz BAĞIROV		19/4/84	M	4		
23	Mähämmäd BAĞIRZADÄ		21/10/93	A		(1)	
13	Comärd BAXŞÄLİYEV		23/2/88	D	3	(3)	1
21	Emin CÄFÄRQULİYEV		17/9/90	D	10		1
1	Amiran GVENTSADZE	GEO	10/4/87	G	13		
7	Nizami HACIYEV		8/2/88	M	12		
2	Räşad HACIZADÄ		21/3/92	D	3	(4)	
2	Namiq HÄSÄNOV		28/9/86	D	1	(1)	
17	Azär HÄŞİMOV		6/11/84	M	11	(1)	1
15	Elçin HÄŞİMOV		9/8/85	D	15		
13	Färid HÄŞİMZADÄ		15/4/88	D	14		
26	Ruslan HÜSEYNOV		28/2/84	M	17		
22	Tariyel HÜSEYNOV		16/2/81	G	6		
7	Zeynalabdin HÜSEYNOV		12/8/87	M	1	(1)	
14	Tural İSGÄNDÄROV		9/2/92	A	13		1
11	Säbuhi İSMAYILOV		27/2/88	A	2	(4)	
12	Davud KÄRİMİ		8/10/84	G	5	(1)	
11	Zaur MÄMMÄDOV		29/3/84	M	4	(9)	
6	Emin MUSTAFAYEV		2/1/90	M	26	(3)	
23	Tural NÄRİMANOV		27/10/89	D	9		
11	Rüstäm NOVRUZOV		19/7/89	M		(1)	
8	Emil PAŞAYEV		22/11/83	M	13		
11	Elvin QÄHRÄMANLI		24/7/92	M		(1)	
10	Anar QASIMOV		16/8/88	M	13		2
18	Rafael QÄVAMİ		16/6/89	M	8	(5)	
19	Nuran QURBANOV		10/8/93	A	16	(1)	2
14	Cavid RÄHİMOV		1/1/88	A	6	(6)	
20	Azär SÄFÄRLİ		5/11/88	M		(1)	
3	Şamil SÄLİMXANOV		22/6/91	D		(2)	
15	Murad SÄTTARLI		9/5/92	A	1	(1)	
9	Nicat TAĞIYEV		15/1/86	A	10	(10)	
13	Ramin TANRIVERDİYEV		25/6/86	D	7	(1)	
8	Ruhid USUBOV		20/1/86	M	9	(3)	1
16	Elçin XÄLİLOV		31/1/87	M	2	(1)	

MUĞAN SALYAN PFK

Coach – Almir Hurtić (BIH); (15/11/10) Bähmän Häsänov

Founded – 2007

Stadium – Salyan Olimpiya İdman Kompleksi (2,000); Şäfa (7,852)

2010				
8/8	MOİK	a	2-3	*Hodžić, Pisla*
15/8	Bakı	h	1-0	*Gutiérrez*

22/8	Turan	a	1-1	*Axundov T.*
28/8	Gäncä	h	1-1	*Igor Souza*
14/9	Neftçi	a	0-1	
18/9	Xäzär Länkäran	h	0-0	
25/9	Simurq	h	1-0	*Gutiérrez*
1/10	İnter	a	0-1	
16/10	Qäbälä	a	0-2	
24/10	Qarabağ	h	0-0	
30/10	Olimpik-Şüvälan	a	0-2	
6/11	Turan	h	0-0	
13/11	Neftçi	h	0-3	
21/11	Xäzär Länkäran	a	0-2	
28/11	İnter	h	1-0	*Gutiérrez*
5/12	Gäncä	a	0-3	
11/12	MOİK	h	1-0	*Zečević (p)*
19/12	Qarabağ	a	0-2	
23/12	Olimpik-Şüvälan	h	3-1	*Mämmädov E. 2, Hodžić*
2011				
12/2	Bakı	a	1-1	*Mämmädov E.*
20/2	Qäbälä	h	1-0	*Mämmädov E.*
27/2	Simurq	a	1-0	*Pelu*
12/3	Simurq	a	3-1	*Mirzäyev, Axundov H., Gulordava*
17/3	Qäbälä	h	1-2	*Igor Souza*
2/4	MOİK	a	0-0	
10/4	Gäncä	a	1-1	*Novruzov*
16/4	Turan	h	2-1	*Barlay, Gutiérrez*
23/4	Simurq	h	3-0	*Pelu 2, Igor Souza*
1/5	Turan	a	1-0	*Novruzov*
8/5	Gäncä	h	2-1	*Zečević (p), Gutiérrez*
12/5	MOİK	h	1-0	*Pelu*
19/5	Qäbälä	a	1-2	*Pelu*

No	Name	Nat	DoB	Pos	Aps	(s)	Gls
21	Ceyhun ABDULLAYEV		25/11/91	A		(3)	
7	Elnur ABDULLAYEV		16/2/86	M	18		
1	Amil AĞACANOV		24/7/83	G	17		
19	Zaur ÄSÄDOV		14/2/82	M	8	(11)	
39	Hüseyn AXUNDOV		30/4/88	M	4	(5)	1
8	Tural AXUNDOV		1/8/88	D	27	(1)	1
18	Samuel BARLAY	SLE	15/9/86	M	6		1
4	Elxan CÄBRAYILOV		21/2/89	D	2	(1)	
	Vadim CRICIMARI	MDA	22/8/88	M	1		
16	Sergey ÇERNIŞEV		27/4/90	M	3	(9)	
22	Irfan FEJZIĆ	BIH	1/7/86	G	13		
23	Giorgi GULORDAVA	GEO	6/4/87	M	8	(2)	1
30	Ángel Gustavo GUTIÉRREZ	URU	12/1/80	A	24	(3)	5
25	Näriman HÄSÄNOV	RUS	4/10/90	M		(2)	
14	Färid HAŞİMZADÄ		15/4/88	D	5	(1)	
26	Ekrem HODŽIĆ	BIH	7/8/79	D	27		2
20	Vüsal HÜSEYNOV		9/8/82	M	4	(4)	
77	Claudinei Reis "IGOR" SOUZA	BRA	27/5/79	M	19	(4)	3
16	Färrux İSMAYILOV		30/8/78	A	3	(2)	
12	Davud KÄRİMİ		8/10/84	G	2		
9	Elşän MÄMMÄDOV		4/5/80	A	17	(6)	4
5	Novruz MÄMMÄDOV		20/3/90	D	23	(1)	
34	Cavad MİRZÄYEV		14/1/82	D	12	(2)	1
6	Taqim NOVRUZOV		21/11/88	M	22	(4)	2
10	Saško PANDEV	MKD	1/5/87	A	9	(7)	
7	Pärvin PAŞAYEV		29/8/88	M	4	(2)	
11	John PELU	SWE	2/2/82	A	6	(5)	5
11	Daniel Petru PISLA	MDA	14/6/86	M	11	(2)	1
23	Ilija PRODANOVIĆ	BIH	16/10/79	D	10	(1)	
15	Anar QASIMOV		16/8/88	M	1		
17	Ravi RÄHMANOV		22/7/86	M	2	(10)	
18	David SVANIDZE	GEO	14/10/79	D	12		
24	Nikola VALEV	BUL	24/4/80	A	3	(4)	
3	Miloš ZEČEVIĆ	SRB	17/5/83	D	29		2

NEFTÇİ PFK

Coach – Arif Äsädov

Founded – 1937

Stadium – Tofiq Bähramov adına Respublika stadionu (29,850)

MAJOR HONOURS: Azerbaijan League – (6) 1992, 1996, 1997, 2004, 2005, 2011;
Azerbaijan Cup – (5) 1995, 1996, 1999, 2002, 2004.

2010				
8/8	Qarabağ	h	1-1	*Nasimov*
15/8	Qäbälä	a	2-0	*Abdullayev R., Nasimov*
21/8	Simurq	h	4-0	*Nasimov 3, Abdullayev R.*
28/8	İnter	a	2-0	*Nasimov, Flavinho (p)*
14/9	Muğan	h	1-0	*Nasimov (p)*
18/9	MOİK	a	4-0	*Quliyev F., Nasimov 2, Hüseynov*
25/9	Xäzär Länkäran	a	0-1	
1/10	Olimpik-Şüvälan	h	1-0	*Mpenza*
17/10	Turan	a	2-2	*Flavinho, Nasimov*
23/10	Gäncä	h	6-2	*Dênis, Flavinho, Nasimov, Mpenza, İmamverdiyev, Abdullayev A.*
31/10	Bakı	a	2-0	*Flavinho, Nasimov*
6/11	İnter	h	1-1	*Mpenza*
13/11	Muğan	a	3-0	*Nasimov 2, Abdullayev R.*
21/11	Qäbälä	h	0-0	
28/11	Qarabağ	a	1-0	*Abışov*
4/12	Olimpik-Şüvälan	a	0-0	
11/12	Bakı	h	0-2	
18/12	Gäncä	a	4-0	*Mpenza, Mitreski, Abdullayev R., Nasimov*
23/12	Turan	h	2-0	*Abdullayev R., Mpenza*
2011				
13/2	Xäzär Länkäran	h	0-0	
19/2	Simurq	a	3-0	*Abdullayev R., Abışov, Flavinho*
25/2	MOİK	h	1-0	*Flavinho*
13/3	Bakı	a	1-0	*Flavinho*
18/3	Xäzär Länkäran	a	1-1	*Rodriguinho*
3/4	Qarabağ	h	2-0	*Rodriguinho, Flavinho*
9/4	İnter	a	1-1	*Flavinho (p)*
17/4	Olimpik-Şüvälan	h	2-1	*Abdullayev R., Mpenza*
23/4	Bakı	h	2-0	*Flavinho 2 (1p)*
1/5	Olimpik-Şüvälan	a	3-1	*Hüseynov, og (Krjauklis), Rodriguinho*
8/5	İnter	h	0-0	
13/5	Qarabağ	a	0-3	
18/5	Xäzär Länkäran	h	1-1	*İmamverdiyev*

No	Name	Nat	DoB	Pos	Aps	(s)	Gls
17	Araz ABDULLAYEV		18/4/92	M	9	(9)	1
27	Räşad ABDULLAYEV		1/10/81	M	26		7
15	Ruslan ABIŞOV		10/10/87	D	24	(1)	2
16	ALESSANDRO Viana da Silva	BRA	10/8/82	D	21	(2)	
18	Ruslan ÄMİRCANOV		1/2/85	D	8	(4)	
8	Elmar BAXŞIYEV		3/8/80	M	9		
30	Vladimir BURDULI	GEO	26/10/80	M		(1)	
3	DÊNIS Silva Cruz	BRA	28/12/85	D	27	(2)	1
9	Flávio Alex Valêncio "FLAVINHO"	BRA	27/7/83	M	20		11
6	Slavco GEORGIEVSKI	MKD	30/3/80	M	29		
24	Paulius GRYBAUSKAS	LTU	2/6/84	G	10	(1)	
4	Yacine HIMA	ALG	25/3/84	M	3	(4)	
11	Cavid HÜSEYNOV		9/3/88	M	10	(17)	2
25	Cavid İMAMVERDİYEV		8/1/90	M	9	(14)	2
22	Ruslan KURBANOV		12/9/91	A	1	(5)	
2	Rail MÄLİKOV		18/12/85	D	19	(1)	
1	Rauf MEHDİYEV		17/10/76	G	19	(1)	
5	Igor MITRESKI	MKD	19/2/79	D	29	(1)	1
10	Émile MPENZA	BEL	4/7/78	A	15	(8)	6
14	Bakhodir NASIMOV	UZB	2/5/87	A	28		15
7	Färid QULİYEV		6/1/86	A	3	(7)	1
26	Tärlan QULİYEV		19/4/92	D	5		
28	Amit QULUZADÄ		20/11/92	M	2	(7)	
7	Rodrigo César Castro Cabral "RODRIGUINHO"	BRA	5/2/82	M	7	(1)	3
12	Elçin SADIQOV		14/6/89	G	3	(1)	
19	Mirhüseyn SEYİDOV		10/8/92	M	16	(5)	

OLIMPIK-ŞÜVÄLAN PFK

Coach – Nazim Süleymanov

Founded – 1996

Stadium – Şäfa (7,852); Olimpik-Şüvälan (3,000)

2010				
7/8	Bakı	a	3-2	*Juška 2, Bunjevčević*
14/8	Turan	h	1-0	*Mandić*
21/8	Gäncä	a	1-1	*Nduka*

29/8	Xäzär Länkäran	h	0-1	
12/9	Simurq	h	2-1	*Juška 2 (1p)*
19/9	Qarabağ	a	0-0	
26/9	MOİK	h	2-0	*Qarayev, Juška*
1/10	Neftçi	a	0-1	
16/10	İnter	h	5-0	*Igbekoyi 2, Juška, Kvirtia, Qarayev*
23/10	Qäbälä	a	0-0	
30/10	Muğan	h	2-0	*Juška, Igbekoyi*
6/11	Simurq	a	1-0	*Benouahi*
12/11	MOİK	a	1-1	*Ikedia*
21/11	Qarabağ	h	2-0	*Benouahi 2*
28/11	Turan	a	2-1	*Benouahi 2*
4/12	Neftçi	h	0-0	
11/12	İnter	a	1-1	*Juška*
19/12	Qäbälä	h	2-2	*Juška, Petrov*
23/12	Muğan	a	1-3	*Qarayev*
2011				
12/2	Gäncä	h	0-0	
20/2	Xäzär Länkäran	a	1-2	*Nduka*
25/2	Bakı	h	0-0	
13/3	Xäzär Länkäran	h	1-0	*Krastovchev*
18/3	Qarabağ	a	0-1	
3/4	İnter	h	1-0	*Bliznyuk*
10/4	Bakı	h	1-0	*Bliznyuk*
17/4	Neftçi	a	1-2	*Benouahi*
23/4	Xäzär Länkäran	a	0-3	
1/5	Neftçi	h	1-3	*Juška*
7/5	Bakı	a	1-2	*Nduka*
13/5	İnter	a	0-0	
18/5	Qarabağ	h	3-1	*Limani, Bunjevčević, Krastovchev*

No	Name	Nat	DoB	Pos	Aps	(s)	Gls
4	Namiq ABDULLAZADÄ		27/7/92	D		(1)	
16	Samir ABDULOV		8/5/87	M	2	(6)	
14	Elvin ÄLİYEV		21/8/84	D	27		
19	Hüseyn AXUNDOV		30/4/88	M		(5)	
11	Zouhir BENOUAHI	MAR	8/3/87	D	22	(4)	6
20	Gennadiy BLIZNYUK	BLR	30/7/80	A	6		2
21	Mirko BUNJEVČEVIĆ	SRB	5/2/78	M	29	(2)	2
22	Anar HÄSÄNOV		14/2/83	M		(8)	
12	Cahangir HÄSÄNZADÄ		4/8/79	G	25		
9	Viktor Kayode IGBEKOYI	NGA	1/9/86	M	29		3
23	Pius Nelson IKEDIA	NGA	11/7/80	M	7	(14)	1
15	Gvidas JUŠKA	LTU	17/8/82	A	24	(7)	10
24	Enyo KRASTOVCHEV	BUL	7/2/84	A	5	(6)	2
6	Ritus KRJAUKLIS	LVA	23/4/86	D	7	(3)	
10	Nugzar KVIRTIA	GEO	16/9/84	M	20	(7)	1
6	Abiodun LAWAL	NGA	25/12/89	D	1	(1)	
16	Mensur LIMANI	SRB	12/4/84	M	7	(2)	1
13	Dragan MANDIĆ	SRB	10/12/76	D	20		1
5	Aqil NÄBİYEV		16/6/82	M	28		
3	Usim NDUKA		23/3/85	D	31		3
8	Eleandro PEMA	ALB	9/2/85	A	8	(6)	
2	Robert PETROV	MKD	2/6/78	D	31		1
96	Elşän POLADOV		30/11/79	G	7		
17	Vüsal QARAYEV		8/7/86	M	12	(12)	3
18	Cavid RÄHİMOV		1/1/88	M		(1)	
7	Tärlan XÄLİLOV		27/8/84	M	4	(5)	

QARABAĞ FK

Coach – Qurban Qurbanov

Founded – 1987

Stadiums – Tofiq Bähramov adına Respublika stadionu (29,850); Tofiq İsmayılov adına Suraxanı qäsäbä stadionu (3,000); Quzanlı Olimpiya İdman Kompleksi (3,000)

MAJOR HONOURS: Azerbaijan League – (1) 1993; Azerbaijan Cup – (3) 1993, 2006, 2009.

2010				
8/8	Neftçi	a	1-1	*Sadiqov R.Ä.*
22/8	MOİK	a	1-0	*Adamia*
11/9	İnter	a	0-1	
19/9	Olimpik-Şüvälan	h	0-0	
22/9	Gäncä	h	3-0	*Sadiqov R.Ä., Äliyev, Adamia*
25/9	Qäbälä	a	1-2	*İmamäliyev*
2/10	Turan	a	1-0	*İmamäliyev*
17/10	Simurq	h	3-2	*Adamia, Äliyev, Sadiqov R.Ä.*
20/10	Bakı	h	2-0	*Adamia 2*
24/10	Muğan	a	0-0	
30/10	Xäzär Länkäran	h	0-1	
5/11	MOİK	h	3-0	*Adamia, Äliyev 2*
13/11	Bakı	a	0-2	
21/11	Olimpik-Şüvälan	a	0-2	
28/11	Neftçi	h	0-1	
4/12	İnter	h	1-0	*Äliyev*
11/12	Simurq	a	1-0	*Hacıyev*
19/12	Muğan	h	2-0	*Sadiqov R.Ä., Nadirov*
23/12	Xäzär Länkäran	a	2-1	*Äliyev 2*
2011				
13/2	Qäbälä	h	3-0	*Äliyev, Adamia, İsmayılov*
20/2	Gäncä	a	1-0	*Adamia*
25/2	Turan	h	5-1	*Mämmädov, Adamia 2, Äliyev, Teli*
12/3	İnter	a	2-0	*Äliyev, Adamia*
18/3	Olimpik-Şüvälan	h	1-0	*Adamia (p)*
3/4	Neftçi	a	0-2	
10/4	Xäzär Länkäran	h	0-0	
16/4	Bakı	a	0-0	
24/4	İnter	h	1-0	*Adamia (p)*
1/5	Bakı	h	2-2	*Adamia, Teli*
7/5	Xäzär Länkäran	a	1-1	*Qurbanov*
13/5	Neftçi	h	3-0	*Adamia 3 (1p)*
18/5	Olimpik-Şüvälan	a	1-3	*Adamia*

No	Name	Nat	DoB	Pos	Aps	(s)	Gls
13	Samir ABASOV		1/2/78	M	9	(5)	
15	Ayxan ABBASOV		25/8/81	M	1		
20	Giorgi ADAMIA	GEO	10/3/81	A	23	(8)	18
25	Ansi AGOLLI	ALB	11/10/82	D	31		
11	Rauf ÄLİYEV		12/2/89	A	25	(6)	10
21	DEVRAN Ayhan	TUR	25/3/78	M	9	(5)	
3	Aftandil HACIYEV		13/8/81	D	3	(2)	1
4	Zaur HÄŞİMOV		24/10/81	D	19		
10	Emin İMAMÄLİYEV		7/8/80	M	8	(1)	2
23	Tural İSGÄNDÄROV		9/2/92	A	1	(5)	
22	Äfran İSMAYILOV		8/10/88	M	9	(3)	1
8	Aslan KÄRİMOV		1/1/73	M	1	(5)	
16	Räşad KÄRİMOV		2/4/86	M	7	(3)	
12	Sahil KÄRİMOV		22/1/79	G	2		
9	Elvin MÄMMÄDOV		18/7/88	M	19	(10)	1
5	Maksim MEDVEDEV		29/9/89	D	18		
17	Vüqar NADİROV		15/6/87	A	18	(12)	1
20	Nderim NEDZIPI	MKD	22/5/84	M	4	(6)	
99	Bojan PAVLOVIĆ	SRB	8/11/86	G	9	(1)	
2	Qara QARAYEV		12/10/92	D	13		
18	İlqar QURBANOV		25/4/86	M	1	(2)	1
31	Andrejs RUBINS	LVA	26/11/78	M	7	(5)	
6	Räşad Ä. SADİQOV		8/10/83	M	29	(3)	4
14	Räşad F. SADIQOV		16/6/82	D	12	(2)	
21	Murad SÄTTARLI		9/5/92	M		(1)	
24	Admir TELI	ALB	2/6/81	D	30		2
1	Färhad VÄLİYEV		1/11/80	G	21		
7	Namiq YUSİFOV		14/8/86	M	23	(4)	

QÄBÄLÄ FK

Coach – Tony Adams (ENG)

Founded – 2005

Stadium – Qäbälä şähär stadionu (2,500); Şäfa (7,852)

2010				
7/8	Xäzär Länkäran	a	0-1	
15/8	Neftçi	h	0-2	
22/8	Bakı	a	1-2	*Burton*
29/8	MOİK	h	0-0	
11/9	Turan	a	1-0	*Yunisoğlu*
19/9	İnter	h	0-1	
25/9	Qarabağ	h	2-1	*Burton, Subašić*
1/10	Simurq	a	2-0	*Yunisoğlu, Cooke*
16/10	Muğan	h	2-0	*Subašić, Burton*
23/10	Olimpik-Şüvälan	h	0-0	
31/10	Gäncä	a	0-0	

6/11	Xäzär Länkäran	h	1-0	*Baranin*
13/11	İnter	a	0-0	
21/11	Neftçi	a	0-0	
27/11	Simurq	h	4-0	*Burton 2 (2p), Torres, İsayev*
4/12	MOİK	a	3-0	*Burton 2 (1p), Bruno Barbosa*
11/12	Turan	h	1-0	*Mämmädov*
19/12	Olimpik-Şüvälan	a	2-2	*İsayev, Antić*
23/12	Bakı	h	0-1	
2011				
13/2	Qarabağ	a	0-3	
20/2	Muğan	a	0-1	
27/2	Gäncä	h	0-0	
13/3	MOİK	a	1-1	*Burton*
17/3	Muğan	a	2-1	*Antić, Hüseynov*
2/4	Gäncä	h	1-1	*Hüseynov*
9/4	Turan	a	2-0	*Yunisoğlu, Burton*
17/4	Simurq	h	3-0	*Antić, Baranin, Torres*
24/4	MOİK	h	0-0	
30/4	Simurq	a	0-0	
8/5	Turan	h	1-0	*Abuzärov*
12/5	Gäncä	a	0-0	
19/5	Muğan	h	2-1	*Hüseynov, Abuzärov*

No	Name	Nat	DoB	Pos	Aps	(s)	Gls
7	Yaşar ABUZÄROV		9/9/77	M	10	(4)	2
26	Namiq ÄLİYEV		29/9/80	M	2	(3)	
14	Milan ANTIĆ	SRB	1/7/81	D	24	(1)	3
21	Alhassan BANGURA	SLE	24/1/88	M	4	(1)	
6	Ljubo BARANIN	SRB	25/8/86	D	27		2
18	Goga BERAIA	RUS	26/1/84	D	14	(3)	
9	BRUNO dos ANJOS	BRA	18/12/91	M	10	(4)	
8	BRUNO da Silva BARBOSA	BRA	15/2/88	M	17	(1)	1
10	Deon BURTON	JAM	25/10/76	A	28		9
24	Tärzin CAHANGİROV		17/1/92	M		(6)	
16	Abdoul Kader CAMARA	GUI	18/3/82	M	19	(6)	
11	Terry COOKE	ENG	5/8/76	M	4	(8)	1
12	Pävels DOROŠEVS	LVA	9/10/80	G	27		
40	Färid HAQVERDİYEV		21/3/89	M		(2)	
22	Murad HÜSEYNOV		25/1/89	A	9	(1)	3
17	Arif İSAYEV		28/7/85	M	12	(13)	2
11	Collins JOHN	NED	17/10/85	A	2		
1	Elnar KÄRİMOV		5/4/85	G		(1)	
3	Nodar MÄMMÄDOV		3/6/88	D	27		1
25	Rähman MUSAYEV		14/12/86	A	2	(3)	
30	Anar NÄZİROV		8/9/85	G	5		
34	Steve OLFERS	NED	25/2/82	M	26		
21	Asäf QÄDİRİ		17/8/84	M		(1)	
4	Ramin QULİYEV		22/6/81	D	1	(4)	
25	Nuran QURBANOV		10/8/93	A	1	(3)	
5	Sergey SOKOLOV		12/3/77	D	6		
19	Branimir SUBAŠIĆ		7/4/82	A	16	(3)	2
20	Cristian Damián TORRES	ARG	18/6/85	M	16	(8)	2
15	Răzvan ŢÂRLEA	ROU	5/8/79	D	16	(5)	
29	Amil YUNANOV		6/1/93	A		(1)	
33	Saşa YUNİSOĞLU		18/12/85	D	27		3

SİMURQ ZAQATALA PFK

Coach – Gjokica Hadzievski (MKD);
(18/5/11) (Böyükağa Ağayev)
Founded – 2005
Stadium – Zaqatala Olimpiya İdman Kompleksi (3,500); Şäfa (7,852)

2010				
7/8	Gäncä	a	1-1	*Tskhadadze*
15/8	Xäzär Länkäran	h	0-2	
21/8	Neftçi	a	0-4	
28/8	Turan	h	2-2	*Tskhadadze, Abbasov Y.*
12/9	Olimpik-Şüvälan	a	1-2	*Rähimov*
19/9	Bakı	h	1-1	*Tskhadadze*
25/9	Muğan	a	0-1	
1/10	Qäbälä	h	0-2	
17/10	Qarabağ	a	2-3	*Tskhadadze, Mikayılov*
24/10	MOİK	a	2-0	*Rähimov, Tskhadadze (p)*
31/10	İnter	h	0-1	
6/11	Olimpik-Şüvälan	h	0-1	
13/11	Xäzär Länkäran	a	0-1	
20/11	Gäncä	h	0-0	
27/11	Qäbälä	a	0-4	
5/12	Bakı	a	1-0	*Äliyev S.*
11/12	Qarabağ	h	0-1	
19/12	Turan	a	1-1	*Äliyev S.*
23/12	MOİK	h	1-1	*Äliyev S.*
2011				
13/2	İnter	a	0-2	
19/2	Neftçi	h	0-3	
27/2	Muğan	h	0-1	
12/3	Muğan	h	1-3	*Souza*
18/3	Gäncä	a	1-0	*og (Mämmädov A.)*
3/4	Turan	h	0-1	
9/4	MOİK	h	1-2	*Yunusov*
17/4	Qäbälä	a	0-3	
23/4	Muğan	a	0-3	
30/4	Qäbälä	h	0-0	
7/5	MOİK	a	0-1	
12/5	Turan	a	1-2	*Qafarov*
19/5	Gäncä	h	4-3	*Bağırov 2, Mikayılov, Yunusov*

No	Name	Nat	DoB	Pos	Aps	(s)	Gls
26	Elnur ABBASOV		7/3/84	D	8	(3)	
11	Yasin ABBASOV		15/9/88	A	5	(10)	1
1	Fuad ÄHMÄDOV		14/1/88	G	5		
21	Näsib ÄLİYEV		24/6/91	M		(1)	
7	Samir ÄLİYEV		14/4/79	A	18	(3)	3
10	Vasif ÄLİYEV		6/8/86	M	22	(5)	
11	Dilqäm ÄSGÄROV		25/1/90	M		(2)	
9	Äli BAĞIROV		23/4/88	A	20	(8)	2
14	Anar HÄSÄNLİ		7/5/88	D	14	(2)	
2	Säbuhi HÄSÄNOV		8/7/87	D	8	(1)	
22	Adnan HODŽIĆ	CRO	25/3/85	G	26		
4	Räşad HÜSEYNOV		9/2/90	D	2		
8	Qärib İBRAHİMOV		11/9/88	M	24	(5)	
23	Camal MÄMMÄDOV		26/12/83	M	2	(3)	
17	Rüstäm MÄMMÄDOV		14/8/84	D	26	(2)	
16	Tofiq MİKAYILOV		11/4/86	A	16	(5)	2
18	Samir MUSAYEV		17/3/79	A	5	(3)	
15	Elvin MUSAZADÄ		25/11/89	M	14	(7)	
19	Ramin NÄSİBOV		20/11/79	A	3	(3)	
13	Paulius PAKNYS	LTU	10/5/84	D	9	(1)	
20	Qafar QAFAROV		15/4/90	M	1	(5)	1
28	İlkin QIRTIMOV		4/11/90	M	11	(2)	
4	Emin QULİYEV		12/4/77	D	3		
24	Färid QULİYEV		6/1/86	A	4	(1)	
3	Rasim RAMALDANOV		24/1/86	D	19	(1)	
6	Mikayıl RÄHİMOV		11/5/87	M	25		2
25	Ramil SAYADOV		11/7/83	M	5	(11)	
19	Azär SÄFÄRLİ		5/11/88	M		(1)	
32	Zabid SÄFÄROV		1/2/87	G	1		
28	Laçın ŞÄKÄROV		23/6/88	D		(1)	
11	Mário Sérgio Aumarante Santana SOUZA	BRA	30/1/77	M	3		1
28	Bachana TSKHADADZE	GEO	23/10/87	A	8		5
23	Elçin XÄLİLOV		31/1/86	M	11	(3)	
5	Elvin YUNUSOV		22/8/94	D	31		2
18	Elnur YUSİFOV		17/1/88	D	1	(2)	
21	Zhivko ZHELEV	BUL	23/7/79	D	2		

TURAN PFK

Coach – Sakit Alıyev; (28/9/10) Revaz Dzodzuashvili (GEO); (27/12/10) Naci Şensoy (TUR); (6/5/11) (Asim İbrahimov); (10/5/11) (Eltay Aslanov)
Founded – 1992
Stadium – Tovuz şähär stadionu (6,350)
MAJOR HONOURS: Azerbaijan League – (1) 1994.

2010				
8/8	İnter	h	0-3	
14/8	Olimpik-Şüvälan	a	0-1	
22/8	Muğan	h	1-1	*Kolawole*
28/8	Simurq	a	2-2	*Modebadze 2*
11/9	Qäbälä	h	0-1	

18/9	Gäncä	a	1-1	*Pirtskhalava (p)*
27/9	Bakı	a	1-3	*Orucov*
2/10	Qarabağ	h	0-1	
17/10	Neftçi	h	2-2	*Gonta, Chedia*
23/10	Xäzär Länkäran	a	0-2	
30/10	MOİK	h	2-0	*Hüseynov (p), Gonta*
6/11	Muğan	a	0-0	
12/11	Gäncä	h	2-1	*Äliyev F., Muammer*
20/11	İnter	a	0-3	
28/11	Olimpik-Şüvälan	h	1-2	*Muammer*
4/12	Xäzär Länkäran	h	1-2	Muammer
11/12	Qäbälä	a	0-1	
19/12	Simurq	h	1-1	*Muammer*
23/12	Neftçi	a	0-2	
2011				
12/2	MOİK	a	2-0	*Chedia, Abbasov Y.*
19/2	Bakı	h	0-1	
25/2	Qarabağ	a	1-5	*Äliyev F.*
13/3	Gäncä	h	1-0	*Abbasov Y.*
18/3	MOİK	h	1-0	*Kondev*
3/4	Simurq	a	1-0	*Beriashvili*
9/4	Qäbälä	h	0-2	
16/4	Muğan	a	1-2	*Tağıyev C.*
24/4	Gäncä	a	0-1	
1/5	Muğan	h	0-1	
8/5	Qäbälä	a	0-1	
12/5	Simurq	h	2-1	*Hüseynov, Muammer*
19/5	MOİK	a	1-4	*Mämmädov A.*

No	Name	Nat	DoB	Pos	Aps	(s)	Gls
6	Elnur ABBASOV		7/3/84	D	5	(1)	
28	Yasin ABBASOV		15/9/88	A	6	(2)	2
7	Kamal ÄLÄKBÄROV		4/3/78	D	6	(1)	
14	Tuqay ALHÜSEYNLİ		18/8/93	A	1		
22	Färmayıl ÄLİYEV		29/8/90	A	15	(7)	2
18	Hafiz ÄLİYEV		17/2/83	M	17		
7	Qalib ÄMRAHOV		31/5/89	A	2	(4)	
27	Qüvvät ÄMRAHOV		7/7/93	D	1		
85	Kamal BAYRAMOV		15/8/85	G	30		
20	Giorgi BERIASHVILI	GEO	10/9/85	A	6	(1)	1
24	Giorgi CHEDIA	GEO	28/8/88	A	16		2
25	Marat DZAKHMISHEV	RUS	25/1/80	A	1		
14	Victor GONTA	MDA	21/9/88	M	23	(3)	2
16	Oleg GVELESIANI	GEO	16/9/80	D	4	(3)	
19	Räşid HÄSÄNOV	RUS	26/6/82	M	9	(5)	
19	Sübhan HÄSÄNOV		23/7/91	A		(1)	
3	Vurğun HÜSEYNOV		25/4/88	D	31		2
2	Hüseyn İSGÄNDÄROV		7/12/84	D	26	(1)	
17	Orxan İSMAYILOV		21/4/89	D	5	(7)	
6	Färman KÄRİMOV		22/8/86	M	1	(1)	
16	Ramil KÄRİMOV		13/5/90	G	1		
25	Martin KERCHEV	BUL	22/10/82	M	10	(1)	
9	Peter KOLAWOLE	NGA	19/11/90	A	5	(2)	1
26	Boris KONDEV	BUL	29/8/79	A	9		1
6	Jurijs KSENZOVS	LVA	5/6/81	D	2	(2)	
11	Azär MÄMMÄDOV		18/6/90	A	11	(12)	1
6	Elmixan MÄMMÄDOV		9/1/94	M		(1)	
8	MARCO TÚLIO Lopes Silva	BRA	28/2/81	M	2		
26	Giorgi MODEBADZE	GEO	27/3/83	M	4	(2)	2
5	MUAMMER Erdoğdu	TUR	7/7/87	D	18		5
16	Mähärräm MÜSLÜMZADÄ		12/8/91	D	6	(8)	
4	Ruslan NAMAZOV		15/2/85	D	13		
78	Romuald ONANA	CMR	11/2/90	M	4	(1)	
21	Räşad ORUCOV		7/10/89	M	21	(2)	1
9	Räşad PİRİYEV		1/10/91	A	2	(2)	
16	Shalva PIRTSKHALAVA	GEO	18/9/84	M	12	(1)	1
10	Xäyal QARAYEV		8/7/86	M	10	(4)	
2	Hüseyn QASIMLI		17/5/94	D		(1)	
12	Shamil SAIDOV	RUS	21/3/82	G	1	(1)	
1	Natiq SÄHRÄTOV		10/10/90	G		(1)	
8	Akif TAĞIYEV		7/6/92	M	3	(2)	
15	Cavid TAĞIYEV		22/7/92	A	10	(6)	1
24	Seymur TAĞIYEV		1992	D	1	(1)	
20	Şähriyar XÄLİLOV		21/8/91	D	2	(3)	

XÄZÄR LÄNKÄRAN FK

Coach – Ağasälim Mircavadov; (15/7/10) Mircea Rednic (ROU)

Founded – 2004

Stadium – Länkäran şähär märkäzi stadionu (15,000); Tofiq İsmayılov adına Suraxanı qäsäbä stadionu (3,000)

MAJOR HONOURS: Azerbaijan League – (1) 2007; Azerbaijan Cup – (3) 2007, 2008, 2011.

2010				
7/8	Qäbälä	h	1-0	*Beqiri*
15/8	Simurq	a	2-0	*Allahverdiyev, Ruiz*
21/8	İnter	h	0-0	
29/8	Olimpik-Şüvälan	a	1-0	*Beqiri*
12/9	MOİK	h	3-0	*Diego Souza, Parks 2*
18/9	Muğan	a	0-0	
25/9	Neftçi	h	1-0	*Ruiz*
2/10	Bakı	h	1-1	*Parks*
17/10	Gäncä	a	1-4	*Doman*
23/10	Turan	h	2-0	*Parks, Doman*
30/10	Qarabağ	a	1-0	*Arbănaş*
6/11	Qäbälä	a	0-1	
13/11	Simurq	h	1-0	*Qurbanov*
21/11	Muğan	h	2-0	*Qurbanov 2*
27/11	Bakı	a	1-1	*Parks*
4/12	Turan	a	2-1	*Lalín, Stancu*
11/12	Gäncä	h	1-0	*Lalín*
18/12	MOİK	a	2-0	*Beqiri 2*
23/12	Qarabağ	h	1-2	*Qurbanov*
2011				
13/2	Neftçi	a	0-0	
20/2	Olimpik-Şüvälan	h	2-1	*Abdullayev, Chiacu*
27/2	İnter	a	3-1	*Chiacu, Piţ, Parks*
13/3	Olimpik-Şüvälan	a	0-1	
18/3	Neftçi	h	1-1	*Wobay (p)*
2/4	Bakı	a	0-0	
10/4	Qarabağ	a	0-0	
16/4	İnter	h	1-1	*Parks*
23/4	Olimpik-Şüvälan	h	3-0	*Opara, Parks, Abdullayev*
30/4	İnter	a	1-1	*Chiacu*
7/5	Qarabağ	h	1-1	*Opara*
13/5	Bakı	h	2-0	*Scarlatache, Opara*
18/5	Neftçi	a	1-1	*Wobay*

No	Name	Nat	DoB	Pos	Aps	(s)	Gls
17	Ramazan ABBASOV		22/9/83	M		(6)	
10	Elnur ABDULLAYEV		16/2/86	M	9	(2)	2
25	Kamran AĞAYEV		9/2/86	G	28		
2	Elnur ALLAHVERDİYEV		2/11/83	D	26	(2)	1
14	Rahid ÄMİRQULİYEV		1/9/89	M	28	(2)	
8	Constantin Dorian ARBĂNAŞ	ROU	28/7/83	M	9	(3)	1
19	Ibrahima BANGOURA	GUI	8/12/82	M	3	(2)	
3	Elvin BEQIRI	ALB	27/9/80	D	21	(3)	4
6	BRUNO Martins SIMÃO	POR	5/5/85	D	8		
55	Tural CÄLİLOV		28/11/78	M		(3)	
17	Hristu CHIACU	ROU	6/9/86	M	5	(7)	3
28	CRISTIAN Martins Cabral	BRA	28/8/79	M	3	(6)	
5	DIEGO SOUZA Gusmão	BRA	12/9/88	M	9	(2)	1
30	Cătălin Petre DOMAN	ROU	30/1/88	M	13	(7)	2
28	Cosmin Valentin FRĂSINESCU	ROU	10/2/85	D	4		
20	Amid HÜSEYNOV		3/2/87	A	1	(3)	
22	David IMEDASHVILI	GEO	15/12/84	M	1		
6	Adrian Gheorghe IORDACHE	ROU	12/9/80	D	15		
12	Yevhen KOPYL	UKR	25/5/86	G	1		
12	Allan LALÍN	HON	5/1/81	A	12	(4)	2
11	Asif MÄMMÄDOV		5/8/86	M	1	(7)	
10	Xaqani MÄMMÄDOV		29/9/76	A	4	(3)	
11	Andrei Iosif MUREŞAN	ROU	1/8/85	M	10	(2)	
8	Nicolae MUŞAT	ROU	4/12/86	M	5	(1)	
15	Emeka OPARA	NGA	2/12/84	A	9	(6)	3
36	Winston Antonio PARKS	CRC	12/10/81	A	23	(2)	8

Adrian Florin PIŢ	ROU	16/7/83	M	12		1
Alexandru PIŢURCĂ	ROU	28/10/83	A	1	(3)	
Ruslan POLADOV		30/11/79	D	11	(4)	
Alim QURBANOV		5/12/77	M	10	(9)	4
Deniss ROMANOVS	LVA	2/9/78	G	3	(1)	
Diego Alejandro RUIZ Scheuschner	ARG	19/12/80	A	5	(3)	2
Manuel Adrian SCARLATACHE	ROU	5/12/86	D	12		1
Stelian STANCU	ROU	22/9/81	M	21	(2)	1
Radomir TODOROV	BUL	11/8/80	D	18		
Şähriyar XÄLİLOV		21/8/91	D		(1)	
Julius Gibrilla WOBAY	SLE	19/5/84	M	11		2

TOP GOALSCORERS 2010/11

18	Giorgi ADAMIA (Qarabağ)
15	Bakhodir NASIMOV (Neftçi)
11	FLAVINHO (Neftçi)
10	Gvidas JUŠKA (Olimpik-Şüvälan) JUNIVAN (Gäncä) Rauf ÄLİYEV (Qarabağ)
9	Sabir ALLAHQULİYEV (Gäncä) Deon BURTON (Qäbälä)
8	Winston PARKS (Xäzär Länkäran)
7	JABÁ (Bakı) Räşad ABDULLAYEV (Neftçi)

PROMOTED CLUBS

RÄVAN BAKI FK

Coach – Vladislav Qädirov
Founded – 2009
Stadium – Şäfa IV meydança (1,000)

SUMQAYIT ŞÄHÄR PFK

Coach – Baba Äsgärov
Founded – 2010
Stadium – Mehdi Hüseynzadä adına Sumqayıt şähär stadionu (15,000)

SECOND LEVEL FINAL TABLE 2010/11

		Pld	W	D	L	F	A	Pts
1	Abşeron Bakı FK	26	23	3	0	75	6	72
2	Rävan Bakı FK	26	19	3	4	54	14	60
3	Bakılı Bakı PFK	26	16	4	6	37	24	52
4	Neftçi İSM Bakı	26	15	5	6	47	24	50
5	MKT Araz İmişli FK	26	15	3	8	49	34	48
6	Şahdağ Qusar FK	26	13	8	5	45	22	47
7	Sumqayıt FK	26	13	5	8	34	26	44
8	Karvan İK	26	6	8	12	26	40	26
9	Şämkir FK	26	5	7	14	15	36	22
10	Neftçala FK	26	5	6	15	28	48	21
11	Göyäzän Qazax PFK	26	5	4	17	22	50	19
12	Energetik Mingäçevir PFK	26	4	6	16	17	50	18
13	Şuşa PFK	26	3	8	15	20	41	17
14	Ädliyyä Bakı PFK	26	3	4	19	13	67	13

NB Abşeron Bakı FK declared defunct at the end of the season; Sumqayit Şähär PFK (formerly Sumqayit FK) invited to 2011/12 Premyer Liqa. Ädliyyä Bakı PFK withdrew after round 14 – their remaining matches being awarded as 0-3 defeats; ANŞAD-Petrol Neftçala FK were renamed Neftçala FK & Şuşa-09 PFK were renamed Şuşa PFK during the season.

DOMESTIC CUP 2010/11

AZÄRBAYCAN KUBOKU

FIRST ROUND

(26/10/10)
Karvan 1, MKT Araz 1 *(aet; 3-4 on pens)*
Bakılı Bakı 0, Neftçi İSM 1
ANŞAD-Petrol Neftçala 0, Şuşa 2
Şämkir 1, Rävan Bakı 3

(27/10/10)
Şahdağ Qusar 0, Gäncä 3
Abşeron Bakı 4, MOİK 0

1/8 FINALS

(7/12/10)
Qarabağ 0, Turan 0 *(aet; 3-4 on pens)*

(8/12/10)
Bakı 1, Muğan 1 *(aet; 5-3 on pens)*
Gäncä 1, Neftçi 3
Qäbälä 2, Neftçi İSM 0
Rävan Bakı 1, Olimpik-Şüvälan 2
Simurq 1, Abşeron Bakı 1 *(aet; 1-4 on pens)*
Şuşa 1, İnter Bakı 4
Xäzär Länkäran 3, MKT Araz 1

QUARTER-FINALS

(2/3/11 & 9/3/11)
Olimpik-Şüvälan 2 *(Juška 39, Kvirtia 43)*, Turan 0
Turan 1 *(Kondev 76)*, Olimpik-Şüvälan 1 *(Pema 63)*
(Olimpik-Şüvälan 3-1)

(3/3/11 & 8/3/11)
Abşeron Bakı 0, İnter Bakı 1 *(Karlsons 79)*
İnter Bakı 0, Abşeron Bakı 0
(İnter Bakı 1-0)

Neftçi 3 *(Flavinho 32p, 63, Georgievski 70)*, Xäzär Länkäran 4 *(Parks 12, Scarlatache 36, Wobay 45+2, Mureşan 61)*
Xäzär Länkäran 1 *(Parks 22)*, Neftçi 1 *(Flavinho 9)*
(Xäzär Länkäran 5-4)

Qäbälä 0, Bakı 0
Bakı 1 *(Jabá 57)*, Qäbälä 0
(Bakı 1-0)

SEMI-FINALS

(27/4/11 & 4/5/11)
İnter Bakı 0, Olimpik-Şüvälan 0
Olimpik-Şüvälan 0, İnter Bakı 1 *(Odikadze 2)*
(İnter Bakı 1-0)

Xäzär Länkäran 1 *(Parks 23)*, Bakı 0
Bakı 2 *(Leo Rocha 49, Fábio 85p)*, Xäzär Länkäran 1 *(Ämirquliyev 57)*
(2-2; Xäzär Länkäran on away goal)

FINAL

(24/5/11)
Tofiq Bähramov adına Respublika stadionu, Baku
XÄZÄR LÄNKÄRAN FK 1 *(Parks 91)*
İNTER BAKI PİK 1 *(Karlsons 100)*
(aet; 4-2 on pens)
Referee – *Yusifov*
XÄZÄR LÄNKÄRAN – *Ağayev, Allahverdiyev, Scarlatache, Diego Souza (Chiacu 74), Muşat, Mureşan, Ämirquliyev, Piţ, Wobay (Doman 105), Opara (Abdullayev 117), Parks.*
İNTER BAKI – *Lomaia, Kruglov, Despotovski (Karlsons 94), Levin, Daşdämirov, Abramidze, Chertoganov (Mzhavanadze 81), Ämiraslanov (Mämmädov A. 71), Červenka, Odikadze, Poškus.*

CLUB COMMUNICATION 2011/12

Bakı FK
9 km of Sumgayit highway
AZ-1060 Bakı

Tel	994 12 497 7173
Fax	994 12 497 7172
Web	fcbaku.com
Email	mail@fcbaku.com
Media Officer	

Gäncä PFK
Ataturk Str. 92A
AZ-374712 Gäncä

Tel	+994 22 650 699
Fax	+994 22 650 699
Web	gancapfk.az
Email	magsad-ragimov@mail.ru
Media Officer	Magsad Ragimov

İnter Bakı PFK
Heydar Aliyev ave., Kondalan 5
AZ-1029 Bakı

Tel	+994 12 567 1021
Fax	+994 12 567 1023
Web	inter.az
Email	pr@inter.az
Media Officer	Sabuhi Mammadov

Muğan Salyan FK
Xatai str, 34
AZ-Salyan

Tel	+99450 447 94 51
Fax	+994 12 447 94 51
Web	muganfc.az
Email	office@muganfc.az
Media Officer	Rovshan Abdullayev

Neftçi PFK
Nobel avenue, 64
AZ-1026 Bakı

Tel	+994 12 424 4640
Fax	
Web	neftchifc.com
Email	neftchi@neftchifc.com
Media Officer	Elnur Eshrefoglu

Olimpik-Şüvälan PFK
H. Aliyev ave 64
AZ-Bakı

Tel	+994 12 514 1316
Fax	+994 12 514 0820
Web	azalpfc.az
Email	info@azalpfc.az
Media Officer	Eldaniz Yusifov

Qarabağ FK
Ali Valiyev 7A, Ruslan-93 Sport Complex
AZ-Bakı

Tel	+994 12 421 5260
Fax	+994 12 421 5260
Web	qarabagh.com
Email	info@qarabagh.com
Media Officer	Nurlan Ibrahimov

Qäbälä FK
E. Karimov 34
AZ-1000 Qäbälä

Tel	+994 12 498 9679
Fax	+994 12 498 9679
Web	gabalafc.az
Email	admin@gabalafc.az
Media Officer	

Rävan Bakı FK
c/o Shafa Stadionu
AZ-Bakı

Tel	
Fax	
Web	
Email	
Media Officer	

Sumqayıt Şähär PFK
Samed Vurgun str. 85
AZ-Sumqayıt

Tel	+99412 521 00 00
Fax	+99412 521 25 34
Web	
Email	info@sumqayitpfc.az
Media Officer	Rashad Mammadov

Turan Tovuz PFK
34, S. Vurgun Str., Tovuz city stadium
AZ-374809 Tovuz

Tel	+994 23 150 304
Fax	+994 23 150 305
Web	turanpfc.com
Email	turan_tovuz@rambler.ru
Media Officer	Suleyman Tagiyev

Xäzär Länkäran FK
Bakı city, T.Aliyev str. 27
AZ-1069 Länkäran

Tel	+994 12 563 6070
Fax	+994 12 562 1340
Web	lankaranfc.com
Email	webmaster@ lankaranfc.com
Media Officer	Yalchin Aliyev

BELARUS

Belarus I Belarus

Belorusskaja Federacija Futbola (BFF)

COMMUNICATION

Address	Prospekt Pobediteli 20/3 BY-220020 Minsk	**President**	Sergei Roumas
Tel	+375 172 545 600	**General Director**	Andrei Sidorenya
Fax	+375 172 544 478	**Media Officer**	Yulia Zenkovich
E-mail	info@bff.by	**Year of Formation**	1989
Website	bff.by	**National Stadium**	Dinamo, Minsk (40,000)

DOMESTIC COMPETITION SUMMARY 2010/11

PREMIER LEAGUE FINAL TABLE

			Home					Away					Total						
		Pld	W	D	L	F	A	W	D	L	F	A	W	D	L	F	A	Pts	Comp
1	FC BATE Borisov	33	11	2	3	32	9	10	7	0	32	9	21	9	3	64	18	72	UCL
2	FC Shakhtyor Soligorsk	33	9	6	2	29	13	10	3	3	22	10	19	9	5	51	23	66	UEL
3	FC Minsk	33	9	4	3	29	15	9	2	6	30	17	18	6	9	59	32	60	UEL
4	FC Dinamo Minsk	33	9	4	4	29	12	8	1	7	20	22	17	5	11	49	34	56	
5	FC Dinamo Brest	33	9	4	3	34	19	3	6	8	14	21	12	10	11	48	40	46	
6	FC Belshina Bobruisk	33	8	4	5	17	15	4	5	7	14	27	12	9	12	31	42	45	
7	FC Naftan Novopolotsk	33	9	4	4	29	16	2	7	7	12	18	11	11	11	41	34	44	
8	FC Dnepr Mogilev	33	7	3	6	19	19	4	4	9	21	34	11	7	15	40	53	40	
9	FC Vitebsk	33	3	5	9	16	29	4	6	6	15	23	7	11	15	31	52	32	
10	FC Neman Grodno	33	4	7	5	13	14	3	3	11	14	28	7	10	16	27	42	31	
11	FC Torpedo Zhodino	33	3	4	9	16	28	4	3	10	17	30	7	7	19	33	58	28	
12	FC Partizan Minsk	33	3	4	10	14	32	2	4	10	10	38	5	8	20	24	70	23	*Relegated*

Top Scorer Renan Bressan (BATE), 15 goals

Promoted Club FC Gomel (UEL)

Cup Final FC Gomel 2, FC Neman Grodno 0

BATE still the best

Belarusian football is on the up. A promising UEFA EURO 2012 qualifying campaign that began with a sensational 1-0 victory in France was backed up by an impressive effort from the Under-21 team, who reached the European semi-finals. Furthermore, the country's top club, FC BATE Borisov, exported their powerful domestic form to reach the knockout phase of the UEFA Europa League.

2010 was a terrific year for BATE. With the Super Cup and Belarusian Cup already in the bag, they cantered to another Premier League title. Their fifth championship win on the trot was never in doubt after a brilliant start in which their goal remained unbreached for 13 matches. Viktor Goncharenko's young team, augmented by the arrival from relegated FC Gomel of classy Brazilian playmaker-cum-goalscorer Renan Bressan, rarely skipped a beat as they strode imperiously towards a seventh domestic title that drew them level in the all-time rankings with FC Dinamo Minsk.

Gomel double

FC Shakhtyor Soligorsk finished second ahead of unheralded FC Minsk. Both were joined in the 2011/12 UEFA Europa League by Gomel, who, not content with winning the second division by 24 points and returning to the top flight, won the 2011 Belarusian Cup, beating FC Neman Grodno 2-0 in the final thanks to two late own goals.

With the new-look 2010 Premier League having fewer teams (12 rather than 14) but more matches (33 rather than 26), it was a marathon campaign for the BATE players even without the extra burden of seven Belarusian Cup matches and another dozen in Europe. By the end of the year the team were showing understandable signs of fatigue, which resulted in a shock defeat by FC Dinamo Brest in the domestic cup and two heavy losses at the end of the UEFA Europa League group phase. As BATE had already accumulated ten points, though, their qualification was secure. They impressed again in the round of 32, falling to Paris Saint-Germain FC on away goals after a 0-0 draw at the Parc des Princes.

The French capital had been the scene of much delight for Belarusian football followers the previous September when Sergei Kislyak's late strike brought a famous 1-0 win in the Stade de France. Alas, Belarus could not back it up in their next two qualifiers, but by the following June, when they held France 1-1 and defeated Luxembourg 2-0 in Minsk, Bernd Stange's team were back on course for a play-off place.

Mixed emotions

Having accounted for Italy in a dramatic play-off win, Georgiy Kondratyev's Under-21s travelled hopefully to Denmark for the UEFA European U21 Championship finals – despite the absence of injured goalscorer-in-chief Vladimir Yurchenko. It was a tournament that would provide a mixture of emotions. Although Belarus reached the last four with just one win and were frustratingly close to eliminating eventual winners Spain in the semi-finals, they signed off from Denmark on a high by defeating the Czech Republic 1-0 to qualify for the 2012 Olympics.

Belarus Under-21s celebrate opening the scoring against Denmark

National Team

Top Five All-time Caps – Aleksandr Kulchiy (92); Sergei Gurenko (80); Sergei Omelyanchuk & Sergei Shtanyuk (71); Maksim Romashchenko (64)

Top Five All-time Goals – Maksim Romashchenko (20); Vitaliy Kutuzov (13); Vyacheslav Hleb (12); Valentin Belkevich, Sergei Kornilenko & Roman Vasilyuk (10)

NATIONAL TEAM RESULTS 2010/11

11/8/10	Lithuania	A	Kaunas	2-0	*Hleb V. (49p, 90+1)*
3/9/10	France (ECQ)	A	Saint-Denis	1-0	*Kislyak (86)*
7/9/10	Romania (ECQ)	H	Minsk	0-0	
8/10/10	Luxembourg (ECQ)	A	Luxembourg	0-0	
12/10/10	Albania (ECQ)	H	Minsk	2-0	*Rodionov (10), Krivets (77)*
17/11/10	Oman	A	Muscat	4-0	*Martynovich (5, 11), Hleb V. (35), Rodionov (57p)*
9/2/11	Kazakhstan	N	Antalya (TUR)	1-1	*Hleb V. (45p)*
26/3/11	Albania (ECQ)	A	Tirana	0-1	
29/3/11	Canada	N	Antalya (TUR)	0-1	
3/6/11	France (ECQ)	H	Minsk	1-1	*Abidal (20og)*
7/6/11	Luxembourg (ECQ)	H	Minsk	2-0	*Kornilenko (48p), Putilo (73)*

NATIONAL TEAM APPEARANCES 2010/11

oach – Bernd STANGE (GER)	14/3/48		Ltu	FRA	ROU	LUX	ALB	Oma	Kaz	ALB	Can	FRA	LUX	Caps	Goals
nton AMELCHENKO	27/3/85	Rostov (RUS)	G46					s46							
		/Lokomotiv Moskva (RUS)							s46		s46			7	-
gor SHITOV	24/10/86	BATE	D	D	D	D	D	D75	D	D	D	D	D	26	1
leksandr MARTYNOVICH	26/8/87	Krasnodar (RUS)	D	D	D	D	D	D80	D87	D	D	D		15	2
ergei OMELYANCHUK	8/8/80	Terek (RUS)	D90	D	D	D	D	D46	D	D	M78	M	D	71	1
mitriy MOLOSH	10/12/81	Sibir (RUS)	D46			s87	D87								
		/Krylya Sovetov (RUS)							D46	D	D			14	-
leksandr KULCHIY	1/11/73	Rostov (RUS)	M46	M	M	M	M75	M							
		/unattached							M46						
		/Krasnodar (RUS)								M62	s78		M87	92	5
an TIGOREV	10/3/84	Metalurh Zaporizhya (UKR)	M	M		M67	M	M	M46						
		/Tom (RUS)								M		M	M	22	-
yacheslav HLEB	12/2/83	Shenzhen Ruby (CHN)	M	M89	M	M67	s83	A							
		/unattached							M 90*	A	M53				
		/Dinamo Minsk										s90	s62	44	12
leksandr HLEB	1/5/81	Barcelona (ESP)	M46												
		/Birmingham (ENG)		M	M73				M 90*					55	6
nton PUTILO	10/6/87	Dinamo Minsk	M83												
		/Freiburg (GER)		s89	s73	s67	M83			M82	s81	M86	M	21	4
Vitaliy RODIONOV	11/12/83	BATE	A60	A85	s76	s67	A	A	A46					28	6
Yuriy ZHEVNOV	17/4/81	Zenit (RUS)	s46	G	G	G	G		G46				G	45	-
Sergei KISLYAK	6/8/87	Dinamo Minsk	s46	s75	M	M	M	s61							
		/Rubin (RUS)							M69	M	M62	s86	s87	17	2
Vitaliy KUTUZOV	20/3/80	Bari (ITA)	s46	A75	A87				s46					52	13
leksandr YUREVICH	8/8/79	BATE	s46	D	D	D87	s87	D61	s46					31	-
Sergei KRIVETS	8/6/86	Lech (POL)	s60		s87		s75	M	s46	M46				14	1
Maksim BORDACHEV	18/6/86	BATE	s83					s46				D	D	11	2
Eduard ZHEVNEROV	1/11/87	Dnepr	s90											1	-
Sergei KORNILENKO	14/6/83	Rubin (RUS)		s85	A76	A 69*									
		/Blackpool (ENG)									s62				
		/Zenit (RUS)											s46	46	10
Timofei KALACHEV	1/5/81	Rostov (RUS)				M	M	M46	s69		M	M90	M	48	7
Sergei VEREMKO	16/10/82	BATE						G46							
		/Sevastopol (UKR)								G	G46	G		8	-
Sergei SOSNOVSKIY	14/8/81	BATE						s46	s87						
		/Tom (RUS)									D			17	-
Denis POLYAKOV	17/4/91	Shakhtyor Soligorsk						s75						1	-
Dmitriy VERKHOVTSOV	10/10/86	Naftan						s80				D	D	18	2
Aleksandr BYCHENOK	30/5/85	Dinamo Minsk							s46	s62	s46			3	-
Leonid KOVEL	29/7/86	Dinamo Minsk								s46	A81			17	3
Pavel SITKO	17/12/85	Shakhtyor Soligorsk								s82	s53			7	1
Maksim ZHAVNERCHIK	9/2/85	Kuban (RUS)									M46			1	-
Vitaliy TRUBILO	7/1/85	Slavia Praha (CZE)										M	M62	2	-
Andrei VORONKOV	8/2/89	Kryvbas (UKR)										A	A46	5	-

BELARUS

CLUB-BY-CLUB

FC BATE BORISOV

Coach – Viktor Goncharenko
Founded – 1996
Stadium – City Stadium (5,392)
MAJOR HONOURS: Belarus League – (7) 1999, 2002, 2006, 2007, 2008, 2009, 2010; Belarus Cup – (2) 2006, 2010.

2010

3/4	Zhodino	a	1-0	*Renan*
10/4	Belshina	h	2-0	*Rodionov, Stasevich*
14/4	Minsk	a	0-0	
18/4	Neman	h	0-0	
24/4	Naftan	a	2-0	*Bordachev, Rodionov*
28/4	Partizan	h	6-0	*Renan 2, Bordachev, Rodionov, Kontsevoi (p), Goharyan (p)*
2/5	Vitebsk	a	0-0	
7/5	Dnepr	h	3-0	*Kontsevoi, Renan, Skavysh*
11/5	Dinamo Minsk	a	1-0	*Renan*
15/5	Shakhtyor	a	0-0	
19/5	Dinamo Brest	h	1-0	*Nekhaichik*
5/6	Zhodino	h	1-0	*Renan*
9/6	Belshina	a	1-0	*og (Druchyk)*
13/6	Minsk	h	1-2	*Nekhaichik*
19/6	Neman	a	5-0	*Kontsevoi 2 (1p), Rodionov, Radkov, Alumona*
23/6	Naftan	h	1-1	*Rodionov*
27/6	Partizan	a	1-1	*Rodionov*
3/7	Vitebsk	h	4-0	*Rodionov, Renan, og (Panasyuk), Shitov*
25/7	Dnepr	a	2-0	*Renan, Pavlov*
14/8	Shakhtyor	h	2-0	*Kontsevoi, Olekhnovich*
22/8	Dinamo Brest	a	4-1	*Skavysh 2, Rodionov, Renan (p)*
29/8	Vitebsk	a	6-1	*Renan, Kontsevoi 2, Skavysh 2, Olekhnovich*
11/9	Naftan	h	1-0	*Skavysh*
19/9	Partizan	a	1-1	*Skavysh*
22/9	Dinamo Minsk	h	1-3	*Renan (p)*
26/9	Minsk	h	2-1	*Baga, Volodko*
3/10	Neman	a	1-1	*Sosnovskiy*
16/10	Dnepr	a	3-2	*Renan, Bordachev, Skavysh*
25/10	Dinamo Brest	h	2-0	*Pavlov, Skavysh*
30/10	Zhodino	a	1-1	*Renan*
8/11	Dinamo Minsk	h	4-0	*Bordachev, Baga, Volodko, Yurevich*
13/11	Belshina	a	3-1	*Renan (p), Bordachev, Nekhaichik*
21/11	Shakhtyor	h	1-2	*Renan*

No	Name	Nat	DoB	Pos	Aps	(s)	Gls
11	Aleksandr ALUMONA	RUS	18/12/83	A	1	(10)	1
25	Dmitriy BAGA		4/1/90	M	11	(4)	2
18	Maksim BORDACHEV		18/6/86	D	25	(4)	5
9	Hovhannes GOHARYAN	ARM	18/3/88	M		(3)	1
30	Aleksandr GUTOR		18/4/89	G	9		
28	Sergei HLEBKO		23/8/92	M		(1)	
7	Artem KONTSEVOI		20/5/83	M	25	(3)	7
2	Dmitriy LIKHTAROVICH		1/3/78	M	23	(3)	
11	MAURO Lucas dos Santos ALONSO	BRA	12/8/88	M	1	(2)	
13	Pavel NEKHAICHIK		15/7/88	M	18	(5)	3
23	Edgar OLEKHNOVICH		17/5/87	M	16	(12)	2
6	Oleg PATOTSKIY		24/6/91	M		(2)	
17	Aleksandr PAVLOV		18/8/84	M	18	(10)	2
14	Artem RADKOV		26/8/85	D	26	(1)	1
10	RENAN Bardini Bressan	BRA	3/11/88	M	31	(1)	15
20	Vitaliy RODIONOV		11/12/83	A	25	(6)	8
4	Igor SHITOV		24/10/86	D	23		1
15	Maksim SKAVYSH		13/11/89	A	11	(15)	9
3	Sergei SOSNOVSKIY		14/8/81	D	22	(1)	1
22	Igor STASEVICH		21/10/85	M	8	(3)	1
16	Sergei VEREMKO		16/10/82	G	24		
8	Aleksandr VOLODKO		18/6/86	M	18	(10)	2
5	Aleksandr YUREVICH		8/8/79	D	28	(3)	1

FC BELSHINA BOBRUISK

Coach – Aleksandr Sednev
Founded – 1976
Stadium – Spartak (3,700)
MAJOR HONOURS: Belarus League – (1) 2001; Belarus Cup – (3) 1997, 1999, 2001.

2010

3/4	Dinamo Minsk	h	0-2	
10/4	BATE	a	0-2	
14/4	Dinamo Brest	h	1-0	*Belousov*
18/4	Zhodino	a	2-1	*Fursin, Lisitsa*
24/4	Shakhtyor	h	1-0	*Druchyk*
28/4	Minsk	h	1-0	*Lanko*
2/5	Neman	a	2-2	*Shchegrikovich (p), Jokšas*
7/5	Naftan	h	1-0	*Kovalenko*
11/5	Partizan	a	2-1	*Sashcheko, Shchegrikovich (p)*
15/5	Vitebsk	h	0-0	
22/5	Dnepr	a	3-1	*Lisitsa, Lanko, Kovalenko*
5/6	Dinamo Minsk	a	0-3	
9/6	BATE	h	0-1	
13/6	Dinamo Brest	a	1-1	*Lanko*
19/6	Zhodino	h	2-0	*Kovalenko, Sashcheko*
23/6	Shakhtyor	a	1-1	*Kovalenko*
27/6	Minsk	a	1-3	*Branfilov (p)*
3/7	Neman	h	0-2	
25/7	Naftan	a	0-4	
31/7	Partizan	h	2-0	*Kuchuk, Durai*
15/8	Vitebsk	a	0-0	
22/8	Dnepr	h	2-1	*Lanko, Sukharev*
28/8	Zhodino	h	1-1	*Branfilov (p)*
12/9	Dinamo Minsk	a	0-4	
18/9	Dnepr	h	1-1	*Yeremchuk*
26/9	Shakhtyor	h	1-3	*Branfilov (p)*
2/10	Vitebsk	a	2-0	*Lisitsa 2*
16/10	Naftan	h	1-1	*Bliznyuk*
23/10	Partizan	a	0-0	
31/10	Minsk	h	2-0	*og (Sachivko), Yeremchuk*
6/11	Neman	a	0-2	
13/11	BATE	h	1-3	*Lebedev*
21/11	Dinamo Brest	a	0-2	

No	Name	Nat	DoB	Pos	Aps	(s)	Gls
15	Aleksei BELOUSOV		26/4/76	D	22		1
19	Gennadiy BLIZNYUK		30/7/80	A	9		1
11	Nikolai BRANFILOV		16/12/77	D	25		3
3	Aleksandr BYLINA		26/3/83	D	14	(1)	
87	Yuriy DRUCHYK	UKR	2/2/87	D	21	(2)	1
5	Taras DURAI	UKR	31/7/84	D	8	(1)	1
15	Nikita FURSIN	RUS	9/3/83	D	15		1
27	Andrius JOKŠAS	LTU	12/1/79	M	6	(8)	1
27	Dmitriy KALACHEV		16/6/78	D	4	(2)	
29	Serhiy KOVALENKO	UKR	10/5/84	A	18	(13)	4
1	Anton KOVALEVSKIY		2/2/86	G	7	(1)	
9	Dmitriy KOVB		20/1/87	A	2	(4)	
9	Aleksei KUCHUK		9/9/86	A	6	(3)	1
14	Yevgeniy KUNTSEVICH		16/8/88	D	9	(5)	
23	Vitaliy LANKO		4/4/77	A	29	(3)	4
77	Aleksandr LEBEDEV		14/4/85	A	15	(8)	1
17	Igor LISITSA		10/4/88	M	12	(11)	4
24	Igor LOGVINOV		23/8/83	G	26		
7	Andrei MISYUK		20/3/81	M	7	(13)	
18	Aleksandr PROKOPENKO		10/5/90	A		(1)	
10	Denis SASHCHEKO		3/10/81	M	29	(2)	2
2	Aleksandr SHAGOIKO		27/7/80	D	6		
11	Dmitriy SHCHEGRIKOVICH		7/12/83	M	31		2
8	Sergei SUKHAREV	RUS	29/1/87	M	13	(9)	1
6	Aleksandr TISHKEVICH		16/2/86	M	2	(8)	
25	Mikhail YEREMCHUK		14/11/80	M	27	(4)	2

FC DINAMO BREST

Coach – Yuriy Puntus

Founded – 1960

Stadium – GOSK Brestskiy (10,080)

MAJOR HONOURS: Belarus Cup – (1) 2007.

10				
4	Shakhtyor	h	1-1	*Berezovskiy*
/4	Zhodino	h	3-2	*Mozolevskiy, Vasilyuk, Chelidze*
/4	Belshina	a	0-1	
/4	Minsk	h	2-1	*Vasilyuk, Mozolevskiy*
/4	Neman	a	0-0	
/4	Naftan	h	0-0	
5	Partizan	a	3-0	*Yanush 2, Chelidze*
5	Vitebsk	h	5-2	*Sokol (p), Makar, Berezovskiy, Kovalyuk, Mozolevskiy*
2/5	Dnepr	a	1-2	*Sokol*
5/5	Dinamo Minsk	h	1-2	*Sokol (p)*
9/5	BATE	a	0-1	
6	Shakhtyor	a	0-2	
6	Zhodino	a	1-0	*Yanush*
3/6	Belshina	h	1-1	*Sokol*
9/6	Minsk	a	1-1	*Chelidze*
3/6	Neman	h	4-0	*og (Shumanskiy), Sokol, Tsevan, Yanush*
7/6	Naftan	a	1-3	*Berezovskiy*
7	Partizan	h	1-1	*Makar*
5/7	Vitebsk	a	1-0	*Kibuk*
8	Dnepr	h	2-3	*Yanush, Vasilyuk (p)*
5/8	Dinamo Minsk	a	2-2	*Tsevan, Mozolevskiy*
2/8	BATE	h	1-4	*Kibuk*
9/8	Shakhtyor	a	1-1	*Yanush*
2/9	Vitebsk	h	2-0	*Mozolevskiy, Khvashchinskiy*
3/9	Naftan	a	0-1	
6/9	Partizan	h	4-0	*Makar, Mozolevskiy, Yanush, og (Vitus)*
/10	Minsk	a	2-2	*Yanush, Khvashchinskiy*
6/10	Neman	h	2-1	*Khvashchinskiy, Makar*
5/10	BATE	a	0-2	
1/10	Dnepr	a	1-1	*Mozolevskiy*
/11	Zhodino	h	3-1	*Khvashchinskiy, Yanush, Mozolevskiy*
3/11	Dinamo Minsk	a	0-2	
1/11	Belshina	h	2-0	*Yanush, Mozolevskiy*

o	Name	Nat	DoB	Pos	Aps	(s)	Gls
6	Aleksei BAGA		4/2/81	D	5	(1)	
1	Vitaliy BEREZOVSKIY	UKR	25/5/84	D	20		3
9	Igor BURKO		8/9/88	D	7		
	Zaza CHELIDZE	GEO	12/5/87	D	29	(1)	3
7	Aleksandr DEMIDOVICH		26/4/89	D	2	(1)	
4	Vitaliy GAIDUCHIK		12/7/89	D	23		
5	Ucha GOGOLADZE	GEO	4/9/90	A		(3)	
9	Aleksei GONCEAROV	MDA	24/2/84	D	1	(1)	
8	Andrei KARASEV		26/5/91	M	1	(4)	
6	Vladimir KHVASHCHINSKIY		10/5/90	A	10	(10)	4
4	Vitaliy KIBUK		7/1/89	A	6	(3)	2
3	Ilya KOLPACHUK		9/10/90	D	1	(2)	
8	Yuriy KOROLYUK		10/1/90	A		(5)	
4	Sergei KOVALYUK		7/1/80	M	11	(5)	1
	Sergei KOZAK		17/10/81	M	11	(6)	
2	Sergei KURGANSKIY		15/5/86	G	1		
1	Sergei KUZNETSOV		3/11/79	D	18	(2)	
	Givi KVARATSKHELIA	GEO	11/5/79	M	4		
20	Dmitriy MAKAR		1/10/81	M	14	(16)	4
18	Dmitriy MOZOLEVSKIY		30/4/85	A	29	(4)	9
3	Vladimir OSIPCHUK		31/5/92	M		(1)	
5	Aleksei PANKOVETS		18/4/81	D	30		
7	Olexandr PAPUSH	UKR	14/1/85	M	1	(9)	
	Aleksandr PLOTNIKOV	RUS	17/2/79	G	32		
54	Yuriy PUDYSHEV		3/4/54	M		(1)	
17	Sergei SHCHEGRIKOVICH		19/12/90	M	5	(3)	
15	Vladimir SHCHERBO		1/4/86	D	13	(3)	
13	Viktor SOKOL		9/5/81	M	26	(1)	5
17	Aleksei TARABANOV		3/5/84	M	4	(4)	
4	Andrei TSEVAN		15/3/86	M	19	(1)	2
10	Roman VASILYUK		23/11/78	A	18	(3)	3
5	Nikolai YANUSH		9/9/84	A	22	(6)	10

FC DINAMO MINSK

Coach – Sergei Gurenko; (12/5/10) Sergei Solodovnikov; (21/5/10) Vladimir Golmak

Founded – 1927

Stadium – Dinamo-Yuni (4,500) & Dinamo (40,000)

MAJOR HONOURS: USSR League – (1) 1982; Belarus League – (7) 1992, 1993, 1994, 1995 (spring), 1995 (autumn), 1997, 2004; Belarus Cup – (3) 1992, 1994, 2003.

2010				
3/4	Belshina	a	2-0	*Strakhanovich, Gavryushko*
10/4	Minsk	h	0-2	
14/4	Neman	a	1-0	*Kislyak*
18/4	Naftan	h	0-0	
24/4	Partizan	a	2-0	*Chukhlei, Sazankov*
28/4	Vitebsk	h	1-1	*Putilo*
2/5	Dnepr	a	0-1	
7/5	Shakhtyor	a	4-2	*Putilo, Martynovich, Sazankov, Strakhanovich*
11/5	BATE	h	0-1	
15/5	Dinamo Brest	a	2-1	*Rekish 2*
19/5	Zhodino	h	5-1	*Kislyak, Martynovich, Montaroup 2 (1p), Rekish*
5/6	Belshina	h	3-0	*Kislyak, Chukhlei, Putilo*
9/6	Minsk	a	2-0	*Putilo 2*
13/6	Neman	h	1-0	*Kislyak*
19/6	Naftan	a	2-0	*Sazankov 2*
23/6	Partizan	h	0-0	
27/6	Vitebsk	a	1-3	*Kislyak (p)*
4/7	Dnepr	h	3-0	*Sazankov, Martynovich, Putilo*
25/7	Shakhtyor	h	0-1	
15/8	Dinamo Brest	h	2-2	*Dragun, Kislyak*
23/8	Zhodino	a	0-2	
29/8	Dnepr	h	2-1	*Chukhlei, Kislyak (p)*
12/9	Belshina	h	4-0	*Lucas, Dragun, Kislyak, Bruno Furlan*
19/9	Shakhtyor	a	0-3	
22/9	BATE	a	3-1	*Chukhlei, Dragun, Lucas*
26/9	Vitebsk	h	0-2	
31/9	Naftan	a	0-2	
16/10	Partizan	h	5-1	*Bruno Furlan 2, Rekish, Veretilo, Chukhlei*
24/10	Minsk	a	0-0	
31/10	Neman	h	1-0	*Dragun*
8/11	BATE	a	0-4	
13/11	Dinamo Brest	h	2-0	*Lucas, Kislyak (p)*
21/11	Zhodino	a	1-3	*Shkabara*

No	Name	Nat	DoB	Pos	Aps	(s)	Gls
33	BRUNO de Oliveira FURLAN	BRA	9/7/92	A	11	(1)	3
24	Artem BULOICHIK		16/6/92	M	1	(7)	
9	Andrei CHUKHLEI		2/10/87	M	24	(1)	5
2	Stanislav DRAGUN		4/6/88	M	30	(1)	4
26	Aleksei GAVRILOVICH		5/1/90	D	4	(3)	
22	Aleksandr GAVRYUSHKO		23/1/86	A	2	(8)	1
35	Andrei GORBUNOV		29/5/83	G	25		
18	Filipp IVANOV		29/5/83	M		(1)	
17	JEFFERSON de Sousa Leite	BRA	7/1/89	M		(3)	
10	Sergei KISLYAK		6/8/87	M	25	(3)	9
13	Sergei KONDRATIYEV		2/2/90	D	21	(2)	
3	Pavel KRUK		3/2/92	D	3	(2)	
7	Aleksandr KUGAN		26/5/91	M		(6)	
16	LEONARDO Ramos dos Santos	BRA	9/6/92	A		(6)	
34	Alves Sotero da Cunha "LUCAS"	BRA	21/5/91	A	9	(4)	3
75	Vitaliy MARAKHOVSKIY	RUS	14/1/88	A	18		
23	Aleksandr MARTYNOVICH		26/8/87	D	18		3
27	Anton MATVEYENKO		3/9/86	M	2	(8)	
19	Aurélien MONTAROUP	FRA	19/12/85	D	22		2
32	Ruslan PIMENOV	RUS	25/11/81	D	1	(3)	
14	Anton PUTILO		10/6/87	M	18	(1)	6
15	Dmitriy REKISH		14/9/88	M	17	(11)	4
32	RENAN Rodrigues da Silva	BRA	9/10/89	M	8	(2)	
11	Aleksandr SAZANKOV		17/4/84	A	20	(2)	5

No	Name	Nat	DoB	Pos	Aps	(s)	Gls
21	Oleg SHKABARA		15/2/83	M	3	(4)	1
8	Oleg STRAKHANOVICH		13/10/79	M	28	(4)	2
1	Aleksandr SULIMA		1/8/79	G	8		
5	Tsyenchen VABHA		19/4/91	D	1	(2)	
5	Yanko Hristov VALKANOV	BUL	25/7/82	D	11		
20	Oleg VERETILO		10/7/88	D	29		1
25	Yuriy VOLOVIK		19/6/93	D	1	(1)	
4	Andrei ZALESKIY		20/1/91	D	3	(2)	

FC DNEPR MOGILEV

Coach – Andrei Skorobogatko

Founded – 1960

Stadium – Spartak (7,300)

MAJOR HONOURS: Belarus League – (1) 1998.

2010				
3/4	Minsk	a	1-2	*Lyasyuk (p)*
10/4	Neman	h	0-0	
14/4	Naftan	a	0-5	
18/4	Partizan	h	3-0	*Lyasyuk 2 (1p), Yurchenko*
24/4	Vitebsk	a	1-1	*Lyasyuk*
28/4	Shakhtyor	a	0-0	
10/5	Dinamo Minsk	h	1-0	*Karpovich*
7/5	BATE	a	0-3	
12/5	Dinamo Brest	h	2-1	*Bychenok, Tereshchenko*
15/5	Zhodino	a	3-2	*Karpovich, Bychenok 2*
22/5	Belshina	h	1-3	*Kalachev*
5/6	Minsk	h	1-5	*Bychenok*
9/6	Neman	a	2-1	*Turlin, Yurchenko*
13/6	Naftan	h	1-0	*Yurchenko*
19/6	Partizan	a	0-1	
23/6	Vitebsk	h	0-0	
27/6	Shakhtyor	h	0-2	
4/7	Dinamo Minsk	a	0-3	
25/7	BATE	h	0-2	
1/8	Dinamo Brest	a	3-2	*Chernykh 2, Yurchenko*
15/8	Zhodino	h	3-1	*Turlin 2, Zenkovich*
22/8	Belshina	a	1-2	*Yurchenko*
29/8	Dinamo Minsk	a	1-2	*Tereshchenko*
12/9	Minsk	h	3-0	*Yurchenko, Shuneiko, Tereshchenko*
18/9	Belshina	a	1-1	*Chernykh*
26/9	Neman	h	1-0	*Shuneiko*
3/10	Shakhtyor	a	2-3	*Yurchenko 2*
16/10	BATE	h	2-3	*Tereshchenko, Yurchenko*
23/10	Vitebsk	a	1-1	*Bychenok*
31/10	Dinamo Brest	h	1-1	*Zenkovich*
6/11	Naftan	a	2-1	*Tereshchenko, Chernykh*
13/11	Zhodino	h	0-1	
21/11	Partizan	a	3-4	*Turlin 3*

No	Name	Nat	DoB	Pos	Aps	(s)	Gls
7	Aleksandr BYCHENOK		30/5/85	M	30		5
15	Fedor CHERNYKH	LTU	21/5/91	A	10	(13)	4
3	Andriy HONCHAR	UKR	15/3/85	D	31		
17	JEFFERSON de Sousa Leite	BRA	7/1/89	M	1	(1)	
92	Dmitriy KALACHEV		16/6/78	M	15	(1)	1
2	Yevgeniy KAPOV		30/1/77	D	29	(1)	
8	Maksim KARPOVICH		27/2/86	M	18	(10)	2
1	Ruslan KOPANTSOV		12/5/81	G	32		
20	Mikhail KOZLOV		12/2/90	D	5	(8)	
17	Andrei LATYPOV		16/3/90	A		(1)	
32	Andrei LYASYUK		14/4/83	A	5	(3)	4
9	Ivan MAGAL		7/1/90	D		(2)	
37	Anton MATVEYENKO		3/9/86	D	5	(7)	
26	Vadim MYTNIK		5/7/88	D	2	(1)	
4	Denis OBRAZOV		24/6/88	D	20	(4)	
12	Andrei PORYVAYEV		3/1/82	D	3	(4)	
24	Andriy RASPOPOV	UKR	25/1/78	D	21	(5)	
31	Anton SHEPELEV		8/11/89	D	2		
6	Vladimir SHUNEIKO		22/4/74	D	22	(3)	2
11	Dmytro TERESHCHENKO	UKR	4/4/87	M	27	(1)	5
20	Olexiy TUPCHIY	UKR	22/8/86	M	14	(4)	
14	Dmitriy TURLIN		8/9/85	M	17	(8)	6
28	Igor YASINSKIY		4/7/90	M		(1)	
10	Vladimir YURCHENKO		26/1/89	A	27	(2)	9
39	Igor ZENKOVICH		17/9/87	A	16	(10)	2
5	Eduard ZHEVNEROV		1/11/87	D	10	(2)	
16	Vladimir ZHUROV		9/3/91	G	1		

FC MINSK

Coach – Vitaliy Tarakanov

Founded – 1995

Stadium – Torpedo (5,200) & Dinamo (40,000)

2010				
3/4	Dnepr	h	2-1	*Soro, Klimovich*
10/4	Dinamo Minsk	a	2-0	*Sheryakov 2*
14/4	BATE	h	0-0	
18/4	Dinamo Brest	a	1-2	*Razin*
24/4	Zhodino	h	2-1	*Razin, Osipenko*
28/4	Belshina	a	0-1	
2/5	Shakhtyor	h	0-2	
7/5	Neman	h	3-1	*Loshankov 2, Razin*
11/5	Naftan	a	0-0	
15/5	Partizan	h	3-0	*Razin, Soro, Khachaturyan*
21/5	Vitebsk	a	3-0	*Razin, Loshankov, Sheryakov (p)*
5/6	Dnepr	a	5-1	*Voronkov 3, Osipenko, Sheryakov*
9/6	Dinamo Minsk	h	0-2	
13/6	BATE	a	2-1	*Sheryakov 2*
19/6	Dinamo Brest	h	1-1	*Voronkov*
23/6	Zhodino	a	4-0	*Razin, Sheryakov 2, Osipenko*
27/6	Belshina	h	3-1	*Loshankov, Razin 2*
4/7	Shakhtyor	a	0-1	
25/7	Neman	a	1-0	*Loshankov*
1/8	Naftan	h	3-1	*Khachaturyan, Osipenko 2 (1p)*
14/8	Partizan	a	4-1	*Osipenko 2, Sheryakov, Razin (p)*
22/8	Vitebsk	h	5-1	*Voronkov, Kirilchik, Loshankov 2, Razin*
28/8	Partizan	a	3-1	*Osipenko 2, Rybak*
12/9	Dnepr	a	0-3	
18/9	Neman	h	2-0	*Klimovich, Gigevich*
26/9	BATE	a	1-2	*Sachivko*
2/10	Dinamo Brest	h	2-2	*Gigevich 2*
16/10	Zhodino	a	1-1	*og (Lavrik)*
24/10	Dinamo Minsk	h	0-0	
31/10	Belshina	a	0-2	
6/11	Shakhtyor	h	1-2	*Osipenko*
13/11	Vitebsk	a	3-1	*Pyatrauskas, Gigevich, Razin*
21/11	Naftan	h	2-0	*Soro, og (Zyulev)*

No	Name	Nat	DoB	Pos	Aps	(s)	Gls
5	Andrei DIVAKOV		7/10/78	D	4	(6)	
8	Sergei GIGEVICH		26/1/87	M	5	(8)	4
9	Andrei KHACHATURYAN		2/9/87	M	4	(16)	2
15	Pavel KIRILCHIK		4/1/81	M	11	(2)	1
13	Dmitriy KLIMOVICH		9/2/84	D	32	(1)	2
18	Sergei KOSHEL		14/3/86	A	1	(9)	
16	Aleksandr LENTSEVICH		2/5/79	G	2		
11	Yevgeniy LOSHANKOV		2/1/79	M	21	(6)	7
22	Donatas NAVIKAS	LTU	30/6/83	M	5	(14)	
26/14	Dmitriy OSIPENKO		12/12/82	A	31	(1)	10
10	Ionas PYATRAUSKAS		18/5/79	D	29		1
24	Artem RAKHMANOV		10/7/90	D	9		
6	Andrei RAZIN		12/8/79	M	28		11
8	Pavel RYBAK		11/9/83	D	28		1
20	Aleksandr SACHIVKO		5/1/86	M	24	(1)	1
19/33	Andrei SHERYAKOV		10/11/82	A	17	(12)	9
1	Simas SKINDERIS	LTU	17/2/81	G	31		
30	Taïna Adama SORO	CIV	20/12/81	M	31		3
2	Ihor VORONKOV	UKR	24/4/81	M	33		5
7	Hidetoshi WAKUI	JPN	12/2/83	M		(2)	
21	Yakiv ZALEVSKIY	UKR	30/5/80	M	17	(9)	
77	Nikolai ZENKO		11/3/89	A		(5)	

FC NAFTAN NOVOPOLOTSK

Coach – Igor Kovalevich

Founded – 1995

Stadium – Atlant (5,300)

MAJOR HONOURS: Belarus Cup – (1) 2009.

10

4	Partizan	h	1-0	*Politevich*
/4	Vitebsk	a	2-4	*Yatskevich, Shakov*
/4	Dnepr	h	5-0	*Stripeikis, Yatskevich, Shakov, Gorbachev, Zyulev*
/4	Dinamo Minsk	a	0-0	
/4	BATE	h	0-2	
/4	Dinamo Brest	a	0-0	
5	Zhodino	h	1-1	*Politevich*
5	Belshina	a	0-1	
/5	Minsk	h	0-0	
/5	Neman	a	0-0	
/5	Shakhtyor	h	0-2	
6	Partizan	a	1-1	*Shakov*
6	Vitebsk	h	0-0	
3/6	Dnepr	a	0-1	
9/6	Dinamo Minsk	h	0-2	
3/6	BATE	a	1-1	*og (Sosnovskiy)*
7/6	Dinamo Brest	h	3-1	*og (Chelidze), Rudik, Zuyev*
5/7	Belshina	h	4-0	*Zhukovskiy, Gavryushko (p), Zuyev, Stripeikis*
8	Minsk	a	1-3	*Gordeichuk*
5/8	Neman	h	4-1	*Rudik, Gordeichuk, Stripeikis, Gavryushko (p)*
8/8	Zhodino	a	4-1	*Zhukovskiy 2, Gavryushko 2*
2/8	Shakhtyor	a	0-0	
3/8	Neman	h	2-1	*Politevich 2*
1/9	BATE	a	0-1	
3/9	Dinamo Brest	h	1-0	*Gordeichuk*
6/9	Zhodino	a	2-0	*Zhukovskiy, Shakov*
10	Dinamo Minsk	h	2-0	*Zhukovskiy, Politevich*
6/10	Belshina	a	1-1	*Rudik*
4/10	Shakhtyor	h	1-0	*Gavryushko*
1/10	Vitebsk	a	0-2	
11	Dnepr	h	1-2	*Rudik (p)*
3/11	Partizan	h	4-4	*Verkhovtsov, Yatskevich 2, Gorbachev*
1/11	Minsk	a	0-2	

o	Name	Nat	DoB	Pos	Aps	(s)	Gls
8	Nikita BUKATKIN		7/3/88	M	28		
	Artem CHELYADINSKIY		29/12/77	D	32		
2	Aleksandr DEGTEREV		20/3/86	M	10	(6)	
	Artem FEDORCHENKO	UKR	13/4/90	D	2	(2)	
4	Aleksandr GAVRYUSHKO		23/1/86	A	14		5
1	Artem GOMELKO		8/12/89	G	22		
	Mikhail GORBACHEV		29/7/83	D	30		2
6	Mikhail GORDEICHUK		23/10/89	M	29	(3)	3
3	JUVENAL Gomes da Silva	BRA	5/6/79	D	24	(1)	
2	Dmytro KOLODIN	UKR	12/4/78	M		(7)	
	Sergei POLITEVICH		9/4/90	D	24	(6)	5
	Nikolai ROMANYUK		2/6/84	G	11		
	Filipp RUDIK	RUS	22/3/87	M	15	(1)	4
5	Vladimir SHAKOV		28/8/84	A	3	(19)	4
0	Nikita SHUGUNKOV		17/4/92	A		(2)	
1	Valeriy STRIPEIKIS		13/11/74	A	13	(10)	3
	Vitaliy TARASHCHIK		18/5/80	M	11		
8	Dmitriy VERKHOVTSOV		10/10/86	D	21	(2)	1
7	Andrei YAKIMOV		17/11/89	M		(3)	
	Aleksandr YATSKEVICH		4/1/85	A	26	(4)	4
	Nikolai YEZERSKIY		17/6/84	D	2	(3)	
25	Valeriy ZHUKOVSKIY		21/5/84	M	32		5
20	Yevgeniy ZUYEV		2/3/83	A	5	(8)	2
33	Igor ZYULEV		5/1/84	M	9	(19)	1

FC NEMAN GRODNO

Coach – Oleg Radushko;

(16/7/10) Aleksandr Koreshkov (RUS)

Founded – 1964

Stadium – Central Sportkomplex Neman (9,000)

MAJOR HONOURS: Belarus Cup – (1) 1993.

2010

3/4	Vitebsk	h	0-0	
10/4	Dnepr	a	0-0	
14/4	Dinamo Minsk	h	0-1	
18/4	BATE	a	0-0	
24/4	Dinamo Brest	h	0-0	
28/4	Zhodino	a	0-2	
2/5	Belshina	h	2-2	*Kovalenok, Nadiyevskiy (p)*
7/5	Minsk	a	1-3	*Kovalenok*
11/5	Shakhtyor	h	0-0	
15/5	Naftan	h	0-0	
22/5	Partizan	a	4-0	*Kovalenok 3, Misyuk*
5/6	Vitebsk	a	2-2	*Kovalenok 2 (1p)*
9/6	Dnepr	h	1-2	*Kovalenok*
13/6	Dinamo Minsk	a	0-1	
19/6	BATE	h	0-5	
23/6	Dinamo Brest	a	0-4	
27/6	Zhodino	h	0-0	
3/7	Belshina	a	2-0	*Demidovich 2*
25/7	Minsk	h	0-1	
1/8	Shakhtyor	a	1-4	*Demidovich*
15/8	Naftan	a	1-4	*Kovalenok*
22/8	Partizan	h	0-1	
28/8	Naftan	a	1-2	*Lebedev*
12/9	Partizan	h	2-0	*Demidovich, Kovalenok*
18/9	Minsk	a	0-2	
26/9	Dnepr	a	0-1	
3/10	BATE	h	1-1	*Savostyanov (p)*
16/10	Dinamo Brest	a	1-2	*Kovalenok*
23/10	Zhodino	h	2-1	*Levitskiy, Kovalenok*
31/10	Dinamo Minsk	a	0-1	
6/11	Belshina	h	2-0	*Lebedev, Sluka*
13/11	Shakhtyor	a	1-0	*Levitskiy*
21/11	Vitebsk	h	3-0	*Pavlov, Demidovich, Nadiyevskiy*

No	Name	Nat	DoB	Pos	Aps	(s)	Gls
33	Ilya ALIYEV		20/5/91	M		(2)	
14	Aleksandr ANYUKEVICH		10/4/92	D	5	(3)	
30	Roman ASTAPENKO		10/3/80	G	21		
25	Dmitriy CHAKA		16/3/90	D		(1)	
16	Sergei CHERNIK		20/7/88	G	12	(3)	
15	Alexandru COVALENCO	MDA	25/3/78	D	13		
7	Vadim DEMIDOVICH		20/9/85	A	19	(10)	5
13	Mohamed Seydou DERA	CIV	9/4/86	M	19	(1)	
13	Artem GONCHARIK		13/4/80	M	1	(4)	
17	Andrei GORBACH		20/5/85	D	24	(2)	
11	Aleksei GURKO		26/6/87	A		(2)	
2	Artem GUZIK		20/3/92	D		(3)	
5	Oleg ICHIM	MDA	27/10/79	D	17		
20	Serghei IEPUREANU	MDA	12/9/76	M	3	(1)	
10	Dmitriy KOVALENOK		3/11/77	A	18	(3)	12
11	Dmitriy LEBEDEV		13/5/86	M	12		2
46	Aleksei LEGCHILIN		11/4/92	M	16	(5)	
6	Sergei LEVITSKIY		17/3/90	M	19	(6)	2
18	Nikolai MISYUK		4/1/87	A	6	(5)	1
4	Vitaliy NADIYEVSKIY		20/10/81	D	20	(2)	2
23	Valeriy PAVLOV	RUS	7/2/86	M	7	(5)	1
21	Pavel PLASKONNIY		29/1/85	D	8		
55	Dmitriy ROVNEIKO		13/5/90	D	33		
3	Yevgeniy SAVOSTYANOV		30/1/88	M	30		1
5	Aleksandr SEMENOV	RUS	11/6/82	A	2	(4)	
8	Yuriy SHUMANSKIY		21/9/80	D	11	(3)	
20	Marián SLUKA	SVK	22/7/79	M	4	(1)	1
15	Valeriy TARASENKO		1/9/81	D	3	(6)	
18	Andrei TSAPLIN	RUS	22/1/77	M	4		
19	Arvidas VEIKUTIS	LTU	19/3/87	M	6	(8)	

No	Name	Nat	DoB	Pos	Aps	(s)	Gls
19	Dmitriy VERSTAK		28/9/80	A	1		
88	Vitaliy VOLODENKOV		25/4/76	M	25	(1)	
77	Aleksandr YEDESHKO		28/1/93	M		(4)	
9	Aleksandr ZAKHAROV	RUS	11/3/87	A	4	(5)	
1	Filipp VOITEKHOVICH		26/3/90	G	2		
16	Dmitriy YUZVOVICH		25/1/89	A	8	(12)	1
14	Yegor ZUBOVICH		1/6/89	M	21	(8)	8

FC PARTIZAN MINSK

Coach – Ludas Rumbutis; (26/5/10) Vladimir Gevorkyan; (16/10/10) Ludas Rumbutis

Founded – 1947

Stadium – Traktor (17,600)

MAJOR HONOURS: Belarus Cup – (2) 2005, 2008.

2010				
2/4	Naftan	a	0-1	
10/4	Shakhtyor	a	0-1	
14/4	Vitebsk	h	0-2	
18/4	Dnepr	a	0-3	
23/4	Dinamo Minsk	h	0-2	
28/4	BATE	a	0-6	
2/5	Dinamo Brest	h	0-3	
7/5	Zhodino	a	2-2	*Činikas, Karpovich*
11/5	Belshina	h	1-2	*Mayevskiy*
15/5	Minsk	a	0-3	
22/5	Neman	h	0-4	
5/6	Naftan	h	1-1	*Yuzvovich*
9/6	Shakhtyor	h	0-2	
13/6	Vitebsk	a	1-0	*Tolkanitsa*
19/6	Dnepr	h	1-0	*Rafael Ledesma*
23/6	Dinamo Minsk	a	0-0	
27/6	BATE	h	1-1	*Rafael Ledesma*
4/7	Dinamo Brest	a	1-1	*Zubovich*
25/7	Zhodino	h	2-3	*Zubovich, Mayevskiy*
31/7	Belshina	a	0-2	
14/8	Minsk	h	1-4	*og (Rybak)*
22/8	Neman	a	1-0	*Kendysh*
28/8	Minsk	h	1-3	*Rafael Ledesma*
12/9	Neman	a	0-2	
19/9	BATE	h	1-1	*Mendy*
26/9	Dinamo Brest	a	0-4	
2/10	Zhodino	h	1-0	*Karpovich*
16/10	Dinamo Minsk	a	1-5	*Zubovich*
23/10	Belshina	h	0-0	
31/10	Shakhtyor	a	0-4	
6/11	Vitebsk	h	0-1	
13/11	Naftan	a	4-4	*Mayevskiy, Zubovich 2, Kendysh*
21/11	Dnepr	h	4-3	*Zubovich 3, Mayevskiy*

No	Name	Nat	DoB	Pos	Aps	(s)	Gls
12	Džugas BARTKUS	LTU	7/11/89	G	7		
21	Anton BUBNOV		23/11/88	M	8	(8)	
6	Aboubacar CAMARA	GUI	3/11/88	M	11	(6)	
13	Marius ČINIKAS	LTU	17/5/86	M	26		1
30	Denis DECHKO		26/4/90	G	4		
33	Maksim GORBACH		14/9/83	D	8	(1)	
9	Mikhail GORNAK		9/3/89	A	3	(2)	
33	Anatoliy KARP		2/10/92	M	2	(1)	
55	Igor KARPOVICH		2/8/88	D	27	(2)	2
27/7	Yuriy KENDYSH		10/6/90	M	26	(3)	2
4	Sergei KHALETSKIY		14/4/84	D	28		
17	Sergei KORSAK		24/2/89	M	8	(14)	
38	Aleksandr MAKAS		8/10/91	A	10	(12)	
20	Ivan MAYEVSKIY		5/5/88	M	29	(2)	4
22	Pascal MENDY	SEN	11/1/79	M	20		1
35	Vladimir PYATIGORETS		12/4/90	G	20	(1)	
21	RAFAEL Pompeo Rodrigues LEDESMA	BRA	31/12/82	M	20	(6)	3
18	Evaldas RAZULIS	LTU	3/4/86	A	6	(3)	
5	Dmitriy SHMATKO		26/7/89	D	8	(1)	
2	Aleksandr SKSHYNETSKIY		28/2/90	D	1	(2)	
3	Aleksandr STASHCHENYUK		23/2/83	D	4	(1)	
77	Donatas STROCKIS	LTU	23/3/87	D	15	(1)	
8	Aleksandr TOLKANITSA		9/5/89	M	25	(7)	1
15	Maksim VITUS		11/2/89	D	16	(3)	

FC SHAKHTYOR SOLIGORSK

Coach – Eduard Malofeyev; (26/4/10) Vladimir Zhuravel

Founded – 1963

Stadium – Stroitel (4,200)

MAJOR HONOURS: Belarus League – (1) 2005; Belarus Cup – (1) 2004.

2010				
3/4	Dinamo Brest	a	1-1	*Ryndyuk*
10/4	Partizan	h	1-0	*Komarovskiy*
14/4	Zhodino	a	1-1	*Rozhkov*
18/4	Vitebsk	h	1-1	*Denisevich (p)*
24/4	Belshina	a	0-1	
28/4	Dnepr	h	0-0	
2/5	Minsk	a	2-0	*Komarovskiy, Sitko*
7/5	Dinamo Minsk	h	2-4	*Balanovich, Denisevich*
11/5	Neman	a	0-0	
15/5	BATE	h	0-0	
21/5	Naftan	a	2-0	*Balanovich, Rios*
5/6	Dinamo Brest	h	2-0	*Sitko, Ryndyuk*
9/6	Partizan	a	2-0	*Komarovskiy, Denisevich*
13/6	Zhodino	h	4-1	*Grenkov, Denisevich, Rynduyk, Rios*
19/6	Vitebsk	a	3-1	*Sitko, Komarovskiy, Ryndyuk*
23/6	Belshina	h	1-1	*Balanovich*
27/6	Dnepr	a	2-0	*Denisevich, Komarovskiy*
4/7	Minsk	h	1-0	*Sitko*
25/7	Dinamo Minsk	a	1-0	*Gukailo*
1/8	Neman	h	4-1	*Alumona 3, Denisevich (p)*
14/8	BATE	a	0-2	
22/8	Naftan	h	0-0	
29/8	Dinamo Brest	h	1-1	*Kirenkin*
12/9	Zhodino	a	1-0	*Rios*
19/9	Dinamo Minsk	h	3-0	*Rios, Sitko, Petrov*
26/9	Belshina	a	3-1	*Komarovskiy, Sitko, Balanovich*
3/10	Dnepr	h	3-2	*Alumona 2, Sitko*
16/10	Vitebsk	h	2-1	*Sitko, Alumona*
24/10	Naftan	a	0-1	
31/10	Partizan	h	4-0	*Yanushkevich, Alumona, Denisevich, Sitko*
6/11	Minsk	a	2-1	*Grenkov, Balanovich*
13/11	Neman	h	0-1	
21/11	BATE	a	2-1	*Alumona, Denisevich*

No	Name	Nat	DoB	Pos	Aps	(s)	Gls
11	Aleksandr ALUMONA	RUS	18/12/83	A	8	(7)	8
2	Sergei BALANOVICH		29/8/87	D	26	(3)	5
8	Ivan DENISEVICH		9/11/84	M	31	(2)	8
9	Aleksandr GRENKOV		20/1/78	M	29	(3)	2
12	Maksim GUKAILO		16/10/79	D	16	(2)	1
30	Roman KIRENKIN		20/2/81	D	16	(1)	1
15	Dmitriy KOMAROVSKIY		10/10/86	A	33		6
20	Sergei KOVALCHUK		9/10/78	D	4	(1)	
22	Eduardas KURSKIS	LTU	17/10/86	G	10		
7	Andrei LEONCHIK		2/1/77	M	27	(2)	
11	Mikhail MARTINOVICH		14/9/79	M		(3)	
10	Sergei NIKIFORENKO		18/2/78	A	1	(8)	
3	Nikolai OSOPOVICH		29/5/86	D	4	(7)	
14	Aleksei PETROV		30/4/91	A		(5)	1
21	Pavel PLASKONNIY		29/1/85	D	8	(2)	
33	Denis POLYAKOV		17/4/91	M	27	(1)	
17	Aleksei RIOS		14/5/87	M	5	(21)	4
4	Igor ROZHKOV		24/6/81	M	31	(1)	1
78	Nikolai RYNDYUK		2/2/78	A	7	(7)	4
24	Pavel SITKO		17/12/85	M	26	(6)	9
70	Yuriy TSYGALKO		27/5/83	G	23	(1)	
23	Kirill VERGEICHIK		23/8/91	A		(4)	
31	Denis YAKUBOVICH		31/3/88	D	1	(1)	
5	Aleksei YANUSHKEVICH		15/1/86	D	30		1

FC TORPEDO ZHODINO

Coach – Aleksandr Lisovskiy; (26/7/10) Sergei Gurenko
Founded – 1961
Stadium – Torpedo (3,020)

10				
4	BATE	h	0-1	
/4	Dinamo Brest	a	2-3	*Brusnikin, Beganskiy*
/4	Shakhtyor	h	1-1	*Karolik*
/4	Belshina	h	1-2	*Levitskiy*
/4	Minsk	a	1-2	*Branovitskiy*
/4	Neman	h	2-0	*Kryvobok, Beganskiy*
5	Naftan	a	1-1	*Levitskiy*
5	Partizan	h	2-2	*Beganskiy, Kontsevoi*
/5	Vitebsk	a	2-0	*Beganskiy (p), Brusnikin*
/5	Dnepr	h	2-3	*Beganskiy 2 (1p)*
/5	Dinamo Minsk	a	1-5	*Kryvobok*
6	BATE	a	0-1	
6	Dinamo Brest	h	0-1	
/6	Shakhtyor	a	1-4	*Beganskiy*
/6	Belshina	a	0-2	
/6	Minsk	h	0-4	
/6	Neman	a	0-0	
/7	Partizan	a	3-2	*Kryvobok 2, Levitskiy*
/7	Vitebsk	h	0-4	
/8	Dnepr	a	1-3	*Lavrik*
/8	Naftan	h	1-4	*Levitskiy*
/8	Dinamo Minsk	h	2-0	*Levitskiy 2 (1p)*
/8	Belshina	a	1-1	*Brusnikin*
2/9	Shakhtyor	h	0-1	
3/9	Vitebsk	a	1-0	*Kryvobok*
5/9	Naftan	h	0-2	
10	Partizan	a	0-1	
5/10	Minsk	h	1-1	*Kryvobok*
3/10	Neman	a	1-2	*Solovei*
0/10	BATE	h	1-1	*Karshakevich*
11	Dinamo Brest	a	1-3	*Kryvobok*
3/11	Dnepr	a	1-0	*Levitskiy (p)*
1/11	Dinamo Minsk	h	3-1	*Lavrik, Levitskiy 2*

o	Name	Nat	DoB	Pos	Aps	(s)	Gls
8	Ilya ALEKSIYEVICH		10/2/91	M	2	(12)	
1	Pavel BEGANSKIY		9/1/81	A	11	(4)	7
	Yevgeniy BRANOVITSKIY		15/5/81	D	7		1
	Anton BRUSNIKIN	RUS	13/1/86	M	19	(9)	3
	Vladimir BUSHMA		24/11/83	G	22		
	Lasha DEKANOSIDZE	GEO	9/7/87	M	1		
0	Nikita FURSIN	RUS	9/3/83	D	7		
0	Ilya GAVRILOV		26/9/88	G	3		
8	Dmitriy GINTOV		14/9/84	M	8	(1)	
	Denis KAROLIK		7/5/79	A	10	(13)	1
1	Valeriy KARSHAKEVICH		15/2/88	D	21	(1)	1
7	Andrei KAZARIN		27/10/84	D	11	(3)	
6	Sergei KONTSEVOI		21/6/86	D	19		1
4	Sergei KOVALYUK		7/1/80	M	13	(1)	
7	Aleksei KOZLOV		11/7/89	M	21	(5)	
5	Aleksandr KRYAKUSHIN		15/3/91	G		(1)	
7	Ihor KRYVOBOK	UKR	28/7/78	A	21	(12)	7
3	Andrei LAVRIK		7/12/74	M	14		2
0	Artur LEVITSKIY		17/3/85	M	32		9
0	Aleksei MARTYNETS		13/5/85	M	16	(7)	
	Vladimir MOROZ		4/9/85	M	7		
3	Simon OGAR Veron	NGA	24/4/87	M	9		
3	Yuriy OSTROUKH		21/1/88	D	15	(2)	
30	Olexandr PAPUSH	UKR	14/1/85	M	10	(3)	
16	Denis PARECHIN		17/11/79	G	8	(1)	
4	Serhiy PONOMARENKO	UKR	8/12/83	A	20		
26	Anton RYABTSEV		19/2/84	D	12		
13	Yuriy RYZHKO		10/10/89	D	3	(2)	
19	Nikolai SHVYDAKOV		6/7/80	A	3	(1)	
2	Artem SOLOVEI		1/11/90	M	8	(13)	1
55	Valeriy TARASENKO		1/9/81	D	9		
14	Vadim YERCHIK		14/7/91	A	1	(4)	

FC VITEBSK

Coach – Yuriy Konoplev
Founded – 1960
Stadium – Central Sportkomplex (CSK) (8,300)
MAJOR HONOURS: Belarus Cup – (1) 1998.

2010				
3/4	Neman	a	0-0	
10/4	Naftan	h	4-2	*Sļesarčuks, Kobets 2, Sorokin*
14/4	Partizan	a	2-0	*Usov, Panasyuk*
18/4	Shakhtyor	a	1-1	*Usov*
24/4	Dnepr	h	1-1	*Trukhov*
28/4	Dinamo Minsk	a	1-1	*Gorovtsov*
2/5	BATE	h	0-0	
7/5	Dinamo Brest	a	2-5	*Sļesarčuks, Trukhov*
11/5	Zhodino	h	0-2	
15/5	Belshina	a	0-0	
21/5	Minsk	h	0-3	
5/6	Neman	h	2-2	*Lebedev (p), Usov*
9/6	Naftan	a	0-0	
13/6	Partizan	h	0-1	
19/6	Shakhtyor	h	1-3	*Usov*
23/6	Dnepr	a	0-0	
27/6	Dinamo Minsk	h	3-1	*Sļesarčuks 2, Sorokin*
3/7	BATE	a	0-4	
25/7	Dinamo Brest	h	0-1	
31/7	Zhodino	a	4-0	*Gorovtsov, Usov, og (Karshakevich), Kholodkov*
15/8	Belshina	h	0-0	
22/8	Minsk	a	1-5	*Kholodkov*
29/8	BATE	h	1-6	*Sļesarčuks*
12/9	Dinamo Brest	a	0-2	
18/9	Zhodino	h	0-1	
26/9	Dinamo Minsk	a	2-0	*Sļesarčuks, Baranok*
2/10	Belshina	h	0-2	
16/10	Shakhtyor	a	1-2	*Sļesarčuks*
23/10	Dnepr	h	1-1	*Sļesarčuks*
31/10	Naftan	h	2-0	*Kobets 2*
6/11	Partizan	a	1-0	*Panasyuk*
13/11	Minsk	h	1-3	*Kholodkov*
21/11	Neman	a	0-3	

No	Name	Nat	DoB	Pos	Aps	(s)	Gls
22	Andrei BARANOK		20/7/79	M	32		1
25	Svyatoslav BOKHAN		26/6/91	M		(2)	
5	Dmitriy CHALEI		4/2/78	D	16		
10	Vitaliy DEIKALO		18/4/84	A		(1)	
20	Andrei GOROVTSOV		2/4/81	D	20	(3)	2
14	Vadims GOSPODARS	LVA	25/12/83	M	20	(11)	
1	Dmitriy GUSHCHENKO		12/5/88	G	21		
21	Aleksei KHALETSKIY		19/6/84	D	12		
17	Igor KHOLODKOV		19/4/91	A	1	(10)	3
18	Aleksandr KOBETS		11/6/81	M	27	(1)	4
4	Yuriy KOLOMYTS		30/4/79	D	15		
15	Aleksandr KOLOTSEI		27/1/88	M	1	(4)	
12	Artem KOSAK		22/2/77	D	11		
3	Jurijs KSENZOVS	LVA	5/6/81	D	9		
24	Dmitriy LEBEDEV		13/5/86	M	4	(6)	1
33	Pavel LYUTKO		1/7/87	D	19	(7)	
8	Igor MAKAROV		26/2/85	M	4		
7	Vitaliy PANASYUK		9/2/80	D	27		2
23	Aleksei PLYASUNOV		3/1/91	M		(2)	
9	Guntars SILAGAILIS	LVA	31/8/84	A	3	(15)	
19	Artem SKITOV		21/1/91	M	3	(8)	
8	Oleg SLAUTIN		21/4/86	A	1	(5)	
13	Igors SĻESARČUKS	LVA	31/3/76	A	26	(3)	8
37	Roman SOROKIN	RUS	17/5/85	M	26	(1)	2
55	Igor TRUKHOV		19/8/76	M	32		2
11	Ruslan USOV		4/8/79	A	21	(5)	5
16	Yuriy VASYUTIN		20/7/78	G	12		

TOP GOALSCORERS 2010

15 RENAN (BATE)

12 Dmitriy KOVALENOK (Neman)

11 Andrei RAZIN (Minsk)

10 Nikolai YANUSH (Dinamo Brest)
Dmitriy OSIPENKO (Minsk)

9 Aleksandr ALUMONA (BATE/Shakhtyor)
Maksim SKAVYSH (BATE)
Dmitriy MOZOLEVSKIY (Dinamo Brest)
Sergei KISLYAK (Dinamo Minsk)
Vladimir YURCHENKO (Dnepr)
Andrei SHERYAKOV (Minsk)
Pavel SITKO (Shakhtyor)
Artur LEVITSKIY (Zhodino)

PROMOTED CLUB

FC GOMEL

Coach – Oleg Kubarev
Founded – 1995
Stadium – Centralnyi (14,307)
MAJOR HONOURS: Belarus League – (1) 2003; Belarus Cup – (2) 2002, 2011.

SECOND LEVEL FINAL TABLE 2010

		Pld	W	D	L	F	A	Pts
1	FC Gomel	30	27	1	2	80	16	82
2	FC SKVICH Minsk	30	17	7	6	52	21	58
3	FC DSK Gomel	30	17	7	6	52	26	58
4	FC Granit Mikashevichi	30	16	8	6	52	23	56
5	FC Rudensk	30	12	7	11	37	39	43
6	FC Baranovichi	30	11	10	9	31	37	43
7	FC Polotsk	30	9	12	9	38	34	39
8	FC Khimik Svetlogorsk	30	10	7	13	37	44	37
9	FC Slaviya Mozyr	30	10	7	13	33	44	37
10	FC Volna Pinsk	30	11	2	17	31	48	35
11	FC Veras Nesvizh	30	9	8	13	31	39	35
12	FC Smorgon	30	8	8	14	33	43	32
13	FC BelCard Grodno	30	8	6	16	25	40	30
14	FC Vedrich-97 Rechitsa	30	8	6	16	29	46	30
15	FC Kommunalnik Slonim	30	5	13	12	23	48	28
16	FC Lida	30	4	7	19	23	59	19

PROMOTION/RELEGATION PLAY-OFFS

(25/11/10 & 28/11/10)
SKVICH 1, Zhodino 3
Zhodino 0, SKVICH 0
(Zhodino 3-1)

DOMESTIC CUP 2010/11

KUBOK BELARUSII

SECOND ROUND

(7/7/10)
Baranovichi 0, BATE 3

(17/7/10)
Gomelzheldortrans 1, Neman 5
Gorodeya 3, Granit 0
Khimik Svetlogorsk 2, Vitebsk 3 *(aet)*
Lida 1, Belshina 3
Molodechno 0, FC Gomel 5
Osipovichi 0, Volna 7
Polotsk 0, DSK Gomel 1
Slutsksahar 0, Minsk 7
Veras 0, Shakhtyor Soligorsk

(18/7/10)
Kommunalnik Slonim 2, Zhodino 0
Rudensk 2, Dnepr 1
SKVICH 1, Partizan 1 *(aet; 2-4 pens)*
Slaviya 0, Naftan 1
Smorgon 1, Dinamo Minsk 2
Vedrich-97 0, Dinamo Brest 2

THIRD ROUND

(22/9/10)
Belshina 2, Kommunalnik Slonim 1 *(aet)*
Minsk 3, DSK Gomel 1 *(aet)*
Naftan 4, Gorodeya 2
Rudensk 0, FC Gomel 5
Shakhtyor Soligorsk 4, Volna 0 *(aet)*
Vitebsk 1, Neman 1 *(aet; 4-5 pens)*

(27/10/10)
Partizan 1, Dinamo Minsk 0

(27/11/10)
BATE 0, Dinamo Brest 1

QUARTER-FINALS

(1/3/11 & 5/3/11)
Shakhtyor Soligorsk 2 *(Kirenkin 19, 56)*, Dinamo Brest 1 *(Tarasenko 79)*
Dinamo Brest 1 *(Chelidze 35)*, Shakhtyor Soligorsk 1 *(Yanushkevich 63)*
(Shakhtyor Soligorsk 3-2)

(2/3/11 & 6/3/11)
Belshina 0, Minsk 1 *(Razin 90+2)*
Minsk 0, Belshina 2 *(Branfilov 30p, Lisovyi 36)*
(Belshina 2-1)

Neman 1 *(Demidovich 65)*, Naftan 1 *(Khlebosolov 90+2)*
Naftan 0, Neman 2 *(Frunza 48, Denisevich 86)*
(Neman 3-1)

Partizan 0, FC Gomel 0
FC Gomel 3 *(Kuzmenok 2, Platonov D. 72p, 90+3)*, Partizan 2 *(Korsak 32, Makas 69)*
(FC Gomel 3-2)

SEMI-FINALS

(13/3/11 & 20/3/11)
Belshina 0, Neman 1 *(Frunza 14)*
Neman 0, Belshina 0
(Neman 1-0)

FC Gomel 2 *(Zuyev 42, Kontsevoi 70)*, Shakhtyor Soligorsk 1 *(Komarovskiy 40)*
Shakhtyor Soligorsk 1 *(Grenkov 17)*, FC Gomel 2 *(Kuzmenok 6, Platonov D. 14p)*
(FC Gomel 4-2)

FINAL

(29/5/11)
Traktor stadium, Minsk
FC GOMEL 2 *(Rybak 87og, Covalenco 90og)*
FC NEMAN GRODNO 0
Referee – *Tsinkevich*
FC GOMEL – *Bushma, Kontsevoi, Stepanov, Kashevskiy, Yevseyenko, Shmakov (Matveichik 90+3), Kozeka, Levitskiy, Stasevich, Timoshenko (Aleksiyevich 77), Zuyev (Kuzmenok 90).*
NEMAN – *Chernik, Covalenco, Plaskonniy, Gorbach (Lebedev 66), Nadiyevskiy (Kovalenok 90+1), Suchkov, Strakhanovich, Demidovich, Rybak, Frunza, Legchilin (Savitskiy 70).*

CLUB COMMUNICATION 2011

C BATE Borisov

-25, Revolution Avenue
-222120 Borisov

l	+375 177 734 123
x	+375 177 734 123
eb	fcbate.by
nail	club@fcbate.by
edia Officer	Sergei Dashkevich

C Belshina Bobruisk

let VLKSM street 26
-213810 Bobruisk

l	+375 225 44 00 56
x	+375 225 43 11 78
eb	fcbelshina.by
nail	fcbelshina@mail.ru
edia Officer	Vladimir Kandybo

C Dinamo Brest

vanevskogo street 7
-224075 Brest

l	+375 162 22 38 342
x	+375 162 23 23 89
eb	dynamo.brest.by
nail	dynamo@brest.by
edia Officer	Anatoli Levanyuk

C Dinamo Minsk

tebskaya str 11
Y-220004 Minsk

el	+375 173 09 20 60
ax	+375 173 09 20 70
eb	dinamo-minsk.by
mail	dinamo@minsk.by
edia Officer	Oleg Sobolevski

FC Dnepr Mogilev

Mogilev region, z/o Lyubuzh, Cheremushki
BY-213112 Mogilev

Tel	+375 222 21 75 72
Fax	+375 222 21 73 90
Web	fcdnepr.by
Email	dnepr@mogilev.by
Media Officer	Anna Titovich

FC Gomel

Voostaniya square 1
BY-246050 Gomel

Tel	+375 232 71 57 41
Fax	+375 232 71 57 39
Web	fcgomel.by
Email	fc_gomel@mail.ru
Media Officer	Ekaterina Alekseevich

FC Minsk

22 Prospekt Pobeditelei
BY-220020 Minsk

Tel	+375 17 250 29 75
Fax	+375 17 250 29 75
Web	fcminsk.by
Email	fc_minsk@tut.by
Media Officer	Aleksandr Tomin

FC Naftan Novopolotsk

Molodezhnaya Street 49 A
BY-211501 Novopolotsk

Tel	+375 214 53 77 40
Fax	+375 214 53 43 77
Web	fcnaftan.com
Email	fcnaftan@naftan.by
Media Officer	Liubov Savko

FC Neman Grodno

Kommunalnaya Street 3
BY-230023 Grodno

Tel	+375 152 72 37 99
Fax	+375 152 72 37 99
Web	fcneman.by
Email	fcgrodno@yandex.ru
Media Officer	Iosif Papko

FC Shakhtyor Soligorsk

51, L. Komsomola, Minsk region
BY-223710 Soligorsk

Tel	+375 174 22 06 21
Fax	+375 174 22 06 21
Web	fcshakhter.by
Email	info@fcshakhter.by
Media Officer	Pavel Martynenkov

FC Torpedo Zhodino

Gagarina str. 1
BY-222160 Zhodino

Tel	+375 177 57 97 22
Fax	+375 177 57 15 79
Web	tarpeda.zhodzina.info
Email	torpedozhodino@tut.by
Media Officer	Sergel Puzankevich

FC Vitebsk

Ludnikova Str. 12
BY-210009 Vitebsk

Tel	+375 212 27 42 30
Fax	+375 212 27 42 30
Web	fc.vitebsk.by
Email	locomotiv-vitebsk@tut.by
Media Officer	Denis Golubev

BELGIUM

Belgique I Belgien

Union Royale Belge des Sociétés de Football Association (URBSFA) / Koninklijke Belgische Voetbalbond (KBVB

COMMUNICATION

Address 145 Avenue Houba de Strooper
BE-1020 Bruxelles
Tel +32 2 477 1211
Fax +32 2 478 2391
E-mail urbsfa.kbvb@footbel.com
Website footbel.com

President François De Keersmaecker
General Secretary Steven Martens
Media Officer Stefan Van Loock
Year of Formation 1895
National Stadium King Baudouin, Brussels (50,024)

DOMESTIC COMPETITION SUMMARY 2010/11

CHAMPIONSHIP PLAY-OFFS FINAL TABLE

			Home					Away					Total						
		Pld	W	D	L	F	A	W	D	L	F	A	W	D	L	F	A	Pts	Comp
1	KRC Genk	10	4	1	0	10	3	2	0	3	6	9	6	1	3	16	12	51	UCL
2	R. Standard de Liège	10	5	0	0	9	2	3	2	0	9	4	8	2	0	18	6	51	UCL
3	RSC Anderlecht	10	2	1	2	10	8	1	1	3	4	8	3	2	5	14	16	44	UEL
4	Club Brugge KV	10	3	2	0	10	1	1	2	2	3	5	4	4	2	13	6	43	UEL
5	KAA Gent	10	0	3	2	7	10	0	1	4	2	12	0	4	6	9	22	33	
6	KSC Lokeren OV	10	0	1	4	2	7	1	2	2	7	10	1	3	6	9	17	31	

NB KRC Genk declared champions as R. Standard Liège benefited from half point rounded upwards after the regular season.

PRO LEAGUE FINAL TABLE

			Home					Away					Total						
		Pld	W	D	L	F	A	W	D	L	F	A	W	D	L	F	A	Pts	Comp
1	RSC Anderlecht	30	11	4	0	39	7	8	4	3	19	13	19	8	3	58	20	65	
2	KRC Genk	30	11	1	3	37	15	8	6	1	27	12	19	7	4	64	27	64	
3	KAA Gent	30	11	1	3	33	21	6	5	4	26	21	17	6	7	59	42	57	
4	Club Brugge KV	30	10	2	3	36	17	6	3	6	24	18	16	5	9	60	35	53	
5	KSC Lokeren OV	30	9	4	2	25	17	4	7	4	18	19	13	11	6	43	36	50	
6	R. Standard de Liège	30	10	3	2	33	15	5	1	9	17	23	15	4	11	50	38	49	
7	KV Mechelen	30	8	6	1	22	8	5	3	7	12	22	13	9	8	34	30	48	
8	KVC Westerlo	30	5	6	4	21	16	6	2	7	20	24	11	8	11	41	40	41	UEL
9	Cercle Brugge KSV	30	7	3	5	20	15	4	3	8	13	19	11	6	13	33	34	39	
10	KV Kortrijk	30	10	2	3	25	11	1	3	11	11	28	11	5	14	36	39	38	
11	SV Zulte Waregem	30	4	6	5	23	19	3	6	6	16	22	7	12	11	39	41	33	
12	K. Sint-Truidense VV	30	6	2	7	12	20	2	3	10	8	31	8	5	17	20	51	29	
13	KFC Germinal Beerschot Antwerpen	30	4	8	3	14	10	1	3	11	10	30	5	11	14	24	40	26	
14	K. Lierse SK	30	3	8	4	17	20	1	4	10	9	38	4	12	14	26	58	24	
15	KAS Eupen	30	3	3	9	15	22	2	5	8	13	28	5	8	17	28	50	23	*Relegated*
16	R. Charleroi SC	30	4	3	8	10	20	0	4	11	10	34	4	7	19	20	54	19	*Relegated*

NB After 30 rounds top six clubs entered championship play-off, carrying forward half of their points total (half points rounded upwards); clubs placed 7-14 entered two play-off groups; clubs placed 15 &16 entered relegation play-off group.

Top Scorer Ivan Perišić (Club Brugge), 22 goals

Promoted Clubs Oud-Heverlee Leuven, RAEC Mons

Cup Final R. Standard de Liège 2, KVC Westerlo 0

Genk prevail in play-off decider

The introduction of a new, multi-stranded format to the Belgian Pro League in 2009/10 engendered much commotion, particularly as its objective of producing an exciting finish failed when RSC Anderlecht romped unopposed to the title. But the experiment was given a re-run in 2010/11 and this time, at the end of a marathon 40-match campaign – the longest in Europe – the play-offs delivered a riveting climax as the top two teams, KRC Genk and R. Standard de Liège, came together in a final-day title face-off.

Although the two clubs went into the game level on points, the advantage lay with home side Genk. This was not because of goal difference or any head-to-head superiority but because at the end of the 30-match regular season, at which juncture the top six clubs entering the championship play-offs had their points totals halved, Standard, unlike Genk, had an odd number of points. Although the regulations stated that half-points would be rounded upwards, they also specified that in the case of two teams or more ending the season level on points, those carrying such a half-point would have to surrender it.

Standard denied

Thus, when the showdown in the Cristal Arena finished all-square, at 1-1, Genk were crowned champions. Evidently both teams knew what was required of them at the start, and when Standard defender Eliaquim Mangala bundled the ball home just before half-time, Les Rouches were on course for their third title in four years. With just 13 minutes remaining, however, Genk substitute Kennedy Nwanganga headed the home side level. The closing stages saw Standard pound at the Genk goal, but they were denied by the brilliance of young 'keeper Thibaut Courtois, who repeatedly kept them at bay.

It was agony at the final whistle for Standard but ecstasy for Genk, champions of Belgium for the third time. It was also a third title as a coach for Frank Vercauteren, twice a winner previously with Anderlecht. Although it had taken a strange quirk of the rules to secure the title, Genk deserved it for their season-long consistency. They won more matches (25) and lost fewer (seven) than any other team and were also the most prolific, scoring 80 times. Their all-Belgian front pairing of Jelle Vossen and Marvin Ogunjimi contributed 35 of those goals and received excellent support from Israeli international Elyaniv Barda, Hungarian midfielder Dániel Tőzsér and multi-talented homegrown teenager Kevin De Bruyne.

Standard eased their pain by winning the Belgian Cup four days later with a comfortable 2-0 win over KVC Westerlo in the Brussels final. Thus concluded a scintillating end to the season for the Liege club. There had been no evidence of such potential in the early part of the campaign. Indeed, they only just scraped into the play-off group, an unlikely late equaliser by Germinal Beerschot Antwerpen's

Jelle Vossen scored 20 league goals for Belgian champions Genk

veteran midfielder Bart Goor against KV Mechelen in the penultimate round of the regular season keeping alive their top-six hopes. Once in the play-offs, though, Dominique D'Onofrio's side opened their account with a brilliant 3-1 win at Anderlecht and were irrepressible thereafter, winning seven of their next eight games leading up to the title decider. Belgian international Axel Witsel was an inspired figure in midfield throughout the run, but ultimately Standard fell just short. Even so, the Belgian Cup and a UEFA Champions League qualifying place – the same European prize on offer to Genk – made their efforts worthwhile.

Talisman sold

By reaching the Cup final, Westerlo were guaranteed a place in the UEFA Europa League, but Jan Ceulemans's side ended up winning a European ticket twice over after defeating Cercle Brugge KV in the mid-table play-off final. Cercle's defeat enabled their stadium-sharing city rivals Club Brugge KV, fourth in the league, to join Westerlo and third-placed Anderlecht in the secondary European club competition. The Brussels club, whose title hopes nosedived after the spring departure of their talismanic playmaker Mbark Boussoufa to Russia, resulting in just three play-off wins, had been Belgium's top performers in Europe in 2010/11, albeit only by reaching the last 32 of the UEFA Europa League – where they were humiliated by AFC Ajax – after missing out on the UEFA Champions League group stage in a penalty shoot-out. Gent and Club Brugge also reached the UEFA Europa League group stage but went no further, while Genk were mown down in the play-offs of the same competition by eventual winners FC Porto.

For much of their disappointing season Club Brugge were carried almost single-handedly by their outstanding young Croatian midfielder Ivan Perišić, who scored 22 goals to edge out Genk's Vossen and win the league's top-scorer prize. R. Charleroi SC managed less than that number as a team in the regular league campaign, and although their goal output improved in the relegation play-off group, they still finished a distant second to newcomers KAS Eupen, which resulted in relegation after 26 years among the elite. Eupen subsequently accompanied Charleroi down after failing to pick up a point in a further play-off series with three second-tier sides, at the end of which RAEC Mons were promoted alongside champions Oud-Heverlee Leuven.

National Team

International Tournament Appearances – FIFA World Cup - (11) 1930, 1934, 1938, 1954, 1970, 1982 (2nd phase), 1986 (4th), 1990 (2nd round), 1994 (2nd round), 1998, 2002 (2nd round). UEFA European Championship - (3) 1972 (3rd), 1980 (runners-up), 2000.

Top Five All-time Caps – Jan Ceulemans (96); Eric Gerets & Franky Van der Elst (86); Vincenzo Scifo (84); Timmy Simons (83)

Top Five All-time Goals – Paul Van Himst & Bernard Voorhoof (30); Marc Wilmots (28); Jef Mermans (27); Raymond Braine & Robert De Veen (26)

High hopes accompanied Belgium into the UEFA EURO 2012 qualifying campaign, but the Red Devils' bid to end a decade in the international wilderness came unstuck immediately with back-to-back defeats against Germany and Turkey. Further points were shed in a remarkable 4-4 draw at home to Austria, and although Georges Leekens' side won the return in Vienna 2-0 with a couple of Witsel goals, the young Standard star went from hero to villain in the last qualifier of the season, a must-win game at home to Turkey, when he blasted a late penalty over the bar, leaving the final result at 1-1 and their opponents much better placed to take the Group A runners-up berth behind Germany. For the most gifted collection of Belgian players in a generation – with Witsel, Vincent Kompany, Eden Hazard and Romelu Lukaku leading the way – failure to reach even the play-offs, albeit from a tough group, was a sour prospect indeed.

Standard and Belgium midfielder Axel Witsel had an eventful season for club and country

NATIONAL TEAM RESULTS 2010/11

11/8/10	Finland	A	Turku	0-1	
3/9/10	Germany (ECQ)	H	Brussels	0-1	
7/9/10	Turkey (ECQ)	A	Istanbul	2-3	*Van Buyten (28, 69)*
8/10/10	Kazakhstan (ECQ)	A	Astana	2-0	*Ogunjimi (52, 70)*
12/10/10	Austria (ECQ)	H	Brussels	4-4	*Vossen (11), Fellaini (47), Ogunjimi (87), Lombaerts (90)*
17/11/10	Russia	A	Voronezh	2-0	*Lukaku (2, 73)*
9/2/11	Finland	H	Ghent	1-1	*Witsel (61)*
25/3/11	Austria (ECQ)	A	Vienna	2-0	*Witsel (6, 50)*
29/3/11	Azerbaijan (ECQ)	H	Brussels	4-1	*Vertonghen (12), Simons (32p), Chadli (45+1), Vossen (74)*
3/6/11	Turkey (ECQ)	H	Brussels	1-1	*Ogunjimi (4)*

NATIONAL TEAM APPEARANCES 2010/11

oach – Georges LEEKENS	**18/5/49**		**Fin**	**GER**	**TUR**	**KAZ**	**AUT**	**Rus**	**Fin**	**AUT**	**AZE**	**TUR**	**Caps**	**Goals**
ogan BAILLY	27/12/85	Mönchengladbach (GER)	G	G	G	G	G						8	-
uillaume GILLET	9/3/84	Anderlecht	D		M82				M58				14	-
incent KOMPANY	10/4/86	Man. City (ENG)	D	D	D 64*		D	D	D	D		D	39	1
homas VERMAELEN	14/11/85	Arsenal (ENG)	D	D	D							s46	32	1
icolas LOMBAERTS	20/3/85	Zenit (RUS)	D46			D	D				D	D	14	1
an VERTONGHEN	24/4/87	Ajax (NED)	M	M	M		D	D	D	D	D	D46	31	2
xel WITSEL	12/1/89	Standard	M73		s76	M	M		M	M	M	M	19	5
elle VAN DAMME	10/10/83	Wolves (ENG) /Standard	M46			M79			 s58		 s80		 29	 -
evin DE BRUYNE	28/6/91	Genk	M46										1	-
den HAZARD	7/1/91	Lille (FRA)	A	A73	s82		s81	A90	A82		s64	A60	20	-
hristian BENTEKE	3/12/90	Standard /Mechelen	A66	 s73									 3	 -
ébastien POCOGNOLI	1/8/87	Standard	s46					s90					6	-
teven DEFOUR	15/4/88	Standard	s46	s73				M		M	M90	M88	30	1
hristophe LEPOINT	24/10/84	Gent	s46 /61										2	1
ernd THIJS	28/6/78	Gent	s61										7	-
omelu LUKAKU	13/5/93	Anderlecht	s66	A73	A76	A46	s73	A75	A82				9	2
jörn VLEMINCKX	1/12/85	NEC (NED)	s73						s82				2	-
oby ALDERWEIRELD	2/3/89	Ajax (NED)		D	D	D	D46					D	11	-
aniel VAN BUYTEN	7/2/78	Bayern (GER)		D	D	D		D	D	D	D80		62	9
arouane FELLAINI	22/11/87	Everton (ENG)		M	M	M	M81	M					26	4
immy SIMONS	11/12/76	Nürnberg (GER)		M83	M	M	M73	M	M	M	M	M	83	4
oussa DEMBÉLÉ	16/7/87	Fulham (ENG)		A	A64			A90		M	M64		33	5
elle VOSSEN	22/3/89	Genk		s83		A	A	s75			A	s88	8	2
evin MIRALLAS	5/10/87	Olympiacos (GRE)			s64					s80			22	4
Olivier DESCHACHT	16/2/81	Anderlecht				D							20	-
arvin OGUNJIMI	12/10/87	Genk				s46	A			A80		A	4	4
Jonathan LEGEAR	13/4/87	Anderlecht				s79	M						2	-
Dedryck BOYATA	28/11/90	Man. City (ENG)					s46						1	-
Jean-François GILLET	31/5/79	Bari (ITA)						G					6	-
Laurent CIMAN	5/8/85	Standard						D	D	D	D		5	-
Vadis ODJIDJA-OFOE	21/2/89	Club Brugge						s90			s90		2	-
Silvio PROTO	23/5/83	Anderlecht							G				13	-
Nacer CHADLI	3/6/88	Twente (NED)							M58	M	M	M	4	1
Dries MERTENS	6/5/87	Utrecht (NED)							s58			s60	2	-
Yassine EL GHANASSY	12/7/90	Gent							s82				1	-
Simon MIGNOLET	6/8/88	Sunderland (ENG)								G	G	G	3	-

CLUB-BY-CLUB

RSC ANDERLECHT

Coach – Ariël Jacobs
Founded – 1908
Stadium – Constant Vanden Stock (28,063)
MAJOR HONOURS: UEFA Cup Winners' Cup – (2) 1976, 1978; UEFA Cup – (1) 1983; UEFA Super Cup – (2) 1976, 1978; Belgian League – (30) 1947, 1949, 1950, 1951, 1954, 1955, 1956, 1959, 1962, 1964, 1965, 1966, 1967, 1968, 1972, 1974, 1981, 1985, 1986, 1987, 1991, 1993, 1994, 1995, 2000, 2001, 2004, 2006, 2007, 2010; Belgian Cup – (9) 1965, 1972, 1973, 1975, 1976, 1988, 1989, 1994, 2008.

2010

31/7	Eupen	h	4-1	*Suárez 2, Legear, Boussoufa*
7/8	Charleroi	a	0-0	
14/8	GBA	h	4-0	*Boussoufa, Suárez, De Sutter, Polák*
21/8	Lokeren	a	3-0	*Kljestan, Kanu, Boussoufa (p)*
28/8	Zulte Waregem	h	0-0	
10/9	Sint-Truiden	a	2-0	*Lukaku 2*
19/9	Kortrijk	h	3-0	*Lukaku, Legear, Boussoufa*
22/9	Lierse	a	1-1	*Mazuch*
26/9	Mechelen	h	5-0	*Boussoufa, Gillet, Suárez, Deschacht, Legear*
3/10	Standard	a	1-5	*Boussoufa*
17/10	Cercle Brugge	a	0-1	
24/10	Westerlo	h	2-0	*Lukaku, og (Mravac)*
31/10	Genk	a	2-1	*Kljestan, Lukaku*
7/11	Club Brugge	h	2-2	*Juhász, Lukaku*
14/11	Gent	a	2-1	*Kanu, Lukaku (p)*
20/11	GBA	a	1-0	*Kanu*
27/11	Charleroi	h	4-1	*De Sutter, Kabananga, Legear, Suárez*
5/12	Zulte Waregem	a	2-1	*Wasilewski, Lukaku*
12/12	Lokeren	h	0-0	
19/12	Club Brugge	a	2-0	*Lukaku, Boussoufa*
26/12	Lierse	h	6-0	*Juhász, Lukaku, Wasilewski (p), Boussoufa 2, Chavarría*
29/12	Kortrijk	a	2-0	*Gillet, og (Gershon)*

2011

23/1	Standard	h	2-0	*Gillet, Legear (p)*
30/1	Mechelen	a	0-0	
5/2	Sint-Truiden	h	2-0	*Kanu, Suárez*
12/2	Cercle Brugge	h	1-0	*Boussoufa*
20/2	Westerlo	a	0-2	
4/3	Genk	h	1-1	*Juhász*
12/3	Eupen	a	1-1	*Lukaku*
20/3	Gent	h	3-2	*De Sutter 2, Lukaku*
3/4	Standard	h	1-3	*Gillet*
10/4	Club Brugge	a	0-3	
15/4	Racing Genk	h	2-0	*Veselinović, Lukaku*
20/4	Gent	a	1-1	*Juhász*
24/4	Lokeren	a	2-1	*Lukaku, Suárez*
1/5	Club Brugge	h	0-0	
6/5	Genk	a	0-1	
11/5	Gent	h	4-1	*Lukaku 2, Badibanga, Suárez*
14/5	Standard	a	1-2	*Juhász*
17/5	Lokeren	h	3-4	*Wasilewski, Kouyaté, Gillet*

No	Name	Nat	DoB	Pos	Aps	(s)	Gls
39	Ziguy BADIBANGA		26/11/91	A	4	(10)	1
26	Víctor BERNÁRDEZ	HON	24/5/82	D	6	(2)	
5	Lucas BIGLIA	ARG	30/1/86	M	25	(1)	
11	Mbark BOUSSOUFA	MAR	15/8/84	M	23		10
12	Thomas CHATELLE		31/3/81	M		(1)	
25	Pablo CHAVARRÍA	ARG	2/1/88	A	1	(4)	1
28	Michaël CORDIER		27/3/84	G		(1)	
21	Tom DE SUTTER		3/7/85	A	7	(9)	4
3	Olivier DESCHACHT		16/2/81	D	13		1
35	Christophe DIANDY	SEN	12/6/89	M	2	(7)	
55	FERNANDO Canesin Matos	BRA	27/2/92	M	1		
30	Guillaume GILLET		9/3/84	M	39		5
23	Roland JUHÁSZ	HUN	1/7/83	D	35		5
38	Junior KABANANGA Kalonji	COD	4/4/89	A		(5)	1
36	Nathan KABASELE		14/1/94	A		(3)	
10	Rubenilson dos Santos da Rocha "KANU"	BRA	23/9/87	A	19	(8)	4
19	Sacha KLJESTAN	USA	9/9/85	M	20	(5)	2
16	Cheikhou KOUYATÉ	SEN	21/12/89	M	21	(2)	1
7	Jan LECJAKS	CZE	9/8/90	D	26	(4)	
13	Jonathan LEGEAR		13/4/87	M	19	(4)	5
36	Romelu LUKAKU		13/5/93	A	34	(3)	16
18	Lukáš MAREČEK	CZE	17/4/90	M	9	(8)	
2	Ondřej MAZUCH	CZE	15/3/89	D	35		1
8	Jan POLÁK	POL	14/3/81	M	14	(1)	1
24	Silvio PROTO		23/5/83	G	37		
44	Nemanja RNIĆ	SRB	30/9/84	D	1	(2)	
22	Davy SCHOLLEN		28/2/78	G	3		
15	Abdoulaye SECK	SEN	10/3/88	D	1		
9	Matías SUÁREZ	ARG	9/5/88	A	23	(11)	8
87	Dalibor VESELINOVIĆ	SRB	21/9/87	A	6	(8)	1
27	Marcin WASILEWSKI	POL	9/6/80	D	16	(1)	3

CERCLE BRUGGE KSV

Coach – Bob Peeters
Founded – 1899
Stadium – Jan Breydel (29,042)
MAJOR HONOURS: Belgian League – (3) 1911, 1927, 1930; Belgian Cup – (2) 1927, 1985.

2010

1/8	Charleroi	h	1-1	*Reynaldo*
8/8	GBA	a	0-0	
15/8	Club Brugge	h	3-1	*Renato Neto, Boi, Evens*
21/8	Zulte Waregem	a	0-4	
28/8	Lokeren	h	1-1	*Reynaldo*
11/9	Standard	a	0-2	
18/9	Sint-Truiden	h	4-2	*Evens, Yashchuk 3*
22/9	Mechelen	a	2-2	*Owusu, Renato Neto*
25/9	Kortrijk	h	2-1	*Renato Neto, Owusu*
2/10	Lierse	a	1-0	*Cornelis*
17/10	Anderlecht	h	1-0	*Yashchuk*
23/10	Eupen	h	2-1	*Owusu, Reynaldo*
30/10	Westerlo	a	1-2	*Reynaldo*
7/11	Gent	h	0-1	
13/11	Genk	a	0-3	
21/11	Club Brugge	a	1-0	*D'Haene*
27/11	GBA	h	1-1	*Boi*
11/12	Zulte Waregem	h	1-3	*Nuno Reis*
26/12	Standard	h	1-0	*Reynaldo*

2011

22/1	Lierse	h	3-0	*Boi, Owusu, Renato Neto*
29/1	Kortrijk	a	1-2	*Yashchuk (p)*
2/2	Lokeren	a	1-2	*Boi*
5/2	Mechelen	h	0-1	
12/2	Anderlecht	a	0-1	
19/2	Eupen	a	0-0	
27/2	Sint-Truiden	a	3-0	*Sergeant, Reynaldo 2*
5/3	Westerlo	h	0-1	
12/3	Gent	a	0-1	
20/3	Genk	h	0-1	
23/3	Charleroi	a	3-0	*Evens, Foley (p), Boi*
2/4	Lierse	h	0-0	
9/4	Sint-Truiden	a	1-1	*Foley*
16/4	Mechelen	a	0-0	
23/4	Mechelen	h	3-1	*Evens, D'Haene, Foley*
30/4	Lierse	a	0-3	
7/5	Sint-Truiden	h	1-0	*Yashchuk*

No	Name	Nat	DoB	Pos	Aps	(s)	Gls
12	Frederik BOI		25/10/81	D	18	(5)	5
37	Jo COPPENS		21/12/90	G	1		
8	Hans CORNELIS		23/10/82	D	34		1
30	Kristof D'HAENE		6/6/90	D	12	(16)	2
4	Bernt EVENS		9/11/78	D	35		4
15	Dominic FOLEY	IRL	7/7/76	A	14	(7)	3

Dejan KELHAR	SVN	5/4/84	D	9		
Nicaise Mulopo KUDIMBANA	COD	21/1/87	G	1		
Gregory MERTENS		2/2/91	M	2	(2)	
Arne NAUDTS		27/11/93	A		(4)	
NUNO Miguel Pereira REIS	POR	31/1/91	D	31		1
Vusumuzi Prince NYONI	ZIM	21/4/84	D		(1)	
William OWUSU Acheampong	GHA	13/9/89	A	21	(8)	4
Anthony PORTIER		1/6/82	D	12	(3)	
Milan PUROVIĆ	MNE	7/5/85	A		(4)	
RENATO Cardoso Porto NETO	BRA	27/9/91	M	31	(3)	4
REYNALDO dos Santos Silva	BRA	24/8/89	A	23	(9)	7
Papa SENE	SEN	13/12/90	A	1	(2)	
Serhiy SEREBRENNIKOV	UKR	1/9/76	M	7	(19)	
Tony SERGEANT		6/6/77	M	3	(1)	1
Lukas VAN EENOO		6/2/91	M	27	(1)	
Karel VAN ROOSE		1/4/90	M	8	(1)	
Bram VERBIST		5/3/83	G	34		
Denis VIANE		2/10/77	D	13		
Arnar Thór VIDARSSON	ISL	15/3/78	M	33		
WANG Yang	CHN	26/7/89	A	7	(7)	
Oleh YASHCHUK	UKR	26/10/77	A	19	(7)	6

CLUB BRUGGE KV

Coach – Adrie Koster (NED)

Founded – 1891

Stadium – Jan Breydel (29,042)

MAJOR HONOURS: Belgian League – (13) 1920, 1973, 1976, 1977, 1978, 1980, 1988, 1990, 1992, 1996, 1998, 2003, 2005; Belgian Cup – (10) 1968, 1970, 1977, 1986, 1991, 1995, 1996, 2002, 2004, 2007.

010				
1/7	Kortrijk	a	0-1	
8	Sint-Truiden	h	4-1	*Perišić 2, Odjidja-Ofoe, Blondel*
5/8	Cercle Brugge	a	1-3	*Hoefkens*
2/8	Mechelen	h	1-2	*Vargas*
9/8	Westerlo	a	2-1	*Vargas 2*
2/9	Genk	h	2-2	*Vargas, Van der Heyden*
9/9	Charleroi	a	5-0	*Perišić, Odjidja-Ofoe, Vargas 2, Lestienne*
2/9	Eupen	h	4-0	*Odjidja-Ofoe 2, Lestienne, Hoefkens (p)*
6/9	GBA	a	1-2	*Geraerts*
10	Gent	h	3-2	*Kouemaha, Geraerts, Vargas*
5/10	Zulte Waregem	a	3-2	*Vargas 2, Kouemaha*
4/10	Lokeren	a	0-1	
1/10	Standard	h	2-2	*Vargas 2*
11	Anderlecht	a	2-2	*Dalmat, Geraerts*
3/11	Lierse	h	2-0	*Vargas, Simaeys*
1/11	Cercle Brugge	h	0-1	
8/11	Sint-Truiden	a	1-2	*Dirar*
/12	Westerlo	h	4-3	*Perišić 2, Odjidja-Ofoe, Dirar*
0/12	Mechelen	a	1-0	*Perišić*
9/12	Anderlecht	h	0-2	
6/12	Gent	a	2-0	*Perišić, Kouemaha*
9/12	Charleroi	h	5-0	*Perišić 4, Dirar*
011				
1/1	Eupen	a	4-1	*Dalmat, Perišić, Vargas 2*
9/1	GBA	h	1-0	*Vargas*
/2	Genk	a	0-1	
2/2	Zulte Waregem	h	2-0	*Dalmat, Akpala*
9/2	Lokeren	h	2-1	*Perišić, Akpala*
/3	Standard	a	2-2	*Perišić, Akpala*
2/3	Kortrijk	h	4-1	*Perišić 2, Blondel, Akpala*
0/3	Lierse	a	0-0	
/4	Gent	a	1-1	*Dalmat*
0/4	Anderlecht	h	3-0	*Geraerts, Perišić (p), Akpala*
7/4	Lokeren	h	0-0	
20/4	Genk	a	1-3	*Akpala*
25/4	Standard	h	1-1	*Simaeys*
/5	Anderlecht	a	0-0	
7/5	Standard	a	0-1	
0/5	Genk	h	3-0	*Perišić 2, Akpala*
4/5	Lokeren	a	1-0	*Perišić*
17/5	Gent	h	3-0	*Perišić 2, Odjidja-Ofoe*

No	Name	Nat	DoB	Pos	Aps	(s)	Gls
15	Joseph AKPALA	NGA	24/8/90	A	18	(10)	7
11	Jonathan BLONDEL		3/4/84	M	20	(7)	2
26	Colin COOSEMANS		3/8/92	G	19		
77	Mohamed DAHMANE	ALG	9/4/82	A		(2)	
6	Wilfried DALMAT	FRA	17/7/82	M	14	(12)	4
13	Geert DE VLIEGER		16/10/71	G	9	(1)	
25	Júnior Enrique DÍAZ Campbell	CRC	12/9/83	D	8	(4)	
10	Nabil DIRAR	MAR	25/2/86	M	30	(3)	3
18	Ryan DONK	NED	30/3/86	D	33	(3)	
22	Karel GERAERTS		5/1/82	M	30		4
4	Carl HOEFKENS		6/10/78	D	38		2
5	Michael KLUKOWSKI	CAN	27/5/81	D	1		
40	Dorge Rostand KOUEMAHA	CMR	28/6/83	A	19	(15)	3
16	Maxime LESTIENNE		17/6/92	A		(15)	2
17	MARCOS Camozzato	BRA	17/6/83	D	20	(2)	
32	Vadis ODJIDJA-OFOE		21/2/89	M	31	(6)	6
44	Ivan PERIŠIĆ	CRO	2/2/89	M	34	(3)	22
8	Stefan ŠĆEPOVIĆ	SRB	10/1/90	A		(4)	
14	Jeroen SIMAEYS		12/5/85	D	22	(4)	2
1	Stijn STIJNEN		7/4/81	G	12		
41	Thibaut VAN ACKER		21/11/91	M	4	(4)	
3	Peter VAN DER HEYDEN		16/7/76	M	30	(1)	1
24	Daan VAN GIJSEGHEM		2/3/88	D	26	(4)	
20	Ronald VARGAS	VEN	2/12/86	M	22	(1)	15
21	Jorn VERMEULEN		16/4/87	D		(8)	

R. CHARLEROI SC

Coach – Jacky Mathijssen; (19/9/10) László Csaba (HUN); (17/3/11) (Tibor Balog (HUN)); (24/3/11) (Zoltán Kovaćs (HUN)); (4/4/11) Luka Peruzović (CRO)

Stadium – Pays de Charleroi (22,000)

2010				
1/8	Cercle Brugge	a	1-1	*Gueye*
7/8	Anderlecht	h	0-0	
15/8	Genk	a	0-5	
22/8	Gent	h	1-3	*Losada*
28/8	Eupen	h	2-0	*Kaya, Serwy*
11/9	GBA	a	0-1	
19/9	Club Brugge	h	0-5	
22/9	Standard	a	1-2	*Losada*
25/9	Lierse	h	0-1	
2/10	Zulte Waregem	a	1-1	*Losada*
16/10	Lokeren	h	1-2	*Vuorinen*
23/10	Sint-Truiden	a	2-3	*Aarab, Losada*
29/10	Kortrijk	h	0-0	
6/11	Mechelen	a	0-2	
13/11	Westerlo	h	0-1	
20/11	Genk	h	1-3	*Orlando*
27/11	Anderlecht	a	1-4	*Kaya*
11/12	Gent	a	1-2	*Losada*
18/12	Eupen	a	0-1	
29/12	Club Brugge	a	0-5	
2011				
22/1	Mechelen	h	0-0	
29/1	Lierse	a	0-1	
2/2	GBA	h	2-0	*Losada, Gueye*
5/2	Zulte Waregem	h	2-0	*Biton, Serwy*
12/2	Lokeren	a	1-1	*Biton*
19/2	Sint-Truiden	h	1-0	*Biton*
5/3	Kortrijk	a	0-3	
12/3	Standard	h	0-2	
20/3	Westerlo	a	2-2	*Kahlon, Cordaro*
23/3	Cercle Brugge	h	0-3	
2/4	Eupen	a	2-3	*Kahlon, Džinič*
9/4	Eupen	h	2-0	*Biton, Cordaro*
16/4	Eupen	a	2-4	*Kahlon 2*
23/4	Eupen	h	2-2	*Kudemor, Biton*

No	Name	Nat	DoB	Pos	Aps	(s)	Gls
19	Naïm AARAB		7/2/88	D	22	(6)	1
23	Cyprien BAGUETTE		12/5/89	G	13		
16	Pierre BINON		8/4/91	M		(1)	
20	Dudu BITON	ISR	1/3/82	A	12		5

21	Mijuško BOJOVIĆ	MNE	9/8/88	D	1	(1)	
55	Maxime BRILLAULT	FRA	25/4/83	D	18		
10	Loris BROGNO		18/9/92	A		(1)	
14	Massimo BRUNO		17/9/93	M	1		
6	Mohamed CHAKOURI	FRA	21/5/86	D	1		
29	Alessandro CORDARO		2/5/86	M	31	(1)	2
6	Thibaut DELPLANK		24/4/92	M	1		
15	Kevin DEWOLF		20/11/90	G	4	(1)	
21	Zakari DIALLO	FRA	13/8/86	D	1	(5)	
3	Elvedin DŽINIČ	SVN	25/8/85	D	12		1
21	Nemanja DŽODŽO	SRB	12/12/86	G	1		
27	EDERSON Tormena	BRA	14/3/86	M	27		
13	Hatem Abd ELHAMED	ISR	18/3/91	A		(1)	
5	Romain ELIE	FRA	6/3/85	D	6		
24	Samuel FABRIS		30/1/91	D	8	(3)	
19	Peter FRANQUART	FRA	4/1/85	D	21		
80	Christophe GRÉGOIRE		20/4/80	M	4	(5)	
18	Moussa GUEYE	SEN	20/2/89	A	9	(11)	2
1	Nicola HATEFI		9/1/91	G	5	(2)	
10	Hervé KAGÉ	COD	10/4/89	M	8	(5)	
10	Tamir KAHLON	ISR	29/10/87	M	10		4
24	Onur KAYA		20/4/86	M	24	(5)	2
2	Médhi KCHAB		14/8/91	D	1		
22	Mory Fallo KEITA	GUI	13/12/92	A	1	(3)	
25	Abraham KUDEMOR	GHA	25/2/85	M	3	(3)	1
20	Mohamed LABIADH	TUN	7/8/89	A	1		
26	Grégory LAZITCH		26/5/92	D	7	(4)	
9	Hernán LOSADA	ARG	9/5/82	M	27	(2)	6
2	Francisco Javier MARTOS Espigares	ESP	4/1/84	D	6		
3	Massimo MOIA		9/3/87	D	6		
6	Matan OHAYON	ISR	25/2/86	D	12		
99	Adékanmi OLUFADÉ	TOG	7/1/80	A	1	(4)	
22	ORLANDO dos Santos Costa	BRA	26/2/81	A	12	(4)	1
4	Pietro PERDICHIZZI		16/12/92	D	7	(2)	
16	Juan Pablo RIAL	ARG	17/10/84	A		(2)	
15	Rudy RIOU	FRA	22/1/80	G	11		
8	Jérémy SERWY		4/6/91	A	6	(18)	2
34	Franck SIGNORINO	FRA	19/9/81	D	15		
77	Cyril THÉRÉAU	FRA	24/4/83	A	3		
2	Eitan TIBI	ISR	16/11/87	D	6	(3)	
16	John TSHIBUMBU	GAB	6/1/89	A	1	(3)	
7	Hermanni VUORINEN	FIN	27/1/85	A	8	(3)	1

KAS EUPEN

Coach – Danny Ost; (6/9/10) Eziolino Capuano (ITA); (24/9/10) Albert Cartier (FRA); (13/4/11) Danny Ost

Founded – 1945

Stadium – Am Kehrweg (6000)

2010				
31/7	Anderlecht	a	1-4	*Alex*
7/8	Westerlo	h	0-1	
14/8	Gent	a	1-2	*Lepiller*
22/8	Genk	h	1-4	*Obradović*
28/8	Charleroi	a	0-2	
11/9	Zulte Waregem	a	0-0	
18/9	GBA	h	0-1	
22/9	Club Brugge	a	0-4	
25/9	Lokeren	h	0-1	
2/10	Kortrijk	a	1-3	*Vandenbergh*
16/10	Sint-Truiden	h	6-0	*Panizzolo, Zukanović, Vandenbergh 2, Lepiller, Milicevic*
23/10	Cercle Brugge	a	1-2	*Milicevic*
30/10	Lierse	h	2-2	*Zukanović, Mombongo-Dues*
6/11	Standard	a	3-1	*Vandenbergh 2, Jadid (p)*
20/11	Kortrijk	h	3-1	*Mombongo-Dues, Jadid 2 (1p)*
27/11	Westerlo	a	1-1	*Vandenbergh*
4/12	Gent	h	0-3	
11/12	Genk	a	1-5	*Vandenbergh*
18/12	Charleroi	h	1-0	*Vandenbergh*
29/12	GBA	a	0-0	
2011				
18/1	Mechelen	h	0-1	
21/1	Club Brugge	h	1-4	*og (Hoefkens)*
29/1	Lokeren	a	2-0	*Milicevic, Vandenbergh*
2/2	Zulte Waregem	h	0-2	
6/2	Standard	h	0-1	
12/2	Sint-Truiden	a	1-1	*Jadid*
19/2	Cercle Brugge	h	0-0	
6/3	Lierse	a	1-1	*Chavarría*
12/3	Anderlecht	h	1-1	*Espinal*
20/3	Mechelen	a	0-2	
2/4	Charleroi	h	3-2	*Chavarría, Zukanović, Jefferson*
9/4	Charleroi	a	0-2	
16/4	Charleroi	h	4-2	*Chavarría 2, Jadid, Jefferson (p)*
23/4	Charleroi	a	2-2	*Obradović 2*

No	Name	Nat	DoB	Pos	Aps	(s)	Gls
20	ALEX Costa dos Santos	BRA	29/1/89	D	18	(5)	1
91	Tarik BHAR		16/7/91	M		(1)	
8	Ibrahima CAMARA	GUI	1/1/85	D	6	(3)	
26	Pablo CHAVARRÍA	ARG	2/1/88	A	8	(1)	4
16	Jérôme COLINET		26/4/83	M	5	(5)	
77	Mohamed DAHMANE	ALG	9/4/82	A	3	(1)	
35	Pape Moussa DIAKHATÈ	SEN	22/4/89	M	8	(4)	
23	José Elpys ESPINAL Marte	DOM	14/11/82	A	2	(17)	1
6	Marc HENDRIKX		2/7/74	M	14	(8)	
25	Yacine HIMA	ALG	25/3/84	M	2	(3)	
3	Allesandro IANDOLI	ITA	29/4/84	D	32		
28	Abderrazzak JADID	MAR	1/6/83	M	27		5
26	JEFFERSON Andrade Siqueira	BRA	6/1/88	A	9	(5)	2
14	Christian KABASELE		24/2/91	A		(3)	
4	Fazli KOCABAS		1/1/90	D	9	(2)	
10	Matthias LEPILLER	FRA	12/6/88	A	21	(6)	2
17	Ibrahim MAAROUFI	MAR	18/1/89	M		(1)	
33	MARCUS Plínio DINIZ Paixão	BRA	1/8/87	D	5		
7	Danijel MILICEVIC	SUI	5/1/86	M	28		3
9	Freddy MOMBONGO-DUES	COD	30/8/85	A	7	(8)	2
15	Marko OBRADOVIĆ	SRB	30/6/91	A	6	(13)	3
22	Daniel PANIZZOLO	SUI	25/3/86	D	23		1
1	Radek PETR	CZE	24/2/87	G	14		
18	Enes SAGLIK		8/7/91	M	22	(6)	
83	Kevin VANDENBERGH		16/5/83	A	27	(1)	9
21	Olivier VINAMONT		15/7/85	M	25	(4)	
12	Olivier WERNER		16/4/85	G	20		
5	Ervin ZUKANOVIĆ	BIH	11/2/87	D	33		3

KRC GENK

Coach – Frank Vercauteren

Founded – 1988

Stadium – Cristal Arena (25,010)

MAJOR HONOURS: Belgian League – (3) 1999, 2002, 2011; Belgian Cup – (3) 1998, 2000, 2009.

2010				
1/8	GBA	h	2-1	*Vossen 2*
8/8	Gent	a	4-0	*De Bruyne, Ngcongca, Vossen, Camus*
15/8	Charleroi	h	5-0	*Vossen, De Bruyne 2, Barda 2*
22/8	Eupen	a	4-1	*og (Camara), Joneleit 2, Vossen*
29/8	Lierse	h	4-1	*Vossen 2, Camus, Ogunjimi*
12/9	Club Brugge	a	2-2	*Vossen, Tőzsér*
18/9	Lokeren	h	3-1	*Ogunjimi, Vossen 2*
21/9	Sint-Truiden	a	2-0	*Vossen 2*
25/9	Zulte Waregem	h	3-0	*Vossen, Barda 2 (1p)*
1/10	Mechelen	a	2-2	*Barda, og (Van Hoevelen)*
17/10	Standard	h	4-2	*Ogunjimi, João Carlos, Vossen, Tőzsér*
22/10	Kortrijk	a	0-1	
31/10	Anderlecht	h	1-2	*Buffel*
5/11	Westerlo	a	1-1	*Barda*
13/11	Cercle Brugge	h	3-0	*Ogunjimi, Barda, Hubert*
20/11	Charleroi	a	3-1	*Ogunjimi 2, og (Fabris)*
26/11	Gent	h	1-2	*Joneleit*
4/12	GBA	a	1-0	*Ogunjimi*
11/12	Eupen	h	5-1	*Barda, Tőzsér, Vossen 2, Ogunjimi*
18/12	Lierse	a	1-1	*Barda (p)*
30/12	Lokeren	a	2-2	*João Carlos, Ogunjimi*
2011				
22/1	Kortrijk	h	3-2	*De Bruyne, Ogunjimi, Tőzsér*
28/1	Zulte Waregem	a	1-0	*Tőzsér*

	Sint-Truiden	h	1-1	*Barda*
	Club Brugge	h	1-0	*Ogunjimi*
2	Standard	a	2-0	*og (Witsel), Nwanganga*
2	Mechelen	h	1-0	*Barda*
	Anderlecht	a	1-1	*Vossen*
/3	Westerlo	h	0-2	
/3	Cercle Brugge	a	1-0	*Ogunjimi*
	Lokeren	h	2-1	*Barda 2*
/4	Standard	a	1-2	*Tőzsér*
/4	Anderlecht	a	0-2	
/4	Club Brugge	h	3-1	*Ogunjimi, Barda (p), Vossen*
/4	Gent	h	3-0	*Tőzsér, Vossen, Nwanganga*
	Lokeren	a	2-0	*Matoukou, Ogunjimi*
5	Anderlecht	h	1-0	*Vossen*
/5	Club Brugge	a	0-3	
/5	Gent	a	3-2	*De Bruyne, Tőzsér, Ogunjimi*
/5	Standard	h	1-1	*Nwanganga*

o	Name	Nat	DoB	Pos	Aps	(s)	Gls
	Elyaniv BARDA	ISR	15/12/81	A	25	(7)	14
	Thomas BUFFEL		19/2/81	M	25	(8)	1
	Fabien CAMUS	TUN	28/2/85	M	2	(16)	2
	Thibaut COURTOIS		11/5/92	G	40		
	Dimitri DAESELEIRE		18/5/90	D		(2)	
	Kevin DE BRUYNE		28/6/91	M	30	(2)	5
	Timothy DURWAEL		24/2/91	D		(2)	
	David HUBERT		12/2/88	D	30	(2)	1
	Stein HUYSEGEMS		16/6/82	A		(1)	
	JOÃO CARLOS Chaves Pinto	BRA	1/1/82	D	19		2
	Torben JONELEIT	GER	17/5/87	D	25	(4)	3
	Leroy LABYLLE		11/3/91	M		(3)	
	Anthony LIMBOMBE		15/7/94	M	1	(12)	
	Eric MATOUKOU	CMR	8/7/83	D	36	(2)	1
	Chris MAVINGA	FRA	26/1/91	D	7	(2)	
	José NÁDSON Ferreira	BRA	18/10/84	D	7	(6)	
	Dugary NDABASHINZE	BDI	8/10/89	M	9	(12)	
	Calvin Anele NGCONGCA	RSA	20/10/87	D	40		1
	Kennedy Ugoala NWANGANGA	NGA	15/8/90	A	4	(11)	3
1	Marvin OGUNJIMI		12/10/87	A	27	(5)	15
3	Daniel PUDIL	CZE	27/9/85	M	32	(5)	
	Dániel TŐZSÉR	HUN	12/5/85	M	39		8
	Anthony VANDEN BORRE		24/10/87	D	9	(7)	
9	Jelle VOSSEN		22/3/89	A	33	(4)	20
3	Samuel YEBOAH	GHA	8/8/86	A		(2)	

KAA GENT

Coach – Francky Dury

Founded – 1898

Stadium – Jules Ottenstadion (12,919)

MAJOR HONOURS: Belgian Cup – (3) 1964, 1984, 2010.

010

1/7	Westerlo	a	1-0	*Coulibaly*
/8	Genk	h	0-4	
4/8	Eupen	h	2-1	*Coulibaly, og (Kocabas)*
2/8	Charleroi	a	3-1	*Soumahoro, De Smet, El Ghanassy*
9/8	GBA	h	1-0	*Ljubijankič*
1/9	Lierse	a	2-2	*Soumahoro, De Smet*
9/9	Zulte Waregem	h	5-3	*Wils, og (Sterckx), Coulibaly, El Ghanassy, Azofeifa*
2/9	Lokeren	a	2-3	*Smolders, Ljubijankič*
5/9	Sint-Truiden	h	2-0	*De Smet, Coulibaly*
/10	Club Brugge	a	2-3	*El Ghanassy, Thijs*
6/10	Kortrijk	h	2-0	*Azofeifa, El Ghanassy*
4/10	Standard	a	1-2	*Coulibaly*
0/10	Mechelen	h	3-1	*Coulibaly, Ljubijankič, Smolders (p)*
/11	Cercle Brugge	a	1-0	*Smolders (p)*
4/11	Anderlecht	h	1-2	*Ljubijankič*
0/11	Westerlo	h	4-4	*Smolders, Arbeitman, De Smet, Conté*
6/11	Genk	a	2-1	*og (João Carlos), Arbeitman*
/12	Eupen	a	3-0	*Thijs, Arbeitman, Soumahoro*
1/12	Charleroi	h	2-1	*Wils, Conté*
6/12	Club Brugge	h	0-2	
0/12	Zulte Waregem	a	2-2	*Ljubijankič, og (Dachelet)*

2011

23/1	Lokeren	h	2-1	*Soumahoro, Lepoint*
30/1	Sint-Truiden	a	1-1	*Lepoint*
4/2	Lierse	h	4-1	*og (Vandooren), Thijs 2 (2p), Ljubijankič*
13/2	Kortrijk	a	1-0	*Mboyo*
16/2	GBA	a	2-2	*Coulibaly, El Ghanassy*
20/2	Standard	h	4-1	*Soumahoro, El Ghanassy, Thijs, og (Kanu)*
5/3	Mechelen	a	1-1	*Coulibaly*
12/3	Cercle Brugge	h	1-0	*Mboyo*
20/3	Anderlecht	a	2-3	*Soumahoro, Thijs*
2/4	Club Brugge	h	1-1	*Coulibaly*
9/4	Lokeren	a	1-1	*Coulibaly*
16/4	Standard	h	1-3	*Thijs*
20/4	Anderlecht	h	1-1	*Smolders*
23/4	Genk	a	0-3	
29/4	Standard	a	0-1	
7/5	Lokeren	h	2-2	*Arbeitman 2*
11/5	Anderlecht	a	1-4	*Arbeitman*
14/5	Genk	h	2-3	*Wils (p), Arbeitman*
17/5	Club Brugge	a	0-3	

No	Name	Nat	DoB	Pos	Aps	(s)	Gls
13	ADRIANO DUARTE Mansur da Silva	BRA	29/1/80	D	3	(1)	
23	Shlomi ARBEITMAN	ISR	14/5/85	A	10	(17)	7
10	Randall AZOFEIFA	CRC	30/12/84	M	13	(3)	2
18	Alpha BA	SEN	31/12/89	D	2		
14	Mario BARIĆ	CRO	15/4/85	D	18	(5)	
1	Frank BOECKX		27/9/86	G	4	(1)	
20	Sébastien BRUZZESE		1/3/89	G	3		
15	CÉSAR ARZO Amposta	ESP	21/1/86	D	14		
28	Ibrahima CONTÉ	SEN	3/4/91	M	14	(16)	2
16	Elimane COULIBALY	SEN	15/3/80	A	26	(5)	10
14	Adnan ČUSTOVIĆ	BIH	14/4/78	A	2		
19	Stijn DE SMET		27/3/85	A	17	(12)	4
11	Yassine EL GHANASSY		12/7/90	A	29	(10)	6
31	Christophe GRONDIN	FRA	2/9/83	M	20	(8)	
5	Erlend HANSTVEIT	NOR	28/1/81	D	10	(4)	
29	Bojan JORGAČEVIĆ	SRB	12/2/82	G	33		
10	Jesper JØRGENSEN	DEN	9/5/84	M	11	(3)	
26	Christophe LEPOINT		24/10/84	M	6	(4)	2
30	Zlatan LJUBIJANKIČ	SVN	15/12/83	A	29	(4)	6
9	Ilombe MBOYO	COD	27/4/87	A	6	(5)	2
21	Edson Eli MONTAÑO Angulo	ECU	15/3/91	A	1	(3)	
2	Zakaria M'SILA	MAR	6/4/92	M		(1)	
4	Roy MYRIE	CRC	21/8/82	D	3		
22	Matija ŠKARABOT	SVN	4/2/88	D	4	(2)	
7	Tim SMOLDERS		26/8/80	M	29	(4)	5
24	Yaya Alfa SOUMAHORO	CIV	28/9/89	A	12	(5)	6
3	Marko ŠULER	SVN	9/3/83	D	31		
8	Bernd THIJS		28/6/78	M	26		7
12	Kenny THOMPSON		26/4/85	D	12	(1)	
17	Hannes VAN DER BRUGGEN		1/4/93	M	1		
25	WALLACE Fernando Pereira	BRA	29/10/86	D	21	(1)	
6	Stef WILS		2/8/82	D	30	(2)	3

KFC GERMINAL BEERSCHOT ANTWERPEN

Coach – Glen De Boeck; (2/12/10) Jacky Mathijssen

Founded – 1999

Stadium – Olympisch Stadion (12,400)

MAJOR HONOURS: Belgian Cup – (2) 1997, 2005.

2010

1/8	Genk	a	1-2	*Haroun*
8/8	Cercle Brugge	h	0-0	
14/8	Anderlecht	a	0-4	
21/8	Westerlo	h	0-0	
29/8	Gent	a	0-1	
11/9	Charleroi	h	1-0	*Čustović*
18/9	Eupen	a	1-0	*Haroun*
22/9	Zulte Waregem	a	3-4	*Júnior Negrão 3*
26/9	Club Brugge	h	2-1	*Haroun, Júnior Negrão*

2/10	Lokeren	a	0-1	
16/10	Lierse	h	1-1	*Júnior Negrão*
23/10	Mechelen	a	1-5	*Júnior Negrão (p)*
30/10	Sint-Truiden	h	0-0	
6/11	Kortrijk	a	0-4	
13/11	Standard	h	0-1	
20/11	Anderlecht	h	0-1	
27/11	Cercle Brugge	a	1-1	*Haroun*
4/12	Genk	h	0-1	
11/12	Westerlo	a	1-1	*Wanyama*
29/12	Eupen	h	0-0	
2011				
22/1	Zulte Waregem	h	3-0	*Čustović, Kagelmacher 2 (2p)*
29/1	Club Brugge	a	0-1	
2/2	Charleroi	a	0-2	
5/2	Lokeren	h	1-1	*Júnior Negrão*
12/2	Lierse	a	2-2	*François, Haroun*
16/2	Gent	h	2-2	*MacDonald, Kagelmacher (p)*
19/2	Kortrijk	h	3-1	*Čustović, MacDonald 2*
5/3	Sint-Truiden	a	0-1	
12/3	Mechelen	h	1-1	*Goor*
20/3	Standard	a	0-1	
2/4	Zulte Waregem	h	2-0	*Nyoni, François*
9/4	Kortrijk	a	1-1	*Čustović*
16/4	Westerlo	h	3-3	*MacDonald, Čustović, Wanyama*
23/4	Westerlo	a	0-1	
30/4	Zulte Waregem	a	0-1	
7/5	Kortrijk	h	0-0	

No	Name	Nat	DoB	Pos	Aps	(s)	Gls
7	Philippe CLEMENT		22/3/74	D	29		
10	Daniel CRUZ	COL	9/5/81	M	22	(9)	
19	Adnan ČUSTOVIĆ	BIH	16/4/78	A	25	(6)	5
6	Wim DE DECKER		6/4/82	M	10	(3)	
31	Mark DE MAN		27/4/83	D	1	(1)	
15	Tosin DOSUNMU	NGA	15/7/80	A		(3)	
24	Guillaume FRANÇOIS		3/6/90	A	10	(5)	2
44	Bart GOOR		9/4/73	M	23	(5)	1
9	Faris HAROUN		22/9/85	M	28		5
13	JEAN Acosta Soares	BRA	27/1/92	M	3	(5)	
18	Gleidionor Figueiredo Pinto JÚNIOR "NEGRÃO"	BRA	30/12/86	A	11	(7)	7
27	Junior KABANANGA Kalonji	COD	4/4/89	A	2	(1)	
4	Gary KAGELMACHER	URU	21/4/88	D	26	(1)	3
26	Thomas KAMINSKI		23/10/92	G	31		
8	Sherjill MacDONALD	NED	20/11/84	A	10	(9)	4
20	Kristof MAES		19/4/88	G		(1)	
15	Tomislav MIKULIĆ	CRO	4/1/82	D	9	(3)	
22	Martijn MONTEYNE		12/11/84	D	22	(1)	
5	Pieterjan MONTEYNE		1/1/83	D	25		
11	Vusumuzi NYONI	ZIM	21/4/84	M	16	(5)	1
1	Tomislav PACOVSKI	MKD	28/6/82	G	5		
33	Roni POROKARA	FIN	12/12/83	M	11	(1)	
86	Mats RITS		18/7/93	M	6	(5)	
3	Nemanja RNIĆ	SRB	30/9/84	D	10		
	Ilias SBAA	MAR	11/3/91	M	1		
14	Mike SMET		6/3/91	D		(1)	
21	Bavon TSHIBUABUA	COD	17/7/91	A	9	(8)	
29	Justice WAMFOR	CMR	5/8/81	M	25	(1)	
12	Victor WANYAMA	KEN	25/6/91	M	26	(3)	2
	Georgiy ZHUKOV	KAZ	19/11/94	A		(1)	

KV KORTRIJK

Coach – Hein Vanhaezebrouck

Founded – 1971

Stadium – Guldensporenstadion (9,500)

2010				
31/7	Club Brugge	h	1-0	*De Beule*
7/8	Lokeren	a	1-1	*Rossini*
14/8	Sint-Truiden	h	2-0	*Pavlović, Rossini*
21/8	Lierse	a	2-1	*Pavlović, El Araichi (p)*
28/8	Standard	a	0-1	
11/9	Mechelen	h	1-0	*Capon*
19/9	Anderlecht	a	0-3	
22/9	Westerlo	h	1-2	*Rossini (p)*
25/9	Cercle Brugge	a	1-2	*Mboyo*
2/10	Eupen	h	3-1	*Rossini (p), Mboyo, Kums*
16/10	Gent	a	0-2	
22/10	Genk	h	1-0	*Rossini*
29/10	Charleroi	a	0-0	
6/11	GBA	h	4-0	*Rossini (p), Gershon, Mboyo (p), Messoudi*
14/11	Zulte Waregem	a	1-1	*Mboyo*
20/11	Eupen	a	1-3	*Belhocine*
4/12	Sint-Truiden	a	0-1	
12/12	Lierse	h	3-1	*De Beule 2, Mboyo*
17/12	Standard	h	2-1	*Mboyo, Rossini*
29/12	Anderlecht	h	0-2	
2011				
18/1	Lokeren	h	0-0	
22/1	Genk	a	2-3	*og (Ngcongca), Rossini*
29/1	Cercle Brugge	h	2-1	*Messoudi 2*
2/2	Mechelen	a	0-1	
5/2	Westerlo	a	1-2	*Šćepović*
13/2	Gent	h	0-1	
19/2	GBA	a	1-3	*De Mets*
5/3	Charleroi	h	3-0	*De Beule 2, Kums*
12/3	Club Brugge	a	1-4	*De Beule*
19/3	Zulte Waregem	h	2-2	*Martin, De Beule*
2/4	Westerlo	a	0-3	
9/4	GBA	h	1-1	*Messoudi*
16/4	Zulte Waregem	h	0-1	
22/4	Zulte Waregem	a	0-2	
30/4	Westerlo	h	1-1	*Capon (p)*
7/5	GBA	a	0-0	

No	Name	Nat	DoB	Pos	Aps	(s)	Gls
5	Karim BELHOCINE	FRA	2/1/83	M	33	(1)	1
7	Leon BENKO	CRO	11/11/83	A	1	(5)	
21	Brecht CAPON		22/4/88	D	29	(2)	2
18	Mario CAREVIĆ	CRO	29/3/82	M	17	(6)	
14	Davy DE BEULE		7/11/81	M	28	(1)	7
17	Gertjan DE METS		2/4/87	D	19	(4)	1
16	Brecht DEJAEGHERE		29/5/91	M	5	(1)	
6	Chemcedine EL ARAICHI		18/5/81	D	13	(6)	1
12	Jonas Malvy FLEURY		8/3/92	D		(1)	
25	Rami GERSHON	ISR	12/8/88	M	31	(1)	1
10	Sven KUMS		26/2/88	M	29		2
30	Damien LAHAYE		30/1/84	G	8		
15	Baptiste MARTIN	FRA	14/5/85	D	17	(4)	1
19	Ilombe MBOYO	COD	27/4/87	A	20	(1)	6
20	Mohamed MESSOUDI		7/1/84	M	16	(11)	4
12	Dieter MEULENYZER		11/4/91	M		(2)	
27	Mustapha OUSSALAH	MAR	19/2/82	M	16	(8)	
8	Nebojša PAVLOVIĆ	SRB	9/4/81	M	28	(1)	2
3	Loris REINA	FRA	10/6/80	D	10	(2)	
9	Giuseppe ROSSINI		23/8/86	A	28	(4)	8
12	Ebrahima Ibou SAWANEH	GAM	7/9/86	A	3	(14)	
19	Stefan ŠĆEPOVIĆ	SRB	10/1/90	A	4	(4)	1
11	Taha SOUHAIL	MAR	7/10/91	A		(1)	
4	Toni ŠUNJIĆ	BIH	15/12/88	D	11	(4)	
24	Tom VANDENBOSSCHE		12/3/89	G	1		
13	Glenn VERBAUWHEDE		19/5/85	G	27		
23	Jonas VERVAEKE		10/1/92	D	2	(1)	
20	Monsef ZNAGUI		30/1/91	A		(2)	

K. LIERSE SK

Coach – Aimé Anthuenis; (19/9/10) Eric Van Meir; (1/1/11) Trond Sollied (NOR)

Founded – 1906

Stadium – Herman Vanderpoortenstadion (14,538)

MAJOR HONOURS: Belgian League (4) 1932, 1942, 1960, 1997; Belgian Cup – (2) 1969, 1999.

2010				
31/7	Sint-Truiden	a	0-1	
6/8	Standard	h	1-4	*Cavens*

/8	Mechelen	a	0-1	
/8	Kortrijk	h	1-2	*Douala*
8	Genk	a	1-4	*Cavens*
9	Gent	h	2-2	*Sonck 2*
/9	Westerlo	a	0-2	
9	Anderlecht	h	1-1	*Sonck*
/9	Charleroi	a	1-0	*Kovács*
0	Cercle Brugge	h	0-1	
/10	GBA	a	1-1	*Radzinski*
/10	Zulte Waregem	h	0-0	
/10	Eupen	a	2-2	*Radzinski, Claasen*
1	Lokeren	h	2-2	*Vandooren, Radzinski*
/11	Club Brugge	a	0-2	
/11	Sint-Truiden	h	1-2	*Kovács*
/11	Standard	a	0-7	
/12	Kortrijk	a	1-3	*Radzinski*
/12	Genk	h	1-1	*Sonck*
/12	Anderlecht	a	0-6	
/12	Westerlo	h	2-1	*Kovács, Radzinski*
11				
/1	Cercle Brugge	a	0-3	
/1	Charleroi	h	1-0	*Sonck*
2	Gent	a	1-4	*Sonck (p)*
/2	GBA	h	2-2	*Thompson, Kovács*
/2	Mechelen	h	2-1	*Claasen, og (Pandža)*
/2	Zulte Waregem	a	1-1	*Abdel Wahed*
3	Eupen	h	1-1	*Davids*
/3	Lokeren	a	1-1	*Cavens*
/3	Club Brugge	h	0-0	
4	Cercle Brugge	a	0-0	
/4	Mechelen	h	1-2	*Mathisen*
/4	Sint-Truiden	a	2-1	*El-Gabbas, Bernárdez (p)*
/4	Sint-Truiden	h	1-1	*El-Gabbas*
/4	Cercle Brugge	h	3-0	*De Wree, Radzinski, El-Gabbas*
5	Mechelen	a	3-4	*Radzinski, El-Gabbas, Cavens*

o	Name	Nat	DoB	Pos	Aps	(s)	Gls
0	Mohamed ABDEL WAHED	EGY	19/1/81	M	6	(8)	1
5	Marcus ANDREASSON	SWE	13/7/78	D	2		
5	Árni Gautur ARASON	ISL	7/5/75	G	2		
0	Abdul Ibrahim AYEW	GHA	16/4/88	M	6	(1)	
	Víctor BERNÁRDEZ	HON	24/5/82	D	8	(1)	1
	Bruno CAMACHO	BRA	28/10/85	D	8	(4)	
	Jurgen CAVENS		19/8/78	A	13	(9)	4
4	Daylon CLAASEN	RSA	28/1/90	M	28	(4)	2
9	Lance DAVIDS	RSA	11/4/85	M	27		1
7	Garry DE GRAEF		21/10/74	D	11	(1)	
	Kris DE WREE		21/5/81	D	16	(1)	1
	Joeri DEQUEVY		27/4/88	M	12	(9)	
9	Roudolphe DOUALA	CMR	25/9/78	M		(5)	1
	Mohamed EL-GABBAS	EGY	21/10/87	A	15	(12)	4
5	Frédéric FRANS		3/1/89	D	11		
6	Siboniso GAXA	RSA	6/4/84	D	14	(5)	
8	Felisberto Sebastião de Graça Amaral "GILBERTO"	ANG	21/9/82	M	16	(5)	
3	Kevin JANSSENS		29/5/86	M	2		
6	Joseph-Désiré JOB	CMR	1/12/77	A	2	(3)	
	Eiji KAWASHIMA	JPN	20/3/83	G	28		
9	Péter KOVÁCS	HUN	7/2/78	A	13	(10)	4
2	Vladan KUJOVIĆ	SRB	23/8/78	G	6		
3	Miloš MARIĆ	SRB	5/3/82	M	13		
23	Alexander MATHISEN	NOR	24/11/86	M	3	(1)	1
3	Akwetey MENSAH	GHA	15/4/83	M	11	(1)	
26	Bejamin NICAISE	FRA	28/9/80	M	8		
4	Mattia NOTARI	ITA	20/5/79	D	2	(1)	
13	Tomasz RADZINSKI	CAN	14/12/73	A	29	(1)	7
5	Youssef SEKOUR	FRA	27/2/88	M	3	(2)	
10	Wesley SONCK		9/8/78	A	20	(2)	6
21	Gunter THIEBAUT		12/1/77	A	6	(9)	
4	Kenny THOMPSON		26/4/85	D	13		1
30	Kurt VAN DOOREN		3/8/78	D	15		
24	Roel VAN HEMERT	NED	21/11/84	D	16	(1)	
11	Gonzague VANDOOREN		17/8/79	D	11	(1)	1

KSC LOKEREN OV

Coach – Peter Maes

Founded – 1970

Stadium – Daknamstadion (9,271)

2010				
31/7	Mechelen	a	0-2	
7/8	Kortrijk	h	1-1	*Mokulu*
14/8	Standard	a	3-3	*Persoons, De Pauw, Tshimanga*
21/8	Anderlecht	h	0-3	
28/8	Cercle Brugge	a	1-1	*Leko*
12/9	Westerlo	h	3-1	*Taravel, Leko 2 (1p)*
18/9	Genk	a	1-3	*Leko*
22/9	Gent	h	3-2	*De Pauw, Mokulu, Deekman*
25/9	Eupen	a	1-0	*Overmeire*
2/10	GBA	h	1-0	*Persoons*
16/10	Charleroi	a	2-1	*De Roover, Leko*
24/10	Club Brugge	h	1-0	*Taravel*
30/10	Zulte Waregem	a	1-1	*De Ceulaer*
6/11	Lierse	a	2-2	*Mokulu, De Ceulaer*
13/11	Sint-Truiden	h	3-0	*og (Mennes), De Ceulaer, Overmeire*
20/11	Mechelen	h	3-1	*De Ceulaer 2, Tiko*
3/12	Standard	h	2-1	*De Ceulaer 2*
12/12	Anderlecht	a	0-0	
30/12	Genk	h	2-2	*Tshimanga, Gueye*
2011				
18/1	Kortrijk	a	0-0	
23/1	Gent	a	1-2	*De Pauw*
29/1	Eupen	h	0-2	
2/2	Cercle Brugge	h	2-1	*Taravel, De Ceulaer*
5/2	GBA	a	1-1	*Maric*
12/2	Charleroi	h	1-1	*Finnbogason*
16/2	Westerlo	a	2-1	*Deekman 2*
19/2	Club Brugge	a	1-2	*Finnbogason*
5/3	Zulte Waregem	h	2-1	*Finnbogason, De Ceulaer*
12/3	Lierse	h	1-1	*De Pauw*
20/3	Sint-Truiden	a	2-0	*Mokulu 2*
3/4	Genk	a	1-2	*De Pauw*
9/4	Gent	h	1-1	*De Pauw*
17/4	Club Brugge	a	0-0	
21/4	Standard	a	0-3	
24/4	Anderlecht	h	1-2	*De Ceulaer*
1/5	Genk	h	0-2	
7/5	Gent	a	2-2	*De Ceulaer, Fevang*
11/5	Standard	h	0-1	
14/5	Club Brugge	h	0-1	
17/5	Anderlecht	a	4-3	*Leko, Tshimanga, Fevang 2*

No	Name	Nat	DoB	Pos	Aps	(s)	Gls
16	Julien BAILLEUL	FRA	15/2/88	M	3	(6)	
30	Boubacar "Copa" BARRY	CIV	30/12/79	G	32		
25	Vegaard BRAATEN	NOR	30/6/87	A		(2)	
28	Laurens DE BOCK		7/11/92	D	19	(6)	
11	Benjamin DE CEULAER		19/12/83	A	34	(3)	11
29	Nill DE PAUW		6/1/90	A	32	(3)	6
2	Sepp DE ROOVER		12/11/84	D	14	(3)	1
20	Donovan DEEKMAN	NED	23/6/88	A	6	(13)	3
3	Hassan EL MOUATAZ	MAR	21/9/81	D	4	(4)	
17	Geir Ludvig FEVANG	NOR	17/11/80	M	3	(9)	3
15	Alfred FINNBOGASON	ISL	1/2/89	A	5	(10)	3
23	Ibrahima GUEYE	SEN	19/2/78	D	10	(6)	1
12	Jugoslav LAZIĆ	SRB	12/12/79	G	8		
78	Ivan LEKO	CRO	7/2/78	M	37	(3)	6
24	Sanharib MALKI	SYR	1/3/84	A		(2)	
4	Mijat MARIC	SUI	30/4/84	D	32		1
10	Marcel MBAYO	COD	23/4/78	M	3	(15)	
14	Benjamin MOKULU Tembe		11/10/89	A	33	(5)	5
7	Killian OVERMEIRE		6/12/85	M	37	(1)	2
9	Jérémy PERBET	FRA	12/12/84	A		(3)	
8	Koen PERSOONS		12/7/83	M	37		2
8	Sulejman SMAJIĆ	BIH	13/4/84	M	1	(2)	
22	Jérémy TARAVEL	FRA	17/4/87	D	36		3
6	Tsholola Tshinyama "TIKO"	COD	12/12/80	M	27	(4)	1
31	Jore TROMPET		30/7/92	M		(7)	
26	Derrick Katuku TSHIMANGA		6/11/88	A	27	(1)	3
18	Ivan YAGAN		11/10/89	M		(1)	

KV MECHELEN

Coach – Marc Brys
Founded – 1904
Stadium – Veolia Stadion (13,123)
MAJOR HONOURS: UEFA Cup Winners' Cup – (1) 1988; UEFA Super Cup – (1) 1989; Belgian League – (4) 1943, 1946, 1948, 1989; Belgian Cup – (1) 1987.

2010				
31/7	Lokeren	h	2-0	*Gorius, Nong*
7/8	Zulte Waregem	a	2-1	*Nong, Pandža*
14/8	Lierse	h	1-0	*Buyens*
22/8	Club Brugge	a	2-1	*Van Hoevelen, Gorius (p)*
28/8	Sint-Truiden	h	0-0	
11/9	Kortrijk	a	0-1	
17/9	Standard	h	1-0	*Pandža*
22/9	Cercle Brugge	h	2-2	*Wilmet, Gorius*
26/9	Anderlecht	a	0-5	
1/10	Genk	h	2-2	*Geudens, Pandža*
16/10	Westerlo	a	1-1	*Gorius*
23/10	GBA	h	5-1	*Gorius 2 (1p), Geudens, Benteke 2*
30/10	Gent	a	1-3	*Wilmet*
6/11	Charleroi	h	2-0	*Destorme, Wilmet*
20/11	Lokeren	a	1-3	*Benteke*
28/11	Zulte Waregem	h	0-0	
10/12	Club Brugge	h	0-1	
2011				
18/1	Eupen	a	1-0	*De Witte*
22/1	Charleroi	a	0-0	
30/1	Anderlecht	h	0-0	
2/2	Kortrijk	h	1-0	*Gorius*
5/2	Cercle Brugge	a	1-0	Gorius
12/2	Westerlo	h	3-1	*Destorme, Sawaneh, Koulibaly*
15/2	Lierse	a	1-2	*Gorius*
19/2	Genk	a	0-1	
23/2	Sint-Truiden	a	1-0	*Benteke*
26/2	Standard	a	0-3	
5/3	Gent	h	1-1	*Destorme*
12/3	GBA	a	1-1	*Diabang*
20/3	Eupen	h	2-0	*Gorius, Destorme*
2/4	Sint-Truiden	h	1-1	*Destorme*
8/4	Lierse	a	2-1	*Kabasele, Benteke*
16/4	Cercle Brugge	h	0-0	
23/4	Cercle Brugge	a	1-3	*Gorius*
30/4	Sint-Truiden	a	1-2	*Benteke*
7/5	Lierse	h	4-3	*Geudens, Diabang, Gorius 2 (1p)*

No	Name	Nat	DoB	Pos	Aps	(s)	Gls
14	Christian BENTEKE		3/12/90	A	13	(5)	6
20	Wouter BIEBAUW		21/5/84	G	1		
19	Maxime BISET		26/3/86	M	2	(5)	
17	Yoni BUYENS		10/3/88	M	35		1
8	Xavier CHEN		5/10/83	D	34		
4	Seth DE WITTE		18/10/87	M	6	(5)	1
18	David DESTORME		30/8/79	M	21	(6)	5
28	Boubacar DIABANG Dialiba	BIH	13/7/88	A	12	(12)	2
13	Antun DUNKOVIĆ	CRO	7/6/81	M	2	(2)	
16	Kevin GEUDENS		2/12/80	M	25	(4)	3
26	Antonio GHOMSY	CMR	22/4/86	D	20	(1)	
15	Julien GORIUS	FRA	17/3/85	M	35		13
24	Abdul-Ganiyu IDDI	GHA	8/1/90	A	3	(1)	
10	Abdul-Yakinu IDDI	GHA	25/5/86	M	5	(4)	
27	Christian KABASELE		24/2/91	A	1	(3)	1
25	Pan Pierre KOULIBALY	BFA	24/3/86	A	1	(5)	1
12	Jonas LAUREYS		2/4/91	M	1	(2)	
11	Joachim MUNUNGA		30/6/88	A	16		
14	Aloys NONG	CMR	16/10/83	A	5		2
3	Boris PANDŽA	BIH	15/12/86	D	34		3
2	Tom PIETERMAAT		6/9/92	M		(1)	
23	Olivier RENARD		24/5/79	G	35		
11	Ebrahima Ibou SAWANEH	GAM	7/9/86	A	7	(4)	1
29	Tom SOETAERS		21/7/80	M	1	(10)	
22	Romeo VAN DESSEL		9/4/89	D		(2)	
5	Kenny VAN HOEVELEN		24/6/83	D	35		1
21	Anthony VAN LOO		5/10/88	D	18	(1)	
6	Bjarni Thór VIDARSSON	ISL	5/3/88	M	1	(15)	
9	Jonathan WILMET		7/1/86	M	27	(7)	3

K. SINT-TRUIDENSE VV

Coach – Guido Brepoels
Founded – 1924
Stadium – Staayen (11,250)

2010				
31/7	Lierse	h	1-0	*Euvrard*
7/8	Club Brugge	a	1-4	*Mennes*
14/8	Kortrijk	a	0-2	
20/8	Standard	h	1-0	*Sidibé*
28/8	Mechelen	a	0-0	
10/9	Anderlecht	h	0-2	
18/9	Cercle Brugge	a	2-4	*Camara 2*
21/9	Genk	h	0-2	
25/9	Gent	a	0-2	
2/10	Westerlo	h	1-2	*Deferm*
16/10	Eupen	a	0-6	
23/10	Charleroi	h	3-2	*Rymenants, Sidibé 2*
30/10	GBA	a	0-0	
6/11	Zulte Waregem	h	0-3	
13/11	Lokeren	a	0-3	
20/11	Lierse	a	2-1	*Sidibé, Mbuyi-Mutombo*
28/11	Club Brugge	h	2-1	*Sidibé, Mennes*
4/12	Kortrijk	h	1-0	*Mennes*
11/12	Standard	a	0-1	
2011				
22/1	Westerlo	a	0-3	
30/1	Gent	h	1-1	*Sidibé*
2/2	Genk	a	1-1	*Schouterden*
5/2	Anderlecht	a	0-2	
12/2	Eupen	h	1-1	*Euvrard*
19/2	Charleroi	a	0-1	
23/2	Mechelen	h	0-1	
27/2	Cercle Brugge	h	0-3	
5/3	GBA	h	1-0	*Dufer*
12/3	Zulte Waregem	a	2-1	*Dufer, Schouterden*
20/3	Lokeren	h	0-2	
2/4	Mechelen	a	1-1	*Rymenants*
9/4	Cercle Brugge	h	1-1	*Sidibé*
16/4	Lierse	h	1-2	*Deferm*
23/4	Lierse	a	1-1	*Proesmans*
30/4	Mechelen	h	2-1	*Odoi, Dufer*
7/5	Cercle Brugge	a	0-1	

No	Name	Nat	DoB	Pos	Aps	(s)	Gls
23	Yorick ANTHEUNIS		26/6/91	A	8	(7)	
21	Christophe BERTJENS		5/1/93	M	2	(7)	
10	Cédric BEUKERS		17/4/94	M		(1)	
6	Ludovic BUYSENS		13/3/86	D	14		
15	Tom CALUWE		11/4/78	M	11	(1)	
7	Pape Abdou CAMARA	SEN	24/9/91	M	6	(5)	2
25	Bram CASTRO		30/9/80	G	6		
10	Grégory CHRIST	FRA	4/10/82	M	8	(5)	
24	Giel DEFERM		30/6/88	D	24	(3)	2
17	Peter DELORGE		19/4/80	M	32		
7	Gregory DUFER		19/12/81	M	10	(2)	3
3	Vincent EUVRARD		12/3/82	D	35		2
11	Carlo EVERTZ		1/8/90	A	2	(5)	
27	Laurent HENKINET		14/9/92	G	6	(1)	
12	Mannaseh ISHIAKU	NGA	9/1/83	A	5		
13	Sasha KOTYSCH	GER	2/10/88	D	16	(1)	
20	Benoit MASSET		29/6/90	D	1	(1)	
9	Andréa MBUYI-MUTOMBO		7/6/90	A	14	(14)	1
2	Wim MENNES		25/1/77	M	31	(1)	3
8	Denis ODOI		27/5/88	D	33		1
12	Hervé Ndjana ONANA	CMR	1/6/87	A	3	(6)	
25	Nikolas PROESMANS		11/5/92	M	5	(1)	1
4	Yannick RYMENANTS		23/1/89	D	17	(8)	2
25	Rob SCHOOFS		23/3/94	M		(1)	
18	Nils SCHOUTERDEN		14/12/88	M	22	(3)	2
19	Ibrahima SIDIBÉ	SEN	10/8/80	A	27	(1)	7
10	Tibor TISZA	HUN	10/11/84	A	3	(5)	
22	Sven VAN DER JEUGT		17/9/80	G	19	(1)	
12	Dylan VAN WELKENHUYSEN		20/1/92	A	3	(10)	
1	Mark VOLDERS		13/4/77	G	5		
14	Marc WAGEMAKERS		7/6/78	M	28	(2)	

R. STANDARD DE LIÈGE

Coach – Dominique D'Onofrio

Founded – 1898

Stadium – Maurice Dufrasne (27,500)

MAJOR HONOURS: Belgian League – (10) 1958, 1961, 1963, 1969, 1970, 1971, 1982, 1983, 2008, 2009; Belgian Cup – (6) 1954, 1966, 1967, 1981, 1993, 2011.

10				
/7	Zulte Waregem	h	1-1	*Defour*
3	Lierse	a	4-1	*Witsel (p), Carcela-González 2, Pocognoli*
/8	Lokeren	h	3-3	*Defour, Carcela-González 2*
/8	Sint-Truiden	a	0-1	
/8	Kortrijk	h	1-0	*Pieroni*
/9	Cercle Brugge	h	2-0	*Tchité, Witsel (p)*
/9	Mechelen	a	0-1	
/9	Charleroi	h	2-1	*Ciman, Defour*
/9	Westerlo	a	2-1	*Cyriac 2*
10	Anderlecht	h	5-1	*Leye, Tchité 2, Bokanga, Carcela-González*
/10	Genk	a	2-4	*Carcela-González, Tchité*
/10	Gent	h	2-1	*Tchité, Carcela-González*
/10	Club Brugge	a	2-2	*og (Simaeys), Cyriac*
11	Eupen	h	1-3	*Cyriac*
3/11	GBA	a	1-0	*Tchité*
/11	Zulte Waregem	a	0-2	
/11	Lierse	h	7-0	*Witsel 2, Pieroni, Cyriac 3, Carcela-González*
12	Lokeren	a	1-2	*Carcela-González*
/12	Sint-Truiden	h	1-0	*Cyriac*
7/12	Kortrijk	a	1-2	*Witsel*
6/12	Cercle Brugge	a	0-1	
011				
3/1	Anderlecht	a	0-2	
9/1	Westerlo	h	2-1	*Goreux, Van Damme*
/2	Eupen	a	1-0	*og (Zukanović)*
3/2	Genk	h	0-2	
0/2	Gent	a	1-4	*Leye*
6/2	Mechelen	h	3-0	*Witsel 2, Leye*
/3	Club Brugge	h	2-2	*Tchité, Carcela-González*
2/3	Charleroi	a	2-0	*Van Damme, Tchité*
0/3	GBA	h	1-0	*og (Kaminski)*
/4	Anderlecht	a	3-1	*Nong 2, og (Juhász)*
0/4	Genk	h	2-1	*Witsel (p), Nong*
6/4	Gent	a	3-1	*Carcela-González, Tchité, Witsel*
1/4	Lokeren	h	3-0	*Carcela-González, Leye 2*
5/4	Club Brugge	a	1-1	*Nong*
9/4	Gent	h	1-0	*Tchité*
7/5	Club Brugge	h	1-0	*Witsel*
0/5	Lokeren	a	1-0	*Goreux*
4/5	Anderlecht	h	2-1	*Carcela-González, Tchité*
7/5	Genk	a	1-1	*Mangala*

o	Name	Nat	DoB	Pos	Aps	(s)	Gls
7	Arnor ANGELI		25/2/91	M	3	(2)	
0	Michy BATSHUAYI		2/10/93	A		(2)	
5	Christian BENTEKE		3/12/90	A	4	(1)	
	Franck BERRIER	FRA	2/2/84	M	3	(3)	
3	Srđan BLAŽIĆ	MNE	26/11/82	G	12	(1)	
0	Eric BOKANGA	COD	9/10/88	A	2	(11)	1
4	Pape Abdou CAMARA	SEN	24/9/91	M	13	(3)	
3	Mehdi CARCELA-GONZÁLEZ	MAR	1/7/89	M	34	(4)	13
	Laurent CIMAN		5/8/85	D	26	(3)	1
9	CYRIAC Gohi Bi Zoro Sede	CIV	15/8/90	A	15	(3)	8
4	Koen DAERDEN		8/3/82	M	7	(7)	
4	Richard DANILO Maciel Sousa Campos	BRA	13/1/90	M	1	(2)	
3	Steven DEFOUR		15/4/88	M	26	(1)	3
17	Hans DIBI	FRA	23/6/88	M		(1)	
26	Francesco D'ONOFRIO		6/10/90	D		(1)	
35	Henry ENINFUL	TOG	22/7/92	M	3		
5	FELIPE Trevizan Martins	BRA	15/5/87	D	11	(1)	
2	Réginal GOREUX		31/12/87	D	10	(7)	2
77	Gheorghe GROZAV	ROU	29/9/90	A	2	(8)	
25	António Eduardo Pereira dos Santos "KANU"	BRA	3/5/84	D	14		
20	Leroy LABYLLE		11/3/91	M		(2)	
99	Mbaye LEYE	SEN	1/12/82	A	21	(11)	5
22	Eliaquim MANGALA	FRA	13/2/91	D	32	(3)	1
13	Aloys NONG	CMR	16/10/83	A	12	(12)	4
4	Daniel OPARE	GHA	18/10/90	D	32	(1)	
9	Luigi PIERONI		8/9/80	A	5	(13)	2
35	Sébastien POCOGNOLI		1/8/87	D	33	(1)	1
38	SİNAN Bolat	TUR	3/9/89	G	24		
10	Mohammed TCHITÉ	COD	31/1/84	A	26	(1)	11
37	Jelle VAN DAMME		10/10/83	M	17		2
1	Kristof VAN HOUT		9/2/87	G	4	(1)	
32	Christopher VERBIST		8/10/91	D	1	(1)	
3	VICTOR RAMOS Ferreira	BRA	5/5/89	D	10	(2)	
28	Axel WITSEL		12/1/89	M	37		10

KVC WESTERLO

Coach – Jan Ceulemans

Founded – 1933

Stadium – Het Kuipje (8,141)

MAJOR HONOURS: Belgian Cup – (1) 2001.

2010				
31/7	Gent	h	0-1	
7/8	Eupen	a	1-0	*Liliu*
14/8	Zulte Waregem	h	1-1	*De Petter (p)*
21/8	GBA	a	0-0	
29/8	Club Brugge	h	1-2	*Brüls*
12/9	Lokeren	a	1-3	*Chávez*
18/9	Lierse	h	2-0	*Farssi, Chávez*
22/9	Kortrijk	a	2-1	*Yakovenko, Corstjens*
25/9	Standard	h	1-2	*Paulo Henrique*
2/10	Sint-Truiden	a	2-1	*Paulo Henrique 2*
16/10	Mechelen	h	1-1	*Paulo Henrique*
24/10	Anderlecht	a	0-2	
30/10	Cercle Brugge	h	2-1	*Dekelver, De Petter*
5/11	Genk	h	1-1	*Dekelver*
13/11	Charleroi	a	1-0	*Brüls*
20/11	Gent	a	4-4	*Paulo Henrique 2, og (Smolders), Chávez*
27/11	Eupen	h	1-1	*Farssi*
5/12	Club Brugge	a	3-4	*Dekelver 2, Annab*
11/12	GBA	h	1-1	*Paulo Henrique*
18/12	Zulte Waregem	a	0-2	
29/12	Lierse	a	1-2	*Dekelver*
2011				
22/1	Sint-Truiden	h	3-0	*Yakovenko, De Petter, Paulo Henrique*
29/1	Standard	a	1-2	*Brüls*
5/2	Kortrijk	h	2-1	*Farssi, De Petter*
12/2	Mechelen	a	1-3	*Ngolok*
16/2	Lokeren	h	1-2	*Brüls*
20/2	Anderlecht	h	2-0	*Yakovenko (p), Dekelver*
5/3	Cercle Brugge	a	1-0	*Dekelver*
12/3	Genk	a	2-0	*Paulo Henrique, Farssi*
20/3	Charleroi	h	2-2	*Liliu, Corstjens*
2/4	Kortrijk	h	3-0	*Paulo Henrique, De Petter, Liliu*
10/4	Zulte Waregem	a	1-1	*Paulo Henrique*
16/4	GBA	a	3-3	*Paulo Henrique 2, Van Hout*
23/4	GBA	h	1-0	*Yakovenko*
30/4	Kortrijk	a	1-1	*Paulo Henrique*
7/5	Zulte Waregem	h	7-1	*Paulo Henrique 2, og (Minne), Dekelver 2, Brüls, Annab*

No	Name	Nat	DoB	Pos	Aps	(s)	Gls
20	Moses ADAMS	NGA	21/7/88	M	1	(2)	
24	Lens ANNAB		20/7/88	M	20	(11)	2
8	Christian BRÜLS		30/9/88	M	24	(8)	5
5	Geoffrey CABEKE		5/11/88	D	7	(2)	
11	Daniël CHÁVEZ	PER	8/1/88	A	12	(13)	3
24	Jens COOLS		16/10/90	M	17	(3)	
4	Wouter CORSTJENS		13/2/87	D	27		2
3	Steven DE PETTER		22/11/85	D	27	(1)	5
1	Yves DE WINTER		25/5/87	G	25		
30	Bart DEELKENS		25/4/78	G	11		
7	Dieter DEKELVER		17/8/79	A	17	(11)	9
18	Jef DELEN		29/6/76	M	29	(1)	
21	Rachid FARSSI		15/1/85	D	29	(4)	4

9	Ellenton António Costa Morais "LILIU"	BRA	1/3/90	A	6	(4)	3
14	Michael MODUBI	RSA	22/4/85	M	2	(4)	
23	Jarno MOLENBERGHS		11/12/89	M	5	(10)	
2	Adnan MRAVAC	BIH	10/4/82	D	32		
28	Evariste NGOLOK	CMR	15/11/88	M	12		1
12	PAULO HENRIQUE Carneiro Filho	BRA	13/3/89	A	23	(7)	16
19	Jaime Alfonso RUIZ	COL	3/1/84	A	1	(1)	
17	Elrio VAN HEERDEN	RSA	11/7/83	M	12	(8)	
16	Joris VAN HOUT		10/11/77	D	8		1
32	Gunther VANAUDENAERDE		23/1/84	D	20	(1)	
15	Jeroen VANTHOURNHOUT		29/6/89	D	3		
22	Olexandr YAKOVENKO	UKR	23/6/87	M	26	(4)	4

SV ZULTE WAREGEM

Coach – Bart De Roover; (27/10/10) Hugo Broos

Founded – 2001

Stadium – Regenboogstadion (8,500)

MAJOR HONOURS: Belgian Cup – (1) 2006.

2010				
30/7	Standard	a	1-1	*Hyland*
7/8	Mechelen	h	1-2	*Hyland*
14/8	Westerlo	a	1-1	*Bokila*
21/8	Cercle Brugge	h	4-0	*Habibou, D'Haene, Sterckx, Meert*
28/8	Anderlecht	a	0-0	
11/9	Eupen	h	0-0	
19/9	Gent	a	3-5	*Vandenbroeck, Hyland, Chevalier*
22/9	GBA	h	4-3	*Sterckx, Matton, N'For, Traoré*
25/9	Genk	a	0-3	
2/10	Charleroi	h	1-1	*Matton*
15/10	Club Brugge	h	2-3	*Traoré, Habibou*
23/10	Lierse	a	0-0	
30/10	Lokeren	h	1-1	*Maréval (p)*
6/11	Sint-Truiden	a	3-0	*Habibou 2, Maréval (p)*
14/11	Kortrijk	h	1-1	*Habibou*
21/11	Standard	h	2-0	*Habibou, Chevalier*
28/11	Mechelen	a	0-0	
5/12	Anderlecht	h	1-2	*Maréval*
11/12	Cercle Brugge	a	3-1	*Habibou 2, Chevalier*
18/12	Westerlo	h	2-0	*Traoré, Bokila*
30/12	Gent	h	2-2	*Hyland, Traoré*

2011				
22/1	GBA	a	0-3	
28/1	Genk	h	0-1	
2/2	Eupen	a	2-0	*Hyland, Chevalier*
5/2	Charleroi	a	0-2	
12/2	Club Brugge	a	0-2	
19/2	Lierse	h	1-1	*Habibou*
5/3	Lokeren	a	1-2	*Matton*
12/3	Sint-Truiden	h	1-2	*Vandenbroeck*
19/3	Kortrijk	a	2-2	*D'Haene, Habibou*
2/4	GBA	a	0-2	
10/4	Westerlo	h	1-1	*Habibou*
16/4	Kortrijk	a	1-0	*Naessens*
22/4	Kortrijk	h	2-0	*Habibou, D'Haene*
30/4	GBA	h	1-0	*Matton*
7/5	Westerlo	a	1-7	*Delaplace*

No	Name	Nat	DoB	Pos	Aps	(s)	Gls
14	Jeremy BOKILA	NED	14/11/88	A	4	(17)	2
1	Sammy BOSSUT		11/8/85	G	32		
23	Bart BUYSSE		16/10/86	D	1		
9	Teddy CHEVALIER	FRA	28/6/87	A	24	(5)	4
3	Steve COLPAERT		13/9/86	D	30	(3)	
15	Miguel DACHELET		16/1/88	D	19		
7	Jonathan DELAPLACE	FRA	20/3/86	M	23	(6)	1
24	Karel D'HAENE		5/9/80	D	22	(2)	3
15	Zakari GUEYE	SEN	22/2/86	M	1	(4)	
77	Mouhamadou Habib HABIBOU	FRA	16/4/87	A	29	(2)	12
21	Khaleem HYLAND	TRI	5/6/89	M	31	(1)	5
5	Rémi MARÉVAL	FRA	24/2/83	D	22		3
12	Thomas MATTON		24/10/85	M	28	(2)	4
11	Stijn MEERT		6/4/78	M	5	(8)	1
2	Stijn MINNE		29/6/78	D	23		
22	Tom MUYTERS		5/12/84	G	4		
26	Jens NAESSENS		1/4/91	A	5	(1)	1
10	Ernest N'FOR	CMR	28/4/86	A	19	(4)	1
9	Kevin ROELANDTS		27/8/82	M	2	(6)	
16	René STERCKX		18/1/91	M	9	(1)	2
19	Nicholas TAMSIN		10/12/89	D	7	(2)	
18	Moussa TRAORÉ	CIV	9/3/90	A	5	(12)	4
4	David VANDENBROECK		12/7/85	D	29	(2)	2
6	Ludwin VAN NIEUWENHUYZE		25/2/78	M	22	(5)	

MID-TABLE/RELEGATION PLAY-OFFS 2010/11

PLAY-OFF 2A FINAL TABLE

			Home					Away					Total					
		Pld	W	D	L	F	A	W	D	L	F	A	W	D	L	F	A	Pts
1	Cercle Brugge KSV	6	2	1	0	4	1	0	2	1	1	4	2	3	1	5	5	9
2	K. Lierse SK	6	1	1	1	5	3	1	1	1	5	5	2	2	2	10	8	8
3	KV Mechelen	6	1	2	0	5	4	1	0	2	4	6	2	2	2	9	10	8
4	K. Sint-Truidense VV	6	1	1	1	4	4	0	2	1	2	3	1	3	2	6	7	6

PLAY-OFF 2B FINAL TABLE

			Home					Away					Total					
		Pld	W	D	L	F	A	W	D	L	F	A	W	D	L	F	A	Pts
1	KVC Westerlo	6	3	0	0	11	1	0	3	0	5	5	3	3	0	16	6	12
2	SV Zulte Waregem	6	2	1	0	4	1	1	0	2	2	9	3	1	2	6	10	10
3	KFC Germinal Beerschot Antwerpen	6	1	2	0	5	3	0	1	2	1	3	1	3	2	6	6	6
4	KV Kortrijk	6	0	2	1	2	3	0	1	2	0	5	0	3	3	2	8	3

UEFA EUROPA LEAGUE QUALIFICATION PLAY-OFF

(13/5/11 & 16/5/11)

Westerlo 3 *(Paulo Henrique 4, 55, Ngolok 90)*, Cercle Brugge 0

Cercle Brugge 2 *(D'Haene 59, Yashchuk 68)*, Westerlo 2 *(Chávez 33, Annab 90)*

(Westerlo 5-2)

PLAY-OFF 3 FINAL TABLE

			Home					Away					Total					
		Pld	W	D	L	F	A	W	D	L	F	A	W	D	L	F	A	Pts
1	KAS Eupen	4	2	0	0	7	4	0	1	1	2	4	2	1	1	9	8	10
2	R. Charleroi SC	4	1	1	0	4	2	0	0	2	4	7	1	1	2	8	9	4

NB KAS Eupen carried 3 pts forward from regular season; KAS Eupen subsequently entered promotion/relegation play-offs.

TOP GOALSCORERS 2010/11

22 Ivan PERIŠIĆ (Club Brugge)

20 Jelle VOSSEN (Genk)

16 Romelu LUKAKU (Anderlecht)
PAULO HENRIQUE (Westerlo)

15 Ronald VARGAS (Club Brugge)
Marvin OGUNJIMI (Genk)

14 Elyaniv BARDA (Genk)

13 Julien GORIUS (Mechelen)
Mehdi CARCELA-GONZÁLEZ (Standard)

12 Mouhamadou HABIBOU (Zulte Waregem)

PROMOTED CLUBS

OUD-HEVERLEE LEUVEN

Coach – Ronny Van Geneugden
Founded – 2002
Stadium – Den Dreef (7,435)

RAEC MONS

Coach – Geert Broeckaert; (25/1/11) Dennis van Wijk (NED)
Founded – 1910
Stadium – Charles Tondreau (9,504))

SECOND LEVEL FINAL TABLE 2010/11

		Pld	W	D	L	F	A	Pts
1	Oud-Heverlee Leuven	34	22	7	5	75	38	73
2	Lommel United	34	20	5	9	73	44	65
3	RAEC Mons	34	17	8	9	63	38	59
4	Waasland-Beveren	34	15	11	8	51	35	56
5	CS Visé	34	14	9	11	52	48	51
6	R. Antwerp FC	34	14	8	12	54	53	50
7	FCV Dender EH	34	15	4	15	54	54	49
8	AFC Tubize	34	13	8	13	46	55	47
9	KV Oostende	34	13	6	15	41	48	45
10	KSK Heist	34	12	7	15	57	67	43
11	FC Molenbeek Brussels	34	12	6	16	50	51	42
12	K. Standaard Wetteren	34	10	12	12	42	51	42
13	R. Boussu Dour Borinage	34	11	8	15	48	52	41
14	KSV Roeselare	34	10	11	13	38	42	41
15	KVK Tienen	34	11	8	15	35	47	41
16	KV Turnhout	34	10	10	14	48	59	40
17	K. Rupel Boom FC	34	10	7	17	36	56	37
18	RFC Tournai	34	5	9	20	38	63	24

PROMOTION/RELEGATION PLAY-OFFS

		Pld	W	D	L	F	A	Pts
1	RAEC Mons	6	4	1	1	18	7	13
2	Waasland-Beveren	6	4	1	1	13	9	13
3	Lommel United	6	3	0	3	12	14	9
4	KAS Eupen	6	0	0	6	5	18	0

(29/5/11)
Mons 2, Waasland-Beveren 1

DOMESTIC CUP 2010/11

COUPE DE BELGIQUE/BEKER VAN BELGIË

SIXTH ROUND

(26/10/10)
Charleroi 1, Waasland-Beveren 2
Kortrijk 2, Virton 1 *(aet)*

(27/10/10)
Club Brugge 3, Lommel 1
Eupen 2, Turnhout 1
GBA 3, Aalst 0
Genk 3, Coxyde 0
Gent 4, Tienen 1
KV Mechelen 7, RC Waregem 0
Lierse 4, Rupel Boom 0
Lille 0, Cercle Brugge 4
Standard 2, Antwerp 1
Tournai 2, Sint-Truiden 1
URS Centre 2, Anderlecht 2
(aet; 1-4 on pens)
Westerlo 2, Roeselare 0
Wetteren 2, Lokeren 4 *(aet)*
WS Woluwe 2, Zulte Waregem 1

FOURTH ROUND

(9/11/10)
Standard 2, Genk 1

(10/11/10)
Cercle Brugge 3, Waasland-Beveren 1
GBA 2, Club Brugge 1
Gent 3, Eupen 1
Kortrijk 1, KV Mechelen 2
Lierse 4, Tournai 1
Westerlo 1, Anderlecht 0
WS Woluwe 1, Lokeren 0

QUARTER-FINALS

(26/1/11 & 2/3/11)
Cercle Brugge 2 *(Wang 6, Cornelis 45)*, GBA 0
GBA 1 *(Cruz 65)*, Cercle Brugge 1 *(Owusu 66)*
(Cercle Brugge 3-1)

Standard 2 *(Tchité 23, Daerden 52)*, KV Mechelen 0
KV Mechelen 1 *(Gorius 68p)*, Standard 4 *(Leye 47, 71, Tchité 63, Witsel 66)*
(Standard 6-1)

Westerlo 1 *(Dekelver 43)*, Lierse 2 *(De Wree 2, Radzinski 83)*
Lierse 2 *(Sonck 27, Cavens 82)*, Westerlo 3 *(De Petter 32, Paulo Henrique 59, Dekelver 68)*
(4-4; Westerlo on away goals)

WS Woluwe 0, Gent 2 *(Thijs 64, Bryssinck 90+3og)*
Gent 1 *(Conté 27)*, Woluwe 0
(Gent 3-0)

SEMI-FINALS

(16/3/11 & 6/4/11)
Gent 1 *(El Ghanassy 28)*, Standard 0
Standard 4 *(Van Damme 17, Tchité 31, 74, Carcela-González 68)*, Gent 2 *(Coulibaly 19, Mboyo 82)*
(Standard 4-3)

Westerlo 0, Cercle Brugge 0
Cercle Brugge 3 *(Renato Neto 24, D'Haene 49, Foley 80)*, Westerlo 3 *(Paulo Henrique 45, 61, Ngolok 58)*
(3-3; Westerlo on away goals)

FINAL

(21/5/11)
Stade Roi Baudouin, Brussels
R. STANDARD DE LIÈGE 2 *(Mangala 34, Mravac 61og)*
KVC WESTERLO 0
Referee – *De Bleeckere*
STANDARD – *Sinan, Opare, Boukhriss, Mangala, Kanu, Van Damme (Nong 85), Goreux (Leye 75), Defour, Witsel, Camara, Tchité (Daerden 88).*
WESTERLO – *Deelkens, Mravac, De Petter, Corstjens, Brüls, Ngolok, Delen, Cools, Yakovenko (Liliu 70), Dekelver (Annab 70), Paulo Henrique.*

CLUB COMMUNICATION 2011/12

RSC Anderlecht
Avenue Théo Verbeeck 2
BE-1070 Bruxelles

Tel +32 2 529 4060
Fax +32 2 520 0740
Web rsca.be
Email secretariat@rsca.be
Media Officer David Steegen

K. Beerschot AC
Atletenstraat 80
BE-2020 Antwerpen

Tel +32 32 48 4845
Fax +32 32 48 4846
Web beerschot.be
Email info@germinal-beerschot.be
Media Officer Danny Geerts

Cercle Brugge KSV
Olympialaan 72
BE-8200 Brugge

Tel +32 50 389 193
Fax +32 50 391 141
Web cerclebrugge.be
Email secretariaat@cerclebrugge.be
Media Officer Pol Van Den Driessche

Club Brugge KV
Olympialaan 72
BE-8200 Brugge

Tel +32 50 40 2121
Fax +32 50 38 1023
Web clubbrugge.be
Email info@clubbrugge.be
Media Officer Wim De Meyer

KRC Genk
Stadionplein 4
BE-3600 Genk

Tel +32 89 848 410
Fax +32 89 848 419
Web krcgenk.be
Email info@krcgenk.be
Media Officer Erik Gerits

KAA Gent
Bruiloftstraat 42
BE-9050 Gentbrugge

Tel +32 9 230 6610
Fax +32 9 210 4589
Web kaagent.be
Email info@kaagent.be
Media Officer Patrick Lips

KV Kortrijk
Morseelstraat 11B
BE-8501 Kortrijk

Tel +32 56 960190
Fax +32 56 374 267
Web kvk.be
Email secretariaat@kvk.be
Media Officer Nathalie Cnudde

K. Lierse SK
Lispersteenweg 237, Herman Vanderpoortenstadion, BE-2500 Lier

Tel +32 3 480 1370
Fax +32 3 488 0659
Web lierse.com
Email info@lierse.be
Media Officer Terry Verbiest

KSC Lokeren OV
Daknamstraat 91
BE-9160 Lokeren

Tel +32 9 348 3905
Fax +32 9 349 1243
Web sporting.be
Email info@sporting.be
Media Officer Leen Ide

KV Mechelen
Kleine Nieuwedijk 53
BE-2800 Mechelen

Tel +32 15 218230
Fax +32 15 219033
Web kvmechelen.be
Email info@kvmechelen.be
Media Officer Jeroen Gobin

RAEC Mons
Avenue du Tir 80, Stade Charles Tondreau
BE-7000 Mons

Tel +32 65 221 114
Fax +32 65 221 138
Web raec-mons.be
Email secretariat@raec-mons.be
Media Officer Gilles Barbera

Oud-Heverlee Leuven
Kardiaal Mercieerlaan 46
BE-3001 Heverlee

Tel +32 16 228 508
Fax +32 16 291 934
Web ohl.be
Email steven.moyens@ohl.be
Media Officer Chris Vandebroeck

K. Sint-Truidense VV
Tiensesteenweg 223
BE-3800 Sint-Truiden

Tel +32 11 683 829
Fax +32 11 692 380
Web stvv.com
Email info@stvv.com
Media Officer Peter Lepez

R. Standard de Liège
Rue de la Centrale 2
BE-4000 Liège

Tel +32 4 252 2122
Fax +32 4 252 1469
Web standard.be
Email secretariat@standard.be
Media Officer Jean-Christophe Bury

KVC Westerlo
De Merodedreef 189
BE-2260 Westerlo

Tel +32 14 545 288
Fax +32 14 542 321
Web kvcwesterlo.be
Email secretariaat@kvcwesterlo.be
Media Officer Roger Verhaert

SV Zulte Waregem
Regenboogstadion, Zuiderlaan 17
BE-8790 Waregem

Tel +32 56 440 042
Fax +32 56 440 342
Web svzw.be
Email onthaal@essevee.be
Media Officer Arne Houtekier

BOSNIA & HERZEGOVINA

Bosnie-Herzégovine I Bosnien-Herzegowina

Nogometni / Fudbalski savez Bosne i Hercegovine (NFSBiH)

COMMUNICATION

Address	Ulica Ferhadija 30 BA-71000 Sarajevo	**President**	vacant
Tel	+387 33 276 660	**General Secretary**	Jasmin Baković
Fax	+387 33 444 332	**Media Officer**	Slavica Pecikoza
E-mail	nsbih@bih.net.ba	**Year of Formation**	1992
Website	nfsbih.ba	**National Stadium**	Olimpijski Asim Ferhatović Hase, Sarajevo (34,630)

DOMESTIC COMPETITION SUMMARY 2010/11

PREMIJER LIGA FINAL TABLE

			Home					Away					Total						
		Pld	W	D	L	F	A	W	D	L	F	A	W	D	L	F	A	Pts	Comp
1	FK Borac Banja Luka	30	11	3	1	25	9	8	4	3	12	6	19	7	4	37	15	64	UCL
2	FK Sarajevo	30	12	2	1	30	7	5	4	6	21	19	17	6	7	51	26	57	UEL
3	FK Željezničar	30	11	1	3	34	9	6	3	6	16	16	17	4	9	50	25	55	UEL
4	NK Široki Brijeg	30	11	1	3	42	18	5	1	9	17	27	16	2	12	59	45	50	UEL
5	FK Olimpik Sarajevo	30	9	4	2	20	11	5	2	8	15	22	14	6	10	35	33	48	
6	FK Sloboda Tuzla	30	10	2	3	19	7	4	2	9	9	22	14	4	12	28	29	46	
7	HŠK Zrinjski	30	11	2	2	29	11	2	1	12	12	28	13	3	14	41	39	42	
8	NK Zvijezda	30	6	8	1	19	10	5	1	9	21	28	11	9	10	40	38	42	
9	FK Rudar Prijedor	30	8	5	2	25	15	3	3	9	12	26	11	8	11	37	41	41	
10	NK Čelik	30	11	2	2	22	8	0	5	10	8	22	11	7	12	30	30	40	
11	FK Slavija Sarajevo	30	10	3	2	27	10	1	2	12	17	36	11	5	14	44	46	38	
12	NK Travnik	30	10	2	3	34	14	1	2	12	10	29	11	4	15	44	43	37	
13	FK Velež	30	9	1	5	22	17	2	2	11	9	26	11	3	16	31	43	36	
14	FK Leotar	30	9	2	4	20	13	1	3	11	9	36	10	5	15	29	49	35	
15	FK Budućnost Banovići	30	4	3	8	15	23	2	4	9	10	21	6	7	17	25	44	25	*Relegated*
16	FK Drina Zvornik	30	6	0	9	12	22	1	2	12	6	31	7	2	21	18	53	23	*Relegated*

Top Scorer Ivan Lendrić (Zrinjski), 16 goals

Promoted Clubs NK GOŠK Gabela
FK Kozara

Cup Final FK Željezničar 1, NK Čelik 0
NK Čelik 0, FK Željezničar 3
(FK Željezničar 4-0)

Capital gains for champions Borac

Traditionally the toughest league in Europe for visiting teams, Bosnia & Herzegovina's Premijer Liga had much less of a home-side bias than usual in 2010/11. One team even managed to win more games on the road than they lost, and not surprisingly that mould-breaking statistic proved decisive in bringing FK Borac Banja Luka their first national championship title.

The addition of eight away wins to their 11 at home enabled Borac to win the Premijer Liga with a record points total for a 16-team contest. They were especially strong on their visits to the capital, Sarajevo, where, remarkably, they collected eight points from a possible 12 and did not concede a single goal. Furthermore, they won home and away against the two teams that finished directly below them in the final table – runners-up FK Sarajevo and defending champions FK Željezničar.

Borac had won the domestic cup in 2009/10 under Serbian coach Zoran Marić, but he lasted only game of the new league campaign, a 3-2 home defeat by NK Široki Brijeg. His replacement Vlado Jugodić subsequently led Borac on a 13-match unbeaten run that – despite being halted unexpectedly by a 2-1 defeat at FK Leotar – gave them a mid-season table-topping lead of five points. Borac were to lose two key players for the spring campaign in midfielder Bojan Puzigaća and skipper Vule Trivunović, but former Bosnia & Herzegovina international Branislav Krunić came in and he, along with current international Darko Maletić, proved highly influential as Borac posted another eight-game unbeaten run that kept them a comfortable distance away from any prospective challengers. The championship was sealed in appropriate style with a 1-0 win away to Željezničar in Sarajevo.

Darko Maletić – a key figure in Borac's title triumph

Trophy exchange

Although Željezničar were deposed as champions, they swapped trophies with Borac, collecting the Bosnia & Herzegovina Cup three days later after beating NK Čelik 3-0 away in Zenica to complete a 4-0 aggregate victory in the two-legged final. It was the second season in succession that Amar Osim's side had gone through their nine-match Cup campaign without defeat, having lost the final on away goals to Borac after two draws 12 months earlier. In 2010/11, furthermore, they conceded just one goal – and it very nearly proved costly in the quarter-final against Široki Brijeg before Željezničar's star midfielder Zajko Zeba saved the day with a last-gasp penalty. Zeba, who returned to the club at the start of the season following a spell in Russia, added further goals in each leg of the final and was also the club's top scorer in the Premijer Liga, striking 11 times. For his efforts he was voted the country's player of the season.

The best young player in the Premijer Liga was Široki Brijeg's 18-year-old starlet Goran Zakarić, whose impressive development for both club and country – at Under-19 and U21 level – was recognised by Croatian champions NK Dinamo Zagreb, who signed him on a seven-year contract. Široki Brijeg joined Sarajevo and Željezničar in the 2011/12 UEFA Europa League by finishing fourth, two points and one place ahead of the season's surprise package, FK Olimpik Sarajevo, who also reached the Cup semi-finals despite their home stadium being out of service all season due to reconstruction. Olimpia were one of several clubs expected to struggle, but the relegation battle proved a non-starter because both of the newly promoted sides, FK Budućnost Banovići and FK Drina Zvornik, were cast adrift early on and never recovered.

National Team

Top Five All-time Caps – Zvjezdan Misimović (58); Elvir Bolić (51); Emir Spahić (49), Sergej Barbarez (47); Vedin Music (45)

Top Five All-time Goals – Elvir Bolić (22); Edin Džeko (18); Sergej Barbarez (17); Zvjezdan Misimović (16); Elvir Baljić (14)

It was another bleak season for the Premijer Liga's European contingent, highlighted by Željezničar's 6-0 aggregate defeat by Hapoel Tel-Aviv FC in the second qualifying round of the UEFA Champions League. On the international stage, however, the Bosnia & Herzegovina national side, now coached by former Yugoslavia striker Safet Sušić, maintained their hopes of a first major tournament qualification with ten points from their first six qualifying matches.

Main man Misimović

Having scored prolifically in 2010 FIFA World Cup qualifying, star striker Edin Džeko was a comparatively subdued figure, which was symptomatic of his struggles at Manchester City FC, where he arrived in mid-season from VfL Wolfsburg. Another absconder from the German club was Zvjezdan Misimović, who moved twice during the season, first to Galatasaray AŞ then to FC Dinamo Moskva, but remained an ever-present for his country to usurp Elvir Bolić and become Bosnia & Herzegovina's most-capped international.

NATIONAL TEAM RESULTS 2010/11

10/8/10	Qatar	H	Sarajevo	1-1	*Ibišević (9)*
3/9/10	Luxembourg (ECQ)	A	Luxembourg	3-0	*Ibričić (6), Pjanić (12), Džeko (16)*
7/9/10	France (ECQ)	H	Sarajevo	0-2	
8/10/10	Albania (ECQ)	A	Tirana	1-1	*Ibišević (21)*
17/11/10	Slovakia	A	Bratislava	3-2	*Medunjanin (28), Pjanić (51), Džeko (60)*
10/12/10	Poland	N	Antalya (TUR)	2-2	*Subašić (23), Misimović (54p)*
9/2/11	Mexico	N	Atlanta (USA)	0-2	
26/3/11	Romania (ECQ)	H	Zenica	2-1	*Ibišević (63), Džeko (83)*
3/6/11	Romania (ECQ)	A	Bucharest	0-3	
7/6/11	Albania (ECQ)	H	Zenica	2-0	*Medunjanin (67), Maletić (90+1)*

NATIONAL TEAM APPEARANCES 2010/11

Coach – Safet SUŠIĆ	**13/4/55**		**Qat**	**LUX**	**FRA**	**ALB**	**Svk**	**Pol**	**Mex**	**ROU**	**ROU**	**ALB**	**Caps**	**Goals**
Kenan HASAGIĆ	1/2/80	İstanbul BB (TUR)	G	G	G	G46			G	G	G	G	40	-
Mensur MUJDŽA	28/3/84	Freiburg (GER)	D	D	D	D			D	D	D	D73	8	-
Safet NADAREVIĆ	30/8/80	Eskişehirspor (TUR)	D68	D	D								30	-
Emir SPAHIĆ	18/8/80	Montpellier (FRA)	D	D	D	D	D		D	D	D	D	49	2
Adnan MRAVAC	10/4/82	Westerlo (BEL)	D			D46			D	D	D		12	-
Sanel JAHIĆ	10/12/81	AEK (GRE)	M61	s68	s74								18	1
Miralem PJANIĆ	2/4/90	Lyon (FRA)	M78	M78	M	M	M86		M	M	M	M77	25	3
Zvjezdan MISIMOVIĆ	5/6/82	Wolfsburg (GER)	M78											
		/Galatasaray (TUR)		M	M	M	M75	M	M					
		/Dinamo Moskva (RUS)								M81	M	M	58	16
Zlatan MUSLIMOVIĆ	6/3/81	PAOK (GRE)	M61				s75		s62	s76	s64	s61	29	11
Vedad IBIŠEVIĆ	6/8/84	Hoffenheim (GER)	A71	A	A74	A	s83		A	A76	s46	A61	32	8
Edin DŽEKO	17/3/86	Wolfsburg (GER)	A	A	A	A89	A83							
		/Man. City (ENG)								A	A64	A	34	18
Senijad IBRIČIĆ	26/9/85	Hajduk (CRO)	s61	M73	M	s89	s86							
		/Lokomotiv Moskva (RUS)								s81	M64		32	4
Haris MEDUNJANIN	8/3/85	M. Tel-Aviv (ISR)	s61	s73		M	M		M70	M70	M46	M	11	2
Boris PANDŽA	15/12/86	Mechelen (BEL)	s68			s46	D					D	13	-
Ermin ZEC	6/6/88	Gençlerbirliği (TUR)	s71	s78	s74								7	1
Mehmed ALISPAHIĆ	24/11/87	Šibenik (CRO)	s78										2	-
Semir ŠTILIĆ	8/10/87	Lech (POL)	s78								s64		4	-
Senad LULIĆ	18/1/86	Young Boys (SUI)		D	D	D	D		M62	D	D	D	8	-

NATIONAL TEAM APPEARANCES 2010/11 (contd.)

			Qat	LUX	FRA	ALB	Svk	Pol	Mex	ROU	ROU	ALB	Caps	Goals
Elvir RAHIMIĆ	4/4/76	CSKA Moskva (RUS)		M68	M74	M	M			M	M	M	28	-
Asmir BEGOVIĆ	20/6/87	Stoke (ENG)				s46							4	-
Ibrahim ŠEHIĆ	2/9/88	Željezničar					G	G46					2	-
Ognjen VRANJEŠ	24/10/89	Sheriff (MDA) /Krasnodar (RUS)					D80		s70				2	-
Sejad SALIHOVIĆ	8/10/84	Hoffenheim (GER)					M62		M77				22	3
Muhamed SUBAŠIĆ	19/3/88	Olimpik					s62	D	s77				3	1
Muhamed BEŠIĆ	10/9/92	Hamburg (GER)					s80		D			s77	3	-
Muhamed DŽAKMIĆ	23/8/85	Sarajevo						D					1	-
Josip BARIŠIĆ	12/8/83	Široki Brijeg						D58					1	-
Jure IVANKOVIĆ	15/11/85	Široki Brijeg						D46					1	-
Semir KERLA	26/9/87	Željezničar						D46					1	-
Darko MALETIĆ	20/10/80	Borac Banja Luka						M		s70		s73	12	1
Edin VIŠĆA	17/2/90	Željezničar						M					1	-
Dario PURIĆ	18/5/86	Čelik						M59					1	-
Adin DŽAFIĆ	12/11/89	Čelik						A46					1	-
Asmir AVDUKIĆ	13/5/81	Borac Banja Luka						s46					2	-
Eldin ADILOVIĆ	8/2/86	Čelik						s46					1	-
Adnan ZAHIROVIĆ	23/3/90	Čelik						s46					1	-
Velibor VASILIĆ	19/10/80	Željezničar						s46					3	-
Sedin TORLAK	12/1/85	Sarajevo						s58					1	-
Boris RASPUDIĆ	11/10/82	Borac Banja Luka						s59					1	-

CLUB-BY-CLUB

FK BORAC BANJA LUKA

Coach – Zoran Marić (SRB); (1/8/10) Vlado Jagodić

Founded – 1926

Stadium – Gradski (10,000)

MAJOR HONOURS: Bosnia & Herzegovina League – (1) 2011; Yugoslav Cup – (1) 1988; Bosnia & Herzegovina Cup – (1) 2010.

2010				
31/7	Široki Brijeg	h	2-3	*Nikolić, og (Renato)*
7/8	Drina	a	2-0	*Stajić, Mikić*
14/8	Velež	h	1-1	*Vukelja*
21/8	Čelik	a	1-0	*Nikolić*
28/8	Slavija	h	4-1	*Nikolić 3, Vukelja*
12/9	Sarajevo	a	1-0	*Stajić*
18/9	Zrinjski	h	2-0	*Nikolić, Puzigaća*
25/9	Budućnost	a	1-0	*Stanceski*
5/10	Sloboda	h	2-0	*Stajić, Nikolić*
16/10	Prijedor	h	0-0	
23/10	Olimpik	a	0-0	
30/10	Zvijezda	h	1-0	*Puzigaća*
6/11	Travnik	a	2-1	*Maletić, Trivunović*
13/11	Željezničar	h	1-0	*Maletić*
20/11	Leotar	a	1-2	*Srećo*
2011				
27/2	Široki Brijeg	a	2-1	*Maletić, Grahovac*
5/3	Drina	h	1-0	*Maletić*
12/3	Velež	a	0-0	
19/3	Čelik	h	1-0	*Nikolić (p)*
3/4	Slavija	a	0-0	
9/4	Sarajevo	h	2-0	*Nikolić, Maletić*
17/4	Zrinjski	a	0-0	
23/4	Budućnost	h	2-1	*Vidaković, Krunić*
30/4	Sloboda	a	0-1	
4/5	Prijedor	a	1-0	*Raspudić*
8/5	Olimpik	h	2-1	*Veljović, Krunić*
14/5	Zvijezda	a	0-1	
19/5	Travnik	h	2-0	*Vidaković, Veljović*
22/5	Željezničar	a	1-0	*Stupar*
28/5	Leotar	h	2-2	*Nikolić, Maletić (p)*

No	Name	Nat	DoB	Pos	Aps	(s)	Gls
1	Asmir AVDUKIĆ		13/5/81	G	29		
3	Vukašin BENOVIĆ		31/7/86	D	6	(4)	
5	Leonid ĆORIĆ		30/4/83	D	20	(1)	
19	Nemanja DAMJANOVIĆ		27/9/86	M	6	(6)	
13	Siniša DUJAKOVIĆ		22/11/91	M		(2)	
11	Srđan GRAHOVAC		19/10/92	M	12	(12)	1
79	Branislav KRUNIĆ		28/1/79	M	15		2
33	Darko MALETIĆ		20/10/80	M	20	(1)	6
10	Dražen MEĐEDOVIĆ	MNE	15/10/82	A	7	(3)	
20	Borislav MIKIĆ		20/12/75	M	19	(5)	1
16	Milan MUMINOVIĆ		13/8/84	M	5	(4)	
9	Stevo NIKOLIĆ		12/7/84	A	23	(3)	10
4	Bojan PETRIĆ		29/11/84	D	8	(5)	
12	Aleksandar PETROVIĆ		8/7/89	G	1		
7	Bojan PUZIGAĆA		10/5/85	M	12		2
14	Boris RASPUDIĆ		11/10/82	M	25	(1)	1
18	Duško SAKAN		3/3/89	M	8	(3)	
23	Milan SREĆO		30/1/84	M	3	(7)	1
27	Duško STAJIĆ		11/7/82	A	21	(5)	3
29	Dragoslav STAKIĆ		20/9/85	D	14		
28	Perica STANCESKI	MKD	29/1/85	D	11	(2)	1
6	Milan STUPAR	SRB	9/1/80	D	21	(1)	1
26	Vule TRIVUNOVIĆ		13/3/83	D	15		1
20	Rade VELJOVIĆ	SRB	9/8/86	A	6	(7)	2
17	Nemanja VIDAKOVIĆ	SRB	29/9/83	A	6	(8)	2
10	Ljubiša VUKELJA	SRB	22/7/83	A	9	(1)	2
22	Draško ŽARIĆ		9/10/78	D	8	(2)	

FK BUDUĆNOST BANOVIĆI

Coach – Munever Rizvić; (19/4/11) Nermin Garić

Founded – 1947

Stadium – Gradski (4,000)

010				
1/7	Drina Zvornik	h	1-1	*Haskić*
/8	Velež	a	0-2	
4/8	Čelik	h	1-1	*Čergič*
2/8	Slavija	a	3-2	*Ikanović, Šmigalović, Haskić*
8/8	Sarajevo	h	1-2	*Haskić*
1/9	Zrinjski	a	0-0	
6/9	Sloboda	h	0-0	
5/9	Borac	h	0-1	
/10	Prijedor	a	1-2	*Zrnanović*
5/10	Olimpik	h	2-1	*Čolić, Omić*
3/10	Zvijezda	a	0-0	
0/10	Travnik	h	3-1	*Sarajlić, Šmigalović, Haskić*
/11	Željezničar	a	0-2	
3/11	Leotar	h	2-1	*Slomić, Haskić*
1/11	Široki Brijeg	a	1-2	*Halilović*
011				
/3	Drina Zvornik	a	0-2	
/3	Velež	h	0-1	
2/3	Čelik	a	1-2	*Haskić*
9/3	Slavija	h	0-1	
2/4	Sarajevo	a	0-2	
/4	Zrinjski	h	0-3	*(w/o; match abandoned after 22 mins at 0-0)*
16/4	Sloboda	a	0-1	
23/4	Borac	a	1-2	*Šmigalović*
30/4	Prijedor	h	1-3	*Sliško*
4/5	Olimpik	a	1-1	*Pirić*
7/5	Zvijezda	h	2-5	*Halilović (p), Haskić*
14/5	Travnik	a	1-0	*Haskić*
19/5	Željezničar	h	1-2	*Halilović*
22/5	Leotar	a	1-1	*Haskić*
28/5	Široki Brijeg	h	1-0	*Pirić*

No	Name	Nat	DoB	Pos	Aps	(s)	Gls
	Vedran BOJIĆ		9/8/74	D	1	(5)	
5	Edi BURO		19/9/87	D	2		
13	Mirel ČAMRKOVIĆ		6/4/84	D	22	(3)	
20	Elvis ČERGIČ		29/8/78	D	27		1
6	Nermin ČOLIĆ		18/6/83	M	20	(4)	1
	Arnel DELIĆ		13/2/92	M	3	(2)	
13	Alija ĐERZIĆ		19/12/91	D		(3)	
	Emir HALILOVIĆ		4/11/89	M	18	(1)	3
17	Nermin HASKIĆ		27/6/89	M	27	(2)	9
1	Muris HUSIČ		12/8/80	G	28		
11	Emir IKANOVIĆ		22/7/85	M	14	(6)	1
15	Nermin IMAMOVIĆ		30/9/92	D	1	(3)	
5	Adnan JAHIĆ		28/2/85	M	18	(8)	
10	Eldar KAVAZOVIĆ		13/9/91	M	4	(8)	
	Adis KOVAČEVIĆ		26/7/89	D	8		
18	Edis KURTIĆ		14/9/76	M	7		
12	Armin LUGAVIĆ		1/12/88	G	2		
4	Kenan LUGAVIĆ		26/2/92	D		(1)	
16	Muhamed OMIĆ		4/4/85	D	18	(2)	1
3	Muris PIRIĆ		27/12/92	M	12	(6)	2
8	Adnan SARAJLIĆ		6/1/81	M	26	(1)	1
	Igor SLIŠKO		18/8/77	M	13	(2)	1
7	Semir SLOMIĆ		14/1/88	A	13	(9)	1
10	Kabir SMAJIĆ		30/5/77	M	6	(7)	
19	Almir ŠMIGALOVIĆ		6/5/90	A	19	(8)	3
14	Dilaver ZRNANOVIĆ		17/11/84	D	21		1

NK ČELIK

Coach – Abdulah Ibraković

Founded – 1945

Stadium – Bilino Polje (15,000)

MAJOR HONOURS: Bosnia & Herzegovina League – (3) 1994, 1996, 1997; Bosnia & Herzegovina Cup – (2) 1995, 1996.

2010				
8/8	Zrinjski	h	2-1	*Brković, Šišić*
14/8	Budućnost	a	1-1	*Isaković*
18/8	Sarajevo	a	0-1	
21/8	Borac	h	0-1	
28/8	Prijedor	a	1-1	*Adilović*
11/9	Olimpik	h	0-1	
18/9	Zvijezda	a	1-1	*Milošević*
25/9	Travnik	h	2-0	*Milošević, Smriko*
5/10	Željezničar	a	1-2	*Purić*
16/10	Leotar	h	3-0	*Džafić, Adilović, Arnaut*
24/10	Široki Brijeg	a	2-2	*Obuća, Duro*
30/10	Drina Zvornik	h	1-0	*Adilović (p)*
6/11	Velež	a	0-1	
13/11	Sloboda	a	0-2	
20/11	Slavija	h	1-0	*Džafić*
2011				
26/2	Sarajevo	h	2-1	*Adilović, Šišić*
6/3	Zrinjski	a	0-1	
12/3	Budućnost	h	2-1	*Hasanović, Adilović*
19/3	Borac	a	0-1	
2/4	Prijedor	h	2-1	*Adilović 2 (1p)*
9/4	Olimpik	a	0-1	
16/4	Zvijezda	h	4-1	*Hadžić, Adilović, Milošević, Purić*
23/4	Travnik	a	0-0	
30/4	Željezničar	h	1-1	*Adilović*
4/5	Leotar	a	1-2	*Hadžić*
8/5	Široki Brijeg	h	0-0	
14/5	Drina Zvornik	a	0-1	
19/5	Velež	h	1-0	*Purić*
22/5	Sloboda	h	1-0	*Ćulov*
28/5	Slavija	a	1-5	*Džafić*

No	Name	Nat	DoB	Pos	Aps	(s)	Gls
9	Eldin ADILOVIĆ		8/2/86	A	26		9
25	Armin ARNAUT		7/2/91	M	1	(5)	1
12	Luka BILOBRK		8/12/85	G	28		
14	Zoran BRKOVIĆ		2/5/84	D	22	(1)	1
4	Mehmedalija ČOVIĆ		16/3/86	D	25		
77	Adis ĆULOV		18/7/87	A	4	(7)	1
19	Haris DILAVER		6/2/90	M	2	(5)	
5	Haris DULJEVIĆ		16/11/93	A		(4)	
6	Samir DURO		18/10/77	M	10		1
10	Adin DŽAFIĆ		12/11/89	A	23		3
17	Ermin GADŽO		19/5/90	M	1	(6)	
11	Emir HADŽIĆ		19/7/84	M	11		2
17	Eldar HASANOVIĆ		12/1/90	M	10	(1)	1
13	Kenan HORIĆ		13/9/90	M	5	(10)	
	Harun HUSEINSPAHIĆ		2/9/92	D		(1)	
18	Aladin ISAKOVIĆ		28/7/85	M	8		1
10	Nermin JAMAK		25/8/86	M	12		
14	Emir JUSIĆ		13/6/86	D	11	(3)	
17	Armin KAPETAN		11/3/86	A	19	(2)	
	Elmir KUDUZOVIĆ		28/2/85	D	7	(1)	
7	Selmir MAHMUTOVIĆ		10/11/92	M		(2)	
15	Semjon MILOŠEVIĆ		21/10/79	D	24		3
16	Kenan NEMELJAKOVIĆ		1/6/83	M	7	(5)	
24	Emir OBUĆA		11/12/78	A	2	(3)	1
1	Amel PJANIĆ		7/9/85	G	2		
8	Dario PURIĆ		18/5/86	M	26	(2)	3
21	Elvis SADIKOVIĆ		29/10/83	D	23		
7	Aldin ŠIŠIĆ		3/12/84	M	5	(11)	2
3	Arnes SKOMORAC		8/3/92	M		(1)	
17	Jasmin SMRIKO		20/1/91	A	1	(3)	1
20	Kenan STUPAR		12/4/89	M	3	(5)	
5	Adnan ZAHIROVIĆ		23/3/90	D	12	(1)	

FK DRINA ZVORNIK

Coach – Mile Milanović; (20/10/10) Darko Vojvodić; (15/3/11) Milenko Milošević & Svetozar Vukašinović; (24/3/11) Dragan Mićić

Founded – 1945

Stadium – Gradski (2,500)

2010				
31/7	Budućnost	a	1-1	*Ninić*
7/8	Borac	h	0-2	
14/8	Prijedor	a	0-1	
21/8	Olimpik	h	1-3	*Obradović*
28/8	Zvijezda	a	1-2	*Protić*
11/9	Travnik	h	0-1	
18/9	Željezničar	a	0-2	
25/9	Leotar	h	2-1	*Ristić, Obradović*
5/10	Široki Brijeg	a	1-5	*Ninić*
16/10	Sloboda	a	0-3	
23/10	Velež	h	2-0	*Đelmić, Ristić*
30/10	Čelik	a	0-1	
6/11	Slavija	h	2-1	*Ninić, Đelmić*
13/11	Sarajevo	a	1-1	*Obradović*
29/11	Zrinjski	h	1-0	*Mihajlović*
2011				
2/3	Budućnost	h	2-0	*Lazarević N., Ležajić*
5/3	Borac	a	0-1	
12/3	Prijedor	h	0-1	
20/3	Olimpik	a	1-2	*Lazarević N. (p)*
2/4	Zvijezda	h	1-2	*Lazarević N.*
9/4	Travnik	a	0-6	
16/4	Željezničar	h	0-2	
23/4	Leotar	a	0-1	
30/4	Široki Brijeg	h	0-2	
4/5	Sloboda	h	0-2	
7/5	Velež	a	0-2	
14/5	Čelik	h	1-0	*Ćulum*
19/5	Slavija	a	1-0	*Sredojević*
22/5	Sarajevo	h	0-5	
28/5	Zrinjski	a	0-3	

No	Name	Nat	DoB	Pos	Aps	(s)	Gls
15	Igor AĆIMOVIČ		21/4/87	A		(6)	
12	Dragan ALEKSIĆ	SRB	1/1/73	G	1		
13	Aleksander Sandro BERIĆ		1/4/88	M		(2)	
6	Roberto Carvalho CAUÊ	BRA	22/4/87	M	7		
11	Danijel ĆULUM		19/8/89	A	24	(2)	1
10	Ognjen ĐELMIĆ	SRB	18/8/88	M	11	(3)	2
16	Boban ĐERIĆ		20/8/93	A	1	(13)	
9	Slobodan ĐURIĆ		13/4/92	A	5	(3)	
	Miloš GALIN		22/4/90	A	2	(1)	
6	Aleksandar IVANOVIĆ	SRB	20/11/88	M	2	(3)	
11	Jasmin JARANOVIĆ		29/2/88	M	5	(2)	
14	Radomir JEREMIĆ		11/1/85	D	3	(4)	
4	Darko KIKANOVIĆ		30/7/87	A	13		
	Žejko KRČMAR		14/1/94	D	1		
8	Dalibor KREZOVIĆ		15/1/83	M	26		
4	Nenad KUTLAČIĆ		4/3/81	D	9		
18	Ivan LAZAREVIĆ		22/1/89	D	21	(2)	
9	Nikola LAZAREVIĆ	SRB	1/8/85	M	9	(4)	3
7	Igor LEŽAJIĆ	SRB	25/4/88	A	12	(1)	1
	Filip LUČIĆ		19/2/92	M		(1)	
1	Goran MAKSIMOVIĆ		4/5/80	G	29		
5	Bojan MIHAJLOVIĆ		15/9/88	D	27		1
4	Darko MITROVIĆ		24/8/85	D	8	(3)	
	Nikola MOJOVIĆ		21/12/91	M		(2)	
	Vladimir MOLEROVIĆ		14/4/92	M	1		
	Semir MUJKANOVIĆ		20/4/88	A		(1)	
	Radan MUMINOVIĆ		4/3/85	A		(2)	
9	Ivan NINIĆ	SRB	8/4/86	M	16	(3)	3
2	Nemanja OBRADOVIĆ	SRB	29/5/89	A	14		3
	Vedran PAPOVIĆ		8/4/85	M	2	(5)	
6	Nikola PREBIRAČEVIĆ	SRB	23/1/87	D	8	(1)	
	Predrag PROTIĆ	SRB	15/2/83	D	8		1
7	Dragan RISTIĆ		27/2/82	A	15		2
11	Edin RUSTEMOVIĆ	MNE	6/9/88	M	7	(1)	
18	Miroslav SAVANOVIĆ	SRB	10/3/85	M	9	(3)	
3	Dušan SREDOJEVIĆ	SRB	6/5/86	M	24		1
17	Đorđe SUŠA	SRB	8/5/90	M		(1)	
14	Aleksandar VASIĆ		4/1/85	M	1	(1)	
8	Radovan VASIĆ		27/7/93	M	5	(11)	
17	Svetozar VUKAŠINOVIĆ		10/3/74	D	2	(4)	
	Nenad ZEČEVIĆ	SRB	7/2/78	M	2		

FK LEOTAR

Coach – Goran Skakić; (1/9/10) Vukašin Višnjevac; (3/11/10) Dragan Spaić

Founded – 1925

Stadium – Police (9,000)

MAJOR HONOURS: Bosnia & Herzegovina League – (1) 2003.

2010				
31/7	Prijedor	a	1-1	*Mijailović*
7/8	Olimpik	h	0-1	
14/8	Zvijezda	a	0-1	
21/8	Travnik	h	1-0	*Stojanović*
28/8	Željezničar	a	0-8	
11/9	Sloboda	a	1-1	*Stojanović (p)*
18/9	Široki Brijeg	h	1-0	*Šaraba*
25/9	Drina	a	1-2	*Mandić*
5/10	Velež	h	2-1	*Šaraba, Rajović*
16/10	Čelik	a	0-3	
23/10	Slavija	h	2-1	*Bošković, Vranešević (p)*
30/10	Sarajevo	a	0-3	
6/11	Zrinjski	h	4-1	*Marjanović 2, Lekić, Rajović*
13/11	Budućnost	a	1-2	*Mandić*
20/11	Borac	h	2-1	*Stojanović 2 (1p)*
2011				
26/2	Prijedor	h	0-0	
6/3	Olimpik	a	0-1	
12/3	Zvijezda	h	3-0	*Vranešević, Bondžić 2*
20/3	Travnik	a	0-1	
2/4	Željezničar	h	0-1	
9/4	Sloboda	h	1-3	*Stojanović (p)*
17/4	Široki Brijeg	a	1-3	*Vranešević*
23/4	Drina	h	1-0	*Kokić*
30/4	Velež	a	2-0	*Kujundžić, Vranešević*
4/5	Čelik	h	2-1	*Radović, Bondžić*
8/5	Slavija	a	0-4	
14/5	Sarajevo	h	0-2	
19/5	Zrinjski	a	0-4	
22/5	Budućnost	h	1-1	*Vranešević*
28/5	Borac	a	2-2	*Marjanović, Vranešević*

No	Name	Nat	DoB	Pos	Aps	(s)	Gls
14	Srđan ANDRIĆ		19/9/85	M	27		
16	Darko BONDŽIĆ	SRB	17/1/84	M	7	(4)	3
7	Rade BOŠKOVIĆ		18/4/84	M	2	(3)	1
	César Alexis CANARIO	ARG	18/8/87	A	2	(1)	
18	Gavrilo ČORLIJA		29/10/79	M	18	(1)	
9	Horacio Fabian CORONEL	ARG	29/6/87	A	1	(4)	
16	Franjo DELIĆ		14/10/85	M	11		
3	Darko DREČ		14/1/80	D	6	(2)	
18	Stevan DURIĆ		10/8/90	M		(1)	
24	Darko DŽAJIĆ		30/8/92	M	3	(2)	
	Slobodan KOKIĆ		9/4/81	M	8	(5)	1
20	Rajko KOMNENIĆ		15/7/84	D	10	(10)	
8	Vladan KUJUNDŽIĆ		26/10/82	A	13	(1)	1
91	Mladen KUKRIKA		11/1/91	G	2		
	Ognjen LEKIĆ	SRB	7/1/82	M	4		1
11	Vladmir MANDIĆ		12/12/76	M	23		2
23	Lazar MARJANOVIČ	SRB	25/3/91	M	20	(6)	3

	Nemanja MIJAILOVIĆ	SRB	22/1/87	A	9	(3)	1
5	Miljan MILJANOVIĆ		15/6/91	M		(4)	
	Boško MILENKOVIĆ	SRB	22/6/78	G	28		
	Milan MILUTINOVIĆ	SRB	20/4/83	M	7	(2)	
0	Miroslav PRELO		14/1/83	M	1	(7)	
	Željko RADOVIĆ		12/12/76	D	9	(3)	1
	Stanko RADULOVIĆ	MNE	16/10/88	D	1	(1)	
	Zoran RAJOVIĆ	SRB	28/10/79	A	7	(1)	2
	Anel RAMIĆ		5/4/87	M	2		
	Zdravko ŠARABA		15/5/80	D	27		2
1	Nenad STOJANOVIĆ	SRB	22/10/79	A	15	(5)	5
	Nikola STOJKOVIĆ	SRB	30/4/89	A		(2)	
9	Vladimir TODOROVIĆ		8/12/86	D	17	(3)	
	Marko TOHOLJ		6/7/90	A		(1)	
	Duško VRANEŠEVIĆ		10/11/80	A	20	(3)	6
7	Bojan VUČINIĆ		29/2/80	M	27		
	Nenad ZEČEVIČ	SRB	7/3/78	A	3	(6)	

FK OLIMPIK SARAJEVO

Coach – Edin Prljača; (20/11/10) Mehmed Janjoš

Founded – 1993

Stadium – Olimpijski Asim Ferhatović Hase (34,630)

2010				
/8	Željezničar	h	0-2	
7/8	Leotar	a	1-0	*Suljević*
15/8	Široki Brijeg	h	1-0	*Suljević*
21/8	Drina Zvornik	a	3-1	*Ćulov, Suljević, Thiago Silva*
29/8	Velež	h	0-1	
11/9	Čelik	a	1-0	*Thiago Silva*
19/9	Slavija	h	0-0	
26/9	Sarajevo	a	1-3	*Kresser*
5/10	Zrinjski	h	2-0	*Durak, Thiago Silva*
16/10	Budućnost	a	1-2	*Ćulov*
23/10	Borac	h	0-0	
30/10	Prijedor	a	1-3	*Vidović*
7/11	Sloboda	h	2-2	*Subašić, Durak*
14/11	Zvijezda	h	1-0	*Alimanović*
20/11	Travnik	a	0-1	
2011				
26/2	Željezničar	a	0-3	
6/3	Leotar	h	1-0	*Vidović*
13/3	Široki Brijeg	a	3-1	*Pliska 2, Kiso*
20/3	Drina Zvornik	h	2-1	*Durak, Raščić (p)*
2/4	Velež	a	0-3	
9/4	Čelik	h	1-0	*Durak*
17/4	Slavija	a	0-0	
23/4	Sarajevo	h	2-1	*Savić, Pliska*
30/4	Zrinjski	a	0-1	
4/5	Budućnost	h	1-1	*Raščić*
8/5	Borac	a	1-2	*Rizvanović*
15/5	Prijedor	h	2-0	*Raščić (p), Durak*
19/5	Sloboda	a	1-0	*Raščić*
22/5	Zvijezda	a	2-2	*og (Prodanović), Harba*
28/5	Travnik	h	5-3	*Pliska, Raščić 2, Rizvanović, Pljevljak*

No	Name	Nat	DoB	Pos	Aps	(s)	Gls
11	Sabit ALIMANOVIĆ		21/7/87	A	15	(5)	1
12	Semir BUKVIĆ		21/8/91	G	4		
21	Adis ĆULOV		18/7/87	A	11	(1)	2
21	Franco Gaspar DALMAO	ARG	21/2/84	M		(1)	
16	Eldin DUČIĆ		6/8/93	M		(2)	
10	Dženan DURAK		4/2/91	M	16	(9)	5
3	Darko GLISIC	MKD	23/9/91	D		(1)	
9	Adis HADŽANOVIĆ		3/1/93	M	1	(5)	
2	Haris HARBA		14/7/88	M	4	(4)	1
7	Nedim HIROŠ		29/9/84	A	11	(1)	
4	Vedran JEŠE	CRO	3/2/81	M	13	(1)	
17	Semir KAPIĆ		28/6/86	A	4	(6)	
8	Nenad KISO		30/3/89	M	12		1
5	Nikola KOLAROV	SRB	14/3/83	M	13		
6	Juan Pablo KRESSER	ARG	17/8/87	M	23	(5)	1
1	Mladen LUČIĆ		1/2/85	G	26		
16	Hatourna MANHOULI	CMR	10/2/92	A		(1)	
18	Muhamed MUJIĆ		26/1/91	A	9	(9)	
23	Almir PLISKA		12/8/87	A	14		4
16	Rijad PLJEVLJAK		31/5/91	A	2	(3)	1
9	Admir RAŠČIĆ		16/9/81	A	14		6
3	Mirza RIZVANOVIĆ		27/9/86	D	15		2
2	Smail ŠADIČ		4/12/91	M	4	(2)	
13	Salem SALKIĆ		11/6/88	D	7	(7)	
15	Boris SAVIĆ		18/1/88	D	9	(1)	1
5	Asim ŠKALJIČ		9/8/81	D	13		
17	Boško STUPIĆ		27/4/84	A	1	(7)	
14	Muhamed SUBAŠIĆ		19/3/88	D	21		1
4	Nihad SULJEVIĆ		5/11/80	D	26		3
7	THIAGO de Andrade Lopes "CARIOCA"	BRA	8/2/88	M	13	(1)	
30	THIAGO Roberto da SILVA	BRA	21/1/88	A	10	(3)	3
19	Azur VELAGIĆ		20/10/91	M	5	(4)	
24	Miloš VIDOVIĆ	SRB	3/10/89	M	14	(3)	2

FK RUDAR PRIJEDOR

Coach – Boris Gavran

Founded – 1928

Stadium – Gradski (5,000)

2010				
31/7	Leotar	h	1-1	*Žerić*
8/8	Široki Brijeg	a	2-1	*Kovačević, Kantar*
14/8	Drina	h	1-0	*Kovačević*
21/8	Velež	a	0-3	
28/8	Čelik	h	1-1	*Džafić*
12/9	Slavija	a	0-3	
18/9	Sarajevo	h	1-1	*Kotaran*
25/9	Zrinjski	a	0-1	
5/10	Budućnost	h	2-1	*Džafić, Žerić*
16/10	Borac	a	0-0	
23/10	Sloboda	h	3-0	*Kušljić, Kovačević, Džafić*
30/10	Olimpik	h	3-1	*Džafić 2, Kantar*
6/11	Zvijezda	a	0-0	
13/11	Travnik	h	1-1	*Žerić*
20/11	Željezničar	a	2-4	*Ljeljak, Kušljić*
2011				
26/2	Leotar	a	0-0	
5/3	Široki Brijeg	h	2-1	*Žerić, Kovačević*
12/3	Drina	a	1-0	*Kantar*
19/3	Velež	h	2-0	*Džafić 2*
2/4	Čelik	a	1-2	*Džafić (p)*
9/4	Slavija	h	2-2	*Kantar, Džafić (p)*
16/4	Sarajevo	a	1-5	*Đorić*
23/4	Zrinjski	h	2-0	*Džafić, Kovaćević*
30/4	Budućnost	a	3-1	*Đorić, Kantar 2*
4/5	Borac	h	0-1	
7/5	Sloboda	a	1-2	*Džafić*
15/5	Olimpik	a	0-2	
19/5	Zvijezda	h	1-3	*Džafić*
22/5	Travnik	a	1-2	*Kecman*
28/5	Željezničar	h	3-2	*Džafić 2, Brkić*

No	Name	Nat	DoB	Pos	Aps	(s)	Gls
16	Arnes BRKIĆ		18/12/78	M	7	(9)	1
	Miodrag BURSAČ		1/4/85	M	2	(5)	
9	Ognjen DAŠIĆ		7/2/78	D	12	(2)	
3	Budimir DESPOTOVIĆ		22/2/85	D	3	(2)	
9	Zlatko ĐORIĆ	SRB	7/9/78	A	6	(6)	2
4	Dalibor DRAGIĆ	SRB	23/6/72	D	20	(1)	
16	Ljubiša DRLJAČA		6/1/79	D	2	(2)	
7	Mirza DŽAFIĆ		30/3/81	A	24		14
	Edvin HAMZIĆ		6/11/90	M		(2)	

5	Marko JEVTIĆ	SRB	21/5/82	D	24		
11	Vedran KANTAR	SRB	1/3/85	D	28		6
17	Ajdin KARIĆ		22/3/89	M	1	(4)	
6	Goran KECMAN		23/1/83	M	6	(7)	1
	Saša KERANOVIĆ		11/7/73	D	4	(1)	
6	Aleksandar KIKIĆ		12/12/81	M	18		
3	Goran KOTARAN		11/1/79	M	23		1
10	Saša KOVAČEVIĆ		4/3/83	D	26		5
18	Goran KUŠLJIĆ		28/7/84	A	3	(5)	2
15	Aner LJELJAK		27/1/85	M	2	(4)	1
14	Zoran LUKAČ		5/3/85	D	6	(4)	
	Nemanja MARINOVIĆ		18/3/93	M		(4)	
15	Boris MUZGONJA		27/8/84	M	6	(5)	
14	Ivan PAVIĆ		1/4/89	M		(3)	
2	Nemanja PEKIJA		27/10/92	M	1		
13	Nedeljko RADIVOJAC		16/6/91	M	1	(6)	
18	Zoran RAJEVIĆ	SRB	28/10/79	A	5	(2)	
12	Zoran RODIĆ	SRB	29/11/81	G	2		
2	Nebojša ŠODIĆ		15/7/85	D	27		
4	Dragoslav STAKIĆ		20/9/85	D	13		
9	Saša STIJEPIĆ		11/7/83	A	1	(10)	
1	Bojan TRIPIĆ		29/9/81	G	28		
8	Nedžad ŽERIĆ		26/8/72	M	29		4

FK SARAJEVO

Coach – Mirza Varešanović

Founded – 1946

Stadium – Olimpijski Asim Ferhatović Hase (34,630)

MAJOR HONOURS: Yugoslav League – (2) 1967, 1985; Bosnia & Herzegovina League – (1) 2007; Bosnia & Herzegovina Cup – (4) 1997, 1998, 2002, 2005.

2010				
8/8	Slavija	a	1-2	*Arsenijević (p)*
14/8	Sloboda	h	3-0	*Torlak, Arsenijević (p), Jahovic*
18/8	Čelik	h	1-0	*Arsenijević*
21/8	Zrinjski	h	1-0	*Ščepanović*
28/8	Budućnost	a	2-1	*Kojašević 2*
12/9	Borac	h	0-1	
18/9	Prijedor	a	1-1	*Avdić*
26/10	Olimpik	h	3-1	*Jahovic 2 (1p), Džakmić*
5/10	Zvijezda	a	1-1	*Avdić*
16/10	Travnik	h	1-0	*Hamzagić*
24/10	Željezničar	a	0-0	
30/10	Leotar	h	3-0	*Ščepanović, Džakmić, Jahovic*
7/11	Široki Brijeg	a	1-2	*Avdić*
13/11	Drina	h	1-1	*Suljić*
20/11	Velež	a	2-1	*Kojašević, Arsenijević (p)*
2011				
26/2	Čelik	a	1-2	*Obuća*
5/3	Slavija	h	4-2	*Kojašević, Jahovic, Pehlić, Handžić A.*
12/3	Sloboda	a	0-0	
20/3	Zrinjski	a	2-4	*Gutić, Pehlić*
2/4	Budućnost	h	2-0	*Obuća, Pehlić*
9/4	Borac	a	0-2	
16/4	Prijedor	h	5-1	*Obuća 3, Muharemović (p), Handžić H.*
23/4	Olimpik	a	1-2	*Avdić*
30/4	Zvijezda	h	2-1	*Ščepanović, Muharemović*
4/5	Travnik	a	2-1	*Muharemović 2*
7/5	Željezničar	h	0-0	
14/5	Leotar	a	2-0	*Avdić, Handžić H.*
19/5	Široki Brijeg	h	3-0	*Ščepanović, Arsenijević (p), Handžić H.*
22/5	Drina	a	5-0	*Obuća 3, Handžić H., Trebinjac*
28/5	Velež	h	1-0	*Handžić K.*

No	Name	Nat	DoB	Pos	Aps	(s)	Gls
22	Muhamed ALAIM		10/2/81	G	1		
20	Branislav ARSENIJEVIĆ	SRB	2/8/82	M	26		5
9	Alen AVDIČ		3/4/77	A	24	(3)	5
21	Zoran BELOŠEVIĆ	SRB	20/6/83	D	13	(1)	
2	Jasmin ČAMPARA		8/5/90	M		(6)	
17	Denis ČOMOR		3/1/90	M	8	(3)	
2	Amer DUPOVAC		30/11/90	D	9		
14	Muhamed DŽAKMIĆ		23/8/85	M	12		2
74	Hilmo GUTIĆ	MNE	3/11/80	D	16		1
11	Damir HADŽIĆ		2/10/78	M	2	(2)	
16	Đenaldin HAMZAGIĆ		28/4/86	A	16		1
1	Dino HAMZIĆ		22/1/88	G	16		
23	Amel HANDŽIČ		23/1/91	A	2	(3)	1
77	Haris HANDŽIĆ		20/6/90	A	3	(7)	4
13	Kemal HANDŽIĆ		23/1/91	M	16	(5)	1
	Ibro HODŽIĆ		21/3/85	G	1		
7	Faruk IHTIJAREVIĆ		1/5/76	M	7	(6)	
18	Adis JAHOVIC	MKD	18/3/87	A	9	(8)	5
34	Bojan JOVIĆ	SRB	1/4/82	G	12		
10	Damir KOJAŠEVIĆ	MNE	3/6/87	M	25	(1)	4
8	Veldin MUHAREMOVIĆ		6/12/84	D	21		4
16	Ajdin NUHIĆ		1/11/91	M	12	(4)	
7	Emir OBUĆA		11/12/78	A	11	(1)	8
27	Edin PEHLIĆ		13/1/84	A	7		3
23	Almir PLISKA		12/8/87	A		(3)	
13	Vučina ŠČEPANOVIĆ	MNE	17/11/82	M	22	(1)	4
15	Nail ŠEHOVIĆ		18/1/90	M		(2)	
19	Asmir SULJIĆ		11/9/91	A	3	(16)	1
3	Mirko TODOROVIĆ	SRB	22/8/85	D	4		
6	Sedin TORLAK		12/1/85	D	25		1
3	Sanel TREBINJAC		1/7/91	D	7		1

NK ŠIROKI BRIJEG

Coach – Ivo Ištuk; (15/3/11) (Mario Bazina); (24/3/11) Blaž Slišković

Founded – 1948

Stadium – Pecara (7,000)

MAJOR HONOURS: Bosnia & Herzegovina League – (2) 2004, 2006; Bosnia & Herzegovina Cup – (1) 2007.

2010				
31/7	Borac	a	3-2	*Zakarić, Varea, Ivanković (p)*
8/8	Prijedor	h	1-2	*Topić*
15/8	Olimpik	a	0-1	
22/8	Zvijezda	h	3-0	*Kožul, Ivanković, Peraica*
28/8	Travnik	a	0-4	
12/9	Željezničar	h	4-1	*Šilić, Roskam 3*
18/9	Leotar	a	0-1	
25/9	Sloboda	a	1-0	*Roskam*
5/10	Drina	h	5-1	*Šilić 3 (1p), Wagner 2*
16/10	Velež	a	5-2	*Roskam, Ćutuk, Wagner 2, Šilić (p)*
24/10	Čelik	h	2-2	*Barišić, Wagner*
21/10	Slavija	a	0-1	
7/11	Sarajevo	h	2-1	*Roskam, Varea*
14/11	Zrinjski	a	3-4	*Mišić, Wagner, Varea*
21/11	Budućnost	h	2-1	*Šilić (p), Wagner*
2011				
27/2	Borac	h	1-2	*Zakarić*
5/3	Prijedor	a	1-2	*Roskam*
13/3	Olimpik	h	1-3	*Roskam*
19/3	Zvijezda	a	1-6	*Ljubić*
2/4	Travnik	h	2-1	*Džidić, Serdarušić*
10/4	Željezničar	a	1-0	*Ivanković*
17/4	Leotar	h	3-1	*Šilić, Zakarić, Wagner*
23/4	Sloboda	h	4-0	*Ćorić, Zakarić, Ivanković, Roskam*
30/4	Drina	a	2-0	*Ivanković, Ćorić*
4/5	Velež	h	4-1	*Zakarić, Roskam, Šilić (p), Pinjuh*
8/5	Čelik	a	0-0	
14/5	Slavija	h	4-1	*Mišić, Varea, Wagner, Glavina*
19/5	Sarajevo	a	0-3	
22/5	Zrinjski	h	4-1	*Roskam 2, Wagner, Pinjuh*
28/5	Budućnost	a	0-1	

No	Name	Nat	DoB	Pos	Aps	(s)	Gls
	Boris BAČAK		17/4/87	G	1		
	Dejan BANDOVIĆ		11/6/83	G	22		
	Josip BARIŠIĆ		12/8/83	D	14		1
	Mateo BERTOŠA	CRO	10/8/88	D	6	(1)	
	Slavko BREKALO		25/2/90	D	14	(1)	
6	Dino ĆORIĆ		30/6/90	D	7	(5)	2
	Josip ĆUTUK		4/5/84	M	10	(2)	1
3	DIOGO Souza dos Anjos	BRA	9/7/86	D	26		
3	Ivica DŽIDIĆ		8/2/84	D	13		1
4	Jure GLAVINA		4/1/89	M	3	(5)	1
5	Vlado HRKAĆ		31/8/82	D	3	(5)	
8	Jure IVANKOVIĆ		15/11/85	M	28		5
	Danijel KOŽUL		1/8/88	M	13	(7)	1
	Mario KVESIĆ		12/1/92	A		(4)	
	Mario LJUBIĆ		5/3/85	M	5	(5)	1
	MARCIANO Jose do Nascimento	BRA	12/7/80	M	5	(6)	
2	Nikola MARIĆ		29/8/79	G	7		
	Toni MARKIĆ		25/10/90	M	1	(2)	
20	Hrvoje MIŠIĆ	CRO	17/8/87	A	7	(7)	2
1	Boško PERAICA		7/12/77	M	2	(2)	1
	Ante PINJUH		9/10/90	A	2	(2)	2
	RENATO Alves Gomides	BRA	12/5/84	M	26	(1)	
9	Mateo ROSKAM	CRO	16/3/87	A	27	(2)	12
7	Ante SERDARUŠIĆ		24/1/83	M	8	(3)	1
0	Dalibor ŠILIĆ		23/1/79	M	22	(2)	8
3	Josip TOPIĆ		22/10/82	D	6		1
4	Juan Manuel VAREA	ARG	23/3/86	M	3	(12)	4
5	WAGNER Santos Lago	BRA	1/1/78	M	22		10
22	Ivor WEITZER	CRO	25/5/88	M	6	(7)	
21	Goran ZAKARIĆ		7/11/92	A	21	(3)	5

FK SLAVIJA SARAJEVO

Coach – Dragan Bjelica

Founded – 1908

Stadium – SC Slavija (4,500)

MAJOR HONOURS: Bosnia & Herzegovina Cup – (1) 2009.

2010				
1/8	Sloboda	h	1-0	*Regoje (p)*
8/8	Sarajevo	h	2-1	*Oglečevac, Popović*
14/8	Zrinjski	a	2-4	*Popović, Šešlija B.*
22/8	Budućnost	h	2-3	*Radovanović I., Regoje (p)*
28/8	Borac	a	1-4	*Rašević*
12/9	Prijedor	h	3-0	*Šešlija B., Kokot, Radovanović I.*
19/9	Olimpik	a	0-0	
26/9	Zvijezda	h	2-0	*Rašević, Todorović*
5/10	Travnik	a	3-5	*Radovanović I., Šešlija B., Regoje (p)*
16/10	Željezničar	h	1-0	*Radovanović I.*
21/10	Široki Brijeg	h	1-0	*Kokot*
23/10	Leotar	a	1-2	*Radovanović I.*
6/11	Drina	a	1-2	*Radovanović I.*
14/11	Velež	h	2-1	*Oglečevac, Regoje (p)*
20/11	Čelik	a	0-1	
2011				
26/2	Sloboda	a	1-2	*Pušara*
5/3	Sarajevo	a	2-4	*Radovanović I., Oglečevac*
13/3	Zrinjski	h	3-2	*Radovanović I. (p), Šešlija B., Popović*
19/3	Budućnost	a	1-0	*Pušara*
3/4	Borac	h	0-0	
9/4	Prijedor	a	2-2	*Šešlija B., Popović*
17/4	Olimpik	h	0-0	
23/4	Zvijezda	a	1-2	*Radovanović I. (p)*
30/4	Travnik	h	1-1	*Radovanović I.*
4/5	Željezničar	a	0-2	
8/5	Leotar	h	4-0	*Šešlija B., Rašević, Zeba, Oglečevac*
14/5	Široki Brijeg	a	1-4	*Radovanović I.*
19/5	Drina	h	0-1	
22/5	Velež	a	1-2	*Pušara*
28/5	Čelik	h	5-1	*Radovanović I., Simić, Šešlija B., Oglečevac, Zeba*

No	Name	Nat	DoB	Pos	Aps	(s)	Gls
22	Nikola AŠĆERIĆ	SRB	19/4/91	M		(1)	
2	Damir BEŠIREVIĆ		11/12/92	M	1	(1)	
1	Ratko DUJKOVIĆ		16/3/73	G	22		
17	Bojan JAMINA		5/2/79	M	5		
18	Zoran KOKOT		9/12/85	A	9		2
3	Đorđe LACKANOVIĆ		26/10/88	D	15	(3)	
2	Nemanja MILENKOVIĆ	SRB	15/1/89	M		(1)	
18	Dušan NESTOROVIĆ	SRB	26/6/86	M	4		
20	Nedim OGLEČEVAC		7/4/91	A	13	(10)	5
16	Marko PERIŠIĆ		25/1/91	M	18	(5)	
6	Goran POPOVIĆ		28/4/89	D	28		4
19	Nemanja PUŠARA		21/8/91	A	2	(12)	3
10	Miljan RADONJA		3/6/84	M	11	(8)	
26	Igor RADOVANOVIĆ		2/8/85	M	26	(2)	12
24	Saša RADOVANOVIĆ		10/7/91	D	8	(4)	
7	Dejan RAŠEVIĆ		25/11/83	A	22	(4)	3
4	Bojan REGOJE		2/12/81	D	24		4
31	Dušan REMIĆ		12/7/84	G	1		
11	Džemal SADIKOVIĆ		20/11/83	D	14		
9	Branko ŠEŠLIJA		26/1/87	A	21	(5)	7
13	Nemanja ŠEŠLIJA		30/7/88	M	11	(10)	
8	Goran SIMIĆ		6/4/73	D	21	(1)	1
21	Ivan STANKOVIĆ		7/7/76	M	25		
15	Ognjen TODOROVIĆ		24/3/89	M	19	(9)	1
23	Stefan TOMOVIĆ		15/1/91	G	7		
14	Emir ZEBA		10/6/89	M	3	(11)	2

FK SLOBODA TUZLA

Coach – Vlatko Glavaš; (1/11/10) Denis Sadiković; (9/3/11) Ibrahim Crnkić

Founded – 1919

Stadium – Tušanj (8,000)

2010				
1/8	Slavija	a	0-1	
7/8	Travnik	h	2-0	*Jogunčić, Smajlović*
14/8	Sarajevo	a	0-3	
21/8	Željezničar	h	2-0	*Dajić, Gavarić*
29/8	Zrinjski	a	0-1	
11/9	Leotar	h	1-1	*Smajlović*
18/9	Budućnost	a	0-0	
25/9	Široki Brijeg	h	0-1	
5/10	Borac	a	0-2	
16/10	Drina	h	3-0	*Jogunčić, Bekić Am., Mujić*
23/10	Prijedor	a	0-3	
30/10	Velež	h	1-0	*Jogunčić*
7/11	Olimpik	a	2-2	*Bekić Am., Zoletić*
13/11	Čelik	h	2-0	*Halilović, Smajlović*
20/11	Zvijezda	a	1-0	*Dajić*
2011				
26/2	Slavija	h	2-1	*Mujić 2 (1p)*
5/3	Travnik	a	0-2	
12/3	Sarajevo	h	0-0	
20/3	Željezničar	a	1-0	*Zoletić*
2/4	Zrinjski	h	0-1	
9/4	Leotar	a	3-1	*Bekić Al., Mujić 2*
16/4	Budućnost	h	1-0	*Bekić Al.*
23/4	Široki Brijeg	a	0-4	
30/4	Borac	h	1-0	*Mujić*
4/5	Drina	a	2-0	*Mujić, Bekić Am.*
7/5	Prijedor	h	2-1	*Mujić, Bošnjak*
14/5	Velež	a	0-2	
19/5	Olimpik	h	0-1	
22/5	Čelik	a	0-1	
28/5	Zvijezda	h	2-1	*Zoletić, Mujić*

No	Name	Nat	DoB	Pos	Aps	(s)	Gls
17	Darko ALEKSIĆ		23/11/85	D	10	(1)	
	Alden ALJUKIĆ		12/6/92	M		(1)	
	Almir BEKIĆ		1/6/89	M	12		2
9	Amer BEKIĆ		5/8/92	M	17	(4)	3
7	Emir BORIĆ		26/1/84	M		(2)	
21	Miljenko BOŠNJAK	CRO	11/4/87	M	11	(3)	1
7	Admir ČEHAJIĆ		12/8/86	M	16	(7)	
19	Jusuf DAJIĆ		21/8/84	M	10	(4)	2
12	Tino DIVKOVIĆ		7/2/91	G	1		
15	Dejan DRAKUL		4/6/86	D	9	(4)	
20	Samir EFENDIĆ		10/5/91	M	17	(7)	
8	Srefan GAVARIĆ	SRB	19/7/81	M	27		1
29	Almir HALILOVIC		30/1/85	M	25	(2)	1
	Maid JAGANJAC		11/6/92	M	2	(5)	
5	Samir JOGUNČIĆ		19/12/80	D	26		3
14	Mersed MALKIĆ		19/7/90	M	17	(5)	
19	Alen MEŠANOVIĆ		26/10/75	M	1	(4)	
	Jasmin MEŠANOVIĆ		6/1/92	M		(4)	
18	Senad MUJIĆ		17/9/81	A	16	(10)	9
1	Denis MUJKIĆ		2/9/83	G	29		
17	Damir MURSELOVIĆ		16/5/91	A		(1)	
15	Staniša NIKOLIĆ		28/11/94	D	14		
11	Tarik OKANOVIĆ		3/6/83	A	1	(5)	
4	Darko RACA		21/5/77	D	20	(1)	
	Amar RAHMANOVIĆ		13/5/94	M	1	(3)	
	Haris RIBIĆ		15/2/95	M		(3)	
	Ilija RISTANIĆ		11/2/86	M	2	(4)	
9	Edin ŠARANOVIČ		8/3/76	A	1		
16	Elmir SELIMOVIĆ		3/3/95	M		(2)	
11	Damir SMAJLOVIĆ		27/3/83	A	14		3
	Branislav VUKOMANOVIĆ	SRB	29/12/81	M	5		
6	Muamer ZOLETIĆ		20/1/83	M	26	(2)	3
13	Adnan ZUKIĆ		29/8/91	M		(3)	

NK TRAVNIK

Coach – Nedžad Selimović

Founded – 1922

Stadium – Pirota (3,000)

2010

31/7	Zvijezda	a	1-2	*Ćurić*
7/8	Sloboda	a	0-2	
14/8	Željezničar	h	2-1	*Mujakić, Varupa E. (p)*
21/8	Leotar	a	0-1	
28/8	Široki Brijeg	h	4-0	*Šiljak, Sarajčić, Fajić 2*
11/9	Drina	a	1-0	*Pranjković*
19/9	Velež	h	5-1	*Mujakić, Fajić 2, Pranjković, Ćurić*
25/9	Čelik	a	0-2	
5/10	Slavija	h	5-3	*Fajić 2, Šiljak 2, Varupa E. (p)*
16/10	Sarajevo	a	0-1	
23/10	Zrinjski	h	2-1	*Fajić, Zatagić*
30/10	Budućnost	a	1-3	*Šiljak*
6/11	Borac	h	1-2	*Helvida*
13/11	Prijedor	a	1-1	*Erić*
20/11	Olimpik	h	1-0	*Fajić*

2011

26/2	Zvijezda	h	2-2	*Rekić, Popović*
5/3	Sloboda	h	2-0	*Popović, Fajić*
12/3	Željezničar	a	0-3	
19/3	Leotar	h	1-0	*Helvida*
2/4	Široki Brijeg	a	1-2	*Fajić*
9/4	Drina	h	6-0	*Popović 2, Fajić 3, Šiljak*
16/4	Velež	a	0-1	
23/4	Čelik	h	0-0	
30/4	Slavija	a	1-1	*Mujakić*
4/5	Sarajevo	h	1-2	*Šiljak*
8/5	Zrinjski	a	1-3	*Hodžić*
14/5	Budućnost	h	0-1	
19/5	Borac	a	0-2	
22/5	Prijedor	h	2-1	*Imširević, Ćurić*
28/5	Olimpik	a	3-5	*Fajić, Mujakić, Kovačević*

No	Name	Nat	DoB	Pos	Aps	(s)	Gls
12	Adi ADILOVIĆ		20/2/83	G	29		
19	Stjepan BADROV		1/12/87	D	23	(4)	
16	Nedžad BEGIĆ		15/7/87	D		(1)	
	Robert ĆORIĆ	CRO	23/1/90	D		(1)	
10	Anel ĆURIĆ		28/7/88	M	24	(3)	3
1	Alen DELIĆ		25/3/83	G	1		
	Anes DELIĆ		8/3/91	M	1	(6)	
	Vedad DŽAFIĆ		19/2/89	A	5	(6)	
4	Nenad ERIĆ	CRO	30/8/89	M	1	(6)	1
118	Nusmir FAJIĆ		12/1/87	M	21	(3)	14
6	Suvad GRABUS	SVN	14/12/81	D	11		
15	Armin HELVIDA		20/2/86	D	26		2
4	Aldin HODŽIĆ		1/2/94	A	1	(7)	1
	Jasmin IMŠIREVIĆ		19/9/92	M		(1)	1
	Kenan KARAĐOZ		1/11/90	M	2	(1)	
21	Jasmin KOLAŠINAC		14/12/88	M	3	(4)	
	Adnan KOVAČEVIĆ		9/9/93	M	1	(2)	1
7	Adin LIHOVAC		22/8/87	D	2	(4)	
7	Sanid MUJAKIĆ		19/4/88	A	13	(2)	4
9	Nebojša POPOVIĆ	CRO	4/4/92	A	10	(1)	4
22	Dario PRANJKOVIĆ		5/2/84	M	26		2
	Haris REDŽEPI		20/7/88	A	5	(4)	
21	Bekir REKIĆ		16/11/86	A		(6)	1
5	Nihad RIBIĆ		10/11/81	D	18	(1)	
20	Midhet SARAJČIĆ		16/9/72	M	18	(3)	1
8	Mirsad ŠILJAK		22/2/81	M	22	(1)	6
11	Sanel TERZIĆ		18/5/91	D		(1)	
2	Sinbad TERZIĆ		22/2/81	D	25	(1)	
3	Elvedin VARUPA		16/11/75	M	27		2
14	Nermin VARUPA		18/4/91	M	6	(8)	
11	Haris ZATAGIĆ		15/3/85	D	9	(11)	1

FK VELEŽ

Coach – Demir Hotić; (3/10/10) Adis Obad; (15/1/11) Milorad Mitrović; (11/2/11) Milomir Odović

Founded – 1922

Stadium – Vrapčići (2,500)

MAJOR HONOURS: Yugoslav Cup – (2) 1981, 1986.

2010

7/8	Budućnost	h	2-0	*Okić, Zaimović*
14/8	Borac	a	1-1	*Duraković*
21/8	Prijedor	h	3-0	*Okić, Duraković, Ćemalović*
25/8	Zrinjski	a	0-2	
29/8	Olimpik	a	1-0	*Okić*
11/9	Zvijezda	h	1-4	*Velagić*
19/9	Travnik	a	1-5	*Zaimović (p)*
25/9	Željezničar	h	1-3	*Velagić*
5/10	Leotar	a	1-2	*Hasanović*
16/10	Široki Brijeg	h	2-5	*Velagić, Okić*
23/10	Drina	a	0-2	
30/10	Sloboda	a	0-1	
6/11	Čelik	h	1-0	*Hasanović*
14/11	Slavija	a	1-2	*Hasanović*
20/11	Sarajevo	h	1-2	*Hasanović*

2011

26/2	Zrinjski	h	1-0	*Velagić*
5/3	Budućnost	a	1-0	*Okić*
12/3	Borac	h	0-0	
19/3	Prijedor	a	0-2	
2/4	Olimpik	h	3-0	*Kodro, Velagić 2*
9/4	Zvijezda	a	0-0	
16/4	Travnik	h	1-0	*Okić*
23/4	Željezničar	a	2-3	*Ćemalović, Jazvin*
30/4	Leotar	h	0-2	
4/5	Široki Brijeg	a	1-4	*Rovčanin*
7/5	Drina	h	2-0	*Okić 2*
14/5	Sloboda	h	2-0	*Kodro, Okić*

9/5	Čelik	a	0-1	
2/5	Slavija	h	2-1	*Demić, Okić*
8/5	Sarajevo	a	0-1	

No	Name	Nat	DoB	Pos	Aps	(s)	Gls
	Amar BALALIĆ		3/3/91	A		(1)	
2	Sanel BORIĆ		23/7/87	G	15		
6	Danijel BRKOVIĆ		3/6/91	A	1	(2)	
	Mustafa BURIĆ		8/11/93	D		(1)	
2	Mirza ĆEMALOVIĆ		6/7/93	M	7	(12)	2
	Elmir ČOPELJ		3/3/92	M		(1)	
3	Rijad DEMIĆ		17/11/89	M	20	(2)	1
0	Dženan DURAKOVIĆ		20/6/90	D	16	(8)	2
4	Ermin GADŽO		19/5/90	M	6	(1)	
6	Goran GANCEV	MKD	4/8/83	D	14		
	Emir HADŽUĐULBIĆ		12/4/76	G	8		
	Eldar HASANOVIČ		1/1/90	A	7		4
4	Perica IVETIĆ		28/11/86	M	21		
3	Armin JAZVIN		11/10/90	M	9	(6)	1
13	Adnan KADRIĆ		7/4/76	D	5	(1)	
3	Admir KAJTAZ		30/3/78	D	17	(1)	
	Zlatko KAZAZIĆ		10/2/89	M	16	(2)	
	Mustafa KODRO		29/8/81	M	28		2
8	Elvis LELO		7/2/85	A	5	(6)	
2	Amer MAHIMIĆ		2/6/90	D	1		
3	Halil MAHMUTOVIĆ		7/8/96	M	2	(2)	
	Fadil MARIĆ		12/8/93	M		(1)	
21	Dalio MEMIĆ		21/3/90	D	1	(2)	
20	Šefko OKIĆ		26/7/88	A	26		10
12	Senedin OŠTRAKOVIĆ		13/4/87	G	7	(1)	
18	Igor REMETIČ		10/9/76	A	2	(4)	
13	Damir ROVČANIN		12/3/88	A	14	(1)	1
9	Arnel ŠKALJIĆ		9/8/81	M	8	(6)	
5	Asim ŠKALJIĆ		9/8/88	D	12		
6	Goran STOKIČ	SRB	17/9/80	D	14		
15	Arnel STUPAC		24/3/82	M	2	(6)	
11	Admir VELAGIĆ		19/10/75	M	18	(1)	6
4	Dženan ZAIMOVIĆ		25/9/73	D	20	(2)	2
19	Amir ZOLJ		24/11/89	D	8	(12)	
18	Denis ZVONIĆ		8/2/92	D		(1)	

FK ŽELJEZNIČAR

Coach – Amar Osim

Founded – 1921

Stadium – Grbavica (14,000)

MAJOR HONOURS: Yugoslav League – (1) 1972; Bosnia & Herzegovina League – (4) 1998, 2001, 2002, 2010; Bosnia & Herzegovina Cup – (4) 2000, 2001, 2003, 2011.

2010				
4/8	Olimpik	a	2-0	*Radovanović, Rovčanin (p)*
8/8	Zvijezda	h	2-0	*Bešlija M., Višća*
14/8	Travnik	a	1-2	*Zeba (p)*
21/8	Sloboda	a	0-2	
28/8	Leotar	h	8-0	*Zeba 2 (1p), Popović 3, Svraka, Rovčanin, Savić*
12/9	Široki Brijeg	a	1-4	*Zeba (p)*
18/9	Drina	h	2-0	*Savić, Zeba*
25/9	Velež	a	3-1	*Zeba (p), Čolić E., Višća*
5/10	Čelik	h	2-1	*Savić, Višća*
16/10	Slavija	a	0-1	
24/10	Sarajevo	h	0-0	
31/10	Zrinjski	a	1-0	*Savić*
7/11	Budućnost	h	2-0	*Višća, Savić*
13/11	Borac	a	0-1	
20/11	Prijedor	h	4-2	*Popović, Zeba 2 (1p), Stanić*
2011				
26/2	Olimpik	h	3-0	*Zeba (p), Višća, Bešlija M.*
5/3	Zvijezda	a	0-0	
12/3	Travnik	h	3-0	*Spahić, Savić, Marković*
20/3	Sloboda	h	0-1	
2/4	Leotar	a	1-0	*Svraka*
9/4	Široki Brijeg	h	0-1	
16/4	Drina	a	2-0	*Višća, Bogičević*
23/4	Velež	h	3-2	*Zeba (p), Višća, Stanić*
30/4	Čelik	a	1-1	*Stanceski*
4/5	Slavija	h	2-0	*Zeba, Bešlija M.*
7/5	Sarajevo	a	0-0	
13/5	Zrinjski	h	3-1	*Bešlija M., Nyema, Svraka*
19/5	Budućnost	a	2-1	*Savić, Ćulum*
22/5	Borac	h	0-1	
28/5	Prijedor	a	2-3	*Višća 2*

No	Name	Nat	DoB	Pos	Aps	(s)	Gls
28	Omar BALJIĆ		5/10/90	A	1	(5)	
7	Haris BEŠLIJA		27/9/86	M		(4)	
20	Mirsad BEŠLIJA		6/7/79	M	20	(4)	4
6	Jadranko BOGIČEVIĆ		11/3/83	D	12		1
17	Benjamin ČOLIĆ		23/7/91	D	7	(4)	
2	Elvir ČOLIĆ		17/7/86	A	10	(6)	1
16	Milan ĆULUM	SRB	28/10/84	D	15	(1)	1
5	Goran GANCEV	MKD	4/8/83	D	1		
7	Nermin JAMAK		25/8/86	M	9	(5)	
22	Elvis KARIĆ		21/5/80	G	1		
15	Semir KERLA		26/9/87	D	9		
4	Goran MARKOVIĆ	MNE	8/2/86	M	21		1
24	Elvis MEŠIĆ		12/9/80	M	17	(1)	
26	Aleksandar NIKOLIČ		25/6/91	A		(2)	
15	Patrick NYEMA Gerhardt	LBR	31/7/85	D	8	(1)	1
25	Goran PERAK		1/6/86	M	1	(7)	
29	Lazar POPOVIĆ	SRB	10/1/83	M	25		4
3	Mirko RADOVANOVIĆ	SRB	5/4/86	D	15	(4)	1
9	Mirsad RAMIĆ		6/12/92	M	1	(1)	
9	Damir ROVČANIN		15/4/89	A	4	(7)	2
8	Srđan SAVIĆ		27/9/85	M	20	(6)	7
12	Ibrahim ŠEHIĆ		2/9/88	G	29		
2	Bajro SPAHIĆ		23/4/84	A	2	(2)	1
27	Perica STANCESKI	MKD	29/1/85	M	3	(5)	1
11	Srđan STANIĆ		6/7/89	A	19	(9)	2
23	Muamer SVRAKA		14/2/88	M	23	(1)	3
19	Velibor VASILIĆ		19/10/80	D	13	(1)	
13	Edin VIŠĆA		17/2/90	M	18	(9)	9
10	Zajko ZEBA		22/5/83	M	25	(2)	11
9	Nermin ZOLOTIĆ		7/7/93	M	1	(2)	

HŠK ZRINJSKI

Coach – Dragan Jović; (20/10/10) Marijan Blodek; (19/11/10) Slaven Musa

Founded – 1912

Stadium – Bijeli Brijeg (15,000)

MAJOR HONOURS: Bosnia & Herzegovina League – (2) 2005, 2009; Bosnia & Herzegovina Cup – (1) 2008.

2010				
8/8	Čelik	a	1-2	*Lendrić*
14/8	Slavija	h	4-2	*Lendrić 2, Salčinović, Ivanković*
21/8	Sarajevo	a	0-1	
25/8	Velež	h	2-0	*Zadro, Sušić*
29/8	Sloboda	h	1-0	*Lendrić*
11/9	Budućnost	h	0-0	
18/9	Borac	a	0-2	
25/9	Prijedor	h	1-0	*Dragičević*
5/10	Olimpik	a	0-2	
16/10	Zvijezda	h	1-2	*Lendrić*
23/10	Travnik	a	1-2	*Lendrić*
31/10	Željezničar	h	0-1	
6/11	Leotar	a	1-4	*Dragičević*
14/11	Široki Brijeg	h	4-3	*Lendrić, Ivanković 2, Dragičević*
20/11	Drina	a	0-1	

2011

26/2	Velež	a	0-1	
6/3	Čelik	h	1-0	*Kutalia*
13/3	Slavija	a	2-3	*Lendrić (p), Stjepanović*
20/3	Sarajevo	h	4-2	*Lendrić 2, Selimović, Kutalia*
2/4	Sloboda	a	1-0	*Popović (p)*
9/4	Budućnost	a	3-0	*(w/o; match abandoned after 22 mins at 0-0)*
17/4	Borac	h	0-0	
23/4	Prijedor	a	0-2	
30/4	Olimpik	h	1-0	*Stjepanović*
4/5	Zvijezda	a	1-1	*Pehar*
8/5	Travnik	h	3-1	*Lendrić 2, Džidić*
13/5	Željezničar	a	1-3	*Selimović*
19/5	Leotar	h	4-0	*Selimović, Lendrić 2, Barišić*
22/5	Široki Brijeg	a	1-4	*Lendrić*
28/5	Drina	h	3-0	*Pehar, Miličević, Lendrić*

No	Name	Nat	DoB	Pos	Aps	(s)	Gls
5	Josip ANIČIĆ		23/10/91	D	1		
27	Marin ANIČIĆ		17/8/89	M	26	(2)	
	Filip AREŽINA		8/11/92	M		(1)	
	Ivan BARIŠIĆ		13/7/93	M		(2)	1
21	Matej BARTULICA		1/2/92	D		(2)	
26	Mateo BENCUN		24/4/91	M		(2)	
18	Mate DRAGIČEVIĆ	CRO	19/11/79	A	5	(5)	3
	Alek ĐURIĆ	CRO	19/1/85	M	2	(5)	
4	Samir DURO		18/10/77	D	13		
3	Damir DŽIDIĆ	CRO	15/2/87	D	24		1
21	Toni GAGRO		3/2/89	D	2	(2)	
	Suvad GRABUS	SVN	14/12/81	D	8	(9)	
1	Adnan HADŽIĆ		15/1/88	G	27		
14	Mario IVANKOVIĆ		8/2/75	M	19	(4)	3
17	Levan KUTALIA	GEO	19/7/89	M	9	(1)	2
24	Ivan LENDRIĆ	CRO	8/8/91	A	25	(3)	16
19	Toni MARKIĆ		25/10/90	D	11	(2)	
18	Davor MARTINOVIĆ		6/11/93	M	1	(2)	
12	Igor MELHER		1/11/79	G	3		
15	Hrvoje MILIČEVIĆ		30/4/93	M	4	(5)	1
11	Mile PEHAR		1/2/91	D	11	(9)	2
18	Ozren PERIĆ		4/4/87	A	1	(7)	
25	Marko POPOVIĆ	SRB	25/8/82	D	13		1
	Ivan PULJIĆ		26/6/91	D	1		
	Marko RAŠO	CRO	25/6/89	M		(1)	
25	Mirza RIZVANOVIĆ		27/9/86	D	12	(2)	
8	Fenan SALČINOVIĆ		26/6/87	M	14		1
9	Vernes SELIMOVIĆ		8/5/83	M	20	(3)	3
16	Josip SESAR		16/10/92	D		(1)	
7	Nemanja STJEPANOVIĆ		7/2/84	D	26		2
16	Pero STOJKIĆ		9/12/86	D	13		
13	Pavle SUŠIĆ		15/4/88	M	8	(6)	1
2	Toni ŠUNJIĆ		15/12/88	D	5		
23	Vlado ZADRO		17/3/87	M	20	(6)	1
17	Ivo ZLATIĆ		20/6/91	D		(2)	
	Pero ZOVKO		1/2/91	M	3	(7)	
18	Mladen ŽIŽOVIĆ		27/12/80	M	3		

NK ZVIJEZDA

Coach – Zoran Ćurguz; (1/1/11) Dragan Jović

Founded – 1922

Stadium – Banja Ilidža (3,500)

2010

31/7	Travnik	h	2-1	*Hamzić, Huseinbašić*
8/8	Željezničar	a	0-2	
14/8	Leotar	h	1-0	*Hamzić (p)*
22/8	Široki Brijeg	a	0-3	
28/8	Drina	h	2-1	*Nikić, Tosunović*
11/9	Velež	a	4-1	*Tosunović 4*
18/9	Čelik	h	1-1	*Nikić*
26/9	Slavija	a	0-2	
5/10	Sarajevo	h	1-1	*Tosunović*
16/10	Zrinjski	a	2-1	*Tosunović 2*
23/10	Budućnost	h	0-0	
30/10	Borac	a	0-1	
6/11	Prijedor	h	0-0	
14/11	Olimpik	a	0-1	
20/11	Sloboda	h	0-1	

2011

26/2	Travnik	a	2-2	*Nikić, Ristić*
5/3	Željezničar	h	0-0	
12/3	Leotar	a	0-3	
19/3	Široki Brijeg	h	6-1	*Hamzić, Nuhanovič 2, Ristić, Delić, Husić*
2/4	Drina	a	2-1	*Nikić, Hamzić*
9/4	Velež	h	0-0	
16/4	Čelik	a	1-4	*Tosunović*
23/4	Slavija	h	2-1	*Nuhanovič, Hasić*
30/4	Sarajevo	a	1-2	*Hamzić*
4/5	Zrinjski	h	1-1	*Ristić*
7/5	Budućnost	a	5-2	*Đelmić, Ristić 2, Tosunović 2*
14/5	Borac	h	1-0	*Hamzić*
19/5	Prijedor	a	3-1	*Đelmić, Tosunović 2*
22/5	Olimpik	h	2-2	*Đelmić, Tosunović*
28/5	Sloboda	a	1-2	*Ristić*

No	Name	Nat	DoB	Pos	Aps	(s)	Gls
11	Mersad BEDAK		18/2/89	M	3	(4)	
18	Armin DELIĆ		19/6/83	M	15	(4)	1
7	Ognjen ĐELMIĆ	SRB	18/8/88	M	10	(4)	3
9	Zlatko ĐORIĆ	SRB	7/9/76	A	7	(6)	
12	Irfan FEJZIĆ		1/7/86	G	6	(1)	
12	Emir HADŽIĐULBIĆ		12/4/76	G	11		
20	Amar HAMZIĆ		5/1/75	M	26		6
6	Šerif HASIĆ		7/1/88	M	11	(1)	1
10	Nermin HUSEINBAŠIĆ		2/6/81	M	4	(7)	1
16	Senad HUSIĆ		12/4/90	A	19	(8)	1
11	Omer JAHIĆ		12/4/93	M		(3)	
15	Rusmir JUSIĆ		20/10/80	D	26	(1)	
22	Alvin KARADŽA		28/5/84	D	8		
23	Milan KNEŽEVIĆ	SRB	1/1/88	D	12		
23	Eldin MAŠIĆ		2/1/87	M	14	(4)	
13	Jasmin MORANJKIĆ		11/10/83	M	25	(1)	
3	Muamer NEZIĆ		18/11/90	M	16	(6)	
19	Branislav NIKIĆ		15/8/83	M	17	(4)	4
10	Samir NUHANOVIČ	SVN	6/11/87	A	19	(6)	3
21	Vedad OMERAGIĆ		31/7/91	A	3	(3)	
5	Ilija PRODANOVIĆ		16/10/79	D	6		
14	Dragan RISTIĆ		27/2/82	A	14		6
7	Sanel ŠEHRIĆ		12/11/90	D		(1)	
17	Saša ŠEST	CRO	5/12/85	M	1	(2)	
1	Raif SMAJIĆ		14/6/85	G	13		
	Joco STOKIĆ		7/4/87	M	2	(4)	
17	Adnan SULJIĆ		16/5/92	D		(1)	
21	Damir TOSUNOVIĆ		5/11/85	A	23	(4)	14
14	Nikola VASILJEVIĆ		19/12/83	D	14		
	Antonio VIDOVIĆ		27/7/89	M	5		

TOP GOALSCORERS 2010/11

16	Ivan LENDRIĆ (Zrinjski)
14	Mirza DŽAFIĆ (Prijedor) Nusmir FAJIĆ (Travnik) Damir TOSUNOVIĆ (Zvijezda)
12	Mateo ROSKAM (Široki Brijeg) Igor RADOVANOVIĆ (Slavija)
11	Zajko ZEBA (Željezničar)
10	Stevo NIKOLIĆ (Borac) WAGNER (Široki Brijeg) Šefko OKIĆ (Velež)

PROMOTED CLUBS

NK GOŠK GABELA
Coach – Damir Borovac
Founded – 1919
Stadium – Podavala (2,000)

FK KOZARA
Coach – Vinko Marinović
Founded – 1945
Stadium – Gradski (6,000)

SECOND LEVEL FINAL TABLES 2010/11

PRVA LIGA FBiH

		Pld	W	D	L	F	A	Pts
1	NK GOŠK Gabela	30	16	8	6	38	21	56
2	HNK Čapljina	30	15	3	12	49	41	48
3	NK Iskra Bugojno	30	13	8	9	45	35	47
4	FK Krajina Cazin	30	14	5	11	41	31	47
5	HNK Orašje	30	14	5	11	40	31	47
6	NK Jedinstvo Bihać	30	14	4	12	38	39	46
7	FK Goražde	30	14	3	13	50	39	45
8	NK Gradina Srebrenik	30	13	5	12	44	39	44
9	NK Krajišnik Velika Kladuša	30	13	5	12	41	40	44
10	FK Rudar Kakanj	30	11	10	9	46	44	43
11	NK SAŠK Napredak Sarajevo	30	13	4	13	49	49	43
12	NK Omladinac Mionica	30	13	3	14	37	39	42
13	NK Bosna Visoko	30	12	5	13	39	44	41
14	NK Slaven Živinice	30	10	4	16	27	42	34
15	NK Igman Konjic	30	9	4	17	34	57	31
16	FK Radnik Hadžići	30	4	8	18	26	53	20

PRVA LIGA RS

		Pld	W	D	L	F	A	Pts
1	FK Kozara	26	18	4	4	46	12	58
2	FK Radnik Bijeljina	26	13	4	9	38	20	43
3	FK Sutjeska Foča	26	12	7	7	37	27	43
4	FK Mladost Gacko	26	13	1	12	35	38	40
5	FK Podrinje Janja	26	11	6	9	39	27	39
6	FK Sloga Doboj	26	10	8	8	35	41	38
7	FK Proleter Teslić	26	11	4	11	30	26	37
8	FK Sloboda Novi Grad	26	9	9	8	37	33	36
9	FK Modriča	26	10	5	11	32	33	35
10	FK Laktaši	26	9	8	9	21	28	35
11	FK Sloboda Mrkonjić Grad	26	8	6	12	30	33	30
12	FK Drina Višegrad	26	8	5	13	26	36	29
13	FK Famos Vojkovići	26	8	4	14	29	42	28
14	BSK Banja Luka	26	4	5	17	15	54	17

DOMESTIC CUP 2010/11

KUP BOSNE I HERCEGOVINE

1/16 FINALS

(14/9/10)
Željezničar 2, Rudar Prijedor 0
Zrinjski 3, Budućnost Banovići 1

(15/9/19)
Borac Banja Luka 2, TOŠK Tešanj 0
Bosna Sarajevo 0, Sloboda Tuzla 1
Branitelj Mostar 7, Doboj Istok Klokotnica 0
BSK Banja Luka 0, Omladinac Mionica 2
Čelik 2, Velež Mostar 0
Leotar 1, Zvijezda Gradačac 0
Proleter Teslić 0, Drina Zvornik 0 *(4-3 on pens)*
Sarajevo 2, Sloga Gornji Vakuf/Uskoplje 1
Široki Brijeg 6, Sutjeska Foča 0
Slavija Sarajevo 3, Jedinstvo Bihać 1
Sloboda Novi Grad 1, Orašje 0
Travnik 0, Kozara 1
UNIS Vogošća 2, Modriča 1
Vitez 0, Olimpik Sarajevo 1

1/8 FINALS

(28/9/10 & 19/10/10)
Proleter Teslić v Zrinjski 4-2; 0-3 *(4-5)*

(29/9/10 & 20/10/10)
Borac Banja Luka v Željezničar 0-0, 0-3 *(0-3)*
Čelik v Slavija Sarajevo 1-1; 1-0 *(2-1)*
Kozara v Sloboda Tuzla 1-1; 2-4 *(3-5)*
Leotar v Branitelj Mostar 1-1; 0-1 *(1-2)*
Omladinac Mionica v Široki Brijeg 2-0; 0-4 *(2-4)*
Sarajevo v Sloboda Novi Grad 4-1; 3-1 *(7-2)*

(30/9/10 & 19/10/10)
Olimpik Sarajevo v UNIS Vogošća 5-1; 2-1 *(7-2)*

QUARTER-FINALS

(3/11/10 & 10/11/10)
Sarajevo 2 *(Arsenijević 36, Jahovic 42)*, Široki Brijeg 2 *(Šilić 22, Wagner 62)*
Široki Brijeg 1 *(Wagner 50)*, Sarajevo 0
(Široki Brijeg 3-2)

Zrinjski 2 *(Lendrić 7, Salčinović 22)*, Čelik 0
Čelik 3 *(Kapetan 23, Adilović 47p, Džafić 70)*, Zrinjski 0
(Čelik 3-2)

(4/11/10 & 10/11/10)
Olimpik Sarajevo *(Thiago Silva 83)*, Sloboda Tuzla 1 *(Bekić 43)*
Sloboda Tuzla 1 *(Zoletić 3)*, Olimpik Sarajevo 1 *(Thiago Carioca 4)*
(2-2; Olimpik Sarajevo 6-5 on pens)

Željezničar 6 *(Zeba 11, 17, 20, Kerla 43, Ćulum 57, Perak 65)*, Branitelj Mostar 0
Branitelj Mostar 0, Željezničar 3 *(Bešlija H. 6, Baljić 55, Perak 75)*
(Željezničar 9-0)

SEMI-FINALS

(16/3/11 & 6/4/11)
Željezničar 0, Široki Brijeg 0
Široki Brijeg 1 *(Roskam 60)*, Željezničar 1 *(Zeba 90p)*
(1-1; Željezničar on away goal)

(30/3/11 & 6/4/11)
Čelik 1 *(Kuduzović 39)*, Olimpik Sarajevo 0
Olimpik Sarajevo 1 *(Raščić 75)*, Čelik 1 *(Hadžić 71)*
(Čelik 2-1)

FINAL

(28/4/11)
Stadion Grbavica, Sarajevo
FK ŽELJEZNIČAR 1 *(Zeba 1)*
NK ČELIK 0
Referee – *Paradžik*
ŽELJEZNIČAR – *Šehić, Ćulum, Vasilić, Nyema, Marković (Čolić B. 80), Svraka, Popović, Višća (Savić 83), Zeba, Bešlija M. (Čolić E. 61), Stanić.*
ČELIK – *Bilobrk, Brković, Kuduzović, Čović, Milošević, Horić (Hasanović 64), Kapetan, Purić (Sadiković 89), Adilović, Džafić (Šišić 82), Hadžić.*

(25/5/11)
Stadion Bilino polje, Zenica
NK ČELIK 0
FK ŽELJEZNIČAR 3 *(Savić 12, Zeba 71, Stanić 74)*
Referee – *Arnautović*
ČELIK – *Bilobrk, Brković, Kuduzović, Čović, Milošević, Isaković, Šišić (Horić 76), Purić, Adilović, Džafić (Hasanović 66), Hadžić (Nemeljaković 79).*
ŽELJEZNIČAR – *Šehić, Čolić B., Nyema, Bogičević, Radovanović (Baljić 78), Svraka, Savić, Bešlija M. (Zolotić 82), Zeba, Popović (Ramić 87), Stanić.*
(ŽELJEZNIČAR 4-0)

CLUB COMMUNICATION 2011/12

FK Borac Banja Luka
Vladike Platona 6
BA-78000 Banja Luka

Tel +387 51 301 793
Fax +387 51 301 793
Web fkborac.net
Email fk borac@teol.net
Media Officer Darko Basara

NK Čelik
Bulever Kulina Bana bb, Bilino polje stadion, BA-72000 Zenica

Tel +387 32 248 002
Fax +387 32 248 002
Web nkcelik.ba
Email n.k.celik@bih.net.ba
Media Officer Mirsad Pripoljac

NK GOŠK Gabela
Put Metkovića 115
BA-88306 Gabela

Tel +387 36 821 015
Fax +387 36 807 235
Web
Email nklubgosk@gmail.com
Media Officer Pero Pavlović

FK Kozara
Dositeja Obradovića 9
BA-78440 Bosanska Gradiška

Tel +387 51 813 070
Fax +387 51 813 070
Web fkkozara.info
Email info@fkkozara.info
Media Officer Zoran Vajkić

FK Leotar
Trg Petral bb
BA-89101 Trebinje

Tel +387 59 224 911
Fax +387 59 224 911
Web fkleotar.com
Email fkleotar1925@gmail.com
Media Officer Čedomir Mucović

FK Olimpik Sarajevo
Trg solidarnosti 17
BA-71000 Sarajevo

Tel +387 33 466 541
Fax +387 33 466 541
Web
Email info@olimpik.ba
Media Officer Nermin Demirović

FK Rudar Prijedor
Majora Milana Tepića 10
BA-79101 Prijedor

Tel +387 52 231 994
Fax +387 52 231 994
Web rudarprijedor.com
Email office@rudarprijedor.com
Media Officer Aleksandar Škorić

FK Sarajevo
Maršala Tita 38b
BA-71000 Sarajevo

Tel +387 33 664 262
Fax +387 33 442 333
Web fcsarajevo.ba
Email info@fcsarajevo.ba
Media Officer Mirza Huskić

NK Široki Brijeg
Fra Didaka Buntica 72
BA-88220 Široki Brijeg

Tel +387 39 704 535
Fax +387 39 705 095
Web nk-sirokibrijeg.com
Email nk.siroki.brijeg@tel.net.ba
Media Officer Mario Marušic

FK Slavija Sarajevo
Jovana Raškovića 16, Lukavica
BA-71123 Istočno Sarajevo

Tel +387 57 342 343
Fax +387 57 342 343
Web fkslavija.com
Email info@fkslavija.com
Media Officer Gordana Šarović

FK Sloboda Tuzla
Rudarska 2, Stadion Tušanj
BA-75000 Tuzla

Tel +387 35 272 281
Fax +387 35 272 281
Web
Email info@fcsloboda.com
Media Officer Nedim Cudic

NK Travnik
Bosanska bb
BA-72270 Travnik

Tel +387 30 511 787
Fax +387 30 511 787
Web
Email nktravnik@bih.net.ba
Media Officer Aldijana Fulurija

FK Velež
Maršala Tita 87
BA-88000 Mostar

Tel +387 36 550 431
Fax +387 36 550 431
Web fkvelez.ba
Email kontakt@fkvelez.ba
Media Officer Nedim Ajanić

FK Željezničar
Zvornička 27
BA-71000 Sarajevo

Tel +387 33 660 133
Fax +387 33 715 201
Web fkzeljeznicar.com
Email zeljo@bih.net.ba
Media Officer Mersiha Drinjaković

HŠK Zrinjski
Stjepana Radica 45, HŠK Zrinjski
BA-88000 Mostar

Tel +387 36 321 507
Fax +387 36 320 222
Web hskzrinjski.ba
Email hsk.zrinjski@tel.net.ba
Media Officer Damir Suton

NK Zvijezda
6. Bataljona bb
BA-76250 Gradačac

Tel +387 35 819 011
Fax +387 35 819 011
Web
Email nk.zvijezda@bih.net.ba
Media Officer Džemal Delić

BULGARIA

Bulgarie I Bulgarien

Bulgarski Futbolen Soyuz (BFS)

COMMUNICATION

Address 26 Tzar Ivan Assen II Street
BG-1124 Sofia
Tel +359 2 942 6202
Fax +359 2 942 6201

E-mail bfu@bfunion.bg
Website bfunion.bg

President Borislav Mihaylov
General Secretary Borislav Popov
Media Officer Pavel Kolev

Year of Formation 1923

National Stadium Vasil Levski, Sofia (43,230)

DOMESTIC COMPETITION SUMMARY 2010/11

A PFG FINAL TABLE

			Home					Away					Total						
		Pld	W	D	L	F	A	W	D	L	F	A	W	D	L	F	A	Pts	Comp
1	PFC Litex Lovech	30	12	3	0	31	5	11	3	1	25	8	23	6	1	56	13	75	UCL
2	PFC Levski Sofia	30	13	0	2	36	8	10	3	2	31	16	23	3	4	67	24	72	UEL
3	PFC CSKA Sofia	30	10	3	2	23	10	8	4	3	30	16	18	7	5	53	26	61	UEL
4	PFC Lokomotiv Sofia	30	10	2	3	31	16	6	2	7	16	17	16	4	10	47	33	52	UEL
5	PFC Lokomotiv Plovdiv 1936	30	9	5	1	37	10	5	5	5	17	18	14	10	6	54	28	52	
6	PFC Cherno More Varna	30	10	2	3	25	9	5	4	6	11	19	15	6	9	36	28	51	
7	PFC Beroe Stara Zagora	30	8	5	2	16	9	5	2	8	17	25	13	7	10	33	34	46	
8	PSFC Chernomorets Burgas	30	5	3	7	10	16	4	7	4	9	12	9	10	11	19	28	37	
9	PFC Minior Pernik	30	7	3	5	19	18	3	3	9	14	27	10	6	14	33	45	36	
10	PFC Montana 1921	30	6	5	4	23	20	2	3	10	7	26	8	8	14	30	46	32	
11	PFC Slavia Sofia	30	5	3	7	15	15	4	2	9	19	23	9	5	16	34	38	32	
12	PFC Kaliakra Kavarna	30	4	4	7	13	18	4	2	9	6	22	8	6	16	19	40	30	
13	PFC Pirin Blagoevgrad	30	6	4	5	23	15	0	5	10	9	24	6	9	15	32	39	27	
14	PFC Vidima-Rakovski Sevlievo	30	5	4	6	18	19	1	3	11	8	33	6	7	17	26	52	25	
15	PFC Akademik Sofia	30	3	3	9	11	24	2	2	11	5	27	5	5	20	16	51	20	*Relegated*
16	OFC Sliven 2000	30	3	4	8	15	19	1	3	11	7	33	4	7	19	22	52	19	*Relegated*

NB PFC Pirin Blagoevgrad expelled from 2011/12 A PFG.

Top Scorer Garra Dembélé (Levski), 26 goals

Promoted Club PFC Ludogorets Razgrad
OFC Botev Vratsa
PFC Svetkavitsa Targovishte

Cup Final PFC CSKA Sofia 1, PFC Slavia Sofia 0

Litex lift title again

Back-to-back Bulgarian champions in 1998 and 1999, PFC Litex Lovech repeated the trick with a successful defence of the title they had won in 2009/10, amassing 75 points on the back of club-record run of 25 league games without defeat to edge out fast-finishing runners-up PFC Levski Sofia. After Bulgarian Cup wins in 2008 and 2009 it brought silverware to Lovech for a fourth successive season.

Things did not look quite so promising at the start of the campaign. The team crashed out of the UEFA Champions League in the third qualifying round to MŠK Žilina, and Angel Chervenkov, the coach who had masterminded the club's 2009/10 A PFG title triumph, paid the price with the sack. His replacement, Petko Petkov, fared no better as the club then lost their UEFA Europa League play-off to Debreceni VSC. With European football off the season's agenda, Litex were forced to sell their major asset, captain Ivelin Popov, who departed to Turkish club Gaziantepsor.

Veteran striker Svetoslav Todorov won his fourth Bulgarian league title with Litex Lovech

Masterstroke

The club pulled off a masterstroke, however, with the acquisition, in mid-September, of PFC CSKA Sofia club legend Luboslav Penev, who became their third coach of the campaign. Under his guidance Litex went on a winning spree that took in 13 consecutive matches and lasted – winter break included – more than six months. Five points clear at Christmas, Litex brushed off the January sale of their top scorer from the previous season, French striker Wilfried Niflore, and surged onwards and upwards. Although their unbeaten run ended when Levski defeated them 2-0 in Sofia in early May, they still retained a five-point advantage with four games left and duly confirmed their successful title defence in the penultimate round with a 3-1 win at PFC Lokomotiv Sofia.

Among the goalscorers that day were veteran striker Svetoslav Todorov – once of the English Premier League – and the club's leading marksman, and principal showman, Brazilian playmaker Doka Madureira. Although he was often a substitute, Todorov notched eight goals and maintained his record of being involved in all of the club's Bulgarian title wins. Doka Madureira was on target 12 times, contributed several assists and succeeded the departed Popov as the A PFG's player of the season.

As usual, the season had begun with Sofia giants Levski and CSKA installed as joint-favourites for the title – despite the fact that both clubs had undergone a major summer overhaul, enlisting new coaches and a welter of new players.

Destroyer Dembélé

Journeyman coach Yasen Petrov was handed the big job at Levski, and he got off to the perfect start with a 1-0 win at CSKA on the opening day. The winning goal was scored by another newcomer, French-born Garra Dembélé who later in the season would launch his international career with Mali. It was the first of 26 league goals that the pacy, powerful striker would score, a tally that

National Team

International Tournament Appearances –
FIFA World Cup – (7) 1962, 1966, 1970, 1974, 1986 (2nd round), 1994 (4th), 1998.
UEFA European Championship – (2) 1996, 2004.

Top Five All-time Caps – Borislav Mihaylov & Stiliyan Petrov (102); Hristo Bonev (96); Krassimir Balakov (92); Dimitar Penev (90)

Top Five All-time Goals – Dimitar Berbatov (48); Hristo Bonev (47); Hristo Stoichkov (37); Emil Kostadinov (26); Lyubomir Angelov, Ivan Kolev & Petar Zhekov (25)

included four hat-tricks. It was not just Bulgarian defences that he destroyed; he also struck eight times in Europe as Levski reached the group stage of the UEFA Europa League for the second season running.

The Blues won five of their six European games in Sofia, drawing the other, but on the domestic front a 2-1 reverse at Litex was followed immediately by a shock home defeat against Dembélé's former club PFC Lokomotiv Plovdiv 1936. Another home loss, to CSKA, in the first match of the spring left them eight points in arrears of Litex, and although they dropped just two further points all season, they could not bridge the gap. A penalty shoot-out defeat by Litex scuppered their Bulgarian Cup hopes, and at the end of a trophy-less campaign Petrov was relieved of his duties. Dembélé also departed, for German Bundesliga club SC Freiburg.

The cup was won by CSKA, thus ending the Sofia Reds' three-year wait for a trophy. Their 1-0 victory in the final against PFC Slavia Sofia brought a gratifying end to a turbulent season that was marked by the early sacking – after three winless league fixtures – of new coach Pavel Dochev and the removal two months later of his successor, Gjore Jovanovski, who oversaw three straight defeats without a goal in the group stage of the UEFA Europa League. CSKA struck third time lucky, however, with the untried Milen Radukanov, who not only steadied the ship but also won at SK Rapid Wien on his European debut and introduced a free-flowing style of football that allowed talents such as striker Spas Delev and Dutchman Gregory Nelson to shine.

Although never in the title hunt, CSKA were good value in the spring, recording that rare away win at Levski and powering to victory in the cup. Prior to seeing off Slavia in the final they eliminated Litex in the semis. Young Delev was CSKA's goalscoring hero in both fixtures, his winner in the final making history as he became the first CSKA player to score in every round of a Cup-winning campaign.

Matthäus moves in

The major story regarding the Bulgarian national team was the arrival of German FIFA World Cup-winning captain Lothar Matthäus as the new head coach. He was appointed following the resignation of Stanimir Stoilov, who stepped down after Bulgaria suffered two traumatic defeats in their opening UEFA EURO 2012 qualifiers, against England and Montenegro. Matthäus got off to a winning start against Wales, but subsequent draws against Switzerland and Montenegro left his new charges with only the faintest hope of reaching the finals.

The loss up front of record goalscorer and 2010 Bulgarian Footballer of the Year Dimitar Berbatov, who had announced his international retirement before the campaign began, was keenly felt, and although his replacement as captain, Stiliyan Petrov, became only the second Bulgarian footballer to win 100 caps – before drawing alongside the record-holder, Borislav Mihaylov, on 102 – the trusty midfielder's landmark achievement was largely overshadowed by the team's disappointing results.

NATIONAL TEAM RESULTS 2010/11

11/8/10	Russia	A	St Petersburg	0-1	
3/9/10	England (ECQ)	A	Wembley	0-4	
7/9/10	Montenegro (ECQ)	H	Sofia	0-1	
8/10/10	Wales (ECQ)	A	Cardiff	1-0	*Popov (48)*
12/10/10	Saudi Arabia	N	Istanbul (TUR)	2-0	*Rangelov (39), Domovchiyski (45)*
17/11/10	Serbia	H	Sofia	0-1	
9/2/11	Estonia	N	Antalya (TUR)	2-2	*Popov (40p, 83p)*
26/3/11	Switzerland (ECQ)	H	Sofia	0-0	
29/3/11	Cyprus	A	Larnaca	1-0	*Petrov M. (35)*
4/6/11	Montenegro (ECQ)	A	Podgorica	1-1	*Popov (66)*

BULGARIA

NATIONAL TEAM APPEARANCES 2010/11

Coach –Stanimir STOILOV /(23/9/10) Lothar MATTHÄUS (GER)	13/2/67 21/3/61		Rus	ENG	MNE	WAL	Ksa	Srb	Est	SUI	Cyp	MNE	Caps	Goals
Nikolay MIHAYLOV	28/6/88	Twente (NED)	G	G	G	G		G	G70	G		G	15	-
Stanislav MANOLEV	16/12/85	PSV (NED)	D	D65					D	M	M64	M	17	-
Ilian STOYANOV	20/1/77	Sanfrecce (JPN)	D	D	D								40	-
Ivan IVANOV	25/2/88	Alania (RUS)	D	D	D	D	D	D	D	D	D	D	18	-
Zhivko MILANOV	15/7/84	Vaslui (ROU)	D	D	D46			D65					20	-
Chavdar YANKOV	29/3/84	Metalurh Donetsk (UKR)	M85											
		/Rostov (RUS)		M		s87	M		M66			s46	48	5
Stiliyan PETROV	5/7/79	Aston Villa (ENG)	M89	M	M	M			M	M	M	M46	102	8
Stanislav ANGELOV	12/4/78	Steaua (ROU)	M61	M	M		M55							
		/Anorthosis (CYP)							D46	s85			39	1
Martin PETROV	15/1/79	Bolton (ENG)	M75	M	M	M		M66			M90	M88	89	19
Ivelin POPOV	26/10/87	Litex	A55											
		/Gaziantepspor (TUR)		A79	A	A	M83	A	A	A85		A	24	7
Valeri BOJINOV	15/2/86	Parma (ITA)	A46	A63	s46			A53					33	5
Dimitar RANGELOV	9/2/83	Dortmund (GER)	s46											
		/M. Tel-Aviv (ISR)		s63	A46	s72	A76	M30	A46				22	2
Martin KAMBUROV	13/10/80	Dalian Shide (CHN)	s55										16	-
Stanislav GENCHEV	20/3/81	Vaslui (ROU)	s61		s46			M					6	1
Ilian MITSANSKI	20/12/85	Kaiserslautern (GER)	s75										1	-
Nikolay DIMITROV	15/10/87	Kasımpaşa (TUR)	s85				M	s30	s46		s64		7	-
Zahari SIRAKOV	8/10/77	Amkar (RUS)	s89										4	-
Veselin MINEV	14/10/80	Levski		s65	D				s89				8	-
Georgi PEEV	11/3/79	Amkar (RUS)		s79	M66	M72	s83						53	-
Valeri DOMOVCHIYSKI	5/10/86	Hertha (GER)			s66		A						11	2
Nikolay BODUROV	30/5/86	Litex				D	s90	s65	s46			D	5	-
Valentin ILIEV	11/8/80	Univ Craiova (ROU)				D37							19	-
Petar ZANEV	18/10/85	Litex				D	D	D	D89	D	D	D	14	-
Blagoy GEORGIEV	21/12/81	Terek (RUS)				M	s55		M86	M			46	5
Dimitar MAKRIEV	7/1/84	Ashdod (ISR)				A87	s76	s53	A	A52			8	1
Pavel VIDANOV	8/1/88	CSKA Sofia				s37	D90						4	-
Vladislav STOYANOV	8/6/87	Sheriff (MDA)					G				G		2	-
Yordan MILIEV	5/10/87	Levski					D	D					3	-
Hristo YANEV	4/5/79	Litex						M	s66		M	M84	11	3
Vladimir GADZHEV	18/7/87	Levski						s66			M		2	-
Boyan PEIKOV	1/5/84	Lokomotov Sofia							s70				1	-
Tsvetan GENKOV	8/2/84	Wisła Kraków (POL)							s86	s52	A	s84	15	-
Ivan BANDALOVSKI	23/11/86	CSKA Sofia								D	D	D	5	-
Kostadin STOYANOV	26/5/86	CSKA Sofia								D	D		5	-
Spas DELEV	22/9/89	CSKA Sofia								M81	s90	s88	3	-
Zdravko LAZAROV	20/2/76	Lokomotiv Plovdiv								s81			31	3
MARQUINHOS	20/8/82	CSKA Sofia										M	1	-

CLUB-BY-CLUB

PFC AKADEMIK SOFIA

Coach – Boris Angelov; (28/2/11) Vasil Ivanski

Founded – 1947

Stadium – Slavia (25,000)

10				
	Chernomorets	a	0-0	
	Vidima-Rakovski	h	1-2	*Redovski*
/8	Cherno More	a	0-1	
/8	Sliven	h	0-1	
8	Litex	a	0-2	
/9	Slavia	h	0-4	
/9	Montana	a	2-2	*Ivanov, Redovski (p)*
/9	Lokomotiv Sofia	h	2-3	*Redovski, Petrov*
0	Kaliakra	a	1-0	*Petrov*
/10	Minior	h	2-0	*Redovski, Petrov (p)*
/10	Beroe	a	0-1	
/10	Pirin	h	1-0	*Dimitrov*
1	Lokomotiv Plovdiv	a	0-3	
/11	Levski	a	0-1	
/11	CSKA	h	1-1	*Mbemba*
11				
/2	Chernomorets	h	1-1	*Vasilev A.*
3	Vidima-Rakovski	a	1-0	*Sakaliev*
/3	Cherno More	h	0-0	
/3	Sliven	a	0-3	
4	Litex	h	0-3	
/4	Slavia	a	0-2	
/4	Montana	h	1-0	*Marcos Bonfim*
3/4	Lokomotiv Sofia	a	0-2	
/4	Kaliakra	h	0-1	
5	Minior	a	0-1	
5	Beroe	h	1-3	*Malindi*
/5	Pirin	a	0-6	
3/5	Lokomotiv Plovdiv	h	1-2	*Vasilev A.*
/5	Levski	h	0-3	
3/5	CSKA	a	1-3	*Vasilev A.*

o	Name	Nat	DoB	Pos	Aps	(s)	Gls
	Samir AESS		24/12/90	M	5	(8)	
7	Mihail ALEKSANDROV		11/6/89	A	7	(4)	
	Nikola ASENOV		15/2/83	D	12	(1)	
	Mirolslav BUDINOV		23/1/86	A	4		
	Nikolay CHAVDAROV		22/4/76	G	3		
	Ivailo DIMITROV		26/3/89	M	9	(8)	1
8	Kiril DINCHEV		8/5/89	D	15	(8)	
	ENDER Günlü	FRA	9/5/84	M	4	(3)	
4	GÜVEN Güneri	TUR	22/9/87	M	5	(1)	
5	Mustafa HABIB		17/1/92	M		(2)	
6	Ivan IVANOV		8/12/89	D	29		1
	Peter KYUMYURDZHIEV		15/12/81	D	25		
	Enco MALINDI	ALB	15/1/87	A	9	(1)	1
	Luchezar MANCHEV		23/1/89	M		(3)	
0	MARCOS da Silva BONFIM	BRA	1/2/88	M	19	(2)	1
1	Pierre MBEMBA	BEL	23/7/88	D	26		1
3	Emil MIHAYLOV		5/5/88	G	12		
4	Lyuben NIKOLOV		8/9/89	D	10	(3)	
3	Yulian PETKOV		20/6/79	D	23	(1)	
9	Mihail PETROV		1/7/86	M	24	(3)	3
2	Troyan RADULOV		8/5/74	M		(2)	
5	Nikola RADULOVIĆ	SRB	23/2/93	M		(5)	
	Ivan REDOVSKI		10/9/81	A	19	(4)	4
3	Stoiko SAKALIEV		25/3/79	A	15	(3)	1
	Martin SECHKOV		17/11/86	D	14		
	Edis SELIMINSKI		6/9/90	D		(12)	
2	SÉRGIO José ORGANISTA Aguiar	POR	26/8/84	M	3	(6)	
33	Bozhidar STOICHEV		5/1/91	G	9	(1)	
85	Borislav STOYANOV		13/2/85	G	6		
13	Kristiyan UZUNOV		4/2/89	D	1		
10	Asparuh VASILEV		14/11/81	M	19	(5)	3
15	Ivailo VASILEV		2/8/83	D	2	(3)	
17	Kristiyan VELINOV		10/11/91	D	1		

PFC BEROE STARA ZAGORA

Coach – Ilian Iliev

Founded – 1916

Stadium – Beroe (15,000)

MAJOR HONOURS: Bulgarian League – (1) 1986; Bulgarian Cup – (1) 2010.

2010				
8/8	Litex	h	1-1	*Zlatinov*
15/8	Slavia	a	2-1	*og (Petkov), Bachev*
21/8	Montana	h	2-1	*Dimitrov, Zlatinov*
29/8	Lokomotiv Sofia	a	0-3	
4/9	Sliven	a	1-0	*Zlatinov*
11/9	Kaliakra	h	2-0	*Yordanov, Zlatinov*
18/9	Minior	a	0-2	
27/9	Levski	a	1-2	*Dimitrov*
2/10	Pirin	h	0-0	
16/10	Lokomotiv Plovdiv	a	1-1	*Zhekov*
23/10	Akademik	h	1-0	*Bachev*
30/10	CSKA	a	2-3	*Velev, Yordanov*
6/11	Chernomorets	h	0-0	
13/11	Vidima-Rakovski	a	2-1	*Zlatinov, Stankov*
27/11	Cherno More	h	0-0	
2011				
26/2	Sliven	h	1-0	Zlatinov
7/3	Litex	a	0-4	
13/3	Slavia	h	2-1	*Hristov, Yamukov*
19/3	Montana	a	1-2	*Hristov*
3/4	Lokomotiv Sofia	h	1-0	*og (Varbanov)*
9/4	Kaliakra	a	2-2	*Tanev, Bachev*
16/4	Minior	h	2-0	*Yordanov, Dimitrov*
24/4	Levski	h	2-3	*Yordanov, Zlatinov (p)*
30/4	Pirin	a	0-2	
3/5	Lokomotiv Plovdiv	h	1-0	*Hristov*
8/5	Akademik	a	3-1	*Dimitrov, Zlatinov, Romário*
15/5	CSKA	h	0-2	
18/5	Chernomorets	a	2-0	*Mechev, Zlatinov*
21/5	Vidima-Rakovski	h	1-1	*Zlatinov*
28/5	Cherno More	a	0-1	

No	Name	Nat	DoB	Pos	Aps	(s)	Gls
27	Atanas APOSTOLOV		11/3/89	A	3	(3)	
24	Stanislav BACHEV		3/1/78	D	26	(1)	3
6	Georgi BOZHANOV		7/10/88	M	3	(12)	
88	Petar DIMITROV		28/2/82	A	22	(2)	4
15	Georgi DINKOV		20/5/91	D	2		
5	Vanja DŽAFEROVIĆ	CRO	19/3/83	D	2	(2)	
25	Miroslav ENCHEV		8/8/91	D	6	(3)	
8	Tsvetan FILIPOV		28/8/88	M	1	(5)	
10	Dian GENCHEV		8/2/75	M	13	(3)	
29	Ivo GYUROV		31/8/92	M		(2)	
21	Todor HRISTOV		25/9/87	M	29	(1)	3
22	Karamfil ILCHEV		7/1/79	G	12		
2	Zdravko ILIEV		19/10/84	D	8		
18	Petar KOSTADINOV		1/4/78	M	17	(2)	
30	Pavel KOVACHEV		27/7/87	D	5	(1)	
44	Simeon MECHEV		16/2/90	M	3	(9)	1
29	Simeon MINCHEV		28/6/82	M		(2)	
11	Stoicho MLADENOV		27/8/85	A	4	(5)	
28	Veselin PENEV		11/8/82	D	24		

No	Name	Nat	DoB	Pos	Aps	(s)	Gls
32	ROMÁRIO da Silva Resende	BRA	3/12/90	A	3	(2)	1
33	Teodor SKORCHEV		4/9/86	G	11		
9	Viktor SOFRONIEV		4/4/81	M	2		
20	Nikolay STANKOV		11/12/84	M	4	(7)	1
71	Milen TANEV		4/3/87	M	7	(2)	1
1	Martin TEMENLIEV		7/9/85	G	7		
3	Todor TODOROV		28/11/82	D	9	(1)	
23	Alexander TOMASH		2/9/78	D	27		
16	Stefan VELEV		2/5/89	M	24	(4)	1
27	Vladislav YAMUKOV		22/3/80	D	11		1
15	Ivan YANCHEV		20/3/88	A		(3)	
14	Evgeni YORDANOV		4/2/78	A	16	(9)	4
7	Slavi ZHEKOV		21/8/76	M	8	(2)	1
19	Vladislav ZLATINOV		23/3/83	A	21	(8)	10

PFC CHERNO MORE VARNA

Coach –Velizar Popov; (25/10/10) Stefan Genov

Founded – 1945

Stadium – Ticha (8,000)

2010				
31/7	Pirin	h	2-1	*Tiago, Atanasov*
7/8	Lokomotiv Plovdiv	a	0-2	
14/8	Akademik	h	1-0	*Yurukov*
22/8	CSKA	a	0-1	
28/8	Chernomorets	h	0-1	
11/9	Vidima-Rakovski	a	1-0	*Iliev*
20/9	Levski	h	2-3	*Bozhilov, Iliev*
26/9	Sliven	h	3-0	*og (Ivanov), Yurukov, Dyakov*
2/10	Litex	a	1-3	*Dimov*
17/10	Slavia	h	3-2	*Georgiev, Iliev, Alexandrov A.E.*
23/10	Montana	a	0-4	
31/10	Lokomotiv Sofia	h	1-0	*Jardel*
7/11	Kaliakra	a	0-4	
14/11	Minior	h	3-0	*Tiago, Ratnikov, Nikolov*
27/11	Beroe	a	0-0	
2011				
26/2	Pirin	a	1-0	*Bozhilov*
6/3	Lokomotiv Plovdiv	h	1-1	*Bozhilov*
12/3	Akademik	a	0-0	
20/3	CSKA	h	1-0	*Atanasov*
1/4	Chernomorets	a	2-1	*Bozhilov, Iliev (p)*
9/4	Vidima-Rakovski	h	5-0	*Iliev, Atanasov 2, Ratnikov, Lazarov*
17/4	Levski	a	0-1	
25/4	Sliven	a	3-1	*og (Georgiev S.), Iliev 2*
30/4	Litex	h	0-1	
4/5	Slavia	a	1-0	*Kolev R.*
8/5	Montana	h	0-0	
14/5	Lokomotiv Sofia	a	1-1	*Nikolov*
18/5	Kaliakra	h	2-0	*Iliev (p), Nikolov*
21/5	Minior	a	1-1	*Kaptiev*
28/5	Beroe	h	1-0	*Iliev*

No	Name	Nat	DoB	Pos	Aps	(s)	Gls
3	ADEMAR José Tavares JÚNIOR	BRA	20/9/80	D	19	(2)	
15	Alexander Dragomirov ALEXANDROV		13/4/86	D	23		
25	Alexander Emilov ALEXANDROV		30/7/86	D	27		1
17	Yancho ANDREEV		8/1/90	M	1	(2)	
8	Doncho ATANASOV		2/4/83	M	19	(2)	4
4	Radoslav BACHEV		9/4/81	D	3	(2)	
14	Georgi BOZHILOV		12/2/87	A	24	(4)	4
9	Mirolslav BUDINOV		23/1/86	A		(3)	
5	Samuel Almeida CAMAZZOLA	BRA	30/8/82	M	13	(1)	
1	Petar DENCHEV		16/3/89	G	4	(2)	
27	Daniel DIMOV		21/1/89	M	15		1
5	Nikolay DOMAKINOV		11/7/80	D	2		
6	Tanko DYAKOV		18/8/84	D	28		1
28	ELIdiano MARQUES Lima	BRA	14/3/82	D	6	(2)	
23	Daniel GEORGIEV		6/11/82	M	21	(4)	1
21	Georgi ILIEV		5/9/81	M	23	(3)	9
16	Mário JARDEL de Almeida Ribeiro	BRA	18/9/73	A		(8)	1
13	Iliyan KAPITANOV		25/1/92	M	1	(1)	
77	Vladimir KAPTIEV		4/7/87	A	1	(6)	1
55	Rosen KOLEV		4/7/90	D	7	(1)	1
11	Todor KOLEV		22/9/89	A	1	(7)	
20	Mihail LAZAROV		31/8/80	D	1	(2)	1
18	Viktor MITEV		15/2/92	M		(1)	
90	Rumen NIKOLOV		5/2/90	D	4	(13)	3
24	Dimitar PETKOV		24/8/87	M	16	(5)	
26	Ilko PIRGOV		23/5/86	G	26		
27	Daniil RATNIKOV	EST	10/2/88	M	10	(6)	2
7	Stanislav STOYANOV		10/9/76	M	4	(6)	
2	Vasil TACHEV		7/1/92	A		(1)	
12	Marco TIAGO Faustino	BRA	23/3/84	D	19	(3)	2
77	Yordan YURUKOV		2/10/83	M	12	(1)	2

PSFC CHERNOMORETS BURGAS

Coach – Krassimir Balakov; (23/12/10) Anton Velkov; (21/3/11) Georgi Vasilev

Founded – 2005

Stadium – Lazur (18,000)

2010				
2/8	Akademik	h	0-0	
8/8	CSKA	a	2-1	*Hajri, Pedrinha*
15/8	Levski	h	2-1	*Andonov, Ricardo André*
21/8	Vidima-Rakovski	h	1-0	*Fernández*
28/8	Cherno More	a	1-0	*Pedrinha*
13/9	Sliven	h	0-0	
18/9	Litex	a	0-0	
27/9	Slavia Sofia	h	2-1	*og (Dimitrov), Hajri*
3/10	Montana	a	0-0	
18/10	Lokomotiv Sofia	h	2-1	*Hajri, Mouithys*
22/10	Kaliakra	a	1-1	*Koïta*
1/11	Minior	h	0-0	
6/11	Beroe	a	0-0	
15/11	Pirin	h	1-0	*Fernández*
28/11	Lokomotiv Plovdiv	a	0-2	
2011				
26/2	Akademik	a	1-1	*Andonov*
5/3	CSKA	h	0-4	
12/3	Levski	a	0-1	
19/3	Vidima-Rakovski	a	0-3	
1/4	Cherno More	h	1-2	*Hajri*
11/4	Sliven	a	0-0	
18/4	Litex	h	0-1	
25/4	Slavia Sofia	a	1-0	*Bragança (p)*
2/5	Montana	h	0-1	
5/5	Lokomotiv Sofia	a	1-2	*Hajri*
9/5	Kaliakra	h	0-1	
14/5	Minior	a	1-0	*Bragança*
18/5	Beroe	h	0-2	
21/5	Pirin	a	1-1	*Andonov*
28/5	Lokomotiv Plovdiv	h	1-2	*Bragança (p)*

No	Name	Nat	DoB	Pos	Aps	(s)	Gls
77	Georgi ANDONOV		28/6/83	A	23	(3)	3
3	ANTÓNIO Carlos dos Santos	BRA	3/10/79	M	12		
3	Ventsislav BONEV		8/5/80	D	6	(4)	
28	Pascal BOREL	GER	26/9/78	G	20		
83	Jaime Celestino Dias BRAGANÇA	POR	9/6/83	M	10		3
20	Michele CRUCIANI	ITA	4/5/86	M	1	(1)	

No	Name	Nat	DoB	Pos	Aps	(s)	Gls
	Nik DASHEV		13/10/91	G	1		
	Kostadin DYAKOV		22/8/85	D	2	(4)	
	Trayan DYANKOV		21/6/76	D	26	(1)	
	Adrián FERNÁNDEZ	ARG	28/11/80	A	11	(3)	2
	Venelin FILIPOV		10/10/89	D	6	(3)	
	Héctor GONZÁLEZ	VEN	11/4/77	M	1	(2)	
	Enis HAJRI	TUN	6/3/83	M	26	(1)	5
	Moussa KOÏTA	FRA	19/11/82	A	11	(8)	1
	Stoyan KOLEV		3/2/76	G	9		
	Branimir KOSTADINOV		4/3/89	M	1	(2)	
	Plamen KRUMOV		23/1/75	A	10	(12)	
	MÁRCIO Nuno Ornelas ABREU	POR	25/4/80	M	14	(1)	
	Matthias MORYS	GER	3/7/87	M		(8)	
	Dyzaiss-Lys MOUITHYS	CGO	4/7/85	A	2	(7)	1
	Savio Magala NSEREKO	GER	27/7/89	A	6	(4)	
	Todor PALANKOV		13/1/84	M	22	(2)	
	Pedro Ricardo Marques Pereira Monteiro "PEDRINHA"	POR	3/5/78	M	9	(1)	2
7	Yani PEHLIVANOV		28/3/88	M	2	(4)	
	Alberto QUADRI	ITA	9/1/83	M	2	(3)	
4	RICARDO ANDRÉ Duarte Pires	POR	24/12/82	M	25	(2)	1
3	Jochen SEITZ	GER	11/10/76	D	19	(1)	
	Orlin STAROKIN		8/1/87	D	30		
6	Georgi TERZIEV		18/4/92	D	9	(1)	
3	Martin TOSHEV		15/8/90	A	7	(8)	
2	Tsvetomir TSONKOV		25/6/81	M	7	(1)	

PFC CSKA SOFIA

Coach – Pavel Dochev; (17/8/10) Gjore Jovanovski (MKD); (19/10/10) Milen Radukanov

Founded – 1948

Stadium – Bulgarska Armia (22,000) & Vasil Levski (43,230)

MAJOR HONOURS: Bulgarian League – (31) 1948, 1951, 1952, 1954, 1955, 1956, 1957, 1958, 1959, 1960, 1961, 1962, 1966, 1969, 1971, 1972, 1973, 1975, 1976, 1980, 1981, 1982, 1983, 1987, 1989, 1990, 1992, 1997, 2003, 2005, 2008; Bulgarian Cup – (20) 1951, 1954, 1955, 1961, 1965, 1969, 1972, 1973, 1974 (as Soviet Army Cup), 1981, 1983, 1985, 1987, 1988, 1989, 1993, 1997, 1999, 2006, 2011.

2010				
/8	Levski	h	0-1	
/8	Chernomorets	h	1-2	*Trifonov*
3/8	Vidima-Rakovski	a	2-2	*Delev, Marquinhos*
2/8	Cherno More	h	1-0	*Marquinhos*
9/8	Sliven	a	3-1	*Aquaro, Tonev, Sheridan*
1/9	Litex	h	1-1	*Marquinhos*
9/9	Slavia	a	0-1	
5/9	Montana	h	2-0	*Sheridan 2*
/10	Lokomotiv Sofia	a	2-2	*Marquinhos 2 (1p)*
17/10	Kaliakra	h	0-0	
23/10	Minior	a	4-2	*Marquinhos 2, Delev, Aquaro*
30/10	Beroe	h	3-2	*Delev 2, Marquinhos*
7/11	Pirin	a	1-0	*Delev*
14/11	Lokomotiv Plovdiv	h	1-0	*Marquinhos*
28/11	Akademik	a	1-1	*Michel*
2011				
26/2	Levski	a	3-1	*Michel 2, Popov*
5/3	Chernomorets	a	4-0	*Michel 2, Delev 2*
13/3	Vidima-Rakovski	h	1-0	*Delev*
20/3	Cherno More	a	0-1	
1/4	Sliven	h	2-0	*Delev 2*
10/4	Litex	a	0-0	
16/4	Slavia	h	1-0	*Nelson*
25/4	Montana	a	4-1	*Nelson, Aquaro, Michel, Tonev*
30/4	Lokomotiv Sofia	h	3-1	*Delev, Michel, Stoyanov K.*
4/5	Kaliakra	a	3-0	*Gargorov, Nelson, Galchev*
7/5	Minior	h	2-0	*Michel 2*
15/5	Beroe	a	2-0	*Michel, Delev*
18/5	Pirin	h	2-2	*Trifonov, Popov*
21/5	Lokomotiv Plovdiv	a	1-4	*Gargorov*
28/5	Akademik	h	3-1	*Kostov, Sheridan, Delev*

No	Name	Nat	DoB	Pos	Aps	(s)	Gls
6	Giuseppe AQUARO	ITA	21/5/83	D	19		3
11	Ivan BANDALOVSKI		23/11/86	D	13	(1)	
1	Zdravko CHAVDAROV		28/5/80	G	2		
27	Martin DECHEV		12/4/90	D	5		
7	Spas DELEV		22/9/89	A	24	(2)	13
22	Marco ESPOSITO	ITA	8/2/80	D	2	(1)	
18	Boris GALCHEV		31/10/83	M	19	(3)	1
23	Emil GARGOROV		15/2/81	M	6	(6)	2
15	Elliot GRANDIN	FRA	17/10/87	A	1		
30	Fabrizio GRILLO	ITA	2/2/87	D	3		
14	Dimitar ILIEV		25/9/88	A	2	(3)	
12	Ivan KARADZHOV		12/6/89	G	17		
3	Tomislav KOSTADINOV		15/3/91	A		(5)	
14	Stanislav KOSTOV		2/10/91	M	2	(1)	1
26	Raïs M'BOLHI	ALG	25/4/86	G	9		
12	Blagoy MAKENDZHIEV		11/7/88	G	2		
28	Marcos Antônio Malachias Júnior "MARQUINHOS"		20/8/82	M	24	(4)	9
32	MICHEL Platini Ferreira Mesquita	BRA	8/9/83	A	15	(3)	10
25	Yordan MINEV		14/10/80	D	6		
29	Gregory NELSON	NED	31/1/88	M	17	(6)	3
16	Apostol POPOV		22/12/82	D	16	(4)	2
10	RUI MIGUEL Marinho Reis	POR	30/1/84	M	1		
17	Chetin SADULA		16/6/87	A	3	(2)	
9	Dormushali SAIDHODZHA		16/5/85	A		(5)	
26	Cillian SHERIDAN	IRL	23/12/89	A	9	(7)	4
4	Kostadin STOYANOV		26/5/86	D	17		1
22	Peta STOYANOV		15/8/85	M	2	(1)	
16	Christian TIBONI	ITA	6/4/88	A	1	(3)	
23	William Kwabena TIERO	GHA	3/12/80	M	3	(1)	
24	Alexander TONEV		3/2/90	M	17	(6)	2
10	Lucas Ezequiel TRECARICHI	ARG	12/2/91	M	1	(4)	
8	Rumen TRIFONOV		21/2/85	M	27	(2)	2
2	Pavel VIDANOV		8/1/88	D	12		
5	Todor YANCHEV		19/5/76	M	27	(1)	
21	Kosta YANEV		27/4/83	M	6	(11)	
27	Stanko YOVCHEV		15/4/88	A		(5)	

PFC KALIAKRA KAVARNA

Coach – Filip Filipov; (6/10/10) Antoni Zdravkov

Founded – 1922

Stadium – Kavarna (5,000)

2010				
31/7	Slavia	a	1-0	*Filipov*
7/8	Montana	h	0-0	
16/8	Lokomotiv Sofia	a	0-4	
22/8	Levski	a	0-3	
4/9	Minior	h	2-1	*Petkov 2*
11/9	Beroe	a	0-2	
18/9	Pirin	h	0-0	
25/9	Lokomotiv Plovdiv	a	0-5	
3/10	Akademik	h	0-1	
17/10	CSKA	a	0-0	
22/10	Chernomorets	h	1-1	*Kichukov*
30/10	Vidima-Rakovski	a	0-1	
7/11	Cherno More	h	4-0	*Sadula 2, Petkov, Markov*
13/11	Sliven	a	1-0	*Filipov*
28/11	Litex	h	0-1	
2011				
27/2	Slavia	h	0-1	
5/3	Montana	a	2-3	*Petkov, Tawiah*
14/3	Lokomotiv Sofia	h	0-1	

19/3	Levski	h	0-3	*(w/o)*
2/4	Minior	a	0-1	
9/4	Beroe	h	2-2	*Markov, Raichev*
16/4	Pirin	a	0-1	
25/4	Lokomotiv Plovdiv	h	1-3	*Dimitrov D.*
30/4	Akademik	a	1-0	*Stanchev*
4/5	CSKA	h	0-3	
9/5	Chernomorets	a	1-0	*Tawiah*
15/5	Vidima-Rakovski	h	1-0	*Dimitrov D.*
18/5	Cherno More	a	0-2	
21/5	Sliven	h	2-1	*Petkov, Raichev*
28/5	Litex	a	0-0	

No	Name	Nat	DoB	Pos	Aps	(s)	Gls
30	Luchezar BALTANOV		11/7/88	M	7	(1)	
30	Milen BONEV		1/7/86	M	5	(4)	
5	Anton DIMITROV		31/10/79	D	22	(1)	
4	Detelin DIMITROV		17/1/83	D	28		2
1	Tsvetan DIMITROV		10/2/87	G	7		
3	Martin DIMOV		1/3/86	D	24	(3)	
31	Georgi FILIPOV		12/8/85	A	8	(11)	2
29	Yordan GOSPODINOV		15/6/78	G	22		
11	Dian KATELIEV		25/3/80	M	7	(4)	
17	Georgi KICHUKOV		8/4/76	M	12	(5)	1
7	Marko MARKOV		11/9/81	M	15	(5)	2
27	Alexander MLADENOV		25/6/82	A	3	(2)	
9	Ivan PETKOV		22/1/85	A	15	(9)	5
15	Anton PETROV		11/3/85	D	26		
10	Nikolay PETROV		30/9/88	M	21	(4)	
77	Svetoslav PETROV		12/2/78	M	8		
8	Ivailo RADENTSOV		29/5/83	M	27	(2)	
14	Ivan RAICHEV		28/2/77	D	12	(2)	2
18	Desislav RUSEV		27/4/79	A	6	(7)	
25	Alexander SABEV		9/4/88	D	3	(2)	
22	Chetin SADULA		16/6/87	A	15		2
16	Daniel SHMEDIN		7/5/91	A	1	(2)	
23	Georgi STANCHEV		27/5/85	A	17	(7)	1
5	Stoyan STEFANOV		28/6/83	D	1	(4)	
18	Delcho STOILOV		31/12/81	M	1	(8)	
6	Michael TAWIAH	GHA	1/12/90	M	6	(5)	2
7	Ivan ZDRAVKOV		25/6/91	D		(1)	

PFC LEVSKI SOFIA

Coach – Yasen Petrov

Founded – 1914

Stadium – Georgi Asparuhov (29,000)

MAJOR HONOURS: Bulgarian League – (26) 1933, 1937, 1942, 1946, 1947, 1949, 1950, 1953, 1965, 1968, 1970, 1974, 1977, 1979, 1984, 1985, 1988, 1993, 1994, 1995, 2000, 2001, 2002, 2006, 2007, 2009; Bulgarian Cup – (26) 1942 (as Tsar's Cup), 1946, 1947, 1949, 1950, 1956, 1957, 1959, 1967, 1970, 1971, 1976, 1977, 1979 (as Soviet Army Cup), 1982, 1984, 1986, 1991, 1992, 1994, 1998, 2000, 2002, 2003, 2005, 2007.

2010				
1/8	CSKA	a	1-0	*Dembélé*
9/8	Lokomotiv Sofia	h	3-1	*Dembélé 3 (1p)*
15/8	Chernomorets	a	1-2	*Alexandrov*
22/8	Kaliakra	h	3-0	*og (Petrov A.), Alexandrov (p), Isa*
30/8	Vidima-Rakovski	a	2-1	*Dembélé (p), Tasevski*
12/9	Minior	h	4-0	*Joãozinho, Dembélé 3 (1p)*
20/9	Cherno More	a	3-2	*Mladenov, Miliev, Dembélé (p)*
27/9	Beroe	h	2-1	*Dembélé, Yovov*
4/10	Sliven	a	1-1	*Tasevski*
16/10	Pirin	h	4-1	*Dembélé 3, Ognyanov*
25/10	Litex	a	1-2	*Dembélé*
30/10	Lokomotiv Plovdiv	h	1-2	*Ognyanov*
7/11	Slavia	a	2-2	*Greene, Joãozinho (p)*
13/11	Akademik	h	1-0	*Isa*
27/11	Montana	a	3-0	*Mladenov, Dembélé 2*

2011				
26/2	CSKA	h	1-3	*og (Stoyanov K.)*
6/3	Lokomotiv Sofia	a	2-0	*Dembélé, og (Dimitrov)*
12/3	Chernomorets	h	1-0	*Tasevski*
19/3	Kaliakra	a	3-0	*(w/o)*
2/4	Vidima-Rakovski	h	2-0	*Dembélé (p), Isa*
10/4	Minior	a	0-0	
17/4	Cherno More	h	1-0	*Ivanov*
24/4	Beroe	a	3-2	*Yovov, Alexandrov, Yulu-Matondo*
1/5	Sliven	h	5-0	*Dembélé 3, Yulu-Matondo, Mladen*
4/5	Pirin	a	3-2	*Yulu-Matondo, Dembélé, Yovov*
8/5	Litex	h	2-0	*Dembélé, Yovov*
14/5	Lokomotiv Plovdiv	a	3-2	*Tasevski, Dembélé 2 (1p)*
18/5	Slavia	h	3-0	*Yovov 2, Gadzhev*
21/5	Akademik	a	3-0	*Gadzhev, Mladenov 2*
28/5	Montana	h	3-0	*Minev, Dembélé, Yovov*

No	Name	Nat	DoB	Pos	Aps	(s)	Gls
85	Kiril AKALSKI		17/10/85	G	3		
7	Alexander Yordanov ALEXANDROV		19/1/75	M	5	(12)	3
30	Luchezar BALTANOV		11/7/88	M	1	(2)	
15	Chakib BENZOUKANE	MAR	7/8/86	D	6		
57	Todor CHAVORSKI		30/3/93	D		(1)	
9	Garra DEMBÉLÉ	MLI	21/2/86	A	23	(1)	26
8	Daniel DIMOV		21/1/89	M	3	(8)	
45	Vladimir GADZHEV		18/7/87	M	22	(1)	2
20	Ivan GORANOV		10/6/92	A		(2)	
3	Serginho GREENE	NED	24/6/82	M	23	(1)	1
18	Georgi HRISTOV		10/1/85	A		(1)	
23	Plamen ILIEV		30/11/91	G	13		
29	Ismail ISA Mustafa		26/6/89	A	11	(8)	3
5	Ivo IVANOV		11/3/85	D	19	(1)	1
20	João Natailton Ramos dos Santos "JOÃOZINHO"	BRA	25/12/88	M	14	(1)	2
28	Alexander KIROV		25/10/90	A	5	(9)	
55	Yordan MILIEV		5/10/87	D	26		1
14	Veselin MINEV		14/10/80	D	23	(1)	1
12	Bozhidar MITREV		31/3/87	G	7		
17	Daniel MLADENOV		25/5/87	M	19	(9)	5
2	Dustley MULDER	NED	27/1/85	D	22		
16	Mariyan OGNYANOV		30/7/88	M	13	(9)	2
1	Georgi PETKOV		14/4/76	G	6		
26	Kalin SHTARKOV		20/5/84	D	1		
23	Andwélé SLORY	NED	27/9/82	M	1	(4)	
4	Stefan STANCHEV		26/4/89	D	6	(1)	
22	Darko TASEVSKI	MKD	20/5/84	M	19	(4)	4
6	Michael TAWIAH	GHA	1/12/90	M		(2)	
32	Dimitar TELKIYSKI		5/5/77	M		(1)	
11	Elin TOPUZAKOV		5/2/77	D		(1)	
25	Borislav TSONEV		29/4/95	M		(1)	
30	Radoslav TSONEV		29/4/95	M		(1)	
11	Marko VIDOVIĆ	MNE	3/6/88	D	7		
10	Hristo YOVOV		4/11/77	A	15	(1)	7
6	Jeanvion YULU-MATONDO	BEL	5/1/86	M	6	(2)	3

PFC LITEX LOVECH

Coach – Angel Chervenkov; (8/8/10) Petko Petkov; (2/9/10) Luboslav Penev

Founded – 1921

Stadium – Gradski (7,000)

MAJOR HONOURS: Bulgarian League – (4) 1998, 1999, 2010, 2011; Bulgarian Cup – (4) 2001, 2004, 2008, 2009.

2010				
31/7	Minior	h	2-1	*Bratu, Petkov (p)*
8/8	Beroe	a	1-1	*Todorov*
15/8	Pirin	h	2-1	*Milanov G., Bodurov*
22/8	Lokomotiv Plovdiv	a	2-2	*Niflore, Sandrinho*

/8	Akademik	h	2-0	*Wellington, Niflore*
/9	CSKA	a	1-1	*Todorov*
/9	Chernomorets	h	0-0	
/9	Vidima-Rakovski	a	3-0	*Niflore 2, Todorov*
10	Cherno More	h	3-1	*Yanev, Bodurov, Bratu (p)*
/10	Sliven	a	1-0	*Niflore (p)*
5/10	Levski	h	2-1	*Yanev, Todorov*
/10	Slavia	h	2-0	*Todorov, Barthe*
11	Montana	a	2-0	*Tsvetanov, Niflore*
3/11	Lokomotiv Sofia	h	1-0	*Doka Madureira*
3/11	Kaliakra	a	1-0	*Doka Madureira*
011				
7/2	Minior	a	3-0	*Doka Madureira 2, Diouf*
3	Beroe	h	4-0	*Doka Madureira 3, Đermanovič*
2/3	Pirin	a	2-1	*Doka Madureira, Diouf*
)/3	Lokomotiv Plovdiv	h	1-0	*Đermanovič*
4	Akademik	a	3-0	*og (Kyumyurdzhiev), Todorov, Milanov G.*
)/4	CSKA	h	0-0	
3/4	Chernomorets	a	1-0	*Yanev*
4/4	Vidima-Rakovski	h	4-0	*Yanev 2, Todorov (p), Doka Madureira*
0/4	Cherno More	a	1-0	*Milanov G.*
5	Sliven	h	4-0	*Barthe, Milanov G., Tsvetanov, Đermanovič*
5	Levski	a	0-2	
3/5	Slavia	a	1-0	*og (Deniran V.)*
8/5	Montana	h	4-1	*Doka Madureira 2, Barthe, Zanev*
1/5	Lokomotiv Sofia	a	3-1	*Tsvetanov, Todorov, Doka Madureira*
8/5	Kaliakra	h	0-0	

lo	Name	Nat	DoB	Pos	Aps	(s)	Gls
0	Evgeni ALEKSANDROV		14/6/88	G	1		
	Alexandre BARTHE	FRA	5/3/86	D	16	(5)	3
	Džemal BERBEROVIĆ	BIH	15/11/81	D	21	(2)	
3	Nikolay BODUROV		30/5/86	D	25		2
1	Florin Daniel BRATU	ROU	2/1/80	A	4	(3)	2
4	Dejan ĐERMANOVIČ	SVN	17/6/88	A	4	(8)	3
1	Pape Alioune DIOUF	SEN	22/6/89	A	9	(5)	2
5	Francisco Lima da Silva "DOKA MADUREIRA"	BRA	11/2/84	M	21	(1)	12
1	Rodrigo José GALATTO	BRA	10/3/83	G	1		
	Uroš GOLUBOVIĆ	SRB	19/8/76	G	2		
23	Nebojša JELENKOVIĆ	SRB	26/5/78	M	22		
7	Georgi MILANOV		19/2/92	M	17	(9)	4
8	Iliya MILANOV		19/2/92	D	4	(3)	
19	Wilfried NIFLORE	FRA	29/4/81	A	10	(2)	6
22	Plamen NIKOLOV		12/6/85	D	23	(1)	
5	Ivailo PETKOV		4/3/76	D	4	(1)	1
71	Ivelin POPOV		26/10/87	A	3		
16	Strahil POPOV		31/8/90	M	1	(2)	
32	Rumen RUMENOV		7/6/93	M	1	(5)	
10	Alessandro Correa "SANDRINHO"	BRA	5/7/80	M	10		1
14	Simeon SLAVCHEV		25/9/93	M		(1)	
9	Svetoslav TODOROV		30/8/78	A	14	(11)	8
27	Momchil TSVETANOV		12/3/90	A	7	(15)	3
21	Alexander TSVETKOV		31/8/90	D	8	(6)	
5	Mihail VENKOV		28/7/83	D	8	(4)	
31	VINÍCIUS Barrivieira	BRA	19/6/85	G	26		
8	WELLINGTON Brito da Silva	BRA	23/7/85	M	17	(1)	1
7	Hristo YANEV		4/5/79	M	26	(1)	5
3	Petar ZANEV		18/10/85	D	25	(2)	1
8	Angel ZDRAVCHEV		10/7/94	M		(1)	

PFC LOKOMOTIV PLOVDIV 1936

Coach – Hristo Bonev; (1/10/10) Nedelcho Matushev; (24/4/11) Saša Nikolić (SRB)

Founded – 1936

Stadium – Lokomotiv (13,000)

MAJOR HONOURS: Bulgarian League – (1) 2004.

2010				
31/7	Vidima-Rakovski	a	1-1	*Bengelloun Y.*
7/8	Cherno More	h	2-0	*Carvalho 2*
14/8	Sliven	a	1-0	*Lazarov*
22/8	Litex	h	2-2	*Lazarov, Carvalho*
28/8	Slavia	a	1-2	*Lazarov*
12/9	Montana	h	4-0	*Lazarov 3 (1p), Erős*
19/9	Lokomotiv Sofia	a	0-3	
25/9	Kaliakra	h	5-0	*Raimondi, Zlatinski 2, Lazarov, Carvalho*
2/10	Minior	a	2-2	*Zlatinski, Lazarov*
16/10	Beroe	h	1-1	*Lazarov*
23/10	Pirin	a	1-1	*Abushev*
30/10	Levski	a	2-1	*Lazarov, Carvalho*
6/11	Akademik	h	3-0	*Kocev, Bengelloun Y., Carvalho*
14/11	CSKA	a	0-1	
28/11	Chernomorets	h	2-0	*Raimondi, Carvalho*
2011				
26/2	Vidima-Rakovski	h	3-0	*Zlatinski, Lazarov, Ogunsoto*
6/3	Cherno More	a	1-1	*Zlatinski (p)*
12/3	Sliven	h	3-0	*Kavdanski, Raimondi, Bengelloun Y.*
20/3	Litex	a	0-1	
2/4	Slavia	h	1-1	*Zlatinski (p)*
10/4	Montana	a	1-1	*Krachunov*
17/4	Lokomotiv Sofia	h	0-0	
25/4	Kaliakra	a	3-1	*Raimondi, Zlatinski (p), Serginho*
30/4	Minior	h	3-0	*Carvalho 2, Zlatinski*
3/5	Beroe	a	0-1	
7/5	Pirin	h	2-2	*Bengelloun Y., Erős*
14/5	Levski	h	2-3	*Carvalho, Lazarov (p)*
18/5	Akademik	a	2-1	*Lazarov (p), og (Sérgio Organista)*
21/5	CSKA	h	4-1	*Kavdanski, Rodrigues, Zlatinski 2*
28/5	Chernomorets	a	2-1	*Zlatinski, Lazarov*

No	Name	Nat	DoB	Pos	Aps	(s)	Gls
21	Rangel ABUSHEV		26/5/89	M	1	(6)	1
25	Emil ARGIROV		4/3/87	D	1	(2)	
25	Juan Manuel BARRIENTOS	ARG	4/3/82	M	1		
24	Samir BENGELLOUN	FRA	2/2/85	D	18		
5	Youness BENGELLOUN	FRA	3/1/83	D	27		4
19	Basile Salomon Pereira de CARVALHO	SEN	31/10/81	A	19	(1)	10
80	Gábor ERŐS	HUN	1/7/80	M	14	(11)	2
14	Kostadin GADZHALOV		10/7/89	D	9		
3	Valeri GEORGIEV		28/7/84	D	14	(5)	
55	Martin KAVDANSKI		13/2/87	D	16	(4)	2
17	Martin KERCHEV		22/10/82	M	4	(6)	
9	Dani KIKI		8/1/88	M	1	(13)	
29	Dragi KOCEV	MKD	25/2/87	M	13	(12)	1
66	Kiril KOTEV		18/4/82	D	2	(2)	
6	Plamen KRACHUNOV		11/1/89	D	12	(2)	1
77	Zdravko LAZAROV		20/12/76	A	29		14
13	Florian LUCCHINI	FRA	13/2/81	G	25		
4	Nenad LUKIĆ	SRB	2/9/92	M		(3)	
21	Blagomir MASTAGARKOV		12/3/92	M		(1)	
88	Patrick OGUNSOTO	NGA	19/4/84	A		(3)	1
99	Nicolás RAIMONDI	URU	5/9/84	A	13	(5)	4
2	Jérémie RODRIGUES	FRA	1/11/80	D	24	(2)	1
18	Bassilia SAKANOKO	CIV	3/6/85	A	2	(3)	
10	Sérgio Filipe Dias Ribeiro "SERGINHO"	POR	16/6/85	M	15		1
28	Todor TODOROV		9/5/82	G	5		
7	Yordan TODOROV		27/7/81	D	14		
20	Éverton Fernando Gílio "TON"	BRA	18/3/86	M	10	(3)	
24	Lyubomir VITANOV		11/5/81	M	12	(1)	
16	Hristo ZLATINSKI		22/8/81	M	29		11

BULGARIA

PFC LOKOMOTIV SOFIA

Coach – Dimitar Vasev; (15/11/10) Diyan Petkov
Founded – 1929
Stadium – Vasil Levski (43,230)
MAJOR HONOURS: Bulgarian League – (4) 1940, 1945, 1964, 1978; Bulgarian Cup – (3) 1948, 1953 (as Soviet Army Cup), 1995.

2010				
1/8	Montana	a	1-0	*Genkov*
9/8	Levski	a	1-3	*Yordanov*
16/8	Kaliakra	h	4-0	*Dafchev, Yordanov, og (Gospodinov), Romanov*
23/8	Minior	a	3-1	*Genkov, Asamoah 2*
29/8	Beroe	h	3-0	*Asamoah 2, Genkov*
11/9	Pirin	a	1-2	*Genkov (p)*
19/9	Lokomotiv Plovdiv	h	3-0	*Genkov 2 (1p), Asamoah*
25/9	Akademik	a	3-2	*Goranov, Yordanov, Genkov*
4/10	CSKA	h	2-2	*Pisarov, Genkov*
18/10	Chernomorets	a	1-2	*Pisarov*
24/10	Vidima-Rakovski	h	2-1	*Genkov, Asamoah*
31/10	Cherno More	a	0-1	
6/11	Sliven	h	3-0	*Genkov, Asamoah, Dyakov*
13/11	Litex	a	0-1	
27/11	Slavia	h	4-3	*Pisarov 2, Dyakov, Genkov*
2011				
1/3	Montana	h	2-0	*Goranov (p), Ivanov*
6/3	Levski	h	0-2	
14/3	Kaliakra	a	1-0	*Idrissi*
21/3	Minior	h	0-3	
3/4	Beroe	a	0-1	
11/4	Pirin	h	2-0	*Dafchev 2*
17/4	Lokomotiv Plovdiv	a	0-0	
23/4	Akademik	h	2-0	*Dafchev (p), Saidhodzha*
30/4	CSKA	a	1-3	*Dafchev*
5/5	Chernomorets	h	2-1	*Yordanov, Pisarov*
8/5	Vidima-Rakovski	a	1-1	*Yordanov*
14/5	Cherno More	h	1-1	*Dafchev (p)*
18/5	Sliven	a	2-0	*Dafchev, Romanov*
21/5	Litex	h	1-3	*Lahchev*
28/5	Slavia	a	1-0	*Johnson*

No	Name	Nat	DoB	Pos	Aps	(s)	Gls
1	Derek ASAMOAH	GHA	1/5/81	A	14		7
28	Atanas ATANASOV		14/7/85	D	14	(3)	
30	Dimo ATANASOV		24/10/85	M	3	(6)	
10	Marcho DAFCHEV		12/5/78	M	13	(6)	7
17	Ivailo DIMITROV		26/6/87	M	20	(3)	
11	Kristiyan DOBREV		23/9/78	D	26		
8	Svetoslav DYAKOV		31/5/84	M	27		2
84	Valentin GALEV		1/1/84	G	7		
37	Iliyan GAROV		24/11/86	D	7	(2)	
9	Tsvetan GENKOV		8/8/84	A	13		11
15	Rumen GORANOV		15/7/84	M	25	(2)	2
77	Youssef IDRISSI	MAR	19/1/88	A	2	(12)	1
23	Ivo IVANOV		30/4/85	M	1	(8)	1
7	Jemal JOHNSON	USA	3/5/85	A	10	(4)	1
18	Kaloyan KARADZHINOV		25/1/77	M	12	(13)	
14	Milen LAHCHEV		1/4/87	D	27		1
77	Vladimir MANCHEV		6/10/77	A		(2)	
20	Alexander MANOLOV		3/3/91	M	1	(1)	
22	Boyan PEIKOV		1/5/84	G	23		
21	Iskren PISAROV		5/10/85	M	22	(1)	5
88	Vladislav ROMANOV		7/2/82	A	18	(6)	2
99	Dormushali SAIDHODZHA		16/5/85	A	7	(5)	1
12	Darko SAVIĆ	SRB	19/1/79	D	24	(1)	
19	Yordan VARBANOV		15/2/80	D	4	(3)	
25	Preslav YORDANOV		21/7/89	A	10	(9)	5

PFC MINIOR PERNIK

Coach – Anton Velkov; (11/9/10) Stoicho Stoev
Founded – 1945
Stadium – Minior (15,000)

2010				
31/7	Litex	a	1-2	*Gospodinov*
7/8	Slavia	h	1-2	*Hazurov*
14/8	Montana	a	1-3	*Stoev*
23/8	Lokomotiv Sofia	h	1-3	*Markov*
4/9	Kaliakra	a	1-2	*Markov*
12/9	Levski Sofia	a	0-4	
18/9	Beroe	h	2-0	*Hazurov, Petrov*
25/9	Pirin	a	1-1	*Vitanov*
2/10	Lokomotiv Plovdiv	h	2-2	*Janković, Rangelov*
16/10	Akademik	a	0-2	
23/10	CSKA	h	2-4	*Janković, Gospodinov*
1/11	Chernomorets	a	0-0	
6/11	Vidima-Rakovski	h	2-1	*Rangelov, Todorov Y.*
14/11	Cherno More	a	0-3	
27/11	Sliven	h	4-1	*Petrov, Rangelov, Janković, Todorov*
2011				
27/2	Litex	h	0-3	
5/3	Slavia	a	2-1	*Vandev, Trajanov*
12/3	Montana	h	1-0	*Iliev*
21/3	Lokomotiv Sofia	a	3-0	*Vasilev, Janković, Brahimi*
2/4	Kaliakra	h	1-0	*Iliev*
10/4	Levski	h	0-0	
16/4	Beroe	a	0-2	
25/4	Pirin	h	1-0	*Zlatkov*
30/4	Lokomotiv Plovdiv	a	0-3	
4/5	Akademik	h	1-0	*Vandev*
7/5	CSKA	a	0-2	
14/5	Chernomorets	h	0-1	
18/5	Vidima-Rakovski	a	2-2	*Brahimi, Pavlov*
21/5	Cherno More	h	1-1	*Vandev*
28/5	Sliven	a	3-0	*Pavlov 2, Adzhov*

No	Name	Nat	DoB	Pos	Aps	(s)	Gls
9	Kostadin ADZHOV		19/5/91	A	1		1
8	Samir AESS		24/12/90	M	1	(5)	
1	Nikolay BANKOV		19/11/90	G	1		
2	Vasil BOZHIKOV		2/6/88	D	19	(4)	
42	Farès BRAHIMI	ALG	22/10/88	M	8	(6)	2
91	Ivan ČVOROVIĆ	SRB	15/6/85	G	17		
23	Hristo GOSPODINOV		19/1/79	M	6	(7)	2
21	Kostadin HAZUROV		5/8/85	A	11	(2)	2
4	Nikolay HRISTOZOV		6/3/82	D	17	(4)	
15	Ilian ILIEV		6/11/88	M	12	(1)	2
99	Ivailo IVANOV		8/12/74	G	12		
28	Velimir IVANOVIĆ	SRB	22/11/78	M	7	(4)	
18	Goran JANKOVIĆ	SRB	10/12/78	A	22	(5)	4
32	Kostadin MARKOV		18/2/79	M	25		2
88	Tomáš OKLEŠTĚK	CZE	21/2/87	M	3	(2)	
3	Adrian OLEGOV		1/5/85	D	16		
10	Tomislav PAVLOV		28/6/91	M	2	(5)	3
24	Dimitar PETKOV		15/7/84	D	1		
19	Petar PETROV		19/4/84	M	11	(6)	2
27	Rumen RANGELOV		30/11/85	A	6	(12)	3
7	Mladen STOEV		26/1/84	M	3	(4)	1
5	Borislav STOICHEV		26/11/86	D	13		
20	David STOYANOV		13/11/91	D	3		
13	Ivailo STOYANOV		13/7/90	A	3	(2)	
77	Lyubomir TODOROV		4/10/88	M	6	(3)	
26	Tsvetomir TODOROV		13/11/91	M	1	(1)	
8	Yordan TODOROV		27/7/81	M	11		2
33	Éverton Fernando Gílio "TON"	BRA	18/3/86	M	5	(4)	
17	Vanco TRAJANOV	MKD	9/8/78	M	19	(1)	1
14	Ivailo TSVETKOV		28/8/79	M	8	(4)	

Yavor VANDEV	29/5/83	A	13	(1)	3
Milen VASILEV	30/1/89	M	11	(3)	1
Lyubomir VITANOV	11/5/81	M	11		1
Yordan YORDANOV	14/4/92	M		(1)	
Angel YOSHEV	1/1/85	D	1		
Tomas ZDRAVKOV	17/2/92	M		(1)	
Daniel ZLATKOV	6/3/89	D	24	(1)	1

PFC MONTANA 1921

Coach – Atanas Dzambazki

Founded – 1921

Stadium – Ogosta (4,000)

10				
3	Lokomotiv Sofia	h	0-1	
3	Kaliakra	a	0-0	
/8	Minior	h	3-1	*Antonov, Iliev, Michev*
'8	Beroe	a	1-2	*Ivanov M.*
/8	Pirin	h	3-0	*Hristov 2, Avramov*
/9	Lokomotiv Plovdiv	a	0-4	
/9	Akademik	h	2-2	*Luiz Eduardo 2 (1p)*
/9	CSKA	a	0-2	
10	Chernomorets	h	0-0	
/10	Vidima-Rakovski	a	1-0	*Chepilov*
/10	Cherno More	h	4-0	*Michev 2, Chepilov, Antonov*
/10	Sliven	a	1-1	*Chepilov*
11	Litex	h	0-2	
3/11	Slavia	a	2-3	*Hristov, Luiz Eduardo*
'/11	Levski	h	0-3	
011				
3	Lokomotiv Sofia	a	0-2	
3	Kaliakra	h	3-2	*Anderson, Chepilov 2*
2/3	Minior	a	0-1	
9/3	Beroe	h	2-1	*Nikolov, Kondev*
4	Pirin	a	0-3	
)/4	Lokomotiv Plovdiv	h	1-1	*Luiz Eduardo (p)*
6/4	Akademik	a	0-1	
5/4	CSKA	h	1-4	*Hristov*
'5	Chernomorets	a	1-0	Iliev
'5	Vidima-Rakovski	h	1-1	*Hristov*
'5	Cherno More	a	0-0	
3/5	Sliven	h	2-2	*Luiz Eduardo, Hristov*
3/5	Litex	a	1-4	*Ivanov G.*
1/5	Slavia	h	1-0	*Domakinov*
8/5	Levski	a	0-3	

No	Name	Nat	DoB	Pos	Aps	(s)	Gls
9	Ventsislav ALDEV		11/8/77	M		(4)	
0	ANDERSON Gonçalves Pedro	BRA	17/5/80	M	6	(4)	1
0	Miroslav ANTONOV		10/3/86	A	12	(2)	2
5	Georgi AVRAMOV		5/10/83	M	6	(5)	1
1	Atanas CHEPILOV		6/2/87	A	25	(3)	5
3	Nikolay DOMAKINOV		11/7/80	D	9	(1)	1
8	Atanas FIDANIN		9/8/86	D	8	(3)	
1	Daniel GADZHEV		21/6/85	M	21		
3	Boyan GAITANOV		2/12/89	A		(5)	
	Moussa GUEYE	SEN	20/2/89	D	3	(1)	
	Ahmet HIKMET		5/10/84	M	1	(2)	
	Ventsislav HRISTOV		9/11/88	A	10	(20)	6
	Dimitar ILIEV		27/7/86	D	26	(2)	2
3	Georgi IVANOV		13/3/80	D	9		1
	Hristo IVANOV		6/4/82	G	23		
20	Miroslav IVANOV		11/9/81	M	10	(3)	1
22	Svetlan KONDEV		23/1/76	A	7	(9)	1
23	Yulian LEVASHKI		2/3/81	G	7		
4	Anton LICHKOV		5/8/80	D	23	(1)	
9	LUIZ EDUARDO Azevedo Dantas	BRA	24/5/85	A	20	(6)	5

2	Georgi MECHECHIEV	27/4/78	D	23		
16	Vladimir MICHEV	20/11/85	M	24	(4)	3
13	Dimitar NAKOV	18/10/80	D	3	(4)	
25	Nikolay NIKOLOV	26/1/81	D	9		1
7	Yordan TODOROV	12/11/81	M	3	(10)	
6	Tihomir TRIFONOV	25/11/86	D	27	(1)	
4	Stanislav ZHEKOV	6/2/80	D	15		

PFC PIRIN BLAGOEVGRAD

Coach – Yordan Bozdanski; (1/9/10) Kostadin Angelov

Founded – 1931

Stadium – Hristo Botev (6,500)

2010				
31/7	Cherno More	a	1-2	*Kondev*
7/8	Sliven	h	2-1	*Yakimov 2*
15/8	Litex	a	1-2	*Stoikov*
21/8	Slavia	h	0-2	
28/8	Montana	a	0-3	
11/9	Lokomotiv Sofia	h	2-1	*Kondev, Kostov*
18/9	Kaliakra	a	0-0	
25/9	Minior	h	1-1	*og (Ivanov)*
2/10	Beroe	a	0-0	
16/10	Levski	a	1-4	*Kondev*
23/10	Lokomotiv Plovdiv	h	1-1	*Kondev*
30/10	Akademik	a	0-1	
7/11	CSKA	h	0-1	
15/11	Chernomorets	a	0-1	
27/11	Vidima-Rakovski	h	1-1	*Sandanski*
2011				
26/2	Cherno More	h	0-1	
5/3	Sliven	a	0-1	
12/3	Litex	h	1-2	*Karachanakov*
19/3	Slavia	a	1-1	*Vodenicharov*
2/4	Montana	h	3-0	*Karachanakov, Bibishkov, Tsvetkov (p)*
11/4	Lokomotiv Sofia	a	0-2	
16/4	Kaliakra	h	1-0	*Bashliev*
25/4	Minior	a	0-1	
30/4	Beroe	h	2-0	*Tsvetkov, Stoikov*
4/5	Levski	h	2-3	*Tsvetkov 2 (1p)*
7/5	Lokomotiv Plovdiv	a	2-2	*Iliev, Tsvetkov*
14/5	Akademik	h	6-0	*Sandanski, Karachanakov 2, Iliev, Tsvetkov, Nakov*
18/5	CSKA	a	2-2	*Iliev, Tsvetkov*
21/5	Chernomorets	h	1-1	*Tsvetkov*
28/5	Vidima-Rakovski	a	1-2	*Vodenicharov*

No	Name	Nat	DoB	Pos	Aps	(s)	Gls
1	Atanas ARSHINKOV		8/4/87	G	12	(1)	
20	Alexander BASHLIEV		16/11/89	D	23		1
11	Ventsislav BENGYUZOV		29/8/79	A	4	(2)	
15	Krum BIBISHKOV		2/9/79	A	8		1
2	Alexander DYULGEROV		19/4/90	M	4	(4)	
22	Veselin GANEV		15/9/87	G	3		
6	Georgi GEORGIEV		25/2/81	D	12		
29	Dimitar ILIEV		25/9/88	A	8	(4)	3
7	Ruslan IVANOV		19/2/87	M	22	(2)	
21	Anton KARACHANAKOV		17/1/92	M	6	(8)	4
16	Kostadin KATSIMERSKI		7/2/87	D	3	(3)	
5	Dimitar KOEMDZIEV		28/9/78	D	13		
29	Boris KONDEV		29/8/79	A	13	(1)	4
8	Anton KOSTADINOV		24/6/82	M	17	(5)	
9	Stanislav KOSTOV		2/10/91	A	9	(3)	1
12	Blagoi MAKENDZHIEV		11/7/88	G	15		
3	Ivan MIHOV		8/6/91	D	2	(3)	
27	Radoslav MITREVSKI		22/4/81	D	16	(3)	
23	Diyan MOLDOVANOV		2/4/85	D	10	(2)	
25	Dimitar NAKOV		18/10/80	D	14		1

33	Atanas NIKOLOV		21/7/77	A	1	(3)	
15	Blagoi PASKOV		2/3/91	A		(3)	
20	Viktor PETAKOV		27/1/89	M		(1)	
26	Yulian POPEV		7/7/86	D	20		
25	Miroslav RIZOV		10/10/76	D	7	(1)	
14	Yanko SANDANSKI		23/11/88	M	24	(5)	2
13	Andrei STOEV		2/11/86	D	1		
9	Veselin STOIKOV		27/8/86	A	11	(12)	2
19	Kaloyan STOYANOV		2/11/86	M		(1)	
13	Miroslav TODOROV		26/6/85	M	1	(1)	
24	Ivan TSVETKOV		31/8/79	A	13		8
6	Dimitar VODENICHAROV		26/12/87	A	14	(9)	2
18	Alexander YAKIMOV		27/4/89	M	12	(9)	2
18	Atanas ZEHIROV		13/2/89	M		(1)	
8	Smilen ZLATANOV		1/2/93	M		(1)	
7	Zoran ZLATKOVSKI	MKD	5/4/87	A	12	(1)	

PFC SLAVIA SOFIA

Coach – Emil Velev; (26/5/11) Vladimir Ivanov

Founded – 1913

Stadium – Slavia (25,000)

MAJOR HONOURS: Bulgarian League – (7) 1928, 1930, 1936, 1939, 1941, 1943, 1996; Bulgarian Cup – (7) 1952, 1963, 1964, 1966, 1975, 1980 (as Soviet Army Cup), 1996.

2010

31/7	Kaliakra	h	0-1	
7/8	Minior	a	2-1	*Tsachev, Bozhov*
15/8	Beroe	h	1-2	*Peev (p)*
21/8	Pirin	a	2-0	*Bozhov 2 (1p)*
28/8	Lokomotiv Plovdiv	h	2-1	*Peev (p), Bozhov*
11/9	Akademik	a	4-0	*Bozhov 2, Ivanov, Kolev*
19/9	CSKA	h	1-0	*Peev*
27/9	Chernomorets	a	1-2	*Kolev*
2/10	Vidima-Rakovski	h	2-0	*Kolev (p), Georgiev*
17/10	Cherno More	a	2-3	*Genev, Ivanov*
23/10	Sliven	h	0-0	
31/10	Litex	a	0-2	
7/11	Levski	h	2-2	*Bozhov, Ivanov*
13/11	Montana	h	3-2	*Hristov 2, Bozhov*
27/11	Lokomotiv Sofia	a	3-4	*Bozhov (p), Bogdanov, Peev (p)*

2011

27/2	Kaliakra	a	1-0	*Hristov*
5/3	Minior	h	1-2	*Peev*
13/3	Beroe	a	1-2	*Iliev*
19/3	Pirin	h	1-1	*Hristov*
2/4	Lokomotiv Plovdiv	a	1-1	*Dimitrov*
11/4	Akademik	h	2-0	*og (Redovski), Genev*
16/4	CSKA	a	0-1	
25/4	Chernomorets	h	0-1	
1/5	Vidima-Rakovski	a	1-2	*José Júnior*
4/5	Cherno More	h	0-1	
8/5	Sliven	a	1-1	*Bozhov*
13/5	Litex	h	0-1	
18/5	Levski	a	0-3	
21/5	Montana	a	0-1	
28/5	Lokomotiv Sofia	h	0-1	

No	Name	Nat	DoB	Pos	Aps	(s)	Gls
11	Francisco Terra ALBERONI	BRA	16/5/84	A	1		
33	Erison da Silva Santos Carnietto "BAIANO"	BRA	19/1/81	D	9	(1)	
15	Galin BOGDANOV		6/9/90	D	1		1
17	Nikolay BOZHOV		18/7/77	A	24	(3)	10
5	Ivan DECHEV		1/5/88	D	1		
25	Ortega DENIRAN	NGA	28/5/86	A		(1)	
25	Victor DENIRAN	NGA	27/9/90	A	22		
20	Radoslav DIMITROV		12/8/88	M	23	(4)	1
2	Atanas DRENOVICHKI		5/4/90	D	3	(1)	
21	Bogomil DYAKOV		12/4/84	D	23		
6	Nikolay DYULGEROV		10/3/88	M	3	(2)	
24	Filip FILIPOV		2/8/88	D	10	(1)	
22	Viktor GENEV		27/10/88	D	24	(1)	2
5	Spas GEORGIEV		21/6/92	A	7	(12)	1
9	Georgi HRISTOV		10/1/85	A	18	(5)	4
7	Iliya ILIEV		20/12/74	M	16	(8)	1
33	Galin IVANOV		15/4/88	M	12	(1)	3
44	JOSÉ Carlos Nogueira JÚNIOR	BRA	18/7/85	A	9	(4)	1
4	JOSIAS BASSO Lisboa	BRA	14/4/89	D	5		
13	Stefan KIKOV		2/4/82	M	1	(2)	
10	Todor KOLEV		2/8/80	A	3	(5)	3
1	Stefano KUNCHEV		20/4/91	G	23		
19	Martin KUSHEV		25/8/73	A	3	(4)	
26	Raïs M'BOLHI	ALG	25/4/86	G	1		
27	Tom MANSHAROV	ISR	15/4/87	M	12	(2)	
44	Simeon MECHEV		16/2/90	M		(2)	
23	Deyan MOLDOVANOV		2/4/85	D	8		
3	Kiril OGNYANOV		12/7/92	D	1		
8	Antonio PAVLOV		2/9/88	M		(3)	
77	Daniel PEEV		6/10/84	M	24	(4)	5
35	Yordan PETKOV		11/3/76	D	13		
12	Emil PETROV		22/7/83	G	6	(1)	
8	Pavle POPARA	SRB	20/5/87	M		(2)	
15	Stoyan PREDEV		19/8/93	D		(1)	
19	RAFAEL BARBOSA do Nascimento	BRA	10/8/83	D	1		
18	Radoslav RANGELOV		18/9/85	D	1		
6	Martin SECHKOV		17/11/86	D	8		
24	Ivan TSACHEV		18/1/89	A	8	(7)	1
14	Bozhidar VASEV		14/3/93	M	1	(2)	
11	Radoslav VASILEV		12/10/90	A		(6)	
7	Ivan VINKOV		8/1/92	M		(1)	
77	Yordan YURUKOV		2/10/83	M	5	(1)	

OFC SLIVEN 2000

Coach – Dragoljub Simonović (SRB); (14/1/11) Dimcho Neno

Founded – 2000

Stadium – Hadzhi Dimitar (14,000)

2010

7/8	Pirin	a	1-2	*Bakalov*
14/8	Lokomotiv Plovdiv	h	0-1	
21/8	Akademik	a	1-0	*Hristov*
29/8	CSKA	h	1-3	*Hristov*
4/9	Beroe	h	0-1	
13/9	Chernomorets	a	0-0	
18/9	Vidima-Rakovski	h	6-1	*Hristov 3 (1p), Yamukov, Filipov F., David*
26/9	Cherno More	a	0-3	
4/10	Levski	h	1-1	*Ignatov*
16/10	Litex	h	0-1	
23/10	Slavia	a	0-0	
30/10	Montana	h	1-1	*Yamukov*
6/11	Lokomotiv Sofia	a	0-3	
13/11	Kaliakra	h	0-1	
27/11	Minior	a	1-4	*Hristov (p)*

2011

26/2	Beroe	a	0-1	
5/3	Pirin	h	1-0	*Hashev*
12/3	Lokomotiv Plovdiv	a	0-3	
19/3	Akademik	h	3-0	*Veselinov 2, Bakalov*
1/4	CSKA	a	0-2	
11/4	Chernomorets	h	0-0	
16/4	Vidima-Rakovski	a	1-2	*Georgiev S.*
25/4	Cherno More	h	1-3	*Marchev*
1/5	Levski	a	0-5	
4/5	Litex	a	0-4	

	Slavia	h	1-1	*Idrizov*
'5	Montana	a	2-2	*Bakalov 2*
'5	Lokomotiv Sofia	h	0-2	
/5	Kaliakra	a	1-2	*Petrov I.*
/5	Minior	h	0-3	

No	Name	Nat	DoB	Pos	Aps	(s)	Gls
	ADRIANO MIRANDA de Carvalho	BRA	22/6/89	M	15		
	Dimo BAKALOV		14/12/88	M	21		4
	Vulchan CHANEV		15/7/92	D		(1)	
	DAVID Rafael Lazari	BRA	30/1/89	A	6	(6)	1
	Nikolay DIMITROV		12/6/90	M	6	(4)	
	Filip FILIPOV		2/8/88	D	15		1
	Hyusein FILIPOV		28/5/92	M		(2)	
	Georgi GEORGIEV		12/10/88	G	7		
	Stoyan GEORGIEV		15/5/86	D	12	(1)	1
	Anatoli GOSPODINOV		21/3/94	G		(1)	
	Georgi HASHEV		26/3/90	D	11	(1)	1
	Deyan HRISTOV		29/8/83	A	15		6
	Yakub IDRIZOV		22/11/90	M	4	(4)	1
	Evgeni IGNATOV		4/6/88	M	10	(3)	1
	Marko ILIĆ	SRB	9/5/85	M	11	(2)	
	Yavor IVANOV		11/9/91	D	7	(3)	
	Evgeni KARAMANOV		26/3/86	G	23		
	Geergi KARANEICHEV		9/6/88	A	3	(6)	
	Ivan KOKONOV		17/8/81	A	6	(7)	
7	Dilyan KOLEV		9/11/88	M	12	(1)	
6	Martin KOVACHEV		12/3/82	D	14		
	MIlcho MAKENDZHIEV		31/10/89	D	7	(1)	
3	Teynur MAREN		23/9/94	D		(2)	
	Veselin MARCHEV		7/2/90	A	14		1
	Antonio MIHAYLOV		9/6/91	A		(2)	
	Miroslav MINDEV		27/7/80	A	14		
	Milen MITEV		28/6/83	M	1		
6	Georgi NEDYALKOV		2/11/89	A	3	(4)	
8	Plamen PENEV		8/7/94	M		(2)	
3	Georgi PETKOV		30/8/88	M		(1)	
2	Georgi PETROV		6/7/91	A	3	(3)	
1	Ivailo PETROV		23/1/91	M	3	(8)	1
	Hristiyan POPOV		5/2/90	D	10	(3)	
6	Stoyan STEFANOV		28/6/83	M	15		
9	Andrei STOEV		2/11/86	D	8	(2)	
2	Petar STOYANOV		15/8/85	M	12		
0	Martin TSIRKOV		29/12/88	D	12	(1)	
	Milen VASILEV		30/1/89	M	6	(5)	
0	Veselin VESELINOV		15/6/92	M	11	(10)	2
7	Vladislav YAMUKOV		22/3/80	D	13		2

PFC VIDIMA-RAKOVSKI SEVLIEVO

Coach – Dimitar Todorov; (10/6/11) Kostadin Angelov

Founded – 1997

Stadium – Rakovski (5,000)

2010				
31/7	Lokomotiv Plovdiv	h	1-1	*Vladinov*
7/8	Akademik	a	2-1	*Rusev, Stoichev*
13/8	CSKA	h	2-2	*Zakov (p), Ashimov*
21/8	Chernomorets	a	0-1	
30/8	Levski	h	1-2	*Zakov*
11/9	Cherno More	h	0-1	
18/9	Sliven	a	1-6	*Rusev*
25/9	Litex	h	0-3	
2/10	Slavia	a	0-2	
16/10	Montana	h	0-1	
24/10	Lokomotiv Sofia	a	1-2	*Zakov*
30/10	Kaliakra	h	1-0	*Rusev*
6/11	Minior	a	1-2	*Zakov*
13/11	Beroe	h	1-2	*Zakov*
27/11	Pirin	a	1-1	*Tsvetkov*
2011				
26/2	Lokomotiv Plovdiv	a	0-3	
5/3	Akademik	h	0-1	
13/3	CSKA	a	0-1	
19/3	Chernomorets	h	3-0	*Andonov, Vladinov, Rusev*
2/4	Levski	a	0-2	
9/4	Cherno More	a	0-5	
16/4	Sliven	h	2-1	*Shtarkov, Stoichev*
24/4	Litex	a	0-4	
1/5	Slavia	h	2-1	*Ivanov A., Gospodinov*
5/5	Montana	a	1-1	*Vladimirov*
8/5	Lokomotiv Sofia	h	1-1	*Branekov*
15/5	Kaliakra	a	0-1	
18/5	Minior	h	2-2	*Branekov, Ivanov A.*
21/5	Beroe	a	1-1	*Andonov*
28/5	Pirin	h	2-1	*Rusev, Gospodinov*

No	Name	Nat	DoB	Pos	Aps	(s)	Gls
8	Stanimir ANDONOV		30/9/89	M	11	(11)	2
3	Samet ASHIMOV		16/5/78	D	23	(2)	1
6	Alexander BRANEKOV		31/5/87	D	27		2
13	Dobri DOBREV		2/5/82	M	1	(1)	
10	Hristo GOSPODINOV		19/1/79	M	13		2
4	Borislav GYULEMETOV		21/4/86	D		(1)	
19	Evgeni IGNATOV		4/6/88	A	5	(5)	
1	Plamen ILIEV		30/11/91	G	12		
20	Atanas IVANOV		21/7/87	M	8	(4)	2
5	Stanislav IVANOV		24/3/84	D	1		
22	Plamen KOLEV		9/2/88	G	10		
2	Hristiyan KOZHUHAROV		6/10/91	D		(1)	
25	Tsvetomir PANOV		17/4/85	D	23		
16	Dimitar PANTEV		18/7/89	G	3		
24	Atanas PASHKULEV		10/7/87	D	5	(1)	
8	Vladimir PEKIN		10/8/86	M	6	(1)	
15	Angel RUSEV		6/1/81	A	22	(6)	5
17	Kalin SHTARKOV		20/5/84	D	13		1
14	Ivan SKERLEV		28/1/86	D	2	(3)	
14	Zdravko STANKOV		1/4/77	D	10	(1)	
19	Emil STOEV		16/3/86	A	3	(4)	
5	Georgi STOICHEV		3/7/77	M	28		2
17	Anatoli TODOROV		24/4/85	A	6		
25	Trayan TRAYANOV		3/8/87	D	18	(7)	
21	Nikolay TSVETKOV		10/8/87	A	15	(6)	1
62	Ivailo VASILEV		15/1/91	G	5		
7	Vasil VELEV		15/1/84	M	22	(4)	
18	Lyubomir VELICHKOV		19/6/83	A	1	(1)	
11	Vladimir VLADIMIROV		21/9/96	M	14	(14)	1
9	Nikolay VLADINOV		1/4/87	A	7	(12)	2
18	Atanas VURGOV		19/5/84	M	2	(5)	
10	Gerasim ZAKOV		7/9/84	A	14		5

TOP GOALSCORERS 2010/11

26	Garra DEMBÉLÉ (Levski)
14	Zdravko LAZAROV (Lokomotiv Plovdiv)
13	Spas DELEV (CSKA)
12	DOKA MADUREIRA (Litex)
11	Hristo ZLATINSKI (Lokomotiv Plovdiv)
	Tsvetan GENKOV (Lokomotiv Sofia)
10	Vladislav ZLATINOV (Beroe)
	MICHEL (CSKA)
	CARVALHO (Lokomotiv Plovdiv)
	Nikolay BOZHOV (Slavia)

PROMOTED CLUBS

PFC LUDOGORETS RAZGRAD

Coach – Ivailo Petev
Founded - 1947
Stadium – Dyanko Stefanov (3,000)

OFC BOTEV VRATSA

Coach – Sasho Angelov
Founded – 1921
Stadium – Hristo Botev (6,000)

PFC SVETKAVITSA TARGOVISHTE

Coach – Plamen Donev
Founded – 1922
Stadium – Dimitar Burkov (5,000)

SECOND LEVEL FINAL TABLE 2010/11

EAST	Pld	W	D	L	F	A	Pts
1 PFC Ludogorets Razgrad	24	12	8	4	38	16	44
2 PFC Chernomorets Pomorie	24	9	9	6	23	19	36
3 FC Spartak Plovdiv	24	10	6	8	26	17	36
4 PFC Svetkavitsa Targovishte	24	8	9	7	24	23	33
5 PFC Nesebar	24	9	5	10	20	22	32
6 FC Lyubimets 2007	24	7	9	8	22	26	30
7 PFC Dorostol 2003 Silistra	24	7	7	10	17	22	28
8 PFC Brestnik 1948 Plovdiv	24	6	8	10	21	30	26
9 PFC Dobrudzha 1919 Dobrich	24	7	5	12	14	30	26

NB PFC Ravda 1954 withdrew after round 10; PFC Dunav Ruse & PFC Chernomorets Balchik withdrew after round 14 – their results annulled.

WEST	Pld	W	D	L	F	A	Pts
1 OFC Botev Vratsa	30	20	2	8	52	28	62
2 PFC Sportist Svoge	30	15	7	8	36	15	52
3 FC Etar 1924 Veliko Tarnovo	30	13	12	5	33	19	51
4 FC Bansko 1951	30	14	6	10	42	35	48
5 PFC Chavdar Etropole	30	13	5	12	37	34	44
6 FC Septemvri Simitli	30	12	7	11	30	31	43
7 FC Vihren Sandanski	30	13	3	14	37	32	42
8 PFC Pirin Gotse Delchev	30	10	6	14	27	38	36
9 PFC Chavdar Byala Slatina	30	9	7	14	27	36	34
10 FC Malesh Mikrevo	30	8	8	14	22	37	32
11 FC Botev Krivodov	30	4	5	21	25	63	17

NB PFC Kom-Minior Berkovitsa withdrew after round 16 – their results annulled.

PROMOTION/RELEGATION PLAY-OFFS

(8/6/11)
Chernomorets Pomorie 2, Sportist Svoge 1

(12/6/11)
Chernomorets Pomorie 3, Vidima-Rakovski 0

NB Chernomorets Pomorie subsequently denied licence to compete in top division; with PFC Pirin Blagoevgrad also expelled from the top division, additional play-offs were therefore required to determine two places in 2011/12 A PFG.

ADDITIONAL PLAY-OFFS

(17/6/11)
Svetkavitsa Targovishte 3, Etar Veliko Tarnovo 1

(26/6/11)
Sportist Svoge 1, Vidima-Rakovski 1 *(aet; 3-4 on pens)*

DOMESTIC CUPS 2010/11

KUPA NA BULGARIYA

SECOND ROUND

(20/11/10)
Bansko 1, Levski 3
Botev Krivodol 0, Kom-Minior Berkovista 2 *(aet)*
Chavdar Byala Slatina 0, Etar 1924 Veliko Turnovo 0 *(aet; 2-4 on pens)*
Chavdar Etropole 0, Beroe 1
Chernomorets Balchik 1, Litex 2
Dobrudzha 1919 Dobrich 1, Botev Vratsa 0
Dorostol 2003 Silistra 0, Pirin Blagoevgrad 0 *(aet; 3-5 pens)*
Ludogorets Razgrad 0, Slavia Sofia 2
Males Mikrevo 0, Vidima-Rakovski 0 *(aet; 5-4 on pens)*
Minior 1, Akademik 1 *(aet; 3-2 on pens)*
Montana 0, Cherno More 1
Sliven 1, CSKA Sofia 3
Sozopol 0, Kaliakra 1
Topolite 0, Chernomorets Pomorie 1
Vihren 0, Chernomorets Burgas 5

(21/11/10)
Lokomotiv Sofia 0, Lokomotiv Plovdiv 0 *(aet; 3-4 on pens)*

THIRD ROUND

(4/12/10)
Chernomorets Pomorie 0, Litex 2
Dobrudzha 1919 Dobrich 0, Chernomorets Burgas 3
Etar 1924 Veliko Turnovo 0, Slavia Sofia 1
Kom-Minior Berkovista 0, Cherno More 1
Lokomotiv Plovdiv 2, Minior 1
Pirin Blagoevgrad 3, Kaliakra 1 *(aet)*

(8/12/10)
Levski 1, Beroe 0

(11/12/10)
Malesh Mikrevo 0, CSKA Sofia 3

QUARTER-FINALS

(5/4/11)
CSKA Sofia 2 *(Delev 34, Marquinhos 67)*, Cherno More 0

(6/4/11)
Litex 1 *(Wellington 34p)*, Levski 1 *(Dembélé 79) (aet; 4-2 on pens)*
Lokomotiv Plovdiv 1 *(Krachunov 48)*, Pirin Blagoevgrad 2 *(Tsvetkov 73, Ivanov 90+2)*

(7/4/11)
Chernomorets Burgas 4 *(Bragança 2p, Andonov 32, 91, Seitz 77)*, Slavia Sofia 4 *(Bozhov 16, 90+2, Kushev 69, Moldovanov 102)* *(aet; 3-5 on pens)*

SEMI-FINALS

(20/4/11)
CSKA Sofia 2 *(Delev 28, 87)*, Litex 1 *(Milanov G. 68)*

(21/4/11)
Slavia Sofia 1 *(Peev 45p)*, Pirin Blagoevgrad 1 *(Nakov 70)* *(aet; 7-6 on pens)*

FINAL

(25/5/11)
Vassil Levski stadium, Sofia
PFC CSKA SOFIA 1 *(Delev 39)*
PFC SLAVIA SOFIA 0
Referee – *Stoyanov*
CSKA SOFIA – *Karadzhov, Bandalovski, Popov, Aquaro, Trifonov, Galchev, Yanchev, Delev, Marquinhos (Stoyanov P. 82), Nelson (Sheridan 90), Michel (Tonev 76).*
SLAVIA SOFIA – *Petrov, Filipov, Moldovanov, Josias Basso, Genev, Mansharov, José Júnior (Kushev 78), Popara (Hristov 58), Iliev (Georgiev 53), Dimitrov, Bozhov.*
Sent off: *Josias Basso (89)*

CLUB COMMUNICATION 2011/12

FC Beroe Stara Zagora
eorgi Kiumiurev 10 str.
G-6000 Stara Zagora

l +359 42 603 492
ax +359 42 603 492
eb beroe.eu
nail beroe.press@gmail.com
edia Officer

FC Botev Vratsa
port Complex Stadium "Hristo Botev"
O Box 51, BG-3000 Vratsa

el +359 92 621 540
ax +359 92 621 540
eb botevvratza.com
mail planik61@abv.bg
edia Officer

FC Cherno More Varna
ikola Vaptzarov Street 9, Ticha Stadium
G-9005 Varna

el +359 52 302 243
ax +359 52 302 243
eb chernomorepfc.bg
mail pfk_chernomore@abv.bg
edia Officer Krassimir Nikolov

SFC Chernomorets Burgas
port Complex Lazur, Complex
G-8000 Burgas

el +359 56 834 444
ax +359 56 834 455
Veb chernomoretz.bg
mail pfcchernomoretsburgas@abv.bg
ledia Officer Evelin Kuzmanov

PFC CSKA Sofia
Dragan Tzankov Boulevard 3
Balgarska Armia, BG-1504 Sofia

Tel +359 2 963 3477
Fax +359 2 963 3902
Web cska.bg
Email info@cska.bg
Media Officer Boyan Denchev

PFC Kaliakra Kavarna
Sava Ganchev 29
BG-9650 Kavarna

Tel +359 57 085 888
Fax +359 57 085 888
Web fckaliakra.com
Email fckaliakra@mail.bg
Media Officer

PFC Levski Sofia
Todorini Kukli Street 47
BG-1517 Sofia

Tel +359 2 945 5160
Fax +359 2 945 4227
Web levski.bg
Email office@levski.bg
Media Officer Kiril Lulev

PFC Litex Lovech
12, Targovska Street, P.B.75
BG-5500 Lovech

Tel +359 68 601 704
Fax +359 28 162 040
Web pfclitex.com
Email pfc_litex@litex.bg
Media Officer Vladislav Trifonov

PFC Lokomotiv Plovdiv 1936
Lokomotiv Stadium, Park Lauta
BG-4000 Plovdiv

Tel +359 32 627 373
Fax +359 32 622 889
Web lokomotivpd.com
Email nina@lportala.net
Media Officer Ivan Zhechev

PFC Lokomotiv Sofia
Rogen Boulevard 23, Lokomotiv stadium
BG-1220 Sofia

Tel +359 2 837 8479
Fax +359 2 936 0341
Web lokomotivsofia.bg
Email lokomotiv1929@abv.bg
Media Officer Kiril Petrov

PFC Ludogorets Razgrad
Blvd. Aprilsko vastanie 68A, et. 7
BG-7200 Razgrad

Tel
Fax +359 846 151 22
Web ludogorets.com
Email office@ludogorets.com
Media Officer

PFC Minior Pernik
1 Fizkulturna Str., Minyor Stadium
BG-2300 Pernik

Tel +359 76 630 513
Fax +359 76 630 513
Web minyor.com
Email admin@minyor-pk.com
Media Officer Miroslav Marinov

PFC Montana 1921
Stadium Ogosta
BG-3400 Montana

Tel +359 96 301 113
Fax +359 96 300 401
Web
Email fk_montana@abv.bg
Media Officer

PFC Slavia Sofia
Koloman 1, Slavia stadium
BG-1618 Sofia

Tel +359 2 856 9197
Fax +359 2 855 2137
Web pfcslavia.com
Email slavia@intech.bg
Media Officer Borislav Konstantinov

PFC Svetkavitsa Targovishte
14 Hristo Botev str.
BG-7700 Targovishte

Tel +359 60 164 529
Fax +359 60 164 206
Web
Email svetkavica1922@abv.bg
Media Officer

PFC Vidima-Rakovski Sevlievo
Marin Popov 53, Rakovski Stadium
BG-5400 Sevlievo

Tel +359 675 33 806
Fax +359 675 33 806
Web vidimarakovski.bg
Email press@vidimarakovski.bg
Media Officer Chudomir Penev

CROATIA

Croatie | Kroatien

Hrvatski Nogometni Savez (HNS)

COMMUNICATION

Address	Rusanova 13 HR-10000 Zagreb	**President**	Vlatko Marković
Tel	+385 1 2361 555	**General Secretary**	Zorislav Srebrić
Fax	+385 1 2441 501	**Media Officer**	Davor Gavran
E-mail	info@hns-cff.hr	**Year of Formation**	1912
Website	hns-cff.hr	**National Stadium**	Maksimir, Zagreb (38,079)

DOMESTIC COMPETITION SUMMARY 2010/11

1.HNL FINAL TABLE

			Home					Away					Total						
		Pld	W	D	L	F	A	W	D	L	F	A	W	D	L	F	A	Pts	Comp
1	NK Dinamo Zagreb	30	11	3	1	25	7	11	3	1	27	5	22	6	2	52	12	72	UCL
2	HNK Hajduk Split	30	10	3	2	33	13	6	4	5	21	19	16	7	7	54	32	55	UEL
3	RNK Split	30	10	2	3	24	10	6	3	6	14	12	16	5	9	38	22	53	UEL
4	HNK Cibalia	30	10	2	3	25	10	2	6	7	8	14	12	8	10	33	24	44	
5	NK Inter Zaprešić	30	8	2	5	21	20	4	4	7	10	15	12	6	12	31	35	42	
6	NK Karlovac	30	8	4	3	16	8	3	4	8	9	19	11	8	11	25	27	41	
7	NK Slaven Koprivnica	30	7	3	5	21	14	3	7	5	13	16	10	10	10	34	30	40	
8	NK Osijek	30	6	8	1	15	10	3	4	8	16	19	9	12	9	31	29	39	
9	HNK Rijeka	30	5	5	5	15	16	4	7	4	14	19	9	12	9	29	35	39	
10	NK Zadar	30	9	4	2	17	9	2	1	12	14	25	11	5	14	31	34	38	
11	NK Varaždin	30	8	5	2	24	12	1	4	10	8	26	9	9	12	32	38	36	UEL
12	NK Zagreb	30	4	4	7	16	20	5	4	6	16	19	9	8	13	32	39	35	
13	HNK Šibenik	30	5	6	4	19	17	3	5	7	18	21	8	11	11	37	38	35	
14	NK Lokomotiva Zagreb	30	5	6	4	14	13	3	3	9	10	24	8	9	13	24	37	33	
15	NK Istra	30	8	1	6	14	13	1	3	11	10	31	9	4	17	24	44	31	
16	NK Hrvatski dragovoljac Zagreb	30	3	6	6	14	26	2	2	11	10	29	5	8	17	24	55	23	*Relegated*

NB NK Lokomotiva Zagreb & NK Istra avoided relegation as HNK Gorica & NK Pomorac Kostrena were denied licences to compete in 2011/12 1.HNL.

Top Scorer Ivan Krstanović (Zagreb), 19 goals

Promoted Club NK Lučko

Cup Final NK Dinamo Zagreb 5, NK Varaždin 1
NK Varaždin 1, NK Dinamo Zagreb 3
(NK Dinamo Zagreb 8-2)

Easy pickings for dominant Dinamo

Croatia's 1.HNL beat to a familiar refrain in 2010/11 as NK Dinamo Zagreb cruised unopposed to their fifth successive championship title. They also won the Croatian Cup with nonchalant ease to seal a fourth double in five seasons. The only disappointment was the club's failure, once again, to make a significant mark in Europe.

The final figures said it all. Dinamo ended the league campaign with a gigantic 17-point victory margin over runners-up HNK Hajduk Split. They won 22 of their 30 matches, lost just twice and conceded the miserly sum of 12 goals, half of which, astonishingly, were registered in their opening four matches. Indeed, it was Dinamo's poor start in the league – just four points from three games – that partly accounted for the early dismissal of the club's new coach, the experienced Velimir Zajec. What sealed his fate was the team's failure to beat Moldovan champions FC Sheriff in the third qualifying round of the UEFA Champions League, a penalty shoot-out defeat in the Maksimir Stadium propelling the club into the UEFA Europa League and Zajec into unemployment.

Vahid Halilhodžić steered Dinamo Zagreb to another Croatian title

The man brought in to revive Dinamo was another coach of considerable experience, Bosnian-Herzegovinian veteran Vahid Halilhodžić, last seen helping Ivory Coast qualify for the 2010 FIFA World Cup. No sooner was he in place than Dinamo suddenly sparked into life, reeling off a long run of league victories that was punctuated only by a 1-1 draw away to Hajduk. The team also picked up in Europe, reaching the group stage of the UEFA Europa League and claiming a couple of choice victories against Villarreal CF and Club Brugge KV.

Symbolic scoreline

Unfortunately, Dinamo were found wanting in their crunch European tie at home to PAOK FC, but at home a five-point mid-season lead served merely as a platform for total dominance in the spring, the club's 13th Croatian title being cemented four rounds from the finish with a 1-0 home win over NK Osijek. It was a symbolic scoreline as Dinamo had become very well practised in winning matches with a solitary goal. By the end of the season their 22 wins included no fewer than ten one-nils. In fact, all but one of the 20 league victories obtained under Halilhodžić's watch were achieved with clean sheets. It was a remarkable defensive effort, at the heart of which were foreign imports Tonel and Leandro Cufré as well as gifted young right back Šime Vršaljko, the only Dinamo player to feature for the Croatian national side in 2010/11.

If the Dinamo defence was virtually watertight, the attack left a lot to be desired. Short of a natural goalscorer following the sale of Mario Mandžukić to VfL Wolfsburg, Dinamo's tally of 72 points was achieved with only 52 goals – two fewer than second-placed Hajduk – and only one player, Brazilian playmaker Sammir, reached double figures. Montenegrin international Fatoš Bećiraj showed up well in the spring, not least in the Croatian Cup, where Dinamo actually let themselves go, scoring 18 goals in their last six ties, including eight in the two-legged final against NK Varaždin. Bećiraj scored twice in the first leg (5-1 at home) and once in the second (3-1 away) and was joined on the scoresheet in both matches by midfielder Milan Badelj, who was arguably the club's most consistently impressive performer over the season and often captained the side in the absence of veteran skipper Igor Bišćan.

Dinamo lifted the Cup without Halilhodžić, who had packed his bags after a furious row with the club's executive president Zdravko Mamić during the half-time interval of the league game at home to NK Inter Zaprešić – five days before the first leg of the Cup final. It was interim coach Mario Tot who stood in to lead the team past Varaždin before Dinamo announced that Krunoslav Jurčić, the club's title-winning coach in 2008/09 and 2009/10, would be returning to duty in 2011/12.

Coaching changes

Hajduk also underwent a couple of coaching changes before they sealed their place as distant runners-up to Dinamo – just two points ahead of their local rivals RNK Split, who enjoyed an outstanding first season in the top flight under ex-Hajduk boss Ivan Katalinić. Stanko Poklepović, who took Hajduk to victory in the 2009/10 Croatian Cup, was sacked in October when Hajduk were eliminated from the 2010/11 competition by NK Istra. His successor, Goran Vučević, received his marching orders six months later following a miserable run in the league, and it was another ex-Hajduk stalwart, Ante Miše, who saw the team through the final games of an indifferent campaign. In truth, Hajduk's best moments had come early on under Poklepović, with a promising start in the league supplemented by fine home wins in Europe against FC Dinamo Bucureşti, FC Unirea Urziceni and RSC Anderlecht.

Ante Vukušić

National Team

International Tournament Appearances – FIFA World Cup – (3) 1998 (3rd), 2002, 2006. UEFA European Championship – (3) 1996 (qtr-finals), 2004, 2008 (qtr-finals).

Top Five All-time Caps – Dario Šimić (100); Josip Šimunić (86); Robert Kovač (84); Niko Kovač & Darijo Srna (83)

Top Five All-time Goals – Davor Šuker (45); Eduardo da Silva & Darijo Srna (19); Niko Kranjčar & Goran Vlaović (15)

The 95th-minute winner against the Belgian champions was scored by Hajduk's player of the season, 19-year-old Ante Vukušić, who struck 14 goals in the league – a tally bettered only by NK Zagreb's beanpole striker Ivan Krstanović, who bagged 19 to help his club avoid relegation. It was the second season in a row that a Zagreb player had won the 1.HNL Golden Boot – after Davor Vugrinec in 2009/10 – and, again, the protagonist was to leave the club, with Krstanović being lured across town to fill the striker void at Dinamo.

Just one domestic league player – Hajduk left back Ivan Strinić – was used by national team coach Slaven Bilić in the first six matches of Croatia's UEFA EURO 2012 qualifying campaign, and even he was an exile by the spring. Results were mixed as the UEFA EURO 2008 quarter-finalists attempted to make up for the disappointment of failing to qualify for the 2010 FIFA World Cup. Wins against Latvia, Israel and Malta were counterbalanced by a goalless draw at home to Greece and a shock defeat to a last-minute goal in Georgia. Fortunately, though, Croatia avoided a further calamity by coming from behind to beat Georgia 2-1 at home in June and maintain a realistic prospect of topping the group.

National team newcomers

Bilić continued to select most of his stalwarts from the previous two campaigns, but the coach was also prepared to give opportunities to other Croatian players performing with distinction at their clubs. These included SK Sturm Graz defender Gordon Schildenfeld, Rangers FC striker Nikica Jelavić, Olympique Lyonnais centre back Dejan Lovren and, notably, Club Brugge attacking midfielder Ivan Perišić, the top goalscorer and player of the year in Belgium.

NATIONAL TEAM RESULTS 2010/11

11/8/10	Slovakia	A	Bratislava	1-1	*Jelavić (54)*
3/9/10	Latvia (ECQ)	A	Riga	3-0	*Petrić (43), Olić (51), Srna (82)*
7/9/10	Greece (ECQ)	H	Zagreb	0-0	
9/10/10	Israel (ECQ)	A	Tel-Aviv	2-1	*Kranjčar (36p, 41)*
12/10/10	Norway	H	Zagreb	2-1	*Mandžukić (36), Kranjčar (49)*
17/11/10	Malta (ECQ)	H	Zagreb	3-0	*Kranjčar (18, 42), Kalinić (81)*
9/2/11	Czech Republic	H	Pula	4-2	*Eduardo (9), Kalinić (13, 61), Iličević (74)*
26/3/11	Georgia (ECQ)	A	Tbilisi	0-1	
29/3/11	France	A	Saint-Denis	0-0	
3/6/11	Georgia (ECQ)	H	Split	2-1	*Mandžukić (76), Kalinić (78)*

NATIONAL TEAM APPEARANCES 2010/11

oach – Slaven BILIĆ	**11/9/68**		**Svk**	**LVA**	**GRE**	**ISR**	**Nor**	**MLT**	**Cze**	**GEO**	**Fra**	**GEO**	**Caps**	**Goals**
edran RUNJE	10/2/76	Lens (FRA)	G	G	G	G		G	G	G	G46	G	22	-
arijo SRNA	1/5/82	Shakhtar (UKR)	D	D	D		D89	D	D	D	M80	D	83	19
edran ĆORLUKA	5/2/86	Tottenham (ENG)	D	D	D	D		D	D46	D	D	D	46	1
ordon SCHILDENFELD	18/3/85	Sturm (AUT)	D			D	D	D					7	-
sip ŠIMUNIĆ	18/2/78	Hoffenheim (GER)	D	D	D	D	D		D		D	D	86	3
ka MODRIĆ	9/9/85	Tottenham (ENG)	M		M	M	M46	M		M	M	M	47	7
gnjen VUKOJEVIĆ	20/12/83	Dynamo Kyiv (UKR)	M	M70	M57	s77	M61		M46		M	M71	31	2
ko KRANJČAR	13/8/84	Tottenham (ENG)	M46	M	M	M	M	M	M	M70	M		64	15
an RAKITIĆ	10/3/88	Schalke (GER) /Sevilla (ESP)	M71	M	s57	M77		M69	M	M61	s46		35	8
ario MANĐŽUKIĆ	21/5/86	Wolfsburg (GER)	M46	s84		s57	M	s78				M	19	3
ca OLIĆ	14/9/79	Bayern (GER)	A46	A	A73	A72							73	14
UARDO da Silva	25/2/83	Shakhtar (UKR)	s46	A62	s73	A57	A61	A78	A46			A	37	19
aden PETRIĆ	1/1/81	Hamburg (GER)	s46	M84	A46			A61	s46	A84	s71		44	12
kica JELAVIĆ	27/8/85	Rapid Wien (AUT) /Rangers (SCO)	s46	s62	s46				s63	s70	A56	A46	12	2
mislav DUJMOVIĆ	26/2/81	Lokomotiv Moskva (RUS) /Dinamo Moskva (RUS)	s71				s61	M	s46	M		s71	11	-
an STRINIĆ	17/7/87	Hajduk /Dnipro (UKR)		D	D	D	D		s46	D	s24 /46		10	-
anijel PRANJIĆ	2/12/81	Bayern (GER)		s70	M	M	M90	D	D46	s84	D24	D	39	-
ate BILIĆ	23/10/80	Sporting Gijón (ESP)				s72	s61						7	3
pe PLETIKOSA	8/1/79	Tottenham (ENG)					G				s46		82	-
ILIČEVIĆ	14/11/86	Kaiserslautern (GER)					s46	s69	M81				3	1
rica BULJAT	19/9/86	Hajduk					s89						2	-
kola POKRIVAČ	26/11/85	Salzburg (AUT)					s90						15	-
kola KALINIĆ	5/1/88	Blackburn (ENG)						s61	A63	A	s56	s46	8	4
ejan LOVREN	5/7/89	Lyon (FRA)							s46	D	D		8	-
me VRSALJKO	10/1/92	Dinamo Zagreb							s81				1	-
an PERIŠIĆ	2/2/89	Club Brugge (BEL)								s61	M71	M71	3	-
omagoj VIDA	29/4/89	Leverkusen (GER)									s80		3	-
an KLASNIĆ	29/1/80	Bolton (ENG)										s71	40	12

CLUB-BY-CLUB

HNK CIBALIA

Coach – Stanko Mršić
Founded – 1919
Stadium – HNK Cibalia (10,000)

2010

25/7	Osijek	h	3-0	*Bartolović, Parmaković, Jurić*
31/7	Šibenik	a	0-0	
7/8	Inter	h	1-0	*Prgomet*
14/8	Zadar	a	0-0	
21/8	Split	h	0-1	
29/8	Dinamo	a	0-2	
11/9	Rijeka	h	4-1	*Kresinger, Baraban, Radotić, Bartolović*
17/9	Varaždin	a	1-2	*Kresinger*
25/9	Karlovac	h	1-0	*Kresinger*
2/10	Slaven	a	1-1	*Bartolović*
16/10	Hrvatski dragovoljac	h	3-0	*Prgomet, Kresinger, Bartolović*
24/10	Hajduk	h	2-1	*Prgomet, Bartolović (p)*
30/10	Zagreb	a	2-0	*Kresinger 2*
6/11	Lokomotiva	h	2-1	*Jurić, Bartolović*
13/11	Istra	a	0-1	
20/11	Osijek	a	0-1	
27/11	Šibenik	h	3-1	*Vitaić, Bartolović (p), Kresinger*
3/12	Inter	a	1-2	*Bartolović*

2011

1/3	Zadar	h	0-0	
5/3	Split	a	1-2	*Kresinger*
12/3	Dinamo	h	0-1	
19/3	Rijeka	a	0-0	
2/4	Varaždin	h	2-0	*Jurić, Kresinger*
9/4	Karlovac	a	0-0	
16/4	Slaven	h	1-2	*Kresinger*
23/4	Hrvatski dragovoljac	a	0-0	
30/4	Hajduk	a	2-1	*Prgomet, Čuljak*
7/5	Zagreb	h	2-2	*Kresinger, Radotić*
13/5	Lokomotiva	a	0-2	
21/5	Istra	h	1-0	*Vitaić*

No	Name	Nat	DoB	Pos	Aps	(s)	Gls
25	Ivan BARABAN		22/1/88	A	6	(7)	1
11	Mladen BARTOLOVIĆ	BIH	10/4/77	A	26	(1)	8
20	Tomislav BOŽIĆ		20/2/87	D	13	(9)	
3	Tomislav ČULJAK		25/5/87	D	21	(6)	1
4	Josip DUVNJAK		11/4/86	D	7	(4)	
10	Ivan GRGIĆ		12/5/88	M	5	(7)	
21	Tomislav JURIĆ		8/4/90	D	25	(2)	3
9	Ivan KOLEDIĆ		27/9/89	A	1	(8)	
7	Dino KRESINGER		20/3/82	A	25		11
8	Stjepan KVESIĆ		31/7/85	M	3	(2)	
30	Mario LUČIĆ		25/6/80	D	29		
23	Mato MASIĆ		11/7/90	G	3		
1	Mladen MATKOVIĆ		12/5/89	G	27	(1)	
28	Tomislav MAZALOVIĆ		10/6/90	M	16	(3)	
15	Ninoslav PARMAKOVIĆ		24/11/82	D	20	(3)	1
19	Krešimir PRGOMET		20/6/86	M	19	(6)	4
16	Tomislav RADOTIĆ		13/12/81	M	23	(1)	2
24	Dario RUGAŠEVIĆ		29/1/91	D	14	(8)	
17	Vlatko ŠIMUNAC		1/2/90	A	6	(10)	
18	Marko TERZIĆ		25/5/91	A	2	(5)	
6	Petar TOMIĆ		29/10/82	D	21	(1)	
22	Frane VITAIĆ		4/6/82	M	18	(2)	2
13	Dario ŽUPARIĆ		3/5/92	M		(2)	

NK DINAMO ZAGREB

Coach – Velimir Zajec; (9/8/10) (Sreten Ćuk); (17/8/10) Vahid Halilhodžić (BIH); (7/5/11) (Mario Tot)
Founded – 1945
Stadium – Maksimir (38,079)

MAJOR HONOURS: Inter Cities Fairs Cup – (1) 1967; Yugoslav League – (4) 1948, 1954, 1958, 1982; Croatian League – (13) 1993, 1996, 1997, 1998, 1999, 2000, 2003 2006, 2007, 2008, 2009, 2010, 2011; Yugoslav Cup – (8) 1951, 1960, 1963, 1965, 1969, 1973, 1980, 198 Croatian Cup – (11) 1994, 1996, 1997, 1998, 2001, 2002, 2004, 2007, 2008, 2009, 2011.

2010

24/7	Hrvatski dragovoljac	h	4-1	*Morales, Sammir, Slepička, Mesari*
31/7	Rijeka	h	1-2	*Sammir*
7/8	Varaždin	a	1-1	*Rukavina*
14/8	Karlovac	h	4-2	*Sammir 2 (1p), Kramarić, Rukavina*
22/8	Slaven	a	2-0	*Rukavina, Sammir*
29/8	Cibalia	h	2-0	*Vrsaljko, Tomečak*
11/9	Hajduk	a	1-1	*Sammir*
19/9	Zagreb	h	1-0	*Barbarić*
26/9	Lokomotiva	a	2-0	*Chago, Tonel*
3/10	Istra	h	4-0	*Sylvestr, Bećiraj, Sammir 2 (1p)*
16/10	Osijek	a	3-1	*Sammir (p), Badelj, Bećiraj*
24/10	Šibenik	h	1-0	*Tomečak*
30/10	Inter	a	3-0	*Tonel, Sammir, Ibáñez*
7/11	Zadar	h	1-0	*Tomečak*
13/11	Split	a	1-0	*Calello*
20/11	Hrvatski dragovoljac	a	6-0	*Tomečak, Chago, Ibáñez, Kovačić, Badelj, Bećiraj*
27/11	Rijeka	a	2-0	*Bećiraj, Badelj*
5/12	Varaždin	h	1-1	*Morales (p)*

2011

26/2	Karlovac	a	1-0	*Šitum*
5/3	Slaven	h	0-0	
12/3	Ciblia	a	1-0	*Bećiraj*
19/3	Hajduk	h	2-0	*Badelj, Bećiraj*
2/4	Zagreb	a	1-0	*Calello*
9/4	Lokomotiva	h	1-0	*Sylvestr*
16/4	Istra	a	1-2	*Bećiraj*
23/4	Osijek	h	1-0	*Badelj*
30/4	Šibenik	a	2-0	*Morales, Rukavina (p)*
6/5	Inter	h	1-0	*Bećiraj*
14/5	Zadar	a	0-0	
21/5	Split	h	1-1	*Badelj*

No	Name	Nat	DoB	Pos	Aps	(s)	Gls
6	Arijan ADEMI		29/5/91	M	16	(5)	
18	Domagoj ANTOLIĆ		30/6/90	M		(1)	
16	Milan BADELJ		25/2/89	M	27	(2)	6
19	Tomislav BARBARIĆ		29/3/89	D	8	(2)	1
21	Fatos BEĆIRAJ	MNE	5/5/88	A	15	(7)	8
22	Igor BIŠĆAN		4/5/78	D	14		
7	Josip BREZOVEC		21/12/86	M	4	(2)	
1	Tomislav BUTINA		30/3/74	G	1		
5	Adrián Daniel CALELLO	ARG	14/5/87	M	14	(4)	2
15	Mathias Dellgoue CHAGO de Confiance	CMR	13/3/83	M	9	(7)	2
25	Leonardo Damián CUFRÉ	ARG	9/5/78	D	25	(1)	
23	Luiz Paulo Hilário "DODÔ"	BRA	16/10/87	A	4	(3)	
7	Oelilton Araújo dos Santos "ETTO"	BRA	8/3/81	D	8	(2)	
3	Luis Ezequiel IBÁÑEZ	ARG	15/7/88	D	16	(6)	2
30	Ivan KELAVA		20/2/88	G	23	(1)	
8	Mateo KOVAČIĆ		6/5/94	M	1	(6)	1
9	Andrej KRAMARIĆ		19/6/91	A	2	(10)	1
12	Filip LONČARIĆ		6/12/86	G	6		
4	Leonard MESARIĆ		10/8/83	D	7	(4)	1
77	Pedro Andrés MORALES Flores	CHI	25/5/85	M	14	(2)	3
33	Antun PALIĆ		25/6/88	M	2	(2)	
55	Ante RUKAVINA		18/6/86	A	14	(7)	4
10	Jorge SAMMIR Cruz Campos	BRA	23/4/87	M	20	(2)	10
24	Ilija SIVONJIĆ		10/7/87	A	3	(2)	
20	Miroslav SLEPIČKA	CZE	10/11/81	A	3		1

7	Jakub SYLVESTR	SVK	2/2/89	A	14	(7)	2
8	Mario ŠITUM		4/4/92	A	4	(1)	1
1	Ivan TOMEČAK		7/12/89	M	18	(4)	4
3	António Leonel Vilar Nogueira de Sousa "TONEL"	POR	13/4/80	D	22		2
4	Šime VRSALJKO		10/1/92	D	16		1

HNK HAJDUK SPLIT

Coach – Stanko Poklepović; (28/10/10) (Joško Španjić); (1/11/10) Goran Vučević; (18/4/11) Ante Miše

Founded – 1911

Stadium – Poljud (34,200)

MAJOR HONOURS: Yugoslav League – (9) 1927, 1929, 1950, 1952, 1955, 1971, 1974, 1975, 1979; Croatian League – (6) 1992, 1994, 1995, 2001, 2004, 2005; Yugoslav Cup – (9) 1967, 1972, 1974, 1975, 1976, 1977, 1984, 1987, 1991; Croatian Cup – (5) 1993, 1995, 2000, 2003, 2010.

2010				
24/7	Istra	h	6-1	*Sharbini An., Oremuš, Andrić, Sharbini Ah., Ljubičić M., Ibričić (p)*
1/8	Osijek	a	2-2	*Buljat J., Ibričić (p)*
8/8	Šibenik	h	2-0	*Ibričić, Vukušić*
14/8	Inter	a	5-0	*Sharbini An., Tomasov, Vukušić 2, Čop*
22/8	Zadar	h	4-1	*Tomasov, Vukušić 2, Ibričić*
29/8	Split	a	1-1	*Vukušić*
11/9	Dinamo	h	1-1	*Sharbini An.*
19/9	Rijeka	a	1-0	*Brkljača*
25/9	Varaždin	h	2-0	*Vukušić, Čop*
3/10	Karlovac	a	1-1	*Vukušić*
16/10	Slaven	h	1-0	*Vukušić*
24/10	Cibalia	a	1-2	*Vukušić (p)*
30/10	Hrvatski dragovoljac	h	2-1	*Buljat J., Tomasov*
7/11	Zagreb	h	4-1	*Trebotić, Sharbini An. 2, Ibričić*
13/11	Lokomotiva	a	1-0	*Oremuš*
20/11	Istra	a	0-2	
27/11	Osijek	h	2-1	*Vukušić, og (Gavrić)*
5/12	Šibenik	a	3-1	*Tomasov, Andrić, Ibričić*
2011				
26/2	Inter	h	0-0	
5/3	Zadar	a	2-0	*Andrić, Ljubičić M.*
12/3	Split	h	3-1	*Andrić 2, Vukušić*
19/3	Dinamo	a	0-2	
2/4	Rijeka	h	1-1	*Vukušić (p)*
9/4	Varaždin	a	0-3	
16/4	Karlovac	h	2-3	*Vejić, Brkljača*
23/4	Slaven	a	2-1	*Vukušić, Čop*
30/4	Cibalia	h	1-2	*Čop*
6/5	Hrvatski dragovoljac	a	0-2	
14/5	Zagreb	a	2-2	*Brkljača, Čop*
21/5	Lokomotiva	h	2-0	*Sharbini Ah., Trebotić*

No	Name	Nat	DoB	Pos	Aps	(s)	Gls
11	Srđan ANDRIĆ		5/1/80	M	16		5
6	Franko ANDRIJAŠEVIĆ		22/6/91	M	4	(3)	
2	Josip BARIŠIĆ	BIH	12/8/83	D	4	(1)	
21	Mario BRKLJAČA		7/2/85	M	11	(11)	3
5	Jurica BULJAT		19/9/86	D	24		2
19	Marijan BULJAT		12/9/81	D	1	(1)	
88	Ervin BULKU	ALB	3/3/81	M	12	(3)	
90	Duje ČOP		1/2/90	A	8	(6)	5
10	Senijad IBRIČIĆ	BIH	26/9/85	M	17		6
27	Matej JONJIĆ		29/1/91	D	4		
29	Goran JOZINOVIĆ		27/8/90	D	15	(7)	
12	Lovre KALINIĆ		3/4/90	G	1		
6	Tonći KUKOČ		25/9/90	M		(1)	
8	Krešo LJUBIČIĆ		26/9/88	M	5	(4)	
4	Marin LJUBIČIĆ		15/6/88	M	15	(5)	2
22	Mario MALOČA		4/5/89	D	26	(1)	
18	Mirko OREMUŠ		6/9/88	M	17	(4)	2
25	Božidar RADOŠEVIĆ		4/4/89	G	9		
20	Ante REŽIĆ		4/6/88	D	6	(3)	
29	Mario SAČER		17/1/90	A	1	(1)	
9	Ahmad SHARBINI		21/2/84	A	4	(9)	2
99	Anas SHARBINI		21/2/87	M	18	(2)	5
17	Ivan STRINIĆ		17/7/87	D	11	(1)	
1	Danijel SUBAŠIĆ		27/10/84	G	20		
24	Mario TIČINOVIĆ		20/8/91	M	8	(1)	
14	Marin TOMASOV		31/8/87	M	15	(11)	4
10	Dinko TREBOTIĆ		30/7/90	M	13	(8)	2
7	Hrvoje VEJIĆ		8/6/77	D	17	(3)	1
13	Ante VUKUŠIĆ		4/6/91	A	28	(1)	14

NK HRVATSKI DRAGOVOLJAC ZAGREB

Coach – Davor Mladina; (19/9/10) Damir Biškup; (3/10/10) Ivan Pudar; (7/11/10) Davor Mladina

Founded – 1975

Stadium – Kranjčevićeva (12,000) & NŠC Stjepan Spajić (5,000)

2010				
24/7	Dinamo	a	1-4	*Kešinović*
30/7	Lokomotiva	h	1-2	*Švarić*
7/8	Rijeka	a	0-3	
13/8	Istra	h	1-1	*Švarić*
21/8	Varaždin	a	0-2	
27/8	Osijek	h	1-1	*Međumurac*
10/9	Karlovac	a	0-2	
17/9	Šibenik	h	0-1	
25/9	Slaven	a	0-3	
1/10	Inter	h	0-0	
16/10	Cibalia	a	0-3	
22/10	Zadar	h	1-4	*Leko*
30/10	Hajduk	a	1-2	*Novak*
6/11	Split	h	0-4	
13/11	Zagreb	a	1-0	*Zlatar*
20/11	Dinamo	h	0-6	
26/11	Lokomotiva	a	2-3	*Janjetović, Zlatar*
3/12	Rijeka	h	2-2	*Žugaj 2*
2011				
26/2	Istra	a	1-0	*Leko*
4/3	Varaždin	h	3-2	*Vrnoga, Janjetović, og (Šimek)*
12/3	Osijek	a	0-0	
18/3	Karlovac	h	1-0	*Brozović*
2/4	Šibenik	a	2-2	*Švarić (p), Jazvić*
9/4	Slaven	h	0-0	
15/4	Inter	a	2-3	*Grgić, Kukoč*
23/4	Cibalia	h	0-0	
30/4	Zadar	a	0-1	
6/5	Hajduk	h	2-0	*Grgić, Jazvić*
14/5	Split	a	0-1	
21/5	Zagreb	h	2-3	*Kešinović, Švarić*

No	Name	Nat	DoB	Pos	Aps	(s)	Gls
7	Ivan BEGOVIĆ		9/2/86	M	11	(3)	
3	Ivan BORZIĆ		28/12/90	M		(2)	
11	Marcelo BROZOVIĆ		16/11/92	M	18	(4)	1
8	Davor ČORDAŠ		16/12/76	A	14	(7)	
8	Ivan ČOSIĆ		13/3/83	D	1	(3)	
12	Ivan ČOVIĆ		17/9/90	G	16		
1	Darko FRANIĆ		22/3/87	G	2		
23	Nikola FRLJUŽEC		29/6/89	A	7	(2)	
13	Mato GRGIĆ		27/9/87	D	26	(1)	2
25	Ivan GRUBIŠIĆ		23/2/92	M		(2)	
11	Sven JAJČINOVIĆ		4/4/93	A		(1)	
5	Marko JANJETOVIĆ		22/4/84	M	11	(3)	2
14	Filip JAZVIĆ		22/10/90	M	17	(7)	2
25	Mario JURIN		10/8/85	M	17		
19	Plumb JUSUFI		10/2/88	M	9	(5)	
24	Karlo KEŠINOVIĆ		12/2/89	D	15	(4)	2
21	Nikola KOVAČEVIĆ		27/4/90	A		(1)	
19	Tonći KUKOČ		25/9/90	M	3	(2)	1
15	Mislav LEKO		19/12/87	D	17	(1)	2
26	Hrvoje LERGA		14/10/89	G	1		
6	Hrvoje MARKOVIĆ		11/11/84	D	14	(2)	

20	Goran MEĐUMURAC		26/9/84	A	8	(5)	1
21	Alen MEŠANOVIĆ	BIH	26/10/75	A	1		
17	Leopold NOVAK		3/12/90	A	6	(5)	1
18	Zoran PLAZONIĆ		1/2/89	M	14	(2)	
10	Mario RAŠIĆ		20/5/89	A	12		
10	SÉRGIO Rúben Lacerda de Oliveira	BRA	27/6/77	M	1	(5)	
2	Dario SMOJE		19/9/78	D	3		
4	Davor ŠPEHAR		9/2/88	M	18		
22	Velimir ŠVARIĆ		19/4/85	A	23	(3)	4
1	Igor VIDAKOVIĆ		20/8/83	G	11		
16	Marin VRNOGA de Gregorio		28/1/91	M	6	(1)	1
9	Danijel ZLATAR		30/8/84	A	26	(2)	2
21	Marin ŽUGAJ		21/9/89	M	2	(14)	2

NK INTER ZAPREŠIĆ

Coach – Ilija Lončarević

Founded – 1929

Stadium – ŠRC Zaprešić (4,500)

MAJOR HONOURS: Croatian Cup – (1) 1992.

2010				
24/7	Karlovac	a	0-3	
30/7	Slaven	h	0-1	
7/8	Cibalia	a	0-1	
14/8	Hajduk	h	0-5	
20/8	Zagreb	a	1-2	*Herceg*
28/8	Lokomotiva	h	5-0	*Oršić, Hrnčević, Bosec 2, Palić*
11/9	Istra	a	1-0	*Palić (p)*
17/9	Osijek	h	1-0	*Šarić*
25/9	Šibenik	a	1-0	*Abilaliaj*
1/10	Hrvatski dragovoljac	a	0-0	
15/10	Zadar	h	1-0	*Palić (p)*
23/10	Split	a	1-1	*Matko*
30/10	Dinamo	h	0-3	
6/11	Rijeka	a	2-0	*Babić, Abilaliaj*
13/11	Varaždin	h	2-0	*Babić, Oršić*
19/11	Karlovac	h	0-0	
27/11	Slaven	a	0-0	
3/12	Cibalia	h	2-1	*Balić, Barišić*
2011				
26/2	Hajduk	a	0-0	
4/3	Zagreb	h	0-2	
11/3	Lokomotiva	a	4-2	*Trajkovski, Kramarić, Budimir, Blažević*
18/3	Istra	h	3-1	*Kramarić, og (Pauletić), Balić*
2/4	Osijek	a	0-1	
8/4	Šibenik	h	3-2	*Budimir, Barišić, Trajkovski*
15/4	Hrvatski dragovoljac	h	3-2	*Trajkovski (p), Oršić, Budimir*
23/4	Zadar	a	0-1	
30/4	Split	h	0-2	
6/5	Dinamo	a	0-1	
13/5	Rijeka	h	1-1	*Trajkovski*
21/5	Varaždin	a	0-3	

No	Name	Nat	DoB	Pos	Aps	(s)	Gls
9	Arbër ABILALIAJ	ALB	6/6/86	A	17	(7)	2
12	Stjepan BABIĆ		4/12/88	M	10	(9)	2
3	Saša BALIĆ	MNE	29/1/90	D	18	(4)	2
4	Josip BARIŠIĆ		7/3/81	D	25	(1)	2
19	Ivan BLAŽEVIĆ		25/7/92	M	5	(5)	1
11	Tomislav BOSEC		14/6/90	A	4	(8)	2
8	Ante BUDIMIR		22/7/91	A	7	(4)	3
13	Mario GRGUROVIĆ		2/2/85	M	6	(1)	
6	Bernard GULIĆ		9/4/80	A	22	(4)	
15	Ivan HERCEG		10/2/90	D	21	(2)	1
18	Antonio HRNČEVIĆ		7/7/84	A	8	(3)	1
17	Hrvoje JANČETIĆ		10/2/81	D	25	(1)	
10	Tomislav JONJIĆ		19/5/83	M	8	(2)	
25	Ivan JURIĆ-BARE		6/5/84	G	2		
22	Mirko KRAMARIĆ		27/1/89	M	8	(2)	2
31	Matija MATKO		20/9/82	A	5	(5)	1
5	Ivan MRŠIĆ	BIH	24/6/91	D	3	(1)	
28	Nenad NIKOLIĆ	SRB	12/8/84	D	6		
20	Mislav ORŠIĆ		29/12/92	A	16	(9)	3
8	Antun PALIĆ		25/6/88	M	15	(1)	3
32	Krševan SANTINI		11/4/87	G	28		
16	Tomislav ŠARIĆ		24/6/90	M	28		1
1	Goran TODORCEV	MKD	21/1/84	M	10	(1)	
21	Aleksandar TRAJKOVSKI	MKD	5/9/92	A	10	(5)	4
23	Adrian VALENTIĆ		10/8/87	D	8	(6)	
7	Armand Dubois YANKEP	CMR	17/12/85	M	15	(7)	

NK ISTRA

Coach – Ante Miše; (4/8/10) Robert Jarni; (19/9/10) (Davor Lasić); (5/10/10) Zoran Vulić; (29/3/11) Igor Pamić

Founded – 1948

Stadium – ŠRC Uljanik Veruda (3,500) & Aldo Drosina (8,923)

2010				
24/7	Hajduk	a	1-6	*Šehić*
31/7	Zagreb	h	0-2	
7/8	Lokomotiva	a	0-1	
13/8	Hrvatski dragovoljac	a	1-1	*Stupić*
21/8	Osijek	h	1-2	*Alimi*
28/8	Šibenik	a	2-2	*Pauletić, Anđelković*
11/9	Inter	h	0-1	
18/9	Zadar	a	0-2	
25/9	Split	h	0-1	
3/10	Dinamo	a	0-4	
16/10	Rijeka	h	0-0	
23/10	Varaždin	a	1-2	*Linić*
30/10	Karlovac	h	1-0	*Sušić*
6/11	Slaven	a	1-2	*Linić*
13/11	Cibalia	h	1-0	*Linić*
20/11	Hajduk	h	2-0	*Alimi, Šehić*
27/11	Zagreb	a	1-0	*Šehić*
4/12	Lokomotiva	h	2-1	*Roce, Linić*
2011				
26/2	Hrvatski dragovoljac	h	0-1	
5/3	Osijek	a	1-2	*Weitzer*
12/3	Šibenik	h	1-4	*Tepurić*
18/3	Inter	a	1-3	*Plantić*
2/4	Zadar	h	1-0	*Sušić*
9/4	Split	a	0-2	
16/4	Dinamo	h	2-1	*Eliomar, Belle*
23/4	Rijeka	a	0-2	
30/4	Varaždin	h	2-0	*Linić, Šehić (p)*
7/5	Karlovac	a	1-1	*Alimi*
14/5	Slaven	h	1-0	*Belle*
21/5	Cibalia	a	0-1	

No	Name	Nat	DoB	Pos	Aps	(s)	Gls
10	Armend ALIMI	MKD	11/12/87	M	26	(3)	3
7	Mislav ANĐELKOVIĆ		22/4/88	M	25	(2)	1
15	Goran BARIŠIĆ		12/12/85	D	10	(3)	
23	Julio BARRABES	FRA	14/8/88	D	1		
13	Kristijan BATELIĆ		26/8/93	M	3	(5)	
25	Henry BELLE	CMR	25/1/89	M	5	(2)	2
23	Gjergj BUSHAJ	SRB	8/3/91	M		(2)	
2	Robert DEAK		31/1/90	D		(1)	
50	ELIOMAR dos Santos Silva	BRA	12/2/87	A	6	(5)	1
8	Paolo GRBAC		9/7/90	M	3	(4)	
16	Emir HADŽIĆ	BIH	19/7/84	A	1	(9)	
16	Mario JURIĆ		8/7/76	A	4		
3	Hasan KACIĆ		29/7/76	D	23	(3)	
19	Hrvoje KOVAČEVIĆ		21/7/82	M	20	(2)	
6	Siniša LINIĆ		23/8/82	M	21		5
1	Igor LOVRIĆ		7/10/87	G	1		
20	Marjan MARKOVIĆ	SRB	28/9/81	M	15	(1)	
4	Ninoslav MILENKOVIĆ		31/12/77	D	8		
11	Dalibor PAULETIĆ		27/10/78	D	29		1
25	Mirko PLANTIĆ		15/1/85	D		(2)	1
10	Nikola PRELČEC		12/11/89	M	4	(3)	
32	Andrej PRSKALO		1/5/87	G	3	(1)	

	Goran ROCE		12/4/86	M	21	(2)	1
)	Ivan RODIĆ		11/11/85	A	5		
5	Dean STOJANOVIĆ		8/6/91	M		(2)	
	Slobodan STRANATIĆ		27/11/85	D	14		
	Boško STUPIĆ	BIH	27/6/84	A	6	(5)	1
	Mateo SUŠIĆ	BIH	18/11/90	D	9	(10)	2
	Asim ŠEHIĆ	BIH	16/6/81	A	21		4
	Josip ŠKORIĆ		13/2/81	G	26		
)	Franjo TEPURIĆ		10/2/90	A	2	(4)	1
3	Ivor WEITZER		24/5/88	M	3		1
7	Dragan ŽUPAN		26/5/82	M	4	(1)	
1	Ivan ŽURŽINOV	SRB	30/5/81	D	11	(9)	

NK KARLOVAC

Coach – Igor Pamić; (23/3/11) Srećko Lušić

Founded – 1919

Stadium – Branko Čavlović-Čavlek (12,000)

010				
4/7	Inter	h	3-0	*Špišić, Husić, Kovačević*
1/7	Zadar	a	0-2	
/8	Split	h	1-0	*Barić*
4/8	Dinamo	a	2-4	*Špišić, Tičinović*
1/8	Rijeka	h	0-1	
8/8	Varaždin	a	0-1	
0/9	Hrvatski dragovoljac	h	2-0	*Jerneić, Batarelo*
8/9	Slaven	h	1-0	*Čejvanović*
5/9	Cibalia	a	0-1	
/10	Hajduk	h	1-1	*Novinić*
5/10	Zagreb	a	2-1	*Novinić, Batarelo*
3/10	Lokomotiva	h	1-2	*Primorac*
0/10	Istra	a	0-1	
/11	Osijek	h	1-0	*Kovačević*
3/11	Šibenik	a	1-2	*Primorac*
9/11	Inter	a	0-0	
27/11	Zadar	h	1-0	*Jerneić*
/12	Split	a	1-0	*Pilipović*
2011				
26/2	Dinamo	h	0-1	
5/3	Rijeka	a	0-0	
12/3	Varaždin	h	1-0	*Primorac*
18/3	Hrvatski dragovoljac	a	0-1	
2/4	Slaven	a	0-4	
9/4	Cibalia	h	0-0	
16/4	Hajduk	a	3-2	*Primorac, Štefančić, Husić*
23/4	Zagreb	h	2-1	*Primorac, Kovačević*
29/4	Lokomotiva	a	0-0	
7/5	Istra	h	1-1	*Štefančić*
14/5	Osijek	a	0-0	
21/5	Šibenik	h	1-1	*Husić*

No	Name	Nat	DoB	Pos	Aps	(s)	Gls
7	Mario BARIĆ		15/4/85	D	6		1
18	Ante BATARELO		21/11/84	M	26	(3)	2
19	Marijan BUDIMIR		19/10/80	D	13	(1)	
7	Kenan ČEJVANOVIĆ	BIH	9/8/86	D	13	(3)	1
27	Romeo FILIPOVIĆ		31/3/86	M		(5)	
17	Kristijan GLAVAŠ		12/1/91	M		(3)	
4	Toni GOLEM		14/1/82	D	2		
5	Edin HUSIĆ	BIH	10/11/85	M	23	(6)	3
10	Josip JERNEIĆ		6/5/80	A	24	(3)	2
2	Goran JUROŠ		9/1/86	M	4	(1)	
28	Jurica KARABATIĆ		22/7/78	D	29		
15	Željko KOVAČEVIĆ		9/8/79	M	28		3
11	Ivan LAJTMAN		7/1/79	M	1	(1)	
12	Igor LOVRIĆ		7/10/87	G	18		
9	Enes NOVINIĆ		18/7/85	A	9	(8)	2
16	Andrea OTTOCHIAN		26/6/88	M	11	(4)	
6	Goran PARACKI		21/1/87	M	22	(1)	
3	Borislav PILIPOVIĆ	BIH	25/3/84	D	24	(2)	1
24	Patrik POLJAK		21/2/94	M		(3)	
22	Karlo PRIMORAC		1/6/84	A	18	(2)	5
20	Miheal SOPČIĆ		8/9/91	A		(5)	
21	Adis STAMBOLIJA	BIH	24/11/83	M	11	(7)	
1	Hrvoje SUNARA		4/8/79	G	12		
17	Slavko ŠIPIĆ		31/8/88	A		(2)	
14	Viktor ŠPIŠIĆ		8/6/82	M	15	(9)	2
8	Matija ŠTEFANČIĆ		13/7/81	A	11	(11)	2
20	Mario TIČINOVIĆ		20/8/91	M	7		1
19	Niko TOKIĆ		7/6/88	A	2	(1)	
2	Ivan ZGRABLIĆ		15/3/91	D	1	(1)	

NK LOKOMOTIVA ZAGREB

Coach – Roy Ferečina; (2/10/10) Ljupko Petrović (SRB); (14/3/11) Krunoslav Jurčić

Founded – 1914

Stadium – Maksimir (37,168)

2010				
23/7	Zagreb	a	1-3	*Peko*
30/7	Hrvatski dragovoljac	a	2-1	*Martinac, Bule (p)*
7/8	Istra	h	1-0	*Antolić*
14/8	Osijek	a	0-0	
21/8	Šibenik	h	0-0	
28/8	Inter	a	0-5	
10/9	Zadar	h	3-2	*Bule 2, Šimić*
18/9	Split	a	0-1	
26/9	Dinamo	h	0-2	
2/10	Rijeka	a	0-3	
16/10	Varaždin	h	1-2	*Bule*
23/10	Karlovac	a	2-1	*Sopić, Bule*
30/10	Slaven	h	0-0	
6/11	Cibalia	a	1-2	*Bule*
13/11	Hajduk	h	0-1	
20/11	Zagreb	h	2-0	*Bule 2 (1p)*
26/11	Hrvatski dragovoljac	h	3-2	*Komorski, Sesar, Peko*
4/12	Istra	a	1-2	*Peko*
2011				
25/2	Osijek	h	0-0	
5/3	Šibenik	a	0-0	
11/3	Inter	h	2-4	*Sopić, Bule*
19/3	Zadar	a	0-1	
1/4	Split	h	0-0	
9/4	Dinamo	a	0-1	
15/4	Rijeka	h	0-0	
23/4	Varaždin	a	1-0	*Bule*
29/4	Karlovac	h	0-0	
7/5	Slaven	a	2-2	*Dodô, Bule (p)*
13/5	Cibalia	h	2-0	*Samateh, Dodô*
21/5	Hajduk	a	0-2	

No	Name	Nat	DoB	Pos	Aps	(s)	Gls
77	Gheorghe ANDRONIC	MDA	25/9/91	M	1		
18	Domagoj ANTOLIĆ		30/6/90	M	6		1
5	Walid ATTA	SWE	30/6/90	D	8		
17	Matej BAGARIĆ		16/1/89	D	6		
15	Almir BEKIĆ	BIH	1/6/89	M	4	(6)	
2	Ivan BORAS		31/10/91	D	11	(4)	
9	Nino BULE		19/3/76	A	27		11
5	Denis CEROVEC		4/4/91	D	1		
77	Luiz Paulo Hilário "DODÔ"	BRA	16/10/87	A	11	(1)	2
19	Tomislav HAVOJIĆ		10/3/89	M	3	(5)	
22	Ivor HORVAT		19/8/91	D	15	(2)	
12	Ivan KELAVA		20/2/88	G	6		
6	Mislav KOMORSKI		17/4/92	D	26		1
39	Miroslav KONOPEK		28/3/91	A	1	(4)	
14	Mirko KRAMARIĆ		27/1/89	M		(3)	
7	Mate MALEŠ		13/1/89	M	13	(4)	
10	Tomislav MARTINAC		27/6/83	M	12	(9)	1
12	Romeo MITROVIĆ	BIH	12/7/79	G	21		
4	Frano MLINAR		30/3/92	M	14	(4)	
20	Ivan MRŠIĆ	BIH	24/6/91	D		(1)	
3	Mario MUSA		6/7/90	D	19	(3)	
99	Dalibor PANDŽA	BIH	23/3/91	A		(3)	
23	Ivan PEKO		5/1/90	M	18	(5)	3
1	Dominik PICAK		12/2/92	G	3		

No	Name	Nat	DoB	Pos	Aps	(s)	Gls
11	Josip PIVARIĆ		30/1/89	D	27	(2)	
8	Mateo POLJAK		10/9/89	M	17	(6)	
20	Lamin SAMATEH	GAM	26/6/92	D	6	(1)	1
21	Ivan SESAR	BIH	29/8/89	M	10	(7)	1
77	Ilija SIVONJIĆ		13/1/87	A	4	(2)	
13	Željko SOPIĆ		26/7/74	M	28		2
16	Filip ŠĆRBEC		3/6/91	M	1	(1)	
99	Marko ŠIMIĆ		23/1/88	A	2	(6)	1
24	Marko TROJAK		28/3/91	M	8	(6)	
14	Dario ZAHORA		21/3/82	A	1	(1)	

NK OSIJEK

Coach – Tomislav Steinbruckner; (16/8/10) Branko Karačić; (9/5/11) Vlado Bilić

Founded – 1947

Stadium – Gradski vrt (19,500)

MAJOR HONOURS: Croatian Cup – (1) 1999.

2010				
25/7	Cibalia	a	0-3	
1/8	Hajduk	h	2-2	*Vidaković, Miličević*
6/8	Zagreb	a	0-0	
14/8	Lokomotiva	h	0-0	
21/8	Istra	a	2-1	*Pušić, Kvržić*
27/8	Hrvatski dragovoljac	a	1-1	*Barišić*
10/9	Šibenik	h	3-1	*Kvržić, Barišić, Smoje*
17/9	Inter	a	0-1	
25/9	Zadar	h	3-2	*Jugović, Miličević, Nikšić*
2/10	Split	a	0-1	
16/10	Dinamo	h	1-3	*Nikšić (p)*
23/10	Rijeka	a	5-1	*Miličević, Smoje, Nikšić, Šorša, Škorić*
30/10	Varaždin	h	0-0	
6/11	Karlovac	a	0-1	
13/11	Slaven	h	1-1	*Špehar*
20/11	Cibalia	h	1-0	*Maglica*
27/11	Hajduk	a	1-2	*Pavličić*
4/12	Zagreb	h	0-0	
2011				
25/2	Lokomotiva	a	0-0	
5/3	Istra	h	2-1	*Maglica, Smoje*
12/3	Hrvatski dragovoljac	h	0-0	
19/3	Šibenik	a	1-2	*Ljubojević*
2/4	Inter	h	1-0	*Lukačević*
9/4	Zadar	a	1-1	*Barišić*
16/4	Split	h	1-0	*Vidaković*
23/4	Dinamo	a	0-1	
30/4	Rijeka	h	0-0	
6/5	Varaždin	a	4-2	*Miličević 2, Maglica, Babić*
14/5	Karlovac	h	0-0	
21/5	Slaven	a	1-2	*Maglica*

No	Name	Nat	DoB	Pos	Aps	(s)	Gls
28	Marko BABIĆ		28/1/81	M	1	(7)	1
20	Josip BARIŠIĆ		14/11/86	A	12	(12)	3
19	Hrvoje BUBALO		30/12/77	D	6		
14	Andrej ČAUŠIĆ		19/2/90	D	8	(1)	
6	Dino GAVRIĆ		11/4/89	M	25	(1)	
15	Ivan IBRIKS		6/10/87	D	10	(1)	
17	Vedran JUGOVIĆ		10/9/89	M	25		1
12	Ivan KARDUM		18/7/87	G	30		
4	Hrvoje KURTOVIĆ		6/10/83	M	15	(6)	
8	Zoran KVRŽIĆ	BIH	7/8/88	M	13	(8)	2
13	Marko LEŠKOVIĆ		27/4/91	D		(2)	
9	Goran LJUBOJEVIĆ		4/5/83	A	11		1
3	Josip LUKAČEVIĆ	BIH	3/11/83	M	20	(2)	1
16	Anton MAGLICA		11/11/91	A	8	(11)	4
26	Ivan MILIČEVIĆ		11/2/88	A	22	(4)	5
7	Vedran NIKŠIĆ		5/5/87	A	7	(4)	3
18	Milan PAVLIČIĆ		20/12/80	M	2	(5)	1
11	Mladen PELAIĆ		20/8/83	D	12	(2)	
27	Antonio PEROŠEVIĆ		6/3/92	D		(1)	
9	Ivan PLUM		6/5/92	A		(1)	
3	Jurica PRANJIĆ		16/12/87	D	2		
7	Igor PRIJIĆ		30/9/89	A	1	(4)	
5	Domagoj PUŠIĆ		24/10/91	M	14		1
24	Ivo SMOJE		21/11/78	D	17		3
27	Pero STOJKIĆ	BIH	9/12/86	D	3	(2)	
7	Mile ŠKORIĆ		19/6/91	M		(5)	1
22	Tomislav ŠORŠA		11/5/89	M	24		1
10	Dino ŠPEHAR		8/2/94	A	13	(2)	1
23	Srđan VIDAKOVIĆ		13/10/86	M	19	(6)	2
2	Branko VRGOČ		18/12/89	D	10	(1)	

HNK RIJEKA

Coach – Nenad Gračan; (8/11/10) Elvis Scoria

Founded – 1946

Stadium – Kantrida (11,000)

MAJOR HONOURS: Yugoslav Cup – (2) 1978, 1979; Croatian Cup – (2) 2005, 2006.

2010				
24/7	Split	h	1-0	*og (Vidić)*
31/7	Dinamo	a	2-1	*Rodić, og (Badelj)*
7/8	Hrvatski dragovoljac	h	3-0	*Štrok 2, Đalović*
14/8	Varaždin	h	1-1	*Rodić*
21/8	Karlovac	a	1-0	*Švrljuga*
28/8	Slaven	h	2-1	*Štrok, Kreilach*
11/9	Cibalia	a	1-4	*Đalović*
19/9	Hajduk	h	0-1	
26/9	Zagreb	a	1-3	*Đalović (p)*
2/10	Lokomotiva	h	3-0	*Rodić, Kreilach, Čaval*
16/10	Istra	a	0-0	
23/10	Osijek	h	1-5	*Štrok*
30/10	Šibenik	a	1-1	*Budicin*
6/11	Inter	h	0-2	
13/11	Zadar	a	0-1	
20/11	Split	a	3-2	*Štrok, Đalović 2 (1p)*
27/11	Dinamo	h	0-2	
3/12	Hrvatski dragovoljac	a	2-2	*Vukman, Štrok (p)*
2011				
26/2	Varaždin	a	0-3	
5/3	Karlovac	h	0-0	
12/3	Slaven	a	1-0	*Čulina*
19/3	Cibalia	h	0-0	
2/4	Hajduk	a	1-1	*Budicin*
9/4	Zagreb	h	1-1	*Pilčić*
15/4	Lokomotiva	a	0-0	
23/4	Istra	h	2-0	*Vukman, Čulina*
30/4	Osijek	a	0-0	
7/5	Šibenik	h	1-1	*Čulina*
13/5	Inter	a	1-1	*Čulina*
21/5	Zadar	h	0-2	

No	Name	Nat	DoB	Pos	Aps	(s)	Gls
22	Duje BAKOVIĆ		7/6/86	D	21		
13	Ivan BIJELIĆ		15/1/90	M		(2)	
16	Fausto BUDICIN		1/5/81	D	28	(2)	2
5	Igor ČAGALJ		8/10/82	D	24		
3	Kristijan ČAVAL		11/10/78	M	22	(2)	1
15	Antonini ČULINA		27/1/92	M	14	(5)	4
21	Radomir ĐALOVIĆ	MNE	29/10/82	A	20		5
19	Milan ĐURIŠIĆ	MNE	11/4/87	M	5	(4)	
9	Vedran GERC		14/2/86	A	3	(8)	
17	Damir KREILACH		16/4/89	M	27	(1)	2
10	Sandi KRIŽMAN		17/8/89	A	7	(11)	
8	Davor LANDEKA	BIH	18/9/84	M	24	(4)	
12	Robert LISJAK		5/2/78	G	30		
4	Denis LJUBOVIĆ		20/3/88	D	5	(1)	
2	Mato MILOŠ		30/6/93	D	1		
11	Dražen PILČIĆ		24/10/89	A	7	(4)	1
18	Ivan RODIĆ		11/11/85	A	12	(1)	3
20	Antonio RUKAVINA		6/5/85	M	4	(7)	
7	Valentino STEPČIĆ		16/1/90	M	2	(14)	
14	Hrvoje ŠTROK		14/7/80	M	29		6
24	Andro ŠVRLJUGA		24/10/85	M	25	(3)	1
27	Neven VUKMAN		14/10/85	M	14	(5)	2
2	Mikael YOURASSOWSKY	BEL	26/2/83	D	5	(2)	
29	Sergio ZIJLER	NED	8/7/87	A	1	(3)	

HNK ŠIBENIK

Coach – Branko Karačić; (23/7/10) (Anđelo Godinić); (11/8/10) Vjekoslav Lokica

Founded – 1932

Stadium – Šubićevac (8,000)

010				
/7	Slaven	a	0-1	
/7	Cibalia	h	0-0	
8	Hajduk	a	0-2	
/8	Zagreb	h	0-1	
/8	Lokomotiva	a	0-0	
/8	Istra	h	2-2	*Alispahić, Bačelić-Grgić*
/9	Osijek	a	1-3	*Alispahić*
7/9	Hrvatski dragovoljac	a	1-0	*Alispahić (p)*
5/9	Inter	h	0-1	
/10	Zadar	a	4-1	*Alispahić 2 (1p), Jelić, Georgievski*
6/10	Split	h	3-0	*Kartelo, Jelić 2*
/10	Dinamo	a	0-1	
/10	Rijeka	h	1-1	*Malčić*
/11	Varaždin	a	2-2	*Tokić, Malčić*
3/11	Karlovac	h	2-1	*Alispahić (p), Jelić*
/11	Slaven	h	3-3	*Kartelo, Alispahić (p), Božić*
7/11	Cibalia	a	1-3	*Malčić*
/12	Hajduk	h	1-3	*Alispahić (p)*
011				
5/2	Zagreb	a	1-1	*Jelić*
/3	Lokomotiva	h	0-0	
2/3	Istra	a	4-1	*Jelić, Tokić, Alispahić, Kartelo*
9/3	Osijek	h	2-1	*Fuštar 2*
/4	Hrvatski dragovoljac	h	2-2	*Jakoliš 2*
/4	Inter	a	2-3	*Bačelić-Grgić, Brečević*
6/4	Zadar	h	2-0	*Alispahić, Krišto*
3/4	Split	a	0-1	
0/4	Dinamo	h	0-2	
/5	Rijeka	a	1-1	*Bačelić-Grgić*
4/5	Varaždin	h	1-0	*Alispahić*
1/5	Karlovac	a	1-1	*Brečević*

No	Name	Nat	DoB	Pos	Aps	(s)	Gls
0	Mehmed ALISPAHIĆ	BIH	24/11/87	M	25		11
4	Stipe BAČELIĆ-GRGIĆ		16/2/88	M	22	(3)	3
8	Ivan BAKOVIĆ		3/9/90	M	1		
8	Zvonimir BLAIĆ		2/1/91	D		(1)	
	Goran BLAŽEVIĆ		7/6/86	G	28		
9	Sandro BLOUDEK		16/2/86	M	3		
21	Ivan BOŽIĆ	BIH	19/11/83	A	11	(12)	1
9	Ivan BREČEVIĆ		28/7/87	A	2	(7)	2
24	Ante BULAT		6/1/85	M	7	(5)	
4	Tarik CERIĆ	BIH	28/1/78	D	7		
5	Marko ČULIĆ		10/2/87	M	10		
8	Ivan ELEZ		9/5/81	M	3		
19	Ivan FUŠTAR		18/8/89	A	18	(4)	2
2	Daniel GEORGIEVSKI	MKD	17/2/88	D	11	(7)	1
20	Dražen GOVIĆ		29/4/81	M	9	(3)	
5	Luka GUSIĆ		27/9/89	D	1		
11	Zeni HUSMANI		28/11/90	M	23	(1)	
17	Antonio JAKOLIŠ		28/2/92	A	23	(5)	2
26	Dražen JELIĆ		9/7/82	A	12	(11)	6
25	Marko JORDAN		27/10/90	A		(1)	
6	Mladen JURČEVIĆ	BIH	4/3/83	D	20	(1)	
9	Ivan JURIĆ		14/1/87	A		(1)	
7	Marko KARTELO		16/2/81	M	23	(1)	3
4	Dario KRIŠTO		5/3/89	M	5	(3)	1
30	Željko MALČIĆ		15/11/81	A	6	(7)	3
16	Josip MALEŠ		17/1/91	M	1	(4)	
18	Ivan MEDVID	BIH	13/10/77	D	21		
13	Boris PEŠIĆ		25/5/87	M		(3)	
26	Anto RADELJIĆ		31/12/90	D	4		
12	Hrvoje SLAVICA		27/4/81	G	2		
27	Hrvoje SPAHIJA		23/3/88	D	10	(3)	
29	Niko TOKIĆ		7/6/88	A	21		2
23	Ante VRČIĆ		20/10/90	A	1	(3)	

NK SLAVEN KOPRIVNICA

Coach – Mile Petković; (14/3/11) Roy Ferečina

Founded – 1907

Stadium – Gradski (3,800)

2010				
25/7	Šibenik	h	1-0	*Kokalović*
30/7	Inter	a	1-0	*Maras*
7/8	Zadar	h	2-0	*Delić, Vojnović (p)*
14/8	Split	a	0-3	
22/8	Dinamo	h	0-2	
28/8	Rijeka	a	1-2	*Delić*
11/9	Varaždin	h	1-0	*Vojnović*
18/9	Karlovac	a	0-1	
25/9	Hrvatski dragovoljac	h	3-0	*Tepurić, Vojnović (p), Bagarić*
2/10	Cibalia	h	1-1	*Bagarić*
16/10	Hajduk	a	0-1	
23/10	Zagreb	h	1-2	*Milardović*
30/10	Lokomotiva	a	0-0	
6/11	Istra	h	2-1	*Nynkeu, Kokalović*
13/11	Osijek	a	1-1	*og (Pelaić)*
20/11	Šibenik	a	3-3	*Milardović, Vojnović, Delić*
27/11	Inter	h	0-0	
4/12	Zadar	a	1-1	*Delić*
2011				
26/2	Split	h	1-2	*Benko*
5/3	Dinamo	a	0-0	
12/3	Rijeka	h	0-1	
19/3	Varaždin	a	1-1	*Benko*
2/4	Karlovac	h	4-0	*Bagarić, Milardović, Benko, Mujanović*
9/4	Hrvatski dragovoljac	a	0-0	
16/4	Cibalia	a	2-1	*Benko 2*
23/4	Hajduk	h	1-2	*Kokalović*
29/4	Zagreb	a	3-1	*Bušić, Vojnović, Benko*
7/5	Lokomotiva	h	2-2	*Papa, Benko*
14/5	Istra	a	0-1	
21/5	Osijek	h	2-1	*Benko, Havojić*

No	Name	Nat	DoB	Pos	Aps	(s)	Gls
19	Davor BAGARIĆ		8/9/85	M	22		3
15	Leon BENKO		11/11/83	A	11		8
21	Petar BRLEK		29/1/94	M		(1)	
30	Tomislav BUŠIĆ		2/2/86	A	12	(3)	1
14	Mateas DELIĆ		17/6/88	M	11	(5)	4
21	Nikola FRLJUŽEC		29/6/89	A	1	(4)	
23	Stjepan GENG		2/3/93	D	2		
20	Mario GREGURINA		23/3/88	M	20	(5)	
14	Tomislav HAVOJIĆ		10/3/89	M	3	(4)	1
15	Marin JAKŠINIĆ		15/5/89	M	1	(4)	
24	Ivica JURAKIĆ		5/7/89	A		(1)	
4	Elvis KOKALOVIĆ		17/7/88	D	25		3
30	Pejo KUPREŠAK		24/10/92	M		(1)	
3	Tomislav LABUDOVIĆ		25/10/85	D	1	(5)	
26	Alen MARAS		27/2/82	M	27		1
23	Filip MARČIĆ		22/2/85	D	2		
18	Josip MILARDOVIĆ		10/1/88	D	26		3
17	Goran MUJANOVIĆ		29/9/83	A	23	(4)	1
1	Adis NURKOVIĆ	BIH	28/4/86	G	1		
22	Nicolás Niverge NYNKEU	CMR	14/12/82	M	11	(4)	1
11	Drago PAPA		3/2/84	M	2	(8)	1
7	Dalibor POLDRUGAČ		23/4/75	D	3	(4)	
8	Stjepan POLJAK		17/11/83	M	20	(8)	
19	Matija POREDSKI		9/11/88	A	4	(10)	
16	Vedran PURIĆ		16/3/86	D	24		
12	Silvio RODIĆ		25/7/87	G	29		
6	Kaja ROGULJ		15/6/86	D	17	(1)	
5	Marin ŠESTAK		30/6/92	D		(3)	
24	Franjo TEPURIĆ		10/2/90	A	5	(7)	1
9	Aljoša VOJNOVIĆ		24/10/85	A	27	(1)	5

RNK SPLIT

Coach – Ivan Katalinić
Founded – 1912
Stadium – Park mladeži (8,000)

2010

24/7	Rijeka	a	0-1	
31/7	Varaždin	h	4-0	*Žužul, Bučan 2, Obilinović (p)*
7/8	Karlovac	a	0-1	
14/8	Slaven	h	3-0	*Obilinović, Serdarušić, Golubović*
21/8	Cibalia	a	1-0	*Serdarušić*
29/8	Hajduk	h	1-1	*Golubović*
10/9	Zagreb	a	2-0	*Šimić Pr., Vitaić*
18/9	Lokomotiva	h	1-0	*Vitaić*
25/9	Istra	a	1-0	*Milović*
2/10	Osijek	h	1-0	*Golubović (p)*
16/10	Šibenik	a	0-3	
23/10	Inter	h	1-1	*Vidić*
30/10	Zadar	a	0-1	
6/11	Hrvatski dragovoljac	a	4-0	*Serdarušić 2, Radnić, Parać*
13/11	Dinamo	h	0-1	
20/11	Rijeka	h	2-3	*Obilinović, Parać*
28/11	Varaždin	a	0-0	
4/12	Karlovac	h	0-1	

2011

26/2	Slaven	a	2-1	*Golubović, Bučan*
5/3	Cibalia	h	2-1	*Golubović 2*
12/3	Hajduk	a	1-3	*og (Vejić)*
19/3	Zagreb	h	2-0	*Budiša, Rašić*
1/4	Lokomotiva	a	0-0	
9/4	Istra	h	2-0	*Vitaić (p), Križanac*
16/4	Osijek	a	0-1	
23/4	Šibenik	h	1-0	*Vitaić*
30/4	Inter	a	2-0	*Vitaić, Serdarušić*
7/5	Zadar	h	3-2	*Vidić, Šimić Pr., Rašić*
14/5	Hrvatski dragovoljac	h	1-0	*Erceg*
21/5	Dinamo	a	1-1	*Rebić*

No	Name	Nat	DoB	Pos	Aps	(s)	Gls
20	Sead BUČAN	BIH	8/3/81	M	25	(1)	3
4	Igor BUDIŠA		23/9/77	D	27		1
22	Ante ĆAPIN		13/12/85	A		(3)	
11	Zvonimir DERANJA		22/9/79	A	1	(7)	
24	Ante ERCEG		12/12/89	M	5	(6)	1
19	Bojan GOLUBOVIĆ	BIH	22/8/83	A	29		6
7	Juraj GRIZELJ		3/5/86	M	3	(15)	
44	Ivica KRIŽANAC		13/4/79	D	11		1
16	Frane LOJIĆ		8/10/85	M	15	(4)	
25	Filip MARČIĆ		22/2/85	D	12		
14	Goran MILOVIĆ		29/1/89	D	19	(1)	1
21	Romano OBILINOVIĆ		27/9/79	A	14	(14)	3
9	Joško PARAĆ		9/3/78	A		(7)	2
17	Mate PEHAR		25/2/88	M	11	(7)	
3	Ivica PIRIĆ		24/1/77	D	4		
22	Shpat QERIMI	FIN	1/6/89	M		(1)	
2	Goran RADNIĆ		4/5/83	D	17		1
13	Damir RAŠIĆ		5/10/88	D	10	(5)	2
11	Ante REBIĆ		21/9/93	A		(1)	1
18	Josip SERDARUŠIĆ		21/11/86	M	19	(5)	5
15	Petar ŠIMIĆ		24/11/81	D	3	(2)	
6	Predrag ŠIMIĆ	BIH	28/6/79	M	22	(3)	2
27	Marko TEŠIJA		14/1/92	M		(2)	
5	Velimir VIDIĆ	BIH	12/4/79	D	25		2
8	Ante VITAIĆ		7/6/82	M	26		5
1	Andrija VUKOVIĆ		3/8/83	G	30		
10	Ante ŽUŽUL		28/10/78	M	2	(6)	1

NK VARAŽDIN

Coach – Samir Toplak
Founded – 1931
Stadium – Anđelko Herjavec (10,800)

2010

24/7	Zadar	h	2-1	*Brezovec 2*
31/7	Split	a	0-4	
7/8	Dinamo	h	1-1	*Glavina*
14/8	Rijeka	a	1-1	*Glavica*
21/8	Hrvatski dragovoljac	h	2-0	*Golubar, Dudić*
28/8	Karlovac	h	1-0	*Brezovec*
11/9	Slaven	a	0-1	
17/9	Cibalia	h	2-1	*Sušac, Brezovec*
25/9	Hajduk	a	0-2	
2/10	Zagreb	h	0-0	
16/10	Lokomotiva	a	2-1	*Škvorc F. 2*
23/10	Istra	h	2-1	*Dudić, og (Pauletić)*
30/10	Osijek	a	0-0	
6/11	Šibenik	h	2-2	*Golubar, Škvorc F.*
13/11	Inter	a	0-2	
20/11	Zadar	a	0-3	
28/11	Split	h	0-0	
5/12	Dinamo	a	1-1	*Škvorc F.*

2011

26/2	Rijeka	h	3-0	*Vugrinec, Škvorc F., Glavina*
4/3	Hrvatski dragovoljac	a	2-3	*Vugrinec (p), Aganović*
12/3	Karlovac	a	0-1	
19/3	Slaven	h	1-1	*Glavina*
2/4	Cibalia	a	0-2	
9/4	Hajduk	h	3-0	*Vugrinec 2, Brlečić*
15/4	Zagreb	a	2-2	*Glavina, Vugrinec*
23/4	Lokomotiva	h	0-1	
30/4	Istra	a	0-2	
6/5	Osijek	h	2-4	*Brlečić, Škvorc F.*
14/5	Šibenik	a	0-1	
21/5	Inter	h	3-0	*Škvorc F., Vugrinec, Glavica*

No	Name	Nat	DoB	Pos	Aps	(s)	Gls
7	Adnan AGANOVIĆ		3/10/87	M	16	(5)	1
4	Josip BREZOVEC		21/12/86	M	16		4
5	Mario BRLEČIĆ		10/1/89	M	13	(4)	2
27	Ivan CONJAR		15/5/88	D	11	(4)	
1	Saša DREVEN		27/1/90	G	4		
13	Feđa DUDIĆ		1/2/83	A	8	(10)	2
8	Dejan GLAVICA		20/8/91	M	12	(9)	2
17	Dominik GLAVINA		6/12/92	A	15	(3)	4
20	Josip GOLUBAR		4/3/85	A	17	(3)	2
3	Jurica GRGEC		1/9/92	D		(1)	
43	Saša HOJSKI		11/5/90	M	1	(4)	
2	Matija KATANEC		4/5/90	D	2		
16	Stjepan KOKOT		9/11/91	A		(3)	
12	Denis KRKLEC		2/4/91	G	26		
19	Josip KVESIĆ	BIH	21/9/90	D	20	(2)	
16	Srebrenko POSAVEC		19/3/80	M		(4)	
6	Roberto PUNČEC		27/10/91	M	24	(1)	
9	Mario SAČER		17/1/90	A	7	(9)	
18	Adam SUŠAC		20/5/89	D	20	(1)	1
10	Nikola ŠAFARIĆ		11/3/81	M	16	(6)	
14	Karlo ŠIMEK		3/6/88	M	25	(1)	
25	Dino ŠKVORC		2/2/90	D	29		
28	Filip ŠKVORC		22/7/91	A	18	(11)	7
15	Nikola TKALČIĆ		3/12/89	D	6	(2)	
30	Davor VUGRINEC		24/3/75	A	24		6
26	Andrej VUK		22/3/89	A		(6)	

NK ZADAR

Coach – Dalibor Zebić
Founded – 1945
Stadium – Stanovi (5,860)

2010

24/7	Varaždin	a	1-2	*Begonja*
31/7	Karlovac	h	2-0	*Terkeš, Santini*
7/8	Slaven	a	0-2	
14/8	Cibalia	h	0-0	
22/8	Hajduk	a	1-4	*Pezo*
28/8	Zagreb	h	2-1	*Šare, Bilaver J.*

0/9	Lokomotiva	a	2-3	*Santini (p), Mršić*
3/9	Istra	h	2-0	*Con, Bilaver J.*
5/9	Osijek	a	2-3	*Santini, Puljić*
/10	Šibenik	h	1-4	*Santini (p)*
5/10	Inter	a	0-1	
2/10	Hrvatski dragovoljac	a	4-1	*Santini, Banović, Mršić, Ćurjurić*
0/10	Split	h	1-0	*Mršić (p)*
/11	Dinamo	a	0-1	
3/11	Rijeka	h	1-0	*Santini*
0/11	Varaždin	h	3-0	*Skočibušić, Terkeš, Jerbić*
7/11	Karlovac	a	0-1	
/12	Slaven	h	1-1	*Santini (p)*
011				
/3	Cibalia	a	0-0	
/3	Hajduk	h	0-2	
1/3	Zagreb	a	0-1	
9/3	Lokomotiva	h	1-0	*Terkeš*
/4	Istra	a	0-1	
/4	Osijek	h	1-1	*Santini*
6/4	Šibenik	a	0-2	
3/4	Inter	h	1-0	*Mršić*
0/4	Hrvatski dragovoljac	h	1-0	*Mršić*
/5	Split	a	2-3	*Santini, Glumac*
4/5	Dinamo	h	0-0	
1/5	Rijeka	a	2-0	*Banović, Santini*

lo	Name	Nat	DoB	Pos	Aps	(s)	Gls
9	Filip ANIĆ		23/5/93	M		(1)	
7	Igor BANOVIĆ		12/5/87	M	22	(5)	2
0	Luka BEGONJA		23/5/92	M	12	(9)	1
	Franko BILAVER		9/2/92	A		(2)	
2	Josip BILAVER		14/2/84	D	21	(1)	2
5	Marin CON		8/2/85	D	23	(1)	1
4	Ivan ĆURJURIĆ		29/9/89	M	4	(15)	1
2	Tomo GLUIĆ		26/7/83	G	11	(1)	
21	Tomislav GLUMAC		14/5/91	D	18	(4)	1
1	Marko GOSPIĆ		27/4/84	A	6	(4)	
4	Šime GREGOV		8/7/89	M	2	(3)	
23	Šime GRŽAN		30/11/93	M		(1)	
15	Jure JERBIĆ		28/6/90	M	13	(14)	1
1	Antonio JEŽINA		5/6/89	G	19		
13	Šime MARUNA		10/10/89	M	6	(1)	
7	Ivan MATOŠEVIĆ		27/2/89	A		(1)	
7	Ferdo MILIN		15/12/77	D	1		
22	Antonio MRŠIĆ		5/6/87	M	27		5
13	Niko PERAIĆ		9/3/88	M	5	(5)	
25	Toni PEZO		14/2/87	M	22	(2)	1
18	Ante PULJIĆ		15/11/87	D	29		1
19	Ivan SANTINI		21/5/89	A	29		10
26	Stjepan SKOČIBUŠIĆ		10/6/79	D	21		1
8	Jakov SURAĆ		12/2/75	M	7	(1)	
5	Perica ŠARE		6/2/91	D	10	(1)	1
20	Želimir TERKEŠ	BIH	8/1/81	A	9	(4)	3
16	Domagoj TORBARINA		1/4/92	M		(1)	
3	Ivan Anton VASILJ		5/4/91	D	13	(1)	
27	Marin ZULIM		26/10/89	M		(3)	

NK ZAGREB

Coach – Ivo Šušak; (14/9/10) Luka Pavlović

Founded – 1903

Stadium – Kranjčevićeva (12,000)

MAJOR HONOURS: Croatian League – (1) 2002.

2010				
23/7	Lokomotiva	h	3-1	*Krstanović 2, Jurendić*
31/7	Istra	a	2-0	*Krstanović, Šovšić*
6/8	Osijek	h	0-0	
14/8	Šibenik	a	1-0	*Jurendić*
20/8	Inter	h	2-1	*Krstanović 2*
28/8	Zadar	a	1-2	*Sukaj*
10/9	Split	h	0-2	
19/9	Dinamo	a	0-1	
26/9	Rijeka	h	3-1	*Krstanović 3*
2/10	Varaždin	a	0-0	
15/10	Karlovac	h	1-2	*Dedić*
23/10	Slaven	a	2-1	*Pavlović, Dedić*
30/10	Cibalia	h	0-2	
7/11	Hajduk	a	1-4	*Krstanović*
13/11	Hrvatski dragovoljac	h	0-1	
20/11	Lokomotiva	a	0-2	
27/11	Istra	h	0-1	
4/12	Osijek	a	0-0	
2011				
25/2	Šibenik	h	1-1	*Krstanović*
4/3	Inter	a	2-0	*Jurendić 2*
11/3	Zadar	h	1-0	*Krstanović (p)*
19/3	Split	a	0-2	
2/4	Dinamo	h	0-1	
9/4	Rijeka	a	1-1	*Krstanović*
15/4	Varaždin	h	2-2	*Krstanović 2 (1p)*
23/4	Karlovac	a	1-2	*Krstanović*
29/4	Slaven	h	1-3	*Chiavarini*
7/5	Cibalia	a	2-2	*Krstanović, Abdurahimi*
14/5	Hajduk	h	2-2	*Krstanović 2 (1p)*
21/5	Hrvatski dragovoljac	a	3-2	*Carlos Santos, Krstanović, Chiavarini*

No	Name	Nat	DoB	Pos	Aps	(s)	Gls
16	Besart ABDURAHIMI		31/7/90	M	18	(7)	1
1	Goran BAŠIĆ		25/5/88	G	12		
2	CARLOS SANTOS de Jesus	BRA	25/2/85	D	5		1
27	Vedran CELIŠČAK		16/7/82	M	10	(1)	
2	Vedran CELJAK		13/8/91	D	13	(1)	
9	Franco CHIAVARINI	ARG	18/2/80	A	6	(5)	2
17	Hrvoje CINDRIĆ		9/1/93	M		(1)	
25	Sven DEDIĆ		15/4/91	A	4	(10)	2
21	Ivica DŽOLAN		11/10/88	D	3	(2)	
20	Vedran IVANKOVIĆ		3/5/83	D	16		
26	JAMES DENS Maia da Silva	BRA	14/8/86	M	21	(2)	
6	JEFTHON Ferreira de Sena	BRA	3/1/82	D	22		
8	Igor JUGOVIĆ		23/1/87	M	21	(4)	
7	Josip JURENDIĆ		26/4/87	M	19	(2)	4
29	Ivan KRSTANOVIĆ		5/1/83	A	28		19
23	Neven MARKOVIĆ	BIH	20/2/87	D	5	(5)	
28	Lovro MEDIĆ		23/10/90	A	11	(7)	
23	Josip MIKULIĆ		12/4/86	D		(2)	
27	Valentino NOVOSEL		14/2/89	M	2		
13	Marin ORŠULIĆ		25/8/87	D	3	(10)	
10	Ivan PARLOV		3/4/84	M	1	(8)	
11	Mateo PAVLOVIĆ		9/6/90	D	26		1
9	Miroslav PEJIĆ	BIH	16/2/86	M	1	(2)	
17	Krunoslav RENDULIĆ		26/9/73	M	9	(1)	
22	Xhevair SUKAJ	ALB	5/10/87	A		(5)	1
10	Damir ŠOVŠIĆ	BIH	5/2/90	M	28		1
14	Matija ŠPIČIĆ		24/2/88	D	3	(1)	
3	Dino ŠTIGLEC		3/10/90	D		(1)	
5	Mario TOKIĆ		23/7/75	D	25		
12	Hrvoje VIŠIĆ		4/2/83	G	18		

TOP GOALSCORERS 2010/11

19	Ivan KRSTANOVIĆ (Zagreb)
14	Ante VUKUŠIĆ (Hajduk)
11	Dino KRESINGER (Cibalia)
	Nino BULE (Lokomotiva)
	Mehmed ALISPAHIĆ (Šibenik)
10	SAMMIR (Dinamo)
	Ivan SANTINI (Zadar)
8	Mladen BARTOLOVIĆ (Cibalia)
	Fatos BEĆIRAJ (Dinamo)
	Leon BENKO (Slaven)

PROMOTED CLUBS

NK LUČKO

Coach – Dražen Biškup
Founded – 1931
Stadium – Lučko (1,500)

SECOND LEVEL FINAL TABLE 2010/11

		Pld	W	D	L	F	A	Pts
1	HNK Gorica	30	20	4	6	54	21	64
2	NK Lučko	30	19	2	9	54	28	59
3	NK Pomorac Kostrena	30	16	8	6	50	23	56
4	NK Rudeš	30	15	7	8	52	39	52
5	NK Imotski	30	14	6	10	35	32	48
6	NK Solin	30	13	6	11	35	33	45
7	NK Međimurje	30	12	6	12	53	49	42
8	NK Dugopolje	30	10	11	9	39	30	41
9	NK Junak Sinj	30	10	10	10	40	34	40
10	NK Vinogradar Jastrebarsko	30	12	4	14	43	38	40
11	NK Croatia Sesvete	30	12	4	14	37	41	40
12	NK MV Croatia	30	11	6	13	42	42	39
13	NK HAŠK Zagreb	30	11	5	14	40	42	38
14	NK Mosor Žrnovnica	30	9	7	14	32	41	34
15	NK Vukovar 91	30	6	2	22	21	83	20
16	HNK Suhopolje	30	5	2	23	22	73	17

NB HNK Gorica & NK Pomorac Kostrena denied promotion after failing to obtain the necessary licences.

DOMESTIC CUP 2010/11

HRVATSKI NOGOMETNI KUP

FIRST ROUND

(24/8/10)
Bjelovar 4, Suhopolje 4 *(aet; 7-8 on pens)*
(25/8/10)
Graničar 2, Olimpija1
Međimurje 2, Hrvace 0
Mladost Petrinja 1, BSK 2
Moslavina 3, Gaj 0
Nosteria 3, Novalja 2
Opatija 2, Velebit 1
Pazinka 1, Zadrugar 2
Podravac 0, Rudar-47 1
Rudeš 4, Borac 1
Slavija 7, Bilogorac 0
Vinogradar 1, Lokomotiva Zagreb 2 *(aet)*
Vrbovec 4, Mladost Cernik 2 *(aet)*
Zagora 3, Jedinstvo Omladinac 0
Zmaj Blato 1, Karlovac 1 *(aet; 2-3 on pens)*
(1/9/10)
MV Croatia 2, Sloboda 0

SECOND ROUND

(21/9/10)
Karlovac 5, Moslavina 0
MV Croatia 1, Osijek 2
Rudar-47 2, Hajduk 10
(22/9/10)
BSK 0, Varaždin 2
Graničar 0, Pomorac 2
Istra 3, Hrvatski dragovoljac 1
Lokomotiva Zagreb 1, Inter Zaprešić 2
Međimurje 3, Konavljanin 1
Nosteria 2, Rijeka 4
Opatija 0, Slaven Koprivnica 1
Rudeš 0, Cibalia 3
Slavija 3, Šibenik 4 *(aet)*
Suhopolje 3, Segesta 1
Vrbovec 0, Zagreb 2
Zadrugar 0, Dinamo Zagreb 6
Zagora 2, HAŠK 4 *(aet)*

THIRD ROUND

(26/10/10)
Pomorac 0, Zagreb 1
Rijeka 3, Međimurje 1
Varaždin 1, HAŠK 0
(27/10/10)
Hajduk 0, Istra 1 *(aet)*
Inter Zaprešić 0, Cibalia 3
Karlovac 0, Dinamo Zagreb 2
Osijek 2, Šibenik 1
Slaven Koprivnica 2, Suhopolje 0

QUARTER-FINALS

(9/11/10 & 24/11/10)
Varaždin 2 *(Brezovec 33p, Punčec 38)*, Rijeka 1 *(Štrok 27)*
Rijeka 2 *(Štrok 42p, 47)* Varaždin 4 *(Šafarić 27, Aganović 51, Škvorc F. 86, 90)*
(Varaždin 6-3)
(10/11/10 & 23/11/10)
Zagreb 1 *(Šovšić 87)*, Slaven Koprivnica 1 *(Milardović 32)*
Slaven Koprivnica 5 *(Ivanković 40og, Maras 55, Milardović 62, Gregurina 66, Poredski 90)*, Zagreb 1 *(Ivanković 15)*
(Slaven Koprivnica 6-2)
(10/11/10 & 24/11/10)
Istra 2 *(Pauletić 48, Alimi 88)*, Cibalia 3 *(Prgomet 27, Kresinger 43, Koledić 84)*
Cibalia 2 *(Šimunac 3, Tomić 39)*, Istra 0
(Cibalia 5-2)
(23/11/10 & 9/12/10)
Dinamo Zagreb 2 *(Tonel 9, Kramarić 48)*, Osijek 0
Osijek 1 *(Špehar 18)*, Dinamo Zagreb 3 *(Bećiraj 27, 73, Biščan 58p)*
(Dinamo Zagreb 5-1)

SEMI-FINALS

(5/4/11 & 20/4/11)
Cibalia 1 *(Kresinger 31)*, Varaždin 0
Varaždin 3 *(Vugrinec 47, 84p, Škvorc F. 80)*, Cibalia 0
(Varaždin 3-1)
(6/4/11 & 20/4/11)
Dinamo Zagreb 4 *(Sammir 7p, Sylvestr 9, Badelj 23p, Tomečak 88)*, Slaven Koprivnica 1 *(Benko 35)*
Slaven Koprivnica 0, Dinamo Zagreb 1 *(Tomečak 86)*
(Dinamo Zagreb 5-1)

FINAL

(11/5/11)
Maksimir, Zagreb
NK DINAMO ZAGREB 5 *(Sammir 10, Tonel 45, Bećiraj 72, 79, Badelj 80)*
NK VARAŽDIN 1 *(Škvorc D. 35)*
Referee – *Bebek*
DINAMO ZAGREB – *Kelava, Vrsaljko, Tonel, Cufré, Ibáñez, Badelj, Calello, Sammir (Brezovec 85), Morales (Tomečak 65), Rukavina (Ademi 81), Bećiraj.*
VARAŽDIN – Krklec, Šimek, Škvorc D., Sušac, Kvesić, Brlečić, Šafarić, Posavec (Glavina 75), Škvorc F., Golubar, Vugrinec (Glavica 65).
(25/5/11)
Anđelko Herjavec, Varazdin
NK VARAŽDIN 1 *(Šafarić 6)*
NK DINAMO ZAGREB 3 *(Ibáñez 62, Badelj 70, Bećiraj 82)*
Referee – *Vučkov*
VARAŽDIN – *Krklec (Mrmić 73), Škvorc D., Kvesić, Tkalčić, Brlečić, Punčec, Aganović, Glavica (Golubar 61), Šafarić (Hojski 77), Glavina, Škvorc F.*
DINAMO ZAGREB – *Kelava, Vrsaljko (Mesarić 73), Tonel, Ademi, Ibáñez, Kovačić (Brezovec 79), Sammir, Chago, Badelj, Tomečak, Rukavina (Bećiraj 57).*
(DINAMO ZAGREB 8-2)

CLUB COMMUNICATION 2011/12

HNK Cibalia
Hansa Dietricha Genschera 10 b
HR-Vinkovci

Tel +385 32 306 088
Fax +385 32 306 085
Web hnk-cibalia.hr
Email cibalia@hnk-cibalia.hr
Media Officer

GNK Dinamo Zagreb
Maksimirska 128
HR-Zagreb

Tel +385 1 23 86 120
Fax +385 1 23 12 316
Web nk-dinamo.hr
Email dinamo@nk-dinamo.hr
Media Officer Morana Đurčević

HNK Hajduk Split
8. Mediteranskih Igara 2
HR-Split

Tel +385 21 323 650
Fax +385 21 381 241
Web hajduk.hr
Email hnk-hajduk@st.t-com.hr
Media Officer Ante Bilić

NK Inter Zaprešić
Vladimira Novaka bb
HR-Zaprešić

Tel +385 1 400 1100
Fax +385 1 400 1102
Web inter.hr
Email inter@inter.hr
Media Officer Maksim Babić

NK Istra
Veli Joze 3
HR-52100 Pula

Tel +385 52 210 496
Fax +385 52 380 863
Web nkistra1961.hr
Email nkistra1961@inet.hr
Media Officer

NK Karlovac
Mekušansko polje bb
HR-Karlovac

Tel + 385 47 654 260
Fax + 385 47 654 272
Web nk-karlovac.hr
Email nk-karlovac@ka.t-com.hr
Media Officer Ivana Rumenović

NK Lokomotiva Zagreb
Maksimirska 128
HR-10000 Zagreb

Tel +385 1 2386 132
Fax +385 1 2386 124
Web nklokomotiva.hr
Email nklokomotiva@nklokomotiva.hr
Media Officer

NK Lučko
F. Puškarića 122
HR-10250 Lučko

Tel +385 1 653 0696
Fax +385 1 653 0696
Web nk-lucko.hr
Email nk@zg-t-com.hr
Media Officer Mislav Marujević

NK Osijek
Wilsonova bb, Gradski Vrt stadium
HR-Osijek

Tel +385 31 570 300
Fax +385 31 570 400
Web nk-osijek.hr
Email nk.osijek@nk-osijek.hr
Media Officer Dalibor Kasač

HNK Rijeka
Portić 3, Kantrida stadium
HR-Rijeka

Tel +385 51 261 622
Fax +385 51 261 174
Web nk-rijeka.hr
Email nk-rijeka@ri.t-com.hr
Media Officer Sandra Nešić

HNK Šibenik
Ulica bana Josipa Jelačića bb
HR-Šibenik

Tel +385 22 212 963
Fax +385 22 218 406
Web hnk-sibenik.hr
Email hnk-sibenik@si.t-com.hr
Media Officer Josip Caleta

NK Slaven Koprivnica
M.P. Miškine 12
HR-Koprivnica

Tel +385 48 623 960
Fax +385 48 210 327
Web nk-slaven-belupo.hr
Email nk-slaven-belupo@kc.t-com.hr
Media Officer Mirko Kvakarić

RNK Split
Hrvatske mornarice 10
HR-Split

Tel +385 21 382 999
Fax +385 21 382 943
Web rnksplit.hr
Email rnksplit@rnksplit.hr
Media Officer Dražen Kuzmanić

NK Varaždin
Zagrebacka 94
HR-Varaždin

Tel +385 42 240 250
Fax +385 42 204 260
Web
Email info@nk-varazdin.hr
Media Officer Siniša Kalajđija

NK Zadar
Hrvoja Ćustića 2, Stanovi stadium
HR-Zadar

Tel +385 23 312792
Fax +385 23 312802
Web nkzadar.hr
Email nk-zadar1@zd.t-com.hr
Media Officer Josip Bajlo

NK Zagreb
Kranjčevićeva 4, NC Zagrebello,
Veslačka bb, HR-Zagreb

Tel +385 1 366 8111
Fax +385 1 366 8111
Web nkzagreb.hr
Email nkzagreb@nkzagreb.hr
Media Officer Zlatko Abramović

CYPRUS

Chypre I Zypern

Kypriaki Omospondia Podosfairon (KOP)
Cyprus Football Association (CFA)

COMMUNICATION

Address	10 Achaion Street 2413-Engomi PO Box 25071 CY-1306 Nicosia
Tel	+357 22 352 341
Fax	+357 22 590 544
E-mail	info@cfa.com.cy
Website	cfa.com.cy

President	Costakis Koutsokoumnis
General Secretary	Phivos Vakis
Media Officer	Kyriacos Giorgallis
Year of Formation	1934
National Stadium	GSP, Nicosia (22,859)

DOMESTIC COMPETITION SUMMARY 2010/11

A KATIGORIA FINAL TABLE

			Home					Away					Total						
		Pld	W	D	L	F	A	W	D	L	F	A	W	D	L	F	A	Pts	Comp
1	APOEL FC	32	14	0	2	37	10	10	2	4	26	12	24	2	6	63	22	74	UCL
2	AC Omonia	32	11	3	2	29	7	7	6	3	16	12	18	9	5	45	19	63	UEL
3	Anorthosis Famagusta FC	32	9	4	3	31	12	7	3	6	20	22	16	7	9	51	34	55	UEL
4	AEK Larnaca FC	32	5	4	7	19	20	7	2	7	18	22	12	6	14	37	42	42	UEL
5	Apollon Limassol FC	32	10	2	4	31	17	4	5	7	24	27	14	7	11	55	44	49	
6	Enosis Neon Paralimni FC	32	8	2	6	18	18	4	6	6	15	16	12	8	12	33	34	44	
7	AEL Limassol FC	32	7	5	4	23	18	3	6	7	14	27	10	11	11	37	45	41	
8	Olympiakos Nicosia FC	32	5	7	4	24	25	5	4	7	24	28	10	11	11	48	53	41	
9	Ethnikos Achnas FC	32	4	4	8	10	20	6	5	5	19	17	10	9	13	29	37	39	
10	Alki Larnaca FC	32	3	4	9	19	29	8	2	6	21	19	11	6	15	40	48	39	
11	Ermis Aradippou FC	32	5	9	2	23	18	4	2	10	15	27	9	11	12	38	45	38	
12	AEP Paphos FC	32	4	6	6	20	17	4	5	7	24	27	8	11	13	44	44	35	*Relegated*
13	Doxa Katokopia FC	26	5	3	5	18	19	0	2	11	7	36	5	5	16	25	55	20	*Relegated*
14	APOP/Kinyras Peyias FC	26	3	2	8	13	24	1	5	7	11	23	4	7	15	24	47	19	*Relegated*

NB After 26 matches the top 12 clubs are split into three groups of four, after which they play exclusively against teams in their group.

Top Scorer	Miljan Mrdaković (Apollon), 21 goals
Promoted Clubs	Aris Limassol FC Nea Salamis FC Anagennisi Derynia FC
Cup Final	AC Omonia 1, Apollon Limassol FC 1 (aet; 4-3 on pens)

Landslide victory for APOEL

Having surrendered the Cypriot championship crown to AC Omonia in 2009/10, APOEL FC recaptured it in style, seeing off their arch-rivals and every other club in the A Katigoria with room to spare. It was the Nicosia club's 21st league title, putting them back on top of the all-time standings, one clear ahead of Omonia, who consoled themselves for a disappointing title defence by winning the Cypriot Cup.

Led again by Serbian coach Ivan Jovanović, whose second tenure at the club began in January 2008, APOEL were an unyielding force from the moment they won the first big Nicosia derby in early October, a 3-0 win over Omonia triggering a run of eight successive victories, the first six without conceding a goal. By the time the 26-match cut-off arrived in late March, APOEL were in an unassailable position. Indeed, their 12-point lead rendered the six-match play-off series all but redundant, and it was in the second of those fixtures, fittingly against Omonia, that they made the title secure, a brace of goals at the end of the first half from Cypriot international midfielder Kostas Charalambides delivering a 2-0 win that stretched their lead at the top to 15 points with four games remaining.

Foreign recruits

Charalambides was one of the few Cypriots to feature regularly in the APOEL starting XI. In fact, the only other native islander to start more than ten matches was veteran defender Savvas Poursaitidis. APOEL's reaction to losing the title in 2009/10 had been to buy in a host of new foreigners, including three top-notch South Americans in Gustavo Manduca, Aílton and the returning Esteban Solari, all of whom proved their worth in attack. Arguably the pick of the new intake, however, was Macedonian international Ivan Trickovski, who scored 11 goals and was a class act throughout the campaign.

UEFA Champions League group stage participants in 2009/10, APOEL were denied access to the equivalent stage of the UEFA Europa League when they narrowly lost their play-off tie against Getafe CF. Anorthosis Famagusta FC also fell at the same hurdle, to PFC CSKA Moskva, and Omonia completed an unwanted hat-trick by going out to FC Metalist Kharkiv. A few weeks earlier Omonia's bid to become the third different Cypriot club in as many seasons to reach the UEFA Champions League proper had perished against FC Salzburg, so when they lost the first domestic derby to APOEL, it was no great surprise that their 2009/10 title-winning coach, Takis Lemonis, was shown the door.

The illustrious Bosnian Serb coach, Dušan Bajević, was brought in to revive Omonia's championship challenge, but despite the frequent goalscoring of Cypriot international striker Michalis Konstantinou, who struck 12 times in ten games during the winter months, APOEL were uncatchable and it soon became clear that Omonia's only hope of silverware was in the Cypriot Cup. By the time they got to the final, however, Bajević was history, his place having been taken by Neophytou Larkou, the assistant coach of the Cypriot national team.

Ivan Jovanovíc led APOEL to the Cypriot championship title

CYPRUS

Within three weeks of taking over Larkou was a trophy winner, Omonia lifting the Cup for the 13th time after a tense final against holders Apollon Limassol FC that ended 1-1 and went to penalties, with Omonia goalkeeper Antonis Georgiallides decisively saving two spot-kicks.

Apollon had reached the final thanks to last-gasp goals in both the quarter-final and semi-final from their Serbian goal machine Miljan Mrdaković, who finished the season as the league's top scorer, with 21 goals. He was helped to that prize, however, by Apollon's failure to reach the four-team championship play-off, scoring a third of his tally in the last six games to overtake Omonia's Konstantinou. Anorthosis and newly promoted AEK Larnaca FC joined the two Nicosia giants in the elite group and were both rewarded with European qualification – despite the latter's failure to pick up a single point in the play-offs.

Yiannis Okkas – the first Cypriot to win 100 international caps

National Team

Top Five All-time Caps – Yiannis Okkas (100); Pambos Pittas (82); Michalis Konstantinou (82); Nicos Panayiotou (75); Giorgos Theodotou (70)

Top Five All-time Goals – Michalis Konstantinou (32); Yiannis Okkas (25); Kostas Charalambides (11); Marios Agathokleous (10); Efstathios Aloneftis, Siniša Gogić, Andros Sotiriou, Milenko Spoljarić & Phivos Vrahimis (8)

Okkas landmark

Cyprus's UEFA EURO 2012 qualifying campaign began with a bang when they held Portugal to a remarkable 4-4 draw in Guimaraes, Omonia defender Andreas Avraam's 89th-minute header securing one of the best results in the island nation's history. Unfortunately, that was as good as it got for Angelos Anastasiadis and his exclusively home-based team, and the coach was relieved of his duties in the spring – nearly six and a half years after taking the job – following a run of eight games without a win, during which the only highlight saw Yiannis Okkas become the first Cypriot footballer to reach 100 international caps. Anastasiadis's fellow Greek, former Panathinaikos FC coach Nikos Nioplias, was subsequently appointed to take Cyprus through the second half of their EURO campaign and onwards into the 2014 FIFA World Cup qualifiers.

NATIONAL TEAM RESULTS 2010/11

11/8/10	Andorra	H	Larnaca	1-0	*Konstantinou (4)*
3/9/10	Portugal (ECQ)	A	Guimaraes	4-4	*Aloneftis (3), Konstantinou (11), Okkas (57), Avraam (89)*
8/10/10	Norway (ECQ)	H	Larnaca	1-2	*Okkas (58)*
12/10/10	Denmark (ECQ)	A	Copenhagen	0-2	
16/11/10	Jordan	A	Amman	0-0	
8/2/11	Sweden	H	Nicosia	0-2	
9/2/11	Romania	H	Paralimni	1-1	*Konstantinou (85) (4-5 on pens)*
26/3/11	Iceland (ECQ)	H	Nicosia	0-0	
29/3/11	Bulgaria	H	Larnaca	0-1	

NATIONAL TEAM APPEARANCES 2010/11

Coach – Angelos ANASTASIADIS (GRE)		**3/10/53**	And	POR	NOR	DEN	Jor	Swe	Rou	ISL	Bul	Caps	Goals
Antonis GEORGALLIDES	30/1/82	Omonia	G	G	G	G	G54	G56		G	G	38	-
Marios ELIA	14/4/79	APOEL	D73	D66			D73	s70	D70	s61	D	50	2
Paraskevas CHRISTOU	2/2/84	Alki	D46			s28	D46					28	-
Siniša DOBRAŠINOVIĆ	17/2/77	Alki	D46	M	M	M	s54		D	M	D46	11	-
Andreas AVRAAM	6/6/87	Omonia	D	D	D	D63		s60	D	D	s46	19	2

NATIONAL TEAM APPEARANCES 2010/11 (contd.)

			And	POR	NOR	DEN	Jor	Swe	Rou	ISL	Bul	Caps	Goals
Marinos SATSIAS	24/5/78	APOEL	M67	M	s46	M	M64	M70			M	60	-
Chrysis MICHAIL	26/5/77	APOEL	M				M	M46	M	M	s46	68	7
Kostas CHARALAMBIDES	25/7/81	APOEL	M73	M76	M46	s55	M	M63	s70	M	s46	59	11
Efstathios ALONEFTIS	29/3/83	Omonia	M	M56	M	M55	s73	M60	s75	M		46	8
Yiannis OKKAS	11/2/77	Anorthosis	A79	s56	A	A		A				100	25
Michalis KONSTANTINOU	19/2/78	Omonia	A	A	A	A	s58		A			82	32
Giorgos MERKIS	30/7/84	Apollon	s46	D	D81	D	s46	D		D	s46	10	-
Elias CHARALAMBOUS	25/9/80	Omonia	s46	D	D86	D28					D	51	-
Konstantinos MAKRIDES	13/1/82	Omonia	s67	M	M	M		M54	M69	M	s65	55	3
Savvas POURSAITIDIS	26/6/76	APOEL	s73	s66	D	D	D	D		D61		8	-
Christos MARANGOS	9/5/83	Anorthosis	s73									19	1
Giorgos EFREM	5/7/89	Omonia	s79		s86		A	s54	A82		M68	9	-
Marios NICOLAOU	4/10/83	AEL		s76								32	1
Dimitris CHRISTOFI	28/9/88	Omonia			s81		M58			A73	s68	16	2
Alexandros GARPOZIS	5/9/80	AEL				s63		D			D	39	1
Giorgos PANAGI	3/11/86	Omonia					D	s46	s69			14	-
Athos SOLOMOU	30/11/85	APOEL					M54					3	-
Anastasios KISSAS	18/1/88	APOEL					s54	s56	G46			4	-
Nestoras MYTIDES	1/6/91	AEK					s64	s63	s82		A65	4	-
Nikos KATSAVAKIS	16/5/79	Apollon						D46				1	-
Jason DEMETRIOU	18/11/87	AEK						s46	M	s46	M46	7	-
Valentinos SIELIS	1/3/90	Anorthosis							D	D46		2	-
Kyriakos PAVLOU	4/9/86	APOP							M75		M46	7	-
Michalis MORFIS	15/1/79	PAEEK							s46			22	-
Nektarios ALEXANDROU	19/12/83	APOEL								s73	M46	12	-

CLUB-BY-CLUB

AEK LARNACA FC

Coach – Ton Caanen (NED)

Founded – 1994

Stadium – Neo GSZ (12,000)

MAJOR HONOURS: Cypriot Cup - (1) 2004.

2010				
30/8	Omonia	h	1-2	*Jean Paulista*
11/9	Apollon	a	2-1	*Schenkel, Van Dijk (p)*
20/9	Doxa	h	2-0	*Kingsley, Arnal*
25/9	Ethnikos	h	1-1	*Oper*
3/10	Alki	a	2-1	*Van Dijk, Gómez*
16/10	APOP	h	3-2	*Van Dijk 3 (1p)*
23/10	APOEL	a	0-1	
31/10	Olympiakos	h	1-1	*Linssen*
7/11	AEL	a	2-1	*Arnal, Lambropoulos*
13/11	Ermis	h	2-1	*Hofland, Mytides*
20/11	Paralimni	a	2-0	*Kingsley, Hofland*
28/11	Anorthosis	h	3-0	*Hofland, Linssen, Oper*
4/12	AEP	a	0-2	
12/12	Omonia	a	0-2	
18/12	Apollon	h	2-2	*Lambropoulos, Hofland*
2011				
8/1	Doxa	a	4-1	*Linssen, Van Dijk, Pintado 2*
16/1	Ethnikos	a	1-0	*Pintado*
23/1	Alki	h	0-2	
29/1	APOP	a	0-0	
5/2	APOEL	h	1-2	*Pintado*
12/2	Olympiakos	a	3-2	*Van Dijk (p), Cabrera, Oper*
19/2	AEL	h	0-0	
26/2	Ermis	a	1-1	*Priso*
5/3	Paralimni	h	0-2	
13/3	Anorthosis	a	1-2	*Hofland (p)*
19/3	AEP	h	2-1	*Caluwé, Priso*
3/4	APOEL	h	0-1	
10/4	Anorthosis	a	0-2	
16/4	Omonia	a	0-3	
30/4	Omonia	h	1-2	*og (Wenzel)*
7/5	APOEL	a	0-3	
14/5	Anorthosis	h	0-1	

No	Name	Nat	DoB	Pos	Aps	(s)	Gls
42	ALAN da Silva Souza	BRA	9/12/87	M	8	(7)	
	Alekos ALEKOU		13/11/83	A		(2)	
1	ALEXANDRE NEGRI	BRA	27/3/81	G	27		
99	ARNAL Llibert Conde Carbó	ESP	21/11/80	A	4	(8)	2
15	Gonzalo Gabriel CABRERA	ARG	15/1/89	M	6	(5)	1
19	Tom CALUWÉ	BEL	11/4/78	M	12	(1)	1
20	Jason DEMETRIOU		18/11/87	M	11	(4)	
6	Luke DIMECH	MLT	11/1/77	M	15	(6)	
2	Michalis DIMITRIOU		23/8/86	D		(2)	
14	Marco FORTIN	ITA	8/7/74	G	5		
17	Lenos GEORGIOU		18/9/92	M		(1)	
27	Rubén Marcelo GÓMEZ	ARG	26/1/84	M	18	(5)	1
4	Kevin HOFLAND	NED	7/1/79	D	25		5
12	Orthodoxos IOANNOU		4/3/86	D	4	(6)	
10	JEAN Francisco Rodrigues "PAULISTA"	BRA	28/11/77	A	6	(2)	1

No	Name	Nat	DoB	Pos	Aps	(s)	Gls
39	Sunny Ekeh KINGSLEY	NGA	9/9/81	A	24	(3)	2
8	Giorgos LAMBROPOULOS	GRE	26/10/84	M	4	(14)	2
7	Edwin LINSSEN	NED	28/8/80	M	26	(2)	3
5	Loukas LOUKA		17/4/78	D	1		
28	Renato João Inácio MARGAÇA	POR	17/7/85	M	31		
29	Nestoras MYTIDES		1/6/91	A	3	(13)	1
9	Andres OPER	EST	7/11/77	A	20	(1)	3
23	Gorka PINTADO del Molino	ESP	24/3/78	A	6		4
99	Njongo Lobe PRISO Doding	CMR	24/12/88	A	20	(6)	2
25	Danny SCHENKEL	NED	1/4/78	D	28		1
21	Christis THEOFILOU		30/4/80	D	16	(6)	
16	Gregoor VAN DIJK	NED	16/11/81	M	32		7

AEL LIMASSOL FC

Coach – Dušan Uhrin Jr (CZE); (22/9/10) Mihai Stoichiţă (ROU); (7/2/11) Raymond Atteveld (NED); (29/3/11) Pambos Christodoulou

Founded – 1930

Stadium – Tsirion (13,000)

MAJOR HONOURS: Cypriot League - (5) 1941, 1953, 1955, 1956, 1968; Cypriot Cup - (6) 1939, 1940, 1948, 1985, 1987, 1989.

2010				
28/8	Olympiakos	a	2-0	*Vargas, Júnior*
12/9	Doxa	a	0-0	
20/9	Ermis	h	1-2	*Vargas*
26/9	Paralimni	a	1-1	*Freddy*
2/10	Anorthosis	h	1-3	*Freddy*
16/10	AEP	a	2-2	*Freddy 2 (1p)*
24/10	Omonia	h	0-0	
30/10	Apollon	a	0-3	
7/11	AEK	h	1-2	*Freddy*
15/11	Ethnikos	a	0-0	
21/11	Alki	h	1-0	*Kerkez*
28/11	APOP	a	4-3	*Zé Vítor 3, Hélio Roque*
4/12	APOEL	h	2-2	*Freddy (p), Zé Vítor*
13/12	Olympiakos	h	3-2	*Zé Vítor, Nicolaou, Kakoyiannis*
18/12	Doxa	h	3-0	*Zé Vítor, González, Masaryk*
2011				
9/1	Ermis	a	0-0	
17/1	Paralimni	h	0-0	
23/1	Anorthosis	a	0-4	
29/1	AEP	h	1-0	*Freddy*
5/2	Omonia	a	0-2	
13/2	Apollon	h	2-3	*Zé Vítor 2*
19/2	AEK	a	0-0	
26/2	Ethnikos	h	2-1	*Freddy 2*
5/3	Alki	a	0-3	
13/3	APOP	h	2-0	*Vargas, Hélio Roque*
19/3	APOEL	a	0-2	
2/4	Apollon	h	1-1	*Freddy (p)*
9/4	Paralimni	a	3-2	*Vargas, Theodorou, Zonneveld*
17/4	Olympiakos	a	1-2	*Vargas*
29/4	Olympiakos	h	2-1	*Silas, Garpozis*
7/5	Apollon	a	1-3	*Andreou*
14/5	Paralimni	h	1-1	*Andreou*

No	Name	Nat	DoB	Pos	Aps	(s)	Gls
99	Kristis ANDREOU		12/8/94	A	1	(2)	2
46	Minas ANTONIOU		22/2/94	D	3		
76	CARLOS Manuel de Oliveira MARQUES	POR	6/2/83	D	9		
4	Matthew CASSIDY	IRL	2/10/88	M		(1)	
17	Martinos CHRISTOFI		26/6/93	M		(1)	
32	Kamil ČONTOFALSKÝ	SVK	3/6/78	G	4		
22	Nicolás Ignacio CROVETTO Aqueveque	CHI	15/3/86	M	9		
40	Haralambos DIONYSIOU		10/12/93	M	1	(3)	
44	Antonis ELEFTHERIOU		1/2/93	M	1		
30	ELldiano MARQUES Lima	BRA	14/3/82	M	2	(3)	
9	Frederico de Castro Roque dos Santos "FREDDY"	ANG	14/8/79	A	26	(3)	10
11	Alexandros GARPOZIS		5/9/80	M	14	(8)	1
19	Silvio Augusto GONZÁLEZ	ARG	8/6/80	A	8	(11)	1
28	HÉLIO José Lopes ROQUE	POR	20/7/85	M	18	(5)	2
36	José HENRIQUE Souto Esteves	POR	31/3/80	A	1	(5)	
10	Nicky HOFS	NED	17/5/83	M	6	(8)	
41	Marios IAKOVIDIS			D	1		
2	Rui Paulo Silva JÚNIOR	POR	16/6/75	D	19	(4)	1
82	Charalambos KAIRINOS		6/6/82	G	16	(1)	
81	Loizos KAKOYIANNIS		2/5/81	D	20		1
13	Dušan KERKEZ	BIH	1/5/79	M	26	(2)	1
39	Vangelis KOUTSOPOULOS	GRE	2/2/80	D	2	(3)	
45	Andreas KYRIAKO		5/2/94	A	1		
21	Maxim LARROQUE	FRA	20/2/89	M	4	(2)	
7	Maximiliano Andrés LASO	ARG	17/2/88	M		(4)	
16	Arkadiusz MALARZ	POL	19/6/80	G	12		
20	Pavol MASARYK	SVK	11/2/80	A	4	(5)	1
6	Hamad NDIKUMANA	RWA	5/10/78	D	10		
23	David NEOPHYTOU		23/2/94	M	1	(1)	
12	Marios NICOLAOU		4/10/83	M	24	(1)	1
29	Edwin OUON	RWA	26/1/81	D	14		
5	Stelios PARPAS		25/7/85	D	21	(1)	
18	Grzegorz RASIAK	POL	12/1/79	A	11	(6)	
77	Jorge Manuel Rebelo Fernandes "SILAS"	POR	1/9/76	M	7	(5)	1
15	Nikolas THEODOROU		22/3/93	A	2	(1)	1
55	Miguel Rodrigo Pereira VARGAS	POR	18/11/78	M	15	(4)	5
8	José "ZÉ" VÍTOR Jardim Vieira	POR	11/2/82	M	21	(4)	8
6	Mike ZONNEVELD	NED	27/10/80	D	18		1

AEP PAPHOS FC

Coach – Angel Slavkov (BUL); (7/12/10) Giorgos Polyviou

Founded – 2000

Stadium – Pafiako (10,000)

2010				
29/8	Ethnikos	a	1-2	*Purje*
12/9	Alki	h	1-2	*Jovanović*
19/9	APOP	a	1-0	*Hugo Carreira*
25/9	APOEL	h	1-1	*Purje*
2/10	Olympiakos	a	2-2	*Purje, Solari*
16/10	AEL	h	2-2	*Ivanov, Efthymiou*
25/10	Ermis	a	2-2	*Buyse, Ivanov (p)*
31/10	Paralimni	h	0-1	
8/11	Anorthosis	a	1-1	*Pedro Moutinho*
14/11	Doxa	a	1-2	*Santamaria*
20/11	Omonia	h	1-1	*Sielis*
27/11	Apollon	a	0-1	
4/12	AEK	h	2-0	*Voskaridis, og (Hofland)*
11/12	Ethnikos	h	0-1	
20/12	Alki	a	3-2	*Grujić, Sampson, Sielis*
2011				
9/1	APOP	h	0-0	
15/1	APOEL	a	1-5	*Ivanov*
22/1	Olympiakos	h	1-3	*Solari*
29/1	AEL	a	0-1	
6/2	Ermis	h	3-1	*Solari 2 (1p), Purje*
12/2	Paralimni	a	1-2	*Solari (p)*
19/2	Anorthosis	h	1-2	*Vasconcelos*
26/2	Doxa	h	5-0	*Vasconcelos 2, Eduardo Marques, Purje, Ivanov*
6/3	Omonia	a	1-1	*Thiago*
13/3	Apollon	h	1-0	*Vasconcelos*
19/3	AEK	a	1-2	*Grujić*
2/4	Ethnikos	h	0-1	
9/4	Alki	a	3-1	*Vasconcelos, Grujić, Solari*
16/4	Ermis	a	3-3	*Vasconcelos, Hugo Carreira, Ivanov (p)*
30/4	Ermis	h	1-1	*Hugo Carreira*
7/5	Ethnikos	a	3-0	*Sampson, Solari, Vasconcelos*
14/5	Alki	h	1-1	*Ivanov*

Name	Nat	DoB	Pos	Aps	(s)	Gls
Ransford ADDO	GHA	21/7/93	D	15		
Fangio BUYSE	BEL	30/6/11	M	16		1
Alexandros DIMITRIOU		12/8/87	M	9	(2)	
Charalambos DIMOSTHENOUS		16/4/90	M	1	(6)	
EDUARDO MARQUES de Jesus Passos	BRA	26/6/76	M	22	(5)	1
Angelos EFTHYMIOU		18/1/84	M	9	(14)	1
Vladan GRUJIĆ	BIH	17/5/81	M	26	(1)	3
HUGO Miguel Martins CARRIERA	POR	10/3/79	D	21		3
Ventsislav IVANOV	BUL	20/5/82	A	14	(13)	6
JONATHAN ASPAS Juncal	ESP	28/2/82	M	10	(1)	
Ivan JOVANOVIĆ	SRB	1/12/78	M	13	(2)	1
Artur KOTENKO	EST	20/8/81	G	6		
Jimmy MODESTE	CPV	8/7/81	D	21		
Jean-Paul NDEKI	CMR	27/10/82	D	14	(2)	
Andrejs PAVLOVS	LVA	22/2/79	G	26		
PEDRO da Silva MOUTINHO	POR	9/9/79	A	1	(2)	1
Ats PURJE	EST	3/8/85	A	15	(10)	5
Yiannis SAMPSON		6/12/81	D	9	(4)	2
Ricardo Jorge Oliveira Ribeiro Duarte "SANTAMARIA"	POR	11/2/82	D	22	(2)	1
Maciej SCHERFCHEN	POL	16/6/79	M	1		
Giorgos SIELIS		23/10/86	M	15	(4)	2
David Eduardo SOLARI	ARG	21/7/86	M	24	(3)	7
THIAGO dos Santos Ferreira	BRA	12/7/87	A	11	(16)	1
Bernardo Lino Castro Paes VASCONCELOS	POR	10/6/79	A	14		7
Stanislav VELICKÝ	SVK	16/4/81	M	6	(1)	
Stefanos VOSKARIDIS		1/2/80	A	11	(5)	1

ALKI LARNACA FC

oach – Marios Konstantinou; (21/10/10) Itzhak Shum (ISR)

Founded – 1948

Stadium – Antonis Papadopoulos (9,782)

010				
9/8	Anorthosis	h	2-3	*Dobrašinović, Krassas*
2/9	AEP	a	2-1	*Kaiafas, Serjão*
8/9	Omonia	h	0-4	
6/9	Apollon	a	2-1	*Serjão 2*
/10	AEK	h	1-2	*Dobrašinović*
7/10	Ethnikos	a	1-2	*Nadé*
3/10	Doxa	h	1-1	*Serjão*
/11	APOP	h	0-0	
/11	APOEL	a	0-1	
4/11	Olympiakos	h	0-0	
1/11	AEL	a	0-1	
9/11	Ermis	h	0-1	
/12	Paralimni	a	2-0	*González, Edmar Silva*
1/12	Anorthosis	a	2-1	*Bashov, Serjão*
0/12	AEP	h	2-3	*Serjão 2 (2p)*
011				
0/1	Omonia	a	0-2	
5/1	Apollon	h	2-3	*González, Serjão*
3/1	AEK	a	2-0	*Roberto Brum, Dobrašinović*
1/1	Ethnikos	h	2-2	*Edmar Silva, Bashov*
/2	Doxa	a	0-3	
3/2	APOP	a	2-1	*Fernández 2*
0/2	APOEL	h	2-1	*Dobrašinović (p), Semedo*
8/2	Olympiakos	a	1-1	*Fernández*
/3	AEL	h	3-0	*Edmar Silva, Fusco, Serjão*
3/3	Ermis	a	1-3	*Bashov*
9/3	Paralimni	h	0-3	
/4	Ermis	a	2-1	*Bashov 2*
/4	AEP	h	1-3	*Bashov*
6/4	Ethnikos	h	2-3	*Dobrašinović (p), Semedo*
30/4	Ethnikos	a	3-0	*Bashov, Magrelashvili, Al-Saify*
/5	Ermis	h	1-0	*González*
4/5	AEP	a	1-1	*Al-Saify*

No	Name	Nat	DoB	Pos	Aps	(s)	Gls
16	Odai AL-SAIFY	JOR	26/4/86	A	13	(8)	2
7	Kostadin BASHOV	BUL	26/11/82	A	18	(6)	7
6	Daniel Alberto BLANCO	ARG	30/7/78	M	13		
3	BRUNO Everton QUADROS	BRA	3/2/77	D	7	(2)	
21	Paraskevas CHRISTOU		2/2/84	D	15		
83	Radosław CIERZNIAK	POL	24/4/83	G	14		
18	Siniša DOBRAŠINOVIĆ		17/2/77	M	29		5
11	EDMAR Lacerda da SILVA	BRA	19/4/82	A	22	(5)	3
19	Lefteris ELEFTHERIOU		12/6/74	M	1	(4)	
78	Darío Ezequiel FERNÁNDEZ	ARG	24/9/78	M	15		3
20	Emiliano Adrián FUSCO	ARG	2/3/86	D	28		1
32	Robbie GIBBONS	IRL	8/10/91	M		(2)	
99	Héctor Augusto GONZÁLEZ	COL	4/11/77	M	25		3
10	Kostas KAIAFAS		22/9/74	M	11		1
24	Andreas KONSTANTINOU		12/10/80	D	4		
23	Christodoulos KOUNTOURETIS		12/10/87	M	3	(11)	
30	Simos KRASSAS		10/7/82	M	4	(16)	1
1	Dimitris LEONIS		13/11/77	G	15		
3	Haim MAGRELASHVILI	ISR	4/6/82	D	25	(2)	1
5	Dimitris MARIS	GRE	24/6/79	M	1	(2)	
9	Christian NADÉ	FRA	18/9/84	A	1	(9)	1
4	Aleksandar PANTIĆ	SRB	1/10/78	D	14	(4)	
88	Nenad RAJIĆ	SRB	28/12/82	G	3		
33	ROBERTO BRUM Vallado	BRA	7/7/78	M	10	(2)	1
22	António Paulo Sanches SEMEDO	POR	1/6/79	M	15		2
50	Sérgio Luis Gardino da Silva "SERJÃO"	BRA	9/12/79	A	18	(6)	9
7	Luka ŽINKO	SVN	23/3/83	D	14	(1)	
8	Anton ŽLOGAR	SVN	24/11/77	A	14	(9)	

ANORTHOSIS FAMAGUSTA FC

Coach – Guillermo Ángel Hoyos (ARG); (19/11/10) Slobodan Krčmarević (SRB); (19/12/10) (Michael Pamporis); (27/12/10) Stanimir Stoilov (BUL)

Founded – 1911

Stadium – Antonis Papadopoulos (9,782)

MAJOR HONOURS: Cypriot League - (13) 1950, 1957, 1958, 1960, 1962, 1963, 1995, 1997, 1998, 1999, 2000, 2005, 2008; Cypriot Cup - (10) 1949, 1959, 1962, 1964, 1971, 1975, 1998, 2002, 2003, 2007.

2010				
29/8	Alki	a	3-2	*Cafú, Laban (p), Frontini*
12/9	APOP	h	3-0	*Leiwakabessy, Cafú 2*
19/9	APOEL	a	1-2	*Okkas*
25/9	Olympiakos	h	2-1	*Cristóvão, Frontini*
2/10	AEL	a	3-1	*Okkas 2, Lizio*
16/10	Ermis	h	4-0	*Cafú 2, Lizio, Cristóvão*
23/10	Paralimni	a	0-0	
30/10	Doxa	a	2-2	*Georgiou, Okkas*
8/11	AEP	h	1-1	*Laban (p)*
13/11	Omonia	a	0-1	
20/11	Apollon	h	1-2	*Michail*
28/11	AEK	a	0-3	
5/12	Ethnikos	h	1-1	*Okkas*
11/12	Alki	h	1-2	*Brachi*
18/12	APOP	a	1-3	*Cristóvão (p)*
2011				
8/1	APOEL	h	2-0	*Laban, Laborde*
16/1	Olympiakos	a	2-2	*Coto, Laban (p)*
23/1	AEL	h	4-0	*Laban, Okkas, Cafú, Cristóvão*
28/1	Ermis	a	0-3	*(w/o; original result 1-2 Cafú)*
6/2	Paralimni	h	3-1	*Laban 2 (1p), Laborde*
13/2	Doxa	h	4-1	*Cafú 2, Marangos, Angelov*
19/2	AEP	a	2-1	*Laban, Fotheringham*
27/2	Omonia	h	0-0	
5/3	Apollon	a	2-1	*Angelov, Okkas*
13/3	AEK	h	2-1	*Cafú, Cristóvão*
19/3	Ethnikos	a	2-0	*Cafú 2*
3/4	Omonia	a	0-1	
10/4	AEK	h	2-0	*Cafú, Perrone*

17/4	APOEL	h	1-2	*Okkas*
30/4	APOEL	a	1-0	*Cafú*
8/5	Omonia	h	0-0	
14/5	AEK	a	1-0	*Michail*

No	Name	Nat	DoB	Pos	Aps	(s)	Gls
4	Stanislav ANGELOV	BUL	12/4/78	D	14	(1)	2
31	Marcos Daniel ARGÜELLO	ARG	28/7/81	G	11		
15	Gabriel "BIEL" MEDINA Piris	ESP	22/3/80	D	3	(2)	
11	Álvaro Rodríguez BRACHI	ESP	16/1/86	D	15	(6)	1
17	Arlindo Gomes Semedo "CAFÚ"	CPV	17/11/77	A	28	(1)	14
37	Adamos CHATZIGEORGIOU		18/9/92	M	1		
26	Christoforos CHRISTOFI		23/3/91	M		(1)	
44	Jürgen COLIN	NED	20/1/81	D	12		
24	Lucas CONSISTRE	ARG	24/2/83	A		(4)	
10	Carlos COTO Pagés	ESP	11/2/88	M	4	(14)	1
16	CRISTÓVÃO da Silva Ramos	POR	25/3/83	M	26		5
55	Richard EROMOIGBE	NGA	26/6/84	M	3	(3)	
34	Mark FOTHERINGHAM	SCO	22/10/83	M	13	(2)	1
18	Pablo Javier FRONTINI	ARG	4/3/83	D	11		2
5	Ronald Lázaro GARCÍA Justiniano	BOL	17/12/80	M	11		
28	Giorgos GEORGIOU	GRE	24/9/79	D	8		1
22	JANÍCIO de Jesus Gomes Martins	CPV	30/11/79	D	29		
77	Wojciech KOWALEWSKI	POL	11/5/77	G	1		
1	Matúš KOZÁČIK	SVK	27/12/83	G	20	(1)	
20	Vincent LABAN	FRA	9/9/84	M	25	(1)	8
21	Ricardo Alexis LABORDE	COL	16/2/88	A	7	(5)	2
12	Jeffrey LEIWAKABESSY	NED	23/2/81	D	26	(2)	1
48	Marko LJUBINKOVIĆ	SRB	7/12/81	M	7	(6)	
7	Damián Emmanuel LIZIO	ARG	30/6/89	M	5	(6)	2
6	Christos MARANGOS		9/5/83	M	22	(1)	1
36	Markos MICHAIL		13/6/91	A	4	(8)	2
9	Yiannis OKKAS		11/2/77	A	22	(4)	8
99	Emanuel PERRONE	ARG	14/6/83	A	1	(8)	1
23	Valentinos SIELIS		1/3/90	D	7	(10)	
25	Christos SOTIRIOU		6/5/91	M	1	(1)	
83	Civard SPROCKEL	NED	10/5/83	D	15		
	Marko VIDOVIĆ	MNE	3/6/88	D		(5)	

APOEL FC

Coach – Ivan Jovanović (SRB)

Founded – 1926

Stadium – GSP (22,859)

MAJOR HONOURS: Cypriot League - (21) 1936, 1937, 1938, 1939, 1940, 1947, 1948, 1949, 1952, 1965, 1973, 1980, 1986, 1990, 1992, 1996, 2002, 2004, 2007, 2009, 2011; Cypriot Cup - (19) 1937, 1941, 1947, 1951, 1963, 1968, 1969, 1973, 1976, 1978, 1979, 1984, 1993, 1995, 1996, 1997, 1999, 2006, 2008.

2010

30/8	Ermis	h	1-0	*Charalambides*
11/9	Paralimni	a	0-1	
19/9	Anorthosis	h	2-1	*Aílton, Solomou*
25/9	AEP	a	1-1	*Trickovski*
3/10	Omonia	h	3-0	*William, Hélio Pinto, Aílton*
17/10	Apollon	a	5-0	*Manduca 2 (1p), Marcinho 2, Solari*
23/10	AEK	h	1-0	*Trickovski*
30/10	Ethnikos	a	1-0	*Trickovski*
7/11	Alki	h	1-0	*Manduca*
13/11	APOP	a	5-0	*Aílton, Trickovski, Grncarov, Alexandrou, Solari*
21/11	Doxa	h	3-1	*William, Manduca (p), Trickovski*
27/11	Olympiakos	h	4-1	*Solari 3, Grncarov*
4/12	AEL	a	2-2	*Trickovski, Grncarov*
12/12	Ermis	a	2-0	*Solari 2*
18/12	Paralimni	h	2-1	*Trickovski, Aílton*

2011

8/1	Anorthosis	a	0-2	
15/1	AEP	h	5-1	*Manduca (p), og (Ndeki), Solar[i], Marcinho, Trickovski*
22/1	Omonia	a	1-0	*Marcinho*
30/1	Apollon	h	2-1	*Manduca, Grncarov*
5/2	AEK	a	2-1	*William, Aílton*
14/2	Ethnikos	h	0-1	
20/2	Alki	a	1-2	*Grncarov*
27/2	APOP	h	6-2	*Aílton, Marcinho, Manduca 3 (2[p]), Grncarov*
6/3	Doxa	a	1-0	*Aílton*
12/3	Olympiakos	a	2-1	*Manduca, Solari*
19/3	AEL	h	2-0	*Paulo Jorge, Solari*
3/4	AEK	a	1-0	*Trickovski*
10/4	Omonia	h	2-0	*Charalambides 2*
17/4	Anorthosis	a	2-1	*Trickovski 2*
30/4	Anorthosis	h	0-1	
7/5	AEK	h	3-0	*Paulo Jorge, Solari, Marcinho*
11/5	Omonia	a	0-1	

No	Name	Nat	DoB	Pos	Aps	(s)	Gls
27	AÍLTON José Almeida	BRA	20/8/84	A	26	(5)	7
29	Nektarios ALEXANDROU		19/12/83	M	9	(11)	1
14	Joost BROERSE	NED	8/5/79	D	2	(6)	
10	Kostas CHARALAMBIDES		25/7/81	M	20	(10)	3
22	Dionissis CHIOTIS	GRE	4/6/77	G	27		
19	Marios ELIA		14/4/79	D	6		
5	Boban GRNCAROV	MKD	12/8/82	D	25	(1)	6
23	HÉLIO José Ribiero PINTO	POR	29/2/84	M	26		1
88	Anastasios KISSAS		18/1/88	G	4		
70	Panos KONSTANTINOU		11/1/85	G	1		
24	Christos KONTIS	GRE	13/5/75	D	22	(1)	
6	Dimitris KYRIAKOU		14/10/86	M		(1)	
21	Gustavo MANDUCA	BRA	8/6/80	M	26	(2)	10
81	Márcio Ivanildo da Silva "MARCINHO"	BRA	23/3/81	M	18	(7)	6
33	Chrysis MICHAIL		26/5/77	M	2	(3)	
30	Nenad MIROSAVLJEVIĆ	SRB	4/9/77	A	1	(9)	
26	NUNO Miguel Barbosa MORAIS	POR	29/1/84	M	30		
3	PAULO JORGE Soares Gomes	POR	16/6/80	D	15		2
7	Savvas POURSAITIDIS		26/6/76	D	27		
17	Marinos SATSIAS		24/5/78	M	4	(7)	
9	Esteban Andrés SOLARI	ARG	20/7/80	A	14	(13)	11
77	Athos SOLOMOU		30/11/85	M	9	(10)	1
11	Ivan TRICKOVSKI	MKD	18/4/87	A	21	(6)	11
98	WILLIAM Cleite Boaventura	BRA	14/2/80	D	17	(1)	3

APOLLON LIMASSOL FC

Coach – Slobodan Krčmarević (SRB); (26/10/10) Andreas Michaelides

Founded – 1954

Stadium – Tsirion (13,000)

MAJOR HONOURS: Cypriot League (3) 1991, 1994, 2006; Cypriot Cup - (6) 1966, 1967, 1986, 1992, 2001, 2010.

2010

29/8	Doxa	h	4-0	*Mrdaković 2, og (Gilvan), Adorno*
11/9	AEK	h	1-2	*Mrdaković (p)*
19/9	Ethnikos	a	2-0	*Adorno, Núñez*
26/9	Alki	h	1-2	*Semedo*
2/10	APOP	a	1-2	*Quinteros (p)*
17/10	APOEL	h	0-5	
24/10	Olympiakos	a	1-2	*Mrdaković*
30/10	AEL	h	3-0	*Bangura 3*
6/11	Ermis	a	2-2	*Mrdaković 2 (1p)*
14/11	Paralimni	h	1-0	*Mrdaković*
20/11	Anorthosis	a	2-1	*Merkis, Semedo*
27/11	AEP	h	1-0	*Núñez*
5/12	Omonia	a	1-3	*Adorno*
11/12	Doxa	a	1-1	*Mrdaković (p)*
18/12	AEK	a	2-2	*Bangura, Semedo*

11				
	Ethnikos	h	1-1	*Bangura (p)*
1	Alki	a	3-2	*Mrdaković 2, Adorno*
1	APOP	h	2-1	*Ion Erice, Mrdaković*
1	APOEL	a	1-2	*Bangura*
	Olympiakos	h	2-1	*Mrdaković, Bangura*
2	AEL	a	3-2	*Mrdaković, Adorno, Semedo*
2	Ermis	h	1-1	*Semedo*
2	Paralimni	a	1-2	*Bangura*
	Anorthosis	h	1-2	*Mrdaković*
3	AEP	a	0-1	
3	Omonia	h	2-0	*Bangura (p), Núñez*
	AEL	a	1-1	*Mrdaković*
	Olympiakos	h	5-1	*Mrdaković 4, Adorno*
4	Paralimni	a	1-2	*Mrdaković*
4	Paralimni	h	3-0	*Katsavakis, Kosowski, Mrdaković*
	AEL	h	3-1	*Merkis, Stavrou, Toni*
5	Olympiakos	a	2-2	*Adorno, Bangura*

	Name	Nat	DoB	Pos	Aps	(s)	Gls
	Aldo ADORNO	PAR	8/4/82	A	24	(3)	7
	Sofronis AVGOUSTI		9/3/77	G	2		
	Mustapha BANGURA	SLE	24/10/89	A	23	(5)	10
	Marios CHARALAMBOUS		24/1/92	M	1	(4)	
	Aleš CHVALOVSKÝ	CZE	29/5/79	G	28		
	Barukh DEGO	ISR	26/3/81	M	1	(4)	
	Stelios DEMITRIOU		13/8/94	M	1		
	Ioannis EFSTATHIOU		14/1/93	D	3		
	Michalis FANI		4/2/81	G	2		
	Raúl GONZÁLEZ	VEN	28/6/85	D	9	(10)	
	ION ERICE Domínguez	ESP	3/11/86	M	20	(5)	1
	Nikos KATSAVAKIS		16/5/79	M	14	(1)	1
	Martin KOLÁŘ	CZE	18/9/83	D	20	(1)	
	Kamil KOSOWSKI	POL	30/8/77	M	11	(6)	1
	Giorgos MERKIS		30/7/84	M	25		2
	Nasief MORRIS	RSA	16/4/81	D	13		
	Miljan MRDAKOVIĆ	SRB	6/5/82	A	24	(6)	21
	Samuel NEVA	FRA	15/5/81	D	15		
	Antonio NÚÑEZ Tena	ESP	15/1/79	M	20	(3)	3
	Felix OGBUKE	NGA	18/9/85	A	1	(8)	
	Waheed OSENI	NGA	17/1/88	M	16		
	Michalis PERIKLEOUS		23/1/92	D	3	(1)	
	Daniel Eduardo QUINTEROS	ARG	10/3/76	M	25	(1)	1
	João Filipe Correia SEMEDO	CPV	26/12/79	A	14	(11)	5
	Andreas STAVROU		27/10/88	M	9	(14)	1
	Stavrinos STYLIANOU		6/8/91	D	2	(1)	
3	Michalis SYKAS		4/11/90	M	1	(2)	
5	Panos THEODOROU		3/9/94	M	1		
	António Pedro de Brito Lopes "TONI"	POR	23/7/79	D	24	(3)	1

APOP/KINYRAS PEYIAS FC

Coach – Giorgos Polyviou; (13/12/10) Sofoklis Sofokleous

Founded – 2003

Stadium – Peyia Municipal (3,500)

MAJOR HONOURS: Cypriot Cup - (1) 2009.

010				
3/8	Paralimni	h	0-2	
2/9	Anorthosis	a	0-3	
9/9	AEP	h	0-1	
6/9	Omonia	a	1-0	*Tall*
'10	Apollon	h	2-1	*Madou 2 (1p)*
6/10	AEK	a	2-3	*Madou (p), Alekou*
3/10	Ethnikos	h	1-0	*Lukman*
/11	Alki	a	0-0	
/11	Doxa	h	1-1	*Madou (p)*
3/11	APOEL	h	0-5	
2/11	Olympiakos	a	1-1	*Matusiwa*
8/11	AEL	h	3-4	*Alekou, Coly, Berville*
/12	Ermis	a	1-1	*Lukman*
2/12	Paralimni	a	0-1	
8/12	Anorthosis	h	3-1	*Alekou, Pavlou 2 (1p)*

2011				
9/1	AEP	a	0-0	
15/1	Omonia	h	0-1	
23/1	Apollon	a	1-2	*Carboni*
29/1	AEK	h	0-0	
6/2	Ethnikos	a	0-0	
13/2	Alki	h	1-2	*Pavlou*
20/2	Doxa	a	3-4	*Sowunmi, Pavlou, og (Okkaridis)*
27/2	APOEL	a	2-6	*Pavlou (p), Ani*
6/3	Olympiakos	h	1-3	*Pavlou*
13/3	AEL	a	0-2	
19/3	Ermis	h	1-3	*Sotiroglou*

No	Name	Nat	DoB	Pos	Aps	(s)	Gls
44	Michalis AGATHANGELOU		14/11/86	M	1		
88	Alekos ALEKOU		13/11/83	A	9	(5)	3
14	Jeremiah ANI	NGA	7/10/85	A	2	(3)	1
30	Louis ANIWETA	RWA	10/7/84	D	17	(4)	
17	Kelly BERVILLE	FRA	5/1/78	D	20	(1)	1
22	Roberto Eduardo CARBONI	ARG	8/4/85	M	6	(3)	1
13	CARLOS Manuel de Oliveira MARQUES	POR	6/2/83	D	10	(4)	
19	CARMELO Yuste Yuste	ESP	3/2/84	M	10	(4)	
32	Stavros CHRISTODOULOU		17/2/92	M		(1)	
3	Mohamed COLY	SEN	5/3/85	D	16	(1)	1
10	EDGAR Carvalho Figueira MARCELINO	POR	10/9/84	M		(3)	
1	Damián FRASCARELLI	URU	2/6/85	G	16		
91	Lambros FYLAKTOU		16/6/91	M	2	(5)	
33	Andreas KARSERAS		14/1/86	G	1		
31	Serge Alain LIRI	CIV	23/3/79	A	17	(6)	
2	Imoro LUKMAN	GHA	4/10/84	M	20		2
99	Franck Olivier MADOU	CIV	15/9/87	A	6	(4)	4
16	MANUEL de Jesus LOPES	POR	19/8/82	M	7	(1)	
21	Diangi MATUSIWA	ANG	21/12/85	A	3	(6)	1
4	MIGUEL ÂNGELO Ferreira da Castro	POR	10/10/84	D	24		
6	Hamad NDIKUMANA	RWA	5/10/78	D	5	(1)	
12	Christos PALATES		13/7/90	A	1		
11	Kyriakos PAVLOU		4/9/86	A	23	(1)	6
18	Konstantinos SAMARAS		18/5/84	D	13		
9	Giannis SOTIROGLOU	GRE	11/6/87	A	2	(12)	1
27	Thomas SOWUNMI	HUN	25/7/78	A	8		1
5	Gora TALL	SEN	20/5/85	D	20		1
7	Yehiel TZAGAI	ISR	27/1/83	M	4	(3)	
8	Kevin VAN DESSEL	BEL	9/4/79	M	14	(4)	
16	Zlatko ZEČEVIĆ	SRB	10/8/83	G	9	(1)	

DOXA KATOKOPIA FC

Coach – Nikos Papavasiliou; (13/1/11) (Panicos Hatzigeorgiou); (21/1/11) Nikos Andronikou

Founded – 1954

Stadium – Peristerona (4,000)

2010				
29/8	Apollon	a	0-4	
12/9	AEL	h	0-0	
18/9	AEK	a	0-2	
25/9	Ermis	h	1-0	*Moyo*
4/10	Ethnikos	a	2-3	*Henrique (p), Okkaridis*
17/10	Paralimni	h	1-0	*Daniel Gomez*
23/10	Alki	a	1-1	*Henrique*
30/10	Anorthosis	h	2-2	*Eleftheriou, Cabrera*
6/11	APOP	a	1-1	*Henrique (p)*
14/11	AEP	h	2-1	*Henrique 2 (1p)*
21/11	APOEL	a	1-3	*Henrique*
27/11	Omonia	h	2-3	*Escobar, Cabrera*
4/12	Olympiakos	a	0-1	
11/12	Apollon	h	1-1	*Cabrera*
18/12	AEL	a	0-3	
2011				
8/1	AEK	h	1-4	*Henrique*
16/1	Ermis	a	1-2	*Henrique*

22/1	Ethnikos	h	0-2	
29/1	Paralimni	a	0-1	
6/2	Alki	h	3-0	*Arnal 2, Eleftheriou*
13/2	Anorthosis	a	1-4	*Galeano*
20/2	APOP	h	4-3	*Arnal, Galeano 2, Moustakas*
26/2	AEP	a	0-5	
6/3	APOEL	h	0-1	
13/3	Omonia	a	0-6	
19/3	Olympiakos	h	1-2	*Arnal (p)*

No	Name	Nat	DoB	Pos	Aps	(s)	Gls
99	ARNAL Llibert Conde Carbó	ESP	21/11/80	A	6	(2)	4
10	Gonzalo Gabriel CABRERA	ARG	15/1/89	M	16	(2)	3
11	DANIEL GOMEZ Puerta	FRA	16/3/79	A	14	(3)	1
22	Giannis DIMITRIOU		23/12/89	D	6	(8)	
27	Giorgos ELEFTHERIOU		30/9/84	M	19	(7)	2
7	ÉLIO Bruno Teixeira Martins	POR	26/3/85	M	5	(3)	
8	Matías Leonardo ESCOBAR	ARG	21/4/82	D	16	(1)	1
28	Diego GALEANO	ARG	24/2/86	A	10	(11)	3
4	GILVAN Rosa da Lima	BRA	26/3/82	D	8	(1)	
36	José HENRIQUE Souto Esteves	POR	31/3/80	A	18		8
23	Carlos IGOR Silveira PITA	POR	31/5/89	D	3	(1)	
15	Andrés Roberto IMPERIALE	ARG	8/7/86	D	9	(2)	
3	IVÁN Alejandro BENÍTEZ	ESP	31/5/88	D	10		
38	Igor KOJIĆ	SRB	30/7/87	G	1		
18	Stelios KONSTANTINOU		7/2/94	A		(4)	
40	Charalambos KYRIAKOU		15/10/89	M	6	(2)	
14	Geri MALAJ	ALB	3/10/89	M		(4)	
2	Mike MAMPUYA	BEL	17/1/83	D	25		
29	MARCO Paulo Amaral BICHO	POR	7/3/80	M	1	(2)	
59	Dimitris MARIS	GRE	24/6/79	M	1	(5)	
5	Pericles MOUSTAKAS		23/6/83	D	20	(1)	1
30	Kypros MOUZOUROS		27/9/94	M		(2)	
24	Thabani MOYO	ZIM	11/5/85	A	3	(6)	1
1	Zoltán NAGY	HUN	30/3/74	G	8		
36	Stelios OKKARIDIS		15/11/77	D	16	(3)	1
6	Francisco José Borrego Campos "PACO"	ESP	6/7/86	D	20		
25	Zsolt POSZA	HUN	11/5/77	G	17		
19	Carlos Manuel Dias SAAVEDRA	POR	1/2/81	M	22	(1)	
17	Rafael SOFOKLEOUS		19/2/93	M		(2)	
26	Seyfo SOLEY	GAM	12/12/80	D	6	(1)	

ENOSIS NEON PARALIMNI FC

Coach – Cedomir Janevski (MKD); (10/1/11) (Slobodan Vučeković (SRB); (18/1/11) Nicos Papavasiliou

Founded – 1936

Stadium – Tasos Markou (8,000)

2010				
28/8	APOP	a	2-0	*Van Tornhout 2*
11/9	APOEL	h	1-0	*Tarumbwa*
18/9	Olympiakos	a	1-1	*Van Tornhout*
26/9	AEL	h	1-1	*De Wulf*
2/10	Ermis	a	0-1	
17/10	Doxa	a	0-1	
23/10	Anorthosis	h	0-0	
31/10	AEP	a	1-0	*Alexandre (p)*
6/11	Omonia	h	0-1	
14/11	Apollon	a	0-1	
20/11	AEK	h	0-2	
28/11	Ethnikos	a	2-2	*Burchill 2*
4/12	Alki	h	0-2	
12/12	APOP	h	1-0	*Krivokapić (p)*
18/12	APOEL	a	1-2	*Krivokapić*
2011				
9/1	Olympiakos	h	1-3	*Imschoot*
17/1	AEL	a	0-0	
22/1	Ermis	h	3-1	*Burchill, Alexandre 2*
29/1	Doxa	h	1-0	*Krivokapić*
6/2	Anorthosis	a	1-3	*Alexandre (p)*
12/2	AEP	h	2-1	*Van Tornhout, Baldovaliev*
21/2	Omonia	a	0-0	
26/2	Apollon	h	2-1	*Alexandre (p), Van Tornhout*
5/3	AEK	a	2-0	*Burchill, Imschoot*
13/3	Ethnikos	h	1-2	*Alexandre*
19/3	Alki	a	3-0	*Onana, Krivokapić, Van Tornhout*
2/4	Olympiakos	a	1-1	*Baldovaliev*
9/4	AEL	h	2-3	*Krivokapić, Burchill*
17/4	Apollon	h	2-1	*Burchill, Mertakas*
30/4	Apollon	a	0-3	
6/5	Olympiakos	h	1-0	*Hugo Faria*
14/5	AEL	a	1-1	*Onana*

No	Name	Nat	DoB	Pos	Aps	(s)	Gls
9	ALEXANDRE Afonso da Silva	BRA	15/8/83	D	27	(3)	6
28	Zoran BALDOVALIEV	MKD	21/5/83	A	7	(3)	2
27	Mark BURCHILL	SCO	18/8/80	A	16	(6)	6
18	Panayiotis CHARALAMBOUS		15/5/76	G		(1)	
14	Jimmy DE WULF	BEL	9/6/80	D	28	(1)	1
88	Matías Leonardo ESCOBAR	ARG	21/4/82	D	8	(2)	
4	Laurent FASSOTTE	BEL	31/12/77	D	16	(2)	
17	Dimos GOUMENOS		25/12/78	M	12	(12)	
93	Jack HARRIS	ENG	4/5/93	M	2	(1)	
6	HUGO Miguel da Encarnação Pires FARIA	POR	15/2/83	M	22	(5)	1
7	Kristof IMSCHOOT	BEL	4/12/80	M	12	(7)	2
22	Andreas KITTOS		9/9/90	G	2	(1)	
21	Konstantinos KONSTANTINOU		11/12/91	A	2	(1)	
39	Paul KPAKA	SLE	7/8/81	A	1	(4)	
8	Radovan KRIVOKAPIĆ	SRB	14/8/78	M	26	(2)	5
5	Bojan MARKOVSKI	MKD	8/8/83	D	26		
30	Lefteris MERTAKAS		16/3/85	D	22	(4)	1
1	Petar MILOSEVSKI	MKD	6/12/73	G	22		
71	Demetris MOULAZIMIS		15/1/92	D	3	(1)	
25	Dimitris OIKONOMOU		10/11/92	D	4		
12	Hervé Anselme Ndjana ONANA	CMR	1/6/87	M	3	(4)	2
99	Ivan PEJČIĆ	SRB	11/9/82	M	2	(9)	
31	Georgi PETKOV	BUL	14/3/76	G	8		
19	Konstantinos PRIS		10/8/90	M		(1)	
33	Panikos SPYROU		17/10/76	D	18		
77	Obadiah TARUMBWA	ZIM	29/11/85	A	16	(6)	1
20	Matthias TRENSON	BEL	3/10/86	D	20	(4)	
23	Dieter VAN TORNHOUT	BEL	18/3/85	A	20	(5)	6
11	Krste VELKOSKI	MKD	20/2/88	A	6	(5)	
29	Marios ZANNETTOU		23/12/92	M	1	(6)	

ERMIS ARADIPPOU FC

Coach – Christos Kassianos; (15/11/10) Dimitris Ioannou; (10/12/10) João Carlos Pereira (POR)

Founded – 1958

Stadium – Ammochostos, Larnaca (4,000)

2010				
30/8	APOEL	a	0-1	
13/9	Olympiakos	h	2-2	*Chailis, Joeano*
20/9	AEL	a	2-1	*Bemba, Fabinho*
25/9	Doxa	a	0-1	
2/10	Paralimni	h	1-0	*Wender*
16/10	Anorthosis	a	0-4	
25/10	AEP	h	2-2	*Joeano (p), Papathanasiou*
31/10	Omonia	a	1-4	*Joeano*
6/11	Apollon	h	2-2	*Joeano, Gómez*
13/11	AEK	a	1-2	*Joeano*
20/11	Ethnikos	h	1-1	*Wender*
29/11	Alki	a	1-0	*Roncatto*
6/12	APOP	h	1-1	*Joeano (p)*

'12	APOEL	h	0-2	
'12	Olympiakos	a	2-3	*Joeano (p), Wender*
11				
	AEL	h	0-0	
'1	Doxa	h	2-1	*Joeano (p), Maghradze*
'1	Paralimni	a	1-3	*Maghradze*
'1	Anorthosis	h	3-0	*(w/o; original result 2-1 Sebastião Nogueira, Papathanasiou)*
2	AEP	a	1-3	*Roncatto*
'2	Omonia	h	0-0	
/2	Apollon	a	1-1	*Wender*
/2	AEK	h	1-1	*Wender*
3	Ethnikos	a	0-1	
/3	Alki	h	3-1	*Joeano 3 (2p)*
/3	APOP	a	3-1	*og (Tall), Roncatto 2 (1p)*
4	Alki	h	1-2	*Maghradze*
4	Ethnikos	a	1-0	*Papathanasiou*
/4	AEP	h	3-3	*Kolanis, Maghradze, Joeano*
/4	AEP	a	1-1	*Maghradze*
5	Alki	a	0-1	
/5	Ethnikos	h	1-0	*Joeano*

o	Name	Nat	DoB	Pos	Aps	(s)	Gls
	Antonis ALEXIOU		6/12/94	M		(1)	
	Marko BARUN	SVN	7/1/78	D	17	(2)	
	Mathieu Yannick BEMBA	FRA	3/3/88	M	11	(13)	1
	Aleksandar ČANOVIĆ	SRB	18/2/83	G	2	(2)	
	Kyriakos CHAILIS		23/2/78	A	3	(7)	1
	Athos CHRYSOSTOMOU		8/7/81	G	26		
	Fábio de Matos Pereira "FABINHO"	BRA	26/2/82	M	6	(3)	1
9	Hélder FILIPE da Costa Soares "PASTEL"	POR	10/2/82	M	14		
0	Cheikh GADIAGA	SEN	30/11/79	M	29	(1)	
	Juan Cruz GILL	ARG	18/7/83	D	19	(3)	
0	Gabriel Enrique GÓMEZ	PAN	29/5/84	M	9	(2)	1
	JOEANO Pinto Chaves	BRA	12/8/79	A	23	(3)	13
3	Ricardo JOEL dos Santos Dias	POR	15/6/80	D	11		
7	Eduardo Tomas Luís JUMISSE	MOZ	6/6/84	M	4	(2)	
	Antonis KATSIS		6/9/89	M	1	(2)	
9	Giorgos KOLANIS		4/11/80	M	11	(4)	1
1	Giorgos KONSTANTI		19/9/80	D	4	(1)	
6	Levan MAGHRADZE	GEO	5/12/77	D	29		5
1	Federico MARTORELL	ARG	26/3/81	D	6	(4)	
6	Pedro MIGUEL dos Santos OLIVEIRA	POR	18/8/83	D	19	(3)	
	MIGUEL António Teixeira Ferreira PEDRO	POR	6/11/83	M	13	(8)	
8	Azubuike OLISEH	NGA	18/11/78	D	12	(2)	
1	Giorgos PAPADOPOULOS		24/4/91	G	2		
2	Andreas PAPATHANASIOU		3/10/83	A	5	(15)	3
9	PAULO Sérgio Cardoso da COSTA	POR	5/12/79	M	3	(1)	
5	Yordan PETKOV	BUL	11/3/76	D	11		
8	Marios POUTZIOURI		8/12/93	D		(1)	
0	RAFAel Antonio PONZO García	VEN	18/10/78	G	2		
9	Evandro RONCATTO	BRA	24/5/86	A	22	(3)	4
8	Konstantinos SAMARAS		18/5/84	D	7	(1)	
7	SEBASTIÃO José Lopes de Melo e NOGUEIRA	POR	9/9/88	M	2	(11)	1
5	WENDERson de Arruda Said	BRA	17/4/75	M	29	(1)	5

ETHNIKOS ACHNAS FC

Coach – Svetozar Šapurić (SRB)

Founded – 1968

Stadium – Dasaki (5,000)

2010				
29/8	AEP	h	2-1	*Cássio, Poyiatzis*
11/9	Omonia	a	0-1	
19/9	Apollon	h	0-2	
25/9	AEK	a	1-1	*Kebadze*
4/10	Doxa	h	3-2	*Sikov, Filaniotis, Kissi*
17/10	Alki	h	2-1	*Gelson, Kebadze*
23/10	APOP	a	0-1	
30/10	APOEL	h	0-1	
6/11	Olympiakos	a	2-3	*Eduardo, Cássio*
15/11	AEL	h	0-0	
20/11	Ermis	a	1-1	*Ignatov*
28/11	Paralimni	h	2-2	*Gelson, Petrović*
5/12	Anorthosis	a	1-1	*Gelson*
11/12	AEP	a	1-0	*Gelson*
19/12	Omonia	h	0-0	
2011				
8/1	Apollon	a	1-1	*Ignatov*
16/1	AEK	h	0-1	
22/1	Doxa	a	2-0	*Gelson, Petrović*
31/1	Alki	a	2-2	*Filaniotis, Poyiatzis (p)*
6/2	APOP	h	0-0	
14/2	APOEL	a	1-0	*Cássio*
19/2	Olympiakos	h	0-1	
26/2	AEL	a	1-2	*Gelson*
5/3	Ermis	h	1-0	*Gelson*
13/3	Paralimni	a	2-1	*Ignatov, Petrović (p)*
19/3	Anorthosis	h	0-2	
2/4	AEP	a	1-0	*Ivanovski*
9/4	Ermis	h	0-1	
16/4	Alki	a	3-2	*Ignatov, Gelson 2*
30/4	Alki	h	0-3	
7/5	AEP	h	0-3	
14/5	Ermis	a	0-1	

No	Name	Nat	DoB	Pos	Aps	(s)	Gls
30	CÁSSIO Magalhães Fernandes	BRA	11/2/87	M	28	(1)	3
11	Slaviša DUGIĆ	SUI	17/1/85	A	2	(16)	
21	EDUARDO Pinceli	BRA	23/4/83	M	15	(1)	1
16	Elpidoforos ELIA		5/8/85	M		(7)	
33	Petros FILANIOTIS		13/4/80	M	22	(6)	2
16	GELSON Rodrigues de Souza	BRA	3/1/82	A	25	(3)	9
23	Stojan IGNATOV	MKD	27/12/79	M	15	(7)	4
9	Filip IVANOVSKI	MKD	5/1/86	A	7	(8)	1
29	Levan KEBADZE	GEO	1/2/75	A	26		2
4	Abdelkarim KISSI	MAR	5/5/80	M	15	(6)	1
6	Christos KOTSONIS		13/6/76	M	5	(1)	
2	LUÍS Filipe Baptista TORRES	POR	15/10/79	D	24		
3	Ivica MILUTINOVIĆ	SRB	20/10/83	D	27		
1	Edin NUREDINOSKI	MKD	21/4/82	G	30		
35	Predrag OCOKOLJIĆ	SRB	29/7/77	D	9	(5)	
22	Michalis PARPA		1/12/92	M		(1)	
20	Ivan PETROVIĆ	SRB	5/9/78	M	13	(8)	3
17	Nikos PITSILLIDIS		17/12/93	D		(1)	
10	Christos POYIATZIS		12/4/78	M	24	(1)	2
8	Lars SCHLICHTING	GER	14/9/82	M	14	(8)	
19	Djelaludin SHARITYAR	AFG	15/3/83	D	1	(3)	
5	Vance SIKOV	MKD	19/7/85	D	25	(1)	1
15	Dimitris SIMOV		9/4/82	D	20	(3)	
38	Elias VATTIS		28/2/86	M	3	(3)	
22	Milan ZAHÁLKA	CZE	13/3/77	G	2		

OLYMPIAKOS NICOSIA FC

Coach – Charalambos Christodoulou
Founded – 1931
Stadium – GSP (22,859)
MAJOR HONOURS: Cypriot League (3) 1967, 1969, 1971; Cypriot Cup - (1) 1977.

2010				
28/8	AEL	h	0-2	
13/9	Ermis	a	2-2	*Fernando, Hélder Sousa*
18/9	Paralimni	h	1-1	*João Paulo*
25/9	Anorthosis	a	1-2	*João Paulo*
2/10	AEP	h	2-2	*Kenmogne, João Paulo*
18/10	Omonia	a	2-2	*Dédé 2*
24/10	Apollon	h	2-1	*Kenmogne (p), João Paulo*
31/10	AEK	a	1-1	*David Caiado*
6/11	Ethnikos	h	3-2	*Chidi 2, Kenmogne (p)*
14/11	Alki	a	0-0	
22/11	APOP	h	1-1	*Chidi*
27/11	APOEL	a	1-4	*Rodrigão*
4/12	Doxa	h	1-0	*João Paulo (p)*
13/12	AEL	a	2-3	*og (Júnior), João Paulo*
19/12	Ermis	h	3-2	*Kenmogne 3*
2011				
9/1	Paralimni	a	3-1	*João Paulo, Hélder Sousa, David Caiado*
16/1	Anorthosis	h	2-2	*João Paulo 2 (1p)*
22/1	AEP	a	3-1	*Kenmogne, Chidi, Júnior*
29/1	Omonia	h	0-2	
5/2	Apollon	a	1-2	*Kenmogne*
12/2	AEK	h	2-3	*João Paulo, Kenmogne*
19/2	Ethnikos	a	1-0	*João Paulo*
28/2	Alki	h	1-1	*Kenmogne*
6/3	APOP	a	3-1	*Hélder Sousa, João Paulo 2*
12/3	APOEL	h	1-2	*João Paulo*
19/3	Doxa	a	2-1	*Chidi, João Paulo (p)*
2/4	Paralimni	h	1-1	*Alkiviadis*
9/4	Apollon	a	1-5	*Chidi*
17/4	AEL	h	2-1	*Chidi 2*
29/4	AEL	a	1-2	*Kenmogne*
6/5	Paralimni	a	0-1	
10/5	Apollon	h	2-2	*João Paulo (p), Alkiviadis*

No	Name	Nat	DoB	Pos	Aps	(s)	Gls
19	Andreas ALKIVIADIS		19/9/91	A	3	(6)	2
5	Carlos ANDRÉ Santos Jesus	BRA	27/2/87	D	6	(1)	
1	Arjan BEQAJ	ALB	25/8/75	G	5		
30	Cristiano Pereira da Souza "BRASÍLIA"	BRA	28/7/77	M	7	(1)	
7	CARLOS ANDRÉ Filipe Martins	POR	15/4/82	M	21	(3)	
15	Philip CHIDI Onyemah	NGA	20/2/84	A	25	(6)	8
10	DAVID CAIADO Dias	POR	2/5/87	M	19	(9)	2
29	Adérito Waldemar Alves Carvalho "DÉDÉ"	ANG	4/7/81	M	20	(5)	2
4	FERNANDO Augusto de Abreu Ferreira	BRA	3/10/84	D	8	(1)	1
31	HÉLDER Bruno Macedo SOUSA	POR	13/10/77	M	28	(1)	3
22	Isli HIDI	ALB	15/10/80	G	7		
80	JOÃO PAULO Pinto Ribeiro	POR	8/4/80	A	20	(5)	16
35	Rui Paulo Silva JÚNIOR	POR	16/6/75	D	15		1
98	Valantis KAPARTIS		26/10/91	D	2	(3)	
93	Giorgos KARKOTIS					(1)	
99	Emmanuel KENMOGNE	CMR	2/9/80	A	23	(4)	11
8	MÉRCIO José Santos da Silva	BRA	26/5/80	M	14	(11)	
11	Nikos NICOLAOU		10/5/79	M	15	(5)	
16	Konstantinos PANAGI		8/10/94	G	2		
77	Panayiotis PANAYIOTOU		27/9/88	D	7	(2)	
2	Paulo Roberto Teles Goes Sobrinho "PAULINHO"	BRA	24/8/83	D	23	(1)	
21	PEDRO Miguel Mimoso DUARTE	POR	22/4/78	M	15	(6)	
18	Paulo Jorge Martins dos Santos PINA	CPV	4/1/83	D	11	(1)	
6	Kyriakos POLYKARPOU		17/3/80	M	8	(14)	
3	Rodrigo Rodrigues Ribeiro "RODRIGÃO"	BRA	18/7/78	D	26	(1)	1
13	Ernestas ŠETKUS	LTU	25/5/85	G	18		
20	Pieros SOTIRIOU		13/1/93	M	4	(2)	

AC OMONIA

Coach – Takis Lemonis (GRE); (13/10/10) Dušan Bajević (SRB); (27/4/11) Neophytos Larkou
Founded – 1948
Stadium – GSP (22,859)
MAJOR HONOURS: Cypriot League - (20) 1961, 1966, 1972, 1974, 1975, 1976, 1977, 1978, 1979, 1981, 1982, 1983, 1984, 1985, 1987, 1989, 1993, 2001, 2003, 2010; Cypriot Cup - (13) 1965, 1972, 1974, 1980, 1981, 1982, 1983, 1988, 1991, 1994, 2000, 2005, 2011.

2010				
30/8	AEK	a	2-1	*Rengifo (p), Rueda*
11/9	Ethnikos	h	1-0	*Rueda*
18/9	Alki	a	4-0	*Iago Bouzón, Konstantinou, Efrem, LuaLua*
26/9	APOP	h	0-1	
3/10	APOEL	a	0-3	
18/10	Olympiakos	h	2-2	*Rueda, LuaLua*
24/10	AEL	a	0-0	
31/10	Ermis	h	4-1	*Konstantinou 2 (1p), Christofi, Rengifo*
6/11	Paralimni	a	1-0	*Avraam*
13/11	Anorthosis	h	1-0	*Leandro*
20/11	AEP	a	1-1	*Konstantinou (p)*
27/11	Doxa	a	3-2	*Konstantinou, Aloneftis (p), Shpungin*
5/12	Apollon	h	3-1	*Konstantinou 3 (1p)*
12/12	AEK	h	2-0	*Konstantinou 2 (1p)*
19/12	Ethnikos	a	0-0	
2011				
10/1	Alki	h	2-0	*Konstantinou 2*
15/1	APOP	a	1-0	*Konstantinou*
22/1	APOEL	h	0-1	
29/1	Olympiakos	a	2-0	*Konstantinou, Karipidis*
5/2	AEL	h	2-0	*Konstantinou, Kaseke*
14/2	Ermis	a	0-0	
21/2	Paralimni	h	0-0	
27/2	Anorthosis	a	0-0	
6/3	AEP	h	1-1	*Aloneftis*
13/3	Doxa	h	6-0	*Konstantinou 2 (1p), Leandro, LuaLua, Christofi, Efrem*
19/3	Apollon	a	0-2	
3/4	Anorthosis	h	1-0	*Leandro*
10/4	APOEL	a	0-2	
16/4	AEK	h	3-0	*Makrides, LuaLua, Aloneftis*
30/4	AEK	a	2-1	*Leandro, Rengifo*
8/5	Anorthosis	a	0-0	
11/5	APOEL	h	1-0	*Bruno Aguiar*

No	Name	Nat	DoB	Pos	Aps	(s)	Gls
2	Rasheed ALABI	NGA	9/1/86	D	8	(2)	
46	Efstathios ALONEFTIS		29/3/83	M	20	(6)	3
9	Andreas AVRAAM		6/6/87	M	18	(10)	1
10	BRUNO João Morais AGUIAR	POR	24/2/81	M	15	(4)	1
18	Christoforos CHARALAMBOUS		9/7/92	M	1		
33	Ilias CHARALAMBOUS		25/9/80	D	14	(2)	
77	Dimitris CHRISTOFI		28/9/88	M	10	(7)	2
3	DAVIDSON de Oliveira Morais	BRA	18/7/71	M	18	(4)	
7	Giorgos EFREM		5/7/89	M	19	(8)	2

Antonis GEORGALLIDES		30/1/82	G	30		
Dimitris GRAMMOZIS	GRE	8/7/78	M	1	(2)	
Dragoslav JEVRIĆ	SRB	8/7/74	G	2	(1)	
IAGO BOUZÓN Amoedo	ESP	17/3/83	D	9		1
Christos KARIPIDIS	GRE	2/12/82	D	23	(1)	1
Noel KASEKE	ZIM	24/12/80	D	10	(4)	1
Michalis KONSTANTINOU		19/2/78	A	24	(2)	17
Theodosis KYPROU		24/2/92	A	1	(1)	
LEANDRO Marcolini Pedroso de Almeida	HUN	19/3/82	D	26	(2)	4
Lomano Trésor LUALUA	COD	28/12/80	A	11	(8)	4
Konstantinos MAKRIDES		13/1/82	M	27	(1)	1
Giorgos PANAGI		3/11/86	M	3	(4)	
Hernán RENGIFO Trigoso	PER	18/4/83	A	7	(9)	3
José Manuel RUEDA Sampedro	ESP	30/1/88	M	7	(10)	3
Yuval SHPUNGIN	ISR	3/4/87	D	15	(3)	1
VÍCTOR Manuel Espasandín Facal	ESP	16/3/85	D	7	(2)	
Timo WENZEL	GER	30/11/77	D	26	(1)	

TOP GOALSCORERS 2010/11

21	Miljan MRDAKOVIĆ (Apollon)
17	Michalis KONSTANTINOU (Omonia)
16	JOÃO PAULO (Olympiakos)
14	CAFÚ (Anorthosis)
13	JOEANO (Ermis)
11	Emmanuel KENMOGNE (Olympiakos) Esteban Andrés SOLARI (APOEL) Ivan TRICKOVSKI (APOEL)
10	FREDDY (AEL) Gustavo MANDUCA (APOEL) Mustapha BANGURA (Apollon)

PROMOTED CLUBS

ARIS LIMASSOL FC

Coach – Tasos Kyriakou; (23/11/10) Dusan Mitošević (SRB)
Founded – 1930
Stadium – Tsirion (13,000)

NEA SALAMIS FC

Coach – Nedim Tutić (BIH); (18/10/10) Stephen Constantine (ENG)
Founded – 1948
Stadium – Ammochostos (4,000)
MAJOR HONOURS: Cypriot Cup - (1) 1990.

ANAGENNISI DERYNIA FC

Coach – Adam Adamou
Founded – 1920
Stadium – Gypedo Anagennisi (4,000)

SECOND LEVEL FINAL TABLE 2010/11

		Pld	W	D	L	F	A	Pts
1	Aris Limassol FC	32	16	9	7	49	25	57
2	Nea Salamis FC	32	14	13	5	50	25	55
3	Anagennisi Derynia FC	32	15	9	8	37	27	54
4	Omonia Aradippou FC	32	15	6	11	42	41	51
5	Othellos Athienou FC	26	10	11	5	28	22	41
6	Atromitos Yeroskipou FC	26	12	4	10	35	26	40
7	PAEEK FC	26	10	6	10	36	36	36
8	Akritas Chloraka FC	26	9	7	10	34	38	34
9	APEP Kyperounda FC	26	8	9	9	33	34	33
10	Chalkanoras Idaliou	26	9	6	11	41	44	33
11	Onisilos Sotira FC	26	8	8	10	26	30	32
12	ASIL FC	26	6	5	15	20	41	23
13	Digenis Akritas Morphou FC	26	5	6	15	24	45	21
14	Adonis Idalion FC	26	4	7	15	24	45	19

NB After 26 rounds top four clubs enter play-off round.

DOMESTIC CUP 2010/11

CYPRUS CUP

SECOND ROUND

(10/11/10 & 24/11/10)
Adonis v Ermis 3-2; 0-3 *(3-5)*
APEP v ASIL 1-0; 1-2 *(2-2; APEP on away goal)*
Chalkanoras v Omonia 0-4; 0-2 *(0-6)*
Digenis v AEK 0-1; 1-2 *(aet) (1-3)*
Nea Salamis v Ethnikos Achnas 0-2; 0-2 *(0-4)*
Omonia Aradippou v Paralimni 0-3; 0-3 *(0-6)*
Othellos v Doxa 1-4; 0-2 *(1-6)*

(10/11/10 & 1/12/10)
Akritas v Anorthosis 0-3; 0-5 *(0-8)*
Anagennisi Derynia v Olympiakos 0-1; 1-2 *(1-3)*
Atromitos v APOP 1-2; 3-2 *(aet) (4-4; Atromitos on away goals)*

(10/11/10 & 8/12/10)
Onisilos v Alki 0-2; 0-4 *(0-6)*

(24/11/10 & 1/12/10)
PAEEK v AEP 2-3; 3-4 *(5-7)*

Byes – AEL, APOEL, Apollon, Aris

THIRD ROUND

(12/1/11 & 19/1/11)
APOEL v Apollon 1-1; 0-2 *(1-3)*
Doxa v AEK 0-1; 1-4 *(1-5)*
Ermis v Ethnikos Achnas 0-1; 1-1 *(1-2)*

(12/1/11 & 26/1/11)
AEL v Aris 0-1; 0-0 *(0-1)*
AEP v Olympiakos 0-0; 1-3 *(1-3)*

(12/1/11 & 2/2/11)
Anorthosis v APEP 2-0; 1-0 *(3-0)*

(19/1/11 & 26/1/11)
Omonia v Atromitos 6-0; 2-2 *(8-2)*

(26/1/11 & 16/2/11)
Paralimni v Alki 0-1; 3-4 *(3-5)*

QUARTER-FINALS

(9/3/11 & 16/3/11)
AEK 1 *(Caluwé 43)*, Anorthosis 2 *(Laban 19, Fotheringham 32)*
Anorthosis 1 *(Cafú 4)*, AEK 1 *(Oper 1)*
(Anorthosis 3-2)

Alki 0, Ethnikos Achnas 3 *(Filaniotis 19, Dugić 80, Petrović 90)*
Ethnikos Achnas 0, Alki 2 *(Edmar Silva 50, Bashov 89)*
(Ethnikos Achnas 3-2)

Olympiakos 1 *(Chidi 65)*, Apollon 1 *(Bangura 58)*
Apollon 3 *(Bangura 80, Mrdaković 87, 90)*, Olympiakos 2 *(João Paulo 34, Dédé 37)*
(Apollon 4-3)

(16/3/11 & 6/4/11)
Omonia 3 *(LuaLua 15, 36p, Avraam 82)*, Aris 0
Aris 1 *(Theofanous 18)*, Omonia 3 *(Rengifo 63, Shpungin 80, Alabi 85)*
(Omonia 6-1)

SEMI-FINALS

(20/4/11 & 4/5/11)
Apollon 1 *(Quinteros 90p)*, Anorthosis 1 *(Perrone 74)*
Anorthosis 1 *(Cafú 7)*, Apollon 2 *(Bangura 77, Mrdaković 90)*
(Apollon 3-2)

Omonia 1 *(Makrides 44)*, Ethnikos Achnas 0
Ethnikos Achnas 1 *(Kebadze 53)*, Omonia 1 *(Leandro 113) (aet)*
(Omonia 2-1)

FINAL

(18/5/11)
Neo GSZ, Larnaca
AC OMONIA 1 *(Konstantinou 12)*
APOLLON LIMASSOL FC 1 *(Charalambous I. 85og)*
(aet; 4-3 on pens)
Referee – *Busacca (ITA)*
OMONIA – *Georgallides, Davidson, Karipidis (Wenzel 77), Charalambous I., Avraam, Leandro, Bruno Aguiar, Makrides, Aloneftis (Rueda 90+4), LuaLua (Efrem 58), Konstantinou.*
APOLLON – *Chvalovský, Merkis, Neva, Toni, Morris (Semedo 58), Quinteros (Núñez 33), Ion Erice, Kosowski (Stavrou 73), Bangura, Adorno, Mrdaković.*

CLUB COMMUNICATION 2011/12

AEK Larnaca FC

7, Kilkis Street, PO Box 40060
CY-6015 Larnaca

Tel	+357 24 655 999
Fax	+357 24 652 464
Web	aek.com.cy
Email	info@aek.com.cy
Media Officer	Nektarios Markettos

AEL Limassol FC

PO Box 51606
CY-3507 Limassol

Tel	+357 25 737 555
Fax	+357 25 737 540
Web	aelfc.com
Email	ael@cytanet.com.cy
Media Officer	Nicolas Leventis

Alki Larnaca FC

51 Georgiou Griva Digheni Ave, Savvides Buildings, Flat 7, CY-6036 Larnaca

Tel	+357 24 652 955
Fax	+357 24 626 984
Web	alkifc.com.cy
Email	info@alkifc.com.cy
Media Officer	Michalis Markou

Anagennisi Derynia FC

PO Box 36081
CY-5385 Deryneia, Famagusta

Tel	+357 23 821 436
Fax	+357 23 741 442
Web	anagennisis1920.net
Email	
Media Officer	Dimitris Martis

Anorthosis Famagusta FC

1, Antonis Papadopoulos Street
PO Box 40756, CY-6307 Larnaca

Tel	+357 24 821 911
Fax	+357 24 635 833
Web	anorthosisfc.com
Email	info@anorthosisfc.com
Media Officer	Dimitris Souglis

APOEL FC

Dimofontos 39, Suite 301
CY-1075 Nicosia

Tel	+357 22 240 200
Fax	+357 22 335 865
Web	apoelfc.com.cy
Email	info@apoelfc.com.cy
Media Officer	Panicos Hatziliasis

Apollon Limassol FC

Mesologgiou 1, 3031 , PO Box 53206
CY-3301 Limassol

Tel	+357 25 746 805
Fax	+357 25 746 808
Web	apollon.com.cy
Email	apollon@apollon.com.cy
Media Officer	Ilias Poniros

Aris Limassol FC

Costa Kouzari, PO Box 50579
CY-3040 Limassol

Tel	+357 25 375 070
Fax	+357 25 341 482
Web	aris-fc.com
Email	aris.fc@live.com
Media Officer	Savvinos Lofitis

Enosis Neon Paralimni FC

17, Antonis Papadopoulos Street,
PO Box 33020, CY-5310 Paralimni

Tel	+357 23 827 329
Fax	+357 23 825 658
Web	enpfc.com
Email	info@enpfc.com
Media Officer	Costas M. Stratis

Ermis Aradippou FC

Georgiou Taoulou 7, Oidipodos 4-6
CY-6058 Larnaca

Tel	+357 24 664 489
Fax	+357 24 664 488
Web	ermisaradippoufc.com
Email	ermisaradippou@ cytanet.com.cy
Media Officer	Thasos Panayiotou

Ethnikos Achnas FC

Griva Digeni Avenue, PO Box 36543
CY-5523 Dasaki Achnas

Tel	+357 24 722 333
Fax	+357 24 721 320
Web	
Email	ethnikosachnas@ cytanet.com
Media Officer	Antonis Orthodoxou

Nea Salamis Famagusta FC

PO Box 40345, Ammochostos Epistrofi Stadium, CY-6303 Larnaca

Tel	+357 24 663 090
Fax	+357 24 663 228
Web	neasalamis.com.cy
Email	neasalamis@ cytanet.com.cy
Media Officer	Pantelis Andronicou

Olympiakos Nicosia FC

Athninas 6A, PO Box 22339
CY-1520 Nicosia

Tel	+357 22 344 080
Fax	+357 22 344 090
Web	olympiakos.com.cy
Email	olympiakos.fc@ cablenet.com.cy
Media Officer	Andreas Chartziotis

AC Omonia

Karpenisiou 18B, PO Box 20617
CY-1661 Nicosia

Tel	+357 22 875 874
Fax	+357 22 377 496
Web	omonoia.com.cy
Email	info@omonoia.com.cy
Media Officer	Theodoros Kafkarides

CZECH REPUBLIC

République Tchèque I Tschechische Republik

Fotbalová asociace České republiky (FAČR)

COMMUNICATION

Address Diskarská 100
CZ-160 17 Praha
Tel +420 2 3302 9111
Fax +420 2 3335 3107
E-mail cmfs@fotbal.cz
Website fotbal.cz

Vice-President Dalibor Kučera
General Secretary Rudolf Řepka
Media Officer Jaroslav Kolář

Year of Formation 1901

DOMESTIC COMPETITION SUMMARY 2010/11

1. LIGA FINAL TABLE

			Home					Away					Total						
		Pld	W	D	L	F	A	W	D	L	F	A	W	D	L	F	A	Pts	Comp
1	FC Viktoria Plzeň	30	11	4	0	39	15	10	2	3	31	13	21	6	3	70	28	69	UCL
2	AC Sparta Praha	30	12	1	2	29	9	10	1	4	25	12	22	2	6	54	21	68	UEL
3	FK Jablonec	30	10	4	1	42	14	7	3	5	23	20	17	7	6	65	34	58	UEL
4	SK Sigma Olomouc	30	11	2	2	34	8	3	3	9	13	21	14	5	11	47	29	47	
5	FK Mladá Boleslav	30	9	2	4	35	20	4	5	6	14	20	13	7	10	49	40	46	UEL
6	Bohemians 1905	30	9	4	2	20	11	3	3	9	13	22	12	7	11	33	33	43	
7	FC Slovan Liberec	30	9	3	3	35	15	3	4	8	10	21	12	7	11	45	36	43	
8	FC Hradec Králové	30	8	6	1	16	10	3	2	10	10	26	11	8	11	26	36	41	
9	SK Slavia Praha	30	7	4	4	25	15	2	9	4	16	21	9	13	8	41	36	40	
10	FK Teplice	30	6	3	6	20	18	4	6	5	19	28	10	9	11	39	46	39	
11	SK Dynamo České Budějovice	30	7	6	2	17	12	0	6	9	13	36	7	12	11	30	48	33	
12	1. FC Slovácko	30	5	4	6	18	17	3	3	9	9	26	8	7	15	27	43	31	
13	1. FK Příbram	30	4	6	5	8	10	4	1	10	14	26	8	7	15	22	36	31	
14	FC Baník Ostrava	30	5	4	6	16	19	2	5	8	15	27	7	9	14	31	46	30	
15	FC Zbrojovka Brno	30	4	2	9	22	25	3	1	11	11	30	7	3	20	33	55	24	*Relegated*
16	FK Ústí nad Labem	30	3	3	9	10	30	1	4	10	12	37	4	7	19	22	67	19	*Relegated*

Top Scorer David Lafata (Jablonec), 19 goals

Promoted Clubs FK Dukla Praha
FK Viktoria Žižkov

Cup Final FK Mladá Boleslav 1, SK Sigma Olomouc 1 (aet; 4-3 on pens)

Perfect 100th birthday present for Plzeň

It took them 100 years to achieve it, but FC Viktoria Plzeň celebrated their centenary in the best possible manner by winning their domestic championship for the first time. Czech Cup winners the previous season, the club from the famous beer town in western Bohemia pulled off a remarkable one-two, bossing the title race virtually from start to finish and trumping record champions AC Sparta Praha with a game to spare.

Plzeň finished fifth in 2009/10 and were clearly a coming force under their wily, adventurous coach Pavel Vrba, but nobody could possibly have foreseen the astonishing start they would make to the 2010/11 championship. After kicking off with a 2-2 draw at home to SK Sigma Olomouc, they then reeled off 11 successive victories, including 1-0 wins in the capital against both Sparta and SK Slavia Praha. By mid-October Vrba's potent blend of cast-offs and wannabes had carved out a formidable lead at the 1. Liga summit. Furthermore, in a league that traditionally favoured defences, Plzeň were a mould-breaking joy to watch, their ceaseless commitment to attack yielding a plethora of goals. By the winter break they had registered 43 – more than in the whole of the previous season.

Renewed gusto

Although a couple of defeats left them with a reduced advantage of four points over Sparta, Plzeň returned after the three-month stoppage with renewed gusto, completing the double over Sparta with another 1-0 win – courtesy of Sparta old boy Pavel Horváth's 16th-minute winner – and refusing steadfastly to fulfil the widely touted predictions that it was simply a matter of time before their challenge came off the rails. Seemingly emboldened, rather than pressurised, by the prospect of giving the club the perfect 100th birthday present, Plzeň kept piling up the points and goals and on 21 May, in the penultimate round, they clinched the biggest prize in the club's history with a 3-1 victory at home to FC Baník Ostrava.

Plzeň lost at Olomouc the following week but it was a mere footnote to an extraordinary campaign. Undefeated at home, their final tally of 69 points was the highest recorded by a Czech champion for 11 years, and their 70 goals were 28 more than Sparta managed in taking the 2009/10 title undefeated. They only failed to score once – away to Bohemians 1905 – and even in that fixture had a goal erroneously disallowed. It was a stunning effort by all and sundry, and although 36-year-old Horváth stood out for his masterful leadership and authority – he was duly voted 1. Liga's player of the season – the Plzeň skipper was surrounded by trusty lieutenants. No fewer than five of them – Milan Petržela, Jan Rezek, David Limberský, Daniel Kolář and mid-season signing Petr Trapp – were honoured with call-ups to the Czech national team.

In any other season Sparta's 68-point haul would have been enough to win the championship. Led again by Jozef Chovanec, they won 22 of their 30 games and had the best defence, but they were massively outgunned by the champions, who defeated them twice, and also suffered from a stuttering start, losing three of their opening six matches – a real shock to the system after the

Pavel Horváth – a pivota[l] figure in Viktoria Plzeň's Czech title triumph

National Team

International Tournament Honours* –
UEFA European Championship - (1) 1976.

International Tournament Appearances* –
FIFA World Cup - (9) 1934 (runners-up), 1938 (qtr-finals), 1954, 1958, 1962 (runners-up), 1970, 1982, 1990 (qtr-finals), 2006.
UEFA European Championship - (7) 1960 (3rd), 1976 (Winners), 1980 (3rd), 1996 (runners-up), 2000, 2004 (semi-finals), 2008.

Top Five All-time Caps (including Czechoslovakia) – Karel Poborský (118); Jan Koller & Pavel Nedvěd (91); Zdeněk Nehoda (90); Pavel Kuka (87)

Top Five All-time Goals (including Czechoslovakia) –
Jan Koller (55); Milan Baroš (39); Antonín Puč (35); Zdeněk Nehoda (32); Oldřich Nejedlý & Pavel Kuka (29)

(before 1996 as Czechoslovakia)*

previous defeat-free campaign. Spearheaded by African strikers Bony Wilfried – who scored ten goals before decamping in mid-season to Dutch club Vitesse – and Léonard Kweuke – 14 goals in just 17 games – they also acquired Czech Under-21 star Tomáš Pekhart in mid-season on loan from FK Jablonec, and with seven goals for Sparta to add to his 11 for Jablonec, the tall centre forward was just edged out for the 1. Liga's Golden Boot by his erstwhile Jablonec team-mate David Lafata.

Runners-up in both domestic competitions in 2009/10, Jablonec enjoyed another excellent season under František Komnacký. Almost on a par with Plzeň in terms of attacking productivity, they finished third – ten points behind Sparta but 11 points clear of fourth-placed Sigma. Like Plzeň, they re-qualified for Europe with the ambition of improving on their 2009/10 performance, when they fell in the third qualifying round of the UEFA Europa League. With Plzeň and Baník also dropping out at the same stage, it was left to Sparta to carry the Czech standard alone. Unfortunately, they suffered an embarrassing defeat to Slovakian champions MŠK Žilina in the UEFA Champions League play-offs but recovered well to qualify for spring football in the UEFA Europa League before narrowly succumbing to Liverpool FC in the round of 32.

Absent coach

Sparta were dumped out of the Czech Cup early after a penalty shoot-out defeat to second-tier FC Baník Sokolov. Holders Plzeň came a cropper in the quarter-finals against Mladá Boleslav, who, with youngster Jan Chramosta scoring freely, went on to reach the final, where they claimed their first major trophy by overcoming Sigma – another undecorated club – 4-3 on penalties after a 1-1 draw in Jihlava. Goalkeeper Miroslav Miller was the hero, saving three spot-kicks, but the coach who had taken Mladá Boleslav to the final, Karel Stanner, was not there to enjoy the celebrations. He had been sacked a week earlier following five successive league defeats and replaced by sporting director Ladislav Minář.

There was a desperate start to the Czech Republic's UEFA EURO 2012 qualifying campaign when they lost 1-0 at home to Lithuania, but a remedial 1-0 win over Scotland in Prague, a couple of routine victories over Liechtenstein and a fighting performance away to Spain left Michal Bílek's team handily placed to take the runners-up berth in Group I – which, given the inclusion of the European/world champions, was all they could reasonably have expected at the outset. There was Czech representation at the UEFA European Under-21 Championship in Denmark, where Jakub Dovalil's young charges, unbeaten in qualification, reached the semi-finals thanks to a dramatic late comeback against England. They returned home empty-handed, however, after losing the semi-final in extra time to Switzerland and then going down 1-0 to Belarus in the play-off for the 2012 Olympics.

NATIONAL TEAM RESULTS 2010/11

11/8/10	Latvia	H	Liberec	4-1	*Bednář (48), Fenin (54), Pospěch (74), Necid (77)*
7/9/10	Lithuania (ECQ)	H	Olomouc	0-1	
8/10/10	Scotland (ECQ)	H	Prague	1-0	*Hubník R. (69)*
12/10/10	Liechtenstein (ECQ)	A	Vaduz	2-0	*Necid (12), Kadlec V. (29)*
17/11/10	Denmark	A	Aarhus	0-0	
9/2/11	Croatia	A	Pula	2-4	*Sivok (20), Rosický (45+1)*
25/3/11	Spain (ECQ)	A	Granada	1-2	*Plašil (29)*
29/3/11	Liechtenstein (ECQ)	H	Ceske Budejovice	2-0	*Baroš (3), Kadlec M. (70)*
4/6/11	Peru	N	Matsumoto (JPN)	0-0	
7/6/11	Japan	A	Yokohama	0-0	

NATIONAL TEAM APPEARANCES 2010/11

Coach – Michal BÍLEK	13/4/65		Lva	LTU	SCO	LIE	Den	Cro	ESP	LIE	Per	Jpn	Caps	Goals
Jaroslav DROBNÝ	18/10/79	Hamburg (GER)	G										4	-
Zdeněk POSPĚCH	14/12/78	København (DEN)	D	D	D	D	D85	D	D	D			26	2
Roman HUBNÍK	6/6/84	Hertha (GER)	D	D	D	D		D	D	D	D	D	16	2
Daniel PUDIL	27/9/85	Genk (BEL)	D46	D84			s85	s68	M78				18	2
Michal KADLEC	13/12/84	Leverkusen (GER)	D	D	D	D	D85	D76	D	D	D	D	25	2
Tomáš HÜBSCHMAN	4/9/81	Shakhtar (UKR)	M	M	M	M	M	M	M	M			36	-
Jan POLÁK	14/3/81	Anderlecht (BEL) /Wolfsburg (GER)	M61	M69	M	M59	M	M81		s84			57	7
Jaroslav PLAŠIL	5/1/82	Bordeaux (FRA)	M77	M	M94	M	M89	M68	M	M			63	5
Tomáš ROSICKÝ	4/10/80	Arsenal (ENG)	M61	M	M	M	M46	M63	M	M84			80	20
Roman BEDNÁŘ	26/3/83	West Brom (ENG)	A61	s84	s59	s64	s65						8	1
Martin FENIN	16/4/87	Eintracht (GER)	A61	A59							M46	A80	16	3
Jan RAJNOCH	30/9/81	Ankaragücü (TUR)	s46		s94		D	s81			D	D	13	-
Mario HOLEK	28/10/86	Dnipro (UKR)	s61		s84								6	-
Jiří ŠTAJNER	27/5/76	Liberec	s61	s69		s59		s63					36	4
Tomáš NECID	13/8/89	CSKA Moskva (RUS)	s61	s59	A84	A89	A65	s46	s84	s59	A66	s80	25	7
David LAFATA	18/9/81	Jablonec	s61							A59	s78	A66	12	2
Milan ČERNÝ	16/3/88	Slavia Praha	s77										3	1
Petr ČECH	20/5/82	Chelsea (ENG)		G	G	G	G	G	G	G	G	G	83	-
Milan BAROŠ	28/10/81	Galatasaray (TUR)		A					A	A			81	39
Marek SUCHÝ	29/3/88	Spartak Moskva (RUS)			D	D	D						3	-
Lukáš MAGERA	17/1/83	Timişoara (ROU)			A59								4	-
Václav KADLEC	20/5/92	Sparta Praha				A64							1	1
Milan PETRŽELA	19/6/83	Plzeň				s89	s89	M57			M46	M83	5	-
Jan REZEK	5/5/82	Plzeň					A65	A46	M84		s46	M90	5	-
Mario LIČKA	30/4/82	Brest (FRA)					s46						3	-
Michal HUBNÍK	1/6/83	Sigma /Legia (POL)					s65	s57			s66	s66	4	-
David LIMBERSKÝ	6/10/83	Plzeň					s85	s76					6	-
Tomáš SIVOK	15/9/83	Beşiktaş (TUR)						D	D	D		D46	16	2
Adam HLOUŠEK	20/12/88	Kaiserslautern (GER)							s78	s56			5	-
Jan MORÁVEK	1/11/89	Kaiserslautern (GER)								M56			3	-
Ondřej KUŠNÍR	5/4/84	Sparta Praha									D46		4	-
Kamil VACEK	18/5/87	Sparta Praha									M	M	2	-
Petr TRAPP	6/12/85	Plzeň									M86		1	-
Daniel KOLÁŘ	27/10/85	Plzeň									M78	M	3	-
Theodor GEBRE SELASSIE	24/12/86	Liberec									s46	s46	2	-
Václav PILAŘ	13/10/88	Hradec Králové									s46	s83	2	-
Petr JANDA	5/1/87	Slavia Praha									s86	s90	2	-

CLUB-BY-CLUB

FC BANÍK OSTRAVA

Coach – Miroslav Koubek; (25/10/10) (Verner Lička); (8/11/10) Karol Marko

Founded – 1922

Stadium – Stadion Bazaly (17,372)

MAJOR HONOURS: Czechoslovakian/Czech League – (4) 1976, 1980, 1981, 2004;

Czechoslovakian/Czech Cup – (4) 1973, 1978, 1991, 2005.

2010

18/7	Příbram	a	0-0	
25/7	Slavia	h	1-1	*Frejlach*
1/8	Brno	h	3-0	*Šmejkal, Varadi, Neves (p)*
8/8	Sparta	a	0-4	
14/8	Sigma	h	1-2	*Šenkeřík*
22/8	Mladá Boleslav	a	0-1	
28/8	Teplice	h	0-1	
10/9	Liberec	a	1-4	*Šmejkal*
18/9	Hradec Králové	h	1-0	*Frejlach*
26/9	Bohemians 1905	a	1-1	*Frejlach*
2/10	Slovácko	h	2-1	*Neves (p), Varadi*
17/10	České Budějovice	a	1-2	*Řezník*
24/10	Jablonec	h	1-3	*Neves (p)*
31/10	Ústí nad Labem	a	4-0	*Koukal 2, Zeher, Frejlach*
6/11	Plzeň	h	0-2	
12/11	Slavia	a	1-1	*Hušbauer*
22/11	Brno	a	2-0	*Neves (p), Šenkeřík*

11

2	Sparta	h 0-2	
	Sigma	a 0-2	
3	Mladá Boleslav	h 1-0	*Varadi*
3	Teplice	a 0-4	
	Liberec	h 0-0	
4	Hradec Králové	a 1-2	*Bolf*
4	Bohemians 1905	h 0-0	
4	Slovácko	a 0-0	
4	České Budějovice	h 3-2	*Bolf, Kraut, Varadi*
	Jablonec	a 3-3	*Šenkeřík, Fantiš, Hušbauer*
5	Ústí nad Labem	h 3-3	*Šenkeřík 2, Lukeš*
5	Plzeň	a 1-3	*og (Limberský)*
5	Příbram	h 0-2	

No	Name	Nat	DoB	Pos	Aps	(s)	Gls
	Vít BARÁNEK		27/9/74	G	8		
	Patrik BOHÁČ		30/4/92	A		(1)	
	René BOLF		25/2/74	D	22	(2)	2
	Antonín BUČEK		24/2/84	G	2		
	Dennis CHRISTU		27/7/89	A		(2)	
	Michal DANĚK		6/7/83	G	17	(1)	
	Antonín FANTIŠ		15/4/92	A	9	(9)	1
	Milan FERENČÍK		13/2/91	M	2	(2)	
	Tomáš FREJLACH		24/11/85	M	22	(2)	4
	Michal FRYDRYCH		27/2/90	D	6	(4)	
	Gligor GLIGOROV	MKD	5/3/87	D		(2)	
	Ján GREGUŠ	SVK	29/1/91	M	15	(6)	
	Josef HUŠBAUER		16/3/90	M	18	(6)	2
	Zdeněk KOUKAL		14/3/84	D	7	(2)	2
	Dominik KRAUT		15/1/90	A	5	(5)	1
	Martin LUKEŠ		17/11/78	M	22	(1)	1
3	Tomáš MAREK		20/4/81	M	23	(2)	
	Aleš NEUWIRTH		4/1/85	D	16		
	Fernando Maria NEVES	CPV	9/6/78	D	28		4
)	Dawid PIETRZKIEWICZ	POL	9/2/88	G	3		
5	Tomáš PILÍK		20/12/88	A	5	(8)	
	Radim ŘEZNÍK		20/1/89	D	21		1
	Zdeněk ŠENKEŘÍK		19/12/80	A	16	(8)	5
2	Zdeněk ŠMEJKAL		29/6/88	M	17		2
4	Adam VARADI		30/4/85	A	25		4
7	Dalibor VAŠENDA		2/6/91	M	1		
4	Tomáš VRŤO		6/9/88	A	1	(3)	
)	Robert ZEHER	SVK	12/2/85	A	12	(11)	1
2	Łukasz ZEJDLER	POL	22/3/92	D	7		

BOHEMIANS 1905

Coach – Pavel Hoftych

Founded – 1905

Stadium – Synot Tip Aréna (20,800)

MAJOR HONOURS: Czechoslovakian League – (1) 1983.

010

6/7	Slavia	h 1-1	*Bartek*
6/7	Hradec Králové	a 1-1	*Škoda*
/8	Plzeň	a 1-2	*Nešpor M.*
/8	Slovácko	h 1-0	*Hartig*
5/8	Jablonec	a 1-3	*Bálek*
2/8	České Budějovice	h 2-2	*Moravec, Kaufman*
9/8	Ústí nad Labem	a 0-1	
2/9	Příbram	h 1-0	*Štohanzl*
9/9	Brno	a 0-1	
6/9	Baník	h 1-1	*Kaufman*
/10	Mladá Boleslav	a 2-3	*Hartig 2*
5/10	Liberec	h 3-1	*Držík, Škoda, Nešpor M.*
4/10	Sigma	a 1-3	*Škoda*
30/10	Sparta	h 0-1	
/11	Teplice	a 2-0	*Škoda, og (Siva)*
4/11	Hradec Králové	h 1-0	*Škoda*
19/11	Plzeň	h 1-0	*Trubilo*

2011

26/2	Slovácko	a 3-1	*Štohanzl 2, Kaufman*
4/3	Jablonec	h 0-1	
13/3	České Budějovice	a 1-1	*Škoda*
20/3	Ústí nad Labem	h 1-0	*Ibragimov*
2/4	Příbram	a 1-0	*Bartek*
10/4	Brno	h 2-1	*Nikl, Škoda*
16/4	Baník	a 0-0	
24/4	Mladá Boleslav	h 3-1	*Nešpor M. 2, Škoda*
29/4	Liberec	a 0-1	
8/5	Sigma	h 2-1	*og (Kučera), Škoda*
13/5	Sparta	a 0-2	
21/5	Teplice	h 1-1	*Sedláček*
28/5	Slavia	a 0-3	

No	Name	Nat	DoB	Pos	Aps	(s)	Gls
31	Vladimír BÁLEK		8/3/81	A	3	(3)	1
13	Benoît BARROS	FRA	6/8/89	M		(1)	
5	David BARTEK		13/2/88	M	15	(5)	2
23	Lukáš BUDÍNSKÝ		27/3/92	M		(1)	
20	Amadou CISSÉ	GUI	23/10/85	M	1	(7)	
27	Martin CSEH	SVK	22/8/88	D	16	(2)	
8	Igor DRŽÍK	SVK	10/4/82	M	22	(3)	1
12	Lukáš HARTIG		28/10/76	A	20	(2)	3
2	Jan HAUER		18/5/90	D		(1)	
22	Aziz IBRAGIMOV	UZB	21/7/86	A	2	(13)	1
4	Josef JINDŘÍŠEK		14/2/81	D	28	(2)	
15	Jiří KAUFMAN		28/11/79	M	14		3
17	Martin KRAUS		30/5/92	M	10	(1)	
3	Pavel LUKÁŠ		20/11/75	D	24	(1)	
20	Josef MAREK		11/6/87	A		(2)	
28	Václav MAREK		16/3/81	G	2	(1)	
16	Jan MORAVEC		13/7/87	M	27	(2)	1
30	Daniel NEŠPOR		28/9/87	D	12	(1)	
14	Martin NEŠPOR		5/6/90	A	12	(10)	4
7	Marek NIKL		20/2/76	D	26		1
31	Roman POTOČNÝ		25/4/91	D		(2)	
9	Jiří RYCHLÍK		24/11/77	D	9	(1)	
30	Michal SEDLÁČEK		27/10/88	M	7	(5)	1
21	Milan ŠKODA		16/1/86	A	20	(8)	9
1	Radek SŇOZÍK		17/10/75	G	28		
6	Jan ŠTOHANZL		20/3/85	M	25	(2)	3
11	Vitaliy TRUBILO	BLR	7/1/85	M	7	(9)	1

SK DYNAMO ČESKÉ BUDĚJOVICE

Coach – Jaroslav Šilhavý

Founded – 1905

Stadium – E.ON stadion (6,746)

2010

18/7	Liberec	h 0-0	
23/7	Mladá Boleslav	a 1-1	*Benát*
1/8	Sparta	h 1-0	*Jarabica*
9/8	Teplice	a 1-1	*Ondrášek*
15/8	Hradec Králové	h 0-0	
22/8	Bohemians 1905	a 2-2	*Ondrášek 2*
29/8	Plzeň	h 0-3	
11/9	Slovácko	a 0-2	
19/9	Ústí nad Labem	a 1-1	*Mezlík*
26/9	Jablonec	h 2-1	*Ondrášek, Otepka*
2/10	Příbram	a 0-2	
17/10	Baník	h 2-1	*Mezlík, Ondrášek*
24/10	Slavia	a 0-4	
31/10	Brno	h 1-0	*Černák*
7/11	Sigma	a 1-5	*Otepka*
15/11	Mladá Boleslav	h 1-3	*Otepka (p)*
21/11	Sparta	a 0-2	

2011

27/2	Teplice	h 2-2	*Hořejš, Ondrášek*
6/3	Hradec Králové	a 0-2	
13/3	Bohemians 1905	h 1-1	*Vulin*
18/3	Plzeň	a 1-2	*Nitrianský*

3/4	Slovácko	h	0-0	
10/4	Ústí nad Labem	h	2-0	*Nitrianský, Ondrášek*
17/4	Jablonec	a	0-5	
24/4	Příbram	h	3-0	*Chirkin, Stráský, Ondrášek*
30/4	Baník	a	2-3	*Stráský, Ondrášek*
8/5	Slavia	h	1-1	*Stráský*
16/5	Brno	a	1-1	*Otepka*
21/5	Sigma	h	1-0	*Hudson*
28/5	Liberec	a	3-3	*Chirkin 2, Ondrášek*

No	Name	Nat	DoB	Pos	Aps	(s)	Gls
19	Rastislav BAKALA	SVK	22/4/90	M	2	(1)	
7	Petr BENÁT		20/5/80	M	7	(1)	1
21	Peter ČERNÁK	SVK	21/1/76	M	21	(2)	1
11	Grigoriy CHIRKIN	RUS	26/2/86	M	11		3
20	Aleš DVOŘÁK		9/3/91	M		(1)	
3	David HOŘEJŠ		19/5/77	D	19	(2)	1
18	Fernando Tobias de Carvalho "HUDSON"	BRA	18/7/86	M	18	(9)	1
22	Marián JARABICA	SVK	27/4/89	D	2	(1)	1
6	Martin JASANSKÝ		4/8/89	M	1		
19	Jindřich KADULA		10/6/94	M		(1)	
11/20	Michal KAŇÁK		16/7/88	A		(2)	
11	Radim KOUTNÝ		3/8/91	D	1	(1)	
30	Zdeněk KŘÍŽEK		16/1/83	G	2		
1	Pavel KUČERA		2/7/76	G	28		
20	Josef LAŠTOVKA		20/2/82	D	26		
6	Roman LENGYEL		3/11/78	D	22		
23	Dmitriy LENTSEVICH	BLR	20/6/83	D	9		
19	Martin LEŠTINA		25/4/81	D	1		
10	Pavel MEZLÍK		25/6/83	M	16	(10)	2
19	František NĚMEC		19/7/92	A		(1)	
4	Milan NITRIANSKÝ		13/12/90	M	12	(1)	2
13	Zdeněk ONDRÁŠEK		22/12/88	A	26	(3)	10
9	Rudolf OTEPKA		13/11/73	M	27	(2)	4
16	Luboš PECKA		19/2/78	A	14	(12)	
17	Michal PETRÁŇ		26/6/92	M	1	(1)	
17	Michal RAKOVAN		15/4/89	M	6	(2)	
15	Jan RIEGEL		3/8/80	D	8	(2)	
28	Tomáš SEDLÁČEK		29/8/80	A	2	(6)	
25	Petr ŠÍMA		25/2/83	M	3	(8)	
22	Borislav SIMIĆ	SRB	15/5/87	D	4	(1)	
14	Tomáš STRÁSKÝ		15/4/87	A	9	(12)	3
11	Marián TIMM	SVK	7/1/90	A		(2)	
23	Lovre VULIN	CRO	2/9/84	D	12		1
12	Michal ŽIŽKA		23/5/81	D	20	(2)	

FC HRADEC KRÁLOVÉ

Coach – Václav Kotal

Founded – 1905

Stadium – Všesportovní stadion (4,000)

MAJOR HONOURS: Czechoslovakian League – (1) 1960; Czech Cup – (1) 1995.

2010				
17/7	Sparta	h	2-1	*Rezek, Pilař*
26/7	Bohemians 1905	h	1-1	*Černý*
31/7	Slovácko	a	1-2	*Dvořák*
9/8	Plzeň	h	0-3	
15/8	České Budějovice	a	0-0	
20/8	Jablonec	h	1-0	*Pilař*
28/8	Příbram	a	0-1	
12/9	Slavia	h	0-0	
18/9	Baník	a	0-1	
26/9	Ústí nad Labem	h	3-3	*Chleboun, Černý (p), og (Franc)*
3/10	Brno	a	2-1	*Dvořák 2*
17/10	Mladá Boleslav	h	0-0	
22/10	Teplice	a	1-2	*Pokorný*
31/10	Sigma	h	1-0	*Poděbradský*
6/11	Liberec	a	0-3	
14/11	Bohemians 1905	a	0-1	
21/11	Slovácko	h	0-0	
2011				
26/2	Plzeň	a	1-2	*Hochmeister*
6/3	České Budějovice	h	2-0	*Fischer (p), Dvořák*
13/3	Jablonec	a	0-7	
21/3	Příbram	h	2-1	*Klapka, Fischer*
3/4	Slavia	a	0-0	
10/4	Baník	h	2-1	*Kasálek, Dvořák*
17/4	Ústí nad Labem	a	2-0	*Jandík 2*
24/4	Brno	h	1-0	*Klapka*
30/4	Mladá Boleslav	a	2-1	*Fischer, Zelený*
8/5	Teplice	h	0-0	
15/5	Sigma	a	0-2	
21/5	Liberec	h	1-0	*Fischer*
28/5	Sparta	a	1-3	*Pilař*

No	Name	Nat	DoB	Pos	Aps	(s)	Gls
9	Pavel ČERNÝ		28/1/85	A	20	(8)	2
15	Jakub CHLEBOUN		24/3/85	D	24	(1)	1
14	Pavel DVOŘÁK		19/2/89	A	19	(9)	5
26	Roman FISCHER		24/3/83	M	30		4
27	Tomáš HÁJOVSKÝ		10/12/82	D	5	(4)	
1	Jan HANUŠ		28/4/88	G	5		
5	Radek HOCHMEISTER		6/9/82	M	18	(5)	1
8	Jan HODAS		14/2/92	A		(1)	
23	Marek JANDÍK		19/4/85	D		(6)	2
13	Jiří JANOUŠEK		17/11/89	M	17		
4	Vlastimil KARAL		26/4/83	M	6	(4)	
17	Martin KASÁLEK		8/9/80	D	18	(2)	1
28	Filip KLAPKA		20/6/81	M	12		2
8	Daniel KOCOUREK		12/12/86	A	8	(7)	
30	Tomáš KOUBEK		26/8/92	G	2		
20	Jiří LINDR		7/8/86	G	20		
10	Vladimír MIŠINSKÝ		8/7/86	A	4	(4)	
3	Pavel NĚMEČEK		12/1/82	D	2		
24	Michal PÁVEK		13/2/85	D	18		
6	Václav PILAŘ		13/10/88	A	25	(3)	3
16	Jiří PODĚBRADSKÝ		9/9/82	D	26		1
19	Vladimír POKORNÝ		30/10/80	A	3	(8)	1
22	Tomáš REZEK		9/5/84	M	16	(9)	1
7	Vojtěch ŠTĚPÁN		8/6/85	M	6	(5)	
10	Petr TOMAŠÁK		20/2/86	M		(5)	
25	Radim WOZNIAK		29/1/78	D	18	(2)	
11	Jaroslav ZELENÝ		20/8/92	D	5	(1)	1
29	Lukáš ZICH		10/1/85	G	3		

FK JABLONEC

Coach – František Komňacký

Founded –1945

Stadium – Chance arena (6,216)

MAJOR HONOURS: Czech Cup – (1) 1998.

2010				
19/7	Brno	h	1-0	*Pekhart*
25/7	Sigma	a	1-4	*Pekhart*
1/8	Teplice	h	1-1	*Pekhart*
8/8	Liberec	a	1-1	*Piták*
15/8	Bohemians 1905	h	3-1	*Vošahlík 2, Jarolím*
20/8	Hradec Králové	a	0-1	
29/8	Slovácko	h	3-0	*og (Mezlík), Haurdić, Eliáš*
11/9	Sparta	a	0-1	
17/9	Plzeň	h	1-2	*Lafata*
26/9	České Budějovice	a	1-2	*Lafata*
3/10	Ústí nad Labem	h	2-0	*Pekhart 2*
17/10	Příbram	h	5-1	*Pekhart 2, Kovařík, Haurdić, Piták*
24/10	Baník	a	3-1	*Pekhart, Loučka, Piták*
1/11	Mladá Boleslav	h	1-1	*Pekhart*
5/11	Slavia	a	3-0	*Pekhart, Lafata, Zábojník*
14/11	Sigma	h	3-2	*Lafata 2 (2p), Pekhart*
22/11	Teplice	a	2-1	*Kovařík 2*
2011				
27/2	Liberec	h	3-0	*Lafata 3*
4/3	Bohemians 1905	a	1-0	*Eliáš*

/3	Hradec Králové	h	7-0	*Lafata 3, Jarolím 2, Piták, Třešňák*
/3	Slovácko	a	1-1	*Jarolím*
	Sparta	h	2-1	*Vošahlík 2*
	Plzeň	a	1-1	*Lafata*
/4	České Budějovice	h	5-0	*Lafata 3 (1p), Vaněk, Kocourek*
/4	Ústí nad Labem	a	1-2	*Piták*
/4	Příbram	a	2-1	*Loučka, Piták*
	Baník	h	3-3	*Lafata 2, Piták*
/5	Mladá Boleslav	a	2-1	*Piták, og (Mach)*
/5	Slavia	h	2-2	*Piták, Třešňák*
/5	Brno	a	4-3	*Lafata 2, Třešňák, Vaněk*

No	Name	Nat	DoB	Pos	Aps	(s)	Gls
	Vít BENEŠ		12/8/88	D	13	(3)	
	Pavel DRSEK		22/9/76	D	8	(11)	
	Pavel ELIÁŠ		26/11/86	M	16	(9)	2
	Anes HAURDIĆ	BIH	1/3/90	M	6	(11)	2
	Lukáš HEJDA		9/3/90	D		(6)	
	Marek HOVORKA		24/10/91	M		(1)	
	Tomáš HUBER		29/8/85	D	5	(2)	
	Tomáš JABLONSKÝ		21/6/87	D	29		
	Marek JAROLÍM		21/5/85	M	22	(4)	4
	Daniel KOCOUREK		12/12/86	M		(2)	1
	Jan KOVAŘÍK		19/6/88	M	27	(2)	3
	Matej KRAJČÍK	SVK	19/3/78	D	9	(1)	
	David LAFATA		18/9/81	A	29		19
	Luboš LOUČKA		25/8/82	M	30		2
	Tomáš MICHÁLEK		27/11/77	M		(4)	
	Petr PAVLÍK		17/7/78	D	29		
	Tomáš PEKHART		26/5/89	A	12	(3)	11
	Karel PITÁK		28/1/80	M	19	(8)	9
	Michal ŠPIT		9/4/75	G	22		
	Lukáš TŘEŠŇÁK		3/5/88	A	1	(11)	3
	Martin UVÍRA		4/4/88	D	1		
	Roman VALEŠ		6/3/90	G	8	(2)	
3	Ondřej VANĚK		5/7/90	M	4	(4)	2
7	Jan VOŠAHLÍK		8/3/89	A	26	(2)	4
	Milan VUKOVIČ		28/4/88	A		(2)	
	Petr ZÁBOJNÍK		3/10/80	D	14		1

FK MLADÁ BOLESLAV

Coach – Karel Stanner; (18/5/11) Ladislav Minář

Founded – 1902

Stadium – Městský stadion (5,000)

MAJOR HONOURS: Czech Cup – (1) 2011.

010				
8/7	Ústí nad Labem	a	2-0	*Sylvestre, og (Polák)*
3/7	České Budějovice	h	1-1	*Táborský*
1/7	Slavia	a	0-1	
/8	Příbram	h	3-0	*Mendy, Fabián, Bulut*
6/8	Brno	a	1-3	*Táborský*
2/8	Baník	h	1-0	*Rolko*
9/8	Liberec	h	3-1	*Chramosta, Procházka, Kulič*
3/9	Sigma	a	0-0	
9/9	Teplice	h	3-3	*Kulič, Chramosta, Rolko*
5/9	Sparta	a	1-1	*Opiela*
/10	Bohemians 1905	h	3-2	*Řezníček 2 (1p), Mendy*
7/10	Hradec Králové	a	0-0	
3/10	Plzeň	h	4-3	*Chramosta, Rolko, Táborský (p), Dimitrovski*
/11	Jablonec	a	1-1	*Řezníček*
/11	Slovácko	h	2-3	*Kulič, Kysela*
5/11	České Budějovice	a	3-1	*Kulič 2, Opiela*
0/11	Slavia	h	3-1	*Procházka, Toleski, Kulič*
2011				
26/2	Příbram	a	0-0	
5/3	Brno	h	5-0	*Kulič 2, Mendy, Procházka, Chramosta*
4/3	Baník	a	0-1	
9/3	Liberec	a	0-4	
/4	Sigma	h	2-0	*Johana, Mendy*
10/4	Teplice	a	2-1	*Chramosta, Fabián*
17/4	Sparta	h	1-2	*Chramosta*
24/4	Bohemians 1905	a	1-3	*Mendy*
30/4	Hradec Králové	h	1-2	*Chramosta*
7/5	Plzeň	a	1-3	*Řezníček*
15/5	Jablonec	h	1-2	*Řezníček*
21/5	Slovácko	a	2-1	*Řezníček 2*
28/5	Ústí nad Labem	h	2-0	*Kulič, Mendy*

No	Name	Nat	DoB	Pos	Aps	(s)	Gls
22	Jan BOŘIL		1/1/91	A		(1)	
17	David BRUNCLÍK		17/4/85	D	4		
9	Kerem BULUT	AUS	3/2/92	A	6	(2)	1
19	Jan CHRAMOSTA		12/10/90	A	23	(2)	7
13	Vladimír DIMITROVSKI	MKD	30/11/88	D	17	(2)	1
14	Elini DIMOUTSOS	GRE	18/6/88	M	5	(7)	
16	Daniel DUDKA		8/1/90	M		(4)	
3	Tomáš FABIÁN		10/9/89	M	20		2
5	Tomáš JANÍČEK		7/9/82	D	3		
2	Petr JOHANA		1/11/76	D	12	(3)	1
6	Václav KALINA		15/7/79	D	20		
23	Liridon KRASNIQI	SRB	1/1/92	M		(1)	
11	Ondřej KÚDELA		26/3/87	M	12	(1)	
10	Marek KULIČ		11/10/75	A	21	(7)	9
20	Jan KYSELA		17/12/85	M	8	(6)	1
17	Petr MACH		22/3/85	D	2	(1)	
18	Alexandre Noël MENDY	FRA	14/12/83	M	30		6
27	Miroslav MILLER		19/8/80	G	25		
33	Lukáš OPIELA	SVK	13/1/86	M	25		2
26	Václav PROCHÁZKA		8/5/84	D	17	(4)	3
7	Jakub ŘEZNÍČEK		26/5/88	A	7	(16)	7
4	Adrian ROLKO		14/9/78	D	28		3
23	Jiří SCHUBERT		18/4/88	A		(1)	
15	Jasmin ŠĆUK	BIH	14/7/90	M	1	(2)	
12	Jan ŠEDA		17/12/85	G	5		
28	Michal SEDLÁČEK		27/10/88	M	1	(12)	
25	Radek ŠÍRL		20/3/81	M	13	(1)	
14	Ludovic SYLVESTRE	FRA	5/2/84	M	4		1
8	Ivo TÁBORSKÝ		10/5/85	A	20	(8)	3
22	Goce TOLESKI	MKD	5/5/77	A	1	(5)	1
16	Marek VOLF		21/12/91	A		(1)	

1. FK PŘÍBRAM

Coach – Martin Hřídel; (28/9/10) (František Kopač); (11/10/10) (Roman Nádvorník); (2/5/11) František Kopač

Founded – 1948

Stadium – Na Litavce (8,200)

2010				
18/7	Baník	h	0-0	
25/7	Teplice	a	2-1	*Jurdík, Huňa*
2/8	Sigma	h	0-0	
8/8	Mladá Boleslav	a	0-3	
13/8	Sparta	h	0-1	
21/8	Liberec	a	0-0	
28/8	Hradec Králové	h	1-0	*Wágner*
12/9	Bohemians 1905	a	0-1	
18/9	Slovácko	h	0-1	
26/9	Plzeň	a	1-2	*og (Limberský)*
2/10	České Budějovice	h	2-0	*Pleško, Šlapák*
17/10	Jablonec	a	1-5	*Klesa*
23/10	Ústí nad Labem	h	0-0	
30/10	Slavia	h	1-1	*Klesa*
7/11	Brno	a	1-0	*Klesa*
14/11	Teplice	h	1-1	*Videgla*
21/11	Sigma	a	1-3	*Huňa*
2011				
26/2	Mladá Boleslav	h	0-0	
6/3	Sparta	a	0-1	
12/3	Liberec	h	1-0	*Štochl M.*
21/3	Hradec Králové	a	1-2	*Koukal*
2/4	Bohemians 1905	h	0-1	
9/4	Slovácko	a	0-2	

15/4	Plzeň	h	0-3	
24/4	České Budějovice	a	0-3	
30/4	Jablonec	h	1-2	*Koukal*
8/5	Ústí nad Labem	a	3-0	*Wágner, Koukal, Papšys*
16/5	Slavia	a	2-3	*Koukal, Wágner*
21/5	Brno	h	1-0	*Wágner*
28/5	Baník	a	2-0	*Koukal, og (Bolf)*

No	Name	Nat	DoB	Pos	Aps	(s)	Gls
23	Tomáš BOREK		4/4/86	M	7	(6)	
24	Josef DIVÍŠEK		24/9/90	M	11	(6)	
22	Aleš HRUŠKA		23/11/85	G	28		
11	Daniel HUŇA		25/6/79	A	22	(5)	2
15	Stanley IBE	NGA	19/7/84	A	2	(2)	
19	Milan JURDÍK		8/11/91	A	9	(6)	1
10	Michal KLESA		13/5/83	M	25	(1)	3
23	Zdeněk KOUKAL		14/3/84	M	11	(2)	5
2	Michal MACEK		19/1/81	M	6	(2)	
2	Jan MOJDL		9/2/89	M		(1)	
17	Stanislav NOHÝNEK		2/8/83	D	28		
5	Marius PAPŠYS	LTU	13/5/89	M	1	(6)	1
14	Pavel PILÍK		13/2/92	A	6	(3)	
13	Tomáš PILÍK		20/12/88	M	11	(2)	
20	Marek PLAŠIL		19/12/85	D	29		
7	Lukáš PLEŠKO		21/5/77	D	27		1
16	Pavel RICKA		28/1/87	D	17	(4)	
1	Jakub RONDZIK	SVK	22/11/86	G	2	(1)	
25	Martin ŠLAPÁK		25/3/87	A		(5)	1
4	Jakub ŠTOCHL		2/2/87	D	28		
18	Matěj ŠTOCHL		4/5/89	A	10	(9)	1
6	Daniel TARCZAL		22/3/85	M	29		
12	Claude Roland VIDEGLA	TOG	14/5/90	M	11	(7)	1
9	Tomáš WÁGNER		6/3/90	A	10	(13)	4

SK SIGMA OLOMOUC

Coach – Zdeněk Psotka

Founded – 1919

Stadium – Andrův stadion (10,212)

2010				
18/7	Plzeň	a	2-2	*Šultes, Janotka*
25/7	Jablonec	h	4-1	*Hubník 3, Petr*
2/8	Příbram	a	0-0	
8/8	Ústí nad Labem	h	3-0	*Petr, Šultes, Vašíček*
14/8	Baník	a	2-1	*Hubník, Daniel Rossi*
22/8	Brno	h	3-0	*Hubník, Šultes, Melinho*
27/8	Slavia	a	1-1	*Hubník*
13/9	Mladá Boleslav	h	0-0	
18/9	Liberec	h	4-0	*Hubník, Petr, Navrátil, Janotka*
27/9	Teplice	a	0-1	
4/10	Sparta	h	0-1	
18/10	Slovácko	a	2-0	*Hořava, Hubník*
24/10	Bohemians 1905	h	3-1	*Navrátil, Petr, Hubník*
31/10	Hradec Králové	a	0-1	
7/11	České Budějovice	h	5-1	*Ordoš, Šultes, Hubník, og (Laštovka), Hořava*
14/11	Jablonec	a	2-3	*Hubník, Šultes*
21/11	Příbram	h	3-1	*Petr, Hubník, Murin*
2011				
27/2	Ústí nad Labem	a	3-0	*Doležal 2, Janotka*
7/3	Baník	h	2-0	*Janotka (p), Přikryl*
11/3	Brno	a	0-2	
20/3	Slavia	h	0-0	
1/4	Mladá Boleslav	a	0-2	
9/4	Liberec	a	0-3	
17/4	Teplice	h	3-0	*Ordoš, Navrátil, Přikryl*
22/4	Sparta	a	0-2	
1/5	Slovácko	h	0-2	
8/5	Bohemians 1905	a	1-2	*Přikryl*
15/5	Hradec Králové	h	2-0	*Šultes 2*
21/5	České Budějovice	a	0-1	
28/5	Plzeň	h	2-1	*Petr 2*

No	Name	Nat	DoB	Pos	Aps	(s)	Gl
9	Lukáš BAJER		15/12/84	M	25	(4)	
1	Martin BLAHA		8/8/85	G	5		
8	DANIEL ROSSI da Silva	BRA	4/1/81	M	25		1
26	Martin DOLEŽAL		3/5/90	A	6	(4)	2
3	Pavel DREKSA		17/9/89	D	10		
18	Petr DROBISZ		14/7/76	G	25		
17	Tomáš HOŘAVA		29/5/88	M	23	(5)	2
10	Michal HUBNÍK		1/6/83	A	17		12
23	Tomáš JANOTKA		4/3/82	D	29		4
2	Tomáš KALAS		15/5/93	D	2	(2)	
5	Marek KAŠČÁK	SVK	22/5/82	M	3	(1)	
24	Václav KOUTNÝ		4/10/91	D	6	(1)	
13	Radim KUČERA		1/3/74	D	17		
6	Milan MACHALICKÝ		1/6/91	D	2	(3)	
30	Rogério Pereira Tarciso "MELINHO"	BRA	26/3/80	M		(5)	1
19	Ondřej MURIN		15/2/91	D	2	(1)	1
25	Jan NAVRÁTIL		13/4/90	M	16	(13)	3
7	Michal ORDOŠ		27/1/83	A	11	(9)	2
22	Jakub PETR		10/4/90	A	24	(2)	7
6	Martin POSPÍŠIL		26/6/91	M	1	(1)	
4	Tomáš PŘIKRYL		4/7/92	M	2	(15)	3
11	Jan SCHULMEISTER		11/3/86	A	3	(2)	
12	Aleš ŠKERLE		14/6/82	D	27		
29	Pavel ŠULTES		15/9/85	A	22	(8)	7
14	Václav TOMEČEK		24/8/91	A		(6)	
26	Václav VAŠÍČEK		10/2/91	A		(8)	1
21	Michal VEPŘEK		17/6/85	D	27		

SK SLAVIA PRAHA

Coach – Karel Jarolím; (29/9/10) Michal Petrouš

Founded – 1892

Stadium – Synot Tip Aréna (20,800)

MAJOR HONOURS: Czechoslovakian/Czech League – (12) 1925, 1929, 1930, 1931, 1933, 1934, 1935, 1937, 1947, 1996, 2008, 200

Czech Cup – (3) 1997, 1999, 2002.

2010				
16/7	Bohemians 1905	a	1-1	*Kisel*
25/7	Baník	a	1-1	*Kisel*
31/7	Mladá Boleslav	h	1-0	*Vlček*
6/8	Brno	a	3-2	*Černý J., Kisel, Jarolím*
15/8	Liberec	h	1-3	*Kisel*
23/8	Teplice	a	1-2	*og (Vidlička)*
27/8	Sigma	h	1-1	*Černý J.*
12/9	Hradec Králové	a	0-0	
20/9	Sparta	h	1-2	*Trapp*
24/9	Slovácko	a	0-3	
1/10	Plzeň	h	0-1	
17/10	Ústí nad Labem	a	1-1	*Kisel (p)*
24/10	České Budějovice	h	4-0	*Kisel, Hora, Čelůstka, Černý M.*
30/10	Příbram	a	1-1	*Hora*
5/11	Jablonec	h	0-3	
12/11	Baník	h	1-1	*Koubský*
20/11	Mladá Boleslav	a	1-3	*Koubský*
2011				
25/2	Brno	h	1-1	*Vlček*
5/3	Liberec	a	2-0	*Pospěch, Koreš*
13/3	Teplice	h	4-1	*Jarolím 2, Pospěch, Milutinović*
20/3	Sigma	a	0-0	
3/4	Hradec Králové	h	0-0	
11/4	Sparta	a	0-2	
18/4	Slovácko	h	2-0	*Kaufman, Jarolím*
25/4	Plzeň	a	2-2	*Kisel, Černý M.*
1/5	Ústí nad Labem	h	3-0	*Pospěch 2, Vlček*
8/5	České Budějovice	a	1-1	*Pospěch*
16/5	Příbram	h	3-2	*Koreš, Trubilo, Pospěch*
21/5	Jablonec	a	2-2	*Koreš, Kaufman*
28/5	Bohemians 1905	h	3-0	*Koreš, Pospěch, Čelůstka*

No	Name	Nat	DoB	Pos	Aps	(s)	Gls
	Tijani BELAID	TUN	6/9/87	M	6	(5)	
	Ondřej ČELŮSTKA		18/6/89	D	28		2
	Jaroslav ČERNÝ		26/6/79	M	11	(2)	2
3	Milan ČERNÝ		16/3/88	M	24	(4)	2
	Bassirou DEMBÉLÉ	MLI	28/1/90	M	6	(1)	
	Martin DOSTÁL		23/9/89	D	6		
	Peter GRAJCIAR	SVK	17/9/83	M	2		
	Adam HLOUŠEK		20/12/88	M	1	(3)	
3	Jakub HORA		23/2/91	A	16	(12)	2
	David HUBÁČEK		23/2/77	D	29		
	Anssi JAAKKOLA	FIN	13/3/87	G	2		
	Petr JANDA		5/1/87	M	20	(8)	
	Lukáš JAROLÍM		29/7/76	M	20	(5)	4
	Josef KAUFMAN		27/3/84	D	11	(1)	2
	Karol KISEL	SVK	15/3/77	M	27		7
	Štěpán KOREŠ		14/2/89	M	17	(3)	4
	Jiří KOUBSKÝ		5/8/82	D	12		2
3	Zoran MILUTINOVIĆ	BIH	1/3/88	M	2	(10)	1
4	Jan PÁZLER		10/1/91	A	1		
3	Ondřej PETRÁK		11/3/92	M		(1)	
7	Zbyněk POSPĚCH		24/10/82	A	12		7
5	Václav PROŠEK		8/4/93	M		(1)	
	Hocine RAGUED	TUN	11/2/83	M	9	(3)	
	Petr TRAPP		6/12/85	D	9	(2)	1
4	Vitaliy TRUBILO	BLR	7/1/85	D	12		1
3	Martin VANIAK		4/10/70	G	19		
	Stanislav VLČEK		26/2/76	A	7	(10)	3
2	Benjamin VOMÁČKA		27/6/78	D	6	(2)	
2	Pavel VYHNAL		25/5/90	A	5	(3)	
7	Jan ZÁKOSTELSKÝ		25/11/91	A	1	(4)	
5	Zdeněk ZLÁMAL		5/11/85	G	9		

1. FC SLOVÁCKO

Coach – Miroslav Soukup

Founded – 2000

Stadium – Městský fotbalový stadion Miroslava Valenty (8,121)

2010				
7/7	Teplice	h	3-0	*Švancara 2 (1p), Kuncl*
4/7	Sparta	a	1-2	*Košút*
1/7	Hradec Králové	h	2-1	*og (Karal), Ondřejka*
/8	Bohemians 1905	a	0-1	
5/8	Plzeň	a	0-3	
1/8	Ústí nad Labem	h	1-1	*Švancara (p)*
9/8	Jablonec	a	0-3	
1/9	České Budějovice	h	2-0	*Nestoroski, Volešák*
8/9	Příbram	a	1-0	*Valenta J.*
4/9	Slavia	h	3-0	*Švancara (p), Volešák, Szmek*
/10	Baník	a	1-2	*Reinberk*
8/10	Sigma	h	0-2	
4/10	Brno	a	0-7	
1/10	Liberec	h	0-1	
/11	Mladá Boleslav	a	3-2	*Fujerik, Švancara, Ondřejka*
3/11	Sparta	h	0-2	
1/11	Hradec Králové	a	0-0	
2011				
6/2	Bohemians 1905	h	1-3	*Kordula*
/3	Plzeň	h	2-2	*Mezlík, Valenta J.*
3/3	Ústí nad Labem	a	0-2	
9/3	Jablonec	h	1-1	*Švancara*
/4	České Budějovice	a	0-0	
/4	Příbram	h	2-0	*Švancara, Košút*
8/4	Slavia	a	0-2	
3/4	Baník	h	0-0	
/5	Sigma	a	2-0	*Valenta J., Szmek*
/5	Brno	h	0-2	
4/5	Liberec	a	0-1	
21/5	Mladá Boleslav	h	1-2	*Ondřejka*
28/5	Teplice	a	1-1	*og (Hošek)*

No	Name	Nat	DoB	Pos	Aps	(s)	Gls
26	Amadou CISSÉ	GUI	23/10/85	M		(1)	
12	Vlastimil DANÍČEK		15/7/91	D	2	(1)	
29	Miroslav FILIPKO	SVK	23/9/73	G	26		
30	Tomáš FRYŠTÁK		18/8/87	G		(1)	
16	Lukáš FUJERIK		9/12/83	A	24	(3)	1
1	Milan HEČA		23/3/91	G	2	(1)	
8	Filip HLÚPIK		30/4/91	M	4	(12)	
4	Tomáš JELEČEK		25/2/92	D		(1)	
5	Michal KORDULA		11/2/78	M	25		1
22	Tomáš KOŠÚT	SVK	13/1/90	D	19	(4)	2
3	Lukáš KUBÁŇ		22/6/87	D	24	(1)	
17	Martin KUNCL		1/4/84	D	25		1
19	Radek MEZLÍK		20/5/82	D	29		1
30	Ilya MOTALYGO	BLR	5/5/84	G	2		
25	Daniel NEŠPOR		28/9/87	D	3		
20	Ilija NESTOROSKI	MKD	12/3/90	A	9	(8)	1
18	Václav ONDŘEJKA		30/4/88	A	20	(5)	3
15	Jiří PERŮTKA		22/2/88	M	8	(4)	
6	Petr REINBERK		23/5/89	D	12	(5)	1
13	Jaroslav STARÝ		9/2/88	D	1	(1)	
9	Petr ŠVANCARA		5/11/77	A	22	(2)	7
10	Jakub SVÍZELA		9/1/92	M		(1)	
14	Radek SZMEK		13/8/86	A	3	(19)	2
21	Aleš URBÁNEK		25/5/80	D	9	(3)	
7	Jiří VALENTA		14/2/88	M	17	(5)	3
2	Vít VALENTA		4/1/84	M	16	(4)	
23	Ladislav VOLEŠÁK		7/4/84	M	28		2

FC SLOVAN LIBEREC

Coach – Josef Petřík; (27/10/10) Petr Rada

Founded – 1921

Stadium – U Nisy (9,900)

MAJOR HONOURS: Czech League – (2) 2002, 2006; Czech Cup – (1) 2000.

2010				
18/7	České Budějovice	a	0-0	
24/7	Plzeň	h	2-3	*Kerić, Bosančić (p)*
30/7	Ústí nad Labem	a	0-0	
8/8	Jablonec	h	1-1	*Papoušek*
15/8	Slavia	a	3-1	*Kerić 2, Štajner*
21/8	Příbram	h	0-0	
29/8	Mladá Boleslav	a	1-3	*Štajner*
10/9	Baník	h	4-1	*Kerić, Nezmar, Fleišman, Papoušek*
18/9	Sigma	a	0-4	
25/9	Brno	h	3-1	*Kelić, Nezmar, Dejmek*
2/10	Teplice	a	0-1	
15/10	Bohemians 1905	a	1-3	*Breznaník*
25/10	Sparta	h	1-2	*Nezmar*
31/10	Slovácko	a	1-0	*Bosančić*
6/11	Hradec Králové	h	3-0	*Štajner 2, Kerić*
13/11	Plzeň	a	1-1	*Kerić*
20/11	Ústí nad Labem	h	3-0	*Breznaník, Nezmar, Bosančić*
2011				
27/2	Jablonec	a	0-3	
5/3	Slavia	h	0-2	
12/3	Příbram	a	0-1	
19/3	Mladá Boleslav	h	4-0	*Nezmar, Breznaník, Dočkal, Vácha*
2/4	Baník	a	0-0	
9/4	Sigma	h	3-0	*Štajner, Nezmar, Kelić*
17/4	Brno	a	1-0	*Nezmar*
24/4	Teplice	h	6-2	*Nezmar 2, Štajner 2, Gecov, Breznaník*
29/4	Bohemians 1905	h	1-0	*Nezmar*
6/5	Sparta	a	2-3	*Hadaščok, Dejmek*
14/5	Slovácko	h	1-0	*Dočkal*
21/5	Hradec Králové	a	0-1	
28/5	České Budějovice	h	3-3	*Štajner 2, Sivrić*

No	Name	Nat	DoB	Pos	Aps	(s)	Gls
30	David BIČÍK		6/4/81	G	30		
12	Miloš BOSANČIĆ	SRB	22/5/88	M	14	(1)	3
20	Michal BREZNANÍK	SVK	16/12/85	M	21		4
21	Radek DEJMEK		2/2/88	D	21	(1)	2
18	Bořek DOČKAL		30/9/88	M	13		2
25	Jiří FLEIŠMAN		2/10/84	D	27		1
32	Theodor GEBRE SELASSIE		24/12/86	D	29	(1)	
10	Marcel GECOV		1/1/88	M	24	(1)	1
15	Vojtěch HADAŠČOK		8/1/92	A	5	(7)	1

11	Miroslav HOLEŇÁK		10/2/76	D	19	(3)	
17	Tomáš JANŮ		17/9/73	D	2	(1)	
2	Renato KELIĆ	CRO	31/3/91	D	21		2
15	Andrej KERIĆ	CRO	11/2/86	A	17		6
22	Jiří KRYSTAN		31/1/90	M	1	(1)	
8	Jiří LIŠKA		13/3/82	D	4	(2)	
14	Ladislav MARTAN		2/10/89	A	2	(6)	
7	Jan NEZMAR		5/7/77	A	17	(6)	10
23	Petr PAPOUŠEK		7/5/77	M	5	(19)	2
3	Matej SIVRIĆ	CRO	27/11/89	A	1	(6)	1
24	Jiří ŠTAJNER		27/5/76	A	29		9
6	Lukáš VÁCHA		13/5/89	M	25	(2)	1
27	Ján VLASKO	SVK	11/1/90	M		(6)	
9	Jakub VOJTA		19/4/91	A	1	(7)	
19	Lovre VULIN	CRO	2/9/84	D	2	(8)	
5	Michal ZEMAN		18/8/84	M		(2)	
29	Petr ZIERIS		19/3/89	D		(3)	

AC SPARTA PRAHA

Coach – Jozef Chovanec

Founded – 1893

Stadium – Letná (18,873)

MAJOR HONOURS: Czechoslovakian/Czech League – (30) 1926, 1927, 1932, 1936, 1938, 1946, 1948, 1952, 1954, 1965, 1967, 1984, 1985, 1987, 1988, 1989, 1990, 1991, 1993, 1994, 1995, 1997, 1998, 1999, 2000, 2001, 2003, 2005, 2007, 2010; Czechoslovakian/Czech Cup – (13) 1964, 1972, 1976, 1980, 1984, 1988, 1989, 1992, 1996, 2004, 2006, 2007, 2008.

2010

17/7	Hradec Králové	a	1-2	*Wilfried*
24/7	Slovácko	h	2-1	*Třešňák, Kadlec*
1/8	České Budějovice	a	0-1	
8/8	Baník	h	4-0	*Wilfried 2, Kladrubský (p), Pamić*
13/8	Příbram	a	1-0	*Wilfried*
21/8	Plzeň	h	0-1	
30/8	Brno	a	5-0	*Kadlec, Pamić, Vacek, Kucka, Sionko*
11/9	Jablonec	h	1-0	*Kucka*
20/9	Slavia	a	2-1	*Kadlec, Wilfried*
25/9	Mladá Boleslav	h	1-1	*Wilfried*
4/10	Sigma	a	1-0	*Kucka (p)*
16/10	Teplice	h	0-2	
25/10	Liberec	a	2-1	*Kweuke, Wilfried*
30/10	Bohemians 1905	a	1-0	*Kweuke*
8/11	Ústí nad Labem	h	4-1	*Pamić, Kweuke, Wilfried, Kadlec*
13/11	Slovácko	a	2-0	*Wilfried (p), Kweuke*
21/11	České Budějovice	h	2-0	*Kweuke, Wilfried*

2011

28/2	Baník	a	2-0	*Kweuke 2*
6/3	Příbram	h	1-0	*Zeman*
12/3	Plzeň	a	0-1	
19/3	Brno	h	2-0	*Pekhart 2*
2/4	Jablonec	a	1-2	*Podaný*
11/4	Slavia	h	2-0	*Kweuke 2*
17/4	Mladá Boleslav	a	2-1	*Kweuke, Sionko*
22/4	Sigma	h	2-0	*Kweuke, Vacek (p)*
2/5	Teplice	a	2-2	*Pekhart (p), Kerić*
6/5	Liberec	h	3-2	*og (Dejmek), Kweuke, Kerić*
13/5	Bohemians 1905	h	2-0	*Sionko, Pekhart*
21/5	Ústí nad Labem	a	3-1	*Pekhart 2, Kweuke*
28/5	Hradec Králové	h	3-1	*Pekhart (p), Kweuke, Zápotočný*

No	Name	Nat	DoB	Pos	Aps	(s)	Gls
4	Martin Achille ABENA	CMR	14/6/86	M	4	(2)	
19	Clovis Guy ADIABA Bondoa	CMR	2/1/87	D	7	(1)	
29	Jaromír BLAŽEK		29/12/72	G	27		
21	Erich BRABEC		24/2/77	D	30		
30	Lukáš HEJDA		9/3/90	D	4	(4)	
4	Niklas HOHENEDER	AUT	17/8/86	D	6	(5)	
27	Luboš HUŠEK		26/1/84	M		(1)	
18	Jiří JESLÍNEK		30/9/87	A	4		
14	Václav KADLEC		20/5/92	A	20	(5)	4
18	Andrej KERIĆ	CRO	11/2/86	A	7	(6)	2
15	Jiří KLADRUBSKÝ		19/11/85	M	18	(5)	1
23	Ladislav KREJČÍ		5/7/92	M		(2)	
5	Jan KROB		27/4/87	D	2		
20	Juraj KUCKA	SVK	26/2/87	M	13		3
13	Ondřej KUŠNÍR		5/4/84	D	13	(1)	
9	Léonard KWEUKE	CMR	12/7/87	A	16	(1)	14
6	Miloš LAČNÝ	SVK	8/3/88	A		(5)	
8	Marek MATĚJOVSKÝ		20/12/81	M	19	(6)	
3	Manuel PAMIĆ	CRO	20/8/86	D	27		3
36	David PAVELKA		18/5/91	M	2	(1)	
11	Tomáš PEKHART		26/5/89	A	5	(4)	7
5	Jakub PODANÝ		15/6/87	M	10	(10)	1
2	Tomáš ŘEPKA		2/1/74	D	22		
7	Libor SIONKO		1/2/77	M	17	(9)	3
26	Lukáš TŘEŠŇÁK		3/5/88	A	2		1
25	Kamil VACEK		18/5/87	M	24		2
28	Štěpán VACHOUŠEK		26/7/79	M	2	(2)	
12	Bony WILFRIED	CIV	10/12/88	A	14		10
20	Tomáš ZÁPOTOČNÝ		13/9/80	D	5	(2)	1
22	Martin ZEMAN		28/3/89	M	5	(4)	1
1	Daniel ZÍTKA		20/6/75	G	3	(1)	
11	Igor ŽOFČÁK	SVK	10/4/83	M	2	(3)	

FK TEPLICE

Coach – Jiří Plíšek

Founded – 1945

Stadium – Na Stínadlech (18,221)

MAJOR HONOURS: Czech Cup – (2) 2003, 2009.

2010

17/7	Slovácko	a	0-3	
25/7	Příbram	h	1-2	*Mareš*
1/8	Jablonec	a	1-1	*Matula*
9/8	České Budějovice	h	1-1	*Mahmutović*
16/8	Ústí nad Labem	a	2-0	*Mahmutović, Došek*
23/8	Slavia	h	2-1	*Kalivoda, Verbíř (I) (p)*
28/8	Baník	a	1-0	*Mareš*
12/9	Brno	h	1-2	*Kalivoda*
19/9	Mladá Boleslav	a	3-3	*Mareš 2, Vondrášek*
27/9	Sigma	h	1-0	*Vidlička*
2/10	Liberec	h	1-0	*Kalivoda (p)*
16/10	Sparta	a	2-0	*og (Brabec), Mahmutović*
22/10	Hradec Králové	h	2-1	*Zoubele, Mahmutović*
29/10	Plzeň	a	2-4	*Matula, Vondrášek*
7/11	Bohemians 1905	h	0-2	
14 /11	Příbram	a	1-1	*Mareš*
22/11	Jablonec	h	1-2	*Mahmutović*

2011

27/2	České Budějovice	a	2-2	*Mareš, Došek*
6/3	Ústí nad Labem	h	2-1	*Mahmutović, Vondrášek*
13/3	Slavia	a	1-4	*Mahmutović*
20/3	Baník	h	4-0	*Vachoušek 2 (1p), Mahmutović, Mareš*
3/4	Brno	a	1-0	*Rosa*
10/4	Mladá Boleslav	h	1-2	*Mahmutović*
17/4	Sigma	a	0-3	
24/4	Liberec	a	2-6	*Vondrášek, Verbíř (I) (p)*
2/5	Sparta	h	2-2	*Čajić, Mahmutović*
8/5	Hradec Králové	a	0-0	
14/5	Plzeň	h	0-1	
21/5	Bohemians 1905	a	1-1	*Vondrášek*
28/5	Slovácko	h	1-1	*Rosa*

No	Name	Nat	DoB	Pos	Aps	(s)	Gls
14	Aldin ČAJIĆ	BIH	11/9/92	M	18	(2)	1
3	Tomáš ČESLÁK		8/6/93	M		(1)	
18	Libor DOŠEK		24/4/78	A	4	(15)	2
30	Tomáš GRIGAR		1/2/83	G	22		
23	Jan HOŠEK		1/4/89	D	18	(2)	
16	Marek JUNGR		11/4/87	M	4	(5)	
27/10	David KALIVODA		25/8/82	M	12	(7)	3
4	Martin KLEIN		2/7/84	D	2		
7	Marek KRÁTKÝ		8/6/93	D		(1)	
12	Patrik LÁCHA		20/1/92	M	2	(7)	
5	Admir LJEVAKOVIĆ	BIH	7/8/84	M	24	(1)	
15	Petr LUKÁŠ		24/4/78	D	3		
25	Aidin MAHMUTOVIĆ	BIH	6/4/86	A	27	(2)	10
19	Jakub MAREŠ		26/1/87	M	25	(3)	7

)	Milan MATULA		22/4/84	D	26		2
3	Alen MELUNOVIĆ	BIH	26/1/90	A	2	(4)	
2	Antonín ROSA		12/11/86	D	29		2
	Matej SIVA	SVK	10/10/84	D	9	(4)	
	Martin SLAVÍK		21/9/79	G	8		
	Michal SMEJKAL		21/2/86	D	21	(1)	
)	Vlastimil STOŽICKÝ		19/8/83	M	4	(5)	
	Štěpán VACHOUŠEK		26/7/79	M	14		2
	Pavel VERBÍŘ (I)		13/11/72	M	12	(9)	2
7	Pavel VERBÍŘ (II)		8/11/92	M		(1)	
	Vlastimil VIDLIČKA		2/7/81	D	20		1
7	Tomáš VONDRÁŠEK		26/10/87	A	19	(8)	5
1	Lukáš ZOUBELE		20/12/85	M	5	(9)	1

FK ÚSTÍ NAD LABEM

Coach – Svatopluk Habanec

Founded – 1927

Stadium – Na Stínadlech, Teplice (18,221)

010				
8/7	Mladá Boleslav	h	0-2	
5/7	Brno	a	3-1	*Doležal 2 (2p), Kraut*
0/7	Liberec	h	0-0	
/8	Sigma	a	0-3	
6/8	Teplice	h	0-2	
1/8	Slovácko	a	1-1	*Volek*
9/8	Bohemians 1905	h	1-0	*Volek*
2/9	Plzeň	a	0-7	
9/9	České Budějovice	h	1-1	*Valenta*
6/9	Hradec Králové	a	3-3	*Kraut 2, Jindráček*
/10	Jablonec	a	0-2	
7/10	Slavia	h	1-1	*Krbeček*
3/10	Příbram	a	0-0	
1/10	Baník	h	0-4	
/11	Sparta	a	1-4	*Volek*
4/11	Brno	h	2-3	*Vrtělka (p), Veverka*
0/11	Liberec	a	0-3	
011				
7/2	Sigma	h	0-3	
/3	Teplice	a	1-2	*Krbeček*
3/3	Slovácko	h	2-0	*Valenta, Martykán*
0/3	Bohemians 1905	a	0-1	
/4	Plzeň	h	0-5	
0/4	České Budějovice	a	0-2	
7/4	Hradec Králové	h	0-2	
24/4	Jablonec	h	2-1	*Veverka, Krbeček*
/5	Slavia	a	0-3	
/5	Příbram	h	0-3	
14/5	Baník	a	3-3	*Veverka, Dvořák, Jindráček*
21/5	Sparta	h	1-3	*Jindráček*
28/5	Mladá Boleslav	a	0-2	

No	Name	Nat	DoB	Pos	Aps	(s)	Gls
17	Ladislav BENČÍK	SVK	13/8/84	M		(10)	
1	Antonín BUČEK		24/2/84	G	5		
7	Michal DOLEŽAL		19/8/77	M	20	(7)	2
3	Pavel DREKSA		17/9/89	D	9		
15	Lukáš DVOŘÁK		30/1/84	D	13		1
4	Pavel DŽUBAN		6/9/80	D	18	(3)	
9	Jan FRANC		12/3/87	M	1	(6)	
8	Miloš GIBALA		21/5/85	M	1	(4)	
14	Martin HOLEK		29/5/89	A	2	(2)	
18	Alois HYČKA		22/7/90	D	12	(4)	
14	Tomáš JANŮ		17/9/73	D	8	(1)	
16/9	Martin JINDRÁČEK		29/11/89	A	25	(4)	3
1	Přemysl KOVÁŘ		14/10/85	G	3		
10	Dominik KRAUT		15/1/90	A	11	(4)	3
13	Tomáš KRBEČEK		27/10/85	A	17	(9)	3
16	Mario LAMESIĆ	BIH	12/4/83	M	5	(4)	
2	Jan MARTYKÁN		17/3/83	M	26	(1)	1
20	Radim NOVÁK		2/4/78	G	13		
3	Jan POLÁK		26/3/89	D	22	(3)	
10	Vlastimil STOŽICKÝ		19/8/83	M	11		
5	Michal VALENTA		8/6/77	M	29		2
19	Richard VEVERKA		20/12/87	A	10	(10)	3
11	Zdeněk VOLEK		12/4/85	M	21	(6)	3
20	Michal VOREL		27/6/75	G	9		
12	Vít VRTĚLKA		21/10/82	M	23		1
6	Milan ZACHARIÁŠ		1/10/83	D	16	(4)	

FC VIKTORIA PLZEŇ

Coach – Pavel Vrba

Founded – 1911

Stadium – Města Plzně (7,300)

MAJOR HONOURS: Czech League – (1) 2011; Czech Cup – (1) 2010.

2010				
18/7	Sigma	h	2-2	*Horváth (p), og (Janotka)*
24/7	Liberec	a	3-2	*Rezek 2, Limberský*
1/8	Bohemians 1905	h	2-1	*Kolář, Horváth*
9/8	Hradec Králové	a	3-0	*Rezek 2 (1p), Rada*
15/8	Slovácko	h	3-0	*Horváth, Rezek, Kolář*
21/8	Sparta	a	1-0	*Jiráček*
29/8	České Budějovice	a	3-0	*Kolář 2, Rezek*
12/9	Ústí nad Labem	h	7-0	*Kolář 2, Bakoš, Petržela, Horváth (p), Limberský, Navrátil*
17/9	Jablonec	a	2-1	*Kolář, Bakoš*
26/9	Příbram	h	2-1	*Jiráček, Střihavka*
1/10	Slavia	a	1-0	*Rezek (p)*
17/10	Brno	h	4-1	*Rezek 2 (1p), Petržela, Kolář*
23/10	Mladá Boleslav	a	3-4	*Petržela, Rada, Rajtoral*
29/10	Teplice	h	4-2	*Petržela 2, Bystroň, Rezek*
6/11	Baník	a	2-0	*Rajtoral, Kolář*
13 /11	Liberec	h	1-1	*Horváth (p)*
19/11	Bohemians 1905	a	0-1	
2011				
26/2	Hradec Králové	h	2-1	*Bakoš, Kolář*
5/3	Slovácko	a	2-2	*Bakoš, Jiráček*
12/3	Sparta	h	1-0	*Horváth*
18/3	České Budějovice	h	2-1	*Bakoš, Ďuriš*
3/4	Ústí nad Labem	a	5-0	*Bakoš 2, Petržela, Bystroň, Ďuriš*
8/4	Jablonec	h	1-1	*Rezek*
15/4	Příbram	a	3-0	*Horváth (p), Jiráček, Ďuriš*
25/4	Slavia	h	2-2	*Kolář, Ševinský*
1/5	Brno	a	1-1	*Petržela*
7/5	Mladá Boleslav	h	3-1	*Kolář, Bakoš, Rajtoral*
14/5	Teplice	a	1-0	*Kolář*
21/5	Baník	h	3-1	*Jiráček, Bakoš, Horváth*
28/5	Sigma	a	1-2	*og (Kučera)*

No	Name	Nat	DoB	Pos	Aps	(s)	Gls
23	Marek BAKOŠ	SVK	15/4/83	A	19	(6)	9
3	Miloš BREZINSKÝ	SVK	2/4/84	D	2	(13)	
18	David BYSTROŇ		18/11/82	D	27		2
16	Vladimír DARIDA		8/8/90	M		(4)	
5	Michal ĎURIŠ	SVK	1/6/88	A	8	(15)	3
9	Martin FILLO		7/2/86	M	2	(8)	
3/4	Tomáš HÁJOVSKÝ	SVK	10/12/82	D		(2)	
10	Pavel HORVÁTH		22/4/75	M	26		8
29	Martin HRUŠKA		11/5/81	M	1	(2)	
20	Petr JIRÁČEK		2/3/86	M	20	(9)	5
26	Daniel KOLÁŘ		27/10/85	M	27	(2)	13
19	Lukáš KRBEČEK		27/10/85	G	6	(1)	
6	Michal KRMENČÍK		15/3/93	A		(1)	
8	David LIMBERSKÝ		6/10/83	D	29		2
24	Bogdan MILIĆ	BIH	24/11/87	A		(1)	
21	Jakub NAVRÁTIL		1/2/84	D	16		1
21	Aleš NEUWIRT		4/1/85	D	6		
33	Roman PAVLÍK		17/1/76	G	22		
11	Milan PETRŽELA		19/6/83	M	26		7
4	Tomáš RADA		15/2/83	D	17		2
27	František RAJTORAL		12/3/86	M	27		3
17	Jan REZEK		5/5/82	A	27	(3)	11
24	Filip RÝDEL		30/3/84	M		(1)	
15	František ŠEVINSKÝ		31/3/79	D	9	(5)	1
22	Martin SLADKÝ		1/3/92	M		(2)	
7	David STŘIHAVKA		4/3/83	A	1	(10)	1

30	Martin TICHÁČEK		15/9/81	G	2		
7	Petr TRAPP		6/12/85	D	10	(1)	
6	David VANĚČEK		9/3/91	M		(2)	
9	Libor ŽŮREK		2/11/79	A		(1)	

FC ZBROJOVKA BRNO

Coach – Karel Večeřa; (15/4/11) René Wagner

Founded – 1913

Stadium – Městský fotbalový stadion Srbská (10,785)

MAJOR HONOURS: Czechoslovakian League – (1) 1978.

2010

19/7	Jablonec	a	0-1	
25/7	Ústí nad Labem	h	1-3	*Dostálek*
1/8	Baník	a	0-3	
6/8	Slavia	h	2-3	*Kalabiška, Střeštík*
16/8	Mladá Boleslav	h	3-1	*Polách, Dostálek (p), Michálek*
22/8	Sigma	a	0-3	
30/8	Sparta	h	0-5	
12/9	Teplice	a	2-1	*Střeštík, Došek*
19/9	Bohemians 1905	h	1-0	*Dostálek*
25/9	Liberec	a	1-3	*Došek*
3/10	Hradec Králové	h	1-2	*Rýdel*
17/10	Plzeň	a	1-4	*Michálek*
24/10	Slovácko	h	7-0	*Michálek 2 (2p), Rýdel, Kalabiška, Střeštík, Polách, Šamánek*
31/10	České Budějovice	a	0-1	
7/11	Příbram	h	0-1	
14/11	Ústí nad Labem	a	3-2	*Šimerský, Kalabiška, Hodek*
22/11	Baník	h	0-2	

2011

25/2	Slavia	a	1-1	*Pernica*
6/3	Mladá Boleslav	a	0-5	
11/3	Sigma	h	2-0	*Dostálek, Rýdel*
19/3	Sparta	a	0-2	
3/4	Teplice	h	0-1	
10/4	Bohemians 1905	a	1-2	*Valenta*
17/4	Liberec	h	0-1	
24/4	Hradec Králové	a	0-1	
1/5	Plzeň	h	1-1	*Rabušic*
7/5	Slovácko	a	2-0	*Došek, Valenta*
16/5	České Budějovice	h	1-1	*og (Simić)*
21/5	Příbram	a	0-1	
28/5	Jablonec	h	3-4	*Došek 2, Dostálek*

No	Name	Nat	DoB	Pos	Aps	(s)	Gls
16	Tomáš BOREK		4/4/86	M	9	(1)	
25	Vladica BRDAROVSKI	MKD	7/2/90	D		(3)	
24	Radek BUCHTA		22/4/89	M	1		
20	Tomáš BUREŠ		27/9/78	G	13		
16	Jakub ČERVÍNEK		4/6/87	D	3		
10	Filip CHLUP		10/6/85	M	3	(1)	
3	Petr ČOUPEK		10/5/82	D	3		
26	Tomáš DOŠEK		12/9/78	A	15	(5)	5
7	Richard DOSTÁLEK		26/4/74	M	23	(3)	5
12	František DŘÍŽĎAL		8/8/78	D	8		
29	Josef DVORNÍK		23/4/78	D	2		
6	Zdeněk FOLPRECHT		1/7/91	M	4	(2)	
9	Josef HAMOUZ		8/4/80	D	13	(4)	
8	Andrej HODEK	SVK	24/5/81	A	5	(10)	1
25	Martin HUDEC		15/4/82	D	8	(1)	
30	Martin HUSÁR	SVK	1/2/85	D	25	(1)	
2	Martin JÍLEK		7/7/86	D	5		
11	Jan KALABIŠKA		22/12/86	A	20	(8)	3
18	Luboš KOŠULIČ		11/5/90	M		(1)	
24	Zdravko KOVAČEVIĆ	SRB	6/8/84	D		(1)	
1	Lukáš KRBEČEK		27/10/85	G	6		
6	Lukáš KŘEČEK		1/10/86	M	3	(2)	
1	Martin LEJSAL		16/9/82	G	11		
3	Lukáš MATYSKA		26/4/92	D	2	(2)	
19	Tomáš MICHÁLEK		9/5/94	M	13		4
18	Lukáš MICHNA		28/4/90	M		(2)	
22	Marco MIGLIORINI	ITA	3/1/92	D	5		
29	Stefan MITROVIĆ	SRB	22/5/90	D	8		
9	Tomáš OKLEŠTĚK		21/2/87	M		(5)	
3	David PAŠEK		27/9/89	D	5	(1)	
19	Matijas PEJIĆ	BIH	18/5/88	D	2	(2)	
4	Luděk PERNICA		16/6/90	D	8		1
21	Tomáš POLÁCH		16/1/77	M	14	(1)	2
10	Daniel PŘEROVSKÝ		5/3/92	M	6	(2)	
14	Michael RABUŠIC		17/9/89	A	15	(7)	1
27	Filip RÝDEL		30/3/84	M	20	(1)	3
28	Rostislav ŠAMÁNEK		9/8/89	A	4	(5)	1
5	Dominik ŠIMERSKÝ		29/9/92	D	14	(4)	1
15	Marek STŘEŠTÍK		1/2/87	M	15	(6)	3
22	Jan TROUSIL		9/4/76	D	16		
21	Róbert VALENTA	SVK	10/1/90	M	3	(4)	2

TOP GOALSCORERS 2010/11

19	David LAFATA (Jablonec)
18	Tomáš PEKHART (Jablonec/Sparta)
14	Léonard KWEUKE (Sparta)
13	Daniel KOLÁŘ (Plzeň)
12	Michal HUBNÍK (Sigma)
11	Jan REZEK (Plzeň)
10	Zdeněk ONDRÁŠEK (České Budějovice)
	Jan NEZMAR (Liberec)
	Bony WILFRIED (Sparta)
	Aidin MAHMUTOVIĆ (Teplice)

PROMOTED CLUBS

FK DUKLA PRAHA

Coach – Luboš Kozel

Founded – 1959

Stadium – Juliska (1,830)

FK VIKTORIA ŽIŽKOV

Coach – Martin Pulpit

Founded – 1903

Stadium – FK Viktoria (5,037)

MAJOR HONOURS: Czechoslovakian League - (1) 1928; Czech Cup - (2) 1994, 2001.

SECOND LEVEL FINAL TABLE 2010/11

		Pld	W	D	L	F	A	Pts
1	FK Dukla Praha	30	18	9	3	55	18	63
2	FK Viktoria Žižkov	30	16	7	7	44	31	55
3	FC Vysočina Jihlava	30	15	8	7	49	29	53
4	MFK OKD Karviná	30	13	7	10	42	36	46
5	FK Fotbal Třinec	30	12	8	10	32	34	44
6	FK Baník Sokolov	30	12	7	11	53	51	43
7	FC Vlašim	30	12	6	12	38	32	42
8	FC Zenit Čáslav	30	11	8	11	37	48	41
9	FK Spartak MAS Sezimovo Ústí	30	11	7	12	42	40	40
10	AC Sparta Praha B	30	11	6	13	35	47	39
11	FC Zlín	30	11	5	14	46	45	38
12	FK Baník Most	30	10	7	13	35	46	37
13	SK Slovan Varnsdorf	30	10	7	13	33	38	37
14	1.SC Znojmo	30	10	6	14	30	40	36
15	SK Kladno	30	8	7	15	42	48	31
16	FC Hlučín	30	6	3	21	36	66	21

DOMESTIC CUP 2010/11

POHÁR ČMFS

ECOND ROUND

25/8/10)
vůr Králové 0, Jablonec 5

31/8/10)
iskra Ústí nad Orlicí 2, Sigma 5
ENCO Doubravka 0, Baník Sokolov 3

1/9/10)
C Písek 1, Příbram 0
C Velim 1, SK Hlavice 2
C Vítkovice 1, Třinec 2
K Hořovicko 0, Vlašim 3
K Litvínov 0, Sokol Ovčáry 3
K OEZ Letohrad 1, Zenit Čáslav 0
K Pardubice 0, Slavia Praha 1
K Trutnov 1, Mladá Boleslav 2
Iorácký Třebíč 2, Znojmo 1
IS Kroměříž 2, Viktoria Otrokovice 1
Králův Dvůr 1, FK Kunice 1 *(4-5 on pens)*
Meteor Praha 0, České Budějovice 2
MSK Břeclav1, Slovácko 1 *(7-6 on pens)*
Přední Kopanina 1, Ústí nad Labem 5
ROSTEX Vyškov 1, 1. HFK Olomouc 3
SFK Vrchovina 2, SK Líšeň 1
SK Uničov 1, Karviná 1 *(1-3 on pens)*
Slovan Varnsdorf 1, Bohemians 1905 1 *(5-4 on pens)*
Sokol Brozany 0, Teplice 5
Sokol Konice 5, TJ Valašské Meziříčí 1
Spartak Hulín 2, FC Hlučín 2 *(5-4 on pens)*
Šumperk 0, SFC Opava 4

(2/9/10)
Slovan Rosice 1, Brno 2

(4/9/10)
Marila Votice 0, Sparta Praha 1

(7/9/10)
Most 1, Plzeň 4
Spartak Sezimovo Ústí 2, Dukla Praha 3
Žižkov 0, Hradec Králové 0 *(4-3 on pens)*

(14/9/10)
FK Kolín 0, Liberec 3
TVD Slavičín 0, Baník 0 *(5-4 on pens)*

THIRD ROUND

(21/9/10)
Dukla Praha 1, Jablonec 1 *(3-4 on pens)*
FC Písek 3, Třinec 1

(22/9/10)
FK Kunice 1, Mladá Boleslav 1 *(2-4 on pens)*
FK OEZ Letohrad 1, Žižkov 3
Horácký Třebíč 1, Teplice 2
Karviná 0, Liberec 0 *(5-3 on pens)*
MSK Břeclav 1, TVD Slavičín 1 *(4-5 on pens)*
SFC Opava 2, Slovan Varnsdorf 1
SFK Vrchovina 2, HS Kroměříž 3
Sokol Konice 0, 1. HFK Olomouc 2
Sokol Ovčáry 2, Brno 2 *(2-4 on pens)*
Spartak Hulín 1, Sigma 3

(6/10/10)
SK Hlavice 1, České Budějovice 3
Vlašim 0, Plzeň 2

(9/10/10)
Baník Sokolov 1, Sparta Praha 1 *(4-1 on pens)*

(12/10/10)
Slavia Praha 3, Ústí nad Labem 2

FOURTH ROUND

(27/10/10 & 9/11/10)
Žižkov v Slavia Praha 1-1; 0-3 *(1-4)*

(27/10/10 & 10/11/10)
1. HFK Olomouc v Jablonec 4-2; 0-5 *(4-7)*
Baník Sokolov v Mladá Boleslav 3-0; 0-3 *(3-3; 5-6 on pens)*
FC Písek v Sigma 3-3; 1-1 *(4-4; Sigma on away goals)*
Karviná v Brno 2-0; 0-4 *(2-4)*

(27/10/10 & 17/11/10)
TVD Slavičín v HS Kroměříž 1-5; 0-0 *(1-5)*

(3/11/10 & 10/11/10)
Teplice v České Budějovice 0-1; 2-0 *(2-1)*

(10/11/10 & 23/11/10)
Plzeň v SFC Opava 3-0; 3-3 *(6-3)*

QUARTER-FINALS

(12/4/11 & 20/4/11)
Mladá Boleslav 2 *(Dimitrovski 30, Chramosta 37)*, Plzeň 1 *(Bakoš 78)*
Plzeň 1 *(Fillo 11)*, Mladá Boleslav 2 *(Chramosta 49, Dimoutsos 85)*
(Mladá Boleslav 4-2)

(13/4/11 & 20/4/11)
Brno 1 *(Šimerský 88)*, HS Kroměříž 2 *(Janča 43, Hromek 46)*
HS Kroměříž 1 *(Hajdarovič 85)*, Brno 0
(HS Kroměříž 3-1)

(13/4/11 & 27/4/11)
Sigma 2 *(Hořava 51, Šultes 66)*, Jablonec 0
Jablonec 2 *(Vošahlík 21, Lafata 69p)*, Sigma 1 *(Ordoš 75)*
(Sigma 3-2)

(14/4/11 & 21/4/11)
Teplice 2 *(Verbíř (I) 45p, 90)*, Slavia Praha 1 *(Vlček 62)*
Slavia Praha 1 *(Kisel 62)*, Teplice 0
(2-2; Slavia Praha on away goal)

SEMI-FINALS

(3/5/11 & 10/5/11)
Mladá Boleslav 1 *(Chramosta 34)*, HS Kroměříž 1 *(Hromek 52)*
HS Kroměříž 1 *(Šilinger 89p)*, Mladá Boleslav 3 *(Chramosta 35, 72, Kulič 67)*
(Mladá Boleslav 4-2)

(5/5/11 & 11/5/11)
Slavia Praha 1 *(Kisel 35)*, Sigma 1 *(Hořava 32) (abandoned at halftime; awarded 0-3)*
Sigma 1 *(Hořava 56)*, Slavia Praha 0
(Sigma 4-0)

FINAL

(25/5/11)
FC Vysočina stadion, Jihlava
FK MLADÁ BOLESLAV 1 *(Táborský 73p)*
SK SIGMA OLOMOUC 1 *(Hořava 59)*
(aet; 4-3 on pens)
Referee – *Kovařík*
MLADÁ BOLESLAV – *Miller, Kysela, Rolko, Johana, Šírl, Táborský (Dimoutsos 80), Opiela, Kúdela (Procházka 8), Mendy, Kulič (Řezníček 57), Chramosta.*
SIGMA – *Drobisz, Vepřek, Škerle, Kučera, Janotka, Bajer, Hořava, Daniel Rossi, Navrátil (Ordoš 67), Schulmeister (Petr 61), Šultes.*

CLUB COMMUNICATION 2011/12

FC Baník Ostrava

Bukovanského 4/1028
CZ-710 00 Ostrava

Tel	+420 596 241 687
Fax	+420 596 241 827
Web	fcb.cz
Email	info@fcb.cz
Media Officer	Adam Januszek

Bohemians 1905

Vršovická 1489/31
CZ-101 00 Praha 10

Tel	+420 245 005 014
Fax	+420 245 005 014
Web	bohemians.cz
Email	info@bohemians1905.cz
Media Officer	Jaroslav Köstl

SK Dynamo České Budějovice

Strelecky Ostrov 3
CZ-370 21 České Budějovice

Tel	+420 387 312 502
Fax	+420 387 312 503
Web	dynamocb.cz
Email	klub@dynamocb.cz
Media Officer	Radim Šupka

FK Dukla Praha

Na Julisce 28
CZ-160 00 Praha-Dejvice

Tel	+420 220 514 312
Fax	+420 220 514 312
Web	fkdukla.cz
Email	fotbal@fkdukla.cz
Media Officer	Petr Voženílek

FC Hradec Králové

Všesportovní stadion, Úprkova 473/1
CZ-500 09 Hradec Králové

Tel	+420 495 515 532
Fax	+420 495 511 485
Web	fchk.cz
Email	fchk@fchk.cz
Media Officer	Milan Šedivý

FK Jablonec

U Stadionu 4904/5,
CZ-466 01 Jablonec nad Nisou

Tel	+420 483 312 139
Fax	+420 483 312 140
Web	fkjablonec.cz
Email	sekretariat@fkjablonec.cz
Media Officer	Tomás Bárta

FK Mladá Boleslav

U stadionu 1118/II, Mestský stadion
CZ-293 01 Mladá Boleslav

Tel	+420 326 719 041
Fax	+420 326 719 044
Web	fkmb.cz
Email	fkmb@fkmb.cz
Media Officer	Jiří Koros

1. FK Příbram

Lazec 60, stadion Na Litavce
CZ-261 01 Příbram

Tel	+420 318 626173
Fax	+420 318 626173
Web	fkpribram.cz
Email	
Media Officer	Radim Horák

SK Sigma Olomouc

Legionářská 1165/12
CZ-779 00 Olomouc

Tel	+420 585 222 956
Fax	+420 585 220 953
Web	sigmafotbal.cz
Email	sekretariat@sigmafotbal.cz
Media Officer	Petr Pelíšek

SK Slavia Praha

Vladivostocká 1460/2
CZ-100 00 Praha

Tel	+420 233 081 753
Fax	+420 233 081 760
Web	slavia.cz
Email	mirka.fouskova@slavia.cz
Media Officer	Ondrej Zlamal

1. FC Slovácko

Stonky 566, Městský fotbalový stadion
CZ-686 01 Uherské Hradiště

Tel	+420 572 551 801
Fax	+420 572 541 202
Web	fcslovacko.cz
Email	info@fcslovacko.cz
Media Officer	Aleš Mazúrek

FC Slovan Liberec

Na Hradbách 1300,
CZ-460 01 Liberec 1

Tel	+420 485 103 714
Fax	+420 485 103 715
Web	fcslovanliberec.cz
Email	info@fcslovanliberec.cz
Media Officer	Lukáš Váňa

AC Sparta Praha

Milady Horákové 1066/98, Letná
CZ-170 82 Praha 7

Tel	+420 2 96 111 111
Fax	+420 2 20 571 665
Web	sparta.cz
Email	football@sparta.cz
Media Officer	Ondřej Kasík

FK Teplice

Na Stínadlech 2796,
CZ-415 01 Teplice

Tel	+420 417 507 401
Fax	+420 417 539 517
Web	fkteplice.cz
Email	info@fkteplice.cz
Media Officer	Petr Heidenreich

FC Viktoria Plzeň

Štruncovy Sady 3,
CZ-301 00 Plzeň

Tel	+420 377 221 507
Fax	+420 377 221 543
Web	fcviktoria.cz
Email	fcviktoria@fcviktoria.cz
Media Officer	Jaromír Hamouz

FK Viktoria Žižkov

Seifertova Tríd
CZ-130 00 Praha 3

Tel	+420 22 142 3427
Fax	+420 22 272 2045
Web	fkvz.cz
Email	berna@fkvz.cz
Media Officer	Jirí Fryc

DENMARK

Danemark I Dänemark

Dansk Boldspil-Union (DBU)

COMMUNICATION

Address House of Football
DBU Allé 1
DK-2605 Brøndby

Tel +45 43 262 222
Fax +45 43 262 245

E-mail dbu@dbu.dk
Website dbu.dk

President Allan Hansen
General Secretary Jim Stjerne Hansen
Media Officer Lars Berendt

Year of Formation 1889

National Stadium Parken, Copenhagen (38,065)

DOMESTIC COMPETITION SUMMARY 2010/11

SUPERLIGA FINAL TABLE

			Home					Away					Total						
		Pld	**W**	**D**	**L**	**F**	**A**	**W**	**D**	**L**	**F**	**A**	**W**	**D**	**L**	**F**	**A**	**Pts**	**Comp**
1	FC København	33	15	2	0	46	11	10	4	2	31	18	25	6	2	77	29	81	UCL
2	Odense BK	33	9	4	4	33	17	7	3	6	22	24	16	7	10	55	41	55	UCL
3	Brøndby IF	33	6	8	3	24	17	7	4	5	28	22	13	12	8	52	39	51	UEL
4	FC Midtjylland	33	8	7	2	31	22	5	3	8	19	20	13	10	10	50	42	49	UEL
5	Silkeborg IF	33	7	6	3	25	21	3	7	7	18	28	10	13	10	43	49	43	
6	FC Nordsjælland	33	6	5	5	26	25	4	4	9	12	25	10	9	14	38	50	39	UEL
7	SønderjyskE	33	6	2	8	18	25	5	4	8	14	21	11	6	16	32	46	39	
8	Lyngby BK	33	7	3	6	22	21	3	5	9	20	31	10	8	15	42	52	38	
9	AC Horsens	33	4	7	5	12	16	5	3	9	17	24	9	10	14	29	40	37	
10	Aalborg BK	33	4	4	9	17	21	4	7	5	21	27	8	11	14	38	48	35	
11	Randers FC	33	5	6	5	21	21	1	10	6	20	27	6	16	11	41	48	34	*Relegated*
12	Esbjerg fB	33	3	6	8	17	24	4	6	6	19	25	7	12	14	36	49	33	*Relegated*

Top Scorer Dame N'Doye (København), 25 goals

Promoted Club AGF Århus
HB Køge

Cup Final FC Nordsjælland 3, FC Midtjylland 2

FC København a class apart

With a show of strength that had researchers repeatedly referring to the Superliga record books, FC København stormed to their ninth Danish title in emphatic style. Their third championship triumph in succession was also the fourth under Norwegian coach Ståle Solbakken, who, in situ since December 2005, could hardly have ended his tenure in grander style as he left to start a new career in Germany with 1. FC Köln.

Largely unchanged from the previous season, FCK pressed home their dominance in ruthless fashion right from the start. A fabulous autumn, during which the club also made history by becoming the first Danish club to qualify for the knockout phase of the UEFA Champions League, yielded 16 wins and three draws, and after 19 games, remarkably, they had constructed an impregnable 19-point lead over second-placed Odense BK. They also went into the winter break with a nice round figure of 50 goals, so it was a very merry Christmas all round for Solbakken and his players.

With the title a foregone conclusion – in retrospect FCK could have won just two of their 14 spring fixtures and remained top – it was perhaps understandable that they would return to Superliga action in early March with a touch of complacency, their unbeaten record ending in the first game back with a 2-0 defeat at FC Midtjylland. Their UEFA Champions League campaign also resumed in disappointing fashion as they lost 2-0 to Chelsea FC in a packed Parken, but they would sign off with a worthy 0-0 draw at Stamford Bridge to end a memorable European jaunt that had brought famous wins over FC BATE Borisov, Rosenborg BK, FC Rubin Kazan and Panathinaikos FC (twice) plus an epic 1-1 draw at home to eventual winners FC Barcelona.

William Kvist Jørgensen, one of FC København's most consistent performers, lifts the Danish Superliga trophy

Records tumble

Out of Europe and also the Danish Cup, FCK were left to concentrate on the league and see how many Superliga records they could break. The final figure was six – most points (81), most wins (25), fewest defeats (two), biggest winning margin (26 points), most consecutive home wins (13) and, by securing the title in round 26 with a 2-1 victory at Lyngby BK, earliest championship triumph.

Needless to say, with 77 goals to their credit, FCK also boasted the Superliga's top individual marksman, Senegalese striker Dame N'Doye carrying on where he had left off the previous season and scoring 25 goals. His Brazilian team-mate César Santin was next in line with 17, both strikers enjoying excellent service from veteran winger Jesper Grønkjær, who announced his retirement at the end of the season. One player absent from the scoresheet was Danish international William Kvist Jørgensen, who nonetheless enjoyed a brilliant season in a new role as the team's deep-lying midfield commander. His namesake, Mathias 'Zanka' Jørgsensen, was another prominent figure, marshalling a defence that contained three Swedes – goalkeeper Johan Wiland, centre back Mikael Antonsson and left back Oscar Wendt – and an outstanding Czech in

National Team

International Honours –
UEFA European Championship – (1) 1992.

International Tournament Appearances –
FIFA World Cup – (4) 1986 (2nd round), 1998 (qtr-finals), 2002 (2nd round), 2010.
UEFA European Championship – (7) 1964 (4th), 1984 (semi-finals), 1988, 1992 (Winners), 1996, 2000, 2004 (qtr-finals).

Top Five All-time Caps – Peter Schmeichel (129); Jon Dahl Tomasson (112); Thomas Helveg & Dennis Rommedahl (108); Michael Laudrup (104)

Top Five All-time Goals – Poul "Tist" Nielsen & Jon Dahl Tomasson (52); Pauli Jørgensen (44); Ole Madsen (42); Preben Elkjær (38)

effervescent right back Zdeněk Pospech. There would be an even greater Swedish influence at the club in 2011/12 following the arrival of Roland Nilsson, an Allsvenskan title winner just across the water with Malmö FF, as the new FCK coach.

Thanks largely to FCK's efforts, the Superliga was granted a second UEFA Champions League place in 2011/12, and it was OB, 2009/10 UEFA Europa League group stage participants, who deservedly claimed it by taking the runners-up spot for the second straight year. Brøndby IF repeated their third-place finish of the previous season and it was also a case of déjà vu in the final of the Danish Cup, where FC Nordsjælland and Midtjylland reconvened at Parken, with the former once more coming out on top to leave the latter nursing the wounds of the vanquished for the fourth time in as many cup final visits. The game looked set to go into extra time – as it had in 2010 – but Nordsjælland midfielder Søren Christensen struck a dramatic winner just before the final whistle to ensure a successful trophy defence for Morten Wieghorst's side.

If the top of the Superliga table lacked excitement, the bottom was full of it as the battle to avoid relegation stretched to the last minute of the season. The bottom two teams going into the final day, Esbjerg fB and Randers FC, ended up going down but only after sharing a 2-2 draw. Randers, great escape artists in 2009/10, were poised to survive once again as they led 2-1 while another relegation candidate, Aalborg BK, trailed 2-0 at champions FCK, but Esbjerg, already doomed and with nothing to play for, dragged their hosts down with them by scoring a last-gasp equaliser. As expected, AGF Århus returned to the Superliga after one season away and were joined in promotion by HB Køge.

Three-way tie

Having topped a tough qualifying group for the 2010 FIFA World Cup, Morten Olsen's Denmark were asked to repeat the feat when they were pitted with Portugal (again) and Norway in the qualifiers for UEFA EURO 2012. At the end of an indifferent season during which 100th caps were awarded to both Dennis Rommedahl – still going strong at the highest level – and Martin Jørgensen – in a special farewell appearance - Denmark were tied with both of their main rivals on ten points from six games, and although it was to their advantage that they still had to host both teams, on the other hand Norway and Portugal had already met twice. With Olsen set to end his 12-year tenure in the summer of 2012, it was far from clear whether he would be bowing out with a bang or a whimper.

Alas, it was a case of the latter for the Danish Under-21 side as they exited the 2011 European finals, staged on the home soil of northern Jutland, in the group stage. Defeated by Switzerland in Aalborg but victorious over Belarus in Aarhus, they needed just a draw back in Aalborg against Iceland to reach the semi-finals, but it was not to be, their fellow Scandinavians consigning Keld Bordingaard's youngsters to a fatal 3-1 defeat.

NATIONAL TEAM RESULTS 2010/11

11/8/10	Germany	H	Copenhagen	2-2	*Rommedahl (74), Junker (87)*
7/9/10	Iceland (ECQ)	H	Copenhagen	1-0	*Kahlenberg (90+1)*
8/10/10	Portugal (ECQ)	A	Porto	1-3	*Ricardo Carvalho (79og)*
12/10/10	Cyprus (ECQ)	H	Copenhagen	2-0	*Rasmussen (48), Lorentzen (81)*
17/11/10	Czech Republic	H	Aarhus	0-0	
9/2/11	England	H	Copenhagen	1-2	*Agger (7)*
26/3/11	Norway (ECQ)	A	Oslo	1-1	*Rommedahl (27)*
29/3/11	Slovakia	A	Trnava	2-1	*Saláta (3og), Krohn-Dehli (72)*
4/6/11	Iceland (ECQ)	A	Reykjavik	2-0	*Schøne (60), Eriksen (75)*

NATIONAL TEAM APPEARANCES 2010/11

Coach – Morten OLSEN	14/8/49		Ger	ISL	POR	CYP	Cze	Eng	NOR	Svk	ISL	Caps	Goals
Thomas SØRENSEN	12/6/76	Stoke (ENG)	G		G32			G	G		G	94	-
Lars JACOBSEN	20/9/79	Blackburn (ENG)	D										
		/West Ham (ENG)		D	D	D		D59	D	D60	D	42	-
Simon KJÆR	26/3/89	Wolfsburg (GER)	D	D	D	D		s46			D	17	-
Daniel AGGER	12/12/84	Liverpool (ENG)	D	D		D39		D	D			40	4
Simon Busk POULSEN	7/10/84	AZ (NED)	D27					D46		D	D	12	-
Mike JENSEN	19/2/88	Brøndby	M46									1	-
William Kvist JØRGENSEN	24/2/85	København	M66		M72			M90	M	M	M60	20	-
Christian ERIKSEN	14/2/92	Ajax (NED)	M	M56	s58	s65	s76	M	M	s61	M	14	1
Nicklas PEDERSEN	10/10/87	Groningen (NED)	A54	A71	A	M		s70				5	-
Dennis ROMMEDAHL	22/7/78	Olympiacos (GRE)	A	A	A	A	A76	A82	A93	A32	A	108	19
Thomas ENEVOLDSEN	27/7/87	Groningen (NED)	A46					s82	s82	s32		11	1
Johnny THOMSEN	26/2/82	SønderjyskE	s27				D			s60		3	-
Michael SILBERBAUER	7/7/81	Utrecht (NED)	s46		D			s59	D			18	1
Lasse SCHØNE	27/5/86	NEC (NED)	s46							M61	s46	4	2
Mads JUNKER	21/4/81	Roda (NED)	s54	s56		A46	A46			s76		6	1
Kasper LORENTZEN	19/11/85	Randers	s66			M				s46		3	1
Anders LINDEGAARD	13/4/84	Aalesund (NOR)		G	s32	G	G					4	-
Leon JESSEN	11/6/86	Kaiserslautern (GER)		D		D						4	-
Christian POULSEN	28/2/80	Liverpool (ENG)		M	M	M	M69	M	M70		s60	84	6
Thomas KAHLENBERG	20/3/83	Wolfsburg (GER)		M			M62					36	4
Michael KROHN-DEHLI	6/6/83	Brøndby		A76		A65	A	A70	A82	A84	A46	12	1
Morten SKOUBO	30/6/80	Roda (NED)		s71						s84		6	1
Martin VINGAARD	20/3/85	København		s76	A			s90				9	1
Per KRØLDRUP	31/7/79	Fiorentina (ITA)			D	s39						33	-
Daniel JENSEN	25/6/79	Werder (GER)			M58		s29					52	3
Peter LØVENKRANDS	29/1/80	Newcastle (ENG)			s72							22	1
Morten "Duncan" RASMUSSEN	31/1/85	Mainz (GER)				s46	s46					5	1
Patrick MTILIGA	28/1/81	Malaga (ESP)					D					5	-
Mathias "Zanka" JØRGENSEN	23/4/90	København					D46	D46	D	D		5	-
Andreas BJELLAND	11/7/88	Nordsjælland					D					1	-
Martin JØRGENSEN	6/10/75	AGF					M29					100	12
Kris STADSGAARD	1/8/85	Málaga (ESP)					s46					2	-
Hans Henrik ANDREASEN	10/1/79	OB					s62					1	-
Niki ZIMLING	19/4/85	NEC (NED)					s69				M	3	-
Nicklas BENDTNER	16/1/88	Arsenal (ENG)						A	A	A76	A	39	12
Daniel WASS	31/5/89	Brøndby						s46	s93			2	-
Jakob POULSEN	7/7/83	Midtjylland							s70	M46		17	1
Stephan ANDERSEN	26/11/81	Brøndby								G		8	-
Bo SVENSSON	4/8/79	Mainz (GER)								D	D	3	-

CLUB-BY-CLUB

AALBORG BK

Coach – Magnus Pehrsson (SWE); (11/10/10) Kent Nielsen
Founded – 1885
Stadium – Energi Nord Arena (13,800)
MAJOR HONOURS: Danish League – (3) 1995, 1999, 2008; Danish Cup – (2) 1966, 1970.

2010

9/7	Lyngby	a	4-2	*Schwartz 3, Marshall*
5/7	Brøndby	h	0-2	
1/7	København	a	1-1	*Bøgelund*
7/8	Silkeborg	h	0-0	
6/8	Midtjylland	a	1-2	*og (Priske)*
1/8	Esbjerg	h	0-2	
9/8	Nordsjælland	a	0-0	
2/9	Horsens	h	2-3	*Dalsgaard, Helenius*
8/9	Randers	a	3-2	*Kusi-Asare, Schwartz, Sørensen*
25/9	SønderjyskE	h	0-2	
4/10	OB	h	1-2	*Nwakaeme*
16/10	SønderjyskE	a	0-1	
24/10	Nordsjælland	h	2-0	*Curth, Helenius*
30/10	Randers	a	0-0	
5/11	Esbjerg	h	1-1	*Helenius*
13/11	Midtjylland	a	2-2	*Helenius 2*
21/11	Brøndby	h	1-2	*Würtz*
29/11	Horsens	a	0-0	
4/12	OB	a	0-6	

2011

5/3	Silkeborg	h	1-1	*Curth*
12/3	København	h	0-1	
20/3	Lyngby	a	2-1	*Due, Wæhler*
2/4	OB	h	0-1	
10/4	Horsens	h	0-0	
17/4	Brøndby	a	2-1	*Rasmussen, Due*
20/4	Randers	h	4-1	*Kayke, Curth, Due, Rasmussen (p)*
24/4	Nordsjælland	a	3-3	*Rasmussen 2, Rolfe*
30/4	Midtjylland	h	2-0	*Nielsen, Rasmussen (p)*
6/5	Lyngby	h	2-1	*Rasmussen, Augustinussen*
15/5	Esbjerg	a	0-0	
20/5	Silkeborg	a	3-4	*Kayke 2, Augustinussen*
25/5	SønderjyskE	h	1-2	*Wæhler*
29/5	København	a	0-2	

No	Name	Nat	DoB	Pos	Aps	(s)	Gls
18	Lucas ANDERSEN		13/9/94	M		(10)	
9	Thomas AUGUSTINUSSEN		20/3/81	M	14		2
16	Kasper BØGELUND		8/10/80	D	14	(1)	1
6	Louay CHANKO	SYR	29/11/79	M	21	(4)	
36	Daniel CHRISTENSEN		19/9/88	M	10	(5)	
10	Jeppe CURTH		21/3/84	A	22	(2)	3
20	Henrik DALSGAARD		27/7/89	A	8	(7)	1
7	Anders DUE		17/3/82	M	15	(4)	3
29	Nicklas HELENIUS Jensen		8/5/91	A	12	(17)	5
21	KAYKE Moreno de Andrade Rodrigues	BRA	1/4/88	A	6	(3)	3
27	Patrick KRISTENSEN		28/4/87	M	16	(2)	
14	Jones KUSI-ASARE	SWE	21/5/80	A	3		1
33	Kasper KUSK		10/11/91	M		(2)	
28	Michael LUMB		9/1/88	D	14		
15	Dennis MARSHALL	CRC	9/8/85	M	11	(6)	1
4	Lasse NIELSEN		8/1/88	D	27		1
9	Dickson NWAKAEME	NGA	21/5/86	A	2	(5)	1
5	Kenneth Emil PETERSEN		15/1/85	D	20	(1)	
11	Morten "Duncan" RASMUSSEN		31/1/85	A	12	(2)	6
17	Chris ROLFE	USA	17/1/83	M	5	(2)	1
32	Ronnie SCHWARTZ		29/8/89	A	9	(7)	4
24	Jens-Kristian SØRENSEN		21/3/87	M	6	(7)	1
30	Mathias WICHMANN		6/8/91	M	20	(8)	
8	Rasmus WÜRTZ		18/9/83	M	31		1
3	Kjetil WÆHLER	NOR	16/3/76	D	32		2
1	Karim ZAZA	MAR	9/1/75	G	33		

BRØNDBY IF

Coach – Henrik Jensen
Founded – 1964
Stadium – Brøndby Stadion (29,000)
MAJOR HONOURS: Danish League – (10) 1985, 1987, 1988, 1990, 1991, 1996, 1997, 1998, 2002, 2005; Danish Cup – (6) 1989, 1994, 1998, 2003, 2005, 2008.

2010

18/7	Randers	a	2-3	*Krohn-Dehli 2 (1p)*
25/7	AaB	a	2-0	*Larsen, Jensen*
1/8	Midtjylland	h	1-0	*Larsen*
8/8	Nordsjælland	a	3-1	*Krohn-Dehli, Wass, Jensen*
15/8	Esbjerg	h	1-1	*Bischoff*
22/8	OB	h	2-2	*Batata (p), Van der Schaaf*
29/8	Lyngby	a	3-3	*Van der Schaaf 3*
12/9	SønderjyskE	h	3-1	*Wass, Krohn-Dehli 2 (1p)*
19/9	København	a	0-2	
26/9	Silkeborg	h	0-2	
3/10	Horsens	h	0-1	
17/10	Nordsjælland	a	1-1	*McGrath*
24/10	Randers	h	2-1	*Wass, Krohn-Dehli*
31/10	Esbjerg	a	2-1	*Frederiksen, Jensen*
7/11	Midtjylland	h	2-2	*Van der Schaaf, Krohn-Dehli (p)*
14/11	Horsens	a	1-2	*Krohn-Dehli (p)*
21/11	AaB	a	2-1	*Agger, Jensen*
28/11	OB	h	2-0	*Farnerud, Krohn-Dehli*
5/12	Silkeborg	a	2-2	*Farnerud 2*

2011

6/3	Lyngby	h	1-1	*Wass*
13/3	SønderjyskE	h	2-0	*Nilsson, Wass*
20/3	København	a	1-3	*Agger*
3/4	Silkeborg	h	2-2	*Gehrt, Krohn-Dehli (p)*
10/4	OB	a	1-1	*Nilsson*
17/4	AaB	h	1-2	*Wass*
21/4	Esbjerg	h	3-0	*Goodson, Jensen, Agger*
25/4	Randers	a	4-0	*Gehrt, Agger 2, Krohn-Dehli*
1/5	Horsens	h	0-0	
8/5	København	h	1-1	*Van der Schaaf*
15/5	Midtjylland	a	0-1	
20/5	Lyngby	a	2-1	*Agger 2*
25/5	Nordsjælland	h	1-1	*Goodson*
29/5	SønderjyskE	a	2-0	*og (Østli), Krohn-Dehli*

No	Name	Nat	DoB	Pos	Aps	(s)	Gls
18	Nicolaj AGGER		23/10/88	A	21	(5)	7
38	Osama AKHARRAZ		26/11/90	A	1	(3)	
16	Stephan ANDERSEN		26/11/81	G	21		
11	Bruno Fressato Cardoso "BATATA"	BRA	26/9/84	A		(4)	1
10	Martin BERNBURG		26/12/85	A	4	(2)	
24	Mikkel BISCHOFF		3/2/82	D	5	(2)	1
9	Alexander FARNERUD	SWE	1/5/84	A	12	(5)	3
5	Jan FREDERIKSEN		20/6/82	D	18	(2)	1
39	Mathias GEHRT		7/6/92	A	10	(2)	2
7	Clarence GOODSON	USA	17/5/82	D	9	(1)	2

No	Name	Nat	DoB	Pos	Aps	(s)	Gls
22	Ousman JALLOW	GAM	21/10/88	A	11	(10)	
28	Paul JATTA	GAM	21/2/91	M	1	(12)	
26	Mike JENSEN		19/2/88	M	32		5
27	Jan KRISTIANSEN		4/8/81	M	19	(9)	
23	Michael KROHN-DEHLI		6/6/83	M	28	(1)	12
39/17	Jens LARSEN		21/2/91	M	13	(7)	2
13	Peter MADSEN		26/4/78	A		(2)	
32	Brent McGRATH	AUS	18/6/91	A	4	(6)	1
36	Kristoffer MUNKSGAARD		1/1/90	M		(1)	
8	Mikael NILSSON	SWE	24/6/78	M	32		2
2	Anders RANDRUP		16/7/88	D	13	(9)	
21	Thomas RASMUSSEN		16/4/77	D	15	(3)	
19	Daniel STENDERUP		31/5/89	D	20	(2)	
1	Michael TØRNES		8/1/86	G	12		
4	Remco VAN DER SCHAAF	NED	28/2/79	D	13	(7)	6
3	Max VON SCHLEBRÜGGE	SWE	1/2/77	D	20	(1)	
29	Daniel WASS		31/5/89	D	29	(3)	6

ESBJERG FB

Coach – Ove Pedersen; (14/3/11) Jess Thorup

Founded – 1924

Stadium – Blue Water Arena (13,282)

MAJOR HONOURS: Danish League – (5) 1961, 1962, 1963, 1965, 1979; Danish Cup – (2) 1964, 1976.

2010

17/7	OB	a	0-3	
24/7	København	h	1-2	*Conboy*
31/7	SønderjyskE	a	0-3	
7/8	Midtjylland	h	0-3	
15/8	Brøndby	a	1-1	*Lange*
21/8	AaB	a	2-0	*Janssen, Lange*
28/8	Silkeborg	h	2-1	*Smárason, Høgh*
12/9	Lyngby	h	2-3	*Rieks, Janssen*
19/9	Horsens	a	3-0	*og (Nøhr), Vendelbo, Janssen*
26/9	Randers	h	2-2	*Lange, Ankersen*
3/10	Nordsjælland	h	1-1	*Vendelbo*
17/10	Horsens	a	1-1	*Rieks*
23/10	Midtjylland	a	2-2	*Vendelbo, Janssen*
31/10	Brøndby	h	1-2	*Janssen*
6/11	AaB	a	1-1	*Ankersen*
13/11	OB	h	1-2	*Rieks*
21/11	Silkeborg	a	1-1	*Janssen*
28/11	Lyngby	h	0-0	
4/12	København	a	1-3	*Lange*

2011

6/3	SønderjyskE	h	0-1	
13/3	Randers	h	1-3	*Rieks*
20/3	Nordsjælland	a	2-1	*Smárason, Lange*
2/4	København	h	1-1	*Janssen*
11/4	Lyngby	a	2-1	*Smárason, Rieks*
16/4	Silkeborg	h	1-1	*Rieks*
21/4	Brøndby	a	0-3	
24/4	Midtjylland	h	0-1	
2/5	OB	a	0-1	
8/5	Nordsjælland	h	2-0	*Lange 2*
15/5	AaB	h	0-0	
19/5	SønderjyskE	a	1-2	*Ankersen*
25/5	Horsens	h	2-1	*Ankersen, Lange*
29/5	Randers	a	2-2	*Lange, Janssen*

No	Name	Nat	DoB	Pos	Aps	(s)	Gls
21	Sebastian Lykke ANDERSEN		23/12/88	M	5	(9)	
19	Jakob ANKERSEN		22/9/90	M	5	(12)	4
32	Martin BRAITHWAITE		5/6/91	A	6	(10)	
20	Kennie CHOPART		1/6/90	A		(2)	
13	Kevin CONBOY		15/10/87	D	28	(2)	1
4	Davidson DROBO-AMPEM	GER	26/3/88	D	1	(4)	
5	Thomas GAARDSØE		23/11/79	D	10		
2	Kian HANSEN		3/3/89	D	15	(4)	
1	Lukas HRADECKY	FIN	24/11/89	G	13		
24	Nicolai HØGH		9/11/83	D	27	(1)	1
10	Tim JANSSEN	NED	6/3/86	A	23	(6)	8
7	Jesper JØRGENSEN		9/5/84	M	18		
6	Morten KARLSEN		25/3/79	M	13	(1)	
23	Jonas KNUDSEN		16/9/92	D	4	(1)	
22	Jesper LANGE		11/1/86	A	15	(14)	9
18	Jeppe MEHL		21/9/86	M	27	(3)	
11	Peter NYMANN Mikkelsen		22/8/82	D	26	(5)	
7	Johan PERSSON	SWE	20/6/84	M	1	(3)	
29	Martin RAUSCHENBERG		15/1/92	D	4		
31	Søren RIEKS		7/4/87	A	27		6
3	Fredrik RISP	SWE	15/12/80	D	22		
6	Mikael RYNELL	SWE	25/2/82	M		(1)	
9	Arnór SMÁRASON	ISL	7/9/88	M	20	(4)	3
17	Kevin Bechmann TIMM		9/7/89	A		(4)	
26	Mikkel VENDELBO		15/8/87	M	32		3
25	Mikkel VESTERGAARD		22/11/92	A	1	(1)	
16	Lars WINDE		3/12/75	G	20		

AC HORSENS

Coach – Johnny Mølby

Founded – 1994

Stadium – Casa Arena (6,000)

2010

18/7	Midtjylland	h	0-2	
24/7	Lyngby	a	0-1	
2/8	OB	h	1-0	*Rasmussen*
8/8	Randers	h	0-0	
15/8	Silkeborg	a	2-1	*Spelmann 2*
22/8	SønderjyskE	a	0-2	
29/8	København	h	1-2	*Lodberg*
12/9	AaB	a	3-2	*Macena 2, Kryger*
19/9	Esbjerg	h	0-3	
26/9	Nordsjælland	a	0-3	
3/10	Brøndby	a	1-0	*Macena*
17/10	Esbjerg	h	1-1	*Kryger*
24/10	Lyngby	a	2-0	*Macena, Nakajima-Farran*
31/10	Midtjylland	h	0-2	
7/11	København	a	0-4	
14/11	Brøndby	h	2-1	*Rasmussen, Kortegaard*
21/11	SønderjyskE	a	3-0	*Macena 2, Nakajima-Farran*
29/11	AaB	h	0-0	
5/12	Nordsjælland	a	1-2	*Nakajima-Farran*

2011

7/3	OB	h	2-1	*Lodberg (p), Kortegaard*
13/3	Silkeborg	a	1-2	*Drachmann*
20/3	Randers	h	0-0	
3/4	Nordsjælland	h	0-0	
10/4	AaB	a	0-0	
17/4	SønderjyskE	h	1-1	*Aslam*
21/4	Midtjylland	a	0-1	
25/4	Lyngby	h	2-0	*Hajdarević, Nakajima-Farran*
1/5	Brøndby	a	0-0	
8/5	Randers	a	0-1	
16/5	København	h	1-1	*Macena*
19/5	OB	a	3-3	*Lodberg (p), Kortegaard, Hajdarević*
25/5	Esbjerg	a	1-2	*Macena*
29/5	Silkeborg	h	1-2	*Lodberg (p)*

No	Name	Nat	DoB	Pos	Aps	(s)	Gls
19	Mads AGESEN		17/3/83	D	11	(2)	
12	Sebastian Lykke ANDERSEN		23/12/88	M	8	(5)	

	Nabil ASLAM		3/8/84	D	21		1
2	Andreas AUGUSTSSON	SWE	26/11/76	D	18		
9	André BJERREGAARD		3/9/91	M	1	(5)	
3	Tonny BROCHMANN		27/11/90	M		(5)	
0	Janus DRACHMANN		11/5/88	M	11	(16)	1
5	Kenan HAJDAREVIĆ	BIH	29/1/90	A	7	(9)	2
6	Troels Kløve HALLSTRØM		23/10/90	M		(4)	
	Allan Kierstein JEPSEN		4/7/77	D	5	(5)	
	Søren JOCHUMSEN		1/8/76	G	33		
6	Alioune KÉBÉ	SEN	24/11/84	A		(1)	
3	Thomas KORTEGAARD		2/7/84	M	32		3
5	Lasse KRYGER		3/11/82	M	16	(6)	2
2	Ulrik LINDKVIST		5/3/81	D	1	(1)	
1	Niels LODBERG		14/10/80	M	25	(4)	4
	Gilberto MACENA	BRA	1/4/84	A	32		8
8	Jimmy MAYASI		6/6/87	A	1	(7)	
	Simon NAGEL		5/7/85	M		(5)	
	Issey NAKAJIMA-FARRAN	CAN	16/5/84	A	19	(9)	4
	Anders NØHR		3/9/81	D	31		
	Morten RASMUSSEN		26/3/85	D	29		2
4	Martin RETOV		5/5/80	M	32	(1)	
0	Martin SPELMANN		21/3/87	M	30		2

FC KØBENHAVN

Coach – Ståle Solbakken (NOR)

Founded – 1992

Stadium – Parken (38,065)

MAJOR HONOURS: Danish League – (9) 1993, 2001, 2003, 2004, 2006, 2007, 2009, 2010, 2011; Danish Cup – (4) 1995, 1997, 2004, 2009.

2010				
18/7	SønderjyskE	a	3-1	*og (Larsen), og (Østli), Vingaard*
24/7	Esbjerg	a	2-1	*César Santin, Vingaard*
31/7	AaB	h	1-1	*César Santin (p)*
8/8	OB	a	3-2	*N'Doye 2, Grønkjær*
14/8	Nordsjælland	h	2-0	*N'Doye 2*
21/8	Lyngby	h	3-0	*Wendt, N'Doye, César Santin*
29/8	Horsens	a	2-1	*Ottesen, Vingaard*
11/9	Silkeborg	h	2-2	*César Santin, N'Doye*
19/9	Brøndby	h	2-0	*César Santin 2 (1p)*
25/9	Midtjylland	a	3-0	*Pospěch, Claudemir, N'Doye*
3/10	Randers	h	1-0	*N'Doye*
17/10	OB	h	5-0	*César Santin 3, Vingaard, N'Doye*
24/10	Silkeborg	a	3-0	*César Santin, Vingaard, Bolaños*
30/10	Lyngby	h	3-2	*Zohore, Nordstrand, Ottesen*
7/11	Horsens	h	4-0	*César Santin, Vingaard, Bolaños, Jørgensen M.*
14/11	SønderjyskE	a	3-3	*N'Doye 2, Vingaard*
21/11	Nordsjælland	h	2-1	*Claudemir, César Santin (p)*
28/11	Randers	a	3-0	*César Santin, Pospěch, Grønkjær*
4/12	Esbjerg	h	3-1	*N'Doye 2, Pospěch*
2011				
6/3	Midtjylland	a	0-2	
12/3	AaB	a	1-0	*Bolaños*
20/3	Brøndby	h	3-1	*César Santin, N'Doye, Grønkjær*
2/4	Esbjerg	a	1-1	*César Santin*
9/4	Randers	h	3-1	*N'Doye 2, Pospěch*
17/4	Nordsjælland	a	3-1	*N'Doye 2, Claudemir*
21/4	Lyngby	a	2-1	*Bolaños, N'Doye*
25/4	Silkeborg	h	2-0	*Claudemir, Bolaños*
1/5	SønderjyskE	h	3-0	*Kristensen, N'Doye 2*
8/5	Brøndby	a	1-1	*N'Doye*
16/5	Horsens	a	1-1	*Delaney*
19/5	Midtjylland	h	5-2	*N'Doye 3, Bolaños, César Santin*
25/5	OB	a	0-3	
29/5	AaB	h	2-0	*César Santin, Grønkjær*

No	Name	Nat	DoB	Pos	Aps	(s)	Gls
22	Johan ABSALONSEN		16/9/85	M	1	(2)	
7	AÍLTON José Almeida	BRA	20/8/84	A	1		
15	Mikael ANTONSSON	SWE	31/5/81	D	28		
3	Pierre BENGTSSON	SWE	12/4/88	D	5	(1)	
7	Martin BERGVOLD		20/2/84	M	1	(5)	
30	Christian BOLAÑOS	CRC	17/5/84	M	22	(2)	6
11	CÉSAR SANTIN	BRA	24/2/81	A	21	(6)	17
1	Kim CHRISTENSEN		16/7/79	G	1		
6	CLAUDEMIR Domingues de Souza	BRA	27/3/88	M	31	(1)	4
27	Thomas DELANEY		3/9/91	M	4	(12)	1
23	Søren FREDERIKSEN		8/7/89	A		(2)	
10	Jesper GRØNKJÆR		12/8/77	M	18	(7)	4
24	Jos HOOIVELD	NED	22/4/83	D	7	(4)	
25	Mathias "Zanka" JØRGENSEN		23/4/90	D	23	(2)	1
8	William Kvist JØRGENSEN		24/2/85	M	29	(4)	
16	Thomas KRISTENSEN		17/4/83	M	15	(12)	1
14	Dame N'DOYE	SEN	21/2/85	A	31		25
9	Morten NORDSTRAND		8/6/83	A		(4)	1
4	Hjalte Bo NØRREGAARD		8/4/81	M	4	(6)	
5	Sölvi Geir OTTESEN	ISL	18/2/84	D	8	(5)	2
19	Bryan OVIEDO	CRC	18/2/90	D		(1)	
28	Saban ÖZDOGAN		14/3/90	M		(4)	
2	Zdeněk POSPĚCH	CZE	14/12/78	D	33		4
20	Martin VINGAARD		20/3/85	M	15	(6)	7
17	Oscar WENDT	SWE	24/10/85	D	28	(1)	1
21	Johan WILAND	SWE	24/1/81	G	32		
18	Kenneth Dahrup ZOHORE		31/1/94	A	5	(10)	1

LYNGBY BK

Coach – Niels Frederiksen

Founded – 1921

Stadium – Lyngby Stadion (12,000)

MAJOR HONOURS: Danish League – (2) 1983, 1992; Danish Cup – (3) 1984, 1985, 1990.

2010				
19/7	AaB	h	2-4	*Bertolt, Brandrup*
25/7	Horsens	h	1-0	*Aabech (p)*
1/8	Silkeborg	a	2-2	*Aabech, Sørensen*
8/8	SønderjyskE	h	1-0	*Aabech*
15/8	Randers	a	1-2	*Rise*
21/8	København	a	0-3	
29/8	Brøndby	h	3-3	*Larsen, Mortensen, Sørensen*
12/9	Esbjerg	a	3-2	*Mortensen 2, Aabech*
20/9	Nordsjælland	h	2-0	*Aabech, Larsen*
27/9	OB	a	1-3	*Larsen*
2/10	Midtjylland	a	2-1	*Aabech, Larsen*
17/10	Silkeborg	h	1-1	*Sørensen*
24/10	Horsens	h	0-2	
30/10	København	a	2-3	*Aabech, Rise*
7/11	SønderjyskE	h	1-0	*Aabech (p)*
14/11	Nordsjælland	a	1-2	*Rise (p)*
20/11	Randers	h	3-3	*Rise, Aabech, Mortensen*
28/11	Esbjerg	a	0-0	
2011				
6/3	Brøndby	a	1-1	*Christiansen*
14/3	OB	a	0-2	
20/3	AaB	h	1-2	*Boysen*
4/4	Midtjylland	a	4-4	*Aabech 2 (1p), Madsen 2*
11/4	Esbjerg	h	1-2	*Fetai*
14/4	Midtjylland	h	1-0	*Bech*
17/4	Randers	a	1-1	*Aabech*
21/4	København	h	1-2	*Madsen*
25/4	Horsens	a	0-2	
1/5	Nordsjælland	h	1-0	*Fetai*

6/5	AaB	a	1-2	*Fetai*
15/5	SønderjyskE	a	0-1	
20/5	Brøndby	h	1-2	*og (Randrup)*
25/5	Silkeborg	a	1-0	*Hamalainen*
29/5	OB	h	2-0	*Hamalainen, Larsen*

No	Name	Nat	DoB	Pos	Aps	(s)	Gls
10	Kim AABECH		31/5/83	A	32		12
12	Emmanuel AKE	KEN	11/6/80	A		(1)	
25	Uffe Manich BECH		13/1/93	A	3	(9)	1
18	Morten BERTOLT		12/2/84	M	30		1
12	David BOYSEN		30/4/91	A	7	(4)	1
20	Jeppe BRANDRUP		3/6/85	D	19	(3)	1
4	Jakob BRESEMANN		22/10/76	D	11	(2)	
21	Anders Bleg CHRISTIANSEN		8/6/90	M	31	(1)	1
6	Jacob EGERIS		19/5/90	D	2		
9	Bajram FETAI	MKD	7/9/85	A	11	(2)	3
23	Brian HAMALAINEN		29/5/89	D	33		2
24	Esben HANSEN		10/8/81	M	7	(11)	
19	Jonas HENRIKSEN		6/3/91	A		(6)	
31	Nicklas Wier HØJLUND		6/3/90	G	7		
8	Kasper KRISTENSEN		27/3/86	M	2	(8)	
15	Emil LARSEN		22/6/91	M	18	(6)	5
8	Peter MADSEN		26/4/78	A	12	(3)	3
13	Nicolai MELCHIORSEN		9/3/84	M		(1)	
6	Mitja MÖREC	SVN	21/2/83	D	3	(2)	
11	Patrick MORTENSEN		13/9/89	A	19	(8)	4
3	Marc MØLLER		7/6/86	D	23	(5)	
1	Rune PEDERSEN		9/10/79	G	26		
5	Morten PETERSEN		27/5/78	D	8	(3)	
9	Lasse RISE		9/6/86	M	17	(1)	4
2	Cheikh SARR		15/3/87	D	14	(2)	
7	Ayoub SØRENSEN		12/4/88	M	6	(13)	3
14	Mathias TAUBER		24/8/84	D	22	(5)	

FC MIDTJYLLAND

Coach – Allan Kuhn; (15/4/11) Glen Riddersholm

Founded – 1999

Stadium – MCH Arena (11,809)

2010				
18/7	Horsens	a	2-0	*Kristensen F. 2*
24/7	Silkeborg	h	2-0	*Olsen (p), Ilsø*
1/8	Brøndby	a	0-1	
7/8	Esbjerg	a	3-0	*Kristensen F., Igboun, Hassan*
16/8	AaB	h	2-1	*Kristensen J.J., Kristensen F.*
23/8	Nordsjælland	h	4-0	*Uzochukwu, Fagerberg, Borring, Kristensen F.*
30/8	OB	a	1-2	*Igboun*
13/9	Randers	h	1-1	*Kristensen F.*
19/9	SønderjyskE	a	2-0	*Kristensen F., Olsen*
25/9	København	h	0-3	
2/10	Lyngby	h	1-2	*Olsen (p)*
18/10	Randers	a	1-1	*Thygesen*
23/10	Esbjerg	h	2-2	*Ilsø 2*
31/10	Horsens	a	2-0	*Thygesen 2*
7/11	Brøndby	a	2-2	*Priske, Thygesen*
13/11	AaB	h	2-2	*Olsen, Igboun*
22/11	OB	a	2-3	*Ilsø, Thygesen*
27/11	Silkeborg	h	2-1	*Albrechtsen, Borring*
2011				
6/3	København	h	2-0	*Poulsen (p), Thygesen*
12/3	Nordsjælland	h	2-2	*Albæk, Uzochukwu*
21/3	SønderjyskE	a	1-2	*Igboun*
4/4	Lyngby	h	4-4	*Thygesen 2, Fagerberg, Nielsen*
9/4	Silkeborg	a	0-1	
14/4	Lyngby	a	0-1	
18/4	OB	h	1-1	*Olsen*
21/4	Horsens	h	1-0	*Sivebæk*
24/4	Esbjerg	a	1-0	*og (Høgh)*
30/4	AaB	a	0-2	
9/5	SønderjyskE	h	2-1	*Igboun, Lauridsen*
15/5	Brøndby	h	1-0	*Igboun*
19/5	København	a	2-5	*Albrechtsen, Albæk (p)*
25/5	Randers	h	2-2	*Poulsen, Thygesen*
29/5	Nordsjælland	a	0-0	

No	Name	Nat	DoB	Pos	Aps	(s)	Gls
5	Martin ALBRECHTSEN		31/3/80	D	20		2
17	Mads Winther ALBÆK		14/1/90	M	16	(4)	2
30	Babajide Collins BABATUNDE	NGA	2/12/88	A		(1)	
8	Jonas BORRING		4/1/85	M	16	(12)	2
41	Rasmus Lynge CHRISTENSEN		12/8/91	M		(1)	
24	Ken FAGERBERG	SWE	9/1/89	A	5	(9)	2
21	Kasper HANSEN		15/2/91	M	4	(1)	
36	Rilwan Olanrewaju HASSAN	NGA	9/2/91	M	17	(11)	1
22	Mads HVILSOM		23/8/92	A	3	(3)	
44	Sylvester IGBOUN	NGA	8/9/90	A	26	(5)	6
7	Ken ILSØ		2/12/86	A	11	(3)	4
20	Kristijan IPŠA	CRO	4/4/86	D	16	(3)	
14	Kasper JENSEN		7/10/82	G	3	(1)	
23	Frank KRISTENSEN		10/3/77	A	13	(1)	7
6	Jesper Juelsgård KRISTENSEN		26/1/89	D	32		1
15	Jesper LAURIDSEN		27/3/91	D	4	(1)	1
1	Jonas LÖSSL		1/2/89	G	30		
33	Alexander LUDWIG		30/6/93	D	1		
32	Kristian Bak NIELSEN		20/10/82	D	17		1
11	Danny OLSEN		11/6/85	M	14	(10)	5
26	Jesper Bøge PEDERSEN		22/2/90	D		(2)	
9	Jakob POULSEN		7/7/83	M	12	(4)	2
3	Brian PRISKE		14/5/77	D	16	(1)	1
29	Winston REID	NZL	3/7/88	D	1		
27	Adigun Taofeek SALAMI	NGA	6/5/88	M	11	(4)	
34	Christian SIVEBÆK		19/2/88	M	10	(9)	1
18	Erik SVIATCHENKO		4/10/91	D	11	(2)	
10	Mikkel THYGESEN		22/10/84	M	28	(2)	9
43	Izunna Arnest UZOCHUKWU	NGA	11/4/90	M	26	(4)	2

FC NORDSJÆLLAND

Coach – Morten Wieghorst

Founded – 2003

Stadium – Farum Park (10,100)

MAJOR HONOURS: Danish Cup – (2) 2010, 2011.

2010				
18/7	Silkeborg	h	4-1	*Nielsen M.L., Nielsen N.B. 2, Stokholm*
25/7	SønderjyskE	h	1-2	*Nielsen M.L.*
1/8	Randers	a	2-0	*Stokholm 2*
8/8	Brøndby	h	1-3	*Fetai*
14/8	København	a	0-2	
23/8	Midtjylland	a	0-4	
29/8	AaB	h	0-0	
11/9	OB	a	1-0	*Gytkjær*
20/9	Lyngby	a	0-2	
26/9	Horsens	h	3-0	*Mikkelsen, Granskov, Lawan*
3/10	Esbjerg	a	1-1	*Mikkelsen*
17/10	Brøndby	h	1-1	*Christensen*
24/10	AaB	a	0-2	
1/11	OB	h	1-4	*Bjelland*
7/11	Silkeborg	a	0-1	
14/11	Lyngby	h	2-1	*Mikkelsen, Bernier*

1/11	København	a	1-2	*Gytkjær*
3/11	SønderjyskE	h	1-1	*Granskov*
/12	Horsens	h	2-1	*Granskov, Due*
011				
/3	Randers	a	0-4	
2/3	Midtjylland	a	2-2	*Christensen, Nordstrand*
0/3	Esbjerg	h	1-2	*Lyng*
/4	Horsens	a	0-0	
0/4	SønderjyskE	a	2-0	*Laudrup 2*
7/4	København	h	1-3	*Mikkelsen*
1/4	OB	a	2-1	*Nielsen M.L. 2*
4/4	AaB	h	3-3	*Nielsen M.L. 2, Gytkjær*
/5	Lyngby	a	0-1	
/5	Esbjerg	a	0-2	
5/5	Silkeborg	h	3-2	*Lawan 2, Stokholm (p)*
8/5	Randers	h	2-1	*Nielsen M.L., Laudrup*
5/5	Brøndby	a	1-1	*Lawan*
9/5	Midtjylland	h	0-0	

lo	Name	Nat	DoB	Pos	Aps	(s)	Gls
	Enoch Kofi ADU	GHA	14/9/90	M	25	(4)	
9	Oguzhan AYNAOGLU		22/3/92	M	1	(1)	
7	Pierre BENGTSSON	SWE	12/4/88	D	19		
	Patrice BERNIER	CAN	23/9/79	M	15	(7)	1
	Andreas BJELLAND		11/7/88	D	23	(1)	1
7	Søren CHRISTENSEN		29/6/86	M	18	(3)	2
4	Anders DUE		17/3/82	M	7	(3)	1
5	Bajram FETAI	MKD	7/9/85	A	6	(7)	1
4	Andreas GRANSKOV		5/3/89	A	11	(16)	3
9	Mark GUNDELACH		7/1/92	D		(1)	
21	Christian GYTKJÆR		6/5/90	A	14	(5)	3
	Jesper HANSEN		31/3/85	G	33		
23	Daniel JENSEN		8/5/85	D	14	(5)	
4	Henrik KILDENTOFT		18/3/85	D	28	(1)	
22	Andreas LAUDRUP		10/11/90	M	10	(13)	3
12	Rawez LAWAN	SWE	4/10/87	A	12	(11)	4
15	Emil LYNG		3/8/89	A	4		1
9	Tobias MIKKELSEN		18/9/86	M	27	(1)	4
30	Mathias NIELSEN		2/3/91	D		(1)	
20	Matti Lund NIELSEN		8/5/88	M	20	(6)	7
16	Nicki Bille NIELSEN		7/2/88	A	4	(1)	2
11	Morten NORDSTRAND		8/6/83	A	3	(6)	1
31	Jores OKORE		11/8/92	M	10	(1)	
14	Bryan OVIEDO	CRC	18/2/90	D	14		
18	Michael PARKHURST	USA	24/1/84	D	20	(1)	
33	Philip RASMUSSEN		12/1/89	M		(1)	
7	Nicolai STOKHOLM		1/4/76	M	24	(1)	4
13	Mads THOMSEN		15/3/89	A	1		

ODENSE BK

Coach – Lars Olsen; (14/9/10) (Uffe Pedersen); (7/11/10) Henrik Clausen

Founded – 1887

Stadium – TRE-FOR Park (15,761)

MAJOR HONOURS: Danish League – (3) 1977, 1982, 1989; Danish Cup – (5) 1983, 1991, 1993, 2002, 2007.

2010				
17/7	Esbjerg	h	3-0	*Johansson, Andreasen, Gíslason*
26/7	Randers	h	1-1	*Andreasen*
2/8	Horsens	a	0-1	
8/8	København	h	2-3	*Gíslason, Andreasen*
14/8	SønderjyskE	a	3-1	*Andreasen 2, Utaka*
22/8	Brøndby	a	2-2	*Andreasen, Utaka*
30/8	Midtjylland	h	2-1	*Andreasen, Utaka*
11/9	Nordsjælland	h	0-1	
19/9	Silkeborg	a	1-3	*Utaka*
27/9	Lyngby	h	3-1	*Andreasen, Sørensen (p), Gíslason*
4/10	AaB	a	2-1	*Utaka 2*
17/10	København	a	0-5	
25/10	SønderjyskE	h	1-2	*Gíslason*
1/11	Nordsjælland	a	4-1	*Absalonsen, Traoré, Ruud, Andreasen*
8/11	Randers	h	1-0	*Utaka*
13/11	Esbjerg	a	2-1	*Traoré, Toft*
22/11	Midtjylland	h	3-2	*Utaka, og (Sviatchenko), Ruud*
28/11	Brøndby	a	0-2	
4/12	AaB	h	6-0	*Utaka 2, Andreasen, Ruud 2, Toft*
2011				
7/3	Horsens	a	1-2	*Kadrii*
14/3	Lyngby	h	2-0	*Jensen, og (Pedersen)*
19/3	Silkeborg	a	1-1	*Ruud*
2/4	AaB	a	1-0	*Utaka*
10/4	Brøndby	h	1-1	*Håland*
18/4	Midtjylland	a	1-1	*Traoré*
21/4	Nordsjælland	h	1-2	*Utaka*
25/4	SønderjyskE	a	2-0	*Traoré, Gíslason*
2/5	Esbjerg	h	1-0	*Johansson*
8/5	Silkeborg	h	0-0	
14/5	Randers	a	2-1	*Utaka, Andreasen (p)*
19/5	Horsens	h	3-3	*Høegh, Andreasen, Johansson*
25/5	København	h	3-0	*Ruud, Johansson, Utaka*
29/5	Lyngby	a	0-2	

No	Name	Nat	DoB	Pos	Aps	(s)	Gls
11	Johan ABSALONSEN		16/9/85	M	13		1
4	Hans Henrik ANDREASEN		10/1/79	M	32		12
17	Lucas de Deus Santos "CACÁ"	BRA	9/10/82	A		(3)	
30	Roy CARROLL	NIR	30/9/77	G	18		
5	Anders Møller CHRISTENSEN		26/7/77	D	33		
22	Njogu DEMBA-NYRÉN	GAM	26/6/79	A	1	(6)	
19	Eric DJEMBA-DJEMBA	CMR	4/5/81	M	24	(2)	
25	Oliver FELDBALLE		3/4/90	A	2	(14)	
21	Rúrik GÍSLASON	ISL	25/2/88	M	19	(3)	5
30	Alexander Lund HANSEN	NOR	6/10/82	G	1	(2)	
8	Henrik HANSEN		28/7/79	M		(3)	
6	Thomas HELVEG		24/6/71	D	3	(3)	
26	Daniel HØEGH		6/1/91	D	10	(2)	1
3	Atle Roar HÅLAND	NOR	26/7/77	D	22		1
9	Rasmus Falk JENSEN		15/1/92	M	7	(5)	1
10	Andreas JOHANSSON	SWE	5/7/78	M	23	(5)	4
24	Bashkim KADRII		9/7/91	A	16	(5)	1
35	Oliver LARSEN		12/11/91	D		(1)	
22	Bernard MENDY	FRA	20/8/81	D	7	(4)	
16	Emil OUSAGER		19/7/87	G		(1)	
2	Espen RUUD	NOR	28/2/84	D	32		6
15	Chris SØRENSEN		27/7/77	D	21	(3)	1
13	Henrik TOFT		15/4/81	A	9	(16)	2
17	Mads TOPPEL		30/1/82	G	1		
18	Mohamed Kalilou TRAORÉ	MLI	9/9/87	M	23	(3)	4
14	Jonas TROEST		4/3/85	D	1	(1)	
7	Peter UTAKA	NGA	12/2/84	A	32		14
33	Stefan WESSELS	GER	28/2/79	G	13		
38	Andreas WINDING		16/2/91	M		(1)	

RANDERS FC

Coach – Ove Christensen; (26/4/11) (Peter Elstrup)

Founded – 1898

Stadium – AutoC Park (12,000)

MAJOR HONOURS: Danish Cup – (4) 1967, 1968, 1973, 2006.

2010				
18/7	Brøndby	h	3-2	*Fischer, Movsisyan, Berg*
26/7	OB	a	1-1	*Cramer*
1/8	Nordsjælland	h	0-2	
8/8	Horsens	a	0-0	
15/8	Lyngby	h	2-1	*Movsisyan, Berg*
22/8	Silkeborg	a	1-1	*Cramer*
29/8	SønderjyskE	h	0-0	
13/9	Midtjylland	a	1-1	*Movsisyan*
18/9	AaB	h	2-3	*Sarr, Ahmed*
26/9	Esbjerg	a	2-2	*Berg, Fischer*
4/10	København	a	0-1	
18/10	Midtjylland	h	1-1	*Movsisyan (p)*
24/10	Brøndby	a	1-2	*Movsisyan*
30/10	AaB	h	0-0	
8/11	OB	a	0-1	
14/11	Silkeborg	h	4-0	*og (Poulsen), Kamper, Sarr 2*
20/11	Lyngby	a	3-3	*Sane, Egholm, Jensen S.*
28/11	København	h	0-3	
5/12	SønderjyskE	a	1-1	*Pedersen S.*
2011				
6/3	Nordsjælland	h	4-0	*Lorentzen, Jensen S., Kristensen, Kamper*
13/3	Esbjerg	a	3-1	*Kamper 3*
20/3	Horsens	a	0-0	
3/4	SønderjyskE	h	0-0	
9/4	København	a	1-3	*Sarr*
17/4	Lyngby	h	1-1	*Beckmann*
20/4	AaB	a	1-4	*Beckmann*
25/4	Brøndby	h	0-4	
1/5	Silkeborg	a	2-2	*Lorentzen, Beckmann*
8/5	Horsens	h	1-0	*Cramer*
14/5	OB	h	1-2	*Lorentzen*
18/5	Nordsjælland	a	1-2	*og (Okore)*
25/5	Midtjylland	a	2-2	*Rise, Jensen S.*
29/5	Esbjerg	h	2-2	*Kamper 2*

No	Name	Nat	DoB	Pos	Aps	(s)	Gls
4	Issah AHMED	GHA	24/5/82	D	16	(6)	1
11/10	Mikkel BECKMANN		24/10/83	A	14	(3)	3
10	Søren BERG		15/5/76	M	19		3
39	Mikkel CRAMER		25/1/92	D	5	(14)	3
12	Jonas DAMBORG		17/4/86	M	5	(5)	
5	Anders EGHOLM		15/5/83	D	26		1
11	Erton FEJZULLAHU	SWE	13/3/88	A	4	(3)	
13	Mads FENGER		10/9/90	D	16		
21	Alexander FISCHER		16/9/86	M	20	(7)	2
6	Rasmus Grønborg HANSEN		12/4/86	M	7	(7)	
24	Tijan JAITEH	GAM	31/12/88	M	11	(2)	
25	Peter Friis JENSEN		2/5/88	G	4		
16	Søren JENSEN		1/3/84	D	31		3
17	Jonas KAMPER		3/5/83	M	16	(10)	7
6	Morten KARLSEN		25/3/79	M	15	(1)	
20	Frank KRISTENSEN		10/3/77	A	6	(3)	1
7	Kasper LORENTZEN		19/11/85	M	31		3
9	Yura MOVSISYAN	ARM	2/8/87	A	15	(2)	5
18	George ODHIAMBO	KEN	31/12/92	A		(1)	
15	Ricki OLSEN		21/10/88	M	2	(9)	
1	David OUSTED		1/2/85	G	29		
3	Marc PEDERSEN		31/7/89	D	3		
8	Søren PEDERSEN		2/11/78	D	31		1
9	Lasse RISE		9/6/86	M	9	(3)	1
31	Tidiane SANE	SEN	10/7/85	M	11	(3)	1
23	Ousmane SARR	SEN	2/9/86	A	11	(10)	4
15	Christian TRAORÉ		18/4/82	D	6	(1)	

SILKEBORG IF

Coach – Troels Bech

Founded – 1917

Stadium – Silkeborg Stadion (9,200)

MAJOR HONOURS: Danish League – (1) 1994; Danish Cup – (1) 2001.

2010				
18/7	Nordsjælland	a	1-4	*Mikkelsen*
24/7	Midtjylland	a	0-2	
1/8	Lyngby	h	2-2	*Lekic, Bech*
7/8	AaB	a	0-0	
15/8	Horsens	h	1-2	*Lekic (p)*
22/8	Randers	h	1-1	*Hansen T.*
28/8	Esbjerg	a	1-2	*Bech*
11/9	København	a	2-2	*Svensson, Saag*
19/9	OB	h	3-1	*Bech, Larsen, Holst*
26/9	Brøndby	a	2-0	*Saag, Holst*
3/10	SønderjyskE	h	3-1	*Bech, Larsen, Svensson*
17/10	Lyngby	a	1-1	*Bech*
24/10	København	h	0-3	
31/10	SønderjyskE	a	2-1	*Bech, og (Østli)*
7/11	Nordsjælland	h	1-0	*Pedersen*
14/11	Randers	a	0-4	
21/11	Esbjerg	h	1-1	*Holst*
27/11	Midtjylland	a	1-2	*Hansen F.*
5/12	Brøndby	h	2-2	*Hansen F., Larsen*
2011				
5/3	AaB	a	1-1	*Lekic (p)*
13/3	Horsens	h	2-1	*Saag, Poulsen*
19/3	OB	h	1-1	*Lekic (p)*
3/4	Brøndby	a	2-2	*Saag, Holst*
9/4	Midtjylland	h	1-0	*Holst*
16/4	Esbjerg	a	1-1	*Bech*
20/4	SønderjyskE	h	1-0	*Svensson*
25/4	København	a	0-2	
1/5	Randers	h	2-2	*Risgård, Saag*
8/5	OB	a	0-0	
15/5	Nordsjælland	a	2-3	*Nielsen, Illum*
20/5	AaB	h	4-3	*og (Petersen), Hansen F., Poulsen, Holst*
25/5	Lyngby	h	0-1	
29/5	Horsens	a	2-1	*Saag 2*

No	Name	Nat	DoB	Pos	Aps	(s)	Gls
10	Jesper BECH		25/5/82	A	23	(1)	7
3	Thomas BÆLUM		5/6/78	D		(5)	
7	Peter DEGN		6/4/77	M		(3)	
14	Dennis FLINTA		14/11/83	D	29		
20	Frank HANSEN		23/2/83	M	33		3
16	Thomas HANSEN		18/1/83	D	10	(14)	1
30	Lasse HEINZE		3/4/86	G	33		
18	Christian Lamhauge HOLST	FRO	25/12/81	M	23	(7)	6
24	Lars HULDGAARD		1/2/89	A	2	(6)	
23	Jeppe ILLUM		25/3/92	A	2	(5)	1
29	Simon JAKOBSEN		17/11/90	D	21	(2)	
4	Jim LARSEN		6/11/85	D	16		3
8	Rajko LEKIC		3/7/81	A	11	(8)	4
2	Jesper MIKKELSEN		26/6/80	M	5	(4)	1
6	Martin Ørnskov NIELSEN		10/10/85	M	30		1
11	Henrik "Tømrer" PEDERSEN		10/6/75	D	20	(11)	1
5	Christopher POULSEN		11/9/81	D	25	(3)	2
26	Thorbjørn Holst RASMUSSEN		21/3/87	D	29		
21	Kasper RISGÅRD		4/1/83	M	7	(1)	1
17	Kaimar SAAG	EST	5/8/88	A	22	(9)	7
27	Simon SKIBSTED		25/11/91	A		(5)	
22	Martin SVENSSON		10/8/89	M	22	(9)	3
28	Mathias VALENTIN		29/3/89	M		(1)	

SØNDERJYSKE

Coach – Michael Hemmingsen

Founded – 2004

Stadium – Haderslev Fodboldstadion (10,000)

10				
/7	København	h	1-3	*Hansen R.G. (p)*
/7	Nordsjælland	a	2-1	*Østli, Frederiksen*
/7	Esbjerg	h	3-0	*Bødker, og (Conboy), Fabricius*
3	Lyngby	a	0-1	
/8	OB	h	1-3	*Fabricius (p)*
/8	Horsens	h	2-0	*Thomsen, Antipas*
/8	Randers	a	0-0	
2/9	Brøndby	a	1-3	*Fabricius*
/9	Midtjylland	h	0-2	
/9	AaB	a	2-0	*Hansen R.G. 2*
10	Silkeborg	a	1-3	*Larsen*
3/10	AaB	h	1-0	*Jessen*
5/10	OB	a	2-1	*og (Christensen), Fabricius*
/10	Silkeborg	h	1-2	*Antipas*
11	Lyngby	a	0-1	
4/11	København	h	3-3	*Hansen R.G. (p), Kucukovic, Fabricius*
/11	Horsens	h	0-3	
8/11	Nordsjælland	a	1-1	*Kucukovic*
12	Randers	h	1-1	*Kucukovic*
011				
/3	Esbjerg	a	1-0	*Antipas*
3/3	Brøndby	a	0-2	
/3	Midtjylland	h	2-1	*Fabricius 2*
4	Randers	a	0-0	
0/4	Nordsjælland	h	0-2	
7/4	Horsens	a	1-1	*Kucukovic*
0/4	Silkeborg	a	0-1	
5/4	OB	h	0-2	
/5	København	a	0-3	
/5	Midtjylland	a	1-2	*Antipas*
5/5	Lyngby	h	1-0	*Antipas*
9/5	Esbjerg	h	2-1	*Hansen H., Hédinsson*
5/5	AaB	a	2-1	*Frederiksen, Hédinsson*
9/5	Brøndby	h	0-2	

No	Name	Nat	DoB	Pos	Aps	(s)	Gls
0	Quincy ANTIPAS	ZIM	20/4/84	A	19	(8)	5
4	Henrik BØDKER		6/6/83	M	8	(8)	1
5	Thomas CALLESEN		5/7/92	D		(2)	
	Nathan COE	AUS	1/6/84	G	33		
6	Hannes EDER	AUT	5/9/83	D	1	(1)	
1	Kenneth FABRICIUS		3/11/81	A	27	(1)	7
/12	Søren FREDERIKSEN		8/7/89	A	19	(1)	2
3	Henrik HANSEN		28/7/79	M	24		1
8	Rasmus Grønborg HANSEN		12/4/86	M	19		4
8	Eyjólfur HÉDINSSON	ISL	1/1/85	M	14		2
7	Anders HOSTRUP		13/4/90	A		(1)	
9	Mads JESSEN		14/10/89	M	13	(7)	1
9	Mustafa KUCUKOVIC	GER	5/11/86	A	11	(6)	4
13	Michael LARSEN		6/2/83	D	13		1
7	Søren MUUSMANN		29/6/93	D		(1)	
5	Anders NIELSEN		28/9/86	D	11	(2)	
20	Bjørn PAULSEN		2/7/91	A	1	(20)	
26	Andrei SIDORENKOV	EST	12/2/84	D	19	(11)	
22	Ólafur Ingi SKÚLASON	ISL	1/4/83	M	28		
23	Jarl André STORBÆK	NOR	21/9/78	D	30	(1)	
3	Michael STRYGER		15/4/83	D	8	(4)	
6	Johnny THOMSEN		26/2/82	M	33		1
14	Jacob TJØRNELUND		31/12/91	M		(5)	
2	Anders ØSTLI	NOR	8/1/83	D	32		1

TOP GOALSCORERS 2010/11

25	Dame N'DOYE (København)
17	CÉSAR SANTIN (København)
14	Peter UTAKA (OB)
12	Michael KROHN-DEHLI (Brøndby)
	Kim AABECH (Lyngby)
	Hans Henrik ANDREASEN (OB)
9	Jesper LANGE (Esbjerg)
	Mikkel THYGESEN (Midtjylland)
8	Tim JANSSEN (Esbjerg)
	Gilberto MACENA (Horsens)
	Frank KRISTENSEN (Midtjylland/Randers)

PROMOTED CLUBS

AGF ÅRHUS

Coach – Peter Sørensen

Founded – 1880

Stadium – NRGi Park (20,032)

MAJOR HONOURS: Danish League – (5) 1955, 1956, 1957, 1960, 1986; Danish Cup - (9) 1955, 1957, 1960, 1961, 1965, 1987, 1988, 1992, 1996.

HB KØGE

Coach – Aurelijus Skarbalius (LTU)

Founded – 2009

Stadium – SEAS-NVE Park (8,000)

SECOND LEVEL FINAL TABLE 2010/11

		Pld	W	D	L	F	A	Pts
1	AGF Århus	30	22	6	2	66	25	72
2	HB Køge	30	19	4	7	58	35	61
3	Vejle BK	30	14	10	6	49	32	52
4	Skive IK	30	13	8	9	55	47	47
5	Brønshøj BK	30	13	7	10	38	38	46
6	FC Fredericia	30	13	6	11	53	41	45
7	FC Vestsjælland	30	10	12	8	58	57	42
8	FC Roskilde	30	11	9	10	45	45	42
9	Akademisk BK	30	9	10	11	48	49	37
10	Næstved BK	30	8	9	13	43	44	33
11	Viborg FF	30	9	6	15	37	43	33
12	Hobro IK	30	8	9	13	41	55	33
13	FC Hjørring	30	8	9	13	40	57	33
14	Kolding FC	30	6	12	12	38	53	30
15	FC Fyn	30	6	8	16	45	60	26
16	Hvidovre IF	30	6	5	19	36	69	23

DOMESTIC CUP 2010/11

LANDSPOKALTURNERINGEN

SECOND ROUND

(24/8/10)
Aabenraa 1, Hobro 4
Birkerød 1, Brønshøj 4
Blokhus 0, AaB 3
Bolbro 0, Hjørring 5
Hirtshals 2, Skive 4
Lystrup 0, Varde 5
Marienlyst 2, B1908 1
NB Bornholm 0, HIK 1
Ringkøbing 0, Viborg 3
Tuse 0, B93 2
ØB 1, Thisted 3

(25/8/10)
Avedøre 3, Lolland-Falster Alliancen 1 *(aet)*
Brabrand 1, Horsens 4
Elite 3000 Helsingør 1, Vestsjælland 3
FB 2, Svendborg 3 *(aet)*
Fredericia 4, SønderjyskE 0
Fremad Valby 2, Nordvest 5
Fyn 0, Lyngby 1
Gladsaxe-Hero 0, Næstved 1
Jægersborg 0, Hvidovre 1
Kastrup 1, Stenløse 1 *(aet; 5-4 on pens)*
Odder 0, AGF 1
Skovbakken 1, Randers 4
Svebølle 2, HB Køge 4
Vejle 2, Silkeborg 4 *(aet)*
Viby 0, Kolding 0 *(aet; 3-2 on pens)*

(26/8/10)
Skanderborg 1, Midtjylland 3 *(aet)*
Vanløse 0, Nordsjælland 5

Byes – Brøndby, Esbjerg, København, OB

THIRD ROUND

(15/9/10)
B93 0, Silkeborg 5

(22/9/10)

AGF 6, Skive 3 (aet)
Avedøre 2, Midtjylland 3
Brønshøj 0, Hvidovre 1
Hobro 0, Viborg 1
Kastrup 1, Lyngby 2
Marienlyst 0, OB 2
Nordvest 1, Randers 5
Næstved 0, AaB 1
Svendborg 0, Esbjerg 3
Thisted 1, HB Køge 3
Varde 4, Brøndby 2
Vestsjælland 2, Horsens 6 *(aet)*
Viby 1, København 4

(23/9/10)
Hjørring 0, Nordsjælland 1

(29/9/10)
HIK 1, Fredericia 2

FOURTH ROUND

(26/10/10)
HB Køge 0, Midtjylland 4

(27/10/10)
Fredericia 1, Randers 2
Hvidovre 2, Lyngby 2 *(aet; 4-5 on pens)*
København 2, Horsens 4
Varde 0, AGF 1
Viborg 1, AaB 1 *(aet; 4-5 on pens)*

(28/10/10)
Esbjerg 2, Silkeborg 0
OB 2, Nordsjælland 3

QUARTER-FINALS

(9/11/10)
AaB 0, Esbjerg 2 *(Lange 83, Mehl 85)*

(10/11/10)
AGF 0, Midtjylland 1 *(Igboun 40)*

(11/11/10)
Horsens 0, Nordsjælland 1 *(Kildentoft 16)*
Randers 3 *(Sane 1, Cramer 80, Sarr 87)*, Lyngby 0

SEMI-FINALS

(27/4/11 & 5/5/11)
Midtjylland 1 *(Hvilsom 68)*, Esbjerg 2 *(Janssen 28, Lange 53p)*
Esbjerg 1 *(Timm 90)*, Midtjylland 2 *(Thygesen 58, Hassan 60) (aet)*
(3-3; Midtjylland 5-4 on pens)

(28/4/11 & 4/5/11)
Nordsjælland 1 *(Lawan 31)*, Randers 0
Randers 0, Nordsjælland 0
(Nordsjælland 1-0)

FINAL

(22/5/11)
Parken, Copenhagen
FC NORDSJÆLLAND 3 *(Lawan 16, 54, Christensen 90)*
FC MIDTJYLLAND 2 *(Thygesen 37, 71)*
Referee – *Larsen*
NORDSJÆLLAND – *Hansen, Kildentoft, Bjelland, Parkhurst, Oviedo, Okore, Adu (Nielsen M.L. 53), Laudrup (Nordstrand 62), Stokholm, Mikkelsen (Christensen 79), Lawan.*
MIDTJYLLAND – *Lössl, Hansen, Nielsen, Ipša, Kristensen J.J., Olsen (Fagerberg 67), Poulsen, Uzochukwu, Hassan (Borring 90), Thygesen, Igboun.*

CLUB COMMUNICATION 2011/12

alborg BK
rnevej 2
-9000 Aalborg

l	+45 96 355 900
x	+45 96 355 910
eb	aabsport.dk
nail	jtg@aab-as.dk
edia Officer	Brian Andersen

GF Århus
ættens Hus Vest, Stadion Alle 70
-8000 Aarhus C

l	+45 89 386 000
ax	+45 87 331 019
eb	agffodbold.dk
nail	info@agf-as.dk
edia Officer	Ole Hall

røndby IF
øndby Stadion 30
K-2605 Brøndby

el	+45 43 630 810
ax	+45 43 432 627
eb	brondby.com
mail	info@brondby.com
edia Officer	Steen Laursen

C Horsens
angmarksvej 59
K-8700 Horsens

el	+45 75 626 020
ax	+45 75 626 241
eb	achorsens.dk
mail	jh@achorsens.dk
edia Officer	Frank Hove

FC København
P.H. Lings Allé 2
DK-2100 København Ø

Tel	+45 35 437 400
Fax	+45 35 437 422
Web	fck.dk
Email	info@fck.dk
Media Officer	Charles Maskelyne

HB Køge
Vordingborgvej 112 C
DK-4600 Køge

Tel	+45 56 276 021
Fax	+45 56 275 575
Web	hb.dk
Email	pr@hbkoge.dk
Media Officer	Per Rud

Lyngby BK
Lundtoftevej 61
DK-2800 Lyngby

Tel	+45 45 884 060
Fax	+45 45 874 445
Web	lyngby-boldklub.dk
Email	dbu@lyngby-boldklub.dk
Media Officer	

FC Midtjylland
Kaj Zartos Vej 5
DK-7400 Herning

Tel	+45 96 271 040
Fax	+45 96 271 041
Web	fcm.dk
Email	fcm@fcm.dk
Media Officer	Torben Kølbæk

FC Nordsjælland
Farum Park 2
DK-3520 Farum

Tel	+45 44 342 500
Fax	+45 44 342 570
Web	fcn.dk
Email	cn@fcn.dk
Media Officer	Christian Wolny

Odense BK
Odense Sport & Event A/S, Ørbækvej 350
DK-5220 Odense

Tel	+45 70 221 887
Fax	+45 63 119 080
Web	ob.dk
Email	ob@ose.dk
Media Officer	Asger Torning

Silkeborg IF
Silkeborg IF Invest, Papirfabrikken 34
1. Sal, Postbox 11, DK-8600 Silkeborg

Tel	+45 86 804 477
Fax	+45 86 804 647
Web	silkeborgif.com
Email	sif@silkeborgif.com
Media Officer	Michael Ravn

SønderjyskE
Sonderjyske Elitesport A/S, Stadionvej 5
DK-6100 Haderslev

Tel	+45 74 521 499
Fax	+45 74 524 699
Web	soenderjyske.dk
Email	ne@soenderjyske.dk
Media Officer	Kell Haugaard

ENGLAND

Angleterre I England

The Football Association (FA)

COMMUNICATION

Address Wembley Stadium
PO Box 1966
GB-London SW1P 9EQ
Tel +44 844 980 8200
Fax +44 207 745 4546

E-mail info@thefa.com
Website thefa.com

Chairman David Bernstein
General Secretary Alex Horne
Media Officer Scott Field

Year of Formation 1863

National Stadium Wembley Stadium, London (90,000)

DOMESTIC COMPETITION SUMMARY 2010/11

PREMIER LEAGUE FINAL TABLE

			Home					Away					Total						
		Pld	W	D	L	F	A	W	D	L	F	A	W	D	L	F	A	Pts	Comp
1	Manchester United FC	38	18	1	0	49	12	5	10	4	29	25	23	11	4	78	37	80	UCL
2	Chelsea FC	38	14	3	2	39	13	7	5	7	30	20	21	8	9	69	33	71	UCL
3	Manchester City FC	38	13	4	2	34	12	8	4	7	26	21	21	8	9	60	33	71	UCL
4	Arsenal FC	38	11	4	4	33	15	8	7	4	39	28	19	11	8	72	43	68	UCL
5	Tottenham Hotspur FC	38	9	9	1	30	19	7	5	7	25	27	16	14	8	55	46	62	UEL
6	Liverpool FC	38	12	4	3	37	14	5	3	11	22	30	17	7	14	59	44	58	
7	Everton FC	38	9	7	3	31	23	4	8	7	20	22	13	15	10	51	45	54	
8	Fulham FC	38	8	7	4	30	23	3	9	7	19	20	11	16	11	49	43	49	UEL
9	Aston Villa FC	38	8	7	4	26	19	4	5	10	22	40	12	12	14	48	59	48	
10	Sunderland AFC	38	7	5	7	25	27	5	6	8	20	29	12	11	15	45	56	47	
11	West Bromwich Albion FC	38	8	6	5	30	30	4	5	10	26	41	12	11	15	56	71	47	
12	Newcastle United FC	38	6	8	5	41	27	5	5	9	15	30	11	13	14	56	57	46	
13	Stoke City FC	38	10	4	5	31	18	3	3	13	15	30	13	7	18	46	48	46	UEL
14	Bolton Wanderers FC	38	10	5	4	34	24	2	5	12	18	32	12	10	16	52	56	46	
15	Blackburn Rovers FC	38	7	7	5	22	16	4	3	12	24	43	11	10	17	46	59	43	
16	Wigan Athletic FC	38	5	8	6	22	34	4	7	8	18	27	9	15	14	40	61	42	
17	Wolverhampton Wanderers FC	38	8	4	7	30	30	3	3	13	16	36	11	7	20	46	66	40	
18	Birmingham City FC	38	6	8	5	19	22	2	7	10	18	36	8	15	15	37	58	39	UEL / *Relegated*
19	Blackpool FC	38	5	5	9	30	37	5	4	10	25	41	10	9	19	55	78	39	*Relegated*
20	West Ham United FC	38	5	5	9	24	31	2	7	10	19	39	7	12	19	43	70	33	*Relegated*

Top Scorer Carlos Tévez (Man. City) & Dimitar Berbatov (Man. United), 20 goals

Promoted Clubs Queens Park Rangers FC
Norwich City FC
Swansea City AFC

FA Cup Final Manchester City FC 1, Stoke City FC 0

League Cup Final Birmingham City FC 2, Arsenal FC 1

European crown eludes domestic kings

Manchester United FC fulfilled a personal ambition of their long-serving manager Sir Alex Ferguson as they won their 19th domestic league title to dislodge arch-rivals Liverpool FC as England's record champions. There would be no fourth European Champion Clubs' Cup for the Old Trafford club, however, as their dreams of returning to the continental summit were dashed by a dazzling display from FC Barcelona in the UEFA Champions League final at Wembley.

As in Rome two years earlier, United came up short against Josep Guardiola's side, but a third final appearance in four seasons was an impressive achievement none the less. The 3-1 defeat at Wembley was simply a case of being beaten by a better team, and there were few, if any, recriminations after the event, with a huge number of the club's followers turning out in pouring rain to line the streets of Manchester a couple of days later and salute the team on their open-top bus ride through the city with the Premier League trophy.

Manchester United defenders Nemanja Vidić (left) and Rio Ferdinand show off the Premier League trophy to their supporters

United make history

The victory bus bore the number 19 – a figure that officially proclaimed United as the most successful club in the history of English football. Already with a record number of FA Cups to their name, the club's 2010/11 Premier League triumph raised their combined total of victories in the country's top two domestic competitions to 30 – no fewer than 17 of them having been claimed during the 25 years of Ferguson's reign.

Although the Scot's 12th Premier League title had historic value, the general consensus was that it was not a vintage triumph. There could be no denying that United deserved it – they led the table for most of the campaign and eventually finished nine points clear – but their 80-point haul was the lowest by an English champion for a decade, and although they reigned supreme at Old Trafford, where they won 18 of their 19 fixtures and drew the other, they managed just five wins on their travels. That shoddy away form was in complete contrast to the team's excellence on the road in Europe, where they did not concede a single goal in six matches, winning five of them.

United drew more games away from home in the Premier League than any other team, but their first defeat did not arrive until early February, when they were humbled 2-1 by Wolverhampton Wanderers FC at Molineux. Two further losses the following month, at Liverpool and – in a rearranged fixture – defending champions Chelsea FC, threatened to reverse their traditional spring title thrust, but a comeback 4-2 victory at West Ham United FC plus late winning goals at home to Bolton Wanderers FC and Everton FC proved pivotal, and when in-form Chelsea, already eliminated by Ferguson's team from the UEFA Champions League, were impressively beaten 2-1 at Old Trafford in early May, giving United a six-point lead with two games remaining, the title race was effectively over. A hard-fought 1-1 draw at Blackburn Rovers FC the following weekend sealed the deal.

Consistent performers

It was a title triumph founded on character and gritty resolve rather than fantasy and flair. The team's most consistent performers were captain Nemanja Vidić – a rock in the centre of an otherwise ever-changing back four – and 40-year-old goalkeeper Edwin van der Sar, whose last season before retirement was as good as any of the many that had gone before. 2010/11 was also the last hurrah for club legends Gary Neville and Paul Scholes, the former retiring during the course of the season, the latter at the conclusion of it. Ryan Giggs, however, opted to carry on, which was no real surprise as the 37-year-old was as fit and influential as ever. Young Mexican striker Javier Hernández proved to be great value for money at just £6m, demonstrating a natural goalscorer's instinct and composure that proved decisive on many an occasion. Dimitar Berbatov also had his moments – such as a brilliant hat-trick in the 3-2 home win over Liverpool and five goals in a 7-1 spree against Blackburn – but although he registered 20 times in the league, the elegant Bulgarian struggled in the big games and eventually became marginalised, missing out altogether on the UEFA Champions League final.

As for United's number one attraction, Wayne Rooney, he experienced a very mixed season, taking the role of Dr Jekyll and Mr Hyde by turns. He actually looked set to leave the club in the autumn when he issued an extraordinary statement questioning the club's ambition, but United agreed terms with the striker and handed him a new, improved contract. Injured and wholly ineffective until the New Year, he finally found his best form in the closing weeks, scoring important UEFA Champions League goals at Chelsea and FC Schalke 04 and also pulling United level temporarily against Barcelona at Wembley, where he was the team's most eye-catching performer by some distance.

Rooney's stunning overhead volley in the derby win at home to Manchester City FC was unquestionably the goal of the Premier League season, but the striker foolishly got himself suspended for the re-

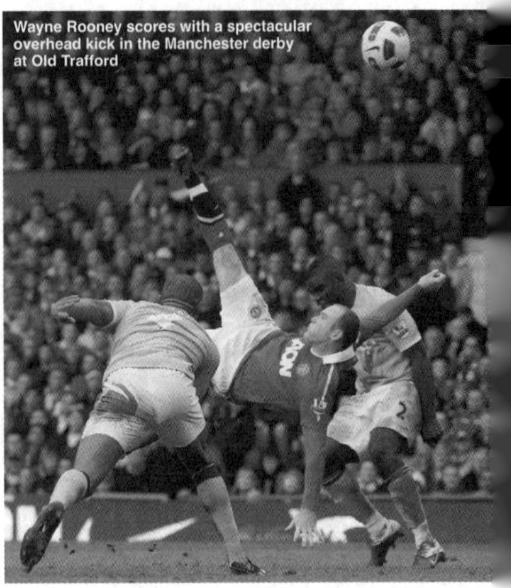
Wayne Rooney scores with a spectacular overhead kick in the Manchester derby at Old Trafford

match with City in the FA Cup semi-final for swearing into a live television camera while celebrating one of his three goals at West Ham. Without him, United lost at Wembley 1-0 to end their double and treble hopes. City went on to win the final, 1-0 against Stoke City FC, with midfielder Yaya Touré, as against United, scoring the only goal. City's first FA Cup win in 42 years ended a trophy drought that had lasted since their League Cup victory in 1976. A provocative banner depicting the number of years City had gone without silverware had long been a fixture on Old Trafford's Stretford End; Touré's 74th-minute strike against Stoke finally brought about its removal.

With the FA Cup final moved forward to accommodate the UEFA Champions League final, City's cup-winning celebrations were rather tempered by the fact that United had claimed the Premier League title earlier the same day. Roberto Mancini's team could not afford to overindulge in victory champagne, however, as they still had two important league matches to play. Although a place in the top four had already been secured with a 1-0 win at home to Tottenham Hotspur FC, direct qualification for the UEFA Champions League would be theirs with six more points. It was a mission they accomplished in style, the first of the two wins coming in a rescheduled fixture against cup final victims Stoke, in which captain Carlos Tévez scored twice to join Berbatov at the top of the Golden Boot standings.

Despite repeated claims that he was desperate to leave Manchester, Tévez was the driving force of City's triumphant campaign. With new signings Mario Balotelli and Edin Džeko failing to shine, the Argentinian was the team's only reliable source of goals. From a defensive perspective, goalkeeper Joe Hart and centre-back Vincent Kompany both enjoyed outstanding campaigns, but, for all the money invested in the team by the club's wealthy Middle Eastern owners, City were little more than functional going forward unless Tévez or the oddly underused Adam Johnson were in possession. Mancini was often accused of betraying his Italian roots by sending his team out to defend first and attack later, but although caution brought calamity against FC Dynamo Kyiv in the last 16 of the UEFA Europa League, his approach ultimately paid dividends on the domestic front. Indeed, had it not been for the stifling tactic he adopted in earning a goalless draw at Arsenal FC in February, City might have finished below, rather than above, the Gunners in the final table.

Driving force

Whereas City's season finished on a high, Arsenal's sank to depths of frustration seldom encountered during manager Arsène Wenger's 15 years in charge. The Frenchman cut a despairing figure during the second half of the campaign as once again, for the sixth season in a row, his team challenged strongly for silverware on several fronts but ended up with nothing. Even with fit-again Dutch striker Robin van Persie scoring goals for fun and young Englishman Jack Wilshere illuminating the midfield, Wenger could not rally his troops sufficiently in the games that mattered. A prime example was the League Cup final at the end of February. Arsenal went into the game as overwhelming favourites to beat Birmingham City FC and lay their trophy hoodoo to rest, but a horrible defensive mix-up gifted their opponents an 89th-minute winner. A couple of weeks later the north London club found themselves having to concentrate on the league after being eliminated from the UEFA Champions League by Barcelona and the FA Cup by Manchester United. More horror stories were to follow in the Premier League as Wenger's weary warriors won only two of their last 11 fixtures to drop out of title contention and down to fourth place.

Chelsea, Premier League and FA Cup winners in 2009/10, also drew a blank in 2010/11, but where repeated failure was seemingly acceptable at Arsenal, the application of zero tolerance by Roman Abramovich, the west London club's Russian owner, led to the end-of-season dismissal of double-winning manager Carlo Ancelotti – and his replacement by one of European football's brightest young coaches, André Villas-Boas. Once Chelsea had gone out of the UEFA Champions League at the quarter-final stage – they lost home and away to United – the affable Ancelotti was clearly living on borrowed time. The club's bid for a hat-trick of FA Cup wins ended early with a penalty shoot-out defeat by Everton, and their Premier League title defence veered wildly off course in the late autumn when, following the unexpected sacking of Ancelotti's assistant Ray Wilkins and a shock 3-0 home defeat by Sunderland AFC three days later, their excellent early-season form completely evaporated.

Fernando Torres was bought from Liverpool for an English record fee in January to reinvigorate Chelsea's title challenge, but while the Spaniard turned out to be a resounding flop, scoring just one goal and losing his place in the team, another expensive new signing, David Luiz from SL Benfica, proved a worthy acquisition, and with stalwarts John Terry, Frank Lampard and Didier Drogba rising to the challenge, Chelsea charged back at United,

Manchester City captain Carlos Tévez (left) and manager Roberto Mancini

claiming 25 points from a possible 27 – only to lose the big game at Old Trafford when a victory would have drawn them level with their hosts at the top of the table.

Euro joyride

If the supporters of Arsenal and Chelsea were entitled to feel short-changed by their teams' efforts in 2010/11, their counterparts at Tottenham were less inclined to show dissatisfaction having been royally entertained during a fabulous debut campaign in the UEFA Champions League. Harry Redknapp's effervescent side failed to re-qualify for the competition after dropping from fourth to fifth in the Premier League but they made the most of their time among Europe's elite, with Welsh wing wizard Gareth Bale, especially, rising to the occasion. After topping their group on the back of a magical 3-1 home win over holders FC Internazionale Milano at White Hart Lane, they then dumped AC Milan out of the competition in the last 16 before succumbing to Real Madrid CF in the quarter-finals. Striker Peter Crouch was the team's hero-turned-villain. Having scored a hat-trick against BSC Young Boys to get Spurs into the group stage, then struck winning goals against both Inter and Milan, he was red-carded for two reckless lunging tackles 15 minutes into the first leg in Madrid, at which point Tottenham's hopes of making further progress were effectively extinguished.

With Stoke and Birmingham claiming two of the 2011/12 UEFA Europa League berths thanks to their cup exploits – the former thus returning to European competition for the first time in 37 years; the latter ending an even longer wait stretching back to 1961/62 – only one qualifying place remained available via the Premier League. Liverpool, who had competed in the event in 2010/11, reaching the round of 16 where they fell to SC Braga, looked favourites to take it, but a home defeat to Spurs on the penultimate weekend enabled their conquerors to snatch it from them, leaving the Reds out of Europe for the first time in 12 years.

Tottenham players congratulate one another after knocking Milan out of the UEFA Champions League

National Team

International Honours –
FIFA World Cup – (1) 1966.

International Tournament Appearances –
FIFA World Cup – (13) 1950, 1954 (qtr-finals), 1958, 1962 (qtr-finals), 1966 (Winners), 1970 (qtr-finals), 1982 (2nd phase), 1986 (qtr-finals), 1990 (4th), 1998 (2nd round), 2002 (qtr-finals), 2006 (qtr-finals), 2010 (2nd round).
UEFA European Championship – (7) 1968 (3rd), 1980, 1988, 1992, 1996 (semi-finals), 2000, 2004 (qtr-finals)

Top Five All-time Caps – Peter Shilton (125); David Beckham (115); Bobby Moore (108); Bobby Charlton (106); Billy Wright (105)

Top Five All-time Goals – Bobby Charlton (49); Gary Lineker (48); Jimmy Greaves (44); Michael Owen (40); Alan Shearer, Nat Lofthouse & Tom Finney (30)

Having parted company with Rafael Benítez after a sorry seventh-place finish in 2009/10, Liverpool placed their faith in Roy Hodgson to get the club going again, but it proved to be an unhappy union, and the man who had just steered Fulham FC to the UEFA Europa League final lasted barely half a season at Anfield. Kenny Dalglish, the revered Kop icon, was summoned from upstairs to take over on the bench – 20 years since he had last served as manager – and, with spirit and harmony restored, the Merseysiders climbed up the table. Sixth place was no mean achievement given that neither of their two principal figures from the Benítez era – Fernando Torres (sold to Chelsea) and skipper Steven Gerrard (injured) – was involved. The money received for the Spaniard was spent on two new strikers in Uruguayan international Luis Suárez (from AFC Ajax) and young English centre-forward Andy Carroll (from Newcastle United FC). Suárez, who took on Dalglish's old No7 shirt, was a big hit virtually from day one, but Carroll, who had scored 11 Premier League goals for Newcastle before Christmas, was hampered by injury. Fortunately, the ever-reliable Dirk Kuyt was still around to help Liverpool finish ahead of local rivals Everton, his

NATIONAL TEAM RESULTS 2010/11

11/8/10	Hungary	H	Wembley	2-1	*Gerrard (69, 73)*
3/9/10	Bulgaria (ECQ)	H	Wembley	4-0	*Defoe (3, 61, 86), Johnson A. (83)*
7/9/10	Switzerland (ECQ)	A	Basel	3-1	*Rooney (10), Johnson A. (69), Bent (88)*
12/10/10	Montenegro (ECQ)	H	Wembley	0-0	
17/11/10	France	H	Wembley	1-2	*Crouch (86)*
9/2/11	Denmark	A	Copenhagen	2-1	*Bent (10), Young (68)*
26/3/11	Wales (ECQ)	A	Cardiff	2-0	*Lampard (7p), Bent (15)*
29/3/11	Ghana	H	Wembley	1-1	*Carroll (43)*
4/6/11	Switzerland (ECQ)	H	Wembley	2-2	*Lampard (37p), Young (51)*

NATIONAL TEAM APPEARANCES 2010/11

›ach – Fabio CAPELLO (ITA)	**18/6/46**		**Hun**	**BUL**	**SUI**	**MNE**	**Fra**	**Den**	**WAL**	**Gha**	**SUI**	**Caps**	**Goals**
e HART	19/4/87	Man. City	G	G	G	G		G	G	G	G	11	-
en JOHNSON	23/8/84	Liverpool	D	D	D	D		D	D	D46	D	34	1
il JAGIELKA	17/8/82	Everton	D	D	D		D		s89	D		9	-
hn TERRY	7/12/80	Chelsea	D46					D	D		D	68	6
shley COLE	20/12/80	Chelsea	D46	D	D	D		D81	D		D31	89	-
areth BARRY	23/2/81	Man. City	M	M	M	M	M46	s46		M		46	2
ank LAMPARD	20/6/78	Chelsea	M46					M46	M		M46	86	22
ieo WALCOTT	16/3/89	Arsenal	M46	M74	M13		M46	M67			M78	17	3
even GERRARD	30/5/80	Liverpool	M82	M	M	M	M85					89	19
dam JOHNSON	14/7/87	Man. City	M	s74	s13	M	s46					6	2
ayne ROONEY	24/10/85	Man. United	A66	A	A79	A		A46	A70			70	26
chael DAWSON	18/11/83	Tottenham	s46	D57				D60	D			4	-
eran GIBBS	26/9/89	Arsenal	s46				D72					2	-
shley YOUNG	9/7/85	Aston Villa	s46	s87		M74	s46	s46	A	A81	s46	15	2
obby ZAMORA	16/1/81	Fulham	s46									1	-
ames MILNER	4/1/86	Aston Villa /Man. City	s66	M	M		M	M	s70	M	A	19	-
ack WILSHERE	1/1/92	Arsenal	s82					M46	M82	M69	M	5	-
ermain DEFOE	7/10/82	Tottenham		A87	A71					s59		46	15
ary CAHILL	19/12/85	Bolton		s57				s60		D		3	-
oleon LESCOTT	16/8/82	Man. City			D	D	D			s46		13	-
arren BENT	6/2/84	Sunderland /Aston Villa			s71			A	A		A	10	3
haun WRIGHT-PHILLIPS	25/10/81	Man. City			s79	s74						36	6
io FERDINAND	7/11/78	Man. United				D	D46				D	81	3
eter CROUCH	30/1/81	Tottenham				A70	s85					42	22
evin DAVIES	26/3/77	Bolton				s70						1	-
en FOSTER	3/4/83	Birmingham					G					5	-
ordan HENDERSON	17/6/90	Sunderland					M					1	-
ndy CARROLL	6/1/89	Newcastle /Liverpool					A72			A59		2	1
licah RICHARDS	24/6/88	Man. City					s46					12	1
tephen WARNOCK	12/12/81	Aston Villa					s72					2	-
ay BOTHROYD	5/5/82	Cardiff (WAL)					s72					1	-
cott PARKER	13/10/80	West Ham						s46	M89		M	6	-
tewart DOWNING	22/7/84	Aston Villa						s67	s82	A	s78	27	-
eighton BAINES	11/12/84	Everton						s81		D	s31	5	-
latt JARVIS	22/5/86	Wolves								s69		1	-
anny WELBECK	26/11/90	Sunderland								s81		1	-

nine goals in eight games featuring a hat-trick against Manchester United and a wildly-celebrated last-gasp penalty at Arsenal.

A tense relegation battle claimed its first victim in West Ham, but there were five candidates to join them on the final day. In the event, Blackburn, Wolves and Wigan Athletic FC all squeezed clear to send League Cup winners Birmingham and neutrals' favourites Blackpool FC plummeting down to the Football League Championship. Blackpool, appropriately for a club from a seaside resort, had been a breath of fresh air for the Premier League with their quixotic manager Ian Holloway and their cavalier style of play, but despite scoring as many goals as Spurs and boasting arguably the revelation of the season in Scottish playmaker Charlie Adam, their leaky defence let them down. West Bromwich Albion FC, another newly-promoted team, also struggled to keep the goals out, but the appointment of Liverpool reject Hodgson in February settled things down, and with Nigerian striker Peter Odemwingie scoring 15 goals in his debut Premier League campaign, the Baggies made an impressive recovery, finishing 11th. Hodgson's old club Fulham did even better, taking ninth spot and returning to the UEFA Europa League via the Respect Fair Play route.

Last-day drama

Although West Ham went down, London's 25 % membership of the Premier League was maintained as Queens Park Rangers FC won the Championship to return to the top flight after 15 years away. Norwich City FC put East Anglia back on the Premier League map by finishing runners-up, while the division's geographical reach extended to beyond English borders when Swansea City AFC defeated Reading FC in an exciting play-off final to become the first Welsh team to compete in England's top flight since they dropped out of the old First Division in 1983.

There was a trip to the south of Wales for Fabio Capello's England in the spring of 2011, and it proved to be a profitable visit as three important points were claimed to keep the Three Lions on top of their UEFA EURO 2012 qualifying group. England's standout performer in that 2-0 win was 30-year-old midfielder Scott Parker, who, despite his club West Ham's relegation, was voted by the nation's journalists as England's Footballer of the Year. Parker was one of several newcomers to the team following the FIFA World Cup flop in South Africa, with the Manchester City pair of Hart and Johnson also making a positive impression and Darren Bent scoring on each of his appearances until he blotted his copybook by missing an open goal in the final EURO qualifier of the season, a 2-2 draw at home to Switzerland.

Wilshere missed

With points having also been conceded at Wembley in a 0-0 draw against Group G giant-killers Montenegro, England were grateful for their excellent start to the campaign, when they banished their World Cup blues with impressive victories over Bulgaria (4-0 at Wembley) and Switzerland (3-1 in Basel). Performances, and results, in the season's friendly internationals were mixed, with Capello suffering his first Wembley defeat as France played an experimental England XI off the park in November but good form on the road continuing with a 2-1 win in Copenhagen during which 19-year-old Wilshere made an impressive first full international start. The gifted Arsenal schemer is sure to become a major star for England, but he was denied the opportunity to return to Denmark and further his international education at the UEFA European Under-21 Championship finals in June when his club, brandishing statistics to prove that he was too tired to take part, requested he be withdrawn. Without him, Stuart Pearce's team were made to pay for their lack of midfield creativity and exited the competition at the end of the first round. Another tournament, another missed opportunity for England.

Jack Wilshere – England's brightest hope for the future

CLUB-BY-CLUB

ARSENAL FC

Manager – Arsène Wenger (FRA)
Founded – 1886
Stadium – Emirates Stadium (60,361)
MAJOR HONOURS: UEFA Cup Winners' Cup – (1) 1994;
Inter Cities Fairs Cup – (1) 1970;
nglish League – (13) 1931, 1933, 1934, 1935, 1938, 1948, 1953, 1971, 1989, 1991, 1998, 2002, 2004;
A Cup – (10) 1930, 1936, 1950, 1971, 1979, 1993, 1998, 2002, 2003, 2005; League Cup – (2) 1987, 1993.

10

8	Liverpool	a	1-1	*og (Reina)*
'8	Blackpool	h	6-0	*Walcott 3, Arshavin (p), Diaby, Chamakh*
8	Blackburn	a	2-1	*Walcott, Arshavin*
9	Bolton	h	4-1	*Koscielny, Chamakh, Song, Vela*
'9	Sunderland	a	1-1	*Fàbregas*
'9	West Brom	h	2-3	*Nasri 2*
0	Chelsea	a	0-2	
'10	Birmingham	h	2-1	*Nasri (p), Chamakh*
'10	Man. City	a	3-0	*Nasri, Song, Bendtner*
'10	West Ham	h	1-0	*Song*
1	Newcastle	h	0-1	
'11	Wolves	a	2-0	*Chamakh 2*
'11	Everton	a	2-1	*Sagna, Fàbregas*
/11	Tottenham	h	2-3	*Nasri, Chamakh*
/11	Aston Villa	a	4-2	*Arshavin, Nasri, Chamakh, Wilshere*
2	Fulham	h	2-1	*Nasri 2*
/12	Man. United	a	0-1	
'/12	Chelsea	h	3-1	*Song, Fàbregas, Walcott*
/12	Wigan	a	2-2	*Arshavin, Bendtner*
11				
1	Birmingham	a	3-0	*Van Persie, Nasri, og (Johnson)*
1	Man. City	h	0-0	
/1	West Ham	a	3-0	*Van Persie 2 (1p), Walcott*
2/1	Wigan	h	3-0	*Van Persie 3*
2	Everton	h	2-1	*Arshavin, Koscielny*
2	Newcastle	a	4-4	*Walcott, Djourou, Van Persie 2*
2/2	Wolves	h	2-0	*Van Persie 2*
3/2	Stoke	h	1-0	*Squillaci*
3	Sunderland	h	0-0	
9/3	West Brom	a	2-2	*Arshavin, Van Persie*
'4	Blackburn	h	0-0	
0/4	Blackpool	a	3-1	*Diaby, Eboué, Van Persie*
7/4	Liverpool	h	1-1	*Van Persie (p)*
0/4	Tottenham	a	3-3	*Walcott, Nasri, Van Persie*
4/4	Bolton	a	1-2	*Van Persie*
'5	Man. United	h	1-0	*Ramsey*
'5	Stoke	a	1-3	*Van Persie*
5/5	Aston Villa	h	1-2	*Van Persie*
2/5	Fulham	a	2-2	*Van Persie, Walcott*

lo	Name	Nat	DoB	Pos	Aps	(s)	Gls
	Manuel ALMUNIA Rivero	ESP	16/5/77	G	8		
'3	Andrey ARSHAVIN	RUS	29/5/81	A	25	(12)	6
2	Nicklas BENDTNER	DEN	16/1/88	A	3	(14)	2
9	Marouane CHAMAKH	MAR	10/1/84	A	18	(11)	7
2	Gaël CLICHY	FRA	26/7/85	D	33		
5	DENÍLSON Pereira Neves	BRA	16/2/88	M	6	(10)	
	Abou DIABY	FRA	11/5/86	M	13	(3)	2
0	Johan DJOUROU	SUI	18/1/87	D	20	(2)	1
7	Emmanuel EBOUÉ	CIV	4/6/83	D	8	(5)	1
1	Jay EMMANUEL-THOMAS		27/12/90	M		(1)	
1	Łukasz FABIAŃSKI	POL	18/4/85	G	14		
	Francesc "Cesc" FÀBREGAS I Soler	ESP	4/5/87	M	22	(3)	3
28	Kieran GIBBS		26/9/89	D	4	(3)	
6	Laurent KOSCIELNY	FRA	10/9/85	D	30		2
13	Jens LEHMANN	GER	10/11/69	G	1		
8	Samir NASRI	FRA	26/6/87	M	28	(1)	10
16	Aaron RAMSEY	WAL	26/12/90	M	5	(2)	1
7	Tomáš ROSICKÝ	CZE	4/10/80	M	8	(13)	
3	Bacary SAGNA	FRA	14/2/83	D	33		1
17	Alex SONG	CMR	9/9/87	M	30	(1)	4
18	Sébastien SQUILLACI	FRA	11/8/80	D	20	(2)	1
53	Wojciech SZCZĘSNY	POL	18/4/90	G	15		
10	Robin VAN PERSIE	NED	6/8/83	A	19	(6)	18
11	Carlos Alberto VELA	MEX	1/3/89	A		(4)	1
5	Thomas VERMAELEN	BEL	14/11/85	D	5		
14	Theo WALCOTT		16/3/89	A	19	(9)	9
19	Jack WILSHERE		1/1/92	M	31	(4)	1

ASTON VILLA FC

Manager – (Kevin McDonald (SCO)); (8/9/10) Gérard Houllier (FRA); (21/4/11) (Gary McAllister (SCO))
Founded – 1874
Stadium – Villa Park (42,640)
MAJOR HONOURS: European Champion Clubs' Cup – (1) 1982;
UEFA Super Cup – (1) 1982;
English League – (7) 1894, 1896, 1897, 1899, 1900, 1910, 1981;
FA Cup – (7) 1887, 1895, 1897, 1905, 1913, 1920, 1957;
League Cup – (5) 1961, 1975, 1977, 1994, 1996.

2010

14/8	West Ham	h	3-0	*Downing, Petrov, Milner*
22/8	Newcastle	a	0-6	
29/8	Everton	h	1-0	*Young L.*
13/9	Stoke	a	1-2	*Downing*
18/9	Bolton	h	1-1	*Young A.*
26/9	Wolves	a	2-1	*Downing, Heskey*
2/10	Tottenham	a	1-2	*Albrighton*
16/10	Chelsea	h	0-0	
23/10	Sunderland	a	0-1	
31/10	Birmingham	h	0-0	
6/11	Fulham	a	1-1	*Albrighton*
10/11	Blackpool	h	3-2	*Downing, Delfouneso, Collins*
13/11	Man. United	h	2-2	*Young A. (p), Albrighton*
21/11	Blackburn	a	0-2	
27/11	Arsenal	h	2-4	*Clark 2*
6/12	Liverpool	a	0-3	
11/12	West Brom	h	2-1	*Downing, Heskey*
26/12	Tottenham	h	1-2	*Albrighton*
28/12	Man. City	a	0-4	
2011				
2/1	Chelsea	a	3-3	*Young A. (p), Heskey, Clark*
5/1	Sunderland	h	0-1	
16/1	Birmingham	a	1-1	*Collins*
22/1	Man. City	h	1-0	*Bent*
25/1	Wigan	a	2-1	*Agbonlahor, Young A. (p)*
1/2	Man. United	a	1-3	*Bent*
5/2	Fulham	h	2-2	*og (Pantsil), Walker*
12/2	Blackpool	a	1-1	*Agbonlahor*
26/2	Blackburn	h	4-1	*Young A. 2 (1p), og (Hanley), Downing*
5/3	Bolton	a	2-3	*Bent, Albrighton*
19/3	Wolves	h	0-1	
2/4	Everton	a	2-2	*Bent 2*
10/4	Newcastle	h	1-0	*Collins*
16/4	West Ham	a	2-1	*Bent, Agbonlahor*
23/4	Stoke	h	1-1	*Bent*
30/4	West Brom	a	1-2	*og (Méïté)*
7/5	Wigan	h	1-1	*Young A.*
15/5	Arsenal	a	2-1	*Bent 2*
22/5	Liverpool	h	1-0	*Downing*

No	Name	Nat	DoB	Pos	Aps	(s)	Gls
11	Gabriel AGBONLAHOR		13/10/86	A	17	(9)	3
12	Marc ALBRIGHTON		18/11/89	M	20	(9)	5
48	Nathan BAKER		23/4/91	D	4		
25	Barry BANNAN	SCO	1/12/89	M	7	(5)	
39	Darren BENT		6/2/84	A	16		9
23	Habib BEYE	SEN	19/10/77	D	2	(1)	
26	Michael BRADLEY	USA	31/7/87	M		(3)	
10	John CAREW	NOR	5/9/79	A	6	(4)	
21	Ciaran CLARK	IRL	26/9/89	D	16	(3)	3
29	James COLLINS	WAL	23/8/83	D	31	(1)	3
24	Carlos Javier CUÉLLAR Jiménez	ESP	23/8/81	D	10	(2)	
14	Nathan DELFOUNESO		2/2/91	A	2	(9)	1
16	Fabian DELPH		21/11/89	M	4	(3)	
6	Stewart DOWNING		22/7/84	M	38		7
5	Richard DUNNE	IRL	21/9/79	D	32		
1	Brad FRIEDEL	USA	18/5/71	G	38		
49	Chris HERD	AUS	4/4/89	M	1	(5)	
18	Emile HESKEY		11/1/78	A	11	(8)	3
50	Jonathan HOGG		6/12/88	M	5		
9	Stephen IRELAND	IRL	22/8/86	M	6	(4)	
30	Eric LICHAJ	USA	17/11/88	D	3	(2)	
17	Jean II MAKOUN	CMR	29/5/83	M	7		
8	James MILNER		4/1/86	M	1		1
19	Stiliyan PETROV	BUL	5/7/79	M	23	(4)	1
8	Robert PIRÈS	FRA	29/10/73	M	2	(7)	
20	Nigel REO-COKER		14/5/84	M	24	(6)	
4	Steve SIDWELL		14/12/82	M	1	(3)	
36	Kyle WALKER		28/5/90	D	15		1
3	Stephen WARNOCK		12/12/81	D	19		
42	Andreas WEIMANN	AUT	5/8/91	A		(1)	
7	Ashley YOUNG		9/7/85	M	34		7
2	Luke YOUNG		19/7/79	D	23		1

BIRMINGHAM CITY FC

Coach – Alex McLeish (SCO)

Founded – 1875

Stadium – St Andrews (30,079)

MAJOR HONOURS: League Cup – (2) 1963, 2011.

2010				
14/8	Sunderland	a	2-2	*Dann, Ridgewell*
21/8	Blackburn	h	2-1	*Gardner 2*
29/8	Bolton	a	2-2	*Johnson, Gardner*
12/9	Liverpool	h	0-0	
18/9	West Brom	a	1-3	*Jerome*
25/9	Wigan	h	0-0	
2/10	Everton	h	0-2	
16/10	Arsenal	a	1-2	*Žigić*
23/10	Blackpool	h	2-0	*Ridgewell, Žigić*
31/10	Aston Villa	a	0-0	
6/11	West Ham	h	2-2	*Jerome, Ridgewell*
9/11	Stoke	a	2-3	*Fahey, Jerome*
13/11	Man. City	a	0-0	
20/11	Chelsea	h	1-0	*Bowyer*
27/11	Fulham	a	1-1	*Larsson*
4/12	Tottenham	h	1-1	*Gardner*
12/12	Wolves	a	0-1	
28/12	Man. United	h	1-1	*Bowyer*
2011				
1/1	Arsenal	h	0-3	
4/1	Blackpool	a	2-1	*Hleb, Dann*
16/1	Aston Villa	h	1-1	*Johnson*
22/1	Man. United	a	0-5	
2/2	Man. City	h	2-2	*Žigić, Gardner (p)*
6/2	West Ham	a	1-0	*Žigić*
12/2	Stoke	h	1-0	*Žigić*
15/2	Newcastle	h	0-2	
5/3	West Brom	h	1-3	*Beausejour*
9/3	Everton	a	1-1	*Beausejour*
19/3	Wigan	a	1-2	*Ridgewell*
2/4	Bolton	h	2-1	*Phillips, Gardner*
9/4	Blackburn	a	1-1	*Bowyer*
16/4	Sunderland	h	2-0	*Larsson, Gardner*
20/4	Chelsea	a	1-3	*Larsson (p)*
23/4	Liverpool	a	0-5	
1/5	Wolves	h	1-1	*Larsson*
7/5	Newcastle	a	1-2	*Bowyer*
15/5	Fulham	h	0-2	
22/5	Tottenham	a	1-2	*Gardner*

No	Name	Nat	DoB	Pos	Aps	(s)	Gls
23	Jean BEAUSEJOUR	CHI	1/6/84	M	9	(8)	2
11	David BENTLEY		27/8/84	M	9	(4)	
4	Lee BOWYER		3/1/77	M	24	(5)	4
2	Stephen CARR	IRL	29/8/76	D	38		
15	Scott DANN		14/2/87	D	20		2
32	Curtis DAVIES		15/3/85	D	2	(4)	
14	Matt DERBYSHIRE		14/4/86	A	4	(9)	
13	Colin DOYLE	IRL	12/6/85	G		(1)	
18	Keith FAHEY	IRL	15/1/83	M	19	(5)	1
12	Barry FERGUSON	SCO	2/2/78	M	35		
26	Ben FOSTER		3/4/83	G	38		
8	Craig GARDNER		25/11/86	M	25	(4)	8
22	Aleksandr HLEB	BLR	1/5/81	M	13	(6)	1
10	Cameron JEROME		14/8/86	A	30	(4)	3
28	Martin JIRÁNEK	CZE	25/5/79	D	10		
5	Roger JOHNSON		28/4/83	D	38		2
7	Sebastian LARSSON	SWE	6/6/85	M	31	(4)	4
17	Obafemi MARTINS	NGA	28/10/84	A	3	(1)	
16	James McFADDEN	SCO	14/4/83	A	3	(1)	
3	David MURPHY		1/3/84	D	3	(7)	
25	Jordan MUTCH		2/12/91	M	3		
8	Garry O'CONNOR	SCO	7/5/83	A	2	(1)	
21	Stuart PARNABY		19/7/82	D	5		
9	Kevin PHILLIPS		25/7/73	A	5	(9)	1
6	Liam RIDGEWELL		21/7/84	D	36		4
19	Nikola ŽIGIĆ	SRB	25/9/80	A	13	(12)	5

BLACKBURN ROVERS FC

Manager – Sam Allardyce; (13/12/10) Steve Kean (SCO)

Founded – 1875

Stadium – Ewood Park (31,154)

MAJOR HONOURS: English League – (3) 1912, 1914, 1995; FA Cup – (6) 1884, 1885, 1886, 1890, 1891, 1928; League Cup – (1) 2002.

2010				
14/8	Everton	h	1-0	*Kalinić*
21/8	Birmingham	a	1-2	*N'Zonzi*
28/8	Arsenal	h	1-2	*Diouf M.*
11/9	Man. City	a	1-1	*Kalinić*
18/9	Fulham	h	1-1	*Samba*
25/9	Blackpool	a	2-1	*og (Adam), Emerton*
2/10	Stoke	a	0-1	
18/10	Sunderland	h	0-0	
24/10	Liverpool	a	1-2	*og (Carragher)*
30/10	Chelsea	h	1-2	*Benjani*
6/11	Wigan	h	2-1	*Gamst Pedersen, Roberts*
10/11	Newcastle	a	2-1	*Gamst Pedersen, Roberts*
13/11	Tottenham	a	2-4	*Nelsen, Givet*
21/11	Aston Villa	h	2-0	*Gamst Pedersen 2*
27/11	Man. United	a	1-7	*Samba*
4/12	Wolves	h	3-0	*Dunn, Emerton, Nelsen*
12/12	Bolton	a	1-2	*Diouf M.*
18/12	West Ham	h	1-1	*Nelsen*
26/12	Stoke	h	0-2	
28/12	West Brom	a	3-1	*Kalinić 2, Diouf M.*
2011				
1/1	Sunderland	a	0-3	
5/1	Liverpool	h	3-1	*Olsson, Benjani 2*

1	Chelsea	a	0-2	
1	West Brom	h	2-0	*og (Tamaş), Hoilett*
	Tottenham	h	0-1	
	Wigan	a	3-4	*Roberts, Samba, Dunn (p)*
2	Newcastle	h	0-0	
2	Aston Villa	a	1-4	*Kalinić*
	Fulham	a	2-3	*og (Hangeland), Hoilett*
3	Blackpool	h	2-2	*Samba, Hoilett*
	Arsenal	a	0-0	
	Birmingham	h	1-1	*Hoilett*
4	Everton	a	0-2	
4	Man. City	h	0-1	
4	Bolton	h	1-0	*Olsson*
	West Ham	a	1-1	*Roberts*
5	Man. United	h	1-1	*Emerton*
5	Wolves	a	3-2	*Roberts, Emerton, Hoilett*

	Name	Nat	DoB	Pos	Aps	(s)	Gls
	Keith ANDREWS	IRL	13/9/80	M	2	(3)	
	Benjamin Mwaruwari "BENJANI"	ZIM	13/8/78	A	6	(12)	3
	Mark BUNN		16/11/84	G	2	(1)	
	Pascal CHIMBONDA	FRA	21/2/79	D	3	(3)	
	El Hadji DIOUF	SEN	15/1/81	A	18	(2)	
	Mame Biram DIOUF	SEN	16/12/87	A	17	(10)	3
	David DUNN		27/12/79	M	17	(10)	2
	Brett EMERTON	AUS	22/2/79	M	24	(6)	4
	Morten GAMST PEDERSEN	NOR	8/9/81	M	27	(8)	4
	Gaël GIVET	FRA	9/10/81	D	29		1
	Hérold GOULON	FRA	12/6/88	M	1	(3)	
	Vince GRELLA	AUS	5/10/79	M	4	(1)	
	Grant HANLEY	SCO	20/11/91	D	5	(2)	
	David HOILETT	CAN	5/6/90	A	17	(7)	5
	Jermaine JONES	USA	3/11/81	M	15		
	Phil JONES		21/2/92	D	24	(2)	
	Nikola KALINIĆ	CRO	5/1/88	A	15	(3)	5
4	Amine LINGANZI	ALG	16/11/89	M		(1)	
5	Jason LOWE		2/9/91	M		(1)	
7	Miguel Ángel "MÍCHEL" SALGADO Fernández	ESP	22/10/75	D	36		
3	Josh MORRIS		30/9/91	D		(4)	
	Ryan NELSEN	NZL	18/10/77	D	28		3
5	Steven N'ZONZI	FRA	15/12/88	M	13	(8)	1
	Martin OLSSON	SWE	17/5/88	D	25	(4)	2
0	Jason ROBERTS	GRN	25/1/78	A	13	(12)	5
	Paul ROBINSON		15/10/79	G	36		
0	RUBÉN ROCHINA Naixes	ESP	23/3/91	A	1	(3)	
	Christopher SAMBA	CGO	28/3/84	D	33		4
8	Roque SANTA CRUZ	PAR	16/8/81	A	7	(2)	

BLACKPOOL FC

Manager – Ian Holloway

Founded – 1887

Stadium – Bloomfield Road (12,555)

MAJOR HONOURS: FA Cup – (1) 1953.

2010				
14/8	Wigan	a	4-0	*Taylor-Fletcher, Harewood 2, Baptiste*
21/8	Arsenal	a	0-6	
28/8	Fulham	h	2-2	*og (Pantsil), Varney*
11/9	Newcastle	a	2-0	*Adam (p), Campbell*
19/9	Chelsea	a	0-4	
25/9	Blackburn	h	1-2	*Phillips*
3/10	Liverpool	a	2-1	*Adam (p), Varney*
17/10	Man. City	h	2-3	*Harewood, Taylor-Fletcher*
23/10	Birmingham	a	0-2	
1/11	West Brom	h	2-1	*Adam (p), Varney*
6/11	Everton	h	2-2	*Eardley, Vaughan*
10/11	Aston Villa	a	2-3	*Harewood, Campbell*
13/11	West Ham	a	0-0	
20/11	Wolves	h	2-1	*Varney, Harewood*
27/11	Bolton	a	2-2	*Evatt, Varney*
11/12	Stoke	a	1-0	*Campbell*
28/12	Sunderland	a	2-0	*Campbell 2*
2011				
1/1	Man. City	a	0-1	
4/1	Birmingham	h	1-2	*Campbell*
12/1	Liverpool	h	2-1	*Taylor-Fletcher, Campbell*
15/1	West Brom	a	2-3	*Vaughan, Taylor-Fletcher*
22/1	Sunderland	h	1-2	*Adam (p)*
25/1	Man. United	h	2-3	*Cathcart, Campbell*
2/2	West Ham	h	1-3	*Adam*
5/2	Everton	a	3-5	*Baptiste, Puncheon, Adam*
12/2	Aston Villa	h	1-1	*Grandin*
22/2	Tottenham	h	3-1	*Adam (p), Campbell, Ormerod*
26/2	Wolves	a	0-4	
7/3	Chelsea	h	1-3	*Puncheon*
19/3	Blackburn	a	2-2	*Adam 2 (1p)*
3/4	Fulham	a	0-3	
10/4	Arsenal	h	1-3	*Taylor-Fletcher*
16/4	Wigan	h	1-3	*Campbell*
23/4	Newcastle	h	1-1	*Campbell*
30/4	Stoke	h	0-0	
7/5	Tottenham	a	1-1	*Adam (p)*
14/5	Bolton	h	4-3	*Campbell 2, Puncheon, Adam*
22/5	Man. United	a	2-4	*Adam, Taylor-Fletcher*

No	Name	Nat	DoB	Pos	Aps	(s)	Gls
26	Charlie ADAM	SCO	10/12/85	M	34	(1)	12
15	Alex BAPTISTE		31/1/86	D	19	(2)	2
17	Chris BASHAM		20/7/88	M	1	(1)	
44	James BEATTIE		27/2/78	A	5	(4)	
39	Dudley Junior "DJ" CAMPBELL		12/11/81	A	30	(1)	13
29	David CARNEY	AUS	30/11/83	D	5	(6)	
20	Craig CATHCART	NIR	6/2/89	D	28	(2)	1
3	Stephen CRAINEY	SCO	22/6/81	D	31		
27	Ishmel DEMONTAGNAC		15/6/88	M		(1)	
5	Neil EARDLEY	WAL	6/11/88	D	30	(1)	1
24	Rob EDWARDS	WAL	25/12/82	D	1	(1)	
18	Jason EUELL	JAM	6/2/77	A	1	(2)	
6	Ian EVATT		19/11/81	D	36	(2)	1
21	Matthew GILKS	SCO	4/6/82	G	18		
14	Elliott GRANDIN	FRA	17/10/87	A	21	(2)	1
13	Mark HALSTEAD		1/1/90	G		(1)	
9	Marlon HAREWOOD		25/8/79	A	7	(9)	5
31	Dekel KEINAN	ISR	15/9/84	D	3	(3)	
28	Richard KINGSON	GHA	13/6/78	G	19	(1)	
41	Sergei KORNILENKO	BLR	14/6/83	A	3	(3)	
10	Brett ORMEROD		18/10/76	A	6	(13)	1
23	Matt PHILLIPS		13/3/91	M	6	(21)	1
42	Jason PUNCHEON		26/6/86	M	6	(5)	3
1	Paul RACHUBKA		21/5/81	G	1	(1)	
43	Andy REID	IRL	29/7/82	M	2	(3)	
4	Keith SOUTHERN		21/4/81	M	11	(10)	
19	Ludovic SYLVESTRE	FRA	5/2/84	M	6	(2)	
12	Gary TAYLOR-FLETCHER		4/6/81	A	29	(2)	6
16	Luke VARNEY		28/9/82	A	24	(6)	5
11	David VAUGHAN	WAL	18/2/83	M	35		2

BOLTON WANDERERS FC

Manager – Owen Coyle (IRL)

Founded – 1874

Stadium – Reebok Stadium (28,101)

MAJOR HONOURS: FA Cup – (4) 1923, 1926, 1929, 1958.

2010				
14/8	Fulham	h	0-0	
21/8	West Ham	a	3-1	*og (Upson), Elmander 2*
29/8	Birmingham	h	2-2	*Davies K. (p), Blake*
11/9	Arsenal	a	1-4	*Elmander*
18/9	Aston Villa	a	1-1	*Davies K.*
26/9	Man. United	h	2-2	*Knight, Petrov*

2/10	West Brom	a	1-1	*Elmander*
16/10	Stoke	h	2-1	*Lee, Klasnić*
23/10	Wigan	a	1-1	*Elmander*
31/10	Liverpool	h	0-1	
6/11	Tottenham	h	4-2	*Davies K. 2 (1p), Steinsson, Petrov*
10/11	Everton	a	1-1	*Klasnić*
13/11	Wolves	a	3-2	*og (Stearman), Elmander, Holden*
20/11	Newcastle	h	5-1	*Davies K. 2 (2p), Lee, Elmander 2*
27/11	Blackpool	h	2-2	*Petrov, Davies M.*
4/12	Man. City	a	0-1	
12/12	Blackburn	h	2-1	*Muamba, Holden*
18/12	Sunderland	a	0-1	
26/12	West Brom	h	2-0	*Taylor, Elmander*
29/12	Chelsea	a	0-1	
2011				
1/1	Liverpool	a	1-2	*Davies K.*
5/1	Wigan	h	1-1	*Rodrigo*
15/1	Stoke	a	0-2	
24/1	Chelsea	h	0-4	
2/2	Wolves	h	1-0	*Sturridge*
5/2	Tottenham	a	1-2	*Sturridge*
13/2	Everton	h	2-0	*Cahill, Sturridge*
26/2	Newcastle	a	1-1	*Sturridge*
5/3	Aston Villa	h	3-2	*Cahill 2, Klasnić*
19/3	Man. United	a	0-1	
2/4	Birmingham	a	1-2	*Elmander*
9/4	West Ham	h	3-0	*Sturridge 2, Lee*
24/4	Arsenal	h	2-1	*Sturridge, Cohen*
27/4	Fulham	a	0-3	
30/4	Blackburn	a	0-1	
7/5	Sunderland	h	1-2	*Klasnić*
14/5	Blackpool	a	3-4	*Davies K., Taylor, Sturridge*
22/5	Man. City	h	0-2	

No	Name	Nat	DoB	Pos	Aps	(s)	Gls
20	Robbie BLAKE		4/3/76	M		(8)	1
1	Ádám BOGDÁN	HUN	27/9/87	G	3	(1)	
5	Gary CAHILL		19/12/85	D	36		3
21	Tamir COHEN	ISR	4/3/84	M	3	(5)	1
14	Kevin DAVIES		26/3/77	A	38		8
16	Mark DAVIES		18/2/88	M	9	(15)	1
9	Johan ELMANDER	SWE	27/5/81	A	37		10
11	Ricardo GARDNER	JAM	25/9/78	M	3	(2)	
8	Stuart HOLDEN	USA	1/8/85	M	26		2
22	Jussi JÄÄSKELÄINEN	FIN	19/4/75	G	35		
17	Ivan KLASNIĆ	CRO	29/1/80	A		(22)	4
12	Zat KNIGHT		2/5/80	D	34		1
27	LEE Chung-yong	KOR	2/7/88	M	25	(6)	3
25	MARCOS ALONSO Mendoza	ESP	28/12/90	D	4		
6	Fabrice MUAMBA		6/4/88	M	32	(4)	1
31	Andy O'BRIEN	IRL	26/6/79	D	1	(1)	
10	Martin PETROV	BUL	15/1/79	M	18	(10)	3
18	Sam RICKETTS	WAL	11/10/81	D	14	(3)	
4	Paul ROBINSON		14/12/78	D	35		
19	RODRIGO Moreno Machado	ESP	6/3/91	A	4	(13)	1
2	Grétar Rafn STEINSSON	ISL	9/1/82	D	23		1
15	Daniel STURRIDGE		1/9/89	A	11	(1)	8
7	Matthew TAYLOR		27/11/81	M	22	(14)	2
31	David WHEATER		14/2/87	D	5	(2)	

CHELSEA FC

Manager – Carlo Ancelotti (ITA)

Founded – 1905

Stadium – Stamford Bridge (41,841)

MAJOR HONOURS: UEFA Cup Winners' Cup – (2) 1971, 1998;
UEFA Super Cup – (1) 1998;
English League – (4) 1955, 2005, 2006, 2010;
FA Cup – (6) 1970, 1997, 2000, 2007, 2009, 2010;
League Cup – (4) 1965, 1998, 2005, 2007.

2010				
14/8	West Brom	h	6-0	*Malouda 2, Drogba 3, Lampard*
21/8	Wigan	a	6-0	*Malouda, Anelka 2, Kalou 2, Benayoun*
28/8	Stoke	h	2-0	*Malouda, Drogba (p)*
11/9	West Ham	a	3-1	*Essien 2, Kalou*
19/9	Blackpool	h	4-0	*Kalou, Malouda 2, og (Evatt)*
25/9	Man. City	a	0-1	
3/10	Arsenal	h	2-0	*Drogba, Alex*
16/10	Aston Villa	a	0-0	
23/10	Wolves	h	2-0	*Malouda, Kalou*
30/10	Blackburn	a	2-1	*Anelka, Ivanović*
7/11	Liverpool	a	0-2	
10/11	Fulham	h	1-0	*Essien*
14/11	Sunderland	h	0-3	
20/11	Birmingham	a	0-1	
28/11	Newcastle	a	1-1	*Kalou*
4/12	Everton	h	1-1	*Drogba (p)*
12/12	Tottenham	a	1-1	*Drogba*
27/12	Arsenal	a	1-3	*Ivanović*
29/12	Bolton	h	1-0	*Malouda*
2011				
2/1	Aston Villa	h	3-3	*Lampard (p), Drogba, Terry*
6/1	Wolves	a	0-1	
15/1	Blackburn	h	2-0	*Ivanović, Anelka*
24/1	Bolton	a	4-0	*Drogba, Malouda, Anelka, Ramires*
1/2	Sunderland	a	4-2	*Lampard (p), Kalou, Terry, Anelka*
6/2	Liverpool	h	0-1	
14/2	Fulham	a	0-0	
1/3	Man. United	h	2-1	*David Luiz, Lampard (p)*
7/3	Blackpool	a	3-1	*Terry, Lampard 2 (1p)*
20/3	Man. City	h	2-0	*David Luiz, Ramires*
2/4	Stoke	a	1-1	*Drogba*
9/4	Wigan	h	1-0	*Malouda*
16/4	West Brom	a	3-1	*Drogba, Kalou, Lampard*
20/4	Birmingham	h	3-1	*Malouda 2, Kalou*
23/4	West Ham	h	3-0	*Lampard, Fernando Torres, Malouda*
30/4	Tottenham	h	2-1	*Lampard, Kalou*
8/5	Man. United	a	1-2	*Lampard*
15/5	Newcastle	h	2-2	*Ivanović, Alex*
22/5	Everton	a	0-1	

No	Name	Nat	DoB	Pos	Aps	(s)	Gls
33	ALEX Rodrigo Dias da Costa	BRA	17/6/82	D	12	(3)	2
39	Nicolas ANELKA	FRA	14/3/79	A	27	(5)	6
10	Yossi BENAYOUN	ISR	5/5/80	M	1	(6)	1
34	Ryan BERTRAND		5/8/89	D		(1)	
17	José BOSINGWA da Silva	POR	24/8/82	D	13	(7)	
43	Jeffrey BRUMA	NED	13/11/91	D	1	(1)	
1	Petr ČECH	CZE	20/5/82	G	38		
3	Ashley COLE		20/12/80	D	38		
4	DAVID LUIZ Moreira Marinho	BRA	22/4/87	D	11	(1)	2
11	Didier DROGBA	CIV	11/3/78	A	30	(6)	11
5	Michael ESSIEN	GHA	3/12/82	M	32	(1)	3
9	FERNANDO José TORRES Sanz	ESP	20/3/84	A	8	(6)	1
2	Branislav IVANOVIĆ	SRB	22/2/84	D	32	(2)	4
44	Gaël KAKUTA	FRA	21/6/91	M	1	(4)	
21	Salomon KALOU	CIV	5/8/85	A	16	(15)	10
8	Frank LAMPARD		20/6/78	M	23	(1)	10
15	Florent MALOUDA	FRA	13/6/80	M	33	(5)	13
46	Josh McEACHRAN		1/3/93	M	1	(8)	
12	John Obi MIKEL	NGA	22/4/87	M	28		
19	PAULO Renato Rebocho FERREIRA	POR	18/1/79	D	12	(9)	
7	RAMIRES Santos do Nascimento	BRA	24/3/87	M	22	(7)	2
23	Daniel STURRIDGE		1/9/89	A		(13)	
26	John TERRY		7/12/80	D	33		3
18	Yuriy ZHIRKOV	RUS	20/8/83	D	6	(6)	

EVERTON FC

Manager – David Moyes (SCO)
Founded – 1878
Stadium – Goodison Park (40,157)
MAJOR HONOURS: UEFA Cup Winners' Cup – (1) 1985; English League – (9) 1891, 1915, 1928, 1932, 1939, 1963, 1970, 1985, 1987; FA Cup – (5) 1906, 1933, 1966, 1984, 1995.

10				
8	Blackburn	a	0-1	
'8	Wolves	h	1-1	*Cahill*
'8	Aston Villa	a	0-1	
'9	Man. United	h	3-3	*Pienaar, Cahill, Arteta*
'9	Newcastle	h	0-1	
'9	Fulham	a	0-0	
0	Birmingham	a	2-0	*og (Johnson), Cahill*
'10	Liverpool	h	2-0	*Cahill, Arteta*
/10	Tottenham	a	1-1	*Baines*
/10	Stoke	h	1-0	*Yakubu*
1	Blackpool	a	2-2	*Cahill, Coleman*
/11	Bolton	h	1-1	*Beckford*
/11	Arsenal	h	1-2	*Cahill*
/11	Sunderland	a	2-2	*Cahill, Arteta*
/11	West Brom	h	1-4	*Cahill*
2	Chelsea	a	1-1	*Beckford*
/12	Wigan	h	0-0	
/12	Man. City	a	2-1	*Cahill, Baines*
/12	West Ham	a	1-1	*Coleman*
)11				
1	Stoke	a	0-2	
1	Tottenham	h	2-1	*Saha, Coleman*
/1	Liverpool	a	2-2	*Distin, Beckford*
2/1	West Ham	h	2-2	*Bilyaletdinov, Fellaini*
2	Arsenal	a	1-2	*Saha*
2	Blackpool	h	5-3	*Saha 4, Beckford*
3/2	Bolton	a	0-2	
5/2	Sunderland	h	2-0	*Beckford 2*
'3	Newcastle	a	2-1	*Osman, Jagielka*
'3	Birmingham	h	1-1	*Heitinga*
9/3	Fulham	h	2-1	*Coleman, Saha*
'4	Aston Villa	h	2-2	*Osman, Baines (p)*
'4	Wolves	a	3-0	*Beckford, Neville, Bilyaletdinov*
6/4	Blackburn	h	2-0	*Osman, Baines (p)*
3/4	Man. United	a	0-1	
0/4	Wigan	a	1-1	*Baines (p)*
/5	Man. City	h	2-1	*Distin, Osman*
4/5	West Brom	a	0-1	
2/5	Chelsea	h	1-0	*Beckford*

lo	Name	Nat	DoB	Pos	Aps	(s)	Gls
8	Victor ANICHEBE	NGA	23/4/88	A	8	(8)	
0	Mikel ARTETA Amatriain	ESP	26/3/82	M	29		3
	Leighton BAINES		11/12/84	D	38		5
7	Jose BAXTER		7/2/92	M		(1)	
6	Jermaine BECKFORD		9/12/83	A	14	(18)	8
	Diniyar BILYALETDINOV	RUS	27/2/85	M	10	(16)	2
7	Tim CAHILL	AUS	6/12/79	M	22	(5)	9
3	Séamus COLEMAN	IRL	11/10/88	D	25	(9)	4
5	Sylvain DISTIN	FRA	16/12/77	D	38		2
25	Marouane FELLAINI	BEL	22/11/87	M	19	(1)	1
29	Adam FORSHAW		8/10/91	M		(1)	
19	Magaye GUEYE	FRA	6/7/90	M	2	(3)	
5	John HEITINGA	NED	15/11/83	D	23	(4)	1
2	Tony HIBBERT		20/2/81	D	17	(3)	
24	Tim HOWARD	USA	6/3/79	G	38		
6	Phil JAGIELKA		17/8/82	D	31	(2)	1
18	Phil NEVILLE		21/1/77	D	31		1
21	Leon OSMAN		17/5/81	M	20	(6)	4
20	Steven PIENAAR	RSA	17/3/82	M	18		1
26	Jack RODWELL		11/3/91	M	14	(10)	
8	Louis SAHA	FRA	8/8/78	A	14	(8)	7
14	James VAUGHAN		14/7/88	A		(1)	
27	Apostolos VELLIOS	GRE	8/1/92	A		(3)	
22	YAKUBU Aiyegbeni	NGA	22/11/82	A	7	(7)	1

FULHAM FC

Manager – Mark Hughes (WAL)
Founded – 1879
Stadium – Craven Cottage (25,478)

2010				
14/8	Bolton	a	0-0	
22/8	Man. United	h	2-2	*Davies, Hangeland*
28/8	Blackpool	a	2-2	*Zamora, Etuhu*
11/9	Wolves	h	2-1	*Dembélé 2*
18/9	Blackburn	a	1-1	*Dempsey*
25/9	Everton	h	0-0	
2/10	West Ham	a	1-1	*Dempsey*
16/10	Tottenham	h	1-2	*Kamara*
23/10	West Brom	a	1-2	*og (Carson)*
30/10	Wigan	h	2-0	*Dempsey 2*
6/11	Aston Villa	h	1-1	*Hangeland*
10/11	Chelsea	a	0-1	
13/11	Newcastle	a	0-0	
21/11	Man. City	h	1-4	*Gera*
27/11	Birmingham	h	1-1	*Dempsey*
4/12	Arsenal	a	1-2	*Kamara*
11/12	Sunderland	h	0-0	
26/12	West Ham	h	1-3	*Hughes*
28/12	Stoke	a	2-0	*Baird 2*
2011				
1/1	Tottenham	a	0-1	
4/1	West Brom	h	3-0	*Davies, Dempsey, Hangeland*
15/1	Wigan	a	1-1	*Johnson A.*
22/1	Stoke	h	2-0	*Dempsey 2 (1p)*
26/1	Liverpool	a	0-1	
2/2	Newcastle	h	1-0	*Duff*
5/2	Aston Villa	a	2-2	*Johnson A., Dempsey*
14/2	Chelsea	h	0-0	
27/2	Man. City	a	1-1	*Duff*
5/3	Blackburn	h	3-2	*Duff 2, Zamora (p)*
19/3	Everton	a	1-2	*Dempsey*
3/4	Blackpool	h	3-0	*Zamora 2, Etuhu*
9/4	Man. United	a	0-2	
23/4	Wolves	a	1-1	*Johnson A.*
27/4	Bolton	h	3-0	*Dempsey 2, Hangeland*
30/4	Sunderland	a	3-0	*Kakuta, Davies 2*
9/5	Liverpool	h	2-5	*Dembélé, Sidwell*
15/5	Birmingham	a	2-0	*Hangeland 2*
22/5	Arsenal	h	2-2	*Sidwell, Zamora*

No	Name	Nat	DoB	Pos	Aps	(s)	Gls
6	Chris BAIRD	NIR	25/2/82	D	25	(4)	2
28	Matthew BRIGGS		19/3/91	D	3		
29	Simon DAVIES	WAL	23/10/79	M	25	(5)	4
30	Moussa DEMBÉLÉ	BEL	16/7/87	A	22	(2)	3
23	Clint DEMPSEY	USA	9/3/83	M	35	(2)	12
26	Kagisho DIKGACOI	RSA	24/11/84	M		(1)	
16	Damien DUFF	IRL	2/3/79	M	22	(2)	4
20	Dickson ETUHU	NGA	8/6/82	M	23	(5)	2
11	Zoltán GERA	HUN	22/4/79	M	10	(17)	1
27	Jonathan GREENING		2/1/79	M	6	(4)	
22	Eidur Smári GUDJOHNSEN	ISL	15/9/78	A	4	(6)	
32	Rafik HALLICHE	ALG	2/9/86	D		(1)	
5	Brede Paulsen HANGELAND	NOR	20/6/81	D	37		6
18	Aaron HUGHES	NIR	8/11/79	D	38		1
8	Andrew JOHNSON		10/2/81	A	15	(12)	3
21	Eddie JOHNSON	USA	31/3/84	A	1	(10)	
24	Gaël KAKUTA	FRA	21/6/91	M	2	(5)	1
15	Diomansy KAMARA	SEN	8/11/80	A	7	(3)	2
2	Stephen KELLY	IRL	6/9/83	D	8	(2)	
3	Paul KONCHESKY		15/5/81	D	1		
13	Danny MURPHY		18/3/77	M	37		

4	John PANTSIL	GHA	15/6/81	D	15	(1)	
17	Bjørn Helge RIISE	NOR	21/6/83	M		(3)	
3	Carlos Arnaldo SALCIDO	MEX	2/4/80	D	22	(1)	
1	Mark SCHWARZER	AUS	6/10/72	G	31		
14	Philippe SENDEROS	SUI	14/2/85	D	3		
7	Steve SIDWELL		14/12/82	M	10	(2)	2
12	David STOCKDALE		20/9/85	G	7		
25	Bobby ZAMORA		16/1/81	A	9	(5)	5

LIVERPOOL FC

Manager – Roy Hodgson; (8/1/11) Kenny Dalglish (SCO)

Founded – 1892

Stadium – Anfield (45,362)

MAJOR HONOURS: European Champion Clubs' Cup/ UEFA Champions League – (5) 1977, 1978, 1981, 1984, 2005; UEFA Cup – (3) 1973, 1976, 2001; UEFA Super Cup – (3) 1977, 2001, 2005; English League – (18) 1901, 1906, 1922, 1923, 1947, 1964, 1966, 1973, 1976, 1977, 1979, 1980, 1982, 1983, 1984, 1986, 1988, 1990; FA Cup – (7) 1965, 1974, 1986, 1989, 1992, 2001, 2006; League Cup – (7) 1981, 1982, 1983, 1984, 1995, 2001, 2003.

2010				
15/8	Arsenal	h	1-1	*N'Gog*
23/8	Man. City	a	0-3	
29/8	West Brom	h	1-0	*Fernando Torres*
12/9	Birmingham	a	0-0	
19/9	Man. United	a	2-3	*Gerrard 2 (1p)*
25/9	Sunderland	h	2-2	*Kuyt, Gerrard*
3/10	Blackpool	h	1-2	*Kyrgiakos*
17/10	Everton	a	0-2	
24/10	Blackburn	h	2-1	*Kyrgiakos, Fernando Torres*
31/10	Bolton	a	1-0	*Maxi*
7/11	Chelsea	h	2-0	*Fernando Torres 2*
10/11	Wigan	a	1-1	*Fernando Torres*
13/11	Stoke	a	0-2	
20/11	West Ham	h	3-0	*Johnson, Kuyt (p), Maxi*
28/11	Tottenham	a	1-2	*Škrtel'*
6/12	Aston Villa	h	3-0	*N'Gog, Babel, Maxi*
11/12	Newcastle	a	1-3	*Kuyt*
29/12	Wolves	h	0-1	
2011				
1/1	Bolton	h	2-1	*Fernando Torres, Cole*
5/1	Blackburn	a	1-3	*Gerrard*
12/1	Blackpool	a	1-2	*Fernando Torres*
16/1	Everton	h	2-2	*Raul Meireles, Kuyt (p)*
22/1	Wolves	a	3-0	*Fernando Torres 2, Raul Meireles*
26/1	Fulham	h	1-0	*og (Pantsil)*
2/2	Stoke	h	2-0	*Raul Meireles, Suárez*
6/2	Chelsea	a	1-0	*Raul Meireles*
12/2	Wigan	h	1-1	*Raul Meireles*
27/2	West Ham	a	1-3	*Johnson*
6/3	Man. United	h	3-1	*Kuyt 3*
20/3	Sunderland	a	2-0	*Kuyt (p), Suárez*
2/4	West Brom	a	1-2	*Škrtel'*
11/4	Man. City	h	3-0	*Carroll 2, Kuyt*
17/4	Arsenal	a	1-1	*Kuyt (p)*
23/4	Birmingham	h	5-0	*Maxi 3, Kuyt, Cole*
1/5	Newcastle	h	3-0	*Maxi, Kuyt (p), Suárez*
9/5	Fulham	a	5-2	*Maxi 3, Kuyt, Suárez*
15/5	Tottenham	h	0-2	
22/5	Aston Villa	a	0-1	

No	Name	Nat	DoB	Pos	Aps	(s)	Gls
5	Daniel AGGER	DEN	12/12/84	D	12	(4)	
19	Ryan BABEL	NED	19/12/86	M	1	(8)	1
23	Jamie CARRAGHER		28/1/78	D	28		
9	Andy CARROLL		6/1/89	A	5	(2)	2
10	Joe COLE		8/11/81	M	9	(11)	2
12	DANIel PACHECO Lobato	ESP	5/1/91	A		(1)	
39	Nathan ECCLESTON		30/12/90	A		(1)	
12	FÁBIO AURÉLIO Rodrigues	BRA	24/9/79	D	7	(7)	
9	FERNANDO José TORRES Sanz	ESP	20/3/84	A	22	(1)	9
38	John FLANAGAN		21/1/93	D	7		
8	Steven GERRARD		30/5/80	M	20	(1)	4
2	Glen JOHNSON		23/8/84	D	28		2
14	Milan JOVANOVIĆ	SRB	18/4/83	A	5	(5)	
34	Martin KELLY		27/4/90	D	10	(1)	
3	Paul KONCHESKY		15/5/81	D	15		
18	Dirk KUYT	NED	22/7/80	A	32	(1)	13
16	Sotirios KYRGIAKOS	GRE	23/7/79	D	10	(6)	2
21	LUCAS Pezzini Leiva	BRA	9/1/87	M	32	(1)	
20	Javier MASCHERANO	ARG	8/6/84	M	1		
17	MAXImiliano Rubén Rodríguez	ARG	2/1/81	M	24	(4)	10
24	David N'GOG	FRA	1/4/89	A	9	(16)	2
28	Christian POULSEN	DEN	28/2/80	M	9	(3)	
4	RAUL José Trindade MEIRELES	POR	17/3/83	M	32	(1)	5
25	José Manuel "Pepe" REINA	ESP	31/8/82	G	38		
49	Jack ROBINSON		1/9/93	D	1	(1)	
33	Jonjo SHELVEY		27/2/92	M		(15)	
37	Martin ŠKRTEL'	SVK	15/12/84	D	38		2
26	Jay SPEARING		25/11/88	M	10	(1)	
7	Luis Alberto SUÁREZ	URU	24/1/87	A	12	(1)	4
22	Danny WILSON	SCO	27/12/91	D	1	(1)	

MANCHESTER CITY FC

Manager – Roberto Mancini (ITA)

Founded – 1894

Stadium – City of Manchester Stadium (47,715)

MAJOR HONOURS: UEFA Cup Winners' Cup – (1) 1970; English League – (2) 1937, 1968; FA Cup – (5) 1904, 1934, 1956, 1969, 2011; League Cup – (2) 1970, 1976.

2010				
14/8	Tottenham	a	0-0	
23/8	Liverpool	h	3-0	*Barry, Tévez 2 (1p)*
29/8	Sunderland	a	0-1	
11/9	Blackburn	h	1-1	*Vieira*
19/9	Wigan	a	2-0	*Tévez, Touré Y.*
25/9	Chelsea	h	1-0	*Tévez*
3/10	Newcastle	h	2-1	*Tévez (p), Johnson*
17/10	Blackpool	a	3-2	*Tévez 2, David Silva*
24/10	Arsenal	h	0-3	
30/10	Wolves	a	1-2	*Adebayor (p)*
7/11	West Brom	a	2-0	*Balotelli 2*
10/11	Man. United	h	0-0	
13/11	Birmingham	h	0-0	
21/11	Fulham	a	4-1	*Tévez 2, Zabaleta, Touré Y.*
27/11	Stoke	a	1-1	*Richards*
4/12	Bolton	h	1-0	*Tévez*
11/12	West Ham	a	3-1	*Touré Y. 2, Johnson*
20/12	Everton	h	1-2	*Touré Y.*
26/12	Newcastle	a	3-1	*Barry, Tévez, og (Coloccini)*
28/12	Aston Villa	h	4-0	*Balotelli 3 (2p), Lescott*
2011				
1/1	Blackpool	h	1-0	*Johnson*
5/1	Arsenal	a	0-0	
15/1	Wolves	h	4-3	*Touré K., Tévez 2, Touré Y.*
22/1	Aston Villa	a	0-1	
2/2	Birmingham	a	2-2	*Tévez, Kolarov*
5/2	West Brom	h	3-0	*Tévez 3 (2p)*
12/2	Man. United	a	1-2	*David Silva*
27/2	Fulham	h	1-1	*Balotelli*
5/3	Wigan	h	1-0	*David Silva*
20/3	Chelsea	a	0-2	
3/4	Sunderland	h	5-0	*Johnson, Tévez (p), David Silva, Vieira, Touré Y.*
11/4	Liverpool	a	0-3	
25/4	Blackburn	a	1-0	*Džeko*
1/5	West Ham	h	2-1	*De Jong, Zabaleta*

	Everton	a	1-2	*Touré Y.*
5	Tottenham	h	1-0	*og (Crouch)*
5	Stoke	h	3-0	*Tévez 2, Lescott*
5	Bolton	a	2-0	*Lescott, Džeko*

Name	Nat	DoB	Pos	Aps	(s)	Gls
Emmanuel ADEBAYOR	TOG	26/2/84	A	2	(6)	1
Mario BALOTELLI	ITA	12/8/90	A	12	(5)	6
Gareth BARRY		23/2/81	M	31	(2)	2
Jérôme BOATENG	GER	3/9/88	D	14	(2)	
Dedryck BOYATA	BEL	28/11/90	D	5	(2)	
Wayne BRIDGE		5/8/80	D	1	(2)	
DAVID Jiménez SILVA	ESP	8/1/86	M	30	(5)	4
Nigel DE JONG	NED	30/11/84	M	30	(2)	1
Edin DŽEKO	BIH	17/3/86	A	8	(7)	2
Joe HART		19/4/87	G	38		
João Alves de Assis Silva "JÔ"	BRA	20/3/87	A	3	(9)	
Adam JOHNSON		14/7/87	M	15	(16)	4
Aleksandar KOLAROV	SRB	10/11/85	D	20	(4)	1
Vincent KOMPANY	BEL	10/4/86	D	37		
Joleon LESCOTT		16/8/82	D	20	(2)	3
Ryan McGIVERN	NIR	8/1/90	D		(1)	
James MILNER		4/1/86	M	23	(9)	
Abdul RAZAK	CIV	11/11/92	D		(1)	
Micah RICHARDS		24/6/88	D	16	(2)	1
Roque SANTA CRUZ	PAR	16/8/81	A		(1)	
Carlos Alberto TÉVEZ	ARG	5/2/84	A	30	(1)	20
Kolo TOURÉ	CIV	19/3/81	D	21	(1)	1
Yaya TOURÉ	CIV	13/5/83	M	35		8
Patrick VIEIRA	FRA	23/6/76	M	4	(11)	2
Reece WABARA		28/12/91	D		(1)	
Shaun WRIGHT-PHILLIPS		25/10/81	M	2	(5)	
Pablo Javier ZABALETA	ARG	16/1/85	D	21	(5)	2

MANCHESTER UNITED FC

Manager – Sir Alex Ferguson (SCO)

Founded – 1878

Stadium – Old Trafford (76,212)

MAJOR HONOURS: European Champion Clubs' Cup/ UEFA Champions League – (3) 1968, 1999, 2008; UEFA Cup Winners' Cup – (1) 1991; UEFA Super Cup – (1) 1991; World Club Cup/FIFA Club World Cup – (2) 1999, 2008; English League – (19) 1908, 1911, 1952, 1956, 1957, 1965, 1967, 1993, 1994, 1996, 1997, 1999, 2000, 2001, 2003, 2007, 2008, 2009, 2011; FA Cup – (11) 1909, 1948, 1963, 1977, 1983, 1985, 1990, 1994, 1996, 1999, 2004; League Cup – (4) 1992, 2006, 2009, 2010.

2010				
16/8	Newcastle	h	3-0	*Berbatov, Fletcher, Giggs*
22/8	Fulham	a	2-2	*Scholes, og (Hangeland)*
28/8	West Ham	h	3-0	*Rooney (p), Nani, Berbatov*
1/9	Everton	a	3-3	*Fletcher, Vidić, Berbatov*
19/9	Liverpool	h	3-2	*Berbatov 3*
26/9	Bolton	a	2-2	*Nani, Owen*
2/10	Sunderland	a	0-0	
16/10	West Brom	h	2-2	*Hernández, Nani*
23/10	Stoke	a	2-1	*Hernández 2*
30/10	Tottenham	h	2-0	*Vidić, Nani*
6/11	Wolves	h	2-1	*Park 2*
10/11	Man. City	a	0-0	
13/11	Aston Villa	a	2-2	*Macheda, Vidić*
20/11	Wigan	h	2-0	*Evra, Hernández*
27/11	Blackburn	h	7-1	*Berbatov 5, Park, Nani*
13/12	Arsenal	h	1-0	*Park*
26/12	Sunderland	h	2-0	*Berbatov, og (Ferdinand)*
28/12	Birmingham	a	1-1	*Berbatov*
2011				
1/1	West Brom	a	2-1	*Rooney, Hernández*
4/1	Stoke	h	2-1	*Hernández, Nani*
16/1	Tottenham	a	0-0	
22/1	Birmingham	h	5-0	*Berbatov 3, Giggs, Nani*
25/1	Blackpool	a	3-2	*Berbatov 2, Hernández*
1/2	Aston Villa	h	3-1	*Rooney 2, Vidić*
5/2	Wolves	a	1-2	*Nani*
12/2	Man. City	h	2-1	*Nani, Rooney*
26/2	Wigan	a	4-0	*Hernández 2, Rooney, Fábio*
1/3	Chelsea	a	1-2	*Rooney*
6/3	Liverpool	a	1-3	*Hernández*
19/3	Bolton	h	1-0	*Berbatov*
2/4	West Ham	a	4-2	*Rooney 3 (1p), Hernández*
9/4	Fulham	h	2-0	*Berbatov, Valencia*
19/4	Newcastle	a	0-0	
23/4	Everton	h	1-0	*Hernández*
1/5	Arsenal	a	0-1	
8/5	Chelsea	h	2-1	*Hernández, Vidić*
14/5	Blackburn	a	1-1	*Rooney (p)*
22/5	Blackpool	h	4-2	*Park, Anderson, og (Evatt), Owen*

No	Name	Nat	DoB	Pos	Aps	(s)	Gls
8	ANDERSON Luís de Abreu Oliveira	BRA	13/4/88	M	14	(4)	1
33	Tiago Manuel Dias Correia "BÉBÉ"	POR	12/7/90	A		(2)	
9	Dimitar BERBATOV	BUL	30/1/81	A	24	(8)	20
6	Wes BROWN		13/10/79	D	4	(3)	
16	Michael CARRICK		28/7/81	M	23	(5)	
23	Jonny EVANS	NIR	3/1/89	D	11	(2)	
3	Patrice EVRA	FRA	15/5/81	D	34	(1)	1
20	FÁBIO Pereira da Silva	BRA	9/7/90	D	5	(6)	1
5	Rio FERDINAND		7/11/78	D	19		
24	Darren FLETCHER	SCO	1/2/84	M	24	(2)	2
28	Darron GIBSON	IRL	25/10/87	M	6	(6)	
11	Ryan GIGGS	WAL	29/11/73	M	19	(6)	2
4	Owen HARGREAVES		20/1/81	M	1		
14	Javier HERNÁNDEZ Balcázar	MEX	1/6/98	A	15	(12)	13
29	Tomasz KUSZCZAK	POL	20/3/82	G	5		
27	Federico MACHEDA	ITA	22/8/91	A	2	(5)	1
17	Luís Carlos Almeida da Cunha "NANI"	POR	17/11/86	M	31	(2)	9
2	Gary NEVILLE		18/2/75	D	3		
26	Gabriel OBERTAN	FRA	26/2/89	A	3	(4)	
22	John O'SHEA	IRL	30/4/81	D	18	(2)	
7	Michael OWEN		14/12/79	A	1	(10)	2
13	PARK Ji-sung	KOR	25/2/81	M	13	(2)	5
21	RAFAEL Pereira da Silva	BRA	9/7/90	D	15	(1)	
10	Wayne ROONEY		24/10/85	A	25	(3)	11
18	Paul SCHOLES		16/11/74	M	16	(6)	1
12	Chris SMALLING		22/11/89	D	11	(5)	
25	Luis Antonio VALENCIA	ECU	4/8/85	M	8	(2)	1
1	Edwin VAN DER SAR	NED	29/10/70	G	33		
15	Nemanja VIDIĆ	SRB	21/10/81	D	35		5

NEWCASTLE UNITED FC

Manager – Chris Hughton (IRL); (9/12/10) Alan Pardew

Founded – 1881

Stadium – St. James' Park (52,387)

MAJOR HONOURS: Inter Cities Fairs Cup – (1) 1969; English League – (4) 1905, 1907, 1909, 1927; FA Cup – (6) 1910, 1924, 1932, 1951, 1952, 1955.

2010				
16/8	Man. United	a	0-3	
22/8	Aston Villa	h	6-0	*Barton, Nolan 2, Carroll 3*
28/8	Wolves	a	1-1	*Carroll*
11/9	Blackpool	h	0-2	
18/9	Everton	a	1-0	*Ben Arfa*
26/9	Stoke	h	1-2	*Nolan (p)*
3/10	Man. City	a	1-2	*Gutiérrez*
16/10	Wigan	h	2-2	*Ameobi Sh., Coloccini*
23/10	West Ham	a	2-1	*Nolan, Carroll*
31/10	Sunderland	h	5-1	*Nolan 3, Ameobi Sh. 2 (1p)*

7/11	Arsenal	a	1-0	*Carroll*
10/11	Blackburn	h	1-2	*Carroll*
13/11	Fulham	h	0-0	
20/11	Bolton	a	1-5	*Carroll*
28/11	Chelsea	h	1-1	*Carroll*
5/12	West Brom	a	1-3	*Løvenkrands*
11/12	Liverpool	h	3-1	*Nolan, Barton, Carroll*
26/12	Man. City	h	1-3	*Carroll*
28/12	Tottenham	a	0-2	
2011				
2/1	Wigan	a	1-0	*Ameobi Sh.*
5/1	West Ham	h	5-0	*Best 3, Nolan, Løvenkrands*
16/1	Sunderland	a	1-1	*Nolan*
22/1	Tottenham	h	1-1	*Coloccini*
2/2	Fulham	a	0-1	
5/2	Arsenal	h	4-4	*Barton 2 (2p), Best, Tioté*
12/2	Blackburn	a	0-0	
15/2	Birmingham	a	2-0	*Løvenkrands, Best*
26/2	Bolton	h	1-1	*Nolan*
5/3	Everton	h	1-2	*Best*
19/3	Stoke	a	0-4	
2/4	Wolves	h	4-1	*Nolan, Ameobi Sh., Løvenkrands, Gutiérrez*
10/4	Aston Villa	a	0-1	
19/4	Man. United	h	0-0	
23/4	Blackpool	a	1-1	*Løvenkrands*
1/5	Liverpool	a	0-3	
7/5	Birmingham	h	2-1	*Ameobi Sh. (p), Taylor S.*
15/5	Chelsea	a	2-2	*Gutiérrez, Taylor S.*
22/5	West Brom	h	3-3	*Taylor S., Løvenkrands, og (Olsson)*

No	Name	Nat	DoB	Pos	Aps	(s)	Gls
44	Sammy AMEOBI	NGA	1/5/92	A		(1)	
23	Shola AMEOBI		12/10/81	A	21	(7)	6
7	Joey BARTON		2/9/82	M	32		4
37	Hatem BEN ARFA	FRA	7/3/87	M	3	(1)	1
20	Leon BEST	IRL	10/9/86	A	9	(2)	6
5	Sol CAMPBELL		18/9/74	D	4	(3)	
9	Andy CARROLL		6/1/89	A	18	(1)	11
2	Fabricio COLOCCINI	ARG	22/1/82	D	35		2
31	Shane FERGUSON	NIR	12/7/91	M	3	(4)	
15	Dan GOSLING		2/2/90	M		(1)	
8	Danny GUTHRIE		18/4/87	M	11	(3)	
18	Jonás Manuel GUTIÉRREZ	ARG	5/7/82	M	34	(3)	3
1	Steve HARPER		14/3/75	G	18		
9	Stephen IRELAND	IRL	22/8/86	M		(2)	
3	JOSÉ ENRIQUE Sánchez Díaz	ESP	23/1/86	D	36		
20	Tim KRUL	NED	3/4/88	G	20	(1)	
42	Shefki KUQI	FIN	10/11/76	A		(6)	
11	Peter LØVENKRANDS	DEN	29/1/80	A	18	(7)	6
25	Kazenga LUALUA	COD	10/12/90	M		(2)	
4	Kevin NOLAN		24/6/82	M	30		12
14	James PERCH		28/9/85	D	9	(3)	
30	Nile RANGER		11/4/91	A	1	(23)	
10	Wayne ROUTLEDGE		7/1/85	M	10	(7)	
12	Danny SIMPSON		4/1/87	D	30		
17	Alan SMITH		28/10/80	M	7	(4)	
16	Ryan TAYLOR		19/8/84	M	3	(3)	
27	Steven TAYLOR		23/1/86	D	12	(2)	3
24	Cheik TIOTÉ	CIV	21/6/86	M	26		1
6	Mik WILLIAMSON		8/11/83	D	28	(1)	
19	Francisco Jiménez Tejada "XISCO"	ESP	27/6/86	A		(2)	

STOKE CITY FC

Manager – Tony Pulis (WAL)

Founded – 1868

Stadium – Britannia Stadium (28,218)

MAJOR HONOURS: League Cup – (1) 1972.

2010				
14/8	Wolves	a	1-2	*Faye*
21/8	Tottenham	h	1-2	*Fuller*
28/8	Chelsea	a	0-2	
13/9	Aston Villa	h	2-1	*Jones, Huth*
18/9	West Ham	h	1-1	*Jones*
26/9	Newcastle	a	2-1	*Jones, og (Perch)*
2/10	Blackburn	h	1-0	*Walters*
16/10	Bolton	a	1-2	*Delap*
24/10	Man. United	h	1-2	*Tuncay*
30/10	Everton	a	0-1	
6/11	Sunderland	a	0-2	
9/11	Birmingham	h	3-2	*Huth, Fuller, Whitehead*
13/11	Liverpool	h	2-0	*Fuller, Jones*
20/11	West Brom	a	3-0	*Etherington (p), Walters 2 (1p)*
27/11	Man. City	h	1-1	*Etherington*
4/12	Wigan	a	2-2	*Huth, Etherington*
11/12	Blackpool	h	0-1	
26/12	Blackburn	a	2-0	*Huth, Wilson*
28/12	Fulham	h	0-2	
2011				
1/1	Everton	h	2-0	*Jones, og (Jagielka)*
4/1	Man. United	a	1-2	*Whitehead*
15/1	Bolton	h	2-0	*Higginbotham, Etherington (p)*
22/1	Fulham	a	0-2	
2/2	Liverpool	a	0-2	
5/2	Sunderland	h	3-2	*Carew, Huth 2*
12/2	Birmingham	a	0-1	
23/2	Arsenal	a	0-1	
28/2	West Brom	h	1-1	*Delap*
5/3	West Ham	a	0-3	
19/3	Newcastle	h	4-0	*Walters, Pennant, Higginbotham, Fuller*
2/4	Chelsea	h	1-1	*Walters*
9/4	Tottenham	a	2-3	*Etherington, Jones*
23/4	Aston Villa	a	1-1	*Jones*
26/4	Wolves	h	3-0	*Jones, Shawcross, Pennant*
30/4	Blackpool	a	0-0	
8/5	Arsenal	h	3-1	*Jones, Pennant, Walters*
17/5	Man. City	a	0-3	
22/5	Wigan	h	0-1	

No	Name	Nat	DoB	Pos	Aps	(s)	Gls
1	Asmir BEGOVIĆ	BIH	20/6/87	G	28		
2	John CAREW	NOR	5/9/79	A	7	(3)	1
5	Danny COLLINS	WAL	6/8/80	D	23	(2)	
24	Rory DELAP	IRL	6/7/76	M	33	(4)	2
15	Salif DIAO	SEN	10/2/77	M	3	(5)	
26	Matthew ETHERINGTON		14/8/81	M	30	(2)	5
25	Abdoulaye FAYE	SEN	26/2/78	D	12	(2)	1
10	Ricardo FULLER	JAM	31/10/79	A	9	(19)	4
7	Eidur Smári GUDJOHNSEN	ISL	15/9/78	A		(4)	
3	Danny HIGGINBOTHAM		29/12/78	D	9	(1)	2
4	Robert HUTH	GER	18/8/84	D	35		6
9	Kenwyne JONES	TRI	5/10/84	A	33	(1)	9
16	Jermaine PENNANT		15/1/83	M	26	(3)	3
14	Danny PUGH		19/10/82	M	5	(5)	
17	Ryan SHAWCROSS		4/10/87	D	36		1
30	Ryan SHOTTON		30/10/88	D		(2)	
11	Mamady SIDIBÉ	MLI	18/12/79	A		(2)	
29	Thomas SØRENSEN	DEN	12/6/76	G	10		
23	Michael TONGE		7/4/83	M		(2)	
20	TUNCAY Şanlı	TUR	16/1/82	A	5	(9)	1
19	Jonathan WALTERS	IRL	20/9/83	A	27	(9)	6
6	Glenn WHELAN	IRL	13/1/84	M	14	(15)	
18	Dean WHITEHEAD		12/1/82	M	31	(6)	2
28	Andy WILKINSON		6/8/84	D	21	(1)	
12	Marc WILSON	IRL	17/8/87	D	21	(7)	1

SUNDERLAND AFC

Manager – Steve Bruce
Founded – 1879
Stadium – Stadium of Light (49,000)
MAJOR HONOURS: English League – (6) 1892, 1893, 1895, 1902, 1913, 1936; FA Cup – (2) 1937, 1973.

10				
/8	Birmingham	h	2-2	*Bent, og (Carr)*
/8	West Brom	a	0-1	
/8	Man. City	h	1-0	*Bent (p)*
/9	Wigan	a	1-1	*Gyan*
/9	Arsenal	h	1-1	*Bent*
/9	Liverpool	a	2-2	*Bent 2 (1p)*
10	Man. United	h	0-0	
/10	Blackburn	a	0-0	
3/10	Aston Villa	h	1-0	*og (Dunne)*
1/10	Newcastle	a	1-5	*Bent*
11	Stoke	h	2-0	*Gyan 2*
11	Tottenham	a	1-1	*Gyan*
4/11	Chelsea	a	3-0	*Onuoha, Gyan, Welbeck*
2/11	Everton	h	2-2	*Welbeck 2*
7/11	Wolves	a	2-3	*Bent, Welbeck*
12	West Ham	h	1-0	*Henderson*
1/12	Fulham	a	0-0	
3/12	Bolton	h	1-0	*Welbeck*
6/12	Man. United	a	0-2	
8/12	Blackpool	h	0-2	
011				
/1	Blackburn	h	3-0	*Welbeck, Bent, Gyan*
/1	Aston Villa	a	1-0	*Bardsley*
6/1	Newcastle	h	1-1	*Gyan*
2/1	Blackpool	a	2-1	*Richardson 2*
/2	Chelsea	h	2-4	*Bardsley, Richardson*
/2	Stoke	a	2-3	*Richardson, Gyan*
2/2	Tottenham	h	1-2	*Gyan*
6/2	Everton	a	0-2	
/3	Arsenal	a	0-0	
0/3	Liverpool	h	0-2	
/4	Man. City	a	0-5	
/4	West Brom	h	2-3	*og (Shorey), Bardsley*
6/4	Birmingham	a	0-2	
3/4	Wigan	h	4-2	*Gyan, Henderson 2, Sessegnon (p)*
0/4	Fulham	h	0-3	
/5	Bolton	a	2-1	*Zenden, og (Knight)*
4/5	Wolves	h	1-3	*Sessegnon*
22/5	West Ham	a	3-0	*Zenden, Sessegnon, Riveros*

No	Name	Nat	DoB	Pos	Aps	(s)	Gls
2	Marcos Alberto ANGELERI	ARG	4/7/83	D		(2)	
2	Phil BARDSLEY	SCO	28/6/85	D	32	(2)	3
11	Darren BENT		6/2/84	A	20		8
19	Titus BRAMBLE		21/7/81	D	22	(1)	
9	Fraizer CAMPBELL		13/9/87	A	3		
6	Lee CATTERMOLE		21/3/88	M	22	(1)	
25	Jack COLBACK		24/10/89	M	6	(5)	
26	Jordan COOK		20/3/90	A		(3)	
14	Paulo DA SILVA	PAR	1/2/80	D	1		
27	Ahmed ELMOHAMADY	EGY	9/9/87	M	26	(10)	
29	Anton FERDINAND		18/2/85	D	23	(4)	
1	Craig GORDON	SCO	31/12/82	G	15		
33	Asamoah GYAN	GHA	22/11/85	A	20	(11)	10
10	Jordan HENDERSON		17/6/90	M	37		3
40	Louis LAING		6/3/93	D		(1)	
38	Craig LYNCH		25/3/92	A		(2)	
8	Steed MALBRANQUE	FRA	6/1/80	M	24	(11)	
5	John MENSAH	GHA	29/11/82	D	15	(3)	
18	David MEYLER	IRL	29/5/89	M	4	(1)	
22	Simon MIGNOLET	BEL	6/8/88	G	23		
11	Sulley Ali MUNTARI	GHA	27/8/84	M	7	(2)	
31	Ryan NOBLE		1/11/92	A		(3)	
15	Nedum ONUOHA		12/11/86	D	31		1
20	Andy REID	IRL	29/7/82	M		(2)	
3	Kieran RICHARDSON		21/10/84	M	23	(3)	4
16	Cristian RIVEROS	PAR	16/10/82	M	5	(7)	1
28	Stéphane SESSEGNON	BEN	1/6/84	M	13	(1)	3
4	Michael TURNER		9/11/83	D	15		
27	Martyn WAGHORN		23/1/90	A		(2)	
17	Danny WELBECK		26/11/90	A	21	(5)	6
7	Boudewijn ZENDEN	NED	15/8/76	M	10	(17)	2

TOTTENHAM HOTSPUR FC

Manager – Harry Redknapp
Founded – 1882
Stadium – White Hart Lane (36,310)
MAJOR HONOURS: UEFA Cup Winners' Cup – (1) 1963; UEFA Cup – (2) 1972, 1984; English League – (2) 1951, 1961; FA Cup – (8) 1901, 1921, 1961, 1962, 1967, 1981, 1982, 1991; League Cup – (4) 1971, 1973, 1999, 2008.

2010				
14/8	Man. City	h	0-0	
21/8	Stoke	a	2-1	*Bale 2*
28/8	Wigan	h	0-1	
11/9	West Brom	a	1-1	*Modrić*
18/9	Wolves	h	3-1	*Van der Vaart (p), Pavlyuchenko, Hutton*
25/9	West Ham	a	0-1	
2/10	Aston Villa	h	2-1	*Van der Vaart 2*
16/10	Fulham	a	2-1	*Pavlyuchenko, Huddlestone*
23/10	Everton	h	1-1	*Van der Vaart*
30/10	Man. United	a	0-2	
6/11	Bolton	a	2-4	*Hutton, Pavlyuchenko*
9/11	Sunderland	h	1-1	*Van der Vaart*
13/11	Blackburn	h	4-2	*Bale 2, Pavlyuchenko, Crouch*
20/11	Arsenal	a	3-2	*Bale, Van der Vaart (p), Kaboul*
28/11	Liverpool	h	2-1	*og (Škrtel), Lennon*
4/12	Birmingham	a	1-1	*Bassong*
12/12	Chelsea	h	1-1	*Pavlyuchenko*
26/12	Aston Villa	a	2-1	*Van der Vaart 2*
28/12	Newcastle	h	2-0	*Lennon, Bale*
2011				
1/1	Fulham	h	1-0	*Bale*
5/1	Everton	a	1-2	*Van der Vaart*
16/1	Man. United	h	0-0	
22/1	Newcastle	a	1-1	*Lennon*
2/2	Blackburn	a	1-0	*Crouch*
5/2	Bolton	h	2-1	*Van der Vaart (p), Kranjčar*
12/2	Sunderland	a	2-1	*Dawson, Kranjčar*
22/2	Blackpool	a	1-3	*og (Cathcart)*
6/3	Wolves	a	3-3	*Defoe 2, Pavlyuchenko*
19/3	West Ham	h	0-0	
2/4	Wigan	a	0-0	
9/4	Stoke	h	3-2	*Crouch 2, Modrić*
20/4	Arsenal	h	3-3	*Van der Vaart 2 (1p), Huddlestone*
23/4	West Brom	h	2-2	*Pavlyuchenko, Defoe*
30/4	Chelsea	a	1-2	*Sandro*
7/5	Blackpool	h	1-1	*Defoe*
10/5	Man. City	a	0-1	
15/5	Liverpool	a	2-0	*Van der Vaart, Modrić (p)*
22/5	Birmingham	h	2-1	*Pavlyuchenko 2*

No	Name	Nat	DoB	Pos	Aps	(s)	Gls
32	Benoît ASSOU-EKOTTO	CMR	24/3/84	D	30		
3	Gareth BALE	WAL	16/7/89	M	29	(1)	7
19	Sébastien BASSONG	CMR	9/7/86	D	7	(5)	1
5	David BENTLEY		27/8/84	M	1	(1)	
22	Vedran ĆORLUKA	CRO	5/2/86	D	13	(2)	
15	Peter CROUCH		30/1/81	A	20	(14)	4
23	Carlo CUDICINI	ITA	6/9/73	G	8		
20	Michael DAWSON		18/11/83	D	24		1
18	Jermain DEFOE		7/10/82	A	16	(6)	4
13	William GALLAS	FRA	17/8/77	D	26	(1)	
17	GIOVANI dos Santos Ramírez	MEX	11/5/89	M		(3)	

1	Heurelho da Silva GOMES	BRA	15/2/81	G	30		
6	Tom HUDDLESTONE		28/12/86	M	13	(1)	2
2	Alan HUTTON	SCO	30/11/84	D	19	(2)	2
8	Jermaine JENAS		18/2/83	M	14	(5)	
4	Younes KABOUL	FRA	4/1/86	D	19	(2)	1
10	Robbie KEANE	IRL	8/7/80	A	2	(5)	
26	Ledley KING		12/10/80	D	6		
21	Niko KRANJČAR	CRO	13/8/84	M	2	(11)	2
7	Aaron LENNON		16/4/87	M	25	(9)	3
14	Luka MODRIĆ	CRO	9/9/85	M	32		3
12	Wilson PALACIOS	HON	29/7/84	M	16	(5)	
9	Roman PAVLYUCHENKO	RUS	15/12/81	A	18	(11)	9
40	Steven PIENAAR	RSA	17/3/82	M	5	(3)	
25	Danny ROSE		2/6/90	D	4		
30	SANDRO Ranieri Guimarães Cordeiro	BRA	15/3/89	M	11	(8)	1
11	Rafael VAN DER VAART	NED	11/2/83	M	28		13
28	Kyle WALKER		28/5/90	D		(1)	

WEST BROMWICH ALBION FC

Manager – Roberto Di Matteo (ITA); (11/2/11) Roy Hodgson
Founded – 1878
Stadium – The Hawthorns (27,877)
MAJOR HONOURS: English League – (1) 1920; FA Cup – (5) 1888, 1892, 1931, 1954, 1968; League Cup – (1) 1966.

2010				
14/8	Chelsea	a	0-6	
21/8	Sunderland	h	1-0	*Odemwingie*
29/8	Liverpool	a	0-1	
11/9	Tottenham	h	1-1	*Brunt*
18/9	Birmingham	h	3-1	*og (Dann), Odemwingie, Olsson*
25/9	Arsenal	a	3-2	*Odemwingie, Jara, Thomas*
2/10	Bolton	h	1-1	*Morrison*
16/10	Man. United	a	2-2	*og (Evra), Tchoyi*
23/10	Fulham	h	2-1	*Mulumbu, Fortuné*
1/11	Blackpool	a	1-2	*Mulumbu*
7/11	Man. City	h	0-2	
10/11	West Ham	a	2-2	*Odemwingie (p), Pablo*
13/11	Wigan	a	0-1	
20/11	Stoke	h	0-3	
27/11	Everton	a	4-1	*Scharner, Brunt, Tchoyi, Mulumbu*
5/12	Newcastle	h	3-1	*Tchoyi, Odemwingie 2*
11/12	Aston Villa	a	1-2	*Scharner*
26/12	Bolton	a	0-2	
28/12	Blackburn	h	1-3	*Thomas*
2011				
1/1	Man. United	h	1-2	*Morrison*
4/1	Fulham	a	0-3	
15/1	Blackpool	h	3-2	*Odemwingie 2, Morrison*
23/1	Blackburn	a	0-2	
1/2	Wigan	h	2-2	*Odemwingie, Fortuné*
5/2	Man. City	a	0-3	
12/2	West Ham	h	3-3	*Dorrans, Thomas, og (Reid)*
20/2	Wolves	h	1-1	*Vela*
28/2	Stoke	a	1-1	*Vela*
5/3	Birmingham	a	3-1	*Mulumbu, Morrison, Scharner*
19/3	Arsenal	h	2-2	*Reid, Odemwingie*
2/4	Liverpool	h	2-1	*Brunt 2 (2p)*
9/4	Sunderland	a	3-2	*Odemwingie, Mulumbu, Scharner*
16/4	Chelsea	h	1-3	*Odemwingie*
23/4	Tottenham	a	2-2	*Odemwingie, Cox*
30/4	Aston Villa	h	2-1	*Odemwingie, Mulumbu*
8/5	Wolves	a	1-3	*Odemwingie (p)*
14/5	Everton	h	1-0	*Mulumbu*
22/5	Newcastle	a	3-3	*Tchoyi 3*

No	Name	Nat	DoB	Pos	Aps	(s)	Gls
8	Giles BARNES		5/8/88	M	1	(13)	
9	Roman BEDNÁŘ	CZE	26/3/83	A	1	(3)	
11	Chris BRUNT	NIR	14/12/84	M	34		4
1	Scott CARSON		3/9/85	G	32		
4	Marek ČECH	SVK	26/1/83	D	14	(1)	
31	Simon COX	IRL	28/4/87	A	8	(11)	1
17	Graham DORRANS	SCO	5/5/87	M	16	(5)	1
28	Marc-Antoine FORTUNÉ	FRA	2/7/81	A	14	(11)	2
26	James HURST		31/1/92	D	1		
36	Gonzalo Alejandro JARA	CHI	29/8/85	D	24	(5)	1
23	Abdoulaye MÉÏTÉ	CIV	6/10/80	D	10		
10	Ishmael MILLER		5/3/87	A		(6)	
7	James MORRISON	SCO	25/5/86	M	26	(5)	4
21	Youssuf MULUMBU	COD	25/1/87	M	34		7
13	Boaz MYHILL	WAL	9/11/82	G	6		
24	Peter ODEMWINGIE	NGA	15/7/81	A	29	(3)	15
3	Jonas OLSSON	SWE	10/3/83	D	24		1
6	PABLO Ibáñez Tébar	ESP	3/8/81	D	8	(2)	1
12	Steven REID	IRL	10/3/81	M	13	(10)	1
33	Paul SCHARNER	AUT	11/3/80	M	33		4
20	Nicky SHOREY		19/2/81	D	25	(3)	
30	Gabriel Sebastian TAMAŞ	ROU	9/11/83	D	22	(4)	
5	Somen TCHOYI	CMR	29/3/83	M	7	(16)	6
14	Jerome THOMAS		23/3/83	M	32	(1)	3
21	George THORNE		4/1/93	M		(1)	
18	Carlos Alberto VELA	MEX	1/3/89	A	3	(5)	2
15	Chris WOOD	NZL	7/12/91	A		(1)	
22	Gianni ZUIVERLOON	NED	30/12/86	D	1	(1)	

WEST HAM UNITED FC

Manager – Avram Grant (ISR); (16/5/11) (Kevin Keen)
Founded – 1900
Stadium – Upton Park (35,303)
MAJOR HONOURS: UEFA Cup Winners' Cup – (1) 1965; FA Cup – (3) 1964, 1975, 1980.

2010				
14/8	Aston Villa	a	0-3	
21/8	Bolton	h	1-3	*Noble (p)*
28/8	Man. United	a	0-3	
11/9	Chelsea	h	1-3	*Parker*
18/9	Stoke	a	1-1	*Parker*
25/9	Tottenham	h	1-0	*Piquionne*
2/10	Fulham	h	1-1	*Piquionne*
16/10	Wolves	a	1-1	*Noble*
23/10	Newcastle	h	1-2	*Cole*
30/10	Arsenal	a	0-1	
6/11	Birmingham	a	2-2	*Piquionne, Behrami*
10/11	West Brom	h	2-2	*Parker, Piquionne (p)*
13/11	Blackpool	h	0-0	
20/11	Liverpool	a	0-3	
27/11	Wigan	h	3-1	*Behrami, Obinna, Parker*
5/12	Sunderland	a	0-1	
11/12	Man. City	h	1-3	*Tomkins*
18/12	Blackburn	a	1-1	*Stanislas*
26/12	Fulham	a	3-1	*Cole 2, Piquionne*
28/12	Everton	h	1-1	*og (Hibbert)*
2011				
1/1	Wolves	h	2-0	*og (Zubar), Sears*
5/1	Newcastle	a	0-5	
15/1	Arsenal	h	0-3	
22/1	Everton	a	2-2	*Spector, Piquionne*
2/2	Blackpool	a	3-1	*Obinna 2, Keane*
6/2	Birmingham	h	0-1	
12/2	West Brom	a	3-3	*Ba 2, Cole*
27/2	Liverpool	h	3-1	*Parker, Ba, Cole*
5/3	Stoke	h	3-0	*Ba, Da Costa, Hitzlsperger*
19/3	Tottenham	a	0-0	
2/4	Man. United	h	2-4	*Noble 2 (2p)*
9/4	Bolton	a	0-3	
16/4	Aston Villa	h	1-2	*Keane*
23/4	Chelsea	a	0-3	
1/5	Man. City	a	1-2	*Ba*
7/5	Blackburn	h	1-1	*Hitzlsperger*
15/5	Wigan	a	2-3	*Ba 2*
22/5	Sunderland	h	0-3	

No	Name	Nat	DoB	Pos	Aps	(s)	Gls
21	Demba BA	SEN	25/5/85	A	10	(2)	7
2	Pablo BARRERA	MEX	21/6/87	M	6	(8)	
21	Valon BEHRAMI	SUI	19/4/85	M	6	(1)	2
	Tal BEN HAIM	ISR	31/3/82	D	8		
3	Luís BOA MORTE Pereira	POR	4/8/77	M	19	(3)	
31	Ruud BOFFIN	BEL	5/11/87	G	1		
36	Wayne BRIDGE		5/8/80	D	15		
	Carlton COLE		12/10/83	A	21	(14)	5
10	Jack COLLISON	WAL	2/10/88	M	2	(1)	
22	Manuel DA COSTA	POR	6/5/86	D	14	(2)	1
32	Alessandro DIAMANTI	ITA	2/5/83	A		(1)	
7	Kieron DYER		29/12/78	M	8	(3)	
20	Julien FAUBERT	FRA	1/8/83	D	7	(2)	
4	Danny GABBIDON	WAL	8/8/79	D	24	(2)	
	Robert GREEN		18/1/80	G	37		
26	Zavon HINES	JAM	27/12/88	A	4	(5)	
11	Thomas HITZLSPERGER	GER	5/4/82	M	11		2
23	Hérita ILUNGA	COD	25/2/82	D	10	(1)	
37	Lars JACOBSEN	DEN	20/9/79	D	22	(2)	
34	Robbie KEANE	IRL	8/7/80	A	5	(4)	2
14	Radoslav KOVÁČ	CZE	27/11/79	D	7	(6)	
17	Benni McCARTHY	RSA	12/11/77	A		(6)	
16	Mark NOBLE		8/5/87	M	25	(1)	4
24	Frank NOUBLE		24/9/91	A		(2)	
33	Victor Nsofor OBINNA	NGA	25/3/87	A	17	(8)	3
32	Gary O'NEIL		18/5/83	M	7	(1)	
8	Scott PARKER		13/10/80	M	30	(2)	5
30	Frédéric PIQUIONNE	FRA	8/12/78	A	26	(8)	6
2	Winston REID	NZL	3/7/88	D	3	(4)	
19	Freddie SEARS		27/11/89	A	9	(2)	1
18	Jonathan SPECTOR	USA	1/3/86	D	10	(4)	1
27	Jordan SPENCE		24/5/90	D	2		
25	Junior STANISLAS		26/11/89	M	4	(2)	1
5	James TOMKINS		29/3/89	D	18	(1)	1
15	Matthew UPSON		18/4/79	D	30		

WIGAN ATHLETIC FC

Manager – Roberto Martínez (ESP)

Founded – 1932

Stadium – DW Stadium (25,138)

2010				
14/8	Blackpool	h	0-4	
21/8	Chelsea	h	0-6	
28/8	Tottenham	a	1-0	*Rodallega*
11/9	Sunderland	h	1-1	*Alcaraz*
19/9	Man. City	h	0-2	
25/9	Birmingham	a	0-0	
2/10	Wolves	h	2-0	*Jordi Gómez, Rodallega*
16/10	Newcastle	a	2-2	*N'Zogbia 2*
23/10	Bolton	h	1-1	*Rodallega*
30/10	Fulham	a	0-2	
6/11	Blackburn	a	1-2	*N'Zogbia*
10/11	Liverpool	h	1-1	*Rodallega*
13/11	West Brom	h	1-0	*Moses*
20/11	Man. United	a	0-2	
27/11	West Ham	a	1-3	*Cleverley*
4/12	Stoke	h	2-2	*og (Collins), og (Delap)*
11/12	Everton	a	0-0	
26/12	Wolves	a	2-1	*Rodallega, Cleverley*
29/12	Arsenal	h	2-2	*Watson (p), og (Squillaci)*
2011				
2/1	Newcastle	h	0-1	
5/1	Bolton	a	1-1	*Stam*
15/1	Fulham	h	1-1	*Rodallega*
22/1	Arsenal	a	0-3	
25/1	Aston Villa	h	1-2	*McCarthy*
1/2	West Brom	a	2-2	*N'Zogbia, Watson*
5/2	Blackburn	h	4-3	*McCarthy 2, Rodallega, Watson (p)*
12/2	Liverpool	a	1-1	*Gohouri*
26/2	Man. United	h	0-4	
5/3	Man. City	a	0-1	
19/3	Birmingham	h	2-1	*Cleverley, Figueroa*
2/4	Tottenham	h	0-0	
9/4	Chelsea	a	0-1	
16/4	Blackpool	a	3-1	*Rodallega, N'Zogbia, og (Eardley)*
23/4	Sunderland	a	2-4	*Diamé, Di Santo*
30/4	Everton	h	1-1	*N'Zogbia*
7/5	Aston Villa	a	1-1	*N'Zogbia*
15/5	West Ham	h	3-2	*N'Zogbia 2, Sammon*
22/5	Stoke	a	1-0	*Rodallega*

No	Name	Nat	DoB	Pos	Aps	(s)	Gls
26	Ali AL HABSI	OMA	30/12/81	G	34		
3	Antolín ALCARAZ	PAR	30/7/82	D	34		1
9	Mauro BOSELLI	ARG	22/5/85	A	5	(3)	
17	Emmerson BOYCE	BRB	24/9/79	D	20	(2)	
5	Gary CALDWELL	SCO	12/4/82	D	23		
13	Steven CALDWELL	SCO	12/9/80	D	8	(2)	
15	Tom CLEVERLEY		12/8/89	M	19	(6)	3
7	Franco DI SANTO	ARG	7/4/89	A	9	(16)	1
21	Mohamed DIAMÉ	SEN	14/6/87	M	30	(6)	1
31	Maynor FIGUEROA	HON	2/5/83	D	32	(1)	1
2	Steve GOHOURI	CIV	8/2/81	D	26	(1)	1
14	JORDI GÓMEZ Garcia-Penche	ESP	24/5/85	M	9	(4)	1
1	Chris KIRKLAND		2/5/81	G	4		
16	James McARTHUR	SCO	7/10/87	M	3	(15)	
4	James McCARTHY	IRL	12/11/90	M	24		3
38	Callum McMANAMAN		25/4/91	A		(3)	
11	Victor MOSES		12/12/90	A	8	(13)	1
10	Charles N'ZOGBIA	FRA	28/5/86	M	32	(2)	9
24	Adrián López Rodríguez "PISCU"	ESP	25/2/87	D	1		
12	Mike POLLITT		29/2/72	G		(1)	
20	Hugo RODALLEGA	COL	25/7/85	A	34	(2)	9
18	Conor SAMMON	IRL	6/11/86	A	1	(6)	1
23	Ronnie STAM	NED	18/6/84	M	17	(8)	1
6	Hendry THOMAS	HON	23/2/85	M	22	(2)	
8	Ben WATSON		9/7/85	M	23	(6)	3

WOLVERHAMPTON WANDERERS FC

Manager – Mick McCarthy (IRL)

Founded – 1877

Stadium – Molineux (28,576)

MAJOR HONOURS: English League – (3) 1954, 1958, 1959; FA Cup – (4) 1893, 1908, 1949, 1960; League Cup – (2) 1974, 1980.

2010				
14/8	Stoke	h	2-1	*Jones, Fletcher*
21/8	Everton	a	1-1	*Ebanks-Blake*
28/8	Newcastle	h	1-1	*Ebanks-Blake*
11/9	Fulham	a	1-2	*Van Damme*
18/9	Tottenham	a	1-3	*Fletcher*
26/9	Aston Villa	h	1-2	*Jarvis*
2/10	Wigan	a	0-2	
16/10	West Ham	h	1-1	*Jarvis*
23/10	Chelsea	a	0-2	
30/10	Man. City	h	2-1	*Milijaš, Edwards*
6/11	Man. United	a	1-2	*Ebanks-Blake*
10/11	Arsenal	h	0-2	
13/11	Bolton	h	2-3	*Foley, Fletcher*
20/11	Blackpool	a	1-2	*Doyle*
27/11	Sunderland	h	3-2	*Foley, Hunt, Ebanks-Blake*
4/12	Blackburn	a	0-3	
12/12	Birmingham	h	1-0	*Hunt*
26/12	Wigan	h	1-2	*Fletcher*
29/12	Liverpool	a	1-0	*Ward*

2011

1/1	West Ham	a	0-2	
5/1	Chelsea	h	1-0	*og (Bosingwa)*
15/1	Man. City	a	3-4	*Milijaš, Doyle (p), Zubar*
22/1	Liverpool	h	0-3	
2/2	Bolton	a	0-1	
5/2	Man. United	h	2-1	*Elokobi, Doyle*
12/2	Arsenal	a	0-2	
20/2	West Brom	a	1-1	*O'Hara*
26/2	Blackpool	h	4-0	*Jarvis, O'Hara, Ebanks-Blake 2*
6/3	Tottenham	h	3-3	*Doyle 2 (1p), Fletcher*
19/3	Aston Villa	a	1-0	*Jarvis*
2/4	Newcastle	a	1-4	*Ebanks-Blake*
9/4	Everton	h	0-3	
23/4	Fulham	h	1-1	*Fletcher*
26/4	Stoke	a	0-3	
1/5	Birmingham	a	1-1	*Fletcher (p)*
8/5	West Brom	h	3-1	*Fletcher 2, Guedioura*
14/5	Sunderland	a	3-1	*Craddock, Fletcher, Elokobi*
22/5	Blackburn	h	2-3	*O'Hara, Hunt*

No	Name	Nat	DoB	Pos	Aps	(s)	Gls
19	Marcus BENT		19/5/78	A		(3)	
16	Christophe BERRA	SCO	31/1/85	D	31	(1)	
6	Jody CRADDOCK		25/7/75	D	14	(1)	1
29	Kevin DOYLE	IRL	18/9/83	A	25	(1)	5
9	Sylvan EBANKS-BLAKE		29/3/86	A	11	(19)	7
4	David EDWARDS	WAL	3/2/86	M	12	(3)	1
3	George ELOKOBI	CMR	31/1/86	D	23	(4)	2
10	Steven FLETCHER	SCO	26/3/87	A	15	(14)	10
32	Kevin FOLEY	IRL	1/11/84	D	30	(3)	2
34	Adlène GUEDIOURA	ALG	12/11/85	M	4	(6)	1
1	Marcus HAHNEMANN	USA	15/6/72	G	14		
15	Greg HALFORD		8/12/84	D		(2)	
10	Adam HAMMILL		25/1/88	M	7	(3)	
13	Wayne HENNESSEY	WAL	24/1/87	G	24		
8	Karl HENRY		26/11/82	M	28	(1)	
12	Stephen HUNT	IRL	1/8/81	M	14	(6)	3
17	Matthew JARVIS		22/5/86	M	34	(3)	4
14	David JONES		4/11/84	M	11	(1)	1
19	Andy KEOGH	IRL	16/5/86	A		(1)	
7	Michael KIGHTLY		24/1/86	M	1	(3)	
21	Michael MANCIENNE		8/1/88	D	13	(3)	
20	Nenad MILIJAŠ	SRB	30/4/83	M	20	(3)	2
22	Steven MOUYOKOLO	FRA	24/1/87	D	2	(2)	
25	Geoffrey MUJANGI BIA	BEL	12/8/89	M		(1)	
24	Jamie O'HARA		25/9/86	M	13	(1)	3
5	Richard STEARMAN		19/8/87	D	27	(4)	
2	Jelle VAN DAMME	BEL	10/10/83	D	4	(2)	1
18	Sam VOKES	WAL	21/10/89	A		(2)	
11	Stephen WARD	IRL	20/8/85	D	27	(7)	1
23	Ronald ZUBAR	FRA	20/9/85	D	14	(1)	1

TOP GOALSCORERS 2010/11

20	Carlos TÉVEZ (Man City)
	Dimitar BERBATOV (Man. United)
18	Robin VAN PERSIE (Arsenal)
17	Darren BENT (Sunderland/Aston Villa)
15	Peter ODEMWINGIE (West Brom)
13	DJ CAMPBELL (Blackpool)
	Florent MALOUDA (Chelsea)
	Dirk KUYT (Liverpool)
	Javier HERNÁNDEZ (Man. United)
	Andy CARROLL (Newcastle/Liverpool)
	Rafael VAN DER VAART (Tottenham)

PROMOTED CLUBS

QUEENS PARK RANGERS FC

Manager – Neil Warnock
Founded – 1882
Stadium – Loftus Road (18,682)
MAJOR HONOURS: League Cup – (1) 1967.

NORWICH CITY FC

Manager – Paul Lambert (SCO)
Founded – 1902
Stadium – Carrow Road (26,034)
MAJOR HONOURS: League Cup – (2) 1962, 1985.

SWANSEA CITY AFC

Manager – Brendan Rodgers (NIR)
Founded – 1912
Stadium – Liberty Stadium (20,520)
MAJOR HONOURS: Welsh Cup – (10) 1913, 1932, 1950, 1961, 1966, 1981, 1982, 1983, 1989, 1991.

SECOND LEVEL FINAL TABLE 2010/11

		Pld	W	D	L	F	A	Pts
1	Queens Park Rangers FC	46	24	16	6	71	32	88
2	Norwich City FC	46	23	15	8	83	58	84
3	Swansea City AFC	46	24	8	14	69	42	80
4	Cardiff City FC	46	23	11	12	76	54	80
5	Reading FC	46	20	17	9	77	51	77
6	Nottingham Forest FC	46	20	15	11	69	50	75
7	Leeds United AFC	46	19	15	12	81	70	72
8	Burnley FC	46	18	14	14	65	61	68
9	Millwall FC	46	18	13	15	62	48	67
10	Leicester City FC	46	19	10	17	76	71	67
11	Hull City AFC	46	16	17	13	52	51	65
12	Middlesbrough FC	46	17	11	18	68	68	62
13	Ipswich Town FC	46	18	8	20	62	68	62
14	Watford FC	46	16	13	17	77	71	61
15	Bristol City FC	46	17	9	20	62	65	60
16	Portsmouth FC	46	15	13	18	53	60	58
17	Barnsley FC	46	14	14	18	55	66	56
18	Coventry City FC	46	14	13	19	54	58	55
19	Derby County FC	46	13	10	23	58	71	49
20	Crystal Palace FC	46	12	12	22	44	69	48
21	Doncaster Rovers FC	46	11	15	20	55	81	48
22	Preston North End FC	46	10	12	24	54	79	42
23	Sheffield United FC	46	11	9	26	44	79	42
24	Scunthorpe United FC	46	12	6	28	43	87	42

PROMOTION PLAY-OFFS

(12/5/11)
Nottingham Forest 0, Swansea 0
(16/5/11)
Swansea 3, Nottingham Forest 1
(Swansea 3-1)

(13/5/11)
Reading 0, Cardiff 0
(17/5/11)
Cardiff 0, Reading 3
(Reading 3-0)

(30/5/11)
Swansea 4, Reading 2

DOMESTIC CUPS 2010/11

FA CUP

THIRD ROUND

(8/1/11)
Arsenal 1, Leeds 1
Blackburn 1, QPR 0
Bolton 2, York 0
Brighton 3, Portsmouth 1
Bristol City 0, Sheffield Wednesday 3
Burnley 4, Port Vale 2
Burton 2, Middlesbrough 1
Coventry 2, Crystal Palace 1
Doncaster 2, Wolves 2
Fulham 6, Peterborough 2
Huddersfield 2, Dover 0
Hull 2, Wigan 3
Millwall 1, Birmingham 4
Norwich 0, Leyton Orient 1
Preston 1, Nottingham Forest 2
Reading 1, West Brom 0
Scunthorpe 1, Everton 5
Sheffield United 1, Aston Villa 3
Southampton 2, Blackpool 0
Stevenage 3, Newcastle 1
Stoke 1, Cardiff 1
Sunderland 1, Notts County 2
Swansea 4, Colchester 0
Torquay 1, Carlisle 0
Watford 4, Hartlepool 1
West Ham 2, Barnsley 0

(9/1/11)
Chelsea 7, Ipswich 0
Leicester 2, Man. City 2
Man. United 1, Liverpool 0
Tottenham 3, Charlton 0

(10/1/11)
Crawley 2, Derby 1

(11/1/11)
Wycombe 0, Hereford 1

Replays

(18/1/11)
Cardiff 0, Stoke 2 (aet)
Man. City 4, Leicester 2
Wolves 5, Doncaster 0

(19/1/11)
Leeds 1, Arsenal 3

FOURTH ROUND

(29/1/11)
Aston Villa 3, Blackburn 1
Birmingham 3, Coventry 2
Bolton 0, Wigan 0
Burnley 3, Burton 1
Everton 1, Chelsea 1
Sheffield Wednesday 4, Hereford 1
Southampton 1, Man. United 2
Stevenage 1, Reading 2
Swansea 1, Leyton Orient 2
Torquay 0, Crawley 1
Watford 0, Brighton 1

(30/1/11)
Arsenal 2, Huddersfield 1
Fulham 4, Tottenham 0
Notts County 1, Man. City 1
West Ham 3, Nottingham Forest 2
Wolves 0, Stoke 1

Replays

(16/2/11)
Wigan 0, Bolton 1

(19/2/11)
Chelsea 1, Everton 1 *(aet; 3-4 on pens)*

(20/2/11)
Man. City 5, Notts County 0

FIFTH ROUND

(19/2/11)
Birmingham 3, Sheffield Wednesday 0
Man. United 1, Crawley 0
Stoke 3, Brighton 0

(20/2/11)
Fulham 0, Bolton 1
Leyton Orient 1, Arsenal 1

(21/2/11)
West Ham 5, Burnley 1

(1/3/11)
Everton 0, Reading 1

(2/3/11)
Man. City 3, Aston Villa 0

Replay

(2/3/11)
Arsenal 5, Leyton Orient 0

QUARTER-FINALS

(12/3/11)
Birmingham 2 *(Jerome 38, Phillips 80)*, Bolton 3 *(Elmander 21, Davies K. 66p, Lee 90)*
Man. United 2 *(Fábio 28, Rooney 49)*, Arsenal 0

(13/3/11)
Man. City 1 *(Richards 74)*, Reading 0
Stoke 2 *(Huth 12, Higginbotham 63)*, West Ham 1 *(Piquionne 30)*

SEMI-FINALS

(16/4/11)
Man. City 1 *(Touré Y. 52)*, Man. United 0

(17/4/11)
Stoke 5 *(Etherington 11, Huth 17, Jones 30, Walters 68, 81)*, Bolton 0

FINAL

(14/5/11)
Wembley Stadium, London
MANCHESTER CITY FC 1 *(Touré Y. 74)*
STOKE CITY FC 0
Referee – *Atkinson*
MAN. CITY – *Hart, Richards, Kompany, Lescott, Kolarov, De Jong, Barry (Johnson 73), David Silva (Vieira 90), Touré Y., Balotelli, Tévez (Zabaleta 87).*
STOKE – *Sørensen, Wilkinson, Huth, Shawcross, Wilson, Pennant, Whelan (Pugh 84), Delap (Carew 80), Etherington (Whitehead 62), Walters, Jones.*

LEAGUE CUP

QUARTER-FINALS

(30/11/10)
Arsenal 2 *(Alcáraz 42og, Bendtner 67)*, Wigan 0
West Ham 4 *(Spector 22, 37, Cole 56, 66)*, Man. United 0

(1/12/10)
Birmingham 2 *(Larsson 12p, Žigić 84)*, Aston Villa 1 *(Agbonlahor 30)*
Ipswich 1 *(Leadbitter 69p)*, West Brom 0

SEMI-FINALS

(11/1/11 & 26/1/11)
West Ham 2 *(Noble 13, Cole 78)*, Birmingham 1 *(Ridgewell 56)*
Birmingham 3 *(Bowyer 59, Johnson 79, Gardner 94)*, West Ham 1 *(Cole 31) (aet)*
(Birmingham 4-3)

(12/1/11 & 25/1/11)
Ipswich 1 *(Priskin 78)*, Arsenal 0
Arsenal 3 *(Bendtner 61, Koscielny 64, Fàbregas 77)*, Ipswich 0
(Arsenal 3-1)

FINAL

(27/2/11)
Wembley Stadium, London
BIRMINGHAM CITY FC 2 *(Žigić 28, Martins 89)*
ARSENAL FC 1 *(Van Persie 39)*
Referee – *Dean*
BIRMINGHAM – *Foster, Carr, Johnson, Jiránek, Ridgewell, Larsson, Ferguson, Fahey (Martins 83), Gardner (Beausejour 50), Bowyer, Žigić (Jerome 90+2).*
ARSENAL – *Szczęsny, Sagna, Djourou, Koscielny, Clichy, Song, Wilshere, Nasri, Rosický, Arshavin (Chamakh 77), Van Persie (Bendtner 69).*

CLUB COMMUNICATION 2011/12

Arsenal FC
Highbury House, 75 Drayton Park
GB-London N5 1BU

Tel	+44 20 7619 5003
Fax	+44 20 7704 4001
Web	arsenal.com
Email	info@arsenal.co.uk
Media Officer	Dan Tolhurst

Aston Villa FC
Villa Park, Trinity Road
GB-Birmingham B6 6HE

Tel	+44 121 327 2299
Fax	+44 121 322 2107
Web	avfc.co.uk
Email	postmaster@avfc.co.uk
Media Officer	Brian Doogan

Blackburn Rovers FC
Ewood Park, Blackburn, Lancashire
GB-Blackburn BB2 4JF

Tel	+44 871 702 1875
Fax	+44 125 467 1042
Web	rovers.co.uk
Email	enquiries@rovers.co.uk
Media Officer	Paul Agnew

Bolton Wanderers FC
Reebok Stadium, Burnden Way
GB-Bolton BL6 6JW

Tel	+44 1204 673 673
Fax	+44 1204 469 046
Web	bwfc.co.uk
Email	reception@bwfc.co.uk
Media Officer	Mark Alderton

Chelsea FC
Stamford Bridge, Fulham Road
GB-London SW6 1HS

Tel	+44 207 835 6000
Fax	+44 193 258 8230
Web	chelseafc.com
Email	enquiries@chelseafc.com
Media Officer	Steve Atkins

Everton FC
Goodison Park, Goodison Road
GB-Liverpool L4 4EL

Tel	+44 871 663 1878
Fax	+44 151 286 9112
Web	evertonfc.com
Email	everton@evertonfc.com
Media Officer	Darren Griffiths

Fulham FC
Training Ground, Motspur Park
GB-New Malden, Surrey KT3 6PT

Tel	+44 843 208 1234
Fax	+44 208 336 7526
Web	fulhamfc.com
Email	enquiries@fulhamfc.com
Media Officer	Carmelo Mifsud

Liverpool FC
Anfield Road
GB-Liverpool L4 0TH

Tel	+44 151 263 2361
Fax	+44 151 260 8813
Web	liverpoolfc.tv
Email	customerservices@ liverpoolfc.tv
Media Officer	Paul Tyrrell

Manchester City FC
City of Manchester Stadium, SportCity
Rowsley Street, GB-Manchester M11 3FF

Tel	+44 161 444 1894
Fax	+44 161 438 7999
Web	mcfc.co.uk
Email	mcfc@mcfc.co.uk
Media Officer	Simon Heggie

Manchester United FC
Sir Matt Busby Way, Old Trafford
GB-Manchester M16 0RA

Tel	+44 161 868 8000
Fax	+44 161 868 8804
Web	manutd.com
Email	enquiries@manutd.co.uk
Media Officer	Karen Shotbolt

Newcastle United FC
St James' Park, Newcastle upon Tyne
GB-Newcastle NE1 4ST

Tel	+44 844 372 1892
Fax	+44 191 201 8600
Web	nufc.co.uk
Email	admin@nufc.co.uk
Media Officer	Wendy Taylor

Norwich City FC
Carrow Road
GB-Norwich NR1 1JE

Tel	+44 1603 760 760
Fax	+44 1603 613 886
Web	canaries.co.uk
Email	reception@ ncfc-canaries.co.uk
Media Officer	Joe Ferrari

Queens Park Rangers FC
Loftus Road Stadium, South Africa Road,
GB-London W12 7PJ

Tel	+44 20 8743 0262
Fax	+44 20 8749 0994
Web	qpr.co.uk
Email	terry.s@qpr.co.uk
Media Officer	Ian Taylor

Stoke City FC
Clayton Wood Training Ground
Rosetree Avenue, Trent Vale
GB-Stoke on Trent ST4 6NL

Tel	+44 871 663 2008
Fax	+44 178 264 6988
Web	stokecityfc.com
Email	info@stokecityfc.com
Media Officer	Nick Lucy

Sunderland AFC
Stadium of Light
GB-Sunderland SR5 1SU

Tel	+44 191 551 5000
Fax	+44 191 542 8010
Web	safc.com
Email	enquiries@safc.com
Media Officer	Louise Wanless

Swansea City AFC
Liberty Stadium, Landore
GB-Swansea SA1 2FA

Tel	+44 1792 616 600
Fax	+44 1792 616 606
Web	swanseacity.net
Email	info@swanseacityfc.co.uk
Media Officer	Jonathan Wilsher

Tottenham Hotspur FC
White Hart Lane, Bill Nicholson Way
Tottenham, GB-London N17 0AP

Tel	+44 844 499 5000
Fax	+44 208 506 9048
Web	tottenhamhotspur.com
Email	email@ tottenhamhotspur.com
Media Officer	Simon Felstein

West Bromwich Albion FC
The Hawthorns, West Midlands
GB-West Bromwich B71 4LF

Tel	+44 871 271 1100
Fax	+44 871 271 9861
Web	wba.co.uk
Email	enquiries@wbafc.co.uk
Media Officer	John Simpson

Wigan Athletic FC
DW Stadium, Loire Drive, Newtown
Wigan, GB-Lancashire WN5 0UZ

Tel	+44 1942 774 400
Fax	+44 1942 770 477
Web	wiganlatics.co.uk
Email	info@wiganathletic.com
Media Officer	Ed Jones

Wolverhampton Wanderers FC
Molineux Stadium, Waterloo Road
GB-Wolverhampton WV1 4QR

Tel	+44 871 222 2220
Fax	+44 190 268 7006
Web	wolves.co.uk
Email	info@wolves.co.uk
Media Officer	Paul Berry

ESTONIA

Estonie I Estland

Eesti Jalgpalli Liit (EJL)

COMMUNICATION

Address	Lilleküla staadion, Asula 4c EE-11312 Tallinn	**President**	Aivar Pohlak
		General Secretary	Tõnu Sirel
Tel	+372 627 9960	**Media Officer**	Mihkel Uiboleht
Fax	+372 627 9969	**Year of Formation**	1921
E-mail	efa@jalgpall.ee	**National Stadium**	Lilleküla staadion, Tallinn (9,692)
Website	jalgpall.ee		

DOMESTIC COMPETITION SUMMARY 2010/11

MEISTRILIIGA FINAL TABLE

			Home					Away					Total						
		Pld	W	D	L	F	A	W	D	L	F	A	W	D	L	F	A	Pts	Comp
1	FC Flora Tallinn	36	16	2	0	56	14	13	2	3	48	18	29	4	3	104	32	91	UCL
2	FC Levadia Tallinn	36	13	5	0	52	8	13	3	2	48	8	26	8	2	100	16	86	UEL
3	JK Trans Narva	36	10	4	4	31	17	13	3	2	36	14	23	7	6	67	31	76	UEL
4	JK Nõmme Kalju	36	8	4	6	22	23	10	4	4	37	19	18	8	10	59	42	62	UEL
5	JK Sillamäe Kalev	36	9	3	6	38	24	9	2	7	41	28	18	5	13	79	52	59	
6	JK Tammeka Tartu	36	5	4	9	21	23	6	3	9	29	43	11	7	18	50	66	40	
7	JK Tulevik Viljandi	36	7	1	10	21	26	1	4	13	12	36	8	5	23	33	62	29	
8	Paide Linnameeskond	36	3	3	12	17	43	3	4	11	13	36	6	7	23	30	79	25	
9	FC Kuressaare	36	4	1	13	22	48	3	2	13	10	45	7	3	26	32	93	24	
10	FC Lootus Kohtla-Järve	36	3	1	14	12	58	3	1	14	10	45	6	2	28	22	103	20	*Relegated*

Top Scorer Sander Post (Flora), 24 goals

Promoted Club FC Ajax Lasnamäe

Cup Final FC Flora Tallinn 2, JK Trans Narva 0

Flora blossom again under Reim

The four-year reign of FC Levadia Tallinn was brought to an end in 2010 as capital city rivals FC Flora Tallinn usurped them to become the Baltic country's record champions with an eighth Meistriliiga title triumph. The man to end Flora's seven-year barren run was former player – and Estonia's most-capped international – Martin Reim, who, in his first job as a senior coach, brilliantly steered his young team to victory, shrugging off the club's financial problems to see off Levadia with a couple of games to spare.

A mere fourth in 2009, Flora were a team transformed by Reim, a legendary figure who had won seven Meistriliiga titles with the club as a player. Commanding respect from all and sundry at the club – even during a spell when the players did not receive their wages – Reim oversaw a campaign that peaked with crucial home wins over Levadia in May and October and accelerated with the mid-season return from two years at Dutch club Go Ahead Eagles of lanky centre forward Sander Post, whose voracious appetite for goals brought him a hat-trick on his debut, two more in his next five games and, to cap it all, a double hat-trick in an 8-0 away win at bottom club FC Lootus Kohtla-Järve.

Post haste

Post, who claimed the Meistrilliga Golden Boot in double-quick time with his 24 goals (in 17 games), was, at 26, one of the senior citizens in a Flora side packed with Estonian colts. Among those was 19-year-old Henri Anier, who also notched up goals at an impressive rate of frequency – 13 in 16 games – and was one of five Flora players to make their senior debut for the Estonian national team – coached by ex-Flora boss Tarmo Rüütli – during the 2010/11 international season.

Reim's fledglings would add to their trophy collection in the spring of 2011 when they won the Estonian Cup, defeating the 2010 Meistriliiga's third-placed club, JK Trans Narva, 2-0 in the final. It was Flora's third cup win in four years, the only interruption to their monopoly having come 12 months earlier when Levadia defeated them 3-0 in the final.

Led at the time of that 2010 Cup final triumph by their 2008 and 2009 Meistriliiga-winning coach Igor Prins, Levadia decided to do away with his services in August after a couple of painful knockout blows – the first in the second qualifying round of the UEFA Champions League by the Hungarians of Debreceni VSC; the second, rather more embarrassingly, in the third round of the 2010/11 Estonian Cup after an extra-time defeat to second-tier JK Tallinna Kalev. Although, like Flora, Levadia managed to reach a century of goals and remain unbeaten at home in the Meistriliiga, those two losses away to Flora – the club's only league defeats of the entire campaign – ultimately prevented them from racking up a fifth straight championship triumph.

Levadia's leading scorer in the league, 20-goal Tarmo Neemelo, was the only player from an Estonian club to score on home soil in 2010/11 UEFA club competition, and although both Levadia – against Debrecen – and Flora – in the UEFA Europa League against FC Dinamo Tbilisi – were

Martin Reim's return to Flora, as coach, heralded a first Meistriliiga title for the Tallinn club in seven years

National Team

Top Five All-time Caps – Martin Reim (157); Marko Kristal (143); Andres Oper (121); Mart Poom (120); Kristen Viikmäe (114)

Top Five All-time Goals – Andres Oper (36); Indrek Zelinski (27); Eduard Ellmen-Eelma (21); Arnold Pihlak (17); Richard Kuremaa (16)

just one goal away from winning their respective ties, the immediate dismissal from Europe of all four Estonian teams was a major disappointment.

Sensation in Serbia

There was brighter news to report from the UEFA EURO 2012 qualifying campaign as Rüütli's Estonia got off to a very encouraging start, scoring two added-time goals to win the competition's opening tie at home to the Faroe Islands, taking the lead at home to Italy, and then recording one of the country's greatest ever victories with a sensational 3-1 win over Serbia in Belgrade. A subsequent 1-1 draw at home to the same opponents, in which midfielder Konstantin Vassiljev scored his eighth goal of an unexpectedly prolific international season, was also viewed as a positive result, but the month of June dampened spirits as Estonia lost four successive matches without scoring, the worst of them in their seventh qualifier of the EURO campaign, 2-0 away to the Faroe Islands. The season also saw skipper Raio Piiroja become the seventh Estonian footballer to reach a century of international caps – a landmark he celebrated in March 2011 with a memorable 2-0 victory in a friendly against 2010 FIFA World Cup semi-finalists Uruguay.

NATIONAL TEAM RESULTS 2010/11

11/8/10	Faroe Islands (ECQ)	H	Tallinn	2-1	Saag (90+1), Piiroja (90+3)
3/9/10	Italy (ECQ)	H	Tallinn	1-2	Zenjov (31)
7/9/10	Uzbekistan	H	Tallinn	3-3	Purje (25), Vassiljev (63, 72p)
8/10/10	Serbia (ECQ)	A	Belgrade	3-1	Kink (63), Vassiljev (73), Luković (90+1og)
12/10/10	Slovenia (ECQ)	H	Tallinn	0-1	
17/11/10	Liechtenstein	H	Tallinn	1-1	Vassiljev (57p)
18/12/10	China	A	Zhuhai	0-3	
22/12/10	Qatar	A	Doha	0-2	
9/2/11	Bulgaria	N	Antalya (TUR)	2-2	Vassiljev (20p, 80p)
25/3/11	Uruguay	H	Tallinn	2-0	Vassiljev (61), Zahovaiko (65)
29/3/11	Serbia (ECQ)	H	Tallinn	1-1	Vassiljev (84)
3/6/11	Italy (ECQ)	A	Modena	0-3	
7/6/11	Faroe Islands (ECQ)	A	Toftir	0-2	
19/6/11	Chile	A	Santiago	0-4	
23/6/11	Uruguay	A	Rivera	0-3	

NATIONAL TEAM APPEARANCES 2010/11

Coach – Tarmo RÜÜTLI	11/8/54		FRO	ITA	Uzb	SRB	SVN	Lie	Chn	Qat	Bul	Uru	SRB	ITA	FRO	Chi	Uru	Caps	Goals
Sergei PAREIKO	31/1/77	Tom (RUS)	G	G		G	G												
		/Wisła Kraków (POL)										G	G	G	G			26	-
Raio PIIROJA	11/7/79	Fredrikstad (NOR)	D	D		D						D	D	D	D			103	8
Ragnar KLAVAN	30/10/85	AZ (NED)	D	D		D	D				D		D	M				69	1
Enar JÄÄGER	18/11/84	Aalesund (NOR)	D	D		D	D	D			D	D	D	M	D			79	-
Alo BÄRENGRUB	12/2/84	Bodø/Glimt (NOR)	D		D													34	-
Aleksandr DMITRIJEV	18/2/82	Hønefoss (NOR)	M	M	M	M	M	M	M	M									
		/Ural (RUS)									M	M79	M					67	-
Sander PURI	7/5/88	Larissa (GRE)	M76	M77		M70	M69	s61											
		/Korona (POL)									s39	s56	M29	M	M 57*	M	M	34	2
Konstantin VASSILJEV	16/8/84	Nafta (SVN)	M	M	s58	M	M	M											
		/Koper (SVN)									M	s58	M		M			42	11
Dmitri KRUGLOV	24/5/84	İnter Bakı (AZE)	M70	M82	s65	M	M	M61			M91	M62	M	D	D	D	D	65	1
Tarmo KINK	6/10/85	Middlesbrough (ENG)	A	s82	A	A64	A59	A76			M39	s62	s66	M79	M			53	4
Andres OPER	7/11/77	unattached	A62																
		/AEK (CYP)								A	A63	s79	s55					121	36
Kaimar SAAG	5/8/88	Silkeborg (DEN)	s62	s63	A65	s64	A	A88				A58	A66	s58	A82			32	2

NATIONAL TEAM APPEARANCES 2010/11 (contd.)

			FRO	ITA	Uzb	SRB	SVN	Lie	Chn	Qat	Bul	Uru	SRB	ITA	FRO	Chi	Uru	Caps	Goals
Sander POST	10/9/84	Flora	s70		s65			s63	A62	s57								10	1
Ats PURJE	3/8/85	AEP (CYP)	s76	s77	M65	s70	s69	M63			s63	M56	s29					28	3
Martin VUNK	21/8/84	Syrianska (SWE) /Nea Salamis (CYP)		M	M58	s87			M	M	M	M		M				34	-
Taavi RÄHN	16/5/81	Baltika (RUS) /Tianjin Songjiang (CHN)		D		D	D55	D			D	D	D	D	D			61	-
Sergei ZENJOV	20/4/89	Karpaty (UKR)		A63	s58	A87	s59							A58	M			17	4
Artur KOTENKO	20/8/81	AEP (CYP)			G46					G	s46							25	-
Igor MOROZOV	27/5/89	Levadia			D				D	D	D					s80	s62	11	-
Andrei SIDORENKOV	12/2/84	SønderjyskE (DEN)			D		D	D				D						21	-
Gert KAMS	25/5/85	Flora			D83									s79	s66	D63	D88	19	-
Vjatšeslav ZAHOVAIKO	29/12/81	Leiria (POR)			A58							s57						39	8
Mihkel AKSALU	7/11/84	Sheffield United (ENG)			s46													9	-
Tihhon ŠIŠOV	11/2/83	Xäzär Länkäran (AZE)			s83				D	D	s91					D80	D	29	-
Karl PALATU	5/12/82	Flora					s55		s72	D						D	D	7	-
Pavel LONDAK	14/5/80	Bodø/Glimt (NOR) /Bucaspor (TUR)						G	G89		G46						G	21	-
Andrei STEPANOV	16/3/79	Khimki (RUS)						D	D									83	1
Siim LUTS	12/3/89	Flora						s76	M72							M63	M64	4	-
Sergei MOŠNIKOV	7/1/88	Flora						s88		s46					s82	M75	s62	7	-
Markus JÜRGENSON	9/9/87	Flora							D	D								2	-
Oliver KONSA	4/3/85	Kalju							M	s46								17	-
Rauno ALLIKU	2/3/90	Flora							A46	M46								2	-
Alo DUPIKOV	5/11/85	Flora							s46	A46								5	-
Vladimir VOSKOBOINIKOV	2/2/83	Levadia							s62	M57								27	3
Marko MEERITS	26/4/92	Flora							s89							G		2	-
Jarmo AHJUPERA	13/4/84	Újpest (HUN)										A57	A55	s58	A66			9	-
Taijo TENISTE	31/1/88	Levadia												D58				7	-
Mikk REINTAM	22/5/90	JJK (FIN)														D	D62	2	-
Siim TENNO	4/8/90	Tammeka														M63	M62	2	-
Joonas TAMM	2/2/92	Norrköping (SWE)														A63	A80	2	-
Joel INDERMITTE	27/12/92	Viljandi														s63	s80	2	-
Meelis PEITRE	27/3/90	Flora														s63	s64	2	-
Albert PROSA	1/10/90	Tammeka														s63	s64	2	-
Andrei VEIS	6/4/90	Viljandi														s63	s88	2	-
Henri ANIER	17/12/90	Flora														s75	A64	2	-

CLUB-BY-CLUB

FC FLORA TALLINN

Coach – Martin Reim

Founded – 1990

Stadium – A. Le Coq Arena (9,692)

MAJOR HONOURS: Estonian League – (8) 1994, 1995, 1998, 1998 (autumn), 2001, 2002, 2003, 2010; Estonian Cup – (5) 1995, 1998, 2008, 2009, 2011.

2010

9/3	Sillamäe Kalev	a	2-1	*Konsa, Minkenen (p)*
13/3	Trans	a	0-1	
20/3	Lootus	h	2-1	*Mošnikov, Alliku*
23/3	Tulevik	a	1-0	*Dupikov*
27/3	Tammeka	h	3-2	*Kasimir, Konsa, Alliku*
3/4	Levadia	a	1-2	*Mašitšev*
10/4	Kuressaare	h	4-0	*Konsa, Palatu, Beglarishvili, Kasimir*
17/4	Kalju	a	2-1	*Alliku, Minkenen*
24/4	Paide	h	2-1	*Mašitšev, Kasimir*
1/5	Paide	a	2-0	*Dupikov, Minkenen*
8/5	Kalju	h	1-0	*Jahhimovitš*
15/5	Kuressaare	a	2-1	*Minkenen, Luts*
29/5	Levadia	h	2-1	*Mošnikov, Kams*
1/6	Tammeka	a	1-0	*Alliku*
5/6	Tulevik	h	1-1	*Konsa*
12/6	Lootus	a	4-0	*og (Vaštšenko), Kams, Beglarishvili, Dupikov*
15/6	Trans	h	1-1	*og (Kitto)*
17/7	Kuressaare	h	6-0	*Post 3, Luts, Kasimir, Beglarishvili*
25/7	Levadia	a	2-2	*Anier, Post*
31/7	Tammeka	h	6-3	*Kams 2, Post, Anier, Luts, Mašitšev*
7/8	Tulevik	a	6-1	*Post 3, Kams, Mošnikov, Mašitšev*
14/8	Lootus	h	5-0	*Anier 3, Tamm, Beglarishvili*
17/8	Sillamäe Kalev	h	4-2	*Post 3, Alliku*
21/8	Trans	a	2-1	*Minkenen (p), Post*
24/8	Paide	h	6-2	*Luts 2, Post 2, Beglarishvili, Anier*
28/8	Sillamäe Kalev	a	5-2	*Minkenen 2, Mašitšev, Mošnikov, Palatu*
11/9	Sillamäe Kalev	h	3-0	*Anier 2, Post*
14/9	Trans	h	4-0	*og (Gorškov), Alliku, Palatu 2*

8/9	Lootus	a	8-0	*Post 6, Anier, Tamm*
5/9	Tulevik	h	1-0	*Anier*
/10	Tammeka	a	1-2	*Post (p)*
6/10	Levadia	h	2-0	*Jürgenson, Minkenen*
3/10	Kuressaare	a	2-0	*Kams, Jürgenson*
0/10	Kalju	h	3-0	*Post 2, Palatu*
/11	Kalju	a	3-3	*Luts, Anier, Beglarishvili*
/11	Paide	a	4-1	*Anier 2, Alliku 2*

lame	Nat	DoB	Pos	Aps	(s)	Gls
eet ALLAS		2/6/77	D	10		
auno ALLIKU		2/3/90	A	16	(12)	8
lenri ANIER		17/12/90	A	13	(3)	13
ivar ANNISTE		18/2/80	M	1		
likita BARANOV		19/8/92	D	2		
akaria BEGLARISHVILI	GEO	30/4/90	M	10	(12)	6
lo DUPIKOV		5/11/85	A	13	(12)	3
ndre FROLOV		18/4/88	D	7	(9)	
leksei JAHHIMOVITŠ		30/3/90	D	30	(1)	1
larkus JÜRGENSON		9/9/87	D	33		2
ert KAMS		25/5/85	D	34	(1)	6
iksten KASIMIR		23/7/80	M	16	(2)	4
liver KONSA		4/3/85	M	12	(4)	4
iim LUTS		12/3/89	M	25	(6)	6
likolai MAŠITŠEV		5/12/88	M	20	(8)	5
larko MEERITS		26/4/92	G	10		
aleri MINKENEN	FIN	9/4/89	M	30	4	8
Sergei MOŠNIKOV		7/1/88	M	29	(3)	4
Karl PALATU		5/12/82	D	31		5
Stanislav PEDÕK		6/6/88	G	26	(1)	
Meelis PEITRE		27/3/90	M	1	(4)	
Sander POST		10/9/84	A	14	(3)	24
Albert TAAR		15/1/90	M	3		
Joonas TAMM		2/2/92	A	4	(9)	2
Andrei VEIS		6/4/90	D	6	(7)	

FC KURESSAARE

Coach – Sergei Zamogilnõi
Founded – 1997
Stadium – Kuressaare Linnastaadion (2,000)

2010

9/3	Tammeka	h	2-3	*Pukk, Skiperski*
13/3	Levadia	a	1-1	*Kluge (p)*
20/3	Trans	h	0-1	
23/3	Kalju	h	1-2	*Pukk*
27/3	Paide	a	2-1	*Skiperski, Petrovitš*
3/4	Sillamäe Kalev	h	0-4	
10/4	Flora	a	0-4	
17/4	Lootus	h	1-2	*Skiperski*
24/4	Tulevik	a	0-0	
1/5	Tulevik	h	3-2	*Kuusik, Kluge (p), Skiperski*
8/5	Lootus	a	2-5	*Laht, Skiperski*
15/5	Flora	h	1-2	*Laht*
29/5	Sillamäe Kalev	a	0-0	*(w/o; awarded as away win; original result 0-6)*
1/6	Paide	h	1-0	*Rajaver*
5/6	Kalju	a	1-2	*Pukk*
12/6	Trans	a	0-3	
15/6	Levadia	h	0-7	
29/6	Tammeka	a	0-2	
3/7	Tulevik	a	1-4	*Valmas*
10/7	Lootus	h	0-1	
17/7	Flora	a	0-6	
31/7	Paide	a	0-3	
7/8	Kalju	h	1-5	*Valmas*
14/8	Trans	h	1-4	*Laht*
21/8	Levadia	a	0-4	
28/8	Tammeka	h	3-2	*Tovstik A., Skiperski, Pukk*
11/9	Tammeka	a	2-0	*Valmas, Skiperski*
14/9	Levadia	h	0-4	
18/9	Trans	a	1-5	*Pukk*
25/9	Kalju	a	0-1	
28/9	Sillamäe Kalev	h	2-2	*Laht 2*
2/10	Paide	h	2-3	*Skiperski, Valmas*
16/10	Sillamäe Kalev	a	0-2	
23/10	Flora	h	0-2	
30/10	Lootus	a	0-2	
6/11	Tulevik	h	4-2	*Aljas, Pukk, Skiperski, Laht*

Name	Nat	DoB	Pos	Aps	(s)	Gls
Argo AAVA		29/3/86	D	28	(4)	
Sergei AKIMOV		22/10/76	A	4		
Rene ALJAS		18/12/86	A	13	(2)	1
Alari AUNAPUU		23/12/89	A	3	(16)	
Taavi AZAROV		20/4/80	M	9	(6)	
Rait HANSEN		12/11/88	G	8		
Hans HIIUVÄIN		5/7/90	A		(3)	
Endrik JÄGER		13/1/90	M	2	(6)	
Jaanus KAASIK		22/6/90	D	9	(2)	
Arsen KATŠMAZOV		9/7/89	D		(2)	
Märt KLUGE		8/3/84	D	27	(1)	2
Jaanis KRISKA		23/6/88	D		(1)	
Roland KÜTT		22/4/87	G	13		
Reijo KUUSIK		24/6/87	A	11	(1)	1
Sander LAHT		26/9/91	M	24	(7)	6
Aivo LAUL		1/1/84	M	7	(3)	
Joonas LJAŠ		3/9/90	M	1	(2)	
Amor LUUP		18/2/92	A	3	(6)	
Alar PETROVITŠ		7/6/87	A	3	(11)	1
Priit PIKKER		15/3/86	G	13		
Pelle POHLAK		31/12/88	M	9	(5)	
Martti PUKK		20/2/77	A	32		6
Urmas RAJAVER		3/1/88	D	32	(1)	1
Kaarel SAAR		19/3/90	D	34		
Jüris SAHKUR		12/9/90	G	2	(1)	
Sander SEEMAN		12/9/92	M		(1)	
Dmitri SKIPERSKI		29/4/73	A	30	(3)	9
Alari TOVSTIK		31/7/84	M	27	(2)	1
Elar TOVSTIK		31/10/81	A	22		
Taavi TRASBERG		17/7/93	A		(2)	
Elari VALMAS		2/7/88	D	15	(13)	4
Sander `VIIRA		29/8/89	D	15	(2)	

FC LEVADIA TALLINN

Coach – Igor Prins; (5/8/10) Aleksandr Puštov
Founded – 1998
Stadium – Kadriorg (4,700)
MAJOR HONOURS: Estonian League – (7) 1999, 2000, 2004, 2006, 2007, 2008, 2009;
Estonian Cup – (6) 1999, 2000, 2004, 2005, 2007, 2010.

2010

9/3	Trans	h	3-0	*Neemelo 2, Leitan*
13/3	Kuressaare	h	1-1	*Artjunin*
20/3	Kalju	a	3-0	*Puri 2, Nahk (p)*
23/3	Paide	h	6-0	*Neemelo 3, Leitan, Morozov, Ivanov (p)*
27/3	Sillamäe Kalev	a	1-1	*Nahk*
3/4	Flora	h	2-1	*Nahk (p), Neemelo*
10/4	Lootus	a	3-0	*Ivanov 3 (1p)*
17/4	Tulevik	h	2-0	*Leitan, Malov*
24/4	Tammeka	a	0-0	
1/5	Tammeka	h	2-0	*Neemelo, Pebre*
8/5	Tulevik	a	1-0	*Malov*
15/5	Lootus	h	5-1	*Leitan, Nahk (p), Morozov, Ivanov, og (Akhalbedashvili)*
29/5	Flora	a	1-2	*Neemelo*
1/6	Sillamäe Kalev	h	3-1	*Leitan, Neemelo, Nahk*
5/6	Paide	a	4-0	*Leitan 2, Malov, Puri*
8/6	Trans	a	2-1	*Neemelo, Nahk (p)*
12/6	Kalju	h	0-0	
15/6	Kuressaare	a	7-0	*Ivanov 2, Dmitrijev 2, Malov 2 (2p), Leitan*
3/7	Tammeka	a	0-0	
10/7	Tulevik	h	3-0	*Felipe Nunes 2, Malov*
17/7	Lootus	a	5-0	*Dmitrijev 2, Subbotin, Felipe Nunes, Pebre*

25/7	Flora	h	2-2	*Nahk, Neemelo*
31/7	Sillamäe Kalev	a	4-0	*Leitan 2, Neemelo, Nahk*
7/8	Paide	h	4-0	*Neemelo, Dmitrijev, Morozov, Malov*
14/8	Kalju	a	5-1	*Felipe Nunes 2, Teniste, Nahk, Dmitrijev*
21/8	Kuressaare	h	4-0	*Felipe Nunes 2, Neemelo, Dmitriev*
28/8	Trans	h	1-1	*Neemelo*
11/9	Trans	a	3-0	*Nahk (p), Malov, Dmitrijev*
14/9	Kuressaare	a	4-0	*Neemelo 2, Malov, Nahk*
18/9	Kalju	h	1-1	*Leitan*
25/9	Paide	a	4-1	*Nahk (p), Leitan, Malov, og (Kõll)*
2/10	Sillamäe Kalev	h	2-0	*Malov (p), Neemelo*
16/10	Flora	a	0-2	
23/10	Lootus	h	5-0	*Malov 2, Leitan, Neemelo, og (Nesterovski)*
30/10	Tulevik	a	1-0	*Felipe Nunes*
6/11	Tammeka	h	6-0	*Leitan 3, Neemelo, Malov, Subbotin*

Name	Nat	DoB	Pos	Aps	(s)	Gls
Artjom ARTJUNIN		24/1/90	D	13	(1)	1
Yaroslav DMITRIEV	RUS	25/6/88	A	1	(3)	1
Artjom DMITRIJEV		14/11/88	M	6	(19)	7
Tengiz ETERIA	GEO	11/12/89	M		(1)	
FELIPE de Araújo NUNES	BRA	2/3/81	A	14	(3)	8
Vladislav IVANOV	RUS	24/1/86	A	10	(8)	7
Martin KAALMA		14/4/77	G	14		
Andrei KALIMULLIN		6/10/77	D	33		
Aleksandr KULINITŠ		24/5/92	D		(1)	
Vitali LEITAN		1/12/78	M	34		16
Sergei LEPMETS		5/4/87	G	22	(1)	
Deniss MALOV		8/6/80	M	32	(4)	14
Aleks MONES		27/8/90	M	1	(2)	
Igor MOROZOV		27/5/89	D	27	(2)	3
Konstantin NAHK		10/2/75	M	27		12
Tarmo NEEMELO		2/10/82	A	29	(3)	20
Maksim PAPONOV		11/1/90	M	3	(4)	
Andero PEBRE		7/8/91	M	9	(13)	2
Maksim PODHOLJUZIN		13/11/92	D	21	(2)	
Eino PURI		7/5/88	M	19	(3)	3
Eduard RATNIKOV		13/9/83	M	7	(5)	
Tomi Tapani SAARELMA	FIN	30/11/88	M	2	(2)	
Igor SUBBOTIN		26/6/90	M	10	(4)	2
Taijo TENISTE		31/1/88	D	33		1
Aleksandr VOLODIN		29/3/88	D	29	(3)	

FC LOOTUS KOHTLA-JÄRVE

Coach – Aleksei Zhukov; (15/5/10) Andrei Škaleta

Founded – 1998

Stadium – Spordikeskuse Staadion (2,200)

2010

9/3	Paide	a	0-1	
13/3	Sillamäe Kalev	h	0-1	
20/3	Flora	a	1-2	*Kulik*
23/3	Trans	a	1-0	*Kulik*
27/3	Tulevik	h	0-1	
3/4	Tammeka	a	0-1	
10/4	Levadia	h	0-3	
17/4	Kuressaare	a	2-1	*Mamontov, Škaleta*
24/4	Kalju	h	0-5	
1/5	Kalju	a	0-1	
8/5	Kuressaare	h	5-2	*Kulik 3, Plotnikov, Škaleta*
15/5	Levadia	a	1-5	*Smelkov (p)*
29/5	Tammeka	h	1-3	*Mamontov*
1/6	Tulevik	a	0-1	
5/6	Trans	h	0-5	
12/6	Flora	h	0-4	
15/6	Sillamäe Kalev	a	1-3	*Plotnikov*
29/6	Paide	h	2-1	*Semjonov 2*
3/7	Kalju	h	0-6	
10/7	Kuressaare	a	1-0	*Vedehhov*
17/7	Levadia	h	0-5	
24/7	Tammeka	a	1-5	*Semjonov*
31/7	Tulevik	h	0-0	
7/8	Trans	a	1-4	*Kabayev*
14/8	Flora	a	0-5	
21/8	Sillamäe Kalev	h	0-5	
28/8	Paide	a	1-1	*Kulik*
11/9	Paide	h	1-2	*Semjonov*
14/9	Sillamäe Kalev	a	0-4	
18/9	Flora	h	0-8	
25/9	Trans	h	0-4	
16/10	Tammeka	h	1-3	*og (Kaldoja)*
19/10	Tulevik	a	0-4	
23/10	Levadia	a	0-5	
30/10	Kuressaare	h	2-0	*Ametov 2*
6/11	Kalju	a	0-2	

Name	Nat	DoB	Pos	Aps	(s)	Gls
Khampash ABDURASHIDOV	RUS	17/11/87	A	10	(1)	
Sergey AFANASYEV	RUS	5/3/86	A	4	(8)	
Ernest AKHALBEDASHVILI	GEO	28/8/91	D	10	(1)	
Viktor AKSJONOV		7/5/90	M	12	(10)	
Irfan AMETOV	UKR	3/2/80	A	17		2
Vitali BOLŠAKOV		12/6/86	A	12	(3)	
Jan DEMIDOVITŠ		24/8/88	M	13		
Aleksandr GLUHNO		5/5/88	A		(3)	
Pavel GRIBANOV		9/8/89	M		(1)	
Vadim GRITSJUK		16/9/81	D	17	(11)	
Saddam GUSEINOV	UKR	1/2/91	A	7	(1)	
Yevgeniy KABAYEV	RUS	28/2/88	A	3		1
Vassili KULIK		20/12/86	M	33		6
Ivan LIHHAVTSOV		23/6/91	M	5	(6)	
Aleksei MAMONTOV		6/5/85	M	14	(2)	2
Vadim MILLER		22/8/88	M		(1)	
Aleksandr MUTIK	RUS	3/9/86	D	13		
Roman NESTEROVSKI		9/6/89	D	12		
Viktor PLOTNIKOV		14/7/89	A	15	(1)	2
Maksim POZJABIN		2/6/90	D	25	(4)	
Konstantin RUBTSOV		17/6/77	G	9		
Anton SEMJONOV		17/11/80	M	15		4
Valeri SMELKOV		17/11/80	G	27		1
Dmitri SMIRNOV		10/9/89	M	23	(5)	
Vjatšeslav SMIRNOV		27/10/90	D		(5)	
Aleksandr SOJUNEN		6/7/90	M		(2)	
Andrei ŠKALETA		2/8/72	D	12	(12)	2
Aleksandr ZAHHARENKOV		9/2/87	D	30		
Aleksei ZHUKOV		11/1/65	M	8	(3)	
Jaan TARASSU		25/3/83	D	5	(12)	
Vitali VAŠTŠENKO		16/5/77	D	17		
Roman VEDEHHOV		20/7/81	D	28	(2)	1

JK NÕMME KALJU

Coach – Fredo Getúlio Aurélio (BRA); (19/4/10) Karel Voolaid; (1/9/10) Igor Prins

Founded – 1923

Stadium – Hiiu (600)

2010

9/3	Tulevik	h	1-0	*Teever*
13/3	Tammeka	a	3-2	*Jevdokimov, Felipe Nunes, Kallaste*
20/3	Levadia	h	0-3	
23/3	Kuressaare	a	2-1	*Jevdokimov, Teever (p)*
27/3	Trans	h	0-1	
3/4	Paide	h	1-1	*Teever (p)*
10/4	Sillamäe Kalev	a	2-2	*Jevdokimov 2 (2p)*
17/4	Flora	h	1-2	*Kallaste*
24/4	Lootus	a	5-0	*Alemão, Võtti, Terehhov, Jevdokimov, og (Gritsjuk)*
1/5	Lootus	h	1-0	*Jevdokimov*
8/5	Flora	a	0-1	
15/5	Sillamäe Kalev	h	2-1	*Jevdokimov, Tiago Sala (p)*
29/5	Paide	a	3-0	*Jevdokimov 2 (1p), Kaukvere*
1/6	Trans	a	2-2	*Kallaste, Jevdokimov*
5/6	Kuressaare	h	2-1	*Teever, Jevdokimov*
12/6	Levadia	a	0-0	
15/6	Tammeka	h	1-1	*Teever*

9/6	Tulevik	a	4-1	*Vnukov, Jevdokimov, Teever, Kõrtsmik*
/7	Lootus	a	6-0	*Teever 2, Kõrtsmik, Jevdokimov, Kallaste, og (Škaleta)*
4/7	Paide	h	0-0	
1/7	Trans	h	0-2	
/8	Kuressaare	a	5-1	*Kaukvere 3, Jevdokimov (p), Koogas*
4/8	Levadia	h	1-5	*Koogas*
1/8	Tammeka	a	1-0	*Jevdokimov*
4/8	Sillamäe Kalev	a	1-4	*Jevdokimov*
8/8	Tulevik	h	3-0	*Kovtunovitš, Terehhov, Mones*
1/9	Tulevik	a	1-0	*Kouakou*
4/9	Tammeka	h	3-1	*Jevdokimov 2, Koogas*
8/9	Levadia	a	1-1	*Mones*
5/9	Kuressaare	h	1-0	*Jevdokimov*
/10	Trans	a	0-1	
6/10	Paide	a	1-0	*Jevdokimov (p)*
3/10	Sillamäe Kalev	h	0-2	
0/10	Flora	a	0-3	
/11	Flora	h	3-3	*Koogas, Jevdokimov, Kouakou*
/11	Lootus	h	2-0	*Kõlu, Kouakou*

Name	Nat	DoB	Pos	Aps	(s)	Gls
Giovani Albani "ALEMÃO"	BRA	28/3/83	D	9		1
BRUNO Daniel GOMES Gonçalves	POR	6/2/86	A	6	(4)	
FELIPE de Araújo NUNES	BRA	2/3/81	M	5		1
Mikk HAAVISTU		27/3/85	D	27		
Janno HERMANSON		27/6/81	G	1	(1)	
Greeg JAKOBSON		31/10/91	D		(4)	
Jüri JEVDOKIMOV		3/6/88	A	34		21
Deniss JÕGISTE		5/2/90	M		(4)	
Ken KALLASTE		31/8/88	D	35		4
Tõnis KAUKVERE		19/3/86	M	23	(9)	4
Sami-Sander KIVI		11/5/90	D	5	(5)	
Martin KLASEN		13/3/90	M	1	(3)	
Risto KÕGO		4/8/89	D	1	(1)	
Anti KÕLU		19/7/91	A	8	(12)	1
Oliver KONSA		4/3/85	M	13	(2)	
Andres KOOGAS		5/9/87	D	15		4
Christian KÕRTSMIK		7/2/91	M	13	(11)	2
Fabrice Kouadio KOUAKOU Elysee	CIV	3/10/90	A	9	(3)	3
Dmitri KOVTUNOVITŠ		11/5/91	M	18	(1)	1
Kert KÜTT		9/10/80	G	29		
Rait KUUSK		21/5/86	M	7	(4)	
Aleks MONES		27/6/90	M	15	(1)	2
Juan Adriel OCHOA Reyes	MEX	6/4/87	A	4	(2)	
RAFAEL Amaral do Nascimento	BRA	10/10/88	M	3	(3)	
Daniil SAVITSKI		4/5/89	G	6		
Julius STOKAS		25/2/90	D	1		
Ingemar TEEVER		24/2/83	A	16	(2)	8
Sergei TEREHHOV		18/4/75	M	33		2
TIAGO SALA	BRA	3/10/84	D	12		1
Martin TŠEGODAJEV		30/11/90	A	12	(8)	
Denis VNUKOV		1/11/91	M	12	(4)	1
Tanel VÕTTI		16/5/88	D	23	(3)	1

PAIDE LINNAMEESKOND

Coach – Erki Kesküla; (17/7/10) Meelis Rooba

Founded – 1999

Stadium – Paide Ühisgümnaasium (500)

2010

9/3	Lootus	h	1-0	*Rooba M.*
13/3	Tulevik	a	0-1	
20/3	Tammeka	h	1-3	*Mägi*
23/3	Levadia	a	0-6	
27/3	Kuressaare	h	1-2	*Varendi*
3/4	Kalju	a	1-1	*Kööp*
10/4	Trans	h	0-4	
17/4	Sillamäe Kalev	h	0-1	
24/4	Flora	a	1-2	*Nõmme*
1/5	Flora	h	0-2	
8/5	Sillamäe Kalev	a	0-4	
15/5	Trans	a	1-4	*Tubarik*
29/5	Kalju	h	0-3	
1/6	Kuressaare	a	0-1	
5/6	Levadia	h	0-4	
12/6	Tammeka	h	0-0	
15/6	Tulevik	h	2-0	*Kalda, Kõll (p)*
29/6	Lootus	a	1-2	*Raal*
10/7	Sillamäe Kalev	h	1-8	*Nõmme*
17/7	Trans	h	1-1	*Kööp*
24/7	Kalju	a	0-0	
31/7	Kuressaare	h	3-0	*Kõll, Nõmme, og (Kaasik)*
7/8	Levadia	a	0-4	
14/8	Tammeka	h	3-4	*Sillaste 2, Luga*
21/8	Tulevik	a	0-1	
24/8	Flora	a	2-6	*Kööp, Mägi (p)*
28/8	Lootus	h	1-1	*Varendi*
11/9	Lootus	a	2-1	*Ištšuk 2*
14/9	Tulevik	h	1-1	*Sillaste*
18/9	Tammeka	a	2-1	*Ištšuk, Nõmme*
25/9	Levadia	h	1-4	*Ištšuk*
2/10	Kuressaare	a	3-2	*Ellram, Lomp, Ištšuk*
16/10	Kalju	h	0-1	
23/10	Trans	a	0-0	*(w/o; awarded as home win; original result 0-0)*
30/10	Sillamäe Kalev	a	0-0	
6/11	Flora	h	1-4	*Ištšuk*

Name	Nat	DoB	Pos	Aps	(s)	Gls
Lauri ELLRAM		18/2/84	A	6	(4)	1
Volodja ERDEI		12/12/87	A	7	(10)	
Mihhail IŠTŠUK		23/9/86	A	10	(4)	6
Rauno KALD		11/3/91	D	16	(2)	
Janek KALDA		13/9/78	A	31	(1)	1
Roomet KÖHLER		22/12/90	M		(1)	
Ervin KÕLL		18/3/89	M	34		2
Rauno KÖÖP		18/8/89	A	30	(1)	3
Sander KOOSER		24/9/88	D	1		
Kaido KOPPEL		9/5/88	G	8		
Kristo KÜLLJASTINEN		16/2/85	D		(2)	
Timo LOMP		26/7/88	D	21	(2)	1
Anders LUGA		27/3/91	M	7	(3)	1
Andre MÄGI		14/1/88	D	31	(2)	2
Silver NEEMELO		28/11/78	A	5	(10)	
Mait NÕMME		1/7/83	D	28		4
Keio OJA		13/8/88	D	8	(7)	
Herkki ORRO		12/2/88	M	1	(4)	
Priit RAAL		9/2/89	M	14	(4)	1
Madis RAJANDO		25/3/89	G	20		
Margus REINARU		12/11/86	M	1	(11)	
Eerik REINSOO		12/5/88	M	7	(1)	
Rauno RIIKBERG		30/7/88	A	10	(3)	
Meelis ROOBA		20/4/77	M	6	(1)	1
Urmas ROOBA		8/7/78	D	13	(1)	
Martin SAAR		28/9/88	M	19	(5)	
Ats SILLASTE		8/4/88	M	16		3
Alar TOOM		23/11/89	G	8		
Carl TUBARIK		31/7/81	M	25	(2)	1
Vahur VAHTRAMÄE		24/9/76	M	1		
Lauri VARENDI		29/12/88	D	12	(4)	2

JK SILLAMÄE KALEV

Coach – Vladimir Kazachyonok (RUS)

Founded – 1951

Stadium – Sillamäe Kalevi (500)

2010

9/3	Flora	h	1-2	*Tarassenkov*
13/3	Lootus	a	1-0	*Vihrov*
20/3	Tulevik	h	2-1	*Naumov (p), Gruznov*
23/3	Tammeka	a	4-1	*Stankevičius 2, Zubavičius, Vihrov*
27/3	Levadia	h	1-1	*Tarassenkov*

3/4	Kuressaare	a	4-0	*Kabayev, Tarassenkov, Gruznov, og (Kluge)*
10/4	Kalju	h	2-2	*Vasiliauskas, Tarassenkov*
17/4	Paide	a	1-0	*Stankevičius*
24/4	Trans	h	1-2	*Stankevičius (p)*
1/5	Trans	a	2-2	*Gruznov, Tarassenkov*
4/5	Trans	h	1-3	*Gruznov*
8/5	Paide	h	4-0	*Ametov, Kabayev, Kulik, Vihrov*
15/5	Kalju	a	1-2	*Kabayev*
29/5	Kuressaare	h	0-0	*(w/o; awarded as away win; original result 6-0 Vasiliauskas, Kabayev, Gruznov, Gornev, Lipartov, Tarassenkov)*
1/6	Levadia	a	1-3	*og (Podholjuzin)*
5/6	Tammeka	h	4-0	*Kabayev 2, Vasiliauskas 2*
12/6	Tulevik	a	2-1	*Zubavičius, Vasiliauskas*
15/6	Lootus	h	3-1	*Zubavičius, Vasiliauskas, Stankevičius*
10/7	Paide	a	8-1	*Kolyaev 3, Vasiliauskas 2, Kuresoo 2, Stankevičius*
31/7	Levadia	h	0-4	
7/8	Tammeka	a	3-2	*Kolyaev, Dubõkin, Veikutis Au.*
14/8	Tulevik	h	5-2	*Nikulin 2, Gorbunov, Kolyaev, Stankevičius*
17/8	Flora	a	2-4	*Tarassenkov 2*
21/8	Lootus	a	5-0	*Nikulin 2, Dubõkin, Veikutis Ar., Vasiliauskas*
24/8	Kalju	h	4-1	*Veikutis Ar. 2, Dubõkin, Kolyaev*
28/8	Flora	h	2-5	*Kulik, Naumov (p)*
11/9	Flora	a	0-3	
14/9	Lootus	h	4-0	*Kulik, Nikulin, Vasiliauskas, Kolyaev*
18/9	Tulevik	a	2-3	*Vihrov, Kolyaev*
25/9	Tammeka	h	2-0	*Kolyaev, Veikutis Au.*
28/9	Kuressaare	a	2-2	*Nikulin 2*
2/10	Levadia	a	0-2	
16/10	Kuressaare	h	2-0	*Stankevičius, Tarassenkov*
23/10	Kalju	a	2-0	*Nikulin 2*
30/10	Paide	h	0-0	
6/11	Trans	a	1-2	*Veikutis Ar.*

Name	Nat	DoB	Pos	Aps	(s)	Gls
Igor ALEKSANDROV		28/2/94	M		(1)	
Pavel ALEKSEJEV		24/2/91	D	3	(10)	
Irfan AMETOV	UKR	3/2/80	M	5		1
Aleksandr BÕKOV		19/10/92	M		(1)	
Aleksey CHERKASOV	RUS	1/9/94	D		(1)	
Aleksandr DJATŠENKO		3/2/81	G	6		
Aleksandr DUBÕKIN		6/5/83	M	11	(3)	3
Igor DUDAREV	RUS	12/8/93	D	6	(4)	
Sergei GORBUNOV	RUS	5/4/87	D	16		1
Andrei GORNEV		28/7/88	M	8	(3)	1
Maksim GRUZNOV		21/4/74	A	8	(7)	5
Kennet JÄDAL		8/5/90	D	18		
Yevgeniy KABAYEV	RUS	28/2/88	A	17	(1)	6
Nikita KOLYAEV	RUS	23/7/89	A	10	(7)	9
Aleksandr KULIK		23/7/81	A	27	(5)	3
Jürgen KURESOO		11/2/87	M	6	(21)	2
Dmitriy LIPARTOV	RUS	2/4/73	A	1	(1)	1
Igor MOISSEJEV		30/12/84	D		(2)	
Aleksandr MUTIK	RUS	3/9/86	M	7	(3)	
Aleksei NAUMOV	RUS	2/2/72	M	27	(2)	2
Roman NESTEROVSKI		9/6/89	D	14	(3)	
Aleksandr NIKULIN	RUS	19/1/85	A	15	(2)	9
Tadas PAPEČKYS	LTU	8/9/78	D	5		
Vitalis STANKEVIČIUS	LTU	23/6/82	A	28		8
Mihhail STARODUBTSEV		14/8/82	G	30		
Alber TAAR		15/1/90	M	9		
Tanel TAMBERG		6/6/92	D		(4)	
Aleksandr TARASSENKOV		29/9/80	M	28	(4)	9
Nerijus VASILIAUSKAS	LTU	20/6/77	A	19	(2)	10
Arvydas VEIKUTIS	LTU	19/3/87	M	14		4
Audrius VEIKUTIS	LTU	23/7/79	D	15		2
Sergei VIHROV		2/3/86	M	25	(3)	4
Vygantas ZUBAVIČIUS	LTU	14/11/84	M	18	(3)	3

JK TAMMEKA TARTU

Coach – Marko Kristal

Founded – 1989

Stadium – Tamme (800)

2010

9/3	Kuressaare	a	3-2	*Sonn, Tamm (p), Roops*
13/3	Kalju	h	2-3	*Tamm (p), Torop*
20/3	Paide	a	3-1	*Laas, Sonn, Prosa*
23/3	Sillamäe Kalev	h	1-4	*Teniste*
27/3	Flora	a	2-3	*Kiidron 2*
3/4	Lootus	h	1-0	*Laas*
10/4	Tulevik	a	3-0	*Valtna, Tikenberg, Laas*
17/4	Trans	a	0-0	
24/4	Levadia	h	0-0	
1/5	Levadia	a	0-2	
8/5	Trans	h	1-2	*Laas*
15/5	Tulevik	h	2-0	*Laabus, Tamm*
25/5	Trans	a	1-1	*Tikenberg*
29/5	Lootus	a	3-1	*Kiidron, Valtna, Laas*
1/6	Flora	h	0-1	
5/6	Sillamäe Kalev	a	0-4	
12/6	Paide	h	0-0	
15/6	Kalju	a	1-1	*og (Võtti)*
29/6	Kuressaare	h	2-0	*Tenno, Prosa*
3/7	Levadia	h	0-0	
17/7	Tulevik	a	0-4	
24/7	Lootus	h	5-1	*Torop 2, Roops, Laabus, Prosa*
31/7	Flora	a	3-6	*Prosa 3*
7/8	Sillamäe Kalev	h	2-3	*Prosa 2*
14/8	Paide	a	4-3	*Prosa, Tenno, Haljak, og (Lomp)*
21/8	Kalju	h	0-1	
28/8	Kuressaare	a	2-3	*Tenno, Haljak*
11/9	Kuressaare	h	0-2	
14/9	Kalju	a	1-3	*Perlin*
18/9	Paide	h	1-2	*Prosa*
25/9	Sillamäe Kalev	a	0-2	
2/10	Flora	h	2-1	*Laabus, Laas*
16/10	Lootus	a	3-1	*Prosa 2, Laas*
23/10	Tulevik	h	2-2	*Tamm, og (Tutk)*
30/10	Trans	h	0-1	
9'6/11	Levadia	a	0-6	

Name	Nat	DoB	Pos	Aps	(s)	Gls
Chris ANDERSON		5/10/92	D		(1)	
Martin HALJAK		16/5/90	D	10	(2)	2
Mario HANSI		21/5/87	M	8	(14)	
Kaspar KALDOJA		1/1/90	M	16	(3)	
Kaarel KALLANDI		22/3/89	M	19	(3)	
Kaarel KIIDRON		30/4/90	D	33		3
Karli KÜTT		17/2/93	G	11		
Ats KUTTER		28/3/91	G	5		
Reio LAABUS		14/3/90	M	31	(2)	3
Mikk LAAS		30/9/80	M	27	(5)	7
Meelis MEISALU		18/4/94	M		(1)	
Kristjan PAAPSI		30/7/87	A	3	(10)	
Olari PERLIN		28/2/90	D	2	(12)	1
Albert PROSA		1/10/90	M	28	(4)	12
Siim ROOPS		4/3/86	D	35		2
Marko SONN		29/10/88	D	32		2
Heiko TAMM		18/3/87	M	31	(2)	4
Timo TENISTE		27/10/85	D	5		1
Siim TENNO		4/8/90	A	33	(1)	3
Tiit TIKENBERG		28/1/83	A	11	(7)	2
Sebastian TISZAI	GER	7/4/88	G	4		
Mait TOOM		7/5/90	G	16		
Kaarel TOROP		20/9/92	A	10	(12)	3
Siim VALTNA		31/7/87	M	26	(2)	2
Erik VARES		6/7/90	M		(1)	

JK TRANS NARVA

Coach – Valeri Bondarenko; (29/10/10) Aleksei Jagudin

Founded – 1979

Stadium – Kreenholm (1,000)

MAJOR HONOURS: Estonian Cup – (1) 2001.

010

/3	Levadia	a	0-3	
3/3	Flora	h	1-0	*Smirnov*
0/3	Kuressaare	a	1-0	*Bezykornovas (p)*
3/3	Lootus	h	0-1	
7/3	Kalju	a	1-0	*Abramenko*
/4	Tulevik	h	2-0	*Bazjukin, Felipe Lemos*
0/4	Paide	a	4-0	*Abramenko, Mitin, Saulėnas, Bezykornovas*
7/4	Tammeka	h	0-0	
4/4	Sillamäe Kalev	a	2-1	*Bezykornovas (p), Mitin*
/5	Sillamäe Kalev	h	2-2	*Bazjukin, Bezykornovas (p)*
/5	Sillamäe Kalev	a	3-1	*Bazjukin 2, Abramenko*
/5	Tammeka	a	2-1	*Rimas, Bazjukin*
5/5	Paide	h	4-1	*Felipe Lemos 2, Bezykornovas, og (Nõmme)*
5/5	Tammeka	h	1-1	*Leontovitš*
9/5	Tulevik	a	1-0	*Kazakov*
/6	Kalju	h	2-2	*Leontovitš, Bezykornovas*
/6	Lootus	a	5-0	*Smirnov, Rimas, Leontovitš, Bezykornovas, Felipe Lemos*
3/6	Levadia	h	1-2	*Leontovitš*
12/6	Kuressaare	h	3-0	*Mitin, Bezykornovas, Abramenko*
15/6	Flora	a	1-1	*Saulėnas*
17/7	Paide	a	1-1	*Mitin*
24/7	Tulevik	h	2-0	*Bezykornovas, Felipe Lemos*
31/7	Kalju	a	2-0	*Leontovitš, Bezykornovas (p)*
7/8	Lootus	h	4-1	*Gruznov 2 (1p), Rimas, og (Škaleta)*
14/8	Kuressaare	a	4-1	*Ghasaboghlyan, Gruznov (p), Felipe Lemos, Bazjukin*
21/8	Flora	h	1-2	*Gruznov*
28/8	Levadia	a	1-1	*Eessaar*
11/9	Levadia	h	0-3	
14/9	Flora	a	0-4	
18/9	Kuressaare	h	5-1	*Bezykornovas 2 (1p), Felipe Lemos, Ivanov, Ghasaboghlyan*
25/9	Lootus	a	4-0	*Bazjukin 2, Gruznov, Felipe Lemos*
2/10	Kalju	h	1-0	*Mitin*
16/10	Tulevik	a	3-0	*Gorškov, Ivanov, Abramenko*
23/10	Paide	h	0-0	*(w/o; awarded as home win; original result 0-0)*
30/10	Tammeka	a	1-0	*Abramenko*
6/11	Sillamäe Kalev	h	2-1	*Bezykornovas (p), Abramenko*

Name	Nat	DoB	Pos	Aps	(s)	Gls
Aleksandrs ABRAMENKO	LVA	9/1/85	M	28	(4)	7
Reimo AUSTA		24/2/90	D		(1)	
Oliver AVASOO		17/4/90	D		(3)	
Maksim BAZJUKIN	RUS	18/6/83	M	27	(1)	8
Marius BEZYKORNOVAS	LTU	22/8/76	M	33		13
Eero EESSAAR		27/11/89	M	1	(4)	1
FELIPE LEMOS Rodrigues	BRA	6/6/83	A	31	(3)	8
Mantas GALDIKAS	LTU	22/6/89	G	3		
Levon GHASABOGHLYAN	ARM	27/1/86	M		(6)	2
Aleksei GORŠKOV		13/2/85	D	30	(1)	1
Maksim GRUZNOV		21/4/74	A	11		5
Georgi IVANOV		19/6/92	M	1	(8)	2
Sergei KAZAKOV		2/1/80	M	17	(13)	1
Stanislav KITTO		30/11/72	D	30		
Sergei LEONTOVITŠ		4/3/87	M	15	(10)	5
Oleg LEPIK		1/8/73	D	30	(2)	
Armando Tarlazis Viera dos Santos "MANDINHO"	BRA	28/4/84	M	7	(3)	
Serhiy MITIN	UKR	27/7/77	D	30		5
Lauri OTT		16/7/92	M		(1)	
Igor OVSJANNIKOV		23/2/92	D	3	(4)	
Viktor PLOTNIKOV		14/7/89	M	1	(10)	
Tomas RIMAS	LTU	2/5/78	D	34		3
Dainius SAULĖNAS	LTU	13/3/79	A	10	(9)	2
Maksim SMIRNOV		28/12/79	M	8	(7)	2
Sergei STAROVOITOV		26/7/81	D	13	(6)	
Modestas STONYS	LTU	17/1/80	G	20		
Sergei USSOLTSEV		2/4/75	G	13		

JK TULEVIK VILJANDI

Coach – Marko Lelov

Founded – 1912

Stadium – Viljandi Linnastaadion (1,000)

2010

9/3	Kalju	a	0-1	
13/3	Paide	h	1-0	*Luhakooder*
20/3	Sillamäe Kalev	a	1-2	*Indermitte*
23/3	Flora	h	0-1	
27/3	Lootus	a	1-0	*Toomet*
3/4	Trans	a	0-2	
10/4	Tammeka	h	0-3	
17/4	Levadia	a	0-2	
24/4	Kuressaare	h	0-0	
1/5	Kuressaare	a	2-3	*Luhakooder, Kulatšenko*
8/5	Levadia	h	0-1	
15/5	Tammeka	a	0-2	
29/5	Trans	h	0-1	
1/6	Lootus	h	1-0	*Toomet*
5/6	Flora	a	1-1	*Tomson*
12/6	Sillamäe Kalev	h	1-2	*Luigend*
15/6	Paide	a	0-2	
29/6	Kalju	h	1-4	*Kulatšenko (p)*
3/7	Kuressaare	h	4-1	*Tomson 2, Sinilaid, Kulatšenko*
10/7	Levadia	a	0-3	
17/7	Tammeka	h	4-0	*Stüf, Ottis, Luigend, Raudsepp*
24/7	Trans	a	0-2	
31/7	Lootus	a	0-0	
7/8	Flora	h	1-6	*Indermitte*
14/8	Sillamäe Kalev	a	2-5	*Stüf, og (Starodubtsev)*
21/8	Paide	h	1-0	*Tomson*
28/8	Kalju	a	0-3	
11/9	Kalju	h	0-1	
14/9	Paide	a	1-1	*Kulatšenko*
18/9	Sillamäe Kalev	h	3-2	*Kulatšenko 2, Reintam*
25/9	Flora	a	0-1	
16/10	Trans	h	0-3	
19/10	Lootus	h	4-0	*Kulatšenko 2, Reintam, Luigend*
23/10	Tammeka	a	2-2	*Sillaste, Ottis*
30/10	Levadia	h	0-1	
6/11	Kuressaare	a	2-4	*Stüf, Naris*

Name	Nat	DoB	Pos	Aps	(s)	Gls
Henri ERTI		12/12/87	M		(1)	
Joel INDERMITTE		27/12/92	D	6	(24)	2
Rait KASTERPALU		1/9/87	M	5	(4)	
Andres KOOGAS		5/9/87	D	14		
Aleksandr KULATŠENKO		25/5/87	M	24	(1)	8
Elvis LIIVAMÄGI		21/1/92	D	23	(4)	
Rasmus LUHAKOODER		8/12/88	M	9	(1)	2
Karl-Erik LUIGEND		15/1/93	M	25	(5)	3
Karl MÖÖL		4/3/92	M		(7)	
Rasmus MUNSKIND		31/8/89	M		(3)	
Armand NARIS		6/10/88	D	17		1
Aiko ORGLA		24/5/87	G	18		
Ott OTTIS		14/6/89	M	24	(10)	2
Mikk PÄRT		1/4/90	M	8	(8)	
Ivo-Henri PIKKOR		15/6/93	M		(4)	
Andreas RAUDSEPP		13/12/93	M	2	(7)	1
Mikk REINTAM		22/5/90	D	14		2
Mikk SILLASTE		1/3/87	D	35		1
Sander SINILAID		7/10/90	M	34	(1)	1
Edwin STÜF		30/7/89	M	20	(3)	3
Martin TASKA		9/12/86	D	17	(5)	
Rasmus TOMSON		13/8/85	M	33	(1)	4
Janar TOOMET		10/8/89	M	19	(2)	2
Rauno TUTK		10/4/88	D	31	(1)	
Alan VENTSEL		2/9/88	G	18	(1)	

ESTONIA

TOP GOALSCORERS 2010

24	Sander POST (Flora)
21	Jüri JEVDOKIMOV (Kalju)
20	Tarmo NEEMELO (Levadia)
16	Vitali LEITAN (Levadia)
14	Deniss MALOV (Levadia)
13	Henri ANIER (Flora)
	Marius BEZYKORNOVAS (Trans)
12	Konstantin NAHK (Levadia)
	Albert PROSA (Tammeka)
10	Nerijus VASILIAUSKAS (Sillamäe Kalev)
	Maksim GRUZNOV (Sillamäe Kalev/Trans)

PROMOTED CLUB

FC AJAX LASNAMÄE

Coach – Andrei Borissov
Founded – 1993
Stadium – Ajaxi Staadion Kunstmuru (500)

SECOND LEVEL FINAL TABLE 2010

		Pld	W	D	L	F	A	Pts
1	FC Levadia II Tallinn	36	28	5	3	107	28	89
2	FC Flora II Tallinn	36	22	6	8	93	45	72
3	FC Ajax Lasnamäe	36	20	9	7	71	38	69
4	SK Kiviõli Tamme Auto	36	17	6	13	85	72	57
5	JK Tallinna Kalev	36	17	6	13	67	65	53
6	Tallinna JK Legion	36	11	6	19	57	81	39
7	JK Vaprus Pärnu	36	10	7	19	57	78	37
8	FC Warrior Valga	36	10	6	20	57	90	35
9	FC Flora Rakvere	36	10	3	23	45	95	31
10	JK Orbiit Jõhvi	36	6	4	26	35	82	22

NB FC Levadia II Tallinn & FC Flora II Tallinn ineligible for promotion; FC Ajax Lasnamäe promoted directly; SK Kiviõli Tamme Auto entered play-offs; JK Tallinna Kalev – 4 pts deducted; FC Flora Rakvere – 2 pts deducted; FC Warrior Valga – 1 pt deducted.

PROMOTION/RELEGATION PLAY-OFFS

(14/11/10)
Tamme Auto 2, Kuressaare 1

(20/11/10)
Kuressaare 3, Tamme Auto 0
(Kuressaare 4-2)

DOMESTIC CUP 2010/11

EESTI KARIKAS

SECOND ROUND

(3/8/10)
Paide 0, Tulevik 1
Sillamäe Kalev 6, Atli 0
Tääksi 4, Kaitseliit Kalev 3
Tabasalu 2, HaServ 3

(4/8/10)
AameraaS 2, Kalju 6
Aspen 0, Igiliikur 8
Flora Tallinn II 1, Sillamäe Kalev II 3
Joker 2, Lootus II 0
Kiiu 0, Emmaste 9
Kotkad 0, Luunja 1
Kumake 0, Flora Tallinn 5
Laagri 3, TJK Legion 0
Löök 2, A&A Kinnisvara 3 *(aet)*
Noorus 96 0, Kuressaare 3
Saue 3, Otepää 10
Tallinna Kalev 1, Levadia 0 *(aet)*

(5/8/10)
Jalgpallihaigla 1, Alko 7
Flora Rakvere II 8, Suema Cargobus 0
Twister 1, Tammeka II 2

(10/8/10)
Ararat TTÜ 1, Lootus 0
Olympik 1, Tammeka 8
Tallinna Kalev III 0, Trans 7

(12/8/10)
Ajax Lasnamäe 9, Järva-Jääni Rada 3, Lootos 6
Saku 1, EMÜ 3

(18/8/10)
Nõmme United 4, Warrior II 0
Rannamõisa 0, Tarvastu 4
Warrior 0, Atletik 1

(19/8/10)
SK 10 II 0, Ganvix 4

(25/8/10)
Kalju II 3, Kristiine 0

(26/8/10)
Võru 0, Flora Rakvere 4 (w/o; original result 2-4)

(4/9/10)
Tamme Auto 3, Puuma 2

THIRD ROUND

(31/8/10)
Alko 2, Ararat TTÜ 1
Flora Tallinn 5, Flora Rakvere II 0
Kuressaare 1, Sillamäe Kalev 5

(2/9/10)
Otepää 1, Lootos 1 *(aet; 2-3 on pens)*

(4/9/10)
Kalju 0, Trans 1

(8/9/10)
EMÜ 0, Ajax Lasnamäe 2
Igiliikur 1, Nõmme United 2
Tallinna Kalev 2, Luunja 0
Tammeka II 4, Tarvastu 3 *(aet)*

(15/9/10)
Tääksi 1, Joker 5

(21/9/10)
Tammeka 4, Atletik 0

(22/9/10)
Ganvix w/o A&A Kinnisvara
Sillamäe Kalev II 3, Flora Rakvere 0

(29/9/10)
Kalju II 0, Emmaste 4
Laagri 2, Tamme Auto 3

(7/10/10)
HaServ 1, Tulevik 0

1/8 FINALS

(5/10/10)
Tammeka 0, Trans 1

(6/10/10)
Flora Tallinn 4, Lootos 1
Joker 3, Sillamäe Kalev II 0
Tallinna Kalev 2, Tammeka II 1

(14/10/10)
Emmaste 4, Alko 0

(20/10/10)
Sillamäe Kalev 12, Tamme Auto 1

(27/10/10)
HaServ 1, Ganvix 0

(13/11/10)
Ajax Lasnamäe 4, Nõmme United 1

QUARTER-FINALS

Flora Tallinn w/o Joker

(12/4/11)
HaServ 0, Ajax Lasnamäe 4 *(Mones 91, Tasso 106, Dmitriev 108, Starodub 119) (aet)*

(13/4/11)
Emmaste 0, Sillamäe Kalev 1*(Nikulin 20)*
Trans 1 *(Čekulajevs 109)*, Tallinna Kalev 0 *(aet)*

SEMI-FINALS

(26/4/11)
Flora Tallinn 6 *(Alliku 7, Anier Ha. 54, 85, Mošnikov 69, Beglarishvili 77, Jürgenson 81)*, Ajax Lasnamäe 0
Sillamäe Kalev 1 *(Tarassenkov 61)*, Trans 1 *(Čekulajevs 57) (aet; 16-17 on pens)*

FINAL

(10/5/11)
A. Le Coq Arena, Tallinn
FC FLORA TALLINN 2 *(Jürgenson 48, Dupikov 78)*
JK TRANS NARVA 0
Referee – *Kaasik*
FLORA TALLINN – *Meerits, Kams, Palatu, Jahhimovitš, Jürgenson, Minkenen, Frolov, Peitre (Mošnikov 64), Luts, Alliku (Anier Ha. 81), Dupikov.*
TRANS – *Vyalchinov, Grigorjev, Rimas, Kitto (Bezykornovas 14), Kazakov, Abramenko, Bazjukin, Plotnikov (Epikhin 77), Šiškin, Gruznov (Biskys 85), Čekulajevs.*

CLUB COMMUNICATION 2011

'C Ajax Lasnamäe

uslinna 10
E-11415 Tallinn

el	+372 5221 237
ax	+372 6011 229
'eb	fcajax.ee
mail	jkajax@hot.ee
ledia Officer	Ivar Siig

'C Flora Tallinn

sula 4C
E-11312 Tallinn

el	+372 6279 940
ax	+372 6279 941
Veb	fcflora.ee
mail	fcflora@fcflora.ee
ledia Officer	Ege Heeringas

'C Kuressaare

Staadioni 2, Kuressaare, Kuressaare
Staadion, EE-93815 Kuressaare

'el	+372 5156 165
'ax	+372 4576 380
Veb	fckuressaare.ee
Email	priit.penu@ fckuressaare.ee
Media Officer	Miko Pupart

FC Levadia Tallinn

Kose tee 4
EE-12011 Tallinn

Tel	+372 6313 017
Fax	+372 6464 909
Web	fclevadia.ee
Email	sport@levadia.ee
Media Officer	Indrek Petersoo

JK Nõmme Kalju

Harju 6
EE-10130 Tallinn

Tel	+372 5647 0005
Fax	+372 6310 546
Web	jkkalju.ee
Email	kalju@jkkalju.ee
Media Officer	Helen Mahmastol

Paide Linnameeskond

Asula 4c
EE-11312 Tallinn

Tel	+372 5625 1081
Fax	
Web	linnameeskond.com
Email	info@linnameeskond.ee
Media Officer	Urmas Meisner

JK Sillamäe Kalev

Kesk 30
EE-40231 Sillamäe

Tel	+372 5158 795
Fax	+372 3929 177
Web	fcsillamae.ee
Email	jksillamae@gmail.com
Media Officer	Igor Saveljev

JK Tammeka Tartu

Tamme pst 1
EE-50403 Tartu

Tel	+372 7428 038
Fax	+372 7428 038
Web	jktammeka.ee
Email	jktammeka@ jktammeka.ee
Media Officer	Mari Lill

JK Trans Narva

Tiimani str.,3
EE-21004 Narva

Tel	+372 3573 299
Fax	+372 3573 304
Web	fctrans.ee
Email	fctrans@fctrans.ee
Media Officer	Christina Burdakova

FC Viljandi

Ranna pst 6
EE-71003 Viljandi

Tel	+372 55 570 197
Fax	+372 43 48 016
Web	
Email	rain_tolpus@hotmail.com
Media Officer	Urmas Meisner

FAROE ISLANDS

Îles Féroé I Färöer-Inseln

Fótbóltssamband Føroya (FSF)

COMMUNICATION

Address Gundadalur
PO Box 3028
FO-110 Tórshavn

Tel +298 351979
Fax +298 319079

E-mail fsf@football.fo
Website football.fo

President Christian Andreasen
General Secretary Virgar Hvidbro

Year of Formation 1979

National Stadium Tórsvøllur, Torshavn (6,040)

DOMESTIC COMPETITION SUMMARY 2010

FORMULADEILDIN FINAL TABLE

			Home					Away					Total						
		Pld	W	D	L	F	A	W	D	L	F	A	W	D	L	F	A	Pts	Comp
1	HB Tórshavn	27	10	2	2	34	22	6	4	3	15	10	16	6	5	49	32	54	UCL
2	EB/Streymur	27	9	3	2	41	12	5	6	2	24	18	14	9	4	65	30	51	UEL
3	NSÍ Runavík	27	9	2	3	29	13	5	4	4	31	20	14	6	7	60	33	48	UEL
4	ÍF Fuglafjørdur	27	5	4	4	27	26	7	3	4	23	15	12	7	8	50	41	43	UEL
5	Víkingur	27	5	4	5	24	20	7	3	3	20	15	12	7	8	44	35	43	
6	B36 Tórshavn	27	7	3	3	18	16	4	4	6	26	20	11	7	9	44	36	40	
7	B68 Toftir	27	7	6	1	29	17	1	1	11	13	30	8	7	12	42	47	31	
8	B71 Sandoy	27	3	3	7	10	24	2	5	7	14	41	5	8	14	24	65	23	
9	FC Suduroy	27	4	4	5	16	22	1	3	10	17	32	5	7	15	33	54	22	*Relegated*
10	AB Argir	27	2	5	6	12	26	0	3	11	15	39	2	8	17	27	65	14	*Relegated*

Top Scorer Arnbjørn Theodor Hansen (EB/Streymur) & Christian Høgni Jacobsen (NSÍ), 22 goals

Promoted Clubs 07 Vestur
KÍ Klaksvík

Cup Final EB/Streymur 1, ÍF Fuglafjørdur 0

Successful title defence for HB

After a topsy-turvy tussle for the 2010 Faroese championship, during which no fewer than five of the ten competing teams topped the table, it was HB Tórshavn, the defending champions, who emerged triumphant to take the title for a record 21st time.

HB went into the campaign with a new coach, but Kristján Gudmundsson, who had taken over from 2009 title-winning boss Sámal Erik Hentze, did not survive the season. The Icelander was dismissed after a humiliating 4-1 home defeat by lowly FC Suduroy in mid-September and replaced by ex-Faroese international Julian Hansen, who then proceeded to steer the club successfully through the title run-in, collecting 16 points from a possible 18 to see the team home with a three-point winning margin over runners-up EB/Streymur.

Special presentation

HB needed a point from their final game – a derby against mid-table B36 Tórshavn – and although they were second-best for much of the contest, they won the game with goals from inspirational skipper Fródi Benjaminsen and defender Hendrik Rubeksen. As an added bonus, the team were presented with the championship trophy by visiting UEFA president Michel Platini.

HB scored ten goals fewer than in 2009, and their three closest pursuers – EB/Streymur, NSÍ Runavík and ÍF Fuglafjørdur – all outgunned them. But it was the Torshavn club's ability to win the games that really mattered which proved decisive. They took seven points from EB/Streymur and six apiece from NSÍ and ÍF. Their top scorer was veteran Faroese international Benjaminsen, who, as in 2009, enjoyed a magnificent campaign, starting all 27 matches and scoring 13 goals, six of them during that impressive late run under new boss Hansen. As HB finished strongly, NSÍ, who at one stage headed the defending champions by seven points, fell away badly, winning just once in eight matches before signing off with a 9-1 thrashing

Champions HB celebrate with the trophy

of B71 Sandoy in which star striker Christian Høgni Jacobsen scored five goals to end the season as the league's joint-leading marksman alongside another former Golden Boot winner, EB/Streymur's Arnbjørn Theodor Hansen.

EB/Streymur ended a poor first half of the season with a 5-2 defeat by HB, but they were unbeaten after the July break. In early August they won the Faroese Cup for the third time in four years, defeating ÍF 1-0 in the final with a goal from their Romanian-born striker Sorin Anghel, who, a few weeks after obtaining Faroese citizenship, celebrated his 250th game for the club by tapping in the 25th-minute winner. Although ÍF lost the cup final, they did claim European qualification for the first time via the league – but only thanks to a goal in the 93rd minute of their last-day encounter at Víkingur. Bartal Eliasen's last-gasp strike enabled ÍF to take fourth place ahead of their hosts on the number of goals scored after both teams had ended the campaign with the same points total and goal difference.

Irishman Brian Kerr led the Faroe Islands national team into the UEFA EURO 2012 qualifying campaign and was within a couple of minutes of savouring an opening-day win in Estonia, only for the home side to snatch victory from the jaws of defeat with two late goals. Ten months later, however, Kerr's men would have their revenge for that heartbreak when they beat Estonia 2-0 in Toftir. It was the Faroe Islands' first victory in the competition for 16 years and, after an earlier 1-1 draw at the same venue against Northern Ireland, restored some balance to a campaign that had been scarred by early trouncings in Florence and Ljubljana.

National Team

Top Five All-time Caps – Óli Johannesen (83); Jákup Mikkelsen (71); Fródi Benjaminsen & Jens Martin Knudsen (65); Julian Johnsson (62)

Top Five All-time Goals – Rógvi Jacobsen (10); Todi Jónsson (9); Uni Arge (8); John Petersen (6); Fródi Benjaminsen, Julian Johnsson & Jan Allan Müller (4)

NATIONAL TEAM RESULTS 2010/11

11/8/10	Estonia (ECQ)	A	Tallinn	1-2	*Edmundsson (28)*
3/9/10	Serbia (ECQ)	H	Torshavn	0-3	
7/9/10	Italy (ECQ)	A	Florence	0-5	
8/10/10	Slovenia (ECQ)	A	Ljubljana	1-5	*Mouritsen (90+3)*
12/10/10	Northern Ireland (ECQ)	H	Toftir	1-1	*Holst (60)*
16/11/10	Scotland	A	Aberdeen	0-3	
3/6/11	Slovenia (ECQ)	H	Toftir	0-2	
7/6/11	Estonia (ECQ)	H	Toftir	2-0	*Benjaminsen (43p), Hansen A. (47)*

NATIONAL TEAM APPEARANCES 2010/11

Coach – Brian KERR (IRL)	3/3/53		EST	SRB	ITA	SVN	NIR	Sco	SVN	EST	Caps	Goals
Gunnar NIELSEN	7/10/86	Tranmere (ENG)	G	G	G			G68			7	-
Jónas Tór NÆS	27/12/86	B36 /Valur (ISL)	D	D	s74	D	D	D	D81	D	21	-
Atli GREGERSEN	15/6/82	Ross County (SCO) /Víkingur	D	D	D	D	D	D		D	15	-
Jóhan Troest DAVIDSEN	31/1/88	NSÍ /Aarhus Fremad (DEN)	D	D	D		D	D	D		21	-
Hendrik RUBEKSEN	1/11/83	HB	D	D	D	D					4	-
Fródi BENJAMINSEN	14/12/77	HB	M	M	M	M	M		M	M	65	4
Jákup á BORG	26/10/79	B36	M67								61	2
Jann Ingi PETERSEN	7/1/84	NSÍ	M85	M73	M	s81	s68	M60			22	-
Símun SAMUELSEN	21/5/85	HB	M74	M	M		M78			s69	34	1
Christian Lamhauge HOLST	25/12/81	Silkeborg (DEN)	M	M79	s74	M81	M85	M56	M75	M85	27	3
Jóan Símun EDMUNDSSON	26/7/91	Newcastle (ENG)	A	A	A89	A	A	A	A		10	1
Rógvi POULSEN	31/10/89	HB	s67					s56			4	-
Jústinus R. HANSEN	14/5/85	NSÍ	s74	s73		M	s85				4	-
Bogi LØKIN	22/10/88	NSÍ	s85		M74	M41		M79			17	1
Daniel UDSEN	18/3/83	EB/Streymur		M46	s89	M81	M68	M87	M45		6	-
Christian R. MOURITSEN	3/12/88	B36 /Valur (ISL)		s46	M74	s81		s60	s75	s85	9	1
Arnbjørn Theodor HANSEN	27/2/86	EB/Streymur		s79			s78			A69	10	2
Egil á BØ	2/4/74	EB/Streymur			D	D					14	1
Jákup MIKKELSEN	14/8/70	ÍF				G	G		G	G	71	-
Hjalgrím ELTTØR	3/3/83	B36 /KÍ				s41	M	M	M	M91	20	-
Erling D. JACOBSEN	13/2/90	Víkingur					D	D			2	-
Tórdur THOMSEN	11/6/86	HB						s68			1	-
Levi HANSSEN	24/2/88	HB						s79			3	-
Pól Jóhannus JUSTINUSSEN	13/1/89	B68 /Valur (ISL)						s87	M	M 89*	3	-
Rógvi BALDVINSSON	6/12/89	Ålgård (NOR)							D	D	2	-
Einar T. HANSEN	2/4/88	NSÍ							D	D	12	-
Atli DANIELSEN	15/8/83	Roskilde (DEN)							s45	M	38	-
Súni OLSEN	7/3/81	B36							s81	s91	43	3

CLUB-BY-CLUB

AB ARGIR

Coach – Allan Mørkøre; (13/8/10) Allan Mørkøre & Sámal Erik Hentze; (27/8/10) Sámal Erik Hentze

Founded – 1973

Stadium – Inni í Vika (2,000)

10

·	Víkingur	a	3-5	*Søbstad 2, Overgaard*
·	B71	h	3-3	*Haraldsen, Søbstad 2*
/4	HB	a	1-2	*Splidt*
/4	B36	h	2-2	*Søbstad, Overgaard*
·	NSÍ	a	0-3	
·	ÍF	h	0-2	
/5	EB/Streymur	a	1-2	*Blé (p)*
/5	B68	a	1-1	*Eriksen*
/5	Suduroy	h	1-0	*Aristide*
/5	Víkingur	h	1-1	*Søbstad*
/6	B71	a	0-1	
/6	HB	h	1-1	*Mellemgaard*
/6	B36	a	0-1	
/6	NSÍ	h	0-0	
·	ÍF	a	4-4	*Blé 3 (1p), Aristide*
/7	EB/Streymur	h	1-2	*Vang*
·	B68	h	1-2	*Dam*
/8	Suduroy	a	3-3	*Bordoy, Eriksen 2*
/8	ÍF	h	1-4	*Hørg*
/8	EB/Streymur	a	0-6	
/9	Víkingur	a	1-3	*Dam*
/9	B71	h	0-4	
/9	HB	a	0-3	
/9	NSÍ	a	1-2	*Sigurdsson*
10	B36	h	0-5	
/10	B68	a	0-3	
/10	Suduroy	h	1-0	*Sigurdsson (p)*

No	Name	Nat	DoB	Pos	Aps	(s)	Gls
·	Fabrice AMESSAN	CIV	5/6/86	M	4	(4)	
	Téhé ARISTIDE	CIV	31/12/86	D	25	(1)	2
	Evrard BLÉ	CIV	2/1/82	M	20	(2)	4
·	Yohan Andres BORDOY		6/7/88	D	10	(2)	1
·	Jákup Pætursson DAM		28/9/89	A	8	(12)	2
	Rói DANIELSEN		18/2/89	D	3		
·	Gert DRANGASTEIN		25/4/94	M		(1)	
·	Jobin Schrøter DRANGASTEIN		1/11/90	M	17	(1)	
·	Sjúrdur ELLEFSEN		22/10/81	D	1	(7)	
·	Nikolai Lindholm ERIKSEN	DEN	1/8/86	A	19		3
	John HANSEN		14/11/88	M	10	(1)	
	Símun Rógvi HANSEN		10/4/87	G	5		
	Gunnar Højgaard HARALDSEN		21/11/87	M	21	(3)	1
3	Brandur HEINASON		7/1/90	M		(1)	
4	Mortan úr HØRG		21/9/80	D	18	(1)	1
0	Kenneth JACOBSEN		11/5/81	M	20	(3)	
1	Teitur JÓANESARSSON		18/3/89	D	8		
	Tummas JUSTINUSSEN		20/3/90	M	12		
3	Alex MELLEMGAARD		27/11/91	D	22		1
	Martin MIDJORD		25/12/89	D		(1)	
	Rasmus Frídi NIELSEN		22/9/89	M	2		
	Morten OVERGAARD	DEN	24/5/87	D	5		2
0	Dan PETERSEN		2/7/90	A	1	(3)	
·	Tróndur SIGURDSSON		16/12/88	A	6	(4)	2
0	Dion Brynjolf SPLIDT		5/6/89	A	9	(9)	1
6	Hedin STENBERG		14/1/89	G	10	(1)	
3	Jónas STENBERG		7/4/87	D	8	(3)	
·	Stig-Roar SØBSTAD	NOR	12/3/82	A	14	(1)	6
6	Thomas Juul THOMSEN		3/9/91	G	4		
	Tórdur THOMSEN		11/6/86	G	8		
5	Ingvard VANG		11/8/88	M	7	(2)	1

B36 TÓRSHAVN

Coach – Sigfridur Clementsen; (27/8/10) Allan Mørkøre

Founded – 1936

Stadium – Gundadalur (5,000)

MAJOR HONOURS: Faroe Islands League – (8) 1946, 1948, 1950, 1959, 1962, 1997, 2001, 2005; Faroe Islands Cup – (5) 1965, 1991, 2001, 2003, 2006.

2010

1/4	EB/Streymur	a	2-1	*Jacobsen Ró., Mouritsen*
5/4	B68	h	3-1	*Olsen B. 2, Borg*
11/4	B71	a	3-0	*Clementsen, Jacobsen Ró., Mouritsen*
18/4	AB	a	2-2	*Olsen B., Elttør*
2/5	ÍF	h	1-1	*Elttør*
9/5	Suduroy	a	1-1	*Ellingsgaard*
13/5	Víkingur	h	1-2	*Eysturoy*
16/5	NSÍ	h	1-5	*Eysturoy*
24/5	HB	a	2-2	*Borg, Færø*
30/5	EB/Streymur	h	1-1	*Borg*
13/6	B68	a	0-1	
16/6	B71	h	1-1	*Skorini*
20/6	AB	h	1-0	*Borg*
27/6	ÍF	a	5-0	*Olsen B., Mouritsen, Eysturoy, Jacobsen Ró., Olsen M.*
29/7	Víkingur	h	1-3	*Borg*
3/8	NSÍ	a	3-4	*Joensen S., Mouritsen, Borg*
15/8	HB	h	1-0	*Elttør*
22/8	Suduroy	a	1-2	*Matras*
25/8	Suduroy	h	1-0	*Olsen B.*
29/8	Víkingur	a	0-1	
12/9	EB/Streymur	a	1-4	*Skorini*
19/9	B68	h	3-1	*Mouritsen, Elttør 2*
22/9	B71	a	0-0	
26/9	ÍF	h	1-0	*Jacobsen Ró.*
2/10	AB	a	5-0	*Mouritsen, Matras, Jacobsen Ró., Borg, Elttør*
17/10	NSÍ	h	2-1	*Elttør, Matras (p)*
23/10	HB	a	1-2	*Mouritsen*

No	Name	Nat	DoB	Pos	Aps	(s)	Gls
9	Jákup á BORG		26/10/79	A	24		7
13	Sigurd Djurhuus CARLSSON		4/3/89	A		(1)	
17	Fródi CLEMENTSEN		30/11/78	D	8	(4)	1
12	Johan ELLINGSGAARD		12/5/89	M	13	(4)	1
23	Hjalgrím ELTTØR		3/3/83	A	25	(2)	7
20	Høgni EYSTUROY		14/7/90	M	4	(16)	3
5	Odmar FÆRØ		1/11/89	M	23	(4)	1
14	Bárdur HEINASON		21/8/73	A		(1)	
6	Ingi HØJSTED		12/11/85	M		(4)	
28	Herbert í Lon JACOBSEN		1/12/79	D	8		
2	Pól Arni JACOBSEN		22/10/76	A		(1)	
10	Róaldur JACOBSEN		23/1/91	M	24	(2)	5
12	Rúnar í Lon JACOBSEN		13/3/89	D		(2)	
1	Jóan Pauli Dahl JAKOBSEN		26/8/89	G	9		
4	Dmitrije JANKOVIĆ	SRB	5/11/75	D	22	(2)	
16	Meinhard JOENSEN		27/11/79	G	12		
3	Símun JOENSEN		12/7/83	M	15	(1)	1
22	Klæmint MATRAS		20/5/81	M	25		3
7	Bergur MIDJORD		20/4/85	A		(1)	
11	Christian Restorff MOURITSEN		3/12/88	A	26		7
3	Jónas Tór NÆS		27/12/86	D	13		
8	Bárdur OLSEN		5/12/85	M	26	(1)	5
18	Magnus Hendriksson OLSEN		26/10/86	M	4	(7)	1
1	Magnus Emil POULSEN		16/4/80	G	6		
14	Heini í SKORINI		14/5/83	A	4	(10)	2
7	Stig-Roar SØBSTAD	NOR	12/3/82	A	6	(1)	

B68 TOFTIR

Coach – Bill McLeod Jacobsen

Founded – 1962

Stadium – Svangarskard (1,200)

MAJOR HONOURS: Faroe Islands League – (3) 1984, 1985, 1992.

2010				
1/4	B71	h	5-0	*Højgaard O., Gueye, Justinussen, Keita, Joensen*
5/4	B36	a	1-3	*Justinussen*
12/4	ÍF	h	1-0	*Olsen A.*
18/4	Suduroy	a	1-3	*Justinussen*
3/5	Víkingur	h	5-3	*og (Túri), Justinussen, Højgaard O. 3*
9/5	HB	a	3-4	*Højgaard Jóh., Justinussen, Højgaard O.*
12/5	NSÍ	h	0-3	
16/5	AB	h	1-1	*Andreasen*
25/5	EB/Streymur	a	0-3	
30/5	B71	a	0-1	
13/6	B36	h	1-0	*Olsen Ó.*
16/6	ÍF	a	2-4	*Langgaard, Højgaard Jón.*
20/6	Suduroy	h	1-1	*Gueye*
25/6	Víkingur	a	0-0	
27/7	NSÍ	a	1-2	*Keita*
3/8	AB	a	2-1	*Andreasen, Keita*
16/8	EB/Streymur	h	1-1	*Gueye*
22/8	HB	a	0-1	
25/8	HB	h	2-2	*Hansen (p), Keita*
28/8	NSÍ	h	3-2	*Justinussen, Gueye, Hansen (p)*
12/9	B71	h	1-1	*Camara*
19/9	B36	a	1-3	*Keita*
22/9	ÍF	h	3-3	*Justinussen 2 (1p), Keita*
26/9	Víkingur	h	2-0	*Keita, Justinussen*
2/10	Suduroy	a	1-2	*Justinussen*
17/10	AB	h	3-0	*Camara (p), Poulsen J., Olsen A.*
23/10	EB/Streymur	a	1-3	*Poulsen J.*

No	Name	Nat	DoB	Pos	Aps	(s)	Gls
8	Kristian Anthon ANDREASEN		30/8/85	A	15	(6)	2
19	Ibrahima CAMARA	SEN	30/7/89	A	6	(4)	2
1	Vlada FILIPOVIĆ	SRB	18/3/78	G	24	(1)	
6	Ndende Adama GUEYE	SEN	5/1/83	M	23		4
5	Øssur HANSEN		7/1/71	M	18	(2)	2
9	Dánjal Pauli HØJGAARD		27/12/83	D	11	(6)	
20	Jóhan Dávur HØJGAARD		11/6/82	D	23	(1)	1
15	Jónleif HØJGAARD		26/10/88	A	2	(11)	1
16	Oddur Árnason HØJGAARD		12/9/89	D	16	(8)	5
32	Niclas Frídrikur JOENSEN		20/5/86	D	20	(4)	1
2	Pól Jóhannus JUSTINUSSEN		13/1/89	M	24		10
18	Ahmed KEITA	SEN	12/5/87	A	19	(5)	7
7	Remi LANGGAARD		16/12/91	M	21	(2)	1
26	Petur Meinhard MAGNUSSEN		26/3/90	G	3		
23	André OLSEN		23/10/90	A	18	(5)	2
14	Óli Højgaard OLSEN		24/11/85	A	4	(4)	1
11	Jóhan Petur POULSEN		8/5/86	M	23	(3)	2
17	Niklas POULSEN		30/3/89	D		(1)	
10	Poul Narvi POULSEN		22/9/86	A	15		
3	Eli SIMONSEN		3/9/90	M	12	(9)	

B71 SANDOY

Coach – Piotr Krakowski (POL)

Founded – 1970

Stadium – Inni í Dal (1,000)

MAJOR HONOURS: Faroe Islands League – (1) 1989; Faroe Islands Cup – (1) 1993.

2010				
1/4	B68	a	0-5	
5/4	AB	a	3-3	*Hentze Ma. 2, Živić*
11/4	B36	h	0-3	
18/4	ÍF	a	1-1	*Hansen*
2/5	Suduroy	h	3-1	*Hentze Ma. 2, og (Tausen T.)*
9/5	Víkingur	a	0-0	
13/5	HB	h	0-1	
16/5	EB/Streymur	h	2-3	*Midjord, Hentze Mi.*
24/5	NSÍ	a	0-2	
30/5	B68	h	1-0	*Hansen*
13/6	AB	h	1-0	*Thomsen E.*
16/6	B36	a	1-1	*Kovačević*
19/6	ÍF	h	0-2	
26/6	Suduroy	a	1-2	*Hentze Ma.*
28/7	HB	a	2-1	*Hansen, Hentze Ma.*
1/8	EB/Streymur	a	0-8	
15/8	NSÍ	h	1-6	*Živić*
22/8	Víkingur	a	0-5	
25/8	Víkingur	h	0-0	
29/8	HB	h	0-2	
12/9	B68	a	1-1	*Rubeksen*
19/9	AB	a	4-0	*Thomsen E. 2, Hansen, Kovačević*
22/9	B36	h	0-0	
26/9	Suduroy	h	2-2	*Midjord (p), Rubeksen*
2/10	ÍF	a	0-3	
17/10	EB/Streymur	h	0-4	
23/10	NSÍ	a	1-9	*Rubeksen*

No	Name	Nat	DoB	Pos	Aps	(s)	Gls
24	Hanus CLEMENTSEN		9/6/83	D		(1)	
24	Tummas Dam CLEMENTSEN		7/8/90	D	10	(9)	
4	Frits EID		1/5/81	M	15		
10	Símun HANSEN		11/12/82	A	22		4
13	Eli HENTZE		1/9/69	A		(1)	
12	Gustav HENTZE		10/2/92	G	2		
19	Mads Andrias HENTZE		5/1/89	M	18	(9)	6
18	Mikkjal Theodor HENTZE		8/12/86	M	26		1
9	Bogi HERMANSEN		3/6/86	A	4	(4)	
21	Jóhannes Andrias JENSEN		21/1/79	M	23	(1)	
2	Rúni JOENSEN		12/2/84	D	8	(7)	
22	Bárdur JOHANNESEN		14/11/73	G	8		
14	Danilo KOVAČEVIĆ	SRB	26/1/89	A	27		2
22	Predrag MARKOVIĆ	SRB	1/2/77	G	17		
7	Høgni MIDJORD		4/2/91	A	23	(4)	2
13	Jón Koytu PETERSEN		3/12/89	A		(4)	
2	Eirikur POULSEN		5/9/81	D	1	(3)	
3	Anders RASMUSSEN	DEN	7/2/83	D	1		
17	Thomas Hans Lamain RUBEKSEN		13/6/86	A	10	(3)	3
23	Marko STANIĆ	SRB	23/9/89	M	25		
20	Ebbe Kristin THOMSEN		2/8/87	A	10	(13)	3
11	Finn Erik THOMSEN		22/6/92	A		(2)	
32	Tórhallur THOMSEN		10/2/83	M		(3)	
6	Allan Gullbrandsson TUNGÁ		15/4/86	D	24		
28	Bojan ŽIVIĆ	SRB	13/2/81	D	23		2

EB/STREYMUR

Coach – Hedin Askham

Founded – 1993

Stadium – Vid Margáir (1,000)

MAJOR HONOURS: Faroe Islands League – (1) 2008; Faroe Islands Cup – (3) 2007, 2008, 2010.

2010				
1/4	B36	h	1-2	*Alex (p)*
6/4	ÍF	a	1-1	*Jørgensen*
11/4	Suduroy	h	2-0	*Hansen A. 2*
16/4	Víkingur	a	2-2	*Samuelsen, Jakobsen (p)*
2/5	HB	h	0-1	
7/5	NSÍ	a	1-2	*og (Davidsen)*
13/5	AB	h	2-1	*Alex, Hansen G.*
16/5	B71	a	3-2	*Hansen A., Alex (p), Hansen G.*
25/5	B68	h	3-0	*Samuelsen, Hansen A. 2*
30/5	B36	a	1-1	*Nielsen*
12/6	ÍF	h	3-0	*Nielsen, Hansen A. 2*
16/6	Suduroy	a	1-0	*Bø*
20/6	Víkingur	h	2-2	*Niclasen, Udsen*
27/6	HB	a	2-5	*Nielsen, Bø*
27/7	AB	a	2-1	*Hansen A., Anghel*
1/8	B71	h	8-0	*Olsen B. 4, Udsen 2, Hansen G., Samuelsen*
16/8	B68	a	1-1	*Udsen (p)*
20/8	NSÍ	a	0-0	
25/8	NSÍ	h	1-1	*Hansen A.*
29/8	AB	h	6-0	*Hansen A. 5, Samuelsen*
12/9	B36	h	4-1	*Hansen A. 3, Nielsen*
17/9	ÍF	a	3-3	*Udsen 2, Samuelsen*
22/9	Suduroy	h	5-2	*Udsen 2, og (Hørg), Samuelsen, Hansen A. (p)*
27/9	HB	h	1-1	*Hansen A.*
2/10	Víkingur	a	3-0	*Hansen P., Nielsen, Anghel*
17/10	B71	a	4-0	*Samuelsen 2, Hansen A. 2 (1p)*
23/10	B68	h	3-1	*Anghel, Nielsen, Hansen A.*

Name	Nat	DoB	Pos	Aps	(s)	Gls
ALEX José dos Santos	BRA	28/3/81	M	17	(1)	3
Sorin Vasile ANGHEL		16/7/79	A	21	(2)	3
Sam BJARTALÍD		17/10/91	G	1		
Egil á BØ		2/4/74	D	24	(1)	2
Arnar DAM		19/10/91	A		(16)	
Dánjal Scheel DAVIDSEN		17/4/88	D	11	(1)	
Marni DJURHUUS		6/9/85	M	19		
Arnbjørn Theodor HANSEN		27/2/86	A	25	(2)	22
Gert Åge HANSEN		25/7/84	D	27		3
Pauli Gregersen HANSEN		9/4/80	M	13		1
Pætur Dam JACOBSEN		5/12/82	M	20		
Kristoffur JAKOBSEN		7/11/88	A	14	(5)	1
Jens Michael JENSEN		24/1/91	A		(1)	
Bjarni JØRGENSEN		29/8/84	A	4	(3)	1
Leif NICLASEN		1/10/86	D	11	(16)	1
Gudmund NIELSEN		10/10/87	A	22	(4)	6
Brian OLSEN		22/8/85	M	5	(12)	4
Poul Grunnveit OLSEN		30/9/91	M		(2)	
Hans Pauli SAMUELSEN		18/10/84	M	20	(3)	8
René TÓRGARD		3/8/79	G	21		
Daniel UDSEN		18/3/83	M	17	(2)	8
Tróndur VATNHAMAR		12/1/80	G	5		

HB TÓRSHAVN

ach – Kristján Gudmundsson (ISL); (13/9/10) Julian Hansen

Founded – 1904

Stadium – Gundadalur (5,000)

JOR HONOURS: Faroe Islands League – (21) 1955, 1960, 1963, 64, 1965, 1971, 1973, 1974, 1975, 1978, 1981, 1982, 1988, 1990, 1998, 2002, 2003, 2004, 2006, 2009, 2010; Faroe Islands Cup – (26) 1955, 1957, 1959, 1962, 1963, 1964, 68, 1969, 1971, 1972, 1973, 1975, 1976, 1978, 1979, 1980, 1981, 1982, 1984, 1987, 1988, 1989, 1992, 1995, 1998, 2004.

10

	Suduroy	h	4-4	*Nielsen, Fløtum, Poulsen, Hreidarsson*
	Víkingur	a	0-0	
/4	AB	h	2-1	*Benjaminsen 2 (1p)*
/4	NSÍ	h	2-1	*Rubeksen, Fløtum*
5	EB/Streymur	a	1-0	*Poulsen*
5	B68	h	4-3	*Fløtum, Benjaminsen 2, Kuljić*
/5	B71	a	1-0	*Rubeksen*
/5	ÍF	a	1-2	*Poulsen*
/5	B36	h	2-2	*Samuelsen, Hreidarsson*
/5	Suduroy	a	3-0	*Poulsen, Samuelsen (p), Akselsen*
/6	Víkingur	h	2-0	*Akselsen, Hanssen*
/6	AB	a	1-1	*Nolsøe*
/6	NSÍ	a	0-2	
/6	EB/Streymur	h	5-2	*Benjaminsen, Fløtum, Poulsen, Samuelsen 2*
/7	B71	h	1-2	*Benjaminsen (p)*
3	ÍF	h	2-0	*Fløtum, Holm*
/8	B36	a	0-1	
/8	B68	h	1-0	*Hreidarsson*
/8	B68	a	2-2	*Thorleifsson, Fløtum (p)*
/8	B71	a	2-0	*Benjaminsen, Fløtum*
/9	Suduroy	h	1-4	*Kuljić*
/9	Víkingur	a	1-0	*Benjaminsen*
/9	AB	h	3-0	*Benjaminsen, Poulsen 2*
/9	EB/Streymur	a	1-1	*Poulsen*
10	NSÍ	h	3-2	*Benjaminsen 2 (1p), Jespersen*
/10	ÍF	a	2-1	*og (Zachariassen), Benjaminsen (p)*
3/10	B36	h	2-1	*Benjaminsen, Rubeksen*

o	Name	Nat	DoB	Pos	Aps	(s)	Gls
	Tór-Ingar AKSELSEN		1/5/81	A	4	(10)	2
	Fródi BENJAMINSEN		14/12/77	M	27		13
	Jógvan Rói DAVIDSEN		9/10/91	A	1		
	Marcin DAWID	POL	28/1/80	G	18		
	Andrew av FLØTUM		13/6/79	A	25		7
	Símun Rógvi HANSEN		10/4/87	G	2		
	Levi HANSSEN		24/2/88	A	20	(6)	1
	Rógvi Sjúrdarson HOLM		24/1/90	D	16	(1)	1
	Thórdur Steinar HREIDARSSON	ISL	13/12/86	D	27		3
23	Rókur av Fløtum JESPERSEN		16/3/85	M	6	(5)	1
24	Páll Mohr JOENSEN		29/6/86	A		(5)	
22	Pætur Tórstein JØRGENSEN		12/4/88	M	15	(2)	
14	Milan KULJIĆ	SRB	24/12/75	M	18	(4)	2
4	Hans á LAG		26/9/74	D	8	(6)	
20	Vagnur Mohr MORTENSEN		10/2/83	D	17	(3)	
21	Kristin Restorff MOURITSEN		23/4/91	M	4	(2)	
8	Kári NIELSEN		3/3/81	M	9	(7)	1
15	Jógvan Andrias Skeel NOLSØE		20/5/92	A		(8)	1
6	Ólavur Sakarisson í ÓLAVSSTOVU		14/6/88	M		(1)	
18	Rógvi POULSEN		31/10/89	M	26	(1)	8
12	Hendrik RUBEKSEN		1/11/83	D	21	(2)	3
9	Símun SAMUELSEN		21/5/85	A	25	(1)	4
25	Tórdur THOMSEN		11/6/86	G	7		
6	Hanus THORLEIFSSON		19/12/85	M	1	(8)	1

ÍF FUGLAFJØRDUR

Coach – Abraham Løkin

Founded – 1946

Stadium – Fløtugerdi (3,000)

MAJOR HONOURS: Faroe Islands League – (1) 1979.

2010

1/4	NSÍ	a	2-1	*Lakjuni, Olsen*
6/4	EB/Streymur	h	1-1	*Jacobsen*
12/4	B68	a	0-1	
18/4	B71	h	1-1	*Jacobsen*
2/5	B36	a	1-1	*Jacobsen*
9/5	AB	a	2-0	*Dalbúd, Sarić*
13/5	Suduroy	h	2-0	*Ennigard K., Sarić*
16/5	HB	h	2-1	*Dalbúd, Olsen (p)*
24/5	Víkingur	a	3-1	*Olsen (p), Sarić, Poulsen*
28/5	NSÍ	h	3-5	*Sarić, Dalbúd, Lakjuni*
13/6	EB/Streymur	a	0-3	
16/6	B68	h	4-2	*Løkin, Sarić 2, Zachariassen*
19/6	B71	a	2-0	*Dalbúd, Olsen*
27/6	B36	h	0-5	
3/7	AB	h	4-4	*Ellingsgaard J., Ennigard K., Lakjuni, Poulsen*
27/7	Suduroy	a	3-0	*Dalbúd 2, Olsen*
1/8	HB	a	0-2	
15/8	Víkingur	h	0-1	
22/8	AB	a	4-1	*Eliasen B., Ellingsgaard J., Dalbúd, Olsen*
29/8	Suduroy	h	3-1	*Dalbúd, Eliasen B. (p), Poulsen*
13/9	NSÍ	a	0-0	
17/9	EB/Streymur	h	3-3	*Sarić 2, Dalbúd*
22/9	B68	a	3-3	*Eliasen B., Lakjuni, Olsen*
26/9	B36	a	0-1	
2/10	B71	h	3-0	*Eliasen B. (p), Dalbúd 2*
17/10	HB	h	1-2	*Petersen Á.*
23/10	Víkingur	a	3-1	*Eliasen B. 2 (1p), Petersen U.*

No	Name	Nat	DoB	Pos	Aps	(s)	Gls
10	Øssur Meinhardsson DALBÚD		23/3/89	A	23	(2)	11
76	Bartal ELIASEN		23/8/76	D	11		6
28	Hanus ELIASEN		9/5/84	M		(1)	
15	Ari Ólavsson ELLINGSGAARD		3/2/93	M	1	(10)	
3	Jan Ólavsson ELLINGSGAARD		26/6/90	D	23	(2)	2
18	Sverri Sólheim ELLINGSGAARD		16/4/85	M		(2)	
12	Kaj ENNIGARD		6/3/84	D	11	(1)	2
5	Poul ENNIGARD		27/7/77	D	17	(2)	
9	Rógvi JACOBSEN		5/3/79	A	2	(3)	3
7	Aleksandar JOVEVIĆ	SRB	10/4/78	M	8	(11)	
14	Dánjal á LAKJUNI		22/9/90	M	18	(9)	4
8	Fritleif í LAMBANUM		13/4/86	M	24	(1)	
6	Karl LØKIN		19/4/91	M	24	(1)	1
16	Eydun MADSEN		29/7/79	G	1		
1	Jákup MIKKELSEN		16/8/70	G	26		
23	Andy Ólavur OLSEN		3/12/84	M	26	(1)	7
2	Áki PETERSEN		1/12/84	D	19	(1)	1
21	Atli PETERSEN		21/5/85	A		(1)	
13	Uni Reinert PETERSEN		30/1/90	D	7	(8)	1
11	Frank Højbjerg POULSEN		3/11/88	M	13	(11)	3
4	Nenad SARIĆ	SRB	5/7/81	M	24	(2)	8
17	Høgni Justinus ZACHARIASSEN		26/8/82	M	19		1

NSÍ RUNAVÍK

Coach – Pauli Poulsen
Founded – 1957
Stadium – Vid Løkin (4,000)
MAJOR HONOURS: Faroe Islands League – (1) 2007; Faroe Islands Cup – (2) 1986, 2002.

2010

1/4	ÍF	h	1-2	*Jacobsen C.*
5/4	Suduroy	a	1-1	*Jacobsen C. (p)*
11/4	Víkingur	h	0-2	
18/4	HB	a	1-2	*Jacobsen C.*
4/5	AB	h	3-0	*Olsen, Lakjuni H., Jacobsen C.*
7/5	EB/Streymur	h	2-1	*Jacobsen C. 2 (1p)*
12/5	B68	a	3-0	*Jacobsen C. 2, Olsen*
16/5	B36	a	5-1	*Mortensen, Danielsen D. 2, Lakjuni H., Ólavsstovu*
24/5	B71	h	2-0	*Olsen 2*
28/5	ÍF	a	5-3	*Hansen E., Danielsen D., Hansen J., Petersen, Potemkin*
12/6	Suduroy	h	2-1	*Olsen, Danielsen D.*
16/6	Víkingur	a	3-2	*Olsen, Jacobsen C. 2*
19/6	HB	h	2-0	*Jacobsen C. 2 (1p)*
27/6	AB	a	0-0	
27/7	B68	h	2-1	*Petersen 2*
3/8	B36	h	4-3	*og (Jacobsen H.), Davidsen, Petersen, Danielsen E.*
15/8	B71	a	6-1	*Jacobsen C. 2 (1p), Lakjuni H., Olsen 2, Frederiksberg Á.*
20/8	EB/Streymur	h	0-0	
25/8	EB/Streymur	a	1-1	*Frederiksberg Á.*
28/8	B68	a	2-3	*Løkin, Jacobsen C.*
13/9	ÍF	h	0-0	
19/9	Suduroy	a	1-1	*Jacobsen C.*
23/9	Víkingur	h	0-1	
27/9	AB	h	2-1	*Jacobsen C., Joensen J.*
2/10	HB	a	2-3	*Olsen, Hansen E.*
17/10	B36	a	1-2	*Olsen*
23/10	B71	h	9-1	*Joensen J., Jacobsen C. 5, Olsen, Lakjuni H. 2*

No	Name	Nat	DoB	Pos	Aps	(s)	Gls
7	Debes DANIELSEN		12/8/86	M	5	(18)	4
15	Erland Berg DANIELSEN		16/5/90	M	3	(14)	1
8	Jóhan Troest DAVIDSEN		31/1/88	D	25		1
22	Árni FREDERIKSBERG		13/6/92	M		(9)	2
17	Jónhard FREDERIKSBERG		27/8/80	A	27		
1	András GÁNGÓ	HUN	2/3/84	G	27		
12	Einar Tróndargjógv HANSEN		2/4/88	D	25		2
6	Jústinus Ragnhardson HANSEN		14/5/85	M	27		1
10	Christian Høgni JACOBSEN		12/5/80	A	26		22
19	Monrad Holm JACOBSEN		23/4/91	D		(1)	
4	Jens JOENSEN		17/5/89	D	23	(1)	2
20	Kristian JOENSEN		21/12/92	G		(1)	
18	Hedin á LAKJUNI		19/2/78	A	27	5	
23	Oddmar á LAKJUNI		17/10/86	M	1	(1)	
2	Per LANGGAARD		30/5/91	D	2	(1)	
14	Bogi Abrahamsson LØKIN		22/10/88	M	9	(2)	1
5	Jann Martin MORTENSEN		18/7/89	M	18	(3)	1
14	Ólavur Sakarisson í ÓLAVSSTOVU		14/6/88	M	1	(8)	1
13	Klæmint Andrasson OLSEN		17/7/90	A	25		11
11	Jann Ingi PETERSEN		7/1/84	M	24		4
9	Károly POTEMKIN	HUN	19/6/77	A	2	(7)	1

FC SUDUROY

Coach – Jón Pauli Olsen
Founded – 2010
Stadium – Vesturi á Eidinum (3,300)
MAJOR HONOURS: Faroe Islands League – (1) 2000 (as VB Vágur); Faroe Islands Cup – (1) 1974 (as VB Vágur).

2010

1/4	HB	a	4-4	*Ikechukwu, Augustinussen, Tausen T., Poulsen Jón (p)*
5/4	NSÍ	h	1-1	*Poulsen Jón (p)*
11/4	EB/Streymur	a	0-2	
18/4	B68	h	3-1	*Poulsen Jón, Ikechukwu 2*
2/5	B71	a	1-3	*Joensen*
9/5	B36	h	1-1	*Toronjadze*
13/5	ÍF	a	0-2	
16/5	Víkingur	h	1-3	*Vatnsdal*
24/5	AB	a	0-1	
29/5	HB	h	0-3	
12/6	NSÍ	a	1-2	*Poulsen Jón (p)*
16/6	EB/Streymur	h	0-1	
20/6	B68	a	1-1	*Ikechukwu*
26/6	B71	h	2-1	*Poulsen Jón, Ikechukwu*
27/7	ÍF	h	0-3	
2/8	Víkingur	a	1-4	*Augustinussen*
15/8	AB	h	3-3	*Poulsen Jón, Schultz, Joensen*
22/8	B36	h	2-1	*Poulsen Jón, Toronjadze*
25/8	B36	a	0-1	
29/8	ÍF	a	1-3	*Toronjadze*
12/9	HB	a	4-1	*Joensen, Poulsen Jón, Toronjadze 2*
19/9	NSÍ	h	1-1	*Toronjadze*
22/9	EB/Streymur	a	2-5	*Poulsen Jón 2*
26/9	B71	a	2-2	*Djurhuus, Tausen T.*
2/10	B68	h	2-1	*Augustinussen, Djurhuus*
17/10	Víkingur	h	0-2	
23/10	AB	a	0-1	

21/3 Atletas 3-0 *Douglas, Gallo 2*

No	Name	Nat	DoB	Pos	Aps	(s)	G
9	Palli AUGUSTINUSSEN		16/12/80	M	27		
4	Heini BECH		21/6/90	D	13	(9)	
12	Tóki BRATTALÍD		5/3/93	A	1	(8)	
20	Jónar Borg DAHL		13/4/85	M	1	(3)	
14	Dan DJURHUUS		15/8/78	D	15	(2)	
13	Suni úr HØRG		24/12/82	M	25		
11	Charles Obi IKECHUKWU	NGA	6/4/84	A	13	(1)	
17	Henning Gledisheygg JOENSEN		19/12/89	M	14	(9)	
11	Sonni KJÆRBO		8/1/81	M		(4)	
32	Stanislav KUZMA	SVN	16/9/76	G	27		
19	Kári í LÁGABØ		12/6/83	M	19	(7)	
3	Karl LISBERG		14/2/85	A	7		
3	Jákup Flóvin Sigmundarson OLSEN		5/4/85	D		(2)	
20	John Tordar POULSEN		17/9/85	A	1	(6)	
10	Jón Krosslá POULSEN		17/2/88	A	25	10	
2	Kasper SCHULTZ	DEN	15/4/88	D	10	(1)	
18	Brandur SUDUROY		4/7/94	M		(2)	
15	Arthur TAUSEN		17/10/87	A		(7)	
8	Martin TAUSEN		4/5/90	M	25		
6	Teitur TAUSEN		27/3/91	D	23	(2)	
7	Mamuka TORONJADZE	GEO	13/5/86	M	25		
5	Heini VATNSDAL		18/10/91	M	26		

VÍKINGUR

Coach – Jógvan Martin Olsen
Founded – 2008
Stadium – Sarpugerdi (2,000)
MAJOR HONOURS: Faroe Islands League – (6) 1983, 1986, 1. 1994, 1995, 1996 (as GÍ Gøta); Faroe Islands Cup – (7) 1983, 1 1996, 1997, 2000, 2005 (as GÍ Gøta), 2009.

2010

1/4	AB	h	5-3	*Gregersen A. 2, Vatnhamar 2, Justinussen*
7/4	HB	h	0-0	
11/4	NSÍ	a	2-0	*Hansen B., Jacobsen Sa.*
16/4	EB/Streymur	h	2-2	*Olsen S., Vatnhamar*
3/5	B68	a	3-5	*Olsen S., Vatnhamar, Jacobsen Sv.*
9/5	B71	h	0-0	
13/5	B36	a	2-1	*Jacobsen Sa., Olsen S. (p)*
16/5	Suduroy	a	3-1	*Olsen S. 2, Justinussen*
24/5	ÍF	h	1-3	*Vatnhamar*
29/5	AB	a	1-1	*Petersen Á.*
13/6	HB	a	0-2	
16/6	NSÍ	h	2-3	*Vatnhamar, og (Frederiksberg J.)*
20/6	EB/Streymur	a	2-2	*Justinussen 2*
25/6	B68	h	0-0	
29/7	B36	a	3-1	*Jacobsen Sa. (p), Klettskard, Vatnh.*

	Suduroy	h	4-1	*Vatnhamar 2, Klettskard, og (Kuzma)*
8	ÍF	a	1-0	*Vatnhamar*
8	B71	h	5-0	*Jacobsen H., Stanković, Klettskard 2, Justinussen (p)*
8	B71	a	0-0	
/8	B36	h	1-0	*Jacobsen Sa.*
/9	AB	h	3-1	*Justinussen, Klettskard, Jacobsen Sa. (p)*
9	HB	h	0-1	
/9	NSÍ	a	1-0	*og (Danielsen E.)*
/9	B68	a	0-2	
0	EB/Streymur	h	0-3	
/10	Suduroy	a	2-0	*Justinussen, Djurhuus*
/10	ÍF	h	1-3	*Hansen H.*

Name	Nat	DoB	Pos	Aps	(s)	Gls
Kaj Leo í BARTALSSTOVU		23/6/91	M	12	(15)	
Petur Gullstein DALBØ		15/3/91	D	1	(2)	
Hans Jørgin DJURHUUS		29/11/78	D	8	(2)	1
Atli GREGERSEN		15/6/82	D	13		2
Per GREGERSEN		14/6/91	M		(3)	
Bárdur Jógvansson HANSEN		13/3/92	D	25	(2)	1
Hjartvard HANSEN		17/9/88	D	8	(13)	1
Erling Dávidsson JACOBSEN		13/2/90	D	12		
Hanus JACOBSEN		25/5/85	D	16	(2)	1
Sam JACOBSEN		24/2/88	D	23		5
Sverri JACOBSEN		29/3/86	M	24	(1)	1
Finnur JUSTINUSSEN		30/3/89	A	26	(1)	7
Páll Andrasson KLETTSKARD		17/5/90	A	13		5
Dánjal Pauli LERVIG		26/4/91	D		(1)	
Niclas NICLASSEN		26/7/79	D	25		
Martin OLSEN		22/12/89	A		(7)	
Súni OLSEN		7/3/81	M	11	(1)	5
Áslakur Reinert PETERSEN		9/4/78	M	4	(5)	1
Hans Paule PETERSEN		29/7/80	M	1	(3)	
Nenad STANKOVIĆ		8/8/77	M	22		1
Ingi SØRENSEN		24/11/90	M		(4)	
Géza TÚRI	HUN	11/3/74	G	27		
Sølvi VATNHAMAR		5/5/86	M	26		10

PROMOTED CLUBS

07 VESTUR

Coach – Jógvan Hendrik Samuelsen
Founded – 2007
Stadium – Á Dungasandi (1,000)

KÍ KLAKSVÍK

Coach – Aleksandar Đorđević (SRB)
Founded – 1904
Stadium – Djúpumýri (4,000)

MAJOR HONOURS: Faroe Islands League – (17) 1942, 1945, 1952, 1953, 1954, 1956, 1957, 1958, 1961, 1966, 1967, 1968, 1969, 1970, 1972, 1991, 1999;
Faroe Islands Cup – (5) 1966, 1967, 1990, 1994, 1999.

SECOND LEVEL FINAL TABLE 2010

		Pld	W	D	L	F	A	Pts
1	07 Vestur	27	18	7	2	75	23	61
2	KÍ Klaksvík	27	18	4	5	78	26	58
3	TB Tvøroyri	27	15	6	6	62	34	51
4	EB/Streymur II	27	13	6	8	59	42	45
5	HB Tórshavn II	27	12	3	12	53	63	39
6	Víkingur II	27	11	4	12	40	53	37
7	FC Hoyvík	27	9	6	12	40	49	33
8	AB Argir II	27	8	2	17	28	68	26
9	NSÍ Runavik II	27	6	7	14	35	63	25
10	B68 Toftir II	27	1	3	23	19	68	6

NB AB Argir II were relegated as first team entered second level for 2011; NSÍ Runavik II remain at second level.

TOP GOALSCORERS 2010

22 Arnbjørn Theodor HANSEN (EB/Streymur)
Christian Høgni JACOBSEN (NSÍ)

13 Fródi BENJAMINSEN (HB)

11 Øssur Meinhardsson DALBÚD (ÍF)
Klæmint Andrasson OLSEN (NSÍ)

10 Pól Jóhannus JUSTINUSSEN (B68)
Jón Krosslá POULSEN (Suduroy)
Sølvi VATNHAMAR (Víkingur)

8 Hans Pauli SAMUELSEN (EB/Streymur)
Daniel UDSEN (EB/Streymur)
Rógvi POULSEN (HB)
Nenad SARIĆ (ÍF)

DOMESTIC CUP 2010

LØGMANSSTEYPID

SECOND ROUND

(27/3/10)
AB 3, KÍ 1 *(aet)*
B68 3, Vestur 0
B71 2, Víkingur 4 *(aet)*
EB/Streymur 1, NSÍ 0 *(aet)*
HB 0, B36 1
Hoyvík 2, TB 0
Undri 0, ÍF 1

(21/4/10)
Suduroy 6, Skála 1

QUARTER-FINALS

(25/4/10)
Hoyvík 1 *(Midjord 73)*, B36 7 *(Olsen B. 17, Elttør 36, Borg 44, 49, Joensen S. 45, Mouritsen 56, Olsen M. 58)*
ÍF 3 *(Petersen Á 53, Jacobsen 77, Dalbúd 120)*, B68 2 *(Gueye 37, Hansen 81p) (aet)*
Suduroy 1 *(Poulsen Jón 37p)*, EB/Streymur 4 *(Samuelsen 16, Nielsen 46, Hansen A. 56p, Niclasen 90)*
Víkingur 1 *(Olsen S. 20)*, AB 1 *(Aristide 75) (aet; 4-3 on pens)*

SEMI-FINALS

(20/5/10 & 8/6/10)
B36 2 *(Olsen B. 52, Elttør 62)*, EB/Streymur 1 *(Hansen A. 22)*
EB/Streymur 2 *(Anghel 61, Jakobsen 86p)*, B36 0
(EB/Streymur 3-2)
ÍF 1 *(Ennigard P. 19)*, Víkingur 2 *(Olsen S. 23, Justinussen 29)*
Víkingur 0, ÍF 3 *(Lakjuni 25, Ellingsgaard J. 89, Dalbúd 90)*
(ÍF 4-2)

FINAL

(6/8/10)
Djúpumýri stadium, Klaksvik
EB/STREYMUR 1 *(Anghel 25)*
ÍF FUGLAFJØRDUR 0
Referee – *Djurhuus*
EB/STREYMUR – *Tórgard, Bø, Hansen G., Djurhuus, Davidsen, Nielsen (Samuelsen 74), Olsen B. (Jacobsen 66), Hansen P., Udsen, Anghel (Dam 84), Hansen A.*
ÍF – *Mikkelsen, Petersen Á., Eliasen B., Lambanum (Lakjuni 58), Ennigard P., Zachariassen, Jović (Poulsen 65), Løkin, Sarić, Olsen (Ellingsgaard J. 65), Dalbúd.*

CLUB COMMUNICATION 2011

B36 Tórshavn

Gundadalur
FO-100 Tórshavn

Tel +298 311 936
Fax +298 318 036
Web b36.fo
Email b36@b36.fo
Media Officer Hannis Egholm

B68 Toftir

c/o Mr. Jógvan Højgaard, Svangaskarð
Stadium, FO-650 Toftir
Tel +298 449 068
Fax +298 449 050
Web b68.fo
Email b-68@post.olivant.fo
Media Officer Jógvan Højgaard

B71 Sandoy

Sandoyar Ítróttarfelag B71
FO-210 Sandur

Tel +298 361 090
Fax
Web b71-sandoy.com
Email eli.hentze@skulin.fo
Media Officer Ragnar Fossdalsá

EB/Streymur

Postrúm 18
FO-FO-470 Eiði

Tel +298 508 090
Fax +298 422 780
Web eb-streymur.fo
Email ebstreym@olivant.fo
Media Officer Bjarni Arnason

HB Tórshavn

PO Box 1333, Gundadalur stadium
FO-110 Tórshavn

Tel +298 314 046
Fax +298 318 502
Web hb.fo
Email hb@hb.fo
Media Officer Marni Mortensen

ÍF Fuglafjørdur

PO Box 94, Ítróttarfelag Fuglafjørdur
FO-530 Fuglafjørdur

Tel +298 444 636
Fax +298 444 634
Web if.fo
Email if@if.fo
Media Officer Ólavur Larsen

KÍ Klaksvík

Jógvan Waagsteinsgøta, PO Box 204
FO-700 Klaksvík

Tel +298 456 184
Fax +298 456 167
Web ki.fo
Email ki@ki.fo
Media Officer Jóhan Lützen

NSÍ Runavík

PO Box 173
FO-620 Runavík

Tel +298 749 909
Fax +298 449 919
Web nsi.fo
Email nsi@nsi.fo
Media Officer Jákup Øster Vágsheyg

07 Vestur

Box 51
FO-370 Miðvágur

Tel +298 215 180
Fax +298 333 264
Web 07vestur.fo
Email 07vestur@07vestur.fo
Media Officer Jarnhold Nattestad

Vikingur

PO Box 58
FO-512 Leirvík

Tel +298 443 222
Fax +298 443 322
Web vikingur.fo
Email vikingur@vikingur.fo
Media Officer Erik Lervig

FINLAND

Finlande I Finnland

Suomen Palloliitto – Finlands Bollförbund (SPL-FBF)

COMMUNICATION

Address	Urheilukatu 5, PO Box 191 FI-00251 Helsinki	**President**	Sauli Niinistö
		General Secretary	Kimmo J. Lipponen
		Media Officer	Mikko Hyppönen
Tel	+358 9 742 151		
Fax	+358 9 742 15200	**Year of Formation**	1907
E-mail	sami.terava@palloliitto.fi	**National Stadium**	Olympic Stadium, Helsinki (37,500)
Website	palloliitto.fi		

DOMESTIC COMPETITION SUMMARY 2010

VEIKKAUSLIIGA FINAL TABLE

			Home					Away					Total						
		Pld	**W**	**D**	**L**	**F**	**A**	**W**	**D**	**L**	**F**	**A**	**W**	**D**	**L**	**F**	**A**	**Pts**	**Comp**
1	HJK Helsinki	26	8	3	2	22	9	7	4	2	21	10	15	7	4	43	19	52	UCL
2	KuPS Kuopio	26	8	2	3	22	17	7	1	5	23	19	15	3	8	45	36	48	UEL
3	TPS Turku	26	7	3	3	26	17	6	3	4	20	13	13	6	7	46	30	45	UEL
4	FC Honka Espoo	26	7	2	4	26	18	5	3	5	16	16	12	5	9	42	34	41	UEL
5	FF Jaro	26	5	3	5	21	17	6	2	5	21	17	11	5	10	42	34	38	
6	FC Inter Turku	26	5	3	5	14	16	5	4	4	20	16	10	7	9	34	32	37	
7	Tampere United	26	5	3	5	19	19	5	1	7	18	27	10	4	12	37	46	34	
8	Valkeakosken Haka	26	6	3	4	16	15	3	3	7	14	23	9	6	11	30	38	33	
9	Myllykosken Pallo-47	26	4	7	2	22	19	3	4	6	14	20	7	11	8	36	39	32	
10	VPS Vaasa	26	5	2	6	15	22	3	5	5	14	18	8	7	11	29	40	31	
11	AC Oulu	26	3	5	5	14	16	5	1	7	17	28	8	6	12	31	44	30	
12	IFK Mariehamn	26	3	3	7	19	24	4	4	5	19	19	7	7	12	38	43	28	
13	JJK Jyväskylä	26	1	2	10	13	23	7	1	5	21	18	8	3	15	34	41	27	
14	FC Lahti	26	2	3	8	10	22	3	8	2	16	15	5	11	10	26	37	26	*Relegated*

NB AC Oulu excluded from 2011 Veikkausliiga after their licence was revoked; Tampere United excluded from all competitions in 2011 for disciplinary reasons; 2011 Veikkausliiga therefore reduced to 12 clubs.

Top Scorer Juho Mäkelä (HJK), 16 goals

Promoted Club RoPS Rovanieni

Cup Final TPS Turku 2, HJK Helsinki 0

Record champions reign again

A 2010 Veikkausliiga season distinguished by the return to their homeland of several high-profile Finnish internationals – Jonatan Johansson at TPS Turku, Janne Saarinen at HJK Helsinki, Toni Kuivasto at Valkeakosken Haka and, temporarily, Alexei Eremenko Jr at FF Jaro – ended with the shock departure from the league of Finland's greatest ever player, Jari Litmanen, who dropped out of the top flight with his beloved hometown club FC Lahti.

The demise of Litmanen and Lahti almost eclipsed the success of HJK, who retained the Finnish title and therefore raised their record number of domestic championship wins to 23. Antti Muurinen's defending champions made their intentions clear at the outset, thrashing KuPS Kuopio 5–0 away on day one. Striker Juho Mäkelä scored eight goals in the first four matches, and he would need only to double that tally over the remainder of the season to scoop the Veikkausliiga's top-scorer prize with room to spare.

HJK hold off Honka

As in 2009, HJK's main challengers were local rivals FC Honka Espoo. Mika Lehkosuo's side momentarily took the lead after beating HJK 3-1 at home, but they shed points carelessly over the next few weeks to allow HJK to return to the top. At the mid-season point 'Klubi' had a commanding seven-point lead, but in mid-August they lost to Honka again, this time at home at the Sonera Stadium (formerly Finnair Stadium), which enabled their conquerors to move to within three points, Honka, however, lost their next match at home to struggling JJK Jyväskylä and never challenged again, enabling HJK to reclaim their crown with two matches in hand.

The champions' most influential players were Mäkelä, goalkeeper Ville Wallén, young centre-back Juhani Ojala, Brazilian full-back Rafinha and Sierra Leonean midfielder Mohamed Kamara, aka Medo, who left the club in September to join FK Partizan, the team that had ended HJK's European adventure in the third qualifying round of the UEFA Champions League.

Honka dropped to fourth place, with the runners-up position being taken, to universal surprise, by HJK's opening-day punchbags KuPS. Esa Pekonen's pre-season relegation candidates proved to be stubbornly feisty and won their last four matches to ascend to their highest league position for 31 years. Even stronger in the latter stages were TPS, who won nine of their last 11 matches to finish third. They were inspired by the Riski brothers, Riku and Roope, both of whom were rewarded with post-season transfers to greener pastures, Riku to RTS Widzew Łódź and 12-goal Roope to AC Cesena. TPS also ended HJK's double dream by defeating them 2-0 in the Finnish Cup final, with Mika Ääritalo and Riku Riski scoring the decisive goals.

A peculiar feature of the 2010 Veikkausliiga was the abundance of away wins – exactly the same number, in fact, as home wins – 69 apiece. Oddest of all was the record of JJK, victorious just once at home but seven times away. They did, however,

HJK striker Juha Mäkelä was the Veikkausliiga's top scorer with 16 goals

Top Five All-time Caps – Jari Litmanen (137); Sami Hyypiä & Jonatan Johansson (105); Ari Hjelm (100); Joonas Kolkka (98)

Top Five All-time Goals – Jari Litmanen (32); Mikael Forssell (25); Jonatan Johansson (22); Ari Hjelm (20); Mixu Paatelainen (18)

win their most important home fixture – in the promotion/relegation play-off against FC Viikingit – to rescue their Veikkausliiga status, which meant that Lahti, who crucially lost their final game 3-2 at TPS after leading 2-0 at half-time, were the only team relegated while Lapland's RoPS Rovaniemi were promoted alone.

EURO woe

Finland's UEFA EURO 2012 qualifying campaign began badly and never recovered. The opening fixture in Moldova was lost 2-0 after veteran skipper Sami Hyypiä received a first-half red card; then, after a 2-1 defeat by the Netherlands in Rotterdam, Finland fell at home to Hungary by the same scoreline courtesy of a heartbreaking stoppage-time winner. With three defeats out of three and criticism building in the media, coach Stuart Baxter was relieved of his duties in November.

The Finnish FA employed two caretaker coaches while deliberating a permanent solution. Olli Huttunen oversaw an 8–0 victory over San Marino, notable mainly for Mikael Forssell's hat-trick and Litmanen's 32nd (and possibly last) goal for Finland. Markku Kanerva was left with the job of axing the 40-year-old icon from the spring friendlies against Belgium and Portugal before Mixu Paatelainen, of Scottish fame, took over as the new permanent head coach in April. With chronic goalscoring problems now compounded by gaping holes at the back following the retirements of Hyypiä, Hannu Tihinen and Jussi Jääskeläinen, the extent of Paatelainen's rebuilding job – and the long-term goal of guiding Finland to the 24-team finals of UEFA EURO 2016 – was put into perspective by a crushing 5-0 defeat away to neighbours Sweden in June.

NATIONAL TEAM RESULTS 2010/11

11/8/10	Belgium	H	Turku	1-0	*Porokara (13)*
3/9/10	Moldova (ECQ)	A	Chisinau	0-2	
7/9/10	Netherlands (ECQ)	A	Rotterdam	1-2	*Forssell (18)*
12/10/10	Hungary (ECQ)	H	Helsinki	1-2	*Forssell (86)*
17/11/10	San Marino (ECQ)	H	Helsinki	8-0	*Väyrynen (39), Hämäläinen (49, 67), Forssell (51, 59, 78), Litmanen (71p), Porokara (73)*
9/2/11	Belgium	A	Ghent	1-1	*Porokara (90+2)*
29/3/11	Portugal	A	Aveiro	0-2	
3/6/11	San Marino (ECQ)	A	Serravalle	1-0	*Forssell (41)*
7/6/11	Sweden (ECQ)	A	Solna	0-5	

NATIONAL TEAM APPEARANCES 2010/11

			Bel	MDA	NED	HUN	SMR	Bel	Por	SMR	SWE	Caps	Goals
Coach – Stuart BAXTER (ENG)	**16/8/53**												
/(9/11/10) (Olli HUTTUNEN)	**4/8/60**												
/(12/1/11) (Markku KANERVA)	**24/5/64**												
/(31/3/11) Mixu PAATELAINEN	**3/2/67**												
Otto FREDRIKSON	30/11/81	Spartak Nalchik (RUS)	G	G	G		G		G			11	-
Veli LAMPI	18/7/84	Willem II (NED)	D		D		D	D65		D		24	-
Petri PASANEN	24/9/80	Werder (GER)	D	D	D	D	D		D	D	D	65	1
Markus HEIKKINEN	13/10/78	Rapid Wien (AUT)	D87	D	D	D	D		D	M	D46	60	-
Niklas MOISANDER	29/9/85	AZ (NED)	D	D	D	D	D	D		D	D	19	1
Roman EREMENKO	19/3/87	Dynamo Kyiv (UKR)	M46	M	M	M	M	M	M87		M	35	1
Tim SPARV	20/2/87	Groningen (NED)	M	M	M	M72		M83	s73			14	-
Kasper HÄMÄLÄINEN	8/8/86	Djurgården (SWE)	M38	s46	M46		M70	M65		M	M46	14	2
Roni POROKARA	12/12/83	Örebro (SWE)	M62	M75	s46	M71	s70						
		/GBA (BEL)						s56	s46			20	5

NATIONAL TEAM APPEARANCES 2010/11 (contd.)

			Bel	MDA	NED	HUN	SMR	Bel	Por	SMR	SWE	Caps	Goal
Alexei EREMENKO Jr	24/3/83	Jaro /Kilmarnock (SCO)	M62	A81	s80	s71	A80	A55	A46	A68	A80	52	13
Mikael FORSSELL	15/3/81	Hannover (GER)	A80	s81	A80	A	A	A65	s73	A90	A	76	25
Mika VÄYRYNEN	28/12/81	Heerenveen (NED)	s38	s75	M	M	M		M73	M	M	51	5
Teemu TAINIO	27/11/79	Sunderland (ENG)	s46									52	6
Jari LITMANEN	20/2/71	Lahti /unattached	s62	M46		s72	s46					137	32
Daniel SJÖLUND	22/4/83	Djurgården (SWE)	s62		M68	M81	M46		M46	s84		28	2
Paulus ROIHA	3/8/80	Åtvidaberg (SWE)	s80									20	4
Jani LYYSKI	16/3/83	Djurgården (SWE)	s87									3	-
Sami HYYPIÄ	7/10/73	Leverkusen (GER)		D 36*		D						105	5
Jonatan JOHANSSON	16/8/75	TPS		A	s68							105	22
Jussi JÄÄSKELÄINEN	19/4/75	Bolton (ENG)				G						56	-
Shefki KUQI	10/11/76	Derby (ENG)				s81	s80					62	7
Lukas HRADECKY	24/11/89	Esbjerg (DEN)						G		G		3	-
Joona TOIVIO	10/3/88	Djurgården (SWE)						D	s87		D	3	-
Jukka RAITALA	15/9/88	Paderborn (GER)						D	D	D		5	-
Perparim HETEMAJ	12/12/86	Brescia (ITA)						M56	M63	M84	M	6	-
Riku RISKI	16/8/89	Widzew (POL)						s55	s46	s68		3	-
Mika ÄÄRITALO	25/7/85	TPS						s65			s46	3	-
Sebastian MANNSTRÖM	29/10/88	HJK Helsinki						s65	s63			2	-
Hannu PATRONEN	23/5/84	Helsingborg (SWE)						s65				1	-
Ilja VENÄLÄINEN	27/9/80	KuPS						s83				1	-
Kari ARKIVUO	23/6/83	Häcken (SWE)							D			8	1
Berat SADIK	14/9/86	HJK Helsinki							A73	s90		6	-
Anssi JAAKKOLA	13/3/87	Kilmarnock (SCO)									G	1	-
Markus HALSTI	19/3/84	Malmö (SWE)									s46	4	-
Alexander RING	9/4/91	HJK Helsinki									s80	1	

CLUB-BY-CLUB

HJK HELSINKI

Coach – Antti Muurinen

Founded – 1907

Stadium – Sonera Stadium (10,800)

MAJOR HONOURS: Finnish League – (23) 1911, 1912, 1917, 1918, 1919, 1923, 1925, 1936, 1938, 1964, 1973, 1978, 1981, 1985, 1987, 1988, 1990, 1992, 1997, 2002, 2003, 2009, 2010;
Finnish Cup – (10) 1966, 1981, 1984, 1993, 1996, 1998, 2000, 2003, 2006, 2008.

2010

16/4	KuPS	a	5-0	*Fowler, og (Nykänen), Mäkelä 2, Kamara*
26/4	Haka	h	1-1	*Mäkelä*
2/5	VPS	a	3-0	*Mäkelä 3*
10/5	AC Oulu	h	2-0	*Mäkelä 2 (1p)*
16/5	Honka	a	1-3	*Westö*
24/5	Lahti	h	0-0	
29/5	Mariehamn	a	2-1	*Hoesen, Mäkelä (p)*
6/6	Jaro	h	2-1	*Kamara, Mäkelä*
13/6	MyPa	h	2-0	*Zeneli, Bah*
20/6	Inter	a	0-0	
23/6	JJK	h	1-0	*Hoesen*
4/7	TPS	a	1-0	*Parikka*
10/7	Tampere United	h	3-1	*Westö, Parikka, Kamara*
17/7	KuPS	h	1-2	*Zeneli (p)*
24/7	Haka	a	3-0	*Zeneli, Bah, Mäkelä*
31/7	VPS	h	3-0	*Parikka, Pelvas, Westö*
7/8	AC Oulu	a	1-1	*Mäkelä*
14/8	Honka	h	0-1	
22/8	Lahti	a	1-0	*Kamara*
30/8	Mariehamn	h	3-1	*Rafinha, Pelvas, Mäkelä*
12/9	Jaro	a	1-1	*Pukki*
19/9	MyPa	a	1-1	*Mäkelä*
22/9	Inter	h	2-2	*Lindström, Zeneli*
2/10	JJK	a	2-1	*Pukki, Mäkelä*
18/10	TPS	h	2-0	*Mäkelä, Bah*
23/10	Tampere United	a	0-2	

No	Name	Nat	DoB	Pos	Aps	(s)	Gls
	Dawda BAH	GAM	12/11/83	M	24		3
	William de Mattia "DEMA"	BRA	28/4/83	M	3	(2)	
	Cheyne FOWLER	RSA	8/3/82	M	22	(4)	1
	Mikko HAUHIA		3/9/84	D	1		
	Danny HOESEN	NED	15/1/91	A	8	(4)	2
	Mohamed "Medo" KAMARA	SLE	16/11/87	M	16		4
	Tuomas KANSIKAS		15/5/81	D	16		
	Pyry KÄRKKÄINEN		10/11/86	D	7	(2)	
	Mathias LINDSTRÖM		14/1/81	D	7		1
	Peter MAGNUSSON	SWE	16/7/84	D	13	(2)	
	Juho MÄKELÄ		23/6/83	A	18	(6)	16
	Valtteri MOREN		15/6/91	D	1	(1)	
	Juhani OJALA		19/6/89	D	24		
	Jarno PARIKKA		21/7/86	A	5	(10)	3
	Akseli PELVAS		8/2/89	A	6	(7)	2
	Teemu PUKKI		29/3/90	A	3	(4)	2
	Rafael Scapini de Almeida "RAFINHA"	BRA	29/6/82	D	24		1
	David RAMANDINGAYE		14/9/89	M		(1)	
	Aki RIIHILAHTI		9/9/76	M	5	(6)	
	Alexander RING		9/4/91	M		(3)	
	Janne SAARINEN		28/2/77	M	2	(3)	
	Sebastian SORSA		25/1/84	M	16	(5)	
	Mikko SUMUSALO		12/3/90	D	11	(3)	
	Jani VIANDER		18/8/75	G	1		
	Ville WALLÉN		26/6/76	G	25		
	Johannes WESTÖ		1/4/91	A	18	(4)	3
	Erfan ZENELI		28/12/86	M	10	(8)	4

FC HONKA ESPOO

Coach – Mika Lehkosuo

Founded – 1957

Stadium – Tapiolan urheilupuisto (5,000)

2010				
8/4	MyPa	h	3-1	*Puustinen, Vasara, Heilala*
6/4	TPS	a	0-1	
/5	Mariehamn	h	3-0	*og (Gueye), Vasara, Puustinen*
/5	Jaro	a	0-0	
6/5	HJK	h	3-1	*Kokko 2, Puustinen*
3/5	JJK	a	1-0	*Savage*
0/5	VPS	h	0-0	
/6	AC Oulu	a	0-2	
3/6	KuPS	a	2-0	*Simpanen, Vuorinen*
20/6	Tampere United	h	0-2	
30/6	Lahti	a	4-2	*Paatelainen (p), Puustinen 2, Weckström*
4/7	Haka	h	4-2	*Puustinen 2, Paatelainen, Weckström*
9/7	Inter	a	0-2	
18/7	MyPa	a	2-2	*Puustinen, Rasimus*
25/7	TPS	h	1-0	*Puustinen*
1/8	Mariehamn	a	2-2	*Vuorinen 2*
8/8	Jaro	h	3-1	*Savage, Koskinen, Vuorinen*
14/8	HJK	a	1-0	*Schüller*
23/8	JJK	h	2-3	*Paatelainen, Vuorinen*
29/8	VPS	a	3-1	*Vasara, Schüller, Vuorinen*
13/9	AC Oulu	h	3-4	*Vasara, Aalto, og (Hietanen)*
19/9	KuPS	h	2-1	*Schüller, Otaru*
22/9	Tampere United	a	1-2	*Hakanpää*
4/10	Lahti	h	1-2	*Weckström*
16/10	Haka	a	0-2	
23/10	Inter	h	1-1	*Lepola*

No	Name	Nat	DoB	Pos	Aps	(s)	Gls
5	Henri AALTO		20/4/89	D	6	(3)	1
24	DOUGLAS Pereira dos Santos	BRA	8/9/82	A		(1)	
11	Hannu HAARALA		15/8/81	D	12		
19	Rami HAKANPÄÄ		9/10/78	D	19		1
25	Tapio HEIKKILÄ		8/4/90	D	1	(5)	
3	Roope HEILALA		13/8/80	D	21		1
15	Aleksandr KOKKO		4/6/87	A	6	(2)	2
13	Ville KOSKIMAA		21/5/83	D	11	(4)	
2	Sampo KOSKINEN		1/3/79	D	25		1
26	Jaakko LEPOLA		14/3/90	M	12	(6)	1
20	Nicholas OTARU		15/7/86	M	22	(4)	1
8	Markus PAATELAINEN		23/1/83	A	13	(10)	3
1	Tuomas PELTONEN		20/10/77	G	26		
10	Jami PUUSTINEN		9/1/87	A	25	(1)	9
27	Konsta RASIMUS		15/12/90	M	6	(11)	1
17	Demba SAVAGE	GAM	17/6/88	M	15	(3)	2
28	Rasmus SCHÜLLER		18/6/91	M	16	(3)	3
22	Valmir SEFERI		12/2/93	M		(1)	
29	Juuso SIMPANEN		8/6/91	M	13	(2)	1
14	Jussi VASARA		14/5/87	M	19	(1)	4
18	Tim VÄYRYNEN		30/3/93	A		(2)	
6	Hermanni VUORINEN		27/1/85	A	10	(4)	6
7	John WECKSTRÖM		26/12/80	M	8	(10)	3

FC INTER TURKU

Coach – Job Dragtsma (NED)

Founded – 1990

Stadium – Veritas Stadion (9,300)

MAJOR HONOURS: Finnish League – (1) 2008; Finnish Cup – (1) 2009.

2010				
19/4	Mariehamn	h	1-1	*Lehtonen*
25/4	Jaro	a	1-0	*Nwanganga*
3/5	Lahti	h	1-3	*Antunez*
9/5	KuPS	a	1-2	*Grot*
15/5	TPS	a	2-2	*Nyman, Ojala*
24/5	Tampere United	h	0-2	
31/5	AC Oulu	h	0-2	
6/6	JJK	a	3-0	*Lehtonen 2, Ojala*
14/6	VPS	h	1-0	*Lehtonen*
20/6	HJK	h	0-0	
30/6	Haka	a	3-1	*Nwanganga 2, Lehtonen*
4/7	MyPa	a	2-3	*Ojala, Nwanganga*
9/7	Honka	h	2-0	*Paajanen, Grot*
18/7	Mariehamn	a	0-3	
25/7	Jaro	h	2-0	*Lehtonen, Nwanganga*
1/8	Lahti	a	1-1	*Nwanganga*
8/8	KuPS	h	1-3	*Lehtonen*
15/8	TPS	h	1-2	*Ojala*
22/8	Tampere United	a	1-0	*Grot*
29/8	AC Oulu	a	0-1	
13/9	JJK	h	3-2	*Ojala, Grot, Lehtonen*
19/9	VPS	a	3-0	*Lehtonen 2, Ojala (p)*
22/9	HJK	a	2-2	*Lehtonen, Paajanen*
4/10	Haka	h	1-0	*og (Osei)*
18/10	MyPa	h	1-1	*Grot*
23/10	Honka	a	1-1	*Nwanganga*

No	Name	Nat	DoB	Pos	Aps	(s)	Gls
14	Joni AHO		12/4/86	D	18	(1)	
26	Felix ÅKERLUND		12/2/90	M	1	(2)	
20	Andrey ALMEIDA	BRA	10/4/88	A	1	(4)	
5	Daniel ANTUNEZ	USA	10/2/86	M	21	(2)	1
1	Patrick BANTAMOI	SLE	24/5/86	G	9		
4	DAVI Alexandre RANCAN Afonso	BRA	22/9/81	D	2	(1)	
30	Solomon DUAH		7/1/93	A		(1)	
11	Timo FURUHOLM		11/10/87	A		(4)	
21	Pablo GOMEZ-MARTTILA		9/10/88	M	2	(8)	
9	Guilliano GROT	NED	15/3/83	A	14	(9)	5
6	Jermu GUSTAFSSON		22/6/86	D		(2)	
19	Jan-Erik HELJANDER		22/6/92	A		(1)	

31	Thomas KAPLAS		16/3/92	D		(1)	
24	Joni KAUKO		12/7/90	M	15	(1)	
16	Kalle KAUPPI		6/5/92	M		(5)	
29	Henri LEHTONEN		28/7/80	A	26		11
28	Mika MÄKITALO		12/6/85	M	21	(4)	
2	Tero MÄNTYLÄ		18/4/91	D	9	(1)	
12	David MONSALVE	CAN	21/12/88	G	7		
23	Ville NIKKARI		5/11/88	D	20	(1)	
27	Kennedy NWANGANGA	NGA	15/8/90	M	20	(2)	7
7	Ari NYMAN		7/2/84	M	25		1
17	Mika OJALA		21/6/88	A	22	(1)	6
8	Daniel OSINACHI	NGA	25/8/89	A	7	(7)	
15	Severi PAAJANEN		23/10/86	M	23	(2)	2
13	Eemeli REPONEN		6/6/90	G	10	(2)	
22	Sami SANEVUORI		20/2/86	M	13	(1)	

FF JARO

Coach – Alexei Eremenko
Founded – 1965
Stadium – Centralplan (5,000)

2010				
17/4	Lahti	a	3-1	*Sundqvist 2, Eremenko*
25/4	Inter	h	0-1	
30/4	Haka	a	3-4	*Björkstrand, Zézé, Xhaferi (p)*
9/5	Honka	h	0-0	
16/5	VPS	h	3-2	*Björkstrand, Eremenko 2 (1p)*
23/5	Mariehamn	a	0-0	
1/6	Tampere United	h	2-2	*Sundqvist, Mannström*
6/6	HJK	a	1-2	*Haanpää*
11/6	JJK	h	1-3	*Eremenko*
20/6	MyPa	a	1-0	*Zézé*
23/6	TPS	a	3-0	*Grove, Xhaferi 2*
4/7	KuPS	h	0-1	
11/7	AC Oulu	a	1-0	*Mannström*
16/7	Lahti	h	2-0	*Zézé, Niang*
25/7	Inter	a	0-2	
2/8	Haka	h	5-0	*Zézé, Niang, Vasilyev, Eremenko, Björkstrand*
8/8	Honka	a	1-3	*Mannström*
16/8	VPS	a	1-1	*Eremenko*
20/8	Mariehamn	h	2-0	*Zézé, Niang*
30/8	Tampere United	a	4-1	*Matrone, Eremenko, Kronholm, Zézé*
12/9	HJK	h	1-1	*Niang*
19/9	JJK	a	2-1	*Niang 2*
24/9	MyPa	h	3-2	*Niang, Kronholm, Aho*
3/10	TPS	h	1-3	*Niang (p)*
16/10	KuPS	a	1-2	*Zézé*
23/10	AC Oulu	h	1-2	*Xhaferi*

No	Name	Nat	DoB	Pos	Aps	(s)	Gls
3	Heikki AHO		16/3/83	D	23		1
2	Nosh A LODY		17/7/89	D	13	(3)	
11	Jani BÄCKMAN		20/3/88	A	1	(6)	
5	Kåre BJÖRKSTRAND		31/3/87	M	10	(12)	3
14	Alexei Jr. EREMENKO		24/3/83	M	16		7
20	Tillmann GROVE	GER	3/9/88	D	16		1
26	Tommi HAANPÄÄ		21/4/90	A	1	(6)	1
15	Markus KRONHOLM		2/4/91	M	20		2
18	Thomas KULA		24/5/91	M		(7)	
19	Sebastian MANNSTRÖM		29/10/88	M	15	(5)	3
7	Marco MATRONE		2/7/87	M	22	(3)	1
17	Petter MEYER		21/2/85	A	5	(10)	
16	Papa NIANG	SEN	5/12/88	A	14	(3)	8
23	Jevgeni NOVIKOV	EST	28/6/80	M	6		
8	Jari SARA		25/4/89	D	3	(6)	
13	Jani SARAJÄRVI		9/9/79	D	5	(3)	
9	Björn-Erik SUNDQVIST		5/3/88	A	13	(4)	3
1	Vitali TELEŠ	EST	17/10/83	G	26		
4	Maksim VASILYEV	RUS	31/1/87	D	25		1
6	Janne VELLAMO		28/9/84	M	3	(2)	
10	Ymer XHAFERI	ALB	6/11/85	M	25		4
25	Venance ZÉZÉ	CIV	17/6/81	A	24		7

JJK JYVÄSKYLÄ

Coach – Kari Martonen
Founded – 1992
Stadium – Harjun stadion (4,600)

2010				
23/4	Tampere United	a	2-0	*Sund, Lahtinen Mik.*
28/4	VPS	a	1-0	*Pasoja*
2/5	TPS	h	0-2	
8/5	MyPa	a	4-2	*Kari (p), Lahtinen Mik., Linjala, Markkula*
17/5	KuPS	a	0-2	
23/5	Honka	h	0-1	
1/6	Lahti	a	0-0	
6/6	Inter	h	0-3	
11/6	Jaro	a	3-1	*Kari 2, Okkonen*
18/6	Mariehamn	h	0-2	
23/6	HJK	a	0-1	
5/7	AC Oulu	h	6-1	*Linjala, Lahtinen Mik., Hyyrynen, Kari 2, Markkula*
12/7	Haka	a	2-1	*Lahtinen Mik., Hyyrynen*
19/7	VPS	h	0-1	
26/7	Tampere United	h	0-1	
1/8	TPS	a	0-2	
8/8	MyPa	h	1-1	*Poutiainen*
13/8	KuPS	h	1-3	*Kari*
23/8	Honka	a	3-2	*Linjala, Hyyrynen, Lahtinen Mik.*
27/8	Lahti	h	2-2	*Linjala, Kari (p)*
13/9	Inter	a	2-3	*Tuomanen, Hyyrynen*
19/9	Jaro	h	1-2	*Kari*
27/9	Mariehamn	a	2-3	*Tuomanen, Hyyrynen*
2/10	HJK	h	1-2	*Kari (p)*
17/10	AC Oulu	a	2-1	*Hyyrynen, Lahtinen Mik.*
23/10	Haka	h	1-2	*Okkonen*

No	Name	Nat	DoB	Pos	Aps	(s)	Gls
18	Zakaria ABAHASSINE		23/7/88	A	12	(7)	
21	Kim ALONEN		22/2/91	A		(2)	
20	Mikko HYYRYNEN		1/11/77	A	17	(4)	6
10	Tommi KARI		22/9/86	A	23	(1)	9
30	Janne KORHONEN		28/11/79	G	11		
8	Matti LÄHITIE		13/2/85	M	3	(8)	
3	Miikka LAHTINEN		8/6/92	A		(1)	
9	Mika LAHTINEN		30/4/85	A	25	(1)	6
13	Tuomas LATIKKA		20/9/85	D	22	(1)	
17	Lasse LINJALA		15/8/87	A	11	(8)	4
16	Niko MARKKULA		27/6/90	M	5	(18)	2
2	Samu NIEMINEN		14/1/92	D	6	(5)	
4	Jarkko OKKONEN		8/9/78	D	23		2
5	Juha PASOJA		16/11/76	D	24		1
23	Patrick POUTIAINEN		14/6/91	M	19	(3)	1
14	Jukka SINISALO		21/5/82	D	7	(8)	
19	Christian SUND		28/12/78	M	10	(3)	1
1	Mihály SZERÓVAY	HUN	14/4/82	G	15		
15	Antto TAPANINEN		16/6/89	D	1		
11	Touko TUMANTO		6/3/82	M	1		
6	Jukka-Pekka TUOMANEN		4/12/85	M	21	(3)	2
7	Anssi VIREN		10/4/77	D	23		
26	Jani VIRTANEN		6/5/88	M	7	(2)	

KUPS KUOPIO

Coach – Esa Pekonen

Founded – 1923

Stadium – Keskuskentän jalkapallostadion (3,700)

AJOR HONOURS: Finnish League – (5) 1956, 1958, 1966, 1974, 1976; Finnish Cup – (2) 1968, 1989.

010

5/4	HJK	h	0-5	
5/4	Lahti	h	1-1	*Venäläinen*
'5	AC Oulu	a	5-2	*Ilo, Venäläinen 2, Nwakaeme, Ollo (p)*
'5	Inter	h	2-1	*Ilo, Holopainen*
7/5	JJK	h	2-0	*Nwakaeme, Williams*
3/5	VPS	a	0-2	
'6	TPS	h	2-1	*Oravainen, Ollo*
'6	MyPa	a	1-1	*Holopainen*
3/6	Honka	h	0-2	
/6	Haka	a	1-2	*Holopainen*
0/6	Tampere United	h	6-2	*Ilo, Nwakaeme, Udah 3, Turunen M.*
'7	Jaro	a	1-0	*Holopainen*
2/7	Mariehamn	h	0-0	
7/7	HJK	a	2-1	*Nwakaeme 2*
3/7	Lahti	a	1-2	*Kaivonurmi*
0/7	AC Oulu	h	3-1	*Taipale (p), Holopainen, Ilo*
/8	Inter	a	3-1	*Ilo, Dudu, Holopainen*
3/8	JJK	a	3-1	*Ilo, Dudu, Oravainen*
3/8	VPS	h	1-2	*Dudu*
8/8	TPS	a	0-3	
2/9	MyPa	h	2-1	*Venäläinen, Holopainen*
9/9	Honka	a	1-2	*Dudu*
7/9	Haka	h	1-0	*Ilo*
/10	Tampere United	a	3-1	*Dudu 3*
6/10	Jaro	h	2-1	*Venäläinen 2*
3/10	Mariehamn	a	2-1	*og (Trafford), Dudu*

No	Name	Nat	DoB	Pos	Aps	(s)	Gls
	Balázs BALOGH	HUN	21/7/82	D	26		
8	MacPherlin DUDU Omagbeni	NGA	18/7/85	A	10		8
24	Atte HOIVALA		10/2/92	D	24		
	Pietari HOLOPAINEN		26/9/82	D	26		7
25	Antti HYNYNEN		30/5/84	M	10	(2)	
20	Miikka ILO		9/5/82	A	23	(1)	7
6	Samuli KAIVONURMI		3/3/88	A	1	(12)	1
26	Dickson NWAKAEME	NGA	21/4/86	A	14	(2)	5
15	Juho NYKÄNEN		11/9/85	D	26		
22	Jerome OGBUEFI	NGA	26/8/91	M	1	(6)	
23	Patrice OLLO N'Doumba	CMR	10/1/86	M	21		2
11	Petri ORAVAINEN		26/1/83	M	15	(7)	2
13	Aleksi PAANANEN		25/1/93	M		(1)	
12	Joonas PÖNTINEN		19/3/90	G	6	(1)	
28	Oliver RISSER	NAM	19/9/80	D	8		
8	Tero TAIPALE		14/12/72	M	18	(3)	1
7	Miikka TURUNEN		18/8/79	M		(5)	1
4	Patrik TURUNEN		1/7/88	D		(1)	
6	Raphael UDAH	NGA	1/9/89	M	18		3
27	Ilja VENÄLÄINEN		27/9/80	A	10	(8)	6
30	Mikko VILMUNEN		23/8/80	G	20	(2)	
10	Olajide WILLIAMS	NGA	20/7/88	A	9	(8)	1

FC LAHTI

Coach – Ilkka Mäkelä

Founded – 1996

Stadium – Lahden stadion (7,400)

2010

17/4	Jaro	h	1-3	*Länsitalo*
25/4	KuPS	a	1-1	*Litmanen*
3/5	Inter	a	3-1	*Litmanen, Sihvola, Rafael*
10/5	Haka	h	0-1	
14/5	MyPa	h	0-2	
24/5	HJK	a	0-0	
1/6	JJK	h	0-0	
4/6	Tampere United	a	0-0	
12/6	AC Oulu	h	0-3	
21/6	VPS	a	1-1	*Rafael*
30/6	Honka	h	2-4	*Miranda, Shala*
3/7	Mariehamn	a	2-2	*Kemppinen 2*
11/7	TPS	h	1-3	*Sihvola*
16/7	Jaro	a	0-2	
23/7	KuPS	h	2-1	*Rafael 2*
1/8	Inter	h	1-1	*Litmanen*
6/8	Haka	a	0-0	
15/8	MyPa	a	1-1	*Shala*
22/8	HJK	h	0-1	
27/8	JJK	a	2-2	*Sadik, Miranda*
10/9	Tampere United	h	0-1	
18/9	AC Oulu	a	2-1	*Shala, Litmanen*
27/9	VPS	h	2-1	*Korte, Sadik*
4/10	Honka	a	2-1	*Rafael, Shala*
17/10	Mariehamn	h	1-1	*Heini*
23/10	TPS	a	2-3	*Rafael, Litmanen*

No	Name	Nat	DoB	Pos	Aps	(s)	Gls
7	Kalle EEROLA		1/11/83	D	13	(3)	
8	Mohamed FOFANA	GUI	21/10/85	M	17	(3)	
18	Juho-Matti HEIKARI		14/2/91	D	6	(1)	
19	Riku HEINI		9/12/90	M	15	(8)	1
20	Jonne KEMPPINEN		25/8/81	A	3	(9)	2
17	Eero KORTE		20/9/87	M	25		1
14	Ibrahim KÖSE		4/3/92	M	1	(4)	
13	Jussi LÄNSITALO		30/6/90	A	5	(10)	1
1	Janne LEINO		5/4/87	G	12		
10	Jari LITMANEN		20/2/71	M	12	(9)	5
23	Tatu MÄKELÄ		14/6/88	D	2	(1)	
6	Tennant McVEA	NIR	20/1/88	D	26		
29	Hugo MIRANDA	PAR	8/8/80	D	25		2
9	RAFAEL Pires Vieira	BRA	1/8/78	A	23	(2)	6
32	Berat SADIK		14/9/86	A	5		2
11	Drilon SHALA		20/3/87	A	14	(7)	4
16	Pekka SIHVOLA		22/4/84	A	12	(5)	2
3	Henri TOIVOMÄKI		21/2/91	D	7	(2)	
21	Janne TÖRMÄNEN		29/1/89	M	6	(6)	
22	Juha TUOMI		7/11/89	G	14	(1)	
15	Jukka VANNINEN		31/1/77	M	18	(1)	
5	Jarkko VÄRTTÖ		24/2/89	D	25		

IFK MARIEHAMN

Coach – Pekka Lyyski

Founded – 1919

Stadium – Wiklöf Holding Arena (4,000)

2010

19/4	Inter	a	1-1	*Forsell*
25/4	VPS	h	0-3	
1/5	Honka	a	0-3	
9/5	Tampere United	h	2-3	*Paatelainen, Strandvall*
16/5	AC Oulu	a	0-0	
23/5	Jaro	h	0-0	
29/5	HJK	h	1-2	*Okodugha*
6/6	TPS	a	4-1	*Gruborovics 2, Anttilainen, Forsell*
13/6	Haka	h	2-3	*Strandvall, Okodugha*
18/6	JJK	a	2-0	*Okodugha, Olofsson*
23/6	MyPa	h	1-2	*Paatelainen*
3/7	Lahti	h	2-2	*Paatelainen 2*
12/7	KuPS	a	0-0	
18/7	Inter	h	3-0	*Gruborovics, Paatelainen 2 (1p)*
26/7	VPS	a	4-1	*Gruborovics 2, Anttilainen, Paatelainen*
1/8	Honka	h	2-2	*Paatelainen (p), Anttilainen*
8/8	Tampere United	a	4-3	*Forsell, Gruborovics 2, Okodugha*

16/8	AC Oulu	h	0-2	
20/8	Jaro	a	0-2	
30/8	HJK	a	1-3	*Anttilainen*
12/9	TPS	h	2-1	*Okodugha, og (Rähmönen)*
20/9	Haka	a	1-2	*Gruborovics (p)*
27/9	JJK	h	3-2	*Ingves, Trafford, Gruborovics*
2/10	MyPa	a	1-2	*Neagle*
17/10	Lahti	a	1-1	*Neagle*
23/10	KuPS	h	1-2	*Gruborovics*

No	Name	Nat	DoB	Pos	Aps	(s)	Gls
99	ANDRÉ Filipe Saraiva MARTINS	POR	26/3/87	A		(1)	
30	Sasha ANTTILAINEN		19/12/86	A	17	(1)	4
4	Johan CARLSSON	SWE	1/8/81	M	4	(2)	
24	Mate DUJILO	CRO	30/11/81	D	17		
15	Amos EKHALIE	KEN	8/7/88	M	13	(2)	
7	Petteri FORSELL		16/10/90	M	6	(6)	3
23	Giuseppe FUNICELLO	ITA	19/4/87	D	6		
10	Tamás GRUBOROVICS		3/7/84	M	26		10
5	Médoune GUEYE	FRA	28/3/82	D	15	(3)	
18	Boussad HOUCHE	FRA	5/4/78	D	6	(1)	
26	Wilhelm INGVES		10/1/90	A	4	(10)	1
29	Gustav LÅNGBACKA		8/5/84	G	5		
14	Lamar NEAGLE	USA	7/5/87	M	2	(3)	2
11	Mika NISKALA		28/3/81	M	24		
20	Johannes NORDSTRÖM		23/1/93	D	1		
1	Willis OCHIENG	KEN	10/10/81	G	21		
22	Echiabhi OKODUGHA	NGA	12/10/88	D	21	(4)	5
6	Marcus OLOFSSON	SWE	4/8/82	M	13	(12)	1
28	Mikko PAATELAINEN		24/11/80	A	21		8
3	Patrik RIKAMA		8/2/83	D	23		
9	Ante ŠIMUNAC	CRO	12/1/84	M	13	(6)	
8	Sebastian STRANDVALL		16/9/86	M	12	(6)	2
21	Jimmy SUNDMAN		7/3/89	A		(2)	
17	Mason TRAFFORD	CAN	21/8/86	D	7		1
2	Dmytro VOLOSHYN	UKR	29/4/86	D	9	(1)	

MYLLYKOSKEN PALLO -47

Coach – Janne Lindberg

Founded – 1947

Stadium – Saviniemen jalkapallostadion (4,100)

MAJOR HONOURS: Finnish League – (1) 2005; Finnish Cup – (3) 1992, 1995, 2004.

2010

18/4	Honka	a	1-3	*Votinov*
24/4	AC Oulu	h	1-1	*Lindberg*
3/5	Tampere United	a	1-1	*Votinov*
8/5	JJK	h	2-4	*Okkonen, Votinov*
14/5	Lahti	a	2-0	*Koljonen 2*
24/5	TPS	h	2-2	*Äijälä 2*
31/5	Haka	a	1-0	*og (Kuivasto)*
7/6	KuPS	h	1-1	*Hietanen*
13/6	HJK	a	0-2	
20/6	Jaro	h	0-1	
23/6	Mariehamn	a	2-1	*Votinov 2*
4/7	Inter	h	3-2	*Oksanen, Saxman, Koljonen*
11/7	VPS	a	1-2	*Votinov*
18/7	Honka	h	2-2	*Äijälä (p), Felipe Benevides*
1/8	Tampere United	h	3-0	*Ricketts 2, Koljonen*
8/8	JJK	a	1-1	*Lindberg*
12/8	AC Oulu	a	1-1	*Ricketts*
15/8	Lahti	h	1-1	*Äijälä*
22/8	TPS	a	0-3	
30/8	Haka	h	2-1	*Votinov, Oksanen*
12/9	KuPS	a	1-2	*Äijälä*
19/9	HJK	h	1-1	*Votinov*
24/9	Jaro	a	2-3	*Aho, Ricketts*
2/10	Mariehamn	h	2-1	*Oksanen, Lindberg*
18/10	Inter	a	1-1	*Koljonen*
23/10	VPS	h	2-2	*Votinov, Koljonen*

No	Name	Nat	DoB	Pos	Aps	(s)	Gls
8	Adaílton Pereira dos Santos "ADY"	TUN	18/4/73	M	2	(5)	
18	Tuomas AHO		27/5/81	D	19	(2)	1
11	Ilari ÄIJÄLÄ		30/9/86	D	25	(1)	5
23	Kim ALONEN		22/2/91	A		(3)	
25	Stefan DE LAS	TRI	16/3/88	M	2	(3)	
20	FELIPE de Oliveira BENEVIDES	BRA	3/1/89	A	2	(19)	1
2	Konsta HIETANEN		20/7/84	M	19		1
12	Mika JOHANSSON		13/3/84	G	5		
27	Niklas KIVINEN		12/5/91	M		(1)	
19	Pele KOLJONEN		25/7/88	A	15	(9)	6
1	Antti KUISMALA		20/1/76	G	21		
17	Einari KURITTU		27/9/89	A		(7)	
13	Toni LINDBERG		23/9/85	D	18	(6)	3
6	Antti OKKONEN		6/6/82	M	24		1
15	Ville OKSANEN		25/2/87	M	25		3
22	Roope RAUTIAINEN		7/8/89	M		(3)	
14	Tosaint RICKETTS	CAN	6/6/87	A	15	(9)	4
24	Ville SAXMAN		15/11/89	M	23	(3)	1
3	Sampsa TIMOSKA		12/2/79	D	19		
5	Jarno TUUNAINEN		5/11/77	D	4		
4	Antti UIMANIEMI		30/1/86	D	25		
9	Maksim VOTINOV	RUS	29/8/88	A	23	(2)	9

AC OULU

Coach – Juha Malinen

Founded – 2002

Stadium –Oulu-lehti Areena (4,000)

2010

18/4	Tampere United	h	3-0	*Yobe Dom. 2, Yobe Don.*
24/4	MyPa	a	1-1	*Yobe Don.*
2/5	KuPS	h	2-5	*Nurmela, Jonke*
10/5	HJK	a	0-2	
16/5	Mariehamn	h	0-0	
21/5	Haka	a	0-2	
31/5	Inter	a	2-0	*Pennanen, Hietanen*
5/6	Honka	h	2-0	*Kukka, Majava Juh.*
12/6	Lahti	a	3-0	*Ngambe Ngambe, Nurmela 2*
19/6	TPS	h	0-2	
2/7	VPS	a	0-2	
5/7	JJK	a	1-6	*Yobe Don.*
11/7	Jaro	h	0-1	
19/7	Tampere United	a	1-3	*Yobe Don.*
30/7	KuPS	a	1-3	*Jonke*
7/8	HJK	h	1-1	*Kukka (p)*
12/8	MyPa	h	1-1	*Ngambe Ngambe*
16/8	Mariehamn	a	2-0	*Pennanen, Jonke*
21/8	Haka	h	1-1	*Yobe Don.*
29/8	Inter	h	1-0	*Nurmela*
13/9	Honka	a	4-3	*Jonke 4*
18/9	Lahti	h	1-2	*Nurmela*
22/9	TPS	a	0-5	
3/10	VPS	h	1-1	*Jonke*
17/10	JJK	h	1-2	*Hietanen*
23/10	Jaro	a	2-1	*Nurmela, Majava Juu.*

No	Name	Nat	DoB	Pos	Aps	(s)	Gls
9	Davor ČELIĆ	SRB	21/11/82	M		(4)	
21	ETHIÊ Viana Melo SOUSA	BRA	13/5/80	M	4	(9)	
2	Janne HIETANEN		2/6/78	D	24		2
18	Jarkko HURME		4/6/86	D	24		
11	Frank JONKE	CAN	30/1/85	A	22	(2)	8
3	Niko KUKKA		30/9/87	D	24		2
5	Mika LÄHDERINNE		8/5/80	D	7	(7)	

No	Name	Nat	DoB	Pos	Aps	(s)	Gls
	Jani LUUKKONEN		7/6/77	G		(1)	
6	Juha MAJAVA		28/11/82	M	13	(2)	1
9	Juuso MAJAVA		7/4/89	A	10	(8)	1
5	Joni MÄKELÄ		28/9/93	M	1	(9)	
	Juho MERILÄINEN		26/2/88	D	10	(5)	
0	Jean Fridolin NGAMBE NGAMBE	CMR	30/11/87	A	15	(5)	2
3	Mika NURMELA		26/12/71	M	25		6
7	Matias OJALA		28/2/95	M		(1)	
	Antti PEHKONEN		4/3/82	D	19	(4)	
4	Joonas PENNANEN		25/3/88	M	19	(6)	2
2	Dennys RODRIGUES	BRA	18/4/78	G	26		
6	Arttu SIIRA		18/4/93	M		(2)	
	Dominic YOBE	ZAM	4/8/86	M	26		2
0	Donewell YOBE	ZAM	24/8/83	A	17	(8)	5

TAMPERE UNITED

Coach – Ari Hjelm

Founded – 1998

Stadium – Ratinan stadion (16,800)

MAJOR HONOURS: Finnish League – (3) 2001, 2006, 2007; Finnish Cup – (1) 2007.

2010				
18/4	AC Oulu	a	0-3	
23/4	JJK	h	0-2	
3/5	MyPa	h	1-1	*Pirinen*
9/5	Mariehamn	a	3-2	*Pirinen 2, Myntti (p)*
17/5	Haka	h	2-1	*Dema, Savolainen*
24/5	Inter	a	2-0	*Savolainen, Myntti (p)*
1/6	Jaro	a	2-2	*Dema, Kangaskolkka*
4/6	Lahti	h	0-0	
14/6	TPS	h	1-1	*Kojola*
20/6	Honka	a	2-0	*Myntti, Kangaskolkka*
30/6	KuPS	a	2-6	*Hjelm, Kangaskolkka*
5/7	VPS	h	3-0	*Kangaskolkka 2, Emet*
10/7	HJK	a	1-3	*Hjelm*
19/7	AC Oulu	h	3-1	*Kangaskolkka (p), Hjelm, Myntti*
26/7	JJK	a	1-0	*Petrescu*
1/8	MyPa	a	0-3	
8/8	Mariehamn	h	3-4	*Saarinen, Haapala, Kojola*
16/8	Haka	a	0-1	
22/8	Inter	h	0-1	
30/8	Jaro	h	1-4	*Hjelm*
10/9	Lahti	a	1-0	*Kojola*
18/9	TPS	a	3-4	*Ring, Myntti 2*
22/9	Honka	h	2-1	*Petrescu, Ojanperä*
3/10	KuPS	h	1-3	*Kojola*
17/10	VPS	a	1-3	*Hjelm*
23/10	HJK	h	2-0	*Emet, Hjelm*

No	Name	Nat	DoB	Pos	Aps	(s)	Gls
3	William de Mattia "DEMA"	BRA	28/4/83	M	15		2
6	Jonas EMET		13/2/88	M	8	(10)	2
7	Tuomas HAAPALA		20/4/79	M	20	(1)	1
12	Mika HILANDER		17/8/83	G	14	(2)	
21	Jonne HJELM		14/1/88	A	24		6
11	Aleksei KANGASKOLKKA		29/10/88	A	17	(6)	6
14	Jusu KARVONEN		17/1/93	M	1	(7)	
1	Mikko KAVÉN		19/2/75	G	12		
4	Kristian KOJOLA		12/9/86	D	19	(2)	4
23	Jesse-Juho KUUSISTO		27/3/91	D	1	(6)	
25	Aapo LAPPALAINEN		3/11/89	A		(1)	
27	Johannes MONONEN		4/5/91	D	5	(5)	
15	Henri MYNTTI		23/3/82	A	20	(4)	6
30	Jari NIEMI		2/2/77	A	22		
5	Antti OJANPERÄ		6/4/83	D	25		1
10	Tomi PETRESCU		24/7/86	A	16	(4)	2
9	Juha PIRINEN		22/10/91	M	9	(15)	3
8	Antti POHJA		11/1/77	M	4	(1)	
14	Alexander RING		9/4/91	M	3	(1)	1
16	Ilari RUUTH		27/8/90	D		(1)	
13	Sakari SAARINEN		18/7/78	M	25		1
17	Vili SAVOLAINEN		25/10/85	M	26		2

TPS TURKU

Coach – Marko Rajamäki

Founded – 1922

Stadium – Veritas Stadion (9,300)

MAJOR HONOURS: Finnish League – (8) 1928, 1939, 1941, 1949, 1968, 1971, 1972, 1975; Finnish Cup – (3) 1991, 1994, 2010.

2010				
19/4	Haka	a	0-0	
26/4	Honka	h	1-0	*Kolehmainen*
2/5	JJK	a	2-0	*Ääritalo, Wusu*
7/5	VPS	h	1-1	*Johansson (p)*
15/5	Inter	h	2-2	*Johansson 2 (1p)*
24/5	MyPa	a	2-2	*Manninen, Nyberg*
1/6	KuPS	a	1-2	*Johansson (p)*
6/6	Mariehamn	h	1-4	*Johansson*
14/6	Tampere United	a	1-1	*Johansson*
19/6	AC Oulu	a	2-0	*Riski Ri., Wusu*
23/6	Jaro	h	0-3	
4/7	HJK	h	0-1	
11/7	Lahti	a	3-1	*og (McVea), Riski Ro. 2*
18/7	Haka	h	1-1	*Johansson (p)*
25/7	Honka	a	0-1	
1/8	JJK	h	2-0	*Riski Ri., Ääritalo*
8/8	VPS	a	3-0	*Riski Ri., Lähde, Riski Ro.*
15/8	Inter	a	2-1	*Manninen, Riski Ro.*
22/8	MyPa	h	3-0	*og (Lindberg), Ääritalo, Riski Ro.*
28/8	KuPS	h	3-0	*Riski Ro. 2, Johansson*
12/9	Mariehamn	a	1-2	*Riski Ri.*
18/9	Tampere United	h	4-3	*Riski Ro., Riski Ri. 2, Johansson*
22/9	AC Oulu	h	5-0	*Cleaver, Riski Ro. 3, Ääritalo*
3/10	Jaro	a	3-1	*Riski Ro., Heinikangas, Manninen*
18/10	HJK	a	0-2	
23/10	Lahti	h	3-2	*Wusu 2, Johansson*

No	Name	Nat	DoB	Pos	Aps	(s)	Gls
11	Mika ÄÄRITALO		25/7/85	A	18	(7)	4
18	Chris CLEAVER	ENG	24/3/79	M	12	(9)	1
31	Alban FERATI		1/11/91	A		(3)	
8	Jarno HEINIKANGAS		5/3/79	D	24		1
16	Jonatan JOHANSSON		16/8/75	A	15	(5)	10
4	Igor JOVANOVIC	GER	3/5/89	M	15	(5)	
13	Toni KOLEHMAINEN		20/7/88	M	21		1
23	Juho LÄHDE		11/2/91	M	7	(6)	1
12	Jukka LEHTOVAARA		15/3/88	G	20		
2	Mikael LIESPUU		4/3/91	D	1		
19	Patrik LOMSKI		3/2/89	A		(1)	
3	Kalle MÄKINEN		1/2/89	D	13	(1)	
25	Santeri MÄKINEN		9/4/92	M	1	(5)	
28	Leroy MALUKA	RSA	22/12/85	M	1	(4)	
9	Mikko MANNINEN		25/5/85	M	21	(2)	3
5	Robert MILSOM	ENG	2/1/87	M	13	(1)	
35	Henrik MOISANDER		29/9/85	G	5		
6	Jaakko NYBERG		19/12/80	D	25		1
7	Sami RÄHMÖNEN		19/4/87	D	24	(2)	
10	Riku RISKI		16/8/89	M	23	(2)	6
17	Roope RISKI		16/8/91	A	15	(3)	12
1	Jani TUOMALA		3/2/77	G	1		
26	Jani VIRTANEN		6/5/88	M	2	(5)	
20	Babatunde WUSU	NGA	18/4/84	A	9	(9)	4

VALKEAKOSKEN HAKA

Coach – Sami Ristilä

Founded – 1934

Stadium – Tehtaan kenttä (3,500)

MAJOR HONOURS: Finnish League – (9) 1960, 1962, 1965, 1977, 1995, 1998, 1999, 2000, 2004; Finnish Cup – (12) 1955, 1959, 1960, 1963, 1969, 1977, 1982, 1985, 1988, 1997, 2002, 2005.

2010

19/4	TPS	h	0-0	
26/4	HJK	a	1-1	*Parviainen*
30/4	Jaro	h	4-3	*Nam, Parviainen 2, Hynynen (p)*
10/5	Lahti	a	1-0	*Nam*
17/5	Tampere United	a	1-2	*Hynynen*
21/5	AC Oulu	h	2-0	*Nam, Santala*
31/5	MyPa	h	0-1	
7/6	VPS	a	1-2	*Yllaconza*
13/6	Mariehamn	a	3-2	*Nooitmeer, Nam, Hynynen (p)*
21/6	KuPS	h	2-1	*Hynynen, Innanen*
30/6	Inter	h	1-3	*Ikävalko*
4/7	Honka	a	2-4	*Multanen, Santala*
12/7	JJK	h	1-2	*Ikävalko*
18/7	TPS	a	1-1	*Ikävalko*
24/7	HJK	h	0-3	
2/8	Jaro	a	0-5	
6/8	Lahti	h	0-0	
16/8	Tampere United	h	1-0	*Gela (p)*
21/8	AC Oulu	a	1-1	*Nooitmeer*
30/8	MyPa	a	1-2	*Innanen*
11/9	VPS	h	1-1	*Gela (p)*
20/9	Mariehamn	h	2-1	*Innanen, Lehtinen (p)*
27/9	KuPS	a	0-1	
4/10	Inter	a	0-1	
16/10	Honka	h	2-0	*Nooitmeer, Innanen*
23/10	JJK	a	2-1	*Juuti, Multanen*

No	Name	Nat	DoB	Pos	Aps	(s)	Gls
18	Josef CHÁVEZ	PER	12/8/90	D	9	(3)	
10	Xhevdet GELA		14/11/89	M	10	(11)	2
11	Antti HYNYNEN		30/5/84	M	12	(1)	4
9	Niko IKÄVALKO		24/4/88	A	5	(3)	3
7	Mikko INNANEN		8/9/82	M	21	(3)	4
4	Markus JOENMÄKI		11/2/88	D	12	(4)	
15	Jaakko JUUTI		13/8/87	M	18	(4)	1
8	Jani KAUPPILA		16/1/80	M	19	(3)	
1	Janne KORHONEN		28/11/79	G	12		
23	Mohamed KOROMA	SLE	11/6/88	A	7	(6)	
3	Toni KUIVASTO		31/12/75	D	21		
6	Timi LAHTI		28/6/90	D	7		
24	Mikko-Petteri LATOSAARI		25/9/93	D		(1)	
11	Toni LEHTINEN		5/5/84	A	6		1
22	Jarno MATTILA		10/11/84	A	22	(1)	
17	Kalle MULTANEN		7/4/89	A	11	(8)	2
24	NAM Ik-kyung	KOR	26/1/83	A	11		4
2	Regillio NOOITMEER	HAI	16/7/83	D	23		3
20	Quincy OSEI	GHA	8/12/89	M	18	(4)	
5	Kalle PARVIAINEN		3/10/82	D	7	(1)	3
12	Saku PESONEN		30/11/85	G	14		
32	Jukka SANTALA		10/4/85	A	6	(6)	2
6	Sebastian STRANDVALL		16/9/86	M		(1)	
13	Ben Abdoulaye TRAORÉ	MLI	18/4/86	M	10	(5)	
16	Benito YLLACONZA	PER	18/2/91	M	5	(11)	1

VPS VAASA

Coach – Tommi Pikkarainen

Founded – 1924

Stadium – Hietalahden jalkapallostadion (4,600)

MAJOR HONOURS: Finnish League – (2) 1945, 1948.

2010

25/4	Mariehamn	a	3-0	*Kainu, Laaksonen, Inutile*
28/4	JJK	h	0-1	
2/5	HJK	h	0-3	
7/5	TPS	a	1-1	*Inutile*
16/5	Jaro	a	2-3	*Kainu 2*
23/5	KuPS	h	2-0	*Aalto, Savolainen*
30/5	Honka	a	0-0	
7/6	Haka	h	2-1	*Aalto 2*
14/6	Inter	a	0-1	
21/6	Lahti	h	1-1	*Äijälä*
2/7	AC Oulu	h	2-0	*Aalto, Björk*
5/7	Tampere United	a	0-3	
11/7	MyPa	h	2-1	*Kainu, Aalto (p)*
19/7	JJK	a	1-0	*Aalto*
26/7	Mariehamn	h	1-4	*Seppälä*
31/7	HJK	a	0-3	
8/8	TPS	h	0-3	
16/8	Jaro	h	1-1	*Savolainen*
23/8	KuPS	a	2-1	*Kainu 2*
29/8	Honka	h	1-3	*Aalto*
11/9	Haka	a	1-1	*Inutile*
19/9	Inter	h	0-3	
27/9	Lahti	a	1-2	*Inutile*
3/10	AC Oulu	a	1-1	*Hietaharju*
17/10	Tampere United	h	3-1	*Laaksonen, Bernhardt, Kainu*
23/10	MyPa	a	2-2	*Laaksonen, og (Votinov)*

No	Name	Nat	DoB	Pos	Aps	(s)	Gls
9	Jussi AALTO		28/7/83	A	20	(4)	7
4	Jussi ÄIJÄLÄ		27/11/88	D	21	(3)	1
19	Jan BERG		22/5/85	D	1	(4)	
28	Edgar BERNHARDT	GER	30/3/86	M	6		1
22	Tony BJÖRK		25/10/83	M	17	(1)	1
15	Kim BÖLING		4/2/92	A		(14)	
11	Osahon EBOIGBE	NGA	11/9/89	A	5	(1)	
3	Greg ECKHARDT	USA	7/1/89	D	13	(6)	
23	Jyri HIETAHARJU		23/4/81	M	21		1
18	Mikko INKI		15/7/92	D		(1)	
10	Antonio INUTILE		12/5/85	A	9	(4)	4
25	Pekka KAINU		20/12/79	A	23	(1)	7
7	Tero KOSKELA		13/10/76	M	13	(5)	
1	KWON Jung-hyuk	KOR	8/2/78	G	22		
17	Valtter LAAKSONEN		3/5/84	A	10	(3)	3
24	Alessandro MARZUOLI	ITA	26/2/84	G	4		
14	Jens NYGÅRD		8/1/78	M	23	(1)	
20	Sami SALMI		8/6/88	D	15	(3)	
16	Jyrki SARANPÄÄ		30/8/83	A	14	(4)	
6	Jussi-Pekka SAVOLAINEN		25/6/86	M	21	(2)	2
21	Arttu SEPPÄLÄ		18/3/87	A	2	(15)	1
2	Jani TANSKA		29/7/88	D	26		

TOP GOALSCORERS 2010

16	Juho MÄKELÄ (HJK)
12	Roope RISKI (TPS)
11	Henri LEHTONEN (Inter)
10	Tamás GRUBOROVICS (Mariehamn)
	Jonatan JOHANSSON (TPS)
9	Jami PUUSTINEN (Honka)
	Tommi KARI (JJK)
	Maksim VOTINOV (MyPa)
8	Papa NIANG (Jaro)
	MacPherlin DUDU (KuPS)
	Mikko PAATELAINEN (Mariehamn)
	Frank JONKE (AC Oulu)

PROMOTED CLUB

ROPS ROVANIEMI

Coach – John Allen (WAL)
Founded – 1950
Stadium – Keskuskenttä (3,400)
MAJOR HONOURS: Finnish Cup – (1) 1986.

SECOND LEVEL FINAL TABLE 2010

		Pld	W	D	L	F	A	Pts
1	RoPS Rovaniemi	26	15	9	2	61	17	54
2	FC Viikingit	26	15	7	4	49	19	52
3	PoPa Pori	26	15	5	6	48	39	50
4	KPV Kokkola	26	14	5	7	43	31	47
5	OPS-jp Oulu	26	11	7	8	34	29	40
6	FC Espoo	26	10	7	9	32	39	37
7	FC KooTeePee	26	10	5	11	28	24	35
8	PK-35 Vantaa	26	10	4	12	36	30	34
9	PS Kemi	26	7	10	9	31	39	31
10	FC Hämeenlinna	26	9	4	13	33	43	31
11	JIPPO Joensuu	26	7	9	10	23	26	30
12	TPV Tampere	26	6	9	11	26	49	27
13	Klubi 04	26	4	5	17	21	50	17
14	MP Mikkeli	26	5	2	19	17	47	17

PROMOTION/RELEGATION PLAY-OFFS

(27/10/10)
Viikingit 1, JJK 1
(30/10/10)
JJK 2, Viikingit 0
(JJK 3-1)

DOMESTIC CUPS 2010

SUOMEN CUP

FOURTH ROUND

(16/4/10)
SC Riverball 0, JIPPO 3
(17/4/10)
KPV 2, RoPS 1
Viikingit 2, MP 2 *(aet; 4-5 on pens)*
(20/4/10)
GBK 2, PS Kemi 2 *(aet; 3-1 on pens)*
(21/4/10)
LeKi 1, TPV 4
Spartak Kajaani 0, Jaro 6
VPS 3, AC Oulu 1
(22/4/10)
FC Boda 0, Ilves 8
City Stars 2, EIF 3
FC Hämeenlinna 1, Haka 2
(23/4/10)
KPV/2 0, SJK 4
MuSa 0, SoVo 6
(24/4/10)
Ponnistus 2, Gnistan 6 *(aet)*
Pöxyt 1, AC Vantaa 0
(25/4/10)
EsPa 4, PEPO 3
LPS 3, GrIFK 1
PaPe 2, Sudet 4
PPV 2, FC Kuusankoski 0
SalReipas 4, LoPa 1
(27/4/10)
P-Iirot 0, Mariehamn 1
(28/4/10)
HIFK 3, PK-35 4 *(aet)*
I-Kissat 0, FC Jazz-j 3
JPS 0, SC KuFu-98 1
MPS 1, MyPa 4
OPS-j 1, FC YPA 1 *(aet; 6-5 on pens)*
(29/4/10)
Tampere United 1, Lahti 2
ViPa 3, BET 0
(5/5/10)
JJK 1, KuPS 2

FIFTH ROUND

(11/5/10)
Ilves 2, ViPa 1
(12/5/10)
KPV 2, PK-35 1
Pöxyt 0, Inter 6
PPV 1, TPS 3
SalReipas 2, LPS 0
SJK 1, Jaro 2 *(aet)*
SoVo 0, Mariehamn 3
TPV 0, Honka 1
(13/5/10)
EIF 0, Haka 1
EsPa 0, HJK 4
GBK 0, MP 3
Gnistan 3, SC KuFu-98 0 *(aet)*
FC Jazz-j 1, VPS 2
JIPPO 0, KuPS 1
Sudet 4, OPS-j 0
(18/5/10)
Lahti 1, MyPa 2

SIXTH ROUND

(26/5/10)
Gnistan 0, Mariehamn 3
MP 0, KuPS 2
SalReipas 1, Ilves 2
Sudet 0, Haka 1
(27/5/10)
HJK 3, Honka 0
KPV 0, Inter 1 *(aet)*
TPS 3, Jaro 0
VPS 1, MyPa 0

QUARTER-FINALS

(9/6/10)
TPS 2 *(Wusu 32, Johansson 70)*, Ilves 1 *(Pessi 57)*
(10/6/10)
Haka 0, KuPS 1 *(Udah 23)*
HJK 2 *(Parikka 55, 90p)*, VPS 0
Mariehamn 2 *(Paatelainen 47, Gueye 85)*, Inter 1 *(Osinachi 10)*

SEMI-FINALS

(16/6/10)
HJK 3 *(Parikka 5, Ojala 66, Westö 75)*, Mariehamn 0
KuPS 1 *(Ollo 43)*, TPS 2 *(Johansson 32p, Riski Ri. 75)*

FINAL

(25/9/10)
Sonera Stadium, Helsinki
TPS TURKU 2 *(Ääritalo 34, Riski Ri. 90)*
HJK HELSINKI 0
Referee – *Pohjonen*
TPS – *Lehtovaara, Rähmönen, Nyberg, Heinikangas, Mäkinen K., Manninen, Kolehmainen, Johansson (Cleaver 57), Riski Ri., Ääritalo (Lähde 90), Riski Ro. (Wusu 85).*
HJK – *Wallén, Rafinha, Lindström, Ojala, Kansikas, Westö, Dema, Kärkkäinen (Parikka 79), Bah, Zeneli (Mäkelä 46), Pelvas (Pukki 46).*

CLUB COMMUNICATION 2011

HJK Helsinki
Urheilukatu 5, Sonera stadium
FI-00250 Helsinki

Tel +358 9 7421 6600
Fax +358 9 7421 6666
Web hjk.fi
Email hjk@hjk.fi
Media Officer Felix Siivonen

FC Honka Espoo
Urheilupuistontie 2 B
FI-02200 Espoo

Tel +358 9 256 1600
Fax +358 9 256 1600
Web fchonka.fi
Email toimisto@fchonka.fi
Media Officer Kim Sanden

FC Inter Turku
Hippoksentie 21
FI-20720 Turku

Tel +358 22 792 700
Fax +358 22 792 710
Web fcinter.com
Email fcinter.turku@alfonshakans.fi
Media Officer Lauri Kemppainen

FF Jaro
Södermalmsgatan 20, Centralplan stadium, FI-68600 Pietarsaari

Tel +358 67 247 936
Fax +358 67 230 220
Web ffjaro.fi
Email office@ffjaro.fi
Media Officer Jukka Karjalainen

JJK Jyväskylä
Ihantolantie 1, Harjun Stadion
FI-40720 Jyväskylä

Tel +358 14 612 347
Fax +358 14 612 347
Web fcjjk.com
Email joni.vesalainen@fcjjk.com
Media Officer Mikko Hyppönen

KuPS Kuopio
Kaartokatu 6, Kuopion Keskuskenttä
FI-70620 Kuopio

Tel +358 17 266 85 60
Fax +358 17 261 95 98
Web kups.fi
Email toimisto@kups.fi
Media Officer Martti Juurtela

IFK Mariehamn
Wiklöf Holding Arena
FI-22100 Mariehamn

Tel +358 18 163 45
Fax +358 18 237 15
Web ifkmariehamn.com/fotboll
Email henrik.johansson@ifkmariehamn.com
Media Officer Peter Mattsson

Myllykosken Pallo-47
Koulutie 1
FI-46800 Anjalankoski

Tel +358 53 656 686
Fax +358 53 255 292
Web mypa.fi
Email toimisto@mypa.fi
Media Officer Toni Hannula

RoPS Rovaniemi
PL 2254
FI-96201 Rovaniemi

Tel +358 40 137 5110
Fax +358 16 319 837
Web rops.fi
Email antti.hietakangas@rops.fi
Media Officer Jorma Kilpeläinen

TPS Turku
Lemminkäisenkatu 14-18 A, U-kerros
FI-20701 Turku

Tel +358 10 820 1922
Fax +358 10 820 1911
Web fctps.fi
Email fc.toimisto@tps.fi
Media Officer Heikki Mottonen

Valkeakosken Haka
Tehtaankatu 9
FI-37600 Valkeakoski

Tel +358 3 584 5364
Fax +358 3 585 1066
Web fchaka.fi
Email toimisto@fchaka.fi
Media Officer Jukka Malm

VPS Vaasa
Reininkatu 3
FI-65170 Vaasa

Tel +358 6 318 2970
Fax +358 6 318 2971
Web vepsu..fi
Email eero.karhumaki@vepsu.fi
Media Officer Jukka Niemi

FRANCE

France I Frankreich

Fédération Française de Football (FFF)

COMMUNICATION

Address	87 boulevard de Grenelle FR-75738 Paris Cedex 15	**President**	Noël Le Graët
		Chief Executive	Alain Christnacht
		Media Officer	François Manardo
Tel	+33 1 4431 7300		
Fax	+33 1 4431 7373	**Year of Formation**	1919
E-mail	webmaster@fff.fr	**National Stadium**	Stade de France, Saint-Denis (76,474)
Website	fff.fr		

DOMESTIC COMPETITION SUMMARY 2010/11

LIGUE 1 FINAL TABLE

			Home					Away					Total						
		Pld	W	D	L	F	A	W	D	L	F	A	W	D	L	F	A	Pts	• Comp
1	LOSC Lille Métropole	38	13	5	1	40	17	8	8	3	28	19	21	13	4	68	36	76	UCL
2	Olympique de Marseille	38	10	7	2	34	19	8	7	4	28	20	18	14	6	62	39	68	UCL
3	Olympique Lyonnais	38	11	7	1	35	12	6	6	7	26	28	17	13	8	61	40	64	UCL
4	Paris Saint-Germain FC	38	9	8	2	33	20	6	7	6	23	21	15	15	8	56	41	60	UEL
5	FC Sochaux-Montbéliard	38	12	4	3	36	17	5	3	11	24	26	17	7	14	60	43	58	UEL
6	Stade Rennais FC	38	9	6	4	22	13	6	5	8	16	22	15	11	12	38	35	56	UEL
7	FC Girondins de Bordeaux	38	8	6	5	22	17	4	9	6	21	25	12	15	11	43	42	51	
8	Toulouse FC	38	8	4	7	19	13	6	4	9	19	23	14	8	16	38	36	50	
9	AJ Auxerre	38	6	10	3	26	18	4	9	6	19	23	10	19	9	45	41	49	
10	AS Saint-Étienne	38	7	7	5	29	25	5	6	8	17	22	12	13	13	46	47	49	
11	FC Lorient	38	8	8	3	27	13	4	5	10	19	35	12	13	13	46	48	49	
12	Valenciennes FC	38	8	9	2	28	17	2	9	8	17	24	10	18	10	45	41	48	
13	AS Nancy-Lorraine	38	8	3	8	23	21	5	6	8	20	27	13	9	16	43	48	48	
14	Montpellier Hérault SC	38	7	5	7	21	20	5	6	8	11	23	12	11	15	32	43	47	
15	SM Caen	38	6	7	6	22	25	5	6	8	24	26	11	13	14	46	51	46	
16	Stade Brestois 29	38	6	9	4	21	17	5	4	10	15	26	11	13	14	36	43	46	
17	OGC Nice	38	9	5	5	22	22	2	8	9	11	26	11	13	14	33	48	46	
18	AS Monaco FC	38	5	9	5	16	17	4	8	7	20	23	9	17	12	36	40	44	*Relegated*
19	RC Lens	38	5	5	9	20	26	2	9	8	15	32	7	14	17	35	58	35	*Relegated*
20	AC Arles-Avignon	38	2	6	11	14	31	1	5	13	7	39	3	11	24	21	70	20	*Relegated*

Top Scorer Moussa Sow (Lille), 25 goals

Promoted Clubs Évian Thonon Gaillard FC
AC Ajaccio
Dijon FCO

Cup Final LOSC Lille Métropole 1, Paris Saint-Germain FC 0

League Cup Final Olympique de Marseille 1, Montpellier Hérault SC 0

Lille leave the rest standing

Without a major trophy for over half a century, LOSC Lille Métropole brought their long barren run to an end by winning both of French football's most coveted domestic prizes, victory in the Coupe de France being accompanied by a glorious triumph in the Ligue 1 championship.

It was a season of unfettered jubilation for the long-suffering supporters of the northern club. France's top side in the years immediately following the Second World War, during which they won two league titles and five domestic cups, Lille subsequently lost their way. In 2010/11, however, under the shrewd guidance of 47-year-old former player Rudi Garcia, Les Dogues re-established themselves as the pre-eminent power in the land, leaving heavyweight opponents such as Olympique Lyonnais, Olympique de Marseille and Paris Saint-Germain FC trailing in their formidable wake.

Solid foundation

The second coming of Lille was not a complete surprise. After all, they had finished in the top five of the Ligue 1 standings in six of the previous ten seasons. And although they had just missed out on a third UEFA Champions League adventure by finishing fourth in 2009/10, they were evidently a coming force under Garcia, who had joined the club in June 2008 as a replacement for Lyon-bound Claude Puel. With no major changes to the team in 2010/11 other than the arrival, from Stade Rennais FC, of Senegalese striker Moussa Sow, a solid foundation was in place for Lille to mount a serious challenge for honours.

Draws in each of their first four league encounters did not bode well, but after defeating local rivals RC Lens 4-1 in September, their form picked up sufficiently to lift them into contention in a Ligue 1 title race that appeared to be as open and unpredictable as any in recent history. Among the unfancied early table-toppers were AS Saint-Étienne, Rennes and even newly promoted Stade Brestois 29, who secured their place at the summit with eight successive clean sheets. It was anyone's title, with a mere five points separating the top ten teams at the winter break. In pole position, however, were Lille, with a one-point advantage and a game in hand over closest pursuers PSG, Rennes and Lyon.

Despite mixed displays in the group stage of the UEFA Europa League – two wins, two draws and two defeats – Lille reached the round of 32, where they were eliminated by PSV Eindhoven. The exit from Europe, though a setback, served to reinforce their domestic ambitions, and they responded with four successive wins in Ligue 1 plus a penalty shoot-out victory over FC Lorient in the quarter-final of the French Cup (their second in succession, having also overcome FC Nantes by that method in the previous

Rudi Garcia led Lille to a Ligue 1/Coupe de France double

round). With the season building to an exciting climax, and Garcia's key personnel avoiding injuries, the opportunity was there for Lille to make history. They would seize it with aplomb.

Victory in the Coupe de France came first. Lille reached the Stade de France showpiece thanks to a 2-0 away win in the semi-finals against OGC Nice. Their opponents in the final were holders PSG, and it was the Parisians who looked the likelier winners as an even contest entered its latter stages, only for Lille to snatch victory a minute from time when substitute Ludovic Obraniak curled in a free-kick from the right that flew directly into the far corner. There was still time for Lille to miss a penalty – midfielder Mathieu Debuchy the culprit – before the final whistle signalled their first victory in the competition since 1955.

Last-day hat-trick

It was also against PSG, in Paris, at the Parc des Princes, that Lille completed the second part of their historic double seven days later, a 2-2 draw in their penultimate league fixture leaving them six points clear at the top. Obraniak was on target again before Sow added a second. The big striker capped a superb debut season by hitting a hat-trick against his old club Rennes the following weekend as Lille celebrated in front of their fans with a 3-2 victory. That lifted Sow's end-of-term haul to 25 goals, which earned him the Ligue 1 Golden Boot ahead of Lorient's 22-goal Kevin Gameiro. If Sow was the man who made the difference for Lille, he was brilliantly assisted by Ivory Coast winger-cum-striker Gervinho and the dynamic young Belgian playmaker Eden Hazard, who, having twice been voted Ligue 1's Young Player of the Season, scooped the main award in 2010/11. Debuchy, Yohan Cabaye and captain Rio Mavuba also performed with great consistency in midfield while Adil Rami was a rock in central defence and veteran 'keeper Mickaël Landreau an ever-reliable source of security in goal.

Joy for Lille meant pain elsewhere, although defending Ligue 1 champions Marseille did achieve a double of their own by becoming the first team to defend the Coupe de la Ligue – France's secondary domestic cup – and also guaranteeing another season in the UEFA Champions League with a runners-up placing in Ligue 1. That was a decent enough return for Didier Deschamps' side, although a fine run of form in the early months of 2011 –

Taye Taiwo scored Marseille's winning goal in the French League Cup final

spoiled only by a home defeat to Lille – had hinted at an even better outcome. Having recovered well from a poor start, Marseille effectively surrendered the title in early May when a home draw against AJ Auxerre was followed by a 3-2 defeat at Lyon. Long-serving left-back Taye Taiwo – who left for AC Milan in June – was a prominent figure throughout the campaign and also scored the League Cup final winner against Montpellier Hérault SC, while fellow West African André Ayew – son of OM legend Abedi Pelé – did his father proud with some outstanding displays. Of the two new strikers recruited to replace 2009/10 top scorer Mamadou Niang, Loïc Rémy outshone André-Pierre Gignac, scoring 15 goals to the ex-Toulouse FC striker's eight.

Lyon, for whom record signing Yoann Gourcuff was a major disappointment, managed to claw their way to third place but they were upstaged by their female counterparts who lifted the UEFA Women's Champions League trophy. A third successive season without silverware for coach Puel led to his dismissal, with assistant Rémi Garde being promoted from within to take his place. UEFA Champions League semi-finalists in 2009/10, Lyon fell at the last-16 hurdle as Real Madrid CF comfortably avenged their elimination of a year earlier. Marseille also departed the competition at the same juncture, at the hands of Manchester United FC, though an earlier exit had

FRANCE

been on the cards when they lost their opening two group games. Their recovery included a 7-0 win at Slovakian champions MŠK Žilina – the biggest away win in the competition's history.

Arguably the best result recorded by a French club in Europe in 2010/11 was Auxerre's 2-1 aggregate victory over Russian champions-elect FC Zenit St Petersburg in the UEFA Champions League play-offs. Jean Fernandez's side lost five of their subsequent group encounters and also endured a tough season in the league, flirting dangerously with relegation until a nine-game unbeaten run in the spring hoisted them clear and all the way up into the top half of the table.

Last team standing

PSG, who finished fourth in Ligue 1, 16 points behind the champions, were France's last team standing in Europe. With Montpellier eliminated on penalties from the UEFA Europa League in the third qualifying round, and Lille's run ending in the round of 32, Antoine Kombouaré's side reached the last 16 before bowing out to SL Benfica. Inspired by their Brazilian playmaker Nenê, a summer signing from AS Monaco FC, they had done supremely well to top a group containing Sevilla FC and Borussia Dortmund, but as Nenê's form faded in the spring, so did that of his team, a chronic inability to convert draws into victories – evident also in Europe – scuppering their hopes of a first league title in 17 years. Heavy investment from the Middle East, which enabled the club to buy Gameiro from Lorient and bring club legend Leonardo back from FC Internazionale Milano as sporting director, suggested there would be a more sustained challenge for the Ligue 1 crown in 2011/12.

National Team

International Honours –
FIFA World Cup – (1) 1998.
UEFA European Championship – (2) 1984, 2000.
FIFA Confederations Cup – (2) 2001, 2003.

International Tournament Appearances –
FIFA World Cup – (12) 1930, 1938 (2nd round), 1954, 1958 (3rd), 1966, 1978, 1982 (4th), 1986 (3rd), 1998 (Winners), 2002, 2006 (runners-up), 2010.
UEFA European Championship – (7) 1960 (4th), 1984 (Winners), 1992, 1996 (semi-finals), 2000 (Winners), 2004 (qtr-finals), 2008.

Top Five All-time Caps – Lilian Thuram (142); Thierry Henry (123); Marcel Desailly (116); Zinedine Zidane (108); Patrick Vieira (107)

Top Five All-time Goals – Thierry Henry (51); Michel Platini (41); David Trezeguet (34); Zinedine Zidane (31); Just Fontaine & Jean-Pierre Papin (30)

PSG's position as Coupe de France runners-up, allied to Marseille's Coupe de le Ligue victory, opened up two further UEFA Europa League qualifying places in the league. The first of them was claimed by FC Sochaux-Montbéliard, who powered up the table in the closing weeks with seven wins and two draws in their last ten games. Inspired by the midfield creativity of 22-year-old Marvin Martin – who was credited with 17 assists, the highest number in the league – and an all-African strike force of Ideye Brown and Modibo Maïga, who scored 15 goals apiece, Sochaux reached their highest position for seven seasons.

Few could have predicted that Sochaux would end up above Rennes, who, in contrast, petered out in the spring, winning only one of their last 12 matches, when they had looked like genuine title challengers during the autumn and winter. The Bretons led the table for the first time in 40 years during the early stages, but although their defence was the best in

NATIONAL TEAM RESULTS 2010/11

11/8/10	Norway	A	Oslo	1-2	*Ben Arfa (48)*
3/9/10	Belarus (ECQ)	H	Saint-Denis	0-1	
7/9/10	Bosnia & Herzegovina (ECQ)	A	Sarajevo	2-0	*Benzema (72), Malouda (78)*
9/10/10	Romania (ECQ)	H	Saint-Denis	2-0	*Rémy (83), Gourcuff (90+3)*
12/10/10	Luxembourg (ECQ)	H	Metz	2-0	*Benzema (22), Gourcuff (76)*
17/11/10	England	A	Wembley	2-1	*Benzema (16), Valbuena (55)*
9/2/11	Brazil	H	Saint-Denis	1-0	*Benzema (54)*
25/3/11	Luxembourg (ECQ)	A	Luxembourg	2-0	*Mexès (28), Gourcuff (72)*
29/3/11	Croatia	H	Saint-Denis	0-0	
3/6/11	Belarus (ECQ)	A	Minsk	1-1	*Malouda (22)*
6/6/11	Ukraine	A	Donetsk	4-1	*Gameiro (58), Martin (87, 90+2), Kaboul (89)*
9/6/11	Poland	A	Warsaw	1-0	*Jodłowiec (12og)*

NATIONAL TEAM APPEARANCES 2010/11

Coach – Laurent BLANC	19/11/65		Nor	BLR	BIH	ROU	LUX	Eng	Bra	LUX	Cro	BLR	Ukr	Pol	Caps	Goals
Stéphane RUFFIER	27/9/86	Monaco	G												1	-
Rod FANNI	6/12/81	Rennes	D												5	-
Philippe MEXÈS	30/3/82	Roma (ITA)	D	D	D	D	D	D46	D	D	D				22	1
Adil RAMI	27/12/85	Lille	D	D	D	D	D	D	D	D	D90	D		s27	11	-
Aly CISSOKHO	15/9/87	Lyon	D												1	-
Moussa SISSOKO	16/8/89	Toulouse	M46												3	-
Yann M'VILA	29/6/90	Rennes	M74	M	M	M		M	M59	M	s87		M	s46	10	-
Samir NASRI	26/6/87	Arsenal (ENG)	M79			M74	s63	M		M	M87	M			22	2
Charles N'ZOGBIA	28/5/86	Wigan (ENG)	M46											M73	2	-
Loïc RÉMY	2/1/87	Nice /Marseille	A46	 A34		 s68	 s73	 s67	 s66		 s60	 s73	 M64	 s73	 11	 1
Guillaume HOARAU	5/3/84	PSG	A61	A			A73	s85						A78	5	-
Lassana DIARRA	10/3/85	Real Madrid (ESP)	s46												28	-
Hatem BEN ARFA	7/3/87	Marseille	s46												8	2
Jérémy MÉNEZ	7/5/87	Roma (ITA)	s46	M69					M66		M60		M65		5	-
Karim BENZEMA	19/12/87	Real Madrid (ESP)	s61		A	A86	A63	A67	A85	A	A75	A	s65		37	12
Yohan CABAYE	14/1/86	Lille	s74						s85				M76	M46	4	-
Jimmy BRIAND	2/8/85	Lyon	s79												4	-
Hugo LLORIS	26/12/86	Lyon		G	G	G	G	G	G	G	G	G			23	-
Bacary SAGNA	14/2/83	Arsenal (ENG)		D	D			D87	D	D		D		D	30	-
Gaël CLICHY	26/7/85	Arsenal (ENG)		D	D	D	D				D				10	-
Abou DIABY	11/5/86	Arsenal (ENG)		M	M		M		s59			M73	s76	s46	15	-
Florent MALOUDA	13/6/80	Chelsea (ENG)		M	M80	M	M63	M77	M	M	M59	M	s65	s73	68	6
Mathieu VALBUENA	28/9/84	Marseille		s34	M	M68		M68						M73	8	2
Louis SAHA	8/8/78	Everton (ENG)		s69 /80											19	4
Kevin GAMEIRO	9/5/87	Lorient		s80					s85		s75		A65	s78	5	1
Alou DIARRA	15/7/81	Bordeaux			M	M	M	s68	M		M	M		M46	34	-
Blaise MATUIDI	9/4/87	St-Étienne			s80						M87		M76		3	-
Anthony RÉVEILLÈRE	10/11/79	Lyon				D	D	s87			D		D		11	-
Yoann GOURCUFF	11/7/86	Lyon				s74	M	M85	M85	M	s87				28	4
Dimitri PAYET	29/3/87	St-Étienne				s86	s63	s77							3	-
Éric ABIDAL	11/9/79	Barcelona (ESP)						D	D			D	s76	D	55	-
Mamadou SAKHO	13/2/90	PSG						s46			s90	D	D76		4	-
Patrice EVRA	15/5/81	Man. United (ENG)								D			D	D	35	-
Franck RIBÉRY	7/4/83	Bayern (GER)								M	s59	M	s64		52	7
Steve MANDANDA	28/3/85	Marseille											G		14	-
Younes KABOUL	4/1/86	Tottenham (ENG)											D	D27	2	1
Marvin MARTIN	10/6/88	Sochaux											s76	M	2	2
Cédric CARRASSO	30/12/81	Bordeaux												G	1	-

the division, with young holding midfielder Yann M'Vila a colossus in the role, Frédéric Antonetti's side were ultimately made to pay for the pre-season departure of three key strikers in Sow, Asamoah Gyan and Jimmy Briand. Still, despite scoring just 38 goals in as many games, they held on to sixth place, leaving 2008/09 champions FC Girondins de Bordeaux, for whom new boss Jean Tigana did not see out the season, five points adrift in seventh.

Monaco relegated

Bordeaux's second successive failure to qualify for Europe was nothing compared to the shock felt by the relegation of Monaco, whose last-day defeat at home to Lyon ended the Principality club's 34-year sojourn in France's top division. A win for the 2004 UEFA Champions League runners-up would have sent down Côte d'Azur rivals Nice instead, but it was not to be and they dropped to Ligue 2 in the company of Lens and long-doomed AC Arles-Avignon, the fate of the newly-promoted Provençal outfit having virtually been sealed early on when they lost their opening eight matches. Another merger club, Évian Thonon Gaillard FC, won Ligue 2 to achieve a second successive promotion and a first season in the top flight. The Alpine outfit were accompanied up by AC Ajaccio, from Corsica, and another Ligue 1 debutant, Dijon FCO.

A new era for the French national team, under former defender and 1998 FIFA World Cup winner Laurent Blanc, got off to a worrying start when Les Bleus lost their opening UEFA EURO 2012 qualifier at home to Belarus. But the new coach, who led Bordeaux to the 2008/09 Ligue 1 title, soon turned things around, and by the end of the season, after a run of ten games without defeat, the fiasco of the 2010 FIFA World Cup just 12 months earlier had become a dim and distant memory.

Blanc began by excluding every member of the mutinous World Cup squad from his first game – a friendly in Norway. Although Les Bleus lost 2-1, the decision proved beneficial on two counts. Not only did Blanc assert himself straight away as a no-nonsense figure of authority, but several of the players who turned out in Oslo were to become cornerstones of his new-look team, notably the central defensive duo of Rami and Philippe Mexès, anchorman M'Vila and striker Karim Benzema. The latter got the EURO qualifying campaign up and running with the first of France's goals in their 2-0 win over Bosnia & Herzegovina in Sarajevo, and he was also on target in prestige friendly wins over England at Wembley and Brazil at the Stade de France.

Rebels restored

Patrice Evra and Franck Ribéry, who had both received lengthy bans following their World Cup misdemeanours, were restored in the spring, and although the return qualifier against Belarus in June ended in a disappointing 1-1 draw, the four victories that had preceded it left France as strong favourites to top their qualifying group. Furthermore, Blanc's men closed their season with friendly wins away to Ukraine and Poland – the two co-hosts of a tournament that the French public can now look forward to with renewed enthusiasm and confidence.

CLUB-BY-CLUB

AC ARLES-AVIGNON

Coach – Michel Estevan; (16/9/10) (Jean-Louis Saez); (2/10/10) Faruk Hadžibegić (BIH)

Founded – 1913

Stadium – Parc des Sports d'Avignon (17,500)

2010				
7/8	Sochaux	a	1-2	*Dja Djédjé*
14/8	Lens	h	0-1	
21/8	Toulouse	a	1-2	*Dja Djédjé*
28/8	Rennes	h	0-1	
11/9	PSG	a	0-4	
18/9	Marseille	h	0-3	
25/9	Montpellier	a	1-3	*Kermorgant*
2/10	Auxerre	h	0-4	
16/10	Brest	a	0-0	
24/10	Lyon	h	1-1	*Dja Djédjé*
30/10	Lorient	a	0-2	
6/11	Caen	h	3-2	*Germany, Diawara 2 (1p)*
13/11	Monaco	a	0-0	
21/11	Bordeaux	h	2-4	*Meriem, Bouazza*
27/11	Valenciennes	a	0-3	
4/12	Nancy	h	1-1	*Dja Djédjé*
11/12	Lille	h	0-1	
18/12	St-Étienne	a	0-2	
22/12	Nice	h	0-0	
2011				
15/1	Rennes	a	0-4	
29/1	PSG	h	1-2	*N'Diaye*
5/2	Marseille	a	0-1	
12/2	Montpellier	h	0-0	
19/2	Auxerre	a	1-1	*N'Diaye*
26/2	Brest	h	1-1	*Ghilas*
6/3	Lyon	a	0-5	
12/3	Lorient	h	3-3	*Meriem, Kermorgant, Cabella*
20/3	Caen	a	0-2	
2/4	Monaco	h	0-2	
9/4	Bordeaux	a	0-0	
17/4	Valenciennes	h	0-1	

4/4	Nancy	a	0-0	
0/4	Lille	a	0-5	
/5	St-Étienne	h	0-1	
1/5	Nice	a	2-3	*Cabella, Diawara*
5/5	Toulouse	h	1-0	*Ghilas*
1/5	Lens	a	1-0	*Kermorgant*
9/5	Sochaux	h	1-3	*Cabella*

No	Name	Nat	DoB	Pos	Aps	(s)	Gls
3	Loïc ABENZOAR		14/2/89	D	10	(2)	
[illegible]	Jamel AÏT BEN IDIR		10/1/84	M	21	(4)	
3	Rachid ALIAOUI		14/8/86	M		(1)	
7	Thomas AYASSE		17/2/87	M	19	(4)	
[illegible]	Dianbobo BALDÉ	GUI	5/10/75	D	13		
26	Angelos BASINAS	GRE	3/1/76	M	3	(1)	
1	Hameur BOUAZZA	ALG	22/2/85	A	3	(6)	1
20	Rémy CABELLA		8/3/90	M	5	(12)	3
9	Angelos CHARISTEAS	GRE	9/2/80	A	3	(3)	
24	Emmanuel CORRÈZE		9/3/82	M	4	(4)	
9	Kaba DIAWARA	GUI	16/12/75	A	10	(10)	3
29	Franck DJA DJÉDJÉ	CIV	2/6/86	A	30	(4)	4
4	El-Amin ERBATE	MAR	7/7/81	D	8		
23	Jean-Alain FANCHONE		2/9/88	D	16	(5)	
22	Gaël GERMANY		19/5/83	M	16	(3)	1
10	Kamel GHILAS	ALG	9/3/84	A	11	(8)	2
21	Anthony GUISE		5/3/85	A		(1)	
25	JONATHAN Aparecido da Silva	BRA	29/3/90	A		(3)	
18	Yann KERMORGANT		8/11/81	A	20	(6)	3
15	Fabien LAURENTI		8/1/83	D	26		
7	Grégory LORENZI		17/12/83	D	12		
33	Clément MARTÍNEZ		22/9/88	M		(1)	
2	Álvaro Pérez MEJIA	ESP	18/1/82	D	12		
28	Camel MERIEM		18/10/79	M	31	(1)	2
16	Cyrille MERVILLE		14/4/82	G	19		
27	Deme N'DIAYE	SEN	6/2/85	M	25	(8)	2
14	Chafik NAJIH		5/8/83	A	1	(1)	
3	Francisco PAVÓN	ESP	9/1/80	D	26		
8	Sébastien PIOCELLE		10/11/78	M	15	(4)	
1	Vincent PLANTÉ		19/10/80	G	17	(2)	
7	Benjamin PSAUME		12/1/85	A	3	(11)	
7	Romain ROCCHI		2/10/81	M	13	(4)	
5	Bakari SORO	CIV	5/12/85	D	24	(4)	
30	Naby-Moussa YATTARA	GUI	12/1/84	G	2		

AJ AUXERRE

Coach – Jean Fernandez

Founded – 1905

Stadium – Abbé-Deschamps (20,300)

MAJOR HONOURS: French League – (1) 1996; French Cup – (4) 1994, 1996, 2003, 2005.

2010				
7/8	Lorient	h	2-2	*Pedretti, Le Tallec*
14/8	Brest	a	1-1	*Pedretti*
21/8	Valenciennes	h	1-1	*Jeleń*
29/8	Monaco	a	0-2	
11/9	Caen	h	1-1	*Pedretti*
19/9	Lille	a	0-1	
25/9	Nancy	h	2-2	*Oliech 2*
2/10	Arles-Avignon	a	4-0	*Traoré, Pedretti, Contout, Birsa*
16/10	Bordeaux	h	0-1	
24/10	PSG	a	3-2	*Mignot, Contout, Quercia*
30/10	Nice	h	2-0	*Birsa, Pedretti*
6/11	Sochaux	a	1-1	*Sammaritano*
14/11	Rennes	h	2-1	*Birsa, Quercia*
20/11	St-Étienne	a	1-1	*Mignot*
28/11	Toulouse	h	1-2	*Traoré*
4/12	Lens	a	1-1	*Mignot*
11/12	Marseille	h	1-1	*Birsa (p)*
18/12	Montpellier	a	1-1	*Traoré*
22/12	Lyon	a	1-1	*Quercia*

2011				
15/1	Monaco	h	1-1	*Quercia*
29/1	Caen	a	0-2	
6/2	Lille	h	1-1	*Dudka*
12/2	Nancy	a	1-3	*Jeleń*
19/2	Arles-Avignon	h	1-1	*Jeleń*
26/2	Bordeaux	a	0-3	
5/3	PSG	h	1-0	*Chafni*
12/3	Nice	a	0-1	
19/3	Sochaux	h	2-0	*Jeleń 2*
2/4	Rennes	a	0-0	
9/4	St-Étienne	h	2-2	*Oliech, Dudka (p)*
16/4	Toulouse	a	1-0	*Dudka*
24/4	Lens	h	1-1	*Boly*
1/5	Marseille	a	1-1	*Jung*
7/5	Montpellier	h	1-0	*Contout*
11/5	Lyon	h	4-0	*Oliech, Traoré 2, Hengbart*
15/5	Valenciennes	a	1-1	*Jung*
21/5	Brest	h	0-1	
29/5	Lorient	a	2-1	*og (Ecuele Manga), Birsa*

No	Name	Nat	DoB	Pos	Aps	(s)	Gls
23	Jérémy BERTHOD		24/4/84	D	11	(6)	
9	Valter BIRSA	SVN	7/8/86	A	27	(6)	5
3	Willy BOLY		3/2/91	D	8		1
25	Maxime BOURGEOIS		3/2/91	A		(3)	
7	Kamel CHAFNI	MAR	11/6/82	M	16	(6)	1
18	Roy CONTOUT		11/2/85	M	25	(4)	3
6	Adama COULIBALY	MLI	9/10/80	D	38		
5	Dariusz DUDKA	POL	9/12/83	D	29		3
4	Stéphane GRICHTING	SUI	30/3/79	D	24	(1)	
2	Cédric HENGBART		13/7/80	D	27	(1)	1
22	Ireneusz JELEŃ	POL	9/4/81	A	18	(3)	5
24	JUNG Jo-gook	KOR	23/4/84	A	1	(14)	2
21	Steeven LANGIL		4/3/88	M	3	(7)	
8	Anthony LE TALLEC		3/10/84	A	8	(14)	1
12	Jean-Pascal MIGNOT		26/2/81	D	16	(1)	3
29	Delvin NDINGA	CGO	3/4/88	M	25	(1)	
14	Dennis OLIECH	KEN	2/2/85	A	28	(5)	4
33	Bernard ONANGA ITOUA		7/9/88	D	2		
17	Benoît PEDRETTI		12/11/80	M	20		5
11	Julien QUERCIA		17/8/86	A	14	(5)	4
15	Frédéric SAMMARITANO		23/3/85	M	10	(17)	1
34	Kossi Prince SEGBEFIA	TOG	11/3/91	M	3	(1)	
20	Amadou SIDIBÉ	MLI	19/2/86	M	9	(1)	
1	Olivier SORIN		16/4/81	G	38		
27	Alain TRAORÉ	BFA	31/12/88	M	18	(2)	5

FC GIRONDINS DE BORDEAUX

Coach – Jean Tigana; (8/5/11) (Éric Bédouet)

Founded – 1881

Stadium – Chaban-Delmas (34,263)

MAJOR HONOURS: French League – (6) 1950, 1984, 1985, 1987, 1999, 2009; French Cup – (3) 1941, 1986, 1987; League Cup – (3) 2002, 2007, 2009.

2010				
8/8	Montpellier	a	0-1	
15/8	Toulouse	h	1-2	*Plašil*
22/8	PSG	a	2-1	*Diarra, Ciani*
29/8	Marseille	h	1-1	*Modeste*
12/9	Nice	a	1-2	*Modeste (p)*
19/9	Lyon	h	2-0	*Diarra, Jussiê*
25/9	Caen	a	0-0	
2/10	Lorient	h	1-0	*Ciani*
16/10	Auxerre	a	1-0	*Modeste*
23/10	Brest	h	0-2	
2/11	Monaco	a	2-2	*og (Traoré), Jussiê*
6/11	Valenciennes	h	1-1	*Maazou*
13/11	Nancy	h	2-1	*Sané L., Wendel*
21/11	Arles-Avignon	a	4-2	*Modeste 3 (1p), Gouffran*
27/11	Lille	h	1-1	*og (Rami)*
5/12	St-Étienne	a	2-2	*Ben Khalfallah, Fernando*

12/12	Rennes	h	0-0	
19/12	Sochaux	a	1-1	*Jussiê*
22/12	Lens	h	2-2	*Diarra, Gouffran*
2011				
16/1	Marseille	a	1-2	*Modeste (p)*
30/1	Nice	h	2-0	*Sané L., Modeste*
6/2	Lyon	a	0-0	
12/2	Caen	h	1-2	*Modeste*
19/2	Lorient	a	1-5	*Fernando*
26/2	Auxerre	h	3-0	*Diarra, Modeste (p), Plašil*
6/3	Brest	a	3-1	*Wendel, Plašil, Diabaté*
13/3	Monaco	h	0-1	
19/3	Valenciennes	a	2-2	*Jussiê, Ciani*
2/4	Nancy	a	0-0	
9/4	Arles-Avignon	h	0-0	
16/4	Lille	a	1-1	*Savić*
24/4	St-Étienne	h	2-0	*Plašil, Diabaté*
30/4	Rennes	a	0-0	
7/5	Sochaux	h	0-4	
11/5	Lens	a	0-1	
18/5	PSG	h	1-0	*Diabaté (p)*
21/5	Toulouse	a	0-2	
29/5	Montpellier	h	2-0	*Diabaté, Wendel*

No	Name	Nat	DoB	Pos	Aps	(s)	Gls
9	ANDRÉ Felipe Ribeiro de Souza	BRA	27/9/90	A	1	(7)	
14	Floyd AYITÉ	TOG	15/2/88	M		(7)	
11	David BELLION		27/11/82	A		(2)	
8	Fahid BEN KHALFALLAH	TUN	9/10/82	M	26	(6)	1
1	Cédric CARRASSO		30/12/81	G	34	(1)	
9	Fernando CAVENAGHI	ARG	21/9/83	A	2		
21	Mathieu CHALMÉ		7/10/80	D	18	(2)	
36	Evan CHEVALIER		13/5/92	M		(1)	
2	Michaël CIANI		6/4/84	D	27	(2)	3
25	Cheick DIABATÉ	MLI	25/4/88	A	7	(9)	4
4	Alou DIARRA		15/7/81	M	32		4
19	Pierre DUCASSE		7/5/87	M	4	(6)	
37	Rémy ELISSALDE		1/1/91	M		(1)	
5	FERNANDO Menegazzo	BRA	3/5/81	M	34	(1)	2
7	Yoan GOUFFRAN		25/5/86	A	15	(7)	2
8	Yoann GOURCUFF		11/7/86	M	2	(1)	
3	Carlos HENRIQUE dos Santos Souza	BRA	2/5/83	D		(2)	
10	JUSSIÊ Ferreira Vieira	BRA	19/9/83	A	21	(10)	4
26	Ouwo Moussa MAAZOU	NIG	25/8/88	A	5	(10)	1
23	Florian MARANGE		3/3/86	D	11	(1)	
22	Anthony MODESTE		14/4/88	A	27	(10)	10
30	Kevin OLIMPA		10/3/88	G	2		
27	Marc PLANUS		7/3/82	D	9	(2)	
18	Jaroslav PLAŠIL	CZE	5/1/82	M	38		4
16	Ulrich RAMÉ		19/9/72	G	2	(1)	
20	Henri SAIVET		26/10/90	A	1	(5)	
25	Ludovic SANÉ	SEN	22/3/87	M	33		2
33	Salif SANÉ		25/8/90	D	4		
15	Vujadin SAVIĆ	SRB	1/7/90	D	7		1
28	Benoît TRÉMOULINAS		28/12/85	D	30	(1)	
17	WENDEL Geraldo Maurício da Silva	BRA	8/4/82	M	26	(5)	3

STADE BRESTOIS 29

Coach – Alex Dupont

Founded – 1950

Stadium – Francis-Le Blé (16,000)

2010				
7/8	Toulouse	a	0-2	
14/8	Auxerre	h	1-1	*Roux*
21/8	Lyon	a	0-1	
28/8	Caen	a	2-0	*Roux, Lička (p)*
12/9	Lorient	h	0-0	
18/9	Nancy	a	2-0	*Mičola, Touré*
26/9	Valenciennes	h	1-0	*Roux*
2/10	Monaco	a	1-0	*Grougi*
16/10	Arles-Avignon	h	0-0	
23/10	Bordeaux	a	2-0	*Poyet, Lesoimier*
30/10	St-Étienne	h	2-0	*Lička, Poyet*
7/11	Lille	a	1-3	*Poyet*
13/11	Sochaux	h	1-1	*Roux*
20/11	Rennes	a	1-2	*Grougi (p)*
30/11	Lens	h	4-1	*Poyet, Baysse, Grougi 2*
5/12	PSG	a	1-3	*Roux*
11/12	Montpellier	h	0-0	
18/12	Nice	a	1-1	*Martial*
22/12	Marseille	h	0-0	
2011				
15/1	Caen	h	1-3	*Grougi (p)*
29/1	Lorient	a	0-2	
5/2	Nancy	h	2-1	*Ayité, Grougi*
13/2	Valenciennes	a	0-3	
19/2	Monaco	h	2-0	*Ayité 2 (1p)*
26/2	Arles-Avignon	a	1-1	*Touré*
6/3	Bordeaux	h	1-3	*Ferradj*
12/3	St-Étienne	a	0-2	
19/3	Lille	h	1-2	*Lesoimier*
2/4	Sochaux	a	1-2	*Grougi (p)*
9/4	Rennes	h	2-0	*Roux, Grougi*
16/4	Lens	a	1-1	*Ayité*
24/4	PSG	h	2-2	*Touré, Grougi*
1/5	Montpellier	a	0-0	
7/5	Nice	h	0-0	
11/5	Marseille	a	0-3	
16/5	Lyon	h	1-1	*Lička*
21/5	Auxerre	a	1-0	*Touré*
29/5	Toulouse	h	0-2	

No	Name	Nat	DoB	Pos	Aps	(s)	Gls
7	Jonathan AYITÉ	TOG	21/7/85	A	9	(5)	4
2	Paul BAYSSE		18/5/88	D	29	(2)	1
23	Yoann BIGNÉ		23/8/77	M	4	(5)	
33	Anthony BOVA		7/3/90	A		(2)	
18	Moïse BROU APANGA	GAB	4/2/82	D	28	(2)	
22	Ousmane COULIBALY		9/7/89	D	5	(2)	
25	Omar DAF	SEN	12/2/77	D	28		
28	Filippos DARLAS	GRE	23/10/83	D	2		
1	Steeve ELANA		11/7/80	G	38		
5	Oscar EWOLO	CGO	9/10/78	M	32	(3)	
21	Brahim FERRADJ		4/9/87	M	21	(5)	1
6	Bruno GROUGI		26/4/83	M	25	(8)	9
24	Ahmed KANTARI		28/6/85	D	32		
19	Benoît LESOIMIER		21/2/83	M	28	(5)	2
27	Mario LIČKA	CZE	30/4/82	M	27	(8)	3
7	Grégory LORENZI		17/12/84	D		(2)	
4	Johan MARTIAL		30/5/91	D	7		1
15	Tomáš MIČOLA	CZE	26/9/88	A	10	(7)	1
9	Théophile Junior N'TAMÉ	CMR	17/5/85	D		(2)	
8	Granddi NGOYI		17/5/88	M	17	(8)	
20	Romain POYET		25/11/80	A	24	(8)	4
26	Nolan ROUX		1/3/88	A	26	(2)	6
11	Richard SOUMAH	GUI	6/10/86	M	8	(5)	
10	Larsen TOURÉ	GUI	20/7/84	A	17	(5)	4
17	Fodie TRAORÉ		1/3/85	M	1	(3)	

SM CAEN

Coach – Franck Dumas

Founded – 1919

Stadium – Michel-d'Ornano (22,864)

2010				
7/8	Marseille	a	2-1	*Seube, El-Arabi*
15/8	Lyon	h	3-2	*El-Arabi, Yatabaré, N'Diaye*
22/8	Montpellier	a	0-0	
28/8	Brest	h	0-2	
11/9	Auxerre	a	1-1	*El-Arabi*

3/9	Lorient	a	1-0	*El-Arabi*
/9	Bordeaux	h	0-0	
10	Valenciennes	a	1-2	*El-Arabi*
6/10	Monaco	h	0-0	
3/10	St-Étienne	a	1-1	*El-Arabi*
/10	Nancy	h	2-3	*El-Arabi, Traoré*
11	Arles-Avignon	a	2-3	*El-Arabi, Traoré*
3/11	Lille	h	2-5	*El-Arabi, Traoré*
)/11	PSG	a	1-2	*El-Arabi*
3/11	Sochaux	h	0-3	
12	Toulouse	a	0-1	
/12	Nice	h	0-0	
2/12	Rennes	h	1-0	*Hamouma*

011

5/1	Brest	a	3-1	*Nivet, El-Arabi (p), Hamouma*
2/1	Lens	a	0-2	
9/1	Auxerre	h	2-0	*Nivet, Traoré*
2	Lorient	h	0-2	
2/2	Bordeaux	a	2-1	*Traoré, Hamouma*
9/2	Valenciennes	h	2-2	*Nivet, Yatabaré*
6/2	Monaco	a	2-2	*El-Arabi, Mollo*
/3	St-Étienne	h	1-0	*El-Arabi*
2/3	Nancy	a	0-2	
0/3	Arles-Avignon	h	2-0	*Mollo, El-Arabi*
/4	Lille	a	1-3	*El-Arabi*
/4	PSG	h	1-2	*Hamouma*
6/4	Sochaux	a	2-3	*El-Arabi, Hamouma*
4/4	Toulouse	h	1-1	*Hamouma*
/5	Nice	a	4-0	*Hamouma 2, Mollo, El-Arabi*
/5	Lens	h	1-1	*Niang*
1/5	Rennes	a	1-1	*Niang*
5/5	Montpellier	h	2-0	*Hamouma, Traoré*
1/5	Lyon	a	0-0	
9/5	Marseille	h	2-2	*Mollo, Niang*

No	Name	Nat	DoB	Pos	Aps	(s)	Gls
21	Pablo Maximiliano BARZOLA	ARG	17/11/83	D	11	(1)	
30	Thomas BOSMEL		18/4/88	G	3		
7	Anthony DEROIN		15/3/79	M		(4)	
15	Youssef EL-ARABI	MAR	3/2/87	A	36	(2)	17
20	Romain HAMOUMA		29/3/87	M	31	(1)	9
5	Thomas HEURTAUX		3/7/88	D	29	(2)	
3	Romain INEZ		30/4/88	D	18	(2)	
6	Branko LAZAREVIĆ	SRB	14/5/84	D	4	(1)	
24	Grégory LECA		22/8/80	M	24	(2)	
8	Damien MARCQ		8/12/88	M	22	(6)	
26	Yohan MOLLO		18/7/89	M	27	(8)	4
28	Benjamin MOREL		10/6/87	A	2	(6)	
33	Thibault MOULIN		13/1/90	A	4	(13)	
29	Ismaila N'DIAYE		22/1/88	M	5	(6)	1
11	Livio NABAB		14/6/88	A		(8)	
9	M'Baye NIANG		19/12/94	A	4	(3)	3
10	Benjamin NIVET		2/1/77	M	24	(7)	3
12	Grégory PROMENT		10/12/78	M	6	(1)	
22	Alexandre RAINEAU		21/6/86	M	21	(2)	
2	Nicolas SEUBE		11/8/79	D	29		1
19	Jérémy SORBON		5/8/83	D	24	(1)	
23	Grégory TAFFOREAU		29/9/76	D	16		
1	Alexis THÉBAUX		17/3/85	G	35		
18	Kandia TRAORÉ	CIV	5/7/80	A	24	(14)	6
17	Rajiv VAN LA PARRA	NED	4/6/91	M	1	(5)	
25	Sambou YATABARÉ		3/2/89	M	18	(7)	2

RC LENS

Coach – Jean-Guy Wallemme; (2/1/11) László Bölöni (ROU)

Founded – 1906

Stadium – Félix-Bollaert (41,233)

MAJOR HONOURS: French League – (1) 1998; League Cup – (1) 1999.

2010

7/8	Nancy	h	1-2	*Maoulida*
14/8	Arles-Avignon	a	1-0	*Pollet*
21/8	Monaco	h	2-2	*og (Adriano), Roudet*
28/8	St-Étienne	a	1-3	*Jemâa*
11/9	Lille	h	1-4	*Boukari*
18/9	Valenciennes	a	1-1	*Boukari*
26/9	PSG	h	0-2	
2/10	Sochaux	a	0-3	
17/10	Rennes	h	0-0	
23/10	Nice	h	1-0	*Jemâa*
30/10	Toulouse	a	1-1	*Yahia*
7/11	Montpellier	h	2-0	*Hermach, Akalé*
13/11	Marseille	a	1-1	*Eduardo*
21/11	Lyon	h	1-3	*Akalé*
30/11	Brest	a	1-4	*Eduardo*
4/12	Auxerre	h	1-1	*Yahia*
11/12	Lorient	a	0-3	
22/12	Bordeaux	a	2-2	*Eduardo, Boukari*

2011

15/1	St-Étienne	h	2-1	*Roudet (p), og (Perrin)*
22/1	Caen	h	2-0	*Hermach, Maoulida*
29/1	Lille	a	0-1	
5/2	Valenciennes	h	1-1	*Jemâa*
12/2	PSG	a	0-0	
19/2	Sochaux	h	2-3	*Jemâa, Yahia*
26/2	Rennes	a	0-2	
5/3	Nice	a	0-0	
12/3	Toulouse	h	0-1	
19/3	Montpellier	a	4-1	*Akalé, og (Marveaux), Roudet, Jemâa*
3/4	Marseille	h	0-1	
10/4	Lyon	a	0-3	
16/4	Brest	h	1-1	*Hermach*
29/4	Auxerre	a	1-1	*Roudet*
30/4	Lorient	h	2-3	*Demont, Eduardo*
7/5	Caen	a	1-1	*Varane*
11/5	Bordeaux	h	1-0	*Hermach*
15/5	Monaco	a	1-1	*Varane*
21/5	Arles-Avignon	h	0-1	
29/5	Nancy	a	0-4	

No	Name	Nat	DoB	Pos	Aps	(s)	Gls
28	Kanga AKALÉ	CIV	7/3/81	M	21	(9)	3
3	Serge AURIER		5/12/93	M	24	(3)	
6	Henri BEDIMO	CMR	4/6/84	D	31	(4)	
37	Zakarya BERGDICH	MAR	7/1/89	M	2		
7	Razak BOUKARI	TOG	25/4/87	M	14	(4)	3
24	Eric CHELLE	MLI	11/11/77	D	15	(1)	
40	Alexandre COEFF		20/2/92	M		(1)	
26	Yohan DEMONT		15/5/78	M	30	(3)	1
11	EDUARDO Ribeiro dos Santos	BRA	5/8/80	A	24	(8)	4
20	Adil HERMACH	MAR	27/6/86	D	30	(1)	4
22	Issam JEMÂA	TUN	28/1/84	A	20	(6)	5
15	Steven JOSEPH-MONROSE		20/7/90	M	2	(8)	
16	Hamdi KASRAOUI	TUN	18/1/83	G	6	(1)	
21	Sidi Yaya KEITA	MLI	20/3/85	M	6	(2)	
33	Geoffrey KONDOGBIA		15/2/93	M	1	(2)	
23	Nenad KOVAČEVIĆ	SRB	11/11/80	M	13	(3)	
9	Toifilou MAOULIDA		8/6/79	A	20	(12)	2
22	Kévin MONNET-PACQUET		19/8/88	A	3		
34	Abdelhakrim OMRANI		18/2/91	M		(2)	
29	David POLLET	BEL	12/8/88	A	2	(14)	1
4	Franck QUEUDRUE		27/8/78	D	8	(1)	
2	Marco RAMOS	POR	26/4/83	D	2	(1)	
18	Sébastien ROUDET		16/6/81	M	29	(3)	4
1	Vedran RUNJE	CRO	10/2/76	G	32		
19	Romain SARTRE		12/11/82	D	1		
10	Grégory SERTIC		5/8/89	M	11	(12)	
25	Darnel SITU BUYENTE		18/3/92	D		(1)	
27	Samba SOW	MLI	29/4/89	M	7	(3)	
33	Alassane TOURÉ		9/2/89	D	10	(2)	
14	Raphaël VARANE		25/4/93	D	22	(1)	2
5	Alaeddine YAHIA	TUN	26/9/81	D	32	(2)	3

LOSC LILLE MÉTROPOLE

Coach – Rudi Garcia

Founded – 1944

Stadium – Stadium Lille Métropole (17,754)

MAJOR HONOURS: French League – (3) 1946, 1954, 2011; French Cup – (6) 1946, 1947, 1948, 1953, 1955, 2011.

2010

7/8	Rennes	a	1-1	*Sow*
15/8	PSG	h	0-0	
22/8	Sochaux	a	0-0	
29/8	Nice	h	1-1	*Hazard*
11/9	Lens	a	4-1	*Gervinho 2, Frau 2*
19/9	Auxerre	h	1-0	*Sow*
26/9	Toulouse	a	1-1	*Gervinho*
3/10	Montpellier	h	3-1	*Sow 2, Gervinho*
17/10	Lyon	a	1-3	*Sow*
24/10	Marseille	h	1-3	*Cabaye*
31/10	Valenciennes	a	1-1	*og (Penneteau)*
7/11	Brest	h	3-1	*Sow, Gervinho, Hazard*
13/11	Caen	a	5-2	*Sow 3, Gervinho, Béria*
21/11	Monaco	h	2-1	*Frau, Obraniak*
27/11	Bordeaux	a	1-1	*Sow*
5/12	Lorient	h	6-3	*Sow 3, og (Baca), Gervinho, Frau*
11/12	Arles-Avignon	a	1-0	*Túlio de Melo*
22/12	St-Étienne	h	1-1	*Sow*

2011

15/1	Nice	a	2-0	*Gervinho, Sow*
19/1	Nancy	h	3-0	*Gervinho 2, Hazard*
29/1	Lens	h	1-0	*Túlio de Melo*
6/2	Auxerre	a	1-1	*Sow*
13/2	Toulouse	h	2-0	*Gervinho, Túlio de Melo*
20/2	Montpellier	a	0-1	
27/2	Lyon	h	1-1	*Sow*
6/3	Marseille	a	2-1	*Hazard, Frau*
13/3	Valenciennes	h	2-1	*Sow, Hazard*
19/3	Brest	a	2-1	*Gervinho, Sow*
2/4	Caen	h	3-1	*Chedjou, Hazard, Sow*
9/4	Monaco	a	0-1	
16/4	Bordeaux	h	1-1	*Sow*
24/4	Lorient	a	1-1	*Debuchy*
30/4	Arles-Avignon	h	5-0	*Gervinho 2, Debuchy (p), Cabaye, Rozehnal*
7/5	Nancy	a	1-0	*Hazard*
10/5	St-Étienne	a	2-1	*Túlio de Melo, Mavuba*
18/5	Sochaux	h	1-0	*Gervinho*
21/5	PSG	a	2-2	*Obraniak, Sow*
29/5	Rennes	h	3-2	*Sow 3 (1p)*

No	Name	Nat	DoB	Pos	Aps	(s)	Gls
4	Florent BALMONT		2/2/80	M	26	(1)	
18	Franck BÉRIA		23/5/83	D	25	(2)	1
7	Yohan CABAYE		14/1/86	M	36		2
22	Aurélien CHEDJOU	CMR	20/6/85	M	31	(3)	1
2	Mathieu DEBUCHY		28/7/85	M	35		2
29	Stéphane DUMONT		6/9/82	M	1	(11)	
15	EMERSON da Conceição	BRA	23/2/86	D	17	(3)	
17	Pierre-Alain FRAU		15/4/80	A	10	(19)	5
27	Gervais Yao Kouassi "GERVINHO"	CIV	27/5/87	M	33		15
5	Idrissa GUEYE	SEN	26/9/89	M	2	(9)	
26	Eden HAZARD	BEL	7/1/91	M	35	(3)	7
1	Michaël LANDREAU		14/5/79	G	38		
28	Emil LYNG	DEN	3/8/89	A		(1)	
24	Rio MAVUBA		8/3/84	M	38		1
10	Ludovic OBRANIAK	POL	10/11/84	M	5	(21)	2
23	Adil RAMI		27/12/85	D	36		
14	David ROZEHNAL	CZE	5/7/80	D	10	(3)	1
6	Pape N'Diaye SOUARÉ	SEN	6/6/90	D	1	(3)	
8	Moussa SOW	SEN	19/1/86	A	33	(3)	25
9	TÚLIO Vinícius Fróes DE MELO	BRA	31/1/85	A	5	(24)	4
3	Jerry VANDAM		8/12/88	M	1	(1)	
31	Omar WADE	SEN	15/5/90	A		(1)	

FC LORIENT

Coach – Christian Gourcuff

Founded – 1926

Stadium – Moustoir-Yves-Allainmat (18,110)

MAJOR HONOURS: French Cup – (1) 2002.

2010

7/8	Auxerre	a	2-2	*Diarra, Robert*
14/8	Nice	h	1-2	*Jouffre*
21/8	Marseille	a	0-2	
28/8	Lyon	h	2-0	*Gameiro (p), Kitambala*
12/9	Brest	a	0-0	
18/9	Caen	h	0-1	
25/9	Monaco	h	2-1	*Gameiro, Kitambala*
2/10	Bordeaux	a	0-1	
17/10	Valenciennes	h	2-1	*Gameiro (p), Diarra*
23/10	Nancy	a	0-1	
30/10	Arles-Avignon	h	2-0	*Gameiro, Kitambala*
6/11	St-Étienne	a	2-1	*Gameiro 2*
14/11	PSG	h	1-1	*Kitambala*
20/11	Sochaux	a	0-2	
27/11	Rennes	h	2-0	*Romao, Morel*
5/12	Lille	a	3-6	*Gameiro 2, Kitambala*
11/12	Lens	h	3-0	*Amalfitano, Kitambala, Mvuemba*
18/12	Toulouse	a	0-3	
21/12	Montpellier	h	0-0	

2011

15/1	Lyon	a	0-3	
29/1	Brest	h	2-0	*Gameiro 2*
5/2	Caen	a	2-0	*Amalfitano, Gameiro*
12/2	Monaco	a	1-3	*Gameiro*
19/2	Bordeaux	h	5-1	*Amalfitano, Gameiro 3, Mvuemba (p)*
26/2	Valenciennes	a	0-0	
5/3	Nancy	h	0-0	
12/3	Arles-Avignon	a	3-3	*Amalfitano, Diarra, Gameiro*
19/3	St-Étienne	h	0-0	
2/4	PSG	a	0-0	
9/4	Sochaux	h	1-1	*Morel*
16/4	Rennes	a	2-1	*Gameiro, Coquelin*
24/4	Lille	h	1-1	*Gameiro*
30/4	Lens	a	3-2	*Gameiro 2, Amalfitano (p)*
7/5	Toulouse	h	0-0	
11/5	Montpellier	a	1-3	*Ecuele Manga*
15/5	Marseille	h	2-2	*Koné, Gameiro*
21/5	Nice	a	0-2	
29/5	Auxerre	h	1-2	*Gameiro*

No	Name	Nat	DoB	Pos	Aps	(s)	Gls
18	Morgan AMALFITANO		20/3/85	M	38		5
16	Fabien AUDARD		28/3/78	G	29		
23	Mathias AUTRET		1/3/91	M		(7)	
17	Maxime BACA		2/6/83	D	27	(2)	
6	Grégory BOURILLON		1/7/84	D	32	(1)	
1	Lionel CAPPONE		8/2/79	G	9	(2)	
19	Francis COQUELIN		13/5/91	M	13	(11)	1
11	Sigamary DIARRA	MLI	10/1/84	A	28	(6)	3
21	Cheick DOUKOURE		11/9/92	M	1	(3)	
13	Sebastián DUBARBIER	ARG	19/2/86	A	1	(5)	
5	Bruno ECUELE MANGA	GAB	16/7/88	D	31		1
12	James FANCHONE		21/2/90	A	2	(9)	
9	Kevin GAMEIRO		9/5/87	A	36		22
8	Yann JOUFFRE		23/7/84	M	5	(8)	1
27	Lynel KITAMBALA		26/10/88	A	24	(3)	6
3	Lamine KONÉ		1/2/89	D	5	(2)	1
14	Arnaud LE LAN		22/3/78	D	10	(6)	
30	Benjamin LECOMTE		26/4/81	G		(2)	
22	Kévin MONNET-PAQUET		19/8/88	A	22	(9)	
10	Olivier MONTERRUBIO		8/8/76	M		(1)	
15	Jérémy MOREL		2/4/84	D	28	(1)	2
26	Rémi MULUMBU		2/11/92	M		(1)	
7	Arnold MVUEMBA		28/1/85	M	33	(1)	2
29	Fabien ROBERT		6/1/89	A		(4)	1

	Alaixys ROMAO	TOG	18/1/84	M	33		1
	Franco Sebastián SOSA	ARG	4/4/81	D	11	(2)	
	Gilles SUNU		30/3/91	A		(9)	

OLYMPIQUE LYONNAIS

Coach – Claude Puel

Founded – 1950

Stadium – Gerland (40,494)

MAJOR HONOURS: French League – (7) 2002, 2003, 2004, 2005, 2006, 2007, 2008; French Cup – (4) 1964, 1967, 1973, 2008; League Cup – (1) 2001.

010				
8	Monaco	h	0-0	
5/8	Caen	a	2-3	*Gomis 2*
1/8	Brest	h	1-0	*Makoun*
3/8	Lorient	a	0-2	
1/9	Valenciennes	h	1-1	*Pied*
9/9	Bordeaux	a	0-2	
5/9	St-Étienne	h	0-1	
10	Nancy	a	3-2	*Lisandro López, Briand 2*
7/10	Lille	h	3-1	*Lisandro López 2 (1p), Gourcuff*
4/10	Arles-Avignon	a	1-1	*Briand*
0/10	Sochaux	h	2-1	*Michel Bastos, Lacazette*
/11	Rennes	a	1-1	*Michel Bastos*
4/11	Nice	h	1-0	*Pied*
1/11	Lens	a	3-1	*Gomis 2, Lisandro López*
8/11	PSG	h	2-2	*Cissokho, Gomis*
/12	Montpellier	a	2-1	*Lisandro López 2*
2/12	Toulouse	h	2-0	*Lisandro López, Gomis*
9/12	Marseille	a	1-1	*Lisandro López*
2/12	Auxerre	h	1-1	*og (Mignot)*
011				
5/1	Lorient	h	3-0	*Gomis 2, Källström*
9/1	Valenciennes	a	1-2	*Michel Bastos*
/2	Bordeaux	h	0-0	
2/2	St-Étienne	a	4-1	*Gomis, og (Bayal Sall), Michel Bastos, Briand*
8/2	Nancy	h	4-0	*Gourcuff, Pied, Pjanić, Briand*
7/2	Lille	a	1-1	*Källström*
/3	Arles-Avignon	h	5-0	*Lisandro López 3, Pjanić, Michel Bastos*
2/3	Sochaux	a	2-0	*Lisandro López, Pjanić*
9/3	Rennes	h	1-1	*Gomis*
3/4	Nice	a	2-2	*Källström, Lisandro López*
0/4	Lens	h	3-0	*og (Bedimo), Briand, Lisandro López*
17/4	PSG	a	0-1	
27/4	Montpellier	h	3-2	*Ederson, Lisandro López, Gourcuff*
1/5	Toulouse	a	0-2	
3/5	Marseille	h	3-2	*Lisandro López (p), Delgado, Cris*
11/5	Auxerre	a	0-4	
16/5	Brest	a	1-1	*Ederson*
21/5	Caen	h	0-0	
29/5	Monaco	a	2-0	*Diakhaté, Lisandro López*

No	Name	Nat	DoB	Pos	Aps	(s)	Gls
7	Jimmy BRIAND		2/8/85	A	22	(11)	6
20	Aly CISSOKHO		15/9/87	D	29		1
3	CRIStiano Marques Gomes	BRA	3/6/77	D	20	(1)	1
19	César DELGADO	ARG	18/8/81	A	9	(10)	1
4	Pape DIAKHATÉ	SEN	21/6/84	D	23	(1)	1
10	EDERSON Honorato Campos	BRA	13/1/86	M	5	(3)	2
2	Lamine GASSAMA		20/10/89	D	3	(1)	
18	Bafétimbi GOMIS		6/8/85	A	28	(7)	10
21	Maxime GONALONS		10/3/89	M	15	(8)	
29	Yoann GOURCUFF		11/7/86	M	20	(4)	3
22	Clément GRENIER		7/1/91	M	2	(5)	
6	Kim KÄLLSTRÖM	SWE	24/8/82	M	29	(4)	3
12	Thimothée KOLODZIEJCZAK		1/10/91	D	7	(1)	
38	Alexandre LACAZETTE		28/5/91	A		(9)	1
9	LISANDRO LÓPEZ	ARG	2/3/83	A	24	(3)	17
1	Hugo LLORIS		26/12/86	G	37		
5	Dejan LOVREN	CRO	5/7/89	D	26	(2)	
17	Jean II MAKOUN	CMR	29/5/83	M	11	(2)	1
11	MICHEL Fernandes BASTOS	BRA	2/8/83	M	22	(6)	5
15	Harry NOVILLO		11/2/92	A		(1)	
24	Jérémy PIED		23/2/89	A	7	(18)	3
8	Miralem PJANIĆ	BIH	2/4/90	M	16	(14)	3
48	Enzo REALE		7/10/91	D		(1)	
13	Anthony RÉVEILLÈRE		10/11/79	D	35		
28	Jérémy TOULALAN		10/9/83	M	27	(1)	
30	Rémy VERCOUTRE		26/6/80	G	1	(1)	

OLYMPIQUE DE MARSEILLE

Coach – Didier Deschamps

Founded – 1899

Stadium – Vélodrome (60,031)

MAJOR HONOURS: UEFA Champions League – (1) 1993; French League – (9) 1937, 1948, 1971, 1972, 1989, 1990, 1991, 1992, 2010; French Cup – (10) 1924, 1926, 1927, 1935, 1938, 1943, 1969, 1972, 1976, 1989; League Cup – (2) 2010, 2011.

2010				
7/8	Caen	h	1-2	*Samassa*
14/8	Valenciennes	a	2-3	*Taiwo (p), Ayew A.*
21/8	Lorient	h	2-0	*Heinze, Taiwo*
29/8	Bordeaux	a	1-1	*Lucho González*
12/9	Monaco	h	2-2	*Valbuena, og (Adriano)*
18/9	Arles-Avignon	a	3-0	*Cheyrou, Ayew A. 2*
25/9	Sochaux	h	2-1	*Taiwo, Lucho González*
2/10	St-Étienne	a	1-1	*Gignac*
16/10	Nancy	h	1-0	*Rémy*
24/10	Lille	a	3-1	*Rémy 2, Lucho González*
7/11	PSG	a	1-2	*Lucho González*
13/11	Lens	h	1-1	*Mbia*
20/11	Toulouse	a	1-0	*Ayew A.*
27/11	Montpellier	h	4-0	*Lucho González, Cheyrou, Valbuena, Rémy*
1/12	Rennes	h	0-0	
5/12	Nice	a	0-1	
11/12	Auxerre	a	1-1	*Rémy*
19/12	Lyon	h	1-1	*Valbuena*
22/12	Brest	a	0-0	
2011				
16/1	Bordeaux	h	2-1	*Gignac, Brandão*
30/1	Monaco	a	0-0	
5/2	Arles-Avignon	h	1-0	*Gignac*
12/2	Sochaux	a	2-1	*Gignac 2*
19/2	St-Étienne	h	2-1	*Lucho González, Rémy*
27/2	Nancy	a	2-1	*Ayew A. 2*
6/3	Lille	h	1-2	*Rémy*
11/3	Rennes	a	2-0	*Rémy, Lucho González*
20/3	PSG	h	2-1	*Heinze, Ayew A.*
3/4	Lens	a	1-0	*Cheyrou*
10/4	Toulouse	h	2-2	*Rémy, Gignac*
17/4	Montpellier	a	2-1	*Gignac, Taiwo (p)*
27/4	Nice	h	4-2	*Ayew A. 3, Ayew J.*
1/5	Auxerre	h	1-1	*Valbuena*
8/5	Lyon	a	2-3	*Lucho González, Rémy*
11/5	Brest	h	3-0	*Rémy, Ayew J., Heinze*
15/5	Lorient	a	2-2	*Rémy, Gignac*
21/5	Valenciennes	h	2-2	*Ayew A., Rémy*
29/5	Caen	a	2-2	*Rémy 2*

No	Name	Nat	DoB	Pos	Aps	(s)	Gls
18	Fabrice ABRIEL		6/7/79	M	4	(18)	
20	André AYEW	GHA	17/12/89	A	32	(5)	11
15	Jordan AYEW	GHA	11/9/91	M	5	(17)	2
2	César AZPILICUETA Tanco	ESP	28/8/89	D	12	(3)	
37	Hatem BEN ARFA		7/3/87	M		(1)	
9	Evaeverson Lemos da Silva "BRANDÃO"	BRA	16/6/80	A	13	(6)	1
7	Benoît CHEYROU		3/5/81	M	27	(7)	3

6	Edouard CISSÉ		30/3/78	M	21	(2)	
21	Souleymane DIAWARA	SEN	24/12/78	D	27		
24	Rod FANNI		6/12/81	D	19		
10	André-Pierre GIGNAC		12/5/85	A	20	(10)	8
31	Guy Kassa GNABOUYOU		1/12/89	A		(1)	
19	Gabriel HEINZE	ARG	19/4/78	D	31		3
5	Vittorino HILTON da Silva	BRA	13/9/77	D	6	(2)	
12	Charles KABORÉ	BFA	9/2/88	M	22	(12)	
8	Luis Óscar "LUCHO" GONZÁLEZ	ARG	19/1/81	M	33	(3)	8
27	Pape M'BOW	SEN	22/5/88	D		(1)	
30	Steve MANDANDA		28/3/85	G	38		
17	Stéphane MBIA	CMR	20/5/86	M	24	(2)	1
14	Leyti N'DIAYE	SEN	19/8/85	D	3	(1)	
11	Mamadou NIANG	SEN	13/10/79	A	2		
11	Loïc RÉMY		2/1/87	A	24	(7)	15
4	Julien RODRIGUEZ		11/6/78	D		(1)	
27	Mamadou SAMASSA	MLI	1/5/86	A		(1)	1
3	Taye TAIWO	NGA	16/4/85	D	29	(1)	4
28	Mathieu VALBUENA		28/9/84	M	26	(6)	4

AS MONACO FC

Coach – Guy Lacombe; (10/1/11) Laurent Banide

Founded – 1919

Stadium – Louis II (18,523)

MAJOR HONOURS: French League – (7) 1961, 1963, 1978, 1982, 1988, 1997, 2000; French Cup – (5) 1960, 1963, 1980, 1985, 1991; League Cup – (1) 2003.

2010				
7/8	Lyon	a	0-0	
17/8	Montpellier	h	0-0	
21/8	Lens	a	2-2	*Niculae, Aubameyang*
29/8	Auxerre	h	2-0	*Niculae, Aubameyang*
12/9	Marseille	a	2-2	*Niculae, Park*
18/9	Toulouse	h	0-0	
25/9	Lorient	a	1-2	*Mbokani*
2/10	Brest	h	0-1	
16/10	Caen	a	0-0	
23/10	Valenciennes	h	0-2	
2/11	Bordeaux	h	2-2	*Park, Coutadeur*
7/11	Nancy	a	4-0	*og (Gavanon), og (Lotiès), Park 2*
13/11	Arles-Avignon	h	0-0	
21/11	Lille	a	1-2	*Adriano*
27/11	Nice	h	1-1	*Park (p)*
4/12	Rennes	a	0-1	
12/12	St-Étienne	h	0-2	
18/12	PSG	a	2-2	*Puygrenier, Niculae*
22/12	Sochaux	h	2-1	*Malonga, Park*
2011				
15/1	Auxerre	a	1-1	*Adriano*
30/1	Marseille	h	0-0	
6/2	Toulouse	a	0-2	
12/2	Lorient	h	3-1	*Lolo, Mangani, Park (p)*
19/2	Brest	a	0-2	
26/2	Caen	h	2-2	*Park 2 (1p)*
5/3	Valenciennes	a	0-0	
13/3	Bordeaux	a	1-0	*Adriano*
20/3	Nancy	h	0-1	
2/4	Arles-Avignon	a	2-0	*Moukandjo, Park*
9/4	Lille	h	1-0	*Park*
16/4	Nice	a	2-3	*Gosso, Park (p)*
24/4	Rennes	h	1-0	*Welcome*
1/5	St-Étienne	a	1-1	*Welcome*
7/5	PSG	h	1-1	*Adriano*
11/5	Sochaux	a	0-3	
15/5	Lens	h	1-1	*Moukandjo*
21/5	Montpellier	a	1-0	*Moukandjo*
29/5	Lyon	h	0-2	

No	Name	Nat	DoB	Pos	Aps	(s)	Gls
12	ADRIANO Pereira da Silva	BRA	3/4/82	D	32		4
8	Alejandro ALONSO	ARG	3/3/82	M	3	(1)	
11	Pierre-Emerick AUBAMEYANG	GAB	18/6/89	A	17	(2)	2
5	Laurent BONNART		25/12/79	D	24	(1)	
22	Frédéric BULOT		27/9/90	M	3	(5)	
1	Sébastien CHABBERT		15/5/78	G	4	(2)	
20	Mathieu COUTADEUR		20/6/86	M	11	(7)	1
6	Mahamadou DIARRA	MLI	18/5/81	M	9		
14	Pascal FEINDOUNO	GUI	27/2/81	A	2	(3)	
17	Serge GAKPÉ	TOG	7/5/87	A	2	(8)	
34	Valère GERMAIN		17/4/90	A		(2)	
19	Jean-Jacques GOSSO	CIV	15/3/83	M	18	(4)	1
13	Petter HANSSON	SWE	14/12/76	D	28	(2)	
25	Lukman HARUNA	NGA	4/12/90	M	12	(5)	
29	Layvin KURZAWA		4/9/92	D	5		
27	Grégory LACOMBE		11/1/82	M	4	(4)	
32	Igor LOLO	CIV	22/7/82	D	9	(8)	1
26	Ouwo Moussa MAAZOU	NIG	25/8/88	A		(1)	
26	Kévin MALCUIT		31/7/91	A		(1)	
7	Francis Chris MALONGA Ntsayi	CGO	11/7/87	M	9	(7)	1
15	Thomas MANGANI		29/4/87	D	20	(4)	1
9	Dieumerci MBOKANI	COD	22/11/85	A	9	(1)	1
24	Nampalys MENDY		23/6/92	M	13	(1)	
4	Cédric MONGONGU	COD	22/6/89	D	14	(5)	
11	Benjamin MOUKANDJO	CMR	12/11/88	A	13	(3)	3
23	Vincent MURATORI		3/8/87	D	14	(3)	
3	Nicolas N'KOULOU N'Doubena	CMR	27/3/90	D	26	(4)	
21	Daniel George NICULAE	ROU	6/10/82	A	13	(4)	4
10	PARK Chu-young	KOR	10/7/85	A	32	(1)	12
28	Sébastien PUYGRENIER		28/1/82	D	28	(3)	1
16	Stéphane RUFFIER		27/9/86	G	34		
25	Yannick SAGBO		12/4/88	A		(1)	
18	Djimi TRAORÉ	MLI	1/3/80	D	5	(2)	
9	Georgie WELCOME	HON	9/3/85	A	5	(8)	2

MONTPELLIER HÉRAULT SC

Coach – René Girard

Founded – 1974

Stadium – La Mosson (32,950)

MAJOR HONOURS: French Cup – (1) 1990.

2010				
8/8	Bordeaux	h	1-0	*Bocaly*
17/8	Monaco	a	0-0	
22/8	Caen	h	0-0	
28/8	Valenciennes	a	1-0	*Giroud*
11/9	Nancy	h	1-2	*Estrada*
18/9	St-Étienne	a	0-3	
25/9	Arles-Avignon	h	3-1	*Giroud 2 (1p), Camara*
3/10	Lille	a	1-3	*Giroud (p)*
16/10	Sochaux	h	2-0	*Yanga M'Biwa, Belhanda*
23/10	Rennes	a	1-0	*Marveaux*
31/10	PSG	h	1-1	*Estrada*
7/11	Lens	a	0-2	
13/11	Toulouse	h	1-0	*Giroud*
20/11	Nice	a	1-0	*Giroud*
27/11	Marseille	a	0-4	
4/12	Lyon	h	1-2	*Spahić*
11/12	Brest	a	0-0	
18/12	Auxerre	h	1-1	*Belhanda*
21/12	Lorient	a	0-0	
2011				
15/1	Valenciennes	h	2-1	*Giroud (p), El-Kaoutari*
30/1	Nancy	a	2-1	*Camara, Bocaly*
5/2	St-Étienne	h	1-2	*Martin*
12/2	Arles-Avignon	a	0-0	
20/2	Lille	h	1-0	*Belhanda*
26/2	Sochaux	a	0-0	

	Rennes	h	0-1	
/3	PSG	a	2-2	*Giroud 2*
/3	Lens	h	1-4	*Bocaly*
	Toulouse	a	1-0	*Camara*
/4	Nice	h	1-1	*Dernis*
/4	Marseille	h	1-2	*Giroud*
/4	Lyon	a	2-3	*Giroud, Camara*
	Brest	h	0-0	
	Auxerre	a	0-1	
/5	Lorient	h	3-1	*Giroud, Estrada, Saihi*
/5	Caen	a	0-2	
/5	Monaco	h	0-1	
/5	Bordeaux	a	0-2	

No	Name	Nat	DoB	Pos	Aps	(s)	Gls
	Karim AÏT-FANA		25/2/89	M	9	(10)	
	Romain ARMAND		27/2/87	A		(1)	
	Younes BELHANDA	MAR	25/2/90	M	28	(8)	3
	Garry BOCALY		19/4/88	D	27	(2)	3
	Souleymane CAMARA	SEN	22/12/82	A	28	(8)	4
	Xavier COLLIN		17/8/74	D	2	(1)	
	Geoffrey DERNIS		24/12/80	M	14	(11)	1
	Nenad DŽODIĆ	SRB	4/1/77	D	3		
	Abdelhamid EL-KAOUTARI	MAR	17/3/90	D	18	(7)	1
	Marco ESTRADA	CHI	28/5/83	M	26	(4)	3
	Olivier GIROUD		30/9/86	A	33	(4)	12
	HASAN Kabze	TUR	26/5/82	A	16	(6)	
	Cyril JEUNECHAMP		18/12/75	D	31		
	Geoffrey JOURDREN		4/2/86	G	37		
	Bengali Fodé KOÏTA		21/10/90	A	1	(4)	
	Grégory LACOMBE		11/1/82	M		(3)	
3	Jonas MARTIN		9/4/90	M		(5)	1
	Joris Steve MARVEAUX		15/8/82	D	30	(5)	1
	Laurent PIONNIER		24/5/82	G	1		
4	Romain PITAU		8/8/77	M	27	(3)	
3	Jamel SAIHI	TUN	27/1/87	D	5	(9)	1
	Emir SPAHIĆ	BIH	18/8/80	D	23		1
2	Benjamin STAMBOULI		13/8/90	D	14	(12)	
	John UTAKA	NGA	8/1/82	A	9	(2)	
	Mapou YANGA M'BIWA		15/5/89	D	36		1

AS NANCY-LORRAINE

Coach – Pablo Correa (URU)

Founded – 1967

Stadium – Marcel-Picot (20,085)

MAJOR HONOURS: French Cup – (1) 1978; League Cup – (1) 2006.

010

/8	Lens	a	2-1	*Féret, Bérenguer*
4/8	Rennes	h	0-3	
1/8	Nice	a	1-1	*Alo'o Efoulou*
8/8	Toulouse	h	0-2	
1/9	Montpellier	a	2-1	*Bakar, Traoré*
8/9	Brest	h	0-2	
5/9	Auxerre	a	2-2	*Cuvillier, Vahirua*
/10	Lyon	h	2-3	*André Luiz, Féret*
6/10	Marseille	a	0-1	
3/10	Lorient	h	1-0	*Féret*
0/10	Caen	a	3-2	*Hadji (p), og (Tafforeau), Traoré*
/11	Monaco	h	0-4	
3/11	Bordeaux	a	1-2	*Alo'o Efoulou*
0/11	Valenciennes	h	2-0	*André Luiz, Vahirua*
27/11	St-Étienne	h	1-1	*Vahirua*
/12	Arles-Avignon	a	1-1	*Hadji*
1/12	Sochaux	h	1-0	*André Luiz*
22/12	PSG	h	2-0	*Hadji 2*

2011

15/1	Toulouse	a	0-1	
19/1	Lille	a	0-3	
30/1	Montpellier	h	1-2	*Hadji*
5/2	Brest	a	1-2	*og (Brou Apanga)*
12/2	Auxerre	h	3-1	*Féret, Cuvillier, Hadji*
18/2	Lyon	a	0-4	
27/2	Marseille	h	1-2	*Féret*
5/3	Lorient	a	0-0	
12/3	Caen	h	2-0	*N'Guémo, Traoré*
20/3	Monaco	a	1-0	*André Luiz*
2/4	Bordeaux	h	0-0	
9/4	Valenciennes	a	1-1	*Vahirua*
16/4	St-Étienne	a	1-2	*André Luiz*
24/4	Arles-Avignon	h	0-0	
30/4	Sochaux	a	0-1	
7/5	Lille	h	0-1	
10/5	PSG	a	2-2	*N'Guémo (p), Hadji*
15/5	Nice	h	3-0	*Hadji, Bérenguer, Traoré*
21/5	Rennes	a	2-0	*Traoré, Féret*
29/5	Lens	h	4-0	*Bérenguer 2, Traoré, Vahirua*

No	Name	Nat	DoB	Pos	Aps	(s)	Gls
14	Paul ALO'O EFOULOU	CMR	12/11/83	A	3	(5)	2
5	ANDRÉ LUIZ Silva do Nascimento	BRA	27/1/80	D	34		5
11	Djamel BAKAR		6/4/89	A	10	(10)	1
6	Pascal BÉRENGUER		20/5/81	M	15	(3)	4
1	Gennaro BRACIGLIANO		1/3/80	G	7		
23	Jonathan BRISON		7/2/83	M	28	(6)	
9	Aatif CHAHÉCHOUCHE		2/7/86	M	1	(4)	
20	Michaël CHRÉTIEN	MAR	10/7/84	D	26		
22	Alexandre CUVILLIER		17/6/86	M	17	(8)	2
21	Samba DIAKITÉ		24/1/89	M	16	(7)	
18	Julien FÉRET		5/7/82	M	36		6
24	Benjamin GAVANON		9/8/80	M	16	(7)	
16	Damien GRÉGORINI		2/3/79	G	31		
15	Youssouf HADJI	MAR	25/2/80	M	25	(1)	8
17	Massadio HAÏDARA		2/12/92	D	7	(3)	
33	Ziri HAMMAR	ALG	25/7/92	M		(1)	
34	Benjamin JEANNOT		23/1/92	A	5	(4)	
25	Reynald LEMAÎTRE		28/6/83	M	23	(2)	
8	Jordan LOTIÈS		5/8/84	M	24	(1)	
4	Francis Chris MALONGA Ntsayi	CGO	11/7/87	M		(2)	
29	Alfred N'DIAYE		6/3/90	M	10	(4)	
7	Landry N'GUÉMO	CMR	28/11/85	M	30	(3)	2
33	Fouad RACHID		15/11/91	M		(2)	
3	Joël SAMI	COD	13/11/84	D	20	(3)	
12	Bakaye TRAORÉ	MLI	6/3/85	M	19	(10)	6
19	Marama VAHIRUA		12/5/80	A	15	(10)	5

OGC NICE

Coach – Éric Roy

Founded – 1904

Stadium – Ray (18,696)

MAJOR HONOURS: French League – (4) 1951, 1952, 1956, 1959; French Cup – (3) 1952, 1954, 1997.

2010

7/8	Valenciennes	h	0-0	
14/8	Lorient	a	2-1	*Gacé, Rémy*
21/8	Nancy	h	1-1	*Faé*
29/8	Lille	a	1-1	*Faé (p)*
12/9	Bordeaux	h	2-1	*Mouloungui, Bamogo*
18/9	Sochaux	a	0-4	
25/9	Rennes	h	1-2	*Ljuboja*
3/10	PSG	a	0-0	
17/10	St-Étienne	h	2-1	*Mounier, Ben Saada*
23/10	Lens	a	0-1	
30/10	Auxerre	a	0-2	
7/11	Toulouse	h	2-0	*Ljuboja, Ben Saada*
14/11	Lyon	a	0-1	
20/11	Montpellier	h	0-1	
27/11	Monaco	a	1-1	*Mouloungui*
5/12	Marseille	h	1-0	*Faé*
11/12	Caen	a	0-0	

18/12 Brest h 1-1 *Ljuboja*
22/12 Arles-Avignon a 0-0

2011

15/1 Lille h 0-2
30/1 Bordeaux a 0-2
5/2 Sochaux h 1-0 *Pejčinović*
13/2 Rennes a 0-2
20/2 PSG h 0-3
26/2 St-Étienne a 2-0 *Coulibaly, Mounier*
5/3 Lens h 0-0
12/3 Auxerre h 1-0 *Mouloungui*
19/3 Toulouse a 1-1 *og (Cetto)*
3/4 Lyon h 2-2 *Mouloungui (p), Civelli*
10/4 Montpellier a 1-1 *og (Jourdren)*
16/4 Monaco h 3-2 *Mounier, Civelli, Mouloungui*
27/4 Marseille a 2-4 *Traoré, Civelli*
1/5 Caen h 0-4
7/5 Brest a 0-0
11/5 Arles-Avignon h 3-2 *Ljuboja 2, Clerc*
15/5 Nancy a 0-3
21/5 Lorient h 2-0 *Mouloungui 2*
29/5 Valenciennes a 1-2 *Mouloungui*

No	Name	Nat	DoB	Pos	Aps	(s)	Gls
22	ADEILSON Pereira de Mello	BRA	7/10/85	A		(1)	
10	Mamadou BAGAYOKO	MLI	21/5/79	A	1	(4)	
33	Stéphane BAHOKEN	CMR	28/5/92	A		(1)	
21	Habib BAMOGO	BFA	8/5/82	A	2	(9)	1
7	David BELLION		27/11/82	A	9	(1)	
17	Chaouki BEN SAADA	TUN	1/7/84	A	15	(12)	2
3	Alain CANTAREIL		15/8/83	D	1	(3)	
2	Renato CIVELLI	ARG	14/10/83	D	31		3
29	François CLERC		18/4/83	D	29		1
15	Kafoumba COULIBALY	CIV	26/10/85	M	33	(1)	1
23	Drissa DIAKITÉ	MLI	18/2/85	M	24	(5)	
6	Didier DIGARD		12/7/86	M	21	(3)	
14	Emerse FAÉ	CIV	24/1/84	M	23	(1)	3
18	Ismaël GACÉ		19/9/86	D	12	(6)	1
33	Esmaël GONÇALVES	GNB	25/6/91	A		(1)	
8	David HELLEBUYCK		12/5/79	M	4	(5)	
33	Cyril HENNION		3/1/92	M		(1)	
16	Lionel LETIZI		28/5/73	G	3	(1)	
28	Danijel LJUBOJA	SRB	4/9/78	A	22	(8)	5
19	Larrys MABIALA	COD	8/9/87	D	6	(3)	
37	Kévin MALAGA		24/6/87	D		(1)	
11	Eric MOULOUNGUI	GAB	1/4/84	A	26	(8)	8
26	Anthony MOUNIER		27/9/87	M	33	(1)	3
1	David OSPINA	COL	31/8/88	G	35		
5	Grégory PAISLEY		7/5/77	D	8		
36	Lloyd PALUN	GAB	28/11/88	M	3	(3)	
4	Nemanja PEJČINOVIĆ	SRB	4/11/87	D	32	(1)	1
9	Mickaël POTÉ	BEN	24/9/84	A		(8)	
12	Abeiku QUANSAH	GHA	2/11/90	A		(5)	
11	Loïc RÉMY		2/1/87	A	2		1
27	Julien SABLÉ		11/9/80	M	29	(3)	
24	Mahamane TRAORÉ	MLI	31/8/88	M	14	(9)	1

PARIS SAINT-GERMAIN FC

Coach – Antoine Kombouaré

Founded – 1970

Stadium – Parc des Princes (47,428)

MAJOR HONOURS: UEFA European Cup-Winners' Cup – (1) 1996;
French League – (2) 1986, 1994;
French Cup – (8) 1982, 1983, 1993, 1995, 1998, 2004, 2006, 2010;
League Cup – (3) 1995, 1998, 2008.

2010

7/8 St-Étienne h 3-1 *Mevlüt, og (Janot), Nenê*
15/8 Lille a 0-0
22/8 Bordeaux h 1-2 *Hoarau*
29/8 Sochaux a 1-3 *Hoarau*
11/9 Arles-Avignon h 4-0 *Hoarau, Sakho, Nenê 2*
19/9 Rennes h 0-0
26/9 Lens a 2-0 *og (Bedimo), Nenê*
3/10 Nice h 0-0
16/10 Toulouse a 2-0 *Sakho, Mevlüt*
24/10 Auxerre h 2-3 *Nenê 2 (1p)*
31/10 Montpellier a 1-1 *Giuly*
7/11 Marseille h 2-1 *Mevlüt, Hoarau*
14/11 Lorient a 1-1 *Nenê*
20/11 Caen h 2-1 *Hoarau, Mevlüt*
28/11 Lyon a 2-2 *Nenê, Hoarau (p)*
5/12 Brest h 3-1 *Nenê, Bodmer, Giuly*
11/12 Valenciennes a 2-1 *Nenê 2*
18/12 Monaco h 2-2 *Nenê 2*
22/12 Nancy a 0-2

2011

15/1 Sochaux h 2-1 *Sakho, Giuly*
29/1 Arles-Avignon a 2-1 *Mevlüt 2*
5/2 Rennes a 0-1
12/2 Lens h 0-0
20/2 Nice a 3-0 *Giuly, Hoarau, Armand*
27/2 Toulouse h 2-1 *Armand, og (Gunino)*
5/3 Auxerre a 0-1
13/3 Montpellier h 2-2 *Hoarau, og (Yanga M'Biwa)*
20/3 Marseille a 1-2 *Chantôme*
2/4 Lorient h 0-0
9/4 Caen a 2-1 *Jallet, Chantôme*
17/4 Lyon h 1-0 *Camara*
24/4 Brest a 2-2 *Bodmer, og (Kantari)*
30/4 Valenciennes h 3-1 *Nenê, Bodmer, Sakho*
7/5 Monaco a 1-1 *Mevlüt*
10/5 Nancy h 2-2 *Mevlüt, Camara*
18/5 Bordeaux a 0-1
21/5 Lille h 2-2 *Hoarau, Bodmer*
29/5 St-Étienne a 1-1 *Bodmer (p)*

No	Name	Nat	DoB	Pos	Aps	(s)	Gls
22	Sylvain ARMAND		1/8/80	D	31	(2)	2
25	Jean-Christophe BAHEBECK		1/5/93	A	1	(10)	
12	Mathieu BODMER		22/11/82	M	21	(7)	5
6	Zoumana CAMARA		3/4/79	D	14	(3)	2
2	Marcos Venâncio de Albuquerque "CEARÁ"	BRA	18/6/80	D	14	(6)	
20	Clément CHANTÔME		11/9/87	M	26		2
23	Jérémy CLÉMENT		26/8/84	M	8	(16)	
1	Grégory COUPET		31/12/72	G	15		
30	Apoula Edima ÉDEL	ARM	17/6/86	G	23	(1)	
7	Ludovic GIULY		10/7/76	M	30	(5)	4
9	Guillaume HOARAU		5/3/84	A	31	(2)	9
26	Christophe JALLET		31/10/83	D	35		1
32	Neeskens KEBANO		10/3/92	M	1	(2)	
14	Mateja KEŽMAN	SRB	12/4/79	A		(1)	
35	Loïck LANDRE		5/5/92	M		(1)	
8	Péguy LUYINDULA		25/5/79	A	4	(19)	
4	Claude MAKELELE		18/2/73	M	33		
24	Tripy MAKONDA		24/1/90	M	1	(3)	
21	Jean-Eudes MAURICE		21/6/86	A		(10)	
11	MEVLÜT Erdinç	TUR	25/2/87	A	29	(5)	8
19, 10	Anderson Luis de Carvalho "NENÊ"	BRA	19/7/81	M	35		14
3	Mamadou SAKHO		13/2/90	D	35		4
10	Stéphane SESSEGNON	BEN	1/6/84	M	4	(10)	
5	Siaka TIÉNÉ	CIV	22/2/82	D	27	(2)	
13	Sammy TRAORÉ	MLI	25/2/76	D		(2)	

STADE RENNAIS FC

Coach – Frédéric Antonetti

Founded – 1901

Stadium – Route-de-Lorient (29,778)

MAJOR HONOURS: French Cup – (2) 1965, 1971.

10

	Lille	h	1-1	*Bangoura*
8	Nancy	a	3-0	*Montaño, Brahimi, Bangoura*
8	St-Étienne	h	0-0	
8	Arles-Avignon	a	1-0	*Montaño*
9	Sochaux	h	2-1	*Théophile-Catherine, Mangane*
9	PSG	a	0-0	
9	Nice	a	2-1	*Dalmat, Montaño*
0	Toulouse	h	3-1	*Danzé, Mangane, Marveaux (p)*
/10	Lens	a	0-0	
/10	Montpellier	h	0-1	
1	Lyon	h	1-1	*Kembo-Ekoko*
/11	Auxerre	a	1-2	*Kembo-Ekoko*
/11	Brest	h	2-1	*Kembo-Ekoko, Leroy*
/11	Lorient	a	0-2	
2	Marseille	a	0-0	
2	Monaco	h	1-0	*Montaño (p)*
/12	Bordeaux	a	0-0	
/12	Valenciennes	h	1-0	*Kana-Biyik*
/12	Caen	a	0-1	

11

/1	Arles-Avignon	h	4-0	*Tettey, Brahimi 2, M'Vila (p)*
/1	Sochaux	a	1-5	*Boukari*
2	PSG	h	1-0	*Brahimi*
/2	Nice	h	2-0	*Montaño, Boukari (p)*
/2	Toulouse	a	2-1	*M'Vila, Montaño (p)*
/2	Lens	h	2-0	*Boukari, Montaño*
3	Montpellier	a	1-0	*Boukari*
/3	Marseille	h	0-2	
/3	Lyon	a	1-1	*Théophile-Catherine*
4	Auxerre	h	0-0	
4	Brest	a	0-2	
/4	Lorient	h	1-2	*Dalmat*
/4	Monaco	a	0-1	
)/4	Bordeaux	h	0-0	
5	Valenciennes	a	0-2	
/5	Caen	h	1-1	*Mangane*
5/5	St-Étienne	a	2-1	*Montaño, Leroy*
/5	Nancy	h	0-2	
)/5	Lille	a	2-3	*og (Chedjou), Montaño*

o	Name	Nat	DoB	Pos	Aps	(s)	Gls
	Ismaël BANGOURA	GUI	2/1/85	A	1	(3)	2
2	Razak BOUKARI	TOG	25/4/87	M	18		4
5	John BOYE	GHA	23/4/87	D	8	(2)	
0	Yacine BRAHIMI		8/2/90	M	14	(8)	4
2	Abdoul Razzagui CAMARA		20/2/90	A	5	(19)	
6	Johann CARRASSO		7/5/88	G	1		
)	Stéphane DALMAT		16/2/79	M	30	(3)	2
9	Romain DANZÉ		3/7/86	M	38		1
	Nicolas DOUCHEZ		22/4/80	G	37		
8	Tongo Hamed DOUMBIA		6/8/89	M	9	(10)	
2	Rod FANNI		6/12/81	D	11		
	Asamoah GYAN	GHA	22/11/85	A	2	(1)	
2	Yassine JEBBOUR		24/8/91	M	3	(3)	
3	Franck JULIENNE		7/3/91	A		(1)	
5	Jean-Armel KANA-BIYIK		3/7/89	D	27	(1)	1
1	Jirès KEMBO-EKOKO		8/1/88	A	16	(7)	3
8	Fabien LEMOINE		13/3/87	M	7	(11)	
	Jérôme LEROY		4/11/74	M	22	(12)	2
7	Yann M'VILA		29/6/90	M	37		2
4	Georges MANDJECK	CMR	9/12/88	M	7	(15)	
	Abdou Kader MANGANE	SEN	23/3/83	D	29		3
3	Sylvain MARVEAUX		15/4/86	M	9	(1)	1
21	Víctor Hugo MONTAÑO	COL	1/5/84	A	31	(1)	9
13	Samuel SOUPRAYEN		18/2/89	D	14	(2)	
5	Alexander TETTEY	NOR	4/4/86	M	15	(2)	1
26	Kévin THÉOPHILE-CATHERINE		28/10/89	M	25	(1)	2
19	John VERHOEK	NED	25/3/89	A	2	(5)	

AS SAINT-ÉTIENNE

Coach – Christophe Galtier

Founded – 1933

Stadium – Geoffroy-Guichard (35,616)

MAJOR HONOURS: French League – (10) 1957, 1964, 1967, 1968, 1969, 1970, 1974, 1975, 1976, 1981;
French Cup – (6) 1962, 1968, 1970, 1974, 1975, 1977.

2010

7/8	PSG	a	1-3	*Payet*
14/8	Sochaux	h	3-2	*og (Sauget), Perrin 2*
21/8	Rennes	a	0-0	
28/8	Lens	h	3-1	*Payet 3*
11/9	Toulouse	a	1-0	*Batlles*
18/9	Montpellier	h	3-0	*Payet 2, Rivière*
25/9	Lyon	a	1-0	*Payet*
2/10	Marseille	h	1-1	*Batlles*
17/10	Nice	a	1-2	*Payet (p)*
23/10	Caen	h	1-1	*Rivière*
30/10	Brest	a	0-2	
6/11	Lorient	h	1-2	*Sako*
20/11	Auxerre	h	1-1	*Perrin*
27/11	Nancy	a	1-1	*Perrin*
1/12	Valenciennes	a	1-1	*Rivière*
5/12	Bordeaux	h	2-2	*Ébondo, Bocanegra*
12/12	Monaco	a	2-0	*Batlles, Sako*
18/12	Arles-Avignon	h	2-0	*Batlles, Rivière*
22/12	Lille	a	1-1	*Sako (p)*

2011

15/1	Lens	a	1-2	*og (Chelle)*
29/1	Toulouse	h	2-1	*Sako 2*
5/2	Montpellier	a	2-1	*Rivière 2*
12/2	Lyon	h	1-4	*Bocanegra*
19/2	Marseille	a	1-2	*Landrin*
26/2	Nice	h	0-2	
5/3	Caen	a	0-1	
12/3	Brest	h	2-0	*Sako (p), Payet*
19/3	Lorient	a	0-0	
3/4	Valenciennes	h	1-1	*Payet*
9/4	Auxerre	a	2-2	*Rivière, Aubameyang*
16/4	Nancy	h	2-1	*Payet 2*
24/4	Bordeaux	a	0-2	
1/5	Monaco	h	1-1	*Payet*
7/5	Arles-Avignon	a	1-0	*Alonso (p)*
10/5	Lille	h	1-2	*Rivière*
15/5	Rennes	h	1-2	*Sako*
21/5	Sochaux	a	1-2	*Aubameyang*
29/5	PSG	h	1-1	*Guilavogui*

No	Name	Nat	DoB	Pos	Aps	(s)	Gls
8	Alejandro ALONSO	ARG	3/3/82	M	11	(3)	1
15	Yohann ANDREU		3/5/89	D		(1)	
11	Pierre-Emerick AUBAMEYANG	GAB	18/6/89	A	8	(6)	2
10	Laurent BATLLES		23/9/75	M	22	(10)	4
26	Mustapha BAYAL SALL	SEN	30/11/85	D	19		
28	Yohan BENALOUANE		28/3/87	D		(1)	
9	Gonzalo Rubén BERGESSIO	ARG	20/7/84	A	5	(11)	
3	Carlos BOCANEGRA	USA	25/5/79	D	34		2
22	Albin ÉBONDO		23/2/84	D	29	(1)	1
31	Faouzi GHOULAM		1/2/91	M	10	(2)	
27	Josua GUILAVOGUI		19/9/90	M	17	(5)	1
16	Jérémie JANOT		11/10/77	G	36		
19	Christophe LANDRIN		30/6/77	M	11	(14)	1
5	Sylvain MARCHAL		10/2/80	D	19		
12	Blaise MATUIDI		9/4/87	M	34		
6	Sylvain MONSOREAU		20/3/81	D	30	(1)	
30	Jessy MOULIN		13/1/86	G	2	(1)	
8	Guirane NDAW	SEN	24/4/84	M	2	(3)	
27	Loris NÉRY		5/2/91	D	10	(4)	
7	Dimitri PAYET		29/3/87	A	28	(5)	13
24	Loïc PERRIN		7/8/85	M	27		4
21	Yoric RAVET		12/9/89	M		(2)	
29	Emmanuel RIVIÈRE		3/3/90	A	31	(4)	8
33	Idriss SAADI		8/2/92	A		(9)	
11	Bakary SAKO		26/4/88	M	32	(6)	7
18	Boubacar SANOGO	CIV	17/12/82	A	1	(12)	

FC SOCHAUX-MONTBÉLIARD

Coach – Francis Gillot

Founded – 1928

Stadium – Auguste-Bonal (20,005)

MAJOR HONOURS: French League – (2) 1935, 1938; French Cup – (2) 1937, 2007; League Cup – (1) 2004.

2010				
7/8	Arles-Avignon	h	2-1	*Butin, Faty*
14/8	St-Étienne	a	2-3	*Boudebouz, Martin*
22/8	Lille	h	0-0	
29/8	PSG	h	3-1	*Maïga, Brown, Perquis*
11/9	Rennes	a	1-2	*Perquis*
18/9	Nice	h	4-0	*Brown, Boudebouz, Martin, Maïga*
25/9	Marseille	a	1-2	*Maurice-Belay*
2/10	Lens	h	3-0	*Maïga, Brown, Perquis*
16/10	Montpellier	a	0-2	
23/10	Toulouse	h	1-3	*Tulasne*
30/10	Lyon	a	1-2	*Brown*
6/11	Auxerre	h	1-1	*Maïga*
13/11	Brest	a	1-1	*Brown*
20/11	Lorient	h	2-0	*Maïga, Brown*
28/11	Caen	a	3-0	*Perquis, Brown, Maurice-Belay*
4/12	Valenciennes	h	2-1	*Carlão, Maïga*
11/12	Nancy	a	0-1	
19/12	Bordeaux	h	1-1	*Brown*
22/12	Monaco	a	1-2	*og (Lolo)*
2011				
15/1	PSG	a	1-2	*Maïga*
29/1	Rennes	h	5-1	*Maïga 2, Martin, Brown, Boudebouz (p)*
5/2	Nice	a	0-1	
12/2	Marseille	h	1-2	*Brown*
19/2	Lens	a	3-2	*Maurice-Belay, Maïga, Boudebouz*
26/2	Montpellier	h	0-0	
5/3	Toulouse	a	1-0	*Maïga*
12/3	Lyon	h	0-2	
19/3	Auxerre	a	0-2	
2/4	Brest	h	2-1	*Boudebouz (p), Brown*
9/4	Lorient	a	1-1	*Dramé*
16/4	Caen	h	3-2	*Dramé, Maïga 2*
24/4	Valenciennes	a	1-1	*og (Ducourtioux)*
30/4	Nancy	h	1-0	*Butin*
7/5	Bordeaux	a	4-0	*Brown 2, Perquis, Boudebouz*
11/5	Monaco	h	3-0	*Sauget, Maïga, Boudebouz*
18/5	Lille	a	0-1	
21/5	St-Étienne	h	2-1	*Brown 2*
29/5	Arles-Avignon	a	3-1	*Boudebouz (p), Nogueira, Maïga*

No	Name	Nat	DoB	Pos	Aps	(s)	Gls
6	Kévin ANIN		5/7/86	M	23	(1)	
18	Cédric BAKAMBU		11/4/91	A		(9)	
10	Ryad BOUDEBOUZ	ALG	19/2/90	M	37	(1)	8
13	Jérémie BRÉCHET		14/8/79	D	20		
12	Ideye Aide BROWN	NGA	10/10/88	A	33	(2)	15
20	Edouard BUTIN		16/6/88	A	5	(13)	2
8	Carlos Roberto da Cruz Júnior "CARLÃO"	BRA	19/1/86	M	19	(5)	1
1	Pierrick CROS		23/6/91	G	13		
4	Boukary DRAMÉ	SEN	22/7/85	D	23	(3)	2
30	Mathieu DREYER		20/3/89	G	10	(1)	
19	Jacques FATY	SEN	25/2/84	D	23	(1)	1
17	Maxime JOSSE		21/3/87	D	6	(5)	
15	Modibo MAÏGA	MLI	3/9/86	A	35	(1)	15
14	Marvin MARTIN		10/6/88	M	37		3
11	Nicolas MAURICE-BELAY		19/4/85	A	31	(6)	3
22	Yassine MIKARI	TUN	9/1/83	D	5	(1)	
21	Vincent NOGUEIRA		16/1/88	M	4	(19)	1
16	Damien PERQUIS		10/4/84	D	35		5
29	Mathieu PEYBERNES		21/10/90	D	4	(4)	
27	Loïc POUJOL		27/2/89	M	1	(6)	
28	RAFAËL Marques DIAS Brito	POR	29/1/91	A		(2)	
16	Teddy RICHERT		21/9/74	G	15		
23	David SAUGET		23/11/79	D	38		1
25	Václav SVĚRKOŠ	CZE	1/11/83	A		(4)	
7	Geoffrey TULASNE		24/2/88	M	1	(14)	1

TOULOUSE FC

Coach – Alain Casanova

Founded – 1970

Stadium – Stadium de Toulouse (35,472)

2010				
7/8	Brest	h	2-0	*Braaten, Paulo Machado (p)*
15/8	Bordeaux	a	2-1	*Braaten, Didot*
21/8	Arles-Avignon	h	2-1	*Braaten, Didot*
28/8	Nancy	a	2-0	*Capoue, Tabanou*
11/9	St-Étienne	h	0-1	
18/9	Monaco	a	0-0	
26/9	Lille	h	1-1	*Devaux*
3/10	Rennes	a	1-3	*Sissoko*
16/10	PSG	h	0-2	
23/10	Sochaux	a	3-1	*Congré 2, Cetto*
30/10	Lens	h	1-1	*Paulo Machado (p)*
7/11	Nice	a	0-2	
13/11	Montpellier	a	0-1	
20/11	Marseille	h	0-1	
28/11	Auxerre	a	2-1	*Braaten, Santander*
4/12	Caen	h	1-0	*Santander*
12/12	Lyon	a	0-2	
18/12	Lorient	h	3-0	*Paulo Machado 2 (1p), Santander*
22/12	Valenciennes	a	1-2	*Sissoko*
2011				
15/1	Nancy	h	1-0	*Tabanou*
29/1	St-Étienne	a	1-2	*Tabanou*
6/2	Monaco	h	2-0	*Sissoko 2*
13/2	Lille	a	0-2	
20/2	Rennes	h	1-2	*og (Théophile-Catherine)*
27/2	PSG	a	1-2	*Tabanou*
5/3	Sochaux	h	0-1	
12/3	Lens	a	1-0	*Santander*
19/3	Nice	h	1-1	*Santander*
2/4	Montpellier	h	0-1	
10/4	Marseille	a	2-2	*Braaten, Cetto*
16/4	Auxerre	h	0-1	
24/4	Caen	a	1-1	*Sissoko (p)*
1/5	Lyon	h	2-0	*Cetto, og (Cissokho)*
7/5	Lorient	a	0-0	
11/5	Valenciennes	h	0-0	
15/5	Arles-Avignon	a	0-1	
21/5	Bordeaux	h	2-0	*Cetto, Capoue*
29/5	Brest	a	2-0	*Pentecôte 2*

No	Name	Nat	DoB	Pos	Aps	(s)	Gls
40	Ali AHAMADA		14/7/90	G	8	(1)	
26	Wissam BEN YEDDER		12/8/90	M		(4)	
25	Daniel Omoya BRAATEN	NOR	25/5/82	M	21	(11)	5
29	Étienne CAPOUE		11/7/88	M	37		2
4	Mauro CETTO	ARG	14/4/82	D	25		4
3	Daniel CONGRÉ		5/4/85	D	37		2
6	Antoine DEVAUX		21/2/85	M	23	(5)	1
8	Étienne DIDOT		24/7/83	M	36		2
2	Mohamed FOFANA		7/3/85	D	21		
10	André-Pierre GIGNAC		5/12/85	A	1		
21	Adrián Javier GUNINO	URU	3/2/89	D	29		
18	Søren LARSEN	DEN	6/9/81	A		(2)	
12	Cheikh M'BENGUÉ	SEN	23/7/88	D	25		
7	Fodé MANSARÉ	GUI	3/9/81	M	6	(19)	
13	Dany NOUNKEU	CMR	11/4/86	D		(1)	
5	PAULO Ricardo Ribeiro de Jesus MACHADO	POR	31/3/86	M	29	(4)	4
9	Xavier PENTECÔTE		13/8/86	A	2	(4)	2
33	Adrien REGATTIN		22/8/91	M		(3)	
11	Federico Javier SANTANDER	PAR	4/6/91	A	18	(5)	5
14	François SIRIEIX		7/10/80	M	1	(11)	
22	Moussa SISSOKO		16/8/89	M	32	(4)	5
32	Amadou SOUKOUNA		21/6/92	A	1	(1)	

Franck TABANOU		30/1/89	M	32	(2)	4
Yannis TAFER		11/2/91	A	4	(12)	
Matthieu VALVERDE		14/5/83	G	29		
Marc VIDAL		3/6/91	G	1	(1)	

VALENCIENNES FC

Coach – Philippe Montanier
Founded – 1913
Stadium – Nungesser (16,547)

10				
	Nice	a	0-0	
/8	Marseille	h	3-2	*Danic, Pujol 2*
/8	Auxerre	a	1-1	*Danic*
/8	Montpellier	h	0-1	
/9	Lyon	a	1-1	*Bong*
/9	Lens	h	1-1	*Samassa*
/9	Brest	a	0-1	
10	Caen	h	2-1	*Pujol, Samassa*
/10	Lorient	a	1-2	*Danic*
/10	Monaco	a	2-0	*Pujol 2*
/10	Lille	h	1-1	*Pujol*
11	Bordeaux	a	1-1	*Ducourtioux*
/11	Nancy	a	0-2	
/11	Arles-Avignon	h	3-0	*Pujol, Sánchez, Danic*
12	St-Étienne	h	1-1	*Danic*
12	Sochaux	a	1-2	*Sánchez*
/12	PSG	h	1-2	*Aboubakar*
3/12	Rennes	a	0-1	
2/12	Toulouse	h	2-1	*Angoua, Danic*
011				
5/1	Montpellier	a	1-2	*Dossevi*
9/1	Lyon	h	2-1	*Biševac (p), Pujol*
2	Lens	a	1-1	*Dossevi*
3/2	Brest	h	3-0	*Ducourtioux, Biševac, Pujol*
9/2	Caen	a	2-2	*Pujol, Langil*
6/2	Lorient	h	0-0	
3	Monaco	h	0-0	
3/3	Lille	a	1-2	*Pujol*
9/3	Bordeaux	h	2-2	*Danic 2*
4	St-Étienne	a	1-1	*Pujol*
4	Nancy	h	1-1	*Pujol*
7/4	Arles-Avignon	a	1-0	*Pujol*
4/4	Sochaux	h	1-1	*Kadir*
0/4	PSG	a	1-3	*Pujol*
/5	Rennes	h	2-0	*Kadir, Danic*
1/5	Toulouse	a	0-0	
5/5	Auxerre	h	1-1	*Kadir*
1/5	Marseille	a	2-2	*Kadir, Gomis*
9/5	Nice	h	2-1	*Pujol 2*

o	Name	Nat	DoB	Pos	Aps	(s)	Gls
	Vincent ABOUBAKAR	CMR	22/1/92	A	4	(13)	1
0	Benjamin ANGOUA	CIV	28/11/86	D	30	(1)	1
	Dianbobo BALDÉ	GUI	5/10/75	D	12	(3)	
	Fahid BEN KHALFALLAH	TUN	9/10/82	M	2	(1)	
	Milan BIŠEVAC	SRB	31/8/83	D	32		2
3	Lilian BOCHET		4/3/91	M		(1)	
4	Gaëtan BONG	CMR	25/4/88	D	22		1
6	Renaud COHADE		29/9/84	M	27	(4)	
3	Gaël DANIC		19/11/81	M	31	(5)	9
10	Mathieu DOSSEVI		12/2/88	M	17	(7)	2
2	David DUCOURTIOUX		11/4/78	D	33	(4)	2
12	Rémi GOMIS	SEN	14/2/84	M	26	(3)	1
33	Nicolas ISIMAT MIRIN		15/11/91	D	6	(4)	
14	Foued KADIR	ALG	5/12/83	A	11	(1)	4
11	Steeven LANGIL		4/3/88	M		(7)	1
16	Jean-Louis LECA		21/9/85	G		(1)	
22	Guillaume LORIOT		21/5/86	M	3	(1)	
34	Francis Kama MASSAMPU		26/12/91	A		(2)	
25	Rudy MATER		13/10/80	D	26	(3)	
19	NAM Tae-hee	KOR	3/7/91	M	11	(7)	
21	Nicolas PALLOIS		19/9/87	D	4	(7)	
1	Nicolas PENNETEAU		20/2/81	G	38		
28	Grégory PUJOL		25/1/80	A	33		17
5	RAFAEL Schmitz	BRA	17/12/80	D	3	(2)	
23	José SAEZ		7/5/82	M	11	(8)	
27	Mamadou SAMASSA	MLI	1/5/86	A	9	(9)	2
17	Carlos Alberto SÁNCHEZ	COL	6/2/86	M	27	(1)	2

TOP GOALSCORERS 2010/11

25	Moussa SOW (Lille)
22	Kevin GAMEIRO (Lorient)
17	Youssef EL-ARABI (Caen)
	LISANDRO LÓPEZ (Lyon)
	Grégory PUJOL (Valenciennes)
16	Loïc RÉMY (Nice/Marseille)
15	GERVINHO (Lille)
	Ideye BROWN (Sochaux)
	Modibo MAÏGA (Sochaux)
14	NENÊ (PSG)

PROMOTED CLUBS

ÉVIAN THONON GAILLARD FC

Coach – Bernard Casoni
Founded – 2009
Stadium – Parc des Sports d'Annecy (12,000)

AC AJACCIO

Coach – Olivier Pantaloni
Founded – 1910
Stadium –François-Coty (8,219)

DIJON FCO

Coach – Patrice Carteron
Founded – 1998
Stadium – Parc des Sports Gaston-Gérard (15,995)

SECOND LEVEL FINAL TABLE 2010/11

		Pld	W	D	L	F	A	Pts
1	Évian Thonon Gaillard FC	38	18	13	7	63	41	67
2	AC Ajaccio	38	17	13	8	45	37	64
3	Dijon FCO	38	17	11	10	55	40	62
4	Le Mans FC	38	17	11	10	48	37	62
5	CS Sedan Ardennes	38	15	14	9	57	37	59
6	Angers SCO	38	14	15	9	41	32	57
7	Clermont Foot Auvergne	38	12	16	10	51	49	52
8	US Boulogne CO	38	13	13	12	35	41	52
9	Le Havre AC	38	12	13	13	43	38	49
10	Stade de Reims	38	12	13	13	53	51	49
11	FC Istres	38	12	13	13	45	47	49
12	Tours FC	38	13	10	15	52	59	49
13	FC Nantes	38	11	14	13	38	40	47
14	LB Châteauroux	38	12	11	15	41	47	47
15	Stade Lavallois MFC	38	11	14	13	36	43	47
16	ES Troyes AC	38	13	7	18	35	45	46
17	FC Metz	38	10	15	13	43	40	45
18	Vannes OC	38	12	8	18	39	61	44
19	Nîmes Olympique	38	9	10	19	35	46	37
20	Grenoble Foot 38	38	7	12	19	36	60	33

DOMESTIC CUPS 2010/11

COUPE DE FRANCE

1/32 FINALS

(7/1/11)
Toulouse 1, Paris FC 2

(8/1/11)
Angers 2, Valenciennes 1 *(aet)*
Arles-Avignon 1, Sedan 1 *(aet; 2-4 on pens)*
Avranches 1, Fontenay 3
Bordeaux 3, Rouen 1
Caen 0, Lyon 1
Chambéry 1, Monaco 1 *(aet; 3-2 on pens)*
Chauvigny 1, Le Mans 3
Cherbourg 1, Le Poiré-sur-Vie 0
Créteil 1, Nice 1 *(aet; 5-6 on pens)*
Forbach 1, Lille 3
Jarville 0, Sochaux 1
Lorient 4, Vannes 1
Montagnarde 0, Drancy 0 *(aet; 6-7 on pens)*
Nantes 3, Cognac 1
Nîmes 3, Fréjus-St-Raphaël 2
PSG 5, Lens 1
Poissy 1, Strasbourg 2
Reims 1, Montpellier 0
St-Étienne 0, Clermont 2
Trélissac 0, Quevilly 1
Troyes 2, Metz 3 (aet)
Wasquehal 2, Auxerre 1

(9/1/11)
Agen 2, Poitiers 0
Aurillac 2, Nancy 2 *(aet; 3-4 on pens)*
Boulogne 2, Amiens 2 *(aet; 5-4 on pens)*
Évian 3, Marseille 1
Issy-les-Moulineaux 0, Brest 1 *(aet)*
Martigues 2, Cheminots Paray 1
Raon-l'Étape 4, Sézanne 0
Rennes 7, Cannes 0

(15/1/11)
Vaulx-en-Velin 1, Jura Sud 1 *(aet; 5-4 on pens)*

1/16 FINALS

(21/1/11)
Sochaux 2, Paris FC 1

(22/1/11)
Angers 1, Bordeaux 0
Boulogne 0, Drancy 1
Chambéry 1, Brest 1 *(aet; 4-3 on pens)*
Cherbourg 0, Le Mans 1
Clermont 1, Reims 3
Fontenay 0, Lorient 1 *(aet)*
Nantes 2, Raon l'Étape 1
Nîmes 1, Nancy 2 *(aet)*
Quevilly 1, Martigues 1 *(aet; 3-5 on pens)*
Strasbourg 1, Évian 0

(23/1/11)
Agen 2, PSG 3
Lille 1, Wasquehal 0
Nice 1, Lyon 0 *(aet)*
Sedan 0, Metz 1
Vaulx-en-Velin 0, Rennes 2

1/8 FINALS

(1/2/11)
Angers 2, Strasbourg 0
Lorient 3, Metz 0
Rennes 3, Reims 4 *(aet)*

(2/2/11)
Chambéry 2, Sochaux 1
Drancy 0, Nice 1
Lille 1, Nantes 1 *(aet; 3-2 on pens)*
Martigues 1, PSG 4
Nancy 1, Le Mans 2

QUARTER-FINALS

(1/3/11)
Reims 2 *(Amalfitano 32, Fortes 58)*, Nice *(Ljuboja 31, Mouloungui 49, 114) (aet)*

(2/3/11)
Chambéry 0, Angers 3 *(Saivet 45+1, Renouard 63, Gómez 84)*
Lille 0, Lorient 0 *(aet; 5-3 on pens)*
PSG 2 *(Bahebeck 108, Kebano 117)*, Le Mans 0 *(aet)*

SEMI-FINALS

(19/4/11)
Nice 0, Lille 2 *(Hazard 44, Gervinho 46)*

(20/4/11)
Angers 1 *(Renouard 57)*, PSG 3 *(Bodmer 22, Nenê 51, Hoarau 62)*

FINAL

(14/5/11)
Stade de France, Saint-Denis
LOSC LILLE MÉTROPOLE 1 *(Obraniak 90)*
PARIS SAINT-GERMAIN FC 0
Referee – *Turpin*
LILLE – *Landreau, Debuchy, Rami, Chedjou, Béria, Mavuba, Gueye (Túlio de Melo 63), Cabaye, Gervinho, Hazard (Dumont 89), Sow (Obraniak 79).*
PSG – *Coupet, Ceará, Camara, Sakho, Tiéné, Chantôme, Makelele (Clément 48), Giuly (Traoré 90), Bodmer (Mevlüt 69), Nenê, Hoarau.*

COUPE DE LA LIGUE

QUARTER-FINALS

(9/11/10)
Auxerre 2 *(Pedretti 16p, Dudka 49p)*, St-Étienne 0

(10/11/10)
Marseille 2 *(Ayew A. 42, Azpilicueta 60)*, Monaco 1 *(Coutadeur 22p)*
Montpellier 2 *(Hasan 28, 52)*, Lille 1 *(Hazard 68)*
Valenciennes 1 *(Dossevi 3)*, PSG 3 *(Camara 9, Jallet 27, Luyindula 51)*

SEMI-FINALS

(18/1/11)
Montpellier 1 *(Giroud 118)*, PSG 0 *(aet)*

(19/1/11)
Auxerre 0, Marseille 2 *(Brandão 45+2, Gignac 68)*

FINAL

(23/4/11)
Stade de France, Saint-Denis
OLYMPIQUE DE MARSEILLE 1 *(Taiwo 80)*
MONTPELLIER HÉRAULT SC 0
Referee – *Gautier*
MARSEILLE – *Mandanda, Fanni, Diawara, Heinze, Taiwo, Mbia (Kaboré 7), Cheyrou, Lucho González (Abriel 85), Valbuena (Ayew J. 90), Ayew A., Gignac.*
MONTPELLIER – *Pionnier, Bocaly, Yanga M'Biwa, Stambouli, Jeunechamp, Marveaux (Koïta 89), Pitau (Hasan 73), Belhanda, Saihi, Giroud, Camara (Dernis 83).*

CLUB COMMUNICATION 2011/12

C Ajaccio
ade François Coty, ZI du Vazzio, François
ty stadium, FR-20090 Ajaccio

l	+33 4 9520 3252
x	+33 4 9510 0165
eb	ac-ajaccio.com
nail	contact@ac-ajaccio.com
edia Officer	Patrick Vernet

J Auxerre
P 349, Route de Vaux, Stade Abbé
eschamps, FR-89006 Auxerre Cédex

el	+33 3 8672 3232
ax	+33 3 8652 2087
eb	aja.fr
mail	c.rollet@aja.tm.fr
edia Officer	Baptiste Malherbe

C Girondins de ordeaux
ue Joliot-Curie, "Jacques Chaban-Delmas"
adium, FR-33187 Le Haillan Cédex

el	+33 8 9268 3433
ax	+33 5 5628 8334
eb	girondins.com
mail	cberteau@girondins.com
edia Officer	Aurélie Carrey

tade Brestois 29
70 bis rue Alain Colas, Port de plaisance
R-29229 Brest

el	+33 2 9802 2030
ax	+33 2 9802 2741
Veb	sb29.com
mail	
ledia Officer	Régis Lerat

SM Caen
.P. 6138, Boulevard Georges Pompidou,
our 8-9, FR-14064 Caen Cedex

Tel	+33 2 3171 7200
Fax	+33 2 3173 6746
Web	smcaen.fr
Email	
Media Officer	Alexandre Lucas

Dijon FCO
Stade des Poussots, 9, Rue Ernest
Champaux, FR-21000 Dijon

Tel	+33 3 8065 0965
Fax	+33 3 8065 0208
Web	dfco.fr
Email	
Media Officer	Hélène Perdriat

Évian Thonon Gaillard FC
56 avenue du Général de Gaulle,
BP 60122, FR-74207 Thonon-les-Bains

Tel	+33 4 5070 3437
Fax	+33 4 5070 8765
Web	etgfc.com
Email	infos@etgfc.com
Media Officer	Julian Dupraz

LOSC Lille Métropole
Domaine de Luchin, Grand Rue BP 79,
Camphin en Pévèle, FR-59780 Lille

Tel	+33 3 2017 7177
Fax	+33 3 2017 7178
Web	losc.fr
Email	losc@losc.fr
Media Officer	Laetitia Masson

FC Lorient
Stade du Moustoir
FR-56323 Lorient Cedex

Tel	+33 2 97351500
Fax	+33 2 97351502
Web	fclweb.fr
Email	contact@fclweb.fr
Media Officer	Simon Rabaud

Olympique Lyonnais
Avenue Jean Jaurès 350
FR-69007 Lyon

Tel	+33 4 2629 6700
Fax	+33 4 2629 6723
Web	olweb.fr
Email	achambon@olympiquelyonnais.com
Media Officer	Pierre Bideau

Olympique de Marseille
Centre d'entraînement Robert Louis-Dreyfus,
33 Traverse de la Martine, FR-13012 Marseille

Tel	+33 4 9176 5609
Fax	+33 4 9176 9129
Web	om.net
Email	info@omfr.com
Media Officer	Alexandre Rosee

Montpellier Hérault SC
Domaine de Grammont, CS 79041
FR-34967 Montpellier

Tel	+33 4 6715 4600
Fax	+33 4 6715 4626
Web	mhscfoot.com
Email	accueil@mhscfoot.com
Media Officer	Katia Mourad

AS Nancy-Lorraine
Boulevard Jean-Jaurès 90, Stade Marcel-
Picot, FR-54510 Tomblaine

Tel	+33 3 8318 3090
Fax	+33 3 8318 3092
Web	asnl.net
Email	nhumblot@asnl.net
Media Officer	Emmanuel Lafrogne

OGC Nice
Route de Grenoble 177, Parc des Sports
Charles Ehrmann, Stade du Ray
FR-06200 Nice

Tel	+33 8 9270 0238
Fax	+33 4 9318 0679
Web	ogcnice.com
Email	pascale.marrel@ogcnice.com
Media Officer	Virginie Rossetti

Paris Saint-Germain FC
Rue du Commandant Guilbaud 24
FR-75016 Paris

Tel	+33 1 4743 7171
Fax	+33 1 4230 5027
Web	psg.fr
Email	psg@psg.tm.fr
Media Officer	Mathias Barbera

Stade Rennais FC
CS 53909
FR-35 039 Rennes Cedex

Tel	+33 8 2000 0035
Fax	+33 2 9914 3577
Web	staderennais.com
Email	contact@staderennais.fr
Media Officer	Jérôme Poupard

AS Saint-Étienne
11 rue de Verdun, Stade Geoffroy Guichard
FR-42580 L'Etrat

Tel	+33 4 7792 9899
Fax	+33 4 7792 3182
Web	asse.fr
Email	secretariat.club@asse.fr
Media Officer	Eric Fages

FC Sochaux-Montbéliard
Stade Bonal
FR-25200 Montbéliard

Tel	+33 3 8199 7033
Fax	+33 3 8199 3000
Web	fcsochaux.fr
Email	karine.richard@fcsochaux.fr
Media Officer	Fabien Dorier

Toulouse FC
"Stadium", 1 Allée Gabriel-Biénés, PO Box
54023, FR-31028 Toulouse Cedex 4

Tel	+33 39 40
Fax	+33 5 6153 5567
Web	tfc.info
Email	jf.soucasse@tfc.info
Media Officer	Géraldine Courteix

Valenciennes FC
43 avenue de Reims, Stade Nungesser
FR-59303 Valenciennes

Tel	+33 39 40
Fax	+33 3 2729 9507
Web	va-fc.com
Email	contact@va-fc.com
Media Officer	Maxime Parent

GEORGIA

Géorgie I Georgien

Georgian Football Federation (GFF)

COMMUNICATION

Address 76a Chavchavadze Ave.
GE-0162 Tbilisi
Tel +995 32 912 680
Fax +995 32 915 995

E-mail gff@gff.ge
Website gff.ge

President Domenti Sichinava
General Secretary Revaz Arveladze
Media Officer Lasha Dvalishvili

Year of Formation 1990

National Stadium Boris Paichadze, Tbili
(53,279)

DOMESTIC COMPETITION SUMMARY 2010/11

UMAGLESI LIGA FINAL TABLE

			Home					Away					Total						
		Pld	W	D	L	F	A	W	D	L	F	A	W	D	L	F	A	Pts	Comp
1	FC Zestafoni	36	15	2	1	46	4	9	4	5	26	15	24	6	6	72	19	78	UCL
2	FC Dinamo Tbilisi	36	12	5	1	36	12	9	4	5	19	10	21	9	6	55	22	72	UEL
3	FC Olimpi Rustavi	36	14	2	2	30	8	6	4	8	22	23	20	6	10	52	31	66	UEL
4	FC Torpedo Kutaisi	36	9	8	1	15	5	5	5	8	16	17	14	13	9	31	22	55	
5	FC WIT Georgia	36	8	3	7	23	20	6	3	9	12	21	14	6	16	35	41	48	
6	FC Baia Zugdidi	36	12	3	3	27	14	1	2	15	9	37	13	5	18	36	51	44	
7	FC Kolkheti Poti	36	8	4	6	18	18	2	6	10	7	29	10	10	16	25	47	40	
8	FC Sioni Bolnisi	36	9	4	5	21	16	1	5	12	6	29	10	9	17	27	45	39	
9	FC Spartaki Tskhinvali	36	6	5	7	27	20	1	6	11	5	22	7	11	18	32	42	32	
10	FC Samtredia	36	6	5	7	15	17	0	2	16	12	55	6	7	23	27	72	25	*Relegated*

Top Scorer Nikoloz Gelashvili (Zestafoni), 18 goals

Promoted Clubs FC Gagra (UEL)
FC Merani Martvili
FC Dila Gori

Cup Final FC Gagra 1, FC Torpedo Kutaisi 0 (aet)

Zestafoni spearhead season of surprises

There was a fourth different winner of the Umaglesi Liga in as many seasons as FC Zestafoni became the champions of Georgia for the first time, seeing off the dual challenge of record champions FC Dinamo Tbilisi and title-holders FC Olimpi Rustavi. A major upset occurred too in the Georgian Cup, which was won by second-division FC Gagra, who had a double cause for celebration after also winning promotion back to the top flight after a year's absence.

Zestafoni's success was founded on a very settled side – only 22 players were used for the 36-match campaign – and an excellent home record – 15 wins and just one defeat in their 18 fixtures at the David Abashidze Stadium – as well as a decisive 20-match run without defeat that lasted from early November through to the 4-1 win at home to FC Samtredia in mid-May that secured the title with two games still to play. Formed only in 2004, Zestafoni thus added the league title to the Georgian Cup they had won in 2008.

Hot shot Gelashvili

The provincial club from Georgia's central heartland were led to victory by coach Giorgi Geguchadze, once of Dinamo Tbilisi, who joined the club in November 2008. There was continuity also in the prolific goalscoring of the club's 26-year-old striker Nikoloz Gelashvili, who topped the Umaglesi Liga goal charts for the second time in three seasons (having finished runner-up in 2009/10). Zestafoni scored 72 goals – an average of exactly two per game – and Gelashvili was responsible for 18 of them, thereby taking his three-season aggregate to 54. His main strike partner, Jaba Dvali, also contributed 12 goals but was marginally outgunned by the team's supersub Rati Tsinamdzgvrishvili, whose lengthy surname found its way on to the scoresheet no fewer than 13 times after he had been introduced from the bench. Curiously, in each of the six games he started he failed to find the target.

Although Zestafoni's long unbeaten run ended four days after their title win, with a 1-0 defeat at FC Sioni Bolnisi, they still ended up with a six-point winning margin over runners-up Dinamo Tbilisi. The team that won the first ten Georgian league titles during the 1990s had the better of their four head-to-head meetings with Zestafoni, winning two and drawing one, but it was the solitary defeat, in April, that effectively scuppered their title hopes. Coach Kakha Kancharava was sacked after a poor run in November but reinstated a month later, and although he rallied the troops well, the lack of a reliable goalscorer proved to be a handicap for him and the team, with not one player claiming a goal tally in double figures.

2009/10 champions Olimpi had a very different look to their side in 2010/11, with all of the Brazilians who had helped them to the title, including top scorer Anderson Aquino, having hot-footed it back to South America when their loan contracts came to an end. Despite the use of three coaches and a playing squad that was exclusively Georgian, Olimpi were level on points with Zestafoni at the head of the winter-break standings

Nikoloz Gelashvili of champions Zestafoni was the Umaglesi Liga's top scorer with 18 goals

and never likely to finish lower than third – which ensured them a place alongside Dinamo Tbilisi in the 2011/12 UEFA Europa League, albeit under the new name of FC Rustavi Metallurgist following a post-season identity switch.

Giant-killing Gagra

Gagra, originally from the Black Sea coastal town of the same name in the country's volatile north-west but now based in Tbilisi, snatched the final UEFA Europa League berth from fourth-placed FC Torpedo Kutaisi by defeating them in the Georgian Cup final to complete a dream double after claiming the Pirveli Liga (second division) title to secure promotion. Led by Ukrainian coach Anatoliy Piskovets, Gagra eliminated three top-flight teams, including Dinamo with a brilliant quarter-final second-leg comeback win, to reach the final before accounting for a fourth – and previous three-time winner – thanks to an own goal from Torpedo's veteran ex-Georgian international defender Sevasti Todua at the end of the first period of extra time.

With the Umaglesi Liga increasing its membership from ten teams to a dozen in 2011/12, Gagra were one of three teams promoted. Pirveli Liga runners-up FC Merani Martvili accompanied them up automatically before FC Dila Gori joined the throng with a play-off win over Samtredia. FC Spartaki Tskhinvali salvaged their top-division status by winning the other play-off, at home to FC Chikhura Sachkhere.

Both Dinamo Tbilisi and Zestafoni came through two UEFA Europa League ties before perishing in the third qualifying round against, respectively, SK Sturm Graz and FC Karpaty Lviv, but while Georgian clubs continued to tread water in Europe, the country at long last made something of a mark at international level in the UEFA EURO 2012 qualifying campaign under new head coach Temur Ketsbaia.

National Team

Top Five All-time Caps – Levan Kobiashvili (95); Kakha Kaladze (79); Zurab Khizanishvili (75); Giorgi Nemsadze (69); Aleksandre Iashvili (64)

Top Five All-time Goals – Shota Arveladze (26); Temur Ketsbaia (17); Aleksandre Iashvili (15); Giorgi Demetradze & Levan Kobiashvili (12)

Late winners

The celebrated former Georgia midfielder, who replaced Héctor Cúper in November 2009 after a lamentable 2010 FIFA World Cup qualifying series that yielded just three points, managed to steer the team through a ten-match unbeaten run. Although half of those games were drawn, and three of the five wins came in friendlies, it was the 1-0 victory over UEFA EURO 2008 quarter-finalists Croatia in Tbilisi in March that really lifted the spirits of the long-suffering Georgian fans. As in their previous qualifying victory at home to Malta, the three points were claimed with a late winner, Levan Kobiashvili striking home his 12th international goal – on his record-extending 95th appearance – in the 90th minute of play.

Unfortunately, no sooner had hopes been raised of a possible qualification for the finals in Poland/Ukraine than they were lowered again three days later when the team succumbed to their first defeat under Ketsbaia, going down 1-0 to Israel in Tel-Aviv. Worse was to follow in June when Georgia failed to hold on to a first-half lead in the re-match against Croatia in Split and ended up with a second successive defeat that left them probably needing to win all three of their remaining fixtures to finish as one of the top two teams in Group F.

NATIONAL TEAM RESULTS 2010/11

11/8/10	Moldova	A	Chisinau	0-0	
3/9/10	Greece (ECQ)	A	Piraeus	1-1	*Iashvili (3)*
7/9/10	Israel (ECQ)	H	Tbilisi	0-0	
8/10/10	Malta (ECQ)	H	Tbilisi	1-0	*Siradze (90+1)*
12/10/10	Latvia (ECQ)	A	Riga	1-1	*Siradze (74)*
17/11/10	Slovenia	A	Koper	2-1	*Guruli (67), Ananidze (68)*
9/2/11	Armenia	N	Limassol (CYP)	2-1	*Iashvili (23), Siradze (34)*
26/3/11	Croatia (ECQ)	H	Tbilisi	1-0	*Kobiashvili (90)*
29/3/11	Israel (ECQ)	A	Tel-Aviv	0-1	
3/6/11	Croatia (ECQ)	A	Split	1-2	*Kankava (17)*

NATIONAL TEAM APPEARANCES 2010/11

oach – Temur KETSBAIA	18/3/68		Mda	GRE	ISR	MLT	LVA	Svn	Arm	CRO	ISR	CRO	Caps	Goals
iorgi LORIA	27/1/86	Dinamo Tbilisi	G					G	G46			G	9	-
cha LOBJANIDZE	23/2/87	Dnipro (UKR)	D	D	D		D						19	-
			75*											
eksandre AMISULASHVILI	20/8/82	Kayserispor (TUR)	D46	D	D	D	D		s46					
		/Krasnodar (RUS)								D	D		19	1
alkhaz ASATIANI	4/8/81	Lokomotiv Moskva (RUS)	D69	D	D	D	D						42	4
akha KALADZE	27/2/78	Milan (ITA)	D											
		/Genoa (ITA)		D	D	D	D	D	D46	D	D	D	79	1
ogita GOGUA	4/10/83	Spartak Nalchik (RUS)	M64	M87	M75	M	s69							
		/Volga (RUS)							M46	s73			27	1
urab KHIZANISHVILI	6/10/81	Blackburn (ENG)	M											
		/Reading (ENG)		M	M	M		M	M57	M	M	M	75	1
evan KOBIASHVILI	10/7/77	Hertha (GER)	M	M	M	M	M		D46	M	M		95	12
leksandre IASHVILI	23/10/77	Karlsruhe (GER)	M46	M54	M46	s46	M88		M50	M62	M63	M62	64	15
avid SIRADZE	21/10/81	Spartak Nalchik (RUS)	A56		s46	s46	A		A	s46	s73	A56	27	8
ladimer DVALISHVILI	20/4/86	M. Haifa (ISR)	A78	A60	A63	A46				A46	s63	s56	16	4
ikoloz GELASHVILI	5/8/85	Zestafoni	s46	s60				A61					8	-
avid KVIRKVELIA	27/6/80	Rubin (RUS)	s46	M			M69	D						
		/Panionios (GRE)							s46		s46	M	45	-
iorgi MEREBASHVILI	15/8/86	Vojvodina (SRB)	s56	s87	s63	M46			s50				17	-
ornike APTSIAURI	28/11/79	Zestafoni	s64		s75								5	-
asha SALUKVADZE	21/12/81	Rubin (RUS)	s69			D	s79							
		/Volga (RUS)							D	D	D	D	36	1
Aleksandre KOSHKADZE	4/12/81	Dinamo Tbilisi	s78				s88	s89					3	-
Nukri REVISHVILI	2/3/87	Anzhi (RUS)		G	G	G	G		s46	G	G		16	-
Zhano ANANIDZE	10/10/92	Spartak Moskva (RUS)		s54	M	M73	M79	M89	M			s80	9	1
Murtaz DAUSHVILI	1/5/89	Zestafoni				s73	M		M	M73	M46	s62	9	-
Guram KASHIA	4/7/87	Vitesse (NED)						D				D80	7	-
Akaki KHUBUTIA	17/3/86	Gaz Metan (ROU)						D	D	D	D	D	5	-
Gocha KHOJAVA	16/3/85	Volga (RUS)						M46					1	-
Jaba KANKAVA	18/3/86	Dnipro (UKR)						M73						
		/Kryvbas (UKR)								M	M	M	28	3
Irakli MODEBADZE	4/10/84	Olimpi						A46					2	-
Aleksandre GURULI	9/11/85	Karpaty (UKR)						s46					1	1
Mate VATSADZE	17/12/88	Dinamo Tbilisi						s46						
		/Volga (RUS)							s46				4	-
Tornike OKRIASHVILI	12/2/92	Shakhtar (UKR)						s61					1	-
Levan KAKUBAVA	15/10/90	Dinamo Tbilisi						s73	s57				2	-
Otar MARTSVALADZE	14/7/84	Volga (RUS)								s62	A73		15	2
Gia GRIGALAVA	5/8/89	Volga (RUS)										D	1	-

CLUB-BY-CLUB

FC BAIA ZUGDIDI

Coach – Elguja Kometiani
Founded – 2005
Stadium – Gulia Tutberidze (4,200)

2010

15/8	WIT Georgia	a	1-2	*Megreladze*
20/8	Torpedo	h	1-0	*Guguchia*
29/8	Dinamo	h	0-0	
11/9	Zestafoni	h	2-1	*Megreladze 2*
15/9	Sioni	h	2-2	*Megreladze 2 (1p)*
19/9	Olimpi	a	0-2	
25/9	Spartaki	h	1-1	*Guguchia (p)*
29/9	Kolkheti	h	2-1	*Megreladze, Kvekveskiri*
3/10	Samtredia	a	1-3	*Akhalaia L.*
17/10	Sioni	a	3-1	*Rigvava 2, og (Didava)*
23/10	WIT Georgia	h	1-0	*Rigvava*
27/10	Zestafoni	h	1-3	*Malichava*
31/10	Torpedo	a	0-1	
5/11	Dinamo	a	0-0	
20/11	Olimpi	h	0-1	
27/11	Spartaki	a	0-2	
5/12	Kolkheti	a	0-1	
11/12	Samtredia	h	3-1	*Ekhvaia 2, Malichava (p)*

2011

13/2	Sioni	h	1-0	*Kobalia*
19/2	WIT Georgia	a	1-1	*Kobalia*
23/2	Torpedo	h	1-0	*Ekhvaia*
7/3	Zestafoni	a	1-6	*Kobalia*
12/3	Olimpi	a	0-2	
16/3	Spartaki	h	2-0	*Kobalia, Apakidze*
20/3	Kolkheti	h	1-0	*Kobalia*
2/4	Samtredia	a	0-3	
6/4	Sioni	a	0-1	
10/4	WIT Georgia	h	1-0	*Apakidze*
15/4	Torpedo	a	0-2	
19/4	Dinamo	a	1-2	*Ekhvaia*
23/4	Dinamo	h	1-2	*Sikharulia*
30/4	Zestafoni	a	0-3	
8/5	Olimpi	h	3-1	*Ekhvaia 2, Lomia*
14/5	Spartaki	a	0-3	
18/5	Kolkheti	a	1-2	*Lomia*
22/5	Samtredia	h	4-1	*Ekhvaia, Apakidze, Kobalia 2*

Name	Nat	DoB	Pos	Aps	(s)	Gls
Konstantine AKHALAIA		8/8/91	M		(3)	
Lado AKHALAIA		26/6/82	M	2	(1)	1
Nikoloz AKHVLEDIANI		20/5/95	M		(1)	
Levan AKOBIA		11/2/80	D	16		
Tamaz AKOBIA		1/1/92	M	6	(1)	
Makar AKUBARDIA		20/1/88	D	14		
Nikoloz APAKIDZE		4/4/92	M	16	(5)	3
Murtaz CHANGELIA		26/6/92	A	2	(9)	
David CHICHVEISHVILI		23/10/75	D	8		
Kakhaber CHKHETIANI		24/2/78	M	6		
Grigol DOLIDZE		25/10/82	M	7	(1)	
Irakli EKHVAIA		9/1/91	A	21	(7)	7
Avto ENDELADZE		17/9/94	M	1	(2)	
Ilia GAMREKLIDZE		3/12/90	D	14		
Aleksandre GOGOBERISHVILI		26/2/77	M	9		
Luka GUGUCHIA		10/12/91	M	10	(2)	2
Ivane KANDELAKI		2/1/90	D	8	(1)	
Giorgi KHIDESHELI		21/11/85	M	2	(3)	
Gela KHUBUA		25/1/84	M		(4)	
Giorgi KIRIA		10/5/83	M		(3)	
Irakli KOBALIA		10/3/92	A	16	(1)	7
Lasha KUKAVA		12/1/92	M	1	(13)	
Giorgi KVARTSKHAVA		1/9/92	D	6	(2)	
Zurab KVARTSKHAVA		20/10/93	M		(1)	
Nika KVEKVESKIRI		29/5/92	D	14		1
Giorgi KVESIESHVILI		1/12/85	D	12	(2)	
Shota LOMIA		13/2/84	M	24	(4)	2
Archil MAKATSARIA		19/3/92	G	1		
Mamuka MAKATSARIA		7/2/90	M		(2)	
Irakli MALICHAVA		3/7/84	M	8	(1)	2
Giorgi MEGRELADZE		21/7/78	A	8		6
Roin ONIANI		14/6/75	D	27		
Data RIGVAVA		8/10/91	M	24	(3)	3
Guram SAMUSHIA		5/9/94	M	2	(9)	
Nika SHONIA		14/10/91	M	7	(6)	
Zviad SIKHARULIA		1/8/92	M	19	(10)	1
Giorgi SOMKHISHVILI		27/11/80	G	22		
Lasha SVIRAVA		8/3/89	D	6	(2)	
Levan TSURTSUMIA		28/1/89	A	26	(4)	
Levan VARTAGAVA		10/8/81	M	18	(2)	
Tornike ZARKUA		1/9/90	G	9		
Vladimer ZUKHBAIA		31/1/86	G	4		

FC DINAMO TBILISI

Coach – Kakha Kacharava; (21/11/10) Tamaz Samkharadze; (20/12/10) Kakha Kacharava
Founded – 1925
Stadium – Boris Paichadze (53,279)
MAJOR HONOURS: UEFA Cup Winners' Cup – (1) 1981; USSR League – (2) 1964, 1978; Georgian League – (13) 1990, 1991, 1992, 1993, 1994, 1995, 1996, 1997, 1998, 1999, 2003, 2005, 2008; USSR Cup – (2) 1976, 1979; Georgian Cup – (9) 1992, 1993, 1994, 1995, 1996, 1997, 2003, 2004, 2009.

2010

15/8	Zestafoni	h	2-1	*Vatsadze, Pirtskhalava*
22/8	Olimpi	a	0-1	
29/8	Baia	a	0-0	
11/9	Kolkheti	a	3-1	*Khmaladze, Koshkadze, Mujiri*
15/9	Spartaki	h	1-0	*Khmaladze (p)*
19/9	Samtredia	h	3-2	*Liluashvili, Koshkadze, Kakubava*
24/9	Sioni	a	0-1	
28/9	WIT Georgia	h	2-0	*Kvaratskhelia, Khmaladze (p)*
2/10	Torpedo	a	1-1	*Djousse*
16/10	Spartaki	a	0-0	
23/10	Zestafoni	a	1-0	*Koshkadze*
27/10	Kolkheti	h	5-0	*Kvaratskhelia, Lekvtadze 2, Mujiri, Khmaladze*
31/10	Olimpi	h	1-1	*Lekvtadze*
5/11	Baia	h	0-0	
21/11	Samtredia	a	0-1	
26/11	Sioni	h	2-0	*Vatsadze, Lekvtadze*
5/12	WIT Georgia	a	1-0	*Mujiri*
12/12	Torpedo	h	1-0	*Mujiri*

2011

13/2	Spartaki	h	1-1	*Hadžibulić*
19/2	Zestafoni	h	0-0	
23/2	Olimpi	a	0-1	
6/3	Kolkheti	a	2-0	*Koshkadze, Jelić*
11/3	Samtredia	h	7-1	*Jelić, Khmaladze 2, og (Khumarashvili), Djousse 2, Arziani*
16/3	Sioni	a	2-0	*Khmaladze (p), Djousse*
2/4	Torpedo	a	0-0	
6/4	Spartaki	a	3-1	*Koshkadze 2, Tatanashvili*
10/4	Zestafoni	a	0-1	
15/4	Olimpi	h	2-0	*Robertinho, Koshkadze*
19/4	Baia	h	2-1	*Koshkadze, Khmaladze (p)*
23/4	Baia	a	2-1	*Kvaratskhelia 2*
27/4	WIT Georgia	h	1-1	*Pantskhava*
1/5	Kolkheti	h	4-2	*Pantskhava, Arziani, Kakubava, Djousse*
8/5	Samtredia	a	2-1	*Tatanashvili, Tomashvili*
14/5	Sioni	h	1-0	*Tatanashvili*

/5	WIT Georgia	a	2-0	*Lekvtadze, Tatanashvili*
/5	Torpedo	h	1-2	*Jigauri*

ame	Nat	DoB	Pos	Aps	(s)	Gls
rab ARZIANI	RUS	19/10/87	M	14		2
sha CHADUNELI		14/1/90	D		(1)	
nald Dering DJOUSSE	CMR	18/3/90	A	22	(8)	5
NILSON Pedro Rocha drade Mendes	POR	25/9/82	M	15	(2)	
orgi GAVASHELISHVILI		31/10/89	D	4	(1)	
mur GONGADZE		8/9/85	D	6	(2)	
orgi GVELESIANI		5/5/91	D	2		
emir HADŽIBULIĆ	SRB	16/8/86	M	8		1
í HOMOLA	CZE	2/7/80	D	13		
etar JELIĆ	BIH	18/10/86	A	6		2
mbul JIGAURI		8/7/92	M	1		1
iorgi KAKHELISHVILI		22/5/87	M	20	(12)	
evan KAKUBAVA		15/10/90	D	34		2
viad KANTARIA		3/6/90	A		(2)	
uram KASHIA		4/7/87	D	3		
hota KASHIA		22/10/84	D	1		
evan KHMALADZE		6/4/85	M	32		8
leksandre KOSHKADZE		4/12/81	M	31		8
evan KUKHALEISHVILI		24/2/92	M		(1)	
ivi KVARATSKHELIA		11/5/79	D	16	(4)	4
ika KVEKVESKIRI		29/5/92	D	5	(12)	
akli LEKVTADZE		30/8/91	M	7	(6)	5
akli LILUASHVILI		13/10/84	M	4	(3)	1
iorgi LORIA		27/1/86	G	35		
iorgi MAMUCHASHVILI		12/4/90	M		(2)	
larko MAROVIĆ	SRB	30/1/83	D	4		
viad METREVELI		28/11/85	A	5	(7)	
avid MUJIRI		2/1/78	M	6	(6)	4
iorgi OTARISHVILI		12/12/90	M	3		
akhtang PANTSKHAVA		8/10/89	A	6	(1)	2
ikoloz PIRTSKHALAVA		15/5/87	M	8	(7)	1
oberto Soares Anghinetti ROBERTINHO"	BRA	13/6/88	M	24	(1)	1
akli SIKHARULIDZE		18/7/90	A	2	(4)	
imitri TATANASHVILI		19/10/83	A	6	(9)	4
iorgi TEKTURMANIDZE		17/9/90	M	13	(11)	
ulverd TOMASHVILI		13/10/88	D	30	(1)	1
iorgi TSIMAKURIDZE		10/11/83	D	2		
Mate VATSADZE		17/12/88	A	7	(1)	2
ornike ZARKUA		1/9/90	G	1		

FC KOLKHETI POTI

Coach – Besik Sherozia; (12/3/11) (David Makharadze); (16/3/11) Soso Pilia

Founded – 1913

Stadium – Phazisi (6,000)

2010				
14/8	Sioni	a	0-0	
21/8	WIT Georgia	h	2-0	*Sichinava (p), Gulua*
29/8	Torpedo	a	0-0	
11/9	Dinamo	h	1-3	*Gvalia*
15/9	Samtredia	h	1-0	*Tskhvitaria*
19/9	Zestafoni	a	0-2	
25/9	Olimpi	h	5-1	*Tsitskhvaia 2, Silagava, Gvalia, Gulua*
29/9	Baia	a	1-2	*Sichinava*
3/10	Spartaki	h	1-0	*Jikia*
16/10	Samtredia	a	1-1	*Sichinava*
24/10	Sioni	h	0-0	
27/10	Dinamo	a	0-5	
31/10	WIT Georgia	a	1-5	*Tskhvitaria*
5/11	Torpedo	h	0-1	
21/11	Zestafoni	h	0-2	
26/11	Olimpi	a	0-2	
5/12	Baia	h	1-0	*Megrelishvili*
11/12	Spartaki	a	0-4	

2011				
12/2	Samtredia	h	2-1	*Tskhvitaria, Kverenchkhiladze*
19/2	Sioni	a	0-2	
23/2	WIT Georgia	h	0-2	
27/2	Torpedo	a	0-1	
6/3	Dinamo	h	0-2	
12/3	Zestafoni	a	0-0	
16/3	Olimpi	h	0-0	
20/3	Baia	a	0-1	
2/4	Spartaki	h	0-0	
6/4	Samtredia	a	0-0	
10/4	Sioni	h	1-0	*Gavashelishvili*
15/4	WIT Georgia	a	1-0	*Mdivnishvili*
23/4	Torpedo	h	1-1	*Mdivnishvili*
1/5	Dinamo	a	2-4	*Gvalia, Mdivnishvili*
8/5	Zestafoni	h	1-4	*Kverenchkhiladze*
14/5	Olimpi	a	1-0	*Mdivnishvili*
18/5	Baia	h	2-1	*Sichinava, Samadashvili*
22/5	Spartaki	a	0-0	

Name	Nat	DoB	Pos	Aps	(s)	Gls
Konstantine BARAMIDZE		12/7/91	D	2		
Tsotne BUKIA		3/1/90	M	4		
Zviad CHEDIA		16/1/92	M	1	(1)	
David CHITANAVA		2/4/82	D	13	(1)	
Pavle DATUNAISHVILI		25/8/83	M	6	(1)	
Giorgi DEKANOSIDZE		2/1/81	M		(2)	
Lasha DZAGANIA		14/1/88	G	18		
Zurab EKONIA		7/6/84	D		(2)	
Shota GABUNIA		31/5/90	M		(2)	
Giorgi GAVASHELISHVILI		31/10/89	M	11	(1)	1
Amiran GEGELIA		29/6/91	D	3	(2)	
Boris GELACHEISHVILI		30/1/88	D	7	(4)	
Omar GOGONAIA		24/1/90	M	21		
Levan GORDEZIANI		23/3/88	G	5		
Levan GULUA		6/5/91	M	14	(12)	2
Lasha GVALIA		6/10/91	M	33	(1)	3
OlegGVELESIANI		16/9/80	D	13		
Aleksandre INTSKIRVELI		24/8/81	D	30		
Zamir JANASHIA		26/2/88	M	7	(3)	
Rezo JIKIA		1/9/80	A	8	(3)	1
Vladimer JOJUA		5/12/80	M	13		
Levan KASHIBADZE		15/5/93	M		(1)	
Aleksandre KORCHILAVA		11/9/91	M		(3)	
David KUKULADZE		16/11/90	M	1	(2)	
GigaKVERENCHKHILADZE		21/2/85	A	10	(4)	2
Giorgi LEMONJAVA		25/11/90	D	6	(1)	
Mikheil MAKHVILADZE		22/7/78	D	28		
Levan MDIVNISHVILI		3/10/82	A	14	(4)	4
David MEGRELISHVILI		25/8/91	M	19	(1)	1
IrakliMOISTSRAPISHVILI		11/5/91	M	5	(3)	
Guram SAMADASHVILI		6/2/86	A	3	(6)	1
Lasha SATSERADZE		10/5/90	A	2	(1)	
Gizo SHENGELIA		17/8/83	G	13		
Data SICHINAVA		21/3/89	A	23	(4)	4
Giorgi SILAGAVA		26/5/84	M	13	(1)	1
Levan TEDIASHVILI		1/6/86	M	10	(4)	
Manuchar TSIKARISHVILI		28/4/85	A	6	(22)	
David TSITSKHVAIA		30/11/83	A	11	(2)	2
Paata TSKHVITARIA		17/9/89	D	23	(9)	3

FC OLIMPI RUSTAVI

Coach – Temur Makharadze; (16/10/10) Nestor Mumladze; (11/12/10) Armaz Jeladze

Founded – 1991

Stadium – Poladi (4,656)

MAJOR HONOURS: Georgian League – (2) 2007, 2010.

2010				
14/8	Torpedo	a	1-1	*Razmadze*
22/8	Dinamo	h	1-0	*Rekhviashvili*
29/8	Zestafoni	a	0-1	

11/9	Spartaki	h	2-0	*Beriashvili, Getsadze*
15/9	WIT Georgia	h	2-1	*Kavtaradze, Beriashvili*
19/9	Baia	h	2-0	*Razmadze (p), Kazaishvili*
25/9	Kolkheti	a	1-5	*Modebadze*
29/9	Samtredia	h	3-0	*Modebadze 3 (1p)*
3/10	Sioni	a	1-2	*Modebadze*
16/10	WIT Georgia	a	4-0	*og (Adamadze), Modebadze 2, Dobrovolski*
23/10	Torpedo	h	0-0	
27/10	Spartaki	a	3-2	*Bolkvadze, Kvakhadze, Modebadze*
31/10	Dinamo	a	1-1	*Getsadze*
6/11	Zestafoni	h	1-0	*Kvakhadze*
20/11	Baia	a	1-0	*Modebadze*
26/11	Kolkheti	h	2-0	*Razmadze (p), Rekhviashvili*
5/12	Samtredia	a	1-1	*Razmadze (p)*
11/12	Sioni	h	3-1	*Kavtaradze, Bolkvadze, Razmadze (p)*
2011				
13/2	WIT Georgia	h	2-1	*og (Bechvaia), Modebadze*
19/2	Torpedo	h	1-1	*Tkemaladze*
23/2	Dinamo	h	1-0	*Maisuradze*
27/2	Zestafoni	a	0-2	
7/3	Spartaki	h	1-0	*Getsadze*
12/3	Baia	h	2-0	*Modebadze, Getsadze*
16/3	Kolkheti	a	0-0	
20/3	Samtredia	h	4-0	*Modebadze, Bolkvadze 2, Pavliashvili*
2/4	Sioni	a	0-1	
6/4	WIT Georgia	a	1-0	*Getsadze*
10/4	Torpedo	a	1-2	*Maisuradze*
15/4	Dinamo	a	0-2	
23/4	Zestafoni	h	1-2	*Murvelashvili*
30/4	Spartaki	a	2-0	*Modebadze 2*
8/5	Baia	a	1-3	*Getsadze*
14/5	Kolkheti	h	0-1	
18/5	Samtredia	a	4-0	*Tkemaladze 2, Modebadze, Bolkvadze*
22/5	Sioni	h	2-1	*Modebadze, Bolkvadze*

Name	Nat	DoB	Pos	Aps	(s)	Gls
Giorgi ABURJANIA		2/1/95	M	2	(1)	
Roman AKHALKATSI		20/2/81	M		(4)	
Tornike BAKHTADZE		18/4/88	M		(2)	
Revaz BARABADZE		4/10/88	A		(2)	
Zurab BATIASHVILI		6/2/80	G	9	(1)	
Grigol BEDIASHVILI		7/2/80	G	23		
Giorgi BERIASHVILI		10/9/86	A	15	(1)	2
David BOLKVADZE		5/6/80	M	32		6
Grigol CHANTURIA		25/9/73	G	4		
Giorgi CHEDIA		28/8/88	A	2	(1)	
Giorgi CHELIDZE		29/11/84	M	7	(19)	
Denis DOBROVOLSKI		10/10/85	M	26	(5)	1
Revaz GETSADZE		11/1/85	M	26	(4)	6
Temur GONGADZE		8/9/85	D	16		
Giorgi GORDEZIANI		2/5/91	M		(2)	
Sandro IASHVILI		3/1/85	A	2	(3)	
Lasha JAPARIDZE		16/4/85	D	23	(4)	
Ivane KANDELAKI		2/1/90	D	1	(2)	
Giorgi KAVTARADZE		1/1/89	M	24	(7)	2
Valeri KAZAISHVILI		29/1/93	M		(7)	1
Revaz KEMOKLIDZE		13/3/79	D	15	(9)	
Ilia KERDZEVADZE		19/1/96	M		(1)	
David KHOCHOLAVA		8/2/93	M		(2)	
Lasha KOCHLADZE		22/8/95	M		(1)	
David KURDOBADZE		31/5/91	M		(2)	
Aleksandre KVAKHADZE		17/8/84	D	29		2
Irakli MAISURADZE		22/8/88	M	14		2
Irakli MODEBADZE		4/10/84	A	32	(2)	16
Giorgi MURVELASHVILI		23/8/88	D	13		1
Ilia PAVLIASHVILI		12/8/89	A	9	(4)	1
Luka RAZMADZE		30/12/83	M	28		5
Giorgi REKHVIASHVILI		1/2/88	D	32		2
Levan SETURIDZE		16/10/90	M		(2)	
Valiko TKEMALADZE		14/11/87	M	11	(3)	3
Jaba UGULAVA		8/4/92	M	1	(6)	

FC SAMTREDIA

Coach – Gela Sanaia; (25/1/11) Levan Anjaparidze

Founded – 1936

Stadium – Erosi Manjgaladze (2,000)

2010				
14/8	Spartaki	a	2-2	*Bakuradze, Etsadeishvili*
20/8	Sioni	h	0-1	
29/8	WIT Georgia	a	2-4	*Kverenchkhiladze, Pavliashvili*
10/9	Torpedo	h	1-0	*Kakaladze*
15/9	Kolkheti	a	0-1	
19/9	Dinamo	a	2-3	*Tkemaladze, Chomakhidze*
24/9	Zestafoni	h	1-3	*Chomakhidze*
29/9	Olimpi	a	0-3	
3/10	Baia	h	3-1	*Bakuradze, Bakarandze, Kirkitadze*
16/10	Kolkheti	h	1-1	*Kverenchkhiladze*
24/10	Spartaki	h	1-0	*Kirkitadze*
27/10	Torpedo	a	0-0	
31/10	Sioni	a	0-1	
6/11	WIT Georgia	h	1-0	*Chomakhidze*
21/11	Dinamo	h	1-0	*Bakuradze (p)*
26/11	Zestafoni	a	0-7	
5/12	Olimpi	h	1-1	*Kebadze*
11/12	Baia	a	1-3	*Kebadze*
2011				
12/2	Kolkheti	a	1-2	*Khumarashvili*
23/2	Sioni	h	1-1	*Tskhadaia*
27/2	WIT Georgia	a	0-2	
3/3	Spartaki	a	0-1	
7/3	Torpedo	h	0-1	
11/3	Dinamo	a	1-7	*Gogishvili*
16/3	Zestafoni	h	0-1	
20/3	Olimpi	a	0-4	
2/4	Baia	h	3-0	*Khumarashvili, Burjanadze, Lomashvili*
6/4	Kolkheti	h	0-0	
10/4	Spartaki	h	0-0	
15/4	Sioni	a	0-5	
23/4	WIT Georgia	h	0-1	
30/4	Torpedo	a	1-2	*Mikaberidze*
8/5	Dinamo	h	1-2	*Lomashvili*
14/5	Zestafoni	a	1-4	*Dvalishvili*
18/5	Olimpi	h	0-4	
22/5	Baia	a	1-4	*Kerdzevadze*

Name	Nat	DoB	Pos	Aps	(s)	Gls
Bakar AKHOBADZE		7/9/90	M	1	(2)	
Giorgi ALAVERDASHVILI		21/11/87	A	9	(3)	
Paata BAKARANDZE		20/3/82	A	13	(6)	1
Levan BAKURADZE		18/1/86	M	12	(3)	3
Nika BANDZAVA		23/8/93	G	3	(1)	
Giga BURJANADZE		19/5/87	M	13	(1)	1
David CHACHUA		14/4/92	M		(1)	
David CHKHIKVADZE		27/11/86	M	20	(3)	
Shota CHOMAKHIDZE		17/11/78	M	18	(1)	3
Akaki DVALISHVILI		30/6/91	D	7	(2)	1
Lasha DZAGANIA		14/1/88	G	16		
Zurab ENDELADZE		23/4/91	D	7	(1)	
Zurab ETSADEISHVILI		6/10/85	A		(4)	1
Spartak GOGIA		11/12/78	D	25		
Murad GOGISHVILI		15/6/92	A	5	(5)	1
Valter GUCHUA		6/7/75	M	3	(3)	
Grigol IMEDADZE		2/10/80	A	2	(2)	
Kakhaber JINCHARADZE		25/3/85	G	13		
Mikheil KAKALADZE		6/6/82	A	11	(3)	1
Tornike KAPANADZE		4/6/92	M		(1)	
Levan KEBADZE		27/8/83	M	16		2
David KEKELIDZE		6/5/89	G	4	(1)	
Shota KERDZEVADZE		20/3/93	M	1	(1)	1
Lasha KHACHAPURIDZE		11/6/92	D	2	(1)	
Tsotne KHARABADZE		16/5/93	D	1		
Giorgi KHUMARASHVILI		24/8/89	D	26	(1)	2
Irakli KHVADAGIANI		17/6/90	M	4	(10)	

avid KIRKITADZE		3/9/92	M	4	(13)	2
akhaber KIRTADZE		28/7/86	D	19	(2)	
kaki KUPREISHVILI		1/4/83	D	11		
ga KVERENCHKHILADZE		21/2/85	A	11	(2)	2
aja LOMASHVILI		4/9/85	M	13		2
iorgi MIKABERIDZE		17/2/88	M	15		1
aza MIKELTADZE		25/5/92	D	1		
ezo NINUA		3/1/86	M	6	(3)	
a PAVLIASHVILI		12/8/89	A	14	(2)	1
eimuraz PURTUKHIA		23/9/84	M	2	(4)	
ariel RUKHAIA		4/6/91	M	8	(7)	
akli SHALIKASHVILI		24/10/90	M	2	(3)	
ornike SHALIKASHVILI		24/10/90	D	19	(1)	
rchil SHENGELIA		22/9/89	M	1	(5)	
uchuna SOKHANEISHVILI		19/12/92	M		(1)	
iorgi SOSELIA		1/1/91	M	8	(1)	
evan SUTIDZE		28/4/92	M		(1)	
akhtang TEVZADZE		31/1/91	M		(1)	
aliko TKEMALADZE		14/11/87	M	14		1
iorgi TSKHADAIA		23/4/88	M	15		1
halva TSKIPURISHVILI		15/1/92	M	1		

FC SIONI BOLNISI

Coach – Giorgi Kipshidze; (20/3/11) Khvicha Kasrashvili

Founded – 1936

Stadium – Teimuraz Stepania (3,500)

MAJOR HONOURS: Georgian League – (1) 2006.

2010				
4/8	Kolkheti	h	0-0	
20/8	Samtredia	a	1-0	*og (Dvalishvili)*
29/8	Spartaki	a	0-3	
11/9	WIT Georgia	h	0-0	
15/9	Baia	a	2-2	*Gotsiridze, Isiani*
19/9	Torpedo	a	0-0	
24/9	Dinamo	h	1-0	*Vashakidze*
28/9	Zestafoni	h	1-3	*Nozadze*
3/10	Olimpi	h	2-1	*Gotsiridze, Ugrekhelidze*
17/10	Baia	h	1-3	*Melkadze*
24/10	Kolkheti	a	0-0	
27/10	WIT Georgia	a	0-1	
31/10	Samtredia	h	1-0	*Orbeladze*
5/11	Spartaki	h	2-0	*Isiani, Chelidze L.*
20/11	Torpedo	h	0-0	
26/11	Dinamo	a	0-2	
5/12	Zestafoni	a	0-4	
11/12	Olimpi	a	1-3	*Bobokhidze (p)*
2011				
13/2	Baia	a	0-1	
19/2	Kolkheti	h	2-0	*Chirikashvili, Jikia*
23/2	Samtredia	a	1-1	*Jikia*
28/2	Spartaki	a	0-3	
6/3	WIT Georgia	h	1-2	*Svanidze*
12/3	Torpedo	a	0-2	
16/3	Dinamo	h	0-2	
20/3	Zestafoni	a	0-0	
2/4	Olimpi	h	1-0	*Shalamberidze*
6/4	Baia	h	1-0	*Chirikashvili*
10/4	Kolkheti	a	0-1	
15/4	Samtredia	h	5-0	*Jikia 2, Didava (p), Isiani, Gogoberishvili*
23/4	Spartaki	h	1-1	*Didava (p)*
30/4	WIT Georgia	a	0-3	
8/5	Torpedo	h	1-4	*Orbeladze*
14/5	Dinamo	a	0-1	
18/5	Zestafoni	h	1-0	*Jikia*
22/5	Olimpi	a	1-2	*Shalamberidze*

Name	Nat	DoB	Pos	Aps	(s)	Gls
Saba ADAMASHVILI		29/9/92	M	7	(2)	
Mindia BOBGIASHVILI		2/8/83	G	22	(1)	
Mikheil BOBOKHIDZE		23/11/81	A	3	(8)	1
Giorgi CHELIDZE		24/10/86	A	1		
Lasha CHELIDZE		13/3/85	D	12	(1)	1
Irakli CHIRIKASHVILI		10/1/87	M	14	(1)	2
Giorgi CHIVADZE		14/6/84	M	6		
Levan CHKHETIANI		17/8/87	M	3	(2)	
Givi DIDAVA		21/3/76	D	31		2
Aleksandre GOGOBERISHVILI		26/2/77	M	17		1
Revaz GOTSIRIDZE		17/1/81	A	14	(2)	2
Vili ISIANI		22/3/91	M	7	(21)	3
Rezo JIKIA		1/9/80	A	15		5
Mikheil KOBAURI		11/6/82	D	27		
Vaja KORIDZE		5/1/87	D	9	(3)	
Murman KURASBEDIANI		11/4/88	M	11	(3)	
Giorgi KUTSURUA		19/7/86	M	6	(3)	
Nika KVAKHADZE		15/4/88	M	5	(5)	
David LEGASHVILI		9/2/93	G	1		
David LOMAIA		18/5/85	D	6	(2)	
Giorgi MELKADZE		24/11/84	M	4	(3)	1
Mirza MERLANI		5/10/80	G	10		
Vaja NEMSADZE		7/12/90	M	4	(4)	
Lasha NOZADZE		18/3/80	M	35		1
Giorgi OKROPIRIDZE		1/3/86	M	3	(6)	
Manuchar OKROPIRIDZE		19/2/90	M	3	(6)	
Sergo ORBELADZE		1/5/82	D	30		2
Teimuraz RAKVIASHVILI		15/10/83	D	9		
Giorgi REKHVIASHVILI		15/4/86	A	9	(5)	
Levan SANIKIDZE		9/6/82	M	2	(4)	
Koba SHALAMBERIDZE		15/10/84	M	2	(7)	2
David SVANIDZE		14/10/79	D	14		1
Giorgi TARGAMADZE		11/1/90	M	16	(3)	
Gia TODUA		7/6/82	A	9	(3)	
Vladimer UGREKHELIDZE		29/11/85	M	15	(2)	1
Lasha VASHAKIDZE		19/11/85	M	11	(6)	1
Vladimer ZUKHBAIA		31/1/86	G	3	(1)	

FC SPARTAKI TSKHINVALI

Coach – Gocha Chikovani; (3/10/10) Badri Kvaratskhelia

Founded – 2007

Stadium – Kartli, Gori (400)

2010				
14/8	Samtredia	h	2-2	*Clovis, Dekanoidze*
21/8	Zestafoni	a	0-4	
29/8	Sioni	h	3-0	*Shonia 2, Clovis*
11/9	Olimpi	a	0-2	
15/9	Dinamo	a	0-1	
19/9	WIT Georgia	h	1-2	*Shonia (p)*
25/9	Baia	a	1-1	*og (Chichveishvili)*
29/9	Torpedo	h	1-2	*Mgeladze*
3/10	Kolkheti	a	0-1	
16/10	Dinamo	h	0-0	
24/10	Samtredia	a	0-1	
27/10	Olimpi	h	2-3	Bolkvadze, Shonia
31/10	Zestafoni	h	1-1	*Dekanoidze*
5/11	Sioni	a	0-2	
21/11	WIT Georgia	a	1-0	*Bolkvadze*
27/11	Baia	h	2-0	*Barabadze 2*
5/12	Torpedo	a	0-1	
11/12	Kolkheti	h	4-0	*Clovis 2, Maisuradze, Kashia (p)*
2011				
13/2	Dinamo	a	1-1	*Metreveli*
23/2	Zestafoni	h	1-2	*Buzaladze*
28/2	Sioni	h	3-0	*Metreveli 3*
3/3	Samtredia	h	1-0	*Mamuchashvili*
7/3	Olimpi	a	0-1	
12/3	WIT Georgia	h	0-1	
16/3	Baia	a	0-2	
20/3	Torpedo	h	2-2	*Metreveli 2*
2/4	Kolkheti	a	0-0	
6/4	Dinamo	h	1-3	*Jakobia*
10/4	Samtredia	a	0-0	

15/4	Zestafoni	a	0-2	
23/4	Sioni	a	1-1	*Metreveli*
30/4	Olimpi	h	0-2	
8/5	WIT Georgia	a	1-1	*Dekanoidze*
14/5	Baia	h	3-0	*Shonia, Jakobia (p), Dekanoidze*
18/5	Torpedo	a	0-1	
22/5	Kolkheti	h	0-0	

Name	Nat	DoB	Pos	Aps	(s)	Gls
Makar AKUBARDIA		20/1/88	D	4	(1)	
Giorgi ALAVIDZE		28/11/89	D	11	(3)	
Giorgi BABULAIDZE		1/2/89	M	6	(2)	
Mikheil BARABADZE		23/9/88	A	9	(6)	2
Valeri BOLKVADZE		25/2/88	M	12	(7)	2
Fridolin BOYOMO	CMR	4/8/82	D	32		
Ucha BURDZENADZE		23/4/93	D	1	(1)	
Ilia BUZALADZE		29/2/92	A	5	(12)	1
Lasha CHALADZE		5/11/87	M	5	(7)	
Levan CHAPODZE		21/10/88	D	35		
Thierry CLOVIS	CIV	15/8/93	M	15	(9)	4
Nika DAUSHVILI		16/10/89	G	4	(1)	
Besik DEKANOIDZE		1/3/92	M	25	(4)	4
Zurab DZAGANIA		20/7/89	A	8		
Soso GRISHIKASHVILI		25/12/73	G	30		
Vakhtang JAKELI		17/3/92	M		(4)	
Lasha JAKOBIA		20/8/80	A	9	(1)	2
Mikheil JISHKARIANI		31/10/92	M	6	(4)	
Kakhaber KAKASHVILI		26/6/93	M	5	(3)	
Shota KASHIA		22/10/84	D	18		1
Erekle KHACHVANI		31/12/91	D	6	(1)	
Ioseb KHOMERIKI		29/3/88	G	2		
Varlam KILASONIA		9/1/93	M	8	(5)	
Mikheil KORSANTIA		14/12/86	D	8	(1)	
Diego LOBJANIDZE		16/2/91	M	4		
Nikoloz MAISURADZE		29/5/89	A	2	(5)	1
Giorgi MAMUCHASHVILI		12/4/90	M	16		1
David MAMUDOV		3/10/89	M		(2)	
Nukri MANCHKHAVA		5/1/82	M	9		
Zviad METREVELI		28/11/85	A	15		7
Nika MGELADZE		20/12/87	D	20		1
Giorgi NARIMANIDZE		25/11/93	M	3	(2)	
Giorgi OTARISHVILI		12/12/90	D	5	(1)	
Levan SARALIDZE		8/4/86	D	4	(2)	
Giorgi SEPIASHVILI		29/9/90	D	5	(4)	
Teimuraz SHONIA		28/5/90	M	23	(3)	5
Giorgi TAVBERIDZE		7/3/87	D	5		
Badri TETUNASHVILI		9/2/90	D	15	(2)	
Tornike TUKHARELI		11/9/91	D	2		
Vladimer UGREKHELIDZE		29/11/85	M	4	(4)	
David ZEREKIDZE		9/3/91	M		(4)	

FC TORPEDO KUTAISI

Coach – Nestor Mumladze; (29/9/10) Gia Gigatadze

Founded – 1949

Stadium – Central (11,880)

MAJOR HONOURS: Georgian League – (3) 2000, 2001, 2002; Georgian Cup – (2) 1999, 2001.

2010				
14/8	Olimpi	h	1-1	*Khachiperadze*
20/8	Baia	a	0-1	
29/8	Kolkheti	h	0-0	
10/9	Samtredia	a	0-1	
15/9	Zestafoni	a	1-2	*Chikviladze*
19/9	Sioni	h	0-0	
24/9	WIT Georgia	a	0-1	
29/9	Spartaki	a	2-1	*Kemukhtashvili 2*
2/10	Dinamo	h	1-1	*Chikviladze*
17/10	Zestafoni	h	1-0	*Gigauri*
23/10	Olimpi	a	0-0	
27/10	Samtredia	h	0-0	
31/10	Baia	h	1-0	*Sabanadze*
5/11	Kolkheti	a	1-0	*Kvaratskhelia*
20/11	Sioni	a	0-0	
27/11	WIT Georgia	h	0-1	
5/12	Spartaki	h	1-0	*Chikviladze*
12/12	Dinamo	a	0-1	
2011				
19/2	Olimpi	a	1-1	*Kebadze*
23/2	Baia	a	0-1	
27/2	Kolkheti	h	1-0	*Megreladze*
3/3	Zestafoni	a	0-1	
7/3	Samtredia	a	1-0	*Megreladze*
12/3	Sioni	h	2-0	*Megreladze 2*
16/3	WIT Georgia	a	1-2	*Megreladze*
20/3	Spartaki	a	2-2	*Sabanadze 2*
2/4	Dinamo	h	0-0	
6/4	Zestafoni	h	0-0	
10/4	Olimpi	h	2-1	*Megreladze, Kebadze*
15/4	Baia	h	2-0	*Kvaratskhelia, Megreladze (p)*
23/4	Kolkheti	a	1-1	*Gotsiridze*
30/4	Samtredia	h	2-1	*Digmelashvili, Datunaishvili*
8/5	Sioni	a	4-1	*Gotsiridze 3, Kemukhtashvili*
14/5	WIT Georgia	h	0-0	
18/5	Spartaki	h	1-0	*Chikviladze*
22/5	Dinamo	a	2-1	*Gotsiridze, Guguchia*

Name	Nat	DoB	Pos	Aps	(s)	Gls
Levan BAKURADZE		18/1/86	M	3	(3)	
Tengiz CHIKVILADZE		12/8/83	D	32		4
Givi CHKHETIANI		14/3/84	M	10	(8)	
Giorgi DATUNAISHVILI		9/2/85	M	31		1
David DIGMELASHVILI		18/1/80	M	29	(1)	1
Grigol DOLIDZE		25/10/82	M	7	(9)	
Merab GIGAURI		5/6/93	M	13	(7)	1
Revaz GOTSIRIDZE		17/1/81	A	7	(3)	5
Luka GUGUCHIA		10/12/91	M		(4)	1
Giorgi GURULI		31/7/88	M	10	(2)	
Lasha KEBADZE		27/8/83	M	10	(6)	2
Lasha KEMUKHTASHVILI		9/4/92	A	5	(9)	3
Zaur KHACHIPERADZE		19/9/86	A	4	(3)	1
David KIRKITADZE		3/3/92	M		(4)	
Levan KIRKITADZE		17/3/88	M		(2)	
Vakhtang KVARATSKHELIA		30/3/88	A	20	(2)	2
Nika KVASKHVADZE		15/4/88	M	7	(3)	
Revaz KVERNADZE		25/8/81	A		(4)	
Maksime KVILITAIA		17/9/85	G	6		
Vaja LOMASHVILI		4/9/85	M	1	(8)	
Nodar MACHAVARIANI		14/1/87	D	9		
Nikoloz MAISURADZE		29/5/89	A	1	(1)	
Giorgi MEGRELADZE		21/7/78	A	10	(1)	7
Omar MIGINEISHVILI		2/6/84	G	30	(1)	
Teimuraz PARULAVA		20/7/83	D	27		
Dachi POPKHADZE		27/1/84	D	33	(1)	
Mikheil ROSTIASHVILI		21/9/90	M		(3)	
Nikoloz SABANADZE		2/5/91	A	16	(7)	3
Temur SANIKIDZE		4/3/92	M		(1)	
Giorgi SETURIDZE		1/4/85	M	17		
Tornike TARKHNISHVILI		30/6/90	M	21	(8)	
Sevasti TODUA		13/5/76	D	36		
Irakli TSNOBILADZE		28/8/84	A	1	(4)	

FC WIT GEORGIA

Coach – Merab Kochlashvili; (27/4/11) Zurab Beridze

Founded – 1968

Stadium – Poladi, Rustavi (4,656); Sikharuli (2,000)

MAJOR HONOURS: Georgian League – (2) 2004, 2009; Georgian Cup – (1) 2010.

2010				
15/8	Baia	h	2-1	*Lipartia (p), Kvaratskhelia*
21/8	Kolkheti	a	0-2	

9/8	Samtredia	h	4-2	*Kvaratskhelia 2, Lipartia, Zakradze*
/9	Sioni	a	0-0	
5/9	Olimpi	a	1-2	*Lipartia*
9/9	Spartaki	a	2-1	*Lipartia 2*
4/9	Torpedo	h	1-0	*Chimakadze*
8/9	Dinamo	a	0-2	
/10	Zestafoni	h	0-2	
6/10	Olimpi	h	0-4	
3/10	Baia	a	0-1	
7/10	Sioni	h	1-0	*Bechvaia*
1/10	Kolkheti	h	5-1	*Bechvaia, Chimakadze, Klimiashvili, Janelidze, Zakradze*
/11	Samtredia	a	0-1	
1/11	Spartaki	h	0-1	
7/11	Torpedo	a	1-0	*Lipartia*
/12	Dinamo	h	0-1	
1/12	Zestafoni	a	0-3	
011				
3/2	Olimpi	a	1-2	*Chimakadze*
9/2	Baia	h	1-1	*og (Oniani)*
3/2	Kolkheti	a	2-0	*Chimakadze, Bechvaia*
27/2	Samtredia	h	2-0	*Bechvaia, Rostiashvili*
/3	Sioni	a	2-1	*Gureshidze Gu., Vasadze*
12/3	Spartaki	a	1-0	*Bechvaia*
16/3	Torpedo	h	2-1	*Korifadze, Chimakadze*
2/4	Zestafoni	h	1-1	*Bechvaia*
6/4	Olimpi	h	0-1	
10/4	Baia	a	0-1	
15/4	Kolkheti	h	0-1	
23/4	Samtredia	a	1-0	*Ganiashvili*
27/4	Dinamo	a	1-1	*Adamadze*
30/4	Sioni	h	3-0	*Bechvaia, Chimakadze, Gureshidze Gi.*
8/5	Spartaki	h	1-1	*Khurtsilava*
14/5	Torpedo	a	0-0	
18/5	Dinamo	h	0-2	
22/5	Zestafoni	a	0-4	

Name	Nat	DoB	Pos	Aps	(s)	Gls
Guram ADAMADZE		31/8/88	D	34		1
Giga BECHVAIA		29/8/86	D	29		7
Irakli CHAKVETADZE		2/2/88	D	7		
Besik CHIMAKADZE		24/6/88	A	29	(6)	6
Giorgi DZADZAMIA		12/12/88	G	12	(1)	
Lasha GABRICHIDZE		21/2/89	M		(4)	
Revaz GANIASHVILI		27/5/90	A	31	(2)	1
Jemal GOGIASHVILI		6/5/88	D	5	(11)	
Giorgi GURESHIDZE		21/1/91	M	1	(5)	1
Guram GURESHIDZE		8/10/89	M	32		1
Giorgi JANELIDZE		25/9/89	M	30	(4)	1
Giga JUGELI		8/11/91	M		(1)	
Lasha KASRADZE		28/7/89	M	28	(4)	
David KHURTSILAVA		9/3/88	D	20	(3)	1
Irakl KLIMIASHVILI		30/5/88	M	16		1
Giorgi KORIFADZE		10/3/89	M	16	(8)	1
Vakhtang KVARATSKHELIA		30/3/88	A	3		3
Jaba LIPARTIA		16/11/87	A	18		6
David LOMAIA		18/5/85	D	9		
David MAISASHVILI		18/2/89	M	20		
Ardalion MIKABERIDZE		2/6/86	G	24		
Mikheil ROSTIAȘHVILI		21/9/90	A	2	(11)	1
Giorgi VASADZE		14/6/89	M	23	(4)	1
Beka ZAKRADZE		30/5/90	M	7	(24)	2

FC ZESTAFONI

Coach – Giorgi Geguchadze

Founded – 1936

Stadium – David Abashidze (5,000)

MAJOR HONOURS: Georgian League – (1) 2011; Georgian Cup – (1) 2008.

2010				
15/8	Dinamo	a	1-2	*Aladashvili*
21/8	Spartaki	h	4-0	*Dzaria, Tsinamdzgvrishvili 2, Grigalashvili*
29/8	Olimpi	h	1-0	*Gelashvili*
11/9	Baia	a	1-2	*Tsinamdzgvrishvili*
15/9	Torpedo	h	2-1	*Daushvili 2*
19/9	Kolkheti	h	2-0	*Tsinamdzgvrishvili, Dvali*
24/9	Samtredia	a	3-1	*Aptsiauri 2, Oniani*
28/9	Sioni	a	3-1	*Aptsiauri, Dvali, Gorgiashvili*
2/10	WIT Georgia	a	2-0	*Gelashvili, Dvali*
17/10	Torpedo	a	0-1	
23/10	Dinamo	h	0-1	
27/10	Baia	a	3-1	*Gelashvili 2, Grigalashvili*
31/10	Spartaki	a	1-1	*Aladashvili*
5/11	Olimpi	a	0-1	
21/11	Kolkheti	a	2-0	*Tsinamdzgvrishvili 2*
26/11	Samtredia	h	7-0	*Gelashvili 3, Tsinamdzgvrishvili 2 (1p), Dvali 2*
5/12	Sioni	h	4-0	*Dvali 2, Tsinamdzgvrishvili 2*
11/12	WIT Georgia	h	3-0	*Gelashvili 3 (1p)*
2011				
19/2	Dinamo	a	0-0	
23/2	Spartaki	a	2-1	*Daushvili, Tsinamdzgvrishvili*
27/2	Olimpi	h	2-0	*Grigalashvili, Gelashvili*
3/3	Torpedo	h	1-0	*Dvali*
7/3	Baia	h	6-1	*Grigalashvili, Gelashvili, Dvali 2, Aptsiauri, Oniani*
12/3	Kolkheti	h	0-0	
16/3	Samtredia	a	1-0	*Gelashvili*
20/3	Sioni	h	0-0	
2/4	WIT Georgia	a	1-1	*Gelashvili*
6/4	Torpedo	a	0-0	
10/4	Dinamo	h	1-0	*Chankotadze*
15/4	Spartaki	h	2-0	*Gelashvili, Tsinamdzgrishvili*
23/4	Olimpi	a	2-1	*Gelashvili, Dzaria*
30/4	Baia	h	3-0	*Dvali, Grigalashvili, Khidesheli*
8/5	Kolkheti	a	4-1	*Gorgiashvili, Kobakhidze, Daushvili, Aptsiauri*
14/5	Samtredia	h	4-1	*Gelashvili, Dvali, Oniani, Tsinamdzgvrishvili*
18/5	Sioni	a	0-1	
22/5	WIT Georgia	h	4-0	*Gorgiashvili, Gelashvili, Kobakhidze, og (Ganiashvili)*

Name	Nat	DoB	Pos	Aps	(s)	Gls
Kakhaber ALADASHVILI		11/8/83	M	26	(3)	2
Tornike APTSIAURI		28/11/79	M	28	(6)	5
Shota BABUNASHVILI		17/11/80	M	17	(14)	
Aleksi BENASHVILI		20/3/89	M	16	(10)	
Giorgi CHANKOTADZE		6/5/91	A		(3)	1
Murtaz DAUSHVILI		1/5/89	M	30		4
Jaba DVALI		8/2/85	A	28	(6)	12
Irakli DZARIA		1/12/87	M	25	(2)	2
Zaal ELIAVA		2/1/85	D	31		
Nikoloz GELASHVILI		5/8/85	A	30	(3)	18
Rostom GETSADZE		18/1/92	M		(1)	
Tornike GORGIASHVILI		27/4/88	M	15	(13)	3
Shota GRIGALASHVILI		21/6/86	M	31	(3)	5
Giorgi KHIDESHELI		23/1/88	D	21	(2)	1
Mamuka KOBAKHIDZE		23/8/92	D	16	(2)	2
Roin KVASKHVADZE		31/5/89	G	35		
Saba LOMIA		7/7/90	A		(4)	
Zurab MAMALADZE		10/2/82	G	1		
Giorgi ONIANI		23/11/83	D	34	(1)	3
Gogi PIPIA		4/2/85	A	1	(10)	
Giorgi POPKHADZE		25/9/86	D	5	(1)	
Rati TSINAMDZGVRISHVILI		22/3/88	A	6	(24)	13

TOP GOALSCORERS 2010/11

18 Nikoloz GELASHVILI (Zestafoni)

16 Irakli MODEBADZE (Olimpi)

13 Giorgi MEGRELADZE (Baia/Torpedo)
Rati TSINAMDZGVRISHVILI (Zestafoni)

12 Jaba DVALI (Zestafoni)

8 Levan KHMALADZE (Dinamo)
Aleksandre KOSHKADZE (Dinamo)

7 Irakli EKHVAIA (Baia)
Irakli KOBALIA (Baia)
Zviad METREVELI (Spartaki)
Giga BECHVAIA (WIT Georgia)

PROMOTED CLUBS

FC GAGRA

Coach – Anatoliy Piskovets (UKR)
Founded – 2004
Stadium – Merani, Tbilisi (1,000)
MAJOR HONOURS: Georgian Cup – (1) 2011.

FC MERANI MARTVILI

Coach – Malkhaz Jvania
Founded – 2006
Stadium – Central (2,000)

FC DILA GORI

Coach – Giorgi Tsetsadze
Founded – 1936
Stadium – Tengiz Burjanadze (5,000)

SECOND LEVEL FINAL TABLE 2010/11

		Pld	W	D	L	F	A	Pts
1	FC Gagra	32	23	6	3	73	19	75
2	FC Merani Martvili	32	22	7	3	60	15	73
3	FC Dila Gori	32	20	9	3	58	21	69
4	FC Chikhura Sachkhere	32	20	6	6	58	25	66
5	FC Dinamo Batumi	32	18	9	5	66	18	63
6	FC Guria Lanchkhuti	32	14	4	14	50	59	46
7	FC Kolkheti Khobi	32	12	10	10	30	34	46
8	FC Imereti Khoni	32	11	4	17	36	43	37
9	FC Meshakhte Tkibuli	32	10	5	17	32	48	35
10	FC Norchi Dinamo Tbilisi	32	10	5	17	39	58	35
11	FC Chkherimela Kharagauli	32	7	14	11	35	45	35
12	FC Adeli Batumi	32	10	2	20	38	54	32
13	FC Mertskhali Ozurgeti	32	8	8	16	41	68	32
14	FC Samgurali Tskhaltubo	32	8	6	18	38	64	30
15	FC Skuri Tsalenjikha	32	8	5	19	28	52	29
16	FC Chiatura	32	8	5	19	28	69	29
17	FC Lokomotivi Tbilisi	32	7	7	18	30	48	28

PROMOTION/RELEGATION PLAY-OFFS

(29/5/11)
Spartaki 2, Chikhura 1
(30/5/11)
Dila Gori 2, Samtredia 0

DOMESTIC CUP 2010/11

SAKARTVELOS TASI

FIRST ROUND

(24/8/10)
Chiatura 1, Samtredia 6
Dila 0, Lokomotivi Tbilisi 0 *(aet; 3-4 on pens)*
Imereti 0, Baia Zugdidi 1
Mertskhali 0, Torpedo 4
Norchi Dinamo 1, Gagra 3
Samgurali 0, Merani Martvili 2
Zooveti 0, Sioni 2

(25/8/10)
Adeli 0, Kolkheti Poti 2
Iveria 0, Spartaki Tskhinvali 2
Kolkheti Khobi 1, Dinamo Batumi 2
Meshakhte 1, Chikhura 3
Skuri 2, Guria 0

Byes – Dinamo Tbilisi, Olimpi, WIT Georgia, Zestafoni

SECOND ROUND

(10/11/10)
Dinamo Batumi 1, Zestafoni 2
Chikhura 0, Dinamo Tbilisi 4
Gagra 1, Kolkheti Poti 0
Lokomotivi Tbilisi 0, Olimpi 2
Merani Martvili 0, Sioni 0 *(aet; 2-4 on pens)*
Skuri 1, WIT Georgia 2 *(aet)*
Spartaki Tskhinvali 1, Samtredia 0
Torpedo 1, Baia Zugdidi 0 *(aet)*

QUARTER-FINALS

(1/12/10 & 15/12/10)
WIT Georgia 2 *(Bechvaia 34p, Kasradze 78),* Spartaki Tskhinvali 1 *(Bolkvadze 90p)*
Spartaki Tskhinvali 0, WIT Georgia 1 *(Adamadze 47)*
(WIT Georgia 3-1)

Zestafoni 3 *(Gelashvili 31, 80, Aptsiauri 64),* Olimpi 0
Olimpi 0, Zestafoni 0
(Zestafoni 3-0)

(1/12/10 & 16/12/10)
Gagra 1 *(Sharikadze 45),* Dinamo Tbilisi 2 *(Metreveli 7, 14)*
Dinamo Tbilisi 1 *(Mujiri 53),* Gagra 2 *(Owonikoko 14, Tkeshelashvili 77) (aet)*
(3-3; Gagra 4-2 on pens)

Sioni 0, Torpedo 1 *(Kvaratskhelia 46)*
Torpedo 0, Sioni 0
(Torpedo 1-0)

SEMI-FINALS

(19/4/11 & 4/5/11)
Gagra 3 *(Kvantaliani 16, Owonikoko 30, 79),* WIT Georgia 0
WIT Georgia 2 *(Chimakadze 45, 80),* Gagra 4 *(Kvantaliani 42, Owonikoko 56, 69, Tsitskhvaia 90)*
(Gagra 7-2)

Torpedo 1 *(Megreladze 65),* Zestafoni 0
Zestafoni 0, Torpedo 0
(Torpedo 1-0)

FINAL

(26/5/11)
Boris Paichadze National stadium, Tbilisi
FC GAGRA 1 *(Todua 105og)*
FC TORPEDO KUTAISI 0
(aet)
Referee – *Kvaratskhelia*
GAGRA – *Sepiashvili, Kalandadze, Tkeshelashvili, Chkhetiani, Jishkariani Ni., Khutsidze, Nakonechniy, Sharikadze, Kvantaliani, Ordinskiy (Koberidze 91; Tsitskhvaia 120), Gabedava (Gigauri 118).*
TORPEDO – *Migineishvili, Popkhadze, Parulava, Todua, Chikviladze, Datunaishvili, Seturidze, Dolidze (Kebadze 97), Tarkhnishvili (Guguchia 118), Megreladze, Gotsiridze (Kvaratskhelia 72).*

CLUB COMMUNICATION 2011/12

FC Baia Zugdidi

7 Mtskheta Street, 92 Rustaveli Street
GE-2100 Zugdidi

Tel +995 415 222 66
Fax +995 415 222 66
Web
Email mglebi@yahoo.com
Media Officer Lasha Jikia

FC Dila Gori

Guramishvili Street
GE-1400 Gori

Tel +995 370 270 801
Fax
Web
Email fcdila.gori@mail.ru
Media Officer David Chanturia

FC Dinamo Tbilisi

III Block, Digomy Township
Digmis Masivi, Paichadze Street
GE-0159 Tbilisi

Tel +995 32 251 6688
Fax +995 32 252 2784
Web fcdinamo.ge
Email webmaster@fcdinamo.ge
Media Officer Grigol Gventsadze

FC Gagra

51 Lomtatidze Street, V Block
GE-0159 Tbilisi

Tel +995 32 269 9780
Fax +995 32 296 7546
Web fcgagra.ge
Email gundi@fcgagra.ge
Media Officer Inga Koridze

FC Kolkheti Poti

20/11 Gegidze Street, 23 Petre Iberi Street
GE-Poti

Tel +995 493 703 70
Fax +995 493 703 71
Web
Email potistadioni@mail.ru
Media Officer

FC Merani Martvili

7 Tbilisi Street
GE-3100 Martvili

Tel +995 58 36 6336
Fax +995 32 277 9557
Web
Email elodanelia@mail.ru
Media Officer Nugzar Moniava

FC Metalurgi Rustavi

5 Mshenebelta Street
GE-3700 Rustavi

Tel +995 34 192 010
Fax +995 34 192 010
Web fcml.ge
Email shotashermadini@yahoo.com
Media Officer Shota Shermadini

FC Sioni Bolnisi

115 S.S. Orbeliani Street, 99 S.S.
Orbeliani Street, GE-1100 Bolnisi

Tel +995 90 579 399
Fax +995 32 922 493
Web
Email fcbolsioni@yahoo.de
Media Officer Jemal Chipashvili

FC Spartaki Tskhinvali

4 Galaktion Tabidze Street
GE-0105 Tbilisi

Tel +995 32 299 0216
Fax +995 32 299 0216
Web
Email nwn108@gmail.com
Media Officer Mikheil Egikov

FC Torpedo Kutaisi

1 Akaki Khorava Street
GE-4600 Kutaisi

Tel +995 43 162 787
Fax +995 43 162 787
Web fctorpedo.ge
Email info@fctorpedo.ge
Media Officer Ramaz Chkhikvadze

FC WIT Georgia

24 Al. Kazbegi Avenue
GE-0177 Tbilisi

Tel +995 32 312 400
Fax +995 32 312 400
Web witgeorgia.ge
Email witgeorgia@gmail.com
Media Officer David Tavartkiladze

FC Zestafoni

Staroselskiy str.2, 2 Gunia Street
GE-2000 Zestafoni

Tel +995 32 987 002
Fax +995 32 987 004
Web fczestafoni.ge
Email fczestafoni@rambler.ru
Media Officer Sergo Putkaradze

GERMANY

Allemagne I Deutschland

Deutscher Fussball-Bund (DFB)

COMMUNICATION

Address	Otto-Fleck-Schneise 6 Postfach 710265 DE-60492 Frankfurt am Main	**President**	Theo Zwanziger
		General Secretary	Wolfgang Niersbach
		Media Officer	Ralf Köttker
Tel	+49 69 67 880	**Year of Formation**	1900
Fax	+49 69 67 88266		
E-mail	info@dfb.de		
Website	dfb.de		

DOMESTIC COMPETITION SUMMARY 2010/11

BUNDESLIGA FINAL TABLE

			Home					Away					Total						
		Pld	**W**	**D**	**L**	**F**	**A**	**W**	**D**	**L**	**F**	**A**	**W**	**D**	**L**	**F**	**A**	**Pts**	**Comp**
1	Borussia Dortmund	34	12	4	1	35	8	11	2	4	32	14	23	6	5	67	22	75	UCL
2	Bayer 04 Leverkusen	34	9	5	3	33	24	11	3	3	31	20	20	8	6	64	44	68	UCL
3	FC Bayern München	34	13	2	2	48	13	6	6	5	33	27	19	8	7	81	40	65	UCL
4	Hannover 96	34	12	1	4	32	17	7	2	8	17	28	19	3	12	49	45	60	UEL
5	1. FSV Mainz 05	34	8	2	7	22	16	10	2	5	30	23	18	4	12	52	39	58	UEL
6	1. FC Nürnberg	34	9	2	6	28	19	4	6	7	19	26	13	8	13	47	45	47	
7	1. FC Kaiserslautern	34	6	6	5	25	19	7	1	9	23	32	13	7	14	48	51	46	
8	Hamburger SV	34	7	5	5	29	24	5	4	8	17	28	12	9	13	46	52	45	
9	SC Freiburg	34	8	2	7	24	24	5	3	9	17	26	13	5	16	41	50	44	
10	1. FC Köln	34	11	2	4	30	21	2	3	12	17	41	13	5	16	47	62	44	
11	TSG 1899 Hoffenheim	34	7	5	5	28	21	4	5	8	22	29	11	10	13	50	50	43	
12	VfB Stuttgart	34	7	2	8	33	27	5	4	8	27	32	12	6	16	60	59	42	
13	SV Werder Bremen	34	6	6	5	26	23	4	5	8	21	38	10	11	13	47	61	41	
14	FC Schalke 04	34	7	3	7	24	18	4	4	9	14	26	11	7	16	38	44	40	UEL
15	VfL Wolfsburg	34	5	6	6	27	26	4	5	8	16	22	9	11	14	43	48	38	
16	VfL Borussia Mönchengladbach	34	5	3	9	26	31	5	3	9	22	34	10	6	18	48	65	36	
17	Eintracht Frankfurt	34	5	4	8	13	24	4	3	10	18	25	9	7	18	31	49	34	*Relegated*
18	FC St Pauli	34	4	3	10	21	35	4	2	11	14	33	8	5	21	35	68	29	*Relegated*

Top Scorer Mario Gomez (Bayern), 28 goals

Promoted Clubs Hertha BSC Berlin
FC Augsburg

Cup Final FC Schalke 04 5, MSV Duisburg 0

Young guns fire Dortmund to title

The German Bundesliga had a champion to savour in 2010/11 as Borussia Dortmund – youthful, attractive and the best supported team in the land – cruised to their first league title in nine years. Dominant and defiant, the club from the Ruhr held sway for virtually the entire season, their charismatic coach Jürgen Klopp masterminding a triumph that was as worthy as it was universally popular.

At the core of Dortmund's success was a group of fast-developing, talented players in their early 20s and late teens. The simultaneous blossoming of centre-backs Mats Hummels and Neven Subotić, left-back Marcel Schmelzer, midfielders Nuri Şahin, Sven Bender and Shinji Kagawa, playmaker Mario Götze and winger Kevin Grosskreutz – all 23 or under at the start of 2011 – provided the club with a source of youthful energy and stamina that the other teams in the Bundesliga did not see coming. A mere fifth in the 2009/10 Bundesliga, Klopp's team of colts matured so rapidly that by the halfway point in the 2010/11 campaign Dortmund were ten points clear at the top of the standings.

Victory charge

Defeated in their opening fixture – 2-0 at home to Bayer 04 Leverkusen, the team that would eventually finish seven points behind them as runners-up – Klopp's young guns responded by reeling off 15 wins in their next 16 games, the only interruption to their victory charge coming in late October with a 1-1 draw at home to TSG 1899 Hoffenheim. Forceful and aggressive up front, where Argentina-born Paraguayan international Lucas Barrios, a 19-goal marksman the previous season, once again provided a formidable spearhead, Dortmund were close to impenetrable at the back, where goalkeeper/captain Roman Weidenfeller, at 30 the team's senior figure, conceded just seven goals – and no more than one in any game – during that remarkable run.

Dortmund players celebrate their Bundesliga triumph with the championship shield

Although Dortmund lost their last game before Christmas – 1-0 away to Eintracht Frankfurt – they reasserted their authority on the league's resumption in mid-January with a brilliant 3-1 win at Leverkusen, two goals from Grosskreutz and one from Götze effectively killing the title race stone dead. Outgoing champions FC Bayern München were also put to the sword at the end of February as Klopp's rampant young team – minus Japanese revelation Kagawa, who was ruled out of the spring campaign after picking up a serious injury at the Asian Cup – triumphed 3-1 in Munich to stretch their lead at the top to 12 points with just ten matches remaining. Dortmund could afford to ease off during the run-in, and the club's seventh German title was secured on the last day of April with a 2-0 home win over 1. FC Nürnberg, Barrios and Polish striker Robert Lewandowski scoring the goals that gave the Schwarzgelben an eight-point lead over Leverkusen – defeated the same day at local rivals 1. FC Köln – with two matches to spare.

Consistently cheered on by crowds of 80,000-plus at their hyper-atmospheric Westfalenstadion home, Dortmund's championship party really got going a couple of weeks later, after their final home game of the season, a 3-1 win over Frankfurt, when the B1 motorway just next to the stadium had to be closed for the entire weekend as hordes of yellow-and-black-bedecked fans over-indulged in the title celebrations.

Runners-up Leverkusen

Leverkusen needed something from their final fixture, away to SC Freiburg, to ensure second place and guaranteed participation alongside Dortmund in the group stage of the 2011/12 UEFA Champions League. A 1-0 win – secured by a fortuitous goal generously credited to midfielder Hanno Balitsch – did the trick, enabling coach Jupp Heynckes to leave the club on a positive note as he packed his bags for a third stint at Bayern – the club Leverkusen had just edged into third place. Although it was also the last game in charge for Freiburg coach Robin Dutt, the result was a handy one for him too as he had already agreed to become Heynckes' replacement at Leverkusen.

Given that Michael Ballack, who had rejoined Leverkusen from Chelsea FC the previous summer, barely played because of injury, the Rhinelanders did extremely well to finish second. Although they were never close enough to worry Dortmund, they accumulated points at a steady rate and unearthed a jewel in Chilean midfield all-rounder Arturo Vidal, who was the club's top scorer with ten goals. Leverkusen also performed creditably in the UEFA Europa League, going unbeaten in ten matches until they encountered Villarreal CF in the round of 16. That was two rounds further than Dortmund went, Klopp's side surprisingly failing to export their autumn Bundesliga form into Europe, where they could only finish third in their UEFA Europa League group behind Paris Saint-Germain FC and Sevilla FC.

Bayern, who won the German double and reached the UEFA Champions League final under new coach Louis van Gaal in 2009/10, fell well short of a repeat performance on all three fronts, which led to a parting of the ways with the Dutchman after less than two full seasons in charge. It was announced first of all, in early March, that Van Gaal would be leaving at the end of the season, but when a fatal home defeat to FC Internazionale Milano in the first knockout round of the UEFA Champions League followed hot on the heels of another couple of vitally important home losses – in the league against Dortmund and the semi-final of the German Cup

National Team

International Honours* –
FIFA World Cup – (3) 1954, 1974, 1990.
UEFA European Championship – (3) 1972, 1980, 1996.

International Tournament Appearances* –
FIFA World Cup – (17) 1934 (3rd), 1938, 1954 (Winners), 1958 (4th), 1962 (qtr-finals), 1966 (runners-up), 1970 (3rd), 1974 (Winners), 1978 (2nd phase), 1982 (runners-up), 1986 (runners-up), 1990 (Winners), 1994 (qtr-finals), 1998 (qtr-finals), 2002 (runners-up), 2006 (3rd), 2010 (3rd).
UEFA European Championship – (10) 1972 (Winners), 1976 (runners-up), 1980 (Winners), 1984, 1988 (semi-finals), 1992 (runners-up), 1996 (Winners), 2000, 2004, 2008 (runners-up).

Top Five All-time Caps – Lothar Matthäus (150); Miroslav Klose (109); Jürgen Klinsmann (108); Jürgen Kohler (105); Franz Beckenbauer (103)

Top Five All-time Goals – Gerd Müller (68); Miroslav Klose (61); Jürgen Klinsmann & Rudi Völler (47); Karl-Heinz Rummenigge (45)

(before 1992 as West Germany)*

NATIONAL TEAM RESULTS 2010/11

11/8/10	Denmark	A	Copenhagen	2-2	*Gomez (19), Helmes (73)*
3/9/10	Belgium (ECQ)	A	Brussels	1-0	*Klose (51)*
7/9/10	Azerbaijan (ECQ)	H	Cologne	6-1	*Westermann (28), Podolski (45+1), Klose (45+2, 90+2), Sadıqov R.F. (53og), Badstuber (86)*
8/10/10	Turkey (ECQ)	H	Berlin	3-0	*Klose (42, 87), Özil (79)*
12/10/10	Kazakhstan (ECQ)	A	Astana	3-0	*Klose (48), Gomez (76), Podolski (85)*
17/11/10	Sweden	A	Gothenburg	0-0	
9/2/11	Italy	H	Dortmund	1-1	*Klose (16)*
26/3/11	Kazakhstan (ECQ)	H	Kaiserslautern	4-0	*Klose (3, 88), Müller (25, 43)*
29/3/11	Australia	H	Monchengladbach	1-2	*Gomez (26)*
29/5/11	Uruguay	H	Sinsheim	2-1	*Gomez (20), Schürrle (35)*
3/6/11	Austria (ECQ)	A	Vienna	2-1	*Gomez (44, 90)*
7/6/11	Azerbaijan (ECQ)	A	Baku	3-1	*Özil (29), Gomez (40), Schürrle (90+3)*

NATIONAL TEAM APPEARANCES 2010/11

Coach – Joachim LÖW	3/2/60		Den	BEL	AZE	TUR	KAZ	Swe	Ita	KAZ	Aus	Uru	AUT	AZE	Caps	Goals
Tim WIESE	17/12/81	Werder	G								G				4	-
Andreas BECK	13/3/87	Hoffenheim	D56					s46							9	-
Jérôme BOATENG	3/9/88	Man. City (ENG)	D78					D46	s64						13	-
Serdar TAŞÇI	24/4/87	Stuttgart	D												14	-
Marcel SCHÄFER	7/6/84	Wolfsburg	D												8	-
Christian GENTNER	14/8/85	Stuttgart	M												5	-
Thomas HITZLSPERGER	5/4/82	West Ham (ENG)	M66												52	6
Christian TRÄSCH	1/9/87	Stuttgart	M			s86		s60			D	s79			7	-
Toni KROOS	4/1/90	Bayern	M	s70		M	M	s60		s77	s64	M79	M93	M	18	-
Marko MARIN	13/3/89	Werder	M56		s61	s90	s71	M60							16	1
Mario GOMEZ	10/7/85	Bayern	A				s55	A		s65	A73	A	A	A	46	19
Sascha RIETHER	23/3/83	Wolfsburg	s56		D										2	-
Aaron HUNT	4/9/86	Werder	s56												2	-
Patrick HELMES	1/3/84	Leverkusen	s66												13	2
Christian SCHULZ	1/4/83	Hannover	s78												4	-
Manuel NEUER	27/3/86	Schalke		G	G	G	G		G	G		G	G	G	20	-
Philipp LAHM	11/11/83	Bayern		D	D	D	D		D64	D		D66	D	M	80	4
Per MERTESACKER	29/9/84	Werder		D	D11	D	D		D	D					75	1
Holger BADSTUBER	13/3/89	Bayern		D	D	D	D		D64	D		s66	s69	D	13	1
Marcell JANSEN	4/11/85	Hamburg		D46											36	3
Sami KHEDIRA	4/4/87	Real Madrid (ESP)		M	M	M	M	M60	M	M			M69		20	1
Bastian SCHWEINSTEIGER	1/8/84	Bayern		M	M78			M60	M	M77	M64				87	21
Thomas MÜLLER	13/9/89	Bayern		M	M61	M	M71		M46	M78	M64	M79	M	M88	18	7
Mesut ÖZIL	15/10/88	Real Madrid (ESP)		M88	M	M90	M79		M	M		M46	M	M81	26	4
Lukas PODOLSKI	4/6/85	Köln		A70	M	M86	M		M	M65	M	s58	M67	M75	89	42
Miroslav KLOSE	9/6/78	Bayern		A	A	A90	A55		A75	A	s73	s46			109	61
Heiko WESTERMANN	14/8/83	Hamburg		s46	s11	D	D	D							24	3
Jerónimo da Silva "CACAU"	27/3/81	Stuttgart		s88	s78	s90	s79	s60							17	4
René ADLER	15/1/85	Leverkusen						G							10	-
Mats HUMMELS	16/12/88	Dortmund						D	s64		D	D	D	D	7	-
Marcel SCHMELZER	22/1/88	Dortmund						D			D	D	D		4	-
Kevin GROSSKREUTZ	19/7/88	Dortmund						M78	s75						3	-
Lewis HOLTBY	18/9/90	Mainz						M78						s88	2	-
André SCHÜRRLE	6/11/90	Mainz						s78			M	M58	s67	s75	5	2
Mario GÖTZE	3/6/92	Dortmund						s78	s46	s78	s64	s79		s81	6	-
Dennis AOGO	14/1/87	Hamburg							D	D			s93	D	7	-
Arne FRIEDRICH	29/5/79	Wolfsburg									D	D66	D		82	1
Sven BENDER	27/4/89	Dortmund									M				1	-
Simon ROLFES	21/1/82	Leverkusen										M			22	1
Benedikt HÖWEDES	29/2/88	Schalke										s66		D	2	-

against FC Schalke 04 – the coach's borrowed time was cut short. For the last five games of the season Bayern were led by Van Gaal's assistant, Andries Jonker, and they did enough to finish third, which guaranteed their participation in the qualifying phase of a 2011/12 UEFA Champions League that will end with the final in their home stadium.

Robben missed

Bayern's campaign was not quite trophyless as they did defeat Schalke 2-0 in the pre-season German Super Cup, but it was hugely disappointing nonetheless. Arjen Robben, the Bundesliga Player of the Year in 2009/10, missed the first half of the season with a hamstring injury aggravated while playing for the Netherlands at the 2010 FIFA World Cup, and although he was in scintillating form in the spring, scoring a dozen goals in 14 games, his efforts came too late. Several of the team's World Cup performers, among them German heroes Thomas Müller and Bastian Schweinsteiger, were underpowered at the start, and although 2009/10 outcast Mario Gomez came thrillingly to the fore to claim the Bundesliga Golden Boot with 28 goals and help to make Bayern's attack the strongest in the league, the team's defence was repeatedly found wanting. Only Philipp Lahm stood up to be counted in the back four, and Van Gaal came in for some strong criticism both for promoting young goalkeeper Thomas Kraft ahead of old stager Hans-Jörg Butt and allowing experienced holding midfielder Mark van Bommel to leave in mid-season for AC Milan.

Manuel Neuer shone for Schalke in the German Cup and UEFA Champions League before leaving his hometown club for Bayern

Bayern's shaky rearguard was shown up most obviously when they conceded three goals at home to Inter in a re-match of the previous season's UEFA Champions League final. Having won the first leg 1-0 in Milan with a late Gomez goal, then gone 2-1 up in Munich, revenge seemed assured, Instead that task was carried out for them a round later when Schalke, who had impressively eliminated Valencia CF, slayed the holders with an astonishing 5-2 victory at San Siro before completing the job with a 2-1 win in Gelsenkirchen. The club's first qualification for the UEFA Champions League semi-finals was all the more remarkable for the fact that they had just changed coach, Ralf Rangnick having been appointed in place of Felix Magath, who, a season after steering the club to a runners-up spot, paid the price for the team's miserable efforts in the Bundesliga, where they would eventually end up in 14th place, just four points clear of the relegation zone.

Schalke storm Berlin

Before he left, Magath guided Schalke into the German Cup final, the club's 1-0 win at Bayern reversing the outcome of the previous season's fixture. The goalscorer in Munich was legendary ex-Real Madrid CF striker Raúl, who had left the Spanish capital the previous summer for a new challenge in Germany. His UEFA Champions League pedigree proved crucial – he added another five goals to his record tally in the competition – but although he could not steer Schalke past a dominant Manchester United FC in the semi-finals, he did get to enjoy the first domestic cup triumph of his illustrious career as the Königsblauen completed a one-two of domestic trophies for the Ruhr region by hammering second division MSV Duisburg 5-0 in the final. Dutchman Klaas Jan Huntelaar, another high-profile pre-season signing, scored twice in Berlin to end his injury-blighted first campaign in German football on a high. It was also a fitting farewell for Schalke's Gelsenkirchen-born German international goalkeeper Manuel Neuer, who subsequently left for Bayern.

Miroslav Klose steered Germany towards the UEFA EURO 2012 finals with eight qualifying goals

While Schalke's DFB-Pokal triumph secured a return ticket to Europe, there was no such consolation for some of the Bundesliga's other big-budget clubs, such as SV Werder Bremen, VfB Stuttgart and VfL Wolfsburg, all of whom finished alongside Schalke in the nether reaches of the table. Werder stayed loyal to long-serving Thomas Schaaf, but three coaches were required at both Stuttgart and Wolfsburg before relegation fears were finally banished. Bremen began the season by thrillingly overcoming UC Sampdoria to reach the UEFA Champions League group stage but ended it a lowly 13th in the Bundesliga, the departure of playmaker Mesut Özil to Real Madrid and – in January – striker Hugo Almeida to Beşiktaş JK having created two gaping voids. Stuttgart were rescued from relegation by four late wins under ex-Hamburger SV boss Bruno Labbadia while Magath, who returned to Wolfsburg two days after leaving Schalke, kept up the team he had led to the 2008/09 title only with a last-day 3-1 win at Hoffenheim, the late-season goalscoring form of Croatian international Mario Mandžukić proving crucial to the Lower Saxony club's salvation.

Frankfurt also brought in a famous coach to help them avoid the drop, but Christoph Daum was unable to rescue a team that had forgotten how to score – despite possessing in their ranks the Bundesliga's leading marksman at Christmas, Greek international Theofanis Gekas. They went down with new boys FC St Pauli, who were simply not up to Bundesliga standard. VfL Borussia Mönchengladbach retained their top-flight status thanks to the sterling efforts of their new coach Lucien Favre and a play-off win over VfL Bochum 1848. That left just the top two in the 2. Bundesliga – champions Hertha BSC Berlin and runners-up FC Augsburg – celebrating promotion. Hertha had been absent for just 12 months but Augsburg, who lost the previous season's play-off to Nürnberg, moved up to the Bundesliga for the very first time, becoming the league's 51st participant since its inception in 1963/64.

Nürnberg and newly-promoted 1. FC Kaiserslautern both enjoyed positive 2010/11 campaigns, finishing sixth and seventh respectively, but they were outshone by the two teams that finished above them and qualified for the UEFA Europa League – Hannover 96 and 1. FSV Mainz 05. Hannover jumped 11 places to finish fourth and for a long time challenged Bayern for third. Mirko Slomka's team possessed two fine foreign strikers in Mohammed Abdellaoue and Didier Konan Ya, while the star performers for a Mainz side led by the Bundesliga's youngest coach, Thomas Tuchel, were up-and-coming Germans Lewis Holtby and André Schürrle. Mainz had a phenomenal start to the season, winning their first seven matches, including a 2-1 win at Bayern.

Serene progress

Joachim Löw's German national team made smooth and serene progress towards the UEFA EURO 2012 finals, winning all of their first seven qualifiers. The Bundestrainer kept the bulk of his bronze medal-winning World Cup team intact while introducing fresh faces such as Holtby, Schürrrle, Schalke centre-back Benedikt Höwedes and the young Dortmund quintet of Bender, Götze, Grosskreutz, Hummels and Schmelzer. With Miroslav Klose, underused at Bayern, continuing to score prolifically for his country – another nine goals in 2010/11 took his cumulative tally to 61, just seven behind Gerd Müller's record haul – and Gomez also joining in with five goals in four games during the spring, the Nationalmannschaft appears to be better equipped now than for many years and will travel to Poland/Ukraine high on confidence and full of determination to unseat holders Spain and claim a record fourth continental crown.

CLUB-BY-CLUB

BAYER 04 LEVERKUSEN

Coach – Jupp Heynckes
Founded – 1904
Stadium – BayArena (30,210)
MAJOR HONOURS: UEFA Cup – (1) 1988; German Cup – (1) 1993.

2010

22/8	Dortmund	a	2-0	*Barnetta, Renato Augusto*
29/8	Mönchengladbach	h	3-6	*Derdiyok, Vidal (p), Kiessling*
11/9	Hannover	a	2-2	*Derdiyok, Helmes*
19/9	Nürnberg	h	0-0	
22/9	Eintracht	h	2-1	*Bender, Vidal (p)*
25/9	Stuttgart	a	4-1	*Hyypiä, Vidal, Balitsch, Sam*
3/10	Werder	h	2-2	*Helmes, Derdiyok*
16/10	Wolfsburg	a	3-2	*Rolfes 2, Vidal (p)*
24/10	Mainz	h	0-1	
30/10	Schalke	a	1-0	*Sam*
7/11	Kaiserslautern	h	3-1	*Sam 2, Helmes*
13/11	St Pauli	a	1-0	*Renato Augusto*
20/11	Bayern	h	1-1	*Vidal (p)*
27/11	Hoffenheim	a	2-2	*Sam, Vidal (p)*
5/12	Köln	h	3-2	*Helmes, Barnetta, Reinartz*
11/12	Hamburg	a	4-2	*Sam, Vidal, Renato Augusto 2*
19/12	Freiburg	h	2-2	*Vidal (p), Helmes*

2011

14/1	Dortmund	h	1-3	*Kiessling*
23/1	Mönchengladbach	a	3-1	*Kadlec, Castro 2*
28/1	Hannover	h	2-0	*Vidal, Rolfes*
5/2	Nürnberg	a	0-1	
12/2	Eintracht	a	3-0	*Rolfes, Renato Augusto, Balitsch*
20/2	Stuttgart	h	4-2	*Kiessling 2, Castro, Reinartz*
27/2	Werder	a	2-2	*Derdiyok, Rolfes*
5/3	Wolfsburg	h	3-0	*Bender, Renato Augusto, Kiessling*
13/3	Mainz	a	1-0	*Renato Augusto*
20/3	Schalke	h	2-0	*Derdiyok, og (Metzelder)*
2/4	Kaiserslautern	a	1-0	*Sam*
10/4	St Pauli	h	2-1	*Kiessling, Bender*
17/4	Bayern	a	1-5	*Derdiyok*
23/4	Hoffenheim	h	2-1	*Kadlec, Vidal*
30/4	Köln	a	0-2	
7/5	Hamburg	h	1-1	*Kiessling*
14/5	Freiburg	a	1-0	*Balitsch*

No	Name	Nat	DoB	Pos	Aps	(s)	Gls
1	René ADLER		15/1/85	G	32		
14	Hanno BALITSCH		2/1/81	M	9	(15)	3
13	Michael BALLACK		26/9/76	M	13	(4)	
7	Tranquillo BARNETTA	SUI	22/5/85	M	19	(5)	2
8	Lars BENDER		27/4/89	M	10	(17)	3
27	Gonzalo CASTRO		11/6/87	D	19	(4)	3
19	Eren DERDIYOK	SUI	12/6/88	A	18	(14)	6
5	Manuel FRIEDRICH		13/9/79	D	17	(2)	
36	Fabian GIEFER		17/5/90	G	2		
9	Patrick HELMES		1/3/84	A	8	(3)	5
4	Sami HYYPIÄ	FIN	7/10/73	D	20	(1)	1
31	Nicolai JØRGENSEN	DEN	15/1/91	A	1	(8)	
24	Michal KADLEC	CZE	13/12/84	D	30	(2)	2
11	Stefan KIESSLING		25/1/84	A	15	(7)	7
3	Stefan REINARTZ		1/1/89	D	29	(2)	2
10	RENATO Soares de Oliveira AUGUSTO	BRA	8/2/88	M	26	(1)	7
6	Simon ROLFES		21/1/82	M	21	(7)	5
18	Sidney SAM		31/1/88	M	26	(4)	7
2	Daniel SCHWAAB		23/8/88	D	28	(2)	
17	Domagoj VIDA	CRO	29/4/89	D		(1)	
23	Arturo VIDAL	CHI	22/5/87	M	31	(2)	10

FC BAYERN MÜNCHEN

Coach – Louis van Gaal (NED);
(10/4/11) (Andries Jonker (NED))
Founded – 1900
Stadium – Allianz-Arena (69,000)
MAJOR HONOURS: European Champion Clubs' Cup/ UEFA Champions League – (4) 1974, 1975, 1976, 2001; UEFA Cup – (1) 1996; World Club Cup – (2) 1976, 2001; German League – (22) 1932, 1969, 1972, 1973, 1974, 1980, 1981, 1985, 1986, 1987, 1989, 1990, 1994, 1997, 1999, 2000, 2001, 2003, 2005, 2006, 2008, 2010; German Cup – (15) 1957, 1966, 1967, 1969, 1971, 1982, 1984, 1986, 1998, 2000, 2003, 2005, 2006, 2008, 2010.

2010

20/8	Wolfsburg	h	2-1	*Müller, Schweinsteiger*
27/8	Kaiserslautern	a	0-2	
11/9	Werder	h	0-0	
18/9	Köln	h	0-0	
21/9	Hoffenheim	a	2-1	*Müller, Van Buyten*
25/9	Mainz	h	1-2	*og (Svensson)*
3/10	Dortmund	a	0-2	
16/10	Hannover	h	3-0	*Gomez 3*
22/10	Hamburg	a	0-0	
29/10	Freiburg	h	4-2	*Demichelis, Gomez, Tymoshchuk, Kroos*
6/11	Mönchengladbach	a	3-3	*Gomez, Schweinsteiger, Lahm*
14/11	Nürnberg	h	3-0	*Gomez 2, Lahm (p)*
20/11	Leverkusen	a	1-1	*Gomez*
27/11	Eintracht	h	4-1	*Tymoshchuk 2, Müller, Gomez*
4/12	Schalke	a	0-2	
11/12	St Pauli	h	3-0	*Hamit, Lahm (p), Ribéry*
19/12	Stuttgart	a	5-3	*Gomez 3, Müller, Ribéry*

2011

15/1	Wolfsburg	a	1-1	*Müller*
22/1	Kaiserslautern	h	5-1	*Robben, Gomez 3, Müller*
29/1	Werder	a	3-1	*Robben, og (Mertesacker), Klose*
5/2	Köln	a	2-3	*Gomez, Hamit*
12/2	Hoffenheim	h	4-0	*Gomez, Müller, Robben 2*
19/2	Mainz	a	3-1	*Schweinsteiger, Müller, Gomez*
26/2	Dortmund	h	1-3	*Luiz Gustavo*
5/3	Hannover	a	1-3	*Robben*
12/3	Hamburg	h	6-0	*Robben 3, Ribéry, Müller, og (Westermann)*
19/3	Freiburg	a	2-1	*Gomez, Ribéry*
2/4	Mönchengladbach	h	1-0	*Robben*
9/4	Nürnberg	a	1-1	*Müller*
17/4	Leverkusen	h	5-1	*og (Rolfes), Gomez 3, Ribéry*
23/4	Eintracht	a	1-1	*Gomez (p)*
30/4	Schalke	h	4-1	*Robben, Müller 2, Gomez*
7/5	St Pauli	a	8-1	*Gomez 3, Van Buyten, Robben 2, Ribéry 2*
14/5	Stuttgart	h	2-1	*Gomez, Schweinsteiger*

No	Name	Nat	DoB	Pos	Aps	(s)	Gls
27	David ALABA	AUT	24/6/92	M		(2)	
28	Holger BADSTUBER		13/3/89	D	21	(2)	
4	Edson BRAAFHEID	NED	8/4/83	D	2	(1)	
2	BRENO Vinícius Rodrigues Borges	BRA	13/10/89	D	7	(6)	
1	Hans-Jörg BUTT		28/5/74	G	22	(1)	
26	Diego CONTENTO		1/5/90	D	11	(2)	
6	Martín DEMICHELIS	ARG	20/12/80	D	3	(3)	1
33	Mario GOMEZ		10/7/85	A	27	(5)	28
8	HAMİT Altıntop	TUR	8/12/82	M	8	(6)	2
18	Miroslav KLOSE		9/6/78	A	9	(11)	1
35	Thomas KRAFT		22/7/88	G	12		
39	Toni KROOS		4/1/90	M	19	(8)	1
21	Philipp LAHM		11/11/83	D	34		3

0	LUIZ GUSTAVO Dias	BRA	23/7/87	M	13	(1)	1
5	Thomas MÜLLER		13/9/89	A	32	(2)	12
	Ivica OLIĆ	CRO	14/9/79	A	3	(3)	
6	Andreas OTTL		1/3/85	M	9	(6)	
3	Danijel PRANJIĆ	CRO	2/12/81	M	22	(6)	
	Franck RIBÉRY	FRA	7/4/83	M	22	(3)	7
0	Arjen ROBBEN	NED	23/1/84	M	13	(1)	12
1	Bastian SCHWEINSTEIGER		1/8/84	M	32	(1)	4
4	Anatoliy TYMOSHCHUK	UKR	30/3/79	M	23	(3)	3
7	Mark VAN BOMMEL	NED	22/4/77	M	12	(1)	
	Daniel VAN BUYTEN	BEL	7/2/78	D	18	(3)	2

BORUSSIA DORTMUND

Coach – Jürgen Klopp

Founded – 1909

Stadium – Signal-Iduna-Park (80,720)

MAJOR HONOURS: UEFA Champions League – (1) 1997; UEFA Cup Winners' Cup – (1) 1966; World Club Cup – (1) 1997; German League – (7) 1956, 1957, 1963, 1995, 1996, 2002, 2011; German Cup – (2) 1965, 1989.

010				
2/8	Leverkusen	h	0-2	
9/8	Stuttgart	a	3-1	*og (Boulahrouz), Barrios, Götze*
1/9	Wolfsburg	h	2-0	*Nuri, Kagawa*
9/9	Schalke	a	3-1	*Kagawa 2, Lewandowski*
2/9	Kaiserslautern	h	5-0	*Barrios 2, Grosskreutz, Hummels, Lewandowski*
5/9	St Pauli	a	3-1	*Grosskreutz 2, Kagawa*
/10	Bayern	h	2-0	*Barrios, Nuri*
5/10	Köln	a	2-1	*Błaszczykowski, Nuri*
4/10	Hoffenheim	h	1-1	*Antônio da Silva*
1/10	Mainz	a	2-0	*Götze, Barrios*
/11	Hannover	a	4-0	*Kagawa, Barrios, Lewandowski, Błaszczykowski*
12/11	Hamburg	h	2-0	*Kagawa, Barrios*
20/11	Freiburg	a	2-1	*Lewandowski, og (Mujdža)*
27/11	Mönchengladbach	h	4-1	*Subotić, Kagawa, Grosskreutz, Barrios*
5/12	Nürnberg	a	2-0	*Hummels, Lewandowski*
11/12	Werder	h	2-0	*Nuri, Kagawa*
18/12	Eintracht	a	0-1	
2011				
14/1	Leverkusen	a	3-1	*Grosskreutz 2, Götze*
22/1	Stuttgart	h	1-1	*Götze*
29/1	Wolfsburg	a	3-0	*Barrios, Nuri, Hummels*
4/2	Schalke	h	0-0	
12/2	Kaiserslautern	a	1-1	*Bender*
19/2	St Pauli	h	2-0	*Barrios, og (Gunesch)*
26/2	Bayern	a	3-1	*Barrios, Nuri, Hummels*
4/3	Köln	h	1-0	*Lewandowski*
12/3	Hoffenheim	a	0-1	
19/3	Mainz	h	1-1	*Hummels*
2/4	Hannover	h	4-1	*Götze, Barrios 2, Grosskreutz*
9/4	Hamburg	a	1-1	*Błaszczykowski*
17/4	Freiburg	h	3-0	*Götze, Lewandowski, Grosskreutz*
23/4	Mönchengladbach	a	0-1	
30/4	Nürnberg	h	2-0	*Barrios, Lewandowski*
7/5	Werder	a	0-2	
14/5	Eintracht	h	3-1	*Barrios 2, og (Russ)*

No	Name	Nat	DoB	Pos	Aps	(s)	Gls
32	ANTÔNIO DA SILVA	BRA	13/6/78	M	5	(17)	1
18	Lucas BARRIOS	PAR	13/11/84	A	29	(3)	16
22	Sven BENDER		27/4/89	M	29	(2)	1
16	Jakub BŁASZCZYKOWSKI	POL	14/12/85	M	15	(14)	3
17	Leonardo de Déus Santos "DEDÊ"	BRA	18/4/78	D		(4)	
27	FELIPE Augusto SANTANA	BRA	17/3/86	D	5	(8)	
14	Markus FEULNER		12/2/82	M		(6)	
31	Mario GÖTZE		3/6/92	M	29	(4)	6
19	Kevin GROSSKREUTZ		19/7/88	M	32	(2)	8
15	Mats HUMMELS		16/12/88	D	32		5
23	Shinji KAGAWA	JPN	17/3/89	M	17	(1)	8
5	Sebastian KEHL		13/2/80	M	3	(3)	
20	Mitchell LANGERAK	AUS	22/8/88	G	1		
7	Robert LEWANDOWSKI	POL	21/8/88	A	15	(18)	8
8	NURI Şahin	TUR	5/9/88	M	30		6
25	Patrick OWOMOYELA		5/11/79	D	5	(1)	
26	Łukasz PISZCZEK	POL	3/6/85	D	29	(4)	
11	Dimitar RANGELOV	BUL	9/2/83	A		(1)	
29	Marcel SCHMELZER		22/1/88	D	34		
39	Marco STIEPERMANN		9/2/91	A		(4)	
4	Neven SUBOTIĆ	SRB	10/12/88	D	31		1
1	Roman WEIDENFELLER		6/8/80	G	33		
10	Mohamed ZIDAN	EGY	11/12/81	A		(8)	

VFL BORUSSIA MÖNCHENGLADBACH

Coach – Michael Frontzeck; (14/2/11) Lucien Favre (SUI)

Founded – 1900

Stadium – Borussia-Park (54,057)

MAJOR HONOURS: UEFA Cup – (2) 1975, 1979; German League – (5) 1970, 1971, 1975, 1976, 1977; German Cup – (3) 1960, 1973, 1995.

2010				
21/8	Nürnberg	h	1-1	*Idrissou*
29/8	Leverkusen	a	6-3	*Herrmann 2, Brouwers, Juan Arango, Idrissou, Reus*
11/9	Eintracht	h	0-4	
18/9	Stuttgart	a	0-7	
22/9	St Pauli	h	1-2	*Juan Arango*
25/9	Schalke	a	2-2	*Daems (p), Bradley*
2/10	Wolfsburg	h	1-1	*Marx*
17/10	Hoffenheim	a	2-3	*Bobadilla, Idrissou*
23/10	Werder	h	1-4	*og (Mertesacker)*
30/10	Kaiserslautern	a	0-3	
6/11	Bayern	h	3-3	*Herrmann, Reus, De Camargo*
13/11	Köln	a	4-0	*Bobadilla 2, Bradley, De Camargo*
20/11	Mainz	h	2-3	*Reus 2*
27/11	Dortmund	a	1-4	*Reus*
4/12	Hannover	h	1-2	*Bradley*
12/12	Freiburg	a	0-3	
17/12	Hamburg	h	1-2	*De Camargo*
2011				
15/1	Nürnberg	a	1-0	*Neustädter*
23/1	Leverkusen	h	1-3	*Stranzl*
30/1	Eintracht	a	1-0	*De Camargo*
5/2	Stuttgart	h	2-3	*Dante, De Camargo*
12/2	St Pauli	a	1-3	*De Camargo*
20/2	Schalke	h	2-1	*Reus, Idrissou*
25/2	Wolfsburg	a	1-2	*Daems (p)*
5/3	Hoffenheim	h	2-0	*Daems (p), De Camargo*
12/3	Werder	a	1-1	*Dante*
18/3	Kaiserslautern	h	0-1	
2/4	Bayern	a	0-1	
10/4	Köln	h	5-1	*Juan Arango, Reus 2, Daems (p), Nordtveit*
15/4	Mainz	a	0-1	
23/4	Dortmund	h	1-0	*Idrissou*
30/4	Hannover	a	1-0	*Reus*
7/5	Freiburg	h	2-0	*Hanke, Reus*
14/5	Hamburg	a	1-1	*Juan Arango*

No	Name	Nat	DoB	Pos	Aps	(s)	Gls
5	ANDERSON Soares de Oliveira "BAMBA"	BRA	10/1/88	D	11	(2)	
30	Logan BAILLY	BEL	27/12/85	G	15		
10	Raúl Marcelo BOBADILLA	ARG	18/6/87	A	8	(6)	3
26	Michael BRADLEY	USA	31/7/87	M	17	(2)	3
4	Roel BROUWERS	NED	28/11/81	D	10	(5)	1
6	Jan-Ingwer CALLSEN-BRACKER		23/9/84	D	3	(1)	
3	Filip DAEMS	BEL	31/10/78	D	34		4

No	Name	Nat	DoB	Pos	Aps	(s)	Gls
31	DANTE Bonfim Costa Santos	BRA	18/10/83	D	17	(1)	2
10	Igor DE CAMARGO	BEL	12/5/83	A	14	(5)	7
6	Michael FINK		1/2/82	M	4	(2)	
19	Mike HANKE		5/11/83	A	10	(4)	1
1	Christofer HEIMEROTH		1/8/81	G	13		
15	Patrick HERRMANN		12/2/91	M	15	(9)	3
25	Mohamadou IDRISSOU	CMR	8/3/80	A	26	(7)	5
24	Tony JANTSCHKE		7/4/90	M	10	(1)	
18	JUAN Fernando ARANGO Sáenz	VEN	17/5/80	M	24	(1)	4
32	Elias KACHUNGA		22/4/92	A		(2)	
22	Tobias LEVELS		22/11/86	M	22		
14	Thorben MARX		1/6/81	M	19	(8)	1
40	Karim MATMOUR	ALG	25/6/85	A	3	(15)	
8	Marcel MEEUWIS	NED	31/10/80	M		(2)	
13	Roman NEUSTÄDTER		18/2/88	M	20	(4)	1
16	Håvard NORDTVEIT	NOR	21/6/90	D	15	(1)	1
11	Marco REUS		31/5/89	M	32		10
2	Sebastian SCHACHTEN		6/11/84	D	7	(6)	
39	Martin STRANZL	AUT	16/6/80	D	17		1
21	Marc-André TER STEGEN		30/4/92	G	6		
27	Jens WISSING		2/1/88	D	2	(1)	

EINTRACHT FRANKFURT

Coach – Michael Skibbe; (22/3/11) Christoph Daum

Founded – 1899

Stadium – Commerzbank-Arena (51,500)

MAJOR HONOURS: UEFA Cup – (1) 1980;
German League – (1) 1959;
German Cup – (4) 1974, 1975, 1981, 1988.

2010				
21/8	Hannover	a	1-2	*Köhler*
28/8	Hamburg	h	1-3	*Ochs*
11/9	Mönchengladbach	a	4-0	*Köhler, Gekas 2, Ochs*
17/9	Freiburg	h	0-1	
22/9	Leverkusen	a	1-2	*Gekas*
25/9	Nürnberg	h	2-0	*Gekas, Chris*
3/10	Stuttgart	a	2-1	*Gekas, Chris*
17/10	Kaiserslautern	a	3-0	*Gekas 2, Meier*
23/10	Schalke	h	0-0	
30/10	St Pauli	a	3-1	*Gekas 2 (1p), Caio*
6/11	Wolfsburg	h	3-1	*Gekas 2 (1p), Schwegler*
13/11	Werder	a	0-0	
20/11	Hoffenheim	h	0-4	
27/11	Bayern	a	1-4	*Gekas*
4/12	Mainz	h	2-1	*Russ, Gekas (p)*
11/12	Köln	a	0-1	
18/12	Dortmund	h	1-0	*Gekas*
16/12	Hannover	h	0-3	
2011				
21/1	Hamburg	a	0-1	
30/1	Mönchengladbach	h	0-1	
6/2	Freiburg	a	0-0	
12/2	Leverkusen	h	0-3	
18/2	Nürnberg	a	0-3	
27/2	Stuttgart	h	0-2	
5/3	Kaiserslautern	h	0-0	
12/3	Schalke	a	1-2	*Tzavelas*
19/3	St Pauli	h	2-1	*Gekas 2 (1p)*
3/4	Wolfsburg	a	1-1	*Meier*
8/4	Werder	h	1-1	*Fenin*
16/4	Hoffenheim	a	0-1	
23/4	Bayern	h	1-1	*Rode*
30/4	Mainz	a	0-3	
7/5	Köln	h	0-2	
14/5	Dortmund	a	1-3	*Rode*

No	Name	Nat	DoB	Pos	Aps	(s)	Gls
18	Ioannis AMANATIDIS	GRE	3/12/81	A	6	(13)	
30	CAIO César Alves dos Santos	BRA	29/5/86	M	12	(15)	1
29	CHRIStian Maicon Hening	BRA	25/8/78	D	5	(2)	2
13	Ricardo CLARK	USA	10/2/83	M	8	(3)	
39	Julian DUDDA		8/4/93	D	1		
22	Ralf FÄHRMANN		27/9/88	G	14	(1)	
17	Martin FENIN	CZE	16/4/87	A	6	(18)	1
4	Maik FRANZ		5/8/81	D	23		
21	Theofanis GEKAS	GRE	23/5/80	A	31	(3)	16
10	HALİL Altıntop	TUR	8/12/82	A	26	(8)	
25	Marcel HELLER		12/2/86	A	3	(7)	
24	Sebastian JUNG		22/6/90	D	33		
28	Sonny KITTEL		6/1/93	M	2	(6)	
7	Benjamin KÖHLER		4/8/80	M	28	(2)	2
11	Ümit KORKMAZ	AUT	17/9/85	A		(2)	
19	Kevin KRAUS		12/8/92	D	1		
14	Alexander MEIER		17/1/83	M	20	(4)	2
1	Oka NIKOLOV	MKD	25/5/74	G	20		
2	Patrick OCHS		14/5/84	M	29		2
3	Nikola PETKOVIĆ	SRB	28/3/86	D	1		
20	Sebastian RODE		11/10/90	M	11		2
23	Marco RUSS		4/8/85	D	31		1
27	Pirmin SCHWEGLER	SUI	9/3/87	M	32		1
13	Markus STEINHÖFER		7/3/86	M		(4)	
36	Marcel TITSCH-RIVERO		2/11/89	M		(1)	
31	Georgios TZAVELAS	GRE	26/11/87	D	25		1
5	Aleksandar VASOSKI	MKD	21/11/79	D	6	(5)	

SC FREIBURG

Coach – Robin Dutt

Founded – 1904

Stadium – Badenova-Stadion (24,000)

2010				
21/8	St Pauli	h	1-3	*Cissé*
28/8	Nürnberg	a	2-1	*Cissé 2 (1p)*
11/9	Stuttgart	h	2-1	*Cissé, Schuster*
17/9	Eintracht	a	1-0	*Rosenthal*
22/9	Schalke	h	1-2	*Cissé*
26/9	Wolfsburg	a	1-2	*Cissé*
2/10	Köln	h	3-2	*Rosenthal 2, Cissé*
16/10	Werder	a	1-2	*Schuster*
23/10	Kaiserslautern	h	2-1	*Cissé, Reisinger*
29/10	Bayern	a	2-4	*Reisinger, og (Braafheid)*
6/11	Mainz	h	1-0	*Cissé (p)*
14/11	Hoffenheim	a	1-0	*Cissé*
20/11	Dortmund	h	1-2	*og (Hummels)*
27/11	Hannover	a	0-3	
4/12	Hamburg	h	1-0	*Cissé*
12/12	Mönchengladbach	h	3-0	*Cissé 2, Barth*
19/12	Leverkusen	a	2-2	*Rosenthal, Reisinger*
2011				
15/1	St Pauli	a	2-2	*Cissé 2*
22/1	Nürnberg	h	1-1	*Flum*
30/1	Stuttgart	a	1-0	*Flum*
6/2	Eintracht	h	0-0	
12/2	Schalke	a	0-1	
19/2	Wolfsburg	h	2-1	*Reisinger, Cissé*
26/2	Köln	a	0-1	
6/3	Werder	h	1-3	*Cissé (p)*
12/3	Kaiserslautern	a	1-2	*og (Nemec)*
19/3	Bayern	h	1-2	*Cissé*
2/4	Mainz	a	1-1	*Cissé*
9/4	Hoffenheim	h	3-2	*Schuster, Cissé (p), Butscher*
17/4	Dortmund	a	0-3	
21/4	Hannover	h	1-3	*Rosenthal*
30/4	Hamburg	a	2-0	*Cissé 2*
7/5	Mönchengladbach	a	0-2	
14/5	Leverkusen	h	0-1	

No	Name	Nat	DoB	Pos	Aps	(s)	Gls
6	Yacine ABDESSADKI	MAR	1/1/81	M	20	(1)	
20	Ivica BANOVIĆ	CRO	2/8/80	M	1	(1)	
15	Oliver BARTH		6/10/79	D	28	(1)	1

No	Name	Nat	DoB	Pos	Aps	(s)	Gls
	Felix BASTIANS		9/5/88	D	29		
	Oliver BAUMANN		2/6/90	G	30		
4	Squipon BEKTASI	ALB	14/9/90	A		(1)	
	Heiko BUTSCHER		28/7/80	D	22	(3)	1
0	Daniel CALIGIURI		15/1/88	M	11	(12)	
	Papiss Demba CISSÉ	SEN	3/6/85	A	32		22
3	Johannes FLUM		14/12/87	M	10	(2)	2
	Jonathan JÄGER	FRA	23/5/78	M	4	(8)	
9	Erik JENDRIŠEK	SVK	26/10/86	A	5	(3)	
	Pavel KRMAŠ	CZE	3/3/80	D	5	(1)	
	Cédric MAKIADI	COD	23/2/84	M	34		
4	Mensur MUJDŽA	BIH	28/3/84	D	32		
0	Maximilian NICU	ROU	25/11/82	M	17	(6)	
4	Zvonko PAMIĆ	CRO	4/2/91	M		(2)	
	Simon POUPLIN	FRA	28/5/85	G	4		
1	Anton PUTILO	BLR	10/6/87	M	21	(4)	
7	Stefan REISINGER		14/9/81	A	3	(19)	4
	Jan ROSENTHAL		7/4/86	M	19	(3)	5
2	Jonathan SCHMID	FRA	26/6/90	M		(1)	
3	Julian SCHUSTER		15/4/85	M	26		3
5	Daniel SEREINIG	SUI	10/5/82	D		(2)	
8	Ömer TOPRAK		21/7/89	D	18	(6)	
8	Daniel WILLIAMS		8/3/89	M	1	(6)	
2	Kisho YANO	JPN	5/4/84	A	2	(13)	

HAMBURGER SV

Coach – Armin Veh; (13/3/11) Michael Oenning

Founded – 1919

Stadium – Imtech-Arena (57,000)

MAJOR HONOURS: European Champion Clubs' Cup – (1) 1983; UEFA Cup Winners' Cup – (1) 1977; German League – (6) 1923, 1928, 1960, 1979, 1982, 1983; German Cup – (3) 1963, 1976, 1987.

2010				
21/8	Schalke	h	2-1	*Van Nistelrooy 2*
28/8	Eintracht	a	3-1	*Mathijsen, Van Nistelrooy, Guerrero*
11/9	Nürnberg	h	1-1	*Mathijsen*
19/9	St Pauli	a	1-1	*Petrić*
22/9	Wolfsburg	h	1-3	*Choupo-Moting*
25/9	Werder	a	2-3	*Van Nistelrooy, Pitroipa*
2/10	Kaiserslautern	h	2-1	*Kačar, Choupo-Moting*
16/10	Mainz	a	1-0	*Guerrero*
22/10	Bayern	h	0-0	
30/10	Köln	a	2-3	*Petrić, Son*
6/11	Hoffenheim	h	2-1	*Westermann, Petrić*
12/11	Dortmund	a	0-2	
20/11	Hannover	a	2-3	*Son 2*
27/11	Stuttgart	h	4-2	*Trochowski, Pitroipa, Petrić, Van Nistelrooy*
4/12	Freiburg	a	0-1	
11/12	Leverkusen	h	2-4	*og (Vidal), Elia*
17/12	Mönchengladbach	a	2-1	*Elia, Trochowski*
2011				
15/1	Schalke	a	1-0	*Van Nistelrooy*
21/1	Eintracht	h	1-0	*Petrić*
29/1	Nürnberg	a	0-2	
12/2	Wolfsburg	a	1-0	*Petrić (p)*
16/2	St Pauli	h	0-1	
19/2	Werder	h	4-0	*Petrić, Guerrero 2, Ben-Hatira*
26/2	Kaiserslautern	a	1-1	*Jansen*
6/3	Mainz	h	2-4	*Jansen, Petrić*
12/3	Bayern	a	0-6	
19/3	Köln	h	6-2	*Petrić 3, Ben-Hatira, Kačar, Zé Roberto (p)*
2/4	Hoffenheim	a	0-0	
9/4	Dortmund	h	1-1	*Van Nistelrooy (p)*
16/4	Hannover	h	0-0	
23/4	Stuttgart	a	0-3	
30/4	Freiburg	h	0-2	
7/5	Leverkusen	a	1-1	*Westermann*
14/5	Mönchengladbach	h	1-1	*Ben-Hatira*

No	Name	Nat	DoB	Pos	Aps	(s)	Gls
6	Dennis AOGO		14/1/87	D	20		
31	Änis BEN-HATIRA		18/7/88	M	12	(6)	3
30	Collin BENJAMIN	NAM	3/8/78	D	3	(5)	
34	Muhamed BEŠIĆ	BIH	10/9/92	D	2	(1)	
17	Eric Maxim CHOUPO-MOTING	CMR	23/3/89	A	4	(6)	2
20	Guy DEMEL	CIV	13/6/81	D	19	(2)	
2	Dennis DIEKMEIER		20/10/89	D	8		
45	Jaroslav DROBNÝ	CZE	18/10/79	G	4	(1)	
11	Eljero ELIA	NED	13/2/87	M	18	(6)	2
9	José Pablo GUERRERO	PER	1/1/84	A	18	(7)	4
7	Marcell JANSEN		4/11/85	M	12	(4)	2
14	David JAROLÍM	CZE	17/5/79	M	23	(1)	
44	Gojko KAČAR	SRB	26/1/87	M	18	(5)	2
5	Joris MATHIJSEN	NED	5/4/80	D	19		2
10	Mladen PETRIĆ	CRO	1/1/81	A	18	(4)	11
21	Jonathan PITROIPA	BFA	12/4/86	M	20	(6)	2
25	Tomás Eduardo RINCÓN	VEN	13/1/88	M	12	(7)	
1	Frank ROST		30/6/73	G	30		
40	SON Heung-min	KOR	8/7/92	A	8	(5)	3
13	Robert TESCHE		27/5/87	M	5	(6)	
15	Piotr TROCHOWSKI		22/3/84	M	13	(8)	2
35	TUNAY Torun	TUR	21/4/90	A	4	(1)	
22	Ruud VAN NISTELROOY	NED	1/7/76	A	19	(6)	7
4	Heiko WESTERMANN		14/8/83	D	34		2
8	José "ZÉ" ROBERTO da Silva Júnior	BRA	6/7/74	M	31		1

HANNOVER 96

Coach – Mirko Slomka

Founded – 1896

Stadium – AWD-Arena (49,000)

MAJOR HONOURS: German League – (2) 1938, 1954; German Cup – (1) 1992.

2010				
21/8	Eintracht	h	2-1	*Rausch, Konan Ya*
28/8	Schalke	a	2-1	*Rausch, Abdellaoue*
11/9	Leverkusen	h	2-2	*Konan Ya, Abdellaoue*
18/9	Wolfsburg	a	0-2	
21/9	Werder	h	4-1	*og (Fritz), Konan Ya, Schulz, Abdellaoue*
26/9	Kaiserslautern	a	1-0	*Abdellaoue*
1/10	St Pauli	h	0-1	
16/10	Bayern	a	0-3	
23/10	Köln	h	2-1	*Konan Ya 2*
31/10	Hoffenheim	a	0-4	
7/11	Dortmund	h	0-4	
13/11	Mainz	a	1-0	*Pinto*
20/11	Hamburg	h	3-2	*Stindl, Schulz, Hanke*
27/11	Freiburg	h	3-0	*Schlaudraff, Konan Ya, Hanke*
4/12	Mönchengladbach	a	2-1	*Hanke, Konan Ya*
10/12	Stuttgart	h	2-1	*Konan Ya 2*
18/12	Nürnberg	a	1-3	*Pinto (p)*
2011				
16/1	Eintracht	a	3-0	*Abdellaoue, Schulz, Konan Ya*
22/1	Schalke	h	0-1	
28/1	Leverkusen	a	0-2	
5/2	Wolfsburg	h	1-0	*Pinto*
13/2	Werder	a	1-1	*Konan Ya*
19/2	Kaiserslautern	h	3-0	*Schlaudraff 2, Abdellaoue*
26/2	St Pauli	a	1-0	*Schulz*
5/3	Bayern	h	3-1	*Abdellaoue, Rausch, Pinto*
11/3	Köln	a	0-4	
19/3	Hoffenheim	h	2-0	*Konan Ya, Abdellaoue*
2/4	Dortmund	a	1-4	*Abdellaoue*
9/4	Mainz	h	2-0	*Konan Ya (p), Pinto*
16/4	Hamburg	a	0-0	
21/4	Freiburg	a	3-1	*Abdellaoue, Schlaudraff, Rausch*
30/4	Mönchengladbach	h	0-1	
7/5	Stuttgart	a	1-2	*Stindl*
14/5	Nürnberg	h	3-1	*Haggui, Rausch, Konan Ya (p)*

No	Name	Nat	DoB	Pos	Aps	(s)	Gls
25	Mohammed ABDELLAOUE	NOR	23/10/85	A	26		10
35	Christopher AVEVOR		11/2/92	D	3	(2)	
16	DeMarcus BEASLEY	USA	24/5/82	M		(4)	
30	Carlos Alberto Alves Garcia "CARLITOS"	POR	6/9/82	M	2	(4)	
23	Sofian CHAHED	TUN	18/4/83	M	2	(16)	
6	Steve CHERUNDOLO	USA	19/2/79	D	33		
15	Constant DJAKPA	CIV	17/10/86	M	5	(9)	
5	Mario EGGIMANN	SUI	24/1/81	D	7	(5)	
32	Mikael FORSSELL	FIN	15/3/81	A	1	(11)	
1	Florian FROMLOWITZ		2/7/86	G	19	(1)	
21	Karim HAGGUI	TUN	20/1/84	D	25		1
9	Mike HANKE		5/11/83	A		(7)	3
11	Didier KONAN YA	CIV	22/5/84	A	28		14
8	Altin LALA	ALB	18/11/75	M	2	(8)	
7	Sérgio PINTO		16/10/80	M	31		5
4	Emanuel POGATETZ	AUT	16/1/83	D	28		
34	Konstantin RAUSCH		15/3/90	D	34		5
13	Jan SCHLAUDRAFF		18/7/83	A	16	(5)	4
33	Manuel SCHMIEDEBACH		5/12/88	M	31	(1)	
19	Christian SCHULZ		1/4/83	D	33		4
28	Lars STINDL		26/8/88	M	23	(10)	2
17	Moritz STOPPELKAMP		11/12/86	A	10	(13)	
20	Ron-Robert ZIELER		12/2/89	G	15		

TSG 1899 HOFFENHEIM

Coach – Ralf Rangnick; (2/1/11) Marco Pezzaiuoli

Founded – 1899

Stadium – Rhein-Neckar-Arena, Sinsheim (30,150)

2010				
21/8	Werder	h	4-1	*Ba, Mlapa, Ibišević, Salihović*
28/8	St Pauli	a	1-0	*Vorsah*
10/9	Schalke	h	2-0	*Vorsah, Salihović*
18/9	Kaiserslautern	a	2-2	*Luiz Gustavo, Sigurdsson*
21/9	Bayern	h	1-2	*Ibišević*
24/9	Köln	a	1-1	*Ba*
2/10	Mainz	a	2-4	*Ba, Sigurdsson*
17/10	Mönchengladbach	h	3-2	*Ba, og (Anderson Bamba), Salihović (p)*
24/10	Dortmund	a	1-1	*Ba*
31/10	Hannover	h	4-0	*Sigurdsson 2 (1p), Ba, Mlapa*
6/11	Hamburg	a	1-2	*Salihović (p)*
14/11	Freiburg	h	0-1	
20/11	Eintracht	a	4-0	*Vukčević, Ibišević 2, Mlapa*
27/11	Leverkusen	h	2-2	*Ibišević, Sigurdsson (p)*
4/12	Stuttgart	a	1-1	*Salihović*
11/12	Nürnberg	h	1-1	*Compper*
18/12	Wolfsburg	a	2-2	*Luiz Gustavo, Sigurdsson*
2011				
15/1	Werder	a	1-2	*Vukčević*
23/1	St Pauli	h	2-2	*Compper, Alaba*
29/1	Schalke	a	1-0	*Vorsah*
5/2	Kaiserslautern	h	3-2	*Sigurdsson, Rudy, Ibišević*
12/2	Bayern	a	0-4	
19/2	Köln	h	1-1	*og (Novakovič)*
26/2	Mainz	h	1-2	*Alaba*
5/3	Mönchengladbach	a	0-2	
12/3	Dortmund	h	1-0	*Ibišević*
19/3	Hannover	a	0-2	
2/4	Hamburg	h	0-0	
9/4	Freiburg	a	2-3	*Ibišević (p), Babel*
16/4	Eintracht	h	1-0	*Roberto Firmino*
23/4	Leverkusen	a	1-2	*Sigurdsson*
30/4	Stuttgart	h	1-2	*Mlapa*
7/5	Nürnberg	a	2-1	*Roberto Firmino, Sigurdsson*
14/5	Wolfsburg	h	1-3	*Roberto Firmino*

No	Name	Nat	DoB	Pos	Aps	(s)	Gls
8	David ALABA	AUT	24/6/92	M	17		2
9	Demba BA	SEN	25/5/85	A	15	(2)	6
10	Ryan BABEL	NED	19/12/86	A	15		1
2	Andreas BECK		13/3/87	D	33		
28	Edson BRAAFHEID	NED	8/4/83	D	9	(1)	
5	Marvin COMPPER		14/6/85	D	32		2
8	Christian EICHNER		24/11/82	D	2	(2)	
37	Manuel GULDE		12/2/91	D		(1)	
1	Daniel HAAS		1/8/83	G	9		
26	Andreas IBERTSBERGER	AUT	27/7/82	D	18	(2)	
19	Vedad IBIŠEVIĆ	BIH	6/8/84	A	25	(6)	8
3	Matthias JAISSLE		5/4/88	D	4	(5)	
36	Dominik KAISER		16/9/88	M		(1)	
21	LUIZ GUSTAVO Dias	BRA	23/7/87	M	17		2
15	Peniel Kokou MLAPA		20/2/91	A	18	(12)	4
20	Chinedu OBASI	NGA	1/6/86	A	2	(3)	
22	ROBERTO FIRMINO Barbosa de Oliveira	BRA	2/10/91	M	5	(6)	3
6	Sebastian RUDY		28/2/90	M	29	(3)	1
23	Sejad SALIHOVIĆ	BIH	8/10/84	M	24	(2)	5
11	Gylfi Thór SIGURDSSON	ISL	8/9/89	M	10	(19)	9
14	Josip ŠIMUNIĆ	CRO	18/2/78	D	7	(3)	
33	Tom STARKE		18/3/81	G	25		
18	Prince TAGOE	GHA	9/11/86	A		(6)	
34	Denis THOMALLA		16/8/92	A		(4)	
29	Jannik VESTERGAARD	DEN	3/8/92	D		(1)	
25	Isaac VORSAH	GHA	21/6/88	D	29	(1)	3
7	Boris VUKČEVIĆ		16/3/90	M	16	(10)	2
17	Tobias WEIS		30/7/85	M	13	(4)	

1. FC KAISERSLAUTERN

Coach – Marco Kurz

Founded – 1900

Stadium – Fritz-Walter-Stadion (49,780)

MAJOR HONOURS: German League – (4) 1951, 1953, 1991, 1998; German Cup – (2) 1990, 1996.

2010				
21/8	Köln	a	3-1	*Lakić 2, Iličević*
27/8	Bayern	h	2-0	*Iličević, Lakić*
12/9	Mainz	a	1-2	*Lakić*
18/9	Hoffenheim	h	2-2	*Hoffer 2*
22/9	Dortmund	a	0-5	
26/9	Hannover	h	0-1	
2/10	Hamburg	a	1-2	*Lakić*
17/10	Eintracht	h	0-3	
23/10	Freiburg	a	1-2	*Morávek*
30/10	Mönchengladbach	h	3-0	*Tiffert, Nemec, Lakić*
7/11	Leverkusen	a	1-3	*Dick*
13/11	Stuttgart	h	3-3	*Mitsanski, Iličević, Abel*
20/11	Nürnberg	a	3-1	*Rivić, Iličević, Lakić*
27/11	Schalke	h	5-0	*Lakić 2, Amedick, Iličević (p), Morávek*
3/12	St Pauli	a	0-1	
11/12	Wolfsburg	h	0-0	
18/12	Werder	a	2-1	*Lakić 2*
2011				
16/1	Köln	h	1-1	*Morávek*
22/1	Bayern	a	1-5	*Morávek*
29/1	Mainz	h	0-1	
5/2	Hoffenheim	a	2-3	*Hoffer, Rodnei*
12/2	Dortmund	h	1-1	*Morávek*
19/2	Hannover	a	0-3	
26/2	Hamburg	h	1-1	*Hloušek*
5/3	Eintracht	a	0-0	
12/3	Freiburg	h	2-1	*Nemec, Hoffer*
18/3	Mönchengladbach	a	1-0	*og (Bailly)*
2/4	Leverkusen	h	0-1	
9/4	Stuttgart	a	4-2	*Lakić 2, Hoffer, Rivić*
16/4	Nürnberg	h	0-2	
23/4	Schalke	a	1-0	*Lakić*
29/4	St Pauli	h	2-0	*Tiffert, Abel*
7/5	Wolfsburg	a	2-1	*Lakić, Amedick*
14/5	Werder	h	3-2	*Nemec, Rodnei, Lakić*

No	Name	Nat	DoB	Pos	Aps	(s)	Gls
	Mathias ABEL		22/6/91	D	19		2
	Martin AMEDICK		6/9/82	D	23	(3)	2
	Chadli AMRI	ALG	14/12/84	M	1	(5)	
	Jiří BÍLEK	CZE	4/11/83	M	14	(1)	
	Alexander BUGERA		8/8/78	D	11	(1)	
	Pierre DE WIT		26/9/87	M	7	(6)	
	Florian DICK		9/11/84	D	27		1
	Danny FUCHS		25/2/76	M		(1)	
	Adam HLOUŠEK	CZE	20/12/88	M	12	(1)	1
	Erwin HOFFER	AUT	14/4/87	A	11	(13)	5
	Ivo ILIČEVIĆ	CRO	14/11/86	M	19	(2)	5
	Leon JESSEN	DEN	11/6/86	D	23	(4)	
	Oliver KIRCH		21/8/82	M	23	(6)	
	Srđan LAKIĆ	CRO	2/10/83	A	30	(1)	16
	Ilian MITSANSKI	BUL	20/12/85	A	2	(8)	1
	Jan MORÁVEK	CZE	1/11/89	M	23	(6)	5
	Adam NEMEC	SVK	2/9/85	A	7	(17)	3
	Athanasios PETSOS	GRE	5/6/91	D	16	(4)	
	Stiven RIVIĆ	CRO	9/8/85	M	7	(5)	2
	RODNEI Francisco de Lima	BRA	11/9/85	D	26		2
	Bastian SCHULZ		10/7/85	M	1	(2)	
	Tobias SIPPEL		22/3/88	G	25		
	Christian TIFFERT		18/2/82	M	33		2
	Kevin TRAPP		8/7/90	G	9		
	Clemens WALCH	AUT	10/7/87	M	5	(7)	

1. FC KÖLN

Coach – Zvonimir Soldo (CRO); (25/10/10) Frank Schaefer; (27/4/11) Volker Finke

Founded – 1948

Stadium – Rhein-Energie-Stadion (50,000)

MAJOR HONOURS: German League – (3) 1962, 1964, 1978; German Cup – (4) 1968, 1977, 1978, 1983.

2010				
1/8	Kaiserslautern	h	1-3	*Novakovič*
8/8	Werder	a	2-4	*Podolski, McKenna*
2/9	St Pauli	h	1-0	*Yalçin*
8/9	Bayern	a	0-0	
1/9	Mainz	a	0-2	
4/9	Hoffenheim	h	1-1	*Podolski*
/10	Freiburg	a	2-3	*Mohamad, Matuszczyk*
5/10	Dortmund	h	1-2	*Podolski*
3/10	Hannover	a	1-2	*Lanig*
0/10	Hamburg	h	3-2	*Novakovič 3*
/11	Nürnberg	a	1-3	*Geromel*
3/11	Mönchengladbach	h	0-4	
1/11	Stuttgart	a	1-0	*Podolski (p)*
8/11	Wolfsburg	h	1-1	*Novakovič*
5/12	Leverkusen	a	2-3	*Geromel, Lanig*
1/12	Eintracht	h	1-0	*Clemens*
8/12	Schalke	a	0-3	
2011				
16/1	Kaiserslautern	a	1-1	*Podolski*
22/1	Werder	h	3-0	*Podolski 2, Matuszczyk*
29/1	St Pauli	a	0-3	
5/2	Bayern	h	3-2	*Clemens, Novakovič 2*
13/2	Mainz	h	4-2	*Podolski 2, Novakovič 2*
19/2	Hoffenheim	a	1-1	*Mohamad*
26/2	Freiburg	h	1-0	*Podolski*
4/3	Dortmund	a	0-1	
11/3	Hannover	h	4-0	*Petit, Podolski, Novakovič 2*
19/3	Hamburg	a	2-6	*Jajalo, Podolski*
3/4	Nürnberg	h	1-0	*Novakovič*
10/4	Mönchengladbach	a	1-5	*Novakovič*
16/4	Stuttgart	h	1-3	*Novakovič*
24/4	Wolfsburg	a	1-4	*Freis*
30/4	Leverkusen	h	2-0	*Novakovič 2*
7/5	Eintracht	a	2-0	*Chihi, Podolski (p)*
14/5	Schalke	h	2-1	*Novakovič, Jajalo*

No	Name	Nat	DoB	Pos	Aps	(s)	Gls
12	André Ricardo Soares "ANDREZINHO"	BRA	9/10/81	D	6	(2)	
2	Mišo BREČKO	SVN	1/5/84	D	28	(1)	
20	Adil CHIHI	MAR	21/2/88	A	4	(7)	1
27	Christian CLEMENS		4/8/91	M	22	(5)	2
22	Fabrice EHRET	FRA	22/9/79	D	16	(5)	
4	Christian EICHNER		24/11/82	D	17		
7	Sebastian FREIS		23/4/85	A	8	(5)	1
21	Pedro Tonon GEROMEL	BRA	21/9/85	D	27		2
14	Alexandru IONIŢĂ	ROU	5/8/89	A		(7)	
19	Mato JAJALO	CRO	24/5/88	M	24	(6)	2
5	Martin LANIG		11/7/84	M	24	(4)	2
43	Tomoaki MAKINO	JPN	11/5/87	D	1	(4)	
25	Adam MATUSZCZYK	POL	14/2/89	M	16	(8)	2
23	Kevin McKENNA	CAN	21/1/80	D	2	(5)	1
3	Youssef MOHAMAD	LIB	1/7/80	D	28		2
1	Faryd Aly Camilo MONDRAGÓN	COL	21/6/71	G	12		
11	Milivoje NOVAKOVIČ	SVN	18/5/79	A	24	(4)	17
15	Sławomir PESZKO	POL	19/2/85	M	11		
8	Armando Gonçalves Teixeira "PETIT"	POR	25/9/76	M	23	(1)	1
17	Kevin PEZZONI		22/3/89	M	15	(5)	
10	Lukas PODOLSKI		4/6/85	A	32		13
1	Michael RENSING		14/5/89	G	17		
32	Stephan SALGER		30/1/90	D	5		
13	Wilfried SANOU	BFA	16/3/84	M		(3)	
16	Christopher SCHORCH		30/1/89	D	1	(3)	
30	Simon TERODDE		2/3/88	A		(5)	
34	Miro VARVODIĆ	CRO	15/5/89	G	5		
27	José Pierre VUNGUIDICA	ANG	3/1/90	A		(1)	
37	Reinhold YABO		10/2/92	M	1	(3)	
6	Taner YALÇIN		18/2/90	M	5	(11)	1

1. FSV MAINZ 05

Coach – Thomas Tuchel

Founded – 1905

Stadium – Bruchwegstadion (20,300)

2010				
22/8	Stuttgart	h	2-0	*Allagui, Rasmussen*
28/8	Wolfsburg	a	4-3	*Rasmussen, Soto, Schürrle, Szalai*
12/9	Kaiserslautern	h	2-1	*Bungert, Schürrle*
18/9	Werder	a	2-0	*Risse, Schürrle*
21/9	Köln	h	2-0	*Holtby 2*
25/9	Bayern	a	2-1	*Allagui, Szalai*
2/10	Hoffenheim	h	4-2	*Allagui, Szalai, og (Luiz Gustavo), Schürrle (p)*
16/10	Hamburg	h	0-1	
24/10	Leverkusen	a	1-0	*Ivanschitz*
31/10	Dortmund	h	0-2	
6/11	Freiburg	a	0-1	
13/11	Hannover	h	0-1	
20/11	Mönchengladbach	a	3-2	*Schürrle, Allagui 2*
26/11	Nürnberg	h	3-0	*Schürrle, Noveski, Allagui*
4/12	Eintracht	a	1-2	*Schürrle (p)*
12/12	Schalke	h	0-1	
18/12	St Pauli	a	4-2	*Schürrle 2, Szalai, Caligiuri*
2011				
15/1	Stuttgart	a	0-1	
22/1	Wolfsburg	h	0-1	
29/1	Kaiserslautern	a	1-0	*Holtby*
5/2	Werder	h	1-1	*Schürrle*
13/2	Köln	a	2-4	*Allagui, Slišković*
19/2	Bayern	h	1-3	*Allagui*
26/2	Hoffenheim	a	2-1	*Ivanschitz, Soto*
6/3	Hamburg	a	4-2	*Schürrle 2, Risse, Heller*
13/3	Leverkusen	h	0-1	
19/3	Dortmund	a	1-1	*Slišković*
2/4	Freiburg	h	1-1	*Allagui*
9/4	Hannover	a	0-2	

15/4	Mönchengladbach	h	1-0	*Schürrle*
24/4	Nürnberg	a	0-0	
30/4	Eintracht	h	3-0	*Ivanschitz, Soto 2*
7/5	Schalke	a	3-1	*Schürrle, Holtby, Noveski*
14/5	St Pauli	h	2-1	*Schürrle (p), Allagui*

No	Name	Nat	DoB	Pos	Aps	(s)	Gls
9	Sami ALLAGUI	TUN	28/5/86	A	18	(10)	10
17	Haruna BABANGIDA	NGA	1/10/82	A	1		
26	Niko BUNGERT		24/10/86	D	26	(2)	1
6	Marco CALIGIURI		14/4/84	M	17	(5)	1
3	Malik FATHI		29/10/83	D	17	(2)	
22	Christian FUCHS	AUT	7/4/86	D	30	(1)	
5	Eugen GOPKO		5/1/91	D		(1)	
16	Florian HELLER		10/3/82	M	7	(12)	1
18	Lewis HOLTBY		18/9/90	M	23	(7)	4
25	Andreas IVANSCHITZ	AUT	15/10/83	M	13	(7)	3
21	Miroslav KARHAN	SVK	21/6/76	M	9	(4)	
15	Jan KIRCHHOFF		1/10/90	D	8	(2)	
33	Heinz MÜLLER		30/5/78	G	10		
4	Nikolce NOVESKI	MKD	28/4/79	D	32		2
1	Martin PIECKENHAGEN		15/11/71	G		(1)	
7	Eugen POLANSKI		17/3/86	M	25	(3)	
11	Morten "Duncan" RASMUSSEN	DEN	31/1/85	A	3	(2)	2
23	Marcel RISSE		17/12/89	M	12	(13)	2
12	André SCHÜRRLE		6/11/90	A	26	(7)	15
10	Jan ŠIMÁK	CZE	13/10/78	M		(1)	
35	Petar SLIŠKOVIĆ	CRO	21/2/91	A	1	(8)	2
19	Elkin SOTO	COL	4/8/80	M	21	(5)	4
2	Bo SVENSSON	DEN	4/8/79	D	19		
28	Ádám SZALAI	HUN	9/12/87	A	14	(6)	4
29	Christian WETKLO		11/1/80	G	24		
8	Radoslav ZABAVNÍK	SVK	16/9/80	D	18	(2)	

1. FC NÜRNBERG

Coach – Dieter Hecking

Founded – 1900

Stadium – Easy-Credit-Stadion (48,548)

MAJOR HONOURS: German League – (9) 1920, 1921, 1924, 1925, 1927, 1936, 1948, 1961, 1968; German Cup – (4) 1935, 1939, 1962, 2007.

2010				
21/8	Mönchengladbach	a	1-1	*Hegeler*
28/8	Freiburg	h	1-2	*Schieber*
11/9	Hamburg	a	1-1	*Pinola (p)*
19/9	Leverkusen	a	0-0	
22/9	Stuttgart	h	2-1	*Schieber, Pinola*
25/9	Eintracht	a	0-2	
2/10	Schalke	h	2-1	*Frantz, Wolf*
16/10	St Pauli	a	2-3	*Mehmet, Wolf*
23/10	Wolfsburg	h	2-1	*Gündoğan, Frantz*
30/10	Werder	a	3-2	*Gündoğan 2, Mehmet*
6/11	Köln	h	3-1	*Hegeler, Gündoğan, Schieber*
14/11	Bayern	a	0-3	
20/11	Kaiserslautern	h	1-3	*Mak*
26/11	Mainz	a	0-3	
5/12	Dortmund	h	0-2	
11/12	Hoffenheim	a	1-1	*Eigler*
18/12	Hannover	h	3-1	*og (Cherundolo), Wolf, Schieber*
2011				
15/1	Mönchengladbach	h	0-1	
22/1	Freiburg	a	1-1	*Schieber*
29/1	Hamburg	h	2-0	*Simons (p), Cohen*
5/2	Leverkusen	h	1-0	*Eigler*
12/2	Stuttgart	a	4-1	*Simons, Schieber, Chandler, Mehmet*
18/2	Eintracht	h	3-0	*Schieber, Mak, Cohen*
26/2	Schalke	a	1-1	*Hegeler*
5/3	St Pauli	h	5-0	*Wollscheid, Eigler 4*
12/3	Wolfsburg	a	2-1	*Wollscheid, Nilsson*
19/3	Werder	h	1-3	*Gündoğan*
3/4	Köln	a	0-1	
9/4	Bayern	h	1-1	*Eigler*
16/4	Kaiserslautern	a	2-0	*Eigler, Mak*
24/4	Mainz	h	0-0	
30/4	Dortmund	a	0-2	
7/5	Hoffenheim	h	1-2	*Wollscheid*
14/5	Hannover	a	1-3	*Wiessmeier*

No	Name	Nat	DoB	Pos	Aps	(s)	Gls
19	Nassim BEN KHALIFA	SUI	13/1/92	A		(1)	
20	Pascal BIELER		26/2/86	D	3	(1)	
19	Isaac BOAKYE	GHA	26/11/81	A		(2)	
10	Albert BUNJAKU	SUI	29/11/83	A	3		
26	Timothy CHANDLER	USA	29/3/90	M	11	(3)	1
18	Almog COHEN	ISR	1/9/88	M	19	(6)	2
8	Christian EIGLER		1/1/84	A	21	(11)	8
17	Mike FRANTZ		14/10/86	M	10	(4)	2
22	İlkay GÜNDOĞAN		24/10/90	M	21	(4)	5
13	Jens HEGELER		22/1/88	M	29	(5)	3
16	Juri JUDT		24/7/86	D	24		
14	Róbert MAK	SVK	8/3/91	A	6	(16)	3
6	Dominic MAROH		4/3/87	D	6	(2)	
37	MEHMET Ekici	TUR	25/3/90	M	29	(3)	3
27	Markus MENDLER		7/1/93	M	1	(5)	
11	Marek MINTÁL	SVK	2/9/77	M		(17)	
3	Per NILSSON	SWE	15/9/82	D	14	(5)	1
29	Rubin OKOTIE	AUT	6/6/87	A		(4)	
25	Javier Horacio PINOLA	ARG	24/2/83	D	27	(1)	2
40	Marvin PLATTENHARDT		26/1/92	D	4	(5)	
1	Raphael SCHÄFER		30/1/79	G	34		
23	Julian SCHIEBER		13/2/89	A	28	(1)	7
2	Timmy SIMONS	BEL	11/12/76	M	34		2
30	Alexander STEPHAN		15/9/86	G		(1)	
21	Dario VIDOSIC	AUS	8/4/87	M	1	(4)	
31	Julian WIESSMEIER		4/11/92	A	1		1
5	Andreas WOLF		12/6/82	D	30		3
38	Philipp WOLLSCHEID		6/3/89	D	18	(1)	3

FC SCHALKE 04

Coach – Felix Magath; (16/3/11) (Seppo Eichkorn); (21/3/11) Ralf Rangnick

Founded – 1904

Stadium – Veltins-Arena (61,673)

MAJOR HONOURS: UEFA Cup – (1) 1997; German League – (7) 1934, 1935, 1937, 1939, 1940, 1942, 1958; German Cup – (5) 1937, 1972, 2001, 2002, 2011.

2010				
21/8	Hamburg	a	1-2	*Farfán*
28/8	Hannover	h	1-2	*Jones*
10/9	Hoffenheim	a	0-2	
19/9	Dortmund	h	1-3	*Huntelaar*
22/9	Freiburg	a	2-1	*Rakitić, Huntelaar*
25/9	Mönchengladbach	h	2-2	*Huntelaar, Raúl*
2/10	Nürnberg	a	1-2	*Huntelaar*
16/10	Stuttgart	h	2-2	*Edu, Huntelaar (p)*
23/10	Eintracht	a	0-0	
30/10	Leverkusen	h	0-1	
5/11	St Pauli	h	3-0	*Raúl 2, Huntelaar*
13/11	Wolfsburg	a	2-2	*Edu, Huntelaar*
20/11	Werder	h	4-0	*Metzelder, Raúl 3*
27/11	Kaiserslautern	a	0-5	
4/12	Bayern	h	2-0	*Jurado, Höwedes*
12/12	Mainz	a	1-0	*Farfán*
18/12	Köln	h	3-0	*Raúl 3*
2011				
15/1	Hamburg	h	0-1	
22/1	Hannover	a	1-0	*Raúl*
29/1	Hoffenheim	h	0-1	
4/2	Dortmund	a	0-0	
12/2	Freiburg	h	1-0	*Farfán*
20/2	Mönchengladbach	a	1-2	*Kluge*

2	Nürnberg	h	1-1	*Raúl*
	Stuttgart	a	0-1	
3	Eintracht	h	2-1	*Jurado (p), Charisteas*
3	Leverkusen	a	0-2	
	St Pauli	a	2-0	*Raúl, Draxler (match abandoned after 87 mins; result stood)*
	Wolfsburg	h	1-0	*Jurado*
4	Werder	a	1-1	*Edu*
4	Kaiserslautern	h	0-1	
4	Bayern	a	1-4	*og (Badstuber)*
	Mainz	h	1-3	*Huntelaar*
5	Köln	a	1-2	*Raúl*

Name	Nat	DoB	Pos	Aps	(s)	Gls
Anthony ANNAN	GHA	21/7/86	M	8	(1)	
Alexander BAUMJOHANN		23/1/87	M	3	(6)	
Angelos CHARISTEAS	GRE	9/2/80	A	1	(3)	1
DANILO Fernando AVELAR	BRA	9/6/89	M	2	(1)	
Ciprian Ioan DEAC	ROU	16/2/86	M	2		
Julian DRAXLER		20/9/93	M	3	(12)	1
Sergio ESCUDERO Palomo	ESP	2/9/89	D	5	(1)	
EDUardo Gonçalves de Oliveira	BRA	30/11/81	A	15	(13)	3
Jefferson FARFÁN	PER	26/10/84	A	26	(2)	3
Mario GAVRANOVIC	SUI	24/11/89	A	4	(4)	
HAO Junmin	CHN	24/3/87	M	2	(4)	
Klaas Jan HUNTELAAR	NED	12/8/83	A	22	(2)	8
Benedikt HÖWEDES		29/2/88	D	30		1
Erik JENDRIŠEK	SVK	26/10/86	A		(3)	
Jermaine JONES	USA	3/11/81	M	10		1
José Manuel JURADO Marín	ESP	29/6/86	M	21	(7)	3
Ali KARIMI	IRN	8/11/78	M		(1)	
Peer KLUGE		22/11/80	M	18	(4)	1
Joël MATIP	CMR	8/8/91	D	14	(12)	
Christoph METZELDER		5/11/80	D	32		1
Christoph MORITZ		27/1/90	M	8	(4)	
Manuel NEUER		27/3/86	G	34		
Christian PANDER		28/8/83	D	1	(3)	
Kyriakos PAPADOPOULOS	GRE	23/2/92	D	10	(8)	
Nicolas PLESTAN	FRA	2/6/81	D	3		
Vasilios PLIATSIKAS	GRE	14/4/88	M	1		
Ivan RAKITIĆ	CRO	10/3/88	M	14	(2)	1
RAÚL González Blanco	ESP	27/6/77	A	34		13
Hans SARPEI	GHA	28/6/76	D	6	(3)	
Lukas SCHMITZ		13/10/88	M	21	(2)	
Atsuto UCHIDA	JPN	27/3/88	D	24	(2)	

FC ST PAULI

Coach – Holger Stanislawski

Founded – 1910

Stadium – Millerntor-Stadion (24,487)

010				
1/8	Freiburg	a	3-1	*Boll, Sukuta-Pasu, Bartels*
8/8	Hoffenheim	h	0-1	
2/9	Köln	a	0-1	
9/9	Hamburg	h	1-1	*Boll*
2/9	Mönchengladbach	a	2-1	*Asamoah, Bruns (p)*
5/9	Dortmund	h	1-3	*Hennings*
/10	Hannover	a	1-0	*Ebbers*
6/10	Nürnberg	h	3-2	*Asamoah, Ebbers, Bruns*
4/10	Stuttgart	a	0-2	
0/10	Eintracht	h	1-3	*Zambrano*
/11	Schalke	a	0-3	
3/11	Leverkusen	h	0-1	
1/11	Wolfsburg	h	1-1	*Thorandt*
8/11	Werder	a	0-3	
/12	Kaiserslautern	h	1-0	*og (Tiffert)*
1/12	Bayern	a	0-3	
8/12	Mainz	h	2-4	*Lehmann 2 (1p)*

2011				
15/1	Freiburg	h	2-2	*Ebbers, Asamoah*
23/1	Hoffenheim	a	2-2	*Kruse, Asamoah*
29/1	Köln	h	3-0	*Takyi 2, Bruns (p)*
12/2	Mönchengladbach	h	3-1	*Kruse, Asamoah, Lehmann*
16/2	Hamburg	a	1-0	*Asamoah*
19/2	Dortmund	a	0-2	
26/2	Hannover	h	0-1	
5/3	Nürnberg	a	0-5	
13/3	Stuttgart	h	1-2	*Boll*
19/3	Eintracht	a	1-2	*Takyi*
1/4	Schalke	h	0-2	*(match abandoned after 87 mins; result stood)*
10/4	Leverkusen	a	1-2	*Takyi*
16/4	Wolfsburg	a	2-2	*Naki, Lehmann*
23/4	Werder	h	1-3	*Bartels*
29/4	Kaiserslautern	a	0-2	
7/5	Bayern	h	1-8	*Eger*
14/5	Mainz	a	1-2	*Lehmann*

No	Name	Nat	DoB	Pos	Aps	(s)	Gls
13	Gerald ASAMOAH		3/10/78	A	21	(6)	6
22	Fin BARTELS		7/2/87	M	23	(8)	2
17	Fabian BOLL		16/6/79	M	28		3
8	Florian BRUNS		21/8/79	M	11	(19)	3
30	Dennis DAUBE		11/7/89	M	7	(6)	
32	Davidson DROBO-AMPEM		26/3/88	D		(1)	
9	Marius EBBERS		4/1/78	A	21	(10)	3
14	Marcel EGER		23/3/63	D	4	(3)	1
35	Petar FILIPOVIC		14/9/90	M		(1)	
11	Ralph GUNESCH		2/9/83	D	20		
25	Mathias HAIN		31/12/72	G	3	(1)	
7	Rouwen HENNINGS		28/8/87	A	10	(6)	1
27	Jan-Phillipp KALLA		6/8/86	M	4	(1)	
26	Thomas KESSLER		20/1/86	G	26		
18	Max KRUSE		19/3/88	M	27	(6)	2
2	Florian LECHNER		3/3/81	D	9	(1)	
20	Matthias LEHMANN		28/5/83	M	33		5
4	Fabio MORENA		19/3/80	D	7		
23	Deniz NAKI		9/7/89	M	6	(14)	1
6	Bastian OCZIPKA		12/1/89	D	20		
1	Benedikt PLIQUETT		20/12/84	G	5		
24	Carsten ROTHENBACH		3/9/80	D	13		
12	Timo SCHULTZ		26/8/77	M		(4)	
19	Richard SUKUTA-PASU		24/6/90	A	1	(8)	1
10	Charles TAKYI		12/11/84	M	19	(5)	4
16	Markus THORANDT		1/4/81	D	29		1
28	Moritz VOLZ		21/1/83	D	8	(1)	
5	Carlos ZAMBRANO	PER	10/7/89	D	19	(1)	1

VFB STUTTGART

Coach – Christian Gross (SUI); (13/10/10) Jens Keller; (12/12/10) Bruno Labbadia

Founded – 1893

Stadium – Mercedes-Benz-Arena (44,950)

MAJOR HONOURS: German League – (5) 1950, 1952, 1984, 1992, 2007; German Cup – (3), 1954, 1958, 1997.

2010				
22/8	Mainz	a	0-2	
29/8	Dortmund	h	1-3	*Cacau*
11/9	Freiburg	a	1-2	*Pogrebnyak*
18/9	Mönchengladbach	h	7-0	*Pogrebnyak 3, Niedermeier, Kuzmanović, Delpierre, Marica*
22/9	Nürnberg	a	1-2	*Cacau*
25/9	Leverkusen	h	1-4	*Kuzmanović*
3/10	Eintracht	h	1-2	*Pogrebnyak*
16/10	Schalke	a	2-2	*Gebhart, Harnik*
24/10	St Pauli	h	2-0	*Niedermeier, Kuzmanović*
30/10	Wolfsburg	a	0-2	
7/11	Werder	h	6-0	*Marica, Cacau 2, Gentner, Niedermeier, Boka*

13/11	Kaiserslautern	a	3-3	*Boka, Cacau, Gentner (p)*
21/11	Köln	h	0-1	
27/11	Hamburg	a	2-4	*Marica, Gentner*
4/12	Hoffenheim	h	1-1	*Harnik*
10/12	Hannover	a	1-2	*Niedermeier*
19/12	Bayern	h	3-5	*Harnik 2, Gentner*
2011				
15/1	Mainz	h	1-0	*Harnik*
22/1	Dortmund	a	1-1	*Pogrebnyak*
30/1	Freiburg	h	0-1	
5/2	Mönchengladbach	a	3-2	*Pogrebnyak, Harnik, Gebhart (p)*
12/2	Nürnberg	h	1-4	*Funk*
20/2	Leverkusen	a	2-4	*Harnik, Kuzmanović*
27/2	Eintracht	a	2-0	*Harnik, Hajnal*
5/3	Schalke	h	1-0	*Kuzmanović (p)*
13/3	St Pauli	a	2-1	*Kuzmanović, Schipplock*
20/3	Wolfsburg	h	1-1	*Niedermeier*
2/4	Werder	a	1-1	*Hajnal*
9/4	Kaiserslautern	h	2-4	*Kuzmanović (p), Pogrebnyak*
16/4	Köln	a	3-1	*Träsch, Harnik, Kuzmanović (p)*
23/4	Hamburg	h	3-0	*Cacau 2, Gentner*
30/4	Hoffenheim	a	2-1	*Cacau, Kuzmanović (p)*
7/5	Hannover	h	2-1	*Hajnal, Okazaki*
14/5	Bayern	a	1-2	*Okazaki*

No	Name	Nat	DoB	Pos	Aps	(s)	Gls
11	Johan AUDEL	FRA	12/12/83	M		(3)	
24	Mamadou BAH	GUI	25/4/88	M	2		
38	Ermin BIČAKČIĆ	BIH	24/1/90	D	1		
15	Arthur BOKA	CIV	2/4/83	D	18	(5)	2
21	Khalid BOULAHROUZ	NED	28/12/81	D	13	(3)	
18	Jerónimo Maria Barreto Claudemir da Silva "CACAU"		27/3/81	A	24	(3)	8
16	Mauro CAMORANESI	ITA	4/10/76	M	3	(4)	
27	Stefano CELOZZI		2/11/88	D	6	(1)	
2	Philipp DEGEN	SUI	15/2/83	D	4	(1)	
17	Matthieu DELPIERRE	FRA	26/4/81	D	15	(3)	1
26	Daniel DIDAVI		21/2/90	M	4	(4)	
25	ÉLSON Falcão da Silva	BRA	16/11/81	M	2	(1)	
14	Patrick FUNK		11/2/90	M	7	(2)	1
13	Timo GEBHART		12/4/89	M	15	(10)	2
20	Christian GENTNER		14/8/85	M	23	(8)	5
28	Tamás HAJNAL	HUN	15/3/81	M	11	(1)	3
7	Martin HARNIK	AUT	10/6/87	A	17	(15)	9
8	Zdravko KUZMANOVIĆ	SRB	22/9/87	M	27	(5)	9
9	Ciprian Andrei MARICA	ROU	2/10/85	A	8	(5)	3
3	Cristian MOLINARO	ITA	30/7/83	D	24	(3)	
6	Georg NIEDERMEIER		26/2/86	D	25	(4)	5
31	Shinji OKAZAKI	JPN	16/4/86	M	12		2
29	Pavel POGREBNYAK	RUS	8/11/83	A	18	(8)	8
36	Sven SCHIPPLOCK		8/11/88	A	1	(11)	1
5	Serdar TAŞÇI		24/4/87	D	26		
35	Christian TRÄSCH		1/9/87	M	34		1
1	Sven ULREICH		3/8/88	G	34		

SV WERDER BREMEN

Coach – Thomas Schaaf

Founded – 1899

Stadium – Weserstadion (40,500)

MAJOR HONOURS: UEFA Cup Winners' Cup – (1) 1992; German League – (4) 1965, 1988, 1993, 2004; German Cup – (6) 1961, 1991, 1994, 1999, 2004, 2009.

2010				
21/8	Hoffenheim	a	1-4	*Frings (p)*
28/8	Köln	h	4-2	*Frings (p), Arnautovic 2, Hugo Almeida*
11/9	Bayern	a	0-0	
18/9	Mainz	h	0-2	
21/9	Hannover	a	1-4	*Frings (p)*
25/9	Hamburg	h	3-2	*og (Demel), Hugo Almeida 2*
3/10	Leverkusen	a	2-2	*Hugo Almeida, Marin*
16/10	Freiburg	h	2-1	*Hunt, Hugo Almeida*
23/10	Mönchengladbach	a	4-1	*Marin, Wesley, Hunt, Pizarro*
30/10	Nürnberg	h	2-3	*Hugo Almeida, Pizarro*
7/11	Stuttgart	a	0-6	
13/11	Eintracht	h	0-0	
20/11	Schalke	a	0-4	
28/11	St Pauli	h	3-0	*Hugo Almeida 3*
4/12	Wolfsburg	a	0-0	
11/12	Dortmund	a	0-2	
18/12	Kaiserslautern	h	1-2	*Hunt (p)*
2011				
15/1	Hoffenheim	h	2-1	*Pizarro, Frings*
22/1	Köln	a	0-3	
29/1	Bayern	h	1-3	*Mertesacker*
5/2	Mainz	a	1-1	*Pizarro*
13/2	Hannover	h	1-1	*Mertesacker*
19/2	Hamburg	a	0-4	
27/2	Leverkusen	h	2-2	*og (Kiessling), Prödl*
6/3	Freiburg	a	3-1	*Wagner, Pizarro, Marin*
12/3	Mönchengladbach	h	1-1	*Wagner*
19/3	Nürnberg	a	3-1	*Wagner 2 (2p), Pizarro*
2/4	Stuttgart	h	1-1	*Frings*
8/4	Eintracht	a	1-1	*og (Halil)*
16/4	Schalke	h	1-1	*Wagner*
23/4	St Pauli	a	3-1	*og (Thorandt), Pizarro 2*
29/4	Wolfsburg	h	0-1	
7/5	Dortmund	h	2-0	*Silvestre, Pizarro*
14/5	Kaiserslautern	a	2-3	*Frings, Arnautovic*

No	Name	Nat	DoB	Pos	Aps	(s)	Gl.
7	Marko ARNAUTOVIC	AUT	19/4/89	A	15	(10)	3
9	Denni AVDIC	SWE	5/9/88	A	2	(5)	
46	Onur AYIK	TUR	28/1/90	A		(1)	
37	Leon BALOGUN		28/6/88	D		(3)	
44	Philipp BARGFREDE		3/3/89	M	23	(5)	
2	Sebastian BOENISCH	POL	1/2/87	D	1		
6	Tim BOROWSKI		2/5/80	M	10	(2)	
22	Torsten FRINGS		22/11/76	M	32		6
8	Clemens FRITZ		7/12/80	D	29		
34	HUGO Miguel Pereira de ALMEIDA	POR	23/5/84	A	7	(6)	9
14	Aaron HUNT		4/9/86	M	21	(8)	3
17	Said HUSEJINOVIĆ		13/5/88	M		(4)	
20	Daniel JENSEN	DEN	25/6/79	M	3	(8)	
18	Felix KROOS		12/3/91	M	3	(2)	
10	Marko MARIN		13/3/89	M	28	(6)	3
29	Per MERTESACKER		29/9/84	D	30		2
21	Sebastian MIELITZ		18/7/89	G	5	(1)	
3	Petri PASANEN	FIN	24/9/80	D	23	(1)	
24	Claudio PIZARRO	PER	3/10/78	A	20	(2)	9
15	Sebastian PRÖDL	AUT	21/6/87	D	25		1
41	Dominik SCHMIDT		1/7/87	D	7	(5)	
16	Mikaël SILVESTRE	FRA	9/8/77	D	26		1
31	Predrag STEVANOVIĆ	SRB	3/3/91	M	1	(2)	
36	Lennart THY		25/2/92	A		(2)	
35	Florian TRINKS		11/3/92	M	4	(4)	
19	Sandro WAGNER		29/11/87	A	12	(11)	5
5	WESLEY Lopes Beltrame	BRA	24/6/87	M	18	(2)	1
1	Tim WIESE		17/12/81	G	29	(1)	

VFL WOLFSBURG

Coach – Steve McClaren (ENG); (7/2/11) (Pierre Littbarski); (18/3/11) Felix Magath

Founded – 1945

Stadium – Volkswagen-Arena (30,000)

MAJOR HONOURS: German League – (1) 2009.

10				
'8	Bayern	a	1-2	*Džeko*
'8	Mainz	h	3-4	*Džeko 2, Diego*
9	Dortmund	a	0-2	
'9	Hannover	h	2-0	*Diego, Džeko*
'9	Hamburg	a	3-1	*Džeko, Grafite 2*
9	Freiburg	h	2-1	*Grafite 2*
0	Mönchengladbach	a	1-1	*Kahlenberg*
'10	Leverkusen	h	2-3	*Diego, Grafite*
'10	Nürnberg	a	1-2	*Grafite*
'10	Stuttgart	h	2-0	*Džeko 2*
1	Eintracht	a	1-3	*Dejagah*
'11	Schalke	h	2-2	*Grafite, Džeko*
/11	St Pauli	a	1-1	*Džeko*
/11	Köln	a	1-1	*Cícero*
2	Werder	h	0-0	
'12	Kaiserslautern	a	0-0	
/12	Hoffenheim	h	2-2	*Diego, Džeko*
11				
/1	Bayern	h	1-1	*Riether*
/1	Mainz	a	1-0	*Kjær*
/1	Dortmund	h	0-3	
2	Hannover	a	0-1	
/2	Hamburg	h	0-1	
/2	Freiburg	a	1-2	*Helmes*
/2	Mönchengladbach	h	2-1	*Diego 2*
3	Leverkusen	a	0-3	
/3	Nürnberg	h	1-2	*Mandžukić*
/3	Stuttgart	a	1-1	*Grafite*
4	Eintracht	h	1-1	*Mandžukić*
4	Schalke	a	0-1	
/4	St Pauli	h	2-2	*Mandžukić, Polák*
/4	Köln	h	4-1	*Mandžukić 2, Dejagah 2*
/4	Werder	a	1-0	*Riether*
5	Kaiserslautern	h	1-2	*Mandžukić*
/5	Hoffenheim	a	3-1	*Mandžukić 2, Grafite*

o	Name	Nat	DoB	Pos	Aps	(s)	Gls
5	Andrea BARZAGLI	ITA	8/5/81	D	17		
	Diego BENAGLIO	SUI	8/9/83	G	28		
1	CÍCERO Santos	BRA	26/8/84	M	14	(7)	1
4	Tolga CIĞERCI		23/3/92	M	5	(1)	
4	Ashkan DEJAGAH		5/7/86	M	10	(13)	3
8	DIEGO Ribas da Cunha	BRA	28/2/85	M	30		6
0	Edin DŽEKO	BIH	17/3/86	A	17		10
	Arne FRIEDRICH		29/5/79	D	15		
3	Edinaldo Batista Libano "GRAFITE"	BRA	2/4/79	A	22	(6)	9
3	Makoto HASEBE	JPN	18/1/84	M	19	(4)	
3	Patrick HELMES		1/3/84	A	5	(3)	1
5	Marwin HITZ	SUI	18/9/87	G	5	(1)	
6	Fabian JOHNSON		11/12/87	D	1	(5)	
	JOSUÉ Anunciado de Oliveira	BRA	19/7/79	M	26		
	Thomas KAHLENBERG	DEN	20/3/83	M	8	(6)	1
4	Simon KJÆR	DEN	26/3/89	D	32		1
	KOO Ja-cheol	KOR	27/2/89	M	1	(9)	
2	André LENZ		19/11/73	G	1		
7	Alexander MADLUNG		11/7/82	D	4	(16)	
8	Mario MANDŽUKIĆ	CRO	21/5/86	A	15	(9)	8
5	Dieumerci MBOKANI	COD	22/11/85	A	2	(5)	
0	Zvjezdan MISIMOVIĆ	BIH	5/6/82	M		(1)	
9	Peter PEKARÍK	SVK	30/10/86	D	19	(4)	
9	Jan POLÁK	CZE	14/3/81	M	9	(3)	1
0	Sascha RIETHER		23/3/83	D	28		2
4	Marcel SCHÄFER		7/6/84	D	34		
3	TUNCAY Şanlı	TUR	16/1/82	M	3	(1)	
5	Karim ZIANI	ALG	17/8/82	M	4	(1)	

TOP GOALSCORERS 2010/11

28	Mario GOMEZ (Bayern)
22	Papiss Demba CISSÉ (Freiburg)
17	Milivoje NOVAKOVIČ (Köln)
16	Lucas BARRIOS (Dortmund) Theofanis GEKAS (Eintracht) Srđan LAKIĆ (Kaiserslautern)
15	André SCHÜRRLE (Mainz)
14	Didier KONAN YA (Hannover)
13	Lukas PODOLSKI (Köln) RAÚL (Schalke)

PROMOTED CLUBS

HERTHA BSC BERLIN

Coach – Markus Babbel
Founded – 1892
Stadium – Olympiastadion (74,244)
MAJOR HONOURS: German League – (2) 1930, 1931.

FC AUGSBURG

Coach – Jos Luhukay (NED)
Founded – 1907
Stadium – Impuls-Arena (30,660)

SECOND LEVEL FINAL TABLE 2010/11

		Pld	W	D	L	F	A	Pts
1	Hertha BSC Berlin	34	23	5	6	69	28	74
2	FC Augsburg	34	19	8	7	58	27	65
3	VfL Bochum 1848	34	20	5	9	49	35	65
4	SpVgg Greuther Fürth	34	17	10	7	47	27	61
5	FC Erzgebirge Aue	34	16	8	10	40	37	56
6	FC Energie Cottbus	34	16	7	11	65	52	55
7	Fortuna Düsseldorf	34	16	5	13	49	39	53
8	MSV Duisburg	34	15	7	12	53	38	52
9	TSV 1860 München	34	14	10	10	50	36	50
10	Alemannia Aachen	34	13	9	12	58	60	48
11	1. FC Union Berlin	34	11	9	14	39	45	42
12	SC Paderborn 07	34	10	9	15	32	47	39
13	FSV Frankfurt	34	11	5	18	42	54	38
14	FC Ingolstadt 04	34	9	10	15	40	46	37
15	Karlsruher SC	34	8	9	17	46	72	33
16	VfL Osnabrück	34	8	7	19	40	62	31
17	Rot-Weiss Oberhausen	34	7	7	20	30	65	28
18	DSC Arminia Bielefeld	34	4	8	22	28	65	17

NB DSC Arminia Bielefeld – 3 pts deducted;
TSV 1860 München – 2 pts deducted.

PROMOTION/RELEGATION PLAY-OFFS

(19/5/11 & 24/5/11)
Mönchengladbach 1, Bochum 0
Bochum 1, Mönchengladbach 1
(Mönchengladbach 2-1)

DOMESTIC CUP 2010/11

DFB-POKAL

FIRST ROUND

(13/8/10)
FSV Frankfurt 2, Paderborn 0
Ingolstadt 2, Karlsruhe 0
Lübeck 0, Duisburg 2
Osnabrück 2, Kaiserslautern 3 *(aet)*
Regensburg 1, Arminia 1 *(aet; 5-6 on pens)*
Wilhelmshaven 0, Eintracht 4

(14/8/10)
Ahlen 0, Werder 4
Babelsberg 1, Stuttgart 2
Braunschweig 1, Greuther Fürth 2 *(aet)*
Burghausen 0, Dortmund 3
Chemnitz 1, St Pauli 0
Elversberg 0, Hannover 0 *(aet; 5-4 on pens)*
Erzgebirge Aue 1, Mönchengladbach 3
Oberneuland 0, Freiburg 1
Pfullendorf 0, Hertha 2
Pirmasens 1, Leverkusen 11
Rostock 0, Hoffenheim 4
Sandhausen 4, Augsburg 4 *(aet; 1-3 on pens)*
Verl 1, 1860 München 2

(15/8/10)
Berliner AK 1, Mainz 2
Halle 1, Union Berlin 0
Heeslingen 1, Energie 2
Koblenz 1, Düsseldorf 0
Meuselwitz 0, Köln 2
Münster 1, Wolfsburg 2
Offenbach 3, Bochum 0
Schwarz-Weiss Essen 1, Aachen 2
Torgelow 1, Hamburg 5
Trier 0, Nürnberg 2
Victoria Hamburg 1, Oberhausen 0

(16/8/10)
Aalen 1, Schalke 2
Germania Windeck 0, Bayern 4

SECOND ROUND

(26/10/10)
Bayern 2, Werder 1
Energie 2, Freiburg 1
FSV Frankfurt 0, Schalke 1
Greuther Fürth 2, Augsburg 4 *(aet)*
Kaiserslautern 3, Arminia 0
Koblenz 2, Hertha 1
Köln 3, 1860 München 0
Victoria Hamburg 1, Wolfsburg 3

(27/10/10)
Aachen 2, Mainz 1
Chemnitzer 1, Stuttgart 3 *(aet)*
Eintracht 5, Hamburg 2
Elversberg 0, Nürnberg 3
Halle 0, Duisburg 3
Hoffenheim 1, Ingolstadt 0
Mönchengladbach 1, Leverkusen 1 *(aet; 5-4 on pens)*
Offenbach 0, Dortmund 0 *(aet; 4-2 on pens)*

THIRD ROUND

(21/12/10)
Augsburg 0, Schalke 1
Hoffenheim 2, Mönchengladbach 0

(22/12/10)
Aachen 1, Eintracht 1 *(aet; 5-3 on pens)*
Köln 1, Duisburg 2
Stuttgart 3, Bayern 6
Wolfsburg 1, Energie 3

(19/1/11)
Koblenz 1, Kaiserslautern 4
Offenbach 0, Nürnberg 2

QUARTER-FINALS

(25/1/11)
Schalke 3 *(Gavranovic 14, Rakitić 58, Draxler 119)*, Nürnberg 2 *(Schieber 4, 32) (aet)*

(26/1/11)
Aachen 0, Bayern 4 *(Gomez 26, Müller 75, 80, Robben 88)*
Duisburg 2 *(Bajić 36, Šukalo 58)*, Kaiserslautern 0
Energie 1 *(Shao 84)*, Hoffenheim 0

SEMI-FINALS

(1/3/11)
Duisburg 2 *(Maierhofer 24, Baljak 54)*, Energie 1 *(Petersen 78p)*

(2/3/11)
Bayern 0, Schalke 1 *(Raúl 15)*

FINAL

(21/5/11)
Olympiastadion, Berlin
FC SCHALKE 04 5 *(Draxler 18, Huntelaar 22, 70, Höwedes 42, Jurado 55)*
MSV DUISBURG 0
Referee – *Stark*
SCHALKE – *Neuer, Höwedes, Papadopoulos, Metzelder, Sarpei (Escudero 43), Kluge (Uchida 81), Jurado, Farfán, Draxler (Matip 72), Raúl, Huntelaar.*
DUISBURG – *Yelldell, Kern (Exslager 77), Reiche (Trojan 60), Bajić, Veigneau, Šukalo, Yilmaz, Grlić, Banović, Sahan, Schäffler.*

CLUB COMMUNICATION 2011/12

C Augsburg
nauwörther Strasse 170
-86154 Augsburg

l	++49 821 4554 77 0
x	++49 821 4554 77 70
eb	fcaugsburg.de
nail	info@fcaugsburg.de
edia Officer	Dominik Schmitz

ayer 04 Leverkusen
smarckstrasse 122-124
-51373 Leverkusen

l	+49 214 8660 0
x	+49 214 8660 512
eb	bayer04.de
nail	info@bayer04.de
edia Officer	Dirk Mesch

C Bayern München
äbener Strasse 51
E-81547 München

l	+49 89 699 310
ax	+49 89 644 165
eb	fcbayern.telekom.de
mail	info@fcb.de
edia Officer	Markus Hörwick

orussia Dortmund
heinlanddamm 207-209
E-44137 Dortmund

el	+49 231 902 00
ax	+49 231 902 0105
eb	bvb.de
mail	verein@bvb.de
ledia Officer	Josef Schneck

fL Borussia Mönchengladbach
ennes-Weisweiler-Allee 1
E-Mönchengladbach

el	+49 2161 9293 1000
ax	+49 2161 9293 1009
eb	borussia.de
mail	info@borussia.de
ledia Officer	Markus Aretz

SC Freiburg
Schwarzwaldstrasse 193
DE-79117 Freiburg

Tel	+49 761 385 510
Fax	+49 761 385 515 0
Web	scfreiburg.com
Email	scf@scfreiburg.com
Media Officer	Rudi Raschke

Hamburger SV
Sylvesterallee 7
DE-22525 Hamburg

Tel	+49 48 0547 8478
Fax	+49 40 4155 1234
Web	hsv.de
Email	info@hsv.de
Media Officer	Joern Wolf

Hannover 96
Arthur-Menge-Ufer 5, AWD-Arena
DE-30169 Hannover

Tel	+49 511 969 00 96
Fax	+49 511 969 00 796
Web	hannover96.de
Email	info@hannover96.de
Media Officer	Andreas Kuhnt

Hertha BSC Berlin
Hanns-Braun-Strasse, Friesenhaus 2
DE-14053 Berlin

Tel	+49 30 300 9280
Fax	+49 30 300 9289 9
Web	herthabsc.de
Email	info@herthabsc.de
Media Officer	

TSG 1899 Hoffenheim
Dietmar-Hopp-Sportpark, Horrenberger Strasse 58, DE-74939 Zuzenhausen

Tel	++49 7261 9493 100
Fax	++49 7261 9493 102
Web	achtzehn99.de
Email	info@achtzehn99.de
Media Officer	Markus Sieger

1. FC Kaiserslautern
Fritz-Walter-Strasse 1, Postfach 2427
DE-67663 Kaiserslautern

Tel	+49 631 3188 218
Fax	+49 631 3188 290
Web	fck.de
Email	info@fck.de
Media Officer	Christian Gruber

1. FC Köln
Postfach 450456
DE-50879 Köln

Tel	+49 221 716 1630 0
Fax	+49 221 430 1851
Web	fc-koeln.de
Email	info@fc-koeln.de
Media Officer	Christopher Lymberopoulos

1. FSV Mainz 05
Dr. Martin-Luther-King-Weg 20
DE-55122 Mainz

Tel	+49 6131 375 500
Fax	+49 6131 375 5033
Web	mainz05.de
Email	info@mainz05.de
Media Officer	Tobias Sparwasser

1. FC Nürnberg
Valznerweiherstrasse 200
DE-90480 Nürnberg

Tel	+49 911 940 790
Fax	+49 911 940 797 7
Web	fcn.de
Email	info@fcn.de
Media Officer	Katharina Wildermuth

FC Schalke 04
Ernst-Kuzorra-Weg 1
DE-45891 Gelsenkirchen

Tel	+49 209 3618 0
Fax	+49 209 3618 109
Web	schalke04.de
Email	post@schalke04.de
Media Officer	Thomas Spiegel

VfB Stuttgart
Mercedesstrasse 109
DE-70372 Stuttgart

Tel	+49 711 5500 7195
Fax	+49 711 5500 7196
Web	vfb.de
Email	info@vfb-stuttgart.de
Media Officer	Oliver Schraft

SV Werder Bremen
Franz-Böhmert-Strasse 1C
DE-28205 Bremen

Tel	+49 180 593 733 7
Fax	+49 421 493 555
Web	werder.de
Email	info@werder.de
Media Officer	Tino Polster

VfL Wolfsburg
In den Allerwiesen 1
DE-38446 Wolfsburg

Tel	+49 5361 8903 0
Fax	+49 5361 8903 100
Web	vfl-wolfsburg.de
Email	fussball@vfl-wolfsburg.de
Media Officer	Gerd Voss

GREECE

Grèce I Griechenland

Elliniki Podosfairiki Omospondia (EPO)

COMMUNICATION

Address Goudi Park
PO Box 14161
GR-11510 Athens

Tel +30 210 930 6000
Fax +30 210 935 9666

E-mail epo@epo.gr
Website epo.gr

President Sofoklis Pilavios
General Secretary Ioannis Economides
Media Officer Michael Tsapidis

Year of Formation 1926

National Stadium OACA Spyro Louis, Athens (72,080)

DOMESTIC COMPETITION SUMMARY 2010/11

SUPER LEAGUE FINAL TABLE

			Home					Away					Total						
		Pld	W	D	L	F	A	W	D	L	F	A	W	D	L	F	A	Pts	Comp
1	Olympiacos FC	30	15	0	0	46	6	9	1	5	19	12	24	1	5	65	18	73	UCL
2	Panathinaikos FC	30	11	3	1	27	12	7	3	5	20	14	18	6	6	47	26	60	UCL
3	AEK Athens FC	30	9	4	2	22	10	6	1	8	24	27	15	5	10	46	37	50	UEL
4	PAOK FC	30	10	1	4	20	12	4	5	6	12	17	14	6	10	32	29	48	UEL
5	Olympiacos Volou FC	30	6	6	3	20	13	6	5	4	20	15	12	11	7	40	28	47	UEL
6	Aris Thessaloniki FC	30	7	2	6	14	15	6	4	5	15	14	13	6	11	29	29	45	
7	Kavala FC	30	7	4	4	17	11	3	6	6	12	16	10	10	10	29	27	40	
8	Ergotelis FC	30	7	3	5	18	15	4	3	8	14	23	11	6	13	32	38	39	
9	Xanthi FC	30	6	4	5	16	16	3	5	7	13	19	9	9	12	29	35	36	
10	Panionios GSS	30	4	6	5	10	12	4	5	6	15	23	8	11	11	25	35	35	
11	Iraklis FC	30	5	8	2	12	9	2	6	7	10	19	7	14	9	22	28	35	
12	Atromitos FC	30	4	9	2	21	15	3	4	8	9	19	7	13	10	30	34	34	
13	Kerkyra FC	30	6	3	6	20	20	3	3	9	10	20	9	6	15	30	40	33	
14	Asteras Tripolis FC	30	3	5	7	12	17	4	5	6	9	12	7	10	13	21	29	31	
15	Larissa FC	30	5	4	6	20	19	0	6	9	9	28	5	10	15	29	47	25	
16	Panserraikos FC	30	5	3	7	12	19	1	3	11	10	29	6	6	18	22	48	24	

NB Asteras Tripolis FC, Larissa FC and Panserraikos FC subsequently avoided relegation as Olympiacos Volou FC, Kavala FC and Iraklis FC were excluded from the 2011/12 Super League.

Top Scorer Djibril Cissé (Panathinaikos), 20 goals

Promoted Clubs Panaitolikos GFS
PAS Giannina FC
OFI Crete FC

Cup Final AEK Athens FC 3, Atromitos FC 0

Olympiacos enjoy home comforts

Eliminated embarrassingly early from Europe, Olympiacos FC made peace with their supporters by cruising to victory in the 2010/11 Greek Super League and claiming their record 38th domestic title. The cornerstone of their triumph was a perfect home record, a feat achieved only twice before in Greece's top division and never by Olympiacos themselves.

In racking up those 15 wins out of 15 at the Georgios Karaiskakis Stadium, Olympiacos scored 46 goals and conceded just six. Fittingly it was with their biggest home win of the season, against AEK Athens FC on 20 March, that they made mathematically certain of the title with three rounds to spare, hammering their local rivals 6-0. Olympiacos's 13th championship win in 15 years was also the second in as many attempts for coach Ernesto Valverde.

A double winner with Olympiacos in 2008/09, Valverde had returned to his native Spain to take charge of Villarreal CF, only to be relieved of his duties after half a season. So when Olympiacos were dumped out of the UEFA Europa League at the third qualifying round stage by Maccabi Tel-Aviv FC in the summer of 2010, costing freshly hired German coach Ewald Lienen his job, new club president Vangelis Marinakis decided to re-appoint Valverde.

Ernesto Valverde – a Greek Super League champion with Olympiacos for the second time

It was not all plain sailing from the start, with Olympiacos losing their opening league fixture at Iraklis FC and then going down to defending champions and arch-rivals Panathinaikos FC in the first big derby, but with the team so imperious at home, by the time the short winter break arrived they held a five-point lead over sole challengers Panathinaikos. After the turn of the year Valverde's men reeled off eight successive victories, the last of them a controversial 2-1 success at home to Pana that ended the title race as a contest, enabling Olympiacos to freewheel to victory over the closing weeks of the campaign.

Spanish influence

With Marinakis, unlike many Greek club presidents, allowing Valverde complete sovereignty with regard to running the team, Olympiacos were a happy ship. There was a strong Spanish influence in the team, with no fewer than five of the coach's compatriots in the squad, the most effective of them, 13-goal attacking midfielder David Fuster, having followed Valverde to Piraeus from Villarreal – as had Argentine schemer Ariel Ibagaza. Young Belgian striker Kevin Mirallas also proved an astute buy, scoring 14 goals, many of them spectacular, while Algerian forward Rafik Djebbour turned out to be a valuable mid-season acquisition from AEK, even scoring twice against his former club in that title-clinching 6-0 win.

Although Olympiacos's foreign legion had a profound bearing on the club's success, Greek internationals Avraam Papadopoulos – a rock in central defence – and Vassilis Torosidis – versatile and dependable – both enjoyed excellent campaigns, while 20-year-old Ioannis Fetfatzidis displayed enormous potential. If Fetfatzidis was just starting out on the road to stardom, one man bowing out of the spotlight, at the age of 40, was goalkeeper Antonios Nikopolidis, who, having lost his place to Spaniard Urko Pardo, announced his retirement at the end of the season.

GREECE

As champions, Olympiacos's season ended in mid-April, but for the teams placed second to fifth in the Super League there was another month of overtime to complete in the UEFA Champions League qualification play-offs. Panathinaikos finished a clear second in the regular table, ten points ahead of AEK, and it was the three points they carried forward into the play-offs that would enable them to pip PAOK FC for the second UEFA Champions League place. In fact, Pana were the first team since the introduction of the play-offs in 2007/08 to maintain their runners-up position from the regular campaign after the additional six-match mini-league.

Prolific Cissé

It was a double from Djibril Cissé that brought Pana a decisive 2-0 win over AEK in their final play-off fixture. The French international striker had scored 20 goals in the Super League to retain the Golden Boot he had won in his debut season for Panathinaikos in 2009/10. Although a controversial figure at times – he became involved in a legal spat with Olympiacos president Marinakis as a result of the pitch invasion that followed the February derby in Piraeus – Cissé was indispensable to a Pana side that struggled almost as much on the pitch as off it, where disorder reigned among directors and shareholders. Double-winning coach Nikos Nioplias was sacked in November and replaced by ex-FC Porto boss Jesualdo Ferreira, who never quite got to grips with the job. Still, the team's re-qualification for the UEFA Champions League was not to be sneezed at – even if, as Greece's sole participants in 2010/11, they had put up a poor show, failing to win any of their six group fixtures and scoring just two goals.

Greece had three teams in the group stage of the 2010/11 UEFA Europa League. AEK went no further, eliminated jointly by FC Zenit St Petersburg and RSC Anderlecht, but the two Salonika teams, PAOK and Aris Thessaloniki FC, both progressed into the round of 32. The former, who lost out on away goals to AFC Ajax in the third qualifying round of the UEFA Champions League, put out Fenerbahçe in the play-offs of the secondary competition before finishing runners-up in their group and unluckily exiting in the round of 32 to PFC CSKA Moskva on a freezing night in the Russian capital, having lost just two of their 12 European matches. Aris had the distinction of eliminating holders Club Atlético de Madrid in the group stage, beating them home and away, before they lost in the first round of the knockout phase to Manchester City FC. The club did, however, keep alive their extraordinary record of never having lost a UEFA game at their Kleanthis Vikelidis Stadium, a run now extended to 25 matches.

By narrowly missing out on the end-of-season play-offs, Aris failed to return to Europe in 2011/12. AEK, however, secured a UEFA Europa League ticket prior to the play-offs by winning the Greek Cup. Easy 3-0 winners over Atromitos FC in the final, the hard work for the Yellow-and-Blacks had come in the previous two rounds, when they edged past Panathinaikos and PAOK with impressive away wins

National Team

International Honours –
UEFA European Championship – (1) 2004.

International Tournament Appearances –
FIFA World Cup – (2) 1994, 2010.
UEFA European Championship – (3) 1980, 2004 (Winners), 2008.

Top Five All-time Caps – Theodoros Zagorakis (120); Georgios Karagounis (107); Angelos Basinas (100); Efstratios Apostolakis (96); Antonis Nikopolidis (90)

Top Five All-time Goals – Nikolaos Anastopoulos (29); Angelos Charisteas (24); Dimitrios Saravakos (22); Theofanis Gekas & Dimitrios "Mimis" Papaioannou (20)

NATIONAL TEAM RESULTS 2010/11

11/8/10	Serbia	A	Belgrade	1-0	*Salpingidis (45)*
3/9/10	Georgia (ECQ)	H	Piraeus	1-1	*Spiropoulos (72)*
7/9/10	Croatia (ECQ)	A	Zagreb	0-0	
8/10/10	Latvia (ECQ)	H	Piraeus	1-0	*Torosidis (58)*
12/10/10	Israel (ECQ)	H	Piraeus	2-1	*Salpingidis (22), Karagounis (63p)*
17/11/10	Austria	A	Vienna	2-1	*Samaras (49), Fotakis (81)*
9/2/11	Canada	H	Larissa	1-0	*Fetfatzidis (63)*
26/3/11	Malta (ECQ)	A	Ta' Qali	1-0	*Torosidis (90+2)*
29/3/11	Poland	H	Piraeus	0-0	
4/6/11	Malta (ECQ)	H	Piraeus	3-1	*Fetfatzidis (7, 63), Papadopoulos K. (26)*
7/6/11	Ecuador	N	New York (USA)	1-1	*Tziolis (16)*

NATIONAL TEAM APPEARANCES 2010/11

oach – FERNANDO SANTOS (POR)	10/10/54		Srb	GEO	CRO	LVA	ISR	Aut	Can	MLT	Pol	MLT	Ecu	Caps	Goals
ihail SIFAKIS	9/9/84	Aris	G	G	G	G	G		G46					8	-
oukas VYNTRA	5/2/81	Panathinaikos	D81		D		D	s46	s46		D		D	39	-
ikolaos SPIROPOULOS	10/10/83	Panathinaikos	D	D			D					D	s89	25	1
otirios KYRGIAKOS	23/7/79	Liverpool (ENG)	D46											61	4
okratis PAPASTATHOPOULOS	9/6/88	Milan (ITA)	D	D	D	D	D	D	D	D 84*				20	-
ostas KATSOURANIS	21/6/79	Panathinaikos	M	M	M	M	M	M74	M46	M	s73	M	s78	83	8
'assilis TOROSIDIS	10/6/85	Olympiacos	M66	M	M92	D		D46	D46	D	s77	D		38	5
ieorgios KARAGOUNIS	6/3/77	Panathinaikos	M87	M	M70	M90	M	M91	M	M	M73	M70	s64	107	7
iotirios NINIS	3/4/90	Panathinaikos	M74	s59	s70	M82	M15		M	M81	s58	M80	s63	16	1
imitris SALPINGIDIS	18/8/81	PAOK	A46	A	A59	s77	A87	A71	A46	A61	s77	A89		48	6
ieorgios SAMARAS	21/2/85	Celtic (SCO)	A	A59	A	A	A81	A		A	A77			45	6
vraam PAPADOPOULOS	3/12/84	Olympiacos	s46	D	D	D	D	D		D	D			25	-
heofanis GEKAS	23/5/80	Eintracht (GER)	s46	A	s59									52	20
antelis KAFES	24/6/78	AEK	s66			s90	M	s74	s46		M	s70	M64	39	3
oannis PAPADOPOULOS	9/3/89	Olympiacos	s74											1	-
oannis MANIATIS	12/10/86	Panionios /Olympiacos	s81				s87						D89	3	-
Stergos MARINOS	17/9/87	Panathinaikos	s87											1	-
Giourkas SEITARIDIS	4/6/81	Panathinaikos		D71	s92									72	1
Konstantinos MITROGLOU	12/3/88	Olympiacos /Panionios		s71		A77	s81		s46 /69	s70	A58	s89	A65	9	-
Georgios TZAVELAS	26/11/87	Eintracht (GER)			D	D		D	D	D				5	-
Alexandros TZIOLIS	13/2/85	Racing (ESP)			M	M						M	M	26	1
Ioannis FETFATZIDIS	21/12/90	Olympiacos				s82	s15	s71	M	s61	M77	M	s64	8	3
Alexandros TZORVAS	12/8/82	Panathinaikos						G		G				13	-
Panagiotis KONE	26/7/87	Brescia (ITA)						M46	s61	s81	M66		M64	5	-
Lazaros HRISTODOULOPOULOS	19/12/86	Panathinaikos						M84				s80	M63	6	-
Georgios FOTAKIS	29/10/81	PAOK						s46					M78	3	1
Georgios K. GEORGIADIS	14/11/87	Panserraikos						s84	s69					2	-
Grigorios MAKOS	18/1/87	AEK						s91						4	-
Vangelis MORAS	26/8/81	Bologna (ITA)							D		D	D	D	16	-
Nikos LIBEROPOULOS	4/8/75	AEK							A61	A70	s66			70	13
Kostas CHALKIAS	30/5/74	PAOK							s46		G			29	-
Panagiotis LAGOS	18/7/85	AEK									D			9	-
Dimitrios KONSTANTOPOULOS	29/11/78	Kerkyra										G		1	-
Kyriakos PAPADOPOULOS	23/2/92	Schalke (GER)										D	D	2	1
Stefanos KOTSOLIS	6/5/79	Panathinaikos											G	5	-
Stefanos ATHANASIADIS	24/12/88	PAOK											s65	1	-

in the two-legged ties. The Cup win was the club's first trophy success in nine years, thus ending their longest barren run in over half a century, and was achieved, like Olympiacos's championship triumph, under the direction of a Spanish coach, ex-Sevilla FC boss Manuel 'Manolo' Jiménez having arrived the previous October following the resignation of club legend Dušan Bajević.

Valiant Volou

It was as a consequence of a 3-1 defeat away to newly promoted Olympiacos Volou FC that Bajević decided to turn his back on AEK. The Super League newcomers – back in the top flight after a 21-year absence – were widely expected to struggle against relegation but they proved to be the revelation of the season, reaching the semi-finals of the Cup and also – thanks to an astonishing fifth-place finish in the Super League achieved with home and away wins over both AEK and Panathinaikos – the play-offs, which earned them European qualification for the first time.

A new era for the Greek national team, with Fernando Santos replacing long-serving Otto Rehhagel as coach, began on a positive note. Not only did the Portuguese go unbeaten through his first 11 matches at the helm, but by the end of the season Greece sat on top of the standings in their UEFA EURO 2012 qualifying group on the back of four successive victories. The pragmatic, safety-first style of the team's play did not differ greatly from that of the previous regime, and overall the results were arguably no better nor worse than expected – a fine 0-0 draw in Croatia having offset a disappointing opening home draw with Georgia - but, as debut seasons go, Fernando Santos had every reason to feel pleased with his endeavours.

There was no wholesale turnover of personnel, but in giving young talent-in-waiting Sotirios Ninis an extended opportunity in the side and introducing other gifted colts such as Fetfatzidis and FC Schalke 04 defender Kyriakos Papadopoulos, the new coach was gradually trying to manoeuvre the team in a forward-looking direction. There was still room, though, for the odd hero of 2004, with 34-year-old Georgios Karagounis becoming only the third Greek footballer to reach a century of international appearances. He won his 100th cap in the October 2010 qualifier against Latvia and celebrated four days later by scoring the winning penalty against Israel.

CLUB-BY-CLUB

AEK ATHENS FC

Coach – Dušan Bajević (SRB); (27/9/10) (Bledar Kola (ALB)); (7/10/10) Manuel Jiménez (ESP)

Founded – 1924

Stadium – OACA Spyro Louis (72,080)

MAJOR HONOURS: Greek League – (11) 1939, 1940, 1963, 1968, 1971, 1978, 1979, 1989, 1992, 1993, 1994;
Greek Cup – (14) 1932, 1939, 1949, 1950, 1956, 1964, 1966, 1978, 1983, 1996, 1997, 2000, 2002, 2011.

2010				
29/8	Kerkyra	a	1-2	*Djebbour*
12/9	Panserraikos	h	2-0	*Djebbour, Kafes*
19/9	Tripolis	h	2-2	*Djebbour, Scocco*
26/9	Olympiacos Volou	a	1-3	*Liberopoulos*
3/10	Xanthi	h	1-0	*Leonardo*
17/10	Aris	a	4-0	*Kafes, Scocco 2, Djebbour*
24/10	Panathinaikos	h	1-0	*Djebbour*
31/10	Panionios	a	0-1	
8/11	Ergotelis	h	3-1	*Kafes, Blanco, Éder*
13/11	PAOK	a	1-2	*Leonardo (p)*
21/11	Kavala	a	1-2	*Scocco*
27/11	Olympiacos	h	1-0	*Blanco*
5/12	Atromitos	a	1-1	*Blanco*
12/12	Larissa	h	4-0	*Blanco 2, Liberopoulos, Dellas*
19/12	Iraklis	a	0-2	
2011				
5/1	Kerkyra	h	0-0	
9/1	Panserraikos	a	3-1	*Blanco, Liberopoulos 2 (1p)*
16/1	Tripolis	a	3-0	*Liberopoulos, Blanco, Scocco (p)*
22/1	Olympiacos Volou	h	0-4	
29/1	Xanthi	a	2-0	*Leonardo, Liberopoulos*
5/2	Aris	h	1-2	*Blanco*
13/2	Panathinaikos	a	1-3	*Scocco*
20/2	Panionios	h	1-1	*Liberopoulos*
27/2	Ergotelis	a	3-2	*Blanco, Burns, Georgeas*
6/3	PAOK	h	4-0	*Diop, Scocco 2, Dellas*
13/3	Kavala	h	1-0	*Scocco*
20/3	Olympiacos	a	0-6	
3/4	Atromitos	h	1-0	*Roger*
10/4	Larissa	a	3-2	*Manolas, Lagos 2*
17/4	Iraklis	h	0-0	

No	Name	Nat	DoB	Pos	Aps	(s)	Gl
99	Serxhio ABDURAHMANI	ALB	17/7/92	A		(1)	
22	Ioannis ARABATZIS		28/5/84	G	9		
27	Anestis ARGIRIOU		4/1/88	D	4	(1)	
39	Nabil BAHA	MAR	12/8/81	A	6	(3)	
18	Ismael BLANCO	ARG	19/1/83	A	16	(6)	9
24	Nathan BURNS	AUS	7/5/88	A	10	(7)	1
13	Claudio Martín DADÓMO	URU	10/2/82	D	5		
6	DAVID MATEOS Ramajo	ESP	22/4/87	D	7		
5	Traianos DELLAS		31/1/76	D	19		2
21	Papa Bouba DIOP	SEN	28/1/78	M	12	(7)	1
10	Rafik DJEBBOUR	ALG	8/3/84	A	9	(2)	5
26	Dino DRPIĆ	CRO	26/5/81	D		(1)	
20	ÉDER Luiz Lima de Sousa	BRA	9/1/87	A	4	(6)	1
90	Savvas GENTSOGLOU		19/9/90	M	8	(7)	
31	Nikolaos GEORGEAS		27/12/76	D	7		1
12	Sanel JAHIĆ	BIH	10/12/81	D	14	(3)	
1	Pantelis KAFES		24/6/78	M	16	(4)	3
15	Nikolaos KARABELAS		20/12/84	D	15	(2)	
19	Panagiotis LAGOS		18/7/85	M	19	(2)	2
9	LEONARDO Rodrigues Pereira	BRA	22/9/86	M	12	(10)	3
33	Nikolaos LIBEROPOULOS		4/8/75	A	16	(6)	7
14	Grigorios MAKOS		18/1/87	D	22		

No	Name	Nat	DoB	Pos	Aps	(s)	Gls
	Kostas MANOLAS		14/6/91	D	20	(2)	1
	Miguel Marcos Madera "MICHEL"	ESP	8/11/85	M	8	(2)	
	Cristian Javier NASUTI	ARG	6/9/82	D	15	(3)	
	Georgios NIKOLTSIS		6/4/92	A		(1)	
	Christos PATSATZOGLOU		19/3/79	D	5	(2)	
	ROGER Guerreiro	POL	25/5/82	M	12	(7)	1
	Diego Sebastián SAJA	ARG	5/6/79	G	21		
	Ignacio Martín SCOCCO	ARG	29/5/85	A	19	(4)	9

ARIS THESSALONIKI FC

Coach – Héctor Cúper (ARG); (19/1/11) (Ioannis Mihalitsios); (10/3/11) Athanasios Tsiolis

Founded – 1914

Stadium – Kleanthis Vikelidis (22,800)

MAJOR HONOURS: Greek League – (3) 1928, 1932, 1946; Greek Cup – (1) 1970.

010

9/8	Kavala	a	1-0	*Oriol*
/9	Panathinaikos	h	0-1	
9/9	Panionios	a	0-1	
6/9	Ergotelis	h	1-0	*Cesarec*
10	PAOK	a	1-0	*Javito*
7/10	AEK	h	0-4	
4/10	Olympiacos	a	0-1	
0/10	Atromitos	h	2-0	*Javito, Lazaridis*
11	Larissa	h	1-1	*Lazaridis*
5/11	Iraklis	a	0-1	
1/11	Kerkyra	h	2-0	*Cesarec, Portilla A.*
8/11	Panserraikos	a	0-1	
/12	Tripolis	h	1-0	*Neto*
1/12	Olympiacos Volou	a	1-1	*Neto*
9/12	Xanthi	h	0-2	

011

/1	Kavala	h	1-0	*Ruiz*
/1	Panathinaikos	a	0-1	
6/1	Panionios	h	0-2	
3/1	Ergotelis	a	0-0	
0/1	PAOK	h	0-0	
/2	AEK	a	2-1	*Neto 2*
2/2	Olympiacos	h	1-2	*Neto*
20/2	Atromitos	a	0-0	
27/2	Larissa	a	2-2	*Danilo Pereira, Bobadilla*
5/3	Iraklis	h	0-1	
13/3	Kerkyra	a	4-3	*Faty, Lazaridis, Castillo, Koke*
20/3	Panserraikos	h	3-1	*Bobadilla, Castillo, Neto*
3/4	Tripolis	a	2-1	*Koke (p), Lazaridis*
10/4	Olympiacos Volou	h	2-1	*Portilla C., Neto*
17/4	Xanthi	a	2-1	*Neto, Danilo Pereira*

No	Name	Nat	DoB	Pos	Aps	(s)	Gls
23	Christos ARAVIDIS		13/3/87	A	1	(3)	
22	Raúl Marcelo BOBADILLA	ARG	18/6/87	A	7		2
77	Nery Alberto CASTILLO	MEX	13/6/84	M	5	(5)	2
9	Danijel CESAREC	CRO	8/1/83	A	15	(8)	2
33	Deividas ČESNAUSKIS	LTU	30/6/81	M	2	(7)	
26	DANILO Luís Hélio PEREIRA	POR	9/9/91	M	4	(1)	2
28	FABIANO de Lima Campos Maria	BRA	24/11/85	A		(3)	
14	Ricardo FATY	FRA	4/8/86	M	15	(5)	1
27	Haralambos IKONOMOPOULOS		9/1/91			(1)	
20	Francisco Javier Peral Periane "JAVITO"	ESP	4/11/83	A	16	(3)	2
25	Juan Manuel Barrero Barrero "JUANMA"	ESP	27/6/80	G	4	(1)	
12	Georgios KATIDIS		12/2/93	M	1	(2)	
17	Konstantinos KAZNAFERIS		22/6/87	M	4	(7)	
10	Sergio Contreras Pardo "KOKE"	ESP	27/4/83	A	17	(3)	2
4	Efthimios KOULOUHERIS		10/3/81	D	7		
24	Nikolaos LAZARIDIS		12/7/79	D	28		4
19	Konstantinos MENDRINOS		28/5/85	M	11	(9)	
16	MICHEL Garbini Pereira	BRA	9/6/81	D	25		
6	Mehdi NAFTI	TUN	28/11/78	M	9	(1)	
2	Darcy Dolce NETO	BRA	7/2/81	D	25		8
3	Lozano ORIOL Farrán	ESP	23/5/81	D	8		1
21	Grigorios PAPAZAHARIAS		20/3/85	D	2	(1)	
15	Álvaro PORTILLA Suárez	ESP	28/4/86	M		(4)	1
18	Cristian PORTILLA Rodríguez	ESP	28/8/88	M	6	(3)	1
55	Athanasios PRITTAS		9/1/79		13	(2)	
5	RONALDO Guiaro	BRA	18/2/74	D	16		
11	Carlos Humberto RUIZ Gutiérrez	GUA	15/9/79	A	11	(5)	1
88	Daisuke SAKATA	JPN	16/1/83	A	3	(3)	
13	Mihail SIFAKIS		9/9/84	G	22		
8	Juan Carlos TOJA	COL	24/5/85	M	20	(4)	
7	Antonio "TONI" CALVO Arandes	ESP	28/3/87	M	7	(2)	
32	Kristi VANGJELI	ALB	5/9/85	D	22		
1	Markos VELLIDIS		4/4/87	G	4		

ASTERAS TRIPOLIS FC

Coach –Evangelos Vlahos; (17/1/11) (Horácio Gonçalves (POR)); (21/1/11) Pavlos Dermitzakis

Founded – 1931

Stadium – Asteras Tripolis (6,000)

2010

29/8	Ergotelis	a	1-0	*Ladakis*
11/9	PAOK	h	0-0	
19/9	AEK	a	2-2	*Arrache, Fortounis*
25/9	Olympiacos	a	0-3	
2/10	Atromitos	h	1-1	*Pulido*
17/10	Larissa	a	2-0	*Cris, Roberto*
23/10	Iraklis	h	0-0	
31/10	Kerkyra	a	2-1	*Pulido, Udoji*
6/11	Panserraikos	h	0-2	
15/11	Kavala	h	0-1	
22/11	Olympiacos Volou	a	1-1	*Orozco*
28/11	Xanthi	h	1-2	*Bastía*
5/12	Aris	a	0-1	
12/12	Panathinaikos	h	0-0	
18/12	Panionios	a	0-0	

2011

5/1	Ergotelis	h	3-0	*Udoji, Fernandes Francou 2*
9/1	PAOK	a	0-1	
16/1	AEK	h	0-3	
23/1	Olympiacos	h	0-1	
30/1	Atromitos	a	0-0	
5/2	Larissa	h	1-1	*Carrera*
13/2	Iraklis	a	0-0	
19/2	Kerkyra	h	0-2	
27/2	Panserraikos	a	1-0	*Rogério (p)*
6/3	Kavala	a	0-1	
12/3	Olympiacos Volou	h	2-1	*Bastía, Bartolini*
20/3	Xanthi	a	0-1	
3/4	Aris	h	1-2	*Orozco*
10/4	Panathinaikos	a	0-1	
17/4	Panionios	h	3-1	*Pulido 2, Ladakis*

No	Name	Nat	DoB	Pos	Aps	(s)	Gls
79	Nikolaos ANASTASOPOULOS		5/8/79	G	5		
13	Leonidas ARGIROPOULOS		29/5/90	D	11	(1)	
21	Salim ARRACHE	ALG	14/7/82	M	15	(2)	1
86	Nemanja ARSENIJEVIĆ	SRB	29/3/86	M	6	(6)	
34	Anastasios BAKASETAS		28/6/93	A	1	(4)	
22	Sebastián BARTOLINI	ARG	1/2/82	D	17	(1)	1
14	Adrián Jesús BASTÍA	ARG	20/12/78	M	25	(1)	2
18	Sebastián CARRERA	ARG	25/5/78	M	19	(3)	1
17	Bruno CRIStiano da Carvalho Santos	POR	17/1/84	M	8	(1)	1
32	Matías Omar DEGRA	ARG	18/6/83	G	25		
33	Emmanuel FERNANDES FRANCOU	ARG	31/1/86	A	7	(6)	2
5	Sokratis FITANIDIS		25/5/84	D	22	(2)	
19	Konstantinos FORTOUNIS		16/10/92	A	3	(21)	1
7	Mark KERR	SCO	2/3/82	M	3	(6)	
84	Antonios LADAKIS		25/1/82	M	28		2

No	Name	Nat	DoB	Pos	Aps	(s)	Gls
4	Vasilios LAMBROPOULOS		31/3/90	D		(1)	
28	MARCELO Rodrigues Alves "GOIANIRA"	BRA	6/8/80	M	2	(2)	
8	Radosław MATUSIAK	POL	1/1/82	A	3	(1)	
24	Daniel OROZCO Álvarez	ESP	1/2/87	D	18	(1)	2
90	Athanasios PAPAZOGLOU		30/3/88	A	7	(2)	
3	Christos PIPINIS		1/11/84	D	4		
44	Rubén Martín PULIDO	ESP	2/2/79	D	20	(1)	4
83	Artūras RIMKEVIČIUS	LTU	14/4/83	A		(1)	
30	Leonel RÍOS	ARG	17/11/82	M	1	(3)	
9	ROBERTO Calmon Félix	BRA	29/7/78	A	7	(2)	1
10	ROGÉRIO Gonçalves Martins	BRA	19/11/84	M	25	(5)	1
20	Goran RUBIL	CRO	9/3/81	D	7	(4)	
15	Nikolaos SKONDRAS		16/11/92	M		(1)	
11	Savvas TSABOURIS		16/7/86	M	1	(5)	
23	Shikoze UDOJI	NGA	16/7/86	M	16	(7)	2
6	Bruno Saul URRIBARRI	ARG	6/11/86	D	24		

ATROMITOS FC

Coach – Georgios Donis

Founded – 1923

Stadium – Dimotiko Peristeriou (9,000)

2010				
28/8	Larissa	a	0-1	
11/9	Iraklis	h	1-1	*Perrone*
19/9	Kerkyra	a	1-3	*Perrone*
25/9	Panserraikos	h	2-1	*Camara, Perrone*
2/10	Tripolis	a	1-1	*Karalis*
17/10	Olympiacos Volou	h	2-2	*Brito, Sambou*
23/10	Xanthi	h	1-1	*Perrone (p)*
30/10	Aris	a	0-2	
8/11	Panathinaikos	h	0-1	
13/11	Panionios	a	1-0	*Tatos*
21/11	Ergotelis	h	1-1	*Saganowski*
28/11	PAOK	a	1-0	*Sfakianakis*
5/12	AEK	h	1-1	*Anastasakos*
12/12	Olympiacos	a	1-2	*Favalli*
18/12	Kavala	a	1-1	*Saganowski*
2011				
4/1	Larissa	h	3-0	*Nastos, Saganowski, Sarmiento*
9/1	Iraklis	a	0-1	
15/1	Kerkyra	h	4-2	*Anastasakos 2, Camara, Sarmiento*
23/1	Panserraikos	a	1-0	*Anastasakos*
30/1	Tripolis	h	0-0	
6/2	Olympiacos Volou	a	0-2	
13/2	Xanthi	a	0-3	
20/2	Aris	h	0-0	
26/2	Panathinaikos	a	1-1	*Brito*
6/3	Panionios	h	1-2	*Sfakianakis*
13/3	Ergotelis	a	1-1	*Anastasakos*
20/3	PAOK	h	2-2	*Sfakianakis 2*
3/4	AEK	a	0-1	
10/4	Olympiacos	h	3-1	*Sfakianakis, Anastasakos, Camara*
17/4	Kavala	h	0-0	

No	Name	Nat	DoB	Pos	Aps	(s)	Gls
8	Ilias ANASTASAKOS		3/3/78	A	9	(8)	6
25	Vasilios APOSTOLOPOULOS		13/8/88	D		(1)	
28	Antonios ATHANASIOU		21/9/92	M		(1)	
27	Panagiotis BALLAS		6/9/93	M	1		
4	Marcin BASZCZYŃSKI	POL	7/6/77	D	25		
11	Luiz Eduardo de Santana BRITO	BRA	21/9/82	M	14	(8)	2
7	Henri CAMARA	SEN	10/5/77	A	26	(2)	3
31	Filippos DARLAS		23/10/83	D	5	(1)	
10	Lucas Gabriel FAVALLI	ARG	16/7/85	M	9	(8)	1
1	Charles ITANDJE	FRA	2/11/82	G	6	(1)	
21	Athanasios KARAGOUNIS		25/9/91	A	9	(4)	
40	Ioannis KARALIS		6/11/88	M	4	(9)	1
26	MARCELO José de OLIVEIRA	BRA	5/9/81	D	27		
3	Pashalis MELISSAS		9/3/82	M	14	(4)	
23	Hristostomos MIHAILIDIS		15/1/75	G	23		
2	Evangelos NASTOS		13/9/80	D	25	(1)	1
6	Konstantinos NEBEGLERAS		14/4/75	M	28		
9	Emanuel PERRONE	ARG	14/6/83	A	9	(8)	4
20	Marek SAGANOWSKI	POL	31/10/78	A	18	(7)	3
5	Massamba SAMBOU	SEN	14/4/86	D	11		1
1	Jonas SANDQVIST	SWE	6/5/81	G	1		
17	Marcelo SARMIENTO	ARG	3/11/79	M	14	(7)	2
19	Stilianos SFAKIANAKIS		19/3/76	M	22	(5)	5
32	Ioannis SKONDRAS		21/2/90	D	9	(3)	
22	Andreas TATOS		11/5/89	M	17	(6)	1
14	Grégory VIGNAL	FRA	19/7/81	D	4		

ERGOTELIS FC

Coach – Nikolaos Karageorgiou

Founded – 1929

Stadium – Pagrition (27,574)

2010				
29/8	Tripolis	h	0-1	
12/9	Olympiacos Volou	a	1-0	*Budimir*
18/9	Xanthi	h	1-0	*Romano*
26/9	Aris	a	0-1	
3/10	Panathinaikos	h	1-4	*Budimir*
16/10	Panionios	a	1-0	*Leal*
24/10	Kavala	a	1-3	*Leal*
31/10	PAOK	h	1-2	*Budimir*
8/11	AEK	a	1-3	*Fragoulakis*
21/11	Atromitos	a	1-1	*Leal*
24/11	Olympiacos	h	0-2	(first half played on 13/11)
27/11	Larissa	h	2-1	*Romano, Leal (p)*
4/12	Iraklis	a	1-1	*Romano*
12/12	Kerkyra	h	3-0	*Oliseh, Verpakovskis, Budimir*
18/12	Panserraikos	h	2-0	*Budimir, Wisio*
2011				
5/1	Tripolis	a	0-3	
9/1	Olympiacos Volou	h	0-0	
16/1	Xanthi	a	1-0	*Romano*
23/1	Aris	h	0-0	
29/1	Panathinaikos	a	0-2	
6/2	Panionios	h	2-0	*Shashiashvili, Júnior*
12/2	Kavala	h	2-1	*Beto, Leal (p)*
27/2	AEK	h	2-3	*Leal (p), Fragoulakis*
6/3	Olympiacos	a	0-3	
9/3	PAOK	a	0-2	
13/3	Atromitos	h	1-1	*Romano*
20/3	Larissa	a	3-3	*Verpakovskis 2, Hieblinger*
3/4	Iraklis	h	1-0	*Hieblinger*
10/4	Kerkyra	a	0-1	
17/4	Panserraikos	a	4-0	*Verpakovskis, Orfanos, Budimir, Karelis (p)*

No	Name	Nat	DoB	Pos	Aps	(s)	Gls
17	Angelos ABDELCHADI		7/9/89	A	3	(3)	
4	Georgios ALEXOPOULOS		7/2/77	D	10		
84	Grigorios ATHANASIOU		9/3/84	G	2		
11	Gilberto Galdino dos Santos "BETO"	BRA	20/11/76	M	18	(9)	1
25	Mario BUDIMIR	CRO	13/2/86	A	28	(1)	6
24	Christos CHRISOFAKIS		18/1/90	M	1	(8)	
1	Iosif DASKALAKIS		7/8/82	G	28		
31	Mihail FRAGOULAKIS		15/7/83	M	14	(6)	2
27	Eleftherios GIALOUSIS		18/7/85	D	18	(2)	
5	Mario HIEBLINGER	AUT	5/7/77	D	28		2
15	Manuel Oliveira Silva "JÚNIOR"	BRA	24/9/76	M	21	(1)	1
14	Nikolaos KARELIS		24/2/92	A	1	(11)	1
2	Ilias KIRIAKIDIS		5/8/85	M	3	(6)	
10	Sergio William LEAL	URU	25/9/82	A	16	(6)	6
23	Egutu OLISEH	NGA	18/11/80	M	24	(1)	1
12	Dimitrios ORFANOS		2/11/82	M	5	(15)	1
8	Diego Sebastián ROMANO	ARG	2/3/80	M	27	(1)	5
7	Emmanouil ROUMBAKIS		6/1/79	M	24	(2)	
89	Georgios SARRIS		8/9/89	D	3	(5)	
37	Giorgi SHASHIASHVILI	GEO	1/9/79	D	23	(1)	1
9	Māris VERPAKOVSKIS	LVA	15/10/79	A	16	(9)	4
4	Tomasz WISIO	POL	20/1/82	D	17	(4)	1

IRAKLIS FC

:oach – Jozef Bubenko (SVK); (9/8/10) Marinos Ouzounidis; (31/1/11) Georgios Parashos

Founded – 1908

Stadium – Kaftanzoglion (29,080)

MAJOR HONOURS: Greek Cup – (1) 1976.

010				
/8	Olympiacos	h	2-1	*Mara (p), Vellios*
/9	Atromitos	a	1-1	*Soltani*
/9	Larissa	h	1-0	*og (Cousin)*
/9	Kavala	h	0-1	
10	Kerkyra	a	0-0	
/10	Panserraikos	h	1-1	*Soltani*
/10	Tripolis	a	0-0	
/10	Olympiacos Volou	h	0-0	
11	Xanthi	a	2-2	*Mara, Soltani*
/11	Aris	h	1-0	*Soltani*
/11	Panathinaikos	a	2-4	*Mara, Pitu*
/11	Panionios	a	0-1	
12	Ergotelis	h	1-1	*Pablo Lima*
/12	PAOK	a	0-1	
9/12	AEK	h	2-0	*Dani, Papasterianos*
011				
1	Olympiacos	a	0-2	
1	Atromitos	h	1-0	*Iacob*
6/1	Larissa	a	1-2	*Vellios*
3/1	Kavala	a	0-3	
9/1	Kerkyra	h	0-0	
2	Panserraikos	a	2-1	*Ngwat-Mahop, Mara (p)*
3/2	Tripolis	h	0-0	
0/2	Olympiacos Volou	a	1-1	*Mara (p)*
6/2	Xanthi	h	1-1	*Dani*
/3	Aris	a	1-0	*Iacob*
2/3	Panathinaikos	h	1-3	*Ngwat-Mahop*
0/3	Panionios	h	1-1	*Ngwat-Mahop*
/4	Ergotelis	a	0-1	
0/4	PAOK	h	0-0	
7/4	AEK	a	0-0	

lo	Name	Nat	DoB	Pos	Aps	(s)	Gls
9	Nikolaos ARABATZIS		10/3/84	D	26		
7	Georgios BANDIS		30/4/85	G	3	(1)	
1	Carlos César Matheus "CARLINHOS"	BRA	2/8/84	M	5	(5)	
6	DANIel Ricardo da Silva Soares	POR	30/1/82	M	24		2
3	Dimitrios ELEFTHEROPOULOS		7/8/76	G	26		
0	Joël Dieudonné EPALLE	CMR	20/2/78	M	6	(4)	
20	Victoraş Constantin IACOB	ROU	14/10/80	A	17	(2)	2
3	Stilianos ILIADIS		3/6/86	M	2	(5)	
6	José Miguel González Rey "JOSEMI"	ESP	15/11/79	D	26		
5	Sani KAITA	NGA	2/5/86	M	2	(4)	
5	Petros KANAKOUDIS		16/4/84	M	13	(1)	
4	Anastasios KATSABIS		30/7/73	D	17		
5	Georgios KATSIKAS		14/6/90	D	10	(3)	
2	Georgios KIRIAZIS		28/2/80	D	12	(2)	
30	Daigo KOBAYASHI	JPN	19/2/83	M	3	(3)	
10	Bogdan Ion MARA	ROU	29/9/77	M	22	(5)	5
29	Louis Clement NGWAT-MAHOP	CMR	16/9/87	A	7	(3)	3
13	PABLO Martín LIMA Olid	URU	26/3/81	D	19	(2)	1
17	Emmanouil PAPASTERIANOS		15/8/87	M	16	(4)	1
19	Miguel Sebastián García "PITU"	ARG	27/1/84	M	23	(2)	1
30	Javier Sebastián ROBLES	ARG	18/1/85	M	2	(4)	
14	Marcel Nicolás ROMÁN Nuñez	URU	7/2/88	M		(3)	
32	Mirnes ŠIŠIČ	SVN	8/8/81	M	12	(3)	
77	Karim SOLTANI	ALG	29/8/84	A	20	(3)	4
91	Dimitrios STAMOU		27/4/91	M	2	(1)	
7	Robert SZCZOT	POL	31/1/82	D	6	(3)	
18	Thomas TSITAS		30/7/91	A		(3)	
9	Apostolos VELLIOS		8/1/92	A	1	(11)	2
36	Pashalis VOUTSIAS		23/3/90	M		(10)	
33	Norbert WITKOWSKI	POL	5/8/81	G	1		
12	Monsef ZERKA	MAR	31/8/81	A	7	(2)	

KAVALA FC

Coach – Dragomir Okuka (SRB); (17/11/10) Henryk Kasperczak (POL); (18/3/11) Ioannis Matzourakis

Founded – 1965

Stadium – Dimotiko Stadio Anthi Karagianni (12,600)

2010				
29/8	Aris	h	0-1	
12/9	Larissa	a	0-0	
18/9	Panathinaikos	h	2-2	*Douglão, Darcheville*
26/9	Iraklis	a	1-0	*Onwuachi*
2/10	Panionios	h	2-1	*Onwuachi, Vučićević*
17/10	Kerkyra	a	1-1	*Onwuachi*
24/10	Ergotelis	h	3-1	*Dié, Darcheville, Onwuachi*
31/10	Panserraikos	a	0-1	
8/11	PAOK	h	0-1	
15/11	Tripolis	a	1-0	*Onwuachi*
21/11	AEK	h	2-1	*Vučićević, Onwuachi*
28/11	Olympiacos Volou	a	1-1	*Onwuachi*
5/12	Olympiacos	h	0-1	
12/12	Xanthi	a	1-1	*Onwuachi*
18/12	Atromitos	h	1-1	*Ogbeche*
2011				
4/1	Aris	a	0-1	
8/1	Larissa	h	1-0	*Dié*
16/1	Panathinaikos	a	2-4	*Abdoun 2 (1p)*
23/1	Iraklis	h	3-0	*Tomašić, Onwuachi, Pfertzel*
30/1	Panionios	a	1-1	*Dié*
6/2	Kerkyra	h	1-0	*Niculae*
12/2	Ergotelis	a	1-2	*Onwuachi*
19/2	Panserraikos	h	0-0	
27/2	PAOK	a	2-0	*Niculae, Ríos*
6/3	Tripolis	h	1-0	*Abdoun*
13/3	AEK	a	0-1	
20/3	Olympiacos Volou	h	0-1	
3/4	Olympiacos	a	1-3	*Niculae*
10/4	Xanthi	h	1-1	*Niculae*
17/4	Atromitos	a	0-0	

No	Name	Nat	DoB	Pos	Aps	(s)	Gls
93	Djamel ABDOUN	ALG	14/2/86	M	26		3
17	Patryk ALEKSANDROWICZ	POL	5/6/83	A	1	(5)	
30	Horacio Ramón CARDOZO	ARG	29/11/79	M	22		
19	Jean-Claude DARCHEVILLE	FRA	25/7/75	A	6	(3)	2
77	Serge DIÉ	CIV	4/10/77	M	27		3
40	Douglas Ferreira "DOUGLÃO"	BRA	15/8/86	D	24		1
12	Dimitrios DROSOS		26/6/89	A	3	(3)	
14	Pierre DUCROCQ	FRA	18/12/76	M	12	(13)	
91	Christos ELEFTHERIADIS		14/2/91	M		(2)	
1	Mario GALINOVIĆ	CRO	15/11/76	G	27		
99	Apostolos GIANNOU		25/1/90	A		(10)	
33	Mirko HRGOVIĆ	BIH	5/2/79	M	22	(1)	
18	Evangelos IKONOMOU		18/7/87	D	4		
44	Ilias IOANNOU		23/10/79	A		(1)	
22	Georgios KAPNOPOULOS		26/9/92	M		(1)	
15	Theofanis KATERGIANNAKIS		16/2/74	G		(1)	
25	Javier LÓPEZ VALLEJO	ESP	22/9/75	G	3		
23	Thomas NAZLIDIS		23/10/87	A	3	(8)	
29	Marius Constantin NICULAE	ROU	16/5/81	A	12		4
9	Bartholomew OGBECHE	NGA	1/10/84	A	13	(7)	1
80	Benjamin ONWUACHI	NGA	9/4/84	A	27		10
7	Bruno Alexandre Marques PEREIRINHA	POR	2/3/88	M	5	(8)	
50	Enoc Abraham PÉREZ Matamoros	CRC	22/1/82	A		(2)	
21	Dimitrios PETKAKIS		1/8/83	M	19		
6	Marc PFERTZEL	FRA	21/5/81	D	10	(1)	1
11	Leonel RÍOS	ARG	17/11/82	M	10		1
5	Stefanos SIONDIS		4/9/87	D	4	(7)	
88	Lazaros THEODORELIS		14/1/82	D	8	(4)	
4	Igor TOMAŠIĆ	BUL	14/12/76	D	27	(1)	1
37	Valentinos VLAHOS		14/2/92	M		(1)	
10	Nemanja VUČIĆEVIĆ	SRB	11/8/79	M	15	(8)	2

KERKYRA FC

Coach – Haralambos Tennes; (29/11/10) Božidar Bandović (SRB)

Founded – 1967

Stadium – Ethniko Athlitiko Kentro (EAK) Kerkyras (2,685)

2010				
29/8	AEK	h	2-1	*Tsingas, Epstein*
11/9	Olympiacos	a	0-2	
19/9	Atromitos	h	3-1	*Epstein 2, Tsingas*
26/9	Larissa	a	1-1	*Flavinho*
3/10	Iraklis	h	0-0	
17/10	Kavala	h	1-1	*Epstein*
24/10	Panserraikos	a	2-0	*Epstein, Ioannou I.*
31/10	Tripolis	h	1-2	*Tsingas*
6/11	Olympiacos Volou	a	0-1	
13/11	Xanthi	h	1-1	*Majstorović*
21/11	Aris	a	0-2	
28/11	Panathinaikos	h	0-2	
4/12	Panionios	a	1-0	*Flavinho*
12/12	Ergotelis	a	0-3	
19/12	PAOK	h	2-1	*Ioannou I., Stoltidis*
2011				
5/1	AEK	a	0-0	
9/1	Olympiacos	h	0-2	
15/1	Atromitos	a	2-4	*Kalantzis, Tsingas*
22/1	Larissa	h	1-0	*Maznov*
29/1	Iraklis	a	0-0	
6/2	Kavala	a	0-1	
13/2	Panserraikos	h	3-0	*Epstein, Ioannou I., Gustavo*
19/2	Tripolis	a	2-0	*Epstein (p), Kalantzis*
26/2	Olympiacos Volou	h	1-3	*Kalantzis*
5/3	Xanthi	a	1-2	*Epstein (p)*
13/3	Aris	h	3-4	*Maznov, Grammozis, Gustavo*
20/3	Panathinaikos	a	1-2	*Stoltidis*
3/4	Panionios	h	1-2	*Epstein (p)*
10/4	Ergotelis	h	1-0	*Kalantzis*
17/4	PAOK	a	0-2	

No	Name	Nat	DoB	Pos	Aps	(s)	Gls
9	Athanasios DEINOPAPAS		24/11/88	A		(6)	
26	Denis EPSTEIN	GER	2/7/86	M	27		9
10	Flávio Silveiro José de Carvalho "FLAVINHO"	BRA	20/6/81	D	11	(7)	2
12	Dimitrios GIANTSIS		4/3/88	A	6	(15)	
30	Dimitrios GRAMMOZIS		8/7/78	M	8	(1)	1
25	GUSTAVO Nacarato Veronesi	BRA	7/5/82	D	25		2
20	Jan HABLE	CZE	4/1/89	M	6	(10)	
4	Dimitrios IOANNOU		15/3/77	D	5	(5)	
44	Ilias IOANNOU		23/10/79	A	8	(11)	3
21	Hristos KALANTZIS		1/12/82	A	24	(2)	4
23	Dimitrios KONSTANTOPOULOS		29/11/78	G	30		
21	Dimitrios KONTODIMOS		21/4/82	D	25		
13	Andreas LAMBROPOULOS		30/7/88	A	3	(8)	
19	Ivica MAJSTOROVIĆ	CRO	20/9/81	M	28		1
32	Dionisios MAKRIDIMITRIS		26/1/85	D	1	(4)	
54	Georgios MAKRIS		15/11/84	M	27		
90	Constantinos MAMALOS		5/1/90	M		(1)	
27	Neven MARKOVIĆ	SRB	20/2/87	D	1	(1)	
24	Goran MAZNOV	MKD	22/4/81	A	6	(3)	2
8	Haridimos MIHOS		15/3/81	D	6	(2)	
22	Emmanouil MONIAKIS		9/11/88	D	2		
16	Georgios PARASKEVAIDIS		9/10/82	D	9	(2)	
18	Antonios RIKKA		3/3/86	M	2		
6	Ieroklis STOLTIDIS		2/2/75	M	27	(1)	2
11	Athanasios TSINGAS		20/9/82	A	21	(6)	4
5	Anastasios VENETIS		24/3/80	D	22		
94	Petros VIOPOULOS		9/7/94	A		(1)	

LARISSA FC

Coach – Giannis Papakostas; (29/11/10) (Konstantinos Katsaras (17/12/10) Jørn Andersen (NOR); (9/1/11) Nikolaos Kostenoglc

Founded – 1964

Stadium – Alkazar (13,108); AEL FC Arena (16,118)

MAJOR HONOURS: Greek League – (1) 1988; Greek Cup – (2) 1985, 2007.

2010				
28/8	Atromitos	h	1-0	*Cousin*
12/9	Kavala	h	0-0	
18/9	Iraklis	a	0-1	
26/9	Kerkyra	h	1-1	*Tümer (p)*
3/10	Panserraikos	a	0-1	
17/10	Tripolis	h	0-2	
23/10	Olympiacos Volou	a	1-1	*Tümer,*
30/10	Xanthi	h	3-0	*Canobbio 2 (1p), Iglesias*
8/11	Aris	a	1-1	*Makinwa*
13/11	Panathinaikos	a	1-1	*Cousin*
21/11	Panionios	h	0-1	
27/11	Ergotelis	a	1-2	*Canobbio*
5/12	PAOK	h	1-2	*Cousin*
12/12	AEK	a	0-4	
19/12	Olympiacos	h	0-1	
2011				
4/1	Atromitos	a	0-3	
8/1	Kavala	a	0-1	
16/1	Iraklis	h	2-1	*Blažek, Tshibamba*
22/1	Kerkyra	a	0-1	
30/1	Panserraikos	h	2-1	*Tümer 2*
5/2	Tripolis	a	1-1	*Romeu*
13/2	Olympiacos Volou	h	1-2	*Tümer (p)*
20/2	Xanthi	a	1-1	*Romeu*
27/2	Aris	h	2-2	*Cousin, Romeu*
6/3	Panathinaikos	h	2-0	*Pancrate, Tshibamba*
13/3	Panionios	a	3-3	*Tümer 2 (1p), Dabizas*
20/3	Ergotelis	h	3-3	*Abubakari, Tshibamba, Cousin*
3/4	PAOK	a	0-1	
10/4	AEK	h	2-3	*Tümer, Cousin*
17/4	Olympiacos	a	0-6	

No	Name	Nat	DoB	Pos	Aps	(s)	Gls
40	Georgios ABARIS		23/4/82	G	16		
28	Mohammed ABUBAKARI	GHA	15/2/86	M	8	(1)	1
99	Shimon ABUHAZEIRA	ISR	10/10/86	A	1	(5)	
88	Jan BLAŽEK	CZE	20/3/88	A	13	(7)	1
27	Néstor Fabián CANOBBIO Bentaberry	URU	8/3/80	A	13	(5)	3
32	Kamil ČONTOFALSKÝ	SVK	3/6/78	G	8		
9	Daniel COUSIN	GAB	7/2/77	A	24	(3)	6
4	Nikolaos DABIZAS		3/8/73	D	24		1
45	Mattheos FALANGAS		24/1/92	A		(2)	
8	GEREMI Njitap	CMR	20/12/78	M	5	(5)	
42	Walter Matías IGLESIAS	ARG	18/4/85	M	19	(2)	1
77	Panagiotis KATSIAROS		8/5/78	D	12	(2)	
26	Dimitrios KOLOVETSIOS		16/10/91	D	11	(1)	
31	Ján KOZÁK	SVK	22/4/80	D	2	(1)	
30	Sanel KULJIC	AUT	10/10/77	A	1	(4)	
82	Stephen Ayodele MAKINWA	NGA	26/7/83	A	2	(8)	1
2	Hristos MELISSIS		1/12/82	D	8	(1)	
12	Fabrice PANCRATE	FRA	2/5/80	M	8		1
33	Dimitrios PLIAGAS		26/3/85	A	1	(1)	
28	Sander PURI	EST	7/5/88	A	6	(4)	
14	Vasilios RENTZAS		16/4/92	A	2	(5)	
21	ROMEU Pereira dos Santos	BRA	13/2/85	M	21	(1)	3
92	Savvas SIATRAVANIS		24/11/92	M		(1)	
7	Aleksandar SIMIĆ	SRB	31/1/80	M	15	(5)	
6	Ibrahim TALL	SEN	23/6/81	D	15	(6)	
5	Efstathios TAVLARIDIS		25/1/80	D	24		
22	Joël Omari TSHIBAMBA	COD	22/9/88	A	7	(5)	3
11	TÜMER Metin	TUR	14/10/74	M	22	(6)	8
23	Juan VELASCO Damas	ESP	15/5/77	D	10	(5)	
3	Stilianos VENETIDIS		19/11/76	D	24		
83	Mario Sebastián VIERA Galain	URU	7/3/83	G	6		
17	Antonios VOUZAS		3/2/93	A	2	(1)	

OLYMPIACOS FC

oach – Ewald Lienen (GER); (8/8/10) Ernesto Valverde (ESP)

Founded – 1925

Stadium – Georgios Karaiskakis (32,130)

AJOR HONOURS: Greek League – (38) 1931, 1933, 1934, 1936, 937, 1938, 1947, 1948, 1951, 1954, 1955, 1956, 1957, 1958, 1959, 966, 1967, 1973, 1974, 1975, 1980, 1981, 1982, 1983, 1987, 1997, 998, 1999, 2000, 2001, 2002, 2003, 2005, 2006, 2007, 2008, 2009, 011; Greek Cup – (24) 1947, 1951, 1952, 1953, 1954, 1957, 1958, 959, 1960, 1961, 1963, 1965, 1968, 1971, 1973, 1975, 1981, 1990, 1992, 1999, 2005, 2006, 2008, 2009.

)10				
3/8	Iraklis	a	1-2	*Mitroglou*
/9	Kerkyra	h	2-0	*Mellberg, Riera*
9/9	Panserraikos	a	1-0	*Pantelić*
5/9	Tripolis	h	3-0	*Pantelić, David Fuster, og (Fitanidis)*
/10	Olympiacos Volou	h	3-1	*Torosidis, Mirallas 2*
6/10	Xanthi	a	3-0	*Riera, Torosidis, Fetfatzidis*
4/10	Aris	h	1-0	*Riera*
0/10	Panathinaikos	a	1-2	*Mirallas*
11	Panionios	h	5-0	*Mirallas 2, Torosidis, Pantelić, Riera*
1/11	PAOK	h	3-0	*Mirallas 2, Rommedahl*
4/11	Ergotelis	a	2-0	*Pantelić, David Fuster (first half played on 13/11)*
7/11	AEK	a	0-1	
/12	Kavala	a	1-0	*David Fuster (p)*
2/12	Atromitos	h	2-1	*David Fuster (p), Mirallas*
9/12	Larissa	a	1-0	*og (Katsiaros)*
011				
/1	Iraklis	h	2-0	*David Fuster, Pantelić*
/1	Kerkyra	a	2-0	*og (Tsingas), Mirallas*
5/1	Panserraikos	h	4-2	*Pantelić 2, Riera 2 (1p)*
3/1	Tripolis	a	1-0	*David Fuster (p)*
0/1	Olympiacos Volou	a	1-0	*David Fuster*
/2	Xanthi	h	1-0	*David Fuster*
2/2	Aris	a	2-1	*Djebbour, David Fuster*
9/2	Panathinaikos	h	2-1	*Mirallas, Djebbour*
7/2	Panionios	a	1-1	*Mirallas*
/3	Ergotelis	h	3-0	*Modesto, Pantelić, Mirallas*
3/3	PAOK	a	1-2	*Djebbour*
0/3	AEK	h	6-0	*Djebbour 2, Mellberg, David Fuster, Mirallas, Holebas*
/4	Kavala	h	3-1	*David Fuster, Djebbour, Mirallas*
0/4	Atromitos	a	1-3	*Modesto*
7/4	Larissa	h	6-0	*Djebbour, David Fuster 2, Mellberg, Pantelić, Fetfatzidis*

No	Name	Nat	DoB	Pos	Aps	(s)	Gls
19	DAVID FUSTER Torrijos	ESP	3/2/82	M	27	(2)	13
10	Rafik DJEBBOUR	ALG	8/3/84	A	8	(2)	7
20	Alexandro Silva de Souza "DUDU CEARENSE"	BRA	15/4/83	M	16	(3)	
18	Ioannis FETFATZIDIS		21/12/90	M	10	(9)	2
5	Georgios GALITSIOS		6/7/86	D	1	(2)	
20	José HOLEBAS	GER	27/6/84	D	14	(10)	1
7	Ariel Santiago IBAGAZA	ARG	27/10/76	M	20	(4)	
2	Ioannis MANIATIS		12/10/86	D	8	(1)	
42	Balázs MEGYERI	HUN	31/3/90	G	2	(1)	
4	Olof MELLBERG	SWE	3/9/77	D	23		3
14	Kevin MIRALLAS	BEL	5/10/87	A	24	(3)	14
22	Konstantinos MITROGLOU		12/3/88	A	2	(3)	1
3	François Joseph MODESTO	FRA	19/8/78	D	20	(4)	2
30	MOISÉS HURTADO Pérez	ESP	2/1/82	M	10	(6)	
29	Krisztián NÉMETH	HUN	5/1/89	A		(3)	
71	Antonios NIKOPOLIDIS		14/1/71	G	6		
9	Marko PANTELIĆ	SRB	15/9/78	A	9	(11)	9
21	Avraam PAPADOPOULOS		3/12/84	D	25	(1)	
33	Ioannis PAPADOPOULOS		9/3/89	M	3	(5)	
92	Ioannis POTOURIDIS		27/2/92	D	4	(2)	
15	RAÚL BRAVO Sanfélix	ESP	14/4/81	D	17	(1)	
77	Albert RIERA Ortega	ESP	15/4/82	M	25	(1)	6
24	Dennis ROMMEDAHL	DEN	22/7/78	A	10	(8)	1
35	Vassilis TOROSIDIS		10/6/85	D	19	(1)	3
78	URKO Rafael PARDO Goas	ESP	28/1/83	G	22		
11	Jaouad ZAIRI	MAR	14/4/82	A	5	(8)	

OLYMPIACOS VOLOU FC

Coach – Athanasios Tsiolis; (22/2/11) Thomas Katsavakis

Founded – 1937

Stadium – Panthessaliko (22,700)

2010				
28/8	Panionios	a	1-0	*Breška*
12/9	Ergotelis	h	0-1	
19/9	PAOK	a	1-1	*Martín*
26/9	AEK	h	3-1	*Sankaré, Breška, Umbides (p)*
2/10	Olympiacos	a	1-3	*Umbides*
17/10	Atromitos	a	2-2	*Breška, Doležaj*
23/10	Larissa	h	1-1	*Monje*
31/10	Iraklis	a	0-0	
6/11	Kerkyra	h	1-0	*Solakis*
15/11	Panserraikos	a	2-2	*Martín, Umbides (p)*
20/11	Tripolis	h	1-1	*Martín*
28/11	Kavala	h	1-1	*Kapetanos*
5/12	Xanthi	a	0-1	
11/12	Aris	h	1-1	*Doležaj*
18/12	Panathinaikos	a	1-0	*Monje*
2011				
5/1	Panionios	h	0-0	
9/1	Ergotelis	a	0-0	
15/1	PAOK	h	0-3	
22/1	AEK	a	4-0	*Sankaré, Umbides, Monje, Kapetanos*
30/1	Olympiacos	h	0-1	
6/2	Atromitos	h	2-0	*Martín, Doležaj*
13/2	Larissa	a	2-1	*Breška 2*
20/2	Iraklis	h	1-1	*Kapetanos*
26/2	Kerkyra	a	3-1	*Solakis 2, Breška*
5/3	Panserraikos	h	3-0	*Németh, Breška, Tomas*
12/3	Tripolis	a	1-2	*Solakis*
20/3	Kavala	a	1-0	*Martín*
3/4	Xanthi	h	3-0	*Sankaré, Solakis, Tomas*
10/4	Aris	a	1-2	*Umbides (p)*
17/4	Panathinaikos	h	3-2	*Martín 2 (1p), Breška*

No	Name	Nat	DoB	Pos	Aps	(s)	Gls
20	Noé ACOSTA Rivera	ESP	10/12/83	M	3	(8)	
13	Leandro Miguel ÁLVAREZ	ARG	4/6/81	M	24	(1)	
10	Mário BREŠKA	SVK	27/12/79	A	16	(14)	8
3	Peter DOLEŽAJ	SVK	5/4/81	D	20	(1)	3
17	Paolo Daniel FRANGIPANE	ARG	11/7/79	M	1	(1)	
33	Evangelos GOTOVOS		13/8/86	M	1		
1	Eldin JAKUPOVIC	SUI	2/10/84	G	27		
79	Leonidas KABADAIS		8/3/82	A	2	(3)	
11	Konstantinos KAPETANOS		27/10/84	M	16	(7)	3
28	Ilias MAROULIS		28/6/89	G	1		
9	Juan Eduardo MARTÍN	ARG	27/4/82	A	22	(6)	7
30	Pavlos MITROPOULOS		4/4/90	M	9	(2)	
26	Vicente Alfredo MONJE	ARG	22/6/81	A	21		3
29	Krisztián NÉMETH	HUN	5/1/89	A	3	(3)	1
5	Facundo Javier PÉREZ Castro	ARG	7/8/81	D	3	(3)	
7	Dimitrios PLIAGAS		26/3/85	A	1	(5)	
36	Nikolaos PSIHOGIOS		25/2/89	D	8	(3)	
18	Antonios RIKKA		3/3/86	M	6	(1)	
22	José Manuel ROCA Cases	ESP	28/2/76	G	2	(1)	
7	Gabriel Nicolás RODRÍGUEZ	ARG	5/2/89	A		(3)	
21	Efstathios ROKAS		18/9/84	M	19	(7)	
19	Khalifa Papa SANKARÉ	SEN	15/8/84	D	24	(1)	3
77	Ilias SOLAKIS		15/12/74	A	14	(10)	5
25	Zoltán SZÉLESI	HUN	22/11/81	D	23		
50	Carlos Augusto Bertoldi "TICÃO"	BRA	7/2/85	M	2	(2)	
4	Xavier TOMAS	FRA	4/1/86	D	16	(6)	2
8	Javier Horacio UMBIDES	ARG	9/2/82	M	24		5
31	Ioannis ZARADOUKAS		12/12/85	M	22	(2)	

PANATHINAIKOS FC

Coach – Nikolaos Nioplias; (15/11/10) (Jacek Gmoch (POL)); (21/11/10) Jesualdo Ferreira (POR)

Founded – 1908

Stadium – OACA Spyro Louis (72,080)

MAJOR HONOURS: Greek League – (20) 1930, 1949, 1953, 1960, 1961, 1962, 1964, 1965, 1969, 1970, 1972, 1977, 1984, 1986, 1990, 1991, 1995, 1996, 2004, 2010; Greek Cup – (17) 1940, 1948, 1955, 1967, 1969, 1977, 1982, 1984, 1986, 1988, 1989, 1991, 1993, 1994, 1995, 2004, 2010.

2010				
27/8	Xanthi	h	1-1	*Petropoulos*
11/9	Aris	a	1-0	*Cissé (p)*
18/9	Kavala	a	2-2	*Cissé 2*
25/9	Panionios	h	2-1	*Ninis, Katsouranis*
3/10	Ergotelis	a	4-1	*Spiropoulos, Cissé 2, Katsouranis*
16/10	PAOK	h	1-0	*Vyntra*
24/10	AEK	a	0-1	
30/10	Olympiacos	h	2-1	*Cissé 2 (1p)*
8/11	Atromitos	a	1-0	*Hristodoulopoulos*
13/11	Larissa	h	1-1	*Cissé*
20/11	Iraklis	h	4-2	*Luis García, Cissé 2, Petropoulos*
28/11	Kerkyra	a	2-0	*Cissé 2 (1p)*
4/12	Panserraikos	h	2-0	*Boumsong, Cissé*
12/12	Tripolis	a	0-0	
18/12	Olympiacos Volou	h	0-1	
2011				
4/1	Xanthi	a	2-0	*Cissé, Hristodoulopoulos*
8/1	Aris	h	1-0	*Ninis*
16/1	Kavala	h	4-2	*Katsouranis, Cissé 2 (1p), Hristodoulopoulos*
23/1	Panionios	a	1-1	*Cissé (p)*
29/1	Ergotelis	h	2-0	*Gilberto Silva, Kanté*
6/2	PAOK	a	1-0	*Ninis*
13/2	AEK	h	3-1	*Katsouranis, Vyntra, Cissé*
19/2	Olympiacos	a	1-2	*Leto*
26/2	Atromitos	h	1-1	*Govou*
6/3	Larissa	a	0-2	
12/3	Iraklis	a	3-1	*Petropoulos 2, Hristodoulopoulos*
20/3	Kerkyra	h	2-1	*Hristodoulopoulos, Cissé*
3/4	Panserraikos	a	0-1	
10/4	Tripolis	h	1-0	*Sarriegi*
17/4	Olympiacos Volou	a	2-3	*Katsouranis, Cissé*

No	Name	Nat	DoB	Pos	Aps	(s)	Gls
4	Jean-Alain BOUMSONG	FRA	14/12/79	D	21		1
9	Djibril CISSÉ	FRA	12/8/81	A	27		20
38	Alexandre Henri Marco CLEYTON Silva	BRA	8/3/83	M		(5)	
21	Elini DIMOUTSOS		18/6/88	M		(5)	
15	GILBERTO Aparecido da SILVA	BRA	7/10/76	M	25		1
10	Sidney GOVOU	FRA	27/7/79	A	15	(3)	1
20	Lazaros HRISTODOULOPOULOS		19/12/86	M	18	(4)	5
8	Georgios IOANNIDIS		4/5/88	M	4	(6)	
5	Cédric KANTÉ	MLI	6/7/79	D	22		1
26	Georgios KARAGOUNIS		6/3/77	M	13	(10)	
29	Kostas KATSOURANIS		21/6/79	M	24	(4)	5
20	Stefanos KOTSOLIS		6/5/79	G	1		
11	Sebastián Eduardo LETO	ARG	30/8/86	M	16	(2)	1
14	LUIS Javier GARCÍA Sanz	ESP	24/6/78	M	7	(7)	1
22	Stergos MARINOS		17/9/87	D	10	(12)	
35	Haralambos MAVRIAS		21/2/94	A		(4)	
7	Sotirios NINIS		3/4/90	M	15	(3)	3
28	Antonios PETROPOULOS		28/1/86	A	4	(7)	4
19	Damien PLESSIS	FRA	18/6/86	A	4		
3	Josu SARRIEGI Zumárraga	ESP	19/1/79	D	16		1
2	Georgios SEITARIDIS		4/6/81	D	4	(3)	
23	SIMÃO Mate Júnior	MOZ	23/7/88	M	8	(10)	
31	Nikolaos SPIROPOULOS		10/10/83	D	22		1
30	Alexandros TZORVAS		12/8/82	G	29		
24	Loukas VYNTRA		5/2/81	D	25		2

PANIONIOS GSS

Coach – Mikael Stahre (SWE); (28/10/10) (Apostolos Mantzios (8/11/10) Georgios Parashos; (16/11/10) (Apostolos Mantzios (10/12/10) Panagiotis Lemonis

Founded – 1890

Stadium – Panionios GSS (16,800)

MAJOR HONOURS: Greek Cup – (2) 1979, 1998.

2010				
28/8	Olympiacos Volou	h	0-1	
12/9	Xanthi	a	1-1	*Sito Riera*
19/9	Aris	h	1-0	*Balaban*
25/9	Panathinaikos	a	1-2	*Yao Kumordzi*
2/10	Kavala	a	1-2	*Vaz Té*
16/10	Ergotelis	h	0-1	
24/10	PAOK	a	1-3	*Maniatis*
31/10	AEK	h	1-0	*Sito Riera*
6/11	Olympiacos	a	0-5	
13/11	Atromitos	h	0-1	
21/11	Larissa	a	1-0	*Samaris*
28/11	Iraklis	h	1-0	*Kukec*
4/12	Kerkyra	h	0-1	
12/12	Panserraikos	a	1-1	*Siovas*
18/12	Tripolis	h	0-0	
2011				
5/1	Olympiacos Volou	a	0-0	
9/1	Xanthi	h	0-2	
16/1	Aris	a	2-0	*Mitroglou 2*
23/1	Panathinaikos	h	1-1	*Mitroglou*
30/1	Kavala	h	1-1	*Balaban*
6/2	Ergotelis	a	0-2	
12/2	PAOK	h	1-0	*Balaban (p)*
20/2	AEK	a	1-1	*Mitroglou*
27/2	Olympiacos	h	1-1	*Svěrkoš*
6/3	Atromitos	a	2-1	*Goundoulakis, Mitroglou*
13/3	Larissa	h	3-3	*Galitsios, Mitroglou (p), Balaban*
20/3	Iraklis	a	1-1	*Mitroglou*
3/4	Kerkyra	a	2-1	*Mitroglou, Siovas*
10/4	Panserraikos	h	0-0	
17/4	Tripolis	a	1-3	*Galitsios*

No	Name	Nat	DoB	Pos	Aps	(s)	Gls
24	Dimitrios ANASTASOPOULOS		11/4/90	M	6	(7)	
10	Boško BALABAN	CRO	15/10/78	A	21	(5)	4
1	Tomáš BELIC	SVK	2/7/78	G	1		
28	Mohamed CHALALI	ALG	4/4/89	A	5	(7)	
26	Edin COCALIĆ	BIH	5/12/87	M	26		
13	Georgios GALITSIOS		6/7/86	D	9		2
20	Fanourios GOUNDOULAKIS		13/7/83	M	22	(5)	1
19	Jahmir HYKA	ALB	8/3/88	M	1	(8)	
4	Markus JONSSON	SWE	9/3/81	D	10	(3)	
16	Dimitrios KOLOVOS		7/4/93	M		(2)	
25	Ioannis KONTOES		24/5/86	D	24	(1)	
14	Davor KUKEC	CRO	16/3/86	M	5	(10)	1
27	Amir KURDI		11/9/91	M	2		
2	David KVIRKVELIA	GEO	27/6/80	D	7		
5	Martin LATKA	CZE	28/9/84	D	22	(2)	
77	Jürgen MACHO	AUT	24/8/77	G	27		
2	Ioannis MANIATIS		12/10/86	D	14		1
11	Konstantinos MITROGLOU		12/3/88	A	11		8
17	Solomon OKPAKO	NGA	1/5/90	M		(3)	
87	Leonidas PANAGOPOULOS		3/1/87	G	1		
3	Patrick PHUNGWAYO	RSA	6/1/88	D	2	(1)	
19	Markus PRÖLL	GER	28/8/79	G	1		
40	Isaac PUPO	LBR	23/10/85	M		(2)	
22	Andreas SAMARIS		13/6/89	M	12	(8)	1
9	Vasilaq SHKURTAJ	ALB	27/2/92	A		(3)	
23	Dimitrios SIOVAS		16/9/88	D	28	(1)	2
8	Lorenç "SITO" RIERA Ortega	ESP	5/1/87	A	20	(2)	2
6	SULEIMAN Akim OMOlade	NGA	15/12/85	D	14	(4)	
99	Václav SVĚRKOŠ	CZE	1/11/83	A	3	(8)	1
12	Cédric VARRAULT	FRA	30/1/80	D	10	(2)	
39	Ricardo VAZ TÉ	POR	1/10/86	A	5	(3)	1
14	Bernard YAO KUMORDZI	GHA	21/3/85	M	21	(2)	1

PANSERRAIKOS FC

Coach – Dragan Kokotović (SRB); (28/1/11) Momčilo Vukotić (SRB); (8/3/11) (Pavlos Dimitriou)
Founded – 1963
Stadium – Dimotiko Serron (9,500)

2010				
29/8	PAOK	a	2-3	*Beljić 2*
12/9	AEK	a	0-2	
19/9	Olympiacos	h	0-1	
25/9	Atromitos	a	1-2	*Georgiadis*
/10	Larissa	h	1-0	*Dalé*
17/10	Iraklis	a	1-1	*Papazoglou*
24/10	Kerkyra	h	0-2	
31/10	Kavala	h	1-0	*Leozinho*
6/11	Tripolis	a	2-0	*Panteliadis, Georgiadis*
15/11	Olympiacos Volou	h	2-2	*Beljić, Leozinho (p)*
20/11	Xanthi	a	0-2	
28/11	Aris	h	1-0	*Chumbinho*
4/12	Panathinaikos	a	0-2	
12/12	Panionios	h	1-1	*Leozinho (p)*
18/12	Ergotelis	a	0-2	
2011				
5/1	PAOK	h	1-1	*Georgiadis*
9/1	AEK	h	1-3	*Georgiadis*
15/1	Olympiacos	a	2-4	*Georgiadis 2 (1p)*
23/1	Atromitos	h	0-1	
30/1	Larissa	a	1-2	*Leozinho*
5/2	Iraklis	h	1-2	*Leozinho*
13/2	Kerkyra	a	0-3	
19/2	Kavala	a	0-0	
27/2	Tripolis	h	0-1	
5/3	Olympiacos Volou	a	0-3	
12/3	Xanthi	h	2-1	*Papazoglou, Dalé*
20/3	Aris	a	1-3	*Parker*
3/4	Panathinaikos	h	1-0	*Georgiadis*
10/4	Panionios	a	0-0	
17/4	Ergotelis	h	0-4	

No	Name	Nat	DoB	Pos	Aps	(s)	Gls
28	Mohammed ABUBAKARI	GHA	15/2/86	M	6	(3)	
27	Pablo ÁLVAREZ Menéndez	URU	7/2/85	D	15	(1)	
22	Dimitrios ANAKOGLOU		6/9/91	M	6	(12)	
21	Nikolaos ASLANIDIS		1/6/93	A		(3)	
8	Nikola BELJIĆ	SRB	14/5/83	M	26	(1)	3
15	Jorge Orlando BRÍTEZ	PAR	8/2/81	M		(1)	
5	César Alberto CASTRO Pérez	VEN	10/4/83	D	24	(1)	
25	Marinaldo Cícero da Silva "CHUMBINHO"	BRA	21/9/86	M	19	(5)	1
18	Maurice Junior DALÉ	FRA	12/7/85	A	25	(4)	2
66	DANIEL Márcio FERNANDES	POR	25/9/83	G	7		
14	Jordão da Encarnação Tackey DIOGO	POR	12/11/85	D	6	(3)	
2	Aristidis GALANOPOULOS		29/9/81	D	4	(3)	
7	Georgios K. GEORGIADIS		14/11/87	A	22	(6)	7
32	Panagiotis GIANNOPOULOS		21/7/94	M		(2)	
29	Semir KERLA	BIH	26/9/87	D	5	(1)	
10	Zoltán KISS	HUN	18/8/80	M	5	(3)	
19	Alexandros KONTOS		12/9/86	M		(2)	
26	Leandro Salesde Santana "LEOZINHO"	BRA	12/12/85	M	20	(7)	5
35	Bojan MARKOVIĆ	BIH	12/11/85	D	1		
20	Youl MAWÉNÉ	FRA	16/7/79	D	20		
24	Konstantinos MOUSIKAKIS		11/1/89	M	1	(1)	
3	PABLO AMO Aguado	ESP	15/1/78	D	19		
11	Athanasios PANTELIADIS		6/9/87	M	16	(2)	1
17	Georgios PAPADOPOULOS		26/2/91	M		(2)	
23	Anastasios PAPAZOGLOU		24/9/88	D	24		2
37	Bernard PARKER	RSA	16/3/86	A	12		1
30	Velimir RADMAN	CRO	28/5/83	G	22		
31	Uroš SINĐIĆ	SRB	19/1/86	M	5	(4)	
10	Bozidar TADIĆ	SRB	14/7/83	M	4	(7)	
6	Konstantinos TRIANTAFILLOU		2/4/91	M	8	(3)	
13	Georgios VALSAMAKIS		1/5/86	G	1		
4	Ioannis VOSKOPOULOS		24/10/87	D	4	(3)	
9	Bojan VRUČINA	CRO	8/11/84	A	3	(2)	

PAOK FC

Coach – Mario Beretta (ITA); (23/7/10) Pavlos Dermitzakis; (18/10/10) Ioakim Havos
Founded – 1926
Stadium – Toumbas (31,060)
MAJOR HONOURS: Greek League – (2) 1976, 1985; Greek Cup – (4) 1972, 1974, 2001, 2003.

2010				
29/8	Panserraikos	h	3-2	*Vieirinha, Cirillo, Papazoglou*
11/9	Tripolis	a	0-0	
19/9	Olympiacos Volou	h	1-1	*Ivić*
26/9	Xanthi	a	0-1	
3/10	Aris	h	0-1	
16/10	Panathinaikos	a	0-1	
24/10	Panionios	h	3-1	*Muslimović, Salpingidis, Fotakis*
31/10	Ergotelis	a	2-1	*Salpingidis, Contreras*
8/11	Kavala	a	1-0	*Pablo García*
13/11	AEK	h	2-1	*Fotakis, Vieirinha*
21/11	Olympiacos	a	0-3	
28/11	Atromitos	h	0-1	
5/12	Larissa	a	2-1	*Contreras, Athanasiadis*
11/12	Iraklis	h	1-0	*Vieirinha*
19/12	Kerkyra	a	1-2	*Athanasiadis*
2011				
5/1	Panserraikos	a	1-1	*Salpingidis*
9/1	Tripolis	h	1-0	*Salpingidis*
15/1	Olympiacos Volou	a	3-0	*Lino, Vieirinha, Salpingidis*
22/1	Xanthi	h	2-1	*Athanasiadis, Salpingidis*
30/1	Aris	a	0-0	
6/2	Panathinaikos	h	0-1	
12/2	Panionios	a	0-1	
27/2	Kavala	h	0-2	
6/3	AEK	a	0-4	
9/3	Ergotelis	h	2-0	*Contreras, Tsoukalas*
13/3	Olympiacos	h	2-1	*Koutsianikoulis, Vitolo (p)*
20/3	Atromitos	a	2-2	*Lino, El Zhar*
3/4	Larissa	h	1-0	*Athanasiadis*
10/4	Iraklis	a	0-0	
17/4	Kerkyra	h	2-0	*Ivić, Athanasiadis*

No	Name	Nat	DoB	Pos	Aps	(s)	Gls
85	Diego Alejandro ARIAS Hincapie	COL	16/6/85	M	1	(4)	
33	Stefanos ATHANASIADIS		24/12/88	A	9	(7)	5
4	Sotirios BALAFAS		19/8/86	M	2	(3)	
3	Anis BOUSSAÏDI	TUN	10/4/81	D	10	(2)	
1	Kostas CHALKIAS		30/5/74	G	14		
8	Bruno CIRILLO	ITA	21/3/77	D	21		1
15	Pablo CONTRERAS	CHI	11/9/78	D	22		3
80	CRISTIANO Morães de Oliveira	BRA	28/9/83	A	2	(5)	
7	Nabil EL ZHAR	MAR	27/8/86	A	12	(7)	1
77	Oélilton Araújo dos Santos "ETTO"	BRA	8/3/81	D	8	(1)	
31	Lucio Alejo FILOMENO	ARG	8/5/80	A	2	(8)	
18	Georgios FOTAKIS		29/10/81	M	16	(2)	2
21	Vladimir IVIĆ	SRB	7/5/77	M	20	(2)	2
26	Ergys KACE	ALB	8/7/93	M		(1)	
19	Vasilios KOUTSIANIKOULIS		9/8/88	M	3	(5)	1
91	Dario KREŠIĆ	CRO	11/1/84	G	16	(1)	
16	DorvaLINO Alves Maciel	BRA	1/7/77	D	15	(3)	2
13	Stilianos MALEZAS		11/3/85	D	15		
11	Zlatan MUSLIMOVIĆ	BIH	6/3/81	A	8	(8)	1
5	PABLO Gabriel GARCÍA Pérez	URU	11/5/77	M	23	(1)	1
14	Athanasios PAPAZOGLOU		30/3/88	A		(8)	1
23	Eleftherios SAKELLARIOU		17/2/87	D	8	(2)	

9	Dimitris SALPINGIDIS		18/8/81	A	26	(4)	6
36	Mirko SAVINI	ITA	11/3/79	D	4	(3)	
10	Olivier SORLIN	FRA	9/4/79	M	1		
27	Mirosław SZNAUCNER	POL	9/5/79	D	16	(1)	
28	Stavros TSOUKALAS		23/5/88	M	10	(2)	1
20	Adelino André Vieira Freitas "VIEIRINHA"	POR	14/1/86	A	25	(1)	4
6	Víctor José Añino Bermúdez "VITOLO"	ESP	9/9/83	M	18	(1)	1
42	José Luís Francisco ZUELA dos Santos	ANG	3/8/83	D	3	(4)	

XANTHI FC

Coach – Nikolaos Kehagias; (20/9/10) Georgios Parashos; (8/11/10) (Nikolaos Papadopoulos)

Founded – 1967

Stadium – Skoda Xanthi Arena (7,500)

2010				
27/8	Panathinaikos	a	1-1	*Ellington*
12/9	Panionios	h	1-1	*Marcelinho (p)*
18/9	Ergotelis	a	0-1	
26/9	PAOK	h	1-0	*Poy (p)*
3/10	AEK	a	0-1	
16/10	Olympiacos	h	0-3	
23/10	Atromitos	a	1-1	*Ellington (p)*
30/10	Larissa	a	0-3	
6/11	Iraklis	h	2-2	*Vallas, Stewart*
13/11	Kerkyra	a	1-1	*Vasilakakis*
20/11	Panserraikos	h	2-0	*Marcelinho, Ellington*
28/11	Tripolis	a	2-1	*Katongo, Quintana (p)*
5/12	Olympiacos Volou	h	1-0	*Marcelinho*
12/12	Kavala	h	1-1	*Poy*
19/12	Aris	a	2-0	*Souanis 2*
2011				
4/1	Panathinaikos	h	0-2	
9/1	Panionios	a	2-0	*Katongo, Boateng*
16/1	Ergotelis	h	0-1	
22/1	PAOK	a	1-2	*Poy*
29/1	AEK	h	0-2	
6/2	Olympiacos	a	0-1	
13/2	Atromitos	h	3-0	*Adefemi, Kazakis, Poy*
20/2	Larissa	h	1-1	*Boateng*
26/2	Iraklis	a	1-1	*Kazakis*
5/3	Kerkyra	h	2-1	*Adefemi, Vallas*
12/3	Panserraikos	a	1-2	*Marcelinho (p)*
20/3	Tripolis	h	1-0	*Marcelinho*
3/4	Olympiacos Volou	a	0-3	
10/4	Kavala	a	1-1	*Kazakis*
17/4	Aris	h	1-2	*Stathakis*

No	Name	Nat	DoB	Pos	Aps	(s)	Gls
13	Olubayo ADEFEMI	NGA	13/8/85	D	21	(3)	2
88	Marijan ALTIPARMAKOVSKI	MKD	18/7/91	A		(2)	
90	Christian BEKAMENGA	CMR	9/5/86	A		(3)	
35	Emmanouil BERTOS		13/5/89	D	17	(4)	
20	George BOATENG	NED	5/9/75	M	16	(3)	2
29	Mugurel Mihai BUGA	ROU	16/12/77	A	2	(9)	
99	Nathan ELLINGTON	ENG	2/7/81	A	6	(3)	3
21	Konstantinos FLISKAS		22/12/80	D	20	(1)	
5	GLEISON Pinto dos Santos	BRA	18/8/81	D	12	(1)	
24	Michael GSPURNING	AUT	2/5/81	G	19	(1)	
15	Kim JAGGY	SUI	14/11/82	D	17		
22	JEAN Agostinho da Silva "CARIOCA"	BRA	1/6/88	A		(1)	
77	Pavlos KATHARIOS		11/3/92	M		(2)	
8	Christopher KATONGO	ZAM	31/8/82	A	24	(4)	2
34	Vlassios KAZAKIS		17/6/83	A	5	(5)	3
23	Dimitrios KOMESIDIS		2/2/88	D	12	(2)	
28	Athanasios KOSTOULAS		24/3/76	D	22	(1)	
33	Sotirios LIBEROPOULOS		29/6/77	G	11		
14	Petros MANTALOS		31/8/91	M		(4)	
11	Marcelo Leite Pereira "MARCELINHO"	BRA	22/6/87	M	21	(5)	5
7	Mauro POY	ARG	7/2/81	A	23	(3)	4
10	Diego QUINTANA	ARG	24/4/78	M	9	(8)	1
19	Dimitrios SOUANIS		17/11/85	A	14	(9)	2
18	Stavros STATHAKIS		30/11/87	D	2	(1)	1
3	Jordan STEWART	ENG	3/3/82	D	13	(1)	1
66	Zdeno ŠTRBA	SVK	9/6/76	M	7	(2)	
31	Nikolaos TSOUMANIS		8/6/90	M	1	(1)	
25	Spiridon VALLAS		26/8/81	D	23	(1)	2
16	Theodoros VASILAKAKIS		20/7/88	M	13	(10)	1

TOP GOALSCORERS 2010/11

20	Djibril CISSÉ (Panathinaikos)
14	Kevin MIRALLAS (Olympiacos)
13	DAVID FUSTER (Olympiacos)
12	Rafik DJEBBOUR (AEK/Olympiacos)
10	Benjamin ONWACHI (Kavala)
9	Ismael BLANCO (AEK)
	Ignacio Martín SCOCCO (AEK)
	Denis EPSTEIN (Kerkyra)
	Konstantinos MITROGLOU (Olympiacos/Panionios)
	Marko PANTELIĆ (Olympiacos)

SUPERLEAGUE PLAY-OFFS 2010/11 : UEFA CHAMPIONS LEAGUE QUALIFICATION

(8/5/11)
AEK 1 *(Leonardo 38p)*, Olympiacos Volou 0
PAOK 2 *(Athanasiadis 57, El Zhar 75)*, Panathinaikos 1 *(Cissé 79)*

(12/5/11)
Olympiacos Volou 1 *(Martín 62)*, PAOK 2 *(Vieirinha 33, Salpingidis 53)*
Panathinaikos 1 (Blanco 24og), AEK 1 (Leonardo 3)

(15/5/11)
AEK 3 *(Dellas 21, Diop 47, 67)*, PAOK 0
Olympiacos Volou 2 *(Solakis 52, Martín 64)*, Panathinaikos 1 *(Leto 33)*

(18/5/11)
Panathinaikos 3 *(Luis García 28, Cissé 58, Katsouranis 85)*, Olympiacos Volou 0
PAOK 2 *(Pablo García 29, Vitolo 37p)*, AEK 1 *(Scocco 14)*

(22/5/11)
Olympiacos Volou 1 *(Doležaj 84)*, AEK 0
Panathinaikos 1 *(Gilberto Silva 74)*, PAOK 0

(25/5/11)
AEK 0, Panathinaikos 2 *(Cissé 58, 67)*
PAOK 5 *(Salpingidis 1, 53, Vieirinha 12, Arias 38, Muslimović 67)*, Olympiacos Volou 1 *(Martín 83p)*

			Home					Away					Total					
		Pld	W	D	L	F	A	W	D	L	F	A	W	D	L	F	A	Pts
2	Panathinaikos FC	6	2	1	0	5	1	1	0	2	4	4	3	1	2	9	5	13
3	PAOK FC	6	3	0	0	9	3	1	0	2	2	5	4	0	2	11	8	12
4	AEK Athens FC	6	2	0	1	4	2	0	1	2	2	4	2	1	3	6	6	8
5	Olympiacos Volou FC	6	2	0	1	4	3	0	0	3	1	9	2	0	4	5	12	6

NB Points carried forward from regular league: Panathinaikos 3 pts, AEK 1 pts, PAOK 0 pts, Olympiacos Volou 0 pts.

PROMOTED CLUBS

PANAITOLIKOS GFS

Coach – Ioannis Dalakouras; (10/1/11) Haralambos Tennes
Founded – 1926
Stadium – Panaitolikou (3,985)

PAS GIANNINA FC

Coach – Stéphane Demol (BEL)
Founded – 1966
Stadium – Oi Zosimades (7,652)

OFI CRETE FC

Coach – Ioannis Hatzinikolaou; (28/9/10) Nikolaos Anastopoulos
Founded – 1925
Stadium – Thodoros Vardinoyannis (8,700)
MAJOR HONOURS: Greek Cup – (1) 1987.

SECOND LEVEL FINAL TABLE 2010/11

		Pld	W	D	L	F	A	Pts
1	Panaitolikos GFS	34	23	6	5	47	19	75
2	PAS Giannina FC	34	22	8	4	55	17	74
3	OFI Crete FC	34	21	6	7	42	20	69
4	Trikala FC	34	18	6	10	42	23	60
5	Levadiakos FC	34	17	9	8	48	33	60
6	Doxa Dramas FC	34	16	8	10	51	28	56
7	Diagoras FC	34	15	7	12	36	36	52
8	Panthrakikos FC	34	13	8	13	36	38	47
9	Veria FC	34	12	8	14	37	42	44
10	Pierikos FC	34	11	10	13	39	43	43
11	Agrotikos Asteras FC	34	11	7	16	34	41	40
12	Ethnikos Asteras FC	34	9	11	14	27	38	38
13	GS Ilioupoli	34	10	6	18	29	50	36
14	Thrasivoulos Fylis FC	34	9	9	16	33	36	36
15	Anagennisi Karditsas FC	34	9	6	19	23	42	33
16	Ionikos FC	34	8	9	17	25	51	33
17	Ethnikos Piraeus FC	34	8	8	18	28	48	32
18	Kallithea FC	34	3	10	21	27	54	19

NB Trikala FC excluded from league and play-offs; Diagoras FC took their play-off place.
Ionikos FC, Anagennisi Karditsas FC & Ethnikos Piraeus FC were excluded for 2011/12; Kallithea FC subsequently avoided relegation.

PROMOTION PLAY-OFF FINAL TABLE

		Pld	W	D	L	F	A	Pts
1	OFI Crete FC	6	4	2	0	13	5	18
2	Levadiakos FC	6	4	1	1	12	2	15
3	Doxa Dramas FC	6	1	2	3	5	13	6
4	Diagoras FC	6	0	1	5	2	12	1

NB Points carried forward from regular league – OFI Crete FC 4 pts, Levadiakos FC 2 pts, Doxa Dramas FC 1 pt, Diagoras FC 0 pts.

DOMESTIC CUP 2010/11

KYPELLO ELLADOS

FOURTH ROUND

(26/10/10)
Anagennisi Giannitson 1, Atromitos 3
Ethnikos Asteras 0, Xanthi 0 *(aet; 4-2 on pens)*
Ethnikos Piraeus 0, Larissa 1
OFI 0, Olympiacos Volou 1 *(aet)*
Pierikos 1, Tripolis 3

(27/10/10)
Aetos Skidras 0, Panserraikos 2 *(aet)*
Diagoras Rodou 3, Panionios 1
Giannina 1, Ergotelis 0
Kozani 0, Panathinaikos 5
Panachaiki 0, Kavala 2
Panaitolikos 0, Iraklis 2
Trikala 1, Aris 1 *(aet; 4-2 on pens)*

(28/10/10)
Eordaikos 0, PAOK 1 *(aet)*
Panthrakikos 1, AEK 5
Veria 0, Kerkyra 1

(3/11/10)
Ilioupoli 0, Olympiacos 1

FIFTH ROUND

(21/12/10)
Atromitos 1, Kavala 0
Olympiacos Volou 2, Panserraikos 0

(22/12/10)
Panathinaikos 3, Trikala 2
PAOK 2, Giannina 1
Tripolis 0, Olympiacos 1

(23/12/10)
Ethnikos Asteras 1, Diagoras Rodou 1
Iraklis 1, Kerkyra 1
Larissa 0, AEK 4

Replays

(12/1/11)
Diagoras Rodou 1, Ethnikos Asteras 0
Kerkyra 0, Iraklis 0 *(aet; 5-3 on pens)*

QUARTER-FINALS

(18/1/11 & 3/2/11)
Kerkyra 0, Olympiacos Volou 2 *(Monje 26p, Martín 80)*
Olympiacos Volou 1 *(Martín 28)*, Kerkyra 2 *(Paraskevaidis 17, Ioannou I. 74p)*
(Olympiacos Volou 3-2)

(19/1/11 & 2/2/11)
Olympiacos 1 *(Modesto 45)*, PAOK 1 *(Vieirinha 82)*
PAOK 1 *(Salpingidis 57)*, Olympiacos 0
(PAOK 2-1)

Panathinaikos 0, AEK 2 *(Liberopoulos 64, 80)*
AEK 2 *(Lagos 13, Míchel 90)*, Panathinaikos 3 *(Cissé 21, Gilberto Silva 45, Vintra 63)*
(AEK 4-3)

(20/1/11 & 3/2/11)
Atromitos 2 *(Perrone 41, Camara 78)*, Diagoras Rodou 0
Diagoras Rodou 0, Atromitos 1 *(Saganowski 34)*
(Atromitos 3-0)

SEMI-FINALS

(2/3/11 & 16/3/11)
AEK 0, PAOK 0
PAOK 0, AEK 1 *(Dellas 48)*
(AEK 1-0)

Atromitos 2 *(Saganowski 10, Nebegleras 61)*, Olympiacos Volou 1 *(Sankaré 79)*
Olympiacos Volou 0, Atromitos 0
(Atromitos 2-1)

FINAL

(30/4/11)
OACA Spyro Louis, Athens
AEK ATHENS FC 3 *(Liberopoulos 28, Baha 78, Kafes 85)*
ATROMITOS FC 0
Referee – *Kakos*
AEK – *Saja, Georgeas, Karabelas, Manolas, Dellas, Diop, Makos, Lagos, Scocco (Baha 33), Blanco (Kafes 70), Liberopoulos.*
ATROMITOS – *Itandje, Nastos, Skondras, Baszczyński, Marcelo Oliveira (Sarmiento 83), Nebegleras, Sfakianakis, Tatos, Camara (Sambou 89), Anastasakos, Saganowski (Brito 66).*

CLUB COMMUNICATION 2011/12

AEK Athens FC
Lane of the street Rethimnis, Area Mazareko, GR-190 04 Spata

Tel +30 210 6673 700
Fax +30 210 6673 895
Web aekfc.gr
Email info@aekfc.gr
Media Officer Aggeliki Arkadi

Aris Thessaloniki FC
69, Alkminis str.
GR-54249 Thessaloniki

Tel +30 2310 325 044
Fax +30 2310 309 035
Web arisfc.gr
Email info@arisfc.gr
Media Officer Crisanthos Tsaltidis

Asteras Tripolis FC
Terma Tertseti
GR-22100 Tripoli

Tel +30 27102 30400
Fax +30 27102 39526
Web asterastripolis.gr
Email info@asterstripolis.gr
Media Officer Stavros Koukakis

Atromitos FC
94-96 Paparigopoulou Str.
GR-121 32 Peristeri (Athens)

Tel +30 210 577 4003
Fax +30 210 577 4734
Web atromitosfc.gr
Email atromitos@atromitosfc.gr
Media Officer Paulos Katonis

Ergotelis FC
Steriogianni 1
GR-71305 Heraklion Kritis

Tel +30 2810 313 959
Fax +30 2810 311 146
Web ergotelis.gr
Email info@ergotelis.gr
Media Officer Giannis Trelakas

Kerkyra FC
Samara 22
GR-49100 Kerkyra

Tel +30 26610 35073
Fax +30 26610 43583
Web aokerkyra.com.gr
Email info@aokerkyra.com.gr
Media Officer Fotis Skourtis

Larissa FC
AEL FC ARENA, Mezourlo
Neapoli Larissas, GR-Larissa 41 000

Tel +30 2410 681964
Fax +30 2410 681801
Web ael1964.gr
Email ael1964@lar.forthnet.gr
Media Officer Giorgos Mantaios

OFI Crete FC
Skafidaras, Gazi
GR-71500 Heraklion

Tel +30 2810 823650-3
Fax +30 2810 823660
Web ofi.gr
Email team@ofifc.gr
Media Officer Stelios Katergiannakis

Olympiacos FC
Alexandra Square
GR-18534 Piraeus

Tel +30 210 4143 000
Fax +30 210 4143 113
Web olympiacos.org
Email footballdpt@olympiacos.org
Media Officer Evgenia Lagou

Panaitolikos GFS
Prousiotisis 15
GR-30100 Agrinio

Tel +30 26410 29584
Fax +30 26410 54957
Web panaitolikos.gr
Email panaitolikos@otenet.gr
Media Officer Christos Stoumbos

Panathinaikos FC
168 Kifissias Ave & Sofokleous
GR-15126 Marousi-Athens

Tel +30 210 8709 000
Fax +30 210 8093 644
Web pao.gr
Email paepao@hellasnet.gr
Media Officer Andreas Droukopoulos

Panionios GSS
1 Chrisostomou Street
GR-17122 Nea Smyrni

Tel +30 210 9311 189
Fax +30 210 9332 036
Web pgss.gr
Email info@panionios.gr
Media Officer Kostas Papadakos

Panserraikos FC
Municipal Stadium
GR-62125 Serres

Tel +30 23210 35745
Fax +30 23210 35788
Web panserraikos.eu
Email fcpanser@otenet.gr
Media Officer Eirini Papadaki

PAOK FC
Mikras Asias, Toumba's stadium
GR-54351 Thessaloniki

Tel +30 2310 954 050
Fax +30 2310 951 000
Web paokfc.gr
Email info@paokfc.gr
Media Officer Stavros Sountoulidis

PAS Giannina FC
P.E.A.K.I – Anatoli -Ioannina
GR-45500 Ioannina

Tel +30 26510 70340
Fax +30 26510 75570
Web pasgiannina.gr
Email info@pasgiannina.gr
Media Officer Cristos Lemonias

Xanthi FC
Skoda Xanthi Arena, Kimmeria – Pigadia Xanthi, GR-67100 Xanthi

Tel +30 254 1022 977
Fax +30 254 1025 852
Web skodaxanthifc.gr
Email office@skodaxanthifc.gr
Media Officer Babis Kirlidis

HUNGARY

Hongrie I Ungarn

Magyar Labdarúgó Szövetség (MLSZ)

COMMUNICATION

Address Kánal St. 2.D
HU-1112 Budapest
Tel +36 1 577 9500
Fax +36 1 577 9503

E-mail mlsz@mlsz.hu
Website mlsz.hu

President Sándor Csányi
General Secretary Márton Vági
Media Officer László Pajor-Gyulai

Year of Formation 1901

National Stadium Ferenc Puskás, Budapest (39,111)

DOMESTIC COMPETITION SUMMARY 2010/11

NB I LEAGUE FINAL TABLE

			Home					Away					Total						
		Pld	W	D	L	F	A	W	D	L	F	A	W	D	L	F	A	Pts	Comp
1	Videoton FC	30	12	2	1	33	12	6	5	4	26	17	18	7	5	59	29	61	UCL
2	Paksi SE	30	9	4	2	29	15	8	1	6	25	23	17	5	8	54	38	56	UEL
3	Ferencvárosi TC	30	9	2	4	25	19	6	3	6	25	24	15	5	10	50	43	50	UEL
4	Zalaegerszegi TE	30	10	3	2	26	18	4	3	8	25	29	14	6	10	51	47	48	
5	Debreceni VSC	30	10	3	2	37	18	2	7	6	16	25	12	10	8	53	43	46	
6	Újpest FC	30	10	4	1	34	17	3	2	10	16	21	13	6	11	50	38	45	
7	Kaposvári Rákóczi FC	30	8	2	5	20	15	5	2	8	21	27	13	4	13	41	42	43	
8	Szombathelyi Haladás	30	9	4	2	27	10	2	4	9	15	26	11	8	11	42	36	41	
9	Győri ETO FC	30	8	4	3	23	12	2	7	6	17	23	10	11	9	40	35	41	
10	Budapest Honvéd FC	30	5	4	6	15	18	6	3	6	21	21	11	7	12	36	39	40	
11	Vasas SC	30	7	4	4	24	21	4	3	8	10	25	11	7	12	34	46	40	
12	Kecskeméti TE	30	9	1	5	33	22	2	2	11	18	34	11	3	16	51	56	36	UEL
13	Lombard-Pápa TFC	30	6	3	6	24	23	4	2	9	15	29	10	5	15	39	52	35	
14	BFC Siófok	30	1	8	6	11	19	7	2	6	18	22	8	10	12	29	41	34	
15	MTK Budapest	30	6	2	7	23	25	2	4	9	12	24	8	6	16	35	49	30	*Relegated*
16	Szolnoki MÁV FC	30	4	3	8	16	26	1	3	11	10	30	5	6	19	26	56	21	*Relegated*

Top Scorer André Alves (Videoton), 24 goals

Promoted Clubs Diósgyőri VTK
Pécsi MFC

Cup Final Kecskeméti TE 3, Videoton FC 2

New names on the trophies

Veteran coach György Mezey led Videoton to the Hungarian title – but was dismissed at the end of the season

The 2010/11 Hungarian season provided a number of unlikely stories, with 2009/10 treble winners Debreceni VSC failing to defend any of their trophies, the fortunes of the big Budapest clubs continuing to fade, and several unheralded provincial clubs coming unexpectedly to the fore. There were maiden victors in both the NB I championship and the Hungarian Cup, plus two first-time qualifiers for European competition. Continuity, alas, remained on the international front where the long-awaited breakthrough for the Hungarian national team once again failed to materialise.

That Videoton FC dethroned Debrecen to become Hungarian champions for the first time was not strictly a surprise. The team from Szekesfehervar had been a close second the previous season, finishing just a point in arrears after a fatal final-day defeat. Furthermore, they had retained their wily veteran coach György Mezey, the man who had led Hungary to their last major tournament, the 1986 FIFA World Cup. Near to bankruptcy in 2007, the club then known as FC Fehérvár had been rescued by wealthy businessman István Garancsi, who restored the old name of Videoton and provided generous investment, from which he demanded the dividend of a first national title within three years.

Mission accomplished

Under Mezey's shrewd command, Videoton fulfilled their owner's objective, displaying a season-long consistency that enabled the club to emerge as domestic champions more than a quarter of a century after gracing the final of the UEFA Cup (they lost the 1985 showpiece to Real Madrid CF after knocking out Manchester United FC in the quarter-finals on penalties). Worthy champions in every respect – most wins, fewest defeats, most goals scored, fewest conceded – and popular with the neutrals as well as Hungarian Prime Minister Viktor Orbán (a long-time fan and regular visitor to the Sóstói stadium in the spring), Videoton were heavily indebted to the contributions of two outstanding foreign imports – Montenegrin international goalkeeper Mladen Božović, a new signing from Serbian champions FK Partizan, and free-scoring Brazilian striker André Alves, who, having found the net 15 times in 2009/10, increased his output to 24 goals, which not only earned him the NB I Golden Boot but did so with the highest winning total for nine years. Of the locals in the team the standout figure was 22-year-old midfield schemer Ákos Elek, closely followed by defenders Zoltán Lipták and Pál Lázár. All three featured regularly during the season for the Hungarian national side.

Videoton collected the title two rounds before the end, with a 3-1 home win over Kaposvári Rákóczi FC, which allowed them to focus on the Hungarian Cup final six days later. The build-up to the match with Kecskeméti TE in Budapest, where Videoton were firm favourites to complete the double, was soured, however, by the news that the club would not be extending Mezey's contract at the end of the season, appointing ex-Portuguese international midfielder Paulo Sousa instead. With the coach in understandably downbeat mood, Videoton lost an exciting final 3-2, victims of a fabulous hat-trick from African striker Foxi Kethevoama, who thus delivered Kecskemét's first major trophy in the year of their centenary.

National Team

International Tournament Appearances – FIFA World Cup – (9) 1934 (2nd round), 1938 (runners-up), 1954 (runners-up), 1958, 1962 (qtr-finals), 1966 (qtr finals), 1978, 1982, 1986. UEFA European Championship – (2) 1964 (3rd), 1972 (4th).

Top Five All-time Caps – József Bozsik (101); László Fazekas (92); Gyula Grosics (86); Ferenc Puskás (85); Imre Garaba (82)

Top Five All-time Goals – Ferenc Puskás (84); Sándor Kocsis (75); Imre Schlosser (59); Lajos Tichy (51); György Sárosi (42)

A mere 12th in the league, just six points clear of a relegation zone that consumed once-mighty MTK Budapest as well as Szolnoki MÁV FC, Kecskemét's Cup win earned them a first crack at European football, in the 2011/12 UEFA Europa League. The same reward went to unheralded Paksi SE, who pulled off an even bigger coup by finishing runners-up to Videoton in the NB I – and also winning the League Cup after reversing the outcome of the previous season's final with a 4-2 aggregate victory over Debrecen. Paks, from the town on the banks of the Danube known primarily for its nuclear power plant, were the only team in the NB I without a foreigner in their squad. This Hungarian-only policy paid off handsomely as coach Károly Kiss led his well-drilled, ego-free team to a series of remarkable wins, the best of them arguably in the last match before the winter break when they overcame Ferencvárosi TC 3-2.

Ferencváros were the best of a bad bunch from Budapest, finishing in third place to secure a long-awaited return to Europe. They succumbed to a couple of shocking defeats – 0-6 at Újpest FC in September and 0-5 at Videoton in March – but generally performed well under new coach László Prukner (ex-Kaposvár). Újpest ended up sixth, with two other clubs from the capital, Budapest Honvéd FC and Vasas SC, finishing discreetly low in 10th and 11th, respectively, albeit both ten points ahead of doomed local rivals MTK.

Disappointing Debrecen

As for Debrecen, champions in five of the previous six seasons, they could do no better than fifth place – their lowest position for a decade. Inevitably, the club's title-winning coach from 2008/09 and 2009/10, András Herczeg, did not see out the season. He was dismissed halfway through, going out at least on a relative high with a 2-0 home win over UC Sampdoria in the UEFA Europa League. Unfortunately Debrecen had lost all five of their previous group games, so the victory had no significant value. Herczeg's successor, Czech coach Zdeněk Ščasný, was unable to relaunch Debrecen's domestic title bid so he too was removed from office midway through the spring campaign.

Hungary's UEFA EURO 2012 qualifying campaign ran along predictable lines, with victories over lesser-ranked teams counterbalanced by defeats to those seeded above them, the only variation on that theme coming when star winger Balázs Dzsudzsák scored a stoppage-time goal to deliver a 2-1 victory over Finland in Helsinki. Earlier, Sándor Egervári's team had opened their campaign with a 2-0 defeat to bogey side Sweden, but it was the back-to-back losses in March against the Netherlands – 0-4 in Budapest, 3-5 in Amsterdam – that all but extinguished Hungary's hopes of claiming a top-two berth and thus ending the country's achingly long penance in the international wilderness.

NATIONAL TEAM RESULTS 2010/11

11/8/10	England	A	Wembley	1-2	*Jagielka (62og)*
3/9/10	Sweden (ECQ)	A	Solna	0-2	
7/9/10	Moldova (ECQ)	H	Budapest	2-1	*Rudolf (50), Koman (66)*
8/10/10	San Marino (ECQ)	H	Budapest	8-0	*Rudolf (11, 25), Szalai (18, 27, 48), Koman (60), Dzsudzsák (89), Gera (90+4p)*
12/10/10	Finland (ECQ)	A	Helsinki	2-1	*Szalai (50), Dzsudzsák (90+4)*
17/11/10	Lithuania	H	Szekesfehervar	2-0	*Priskin (61), Dzsudzsák (80)*
9/2/11	Azerbaijan	N	Dubai (UAE)	2-0	*Rudolf (37), Hajnal (81)*
25/3/11	Netherlands (ECQ)	H	Budapest	0-4	
29/3/11	Netherlands (ECQ)	A	Amsterdam	3-5	*Rudolf (46), Gera (50, 75)*
3/6/11	Luxembourg	A	Luxembourg	1-0	*Szabics (53)*
7/6/11	San Marino (ECQ)	A	Serravalle	3-0	*Lipták (40), Szabics (49), Koman (83)*

HUNGARY

NATIONAL TEAM APPEARANCES 2010/11

Coach – Sándor EGERVÁRI	15/7/50		Eng	SWE	MDA	SMR	FIN	Ltu	Aze	NED	NED	Lux	SMR	Caps	Goals
Gábor KIRÁLY	1/4/76	1860 München (GER)	G	G	G	G	G		G46	G			G	81	-
Zoltán SZÉLESI	22/11/81	Olympiacos Volou (GRE)	D											27	-
Roland JUHÁSZ	1/7/83	Anderlecht (BEL)	D	D	D	D	D	D78	D	D	D	D	D	64	5
Zoltán LIPTÁK	10/12/84	Videoton	D55	D	D		D	D		D		D	D87	8	1
Vilmos VANCZÁK	20/6/83	Sion (SUI)	D46		s64	D	s86		D	D	D	D	D	56	1
Balázs DZSUDZSÁK	23/12/86	PSV (NED)	M46	M46	M	M	M	M	M	M	M	M	M	37	5
Krisztián VADÓCZ	30/5/85	Osasuna (ESP)	M	M	s88	s64	M75		s46	s46	M90	M68		37	2
Ákos ELEK	21/7/88	Videoton	M60	M59	M	M64	M	M46	M84	M79		M46	M	11	-
Szabolcs HUSZTI	18/4/83	Zenit (RUS)	M46	s46										51	7
Zoltán GERA	22/4/79	Fulham (ENG)	M	M	M	M	M		M	M	M			71	21
Gergely RUDOLF	9/3/85	Genoa (ITA)	A83	A82	A64	A	M46	A46							
		/Bari (ITA)							A46	A	A			20	6
Tamás HAJNAL	15/3/81	Dortmund (GER)	s46	s82				s73							
		/Stuttgart (GER)							s46			M80	M71	40	5
Vladimir KOMAN	16/3/89	Sampdoria (ITA)	s46	M	M88	M79	s46	M	M46	M46	s46	M68	M	12	3
Zsolt LACZKÓ	18/12/86	Debrecen	s46	D	D	D	D86	D46							
		/Sampdoria (ITA)							D70	D	D	D	D	13	-
Ádám KOMLÓSI	6/12/77	Debrecen	s55											10	-
Balázs TÓTH	24/9/81	VVV (NED)	s60											34	-
Tamás PRISKIN	27/9/86	Ipswich (ENG)	s83	s59		s64		s46	A46						
		/Swansea (WAL)								s79	A73			33	8
Pál LÁZÁR	11/3/88	Videoton		D	D			D73	D		D			5	-
Péter CZVITKOVICS	10/2/83	Debrecen			M46	s79		M73		s46	s90	s68	s71	8	-
Ádám SZALAI	9/12/87	Mainz (GER)			s46	A64	A	A						6	4
Krisztián VERMES	7/7/85	Újpest				D	D	s73	s70					6	-
Ádám PINTÉR	12/6/88	Zaragoza (ESP)					s75	s78			M46	s68	s87	5	-
Márton FÜLÖP	3/5/83	Ipswich (ENG)						G	s46		G			24	-
Tamás KÁDÁR	14/3/90	Newcastle (ENG)						s46						1	-
József VARGA	6/6/88	Debrecen						s46	s84	M46				5	-
Attila TÖKÖLI	14/5/76	Kecskemét							s46		s73	A46		25	3
Ádám BOGDÁN	27/9/87	Bolton (ENG)										G		1	-
Krisztián NÉMETH	5/1/89	Olympiacos (GRE)										s46	A	3	-
Imre SZABICS	22/3/81	Sturm (AUT)										s46	A83	23	11
Tamás KOLTAI	30/4/87	Győr										s80	s83	4	-

CLUB-BY-CLUB

BUDAPEST HONVÉD FC

Coach – Massimo Morales (ITA); (13/11/10) László Szalai; (1/1/11) Attila Supka

Founded – 1909

Stadium – Bozsik József (13,500)

MAJOR HONOURS: Hungarian League – (13) 1950, 1950 (autumn), 1952, 1954, 1955, 1980, 1984, 1985, 1986, 1988, 1989, 1991, 1993; Hungarian Cup – (7) 1926, 1964, 1985, 1989, 1996, 2007, 2009.

2010

31/7	Vasas	a	2-3	*Abass, Takács*
7/8	MTK	h	1-2	*Botiş*
15/8	Ferencváros	a	3-1	*Rufino, Hajdu (p), Rouani*
22/8	Debrecen	h	1-0	*Pablo Coira*
28/8	Szolnok	a	2-0	*Sadjo, Rufino*
11/9	ZTE	h	1-0	*Abass*
18/9	Haladás	a	1-1	*Pablo Coira*
25/9	Pápa	h	2-4	*Abass 2*
2/10	Paks	a	1-0	*Bojtor*
16/10	Kecskemét	h	1-2	*Rouani*
23/10	Kaposvár	a	0-0	
29/10	Videoton	a	2-0	*Danilo 2*
5/11	Győr	h	1-1	*Hajdu (p)*
13/11	Újpest	a	1-3	*Bajner*
19/11	Siófok	h	0-1	
26/11	Vasas	h	0-0	

2011

26/2	MTK	a	1-3	*Lovrić*
6/3	Ferencváros	h	0-1	
12/3	Debrecen	a	2-2	*Debreceni, Hajdu*
19/3	Szolnok	h	0-0	
2/4	ZTE	a	1-2	*Akassou (p)*
9/4	Haladás	h	3-1	*Lovrić 2, Ivancsics*
16/4	Pápa	a	1-0	*Bright*
23/4	Paks	h	1-0	*Lovrić*
26/4	Kecskemét	a	1-2	*Zelenka*

)/4	Kaposvár	h	1-0	*Danilo*
'5	Videoton	h	2-2	*Zelenka, Ivancsics*
/5	Győr	a	0-3	
4/5	Újpest	h	1-4	*Danilo*
2/5	Siófok	a	3-1	*Danilo, og (Délczeg), Czár*

No	Name	Nat	DoB	Pos	Aps	(s)	Gls
7	Dieng Cheikh ABASS	SEN	1/1/85	A	12	(4)	4
5	Jean-Baptiste AKASSOU Akra	CIV	5/11/85	M	19	(5)	1
	Bálint BAJNER		18/11/90	A	1	(5)	1
4	László BOJTOR		17/9/85	A	4	(5)	1
	Sorin BOTIŞ	ROU	14/4/78	D	26	(1)	1
5	Kris BRIGHT	NZL	5/9/86	A	7	(2)	1
1	Alfi CONTEH Lacalle	SLE	18/1/85	A	1	(6)	
	György CSÉKE		7/4/83	D	1		
2	Richárd CZÁR		13/8/92	M		(2)	1
9	DANILO Carino de Oliviera	BRA	11/11/86	A	18	(6)	5
	András DEBRECENI		21/4/89	D	24		1
	László ERDÉLYI		10/7/93	A		(1)	
0	FERNANDO Cuerda Peña	ESP	6/3/84	D	7		
7	Péter FIEBER	SVK	10/12/89	D		(1)	
7	GUILHERME Rodrigues Moreira	BRA	11/4/87	A	17	(2)	
	Norbert HAJDU		1/10/82	M	29		3
6	Patrik HIDI		27/11/90	M	11	(2)	
4	Adrián HORVÁTH		20/11/87	M	14	(3)	
0	Gellért IVANCSICS		23/2/87	M	14		2
3	Valér KAPACINA		14/7/93	M		(1)	
1	Szabolcs KEMENES		18/5/86	G	27		
9	Tomislav LABUDOVIĆ	CRO	25/10/85	D		(1)	
5	Ivan LOVRIĆ	CRO	11/7/85	D	13		4
35	Sergiu MOGA	ROU	7/1/92	M	1		
77	Gergő NAGY		7/1/93	M	3	(10)	
33	Gábor NÉMETH		21/5/75	G	1		
18	PABLO COIRA Lojo	ESP	18/10/79	M	13		2
23	Karim ROUANI	FRA	8/3/82	A	15	(2)	2
11	RUFINO Segovia del Burgo	ESP	1/3/85	A	8	(6)	2
3	Haman SADJO	CMR	28/11/84	D	13	(7)	1
28	Márkó SÓS		29/12/90	M	1		
13	Jovica STOKIĆ	BIH	7/4/87	M		(1)	
29	Ákos TAKÁCS		14/2/82	M	15		1
1	Iván TÓTH		22/3/71	G	2		
28	Bálint VÉCSEI		13/7/93	A	1	(2)	
18	Richárd VERNES		24/2/92	M	1		
7	Roland VÓLENT		23/9/92	A		(7)	
30	Lukáš ZELENKA	CZE	5/10/79	M	11	(1)	2

DEBRECENI VSC

Coach – András Herczeg; (30/12/10) Zdeněk Ščasný (CZE); (20/4/11) Elemér Kondás

Founded – 1902

Stadium – Oláh Gábor utcai (11,500)

MAJOR HONOURS: Hungarian League – (5) 2005, 2006, 2007, 2009, 2010; Hungarian Cup – (4) 1999, 2001, 2008, 2010.

2010

31/7	Pápa	h	2-0	*Szilágyi, Kulcsár*
8/8	Paks	a	2-2	*Kabát, Simac*
14/8	Kecskemét	h	6-2	*Czvitkovics 2, Kiss, Coulibaly, Kabát, Dombi*
22/8	Honvéd	a	0-1	
29/8	Videoton	h	3-1	*Czvitkovics (p), Yannick, og (Horváth)*
10/9	Győr	a	0-3	
19/9	Újpest	h	1-1	*Laczkó*
25/9	Siófok	a	1-4	*Szakály (p)*
3/10	Vasas	h	3-1	*Coulibaly 2 (1p), Kabát*
16/10	MTK	a	0-0	
24/10	Ferencváros	h	2-1	*Kabát (p), Czvitkovics*
29/10	Kaposvár	h	3-1	*Bódi, Czvitkovics 2*
7/11	Szolnok	h	4-0	*Szakály 2, Coulibaly, Simac*
13/11	ZTE	h	2-1	*og (Varga), Coulibaly*
20/11	Haladás	a	0-3	
26/11	Pápa	a	1-1	*Mijadinoski*

2011

4/3	Kecskemét	a	0-3	
8/3	Paks	h	2-1	*og (Éger), Czvitkovics (p)*
12/3	Honvéd	h	2-2	*Czvitkovics, Salami*
18/3	Videoton	a	1-2	*Coulibaly*
3/4	Győr	h	1-1	*Czvitkovics (p)*
10/4	Újpest	a	2-2	*Coulibaly, Czvitkovics (p)*
16/4	Siófok	h	2-3	*Coulibaly, Bódi*
23/4	Vasas	a	5-1	*Simac, Bódi 2, Coulibaly 2*
27/4	MTK	h	3-1	*Simac, Ramos, Coulibaly*
1/5	Ferencváros	a	1-1	*Coulibaly*
7/5	Kaposvár	a	0-0	
10/5	Szolnok	a	2-1	*Szakály, Coulibaly*
13/5	ZTE	a	1-1	*Bódi (p)*
22/5	Haladás	h	1-2	*Coulibaly (p)*

No	Name	Nat	DoB	Pos	Aps	(s)	Gls
91	Ádám BALAJTI		7/3/91	A		(1)	
22	Csaba BERNÁTH		26/3/79	D	12		
27	Ádám BÓDI		18/10/90	M	18	(2)	5
39	Adamo COULIBALY	FRA	14/8/81	A	21	(5)	14
77	Péter CZVITKOVICS		10/2/83	M	22	(3)	10
7	Tibor DOMBI		11/11/73	M		(19)	1
10	Balázs FARKAS		24/4/88	A	2	(8)	
21	Marcell FODOR		27/10/87	D	14	(2)	
5	Gyula ILLÉS		9/11/82	M	6	(1)	
11	Péter KABÁT		25/9/77	A	10	(6)	4
30	Zoltán KISS		18/8/80	M	6	(3)	1
16	Ádám KOMLÓSI		6/12/77	D	12		
69	Mihály KORHUT		1/12/88	D	1		
70	Tamás KULCSÁR		13/10/82	A	4	(1)	1
86	Zsolt LACZKÓ		18/12/86	M	12		1
31	Mindaugas MALINAUSKAS	LTU	11/8/83	G	14		
50	Ştefan MARDARE	ROU	3/12/87	D	4		
18	Péter MÁTÉ		2/12/84	D	1		
24	Mirsad MIJADINOSKI	MKD	1/10/81	D	22	(1)	1
28	Zoltán NAGY		25/10/85	D	15	(2)	
8	Balázs NIKOLOV		4/7/77	M	2	(1)	
45	Nenad NOVAKOVIĆ	SRB	17/7/82	G	8		
6	Luis Arcangel RAMOS	HON	11/4/85	M	16	(3)	1
15	László REZES		12/8/87	M	2	(1)	
14	Eugène SALAMI	NGA	5/2/89	A	4	(5)	1
4	Dajan SIMAC	GER	4/1/82	D	19	(1)	4
29	Mihály SPITZMÜLLER		14/5/86	M	1	(4)	
55	Péter SZAKÁLY		17/8/86	M	26	(1)	4
23	Péter SZILÁGYI		26/1/88	A	4	(5)	1
2	István SZŰCS		3/5/85	D	5		
33	József VARGA		6/6/88	M	19	(2)	
87	István VERPECZ		4/2/87	G	8	(1)	
20	Mbengono Ondoa YANNICK	CMR	11/6/87	A	20	(2)	1

FERENCVÁROSI TC

Coach – László Prukner

Founded – 1899

Stadium – Albert Flórián (18,100)

MAJOR HONOURS: Inter Cities Fairs Cup – (1) 1965; Hungarian League – (28) 1903, 1905, 1907, 1909, 1910, 1911, 1912, 1913, 1926, 1927, 1928, 1932, 1934, 1938, 1940, 1941, 1949, 1963, 1964, 1967, 1968, 1976, 1981, 1992, 1995, 1996, 2001, 2004; Hungarian Cup – (20) 1913, 1922, 1927, 1928, 1933, 1935, 1942, 1943, 1944, 1958, 1972, 1974, 1976, 1978, 1991, 1993, 1994, 1995, 2003, 2004.

2010

30/7	Paks	h	2-1	*Heinz, og (Szabó)*
7/8	Kecskemét	a	2-1	*Rósa, Abdi*
15/8	Honvéd	h	1-3	*Kulcsár*
21/8	Videoton	a	1-1	*Andrezinho*
1/9	Győr	h	3-0	*Heinz 2, Schembri*
11/9	Újpest	a	0-6	
18/9	Siófok	h	1-2	*Schembri*
26/9	Vasas	a	3-1	*Schembri 3*

1/10	MTK	h	3-0	*og (Sütő) 2, Csizmadia*
16/10	Kaposvár	h	1-0	*Rósa (p)*
24/10	Debrecen	a	1-2	*Rodenbücher*
30/10	Szolnok	h	1-0	*Rodenbücher*
6/11	ZTE	a	1-2	*Rósa*
14/11	Haladás	h	2-1	*Heinz, Maróti*
20/11	Pápa	a	5-0	*Schembri 3, Heinz, Morales*
30/11	Paks	a	2-3	*Maróti, Miljković*
2011				
25/2	Kecskemét	h	2-1	*og (Preklet), Rósa (p)*
6/3	Honvéd	a	1-0	*Stanić*
12/3	Videoton	h	0-5	
19/3	Győr	a	0-1	
1/4	Újpest	h	1-0	*Heinz*
9/4	Siófok	a	1-1	*Schembri*
15/4	Vasas	h	0-1	
24/4	MTK	a	3-1	*Schembri, Csizmadia, Maróti*
27/4	Kaposvár	a	1-2	*Schembri*
1/5	Debrecen	h	1-1	*og (Mijadinoski)*
7/5	Szolnok	a	3-2	*Pölöskey, Schembri, Rósa (p)*
10/5	ZTE	h	4-4	*Schembri 2, Pölöskey, Heinz*
15/5	Haladás	a	1-1	*Rósa*
22/5	Pápa	h	3-0	*Schembri, Morales, Dragóner*

No	Name	Nat	DoB	Pos	Aps	(s)	Gls
19	Liban ABDI	SOM	5/10/88	A	6	(11)	1
5	ADRIANO Alves dos Santos	BRA	1/7/85	D	4	(6)	
13	AÍLTON José Pereira Júnior	BRA	23/7/87	A	15	(1)	
10	André Francisco Williams Rocha da Silva "ANDREZINHO"	BRA	12/2/86	M	19	(2)	1
78	Zoltán BALOG		22/2/78	D	24		
85	Csaba CSIZMADIA		30/5/85	D	29		2
26	Attila DRAGÓNER		15/11/74	D	4	(6)	1
23	Justin HABER	MLT	9/6/81	G	10		
18	Marek HEINZ	CZE	4/8/77	A	22	(1)	7
7	Nikola JAKIMOVSKI	MKD	26/2/90	M		(1)	
8	György JÓZSI		31/1/83	M	16	(9)	
88	Dávid KULCSÁR		25/2/88	M	1	(6)	1
25	Béla MARÓTI		7/5/79	M	25		3
21	Emil MILJKOVIĆ	BIH	26/5/88	A	9	(7)	1
35	Héctor Gabriel MORALES	ARG	30/11/89	A	12	(4)	2
36	Igor PISANJUK	CAN	28/10/89	A		(1)	
60	Péter PÖLÖSKEY		11/8/88	A	3	(6)	2
1	Marko RANILOVIČ	SVN	25/11/86	G	20		
22	István RODENBÜCHER		22/2/84	D	16	(3)	2
20	Dénes RÓSA		7/4/77	M	28		6
27	André SCHEMBRI	MLT	27/5/86	A	27		15
14	Srđan STANIĆ	SRB	7/6/82	M	16	(6)	1
32	Sam STOCKLEY	ENG	5/9/77	D	1	(1)	
30	Bence TÓTH		27/7/89	M	6	(14)	
15	Đorđe TUTORIĆ	SRB	5/3/83	D	17		

GYŐRI ETO FC

Coach – Attila Pintér; (7/3/11) Aurél Csertői

Founded – 1904

Stadium – ETO Park (16,000)

MAJOR HONOURS: Hungarian League – (3) 1963 (autumn), 1982, 1983; Hungarian Cup – (4) 1965, 1966, 1967, 1979.

2010				
1/8	Újpest	a	0-0	
8/8	Siófok	h	1-0	*Aleksidze*
13/8	Vasas	a	1-2	*Tokody*
22/8	MTK	h	1-1	*Trajković*
1/9	Ferencváros	a	0-3	
10/9	Debrecen	h	3-0	*Koltai 2, Aleksidze*
18/9	Szolnok	a	3-0	*Ceolin 2, Koltai*
25/9	ZTE	h	0-1	
2/10	Haladás	a	3-3	*Pilibaitis, Trajković, Aleksidze*
15/10	Pápa	h	0-1	
22/10	Paks	a	1-2	*Bouguerra*
30/10	Kecskemét	h	2-1	*Pilibaitis, Bouguerra*
5/11	Honvéd	a	1-1	*Völgyi*
12/11	Videoton	h	1-1	*Ganugrava*
19/11	Kaposvár	a	0-3	
28/11	Újpest	h	2-1	*Bouguerra, Ceolin*
2011				
25/2	Siófok	a	1-0	*Aleksidze*
5/3	Vasas	h	0-1	
11/3	MTK	a	0-0	
19/3	Ferencváros	h	1-0	*Aleksidze*
3/4	Debrecen	a	1-1	*Dinjar*
9/4	Szolnok	h	4-2	*Dinjar, Ji-Paraná, Đorđević, Dudás*
16/4	ZTE	a	1-1	*Völgyi*
22/4	Haladás	h	2-2	*Aleksidze 2*
26/4	Pápa	a	1-2	*Totadze*
29/4	Paks	h	1-1	*Trajković*
6/5	Kecskemét	a	3-3	*Dinjar, Pilibaitis (p), Dudás*
11/5	Honvéd	h	3-0	*Völgyi, Kiss, Aleksidze*
14/5	Videoton	a	1-2	*Dudás*
21/5	Kaposvár	h	2-0	*Aleksidze, Dinjar*

No	Name	Nat	DoB	Pos	Aps	(s)	Gls
10	Rati ALEKSIDZE	GEO	3/8/78	A	21	(4)	9
22	Valentin BABIĆ	CRO	6/7/81	D	10	(1)	
19	Fouad BOUGUERRA	ALG	7/5/81	A	13	(7)	3
25	Juan Ignácio BRIONES	ARG	16/1/86	M		(1)	
11	Nicolas CEOLIN	BRA	10/4/86	A	5	(10)	3
8	Đorđe ĆETKOVIĆ	MNE	3/1/83	A	1	(4)	
13	Arsène COPA	GAB	7/6/88	A	5	(5)	
5	Marko DINJAR	CRO	21/5/86	M	19	(2)	4
28	Vladimir ĐORĐEVIĆ	SRB	25/12/82	D	19		1
8	Ádám DUDÁS		12/2/89	M	2	(8)	3
6	Zoltán FEHÉR		12/6/81	D	21	(1)	
2	Eugène FOMUMBOD	CMR	22/2/85	M	7	(1)	
30	Giorgi GANUGRAVA	GEO	21/2/88	M	8	(4)	1
16	Júnior Felício Marques "JI-PARANÁ"	BRA	11/6/87	M	11	(6)	1
14	Máté KISS		30/4/91	M	15	(3)	1
29	Tamás KOLTAI		30/4/87	M	26	(3)	3
2	Carlos Ariel MARINELLI	ARG	14/3/82	M		(2)	
20	Onişor Mihai NICOREC	ROU	28/3/86	A	4		
18	Vedran NIKŠIĆ	CRO	5/5/87	M	1	(2)	
7	Linas PILIBAITIS	LTU	5/4/85	M	25		3
26	Aleksandar RADOSAVLJEVIĆ	SRB	21/12/82	G	2	(1)	
24	András SÁNTA	ROU	1/7/85	G	1		
17	Teimuraz SHARASHENIDZE	GEO	21/1/92	A	1	(5)	
4	Lazar STANIŠIĆ	SRB	21/7/82	D	17	(1)	
1	Saša STEVANOVIĆ	SRB	4/8/74	G	27		
9	Ottó SZABÓ	SVK	1/3/81	M	8	(1)	
2	Ákos TAKÁCS		14/2/82	D	9		
23	Tibor TOKODY		1/9/80	M	11	(4)	1
3	Lasha TOTADZE	GEO	24/8/88	D	4	(3)	1
12	Nikola TRAJKOVIĆ	SRB	5/1/81	M	12	(7)	3
15	Dániel VÖLGYI		7/6/87	M	24	(1)	3
43	József WINDECKER		2/12/92	M	1		

KAPOSVÁRI RÁKÓCZI FC

Coach – Tibor Sisa

Founded – 1923

Stadium – Városi (7,000)

2010				
31/7	ZTE	a	5-3	*Pavlović 2, og (Kovács), Oláh, Grúz*
6/8	Újpest	h	0-1	
14/8	Haladás	h	1-0	*Jawad*
21/8	Siófok	a	0-0	
28/8	Pápa	h	3-2	*Grúz, Kulcsár, Zsók*
10/9	Vasas	a	3-1	*Pavlović (p), Jawad, Gujić (p)*
17/9	Paks	h	1-2	*Oláh (p)*
2/10	Kecskemét	h	2-1	*Jawad, Oláh*
9/10	MTK	a	2-0	*Perić, Oláh*
16/10	Ferencváros	a	0-1	
23/10	Honvéd	h	0-0	

9/10	Debrecen	a	1-3	*Oláh*
/11	Videoton	h	1-4	*Oláh*
3/11	Szolnok	a	2-1	*Szepessy, Perić*
9/11	Győr	h	3-0	*Oláh 2, Pedro*
7/11	ZTE	h	2-1	*Oláh, Perić*
011				
6/2	Újpest	a	2-3	*Perić, Hegedűs*
/3	Haladás	a	0-2	
2/3	Siófok	h	3-0	*Perić, Oláh (p), Balázs*
9/3	Pápa	a	1-1	*Hegedűs*
/4	Vasas	h	0-1	
/4	Paks	a	3-2	*Perić 2, Oláh*
6/4	MTK	h	2-1	*Oláh, Máté*
3/4	Kecskemét	a	1-4	*Perić*
7/4	Ferencváros	h	2-1	*Oláh (p), Zsók*
0/4	Honvéd	a	0-1	
/5	Debrecen	h	0-0	
1/5	Videoton	a	1-3	*Grumić*
4/5	Szolnok	h	0-1	
1/5	Győr	a	0-2	

lo	Name	Nat	DoB	Pos	Aps	(s)	Gls
9	ANDRÉ Cabete PORTULEZ	POR	29/4/86	M	1		
8	Benjámin BALÁZS		26/4/90	M	25	(5)	1
	István BANK		14/4/84	M	10		
	Lukács BÖLE		27/3/90	M		(2)	
20	Zoltán FARKAS		7/10/89	M	2	(8)	
	Ukwoma Egejuru GODSLOVE	NGA	4/12/86	A	1	(6)	
	Miroslav GRUMIĆ	SRB	29/6/84	A	1	(5)	1
26	Tamás GRÚZ		8/11/85	D	19	(2)	2
7	Boris GUJIĆ	BIH	9/7/86	D	23	(1)	1
24	Dávid HEGEDŰS		6/6/85	M	20	(3)	2
1	László HORVÁTH		23/2/88	G	1		
11	Daniane JAWAD	MAR	14/4/86	A	15	(8)	3
30	Mihály KORHUT		1/12/88	D	7	(3)	
15	Olivér KOVÁCS		22/12/90	M		(1)	
29	Zoltán KOVÁCS		29/10/84	G	24		
6	Róbert KOVÁCSEVICS		19/3/79	D	2	(1)	
8	Kornél KULCSÁR		11/11/91	M	9	(11)	1
30	Mátyás LELKES	SVK	15/2/84	D	1		
16	Norbert LIPUSZ		23/4/86	M	1		
16	Péter MÁTÉ		15/11/79	M	6	(1)	1
1	Árpád MILINTE		4/5/76	G	5		
13	Dražen OKUKA	SRB	5/3/86	D	25		
14	Lóránt OLÁH		23/11/79	A	24	(3)	13
22	Bojan PAVLOVIĆ	SRB	1/2/85	A	23	(3)	3
33	PEDRO Sass Petrazzi	BRA	15/9/90	M	23	(3)	1
3	Milan PERIĆ	SRB	16/4/84	A	20	(7)	8
17	Vikto PETRÓK		3/4/81	D	1		
17	Gábor RESZLI		20/1/88	A	1		
10	Róbert SZEPESSY		12/8/85	A	6	(9)	1
2	Zalán VADAS		23/4/91	D	1		
28	Krisztián ZAHORECZ		28/10/75	D	6	(1)	
31	József ZSÓK		2/10/84	D	27	(1)	2
15	Róbert ZSOLNAI		11/4/82	A		(4)	

KECSKEMÉTI TE

Coach – István Urbányi; (13/10/10) Tomislav Sivić (SRB)

Founded – 1911

Stadium – Széktói (6,500)

MAJOR HONOURS: Hungarian Cup – (1) 2011.

2010				
31/7	MTK	a	2-4	*Litsingi, Tököli*
7/8	Ferencváros	h	1-2	*Tököli*
14/8	Debrecen	a	2-6	*Foxi 2*
21/8	Szolnok	h	4-2	*Litsingi 2, Simon (p), Balogh*
28/8	ZTE	a	1-2	*Némedi (p)*
18/9	Pápa	a	1-4	*Gyagya*
25/9	Paks	h	0-1	
2/10	Kaposvár	a	1-2	*Gyagya*
9/10	Haladás	h	1-0	*Némedi (p)*
16/10	Honvéd	a	2-1	*Tököli 2*
23/10	Videoton	h	2-4	*Némedi (p), Csordás*
30/10	Győr	a	1-2	*Némedi (p)*
5/11	Újpest	h	4-3	*Foxi, Alempijević, Tököli, Čukić*
13/11	Siófok	a	2-1	*Foxi, Tököli*
20/11	Vasas	h	3-1	*Alempijević, Ebala, Litsingi*
27/11	MTK	h	3-0	*Tököli 2, Savić*
2011				
25/2	Ferencváros	a	1-2	*Tököli*
4/3	Debrecen	h	3-0	*Balogh (p), Vujović (p), og (Salami)*
12/3	Szolnok	a	1-2	*Tököli*
18/3	ZTE	h	1-0	*Gyagya*
2/4	Haladás	a	0-1	
9/4	Pápa	h	0-1	
16/4	Paks	a	0-2	
23/4	Kaposvár	h	4-1	*Bori, Tököli, Litsingi, Foxi*
26/4	Honvéd	h	2-1	*Mohl, og (Sadjo)*
29/4	Videoton	a	2-2	*Litsingi, Ebala*
6/5	Győr	h	3-3	*Vujović, Tököli, Foxi*
11/5	Újpest	a	1-2	*Tököli*
14/5	Siófok	h	2-3	*Bori, Bertus*
20/5	Vasas	a	1-1	*Dosso*

No	Name	Nat	DoB	Pos	Aps	(s)	Gls
7	Aleksandar ALEMPIJEVIĆ	SRB	25/7/88	M	16	(1)	2
31	Botond ANTAL		22/8/91	G	3		
22	István BAGI		23/3/89	D	1		
9	Marcell BALOG		23/2/88	A		(1)	
6	Béla BALOGH		30/12/84	D	27		2
26	Lajos BERTUS		26/9/90	M	7	(9)	1
21	Gábor BORI		16/1/84	A	23	(5)	2
11	Csaba CSORDÁS		9/8/77	A	3	(10)	1
14	Vladan ČUKIĆ	SRB	27/6/80	M	24	(3)	1
19	Sindou DOSSO	CIV	23/4/86	A	2	(13)	1
17	Bodiong Christian EBALA	CMR	17/3/88	M	19	(4)	2
22	András FARKAS		3/12/92	A	1		
5	István FARKAS		16/1/84	D	8		
20	FOXI Kethevoama	CTA	30/5/86	M	23	(3)	6
15	Attila GYAGYA	ROU	30/3/82	D	19	(1)	3
13	Ádám HOLCZER		28/3/88	G	4	(1)	
8	Zsolt KONCZ		18/9/77	M	5	(1)	
2	Balázs Tibor KOSZÓ		20/3/88	D	3	(2)	
4	Mladen LAMBULIĆ	SRB	9/7/72	D	8	(1)	
18	Francis LITSINGI	CGO	9/10/86	A	24	(5)	6
3	Gergő MÁTÉ		13/7/90	D		(2)	
85	Dávid MOHL		28/4/85	D	20	(2)	1
12	Norbert NÉMEDI		1/6/77	M	11	(1)	4
2	Zsolt PATVAROS		18/2/93	D	1	(2)	
32	Csaba PREKLET		25/1/91	D	1	(1)	
4	Siniša RADANOVIĆ	SRB	23/11/79	D	10		
28	Ladislav RYBÁNSKY	SVK	19/12/84	G	23		
23	Attila SÁNTA		22/8/88	M		(1)	
10	Vladan SAVIĆ	MNE	26/7/79	M	11	(6)	1
9	Attila SIMON		4/2/83	A	1	(2)	1
55	Attila TÖKÖLI		14/5/76	A	25	(3)	13
88	Viktor TÖLGYESI		18/1/92	M		(1)	
16	Pál URBÁN		14/1/89	D	1		
9	Goran VUJOVIĆ	MNE	3/5/87	A	6	(4)	2
3	Electo WILSON		19/2/89	M		(3)	

LOMBARD-PÁPA TFC

Coach – György Véber

Founded – 2004

Stadium – Perutz (8,000)

2010				
31/7	Debrecen	a	0-2	
7/8	Szolnok	h	0-0	
20/8	Haladás	h	5-1	*Bárányos (p), Marić 2, Germán, Gyömbér (p)*
28/8	Kaposvár	a	2-3	*Abwo, Takács*
1/9	ZTE	a	1-3	*Abwo*
18/9	Kecskemét	h	4-1	*Gyömbér, Takács, Rebryk, Heffler*

25/9	Honvéd	a	4-2	*Marić, Bárányos 2, Heffler*
1/10	Videoton	h	1-2	*Heffler*
9/10	Paks	a	0-4	
15/10	Győr	a	1-0	*Abwo*
23/10	Újpest	h	3-1	*og (Vermes), Marić, Heffler*
30/10	Siófok	a	1-0	*Marić*
6/11	Vasas	h	2-1	*og (Lázok), Marić*
12/11	MTK	a	1-2	*Abwo*
20/11	Ferencváros	h	0-5	
26/11	Debrecen	h	1-1	*Rajnay*
2011				
5/3	ZTE	h	4-3	*Takács 2, Marić 2 (1p)*
8/3	Szolnok	a	2-2	*Marić, Bárányos*
12/3	Haladás	a	0-1	
19/3	Kaposvár	h	1-1	*Marić*
2/4	Paks	h	1-2	*Bárányos*
9/4	Kecskemét	a	1-0	*Rebryk*
16/4	Honvéd	h	0-1	
23/4	Videoton	a	0-4	
26/4	Győr	h	2-1	*Bárányos, Marić*
30/4	Újpest	a	1-2	*Quintero*
7/5	Siófok	h	0-1	
10/5	Vasas	a	1-1	*Bali*
14/5	MTK	h	0-2	
22/5	Ferencváros	a	0-3	

No	Name	Nat	DoB	Pos	Aps	(s)	Gls
10	David Salomon ABWO	NGA	10/5/86	M	15	(1)	4
39	Péter BALI		6/1/84	A	2	(12)	1
19	Zsolt BÁRÁNYOS		15/12/75	M	29		6
24	Péter BÍRÓ		20/9/85	D	7	(1)	
5	András DLUSZTUS		22/7/88	D	15		
23	Attila FARKAS		5/10/78	D	20	(2)	
7	Tamás GERMÁN		26/3/87	A	1	(3)	1
13	Gábor GYÖMBÉR		27/2/88	M	28		2
8	Norbert HEFFLER		24/5/90	M	18	(2)	4
12	Zoltán JOVÁNCZAI		8/12/84	A	1	(5)	
21	Goran MARIĆ	SRB	23/3/84	A	26		11
2	Sándor NAGY		1/1/88	D	13		
29	Milán NÉMETH		29/5/88	A	19		
64	Dávid PALKÓ		7/2/89	A	3	(2)	
30	César Alexander QUINTERO Jiménez	COL	9/11/88	D	17	(9)	1
14	Attila RAJNAY		3/6/79	D	10	(1)	1
17	Denys REBRYK	UKR	4/4/85	A	15	(11)	2
26	Zoran ŠUPIĆ	SRB	21/7/84	D	20		
9	Zsolt SZABÓ		30/4/86	A	1	(7)	
27	Lajos SZŰCS		8/8/73	G	30		
11	Péter TAKÁCS		25/1/90	M	17	6	4
4	Gábor TÓTH		26/3/87	D	6	(4)	
20	Norbert TÓTH		11/8/76	M	6	(7)	
18	Gábor VARGA		20/8/85	D		(1)	
6	Balázs VENCZEL		6/9/86	M	2	(5)	
15	Vadims ŽUĻEVS	LVA	1/3/88	M	9	(3)	

MTK BUDAPEST

Coach – József Garami

Founded – 1888

Stadium – Hidegkuti Nándor (7,702)

MAJOR HONOURS: Hungarian League – (23) 1904, 1908, 1914, 1917, 1918, 1919, 1920, 1921, 1922, 1923, 1924, 1925, 1929, 1936, 1937, 1951, 1953, 1958, 1987, 1997, 1999, 2003, 2008; Hungarian Cup – (12) 1910, 1911, 1912, 1914, 1923, 1925, 1932, 1952, 1968, 1997, 1998, 2000.

2010				
31/7	Kecskemét	h	4-2	*Tischler, Kanta, Pintér, Könyves*
7/8	Honvéd	a	2-1	*Kanta (p), Tischler*
14/8	Videoton	h	0-3	
22/8	Győr	a	1-1	*Kanta*
27/8	Újpest	h	1-0	*Tischler*
11/9	Siófok	a	0-0	
16/9	Vasas	h	4-0	*Tischler 2 (1p), Gál, Pál*
1/10	Ferencváros	a	0-3	
9/10	Kaposvár	h	0-2	
16/10	Debrecen	h	0-0	
23/10	Szolnok	a	1-2	*Tischler*
30/10	ZTE	h	3-4	*Könyves, Ladányi, Eppel*
6/11	Haladás	a	0-2	
12/11	Pápa	h	2-1	*Könyves, Eppel*
20/11	Paks	a	1-1	*Könyves*
27/11	Kecskemét	a	0-3	
2011				
26/2	Honvéd	h	3-1	*Sütő, Urbán, Eppel*
5/3	Videoton	a	1-2	*Frank*
11/3	Győr	h	0-0	
20/3	Újpest	a	1-2	*Kanta*
2/4	Siófok	h	1-2	*Sütő*
8/4	Vasas	a	1-1	*Tischler*
16/4	Kaposvár	a	1-2	*Tischler*
24/4	Ferencváros	h	1-3	*Könyves*
27/4	Debrecen	a	1-3	*Pátkai*
30/4	Szolnok	h	1-0	*Pál*
6/5	ZTE	a	0-1	
11/5	Haladás	h	0-3	
14/5	Pápa	a	2-0	*Tischler, Pátkai*
21/5	Paks	h	3-4	*Tischler 3*

No	Name	Nat	DoB	Pos	Aps	(s)	Gls
8	Norbert CSIKI		21/5/91	A		(1)	
17	Márton EPPEL		26/10/91	A	3	(18)	3
27	Richárd FRANK		28/9/90	A	5		1
2	András GÁL		20/4/89	M	12	(3)	1
3	Sándor HAJDÚ		21/1/85	M	8	(2)	
1	Lajos HEGEDŰS		19/12/87	G	6	(1)	
33	Ádám HREPKA		15/4/87	A	2	(5)	
12	Dávid KÁLNOKI KIS		6/8/91	D	4	(1)	
19	József KANTA		24/3/84	M	26		4
14	Dávid KELEMEN		24/5/92	M	1	(2)	
15	Norbert KÖNYVES		10/6/89	A	18	(7)	5
11	Tibor LADÁNYI		21/11/91	M	11	(13)	1
21	Marcell MOLNÁR		26/8/90	A		(1)	
25	Márk NIKHÁZI		2/2/89	M	4	(7)	
9	András PÁL		19/8/85	A	23	(4)	2
6	Máté PÁTKAI		6/3/88	M	25	(1)	2
27	Ádám PINTÉR		12/6/88	D	4		1
16	Máté SKRIBA		13/3/92	A		(2)	
5	László SÜTŐ		18/4/86	D	25		2
23	Ádám SZABÓ		2/1/88	M	12	(2)	
1	Levente SZÁNTAI		15/11/82	G	1		
29	Zoltán SZATMÁRI		2/5/79	G	23	(1)	
13	Adrián SZEKERES		21/4/89	D	28		
30	Patrik TISCHLER		30/7/91	A	26	(3)	12
31	Gábor URBÁN		30/12/84	A		(4)	1
4	Dániel VADNAI		19/2/88	D	20	(1)	
7	Dejan VUKADINOVIĆ	SRB	3/9/82	D	24	(1)	
20	Dragan VUKMIR	SRB	2/8/78	D	14	(2)	
39	Rafe Raccini WOLFE	JAM	19/12/85	D	5		
24	Bence ZÁMBÓ		17/8/89	D		(1)	

PAKSI SE

Coach – Károly Kiss

Founded – 1952

Stadium – Városi (5,000)

2010				
30/7	Ferencváros	a	1-2	*Bartha*
8/8	Debrecen	h	2-2	*Montvai, Heffler (p)*
14/8	Szolnok	a	1-3	*Sipeki*
21/8	ZTE	h	2-2	*Montvai, Kiss*
28/8	Haladás	a	2-1	*Sifter, Vayer*
17/9	Kaposvár	a	2-1	*Böde, Montvai*
25/9	Kecskemét	a	1-0	*Montvai*
2/10	Honvéd	h	0-1	

'10	Pápa	h	4-0	*Bartha 2, Vayer, Montvai*
'/10	Videoton	a	1-2	*Éger (p)*
2/10	Győr	h	2-1	*Vayer, Böde*
/10	Újpest	a	3-2	*Éger, Böde, Bartha*
'11	Siófok	h	0-0	
3/11	Vasas	a	3-2	*Kiss, Heffler, Böde*
)/11	MTK	h	1-1	*Böde*
)/11	Ferencváros	h	3-2	*Vayer, Böde, Montvai*
011				
'3	Szolnok	h	3-1	*Böde, Bartha, Montvai*
'3	Debrecen	a	1-2	*Éger*
2/3	ZTE	a	0-1	
9/3	Haladás	h	2-1	*Kiss, Vayer*
'4	Pápa	a	2-1	*Böde, Magasföldi*
'4	Kaposvár	h	2-3	*Bartha, Magasföldi*
6/4	Kecskemét	h	2-0	*Montvai, Bartha*
3/4	Honvéd	a	0-1	
6/4	Videoton	h	1-0	*Bartha*
9/4	Győr	a	1-1	*Magasföldi*
/5	Újpest	h	2-1	*Vayer, Böde*
0/5	Siófok	a	3-1	*Sifter, Böde, Éger (p)*
3/5	Vasas	h	3-0	*Böde 3 (1p)*
1/5	MTK	a	4-3	*Csehi, Magasföldi, Böde 2*

lo	Name	Nat	DoB	Pos	Aps	(s)	Gls
	Tamás BÁLÓ		12/1/84	M	9	(8)	
9	László BARTHA		9/2/87	A	26		8
3	Dániel BÖDE		24/10/86	M	19	(5)	15
	Tamás CSEHI		6/2/84	D	21	(4)	1
7	Norbert CSERNYÁNSZKI		1/2/76	G	27	(1)	
6	Ádám DUDÁS		12/2/89	M		(1)	
3	László ÉGER		7/5/77	D	24		4
8	Attila FIOLA		17/2/90	D	27		
5	Zsolt GÉVAY		19/11/87	D	2	(3)	
1	Zsolt HARASZTI		4/11/91	A	1	(7)	
16	Tibor HEFFLER		17/5/87	M	30		2
0	Tamás KISS		27/9/79	M	24	(6)	3
1	Attila KOVÁCS		17/2/81	G	2		
33	Krisztián LISZTES		2/7/76	M	2	(4)	
17	József MAGASFÖLDI		10/11/84	A	12	(11)	4
19	István MÉSZÁROS		3/3/80	M	3	(4)	
12	László MISKOLCZI		12/3/86	M	2	(1)	
53	Tibor MONTVAI		23/11/78	A	18	(5)	8
2	István NAGY		16/5/86	M		(2)	
63	Norbert PALÁSTHY		10/2/81	A		(1)	
28	Péter POKORNI		22/11/89	G	1		
6	Tamás SIFTER		3/3/81	M	26	(1)	2
22	István SIPEKI		17/2/79	M	25		1
30	János SZABÓ		11/7/89	D	10	(5)	
26	Gábor TAMÁSI		26/8/81	M		(1)	
37	Balázs B. TÓTH		14/7/86	M		(1)	
87	Barnabás VÁRI		15/9/87	A		(5)	
11	Gábor VAYER		18/5/77	M	19	(6)	6

BFC SIÓFOK

Coach – István Mihalecz jr.

Founded – 1921

Stadium – Városi (12,000)

MAJOR HONOURS: Hungarian Cup – (1) 1984.

2010				
1/8	Videoton	h	1-1	*Sowunmi*
8/8	Győr	a	0-1	
14/8	Újpest	h	1-1	*Graszl (p)*
21/8	Kaposvár	h	0-0	
27/8	Vasas	a	0-3	
11/9	MTK	h	0-0	
18/9	Ferencváros	a	2-1	*Homma, Sowunmi*
25/9	Debrecen	h	4-1	*Sowunmi 2, Tusori 2*
2/10	Szolnok	a	4-0	*Homma, Lukács, Novák, Graszl*
16/10	ZTE	h	0-4	
23/10	Haladás	a	0-4	
30/10	Pápa	h	0-1	
6/11	Paks	a	0-0	
13/11	Kecskemét	h	1-2	*og (Mohl)*
19/11	Honvéd	a	1-0	*Délczeg*
27/11	Videoton	a	0-2	
2011				
25/2	Győr	h	0-1	
4/3	Újpest	a	1-1	*Novák*
12/3	Kaposvár	a	0-3	
19/3	Vasas	h	0-0	
2/4	MTK	a	2-1	*Délczeg 2*
9/4	Ferencváros	h	1-1	*Délczeg*
16/4	Debrecen	a	3-2	*Délczeg, Homma, Tusori*
23/4	Szolnok	h	1-1	*Délczeg*
27/4	ZTE	a	1-2	*Csordás*
30/4	Haladás	h	0-0	
7/5	Pápa	a	1-0	*Csermelyi*
10/5	Paks	h	1-3	*Homma*
14/5	Kecskemét	a	3-2	*Homma 3*
22/5	Honvéd	h	1-3	*Homma*

No	Name	Nat	DoB	Pos	Aps	(s)	Gls
16	Imre CSERMELYI		29/8/88	A	5	(10)	1
20	Csaba CSORDÁS		9/8/77	A	8	(4)	1
9	Gergely DÉLCZEG		9/8/87	A	18	(7)	6
3	Zsolt FEHÉR		13/9/85	D	25		
28	Károly GRASZL		8/1/85	D	26	(1)	2
18	Kazuo HOMMA	JPN	17/3/80	A	22	(3)	8
24	Attila HORVÁTH		30/12/88	M		(6)	
10	Henry ISAAC Osaro Nwosu Kanu	NGA	14/2/80	A	1	(6)	
7	Gellért IVANCSICS		23/2/87	M	10	(1)	
11	Szabolcs KANTA		29/1/82	M	1		
23	Attila KATONA		16/6/81	D	4	(1)	
13	Tamás KECSKÉS		15/1/86	M	23	(1)	
23	Gábor KOCSIS		30/11/85	D	3	(6)	
4	András LÁSZLÓ		16/8/76	D	2	(2)	
18	István LUDÁNSZKI		26/7/87	M	9	(10)	
8	Tihamér LUKÁCS		18/7/80	M	19	(5)	1
25	Dávid MÁRTON		17/10/87	D	6	(1)	
5	Vilmos MELCZER		25/2/86	M	11	(3)	
2	József MOGYORÓSI		1/11/78	D	27		
12	Péter MOLNÁR	SVK	14/12/83	G	30		
15	Jean-Paul NOMEL	CIV	23/6/88	A	1		
29	Alexisz NOVÁK		22/11/87	D	28		2
19	Szilárd PÉCSELI		2/2/92	A		(1)	
20	József PILLER		16/8/88	M	2	(5)	
7	Ronaldo Ribeiro da Silva "RONI"	BRA	30/6/80	A		(3)	
21	Thomas SOWUNMI		25/7/80	A	16		4
10	THIAGO Vasconcelos Ribeiro da Silva	BRA	23/1/85	M	5	(7)	
14	Róbert TÓTH		9/8/89	M		(1)	
6	Richárd TUSORI		12/7/84	D	28	(1)	3

SZOLNOKI MÁV FC

Coach – Attila Vágó; (18/10/10) Antal Simon

Founded – 1910

Stadium – Tiszaligeti (4,000)

2010				
7/8	Pápa	a	0-0	
14/8	Paks	h	3-1	*Alex, Remili (p), Lengyel*
21/8	Kecskemét	a	2-4	*Alex, Remili (p)*
28/8	Honvéd	h	0-2	
4/9	Haladás	h	0-0	
12/9	Videoton	a	1-3	*Alex (p)*
18/9	Győr	h	0-3	
24/9	Újpest	a	0-1	
2/10	Siófok	h	0-4	
16/10	Vasas	a	0-3	
23/10	MTK	h	2-1	*Stanišić, Remili (p)*

30/10	Ferencváros	a	0-1	
7/11	Debrecen	a	0-4	
13/11	Kaposvár	h	1-2	*Ngalle*
20/11	ZTE	a	1-2	*Remili*
27/11	Haladás	a	1-3	*Remili*
2011				
5/3	Paks	a	1-3	*Némedi*
8/3	Pápa	h	2-2	*Némedi 2 (1p)*
13/3	Kecskemét	h	2-1	*Remili 2 (1p)*
19/3	Honvéd	a	0-0	
2/4	Videoton	h	1-1	*Zsolnai*
9/4	Győr	a	2-4	*Némedi, Đurović*
15/4	Újpest	h	1-0	*Fitos*
23/4	Siófok	a	1-1	*Miličić*
27/4	Vasas	h	0-1	
30/4	MTK	a	0-1	
7/5	Ferencváros	h	2-3	*Zsolnai 2*
10/5	Debrecen	h	1-2	*Tchami*
14/5	Kaposvár	a	1-0	*Tchami*
22/5	ZTE	h	1-3	*Miličić*

No	Name	Nat	DoB	Pos	Aps	(s)	Gls
9	ALEX Jose de Paula	BRA	13/9/81	A	9	(3)	3
17	Gábor ANTAL		18/1/78	D	4	(13)	
15	Pál BALOGH		5/10/74	D	11	(4)	
20	Zoltán BÚRÁNY		26/7/89	M	23	(1)	
19	Claudiu CORNACI	ROU	19/7/75	D	8		
9	Nenad ĐUROVIĆ	MNE	17/1/86	D	12	(1)	1
13	László FITOS		27/2/87	M	12	(2)	1
55	Dragan GOŠIĆ	SRB	10/6/81	A	3	(4)	
33	Gyula HEGEDŰS		25/2/80	D	4		
11	Tamás HEVESI-TÓTH		29/9/84	M	9	(1)	
19	Miloš JOKIĆ	SRB	7/6/87	M	12	(1)	
29	Gábor KOÓS		9/2/86	A	11	(4)	
66	István KÖVESFALVI		5/12/68	G	3		
8	Béla LENGYEL		29/10/90	M	4	(15)	1
4	Eimantas MAROZAS	LTU	29/12/85	A		(2)	
14	Péter MÁTÉ		2/12/84	D	13		
85	Vitālijs MEĻNIČENKO	LVA	11/11/87	G	13		
7	Krisztián MILE		11/4/83	M	4		
33	Boris MILIČIĆ	SRB	4/4/79	D	14		2
2	Zoltán MOLNÁR		4/11/73	D	13		
7	Norbert NÉMEDI		1/6/77	M	13		4
10	Joseph NGALLE	CMR	13/3/85	M	6	(13)	1
27	Zoltán PETŐ		19/9/74	D	13		
6	Igor PISANJUK	CAN	28/10/89	A	9	(2)	
77	Mohamed REMILI		30/5/86	M	20		7
70	Péter RÉZSÓ		3/10/70	G	7		
36	Szabolcs SCHINDLER		26/10/74	D	9	(1)	
13	Petar STANIŠIĆ	MNE	23/9/84	D	8		1
5	Botond SZALAI		26/10/77	M	13	(6)	
85	Pál TARCZY		10/10/85	G	7		
21	Hervé-Christian TCHAMI	CMR	20/2/88	A	13	(7)	2
14	Péter VŐRÖS		14/12/77	M	3	(7)	
27	Branislav VUKOMANOVIĆ	SRB	29/12/81	D	14		
11	Róbert ZSOLNAI		11/4/82	A	13	(1)	3

SZOMBATHELYI HALADÁS

Coach – Aurél Csertői; (17/10/10) Zoltán Aczél

Founded – 1919

Stadium – Rohonci úti (12,500)

2010				
7/8	ZTE	h	0-0	
14/8	Kaposvár	a	0-1	
20/8	Pápa	a	1-5	*Tóth*
28/8	Paks	h	1-2	*Kenesei*
4/9	Szolnok	a	0-0	
18/9	Honvéd	h	1-1	*Tóth*
24/9	Videoton	a	1-3	*Kenesei (p)*
2/10	Győr	h	3-3	*Sipos, Lengyel, Schimmer*
9/10	Kecskemét	a	0-1	
15/10	Újpest	a	1-3	*Lattenstein*
23/10	Siófok	h	4-0	*Kenesei (p), Tóth, Nagy (II) 2*
30/10	Vasas	a	1-2	*Sipos*
6/11	MTK	h	2-0	*Simon Á., Kenesei*
14/11	Ferencváros	a	1-2	*Kenesei*
20/11	Debrecen	h	3-0	*Fodrek 2, Tóth (p)*
27/11	Szolnok	h	3-1	*Oross, Nagy (II), Kenesei*
2011				
26/2	ZTE	a	1-1	*Kenesei (p)*
5/3	Kaposvár	h	2-0	*Oross, Irhás*
12/3	Pápa	h	1-0	*Kenesei*
19/3	Paks	a	1-2	*Halmosi*
2/4	Kecskemét	h	1-0	*Tóth*
9/4	Honvéd	a	1-3	*Halmosi*
17/4	Videoton	h	2-0	*Halmosi, Kenesei*
22/4	Győr	a	2-2	*Kenesei, Tóth*
26/4	Újpest	h	0-2	
30/4	Siófok	a	0-0	
7/5	Vasas	h	3-0	*Oross 3*
11/5	MTK	a	3-0	*Kenesei, Fodrek, Halmosi*
15/5	Ferencváros	h	1-1	*Iszlai (p)*
22/5	Debrecen	a	2-1	*Sipos, Halmosi*

No	Name	Nat	DoB	Pos	Aps	(s)	Gls
2	Zoltán CSONTOS		30/5/86	D		(6)	
12	Szilárd DEVECSERI		13/2/90	D	2		
33	Márk FARKAS		13/1/92	D		(1)	
25	Branislav FODREK	SVK	5/2/81	M	9	(11)	3
22	Richard GUZMICS		16/4/87	D	28		
19	Bence GYURJÁN		21/2/92	M		(1)	
13	Péter HALMOSI		25/9/79	M	12		5
11	Ignác IRHÁS		18/3/85	M	11	(10)	1
90	Bence ISZLAI		29/5/90	D	7		1
26	Márk JAGODICS		12/4/92	M		(1)	
20	Krisztián KENESEI		7/1/77	A	22	(1)	11
5	Gábor KOROLOVSZKY		11/7/79	M	20		
10	István KOVÁCS		27/3/92	M		(1)	
84	Norbert LATTENSTEIN		13/2/84	M	2	(7)	1
6	Dániel LENGYEL		1/3/89	D	12	(1)	1
7	Balázs MOLNÁR		1/7/77	M	10	(2)	
3	Gábor NAGY (I)		30/9/81	D	5	(4)	
8	Gábor NAGY (II)		16/10/85	M	25	(1)	3
13	Nemanja OBRIĆ	SRB	15/4/84	M		(3)	
9	Márton OROSS		3/3/81	A	21	(4)	5
32	Ferenc RÁCZ		28/3/91	A	1	(3)	
4	Gábor RAJOS		17/3/84	M	9	(6)	
66	Dániel RÓZSA		24/11/84	G	30		
23	Szabolcs SCHIMMER		24/2/84	M	26		1
46	Ádám SIMON		30/3/90	M	27		1
17	Attila SIMON		23/9/88	A		(5)	
18	Norbert SIPOS		21/3/81	M	17	(6)	3
29	Marián SLUKA	SVK	22/7/79	M	4	(4)	
15	Péter TÓTH		25/6/77	M	28		6
14	Roland UGRAI		13/11/92	A	2	(2)	

ÚJPEST FC

Coach – Géza Mészöly

Founded – 1885

Stadium – Szusza Ferenc (13,500)

MAJOR HONOURS: Hungarian League – (20) 1930, 1931, 1933, 1935, 1939, 1945, 1946, 1947, 1960, 1969, 1970, 1971, 1972, 1973, 1974, 1975, 1978, 1979, 1990, 1998;

Hungarian Cup – (8) 1969, 1970, 1975, 1982, 1983, 1987, 1992, 2002.

2010				
1/8	Győr	h	0-0	
6/8	Kaposvár	a	1-0	*og (Grúz)*
14/8	Siófok	a	1-1	*Tajthy*
21/8	Vasas	h	2-2	*Rajczi, Tisza*
27/8	MTK	a	0-1	
11/9	Ferencváros	h	6-0	*Simon, Tisza 2, Mitrović, Rajczi 2*
19/9	Debrecen	a	1-1	*Simek*

4/9	Szolnok	h	1-0	*Balogh*
10	ZTE	a	1-2	*Rajczi (p)*
5/10	Haladás	h	3-1	*Tisza, Rajczi, Barczi*
3/10	Pápa	a	1-3	*Tisza*
1/10	Paks	h	2-3	*Tisza, Böőr*
11	Kecskemét	a	3-4	*Böőr, Rajczi (p), Barczi*
3/11	Honvéd	h	3-1	*og (Hajdu), Böőr, Rajczi (p)*
1/11	Videoton	a	0-1	
3/11	Győr	a	1-2	*Simon*
011				
6/2	Kaposvár	h	3-2	*Rubus, Lázár 2*
3	Siófok	h	1-1	*Lázár*
3/3	Vasas	a	0-1	
0/3	MTK	h	2-1	*Ahjupera, Balajti*
/4	Ferencváros	a	0-1	
0/4	Debrecen	h	2-2	*Ahjupera 2*
5/4	Szolnok	a	0-1	
2/4	ZTE	h	4-2	*Ahjupera 2, Lázár, Balogh*
6/4	Haladás	a	2-0	*Lázár, Balajti*
0/4	Pápa	h	2-1	*Lázár, Ahjupera*
/5	Paks	a	1-2	*Lázár*
1/5	Kecskemét	h	2-1	*Takács (p), Lázár (p)*
4/5	Honvéd	a	4-1	*Ahjupera, Balogh, Balajti, Rajczi*
2/5	Videoton	h	1-0	*Ahjupera*

lo	Name	Nat	DoB	Pos	Aps	(s)	Gls
2	Jarmo AHJUPERA	EST	13/4/84	A	15		8
	Szabolcs BALAJCZA		14/7/79	G	29		
1	Ádám BALAJTI		7/3/91	A	8	(6)	3
9	Balázs BALOGH		11/6/90	M	12	(4)	3
20	Balázs BANAI		9/12/92	D		(1)	
31	Dávid BARCZI		1/2/89	M	1	(8)	2
17	István BOGNÁR		6/5/91	M		(1)	
13	Zoltán BÖŐR		14/8/78	M	12	(9)	3
25	Gábor DVORSCHÁK		14/9/89	D	2	(1)	
22	Tamás EGERSZEGI		2/8/91	M	17	(3)	
36	Tamás HORVÁTH		18/6/87	G	1		
6	JHONNES Marques de Souza	BRA	22/4/84	D	1		
15	Zoltán KISS		12/7/86	D	6	(7)	
27	Dániel KOVÁCS		16/6/90	M	2	(1)	
16	Bence LÁZÁR		21/3/91	A	10	(3)	8
29	Róbert LITAUSZKI		15/3/90	D	3	(1)	
21	Mátyás MAGOS		14/3/92	M	1	(3)	
5	Marin MATOŠ	CRO	26/1/89	M	3	(8)	
14	Nikola MITROVIĆ	SRB	2/1/87	M	29		1
24	Zoltán POLLÁK		13/1/84	D	26		
8	Péter RAJCZI		3/4/81	A	16	(6)	8
3	Tamás RUBUS		13/7/89	D	9	(1)	1
11	Péter SIMEK		30/1/80	M	10	(8)	1
7	Krisztián SIMON		10/6/91	M	13	(2)	2
9	Illés SITKU		5/2/78	A	4	(6)	
2	Vilmos SZALAI		11/8/91	D		(1)	
26	Zsolt SZOKOL		16/3/90	D	28		
34	Tamás TAJTHY		29/8/91	M	13	(8)	1
4	Zoltán TAKÁCS		26/11/83	D	28		1
10	Tibor TISZA		10/11/84	A	15		6
18	Krisztián VERMES		7/7/85	D	16		

VASAS SC

Coach – Giovanni Dellacasa (ITA); (6/10/10) András Komjáti

Founded – 1911

Stadium – Illovszky Rudolf (18,000)

MAJOR HONOURS: Hungarian League – (6) 1957, 1961, 1962, 1965, 1966, 1977; Hungarian Cup – (4) 1955, 1973, 1981, 1986.

2010				
31/7	Honvéd	h	3-2	*Gáspár 2, Arnaut*
8/8	Videoton	a	0-3	
13/8	Győr	h	2-1	*Ferenczi (p), Benounes*
21/8	Újpest	a	2-2	*Lázok, Ferenczi*
27/8	Siófok	h	3-0	*Ferenczi 2, Katona*
10/9	Kaposvár	h	1-3	*Ferenczi (p)*
16/9	MTK	a	0-4	
26/9	Ferencváros	h	1-3	*Lázok*
3/10	Debrecen	a	1-3	*Ferenczi*
16/10	Szolnok	h	3-0	*og (Pető), Lázok 2*
22/10	ZTE	a	1-2	*Mileusnić*
30/10	Haladás	h	2-1	*Pantskhava, Németh N.*
6/11	Pápa	a	1-2	*Ferenczi*
13/11	Paks	h	2-3	*Ferenczi, Németh N.*
20/11	Kecskemét	a	1-3	*Németh N.*
25/11	Honvéd	a	0-0	
2011				
27/2	Videoton	h	0-0	
5/3	Győr	a	1-0	*Gáspár*
13/3	Újpest	h	1-0	*Rezes*
19/3	Siófok	a	0-0	
1/4	Kaposvár	a	1-0	*Ferenczi*
8/4	MTK	h	1-1	*Ferenczi (p)*
15/4	Ferencváros	a	1-0	*og (Maróti)*
23/4	Debrecen	h	1-5	*Németh N.*
27/4	Szolnok	a	1-0	*Ferenczi*
30/4	ZTE	h	2-0	*Lisztes, Ponczók*
7/5	Haladás	a	0-3	
10/5	Pápa	h	1-1	*Beliczky*
13/5	Paks	a	0-3	
20/5	Kecskemét	h	1-1	*Ponczók*

No	Name	Nat	DoB	Pos	Aps	(s)	Gls
4	Goran ARNAUT	SRB	27/8/79	D	14	(1)	1
14	Lazar ARSIĆ	SRB	24/9/91	M	11	(11)	
8	Szabolcs BAKOS		4/2/87	M	13	(1)	
27	Zsolt BALOG		10/11/78	D	21	(3)	
11	Gergő BELICZKY		3/7/90	A	4	(12)	1
59	Karim BENOUNES	FRA	9/2/84	M	7		1
25	Saša DOBRIĆ	SRB	21/1/82	M	2	(1)	
13	István FERENCZI		14/9/77	A	24		11
36	József GÁSPÁR	SVK	23/8/77	D	28		3
7	Ádám HREPKA		15/4/87	A	4	(3)	
15	Máté KATONA		16/2/90	M	19	(5)	1
6	Gábor KOVÁCS		4/9/87	D	21	(1)	
7	Dávid KULCSÁR		25/2/88	M	14		
11	János LÁZOK		4/10/84	M	25	(4)	4
28	Krisztián LISZTES		2/7/76	M	14		1
5	Helmi LOUSSAÏEF	TUN	12/2/86	M	2	(1)	
3	Dušan MILEUSNIĆ	SRB	10/4/84	D	20	(5)	1
31	Roland MUNDI		9/6/88	M	5	(4)	
29	Patrik NAGY		16/2/91	M	1		
33	Gábor NÉMETH		21/5/75	G	13		
21	Norbert NÉMETH		5/5/81	M	8	(6)	4
19	Vakhtang PANTSKHAVA	GEO	3/10/89	A	2	(9)	1
10	Čedomir PAVIĆEVIĆ	SRB	23/5/78	M	12	(4)	
22	Gábor POLÉNYI		2/7/91	D	6	(3)	
29	Csaba PONCZÓK		29/1/92	A	1	(6)	2
24	Ádám PRÉSINGER		26/1/89	D	4	(2)	
9	László REZES		12/8/87	M	12		1
25	Péter SZILÁGYI		26/1/88	A	6	(3)	
30	Zoltán VÉGH		7/4/71	G	17		

VIDEOTON FC

Coach – György Mezey

Founded – 1941

Stadium – Sóstói (15,000)

MAJOR HONOURS: Hungarian League – (1) 2011; Hungarian Cup – (1) 2006.

2010				
1/8	Siófok	a	1-1	*Vujović*
8/8	Vasas	h	3-0	*André Alves, Elek, Vujović*
14/8	MTK	a	3-0	*André Alves 2, Vasiljević*
21/8	Ferencváros	h	1-1	*Nikolić*
29/8	Debrecen	a	1-3	*Sándor*
12/9	Szolnok	h	3-1	*Lipták, Sándor, André Alves (p)*

24/9	Haladás	h	3-1	*André Alves 2, Gosztonyi*
28/9	ZTE	a	2-1	*Polonkai, André Alves*
1/10	Pápa	a	2-1	*Elek, André Alves*
17/10	Paks	h	2-1	*Gosztonyi, André Alves (p)*
23/10	Kecskemét	a	4-2	*André Alves 2, Polonkai, Nikolić*
29/10	Honvéd	h	0-2	
6/11	Kaposvár	a	4-1	*André Alves 2 (1p), Vasiljević, Elek*
12/11	Győr	a	1-1	*André Alves (p)*
21/11	Újpest	h	1-0	*Nikolić*
27/11	Siófok	h	2-0	*Sándor, Nikolić*
2011				
27/2	Vasas	a	0-0	
5/3	MTK	h	2-1	*André Alves (p), Elek*
12/3	Ferencváros	a	5-0	*André Alves, Vasiljević, Lencse, Andić, Polonkai*
18/3	Debrecen	h	2-1	*Lencse, André Alves*
2/4	Szolnok	a	1-1	*André Alves*
8/4	ZTE	h	3-0	*Vasiljević, André Alves 2 (1p)*
17/4	Haladás	a	0-2	
23/4	Pápa	h	4-0	*André Alves 2, Nikolić, Lencse*
26/4	Paks	a	0-1	
29/4	Kecskemét	h	2-2	*Nikolić, André Alves (p)*
8/5	Honvéd	a	2-2	*André Alves, Gosztonyi*
11/5	Kaposvár	h	3-1	*Nikolić, Polonkai, Szakály*
14/5	Győr	h	2-1	*Nikolić, Polonkai*
22/5	Újpest	a	0-1	

No	Name	Nat	DoB	Pos	Aps	(s)	Gls
2	Marko ANDIĆ	SRB	14/12/83	D	23		1
21	ANDRÉ ALVES dos Santos	BRA	15/10/83	A	28	(1)	24
22	Mladen BOŽOVIĆ	MNE	1/8/84	G	25		
10	Bojan DJORDJIĆ	SWE	6/2/82	M	1	(3)	
25	Ákos ELEK		21/7/88	M	25	(1)	4
14	Balázs FARKAS		15/10/79	M	12	(8)	
16	András GOSZTONYI		7/11/90	M	13	(10)	3
18	Ádám GYURCSÓ		6/3/91	A		(1)	
4	Sándor HIDVÉGI		9/4/83	D	9	(1)	
3	Gábor HORVÁTH		4/7/85	D	5		
28	Martin ÍZING		11/1/92	D	1		
27	Martin KAYONGO-MUTUMBA	SWE	15/6/85	M		(3)	
20	Pál LÁZÁR		11/3/88	D	27		
19	László LENCSE		2/7/88	A	9	(5)	3
5	Zoltán LIPTÁK		10/12/84	D	28		1
26	Damir MILANOVIĆ	CRO	19/7/82	M	1	(3)	
15	Dániel NAGY		22/11/84	A	16	(3)	
17	Nemanja NIKOLIĆ	SRB	31/12/87	A	9	(15)	8
8	Attila POLONKAI		12/6/79	M	18	(6)	5
11	György SÁNDOR		20/3/84	M	27	(2)	3
1	Zsolt SEBŐK		3/4/79	G	1		
7	Dénes SZAKÁLY		15/3/88	M	2	(13)	1
12	Tomáš TUJVEL	SVK	19/9/83	G	4		
6	Dušan VASILJEVIĆ	SRB	7/5/82	M	16	(11)	4
23	Tamás VASKÓ		20/2/84	D	25	(1)	
18	Goran VUJOVIĆ	MNE	3/5/87	A	5	(1)	2

ZALAEGERSZEGI TE

Coach – János Csank
Founded – 1920
Stadium – Városi (16,000)
MAJOR HONOURS: Hungarian League – (1) 2002.

2010				
31/7	Kaposvár	h	3-5	*Rudņevs 2, Balázs*
7/8	Haladás	a	0-0	
21/8	Paks	a	2-2	*Kamber, Rajcomar*
28/8	Kecskemét	h	2-1	*Rajcomar 2 (1p)*
1/9	Pápa	h	3-1	*Rajcomar, Pavićević 2*
11/9	Honvéd	a	0-1	
25/9	Győr	a	1-0	*Bogunović*
28/9	Videoton	h	1-2	*Varga*
2/10	Újpest	h	2-1	*Pavićević, Rajcomar*
16/10	Siófok	a	4-0	*Balázs, Simon, og (Mogyorósi), Kamber*
22/10	Vasas	h	2-1	*Rajcomar, Miljatovič*
30/10	MTK	a	4-3	*Balázs, Simon, Rajcomar, Panikvar*
6/11	Ferencváros	h	2-1	*Balázs, Delić A. (p)*
13/11	Debrecen	a	1-2	*Simon*
20/11	Szolnok	h	2-1	*Miljatovič, Kamber*
27/11	Kaposvár	a	1-2	*Simon*
2011				
26/2	Haladás	h	1-1	*Balázs*
5/3	Pápa	a	3-4	*Bogunović, Rajcomar, Balázs*
12/3	Paks	h	1-0	*Horváth*
18/3	Kecskemét	a	0-1	
2/4	Honvéd	h	2-1	*Turkovs, Kamber*
8/4	Videoton	a	0-3	
16/4	Győr	h	1-1	*og (Ganugrava)*
22/4	Újpest	a	2-4	*Rajcomar (p), Delić I.*
27/4	Siófok	h	2-1	*Turkovs, Simon (p)*
30/4	Vasas	a	0-2	
6/5	MTK	h	1-0	*Turkovs*
10/5	Ferencváros	a	4-4	*Szalai, Balázs, Turkovs, Kamber*
13/5	Debrecen	h	1-1	*og (Ramos)*
22/5	Szolnok	a	3-1	*Kamber, Balázs, og (Máté)*

No	Name	Nat	DoB	Pos	Aps	(s)	Gls
17	Zsolt BALÁZS		11/8/88	A	20	(3)	8
13	Zsolt BARNA		10/9/87	M	1	(5)	
3	Milan BOGUNOVIĆ	SRB	31/5/83	D	15	(2)	2
6	Stefan CEBARA	CAN	12/4/91	M		(2)	
20	Ahmet DELIĆ	SRB	17/2/86	A	7	(10)	1
10	Ivan DELIĆ	MNE	15/2/86	M	3	(8)	1
21	András HORVÁTH		6/8/80	M	17	(12)	1
7	Gyula ILLÉS		9/11/82	M	11	(3)	
19	Đorđe KAMBER	SRB	20/11/83	M	29		6
2	Gergely KOCSÁRDI		24/11/75	D	17	(5)	
28	Adrián KOCSIS		25/3/91	D		(1)	
18	Gergő KOVÁCS		30/10/89	D	16	(2)	
6	József MAGASFÖLDI		10/11/84	M	1	(1)	
16	Péter MÁTÉ		15/11/79	M	8	(1)	
22	Matej MILJATOVIČ	SVN	23/6/79	D	27	(1)	2
8	Leon PANIKVAR	SVN	28/1/83	D	24	(2)	1
5	Darko PAVIĆEVIĆ	MNE	24/6/85	A	8		3
25	Prince RAJCOMAR	NED	25/4/85	A	21	(6)	9
11	Artjoms RUDŅEVS	LVA	13/1/88	A	1		2
15	Attila SIMON		4/2/83	A	13	(8)	5
29	Gábor SIMONFALVI		20/7/87	M	5	(7)	
23	Gábor SIPOS		29/6/81	G	3	(1)	
14	Tamás SZALAI		10/1/80	M	26	(1)	1
27	Tamás TURCSIK		31/10/90	D	2	(4)	
11	Daniils TURKOVS	LVA	17/2/88	A	11	(2)	4
4	Róbert VARGA		25/11/86	D	17	(1)	1
26	Ádám VITTMAN		23/11/91	A		2	
1	Géza VLASZÁK		3/9/73	G	27		

TOP GOALSCORERS 2010/11

24	ANDRÉ ALVES (Videoton)
15	André SCHEMBRI (Ferencváros)
	Dániel BÖDE (Paks)
14	Adamo COULIBALY (Debrecen)
13	Lóránt OLÁH (Kaposvár)
	Attila TŐKÖLI (Kecskemét)
12	Patrik TISCHLER (MTK)
11	Goran MARIĆ (Pápa)
	Krisztián KENESEI (Haladás)
	István FERENCZI (Vasas)

PROMOTED CLUBS

DIÓSGYŐRI VTK
Coach – Miklós Benczés
Founded – 1910
Stadium – Borsodi (12,000)
MAJOR HONOURS: Hungarian Cup – (2) 1977, 1980.

PÉCSI MFC
Coach – László Kiss; (13/3/11) Ferenc Mészáros
Founded – 1973
Stadium – PMFC (10,000)
MAJOR HONOURS: Hungarian Cup – (1) 1990.

SECOND LEVEL FINAL TABLES 2010/11

EAST		Pld	W	D	L	F	A	Pts
1	Diósgyőri VTK	30	22	2	6	66	23	68
2	Mezőkövesdi SE	30	19	5	6	48	20	62
3	Nyíregyháza Spartacus FC	30	18	6	6	66	23	60
4	Dunakanyar-Vác FC	30	18	6	6	47	27	60
5	MTK Budapest II	30	16	7	7	48	34	55
6	Békéscsabai Előre SE	30	11	10	9	45	40	43
7	Vecsési FC	30	10	8	12	36	37	38
8	Debreceni VSC II	30	10	7	13	37	45	37
9	Újpest FC II	30	9	8	13	43	58	35
10	Rákospalotai EAC	30	9	6	15	30	38	33
11	Kazincbarcikai SC	30	8	8	14	37	60	31
12	Ceglédi VSE	30	8	6	16	46	61	30
13	Makói FC	30	8	6	16	30	54	30
14	Hajdúböszörményi TE	30	7	9	14	29	42	30
15	Orosházai SE	30	7	9	14	32	52	30
16	Böcs KSC	30	5	7	18	27	53	22

NB Kazincbarcikai SC – 1 pt deducted.

WEST		Pld	W	D	L	F	A	Pts
1	Pécsi MFC	30	21	3	6	55	17	66
2	Gyirmót SE	30	19	6	5	62	29	63
3	Videoton FC II	30	18	4	8	58	32	58
4	Bajai LSE	30	17	3	10	51	38	54
5	BKV Előre SC	30	13	9	8	38	37	48
6	FC Ajka	30	13	7	10	47	35	46
7	FC Tatabánya	30	13	7	10	47	39	46
8	Kozármislenyi SE	30	13	6	11	41	37	45
9	Győri ETO FC II	30	13	3	14	42	47	42
10	Szigetszentmiklósi TK	30	12	6	12	45	40	42
11	Budaörsi SC	30	11	8	11	42	41	41
12	Ferencvárosi TC II	30	10	4	16	36	35	34
13	Barcsi SC	30	9	6	15	35	61	33
14	Veszprém FC	30	10	0	20	33	54	30
15	Budapest Honvéd FC II	30	4	6	20	24	57	18
16	Kaposvölgye VSC	30	4	2	24	21	78	14

DOMESTIC CUP 2010/11

MAGYAR KUPA

THIRD ROUND

(21/9/10)
Győrszemere 1, Haladás 2
Tisza Volán 2, Szolnok 1

(22/9/10)
Balatonlelle 0, Paks 4
Báránd 1, Nagyecsed 2
Békéscsaba 1, Kecskemét 2
BKV Előre 1, Dunakanyar-Vác 0 *(aet)*
Bonyhád 0, Siófok 2
Budaörs 1, Honvéd 2
Cegléd 1, Makó 0
Dunaharaszti 2, MTK II 1
Eger 2, Mezőkövesd 0
Győr II 1, Pápa 2
Honvéd II 2, Tatabánya 1
Kakasd 1, Baja 7
Lipót 2, Veszprém 1 *(aet)*
Pécs 7, Kaposvölgye 1
Pétervására 0, Bőcs 3
Putnok 2, Felsőtárkány 1
REAC 3, SZTK 0
Szekszárd 1, Kaposvár 3
Technoroll 0, Barcs 1
Tiszabecs 4, Nyíregyháza 1
Tiszakanyár 2, DVSC-DEAC 1
Tököl 2, Vasas 4
Újbuda 1, Ferencváros 8
Videoton PFA 0, MTK 4

(5/10/10)
Sopron 0, Gyirmót 1

Byes – Újpest, Debrecen, Videoton, Győr, ZTE

FOURTH ROUND

(6/10/10)
Honvéd II 1, ZTE 2

(20/10/10)
Putnok 1, Honvéd 3 *(aet)*

(26/10/10)
Barcs 1, Győr 7
Cegléd 0, MTK 5
Dunaharaszti 1, Kaposvár 2 *(aet)*

(27/10/10)
BKV Előre 1, Siófok 2
Böcs 1, Újpest 5
Gyirmót 1, Pápa 1 *(aet; 2-3 on pens)*
Lipót 2, Haladás 5
Nagyecsed 1, Debrecen 1 *(aet; 8-9 on pens)*
Pécs 0, Paks 1
REAC 0, Ferencváros 5
Tisza Volán 1, Vasas 3
Tiszabecs 1, Eger 3
Tiszakanyár 0, Kecskemét 3

(2/11/10)
Baja 2, Videoton 4

FIFTH ROUND

(9/11/10 & 23/11/10)
Eger v Honvéd 0-3; 0-7 *(0-10)*

(9/11/10 & 1/3/11)
Pápa v Újpest 1-3; 1-3 *(2-6)*

(9/11/10 & 2/3/11)
MTK v Győr 0-0; 1-1 *(1-1; MTK on away goal)*
Videoton v Haladás 3-0; 3-1 *(6-1)*

(10/11/10 & 1/3/11)
Debrecen v Kecskemét 0-3; 1-3 *(1-6)*
Siófok v Ferencváros 3-1; 1-2 *(4-3)*

(10/11/10 & 2/3/11)
Vasas v ZTE 0-6; 0-3 *(0-9)*

(16/2/11 & 2/3/11)
Kaposvár v Paks 1-0, 1-0 *(2-0)*

QUARTER-FINALS

(8/3/11 & 15/3/11)
MTK 0, ZTE 0
ZTE 2 *(Delić A. 36, Turkovs 48)*, MTK 1 *(Könyves 43)*
(ZTE 2-1)

(8/3/11 & 16/3/11)
Újpest 2 *(Lázár 33, Ahjupera 60)*, Kaposvár 3 *(Grumić 21, 38, Balázs 64)*
Kaposvár 2 *(Zsók 20, Kulcsár 73)*, Újpest 2 *(Bőőr 62, Sitku 86)*
(Kaposvár 5-4)

(9/3/11 & 15/3/11)
Honvéd 1 *(Zelenka 22)*, Videoton 1 *(Nikolić 71)*
Videoton 4 *(Gosztonyi 3, Lencse 27, 80, Gyurcsó 90)*, Honvéd 0
(Videoton 5-1)

Kecskemét 5 *(Tököli 8, Vujović 10, 22, Savić 42, Foxi 49)*, Siófok 1 *(Márton 47)*
Siófok 1 *(Melczer 15)*, Kecskemét 1 *(Dosso 12)*
(Kecskemét 6-2)

SEMI-FINALS

(19/4/11 & 3/5/11)
Kecskemét 5 *(Foxi 7, 59, Tököli 18, Litsingi 29, 34)*, ZTE 1 *(Kamber 79)*
ZTE 0, Kecskemét 0
(Kecskemét 5-1)

(20/4/11 & 4/5/11)
Kaposvár 0, Videoton 1 *(Lipták 48)*
Videoton 4 *(Vasiljević 11, 56, Vaskó 17, Nikolić 90+2)*, Kaposvár 0
(Videoton 5-0)

FINAL

(17/5/11)
Puskás Ferenc stadium, Budapest
KECSKEMÉTI TE 3 *(Foxi 2, 14, 80)*
VIDEOTON FC 2 *(Čukić 47og, Nikolić 82)*
Referee – *Ványi*
KECSKEMÉT – *Rybánsky, Gyagya, Radanović, Balogh, Mohl, Bori, Ebala, Čukić (Bertus 90+1), Foxi (Savić 90+3), Litsingi, Tököli (Dosso 87).*
VIDEOTON – *Sebők, Lázár, Lipták, Vaskó, Elek, Sándor, Farkas (Szakály 60), Polonkai (Vasiljević 46), Gosztonyi (Lencse 70), Nikolić, André Alves.*

CLUB COMMUNICATION 2011/12

Budapest Honvéd FC
Puskás F. u. 1-3
HU-1194 Budapest

Tel +36 1 357 6738
Fax +36 1 357 6737
Web honvedfc.hu
Email office@bhfc.hu
Media Officer Zoltan Simon

Debreceni VSC
Oláh Gábor utca 5
HU-4032 Debrecen

Tel +36 52 535 408
Fax +36 52 340 817
Web dvsc.hu
Email dvscrt@dvsc.hu
Media Officer Zoltan Csubak

Diósgyőri VTK
Andrássy út 61.
HU-3533 Miskolc

Tel +36 46 530 440
Fax +36 46 530 440
Web dvtk.eu
Email info@dvtk.eu
Media Officer

Ferencvárosi TC
Üllői út 129
HU-1091 Budapest

Tel +36 1 215 3856
Fax +36 1 215 3698
Web ftc.hu
Email ftcrt@ftc.hu
Media Officer Andrea Féderer

Győri ETO FC
Nagysándor József u. 31
HU-9027 Győr

Tel +36 96 529 005
Fax +36 96 529 008
Web eto.hu
Email titkarsag@eto.hu
Media Officer Henriett Kővári

Kaposvári Rákóczi FC
Pécsi u.4
HU-7400 Kaposvár

Tel +36 82 319 650
Fax +36 82 319 650
Web rakoczifc.hu
Email k.rakoczfc@gmail.com
Media Officer Ferenc Orosz

Kecskeméti TE
Csabai Géza krt.1/a
HU-6000 Kecskemét

Tel +36 76 415 812
Fax +36 76 415 812
Web kecskemetite.hu
Email irodavezeto@kecskemetite.hu
Media Officer Angéla Forczek

Lombard-Pápa TFC
2 Str. Varkert
HU-8500 Pápa

Tel +36 89 512 020
Fax +36 89 512 021
Web lombardfcpapa.hu
Email info@lombardpapafc.hu
Media Officer Imre Matyas

Paksi SE
Fehérvári út 29.
HU-7030 Paks

Tel +36 75 510 618
Fax +36 75 510 619
Web paksise.hu
Email pse@enternet.hu
Media Officer Zoltán Zomborka

Pécsi MFC
Stadion u. 2
HU-7633 Pécs

Tel +36 72 552 880
Fax +36 72 552 881
Web pmfc.hu
Email pmfc@pmfc.hu
Media Officer Attila Brassói

BFC Siófok
Révész G. u. 11.
HU-8600 Siófok

Tel +36 84 311 536
Fax +36 84 311 536
Web bfc-siofok.hu
Email info@bfc-siofok.hu
Media Officer

Szombathelyi Haladás
Rohonci út 3
HU-9700 Szombathely

Tel +36 94 510 200
Fax +36 94 510 200
Web haladas.hu
Email titkarsag@haladas.hu
Media Officer Adam Starcsevics

Újpest FC
Megyeri út 13
HU-1044 Budapest

Tel +36 1 231 0088
Fax +36 1 213 0089
Web ujpestfc.hu
Email ujpestfc@ujpestfc.hu
Media Officer Károly Nemes

Vasas SC
Fáy utca 58.
HU-1139 Budapest XIII

Tel +36 1 4500 162
Fax +36 1 9991 094
Web vasassc.hu
Email info@fcvasas.com
Media Officer Gábor Sinkovits

Videoton FC
Csíkvári utca 10.
HU-8000 Székesfehérvár

Tel +36 22 379 493
Fax +36 22 500 009
Web vidi.hu
Email titkarsag@videotonfc.hu
Media Officer Ferenc Maurer

Zalaegerszegi TE
Október 6. Tér 16
HU-8900 Zalaegerszeg

Tel +36 92 596 303
Fax +36 92 314 093
Web ztefc.hu
Email ztefc@zelkanet.hu
Media Officer Krisztian Toth

ICELAND

Islande I Island

Knattspyrnusamband Íslands (KSÍ)

COMMUNICATION

Address Laugardal
IS-104 Reykjavík

Tel +354 5 102 900

Fax +354 5 6897 93

E-mail ksi@ksi.is

Website ksi.is

President Geir Thorsteinsson

General Secretary Thórir Hákonarson

Media Officer Ómar Smárason

Year of Formation 1947

National Stadium Laugardalsvöllur, Reykjavik (15,427)

DOMESTIC COMPETITION SUMMARY 2010

ÚRVALSDEILD FINAL TABLE

			Home					Away					Total						
		Pld	W	D	L	F	A	W	D	L	F	A	W	D	L	F	A	Pts	Comp
1	Breidablik	22	6	2	3	22	10	7	3	1	25	13	13	5	4	47	23	44	UCL
2	FH Hafnarfjördur	22	7	2	2	28	19	6	3	2	20	12	13	5	4	48	31	44	UEL
3	ÍBV Vestmannaeyjar	22	7	1	3	19	14	6	2	3	17	13	13	3	6	36	27	42	UEL
4	KR Reykjavík	22	5	2	4	15	12	6	3	2	30	19	11	5	6	45	31	38	UEL
5	Fram Reykjavík	22	6	2	3	19	14	3	3	5	16	21	9	5	8	35	35	32	
6	Keflavík	22	4	5	2	17	13	4	1	6	13	19	8	6	8	30	32	30	
7	Valur Reykjavík	22	3	4	4	19	20	4	3	4	15	21	7	7	8	34	41	28	
8	Stjarnan	22	4	4	3	21	17	2	3	6	18	25	6	7	9	39	42	25	
9	Fylkir	22	4	2	5	22	20	3	1	7	14	22	7	3	12	36	42	24	
10	Grindavík	22	2	4	5	17	18	3	2	6	11	21	5	6	11	28	39	21	
11	Haukar	22	3	2	6	16	25	1	6	4	13	20	4	8	10	29	45	20	*Relegated*
12	Selfoss	22	3	1	7	18	24	2	1	8	14	27	5	2	15	32	51	17	*Relegated*

Top Scorer Alfred Finnbogason (Breidablik), Atli Vidar Björnsson (FH) & Gilles Mbang Ondo (Grindavik), 14 goals

Promoted Clubs Víkingur Reykjavík
Thór Akureyri

Cup Final FH Hafnarfjördur 4, KR Reykjavík 0

Underdogs Breidablik upset the odds

At the outset of the 2010 Úrvalsdeild season the general feeling was that the title race would be dominated by major rivals FH Hafnarfjördur and KR Reykjavík. The reality, however, would prove to be quite different. In an exraordinarily open and entertaining contest no fewer than seven of the 12 participating teams occupied top spot in the table. Remarkably, neither FH nor KR were among them.

The co-favourites both endured difficult starts, and the other clubs took advantage, creating a championship that was never short of excitement and unpredictability. Goals and upsets abounded, and there was uncertainty as to the outcome right through to the final whistle of the final game.

Nip and tuck

In the middle of the campaign Breidablik, the 2009 Icelandic Cup winners, moved to the top of the table for the first time in 28 years. ÍBV Vestmannaeyjar, relegation strugglers the year before, soon dislodged them, and thereafter it became nip and tuck between the two clubs at the top. ÍBV held on to first place for four rounds, but in round 19 (out of 22) Breidablik returned to the driving seat, with their sights fixed firmly on a first ever Úrvalsdeild title.

It was only in the latter stages of competition that FH and KR roused themselves from their slumber. Both teams came storming back into contention and threatened to overtake the two unheralded front-runners. But Breidablik's youngsters, led by coach Ólafur H. Kristjánsson, were made of stern stuff and they eliminated KR from the race with a brilliant 3-1 away win in round 20.

As the season entered its final act, in late September, there were three possible champions - Breidablik, ÍBV and FH. The permutations were many and varied, but at the outset the tasks for each club seemed straightforward - Breidablik had to win away to Stjarnan; ÍBV had to beat Keflavík away and hope for a slip-up by Breidablik; and FH had to beat Fram Reykjavík away and hope that Breidablik lost and ÍBV failed to win. In the event, a 0-0 draw proved to be enough for Breidablik as ÍBV, missing suspended talisman Tryggvi Gudmundsson, lost 4-1 at Keflavík, their penalty-taking goalkeeper Albert Sæversson missing a spot-kick when they were 2-1 down close to the end . FH, alone, kept their side of the bargain, beating Fram 3-0 to record their sixth successive victory, but that was not enough for the club to retain their title. Although they had moved level on points with Breidablik, their goal difference was vastly inferior.

Anniversary triumph

Breidablik's triumph was a remarkable story, and it came in the year of their 60th anniversary. The club

Albert Finnbogason spearheaded Breidablik to their first league title

National Team

Top Five All-time Caps – Rúnar Kristinsson (104); Hermann Hreidarsson (88); Gudni Bergsson (80); Brynjar Björn Gunnarsson & Birkir Kristinsson (74)

Top Five All-time Goals – Eidur Smári Gudjohnsen (24); Ríkhardur Jónsson (17); Ríkhardur Dadason & Arnór Gudjohnsen (14); Thórdur Gudjónsson (13)

om Kopavogur had won nothing until 2009 when they efeated Fram on penalties in the Cup final; now, a ear later, they were champions. What made their udden surge to prominence even more remarkable as that after the 2008 season they lost the bulk of eir team, including six foreigners, as a result of the celandic financial crisis. Their places were filled by oung homegrown players, many of them Icelandic outh internationals, and coach Kristjánsson managed mould them into an exciting, free-scoring team that ould challenge the best the country had to offer.

lfred Finnbogason was the player who made the ifference for Breidablik in 2010. The 21-year-old orward was directly involved in 29 of the team's 47 eague goals, scoring 14 himself, which enabled him to share the Úrvalsdeild Golden Boot with Atli Vidar Björnsson of FH and Grindavík's Gabonese striker Gilles Mbang Ondo. Finnbogason received another accolade when he was honoured as Iceland's player of the year. Shortly after the season he made the nevitable move to the European mainland, joining Belgian outfit KSC Lokeren OV.

FH had not had a trophy-less season since 2003, and although they fell just short of collecting their sixth league title in seven years, they did manage to prolong that run by winning the Icelandic Cup. Having eliminated Breidablik on penalties in an early round, Heimir Gudjónsson's team cruised into the final, in mid-August, and demolished KR 4-0 at the Laugardalsvöllur. The outcome was effectively settled by two first-half penalties from Matthías Vilhjálmsson before top-scorer Björnsson and Atli Gudnason got in on the act with two late goals. Although heavily defeated on that occasion, KR were a team transformed in the second half of the season following the arrival of new coach Rúnar Kristinsson, Iceland's most-capped international, who guided the team to eight victories in their last 11 league matches.

In Europe, it was KR again who did Iceland proud, beating Glentoran FC of Northern-Ireland soundly, 5-2 on aggregate, in the first qualifying round of the UEFA Europe League before bowing out to FC Karpaty Lviv of Ukraine. Breidablik made a decent fist of their first European adventure but lost two even matches against Scotland's Motherwell FC 1-0. FC BATE Borisov proved too strong for FH, and Fylkir lost 6-1 on aggegate to another Belarusian team, FC Torpedo Zhodino.

Under-21 success

On the international front, it was Iceland's Under-21 team that grabbed the headlines. Having eliminated European champions Germany in the group stage, beating them 4-1 on an unforgettable evening in Hafnarfjordur, they then overcame Scotland 2-1 in both legs of the play-offs to qualify for the UEFA European U21 Championship for the first time. Sadly, despite high expectations, they lost their first two matches in Denmark – to Belarus and Switzerland - before recovering to defeat the hosts 3-1 and narrowly miss out on the semi-finals.

Several members of Eyjólfur Sverrisson's team were also called up to serve the senior national side at the start of the UEFA EURO 2012 qualifying campaign. With seven players from the U21s, Iceland were unlucky to lose 2-1 at home to Norway and 1-0 to Denmark in Copenhagen. But when Iceland hosted Portugal the following month, the Icelandic FA decided that the U21 team should keep all their players for the play-off matches against Scotland, forcing senior head coach Ólafur Jóhannesson to field a weakened side, which went down 3-1. Iceland's first point would not come until the spring of 2011 when they held Cyprus to a goalless draw in Nicosia, but the international season closed disappointingly with a third home defeat, 2-0 to Denmark.

NATIONAL TEAM RESULTS 2010/11

11/8/10	Liechtenstein	H	Reykjavik	1-1	*Gíslason (20)*
3/9/10	Norway (ECQ)	H	Reykjavik	1-2	*Helguson (38)*
7/9/10	Denmark (ECQ)	A	Copenhagen	0-1	
12/10/10	Portugal (ECQ)	H	Reykjavik	1-3	*Helguson (17)*
17/11/10	Israel	A	Tel-Aviv	2-3	*Finnbogason (79), Sigthórsson (85)*
26/3/11	Cyprus (ECQ)	A	Nicosia	0-0	
4/6/11	Denmark (ECQ)	H	Reykjavik	0-2	

ICELAND

NATIONAL TEAM APPEARANCES 2010/11

Coach – Ólafur JÓHANNESSON	**30/6/57**		Lie	NOR	DEN	POR	Isr	CYP	DEN	Caps	Goals
Árni Gautur ARASON	7/5/75	Odd Grenland (NOR)	G							71	-
Grétar Rafn STEINSSON	9/1/82	Bolton (ENG)	D74	D76		D				41	4
Kristján Örn SIGURDSSON	7/10/80	Hønefoss (NOR)	D	D	D	D	D57	D	D	51	4
Sölvi Geir OTTESEN	18/2/84	København (DEN)	D49	D	D					14	-
Indridi SIGURDSSON	12/10/81	Viking (NOR)	D	D	D	D85	D76	D		59	2
Rúrik GÍSLASON	25/2/88	OB (DEN)	M	s87	M			M63		10	1
Ólafur Ingi SKÚLASON	1/4/83	SønderjyskE (DEN)	M77			M	s46		M66	16	1
Eidur Smári GUDJOHNSEN	15/9/78	Monaco (FRA) /Stoke (ENG) /Fulham (ENG)	M65			M			M	64	24
Aron Einar GUNNARSSON	22/4/89	Coventry (ENG)	M65	M	M		M	M	M	23	-
Arnór SMÁRASON	7/9/88	Esbjerg (DEN)	M84					s59		10	1
Heidar HELGUSON	22/8/77	QPR (ENG)	A	A	A77	A		A	A77	54	12
Ragnar SIGURDSSON	19/6/86	Göteborg (SWE)	s49			D				16	-
Veigar Páll GUNNARSSON	21/3/80	Stabæk (NOR)	s65	M76		s85				33	6
Gudmundur KRISTJÁNSSON	1/3/89	Breidablik	s65							4	-
Arnór Sveinn ADALSTEINSSON	26/1/86	Breidablik	s74	s76		s85	s76			9	-
Matthías VILHJÁLMSSON	30/1/87	FH	s77				s82			6	1
Ólafur Páll SNORRASON	22/4/82	FH	s84							1	-
Gunnleifur GUNNLEIFSSON	14/7/75	FH		G	G	G	G71			21	-
Gylfi Thór SIGURDSSON	8/9/89	Hoffenheim (GER)		M	M			M91	A	5	-
Eggert Gunnthór JÓNSSON	18/8/88	Hearts (SCO)		M	M		M	M		9	-
Jóhann Berg GUDMUNDSSON	27/10/90	AZ (NED)		M87	M92			M59	s77	10	-
Birkir BJARNASON	27/5/88	Viking (NOR)		s76	s92		M82	s91		5	-
Birkir Már SÆVARSSON	11/11/84	Brann (NOR)			D	M85	D	D	D	23	-
Kolbeinn SIGTHÓRSSON	14/3/90	AZ (NED)			s77		A		A	6	3
Helgi Valur DANÍELSSON	13/7/81	AIK (SWE)				M				16	-
Theodór Elmar BJARNASON	4/3/87	Göteborg (SWE)				M68				10	-
Gunnar Heidar THORVALDSSON	1/4/82	Fredrikstad (NOR)				s68				22	5
Hermann HREIDARSSON	11/7/74	Portsmouth (ENG)					D46	D	D	88	5
Alfred FINNBOGASON	1/2/89	Breidablik /Lokeren (BEL)					M	s63	s66	4	1
Steinthór Freyr THORSTEINSSON	29/7/85	Örgryte (SWE)					M			5	-
Jón Gudni FJÓLUSON	10/4/89	Fram					s57			4	-
Stefán Logi MAGNÚSSON	5/9/80	Lillestrøm (NOR)					s71	G	G	6	-
Bjarni Ólafur EIRÍKSSON	28/3/82	Stabæk (NOR)							D	17	-

CLUB-BY-CLUB

BREIDABLIK
Coach – Ólafur H. Kristjánsson
Founded – 1950
Stadium – Kópavogsvöllur (5,039)
MAJOR HONOURS: Icelandic League – (1) 2010; Icelandic Cup – (1) 2009.

)10

1/5	Keflavík	h	0-1	
6/5	Fram	h	2-2	*Pétursson, Finnbogason*
0/5	Valur	a	2-0	*Steindórsson, Finnbogason*
4/5	FH	h	2-0	*Steindórsson 2*
0/5	ÍBV	a	1-1	*Baldvinsson*
/6	Haukar	a	4-2	*Kristjánsson, Ársælsson, Yeoman, og (Jóhannsson T.)*
4/6	Grindavík	h	2-3	*Adalsteinsson, Finnbogason*
0/6	Fylkir	a	4-2	*Finnbogason 2, Sigurgeirsson, Steindórsson*
7/6	KR	h	2-1	*Sigurgeirsson, Pétursson*
/7	Selfoss	a	3-1	*Steindórsson 2, Pétursson*
/7	Stjarnan	h	4-0	*Finnbogason 3 (2p), Baldvinsson*
8/7	Keflavík	a	2-0	*Steindórsson, Finnbogason*
5/7	Fram	a	1-3	*Kristjánsson*
/8	Valur	h	5-0	*Finnbogason 2, Elísabetarson, Steindórsson, Kristjánsson*
3/8	FH	a	1-1	*Elísabetarson*
16/8	ÍBV	h	1-1	*Finnbogason*
23/8	Haukar	h	0-2	
29/8	Grindavík	a	4-2	*Steindórsson 2, Kristjánsson, Yeoman*
12/9	Fylkir	h	1-0	*Steindórsson*
16/9	KR	a	3-1	*Baldvinsson, Steindórsson, Finnbogason*
19/9	Selfoss	h	3-0	*Kristjánsson, Helgason, Finnbogason*
25/9	Stjarnan	a	0-0	

No	Name	Nat	DoB	Pos	Aps	(s)	Gls
22	Arnór ADALSTEINSSON		26/1/86	D	18	(1)	1
6	Kári ÁRSÆLSSON		2/7/85	D	21		1
9	Haukur BALDVINSSON		5/5/90	A	15	(5)	3
17	Jökull Ingason ELÍSABETARSON		26/4/84	M	21		2
10	Alfred FINNBOGASON		1/2/89	A	21		14
27	Tómas Óli GARDARSSON		25/10/93	M		(2)	
2	Árni Kristinn GUNNARSSON		10/4/80	D	5	(7)	
5	Elfar Freyr HELGASON		27/7/89	D	19		1
19	Kristinn JÓNSSON		4/8/90	D	20		
1	Ingvar Thór KALE		8/12/83	G	22		
16	Gudmundur KRISTJÁNSSON		1/3/89	M	19	(2)	5
3	Finnur Orri MARGEIRSSON		8/3/91	M	18	(4)	
24	Gudmundur PÉTURSSON		24/11/86	A	10	(9)	3
26	Elvar Páll SIGURDSSON		30/7/91	A		(2)	
11	Olgeir SIGURGEIRSSON		22/10/82	M	9	(11)	2
15	Rannver SIGURJÓNSSON		11/8/84	A		(3)	
7	Kristinn STEINDÓRSSON		29/4/90	A	22		12
30	Andri Rafn YEOMAN		18/4/92	A	2	(15)	2

FH HAFNARFJÖRDUR
Coach – Heimir Gudjónsson
Founded – 1929
Stadium – Kaplakriki (6,390)
MAJOR HONOURS: Icelandic League – (5) 2004, 2005, 2006, 2008, 2009; Icelandic Cup – (2) 2007, 2010.

2010

10/5	Valur	a	2-2	*Björnsson, Gudmundsson (p)*
16/5	Haukar	a	1-0	*Sverrisson*
20/5	ÍBV	h	2-3	*Motland, Ásgeirsson*
24/5	Breidablik	a	0-2	
31/5	Grindavík	h	2-1	*Vilhjálmsson, Björnsson*
7/6	Fylkir	a	2-2	*Björnsson 2*
14/6	KR	h	3-2	*Vilhjálmsson, Nielsen (p), Valgardsson*
21/6	Selfoss	a	2-0	*Snorrason, Vilhjálmsson*
27/6	Stjarnan	h	1-3	*Snorrason*
4/7	Keflavík	a	1-1	*Snorrason*
8/7	Fram	h	4-1	*Gudnason, Vidarsson, Sverrisson, Björnsson*
18/7	Valur	h	1-1	*Motland*
25/7	Haukar	h	3-1	*Björnsson 2, Snorrason*
5/8	ÍBV	a	3-1	*Bjarnason, Gudmundsson, og (Ásgeirsson)*
8/8	Breidablik	h	1-1	*Motland*
19/8	Grindavík	a	1-3	*Björnsson*
22/8	Fylkir	h	4-2	*Björnsson 2, Bjarnason, Gudmundsson*
30/8	KR	a	1-0	*Björnsson*
12/9	Selfoss	h	2-1	*Sverrisson, Vilhjálmsson (p)*
16/9	Stjarnan	a	4-1	*Sverrisson, Vilhjálmsson, Snorrason, Gudnason*
19/9	Keflavík	h	5-3	*Björnsson 2, Sverrisson 2, Vilhjálmsson (p)*
25/9	Fram	a	3-0	*Kristjánsson 2, Björnsson*

No	Name	Nat	DoB	Pos	Aps	(s)	Gls
6	Ásgeir Gunnar ÁSGEIRSSON		3/6/80	M	5	(4)	1
5	Freyr BJARNASON		30/6/77	D	13	(2)	2
17	Atli Vidar BJÖRNSSON		4/1/80	A	22		14
2	Gunnar Már GUDMUNDSSON		15/12/83	M	5	(7)	3
11	Atli GUDNASON		28/9/84	A	19	(1)	2
13	Bjarki GUNNLAUGSSON		6/3/73	M	5	(1)	
1	Gunnleifur GUNNLEIFSSON		14/7/75	G	22		
19	Hákon Atli HALLFREDSSON		30/3/90	M	8	(3)	
25	Einar Karl INGVARSSON		8/10/93	M		(2)	
16	Jón Ragnar JÓNSSON		30/10/85	D		(3)	
3	Gunnar KRISTJÁNSSON		2/3/87	A		(8)	2
8	Torger MOTLAND	NOR	26/3/85	A	6	(8)	3
28	Jacob NEESTRUP	DEN	8/3/88	M	2	(4)	
4	Tommy NIELSEN	DEN	11/6/72	D	19		1
24	Helgi Valur PÁLSSON		28/11/92	D		(1)	
12	Gunnar SIGURDSSON		14/8/75	G		(1)	
22	Ólafur Páll SNORRASON		22/4/82	A	19	(1)	5
9	Björn Daníel SVERRISSON		29/5/90	M	19		6
14	Gudmundur SÆVARSSON		31/7/78	D	16		
21	Hafthór THRASTARSON		14/2/90	D	6	(2)	
27	Hjörtur Logi VALGARDSSON		27/9/88	D	18	(3)	1
7	Pétur VIDARSSON		25/11/87	D	19		1
10	Matthías VILHJÁLMSSON		30/1/87	M	19	(2)	6

FRAM REYKJAVÍK
Coach – Thorvaldur Örlygsson
Founded – 1908
Stadium – Laugardalsvöllur (15,427)
MAJOR HONOURS: Icelandic League – (18) 1913, 1914, 1915, 1916, 1917, 1918, 1921, 1922, 1923, 1925, 1939, 1946, 1947, 1962, 1972, 1986, 1988, 1990; Icelandic Cup – (7) 1970, 1973, 1979, 1980, 1985, 1987, 1989.

2010

11/5	ÍBV	h	2-0	*Leifsson, Björnsson*
16/5	Breidablik	a	2-2	*Magnússon G., Björnsson*
20/5	Grindavík	h	2-0	*Björnsson, Magnússon H.A.*
24/5	Fylkir	a	2-2	*Thórarinsson H. 2*
6/6	Selfoss	a	2-1	*Tillen J., Thórarinsson H.*
10/6	KR	h	2-3	*Björnsson, Fjóluson*
14/6	Stjarnan	h	2-1	*Björnsson, Leifsson*

21/6	Keflavík	a	1-1	*Hauksson*
27/6	Haukar	h	0-0	
5/7	Valur	h	2-2	*Fjóluson, Tillen S.*
8/7	FH	a	1-4	*Ormarsson*
17/7	ÍBV	a	0-1	
25/7	Breidablik	h	3-1	*Thórarinsson H., Ormarsson, Fjóluson*
5/8	Grindavík	a	0-3	
8/8	Fylkir	h	1-2	*Fjóluson (p)*
19/8	KR	a	1-2	*Ormarsson*
23/8	Selfoss	h	3-1	*Ormarsson 3*
29/8	Stjarnan	a	3-2	*Björnsson 2, Fjóluson*
13/9	Keflavík	h	2-1	*Jónsson, Ormarsson*
16/9	Haukar	a	1-2	*Björnsson*
19/9	Valur	a	3-1	*Tillen J., Ormarsson, Gudmundsson*
25/9	FH	h	0-3	

No	Name	Nat	DoB	Pos	Aps	(s)	Gls
22	Ívar BJÖRNSSON		12/1/85	A	17	(2)	8
8	Jón Gunnar EYSTEINSSON		3/7/86	M	21		
23	Jón Gudni FJÓLUSON		10/4/89	D	17		5
7	Dadi GUDMUNDSSON		11/2/81	D	19	(2)	1
1	Hannes Thór HALLDÓRSSON		27/4/84	G	22		
5	Kristinn Ingi HALLDÓRSSON		8/4/89	M	2	(7)	
4	Kristján HAUKSSON		3/2/86	D	19		1
6	Halldór Hermann JÓNSSON		1/10/84	M	21		1
24	Tómas LEIFSSON		1/5/85	A	17	(3)	2
21	Gudmundur MAGNÚSSON		10/6/91	A	1	(14)	1
14	Hlynur Atli MAGNÚSSON		11/9/90	D	7	(8)	1
17	Hördur Björgvin MAGNÚSSON		11/2/93	D	1	(2)	
11	Almarr ORMARSSON		25/2/88	M	21	(1)	8
26	Jón Orri ÓLAFSSON		11/3/85	D	11	(7)	
20	Alexander THÓRARINSSON		14/12/88	A	1	(3)	
10	Hjálmar THÓRARINSSON		16/2/86	A	15	(2)	4
29	Joe TILLEN	ENG	15/12/86	M	11	(9)	2
9	Sam TILLEN	ENG	16/4/85	D	19		1

FYLKIR

Coach – Ólafur Thórdarson

Founded – 1967

Stadium – Fylkisvöllur (2,832)

MAJOR HONOURS: Icelandic Cup – (2) 2001, 2002.

2010

11/5	Selfoss	a	3-1	*Stígsson, Faye, Thórhallsson*
16/5	Stjarnan	h	3-1	*Óskarsson, Ingason, Thórhallsson*
20/5	Keflavík	a	1-2	*Breiddal*
24/5	Fram	h	2-2	*Ingason (p), Pétursson*
31/5	Valur	a	2-5	*Ingason, Faye*
7/6	FH	h	2-2	*Ingason 2 (1p)*
13/6	ÍBV	a	0-1	
20/6	Breidablik	h	2-4	*Ingason, Óskarsson*
27/6	Grindavík	a	2-1	*Thórhallsson 2*
5/7	Haukar	a	1-1	*Ingason*
18/7	Selfoss	h	5-2	*Thórhallsson 2, Faye, Jóhannesson, Arnthórsson*
25/7	Stjarnan	a	1-2	*Ásgeirsson*
5/8	Keflavík	h	1-2	*Ingason (p)*
8/8	Fram	a	2-1	*Faye, Óskarsson*
16/8	Valur	h	0-1	
22/8	FH	a	2-4	*Jóhannesson, Thórhallsson*
26/8	KR	h	1-4	*Thórhallsson*
29/8	ÍBV	h	1-2	*Thórhallsson (p)*
12/9	Breidablik	a	0-1	
16/9	Grindavík	h	2-0	*Ásbjörnsson, Óskarsson*
19/9	Haukar	h	3-0	*Jóhannesson 2, Óskarsson*
25/9	KR	a	0-3	

No	Name	Nat	DoB	Pos	Aps	(s)	Gls
17	Ásgeir Örn ARNTHÓRSSON		2/5/90	M	10	(9)	1
30	Davíð Thór ÁSBJÖRNSSON		24/2/92	D	3	(5)	1
3	Ásgeir Börkur ÁSGEIRSSON		16/4/87	M	17	(1)	1
15	Baldur BETT		12/4/80	M		(2)	
11	Kjartan Ágúst BREIDDAL		20/3/86	M	14	(3)	1
10	Pape Mamadou FAYE		6/3/91	A	10	(8)	4
4	Valur Fannar GÍSLASON		8/9/77	M	20	(1)	
6	Thórir HANNESSON		8/10/86	D	17	(3)	
22	Andri Már HERMANNSSON		2/3/93	M	2	(3)	
14	Albert Brynjar INGASON		16/1/86	M	18	(1)	8
8	Andrés Már JÓHANNESSON		21/12/88	D	20		4
26	Andri Thór JÓNSSON		24/2/91	D	7		
7	Ingimundur Níels ÓSKARSSON		4/2/86	A	19	(1)	5
23	Einar PÉTURSSON		8/2/86	D	9		1
5	Ólafur Ingi STÍGSSON		16/12/75	M	8	(6)	1
20	Ragnar Bragi SVEINSSON		18/12/94	A		(1)	
18	Fjalar THORGEIRSSON		18/1/77	G	22		
16	Tómas THORSTEINSSON		8/12/88	D	16	(2)	
9	Jóhann THÓRHALLSSON		7/1/80	A	11	(9)	9
24	Fridrik Ingi THRÁINSSON		16/1/90	M		(5)	
2	Kristján VALDIMARSSON		12/5/84	D	19	(2)	

GRINDAVÍK

Coach – Lúkas Kostic; (29/5/10) Milan Stefán Jankovic; (10/6/10) Ólafur Örn Bjarnason

Founded – 1935

Stadium – Grindavíkurvöllur (1,750)

2010

11/5	Stjarnan	a	0-4	
17/5	Keflavík	h	0-1	
20/5	Fram	a	0-2	
25/5	Valur	h	1-2	*Ondo G.*
31/5	FH	a	1-2	*Hjartarson*
6/6	ÍBV	h	1-2	*Fridriksson*
14/6	Breidablik	a	3-2	*Ondo G. 2, Gudmundsson*
21/6	Haukar	a	3-2	*Ondo G. 2, Hjaltalín*
27/6	Fylkir	h	1-2	*Hjartarson*
4/7	KR	a	0-1	
8/7	Selfoss	h	1-1	*Hjartarson*
19/7	Stjarnan	h	1-1	*Manevski*
26/7	Keflavík	a	1-1	*Ondo G.*
5/8	Fram	h	3-0	*Ondo G. 2, Vilhjálmsson*
8/8	Valur	a	0-0	
19/8	FH	h	3-1	*Ondo G. 2, Bjarnason Ó.B.*
22/8	ÍBV	a	1-0	*Vilhjálmsson*
29/8	Breidablik	h	2-4	*Manevski, Símonarson*
12/9	Haukar	h	1-1	*Helgason A.*
16/9	Fylkir	a	0-2	
19/9	KR	h	3-3	*Ondo G. 2, Hjaltalín*
25/9	Selfoss	a	2-5	*Ondo G. 2*

No	Name	Nat	DoB	Pos	Aps	(s)	Gls
25	Jóhann Helgi ADALGEIRSSON		16/3/80	M	2		
21	Gudmundur BERGSTEINSSON		26/4/92	A		(2)	
18	Gudmundur Andri BJARNASON		8/8/81	D	3	(1)	
16	Ólafur Örn BJARNASON		15/5/75	D	8	(1)	
2	Óli Baldur BJARNASON		31/10/89	M	6	(13)	1
12	Rúnar Dór DANÍELSSON		19/7/84	G	8		
18	Vilhjálmur Darri EINARSSON		6/5/91	M		(2)	
9	Matthías Örn FRIDRIKSSON		9/9/86	M	13	(3)	1
8	Páll GUDMUNDSSON		22/10/86	M	3	(1)	1
4	Audun HELGASON		18/6/74	D	20	(1)	1
7	Jóhann HELGASON		19/4/84	M	21		
11	Orri Freyr HJALTALÍN		1/7/80	D	21		2
24	Grétar Ólafur HJARTARSON		26/11/77	A	14	(6)	3
6	Sveinbjörn JÓNASSON		17/7/86	A		(2)	
3	Ray Anthony JÓNSSON	PHI	3/2/79	M	11	(9)	
23	Jósef Kristinn JÓSEFSSON		12/9/89	D	22		

Alexander MAGNÚSSON		10/11/89	D	10	(5)	
Gjorgi MANEVSKI	MKD	17/9/86	A		(2)	2
Gilles Mbang ONDO	GAB	10/10/85	A	20		14
Loic Mbang ONDO	GAB	5/10/90	D	12	(5)	
Óskar PÉTURSSON		26/1/89	G	14		
Scott RAMSAY	SCO	2/10/75	M	18		
Emil Dadi SÍMONARSON		2/6/88	A		(2)	1
Marko Valdimar STEFÁNSSON		18/9/90	D	8		
Hafthór Ægir VILHJÁLMSSON		29/9/86	M	8	(2)	2

HAUKAR

Coach – Andri Marteinsson

Founded – 1931

Stadium – Vodafonevöllurinn ad Hlídarenda (2,225)

)10				
1/5	KR	a	2-2	*Pálsson, Sæmundsson*
6/5	FH	h	0-1	
0/5	Selfoss	a	0-3	
4/5	ÍBV	h	0-3	
1/5	Stjarnan	a	2-2	*Eidsson 2*
6	Breidablik	h	2-4	*Mantom, Gunnlaugsson (p)*
4/6	Keflavík	a	1-1	*Mantom*
1/6	Grindavík	h	2-3	*Gunnlaugsson, Eidsson*
7/6	Fram	a	0-0	
/7	Fylkir	h	1-1	*Björnsson*
/7	Valur	a	2-2	*Eidsson, Gunnlaugsson*
8/7	KR	h	3-3	*Gunnlaugsson (p), Emilsson, Lýdsson*
5/7	FH	a	1-3	*Gunnlaugsson (p)*
/8	Selfoss	h	2-3	*García, Lýdsson*
/8	ÍBV	a	2-3	*Emilsson, Einarsson*
6/8	Stjarnan	h	0-5	
3/8	Breidablik	a	2-0	*Einarsson, og (Ársælsson)*
8/8	Keflavík	h	2-0	*Björgvinsson, Lýdsson*
2/9	Grindavík	a	1-1	*Gunnlaugsson*
6/9	Fram	h	2-1	*Gunnlaugsson (p), Arnarsson*
9/9	Fylkir	a	0-3	
25/9	Valur	h	2-1	*Gunnlaugsson (p), Pálsson*

No	Name	Nat	DoB	Pos	Aps	(s)	Gls
)	Hilmar Trausti ARNARSSON		16/10/86	M	5	(3)	1
15	Gunnar Ormslev ÁSGEIRSSON		28/11/84	D	13	(3)	
7	Jónas BJARNASON		5/6/86	D		(2)	
30	Magnús BJÖRGVINSSON		12/9/87	A	6	(4)	1
4	Kristján Ómar BJÖRNSSON		14/11/80	D	20	(1)	1
10	Hilmar Geir EIDSSON		5/10/85	M	21		4
20	Daníel EINARSSON		20/8/83	D	18	(1)	2
8	Hilmar Rafn EMILSSON		12/9/86	A	14	(5)	2
28	Alexandre GARCÍA Canedo	ESP	25/5/86	A	3	(2)	1
22	Gardar Ingvar GEIRSSON		12/3/88	A		(6)	
3	Pétur Örn GÍSLASON		11/4/87	D	4	(3)	
26	Grétar Atli GRÉTARSSON		5/11/88	D	7	(2)	
19	Jónmundur GRÉTARSSON		12/11/85	A	1	(3)	
13	Arnar GUNNLAUGSSON		6/3/73	A	18		8
17	Ásgeir Thór INGÓLFSSON		31/8/90	M	14	(3)	
27	Aron JÓHANNSSON		11/1/94	D		(1)	
11	Thórhallur Dan JÓHANNSSON		5/12/72	D	7	(1)	
28	Stefán Daníel JÓNSSON		5/4/88	D		(1)	
1	Dadi LÁRUSSON		19/6/73	G	20		
5	Gudjón Pétur LÝDSSON		28/12/87	M	21		3
27	Sam MANTOM	ENG	20/2/92	M	6	(1)	2
2	Jamie McCUNNIE	SCO	15/4/83	D	10		
25	Amir MEHICA	BIH	21/2/80	G	2		
21	Gudmundur Vidar METE		4/2/81	D	12	(1)	
6	Úlfar Hrafn PÁLSSON		16/10/88	M	15	(4)	2
24	Kristján Óli SIGURDSSON		29/6/80	M	1	(4)	
23	Pétur Ásbjörn SÆMUNDSSON		5/1/89	D	4	(4)	1

ÍBV VESTMANNAEYJAR

Coach – Heimir Hallgrímsson

Founded – 1945

Stadium – Hásteinsvöllur (2,834)

MAJOR HONOURS: Icelandic League – (3) 1979, 1997, 1998; Icelandic Cup – (4) 1968, 1972, 1981, 1998.

2010				
11/5	Fram	a	0-2	
17/5	Valur	a	1-1	*Sytnyk*
20/5	FH	a	3-2	*Birgisson, Sigurbjörnsson, Gudmundsson (p)*
24/5	Haukar	a	3-0	*Garner, Ólafsson An. 2*
30/5	Breidablik	h	1-1	*Gudmundsson (p)*
6/6	Grindavík	a	2-1	*Birgisson, Sytnyk*
13/6	Fylkir	h	1-0	*Valdimarsson*
20/6	KR	a	0-1	
25/6	Selfoss	h	3-0	*Gudmundsson 2, Mawejje*
4/7	Stjarnan	a	2-0	*Gudmundsson, Sytnyk*
8/7	Keflavík	h	2-1	*Ólafsson An., Sigurbjörnsson*
17/7	Fram	h	1-0	*Warlem*
25/7	Valur	h	3-1	*Gudmundsson 2 (1p), Warlem*
5/8	FH	h	1-3	*Gudmundsson*
8/8	Haukar	h	3-2	*Warlem 2, Sytnyk*
16/8	Breidablik	a	1-1	*Gudmundsson (p)*
22/8	Grindavík	h	0-1	
29/8	Fylkir	a	2-1	*Valdimarsson, Hurst*
12/9	KR	h	2-4	*Mawejje, Valdimarsson*
16/9	Selfoss	a	2-0	*Valdimarsson, Sævarsson (p)*
19/9	Stjarnan	h	2-1	*Sytnyk, Valdimarsson*
25/9	Keflavík	a	1-4	*Sytnyk*

No	Name	Nat	DoB	Pos	Aps	(s)	Gls
18	Ásgeir Aron ÁSGEIRSSON		12/6/86	M	4	(10)	
16	Eythór Helgi BIRGISSON		24/2/89	A	10	(10)	2
11	Anton BJARNASON		25/7/87	M		(5)	
8	Yngvi Magnús BORGTHÓRSSON		26/3/75	D	3	(12)	
28	Rasmus CHRISTIANSEN	DEN	6/1/89	D	20	(1)	
3	Matt GARNER	ENG	9/4/84	D	21		1
9	Tryggvi GUDMUNDSSON		30/7/74	M	21		9
2	James HURST	ENG	31/1/92	D	16		1
15	Tony MAWEJJE	UGA	15/12/86	M	22		2
6	Andri ÓLAFSSON		26/6/85	M	19		3
19	Arnór Eyvar ÓLAFSSON		27/11/89	D	6	(4)	
4	Finnur ÓLAFSSON		30/1/84	M	19		
23	Eidur Aron SIGURBJÖRNSSON		26/2/90	D	22		2
30	Elías Fannar STEFNISSON		17/10/90	G	1	(1)	
21	Denys SYTNYK	UKR	14/1/86	A	12	(5)	6
7	Albert SÆVARSSON		18/10/73	G	21		1
22	Gauti THORVARDARSON		19/2/89	A		(9)	
5	Thórarinn Ingi VALDIMARSSON		23/4/90	M	21		5
20	Hjálmar VIDARSSON		18/1/91	A		(1)	
27	Danien Justin WARLEM	RSA	8/11/87	A	4	(7)	4

KEFLAVÍK

Coach – Willum Thór Thórsson

Founded – 1929

Stadium – Sparisjódsvöllurinn (2,872) & Njardvíkurvöllur (495)

MAJOR HONOURS: Icelandic League – (4) 1964, 1969, 1971, 1973; Icelandic Cup – (4) 1975, 1997, 2004, 2006.

2010				
11/5	Breidablik	a	1-0	*Sutej*
17/5	Grindavík	a	1-0	*Gudmundsson J.*
20/5	Fylkir	h	2-1	*Steinarsson (p), Thorsteinsson*
25/5	KR	a	0-0	
31/5	Selfoss	h	2-1	*McShane, Sveinsson*
7/6	Stjarnan	a	0-4	

14/6	Haukar	h	1-1	*Gudmundsson B.*
21/6	Fram	h	1-1	*Thorsteinsson*
27/6	Valur	a	2-0	*Antoníusson, Gudmundsson B.*
4/7	FH	h	1-1	*Steinarsson*
8/7	ÍBV	a	1-2	*Matthíasson*
18/7	Breidablik	h	0-2	
26/7	Grindavík	h	1-1	*Gudmundsson J.*
5/8	Fylkir	a	2-1	*Steinarsson (p), Gudmundsson J.*
8/8	KR	h	0-1	
19/8	Selfoss	a	2-3	*Matthíasson, Sveinsson*
23/8	Stjarnan	h	2-2	*Sveinsson 2*
18/8	Haukar	a	0-2	
13/9	Fram	a	1-2	*og (Fjóluson)*
16/9	Valur	h	3-1	*Sveinsson 2, Birgisson*
19/9	FH	a	3-5	*Gudnason, Adalsteinsson, Gudmundsson B.*
25/9	ÍBV	h	4-1	*Sveinsson, Traustason, Thorsteinsson, Ljubicic*

No	Name	Nat	DoB	Pos	Aps	(s)	Gls
20	Bjarni Hólm ADALSTEINSSON		5/10/84	D	21		1
3	Gudjón Árni ANTONÍUSSON		3/9/83	D	21		1
12	Árni Freyr ÁSGEIRSSON		10/3/92	G	2	(1)	
8	Andri Steinn BIRGISSON		23/12/83	M	6	(2)	1
6	Einar Orri EINARSSON		28/10/89	M	9	(3)	
23	Sigurbergur ELÍSSON		10/6/92	M		(1)	
16	Brynjar Örn GUDMUNDSSON		9/10/82	M	5	(10)	3
4	Haraldur Freyr GUDMUNDSSON		14/12/81	D	21		
7	Jóhann Birnir GUDMUNDSSON		5/12/77	M	9	(7)	3
10	Haukur Ingi GUDNASON		8/9/78	A	4	(3)	1
1	Ómar JÓHANNSSON		2/3/81	G	14		
21	Lasse JØRGENSEN	DEN	23/4/84	G	6	(1)	
15	Bojan Stefán LJUBICIC		22/6/92	A		(3)	1
22	Magnús Thór MAGNÚSSON		20/2/92	M		(2)	
18	Magnús Thórir MATTHÍASSON		22/1/90	M	13	(6)	2
5	Paul McSHANE	SCO	13/4/78	M	12	(2)	1
25	Hólmar Örn RÚNARSSON		10/12/81	M	22		
26	Ómar Karl SIGURDSSON		24/8/82	A		(5)	
9	Gudmundur STEINARSSON		20/10/79	A	21		3
2	Alen SUTEJ	SVN	10/9/85	D	22		1
27	Hördur SVEINSSON		24/3/83	A	14	(4)	7
24	Sigurdur Gunnar SÆVARSSON		25/7/90	D		(2)	
11	Magnús Sverrir THORSTEINSSON		22/9/82	A	19	(2)	3
17	Arnór Ingvi TRAUSTASON		30/4/93	M	1	(2)	1

KR REYKJAVÍK

Coach – Logi Ólafsson; (19/7/10) Rúnar Kristinsson

Founded – 1899

Stadium – KR-völlur (2,781)

MAJOR HONOURS: Icelandic League – (24) 1912, 1919, 1926, 1927, 1928, 1929, 1931, 1932, 1934, 1941, 1948, 1949, 1950, 1952, 1955, 1959, 1961, 1963, 1965, 1968, 1999, 2000, 2002, 2003;
Icelandic Cup – (11) 1960, 1961, 1962, 1963, 1964, 1966, 1967, 1994, 1995, 1999, 2008.

2010

11/5	Haukar	h	2-2	*Takefusa, Baldvinsson*
16/5	Selfoss	h	1-2	*Sigurdsson B.*
20/5	Stjarnan	a	2-2	*Finnbogason 2*
25/5	Keflavík	h	0-0	
7/6	Valur	h	1-2	*Hauksson*
10/6	Fram	a	3-2	*Takefusa 2, Sigurdarson*
14/6	FH	a	2-3	*Hauksson, Takefusa*
20/6	ÍBV	h	1-0	*Sigurdsson B.*
27/6	Breidablik	a	1-2	*Arnarsson*
4/7	Grindavík	h	1-0	*Gudjónsson*
18/7	Haukar	a	3-3	*Sigurdarson, Takefusa (p), Baldvinsson*
25/7	Selfoss	a	3-0	*Baldvinsson 2, Rutgers*
5/8	Stjarnan	h	3-1	*Finnbogason, Takefusa, Gunnarssc*
8/8	Keflavík	a	1-0	*Finnbogason*
19/8	Fram	h	2-1	*Sigurdsson B., Finnbogason*
23/8	Valur	a	4-1	*Hauksson 2, Finnbogason, Rutgers*
26/8	Fylkir	a	4-1	*Baldvinsson 2, Finnbogason, Gunnarsson*
30/8	FH	h	0-1	
12/9	ÍBV	a	4-2	*Baldvinsson 2, Rutgers, Finnbogasc (p)*
16/9	Breidablik	h	1-3	*Baldvinsson*
19/9	Grindavík	a	3-3	*Sigurdsson B. 3*
25/9	Fylkir	h	3-0	*Jónsson E., Baldvinsson, Sigurdssc B.*

No	Name	Nat	DoB	Pos	Aps	(s)	Gls
14	Viktor Bjarki ARNARSSON		22/1/83	M	16	(3)	1
23	Gudjón BALDVINSSON		15/2/86	A	11	(2)	10
30	Jordão da Encarnação Tackey DIOGO	POR	12/11/85	D	10	(3)	
26	Davíd EINARSSON		24/8/92	A		(1)	
25	Eggert Rafn EINARSSON		28/1/90	D	3	(2)	
6	Kjartan Henry FINNBOGASON		9/7/86	A	18	(3)	8
7	Skúli Jón FRIDGEIRSSON		30/7/88	D	19	(1)	
4	Bjarni GUDJÓNSSON		26/2/79	M	20		1
21	Gudmundur Reynir GUNNARSSON		21/1/89	D	16	(3)	2
16	Auðunn Örn GYLFASON		11/10/91	D		(1)	
9	Óskar Örn HAUKSSON		22/8/84	M	21		4
1	Thórdur INGASON		30/3/88	G	1	(1)	
15	Egill JÓNSSON		15/2/91	M	4	(2)	1
20	Gunnar Örn JÓNSSON		30/4/85	M	7	(9)	
11	Gunnar KRISTJÁNSSON		2/3/87	A		(6)	
29	Lars Ivar MOLDSKRED	NOR	12/11/78	G	21		
18	Mark RUTGERS	NED	29/6/86	D	18		3
2	Grétar Sigfinnur SIGURDARSON		9/10/82	D	18		2
8	Baldur SIGURDSSON		24/4/85	M	22		7
17	Hróar SIGURDSSON		13/5/92	D		(2)	
12	Dofri SNORRASON		21/7/90	D	5	(4)	
10	Björgólfur TAKEFUSA		11/5/80	A	12	(8)	6

SELFOSS

Coach – Gudmundur Benediktsson

Founded – 1936

Stadium – Selfossvöllur (950)

2010

11/5	Fylkir	h	1-3	*Gíslason*
16/5	KR	a	2-1	*Thórarinsson I. (p), Bödvarsson*
20/5	Haukar	h	3-0	*og (Lárusson), Bödvarsson, Gudbrandsson*
25/5	Stjarnan	h	2-2	Gudbrandsson, Thórarinsson G. (p)
31/5	Keflavík	a	1-2	*Gíslason*
6/6	Fram	h	1-2	*Gudbrandsson*
14/6	Valur	a	1-2	*Birgisson*
21/6	FH	h	0-2	
25/6	ÍBV	a	0-3	
5/7	Breidablik	h	1-3	*Antonsson*
8/7	Grindavík	a	1-1	*og (Helgason A.)*
18/7	Fylkir	a	2-5	*Marteinsson 2*
25/7	KR	h	0-3	
5/8	Haukar	a	3-2	*Gudlaugsson S.R., N'Guessan, Magnússon*
8/8	Stjarnan	a	2-3	*Bödvarsson, Sigurdsson K.*
19/8	Keflavík	h	3-2	*Gudbrandsson, Illugason (p), Kjartansson*
23/8	Fram	a	1-3	*Gíslason*
30/8	Valur	h	2-3	*Illugason (p), Gíslason*
12/9	FH	a	1-2	*Kjartansson*

/9	ÍBV	h	0-2	
/9	Breidablik	a	0-3	
/9	Grindavík	h	5-2	*Illugason, Gíslason, Gudmundsson, Kjartansson, Birgisson*

No	Name	Nat	DoB	Pos	Aps	(s)	Gls
	Einar Ottó ANTONSSON		28/8/84	M	7	(8)	1
	Davíð BIRGISSON		23/11/90	A	6	(5)	2
	Andri Freyr BJÖRNSSON		12/8/86	D	17	(1)	
	Gunnar Rafn BORGTHÓRSSON		3/12/81	M	3		
	Jón Dadi BÖDVARSSON		25/5/92	A	20	(1)	3
	Martin DOHLSTEN	SWE	29/4/86	M	10		
	Elías Örn EINARSSON		30/3/82	G		(1)	
	Sævar Thór GÍSLASON		26/12/75	A	17	(3)	5
	Jón GUDBRANDSSON		18/4/85	D	18	(1)	4
	Sigurdur Eyberg GUDLAUGSSON		2/10/90	D	10		
	Stefán Ragnar GUDLAUGSSON		19/3/91	D	18		1
	Ingthór Jóhann GUDMUNDSSON		6/10/84	M	5	(6)	1
	Viktor Unnar ILLUGASON		25/1/90	A	10		3
3	Ingi Rafn INGIBERGSSON		30/11/83	M	2	(10)	
	Henning JÓNASSON		24/6/83	M	1		
	Vidar Örn KJARTANSSON		11/3/90	A	3	(9)	3
	Agnar Bragi MAGNÚSSON		3/2/87	D	19	(1)	1
	Arilíus MARTEINSSON		31/5/84	M	13	(6)	2
7	Bi Hverve N'GUESSAN	CIV	6/4/91	A	1	(3)	1
2	Jóhann Ólafur SIGURDSSON		21/8/86	G	22		
	Kjartan SIGURDSSON		14/1/89	D	6	(2)	1
	Jón Steindór SVEINSSON		5/9/78	D	2	(1)	
0	Gudmundur THÓRARINSSON		15/4/92	M	16		1
	Ingólfur THÓRARINSSON		31/5/86	M	10	(3)	1
8	Jean Stéphane YAO YAO	CIV	6/10/90	M	6	(1)	

STJARNAN

Coach – Bjarni Jóhannsson

Founded – 1960

Stadium – Stjörnuvöllur (1,080)

2010				
11/5	Grindavík	h	4-0	*Björnsson 2 (1p), Thorsteinsson, Laxdal J.*
16/5	Fylkir	a	1-3	*Björnsson*
20/5	KR	h	2-2	*Sturluson, Finsen*
24/5	Selfoss	a	2-2	*Thorsteinsson, Árnason*
31/5	Haukar	h	2-2	*Bjarnason, Árnason (p)*
7/6	Keflavík	h	4-0	*Björnsson 2 (1p), Thorsteinsson, Danry*
14/6	Fram	a	1-2	*Hilmarsson*
20/6	Valur	h	1-1	Hreinsson
27/6	FH	a	3-1	*Björnsson (p), Hreinsson, Sturluson*
4/7	ÍBV	h	0-2	
8/7	Breidablik	a	0-4	
19/7	Grindavík	a	1-1	*Hreinsson*
25/7	Fylkir	h	2-1	*Björgvinsson, Björnsson (p)*
5/8	KR	a	1-3	*Árnason*
8/8	Selfoss	h	3-2	*Hreinsson, Jóhannsson A., Björnsson*
16/8	Haukar	a	5-0	*Finsen 3, Björnsson 2 (1p)*
23/8	Keflavík	a	2-2	*Björgvinsson, Björnsson*
29/8	Fram	h	2-3	*Jóhannsson A., Árnason*
12/9	Valur	a	1-5	*Björnsson (p)*
16/9	FH	h	1-4	*Björnsson (p)*
19/9	ÍBV	a	1-2	*Laxdal J.*
25/9	Breidablik	h	0-0	

No	Name	Nat	DoB	Pos	Aps	(s)	Gls
15	Thorvaldur ÁRNASON		25/6/80	A	20	(2)	4
19	Hreidar Ingi ÁRSÆLSSON		14/2/93	A		(1)	
8	Birgir Rafn BALDURSSON		18/10/92	M		(1)	
30	Marel Jóhann BALDVINSSON		18/12/80	A	7		
14	Birgir Hrafn BIRGISSON		6/10/85	M		(3)	
3	Tryggvi Sveinn BJARNASON		16/1/83	D	19	(1)	1
18	Arnar Már BJÖRGVINSSON		10/2/90	A	8	(4)	2
10	Halldór Orri BJÖRNSSON		2/3/87	M	21		13
12	Dennis DANRY	DEN	5/12/78	M	13	(2)	1
11	Bjarki Páll EYSTEINSSON		1/4/86	M	13	(6)	
17	Ólafur Karl FINSEN		30/3/92	A	7	(8)	4
1	Bjarni Thórdur HALLDÓRSSON		26/7/83	G	21		
23	Hafsteinn Rúnar HELGASON		9/6/85	D	2	(2)	
16	Hilmar Thór HILMARSSON		20/9/90	D	7	(5)	1
22	Ellert HREINSSON		12/10/86	A	8	(2)	4
7	Atli JÓHANNSSON		5/10/82	M	16	(2)	2
24	Gardar JÓHANNSSON		1/4/80	A		(3)	
9	Daníel LAXDAL		22/9/86	D	22		
4	Jóhann LAXDAL		27/1/90	D	20		2
5	Björn PÁLSSON		28/12/86	M	11	(3)	
13	Magnús Karl PÉTURSSON		30/9/79	G	1	(1)	
21	Baldvin STURLUSON		9/4/89	D	12		2
20	Steinthór THORSTEINSSON		29/7/85	M	12		3
29	Vídir THORVARDARSON		7/7/92	A	2	(4)	

VALUR REYKJAVÍK

Coach – Gunnlaugur Jónsson

Founded – 1911

Stadium – Vodafonevöllurinn ad Hlídarenda (2,225)

MAJOR HONOURS: Icelandic League – (20) 1930, 1933, 1935, 1936, 1937, 1938, 1940, 1942, 1943, 1944, 1945, 1956, 1966, 1967, 1976, 1978, 1980, 1985, 1987, 2007; Icelandic Cup – (9) 1965, 1974, 1976, 1977, 1988, 1990, 1991, 1992, 2005.

2010				
10/5	FH	h	2-2	*König, Geirsson*
17/5	ÍBV	h	1-1	*Thórarinsson*
20/5	Breidablik	h	0-2	
25/5	Grindavík	a	2-1	*König, Ákason*
31/5	Fylkir	h	5-2	*König 2, Sigurdsson, Adalsteinsson, Jeffs*
7/6	KR	a	2-1	*Adalsteinsson, Geirsson*
14/6	Selfoss	h	2-1	*Jeffs, Hafsteinsson*
20/6	Stjarnan	a	1-1	*Sigurjónsson*
27/6	Keflavík	h	0-2	
5/7	Fram	a	2-2	*Hafsteinsson, König*
8/7	Haukar	h	2-2	*Jeffs, Hreidarsson*
18/7	FH	a	1-1	*Sigurdsson*
25/7	ÍBV	a	1-3	*Adalsteinsson*
4/8	Breidablik	a	0-5	
8/8	Grindavík	h	0-0	
16/8	Fylkir	a	1-0	*Sigurdsson*
23/8	KR	h	1-4	*Ákason*
30/8	Selfoss	a	3-2	*Ákason, Geirsson, Hafsteinsson*
12/9	Stjarnan	h	5-1	*Pedersen (p), Hafsteinsson, Geirsson, Ákason, Gudmundsson*
16/9	Keflavík	a	1-3	*Pedersen (p)*
19/9	Fram	h	1-3	*Hafsteinsson*
25/9	Haukar	a	1-2	*Hreidarsson*

No	Name	Nat	DoB	Pos	Aps	(s)	Gls
10	Baldur Ingimar ADALSTEINSSON		12/2/80	A	13	(4)	3
16	Jón Vilhelm ÁKASON		20/11/86	M	14	(3)	4
2	Stefán Jóhann EGGERTSSON		3/5/84	D	17	(2)	
18	Arnar Sveinn GEIRSSON		30/8/91	A	20		4
27	Thórir GUDJÓNSSON		7/4/91	A	3	(9)	
11	Matthías GUDMUNDSSON		1/8/80	A		(5)	1
17	Gudmundur Steinn HAFSTEINSSON		14/6/89	A	8	(7)	5
7	Sigurbjörn HREIDARSSON		25/11/75	M	12	(6)	2
19	Viktor Unnar ILLUGASON		25/1/90	A		(5)	
20	Ian JEFFS	ENG	12/10/82	M	15	(5)	3
30	Danni KÖNIG	DEN	17/12/86	A	13		5

4	Reynir LEÓSSON		20/8/79	D	12		
19	Diarmuid O'CARROLL	IRL	16/3/87	A	4	(2)	
3	Martin Meldgaard PEDERSEN	DEN	9/10/83	D	19		2
6	Greg ROSS	SCO	2/5/87	D	17	(1)	
21	Haukur Páll SIGURDSSON		5/8/87	M	16		3
15	Rúnar Már SIGURJÓNSSON		18/6/90	M	15	(5)	1
1	Kjartan STURLUSON		27/12/75	G	22		
5	Atli Sveinn THÓRARINSSON		24/1/80	D	21		1
9	Hafthór Ægir VILHJÁLMSSON		29/9/86	A	1	(3)	

TOP GOALSCORERS 2010

14 Alfred FINNBOGASON (Breidablik)
Atli Vidar BJÖRNSSON (FH)
Gilles Mbang ONDO (Grindavík)

13 Halldór Orri BJÖRNSSON (Stjarnan)

12 Kristinn STEINDÓRSSON (Breidablik)

10 Gudjón BALDVINSSON (KR)

9 Jóhann THÓRHALLSSON (Fylkir)
Tryggvi GUDMUNDSSON (ÍBV)

8 Ívar BJÖRNSSON (Fram)
Almarr ORMARSSON (Fram)
Albert Brynjar INGASON (Fylkir)
Arnar GUNNLAUGSSON (Haukar)
Kjartan Henry FINNBOGASON (KR)

PROMOTED CLUBS

VÍKINGUR REYKJAVÍK

Coach – Leifur Gardarsson
Founded – 1908
Stadium – Víkingsvöllur (1,249)
MAJOR HONOURS: Icelandic League – (5) 1920, 1924, 1981, 1982, 1991; Icelandic Cup – (1) 1971.

THÓR AKUREYRI

Coach – Lárus Orri Sigurdsson; (31/5/10) Páll Vidar Gíslason
Founded – 1915
Stadium – Thórsvöllur (984)

SECOND LEVEL FINAL TABLE 2010

		Pld	W	D	L	F	A	Pts
1	Víkingur Reykjavík	22	15	3	4	46	23	48
2	Thór Akureyri	22	12	7	3	53	23	43
3	Leiknir Reykjavík	22	13	4	5	32	19	43
4	Fjölnir	22	12	4	6	42	28	40
5	ÍA Akranes	22	9	8	5	44	28	35
6	ÍR Reykjavík	22	8	6	8	31	38	30
7	Thróttur Reykjavík	22	8	5	9	32	37	29
8	HK Kópavogur	22	7	4	11	30	38	25
9	KA Akureyri	22	6	6	10	29	43	24
10	Grótta	22	4	6	12	29	47	18
11	Fjardabyggd	22	4	5	13	26	47	17
12	Njardvík	22	3	4	15	14	37	1

DOMESTIC CUP 2010

BIKAR

THIRD ROUND

(2/6/10)
BÍ/Bolungarvík 2, Völsungur 0
Fjardabyggd 3, Njardvík 2 *(aet)*
Fram 2, ÍR 1
ÍBV 0, KR 1
KA 3, HK 2 *(aet)*
KB 0, Víkingur Ólafsvík 1
Víkingur Reykjavík 7, Sindri 0

(3/6/10)
Breidablik 1, FH 1 *(aet; 1-3 on pens)*
Grindavík 2, Thór 1
Haukar 0, Fjölnir 2
ÍA 2, Selfoss 1
Keflavík 1, KS/Leiftur 0
Leiknir Reykjavík 1, Stjarnan 3
Thróttur Reykjavík 3, Grótta 1
Valur 2, Afturelding 1
Vídir 0, Fylkir 2

FOURTH ROUND

(23/6/10)
BÍ/Bolungarvík 0, Stjarnan 2
Fjölnir 1, KR 2
ÍA 0, Thróttur Reykjavík 1
Víkingur Ólafsvík 3, Fjardabyggd 2
Víkingur Reykjavík 1, Valur 3 *(aet)*

(24/6/10)
Fylkir 0, Fram 2
Grindavík 1, KA 1 *(aet; 4-5 on pens)*
Keflavík 2, FH 3

QUARTER-FINALS

(1/7/10)
FH 3 *(Snorrason 52, 75, Vilhjálmsson 68)*, KA 0

(12/7/10)
Fram 3 *(Jónsson 50, Leifsson 54, Tillen J. 58)*, Valur 1 *(Sigurjónsson 66)*
KR 3 *(Sigurdsson B. 11, 73, Takefusa 31p)*, Thróttur Reykjavík 2 *(Vilhjálmsson 86, Tanasić 90)*
Víkingur Ólafsvík 3 *(Emilsson 10, Beslija 86, Sigurthórsson 93)*, Stjarnan 3 *(Eysteinsson 89, Hreinsson 90, Björgvinsson 100) (aet; 5-4 on pens)*

SEMI-FINALS

(28/7/10)
FH 3 *(Gudmundsson 40, Björnsson 57, Vilhjálmsson 75p)*, Víkingur Ólafsvík 1 *(Nielsen 42og)*

(29/7/10)
KR 4 *(Hauksson 40, Sigurdarson 58, Takefusa 70, 80)*, Fram 0

FINAL

(14/8/10)
Laugardalsvöllur, Reykjavik
FH HAFNARFJÖRDUR 4 *(Vilhjálmsson 35p, 41p, Björnsson 75, Gudnason 86)*
KR REYKJAVÍK 0
Referee – *Eiríksson*
FH – *Gunnleifsson, Sævarsson (Ásgeirsson 46), Bjarnason, Nielsen, Valgardsson (Pálsson 90), Sverrisson, Vidarsson, Vilhjálmsson, Snorrason, Björnsson, Gudnason (Gudmundsson 86).*
KR – *Moldskred, Fridgeirsson, Rutgers, Sigurdarson, Gunnarsson (Diogo 68), Gudjónsson, Sigurdsson B., Hauksson (Arnarsson 83), Finnbogason, Takefusa, Baldvinsson (Snorrason 68).*

CLUB COMMUNICATION 2011

reidablik

alsmára 5
-201 Kópavogur

el	+354 510 6404
ax	+354 554 0050
eb	breidablik.is
mail	knattspyrna@breidablik.is
edia Officer	Helgi Thor Jonasson

H Hafnarfjördur

aplakrika
-220 Hafnarfirdi

el	+354 565 0711
ax	+354 568 4222
eb	fh.is
mail	gassi@fh.is
edia Officer	Gunnar Gunnarsson

ram Reykjavík

afamýri 26, Laugardalsvöllur stadium
S-108 Reykjavík

el	+354 533 5600
ax	+354 568 0495
Veb	fram.is
mail	knattspyrna@fram.is
ledia Officer	Gudmundur Magnússon

Fylkir

thróttafélagid Fylkir, knattspyrnudeild
ylkishöll, IS-110 Reykjavík

Tel	+354 567 6467
Fax	+354 567 6091
Web	fylkir.com
Email	fylkir@fylkir.com
Media Officer	Thórdur Gíslason

Grindavík

Ungmennafélag Grindavíkur, Austurvegi 3
IS-240 Grindavík

Tel	+354 426 8605
Fax	+354 426 7605
Web	umfg.is
Email	umfg@centrum.is
Media Officer	Sigurdur Enoksson

ÍBV Vestmannaeyjar

Tysheimili v/ Hastein
IS-902 Vestmannaeyjar

Tel	+354 481 2060
Fax	+354 481 1260
Web	ibvsport.is
Email	ibv@ibv.is
Media Officer	Olafur Björgvin Jóhannsson

Keflavík

Skólavegur 32, PO Box 122
IS-230 Reykjanesbær

Tel	+354 421 5188
Fax	+354 421 4137
Web	keflavik.is
Email	kef-fc@keflavik.is
Media Officer	Hjordis Baldursdottir

KR Reykjavík

Frostaskjól 2, Knattspyrnufélag Reykjavíkur
IS-107 Reykjavik

Tel	+354 510 5307
Fax	+354 510 5309
Web	kr.is
Email	jonas@kr.is
Media Officer	Otthar Johannsson

Stjarnan

Ungmennafelagid Stjarnan, Stjornuheimilinu
v/Asgard, IS-210 Gardabær

Tel	+354 565 1940
Fax	+354 565 1714
Web	stjarnan.is
Email	knattspyrna@stjarnan.is
Media Officer	Sara Rut Unnarsdóttir

Thór Akureyri

Ithróttafélagid Thór, Knattspyrnudeild
Hamri v/Skardshlíd, IS-603 Akureyri

Tel	+354 461 2080
Fax	+354 462 2381
Web	thorsport.is
Email	boltinn@thorsport.is
Media Officer	Bjarni Gudmundsson

Valur Reykjavík

Hlidarendi v/Laufásveg, Valsvöllur stadium
IS-101 Reykjavík

Tel	+354 414 8000
Fax	+354 414 8010
Web	valur.is
Email	valur@valur.is
Media Officer	Björgvin Brynjólfsson

Víkingur Reykjavík

Knattspyrnufélagid Víkingur, Tradarlandi 1
IS-108 Reykjavík

Tel	+354 581 3245
Fax	+354 588 7845
Web	vikingur.is
Email	knattspyrna@vikingur.is
Media Officer	Halldor Sæmundsson

ISRAEL

Israël I Israel

Israel Football Association (IFA)

COMMUNICATION

Address Ramat Gan Stadium
299 Aba Hilell Street
PO Box 3591
IL-52134 Ramat Gan

Tel +972 3 617 1500
Fax +972 3 570 2044

E-mail info@football.org.il
Website football.org.il

President Avraham Luzon
Chief Executive Ori Shilo
Media Officer Michal Grundland

Year of Formation 1928

National Stadium Ramat Gan (41,583)

DOMESTIC COMPETITION SUMMARY 2010/11

LIGAT HA'AL FINAL TABLE

			Home					Away					Total						
		Pld	W	D	L	F	A	W	D	L	F	A	W	D	L	F	A	Pts	Comp
1	Maccabi Haifa FC	35	12	4	2	34	15	12	4	1	29	13	24	8	3	63	28	45	UCL
2	Hapoel Tel-Aviv FC	35	12	3	3	41	18	9	4	4	31	18	21	7	7	72	36	38	UEL
3	Maccabi Tel-Aviv FC	35	9	3	6	28	18	9	3	5	25	22	18	6	11	53	40	35	UEL
4	Bnei Yehuda Tel-Aviv FC	35	9	5	3	24	13	6	5	7	18	21	15	10	10	42	34	31	UEL
5	Hapoel Kiryat Shmona FC	35	8	5	4	30	18	6	5	7	27	27	14	10	11	57	45	28	
6	Maccabi Netanya FC	35	6	7	4	26	24	6	6	6	21	23	12	13	10	47	47	27	
7	Maccabi Petach-Tikva FC	33	6	5	6	32	23	7	5	4	25	18	13	10	10	57	41	28	
8	Hapoel Akko FC	33	8	5	3	26	14	4	6	7	23	31	12	11	10	49	45	27	
9	Hapoel Beer Sheva FC	33	5	3	8	17	19	6	6	5	24	24	11	9	13	41	43	23	
10	Hapoel Haifa FC	33	6	4	7	21	22	6	4	6	19	21	12	8	13	40	43	22	
11	Beitar Jerusalem FC	35	9	5	4	26	11	3	4	10	12	24	12	9	14	38	35	26	
12	FC Ashdod	35	6	6	6	27	25	4	5	8	15	30	10	11	14	42	55	25	
13	Bnei Sakhnin FC	35	5	4	8	15	21	4	4	10	10	23	9	8	18	25	44	23	
14	Hapoel Petach-Tikva FC	35	6	4	8	22	27	4	4	9	20	31	10	8	17	42	58	22	
15	Hapoel Ashkelon FC	35	5	4	8	18	27	4	1	13	15	39	9	5	21	33	66	19	*Relegated*
16	Hapoel Ramat Gan FC	35	2	4	11	13	30	1	5	12	11	35	3	9	23	24	65	10	*Relegated*

NB After 30 matches clubs were split into three groups, after which they played exclusively against teams in their group. Points obtained during the regular season were halved (and rounded upwards).
Hapoel Ramat Gan FC – 4 pts deducted; Beitar Jerusalem FC – 1 pt deducted.

Top Scorer Toto Tamuz (H. Tel-Aviv), 21 goals

Promoted Club Hapoel Ironi Nir Ramat HaSharon FC
Hapoel Ironi Rishon-LeZion FC

Cup Final Hapoel Tel-Aviv FC 1, Maccabi Haifa FC 0

Big Two share the spoils

For the second season running there was little to choose between Israel's two leading clubs, Maccabi Haifa FC and Hapoel Tel-Aviv FC. Another private duel for the Ligat Ha'al title ended in victory for the former, who thus avenged their last-minute heartbreak of the previous campaign, but it was Hapoel who denied Haifa their first domestic double in 20 years by defeating them 1-0 in the final of the State Cup. Furthermore, Hapoel shone again in Europe, reaching the group stage of the UEFA Champions League.

Of the two teams the Reds of Hapoel, led by the experienced Eli Gutman, arguably played the better, more fluent football, but it was the Greens of Haifa, with Elisha Levi in charge, who trumped them to the bigger prize. This was largely because they were more difficult to beat, losing only three matches, two of which were to their direct rivals. The third loss, at home to Maccabi Netanya FC in the first round of the five-match play-off series, had potentially dire consequences as it enabled Hapoel, five points in arrears of Haifa at the end of the regular 30-match campaign a week earlier, to leapfrog their rivals to the top of the table – thanks to the point-halving rule at the cut-off, the fact that odd-numbered points were rounded up, and a 2-1 home win over Bnei Yehuda Tel-Aviv FC.

Initiative regained

Haifa seized back the initiative the following weekend, however, by defeating Hapoel 2-0 at home – with goals from skipper Yaniv Katan and Georgian striker Vladimer Dvalishvili – and that proved to be the turning point of the campaign. Haifa won their next two matches while Hapoel were held to draws, enabling Levi's men to clinch the title with a game to spare, a brace of second-half goals from their talented playmaker Lior Refaelov wrapping up their all-important 24th victory of the season, at home to Hapoel Kiryat Shmona FC.

It was Haifa's seventh league title since the turn of the century, but the club had not won the State Cup since 1998 so there was a steely determination among Levi's troops to seal the double when they re-encountered Hapoel in front of 38,000 spectators in Ramat Gan ten days after their title triumph. But, despite dominating much of the game, the Greens could not come back from the early goal scored by Hapoel midfielder Salim Tuaama, so the trophy went, for the second year in a row and the 14th time in all, to the Tel-Aviv side. Afterwards an emotional Gutman, who had missed several weeks of the season after suffering a heart attack, announced his departure from the club, the mantle eventually being passed on to former Israel coach Dror Kashtan, who had worked at the club three times previously.

Yaniv Katan captained Maccabi Haifa to victory in the Israeli championship

ISRAEL

One of the legacies of Gutman's four-year reign was to have put Hapoel on the European map. Having played a dozen matches in the UEFA Europa League in 2009/10, they negotiated the same number in the 2010/11 UEFA Champions League, overcoming FC Salzburg to reach the group stage and finishing their campaign strongly with draws against FC Schalke 04 and Olympique Lyonnais and a magnificent 3-0 home win over SL Benfica. Eran Zahavi struck five goals in Europe, including one spectacular strike in Lyon, but it was his fellow Israeli internationals Toto Tamuz and Ben Sahar who outgunned him on the domestic front, the former topping the Ligat Ha'al standings with 21 goals.

Spring revival

While Hapoel were flying the flag for Israel in Europe, the national team made a poor start to their UEFA EURO 2012 qualifying campaign under new coach Luis Fernandez, collecting just four points from their opening four ties. The Frenchman was temporarily suspended by FIFA because of an unresolved financial issue with his former club in Qatar, but he was back on duty in the spring to lead Israel to three successive qualifying victories, which rekindled their challenge for a top-two finish in the autumn. Fernandez's selections were a mixture of Hapoel Tel-Aviv, Maccabi Haifa and overseas-based players. While the most high-profile Israeli footballer, Yossi Benayoun, missed virtually the whole of the season at his new club Chelsea FC with a ruptured Achilles, the country's standout expatriate turned out to be striker Elyaniv Barda, a Belgian champion with KRC Genk.

National Team

International Tournament Appearances – FIFA World Cup - (1) 1970.

Top Five All-time Caps – Arik Benado (94); Alon Harazi (88); Amir Shelache (85); Mordechay Shpiegler (84); Nir Klinger (83)

Top Five All-time Goals – Mordechay Shpiegler (33); Yossi Benayoun & Yehushua Feigenboim (24); Ronen Harazi (23); Nahum Stelmach (22)

NATIONAL TEAM RESULTS 2010/11

2/9/10	Malta (ECQ)	H	Tel-Aviv	3-1	*Benayoun (7, 64p, 75)*
7/9/10	Georgia (ECQ)	A	Tbilisi	0-0	
9/10/10	Croatia (ECQ)	H	Tel-Aviv	1-2	*Shechter (81)*
12/10/10	Greece (ECQ)	A	Piraeus	1-2	*Spiropoulos (59og)*
17/11/10	Iceland	H	Tel-Aviv	3-2	*Damari (6, 14), Refaelov (27)*
9/2/11	Serbia	H	Tel-Aviv	0-2	
26/3/11	Latvia (ECQ)	H	Tel-Aviv	2-1	*Barda (16), Kayal (81)*
29/3/11	Georgia (ECQ)	H	Tel-Aviv	1-0	*Ben Haim (II) (59)*
4/6/11	Latvia (ECQ)	A	Riga	2-1	*Benayoun (19), Ben Haim (I) (43p)*

NATIONAL TEAM APPEARANCES 2010/11

Coach – Luis FERNANDEZ (FRA) 2/10/59			MLT	GEO	CRO	GRE	Isl	Srb	LVA	GEO	LVA	Caps	Goals
Dudu AWAT	17/10/77	Mallorca (ESP)	G	G	G	G	G	G	G	G	G	60	-
Dani BONDARV	7/2/87	H. Tel-Aviv	D	D		D	D	D		D		6	-
Tal BEN HAIM (I)	31/3/82	West Ham (ENG)	D	D	D								
		/Portsmouth (ENG)						D46	D	D	D	61	1
Tamir COHEN	4/3/84	Bolton (ENG)	D	M61	M51	M69						20	-
Dedi BEN DAYAN	27/11/78	H. Tel-Aviv	D	D				s46				26	1
Biram KAYAL	2/5/88	Celtic (SCO)	M86	M				M56	M	M		18	1
Almog COHEN	1/9/88	Nürnberg (GER)	M	M	M	M	M71	s46		M	M	8	-
Lior REFAELOV	26/4/86	M. Haifa	M	M75	s56	M	M53		M84	M63	M79	11	2
Yossi BENAYOUN	5/5/80	Chelsea (ENG)	M	M						s71	M	82	24
Eran ZAHAVI	25/7/87	H. Tel-Aviv	M51	s61			s71	M			M89	5	-
Ben SAHAR	10/8/89	H. Tel-Aviv	A73	A53			s60	s56	s66			24	5
Gil VERMOUTH	5/8/85	H. Tel-Aviv	s51	s75	M	s63	s53	s46	s84	s63		14	-
Shlomi ARBEITMAN	14/5/85	Gent (BEL)	s73	s53								10	3
Eyal GOLASA	7/10/91	M. Haifa	s86		s69	M		M56			s89	5	-

NATIONAL TEAM APPEARANCES 2010/11 (contd.)

			MLT	GEO	CRO	GRE	Isl	Srb	LVA	GEO	LVA	Caps	Goals
Dekel KEINAN	15/9/84	Blackpool (ENG) /Cardiff (WAL)		D	D	D				D	D	20	-
Yoav ZIV	16/3/81	M. Tel-Aviv			D				D66			28	-
Elroi COHEN	7/1/89	H. Kiryat Shmona /H. Tel-Aviv			D69	s69	s68	M46				4	-
Bibras NATCHO	18/2/88	Rubin (RUS)			M	M63	M65	M46	M	M52	s69	10	-
Elyaniv BARDA	15/12/81	Genk (BEL)			A56	s75	A60	A56	A69	A71		28	12
Itay SHECHTER	22/2/87	H. Tel-Aviv			A	A						8	1
Roberto COLAUTTI	24/5/82	M. Tel-Aviv			s51	A75						21	6
Rami GERSHON	12/8/88	Kortrijk (BEL)				D	D	D	D	D	D	6	-
Gal ALBERMAN	17/4/83	M. Tel-Aviv					D					27	1
Yuval SHPUNGIN	3/4/87	Omonia (CYP)					D78				D	11	-
Maor Bar BUZAGLO	14/1/88	M. Tel-Aviv					M68	s56	s69	M	M69	13	-
Omer DAMARI	24/3/89	M. Petach-Tikva					A		A			2	2
Kobi DAJANI	5/11/84	M. Netanya					s65					1	-
Orel DGANI	8/1/89	M. Netanya					s78					1	-
Itzhak COHEN	22/4/83	H. Akko						D	D			2	-
Nir BITON	30/10/91	Ashdod						s56				3	-
Taleb TAWATHA	21/6/92	M. Haifa							D			1	-
Tal BEN HAIM (II)	5/8/89	M. Petach-Tikva								s52	s79	2	1
Tomer HEMED	2/5/87	M. Haifa									A	1	-

CLUB-BY-CLUB

FC ASHDOD

Coach – John Gregory (ENG); (18/4/11) Yossi Mizrahi

Founded – 1999

Stadium – Yud Alef (7,420)

2010				
21/8	H. Akko	a	2-1	*Makriev, Shriki*
28/8	H. Kiryat Shmona	h	2-2	*Ohayon Mo. 2 (2p)*
11/9	M. Netanya	a	0-2	
27/9	M. Tel-Aviv	h	1-2	*Ohayon Mo. (p)*
2/10	M. Petach-Tikva	a	2-2	*Ohayon Mo. (p), Mizrahi*
17/10	H. Beer Sheva	h	0-3	*(w/o; original result 3-3 Makriev, og (Yehiel), Werta)*
23/10	M. Haifa	a	1-1	*Ohayon Mo.*
30/10	Beitar	h	3-0	*Ohayon Mo., Biton, Makriev*
6/11	Bnei Sakhnin	a	2-0	*Ohayon Mo., Shriki*
13/11	Bnei Yehuda	a	0-0	
20/11	H. Petach-Tikva	h	1-2	*Sarki*
28/11	H. Tel-Aviv	a	2-0	*Kingue, Ohayon Mo. (p)*
4/12	H. Ramat Gan	h	2-2	*Ohayon Mo. 2 (1p)*
11/12	H. Haifa	a	0-2	
18/12	H. Ashkelon	h	3-2	*Biton 2, Ohayon Mo.*
2011				
1/1	H. Akko	h	3-1	*Ohayon Mo., Mizrahi, Lavie*
8/1	H. Kiryat Shmona	a	0-3	
16/1	M. Netanya	h	1-0	*Mizrahi*
22/1	M. Tel-Aviv	a	1-4	*Ambrose*
29/1	M. Petach-Tikva	h	1-3	*Makriev*
5/2	H. Beer Sheva	a	0-5	
12/2	M. Haifa	h	1-2	*Kapiloto*
19/2	Beitar	a	0-0	
26/2	Bnei Sakhnin	h	0-0	
5/3	Bnei Yehuda	h	1-2	*Kingue*
12/3	H. Petach-Tikva	a	1-3	*Ohayon Mo.*
20/3	H. Tel-Aviv	h	3-3	*Makriev 2, Ohayon Mo. (p)*
2/4	H. Ramat Gan	a	2-1	*Biton 2*
9/4	H. Haifa	h	0-0	
16/4	H. Ashkelon	a	1-4	*Makriev (p)*
23/4	H. Ashkelon	h	4-1	*Shriki, Makriev 2, Ohayon Mo.*
30/4	Bnei Sakhnin	a	0-1	
7/5	Beitar	h	0-0	
14/5	H. Petach-Tikva	a	1-1	*Ohayon Mo.*
21/5	H. Ramat Gan	h	1-0	*Ohayon Mo. (p)*

No	Name	Nat	DoB	Pos	Aps	(s)	Gls
3	Matti AFLLALO		26/4/85	D	2	(2)	
28	Efe AMBROSE	NGA	18/10/88	D	30		1
18	Timor AVITAN		27/11/91	A	1	(1)	
12	Eden BATIT		21/3/79	D	3	(4)	
4	Nir BITON		30/10/91	M	33	(1)	5
15	Christopher BOMBELE	BEL	26/12/91	A	1	(1)	
16	Ben BUTBUL		22/5/90	M	3	(11)	
8	Rahamim CHECKUL		8/5/88	D	30	(1)	
12	Izthak COHEN		1/1/90	A	4	(1)	
17	Muhamad DARWISH		2/6/91	M		(2)	
2	Cristian GONZÁLEZ	URU	19/12/76	D	2		
5	Nisso KAPILOTO		10/1/89	D	10		1
6	Stéphane KINGUE	CMR	2/6/85	M	29		2
11	Amir LAVIE		8/9/89	M	6	(11)	1
20	Ori MAJABI		12/9/87	D	11	(5)	
7	Dimitar Ivanov MAKRIEV	BUL	7/1/84	A	24	(4)	9
1	Offir MARCIANO		7/10/89	G	9		
19	Nevo MIZRAHI		26/7/87	A	5	(21)	3
17	Mattan OHAYON		25/2/86	D	16		
9	Moshe OHAYON		24/5/83	M	33	(1)	17
2	Isreal ROSH		5/3/88	D	13	(5)	
27	Idan SADE		8/5/88	D	4	(10)	
25	Emmanuel SARKI	NGA	26/12/87	M	26	(5)	1
33	Youssi SHEKEL		24/9/84	G	21	(1)	
14	Idan SHRIKI		30/11/81	A	31	(2)	3
15	Idan SROR		5/10/86	M	2	(3)	
22	Dragan STOJKIĆ	BIH	7/10/75	G	5		
5	Loai TAHA		26/11/89	D	1		
24	Yom-Tov Ofer WERTA		23/5/90	D	30	(2)	1

BEITAR JERUSALEM FC

Coach – Uri Malmilian; (17/1/11) Roni Levi

Founded – 1939

Stadium – Teddy (21,600)

MAJOR HONOURS: Israeli League – (6) 1987, 1993, 1997, 1998, 2007, 2008; Israeli Cup – (7) 1976, 1979, 1985, 1986, 1989, 2008, 2009.

2010				
21/8	M. Netanya	a	1-4	*Ben Shoshan*
29/8	M. Tel-Aviv	h	0-1	
11/9	M. Petach-Tikva	a	1-2	*Yeboah*
25/9	H. Beer Sheva	h	5-1	*Ben Shoshan 2, Baruchyan A., Tal (p), Azriel*
3/10	M. Haifa	a	3-3	*González, Yeboah, Azriel*
18/10	Bnei Yehuda	a	1-2	*Tal*
25/10	Bnei Sakhnin	h	0-0	
30/10	Ashdod	a	0-3	
6/11	H. Petach-Tikva	h	0-2	
14/11	H. Tel-Aviv	a	0-0	
20/11	H. Ramat Gan	h	3-2	*Azriel 2, Baruchyan A.*
27/11	H. Haifa	a	2-0	*Azriel 2*
4/12	H. Ashkelon	h	4-0	*Azriel 2, Ayeli, Ben Shoshan*
11/12	H. Akko	a	0-3	
18/12	H. Kiryat Shmona	h	1-0	*Baruchyan A.*
2011				
1/1	M. Netanya	h	0-0	
10/1	M. Tel-Aviv	a	0-1	
15/1	M. Petach-Tikva	h	0-2	
22/1	H. Beer Sheva	a	2-1	*Tal, González*
30/1	M. Haifa	h	0-0	
5/2	Bnei Yehuda	h	1-1	*Baruchyan A. (p)*
12/2	Bnei Sakhnin	a	0-1	
19/2	Ashdod	h	0-0	
26/2	H. Petach-Tikva	a	0-1	
7/3	H. Tel-Aviv	h	1-0	*Yeboah*
12/3	H. Ramat Gan	a	0-0	
19/3	H. Haifa	h	1-0	*Ben Lulu*
2/4	H. Ashkelon	a	1-2	*Azriel (p)*
9/4	H. Akko	h	2-0	*Tal, Moyal*
16/4	H. Kiryat Shmona	a	1-0	*Moyal*
23/4	H. Ramat Gan	h	5-1	*Baruchyan A., Azriel, Tal (p), Yeboah, Hadad*
30/4	H. Petach-Tikva	h	3-0	*Baruchyan A. 2, Cohen*
7/5	Ashdod	a	0-0	
14/5	H. Ashkelon	h	0-1	
21/5	Bnei Sakhnin	a	0-1	

No	Name	Nat	DoB	Pos	Aps	(s)	Gls
4	Cristián Valenzuela ÁLVAREZ	CHI	20/1/80	D	9		
12	Serge AYELI	CIV	23/8/81	A	4	(5)	1
10	Chen AZRIEL		26/6/88	A	20	(10)	10
8	Aviram BARUCHYAN		20/3/85	M	23	(5)	7
16	Evitar BARUCHYAN		24/8/89	D	11	(1)	
29	Moshe BEN LULU		13/4/88	M	6	(10)	1
7	Amit BEN SHOSHAN		23/5/85	A	25	(3)	4
6	Tomer BEN YOSSEF		2/9/79	D	19	(1)	
25	Matan BRASHI		6/5/88	D	1	(2)	
26	Steven COHEN	FRA	27/2/86	M	12	(13)	1
24	Elazar DASA		3/12/92	D	17	(1)	
9	Dan EINBINDER		16/8/89	M	16	(2)	
12	Tal ELMISHALI		8/10/89	A		(2)	
23	Darío Ezequiel FERNÁNDEZ	ARG	24/9/78	M	4	(4)	
5	Shimon GERSHON		6/10/77	D	2		
2	Cristian GONZÁLEZ	URU	19/12/76	D	33		2
15	Shay HADAD		2/7/87	D	7	(15)	1
1	Ariel HAROSH		25/5/88	G	35		
4	Hervé KAGE	COD	10/4/89	D	6		
23	Gal LEVI		19/11/87	M		(2)	
55	Moshe MISHAELOV		14/9/83	D	24	(3)	
21	Kobi MOYAL		12/6/87	M	18	(3)	2
27	Eden NACHMANI		13/10/90	A		(1)	
28	Lior REUBEN		12/12/80	D	13	(4)	
18	Avi RIKAN		10/9/88	D	25	(4)	
11	Idan TAL		13/9/75	M	29	(3)	5
10	Toto TAMUZ		1/4/88	A	1	(1)	
17	Samuel YEBOAH	GHA	8/8/86	A	25	(5)	4

BNEI SAKHNIN FC

Coach – Yuval Naim; (14/8/10) Haim Levi; (27/9/10) Slobodan Drapić (SRB); (4/4/11) Shlomi Dora

Founded – 1993

Stadium – Doha (6,000)

MAJOR HONOURS: Israeli Cup – (1) 2004.

2010				
21/8	H. Kiryat Shmona	a	0-2	
28/8	M. Netanya	h	1-1	*Abu Ria*
11/9	M. Tel-Aviv	a	0-4	
25/9	M. Petach-Tikva	h	2-3	*Zahora, Kiel*
2/10	H. Beer Sheva	a	0-1	
16/10	M. Haifa	h	1-2	*Zbedat*
25/10	Beitar	a	0-0	
30/10	Bnei Yehuda	a	0-2	
6/11	Ashdod	h	0-2	
15/11	H. Petach-Tikva	a	1-0	*Čeh*
20/11	H. Tel-Aviv	h	1-3	*Dănălache*
27/11	H. Ramat Gan	a	2-1	*Kasum, Dănălache*
4/12	H. Haifa	h	1-3	*Čeh*
11/12	H. Ashkelon	a	0-1	
18/12	H. Akko	h	0-1	
2011				
1/1	H. Kiryat Shmona	h	1-0	*Abu Ria*
8/1	M. Netanya	a	0-1	
15/1	M. Tel-Aviv	h	1-3	*Abu Salah*
23/1	M. Petach-Tikva	a	2-1	*Abu Ria, Hazurov*
29/1	H. Beer Sheva	h	1-1	*Hazurov*
5/2	M. Haifa	a	0-1	
12/2	Beitar	h	1-0	*Kasum*
19/2	Bnei Yehuda	h	0-1	
26/2	Ashdod	a	0-0	
5/3	H. Petach-Tikva	h	1-1	*Hazurov*
12/3	H. Tel-Aviv	a	0-1	
21/3	H. Ramat Gan	h	0-0	
3/4	H. Haifa	a	1-4	*Zbedat*
9/4	H. Ashkelon	h	2-0	*Yeye, Ganaym H.*
16/4	H. Akko	a	0-0	
23/4	H. Petach-Tikva	a	1-1	*Kasum*
30/4	Ashdod	h	1-0	*Hazurov*
7/5	H. Ashkelon	a	1-2	*Čeh (p)*
14/5	H. Ramat Gan	a	2-1	*Hazurov, Ganaym H.*
21/5	Beitar	h	1-0	*Abu Ria*

No	Name	Nat	DoB	Pos	Aps	(s)	Gls
27	Mahran ABU RIA		22/1/83	D	31	(1)	4
8	Ala'a ABU SALAH		25/6/87	M	30	(1)	1
14	Haim BANOON		26/7/80	M	4	(1)	
16	Emad BDARNH		18/3/89	M		(1)	
26	Atanas BORNOSUZOV	BUL	5/10/79	M	4	(4)	
10	Nastja ČEH	SVN	26/1/78	M	26	(4)	3
18	Liran COHEN		4/2/83	M	13	(14)	
1	Meir COHEN		8/6/72	G	17		
9	Cristian Costin DĂNĂLACHE	ROU	15/7/82	A	9	(1)	2
12	Bassem GANAYM		7/10/78	D	12	(5)	
17	Hamed GANAYM		8/7/87	M	25	(5)	2
15	Haled HALAILA		16/12/82	M	31	(2)	
19	Kostadin HAZUROV	BUL	5/8/85	A	18		5
3	Tal HEN		4/8/79	D	14	(1)	
22	Mahmod KANDALI		11/8/88	G	18		
21	Ahmed KASUM		25/1/85	A	26	(7)	3
7	Lohab KIEL		3/5/88	M	31	(3)	1

No	Name	Nat	DoB	Pos	Aps	(s)	Gls
[illegible]	Yaniv LUZON		26/8/81	M	5	(5)	
8	Darijan MATIČ	SVN	28/5/83	M	12		
4	Danail MITEV	BUL	11/1/84	A	6	(2)	
0	Anan NASSER AL DIN		20/11/88	M		(1)	
5	Ahmed Ibrahem SAID		2/7/90	A		(3)	
0	Kenny SEIT		17/12/93	A	1	(5)	
0	Idan WEITZMAN		20/4/85	M	13	(2)	
	Lenkebe Paty YEYE	COD	2/2/82	D	33		1
9	Dario ZAHORA	CRO	21/3/82	A	1	(4)	1
3	Obada ZBEDAT		30/7/90	A	5	(21)	2

BNEI YEHUDA TEL-AVIV FC

Coach – Dror Kashtan

Founded – 1936

Stadium – Bloomfield (15,700)

MAJOR HONOURS: Israeli League – (1) 1990; Israeli Cup – (2) 1968, 1981.

2010				
21/8	H. Ramat Gan	h	0-0	
28/8	H. Beer Sheva	a	1-0	*Yavruyan*
12/9	H. Haifa	a	0-2	
25/9	M. Haifa	h	2-3	*Galván 2*
2/10	H. Ashkelon	a	0-0	
18/10	Beitar	h	2-1	*Galván, Ivaškevičius*
23/10	H. Akko	a	1-3	*Yavruyan*
30/10	Bnei Sakhnin	h	2-0	*Abu Zeid, Menashe*
6/11	H. Kiryat Shmona	a	2-2	*Balili, Biton*
13/11	Ashdod	h	0-0	
20/11	M. Netanya	a	0-0	
27/11	H. Petach-Tikva	h	2-0	*Galván 2*
4/12	M. Tel-Aviv	a	0-2	
15/12	H. Tel-Aviv	h	0-1	
18/12	M. Petach-Tikva	a	0-3	
2011				
1/1	H. Ramat Gan	a	1-1	*Balili*
8/1	H. Beer Sheva	h	0-0	
15/1	H. Haifa	h	3-2	*Levi, Galván, Edri (p)*
22/1	M. Haifa	a	0-1	
29/1	H. Ashkelon	h	2-0	*Menashe, Galván*
5/2	Beitar	a	1-1	*Amsis*
12/2	H. Akko	h	1-0	*Zairi L.*
19/2	Bnei Sakhnin	a	1-0	*Galván*
26/2	H. Kiryat Shmona	h	3-1	*Galván 2, Balili*
5/3	Ashdod	a	2-1	*Rali, Balili*
13/3	M. Netanya	h	1-1	*Galván*
20/3	H. Petach-Tikva	a	1-2	*Galván*
2/4	M. Tel-Aviv	h	2-0	*Galván 2*
9/4	H. Tel-Aviv	a	1-0	*Zairi L.*
17/4	M. Petach-Tikva	h	2-0	*Zairi L., Galván*
25/4	H. Tel-Aviv	a	1-2	*Marinković*
30/4	M. Tel-Aviv	h	1-3	*Ivaškevičius*
7/5	H. Kiryat Shmona	a	2-1	*Zairi L. 2*
14/5	M. Netanya	a	4-0	*Hadad, Menashe, Marinković, Galván*
21/5	M. Haifa	h	1-1	*Menashe*

No	Name	Nat	DoB	Pos	Aps	(s)	Gls
15	Hassan ABU ZEID		4/4/91	M	11	(9)	1
18	Omri AFEK		31/3/79	M	4	(2)	
14	Amir AGAIOV		10/2/92	M		(5)	
1	Bamidele AIYENUGBA	NGA	20/11/83	G	35		
9	George AMSIS		17/12/90	A	5	(3)	1
17	Itzhak AZOZ		30/11/85	D	27	(3)	
8	Asi BALDUT		21/10/81	M	3	(12)	
11	Pini BALILI		18/6/79	A	24	(4)	4
14	Moshe BITON		18/11/82	A	6	(8)	1
23	Kfir EDRI		12/10/76	D	33	(2)	1
20	Pedro Joaquín GALVÁN	ARG	18/8/85	M	27	(2)	16
6	Iván Alonso GARRIDO	COL	2/6/81	D	12		
13	Nitzan HA'ARONOVIC		8/9/89	D		(3)	
21	Aviv HADAD		4/2/84	D	33		1
19	Gil ITZHAK		29/3/93	A	1		
16	Kęstutis IVAŠKEVIČIUS	LTU	17/4/85	M	33		2
25	Shlomi LEVI		29/7/91	A	7	(7)	1
19	Nenad MARINKOVIĆ	SRB	22/9/88	M	13		2
26	Shalev MENASHE		23/5/82	M	20	(14)	4
4	Din MORI		8/11/88	D	25	(1)	
7	Oz RALI		22/12/87	D	20	(9)	1
19	Yeghia YAVRUYAN	ARM	18/10/81	A	12	(4)	2
27	Ben ZAIRI		17/5/92	M	4	(1)	
10	Liroy ZAIRI		2/3/89	M	30	(3)	5

HAPOEL AKKO FC

Coach – Eli Cohen

Founded – 1946

Stadium – Green, Nazareth Ilit (3,000)

2010				
21/8	Ashdod	h	1-2	*Dayan*
28/8	H. Petach-Tikva	a	2-2	*Kalebat, og (Assous)*
11/9	H. Tel-Aviv	h	2-2	*Djako, Falczuk*
26/9	H. Ramat Gan	a	2-3	*Dayan 2 (1p)*
2/10	H. Haifa	h	2-1	*Djako 2*
16/10	H. Ashkelon	a	0-0	
23/10	Bnei Yehuda	h	3-1	*Dayan, Djako 2*
30/10	H. Kiryat Shmona	h	3-0	*Dayan, Djako, Kalebat*
7/11	M. Netanya	a	3-1	*Dayan 2, Kalebat*
13/11	M. Tel-Aviv	h	3-1	*Djako 2, Dayan*
20/11	M. Petach-Tikva	a	1-1	*Djako*
27/11	H. Beer Sheva	h	2-3	*Djako, Dayan (p)*
6/12	M. Haifa	a	1-3	*Gita*
11/12	Beitar	h	3-0	*Dayan, Radi, Kalebat*
18/12	Bnei Sakhnin	a	1-0	*og (Dănălache)*
2011				
1/1	Ashdod	a	1-3	*Dayan*
8/1	H. Petach-Tikva	h	3-0	*Radi 2, Dayan*
17/1	H. Tel-Aviv	a	1-4	*Harosh*
22/1	H. Ramat Gan	h	0-0	
29/1	H. Haifa	a	1-1	*Falczuk*
5/2	H. Ashkelon	h	1-0	*Dayan*
12/2	Bnei Yehuda	a	0-1	
20/2	H. Kiryat Shmona	a	2-2	*Knafo, Falczuk*
26/2	M. Netanya	h	0-0	
5/3	M. Tel-Aviv	a	2-2	*Dayan, Falczuk*
12/3	M. Petach-Tikva	h	1-1	*Barkai*
19/3	H. Beer Sheva	a	2-0	*Radi, Zome*
2/4	M. Haifa	h	0-2	
9/4	Beitar	a	0-2	
16/4	Bnei Sakhnin	h	0-0	
23/4	M. Petach-Tikva	a	1-4	*Cohen S.*
30/4	H. Beer Sheva	a	3-2	*og (Adeleye), Knafo, Zome*
7/5	H. Haifa	h	2-1	*Radi (p), Kalebat*

No	Name	Nat	DoB	Pos	Aps	(s)	Gls
11	Ibrahim ABDUL RAZAK	GHA	18/4/83	A	11	(3)	
17	Samed Abdul AWUDU	GHA	15/9/84	A		(2)	
24	Geva BARKAI		29/6/78	D	15	(4)	1
19	Ben BENJAMIN		17/12/85	M	31		
3	Itzhak COHEN		22/4/83	D	26		
10	Sagiv COHEN		20/9/87	D	3	(8)	1
9	Roei DAYAN		19/9/84	A	27	(3)	14
25	Fidelis Tochukwu DIMAKU	NGA	22/4/89	D	24	(2)	
32	Arafat DJAKO	TOG	30/6/91	A	16		10
20	Liad ELMALIAH		21/2/89	M	22	(7)	
5	Ilay ERLIKH		14/1/89	D	3	(4)	
18	Nicolás Gastón FALCZUK	ARG	16/11/86	A	19	(10)	4
15	Oshri GITA		2/7/85	A	7	(7)	1
1	Dudu GORESH		1/2/80	G	33		
23	Shimon HAROSH		20/2/87	D	23		1
34	Mohamd KALEBAT		15/6/90	A	11	(14)	5

11	Avi KNAFO		4/8/82	A	8	(4)	2
35	Ran KOJOK		12/1/81	D	26	(4)	
8	Roy LEVI		4/9/87	D	13	(6)	
7	Hana NASSER		27/3/91	D	6	(1)	
14	Maharan RADI		1/7/82	M	29	(1)	5
13	Kevin RAYNSHTEIN		22/2/91	M		(3)	
20	Elior SAIDER		17/11/91	A		(1)	
7	Shachar SIMANTOV		18/4/79	M	1	(1)	
21	Jonatan TENENBAUM		1/9/79	D		(1)	
21	Alexander ZAHAVI	USA	21/1/91	A	2	(8)	
30	Louis René ZOME	CMR	6/4/88	A	7	(2)	2

HAPOEL ASHKELON FC

Coach – Guy Azuri; (18/3/11) Eli Mahpud

Founded – 1955

Stadium – Sala Stadium (10,000)

2010				
21/8	H. Petach-Tikva	h	3-1	*Abass, Gawu 2*
28/8	H. Tel-Aviv	a	1-5	*Levi*
11/9	H. Ramat Gan	h	1-1	*Levi*
25/9	H. Haifa	a	2-1	*Levi, Gawu*
2/10	Bnei Yehuda	h	0-0	
16/10	H. Akko	h	0-0	
23/10	H. Kiryat Shmona	a	2-2	*Levi 2*
30/10	M. Netanya	h	0-4	
6/11	M. Tel-Aviv	a	0-2	
13/11	M. Petach-Tikva	h	0-1	
21/11	H. Beer Sheva	a	0-1	
27/11	M. Haifa	h	0-3	
4/12	Beitar	a	0-4	
11/12	Bnei Sakhnin	h	1-0	*Fadida*
18/12	Ashdod	a	2-3	*Abass 2*
2011				
2/1	H. Petach-Tikva	a	2-0	*Tobul, Goata*
8/1	H. Tel-Aviv	h	0-2	
15/1	H. Ramat Gan	a	4-0	*Ayeli, Gawu, Goata, Abass*
22/1	H. Haifa	h	0-0	
29/1	Bnei Yehuda	a	0-2	
5/2	H. Akko	a	0-1	
13/2	H. Kiryat Shmona	h	0-1	
19/2	M. Netanya	a	0-3	
26/2	M. Tel-Aviv	h	2-4	*Goata, Gawu*
5/3	M. Petach-Tikva	a	0-4	
12/3	H. Beer Sheva	h	3-4	*Abass, Yavruyan, og (Gan)*
19/3	M. Haifa	a	0-3	
2/4	Beitar	h	2-1	*Gawu 2*
9/4	Bnei Sakhnin	a	0-2	
16/4	Ashdod	h	4-1	*Goata, Abass 2, Gazal*
23/4	Ashdod	a	1-4	*Filekovič*
30/4	H. Ramat Gan	a	0-2	
7/5	Bnei Sakhnin	h	2-1	*Gazal, Yavruyan*
14/5	Beitar	a	1-0	*Biruk*
21/5	H. Petach-Tikva	h	0-3	

No	Name	Nat	DoB	Pos	Aps	(s)	Gls
11	Mahmod ABASS		29/7/88	M	26	(4)	7
22	Stephen AHORLU	GHA	5/9/88	G	32		
14	Or ALAWA		27/12/90	D		(13)	
20	Serge AYELI	CIV	23/8/81	A	6	(6)	1
18	Osman BASHIRU	GHA	5/5/89	A	9	(5)	
8	Eshetu BIRUK		15/6/84	M	1	(10)	1
5	Mor DAHAN		19/3/89	D	3	(1)	
21	Yaniv ELUL		17/9/78	D	27	(4)	
7	Hanan FADIDA		1/12/81	A	5	(6)	1
17	Suad FILEKOVIČ	SVN	16/9/78	D	14		1
27	Eric GAWU	GHA	10/11/82	A	32		7
6	Ravid GAZAL		9/6/82	M	27	(2)	2
1	Itzhak GIGI		1/12/88	G	3	(1)	
18	Oshri GITA		2/7/85	A	8	(5)	
9	Snir GOATA		7/1/88	M	20	(11)	4
26	Daniel HEIDMAN		10/11/82	M	14	(5)	
20	Michael KIRTAVA		21/8/85	M		(5)	
10	Eran LEVI		4/8/85	M	11		5
28	Darko LOVRIĆ	SRB	24/11/80	D	30		
2	Tal MACHLUF		31/8/91	D		(1)	
30	Zurab MENTESHASHVILI	GEO	30/1/80	M	15		
4	Kobi MUSA		18/4/82	D	8	(2)	
12	Eric NYARKO	GHA	2/10/83	M	2		
7	Raz OHAYON		8/3/93	M		(2)	
23	Shay PATLACH		25/8/86	D	20	(11)	
15	Amaya TAGA		4/2/85	M	29		
16	Adir TOBUL		3/6/79	D	24		1
10	Yeghia YAVRUYAN	ARM	18/10/81	A	16	(1)	2
8	Majd YOUNIS		15/3/89	D	3	(5)	

HAPOEL BEER SHEVA FC

Coach – Nir Klinger

Founded – 1949

Stadium – Artur Vasermil (13,000)

MAJOR HONOURS: Israeli League – (2) 1975, 1976; Israeli Cup – (1) 1997.

2010				
23/8	M. Petach-Tikva	a	1-0	*Asulin L.*
28/8	Bnei Yehuda	h	0-1	
13/9	M. Haifa	h	1-1	*Gan*
25/9	Beitar	a	1-5	*Yehiel*
2/10	Bnei Sakhnin	h	1-0	*Vasconcelos*
17/10	Ashdod	a	3-0	*(w/o; original result 3-3 Revivo 2, Asulin L.)*
23/10	H. Petach-Tikva	h	0-0	
30/10	H. Tel-Aviv	a	2-3	*Asulin L., Meliksson*
6/11	H. Ramat Gan	h	2-0	*og (Ben Lolo), Asulin L.*
13/11	H. Haifa	a	1-1	*Revivo*
21/11	H. Ashkelon	h	1-0	*Gavish*
27/11	H. Akko	a	3-2	*Asulin L. 2, Meliksson*
6/12	H. Kiryat Shmona	h	1-1	*Meliksson*
11/12	M. Netanya	a	0-1	
20/12	M. Tel-Aviv	h	0-1	
2011				
1/1	M. Petach-Tikva	h	2-1	*Meliksson (p), William*
8/1	Bnei Yehuda	a	0-0	
15/1	M. Haifa	a	2-2	*Asulin L., Levi*
22/1	Beitar	h	1-2	*Levi*
29/1	Bnei Sakhnin	a	1-1	*William*
5/2	Ashdod	h	5-0	*Levi, Gabay 3, Gavish*
12/2	H. Petach-Tikva	a	1-3	*Yehiel*
19/2	H. Tel-Aviv	h	0-3	
26/2	H. Ramat Gan	a	0-0	
5/3	H. Haifa	h	0-2	
12/3	H. Ashkelon	a	4-3	*Revivo (p), William, og (Taga), Gavish*
19/3	H. Akko	h	0-2	
2/4	H. Kiryat Shmona	a	0-1	
9/4	M. Netanya	h	1-2	*Naser*
16/4	M. Tel-Aviv	a	2-0	*Gavish, Revivo (p)*
23/4	H. Haifa	a	2-1	*Basit, Naser*
30/4	H. Akko	h	2-3	*Gabay, Uzan*
7/5	M. Petach-Tikva	a	1-1	*Uzan*

No	Name	Nat	DoB	Pos	Aps	(s)	Gls
8	Ibrahim ABDUL RAZAK	GHA	18/4/83	A	8	(3)	
23	Moshe ABUHAZEIRA		24/12/92	A		(1)	
28	Ryan ADELEYE	USA	28/4/87	D	10	(8)	
7	Lior ASULIN		6/10/80	A	20	(7)	7
21	Moshe ASULIN		11/10/88	M	4	(5)	
16	Zach BARBI		27/3/93	M	1		
23	Ibrahim BASIT	GHA	13/10/90	A	7	(15)	1
11	James BISSUE	GHA	15/6/91	A	3	(4)	

2	Ohad COHEN		10/6/75	G	29		
3	Ofir DAVIDAZE		5/5/91	D	30		
	Dor DAVIDI		20/10/87	G	1		
	Yossi ELKAYAM		26/3/89	M		(2)	
6	Dovev GABAY		1/4/87	A	12	(1)	4
0	Lior GAN		21/8/86	D	18	(1)	1
6	Oded GAVISH		23/6/89	D	28	(1)	4
4	Aviatar ILOUZ		4/11/83	D	26	(3)	
	Nadav KEDAR		9/1/87	D	2	(3)	
9	Eran LEVI		4/8/85	M	9	(3)	3
2	Daniel LIFSHITZ		24/4/88	G	1	(1)	
2	Shai LOOK		24/4/90	D	3		
6	Uri MACHLUF		6/4/88	G	2		
6	Zahi MACHLUF		14/3/91	M		(2)	
4	Maor MELIKSSON		30/10/84	M	19		4
7	Siraj NASER		2/9/90	M	10	(11)	2
0	David REVIVO		5/12/77	M	29	(3)	5
	RICARDO Ribeiro FERNANDES	POR	21/4/78	M	14	(1)	
5	Eyal SHEN		29/1/80	M	2		
7	Yossi TURGEMAN		16/11/86	D	3	(3)	
5	Yehiel TZAGAI		27/1/83	M	2	(7)	
7	Yonatan UZAN		11/2/93	A		(2)	2
0	Bernardo Lino Castro Paes VASCONCELOS	POR	10/6/79	A	10	(3)	1
25	WILLIAM Ribeiro Soares	BRA	7/2/85	M	32		3
12	Avi YEHIEL		26/9/79	D	28		2
18	Liel ZAGURI		10/11/90	D		(1)	

HAPOEL HAIFA FC

Coach – Nitzan Shirazi

Founded – 1924

Stadium – Kiriat Eliezer (17,000)

MAJOR HONOURS: Israeli League – (1) 1999; Israeli Cup – (3) 1963, 1966, 1974.

2010				
21/8	H. Tel-Aviv	h	1-0	*Stojanović*
28/8	H. Ramat Gan	a	2-1	*Ben Basat, Stojanović (p)*
12/9	Bnei Yehuda	h	2-0	*Arel 2*
25/9	H. Ashkelon	h	1-2	*Stojanović*
2/10	H. Akko	a	1-2	*Buzorgi*
16/10	H. Kiryat Shmona	h	1-4	*Grubješić*
23/10	M. Netanya	a	1-1	*Abu-El-Nir*
1/11	M. Tel-Aviv	h	0-0	
6/11	M. Petach-Tikva	a	3-2	*Ben Basat 2, Maman*
13/11	H. Beer Sheva	h	1-1	*Ben Basat*
22/11	M. Haifa	a	0-0	
27/11	Beitar	h	0-2	
4/12	Bnei Sakhnin	a	3-1	*Ben Basat 2, Arel*
11/12	Ashdod	h	2-0	*Maman, Ben Basat*
19/12	H. Petach-Tikva	a	0-2	
2011				
1/1	H. Tel-Aviv	a	0-5	
8/1	H. Ramat Gan	h	2-0	*Ben Basat 2*
15/1	Bnei Yehuda	a	2-3	*Ben Basat, Maman*
22/1	H. Ashkelon	a	0-0	
29/1	H. Akko	h	1-1	*Ben Basat*
5/2	H. Kiryat Shmona	a	3-1	*Ben Basat 2, Baldut*
12/2	M. Netanya	h	1-2	*Ben Basat (p)*
19/2	M. Tel-Aviv	a	1-0	*Maman*
26/2	M. Petach-Tikva	h	1-1	*Abu-El-Nir*
5/3	H. Beer Sheva	a	2-0	*Ben Basat (p), Abu-El-Nir*
14/3	M. Haifa	h	0-2	
19/3	Beitar	a	0-1	
3/4	Bnei Sakhnin	h	4-1	*Baldut, Maman, Vered, Ben Basat*
9/4	Ashdod	a	0-0	
16/4	H. Petach-Tikva	h	3-2	*Ben Basat, Abu-El-Nir, Maman*
23/4	H. Beer Sheva	h	1-2	*Ben Basat*
30/4	M. Petach-Tikva	h	0-2	
7/5	H. Akko	a	1-2	*Buzorgi*

No	Name	Nat	DoB	Pos	Aps	(s)	Gls
23	Amir ABU-EL-NIR		27/2/89	A	9	(19)	4
20	Ran ABUKARAT		14/12/88	M	13	(13)	
22	Gad AMOS		24/12/88	G	6		
18	Gal AREL		9/7/89	M	19	(3)	3
16	Asi BALDUT		21/10/81	M	12	(1)	2
9	Eden BEN BASAT		8/9/86	A	30		18
11	Alon BUZORGI		29/3/90	A		(7)	2
26	Yossi DORA		25/8/81	M	29	(1)	
5	Oded ELKAYAM		9/2/88	D	2	(1)	
14	Nikola GRUBJEŠIĆ	SRB	29/6/84	A	4	(1)	1
25	Golan HERMON		26/9/77	D	24	(1)	
1	Tvrtko KALE	CRO	5/6/74	G	27		
8	Hiasham KIWAN		17/5/87	M	12	(11)	
17	Sharon LEVI		1/6/87	D	3	(1)	
24	Savity LIPENIA	COD	17/4/79	D	31		
15	Hanan MAMAN		28/8/89	M	22	(7)	6
21	Oshri ROASH		25/7/88	D	28	(3)	
6	Roee SHUKRANI		26/6/90	M	8	(7)	
10	Saša STOJANOVIĆ	SRB	21/1/83	M	22	(5)	3
13	Eyal TARTAZKI		13/9/77	D	29		
19	Omer VERED		25/1/90	D	30		1
55	Idan WEITZMAN		20/4/85	M	3	(8)	

HAPOEL KIRYAT SHMONA FC

Coach – Ran Ben Shimon

Founded – 2000

Stadium – Municipal (5,300)

2010				
21/8	Bnei Sakhnin	h	2-0	*Rochet, Hemo*
28/8	Ashdod	a	2-2	*Amasha V. 2*
11/9	H. Petach-Tikva	h	3-1	*Hasarma, Cohen 2*
25/9	H. Tel-Aviv	a	4-2	*Amasha V. 3, Njovu*
4/10	H. Ramat Gan	h	1-0	*Baldovaliev (p)*
16/10	H. Haifa	a	4-1	*Amasha V. 2., Njovu, Shitrit*
23/10	H. Ashkelon	h	2-2	*Cohen, Lavie*
30/10	H. Akko	a	0-3	
6/11	Bnei Yehuda	h	2-2	*Cohen, Elisha*
13/11	M. Netanya	h	3-0	*Cohen 2, Amasha V.*
20/11	M. Tel-Aviv	a	1-0	*Badash*
27/11	M. Petach-Tikva	h	2-2	*Badash, Hasarma (p)*
6/12	H. Beer Sheva	a	1-1	*Elisha*
13/12	M. Haifa	h	0-1	
18/12	Beitar	a	0-1	
2011				
1/1	Bnei Sakhnin	a	0-1	
8/1	Ashdod	h	3-0	*Swissa, Elisha, Hemo*
15/1	H. Petach-Tikva	a	3-1	*Gabai, Njovu, Swissa*
24/1	H. Tel-Aviv	h	1-1	*Njovu*
29/1	H. Ramat Gan	a	3-0	*Cohen, Abuhazeira 2*
5/2	H. Haifa	h	1-3	*Abuhazeira*
13/2	H. Ashkelon	a	1-0	*Hasarma*
20/2	H. Akko	h	2-2	*Rochet, Njovu*
26/2	Bnei Yehuda	a	1-3	*Abuhazeira*
5/3	M. Netanya	a	1-1	*Abuhazeira*
12/3	M. Tel-Aviv	h	4-0	*Badash, Amasha V., Rochet, Lavie*
19/3	M. Petach-Tikva	a	0-0	
2/4	H. Beer Sheva	h	1-0	*Amasha V.*
11/4	M. Haifa	a	2-3	*Amasha V., Badash*
16/4	Beitar	h	0-1	
23/4	M. Tel-Aviv	a	1-3	*Abuhazeira (p)*
30/4	M. Netanya	a	3-3	*Amasha V. 2, Hemo*
7/5	Bnei Yehuda	h	1-2	*Shitrit*
16/5	M. Haifa	a	0-2	
21/5	H. Tel-Aviv	h	2-1	*Abuhazeira, Amasha V.*

No	Name	Nat	DoB	Pos	Aps	(s)	Gls
19	Shimon ABUHAZEIRA		10/10/86	A	11	(2)	7
14	Asa'ad AMASHA		31/7/91	D	2	(1)	
14	Viam AMASHA		8/8/85	A	20	(2)	14
22	Dani AMOS		2/2/87	G	11		

10	Shlomi AVISIDRIS		14/5/89	A	2	(12)	
2	Barak BACHAR		1/9/90	M	8		
20	Barak BADASH		30/8/82	A	13	(11)	4
25	Zoran BALDOVALIEV	MKD	21/5/83	A	5	(6)	1
7	Beni BEN ZAKEN		18/10/82	D	3	(17)	
19	Tomer BROCKS		20/12/85	D	3	(2)	
11	Elroi COHEN		7/1/89	M	16	(2)	7
27	Caleb Tochukwu EKWENUGO	NGA	1/8/88	A	1	(7)	
16	Adi ELISHA		28/1/90	M	20	(7)	3
15	Elad GABAI		15/11/85	D	27	(1)	1
18	Bryan Paul GERZICICH	USA	20/3/84	M	34		
55	Guy HAIMOV		9/3/86	G	24		
17	Salah HASARMA		24/2/74	D	32	(2)	3
24	Offir HEMO		10/12/87	M	13	(12)	3
5	Yaniv LAVIE		9/9/77	D	29		2
11	Wahil MARISAT		6/5/92	M	1	(1)	
8	William NJOVU	ZAM	4/3/87	M	26	(4)	5
23	Adrian ROCHET		26/5/87	M	34		3
26	Uri SHITRIT		21/1/86	D	31		2
9	Tomer SWISSA		22/12/88	M	9	(6)	2
27	Eitan TIBT		16/11/87	D	6	(2)	
3	Shir TZEDEK		22/8/89	D	4	(6)	

HAPOEL PETACH-TIKVA FC

Coach – Eli Mahpud; (17/10/10) Yuval Naim; (14/4/11) (Itzhak Shaki); (1/5/11) Gili Landau

Founded – 1935

Stadium – Ramat Gan (41,583)

MAJOR HONOURS: Israeli League – (6) 1955, 1959, 1960, 1961, 1962, 1963; Israeli Cup – (2) 1957, 1992.

2010				
21/8	H. Ashkelon	a	1-3	*Biton*
28/8	H. Akko	h	2-2	*Biton 2 (1p)*
11/9	H. Kiryat Shmona	a	1-3	*Biton*
25/9	M. Netanya	h	1-1	*og (Krupnik)*
2/10	M. Tel-Aviv	a	1-2	*Biton*
16/10	M. Petach-Tikva	h	1-4	*Biton*
23/10	H. Beer Sheva	a	0-0	
31/10	M. Haifa	h	0-1	
6/11	Beitar	a	2-0	*Biton 2 (1p)*
15/11	Bnei Sakhnin	h	0-1	
20/11	Ashdod	a	2-1	*Biton (p), Turgeman*
27/11	Bnei Yehuda	a	0-2	
4/12	H. Tel-Aviv	h	1-5	*og (Fransman)*
11/12	H. Ramat Gan	a	1-1	*Biton*
19/12	H. Haifa	h	2-0	*Biton 2*
2011				
2/1	H. Ashkelon	h	0-2	
8/1	H. Akko	a	0-3	
15/1	H. Kiryat Shmona	h	1-3	*Turgeman*
22/1	M. Netanya	a	3-3	*Kadusi 3*
29/1	M. Tel-Aviv	h	0-1	
5/2	M. Petach-Tikva	a	3-2	*Zaguri, Exbard, Dayan*
12/2	H. Beer Sheva	h	3-1	*Exbard, Dahan, Dayan*
21/2	M. Haifa	a	0-2	
26/2	Beitar	h	1-0	*Exbard*
5/3	Bnei Sakhnin	a	1-1	*Zaguri*
12/3	Ashdod	h	3-1	*Turgeman 2, Luzon*
20/3	Bnei Yehuda	h	2-1	*Stoller, Dayan*
4/4	H. Tel-Aviv	a	0-2	
10/4	H. Ramat Gan	h	2-0	*Turgeman, Kadusi*
16/4	H. Haifa	a	2-3	*Dayan, Tzarfati*
23/4	Bnei Sakhnin	h	1-1	*Dahan*
30/4	Beitar	a	0-3	
7/5	H. Ramat Gan	h	1-2	*Antebi*
14/5	Ashdod	h	1-1	*Exbard*
21/5	H. Ashkelon	a	3-0	*Tzarfati, Turgeman, Dahan*

No	Name	Nat	DoB	Pos	Aps	(s)	Gls
26	Daniel ADDO	GHA	6/3/84	D	23	(4)	
30	William Amartey AMAMOO	GHA	4/4/85	G	2	(1)	
23	Igal ANTEBI		1/8/74	D	12	(2)	1
4	Jonathan ASSOUS	FRA	2/9/86	M	15		
19	Sholmi Yossef AZULAY		30/3/90	M		(1)	
14	Or BEN HEMO		22/5/90	M	1	(2)	
20	Dudu BITON		1/3/88	A	15		12
6	Gal COHEN		14/8/82	D	31		
7	Rafael DAHAN		28/9/89	M	21	(7)	3
22	Guy DAYAN		20/8/86	A	24	(7)	4
13	Snir DORI		4/8/87	G	17		
12	Austin EJIDE	NGA	8/4/84	G	16		
24	Nizan ELKALAY		2/5/90	D	11	(2)	
77	Ido EXBARD		16/12/88	A	11	(11)	4
21	Or FISHBEIN		20/6/89	A		(1)	
21	Roy GORDANA		6/7/90	M	12	(1)	
4	Yehuda HUTA		19/2/89	D		(2)	
11	Ohad KADUSI		24/9/85	A	5	(17)	4
29	Elad KHOTABA		20/11/87	M	32		
8	Yaniv LUZON		26/8/81	M	15	(1)	1
23	Adi MAHPUD		30/1/89	D	1		
3	Emmanuel MATHIAS	TOG	3/4/86	D	5		
23	Mirlan MURZAEV	KGZ	29/3/90	A		(8)	
25	Mohamad NATOR		9/9/91	G		(1)	
15	Eyal SHEN		29/1/80	M	12	(6)	
16	Amiran SHKALIM		23/3/88	D	15	(1)	
27	Fabian STOLLER	SUI	31/3/88	M	15		1
17	Alon TURGEMAN		9/7/91	A	14	(11)	6
10	Guy TZARFATI		28/4/79	M	22	(10)	2
27	César Junior VIZA	PER	3/4/85	M	12	(2)	
9	Israel ZAGURI		29/1/90	M	26	(2)	2

HAPOEL RAMAT GAN FC

Coach – Shlomi Dora; (15/11/10) Tzvika Tzemach; (19/1/11) (Itzhak Baruch); (3/2/11) Yaron Hochenboym

Founded – 1927

Stadium – Winter (4,000)

MAJOR HONOURS: Israeli League – (1) 1964; Israeli Cup – (1) 2003.

2010				
21/8	Bnei Yehuda	a	0-0	
28/8	H. Haifa	h	1-2	*Telkiyski*
11/9	H. Ashkelon	a	1-1	*Haim*
26/9	H. Akko	h	3-2	*Telkiyski, Bibishkov 2*
4/10	H. Kiryat Shmona	a	0-1	
16/10	M. Netanya	h	0-1	
23/10	M. Tel-Aviv	a	0-2	
30/10	M. Petach-Tikva	h	0-2	
6/11	H. Beer Sheva	a	0-2	
13/11	M. Haifa	h	1-3	*Haim*
20/11	Beitar	a	2-3	*Telkiyski, Diamant*
27/11	Bnei Sakhnin	h	1-2	*Sror*
4/12	Ashdod	a	2-2	*Telkiyski (p), Bibishkov*
11/12	H. Petach-Tikva	h	1-1	*Telkiyski (p)*
18/12	H. Tel-Aviv	a	0-4	
2011				
1/1	Bnei Yehuda	h	1-1	*Chacana*
8/1	H. Haifa	a	0-2	
15/1	H. Ashkelon	h	0-4	
22/1	H. Akko	a	0-0	
29/1	H. Kiryat Shmona	h	0-3	
5/2	M. Netanya	a	0-2	
12/2	M. Tel-Aviv	h	0-3	
19/2	M. Petach-Tikva	a	1-4	*Tzemah*
26/2	H. Beer Sheva	h	0-0	
6/3	M. Haifa	a	2-3	*Chacana, Topuzakov*
12/3	Beitar	h	0-0	
21/3	Bnei Sakhnin	a	0-0	

4	Ashdod	h	1-2	*Topuzakov*
)/4	H. Petach-Tikva	a	0-2	
6/4	H. Tel-Aviv	h	1-2	*Shina*
3/4	Beitar	a	1-5	*Tzemah*
)/4	H. Ashkelon	h	2-0	*Chacana, Simantov*
'5	H. Petach-Tikva	a	2-1	*og (Cohen), Haim*
4/5	Bnei Sakhnin	h	1-2	Tzemah
1/5	Ashdod	a	0-1	

lo	Name	Nat	DoB	Pos	Aps	(s)	Gls
5	Shlomi ADREI		29/5/82	A	1	(6)	
	Itai ARKIN		7/7/88	G	34		
	Jonathan ASSOUS	FRA	2/9/86	M	8	(1)	
7	Samed Abdul AWUDU	GHA	15/9/84	A	5	(3)	
8	Tamir BEN AMI		28/2/79	M	19	(1)	
8	Hai BEN LOLO		28/1/82	D	16	(1)	
2	Ori BIBI		27/7/91	M	8	(5)	
9	Krum Georgiev BIBISHKOV	BUL	2/9/82	A	10	(2)	3
0	Omer BUKSENBAUM		12/11/82	M	13	(2)	
4	Carlos CHACANA	ARG	23/6/76	A	32	(2)	3
	Liron DIAMANT		4/4/90	A	24	(7)	1
	Oded ELKAYAM		9/2/88	D	18		
5	Dudu FADLON		16/9/76	D	13	(3)	
	Tamir FOR		19/8/82	D	17	(2)	
7	Offir HAIM		21/4/75	A	2	(16)	3
21	Tal HEN		4/8/79	D	15	(1)	
1	Amit KAMHAZI		7/4/91	M		(3)	
	Eli LEVI		15/5/75	D	11	(4)	
20	Gal LEVI		19/11/87	M	6	(7)	
32	Eliran OHAION		12/8/81	G	1		
5	PABLO Buendía Elvira	ESP	2/1/86	D	1		
28	Tamir RABACH		19/2/92	A		(1)	
23	Claudio Domingo RIVERO Rodríguez	URU	14/4/85	M	9		
3	Dan ROMANN		27/8/82	M	10	(2)	
15	Vladimir Broun ROZENFELD		6/5/89	M	7	(9)	
5	Yakir SHINA		25/9/85	D	27	(3)	1
24	Shachar SIMANTOV		18/4/79	M	5	(8)	1
11	Idan SROR		5/10/86	M	12	(6)	1
19	Aurelijus STAPONKA	LTU	9/11/83	A	1	(3)	
31	Dimitar TELKIYSKI	BUL	5/5/77	M	19	(3)	5
3	Elin TOPUZAKOV	BUL	5/2/77	D	25		2
16	Tzion TZEMAH		19/6/90	M	16		3

HAPOEL TEL-AVIV FC

Coach – Eli Gutman; (29/1/11) (Yossi Abuksis); (7/3/11) Eli Gutman

Founded – 1927

Stadium – Bloomfield (15,700)

MAJOR HONOURS: Israeli League – (14) 1934, 1935, 1936, 1938, 1940, 1943, 1957, 1966, 1969, 1981, 1986, 1988, 2000, 2010; Israeli Cup – (14) 1928, 1934, 1937, 1938, 1939, 1960, 1972, 1983, 1999, 2000, 2006, 2007, 2010, 2011.

2010

21/8	H. Haifa	a	0-1	
28/8	H. Ashkelon	h	5-1	*Zahavi 2, Shivhon, Vermouth 2*
11/9	H. Akko	a	2-2	*Maree, Tamuz*
25/9	H. Kiryat Shmona	h	2-4	*Shechter 2*
2/10	M. Netanya	a	3-1	*Tamuz, Sahar, Shechter*
16/10	M. Tel-Aviv	h	1-0	*Zahavi*
24/10	M. Petach-Tikva	a	2-1	*Douglas, Tuaama*
30/10	H. Beer Sheva	h	3-2	*Tamuz 2, Zahavi*
8/11	M. Haifa	a	2-0	*Abutbol, Vermouth*
14/11	Beitar	h	0-0	
20/11	Bnei Sakhnin	a	3-1	*Tamuz 2, Zahavi*
28/11	Ashdod	h	0-2	
4/12	H. Petach-Tikva	a	5-1	*Tamuz 2, Douglas, Zahavi, Abutbol*
15/12	Bnei Yehuda	a	1-0	*Vermouth*
18/12	H. Ramat Gan	h	4-0	*Sahar, Douglas, Tamuz, Abutbol*

2011

1/1	H. Haifa	h	5-0	*Sahar 2, Tuaama, Zahavi, Shechter (p)*
8/1	H. Ashkelon	a	2-0	*Bondarv, Tuaama*
17/1	H. Akko	h	4-1	*Sahar 2, Tamuz, Vermouth*
24/1	H. Kiryat Shmona	a	1-1	*Sahar*
29/1	M. Netanya	h	2-1	*og (Caporale), Sahar*
6/2	M. Tel-Aviv	a	1-1	*Badir*
14/2	M. Petach-Tikva	h	2-0	*Tamuz, Sahar*
19/2	H. Beer Sheva	a	3-0	*Tamuz, Sahar 2*
27/2	M. Haifa	h	4-1	*Sahar, Zahavi, Tamuz, Tuaama*
7/3	Beitar	a	0-1	
12/3	Bnei Sakhnin	h	1-0	*Tamuz*
20/3	Ashdod	a	3-3	*Tamuz 2, Sahar*
4/4	H. Petach-Tikva	h	2-0	*Tamuz (p), Sahar (p)*
9/4	Bnei Yehuda	h	0-1	
16/4	H. Ramat Gan	a	2-1	*Sahar, Badir*
25/4	Bnei Yehuda	h	2-1	*Zahavi, Tamuz*
30/4	M. Haifa	a	0-2	
7/5	M. Netanya	h	2-2	*Tamuz 2*
14/5	M. Tel-Aviv	h	2-2	*Fransman, Sahar*
21/5	H. Kiryat Shmona	a	1-2	*Tamuz (p)*

No	Name	Nat	DoB	Pos	Aps	(s)	Gls
18	Shay ABUTBOL		16/1/83	M	26	(5)	3
17	Ma'aran AL LALA		7/3/82	A	1	(4)	
10	Walid BADIR		12/3/74	D	24	(2)	2
19	Dedi BEN DAYAN		27/11/78	D	27		
22	Galil BEN SENAN		27/6/82	G	1		
4	Dani BONDARV		7/2/87	D	16		1
30	Elroi COHEN		7/1/89	M	4	(9)	
3	DOUGLAS da Silva	BRA	7/3/84	D	11	(1)	3
1	Vincent ENYEAMA	NGA	29/8/82	G	29		
17	Bevan FRANSMAN	RSA	31/10/83	D	30	(1)	1
21	Roy GORDANA		6/7/90	M	1		
24	Kfir IZENSTEIN		18/2/93	M		(1)	
23	Omri KENDA		6/7/86	D	19	(5)	
12	Victor MAREE		31/5/89	A	2	(17)	1
22	Itamar NITZAN		23/6/87	G	5		
3	Mário PEČALKA	SVK	28/12/80	D	6	(2)	
21	Shay REVIVO		13/12/86	M	1	(1)	
27	Romain ROCCHI	FRA	2/10/81	M	1	(2)	
11	Ben SAHAR		10/8/89	A	29	(5)	16
9	Itay SHECHTER		22/2/87	A	7	(4)	4
25	Gal SHISH		28/1/89	D	7	(4)	
7	Yossi SHIVHON		22/3/82	M	7	(18)	1
99	Toto TAMUZ		1/4/88	A	31	(2)	21
15	Salim TUAAMA		9/8/79	M	12	(15)	4
14	Gil VERMOUTH		5/8/85	M	30	(2)	5
26	Avihai YADIN		26/10/86	M	25	(3)	
16	Eran ZAHAVI		25/7/87	A	33		9

MACCABI HAIFA FC

Coach – Elisha Levi

Founded – 1913

Stadium – Kiriat Eliezer (17,000)

MAJOR HONOURS: Israeli League – (12) 1984, 1985, 1989, 1991, 1994, 2001, 2002, 2004, 2005, 2006, 2009, 2011; Israeli Cup – (5) 1962, 1991, 1993, 1995, 1998.

2010

22/8	M. Tel-Aviv	a	1-0	*Ghdir*
28/8	M. Petach-Tikva	h	1-0	*Ghdir*
13/9	H. Beer Sheva	a	1-1	*Dvalishvili*
25/9	Bnei Yehuda	a	3-2	*Refaelov 2, Dvalishvili (p)*
3/10	Beitar	h	3-3	*Golasa, Azulay 2*
16/10	Bnei Sakhnin	a	2-1	*Azulay, Katan (p)*
23/10	Ashdod	h	1-1	*Refaelov*
31/10	H. Petach-Tikva	a	1-0	*Dvalishvili*
8/11	H. Tel-Aviv	h	0-2	
13/11	H. Ramat Gan	a	3-1	*Meshumar, Culma, Azulay*

22/11	H. Haifa	h	0-0	
27/11	H. Ashkelon	a	3-0	*Dvalishvili, Refaelov, Meshumar*
6/12	H. Akko	h	3-1	*Ghdir, Refaelov, Katan (p)*
13/12	H. Kiryat Shmona	a	1-0	*Katan (p)*
18/12	M. Netanya	h	3-0	*Hemed, Meshumar, Dvalishvili*
2011				
3/1	M. Tel-Aviv	h	3-0	*Tawatha, Golasa, Dvalishvili*
9/1	M. Petach-Tikva	a	3-1	*Dvalishvili 2 (1p), Hemed*
15/1	H. Beer Sheva	h	2-2	*Dvalishvili, og (William)*
22/1	Bnei Yehuda	h	1-0	*Dvalishvili*
30/1	Beitar	a	0-0	
5/2	Bnei Sakhnin	h	1-0	*Hemed*
12/2	Ashdod	a	2-1	*Hemed 2*
21/2	H. Petach-Tikva	h	2-0	*Vered, Ghdir*
27/2	H. Tel-Aviv	a	1-4	*Ghdir*
6/3	H. Ramat Gan	h	3-2	*Refaelov, Hemed, Vered*
14/3	H. Haifa	a	2-0	*Refaelov, Dvalishvili*
19/3	H. Ashkelon	h	3-0	*Maymon, Hemed 2*
2/4	H. Akko	a	2-0	*Hemed, Azulay*
11/4	H. Kiryat Shmona	h	3-2	*Azulay, Refaelov, Hemed*
17/4	M. Netanya	a	1-1	*Hemed*
23/4	M. Netanya	h	1-2	*Refaelov*
30/4	H. Tel-Aviv	h	2-0	*Katan, Dvalishvili*
7/5	M. Tel-Aviv	a	2-0	*Hemed 2*
16/5	H. Kiryat Shmona	h	2-0	*Refaelov 2 (1p)*
21/5	Bnei Yehuda	a	1-1	*Ghdir*

No	Name	Nat	DoB	Pos	Aps	(s)	Gls
6	ADRIEN Sebastian Perruchet SILVA	POR	15/3/89	M	3	(3)	
19	Shlomi AZULAY		18/10/89	A	9	(14)	6
4	Arik BENADO		5/12/73	D	24		
7	Gustavo BOCCOLI	BRA	16/2/78	M	28	(4)	
3	Ignacio CANUTO	ARG	20/2/86	D	9	(1)	
8	John Jairo CULMA	COL	17/3/81	M	22	(4)	1
11	Nir DAVIDOVICH		17/12/76	G	26		
9	Vladimer DVALISHVILI	GEO	20/4/86	A	27	(3)	12
22	Amir EDREE		26/7/85	G	9	(1)	
2	Sari FALACH		27/3/91	D	1		
16	Muhammad GHDIR		21/1/91	M	10	(12)	6
15	Eyal GOLASA		7/10/91	M	20	(6)	2
21	Tomer HEMED		2/5/87	A	22	(9)	13
20	Yaniv KATAN		27/1/81	A	22	(5)	4
17	Tsepo MASILELA	RSA	5/5/85	D	19	(1)	
5	Shai MAYMON		18/3/86	D	21	(1)	1
27	Eyal MESHUMAR		10/8/83	D	25	(1)	3
18	Ali OSMAN		8/2/87	D	9	(5)	
25	Andriy PYLYAVSKIY	UKR	4/12/88	D	16		
10	Lior REFAELOV		26/4/86	M	21	(6)	11
28	Sintiyahu SALALIK		1/1/91	A	1	(9)	
12	Sadi SHABEN		4/3/92	M		(1)	
13	Taleb TAWATHA		21/6/92	D	16	(2)	1
11	Idan VERED		25/5/89	M	16	(14)	2
6	Seydou YAHAYA	GHA	31/12/89	M	9	(3)	

MACCABI NETANYA FC

Coach – Reuvan Atar

Founded – 1934

Stadium – Sar-Tov (7,500)

MAJOR HONOURS: Israeli League – (5) 1971, 1974, 1978, 1980, 1983; Israeli Cup – (1) 1978.

2010				
21/8	Beitar	h	4-1	*Saba'a, Ezra, Asor, Yampolski*
28/8	Bnei Sakhnin	a	1-1	*Yampolski*
11/9	Ashdod	h	2-0	*Peretz, Dgani*
25/9	H. Petach-Tikva	a	1-1	*Saba'a*
2/10	H. Tel-Aviv	h	1-3	*Dgani (p)*
16/10	H. Ramat Gan	a	1-0	*Saba'a*
23/10	H. Haifa	h	1-1	*Ezra*
30/10	H. Ashkelon	a	4-0	*Magharbeh, Saba'a 2, Yampolski*
7/11	H. Akko	h	1-3	*Asor*
13/11	H. Kiryat Shmona	a	0-3	
20/11	Bnei Yehuda	h	0-0	
29/11	M. Tel-Aviv	h	0-2	
5/12	M. Petach-Tikva	a	0-2	
11/12	H. Beer Sheva	h	1-0	*Yampolski*
18/12	M. Haifa	a	0-3	
2011				
1/1	Beitar	a	0-0	
8/1	Bnei Sakhnin	h	1-0	*Nachum*
16/1	Ashdod	a	0-1	
22/1	H. Petach-Tikva	h	3-3	*Nachum, Dajani, Yampolski*
29/1	H. Tel-Aviv	a	1-2	*Tretyak*
5/2	H. Ramat Gan	h	2-0	*Nachum, Tretyak*
12/2	H. Haifa	a	2-1	*Nachum, Yampolski*
19/2	H. Ashkelon	h	3-0	*Nachum, Magharbeh, Peretz*
26/2	H. Akko	a	0-0	
5/3	H. Kiryat Shmona	h	1-1	*Tretyak*
13/3	Bnei Yehuda	a	1-1	*Nachum*
19/3	M. Tel-Aviv	a	3-0	*Nachum, Saba'a, Dajani*
2/4	M. Petach-Tikva	h	2-2	*Yampolski, Magharbeh*
9/4	H. Beer Sheva	a	2-1	*Saba'a 2*
17/4	M. Haifa	h	1-1	*Saba'a*
23/4	M. Haifa	a	2-1	*Saba'a, Tretyak*
30/4	H. Kiryat Shmona	h	3-3	*Tretyak 2, Ezra*
7/5	H. Tel-Aviv	a	2-2	*Saba'a, Tretyak*
14/5	Bnei Yehuda	h	0-4	
21/5	M. Tel-Aviv	a	1-4	*Saba'a*

No	Name	Nat	DoB	Pos	Aps	(s)	Gls
19	Hasib ABU ROKON		11/2/91	A	1	(10)	
23	Offir AMRAM		19/6/86	D		(3)	
1	Carlos Erwin ARIAS Eguez	BOL	18/2/80	G	34		
10	Meir ASOR		25/8/88	A	11	(21)	2
24	Matan BALESTRA		4/6/92	M		(2)	
20	Omri BEN HARUSH		7/3/90	D	25	(1)	
2	Mariano Carlos CAPORALE	ARG	11/1/85	D	21	(1)	
7	Gaga CHKHETIANI	GEO	24/6/83	A		(8)	
17	Kobi DAJANI		5/11/84	M	32		2
12	Orel DGANI		8/1/89	D	32		2
8	Hen EZRA		19/1/89	M	23	(5)	3
14	Gal GENISH		16/12/91	M		(1)	
22	Guy GOMBERG		24/9/90	M	1	(3)	
5	Leonid KRUPNIK	UKR	15/7/79	D	29	(2)	
3	Tal MA'ABI		15/5/85	D	33		
16	Feras MAGHARBEH		24/7/91	A	29	(3)	3
18	Nir NACHUM		9/9/83	M	24	(6)	7
25	Adi NIMNI		27/8/91	D	6	(9)	
15	Omer PERETZ		30/3/90	M	4	(13)	2
9	Ahmed SABA'A		24/5/80	A	35		12
27	Guy SALEM		23/8/84	G	1		
14	Amit SHUMOWITZ		29/7/92	D	1		
7	Serhiy TRETYAK	UKR	28/11/84	A	15	(1)	7
11	Bamidele YAMPOLSKI		28/7/88	A	28	(6)	7

MACCABI PETACH-TIKVA FC

Coach – Fredi David

Founded – 1912

Stadium – Ramat Gan (41,583)

MAJOR HONOURS: Israeli Cup – (2) 1935, 1952.

2010				
23/8	H. Beer Sheva	h	0-1	
28/8	M. Haifa	a	0-1	
11/9	Beitar	h	2-1	*Marinković, Uzan*
25/9	Bnei Sakhnin	a	3-2	*Uzan (p), Ben Haim (p), Damari O.*
2/10	Ashdod	h	2-2	*Ben Haim 2*
16/10	H. Petach-Tikva	a	4-1	*Golan 2, Zandberg, Damari O.*
24/10	H. Tel-Aviv	h	1-2	*Ben Haim (p)*

ı/10	H. Ramat Gan	a	2-0	*Damari O., Ben Haim*
11	H. Haifa	h	2-3	*Golan, Marinković*
ı/11	H. Ashkelon	a	1-0	*Ben Haim*
ı/11	H. Akko	h	1-1	*Damari O.*
'/11	H. Kiryat Shmona	a	2-2	*Damari O., Bekel*
12	M. Netanya	h	2-0	*Sansoni, Damari O.*
/12	M. Tel-Aviv	a	1-1	*Sansoni*
ı/12	Bnei Yehuda	h	3-0	*Golan, Ofir, Sansoni*
)11				
1	H. Beer Sheva	a	1-2	*Mashiach*
1	M. Haifa	h	1-3	*Sansoni*
i/1	Beitar	a	2-0	*Ofir, Golan*
ı/1	Bnei Sakhnin	h	1-2	*Gabay*
ı/1	Ashdod	a	3-1	*Bizera, Golan, Marinković*
2	H. Petach-Tikva	h	2-3	*Ben Haim (p), Zandberg*
ı/2	H. Tel-Aviv	a	0-2	
ı/2	H. Ramat Gan	h	4-1	*Damari O. 2, Abu Anzeh, Bekel*
i/2	H. Haifa	a	1-1	*Golan*
3	H. Ashkelon	h	4-0	*Golan, Uzan (p), Ben Haim, Abu Anzeh*
2/3	H. Akko	a	1-1	*Damari O.*
ı/3	H. Kiryat Shmona	h	0-0	
4	M. Netanya	a	2-2	*Damari O. 2*
4	M. Tel-Aviv	h	2-2	*Uzan (p), Damari O.*
'/4	Bnei Yehuda	a	0-2	
ı/4	H. Akko	h	4-1	*Damari O. 2, Ben Haim (p), Abu Anzeh*
)/4	H. Haifa	a	2-0	*Ben Haim, Damari O.*
5	H. Beer Sheva	h	1-1	*Abu Anzeh*

o	Name	Nat	DoB	Pos	Aps	(s)	Gls
ı	Murad ABU ANZEH		8/11/86	A	5	(6)	4
5	Roee BEKEL		7/10/87	M	18	(7)	2
4	Tal BEN HAIM		5/8/89	A	29	(1)	10
4	Joe Émerson BIZERA Bastos	URU	17/5/80	D	30		1
	Nitzan DAMARI		13/1/87	D	15	(2)	
0	Omer DAMARI		24/3/89	A	29	(1)	15
7	Eliran DANIN		29/3/84	D	19	(3)	
6	Dror DEGO		8/5/92	A		(2)	
5	Tomer ELBAZ		3/7/89	D	2	(3)	
	Dovev GABAY		1/4/87	A	1	(10)	1
2	Kobi GANON		17/5/76	D	14	(3)	
5	Omer GOLAN		4/10/83	A	22	(2)	8
0	Hagai GOLDENBERG		15/9/90	D	4		
3	Marwan KABAHA		23/2/91	M	2	(2)	
	Robi LEVKOVICH		31/8/88	G	29		
	Dor MALICHI		28/8/91	D		(1)	
2	Ivan MANCE	CRO	4/2/83	G	4	(1)	
ı	Nebojša MARINKOVIĆ	SRB	19/6/86	M	5	(15)	3
6	Asi MASHIACH		10/10/81	M	10	(9)	1
-	Merad MEGAMADOV		25/9/73	D	19	(2)	
8	Yossi OFIR		18/11/78	M	30	(2)	2
6	Dani PRADA		1/4/87	M	8	(7)	
-	Sébastien SANSONI	FRA	30/1/78	D	23	(4)	4
1	Rubil SARSOR		17/8/83	A		(2)	
-	Ori UZAN		27/12/78	D	25	(1)	4
:1	Michael ZANDBERG		16/4/80	M	20	(9)	2

MACCABI TEL-AVIV FC

Coach – Avi Nimni; (9/1/11) Motti Iwanir

Founded – 1906

Stadium – Bloomfield (15,700)

MAJOR HONOURS: Israeli League – (18) 1937, 1939, 1941, 1947, 1950, 1952, 1954, 1956, 1958, 1968, 1970, 1972, 1977, 1979, 1992, 1995, 1996, 2003; Israeli Cup – (22) 1929, 1930, 1933, 1941, 1946, 1947, 1954, 1955, 1958, 1959, 1964, 1965, 1967, 1970, 1977, 1987, 1988, 1994, 1996, 2001, 2002, 2005.

2010				
22/8	M. Haifa	h	0-1	
29/8	Beitar	a	1-0	*Medunjanin*
11/9	Bnei Sakhnin	h	4-0	*Medunjanin (p), Colautti, Avidor, Atar*
27/9	Ashdod	a	2-1	*Medunjanin (p), Atar*
2/10	H. Petach-Tikva	h	2-1	*Atar, Medunjanin*
16/10	H. Tel-Aviv	a	0-1	
23/10	H. Ramat Gan	h	2-0	*Buzaglo, Colautti*
1/11	H. Haifa	a	0-0	
6/11	H. Ashkelon	h	2-0	*Rangelov, Sidibé*
13/11	H. Akko	a	1-3	*Atar*
20/11	H. Kiryat Shmona	h	0-1	
29/11	M. Netanya	a	2-0	*Atar 2*
4/12	Bnei Yehuda	h	2-0	*Atar, Israilevich*
11/12	M. Petach-Tikva	h	1-1	*Medunjanin*
18/12	H. Beer Sheva	a	1-0	*Sidibé*
2011				
3/1	M. Haifa	a	0-3	
10/1	Beitar	h	1-0	*Colautti*
15/1	Bnei Sakhnin	a	3-1	*Medunjanin, Colautti 2*
22/1	Ashdod	h	4-1	*Atar, Strul, Buzaglo, Medunjanin*
29/1	H. Petach-Tikva	a	1-0	*og (Cohen)*
6/2	H. Tel-Aviv	h	1-1	*Rangelov*
12/2	H. Ramat Gan	a	3-0	*Atar 2, Micha*
19/2	H. Haifa	h	0-1	
26/2	H. Ashkelon	a	4-2	*Atar 2, Colautti, Medunjanin*
5/3	H. Akko	h	2-2	*Pavićević, Atar*
12/3	H. Kiryat Shmona	a	0-4	
19/3	M. Netanya	h	0-3	
2/4	Bnei Yehuda	a	0-2	
9/4	M. Petach-Tikva	a	2-2	*Atar 2 (1p)*
16/4	H. Beer Sheva	h	0-2	
23/4	H. Kiryat Shmona	h	3-1	*Israilevich, Atar 2*
30/4	Bnei Yehuda	a	3-1	*Buzaglo 2, Atar*
7/5	M. Haifa	h	0-2	
14/5	H. Tel-Aviv	a	2-2	*Colautti 2*
21/5	M. Netanya	h	4-1	*Alberman, Yeini, Colautti, Itzhaki (p)*

No	Name	Nat	DoB	Pos	Aps	(s)	Gls
27	Gal ALBERMAN		17/4/83	M	21	(9)	1
16	Eliran ATAR		17/2/87	A	31	(2)	18
10	Yuval AVIDOR		19/10/86	A	2	(17)	1
3	Albert BANING	CMR	19/3/85	M		(1)	
11	Maor Bar BUZAGLO		14/1/88	M	31	(3)	4
28	Uri COHEN		26/5/92	D	3		
24	Roberto Damián COLAUTTI		24/5/82	A	18	(11)	9
18	Ronni GAFNI		11/3/80	D	8	(2)	
3	Eliran GEORGE		15/3/92	D	4		
25	Maor HALABI		30/5/90	M	1		
7	Guillermo ISRAILEVICH	ARG	10/9/82	M	18	(8)	2
9	Barak ITZHAKI		25/9/84	A	1	(3)	1
28	Tamir KAHLON		29/10/87	M		(2)	
5	Nisso KAPILOTO		10/1/89	D	1		
15	Roi KEHAT		12/5/92	A		(1)	
31	Barak LEVI		7/1/93	G	3		
30	Moshe LUGASI		4/2/91	M	6	(1)	
19	Dor MALUL		30/4/89	D	14	(10)	
34	Gae MARGOULIS		3/4/94	A		(1)	
6	Haris MEDUNJANIN	BIH	8/3/85	M	22	(10)	8
23	Dor MICHA		10/2/92	M	4	(4)	1
4	NIVALDO Batista Santana	BRA	23/6/80	D	11		
17	Savo PAVIĆEVIĆ	MNE	11/12/80	D	31		1
29	Reef PERETZ		25/2/91	M	6	(2)	
13	Dimitar RANGELOV	BUL	9/2/83	A	14	(8)	2
2	Klimi SABAN		17/2/80	D	22	(1)	
20	Djibril SIDIBÉ	MLI	23/3/82	M	21		2
22	Guy SOLOMON		23/9/77	G	1		
1	Liran STRAUBER		20/8/74	G	31		
26	Avi STRUL		18/9/80	D	17		1
21	Sherran YEINI		8/12/86	M	13	(6)	1
14	Yoav ZIV		16/3/81	D	30	(3)	

TOP GOALSCORERS 2010/11

21 Toto TAMUZ (H. Tel-Aviv)

18 Eliran ATAR (M. Tel-Aviv)
Eden Ben BASAT (H. Haifa)

17 Moshe OHAYON (Ashdod)

16 Pedro GALVÁN (Bnei Yehuda)
Ben SAHAR (H. Tel-Aviv)

15 Omer DAMARI (M. Petach-Tikva)

14 Roei DAYAN (H. Akko)
Viam AMASHA (H. Kiryat Shmona)

13 Tomer HEMED (M. Haifa)

PROMOTED CLUBS

HAPOEL IRONI NIR RAMAT HASHARON

Coach – Guy Levi; (7/9/10) Salmon Zaafran
Founded – 1995
Stadium – Ya'akov Grundman (2,000)

HAPOEL IRONI RISHON-LEZION FC

Coach – Nissan Yehezekel
Founded – 1940
Stadium – Haberfeld (6,000)

SECOND LEVEL FINAL TABLE 2010/11

		Pld	W	D	L	F	A	Pts
1	Hapoel Ironi Nir Ramat HaSharon	35	19	11	5	55	28	38
2	Hapoel Ironi Rishon-LeZion FC	35	18	8	9	57	31	36
3	Hapoel Kfar-Saba FC	35	20	9	6	54	36	36
4	Maccabi Herzliya FC	35	17	10	8	41	21	35
5	Hapoel Ra'anana FC	35	14	11	10	43	27	30
6	Sektzya Ness Ziona FC	35	13	11	11	31	29	27
7	Hapoel Herzliya FC	33	15	8	10	46	37	30
8	Hapoel Bnei Lod FC	33	11	13	9	36	31	24
9	Maccabi Ahi Nazareth FC	33	12	11	10	46	41	22
10	Beitar Shimshon Tel-Aviv FC	33	9	9	15	44	47	19
11	Hapoel Nazareth Ilit FC	35	12	7	16	43	46	23
12	Maccabi Beer Sheva FC	35	8	14	13	33	42	22
13	Maccabi Irony Bat-Yam FC	35	7	15	13	29	44	22
14	Hakoach Amidar Ramat Gan FC	35	7	12	16	32	50	21
15	Maccabi Irony Jat FC	35	4	11	20	27	66	14
16	Ahva Arabe FC	35	6	8	21	21	62	10

NB After 30 matches clubs were split into three groups, after which they played exclusively against teams in their group. Points obtained during the regular season were halved (and rounded upwards); Ahava Arabe FC – 10 pts deducted; Hapoel Nazareth Ilit FC & Maccabi Ahi Nazareth FC – 9 pts deducted.

PROMOTION/RELEGATION PLAY-OFFS

(24/5/11 & 27/5/11)
H. Petach-Tikva 4, H. Kfar-Saba 1
H. Kfar-Saba 0, H. Petach-Tikva 1
(H. Petach-Tikva 5-1)

DOMESTIC CUPS 2010/11

G'VIAA HAMEDINA (STATE CUP)

THRID ROUND

(1/2/11)
Hakoach Amidar 0, H. Ra'anana 2 *(aet)*
H. Afula 1, H. Beer Sheva 4
H. Akko 0, M. Jat Al-Ahli 2
H. Ashkelon 1, M. Bat-Yam 0
H. Jerusalem 2, M. Beer Sheva 0
H. Petach-Tikva 3, M. Tel-Aviv 1
M. Herzliya 2, M. Tamra 0
M. Netanya 4, Bnei Yehuda 1
Ness Ziona 1, M. Netovot 0

(2/2/11)
H. Haifa 2, M. Daliat El Carmel 0 *(aet)*
H. Kfar-Saba 0, M. Haifa 3
H. Kiryat Shmona 1, M. Ahi Nazareth 0
H. Ramat Gan 0, Beitar Jerusalem 1
H. Rishon-LeZion 3, Bnei Sakhnin 1
M. Kiryat-Ata 0, H. Tel-Aviv 7
M. Petach-Tikva 0, Ashdod 1

FOURTH ROUND

(1/3/11)
Beitar Jerusalem 2, H. Rishon-LeZion 0
H. Kiryat Shmona 4, H. Beer Sheva 0
H. Ra'anana 3, M. Jat Al-Ahli 0
M. Herzliya 0, Ashdod 2
M. Netanya 1, H. Petach-Tikva 0
Ness Ziona 1, H. Haifa 3 (aet)

(2/3/11)
H. Tel-Aviv 2, H. Ashkelon 1
M. Haifa 2, H. Jerusalem 1

QUARTER-FINALS

(19/4/11)
H. Tel-Aviv 1 *(Tamuz 89p)*, Beitar Jerusalem 0

(20/4/11)
H. Haifa 1 *(Ben Basat 30p)*, M. Haifa 3 *(Vered 38, Refaelov 58p, 71)*
H. Ra'anana 0, H. Kiryat Shmona 1 *(Amasha V. 59)*
M. Netanya 1 *(Magharbeh 80)*, Ashdod 1 *(Makriev 59)*
(aet; 4-1 on pens)

SEMI-FINALS

(11/5/11)
H. Tel-Aviv 2 *(Zahavi 80, Sahar 87)*, H. Kiryat Shmona 0
M. Haifa 3 *(Hemed 37, Dvalishvili 56, Refaelov 69p)*, M. Netanya 2 *(Magharbeh 39, Saba'a 69p)*

FINAL

(26/5/11)
Ramat Gan stadium, Ramat Gan
HAPOEL TEL-AVIV FC 1 *(Tuaama 2)*
MACCABI HAIFA FC 0
Refree – *Levi*
H. TEL-AVIV – *Enyeama, Kenda, Badir, Fransman, Ben Dayan, Yadin, Abutbol, Zahavi, Tuaama (Maree 79), Tamuz (Cohen 77), Sahar (Al Lala 90).*
M. HAIFA – *Davidovich, Meshumar, Benado, Pylyavskiy, Masilela, Boccoli (Ghdir 72), Yahaya, Katan, Refaelov (Azulay 79), Hemed, Dvalishvili (Vered 52).*

CLUB COMMUNICATION 2011/12

'C Ashdod

5 Zabutinski Street, PO Box 2114
-77130 Ashdod

el	+972 8 868 6130
ax	+972 8 868 6131
'eb	fcashod.com
mail	bhaim@bezeqint.net
edia Officer	Ohad Zwick

3eitar Jerusalem FC

shmoel beit st', PO Box 3334
-91033 Jerusalem

el	+972 2 679 2000
ax	+972 2 651 5419
'eb	beitarfc.co.il
mail	korenfine@ bjerusalem.co.il
ledia Officer	Asaf Shaked

3nei Sakhnin FC

akhnin Stadium, POB 17
-30810 Sakhnin

el	+972 4 674 7792
ax	+972 4 674 6017
/eb	
:mail	bneisakhnin@gmail.com
ledia Officer	Halaila Monder

3nei Yehuda Tel-Aviv FC

:abir Street 20, POB 19069
L-67750 Tel-Aviv

'el	+972 3 687 644 5
'ax	+972 3 537 787 7
Veb	bneiyehuda.com
:mail	info@fc-bnei-yehuda.co.il
ledia Officer	Maya Damayo

Hapoel Akko FC

zhfat road, POB 2877
L-24127 Akko

Tel	972 50 981 3467
Fax	972 4 995 6035
Web	
Email	hapoel_akko@walla.com
Media Officer	Shanholsz David

Hapoel Beer Sheva FC

Yehuda Ha'levi 1, PO Box 3242
IL-84142 Beer Sheva

Tel	+972 8 642 2986
Fax	+972 1538 642 2987
Web	hapoelb7.co.il
Email	office@hapoelb7.com
Media Officer	Tsipora Halfon

Hapoel Haifa FC

Kiriat Haim - The stadium 1
IL-26248 Haifa

Tel	+972 4 872 1403
Fax	+972 4 849 1423
Web	hapoel-haifa.org.il
Email	Mielpt@gmail.com
Media Officer	Noam Regev

Hapoel Ironi Nir Ramat HaSharon FC

48 Hachalutz st., POB 91
IL-47100 Ramat Hasharon

Tel	972 3 540 0515
Fax	972 3 540 0518
Web	rhfc.co.il
Email	rhfc@014.net.il
Media Officer	Avishay Ran

Hapoel Ironi Rishon-LeZion FC

POB 4021
IL-75140 Rishon Letzion

Tel	972 3 951 6020
Fax	972 3 962 1050
Web	rishonia.co.il
Email	ravivs@davids.co.il
Media Officer	Efraim Vieman

Hapoel Kiryat Shmona FC

11 Ha'yarden St', PO Box 961
IL-10200 Kiryat Shmona

Tel	+972 4 681 7833
Fax	+972 4 681 7834
Web	iturank8.co.il
Email	merchi29@hotmail.com
Media Officer	Faraj Adi

Hapoel Petach-Tikva FC

Kibutzh Einat, PO Box 241
IL-48805 Kibutzh Einat

Tel	+972 3 924 8353
Fax	+972 3 921 8352
Web	
Email	hpt-fc@012.net.il
Media Officer	Alon Hakmon

Hapoel Tel-Aviv FC

8 Halohamim St., PO Box 8402
IL-61084 Tel-Aviv

Tel	+972 3 682 1275
Fax	+972 3 682 7722
Web	hapoelta-fc.co.il
Email	rachel@hapoelta-fc.co.il
Media Officer	Geva Telem

Maccabi Haifa FC

4 Kiryat Seffer St., PO Box 7744
IL-34676 Haifa

Tel	+972 4 834 6626
Fax	+972 4 834 6630
Web	maccabi-haifafc.walla.co.il
Email	info@maccabihaifafc.com
Media Officer	Dudu Bazak

Maccabi Netanya FC

26 Giborey Israel, PO Box 2242
IL-42122 Netanya

Tel	+972 9 865 1336
Fax	+972 9 885 8690
Web	fcmn.co.il
Email	mn@fcmn.co.il
Media Officer	Itzik Genish

Maccabi Petach-Tikva FC

1 Ben Dror St' Petach-Tikva, PO Box 67
IL-49100 Petach-Tikva

Tel	+972 3 934 7561
Fax	+972 3 934 7560
Web	www.m-pt.co.il
Email	m-pt@zahav.net.il
Media Officer	Liran Zilberman

Maccabi Tel-Aviv FC

106 Ben Tzvi Road Tel Aviv, POB 12069
IL-61120 Tel-Aviv

Tel	+972 3 681 7233
Fax	+972 3 681 7242
Web	maccabi-tlv.co.il
Email	liran@maccabi-tlv.co.ilil
Media Officer	Ofer Ronen

ITALY

Italie I Italien

Federazione Italiana Giuoco Calcio (FIGC

COMMUNICATION

Address Via Gregorio Allegri 14
CP 2450
IT-00198 Roma

Tel +39 06 84 911
Fax +39 06 84 912 526

E-mail international@figc.it
Website figc.it

President Giancarlo Abete
General Secretary Antonio Di Sebastiano
Media Officer Antonello Valentini

Year of Formation 1898

National Stadium Stadio Olimpico, Rom
(82,307)

DOMESTIC COMPETITION SUMMARY 2010/11

SERIE A FINAL TABLE

			Home					Away					Total						
		Pld	W	D	L	F	A	W	D	L	F	A	W	D	L	F	A	Pts	Comp
1	AC Milan	38	13	4	2	42	12	11	6	2	23	12	24	10	4	65	24	82	UCL
2	FC Internazionale Milano	38	15	3	1	48	20	8	4	7	21	22	23	7	8	69	42	76	UCL
3	SSC Napoli	38	12	4	3	33	15	9	3	7	26	24	21	7	10	59	39	70	UCL
4	Udinese Calcio	38	11	4	4	27	16	9	2	8	38	27	20	6	12	65	43	66	UCL
5	S.S. Lazio	38	13	3	3	31	15	7	3	9	24	24	20	6	12	55	39	66	UEL
6	AS Roma	38	11	5	3	31	18	7	4	8	28	34	18	9	11	59	52	63	UEL
7	Juventus	38	8	6	5	35	31	7	7	5	22	16	15	13	10	57	47	58	
8	US Città di Palermo	38	11	3	5	33	28	6	2	11	25	35	17	5	16	58	63	56	UEL
9	ACF Fiorentina	38	9	6	4	28	18	3	9	7	21	26	12	15	11	49	44	51	
10	Genoa CFC	38	10	3	6	29	24	4	6	9	16	23	14	9	15	45	47	51	
11	AC Chievo Verona	38	6	8	5	15	13	5	5	9	23	27	11	13	14	38	40	46	
12	Parma FC	38	7	7	5	21	16	4	6	9	18	31	11	13	14	39	47	46	
13	Calcio Catania	38	11	4	4	27	19	1	6	12	13	33	12	10	16	40	52	46	
14	Cagliari Calcio	38	8	3	8	27	23	4	6	9	17	28	12	9	17	44	51	45	
15	AC Cesena	38	7	5	7	17	21	4	5	10	21	29	11	10	17	38	50	43	
16	Bologna FC	38	7	7	5	17	20	4	5	10	18	32	11	12	15	35	52	42	
17	US Lecce	38	7	5	7	28	29	4	3	12	18	37	11	8	19	46	66	41	
18	UC Sampdoria	38	5	6	8	21	21	3	6	10	12	28	8	12	18	33	49	36	*Relegated*
19	Brescia Calcio	38	6	5	8	22	24	1	6	12	12	28	7	11	20	34	52	32	*Relegated*
20	AS Bari	38	2	6	11	12	28	3	3	13	15	28	5	9	24	27	56	24	*Relegated*

NB Bologna FC – 3 pts deducted.

Top Scorer Antonio Di Natale (Udinese), 28 goals

Promoted Clubs Atalanta BC
AC Siena
Novara Calcio

Cup Final FC Internazionale Milano 3, US Città di Palermo 1

Milan keep the home fires burning

FC Internazionale Milano's five-year reign as champions of Italy came to a halt in 2010/11 as AC Milan, led by unheralded new coach Massimiliano Allegri, dethroned their city rivals to win the scudetto for the first time since 2003/04. It was the Rossoneri's 18th title, putting them back on level terms historically with Inter, who had crept ahead of them during their memorable treble-winning campaign the previous season.

There would be no repeat Italian triumph in the UEFA Champions League, however, as both Inter and Milan struggled to impose themselves in an extremely bleak European campaign for Serie A's finest, with not one of the seven participants from the Peninsula managing to reach the semi-finals of either competition. Indeed, it was only Inter's determination to hang on to their UEFA Champions League crown that extended Italian involvement into the quarter-finals – before they were demolished by mid-table German side FC Schalke 04, an outcome of no little symbolical significance in a season that saw Serie A surrender its fourth UEFA Champions League place to the Bundesliga from 2012/13.

Top priority

Milan, who were deposited from the UEFA Champions League by competition debutants Tottenham Hotspur FC in the round of 16 – after a 1-0 defeat at San Siro and a 0-0 draw at White Hart Lane – did not take too long to shrug off that disappointment and proceed on their merry way in Serie A. Indeed, their mid-season transfer policy had provided strong evidence that the scudetto was their top prioirity, their three major new signings – Mark van Bommel from FC Bayern München, Urby Emanuelson from AFC Ajax and Antonio Cassano from UC Sampdoria – all being ineligible for Europe.

Allegri's team recovered from a modest start to the domestic campaign – just one win in their opening four fixtures – with a powerful four-game winning streak in November that enabled them to unseat early pacesetters S.S. Lazio at the top of the Serie A table, and stay there. Despite the odd hiccup – such as a home defeat to AS Roma in the last game before Christmas – the Rossoneri displayed a consistency that their pursuers – Lazio, SSC Napoli and, belatedly, Inter – were unable to match. The big test of their title resolve came on the first Saturday of April, when they took on an in-form Inter side that were now just two points behind them. They passed it with flying colours, two goals from young Brazilian striker Pato – the first after just 43 seconds – catapulting Milan to a handsome 3-0 win that not only completed the double over their stadium-sharing rivals but also gave them clear breathing space at the top of the table with seven matches remaining.

Massimiliano Allegri is hoisted aloft by Milan players following the club's Serie A triumph

If that result effectively decided the title, the transition of power from Inter to Milan was formally confirmed five weeks later when the Rossoneri drew 0-0 against Roma at the Stadio Olimpico. It was not wholly unsurprising that Allegri's men should claim their prize in a match short on spectacle and devoid of goals. Despite the presence in their ranks of several gifted attacking players – Pato, his compatriot Robinho and ex-Inter striker Zlatan Ibrahimović, each of whom contrbuted 14 goals to the title-winning effort – it was Milan's rock-solid defence that was at the heart of their triumph. While all of the other 19 teams in the league conceded an average of more than one goal per game, the Rossoneri rearguard was breached just 24 times in 38 matches, keeping 20 clean sheets.

Terrific Thiago Silva

Nobody was more responsible for that statistic than centre-back Thiago Silva, who enjoyed a phenomenally consistent campaign. Alessandro Nesta, 35, also demonstrated his evergreen class alongside the Brazilian, while long-serving Christian Abbiati, a scudetto-winner with the club back in 1998/99, was a pillar of strength in goal. Another veteran, Dutchman Clarence Seedorf – who turned 35 in April – rolled back the years with some vintage displays in midfield as he bypassed the legendary Nils Liedholm to become the club's most frequently used foreigner.

Samuel Eto'o enjoyed a prolific season in front of goal for Inter

Milan's success fully vindicated the decision, much debated among fans at the time, to bring in Allegri as coach. Before his arrival at San Siro the 43-year-old's CV – both as a player and coach – was lacking in lustre and achievement, but two impressive seasons in Sardinia at Cagliari Calcio had earned him his big chance, and in the season that marked the 25th anniversary of Silvio Berlusconi's takeover of the club he seized the opportunity and delivered.

It was the man Allegri replaced in the Milan hot seat, Leonardo, who ended up carrying the fight to him from the blue-and-black corner as the battle for the scudetto intensified in the spring. The Brazilian, who endured a disappointing 2009/10 season as Rossoneri coach, was appointed in mid-season by Inter following the departure of Rafael Benítez. The Spaniard, dismissed by Liverpool FC after a six-year spell at Anfield and brought in to replace Real Madrid CF-bound José Mourinho, lasted barely six months at San Siro. Despite winning two trophies during his brief tenure – the Italian Super Cup (3-1 against Roma) and the FIFA Club World Cup (3-0 in the final against African champions TP Mazembe) – he was sacked just before Christmas after a dispute with owner Massimo Moratti over transfer policy.

Inter intact

It did not help Benítez's cause, of course, that at the time of his leaving Inter were way off the pace in Serie A – 13 points behind Milan in sixth place, albeit with a couple of games in hand – or that they had failed to win their UEFA Champions League group, losing their final game 3-0 at already eliminated SV Werder Bremen to cede top spot to Tottenham. Although Mourinho had gone, Inter's treble-winning team remained intact almost to a man. Admittedly there were injuries – not least to their goalscoring star of the previous campaign, Diego Milito – but although Samuel Eto'o upped his game brilliantly under Benítez, the Cameroonian striker was very much an exception to the rule.

Under Leonardo, however, Inter collectively returned to form, his first eight league games yielding seven wins and 24 goals – four more than in 15 Serie A outings under his predecessor. By the time they came face to face with Milan for the scudetto showdown in April, the Nerazzurri had not only pocketed 37 points from a possible 45 under the Brazilian but had also staged a majestic comeback

dinson Cavani
cored 26 Serie A
oals for Napoli –
club record

in the UEFA Champions League to knock out FC Bayern München – their vanquished opponents in the previous season's final – with an epic 3-2 win in Bavaria. But then came the crushing 3-0 defeat in the Derby della Madonnina and, four days later, an even more devastating loss in Europe as Schalke thrashed them 5-2 at San Siro.

Coppa consolation

All of a sudden Inter's hopes of a repeat treble under Leonardo had been reduced to a face-saving exercise in the Coppa Italia. They duly retained that trophy, eliminating regular cup sparring partners Roma in the semi-finals before edging an entertaining final against US Città di Palermo, with Eto'o denying the plucky Sicilians a first major honour – and giving Inter their fourth Italian Cup win in seven years – by scoring his 36th and 37th goals of the season in a 3-1 win. Although Leonardo had his first trophy as a coach, it would be his last game in charge. As he left for France, and a new job as sporting director at Paris Saint-Germain FC, Inter decided to follow Milan's example by appointing in his place a relatively low-profile Italian, 53-year-old ex-Genoa CFC coach Gian Piero Gasperini.

With Inter finishing runners-up to Milan in Serie A, Gasperini could look forward to leading a team in the UEFA Champions League for the first time. So, too, could Walter Mazzarri, the coach of SSC Napoli, who finished third in Serie A and thus returned to Europe's top club competition for the first time since the halcyon days of Diego Maradona. The Neapolitan fans had a new South American star to worship in 2010/11 as Uruguayan international striker Edinson Cavani, freshly recruited from Palermo, set new club records for goalscoring, finding the net 26 times in Serie A – a tally that included hat-tricks at home to Juventus, Sampdoria and Lazio – and seven times in the UEFA Europa League. Mazzarri's men were the only one of Italy's four representatives to progress through the group stage of that competition, eventually falling in the round of 32 after a closely contested tie against Villarreal CF.

Cavani, who had skilful accomplices Marek Hamšík and Ezequiel Lavezzi to thank for many of his goals, was suspended for the final two Serie A games and therefore missed out on the chance to take the Serie A capocannoniere crown. It went instead – for a second successive season – to Udinese Calcio's Antonio Di Natale. In 2009/10 the diminutive Italian international striker's 29 goals had saved Udinese from relegation; in 2010/11 his tally of 28, backed by a dozen from Chilean trick merchant Alexis Sánchez, carried the team all the way to fourth place and into the 2011/12 UEFA Champions League play-offs. With the experienced Francesco Guidolin at the helm, Udinese played richly entertaining football, but it was with an uncharacteristic goalless draw, against champions Milan, that they clinched fourth spot in the final game of the season.

That stalemate at the Stadio Friuli was bad news for Lazio, who, despite finishing level on points with Udinese thanks to a closing 4-2 win at US Lecce, finished below them on the head-to-head rule, with away goals the deciding factor after Lazio had won 3-2 in Rome in December and Udinese had prevailed 2-1 – thanks to a Di Natale double – on home turf in May. Lazio's fans at least had the satisfaction of seeing their team finish above the old enemy, Roma – despite going down 2-0 in both of the derbies. With a crafty coach in Edoardo 'Edy' Reja and a productive new Brazilian playmaker in Hernanes, Lazio matched Napoli and Udinese for overachievement – albeit with the lesser reward of a UEFA Europa League berth.

ITALY

Roma's fall from second place to sixth was a disappointment – as was their performance in the UEFA Champions League, where, like Milan and Inter, they failed to win their group before crashing out prematurely in the knockout phase. FC Shakhtar Donetsk gave them a going-over both in the Stadio Olimpico and the Donbass Arena, although it was a devastating domestic defeat in between the two legs – 4-3 at Genoa after Roma had led 3-0 early in the second half – that prompted the resignation of coach Claudio Ranieri. The Roma board caught everybody off-guard when they announced that just-retired striker Vincenzo Montella would step in to the breach, but by the end of the season, at which stage resident superstar Francesco Totti had become only the sixth player to amass over 200 Serie A goals, another surprise was in store when former Spanish international midfielder Luis Enrique, the coach of FC Barcelona's B team, was installed as the new Giallorossi coach on a two-year contract.

Juve meltdown

Not surprisingly, there was a post-season change of coach too at Juventus, who had finished the Serie A campaign out of the European places in seventh place, 24 points in arrears of the champions. Luigi Delneri, recruited from Sampdoria, was probably fortunate to remain in situ for the whole of a grim campaign that featured an early exit from Europe – Juve drew all six of their UEFA Europa League group games – and a post-Christmas meltdown on the domestic front that brought six Serie A defeats in quick succession plus a home defeat by Roma in the quarter-final of the Coppa Italia. A 13-match unbeaten run in the autumn, which included a 2-1 win away to Milan, had put Juve in the title frame, but a nightmare start to the New Year, with top scorer Fabio Quagliarella sustaining cruciate knee ligament damage during a 4-1 drubbing in Turin by Parma FC, completely took the wind out of the Bianconeri sails. Replacement striker Alessandro Matri, hired on loan from Cagliari, did well, matching Quagliarella's nine-goal total, but Delneri could not re-energise the team in the closing weeks and he was duly dismissed, the black-and-white baton being handed on to ex-Juve midfielder Antonio Conte, who had just strengthened his case for enrolment by guiding AC Siena to promotion.

Siena returned to Serie A after just one year away – as did Serie B champions Atalanta BC. However, the third team relegated in 2009/10, AS Livorno Calcio, finished just outside the promotion play-offs, which were eventually won by third-placed Novara Calcio, who returned to top-flight football after a 55-year absence. Brescia Calcio were the only one of the three teams promoted in 2009/10 to go straight back down. They were joined by AS Bari and, to universal

National Team

International Honours –
FIFA World Cup – (4) 1934, 1938, 1982, 2006.
UEFA European Championship – (1) 1968.

International Tournament Appearances –
FIFA World Cup – (17) 1934 (Winners), 1938 (Winners), 1950, 1958, 1962, 1966, 1970 (runners-up) 1974, 1978 (4th), 1982 (Winners), 1986 (2nd round), 1990 (3rd), 1994 (runners-up), 1998 (qtr-finals), 2002 (2nd round), 2006 (Winners), 2010.
UEFA European Championship – (7) 1968 (Winners), 1980 (4th), 1988 (semi-finals), 1996, 2000 (runners-up), 2004, 2008 (qtr-finals).

Top Five All-time Caps – Fabio Cannavaro (136); Paolo Maldini (126); Dino Zoff (112); Gianluigi Buffon (105); Gianluca Zambrotta (98)

Top Five All-time Goals – Luigi Riva (35); Giuseppe Meazza (33); Silvio Piola (30); Roberto Baggio & Alessandro Del Piero (27)

NATIONAL TEAM RESULTS 2010/11

10/8/10	Ivory Coast	N	London (ENG)	0-1	
3/9/10	Estonia (ECQ)	A	Tallinn	2-1	*Cassano (60), Bonucci (63)*
7/9/10	Faroe Islands (ECQ)	H	Florence	5-0	*Gilardino (11), De Rossi (22), Cassano (27), Quagliarella (81), Pirlo (90)*
8/10/10	Northern Ireland (ECQ)	A	Belfast	0-0	
12/10/10	Serbia (ECQ)	H	Genoa	3-0	*(w/o; original match abandoned after 6 mins)*
17/11/10	Romania	N	Klagenfurt (AUT)	1-1	*Marica (82og)*
9/2/11	Germany	A	Dortmund	1-1	*Rossi (81)*
25/3/11	Slovenia (ECQ)	A	Ljubljana	1-0	*Thiago Motta (73)*
29/3/11	Ukraine	A	Kyiv	2-0	*Rossi (27), Matri (81)*
3/6/11	Estonia (ECQ)	H	Modena	3-0	*Rossi (21), Cassano (39), Pazzini (68)*
7/6/11	Republic of Ireland	N	Liege (BEL)	0-2	

NATIONAL TEAM APPEARANCES 2010/11

oach – Cesare PRANDELLI	19/8/57		Civ	EST	FRO	NIR	SRB	Rou	Ger	SVN	Ukr	EST	Irl	Caps	Goals
alvatore SIRIGU	12/1/87	Palermo	G	G										2	-
arco MOTTA	14/5/86	Juventus	D70											1	-
eonardo BONUCCI	1/5/87	Juventus	D	D	D	D	D	D	D	D	s76			11	2
iorgio CHIELLINI	14/8/84	Juventus	D	D	D	D	D		D78	D	D17	D	D	42	2
ristian MOLINARO	30/7/83	Stuttgart (GER)	D	D										2	-
ngelo PALOMBO	25/9/81	Sampdoria	M81	s75	s76		M						s46	22	-
aniele DE ROSSI	24/7/83	Roma	M	M	M76	M		s46 /80	M					63	10
imone PEPE	30/8/83	Juventus	M73	A60		A84								21	-
ntonio CASSANO	12/7/82	Sampdoria /Milan	M70	A80	A	A	A		A46	A74		A65		23	6
ario BALOTELLI	12/8/90	Inter /Man. City (ENG)	M59					A60						2	-
MAURI Carvalho	3/6/80	Juventus	A59											1	-
arco BORRIELLO	18/6/82	Milan /Roma	s59			A74			s46					7	-
abio QUAGLIARELLA	31/1/83	Napoli /Juventus	s59	s60	s59			s60						25	6
attia CASSANI	26/8/83	Palermo	s70	D		D		s60	D53				D	8	-
iuseppe ROSSI	1/2/87	Villarreal (ESP)	s70		A59	s84		A46	s46	s74	A62	A79	A46	23	6
laudio MARCHISIO	19/1/86	Juventus	s73			s79	M			s87	M88	M	M	13	-
iccardo MONTOLIVO	18/1/85	Fiorentina	s81	M75	M				M	M87	M	M	M	24	-
ndrea PIRLO	19/5/79	Milan		M	M	M	M	s46				M	M46	74	10
iampaolo PAZZINI	2/8/84	Sampdoria /Inter		A	s59	s74	A	s80	A46	A		s65	A59	18	2
uca ANTONELLI	11/2/87	Parma		s80	D									2	-
miliano VIVIANO	1/12/85	Bologna			G	G	G	G			G		G	6	-
orenzo DE SILVESTRI	23/5/88	Fiorentina			D									1	-
Alberto GILARDINO	5/7/82	Fiorentina			A59			s46			A76		s59	47	17
Domenico CRISCITO	30/12/86	Genoa				D	D		s78		D		D65	15	-
Stefano MAURI	8/1/80	Lazio				M79	M	M	M74	M63				11	-
Gianluca ZAMBROTTA	19/2/77	Milan					D							98	2
Davide SANTON	2/1/91	Inter /Cesena						D60			s46			7	-
Andrea RANOCCHIA	16/2/88	Genoa /Inter						D	D			D		3	-
Federico BALZARETTI	6/12/81	Palermo						D		D		D	s65	4	-
Alberto AQUILANI	7/7/84	Juventus						M	s63	M	M46	M24		16	2
Cristian Daniel LEDESMA	24/9/82	Lazio						M46						1	-
Alessandro DIAMANTI	2/5/83	Brescia						M46						1	-
Gianluigi BUFFON	28/1/78	Juventus							G	G		G		105	-
THIAGO MOTTA	28/8/82	Inter							M63	M				2	1
Christian MAGGIO	11/2/82	Napoli							s53	D	D46	D		10	-
Sebastian GIOVINCO	26/1/87	Parma							s74		s46	s79	s59	4	-
Antonio NOCERINO	9/4/85	Palermo								s63	M	s24	M59	5	-
Daniele GASTALDELLO	25/6/83	Sampdoria									D			1	-
Davide ASTORI	7/1/87	Cagliari									s17 74*			1	-
Alessandro MATRI	19/8/84	Juventus									s62		s46	2	1
Marco PAROLO	25/1/85	Cesena									s88			1	-
Alessandro GAMBERINI	27/8/81	Fiorentina											D	8	-

NB The Italian FA (FIGC) awarded caps for the abandoned match against Serbia.

amazement, Sampdoria. The Genoese club, fourth in 2009/10 under Delneri, had started the season by narrowly missing out on a place in the UEFA Champions League after a tightly-contested play-off against Bremen, but the mid-season departure of their two celebrated strikers – Cassano, to Milan, and Giampaolo Pazzini, to Inter – left them in freefall, and by the end of a spring campaign that yielded just ten points from 19 games, they were a full five points from safety.

New-look Azzurri

Cassano, who left Samp under a cloud over a disciplinary issue, would not only experience scudetto success with Milan but also emerge as a key figure in the new-look Italian national team. Given a complete makeover by new coach Cesare Prandelli following the FIFA World Cup blow-out in South Africa, the Azzurri lost their first and last matches of the season – neutral-ground friendlies against the Ivory Coast and the Republic of Ireland – but in between took a firm grip of their UEFA EURO 2012 qualifying group, collecting 16 points from their six matches and conceding just one goal, in their opening fixture against Estonia in Tallinn.

The all-Juve centre-back pairing of Leonardo Bonucci and Giorgio Chiellini deserved credit for that impressive defensive record – even if one of the team's five clean sheets was the result of just six minutes' work in the abandoned home tie against Serbia. Handed a 3-0 forfeit for that game because of the visiting fans' unruly behaviour, Italy saved their best results on the field of play for the spring, when a winning goal from newly-naturalised Brazilian-born midfielder Thiago Motta sealed a hard-earned 1-0 win in Slovenia that was followed by an entertaining 3-0 victory in Modena over Estonia. Villarreal striker Giuseppe Rossi, who, like Cassano, had missed the 2010 World Cup, re-established his international credentials with the opening goal against Estonia and two more in friendlies away to Germany (1-1) and Ukraine (2-0). With Rossi, Cassano, Pazzini and Matri jostling for places up front, the Azzurri could well have a potent new attack – as well as their usual solid defence – on show next summer as they bid for EURO glory in Poland/Ukraine.

CLUB-BY-CLUB

AS BARI

Coach – Giampiero Ventura; (10/2/11) Bortolo Mutti
Founded – 1908
Stadium – San Nicola (58,270)

2010				
29/8	Juventus	h	1-0	*Donati*
12/9	Napoli	a	2-2	*Barreto, Castillo*
19/9	Cagliari	h	0-0	
22/9	Inter	a	0-4	
26/9	Brescia	h	2-1	*Rivas, Barreto (p)*
3/10	Genoa	a	1-2	*Barreto (p)*
17/10	Lazio	h	0-2	
23/10	Fiorentina	a	1-2	*Parisi*
31/10	Udinese	h	0-2	
7/11	Milan	h	2-3	*Kutuzov, Barreto*
10/11	Chievo	a	0-0	
14/11	Parma	h	0-1	
21/11	Catania	a	0-1	
28/11	Cesena	h	1-1	*Caputo*
5/12	Sampdoria	a	0-3	
12/12	Roma	a	0-1	
19/12	Palermo	h	1-1	*Masiello A. (p)*
2011				
6/1	Lecce	a	1-0	*Okaka Chuka*
9/1	Bologna	h	0-2	
16/1	Juventus	a	1-2	*Rudolf*
23/1	Napoli	h	0-2	
30/1	Cagliari	a	1-2	*Okaka Chuka*
3/2	Inter	h	0-3	
6/2	Brescia	a	0-2	
13/2	Genoa	h	0-0	
20/2	Lazio	a	0-1	
27/2	Fiorentina	h	1-1	*Ghezzal*
6/3	Udinese	a	0-1	
13/3	Milan	a	1-1	*Rudolf*
20/3	Chievo	h	1-2	*Ghezzal (p)*
3/4	Parma	a	2-1	*Parisi, Álvarez*
10/4	Catania	h	1-1	*Gazzi*
17/4	Cesena	a	0-1	
23/4	Sampdoria	h	0-1	
1/5	Roma	h	2-3	*Bentivoglio (p), Huseklepp*
7/5	Palermo	a	1-2	*Bentivoglio*
15/5	Lecce	h	0-2	
22/5	Bologna	a	4-0	*Grandolfo 3, Huseklepp*

No	Name	Nat	DoB	Pos	Aps	(s)	Gls
4	Sergio Bernardo ALMIRÓN	ARG	7/11/80	M	21	(4)	
90	Edgar Anthony ÁLVAREZ	HON	18/1/80	M	18	(11)	1
10	Paulo Vítor BARRETO de Souza	BRA	12/7/85	A	13		4
15	Nicola BELMONTE		15/4/87	D	25	(1)	
27	Simone BENTIVOGLIO		29/5/85	M	16		2
18	Francesco CAPUTO		6/8/87	A	5	(7)	1
9	José Ignacio CASTILLO	ARG	4/11/75	A	4	(10)	1
3	Paul Constantin CODREA	ROU	4/4/81	M	4	(2)	
19	Marco CRIMI		17/3/90	M	1	(2)	
91	Marco D'ALESSANDRO		17/2/91	A	1	(10)	
8	Massimo DONATI		26/3/81	M	23	(8)	1
28	Gianluca GALASSO		18/1/84	M	3	(1)	
14	Alessandro Carlo GAZZI		28/1/83	M	29	(2)	1
11	Abdelkader GHEZZAL	ALG	5/12/84	A	15	(5)	2
1	Jean-François GILLET	BEL	31/5/79	G	36		
52	Kamil GLIK	POL	3/2/88	D	15	(1)	
39	Francesco GRANDOLFO		26/7/92	A	1	(2)	3
22	Erik HUSEKLEPP	NOR	5/9/84	A	12	(2)	2
32	JAIME Romero Gómez	ESP	31/7/90	M	5	(5)	
24	Kamil KOPÚNEK	SVK	18/5/84	M	4	(1)	
20	Vitaliy KUTUZOV	BLR	20/3/80	A	13	(1)	1

No	Name	Nat	DoB	Pos	Aps	(s)	Gls
	Andrea MASIELLO		5/2/86	D	36		1
	Salvatore MASIELLO		31/1/82	M	6		
	Stefano OKAKA CHUKA		9/8/89	A	6	(4)	2
	Daniele PADELLI		25/10/85	G	2		
	Alessandro PARISI		15/4/77	D	27		2
	Nico PULZETTI		13/2/84	M	11	(4)	
	Andrea RAGGI		24/6/84	D	14	(2)	
	Luigi RANA		6/11/86	A	2	(1)	
	Michele RINALDI		9/1/87	D	2	(4)	
	Emanuel Benito RIVAS	ARG	17/3/83	M	9	(13)	1
	Marco ROSSI		30/9/87	D	27	(3)	
	Gergely RUDOLF	HUN	9/3/85	A	11	(2)	2
	Nicola STRAMBELLI		6/9/88	M	1	(2)	

BOLOGNA FC

Coach – Franco Colomba; (29/8/10) (Paolo Magnani); (1/9/10) Alberto Malesani

Founded – 1909

Stadium – Renato Dall'Ara (39,444)

MAJOR HONOURS: Italian League – (7) 1925, 1929, 1936, 1937, 1939, 1941, 1964; Italian Cup – (2) 1970, 1974.

010				
0/8	Inter	h	0-0	
2/9	Lazio	a	1-3	*Mudingayi*
9/9	Roma	a	2-2	*Di Vaio 2*
2/9	Udinese	h	2-1	*Giménez, Di Vaio*
6/9	Catania	a	1-1	*Di Vaio*
/10	Sampdoria	h	1-1	*Britos*
7/10	Palermo	a	1-4	*Di Vaio*
4/10	Juventus	h	0-0	
1/10	Cagliari	a	0-2	
/11	Lecce	h	2-0	*Di Vaio, Giménez*
0/11	Genoa	a	0-1	
4/11	Brescia	h	1-0	*Di Vaio*
1/11	Napoli	a	1-4	*Meggiorini*
/12	Cesena	a	2-0	*Di Vaio, Britos*
/12	Chievo	h	2-1	*Britos, Di Vaio*
2/12	Milan	h	0-3	
9/12	Parma	a	0-0	
011				
/1	Fiorentina	h	1-1	*Di Vaio*
/1	Bari	a	2-0	*Ekdal, Di Vaio*
5/1	Inter	a	1-4	*Giménez*
3/1	Lazio	h	3-1	*Ramírez, Di Vaio 2*
/2	Udinese	a	1-1	*Di Vaio*
/2	Catania	h	1-0	*Portanova*
3/2	Sampdoria	a	1-3	*Paponi*
9/2	Palermo	h	1-0	*Paponi*
3/2	Roma	h	0-1	*(first 17 mins played on 30/1)*
26/2	Juventus	a	2-0	*Di Vaio 2*
/3	Cagliari	h	2-2	*Di Vaio (p), Ramírez*
13/3	Lecce	a	1-0	*Ramírez*
20/3	Genoa	h	1-1	*Di Vaio*
2/4	Brescia	a	1-3	*Di Vaio*
10/4	Napoli	h	0-2	
17/4	Chievo	a	0-2	
23/4	Cesena	h	0-2	
1/5	Milan	a	0-1	
8/5	Parma	h	0-0	
15/5	Fiorentina	a	1-1	*Ramírez*
22/5	Bari	h	0-4	

No	Name	Nat	DoB	Pos	Aps	(s)	Gls
6	Miguel Ángel BRITOS	URU	17/7/85	D	33		3
24	Antonio BUSCÈ		12/12/75	M	10	(6)	
32	Federico CASARINI		7/8/89	M	18	(14)	
21	Nicolò CHERUBIN		2/12/86	D	9	(3)	
7	Francesco DELLA ROCCA		14/9/87	M	23	(4)	
9	Marco DI VAIO		15/7/76	A	38		19
15	DIEGO Fernando PÉREZ Aguado	URU	18/5/80	M	27		
12	Albin EKDAL	SWE	28/7/89	M	19	(3)	1
16	Andrea ESPOSITO		17/5/86	D	8	(3)	
8	György GARICS	AUT	8/3/84	D	15		
20	Henry Damián GIMÉNEZ	URU	13/3/86	A	8	(18)	3
4	René KRHIN	SVN	21/5/90	M	2	(2)	
22	Cristiano LUPATELLI		21/6/78	G		(1)	
69	Riccardo MEGGIORINI		4/9/85	A	14	(15)	1
18	Vangelis MORAS	GRE	26/8/81	D	17	(2)	
3	Archimede MORLEO		26/9/83	D	7	(2)	
26	Gaby MUDINGAYI	BEL	1/10/81	M	32		1
5	Massimo MUTARELLI		13/1/78	M	7	(8)	
35	Daniele PAPONI		16/4/88	A	6	(8)	2
13	Daniele PORTANOVA		17/12/78	D	33		1
17	Ivan RADOVANOVIĆ	SRB	29/8/88	M	6	(4)	
10	Gastón Exequiel RAMÍREZ	URU	2/12/90	M	16	(9)	4
19	Matteo RUBIN		9/7/87	D	28	(1)	
77	Luca SILIGARDI		26/1/88	M	4	(8)	
1	Emiliano VIVIANO		1/12/85	G	38		

BRESCIA CALCIO

Coach – Giuseppe Iachini; (6/12/10) Mario Beretta; (30/1/11) Giuseppe Iachini

Founded – 1911

Stadium – Mario Rigamonti (27,547)

2010				
29/8	Parma	a	0-2	
12/9	Palermo	h	3-2	*Dallamano, Éder, Caracciolo (p)*
19/9	Chievo	a	1-0	*Diamanti*
22/9	Roma	h	2-1	*Hetemaj, Caracciolo (p)*
26/9	Bari	a	1-2	*Kone*
3/10	Lazio	a	0-1	
17/10	Udinese	h	0-1	
24/10	Lecce	a	1-2	*Caracciolo*
31/10	Napoli	h	0-1	
6/11	Inter	a	1-1	*Caracciolo*
10/11	Juventus	h	1-1	*Diamanti*
14/11	Bologna	a	0-1	
21/11	Cagliari	h	1-2	*Caracciolo (p)*
28/11	Genoa	h	0-0	
4/12	Milan	a	0-3	
12/12	Sampdoria	h	1-0	*Córdova*
19/12	Catania	a	0-1	
2011				
6/1	Cesena	h	1-2	*Éder*
9/1	Fiorentina	a	2-3	*Diamanti, Córdova*
16/1	Parma	h	2-0	*Bega, Diamanti*
22/1	Palermo	a	0-1	
30/1	Chievo	h	0-3	
2/2	Roma	a	1-1	*Éder*
6/2	Bari	h	2-0	*Diamanti (p), Caracciolo*
13/2	Lazio	h	0-2	
20/2	Udinese	a	0-0	
27/2	Lecce	h	2-2	*Caracciolo, Zoboli*
6/3	Napoli	a	0-0	
11/3	Inter	h	1-1	*Caracciolo*
20/3	Juventus	a	1-2	*Éder*
2/4	Bologna	h	3-1	*Hetemaj, Zoboli, Caracciolo (p)*
10/4	Cagliari	a	1-1	*Caracciolo*
17/4	Genoa	a	0-3	
23/4	Milan	h	0-1	
1/5	Sampdoria	a	3-3	*Éder, Caracciolo 2*
8/5	Catania	h	1-2	*Diamanti*
15/5	Cesena	a	0-1	
22/5	Fiorentina	h	2-2	*Éder, Accardi*

No	Name	Nat	DoB	Pos	Aps	(s)	Gls
20	Pietro ACCARDI		12/9/82	D	6	(2)	1
1	Michele ARCARI		27/6/78	G	22		
17	Davide BAIOCCO		8/5/75	M	13	(8)	
6	Francesco BEGA		26/10/74	D	25	(2)	1
28	Gaetano BERARDI	SUI	21/8/88	D	24	(3)	

19	Alessandro BUDEL		25/2/81	M	4	(8)	
9	Andrea CARACCIOLO		18/9/81	A	30	(3)	12
11	Nicolás Andrés CÓRDOVA	CHI	9/2/79	M	17	(4)	2
23	Simone DALLAMANO		25/11/83	D	12	(2)	1
3	Fabio DAPRELÀ	SUI	19/2/91	D	6	(4)	
21	Sébastien DE MAIO	FRA	5/3/87	D		(2)	
32	Alessandro DIAMANTI		2/5/83	A	29	(3)	6
7	ÉDER Citadin Martins	BRA	15/11/86	A	27	(8)	6
14	Róbert FECZESIN	HUN	22/6/86	A		(2)	
4	Antonio FILIPPINI		3/7/73	M	11	(4)	
56	Perparim HETEMAJ	FIN	12/12/86	M	28	(2)	2
30	JONATHAS Cristian de Jesus	BRA	6/3/89	A	2	(4)	
33	Panagiotis KONE	GRE	26/7/87	M	23	(8)	1
36	Davide LANZAFAME		9/2/87	M	1	(12)	
12	Nicola LEALI		17/2/93	G	1		
16	Víctor Hugo MARECO	PAR	26/2/84	D	6	(2)	
26	Gilberto MARTÍNEZ Vidal	CRC	1/10/79	D	19		
18	Davide POSSANZINI		9/2/76	A	5	(12)	
22	Matteo SERENI		11/2/75	G	15		
31	Riccardo TADDEI		5/9/80	A		(4)	
24	Lorenzo TASSI		12/2/95	M		(1)	
8	Ádám VASS	HUN	9/9/88	M	15	(5)	
38	Maseko Nana Addo WELBECK	GHA	24/11/94	M		(1)	
15	Marco ZAMBELLI		22/8/85	D	25	(3)	
14	Cristiano ZANETTI		14/4/77	M	8		
5	Jonathan ZEBINA	FRA	19/7/78	D	26	(2)	
2	Davide ZOBOLI		8/10/81	D	18		2

CAGLIARI CALCIO

Coach – Pierpaolo Bisoli; (16/11/10) Roberto Donadoni

Founded – 1920

Stadium – Sant'Elia (23,486)

MAJOR HONOURS: Italian League – (1) 1970.

2010				
29/8	Palermo	a	0-0	
11/9	Roma	h	5-1	*Conti, Matri 2 (1p), Acquafresca, Lazzari*
19/9	Bari	a	0-0	
22/9	Sampdoria	h	0-0	
26/9	Juventus	a	2-4	*Matri 2*
3/10	Chievo	a	0-0	
17/10	Inter	h	0-1	
24/10	Lazio	a	1-2	*Matri*
31/10	Bologna	h	2-0	*Nenê, Nainggolan*
7/11	Udinese	a	1-1	*Conti*
10/11	Napoli	h	0-1	
14/11	Genoa	h	0-1	
21/11	Brescia	a	2-1	*Matri, Conti*
28/11	Lecce	h	3-2	*Matri 2, Canini*
5/12	Fiorentina	a	0-1	
12/12	Catania	h	3-0	*Nenê 3*
18/12	Cesena	a	0-1	
2011				
6/1	Milan	h	0-1	
9/1	Parma	a	2-1	*Acquafresca 2*
16/1	Palermo	h	3-1	*Matri, og (Nocerino), Biondini*
22/1	Roma	a	0-3	
30/1	Bari	h	2-1	*Matri 2*
2/2	Sampdoria	a	1-0	*Nainggolan*
5/2	Juventus	h	1-3	*Acquafresca*
13/2	Chievo	h	4-1	*Conti, Canini, Nenê 2*
19/2	Inter	a	0-1	
27/2	Lazio	h	1-0	*og (André Dias)*
6/3	Bologna	a	2-2	*Cossu, Ragatzu*
13/3	Udinese	h	0-4	
20/3	Napoli	a	1-2	*Acquafresca*
3/4	Genoa	a	1-0	*Acquafresca*
10/4	Brescia	h	1-1	*Cossu*
17/4	Lecce	a	3-3	*Acquafresca 2, Conti*
23/4	Fiorentina	h	1-2	*Cossu*
1/5	Catania	a	0-2	
8/5	Cesena	h	0-2	
14/5	Milan	a	1-4	*Cossu*
22/5	Parma	h	1-1	*og (Feltscher)*

No	Name	Nat	DoB	Pos	Aps	(s)	Gls
9	Robert ACQUAFRESCA		11/9/87	A	27	(10)	8
1	Michael AGAZZI		3/7/84	G	38		
31	Alessandro AGOSTINI		23/7/79	D	34		
3	Lorenzo ARIAUDO		11/6/89	D	9	(6)	
13	Davide ASTORI		7/1/87	D	36		
8	Davide BIONDINI		24/1/83	M	35	(2)	1
21	Michele CANINI		5/6/85	D	36		2
32	Pablo Daniel CEPPELINI	URU	11/9/91	M		(3)	
5	Daniele CONTI		9/1/79	M	27	(2)	5
7	Andrea COSSU		3/5/80	M	35		4
20	Simon LANER		28/1/84	M	3	(15)	
10	Andrea LAZZARI		3/12/84	M	20	(10)	1
32	Alessandro MATRI		19/8/84	A	19	(3)	11
23	Simone MISSIROLI		23/5/86	M	5	(11)	
4	Radja NAINGGOLAN	BEL	4/5/88	M	33	(3)	2
18	Anderson Miguel da Silva "NENÊ"	BRA	28/7/83	A	18	(9)	6
25	Ivan PELIZZOLI		18/11/80	G		(1)	
24	Gabriele PERICO		11/3/84	D	21	(6)	
23	Alex PINARDI		5/9/80	A	3	(4)	
14	Francesco PISANO		29/4/86	D	15	(3)	
30	Daniele RAGATZU		21/9/91	A	4	(14)	1
16	Mikhail SIVAKOV	BLR	16/1/88	M		(2)	

CALCIO CATANIA

Coach – Marco Giampaolo; (19/1/11) Diego Simeone (ARG)

Founded – 1946

Stadium – Angelo Massimino (23,420)

2010				
29/8	Chievo	a	1-2	*Ricchiuti*
12/9	Parma	h	2-1	*Mascara (p), Antenucci (p)*
18/9	Milan	a	1-1	*Capuano*
22/9	Cesena	h	2-0	*Silvestre, Maxi López*
26/9	Bologna	h	1-1	*og (Britos)*
3/10	Lecce	a	0-1	
17/10	Napoli	h	1-1	*Gómez*
24/10	Genoa	a	0-1	
31/10	Fiorentina	h	0-0	
7/11	Sampdoria	a	0-0	
10/11	Udinese	h	1-0	*Maxi López*
14/11	Palermo	a	1-3	*Terlizzi*
21/11	Bari	h	1-0	*Terlizzi*
28/11	Lazio	a	1-1	*Silvestre*
5/12	Juventus	h	1-3	*Morimoto*
12/12	Cagliari	a	0-3	
19/12	Brescia	h	1-0	*Maxi López*
2011				
6/1	Roma	a	2-4	*Silvestre, Maxi López*
9/1	Inter	h	1-2	*Gómez*
16/1	Chievo	h	1-1	*Maxi López (p)*
22/1	Parma	a	0-2	
29/1	Milan	h	0-2	
2/2	Cesena	a	1-1	*Maxi López*
6/2	Bologna	a	0-1	
13/2	Lecce	h	3-2	*Silvestre, Lodi 2*
20/2	Napoli	a	0-1	
27/2	Genoa	h	2-1	*Maxi López, Bergessio*
6/3	Fiorentina	a	0-3	
13/3	Sampdoria	h	1-0	*Llama*
20/3	Udinese	a	0-2	
3/4	Palermo	h	4-0	*og (Balzaretti), Bergessio, Ledesma, Pesce*
10/4	Bari	a	1-1	*Maxi López*
17/4	Lazio	h	1-4	*Schelotto*
23/4	Juventus	a	2-2	*Gómez, Lodi*
1/5	Cagliari	h	2-0	*Silvestre, Bergessio*

	Brescia	a	2-1	*Silvestre, Bergessio*
/5	Roma	h	2-1	*Bergessio, Gómez*
/5	Inter	a	1-3	*Ledesma*

Name	Nat	DoB	Pos	Aps	(s)	Gls
Pablo Sebastián ÁLVAREZ	ARG	17/4/84	D	20	(3)	
Mariano Gonzalo ANDÚJAR	ARG	30/7/83	G	37		
Mirko ANTENUCCI		8/9/84	A	2	(12)	1
Błażej AUGUSTYN	POL	26/1/88	D	5	(1)	
Giuseppe BELLUSCI		21/8/89	D	6	(3)	
Gonzalo Rubén BERGESSIO	ARG	20/7/84	A	12	(1)	5
Marco BIAGIANTI		19/4/84	M	15		
Andrea CAMPAGNOLO		17/6/78	G	1		
Ciro CAPUANO		10/7/81	D	22	(1)	1
Ezequiel Alejo CARBONI	ARG	4/4/79	M	24	(4)	
Gennaro DELVECCHIO		25/3/78	M	2	(5)	
Alejandro Darío GÓMEZ	ARG	15/2/88	M	30	(6)	4
Mariano Julio IZCO	ARG	13/3/83	M	11	(7)	
Pablo Martín LEDESMA	ARG	4/2/84	M	25	(7)	2
Cristian Ezequiel LLAMA	ARG	26/6/86	M	5	(10)	1
Francesco LODI		23/3/84	M	10	(6)	3
Giovanni MARCHESE		17/10/84	D	11	(1)	
Giuseppe MASCARA		22/8/79	A	16	(2)	1
MAXImiliano Gastón LÓPEZ	ARG	3/4/84	A	32	(3)	8
Takayuki MORIMOTO	JPN	7/5/88	A	4	(8)	1
Simone PESCE		10/7/82	M	5	(3)	1
Alessandro POTENZA		8/3/84	D	19	(1)	
RAPHAEL MARTINHO Alves de Lima	BRA	15/4/88	M	5	(6)	
Adrián RICCHIUTI		30/6/78	A	19	(12)	1
Ezequiel Matias SCHELOTTO		23/5/89	M	9	(5)	1
Fabio SCIACCA		16/5/89	M	3	(1)	
Matías Augustín SILVESTRE	ARG	25/9/84	D	36		6
Nicolás Federico SPOLLI	ARG	20/2/83	D	23	(2)	
Christian TERLIZZI		10/7/81	D	9	(3)	2

AC CESENA

Coach – Massimo Ficcadenti

Founded – 1940

Stadium – Dino Manuzzi (23,860)

2010				
8/8	Roma	a	0-0	
1/9	Milan	h	2-0	*Bogdani, Giaccherini*
9/9	Lecce	h	1-0	*Bogdani*
2/9	Catania	a	0-2	
6/9	Napoli	h	1-4	*Parolo*
/10	Udinese	a	0-1	
7/10	Parma	h	1-1	*Bogdani*
4/10	Chievo	a	1-2	*og (Guana)*
1/10	Sampdoria	h	0-1	
/11	Juventus	a	1-3	*Jiménez*
0/11	Lazio	h	1-0	*Parolo*
3/11	Fiorentina	a	0-1	
1/11	Palermo	h	1-2	*Bogdani*
8/11	Bari	a	1-1	*Colucci (p)*
/12	Bologna	h	0-2	
8/12	Cagliari	h	1-0	*Jiménez*
2011				
/1	Brescia	a	2-1	*Jiménez, Ceccarelli*
/1	Genoa	h	0-0	
16/1	Roma	h	0-1	
9/1	Inter	a	2-3	*Bogdani, Giaccherini*
23/1	Milan	a	0-2	
30/1	Lecce	a	1-1	*Bogdani*
2/2	Catania	h	1-1	*Jiménez*
/2	Napoli	a	0-2	
13/2	Udinese	h	0-3	
20/2	Parma	a	2-2	*Rosina, Sammarco*
27/2	Chievo	h	1-0	*Jiménez (p)*
6/3	Sampdoria	a	3-2	*Parolo, Giaccherini 2*
12/3	Juventus	h	2-2	*Jiménez (p), Parolo*
19/3	Lazio	a	0-1	
3/4	Fiorentina	h	2-2	*Jiménez, Caserta*
10/4	Palermo	a	2-2	*Parolo, Giaccherini*
17/4	Bari	h	1-0	*Bogdani*
23/4	Bologna	a	2-0	*Giaccherini, Malonga*
30/4	Inter	h	1-2	*Budan*
8/5	Cagliari	a	2-0	*Jiménez, Malonga*
15/5	Brescia	h	1-0	*Giaccherini*
22/5	Genoa	a	2-3	*Bogdani (p), Jiménez*

No	Name	Nat	DoB	Pos	Aps	(s)	Gls
1	Francesco ANTONIOLI		14/9/69	G	37		
4	Stephen APPIAH	GHA	24/12/80	M	13	(1)	
15	Yohan BENALOUANE	FRA	28/3/87	D	10	(5)	
70	Erjon BOGDANI	ALB	14/4/77	A	29	(6)	8
11	Igor BUDAN	CRO	22/4/80	A	6	(11)	1
33	Alex CALDERONI		31/5/76	G	1		
8	Fabio CASERTA		24/9/78	M	19	(6)	1
77	Luca CECCARELLI		24/3/83	D	25	(7)	1
14	Giuseppe COLUCCI		24/8/80	M	32	(1)	1
29	Hernán Paolo DELLAFIORE		2/2/85	D	4	(3)	
13	Ivan FATIĆ	MNE	21/8/88	D		(2)	
5	FELIPE Dias da Silva dal Belo	BRA	31/7/84	D	7		
23	Emanuele GIACCHERINI		5/5/85	A	34	(2)	7
19	Nicolás Martín GOROBSOV	ARG	25/11/89	M	1		
16	Jude Odion IGHALO	NGA	16/6/89	A		(3)	
10	Luis Antonio JIMÉNEZ	CHI	17/6/84	M	30	(1)	9
6	Maurizio LAURO		12/3/81	D	23	(7)	
17	Dominique MALONGA	FRA	8/1/89	A	5	(17)	2
5	Yuto NAGATOMO	JPN	12/9/86	D	16		
18	Marco PAROLO		25/1/85	M	37		5
3	Maximiliano PELLEGRINO	ARG	26/1/80	D	24	(6)	
44	Luigi PIANGERELLI		19/10/73	M		(5)	
7	Roope RISKI	FIN	16/8/91	A		(1)	
30	Alejandro RODRÍGUEZ de Miguel	ESP	30/7/91	A		(1)	
84	Alessandro ROSINA		31/1/84	M	4	(6)	1
24	Paolo SAMMARCO		17/3/83	M	7	(8)	1
46	Davide SANTON		2/1/91	D	9	(2)	
7	Ezequiel Matias SCHELOTTO		23/5/89	M	11	(6)	
25	Steve VON BERGEN	SUI	10/6/83	D	34		

AC CHIEVO VERONA

Coach – Stefano Pioli

Founded – 1929

Stadium – Marc'Antonio Bentegodi (39,211)

2010				
29/8	Catania	h	2-1	*Moscardelli, Pellissier (p)*
12/9	Genoa	a	3-1	*Moscardelli, Marcolini, Pellissier*
19/9	Brescia	h	0-1	
22/9	Napoli	a	3-1	*Pellissier 2, Fernandes*
26/9	Lazio	h	0-1	
3/10	Cagliari	h	0-0	
16/10	Milan	a	1-3	*og (Ibrahimović)*
24/10	Cesena	h	2-1	*Cesar, Théréau*
31/10	Parma	a	0-0	
7/11	Fiorentina	a	0-1	
10/11	Bari	h	0-0	
14/11	Sampdoria	a	0-0	
21/11	Inter	h	2-1	*Pellissier, Moscardelli*
4/12	Roma	h	2-2	*Moscardelli, Granoche*
8/12	Bologna	a	1-2	*Cesar*
12/12	Lecce	a	2-3	*Bogliacino, Mandelli*
19/12	Juventus	h	1-1	*Pellissier*
2011				
6/1	Udinese	a	0-2	
9/1	Palermo	h	0-0	

16/1	Catania	a	1-1	*Pellissier*
23/1	Genoa	h	0-0	
30/1	Brescia	a	3-0	*Pellissier 2, Mandelli*
2/2	Napoli	h	2-0	*Moscardelli, Sardo*
6/2	Lazio	a	1-1	*Cesar*
13/2	Cagliari	a	1-4	*Théréau*
20/2	Milan	h	1-2	*Fernandes*
27/2	Cesena	a	0-1	
6/3	Parma	h	0-0	
13/3	Fiorentina	h	0-1	
20/3	Bari	a	2-1	*Pellissier, Moscardelli*
3/4	Sampdoria	h	0-0	
9/4	Inter	a	0-2	
17/4	Bologna	h	2-0	*Constant, Marcolini*
23/4	Roma	a	0-1	
1/5	Lecce	h	1-0	*Rigoni*
9/5	Juventus	a	2-2	*Uribe, Sardo*
15/5	Udinese	h	0-2	
22/5	Palermo	a	3-1	*Pellissier, Constant, Pulzetti*

No	Name	Nat	DoB	Pos	Aps	(s)	Gls
3	Marco ANDREOLLI		10/6/86	D	27	(1)	
9	Simone BENTIVOGLIO		29/5/85	M	8	(4)	
26	Mariano Adrián BOGLIACINO	URU	2/6/80	M	23	(11)	1
12	Boštjan CESAR	SVN	9/7/82	D	29	(3)	3
23	Kévin CONSTANT	GUI	15/5/87	M	27	(5)	2
8	Miloš DIMITRIJEVIĆ	SRB	16/2/84	M	2		
6	Gelson FERNANDES	SUI	2/9/86	M	24	(5)	2
21	Nicolas FREY	FRA	6/3/84	D	19	(2)	
11	Pablo Mariano GRANOCHE	URU	5/9/83	A	5	(13)	1
14	Roberto GUANA		21/1/81	M	15	(4)	
13	Bojan JOKIČ	SVN	17/5/86	D	13	(2)	
10	LUCIANO Siqueira de Oliveira	BRA	3/12/75	M	3	(1)	
5	Davide MANDELLI		28/6/77	D	16	(4)	2
4	Andrea MANTOVANI		22/6/84	D	31		
7	Michele MARCOLINI		2/10/75	M	14	(12)	2
83	MARCOS Ariel de Paula	BRA	19/12/83	A		(3)	
2	Santiago Eduardo MORERO	ARG	18/4/82	D	3	(2)	
80	Davide MOSCARDELLI		3/2/80	A	21	(13)	6
31	Sergio PELLISSIER		12/4/79	A	35		11
84	Nico PULZETTI		13/2/84	M	3	(4)	1
16	Luca RIGONI		7/12/84	M	27	(2)	1
20	Gennaro SARDO		8/5/79	D	20	(7)	2
28	Stefano SORRENTINO		28/3/79	G	37		
18	Lorenzo SQUIZZI		20/6/74	G	1	(1)	
77	Cyril THÉRÉAU	FRA	24/4/83	A	15	(8)	2
90	Fernando URIBE	COL	1/1/88	A		(7)	1

ACF FIORENTINA

Coach – Siniša Mihajlović (SRB)

Founded – 1926

Stadium – Artemio Franchi (47,282)

MAJOR HONOURS: UEFA Cup Winners' Cup – (1) 1961; Italian League – (2) 1956, 1969; Italian Cup – (6) 1940, 1961, 1966, 1975, 1996, 2001.

2010				
29/8	Napoli	h	1-1	*D'Agostino*
12/9	Lecce	a	0-1	
18/9	Lazio	h	1-2	*Ljajić (p)*
22/9	Genoa	a	1-1	*Gilardino*
26/9	Parma	h	2-0	*Ljajić (p), De Silvestri*
3/10	Palermo	h	1-2	*Gilardino*
17/10	Sampdoria	a	1-2	*Marchionni*
23/10	Bari	h	2-1	*Donadel, Gilardino*
31/10	Catania	a	0-0	
7/11	Chievo	h	1-0	*Cerci*
10/11	Roma	a	2-3	*Gilardino, D'Agostino*
13/11	Cesena	h	1-0	*Gilardino*
20/11	Milan	a	0-1	
27/11	Juventus	a	1-1	*og (Motta)*
5/12	Cagliari	h	1-0	*Mutu*
11/12	Udinese	a	1-2	*Santana*
2011				
6/1	Bologna	a	1-1	*Santana*
9/1	Brescia	h	3-2	*Gilardino, Santana, Ljajić*
15/1	Napoli	a	0-0	
23/1	Lecce	h	1-1	*Gilardino*
29/1	Lazio	a	0-2	
2/2	Genoa	h	1-0	*Santana*
6/2	Parma	a	1-1	*D'Agostino (p)*
13/2	Palermo	a	4-2	*Gilardino, Camporese, og (Bovo), Montolivo*
16/2	Inter	h	1-2	*Pasqual*
20/2	Sampdoria	h	0-0	
27/2	Bari	a	1-1	*Gilardino*
6/3	Catania	h	3-0	*Mutu 2, Gilardino*
13/3	Chievo	a	1-0	*Vargas*
20/3	Roma	h	2-2	*Mutu, Gamberini*
3/4	Cesena	a	2-2	*Gilardino, Montolivo*
10/4	Milan	h	1-2	*Vargas*
17/4	Juventus	h	0-0	
23/4	Cagliari	a	2-1	*Cerci 2*
1/5	Udinese	h	5-2	*Vargas, D'Agostino 2, Cerci 2*
8/5	Inter	a	1-3	*Gilardino*
15/5	Bologna	h	1-1	*Cerci*
22/5	Brescia	a	2-2	*Vargas, Cerci*

No	Name	Nat	DoB	Pos	Aps	(s)	Gls
35	Vlada AVRAMOV	SRB	5/4/79	G	1		
9	Khouma El Hadji BABACAR	SEN	17/3/93	A	3	(15)	
85	Valon BEHRAMI	SUI	19/4/85	M	15	(2)	
28	Mario Ariel BOLATTI	ARG	17/2/85	M	1	(9)	
84	Artur BORUC	POL	20/2/80	G	26		
31	Michele CAMPORESE		19/5/92	D	7	(2)	1
24	Alessio CERCI		23/7/87	A	17	(7)	7
25	Gianluca COMOTTO		16/10/78	D	16	(4)	
21	Gaetano D'AGOSTINO		3/6/82	M	12	(8)	5
29	Lorenzo DE SILVESTRI		23/5/88	D	23	(3)	1
4	Marco DONADEL		21/4/83	M	26	(3)	1
16	FELIPE Dias da Silva dal Belo	BRA	31/7/84	D	2	(3)	
1	Sébastien FREY	FRA	18/3/80	G	11		
5	Alessandro GAMBERINI		27/8/81	D	35		1
11	Alberto GILARDINO		5/7/82	A	35		12
30	Nikola GULAN	SRB	23/3/89	D	3	(3)	
2	Per KRØLDRUP	DEN	31/7/79	D	17	(2)	
22	Adem LJAJIĆ	SRB	29/9/91	M	14	(12)	3
32	Marco MARCHIONNI		22/7/80	M	13	(11)	1
18	Riccardo MONTOLIVO		18/1/85	M	29		2
10	Adrian MUTU	ROU	8/1/79	A	18	(2)	4
14	Cesare NATALI		5/4/79	D	16	(4)	
23	Manuel PASQUAL		13/3/82	D	33	(1)	1
40	Cristiano PICCINI		26/9/92	D		(1)	
17	Amidu SALIFU	GHA	20/9/92	M		(1)	
7	Mario Alberto SANTANA	ARG	23/12/81	M	22	(6)	4
27	Haris SEFEROVIC	SUI	22/2/92	A		(1)	
6	Juan Manuel VARGAS	PER	5/10/83	M	19	(5)	4
20	Papa WAIGO N'Diaye	SEN	20/1/84	A		(1)	
15	Cristiano ZANETTI		14/4/77	M	4	(2)	

GENOA CFC

Coach – Gian Piero Gasperini; (8/11/10) Davide Ballardini

Founded – 1893

Stadium – Luigi Ferraris (36,685)

MAJOR HONOURS: Italian League – (9) 1898, 1899, 1900, 1902, 1903, 1904, 1915, 1923, 1924; Italian Cup – (1) 1937.

2010				
28/8	Udinese	a	1-0	*Mesto*
12/9	Chievo	h	1-3	*Destro*
19/9	Parma	a	1-1	*Toni (p)*

/9	Fiorentina	h	1-1	*Mesto*
/9	Milan	a	0-1	
10	Bari	h	2-1	*Palacio, Toni*
/10	Roma	a	1-2	*Rudolf*
/10	Catania	h	1-0	*Rossi*
/10	Inter	h	0-1	
11	Palermo	a	0-1	
/11	Bologna	h	1-0	*Milanetto*
/11	Cagliari	a	1-0	*Ranocchia*
/11	Juventus	h	0-2	
/11	Brescia	a	0-0	
12	Lecce	a	3-1	*Toni, Ranocchia, Rossi*
/12	Napoli	h	0-1	
011				
1	Lazio	h	0-0	
1	Cesena	a	0-0	
/1	Udinese	h	2-4	*Milanetto, Destro*
/1	Chievo	a	0-0	
/1	Parma	h	3-1	*Palacio (p), og (Paletta), Kaladze*
2	Fiorentina	a	0-1	
2	Milan	h	1-1	*Floro Flores*
/2	Bari	a	0-0	
/2	Sampdoria	a	1-0	*Rafinha*
/2	Roma	h	4-3	*Palacio 2, Paloschi 2*
/2	Catania	a	1-2	*Floro Flores*
3	Inter	a	2-5	*Palacio, Boselli*
3/3	Palermo	h	1-0	*Floro Flores*
0/3	Bologna	a	1-1	*Dainelli*
4	Cagliari	h	0-1	
0/4	Juventus	a	2-3	*og (Bonucci), Floro Flores*
7/4	Brescia	h	3-0	*Rafinha, og (Berardi), Antonelli*
3/4	Lecce	h	4-2	*Floro Flores 2, Palacio 2*
0/4	Napoli	a	0-1	
/5	Sampdoria	h	2-1	*Floro Flores, Boselli*
4/5	Lazio	a	2-4	*Palacio, Floro Flores*
2/5	Cesena	h	3-2	*Floro Flores 2, Palacio*

No	Name	Nat	DoB	Pos	Aps	(s)	Gls
3	Luca ANTONELLI		11/2/87	D	5	(6)	1
5	Richmond Yiadom BOAKYE	GHA	28/1/93	A		(4)	
	Mauro BOSELLI	ARG	22/5/85	A	1	(6)	2
	José Manuel Flores Moreno "CHICO"	ESP	6/3/87	D	7	(8)	
	Domenico CRISCITO		30/12/86	D	36		
	Dario DAINELLI		9/6/79	D	33	(1)	1
22	Mattia DESTRO		20/3/91	A	5	(11)	2
	EDUARDO dos Reis Carvalho	POR	19/9/82	G	37		
33	Antonio FLORO FLORES		18/6/83	A	18		10
71	Boško JANKOVIĆ	SRB	1/3/84	M	3	(3)	
29	Enej JELENIČ	SVN	11/12/92	A		(2)	
13	Kakhaber KALADZE	GEO	27/2/78	D	23	(3)	1
11	Houssine KHARJA	MAR	9/11/82	M	8	(5)	
5	Abdoulay KONKO	FRA	9/3/84	D	11	(2)	
33	Juraj KUCKA	SVK	26/2/87	M	15	(2)	
20	Giandomenico MESTO		25/5/82	M	32	(4)	2
42	MIGUEL Luís Pinto VELOSO	POR	11/5/86	M	16	(4)	
77	Omar MILANETTO		30/11/75	M	28	(3)	2
23	Francesco MODESTO		16/2/82	M		(1)	
24	Emiliano MORETTI		11/6/81	D	9	(9)	
8	Rodrigo Sebastián PALACIO	ARG	5/2/82	A	24	(3)	9
10	Raffaele PALLADINO		17/4/84	M	3	(2)	
43	Alberto PALOSCHI		4/1/90	A	3	(9)	2
88	Mattia PERIN		10/11/92	G	1		
35	Diego Fabián POLENTA	URU	6/2/92	D		(1)	
18	Márcio Rafael Ferreira de Souza "RAFINHA"	BRA	7/9/85	D	28	(6)	2
16	Andrea RANOCCHIA		16/2/88	D	16		2
7	Marco ROSSI		1/4/78	M	32		2
17	Gergely RUDOLF	HUN	9/3/85	A	3	(9)	1
14	Giuseppe SCULLI		23/3/81	A	4	(4)	
9	Luca TONI		26/5/77	A	16		3
36	Franco ZUCULINI	ARG	5/9/90	M	1	(3)	

FC INTERNAZIONALE MILANO

Coach – Rafael Benítez (ESP); (24/12/10) Leonardo (BRA)

Founded – 1908

Stadium – Giuseppe Meazza (82,955)

MAJOR HONOURS: European Champion Clubs' Cup/UEFA Champions League – (3) 1964, 1965, 2010; UEFA Cup – (3) 1991, 1994, 1998; World Club Cup/FIFA Club World Cup – (3) 1964, 1965, 2010; Italian League – (18) 1910, 1920, 1930, 1938, 1940, 1953, 1954, 1963, 1965, 1966, 1971, 1980, 1989, 2006, 2007, 2008, 2009, 2010; Italian Cup – (7) 1939, 1978, 1982, 2005, 2006, 2010, 2011.

2010				
30/8	Bologna	a	0-0	
11/9	Udinese	h	2-1	*Lúcio, Eto'o*
19/9	Palermo	a	2-1	*Eto'o 2*
22/9	Bari	h	4-0	*Milito 2, Eto'o 2 (2p)*
25/9	Roma	a	0-1	
3/10	Juventus	h	0-0	
17/10	Cagliari	a	1-0	*Eto'o*
24/10	Sampdoria	h	1-1	*Eto'o*
29/10	Genoa	a	1-0	*Muntari*
6/11	Brescia	h	1-1	*Eto'o (p)*
10/11	Lecce	a	1-1	*Milito*
14/11	Milan	h	0-1	
21/11	Chievo	a	1-2	*Eto'o*
28/11	Parma	h	5-2	*Stanković 3, Cambiasso, Thiago Motta*
3/12	Lazio	a	1-3	*Pandev*
2011				
6/1	Napoli	h	3-1	*Thiago Motta 2, Cambiasso*
9/1	Catania	a	2-1	*Cambiasso 2*
15/1	Bologna	h	4-1	*Stanković, Milito, Eto'o 2*
19/1	Cesena	h	3-2	*Eto'o, Milito, Chivu*
23/1	Udinese	a	1-3	*Stanković*
30/1	Palermo	h	3-2	*Pazzini 2, Eto'o (p)*
3/2	Bari	a	3-0	*Kharja, Pazzini, Sneijder*
6/2	Roma	h	5-3	*Sneijder, Eto'o 2 (1p), Thiago Motta, Cambiasso*
13/2	Juventus	a	0-1	
16/2	Fiorentina	a	2-1	*og (Camporese), Pazzini*
19/2	Cagliari	h	1-0	*Kharja*
27/2	Sampdoria	a	2-0	*Sneijder, Eto'o*
6/3	Genoa	h	5-2	*Pazzini, Eto'o 2, Pandev, Nagatomo*
11/3	Brescia	a	1-1	*Eto'o*
20/3	Lecce	h	1-0	*Pazzini*
2/4	Milan	a	0-3	
9/4	Chievo	h	2-0	*Cambiasso, Maicon*
16/4	Parma	a	0-2	
23/4	Lazio	h	2-1	*Sneijder, Eto'o*
30/4	Cesena	a	2-1	*Pazzini 2*
8/5	Fiorentina	h	3-1	*Pazzini, Cambiasso, Coutinho*
15/5	Napoli	a	1-1	*Eto'o*
22/5	Catania	h	3-1	*Pazzini 2, Nagatomo*

No	Name	Nat	DoB	Pos	Aps	(s)	Gls
31	Denis ALIBEC	ROU	5/1/91	A		(2)	
88	Jonathan Ludovic BIABIANY	FRA	28/4/88	M	9	(5)	
19	Esteban Matías CAMBIASSO	ARG	18/8/80	M	28	(2)	7
12	Luca CASTELLAZZI		19/7/75	G	13	(2)	
26	Cristian Eugen CHIVU	ROU	26/10/80	D	24		1
2	Iván Ramiro CÓRDOBA	COL	11/8/76	D	15	(7)	
29	Philippe COUTINHO Correia	BRA	12/6/92	M	8	(5)	1
9	Samuel ETO'O	CMR	10/3/81	A	35		21
1	JÚLIO CÉSAR Soares Espindola	BRA	3/9/79	G	25		
14	Houssine KHARJA	MAR	9/11/82	M	10	(5)	2
6	Lucimar Ferreira da Silva "LÚCIO"	BRA	8/5/78	D	30	(1)	1
13	MAICON Douglas Sisenando	BRA	26/7/81	D	28		1
30	Alessandro Faiolhe Amantino "MANCINI"	BRA	1/8/80	M		(2)	

17	McDonald MARIGA	KEN	4/4/87	M	2	(10)	
23	Marco MATERAZZI		19/8/73	D	6	(2)	
22	Diego Alberto MILITO	ARG	12/6/79	A	16	(7)	5
11	Sulley Ali MUNTARI	GHA	27/8/84	M	1	(7)	1
55	Yuto NAGATOMO	JPN	12/9/86	D	10	(3)	2
57	Felice NATALINO		24/3/92	D	1	(1)	
20	Joel Chukwuma OBI	NGA	22/5/91	M	2	(8)	
40	Nwankwo Emeka OBIORA	NGA	12/7/91	M		(2)	
27	Goran PANDEV	MKD	27/7/83	A	17	(10)	2
7	Giampaolo PAZZINI		2/8/84	A	14	(3)	11
15	Andrea RANOCCHIA		16/2/88	D	17	(1)	
25	Walter Adrián SAMUEL	ARG	23/3/78	D	8	(2)	
39	Davide SANTON		2/1/91	D	5	(7)	
10	Wesley SNEIJDER	NED	9/6/84	M	22	(3)	4
5	Dejan STANKOVIĆ	SRB	11/9/78	M	22	(4)	5
8	THIAGO MOTTA		28/8/82	M	15	(4)	4
4	Javier ZANETTI	ARG	10/8/73	D	35		

JUVENTUS

Coach – Luigi Delneri

Founded – 1897

Stadium – Olimpico (27,500)

MAJOR HONOURS: European Champion Clubs' Cup/UEFA Champions League – (2) 1985, 1996; UEFA Cup Winners' Cup – (1) 1984; UEFA Cup – (3) 1977, 1990, 1993; UEFA Super Cup – (2) 1984, 1997; World Club Cup – (2) 1985, 1996; Italian League – (27) 1905, 1926, 1931, 1932, 1933, 1934, 1935, 1950, 1952, 1958, 1960, 1961, 1967, 1972, 1973, 1975, 1977, 1978, 1981, 1982, 1984, 1986, 1995, 1997, 1998, 2002, 2003; Italian Cup – (9) 1938, 1942, 1959, 1960, 1965, 1979, 1983, 1990, 1995.

2010				
29/8	Bari	a	0-1	
12/9	Sampdoria	h	3-3	*Marchisio, Pepe, Quagliarella*
19/9	Udinese	a	4-0	*og (Coda), Quagliarella, Marchisio, Iaquinta*
23/9	Palermo	h	1-3	*Iaquinta*
26/9	Cagliari	h	4-2	*Krasić 3, Bonucci*
3/10	Inter	a	0-0	
17/10	Lecce	h	4-0	*Aquilani, Felipe Melo (p), Quagliarella, Del Piero*
24/10	Bologna	a	0-0	
30/10	Milan	a	2-1	*Quagliarella, Del Piero*
7/11	Cesena	h	3-1	*Del Piero (p), Quagliarella, Iaquinta*
10/11	Brescia	a	1-1	*Quagliarella*
13/11	Roma	h	1-1	*Iaquinta*
21/11	Genoa	a	2-0	*og (Eduardo), Krasić*
27/11	Fiorentina	h	1-1	*Pepe*
5/12	Catania	a	3-1	*Pepe, Quagliarella 2*
12/12	Lazio	h	2-1	*Chiellini, og (Muslera)*
19/12	Chievo	a	1-1	*Quagliarella*
2011				
6/1	Parma	h	1-4	*Legrottaglie*
9/1	Napoli	a	0-3	
16/1	Bari	h	2-1	*Del Piero, Aquilani*
23/1	Sampdoria	a	0-0	
30/1	Udinese	h	1-2	*Marchisio*
2/2	Palermo	a	1-2	*Marchisio*
5/2	Cagliari	a	3-1	*Matri 2, Toni*
13/2	Inter	h	1-0	*Matri*
20/2	Lecce	a	0-2	
26/2	Bologna	h	0-2	
5/3	Milan	h	0-1	
12/3	Cesena	a	2-2	*Matri 2*
20/3	Brescia	h	2-1	*Krasić, Del Piero*
3/4	Roma	a	2-0	*Krasić, Matri*
10/4	Genoa	h	3-2	*og (Rossi), Matri, Toni*
17/4	Fiorentina	a	0-0	
23/4	Catania	h	2-2	*Del Piero 2 (1p)*
2/5	Lazio	a	1-0	*Pepe*
9/5	Chievo	h	2-2	*Del Piero (p), Matri*
15/5	Parma	a	0-1	
22/5	Napoli	h	2-2	*Chiellini, Matri*

No	Name	Nat	DoB	Pos	Aps	(s)	Gl
11	AMAURI Carvalho de Oliveira	BRA	3/6/80	A	5	(4)	
14	Alberto AQUILANI		7/7/84	M	31	(2)	2
15	Andrea BARZAGLI		8/5/81	D	14	(1)	
37	Filippo BONIPERTI		27/9/91	M		(1)	
19	Leonardo BONUCCI		1/5/87	D	32	(2)	1
1	Gianluigi BUFFON		28/1/78	G	16		
3	Giorgio CHIELLINI		14/8/84	D	32		2
29	Paolo DE CEGLIE		17/9/86	D	6	(1)	
10	Alessandro DEL PIERO		9/11/74	A	19	(14)	8
4	FELIPE MELO de Carvalho	BRA	26/6/83	M	28	(1)	1
36	Manuel GIANDONATO		10/10/91	M	2		
41	Niccolò GIANNETTI		12/5/91	A	1		
6	Fabio GROSSO		28/11/77	D	17	(2)	
21	Zdeněk GRYGERA	CZE	14/5/80	D	9	(4)	
9	Vincenzo IAQUINTA		21/11/79	A	8	(11)	4
27	Miloš KRASIĆ	SRB	1/11/84	M	33		6
20	Davide LANZAFAME		9/2/87	M		(3)	
33	Nicola LEGROTTAGLIE		20/10/76	D	2	(3)	1
38	Alberto LIBERTAZZI		1/1/92	A		(1)	
8	Claudio MARCHISIO		19/1/86	M	32		4
25	Jorge Andrés MARTÍNEZ	URU	5/4/83	M	6	(8)	
32	Alessandro MATRI		19/8/84	A	15	(1)	9
2	Marco MOTTA		14/5/86	D	19	(3)	
23	Simone PEPE		30/8/83	M	22	(8)	4
18	Fabio QUAGLIARELLA		31/1/83	A	17		9
26	Leandro RINAUDO		9/5/83	D	1		
7	Hasan SALIHAMIDŽIĆ	BIH	1/1/77	M	1	(9)	
5	Mohamed Lamine SISSOKO	MLI	22/1/85	M	4	(14)	
30	Marco STORARI		7/1/77	G	22	(1)	
43	Frederik SØRENSEN	DEN	14/4/92	D	12	(5)	
20	Luca TONI		26/5/77	A	5	(9)	2
17	Armand TRAORÉ	FRA	8/10/89	D	7	(3)	

S.S. LAZIO

Coach – Edoardo Reja

Founded – 1900

Stadium – Olimpico (82,307)

MAJOR HONOURS: UEFA Cup Winners' Cup – (1) 1999; UEFA Super Cup – (1) 1999; Italian League – (2) 1974, 2000; Italian Cup – (5) 1958, 1998, 2000, 2004, 2009.

2010				
29/8	Sampdoria	a	0-2	
12/9	Bologna	h	3-1	*Mauri, Rocchi, Hernanes (p)*
18/9	Fiorentina	a	2-1	*Ledesma, Kozák*
22/9	Milan	h	1-1	*Floccari*
26/9	Chievo	a	1-0	*Zárate*
3/10	Brescia	h	1-0	*Mauri*
17/10	Bari	a	2-0	*Hernanes, Floccari*
24/10	Cagliari	h	2-1	*Floccari, Mauri*
31/10	Palermo	a	1-0	*André Dias*
7/11	Roma	h	0-2	
10/11	Cesena	a	0-1	
14/11	Napoli	h	2-0	*Zárate, Floccari*
21/11	Parma	a	1-1	*Floccari*
28/11	Catania	h	1-1	*Hernanes*
3/12	Inter	h	3-1	*Biava, Zárate, Hernanes*
12/12	Juventus	a	1-2	*Zárate*
19/12	Udinese	h	3-2	*Hernanes, Biava, og (Zapata)*
2011				
6/1	Genoa	a	0-0	
9/1	Lecce	h	1-2	*Mauri*
16/1	Sampdoria	h	1-0	*Kozák*
23/1	Bologna	a	1-3	*Floccari*
29/1	Fiorentina	h	2-0	*Kozák 2 (1p)*
1/2	Milan	a	0-0	
6/2	Chievo	h	1-1	*Hernanes*
13/2	Brescia	a	2-0	*González, Kozák*
20/2	Bari	h	1-0	*Hernanes*

/2	Cagliari	a	0-1	
3	Palermo	h	2-0	*Sculli 2*
/3	Roma	a	0-2	
/3	Cesena	h	1-0	*Zárate*
4	Napoli	a	3-4	*Mauri, André Dias, og (Aronica)*
)/4	Parma	h	2-0	*Hernanes, Floccari*
/4	Catania	a	4-1	*Hernanes, Mauri, Floccari, Zárate*
/4	Inter	a	1-2	*Zárate (p)*
5	Juventus	h	0-1	
5	Udinese	a	1-2	*Kozák*
4/5	Genoa	h	4-2	*Biava, Rocchi, Hernanes 2*
2/5	Lecce	a	4-2	*Rocchi, Zárate 2 (1p), og (Vives)*

o	Name	Nat	DoB	Pos	Aps	(s)	Gls
	ANDRÉ Gonçalves DIAS	BRA	15/5/79	D	33		2
2	Tommaso BERNI		6/3/83	G	2		
)	Giuseppe BIAVA		8/5/77	D	35		3
3	Mark BRESCIANO	AUS	11/2/80	M	7	(13)	
2	Cristian BROCCHI		30/1/76	M	25	(6)	
9	Luis Pedro CAVENDA	BEL	2/1/90	D	2	(1)	
1	Simone DEL NERO		4/8/81	A	1	(1)	
1	Modibo DIAKITÉ	FRA	2/3/87	D	4	(4)	
2	Sergio FLOCCARI		12/11/81	A	25	(5)	8
7	Pasquale FOGGIA		3/6/83	M	2	(7)	
4	Javier GARRIDO Behobide	ESP	15/3/85	D	8	(2)	
5	Álvaro Rafael GONZÁLEZ	URU	29/10/84	M	8	(11)	1
	Anderson HERNANES de Carvalho Andrade Lima	BRA	29/5/85	M	35	(1)	11
8	Libor KOZÁK	CZE	30/5/89	A	6	(13)	6
24	Cristian Daniel LEDESMA		24/9/82	M	30	(4)	1
2	Stephan LICHTSTEINER	SUI	16/1/84	D	33	(1)	
1	MATUZALÉM Francelino da Silva	BRA	10/6/80	M	18	(4)	
6	Stefano MAURI		8/1/80	M	26	(3)	6
86	Néstor Fernando MUSLERA	URU	16/6/86	G	36		
26	Ştefan Andrei RADU	ROU	22/10/86	D	26		
9	Tommaso ROCCHI		19/9/77	A	6	(11)	3
5	Lionel Sebastián SCALONI	ARG	16/5/78	D	5	(7)	
77	Giuseppe SCULLI		23/3/81	A	11	(2)	2
13	Guglielmo STENDARDO		6/5/81	D	6	(8)	
10	Mauro Matías ZÁRATE	ARG	18/3/87	A	28	(7)	9

US LECCE

Coach – Luigi De Canio

Founded – 1908

Stadium – Via del Mare (36,285)

2010				
29/8	Milan	a	0-4	
12/9	Fiorentina	h	1-0	*Di Michele*
19/9	Cesena	a	0-1	
22/9	Parma	h	1-1	*Jeda (p)*
26/9	Palermo	a	2-2	*Giacomazzi, Corvia*
3/10	Catania	h	1-0	*Corvia*
17/10	Juventus	a	0-4	
24/10	Brescia	h	2-1	*Ofere, Di Michele*
30/10	Roma	a	0-2	
6/11	Bologna	a	0-2	
10/11	Inter	h	1-1	*Olivera*
14/11	Udinese	a	0-4	
21/11	Sampdoria	h	2-3	*Di Michele, Diamoutene*
28/11	Cagliari	a	2-3	*Olivera, Di Michele*
5/12	Genoa	h	1-3	*Ofere*
12/12	Chievo	h	3-2	*Ofere, Piatti 2*
19/12	Napoli	a	0-1	
2011				
6/1	Bari	h	0-1	
9/1	Lazio	a	2-1	*og (Muslera), Grossmüller*
16/1	Milan	h	1-1	*Olivera*
23/1	Fiorentina	a	1-1	*Di Michele*
30/1	Cesena	h	1-1	*Corvia*
2/2	Parma	a	1-0	*Chevantón*
6/2	Palermo	h	2-4	*Giacomazzi, Jeda*
13/2	Catania	a	2-3	*Jeda, Munari*
20/2	Juventus	h	2-0	*Mesbah, Bertolacci*
27/2	Brescia	a	2-2	*Corvia, Munari*
4/3	Roma	h	1-2	*Giacomazzi*
13/3	Bologna	h	0-1	
20/3	Inter	a	0-1	
3/4	Udinese	h	2-0	*Bertolacci 2*
10/4	Sampdoria	a	2-1	*Di Michele, Olivera*
17/4	Cagliari	h	3-3	*Mesbah, Fabiano, Corvia*
23/4	Genoa	a	2-4	*Di Michele 2*
1/5	Chievo	a	0-1	
8/5	Napoli	h	2-1	*Corvia (p), Chevantón*
15/5	Bari	a	2-0	*Jeda, og (Masiello A.)*
22/5	Lazio	h	2-4	*Coppola, Piatti*

No	Name	Nat	DoB	Pos	Aps	(s)	Gls
81	Massimiliano BENASSI		11/11/81	G	1		
91	Andrea BERTOLACCI		11/1/91	M	9		3
28	Davide BRIVIO		17/3/88	D	17	(5)	
23	Ernesto Javier CHEVANTÓN	URU	12/8/80	A	3	(11)	2
32	Manuel COPPOLA		11/5/82	M	1	(13)	1
9	Daniele CORVIA		22/11/84	A	12	(18)	6
17	David DI MICHELE		6/1/76	A	22	(1)	8
30	Souleymane DIAMOUTENE	MLI	30/1/83	D	1	(1)	1
2	Giulio DONATI		5/2/90	D	10	(4)	
14	FABIANO Medina da Silva	BRA	18/1/82	D	28	(1)	1
13	Stefano FERRARIO		28/3/85	D	18	(2)	
18	Guillermo GIACOMAZZI	URU	21/11/77	M	30	(2)	3
3	Alberto GIULIATTO		17/9/83	D	9	(3)	
21	Carlos Javier GROSSMÜLLER	URU	4/5/83	M	18	(5)	1
4	GUSTAVO Franchin Schiavolin	BRA	19/2/82	D	19	(5)	
27	Jedaias Capucho Neves "JEDA"	BRA	15/4/79	A	22	(3)	4
11	Djamel MESBAH	ALG	9/10/84	M	29	(5)	2
8	Gianni MUNARI		24/6/83	M	27	(7)	2
15	Edward OFERE	NGA	28/3/86	A	6	(5)	3
10	Rubén OLIVERA	URU	4/5/83	M	30	(1)	4
19	Ignacio PIATTI	ARG	4/2/85	M	14	(11)	3
33	Andrea RISPOLI		29/9/88	D	9	(4)	
22	Antonio ROSATI		26/6/83	G	37	(1)	
5	Simone SINI		9/4/92	D	1	(1)	
40	Nenad TOMOVIĆ	SRB	30/8/87	D	16		
20	Giuseppe VIVES		14/7/80	M	29	(4)	

AC MILAN

Coach – Massimiliano Allegri

Founded – 1899

Stadium – Giuseppe Meazza (82,955)

MAJOR HONOURS: European Champion Clubs' Cup/UEFA Champions League – (7) 1963, 1969, 1989, 1990, 1994, 2003, 2007; UEFA Cup Winners' Cup – (2) 1968, 1973; UEFA Super Cup – (5) 1989, 1990, 1995, 2003, 2007; World Club Cup/FIFA Club World Cup – (4) 1969, 1989, 1990, 2007; Italian League – (18) 1901, 1906, 1907, 1951, 1955, 1957, 1959, 1962, 1968, 1979, 1988, 1992, 1993, 1994, 1996, 1999, 2004, 2011; Italian Cup – (5) 1967, 1972, 1973, 1977, 2003.

2010				
29/8	Lecce	h	4-0	*Pato 2, Thiago Silva, Inzaghi*
11/9	Cesena	a	0-2	
18/9	Catania	h	1-1	*Inzaghi*
22/9	Lazio	a	1-1	*Ibrahimović*
25/9	Genoa	h	1-0	*Ibrahimović*
2/10	Parma	a	1-0	*Pirlo*
16/10	Chievo	h	3-1	*Pato 2, Robinho*
25/10	Napoli	a	2-1	*Robinho, Ibrahimović*
30/10	Juventus	h	1-2	*Ibrahimović*

7/11	Bari	a	3-2	*Ambrosini, Flamini, Pato*
10/11	Palermo	h	3-1	*Pato, Ibrahimović (p), Robinho*
14/11	Inter	a	1-0	*Ibrahimović (p)*
20/11	Fiorentina	h	1-0	*Ibrahimović*
27/11	Sampdoria	a	1-1	*Robinho*
4/12	Brescia	h	3-0	*Boateng, Robinho, Ibrahimović*
12/12	Bologna	a	3-0	*Boateng, Robinho, Ibrahimović*
18/12	Roma	h	0-1	
2011				
6/1	Cagliari	a	1-0	*Strasser*
9/1	Udinese	h	4-4	*Pato 2, og (Benatia), Ibrahimović*
16/1	Lecce	a	1-1	*Ibrahimović*
23/1	Cesena	h	2-0	*og (Pellegrino), Ibrahimović*
29/1	Catania	a	2-0	*Robinho, Ibrahimović*
1/2	Lazio	h	0-0	
6/2	Genoa	a	1-1	*Pato*
12/2	Parma	h	4-0	*Seedorf, Cassano, Robinho 2*
20/2	Chievo	a	2-1	*Robinho, Pato*
28/2	Napoli	h	3-0	*Ibrahimović (p), Boateng, Pato*
5/3	Juventus	a	1-0	*Gattuso*
13/3	Bari	h	1-1	*Cassano*
19/3	Palermo	a	0-1	
2/4	Inter	h	3-0	*Pato 2, Cassano (p)*
10/4	Fiorentina	a	2-1	*Seedorf, Pato*
16/4	Sampdoria	h	3-0	*Seedorf, Cassano (p), Robinho*
23/4	Brescia	a	1-0	*Robinho*
1/5	Bologna	h	1-0	*Flamini*
7/5	Roma	a	0-0	
14/5	Cagliari	h	4-1	*Robinho 2, Gattuso, Seedorf*
22/5	Udinese	a	0-0	

No	Name	Nat	DoB	Pos	Aps	(s)	Gls
20	Ignazio ABATE		12/11/86	D	26	(3)	
32	Christian ABBIATI		8/7/77	G	35		
23	Massimo AMBROSINI		29/5/77	M	16	(2)	1
1	Marco AMELIA		2/4/82	G	3	(1)	
77	Luca ANTONINI		4/8/82	D	18	(4)	
51	Giacomo BERETTA		14/3/92	A		(1)	
27	Kevin-Prince BOATENG	GHA	6/3/87	M	18	(8)	3
25	Daniele BONERA		31/5/81	D	15	(1)	
22	Marco BORRIELLO		18/6/82	A	1		
99	Antonio CASSANO		12/7/82	A	9	(8)	4
35	DÍDAC Vilà Roselló	ESP	9/6/89	D	1		
28	Urby EMANUELSON	NED	16/6/86	M	2	(7)	
16	Mathieu FLAMINI	FRA	7/3/84	M	14	(8)	2
8	Gennaro Ivan GATTUSO		9/1/78	M	28	(3)	2
11	Zlatan IBRAHIMOVIĆ	SWE	3/10/81	A	29		14
9	Filippo INZAGHI		9/8/73	A	1	(5)	2
18	Marek JANKULOVSKI	CZE	9/5/77	D	3	(2)	
66	Nicola LEGROTTAGLIE		20/10/76	D		(1)	
52	Alexander MERKEL	GER	22/2/92	M	6		
13	Alessandro NESTA		19/3/76	D	26		
17	Massimo ODDO		14/6/76	D	3	(4)	
90	Nnamdi ODUAMADI	NGA	17/10/90	A		(1)	
15	Sokratis PAPASTATHOPOULOS	GRE	9/6/88	D	3	(2)	
7	Alexandre Rodrigues da Silva "PATO"	BRA	2/9/89	A	19	(6)	14
21	Andrea PIRLO		19/5/79	M	12	(5)	1
70	Robson de Souza "ROBINHO"	BRA	25/1/84	A	26	(8)	14
30	Flavio ROMA		21/6/74	G		(1)	
80	Ronaldo de Assis Moreira "RONALDINHO"	BRA	21/3/80	A	7	(4)	
10	Clarence SEEDORF	NED	1/4/76	M	23	(7)	4
14	Rodney STRASSER	SLE	30/3/90	M	1	(2)	1
33	THIAGO Emiliano da SILVA	BRA	22/9/84	D	33		1
4	Mark VAN BOMMEL	NED	22/4/77	M	14		
76	Mario Alberto YEPES	COL	13/1/76	D	11	(2)	
19	Gianluca ZAMBROTTA		19/2/77	D	15		

SSC NAPOLI

Coach – Walter Mazzarri

Founded – 1926

Stadium – San Paolo (60,240)

MAJOR HONOURS: UEFA Cup – (1) 1989;
Italian League – (2) 1987, 1990; Italian Cup – (3) 1962, 1976, 1987

2010				
29/8	Fiorentina	a	1-1	*Cavani*
12/9	Bari	h	2-2	*Cavani, Cannavaro*
19/9	Sampdoria	a	2-1	*Hamšík, Cavani*
22/9	Chievo	h	1-3	*Cannavaro*
26/9	Cesena	a	4-1	*Lavezzi, Hamšík (p), Cavani 2*
3/10	Roma	h	2-0	*Hamšík, og (Juan)*
17/10	Catania	a	1-1	*Cavani*
25/10	Milan	h	1-2	*Lavezzi*
31/10	Brescia	a	1-0	*Lavezzi*
7/11	Parma	h	2-0	*Cavani 2*
10/11	Cagliari	a	1-0	*Lavezzi*
14/11	Lazio	a	0-2	
21/11	Bologna	h	4-1	*Maggio, Hamšík 2, Cavani*
28/11	Udinese	a	1-3	*Hamšík*
6/12	Palermo	h	1-0	*Maggio*
11/12	Genoa	a	1-0	*Hamšík*
19/12	Lecce	h	1-0	*Cavani*
2011				
6/1	Inter	a	1-3	*Pazienza*
9/1	Juventus	h	3-0	*Cavani 3*
15/1	Fiorentina	h	0-0	
23/1	Bari	a	2-0	*Lavezzi, Cavani*
30/1	Sampdoria	h	4-0	*Cavani 3 (1p), Hamšík*
2/2	Chievo	a	0-2	
6/2	Cesena	h	2-0	*Cavani, Sosa*
12/2	Roma	a	2-0	*Cavani 2 (1p)*
20/2	Catania	h	1-0	*Zúñiga*
28/2	Milan	a	0-3	
6/3	Brescia	h	0-0	
13/3	Parma	a	3-1	*Hamšík, Lavezzi, Maggio*
20/3	Cagliari	h	2-1	*Cavani 2 (1p)*
3/4	Lazio	h	4-3	*Dossena, Cavani 3 (1p)*
10/4	Bologna	a	2-0	*Mascara, Hamšík (p)*
17/4	Udinese	h	1-2	*Mascara*
23/4	Palermo	a	1-2	*Cavani (p)*
30/4	Genoa	h	1-0	*Hamšík*
8/5	Lecce	a	1-2	*Mascara*
15/5	Inter	h	1-1	*Zúñiga*
22/5	Juventus	a	2-2	*Maggio, Lucarelli*

No	Name	Nat	DoB	Pos	Aps	(s)	Gls
6	Salvatore ARONICA		20/1/78	D	19	(7)	
80	Manuele BLASI		17/8/80	M	1	(1)	
14	Hugo Armando CAMPAGNARO	ARG	27/6/80	D	30	(1)	
28	Paolo CANNAVARO		26/6/81	D	31	(1)	2
7	Edinson CAVANI	URU	14/2/87	A	32	(3)	26
25	Emílson Sánchez CRIBARI	BRA	6/3/80	D	6	(3)	
26	Morgan DE SANCTIS		26/3/77	G	38		
8	Andrea DOSSENA		11/9/81	D	31	(2)	1
12	Nicolao Manuel DUMITRU		12/10/91	A		(9)	
23	Walter Alejandro GARGANO	URU	23/7/84	M	29	(7)	
2	Gianluca GRAVA		7/3/77	D	12	(1)	
17	Marek HAMŠÍK	SVK	27/7/87	M	36	(1)	11
22	Ezequiel Iván LAVEZZI	ARG	3/5/85	A	29	(2)	6
99	Cristiano LUCARELLI		4/10/75	A	1	(8)	1
11	Christian MAGGIO		11/2/82	M	33		4
91	Raffaele MAIELLO		10/7/91	M	1	(2)	
9	Giuseppe MASCARA		22/8/79	A	4	(10)	3
5	Michele PAZIENZA		5/8/82	M	30	(1)	1
13	Fabiano SANTACROCE		24/8/86	D	10	(1)	
77	José Ernesto SOSA	ARG	19/6/85	M	7	(17)	1
4	VÍCTOR RUIZ Torre	ESP	25/1/89	D	6		

	Luigi VITALE		5/10/87	D	2	(4)	
	Hassan YEBDA	ALG	14/5/84	M	15	(14)	
3	Juan Camilo ZÚÑIGA Mosquera	COL	14/12/85	D	15	(12)	2

US CITTÀ DI PALERMO

Coach – Delio Rossi; (28/2/11) Serse Cosmi; (3/4/11) Delio Rossi

Founded – 1900

Stadium – Renzo Barbera (37,242)

010				
9/8	Cagliari	h	0-0	
2/9	Brescia	a	2-3	*Pastore, Balzaretti*
9/9	Inter	h	1-2	*Iličič*
3/9	Juventus	a	3-1	*Pastore, Iličič, Bovo*
6/9	Lecce	h	2-2	*Pinilla, Maccarone*
/10	Fiorentina	a	2-1	*Iličič, Pastore*
7/10	Bologna	h	4-1	*Pastore, Iličič, Pinilla, Bačinovič*
4/10	Udinese	a	1-2	*Pinilla*
1/10	Lazio	h	0-1	
/11	Genoa	h	1-0	*Pinilla*
0/11	Milan	a	1-3	*Bačinovič*
4/11	Catania	h	3-1	*Pastore 3*
21/11	Cesena	a	2-1	*Iličič, Miccoli*
28/11	Roma	h	3-1	*Miccoli, Iličič, Nocerino*
5/12	Napoli	a	0-1	
11/12	Parma	h	3-1	*Pinilla, Miccoli, og (Zaccardo)*
19/12	Bari	a	1-1	*Iličič*
2011				
6/1	Sampdoria	h	3-0	*Miccoli, Migliaccio, Maccarone*
9/1	Chievo	a	0-0	
16/1	Cagliari	a	1-3	*Pastore*
22/1	Brescia	h	1-0	*Bovo*
30/1	Inter	a	2-3	*Miccoli, Nocerino*
2/2	Juventus	h	2-1	*Miccoli, Migliaccio*
6/2	Lecce	a	4-2	*Miccoli, Pastore, Hernández, Iličič*
13/2	Fiorentina	h	2-4	*Pastore, Nocerino*
19/2	Bologna	a	0-1	
27/2	Udinese	h	0-7	
6/3	Lazio	a	0-2	
13/3	Genoa	a	0-1	
19/3	Milan	h	1-0	*Goian*
3/4	Catania	a	0-4	
10/4	Cesena	h	2-2	*Kurtič, Pinilla*
16/4	Roma	a	3-2	*Pinilla (p), Hernández 2*
23/4	Napoli	h	2-1	*Balzaretti, Bovo (p)*
1/5	Parma	a	1-3	*Pastore*
7/5	Bari	h	2-1	*Miccoli, Bovo*
15/5	Sampdoria	a	2-1	*Miccoli, Pinilla*
22/5	Chievo	h	1-3	*Nocerino*

No	Name	Nat	DoB	Pos	Aps	(s)	Gls
94	Afriyie ACQUAH	GHA	5/1/92	M	3	(8)	
66	Siniša ANĐELKOVIČ	SVN	13/2/86	D	7		
21	Armin BAČINOVIČ	SVN	24/10/89	M	29	(4)	2
42	Federico BALZARETTI		6/12/81	D	33		2
99	Francesco BENUSSI		15/10/81	G	1		
5	Cesare BOVO		14/1/83	D	31	(1)	4
80	Moris CARROZZIERI		16/11/80	D		(1)	
16	Mattia CASSANI		26/8/83	D	32		
36	Matteo DARMIAN		2/12/89	D	6	(5)	
29	Santiago GARCÍA	ARG	8/7/88	D	2	(1)	
3	Dorin Nicolae GOIAN	ROU	12/12/80	D	12	(4)	1
9	Abel Mathías HERNÁNDEZ	URU	8/8/90	A	12	(10)	3
72	Josip ILIČIČ	SVN	29/1/88	M	30	(4)	8
7	JOÃO PEDRO Geraldino dos Santos Galvão	BRA	9/3/92	M		(1)	
4	Pajtim KASAMI	SUI	2/6/92	M	4	(10)	
77	Jasmin KURTIČ	SVN	10/1/89	M	2	(2)	1
11	Fabio LIVERANI		29/4/76	M	4	(8)	
32	Massimo MACCARONE		6/9/79	A	3	(15)	2
10	Fabrizio MICCOLI		27/6/79	A	17	(4)	9
8	Giulio MIGLIACCIO		23/6/81	M	35		2
6	Ezequiel Matías MUÑOZ	ARG	8/10/90	D	32	(2)	
23	Antonio NOCERINO		9/4/85	M	38		4
22	Michele PAOLUCCI		6/2/86	A		(2)	
27	Javier Matías PASTORE	ARG	20/6/89	M	34	(1)	11
51	Mauricio PINILLA	CHI	4/2/84	A	13	(9)	8
24	Nicola RIGONI		12/11/90	M	1	(3)	
46	Salvatore SIRIGU		12/1/87	G	37		

PARMA FC

Coach – Pasquale Marino; (5/4/11) Franco Colomba

Founded – 1913

Stadium – Ennio Tardini (27,906)

MAJOR HONOURS: UEFA Cup Winners' Cup – (1) 1993; UEFA Cup – (2) 1995, 1999; UEFA Super Cup – (1) 1994; Italian Cup – (3) 1992, 1999, 2002.

2010				
29/8	Brescia	h	2-0	*Bojinov, Morrone*
12/9	Catania	a	1-2	*Giovinco*
19/9	Genoa	h	1-1	*Zaccardo*
22/9	Lecce	a	1-1	*Crespo*
26/9	Fiorentina	a	0-2	
2/10	Milan	h	0-1	
17/10	Cesena	a	1-1	*Zaccardo*
24/10	Roma	h	0-0	
31/10	Chievo	h	0-0	
7/11	Napoli	a	0-2	
11/11	Sampdoria	h	1-0	*Bojinov*
14/11	Bari	a	1-0	*Candreva*
21/11	Lazio	h	1-1	*Crespo*
28/11	Inter	a	2-5	*Crespo 2*
5/12	Udinese	h	2-1	*Crespo 2 (1p)*
11/12	Palermo	a	1-3	*Lucarelli*
19/12	Bologna	h	0-0	
2011				
6/1	Juventus	a	4-1	*Giovinco 2, Crespo (p), Palladino*
9/1	Cagliari	h	1-2	*Giovinco*
16/1	Brescia	a	0-2	
22/1	Catania	h	2-0	*Candreva, Giovinco*
30/1	Genoa	a	1-3	*Crespo*
2/2	Lecce	h	0-1	
6/2	Fiorentina	h	1-1	*Amauri*
12/2	Milan	a	0-4	
20/2	Cesena	h	2-2	*Crespo (p), Palladino*
27/2	Roma	a	2-2	*Amauri 2*
6/3	Chievo	a	0-0	
13/3	Napoli	h	1-3	*Palladino*
20/3	Sampdoria	a	1-0	*Zaccardo*
3/4	Bari	h	1-2	*Amauri*
10/4	Lazio	a	0-2	
16/4	Inter	h	2-0	*Giovinco, Amauri*
23/4	Udinese	a	2-0	*Amauri 2*
1/5	Palermo	h	3-1	*Dzemaili, Modesto, Candreva*
8/5	Bologna	a	0-0	
15/5	Juventus	h	1-0	*Giovinco*
22/5	Cagliari	a	1-1	*Bojinov*

No	Name	Nat	DoB	Pos	Aps	(s)	Gls
11	AMAURI Carvalho de Oliveira	BRA	3/6/80	A	11		7
13	ÂNGELO Mariano de Almeida	BRA	12/6/81	D	10	(11)	
3	Luca ANTONELLI		11/2/87	D	12		
86	Valeri BOJINOV	BUL	15/2/86	A	13	(18)	3
7	Antonio CANDREVA		28/2/87	M	23	(8)	3
32	Manuel COPPOLA		11/5/82	M		(1)	
9	Hernán Jorge CRESPO	ARG	5/7/75	A	16	(13)	9
58	Gregoire DEFREL	FRA	17/6/91	A		(1)	
51	Hernán Paolo DELLAFIORE		2/2/85	D		(1)	

10	Blerim DZEMAILI	SUI	12/4/86	M	26	(4)	1
2	Rolf FELTSCHER	SUI	6/10/90	D	2	(1)	
27	FILIPE Vilaça OLIVEIRA	POR	27/5/84	M		(1)	
14	Daniele GALLOPPA		15/5/85	M	5	(6)	
21	Sebastian GIOVINCO		26/1/87	M	28	(2)	7
18	Massimo GOBBI		31/10/80	D	30	(4)	
6	Alessandro LUCARELLI		22/7/77	D	32		1
8	José Fernando MARQUÉS Martínez	ESP	4/12/84	M	12	(1)	
83	Antonio MIRANTE		8/7/83	G	36		
23	Francesco MODESTO		16/2/82	M	13	(2)	1
4	Stefano MORRONE		26/10/78	M	30	(4)	1
40	Nwankwo Emeka OBIORA	NGA	12/7/91	M		(1)	
24	Massimo PACI		9/5/78	D	18	(1)	
29	Gabriel Alejandro PALETTA	ARG	15/2/86	D	26	(1)	
84	Raffaele PALLADINO		17/4/84	M	6	(5)	3
11	Alberto PALOSCHI		4/1/90	A		(1)	
1	Nicola PAVARINI		24/2/74	G	2	(1)	
26	Marco PISANO		13/8/81	D	2	(3)	
20	Antonio "TONI" CALVO Arandes	ESP	28/3/87	M		(3)	
80	Francesco VALIANI		29/10/80	M	31	(4)	
5	Cristian ZACCARDO		21/12/81	D	34		3
22	José "ZÉ" EDUARDO de Araújo	BRA	16/8/91	M		(2)	

AS ROMA

Coach – Claudio Ranieri; (21/2/11) (Vincenzo Montella)

Founded – 1927

Stadium – Olimpico (82,307)

MAJOR HONOURS: Inter Cities Fairs Cup – (1) 1961; Italian League – (3) 1942, 1983, 2001; Italian Cup – (9) 1964, 1969, 1980, 1981, 1984, 1986, 1991, 2007, 2008.

2010

28/8	Cesena	h	0-0	
11/9	Cagliari	a	1-5	*De Rossi*
19/9	Bologna	h	2-2	*Borriello, og (Rubin)*
22/9	Brescia	a	1-2	*Borriello*
25/9	Inter	h	1-0	*Vučinić*
3/10	Napoli	a	0-2	
16/10	Genoa	h	2-1	*Borriello, Brighi*
24/10	Parma	a	0-0	
30/10	Lecce	h	2-0	*Burdisso N., Vučinić*
7/11	Lazio	a	2-0	*Borriello (p), Vučinić (p)*
10/11	Fiorentina	h	3-2	*Fábio Simplício, Borriello, Perrotta*
13/11	Juventus	a	1-1	*Totti (p)*
20/11	Udinese	h	2-0	*Ménez, Borriello*
28/11	Palermo	a	1-3	*Totti*
4/12	Chievo	a	2-2	*Fábio Simplício 2*
12/12	Bari	h	1-0	*Juan*
18/12	Milan	a	1-0	*Borriello*

2011

6/1	Catania	h	4-2	*Borriello 2, Vučinić 2*
9/1	Sampdoria	a	1-2	*Vučinić*
16/1	Cesena	a	1-0	*og (Pellegrino)*
22/1	Cagliari	h	3-0	*Totti (p), Perrotta, Ménez*
2/2	Brescia	h	1-1	*Borriello*
6/2	Inter	a	3-5	*Fábio Simplício, Vučinić, Loria*
12/2	Napoli	h	0-2	
20/2	Genoa	a	3-4	*Mexès, Burdisso N., Totti*
23/2	Bologna	a	1-0	*De Rossi (first 17 mins played on 30/1)*
27/2	Parma	h	2-2	*Totti (p), Juan*
4/3	Lecce	a	2-1	*Vučinić, Pizarro (p)*
13/3	Lazio	h	2-0	*Totti 2 (1p)*
20/3	Fiorentina	a	2-2	*Totti 2 (1p)*
3/4	Juventus	h	0-2	
9/4	Udinese	a	2-1	*Totti 2 (1p)*
16/4	Palermo	h	2-3	*Totti (p), Vučinić*
23/4	Chievo	h	1-0	*Perrotta*
1/5	Bari	a	3-2	*Totti 2 (1p), Rosi*
7/5	Milan	h	0-0	
15/5	Catania	a	1-2	*Loria*
22/5	Sampdoria	h	3-1	*Totti, Vučinić, Borriello*

No	Name	Nat	DoB	Pos	Aps	(s)	Gls
8	ADRIANO Leite Ribeiro	BRA	17/2/82	A	2	(3)	
22	Marco BORRIELLO		18/6/82	A	25	(9)	11
33	Matteo BRIGHI		14/2/81	M	13	(12)	1
25	Guillermo Enio BURDISSO	ARG	26/9/88	D		(2)	
29	Nicolás Andrés BURDISSO	ARG	12/4/81	D	28		2
47	Gianluca CAPRARI		30/7/93	A		(2)	
77	Marco CASSETTI		29/5/77	D	31	(1)	
3	Paolo CASTELLINI		25/3/79	D	5	(2)	
2	Cicero João de Cézare "CICINHO"	BRA	24/6/80	D	3	(3)	
16	Daniele DE ROSSI		24/7/83	M	28		2
32	DONIéber Alexander Marangon	BRA	22/10/79	G	14	(2)	
30	FÁBIO Henrique SIMPLÍCIO	BRA	23/9/79	M	18	(6)	4
48	Alessandro FLORENZI		11/3/91	M		(1)	
23	Leandro GRECO		19/7/86	M	8	(6)	
4	JUAN Silveira dos Santos	BRA	1/2/79	D	28	(2)	2
19	JÚLIO César BAPTISTA	BRA	1/10/81	A		(7)	
27	JÚLIO SÉRGIO Bertagnoli	BRA	8/11/78	G	18		
1	Bogdan Ionuţ LOBONŢ	ROU	18/1/78	G	6		
15	Simone LORIA		28/10/76	D	2	(4)	2
94	Jérémy MÉNEZ	FRA	7/5/87	M	23	(9)	2
5	Philippe MEXÈS	FRA	30/3/82	D	21	(1)	1
89	Stefano OKAKA CHUKA		9/8/89	A		(4)	
20	Simone PERROTTA		17/9/77	M	22	(3)	3
7	David PIZARRO	CHI	11/9/79	M	21	(1)	1
17	John Arne RIISE	NOR	24/9/80	D	32		
87	Aleandro ROSI		17/5/87	M	7	(9)	1
11	Rodrigo TADDEI		6/3/80	M	12	(11)	
10	Francesco TOTTI		27/9/76	A	29	(3)	15
9	Mirko VUČINIĆ	MNE	1/10/83	A	22	(6)	10

UC SAMPDORIA

Coach – Domenico Di Carlo; (7/3/11) Alberto Cavasin

Founded – 1946

Stadium – Luigi Ferraris (36,685)

MAJOR HONOURS: UEFA Cup Winners' Cup – (1) 1990; Italian League – (1) 1991; Italian Cup – (4) 1985, 1988, 1989, 1994.

2010

29/8	Lazio	h	2-0	*Cassano (p), Guberti*
12/9	Juventus	a	3-3	*Pozzi 2, Cassano*
19/9	Napoli	h	1-2	*Cassano (p)*
22/9	Cagliari	a	0-0	
26/9	Udinese	h	0-0	
3/10	Bologna	a	1-1	*og (Portanova)*
17/10	Fiorentina	h	2-1	*Ziegler, Cassano*
24/10	Inter	a	1-1	*Guberti*
31/10	Cesena	a	1-0	*Pazzini*
7/11	Catania	h	0-0	
11/11	Parma	a	0-1	
14/11	Chievo	h	0-0	
21/11	Lecce	a	3-2	*Pazzini 3 (1p)*
27/11	Milan	h	1-1	*Pazzini*
5/12	Bari	h	3-0	*Pazzini (p), Guberti 2*
12/12	Brescia	a	0-1	

2011

6/1	Palermo	a	0-3	
9/1	Roma	h	2-1	*Pozzi (p), Guberti*
16/1	Lazio	a	0-1	
23/1	Juventus	h	0-0	
30/1	Napoli	a	0-4	
2/2	Cagliari	h	0-1	
5/2	Udinese	a	0-2	
13/2	Bologna	h	3-1	*Palombo, Gastaldello, Maccarone*
16/2	Genoa	h	0-1	

0/2	Fiorentina	a	0-0	
7/2	Inter	h	0-2	
/3	Cesena	h	2-3	*Volta, Maccarone (p)*
3/3	Catania	a	0-1	
0/3	Parma	h	0-1	
/4	Chievo	a	0-0	
0/4	Lecce	h	1-2	*Maccarone*
6/4	Milan	a	0-3	
3/4	Bari	a	1-0	*Pozzi (p)*
/5	Brescia	h	3-3	*Pozzi, Tissone, Mannini*
/5	Genoa	a	1-2	*Pozzi*
5/5	Palermo	h	1-2	*Biabiany*
22/5	Roma	a	1-3	*Mannini*

No	Name	Nat	DoB	Pos	Aps	(s)	Gls
5	Pietro ACCARDI		12/9/82	D	4	(5)	
27	Jonathan Ludovic BIABIANY	FRA	28/4/88	M	8	(8)	1
19	Fabrizio CACCIATORE		8/10/86	D	5		
99	Antonio CASSANO		12/7/82	A	7		4
35	Gianluca CURCI		12/7/85	G	35		
4	Daniele DESSENA		10/5/87	M	17	(5)	
23	Bruno FORNAROLI	URU	7/9/87	A		(1)	
28	Daniele GASTALDELLO		25/6/83	D	28	(1)	1
8	Stefano GUBERTI		6/11/84	M	29	(7)	5
1	Angelo Esmael da Costa Júnior "JÚNIOR COSTA"	BRA	12/11/83	G	3	(1)	
11	Vladimir KOMAN	HUN	16/3/89	M	14	(12)	
18	Zsolt LACZKÓ	HUN	18/12/86	D	7	(2)	
6	Stefano LUCCHINI		2/10/80	D	26		
32	Massimo MACCARONE		6/9/79	A	15	(2)	3
41	Federico MACHEDA		22/8/91	A	3	(11)	
7	Daniele MANNINI		25/10/83	M	18	(12)	2
89	Guido MARILUNGO		9/8/89	A	8	(7)	
25	Gilberto MARTÍNEZ Vidal	CRC	1/10/79	D	8	(1)	
20	Marco PADALINO	SUI	8/12/83	M		(1)	
17	Angelo PALOMBO		25/9/81	M	34		1
10	Giampaolo PAZZINI		2/8/84	A	18	(1)	6
14	PEDRO Mba OBIANG Avomo	ESP	27/3/92	M		(4)	
16	Andrea POLI		29/9/89	M	13	(8)	
9	Nicola POZZI		30/6/86	A	14	(8)	6
77	Franco SEMIOLI		20/6/80	M	6	(1)	
12	Fernando Damián TISSONE	ARG	24/7/86	M	20	(2)	1
26	Massimo VOLTA		14/5/87	D	20	(5)	1
78	Luciano ZAURI		20/1/78	D	26	(1)	
91	Simone ZAZA		25/6/91	A		(2)	
3	Reto ZIEGLER	SUI	16/1/86	D	32	(2)	1

UDINESE CALCIO

Coach – Francesco Guidolin

Founded – 1896

Stadium – Friuli (41,652)

2010

28/8	Genoa	h	0-1	
11/9	Inter	a	1-2	*Floro Flores*
19/9	Juventus	h	0-4	
22/9	Bologna	a	1-2	*Di Natale*
26/9	Sampdoria	a	0-0	
2/10	Cesena	h	1-0	*Benatia*
17/10	Brescia	a	1-0	*Corradi*
24/10	Palermo	h	2-1	*Benatia, Di Natale (p)*
31/10	Bari	a	2-0	*Sánchez, Isla*
7/11	Cagliari	h	1-1	*Floro Flores*
10/11	Catania	a	0-1	
14/11	Lecce	h	4-0	*Di Natale 3, Floro Flores*
20/11	Roma	a	0-2	
28/11	Napoli	h	3-1	*Di Natale 3 (1p)*
5/12	Parma	a	1-2	*Di Natale*
11/12	Fiorentina	h	2-1	*Armero, Di Natale*
19/12	Lazio	a	2-3	*Sánchez, Denis*

2011

6/1	Chievo	h	2-0	*Sánchez, Di Natale*
9/1	Milan	a	4-4	*Di Natale 2, Sánchez, Denis*
16/1	Genoa	a	4-2	*Armero, Di Natale, Sánchez, Denis*
23/1	Inter	h	3-1	*Zapata, Di Natale, Domizzi*
30/1	Juventus	a	2-1	*Zapata, Sánchez*
2/2	Bologna	h	1-1	*Domizzi*
5/2	Sampdoria	h	2-0	*Sánchez, Di Natale*
13/2	Cesena	a	3-0	*Di Natale 2, Inler*
20/2	Brescia	h	0-0	
27/2	Palermo	a	7-0	*Di Natale 3 (1p), Sánchez 4*
6/3	Bari	h	1-0	*Di Natale (p)*
13/3	Cagliari	a	4-0	*Benatia, Sánchez, Di Natale 2*
20/3	Catania	h	2-0	*Inler, Di Natale (p)*
3/4	Lecce	a	0-2	
9/4	Roma	h	1-2	*Di Natale*
17/4	Napoli	a	2-1	*Inler, Denis*
23/4	Parma	h	0-2	
1/5	Fiorentina	a	2-5	*Pinzi, Asamoah*
8/5	Lazio	h	2-1	*Di Natale 2*
15/5	Chievo	a	2-0	*Isla, Asamoah*
22/5	Milan	h	0-0	

No	Name	Nat	DoB	Pos	Aps	(s)	Gls
23	Almen ABDI	SUI	21/10/86	M	6	(13)	
19	Emmanuel AGYEMANG-BADU	GHA	2/12/90	M	2	(6)	
45	Gabriele ANGELLA		28/4/89	D	1	(7)	
27	Pablo Estifer ARMERO	COL	2/11/86	D	29	(2)	2
20	Kwadwo ASAMOAH	GHA	9/12/88	M	37	(1)	2
18	Christian BATTOCCHIO		10/2/92	M		(1)	
6	Emanuele BELARDI		9/10/77	G	3		
17	Mehdi BENATIA	MAR	17/4/87	D	34		3
13	Andrea CODA		25/4/85	D	16	(6)	
9	Bernardo CORRADI		30/3/76	A		(18)	1
4	Juan Guillermo CUADRADO	COL	26/5/88	D	3	(6)	
16	Germán Gustavo DENIS	ARG	10/9/81	A	8	(17)	4
10	Antonio DI NATALE		13/10/77	A	35	(1)	28
11	Maurizio DOMIZZI		28/6/80	D	28	(2)	2
22	Joel EKSTRAND	SWE	4/2/89	D		(1)	
83	Antonio FLORO FLORES		18/6/83	A	10	(2)	3
1	Samir HANDANOVIČ	SVN	14/7/84	G	35		
88	Gökhan INLER	SUI	27/6/84	M	35		3
3	Mauricio Aníbal ISLA	CHI	12/6/88	M	34		2
26	Giovanni PASQUALE		5/1/82	D	10	(7)	
66	Giampiero PINZI		11/3/81	M	30	(4)	1
7	Alexis Alejandro SÁNCHEZ	CHI	19/12/88	A	27	(4)	12
21	Matěj VYDRA	CZE	1/5/92	A		(2)	
2	Cristián ZAPATA Valencia	COL	30/9/86	D	35		2

TOP GOALSCORERS 2010/11

28	Antonio DI NATALE (Udinese)
26	Edinson CAVANI (Napoli)
21	Samuel ETO'O (Inter)
20	Alessandro MATRI (Cagliari/Juventus)
19	Marco DI VAIO (Bologna)
17	Giampaolo PAZZINI (Sampdoria/Inter)
15	Francesco TOTTI (Roma)
14	Zlatan IBRAHIMOVIĆ (Milan)
	PATO (Milan)
	ROBINHO (Milan)

PROMOTED CLUBS

ATALANTA BC
Coach – Stefano Colantuono
Founded – 1907
Stadium – Atleti Azzurri d'Italia (26,393)
MAJOR HONOURS: Italian Cup – (1) 1963.

AC SIENA
Coach – Antonio Conte
Founded – 1904
Stadium – Artemio Franchi (15,373)

NOVARA CALCIO
Coach – Attilio Tesser
Founded – 1908
Stadium – Silvio Piola (10,106)

SECOND LEVEL FINAL TABLE 2010/11

		Pld	W	D	L	F	A	Pts
1	Atalanta BC	42	22	13	7	61	35	79
2	AC Siena	42	21	14	7	67	35	77
3	Novara Calcio	42	18	16	8	63	38	70
4	AS Varese	42	16	20	6	51	34	68
5	Calcio Padova	42	15	17	10	63	48	62
6	Reggina Calcio	42	15	16	11	46	40	61
7	AS Livorno Calcio	42	15	14	13	49	46	59
8	Torino FC	42	15	13	14	49	48	58
9	Empoli FC	42	13	18	11	46	39	57
10	Modena FC	42	12	19	11	46	51	55
11	FC Crotone	42	13	15	14	45	50	54
12	Vicenza Calcio	42	15	9	18	44	54	54
13	Pescara Calcio	42	14	11	17	44	48	53
14	AS Cittadella	42	12	15	15	50	54	51
15	US Grosseto	42	12	15	15	43	50	51
16	US Sassuolo Calcio	42	13	12	17	42	46	51
17	Ascoli Calcio	42	14	14	14	44	48	50
18	UC Albinoleffe	42	13	10	19	55	66	49
19	Piacenza Calcio	42	11	13	18	50	63	46
20	US Triestina Calcio	42	8	16	18	34	57	40
21	Calcio Portosummaga	42	10	10	22	39	63	40
22	Frosinone Calcio	42	8	14	20	46	64	38

NB Ascoli Calcio – 6 pts deducted.

PROMOTION PLAY-OFFS
(2/6/11 & 5/6/11)
Reggina 0, Novara 0
Novara 2, Reggina 2
(2-2; Novara on higher position in regular season)

Padova 1, Varese 0
Varese 3, Padova 3
(Padova 4-3)

(9/6/11 & 12/6/11)
Padova 0, Novara 0
Novara 2, Padova 0
(Novara 2-0)

DOMESTIC CUP 2010/11

COPPA ITALIA

THIRD ROUND

(20/10/10)
Genoa 2, Grosseto 1 *(aet)*

(26/10/10)
Fiorentina 1, Empoli 0 *(aet)*

(27/10/10)
Atalanta 0, Livorno 1
Bologna 3, Modena 2
Brescia 1, Cittadella 0
Cagliari 3, Piacenza 0
Catania 4, Varese 3 *(aet)*
Cesena 1, Novara 3 *(aet)*
Crotone 0, AlbinoLeffe 1
Frosinone 2, Reggina 4 *(aet)*
Lazio 3, Portosummaga 0
Lecce 3, Siena 2
Udinese 4, Padova 0
Vicenza 1, Ascoli 0

(28/10/10)
Bari 3, Torino 1
Chievo 2, Sassuolo 0

FOURTH ROUND

(24/11/10)
Genoa 3, Vicenza 1 *(aet)*
Udinese 2, Lecce 1 *(aet)*

(25/11/10)
Cagliari 0, Bologna 3
Catania 5, Brescia 1
Lazio 3, AlbinoLeffe 0

(30/11/10)
Chievo 3, Novara 0
Fiorentina 3, Reggina 0

(1/12/10)
Bari 4, Livorno 1

FIFTH ROUND

(14/12/10)
Parma 2, Fiorentina 1 *(aet)*

(12/1/11)
Inter 3, Genoa 2
Palermo 1, Chievo 0

(13/1/11)
Juventus 2, Catania 0

(18/1/11)
Napoli 2, Bologna 1

(19/1/11)
Roma 2, Lazio 1
Sampdoria 2, Udinese 2 *(aet; 7-6 on pens)*

(20/1/11)
Milan 3, Bari 0

QUARTER-FINALS

(25/1/11)
Palermo 0, Parma 0 *(aet; 5-4 on pens)*

(26/1/11)
Napoli 0, Inter 0 *(aet; 4-5 on pens)*
Sampdoria 1 *(Guberti 51)*, Milan 2 *(Pato 17, 22)*

(27/1/11)
Juventus 0, Roma 2 *(Vučinić 65, Taddei 90+1)*

SEMI-FINALS

(19/4/11 & 11/5/11)
Roma 0, Inter 1 *(Stanković 45)*
Inter 1 *(Eto'o 58)*, Roma 1 *(Borriello 85)*
(Inter 2-1)

(20/4/11 & 10/5/11)
Milan 2 *(Ibrahimović 4, Emanuelson 76)*, Palermo 2 *(Pastore 14, Hernández 53)*
Palermo 2 *(Migliaccio 63, Bovo 72p)*, Milan 1 *(Ibrahimović 90)*
(Palermo 4-3)

FINAL

(29/5/11)
Stadio Olimpico, Rome
FC INTERNAZIONALE MILANO 3 *(Eto'o 26, 77, Milito 90+2)*
US CITTÀ DI PALERMO 1 *(Muñoz 88)*
Referee – *Morganti*
INTER – *Júlio César, Nagatomo, Lúcio, Ranocchia, Chivu, Zanetti, Stanković, Thiago Motta (Mariga 83), Sneijder (Milito 87), Pazzini (Pandev 61), Eto'o.*
PALERMO – *Sirigu, Cassani, Muñoz, Goian (Carrozzieri 24), Balzaretti, Migliaccio, Acquah (Miccoli 55), Nocerino, Iličič, Pastore, Hernández (Pinilla 79).*
Sent off: *Muñoz (90).*

CLUB COMMUNICATION 2011/12

Atalanta BC

Corso Europa - Zingonia
IT-24040 Ciserano-Bergamo

Tel +39 035 4186211
Fax +39 035 4186247
Web atalanta.it
Email info@atalanta.it
Media Officer Andrea Lazzaroni

Bologna FC

Via Casteldebole 10, Stadio "Renato Dall'Ara", IT-40132 Bologna

Tel +39 051 611 1111
Fax +39 051 611 1122
Web bolognafc.it
Email bologna@lega-calcio.it
Media Officer Carlo Caliceti

Cagliari Calcio

Viale La Plaia 15
IT-09123 Cagliari

Tel +39 070 604201
Fax +39 070 6042029
Web cagliaricalcio.net
Email cagliari@lega-calcio.it
Media Officer Sandro Angioini

Calcio Catania

c/o Centro Sportivo Torre del Grifo
Via Magenta, s.n., IT-95030 Mascalucia (CT)

Tel 39 095 754 4411
Fax 39 095 754 4444
Web calciocatania.it
Email info@calciocatania.it
Media Officer Angelo Scaltriti

AC Cesena

Corso Sozzi 5
IT-47521 Cesena (FO)

Tel +39 0547 611 320
Fax +39 0547 611 875
Web cesenacalcio.it
Email info@cesenacalcio.it
Media Officer Andrea Agostini

AC Chievo Verona

Via Luigi Galvani 3, Stadio Marc'Antonio Bentegodi, IT-37138 Verona

Tel +39 045 575 779
Fax +39 045 562 298
Web chievoverona.tv
Email segreteria.generale@chievoverona.it
Media Officer Federica Menegazzi

ACF Fiorentina

Viale Manfredo Fanti 4
IT-50137 Firenze

Tel +39 055 503 011
Fax +39 055 503 0159
Web violachannel.tv
Email segreteria@acffiorentina.it
Media Officer Silvia Berti

Genoa CFC

Villa Rostan, Via Ronchi 67
IT-16155 Genova

Tel +39 010 612 8321
Fax +39 010 612 8344
Web genoacfc.it
Email info@genoacfc.it
Media Officer Dino Storace

FC Internazionale Milano

Corso Vittorio Emanuele II, 9
IT-20122 Milano

Tel +39 02 771 51
Fax +39 02 781 514
Web inter.it
Email inter@inter.it
Media Officer Luigi Crippa

Juventus

Corso Galileo Ferraris 32
IT-10128 Torino

Tel +39 011 656 3431
Fax +39 011 440 7377
Web juventus.com
Email juventus@lega-calcio.it
Media Officer Marco Girotto

S.S. Lazio

Via di Santa Cornelia 1000, Formello
IT-00060 Roma

Tel +39 06 9760 7210
Fax +39 06 9040 0022
Web sslazio.it
Email lazio@lega-calcio.it
Media Officer Stefano De Martino

US Lecce

Via Templari 11, Stadio Via del Mare
IT-73100 Lecce

Tel +39 0832 240 214
Fax +39 0832 243 171
Web uslecce.it
Email lecce@lega-calcio.it
Media Officer Andrea Ferrante

AC Milan

Via Filippo Turati 3
IT-20121 Milano

Tel +39 02 622 81
Fax +39 02 659 8876
Web acmilan.com
Email milan@lega-calcio.it
Media Officer Riccardo Coli

SSC Napoli

Strada Statale Domitiana Km. 35,300
IT-81030 Castel Volturno-Caserta

Tel +39 081 509 53 44
Fax +39 081 509 39 17
Web sscnapoli.it
Email alberto.vallefuoco@sscn.it
Media Officer Monica Scozzafava

Novara Calcio

Viale Kennedy, 8
IT-28100 Novara

Tel +39 0321 555 01
Fax +39 0321 555 0311
Web novaracalcio.com
Email info@novaracalcio.com
Media Officer Francesca Giusti

US Città di Palermo

Viale del Fante 11
IT-90146 Palermo

Tel +39 091 690 1211
Fax +39 091 670 0263
Web ilpalermocalcio.it
Email palermo@lega-calcio.it
Media Officer Fabio Russomando

Parma FC

Viale Partigiani d'Italia, c/o Stadio Tardini
IT-43123 Parma

Tel +39 0521 505 111
Fax +39 0521 505 100
Web fcparma.com
Email parma@lega-calcio.it
Media Officer Maria Luisa Rancati

AS Roma

Via di Trigoria Km 3.600
IT-00128 Roma

Tel +39 06 501 911
Fax +39 06 506 1736
Web asroma.it
Email roma@lega-calcio.it
Media Officer Elena Turra

AC Siena

Via della Sapienza 29
IT-53100 Siena

Tel +39 0577 281 084
Fax +39 0577 281 083
Web acsiena.it
Email info@acsiena.it
Media Officer Orlando Pacchiani

Udinese Calcio

Viale Agostino e Angelo Candolini 2
IT-33100 Udine

Tel +39 0432 544 911
Fax +39 0432 544 933
Web udinese.it
Email udinese@udinesespa.it
Media Officer Mattia Pertoldi

KAZAKHSTAN

Kazakhstan I Kasachstan

Kazakhstanning Futbol Federatsiyasi (KFF)

COMMUNICATION

Address	29 Syganak Street 14th floor KZ-010000 Astana	**President**	Adilbek Jaxybekov
		General Secretary	Sayan Khamitzhanov
		Media Officer	Timur Kamashev
Tel	+7 7172 790780		
Fax	+7 7172 790788	**Year of Formation**	1992
E-mail	kfo@mail.online.kz	**National Stadium**	Astana Arena, Astana (30,000)
Website	kff.kz		

DOMESTIC COMPETITION SUMMARY 2010

PREMIER LIGA TABLE

SECOND PHASE

Championship Pool			Home					Away					Total						
		Pld	**W**	**D**	**L**	**F**	**A**	**W**	**D**	**L**	**F**	**A**	**W**	**D**	**L**	**F**	**A**	**Pts**	**Comp**
1	FC Tobol Kostanay	32	10	3	3	33	14	9	4	3	20	11	19	7	6	53	25	64	UCL
2	FC Aktobe	32	10	3	3	27	12	9	3	4	29	18	19	6	7	56	30	63	UEL
3	FC Irtysh Pavlodar	32	10	3	3	21	11	6	5	5	18	19	16	8	8	39	30	56	UEL
4	FC Lokomotiv Astana	32	10	4	2	26	5	4	4	8	15	23	14	8	10	41	28	50	
5	FC Atyrau	32	8	2	6	18	20	5	3	8	18	24	13	5	14	36	44	44	
6	FC Shakhter Karagandy	32	6	3	7	17	14	5	5	6	15	16	11	8	13	32	30	41	UEL

Relegation Pool			Home					Away					Total						
		Pld	**W**	**D**	**L**	**F**	**A**	**W**	**D**	**L**	**F**	**A**	**W**	**D**	**L**	**F**	**A**	**Pts**	
7	FC Zhetysu Taldykorgan	32	6	6	4	16	13	7	4	5	20	13	13	10	9	36	26	49	
8	FC Ordabasy Shymkent	32	9	4	3	23	14	3	5	8	14	20	12	9	11	37	34	45	
9	FC Taraz	32	5	7	4	21	19	4	3	9	15	21	9	10	13	36	40	37	
10	FC Kairat Almaty	32	5	4	7	9	19	1	7	8	8	19	6	11	15	17	38	29	
11	FC Akzhaiyk Uralsk	32	5	4	7	22	26	2	1	13	11	32	7	5	20	33	58	26	*Relegated*
12	FC Okzhetpes Kokshetau	32	5	4	7	16	24	1	3	12	8	33	6	7	19	24	57	25	*Relegated*

NB League split into top and bottom halves after 22 games, with each team playing a further ten matches exclusively against clubs from its half of the table.

Top Scorer	Ulugbek Bakayev (Tobol), 16 goals
Promoted Clubs	FC Vostok Oskemen FC Kaysar Kyzylorda
Cup Final	FC Lokomotiv Astana 1, FC Shakhter Karagandy 0

Tobol hold off Aktobe to take first title

Runners-up four times in the previous seven seasons, FC Tobol Kostanay finally shed their bridesmaid tag to take Kazkahstan's Premier Liga title for the first time. It was a victory achieved in nerve-shredding circumstances, with Tobol, front-runners for so long, having to hold off a powerful late surge from defending champions and northern rivals FC Aktobe.

Wins in their final three matches, the last of them 2-0 away to FC Atyrau, eventually carried Tobol over the threshold, a point ahead of Aktobe, but the club's long-suffering supporters were made to sweat right through to the moment of deliverance. At the end of the regular 22-match first phase Tobol held a ten-point advantage over Aktobe. With just ten games to go, their sole challengers appeared to be FC Irtysh Pavlodar, just four points in arrears in second place.

Aktobe apply pressure

But as Irtysh slipped off the pace, so did Tobol, a 2-0 loss at Aktobe heralding a horrible five-match winless run that concluded with another defeat by the re-energised champions, 5-2 at home in Kostanay. Aktobe had now closed the gap to one point and had all the momentum. But just when it looked as if Tobol were heading for another heartbreaking near-miss – they had lost the title on penalties to Aktobe in 2008 – they found the strength to resist the pressure. Skipper Nurbol Zhumaskaliyev scored in a 1-0 win five days later at FC Shakhter Karagandy, and when that was followed by another three-pointer, 2-0 at home to FC Lokomotiv Astana, Tobol knew that a third win, at Atyrau, would clinch the title. They took the lead late in the first half before Zhumaskaliyev wrapped up the historic victory 20 minutes from time with a goal direct from a corner.

Tobol's Russian coach, Ravil Sabitov, deserved credit for taking the club to the title in his first season, but Zhumaskaliyev, a Tobol regular for a decade, perhaps had reason to savour the success more. The Kazakhstan international midfielder's 15 goals were crucial – though he was just pipped to the title of Premier Liga top scorer by his team-mate, Uzbekistan striker Ulugbek Bakayev, whose 16 goals included five penalties.

Aktobe were left to rue a poor first phase in which they won only half of their games and were just three points clear of the cut-off line separating the championship and relegation pools. Their best players once again were captain/centre-back Samat Smakov and top-scoring striker Murat Tleshev, although the latter's final tally of ten goals was 50 per cent down on his 2009 output and just one more than Smakov's total. The pair were also among the goals in Europe as, for the second summer running, Aktobe played two qualifying ties in the UEFA Champions League and one in the UEFA Europa League. Unlike Kazakhstan's other three European representatives, Aktobe gave an impressive account of themselves, winning all three home games.

Tobol captain Nurbol Zhumaskaliyev led by example in his club's title triumph

KAZAKHSTAN

Lokomotiv's Cup

Formed as a merger club in 2009, FC Lokomotiv Astana celebrated the second year of their existence with victory in the Kazakhstan Cup, overcoming Shakhter 1-0 in the final – staged in their home stadium, the newly constructed Astana Arena – with a first-half goal from defender Mikhail Rozhkov. It was the second year running that Shakhter had lost the final by a single goal.

A bad start to the UEFA EURO 2012 qualifying campaign – four defeats and no goals – led to the dismissal of Kazakhstan's national team coach Bernd Storck and the appointment of Miroslav Beránek, the man who led his native Czech Republic to victory at the 2002 UEFA European Under-21 Championship. Beránek was thrown into the deep end with a first competitive fixture away to Germany, which predictably resulted in a 4-0 defeat, but he was victorious in his second, at home to Azerbaijan, with Tobol's new 24-year-old striker Sergei Gridin scoring twice on his debut in a 2-1 win.

National Team

Top Five All-time Caps – Ruslan Baltiyev (73); Samat Smakov (58); Nurbol Zhumaskaliyev (54); Andrei Karpovich (50); David Loria (38)

Top Five All-time Goals – Ruslan Baltiyev (13); Viktor Zubarev (12); Dmitry Byakov (8); Igor Avdeev, Oleg Litvinenko & Nurbol Zhumaskaliyev (6)

NATIONAL TEAM RESULTS 2010/11

11/8/10	Oman	H	Astana	3-1	*Karpovich (19), Zhumaskaliyev (42), Al Alavi (59og)*
3/9/10	Turkey (ECQ)	H	Astana	0-3	
7/9/10	Austria (ECQ)	A	Salzburg	0-2	
8/10/10	Belgium (ECQ)	H	Astana	0-2	
12/10/10	Germany (ECQ)	H	Astana	0-3	
9/2/11	Belarus	N	Antalya (TUR)	1-1	*Ostapenko (90)*
26/3/11	Germany (ECQ)	A	Kaiserslautern	0-4	
3/6/11	Azerbaijan (ECQ)	H	Astana	2-1	*Gridin (57, 68)*

NATIONAL TEAM APPEARANCES 2010/11

Coach – Bernd STORCK (GER)		**25/1/63**	**Oma**	**TUR**	**AUT**	**BEL**	**GER**					
/(31/1/11) Miroslav BERÁNEK (CZE)		**24/4/57**						**Blr**	**GER**	**AZE**	**Caps**	**Goals**
Andrei SIDELNIKOV	8/3/80	Aktobe	G	G	G	G	G	G46			7	-
Aleksandr KIROV	4/6/84	Lokomotiv Astana	D	D	D	D	D			s82	13	-
Renat ABDULIN	14/4/82	Tobol	D	D	D	D	D					
		/Vostok						D	D		18	1
Aleksandr KISLITSYN	8/3/86	Shakhter Karagandy	D	D85	D75	D 68*						
		/Tobol						s85			14	-
Mikhail ROZHKOV	27/12/83	Lokomotiv Astana	D	s85	s75	s74	s68			s65	7	-
Sergei KARIMOV	21/12/86	Wolfsburg (GER)	M84								1	-
Azat NURGALIYEV	30/6/86	Tobol	M	M	M59	M74	M63					
		/Ordabasy						M85	M60		11	-
Nurbol ZHUMASKALIYEV	11/5/81	Tobol	M	M	M	M87	M					
		/Lokomotiv Astana						M46	M46		54	6
Andrei KARPOVICH	18/1/81	Aktobe	M80	M64	M	M						
		/Lokomotiv Astana						M			50	3
Maksim AZOVSKI	4/6/86	Lokomotiv Astana	M	M	s59		M	M66			16	-
Sergei OSTAPENKO	23/2/86	Lokomotiv Astana	A68	A72								
		/Zhetysu						s46	s81	A79	25	5
Sergei KHIZHNICHENKO	17/7/91	Atyrau	s68		s46	A	A79	A80				
		/Shakhter Karagandy							A	s79	12	3
Sergei SKORYKH	25/5/84	Shakhter Karagandy	s80									
		/Zhetysu						s66			28	-
Farhadbek IRISMETOV	10/8/81	Tobol	s84				D68					
		/Ordabasy							D		35	-

NATIONAL TEAM APPEARANCES 2010/11 (contd.)

			Oma	TUR	AUT	BEL	GER	Blr	GER	AZE	Caps	Goals
leksei POPOV	7/7/78	Amkar (RUS)		D	D	D	D				4	-
eynrich SCHMIDTGAL	20/11/85	Oberhausen (GER)		M		M	M			M	4	-
enis RODIONOV	26/7/85	Zhetysu		s64							13	1
leb MALTSEV	7/3/88	Irtysh		s72	A46						3	-
evgeniy AVERCHENKO	6/4/82	Aktobe			M	s87	s63				9	-
azbek GETERIYEV	30/6/85	Spartak Nalchik (RUS) /Zhemchuzhina (RUS)			M	M	M		M81	M	5	-
ndrei FINONCHENKO	21/6/82	Shakhter Karagandy					s79	s80			15	2
amat SMAKOV	8/12/78	Aktobe						D		D	58	1
ladislav CHERNYSHEV	16/3/81	Irtysh						D85	D		2	-
nton CHICHULIN	27/10/84	Aktobe						D85	D		24	1
lan KONYSBAYEV	28/5/89	Lokomotiv Astana						M	M	M	3	-
avid LORIA	31/10/81	Irtysh						s46	G		38	-
ayrat NURDAULETOV	6/11/82	Lokomotiv Astana						s85	M	D	16	1
mitriy SHOMKO	19/3/90	Lokomotiv Astana						s85			1	-
Maksat BAYZHANOV	6/8/84	Shakhter Karagandy							s46		12	-
Zhambyl KUKEEV	20/9/88	Shakhter Karagandy							s60		21	1
Roman NESTERENKO	22/3/77	Ordabasy								G	1	-
Yuriy LOGVINENKO	22/7/88	Aktobe								D65	10	-
Mukhtar MUKHTAROV	6/1/86	Ordabasy								D	4	-
Marat KHAIRULLIN	26/4/84	Aktobe								M82	1	-
Sergei GRIDIN	20/5/87	Tobol								A	1	2

CLUB-BY-CLUB

FC AKTOBE

Coach – Vladimir Mukhanov (RUS)

Founded – 1967

Stadium – Aktobe Central Stadium (13,500)

MAJOR HONOURS: Kazakhstan League – (4) 2005, 2007, 2008, 2009; Kazakhstan Cup – (1) 2008.

2010

28/3	Shakhter	a	0-2	
3/4	Zhetysu	a	1-0	*Karpovich*
9/4	Tobol	h	1-3	*Tleshev*
15/4	Akzhaiyk	a	1-1	*Lisenkov*
20/4	Ordabasy	h	1-1	*Ba*
25/4	Lokomotiv	a	1-0	*Strukov*
28/4	Atyrau	h	3-0	*Golovskoy 2, Dosmagambetov*
1/5	Kairat	h	1-0	*Logvinenko*
7/5	Okzhetpes	a	1-0	*Smakov*
12/5	Irtysh	h	0-0	
20/5	Taraz	a	2-2	*Kenzhesariev, Karpovich*
25/5	Shakhter	h	0-1	
30/5	Zhetysu	h	2-1	*Essomba, Smakov*
8/6	Tobol	a	1-2	*Smakov*
13/6	Akzhaiyk	h	4-1	*Kenzhesariev, Essomba, Tleshev, Darabaev*
17/6	Ordabasy	a	2-0	*Darabaev, Essomba*
22/6	Lokomotiv	h	1-2	*Kurmaschev*
27/6	Kairat	a	2-0	*Smakov (p), Tleshev*
17/7	Okzhetpes	h	4-1	*Tleshev 3, Mokrousov*
24/7	Irtysh	a	1-2	*Tleshev*
31/7	Taraz	h	2-1	*Smakov, Kenzhesariev*
14/8	Atyrau	a	1-2	*Smakov*
22/8	Shakhter	h	2-0	*Smakov (p), Kenzhesariev*
11/9	Lokomotiv	a	2-2	*Tleshev, Kenzhesariev*
17/9	Tobol	h	2-0	*Smakov (p), Averchenko*
22/9	Irtysh	h	1-0	*Darabaev*
30/9	Atyrau	a	5-2	*Tleshev 2, Khairullin, Karpovich, Averchenko*
15/10	Lokomotiv	h	1-1	*Kenzhesariev*
22/10	Tobol	a	5-2	*Khairullin 2, Perić 2, Darabaev*
27/10	Irtysh	a	3-1	*Khairullin, Perić, Darabaev*
1/11	Atyrau	h	2-0	*Smakov (p), Khairullin*
6/11	Shakhter	a	1-0	*Khairullin*

No	Name	Nat	DoB	Pos	Aps	(s)	Gls
30	Yevgeniy AVERCHENKO		6/4/82	M	10	(14)	2
2	Khalifa Elhadji BA	SEN	12/10/85	D	21	(2)	1
5	Pyotr BADLO		24/5/76	D	13	(4)	
20	Damir BAYMAGAMBETOV		20/10/92	A		(1)	
7	Maksat BAYZHANOV		6/8/84	M		(3)	
3	Alain BONO	CMR	19/12/83	M	13	(2)	
29	Sergei BOYCHENKO		27/9/77	G	5		
6	Anton CHICHULIN		27/10/84	D	17	(3)	
14	Aslan DARABAYEV		21/1/89	M	32		5
11	Timur DOSMAGAMBETOV		1/5/89	M	10	(2)	1
22	Titi ESSOMBA	CMR	23/5/86	A	21	(3)	3
17	Konstantin GOLOVSKOY		25/4/75	M	13	(1)	2
12	Andrei KARPOVICH		18/1/81	M	29	(1)	3
10	Emil KENZHESARIEV		26/3/87	D	25	(1)	6
7	Marat KHAIRULLIN		26/4/84	M	14		6
4	Nikita KHOKHLOV		27/10/83	D	4	(12)	
32	Maksat KURMASCHEV		14/8/91	A	5	(5)	1
91	Sergei LISENKOV		17/6/91	A	4	(5)	1
23	Yuriy LOGVINENKO		22/7/88	M	10		1
12	Yuriy MOKROUSOV		21/4/89	D	12	(2)	1
55	Ivan PERIĆ	SRB	5/5/82	A	5	(5)	3
25	Maksim SEMENYOV		22/7/88	D	1		
18	Akzhol SERIKZHANOV		6/5/90	M	2	(2)	
55	Andrei SIDELNIKOV		8/3/80	G	27	(1)	

8	Samat SMAKOV		8/12/78	D	32		9
27	Sergei STRUKOV	RUS	17/9/82	A	7	(8)	1
9	Murat TLESHEV		12/4/80	A	20	(6)	10

FC AKZHAIYK URALSK

Coach – Andrei Chernyshov (RUS)

Founded – 1968

Stadium – Pyotr Atoyan (8,320)

2010				
22/3	Irtysh	h	1-4	*Abdrakhmanov*
28/3	Taraz	a	0-3	
3/4	Atyrau	h	1-1	*Sakyi (p)*
9/4	Shakhter	a	2-3	*Sakyi, Maltsev*
15/4	Aktobe	h	1-1	*Gubaydullin*
20/4	Tobol	a	1-3	*Sakyi (p)*
25/4	Zhetysu	a	1-2	*Maltsev*
1/5	Ordabasy	h	2-1	*Sakyi 2*
7/5	Lokomotiv	a	0-2	
12/5	Kairat	h	2-2	*Maltsev 2*
20/5	Okzhetpes	a	1-0	*Zabrodin*
25/5	Taraz	h	2-3	*Sakyi, Kozlov*
30/5	Atyrau	a	0-2	
8/6	Shakhter	h	0-3	
13/6	Aktobe	a	1-4	*Nyukhalov*
17/6	Tobol	h	0-2	
22/6	Zhetysu	h	0-2	
27/6	Ordabasy	a	0-2	
18/7	Lokomotiv	h	2-2	*Maltsev, Sakyi*
25/7	Kairat	a	0-0	
1/8	Okzhetpes	h	2-0	*Gubaydullin, Maltsev*
14/8	Irtysh	a	0-1	
22/8	Ordabasy	a	2-1	*Zabrodin, Sakyi (p)*
11/9	Kairat	h	2-0	*Comleonoc, Sakyi*
17/9	Taraz	a	0-2	
22/9	Okzhetpes	a	0-1	
30/9	Zhetysu	h	0-3	
15/10	Kairat	a	1-2	*Mekang*
22/10	Taraz	h	1-2	*Mekang*
27/10	Okzhetpes	h	2-0	*Sakyi 2 (2p)*
1/11	Zhetysu	a	2-4	*Sakyi, Maltsev*
6/11	Ordabasy	h	4-0	*Sakyi 2, Khairov, Avakyants*

No	Name	Nat	DoB	Pos	Aps	(s)	Gls
7	Eldar ABDRAKHMANOV		16/1/87	M	25	(5)	1
10	Andrei ARBEKOV		12/9/86	M		(2)	
11	Artur AVAKYANTS		30/9/72	M	5	(16)	1
1	Ilya BAYTERYAKOV		13/8/84	G	10	(1)	
10	Victor COMLEONOC	MDA	23/2/79	D	15	(2)	1
3	Nikica GACEŠA	CRO	20/7/83	D	29	(1)	
41	Miraly GALIYEV		14/5/89	M		(4)	
77	Ivan GRABOVAC	CRO	12/7/83	G	16		
9	Aybek GUBAYDULLIN		19/5/88	M	21	(6)	2
18	Ruslan KHAIROV		18/1/90	M	28		1
13	Aslan KIRIYEV		5/1/89	D	7	(8)	
20	Valeriy KORZH		3/6/92	D		(1)	
12	Dmitriy KOZLOV	RUS	22/10/84	A	6	(6)	1
5	Mikhail LYBYUMKIN		26/8/83	D	30	(1)	
8	Aleksei MALTSEV		25/10/86	A	32		7
88	Gock Habib MEKANG	CMR	23/4/82	D	14		2
25	Viktor MYAGKOV	RUS	2/2/85	M	15	(1)	
33	Sergei NYUKHALOV	RUS	30/5/86	D	17		1
14	Bayrzhan OMAROV		3/8/90	D	9	(3)	
16	Moses SAKYI	GHA	12/3/81	A	25	(3)	14
17	Sergei SHEVTSOV		20/10/90	M	15	(11)	
22	Ivan SIVOZHELEZOV		12/3/85	G	6		
6	Ruslan YESENBAYEV		15/1/90	M		(3)	
23	Nikolay ZABRODIN		23/7/90	A	27	(2)	2

FC ATYRAU

Coach – Viktor Pasulko (UKR); (1/8/10) Kairat Aymanov

Founded – 1980

Stadium – Munayshi (8,660)

MAJOR HONOURS: Kazakhstan Cup – (1) 2009.

2010				
28/3	Tobol	h	1-3	*Aliyev (p)*
3/4	Akzhaiyk	a	1-1	*Sedelnikov*
9/4	Ordabasy	h	1-0	*Tatishev*
15/4	Lokomotiv	a	0-1	
20/4	Kairat	h	2-0	*Dzholchiyev, Sakhalbayev*
25/4	Okzhetpes	a	6-0	*Zununov 2, Dzholchiyev 2, Croitoru, Sakhalbayev*
28/4	Aktobe	a	0-3	
1/5	Irtysh	h	0-3	
7/5	Taraz	a	2-1	*Croitoru, og (Khaidarov)*
12/5	Zhetysu	h	1-2	*Peikrishvili*
20/5	Shakhter	h	1-0	*Peikrishvili (p)*
25/5	Tobol	a	2-2	*Frunza, Sedelnikov*
30/5	Akzhaiyk	h	2-0	*Croitoru 2*
8/6	Ordabasy	a	1-2	*Zhumabayev*
13/6	Lokomotiv	h	2-1	*Frunza 2 (1p)*
17/6	Kairat	a	0-1	
22/6	Okzhetpes	h	1-0	*Frunza*
27/6	Irtysh	a	0-3	
18/7	Taraz	h	1-0	*Peikrishvili*
25/7	Zhetysu	a	2-1	*Sakhalbayev, Peikrishvili*
1/8	Shakhter	a	1-1	*Sakhalbayev*
14/8	Aktobe	h	2-1	*Frunza, Khizhnichenko*
22/8	Tobol	a	0-3	
11/9	Shakhter	h	1-1	*Aliyev (p)*
17/9	Irtysh	a	2-1	*Frunza, Shakin*
22/9	Lokomotiv	h	0-0	
30/9	Aktobe	h	2-5	*Peikrishvili, Frunza*
15/10	Shakhter	a	1-0	*Shakin*
22/10	Irtysh	h	1-2	*Sakhalbayev*
27/10	Lokomotiv	a	0-2	
1/11	Aktobe	a	0-2	
6/11	Tobol	h	0-2	

No	Name	Nat	DoB	Pos	Aps	(s)	Gls
14	Almat ABDRAMANOV		12/3/90	M	1		
17	Bakhyt ABUOV		24/1/89	D	7	(3)	
7	Piraly ALIYEV		13/1/84	D	26		2
8	Valentin CHUREYEV		29/8/86	D	29	(1)	
5	Gradimir CRNOGORAC	BIH	14/11/82	D	13		
25	Marius Marian CROITORU	ROU	2/10/80	A	22	(5)	4
22	Baurzhan DZHOLCHIYEV		8/5/90	A	18	(3)	3
24	Viorel FRUNZA	MDA	6/12/79	A	20	(6)	7
8	Sergei KHIZHNICHENKO		17/7/91	A	10	(4)	1
23	Yevgeniy KOSTRUB		27/8/82	M	20	(4)	
77	Sergei LARIN		22/7/86	M	11	(2)	
88	Dmitriy MAMONOV		26/4/78	M	10	(8)	
10	Giorgi PEIKRISHVILI	GEO	28/2/83	M	11	(11)	5
11	Ruslan SAKHALBAYEV		27/6/84	M	28		5
19	Vladimir SEDELNIKOV		15/10/91	D	9	(12)	2
1	Andrei SHABANOV		17/11/86	G	29		
6	Aleksei SHAKIN		6/8/84	M	9	(10)	2
5	Vitaliy SHUMEYKO	UKR	6/10/81	D	12		
22	Ivan SIVOZHELEZOV		12/3/85	G	3		
9	Beybit TATISHEV		24/7/84	A		(11)	1
2	Vasile TUGUTSCHI	MDA	14/1/87	D	4	(1)	
4	Ilya VOROTNIKOV		1/2/86	D	28		
3	Abzal ZHUMABAYEV		28/5/86	D	12	(6)	1
15	Telman ZUNUNOV		17/8/89	M	20	(5)	2

FC IRTYSH PAVLODAR

Coach – Talgat Baysufinov

Founded – 1965

Stadium – Pavlodar Centralny (12,000)

MAJOR HONOURS: Kazakhstan League – (5) 1993, 1997, 1999, 2002, 2003; Kazakhstan Cup – (1) 1998.

2010				
22/3	Akzhaiyk	a	4-1	*Nikolić, Daskalov 2, Maltsev*
28/3	Ordabasy	h	0-0	
3/4	Lokomotiv	a	0-3	
9/4	Kairat	h	0-0	
20/4	Zhetysu	h	1-0	*Maltsev*
25/4	Taraz	h	2-1	*Ivanov, Shabalin*

3/4	Okzhetpes	a	4-2	*Daskalov (p), Maltsev 2, Shabalin*
5	Atyrau	a	3-0	*Chernyshev, Shabalin, Maltsev*
5	Shakhter	h	3-1	*Daskalov 2, Goloveshkin*
2/5	Aktobe	a	0-0	
0/5	Tobol	h	0-0	
5/5	Ordabasy	a	0-1	
0/5	Lokomotiv	h	3-1	*Daskalov 2, Ivanov*
6	Kairat	a	0-0	
3/6	Okzhetpes	h	1-0	*og (Ulchyin)*
7/6	Zhetysu	a	0-0	
2/6	Taraz	a	1-1	*Maltsev*
7/6	Atyrau	h	3-0	*Daskalov 2, Zarechni*
8/7	Shakhter	a	1-0	*Ivanov*
4/7	Aktobe	h	2-1	*Maltsev 2*
1/7	Tobol	a	1-4	*Chernyshev*
4/8	Akzhaiyk	h	1-0	*Maltsev*
2/8	Lokomotiv	h	0-1	
1/9	Tobol	a	0-4	
7/9	Atyrau	h	1-2	*Daskalov*
2/9	Aktobe	a	0-1	
0/9	Shakhter	a	1-1	*Shabalin*
5/10	Tobol	h	2-1	*Daskalov, Shomko*
2/10	Atyrau	a	2-1	*Daskalov 2*
7/10	Aktobe	h	1-3	*Daskalov (p)*
/11	Shakhter	h	1-0	*Daskalov*
/11	Lokomotiv	a	1-0	*Goloveshkin*

No	Name	Nat	DoB	Pos	Aps	(s)	Gls
	Eldos AKHMETOV		1/6/90	D	21	(1)	
	Aleksandr ANDREYEV		9/9/86	M	2		
	Arman BIRKURMANOV		31/1/82	M	1	(11)	
	Vladislav CHERNYSHEV		16/3/81	D	29		2
9	Georgi DASKALOV	BUL	3/8/81	A	29		15
57	Borivoje FILIPOVIĆ	SRB	28/8/82	A	9	(4)	
25	Vitaliy GOLOVESHKIN		10/11/89	A	2	(14)	2
55	Predrag GOVEDARICA	SRB	21/10/84	M	28		
28	Ruslan GUMAR		18/11/73	D	9	(6)	
1	Sergei IVANOV		30/5/80	M	27	(4)	3
4	Viktor KRYUKOV		30/6/90	M	12		
9	Yevgeniy KUZNETSOV		10/5/86	M		(4)	
	David LORIA		31/10/81	G	32		
17	Gleb MALTSEV		7/3/88	M	15	(11)	9
23	Aleksei MIKHAUYLYK		23/7/82	D	18		
37	Milan NIKOLIĆ	SRB	30/3/83	M	12	(4)	1
8	Vladimir NOSKOV		28/1/86	M	1	(5)	
24	Dmitriy PARKHOMCHUK		7/3/87	M	1	(1)	
22	ROBERT de Jesus Daniel	BRA	14/2/82	A		(1)	
7	Pavel SHABALIN		23/10/88	M	27	(2)	4
13	Andrei SHETLE		27/4/91	M		(1)	
20	Dmitriy SHOMKO		19/3/90	M	29	(1)	1
33	Aleksandar VASILJEVIĆ	SRB	19/6/82	D	13	(6)	
12	Konstantin ZARECHNI		14/2/84	M	11	(11)	1
4	Maksim ZHALMAGAMBETOV		11/7/83	D	24		

FC KAIRAT ALMATY

Coach – Sergei Volgin; (22/9/10) Yevgeniy Kuznetsov

Founded – 1954

Stadium – Almaty Centralny (25,057)

MAJOR HONOURS: Kazakhstan League – (2) 1992, 2004; Kazakhstan Cup – (5) 1992, 1996, 1999, 2001 (autumn), 2003.

2010				
22/3	Lokomotiv	a	0-0	
28/3	Zhetysu	h	0-3	
3/4	Okzhetpes	h	1-0	*Nurdauletov (p)*
9/4	Irtysh	a	0-0	
15/4	Taraz	h	0-0	
20/4	Atyrau	a	0-2	
25/4	Shakhter	h	0-1	
1/5	Aktobe	a	0-1	
7/5	Tobol	h	0-1	
12/5	Akzhaiyk	a	2-2	*Kutsov, Abugaliyev*
20/5	Ordabasy	h	1-0	*Fomin*
25/5	Zhetysu	a	0-1	
30/5	Okzhetpes	a	1-0	*Beysenov*
8/6	Irtysh	h	0-0	
13/6	Taraz	a	1-2	*Đorđević*
17/6	Atyrau	h	1-0	*Đorđević*
22/6	Shakhter	a	0-1	
27/6	Aktobe	h	0-2	
18/7	Tobol	a	1-3	*Sabalakov*
25/7	Akzhaiyk	h	0-0	
1/8	Ordabasy	a	1-1	*Gošić*
14/8	Lokomotiv	h	2-2	*Fomin, Abugaliyev*
22/8	Taraz	h	0-3	
11/9	Akzhaiyk	a	0-2	
17/9	Zhetysu	h	0-1	
22/9	Ordabasy	h	1-5	*Gošić*
30/9	Okzhetpes	a	1-1	*Noskov*
15/10	Akzhaiyk	h	2-1	*Rozybakiev, Abugaliyev*
22/10	Zhetysu	a	0-2	
27/10	Ordabasy	a	1-1	*Abugaliyev*
1/11	Okzhetpes	h	1-0	*Fomin*
6/11	Taraz	a	0-0	

No	Name	Nat	DoB	Pos	Aps	(s)	Gls
11	Chingiz ABUGALIYEV		11/10/86	M	16	(7)	4
29	Arman ALIMBETOV		20/5/88	D		(1)	
13	Ilyas AMIRSEITOV		22/10/89	D	28	(2)	
9	Abzal BEYSEBEKOV		30/11/92	A	5	(6)	
41	Bekzat BEYSENOV		18/2/88	M	13	(5)	1
47	Andrei BOGOMOLOV		11/4/77	M	11	(5)	
10	Dragan ĐORĐEVIĆ	SRB	18/4/81	A	20	(8)	2
1	Nenad ERIĆ	SRB	26/5/82	G	31		
7	Artem FOMIN		8/7/88	M	20	(3)	3
81	Dragan GOŠIĆ	SRB	10/6/81	A	11	(3)	2
8	Sabyrkhan IBRAYEV		22/3/88	M	6	(14)	
21	Arman KHALYKOV		1/3/90	M	23	(6)	
20	Sergei KUTSOV		23/4/77	D	23		1
28	Ruslan MANSUROV		23/11/90	A	2	(3)	
8	Vladimir NOSKOV		28/1/86	M	6	(1)	1
44	Kayrat NURDAULETOV		6/11/82	M	10		1
17	Yevgeniy OVSHINOV		17/10/80	D	24	(1)	
23	Oral PAVIZ		6/5/87	M	16	(5)	
15	Rakhimzhan ROZYBAKIEV		2/1/91	M	7	(4)	1
12	Talgat SABALAKOV		9/7/86	A	2	(7)	1
6	Vyatcheslav SOBOLEV		13/10/84	D	25	(2)	
19	Bojan TRKULJA	SRB	20/2/82	D	26		
14	Kayrat UTABAYEV		16/7/80	D	12	(2)	
18	Ilya YUROV		10/9/81	G	1		
5	Konstantin ZOTOV		14/1/86	M	14	(3)	

FC LOKOMOTIV ASTANA

Coach – Holger Fach (GER)

Founded – 2009

Stadium – Astana Arena (30,000)

MAJOR HONOURS: Kazakhstan Cup – (1) 2010.

2010				
22/3	Kairat	h	0-0	
28/3	Okzhetpes	a	1-2	*Bugaiov*
3/4	Irtysh	h	3-0	*Bugaiov 2, Ostapenko*
9/4	Taraz	a	0-1	
15/4	Atyrau	h	1-0	*Bugaiov*
20/4	Shakhter	a	1-3	*Khizhnichenko*
25/4	Aktobe	h	0-1	
1/5	Tobol	a	1-0	*Andronic*
7/5	Akzhaiyk	h	2-0	*Pakholyuk, Ostapenko*
12/5	Ordabasy	a	1-3	*Khizhnichenko*
20/5	Zhetysu	a	0-1	
25/5	Okzhetpes	h	4-0	*Kirov, Andronic, Pakholyuk, Kukeev (p)*
30/5	Irtysh	a	1-3	*Pakholyuk*
8/6	Taraz	h	3-0	*Andronic 2, Bugaiov*
13/6	Atyrau	a	1-2	*Andronic*
17/6	Shakhter	h	4-0	*Kirov, Spanov, Bugaiov, Bozinovski*
22/6	Aktobe	a	2-1	*Bugaiov (p), Ostapenko*
27/6	Tobol	h	2-0	*Andronic, Bugaiov*
18/7	Akzhaiyk	a	2-2	*Spanov, Bugaiov (p)*
26/7	Ordabasy	h	1-0	*Shakhmetov*
1/8	Zhetysu	h	1-0	*Andronic*

14/8	Kairat	a	2-2	*Pakholyuk, Ostapenko*
22/8	Irtysh	a	1-0	*Rozhkov*
11/9	Aktobe	h	2-2	*Ostapenko, Nurdauletov*
17/9	Shakhter	a	1-0	*Kirov*
22/9	Atyrau	a	0-0	
30/9	Tobol	h	0-0	
15/10	Aktobe	a	1-1	*Pakholyuk*
22/10	Shakhter	h	1-1	*Bugaiov*
27/10	Atyrau	h	2-0	*Bugaiov, Dautov*
1/11	Tobol	a	0-2	
6/11	Irtysh	h	0-1	

No	Name	Nat	DoB	Pos	Aps	(s)	Gls
19	Renat ABDULIN		14/4/82	D	4	(4)	
9	Valeriu ANDRONIC	MDA	21/12/82	M	25	(3)	7
18	Maksim AZOVSKI		4/6/86	A	18	(12)	
1	Aleksei BELKIN		25/11/81	G	9		
17	Bobi BOZINOVSKI	MKD	24/2/81	M	4	(10)	1
10	Igor BUGAIOV	MDA	26/6/84	A	30	(1)	11
2	Damir DAUTOV		3/3/90	D		(5)	1
15	Vyacheslav ERBES		14/1/88	M	1	(1)	
77	Roman GERUS	RUS	14/9/80	G	23		
19	Mark GURMAN		9/2/89	D	8	(4)	
4	Denis ILESCU	MDA	20/1/87	D	16		
31	Olzhas KERIMZHANOV		1/1/89	D	6	(3)	
8	Sergei KHIZHNICHENKO		17/7/91	A	11	(4)	2
3	Aleksandr KIROV		4/6/84	D	28	(3)	3
7	Zhambyl KUKEEV		20/9/88	M	11	(7)	1
4	Vlade LAZAREVSKI	MKD	9/6/83	D	4	(4)	
44	Kayrat NURDAULETOV		6/11/82	M	17		1
23	Sergei OSTAPENKO		23/2/86	A	10	(17)	5
11	Roman PAKHOLYUK		3/10/79	M	28	(2)	5
27	Mikhail ROZHKOV		27/12/83	D	30		1
5	Maksim SAMCHENKO		5/5/79	D	25	(1)	
22	Marat SHAKHMETOV		6/2/89	M	28	(1)	1
8	Ivan SHEVCHENKO		10/9/87	D	3	(3)	
32	Olzhas SPANOV		30/11/89	M	13	(2)	2

FC OKZHETPES KOKSHETAU

Coach – Sergei Gerasimets (BLR); (25/5/10) Aleksei Klishin; (14/8/10) Vyacheslav Ledovskikh

Founded – 1968

Stadium – Torpedo (6,000)

2010

22/3	Ordabasy	a	1-1	*og (Trajković)*
28/3	Lokomotiv	h	2-1	*Kuchma, Samokhin*
3/4	Kairat	a	0-1	
9/4	Zhetysu	h	0-0	
20/4	Taraz	a	2-1	*Novikov, Samokhin*
25/4	Atyrau	h	0-6	
28/4	Irtysh	h	2-4	*Dyuk, Chudinov (p)*
1/5	Shakhter	a	0-2	
7/5	Aktobe	h	0-1	
12/5	Tobol	a	0-4	
20/5	Akzhaiyk	h	0-1	
25/5	Lokomotiv	a	0-4	
30/5	Kairat	h	0-1	
8/6	Zhetysu	a	2-2	*Abdukarimov, Krutskevich*
13/6	Irtysh	a	0-1	
17/6	Taraz	h	2-2	*Solochenko, Dyuk (p)*
22/6	Atyrau	a	0-1	
27/6	Shakhter	h	0-1	
17/7	Aktobe	a	1-4	*Abdukarimov*
25/7	Tobol	h	1-3	*Abdukarimov*
1/8	Akzhaiyk	a	0-2	
14/8	Ordabasy	h	3-2	*Pilipović, Chudinov, Abdukarimov*
22/8	Zhetysu	a	0-0	
11/9	Taraz	h	0-0	
17/9	Ordabasy	a	1-4	*Abdukarimov*
22/9	Akzhaiyk	h	1-0	*Chudinov*
30/9	Kairat	h	1-1	*Dyuk (p)*
15/10	Taraz	a	1-3	*Samokhin*
22/10	Ordabasy	h	3-1	*Dragutinović, Dyuk (p), Pilipović*
27/10	Akzhaiyk	a	0-2	
1/11	Kairat	a	0-1	
6/11	Zhetysu	h	1-0	*Dyuk*

No	Name	Nat	DoB	Pos	Aps	(s)	Gls
29	Khasan ABDUKARIMOV		10/3/90	A	24	(3)	5
17	Talgat ADYRBEKOV		26/1/89	D	14	(2)	
17	Kanat ALIYEV		9/2/85	M	26	(1)	
18	Akhmet ALLABERDYEV	TKM	8/3/84	M	5	(5)	
9	Aleksandr ANDREEV		9/9/86	M	5	(9)	
	Aleksandr CHEPUKYAVICIUS		31/8/78	M	2		
4	Maksim CHUDINOV		12/9/88	D	9	(1)	3
12	Dragan DRAGUTINOVIĆ	SRB	17/1/80	M	11	(2)	1
5	Yuriy DYUK		4/7/84	M	28		5
50	Ruslan GARIFULLIN		22/12/89	M	3	(3)	
21	Bakhyt GAYNULLIN		27/9/87	D	22	(1)	
26	Miroslav GEGIĆ	SRB	27/8/84	D	15	(1)	
13	Sergei GLAZYUKOV	RUS	23/9/86	A	11	(3)	
47	Sergei GRIGORYEV		2/8/92	D		(2)	
50	Erzhan KABYLBEKOV		10/8/89	M	11	(3)	
79	Daniyar KENZHEKHANOV		20/1/83	A	2	(1)	
70	Olzhas KERIMZHANOV		16/5/89	D	1	(1)	
35	Artem KIRBITYUEV		18/8/84	G	1		
26	Olexandr KRUTSKEVICH	UKR	13/11/80	D	9	(2)	1
3	Aleksandr KUCHMA		9/12/80	D	9	(1)	1
10	Denis LEDENEV		22/12/87	A	3	(7)	
22	Yevgeniy LUNEV		26/4/76	A	4	(2)	
	Aleksandr MAKSIMOV		8/7/82	A	1	(3)	
8	Maksim MALAKHOVSKY	RUS	28/2/84	M	13		
9	Yuriy MOKROUSOV		21/4/89	D	6		
19	Jevgeni NOVIKOV	EST	28/6/80	M	13		1
14	Yermek NURGALIYEV		8/8/86	D	11	(9)	
25	Nurgazy NURZHIGIT		2/8/91	M	1		
24	Dmitriy PARKHOMCHUK		7/3/87	M	12	(1)	
18	Stojan PILIPOVIĆ	SRB	2/2/87	M	15	(1)	2
1	Daniil RIKHARD		27/2/74	G	31		
52	Yevgeniy SAMOKHIN		3/9/90	A	4	(18)	3
57	Igor SOLOCHENKO		22/5/79	D	14		1
6	Vitaliy STARNOVSKY		7/5/83	D	2	(2)	
15	Aleksandr ULCHYIN		15/10/92	M	1	(2)	
7	Bojan ZAVISIĆ	SRB	9/8/79	D	13	(1)	

FC ORDABASY SHYMKENT

Coach – Anatoliy Yurevich (BLR); (23/8/10) Sergei Kogay

Founded – 1998

Stadium – Kazhimukan (17,000)

2010

22/3	Okzhetpes	h	1-1	*Muminov*
28/3	Irtysh	a	0-0	
3/4	Taraz	h	1-0	*Mitrofanov*
9/4	Atyrau	a	0-1	
15/4	Shakhter	h	1-0	*Vagner*
20/4	Aktobe	a	1-1	*Vagner*
25/4	Tobol	h	1-2	*Tazhimbetov*
1/5	Akzhaiyk	a	1-2	*Trajković (p)*
7/5	Zhetysu	a	0-0	
12/5	Lokomotiv	h	3-1	*Trajković, Asanbaev, Mitrofanov*
20/5	Kairat	a	0-1	
25/5	Irtysh	h	1-0	*Kasyanov (p)*
30/5	Taraz	a	0-0	
8/6	Atyrau	h	2-1	*Vagner, Mitrofanov*
13/6	Shakhter	a	1-0	*Mitrofanov*
17/6	Aktobe	h	0-2	
22/6	Tobol	a	0-2	
27/6	Akzhaiyk	h	2-0	*Akopyan, Mukhtarov*
18/7	Zhetysu	h	2-1	*Yevstigneev, Ashirbekov*
26/7	Lokomotiv	a	0-1	
1/8	Kairat	h	1-1	*Tadzhiev*
14/8	Okzhetpes	a	2-3	*Muminov, Vagner*
22/8	Akzhaiyk	h	1-2	*Kasyanov*
11/9	Zhetysu	a	2-0	*Tazhimbetov, Chikrizov*
17/9	Okzhetpes	h	4-1	*Vagner 2, Tazhimbetov 2 (1p)*
22/9	Kairat	a	5-1	*Tazhimbetov, Zholdasov, Ashirbekov 2, Asanbaev*

)/9	Taraz	a	1-1	*Tazhimbetov*
5/10	Zhetysu	h	1-1	*Tazhimbetov*
2/10	Okzhetpes	a	1-3	*Trajković (p)*
7/10	Kairat	h	1-1	*Vagner*
11	Taraz	h	1-0	*Tazhimbetov*
11	Akzhaiyk	a	0-4	

o	Name	Nat	DoB	Pos	Aps	(s)	Gls
5	Armen AKOPYAN	UKR	15/1/80	M	1	(4)	1
	Mohamed Larbi AROURI	TUN	13/5/83	D	3	(1)	
2	Ulugbek ASANBAEV		13/9/79	M	22	(5)	2
0	Kayrat ASHIRBEKOV		21/10/82	M	24	(2)	3
6	Almat BEKBAYEV		14/7/84	G	1	(1)	
4	Yaroslav BONDARENKO		15/3/92	G		(1)	
1	Yevgeniy CHIKRIZOV		30/7/90	A		(6)	1
3	Daulet DYISEKULOV		2/4/93	D	1		
7	Galymzhan ERMUZAYEV		1/4/91	A		(1)	
4	Boris FOMENKOV		29/9/91	M	1		
2	Abylaykhan ISKANEDIROV		24/7/91	A	1	(4)	
2	Artem KASYANOV	UKR	20/4/83	M	29		2
8	Bakdaulet KOZHABAYEV		19/6/92	D	7		
	Sergei KOZULIN		2/8/80	D	1	(5)	
0	Yevgeniy LEVIN		12/7/92	M	2		
1	Ablaykhan MAKHAMBETOV		3/8/91	M		(1)	
	Aleksandr MITROFANOV		1/11/77	M	13	(14)	4
	Aleksandr MOKIN		19/6/81	G	29		
	Mukhtar MUKHTAROV		6/1/86	D	24	(1)	1
	Madiyar MUMINOV		18/10/80	D	22	(8)	2
	Tanat NUSERBAYEV		1/1/88	A	2	(3)	
2	Samat OTARBAYEV		18/2/90	G	2		
3	Taofik SALHI	TUN	21/8/79	M	2	(5)	
3	Bekseit SHULANBEKOV		1/1/87	A	1		
8	Gafurzhan SYUMBAYEV		19/8/90	A	15		
9	Zeynutdin TADZHIEV	UZB	21/6/77	A	5	(1)	1
8	Daurenbek TAZHIMBETOV		2/7/85	A	19	(9)	8
0	Mardan TOLEBEK		18/12/90	D	1	(1)	
	Aleksandar TRAJKOVIĆ	SRB	16/1/81	D	30		3
5	Serikbolsyn TUREKHANOV		26/7/92	D		(1)	
1	VAGNER Pereira Costa	BRA	1/6/87	A	28		7
7	Abzal YESHMANOV		5/2/90	M	12	(9)	
3	Vitaliy YEVSTIGNEEV		8/8/85	M	24	(2)	1
9	Igor ZAITSEV		29/6/90	D	1		
7	Malik ZHANTLEYOV		2/2/89	M		(1)	
4	Nursayun ZHOLDASOV		11/5/91	M	29	(1)	1

FC SHAKHTER KARAGANDY

Coach – Vladimir Cheburin; (22/10/10) Askar Abildayev

Founded – 1958

Stadium – Shakhter (19,500)

2010				
28/3	Aktobe	h	2-0	*Suchkov, Džidić*
3/4	Tobol	a	0-0	
9/4	Akzhaiyk	h	3-2	*Finonchenko, Suchkov, Vičius*
15/4	Ordabasy	a	0-1	
20/4	Lokomotiv	h	3-1	*Skorykh, Vičius, Shaff*
25/4	Kairat	a	1-0	*Bildinov*
28/4	Zhetysu	a	0-0	
1/5	Okzhetpes	h	2-0	*Finonchenko, Tattybayev*
7/5	Irtysh	a	1-3	*Vičius*
12/5	Taraz	h	2-0	*Finonchenko, Vičius*
20/5	Atyrau	a	0-1	
25/5	Aktobe	a	1-0	*Suchkov*
30/5	Tobol	h	1-1	*Džidić*
8/6	Akzhaiyk	a	3-0	*Džidić, Vičius, Tattybayev*
13/6	Ordabasy	h	0-1	
17/6	Lokomotiv	a	0-4	
22/6	Kairat	h	1-0	*Finonchenko*
27/6	Okzhetpes	a	1-0	*Džidić*
18/7	Irtysh	h	0-1	
25/7	Taraz	a	5-1	*Finonchenko 2, Džidić 2, Tattybayev*
1/8	Atyrau	h	1-1	*Finonchenko*
14/8	Zhetysu	h	1-2	*Džidić*
22/8	Aktobe	a	0-2	
11/9	Atyrau	a	1-1	*Tattybayev*
17/9	Lokomotiv	h	0-1	
25/9	Tobol	a	1-1	*Finonchenko*
30/9	Irtysh	h	1-1	*Pikalkin*
15/10	Atyrau	h	0-1	
22/10	Lokomotiv	a	1-1	*Džidić*
27/10	Tobol	h	0-1	
1/11	Irtysh	a	0-1	
6/11	Aktobe	h	0-1	

No	Name	Nat	DoB	Pos	Aps	(s)	Gls
47	Vladislav AKHMEEV		19/12/92	M		(2)	
23	Nikita BILDINOV		12/1/90	M	10	(2)	1
15	Anatoliy BOGDANOV		7/8/81	A	27	(2)	
7	Askhat BORANTAYEV		22/8/78	D	4	(10)	
8	Vadim BOROVSKIY		30/10/86	A	2	(8)	
4	Aleksei DANAEV		1/9/79	D	20		
2	Saša ĐORĐEVIĆ	SRB	4/8/81	D	27	(1)	
21	Grigory DUBKOV		22/11/90	M	19	(3)	
20	Aldin DŽIDIĆ	BIH	30/8/83	D	26	(1)	8
14	Andrei FINONCHENKO		21/6/82	A	25	(2)	8
22	Yevgeniy GORYUTCHI		2/2/91	D	5	(1)	
1	Aleksandr GRIGORENKO		6/2/85	G	30		
11	Mladen HASIJA	CRO	28/6/86	M		(3)	
27	Ayan KHUSAINOV		10/6/90	D	1		
5	Aleksandr KISLITSYN		8/3/86	D	28		
6	Sergei KOZULIN		2/8/80	D	4	(5)	
6	Ilnur MANGUTKIN		16/9/86	M	1		
11	Jimmy MULISA	RWA	3/4/85	A	8	(5)	
12	Igor PIKALKIN		19/3/92	M	11		1
40	Fedor RUDENKO		28/3/90	D	8	(1)	
16	Sergei SARANA		7/12/78	G	2		
10	Sergei SHAFF		15/4/88	A	7	(13)	1
9	Sergei SKORYKH		25/5/84	M	17	(3)	1
17	Aleksei SUCHKOV	BLR	10/6/81	M	26	(4)	3
13	Yevgeniy TARASOV		16/4/85	D	14	(2)	
43	Aydos TATTYBAYEV		26/4/90	A	10	(8)	4
3	Gediminas VIČIUS	LTU	5/7/85	M	20	(5)	5

FC TARAZ

Coach – Oyrat Saduov; (27/6/10) Igor Ursaki (MDA); (22/8/10) Anatoliy Belsky; (11/9/10) Dmitriy Ogai

Founded – 1961

Stadium – Taraz Centralny (12,000)

MAJOR HONOURS: Kazakhstan League – (1) 1996; Kazakhstan Cup – (1) 2004.

2010				
22/3	Tobol	a	0-1	
28/3	Akzhaiyk	h	3-0	*Buleshev, Tonev, Jovanović*
3/4	Ordabasy	a	0-1	
9/4	Lokomotiv	h	1-0	*Nedashkovsky*
15/4	Kairat	a	0-0	
20/4	Okzhetpes	h	1-2	*Milosavljević (p)*
25/4	Irtysh	a	1-2	*Jovanović*
1/5	Zhetysu	h	2-2	*Zemlyunukhin, Jovanović*
7/5	Atyrau	h	1-2	*Zemlyunukhin*
12/5	Shakhter	a	0-2	
20/5	Aktobe	h	2-2	*Kenbayev, Baytana*
25/5	Akzhaiyk	a	3-2	*Konysbayev, Zemlyunukhin, Yevstigneev*
30/5	Ordabasy	h	0-0	
8/6	Lokomotiv	a	0-3	
13/6	Kairat	h	2-1	*Konysbayev, Suley*
17/6	Okzhetpes	a	2-2	*Kenbayev, Milosavljević (p)*
22/6	Irtysh	h	1-1	*Nedashkovsky*
27/6	Zhetysu	a	0-1	
18/7	Atyrau	a	0-1	
25/7	Shakhter	h	1-5	*Yevstigneev*
31/7	Aktobe	a	1-2	*Nedashkovsky*
14/8	Tobol	h	0-1	
22/8	Kairat	a	3-0	*Nedashkovsky, Zemlyunukhin, Konysbayev*
11/9	Okzhetpes	a	0-0	
17/9	Akzhaiyk	h	2-0	*Kenbayev, Jovanović*
22/9	Zhetysu	a	3-2	*Jovanović, Zemlyunukhin, Nedashkovsky*

30/9	Ordabasy	h	1-1	*Jovanović*
15/10	Okzhetpes	h	3-1	*Zemlyunukhin, Suley, Jovanović*
22/10	Akzhaiyk	a	2-1	*Zemlyunukhin, Kenbayev*
27/10	Zhetysu	h	1-1	*Suley*
1/11	Ordabasy	a	0-1	
6/11	Kairat	h	0-0	

No	Name	Nat	DoB	Pos	Aps	(s)	Gls
8	Zhandos AKHMETOV		4/2/87	D	5	(1)	
23	Galymzhan ALIMBAYEV		9/5/89	M	1	(3)	
2	Maksat AMIRKHANOV		10/2/92	D		(2)	
22	Aziz ANARMETOV		30/7/82	M	19	(8)	
9	Baurzhan BAYTANA		6/6/92	M	24	(3)	1
24	Dmitriy BOGDAN		4/3/89	D	6	(1)	
10	Alibek BULESHEV		9/4/81	A	6	(5)	1
13	Ruslan ISLAMOV		5/3/91	M		(1)	
24	Milan JOVANOVIĆ	SRB	14/10/83	A	16	(15)	7
11	Erzat KENBAYEV		22/4/88	M	16	(12)	4
27	Alik KHAIDAROV		27/4/81	D	17	(5)	
7	Ulan KONYSBAYEV		28/5/89	A	32		3
5	Nurtas KURGULIN		20/9/86	D	25		
21	Uroš MILOSAVLJEVIĆ	SRB	13/7/82	M	29	(1)	2
20	Мурат MUKASHEV		18/9/82	G	29		
17	Oleg NEDASHKOVSKY		9/9/87	M	30	(1)	5
77	Arslan SATYBALDIN		14/8/84	G	3		
4	Igor SOLTANICI	MDA	4/5/84	D	12		
18	Kayrat SULEY		26/10/85	A	3	(8)	3
14	Vaid TALGAYEV		21/12/90	M	2	(14)	
15	Nikola TONEV	MKD	12/11/85	D	26	(1)	1
2	Vasile TUGUTSCHI	MDA	14/1/87	D	2		
19	Dmitriy YEVSTIGNEEV		27/11/86	D	20	(4)	2
44	Anton ZEMLYUNUKHIN	KGZ	11/12/90	A	24	(3)	7
6	Amangeldy ZHUSUPOV		18/7/88	D	5		

FC TOBOL KOSTANAY

Coach – Ravil Sabitov (RUS)

Founded – 1967

Stadium – Kostanay Centralny (5,720)

MAJOR HONOURS: Kazakhstan League – (1) 2010; Kazakhstan Cup – (1) 2007.

2010

22/3	Taraz	h	1-0	*Zhumaskaliyev*
28/3	Atyrau	a	3-1	*Bakayev, Nurgaliyev, Yurin*
3/4	Shakhter	h	0-0	
9/4	Aktobe	a	3-1	*Bakayev 2, Zhumaskaliyev*
15/4	Zhetysu	a	0-0	
20/4	Akzhaiyk	h	3-1	*Zhumaskaliyev, Nurgaliyev 2*
25/4	Ordabasy	a	2-1	*Suyumagambetov, Bakayev (p)*
1/5	Lokomotiv	h	0-1	
7/5	Kairat	a	1-0	*Zhumaskaliyev*
12/5	Okzhetpes	h	4-0	*Zhumaskaliyev 2, Bakayev 2 (1p)*
20/5	Irtysh	a	0-0	
25/5	Atyrau	h	2-2	*Bakayev, Lotov*
30/5	Shakhter	a	1-1	*Parkhachev*
8/6	Aktobe	h	2-1	*Zhumaskaliyev 2*
13/6	Zhetysu	h	0-1	
17/6	Akzhaiyk	a	2-0	*Bakayev (p), Suyumagambetov*
22/6	Ordabasy	h	2-0	*Zhumaskaliyev 2*
27/6	Lokomotiv	a	0-2	
18/7	Kairat	h	3-1	*Beganskiy 2, Klapka*
25/7	Okzhetpes	a	3-1	*Suyumagambetov, Kuantayev, Bakayev*
31/7	Irtysh	h	4-1	*Leviha, Bakayev, Beganskiy, Klapka*
14/8	Taraz	a	1-0	*Malyshev*
22/8	Atyrau	h	3-0	*Bakayev 2 (1p), Kuantayev*
11/9	Irtysh	h	4-0	*Zhumaskaliyev 2, Bakayev 2 (1p)*
17/9	Aktobe	a	0-2	
25/9	Shakhter	h	1-1	*Lotov*
30/9	Lokomotiv	a	0-0	
15/10	Irtysh	a	1-2	*Klapka*
22/10	Aktobe	h	2-5	*Zhumaskaliyev, Bakayev*
27/10	Shakhter	a	1-0	*Zhumaskaliyev*
1/11	Lokomotiv	h	2-0	*Bakayev (p), Kuantayev*
6/11	Atyrau	a	2-0	*Turtenwald, Zhumaskaliyev*

No	Name	Nat	DoB	Pos	Aps	(s)	Gls
19	Renat ABDULIN		14/4/82	D	10		
1	Yaroslav BAGINSKY		3/10/87	G	3	(3)	
10	Ulugbek BAKAYEV	UZB	28/11/78	A	22	(5)	16
17	Pavel BEGANSKIY	BLR	9/1/81	A	5	(4)	3
17	Andrey CORNEENCOV	MDA	1/4/82	M	3	(1)	
40	Artem DELI		2/3/89	M		(2)	
14	Farhadbek IRISMETOV		10/8/81	D	19	(4)	
26	Aleksei JOSIPENKO		9/2/91	D		(1)	
8	Andrei KHARABARA		1/9/85	M	9	(7)	
23	Filip KLAPKA	CZE	20/6/81	M	13		3
20	Yermek KUANTAYEV		13/10/90	M	26	(1)	3
99	Ruslan LEVIHA	UKR	31/1/83	A	8	(3)	1
15	Oleg LOTOV		21/11/75	D	30	(1)	2
21	Aleksei MALYSHEV		24/6/89	M	23	(3)	1
18	Daniyar MUKANOV		26/9/76	D	22	(3)	
7	Azat NURGALIYEV		30/6/86	M	22	(4)	3
23	Dmitriy PARKHACHEV	BLR	2/1/85	A	3	(9)	1
35	Aleksandr PETUKHOV		11/1/85	G	29		
13	Oleg SABIROV		13/3/81	D	15	(2)	
22	Sanat SCHALEKENOV		4/4/89	D	14	(2)	
12	Vyacheslav SERDYUKOV		16/8/89	A	1		
11	Murat SUYUMAGAMBETOV		14/10/83	A	10	(13)	3
27	Andrei TRAVIN		27/4/79	M	4	(4)	
3	Vit TURTENWALD	CZE	5/3/80	D	14	(2)	1
24	Igor YURIN		3/7/82	M	15	(11)	1
9	Nurbol ZHUMASKALIYEV		11/5/81	M	32		15

FC ZHETYSU TALDYKORGAN

Coach – Voit Talgayev; (11/9/10) Askhat Kozhabergenov

Founded – 1981

Stadium – Zhetysu (4,000)

2010

28/3	Kairat	a	3-0	*Belić 2, Perić*
3/4	Aktobe	h	0-1	
9/4	Okzhetpes	a	0-0	
15/4	Tobol	h	0-0	
20/4	Irtysh	a	0-1	
25/4	Akzhaiyk	h	2-1	*Belić, Dosmanbetov*
28/4	Shakhter	h	0-0	
1/5	Taraz	a	2-2	*Belić, Dosmanbetov*
7/5	Ordabasy	h	0-0	
12/5	Atyrau	a	2-1	*Muzhikov, Perić*
20/5	Lokomotiv	h	1-0	*Muzhikov*
25/5	Kairat	h	1-0	*Kostyuk (p)*
30/5	Aktobe	a	1-2	*Muzhikov*
8/6	Okzhetpes	h	2-2	*Kostyuk (p), Belić*
13/6	Tobol	a	1-0	*Yakovlev*
17/6	Irtysh	h	0-0	
22/6	Akzhaiyk	a	2-0	*Tshetkin 2*
27/6	Taraz	h	1-0	*Belić (p)*
18/7	Ordabasy	a	1-2	*Tshetkin*
25/7	Atyrau	h	1-2	*Tshetkin*
1/8	Lokomotiv	a	0-1	
14/8	Shakhter	a	2-1	*Muzhikov 2*
22/8	Okzhetpes	h	0-0	
11/9	Ordabasy	h	0-2	
17/9	Kairat	a	1-0	*Belić*
22/9	Taraz	h	2-3	*Dosmanbetov, Tshetkin*
30/9	Akzhaiyk	a	3-0	*Muzhikov, Tshetkin, Bayzhanov*
15/10	Ordabasy	a	1-1	*Cvetković*
22/10	Kairat	h	2-0	*Tshetkin, Belić*
27/10	Taraz	a	1-1	*Belić*
1/11	Akzhaiyk	h	4-2	*Belić 4 (2p)*
6/11	Okzhetpes	a	0-1	

No	Name	Nat	DoB	Pos	Aps	(s)	Gls
7	Maksat BAYZHANOV		6/8/84	M	13		1
13	Danilo BELIĆ	SRB	10/11/80	A	28	(2)	13
27	Josip BONACIN	CRO	2/7/84	D	17		
31	Ivan CVETKOVIĆ	SRB	12/2/81	M	14		1
10	Serik DOSMANBETOV		8/3/82	M	11	(14)	3

	Ilya FOMICHEV		14/4/82	D	11	(10)	
3	Zakhar KOROBOV		18/5/88	D	20	(3)	
	Sergei KOSTYUK		30/11/78	M	19	(4)	2
4	Viktor KOVALEV		25/8/80	D	19	(5)	
	Aydar KUMISBEKOV		9/2/79	D	32		
2	Vladimir LOGINOSKIY		8/10/85	G	3	(2)	
9	Aset MENLIKHOZHA		13/3/89	M	9	(1)	
	MUHARREM Uz	TUR	10/12/80	M	1	(3)	
5	Ruslan MUKHAMEDZHANOV		25/1/89	M	9	(4)	
	Serikzhan MUZHIKOV		17/6/89	M	27	(2)	6
4	Askhat MYNBAYEV		21/2/91	D		(2)	
3	Dmitriy PARKHACEV		2/1/85	A	7	(5)	
55	Ivan PERIĆ	SRB	5/5/82	A	14	(1)	2
2	Denis RODIONOV		26/7/85	M	7	(3)	
12	Talgat SABALAKOV		9/7/86	A		(3)	
8	Sauyat SARIYEV		15/10/92	M	1	(3)	
	Ruslan SOLYANYK	UKR	8/8/84	D	17	(1)	
6	Sergei STEPANENKO		25/1/81	G	27		
1	Aleksei TSHETKIN		21/5/91	A	17	(5)	7
7	Vladimir YAKOVLEV		2/8/84	D	26	(1)	1
37	Asan ZAMANBEKYLY		24/1/93	M		(1)	
8	Malik ZHANTLEYOV		2/2/89	M	1	(9)	
	Andrei ZVETKOV		20/3/80	G	2		

TOP GOALSCORERS 2010

16	Ulugbek BAKAYEV (Tobol)
15	Georgi DASKALOV (Irtysh)
	Nurbol ZHUMASKALIYEV (Tobol)
14	Moses SAKYI (Akzhaiyk)
13	Danilo BELIĆ (Zhetysu)
11	Igor BUGAIOV (Lokomotiv)
10	Murat TLESHEV (Aktobe)
9	Samat SMAKOV (Aktobe)
	Gleb MALTSEV (Irtysh)
8	Daurenbek TAZHIMBETOV (Ordabasy)
	Aldin ĐIDIĆ (Shakhter)
	Andrei FINONCHENKO (Shakhter)

PROMOTED CLUBS

FC VOSTOK OSKEMEN

Coach – Vakhid Masudov

Founded – 1963

Stadium – Vostok (8,500)

MAJOR HONOURS: Kazakhstan Cup – (1) 1994.

FC KAYSAR KYZYLORDA

Coach – Vladimir Linchevskiy

Founded – 1968

Stadium – Gany Muratbayev (7,300)

MAJOR HONOURS: Kazakhstan Cup – (1) 1999.

SECOND LEVEL FINAL TABLE 2010

		Pld	W	D	L	F	A	Pts
1	FC Vostok Oskemen	34	27	6	1	91	15	87
2	FC Kaysar Kyzylorda	34	25	6	3	74	23	81
3	FC Sunkar Kaskelen	34	22	7	5	73	28	73
4	FC Spartak Semey	34	19	7	8	68	40	64
5	FC Ilie-Saulet Almatinskaya oblast	34	18	9	7	73	38	63
6	FC Zesna Almaty	34	18	5	11	56	34	59
7	FC Kazakhmys	34	17	6	11	80	45	57
8	FC Ekibastuz	34	14	9	11	44	37	51
9	FC Ak Bulak Talgar	34	14	9	11	48	39	51
10	FC Kyzylzhar Petropavlovsk	34	14	4	16	44	57	46
11	FC Lashyn Taraz	34	12	8	14	46	54	44
12	FC Aktobe-Jas	34	13	4	17	40	66	43
13	FC Gefest Karagandy	34	12	2	20	52	83	38
14	FC Bolat Temirtau	34	10	8	16	44	58	38
15	FC Astana	34	9	4	21	41	75	28
16	FC Kaspiy Aktau	34	5	5	24	40	79	20
17	FC CSKA Almaty	34	5	3	26	32	76	18
18	FC Asbest Zhitikara	34	0	2	32	11	110	2

NB FC Astana – 3 pts deducted; FC Asbest Zhitikara withdrew after round 17 – their remaining matches were awarded as 0-3 defeats.

DOMESTIC CUP 2010

KUBOK KAZAKHSTANA

THIRD ROUND

(16/5/10)
Atyrau 0, Okzhetpes 2
Gefest 0, Shakhter Karagandy 4
Lashyn 0, Aktobe 2
Ordabasy 5, Akzhaiyk 0
Taraz 1, Irtysh 0
Vostok 1, Tobol 2
Zesna 0, Lokomotiv Astana 3
Zhetysu 1, Kairat 0

QUARTER-FINALS

(26/9/10)
Lokomotiv Astana 1 *(Bugaiov 39)*, Taraz 0
Shakhter Karagandy 2 *(Suchkov 68, Finonchenko 76)*, Aktobe 1 *(Khairullin 52)*
Tobol 1 *(Akhanov 7)*, Ordabasy 4 *(Zholdasov 26, Tazhimbetov 48, 56, Vagner 71)*
Zhetysu 3 *(Tshetkin 30, 31, Kostyuk 51)*, Atyrau 0

SEMI-FINALS

(19/10/10 & 10/11/10)
Shakhter Karagandy 0, Ordabasy 1 *(Trajković 62)*
Ordabasy 1 *(Trajković 12p)*, Shakhter Karagandy 2 *(Finonchenko 34, Bogdanov 88)*
(2-2; Shakhter Karagandy on away goals)

Zhetysu 0, Lokomotiv Astana 1 *(Bugaiov 51p)*
Lokomotiv Astana 1 *(Bugaiov 24)*, Zhetysu 0
(Lokomotiv Astana 2-0)

FINAL

(14/11/10)
Astana Arena, Astana
FC LOKOMOTIV ASTANA 1 *(Rozhkov 35)*
FC SHAKHTER KARAGANDY 0
Referee – *Khisamutdinov*
LOKOMOTIV ASTANA – *Belkin, Samchenko, Nurdauletov, Rozhkov, Kirov, Gurman (Dautov 90+2), Shakhmetov, Pakholyuk (Ostapenko 81), Andronic (Bozinovski 89), Azovski, Bugaiov.*
SHAKHTER KARAGANDY – *Grigorenko, Kislitsyn, Kozulin, Rudenko, Đorđević, Pikalkin, Shaff, Finonchenko, Vičius (Džidić 69), Bogdanov, Mulisa.*

CLUB COMMUNICATION 2011

FC Aktobe
56, Abylkhair-khan Av.
KZ-30019 Aktobe

Tel +7 7132 550 078
Fax +7 7132 570 953
Web fc-aktobe.kz
Email fk-aktobe@mail.ru
Media Officer Marat Jumabayev

FC Astana
office 2, 11 Kabanbay batyr str. BE-3
KZ-10000 Astana

Tel +7 7172 689 074
Fax +7 7172 689 074
Web fca.kz
Email fcastana@list.ru
Media Officer Zhamalleil Tangiev

FC Atyrau
Auezov Avenue 28a, stadium
"Sudoremontnik", Balykshy, KZ-060014 Atyrau

Tel +7 7122 244 547
Fax +7 7122 244 350
Web rfcatyrau.kz
Email fc_atyrau@mail.ru
Media Officer Altynbek Nsangaliyev

FC Irtysh Pavlodar
Lunacharsky street 50
KZ-140003 Pavlodar

Tel +7 7182 619 166
Fax +7 7182 619 143
Web fcirtysh.kz
Email irtysh-fc@mail.ru
Media Officer Aleksandr Prasolenko

FC Kairat Almaty
Abay ave, 48, Shevchenko str., 118, office 128, 130, KZ-50022 Almaty

Tel +7 7272 390 700
Fax +7 7272 390 700
Web fckairat.kz
Email fckairat@mail.ru
Media Officer Askat Zhakayev

FC Kaysar Kyzylorda
Zheltoksan street 162, Muratbayev str, 1
KZ-467021 Kyzylorda

Tel +7 7242 270 619
Fax +7 7242 270 619
Web fc-kaysar.kz
Email fc_kaysar@rambler.ru
Media Officer Sergel Neudachin

FC Ordabasy Shymkent
Madely Kozha street, 1.
KZ-160000 Shymkent

Tel +7 7252 222 390
Fax +7 7252 314 490
Web fcordabasy.kz
Email pfk_ordabasy@mail.ru
Media Officer Iliyas Zholdas

FC Shakhter Karagandy
Kazakhstanskaya Street 1
KZ-100019 Karagandy

Tel +7 7212 411 831
Fax +7 7212 411 831
Web shahter.kz
Email shahter56@mail.ru
Media Officer Sergei Kikolenko

FC Taraz
Abay Str. 113
KZ-080000 Taraz

Tel +7 7262 431 092
Fax +7 7262 457 146
Web fctaraz.kz
Email fc_taraz@mail.ru
Media Officer Zhanna Nuspekova

FC Tobol Kostanay
1 May str. 153
KZ-110000 Kostanay

Tel +7 7142 578 582
Fax +7 7142 578 582
Web fc-tobol.kz
Email fc-tobol@mail.ru
Media Officer Sairan Bupezhanov

FC Vostok Oskemen
Gagarin Ave 1
KZ-070018 Oskemen

Tel +7 7232 772 841
Fax +7 7232 772 841
Web fc-vostok.kz
Email fkvostok@list.ru
Media Officer Renat Suurov

FC Zhetysu Taldykorgan
Kabanbay-Batyr Street 88/90
KZ-040000 Taldykorgan

Tel +7 7282 244 450
Fax +7 7282 247 977
Web fc-zhetisu.kz
Email pfc_zhetisu@mail.ru
Media Officer Yuriy Pak

LATVIA

Lettonie I Lettland

Latvijas Futbola Federācija (LFF)

COMMUNICATION

Address	Olympic Sports Centre Grostonas Street 6b LV-1013 Rīga	**President**	Guntis Indriksons
		General Secretary	Jānis Mežeckis
		Media Officer	Martins Hartmanis
Tel	+371 67 292988	**Year of Formation**	1921
Fax	+371 67 315604		
E-mail	futbols@lff.lv	**National Stadium**	Skonto, Riga (9,500)
Website	lff.lv		

DOMESTIC COMPETITION SUMMARY 2010/11

VIRSLĪGA FINAL TABLE

			Home					Away					Total						
		Pld	W	D	L	F	A	W	D	L	F	A	W	D	L	F	A	Pts	Comp
1	Skonto FC	27	11	2	1	48	8	11	1	1	38	8	22	3	2	86	16	69	UCL
2	FK Ventspils	27	11	1	2	37	10	9	2	2	31	8	20	3	4	68	18	63	UEL
3	SK Liepājas Metalurgs	27	8	2	4	33	9	11	2	0	37	11	19	4	4	70	20	61	UEL
4	FC Daugava Daugavpils	27	10	3	1	21	6	6	5	2	14	10	16	8	3	35	16	56	UEL
5	FK Jūrmala-VV	27	2	3	9	10	27	6	1	6	20	18	8	4	15	30	45	28	
6	FK Jelgava	27	5	2	7	25	23	1	5	7	11	22	6	7	14	36	45	25	
7	SK Blāzma Rēzekne	27	4	2	7	16	28	3	1	10	11	29	7	3	17	27	57	24	
8	JFK Olimps/RFS	27	2	2	8	8	24	3	4	8	23	39	5	6	16	31	63	21	
9	FC Tranzit	27	2	3	8	11	32	3	1	10	6	24	5	4	18	17	56	19	*Relegated*
10	FK Jaunība Rīga	27	1	3	9	7	33	3	1	10	9	47	4	4	19	16	80	16	*Relegated*

Top Scorer Deniss Rakeļs (Liepājas Metalurgs) & Júnior (Skonto), 18 goals

Promoted Clubs FB Gulbene 2005
FC Jūrmala

Cup Final FK Ventspils 3, SK Liepājas Metalurgs 1

Starkovs restores Skonto to summit

Reappointed as head coach of Skonto FC in January 2010, Aleksandrs Starkovs, the man responsible for the majority of the club's 14 successive domestic titles from 1991-2004, rediscovered his magic touch to end the Riga outfit's six-year wait for the Virslīga title.

It was no coincidence that Skonto's return to power should come in the year that Starkovs decided to supplement his duties as Latvian national team coach with a second stint at his former club. His impact was immediate. Skonto powered out of the blocks, collecting maximum points from their opening seven matches and scoring an average of four goals a game. Although chief rivals SK Liepājas Metalurgs and FK Ventspils ended their barnstorming run, Skonto's momentum was unchecked and they continued to pile up the high-scoring victories.

Rivals defeated

Wins over both Liepājas Metalurgs and Ventspils in the middle third of the 27-match campaign reinforced Skonto's position, and after defeating the former again, they headed into their penultimate fixture, at home to Ventspils, with a six-point lead. One point was all they required to take the Virslīga title for the 15th time, and they duly achieved it, twice coming from behind to claim a 2-2 draw. A week later they celebrated with a 6-0 thrashing of bottom-of-the-table FK Jaunība Riga. Three of the goals came from Brazilian defender-turned-striker Júnior, who thus took his tally for the season to 18 and claimed a share of the Virslīga Golden Boot with Liepājas Metalurgs' teenage scoring sensation Deniss Rakeļs.

Skonto's end-of-season statistics were impressive. They won 22 matches and scored 86 goals while conceding only 16. There was a collective spirit in the camp that warded against complacency, and in players such as Andrejs Pereplotkins, Aleksandrs Cauņa, Vitālijs Smirnovs, Daniils Turkovs and Latvian international veterans Vitālijs Astafjevs and Juris Laizāns they possessed individuals who could make the difference whenever Skonto's superiority was under threat.

The return of the title to Riga was a blow to the region of Kurzeme, home to both Liepājas Metalurgs and Ventspils. The two teams started and finished the season with foreign coaches, although Rüdiger Abramczik (Liepājas Metalurgs) and Nunzio Zavettieri (Ventspils) both left at the close of the campaign. Consequently there were new men in place when the two rivals met in the 2011 Latvian Cup final. It was Ventspils' new boss, Russian Sergei Podpaliy, who emerged victorious over his counterpart Vladimirs Osipovs as the club collected the trophy for the fifth time with a 3-1 victory.

Play-off declined

Skonto's Cup run ended at the quarter-final stage with a penalty shoot-out defeat by FC Daugava Daugavpils, the only team to have beaten them in Riga during the league campaign. Appearing in the

Latvia head coach Aleksandrs Starkovs led Skonto to the Virslīga title

National Team

International Tournament Appearances – UEFA European Championship – (1) 2004.

Top Five All-time Caps – Vitālijs Astafjevs (167); Andrejs Rubins (115); Juris Laizāns (108); Imants Bleidelis (106); Mihails Zemļinskis (105)

Top Five All-time Goals – Māris Verpakovskis (28); Eriks Petersons (24); Vitālijs Astafjevs (16); Juris Laizāns & Marians Pahars (15)

2010 Virslīga as specially invited guests, Daugava did well to finish fourth and qualify for Europe. Indeed they managed twice as many points as the team directly below them, FK Jūrmala-VV. FC Tranzit were relegated alongside Jaunība but only after they declined a play-off with second level runners-up FC Jūrmala. Top spot in the 1. līga went to FB Gulbene 2005, who celebrated their fifth anniversary by winning 21 of their 22 matches and drawing the other.

All four Latvian teams exited the 2010/11 European club competitions at the first attempt, including Skonto, who surprisingly lost at home to Portadown FC. Starkovs fared little better on the international stage with Latvia as the team picked up just four points from six UEFA EURO 2012 qualifiers, thereby ensuring that there would be no reappearance on European football's grandest stage for the coach and his team eight years after their unexpected appearance in Portugal.

As Astafjevs finally called it a day with a European-record haul of 167 caps, the emergence at international level of Skonto midfielder Cauņa and Virslīga Player of the Year Jurijs Žigajevs offered encouragement for the future, and there were successes at foreign clubs for other Latvian internationals. Striker Artjoms Rudņevs scored four goals for KKS Lech Poznań against Juventus in the UEFA Europa League, while goalkeeper Andris Vaņins won the Swiss Cup with FC Sion and national team skipper Kaspars Gorkšs, the 2010 Latvian Footballer of the Year, earned promotion to the English Premier League with Queens Park Rangers FC.

NATIONAL TEAM RESULTS 2010/11

11/8/10	Czech Republic	A	Liberec	1-4	*Cauņa (90)*
3/9/10	Croatia (ECQ)	H	Riga	0-3	
7/9/10	Malta (ECQ)	A	Ta' Qali	2-0	*Gorkšs (43), Verpakovskis (85)*
8/10/10	Greece (ECQ)	A	Piraeus	0-1	
12/10/10	Georgia (ECQ)	H	Riga	1-1	*Cauņa (90+1)*
17/11/10	China	A	Kunming	0-1	
9/2/11	Bolivia	N	Antalya (TUR)	2-1	*Verpakovskis (42p), Cauņa (51p)*
26/3/11	Israel (ECQ)	A	Tel-Aviv	1-2	*Gorkšs (62)*
4/6/11	Israel (ECQ)	H	Riga	1-2	*Cauņa (62p)*
7/6/11	Austria	A	Graz	1-3	*Mihadjuks (49)*

NATIONAL TEAM APPEARANCES 2010/11

Coach – Aleksandrs STARKOVS	**26/7/55**		**Cze**	**CRO**	**MLT**	**GRE**	**GEO**	**Chn**	**Bol**	**ISR**	**ISR**	**Aut**	**Caps**	**Goals**
Andris VAŅINS	30/4/80	Sion (SUI)	G	G	G	G	G		G	G	G	G	40	-
												93*		
Oskars KĻAVA	8/8/83	Anzhi (RUS)	D	D	D	D	D		D		D	D	48	1
												97*		
Kaspars GORKŠS	6/11/81	QPR (ENG)	D	D	D	D	D		D	D	D		38	4
Deniss IVANOVS	11/1/84	Sivasspor (TUR)	D	D	D	D	D			D	D	D	43	2
Pāvels MIHADJUKS	27/5/80	Liepājas Metalurgs	D	D	D			D				D	11	1
												88*		
Andrejs PEREPĻOTKINS	27/12/84	Skonto	M74		s92	s82	s86	M88						
		/Nasaf Qarshi (UZB)							s71	s57	M60	s71	32	3
Juris LAIZĀNS	6/1/79	Salyut Belgorod (RUS)	M59	M87	M	M82	M82						108	15
Maksims RAFAĻSKIS	14/5/84	Liepājas Metalurgs	M80	M	M82			M71	M					
		/Baltika (RUS)								M58	M28		13	-
Andrejs RUBINS	26/11/78	Qarabağ (AZE)	M46	M85	M	M65	M		M71	M57			115	10
Māris VERPAKOVSKIS	15/10/79	Ergotelis (GRE)	A70	A	A92	A			A67	A73			86	28
Ģirts KARLSONS	7/6/81	İnter Bakı (AZE)	A59	A63	s70	s73			s78				49	9

NATIONAL TEAM APPEARANCES 2010/11(contd.)

			Cze	CRO	MLT	GRE	GEO	Chn	Bol	ISR	ISR	Aut	Caps	Goal
Jurijs ŽIGAJEVS	14/11/85	Ventspils /Widzew (POL)	s46	s85		s65	M86	M90		s58	s28	M86	24	1
Aleksandrs CAUŅA	19/1/88	Skonto /CSKA Moskva (RUS)	s59	M	M	M	M		M		M	M79	24	6
Artis LAZDIŅŠ	3/5/86	Jelgava	s59					M90	M	M	M	M	7	-
Kristaps GREBIS	13/12/80	Liepājas Metalurgs	s70				s82						13	2
Genādijs SOLOŅICINS	3/1/80	Liepājas Metalurgs	s74										44	1
Aleksandrs FERTOVS	16/6/87	Skonto	s80					M82					5	-
Artjoms RUDŅEVS	13/1/88	Lech (POL)		s63	A70	A73	A		A78	A	A	A93	12	-
Vitālijs ASTAFJEVS	3/4/71	Skonto		s87	s82	M	M	s71					167	16
Dzintars ZIRNIS	25/4/77	Liepājas Metalurgs				D	D	D					68	-
Deniss ROMANOVS	2/9/78	Xäzär Länkäran (AZE) /Cendrawasih (IDN)						G				s93	5	-
Ritus KRJAUKLIS	23/4/86	Ventspils /Olimpik-Şüvälan (AZE)						D	D	D	D	D	12	-
Vitālijs SMIRNOVS	28/6/86	Skonto						D	D				2	-
Daniils TURKOVS	17/2/88	Skonto /ZTE (HUN)						A77	s67	s73		s86	4	-
Vladislavs KOZLOVS	30/11/87	Jelgava						s77					1	-
Andrejs KOVAĻOVS	23/3/89	Daugava Daugavpils						s82					1	-
Ritvars RUGINS	17/10/89	Ventspils						s88			s71	M	3	-
Vladimirs BESPALOVS	22/6/88	Ventspils						s90					1	-
Kaspars DUBRA	20/12/90	Skonto						s90					1	-
Deniss KAČANOVS	27/11/79	Skonto								D			29	-
Ivans LUKJANOVS	24/1/87	Lechia Gdańsk (POL)								M			2	-
Aleksejs VIŠŅAKOVS	3/2/84	Cracovia (POL)									M71		36	5
Edgaars GAURAČS	10/3/88	Yenisey Krasnoyarsk (RUS)									s60	A71	2	-
Igors TARASOVS	16/1/88	Skonto										s79	2	-

CLUB-BY-CLUB

SK BLĀZMA RĒZEKNE

Coach – Eriks Grigjans
Founded – 2004
Stadium – RSP (2,000)

2010

10/4	Liepājas Metalurgs	a	0-4	
17/4	Jaunība	a	1-0	*Volkovs (p)*
24/4	Daugava	h	3-1	*Ryzhevskiy, Osipovs, Volkovs (p)*
1/5	Ventspils	a	0-1	
8/5	Skonto	h	1-3	*Volkovs (p)*
15/5	Olimps/RFS	h	2-0	*Ryzhevskiy, Osipovs*
29/5	Jelgava	a	0-4	
5/6	Tranzit	a	1-3	*Volkovs*
12/6	Jūrmala-VV	h	0-4	
26/6	Liepājas Metalurgs	h	1-4	*Vaskov*
3/7	Jaunība	h	1-2	*Vaskov*
9/7	Ventspils	h	0-5	
25/7	Daugava	a	0-2	
7/8	Olimps/RFS	a	1-2	*Kuzmickis*
14/8	Jelgava	h	0-0	
22/8	Skonto	a	0-6	
28/8	Tranzit	h	2-0	*Adamenoks, Ryzhevskiy (p)*
12/9	Jūrmala-VV	a	0-0	
15/9	Liepājas Metalurgs	h	2-3	*Silagailis, Silovs*
19/9	Ventspils	a	0-2	
23/9	Skonto	h	1-4	*Sokoļskis*
2/10	Tranzit	a	3-0	*Sokoļskis, Ryzhevskiy, Silovs*
17/10	Olimps/RFS	h	1-1	*Ryzhevskiy*
23/10	Jaunība	a	4-0	*Silagailis, Ryzhevskiy 3*
27/10	Jelgava	a	0-2	
31/10	Jūrmala-VV	h	2-1	*Silagailis 2*
7/11	Daugava	a	1-3	*Silagailis*

No	Name	Nat	DoB	Pos	Aps	(s)	Gls
22	Jevgenijs ADAMENOKS		15/4/90	D	12	(1)	1
2	Dmitrijs HALVITOVS		3/4/86	D	14		
88,9	Vadims JAVOIŠS		19/4/84	D	15		
6	Valdis KAĻVA		3/4/91	D	16	(1)	
3	Ilja KIRILOVS		12/1/85	D	5	(3)	
14	Edgars KLEINS		14/2/90	D	10	(11)	
7	Vjačeslavs KONDAKOVS		1/1/80	M	12		
5	Ervīns KRAINIS		19/2/85	M	20	(5)	
11	Deniss KUZMICKIS		8/7/90	M	4	(3)	1
24	Ritvars LINUŽS		16/8/92	M	1		
2	Rolands LUBGĀNS		7/6/91	M		(1)	
1	Vitālijs MEĻNIČENKO		11/11/87	G	14		
11	Go NAGAOKA	JPN	23/5/84	M	9	(5)	
15	Artis NOVICKIS		9/11/86	M	2	(8)	
7	Artjoms OSIPOVS		8/1/89	A	8		2
17	Māris RANCĀNS		21/9/86	M	20	(3)	
27	Otto RIHTERS		15/5/92	M		(3)	
23	Pavel RYZHEVSKIY	BLR	3/3/81	A	26		8
12	Aigars SELECKIS		13/5/92	G	8		
10	Guntars SILAGAILIS		31/8/84	A	10		5
21	Dmitrijs SILOVS		7/6/85	A	10	(12)	2

	Deniss SOKOĻSKIS		25/8/81	D	21	(1)	2
0	Dmitrijs SUVOROVS		13/6/92	M	17	(6)	
	Artem VASKOV	BLR	21/10/88	M	11	(1)	2
	Edgars VJALKINS		17/2/94	M		(3)	
	Vladimirs VOLKOVS		10/8/84	A	13		4
1	Vitālijs VORONOVS		18/9/88	G	5	(1)	
	Vitaliy ZAYTSEV	RUS	13/5/91	M	14		

FC DAUGAVA DAUGAVPILS

Coach – Tamaz Pertia (GEO)

Founded – 1944

Stadium – Daugava (2,000)

MAJOR HONOURS: Latvian Cup – (1) 2008.

10

/4	Olimps/RFS	a	1-1	*Hong*
/4	Tranzit	a	1-0	*Jaliashvili*
/4	Blāzma	a	1-3	*Afanasjevs (p)*
5	Liepājas Metalurgs	h	1-1	*Ramazanov (p)*
5	Jaunība	a	1-1	*Poroshin*
/5	Ventspils	h	1-0	*Poroshin*
/5	Jūrmala-VV	a	1-0	*Ramazanov (p)*
6	Skonto	a	0-1	
/6	Jelgava	h	1-1	*Jaliashvili*
/6	Olimps/RFS	h	2-0	*Kovaļovs, Afanasjevs*
/6	Tranzit	h	2-0	*Poroshin, Ramazanov (p)*
7	Liepājas Metalurgs	a	1-0	*Ramazanov (p)*
5/7	Blāzma	h	2-0	*Gongadze, Afanasjevs*
'8	Ventspils	a	1-1	*Logins*
5/8	Jūrmala-VV	h	1-0	*Sokolovs (p)*
1/8	Jaunība	h	1-0	*Gongadze*
7/8	Skonto	h	1-1	*Kokins*
2/9	Jelgava	a	3-3	*Afanasjevs, Volkovs, Gongadze*
5/9	Jelgava	a	1-0	*Gongadze*
9/9	Jūrmala-VV	h	2-0	*Logins, Ziziļevs*
3/9	Jaunība	h	3-1	*Shelenkov, Kotyukov, Chikhradze*
/10	Liepājas Metalurgs	a	0-0	
7/10	Ventspils	h	0-1	
2/10	Skonto	a	1-0	*Logins*
7/10	Tranzit	h	1-0	*Gongadze*
1/10	Olimps/RFS	a	2-0	*Gongadze, Volkovs*
/11	Blāzma	h	3-1	*Kovaļovs, Kokins 2*

No	Name	Nat	DoB	Pos	Aps	(s)	Gls
9	Valērijs AFANASJEVS		20/9/82	M	27		4
	Giorgi CHIKHRADZE	GEO	4/8/87	D	21	(1)	1
2	Maksims DEŅISEVIČS		2/1/87	M		(3)	
21	Lionnel Franck DJIMGOU TCHOMBOU	CMR	27/3/87	A	1	(4)	
18	Ihor DUDNYK	UKR	9/8/85	M	2	(1)	
	Māris ELTERMANIS		16/10/81	G	27		
20	Mamuka GONGADZE	GEO	25/11/85	A	14		6
36	HONG Kum-song	PRK	3/1/90	M	3	(2)	1
10	Jemal JALIASHVILI	GEO	27/10/90	A	9	(3)	2
16	Māris JASVINS		8/1/94	D		(2)	
16	Eriks KOKINS		11/1/91	A	4	(11)	3
4	Pāvels KOĻCOVS		1/9/82	D	1		
4	Yuriy KOTYUKOV	RUS	21/4/90	M	9	(3)	1
6	Andrejs KOVAĻOVS		23/3/89	A	23	(2)	2
21	Aleksejs KUPLOVS-OGINSKIS		21/1/88	M	1	(1)	
30	Vadims LOGINS		30/12/81	D	24	(1)	3
10	Davit PAILODZE	GEO	19/3/90	M	2	(2)	
21	Andriy POROSHIN	UKR	30/7/78	D	6	(2)	3
3	Murad RAMAZANOV	RUS	10/3/79	M	7	(3)	4
21,10	Ričards RAŠČEVSKIS		2/4/92	M		(5)	
20	RI Myong-jun	PRK	16/8/90	A	7	(1)	
15	Yuriy SHELENKOV	RUS	6/6/81	M	22		1
22	Jevgenijs SIMONOVS		29/3/84	M	18		
11	Jurijs SOKOLOVS		12/9/83	M	27		1
5	Oļegs TIMOFEJEVS		28/11/88	M	15	(3)	
5,30,22	Vladimirs VOLKOVS		10/8/84	A	6	(6)	2
13	Vitālijs ZIĻS		19/8/87	A		(1)	
9	Mihails ZIZIĻEVS		27/12/73	M	21	(3)	1

FK JAUNĪBA RĪGA

Coach – Sergejs Davidovs

Founded – 2006

Stadium – Daugava (5,500)

2010

11/4	Tranzit	a	0-2	
17/4	Blāzma	h	0-1	
24/4	Liepājas Metalurgs	h	2-3	*Astrahancevs (p), Cigankovs*
1/5	Jūrmala-VV	a	1-0	*Cigankovs*
8/5	Daugava	h	1-1	*Astrahancevs (p)*
15/5	Skonto	a	0-7	
29/5	Ventspils	a	0-5	
6/6	Jelgava	a	1-4	*Cigankovs*
12/6	Olimps/RFS	h	0-9	
19/6	Tranzit	h	1-0	*Alijev*
3/7	Blāzma	a	2-1	*Magdilevičs, Cigankovs*
17/7	Jūrmala-VV	h	0-2	
24/7	Liepājas Metalurgs	a	0-4	
6/8	Skonto	h	0-3	
15/8	Ventspils	h	0-5	
21/8	Daugava	a	0-1	
28/8	Jelgava	h	1-1	*Astrahancevs (p)*
12/9	Olimps/RFS	a	2-2	*Savinovs Māris 2*
15/9	Jūrmala-VV	a	1-0	*Savinovs Māris*
19/9	Tranzit	h	0-1	
23/9	Daugava	a	1-3	*Hromovs*
2/10	Olimps/RFS	h	2-2	*Alijev, Kulikov*
17/10	Liepājas Metalurgs	a	0-8	
23/10	Blāzma	h	0-4	
27/10	Ventspils	a	1-4	*Astrahancevs (p)*
31/10	Jelgava	h	0-1	
7/11	Skonto	a	0-6	

No	Name	Nat	DoB	Pos	Aps	(s)	Gls
9	Rejal ALIJEV	EST	14/6/89	A	11	(8)	2
35	Antons ASTRAHANCEVS		28/7/86	G	24		4
14	Mihails CIGANKOVS		30/3/90	A	11		4
17	Viktors GOLOVIZINS		5/3/90	D	22		
20	Andrejs GUSEVS		5/7/90	M	6	(2)	
10	Deniss HROMOVS		26/10/85	M	26		1
20	Pāvels KOĻCOVS		1/9/82	D	14		
21	Jurijs KRASŅAKOVS		21/4/87	M	10	(5)	
6	Dmitri KULIKOV	EST	23/9/77	D	15	(1)	1
14	Aleksejs KUPLOVS-OGINSKIS		21/1/88	M	9		
1	Vladimirs LUKOŅINS		29/6/76	G	3	(3)	
7	Deniss MAGDILEVIČS		25/10/84	M	19	(3)	1
8	Oleg MAKSIMOV	EST	29/1/86	M	10		
3	Marks MOLČANOVS		15/5/92	M	17	(8)	
1	Jurijs NADEŽDINS		16/1/89	G		(1)	
11	Jurijs NADEŽDINS (same player)		16/1/89	A	2	(1)	
5	Pēteris NAGLA		2/5/79	D	17	(1)	
19	Filips PAVĻIKS		11/3/92	A		(1)	
2	Nikita PAVĻIKS		11/3/92	M	1	(5)	
18	Armands PRUTĀNS		6/6/89	A	8	(1)	
8	Mārcis SAVINOVS		3/5/87	D	3	(2)	
6	Māris SAVINOVS		3/5/87	D	10		3
13	Jānis SKRIBIS		19/8/76	M	19		
18	Ilja SOLOMATINS		13/10/90	A	5	(2)	
11	Alen STEPANYAN	EST	23/7/91	A	4	(9)	
4	Igors ŠKIRJATOVS		31/3/90	D	18	(4)	
15	Antons TRUŠEVS		4/7/84	D	13	(7)	

FK JELGAVA

Coach – Dainis Kazakevičs

Founded – 2004

Stadium – Ozolnieki (800)

MAJOR HONOURS: Latvian Cup – (1) 2010.

2010

10/4	Ventspils	h	1-2	*Kozlovs*
18/4	Skonto	a	1-4	*Redjko*
22/4	Jūrmala-VV	h	1-2	*Weiss*

2/5	Olimps/RFS	h	4-0	*Redjko, Malašenoks 3 (1p)*
8/5	Tranzit	a	1-1	*Bormakovs*
15/5	Liepājas Metalurgs	a	1-3	*Redjko*
30/5	Blāzma	h	4-0	*Malašenoks 3, Bogdaškins*
6/6	Jaunība	h	4-1	*Redjko (p), og (Skribis), Malašenoks, Bormakovs*
13/6	Daugava	a	1-1	*Bogdaškins*
25/6	Ventspils	a	1-2	*Malašenoks*
7/7	Olimps/RFS	h	1-2	*Kozlovs*
25/7	Jūrmala-VV	a	1-2	*Lapkovskis I.*
1/8	Skonto	h	0-5	
7/8	Liepājas Metalurgs	h	1-2	*Redjko*
14/8	Blāzma	a	0-0	
22/8	Tranzit	h	2-1	*Malašenoks 2*
28/8	Jaunība	a	1-1	*Savčenkovs*
12/9	Daugava	h	3-3	*Kozlovs 3*
15/9	Daugava	h	0-1	
19/9	Liepājas Metalurgs	a	0-3	
26/9	Ventspils	h	2-4	*Hohlovs, Bogdaškins*
1/10	Skonto	a	1-2	*Bogdaškins*
17/10	Tranzit	h	0-0	
23/10	Olimps/RFS	a	1-2	*Gubins*
27/10	Blāzma	h	2-0	*Redjko (p), Savčenkovs*
31/10	Jaunība	a	1-0	*Kozlovs*
7/11	Jūrmala-VV	a	1-1	*Malašenoks*

No	Name	Nat	DoB	Pos	Aps	(s)	Gls
9	Aleksejs BESPALOVS		4/12/85	M		(1)	
81	Marks BOGDANOVS		2/12/86	G	27		
32	Boriss BOGDAŠKINS		21/12/90	M	20	(6)	4
12	Dmitrijs BORISOVS		20/12/87	A		(5)	
6	Pāvels BORMAKOVS		1/9/77	M	10	(2)	2
77	Aleksandrs GUBINS		16/5/88	D	26		1
89	Pāvels HOHLOVS		19/12/89	M	9	(5)	1
4	Oļegs IVAŅICA		6/9/87	M	3	(1)	
44	Jevgenijs KAZURA		24/1/88	D	22	(1)	
10	Aivars KERIS		2/4/85	M	4	(5)	
21	Vladislavs KOZLOVS		30/11/87	A	22	(3)	6
17	Igors LAPKOVSKIS		24/2/87	M	17	(4)	1
5	Vitālijs LAPKOVSKIS		7/11/83	D	17		
22	Artis LAZDIŅŠ		3/5/86	M	24		
99	Oļegs MALAŠENOKS		27/4/86	A	23		11
3	Eduards MARTINS		3/2/92	M		(1)	
20	Dmitrijs MEDECKIS		24/3/85	M	14	(8)	
8	Eriks PELCIS		25/6/78	A	1	(8)	
19	Vitālijs PETKEVIČS		24/7/88	D	5	(7)	
7	Valērijs REDJKO		10/3/83	M	26		6
11	Viktors REZJAPKINS		6/1/78	M	1	(4)	
25	Igors SAVČENKOVS		3/11/82	D	11		2
69	Mārcis SAVINOVS		3/5/87	D	3	(2)	
18	Māris SAVINOVS		3/5/87	D	2	(1)	
14	Jumpei SHINMURA	JPN	13/10/88	M	7	(3)	
23	Nathaniel WEISS	USA	16/7/87	M	3	(8)	1
12	Jaroslavs ZORICOVS		1/4/90	M		(2)	

FK JŪRMALA-VV

Coach – Vladimirs Babičevs

Founded – 2003

Stadium – Sloka (2,000)

2010

11/4	Skonto	a	2-4	*Melnyk, Bezzubovs*
18/4	Liepājas Metalurgs	h	1-2	*Kalniņš*
22/4	Jelgava	a	2-1	*Kalniņš, Matsion*
1/5	Jaunība	h	0-1	
8/5	Olimps/RFS	a	2-0	*Zuntners 2 (2p)*
15/5	Tranzit	a	1-1	*Paplavskis*
29/5	Daugava	h	0-1	
2/6	Ventspils	h	1-4	*Paplavskis*
12/6	Blāzma	a	4-0	*Bezzubovs, Zuntners, Kalniņš, Čistjakovs*
22/6	Skonto	h	0-4	
30/6	Liepājas Metalurgs	a	2-1	*Bezzubovs (p), Semjonovs*
17/7	Jaunība	a	2-0	*og (Maksimov), Jermolajevs*
25/7	Jelgava	h	2-1	*Kalniņš, Semjonovs*
8/8	Tranzit	h	2-1	*Kalniņš, Paplavskis*
15/8	Daugava	a	0-1	
21/8	Olimps/RFS	h	2-2	*Krjauklis 2*
27/8	Ventspils	a	0-1	
12/9	Blāzma	h	0-0	
15/9	Jaunība Riga	h	0-1	
19/9	Daugava	a	0-2	
23/9	Liepājas Metalurgs	h	1-4	*Zuntners (p)*
2/10	Ventspils	a	1-3	*Žatkins*
17/10	Skonto	h	0-2	
23/10	Tranzit	a	3-2	*Stepanovs, Žatkins, Čistjakovs*
27/10	Olimps/RFS	h	0-3	
31/10	Blāzma	a	1-2	*Matsion*
7/11	Jelgava	h	1-1	*Kalniņš*

No	Name	Nat	DoB	Pos	Aps	(s)	Gl
8	Ruslans AGAFONOVS		18/4/89	M	4	(1)	
16	Georgs ATVARS		16/9/66	G	1		
18	Alberts BARBALIS		5/3/88	D	9	(3)	
8	Romans BEZZUBOVS		15/5/79	M	10	(1)	3
1	Artūrs BIEZAIS		8/11/86	G	24		
14	Valērijs ČISTJAKOVS		27/11/92	M	8	(7)	2
3	Sergejs GOLUBEVS		24/2/85	D	24	(1)	
2,12	Vitālijs JAGODINSKIS		28/2/92	M	18		
22	Edgars JERMOLAJEVS		16/1/92	M	4	(10)	1
2,23	Gatis KALNIŅŠ		12/8/81	A	22	(1)	6
5	Maksims KOLOKOĻENKINS		30/1/84	M	3	(2)	
19	Rolands KRJAUKLIS		17/10/82	M	24		2
6	Kostyantyn MATSION	UKR	9/2/82	M	23		2
7	Volodymyr MELNYK	UKR	21/11/79	M	21	(2)	1
17	Roman NAGUMANOV	RUS	5/6/85	A	9		
20	Dmitrijs PAPLAVSKIS		10/4/88	M	14	(8)	3
12	Mihails POĻAKOVS		16/5/83	D		(1)	
9	Igors SEMJONOVS		3/7/85	M	8	(2)	2
16	Igors SERKOVS		17/4/92	G	2	(1)	
4	Igors STEPANOVS		21/1/76	D	22	(1)	1
5	Ingus ŠLAMPE		31/1/89	M	7		
17	Vladislav TŠURILKIN	EST	30/5/89	M		(2)	
11	Aleksandrs ZEŅKOVS		23/10/88	A	2	(8)	
18,24	Mareks ZUNTNERS		13/2/83	A	18	(3)	4
10	Oļegs ŽATKINS		13/4/87	A	20	(6)	2

SK LIEPĀJAS METALURGS

Coach – Rüdiger Abramczik (GER)

Founded – 1997

Stadium – Daugava (6,000)

MAJOR HONOURS: Latvian League – (2) 2005, 2009; Latvian Cup – (1) 2006.

2010

10/4	Blāzma	h	4-0	*Rakeļs 2, Spasojević, Grebis*
18/4	Jūrmala-VV	a	2-1	*Rakeļs 2*
24/4	Jaunība	a	3-2	*Kavaliauskas, Kalns, Jemeļins*
1/5	Daugava	a	1-1	*Jemeļins (p)*
9/5	Ventspils	h	0-0	
15/5	Jelgava	h	3-1	*Kavaliauskas, Rakeļs, Grebis*
29/5	Skonto	a	0-0	
2/6	Olimps/RFS	a	3-0	*Rakeļs, Kavaliauskas, Spasojević*
12/6	Tranzit	h	2-0	*Grebis, Spasojević*
26/6	Blāzma	a	4-1	*Rakeļs 2, Kavaliauskas, Spasojević (p)*
30/6	Jūrmala-VV	h	1-2	*og (Kalniņš)*
8/7	Daugava	h	0-1	
24/7	Jaunība	h	4-0	*Kalns, Puljiz 2, Grebis*
7/8	Jelgava	a	2-1	*Rakeļs, Jhonnes*
15/8	Skonto	h	1-2	*Kalns (p)*
22/8	Ventspils	a	4-2	*Grebis 2, Akahoshi, Kalns*
27/8	Olimps/RFS	h	4-0	*Grebis, Rakeļs, Kavaliauskas 2*
12/9	Tranzit	a	4-0	*Rakeļs, Jhonnes, Mihadjuks, og (Barinovs V.)*
15/9	Blāzma	a	3-2	*Rakeļs, Grebis 2*
19/9	Jelgava	h	3-0	*Jemeļins, Rakeļs, Akahoshi*
23/9	Jūrmala-VV	a	4-1	*Prohorenkovs, og (Matsion), Grebis (p), Kirhners*

0	Daugava	h	0-0	
/10	Jaunība	h	8-0	*Prohorenkovs, Akahoshi 2, Grebis 2, Kavaliauskas, Rakeļs 2*
/10	Ventspils	a	1-0	*Akahoshi*
/10	Skonto	h	1-2	*Rakeļs*
/10	Tranzit	a	6-0	*Jemeļins (p), Rakeļs 2, Kavaliauskas 2, Golovins*
11	Olimps/RFS	h	2-1	*Akahoshi, Jemeļins (p)*

o	Name	Nat	DoB	Pos	Aps	(s)	Gls
	Takafumi AKAHOSHI	JPN	27/5/86	M	15		6
	Igors AĻEKSEJEVS		31/7/88	M	8	(4)	
	Jevgenijs GOLOVINS		6/3/89	M	4	(3)	1
	Kristaps GREBIS		13/12/80	A	16	(7)	12
3	Antons JEMEĻINS		19/2/84	D	16	(2)	5
	JHONNES Marques de Souza	BRA	22/4/84	D	8		2
5	Jurģis KALNS		5/10/82	A	27		4
2	Vladimirs KAMEŠS		28/10/88	A		(1)	
	Vitalijus KAVALIAUSKAS	LTU	2/7/83	A	15	(10)	9
4	Intars KIRHNERS		9/4/83	M	11	(9)	1
	Oskars KĻAVA		8/8/83	D	12		
	Artjoms KUZŅECOVS		5/3/86	D	2	(1)	
5	Darius MICEIKA	LTU	22/2/83	M	10		
3	Pāvels MIHADJUKS		27/5/80	D	8	(3)	1
7	Andrejs PROHORENKOVS		5/2/77	M	5	(7)	2
	Jurica PULJIZ	CRO	13/12/79	D	15		2
	Maksims RAFAĻSKIS		14/5/84	M	11	(3)	
0	Deniss RAKEĻS		20/8/92	A	23	(3)	18
	Roberts SAVAĻNIEKS		6/5/87	M	5	(6)	
0	Genādijs SOLOŅICINS		3/1/80	M	7	(3)	
7	Ilija SPASOJEVIĆ	MNE	11/9/87	A	4	(5)	4
1	Viktors SPOLE		5/7/72	G	25		
3	Pāvels SURŅINS		4/8/85	M	7	(3)	
1	Pāvels ŠTEINBORS		21/9/85	G	2	(1)	
	Tomas TAMOŠAUSKAS	LTU	22/5/83	D	24		
2	WELLINGTON Santos da Silva	BRA	11/8/85	D	4		
	Toms VIKSNA		14/1/95	G		(1)	
	Dzintars ZIRŅIS		25/4/77	D	13	(3)	

JFK OLIMPS/RFS

Coach – Mihails Miholaps

Founded – 2005

Stadium – Daugava (2,000)

2010

1/4	Daugava	h	1-1	*Gongadze*
8/4	Ventspils	a	0-7	
3/4	Skonto	h	1-3	*Šabala*
2/5	Jelgava	a	0-4	
3/5	Jūrmala-VV	h	0-2	
5/5	Blāzma	a	0-2	
29/5	Tranzit	h	0-1	
2/6	Liepājas Metalurgs	h	0-3	
12/6	Jaunība	a	9-0	*Gongadze, Kurma, Kļimovs, Budilovs, Šabala 2, Siņicins, Janelidze, Stugļis*
19/6	Daugava	a	0-2	
30/6	Ventspils	h	0-3	
7/7	Jelgava	a	2-1	*Šabala, Janelidze*
25/7	Skonto	a	1-6	*Gongadze*
7/8	Blāzma	h	2-1	*Janelidze, Siņicins (p)*
15/8	Tranzit	a	2-2	*Stugļis, Gongadze*
21/8	Jūrmala-VV	a	2-2	*Nazarchuk, Daņilovs*
27/8	Liepājas Metalurgs	a	0-4	
12/9	Jaunība	h	2-2	*Nazarchuk, Šabala*
15/9	Ventspils	h	0-3	
18/9	Skonto	a	0-4	
23/9	Tranzit	h	0-2	
2/10	Jaunība	a	2-2	*Siņicins (p), Stugļis*
17/10	Blāzma	a	1-1	*Šabala*
23/10	Jelgava	h	2-1	*Stugļis, Siņicins (p)*
27/10	Jūrmala-VV	a	3-0	*Gongadze 2, Siņicins (p)*
31/10	Daugava	h	0-2	
7/11	Liepājas Metalurgs	a	1-2	*Siņicins*

Name	Nat	DoB	Pos	Aps	(s)	Gls
Vitālijs ARTJOMENKO		26/8/90	G	10		
Artūrs BLUMS		21/4/94	M		(4)	
Reinis BRODERS		17/7/92	M	21	(1)	
Konstantīns BUDILOVS		21/3/91	A	25		1
Giorgi CHKHIKVISHVILI	GEO	25/2/93	D	5	(6)	
Dmitrijs DAŅILOVS		25/1/91	D	22	(1)	1
Oskars DARĢIS		6/3/93	G	12		
Lasha GONGADZE	GEO	1/3/90	M	25		6
Vjačeslavs ISAJEVS		27/8/93	M	1	(2)	
David JANELIDZE	GEO	12/9/89	A	10	(1)	3
Artūrs KĻIMOVIČS		31/8/91	D	15	(4)	
Aleksandrs KĻIMOVS		16/11/91	A	24	(3)	1
Andrejs KOSTJUKS		17/2/88	M	5		
Jānis KRUMIŅŠ		9/1/92	G	2	(1)	
Viktors KURMA		4/7/91	A	15	(5)	1
Artūrs MAGEJENKOVS		19/3/90	A	14	(1)	
Anatolijs MAKSIMENKO		9/5/93	D	2	(8)	
Vitālijs MEĻNIČENKO		11/11/87	G	3		
Olexandr NAZARCHUK	UKR	1/2/89	A	12		2
Andrejs OMELJANOVIČS		16/6/92	M	3	(8)	
Deniss OSTROVSKIS		5/2/92	M		(3)	
Armands PRUTĀNS		6/6/89	A	2	(1)	
Sergejs REBIZOVS		11/10/93	D	2	(2)	
Andrejs SIŅICINS		30/1/91	M	22	(1)	6
Elvis STUGĻIS		4/7/93	M	8	(12)	4
Valērijs ŠABALA		12/10/94	A	19	(2)	6
Sergejs TJURIKOVS		27/5/89	M	1		
Konstantin ZARNADZE	GEO	13/1/93	D	17	(2)	

SKONTO FC

Coach – Aleksandrs Starkovs

Founded – 1991

Stadium – Skonto (9,500)

MAJOR HONOURS: Latvian League - (15) 1991, 1992, 1993, 1994, 1995, 1996, 1997, 1998, 1999, 2000, 2001, 2002, 2003, 2004, 2010; Latvian Cup - (7) 1992, 1995, 1997, 1998, 2000, 2001, 2002.

2010

11/4	Jūrmala-VV	h	4-2	*Karašauskas 2, Júnior, Rode*
18/4	Jelgava	h	4-1	*Karašauskas 3, Júnior*
23/4	Olimps/RFS	a	3-1	*Rode, Karašauskas 2*
1/5	Tranzit	h	5-0	*Júnior, Astafjevs, Mingazov, Siņeļņikovs 2*
8/5	Blāzma	a	3-1	*Júnior, Perepļotkins, Siņeļņikovs*
15/5	Jaunība	h	7-0	*Júnior 4 (1p), Mingazov, Karašauskas, Perepechko*
19/5	Tranzit	a	2-0	*Laizāns, Perepļotkins*
29/5	Liepājas Metalurgs	h	0-0	
2/6	Daugava	h	1-0	*Perepļotkins (p)*
12/6	Ventspils	a	1-2	*Pētersons*
22/6	Jūrmala-VV	a	4-0	*Tarasovs, Júnior, Perepļotkins, Fertovs*
25/7	Olimps/RFS	h	6-1	*Turkovs, Mingazov, Júnior 2, Fertovs, Pētersons*
1/8	Jelgava	a	5-0	*Dubra 2, Turkovs, Rode, Cauņa*
6/8	Jaunība	a	3-0	*Dubra, Tarasovs, Mingazov*
15/8	Liepājas Metalurgs	a	2-1	*Júnior (p), Mingazov*
22/8	Blāzma	h	6-0	*Júnior 2, Perepļotkins, Cauņa 2, Siņeļņikovs*
27/8	Daugava	a	1-1	*Mingazov*
12/9	Ventspils	h	1-0	*Mingazov*
15/9	Tranzit	a	6-0	*Siņeļņikovs, Tarasovs, Turkovs 3, Perepechko*
18/9	Olimps/RFS	h	4-0	*Astafjevs, Mingazov, Dubra, Cauņa*
23/9	Blāzma	a	4-1	*Perepļotkins 2, Cauņa, Pētersons*
1/10	Jelgava	h	2-1	*Turkovs, Perepļotkins*
17/10	Jūrmala-VV	a	2-0	*Júnior, Turkovs*
22/10	Daugava	h	0-1	

27/10	Liepājas Metalurgs	a	2-1	*Turkovs, Smirnovs*
31/10	Ventspils	h	2-2	*Dubra, Tarasovs*
7/11	Jaunība	h	6-0	*Siņeļņikovs, Júnior 3 (1p),* Team

No	Name	Nat	DoB	Pos	Aps	(s)	Gls
3	Vitālijs ASTAFJEVS		3/4/71	M	10	(4)	2
9	Kristaps BLANKS		30/1/86	A		(4)	
10	Aleksandrs CAUŅA		19/1/88	M	9	(3)	5
12	Kaspars DUBRA		20/12/90	D	19		5
15	Aleksandrs FERTOVS		16/6/87	M	19	(4)	2
2	Vadims GAIĻUS		27/5/88	D	4		
1	Kaspars IKSTENS		5/6/88	G	24		
24	David JANELIDZE	GEO	12/9/89	A	1	(5)	1
7	Nathan JÚNIOR Soares de Carvalho	BRA	10/3/89	A	24		18
20	Artūrs KARAŠAUSKAS		29/1/92	A	11	(1)	8
5	Juris LAIZĀNS		6/1/79	M	11		1
17	Vitālijs MAKSIMENKO		8/12/90	D	25		
16	Germans MĀLIŅŠ		12/10/87	G	3		
6	Ruslan MINGAZOV	TKM	23/11/91	A	15	(1)	8
21	Aleksandr PEREPECHKO	BLR	7/4/89	A	1	(10)	2
11	Andrejs PEREPĻOTKINS		27/12/84	A	24	(1)	8
8	Armands PĒTERSONS		5/12/90	A	4	(14)	3
22	Deniss PETRENKO		14/3/88	D		(1)	
14	Renārs RODE		6/4/89	M	14	(2)	3
23	Alans SIŅEĻŅIKOVS		14/5/90	A	14	(11)	6
4	Vitālijs SMIRNOVS		28/6/86	D	26		1
18	Kirils ŠEVEĻOVS		2/6/90	D	5	(9)	
19	Igors TARASOVS		16/1/88	M	18	(6)	5
13	Danils TURKOVS		17/2/88	A	16	(1)	8

FC TRANZIT

Coach - Igor Kichigin (RUS)

Founded - 2006

Stadium – 2. pamatskolas (500)

2010

11/4	Jaunība	h	2-0	*Kozačuks, Rullier*
18/4	Daugava	h	0-1	
23/4	Ventspils	h	0-2	
1/5	Skonto	a	0-5	
8/5	Jelgava	h	1-1	*Smirnovs*
15/5	Jūrmala-VV	h	1-1	*Cañas*
19/5	Skonto	h	0-2	
29/5	Olimps/RFS	a	1-0	*Ogunnupe*
5/6	Blāzma	h	3-1	*Kozačuks 2, Kārkliņš*
12/6	Liepājas Metalurgs	a	0-2	
19/6	Jaunība	a	0-1	
30/6	Daugava	a	0-2	
25/7	Ventspils	a	0-2	
8/8	Jūrmala-VV	a	1-2	*Mukins*
15/8	Olimps/RFS	h	2-2	*Bremza, Smirnovs*
22/8	Jelgava	a	1-2	*Visockis*
28/8	Blāzma	a	0-2	
12/9	Liepājas Metalurgs	h	0-4	
15/9	Skonto	h	0-6	
19/9	Jaunība	a	1-0	*Barinovs V. (p)*
23/9	Olimps/RFS	a	2-0	*Kārkliņš, Ļahovs*
2/10	Blāzma	h	0-3	
17/10	Jelgava	a	0-0	
23/10	Jūrmala-VV	h	2-3	*Mukins, Vērdiņš*
27/10	Daugava	a	0-1	
31/10	Liepājas Metalurgs	h	0-6	
7/11	Ventspils	a	0-5	

No	Name	Nat	DoB	Pos	Aps	(s)	Gls
13	Toms AIZGRĀVIS		30/4/89	M	1	(1)	
23,5	Igors BARINOVS		1/6/94	M	3	(3)	
7	Vitālijs BARINOVS		4/5/93	M	21		1
26	Aleksandrs BATURINSKIS		15/12/91	D	18	(2)	
18,10	Romans BESPALOVS		18/10/88	A	8	(2)	
13	Dmitrijs BREMZA		22/2/94	A	9	(2)	1
23,11	Daniels CALKOVSKIS		23/1/93	M	2	(3)	
6,11	Roger CAÑAS Henao	COL	27/3/90	A	4		1
6,4	Aigars CATLAKŠS		9/2/93	D	5	(2)	
10	Imran CHAMKHANOV	FRA	14/6/91	D	4	(5)	
16	Pavel CHESNOVSKIY	BLR	4/3/86	G	3		
20	Aleksejs DIMČUKS		7/2/91	M	8		
22	Pāvels HOHLOVS		19/12/89	M	3	(1)	
3,23	Edgars KĀRKLIŅŠ		21/7/91	A	16	(7)	2
17	Nikolajs KOZAČUKS		7/8/85	A	9		3
8	Andris KUVŠINOVS		31/10/84	D	10		
4,5	Igors ĻAHOVS		27/4/91	M	12	(1)	1
16	Arbi MEZHIYEV	RUS	29/6/93	G	11		
17	Romans MICKEVIČS		29/3/93	M	11	(4)	
19,10,7	Vladimirs MUKINS		29/1/93	M	20	(4)	2
27	Jojo OGUNNUPE	NGA	23/2/92	A	2	(3)	1
8	Bogdans ONIŠČUKS		28/3/93	M	1	(5)	
9,18	Vladas RIMKUS		28/5/93	A	11	(2)	
15	Julian RULLIER	FRA	4/4/90	D	2		1
1	Jevgenijs SAZONOVS		31/7/88	G	6		
12	Māris SMIRNOVS		2/6/76	D	24		2
5	Aleksejs SOĻEIČUKS		12/8/80	D	3	(1)	
14	Artjoms SOLOMATOVS		9/8/94	M	1	(2)	
4	Ivan STAIN	RUS	7/2/89	D	2		
21,2	Vitālijs STOLS		1/6/91	D	9	(1)	
9	Kaspars SVĀRUPS		28/1/94	A	9	(8)	
4	Aleksejs TARASOVS		24/6/93	A		(2)	
25	Serge TATIEFANG	CMR	25/8/87	M	10		
20	Daniels VASILJEVS		7/4/93	M		(3)	
22	Maksims VASILJEVS		27/1/94	M	4	(1)	
14,27	Edgars VĒRDIŅŠ		29/3/93	A	17	(1)	1
7,11, 24,4	Ivans VISOCKIS		8/4/93	M	8	(4)	1
16	Andris ZABUSOVS		5/9/93	G	7	(1)	
7	Nikolajs ZAICEVS		3/1/92	M	1		
5	Ervins ZIEMELIS		27/5/93	D	2	(2)	

FK VENTSPILS

Coach – Nunzio Zavettieri (ITA)

Founded – 1997

Stadium – OSC Ventspils (3,200)

MAJOR HONOURS: Latvian League – (3) 2006, 2007, 2008; Latvian Cup - (5) 2003, 2004, 2005, 2007, 2011.

2010

10/4	Jelgava	a	2-1	*Shumilin, Žigajevs (p)*
18/4	Olimps/RFS	h	7-0	*Shpakov 2, Rugins, Chirkin, Shumilin, Višņakovs E., Solovjovs*
23/4	Tranzit	a	2-0	*Solovjovs 2*
1/5	Blāzma	h	1-0	*Shpakov*
9/5	Liepājas Metalurgs	a	0-0	
15/5	Daugava	a	0-1	
29/5	Jaunība	h	5-0	*Bespalovs V., Višņakovs E., Rugins, Žigajevs 2*
2/6	Jūrmala-VV	a	4-1	*Rugins, Višņakovs A. 2 (1p), Tukura*
12/6	Skonto	h	2-1	*Višņakovs A., Chirkin*
25/6	Jelgava	h	2-1	*Žigajevs (p), Višņakovs E.*
30/6	Olimps/RFS	a	3-0	*Shumilin, Višņakovs E., Žigajevs*
9/7	Blāzma	a	5-0	*Višņakovs E. 3, Žigajevs, Bespalovs V.*
25/7	Tranzit	h	2-0	*Višņakovs A., Bespalovs R.*
8/8	Daugava	h	1-1	*Žigajevs*
15/8	Jaunība	a	5-0	*og (Golovizins), Žigajevs 2, Butriks, Postnikov*
22/8	Liepājas Metalurgs	h	2-4	*Žigajevs 2*
27/8	Jūrmala-VV	h	1-0	*Žigajevs*
12/9	Skonto	a	0-1	
15/9	Olimps/RFS	a	3-0	*Ignatāns, Tatiefang, Maki (p)*
19/9	Blāzma	h	2-0	*Tarasovs, Žigajevs*
26/9	Jelgava	a	4-2	*Zjuzins, Chirkin, Višņakovs E., Gabovs*
2/10	Jūrmala-VV	h	3-1	*Višņakovs E., Višņakovs A., Žigajevs*
17/10	Daugava	a	1-0	*Chirkin*
23/10	Liepājas Metalurgs	h	0-1	

'/10	Jaunība	h	4-1	*Maki 3, Višņakovs A.*
'/10	Skonto	a	2-2	*Zjuzins, Žigajevs*
1	Tranzit	h	5-0	*Ignatāns 2, Tatiefang, Maki 2*

o	Name	Nat	DoB	Pos	Aps	(s)	Gls
	Ahmed ABDULTAOFIK	NGA	25/4/92	M	1	(1)	
	Oļegs BAIKOVS		28/12/84	M	2		
	Romans BESPALOVS		18/10/88	A	5	(2)	1
	Vladimirs BESPALOVS		22/6/88	D	15	(2)	2
1	Nauris BULVITIS		8/3/91	D	9	(1)	
	Andrejs BUTRIKS		20/12/82	A		(4)	1
	Grigoriy CHIRKIN	RUS	26/2/86	M	16	(2)	4
	Alexandru DEDOV	MDA	26/7/89	A	8	(3)	
	Vladislavs GABOVS		13/7/87	D	10	(3)	1
	Visvaldis IGNATĀNS		3/8/91	M	3	(4)	3
	Aleksandrs KOĻIŅKO		18/6/75	G	11		
	Jevgenijs KOSMAČOVS		18/2/88	M	9	(9)	
	Ritus KRJAUKLIS		23/4/86	D	23	(2)	
	Vladislav KRYUCHKOV	RUS	23/4/89	D	5	(1)	
3	Bertrand Michel MAKI Mvondo	GHA	4/8/87	A	4	(6)	6
	Mikhail MISHCHENKO	RUS	27/6/89	D	5	(1)	
	Yevgeniy POSTNIKOV	RUS	16/4/86	D	17	(2)	1
0	Valentins RAĻKEVIČS		8/3/91	G	1		
5	Ritvars RUGIŅS		17/10/89	M	16	(6)	3
2	Igors SAVČENKOVS		3/11/82	D		(1)	
4	Ivan SHPAKOV	RUS	8/6/86	A	4	(3)	3
2	Sergei SHUMILIN	RUS	21/2/90	A	11	(2)	3
	Artūrs SILAGAILIS		3/5/87	D	2	(3)	
4	Aleksandrs SOLOVJOVS		25/2/88	M	9	(1)	3
	Vitālijs STOLS		1/6/91	D	2	(1)	
9	Deniss TARASOVS		14/9/90	M	7	(3)	1
	Serge TATIEFANG	CMR	25/8/87	A	3	(2)	2
3	Michael TUKURA	NGA	19/10/88	M	14		1
0	Aleksejs VIŠŅAKOVS		3/2/84	M	16	(2)	6
	Eduards VIŠŅAKOVS		10/5/90	A	21	(4)	9
6	Aleksandrs VLASOVS		7/5/86	G	15	(2)	
7	Artūrs ZJUZINS		18/6/91	M	19	(1)	2
	Jurijs ŽIGAJEVS		14/11/85	M	14	(4)	15

PROMOTED CLUBS

FB GULBENE 2005

Coach – Mihails Koņevs
Founded – 2005
Stadium – Municipal (2,000)

FC JŪRMALA

Coach – Andrejs Kolidzejs
Founded – 2008
Stadium – Sloka (2,000)

SECOND LEVEL FINAL TABLE 2010

		Pld	W	D	L	F	A	Pts
1	FB Gulbene 2005	22	21	1	0	85	14	64
2	FC Jūrmala	22	14	4	4	47	19	46
3	Daugava/RFS Rīga	22	13	5	4	51	27	44
4	SK Liepājas Metalurgs II	22	13	4	5	55	31	43
5	FS Metta/Latvijas Universitāte Rīga	22	10	6	6	42	25	36
6	FK Valmiera	22	9	4	9	33	40	31
7	FC Daugava Daugavpils II	22	7	3	12	28	35	24
8	FK Auda Rīga	22	6	6	10	21	33	24
9	FK Spartaks Jūrmala	22	6	4	12	32	41	22
10	FK Tukums-2000/TSS	22	4	7	11	33	46	19
11	FK Jelgava II	22	4	3	15	21	42	15
12	FK Kuldīga	22	1	1	20	14	109	4

TOP GOALSCORERS 2010

18	Deniss RAKEĻS (Liepājas Metalurgs)
	JÚNIOR (Skonto)
15	Jurijs ŽIGAJEVS (Ventspils)
12	Kristaps GREBIS (Liepājas Metalurgs)
11	Oļegs MALAŠENOKS (Jelgava)
9	Vitalijus KAVALIAUSKAS (Liepājas Metalurgs)
	Eduards VIŠŅAKOVS (Ventspils)
8	Pavel RYZHEVSKIY (Blāzma)
	Artūrs KARAŠAUSKAS (Skonto)
	Ruslan MINGAZOV (Skonto)
	Andrejs PEREPĻOTKINS (Skonto)
	Danils TURKOVS (Skonto)

DOMESTIC CUP 2010/11

LATVIJAS KAUSS

FOURTH ROUND

(26/9/10)
Blāzma 0, Liepājas Metalurgs 1
Daugava/RFS Rīga 3, Tranzit 1
Gulbene 2, Skonto 3
Olimps/RFS 0, Jūrmala-VV 0 *(aet; 6-7 on pens)*
Salaspils 0, Daugava Daugavpils 10

(10/10/10)
Spartaks Jūrmala 1, Ventspils 2
Valmiera 0, Jaunība 0 *(aet; 7-6 on pens)*

(20/10/10)
Metta/LU Rīga 1, Jelgava 2

QUARTER-FINALS

(19/3/11)
Skonto 0, Daugava Daugavpils 0 *(aet; 0-3 on pens)*

(20/3/11)
Jelgava 0, Liepājas Metalurgs 1 *(Kamešs 23)*

(26/3/11)
Daugava/RFS Rīga 1 *(Priedēns 39p)*, Ventspils 2 *(Višņakovs E. 14, Makovskis 83og)*
Jūrmala-VV 3 *(Krjauklis 17, 85, 90)*, Valmiera 1 *(Gaigals 4)*

SEMI-FINALS

(30/3/11)
Daugava Daugavpils 0, Ventspils 2 *(Sukhanov 49, Laizāns 55)*
Liepājas Metalurgs 2 *(Soloņicins 87, Valskis 111)*, Jūrmala-VV 1 *(Bezzubovs 2p) (aet)*

FINAL

(15/5/11)
Skonto stadium, Riga
FK VENTSPILS 3 *(Laizāns 35, Abdultaofik 44, 71)*
SK LIEPĀJAS METALURGS 1 *(Jemeļins 78p)*
Referee – *Treimanis*
VENTSPILS – *Vlasovs, Bespalovs V. (Shibamura 77), Postnikov, Savčenkovs, Rugins, Laizāns, Sato, Sukhanov (Kosmačovs 70), Gabovs, Višņakovs E., Abdultaofik (Maki 75).*
LIEPĀJAS METALURGS – *Šteinbors, Čirikas, Mihadjuks, Jemeļins, Zirņis (Soloņicins 68), Kalns, Tamošauskas, Valskis, Prohorenkovs, Kamešs, Kavaliauskas.*
Sent off: *Tamošauskas 63*

CLUB COMMUNICATION 2011

FC Daugava Daugavpils
Rīgas iela 75
LV-5403 Daugavpils

Tel	+371 654 39 235
Fax	+371 654 39 235
Web	fcdaugava.lv
Email	zodziks@inbox.lv
Media Officer	Vladislavs Jurkevičs

FB Gulbene 2005
O. Kalpaka iela 1a
LV-4401 Gulbene

Tel	+371 292 29 135
Fax	+371 644 72 058
Web	
Email	gulbene2005@inbox.lv
Media Officer	

FK Jelgava
Raiņa iela 6, Jelgava
LV-3001 Jelgava

Tel	+371 292 34 040
Fax	+371 630 27 540
Web	fkjelgava.lv
Email	kazakevics@inbox.lv
Media Officer	

FC Jūrmala
Skolas iela 32-64, Jūrmala
LV-2011 Jūrmala

Tel	+371 291 40 721
Fax	
Web	jurmalafc.lv
Email	fcjurmala@gmail.com
Media Officer	

FK Jūrmala-VV
Jomas street 61, SIA "Inter Haus"
LV-2015 Jūrmala

Tel	+371 291 04 340
Fax	+371 678 43 413
Web	fcjurmala.lv
Email	fkjurmala1@inbox.lv
Media Officer	Liga Goldmane

SK Liepājas Metalurgs
Brivibas street 93, Brivibas street 3/7
LV-3401 Liepāja

Tel	+371 634 80 927
Fax	+371 634 80 927
Web	skliepajasmetalurgs.lv
Email	fhklubs@inbox.lv
Media Officer	Simona Laiveniece

JFK Olimps/RFS
Ezermalas iela 24/26, Daugavas Stadiur
LV-1014 Rīga

Tel	+371 295 20 530
Fax	+371 675 30 503
Web	
Email	jfk_olimps@inbox.lv
Media Officer	Diana Lange

Skonto FC
1a, Melngaila str., Elizabetes street 75
LV-1010 Rīga

Tel	+371 672 82 669
Fax	+371 672 82 669
Web	skontofc.lv
Email	info@skontofc.lv
Media Officer	Uldis Strautmanis

FK Ventspils
Sporta iela 7/9
LV-3600 Ventspils

Tel	+371 636 81 354
Fax	+371 636 07 555
Web	fkventspils.lv
Email	office@fkventspils.lv
Media Officer	Mihail Korolev

LIECHTENSTEIN

Liechtenstein | Liechtenstein

Liechtensteiner Fussballverband (FLV)

COMMUNICATION

Address	Landstrasse 149 FL-9494 Schaan	**President**	Reinhard Walser
Tel	+423 237 4747	**General Secretary**	Roland Ospelt
Fax	+423 237 4748	**Media Officer**	Judith Frommelt
E-mail	info@lfv.li	**Year of Formation**	1934
Website	lfv.li	**National Stadium**	Rheinpark, Vaduz (7,789)

Vaduz coast to 40th Cup triumph

For the third year in a row the final of the FL1 Cup, Liechtenstein's only major domestic trophy, was disputed by FC Vaduz and USV Eschen/Mauren. Although Vaduz had triumphed on each of the previous two occasions, they had been hard pushed by their rivals, who even stretched them to a penalty shoot-out in 2009/10. But there was only one team in it in 2010/11 as Vaduz claimed their 40th victory in the competition – and 14th in succession – with a thumping 5-0 win.

Victory ensured the continuation of Vaduz's long unbroken participation in Europe, but there was disappointment for Eric Orie's side as they narrowly missed out on promotion from Switzerland's Challenge League (second tier) after finishing in fourth place – five points behind winners FC Lausanne-Sport and two in arrears of runners-up Servette FC, who went up after a play-off.

Long-awaited win

The highlight of the season for three Vaduz players – Marco Ritzberger, Franz Burgmeier and Benjamin Fischer – came at the very end of the season when they helped the Liechtenstein national team claim their first competitive victory for almost four years with a 2-0 win at home to Lithuania in a UEFA EURO 2012 qualifier.

Having lost each of their previous four ties, one of them in excruciating circumstances when they conceded a last-gasp goal to Scotland at Hampden Park, Hans-Peter Zaugg's side were in need of a pick-me-up. First-half goals from Philippe Erne and Michele Polverino – who had also scored the winner in a friendly away to fellow minnows San Marino four months earlier – gave them just that, and with stand-in goalkeeper Benjamin Büchel, who was deputising for the injured Peter Jehle, performing wonders at the other end,

Mario Frick (No10) in action against Scotland – a match in which he scored his 15th international goal for Liechtenstein

LIECHTENSTEIN

Liechtenstein held on to record only their eighth win in 123 competitive matches. The result was even more surprising as Liechtenstein were without their suspended star player Mario Frick, who thus missed out on collecting his 100th cap.

National Team

Top Five All-time Caps – Mario Frick (99); Martin Stocklasa (93); Peter Jehle (85); Daniel Hasler (78); Thomas Beck (77)

Top Five All-time Goals – Mario Frick (16); Franz Burgmeier (7); Thomas Beck & Martin Stocklasa (5); Michele Polverino (3)

NATIONAL TEAM RESULTS 2010/11

11/8/10	Iceland	A	Reykjavik	1-1	*Stocklasa Mi. (69)*
3/9/10	Spain (ECQ)	H	Vaduz	0-4	
7/9/10	Scotland (ECQ)	A	Glasgow	1-2	*Frick (47)*
12/10/10	Czech Republic (ECQ)	H	Vaduz	0-2	
17/11/10	Estonia	A	Tallinn	1-1	*Frick (35)*
9/2/11	San Marino	A	Serravalle	1-0	*Polverino (57)*
29/3/11	Czech Republic (ECQ)	A	Ceske Budejovice	0-2	
3/6/11	Lithuania (ECQ)	H	Vaduz	2-0	*Erne (7), Polverino (36)*

NATIONAL TEAM APPEARANCES 2010/11

Coach – Hans-Peter ZAUGG (SUI)	**2/12/52**		**Isl**	**ESP**	**SCO**	**CZE**	**Est**	**Smr**	**CZE**	**LTU**	**Caps**	**Goals**
Cengiz BIÇER	11/12/87	Mersin İdman Yurdu (TUR)	G								1	-
Franz-Josef VOGT	30/10/85	Eschen/Mauren	D46	s46			s93	D57			26	-
Michael STOCKLASA	2/12/80	Eschen/Mauren	D	D	D	D		D	D		66	2
Martin STOCKLASA	29/5/79	Ried (AUT)	D	D	D	D		D	D	D	93	5
Yves OEHRI	15/3/87	Vaduz	D46	D46	D	D	D				24	-
Marco RITZBERGER	27/12/86	Vaduz	M							D	31	-
Michele POLVERINO	26/9/84	Aarau (SUI)	M	M	M	M		M		M	21	3
Sandro WIESER	3/2/93	Basel (SUI)	M	M82	M71	M84	M85	s57			6	-
Philippe ERNE	14/12/86	Eschen/Mauren /Vaduz	M64	M	M	M78		M	M	M87	8	1
Mario FRICK	7/9/74	St Gallen (SUI) /Grasshoppers (SUI)	M	M	M79	M	M	M	M		99	16
Fabio D'ELIA	19/1/83	Eschen/Mauren	A46		s79						49	2
Martin RECHSTEINER	15/2/89	Vaduz	s46	s45	D	D	D		D		13	-
Lucas EBERLE	13/10/90	Eschen/Mauren	s46	D45				D57			5	-
Mathias CHRISTEN	18/8/87	Vaduz /Linth (SUI)	s46				s86	s85		s72	16	-
Nicolas HASLER	4/5/91	Eschen/Mauren	s64		s92	s66			M	M	5	-
Peter JEHLE	22/1/82	Vaduz		G	G	G	G	G	G		85	-
Franz BURGMEIER	7/4/82	Vaduz		M	M	M	M		D	D	64	7
David HASLER	4/5/90	Vaduz		A	A92		A93	A85	A		14	-
Ronny BÜCHEL	19/3/82	Eschen/Mauren		s82	s71	s84	D				73	-
Thomas BECK	21/2/81	Balzers				A66	M86	M	M	M84	77	5
Rony HANSELMANN	25/6/91	Balzers				s78	s85			s87	3	-
Daniel KAUFMANN	22/12/90	Balzers					D			D	2	-
Martin BÜCHEL	19/2/87	Zürich (SUI) /Deportivo (ESP)					M	M	M10	M	33	-
Wolfgang KIEBER	22/7/84	Balzers						s57	s10 /81		10	-
Andreas CHRISTEN	29/8/89	Eschen/Mauren							s81	s84	2	-
Benjamin BÜCHEL	4/7/89	Eschen/Mauren								G	3	-
Benjamin FISCHER	19/10/80	Vaduz								A72	22	2

DOMESTIC CUP 2010/11

FL1 CUP

IRST ROUND

17/8/10)
alzers III 4, Ruggell II 2
schen/Mauren III 5, Triesenberg II 1
'aduz Portugues 1, Triesen II 3

18/8/10)
chaan Azzurri 5, Balzers II 2
'aduz III 0, Triesen 5

ECOND ROUND

14/9/10)
chaan Azzurri 1, Ruggell 2
riesen II 1, Balzers III 4

15/9/10)
schen/Mauren III 1, Triesen 4
chaan 0, Triesenberg 1

QUARTER-FINALS

19/10/10)
Balzers III 1, Eschen/Mauren 8

(20/10/10)
Ruggell 0, Vaduz 6
Triesen 1, Balzers 13
Eschen/Mauren II 1, Triesenberg 2

SEMI-FINALS

(5/4/11)
Vaduz 8 *(Arlan 3, Merenda 10, 31, 43, Schwegler 13, Sabia 21, 61, Fischer 57)*, Triesenberg 0

(12/4/11)
Eschen/Mauren 2 *(D'Elia 29, Rohrer 84)*, Balzers 1 *(Piperno 90+2)*

FINAL

(25/4/11)
Rheinparkstadion, Vaduz
FC VADUZ 5 *(Harrer 38, Sara 52, Schwegler 64, Arlan 73, Ciccone 90+3)*
USV ESCHEN/MAUREN 0
Referee – *Hänni*
VADUZ – *Jehle, Zanni (Rechsteiner 69), Schwegler, Bader, Cerrone, Arlan, Ciccone, Sara (Ritzberger 69), Harrer, Burgmeier, Merenda (Fischer 9).*
ESCHEN/MAUREN – *Büchel, Vogt (Pelizzatti 41), D'Elia, Stocklasa, Barandun, Christen, Clemente G., Rohrer, Demirci, Hasler, Huber.*

CLUB COMMUNICATION 2011/12

FC Balzers

PO Box 114
FL-9496 Balzers

Tel +423 384 3033
Fax +423 384 3069
Web fcbalzers.li
Email info@fcbalzers.li
Media Officer Christoph Foser

FC USV Eschen/Mauren

Sportpark, PO Box 12
FL-9492 Eschen

Tel +423 371 1700
Fax +423 371 1701
Web usv.li
Email info@usv.li
Media Officer Herbert Marxer

FC Ruggell

Freizeitpark WIdau
FL-9491 Ruggell

Tel +423 373 6168
Fax +423 373 6138
Web fcruggell.li
Email info@fcruggell.li
Media Officer Helmut Allgäuer

FC Schaan

PO Box 213
FL-9494 Schaan

Tel +41 78 831 2248
Fax +423 232 3035
Web fcschaan.li
Email fcschaan@powersurf.li
Media Officer

FC Triesen

PO Box 208
FL-9495 Triesen

Tel +423 392 2333
Fax +423 392 2333
Web fctriesen.li
Email info@fctriesen.li
Media Officer Margrit Beck-Miller

FC Triesenberg

PO Box 1243, Sportplatz Leitawis
FL-9497 Triesenberg

Tel +423 268 1040
Fax +423 268 1010
Web fctriesenberg.li
Email info@fctriesenberg.li
Media Officer Franz Schädler

FC Vaduz

Rheinpark Stadion, PF 158, Lettstrasse 74
FL-9490 Vaduz

Tel +423 375 1800
Fax +423 375 1809
Web fcvaduz.li
Email info@fcvaduz.li
Media Officer Pirol Bont

LITHUANIA

Lituanie I Litauen

Lietuvos futbolo federacija (LFF)

COMMUNICATION

Address Seimyniskiu 15
LT-09312 Vilnius

Tel +370 5 2638741

Fax +370 5 2638740

E-mail media@lff.lt

Website lff.lt

President Liutauras Varanavičius

General Secretary Julius Kvedaras

Media Officer Jurga Chomskyte-McGeever

Year of Formation 1922

National Stadium S.Darius ir S.Girėnas SK, Kaunas (8,248)

DOMESTIC COMPETITION SUMMARY 2010/11

A LYGA FINAL TABLE

			Home					Away					Total						
		Pld	W	D	L	F	A	W	D	L	F	A	W	D	L	F	A	Pts	Comp
1	FK Ekranas	27	10	2	1	35	11	10	1	3	29	8	20	3	4	64	19	63	UCL
2	FK Sūduva	27	8	4	2	28	8	8	4	1	28	8	16	8	3	56	16	56	UEL
3	VMFD Žalgiris	27	11	2	1	28	4	5	6	2	19	12	16	8	3	47	16	56	
4	FK Tauras	27	7	4	3	22	10	7	1	5	19	17	14	5	8	41	27	47	UEL
5	FC Šiauliai	27	5	4	4	14	13	6	4	4	23	15	11	8	8	37	28	41	
6	FK Banga	27	6	3	4	19	16	4	6	4	15	14	10	9	8	34	30	39	UEL
7	FK Kruoja	27	2	8	3	19	21	6	3	5	22	24	8	11	8	41	45	35	
8	FK Klaipėda	27	1	3	9	10	38	2	3	9	9	36	3	6	18	19	74	15	
9	FK Mažeikiai	27	1	4	9	10	26	1	2	10	7	33	2	6	19	17	59	12	
10	FK Atletas	27	0	1	13	6	32	0	5	8	8	24	0	6	21	14	56	0	*Relegated*

NB FK Vėtra withdrew after 16 games - all results annulled; FK Atletas – 6 pts deducted.

Top Scorer Povilas Lukšys (Sūduva), 16 goals

Promoted Clubs FBK Kaunas
FK Dainava
FK Atlantas

Cup Final FK Ekranas 4, FK Banga 2 (aet)

Ekranas complete title hat-trick

In a year that saw former serial champions FBK Kaunas achieve promotion with a clean sweep of victories and a ton of goals, FK Ekranas maintained their position of prominence in Lithuanian football by winning the A Lyga championship for the third successive year. The club's triumph was also a third in three attempts for coach Valdas Urbonas, who subsequently added to his growing reputation by leading the Panevezys club to a successful defence of the Lithuanian Cup.

Not for the first time the composition of the A Lyga was affected by off-the-field issues. An eight-team division in 2009, it increased its membership to an ungainly 11 in 2010 - only to be reduced to ten midway through following the expulsion, after 16 games, of 2009 runners-up FK Vėtra for financial irregularities. With all the Vilnius club's results being retrospectively annulled, the standings had to be readjusted with less than half of the campaign to run.

Title procession

Ekranas were obliged to relinquish the three points they had claimed from Vėtra in a 3-2 win in May – four days after they had defeated the same opponents 2-1 in the 2010 Cup final – but the concession was of little consequence as they went on to win their next eight league fixtures. Their title procession was briefly interrupted when they surrendered points to closest challengers FK Sūduva and VMFD Žalgiris, but by the penultimate round they had secured their title hat-trick with a 2-1 home win over FC Šiauliai in front of 4,700 celebrating spectators.

Fittingly, Ekranas's winning goal was supplied by veteran skipper Deimantas Bička, and it was another old-timer, Latvian goal machine Vīts Rimkus, who ended the campaign as the club's top scorer, his 15-goal tally eclipsing that of A Lyga player of the season, 24-year-old Dominykas Galkevičius, who struck a dozen times from midfield to earn himself a recall to the Lithuanian national team. The only other regular international in Ekranas's ranks was defensive midfielder Ramūnas Radavičius.

Radavičius's former clubs Žalgiris and Sūduva waged an entertaining battle for second place, with the latter emerging victorious only on the head-to-head rule – by virtue of a single away goal in three draws – after the two teams had both finished seven points adrift of the champions. A UEFA Europa League ticket should have been the reward for both clubs but Žalgiris, back in the A Lyga under new ownership following an enforced year away, failed to obtain the necessary licence so their berth went to fourth-placed FK Tauras. Another place open to the 2011 Lithuanian Cup winners actually went to the runners-up, FK Banga, who, despite taking a 2-0 lead in the final against Ekranas, missed out on a first major trophy as the champions came back to win 4-2 in extra time.

Extra-time elimination

Several months earlier Ekranas had been unfortunate victims of an extra-time defeat themselves when HJK Helsinki eliminated them from the UEFA Champions League with a 119th-minute

Ekranas coach Valdas Urbonas captured his third A Lyga title in as many years

own goal. Extra time, however, did produce Lithuania's only European winner in 2010/11 as Tauras overcame Llanelli FC in the first qualifying round of the UEFA Europa League.

The Lithuanian national team's UEFA EURO 2012 qualifying campaign ranged from the sublime – a 1-0 win in the Czech Republic – to the ridiculous – a 2-0 defeat in Liechtenstein - as rookie coach Raimondas Žutautas got to grips with his new job. Two 3-1 defeats by Spain were no disgrace, but the shock submission in Vaduz appeared to scupper the team's last remaining hopes of claiming a play-off place.

National Team

Top Five All-time Caps – Andrius Skerla (82); Deividas Šemberas (73); Tomas Danilevičius (67); Aurelijus Skarbalius (65); Gintaras Staučė (61)

Top Five All-time Goals – Tomas Danilevičius (19); Antanas Lingis (12); Edgaras Jankauskas & Robertas Poškus (10); Virginijus Baltušnikas (9)

NATIONAL TEAM RESULTS 2010/11

11/8/10	Belarus	H	Kaunas	0-2	
3/9/10	Scotland (ECQ)	H	Kaunas	0-0	
7/9/10	Czech Republic (ECQ)	A	Olomouc	1-0	*Šernas (27)*
8/10/10	*Spain (ECQ)*	*A*	*Salamanca*	*1-3*	*Šernas (54)*
17/11/10	Hungary	A	Szekesfehervar	0-2	
25/3/11	Poland	H	Kaunas	2-0	*Mikoliūnas (18), Česnauskis E. (29)*
29/3/11	Spain (ECQ)	H	Kaunas	1-3	*Stankevičius (57)*
3/6/11	Liechtenstein (ECQ)	A	Vaduz	0-2	
7/6/11	Norway	A	Oslo	0-1	

NATIONAL TEAM APPEARANCES 2010/11

Coach – Raimondas ŽUTAUTAS	**4/9/72**		**Blr**	**SCO**	**CZE**	**ESP**	**Hun**	**Pol**	**ESP**	**LIE**	**Nor**	**Caps**	**Goals**
Giedrius ARLAUSKIS	1/12/87	Unirea Urziceni (ROU)	G									5	-
Tadas KIJANSKAS	6/9/85	Jagiellonia (POL)	D	D	D	D	D	D	D	D	D	13	-
Andrius SKERLA	29/4/77	Jagiellonia (POL)	D46	D	D	D		D46	D	D		82	1
Ramūnas RADAVIČIUS	20/1/81	Ekranas	D46	D	D	D	D		s71	D	D	11	-
Marius STANKEVIČIUS	15/7/81	Sampdoria (ITA)	D										
		/Valencia (ESP)		D	D	D	D	D	D	D46		58	5
Deividas ŠEMBERAS	2/8/78	CSKA Moskva (RUS)	M80	M	M	M			M	M		73	-
Kęstutis IVAŠKEVIČIUS	17/4/85	Bnei Yehuda (ISR)	M46	s90	s90	s82	M	M				19	-
Saulius MIKOLIŪNAS	2/5/84	Arsenal Kyiv (UKR)	M62	M71	M79	M59		M46	M71	M		45	3
Deividas ČESNAUSKIS	30/6/81	Aris (GRE)	M55			s59		s46		s46	D	44	4
Darvydas ŠERNAS	22/7/84	Widzew (POL)	A	A80	A61	A	A58		A74	A		23	3
Tomas DANILEVIČIUS	18/7/78	Livorno (ITA)	A	A90	A90	A82		A71	A85	A46		67	19
Irmantas ZELMIKAS	3/1/80	unattached	s46									13	-
Arūnas KLIMAVIČIUS	5/10/82	Sibir (RUS)	s46				D						
		/Zhetysu (KAZ)									D	31	2
Mantas SAVĖNAS	27/8/82	Sibir (RUS)	s46										
		/Gazovik (RUS)								s68	M61	36	5
Mindaugas KALONAS	28/2/84	Metalurh Zaporizhya (UKR)	s55									35	2
Vytautas LUKŠA	14/8/84	Arsenal Kyiv (UKR)	s62	s80	s79							11	-
Linas PILIBAITIS	5/4/85	Győr (HUN)	s80				M67				M	19	-
Žydrūnas KARČEMARSKAS	24/5/83	Gaziantepspor (TUR)		G	G	G	G	G46	G			54	-
Mindaugas PANKA	1/5/84	Widzew (POL)		M	M	M		M87	M	M	M71	13	-
Edgaras ČESNAUSKIS	5/2/84	Dinamo Moskva (RUS)		M	M	M85							
		/Rostov (RUS)						M81	M	M68	M58	33	2
Robertas POŠKUS	5/5/79	İnter Bakı (AZE)		s71	s61	s85	A46					49	10
Dominykas GALKEVIČIUS	16/10/86	Ekranas					M						
		/Zagłębie Lubin (POL)						s71	s85		s61	7	-
Arvydas NOVIKOVAS	18/12/90	Hearts (SCO)					M82					2	-
Mantas FRIDRIKAS	13/9/88	Kaunas					s46					1	-

NATIONAL TEAM APPEARANCES 2010/11 (contd.)

			Blr	SCO	CZE	ESP	Hun	Pol	ESP	LIE	Nor	Caps	Goals
Andrius VELIČKA	5/4/79	Aberdeen (SCO)					s58					22	2
Tadas ELIOŠIUS	1/3/90	Kruoja					s67					1	-
Artūras JERŠOVAS	10/7/86	Žalgiris					s82					1	-
Marius ŽALIUKAS	10/11/83	Hearts (SCO)						D	D			11	-
Tadas LABUKAS	10/1/84	Arka Gdynia (POL)						A	s74	s46	A78	12	-
Ernestas ŠETKUS	25/5/85	Olympiakos (CYP)						s46		G	G	3	-
Tomas ŽVIRGŽDAUSKAS	18/3/75	Halmstad (SWE)						s46				56	-
Valdemar BOROVSKIJ	2/5/84	Sūduva						s81				1	-
Tomas RAŽANAUSKAS	7/1/76	Sūduva						s87				41	7
Marius PAPŠYS	13/5/89	Příbram (CZE)									M	1	-
Vitalijus KAVALIAUSKAS	2/7/83	Liepājas Metalurgs (LVA)									s58	17	3
Povilas LEIMONAS	16/11/87	Sūduva									s71	1	-
Nerijus ASTRAUSKAS	18/10/80	Žalgiris									s78	2	-

CLUB-BY-CLUB

FK ATLETAS

Coach – Viačeslavas Novikovas
Founded – 2005
Stadium – S.Darius ir S.Girėnas SK (8,248)

2010

21/3	Banga	a	0-3	
3/4	Tauras	a	0-2	
11/4	Šiauliai	h	1-2	*Marozas*
18/4	Sūduva	h	0-5	
25/4	Vėtra	h	0-3	*(result annulled)*
28/4	Ekranas	h	0-3	
2/5	Klaipėda	a	0-1	
9/5	Mažeikiai	a	2-2	*Smaryginas, Mikalauskas*
12/5	Kruoja	h	1-2	*Marozas (p)*
19/5	Žalgiris	a	1-4	*Marozas*
30/5	Banga	h	0-0	
13/6	Tauras	h	0-1	
22/6	Šiauliai	a	1-1	*Mačianskas*
27/6	Sūduva	a	1-3	*Smaryginas*
4/7	Vėtra	a	0-0	*(result annulled)*
25/7	Ekranas	a	0-1	
1/8	Klaipėda	h	0-1	
8/8	Mažeikiai	h	1-2	*Rūškys*
14/8	Kruoja	a	1-1	*Rūškys*
18/8	Žalgiris	h	0-2	
22/8	Banga	a	0-1	
29/8	Tauras	h	0-1	
12/9	Šiauliai	a	1-1	*Mačianskas*
17/9	Sūduva	h	1-4	*Rūškys*
3/10	Ekranas	h	0-5	
17/10	Žalgiris	a	0-3	
23/10	Klaipėda	h	2-3	*Smaryginas, Petkevičius (p)*
31/10	Mažeikiai	a	1-1	*Juozaitis J.*
7/11	Kruoja	h	0-1	

No	Name	Nat	DoB	Pos	Aps	(s)	Gls
12	Aivaras BRAŽINSKAS		1/11/90	G	26		
18	Eringas DEGUTIS		25/4/87	D		(2)	
13	Rokas GARASTAS		17/8/88	M	8	(7)	
22	Mantas GINTALAS		4/4/88	G		(1)	
14	Mindaugas GRUŠAUSKAS		16/1/88	A	9	(8)	
20	Aleksandras JEFIŠOVAS		24/11/84	M	19	(1)	
25	Arnas JUOZAITIS		30/12/89	M	1	(1)	
19	Audrius JUOZAITIS		13/8/86	D	6	(4)	
11	Jaunius JUOZAITIS		30/1/90	D	17	(3)	1
27	Mantas JUOZAPAITIS		13/3/92	M		(2)	
7	Deividas LATUŠENKA		2/2/87	M	1	(2)	
4	Gediminas MACEVIČIUS		27/11/86	D	4	(2)	
21	Paulius MACEVIČIUS		9/5/89	D	1		
16	Vaidas MAČIANSKAS		20/8/85	M	26		2
9	Eimantas MAROZAS		29/12/85	A	13		3
7	Tadas MAZILIAUSKAS		30/3/90	A		(5)	
10	Jaunius MIKALAUSKAS		12/3/83	A	25	(3)	1
30	Vladas PETKEVIČIUS		2/8/89	M	15	(8)	1
6	Kęstutis PETKUS		22/7/88	D		(1)	
4	Marius PRIESKENIS		29/9/90	M	4	(7)	
11	Edmundas PUKYS		10/10/90	M		(1)	
17	Erikas RŪŠKYS		12/9/87	A	18	(9)	3
2	Mantas SIRVIDAS		24/2/85	D	29		
8	Paulius SMARYGINAS		30/10/86	M	28		3
1	Algirdas SURGAUTAS		17/1/84	G	2		
32	Mantas TAMULIONIS		7/7/89	G	1		
5	Darius URBELIONIS		30/9/78	M	8	(2)	
23	Eisvinas UTYRA		14/9/90	M	17	(5)	
15	Karolis VASILIAUSKAS		8/5/89	D	21	(2)	
3	Gediminas ZABORSKIS		4/4/88	D	5		
33	Marius ŽUKOVAS		7/11/91	D	15	(1)	

FK BANGA

Coach – Arminas Narbekovas
Founded – 1966
Stadium – Gargždai (3,250)

2010

21/3	Atletas	h	3-0	*Douglas, Gailius 2*
27/3	Tauras	a	0-2	
3/4	Šiauliai	a	0-1	
10/4	Sūduva	a	0-0	
18/4	Vėtra	a	1-2	*Gedgaudas (result annulled)*
25/4	Ekranas	a	0-0	
28/4	Klaipėda	a	3-0	*Juška 2, Gailius*
2/5	Mažeikiai	a	2-2	*Gailius, og (Grigutis)*
9/5	Kruoja	a	3-2	*Staponka, Juška 2*
12/5	Žalgiris	a	0-2	
30/5	Atletas	a	0-0	
4/6	Tauras	h	2-1	*Staponka, Juška*
11/6	Šiauliai	h	2-1	*Staponka, Juška*
23/6	Sūduva	h	0-2	
27/6	Vėtra	h	1-1	*og (Ngapounou) (result annulled)*
2/7	Ekranas	h	0-3	
23/7	Klaipėda	h	1-1	*Gudauskas*
30/7	Mažeikiai	h	2-1	*Staponka, Choruži*
6/8	Kruoja	h	0-3	
13/8	Žalgiris	h	1-1	*Staponka*

22/8	Atletas	h	1-0	*Gudauskas*
12/9	Tauras	a	2-0	*Mižigurskis 2*
18/9	Šiauliai	h	0-1	
26/9	Sūduva	a	0-1	
17/10	Ekranas	a	3-2	*Staponka, Mižigurskis, Choruži*
24/10	Žalgiris	h	1-1	*Ostap*
31/10	Klaipėda	a	1-1	*Choruži*
7/11	Mažeikiai	h	6-1	*Staponka 2, Mižigurskis 2, Gailius, Kulbis*
14/11	Kruoja	a	1-1	*Staponka*

No	Name	Nat	DoB	Pos	Aps	(s)	Gls
19	Ignas BAGDONAS		21/5/92	A		(13)	
27	Edvinas BRAČKUS		11/9/90	D	9	(1)	
55	Marjan CHORUŽI		29/3/80	M	12		3
24	Israel Awenayeri DOUGLAS	NGA	24/7/84	A	1		1
15	Gytis GAILIUS		20/11/90	M	15	(10)	5
55	Andrius GEDGAUDAS		18/9/78	M	6	(1)	1
49	Žygimantas GEDRIMAS		16/6/91	M		(2)	
32	Denis GORDEJ		22/7/89	D	15		
7	Rimvydas GRUDYS		20/9/82	M	25	(1)	
13	Mantas GUDAUSKAS		4/1/89	D	13	(9)	2
12	Aleksandras IVANAUSKAS		5/12/87	D	23		
18	Andrius JOKŠAS		12/1/79	D	11		
77	Gvidas JUŠKA		17/8/82	A	15		6
23	Giedrius KOŽIKIS		29/3/89	M	2	(1)	
25	Gajus KULBIS		5/7/89	M	6	(4)	1
10	Mikas KURA		1/4/89	M	3	(3)	
9	Andrius LIPSKIS		16/2/88	M	23	(2)	
47	Valerijus MIŽIGURSKIS		22/4/83	A	12	(5)	5
23	Anatol OSTAP	MDA	22/11/79	M	7	(2)	1
2	Deividas PADAIGIS		2/2/86	D	22	(2)	
26	Vladislavs PAVĻUČENKO	LVA	14/3/92	M		(3)	
1	Paulius POCIUS		9/11/88	G	3		
24	Giedrius RATKUS		1/12/81	D	5	(1)	
8	Donatas REMĖZA		12/5/88	M	6	(6)	
99	Igor SPIRIDONOV		27/8/88	G	26	(1)	
21	Aurelijus STAPONKA		9/11/83	A	25	(2)	9
17	Aurimas ŠLUŠNYS		21/6/84	D	6	(3)	
11	Julius TRIUŠKA		22/3/89	M	4	(3)	
5	Karolis URBAITIS		12/12/90	D	24	(2)	

FK EKRANAS

Coach – Valdas Urbonas

Founded – 1964

Stadium – Aukštaitija (4,000)

MAJOR HONOURS: Lithuanian League - (5) 1993, 2005, 2008, 2009, 2010; Lithuanian Cup - (4) 1998, 2000, 2010, 2011.

2010

27/3	Klaipėda	a	4-1	*Galkevičius, Rimkus 2, Pogreban*
3/4	Mažeikiai	a	2-0	*Gleveckas, Rimkus*
10/4	Kruoja	h	4-1	*Matović, Tomkevičius, Varnas, Banys*
18/4	Žalgiris	h	3-0	*Galkevičius 2, Bička (p)*
25/4	Banga	h	0-0	
28/4	Atletas	a	3-0	*Varnas 2, Galkevičius*
1/5	Tauras	a	1-2	*Sasnauskas*
9/5	Šiauliai	h	3-1	*Rimkus, Kučys, Matović*
12/5	Sūduva	a	1-1	*Galkevičius*
19/5	Vėtra	h	3-2	*Kučys 2, Radavičius (p) (result annulled)*
5/6	Klaipėda	h	2-1	*Matović, Rimkus*
12/6	Mažeikiai	h	5-0	*Rimkus 2, Radavičius 2, Varnas*
23/6	Kruoja	a	2-0	*Radavičius, Rimkus*
27/6	Žalgiris	a	1-0	*og (Arlauskis)*
2/7	Banga	a	3-0	*Kučys, Radavičius (p), Rimkus*
25/7	Atletas	h	1-0	*Galkevičius*
1/8	Tauras	h	4-1	*Varnas, Rimkus, Ademolu, Radavičius*
8/8	Šiauliai	a	2-1	*Varnas, Pogreban*
15/8	Sūduva	h	1-1	*Radavičius (p)*
29/8	Žalgiris	a	0-1	
12/9	Klaipėda	h	5-0	*Galkevičius 3, Sasnauskas, Rimkus*
18/9	Mažeikiai	a	3-0	*Ademolu, Galkevičius 2*
26/9	Kruoja	h	3-2	*Radavičius, Kučys, Pogreban*
3/10	Atletas	a	5-0	*Arlauskas, Ademolu, Rimkus 2, Galkevičius*
17/10	Banga	h	2-3	*Rimkus 2*
23/10	Tauras	a	2-0	*Varnas, Bička*
31/10	Šiauliai	h	2-1	*Varnas, Bička*
7/11	Sūduva	a	0-2	

No	Name	Nat	DoB	Pos	Aps	(s)	Gls
7	Stephen ADEMOLU	CAN	20/11/82	A	17	(4)	3
17	Andrius ARLAUSKAS		16/1/86	M	14	(4)	1
10	Žilvinas BANYS		25/2/86	M	5	(10)	1
22	Deimantas BIČKA		19/2/72	M	13	(1)	3
2	Yamoudou CAMARA	FRA	12/8/87	D	4	(2)	
29	Vytautas ČERNIAUSKAS		12/3/89	G	15		
88	Dominykas GALKEVIČIUS		16/10/86	M	21	(1)	12
3	Dainius GLEVECKAS		5/3/77	D	26		1
70	Olexandr KABLASH	UKR	5/9/89	A	1	(8)	
12	Tadas KAUNECKAS		31/3/86	G	13		
30	Aurimas KUČYS		22/2/81	M	24		5
25	Egidijus MAJUS		5/1/84	D	1	(4)	
28	Tadas MARKEVIČIUS		10/4/85	A	2	(9)	
58	Dušan MATOVIĆ	SRB	8/7/83	D	23		3
78	Serghei POGREBAN	MDA	13/5/78	A	12	(13)	3
7	Ramūnas RADAVIČIUS		20/1/81	M	26	(1)	8
23	Arnas RIBOKAS		14/1/93	M		(2)	
29	Vīts RIMKUS	LVA	21/6/73	A	24	(2)	15
15	Nerijus SASNAUSKAS		20/4/80	D	11	(2)	2
5	Marius SKINDERIS		13/10/74	D	4	(9)	
11	Andrius ŠIDLAUSKAS		30/10/84	D	15	(1)	
77	Giedrius TOMKEVIČIUS		29/2/84	M	25	(2)	1
19	Egidijus VARNAS		31/7/75	A	12	(8)	8

FK KLAIPĖDA

Coach – Saulius Mikalajūnas; (19/5/10) Rimantas Skersys

Founded – 2005

Stadium – Klaipėda (4,940)

2010

20/3	Vėtra	a	1-1	*Papšys (result annulled)*
27/3	Ekranas	h	1-4	*Papšys*
10/4	Mažeikiai	h	2-2	*Vishnyakov, Kruša*
18/4	Kruoja	h	1-2	*Vishnyakov*
25/4	Žalgiris	a	0-3	
28/4	Banga	h	0-3	
2/5	Atletas	h	1-0	*Grigaravičius*
9/5	Tauras	a	0-2	
12/5	Šiauliai	a	1-2	*Vishnyakov*
19/5	Sūduva	h	1-6	*Vishnyakov*
30/5	Vėtra	h	1-3	*Stotskiy (result annulled)*
5/6	Ekranas	a	1-2	*Surblys*
23/6	Mažeikiai	a	1-1	*Papšys*
4/7	Žalgiris	h	0-3	
23/7	Banga	a	1-1	*Lukošius D.*
1/8	Atletas	a	1-0	*Lukošius A.*
7/8	Tauras	h	2-3	*Papšys, og (Kuzņecovs)*
15/8	Šiauliai	h	0-2	
18/8	Sūduva	a	0-4	
22/8	Sūduva	a	0-7	
12/9	Ekranas	a	0-5	
15/9	Kruoja	a	1-1	*Šarūnas*
19/9	Žalgiris	h	0-4	
3/10	Mažeikiai	a	0-1	
17/10	Kruoja	h	1-1	*Šarūnas*
24/10	Atletas	a	3-2	*Abramavičius, Papšys (p), Lukošius D.*
31/10	Banga	h	1-1	*Papšys (p)*
7/11	Tauras	a	0-5	
14/11	Šiauliai	h	0-7	

No	Name	Nat	DoB	Pos	Aps	(s)	Gls
20	Orestas ABRAMAVIČIUS		20/6/88	M	8	(3)	1
18	Tomas ADOMAUSKAS		26/7/90	D	2	(3)	
3	Anatolij ANISIMENKO		14/4/83	M	13		
5	Vytautas BIRŠKYS		6/12/88	D	10	(1)	
17	Brunas BISKYS		31/3/90	A	15	(4)	
27	Ernestas BISKYS		31/3/90	M	13		

0	Rimantas BOGUŽAS		11/1/93	G	4		
5	Paulius BUDRYS		10/4/93	M	2	(4)	
	Vilius BUNDULAS		23/1/92	M	5	(8)	
	Bartas BUTINAS		12/8/93	A		(5)	
	Tomas DARGUŽAS		2/1/92	D		(1)	
4	Emilijus GRABYS		2/4/93	A		(2)	
3	Mindaugas GRIGARAVIČIUS		15/7/92	M	16	(6)	1
	Gediminas JACKUS		20/1/88	D	20		
	Giedrius KOŽIKIS		29/3/89	M	10	(1)	
	Gediminas KRUŠA		31/10/90	D	9	(6)	1
	Nerijus KUMŽA		21/11/82	M	5	(1)	
7	Edvinas LUKOŠEVIČIUS		22/5/78	D	3		
5	Aivaras LUKOŠIUS		16/4/88	D	22	(2)	1
	Deividas LUKOŠIUS		24/1/91	A	15	(6)	2
0	Marius PAPŠYS		13/5/89	M	14	(5)	6
4	Giedrius RATKUS		1/12/81	D	8		
9	Edvinas RAZUTIS		4/9/92	G	2		
9	Eimantas RUDAVIČIUS		3/2/88	D	6	(3)	
5	Vitalij SAVICKAS		2/6/89	D	8	(2)	
26	Vismantas SKERSYS		19/9/92	M		(5)	
3	Dmitriy STOTSKIY	RUS	1/12/89	A	13		1
6	Donatas SURBLYS		15/7/87	M	12		1
2	Povilas ŠARŪNAS		14/11/85	D	12		2
23	Darius TAMAŠAUSKAS		29/6/87	D	12	(1)	
	Liudvikas VALIUS		15/8/78	G	23		
22	Justas VILAVIČIUS		20/12/92	A	13	(11)	
20	Vitaliy VISHNYAKOV	RUS	8/8/90	A	12	(1)	4
21	Giedrius ZANIAUSKAS		12/3/87	D	12	(1)	

FK KRUOJA

Coach – Albertas Klimavičius

Founded – 2001

Stadium – Pakruojis (1,000)

2010				
20/3	Šiauliai	a	2-2	*Gardzijauskas, Švelna*
27/3	Sūduva	a	1-2	*Rimavičius*
3/4	Vėtra	a	0-3	*(result annulled)*
10/4	Ekranas	a	1-4	*Šimkus*
18/4	Klaipėda	a	2-1	*og (Ratkus), Mykolaitis*
25/4	Mažeikiai	h	1-0	*Šimkus*
2/5	Žalgiris	a	1-3	*Mykolaitis*
9/5	Banga	h	2-3	*Švelna 2*
12/5	Atletas	a	2-1	*Švelna, Šimkus*
19/5	Tauras	a	0-4	
30/5	Šiauliai	h	3-3	*Šimkus, Mykolaitis 2*
5/6	Sūduva	h	0-2	
12/6	Vėtra	h	1-1	*Petrauskas (result annulled)*
23/6	Ekranas	h	0-2	
4/7	Mažeikiai	a	2-0	*Mykolaitis, Gardzijauskas*
1/8	Žalgiris	h	1-1	*Slavickas*
6/8	Banga	a	3-0	*Gardzijauskas, Eliošius, Slavickas*
14/8	Atletas	h	1-1	*Krasnovskis*
18/8	Tauras	h	3-3	*Petrauskas, Krasnovskis, Slavickas*
21/8	Tauras	a	2-2	*Švelna, Eliošius*
29/8	Šiauliai	h	2-2	*Rimavičius, Švelna*
12/9	Sūduva	a	2-1	*Eliošius, Žulpa*
15/9	Klaipėda	h	1-1	*Eliošius*
26/9	Ekranas	a	2-3	*Mykolaitis, Slepakovas*
3/10	Žalgiris	h	2-2	*Gardzijauskas, Ngapounou*
17/10	Klaipėda	a	1-1	*Švelna*
24/10	Mažeikiai	h	2-0	*Švelna, Veliulis*
7/11	Atletas	a	1-0	*Gardzijauskas*
14/11	Banga	h	1-1	*Eliošius*

No	Name	Nat	DoB	Pos	Aps	(s)	Gls
8	Aivaras BAGOČIUS		10/10/87	A	4	(10)	
4	Kęstutis ČYBAS		30/12/90	M		(6)	
32	Kristaps DZELME	LVA	30/1/90	G	2		
20	Tadas ELIOŠIUS		1/3/90	A	12		5
51	Mindaugas GARDZIJAUSKAS		28/9/78	M	27		5
17	Aurimas GARUCKAS		5/6/86	D	14	(1)	
5	Karolis JARMALAVIČIUS		12/1/91	D	14	(2)	
82	Nerijus KĘSTENIS		18/5/82	M	27	(1)	
33	Ruslan KLIUKOITIS		2/7/83	D		(3)	
29	Povilas KRASNOVSKIS		29/4/89	M	5		2
2	Giedrius KVEDARAS		9/7/91	G	26		
3	Gediminas MAZILIAUSKAS		28/9/90	D		(2)	
19	Kęstutis MYKOLAITIS		4/7/83	M	24	(6)	6
32	Bertrand NGAPOUNOU	CMR	20/11/82	D	12		1
16	Donatas PAULAUSKAS		20/2/87	D	17	(6)	
9	Donatas PETRAUSKAS		16/3/84	A	20	(1)	2
31	Laurynas RIMAVIČIUS		21/10/85	D	21	(1)	2
10	Aleksandras ROMAŠOVAS		28/9/85	A	3	(4)	
99	Giedrius SLAVICKAS		3/10/82	M	13		3
6	Rolandas SLEPAKOVAS		29/6/86	D	23	(3)	1
1	Marius ŠALKAUSKAS		22/5/89	G	1		
13	Virginijus ŠIMKUS		25/7/83	M	17	(6)	4
11	Tautvydas ŠVELNA		13/5/91	M	20	(3)	8
18	Domas TAMOŠAUSKAS		17/3/93	D		(1)	
77	Ernestas VELIULIS		22/8/92	A	2	(4)	1
23	Vilius ZABARAUSKAS		3/2/89	M	11	(2)	
10	Artūras ŽULPA		10/6/90	M	4	(1)	1

FK MAŽEIKIAI

Coach – Nerijus Gudaitis; (20/9/10) Ričardas Grigaliūnas

Founded – 1947

Stadium – Mažeikiai (748)

MAJOR HONOURS: Lithuanian League - (1) 1994.

2010				
20/3	Sūduva	a	0-3	
27/3	Vėtra	a	0-3	*(result annulled)*
3/4	Ekranas	h	0-2	
10/4	Klaipėda	a	2-2	*og (Savickas), Šiaulys*
25/4	Kruoja	a	0-1	
28/4	Žalgiris	h	0-1	
2/5	Banga	h	2-2	*Labžentis, Bulošas*
9/5	Atletas	h	2-2	*Tautvydas, Dargevičius*
12/5	Tauras	a	0-0	
19/5	Šiauliai	a	1-2	*Tautvydas (p)*
30/5	Sūduva	h	1-2	*Tautvydas*
5/6	Vėtra	h	1-4	*Tautvydas (result annulled)*
12/6	Ekranas	a	0-5	
23/6	Klaipėda	h	1-1	*Šluta*
4/7	Kruoja	h	0-2	
24/7	Žalgiris	a	0-6	
30/7	Banga	a	1-2	*Podelis*
8/8	Atletas	a	2-1	*Podelis 2*
15/8	Tauras	h	1-3	*Kumža*
18/8	Šiauliai	h	0-1	
22/8	Šiauliai	a	0-1	
29/8	Sūduva	h	1-3	*Kumža*
18/9	Ekranas	h	0-3	
25/9	Žalgiris	a	0-2	
3/10	Klaipėda	h	1-0	*Gladilins (p)*
24/10	Kruoja	a	0-2	
31/10	Atletas	h	1-1	*Podelis*
7/11	Banga	a	1-6	*Podelis*
14/11	Tauras	h	0-3	

No	Name	Nat	DoB	Pos	Aps	(s)	Gls
15	Marius BIRŠKYS		16/7/87	M	12		
9	Antanas BULOŠAS		12/6/78	A	29		1
20	Nerijus DARGEVIČIUS		7/6/87	A	8	(3)	1
16	DIOGO Porcino Braga "TILICO"	BRA	1/8/85	A	11	(1)	
7	Nerijus GARUCKAS		5/6/86	D	11		
12	Renaldas GIRGŽDYS		21/9/91	M	2	(2)	
21	Romans GLADILINS	LVA	28/10/88	D	28		1
16	Mindaugas GRIGUTIS		3/4/85	D	9	(4)	
18	Marijus JASAS		22/3/89	D	8	(2)	
15	Luiz Carlos Silva dos Santos "JÚNIOR"	BRA	9/6/88	D	10		
2	Gintaras JUODEIKIS		30/1/73	D	17		
1	Paulius KAKTAVIČIUS		9/4/85	G	9		

22	Irmantas KANCĖ		3/3/93	M	1	(1)	
11	Tomas KIZEVIČIUS		21/4/90	M	13	(8)	
14	Nerijus KUMŽA		21/11/82	M	11	(1)	2
19	Nerijus LABŽENTIS		3/1/87	M	21	(1)	1
1	Martynas MATUZAS		28/8/89	G	14		
6	Augustinas MONTVYDAS		8/6/93	M	1	(14)	
17	Tomas NORKUS		12/6/05	D		(1)	
18	Andrejus ORIOL		17/6/78	D	6		
14	Linas PETKEVIČIUS		29/6/86	M	3	(7)	
10	Deividas PILIUKAITIS		22/2/89	D	7	(4)	
88	Gintas PODELIS		1/12/86	A	11		5
20	Donatas REMĖZA		12/5/88	M	8	(1)	
23	Erlandas ŠIAULYS		23/4/89	A	10	(5)	1
5	Marius ŠLUTA		21/6/84	M	21	(7)	1
13	Antanas TAUTVYDAS		14/2/82	M	17		4
3	Paulius VAIKASAS		13/11/87	D	13		
77	Maksims VITKOVSKIJS	LVA	16/1/89	G	6	(1)	
4	Mindaugas ŽLIBINAS		12/5/90	D	2	(1)	

FC ŠIAULIAI

Coach – Deivis Kančelskis; (12/8/10) Valdas Ivanauskas

Founded – 1995

Stadium – Šiauliai Municipal (3,000)

2010				
20/3	Kruoja	h	2-2	*Viktoravičius, Kuklys*
28/3	Žalgiris	a	0-1	
3/4	Banga	h	1-0	*Kozlovs*
11/4	Atletas	a	2-1	*Jasaitis 2*
17/4	Tauras	a	0-0	
28/4	Sūduva	a	1-1	*Raskov*
1/5	Vėtra	h	0-0	*(result annulled)*
9/5	Ekranas	a	1-3	*Birškys*
12/5	Klaipėda	h	2-1	*Raskov, Kuklys*
19/5	Mažeikiai	h	2-1	*Raskov 2*
30/5	Kruoja	a	3-3	*Kuklys (p), Viktoravičius, Raskov*
6/6	Žalgiris	h	1-3	*Raskov*
11/6	Banga	a	1-2	*Viktoravičius*
22/6	Atletas	h	1-1	*Kuklys*
26/6	Tauras	h	0-1	
25/7	Sūduva	h	0-0	
8/8	Ekranas	h	1-2	*Vėževičius*
15/8	Klaipėda	a	2-0	*Viktoravičius, Kuklys*
18/8	Mažeikiai	a	1-0	*Raskov*
22/8	Mažeikiai	h	1-0	*Vėževičius*
29/8	Kruoja	a	2-2	*Raskov, Kuklys (p)*
12/9	Atletas	h	1-1	*Vėževičius*
18/9	Banga	a	1-0	*Kuklys*
26/9	Tauras	h	0-1	
17/10	Sūduva	a	1-0	*Kozlovs*
31/10	Ekranas	a	1-2	*Kozlovs (p)*
7/11	Žalgiris	h	2-0	*Lapeikis, Kozlovs*
14/11	Klaipėda	a	7-0	*Šilėnas 2, Vėževičius 2, Urbelis 2, Jasaitis*

No	Name	Nat	DoB	Pos	Aps	(s)	Gls
21	Tomas BIRŠKYS		5/11/92	M	5	(2)	1
33	Valdemar BOROVSKIJ		2/5/84	D	12		
10	Saimonas BURKŠAITIS		21/1/90	M	5	(4)	
23	Paulius DRUBLIONIS		17/12/91	D	1	(2)	
18	Tautvydas ELIOŠIUS		3/11/91	M	2	(10)	
3	Georgas FREIDGEIMAS		10/8/87	D	7	(1)	
2	Robertas FREIDGEIMAS		2/2/89	D	3	(1)	
4	Klimas GUSOČENKO		9/3/89	D	7	(4)	
16	Paulius JANUŠAUSKAS		28/2/89	M	3	(1)	
7	Edvinas JASAITIS		11/4/90	M	8	(12)	3
5	Tomas KANČELSKIS		19/8/75	D	20	(1)	
27	Saša KOLIĆ	CRO	19/11/81	M	11		
37	Sergei KOSOV	RUS	31/1/86	G	9		
13	Igors KOZLOVS	LVA	26/3/87	M	26		4
13	Justinas KUIZINAS		9/10/91	M		(4)	
8	Mantas KUKLYS		10/6/87	M	25	(1)	7
14	Dovydas KVEINYS		8/4/90	M		(3)	
25	Vilius LAPEIKIS		30/6/83	D	21	(5)	1
15	Deivydas LUNSKIS		12/7/77	D	26		
88	Jevgenij MOROZ		20/1/90	M	2	(4)	
37	Pavels NAGLIS	LVA	29/4/87	G	12		
66	Ernestas PILYPAS		17/5/90	D	12	(1)	
19	Edvardas PŠELENSKIS		11/2/88	D	13	(3)	
31	Marius RAPALIS		22/5/89	G	4		
29	Viktor RASKOV	UKR	8/5/84	A	23	(1)	8
90	Tadas SIMAITIS		29/12/90	G	3		
20	Vaidas ŠILĖNAS		16/7/85	M	24	(1)	2
9	Rokas URBELIS		27/1/90	A		(11)	2
32	Robertas VĖŽEVIČIUS		5/1/86	M	11		5
11	Vaidas VIKTORAVIČIUS		8/5/87	A	13	(10)	4

FK SŪDUVA

Coach – Donatas Vencevičius

Founded – 1968

Stadium – Marijampolė FC (6,250)

MAJOR HONOURS: Lithuanian Cup - (2) 2006, 2009.

2010				
20/3	Mažeikiai	h	3-0	*Lukšys 2, Grigaitis*
27/3	Kruoja	h	2-1	*Lukšys 2*
4/4	Zalgiris	h	0-0	
10/4	Banga	h	0-0	
18/4	Atletas	a	5-0	*Chao, Lukšys, Esaú 3*
25/4	Tauras	a	1-0	*Radžius*
28/4	Šiauliai	h	1-1	*Kijanskas*
9/5	Vėtra	a	1-3	*Grande (result annulled)*
12/5	Ekranas	h	1-1	*Esaú*
19/5	Klaipėda	a	6-1	*Urbšys 2, Lukšys 2, Chvedukas, Brokas*
30/5	Mažeikiai	a	2-1	*Slavickas V., Valaitis*
5/6	Kruoja	a	2-0	*Lukšys, Grigaitis*
13/6	Žalgiris	a	1-1	*Chvedukas*
23/6	Banga	a	2-0	*Valaitis, Lukšys*
27/6	Atletas	h	3-1	*Kozyuberda, Radžius, Lukšys (p)*
25/7	Šiauliai	a	0-0	
15/8	Ekranas	a	1-1	*Lukšys*
18/8	Klaipėda	h	4-0	*Urbšys 2, Beniušis, Gogberashvili*
22/8	Klaipėda	h	7-0	*Urbšys 3, Lukšys 2, Chao, Beniušis*
25/8	Tauras	h	3-1	*Urbšys, og (Buitkus), Brokas*
29/8	Mažeikiai	a	3-1	*Lukšys, Grigaitis, Urbšys*
12/9	Kruoja	h	1-2	*Beniušis*
17/9	Atletas	a	4-1	*Chao, Radžius, Beniušis, Brokas*
26/9	Banga	h	1-0	*Grigaitis*
3/10	Tauras	a	1-2	*Lukšys*
17/10	Šiauliai	h	0-1	
7/11	Ekranas	h	2-0	*Urbšys, Lukšys*
14/11	Žalgiris	a	0-0	

No	Name	Nat	DoB	Pos	Aps	(s)	Gls
88	Ričardas BENIUŠIS		23/4/80	A	2	(10)	4
16	Audrius BROKAS		20/8/90	A		(16)	3
11	CHAO Liu	CHN	7/9/87	M	25	(1)	3
13	Karolis CHVEDUKAS		21/4/91	M	17	(4)	2
23	ESAÚ García Álvarez	ESP	2/1/87	M	7	(6)	4
25	Vladimir GOGBERASHVILI	RUS	16/4/87	A	6	(6)	1
15	Sandro GRANDE	CAN	29/9/77	M	22	(2)	1
20	Evaldas GRIGAITIS		28/9/87	A	26	(1)	4
3	Tadas KIJANSKAS		6/9/85	D	12		1
5	Giedrius KLEVINSKAS		4/10/81	D	1	(3)	
14	Aldas KLIUČINYKAS		3/1/92	M		(1)	
10	Serhiy KOZYUBERDA	UKR	21/3/80	M	8	(8)	1
12	Povilas LEIMONAS		16/11/87	D	13	(3)	
7	Povilas LUKŠYS		7/7/79	A	27	(1)	16
2	Nerijus RADŽIUS		27/8/76	D	25	(1)	3
21	Marius RAPALIS		23/3/89	G	9		
8	Alfredas SKROBLAS		11/3/84	D	24	(3)	
9	Giedrius SLAVICKAS		13/10/82	M	1	(1)	
19	Vaidas SLAVICKAS		26/2/86	D	26		1
18	Andrew Eugene SSEPPUYA	UGA	1/4/83	A	2	(1)	
17	Andrius URBŠYS		22/8/86	M	19	(8)	10
5	Eimantas VALAITIS		3/6/82	D	17	(5)	2
30	Povilas VALINČIUS		16/5/89	G	11		
1	Armantas VITKAUSKAS		23/3/89	G	8		

FK TAURAS

Coach – Gedeminas Jarmalavičius
Founded – 1922
Stadium – Vytautas (1,600)

2010				
21/3	Žalgiris	h	1-1	*Savastas*
27/3	Banga	h	2-0	*Daunoravičius, Vide*
3/4	Atletas	h	2-0	*Jasaitis, Savastas*
17/4	Šiauliai	h	0-0	
25/4	Sūduva	h	0-1	
28/4	Vėtra	h	0-0	*(result annulled)*
1/5	Ekranas	h	2-1	*Daunoravičius, Kižys*
9/5	Klaipėda	h	2-0	*Kižys, Bielskis*
12/5	Mažeikiai	h	0-0	
19/5	Kruoja	h	4-0	*Vyšniauskas (p), Kižys, Vide, Mačiulis*
29/5	Žalgiris	a	0-1	
4/6	Banga	a	1-2	*Vyšniauskas*
13/6	Atletas	a	1-0	*Irkha*
26/6	Šiauliai	a	1-0	*Jasaitis*
1/8	Ekranas	a	1-4	*Ražanauskas*
7/8	Klaipėda	a	3-2	*Ražanauskas, Irkha, Gedgaudas*
15/8	Mažeikiai	a	3-1	*og (Kizevičius), Mačiulis, Bielskis*
18/8	Kruoja	a	3-3	*Ražanauskas (p), Savastas, Irkha*
21/8	Kruoja	h	2-2	*Mačiulis, Grigalevičius*
25/8	Sūduva	a	1-3	*Mačiulis*
29/8	Atletas	a	1-0	*Buitkus*
12/9	Banga	h	0-2	
26/9	Šiauliai	a	1-0	*Gedgaudas (p)*
3/10	Sūduva	h	2-1	*Rečickis, Buitkus*
23/10	Ekranas	h	0-2	
31/10	Žalgiris	a	0-1	
7/11	Klaipėda	h	5-0	*Ražanauskas, Grigalevičius, Savastas, Bielskis, Mačiulis*
11/11	Mažeikiai	a	3-0	*Gražiūnas, Buitkus 2*

No	Name	Nat	DoB	Pos	Aps	(s)	Gls
32	Egidijus AURYLA		26/7/92	D		(1)	
25	Simonas BABILIUS		16/9/91	A		(3)	
15	Lukas BIELSKIS		11/5/92	M	3	(16)	3
16	Olexandr BORYSENKO	UKR	1/1/85	G	2		
24	Orestas BUITKUS		11/4/75	M	10	(2)	4
66	Mindaugas DAUNORAVIČIUS		25/1/85	A	16	(5)	2
23	Igor DAYNEKO	RUS	20/5/89	G	2		
36	Andrius GEDGAUDAS		18/9/78	M	13		2
13	Artjoms GONČARS	LVA	24/9/84	D	7		
4	Tadas GRAŽIŪNAS		18/4/78	D	14		1
13	Mindaugas GRIGALEVIČIUS		3/12/81	A	11	(1)	2
35	Sergei IRKHA	BLR	25/3/84	M	16	(10)	3
11	Karolis JASAITIS		1/11/82	M	14	(8)	2
1	Šarūnas KILIJONAS		18/1/85	G	24		
27	Marius KIŽYS		21/2/82	M	9		3
10	Artjoms KUZŅECOVS	LVA	15/11/86	D	3		
3	Mantas LĖKIS		15/11/86	D	22		
14	Nerijus MAČIULIS		1/4/83	M	26	(2)	5
91	Deividas MALKEVIČIUS		16/2/91	M		(1)	
22	Lukas MARTIŠAUSKAS		3/1/90	D	6	(8)	
18	Jaunius MOCKUS		1/1/85	D	19	(1)	
34	Tomas RAŽANAUSKAS		7/1/76	M	12	(2)	4
27	Vitālijs REČICKIS	LVA	8/9/86	M	6	(1)	1
8	Darius REGELSKIS		15/4/76	D	16		
17	Linas SAVASTAS		24/1/86	M	17		4
36	Olegs SEMJONOVS	LVA	1/4/84	A	10	(3)	
13	Jānis VAITKUS	LVA	24/10/84	D	14		
16	José López VIDE	POR	4/2/87	M	5	(7)	2
9	Tomas VYŠNIAUSKAS		7/3/88	M	11	(3)	2

FK VĖTRA

Coach – Virginijus Liubšys
Founded – 1996
Stadium – Vėtra (5,900)

2010				
20/3	Klaipėda	h	1-1	*Eliošius*
27/3	Mažeikiai	h	3-0	*Ražanauskas (p), Rimkevičius 2*
3/4	Kruoja	h	3-0	*Ražanauskas 2, Rimkevičius*
10/4	Žalgiris	a	1-2	*Ražanauskas*
18/4	Banga	h	2-1	*Veikutis, Gogberashvili*
25/4	Atletas	a	3-0	*Rimkevičius 2, Gogberashvili*
28/4	Tauras	a	0-0	
1/5	Šiauliai	a	0-0	
9/5	Sūduva	h	3-1	*Rimkevičius 2, Ražanauskas (p)*
19/5	Ekranas	a	2-3	*Ražanauskas, Eliošius*
30/5	Klaipėda	a	3-1	*Eliošius 2, Jankauskas*
5/6	Mažeikiai	a	4-1	*Gogberashvili, Eliošius 2, Rimkevičius*
12/6	Kruoja	a	1-1	*Lyakh*
23/6	Žalgiris	h	3-1	*Lyakh, Gogberashvili 2*
27/6	Banga	a	1-1	*Gogberashvili*
4/7	Atletas	h	0-0	

NB All results annulled.

No	Name	Nat	DoB	Pos	Aps	(s)	Gls
3	Valdemar BOROVSKIJ		2/5/84	D	15		
9	Tadas ELIOŠIUS		1/3/90	A	14	(1)	6
2	Georgas FREIDGEIMAS		10/8/87	D	3	(2)	
69	Robertas FREIDGEIMAS		2/2/89	D		(1)	
1	Mantas GALDIKAS		22/6/89	G	6		
25	Vladimir GOGBERASHVILI	RUS	16/4/87	A	13	(2)	6
5	Algis JANKAUSKAS		27/9/82	D	13		1
11	Povilas KRASNOVSKIS		29/4/89	M	7	(3)	
10	Gajus KULBIS		5/7/89	M		(3)	
90	Andrey LYAKH	RUS	24/9/90	M	7	(3)	2
26	Jevgenij MOROZ		20/1/90	M		(8)	
4	Bertrand NGAPOUNOU	CMR	20/11/82	D	4	(1)	
34	Tomas RAŽANAUSKAS		7/1/76	M	16		6
77	Artūras RIMKEVIČIUS		14/4/83	A	13		8
26	Marius STANAITIS		26/12/87	M	10	(5)	
22	Andrei USACHEV	RUS	29/4/86	D	15		
30	Povilas VALINČIUS		16/5/89	G	10	(1)	
23	Audrius VEIKUTIS		23/7/79	D	14		1
19	Robertas VĖŽEVIČIUS		5/1/86	M	12	(2)	
8	Artūras ŽULPA		10/6/90	M	4	(12)	

VMFD ŽALGIRIS

Coach – Igoris Pankratjevas
Founded – 1947
Stadium – Žalgiris (15,030)
MAJOR HONOURS: Lithuanian League - (3) 1991, 1992, 1999; Lithuanian Cup - (5) 1991, 1993, 1994, 1997, 2003 (autumn).

2010				
21/3	Tauras	a	1-1	*Morinas (p)*
28/3	Šiauliai	h	1-0	*Komolov*
4/4	Sūduva	a	0-0	
10/4	Vėtra	h	2-1	*Vilėniškis, Nagumanov A. (result annulled)*
18/4	Ekranas	a	0-3	
25/4	Klaipėda	h	3-0	*Morinas, Nagumanov A., Barevičius*
28/4	Mažeikiai	a	1-0	*Vaitkūnas*
2/5	Kruoja	h	3-1	*Morinas (p), Gražiūnas, Vilėniškis*
12/5	Banga	h	2-0	*Mastianica 2*
19/5	Atletas	h	4-1	*Komolov, Jeršovas, Nagumanov A., Jerkovic (p)*
29/5	Tauras	h	1-0	*Vilėniškis*
6/6	Šiauliai	a	3-1	*Vilėniškis, Komolov, Jeršovas*
13/6	Sūduva	h	1-1	*Komolov*
23/6	Vėtra	a	1-3	*Nagumanov A. (result annulled)*
27/6	Ekranas	h	0-1	
4/7	Klaipėda	a	3-0	*Jeršovas 3*
24/7	Mažeikiai	h	6-0	*Jeršovas 4, Astrauskas, Morinas*
1/8	Kruoja	a	1-1	*Vilėniškis*
13/8	Banga	a	1-1	*Astrauskas*
18/8	Atletas	a	2-0	*Vaskėla, Jankauskas*
29/8	Ekranas	h	1-0	*Gnedojus*
19/9	Klaipėda	a	4-0	*Astrauskas 2, Jankauskas, Vaitkūnas*
25/9	Mažeikiai	h	2-0	*Vilėniškis 2*
3/10	Kruoja	a	2-2	*Komolov, Jeršovas*
17/10	Atletas	h	3-0	*Astrauskas, Jeršovas, Nagumanov A.*

24/10	Banga	a	1-1	*Sirevičius*
31/10	Tauras	h	1-0	*Vaskėla*
7/11	Šiauliai	a	0-2	
14/11	Sūduva	h	0-0	

No	Name	Nat	DoB	Pos	Aps	(s)	Gls
29	Davydas ARLAUSKIS		18/11/86	D	23		
24	Nerijus ASTRAUSKAS		18/10/80	A	14		5
77	Giedrius BAREVIČIUS		9/8/76	M	16	(4)	1
11	Yan BOBROVSKIY	RUS	18/9/89	D	10		
3	Kazimieras GNEDOJUS		28/2/86	D	14	(3)	1
18	Tadas GRAŽIŪNAS		18/4/78	D	10	(1)	1
5	Algis JANKAUSKAS		27/9/82	D	11		2
9	Goran JERKOVIC	FRA	10/11/86	A	3	(4)	1
13	Artūras JERŠOVAS		10/7/86	M	26		11
7	Egidijus JUŠKA		12/3/75	M	2	(9)	
1	Saulius KLEVINSKAS		2/4/84	G	10		
10	Pavel KOMOLOV	RUS	10/3/89	M	27		5
12	Pavel LEUS		15/9/78	G	3		
9	Edgar MASTIANICA		26/10/88	M	9	(18)	2
11	Igoris MORINAS		21/2/75	A	9	(8)	4
38	Andrei NAGUMANOV	RUS	21/2/87	M	27		5
18	Roman NAGUMANOV	RUS	5/6/85	M		(2)	
4	Roman ROMANCHUK	UKR	19/8/86	M	8	(12)	
20	Tomas SIREVIČIUS		23/3/79	D	15	(1)	1
6	Artūras SOBOLIS		24/11/80	D	2	(1)	
1	Ernestas ŠETKUS		25/5/85	G	16		
8	Egidijus VAITKŪNAS		8/8/88	D	27		2
21	Arminas VASKĖLA		12/8/90	M	12	(9)	2
17	Raimondas VILĖNIŠKIS		10/6/76	M	25	(2)	7
32	Daumantas ŽUKAUSKAS		4/2/92	A		(3)	

PROMOTED CLUBS

FBK KAUNAS

Coach – Darius Gvildys
Founded – 1960
Stadium – S.Darius ir S.Girėnas SK (8,248)
MAJOR HONOURS: Lithuanian League – (8) 1999 (autumn), 2000, 2001, 2002, 2003, 2004, 2006, 2007; Lithuanian Cup – (4) 2002, 2004, 2005, 2006.

FK DAINAVA

Coach – Virginijus Sinkevičius
Founded – 2010
Stadium – Centrinis (3,500)

FK ATLANTAS

Coach – Šenderis Giršovičius
Founded – 1962
Stadium – Klaipeda (4,940)
MAJOR HONOURS: Lithuanian Cup – (2) 2001, 2003.

SECOND LEVEL FINAL TABLE 2010

		Pld	W	D	L	F	A	Pts
1	FBK Kaunas	27	27	0	0	108	16	81
2	FK Alytis	27	16	3	8	47	35	51
3	FK Vidzgiris	27	14	4	9	69	46	46
4	FK Nevėžis	27	14	3	10	47	47	45
5	FK Lietava	27	11	4	12	54	60	37
6	FK Lifosa	27	10	4	13	48	66	34
7	FK Atlantas	27	9	6	12	35	33	33
8	FK Šilutė	27	5	8	14	27	61	23
9	FK Minija	27	6	4	17	29	51	22
10	Lithuania U-19	27	3	4	20	24	73	13

NB FK Dainava (a merger between FK Alytis and FK Vidzgiris) and FK Atlantas were invited to 2011 A Lyga.

TOP GOALSCORERS 2010

16	Povilas LUKŠYS (Sūduva)
15	Vīts RIMKUS (Ekranas)
12	Dominykas GALKEVIČIUS (Ekranas)
11	Artūras JERŠOVAS (Žalgiris)
10	Andrius URBŠYS (Sūduva)
9	Aurelijus STAPONKA (Banga)
8	Ramūnas RADAVIČIUS (Ekranas)
	Egidijus VARNAS (Ekranas)
	Tautvydas ŠVELNA (Kruoja)
	Viktor RASKOV (Šiauliai)
	Artūras RIMKEVIČIUS (Vėtra)

DOMESTIC CUP 2010/11

LFF TAURĖ

FIFTH ROUND

(24/8/10)
FBK Kaunas 1, Šilutė 0
Lifosa 0, Vidzgiris 2

(25/8/10)
91 United Kaunas 2, Granitas Vilnius 3 *(aet)*
Atletas 5, Alytis 0
Kruoja 2, Atlantas 0
Mažeikiai 1, Klaipėda 3
Tauras Šiauliai 0, Nevėžis 7
Žalgiris 2, Banga 2 *(aet; 2-3 on pens)*

SIXTH ROUND

(29/9/10)
FBK Kaunas 3, Atletas 0
Granitas Vilnius 1, Klaipėda 2
Vidzgiris 4, Kruoja 2

(2/10/10)
Banga 4, Nevėžis 3 *(aet)*

QUARTER-FINALS

(3/11/10)
Banga 2 *(Lipskis 30, Choruži 36)*, Klaipėda 0
Šiauliai 1 *(Vėževičius 68)*, Sūduva 0
Tauras Tauragė 2 *(Grigalevičius 5, Rečickis 64)*, FBK Kaunas 3 *(Razulis 4, Valskis 30, Pehlić 114) (aet)*
Vidzgiris 0, Ekranas 1 *(Pogreban 14)*

SEMI-FINALS

(16/3/11 & 13/4/11)
FBK Kaunas 0, Banga 5 *(Gailius 64, Ostap 75p, 79, Kura 88, Bagdonas 90)*
Banga 1 *(Bagdonas 14)*, FBK Kaunas 1 *(Daukša 85)*
(Banga 6-1)

Šiauliai 0, Ekranas 2 *(Varnas 16, Veikutis Au. 81og)*
Ekranas 2 *(Anđelkovic 95, Varnas 113)*, Šauliai 2 *(Janušauskas 19, Veikutis Ar. 36) (aet)*
(Ekranas 4-2)

FINAL

(14/5/11)
Alytus stadium, Alytus
FK EKRANAS 4 *(Radavičius 30, Varnas 55, Matović 107, Velička 115)*
FK BANGA 2 *(Zelmikas 11, Urbaitis 13)*
(aet)
Referee – *Atmanavičius*
EKRANAS – *Zubas, Jokšas, Gleveckas, Dedura, Sasnauskas (Matović 76), Arlauskas (Markevičius 33), Kučys, Radavičius, Mauro Alonso, Ribokas (Velička 56), Varnas.*
BANGA – *Spiridonov, Zelmikas, Kazlauskas, Bitinas (Ratkus 78), Padaigis, Grudys, Urbaitis (Rodkin 75), Lipskis, Choruži, Kura (Gudauskas 67), Gailius.*

CLUB COMMUNICATION 2011

FK Atlantas
Gintaro str.9
LT-5800 Klaipėda

Tel	+370 46 21 41 53
Fax	+370 46 21 41 53
Web	atlantas.lt
Email	atlantas.akademija@gmail.com
Media Officer	Ineta Mineikiene

FK Banga
Kvietiniu str. 26
LT-96136 Gargždai

Tel	+370 46 45 27 82
Fax	+370 46 45 27 82
Web	fkbanga.lt
Email	rimas@fkbanga.lt
Media Officer	Remigijus Riekašius

FK Dainava
Naujoji str.3
LT-4580 Alytus

Tel	+370 35 53 99 0
Fax	+370 31 56 34 23
Web	fkdainava.lt
Email	darius@alytis.lt
Media Officer	

FK Ekranas
Panevėžys City, Elektronikos Str. 1
LT-35116 Panevėžys

Tel	+370 45 50 64 03
Fax	+370 45 50 64 14
Web	fkekranas.lt
Email	info@fkekranas.lt
Media Officer	Linas Jocius

FBK Kaunas
Raudondvario pl. 70
LT-47184 Kaunas

Tel	+370 37 36 16 13
Fax	+370 37 36 16 13
Web	fbk.lt
Email	info@fbk.lt
Media Officer	Eimantas Puras

FK Klaipėda
Sauliu str.3-2
LT-Klaipėda

Tel	+370 65 25 44 54
Fax	
Web	klaipeda-fc.lt
Email	fkglestum@yahoo.com
Media Officer	

FK Kruoja
Statybininku str. 3
LT-83163 Pakruojis

Tel	+370 42 16 01 32
Fax	+370 42 16 40 10
Web	fkkruoja.lt
Email	info@fkkruoja.lt
Media Officer	Arūnas Balčiūnas

FK Mažeikiai
Laisves str. 32-2
LT-89223 Mažeikiai

Tel	+370 44 33 51 81
Fax	+370 44 33 51 81
Web	fkmazeikiai.lt
Email	aldaras@saurida.lt
Media Officer	

FC Šiauliai
S. Daukanto street 23
LT-76331 Šiauliai

Tel	+370 70 00 50 53
Fax	+370 70 00 50 53
Web	fcsiauliai.lt
Email	fcsiauliai@fcsiauliai.lt
Media Officer	Egidijus Angličkis

FK Sūduva
P. Armino Str. 27
LT-68290 Marijampolė

Tel	+370 34 37 11 78
Fax	+370 34 37 11 78
Web	fksuduva.lt
Email	fksuduva@takas.lt
Media Officer	Arūnas Reinikis

FK Tauras
Svyturio str. 4A
LT-72252 Tauragė

Tel	+370 44 65 10 66
Fax	+370 44 65 10 66
Web	fktauras.lt
Email	info@fktauras.lt
Media Officer	Eugenijus Naujokas

VMFD Žalgiris
Algirdo str. 31
LT-Vilnius

Tel	+370 61 59 37 00
Fax	
Web	zalgiris-vilnius.lt
Email	info@zalgiris-vilnius.lt
Media Officer	Artūras Gimžauskas

LUXEMBOURG

Luxembourg I Luxemburg

Fédération Luxembourgeoise de Football (FLF)

COMMUNICATION

Address BP5
Rue de Limpach
LU-3901 Mondercange
Tel +352 488 665 1
Fax +352 488665 82

E-mail flf@football.lu
Website football.lu

President Paul Philipp
General Secretary Joël Wolff
Media Officer Marc Diederich

Year of Formation 1908

National Stadium Josy Barthel, Luxembourg (8,000)

DOMESTIC COMPETITION SUMMARY 2010/11

NATIONAL DIVISION FINAL TABLE

			Home					Away					Total						
		Pld	**W**	**D**	**L**	**F**	**A**	**W**	**D**	**L**	**F**	**A**	**W**	**D**	**L**	**F**	**A**	**Pts**	**Comp**
1	F91 Dudelange	26	10	0	3	46	16	9	2	2	29	8	19	2	5	75	24	59	UCL
2	CS Fola Esch	26	6	4	3	27	15	8	1	4	21	13	14	5	7	48	28	47	UEL
3	UN Käerjéng 97	26	6	4	3	35	17	7	1	5	19	17	13	5	8	54	34	44	UEL
4	FC Differdange 03	26	5	3	5	24	19	7	4	2	27	18	12	7	7	51	37	43	UEL
5	FC Progrès Niedercorn	26	7	0	6	23	24	5	5	3	20	19	12	5	9	43	43	41	
6	CS Grevenmacher	26	3	3	7	14	20	8	3	2	29	19	11	6	9	43	39	39	
7	CS Pétange	26	6	3	4	22	22	4	5	4	15	14	10	8	8	37	36	38	
8	AS Jeunesse Esch	26	6	2	5	20	15	4	5	4	20	22	10	7	9	40	37	37	
9	FC RM Hamm Benfica	26	6	1	6	21	18	5	2	6	26	28	11	3	12	47	46	36	
10	FC Swift Hesper	26	5	3	5	21	21	4	1	8	17	28	9	4	13	38	49	31	
11	Racing FC Union Lëtzebuerg	26	3	3	7	16	19	5	2	6	22	19	8	5	13	38	38	29	
12	FC Wiltz 71	26	3	1	9	16	32	5	1	7	22	46	8	2	16	38	78	26	*Relegated*
13	FC Etzella Ettelbruck	26	0	6	7	14	26	5	0	8	17	34	5	6	15	31	60	21	*Relegated*
14	Jeunesse Canach	26	3	2	8	17	31	2	3	8	11	31	5	5	16	28	62	20	*Relegated*

Top Scorer Sanel Ibrahimović (Wiltz), 18 goals

Promoted Clubs FC Union 05 Kayl/Tétange
US Rumelange
US Hostert

Cup Final FC Differdange 03 1, F91 Dudelange 0

Dudelange storm back to summit

F91 Dudelange's reaction to losing the Luxembourg National Division title to AS Jeunesse Esch in 2009/10 was to reassert their superiority in emphatic style, winning their first 11 matches, posting a record winning scoreline and galloping to victory with five matches in hand. Their ninth championship triumph since the turn of the century was not, however, accompanied by a fifth Luxembourg Cup win over the same period as FC Differdange 03, fourth in the league, defeated them 1-0 in the final to retain the trophy.

Dudelange's Luxembourg striker Daniel Da Mota made headlines for club and country in 2010/11

Led from the sidelines by Belgian coach Marc Grosjean and spearheaded on the field by a prolific strike force of Daniel Da Mota and Tomasz Gruszczyński, Dudelange were on fire from the off. They raced into an early lead, never to be challenged, and even when their winning run was ended by a shock defeat at CS Pétange, they responded with an incredible 15-0 win at home to FC Wiltz 71 – the biggest victory in the history of the National Division – in which Gruszczyński bagged five goals and Da Mota four. With the title all but wrapped up by Christmas, Dudelange were able to coast home in the spring, although the Cup final defeat to Differdange took some shine off a memorable campaign.

As title-holders Jeunesse dropped to a dismal eighth place, the runners-up spot was taken, to considerable surprise, by their local rivals CS Fola Esch, who won nine of their 14 games after national team legend Jeff Strasser took over as coach. Fola were joined in the 2011/12 UEFA Europa League by another unlikely qualifier, UN Käerjéng, who, a year after surviving the promotion/relegation play-off, finished third. Jeunesse Canach and FC Etzella Ettelbruck were relegated automatically, to be joined later by Wiltz, who lost their play-off against US Hostert on penalties. Ironically, the decisive spot-kick was missed by Sanel Ibrahimović, who had ended the regular National Division campaign as the league's top scorer, with 18 goals.

Da Mota double

Although, as usual, all four Luxembourg representatives bowed out of European club competition at the first time of asking, not one of them lost at home, with Dudelange even claiming a 2-1 win against Randers FC – albeit after a 6-1 reverse in Denmark. There were no victories for the Luxembourg national team in their first seven UEFA EURO 2012 qualifiers, but they did pick up one point – in a 0-0 draw at home to Belarus – and also managed a goal, scored by their only far-flung exile, Norway-based midfielder Lars Gerson, in a 3-1 defeat away to Romania. The team's best performance under new coach Luc Holtz came in a February friendly at home to Slovakia, in which Dudelange striker Da Mota scored twice as Luxembourg came from behind to win 2-1.

National Team

Top Five All-time Caps – Jeff Strasser (98); Carlo Weis (88); René Peters (82); François Konter (77); Eric Hoffmann & Roby Langers (73)

Top Five All-time Goals – Léon Mart (16); Gusty Kemp (15); Camille Libar (14); Nicolas Kettel (13); François Müller (12)

LUXEMBOURG

NATIONAL TEAM RESULTS 2010/11

11/8/10	Wales	A	Llanelli	1-5	*Kitenge (44)*
3/9/10	Bosnia & Herzegovina (ECQ)	H	Luxembourg	0-3	
7/9/10	Albania (ECQ)	A	Tirana	0-1	
8/10/10	Belarus (ECQ)	H	Luxembourg	0-0	
12/10/10	France (ECQ)	A	Metz	0-2	
17/11/10	Algeria	H	Luxembourg	0-0	
9/2/11	Slovakia	H	Luxembourg	2-1	*Da Mota (61, 81)*
25/3/11	France (ECQ)	H	Luxembourg	0-2	
29/3/11	Romania (ECQ)	A	Piatra Neamt	1-3	*Gerson (22)*
3/6/11	Hungary	H	Luxembourg	0-1	
7/6/11	Belarus (ECQ)	A	Minsk	0-2	

NATIONAL TEAM APPEARANCES 2010/11

Coach –Luc HOLTZ /(Mike NEY)	**14/6/69 23/6/69**		**Wal**	**BIH**	**ALB**	**BLR**	**FRA**	**Alg**	**Svk**	**FRA**	**ROU**	**Hun**	**BLR**	**Caps**	**Goals**
Jonathan JOUBERT	12/9/79	Dudelange	G	G	G	G	G	G	G	G	G	G	G	45	-
Kim KINTZIGER	2/4/87	Differdange	D	D	D	D		D						40	1
Tom SCHNELL	8/10/85	Racing Union /Fola	D	D	D	D	D	D	D	D	D90	D	D	21	-
Eric HOFFMANN	21/6/84	Jeunesse Esch	D	D	D	D	D	D	D	D	D	D	D	73	-
Mathias JÄNISCH	27/8/90	Differdange	D79	D				s82						12	-
Mario MUTSCH	3/9/84	Metz (FRA)	M 77*	M	M 58*		D	M	D	D	D	D		49	1
Daniel DA MOTA	11/9/85	Dudelange	M68	s76	A	s66	s84	s46	s58	s71	s59	A62	A77	30	2
Lars GERSON	5/2/90	Kongsvinger (NOR)	M59	M		s62			M	M71	M59	M59	M	14	1
René PETERS	15/6/81	Jeunesse Esch	M	M	M	M	M 54*		M58		M	M79	M	82	3
Gilles BETTMER	31/3/89	Differdange	M86	M86	M91	M62	M84	M	M	M	M81	M18		42	-
Joël KITENGE	12/11/87	Fola	A	s46			s53					s62	s60	27	2
Joël PEDRO de Almeida	10/4/92	Sedan (FRA)	s59									s79		4	-
Tom LATERZA	9/5/92	Sedan (FRA)	s68	s86	M81	M	M69			M54	s81	s18	s77	11	-
Dan COLLETTE	2/4/85	Jeunesse Esch	s79	M76	s91							s85	s84	29	-
Billy BERNARD	9/4/91	Fola	s86											1	-
Stefano BENSI	11/8/88	Dudelange		A46										6	-
Guy BLAISE	12/12/80	Virton (BEL)			D	D	D	D	D36	D	D	D85	D	17	-
Ben PAYAL	8/9/88	Dudelange			M	M77	M	M	M	M	M	M	M	40	-
Massimo MARTINO	18/9/90	Hamm			s81			s64	s36	s54	s90	s59	D	12	-
Charles LEWECK	19/7/83	Jeunesse Esch				M	M	M82	M	M90	M	M85	M84	28	-
Aurélien JOACHIM	10/8/86	Differdange				A66	A53	A64	A90	A	A			27	1
Michel KETTENMEYER	7/2/89	Differdange				s77		M46						2	-
Jeff STRASSER	5/10/74	Fola					s69							98	7
Tom SIEBENALER	28/9/90	Differdange							s90					1	-
Jacques PLEIN	17/2/87	Etzella								s90				2	-
Kevin MALGET	15/1/91	Aachen (GER)										s85	D60	3	-

CLUB-BY-CLUB

FC DIFFERDANGE 03

Coach – Dan Theis; (11/4/11) Maurice Spitoni
Founded – 2003
Stadium – Thillenberg (6,000)
MAJOR HONOURS: Luxembourg Cup – (2) 2010, 2011.

010				
8	Dudelange	h	0-1	
5/8	Käerjéng	a	2-2	*Piskor, Franzoni*
2/8	Racing Union	h	0-2	
8/8	Progrès	a	4-2	*Albanese 2, Marcolino, Jänisch*
2/9	Jeunesse Esch	h	3-0	*Albanese 2, Joachim*
8/9	Grevenmacher	a	2-0	*Siebenaler, Joachim*
2/9	Etzella	h	1-2	*Lebresne*
6/9	Pétange	a	4-1	*Joachim 2, Franzoni, Kintziger*
/10	Hamm	h	3-1	*Kettenmeyer (p), Kintziger, May*
7/10	Jeunesse Canach	a	3-1	*Joachim 3*
3/10	Fola	a	2-1	*og (Pompière), Albanese*
1/10	Wiltz	h	4-4	*Albanese 4 (1p)*
/11	Hesper	a	0-0	
1/11	Racing Union	a	1-1	*Kettenmeyer*
8/11	Progrès	h	1-2	*Jänisch*
011				
0/2	Käerjéng	h	2-1	*Rodrigues, Kintziger*
6/2	Jeunesse Esch	a	2-1	*Joachim, Bettmer*
/3	Grevenmacher	h	2-2	*Piskor, Joachim*
3/3	Etzella	a	2-2	*Piskor, Siebenaler*
9/3	Pétange	h	1-1	*Jänisch*
0/4	Hamm	a	0-2	
17/4	Jeunesse Canach	h	4-0	*Joachim 2, Pedro Ribeiro, Bettmer*
/5	Fola	h	0-3	
8/5	Wiltz	a	1-2	*Joachim (p)*
15/5	Hesper	h	3-0	*Joachim 2, Franzoni*
21/5	Dudelange	a	4-3	*Joachim 2, Piskor, Siebenaler*

No	Name	Nat	DoB	Pos	Aps	(s)	Gls
22	Mirko ALBANESE		4/9/89	A	15	(6)	9
12	Alessandro ALUNNI		19/12/91	M	1	(7)	
13	Gilles BETTMER		31/3/89	M	23	(2)	2
4	Ante BUKVIC		14/11/87	D	17	(2)	
15	Ibrahim DIOP	FRA	20/11/83	M	4	(9)	
23	Geoffrey FRANZONI	FRA	18/2/91	A	8	(13)	3
1	Thomas HYM	FRA	29/8/87	G	6		
16	Mathias JÄNISCH		27/8/90	M	20	(2)	3
24	Aurélien JOACHIM		10/8/86	A	22	(1)	16
17	Michel KETTENMEYER		7/2/89	M	16	(3)	2
5	Kim KINTZIGER		2/4/87	D	26		3
18	Philippe LEBRESNE	FRA	29/7/78	M	16	(2)	1
31	Stéphane LEONI	FRA	5/3/76	M	21	(1)	
6	Jérôme MARCOLINO Rodrigues		27/3/89	D	14		1
8	Andy MAY		2/9/89	D	12	(5)	1
26	Alain MENDES		9/9/76	D		(1)	
20	PEDRO RIBEIRO Alves	POR	17/1/89	M	6	(7)	1
25	Pierre PISKOR	FRA	2/5/87	A	7	(2)	4
10	André RODRIGUES Almeida		6/12/87	D	14	(3)	1
11	Tom SIEBENALER		28/9/90	D	16	(5)	3
21	Dario SORAIRE	ARG	31/3/78	M	2	(1)	
2	Julien WEBER	FRA	12/10/85	G	20		

F91 DUDELANGE

Coach – Marc Grosjean (BEL)
Founded – 1991
Stadium – Jos Nosbaum (4,500)
MAJOR HONOURS: Luxembourg League – (9) 2000, 2001, 2002, 2005, 2006, 2007, 2008, 2009, 2011; Luxembourg Cup – (4) 2004, 2006, 2007, 2009.

2010				
8/8	Differdange	a	1-0	*Gruszczyński (p)*
15/8	Fola	h	3-0	*Benzouien, Bensi, Da Mota*
21/8	Wiltz	a	5-1	*Bensi, Karaca, Da Mota, Guthleber, Mélisse*
28/8	Hesper	h	2-0	*Benzouien, Bensi*
12/9	Jeunesse Canach	h	2-0	*Rentmeister, Da Mota*
19/9	Käerjéng	a	3-1	*Wiggers, Benzouien, Bensi*
22/9	Racing Union	h	3-2	*Da Mota, Benzouien, Gruszczyński*
26/9	Progrès	a	5-1	*Da Mota 2, Somé 2, Bensi*
2/10	Jeunesse Esch	h	2-0	*Mélisse, Da Mota (p)*
17/10	Grevenmacher	a	3-0	*Somé 2, Benzouien*
24/10	Etzella	h	4-1	*Bensi, Benzouien, Rentmeister (p), Da Mota*
31/10	Pétange	a	0-1	
7/11	Hamm	h	4-2	*Ollé-Nicole, og (Martino), Benzouien, Gruszczyński*
21/11	Wiltz	h	15-0	*Gruszczyński 5, Benzouien 2, Da Mota 4, Karaca, Remy 2 (1p), Hareau*
28/11	Hesper	a	3-0	*Gruszczyński 2, Benzouien*
2011				
19/2	Fola	a	3-0	*Mélisse, Da Mota, Somé*
27/2	Jeunesse Canach	a	2-2	*Benzouien, Da Mota*
5/3	Käerjéng	h	0-3	*(w/o; match abandoned after 75 mins at 1-2 Gruszczyński)*
13/3	Racing Union	a	2-0	*Benzouien, Karaca*
19/3	Progrès	h	5-1	*Somé 2, Guthleber, Da Mota 2*
9/4	Jeunesse Esch	a	0-1	
16/4	Grevenmacher	h	0-3	
29/4	Etzella	a	1-1	*Gruszczyński*
7/5	Pétange	h	3-0	*Mélisse, Gruszczyński (p), Sanchez*
14/5	Hamm	a	1-0	*Caillet*
21/5	Differdange	h	3-4	*Gruszczyński 2, Guthleber*

No	Name	Nat	DoB	Pos	Aps	(s)	Gls
27	Stefano BENSI		11/8/88	A	6	(10)	6
16	Sofian BENZOUIEN	BEL	11/8/86	M	24	(1)	12
5	Jean-Philippe CAILLET	FRA	24/6/77	D	20		1
1	Lou CONSBRÜCK		29/4/90	G		(1)	
28	Daniel DA MOTA		11/9/85	A	23	(1)	16
32	Abdoul DIAKITE	FRA	11/1/86	M	4	(1)	
29	Tomasz GRUSZCZYŃSKI	FRA	4/12/80	A	16	(2)	15
8	Laurent GUTHLEBER	FRA	26/10/80	D	23		3
18	Sébastien HAREAU	FRA	25/9/81	M	2	(4)	1
3	Jonathan JOUBERT		12/9/79	G	26		
33	Emko KALABIĆ	BIH	30/3/89	A		(5)	
20	Yasin KARACA	BEL	16/12/83	M	14	(3)	3
21	Bryan MÉLISSE	FRA	25/3/89	M	20	(1)	4
9	Loïc MOUNY	FRA	28/3/81	D	24		
10	Romain OLLÉ-NICOLLE	FRA	18/8/87	D	9		1
22	Ben PAYAL		8/9/88	M	9	(8)	
23	Sébastien REMY		19/4/74	M	9	(14)	2
11	Jeffrey RENTMEISTER	FRA	11/7/84	D	10		2
30	Francisco SANCHEZ D'Avolio	BEL	16/5/86	A	15	(2)	1
6	Fahret SELIMOVIĆ	BIH	26/9/93	D		(2)	
31	Ibrahim SOMÉ	COD	14/5/88	A	9	(4)	7
25	Juncai WANG		5/4/90	M	1	(8)	
12	Michaël WIGGERS	BEL	8/2/80	D	22		1
33	Lehit ZEGHDANE	FRA	3/10/77	M		(1)	

FC ETZELLA ETTELBRUCK

Coach – Gauthier Remacle (BEL)
Founded – 1917
Stadium – Deich (4,500)
MAJOR HONOURS: Luxembourg Cup – (1) 2001.

2010				
8/8	Progrès	h	2-2	*Alves, Nilton (p)*
15/8	Jeunesse Esch	a	1-0	*André Bastos*
22/8	Grevenmacher	h	0-4	
29/8	Jeunesse Canach	a	2-1	*Nilton, André Bastos*
12/9	Pétange	a	1-2	*Da Luz*
19/9	Hamm	h	2-2	*Alves, Pietrasik*
22/9	Differdange	a	2-1	*Nilton 2 (1p)*
26/9	Fola	h	1-2	*Nilton*
2/10	Wiltz	a	2-1	*Remacle, Centrone*
16/10	Hesper	h	2-3	*Engeldinger, Kopecky*
24/10	Dudelange	a	1-4	*André Bastos (p)*
31/10	Käerjéng	h	0-1	
7/11	Racing Union	a	1-5	*Alves*
21/11	Grevenmacher	a	2-1	*Cleudir, Alves*
28/11	Jeunesse Canach	h	1-1	*Cleudir*

2011				
20/2	Jeunesse Esch	h	0-0	
27/2	Pétange	h	0-2	
4/3	Hamm	a	0-1	
13/3	Differdange	h	2-2	*og (Leoni), Cleudir*
19/3	Fola	a	0-5	
9/4	Wiltz	h	1-3	*Nilton*
17/4	Hesper	a	2-4	*Cleudir 2*
29/4	Dudelange	h	1-1	*Da Luz*
8/5	Käerjéng	a	1-6	*Nilton (p)*
14/5	Racing Union	h	2-3	*André Bastos (p), Turpel*
21/5	Progrès	a	2-3	*Nilton 2 (1p)*

No	Name	Nat	DoB	Pos	Aps	(s)	Gls
19	Bruno ALVES		9/1/89	A	18	(3)	4
11	ANDRÉ BASTOS Silva	POR	18/3/91	M	17	(5)	4
20	Michael BARRELA		12/5/88	A	9	(6)	
12	Anouar BELLI	BEL	21/4/80	M		(2)	
27	Maxime BIAUDET	FRA	2/2/89	D	5		
4	Gianni BUTTAZZONI	BEL	26/5/79	D	15	(6)	
13	Ricardo CENTRONE	ITA	3/6/90	M	4	(4)	1
22	CLEUDIR Lopes	CPV	4/1/83	A	16	(1)	5
21	Claudio DA LUZ		27/5/79	A	20	(1)	2
14	Gilson DELGADO	CPV	19/10/92	M		(1)	
6	Gilles ENGELDINGER		4/5/84	D	11	(6)	1
15	Carlos FERREIRA		24/8/80	M	22	(3)	
1	Joé FLICK		16/7/79	G	25		
7	Tom KOPECKY		16/5/82	D	15	(3)	1
29	Philippe HAHM		13/1/90	G	1		
28	Kevin HOLTZ		6/3/93	M		(4)	
23	Didier NILTON Rocha	CPV	19/1/79	A	19	(2)	9
16	Ugur OKAY	TUR	29/9/84	M	2	(3)	
8	Bartłomiej PIETRASIK	POL	25/5/84	D	23	(1)	1
26	Jacques PLEIN		17/2/87	M	11		
17	Gauthier REMACLE	BEL	26/5/77	M	20	(4)	1
24	Michael SARFATI	FRA	19/7/87	M	18	(5)	
10	Tom SCHEIER		25/11/88	D	1	(3)	
25	David TURPEL		19/10/92	M	3	(6)	1
18	Gabriel VIEIRA	POR	6/10/84	M	11	(3)	

CS FOLA ESCH

Coach – Philippe Guerard (BEL); (31/10/10) Jeff Strasser

Founded – 1906

Stadium – Emile Mayrisch (6,000)

MAJOR HONOURS: Luxembourg League – (5) 1918, 1920, 1922, 1924, 1930; Luxembourg Cup – (3) 1923, 1924, 1955.

2010				
8/8	Hesper	h	4-2	*Ronny (p), Dallevedove, Mazurier, Di Gregorio*
15/8	Dudelange	a	0-3	
22/8	Käerjéng	h	2-0	*Hornuss (p), Dallevedove*
29/8	Racing Union	a	2-0	*Hornuss, Kitenge*
12/9	Progrès	h	1-1	*Mazurier*
19/9	Jeunesse Esch	a	1-1	*Dallevedove*
22/9	Grevenmacher	h	1-1	*Di Gregorio*
26/9	Etzella	a	2-1	*Ronny, Omolo*
2/10	Pétange	h	1-1	*Hornuss (p)*
17/10	Hamm	a	2-1	*Dallevedove, Omolo*
23/10	Differdange	h	1-2	*Mazurier*
29/10	Jeunesse Canach	h	1-2	*Kitenge*
7/11	Wiltz	a	1-2	*Dallevedove*
21/11	Käerjéng	a	2-1	*Hornuss, Klein*
28/11	Racing Union	h	3-0	*Mazurier, Di Gregorio 2 (1p)*
2011				
19/2	Dudelange	h	0-3	
27/2	Progrès	a	1-2	*Schnell (p)*
5/3	Jeunesse Esch	h	3-2	*Dallevedove, Ronny (p), Di Gregorio*
12/3	Grevenmacher	a	2-1	*Hornuss, Milak*
19/3	Etzella	h	5-0	*Dallevedove 2, Di Gregorio, Ronny 2*
8/4	Pétange	a	0-1	
16/4	Hamm	h	1-1	*Kitenge*
1/5	Differdange	a	3-0	*Ronny (p), Kitenge (p), Dallevedove*
8/5	Jeunesse Canach	a	3-0	*Ronny (p), Hornuss, Kitenge*
15/5	Wiltz	h	4-0	*Dallevedove, Hornuss 2, Kitenge*
21/5	Hesper	a	2-0	*Helena, Kitenge*

No	Name	Nat	DoB	Pos	Aps	(s)	Gls
5	Billy BERNARD		9/4/91	D	4		
1	Alija BESIC		30/3/75	G	14		
30	Luciano CRAPA	ITA	10/1/74	M		(1)	
24	Jakob DALLEVEDOVE	GER	21/11/87	A	24	(1)	10
25	Joris DI GREGORIO	FRA	4/9/82	A	18	(6)	6
26	Carlos FERREIRA Doria	POR	4/6/83	A		(6)	
6	Gérard GEISBUSCH		4/5/88	D	6	(4)	
12	Carlos Silva HELENA	POR	6/11/74	D	24		1
27	Julien HORNUSS	FRA	1/1/87	A	22	(4)	8
31	Tarik KHARIF	FRA	16/9/77	M		(2)	
28	Joël KITENGE		12/11/87	A	16	(9)	7
18	Julien KLEIN	FRA	7/4/87	M	18	(2)	1
19	Sébastien MAZURIER	FRA	13/4/81	M	23	(1)	4
32	Alen MILAK		23/5/85	D		(4)	1
21	Johanna OMOLO	KEN	13/5/88	M	19	(2)	2
8	Dimitri PARKER	BEL	10/3/90	D	6	(1)	
22	Christophe PAZOS de Matos	ESP	19/5/90	M	9	(7)	
9	Jérémie PEIFFER		7/4/80	D	16		
29	Marco PIRES		13/12/82	A		(11)	
10	Bruno POMPIÈRE	FRA	10/6/80	D	15	(1)	
33	David RODRIGUES Monteiro		13/6/93	M		(1)	
23	Walder Alves Souto Amado "RONNY"	CPV	7/12/78	M	23		7
29	Tom SCHNELL		8/10/85	D	10		1
11	Alex SEMEDO Borges		22/8/89	D	7	(7)	
13	Jeff STRASSER		5/10/74	D		(1)	
4	Pit THEIS		25/1/79	G	12		

CS GREVENMACHER

Coach – Marc Thomé

Founded – 1909

Stadium – Op Flohr (4,000)

MAJOR HONOURS: Luxembourg League – (1) 2003; Luxembourg Cup – (4) 1995, 1998, 2003, 2008.

2010				
8/8	Jeunesse Esch	h	2-2	*Habte 2*
15/8	Jeunesse Canach	a	1-0	*Almeida*
22/8	Etzella	a	4-0	*Brzyski 2, Louadj (p), Boussi*
27/8	Pétange	h	1-0	*Hoffmann*
11/9	Hamm	a	2-3	*Boussi, Louadj*
18/9	Differdange	h	0-2	
22/9	Fola	a	1-1	*Traoré*
26/9	Wiltz	h	4-1	*Müller, Traoré, Louadj 2*
2/10	Hesper	a	3-2	*Louadj 3*
17/10	Dudelange	h	0-3	
24/10	Käerjéng	a	1-5	*Traoré*
31/10	Racing Union	h	1-0	*Baur*
7/11	Progrès	a	3-1	*Louadj 2, Almeida*
21/11	Etzella	h	1-2	*Louadj (p)*
28/11	Pétange	a	2-2	*Louadj 2 (1p)*
2011				
18/2	Jeunesse Canach	h	1-1	*Benichou*
27/2	Hamm	h	1-2	*Almeida*
6/3	Differdange	a	2-2	*Traoré, Hoffmann (p)*
12/3	Fola	h	1-2	*Almeida*
19/3	Wiltz	a	3-2	*Huss, Almeida, Louadj*
10/4	Hesper	h	1-3	*Huss (p)*
16/4	Dudelange	a	3-0	*Huss, Benichou, Louadj*
30/4	Käerjéng	h	0-0	
8/5	Racing Union	a	1-0	*Huss*
15/5	Progrès	h	1-2	*Gaspar G.*
21/5	Jeunesse Esch	a	3-1	*Almeida, Gaspar F., Hoffmann*

No	Name	Nat	DoB	Pos	Aps	(s)	Gls
12	Gonzalo ALMEIDA		26/11/90	M	16	(5)	6
13	Adrien BAUR	FRA	20/5/88	M	10	(2)	1
4	Khalid BENICHOU	FRA	28/3/88	D	20	(3)	2
21	Achmed BOUSSI	GER	23/10/88	A	4	(4)	2
14	Christian BRAUN		12/8/86	M	10	(3)	
5	Dariusz BRZYSKI	POL	6/9/86	D	16		2
6	Jonathan FURST	FRA	23/3/87	D	18	(4)	
22	Florian GASPAR	GER	7/7/87	M	2	(2)	1
15	Gabriel GASPAR Pereira		20/7/90	M	19	(5)	1
7	Sammy HABTE	GER	14/10/83	D	9		2
16	Sebastian HARTUNG	GER	6/12/80	M	23	(2)	

	Tim HEINZ		5/2/84	D	15		
	Sébastien HOFFMANN	FRA	18/12/78	M	22	(1)	3
	Daniel HUSS		8/10/79	A	6	(3)	4
	Tobias LORIG	GER	11/2/81	D	4	(1)	
3	Samir LOUADJ	FRA	9/12/85	M	22	(1)	14
)	Bobby MENDES		7/6/88	M	19	(6)	
3	Christian MÜLLER	GER	17/1/81	A	3	(5)	1
)	Adis OMEROVIC		14/6/80	D	3	(3)	
5	Richard PAUL		12/2/84	M	1		
	Marc PLEIMLING	GER	11/6/89	G	12		
	Arnaud SCHAAB	FRA	3/9/90	G	14		
)	Igor STOJADINOVIC		18/11/85	M	11	(10)	
4	Malick TRAORÉ	GER	21/1/87	A	7	(10)	4

FC RM HAMM BENFICA

Coach – Alvaro Da Cruz; (22/2/11) Felipe Villaverde

Founded – 2004

Stadium – Cents (3,000)

010				
/8	Käerjéng	h	1-2	*Ramires*
5/8	Racing Union	a	1-0	*Di Domenico*
2/8	Progrès	h	0-1	
9/8	Jeunesse Esch	a	1-2	*Kitenge*
1/9	Grevenmacher	h	3-2	*Belabed 2, Kehal*
9/9	Etzella	a	2-2	*Alomerovic, Benhamza*
2/9	Pétange	h	2-2	*Eriton Sousa, Lara*
6/9	Jeunesse Canach	a	4-2	*Kitenge, Alomerovic, Belabed (p), Kehal*
/10	Differdange	a	1-3	*Di Domenico*
7/10	Fola	h	1-2	*Ramires*
4/10	Wiltz	a	3-1	*Lara, Kehal 2*
31/10	Hesper	h	2-0	*Belabed (p), Kehal*
/11	Dudelange	a	2-4	*Lourenço, Martino*
1/11	Progrès	a	2-5	*Di Domenico (p), Kehal*
28/11	Jeunesse Esch	h	1-3	*Niabaly*
2011				
20/2	Racing Union	h	0-4	
27/2	Grevenmacher	a	2-1	*Ramires, Pereira*
4/3	Etzella	h	1-0	*Pereira*
13/3	Pétange	a	5-2	*Di Domenico 2 (1p), Kehal, Ramires, Pereira*
18/3	Jeunesse Canach	h	4-1	*Ramires, Di Domenico, Pereira 2*
10/4	Differdange	h	2-0	*Di Domenico, Kehal*
16/4	Fola	a	1-1	*Kehal*
30/4	Wiltz	h	4-0	*Pereira 2, Kehal, Lara*
8/5	Hesper	a	2-4	*Kehal, Di Domenico*
14/5	Dudelange	h	0-1	
21/5	Käerjéng	a	0-1	

No	Name	Nat	DoB	Pos	Aps	(s)	Gls
3	Assim ALOMEROVIC		25/1/83	D	25		2
27	Cristiano ALVES de Sousa		3/6/90	D		(1)	
30	Aouëd AOUAICHIA	FRA	20/6/77	A		(4)	
11	Rachid BELABED	BEL	20/10/80	M	9	(2)	4
12	Nabil BENHAMZA	FRA	22/8/88	M	14	(6)	1
4	Abdellah BETTAHAR	FRA	31/10/79	D	18		
19	Andrea BORRELLI	ITA	15/11/85	M	1	(1)	
1	Jailson Emanuel da Pina Duarte Moreira "CADABRA"	CPV	26/6/84	G	6		
5	Christopher COLITO Pereira	CPV	4/10/85	D	7	(2)	
15	David DA MOTA	POR	12/5/89	M	8	(3)	
13	Sven DI DOMENICO		15/3/82	M	24	(1)	8
18	ERITON SOUSA Lacerda	BRA	21/11/83	M	4	(5)	1
29	Maurice FLANDER		24/6/91	D		(1)	
28	Antonio FORTES Oliveira		24/12/89	M	1	(2)	
14	Djilali KEHAL	FRA	1/10/78	M	23		11
21	Dimitri KITENGE		2/1/91	A	10	(8)	2
20	Daniel LARA Costa	POR	14/4/87	A	13	(8)	3
26	José LIMA dos Santos	POR	2/10/77	M		(4)	
8	Miguel António LOPES RODRIGUES	POR	23/10/91	D	4	(3)	
7	David LOPEZ	FRA	10/10/75	D	24		
16	Kevin LOURENÇO	POR	12/5/92	M	5	(7)	1
23	Pierre Singa MANZANGALA	BEL	1/8/81	A	1	(7)	
9	Massimo MARTINO		18/9/90	D	25		1
25	Alen MILAK		23/5/84	A	1	(1)	
24	Mohamed NAGUEZ	TUN	26/1/87	M	8		
10	Ousmane NIABALY	FRA	25/6/79	D	13		1
22	Cristiano PEREIRA Fereira		21/11/89	A	9	(2)	7
17	Ricardo RAMIRES Santos Lopes	POR	22/3/76	M	13	(8)	5
2	Jérôme WINCKEL		20/12/85	G	20		

JEUNESSE CANACH

Coach – Patrick Maurer

Founded – 1930

Stadium – Stade rue de Lenningen (1,000)

2010				
8/8	Wiltz	h	1-5	*Danhach*
15/8	Grevenmacher	h	0-1	
22/8	Hesper	a	0-2	
29/8	Etzella	h	1-2	*Sousa*
12/9	Dudelange	a	0-2	
19/9	Pétange	h	1-3	*Ferro*
22/9	Käerjéng	a	0-5	
26/9	Hamm	h	2-4	*Sousa, Ntabala*
2/10	Racing Union	a	2-4	*Vural 2*
17/10	Differdange	h	1-3	*Titon (p)*
24/10	Progrès	a	0-2	
29/10	Fola	a	2-1	*Sousa, Ferro*
7/11	Jeunesse Esch	a	0-2	
21/11	Hesper	h	2-1	*Ferro, Sousa*
28/11	Etzella	a	1-1	*Lang*
2011				
18/2	Grevenmacher	a	1-1	*Ferro*
27/2	Dudelange	h	2-2	*Sözen 2*
6/3	Pétange	a	3-2	*Alvites, Sözen, Ferro*
13/3	Käerjéng	h	2-4	*Sözen, Ferro*
18/3	Hamm	a	1-4	*Ntabala*
10/4	Racing Union	h	3-2	*Abdelkadous, Alvites, Sözen*
17/4	Differdange	a	0-4	
30/4	Progrès	h	1-0	*Sözen*
8/5	Fola	h	0-3	
15/5	Jeunesse Esch	h	1-1	*Ferro*
21/5	Wiltz	a	1-1	*Hoeser*

No	Name	Nat	DoB	Pos	Aps	(s)	Gls
35	Cherif ABDELKADOUS	FRA	17/12/77	A	4	(1)	1
18	Mohaman ABDOULAYE	FRA	2/3/83	M	6		
19	Luis Carlos ALVITES		9/11/87	M	8	(8)	2
20	Abdelghani AMRANE	FRA	23/1/85	M	18	(3)	
5	Yves CANDIDA		6/11/79	D	1		
6	Noureddine DANHACH	FRA	30/10/73	D	18		1
21	Aldi DERVIŠEVIĆ	SRB	19/8/89	M	17	(4)	
22	Din DERVISEVIC		19/5/91	M	6	(14)	
36	Pedro Miguel FERRO	POR	21/7/87	A	14	(2)	7
1	Julien GUTHLEBER	FRA	23/9/87	G	24		
23	Laurent HOESER		20/10/86	M	15	(3)	1
24	Frank JÄGER	FRA	26/8/76	M	6	(3)	
31	João Tavares "KALU"	POR	8/9/84	M	9		
8	Tim KARIUS		20/10/83	D	1		
9	Gueton KREMER	FRA	25/4/85	D	18		
10	Renaud KREMER	FRA	5/4/84	D	10	(1)	
11	Benoît LANG		19/12/83	D	7	(1)	1
34	Andy LOMMEL		31/7/87	M		(2)	
40	Bonny NTABALA	CGO	15/5/85	A	10	(4)	2
12	Patrick OSSAMBA	FRA	25/9/86	D	9		
3	Steve RAACH		24/8/83	G	2		
37	Pol REDINGER		16/7/93	M		(1)	
28	Christian RODRIGUES		17/12/79	M	14	(2)	
41	Fabiano SCHIAVO	BRA	8/3/77	A	2	(5)	
29	Admir SKRIJELJ	BIH	3/6/92	M	12	(5)	
42	Roger SOUSA	BRA	30/8/71	A	11	(5)	4
13	Fatih SÖZEN	GER	7/5/82	A	11		6
30	Waldino Borges TAVARES	CPV	1/10/80	M	5	(7)	
15	Marcos Aurélio TITON	POR	19/7/76	D	15		1
16	Roberto VALAITIS	LTU	11/5/87	D	7		
17	Hasan VURAL	GER	17/12/73	D	5	(1)	2
33	Pieter WEIRIG		17/5/91	M	1	(5)	

AS JEUNESSE ESCH

Coach – Jacques Muller; (13/9/10) (Vinicio Monacelli); (21/9/10) Fernando Gutiérrez (ARG); (14/3/11) (Vinicio Monacelli); (21/3/11) Sébastien Grosjean (BEL)
Founded – 1907
Stadium – Stade de la Frontière (7,000)
MAJOR HONOURS: Luxembourg League – (28) 1921, 1937, 1951, 1954, 1958, 1959, 1960, 1963, 1967, 1968, 1970, 1973, 1974, 1975, 1976, 1977, 1980, 1983, 1985, 1987, 1988, 1995, 1996, 1997, 1998, 1999, 2004, 2010;
Luxembourg Cup – (12) 1935, 1937, 1946, 1954, 1973, 1974, 1976, 1981, 1988, 1997, 1999, 2000.

2010				
8/8	Grevenmacher	a	2-2	*Piron, Cantonnet*
15/8	Etzella	h	0-1	
22/8	Pétange	a	1-1	*Fullenwarth*
29/8	Hamm	h	2-1	*Gonçalves, Fullenwarth*
12/9	Differdange	a	0-3	
19/9	Fola	h	1-1	*og (Klein)*
22/9	Wiltz	a	4-2	*Pupovac 4*
26/9	Hesper	h	4-1	*Pupovac, Piron, Cantonnet, Leweck C.*
2/10	Dudelange	a	0-2	
17/10	Käerjéng	h	4-0	*Piron 2, Deidda, Leweck C.*
24/10	Racing Union	a	1-4	*Fullenwarth*
31/10	Progrès	h	2-2	*Peters, Cantonnet (p)*
7/11	Jeunesse Canach	h	2-0	*Leweck C., Piron*
21/11	Pétange	h	2-1	*Servais, Leweck C.*
28/11	Hamm	a	3-1	*Servais, Pupovac, Hoffmann (p)*
2011				
20/2	Etzella	a	0-0	
26/2	Differdange	h	1-2	*og (Leoni)*
5/3	Fola	a	2-3	*Benajiba 2*
13/3	Wiltz	h	0-2	
19/3	Hesper	a	2-1	*Gonçalves, Hoffmann (p)*
9/4	Dudelange	h	1-0	*Gonçalves*
17/4	Käerjéng	a	1-1	*og (Martins da Silva)*
29/4	Racing Union	h	0-1	
8/5	Progrès	a	3-1	*Piron 2, Benajiba*
15/5	Jeunesse Canach	a	1-1	*Pupovac*
21/5	Grevenmacher	h	1-3	*Cantonnet*

No	Name	Nat	DoB	Pos	Aps	(s)	Gls
4	Edis AGOVIC		12/7/93	D	2		
10	Cédric BASTOS		7/5/89	M	1	(5)	
34	Jimmy BAZZUCCHI		29/3/92	A		(1)	
3	Yassine BENAJIBA	MAR	1/11/84	M	10		3
11	Loïc CANTONNET	FRA	6/9/80	M	10		4
28	Luca COGONI		21/10/91	D	1		
5	Dan COLLETTE		2/4/85	D	13	(3)	
6	Clayton DE SOUSA Moreira		24/2/88	D	21	(2)	
23	Andrea DEIDDA		15/12/93	A	12	(8)	1
29	Ricardo DELGADO		22/2/94	D		(1)	
31	Philippe FREITAS Morgado		29/12/92	M	1		
14	Thomas FULLENWARTH	FRA	21/1/87	M	15	(1)	3
25	Keiven GONÇALVES Fernandes	POR	26/8/86	A	6	(12)	3
7	Eric HOFFMANN		21/6/84	D	22	(1)	2
17	Alphonse "Fons" LEWECK		16/12/81	M	2	(8)	
16	Charles LEWECK		19/7/83	M	24		4
18	Kevin MARTIN	FRA	17/2/80	M	20	(2)	
2	Marc OBERWEIS		6/11/82	G	25		
1	Steve PFEIFFER		1/9/92	G	1		
19	René PETERS		15/6/81	M	21		1
26	Stéphane PIRON	BEL	17/1/84	A	16	(4)	7
20	Adrien PORTIER	FRA	2/2/88	M	18		
27	Sergio PUPOVAC		5/7/79	A	13	(5)	7
8	Dzenid RAMDEDOVIĆ	MNE	25/2/92	D	4	(3)	
21	Roxan RODRÍGUEZ	FRA	15/1/88	M	7	(10)	
33	Yannick RUIZ GOMES	POR	7/12/88	A	1		
22	Grégory SERVAIS	BEL	30/11/88	M	19	(2)	2
32	Jeffrey TAVARES Gomes		12/3/92	M		(1)	
30	Hugo Filipe VIEIRA Castro		22/4/92	D	1		

UN KÄERJÉNG 97

Coach – Roland Schaack
Founded – 1997
Stadium – Bëchel (3,000)

2010				
8/8	Hamm	a	2-1	*Da Cruz, Sabotic*
15/8	Differdange	h	2-2	*Zewe 2*
22/8	Fola	a	0-2	
29/8	Wiltz	h	5-1	*Da Cruz 3, Zewe 2 (1p)*
12/9	Hesper	a	3-2	*Boulahfari, Zewe (p), Rolandi (p)*
19/9	Dudelange	h	1-3	*Andres*
22/9	Jeunesse Canach	h	5-0	*Zewe 3 (1p), Polidori, Andres*
26/9	Racing Union	a	3-1	*Martins da Silva, Ramdedovic, Boulahfari*
2/10	Progrès	h	3-4	*Polidori, Zewe 2 (1p)*
17/10	Jeunesse Esch	a	0-4	
24/10	Grevenmacher	h	5-1	*Da Cruz, Zewe 2, Sabotic, Andres*
31/10	Etzella	a	1-0	*Zewe*
7/11	Pétange	h	0-0	
21/11	Fola	h	1-2	*Rolandi*
28/11	Wiltz	a	1-0	*Boulahfari*
2011				
20/2	Differdange	a	1-2	*Da Cruz*
26/2	Hesper	h	4-1	*Zewe 3, Polidori*
5/3	Dudelange	a	3-0	*(w/o; match abandoned after 75 mins a 2-1 Da Cruz, Boulahfari)*
13/3	Jeunesse Canach	a	4-2	*Andres 2, Rolandi (p), Ngasseu (p)*
18/3	Racing Union	h	1-1	*Leite*
10/4	Progrès	a	1-2	*Boulahfari*
17/4	Jeunesse Esch	h	1-1	*Andres*
30/4	Grevenmacher	a	0-0	
8/5	Etzella	h	6-1	*Rolandi 2 (1p), Corral 2, Boulahfari, Ngasseu*
14/5	Pétange	a	0-1	
21/5	Hamm	h	1-0	*Marinelli*

No	Name	Nat	DoB	Pos	Aps	(s)	Gls
12	Jean-Batiste de ANDRADE	BRA	6/3/92	M	1	(8)	
11	Romain ANDRES	FRA	20/1/88	M	21	(4)	6
19	Rachid BOULAHFARI	FRA	17/4/84	A	20	(3)	6
1	Fabiano CASTELLANI		11/5/89	G	18		
17	CLEYTON Santos Pires	CPV	20/8/90	M	1	(2)	
24	Ken CORRAL Garcia		8/5/92	A	6	(2)	2
4	Paulo DA COSTA	POR	24/4/81	D	22		
20	Stéphane DA CRUZ	FRA	1/3/88	A	21	(3)	7
5	Jeff FELLER		18/4/85	D	8	(5)	
21	Alessandro FIORANI	ITA	19/2/89	A	4	(10)	
6	Lars HELLER	GER	2/4/77	D	18	(2)	
7	Kevin LEITE		15/2/89	D	20		1
8	Vito MARINELLI		7/8/80	D	20		1
13	Gilles MARTINS DA SILVA		3/6/82	M	20	(3)	1
25	Yves NGASSEU	CMR	25/10/85	A	2	(7)	2
14	Andy PESCHEUX		17/12/91	M		(1)	
22	Ben POLIDORI		13/11/89	A	3	(7)	3
9	Henid RAMDEDOVIC		20/7/87	D	16	(2)	1
15	Julien ROLANDI	FRA	28/3/86	M	16	(5)	5
16	Ernad SABOTIC		13/10/79	M	18	(1)	2
18	Fabiano SPINELLI		30/11/87	M	1	(2)	
2	Philippe STELLETTA	ITA	24/2/84	G	8	(1)	
10	Cyrille WELTER		24/2/91	D	4	(7)	
23	Romain ZEWE	FRA	21/4/88	A	18		16

CS PÉTANGE

Coach – Carlo Weis
Founded – 1910
Stadium – Stade Municipal (2,400)
MAJOR HONOURS: Luxembourg Cup – (1) 2005.

2010				
8/8	Racing Union	h	2-2	*Camara, Pjanić*
14/8	Progrès	a	2-1	*Steger, Neger*
22/8	Jeunesse Esch	h	1-1	*Sagramola*
27/8	Grevenmacher	a	0-1	
12/9	Etzella	h	2-1	*Thonon, Camara*
19/9	Jeunesse Canach	a	3-1	*Mutuale, Pjanić (p), Thonon*
22/9	Hamm	a	2-2	*Camara, Steger*
26/9	Differdange	h	1-4	*Neger*
2/10	Fola	a	1-1	*Kirchen*
17/10	Wiltz	h	5-1	*Kruser 2, Kirchen, Pjanić, Thonon*
24/10	Hesper	h	0-0	
31/10	Dudelange	h	1-0	*Pjanić (p)*
7/11	Käerjéng	a	0-0	

/11	Jeunesse Esch	a	1-2	*Sagramola*
/11	Grevenmacher	h	2-2	*Mutuale, Kirchen*
11				
/2	Progrès	h	1-0	*Boukellal*
/2	Etzella	a	2-0	*og (Ferreira), Mutuale*
3	Jeunesse Canach	h	2-3	*Mutuale, Molitor*
/3	Hamm	h	2-5	*Camara, Eriton Sousa*
/3	Differdange	a	1-1	*Boukellal*
4	Fola	h	1-0	*Dione P.*
/4	Wiltz	a	1-2	*Sissoko*
/4	Hesper	h	1-3	*Pjanić*
5	Dudelange	a	0-3	
/5	Käerjéng	h	1-0	*Thonon*
/5	Racing Union	a	2-0	*Mutuale, Pjanić*

o	Name	Nat	DoB	Pos	Aps	(s)	Gls
5	ADAÍLTON de Oliveira Rodrigues	BRA	11/6/77	M	6	(2)	
9	Claudio BERETTA		19/10/93	M	6	(3)	
1	Mourad BOUKELLAL	ALG	17/1/76	M	3	(2)	2
1	Soriba CAMARA	GUI	5/2/74	A	9	(10)	4
2	CARLO Dinis ANTUNES do Carmo	POR	12/10/82	M	9	(5)	
4	DAVID TEIXEIRA Caçador		17/12/86	M	5	(6)	
	El Hadji DIONE	SEN	25/3/73	D	17	(2)	
	Papa Aye DIONE	SEN	8/3/86	D	21	(2)	1
4	ERITON SOUSA Lacerda	BRA	21/11/83	M		(3)	1
	Philippe FELGEN		8/10/75	G	17		
3	Mino FIORENTINO	ITA	17/7/88	A		(2)	
4	Jens KIRCHEN	GER	13/2/89	A	16	(2)	3
	Arthur KRUSER	GER	12/3/89	D	18		2
	Tim LEHNEN		17/6/86	D	26		
0	Steven MARTINS Reis		15/3/93	D	5	(2)	
3	Grégory MOLITOR		12/3/80	M	9		1
	Yamukile MUTUALE	FRA	25/8/87	D	19		5
7	Denis NEGER	GER	22/5/88	M	6	(5)	2
	Jérémy NEVES		18/8/93	D	4	(3)	
8	Dylan NISSAN	IRL	7/11/88	M	8	(5)	
5	Anel PJANIĆ	BIH	26/12/83	A	10	(6)	6
	Samin REDZEPAGIC		1/10/91	G	9	(1)	
6	Chris SAGRAMOLA		25/2/88	A	14	(2)	2
0	Noumeke SISSOKO	FRA	8/11/79	D	17	(1)	1
7	André STEGER	GER	27/5/86	A	7	(1)	2
32	Sébastien THILL		29/12/93	M	7	(4)	
28	Thibaut THONON	FRA	5/2/87	A	18	(3)	4

FC PROGRÈS NIEDERCORN

Coach – Henri Bossi

Founded – 1919

Stadium – Jos Haupert (4,000)

MAJOR HONOURS: Luxembourg League – (3) 1953, 1978, 1981; Luxembourg Cup – (4) 1933, 1945, 1977, 1978.

2010				
8/8	Etzella	a	2-2	*Proietti (p), Kabran*
14/8	Pétange	h	1-2	*Bilon*
22/8	Hamm	a	1-0	*Caldieri*
28/8	Differdange	h	2-4	*Caldieri (p), Gilgemann*
12/9	Fola	a	1-1	*Marques*
18/9	Wiltz	h	0-1	
22/9	Hesper	a	2-2	*Bossi, Bilon*
26/9	Dudelange	h	1-5	*Mondon-Konan*
2/10	Käerjéng	a	4-3	*Caldieri 3, Kabran*
17/10	Racing Union	h	1-0	*Rigo*
24/10	Jeunesse Canach	h	2-0	*Caldieri, Colleatte*
31/10	Jeunesse Esch	a	2-2	*Colleatte (p), Rigo*
7/11	Grevenmacher	h	1-3	*Caldieri*
21/11	Hamm	h	5-2	*Caldieri 2, Bossi, Rigo, Vieira C.*
28/11	Differdange	a	2-1	*Jorge Ribeiro, Gilgemann*
2011				
20/2	Pétange	a	0-1	
27/2	Fola	h	2-1	*De Sousa, Caldieri*
6/3	Wiltz	a	3-0	*Caldieri 2, De Sousa*
12/3	Hesper	h	2-0	*Gilgemann, Caldieri*
19/3	Dudelange	a	1-5	*Gilgemann*
10/4	Käerjéng	h	2-1	*Caldieri (p), Mondon-Konan*
15/4	Racing Union	a	0-0	
30/4	Jeunesse Canach	a	0-1	
8/5	Jeunesse Esch	h	1-3	*Jorge Ribeiro*
15/5	Grevenmacher	a	2-1	*Da Graça, Jorge Ribeiro*
21/5	Etzella	h	3-2	*Kabran, Vieira de Sousa, Jorge Ribeiro*

No	Name	Nat	DoB	Pos	Aps	(s)	Gls
29	Yusef ALIMLI	FRA	9/3/84	A	1	(1)	
1	Jérémie BANDEL	FRA	3/4/85	G	19		
21	Sully BILON	FRA	15/10/80	A	5	(4)	2
22	Paul BOSSI		22/7/91	A	22	(3)	2
23	Nicolas CALDIERI	FRA	1/12/82	A	19	(3)	14
15	François COLLEATTE	FRA	25/2/85	M	15		2
25	Jeffrey DA GRAÇA Dias		27/7/94	A	9	(6)	1
16	Marco DE SOUSA		17/8/86	M	15	(9)	2
6	Enzo GHIN	FRA	21/2/75	D	18		
7	Thomas GILGEMANN	FRA	15/9/83	D	25		4
20	JORGE Manuel RIBEIRO Magalhães	POR	24/10/92	M	16	(6)	4
17	Gilles JUNGBLUTH		7/4/88	M		(7)	
26	Lambert KABRAN Anguoa	CPV	18/10/89	A	10	(14)	3
9	Yi LIN		6/10/82	D	1		
2	Moreno LOMBARDELLI		16/9/91	G		(1)	
12	David MARQUES Soares	POR	20/2/91	D	20	(3)	1
3	Laurent MOND		31/1/83	G	7		
14	Patrice MONDON-KONAN	FRA	17/3/83	M	25		2
18	Tarek NOUIDRA	FRA	9/5/87	M	23		
33	Michael OLIVEIRA Martins	POR	21/9/93	D		(5)	
34	Bruno PINTO da Costa		3/10/94	M		(2)	
19	Jonathan PROIETTI		17/7/82	M	4	(2)	1
28	Mike REA	FRA	2/5/80	A		(1)	
10	Jonathan RIGO	FRA	16/9/87	D	26		3
11	Cédric VIEIRA Gonçalves	POR	12/2/93	M	1	(3)	1
33	Daniel VIEIRA Sousa Teixeira		8/4/90	D	2		
31	José VIEIRA DE SOUSA	POR	19/12/86	M		(5)	1
30	Serge Guy YEMBA Mahop	BEL	20/1/82	D	1	(1)	
32	Nico ZHAN		10/1/85	M	2	(2)	

RACING FC UNION LËTZEBUERG

Coach – Sébastien Allieri (FRA)

Founded – 2005

Stadium – Achille Hammerel (6,000)

2010				
8/8	Pétange	a	2-2	*Bellini, Schnell*
15/8	Hamm	h	0-1	
22/8	Differdange	a	2-0	*Romero, D'Exelle*
29/8	Fola	h	0-2	
12/9	Wiltz	a	4-1	*Romero 2, Rougeaux 2*
19/9	Hesper	h	0-0	
22/9	Dudelange	a	2-3	*Romero, Valente*
26/9	Käerjéng	h	1-3	*Rougeaux*
2/10	Jeunesse Canach	h	4-2	*Rougeaux 2, D'Exelle 2*
17/10	Progrès	a	0-1	
24/10	Jeunesse Esch	h	4-1	*Schnell (p), D'Exelle 2, Centrone*
31/10	Grevenmacher	a	0-1	
7/11	Etzella	h	5-1	*D'Exelle 2, Romero 2, Antonicelli*
21/11	Differdange	h	1-1	*D'Exelle*
28/11	Fola	a	0-3	
2011				
20/2	Hamm	a	4-0	*Romero, Rougeaux 2, Centrone*
27/2	Wiltz	h	1-3	*D'Exelle*
6/3	Hesper	a	1-2	*Rougeaux*
13/3	Dudelange	h	0-2	
18/3	Käerjéng	a	1-1	*D'Exelle*
10/4	Jeunesse Canach	a	2-3	*Rougeaux 2*
15/4	Progrès	h	0-0	
29/4	Jeunesse Esch	a	1-0	*Rani*
8/5	Grevenmacher	h	0-1	
14/5	Etzella	a	3-2	*Rougeaux 2, Valente*
21/5	Pétange	h	0-2	

No	Name	Nat	DoB	Pos	Aps	(s)	Gls
1	Alexandre ABELLO	FRA	22/8/82	G	22		
10	Pasquale ANTONICELLI		16/11/82	M	5	(13)	1
26	Almin BABACIC		16/1/84	D	10		
23	Olivier BAUDRY	FRA	13/4/70	D	4	(1)	
11	Johan BELLINI	FRA	2/6/83	M	23	(1)	1
24	Yannick BIANCHINI		13/11/80	A		(3)	
12	Michael CARVALHO Gonçalves	POR	5/8/86	M	1	(1)	

No	Name	Nat	DoB	Pos	Aps	(s)	Gls
25	Adriano CENTRONE		29/10/93	M	4	(4)	2
2	Chris CLEMENT		29/12/91	G	4		
20	Kris D'EXELLE	BEL	13/7/89	A	16	(7)	10
3	Karim DJELLAL	FRA	27/1/82	D	24	(1)	
14	Sami FONTES		1/2/89	M	5	(9)	
15	Gaël HUG	FRA	8/1/80	M	15		
28	Sydney LOES		21/10/93	A		(1)	
29	Alexandre LOPES		15/1/92	A		(1)	
16	Kevin MOLINERO	FRA	9/1/85	M	14	(2)	
17	Damir MUHOVIC		19/2/85	M	13	(7)	
18	Ahmed RANI	FRA	20/8/87	M	25	(1)	1
5	Jonathan RODRIGUES Monteiro		8/1/91	D	5	(2)	
21	Nicolas ROMERO	FRA	18/8/88	A	19	(4)	7
22	Lévy ROUGEAUX	FRA	8/5/85	A	25	(1)	12
6	Tom SCHNELL		8/10/85	D	13		2
7	Marco SIMOES		1/8/86	D	3		
19	Ramiro VALENTE Soares	POR	26/1/89	M	6	(9)	2
8	Alexandre VITALI	FRA	17/1/89	D	25		
27	Saber ZENNANE	MAR	27/7/76	D	5		

FC SWIFT HESPER

Coach – Angelo Fiorucci; (14/3/11) Nedzib Selimovic

Founded – 1916

Stadium – Alphonse Theis (5,000)

MAJOR HONOURS: Luxembourg Cup – (1) 1990.

2010

8/8	Fola	a	2-4	*Munoz, Schulz (p)*
15/8	Wiltz	h	2-1	*Schulz, Sampaio*
22/8	Jeunesse Canach	h	2-0	*Sampaio 2*
28/8	Dudelange	a	0-2	
12/9	Käerjéng	h	2-3	*Schulz (p), Touré*
19/9	Racing Union	a	0-0	
22/9	Progrès	h	2-2	*Schulz 2*
26/9	Jeunesse Esch	a	1-4	*Willemin*
2/10	Grevenmacher	h	2-3	*Bozic, Sampaio (p)*
16/10	Etzella	a	3-2	*Bozic 2, Stoklosa*
24/10	Pétange	h	0-0	
31/10	Hamm	a	0-2	
7/11	Differdange	h	0-0	
21/11	Jeunesse Canach	a	1-2	*Schäfer*
28/11	Dudelange	h	0-3	

2011

19/2	Wiltz	a	3-1	*Touré (p), Sampaio 2*
26/2	Käerjéng	a	1-4	*Sampaio*
6/3	Racing Union	h	2-1	*Sampaio, Touré*
12/3	Progrès	a	0-2	
19/3	Jeunesse Esch	h	1-2	*Bozic*
10/4	Grevenmacher	a	3-1	*Schulz 2, Bozic*
17/4	Etzella	h	4-2	*Schulz 3, Touré*
30/4	Pétange	a	3-1	*Sampaio 2, Casafina*
8/5	Hamm	h	4-2	*Sampaio, Schulz, Touré, Schiltz*
15/5	Differdange	a	0-3	
21/5	Fola	h	0-2	

No	Name	Nat	DoB	Pos	Aps	(s)	Gls
11	Patrick AQUARO		5/6/91	M	4	(2)	
1	Alex BOUKHETAIA	FRA	19/11/79	G	20		
12	Anton BOZIC		15/2/86	M	23	(2)	5
4	Denis CABRILLON		22/5/90	D	12	(1)	
20	Antonio CASAFINA		15/1/91	A		(14)	1
3	Esteban DELAPORTE		12/8/90	G		(2)	
13	Fabio GASPAR Morais	POR	11/2/86	M	5	(1)	
31	Dorian HELLINCKS		11/5/93	A	1		
5	Pit HILBERT		18/2/90	D	20		
29	Kevin LACROIX	GER	13/10/84	D	11		
6	Olivier LICKES		27/6/88	D	7	(3)	
27	Joé LUX		18/4/92	M		(3)	
21	Matondo MAKIADI	GER	14/7/88	A	8		
2	Celso Gabriel Gonçalves MALHEIRO	POR	25/2/86	G	6	(1)	
14	Hugo MARTINS ALVES	POR	16/2/93	M		(4)	
28	Jordan MOROCUTTI		26/9/92	A		(2)	
15	Tom MUNOZ		2/8/81	M	11	(7)	1
30	Thomas PANEL	FRA	13/10/86	A		(1)	
16	Pedro RODRIGUES Pinto	POR	3/1/84	M	10	(1)	
22	Johan Carlos SAMPAIO Miranda	POR	20/7/80	A	20	(2)	11
17	Lars SCHÄFER	GER	27/8/82	M	20	(5)	1
23	Laurent SCHILTZ		17/2/82	A	7	(8)	1
18	Gustav SCHULZ	GER	27/6/85	M	13	(2)	11
24	Fatih SÖZEN	GER	7/5/82	A	5	(5)	
9	Damian STOKLOSA	GER	30/8/79	D	18		1
10	Armando TAVARES	CPV	25/10/76	D	22		
25	Moussa TOURÉ	FRA	22/12/88	A	15	(5)	5
26	Naby TWIMUMU		24/8/90	A	2	(5)	
19	Michael WILLEMIN	FRA	22/10/82	M	26		1

FC WILTZ 71

Coach – Steve Majerus; (29/10/10) (Samir Kalabić (BIH)); (7/11/10) Pascal Lebrun (BEL)

Founded – 1971

Stadium – Géitzt (2,000)

2010

8/8	Jeunesse Canach	a	5-1	*Mujkic M., Osmanović, Ibrahimović 2, og (Lang)*
15/8	Hesper	a	1-2	*Osmanović*
21/8	Dudelange	h	1-5	*Ibrahimović*
29/8	Käerjéng	a	1-5	*Osmanović*
12/9	Racing Union	h	1-4	*Kouayep*
18/9	Progrès	a	1-0	*Ibrahimović*
22/9	Jeunesse Esch	h	2-4	*Osmanović, Mujkic M. (p)*
26/9	Grevenmacher	a	1-4	*Faljic*
2/10	Etzella	h	1-2	*Kouayep*
17/10	Pétange	a	1-5	*Ibrahimović*
24/10	Hamm	h	1-3	*Ibrahimović*
31/10	Differdange	a	4-4	*Ibrahimović 3, Osmanović*
7/11	Fola	h	2-1	*Ibrahimović 2*
21/11	Dudelange	a	0-15	
28/11	Käerjéng	h	0-1	

2011

19/2	Hesper	h	1-3	*Ibrahimović*
27/2	Racing Union	a	3-1	*Mujkic M., Osmanović, Ibrahimović*
6/3	Progrès	h	0-3	
13/3	Jeunesse Esch	a	2-0	*Kouayep, Ibrahimović*
19/3	Grevenmacher	h	2-3	*Ibrahimović 2 (1p)*
9/4	Etzella	a	3-1	*Ibrahimović 2, Osmanović*
17/4	Pétange	h	2-1	*Kouayep, Mujkic M.*
30/4	Hamm	a	0-4	
8/5	Differdange	h	2-1	*Omerović, Osmanović*
15/5	Fola	a	0-4	
21/5	Jeunesse Canach	h	1-1	*Chionna*

No	Name	Nat	DoB	Pos	Aps	(s)	Gls
1	Jan ARNOLD		3/11/88	G	6	(2)	
5	Adnan BATKIC		4/7/84	D		(3)	
26	Randy CHIONNA	ITA	8/9/89	A	3	(8)	1
27	Amel COSIC		19/11/89	A	1	(5)	
8	Esmir COSIC		14/11/83	D		(2)	
16	Haris FALJIC		1/6/91	M	17	(3)	1
9	Sébastien FISCHETTI	FRA	11/5/91	D	9	(1)	
6	FLÁVIO Campos	POR	16/8/86	D	3		
10	Ben HEIDERSCHEID		9/4/89	D	17	(2)	
17	Claude HENTZ		9/6/85	M	22	(3)	
28	Sanel IBRAHIMOVIĆ	BIH	24/11/87	A	24		18
18	Malick KORODOWOU	TOG	15/12/90	M	4	(2)	
19	Rodrigue KOUAYEP	CMR	7/12/86	M	23		4
11	Guy LIBAMBU	BEL	19/9/76	D	4	(4)	
30	Arnaud LUNSI Diyakame	FRA	13/3/87	D	11		
31	Nicolas MAZOYER	FRA	21/10/79	M	10		
20	Mehmet MUJKIC		26/9/83	M	21	(1)	4
12	Sevad MUJKIC		13/6/85	D	25		
13	Aldin MUSTIC		8/9/90	D		(1)	
21	Alen OMEROVIĆ	BIH	24/8/84	M	8	(7)	1
29	Edis OSMANOVIĆ	BIH	30/8/88	A	22	(1)	8
22	Chris PATINI		18/12/86	M	6	(8)	
24	Jos PELKES		16/7/93	M	2	(3)	
4	RUI BATISTA	POR	3/2/83	D	11	(4)	
25	Nihad SEJDOVIĆ	SRB	25/7/75	M	14	(2)	
3	Fred VAN DE SANDE	BEL	20/11/70	G	20		
15	Ediz VATANSEVER	BEL	12/2/87	D	3		

TOP GOALSCORERS 2010/11

18 Sanel IBRAHIMOVIĆ (Wiltz)

16 Aurélien JOACHIM (Differdange)
Daniel DA MOTA (Dudelange)
Romain ZEWE (Käerjéng)

14 Thomas GRUSZCZYŃSKI (Dudelange)
Samir LOUADJ (Grevenmacher)
Nicolas CALDIERI (Progrès)

12 Sofian BENZOUIEN (Dudelange)
Lévy ROUGEAUX (Racing Union)

11 Djilali KEHAL (Hamm)
Johan Carlos SAMPAIO (Hesper)
Gustav SCHULZ (Hesper)

PROMOTED CLUBS

FC UNION 05 KAYL/TETANGE
Coach – Manuel Correia
Founded – 2005
Stadium – "An der Gennerwiss" (1,200)

US RUMELANGE
Coach – Manuel Cardoni
Founded – 1908
Stadium – Municipal (2,950)
MAJOR HONOURS: Luxembourg Cup - (2) 1968, 1975.

US HOSTERT
Coach – Carlos Texeira
Founded – 1946
Stadium – Jos Becker (1,500)

SECOND LEVEL FINAL TABLE 2010/11

		Pld	W	D	L	F	A	Pts
1	FC Union 05 Kayl/Tétange	26	20	2	4	59	31	62
2	US Rumelange	26	20	2	4	47	22	62
3	US Hostert	26	16	4	6	50	32	52
4	FC Victoria Rosport	26	15	4	7	61	39	49
5	CS Obercorn	26	14	5	7	49	30	47
6	FC Young Boys Diekirch	26	12	4	10	41	39	40
7	FC Erpeldange 72	26	11	4	11	57	46	37
8	FC Mondercange	26	10	4	12	40	34	34
9	US Mondorf-les-Bains	26	6	7	13	34	45	25
10	FC Koeppchen Wormeldange	26	6	7	13	32	46	25
11	Sporting Club Steinfort	26	6	5	15	24	45	23
12	FC GB 77 Harlange/ Tarchamps	26	4	9	13	31	67	21
13	FC Avenir Beggen	26	5	4	17	30	54	19
14	FC Minerva Lintgen	26	3	7	16	25	50	16

PROMOTION/RELEGATION PLAY-OFF

(28/5/11)
Hostert 1, Wiltz 1
(aet; 5-3 on pens)

DOMESTIC CUP 2010/11

COUPE DE LUXEMBOURG

FIFTH ROUND

(1/4/11)
Sanem 0, Jeunesse Canach 2

(2/4/11)
Belvaux 0, Rumelange 1
Beggen 0, Racing Union 3
Mertert/Wasserbillig 0, Jeunesse Esch 1

(3/4/11)
Flaxweiler/Beyren 3, Pétange 3 *(aet; 9-8 on pens)*
Hostert 3, Hamm 5 *(aet)*
Jeunesse Schieren 2, Differdange 4 *(aet)*
Junglinster 0, Fola 2
Kayl/Tétange 1, Muhlenbach 0
Kehlen 1, Käerjéng 6
Mamer 1, Grevenmacher 3
Mertzig 0, Hesper 3
Mondercange 0, Etzella 3
Mondorf 2, Progrès 2 *(aet; 2-5 on pens)*
Steinfort 3, Wiltz 1 *(aet)*
Strassen 0, Dudelange 1 *(aet)*

SIXTH ROUND

(22/4/11)
Differdange 3, Hamm 1 *(aet)*
Dudelange 2, Hesper 1
Etzella 1, Fola 2
Flaxweiler/Beyren 1, Kayl/Tétange 2 *(aet)*
Käerjéng 0, Grevenmacher 2
Progrès 2, Racing Union 3 *(aet)*
Rumelange 0, Jeunesse Canach 2
Steinfort 1, Jeunesse Esch 4

QUARTER-FINALS

(4/5/11)
Differdange 5 *(Franzoni 36, 73, Alunni 46, Joachim 61, May 63)*, Jeunesse Canach 0
Fola 1 *(Helena 72)*, Dudelange 2 *(Benzouien 4, 90)*
Kayl/Tétange 1 *(Deidda I. 64)*, Jeunesse Esch 4 *(Gonçalves 23, Benajiba 45, Pupovac 72, 75)*
Racing Union 4 *(D'Exelle 18, Vitali 49, 89, Valente 90+3)*, Grevenmacher 1 *(Gaspar F. 88)*

SEMI-FINALS

(24/5/11)
Jeunesse Esch 0, Dudelange 2 (Da Mota 13, Gruszczyński 83)

(25/5/11)
Racing Union 0, Differdange 2 (Muhovic 18og, Piskor 72)

FINAL

(29/5/11)
Stade Josy Barthel, Luxembourg
FC DIFFERDANGE 03 1 *(Pedro Ribeiro 24)*
F91 DUDELANGE 0
Referee – *Bourgnon*
DIFFERDANGE – *Hym, Kintziger, Bukvic, Siebenaler, Rodrigues, Jänisch, Lebresne, Pedro Ribeiro (May 76), Bettmer, Joachim (Franzoni 88), Piskor (Kettenmeyer 90).*
DUDELANGE – *Joubert, Mouny, Caillet, Guthleber, Wiggers, Payal (Remy 73), Sanchez, Benzouien, Mélisse, Somé (Gruszczyński 46), Da Mota (Bensi 58).*

LUXEMBOURG

CLUB COMMUNICATION 2011/12

FC Differdange 03
PO Box 38
LU-4501 Differdange

Tel +352 6212 77827
Fax +352 585 128
Web fcd03.lu
Email breden@pt.lu
Media Officer Fabrizio Bei

F91 Dudelange
PO Box 278
LU-3403 Dudelange

Tel +352 621 231 553
Fax +352 265 111 44
Web f91.lu
Email thfelle@pt.lu
Media Officer Romain Schumacher

CS Fola Esch
PO Box 83
LU-4001 Esch-sur-Alzette

Tel +352 530 995
Fax +352 530 994
Web csfola.lu
Email pimknaff@pt.lu
Media Officer Mauro Mariani

CS Grevenmacher
Boîte Postale 60
LU-6701 Grevenmacher

Tel +352 769 370
Fax +352 759 753
Web csg.lu
Email schoux@pt.lu
Media Officer Guy Fusenig

FC RM Hamm Benfica
83A, rue Tawioun
LU-2612 Luxembourg

Tel +352 432 223
Fax +352 432 223
Web rmhb.lu
Email rmhamm@pt.lu
Media Officer laurent Jaquemart

US Hostert
19, rue Andethana
LU-6970 Oberanven

Tel +352 348 163
Fax +352 348 133
Web ushostert.lu
Email fcush@pt.lu
Media Officer

AS Jeunesse Esch
PO Box 45
LU-4001 Esch-sur-Alzette

Tel +352 6211 59292
Fax +352 2656 0047
Web jeunesse-esch.lu
Email jeunesch@pt.lu
Media Officer Romain Wantz

UN Käerjéng 97
PO Box 94
LU-4901 Bascharage

Tel +352 691 240 250
Fax +352 236 517 31
Web un-kaerjeng.lu
Email un97@pt.lu
Media Officer Nico Zenner

CS Pétange
BP 63
LU-4701 Pétange

Tel +352 504 6991
Fax +352 507 385
Web cspetange.lu
Email pwagner@pt.lu
Media Officer Pascal Wagner

FC Progrès Niedercorn
B.P. 121
LU-4502 Differdange

Tel +352 265 801 16
Fax +352 265 801 16
Web progres.lu
Email progres@pt.lu
Media Officer Fabio Marochi

Racing FC Union Lëtzebuerg
PO Box 1614
LU-1016 Luxembourg

Tel +352 483 498
Fax +352 404 747
Web racing-fc.lu
Email racing-fc-union-lux@pt.lu
Media Officer

US Rumelange
PO Box 3
LU-3701 Rumelange

Tel +352 691 162 367
Fax +352 563 782
Web usrumelange.lu
Email info@usrumelange.lu
Media Officer Boris Kirsch

FC Swift Hesper
19, Gruewereck
LU-6734 Grevenmacher

Tel +352 758 893
Fax +352 263 603 41
Web swifthesper.lu
Email mullerfu@pt.lu
Media Officer Fernand Laroche

FC Union 05 Kayl/Tétange
PO Box 33
LU-3705 Tétange

Tel +352 548 368
Fax +352 541 336
Web union05.lu
Email info@union05.lu
Media Officer

FORMER YUGOSLAV REPUBLIC OF

MACEDONIA

ARY de Macédoine I EJR Mazedonien

Futbalska Federacija na Makedonija (FFM)

COMMUNICATION

Address 8-ma Udarna Brigada 31 A
PO Box 84
MK-1000 Skopje
Tel +389 3 222 603
Fax +389 3 165 448
E-mail ffm@ffm.com.mk
Website ffm.com.mk

President Haralampie Hadji-Risteski
General Secretary Igor Klimper
Media Officer Zoran Nikolovski

Year of Formation 1948

National Stadium Philip II Arena, Skopje (33,460)

DOMESTIC COMPETITION SUMMARY 2010/11

PRVA LIGA FINAL TABLE

			Home					Away					Total						
		Pld	W	D	L	F	A	W	D	L	F	A	W	D	L	F	A	Pts	Comp
1	FK Shkëndija 79	33	15	2	0	43	8	6	7	3	22	15	21	9	3	65	23	72	UCL
2	FK Metalurg Skopje	33	10	4	3	30	9	7	6	3	18	15	17	10	6	48	24	61	UEL
3	FK Renova	33	12	5	0	36	11	5	4	7	18	20	17	9	7	54	31	60	UEL
4	FK Rabotnicki	33	7	8	2	31	15	8	2	6	22	16	15	10	8	53	31	55	UEL
5	FK Sileks	33	9	4	3	21	10	4	4	9	18	28	13	8	12	39	38	47	
6	FK Turnovo	33	9	3	5	22	12	4	3	9	13	23	13	6	14	35	35	45	
7	FK Teteks	33	10	3	3	26	14	2	5	10	12	22	12	8	13	38	36	44	
8	FK Bregalnica Stip	33	9	3	4	23	16	3	2	12	10	33	12	5	16	33	49	41	
9	FK Skopje	33	8	4	4	23	15	1	6	10	13	24	9	10	14	36	39	37	Relegated
10	FK Napredok	33	9	3	5	19	16	1	4	11	11	32	10	7	16	30	48	37	
11	FK Vardar	33	7	3	6	15	16	2	2	13	9	28	9	5	19	24	44	29	
12	FK Pelister	33	4	3	9	18	31	1	0	16	7	51	5	3	25	25	82	18	Relegated

NB FK Vardar – 3 pts deducted.

Top Scorer Hristijan Kirovski (Skopje), 20 goals

Promoted Clubs FK 11 Oktomvri
FK Ohrid 2004

Cup Final FK Metalurg Skopje 2, FK Teteks 0

Promoted Shkëndija scoop top prize

The Prva Liga of the Former Yugoslav Reublic of Macedonia (FYROM) has thrown up a number of surprises in recent years, and that trend continued in 2010/11 as FK Shkëndija 79, from Tetovo, became the league's third successive first-time title winners (after FK Makedonija GP Skopje in 2008/09 and FK Renova in 2009/10). Moreover, they did so in their first year after promotion – an unprecedented feat. Other unexpected outcomes were the Macedonian Cup triumph of league runners-up FK Metalurg Skopje and the relegation – before a belated rescue – of the country's most distinguished and decorated club, FK Vardar.

Shkëndija had returned to the Prva Liga after two seasons away by winning the second division in 2009/10. The club's previous best achievement had been to reach the 2006 domestic cup final, but they soared to new heights in 2010/11, claiming their maiden title in emphatic fashion. Promotion-winning coach Qatip Osmani was dismissed early in the season after a 1-0 defeat to reigning champions Renova but reinstated a few weeks later after his successor Edmond Miha oversaw another single-goal defeat to stadium-sharing local rivals, FK Teteks. Osmani's return proved a smart move because thereafter Shkëndija did not lose another game, going undefeated through 21 matches and clinching the title in round 31 (of 33) with a 2-1 home win over FK Rabotnicki.

Impressive debut

The town of Tetovo sits close to the Albanian border in the north-west of the country, and Shkëndija's title-winning squad included many local players of Albanian ethinicity, including their three leading marksman – Ferhan Hasani (13 goals), Ersen Sali (12) and Izair Emini (11). Twenty-year-old Hasani was especially impressive in his first season of top-flight football, with ten of his goals coming in the spring after he had been awarded his first international cap in a friendly away to China.

Shkëndija were able to concentrate on the league after being despatched from the Macedonian Cup by second-division FK Vlaznimi in August. Metalurg, in contrast, sustained a challenge on two fronts, and although they ultimately failed to live with Shkëndija's pace in the Prva Liga, the club's finest season yet was crowned by their first major honour as they defeated holders Teteks 2-0 in Prilep to win the Macedonian Cup. A goal in each half from midfielders Marko Kostencoski and Aleksandar Tenekedziev enabled Metalurg boss Zikica Tanevski to become, at 33, the youngest coach to lift the trophy.

Metalurg's success was in stark contrast to the fortunes of their city rivals. Although Rabotnicki claimed fourth place in the league, five points behind outgoing champions Renova, to make a quick return to the UEFA Europa League – from which they had been eliminated by Liverpool FC in the 2010/11 competition – there was despair for both FK Skopje, who were relegated after a play-off despite possessing the Prva Liga's leading scorer in 20-goal Hristijan Kirovski, and, initially, for five-time champions Vardar, who went down automatically, with bottom club Pelister, after using

FYROM striker Ivan Trickovski (right, after scoring in Dublin) was his country's star performer in 2010/11

National Team

Top Five All-time Caps – Goce Sedloski (100); Artim Sakiri (73); Velice Sumulikoski (66); Igor Mitreski (62); Petar Milosevski (59)

Top Five All-time Goals – Goran Pandev (23); Georgi Hristov (16); Artim Sakiri (15); Goran Maznov (10); Sasa Ciric & Goce Sedloski (8)

three coaches and 42 players. Back in 1998/99 the nation's capital had been home to seven Prva Liga teams (50 % of its membership). In 2011/12 that number should have been down to just two, but FK Skopje's play-off conquerors FK Miravci, a team from a small south-eastern village, traded their top-flight place with Vardar, who consequently gained a reprieve and stayed up.

Vardar's home stadium, the rebuilt Philip II Arena, brought little cheer when the FYROM national team came to town in 2010/11, four matches there bringing three defeats and a draw, the latter achieved only thanks to a last-gasp penalty in a UEFA EURO 2012 qualifier against Armenia.

Although Mirsad Jonuz's team went into the EURO campaign buoyed by a run of five wins and two draws in seven warm-up games, they faltered when it mattered, collecting just four points from their first six qualifiers, three of those at the expense of Andorra.

Trickovski emerges

Record marksman Goran Pandev did not score for his country all season. He also had a subdued campaign in Italy with FC Internazionale Milano, his winning goal in the UEFA Champions League at FC Bayern München a rare highlight, but one Macedonian player who did enjoy 2010/11 was former Vardar and Rabotnicki striker Ivan Trickovski, The 24-year-old not only established himself in the national side, scoring a fine goal against the Republic of Ireland in Dublin, but also starred in helping APOEL FC to victory in the Cypriot championship.

NATIONAL TEAM RESULTS 2010/11

11/8/10	Malta	A	Ta' Qali	1-1	*Trickovski (37)*
3/9/10	Slovakia (ECQ)	A	Bratislava	0-1	
7/9/10	Armenia (ECQ)	H	Skopje	2-2	*Gjurovski (42), Naumoski (90+6p)*
8/10/10	Andorra (ECQ)	A	Andorra la Vella	2-0	*Naumoski (42), Sikov (60)*
12/10/10	Russia (ECQ)	H	Skopje	0-1	
17/11/10	Albania	A	Korce	0-0	
22/12/10	China	A	Guangzhou	0-1	
9/2/11	Cameroon	H	Skopje	0-1	
26/3/11	Republic of Ireland (ECQ)	A	Dublin	1-2	*Trickovski (45)*
4/6/11	Republic of Ireland (ECQ)	H	Skopje	0-2	

NATIONAL TEAM APPEARANCES 2010/11

Coach – Mirsad JONUZ /(Vlatko KOSTOV)	**9/4/62 1/9/65**		**Mlt**	**SVK**	**ARM**	**AND**	**RUS**	**Alb**	**Chn**	**Cmr**	**IRL**	**IRL**	**Caps**	**Goals**
Tomislav PACOVSKI	28/6/82	GBA (BEL)	G78										19	-
Vlade LAZAREVSKI	9/6/83	Lokomotiv Astana (KAZ) /Tobol (KAZ)	D64			D		D68		s59			41	-
Igor MITRESKI	19/2/79	Neftçi (AZE)	D56	D	D	D	D	D		D62			69	1
Nikolce NOVESKI	28/4/79	Mainz (GER)	D	D	D	D	D			D56	D	D	45	2
Goran POPOV	2/10/84	Dynamo Kyiv (UKR)	D	D	D						D	D	37	2
Filip DESPOTOVSKI	18/11/82	Vorskla (UKR) /İnter Bakı (AZE)	M	M73	s67	M	M78			s46		M57	17	1
Mario GJUROVSKI	11/12/85	Vojvodina (SRB) /Metalurh Donetsk (UKR)	M68		M75	s34	M79	M58			s61	s57	9	2
Slavco GEORGIEVSKI	30/3/80	Neftçi (AZE)	M75	M	M67	M34	s78				s84		20	-
Goran PANDEV	27/7/83	Inter (ITA)	A	M	M					A46	M	A	59	23
Ilco NAUMOSKI	29/7/83	Mattersburg (AUT)	A71	A61	s62	A73	A			A	A68	A10	44	9

NATIONAL TEAM APPEARANCES 2010/11 (contd.)

			Mlt	SVK	ARM	AND	RUS	Alb	Chn	Cmr	IRL	IRL	Caps	Goals
Ivan TRICKOVSKI	18/4/87	APOEL (CYP)	A55	A80	A	A	M	A66		A	A	A	11	3
Aco STOJKOV	29/4/83	Aarau (SUI)	s55										40	5
Boban GRNCAROV	12/8/82	APOEL (CYP)	s56	s80		s83					D	D	21	1
Vance SIKOV	19/7/85	Ethnikos Achnas (CYP)	s64	D 85*		D	D	D64		s56	D	D	12	2
Armend ALIMI	11/12/87	Istra (CRO)	s68				s79		M46				9	-
Besart IBRAIMI	17/12/86	Schalke (GER)	s71										7	-
Nikola GLIGOROV	15/8/83	Rabotnicki	s75					M	M				3	-
Edin NUREDINOSKI	21/4/82	Ethnikos Achnas (CYP)	s78	G	G	G	G	G85		G80	G		11	-
Velice SUMULIKOSKI	24/4/81	Sibir (RUS)		M	M	M83	M	M		M	M	M	74	1
Stevica RISTIC	23/5/82	Amkar (RUS)		s61	A62	A	s49			s46	s68		15	1
Aleksandar LAZEVSKI	21/1/88	Partizan (SRB)		s73			D	D	D	D			5	-
Aleksandar TODOROVSKI	26/2/84	Rad (SRB)			D			s68	D	D59			6	-
Blaze ILIJOSKI	9/7/84	Gangwon (KOR)			s75			s66					6	1
Agim IBRAIMI	29/8/88	Eskişehirspor (TUR)				s73	A49						4	-
Hristijan KIROVSKI	12/10/85	Skopje						A61	A46				2	-
Bajram FETAI	7/9/85	Nordsjælland (DEN)						A	A46				2	-
Agron MEMEDI	5/12/80	Renova						s58					1	-
Dusan SAVIC	1/10/85	Incheon (KOR) /Pakhtakor (UZB)						s61				s72	8	-
Daniel MOJSOV	25/12/87	Vojvodina (SRB)						s64	D46	s62			9	-
Martin BOGATINOV	26/4/86	Rabotnicki /Karpaty (UKR)						s85	G	s80		G	4	-
Zlatko TANEVSKI	3/8/83	Bełchatów (POL)							D46				1	-
Muhamed DEMIRI	20/11/85	Thun (SUI)							M	M54	M84	M72	4	-
Borce MANEVSKI	5/7/85	Rabotnicki							M46	s54			2	-
Igor KRALEVSKI	10/11/78	Metalurg Skopje							s46				3	-
Nikola KARCEV	31/3/81	Shanghai (CHN)							s46				1	-
Metodija STEPANOVSKI	26/5/83	Renova							s46				1	-
Mirko IVANOVSKI	31/10/89	Arka (POL)							s46				1	-
Perica STANCESKI	29/1/85	Željezničar (BIH)							s46				1	-
Ferhan HASANI	18/6/90	Shkëndija							s46			s10	2	-
Darko TASEVSKI	20/5/84	Levski (BUL)								M46	M61		34	-

CLUB-BY-CLUB

FK BREGALNICA STIP

Coach – Nikola Kuzmanov; (25/2/11) Dragan Hristovski

Founded – 1921

Stadium – City (6,000)

2010				
31/7	Napredok	a	0-1	
7/8	Shkëndija	h	2-1	*Novakov 2*
14/8	Teteks	a	0-2	
21/8	Pelister	a	0-2	
28/8	Rabotnicki	h	0-2	
11/9	Metalurg	a	0-1	
18/9	Sileks	h	2-2	*Pop Panev, Bogatinov*
25/9	Renova	a	0-2	
2/10	Turnovo	h	1-0	*Novakov*
16/10	Vardar	a	2-1	*Velinov S., Zdravkov*
23/10	Skopje	h	1-0	*Donev*
30/10	Napredok	h	4-2	*Mandak 2, Cvetanovski, Velinov S.*
7/11	Shkëndija	a	0-2	
13/11	Teteks	h	1-0	*Novakov (p)*
20/11	Pelister	h	2-0	*Zdravkov (p), Trajcov*
27/11	Rabotnicki	a	1-3	*Mandak*
5/12	Metalurg	h	1-2	*Velinov D.*
11/12	Sileks	a	1-3	*Mandak*
2011				
5/3	Renova	h	3-1	*Mitrov, Iliev L., Mandak*
12/3	Turnovo	a	0-2	
15/3	Vardar	h	0-0	
19/3	Skopje	a	3-0	*Cvetanovski, Velkovski S., Trajcov*
2/4	Metalurg	a	0-3	
6/4	Shkëndija	h	0-2	
9/4	Teteks	a	2-0	*Iliev L., Mandak*
16/4	Sileks	a	0-3	*(w/o; match abandoned after 75 mins at 0-1)*
23/4	Skopje	h	0-0	
29/4	Vardar	a	1-1	*Iliev L.*
7/5	Pelister	h	4-0	*Pop Panev, Georgiev, Velinov S., Aleksov (p)*
14/5	Napredok	a	0-0	
17/5	Turnovo	h	1-0	*Trajcov*
21/5	Rabotnicki	a	0-7	
28/5	Renova	h	1-4	*Mitrov*

ame	Nat	DoB	Pos	Aps	(s)	Gls
eksandar ALCINOV		21/2/77	G	24	(2)	
artin ALEKSOV		9/3/95	A		(3)	1
usko ANDONOV		6/2/87	D	20	(8)	
mislav BLAZEVSKI		30/8/89	D	31		
ntonio BOGATINOV		19/6/85	M	3	(5)	1
emanja BRADONJIĆ	SRB	3/8/87	M	4	(4)	
oko CVETANOVSKI		16/7/82	M	22		2
artin DIMOVSKI		18/2/91	M	2	(11)	
ihail DONEV		20/7/81	D	12	(4)	1
kola GEORGIEV		18/12/83	A	9	(6)	1
azar ILIEV		23/5/87	A	12		3
iki ILIEV		12/3/83	D	2	(4)	
upco KOLEV		6/12/78	G	9		
adulé LAKO Losarah	USA	26/3/87	A	1	(2)	
imitar MADZUNAROV		15/6/83	D	2	(4)	
mir MANDAK		11/11/84	M	22	(1)	6
odor MIROSLAVOV		9/6/89	D	4	(6)	
an MITROV		24/10/88	M	15		2
atko NOVAKOV		28/9/78	D	18		4
usan PAVLOV		12/1/91	G		(1)	
oran POP PANEV		13/4/77	D	22	(3)	2
oran PROJKOV		25/11/87	A	3	(4)	
orce RISTOVSKI		12/11/84	D	4	(1)	
drian Francisco de Moura "SALVADOR"	BRA	12/4/88	A	5	(1)	
arko SARAFIMOV		15/6/90	D	1		
artin SISKOV		17/7/87	M	23	(1)	
anco TRAJCOV		5/7/75	M	33		3
ordan TRENDAFILOV		20/6/85	M		(1)	
ejan VELINOV		7/2/91	M	1	(1)	1
tojan VELINOV		3/9/89	A	15	(9)	3
oban VELKOVSKI		3/6/90	M	7	(8)	
lavce VELKOVSKI		5/7/87	M	22		1
oran ZDRAVKOV		11/11/80	A	15		2

FK METALURG SKOPJE

Coach – Zikica Tasevski

Founded – 1964

Stadium – Zelezarnica (3,000)

MAJOR HONOURS: Macedonian Cup – (1) 2011.

2010				
31/7	Vardar	a	2-1	*Krstev, Đurić*
7/8	Skopje	h	3-0	*Kleckarovski, Krstev, Kostencoski*
14/8	Napredok	a	1-0	*Vajs*
21/8	Shkëndija	h	1-1	*Kostencoski*
28/8	Teteks	a	0-0	
11/9	Bregalnica Stip	h	1-0	*Đurić*
18/9	Rabotnicki	a	2-2	*Krstev, Demiri*
25/9	Pelister	a	0-0	
2/10	Sileks	h	1-2	*Petkovski*
16/10	Renova	a	0-1	
23/10	Turnovo	h	3-0	*Simonovski, Krstev, Kleckarovski*
30/10	Vardar	h	1-0	*Ljamcevski*
6/11	Skopje	a	0-0	
13/11	Napredok	h	1-2	*Kralevski (p)*
21/11	Shkëndija	a	0-3	
27/11	Teteks	h	1-0	*Krstev (p)*
5/12	Bregalnica Stip	a	2-1	*Simonovski, Medic*
11/12	Rabotnicki	h	0-1	
2011				
5/3	Pelister	h	4-0	*Kralevski, og (Dragarski), Krstev, Ilijoski*
12/3	Sileks	a	1-0	*Ilijoski*
15/3	Renova	h	2-0	*Krstev, Nacevski*
19/3	Turnovo	a	3-1	*Ejupi, Tenekedziev, Nacevski*
2/4	Bregalnica Stip	h	3-0	*og (Cvetanovski), Ilijoski, Nacevski*
5/4	Sileks	a	1-2	*Ilijoski*
9/4	Skopje	h	2-1	*Krstev, Ejupi*
16/4	Vardar	a	1-0	*Ilijoski*
23/4	Pelister	h	5-0	*Tenekedziev, Ilijoski, Nacevski, Kostencoski, Ilievski*
29/4	Napredok	a	2-1	*Ilijoski (p), Ejupi*
7/5	Turnovo	h	1-1	*Ilijoski*
14/5	Rabotnicki	a	1-1	*Krstev*
17/5	Renova	h	0-0	
21/5	Teteks	h	1-1	*Dodevski*
28/5	Shkëndija	a	2-2	*Nastoski, Kostencoski*

Name	Nat	DoB	Pos	Aps	(s)	Gls
Martin BLAZEVSKI		13/5/92	M	1	(3)	
Goran BOGDANOVIC		9/6/90	D	8		
Blagojce DAMEVSKI		17/10/81	D	11		
Ertan DEMIRI		24/1/79	M	13		1
Ninoslav DODEVSKI		29/11/91	D	1	(3)	1
Milan ĐURIĆ	SRB	3/10/87	M	19	(10)	2
Andreja EFREMOV		2/9/92	G	11	(1)	
Muzafer EJUPI		26/9/88	A	11	(6)	3
Jordan GEORGIEVSKI		3/1/82	G	10		
Lazar ILIEV		25/3/87	A	3	(2)	
Milan ILIEVSKI		21/7/82	D	19	(1)	1
Baze ILIJOSKI		9/7/84	A	13		8
Nikolce KLECKAROVSKI		13/5/83	A	12	(5)	2
Marko KOSTENCOSKI		8/10/89	M	13	(5)	4
Igor KRALEVSKI		10/11/78	D	28		2
Aleksandar KRSTESKI		3/9/83	D	8	(1)	
Mile KRSTEV		13/5/79	M	26		9
Blagoja LJAMCEVSKI		7/4/87	M	20	(10)	1
Vladimir MEDIC		21/10/85	D	3	(5)	1
Agron MEMEDI		5/12/82	M	13		
Bojan MIHAJLOVIĆ	SRB	16/12/73	M	13	(8)	
Vasko MITREV		23/5/84	M	16	(4)	
Dragan NACEVSKI		27/1/80	A	13	(1)	4
Kliment NASTOSKI		20/4/87	M	6	(2)	1
Trajce NIKOV		20/8/87	G	12		
Mile PETKOVSKI		19/9/88	D	27		1
Redzep REDZEP		6/12/94	M		(1)	
Marko SIMONOVSKI		2/1/92	A	5	(11)	2
Aleksandar TENEKEDZIEV		13/3/86	M	15	(11)	2
Miroslav VAJS		27/7/79	D	13		1
Kenan VATIC		30/12/93	D		(1)	

FK NAPREDOK

Coach – Dragan Boceski

Founded – 1928

Stadium – City (5,000)

2010				
31/7	Bregalnica Stip	h	1-0	*Markoski*
9/8	Rabotnicki	a	0-0	
14/8	Metalurg	h	0-1	
21/8	Sileks	a	1-1	*Levkov*
28/8	Renova	h	1-0	*Cvetanoski*
12/9	Turnovo	a	0-1	
18/9	Vardar	h	2-1	*Levkov (p), Ballazhi*
25/9	Skopje	a	0-1	
2/10	Pelister	h	3-1	*Levkov 2, Naumoski*
16/10	Shkëndija	h	1-1	*Stepanovski*
23/10	Teteks	a	1-2	*Levkov*
30/10	Bregalnica Stip	a	2-4	*Markoski, Vrencoski*
6/11	Rabotnicki	h	2-0	*Levkov, Cvetanoski*
13/11	Metalurg	a	2-1	*Mihajloski, Najdoski*
20/11	Sileks	h	1-0	*Naumoski*
27/11	Renova	a	0-5	
4/12	Turnovo	h	0-1	
11/12	Vardar	a	1-2	*Najdoski*
2011				
5/3	Skopje	h	2-0	*Cvetanoski, Veljanoski*
12/3	Pelister	a	1-1	*Ballazhi (p)*
16/3	Shkëndija	a	0-3	
19/3	Teteks	h	1-0	*Markoski*
2/4	Pelister	h	2-0	*Levkov 2*
6/4	Teteks	h	1-1	*Levkov*
9/4	Turnovo	a	0-0	
16/4	Rabotnicki	h	0-5	
23/4	Renova	a	1-4	*Simjanoski*

29/4	Metalurg	h	1-2	*Vrencoski*
8/5	Shkëndija	a	1-4	*Ballazhi (p)*
14/5	Bregalnica Stip	h	0-0	
17/5	Sileks	a	1-2	*Ballazhi*
21/5	Skopje	h	1-3	*Simjanoski*
28/5	Vardar	a	0-1	

Name	Nat	DoB	Pos	Aps	(s)	Gls
Ermedin ADEM		7/7/90	M		(3)	
Pero ANGELESKI		12/7/81	D	26		
Oliver ASKOV		29/8/77	D	19	(5)	
Kushtrim BALLAZHI		9/1/84	D	30	(1)	4
Marjan BILBILOSKI		8/6/86	D	1		
Dejan CVETANOSKI		15/5/90	A	21	(1)	3
Agron IBRAIMI		16/9/91	A		(8)	
Armend IBRAIMI		16/9/91	M		(3)	
Mirsad ISEIN		21/1/93	M	1	(2)	
Sasko LAZAREVSKI		24/3/78	M	14	(1)	
Blagoj LEVKOV		7/2/82	A	25	(4)	9
Riste MARKOSKI		30/4/86	M	26	(3)	3
Gjore MIHAJLOSKI		29/5/90	M	9	(14)	1
Risto MITREVSKI		5/10/91	D	18		
Filip NAJDOSKI		13/9/92	M	16	(5)	2
Goran NAUMOSKI		30/9/85	A	3	(12)	2
Belul NEBIU		26/5/93	M	1		
Goran PASOVSKI		15/2/80	G	29		
Dragan RODIĆ	SRB	23/3/88	D		(4)	
Artan SEJDINI		15/1/90	M		(1)	
Zarko SIMJANOSKI		20/1/88	M	27	(1)	2
Kiril STEPANOVSKI		26/5/83	D	16	(1)	1
Zivko STOJKOSKI		18/10/85	D	2	(5)	
Krste TRPENOSKI		16/9/79	M	28		
Toni VELJANOSKI		12/4/84	D	19	(2)	1
Vecko VRENCOSKI		25/3/91	M	18	(9)	2
Igor ZAFIROSKI		29/3/84	D	4	(1)	
Agron ZEQIRI		17/10/86	A	6	(10)	
Nikola ZERDESKI		26/7/85	G	4		

FK PELISTER

Coach – Naum Ljamcevski; (24/9/10) Nedzat Husein

Founded – 1945

Stadium – Tumbe Kafe (10,000)

MAJOR HONOURS: Macedonian Cup – (1) 2001.

2010

31/7	Renova	a	0-2	
9/8	Teteks	h	1-1	*Iliev*
14/8	Turnovo	a	0-3	
21/8	Bregalnica Stip	h	2-0	*Iliev 2*
28/8	Vardar	a	0-1	
11/9	Rabotnicki	h	0-3	
18/9	Skopje	a	0-2	
25/9	Metalurg	h	0-0	
2/10	Napredok	a	1-3	*Milenkovski*
16/10	Sileks	h	1-3	*Simonovski*
24/10	Shkëndija	a	1-4	*og (Bilbiloski)*
30/10	Renova	h	0-1	
6/11	Teteks	a	0-3	
13/11	Turnovo	h	2-0	*Simonovski, Maglovski*
20/11	Bregalnica Stip	a	0-2	
27/11	Vardar	h	1-2	*Talevski*
4/12	Rabotnicki	a	0-3	
11/12	Skopje	h	5-4	*Maglovski, Talevski, Veljanovski A. 2, Naumoski*

2011

5/3	Metalurg	a	0-4	
12/3	Napredok	h	1-1	*Talevski (p)*
15/3	Sileks	a	1-2	*Bujcevski*
19/3	Shkëndija	h	0-1	
2/4	Napredok	a	0-2	
5/4	Turnovo	h	1-4	*Veljanovski A.*
9/4	Rabotnicki	a	2-1	*Bujcevski, Simonovski*
16/4	Renova	h	0-5	
23/4	Metalurg	a	0-5	
29/4	Shkëndija	h	1-3	*og (Abdullai)*
7/5	Bregalnica Stip	a	0-4	
14/5	Sileks	h	2-3	*Talevski, Bujcevski*
17/5	Skopje	a	1-4	*Ivanovic*
21/5	Vardar	h	1-0	*Talevski*
28/5	Teteks	a	1-6	*Anastasov*

Name	Nat	DoB	Pos	Aps	(s)	Gls
Aleksandar ANASTASOV		4/5/93	M	1	(1)	1
Nikola ANGELKOVSKI		4/9/88	G	1		
Aleksandar ANGELOVSKI		11/7/86	M	3	(1)	
Dejan APOSTOLOVSKI		6/8/90	G	5		
Nemanja BRADONJIĆ	SRB	3/8/87	M	7	(1)	
Vladica BRDAROVSKI		7/2/90	D	14		
Toni BRNJARCEVSKI		7/6/85	A	4	(2)	
Antonio BUJCEVSKI		24/1/90	A	9	(4)	3
Michael CVETKOVSKI		21/11/87	D	5		
Hristijan DRAGARSKI		16/4/92	D	21	(1)	
Nikola GONOVSKI		29/9/92	G	1	(1)	
Antonio GRUJOVSKI		8/10/89	M	1	(2)	
Lazar ILIEV		25/3/87	A	7	(1)	3
Milan IVANOVIC		21/7/88	D	3	(1)	1
Ivica KELESOSKI		17/6/90	A	6	(6)	
Tome KITANOVSKI		1/1/88	M	22		
Vlade KITANOVSKI		16/4/88	A		(3)	
Nenad KOKOVIC		3/12/91	D	2	(1)	
Blagojce KONJARSKI		18/2/89	A	8	(1)	
Mihajlo KORLEVSKI		11/8/86	M		(1)	
Marjan KOTEVSKI		12/5/93	A	1		
Mario LAZARESKI		7/9/90	D	2	(2)	
Petar LJAMCEVSKI		8/8/91	M	9	(3)	
Stefan MAGLOVSKI		17/7/90	M	20		2
Ljupco MICEVSKI		9/6/87	D	4	(1)	
Filip MILENKOVSKI		7/1/90	M	23	(4)	1
Blagojce NAUMOSKI		24/11/93	A	1		1
Nikolce PANOVSKI		19/12/83	D	11		
Nikola PETKOVSKI		14/12/86	M	28	(2)	
Ilce PETROVSKI		22/7/89	G	26		
Toni PITOSKA		27/4/82	A	8	(5)	
Blagojce RALEVSKI		8/10/85	D	6		
Caner RAMADAN		7/4/92	M		(2)	
Aleksandar RISTEVSKI		21/8/89	D	21	(3)	
Blagojce RISTEVSKI		27/2/87	A	5	(6)	
Zoran SALEVSKI		24/7/86	D	9		
Zoran SIMONOVSKI		13/3/89	M	19	(4)	3
Darko STANKOVSKI		26/7/91	M		(1)	
Nikola STOJANOVSKI		18/4/88	M	4	(4)	
Igor TALEVSKI		26/1/79	M	24	(4)	5
Pece TASEVSKI		12/8/92	A	1	(2)	
Aleksandar VASILEV		20/2/83	A	1		
Aleksandar VELJANOVSKI		9/8/91	M	19	(10)	3
Saso VELJANOVSKI		16/1/90	A	1	(5)	
Edmond VESELI		19/7/92	M		(2)	

FK RABOTNICKI

Coach – Zoran Stratev; (28/12/10) Vlatko Kostov; (4/4/11) Goran Petreski

Founded – 1937

Stadium – Philip II Arena (33,460)

MAJOR HONOURS: Macedonian League – (3) 2005, 2006, 2008; Macedonian Cup – (2) 2008, 2009.

2010

2/8	Skopje	a	1-0	*Zé Carlos*
9/8	Napredok	h	0-0	
15/8	Shkëndija	a	0-3	
21/8	Teteks	h	1-2	*Manevski*
28/8	Bregalnica Stip	a	2-0	*Roberto Carlos, Manevski*
11/9	Pelister	a	3-0	*Wandeir, Vujcic, Manevski*
18/9	Metalurg	h	2-2	*Manevski (p), Márcio*
25/9	Sileks	a	0-2	
2/10	Renova	h	1-1	*Manevski*

6/10	Turnovo	a	2-0	*Fernando (p), Gligorov N.*
4/10	Vardar	h	2-0	*Márcio 2*
1/10	Skopje	h	1-1	*Tunevski*
11	Napredok	a	0-2	
3/11	Shkëndija	h	1-1	*Fernando*
0/11	Teteks	a	1-0	*Petrovic*
7/11	Bregalnica Stip	h	3-1	*Manevski, Gligorov N., Sinković*
/12	Pelister	h	3-0	*Manevski 2 (1p), Ivanovski*
1/12	Metalurg	a	1-0	*Manevski*
011				
/3	Sileks	h	0-0	
2/3	Renova	a	1-1	*Manevski*
5/3	Turnovo	h	2-1	*Kjumbev, Andonov*
9/3	Vardar	a	0-1	
/4	Skopje	h	1-1	*Petkovski*
/4	Vardar	a	3-1	*Manevski 3 (1p)*
/4	Pelister	h	1-2	*Manevski*
6/4	Napredok	a	5-0	*Velkovski, Todorovski B. 2, Petrovic, Gligorov N.*
3/4	Turnovo	h	3-1	*Manevski (p), og (Sulev), Todorovski B.*
9/4	Teteks	h	2-1	*Gligorov N., Velkovski (p)*
/5	Renova	a	2-2	*Manevski, Tunevski*
4/5	Metalurg	h	1-1	*Velkovski*
7/5	Shkëndija	a	1-2	*Velkovski*
1/5	Bregalnica Stip	h	7-0	*Velkovski 2, Manevski 3, Petrovic, Petkovski*
8/5	Sileks	a	0-2	

Name	Nat	DoB	Pos	Aps	(s)	Gls
Emir ADEM		21/10/86	D	13	(6)	
Marjan ANDONOV		20/12/85	A	6	(3)	1
Daniel AVRAMOVSKI		20/2/92	A		(1)	
Egzon BELICA		3/9/90	D	15	(2)	
Martin BOGATINOV		26/4/86	G	16		
Stole DIMITRIEVSKI		25/12/93	G	2		
Goran DIMOVSKI		14/10/82	D	18		
Boban DZANGAROVSKI		17/6/83	D	7		
FÁBIO Gilvan da Nascimento Silva	BRA	13/9/83	A	10	(5)	
FERNANDO Alcântara Lopes	BRA	28/3/87	D	9		2
Filip GLIGOROV		31/7/93	D	2		
Nikola GLIGOROV		15/8/83	M	32		4
Bojan IVANOVSKI		18/2/90	M		(1)	1
Pance KJUMBEV		25/12/79	D	12		1
Borce MANEVSKI		5/7/85	M	27		19
MÁRCIO Francisco da Silva	BRA	4/3/82	A	4	(6)	3
Darko MICEVSKI		12/4/92	M		(5)	
Risto MITREVSKI		5/10/91	D	2	(2)	
Gjorgji MOJSOV		27/5/85	M	11	(4)	
Mario NASTEVSKI		10/4/95	M	1		
Nafi OSMANI		6/5/93	M		(1)	
Kristijan PANEV		24/11/93	M		(1)	
Filip PETKOVSKI		24/5/90	A	1	(17)	2
Milovan PETROVIC		23/1/90	M	18	(6)	3
Aleksandar RADOVIĆ	SRB	30/3/87	D	2	(2)	
ROBERTO CARLOS da Silva	BRA	4/4/85	M	4	(6)	1
Vladimir SEKULOSKI		10/7/80	D	11		
Martin SILJANOVSKI		22/2/93	D		(1)	
Kristijan SINKOVIĆ	CRO	2/4/87	M	2	(10)	1
Damjan SISKOVSKI		18/3/95	G	1		
Edin SKENDEROVIC		22/7/94	M	4	(10)	
Zvonimir STANKOVIĆ	SRB	22/11/83	D	13	(1)	
Igor STEFANOVIĆ	SRB	17/7/87	G	14		
Igor STOJANOV		12/2/76	D	13		
Blagoja TODOROVSKI		11/6/85	M	13		3
Goce TODOROVSKI		13/9/82	M	6	(3)	
Vladimir TUNEVSKI		3/8/86	M	19	(1)	2
Krste VELKOVSKI		20/2/88	A	15		6
Stephan VUJCIC	GER	3/1/86	M	25		1
WANDEIR Oliveira dos Santos	BRA	15/5/80	A	12		1
José "ZÉ" CARLOS Gomes Filho	BRA	4/10/79	M	3		1

FK RENOVA

Coach – Nedzat Shabani; (10/11/10) Bylbyl Sokoli

Founded – 2003

Stadium – City, Tetovo (15,000)

MAJOR HONOURS: Macedonian League – (1) 2010.

2010				
31/7	Pelister	h	2-0	*Gafuri, Jancevski*
7/8	Turnovo	h	0-0	
14/8	Vardar	a	2-0	*Ismaili, Statovci*
21/8	Skopje	h	1-1	*Memedi*
28/8	Napredok	a	0-1	
11/9	Shkëndija	h	1-0	*Aliu*
18/9	Teteks	a	1-1	*Emini*
25/9	Bregalnica Stip	h	2-0	*Emurlahu, Aliu*
2/10	Rabotnicki	a	1-1	*Aliu*
16/10	Metalurg	h	1-0	*Stepanovski M.*
23/10	Sileks	a	0-2	
30/10	Pelister	a	1-0	*Jancevski*
6/11	Turnovo	a	0-2	
13/11	Vardar	h	4-0	*Emini, Nuhiu, Emurlahu, Ismaili*
20/11	Skopje	a	1-0	*Aliu (p)*
27/11	Napredok	h	5-0	*Emini, Jancevski 2, og (Veljanoski), Bajrami*
5/12	Shkëndija	a	1-4	*Stepanovski M.*
11/12	Teteks	h	2-1	*Emurlahu, Aliu (p)*
2011				
5/3	Bregalnica Stip	a	1-3	*Jancevski*
12/3	Rabotnicki	h	1-1	*Statovci*
15/3	Metalurg	a	0-2	
19/3	Sileks	h	3-1	*Jancevski 2 (1p), Hyseni*
2/4	Sileks	h	2-1	*Bajrami, Stepanovski M.*
5/4	Skopje	a	0-2	
11/4	Vardar	h	1-0	*Emini*
16/4	Pelister	a	5-0	*Emini, Aliu 2, Emurlahu, Xhaferi*
23/4	Napredok	h	4-1	*Emini 2, Aliu, Stepanovski M.*
29/4	Turnovo	a	1-1	*Aliu (p)*
7/5	Rabotnicki	h	2-2	*Emini, Ristov*
14/5	Teteks	h	4-2	*Emini, Stepanovski M., Ismaili, Jancevski*
17/5	Metalurg	a	0-0	
21/5	Shkëndija	h	1-1	*Jancevski*
28/5	Bregalnica Stip	a	4-1	*Hyseni, Jancevski 2, Ismaili*

Name	Nat	DoB	Pos	Aps	(s)	Gls
Festim ADEMI		10/9/77	M	2	(6)	
Ylber ALIU		7/5/79	A	24	(2)	9
Ersen ASANI		28/5/93	D		(1)	
Muharem BAJRAMI		29/11/85	M	7	(13)	2
Vladimir DESPOTOVSKI		5/10/77	D		(1)	
Armend ELEZI		20/4/80	G	16		
Vulnet EMINI		10/9/78	M	31	(1)	9
Burhan EMURLAHU		11/3/82	A	18	(4)	4
Saimir FETAI		4/4/89	M	1	(5)	
Ardjen GAFURI		1/2/89	M	8	(11)	1
Fisnik GASHI		3/12/80	M	24	(3)	
Abdoulaye GUEYE	SEN	13/9/91	A		(8)	
Genc HYSENI		23/8/84	A	8	(2)	2
Darko IGNJATOVSKI		19/5/81	D	7	(2)	
Ismail ISMAILI		14/11/81	A	10	(15)	4
Boban JANCEVSKI		30/4/78	A	20	(2)	11
Leonard KALABA		3/5/86	D	2	(2)	
Agron MEMEDI		5/12/80	M	16		1
Marjan MICKOV		4/8/81	D	12	(4)	
Kushtrim MUSHICA	ALB	1/5/85	G	17	(2)	
Fisnik NUHIU		26/1/83	M	32		1
Sasko RISTOV		22/12/83	D	14		1
Burim SADIKI		5/8/89	M		(1)	
Faruk STATOVCI		29/11/79	M	27		2
Kiril STEPANOVSKI		26/5/83	D	5	(1)	
Metodija STEPANOVSKI		26/5/83	D	27	(1)	5
Igorce STOJANOV		12/2/76	D	15		
Dragan TRAJKOVSKI		27/11/87	M		(2)	
Arijan VELIU		8/6/90	M	11		
Ymer XHAFERI	ALB	6/11/85	M	9	(4)	1

FK SHKËNDIJA 79

Coach – Qatip Osmani; (16/9/10) Edmond Miha; (6/11/10) Qatip Osmani
Founded – 1979
Stadium – City (15,000)
MAJOR HONOURS: Macedonian League – (1) 2011.

2010				
3/8	Teteks	h	0-0	
7/8	Bregalnica Stip	a	1-2	*Nuhiu*
15/8	Rabotnicki	h	3-0	*Sali, Useini, Lomami*
21/8	Metalurg	a	1-1	*Emini*
29/8	Sileks	h	3-0	*Emini, Andonov, Sali*
11/9	Renova	a	0-1	
19/9	Turnovo	h	3-0	*Hasani, Sali, Emini*
25/9	Vardar	a	2-0	*Sali, Cuculi*
3/10	Skopje	h	1-0	*Sali*
16/10	Napredok	a	1-1	*Andonov*
24/10	Pelister	h	4-1	*Andonov 2, Nafiu, Nuhiu*
3/11	Teteks	a	0-1	
7/11	Bregalnica Stip	h	2-0	*Mustafi, Nuhiu*
13/11	Rabotnicki	a	1-1	*Mustafi*
21/11	Metalurg	h	3-0	*Berisha, og (Petkovski), Sali*
27/11	Sileks	a	1-1	*Emini*
5/12	Renova	h	4-1	*Mustafi, Emini, Nuhiu, Hasani*
11/12	Turnovo	a	1-0	*Hasani*
2011				
6/3	Vardar	h	3-1	*Hasani 2, Alomerovic*
12/3	Skopje	a	3-3	*Nuhiu, Hasani (p), Emini*
16/3	Napredok	h	3-0	*Hasani, Emini, Sali*
19/3	Pelister	a	1-0	*Redzepi*
3/4	Teteks	h	3-1	*Alomerovic, Mustafi, Nuhiu*
6/4	Bregalnica Stip	a	2-0	*Sali, Mustafi*
10/4	Sileks	h	1-0	*Mustafi*
16/4	Skopje	a	2-2	*Emini 2 (1p)*
22/4	Vardar	h	2-0	*Sali, Emini*
29/4	Pelister	a	3-1	*Sali, Hasani 2*
8/5	Napredok	h	4-1	*Emini, Nuhiu, Sali, Hasani (p)*
14/5	Turnovo	a	2-0	*Useini, Hasani (p)*
17/5	Rabotnicki	h	2-1	*Hasani, Mustafi*
21/5	Renova	a	1-1	*Sali*
28/5	Metalurg	h	2-2	*Hasani, Mustafi*

Name	Nat	DoB	Pos	Aps	(s)	Gls
Xhelil ABDULLAI		25/9/91	D	11	(3)	
Betim ALIJU		17/3/89	D		(3)	
Kemal ALOMEROVIC		8/12/80	M	10	(5)	2
Marjan ANDONOV		20/12/85	A	2	(8)	4
Nasir AZIZI		31/5/92	D		(1)	
Sedat BERISHA		3/9/89	D	29	(1)	1
Marjan BILBILOSKI		8/6/86	D	7	(4)	
Ardian CUCULI		19/7/87	D	22	(1)	1
Ilir ELMAZOVSKI		18/11/79	D	31		
Izair EMINI		4/10/85	M	27	(1)	11
Blagojce GLAVEVSKI		6/4/88	A	1	(10)	
Ferhan HASANI		18/6/90	A	24	(4)	13
André LOMAMI	RWA	6/8/87	A	3	(2)	1
Marjan MICKOV		4/8/81	D	1	(3)	
Nebi MUSTAFI		21/8/76	M	31		8
Valmir NAFIU		23/4/94	A	4	(15)	1
Mexhit NEZIRI		2/9/90	M	1	(3)	
Vladimir NIKITOVIĆ	SRB	4/12/80	D	31		
Ardian NUHIU		17/12/78	A	29	(1)	7
Elmedin REDZEPI		30/9/88	M	5	(17)	1
Mumin SALLAI		20/1/85	D	4	(7)	
Ersen SALI		5/10/87	A	30		12
Jasir SELMANI		21/1/91	M	2	(3)	
Muhamed USEINI		21/11/88	M	25	(3)	2
Hadis VELII		20/3/90	G	1	(1)	
Suat ZENDELI		24/2/81	G	32		

FK SILEKS

Coach – Ane Andovski
Founded – 1965
Stadium – Sileks (5,000)
MAJOR HONOURS: Macedonian League – (3) 1996, 1997, 1998; Macedonian Cup – (2) 1994, 1997.

2010				
31/7	Turnovo	a	0-4	
7/8	Vardar	h	1-0	*Temelkov*
14/8	Skopje	a	1-2	*Nasevski S.*
21/8	Napredok	h	1-1	*Temelkov*
29/8	Shkëndija	a	0-3	
11/9	Teteks	h	0-0	
18/9	Bregalnica Stip	a	2-2	*Zarevski, Temelkov*
25/9	Rabotnicki	h	2-0	*Temelkov 2 (1p)*
2/10	Metalurg	a	2-1	*Nacev, Zarevski*
16/10	Pelister	a	3-1	*Stojanovski, Temelkov (p), Zarevski*
23/10	Renova	h	2-0	*Zarevski 2*
30/10	Turnovo	h	0-2	
7/11	Vardar	a	1-2	*Zarevski*
13/11	Skopje	h	0-0	
20/11	Napredok	a	0-1	
27/11	Shkëndija	h	1-1	*Misovski*
4/12	Teteks	a	1-1	*Nasevski S.*
11/12	Bregalnica Stip	h	3-1	*Nacev, Temelkov, Zarevski*
2011				
5/3	Rabotnicki	a	0-0	
12/3	Metalurg	h	0-1	
15/3	Pelister	h	2-1	*Nacev, Temelkov (p)*
19/3	Renova	a	1-3	*Temelkov*
2/4	Renova	a	1-2	*Nasevski S.*
5/4	Metalurg	h	2-1	*Nasevski S., Nikolić*
10/4	Shkëndija	a	0-1	
16/4	Bregalnica Stip	h	3-0	*(w/o; match abandoned after 75 mins at 1-0 Stojanovski)*
23/4	Teteks	a	2-0	*Temelkov, Nacev*
29/4	Skopje	a	1-1	*Zarevski*
7/5	Vardar	h	0-1	
14/5	Pelister	a	3-2	*Nasevski S., Zarevski, Nacev*
17/5	Napredok	h	2-1	*Nacev, Temelkov*
21/5	Turnovo	a	0-2	
28/5	Rabotnicki	h	2-0	*Nacev, Temelkov*

Name	Nat	DoB	Pos	Aps	(s)	Gls
Aleksandar ALEKSOVSKI		10/9/77	A	2	(2)	
Miroslav ATLESKI		13/9/86	M	29	(3)	
Milan BOGDANOVSKI		14/4/88	A		(5)	
Zlatko BOSKOVSKI		10/8/86	D	16		
Daniel BOZINOVSKI		9/7/89	G	31		
Amir ĐURIĆ	BIH	25/2/89	A	17	(3)	
Uroš JANKOVIĆ	SRB	22/9/85	D	2	(1)	
Romeo KOCHOSKI		8/5/91	M	1	(21)	
Nenad KOKOVIC		3/12/90	D	4	(3)	
Darko KOSTADINOVSKI		27/6/87	D	22	(3)	
Daniel LAMPEVSKI		3/9/88	D	20	(1)	
Nemanja MARKOVIĆ	SRB	30/8/89	M	1	(1)	
Darko MINEVSKI		18/3/91	M	3	(2)	
Nikola MISOVSKI		22/10/85	D	30		1
Slagan MITEVSKI		4/5/91	M	15	(12)	
Hristijan MITKOVSKI		9/6/90	G	2		
Angel NACEV		10/10/89	A	20	(11)	7
Ivance NASEVSKI		24/11/92	M		(6)	
Stojance NASEVSKI		12/2/91	A	8	(17)	5
Milan NIKOLIĆ	SRB	19/9/81	M	12		1
Dejan PANOVSKI		17/11/92	G		(1)	
Martin PETROV		5/4/85	D	30		
Saša STOJANOVIĆ	SRB	21/1/83	A		(2)	
Borjan STOJANOVSKI		15/1/90	M	23		2
Aleksandar TEMELKOV		6/10/87	M	31		12
Saša VASOV	SRB	29/3/82	D	13		
Gjorgji ZAREVSKI		30/1/89	A	31		9

FK SKOPJE

Coach – Ljupco Markovski
Founded – 1960
Stadium – Zelezarnica (3,000)

010

8	Rabotnicki	h	0-1	
8	Metalurg	a	0-3	
4/8	Sileks	h	2-1	*Simonovski, Kirovski*
/8	Renova	a	1-1	*Kirovski (p)*
3/8	Turnovo	h	3-0	*Kirovski 2, Koleceski*
/9	Vardar	a	0-1	
3/9	Pelister	h	2-0	*Koleceski, Kirovski (p)*
5/9	Napredok	h	1-0	*Popovski*
10	Shkëndija	a	0-1	
6/10	Teteks	h	1-0	*Jovanovski*
3/10	Bregalnica Stip	a	0-1	
1/10	Rabotnicki	a	1-1	*Kirovski*
'11	Metalurg	h	0-0	
3/11	Sileks	a	0-0	
0/11	Renova	h	0-1	
7/11	Turnovo	a	0-1	
'12	Vardar	h	1-0	*Nakovski (p)*
1/12	Pelister	a	4-5	*Kirovski 4 (1p)*

011

/3	Napredok	a	0-2	
2/3	Shkëndija	h	3-3	*Glisic 2, Argirovski*
5/3	Teteks	a	1-2	*Jovanovski*
9/3	Bregalnica Stip	h	0-3	
/4	Rabotnicki	a	1-1	*Kirovski (p)*
/4	Renova	h	2-0	*Glisic, Serafimovski*
/4	Metalurg	a	1-2	*Kirovski*
6/4	Shkëndija	h	2-2	*Kirovski 2 (1p)*
3/4	Bregalnica Stip	a	0-0	
9/4	Sileks	h	1-1	*Kirovski*
/5	Teteks	a	1-2	*Kirovski*
4/5	Vardar	a	0-0	
7/5	Pelister	h	4-1	*Kirovski 2 (1p), Bajramovski, Antovski*
1/5	Napredok	a	3-1	*Kirovski (p), Shabani, Jasarovski*
8/5	Turnovo	h	1-2	*Kirovski*

Name	Nat	DoB	Pos	Aps	(s)	Gls
Aleksandar ANGELOVSKI		11/7/86	M	19	(2)	
Daniel ANTOVSKI		14/12/89	A		(5)	1
Donco ARGIROVSKI		18/7/84	M	27		1
Bujamin ASANI		10/8/88	M	10	(3)	
Almir BAJRAMOVSKI		21/5/82	M	25	(3)	1
Valmir BELULI		16/3/91	M		(1)	
Antonio BOGATINOV		19/6/85	M	1	(4)	
Aleksandar BOZIKOV		1/3/90	A		(5)	
Dragan BRNJARCEVSKI		17/9/83	M	23	(5)	
Bozidar DIMITROVSKI		5/2/87	D	7	(3)	
Vlatko DROBAROV		2/11/92	D	17	(3)	
Darko GLISIC		23/9/91	D	7	(6)	3
Burim GUGJUFI		28/6/86	A		(1)	
Alen JASAROVSKI		6/11/91	M	21	(5)	1
Goran JOVANOVSKI		26/9/80	D	8	(3)	2
Leonard KALABA		3/5/86	D	14	(2)	
Hristijan KIROVSKI		12/10/85	A	30		20
Filip KOLECESKI		10/6/88	A	5	(8)	2
Dejan KOSTURANOV		9/8/86	G	24	(1)	
Stefan MADZOVSKI		23/11/91	D	1		
Jasmin MECINOVIC		20/10/90	D	16		
Dardan MIFTARI		2/12/83	G	7		
Vladimir MOJSOVSKI		2/3/83	A	1	(1)	
Filip NAKOV		23/5/94	M		(2)	
Riste NAKOVSKI		27/5/81	M	28	(1)	1
Florent OSMANI		28/5/88	M		(6)	
Aleksandar POPOVSKI		3/2/81	A	29		1
Denis RAMADAN		27/11/89	D	3	(8)	
Borjan RISTESKI		20/2/92	G	2	(1)	
Dzunejt SALI		3/9/86	D	1		
Nenad SERAFIMOVSKI		11/7/87	M	1	(4)	1
Bunjamin SHABANI		30/1/90	M	27	(2)	1
Vojislav SIMONOVSKI		4/1/80	D	9		1
Saban SULEJMANI		1/2/88	M		(6)	

FK TETEKS

Coach – Toni Jakimovski
Founded – 1953
Stadium – City (15,000)
MAJOR HONOURS: Macedonian Cup – (1) 2010.

2010

3/8	Shkëndija	a	0-0	
9/8	Pelister	a	1-1	*og (Milenkovski)*
14/8	Bregalnica Stip	h	2-0	*Hyseni, Simovski*
21/8	Rabotnicki	a	2-1	*Gligorovski, Ristevski (p)*
28/8	Metalurg	h	0-0	
11/9	Sileks	a	0-0	
18/9	Renova	h	1-1	*Gligorovski*
26/9	Turnovo	a	0-1	
2/10	Vardar	h	3-2	*Zaharievski, Ristovski 2*
16/10	Skopje	a	0-1	
23/10	Napredok	h	2-1	*Hyseni, Ristovski*
3/11	Shkëndija	h	1-0	*Zaharievski (p)*
6/11	Pelister	h	3-0	*Ristevski, Zaharievski, Hyseni*
13/11	Bregalnica Stip	a	0-1	
20/11	Rabotnicki	h	0-1	
27/11	Metalurg	a	0-1	
4/12	Sileks	h	1-1	*Belcev*
11/12	Renova	a	1-2	*Zaharievski (p)*

2011

5/3	Turnovo	h	1-0	*Jovanovski D.*
12/3	Vardar	a	0-2	
15/3	Skopje	h	2-1	*Siljanovski, Kleckarovski*
19/3	Napredok	a	0-1	
3/4	Shkëndija	a	1-3	*Kleckarovski (p)*
6/4	Napredok	a	1-1	*Kleckarovski (p)*
9/4	Bregalnica Stip	h	0-2	
16/4	Turnovo	a	2-0	*Jovanovski Mi., Jakimovski*
23/4	Sileks	h	0-2	
29/4	Rabotnicki	a	1-2	*Naumovski G.*
9/5	Skopje	h	2-1	*Naumovski G., Jovanovski D.*
14/5	Renova	a	2-4	*Siljanovski, Stolevski*
17/5	Vardar	h	2-1	*Gligorovski 2*
21/5	Metalurg	a	1-1	*Urosevic*
28/5	Pelister	h	6-1	*Siljanovski, Kleckarovski 2 (1p), Jakimovski 2, Ismaili*

Name	Nat	DoB	Pos	Aps	(s)	Gls
Burhan ALIJI		29/9/89	D	11	(3)	
Marjan BELCEV		22/10/82	D	13		1
Toni BRNJARCEVSKI		7/6/85	M	5	(2)	
Toni GJORGJEVSKI		15/9/86	D	12		
Ivica GLIGOROVSKI		15/4/81	A	21	(4)	4
Genc HYSENI		28/3/84	A	14	(1)	3
Nuriman ISMAILI		12/9/88	M	1	(1)	1
Nikola JAKIMOVSKI		26/2/90	A	7	(1)	3
Daniel JOVANOVSKI		12/11/83	D	17	(1)	2
Marko JOVANOVSKI		24/7/88	G	29		
Miroslav JOVANOVSKI		13/5/91	M	13	(13)	1
Nikolce KLECKAROVSKI		13/5/83	A	8	(2)	5
Ljupco KMETOVSKI		8/7/72	G	1		
Nenad MISKOVSKI		19/2/86	D	29		
Dragan NAUMOVSKI		19/7/84	D	24	(4)	
Goran NAUMOVSKI		30/9/85	A	4	(6)	2
Blasko NIKOLOVSKI		28/1/88	D		(1)	
Nemanja PAVLOVIĆ	SRB	23/8/88	G	3	(2)	
Oliver PEEV		8/6/87	M	17		
Živorad RADONJIĆ	SRB	2/10/84	A	16	(7)	
Cengiz REDZEPI		8/7/82	A	1	(1)	
Dimce RISTEVSKI		6/11/82	M	15		2
Sasko RISTOV		22/12/83	D	17		
Milan RISTOVSKI		1/3/89	M	2	(13)	3
Darko SAVESKI		21/6/71	M	3	(7)	
Igor SAVEVSKI		21/3/81	D		(1)	
Goran SILJANOVSKI		1/7/90	M	13		3
Dusan SIMOVSKI		1/5/88	M	26	(1)	1
Aleksandar STOJANOVSKI		4/4/86	A	2		
Jovica STOLEVSKI		20/1/90	A	2	(7)	1
Nikola TASIĆ	SRB	22/5/91	M		(7)	
Dusko TRAJCEVSKI		1/11/90	D	2	(1)	
Aleksandar UROSEVIC		14/9/90	M	6	(9)	1
Srgjan ZAHARIEVSKI		12/9/73	M	29		4

FK TURNOVO

Coach – Sefki Arifovski; (16/4/11) Ljupco Dimovski; (19/5/11) Tome Petrov
Founded – 1950
Stadium – Kukus (3,000)

2010				
31/7	Sileks	h	4-0	*Lazarovski, Bajlozov, Curlinov, Kovacev*
7/8	Renova	a	0-0	
14/8	Pelister	h	3-0	*Curlinov 2, Lazarovski*
23/8	Vardar	h	3-0	*(w/o)*
28/8	Skopje	a	0-3	
12/9	Napredok	h	1-0	*Bajlozov*
19/9	Shkëndija	a	0-3	
26/9	Teteks	h	1-0	*Tasev*
2/10	Bregalnica Stip	a	0-1	
16/10	Rabotnicki	h	0-2	
23/10	Metalurg	a	0-3	
30/10	Sileks	a	2-0	*Tasev, Kovacev*
6/11	Renova	h	2-0	*Mitrev, Bajlozov*
13/11	Pelister	a	0-2	
21/11	Vardar	a	1-1	*Sulev*
27/11	Skopje	h	1-0	*Sulev*
4/12	Napredok	a	1-0	*Sulev*
11/12	Shkëndija	h	0-1	
2011				
5/3	Teteks	a	0-1	
12/3	Bregalnica Stip	h	2-0	*Lazarovski, Stojanov P. (p)*
15/3	Rabotnicki	a	1-2	*Lazarovski*
19/3	Metalurg	h	1-3	*Curlinov*
2/4	Vardar	h	1-1	*Tasev*
5/4	Pelister	a	4-1	*Curlinov 3, Tasev*
9/4	Napredok	h	0-0	
16/4	Teteks	h	0-2	
23/4	Rabotnicki	a	1-3	*Lazarovski (p)*
29/4	Renova	h	1-1	*Kovacev*
7/5	Metalurg	a	1-1	*Milusev*
14/5	Shkëndija	h	0-2	
17/5	Bregalnica Stip	a	0-1	
21/5	Sileks	h	2-0	*Curlinov 2*
28/5	Skopje	a	2-1	*Mitrev, Ristov*

Name	Nat	DoB	Pos	Aps	(s)	Gls
Vangel ALTIPARMAKOVSKI		1/3/88	A	2	(1)	
Sasko BAJLOZOV		31/8/83	A	15	(3)	3
Darko BOZINOV		6/1/89	D	21		
Cvetan CURLINOV		24/7/86	A	19	(4)	9
Stojan DIMOVSKI		19/9/82	G	29		
Stefan ISTATOV		27/12/92	G	3	(2)	
Sasko JOVANOV		20/3/87	M	4	(3)	
Daniel KOVACEV		3/3/90	A	29		3
Robert LAZAROVSKI		19/9/90	M	25	(4)	5
Mitko MAVROV		8/4/91	D	21	(2)	
Aleksandar MILUSEV		5/4/88	D	29		1
Dejan MITREV		20/7/88	D	27		2
Trajche MITROV		19/11/92	D	17	(1)	
Bojan NAJDENOV		27/8/91	M	5	(17)	
Sasko PANDEV		1/5/87	A	2		
Tomica PETROV		16/7/90	D	27		
Aleksandar RISTOV		8/1/92	M		(4)	1
Nabi SHAVLEV		6/8/93	A		(1)	
Aleksandar STOJANOV		14/11/84	M	11	(10)	
Pance STOJANOV		23/6/75	D	29		1
Viktor STOJCEV		24/12/92	M	5	(1)	
Stefan SULEV		24/8/89	M	9	(16)	3
Ilija TANCEV		12/7/88	D	1		
Marjan TASEV		2/5/85	M	22	(5)	4
Borce UZEVSKI		23/1/92	D		(3)	

FK VARDAR

Coach – Gjorgi Todorovski; (1/1/11) Zoran Stratev; (16/5/11) Leones Pereira dos Santos "Chita" (BRA)
Founded – 1947
Stadium – Philip II Arena (33,460)

MAJOR HONOURS: Macedonian League – (5) 1993, 1994, 1995, 2002, 2003; Yugoslav Cup – (1) 1961; Macedonian Cup – (5) 1993, 1995, 1998, 1999, 2007.

2010				
31/7	Metalurg	h	1-2	*Nuhiu*
7/8	Sileks	a	0-1	
14/8	Renova	h	0-2	
23/8	Turnovo	a	0-3	*(w/o)*
28/8	Pelister	h	1-0	*Dzangarovski T.*
11/9	Skopje	h	1-0	*Pandovski*
18/9	Napredok	a	1-2	*Pandovski*
25/9	Shkëndija	h	0-2	
2/10	Teteks	a	2-3	*Gjurgjevic 2*
16/10	Bregalnica Stip	h	1-2	*Stojkovski T.*
24/10	Rabotnicki	a	0-2	
30/10	Metalurg	a	0-1	
7/11	Sileks	h	2-1	*Gjurgjevic, Nastevski*
13/11	Renova	a	0-4	
21/11	Turnovo	h	1-1	*Tripunovski (p)*
27/11	Pelister	a	2-1	*Gjurgjevic 2*
4/12	Skopje	a	0-1	
11/12	Napredok	h	2-1	*Nastevski, Tripunovski (p)*
2011				
6/3	Shkëndija	a	1-3	*Dzangarovski B.*
12/3	Teteks	h	2-0	*Dzangarovski T., Nastevski*
15/3	Bregalnica Stip	a	0-0	
19/3	Rabotnicki	h	1-0	*Nastevski*
2/4	Turnovo	a	1-1	*Nikancevski*
5/4	Rabotnicki	h	1-3	*Wandeir (p)*
11/4	Renova	a	0-1	
16/4	Metalurg	h	0-1	
22/4	Shkëndija	a	0-2	
29/4	Bregalnica Stip	h	1-1	*Dzangarovski T.*
7/5	Sileks	a	1-0	*Fábio*
14/5	Skopje	h	0-0	
17/5	Teteks	a	1-2	*Todorovski*
21/5	Pelister	a	0-1	
28/5	Napredok	h	1-0	*Fábio*

Name	Nat	DoB	Pos	Aps	(s)	Gls
Andrej ACEVSKI		5/6/92	M	16	(1)	
Vebi ALIEVSKI		17/10/84	M	2		
Radenko BOJOVIĆ	SRB	26/12/80	D	11		
Boban DZANGAROVSKI		17/6/83	D	15		1
Toni DZANGAROVSKI		17/6/85	D	29	(1)	3
FÁBIO Gilvan da Nascimento Silva	BRA	13/9/83	A	10	(4)	2
FERNANDO Alcântara Lopes	BRA	28/3/87	D	10		
Dimitar GEORGIEVSKI		13/2/91	A	3	(5)	
Bojan GJORGJIEVSKI		25/1/92	D	19	(1)	
Fahrudin GJURGJEVIC		17/2/92	M	14	(4)	5
Goce GOCEVSKI		15/6/92	G	1		
Ivan IVANOV		20/5/92	D		(1)	
Darko LAZAREVSKI		26/1/92	M	1	(7)	
Marjan MADZAROSKI		30/7/86	G	25		
Blagojce MARKOVSKI		12/12/87	A	2	(1)	
Gjorgji MOJSOV		27/5/85	M	9	(2)	
Ivan NASTEVSKI		30/7/91	M	24	(2)	4
Vladimir NELOSKI		23/5/91	D		(1)	
Adelcio Abrilio Carlos "NENO"	BRA	10/10/79	M	12	(1)	
Nikola NIKANCEVSKI		1/6/87	D	21	(2)	1
Darko NIKOLOV		15/9/93	D		(1)	
Blagoja NIOTIS		10/1/92	M		(1)	
Arben NUHIU		27/2/72	A	3		1
Aleksandar PANDOVSKI		13/8/91	M	12		2
Dimce RISTEVSKI		6/11/82	M	4	(7)	
Zlatko RISTOV		13/6/79	D	18	(1)	
Stefan RISTOVSKI		21/12/92	D	3	(2)	
ROBERTO CARLOS da Silva	BRA	4/4/85	M	11	(1)	
Emir SHABANI		2/1/90	M	1	(1)	
Uros SIKMANOVIC		12/7/92	A	4	(3)	
Goran SILJANOVSKI		1/7/90	M	14		
Goran SIMOV	SRB	31/3/75	G	6		
Kristijan SINKOVIĆ	CRO	2/4/87	M		(6)	
Filip SPASESKI		5/5/88	M	3		
Kristijan STOJKOVSKI		17/9/91	A		(1)	

rajce STOJKOVSKI		23/2/89	D	8	(2)	1
lexzep SULEJMANI		8/1/91	A		(5)	
Goce TODOROVSKI		13/9/82	M	4	(3)	1
likola TRIPUNOVSKI		19/12/82	M	18	(5)	2
'erica VASILEVSKI		28/8/89	A	3	(13)	
VANDEIR Oliveira dos Santos	BRA	15/5/80	A	13		1
osé "ZÉ" CARLOS Gomes Filho	BRA	4/10/79	M	3		

TOP GOALSCORERS 2010/11

20	Hristijan KIROVSKI (Skopje)
19	Borce MANEVSKI (Rabotnicki)
13	Ferhan HASANI (Shkëndija)
12	Aleksandar TEMELKOV (Sileks)
	Ersen SALI (Shkëndija)
11	Boban JANCEVSKI (Renova)
	Izair EMINI (Shkëndija)
9	Mile KRSTEV (Metalurg)
	Blagoj LEVKOV (Napredok)
	Ylber ALIU (Renova)
	Vulnet EMINI (Renova)
	Gjorgji ZAREVSKI (Sileks)
	Cvetan CURLINOV (Turnovo)

PROMOTED CLUBS

FK 11 OKTOMVRI
Coach – Nikolce Zdravevski
Founded – 1951
Stadium – Goce Delcev (15,000)

FK OHRID 2004
Coach – Zoran Gjoreski
Founded – 1921
Stadium – Biljanini Izvori (3,000)

SECOND LEVEL FINAL TABLE 2010/11

		Pld	W	D	L	F	A	Pts
1	FK 11 Oktomvri	26	16	6	4	50	19	54
2	FK Ohrid 2004	26	16	5	5	51	21	53
3	FK Tikves	26	13	9	4	45	27	48
4	FK Miravci	26	14	4	8	43	22	46
5	FK Belasica	26	13	4	9	39	26	43
6	FK Rinija	26	10	9	7	25	19	39
7	FK Drita	26	9	8	9	37	29	35
8	FK Euromilk	26	11	2	13	41	49	35
9	FK Lokomotiva	26	9	4	13	27	46	31
10	FK Ohrid Lote	26	9	2	15	40	49	29
11	FK Vlazrimi	26	8	4	14	28	56	27
11	FK Vlaznimi	26	6	4	16	24	51	22
12	FK Novaci 2005	26	5	7	14	22	37	22
14	FK Cementarnica 55	26	4	10	12	20	41	22

NB FK Vlazrimi – 1 pt deducted.

PROMOTION/RELEGATION PLAY-OFFS

(8/6/11)
Napredok 2, Tikves 0
Skopje 1, Miravci 4

NB FK Miravci subsequently declined promotion, enabling FK Vardar to remain in the Prva Liga.

DOMESTIC CUP 2010/11

KUP NA MAKEDONIJA

FIRST ROUND

(18/8/10)
11 Oktomvri 2, Skopje 1
Bair Krkardas 1, Pelister 3
Bregalnica Stip 3, Ohrid Lote 1
Cementarnica 0, Renova 1
Euromilk 1, Napredok 1 *(1-4 on pens)*
Kamenica1, Teteks 2
Karbinci 0, Turnovo 5
Lokomotiva 1, Belasica 0
Miravci 1, Rabotnicki 0
Novaci 2, Vardar 3
Ohrid 2004 0, Sileks 1
Osogovo 6, Prevalec 0
Prespa 0, Metalurg Skopje 7
Rinia 3, Milano 0 *(w/o)*
Tikves 2, Drita 1
Vlaznimi 3, Shkëndija 3 *(5-4 on pens)*

SECOND ROUND

(15/9/10 & 28/9/10)
Rinia v Turnovo 0-3; 0-1 *(0-4)*
Vardar v Renova 1-1; 1-0 *(2-1)*

(15/9/10 & 29/9/10)
Bregalnica Stip v Pelister 0-0; 2-0 *(2-0)*
Napredok v Vlaznimi 4-0; 0-2 *(4-2)*
Osogovo v Tikves 0-3; 1-0 *(1-3)*
Sileks v Teteks 0-1; 0-2 *(0-3)*

(15/9/10 & 9/10/10)
11 Oktomvri v Metalurg Skopje 1-0; 0-1 *(1-1; 6-7 on pens)*

(15/9/10 & 10/10/10)
Lokomotiva v Miravci 0-0; 0-0 *(0-0; 4-3 on pens)*

QUARTER-FINALS

(20/10/10 & 10/11/10)
Bregalnica Stip 0, Napredok 1 *(Mihajloski 75)*
Napredok 1 *(Stepanovski 75p)*, Bregalnica Stip 0
(Napredok 2-0)

Lokomotiva 0, Metalurg Skopje 3 *(Dameski 45, Krstev 46, 47)*
Metalurg Skopje 1 *(Ejupi 88)*, Lokomotiva 1 *(Shabani 82)*
(Metalurg Skopje 4-1)

Turnovo 1 *(Bajlozov 68)*, Teteks 2 *(Ristovski 71, 89)*
Teteks 1 *(Hyseni 41)*, Turnovo 0
(Teteks 3-1)

Vardar 4 *(Gjurgjevic 8, Nastevski 10, Siljanovski 12, Pandovski 64)*, Tikves 1 *(Rangotov 50)*
Tikves 4 *(Krstev 16, 52, Dimov 40, Stojanovski 73)*, Vardar 0
(Tikves 5-4)

SEMI-FINALS

(20/4/11 & 4/5/11)
Metalurg Skopje 0, Napredok 0
Napredok 0, Metalurg Skopje 2 *(Krstev 21, Tenekedziev 45)*
(Metalurg 2-0)

Tikves 0, Teteks 0
Teteks 6 *(Jovanovski D. 19, Gligorovski 24, 54, Lostov 28og, Simovski 69, Siljanovski 85)*, Tikves 0
(Teteks 6-0)

FINAL

(24/5/11)
Goce Delcev stadion, Prilep
FK METALURG SKOPJE 2 *(Kostencoski 14, Tenekedziev 65)*
FK TETEKS 0
Referee – *Boskov*
METALURG – *Nikov, Petkovski, Krsteski, Kralevski, Memedi, Mitrev, Krstev, Kostencoski (Tenekedziev 55), Ljamcevski (Ejupi 76), Nacevski, Ilijoski (Ilievski 84).*
TETEKS – *Jovanovski Ma., Jovanovski D., Gjorgjevski, Miskovski, Aliji, Simovski, Zaharievski, Naumovski G. (Kleckarovski 53), Siljanovski, Gligorovski (Stolevski 72), Jakimovski (Urosevic 80).*

CLUB COMMUNICATION 2011/12

FK Bregalnica Stip

Ul. Partizanska b.b., PO Box 143
MK-2000 Stip

Tel +389 32 613 866
Fax +389 32 613 866
Web bregalnicastip.tk
Email fcbregalnicastip@yahoo.com
Media Officer Dimitar Djonov

FK Metalurg Skopje

16 makedonska brigada 18
MK-1000 Skopje

Tel +389 2 3287 697
Fax +389 2 3287 697
Web fcmetalurg.com.mk
Email fcmetalurg@yahoo.com
Media Officer Marjan Velevski

FK Napredok

Ul. Marshal Tito – bb, City Stadium Kicevo
MK-6250 Kicevo

Tel +389 45 226 244
Fax +389 45 226 244
Web
Email lazarevski_miroslav@hotmail.com
Media Officer Zoran Antoski

FK Ohrid 2004

Bulevar Turisticka bb
MK-6000 Ohrid

Tel +389 46 254 154
Fax +389 46 254 154
Web fkohrid.weebly.com
Email fk.ohrid-s@hotmail.com
Media Officer

FK 11 Oktomvri

Aleksandar Makedonski BB
MK-7500 Prilep

Tel +389 48 551 138
Fax +389 48 400 801
Web fk11oktomvri.com
Email fk11oktomvri@yahoo.com
Media Officer Boboleski Mende

FK Rabotnicki

Gradski Park, (Kosarkarska sala) bb
MK-1000 Skopje

Tel +389 23 217 408
Fax +389 23 246 516
Web rabotnicki.com
Email vtrajceska@yahoo.com
Media Officer Vesna Trajceska

FK Renova

Naselba Drenovec, City Stadium Tetovo
MK-1220 Tetovo

Tel +389 44 334 684
Fax
Web renova.com.mk
Email kfrenova2008@yahoo.com
Media Officer Djevdet Rustemi

FK Shkëndija 79

Blagoja Toska bb
MK-1220 Tetovo

Tel + 389 44 353 670
Fax + 389 44 353 671
Web
Email kfshkendija@yahoo.com
Media Officer Jusuf Iljazi

FK Sileks

Sileks Stadion bb Kratovo, Str. Goce Delcev - 70, MK-1320 Kratovo

Tel +389 31 481 830
Fax +389 31 481 876
Web
Email sileksfk@yahoo.com
Media Officer Bosko Trpevski

FK Teteks

Star gradski stadion blagoja toskla bb, City Stadium Tetovo, MK-1200 Tetovo

Tel +389 2 215 807
Fax +389 2 215 808
Web
Email stevan.alampioski@ttk.com.mk
Media Officer

FK Turnovo

s. Turnovo bb
MK-2433 Turnovo

Tel +389 34 348 600
Fax +389 34 348 600
Web fkhorizontturnovo.mk
Email marakana_2007@yahoo.com
Media Officer Vanco Mitrov

FK Vardar

ul. Orce Nikolov br. 58-1/2 Skopje
MK-1000 Skopje

Tel +389 72 227 597
Fax
Web
Email fc_vardar.skopje@yahoo.com
Media Officer

MALTA
Malte I Malta

Malta Football Association (MFA)

COMMUNICATION

Address	Millennium Stand Floor 2 National Stadium MT-Ta' Qali ATD 4000
Tel	+356 23 386 000
Fax	+356 23 386 900
E-mail	info@mfa.com.mt
Website	mfa.com.mt

President	Norman Darmanin Demajo
General Secretary	Joseph Gauci
Media Officer	Alex Vella
Year of Formation	1900
National Stadium	National, Ta' Qali (17,797)

DOMESTIC COMPETITION SUMMARY 2010/11

PREMIER LEAGUE FINAL TABLES

FIRST PHASE

		Pld	W	D	L	F	A	Pts	
1	Valletta FC	18	13	5	0	42	11	44	(22)
2	Tarxien Rainbows FC	18	8	5	5	25	22	29	(15)
3	Floriana FC	18	8	3	7	25	20	27	(14)
4	Birkirkara FC	18	7	6	5	25	25	27	(14)
5	Marsaxlokk FC	18	5	9	4	25	25	24	(12)
6	Hamrun Spartans FC	18	7	2	9	31	36	23	(12)
7	Sliema Wanderers FC	18	5	7	6	22	26	22	(11)
8	Qormi FC	18	5	6	7	22	26	21	(11)
9	Hibernians FC	18	3	6	9	23	33	15	(8)
10	Vittoriosa Stars FC	18	2	5	11	20	36	11	(6)

NB Figures in brackets indicate points carried forward to the Second Phase.

SECOND PHASE

Championship Pool		Pld	W	D	L	F	A	Pts	Comp
1	Valletta FC	28	18	10	0	59	17	42	UCL
2	Floriana FC	28	14	5	9	46	32	34	UEL
3	Birkirkara FC	28	11	9	8	42	40	29	UEL
4	Marsaxlokk FC	28	9	11	8	45	43	26	
5	Tarxien Rainbows FC	28	10	7	11	41	45	24	
6	Hamrun Spartans FC	28	7	6	15	44	66	16	

Relegation Pool		Pld	W	D	L	F	A	Pts	
7	Sliema Wanderers FC	24	10	7	7	37	31	26	
8	Qormi FC	24	7	7	10	37	43	18	
9	Hibernians FC	24	6	6	12	34	46	17	
10	Vittoriosa Stars FC	24	3	6	15	26	48	10	*Relegated*

Top Scorer	Alfred Effiong (Marsaxlokk), 17 goals
Promoted Clubs	Balzan Youths FC Mqabba FC Mosta FC
Cup Final	Floriana FC 1, Valletta FC 0

Valletta so close to invincibility

Valletta FC won the 2010/11 Maltese Premier League title by the proverbial street, remaining undefeated at the end of a 28-match campaign that they bossed from first kick to last. An irresistible force under new coach Jesmond Zerafa, the Citizens claimed their 20th title in long-serving captain Gilbert Agius's farewell season, but they were denied a double – and a whole season of invincibility – when they lost the FA Trophy final to a late goal from Floriana FC.

Michael Mifsud – Malta's record international goalscorer

Having opened the season with two draws in Europe against Polish club Ruch Chorzów – insufficient to prevent an away-goals elimination – and claimed 18 wins and ten draws in their Premier League title procession, Valletta were so unaccustomed to losing that when Floriana's veteran striker Ivan Woods drove in an 89th-minute free-kick to break the FA Trophy final stalemate, it left the Valletta players and supporters in a state of shock.

Floriana's wait over

An agonising defeat for Valletta, however, was an ecstatic victory for their great rivals, who thus ended a 17-year wait for silverware under charismatic president Johann Said. Already sure of a UEFA Europa League place as league runners-up before the cup final, Floriana were joined in UEFA's second major club competition by deposed champions Birkirkara FC, who finished third despite a season blighted by injuries and subdued contributions from their overseas players. Qormi FC, third under Zerafa in 2009/10, dropped into the relegation pool before they were steered to safety by Malta's record goalscorer Michael Mifsud, who banged in seven goals in five games. Vittoriosa Stars FC were relegated alone, but a Premier League revamp for 2011/12 enabled three clubs to come up – Balzan Youths FC, Mqabba FC and Mosta FC.

Although the likes of Roderick Briffa, Jonathan Caruana, Jamie Pace and goalkeeper Andrew Hogg made avoiding defeat a habit in the all white of Valletta, it was a very different story when they donned the red of Malta in the UEFA EURO 2012 qualifying campaign. The team's first six matches brought six defeats and just two goals - one from Pace, against Israel, and another for Mifsud to add to his record tally, against Greece. André Schembri, who enjoyed a prolific season in Hungary for Ferencvárosi TC, failed to score for his country in 2010/11, but the biggest frustration for coach John Buttigieg was his side's concession of late winning goals to both Georgia, in Tbilisi, and Greece, at Ta' Qali.

National Team

Top Five All-time Caps – David Carabott (121); Gilbert Agius (120); Carmel Busuttil (111); Joe Brincat (103); John Buttigieg (95)

Top Five All-time Goals – Michael Mifsud (26); Carmel Busuttil (23); David Carabott (12); Gilbert Agius & Hubert Suda (8)

NATIONAL TEAM RESULTS 2010/11

11/8/10	FYROM	H	Ta' Qali	1-1	*Mifsud (47)*
2/9/10	Israel (ECQ)	A	Tel-Aviv	1-3	*Pace (38)*
7/9/10	Latvia (ECQ)	H	Ta' Qali	0-2	
8/10/10	Georgia (ECQ)	A	Tbilisi	0-1	
17/11/10	Croatia (ECQ)	A	Zagreb	0-3	
9/2/11	Switzerland	H	Ta' Qali	0-0	
26/3/11	Greece (ECQ)	H	Ta' Qali	0-1	
4/6/11	Greece (ECQ)	A	Piraeus	1-3	*Mifsud (54)*

NATIONAL TEAM APPEARANCES 2010/11

Coach – John BUTTIGIEG	**5/10/63**		**Mkd**	**ISR**	**LVA**	**GEO**	**CRO**	**Sui**	**GRE**	**GRE**	**Caps**	**Goals**
Andrew HOGG	2/3/85	Valletta	G	G	G		G			G	19	-
Edward HERRERA	14/9/86	Hibernians	D	D80							3	-
Jonathan CARUANA	24/7/86	Valletta	D	D	D	D	D	D	D46	D	18	-
Andrei AGIUS	12/8/86	Melfi (ITA) /Birkirkara	D	D	D	D		D79	D	D	19	-
Carlo MAMO	23/4/79	Marsaxlokk	D46	D	D77	D		D64	D		17	-
Jamie PACE	1/1/77	Valletta	M	M	M	M	M	s56	s46		43	3
Roderick BRIFFA	24/8/81	Valletta	M73	M82	M	D	D	D	D	D	57	-
Shaun BAJADA	19/10/83	Birkirkara	M80	M	M	M	D	M	M78	D80	27	-
Gareth SCIBERRAS	29/3/83	Marsaxlokk	M65	M	M77	M69	M88	M	M	M	21	-
Daniel BOGDANOVIC	26/3/80	Sheffield United (ENG)	M	M57	s59		M82		M	M60	34	1
Michael MIFSUD	17/4/81	unattached /Qormi	A	A	A	A	A	A	A	A	82	26
Clayton FAILLA	8/1/86	Sliema	s46	s82	s77			s64		s80	15	-
Ryan FENECH	20/4/86	Hamrun /Valletta	s65		s77	s69	s70		s78	M	22	-
Andrew COHEN	13/5/81	Hibernians	s73	s57	M	M90		M90	s91	s60	42	1
Paul FENECH	20/12/86	Birkirkara	s80			s80	s88	M56		s87	7	-
Emmanuel MUSCAT	7/12/84	Wellington Phoenix (NZL)		s80	D59						8	-
Justin HABER	9/6/81	Ferencváros (HUN)				G		G	G		41	-
André SCHEMBRI	27/5/86	Ferencváros (HUN)				A80	A70	A85	A91	A	35	3
Massimo GRIMA	5/7/79	Hamrun				s90	D				14	-
John HUTCHINSON	29/12/79	Central Coast Mariners (AUS)					M		M	M87	7	-
Kevin SAMMUT	26/5/81	Valletta					s82	s90			37	-
Joseph ZERAFA	31/5/88	Birkirkara						s79			1	-
Ivan WOODS	31/12/76	Floriana						s85			45	1

CLUB-BY-CLUB

BIRKIRKARA FC

Coach – Paul Zammit

Founded – 1950

MAJOR HONOURS: Maltese League – (3) 2000, 2006, 2010; Maltese Cup – (4) 2002, 2003, 2005, 2008.

2010			
13/9	Sliema	4-1	*Galea M. 2 (1p), Vella, Lattes*
18/9	Floriana	0-2	
24/9	Hibernians	2-1	*Vella, Lattes*
15/10	Valletta	2-2	*Cilia 2*
24/10	Marsaxlokk	2-5	*Vella, Fenech*
29/10	Hamrun	1-1	*Galea M.*
4/11	Vittoriosa	1-1	*Vukanac*
21/11	Qormi	2-0	*Lattes 2*
28/11	Tarxien	0-0	
5/12	Sliema	2-2	*Tabone 2 (1p)*
13/12	Floriana	1-0	*Borg*
18/12	Hibernians	3-1	*Fenech 2, Lattes*
2011			
8/1	Valletta	1-3	*Galea M.*
15/1	Marsaxlokk	0-2	
22/1	Hamrun	2-0	*Lattes, Fenech*
30/1	Vittoriosa	1-0	*Agius*
5/2	Qormi	1-4	*Rodolfo*
12/2	Tarxien	0-0	
19/2	Tarxien	3-1	*Galea M., Lattes, Fenech*
27/2	Hamrun	1-1	*Rodolfo*
5/3	Valletta	0-1	
12/3	Marsaxlokk	4-1	*Scicluna, Babatunde, Galea M., Lattes*
3/4	Floriana	1-5	*Galea M.*
10/4	Tarxien	3-0	*Cilia, Galea M., Babatunde*
17/4	Hamrun	2-2	*Babatunde, Cilia*
25/4	Valletta	1-1	*Rodolfo*
30/4	Marsaxlokk	2-0	*Lattes, Galea M.*
6/5	Floriana	0-3	

No	Name	Nat	DoB	Pos	Aps	(s)	Gls
3	Andrei AGIUS		12/8/86	D	12		1
13	Ibrahim Olalekan BABATUNDE	NGA	29/12/84	A	9	(2)	3
18	Shaun BAJADA		19/10/83	M	16	(2)	
4	Manuel BARTOLO		11/9/82	G	11	(1)	
5	Patrick BORG		13/8/87	D	15		1
11	Angus BUHAGIAR		29/4/87	A	25		
23	Michael CAMILLERI		23/3/93	A		(1)	
17	Ryan CAMENZULI		8/9/94	D	1	(1)	
7	Trevor CILIA		2/1/83	A	14	(2)	4
11	Andrew DECESARE		4/3/84	A	11	(6)	
6	Paul FENECH		20/12/86	M	23		5
22	Michael Alan FRASER	SCO	8/10/83	G	16		
15	Andreas GALEA		23/4/91	D		(2)	
9	Michael GALEA		1/2/79	A	24	(2)	9
27	Ryan HARDING	SCO	27/4/84	D	9		
23	Emiliano LATTES	ARG	28/1/85	A	25	(2)	9
1	Ezequiel LOVIZON	ITA	10/8/81	G	1		
2	Rowen MUSCAT		5/6/91	M	21		
8	Thomas PARIS		15/11/86	A	4	(6)	
16	Karl PULO		30/7/89	M	6	(13)	
	RODOLFO Kumbrevicius Adorno de Oliveira	BRA	13/7/81	A	2	(7)	3
2	Ryan SCICLUNA		30/7/93	M	5	(9)	1
10	Alan TABONE		31/10/81	A	3	(2)	2
8	Terence VELLA		20/4/90	M	9	(11)	3
15	Nikola VUKANAC	SRB	14/1/86	D	16	(1)	1
21	Simon ZAHRA	AUS	26/7/84	M	6	(5)	
19	Joseph ZERAFA		31/5/88	D	24	(1)	

FLORIANA FC

Coach – Todor Raykov (BUL); (20/2/11) Michael Woods

Founded – 1894

MAJOR HONOURS: Maltese League – (25) 1910, 1912, 1913, 1921, 1922, 1925, 1927, 1928, 1929, 1931, 1935, 1937, 1950, 1951, 1952, 1953, 1955, 1958, 1962, 1968, 1970, 1973, 1975, 1977, 1993; Maltese Cup – (19) 1938, 1945, 1947, 1949, 1950, 1953, 1954, 1955, 1957, 1958, 1961, 1966, 1967, 1972, 1976, 1981, 1993, 1994, 2011.

2010			
11/9	Hibernians	1-3	*Darmanin*
18/9	Birkirkara	2-0	*Mecerod, Dzhorov*
26/9	Marsaxlokk	0-1	
17/10	Hamrun	2-1	*Caruana, Woods (p)*
23/10	Vittoriosa	0-0	
29/10	Qormi	1-0	*Mecerod*
6/11	Tarxien	0-2	
20/11	Sliema	1-0	*Woods*
27/11	Valletta	0-0	
4/12	Hibernians	1-1	*Agius*
13/12	Birkirkara	0-1	
19/12	Marsaxlokk	3-0	*Woods 2, Caruana*
2011			
7/1	Hamrun	3-1	*Said, Nwoke 2*
16/1	Vittoriosa	6-1	*Nwoke 2, Woods 2 (1p), Draganov, Micallef*
23/1	Qormi	4-3	*Nwoke 2, Caruana, Farrugia*
30/1	Tarxien	1-3	*Draganov*
6/2	Sliema	0-1	
12/2	Valletta	0-2	
19/2	Marsaxlokk	0-4	
26/2	Tarxien	5-1	*Farrugia 2, Cassar, Draganov, Doffo*
5/3	Hamrun	2-0	*Nwoke 2*
13/3	Valletta	0-3	
3/4	Birkirkara	5-1	*Nwoke 4, Woods*
9/4	Marsaxlokk	1-1	*Cassar*
16/4	Tarxien	2-1	*Draganov, Nwoke*
23/4	Hamrun	2-0	*Woods 2 (2p)*
30/4	Valletta	1-1	*Farrugia*
6/5	Birkirkara	3-0	*Borg J. 2, Draganov*

No	Name	Nat	DoB	Pos	Aps	(s)	Gls
23	Alan ABELA		11/1/92	D		(1)	
19	Luke AGIUS		6/3/88	M	1	(3)	1
24	Clyde BORG		20/3/92	D	15	(8)	
17	Joseph BORG		26/1/87	M	10	(12)	2
21	Sasha BORG		27/5/93	A	5	(11)	
2	Owen BUGEJA		20/2/90	D	7	(6)	
10	Christian CARUANA		21/10/86	M	17	(5)	3
25	Christian CASSAR		20/6/83	M	15	(6)	2
19	Ryan DARMANIN		12/12/85	A	4	(5)	1
8	Pablo César DOFFO	ARG	6/3/83	M	21	(4)	1
81	Dragomir DRAGANOV	BUL	27/9/81	A	13	(2)	5
7	Kiril DZHOROV	BUL	12/8/75	D	4	(2)	1
18	Mohamed EL YAMANI	EGY	1/1/82	A	3	(1)	
22	Tyrone FARRUGIA		22/2/89	D	27		4
13	Marçal Guerreiro FERNANDES	POR	28/11/83	A	3	(5)	
20	Mark GAUCI		7/1/86	M	2	(4)	
	Michael MECEROD	USA	19/7/85	A	9	(3)	2
9	Manolito MICALLEF		16/11/83	A	27		1
11	Daniel NWOKE	NGA	16/6/83	A	12		13
6	Thomas PARIS		15/11/86	A	11	(1)	
16	Duncan PISANI		25/5/88	D	24	(1)	
4	Brian SAID		15/3/73	D	19		1
1	Lofti SAÏDI	TUN	8/6/82	G	26		
11	Ivailo SOKOLOV	BUL	15/9/84	D	5	(1)	
	Matthew TOWNS	ENG	12/9/82	G	2		
14	Ivan WOODS		31/12/76	A	26		9

HAMRUN SPARTANS FC

Coach – Steve D'Amato

Founded – 1907

MAJOR HONOURS: Maltese League – (7) 1914, 1918, 1947, 1983, 1987, 1988, 1991; Maltese Cup – (6) 1983, 1984, 1987, 1988, 1989, 1992.

2010			
11/9	Qormi	3-1	*Mangion, Marcelo, Shields*
19/9	Tarxien	3-1	*Marcelo, Grima, Shields*
26/9	Sliema	1-3	*Grima*
17/10	Floriana	1-2	*Shields*
24/10	Hibernians	4-3	*Marcelo, Anizoba 2, Spiteri*
29/10	Birkirkara	1-1	*Marcelo*
6/11	Marsaxlokk	1-2	*Spiteri*
26/11	Vittoriosa	2-0	*Spiteri 2*
1/12	Valletta	0-2	
5/12	Qormi	2-1	*Spiteri, Fenech Ro. (p)*
10/12	Tarxien	1-3	*Grima*
17/12	Sliema	3-2	*Spiteri 2, Grima*
2011			
7/1	Floriana	1-3	*Spiteri*
14/1	Hibernians	2-4	*Grima, Fenech Ro.*
22/1	Birkirkara	0-2	
28/1	Marsaxlokk	2-3	*Shields (p), Spiteri*
5/2	Valletta	1-1	*Falzon*
13/2	Vittoriosa	3-2	*Kokavessis, Spiteri 2*
20/2	Valletta	1-1	*Falzon*
27/2	Birkirkara	1-1	*Shields*
5/3	Floriana	0-2	
13/3	Tarxien	1-4	*Shields*
2/4	Marsaxlokk	2-4	*Chipev, Agius*
8/4	Valletta	0-5	
17/4	Birkirkara	2-2	*Falzon, Marcelo*
23/4	Floriana	0-2	
29/4	Tarxien	3-3	*Mangion, Anizoba, Spiteri*
6/5	Marsaxlokk	3-6	*Falzon, Spiteri 2*

No	Name	Nat	DoB	Pos	Aps	(s)	Gls
18	Lee James AGIUS		8/12/90	M	12	(7)	1
30	Peter Chizoba ANIZOBA	NGA	6/12/84	A	8	(8)	3
5	Aaron ATTARD		19/9/83	D	2	(5)	
	Glenn AZZOPARDI		8/8/83	M		(1)	
2	Mark Anthony BONNICI		17/1/80	D	7	(1)	

No	Name	Nat	DoB	Pos	Aps	(s)	Gls
	Steve BONNICI		2/2/89	D	18	(3)	
27	Omar BORG		12/2/81	G	19		
29	Clyde CAIMON		31/7/87	M		(1)	
24	David CAMILLERI		21/8/74	M	27	(1)	
	Chris CARDONA		19/4/92	A		(1)	
1	Ivan CASHA		21/6/78	G	7		
	Andrea CASSAR		19/12/92	G	2		
23	Nikolai CHIPEV	BUL	20/2/89	M	9		1
	Craig DEBATTISTA		31/3/91	D		(3)	
20	Dyson FALZON		9/3/86	A	12		4
3	Roderick FENECH		19/12/87	D	20	(1)	2
	Ryan FENECH		20/4/86	M	14		
6	Massimo GRIMA		5/7/79	M	26		5
19	Jonathan HOLLAND		15/7/78	M		(2)	
23	Martin HRUBSA	CZE	9/10/84	D	12		
	Dylan KOKAVESSIS		14/1/89	A	4	(5)	1
6	Karl MAGRO		28/1/90	D	3	(3)	
7	Rupert MANGION		31/3/75	M	17	(2)	2
19	MARCELO Pereira	BRA	6/4/81	A	23	(2)	5
14	Mead MIFSUD		9/6/88	D	2	(10)	
4	Dragan MILOVIĆ	SRB	3/3/65	M	5		
9	Dene SHIELDS	SCO	16/9/82	A	10		6
21	Gaetan SPITERI		5/6/81	A	27		14
22	Jovan VUKANIĆ	SRB	22/6/90	D	21	(1)	
	Daniel ZERAFA		8/4/94	D	1	(2)	

HIBERNIANS FC

Coach – Mark Miller (ENG)

Founded – 1922

MAJOR HONOURS: Maltese League – (10) 1961, 1967, 1969, 1979, 1981, 1982, 1994, 1995, 2002, 2009; Maltese Cup – (8) 1962, 1970, 1971, 1980, 1982, 1998, 2006, 2007.

2010			
11/9	Floriana	3-1	*McManus 2, Caruana*
17/9	Valletta	2-2	*Clarke, Herrera*
24/9	Birkirkara	1-2	*Cohen*
17/10	Marsaxlokk	2-2	*McManus, Cohen*
24/10	Hamrun	3-4	*McManus, Farrugia, Cohen (p)*
31/10	Vittoriosa	0-2	
8/11	Qormi	0-0	
20/11	Tarxien	0-2	
27/11	Sliema	0-0	
4/12	Floriana	1-1	*Pearson*
13/12	Valletta	0-2	
18/12	Birkirkara	1-3	*Pisani*
2011			
8/1	Marsaxlokk	2-2	*Herrera, Pulis*
14/1	Hamrun	4-2	*Herrera, Kristensen, McManus, Pisani*
23/1	Vittoriosa	1-2	*og (Micallef)*
29/1	Qormi	0-1	
6/2	Tarxien	3-1	*Cohen, Herrera, Fairbairn*
13/2	Sliema	0-4	
20/2	Vittoriosa	2-1	*McManus (p), Pulis*
28/2	Sliema	1-0	*Kristensen*
11/3	Qormi	4-3	*Taki (p), McManus (p), Hart, Cohen*
1/4	Vittoriosa	0-1	
10/4	Sliema	2-3	*Cohen, Caruana*
18/4	Qormi	2-5	*Herrera 2*

No	Name	Nat	DoB	Pos	Aps	(s)	Gls
	Ayrton AZZOPARDI		12/9/93	M		(2)	
12	Daniel BALZAN		8/6/91	G	2		
	Johann BEZZINA		30/5/94	A		(1)	
20	Ryan CAMILLERI		22/5/88	D	12		
17	Triston CARUANA		15/9/91	M	10	(4)	2
9	Warren CHIRCOP		15/9/88	A	1	(3)	
22	Matt CLARKE	ENG	18/12/80	D	16	(4)	1
10	Andrew COHEN		13/5/81	M	22	(2)	6
	Rene DUCA		30/11/82	M	1		
13	Brian FAIRBAIRN	SCO	7/4/83	M	5	(1)	1
23	Jean Paul FARRUGIA		22/8/90	A	3	(6)	1
16	Matthew GAUCI		2/9/91	M	13	(3)	
	Richie HART	SCO	30/3/78	M	20	(1)	1
3	Edward HERRERA		14/9/86	D	23	(1)	6
11	Bjorn KRISTENSEN		5/4/93	M	6	(11)	2
	Zoran LEVNAJIĆ	CRO	4/4/87	M	13		
	Paul McMANUS	SCO	26/12/82	A	20	(1)	7
	Brandon MUSCAT		3/11/94	D		(1)	
1	Mario MUSCAT		18/8/76	G	22		
21	Patrick OSEI	GHA	16/9/89	M	9		
	PAULO Jorge Fernandes SERENO	POR	24/10/83	A	2	(1)	
6	Jonathan PEARSON		13/1/87	D	16	(4)	1
7	Steve PISANI		7/8/92	A	7	(5)	2
4	Adrian PULIS		30/3/79	D	14	(3)	2
	Dylan SAMMUT		10/1/92	D	1		
14	Matthew TABONE		29/4/92	D	8	(5)	
	Keith TANTI		11/5/93	D		(1)	
18	Abdelilah TAKI	NED	29/3/84	M	4		1
5	Aaron XUEREB		3/10/79	D	14	(2)	

MARSAXLOKK FC

Coach – Patrick Curmi

Founded – 1949

MAJOR HONOURS: Maltese League – (1) 2007.

2010			
12/9	Tarxien	0-0	
19/9	Sliema	0-0	
26/9	Floriana	1-0	*Alcorsé (p)*
17/10	Hibernians	2-2	*Templeman, Effiong*
24/10	Birkirkara	5-2	*Effiong 4, Kokavessis*
1/11	Valletta	0-2	
6/11	Hamrun	2-1	*Effiong 2*
8/11	Vittoriosa	1-1	*Templeman*
28/11	Qormi	0-1	
4/12	Tarxien	2-4	*Deyanov, Ruben Gravata*
12/12	Sliema	1-1	*Ruben Gravata*
19/12	Floriana	0-3	
2011			
8/1	Hibernians	2-2	*Sciberras, Effiong*
15/1	Birkirkara	2-0	*Licari, Sciberras*
22/1	Valletta	0-0	
28/1	Hamrun	3-2	*Raimy, Ruben Gravata, Templeman*
4/2	Vittoriosa	2-2	*Effiong, Raimy*
13/2	Qormi	2-2	*Ruben Gravata (p), Alcorsé*
19/2	Floriana	4-0	*Effiong 4*
27/2	Valletta	1-1	*Licari*
4/3	Tarxien	1-0	*Alcorsé*
12/3	Birkirkara	1-4	*Alcorsé*
2/4	Hamrun	4-2	*Darmanin 3, Effiong*
9/4	Floriana	1-1	*Darmanin*
17/4	Valletta	0-1	
23/4	Tarxien	2-4	*Alcorsé 2*
30/4	Birkirkara	0-2	
6/5	Hamrun	6-3	*Brincat, Darmanin, Licari, Effiong 3 (2p)*

No	Name	Nat	DoB	Pos	Aps	(s)	Gls
10	Julio César ALCORSÉ	ARG	17/9/81	A	8	(11)	6
16	Clive BRINCAT		31/5/83	M	13	(2)	1
14	Gary CARUANA		3/6/92	M	2	(9)	
	Ryan DARMANIN		12/12/85	A	8	(8)	5
7	Martin DEYANOV	BUL	17/1/80	A	25	(2)	1
6	Sunday EBOH	NGA	30/9/81	D	5	(7)	
11	Alfred EFFIONG	NGA	29/11/84	A	22	(5)	17
22	Dylan KOKAVESSIS		14/1/89	A	8	(1)	1
17	Rumen Angelov GALABOV	BUL	29/7/78	M	24		
1	Reuben GAUCI		28/10/83	G	27		
9	Malcolm LICARI		18/4/78	A	25	(2)	3
	Luca LODETTI	ITA	18/11/89	M	4	(1)	
3	Carlo MAMO		23/4/79	D	23		
	Kevin POLIDANO		21/5/82	M	1		
8	Peter PULLICINO		17/6/76	M	13	(5)	
35	Florent RAIMY	BEN	7/2/86	D	13	(1)	2
25	RUBEN Alexandre						

No	Name	Nat	DoB	Pos	Aps	(s)	Gls
	Guerreiro GRAVATA	POR	7/6/88	M	12	(5)	4
4	Gareth SCIBERRAS		29/3/83	M	26		2
18	Andrew SPITERI		8/8/86	M	7	(6)	
20	Trevor TEMPLEMAN		25/11/81	M	22	(3)	3
24	Emil YANCHEV	BUL	15/9/74	D	19	(3)	
21	Glenn ZAMMIT		5/8/87	G	1		

QORMI FC

Coach – Stephen Azzopardi

Founded – 1961

2010

11/9	Hamrun	1-3	*Mallia*
18/9	Vittoriosa	4-2	*Mallia 2, Farrugia J., Bjedov*
25/9	Valletta	0-1	
18/10	Tarxien	2-1	*Frendo, Bello-Osagie*
25/10	Sliema	0-0	
29/10	Floriana	0-1	
8/11	Hibernians	0-0	
21/11	Birkirkara	0-2	
28/11	Marsaxlokk	1-0	*Frendo*
5/12	Hamrun	1-2	*Chetcuti*
12/12	Vittoriosa	2-2	*Frendo, Camilleri B.*
18/12	Valletta	0-4	

2011

9/1	Tarxien	1-1	*Bello-Osagie*
15/1	Sliema	0-0	
23/1	Floriana	3-4	*Frendo, Josué 2 (1p)*
29/1	Hibernians	1-0	*Josué (p)*
5/2	Birkirkara	4-1	*Mifsud 3, Josué (p)*
13/2	Marsaxlokk	2-2	*Bondin, Farrugia J.*
21/2	Sliema	0-4	
26/2	Vittoriosa	4-1	*Mifsud 2, Bello-Osagie, Josué (p)*
11/3	Hibernians	3-4	*Mifsud 2, Frendo*
2/4	Sliema	1-4	*Karamanolis*
9/4	Vittoriosa	2-2	*Josué, Farrugia J. (p)*
18/4	Hibernians	5-2	*Vandelannoite, Frendo, Borg Olivier 2, og (Tabone)*

No	Name	Nat	DoB	Pos	Aps	(s)	Gls
93	Steve AGIUS		15/5/93	D	1	(4)	
7	Matthew BARTOLO		14/6/86	M	17	(4)	
18	Abubakar BELLO-OSAGIE	NGA	11/8/88	A	16		3
	Kosta BJEDOV	SRB	10/5/86	A	9	(1)	1
22	Jonathan BONDIN		11/10/82	D	19		1
19	Michael BORG OLIVIER		12/4/79	D	4	(1)	2
77	Gabriel BUTTIGIEG		10/9/91	M	2	(8)	
16	Ben CAMILLERI		16/8/88	M	4	(7)	1
14	Matthew CAMILLERI		4/9/79	G	5	(3)	
10	Joseph CHETCUTI		16/8/82	M	13	(7)	1
77	George CHIRCOP		18/7/92	M		(1)	
6	Carmelo FARRUGIA		17/6/92	M		(2)	
11	Joseph FARRUGIA		26/7/81	M	20		3
1	Matthew FARRUGIA		17/4/81	G	19		
8	Keith FENECH		28/2/76	M	15	(4)	
26	Cleavon FRENDO		1/7/85	A	17	(3)	6
91	Jurgen GERADA		8/6/91	M		(1)	
2	Gaetano GESUALDI	CAN	15/2/92	D		(1)	
4	Stefan GIGLIO		26/2/79	M	19		
99	JOSUÉ Souza Santos	BRA	10/7/87	A	11	(1)	6
13	Christos KARAMANOLIS	GRE	17/12/85	M	7	(1)	1
28	KANG Ho-jung	KOR	11/6/86	D	15	(5)	
21	George MALLIA		10/10/78	M	13	(6)	3
9	Michael MIFSUD		17/4/81	A	5		7
5	Roderick SAMMUT		7/12/83	D	10	(2)	
	Ibraima Sumaila Vaz SANI	GNB	6/7/82	M		(2)	
15	Luke SCIBERRAS		15/9/89	A	1	(4)	
3	Jason Lee VANDELANNOITE	BEL	6/11/86	D	20		1
	VINÍCIUS Conceição da Silva	BRA	7/3/77	D	2		

SLIEMA WANDERERS FC

Coach – Mark Marlow; (31/1/11) Danilo Dončić (SRB)

Founded – 1909

MAJOR HONOURS: Maltese League – (26) 1920, 1923, 1924, 1926 1930, 1933, 1934, 1936, 1938, 1939, 1940, 1949, 1954, 1956, 1957, 1964, 1965, 1966, 1971, 1972, 1976, 1989, 1996, 2003, 2004, 2005; Maltese Cup – (20) 1935, 1936, 1937, 1940, 1946, 1948, 1951, 1952 1956, 1959, 1963, 1965, 1968, 1969, 1974, 1979, 1990, 2000, 2004, 2009

2010

13/9	Birkirkara	1-4	*Jackson*
19/9	Marsaxlokk	0-0	
26/9	Hamrun	3-1	*Obiefule, Mifsud Triganza 2*
18/10	Vittoriosa	1-0	*Obiefule*
25/10	Qormi	0-0	
31/10	Tarxien	1-2	*Mifsud Triganza*
5/11	Valletta	0-4	
20/11	Floriana	0-1	
27/11	Hibernians	0-0	
5/12	Birkirkara	2-2	*Obiefule, Scerri*
12/12	Marsaxlokk	1-1	*Jackson*
17/12	Hamrun	2-3	*Mifsud Triganza, Obiefule*

2011

9/1	Vittoriosa	4-3	*Jackson, Lachkham 2, Mifsud Triganza*
15/1	Qormi	0-0	
24/1	Tarxien	1-1	*Jackson*
29/1	Valletta	1-4	*Jackson (p)*
6/2	Floriana	1-0	*Obiefule (p)*
13/2	Hibernians	4-0	*Mifsud Triganza, Barbara 2, Jackson*
21/2	Qormi	4-0	*Mifsud Triganza 2, Scerri, Obiefule*
28/2	Hibernians	0-1	
12/3	Vittoriosa	2-1	*Mifsud Triganza 2*
2/4	Qormi	4-1	*Ciantar, Lachkham, Mifsud Triganza, Obiefule*
10/4	Hibernians	3-2	*Jackson 2 (1p), Mifsud Triganza (p)*
16/4	Vittoriosa	2-0	*Obiefule, Mifsud Triganza*

No	Name	Nat	DoB	Pos	Aps	(s)	Gls
	Valdo Gonçalves ALHINHO	POR	17/12/88	M	1	(2)	
22	Roderick BAJADA		4/1/83	M	16	(3)	
99	Etienne BARBARA		10/7/82	A	5	(1)	2
11	Steven BEZZINA		5/1/87	D	16	(1)	
	Henry BONELLO		13/10/88	G	3		
4	Julian BRIFFA		11/8/81	D	11	(3)	
	Andrew CALIGARI		28/1/92	M		(1)	
10	Miguel CIANTAR		17/10/90	A	6	(13)	1
	Ryan DALLI		18/3/93	M		(1)	
12	Ini Aktpan ETIM	NGA	3/8/94	G	4		
77	Clayton FAILLA		8/1/86	M	14	(2)	
13	Clifford GATT BALDACCHINO		9/2/88	D	21		
17	JACKSON Lima Sequeira	BRA	9/7/82	M	22		8
20	Chakib LACHKHAM	TUN	27/10/85	A	9	(2)	3
5	Josef MIFSUD		7/9/84	D	19		
9	Jean Pierre MIFSUD TRIGANZA		20/11/81	A	17	(4)	13
23	John MINTOFF		23/8/88	M	13	(1)	
2	Alexander MUSCAT		14/12/84	D		(1)	
	Beppe MUSCAT		13/4/89	D	17	(2)	
19	Polycarp Obinna OBIEFULE	NGA	7/1/88	A	14	(7)	8
14	James PARIS		22/5/92	M	5	(9)	
8	Mark SCERRI		16/1/90	M	20		2
	Adam SPITERI		18/2/89	M	2	(5)	
1	Viktor SZENTPÉTERI	HUN	1/11/79	G	17		
	Sekou Souare TIDANE	CIV	9/4/83	D	12		
7	Noel TURNER		9/12/74	M		(9)	

TARXIEN RAINBOWS FC

Coach – Noel Coleiro

Founded – 1944

2010

12/9	Marsaxlokk	0-0	
19/9	Hamrun	1-3	*Cristiano (p)*
25/9	Vittoriosa	1-0	*Ricardo Costa*
18/10	Qormi	1-2	*Cristiano*

3/10	Valletta	2-5	*Ricardo Costa, Daniel Bueno*
31/10	Sliema	2-1	*Ricardo Costa, Daniel Bueno*
/11	Floriana	2-0	*Pacheco 2*
20/11	Hibernians	2-0	*og (Pearson), Pacheco*
28/11	Birkirkara	0-0	
/12	Marsaxlokk	4-2	*Caruana, Pacheco, Cristiano, Daniel Bueno*
10/12	Hamrun	3-1	*Daniel Bueno 2, Ricardo Costa*
19/12	Vittoriosa	1-0	*Éverton*
2011			
9/1	Qormi	1-1	*og (Kang)*
16/1	Valletta	0-2	
24/1	Sliema	1-1	*Cristiano*
30/1	Floriana	3-1	*Cristiano 2, Daniel Bueno*
6/2	Hibernians	1-3	*Cristiano*
12/2	Birkirkara	0-0	
19/2	Birkirkara	1-3	*Pacheco (p)*
26/2	Floriana	1-5	*Pacheco (p)*
4/3	Marsaxlokk	0-1	
13/3	Hamrun	4-1	*Daniel Bueno, Pacheco, Ricardo Costa 2*
3/4	Valletta	0-1	
10/4	Birkirkara	0-3	
16/4	Floriana	1-2	*Daniel Bueno*
23/4	Marsaxlokk	4-2	*Pacheco 2, Daniel Bueno, Cristiano*
29/4	Hamrun	3-3	*Daniel Bueno, Pacheco, Ricardo Costa*
7/5	Valletta	2-2	*Ricardo Costa, Daniel Bueno*

No	Name	Nat	DoB	Pos	Aps	(s)	Gls
6	Orosco ANONAM		15/6/79	M	25		
7	Gianluca CALABRETTA		14/10/87	M	12	(7)	
4	Manuel CARUANA		17/2/85	D	21	(2)	1
12	David CASSAR		24/11/87	G	21	(1)	
9	CRISTIANO dos Santos Rodriques	BRA	3/6/81	A	21	(4)	8
1	Anthony CURMI		20/11/82	G	7		
15	DANIEL Mariano BUENO	BRA	15/12/83	A	19	(2)	11
8	ÉVERTON Antônio Pereira	BRA	15/11/79	M	26		1
	Andre FARRUGIA		6/5/91	M		(4)	
11	Sergio HILI		15/4/89	M		(16)	
66	Lee GALEA		14/2/88	D	19	(3)	
6	Ryan GRECH		3/4/85	M	3	(4)	
87	Justin GRIOLI		20/9/87	D	21	(2)	
20	Ryan MINTOFF		3/7/83	D	12	(12)	
10	Sérgio PACHECO de Oliveira	BRA	7/6/81	M	21	(1)	10
8	RICARDO Mion Varella COSTA	BRA	17/6/82	A	22	(3)	8
2	Steven Marc SADOWSKI		21/1/82	D	17	(2)	
14	Mark TANTI		20/4/81	M	12	(4)	
17	Julian VELLA		12/1/86	M	8	(7)	
16	Luke VELLA CRITIEN		19/3/86	M	21	(2)	

VALLETTA FC

Coach – Jesmond Zerafa

Founded – 1943

MAJOR HONOURS: Maltese League – (20) 1915, 1932, 1945, 1946, 1948, 1959, 1960, 1963, 1974, 1978, 1980, 1984, 1990, 1992, 1997, 1998, 1999, 2001, 2008, 2011; Maltese Cup – (12) 1960, 1964, 1975, 1977, 1978, 1991, 1995, 1996, 1997, 1999, 2001, 2010.

2010			
12/9	Vittoriosa	3-0	*Sammut, Zammit, Falzon*
17/9	Hibernians	2-2	*Denni (p), Scerri*
25/9	Qormi	1-0	*Scerri*
15/10	Birkirkara	2-2	*Sammut, Pace*
23/10	Tarxien	5-2	*Scerri 3 (1p), Sammut, Pace*
1/11	Marsaxlokk	2-0	*Sammut, Falzon*
5/11	Sliema	4-0	*Denni, Scerri (p), Agius G., Agius E.*
27/11	Floriana	0-0	
1/12	Hamrun	2-0	*Borg, Temile*
6/12	Vittoriosa	3-2	*Denni 2, Scerri*
13/12	Hibernians	2-0	*Denni, Scerri*
18/12	Qormi	4-0	*Scerri 2, Agius G., Sammut*
2011			
8/1	Birkirkara	3-1	*Denni 2, Scerri (p)*
16/1	Tarxien	2-0	*Scerri, Denni (p)*
22/1	Marsaxlokk	0-0	
29/1	Sliema	4-1	*Scerri 2, Fenech 2*
5/2	Hamrun	1-1	*Briffa*
12/2	Floriana	2-0	*Denni, Zammit*
20/2	Hamrun	1-1	*Caruana*
27/2	Marsaxlokk	1-1	*Fenech*
5/3	Birkirkara	1-0	*Anderson*
13/3	Floriana	3-0	*Anderson, Denni, Zammit*
3/4	Tarxien	1-0	*Agius E.*
8/4	Hamrun	5-0	*Denni, Briffa 2, Agius E. 2*
17/4	Marsaxlokk	1-0	*Briffa*
25/4	Birkirkara	1-1	*Scerri*
30/4	Floriana	1-1	*Agius G.*
7/5	Tarxien	2-2	*Scerri (p), Agius E.*

No	Name	Nat	DoB	Pos	Aps	(s)	Gls
8	Edmond AGIUS		23/2/87	M	16	(9)	5
7	Gilbert AGIUS		21/2/74	A	16	(7)	3
11	Andrade Antunes ANDERSON	BRA	15/11/81	A	8	(2)	2
	Siraj Eddin ARAB		25/3/94	M		(1)	
3	Ian AZZOPARDI		12/8/82	D	27		
4	Steve BORG		15/5/88	D	26		1
10	Roderick BRIFFA		24/8/81	M	25		4
2	Jonathan CARUANA		24/7/86	D	26		1
19	DENNI Rocha dos Santos	BRA	21/8/82	M	25		11
20	Dyson FALZON		9/3/86	M	5	(9)	2
6	Ryan FENECH		20/4/86	M	9	(2)	3
24	Andrew HOGG		2/3/85	G	27		
16	Kurt MAGRO		4/6/86	M		(3)	
	Joseph OKONKWO	NGA	27/9/89	A	1	(3)	
18	Jamie PACE		1/1/77	M	20	(1)	2
5	Lucas RAMON dos Santos	BRA	28/6/85	D	16	(3)	
23	Kevin SAMMUT		26/5/81	M	20	(7)	5
21	Terence SCERRI		3/4/84	A	24	(4)	16
14	Omonigho TEMILE	NGA	16/7/84	M	13	(8)	1
28	Nicholas VELLA		27/8/89	G	1	(2)	
9	Ian ZAMMIT		9/12/86	A	3	(15)	3

VITTORIOSA STARS FC

Coach – Winston Muscat

Founded – 1906

2010			
12/9	Valletta	0-3	
18/9	Qormi	2-4	*Ewurum 2*
25/9	Tarxien	0-1	
18/10	Sliema	0-1	
23/10	Floriana	0-0	
31/10	Hibernians	2-0	*og (Gauci), Ewurum*
4/11	Birkirkara	1-1	*Jorge Silva*
21/11	Marsaxlokk	1-1	*Jorge Silva*
26/11	Hamrun	0-2	
6/12	Valletta	2-3	*Edison, Micallef*
12/12	Qormi	2-2	*Ewurum, Edison*
19/12	Tarxien	0-1	
2011			
9/1	Sliema	3-4	*Edison (p), Jorge Silva, Ewurum*
16/1	Floriana	1-6	*Grech L.*
23/1	Hibernians	2-1	*Ewurum, Edison (p)*
30/1	Birkirkara	0-1	
4/2	Marsaxlokk	2-2	*Jorge Silva 2*
13/2	Hamrun	2-3	*Edison, Grech L.*
20/2	Hibernians	1-2	*Edison*
26/2	Qormi	1-4	*Carlos*
12/3	Sliema	1-2	*og (Mifsud)*
1/4	Hibernians	1-0	*Jorge Silva*
9/4	Qormi	2-2	*Jorge Silva, Ewurum*
16/4	Sliema	0-2	

MALTA

No	Name	Nat	DoB	Pos	Aps	(s)	Gls
1	Simon AGIUS		12/4/78	G	19		
2	Pierre AQUILINA		3/11/77	D	5		
10	Mauro BRINCAT		3/6/84	M	1	(5)	
18	Dino CACHIA		13/12/76	M	14	(3)	
3	Justin CAMILLERI		23/11/81	D	8		
80	CARLOS Emanuel Campagnoli	BRA	9/6/87	M	16	(1)	1
13	Jeffrey CHETCUTI		24/4/74	D	20	(1)	
20	EDISON Luis dos Santos	BRA	9/12/85	A	15	(2)	6
	Ahmed ELKHASSASI	ENG	20/12/91	A	1	(1)	
8	Anthony EWURUM	NGA	4/4/85	A	21	(3)	7
32	Leighton GRECH		20/3/90	M	15	(4)	2
22	Ryan GRECH		3/4/85	M	9	(1)	
14	JORGE Santos SILVA	BRA	23/4/87	A	24		7
18	Larry LAGANA		10/8/76	M	1	(1)	
5	Murilo MACCARI	BRA	21/9/87	M	10		
	Clayton MICALLEF		21/2/84	M	8	(9)	1
	Kevin MIFSUD		14/3/66	M	10	(1)	
29	Sharlon PACE		29/2/80	D	14		
23	Carl SAMMUT		26/4/85	D	16	(2)	
	Ryan SELL		9/3/87	A		(2)	
7	Johann SPITERI		2/4/83	M		(3)	
9	Alan TABONE		31/10/81	A	4	(5)	
12	Jean Matthias VELLA		1/9/92	G	5	(2)	
31	Stephen WELLMAN		31/8/82	D	19		
	Jonathan XERRI		7/1/90	D	9	(5)	

STADIUMS

Ta' Qali National Stadium (17,797)
Hibernians Ground (2,000)
Victor Tedesco Stadium (2,000)

PROMOTED CLUBS

BALZAN YOUTHS FC
Coach – Ivan Zammit
Founded – 1937

MQABBA FC
Coach – Clive Mizzi
Founded – 1957

MOSTA FC
Coach – Oliver Spiteri
Founded – 1935

SECOND LEVEL FINAL TABLE 2010/11

		Pld	W	D	L	F	A	Pts
1	Balzan Youths FC	18	15	2	1	42	16	47
2	Mqabba FC	18	10	5	3	38	16	35
3	Mosta FC	18	9	5	4	42	22	32
4	Melita FC	18	9	5	4	31	21	32
5	Lija Athletic FC	18	7	3	8	24	25	24
6	St George's FC	18	6	6	6	25	28	24
7	St Andrews FC	18	5	5	8	20	28	20
8	Dingli Swallows FC	18	5	3	10	20	36	18
9	Pietà Hotspurs FC	18	4	4	10	34	37	16
10	Msida St Joseph FC	18	0	2	16	5	52	-2

NB Msida St Joseph FC – 4 pts deducted.

PROMOTION PLAY-OFF

(6/5/11)
Mosta 2, Melita 0

TOP GOALSCORERS 2010/11

17	Alfred EFFIONG (Marsaxlokk)
16	Terence SCERRI (Valletta)
14	Gaetan SPITERI (Hamrun)
13	Daniel NWOKE (Floriana) Jean Pierre MIFSUD TRIGANZA (Sliema)
11	DANIEL BEUNO (Tarxien) DENNI (Valletta)
10	PACHECO (Tarxien)
9	Micheal GALEA (Birkirkara) Emiliano LATTES (Birkirkara) Ivan WOODS (Floriana)

DOMESTIC CUP 2010/11

FA TROPHY

FIRST ROUND

(12/11/10)
Dingli 3, Mosta 5 *(aet)*
Hamrun 5, Melita 0
Lija 0, Floriana 3
Marsaxlokk 1, Mqabba 0

(13/11/10)
Balzan 1, Tarxien 3
Hibernians 4, Pietà 0

(14/11/10)
St George's 1, St Andrews 2
Victoria 2, Vittoriosa 4

SECOND ROUND

(19/1/11)
Floriana 1, Mosta 0 *(aet)*
Hamrun 2, Tarxien 3 *(aet)*
Hibernians 3, St Andrews 2
Marsaxlokk 0, Vittoriosa 3

QUARTER-FINALS

(19/3/11)
Sliema 3 *(Mifsud Triganza 4, 69, Barbara 113)*, Birkirkara 3 *(Vukanac 45, Babatunde 55, Galea M. 118) (aet; 1-3 on pens)*
Valletta 1 *(Denni 99)*, Hibernians 0 *(aet)*

(20/3/11)
Tarxien 4 *(Ricardo Costa 45p, 73, Vella Critien 63, Daniel Bueno 80)*, Vittoriosa 2 *(Edison 26p, Jorge Silva 90p)*
Qormi 1 *(Vandelannoitte 71)*, Floriana 1 *(Borg J. 58)* *(aet; 3-5 on pens)*

SEMI-FINALS

(14/5/11)
Tarxien 0, Valletta 1 *(Denni 116) (aet)*

(15/5/11)
Birkirkara 1 *(Cilia 66p)*, Floriana 2 *(Caruana 23, Farrugia 60)*

FINAL

(22/5/11)
National Stadium, Ta'Qali
FLORIANA FC 1 *(Woods 89)*
VALLETTA FC 0
Referee – *Caruana*
FLORIANA – *Towns, Farrugia, Bugeja, Pisani, Micallef, Woods, Cassar, Doffo, Caruana, Nwoke, Paris (Borg J. 63).*
VALLETTA – *Hogg, Briffa, Caruana, Azzopardi, Borg, Fenech (Temile 74), Agius G. (Anderson 82), Agius E., Pace, Denni, Scerri.*

CLUB COMMUNICATION 2011/12

Balzan Youths FC
olerville, Main Street
MT-Balzan BZN 06

Tel	+356 21 414 187
Fax	+356 21 480 898
Web	balzanyouthsfc.net
Email	balzanfc@go.net.mt
Media Officer	Sandro Azzopardi

Birkirkara FC
[illegible], Old Church Street
MT-Birkirkara

Tel	+356 21 489 214
Fax	+356 21 489 214
Web	birkirkarafc.com
Email	info@birkirkarafc.com
Media Officer	John Borg

Floriana FC
St Publius Square
MT-Floriana FRN 1913

Tel	+356 79 046 744
Fax	+356 21 320 962
Web	florianafc.com
Email	secretary@florianafc.com
Media Officer	Matthew Carbone

Hamrun Spartans FC
143, Triq il-Kbira San Guzepp
MT-Hamrun HMR 1015

Tel	+356 21 241 682
Fax	
Web	hamrunspartansfc.com
Email	hamrunspartans1907@gmail.com
Media Officer	Joe Borg

Hibernians FC
114, Paola Square
MT-Paola PLA 1260

Tel	+356 99 429 707
Fax	+356 21 240 887
Web	hiberniansfc.org
Email	stephenabela7@gmail.com
Media Officer	Stefan Zahra

Marsaxlokk FC
Vendome Tower, Triq il Kavallerizza Road
MT-Marsaxlokk ZTN 10

Tel	+356 99471 169
Fax	
Web	
Email	marsaxlokkfootballclub@gmail.com
Media Officer	Jason Vella

Mosta FC
38/40 Eucharistic Congress Road
MT-Mosta MST 9033

Tel	+356 21 432 252
Fax	+356 23 264 576
Web	mostafootballclub.com
Email	mostafc@gmail.com
Media Officer	Joe Quattromani

Mqabba FC
74/76, Triq il-Madonna tal-Gilju
MT-Mqabba MQB 1306

Tel	+356 21 642 774
Fax	
Web	mqabbafc.com
Email	gedward@maltanet.net
Media Officer	Edward Galea

Qormi FC
Qormi Football Grounds, Valletta Road
MT-Qormi

Tel	+356 27 482 310
Fax	
Web	qormifc.com
Email	qormifc@onvol.net
Media Officer	Kenneth Vella

Sliema Wanderers FC
Tower Road 21
MT-Sliema SLM 1602

Tel	+356 79 799 797
Fax	+356 21 480 205
Web	sliemawfc.org
Email	mdebono@gmail.com
Media Officer	Ivan Calleja

Tarxien Rainbows FC
Tarxien Rainbows Sports Complex,
Triq San Frangisk
MT-Tarxien TXN 1312

Tel	+356 21 692 456
Fax	+356 27 345 346
Web	
Email	kevbon@maltanet.net
Media Officer	John Vella

Valletta FC
Saint Lucia Street 126
MT-Valletta VLT 1183

Tel	+356 21 224 939
Fax	+356 21 654 892
Web	vallettafc.net
Email	woodjoe@maltanet.net
Media Officer	Joe Attard

MOLDOVA

Moldavie I Moldawien

Federatia Moldoveneasca de Fotbal (FMF

COMMUNICATION

Address Str. Tricolorului 39
MD-2012 Chisinau
Tel +373 22 210 413
Fax +373 22 210 432

E-mail fmf@fmf.md
Website fmf.md

President Pavel Cebanu
General Secretary Nicolai Cebotari
Media Officer Victor Daghi

Year of Formation 1990

National Stadium Zimbru, Chisinau (10,400)

DOMESTIC COMPETITION SUMMARY 2010/11

DIVIZIA NATIONALA FINAL TABLE

			Home					Away					Total						
		Pld	W	D	L	F	A	W	D	L	F	A	W	D	L	F	A	Pts	Comp
1	FC Dacia Chisinau	39	14	6	0	41	7	13	5	1	25	9	27	11	1	66	16	92	UCL
2	FC Sheriff	39	16	4	0	48	7	8	7	4	33	9	24	11	4	81	16	83	UEL
3	FC Milsami	39	11	5	4	39	15	12	4	3	32	8	23	9	7	71	23	78	UEL
4	FC Zimbru Chisinau	39	13	5	2	26	7	9	5	5	30	13	22	10	7	56	20	76	
5	FC Iskra-Stal	39	11	5	4	39	16	10	6	3	23	10	21	11	7	62	26	74	UEL
6	FC Olimpia Balti	39	11	5	4	29	20	10	6	3	30	11	21	11	7	59	31	74	
7	FC Tiraspol	39	9	3	7	31	16	8	3	9	26	29	17	6	16	57	45	57	
8	FC Rapid Ghidighici	39	10	5	5	25	16	5	5	9	14	21	15	10	14	39	37	55	
9	FC Academia UTM Chisinau	39	9	5	5	16	9	5	5	10	28	28	14	10	15	44	37	52	
10	FC Costuleni	39	3	4	12	11	34	4	2	14	12	34	7	6	26	23	68	27	
11	FC Nistru Otaci	39	6	1	12	20	34	1	3	16	13	41	7	4	28	33	75	25	
12	FC Sfintul Gheorghe Suruceni	39	3	6	10	16	31	3	1	16	14	52	6	7	26	30	83	25	
13	CF Gagauziya Comrat	39	4	1	14	20	47	3	1	16	18	42	7	2	30	38	89	23	
14	FC Dinamo Bender	39	4	1	14	9	55	2	3	15	16	63	6	4	29	25	118	22	*Relegated*

NB CF Gagauziya Comrat did not receive licence to compete in 2011/12 Divizia Nationala.

Top Scorer Gheorghe Boghiu (Milsami), 26 goals

Promoted Clubs None

Cup Final FC Iskra-Stal 2, FC Olimpia Balti 1

Dacia end Sheriff's long rule

High-fives all round as Dacia players celebrate their first Moldovan title

Champions of Moldova for ten successive seasons, FC Sheriff were finally deposed in 2010/11 as FC Dacia Chisinau, led by former Moldova national coach Igor Dobrovolskiy, claimed their first major honour in style, ending a marathon 39-match campaign – the longest regular season in Europe – with 92 points, nine more than Sheriff, who, exhausted by an extra workload in Europe, were also unable to defend the Moldovan Cup, losing out in the semi-finals to eventual winners FC Iskra-Stal.

Having won the domestic double in each of the previous three seasons, it was a major shock for Sheriff to end up with nothing – particularly as they had done the nation proud once again in Europe, reaching the UEFA Champions League play-offs and UEFA Europa League group stage for the second successive campaign. But when their domestic title hopes faded with three successive away wins in April, coach Andrei Sosnitskiy was shown the door.

Single defeat

Dacia won none of their three matches against Sheriff, but the 3-0 defeat they sustained away to the serial champions in November was their only loss of the entire campaign. It was also the only time their defence conceded more than one goal. Although, like Sheriff, they were unbeaten at home, it was Dacia's ability to accumulate points on their travels that proved decisive. While they collected 44 points away from home, Sheriff managed only 31. In Georgian midfielder Levan Korgalidze, Dacia possessed an excellent maker and taker of goals, his final tally of 13 including the late equaliser at home to Sheriff in mid-March that was arguably the pivotal moment of the campaign. Dacia's top scorer was Moldovan international Ghenadie Orbu, who found the net 22 times to finish second in the Divizia Nationala standings behind Gheorghe Boghiu, a 26-goal marksman for FC Milsami (formerly FC Viitorul Orhei), who qualified for the UEFA Europa League by finishing third.

Like Dacia, Iskra-Stal had never previously lifted a major trophy, but nine years after their formation they entered the winners' enclosure by defeating FC Olimpia Balti – another club without silverware – 2-1 in the cup final, their winner coming from midfielder Evgheny Gorodetschi, a key figure also in the semi-final against Sheriff.

Home-based players had little part to play in Moldova's UEFA EURO 2012 qualifying campaign as the team's Romanian coach Gavril Balint filled the side with expatriates operating in Russia and various other points on the eastern European compass. His policy was vindicated when an all-exile XI defeated Finland 2-0 in Chisinau in the opening qualifier, and although the only points acquired in Moldova's next five matches came against San Marino, it was only in the 4-1 home defeat by Sweden in June that Balint's charges were outclassed. The team's most improved performer was 24-year-old midfielder Alexandru Suvorov, who came off the bench to open the scoring against Finland and started every subsequent game, adding further qualifying goals against Hungary and Sweden.

National Team

Top Five All-time Caps – Radu Rebeja (74); Serghey Clescenco (69); Ivan Testimitanu (56); Valeriu Catinsus (55); Serghey Rogaciov (52)

Top Five All-time Goals – Serghey Clescenco (11); Serghey Rogaciov (9); Igor Bugaiov & Iurie Miterev (8); Serghey Dadu (7)

MOLDOVA

NATIONAL TEAM RESULTS 2010/11

11/8/10	Georgia	H	Chisinau	0-0	
3/9/10	Finland (ECQ)	H	Chisinau	2-0	*Suvorov (69), Doros (74)*
7/9/10	Hungary (ECQ)	A	Budapest	1-2	*Suvorov (79)*
8/10/10	Netherlands (ECQ)	H	Chisinau	0-1	
12/10/10	San Marino (ECQ)	A	Serravalle	2-0	*Josan (20), Doros (86p)*
6/2/11	Poland	N	Vila Real (POR)	0-1	
9/2/11	Andorra	N	Lagos (POR)	2-1	*Picusciac (66), Bugaiov (90+4p)*
29/3/11	Sweden (ECQ)	A	Solna	1-2	*Suvorov (90+2)*
3/6/11	Sweden (ECQ)	H	Chisinau	1-4	*Bugaiov (61)*

NATIONAL TEAM APPEARANCES 2010/11

Coach – Gavril BALINT (ROU) 3/1/63			Geo	FIN	HUN	NED	SMR	Pol	And	SWE	SWE	Caps	Goals
Stanislav NAMASCO	10/11/86	Kuban (RUS)	G	G	G	G	G	G		G	G	27	-
Vitalie BORDIAN	11/8/84	Metalist (UKR)	D	D	D	M	D	D	M45			24	1
Semion BULGARU	26/5/85	Alania (RUS)	D	D	D	D		s63				12	1
Petru RACU	17/7/87	Norrköping (SWE)	D		D	D		D63	D46	D	D	7	-
Vadim BORET	5/9/76	Bakı (AZE)	D	D			D			M		39	1
Igor TIGIRLAS	24/2/84	Metalurh Zaporizhya (UKR) /Chornomorets (UKR)	M	M68	M			M46			s46	18	1
Evgheny CEBOTARI	16/10/84	Ceahlăul (ROU)	M	M	M71	M69		M53	s46	M	M78	23	-
Denis ZMEU	8/5/85	Vaslui (ROU)	M67				s69					17	-
Nicolai JOSAN	18/9/83	Anzhi (RUS)	M73	M58	M59	s78	M69					16	2
Valeriu ANDRONIC	21/12/82	Lokomotiv Astana (KAZ) /SKA-Energia (RUS)	M61	s75		s69	M	s53	s45	s83		34	4
Igor BUGAIOV	26/6/84	Lokomotiv Astana (KAZ)	A45	s68	s84	s46	A62	s59	A	s46	A	37	8
Viorel FRUNZA	6/12/79	Atyrau (KAZ) /Neman (BLR)	s45	A	A84	A46	A			A46		32	6
Alexandru SUVOROV	2/2/87	Cracovia (POL)	s61	s58	M	M	M	M63	M 54*	M	M	31	3
Andrei COJOCARI	21/1/87	Dacia Chisinau	s67		s71		M81					6	1
Anatol DOROS	21/3/83	Chornomorets (UKR) /Irtysh (KAZ)	s73	A75	s59	A78	s62	A	A56	A72	A63	14	2
Alexei SAVINOV	19/4/79	Bakı (AZE)		D			s81					35	-
Alexandru EPUREANU	27/9/86	Dinamo Moskva (RUS)		M	M	M	D	M	M			39	3
Vadim BOLOHAN	15/8/86	Sevastopol (UKR)			D	D		D	D	D	D	9	-
Victor GOLOVATENCO	28/4/84	Kuban (RUS) /Krasnodar (RUS) /Sibir (RUS)				D	D	D76	D	D	D	35	3
Igor PICUSCIAC	27/3/83	Krasnodar (RUS)						A59	s56			7	2
Artur PATRAS	10/1/88	Timişoara (ROU) /Unirea Urziceni (ROU)						s46	M46		s78	3	-
Denis CALINCOV	15/9/85	unattached						s63				20	2
Igor ARMAS	14/7/87	Kuban (RUS)						s76	D	D	D	18	-
Nicolae CALANCEA	29/8/86	Zimbru							G			12	-
Serghey GHEORGHIEV	20/10/91	Sheriff							s46			1	-
Alexandru GATCAN	27/3/84	Rostov (RUS)								M83	M46	22	1
Anatol CHEPTINE	20/5/90	Sheriff								s72		1	-
Stanislav IVANOV	7/10/80	Lokomotiv Moskva (RUS)									M	37	-
Gheorghe BOGHIU	26/10/81	Milsami									s63	1	-

CLUB-BY-CLUB

FC ACADEMIA UTM CHISINAU

Coach – Serghey Stroenco; (16/10/10) Oleg Bejenari
Founded – 2006
Stadium – Complexul sportiv UTM (1,000)

2010

5/7	Olimpia	h	0-1	
8	Nistru	a	1-0	*Nikolaev*
8	Dacia	h	0-0	
5/8	Costuleni	a	5-1	*Nikolaev 3, Ginsari 2 (1p)*
1/8	Gagauziya	h	3-0	*Nikolaev 3*
9/8	Dinamo	a	5-1	*Cuznetov, Nikolaev 2, Marina, Lambarschi*
1/9	Rapid	h	0-0	
8/9	Sfintul Gheorghe	a	1-1	*Slivca*
2/9	Sheriff	h	1-0	*Ginsari*
6/9	Zimbru	h	0-1	
/10	Milsami	a	1-1	*Ginsari*
6/10	Iskra-Stal	h	0-0	
/11	Olimpia	a	2-3	*Indoitu, Ginsari*
/11	Nistru	h	1-0	*Ginsari*
4/11	Dacia	a	1-3	*Bludnov*
0/11	Costuleni	h	0-1	
8/11	Gagauziya	a	3-0	*Ginsari (p), Bludnov, Leuca*
/12	Sheriff	a	1-1	*Leuca*
/12	Tiraspol	a	1-2	*Marina*
2/12	Dianmo	h	1-1	*Leuca*
6/12	Rapid	a	0-2	

2011

6/2	Sfintul Gheorghe	h	2-0	*Potirniche, Potlog*
0/2	Zimbru	a	0-1	
6/2	Milsami	h	1-0	*Ginsari*
2/3	Iskra-Stal	a	0-0	
/3	Tiraspol	h	3-0	*Ginsari, Ciuperca, Potlog*
2/3	Rapid	a	2-4	*Slivca 2*
6/3	Sfintul Gheorghe	a	2-0	*Ciuperca, Potlog*
20/3	Tiraspol	h	1-1	*Ginsari*
2/4	Dinamo	a	1-1	*Ginsari*
6/4	Costuleni	h	1-0	*Ginsari*
9/4	Nistru	a	0-1	
16/4	Gagauziya	h	1-0	*Potirniche*
23/4	Dacia	a	0-2	
26/4	Sheriff	h	1-0	*Cascaval*
8/5	Milsami	a	0-1	
13/5	Olimpia	h	0-2	
17/5	Iskra-Stal	a	2-3	*Triboi, Cascaval*
22/5	Zimbru	h	0-2	

No	Name	Nat	DoB	Pos	Aps	(s)	Gls
27	Artem BLUDNOV	RUS	5/9/88	A	8	(9)	2
2	Adrian CASCAVAL		10/6/87	D	25	(9)	2
20	Vadim CEMIRTAN		21/7/87	A	1	(4)	
5	Alexandru CHICIUC		7/11/88	D	36	(1)	
9	Valeri CIUPERCA		12/6/92	M	17	(13)	2
27	Efim COJUHARI		19/3/88	M	2	(3)	
23	Maxim COPELCIUC		6/8/88	G	18		
3	Serghei CUZNETOV		20/8/74	D	18		1
1	Victor DIMOV		19/1/90	G	20	(1)	
14	Radu GINSARI		10/12/91	A	38		12
25	Serghey IEPUREANU		12/9/76	M	2		
11	Daniel INDOITU		8/9/90	D	37	(2)	1
19	Vladislav IVANOV		7/5/90	D	1	(5)	
8	Igor LAMBARSCHI		26/11/92	M	35	(3)	1
9	Petru LEUCA		19/7/90	A	9	(14)	3
25	Alexei LUCHITA		3/12/90	M	1	(1)	
4	Serhiy LYUBCHAK	UKR	15/4/86	D	19		
10	Andrei MARINA		21/2/90	M	34	(1)	2
7	Daniil NIKOLAEV	RUS	14/10/91	A	12	(6)	9
3	Ghenadie OCHINCA		1/3/84	D	9	(2)	
19	Dmitri OLEINIC		12/3/91	G	1		
21	Maxim POTIRNICHE		13/6/89	D	34		2
25	Vladimir POTLOG		4/4/88	A	14	(10)	3
13	Eugeniu SLIVCA		13/7/89	M	30	(2)	3
6	Alexei SOLOMIN		5/6/93	M	5	(5)	
9	Nicolai TRIBOI		15/9/90	D	3	(5)	1

FC COSTULENI

Coach – Ilie Vieru; (24/10/10) Igor Ursachi; (28/2/11) Serghey Botnaras
Founded – 1983
Stadium – Municipal, Orhei (1,000)

2010

25/7	Nistru	h	2-1	*Starciuc, Tomascov*
1/8	Dacia	a	1-3	*Vrabie*
7/8	Gagauziya	h	2-1	*Orbu, Cuico*
15/8	Academia	h	1-5	*Vrabie*
21/8	Sheriff	a	1-1	*Tomascov*
25/8	Dinamo	h	0-0	
29/8	Rapid	a	0-1	
9/9	Sfintul Gheorghe	h	0-3	
18/9	Zimbru	a	0-1	
26/9	Milsami	h	0-7	
2/10	Iskra-Stal	a	0-5	
16/10	Tiraspol	h	1-2	*Dubac*
23/10	Olimpia	a	1-4	*Tomascov (p)*
31/10	Nistru	a	0-1	
6/11	Dacia	h	1-2	*Tomascov (p)*
14/11	Gagauziya	a	3-0	*Mocanu, Vrabie, Tomascov*
20/11	Academia	a	1-0	*Resitca*
28/11	Sheriff	h	0-0	
4/12	Dinamo	a	0-1	
12/12	Rapid	h	1-2	*Tomascov (p)*
16/12	Sfintul Gheorghe	a	2-1	*Cuico, Barburos (p)*

2011

16/2	Zimbru	h	0-2	
20/2	Milsami	a	0-2	
26/2	Iskra-Stal	h	1-3	*Tomascov*
2/3	Tiraspol	a	0-3	
6/3	Olimpia	h	0-1	
12/3	Olimpia	a	0-0	
16/3	Iskra-Stal	h	0-1	
20/3	Zimbru	a	1-2	*Resitca*
2/4	Rapid	h	0-0	
6/4	Academia	a	0-1	
10/4	Tiraspol	h	0-0	
16/4	Dinamo	a	1-0	*Lavrinovici*
23/4	Sfintul Gheorghe	a	0-2	
30/4	Nistru	h	2-0	*Resitca, Josan*
8/5	Gagauziya	a	1-2	*Resitca*
13/5	Dacia	h	0-1	
17/5	Sheriff	a	0-4	
22/5	Milsami	h	0-3	

No	Name	Nat	DoB	Pos	Aps	(s)	Gls
6	Vladimir AGA		9/11/87	M		(1)	
13	Ruslan BARBUROS		15/11/78	A	1	(7)	1
9	Andrei BEREGHICI		9/12/86	M	2	(3)	
17	Maxim BOGACIC		5/4/86	D	14	(5)	
8	Vlad BOSTAN		23/9/90	D		(1)	
4	Mihai CABAC		9/2/86	D	34	(1)	
14	Ion CASTRAVET		18/5/88	D	23	(4)	
21	Stefan CAZACU		4/5/91	M		(3)	
20	Ion CHESCU		29/5/89	M	2	(9)	
11	Sergiu CUICO		2/2/83	A	22	(11)	2
15	Sergiu DUBAC		15/8/85	M	3	(3)	1
19	Roman GHENCEA		19/6/90	D	1		
8	Anatolie GLADICOV		28/5/87	D	5	(1)	
2	Valeriu GUTU		2/7/91	D	1	(2)	
15	Artur IATKO		27/12/88	D	15	(1)	
16	Alexei JOSAN		28/6/88	M	1	(7)	1
5	Evghenii LAVRINOVICI		13/10/88	M	3	(5)	1
1	Vladimir LEVANOV		14/1/86	G	12		
1	Vladimir LIFSIT		24/3/84	G	15		
1	Andrii MACOVIICIUC		1/11/91	G	3	(3)	
16	Victor MARIAN		10/9/84	M	12	(3)	
2	Alexei MELNIC		20/11/85	D	15	(2)	
12	Alexandru MEREUTA		9/11/79	G	9		
9	Sergiu MOCANU		24/10/87	M	33		1

17	Radu MUNTEAN	31/5/91	M	1		
16	Roman MUNTEAN	31/5/91	M	1		
10	Mihai NARTEA	21/11/90	M		(6)	
3	Vitalie NEGRU	15/1/87	M	4	(10)	
5	Denis ORBU	5/11/83	D	18	(1)	1
7	Marcel RESITCA	4/11/75	A	32	(1)	4
6	Ion SANDU	9/3/93	D	15		
18	Petru SARU	3/1/91	M		(1)	
4	Sergiu SIRBU	1/4/86	D	15	(1)	
17	Maxim SOIMU	17/7/90	A	12	(6)	
17	Oleg SOIMU	1/10/75	M	2	(8)	
9	Andrei SOLODCHI	14/12/85	M	16		
22	Tudor STARCIUC	1/2/90	M	4	(7)	1
2	Vladimir TANURCOV	27/11/77	M	2	(1)	
10	Eduard TOMASCOV	15/2/83	M	28	(2)	7
3	Vasile TUGUTSCHI	14/1/87	D	13		
11	Andrei VRABIE	13/2/88	A	30	(5)	3
4	Alexandru ZISLIS	14/3/86	M	10	(3)	

FC DACIA CHISINAU

Coach – Igor Dobrovolskiy (RUS)
Founded – 1999
Stadium – Zimbru (10,400)
MAJOR HONOURS: Moldovan League – (1) 2011.

2010				
26/7	Gagauziya	h	1-0	*Negrescu*
1/8	Costuleni	h	3-1	*Orbu 2, Dragovozov*
7/8	Academia	a	0-0	
14/8	Sheriff	h	0-0	
21/8	Dinamo	a	2-0	*Orbu, Korgalidze*
25/8	Rapid	h	1-0	*og (Valuta)*
29/8	Sfintul Gheorghe	a	2-0	*Orbu, Gorceac*
11/9	Zimbru	h	1-1	*Gamezardashvili*
18/9	Milsami	a	2-1	*Ledenev 2*
26/9	Iskra-Stal	h	0-0	
2/10	Tiraspol	a	0-0	
17/10	Olimpia	h	3-1	*Orbu, Gamezardashvili 2*
23/10	Nistru	a	1-1	*Gorceac*
31/10	Gagauziya	a	4-1	*Korgalidze 3 (1p), Orbu*
6/11	Costuleni	a	2-1	*Korgalidze (p), Namasco*
14/11	Academia	h	3-1	*Orbu 3*
20/11	Sheriff	a	0-3	
28/11	Dinamo	h	5-0	*Orbu 2, Dragovozov, Molla, Sackey*
4/12	Rapid	a	2-0	*Orbu, Molla*
12/12	Sfintul Gheorghe	h	7-0	*Popovici, Bulat, Orbu 3 (1p), Korgalidze, Sackey*
16/12	Zimbru	a	1-0	*Molla*
2011				
16/2	Milsami	h	0-0	
20/2	Iskra-Stal	a	2-1	*Korgalidze, og (Gafina)*
26/2	Tiraspol	h	2-0	*Korgalidze 2 (1p)*
2/3	Olimpia	a	2-1	*Korgalidze, Onica*
6/3	Nistru	h	1-1	*Orbu*
11/3	Sfintul Gheorghe	h	3-0	*Orbu, og (Bugaichuk), Onica*
16/3	Sheriff	h	1-1	*Korgalidze*
20/3	Milsami	a	0-0	
2/4	Olimpia	h	2-0	*Orbu, Dedov*
6/4	Iskra-Stal	a	1-0	*Gamezardashvili*
10/4	Zimbru	h	1-0	*Korgalidze (p)*
16/4	Rapid	a	0-0	
23/4	Academia	h	2-0	*Gamezardashvili, Orbu*
30/4	Tiraspol	a	1-0	*Bursuc*
8/5	Dinamo	h	3-1	*og (Leghezin), Korgalidze, og (Dragan)*
13/5	Costuleni	a	1-0	*Orbu*
17/5	Nistru	h	2-0	*Nechaev, Orbu (p)*
22/5	Gagauziya	a	2-0	*Orbu, Mihaliov*

No	Name	Nat	DoB	Pos	Aps	(s)	Gls
5	Abdulhamad AKHILGOV	RUS	31/8/80	M		(2)	
13	Babajide Collins BABATUNDE	NGA	2/12/88	A	9	(1)	
13	Victor BULAT		5/1/85	M	13	(5)	1
20	Iulian BURSUC		23/9/76	M	6	(15)	1
21	Stefan CARAULAN		2/2/89	D	4	(1)	
17	Andrei COJOCARI		21/1/87	M	29	(3)	
22	Alexandru DEDOV		26/7/89	A	9	(1)	1
25	Goran DIMOVSKI	MKD	14/10/82	D	16		
6	Lucian Mihai DOBRE	ROU	25/9/78	D	5	(2)	
16	Vladimir DRAGOVOZOV		1/1/84	A	15	(5)	2
25	David GAMEZARDASHVILI	GEO	7/5/82	D	35		5
30	Artem GAUDUCHEVICI		22/4/87	G	7		
8	Eugeniu GORCEAC		10/3/87	M	9	(9)	2
18	Iurie GROSEV		16/5/76	D	30	(2)	
16	Vasili GUCHASHVILI	GEO	25/1/85	A	1	(2)	
6	Denis ILESCU		20/1/87	D	26	(2)	
99	Ruslan KARTOEV	RUS	14/8/88	A		(5)	
10	Levan KORGALIDZE	GEO	21/2/80	M	28	(4)	13
24	Claude Ernest Désiré KUM MAKA	KGZ	16/5/85	M		(1)	
79	Vitaliy LEDENEV	BLR	26/3/79	A	7	(3)	2
15	Mamuka LOMIDZE	GEO	16/6/84	D	20		
24	Abdul Gafar MAMAH	TOG	24/8/85	D	9		
25	Evghenii MATIUGHIN		31/10/81	G	24		
14	Maxim MIHALIOV		22/8/86	A	11	(4)	1
19	Oleg MOLLA		22/2/86	A	5	(10)	3
1	Ghenadie MOSNEAGA		25/4/85	G	8	(1)	
6	Serghei NAMASCO		19/6/86	M	12	(2)	1
17	Aleksandr NECHAEV	RUS	17/7/89	A	9	(4)	1
16	Igor NEGRESCU		17/4/79	D	4	(3)	1
8	Alexandru ONICA		29/7/84	M	16		2
9	Ghenadie ORBU		8/7/82	A	25	(12)	22
5	Dumitru POPOVICI		5/8/83	D	13	(3)	1
11	Rohan RICKETTS	ENG	22/12/82	M	4		
88	Eric SACKEY	GHA	20/8/87	A	12	(6)	2
88	Oleg SISCHIN		7/1/75	M		(3)	
22	Goran STANKOVSKI	MKD	20/11/76	A	5	(3)	
23	Islam TSUROEV	RUS	23/4/89	A	3	(7)	
79	Vadim YERCHIK	BLR	14/7/91	A		(3)	

FC DINAMO BENDER

Coach – Alexandr Veriovchin; (11/9/10) Iuri Hodichin
Founded – 1950
Stadium – Dinamo (5,000); Selcovic (3,000)

2010				
26/7	Iskra-Stal	h	0-1	
1/8	Tiraspol	a	1-4	*Dizov*
7/8	Olimpia	h	0-8	
15/8	Nistru	a	2-0	*Golubovschi, Procopiev*
21/8	Dacia	h	0-2	
25/8	Costuleni	a	0-0	
29/8	Academia	h	1-5	*Tiverenco*
11/9	Sheriff	a	0-2	
18/9	Gagauziya	h	0-4	
26/9	Rapid	h	0-1	
2/10	Sfintul Gheorghe	a	2-1	*Procopiev, Ciobanu*
16/10	Zimbru	h	1-0	*Golubovschi*
23/10	Milsami	a	1-1	*Ichim (p)*
31/10	Iskra-Stal	a	0-4	
6/11	Tiraspol	h	0-3	
14/11	Olimpia	a	0-1	
20/11	Nistru	h	3-2	*Zacon, Golubovschi, Titucenco*
28/11	Dacia	a	0-5	
4/12	Costuleni	h	1-0	*Ciobanu*
12/12	Academia	a	1-1	*Tiverenco*
18/12	Sheriff	h	0-7	
2011				
16/2	Gagauziya	a	4-5	*Zacon 3, Procopiev*
20/2	Rapid	a	0-2	
26/2	Sfintul Gheorghe	h	0-2	
2/3	Zimbru	a	1-6	*Tiverenco*
6/3	Milsami	h	0-3	
12/3	Iskra-Stal	a	1-6	*Zacon*
15/3	Zimbru	h	1-6	*Zacon*
20/3	Rapid	a	0-2	
2/4	Academia	h	1-1	*Agafonov*

4	Tiraspol	a	0-7	
/4	Sfintul Gheorghe	a	0-2	
/4	Costuleni	h	0-1	
/4	Nistru	a	0-4	
/4	Gagauziya	h	1-0	*Svet (p)*
5	Dacia	a	1-3	*Procopiev*
/5	Sheriff	h	0-7	
/5	Milsami	a	2-7	*Zacon, og (Stadiiciuc)*
/5	Olimpia	h	0-2	

No	Name	Nat	DoB	Pos	Aps	(s)	Gls
	Veaceslav AGAFONOV		29/5/85	M	37		1
	Dumitru BAILEVICI		3/1/85	M	6	(8)	
	Alexandr BICOV		15/11/86	M	9	(5)	
	Alexandr BIDIRLAN		9/5/89	M	1	(12)	
	Alexei BOBU		23/9/88	M	8	(1)	
7	Pavel CALININ		15/2/89	G	20	(1)	
	Denis CIOBANU		8/8/87	D	23	(5)	2
	Dmitri CONDARIUC		16/2/90	D	9	(2)	
	Alexei DIORDIEV		15/10/91	M		(2)	
	Alexei DIZOV		20/3/88	M	27		1
	Vladimir DRAGAN		10/4/79	D	26		
3	Evgheny GOLUBOVSCHI		19/3/91	A	30	(3)	3
	Evgheny HMARUC		13/6/77	G	17		
	Alexandru HODICHIN		16/7/84	D	12	(4)	
	Stanislav IASCHIN		8/3/87	M		(1)	
1	Oleg IASTREBOV		30/10/90	D	9	(6)	
	Oleg ICHIM		27/10/79	D	7		1
	Alexandr IURCENCO		25/3/92	M		(1)	
6	Maxim LEGHEZIN		25/4/87	M	8	(2)	
1	Pavel MARTINENCO		28/9/87	A	2	(14)	
	Igor MOTROI		3/5/89	D	8	(4)	
	Evgheny NACUL		2/9/87	G	2	(2)	
4	Alexei PROCOPIEV		15/7/91	A	26	(8)	4
	Victor SEVCENCO		8/9/91	D	2	(4)	
	Artur SPINU		14/1/87	M	24	(9)	
9	Alexandr STAROVOIT		6/2/91	A	1		
18	Alexandru SVET		29/10/82	D	28	(1)	1
	Nicolai TITUCENCO		1/9/81	D	10		1
1	Eugen TIVERENCO		18/4/87	A	34	(2)	3
7	Sergey ZACON		13/10/87	M	37	(2)	7
	Allan ZUZI	BRA	18/3/91	D	6	(11)	

CF GAGAUZIYA COMRAT

Coach – Sergey Botnaras; (31/10/10) Petr Stoianov

Founded – 2002

Stadium – Satesc, Suruceni (1,500)

2010

26/7	Dacia	a	0-1	
1/8	Zimbru	h	0-0	
7/8	Costuleni	a	1-2	*Cojusea (p)*
15/8	Milsami	h	0-2	
21/8	Academia	a	0-3	
25/8	Iskra-Stal	h	0-4	
29/8	Sheriff	a	0-3	
11/9	Tiraspol	h	1-3	*Cojusea*
18/9	Dinamo	a	4-0	*og (Svet), Custurov, Cojusea, Hromtov*
26/9	Olimpia	h	1-2	*Negara*
2/10	Rapid	a	1-2	*Cojusea*
16/10	Nistru	h	5-1	*Hromtov 2, Romaniuc, Kartoev, Marcov*
23/10	Sfintul Gheorghe	a	2-2	*Cojusea 2*
31/10	Dacia	h	1-4	*Hromtov*
6/11	Zimbru	a	0-1	
14/11	Costuleni	h	0-3	
20/11	Milsami	a	1-2	*Kartoev*
28/11	Academia	h	0-3	
4/12	Iskra-Stal	a	0-1	
11/12	Sheriff	h	0-4	
16/12	Tiraspol	a	0-5	

2011

16/2	Dinamo	h	5-4	*Cojusea 4, Stoleru*
21/2	Olimpia	a	0-1	
26/2	Rapid	h	1-2	*Custurov*
2/3	Nistru	a	0-3	
6/3	Sfintul Gheorghe	h	2-1	*Cojusea 2*
12/3	Sheriff	a	1-5	*Cojusea (p)*
16/3	Milsami	h	0-3	
19/3	Olimpia	a	2-4	*Cojusea 2 (1p)*
2/4	Iskra-Stal	h	0-3	
6/4	Zimbru	a	1-3	*Cojusea*
10/4	Rapid	h	1-3	*Mostovei*
16/4	Academia	a	0-1	
23/4	Tiraspol	h	1-2	*Cojusea*
30/4	Dinamo	a	0-1	
8/5	Costuleni	h	2-1	*Okoye, Cojusea (p)*
13/5	Nistru	a	2-1	*Zislis 2*
17/5	Sfintul Gheorghe	a	3-1	*Cojusea, Stoleru 2*
22/5	Dacia	h	0-2	

No	Name	Nat	DoB	Pos	Aps	(s)	Gls
1	Andrei BESLEAGA		18/7/89	G	17	(1)	
23	Firuz BOBIEV	TJK	18/6/86	M	3	(7)	
9	Evgheny BOICENCO		29/10/79	M	24	(2)	
22	Igor CARA		9/12/91	G	4		
5	Djabrail CHAMKHANOV	RUS	14/6/91	M	3		
15	Imran CHAMKHANOV	FRA	14/6/81	M	2		
18	Serghei CHIRNEV		16/11/90	A	16	(8)	
6	Sergiu COJOCARI		15/5/89	D	12	(1)	
17	Mihai COJUSEA		12/8/78	A	37		19
1	Alexei COSELEV		19/11/93	G	10	(1)	
20	Alexandru CUCU		28/9/87	M	17	(1)	
7	Andrei CUSTUROV		25/11/87	A	32	(4)	2
3	Anatol ENI		8/6/71	D		(1)	
24	Alexandr GHEORGHIEV		23/7/82	D	2	(7)	
23	Vadim GHIUZELI		24/12/89	A		(3)	
17	Serghey GRITIUC		6/4/84	A	5	(2)	
12	Oleg HROMTOV		30/5/83	A	8		4
16	Sergiu IABANJI		3/8/79	D	3	(12)	
19	Oleg IASTREBOV		30/10/90	D		(1)	
6	Ruslan KARTOEV	RUS	14/8/88	A	5	(3)	2
24	Claude Ernest Désiré KUM MAKA	KGZ	16/5/85	M	8		
77	Petru MARCOV		1/12/75	A	10	(26)	1
5	Iurie MIRZA		5/3/93	M	11	(2)	
22	Ilie MOSTOVEI		26/10/89	D	28	(4)	1
6	Andrei NEGARA		27/10/85	M	12	(5)	1
9	Denis NENOV		22/6/85	M	4		
4	Stefan OANTA		10/1/90	D	5	(8)	
22	Jude Nonso OKOYE	NGA	21/9/90	M	9	(1)	1
33	Iurie ROMANIUC		27/11/78	M	21		1
12	Mark RYUTIN	RUS	26/3/88	G	8		
19	Andrei SECRIERU		7/6/84	M	9	(5)	
10	Marian STOLERU		20/11/88	M	26	(2)	3
2	Ion TATAR		3/7/82	M	13	(11)	
15	Alexandr TODOROV		15/8/89	M	30	(2)	
3	Vasile TUGUTSCHI		14/1/87	D	16		
77	Michael Chinedu UKAEGO	NGA	20/10/88	M	8	(1)	
12	Iurie UZUN		29/12/84	G		(4)	
15	Alexandru ZISLIS		14/3/86	M	11	(1)	2

FC ISKRA-STAL

Coach – Vlad Goian; (28/12/10) Valeriy Chalyi (UKR)

Founded – 2002

Stadium – Municipal (3,800)

MAJOR HONOURS: Moldovan Cup – (1) 2011.

2010

26/7	Dinamo	a	1-0	*Popovici*
1/8	Rapid	h	1-0	*Kilikevych*
7/8	Sfintul Gheorghe	a	2-2	*Rudac, Popovici*
15/8	Zimbru	h	2-1	*Popovici 2*
21/8	Milsami	a	0-0	
25/8	Gagauziya	a	4-0	*Mihaliov, Burcovschi, Gorodetschi, Popovici*
29/8	Tiraspol	h	4-2	*Gorodetschi, Mihaliov, Kilikevych, Burcovschi*
11/9	Olimpia	a	1-0	*Taranu*

18/9	Nistru	h	1-1	*Popovici*
26/9	Dacia	a	0-0	
2/10	Costuleni	h	5-0	*Kilikevych, Burcovschi, Popovici 2 (1p), Mihaliov*
16/10	Academia	a	0-0	
25/10	Sheriff	h	0-1	
31/10	Dinamo	h	4-0	*Popovici 2 (2p), Dobre, Bulat*
6/11	Rapid	a	0-0	
14/11	Sfintul Gheorghe	h	4-0	*Kilikevych, Novicov 2, Mihaliov (p)*
20/11	Zimbru	a	1-0	*Bulat*
28/11	Milsami	h	0-1	
4/12	Gagauziya	h	1-0	*Novicov*
8/12	Olimpia	h	0-0	
12/12	Tiraspol	a	0-0	
2011				
16/2	Nistru	a	1-0	*Uzbek*
20/2	Dacia	h	1-2	*Suchu*
26/2	Costuleni	a	3-1	*Rudac, Mincev, Suchu*
2/3	Academia	h	0-0	
6/3	Sheriff	a	0-1	
12/3	Dinamo	h	6-1	*Porfireanu 2, Shugladze, Suchu, Gorodetschi, Popovici*
16/3	Costuleni	a	1-0	*Gorodetschi*
20/3	Nistru	h	2-1	*Suchu, Popovici (p)*
2/4	Gagauziya	a	3-0	*Suchu, Novicov, Popovici*
6/4	Dacia	h	0-1	
10/4	Sheriff	a	1-2	*Suchu*
16/4	Milsami	h	2-2	*Gorodetschi, Popovici (p)*
23/4	Olimpia	a	1-2	*Novicov*
30/4	Sfintul Gheorghe	h	3-1	*Suchu, Popovici, Vishnyakov*
8/5	Zimbru	h	0-0	
13/5	Rapid	a	2-1	*Shugladze, Popovici*
17/5	Academia	h	3-2	*Suchu 2, Gorodetschi*
22/5	Tiraspol	a	2-1	*Rudac, Truhanov*

No	Name	Nat	DoB	Pos	Aps	(s)	Gls
18	Dumitru BACINSCHI		5/3/93	A		(1)	
16	Vitalie BULAT		14/9/87	M	11	(2)	2
21	Andrei BURCOVSCHI		7/8/79	M	20	(1)	3
3	Alexei CASIAN		10/1/87	M	10	(1)	
1	Anatol CEBOTARI		29/3/88	G	20		
16	Serhiy CHEBOTAREV	UKR	26/3/91	M	3	(6)	
13	Denis CHIRILIUC		5/8/87	A	2	(18)	
4	Igor COSTROV		3/8/87	A	13	(4)	
24	Lucian Mihai DOBRE	ROU	25/9/78	D	15	(1)	1
17	Olexandr FESHCHENKO	UKR	2/1/85	D	18		
2	Sergei GAFINA		11/11/84	D	32	(3)	
22	Artiom GAIDUCHEVICI		22/4/87	G	19		
7	Evgheny GORODETSCHI		24/9/85	M	12	(16)	6
18	Oleh JURCA	UKR	4/11/77	D	5	(2)	
15	Volodymyr KILIKEVYCH	UKR	30/11/83	A	18	(1)	4
17	Vadym LESHCHUK	UKR	8/10/86	D	14		
11	Maxim MIHALIOV		22/8/86	A	19	(2)	4
21	Nikolae MINCEV		20/10/72	D	12		1
21	Rodion NAGINAYLOV	UKR	6/9/89	M	2	(1)	
5	Andrei NOVICOV		24/4/86	D	27	(2)	5
14	Octavian ONOFREI	ROU	16/5/91	A		(11)	
23	Igor PICUS		7/5/90	M		(11)	
14	Denys PONOMAR	UKR	19/8/89	M	3	(6)	
19	Vasilica POPA	ROU	7/8/84	D		(2)	
9	Alexandru POPOVICI		9/4/77	M	35	(3)	16
8	Andrei PORFIREANU		11/5/83	M	21	(11)	2
10	Nicolai RUDAC		23/3/86	M	20	(10)	3
15	Sandro SHUGLADZE	UKR	24/10/90	M	17	(1)	2
20	Olexandr SUCHU	UKR	22/1/90	A	17		9
20	Vladimir TARANU		27/6/82	A	12	(13)	1
25	Victor TRUHANOV		30/1/91	M	7	(5)	1
24	Viktor UZBEK	UKR	22/2/90	D	11	(1)	1
4	Yevhen VISHNYAKOV	UKR	10/7/89	M	14	(3)	1

FC MILSAMI

Coach – Vladimir Gosperschi; (21/9/10) Ştefan Stoica (ROU)
Founded – 2005
Stadium – Municipal (1,000)

2010				
25/7	Rapid	a	1-0	*Grigoruţă*
1/8	Sfintul Gheorghe	h	2-1	*Boghiu, Stinga*
7/8	Zimbru	a	0-0	
15/8	Gagauziya	a	2-0	*Grigoruţă, Caio*
21/8	Iskra-Stal	h	0-0	
25/8	Tiraspol	a	2-1	*Grigoruţă, Boghiu*
29/8	Olimpia	h	0-0	
11/9	Nistru	a	1-0	*Boghiu*
18/9	Dacia	h	1-2	*Ademar*
26/9	Costuleni	a	7-0	*Boghiu 4, Caio, Cucovei, Sosnovschi*
2/10	Academia	h	1-1	*Caio*
16/10	Sheriff	a	0-2	
23/10	Dinamo	h	1-1	*Golban*
31/10	Rapid	h	3-0	*Golban, Ademar, Grigoruţă*
6/11	Sfintul Gheorghe	a	4-0	*Ademar 2, Sosnovschi, Mohammed*
14/11	Zimbru	h	1-0	*Olexici*
20/11	Gagauziya	h	2-1	*Olexici, Boghiu*
24/11	Nistru	h	5-0	*Grigoruţă, Boghiu 2, Ademar 2*
28/11	Iskra-Stal	a	1-0	*Golban*
4/12	Tiraspol	h	5-1	*Olexici, Ademar, Golban, Grigoruţă 2*
12/12	Olimpia	a	0-0	
2011				
16/2	Dacia	a	0-0	
20/2	Costuleni	h	2-0	*Mohammed, Roman*
26/2	Academia	a	0-1	
2/3	Sheriff	h	0-1	
6/3	Dinamo	a	3-0	*Boghiu 2 (1p), Furdui*
12/3	Nistru	h	1-2	*Boghiu*
16/3	Gagauziya	a	3-0	*Sosnovschi, Golban, Boghiu*
20/3	Dacia	h	0-0	
2/4	Sheriff	a	1-2	*Boghiu*
6/4	Sfintul Gheorghe	h	4-0	*Boghiu 4 (1p)*
10/4	Olimpia	h	2-1	*Sosnovschi, Gârlă*
16/4	Iskra-Stal	a	2-2	*Boghiu, Ionescu*
23/4	Zimbru	h	1-2	*Ionescu*
30/4	Rapid	a	1-0	*Boghiu (p)*
8/5	Academia	h	1-0	*Ademar*
13/5	Tiraspol	a	1-0	*Boghiu (p)*
17/5	Dinamo	h	7-2	*Boghiu 3, Grigoruţă, Sosnovschi, Furdui, Ionescu*
22/5	Costuleni	a	3-0	*Traoré, Boghiu, Roman*

No	Name	Nat	DoB	Pos	Aps	(s)	Gls
23	ADEMAR Aparecido Xavier Júnior	BRA	8/1/85	M	21	(5)	8
2	Igor ANDRONIC		11/3/88	D	7		
23	Alexandr BEZIMOV		8/2/84	A	2	(9)	
11	Gheorghe BOGHIU		26/10/81	A	31		26
11	CAIO García Suguino	ESP	3/11/87	M	23	(7)	3
4	Adrian CUCOVEI		21/4/85	D	17	(11)	1
8	Valentin FURDUI		1/9/87	M	16	(1)	2
7	Valeriu GÂRLĂ	ROU	6/7/86	M	15	(1)	1
12	Vadim GHERASIMOV		22/12/92	A		(1)	
23	Dumitru GLIGA		29/8/84	M	1	(1)	
14	Alexandru GOLBAN		28/2/79	A	16	(16)	5
18	Adrian GRIGORUŢĂ	ROU	8/8/83	A	26	(6)	8
3	Eduard GROSSU		5/1/80	D	21	(1)	
10	Claudiu Mircea IONESCU	ROU	20/3/83	M	14	(3)	3
10	Anton KOVALEVSKIY	UKR	2/8/84	A	7	(5)	
50	Yves Simplice MBOUSSI	CMR	30/5/87	D	6		
17	Ovidiu MENDIZOV	ROU	9/8/86	M	38		
14	Nuridin MOHAMMED	GHA	25/2/87	M	17	(4)	2
21	Mihai MORARU		22/10/78	G	30		
12	Adrian NEGAI		28/1/85	G	9		
24	Ghenadie OLEXICI		23/8/78	D	10	(3)	3
84	Valeriu ONILA		14/4/84	M	11	(5)	
8	Iurie OSIPENCO		6/7/74	M	13	(6)	
7	Naufel PEDRO ZAMBUZZI	BRA	12/1/90	M	4	(7)	
13	Marius ROMAN	ROU	10/2/87	M	5	(10)	2

	Andrian SOSNOVSCHI		13/6/77	D	34		5
	Alexandru STADIICIUC		14/7/81	D	27	(7)	
	Petru STINGA		17/4/87	M	4	(11)	1
	Alexandru STOICA	ROU	10/9/88	D	1	(4)	
	Valentin TERNAVSCHI		16/7/88	D	2	(6)	
	Ousmane TRAORÉ	CIV	8/9/90	A	1	(9)	1

FC NISTRU OTACI

Coach – Lilian Popescu
Founded – 1953
Stadium – Calarasauca (1,000)
MAJOR HONOURS: Moldovan Cup – (1) 2005.

010				
5/7	Costuleni	a	1-2	*Belle*
8	Academia	h	0-1	
8	Sheriff	a	0-1	
5/8	Dinamo	h	0-2	
1/8	Rapid	a	0-1	
5/8	Sfintul Gheorghe	h	1-0	*Dolgov*
9/8	Zimbru	a	0-2	
1/9	Milsami	h	0-1	
8/9	Iskra-Stal	a	1-1	*Caragea*
6/9	Tiraspol	h	4-2	*Caragea 2, Maliarenko 2*
10	Olimpia	a	0-1	
6/10	Gagauziya	a	1-5	*og (Tatar)*
3/10	Dacia	h	1-1	*Murgulet*
1/10	Costuleni	h	1-0	*Dolgov*
/11	Academia	a	0-1	
4/11	Sheriff	h	0-3	
0/11	Dinamo	a	2-3	*Vilcu, Radu*
8/11	Rapid	h	0-4	
/12	Sfintul Gheorghe	a	1-2	*Maliarenko*
2/12	Zimbru	h	1-5	*og (Cravcescu)*
6/12	Milsami	a	0-5	
011				
6/2	Iskra-Stal	h	0-1	
20/2	Tiraspol	a	0-4	
26/2	Olimpia	h	0-2	
2/3	Gagauziya	h	3-0	*Murgulet 2, Iepureanu*
6/3	Dacia	a	1-1	*Turkhashvili*
12/3	Milsami	a	2-1	*Burghiu, Gritiuc*
16/3	Olimpia	h	0-3	
20/3	Iskra-Stal	a	1-2	*Vilcu*
2/4	Zimbru	h	2-4	*Vilcu, Tcaciuc*
6/4	Rapid	a	2-3	*Murgulet, Tcaciuc (p)*
9/4	Academia	h	1-0	*Iepureanu*
16/4	Tiraspol	a	0-1	
23/4	Dinamo	h	4-0	*Gritiuc 3 (1p), Vilcu*
30/4	Costuleni	a	0-2	
8/5	Sfintul Gheorghe	a	1-1	*Vilcu*
13/5	Gagauziya	h	1-2	*Murgulet*
17/5	Dacia	a	0-2	
22/5	Sheriff	h	1-3	*Murgulet*

No	Name	Nat	DoB	Pos	Aps	(s)	Gls
17	Vitalie ANDRIES		5/9/87	M		(2)	
14	Victor ANTONII		26/6/89	M	8	(2)	
10	Titi BELLE	CMR	10/3/85	M	19	(6)	1
25	Ghenadie BOGHIU		26/10/81	D	6	(11)	
11	Vitaly BONDARENCO		5/12/88	D	2	(2)	
23	Serhiy BRONNIKOV	UKR	30/5/86	D	5	(5)	
3	Stefan BURGHIU		28/3/91	D	7	(9)	1
23	Adrian Mihai CARAGEA	ROU	6/10/86	A	12		3
20	Oleg COLTUNOVSCHI		9/2/85	D	8	(2)	
15	Artiom COZACENCO		25/7/92	M	15	(6)	
12	Denis CRISTOFOVICI		26/11/86	G	17	(1)	
1	Olexandr DEADIK	UKR	17/1/88	G	22	(3)	
2	Ion DODON		20/11/91	M	10	(4)	
5	Dmitry DOLGOV		24/8/87	D	19		2
15	Gheorghe EREMIA		20/8/87	D	13	(1)	
2	Vadim GORAS		21/1/94	M		(1)	
10	Serghei GRITIUC		6/4/84	A	17		4
14	Serghey IEPUREANU		12/9/76	M	18		2
8	Felix KUIPOU	CMR	8/9/87	D	9	(5)	
14	Evghenii LAVRINOVICI		13/10/88	M	16	(4)	
21	Igor LEONOV		28/3/89	M		(4)	
7	Ihor MALIARENKO	UKR	9/10/89	A	22	(7)	3
5	Sorin Călin MARIN	ROU	26/2/84	D	25	(2)	
23	Alexandr MIRONET		12/11/89	M	2	(3)	
20	Renat MURGULET		18/4/89	M	29	(1)	6
4	Marcel NAVRUC		7/1/94	D		(1)	
19	Oleg PAVLIV		17/1/92	M	2	(1)	
11	Ivan PETRUK	UKR	10/8/89	D	6	(5)	
11	Serghei POGREBAN		13/5/78	M	16		
9	Ionut Florin RADU	ROU	17/8/91	D	5		1
3	Andrei RILSCHII		17/10/88	M	3	(1)	
4	Igor SOLTANICI		4/5/84	D	9	(3)	
5	Alphonse Denis SOPPO	CMR	15/5/85	M	16		
4	François TAMBELL	CMR	16/2/83	M	6	(4)	
6	Alexandr TCACIUC		10/1/81	M	33	(1)	2
17	Serghey TONOFREI		26/11/89	M	2	(20)	
9	Giorgi TURKHASHVILI	GEO	19/10/88	M	3	(13)	1
14	Claudiu VILCU	ROU	16/1/91	D	26		5
2	Cornel VLADIUC		1/4/94	D	1	(2)	

FC OLIMPIA BALTI

Coach – Nicolae Bunea
Founded – 1984
Stadium – Olimpia (7,000)

2010				
26/7	Academia	a	1-0	*Tcaciuc*
1/8	Sheriff	h	0-0	
7/8	Dinamo	a	8-0	*Kourouma, Khorolskiy, Somide, Adaramola, Repinetschii, Pascenco (p), Tcaciuc, Ovseannicov*
15/8	Rapid	h	3-0	*Tcaciuc, og (Rusu V.), Ovseannicov*
21/8	Sfintul Gheorghe	a	2-0	*Tcaciuc, Santana*
25/8	Zimbru	h	1-1	*Ovseannicov*
29/8	Milsami	a	0-0	
11/9	Iskra-Stal	h	0-1	
18/9	Tiraspol	a	3-1	*Ogoazi, Jerome, Orlovschi*
26/9	Gagauziya	a	2-1	*Adaramola, Tcaciuc*
1/10	Nistru	h	1-0	*Pasecniuc*
16/10	Dacia	a	1-3	*Jerome*
23/10	Costuleni	h	4-1	*Orlovschi, Gusacov, Kourouma, Adaramola*
1/11	Academia	h	3-2	*Somide 2, Adaramola (p)*
7/11	Sheriff	a	1-1	*Adaramola*
14/11	Dinamo	h	1-0	*Repinetschii*
20/11	Rapid	a	1-1	*Orlovschi (p)*
28/11	Sfintul Gheorghe	h	4-1	*Adaramola 2, Ovseannicov, Pasecniuc*
4/12	Zimbru	a	0-0	
12/12	Milsami	h	0-0	
16/12	Iskra-Stal	a	0-0	
2011				
16/2	Tiraspol	h	0-4	
21/2	Gagauziya	h	1-0	*Ovseannicov*
26/2	Nistru	a	2-0	*Tcaciuc, Ternavschi*
1/3	Dacia	h	1-2	*Ovseannicov*
6/3	Costuleni	a	1-0	*Jerome*
12/3	Costuleni	h	0-0	
16/3	Nistru	a	3-0	*Pasecniuc, Ovseannicov, Hovanschii*
20/3	Gagauziya	h	4-2	*Pasecniuc, Adaramola, Ovseannicov, Lichioiu*
2/4	Dacia	a	0-2	
6/4	Sheriff	h	1-0	*Ogada*
10/4	Milsami	a	1-2	*Pasecniuc*
16/4	Sfintul Gheorghe	h	1-1	*Remizovskiy (p)*
23/4	Iskra-Stal	h	2-1	*og (Gafina), Ogada*
30/4	Zimbru	a	0-0	
8/5	Rapid	h	2-1	*Ogada (p), Jerome*
13/5	Academia	a	2-0	*Jerome, Ovseannicov*
17/5	Tiraspol	h	0-3	
22/5	Dinamo	a	2-0	*Sidorov, Gusacov*

No	Name	Nat	DoB	Pos	Aps	(s)	Gls
30	Julius Olumide ADARAMOLA	NGA	4/4/90	M	32	(6)	8
21	Ibrahima Sory CAMARA	GUI	6/10/92	M	25	(6)	
20	Serhiy CHAPKO	UKR	24/1/88	M		(5)	
15	Alexandru CHELTUIALA		5/2/83	M	25	(6)	
7	Mykola GLEGA	UKR	19/6/89	M		(2)	
1	Leonid GROZA		17/4/87	G	8		
4	Serghei GUSACOV		6/4/86	D	33	(1)	2
27	Maxim HOVANSCHII		24/2/90	D	19		1
13	Jean-Robens JEROME	HAI	1/1/81	M	30	(5)	5
16	David KAKULIA	GEO	5/1/91	M		(3)	
20	Yevhen KHOROLSKIY	UKR	31/8/88	M	2	(9)	1
6	Thomas KOUROUMA	GUI	26/6/92	D	19	(11)	2
11	Cătălin LICHIOIU	ROU	20/1/82	A	4	(4)	1
24	Sergiu MAXIMOV		6/7/89	M		(5)	
18	Matthew MUTIU	NGA	3/1/91	M	5	(8)	
2	Jude Iloba OGADA	NGA	15/12/89	D	36	(2)	3
16	David OGOAZI	NGA	15/12/90	M	2	(7)	1
5	Nicolai ORLOVSCHI		1/4/85	D	21		3
9	Gheorghii OVSEANNICOV		12/10/85	A	30	(8)	9
32	Mihail PAIUS		6/2/83	G	11	(2)	
12	Serghey PASCENCO		18/12/82	G	20		1
17	Mihail PASECNIUC		9/3/91	M	29	(8)	5
3	Olexiy REMIZOVSKIY	UKR	11/1/87	D	6	(2)	1
7	Maxim REPINETSCHII		2/7/89	D	2	(17)	2
19	Carlos SANTANA	MEX	4/3/87	M		(3)	1
19	Vitaliy SIDOROV	RUS	6/3/90	A	1	(5)	1
25	Oluwawunmi SOMIDE	NGA	16/5/91	A	15	(23)	3
14	Andrei TCACIUC		10/2/82	M	32	(2)	6
24	Valentin TERNAVSCHI		16/7/88	D	7	(2)	1
3	Victor VERBETSCHI		3/7/83	D	15	(2)	

FC RAPID GHIDIGHICI

Coach – Pavlo Irichuk (UKR); (6/8/10) Petru Efros; (13/9/10) Serghey Sirbu; (1/10/10) Serghei Carmanov; (2/1/11) Pavlo Irichuk (UKR)

Founded – 1992

Stadium – Ghidighici (1,000)

2010				
25/7	Milsami	h	0-1	
1/8	Iskra-Stal	a	0-1	
7/8	Tiraspol	h	2-0	*Japalau 2*
15/8	Olimpia	a	0-3	
21/8	Nistru	h	1-0	*Grosu A. (p)*
25/8	Dacia	a	0-1	
29/8	Costuleni	h	1-0	*Japalau*
11/9	Academia	a	0-0	
26/9	Dinamo	a	1-0	*Frantuz*
2/10	Gagauziya	h	2-1	*Frantuz 2*
10/10	Sheriff	h	1-1	*Luca*
16/10	Sfintul Gheorghe	h	2-0	*Luca, Frantuz*
23/10	Zimbru	a	0-0	
31/10	Milsami	a	0-3	
6/11	Iskra-Stal	h	0-0	
14/11	Tiraspol	a	0-1	
20/11	Olimpia	h	1-1	*Maxim*
28/11	Nistru	a	4-0	*Maxim, Tofan, Grosu A.S., Arabadji*
4/12	Dacia	h	0-2	
12/12	Costuleni	a	2-1	*Frantuz, Maxim*
16/12	Academia	h	2-0	*Pascenco, Maxim*
2011				
16/2	Sheriff	a	0-4	
20/2	Dinamo	h	2-0	*Luca, Bugneac*
25/2	Gagauziya	a	2-1	*Bugneac, Maximov*
2/3	Sfintul Gheorghe	a	0-0	
6/3	Zimbru	h	0-0	
12/3	Academia	h	4-2	*Grosu A.S., Luca, Manaliu, Rusu V.*
16/3	Tiraspol	a	0-0	
20/3	Dinamo	h	2-0	*Rusu V., Bugneac*
2/4	Costuleni	a	0-0	
6/4	Nistru	h	3-2	*Bugneac, Jardan, Calincov*
10/4	Gagauziya	a	3-1	*Luca 2, Calincov*
16/4	Dacia	h	0-0	
23/4	Sheriff	a	1-2	*Pascenco*
30/4	Milsami	h	0-1	
8/5	Olimpia	a	1-2	*Grosu A.*
13/5	Iskra-Stal	h	1-2	*Calincov*
17/5	Zimbru	a	0-1	
22/5	Sfintul Gheorghe	h	1-3	*Pascenco*

No	Name	Nat	DoB	Pos	Aps	(s)	Gls
16	Ion ARABADJI		31/7/84	D	30	(3)	1
13	Dumitru BERBINSCHI		23/2/88	D	17	(4)	
24	Anatolie BOESTEAN		26/3/85	D	6	(7)	
25	Andrei BUGNEAC		30/3/88	A	10	(10)	4
16	Denis CALINCOV		15/9/85	A	3	(6)	3
3	Maxim CEBOTARI		16/11/82	M	21		
1	Alexandru CHIRILOV		28/1/78	G	10	(1)	
7	Marcel CIORTAN		19/1/83	M	9	(4)	
18	Oleg CLONIN		2/4/88	M	11		
22	Ibrahim DAUDA	GHA	20/12/87	M	2	(1)	
1	Sergiu DIACONU		16/2/78	G	1		
23	Maxim FRANTUZ		4/5/86	M	16	(11)	5
22	Alexei GONCEAROV		24/2/84	D	15		
8	Alexandru GROSU		18/4/88	M	31	(4)	2
21	Alexandru Sergiu GROSU		16/5/86	A	9	(17)	2
21	Sergiu JAPALAU		30/4/84	A	3	(9)	3
22	Ion JARDAN		10/1/90	M	20	(2)	1
6	Alexandru LEU		4/5/91	D	16		
9	Iurie LIVANDOVSCHI		17/2/88	A	17	(10)	
10	Stanislav LUCA		28/8/86	M	18	(16)	6
14	Vitalie MANALIU		23/3/85	A	13	(1)	1
11	Alexandru MAXIM		19/1/86	A	9	(4)	4
19	Alexandru MAXIMOV		8/7/82	A	4	(6)	1
5	Daniel NOSA	NGA	3/12/90	M	3	(2)	
17	Stefan OANTA		10/1/90	D		(2)	
4	Ghenadie OCHINCA		1/3/84	D	2	(1)	
17	Alexandr PASCENCO		28/5/89	M	25	(5)	3
12	Denis RUSU		2/8/90	G	28		
5	Vasile RUSU		28/7/85	M	29		2
13	Tudor STARCIUC		1/2/90	A	12	(3)	
7	David TELFER	GHA	1/12/88	M	1	(3)	
20	Alexandru TOFAN		19/8/87	M	22	(6)	1
14	Eduard VALUTA		9/4/79	D	16		

FC SFINTUL GHEORGHE SURUCENI

Coach – Sergiu Caraman

Founded – 2003

Stadium – Satesc (1,000)

2010				
25/7	Zimbru	h	0-3	
1/8	Milsami	a	1-2	*Posmac*
7/8	Iskra-Stal	h	2-2	*Ojog, Martin*
15/8	Tiraspol	a	0-1	
21/8	Olimpia	h	0-2	
25/8	Nistru	a	0-1	
29/8	Dacia	h	0-2	
9/9	Costuleni	a	3-0	*Kakulia, Camacho 2*
18/9	Academia	h	1-1	*Ojog*
26/9	Sheriff	a	0-4	
2/10	Dinamo	h	1-2	*Railean*
16/10	Rapid	a	0-2	
23/10	Gagauziya	h	2-2	*Prepelita (p), Platica M.*
31/10	Zimbru	a	1-2	*Posmac*
6/11	Milsami	h	0-4	
14/11	Iskra-Stal	a	0-4	
20/11	Tiraspol	h	0-2	
28/11	Olimpia	a	1-4	*Chiriloaie*
4/12	Nistru	h	2-1	*Rotaru, Railean*
12/12	Dacia	a	0-7	
16/12	Costuleni	h	1-2	*Posmac (p)*
2011				
16/2	Academia	a	0-2	
21/2	Sheriff	h	1-1	*Platica M.*
26/2	Dinamo	a	2-0	*Kriviy 2*
2/3	Rapid	h	0-0	

3	Gagauziya	a	1-2	*Ojog*
/3	Dacia	a	0-3	
/3	Academia	h	0-2	
/3	Sheriff	a	0-6	
4	Tiraspol	h	0-1	
4	Milsami	a	0-4	
/4	Dinamo	h	2-0	*Ojog, Platica M.*
/4	Olimpia	a	1-1	*Pyatnikov*
3/4	Costuleni	h	2-0	*Kravtsov, Tochilin*
)/4	Iskra-Stal	a	1-3	*Railean*
5	Nistru	h	1-1	*Prepelita*
3/5	Zimbru	a	0-3	
7/5	Gagauziya	h	1-3	*Pyatnikov*
2/5	Rapid	a	3-1	*Prepelita, Pyatnikov, Kriviy*

lo	Name	Nat	DoB	Pos	Aps	(s)	Gls
	Valery BUGAICHUK	UKR	7/7/87	M	11	(1)	
	Cristian CAMACHO	USA	11/7/88	M	32	(4)	2
	Evgheni CELEADNIC		9/10/90	D	32	(1)	
2	Ustin CERGA		25/11/88	G	15	(2)	
6	Dumitru CHIRILOAIE		21/2/91	D	6	(10)	1
1	Maxim COVALI		3/2/93	M	5	(13)	
	Victor CULAI		3/8/93	D	1	(11)	
1	Dmitry DOLGOV		24/8/87	D	10		
	Leonid GROZA		17/4/87	G	17	(1)	
5	Sergiu JAPALAU		30/4/84	A	7	(2)	
5	David KAKULIA	GEO	5/1/91	M	16	(3)	1
	Denis KRAVTSOV	RUS	18/3/90	M	6	(8)	1
1	Dmytro KRIVIY	UKR	7/12/87	A	11		3
6	Valentin LUNGU		11/3/94	M	9	(2)	
	Andrei MARTIN		27/6/74	M	5	(11)	1
	Petr OJOG		17/7/90	M	33	(5)	4
0	Mihai PLATICA		15/3/90	M	34	(1)	3
9	Sergiu PLATICA		5/6/91	M	1		
21	Veaceslav POSMAC		7/11/90	D	39		3
13	Andrei PREPELITA		24/7/89	D	27	(5)	3
7	German PYATNIKOV	RUS	23/1/88	D	12		3
14	Alexandr RAILEAN		4/10/90	A	20	(9)	3
12	Ion RIMBU		3/10/87	G	3	(6)	
3	Dorin ROTARU		23/10/90	M	32		1
11	Yevgeniy TOCHILIN	RUS	7/3/91	M	6	(8)	1
20	Andrei TODOROV		6/6/89	D	4	(8)	
2	Gheorghe TONU		25/11/89	G	4	(2)	
11	Ion URSU		19/8/94	M	3	(1)	
8	Alexandru VREMEA		3/11/91	M	28	(7)	

FC SHERIFF

Coach – Andrei Sosnitskiy (BLR); (30/4/11) Vitaliy Rashkevich (BLR)

Founded – 1997

Stadium – Sheriff (14,000)

MAJOR HONOURS: Moldovan League – (10) 2001, 2002, 2003, 2004, 2005, 2006, 2007, 2008, 2009, 2010; Moldovan Cup – (7) 1999, 2001, 2002, 2006, 2008, 2009, 2010.

2010				
24/7	Tiraspol	h	3-0	*Haceaturov, Hoderean, Jymmy*
1/8	Olimpia	a	0-0	
7/8	Nistru	h	1-0	*Đurović*
14/8	Dacia	a	0-0	
21/8	Costuleni	h	1-1	*Samardžić*
29/8	Gagauziya	h	3-0	*Volkov, Samardžić, Gheorghiev*
11/9	Dinamo	h	2-0	*Jymmy, Adamović*
22/9	Academia	a	0-1	
26/9	Sfintul Gheorghe	h	4-0	*Diedhiou, Gauračs 3*
2/10	Zimbru	a	1-1	*Gheorghiev*
10/10	Rapid	a	1-1	*Gheorghiev*
16/10	Milsami	h	2-0	*Erokhin, Diedhiou*
25/10	Iskra-Stal	a	1-0	*Erokhin*
31/10	Tiraspol	a	3-0	*Gheorghiev, Balima, Volkov (p)*
7/11	Olimpia	h	1-1	*Gauračs*
14/11	Nistru	a	3-0	*Tarkhnishvili (p), Erokhin 2*
20/11	Dacia	h	3-0	*Jymmy, Erokhin, Branković*
28/11	Costuleni	a	0-0	
6/12	Academia	h	1-1	*Diedhiou*
12/12	Gagauziya	a	4-0	*Volkov, Erokhin, Jymmy, Gauračs*
18/12	Dinamo	a	7-0	*Gauračs 5, Gheorghiev, Volkov*
2011				
16/2	Rapid	h	4-0	*Volaš, Zamaliyev, Cheptine, Pešić*
21/2	Sfintul Gheorghe	a	1-1	*Zamaliyev*
26/2	Zimbru	h	1-0	*Gheorghiev*
2/3	Milsami	a	1-0	*Pešić*
6/3	Iskra-Stal	h	1-0	*Pešić*
12/3	Gagauziya	h	5-1	*Diedhiou 3, Tarkhnishvili (p), Volaš*
16/3	Dacia	a	1-1	*Cheptine*
20/3	Sfintul Gheorghe	h	6-0	*Zamaliyev, Gheorghiev, Branković, Volaš, Balima 2*
2/4	Milsami	h	2-1	*Jymmy, Kassenu*
6/4	Olimpia	a	0-1	
10/4	Iskra-Stal	h	2-1	*Cheptine, Pešić*
16/4	Zimbru	a	0-1	
23/4	Rapid	h	2-1	*Diedhiou, Volaš*
26/4	Academia	a	0-1	
8/5	Tiraspol	h	0-0	
13/5	Dinamo	a	7-0	*Balima 3, Diedhiou 2, Zamaliyev, og (Bidirlan)*
17/5	Costuleni	h	4-0	*Diedhiou 4*
22/5	Nistru	a	3-1	*Tommy, Gheorghiev, Mirza*

No	Name	Nat	DoB	Pos	Aps	(s)	Gls
44	Miloš ADAMOVIĆ	SRB	19/6/88	M	10	(7)	1
14	Wilfried Benjamin BALIMA	BFA	20/3/85	M	26	(5)	6
30	Vladimir BRANKOVIĆ	SRB	22/9/85	D	17	(8)	2
27	Anatol CHEPTINE		20/5/90	M	12	(5)	3
4	Vadim COSTANDACHI		22/9/91	M	6	(5)	
21	Amath André DIEDHIOU	SEN	19/11/89	A	26	(8)	13
18	Igor DIMA		11/2/93	D		(1)	
13	Serghei DULGHIER		21/3/91	D	7	(1)	
19	Marko ĐUROVIĆ	MNE	2/5/88	M	4	(3)	1
10	Aleksandr EROKHIN	RUS	13/10/89	A	12	(5)	6
21	Nélson FRED de Oliveira	BRA	22/7/86	M	8	(4)	
11	Edgars GAURAČS	LVA	10/3/88	A	5	(7)	10
26	Serghey GHEORGHIEV		20/10/91	M	26	(9)	8
16	Artem HACEATUROV		18/6/92	M	18	(8)	1
23	Eduard HODEREAN		7/1/90	M	5	(3)	1
9	JYMMY Dougllas França	BRA	15/4/84	A	20	(2)	5
20	Ghandy KASSENU	GHA	9/9/89	A	16	(1)	1
15	Jasmin MECINOVIC	MKD	22/10/90	D	3	(4)	
3	Iurie MIRZA		5/3/93	A	1		1
28	José NÁDSON Fereira	BRA	18/10/84	D	15	(1)	
7	Baćo NIKOLIĆ	MNE	19/1/86	M	6	(7)	
16	Aleksandar PEŠIĆ	SRB	21/5/92	A	5	(6)	4
24	Vadim RATA		5/5/93	M	6	(4)	
17	Florent ROUAMBA	BFA	31/12/86	M	27	(2)	
26	Miral SAMARDŽIČ	SVN	17/2/87	D	21	(5)	2
6	Alexandru SCRIPCENCO		13/1/91	D	6	(5)	
12	Dumitru STAJILA		2/8/91	G	22		
25	Vladislav STOYANOV	BUL	8/6/87	G	17	(1)	
5	Vaja TARKHNISHVILI		25/8/71	D	33		2
22	Abu TOMMY	SLE	13/10/89	M	9		1
20	Rustam TSYNYA	UKR	17/6/91	D	3		
19	Dalibor VOLAŠ	SVN	22/1/87	M	4	(8)	4
3	Vladimir VOLKOV	SRB	6/6/86	M	8	(8)	4
15	Ognjen VRANJEŠ	BIH	24/10/89	D	9		
33	Nail ZAMALIYEV	RUS	9/7/89	M	16	(1)	4

FC TIRASPOL

Coach – Iury Blonari; (19/12/10) Vlad Goian

Founded – 2001

Stadium – Sheriff (14,000)

2010				
24/7	Sheriff	a	0-3	
1/8	Dinamo	h	4-1	*Vornisel 2, Paye, Brydnya*
7/8	Rapid	a	0-2	
15/8	Sfintul Gheorghe	h	1-0	*Mamulashvili*
21/8	Zimbru	a	0-1	
25/8	Milsami	h	1-2	*Verbetschi*

29/8	Iskra-Stal	a	2-4	*Mamulashvili, Vornisel*
11/9	Gagauziya	a	3-1	*Vornisel 2, Verbetschi*
18/9	Olimpia	h	1-3	*Nahirniy*
26/9	Nistru	a	2-4	*Cheptine, Iezhov*
2/10	Dacia	h	0-0	
16/10	Costuleni	a	2-1	*Brydnya, og (Tugutschi)*
31/10	Sheriff	h	0-3	
6/11	Dinamo	a	3-0	*Vornisel, Iezhov, Mamulashvili*
14/11	Rapid	h	1-0	*og (Valuta)*
20/11	Sfintul Gheorghe	a	2-0	*Maxymenko, Radiola*
28/11	Zimbru	h	0-2	
4/12	Milsami	a	1-5	*Iezhov*
9/12	Academia	h	2-1	*Vornisel, Nicologlo*
12/12	Iskra-Stal	h	0-0	
16/12	Gagauziya	h	5-0	*Brydnya, Mamulashvili 2, Vornisel, Soimu*
2011				
16/2	Olimpia	a	4-0	*Corneencov, Kilikevych, Nicologlo, Christopher*
20/2	Nistru	h	4-0	*Nicologlo, Kilikevych, Christopher 2*
26/2	Dacia	a	0-2	
2/3	Costuleni	h	3-0	*Kilikevych 2, Dulghier*
6/3	Academia	a	0-3	
12/3	Zimbru	a	0-1	
16/3	Rapid	h	0-0	
20/3	Academia	a	1-1	*Kilikevych (p)*
2/4	Sfintul Gheorghe	a	1-0	*Fred*
6/4	Dinamo	h	7-0	*Nicologlo 2, Christopher, Fred, Kilikevych 2 (1p), Bondarciuc*
10/4	Costuleni	a	0-0	
16/4	Nistru	h	1-0	*Nicologlo*
23/4	Gagauziya	a	2-1	*Caragea, Hoderean*
30/4	Dacia	h	0-1	
8/5	Sheriff	a	0-0	
13/5	Milsami	h	0-1	
17/5	Olimpia	a	3-0	*Christopher, Hoderean, Kilikevych (p)*
22/5	Iskra-Stal	h	1-2	*Iezhov*

No	Name	Nat	DoB	Pos	Aps	(s)	Gls
16	Maxim ALACEV		6/10/90	D	8	(10)	
19	Iury BONDARCIUC		25/2/89	A	20	(14)	1
18	Ihor BRYDNYA	UKR	20/7/88	A	18	(2)	3
17	Vitalie BULAT		14/9/87	M	14	(1)	
25	Adrian Mihai CARAGEA	ROU	6/10/86	A	6	(5)	1
10	Anatol CHEPTINE		20/5/90	M	18	(1)	1
18	Omosebi Elijah CHRISTOPHER	NGA	19/7/86	A	8	(7)	5
6	Dmitri CONDARIUC		16/2/90	D	10	(1)	
7	Andrei CORNEENCOV		1/4/82	M	6		1
16	Igor COSTROV		3/8/87	A	9	(2)	
22	Serghei DULGHIER		21/3/91	D	8	(2)	1
15	Olexandr FESHCHENKO	UKR	2/1/85	D	14	(1)	
27	Nélson FRED de Oliveira	BRA	22/7/86	M	16	(1)	2
14	Eduard HODEREAN		7/1/90	M	4	(5)	2
20	Ruslan HOLOVANOV	UKR	5/7/89	D	3	(2)	
21	Vitaliy IEZHOV	UKR	30/8/90	M	6	(8)	4
1	Serghei JURIC		3/3/84	G	14		
3	Vitaliy KALYNYCHENKO	UKR	29/3/83	D	16		
9	Volodymyr KILIKEVYCH	UKR	30/11/83	A	15	(2)	8
17	Vyacheslav LEBEDYNSKIY	UKR	9/6/89	D	7	(2)	
15	Giga MAMULASHVILI	RUS	2/10/91	A	14	(7)	5
2	Maxym MAXYMENKO	UKR	28/5/90	D	17		1
18	Ihor NAHIRNIY	UKR	4/6/89	A	3	(5)	1
11	Gheorghe NICOLOGLO		2/1/91	A	21	(15)	6
25	Igor OBLASHEVSKIY	RUS	2/1/87	G	1		
13	Vasile PANAIT	ROU	12/4/83	D	12	(2)	
13	Djibril PAYE	GUI	26/2/90	D	31		1
23	Andrei RADIOLA		13/1/90	D	19	(1)	1
1	Dorin RAILEAN		13/10/93	G	1		
5	Iurii SINITCHIH		9/2/91	D	5	(11)	
9	Maxim SOIMU		17/7/90	A		(15)	1
17	Victor TRUHANOV		30/1/91	M	2	(4)	
11	Rustam TSYNYA	UKR	17/6/91	D	4	(2)	
4	Andrei VERBETSCHI		3/7/83	D	28	(4)	2
8	Dmitri VORNISEL		2/2/90	A	28	(10)	8
12	Alexandr ZVEAGHINTEV		26/7/87	G	23		

FC ZIMBRU CHISINAU

Coach – Ivan Tabanov

Founded – 1947

Stadium – Zimbru (10,400)

MAJOR HONOURS: Moldovan League – (8) 1992, 1993, 1994, 1995, 1996, 1998, 1999, 2000; Moldovan Cup – (5) 1997, 1998, 2003, 2004, 2007.

2010				
28/7	Sfintul Gheorghe	a	3-0	*Andronic, Cojocari, Berco*
1/8	Gagauziya	a	0-0	
7/8	Milsami	h	0-0	
15/8	Iskra-Stal	a	1-2	*Berco*
21/8	Tiraspol	h	1-0	*Turcan*
25/8	Olimpia	a	1-1	*Turcan*
29/8	Nistru	h	2-0	*Turcan, Demerji*
11/9	Dacia	a	1-1	*Salifu*
18/9	Costuleni	h	1-0	*Sischin (p)*
26/9	Academia	a	1-0	*Andronic*
3/10	Sheriff	h	1-1	*Salifu*
16/10	Dinamo	a	0-1	
23/10	Rapid	h	0-0	
31/10	Sfintul Gheorghe	h	2-1	*Furdui, Secrieru*
6/11	Gagauziya	h	1-0	*Salifu*
14/11	Milsami	a	0-1	
20/11	Iskra-Stal	h	0-1	
28/11	Tiraspol	a	2-0	*Sidorenco, Furdui*
4/12	Olimoia	h	0-0	
11/12	Nistru	a	5-1	*Demerji, Antoniuc 2, Hvorosteanov, Muntean*
16/12	Dacia	h	0-1	
2011				
16/2	Costuleni	a	2-0	*Andronic, Salifu*
20/2	Academia	h	1-0	*Andronic*
26/2	Sheriff	a	0-1	
2/3	Dinamo	h	6-1	*Kovalevskiy, Sidorenco 2, Demerji, Antoniuc 2*
6/3	Rapid	a	0-0	
12/3	Tiraspol	h	1-0	*Andronic*
16/3	Dinamo	a	6-1	*Guchashvili, Bălaşa, Sidorenco 2, Burdiyan, Komyahin*
20/3	Costuleni	h	2-1	*Andronic 2 (1p)*
2/4	Nistru	a	4-2	*Sischin, Andronic 2, Sidorenco*
6/4	Gagauziya	h	3-1	*Bălaşa, Turcan, Antoniuc*
10/4	Dacia	a	0-1	
16/4	Sheriff	h	1-0	*Sischin*
23/4	Milsami	a	2-1	*Sischin, Plamadeala*
30/4	Olimpia	h	0-0	
8/5	Iskra-Stal	a	0-0	
13/5	Sfintul Gheorghe	h	3-0	*Komyahin, Guchashvili, Burdiyan*
17/5	Rapid	h	1-0	*Sischin (p)*
22/5	Academia	a	2-0	*Turcan 2*

No	Name	Nat	DoB	Pos	Aps	(s)	Gls
13	Henry Ojotule AGOCHI	NGA	29/4/89	A	2	(8)	
9	Oleg ANDRONIC		6/2/89	A	16	(10)	9
15	Maxim ANTONIUC		15/1/91	A	4	(11)	5
18	Ilie Daniel BĂLAŞA	ROU	6/8/81	M	15	(1)	2
10	Victor BERCO		20/4/79	A	7	(4)	2
11	Alexandr BEZIMOV		8/2/84	A	2	(4)	
3	Maxim BOGHIU		24/5/91	D	8	(2)	
13	Ion BOJII		6/4/90	D		(1)	
16	Andriy BURDIYAN	UKR	18/1/86	D	7	(1)	2
22	Nicolae CALANCEA		29/8/86	G	36		
26	Stefan CARAULAN		2/2/89	D	5	(1)	
22	Anatol CHIRINCIUC		4/2/89	G	2		
6	Sergiu COJOCARI		15/5/89	D	20		1
20	Eugen COLEV		16/5/86	M		(3)	
6	Cornel Flaviu CORNEA	ROU	28/7/81	D	4		
24	Vadim CRAVCESCU		7/3/85	M	17	(1)	
11	Alexandru CUCU		28/9/87	M	6	(9)	
25	Serghei CUZNETOV		20/8/74	D	12		
7	Ion DEMERJI		28/4/89	M	11	(20)	3
29	Viktor DMITRENKO	RUS	4/4/91	D	10		
14	Iulian ERHAN		1/7/86	D	11		
16	Artem FAURIANU		5/9/91	M		(1)	

Valentin FURDUI		1/9/87	M	10	(4)	2
Vasili GUCHASHVILI	GEO	25/1/85	A	5	(5)	2
Piotr HVOROSTEANOV		28/8/86	M	14	(5)	1
Yuriy KOMYAHIN	UKR	6/5/84	M	5	(4)	2
Georgi KORUDZHIEV	BUL	2/3/88	M	8	(7)	
Anton KOVALEVSKIY	UKR	2/8/84	A	15	(2)	1
Alexandru MARDARI		1/9/91	D		(1)	
Anton MUNTEAN		25/12/90	D	3		1
Adrian NEGAI		28/1/85	G	1		
Gheorghe NEGRUŢ	ROU	8/2/87	M	6	(3)	
Victor NOSENCO		10/5/87	D	23	(2)	
Vitalie PLAMADEALA		21/1/85	M	24	(9)	1
Abdul Razak SALIFU	GHA	1/10/88	A	19	(2)	4
Andrei SECRIERU		7/6/84	M	5	(9)	1
Aleš SHUSTER	CZE	26/10/81	D	15		
Eugen SIDORENCO		19/3/89	A	20	(6)	6
Sergiu SIRBU		1/4/86	M	19		
Oleg SISCHIN		7/1/75	M	28	(3)	5
Mihai TURCAN		20/8/89	M	14	(8)	6

TOP GOALSCORERS 2010/11

26	Gheorghe BOGHIU (Milsami)
22	Ghenadie ORBU (Dacia)
19	Mihai COJUSEA (Gagauziya)
16	Alexandru POPOVICI (Iskra-Stal)
13	Levan KORGALIDZE (Dacia) Amath André DIEDHIOU (Sheriff)
12	Radu GINSARI (Academia) Volodymyr KILIKEVYCH (Iskra-Stal/Tiraspol)
10	Edgars GAURAČS (Sheriff)
9	Daniil NIKOLAEV (Academia) Olexandr SUCHU (Iskra-Stal) Gheorghii OVSEANNICOV (Olimpia) Oleg ANDRONIC (Zimbru)

PROMOTED CLUBS

SECOND LEVEL FINAL TABLE 2010/11

		Pld	W	D	L	F	A	Pts
1	CF Locomotiv Balti	28	17	8	3	59	23	59
2	FC Ursidos Chisinau	28	16	10	2	63	17	58
3	FC Dinamo-Auto Tiraspol	28	17	6	5	52	26	57
4	CF Intersport-Aroma Cobusca Noua	28	15	9	4	53	20	54
5	FC Sheriff-2	28	15	5	8	64	26	50
6	RS Lilcora Chisinau	28	14	6	8	55	38	48
7	FC Cahul-2005	28	13	5	10	35	40	44
8	CSCA-Buiucani Chisinau	28	12	6	10	56	45	42
9	FC Zimbru-2 Chisinau	28	9	7	12	38	33	34
10	FC Speranta Crihane Veche	28	9	7	12	32	45	34
11	CS MIPAN-Voran	28	9	2	17	45	72	29
12	FC Sfintul Gheorghe-2 Suruceni	28	7	4	17	28	48	25
13	FC Dinamo-2 Bender	28	5	6	17	27	60	21
14	FC Olimp Ungheni	28	4	7	17	31	75	19
15	FC Olimpia-2 Tiligul	28	4	0	24	16	86	12

NB No promotion as CF Locomotiv Balti failed to obtain licence for Divizia Nationala; FC Academia UTM-2 Chisinau withdrew after round 15 – all their matches annulled.

DOMESTIC CUP 2010/11

CUPA MOLDOVEI

SECOND ROUND

(22/9/10)
Cahul-2005 0, Gagauziya 0 *(aet; 5-4 on pens)*
CSCA-Buiucani 0, Sfintul Gheorghe 3
Intersport-Aroma 0, Nistru 2
Izvoras-67 4, Speranta 1
Locomotiv 0, Lilcora 1
MIPAN-Voran 0, Tiraspol 5
Ursidos 2, Dinamo Bender 0
Viisoara 0, Costuleni 6

1/8 FINALS

(27/10/10)
Cahul-2005 1, Zimbru 1 *(aet; 9-8 on pens)*
Izvoras-67 0, Academia 4
Lilcora 0, Rapid Ghidighici 3
Nistru 1, Dacia Chisinau 4
Olimpia Balti 1, Sfintul Gheorghe 0
Tiraspol 1, Milsami 1 *(aet; 5-4 on pens)*

(28/10/10)
Sheriff 3, Costuleni 0
Ursidos 0, Iskra-Stal 1

QUARTER-FINALS

(10/11/10 & 24/11/10)
Cahul-2005 0, Dacia Chisinau 0
Dacia Chisinau 7 *(Orbu 4, 37, Sackey 32, 67, Stankovski 86, Popovici 89, Guchashvili 90+1)*, Cahul-2005 0
(Dacia Chisinau 7-0)

Iskra-Stal 1 *(Bulat 78)*, Rapid Ghidighici 1 *(Grosu A. 66)*
Rapid Ghidighici 0, Iskra-Stal 2 *(Kilikevych 7, 28)*
(Iskra-Stal 3-1)

Olimpia Balti *2 (Gusacov 61, 90)*, Academia 0
Academia 0, Olimpia Balti 1 *(Orlovschi 24)*
(Olimpia Balti 3-0)

Tiraspol 2 *(Cheptine 21, Soimu 41)*, Sheriff 3 *(Erokhin 40, 80, Diedhiou 83)*
Sheriff 2 *(Adamović 6, Jymmy 35)*, Tiraspol 0
(Sheriff 5-2)

SEMI-FINALS

(20/4/11 & 4/5/11)
Dacia Chisinau 0, Olimpia Balti 1 *(Sidorov 84)*
Olimpia Balti 2 *(Tcaciuc 25, Ogada 35p)*, Dacia Chisinau 1 *(Bursuc 31)*
(Olimpia Balti 3-1)

Sheriff 1 *(Balima 14)*, Iskra-Stal 0
Iskra-Stal 3 *(Rudac 11, Gorodetschi 47, Popovici 68)*, Sheriff 0
(Iskra-Stal 3-1)

FINAL

(26/5/11)
Zimbru stadium, Chisinau
FC ISKRA-STAL 2 *(Suchu 11, Gorodetschi 25)*
FC OLIMPIA BALTI 1 *(Ovseannicov 22)*
Referee – *Gheciu*
ISKRA-STAL – *Cebotari, Novicov, Leshchuk, Uzbek, Vishnyakov, Gorodetschi (Ponomar 71), Porfireanu, Popovici (Gafina 90), Rudac, Shugladze (Naginaylov 59), Suchu (Truhanov 81).*
OLIMPIA BALTI – *Paius, Ogada, Gusacov, Hovanschii, Jerome (Lichioiu 86), Tcaciuc, Cheltuiala (Kourouma 80), Pasecniuc (Mutiu 75), Camara (Somide 70), Ovseannicov, Adaramola.*

CLUB COMMUNICATION 2011/12

FC Academia UTM Chisinau

19/208, Decebal Av.
MD-2002 Chisinau

Tel +373 691 07 911
Fax
Web academia.md
Email info@academia.md
Media Officer Vadim Caraus

FC Costuleni

47/2, Titulescu Str.ap.1
MD-2012 Chisinau

Tel +373 22 844 371
Fax +373 22 240 280
Web fccostuleni.md
Email info@fccostuleni.md
Media Officer Mihai Burciu

CSCA-Rapid Chisinau

21 str. 31 August 1989
MD-2012 Chisinau

Tel +373 22 209 116
Fax +373 22 209 116
Web fcrapid.md
Email info@rapid.md
Media Officer Vadim Gurtovenco

FC Dacia Chisinau

87/7, Madan Str.
MD-2020 Chisinau

Tel +373 22 83 96 41
Fax +373 22 83 96 41
Web fcdacia.md
Email office@fcdacia.md
Media Officer Vladimir Meleca

FC Iskra-Stal

1 Industrialinaia Str.
MD-5500 Ribnita

Tel +373 555 77 889
Fax +373 555 76 084
Web iskra-stal.com
Email iskra.stal@gmail.com
Media Officer Dmitriy Burlaka

FC Milsami-Ursidos

91A, Haiducul Grozescu Str.
MD-3504 Orhei

Tel +373 225 26 060
Fax +373 225 24 427
Web milsami.md
Email info@milsami.md
Media Officer Roman Bogdan

FC Nistru Otaci

Libertatii Street 50
MD-7106 Otaci

Tel +373 271 79 117
Fax +373 271 79 111
Web fc-nistru.dnestr.net
Email fcnistru@mail.ru
Media Officer Victor Macinschi

FC Olimpia Balti

40 Sfintul Nicolae Str.
MD-3100 Balti

Tel +373 231 24 086
Fax +373 231 24 086
Web fcolimpia.md
Email olimpia@tellus.md
Media Officer Maxim Vilcov

FC Sfintul Gheorghe Suruceni

Suruceni village, Ialoveni district
MD-6827 Suruceni

Tel +373 268 336 38
Fax +373 22 23 43 30
Web sgsfc.md
Email marketing@sgsfc.md
Media Officer Sergiu Ipatii

FC Sheriff

81 T. Sevcenco str.
MD-3300 Tiraspol

Tel +373 533 63 530
Fax +373 533 63 541
Web fc-sheriff.com
Email club@sc.sheriff.md
Media Officer Pavel Galtsev

FC Tiraspol

7/60 Lenin str.
MD-3300 Tiraspol

Tel +373 533 63 690
Fax +373 533 63 691
Web fc-tiraspol.com
Email info@fc-tiraspol.com
Media Officer Serghei Ursul

FC Zimbru Chisinau

1 Butucului str.
MD-2062 Chisinau

Tel +373 22 772 400
Fax +373 22 771 553
Web zimbru.md
Email zimbru@zimbru.md
Media Officer Serghei Lisevici

MONTENEGRO

Monténégro I Montenegro

Futbalski savez Crne Gore (FSCG)

COMMUNICATION

Address Ulica 19. dicembra 13
ME-81000 Podgorica
Tel +382 20 445 600
Fax +382 20 445 660
E-mail info@fscg.co.me
Website fscg.co.me

President Dejan Savićević
General Secretary Momir Đurđevac
Media Officer Ivan Radović

Year of Formation 1931

National Stadium Pod Goricom, Podgorica (12,000)

DOMESTIC COMPETITION SUMMARY 2010/11

PRVA LIGA FINAL TABLE

			Home					Away					Total						
		Pld	W	D	L	F	A	W	D	L	F	A	W	D	L	F	A	Pts	Comp
1	FK Mogren	33	12	3	2	33	8	10	4	2	27	16	22	7	4	60	24	73	UCL
2	FK Budućnost Podgorica	33	11	4	2	32	18	11	3	2	26	11	22	7	4	58	29	73	UEL
3	FK Rudar Pljevlja	33	9	5	3	29	16	7	2	7	15	13	16	7	10	44	29	55	UEL
4	FK Zeta	33	11	3	3	25	10	1	10	5	11	19	12	13	8	36	29	49	UEL
5	FK Mladost Podgorica	33	8	5	4	25	16	2	6	8	11	19	10	11	12	36	35	41	
6	FK Dečić	33	9	4	4	16	7	1	5	10	8	26	10	9	14	24	33	39	
7	FK Grbalj	33	5	5	6	17	14	5	3	9	13	21	10	8	15	30	35	38	
8	FK Lovćen	33	5	6	5	15	17	4	4	9	14	19	9	10	14	29	36	37	
9	OFK Petrovac	33	4	6	6	9	13	4	5	8	17	25	8	11	14	26	38	35	
10	FK Mornar	33	7	4	5	15	15	2	3	12	10	30	9	7	17	25	45	34	*Relegated*
11	FK Sutjeska	33	8	3	5	24	19	1	4	12	8	35	9	7	17	32	54	34	
12	OFK Bar	33	4	6	6	17	20	3	5	9	13	23	7	11	15	30	43	32	*Relegated*

Top Scorer Ivan Vuković (Budućnost), 20 goals

Promoted Clubs FK Bokelj
FK Berane

Cup Final FK Rudar Pljevlja 2, FK Mogren 2 (aet; 5-4 on pens)

EURO dream alive and kicking

A 2010/11 season in which FK Mogren became the first team to win the Montenegrin Prva Liga twice and FK Rudar Pljevla successfully defended the domestic cup was utterly eclipsed by the extraordinary efforts of the national team in the UEFA EURO 2012 qualifiers.

Making their UEFA European Championship bow as the lowest-ranked team in a section including England, Switzerland, Bulgaria and Wales, and with a new coach, Croatian Zlatko Kranjčar, who had overseen defeats in each of his first three warm-up games, Montenegro were expected merely to make up the numbers. Instead – and despite depleted resources – they posted three 1-0 wins before holding England to a 0-0 stalemate at Wembley. After that opening burst, a 1-1 home draw with Bulgaria in June was a setback, especially as it involved the concession of a goal – something the defence had avoided all season, friendly internationals included. Nevertheless, Montenegro shared top spot with England, who still had to travel to Podgorica, so automatic qualification for Poland/Ukraine remained in their hands. And with a six-point clearance to third place, a play-off berth seemed all but guaranteed.

Mogren regain title

While goalkeeper Mladen Božović, centre back Stefan Savić and goalscoring skipper Mirko Vučinić were all enhancing their reputations – not only on the international stage but also at their respective clubs – the next generation of potential Montenegrin internationals were striving for recognition in the domestic Prva Liga. Results in UEFA club competition have shown that Montenegro's top clubs struggle to compete on the continental stage, but a domestic title is always something to cherish, and Mogren, from the coastal town of Budva, regained the Prva Liga crown they had won for the first time in 2008/09 by edging out FK Budućnost Podgorica on the head-to-head rule.

Montenegro defender Stefan Savić (left) in UEFA EURO 2012 qualifying action against England

A final-day 2-0 win at home to FK Mornar proved sufficient as Mogren, who had led Budućnost comfortably at the winter break, just clung on to their advantage having lost at home to their title rivals the previous weekend. Mogren and Budućnost finished 18 points clear of third-placed Rudar, who partly made up for a disappointing title defence by retaining the Montenegrin Cup. They did so by denying Mogren the double with a penalty shoot-out victory in the final – despite losing their goalkeeper, Miljan Mijatović, to a red card after just 15 minutes. Mogren's influential skipper Petar Grbić was also sent off in the second half of a contest that was tied 1-1 at 90 minutes and 2-2 at the end of extra time before Mogren midfielder Igor Matić missed the decisive spot-kick, giving Rudar their record fourth domestic trophy in the five years of independent Montenegrin football.

National Team

Top Five All-time Caps – Simon Vukčević (27); Savo Pavićević (26); Milan Jovanović (25); Vladimir Božović & Milorad Peković (24)

Top Five All-time Goals – Mirko Vučinić (11); Radomir Đalović (7); Stevan Jovetić (6); Igor Burzanović, Dejan Damjanović & Simon Vukčević (2)

NATIONAL TEAM RESULTS 2010/11

11/8/10	Northern Ireland	H	Podgorica	2-0	*Đalović (43, 59)*
3/9/10	Wales (ECQ)	H	Podgorica	1-0	*Vučinić (30)*
7/9/10	Bulgaria (ECQ)	A	Sofia	1-0	*Zverotić (36)*
8/10/10	Switzerland (ECQ)	H	Podgorica	1-0	*Vučinić (68)*
12/10/10	England (ECQ)	A	Wembley	0-0	
17/11/10	Azerbaijan	H	Podgorica	2-0	*Pejović (62), Bećiraj (73)*
25/3/11	Uzbekistan	H	Podgorica	1-0	*Vukčević (90)*
4/6/11	Bulgaria (ECQ)	H	Podgorica	1-1	*Đalović (53)*

NATIONAL TEAM APPEARANCES 2010/11

Coach – Zlatko KRANJČAR (CRO)	**15/11/56**		**Nir**	**WAL**	**BUL**	**SUI**	**ENG**	**Aze**	**Uzb**	**BUL**	**Caps**	**Goals**
Mladen BOŽOVIĆ	1/8/84	Videoton (HUN)	G	G	G	G	G	G46	G	G	16	-
Savo PAVIĆEVIĆ	11/12/80	Kavala (GRE) /M. Tel-Aviv (ISR)	D52	D	D			D68	D86	D82	26	-
Milan JOVANOVIĆ	21/7/83	Spartak Nalchik (RUS)	D76	D	D	D	D	s59	D71		25	-
Miodrag DŽUDOVIĆ	6/9/79	Spartak Nalchik (RUS)	D	D	D	D	D				13	1
Luka PEJOVIĆ	31/7/85	Mogren /Jagiellonia (POL)	D56					D76		D	21	1
Elsad ZVEROTIĆ	31/10/86	Luzern (SUI)	M83	M	M68	M	M		s61	M72	22	1
Milorad PEKOVIĆ	5/8/77	Greuther Fürth (GER)	M62	M	M		M	M65	M61	M	24	-
Vladimir BOŽOVIĆ	13/11/81	Rapid Bucureşti (ROU)	M	s74	s64				s20	M76	24	-
Simon VUKČEVIĆ	29/1/86	Sporting (POR)	M	M87	M	M84	M	M	s76		27	2
Radomir ĐALOVIĆ	29/10/82	Rijeka (CRO) /Amkar (RUS)	A78	A83	A77	A92	A77	A56	A76	A	22	7
Mirko VUČINIĆ	1/10/83	Roma (ITA)	A	A	A	A				A	23	11
Draško BOŽOVIĆ	30/6/88	Mogren	s52					s65			2	-
Žarko TOMAŠEVIĆ	22/2/90	Nacional (POR)	s56								2	-
Mitar NOVAKOVIĆ	27/9/81	Amkar (RUS)	s62	s83	s68	M	M62		M20		18	-
Stefan SAVIĆ	8/1/91	Borča (SRB) /Partizan (SRB)	s76			D	D	s68	D	D	6	-
Andrija DELIBAŠIĆ	24/4/81	Hércules (ESP) /Rayo Vallecano (ESP)	s78				s77		s71		8	1
Fatos BEĆIRAJ	5/5/88	Budućnost Podgorica /Dinamo Zagreb (CRO)	s83	s87		s84	s83	s56	A		11	1
Marko BAŠA	29/12/82	Lokomotiv Moskva (RUS)		D	D	D	D	D		D	13	1
Branko BOŠKOVIĆ	21/6/80	DC United (USA)		M74	M64	M46	M83				22	1
Mladen KAŠĆELAN	13/2/83	Jagiellonia (POL)			s77	s46	s62	M	M53	s82	15	-
Radoslav BATAK	15/8/77	Mogren				s92		D	D		22	1
Ivan FATIĆ	21/8/88	Cesena (ITA)						M59		s76	6	-
Dejan DAMJANOVIĆ	27/7/86	Seoul (KOR)						A			8	2
Srđan BLAŽIĆ	26/11/82	Standard (BEL)						s46			2	-
Marko ĆETKOVIĆ	10/7/86	Mogren						s76			1	-
Nikola DRINČIĆ	7/9/84	Krasnodar (RUS)							M	M	20	1
Petar GRBIĆ	7/8/88	Mogren							s53		1	-
Saša BALIĆ	29/1/90	Inter Zaprešić (CRO)							s86		1	-
Stevan JOVETIĆ	2/11/89	Fiorentina (ITA)								s72	14	6

CLUB-BY-CLUB

OFK BAR

Coach – Slavoljub Bubanja; (7/9/10) Zlatko Kostić
Founded – 2001
Stadium – Topolica (2,000)

2010				
14/8	Mogren	h	2-4	*Vuković, Mičeta*
21/8	Petrovac	a	3-0	*Jovančov 2, Fejzić*
25/8	Lovćen	h	2-5	*Nedović, Živković*
28/8	Sutjeska	a	1-3	*Begović*
11/9	Mladost	h	1-2	*Cicović*
18/9	Dečić	h	0-0	
25/9	Rudar	a	0-0	
29/9	Budućnost	h	0-0	
2/10	Grbalj	a	0-3	
16/10	Zeta	h	0-0	
23/10	Mornar	a	0-1	
30/10	Mogren	a	1-3	*Begović*
6/11	Petrovac	h	1-1	*Gačević*
13/11	Lovćen	a	1-0	*Nikezić*
20/11	Sutjeska	h	2-0	*Aković, Nikezić*
27/11	Mladost	a	0-1	
12/12	Dečić	a	1-1	*Nedović*
2011				
26/2	Rudar	h	0-2	
5/3	Budućnost	a	0-1	
9/3	Grbalj	h	1-0	*Savić*
12/3	Zeta	a	0-2	
16/3	Mornar	h	1-0	*Nedović*
19/3	Budućnost	h	1-2	*Savić*
2/4	Mogren	a	2-1	*Nedović, Ivanović*
9/4	Sutjeska	h	0-1	
16/4	Mornar	a	1-1	*Gačević*
23/4	Lovćen	a	0-1	
30/4	Grbalj	h	0-0	
4/5	Petrovac	a	0-0	
7/5	Dečić	h	3-0	*Nedović, Živković 2*
14/5	Mladost	a	1-3	*Ivanović*
21/5	Zeta	h	3-3	*Ivanović, Milić, Cicović*
28/5	Rudar	a	2-2	*Kovač, Kljajević*

Name	Nat	DoB	Pos	Aps	(s)	Gls
Zoran AKOVIĆ		25/11/88	G	13		1
Bojan BEGOVIĆ		1/4/83	M	31	(1)	2
Danko BUBANJA		15/12/88	D	11	(4)	
Nenad BUBANJA		1/7/84	D	1	(3)	
Miško CEKLIĆ		18/2/84	D	29		
Dragan CICOVIĆ	BIH	1/9/78	M	10	(3)	2
Edis ČINDRAK		15/10/81	M	5	(3)	
Arslan DACIĆ		25/8/82	G	10	(1)	
Dejan DAMJANOVIĆ		8/6/86	D	11	(1)	
Jasmin FEJZIĆ		16/9/85	M	1	(3)	1
Nikola GAČEVIĆ		13/11/84	M	20		2
Ivan IVANOVIĆ		6/5/92	M	16	(1)	3
Uroš JANKOVIĆ	SRB	22/9/85	D	9	(2)	
Dejan JOVANČOV		15/7/90	A	11	(6)	2
Miroslav JOVANOVIĆ	SRB	21/2/88	M	12	(3)	
Bojan KALEZIĆ		11/3/88	A	3	(5)	
Stefan KLJAJEVIĆ		19/5/90	M	1	(11)	1
Aleksandar KOVAČ		22/8/83	D	13	(2)	1
Milorad KRIVOKAPIĆ		14/5/85	M	2		
Kristijan KRSTOVIĆ		9/7/89	M	2	(6)	
Edi KUJOVIĆ		19/1/90	M	2	(1)	
Marko LJUMOVIĆ		12/2/79	M	3		
Boris MERDOVIĆ		23/8/90	M	14	(5)	
Rajko MIČETA	BIH	6/10/77	D	19	(1)	1
Dražen MILIĆ		14/9/80	A	13	(7)	1
Aleksandar NEDOVIĆ		5/9/78	M	25	(3)	5
Marko NENEZIĆ		27/4/82	M	1		
Miloš NIKEZIĆ		2/3/87	M	13	(4)	2
Miloš PEPĐONOVIĆ		20/10/90	D	16		
Mileta RADULOVIĆ		29/1/81	G	10	(1)	
Zdravko SAVIĆ	SRB	21/3/84	A	10	(2)	2
Miomir VUKOVIĆ		12/2/79	M	12	(1)	1
Tihomir ŽIVKOVIĆ	CRO	20/2/85	A	14	(10)	3

FK BUDUĆNOST PODGORICA

Coach – Nikola Rakojević; (15/12/10) Saša Petrović
Founded – 1925
Stadium – Gradski (12,000)
MAJOR HONOURS: Montenegrin League – (1) 2008.

2010				
14/8	Grbalj	h	2-1	*Vuković (p), Bećiraj*
21/8	Zeta	a	2-0	*Vuković, Bećiraj*
25/8	Mornar	h	3-1	*Kudemor, Vuković, Brnović*
29/8	Mogren	a	0-2	
11/9	Petrovac	h	4-3	*Mugoša M., Vuković 2, Đikanović*
18/9	Lovćen	a	3-1	*Bošković, Brnović, Vuković*
25/9	Sutjeska	h	2-1	*Vuković, Bošković*
29/9	Bar	a	0-0	
2/10	Dečić	h	2-2	*Vuković, Nikač*
16/10	Rudar	a	2-0	*Perutović, Brnović*
23/10	Mladost	h	3-3	*Vuković (p), Bošković, Golubović*
30/10	Grbalj	a	3-1	*Kudemor, Vuković, Vukčević P.*
6/11	Zeta	h	0-0	
13/11	Mornar	a	2-1	*Mugoša S., Vuković*
20/11	Mogren	h	1-2	*Golubović*
27/11	Petrovac	a	2-0	*Cicmil, Vuković*
4/12	Lovćen	h	2-0	*Perutović, Cicmil*
2011				
27/2	Sutjeska	a	2-1	*Bošković, Vuković*
5/3	Bar	h	1-0	*Kalezić*
9/3	Dečić	a	2-0	*Orahovac, Vukčević N.P.*
12/3	Rudar	h	0-1	
16/3	Mladost	a	2-0	*Vuković, Bošković*
19/3	Bar	a	2-1	*Bošković, Mugoša S.*
2/4	Lovćen	h	1-0	*Vukčević N.P.*
9/4	Grbalj	a	0-1	
16/4	Petrovac	h	1-1	*Vuković*
23/4	Dečić	a	0-0	
30/4	Mladost	h	2-0	*Mugoša S., Orahovac*
4/5	Zeta	a	2-2	*Vuković, Đikanović*
7/5	Rudar	h	2-1	*Bošković, Mugoša S.*
14/5	Mornar	h	3-2	*Vuković 2, Mugoša S.*
21/5	Mogren	a	2-1	*Mugoša S., Vuković (p)*
28/5	Sutjeska	h	3-0	*Vuković, Bošković, Mugoša S.*

Name	Nat	DoB	Pos	Aps	(s)	Gls
Goran ADAMOVIĆ	SRB	24/4/87	D	13		
Jasmin AGOVIĆ		13/2/91	G	3	(2)	
Dražen AJKOVIĆ		25/8/85	M	10	(11)	
Zoran BANOVIĆ		14/10/77	G	6		
Fatos BEĆIRAJ		5/5/88	A	4		2
Dragan BOŠKOVIĆ		27/12/85	M	30		8
Nenad BRNOVIĆ		18/1/80	M	20	(4)	3
Stefan CICMIL		16/8/90	D	6	(5)	2
Đorđe ĐIKANOVIĆ		18/8/84	D	18	(1)	2
Miloš DRAGOJEVIĆ		2/2/89	G	24		
Savo GAZIVODA		18/7/94	M		(1)	
Radivoje GOLUBOVIĆ		22/4/90	M	19	(6)	2
Miloš KALEZIĆ		9/8/93	M	4	(6)	1
Abraham KUDEMOR	GHA	25/2/85	M	14		2
Slobodan MAZIĆ	SRB	15/11/77	D	13	(5)	
Marko MUGOŠA		4/4/84	M	6	(2)	1
Stefan MUGOŠA		26/2/92	A	13	(6)	7
Darko NIKAČ		15/9/90	A	3	(18)	1
Jovan NIKOLIĆ		21/7/91	M	3	(5)	
Franck Michel ONGUÉNÉ	CMR	26/7/87	M	10	(1)	
Sanibal ORAHOVAC		12/12/78	M	12	(2)	2
Blažo PERUTOVIĆ		8/12/83	A	10	(4)	2
Ilija RADOVIĆ		5/9/85	D	13		
Milan RADULOVIĆ		18/8/81	D	5		
Risto RADUNOVIĆ		4/5/92	D	18		
Luka ROTKOVIĆ		5/7/88	A	1	(9)	
Luka TIODOROVIĆ		21/1/86	M	3	(3)	
Darko VUČIĆ		28/8/91	A	2	(4)	
Marko VUKČEVIĆ		7/6/93	M	1	(1)	
Nikola P. VUKČEVIĆ		22/3/84	D	16		2
Nikola S. VUKČEVIĆ		13/12/91	D	6		
Petar VUKČEVIĆ		15/8/87	D	23		1
Ivan VUKOVIĆ		9/2/87	A	33		20
Radule ŽIVKOVIĆ		1/11/90	D	1		

FK DEČIĆ

Coach – Mladen Vukićević
Founded – 1920
Stadium – Tuško polje (1,000)

010				
4/8	Mornar	h	2-0	*Đoković A., Lekić*
1/8	Mogren	a	0-5	
5/8	Petrovac	h	2-0	*Đukić, Šofranac*
3/8	Lovćen	a	0-1	
1/9	Sutjeska	h	1-0	*Grbović*
3/9	Bar	a	0-0	
5/9	Mladost	h	1-0	*Pepić*
9/9	Rudar	h	1-0	*Krnić*
/10	Budućnost	a	2-2	*Đoković A., Živković*
6/10	Grbalj	h	2-0	*Krnić, Grbović*
3/10	Zeta	a	0-0	
0/10	Mornar	a	0-1	
/11	Mogren	h	0-1	
3/11	Petrovac	a	0-2	
0/11	Lovćen	h	1-0	*Lekić*
7/11	Sutjeska	a	1-2	*Đukić*
2/12	Bar	h	1-1	*Đoković A.*
011				
6/2	Mladost	a	0-0	
/3	Rudar	a	0-1	
/3	Budućnost	h	0-2	
2/3	Grbalj	a	2-2	*Ikechukwu, Peličić*
6/3	Zeta	h	0-0	
9/3	Mornar	h	0-1	
/4	Mladost	a	0-1	
/4	Zeta	h	3-0	*Lekić, Pepić, Đukić*
6/4	Rudar	a	0-2	
23/4	Budućnost	h	0-0	
30/4	Mogren	a	1-4	*Grbović*
4/5	Sutjeska	h	0-0	
7/5	Bar	a	0-3	
14/5	Lovćen	h	2-0	*Marković, Lekić*
21/5	Grbalj	a	2-0	*Pepić, Đoković A.*
28/5	Petrovac	h	0-2	

Name	Nat	DoB	Pos	Aps	(s)	Gls
Aldin BEĆOVIĆ		4/1/92	D	2		
Fyodor BOLTUNOV	RUS	23/10/88	D		(1)	
Valjento CAMAJ	ALB	17/9/77	M		(6)	
Adis ĐOKOVIĆ		25/8/91	A	31		4
Edin ĐOKOVIĆ		14/12/84	D	8	(5)	
Enis ĐOKOVIĆ		27/2/87	G	29		
Igor DRAGIĆEVIĆ		20/8/75	M		(5)	
Vedad DREŠEVIĆ		22/8/80	G	1	(1)	
Dalibor ĐUKIĆ		16/9/86	M	28	(1)	3
Boris GRBOVIĆ		31/1/80	D	30		3
Ezeh IKECHUKWU	NGA	20/12/87	A	9	(10)	1
Edis JASAVIĆ		12/3/86	M	1		
Aleksandar KALJAJ		27/3/92	M	1		
Sead KRNIĆ		25/8/86	A	1	(20)	2
Edin LEKIĆ		23/6/79	M	25		4
Darko MARKOVIĆ		15/5/87	M	11		1
Miladin NELEVIĆ		15/3/86	M	27	(2)	
Aleksandar NENADOVIĆ		20/6/88	D		(8)	
Amar NUHODŽIĆ		12/9/90	M	10		
Njazim PADOVIĆ		19/11/87	D	27	(1)	
Milan PAVIĆEVIĆ		25/8/87	G	3		
Vladan PELIČIĆ		24/7/89	D	5		1
Rijad PEPIĆ		19/9/91	D	27	(5)	3
Demir RAMOVIĆ		3/1/82	D	24	(2)	
Nikola ROGOŠIĆ		22/5/80	D		(7)	
Nenad ŠOFRANAC		20/4/83	M	31		1
Mirko TODOROVIĆ	SRB	22/8/85	M	7	(2)	
Denis TUZOVIĆ		12/2/88	A		(9)	
Marko ŽIVKOVIĆ	SRB	1/6/83	M	21	(2)	1
Gojko ŽIŽIĆ		27/1/89	D	4	(8)	

FK GRBALJ

Coach – Saša Petrović; (9/11/10) Zvezdan Milošević (BIH); (12/3/11) Dragan Radojičić (SRB)
Founded – 1970
Stadium – SC Grbalj (1,500)

2010				
14/8	Budućnost	a	1-2	*Jovović (p)*
21/8	Mladost	a	2-1	*Kajević, Marković*
25/8	Zeta	h	1-1	*Uzoma*
28/8	Mornar	a	0-0	
12/9	Mogren	h	0-1	
18/9	Petrovac	a	1-0	*Bošković I.*
25/9	Lovćen	h	0-0	
29/9	Sutjeska	a	2-1	*Bošković I. 2*
2/10	Bar	h	3-0	*Simunović, Vasić, Bošković I.*
16/10	Dečić	a	0-2	
23/10	Rudar	h	0-1	
30/10	Budućnost	h	1-3	*Vuković*
6/11	Mladost	h	0-1	
13/11	Zeta	a	0-1	
20/11	Mornar	h	1-0	*Dragićević*
27/11	Mogren	a	0-0	
4/12	Petrovac	h	1-2	*Martinović*
2011				
27/2	Lovćen	a	0-1	
5/3	Sutjeska	h	0-0	
9/3	Bar	a	0-1	
12/3	Dečić	h	2-2	*Dragićević, Skopljak*
16/3	Rudar	a	1-0	*Mikijelj*
19/3	Zeta	h	1-1	*Radonjić*
2/4	Rudar	a	3-4	*Rossi, Mikijelj, Dragićević*
9/4	Budućnost	h	1-0	*Janković*
17/4	Mogren	a	0-2	
23/4	Sutjeska	h	5-0	*Rossi, Radonjić, Radulović, Nikolić, Dragićević*
30/4	Bar	a	0-0	
4/5	Lovćen	h	1-0	*Mikijelj*
7/5	Mornar	a	0-2	
14/5	Petrovac	a	2-1	*Mikijelj, Baković*
21/5	Dečić	h	0-2	
28/5	Mladost	a	1-3	*Vlaisavljević*

Name	Nat	DoB	Pos	Aps	(s)	Gls
Branko BAKOVIĆ	SRB	31/8/81	M	9		1
Darko BOŠKOVIĆ		16/9/87	M	3	(3)	
Ivan BOŠKOVIĆ		1/1/82	A	10	(2)	4
Nenad BOŠKOVIĆ		17/11/89	M	1	(11)	
Zdravko DRAGIĆEVIĆ		17/6/86	A	24	(2)	4
Ljubomir ĐUROVIĆ	SRB	25/8/89	G	19		
Novica GAČEVIĆ		30/6/90	G	13	(1)	
Ilija GLAVAN	BIH	22/11/90	D	14	(1)	
Bojan GOLUBOVIĆ		28/11/86	M	16		
JAIR Júnior Souto	BRA	26/2/87	M	2	(9)	
Branislav JANKOVIĆ		8/2/92	A	5	(9)	1
Aleksandar JOVANOVIĆ		1/6/92	D	6	(2)	
Miloš JOVANOVIĆ		29/1/88	A		(2)	
Saša JOVOVIĆ	SRB	6/9/86	A	8	(2)	1
Demir KAJEVIĆ		20/4/89	M	16	(1)	1
Miodrag KOPRIVICA		9/4/90	M	1	(5)	
Dušan KOSTIĆ	SRB	13/5/90	G	1		
Đuro MAGUD		24/7/92	M		(1)	
Slaven MARJANOVIĆ		23/11/93	M		(3)	
Stevan MARKOVIĆ		31/1/88	D	12		1
Vuk MARTINOVIĆ		19/9/89	D	26	(2)	1
Zoran MIKIJELJ		23/2/91	D	15	(1)	4
Goran MILOJKO		6/9/93	D		(2)	
Velibor MRŠULJA		5/6/93	M	1	(10)	
Baćo NIKOLIĆ		19/1/86		14	(1)	1
Miloš PEPĐONOVIĆ		10/7/90	D	1		
Saša POPOVIĆ		19/9/81	D	1		
Srđan RADONJIĆ		8/5/81	A	13		2
Nikola RADULOVIĆ		17/12/85	D	28		1
Igor RADUSINOVIĆ		15/3/84	D	27		
Renzo ROSSI	ARG	24/3/89	A	13		2
Andrija SIMUNOVIĆ		21/3/91	D	9	(4)	1
Nebojša SKOPLJAK	SRB	12/5/87	D	28		1
Sixtus UZOMA	NGA	5/2/78	M		(4)	1
Nenad VASIĆ	SRB	28/7/79	A	20		1
Miljan VLAISAVLJEVIĆ		27/8/90	M	3	(9)	1
Aleksandar VUKOVIĆ		30/9/92	D	2	(1)	1
Radovan ZEC		16/7/92	M	2	(4)	

FK LOVĆEN

Coach – Branislav Milačić; (20/12/10) Angelo Lombardo (ITA); (28/1/11) Marko Marković

Founded – 1913

Stadium – Obilica poljana (1,500)

2010

14/8	Mladost	h	0-0	
21/8	Sutjeska	h	1-1	*Jablan*
25/8	Bar	a	5-2	*Šćekić, Jablan, Bogdanović, Pejaković I., Radišić*
28/8	Dečić	h	1-0	*Bogdanović*
11/9	Rudar	a	1-1	*Stevović*
18/9	Budućnost	h	1-3	*Radović*
25/9	Grbalj	a	0-0	
29/9	Zeta	h	0-2	
2/10	Mornar	a	1-2	*Jablan (p)*
16/10	Mogren	h	0-1	
23/10	Petrovac	a	0-1	
30/10	Mladost	a	1-1	*Jablan*
6/11	Sutjeska	a	2-1	*Bogdanović 2 (1p)*
13/11	Bar	h	0-1	
20/11	Dečić	a	0-1	
27/11	Rudar	h	1-0	*Kaluđerović*
4/12	Budućnost	a	0-2	

2011

27/2	Grbalj	h	1-0	*Stevović*
5/3	Zeta	a	0-2	
9/3	Mornar	h	2-2	*Jablan, Radišić*
12/3	Mogren	a	0-0	
16/3	Petrovac	h	0-0	
19/3	Rudar	h	2-2	*Radunović V., Stevović*
2/4	Budućnost	a	0-1	
9/4	Mogren	h	0-1	
16/4	Sutjeska	a	2-0	*Jablan 2*
23/4	Bar	h	1-0	*Aleksić*
30/4	Mornar	a	1-0	*Jablan*
4/5	Grbalj	a	0-1	
7/5	Petrovac	h	3-2	*Jablan, Aleksić, Radović*
14/5	Dečić	a	0-2	
21/5	Mladost	h	2-2	*Jablan 2*
28/5	Zeta	a	1-2	*Vujović N.*

No Name	Nat	DoB	Pos	Aps	(s)	Gls
Zijad ADROVIĆ		17/2/86	M	19	(12)	
Srđan AJKOVIĆ		15/10/91	A	2	(4)	
Marko ALEKSIĆ	SRB	14/4/86	A	9	(1)	2
Žarko BELADA		10/6/77	D	14		
Dejan BOGDANOVIĆ		8/8/90	M	27	(2)	4
Saša ĆETKOVIĆ		29/5/82	D	27	(1)	
Ivan JABLAN		18/7/79	A	30	(1)	11
Andrija KALUĐEROVIĆ		29/10/93	M	21	(3)	1
Veljko KOLINOVIĆ		13/10/90	D	1	(1)	
Srđan LOPIČIĆ		20/11/83	D	13	(1)	
Luka MIRKOVIĆ		1/11/90	D	26	(3)	
Saša PAUNOVIĆ	SRB	3/12/85	M		(1)	
Andrija PEJAKOVIĆ		22/2/86	M	17	(6)	
Ivan PEJAKOVIĆ		22/8/92	M	7	(7)	1
Jovan PEROVIĆ		28/12/89	G	17		
Mirko RADIŠIĆ		1/10/90	D	25	(2)	2
Balša RADOVIĆ		4/1/91	M	3	(14)	2
Mihailo RADULOVIĆ		8/3/87	G	16	(1)	
Miloš RADUNOVIĆ		7/7/90	D	12	(1)	
Vladan RADUNOVIĆ		2/1/89	A	11	(4)	1
Aleksandar ŠĆEKIĆ		12/12/91	M	11	(2)	1
Miodrag STANOJEVIĆ		19/7/81	D	22	(7)	
Miloš STEVOVIĆ		14/9/89	M	25	(1)	3
Nenad VUJOVIĆ		2/1/89	D	7	(3)	1
Stevan VUJOVIĆ		13/12/89	A		(3)	
Luka VUŠUROVIĆ		24/2/90	D	1		

FK MLADOST PODGORICA

Coach – Miodrag Vukotić

Founded – 1950

Stadium – Cvijetni brijeg (1,500)

2010

14/8	Lovćen	a	0-0	
21/8	Grbalj	h	1-2	*Đurišić*
25/8	Sutjeska	a	1-2	*Seratlić*
28/8	Zeta	h	2-0	*Petrović, Seratlić (p)*
11/9	Bar	a	2-1	*Lakić, Jovanović*
18/9	Mornar	h	1-0	*Seratlić*
25/9	Dečić	a	0-1	
29/9	Mogren	h	2-2	*Šofranac, Đurišić*
2/10	Rudar	a	1-2	*Đurišić*
16/10	Petrovac	h	1-1	*Vučić*
23/10	Budućnost	a	3-3	*Đurišić 2, Krkeljić*
30/10	Lovćen	h	1-1	*Rašović*
6/11	Grbalj	a	1-0	*Đurišić (p)*
13/11	Sutjeska	h	5-1	*Šofranac, Krkeljić, Đurišić 2, Rašović*
20/11	Zeta	a	1-2	*Lakić*
27/11	Bar	h	1-0	*og (Živković)*
8/12	Mornar	a	0-0	

2011

26/2	Dečić	h	0-0	
5/3	Mogren	a	0-1	
9/3	Rudar	h	2-0	*Tomić, Savićević*
12/3	Petrovac	a	0-0	
16/3	Budućnost	h	0-2	
19/3	Petrovac	a	0-0	
2/4	Dečić	h	1-0	*Sekulić*
9/4	Mornar	h	0-1	
16/4	Zeta	a	0-1	
23/4	Rudar	h	1-3	*Merdović*
30/4	Budućnost	a	0-2	
4/5	Mogren	h	1-1	*Merdović*
7/5	Sutjeska	a	0-2	
14/5	Bar	h	3-1	*Raičević, Merdović, Sekulić*
21/5	Lovćen	a	2-2	*Merdović, Krkeljić*
28/5	Grbalj	h	3-1	*Merdović, Sekulić, Tomić*

Name	Nat	DoB	Pos	Aps	(s)	Gls
Boban ČABARKAPA		1/12/87	D	5	(3)	
Marko ČOLAKOVIĆ		20/7/80	M	16	(6)	
Milan ĐURIŠIĆ		11/4/87	M	14	(1)	8
Marko JOVANOVIĆ	SRB	2/5/82	A	3	(7)	1
Dušan JOVIĆEVIĆ		16/8/88	A		(1)	
Boris KLADNIK		18/9/90	A	1	(5)	
Nemanja KLJAJEVIĆ		5/3/87	M		(2)	
Đorđije KRKELJIĆ		30/7/90	A	10	(10)	3
Miloš LAKIĆ		21/12/85	D	33		2
Mirza LJUMIĆ		5/8/81	A	2	(4)	
Velimir LONČAR		5/5/90	M	16	(2)	
Nikola MARČELJA		17/8/89	G	8	(1)	
Lazar MARTINOVIĆ		3/7/89	M	1	(3)	
Luka MERDOVIĆ		14/3/89	M	11	(2)	5
Ivan MIJUŠKOVIĆ		15/7/88	A	10	(2)	
Dejan MUSTUR		2/12/86	G	22		
Milan PAVIĆEVIĆ		8/7/87	G	3		
Rade PETROVIĆ		21/9/82	M	31		1
Bracan POPOVIĆ		31/3/82	D	23		
Marko RADULOVIĆ		17/6/85	D	28	(1)	
Marko RAIČEVIĆ		31/5/88	M	9	(3)	1
Miloš RAŠOVIĆ		4/4/86	D	5	(11)	2
Nikola ROGOŠIĆ		22/5/80	D		(1)	
Ognjen ROLOVIĆ		12/6/88	A		(3)	
Vladimir SAVIĆEVIĆ		27/11/89	A	20	(8)	1
Radisav SEKULIĆ		27/9/85	A	8	(1)	3
Ermin SERATLIĆ		21/8/90	M	15		3
Mirko SPASOJEVIĆ		4/3/89	A		(2)	
Aleksandar ŠOFRANAC		21/10/90	M	31	(1)	2
Filip ŠUNDIĆ		7/3/90	M		(1)	
Luka TIODOROVIĆ		21/1/86	M	10	(1)	
Danilo TOMIĆ		18/7/85	M	12	(4)	2
Predrag VIDEKANIĆ		23/8/86	D		(3)	
Bojan VLAHOVIĆ		9/2/89	M		(1)	
Darko VUČIĆ		28/8/91	M	11	(4)	1
Nikola VUKČEVIĆ		16/8/92	D	5	(4)	

FK MOGREN

oach – Stevan Mojsilović (SRB); (13/4/11) Branislav Milačić
Founded – 1920
Stadium – Lugovi (3,000)
MAJOR HONOURS: Montenegrin League – (2) 2009, 2011; Montenegrin Cup – (1) 2008.

10

8	Bar	a	4-2	*Ćetković, Gluščević (p), Grbić, Ćulafić*
8	Dečić	h	5-0	*Božović D., Matić, Đokaj 2, Gluščević (p)*
8	Rudar	a	0-4	
8	Budućnost	h	2-0	*Grbić, Ćetković*
9	Grbalj	a	1-0	*Ćetković*
9	Zeta	h	0-0	
9	Mornar	a	5-0	*Gluščević 2 (1p), Matić 2, Nuhi*
9	Mladost	a	2-2	*Nerić, Gluščević*
0	Petrovac	h	3-1	*Simović, Matić, Gluščević*
10	Lovćen	a	1-0	*Ćetković*
10	Sutjeska	h	4-1	*Gluščević 2 (1p), Tatar, Matić*
10	Bar	h	3-1	*Božović D. 2, Gluščević*
1	Dečić	a	1-0	*Gluščević*
11	Rudar	h	1-0	*Grbić*
/11	Budućnost	a	2-1	*Ćetković, Gluščević*
11	Grbalj	h	0-0	
2	Zeta	a	2-1	*Batak, Ćetković*

11

/2	Mornar	h	2-0	*Ćetković, Batak*
3	Mladost	h	1-0	*Zec R.*
3	Petrovac	a	0-0	
/3	Lovćen	h	0-0	
/3	Sutjeska	a	4-1	*Đokaj, Ćetković, Grbić, Matić*
/3	Sutjeska	a	1-3	*Batak*
4	Bar	h	1-2	*Božović D.*
4	Lovćen	a	1-0	*Ranđelović*
/4	Grbalj	h	2-0	*Jovanović, Matić*
/4	Petrovac	a	1-1	*Simović*
/4	Dečić	h	4-1	*Batak, Ranđelović 2, Grbić*
5	Mladost	a	1-1	*Đokaj*
5	Zeta	h	2-0	*Vujović, Matić*
/5	Rudar	a	1-0	*Ćulafić*
/5	Budućnost	h	1-2	*Zec R.*
/5	Mornar	h	2-0	*Batak, Matić*

ame	Nat	DoB	Pos	Aps	(s)	Gls
arko BAKIĆ		1/11/93	M		(4)	
adoslav BATAK		15/8/77	D	29		5
alša BOŽOVIĆ		1/5/87	M	1	(10)	
raško BOŽOVIĆ		30/6/88	D	26		4
arko ĆETKOVIĆ		10/7/86	M	21	(8)	8
anilo ĆULAFIĆ		1/8/86	M	6	(9)	2
rdian ĐOKAJ		25/3/79	M	14	(5)	4
tefan ĐORĐEVIĆ		16/11/90	A		(2)	
arko ĐUROVIĆ		8/5/88	M	1	(2)	
ladimir GLUŠČEVIĆ		20/10/79	A	16		11
etar GRBIĆ		7/8/88	M	24	(2)	5
emanja JANIČIĆ	BIH	13/7/86	D	2		
an JANJUŠEVIĆ		11/7/87	G	20		
oran JOVANOVIĆ	SRB	8/5/77	M	19	(10)	1
asilije JOVOVIĆ		12/5/86	A	1	(2)	
leksandar KAPISODA		17/9/89	D	3	(1)	
leksandar MADŽAR		21/8/78	M	1	(2)	
azar MARTINOVIĆ		3/7/89	M		(1)	
gor MATIĆ	SRB	22/7/81	M	28	(2)	9
ejan MILOŠEVIĆ		18/8/93	D		(1)	
ndrija MIRKOVIĆ		13/12/83	M	28	(1)	
ilenko NERIĆ		9/2/88	A	2	(3)	1
jazdin NUHI	SRB	10/10/79	M	17	(6)	1
uka PEJOVIĆ		31/7/85	D	14		
emanja POPOVIĆ		20/5/84	G	13		
tefan RAČIĆ		2/7/90	A		(1)	
redrag RANĐELOVIĆ		13/9/76	A	14	(1)	3
anko SIMOVIĆ		2/4/87	D	31		2
ladan TATAR		28/1/84	M	23	(2)	1
ikola VUJOVIĆ		23/6/81	M	6	(2)	1
iodrag ZEC		4/10/82	M	2	(9)	
atko ZEC		24/3/77	A	1	(9)	2

FK MORNAR

Coach – Dušan Jevrić (SRB); (29/9/10) Boris Ljutica
Founded – 1931
Stadium – Topolica (2,000)

2010

14/8	Dečić	a	0-2	
21/8	Rudar	h	0-1	
25/8	Budućnost	a	1-3	*Peričić*
28/8	Grbalj	h	0-0	
11/9	Zeta	a	0-4	
18/9	Mladost	a	0-1	
25/9	Mogren	h	0-5	
29/9	Petrovac	a	1-1	*Čekić*
2/10	Lovćen	h	2-1	*Metović, Nenezić M. (p)*
16/10	Sutjeska	a	0-2	
23/10	Bar	h	1-0	*Vuković*
30/10	Dečić	h	1-0	*Čekić*
6/11	Rudar	a	1-2	*Čekić*
13/11	Budućnost	h	1-2	*Petrović*
20/11	Grbalj	a	0-1	
27/11	Zeta	h	0-0	
8/12	Mladost	h	0-0	

2011

26/2	Mogren	a	0-2	
5/3	Petrovac	h	1-2	*og (Mihailović)*
9/3	Lovćen	a	2-2	*Vujačić, Jovović*
12/3	Sutjeska	h	2-1	*Vuković, Vujačić*
16/3	Bar	a	0-1	
19/3	Dečić	a	1-0	*og (Grbović)*
2/4	Sutjeska	h	3-1	*Kasapi, Jovović 2*
9/4	Mladost	a	1-0	*Lalević*
16/4	Bar	h	1-1	*Mirković*
23/4	Zeta	a	0-3	
30/4	Lovćen	h	0-1	
4/5	Rudar	a	1-1	*Vujačić*
7/5	Grbalj	h	2-0	*Lalević, Vujačić*
14/5	Budućnost	a	2-3	*Vuković, Jovović*
21/5	Petrovac	h	1-0	*Jovović*
28/5	Mogren	a	0-2	

Name	Nat	DoB	Pos	Aps	(s)	Gls
Nikola ALEKSIĆ		28/3/88	G		(1)	
Zoran BANOVIĆ		14/10/77	G	17		
Miloš BOKAN		10/7/88	M	21	(2)	
Slobodan ČABARKAPA		22/8/91	D		(1)	
Emir ČEKIĆ		30/12/84	M	16	(1)	3
Marko DABOVIĆ		31/1/91	G	3		
Boško DOPUĐ		9/12/90	D	12	(5)	
Salih HAMIDOVIĆ		23/6/90	M	6	(2)	
Aleksandar JELENIĆ		6/12/89	D	9	(2)	
Saša JOVOVIĆ		6/9/86	A	11		5
Vuk JOVOVIĆ		9/7/93	A	4	(1)	
Fitim KASAPI	ALB	19/5/83	A	11		1
Ilija LALEVIĆ		26/11/87	A	26	(1)	2
Lazar LALOŠEVIĆ		7/5/95	A		(2)	
Dragiša LAZIĆ	BIH	1/6/83	A	3	(2)	
Nemanja LEVERDA		15/3/92	A	1	(2)	
Aleksandar MADŽAR		21/8/78	A	5	(2)	
Vuko MADŽGALJ		16/7/93	M		(3)	
Danijel MARKOLOVIĆ		21/7/90	M	1	(3)	
Ivan MAŠANOVIĆ		25/4/88	D		(9)	
Dragan MASONČIĆ		1/11/88	G	13		
Mustafa METOVIĆ		6/11/92	M	10	(10)	1
Uroš MILOŠEVIĆ		19/10/93	M		(5)	
Ivan MIRKOVIĆ		9/8/81	M	7	(6)	1
Željko MRVALJEVIĆ		8/4/81	D	8	(3)	
Dejan NENEZIĆ		17/11/80	D	13		
Marko NENEZIĆ		27/4/82	M	12		1
Boban OBRADOVIĆ	BIH	4/6/79	D	9	(4)	
Ervin PERIČIĆ		9/7/88	M	8	(7)	1
Mihailo PETROVIĆ		12/12/89	D	26	(3)	1
Mirko SPASOJEVIĆ		7/9/92	A		(3)	
Goran STOJKOVIĆ	SRB	6/12/83	D	7	(1)	
Željko TOMAŠEVIĆ		5/4/88	D	28	(2)	
Đorđe VOJVODIĆ		31/5/86	D	27		
Miloš VRANEŠ		27/7/88	M	8	(8)	
Nemanja VUČEVIĆ		1/2/90	A	2	(1)	
Vule VUJAČIĆ		20/3/88	A	9	(3)	4
Zoran VUKOVIĆ		7/7/79	D	30		3

OFK PETROVAC

Coach – Dejan Mrvaljević; (1/9/10) Dragoljub Đuretić; (1/10/10) Milorad Malovrazić

Founded – 1969

Stadium – Pod Malim brdom (1,500)

MAJOR HONOURS: Montenegrin Cup – (1) 2009.

2010				
14/8	Sutjeska	a	1-1	*Rotković*
21/8	Bar	h	0-3	
25/8	Dečić	a	0-2	
28/8	Rudar	h	0-2	
11/9	Budućnost	a	3-4	*Milić, Rotković 2*
18/9	Grbalj	h	0-1	
25/9	Zeta	a	0-1	
29/9	Mornar	h	1-1	*Radović*
2/10	Mogren	a	1-3	*Ljumić*
16/10	Mladost	a	1-1	*Rotković*
23/10	Lovćen	h	1-0	*Čarapić*
30/10	Sutjeska	h	1-0	*Rotković*
6/11	Bar	a	1-1	*Radović*
13/11	Dečić	h	2-0	*Milić, Rotković*
20/11	Rudar	a	0-3	
27/11	Budućnost	h	0-2	
4/12	Grbalj	a	2-1	*Milić, Rotković*
2011				
26/2	Zeta	h	2-0	*Muhović, Zvicer*
5/3	Mornar	a	2-1	*Milić, Jovanović*
9/3	Mogren	h	0-0	
12/3	Mladost	h	0-0	
16/3	Lovćen	a	0-0	
19/3	Mladost	h	0-0	
3/4	Zeta	a	1-0	*Mikijelj*
9/4	Rudar	h	0-1	
16/4	Budućnost	a	1-1	*Jovanović*
23/4	Mogren	h	1-1	*Jovanović*
30/4	Sutjeska	a	0-2	
4/5	Bar	h	0-0	
7/5	Lovćen	a	2-3	*Zvicer, Nenezić*
14/5	Grbalj	h	1-2	*Novović*
21/5	Mornar	a	0-1	
28/5	Dečić	a	2-0	*Muhović, Vujačić A.*

Name	Nat	DoB	Pos	Aps	(s)	Gls
Vladimir BARAĆ	SRB	29/8/81	M	4	(4)	
Aleksandar BRAIĆ		19/2/85	G	2		
Ivan ČARAPIĆ		18/2/81	D	9	(2)	1
Nikola ČELEBIĆ		4/7/89	D	28	(1)	
Miloš DELIĆ		22/5/83	M	1		
Bojan GOLUBOVIĆ		28/11/86	M	15		
Siniša GRAOVAC	BIH	1/9/84	D	24		
Aleksandar JELENIĆ		6/12/89	M	1	(1)	
Nenad JOVANOVIĆ	SRB	3/10/84	M	14	(1)	3
Vasilije JOVOVIĆ		12/5/86	M	5	(6)	
Benjamin KACIĆ		28/6/91	M	17	(10)	
Boris KLADNIK		26/10/90	A	1	(10)	
Mirza LJUMIĆ		5/8/81	A	1	(10)	1
Marko MARKOVIĆ		5/9/87	M	14	(8)	
Toni MEGLENSKI	MKD	22/5/81	M	3	(2)	
Nikola MIHAILOVIĆ		15/9/84	D	27		
Aleksandar MIKIJELJ		5/2/79	D	25	(2)	1
Božo MILIĆ		10/10/81	A	28		4
Jasmin MUHOVIĆ		2/4/89	M	11	(12)	2
Dejan NENEZIĆ		17/11/80	M	3	(4)	1
Milivoje NOVOVIĆ		29/2/84	D	10	(4)	1
Boban OBRADOVIĆ	BIH	4/6/79	M	3	(5)	
Davor POPOVIĆ		18/7/85	M	10	(3)	
Miljan RADOVIĆ		18/10/75	M	16	(1)	2
Marko RAIČEVIĆ		31/5/88	M	8	(3)	
Luka ROTKOVIĆ		5/7/88	A	17		7
Petar STANIŠIĆ		23/9/84	D	13		
Pavle VELIMIROVIĆ		4/11/90	G	31		
Bojan VLAHOVIĆ		9/2/89	M		(2)	
Milan VUČKOVIĆ		23/1/87	D	6	(4)	
Aleksandar VUJAČIĆ		9/7/90	A		(3)	1
Nenad VUJAČIĆ		15/1/92	M	1		
Krsto ZVICER		10/6/87	A	15		2

FK RUDAR PLJEVLJA

Coach – Nebojša Vignjević (SRB)

Founded – 1914

Stadium – Pod Golubinjom (8,000)

MAJOR HONOURS: Montenegrin League – (1) 2010; Montenegrin Cup – (3) 2007, 2010, 2011.

2010				
15/8	Zeta	h	2-1	*Jovanović I., Mićić*
21/8	Mornar	a	1-0	*Jovanović I.*
25/8	Mogren	h	4-0	*Ranđelović 2, Jovanović I. 2*
28/8	Petrovac	a	2-0	*Bojić, Mićić*
11/9	Lovćen	h	1-1	*Jovanović I.*
18/9	Sutjeska	a	0-0	
25/9	Bar	h	0-0	
29/9	Dečić	a	0-1	
2/10	Mladost	h	2-1	*Idrizović, Jovanović I.*
16/10	Budućnost	h	0-2	
23/10	Grbalj	a	1-0	*Jovanović I.*
31/10	Zeta	a	0-1	
6/11	Mornar	h	2-1	*Useni, Ranđelović (p)*
14/11	Mogren	a	0-1	
20/11	Petrovac	h	3-0	*Mrdak 2, Franciśković*
27/11	Lovćen	a	0-1	
4/12	Sutjeska	h	3-0	*Ranđelović, Bojović, Jovanović M.*
2011				
26/2	Bar	a	2-0	*Bojić, Mrdak*
5/3	Dečić	h	1-0	*Bojić (p)*
9/3	Mladost	a	0-2	
12/3	Budućnost	a	1-0	*Bojić*
16/3	Grbalj	h	0-1	
19/3	Lovćen	a	2-2	*Jovanović I. 2*
2/4	Grbalj	h	4-3	*Jovanović I., Franciśković 2, Adžić*
9/4	Petrovac	a	1-0	*Franciśković*
16/4	Dečić	h	2-0	*Lutovac, Useni*
23/4	Mladost	a	3-1	*Mićić, Mrdak, Jovanović I.*
30/4	Zeta	h	2-2	*og (Petrović), Vlahović*
4/5	Mornar	h	1-1	*Jovanović I.*
7/5	Budućnost	a	1-2	*Bojić*
14/5	Mogren	h	0-1	
21/5	Sutjeska	a	1-2	*Mrdak*
28/5	Bar	h	2-2	*Jovanović I., Mrdak*

Name	Nat	DoB	Pos	Aps	(s)	Gls
Vladan ADŽIĆ		5/7/87	D	16	(1)	1
Aldin AGOVIĆ		18/4/93	D	2	(1)	
Slobodan ASANOVIĆ		27/8/93	G	1		
Veselin BOJIĆ		16/6/77	D	26		5
Mijuško BOJOVIĆ		9/8/88	D	14		1
Predrag BRNOVIĆ		22/10/86	M	28	(4)	
Dejan DAMJANOVIĆ		8/7/86	D	1	(1)	
Ivica FRANCIŠKOVIĆ	SRB	28/9/78	M	21	(3)	4
Serge GUEÏ	CIV	30/5/91	A	3		
Ferid IDRIZOVIĆ		10/9/82	M	3	(12)	1
Blažo IGUMANOVIĆ		19/1/86	D	26	(1)	
Bojan IVANOVIĆ		3/12/81	D	25	(2)	
Igor VANOVIĆ		5/7/92	D	7	(1)	
Vojin JEKNIĆ		13/6/93	M		(1)	
Ivica JOVANOVIĆ	SRB	4/12/87	A	22	(9)	13
Miroje JOVANOVIĆ		10/3/87	A	18	(14)	1
Darko KARADŽIĆ		17/4/89	M		(4)	
Nemanja KLJAJEVIĆ		5/3/87	D	6	(1)	
Stefan LUTOVAC		15/4/86	D	7	(1)	1
Dušan MIĆIĆ	SRB	29/11/84	M	19	(4)	3
Milan MIJATOVIĆ		26/7/87	G	28		
Aleksandar MINIĆ		13/11/75	A	2	(5)	
Milivoje MRDAK		17/2/93	A	10	(9)	6
Miloš POPOVIĆ		8/12/92	M	11	(5)	
Miloš RADANOVIĆ		5/11/80	G	4		
Predrag RANĐELOVIĆ	SRB	13/9/76	A	15	(1)	4
Edi RUSTEMOVIĆ	SRB	7/12/89	M	1		
Nikola SEKULIĆ		10/4/81	M	15	(6)	
Jovan ŠLJIVANČANIN		8/3/94	M	1		
Danilo TOMIĆ		23/6/86	M	1	(3)	
Nermin USENI	SRB	13/3/80	M	22	(2)	2
Nedeljko VLAHOVIĆ		15/1/84	M	8	(6)	1

FK SUTJESKA

Coach – Pero Giljen; (1/1/11) Nikola Rakojević; (5/4/11) Dragan Mijanović

Founded – 1927

Stadium – Kraj Bistrice (8,000)

10				
/8	Petrovac	h	1-1	*Dževerdanović M.*
/8	Lovćen	a	1-1	*Banda*
/8	Mladost	h	2-1	*Međedović, Marković*
/8	Bar	h	3-1	*Marković 3*
/9	Dečić	a	0-1	
/9	Rudar	h	0-0	
/9	Budućnost	a	1-2	*Marković*
/9	Grbalj	h	1-2	*Ćiraković*
10	Zeta	a	1-3	*Marković*
/10	Mornar	h	2-0	*Pejović, Marković*
/10	Mogren	a	1-4	*Bulajić B.R.*
/10	Petrovac	a	0-1	
11	Lovćen	h	1-2	*Međedović (p)*
/11	Mladost	a	1-5	*Marković*
/11	Bar	a	0-2	
/11	Dečić	h	2-1	*Marković 2*
12	Rudar	a	0-3	
011				
/2	Budućnost	h	1-2	*Marković*
3	Grbalj	a	0-0	
3	Zeta	h	1-1	*Bulajić B.R.*
2/3	Mornar	a	1-2	*Marković*
6/3	Mogren	h	1-4	*Vuković*
9/3	Mogren	h	3-1	*Bakoč 2, Marković*
4	Mornar	a	1-3	*Marković*
4	Bar	a	1-0	*Marković*
6/4	Lovćen	h	0-2	
3/4	Grbalj	a	0-5	
0/4	Petrovac	h	2-0	*Dubljević 2*
/5	Dečić	a	0-0	
/5	Mladost	h	2-0	*Marković, Bulajić B.R.*
4/5	Zeta	a	0-0	
1/5	Rudar	h	2-1	*Ćuković, Vuković*
8/5	Budućnost	a	0-3	

Name	Nat	DoB	Pos	Aps	(s)	Gls
uka BAKOČ		23/11/86	A	11		2
ojan BAKRAČ		10/4/93	G	1		
ead BANDA		16/6/90	A	6	(6)	1
oris R. BULAJIĆ		27/4/88	M	31		3
oris V. BULAJIĆ		25/12/90	G	1		
arko BULATOVIĆ		5/9/89	D	13	(2)	
omislav ĆIRAKOVIĆ		10/10/84	M	10	(1)	1
gor ĆUKOVIĆ		6/6/93	D	3	(3)	1
Mitar DAKOVIĆ		20/7/91	M	1	(1)	
Milivoje DELIĆ		14/5/88	D	4		
Bojan DRINČIĆ		11/6/93	D	1		
Aleksandar DUBLJEVIĆ		9/3/84	D	9		2
Mirko DURUTOVIĆ		13/3/89	M	9	(2)	
Marko DŽEVERDANOVIĆ		3/11/81	D	16	(3)	1
Nikola DŽEVERDANOVIĆ		23/10/80	D	28	(1)	
Vukajlo ĐUKIĆ		12/10/83	M	6	(4)	
Dragan JAKOVLJEVIĆ		9/4/92	A		(2)	
Božidar JANJUŠEVIĆ		30/3/94	D		(1)	
Stefan JAREDIĆ		29/11/93	M	1	(1)	
Bojan KALEZIĆ		11/3/88	M	5	(2)	
Marko KASALICA		13/10/86	A	7	(10)	
Nemanja KOSOVIĆ		15/5/93	D	1		
Milorad KRIVOKAPIĆ		14/5/85	D	14		
Boris LAKIĆEVIĆ		24/10/88	G	31		
Nikola LONČAR		2/3/91	A		(3)	
Božo MARKOVIĆ		26/10/89	A	28	(1)	16
Dražen MEĐEDOVIĆ		15/10/82	M	15		2
Jovan NIKOLIĆ		21/7/91	M	13		
Miloš NIKOLIĆ		28/2/93	A	2	(5)	
Milovan NIKOLIĆ		16/8/93	M	5	(6)	
Nemanja OSTOJIĆ		30/7/91	M	1		
Andrija PEJOVIĆ		8/7/91	M	21	(8)	1
Petar PEROŠEVIĆ		14/1/89	M	4	(12)	
Marko SPASOJEVIĆ		3/7/88	M	5	(10)	
Nikola STIJEPOVIĆ		8/9/94	D	1		
Miroslav TODOROVIĆ		29/3/87	M	16	(4)	
Nikola VUČINIĆ		23/6/93	M		(1)	
Ivan VUJAČIĆ		22/6/85	D	1		
Danilo VUKOVIĆ	SRB	1/4/89	D	31		2
Darko ZORIĆ		12/9/93	M	7		
Krsto ZVICER		10/6/87	A	4	(7)	

FK ZETA

Coach – Dragoljub Đuretić; (31/8/10) Dejan Vukićević

Founded – 1927

Stadium – Trešnjica (4,000)

MAJOR HONOURS: Montenegrin League – (1) 2007.

2010				
15/8	Rudar	a	1-2	*Došljak*
21/8	Budućnost	h	0-2	
25/8	Grbalj	a	1-1	*Korać*
28/8	Mladost	a	0-2	
11/9	Mornar	h	4-0	*Zlatičanin, Lađić, Korać, Burzanović*
18/9	Mogren	a	0-0	
25/9	Petrovac	h	1-0	*Lađić*
29/9	Lovćen	a	2-0	*Korać 2*
2/10	Sutjeska	h	3-1	*Boljević, Lađić, Korać*
16/10	Bar	a	0-0	
23/10	Dečić	h	0-0	
31/10	Rudar	h	1-0	*Korać (p)*
6/11	Budućnost	a	0-0	
13/11	Grbalj	h	1-0	*Korać*
20/11	Mladost	h	2-1	*Korać, Orlandić*
27/11	Mornar	a	0-0	
5/12	Mogren	h	1-2	*Došljak*
2011				
26/2	Petrovac	a	0-2	
5/3	Lovćen	h	2-0	*Korać, Božović*
9/3	Sutjeska	a	1-1	*Korać*
12/3	Bar	h	2-0	*Škuletić, Knežević*
16/3	Dečić	a	0-0	
19/3	Grbalj	a	1-1	*Korać*
3/4	Petrovac	h	0-1	
9/4	Dečić	a	0-3	
16/4	Mladost	h	1-0	*Došljak*
23/4	Mornar	h	3-0	*Korać 2, Škuletić*
30/4	Rudar	a	2-2	*Korać 2*
4/5	Budućnost	h	2-2	*Korać 2*
7/5	Mogren	a	0-2	
14/5	Sutjeska	h	0-0	
21/5	Bar	a	3-3	*Korać 2, Petrović*
28/5	Lovćen	h	2-1	*Ćetković, Peličić*

Name	Nat	DoB	Pos	Aps	(s)	Gls
Veljko BATROVIĆ		10/10/94	A	1		
Vladimir BOLJEVIĆ		17/1/88	M	17		1
Balša BOŽOVIĆ		1/5/87	M	11	(2)	1
Davor BRNOVIĆ		17/1/88	G	2		
Goran BURZANOVIĆ		4/8/84	M	28	(2)	1
Đorđije ĆETKOVIĆ		3/1/83	M	7	(2)	1
Aleksandar DABIĆ	SRB	1/5/91	D	1	(1)	
Miroslav DABIĆ	SRB	1/5/91	A		(5)	
Boris DOŠLJAK		4/6/89	M	3	(28)	3
Marko ĐURETIĆ		17/2/86	M	2	(2)	
Saša IVANOVIĆ		26/6/84	G	31		
Filip KALAČEVIĆ		12/3/94	A		(2)	
Momčilo KALEZIĆ		19/4/89	A	4	(1)	
Miroslav KALUĐEROVIĆ		4/2/86	D	27		
Ivan KNEŽEVIĆ		22/2/86	A	3	(6)	1
Žarko KORAĆ		11/6/87	A	32		19
Miloš KRKOTIĆ		29/9/87	M	10	(12)	
Kristijan KRSTOVIĆ		9/7/89	M	8	(5)	
Aleksa LAĐIĆ		7/7/86	M	21	(1)	3
Igor LAMBULIĆ		21/8/88	A		(1)	
Nenad MATIĆ		20/11/91	D	4	(3)	
Ivan NOVOVIĆ		26/4/89	M	11	(3)	
Petar ORLANDIĆ		6/8/90	A	2	(8)	1
Zarija PELIČIĆ		22/1/89	M	25	(2)	1
Gavrilo PETROVIĆ		21/5/84	D	29		1
Milan RADULOVIĆ		18/8/81	D	4		
Miloš B. RADULOVIĆ		23/2/90	D	9	(3)	
Miloš M. RADULOVIĆ		6/8/90	D	25		
Jovan SIMOVIĆ		4/11/82	D	4	(6)	
Petar ŠKULETIĆ		29/6/90	M	13	(2)	2
Miroslav ZLATIČANIN	SRB	26/5/85	D	29	(1)	1

TOP GOALSCORERS 2010/11

20	Ivan VUKOVIĆ (Budućnost)
19	Žarko KORAĆ (Zeta)
16	Božo MARKOVIĆ (Sutjeska)
13	Ivica JOVANOVIĆ (Rudar)
11	Ivan JABLAN (Lovćen) Vladimir GLUŠČEVIĆ (Mogren)
9	Igor MATIĆ (Mogren)
8	Dragan BOŠKOVIĆ (Budućnost) Milan ĐURIŠIĆ (Mladost) Marko ĆETKOVIĆ (Mogren)

PROMOTED CLUBS

FK BOKELJ

Coach – Slobodan Drašković
Founded – 1922
Stadium – Pod Vrmcem (5,000)

FK BERANE

Coach – Slobodan Đukić
Founded – 1920
Stadium – Gradski (7,000)

SECOND LEVEL FINAL TABLE 2010/11

		Pld	W	D	L	F	A	Pts
1	FK Bokelj	33	24	5	4	61	22	77
2	FK Jedinstvo Bijelo Polje	33	14	11	8	33	28	53
3	FK Berane	33	15	6	12	46	32	51
4	FK Bratstvo	33	14	6	13	46	34	48
5	FK Iskra	33	12	11	10	39	40	47
6	FK Kom	33	12	9	12	37	31	45
7	FK Ibar	33	10	14	9	33	33	44
8	FK Čelik Nikšić	33	11	9	13	37	34	42
9	FK Jezero	33	10	10	13	38	57	39
10	FK Zabjelo	33	7	13	13	34	48	34
11	FK Otrant	33	6	12	15	36	56	30
12	FK Pljevlja	33	5	10	18	25	50	25

NB FK Jezero - 1 pt deducted.

PROMOTION/RELEGATION PLAY-OFFS

(1/6/11 & 5/6/11)
Jedinstvo 0, Sutjeska 0
Sutjeska 1, Jedinstvo 0
(Sutjeska 1-0)

Mornar 1, Berane 1
Berane 0, Mornar 0
(1-1; Berane on away goal)

DOMESTIC CUP 2010/11

KUPA CRNE GORE

FIRST ROUND

(14/9/10)
Petnjica 0, Mornar 2

(15/9/10)
Arsenal 0, Bar 1
Berane 2, Pljevlja 1997 2 *(aet; 3-4 on pens)*
Bokelj 0, Lovćen 0 *(aet; 2-0 on pens)*
Cetinje 0, Jezero 2
Crvena stijena 0, Čelik 0 *(aet; 7-6 on pens)*
Gornja Zeta 1, Grbalj 1 *(aet; 9-8 on pens)*
Ibar 1, Zeta 5
Mladost Podgorica 3, Bratstvo
Mogren 3, Jedinstvo 0
Polimlje 0, Dečić 5
Sutjeska 7, Otrant 0
Zabjelo 0, Iskra 2

(22/9/10)
Kom 0, Petrovac 0 *(aet; 8-9 on pens)*

Byes – Budućnost Podgorica, Rudar Pljevlja

SECOND ROUND

(20/10/10 & 3/11/10)
Bar v Mornar 1-0; 1-1 *(2-1)*
Bokelj v Mogren 0-3; 0-1 *(0-4)*
Gornja Zeta v Budućnost Podgorica 0-4; 0-6 *(0-10)*
Iskra v Sutjeska 1-2; 0-2 *(1-4)*
Mladost Podgorica v Dečić 0-0; 1-2 *(1-2)*
Petrovac v Jezero 3-0; 2-0 *(5-0)*
Rudar Pljevlja v Crvena stijena 2-0; 2-1 *(4-1)*
Zeta v Pljevlja 1997 1-0; 3-0 *(4-0)*

QUARTER-FINALS

(24/11/10 & 8/12/10)
Bar 1 *(Vuković 89p)*, Mogren 1 *(Jovanović 24)*
Mogren 2 *(Batak 16, Nerić 43)*, Bar 1 *(Jovančov 45)*
(Mogren 3-2)

Budućnost Podgorica 0, Petrovac 0
Petrovac 2 *(Cicmil 16og, Rotković 28)*, Budućnost Podgorica 0
(Petrovac 2-0)

(24/11/10 & 9/12/10)
Rudar Pljevlja 0, Sutjeska 0
Sutjeska 1 *(Kasalica 50p)*, Rudar Pljevlja 2 *(Bojić 33p, Mićić 50)*
(Rudar Pljevlja 2-1)

(1/12/10 & 8/12/10)
Dečić 0, Zeta 0
Zeta 2 *(Došljak 1, Burzanović 19)*, Dečić 0
(Zeta 2-0)

SEMI-FINALS

(13/4/11 & 27/4/11)
Mogren 2 *(Ćetković 51, Matić 60)*, Petrovac 0
Petrovac 0, Mogren 2 *(Bakić 39, 85)*
(Mogren 4-0)

(20/4/11 & 27/4/11)
Rudar Pljevlja 1 *(Mićić 65)*, Zeta 0
Zeta 2 *(Škuletić 71, Lađić 85)*, Rudar Pljevlja 2 *(Jovanović I. 11, Popović 15)*
(Rudar Pljevlja 3-2)

FINAL

(25/5/11)
Stadion pod Goricom, Podgorica
FK RUDAR PLJEVLJA 2 *(Vlahović 53, Bojić 97p)*
FK MOGREN 2 *(Đokaj 15p, Ćetković 112)*
(aet; 5-4 on pens)

Referee – *Spasojević*
RUDAR PLJEVLJA – *Mijatović, Ivanović I. (Asanović 15), Adžić, Igumanović, Ivanović B., Vlahović, (Popović 63), Bojić, Useni (Lutovac 75), Franciškovič, Jovanović I., Jovanović M.*
Sent off: *Mijatović (15)*
MOGREN – *Janjušević, Kapisoda (Ćetković 63), Simović, Batak, Božović D., Đokaj, Tatar, Jovanović (Mirković 71), Matić, Ranđelović (Vujović 66), Grbić.*
Sent off: *Grbić (63)*

CLUB COMMUNICATION 2011/12

K Berane
'adski stadion bb
E-84300 Berane

el +382 69 049 726
ax +382 51 236 530
'eb
mail fkberane@t-com.me
edia Officer Fuad Ramusović

'K Bokelj
lica Njegoševa bb, p.fah: 5
'E-85300 Kotor

el +382 69 865 411
ax +382 32 322 197
/eb
:mail
ledia Officer Draško Braunović

'K Budućnost Podgorica
:amp FK Budućnost
1E-81000 Podgorica

'el +382 67 900 9900
'ax +382 20 664 304
Veb fkbuducnost.co.me
:mail fkbuducnost@t-com.me
Media Officer Nikola Prentić

FK Dečić
FK Dečić
ME-81206 Tuzi

Tel +382 69 451 182
Fax +382 78 102 402
Web fkdecictuzi.com
Email s_p@t-com.me
Media Officer Senad Padović

FK Grbalj
Radanovići bb
ME-85318 Radanovići

Tel +382 67 810 634
Fax +382 32 363 033
Web
Email ofkgrbalj@t-com.me
Media Officer Dušan Davidović

FK Lovćen
Obilića poljana bb
ME-81250 Cetinje

Tel +382 69 232 196
Fax +382 41 232 016
Web fklovcen.co.me
Email f.k.lovcen@t-com.me
Media Officer Borislav Cimeša

FK Mladost Podgorica
Kamp FK Mladost
ME-81000 Podgorica

Tel +382 67 636 603
Fax
Web
Email orolovic@yahoo.com
Media Officer Miodrag Vukićević

FK Mogren
Jadranski put bb
ME-85310 Budva

Tel +382 67 270 507
Fax +382 33 452 279
Web fkmogren.com
Email fkmogren@t-com.me
Media Officer Ilija Radenovic

OFK Petrovac
Stadion pod Malim brdom
ME-85300 Petrovac

Tel +382 69 332 775
Fax +382 33 452 582
Web ofkpetrovac.com
Email z.o.c.a.p@t-com.me
Media Officer Mihailo Đurović

FK Rudar Pljevlja
Ulica Dušana Obradovića bb
ME-84210 Pljevlja

Tel +382 69 045 420
Fax +382 52 356 186
Web fcrudarpljevlja.com
Email mitrovicradmilo@yahoo.fr
Media Officer Aldin Kordić

FK Sutjeska
Dragova luka bb
ME-81400 Nikšić

Tel +382 69 416 443
Fax +382 40 247 758
Web
Email info@fksutjeska.co.me
Media Officer Milojica Srdanović

FK Zeta
Trešnjica bb
ME-81304 Golubovci

Tel +382 67 572 736
Fax +382 20 873 142
Web fkzeta.me
Email fkzeta@t-com.me
Media Officer Bojan Božović

NETHERLANDS

Pays-Bas | Niederlande

Koninklijke Nederlandse Voetbalbond (KNVB)

KNVB

COMMUNICATION

Address	Woudenbergseweg 56-58 Postbus 515 NL-3700 AM Zeist	**President**	Michael van Praag
		General Secretary	Harry Been
		Media Officer	Rob de Leede
Tel	+31 343 499 201	**Year of Formation**	1889
Fax	+31 343 499 189		
E-mail	concern@knvb.nl		
Website	knvb.nl		

DOMESTIC COMPETITION SUMMARY 2010/11

EREDIVISIE FINAL TABLE

			Home					Away					Total						
		Pld	W	D	L	F	A	W	D	L	F	A	W	D	L	F	A	Pts	Comp
1	AFC Ajax	34	13	2	2	38	9	9	5	3	34	21	22	7	5	72	30	73	UCL
2	FC Twente	34	12	4	1	38	13	9	4	4	27	21	21	8	5	65	34	71	UCL
3	PSV Eindhoven	34	12	3	2	49	15	8	6	3	30	19	20	9	5	79	34	69	UEL
4	AZ Alkmaar	34	10	5	2	37	20	7	3	7	18	24	17	8	9	55	44	59	UEL
5	FC Groningen	34	12	2	3	37	20	5	4	8	28	32	17	6	11	65	52	57	
6	Roda JC	34	7	9	1	34	16	7	4	6	31	34	14	13	7	65	50	55	
7	ADO Den Haag	34	10	3	4	36	25	6	3	8	27	30	16	6	12	63	55	54	UEL
8	Heracles Almelo	34	11	4	2	39	17	3	3	11	26	39	14	7	13	65	56	49	
9	FC Utrecht	34	10	4	3	38	21	3	4	10	17	30	13	8	13	55	51	47	
10	Feyenoord	34	10	3	4	36	16	2	5	10	17	38	12	8	14	53	54	44	
11	NEC Nijmegen	34	7	7	3	30	19	3	6	8	27	37	10	13	11	57	56	43	
12	sc Heerenveen	34	8	3	6	35	23	2	8	7	25	31	10	11	13	60	54	41	
13	NAC Breda	34	9	2	6	27	21	3	3	11	17	39	12	5	17	44	60	40	
14	De Graafschap	34	7	7	3	22	22	2	4	11	9	34	9	11	14	31	56	38	
15	Vitesse	34	7	5	5	23	22	2	3	12	19	39	9	8	17	42	61	35	
16	SBV Excelsior	34	7	3	7	28	30	3	2	12	17	36	10	5	19	45	66	35	
17	VVV-Venlo	34	5	2	10	20	35	1	1	15	14	41	6	3	25	34	76	21	
18	Willem II	34	3	3	11	28	48	0	3	14	9	50	3	6	25	37	98	15	*Relegated*

NB NAC Breda – 1 pt deducted.

Top Scorer Björn Vleminckx (NEC), 23 goals

Promoted Club RKC Waalwijk

Cup Final FC Twente 3, AFC Ajax 2 (aet)

Champions Ajax earn their third star

A gripping three-horse race for the 2010/11 Eredivisie title culminated in an unexpected triumph for AFC Ajax as they came up on the rails with a powerful finishing sprint to overtake long-time pacesetters FC Twente and PSV Eindhoven. The victory ended the Amsterdammers' seven-year wait for their record 30th Dutch title – an achievement that enabled them to embroider a third star on to their famous red and white shirts.

Pipped to the post the previous season by Twente, Ajax gained their revenge by defeating the Enschede club 3-1 on a dramatic final day at the Amsterdam ArenA. The two clubs had met the previous weekend in an epic Dutch Cup final, which Twente won late in extra time after coming back from a two-goal deficit. In front of their expectant fans, Ajax could not afford an encore. It was a simple case of win or bust. If they took all three points, the title was theirs, whereas a draw was sufficient for Twente to retain their crown. The atmosphere was electric, and the Ajax players did not let their fans down, two fabulous goals from their gifted No10 Siem de Jong – whose brother Luuk was in the Twente line-up – sealing a victory that was celebrated long into the night and beyond in traditional style on and around the Amsterdam canals.

Birthday joy

The sight of skipper Jan Vertonghen lifting the championship shield was doubly sweet for Ajax coach Frank de Boer as it came on his 41st birthday. The club legend, a UEFA Champions League winner in 1995, had been in situ less than six months, promoted from youth-team duties in December when an under-pressure Martin Jol quit after a poor run of form in both the Eredivisie and the UEFA Champions League, from which Ajax were eliminated after five group games. With De Boer in charge, they won the sixth – away to AC Milan – to ensure continued European participation, in the UEFA Europa League, and after De Boer had been confirmed in the job with a long-term contract during the Christmas break, Ajax set about making up the ground on PSV and Twente at the top of the Eredivisie table.

Ajax had ended the previous league campaign, under Jol, with 16 straight victories, but although De Boer could not match that feat, it was another late surge - eight wins in nine games – that hoisted them all the way up to the summit. Ajax succeeded despite the winter sale of two key players – captain Luis Suárez, to Liverpool FC, and Dutch international Urby Emanuelson, to AC Milan – but other players filled the gaps admirably, with De Jong, Vertonghen and skilful young Danish schemer Christian Eriksen particularly coming to the fore. Curiously, Ajax's winning total of 73 points was 12 fewer than they had managed, as runners-up, the previous season. Like their two title challengers, they lost five times – including home and away defeats to the season's surprise package ADO Den Haag – but, crucially, claimed one win more than Twente and two more than PSV.

Ajax's Siem de Jong celebrates one of his two goals in the Eredivisie title decider against FC Twente

NETHERLANDS

KNVB

Twente, under their new Belgian coach Michel Preud'homme, were 15 points shy of their 2009/10 title-winning tally under Englishman Steve McClaren, but they nevertheless enjoyed another exceptional season. Victory in the KNVB-Beker might have lacked the same kudos as winning the Eredivisie, but the manner of their triumph over Ajax in De Kuip, with Austrian striker Marc Janko heading in Theo Janssen's free-kick three minutes before the end of extra time to complete an astonishing comeback, evoked similar jubilation. It would have been a travesty had Twente finished the campaign empty-handed. Highly competitive on all fronts, they were a particular menace to PSV, beating them twice in the league and also eliminating them from the Dutch Cup on penalties. Although disappointed, like Ajax, to drop out of the UEFA Champions League at the group stage – on their debut appearance – they reached the quarter-finals of the UEFA Europa League, knocking out two fancied Russian teams before succumbing to Villarreal CF.

Star man Janssen

Twente's star attraction was maverick midfielder Janssen, who, in his 30th year, attained previously unscaled heights and was officially voted Eredivisie player of the year. Unfortunately for Twente fans, he left for Ajax at the end of the season. Also on his way was Preud'homme, who, like McClaren before him, was tempted away by the offer of a more lucrative contract elsewhere, in his case from Saudi Arabian club Al-Shabab of Riyadh. Twente responded by appointing experienced Dutchman Co Adriaanse (ex-Ajax and FC Porto) as his replacement.

Although they lost to Ajax in that final-day showdown, Twente's defeat came with the silver lining of PSV's simultaneous failure to win away at FC Groningen, which meant that Enschede rather than Eindhoven would be a UEFA Champions League venue – at least in the qualifying phase – in 2011/12. A third successive season without a league title (after four wins in a row) meant a third successive year without UEFA Champions League football for PSV. For so long Fred Rutten's team looked title-bound. A terrific start, which peaked with an amazing 10-0 home win over Feyenoord, provided a solid foundation for a concerted challenge, but they lost their star player Ibrahim Afellay to FC Barcelona in January and were found wanting in the closing weeks, losing at Twente and then, ironically and crucially, at Feyenoord to relinquish the initiative and eventually drop to third. Like Twente, they reached the last eight of the UEFA Europa League, eliminating LOSC Lille Métropole and Rangers FC – prospective domestic champions both – before falling to SL Benfica. Like Twente again, their outstanding individual, Hungarian international Balázs Dzudzsák, left the club in the summer – not, as expected, to one of Europe's

National Team

International Honours –
UEFA European Championship – (1) 1988.

International Tournament Appearances –
FIFA World Cup – (9) 1934, 1938, 1974 (runners-up), 1978 (runners-up), 1990 (2nd round), 1994 (qtr-finals), 1998 (4th), 2006 (2nd round), 2010 (runners-up).
UEFA European Championship – (8) 1976 (3rd), 1980, 1988 (Winners), 1992 (semi-finals), 1996 (qtr-finals), 2000 (semi-finals), 2004 (semi-finals), 2008 (qtr-finals).

Top Five All-time Caps – Edwin van der Sar (130); Frank de Boer (112); Giovanni van Bronckhorst (106); Phillip Cocu (101); Rafael van der Vaart (90)

Top Five All-time Goals – Patrick Kluivert (40); Dennis Bergkamp (37); Ruud van Nistelrooy & Faas Wilkes (35); Johan Cruijff & Abe Lenstra (33)

NATIONAL TEAM RESULTS 2010/11

11/8/10	Ukraine	A	Donetsk	1-1	*Lens (73)*
3/9/10	San Marino (ECQ)	A	Serravalle	5-0	*Kuyt (16p), Huntelaar (38, 48, 66), Van Nistelrooy (90)*
7/9/10	Finland (ECQ)	H	Rotterdam	2-1	*Huntelaar (7, 16p)*
8/10/10	Moldova (ECQ)	A	Chisinau	1-0	*Huntelaar (37)*
12/10/10	Sweden (ECQ)	H	Amsterdam	4-1	*Huntelaar (4, 55), Afellay (37, 59)*
17/11/10	Turkey	H	Amsterdam	1-0	*Huntelaar (52)*
9/2/11	Austria	H	Eindhoven	3-1	*Sneijder (28), Huntelaar (48), Kuyt (71p)*
25/3/11	Hungary (ECQ)	A	Budapest	4-0	*Van der Vaart (8), Afellay (45), Kuyt (54), Van Persie (62)*
29/3/11	Hungary (ECQ)	H	Amsterdam	5-3	*Van Persie (13), Sneijder (60), Van Nistelrooy (72), Kuyt (78, 81)*
4/6/11	Brazil	A	Goiania	0-0	
8/6/11	Uruguay	A	Montevideo	1-1	*Kuyt (90) (3-4 on pens)*

KNVB

NATIONAL TEAM APPEARANCES 2010/11

Coach – Bert VAN MARWIJK	19/5/52		Ukr	SMR	FIN	MDA	SWE	Tur	Aut	HUN	HUN	Bra	Uru	Caps	Goals
Michel VORM	20/10/83	Utrecht	G							G	G			7	-
Dirk MARCELLIS	13/4/88	AZ	D											3	-
Ron VLAAR	16/2/85	Feyenoord	D											4	-
Jeffrey BRUMA	13/11/91	Chelsea (ENG)	D84										s46	2	-
Vurnon ANITA	4/4/89	Ajax	D46		D									3	-
Urby EMANUELSON	16/6/86	Ajax	M			s90									
		/Milan (ITA)									s64			14	-
Theo JANSSEN	27/7/81	Twente	M					s46	M72					5	-
Siem DE JONG	28/1/89	Ajax	M63											1	-
Jeremain LENS	24/11/87	PSV	M		s74		s29	M46						4	1
Wout BRAMA	21/8/86	Twente	M46				s72							3	-
Ricky VAN WOLFSWINKEL	27/1/89	Utrecht	A70											1	-
Erik PIETERS	7/8/88	PSV	s46	D		D	D	D	D	D	D64	D	D	10	-
Hedwiges MADURO	13/2/85	Valencia (ESP)	s46	D				M87				s64	s65	17	-
Leroy FER	5/1/90	Feyenoord	s63											1	-
Roy BEERENS	22/12/87	Heerenveen	s70											1	-
Glenn LOOVENS	22/10/83	Celtic (SCO)	s84											2	-
Maarten STEKELENBURG	22/9/82	Ajax		G	G	G	G	G	G					40	-
Gregory VAN DER WIEL	3/2/88	Ajax		D	D	D	D	D	D	D	D	D85		24	-
Joris MATHIJSEN	5/4/80	Hamburg (GER)		D	D	D	D	D46	D46	D	D	D	D46	72	3
Mark VAN BOMMEL	22/4/77	Bayern (GER)		M	M	M	M72								
		/Milan (ITA)							M					68	10
Nigel DE JONG	30/11/84	Man. City (ENG)		M46	M					M	M	M64	M65	54	1
Dirk KUYT	22/7/80	Liverpool (ENG)		M67		M	M29		M74	M82	M90	M64	M90	78	22
Wesley SNEIJDER	9/6/84	Inter (ITA)		M	M	M	M	M46	M46	M	M			76	21
Eljero ELIA	13/2/87	Hamburg (GER)		M59	s64				s46	s63	s90	s64	s90	22	2
Klaas Jan HUNTELAAR	12/8/83	Schalke (GER)		A	A82	A	A84	A87	A72			s64	A81	44	26
Rafael VAN DER VAART	11/2/83	Tottenham (ENG)		s46	M64	M	M	M80		M82	M			90	17
Ibrahim AFELLAY	2/4/86	PSV		s59	M74	M90	M	M							
		/Barcelona (ESP)							M	M63	M	M	M	36	3
Ruud VAN NISTELROOY	1/7/76	Hamburg (GER)		s67	s82		s84		s72	s82	s46			70	35
John HEITINGA	15/11/83	Everton (ENG)			D	D	D	D	D	D	D	D	D	70	6
Peter WISGERHOF	19/11/79	Twente						s46	s46					2	-
Robin VAN PERSIE	6/8/83	Arsenal (ENG)						s46		A	A46	A64	M	56	21
Royston DRENTHE	8/4/87	Hércules (ESP)						s80						1	-
Stijn SCHAARS	11/1/84	AZ						s87				s74	s61	15	-
Ryan BABEL	19/12/86	Liverpool (ENG)						s87						40	5
Kevin STROOTMAN	13/2/90	Utrecht							s72	s82		M74	M61	4	-
Luuk DE JONG	27/8/90	Twente							s74				s81	2	-
Tim KRUL	3/4/88	Newcastle (ENG)										G	G	2	-
Arjen ROBBEN	23/1/84	Bayern (GER)										M		53	15
Khalid BOULAHROUZ	28/12/81	Stuttgart (GER)										s85	D	33	-

powerhouses but to the relatively obscure, but rich, Russians of FC Anzhi Makhachkala.

AZ Alkmaar, the champions of 2008/09, took fourth place in the Eredivisie after a season of peaks and troughs under new coach Gertjan Verbeek. A place below them were Pieter Huistra's progressive Groningen, featuring young Slovenian goal-getter Tim Matavž, but the northerners were unable to join AZ in the 2011/12 UEFA Europa League. Forced into a four-team series of qualifying play-offs for that European spot, they reached the final against Den Haag and looked dead and buried after a 5-1 first-leg defeat, but an amazing comeback in the Euroborg stadium reversed that scoreline, only for the visitors to have the final say when they won the ensuing penalty shoot-out.

Although there was widespread sympathy for Groningen, the return of Den Haag to the European arena for the first time in 24 years was warmly greeted, new coach John van den Brom having re-energised the team and made them arguably the most attractive to watch in the land. Their 31-year-old ex-Russian international striker Dmitriy Bulykin was a star reborn, scoring 21 goals in the regular campaign, which put him second in the Eredivisie goal charts behind NEC Nijmegen's Belgian striker Björn Vleminckx, whose 23 strikes were less evenly spread, including one four-goal haul and three hat-tricks.

Van den Brom was subsequently lured away from Den Haag to become the new coach at Vitesse. The Arnhem outfit, under new ambitious Georgian ownership, only just sidestepped the relegation play-off zone thanks to a favourable goal difference. The two teams that did end up there, SBV Excelsior and VVV-Venlo, both survived the play-offs to retain their Eredivisie status, which meant that only rock-bottom Willem II – after 24 consecutive seasons in the top flight – went down. They were replaced by neighbours RKC Waalwijk, who won the Eerste Divisie to renew their Eredivisie membership after a year away.

2010/11 proved to be another tough season for Feyenoord – despite their large, ever-supportive fan base – but another excellent one for former boss Bert van Marwijk, who continued to excel as the head coach of the Dutch national team, leading the Oranje to six wins out of six in the UEFA EURO 2012 qualifying campaign and thereby preserving his 100

Klaas Jan Huntelaar (9) made the most of his opportunity up front for the Netherlands, scoring ten goals in six games

per cent record in qualifying matches. Indeed, with the exception of the 2010 FIFA World Cup final against Spain, Van Marwijk had won all of his competitive assignments going into the summer of 2011. Furthermore, that showdown at Soccer City was his only defeat in 37 outings – and even that game had been all-square after the regulation 90 minutes.

Hit man Huntelaar

The EURO victories, which yielded 21 goals, were achieved without the inspirational Arjen Robben – who missed all six games through injury – and, of course, retired World Cup skipper Giovanni van Bronckhorst, but otherwise the stalwarts of South Africa were still there in force. The key changes saw PSV's Erik Pieters establish himself at left-back, Afellay take Robben's place on the right wing and Klaas Jan Huntelaar come in for the injured Robin van Persie up front. With ten goals in six matches, including eight in the first four EURO qualifiers, Huntelaar more than justified his promotion. Another player in form up front was the ever-dependable Dirk Kuyt, who found the net six times, the last of his goals, in the 90th minute of the June friendly against Uruguay, ensuring that the Netherlands completed the 2010/11 season undefeated – although they did lose the ensuing penalty shoot-out.

CLUB-BY-CLUB

ADO DEN HAAG

Coach – John van den Brom; (27/10/10) (Maurice Steijn); (7/11/10) John van den Brom
Founded – 1971
Stadium – ADO Den Haag (15,000)
MAJOR HONOURS: Dutch Cup – (1) 1975.

010				
/8	Vitesse	a	1-3	*Immers*
5/8	Roda	h	1-3	*Kubík*
2/8	VVV	a	3-2	*Bulykin 2, Verhoek*
9/8	PSV	h	2-2	*Derijck, Kubík*
2/9	De Graafschap	h	2-2	*Bulykin, Visser*
8/9	Willem II	a	4-2	*Kubík 2, Radosavljevič, Bulykin*
5/9	Heracles	h	3-2	*Bulykin 2, Immers*
/10	Heerenveen	a	0-0	
6/10	Excelsior	h	2-1	*Kubík, Bulykin*
4/10	Twente	a	2-3	*Bulykin, Kubík*
7/10	Groningen	a	1-3	*Immers*
31/10	Utrecht	h	1-0	*Immers*
/11	Ajax	a	1-0	*Verhoek*
4/11	NEC	a	1-1	*og (Will)*
21/11	NAC	h	3-0	*Bulykin, Verhoek, Radosavljevič*
28/11	Feyenoord	a	1-2	*Bulykin*
5/12	AZ	h	0-2	
11/12	Roda	a	1-1	*Bulykin*
18/12	Willem II	h	2-1	*og (Vossebelt), og (Lampi)*
2011				
21/1	Heerenveen	h	3-1	*Buijs, Vicento, Immers*
30/1	Excelsior	a	5-1	*Bulykin 2, Kubík, Toornstra, Verhoek*
5/2	PSV	a	1-0	*Verhoek*
12/2	VVV	h	3-0	*Toornstra, Bulykin 2 (1p)*
20/2	Feyenoord	h	2-2	*Vicento, Bulykin*
26/2	NAC	a	2-3	*Verhoek, og (Horváth)*
5/3	NEC	h	5-1	*Immers, Bulykin (p), Verhoek, Toornstra, Brouwer*
13/3	De Graafschap	a	0-1	
20/3	Ajax	h	3-2	*Kubík, Immers, Derijck*
3/4	Utrecht	a	3-2	*Vicento, Radosavljevič, Bulykin (p)*
9/4	Vitesse	h	1-0	*Buijs*
16/4	AZ	a	1-3	*Derijck*
22/4	Twente	h	1-2	*Bulykin*
1/5	Groningen	h	2-4	*Bulykin 2 (1p)*
15/5	Heracles	a	0-3	

No	Name	Nat	DoB	Pos	Aps	(s)	Gls
25	Giorgio ACHTERBERG		1/2/90	A		(2)	
2	Ahmed AMMI	MAR	19/1/81	D	18	(2)	
47	Jarchinio ANTONIA		27/12/90	A		(3)	
10	Ricky VAN DEN BERGH		17/11/80	M	6	(4)	
5	Pascal BOSSCHAART		28/2/80	M	18	(3)	
27	Jordy BROUWER		26/2/88	A		(3)	1
19	Dmitriy BULYKIN	RUS	20/11/79	A	28	(2)	21
8	Danny BUIJS		21/6/82	M	6	(10)	2
1	Gino COUTINHO		5/8/82	G	33		
4	Timothy DERIJCK		25/5/87	D	33		3
26	Roderick GIELISSE		4/2/90	M		(4)	
17	Kai VAN HESE		15/6/89	D		(2)	
20	Santy HULST		27/10/87	A		(1)	
13	Raily IGNACIO		4/6/87	A		(1)	
9	Lex IMMERS		8/6/86	M	30		7
28	František KUBÍK	SVK	14/3/89	A	26	(1)	8
3	Christian KUM		13/9/85	D	27	(2)	
14	Ramon LEEUWIN		1/9/87	D	27	(3)	
34	Chiró Mena Vuza N'TOKO	BEL	31/1/88	D	1	(3)	
15	Mitchell PIQUÉ		20/11/79	D	15	(2)	
12	Aleksandar RADOSAVLJEVIČ	SVN	25/4/79	M	28	(2)	3
6	Aleksandar RANKOVIĆ	SRB	31/8/78	M		(3)	
24	SERHAT Köksal	TUR	18/2/90	M		(1)	
16	Christian SUPUSEPA		2/4/89	D	1	(2)	
7	Jens TOORNSTRA		1/1/89	M	34		3
11	Wesley VERHOEK		25/9/86	A	32		7
36	Charlton VICENTO		19/1/91	A	7	(13)	3
31	Kevin VISSER		19/7/88	M	3	(15)	1
22	Robert ZWINKELS		4/5/83	G	1		

AFC AJAX

Coach – Martin Jol; (6/12/10) Frank de Boer
Founded – 1900
Stadium – Amsterdam ArenA (51,638)
MAJOR HONOURS: European Champion Clubs' Cup/UEFA Champions League – (4) 1971, 1972, 1973, 1995; UEFA Cup Winners' Cup – (1) 1987; UEFA Cup – (1) 1992; UEFA Super Cup – (3) 1972, 1973, 1995; World Club Cup – (2) 1972, 1995; Dutch League – (30) 1918, 1919, 1931, 1932, 1934, 1937, 1939, 1947, 1957, 1960, 1966, 1967, 1968, 1970, 1972, 1973, 1977, 1979, 1980, 1982, 1983, 1985, 1990, 1994, 1995, 1996, 1998, 2002, 2004, 2011; Dutch Cup – (18) 1917, 1943, 1961, 1967, 1970, 1971, 1972, 1979, 1983, 1986, 1987, 1993, 1998, 1999, 2002, 2006, 2007, 2010.

2010				
8/8	Groningen	a	2-2	*El Hamdaoui 2*
14/8	Vitesse	h	4-2	*Vertonghen, Van der Wiel, De Jong, Anita*
21/8	Roda	h	3-0	*El Hamdaoui 2, Suárez*
29/8	De Graafschap	a	5-0	*Suárez 3, Emanuelson, Eriksen*
11/9	Willem II	h	2-0	*Suárez 2 (2p)*
19/9	Feyenoord	a	2-1	*De Jong, El Hamdaoui*
25/9	Twente	a	2-2	*El Hamdaoui, Enoh*
3/10	Utrecht	h	1-2	*De Jong*
16/10	NAC	h	3-0	*Vertonghen, El Hamdaoui, Suárez*
24/10	Excelsior	a	2-2	*El Hamdaoui, Vertonghen*
27/10	Heerenveen	h	3-1	*El Hamdaoui 2, Anita*
30/10	Heracles	a	4-1	*El Hamdaoui, Lindgren, Ooijer, Sulejmani*
7/11	Den Haag	h	0-1	
14/11	AZ	a	0-2	
20/11	PSV	h	0-0	
28/11	VVV	a	2-0	*Mido, Sulejmani*
4/12	NEC	h	1-1	*Mido*
12/12	Vitesse	a	1-0	*Eriksen*
2011				
19/1	Feyenoord	h	2-0	*Alderweireld, Sulejmani (p)*
23/1	Utrecht	a	0-3	
30/1	NAC	a	3-0	*De Jong, og (Penders), Sulejmani*
4/2	De Graafschap	h	2-0	*El Hamdaoui, De Jong*
13/2	Roda	a	2-2	*Sulejmani, De Jong*
20/2	VVV	h	1-0	*El Hamdaoui*
27/2	PSV	a	0-0	
6/3	AZ	h	4-0	*De Zeeuw, De Jong, Ebecilio, Anita*
13/3	Willem II	a	3-1	*De Jong, Vertonghen, Eriksen*
20/3	Den Haag	a	2-3	*Vertonghen, Eriksen*
3/4	Heracles	h	3-0	*Oleguer, De Jong, Özbiliz*
10/4	Groningen	h	2-0	*Sulejmani, Vertonghen*
17/4	NEC	a	2-1	*Sulejmani, Alderweireld*
24/4	Excelsior	h	4-1	*Ebecilio 2, Eriksen, De Jong*
1/5	Heerenveen	a	2-1	*Sulejmani, Eriksen*
15/5	Twente	h	3-1	*De Jong 2, og (Landzaat)*

No	Name	Nat	DoB	Pos	Aps	(s)	Gls
22	Ismael AISSATI		16/8/88	M	1	(1)	
3	Toby ALDERWEIRELD	BEL	2/3/89	D	26		2
5	Vurnon ANITA		4/4/89	D	27	(4)	3
17	Daley BLIND		9/3/90	D	8	(2)	
31	Nicolai Møller BOILESEN	DEN	16/2/92	D	5	(1)	
28	Roly BONEVACIA		18/10/91	M	1		
42	Geoffrey CASTILLION		25/5/91	A		(1)	
20	Darío CVITANICH	ARG	16/5/84	A	1	(5)	

41	Lorenzo EBECILIO		24/9/91	A	14	(2)	3
9	Mounir EL HAMDAOUI	MAR	14/7/84	A	25	(1)	13
11	Urby EMANUELSON		16/6/86	M	17		1
6	Eyong ENOH	CMR	23/3/86	M	23	(4)	1
8	Christian ERIKSEN	DEN	14/2/92	M	21	(7)	6
10	Siem DE JONG		28/1/89	M	31	(1)	12
46	Florian JOZEFZOON		9/2/91	A		(4)	
18	Rasmus LINDGREN	SWE	29/11/84	M	7	(8)	1
37	Jody LUKOKI		15/11/92	A		(2)	
35	Ahmed Hossam Hussein Abdelhamid "MIDO"	EGY	23/2/83	A	1	(4)	2
23	OLEGUER Presas Renom	ESP	2/2/80	D	2	(1)	1
13	André OOIJER		11/7/74	D	8	(5)	1
33	Aras ÖZBILIZ		9/3/90	A	3	(11)	1
1	Maarten STEKELENBURG		22/9/82	G	26		
16	Luis Alberto SUÁREZ	URU	24/1/87	A	13		7
7	Miralem SULEJMANI	SRB	5/12/88	A	22	(10)	8
19	Teemu TAINIO	FIN	27/11/79	M	1	(1)	
30	Jeroen VERHOEVEN		30/4/80	G	2	(1)	
12	Kenneth VERMEER		10/1/86	G	6		
4	Jan VERTONGHEN	BEL	24/4/87	D	32		6
2	Gregory VAN DER WIEL		3/2/88	D	32		1
24	Marvin ZEEGELAAR		12/8/90	A		(2)	
20	Demy DE ZEEUW		26/5/83	M	19	(8)	1

AZ ALKMAAR

Coach – Gertjan Verbeek

Founded – 1967

Stadium – DSB (17,150)

MAJOR HONOURS: Dutch League – (2) 1981, 2009; Dutch Cup – (3) 1978, 1981, 1982.

2010				
8/8	NAC	a	1-1	*Falkenburg*
14/8	Groningen	h	1-1	*Martens*
22/8	PSV	a	1-3	*Falkenburg*
29/8	Excelsior	h	1-1	*Sigthórsson*
11/9	Roda	h	1-2	*Elm*
19/9	NEC	a	1-0	*Jonathas*
25/9	Utrecht	h	1-0	*Elm*
3/10	Heracles	h	2-1	*Sigthórsson, Jonathas*
16/10	VVV	a	1-0	*Pellè*
24/10	Willem II	h	3-0	*Jonathas (p), Martens, Holman*
27/10	De Graafschap	a	1-2	*Pellè*
31/10	Feyenoord	h	2-1	*Holman, Pellè*
7/11	Vitesse	a	1-1	*Pellè*
14/11	Ajax	h	2-0	*Wernbloom, Sigthórsson*
20/11	Twente	a	2-1	*Elm, Ortíz*
27/11	Heerenveen	h	2-2	*Wernbloom, Sigthórsson*
5/12	Den Haag	a	2-0	*Elm (p), Martens*
12/12	Groningen	a	0-2	
2011				
19/1	NEC	h	2-2	*Schaars, Falkenburg*
22/1	Heracles	a	0-0	
29/1	VVV	h	6-1	*Sigthórsson 5, Gudmundsson*
5/2	Excelsior	a	1-2	*Sigthórsson*
12/2	PSV	h	0-4	
19/2	Heerenveen	a	2-0	*Wernbloom, Moreno*
27/2	Twente	h	2-1	*og (Janssen), Falkenburg*
6/3	Ajax	a	0-4	
12/3	Roda	a	2-1	*Sigthórsson, Martens*
18/3	Vitesse	h	3-1	*Wernbloom, Poulsen, Martens*
2/4	Feyenoord	a	1-0	*Benschop*
8/4	NAC	h	1-1	*Elm (p)*
16/4	Den Haag	h	3-1	*Sigthórsson, Holman, Van der Velden*
23/4	Willem II	a	1-2	*Sigthórsson*
1/5	De Graafschap	h	5-1	*Sigthórsson 2, Pellè 2, Holman*
15/5	Utrecht	a	1-5	*Martens*

No	Name	Nat	DoB	Pos	Aps	(s)	Gls
34	Esteban ALVARADO	CRC	28/4/89	G	6		
35	Charlison BENSCHOP		21/8/89	A	7	(9)	1
1	Joey DIDULICA	CRO	14/10/77	G	5		
20	Rasmus ELM	SWE	17/3/88	M	26	(2)	5
7	Erik FALKENBURG		5/5/88	M	13	(6)	4
17	Jóhann Berg GUDMUNDSSON	ISL	27/10/90	A	19	(4)	1
27	Brett HOLMAN	AUS	27/3/84	M	25	(1)	4
2	Kew JALIENS		15/9/78	D	4	(4)	
9	JONATHAS Cristian de Jesus Maurício	BRA	6/3/89	A	8	(3)	3
14	Ragnar KLAVAN	EST	30/10/85	D	27	(1)	
38	Adam MAHER		20/7/93	M		(1)	
3	Dirk MARCELLIS		13/4/88	D	32		
11	Maarten MARTENS	BEL	2/7/84	M	19	(5)	6
25	Niklas MOISANDER	FIN	29/9/85	D	29		
4	Héctor MORENO	MEX	17/1/88	D	27		1
26	Celso ORTÍZ	PAR	26/1/89	M	3	(10)	1
29	Graziano PELLÈ	ITA	15/7/85	A	5	(13)	6
15	Simon Busk POULSEN	DEN	7/10/84	D	8	(5)	1
22	Sergio ROMERO	ARG	22/2/87	G	23		
8	Stijn SCHAARS		11/1/84	M	29		1
19	Kolbeinn SIGTHÓRSSON	ISL	14/3/90	A	19	(13)	15
28	Gill SWERTS	BEL	23/9/82	D		(1)	
23	Nick VAN DER VELDEN		16/12/81	M		(10)	1
5	Nick VIERGEVER		3/8/89	D	11	(5)	
16	Pontus WERNBLOOM	SWE	25/6/86	M	29		4
32	Giliano WIJNALDUM		31/8/92	D		(1)	

SBV EXCELSIOR

Coach – Alex Pastoor; (24/10/10) (John Lammers); (27/10/10) Alex Pastoor

Founded – 1902

Stadium – Woudestein (3,527)

2010				
7/8	De Graafschap	a	0-3	
15/8	Feyenoord	h	3-2	*Fernandez 2, Bovenberg*
20/8	NEC	h	4-2	*Clasie, Bovenberg, Bergkamp, Fernandez*
29/8	AZ	a	1-1	*Fernandez*
11/9	Heracles	h	2-1	*Bergkamp, Van Steensel*
18/9	Groningen	a	0-2	
26/9	Vitesse	h	0-2	
2/10	Roda	h	1-2	*Gudde*
16/10	Den Haag	a	1-2	*Vincken (p)*
24/10	Ajax	h	2-2	*Bovenberg, Wattamaleo*
27/10	Utrecht	a	0-2	
30/10	Heerenveen	h	0-2	
6/11	Twente	a	1-2	*Van Steensel*
13/11	PSV	a	2-4	*Bovenberg, Fernandez*
20/11	VVV	h	1-0	*Bergkamp*
27/11	Willem II	a	1-1	*Ramsteijn*
12/12	Feyenoord	a	0-1	
15/12	NAC	h	1-3	*Vincken*
18/12	Groningen	h	2-2	*Koolwijk (p), Bovenberg*
2011				
23/1	Roda	a	0-3	
30/1	Den Haag	h	1-5	*Vincken*
5/2	AZ	h	2-1	*Vincken (p), Clasie*
13/2	NEC	a	0-2	
19/2	Willem II	h	4-0	*Roorda 2 (1p), Lagouireh, Fernandez*
25/2	VVV	a	0-1	
5/3	PSV	h	2-3	*Fernandez, De Graaf (p)*
12/3	Heracles	a	1-4	*Fernandez*
20/3	Twente	h	0-2	
2/4	Heerenveen	a	3-2	*Roorda 2, Lagouireh*
9/4	De Graafschap	h	0-0	
16/4	NAC	a	2-1	*Bergkamp, Fernandez*
24/4	Ajax	a	1-4	*Bovenberg*
1/5	Utrecht	h	3-1	*Roorda 2, Bergkamp*
15/5	Vitesse	a	4-1	*Roorda 2 (1p), Fernandez, Vincken*

No	Name	Nat	DoB	Pos	Aps	(s)	Gls
10	Adnan ALISIC		10/2/84	M	3	(7)	
22	Benjamin BALTES	GER	22/3/84	M	5	(5)	
11	Roland BERGKAMP		3/4/91	A	21	(7)	5

2	Daan BOVENBERG		25/10/88	D	31		6
5	Jordy CLASIE		27/6/91	M	30	(2)	2
23	Tim EEKMAN		5/8/91	D	3	(2)	
[illegible]	Guyon FERNANDEZ		18/4/86	A	30	(1)	10
8	Andrea FILLECIA	BEL	6/9/91	A	2	(4)	
21	Edwin DE GRAAF		30/4/80	M	4	(1)	1
4	Wouter GUDDE		5/8/84	D	5	(12)	1
16	Lex VAN HAEFTEN		26/6/87	G	1		
20	Shabir ISOUFI		9/3/92	A		(4)	
3	Ryan KOOLWIJK		8/8/85	M	33		1
17	Nayib LAGOUIREH	BEL	6/6/91	A	4	(26)	2
3	Miguel NELOM		22/9/90	D	32		
5	Norichio NIEVELD		25/4/89	D	33		
25	Cees PAAUWE		3/11/77	G	24		
1	Nico PELLATZ	GER	8/7/86	G	9		
19	Kaj RAMSTEIJN		17/1/90	D	22	(3)	1
14	Jerson RIBEIRO		9/3/88	M		(4)	
14	Geert Arend ROORDA		2/3/88	M	11	(2)	8
24	András SIMON	HUN	30/3/90	A		(1)	
6	Leen VAN STEENSEL		20/4/84	D	16	(8)	2
7	Tim VINCKEN		12/9/86	A	22	(2)	5
12	Tobias WAISAPY		8/1/88	D	2	(3)	
13	Kevin WATTAMALEO		25/1/89	M	20	(8)	1
26	Marvin ZEEGELAAR		12/8/90	A	11	(1)	

FEYENOORD

Coach – Mario Been

Founded – 1908

Stadium – De Kuip (51,137)

MAJOR HONOURS: European Champion Clubs' Cup – (1) 1970; UEFA Cup – (2) 1974, 2002; World Club Cup – (1) 1970; Dutch League – (14) 1924, 1928, 1936, 1938, 1940, 1961, 1962, 1965, 1969, 1971, 1974, 1984, 1993, 1999; Dutch Cup – (11) 1930, 1935, 1965, 1969, 1980, 1984, 1991, 1992, 1994, 1995, 2008.

2010				
8/8	Utrecht	h	3-1	*og (Schut), Bruins, Fer*
15/8	Excelsior	a	2-3	*Vlaar, og (Nelom)*
22/8	Heracles	a	1-1	*Wijnaldum*
29/8	Vitesse	h	4-0	*Leerdam, Fer, Castaignos, Wijnaldum (p)*
12/9	NAC	a	0-2	
19/9	Ajax	h	1-2	*André Bahia*
26/9	NEC	a	0-3	
3/10	De Graafschap	a	1-1	*Bruins (p)*
16/10	Twente	h	0-1	
24/10	PSV	a	0-10	
27/10	VVV	h	3-0	*Wijnaldum 2, André Bahia*
31/10	AZ	a	1-2	*Castaignos*
7/11	Roda	h	1-1	*Castaignos*
14/11	Heerenveen	h	2-2	*Castaignos, Cabral*
21/11	Groningen	a	0-2	
28/11	Den Haag	h	2-1	*og (Radosavljevič), Castaignos*
5/12	Willem II	a	1-1	*Leerdam*
12/12	Excelsior	h	1-0	*Castaignos*
2011				
19/1	Ajax	a	0-2	
22/1	De Graafschap	h	0-1	
30/1	Twente	a	1-2	*Swerts*
6/2	Vitesse	a	1-1	*Castaignos*
12/2	Heracles	h	2-1	*Miyaichi, Biseswar*
20/2	Den Haag	a	2-2	*Castaignos 2*
27/2	Groningen	h	5-1	*Wijnaldum 4 (2p), Vlaar*
6/3	Heerenveen	a	1-0	*Castaignos*
13/3	NAC	h	2-1	*Castaignos, De Vrij*
20/3	Roda	a	0-3	
2/4	AZ	h	0-1	
10/4	Utrecht	a	4-0	*Fer, Leerdam, Biseswar, Wijnaldum*
17/4	Willem II	h	6-1	*Wijnaldum 2, Miyaichi 2, Martins Indi, Castaignos (p)*
24/4	PSV	h	3-1	*Wijnaldum 2, Castaignos*
1/5	VVV	a	2-3	*Wijnaldum, Castaignos*
15/5	NEC	h	1-1	*Castaignos*

No	Name	Nat	DoB	Pos	Aps	(s)	Gls
4	ANDRÉ Luiz BAHIA dos Santos Viana	BRA	24/11/83	D	19	(1)	2
14	Adil AUASSAR		6/10/86	M		(3)	
9	Jhonny VAN BEUKERING		29/9/83	A	1	(2)	
22	Diego BISESWAR		8/3/88	A	22	(1)	2
10	Luigi BRUINS		9/3/87	M	18	(2)	2
31	Jerson CABRAL		3/1/91	A	6	(17)	1
30	Luc CASTAIGNOS		27/2/92	A	28	(6)	15
23	Sekou CISSÉ	CIV	23/5/85	A		(1)	
5	Tim DE CLER		8/11/78	D	27	(2)	
18	Rob VAN DIJK		15/1/69	G	17	(1)	
6	Karim EL AHMADI	MAR	27/1/85	M	13	(2)	
8	Leroy FER		5/1/90	M	16	(7)	3
26	Ricky VAN HAAREN		21/1/91	M	4	(8)	
24	Søren LARSEN	DEN	6/9/81	A		(6)	
27	Kelvin LEERDAM		24/6/90	D	20	(2)	3
19	Michael LUMB	DEN	9/1/88	D		(2)	
32	Bruno MARTINS INDI		8/2/92	M	12	(3)	1
6	Marcel MEEUWIS		31/10/80	M	13		
34	Ryo MIYAICHI	JPN	14/12/92	A	12		3
15	Kamohelo MOKOTJO	RSA	11/3/91	M	13	(1)	
17	Erwin MULDER		3/3/89	G	17		
7	Ruben SCHAKEN		3/4/82	A	8	(3)	
19	Krisztián SIMON	HUN	10/6/91	A	4	(4)	
24	Fyodor SMOLOV	RUS	9/2/90	A	5	(6)	
3	Gill SWERTS	BEL	23/9/82	D	10		1
20	Ron VLAAR		16/2/85	D	26		2
2	Stefan DE VRIJ		5/2/92	D	29	(1)	1
25	Georginio WIJNALDUM		11/11/90	M	34		14

DE GRAAFSCHAP

Coach – Darije Kalezić (BIH); (23/4/11) (Jan Vreman)

Founded – 1954

Stadium – De Vijverberg (12,600)

2010				
7/8	Excelsior	h	3-0	*Poepon, Nalbantoğlu, De Ridder*
14/8	PSV	a	0-6	
21/8	Groningen	a	1-2	*Poepon*
29/8	Ajax	h	0-5	
12/9	Den Haag	a	2-2	*Bargas 2*
17/9	Heerenveen	h	3-2	*Poepon 2, Nalbantoğlu*
26/9	VVV	a	0-1	
3/10	Feyenoord	h	1-1	*Bargas*
16/10	Utrecht	a	2-2	*Bargas, De Ridder*
23/10	Heracles	h	1-1	*Hersi*
27/10	AZ	h	2-1	*Poepon, Bargas*
30/10	NAC	a	0-2	
6/11	NEC	h	1-4	*Nalbantoğlu*
20/11	Roda	h	3-1	*Poepon 3*
24/11	Willem II	a	1-0	*Overgoor (first 59 mins played 12/11)*
28/11	Vitesse	h	1-1	*Hersi*
4/12	Twente	a	0-2	
11/12	PSV	h	0-0	
18/12	Heerenveen	a	0-4	
2011				
22/1	Feyenoord	a	1-0	*Broekhof*
1/2	Utrecht	h	0-0	
4/2	Ajax	a	0-2	
13/2	Groningen	h	1-1	*Poepon*
20/2	Vitesse	a	0-2	
26/2	Roda	a	1-1	*De Ridder*
4/3	Willem II	h	2-1	*Poepon, Bargas*
13/3	Den Haag	h	1-0	*Poepon*
19/3	NEC	a	0-1	
2/4	NAC	h	1-3	*Rose*
9/4	Excelsior	a	0-0	
17/4	Twente	h	1-1	*Meijer*
23/4	Heracles	a	0-2	
1/5	AZ	a	1-5	*Jungschläger*
15/5	VVV	h	1-0	*Poepon*

No	Name	Nat	DoB	Pos	Aps	(s)	Gls
22	Hugo Christophe BARGAS	ARG	22/10/86	A	16	(15)	6
34	Gregor BREINBURG		16/9/91	A	5	(2)	
24	Leon BROEKHOF		14/5/88	D	16	(2)	1
23	Jordy BUIJS		28/12/88	D	29		
20	Kaye COPPOOLSE		3/1/91	A	1		
14	Soufian EL HASSNAOUI		28/10/89	A		(4)	
15	Ties EVERS		14/3/91	D	3	(8)	
5	Purrel FRÄNKEL		8/10/76	D	29		
32	Geoffrey HAIREMANS	BEL	21/10/91	M	2	(3)	
10	Youssouf HERSI		20/8/82	M	20	(2)	2
17	Jochem JANSEN		4/1/90	D	1	(1)	
8	Peter JUNGSCHLÄGER		22/5/84	M	30	(1)	1
28	Lion KAAK		26/6/91	M		(2)	
6	Jussie KUJALA	FIN	4/4/83	M	10	(7)	
7	Tyrone LORAN	ANT	29/6/81	D	7		
13	Rogier MEIJER		5/9/81	M	30		1
2	Muslu NALBANTOĞLU		24/11/83	D	15		3
18	Sjoerd OVERGOOR		6/9/88	M	4	(14)	1
31	Ted VAN DE PAVERT		6/1/92	D		(2)	
9	Rydell POEPON		28/8/87	A	32		12
11	Steve DE RIDDER	BEL	25/2/87	A	23	(8)	3
29	Yuri ROSE		8/5/79	A	32		1
4	Jan-Paul SAEIJS		20/6/78	D	10	(4)	
27	Rik SEBENS		27/2/90	A	1	(9)	
1	Joost TEROL		1/2/80	G	1		
12	Boy WATERMAN		24/1/84	G	33		
3	Vito WORMGOOR		16/11/88	D	24	(2)	

FC GRONINGEN

Coach – Pieter Huistra

Founded – 1926

Stadium – Euroborg (22,329)

2010				
8/8	Ajax	h	2-2	*Matavž, Pedersen*
14/8	AZ	a	1-1	*Sparv*
21/8	De Graafschap	h	2-1	*Granqvist, Enevoldsen*
27/8	Willem II	a	3-0	*Hiariej, Enevoldsen, Pedersen*
12/9	Utrecht	h	1-0	*Granqvist (p)*
18/9	Excelsior	h	2-0	*Pedersen, Matavž*
25/9	PSV	a	1-1	*Gonzalo*
3/10	Twente	a	2-4	*Granqvist (p), Matavž*
17/10	Heerenveen	h	1-0	*Granqvist*
23/10	NEC	a	2-3	*Enevoldsen, Andersson*
27/10	Den Haag	h	3-1	*Ivens, Granqvist, Van de Laak*
30/10	VVV	a	5-3	*Matavž 2, Gonzalo, og (De Regt), Van de Laak*
6/11	NAC	h	2-1	*Granqvist 2 (2p)*
14/11	Heracles	a	0-3	
21/11	Feyenoord	h	2-0	*Matavž 2*
27/11	Roda	a	0-1	
3/12	Vitesse	h	4-1	*Granqvist (p), Matavž, Andersson, Sparv*
12/12	AZ	h	2-0	*Matavž 2*
18/12	Excelsior	a	2-2	*Tadić, og (Paauwe)*
2011				
23/1	Twente	h	1-2	*Matavž*
30/1	Heerenveen	a	4-1	*Ivens, Matavž, Tadić 2*
6/2	Willem II	h	7-1	*Granqvist, Stenman, Matavž 3 (1p), Enevoldsen, Tadić*
13/2	De Graafschap	a	1-1	*Holla*
19/2	Roda	h	1-4	*Pedersen*
27/2	Feyenoord	a	1-5	*Pedersen*
6/3	Heracles	h	1-4	*Tadić*
11/3	Utrecht	a	0-1	
19/3	NAC	a	1-0	*Granqvist*
3/4	VVV	h	3-2	*Tadić, Granqvist, og (De Regt)*
10/4	Ajax	a	0-2	
16/4	Vitesse	a	1-2	*Holla*
24/4	NEC	h	3-1	*Enevoldsen, Tadić, Matavž*
1/5	Den Haag	a	4-2	*Andersson 2, Stenman, Hiariej*
15/5	PSV	h	0-0	

No	Name	Nat	DoB	Pos	Aps	(s)	Gls
20	Petter ANDERSSON	SWE	20/2/85	M	6	(11)	4
12	Leandro BACUNA		21/8/91	A	11	(13)	
41	Virgil VAN DIJK		8/7/91	D		(2)	
23	Thomas ENEVOLDSEN	DEN	27/7/87	M	26	(6)	5
16	GONZALO Manuel García García	ESP	13/10/83	A	8	(7)	2
7	Andreas GRANQVIST	SWE	16/4/85	D	32		11
24	Tom HIARIEJ		25/7/88	D	21	(6)	2
6	Danny HOLLA		31/12/87	M	16	(4)	2
3	Jonas IVENS	BEL	14/10/84	D	33		2
2	Maikel KIEFTENBELD		26/6/90	D	29		
13	Koen VAN DE LAAK		3/9/82	M	5	(11)	2
27	Darryl LACHMAN		11/11/89	D	2	(4)	
1	Brian VAN LOO		2/4/75	G	4		
26	LUCIANO José Pereira da Silva	BRA	16/3/80	G	30		
45	Norair MAMEDOV		25/3/91	A		(5)	
11	Tim MATAVŽ	SVN	13/1/89	A	24	(5)	16
19	Shkodran METAJ		5/2/88	M		(4)	
15	Ajilore OLUWAFEMI	NGA	18/1/85	M	4	(14)	
14	Nicklas PEDERSEN	DEN	10/10/87	A	21	(1)	5
17	Danny POST		7/4/89	M		(1)	
8	Tim SPARV	FIN	20/2/87	M	31		2
5	Fredrik STENMAN	SWE	2/6/83	D	34		2
10	Dušan TADIĆ	SRB	20/11/88	M	34		7
21	Jeroen VELDMATE		5/11/88	D	3	(3)	

SC HEERENVEEN

Coach – Ron Jans

Founded – 1920

Stadium – Abe Lenstra (26,100)

MAJOR HONOURS: Dutch Cup – (1) 2009.

2010				
7/8	PSV	h	1-3	*Kopic*
14/8	Twente	a	0-0	
21/8	NAC	h	3-1	*Dost 2, og (Luijckx)*
28/8	NEC	a	2-2	*Grindheim, Beerens*
11/9	Vitesse	h	2-1	*Beerens, Assaidi*
17/9	De Graafschap	a	2-3	*Grindheim, Assaidi*
25/9	Roda	h	2-2	*Dost 2*
3/10	Den Haag	h	0-0	
17/10	Groningen	a	0-1	
23/10	VVV	h	2-0	*Dost, Väyrynen*
27/10	Ajax	a	1-3	*Dost*
30/10	Excelsior	a	2-0	*Dost, Assaidi*
6/11	Heracles	h	3-2	*Breuer, Beerens (p), og (Maertens)*
14/11	Feyenoord	a	2-2	*Väyrynen, Elm*
21/11	Willem II	h	5-0	*Väyrynen, Breuer 2, Beerens 2 (1p)*
27/11	AZ	a	2-2	*Väyrynen, Janmaat*
5/12	Utrecht	a	1-2	*Beerens (p)*
12/12	Twente	h	6-2	*Assaidi 3, Elm, Narsingh, Väyrynen (p)*
18/12	De Graafschap	h	4-0	*Elm, Đuričić, Narsingh 2*
2011				
21/1	Den Haag	a	1-3	*Dost*
30/1	Groningen	h	1-4	*Đuričić*
5/2	NEC	h	0-0	
13/2	NAC	a	2-0	*Narsingh, Assaidi*
19/2	AZ	h	0-2	
26/2	Willem II	a	3-4	*Janmaat, Dost, og (Rigters)*
6/3	Feyenoord	h	0-1	
12/3	Vitesse	a	1-1	*Janmaat*
19/3	Heracles	a	2-4	*Väyrynen, Haglund*
2/4	Excelsior	h	2-3	*Breuer, Dost*
10/4	PSV	a	2-2	*Assaidi, Dost*
15/4	Utrecht	h	3-0	*Assaidi, Narsingh, Dost*
23/4	VVV	a	2-2	*Väyrynen, Dost*
1/5	Ajax	h	1-2	*Väyrynen*
15/5	Roda	a	0-0	

No	Name	Nat	DoB	Pos	Aps	(s)	Gls
2	Oussama ASSAIDI		5/8/88	A	30	(1)	9
	Roy BEERENS		22/12/87	A	23	(5)	6
	Michel BREUER		25/5/80	D	31	(1)	4
2	Bas DOST		31/5/89	A	22	(10)	13
0	Igor ĐURIĆ	SRB	22/2/85	D	4	(1)	
4	Filip ĐURIČIĆ	SRB	30/1/92	A	12	(11)	2
	Youssef EL AKCHAOUI	MAR	18/2/81	D	5	(1)	
	Viktor ELM	SWE	13/11/85	M	23	(6)	3
3	Tarik ELYOUNOUSSI	NOR	23/2/88	A	1		
9	Samir FAZLI	MKD	22/4/91	A		(9)	
1	Jeffrey GOUWELEEUW		10/7/91	D	6		
7	Christian GRINDHEIM	NOR	17/7/83	M	30		2
8	Philip HAGLUND	SWE	22/3/87	M	5	(8)	1
9	Daryl JANMAAT		22/7/89	D	20	(4)	3
23	Calvin JONG-A-PIN		18/7/86	D	28	(1)	
[illegible]	Tobias KAINZ	AUT	31/10/92	M		(1)	
37	Gerry KONING		3/1/80	D	14	(2)	
2	Milan KOPIC	CZE	13/11/85	D	6	(1)	1
3	Arnold KRUISWIJK		2/11/84	D	21		
36	Quenten MARTINUS		7/3/91	A		(1)	
24	Luciano NARSINGH		13/9/90	A	16	(8)	5
21	Michal PAPADOPULOS	CZE	14/4/85	A	1	(3)	
6	Geert Arend ROORDA		2/3/88	M		(4)	
1	Kenny STEPPE	BEL	14/11/88	G	5		
16	Kevin STUHR-ELLEGAARD	DEN	23/5/83	G	28		
15	Michal ŠVEC	CZE	19/3/87	M	12	(7)	
25	Brian VANDENBUSSCHE	BEL	24/9/81	G	1		
10	Mika VÄYRYNEN	FIN	28/12/81	M	30		8

HERACLES ALMELO

Coach – Peter Bosz

Founded – 1903

Stadium – Polman (8,500)

2010				
7/8	Willem II	h	3-0	*Plet 2, Vejinović*
14/8	VVV	a	0-1	
22/8	Feyenoord	h	1-1	*Looms*
28/8	Roda	a	2-4	*Vejinović, og (De Fauw)*
11/9	Excelsior	a	1-2	*Fledderus*
19/9	Twente	h	0-0	
25/9	Den Haag	a	2-3	*Plet, Everton*
3/10	AZ	a	1-2	*Overtoom*
17/10	NEC	h	3-2	*Overtoom (p), Everton, Armenteros*
23/10	De Graafschap	a	1-1	*Plet*
26/10	NAC	h	4-1	*Armenteros, Fledderus, Overtoom, Plet*
30/10	Ajax	h	1-4	*Overtoom*
6/11	Heerenveen	a	2-3	*Overtoom (p), Everton*
14/11	Groningen	h	3-0	*Armenteros, Everton, Looms*
20/11	Vitesse	a	0-2	
28/11	Utrecht	h	2-1	*og (Schut), Overtoom (p)*
4/12	PSV	a	2-5	*Everton 2*
10/12	VVV	h	2-2	*Everton, Armenteros*
2011				
19/1	Twente	a	0-5	
22/1	AZ	h	0-0	
28/1	NEC	a	1-1	*Fledderus*
6/2	Roda	h	1-0	*Overtoom*
12/2	Feyenoord	a	1-2	*Fledderus*
18/2	Utrecht	a	1-1	*Cairo*
26/2	Vitesse	h	6-1	*og (Room), Everton, Fledderus, Overtoom 2 (2p), og (Kashia)*
6/3	Groningen	a	4-1	*Everton 2, Armenteros 2*
12/3	Excelsior	h	4-1	*Fledderus, Quansah, Looms, Plet*
19/3	Heerenveen	h	4-2	*Everton, Armenteros, Van der Linden, Douglas*
3/4	Ajax	a	0-3	
9/4	Willem II	a	6-2	*Everton 3, Overtoom 2 (1p), Quansah*
17/4	PSV	h	0-2	
23/4	De Graafschap	h	2-0	*Everton, Overtoom*
1/5	NAC	a	2-1	*Fledderus, Plet*
15/5	Den Haag	h	3-0	*Overtoom 2 (1p), Armenteros*

No	Name	Nat	DoB	Pos	Aps	(s)	Gls
30	Anmar ALMUBAKARI	IRQ	1/7/91	A		(3)	
18	Samuel ARMENTEROS	SWE	27/5/90	A	27	(5)	8
33	Alexander BANNINK		26/2/90	D		(4)	
2	Tim BREUKERS		4/11/87	D	32		
20	Thomas BRUNS		7/1/92	M		(1)	
19	Ellery CAIRO		3/8/78	A		(6)	1
21	Darl DOUGLAS		5/10/79	A	28	(3)	1
11	EVERTON Ramos da Silva	BRA	8/6/83	A	30	(3)	15
8	Mark-Jan FLEDDERUS		14/12/82	M	27	(4)	7
24	Olivier TER HORST		6/4/89	D	1	(3)	
27	Xander HOUTKOOP		26/3/89	A	1	(5)	
28	Gaby JALLO		1/1/89	D		(1)	
4	Antoine VAN DER LINDEN		17/3/76	D	34		1
5	Mark LOOMS		24/3/81	D	31		3
3	Birger MAERTENS	BEL	28/6/80	D	32		
23	Willie OVERTOOM		2/9/86	A	34		14
22	Remko PASVEER		8/3/83	G	34		
12	Glynor PLET		30/7/87	A	7	(15)	7
17	Kwame QUANSAH	GHA	24/11/82	M	32		2
15	Peter REEKERS		2/6/81	D	2	(3)	
9	Andrej RENDLA	SVK	13/10/90	A	3	(7)	
14	Ben RIENSTRA		5/6/90	M	2	(10)	
10	Marko VEJINOVIĆ		3/2/90	M	15	(12)	2
32	Mike TE WIERIK		8/6/92	D	2	(2)	

NAC BREDA

Coach – Robert Maaskant;
(22/8/10) John Karelse & Gert Aandewiel

Founded – 1912

Stadium – Rat Verlegh (17,254)

MAJOR HONOURS: Dutch League – (1) 1921;
Dutch Cup – (1) 1973.

2010				
8/8	AZ	h	1-1	*Amoah*
15/8	Utrecht	a	1-3	*Amoah*
21/8	Heerenveen	a	1-3	*Amoah*
28/8	VVV	h	2-0	*Amoah, Gorter*
12/9	Feyenoord	h	2-0	*Schilder 2*
18/9	Vitesse	a	0-0	
26/9	Willem II	h	2-1	*Luijckx, Kolkka*
2/10	NEC	h	2-0	*Amoah, Idabdelhay*
16/10	Ajax	a	0-3	
22/10	Roda	h	1-2	*Kolkka*
26/10	Heracles	a	1-4	*Luijckx*
30/10	De Graafschap	h	2-0	*Penders, Gorter (p)*
6/11	Groningen	a	1-2	*og (Granqvist)*
13/11	Twente	h	2-1	*Boussaboun, Amoah*
21/11	Den Haag	a	0-3	
26/11	PSV	h	4-2	*Leonardo, Amoah 2, Boussaboun*
11/12	Utrecht	h	3-1	*Fehér, og (Schut), Luijckx*
15/12	Excelsior	a	3-1	*Amoah, Schilder, Boussaboun*
18/12	Vitesse	h	1-1	*Gudelj*
2011				
22/1	NEC	a	2-2	*Gudelj, Van der Pluijm*
30/1	Ajax	h	0-3	
5/2	VVV	a	0-3	
13/2	Heerenveen	h	0-2	
20/2	PSV	a	1-4	*Lurling*
26/2	Den Haag	h	3-2	*Schilder 2, Fehér*
5/3	Twente	a	0-2	
13/3	Feyenoord	a	1-2	*Jenner*
19/3	Groningen	h	0-1	
2/4	De Graafschap	a	3-1	*Leonardo, Lurling, Gorter (p)*
8/4	AZ	a	1-1	*Gorter (p)*
16/4	Excelsior	h	1-2	*Boussaboun*
23/4	Roda	a	1-5	*Kolkka*
1/5	Heracles	h	1-2	*Amoah*
15/5	Willem II	a	1-0	*Jenner*

No	Name	Nat	DoB	Pos	Aps	(s)	Gls
14	Matthew AMOAH	GHA	24/10/80	A	27	(1)	10
31	Omer BAYRAM		27/9/91	A	1	(5)	
9	Ali BOUSSABOUN	MAR	11/6/79	A	16	(7)	4
24	Tim BOUWMAN		30/1/91	M		(1)	
12	Csaba FEHÉR	HUN	2/9/75	M	22	(3)	2
6	Tim GILISSEN		4/6/82	M	13	(5)	
18	Donny GORTER		15/6/88	M	25	(6)	4
20	Nemanja GUDELJ	SRB	16/11/91	D	19	(10)	2
17	Gábor HORVÁTH	HUN	4/7/85	D	19		
19	Fouad IDABDELHAY		2/5/88	A	5	(12)	1
22	Jens JANSE		1/7/86	D	13	(5)	
5	Julian JENNER		28/2/84	A	3	(8)	2
15	Milano KOENDERS		31/7/86	D	17	(7)	
11	Joonas KOLKKA	FIN	28/9/74	A	16	(4)	3
5	Kees KWAKMAN		10/6/83	M	4		
30	LEONARDO Vítor Santiago	BRA	9/3/83	A	23	(2)	2
4	Tyrone LORAN	ANT	29/6/81	D	7	(3)	
7	Kees LUIJCKX		11/2/86	M	29		3
10	Anthony LURLING		22/4/77	A	19	(4)	2
3	Rob PENDERS		31/12/75	D	29		1
25	Marvin VAN DER PLUIJM		1/6/88	M		(1)	1
1	Jelle TEN ROUWELAAR		24/12/80	G	34		
34	Alex SCHALK		7/8/92	A		(1)	
8	Robbert SCHILDER		18/4/86	M	32		5
29	Ferne SNOYL		8/3/85	D	1		

NEC NIJMEGEN

Coach – Wiljan Vloet

Founded – 1900

Stadium – Goffert (12,500)

2010				
7/8	VVV	h	1-0	*Zomer*
15/8	Willem II	a	5-3	*Vleminckx 3, Schøne, Sibum*
20/8	Excelsior	a	2-4	*Vleminckx, Sibum*
28/8	Heerenveen	h	2-2	*George, Schøne*
11/9	PSV	a	1-3	*Goossens*
19/9	AZ	h	0-1	
26/9	Feyenoord	h	3-0	*Schøne, Ten Voorde, Nuytinck*
2/10	NAC	a	0-2	
17/10	Heracles	a	2-3	*Davids, Schøne*
23/10	Groningen	h	3-2	*Vleminckx 3*
26/10	Roda	a	1-1	*Vleminckx*
31/10	Vitesse	h	0-0	
6/11	De Graafschap	a	4-1	*Vleminckx 3, Will*
14/11	Den Haag	h	1-1	*Zomer*
21/11	Utrecht	a	0-4	
27/11	Twente	h	2-4	*Sibum, Vleminckx*
4/12	Ajax	a	1-1	*Nuytinck*
11/12	Willem II	h	3-1	*Vleminckx, Schøne, Goossens*
2011				
19/1	AZ	a	2-2	*Vleminckx 2*
22/1	NAC	h	2-2	*Vleminckx, Goossens*
28/1	Heracles	h	1-1	*Vleminckx*
5/2	Heerenveen	a	0-0	
13/2	Excelsior	h	2-0	*Zimling 2*
20/2	Twente	a	1-1	*Zimling*
27/2	Utrecht	h	1-1	*Goossens*
5/3	Den Haag	a	1-5	*Vleminckx*
13/3	PSV	h	2-2	*George, Zomer*
19/3	De Graafschap	h	1-0	*George*
3/4	Vitesse	a	1-2	*Goossens*
9/4	VVV	a	4-1	*Davids, Goossens 2, Vleminckx*
17/4	Ajax	h	1-2	*Schøne*
24/4	Groningen	a	1-3	*Zimling*
1/5	Roda JC	h	5-0	*Vleminckx 4, Amieux*
15/5	Feyenoord	a	1-1	*Schøne*

No	Name	Nat	DoB	Pos	Aps	(s)	Gls
5	Rémy AMIEUX	FRA	5/9/86	D	18	(2)	1
1	Gábor BABOS	HUN	24/10/74	G	3		
11	Thomas CHATELLE	BEL	31/3/81	M	13	(14)	
22	Jasper CILLISSEN		22/4/89	G	31		
8	Lorenzo DAVIDS		4/9/86	M	26	(3)	2
3	Rens VAN EIJDEN		3/3/88	D	10	(4)	
9	Erton FEJZULLAHU	SWE	9/4/88	A	1	(7)	
7	Leroy GEORGE		21/4/87	A	15	(7)	3
20	John GOOSSENS		25/7/88	M	28	(3)	7
30	Cayfano LATUPEIRISSA		28/4/91	A	1	(9)	
27	Youri LOEN		27/1/91	M		(1)	
4	Bram NUYTINCK		4/5/90	D	31	(2)	2
13	Mark OTTEN		2/9/85	D	12	(9)	
10	Lasse SCHØNE	DEN	27/5/86	M	34		7
16	Bas SIBUM		26/12/82	M	29	(1)	3
18	Björn VLEMINCKX	BEL	1/12/85	A	32		23
14	Rick TEN VOORDE		20/6/91	A	1	(15)	1
15	Niels WELLENBERG		9/8/82	D	1	(4)	
19	Nathaniel WILL		16/2/89	D	28		1
6	Niki ZIMLING	DEN	19/4/85	M	26		4
2	Ramon ZOMER		13/4/83	D	34		3

PSV EINDHOVEN

Coach – Fred Rutten

Founded – 1913

Stadium – Philips (35,000)

MAJOR HONOURS: European Champion Clubs' Cup – (1) 1988;
UEFA Cup – (1) 1978;
Dutch League – (21) 1929, 1935, 1951, 1963, 1975, 1976, 1978, 1986, 1987, 1988, 1989, 1991, 1992, 1997, 2000, 2001, 2003, 2005, 2006, 2007, 2008;
Dutch Cup – (8) 1950, 1974, 1976, 1988, 1989, 1990, 1996, 2005.

2010				
7/8	Heerenveen	a	3-1	*Toivonen 2, Engelaar*
14/8	De Graafschap	h	6-0	*Toivonen 3, Dzsudzsák, Amrabat, Afellay*
22/8	AZ	h	3-1	*Berg 2, Afellay*
29/8	Den Haag	a	2-2	*Afellay, Rodríguez*
11/9	NEC	h	3-1	*Koevermans, Afellay, Toivonen*
19/9	Roda	a	0-0	
25/9	Groningen	h	1-1	*Toivonen*
3/10	VVV	h	3-0	*Reis 2, Bouma*
17/10	Willem II	a	4-2	*Dzsudzsák, Lens, Afellay, Reis*
24/10	Feyenoord	h	10-0	*Reis 3, og (Martins Indi), Toivonen, Lens 2, Dzsudzsák 2 (1p), Engelaar*
27/10	Vitesse	a	2-0	*Reis, Dzsudzsák (p)*
30/10	Twente	h	0-1	
7/11	Utrecht	a	2-1	*Dzsudzsák 2 (1p)*
13/11	Excelsior	h	4-2	*Lens, Bouma, Toivonen, Marcelo*
20/11	Ajax	a	0-0	
26/11	NAC	a	2-4	*Reis, Dzsudzsák*
4/12	Heracles	h	5-2	*Dzsudzsák, Toivonen 2, Afellay, Berg*
11/12	De Graafschap	a	0-0	
19/12	Roda	h	3-1	*Lens, Berg, Dzsudzsák*
2011				
23/1	VVV	a	3-0	*Bouma, Lens, Hutchinson*
29/1	Willem II	h	2-1	*Toivonen, Zeefuik*
5/2	Den Haag	h	0-1	
12/2	AZ	a	4-0	*Berg 2, Dzsudzsák 2*
20/2	NAC	h	4-1	*Dzsudzsák, Lens, Toivonen, Rodríguez*
27/2	Ajax	h	0-0	
5/3	Excelsior	a	3-2	*Lens, Hutchinson, Dzsudzsák (p)*
13/3	NEC	a	2-2	*Dzsudzsák, Lens*
20/3	Utrecht	h	1-0	*Bakkal*
2/4	Twente	a	0-2	
10/4	Heerenveen	h	2-2	*Lens, Toivonen*
17/4	Heracles	a	2-0	*Dzsudzsák, Berg*
24/4	Feyenoord	a	1-3	*Toivonen*
1/5	Vitesse	h	2-1	*Berg, Marcelo*
15/5	Groningen	a	0-0	

No	Name	Nat	DoB	Pos	Aps	(s)	Gls
20	Ibrahim AFELLAY		2/4/86	M	16	(3)	6
11	Nordin AMRABAT		31/3/87	A		(6)	1
28	Otman BAKKAL		27/2/85	M	12	(13)	1
6	Marcus BERG	SWE	17/8/86	A	17	(8)	8

No	Name	Nat	DoB	Pos	Aps	(s)	Gls
18	Wilfred BOUMA		15/6/78	D	25	(1)	3
31	CÁSSIO Ramos	BRA	6/6/87	G		(2)	
22	Balázs DZSUDZSÁK	HUN	23/12/86	A	33		16
8	Orlando ENGELAAR		24/8/79	M	29	(1)	2
13	Atiba HUTCHINSON	CAN	8/2/83	M	33		2
1	Andreas ISAKSSON	SWE	3/10/81	G	34		
10	Danny KOEVERMANS		1/11/78	A	3	(11)	1
24	Zakaria LABYAD		9/3/93	M	5	(2)	
9	Jeremain LENS		24/11/87	A	31	(2)	10
25	Stanislav MANOLEV	BUL	16/12/85	D	20	(1)	
2	MARCELO Antônio Guedes Filho	BRA	20/5/87	D	26	(2)	2
16	Stefan NIJLAND		10/8/88	A		(4)	
23	Funso OJO	BEL	28/8/91	M		(2)	
14	Erik PIETERS		7/8/88	D	31		
30	Jonathan REIS	BRA	6/6/89	A	10	(1)	8
4	Francisco Javier RODRÍGUEZ	MEX	20/10/81	D	14	(8)	2
47	Abel TAMATA		5/12/90	D	3		
7	Ola TOIVONEN	SWE	3/7/86	A	26	(2)	15
5	Jagoš VUKOVIĆ	SRB	10/6/88	D	3	(1)	
15	Stijn WUYTENS	BEL	8/10/89	M	2	(6)	
36	Género ZEEFUIK		5/4/90	A	1	(6)	1

RODA JC

Coach – Harm Van Veldhoven (BEL)
Founded – 1962
Stadium – Parkstad Limburg (19,979)
MAJOR HONOURS: Dutch Cup – (2) 1997, 2000.

2010				
6/8	Twente	h	0-0	
15/8	Den Haag	a	3-1	*Junker (p), Delorge, Hempte*
21/8	Ajax	a	0-3	
28/8	Heracles	h	4-2	*Skoubo 2, Delorge, Junker*
11/9	AZ	a	2-1	*Delorge, Janssen*
19/9	PSV	h	0-0	
25/9	Heerenveen	a	2-2	*Sutchuin, Junker*
2/10	Excelsior	a	2-1	*Kah, Hadouir*
17/10	Vitesse	h	4-1	*Junker 2, Sutchuin, Janssen*
22/10	NAC	a	2-1	*Sutchuin, Hempte*
26/10	NEC	h	1-1	*Sutchuin*
31/10	Willem II	h	2-2	*Janssen 2*
7/11	Feyenoord	a	1-1	*Junker*
20/11	De Graafschap	a	1-3	*Huysegems*
24/11	Utrecht	h	1-1	*Vormer*
27/11	Groningen	h	1-0	*Sutchuin*
11/12	Den Haag	h	1-1	*Janssen*
14/12	VVV	a	4-0	*Janssen, Delorge, Junker 2*
19/12	PSV	a	1-3	*Hadouir*
2011				
23/1	Excelsior	h	3-0	*Hempte, Kah, Skoubo*
29/1	Vitesse	a	2-5	*Junker, Hempte*
6/2	Heracles	a	0-1	
13/2	Ajax	h	2-2	*Junker, Hadouir*
19/2	Groningen	a	4-1	*Junker 3, Bodor*
26/2	De Graafschap	h	1-1	*Skoubo*
6/3	Utrecht	a	1-1	*Junker (p)*
12/3	AZ	h	1-2	*Hadouir*
20/3	Feyenoord	h	3-0	*Hadouir, Junker, og (Biseswar)*
2/4	Willem II	a	5-4	*Kah, Skoubo, Vormer 2, De Fauw*
10/4	Twente	a	1-1	*Bodor*
16/4	VVV	h	5-2	*Junker 3, Wielaert, Kah*
23/4	NAC	h	5-1	*Junker 2 (1p), Hempte, Skoubo, Hadouir*
1/5	NEC	a	0-5	
15/5	Heerenveen	h	0-0	

No	Name	Nat	DoB	Pos	Aps	(s)	Gls
3	Eric ADDO	GHA	12/11/78	D	9	(4)	
27	Boldizsár BODOR	HUN	27/4/82	M	11	(15)	2
26	Laurent DELORGE	BEL	21/7/79	M	24	(1)	4
29	Collin VAN EIJK		29/8/91	G	1	(1)	
2	Davy DE FAUW	BEL	8/7/81	D	31		1
10	Anouar HADOUIR	MAR	14/9/82	A	29		6
15	Jimmy HEMPTE	BEL	24/3/82	D	30		5
12	Eelco HORSTEN		31/12/89	D		(4)	
20	Guus HUPPERTS		25/4/92	A		(2)	
16	Stein HUYSEGEMS	BEL	16/6/82	A	2	(11)	1
8	Willem JANSSEN		4/7/86	M	34		6
9	Mads JUNKER	DEN	21/4/81	A	32	(1)	20
4	Pa Modou KAH	NOR	30/7/80	D	32		4
5	Vincent LACHAMBRE	BEL	6/11/80	D	3		
17	Rihairo MEULENS		3/6/88	A	3	(15)	
23	Wiljan PLUIM		4/1/89	A		(12)	
21	Mateusz PRUS	POL	9/3/90	G	6		
11	Morten SKOUBO	DEN	30/6/80	A	14	(6)	6
33	Aleksander STANKOV	MKD	19/2/91	D		(1)	
18	Arnaud SUTCHUIN	BEL	2/5/89	M	19	(9)	5
7	Sebastian SVÄRD	DEN	15/1/83	M	4	(2)	
22	Przemysław TYTÓN	POL	4/1/87	G	27		
6	Ruud VORMER		11/5/88	M	33		3
14	Rob WIELAERT		29/12/78	D	30		1
34	Jeanvion YULU-MATONDO	BEL	5/1/86	A		(1)	

FC TWENTE

Coach – Michel Preud'homme (BEL)
Founded – 1965
Stadium – De Grolsch Veste (24,244)
MAJOR HONOURS: Dutch League – (1) 2010; Dutch Cup – (3) 1977, 2001, 2011.

2010				
6/8	Roda	a	0-0	
14/8	Heerenveen	h	0-0	
21/8	Vitesse	a	3-0	*De Jong 2, Janko*
29/8	Utrecht	h	4-0	*Janko 2, De Jong 2*
11/9	VVV	a	2-1	*Ruiz, Rosales*
19/9	Heracles	a	0-0	
25/9	Ajax	h	2-2	*Janssen 2*
3/10	Groningen	h	4-2	*Ruiz 2 (1p), Janko, Janssen*
16/10	Feyenoord	a	1-0	*Landzaat*
24/10	Den Haag	h	3-2	*Janssen, Ruiz (p), Janko*
27/10	Willem II	a	3-1	*De Jong 2, Douglas*
30/10	PSV	a	1-0	*Chadli*
6/11	Excelsior	h	2-1	*Chadli, Janko*
13/11	NAC	a	1-2	*Ruiz*
20/11	AZ	h	1-2	*De Jong*
27/11	NEC	a	4-2	*Ruiz 2 (1p), Janko 2*
4/12	De Graafschap	h	2-0	*Janssen 2*
12/12	Heerenveen	a	2-6	*Chadli 2*
2011				
19/1	Heracles	h	5-0	*Janko 4, De Jong*
23/1	Groningen	a	2-1	*Janko 2*
30/1	Feyenoord	h	2-1	*Brama, Ruiz*
6/2	Utrecht	a	1-1	*Chadli*
12/2	Vitesse	h	1-0	*Chadli*
20/2	NEC	h	1-1	*Bajrami*
27/2	AZ	a	1-2	*De Jong*
5/3	NAC	h	2-0	*De Jong, Chadli*
13/3	VVV	h	2-1	*Brama, John*
20/3	Excelsior	a	2-0	*Janssen 2 (1p)*
2/4	PSV	h	2-0	*Janssen 2 (1p)*
10/4	Roda	h	1-1	*Janssen (p)*
17/4	De Graafschap	a	1-1	*Landzaat*
22/4	Den Haag	a	2-1	*Ruiz, De Jong*
1/5	Willem II	h	4-0	*De Jong, Douglas, og (Jelič), Janssen (p)*
15/5	Ajax	a	1-3	*Janssen*

No	Name	Nat	DoB	Pos	Aps	(s)	Gls
11	Emir BAJRAMI	SWE	7/3/88	M	11	(10)	1
25	Alexander BANNINK		26/2/90	D		(2)	
5	Rasmus BENGTSSON	SWE	26/6/86	D	8	(2)	
50	Steven BERGHUIS		19/12/91	M		(1)	
1	Sander BOSCHKER		20/10/70	G	3	(1)	
6	Wout BRAMA		21/8/86	M	30	(1)	2
17	Arnold BRUGGINK		24/7/77	M		(6)	

No	Name	Nat	DoB	Pos	Aps	(s)	Gls
23	Bart BUYSSE	BEL	16/10/86	D	10	(4)	
2	David CARNEY	AUS	30/11/83	D	2	(1)	
22	Nacer CHADLI	BEL	3/6/88	M	30	(3)	7
25	Anouar DIBA		27/2/83	M		(1)	
19	DOUGLAS Franco Teixeira	BRA	12/1/88	D	28		2
21	Marc JANKO	AUT	25/6/83	A	22	(7)	14
8	Theo JANSSEN		27/7/81	M	29	(1)	13
44	Ola JOHN	LBR	19/5/92	A	3	(10)	1
9	Luuk DE JONG		27/8/90	A	31	(1)	12
3	Nicky KUIPER		7/6/89	D	3	(1)	
7	Denny LANDZAAT		6/5/76	M	19	(8)	2
34	Thilo LEUGERS	GER	9/1/91	D	7	(1)	
13	Nikolay MIHAYLOV	BUL	28/6/88	G	31		
2	Oguchi ONYEWU	USA	13/5/82	D	7	(1)	
14	Bernard PARKER	RSA	16/3/86	A	1	(2)	
15	Roberto José ROSALES Altuve	VEN	20/11/88	D	27	(2)	1
10	Bryan RUIZ	CRC	18/8/85	A	24	(3)	9
36	Michael SCHIMPELSBERGER	AUT	12/2/91	M		(2)	
33	Dwight TIENDALLI		21/10/85	D	13	(5)	
18	Cheik TIOTÉ	CIV	21/6/86	M	2		
27	Dario VUJIČEVIĆ	CRO	1/4/90	M	2	(4)	
4	Peter WISGERHOF		19/11/79	D	31	(1)	

FC UTRECHT

Coach – Ton du Chatinier

Founded – 1970

Stadium – Galgenwaard (24,500)

MAJOR HONOURS: Dutch Cup – (3) 1985, 2003, 2004.

2010

8/8	Feyenoord	a	1-3	*Van Wolfswinkel*
15/8	NAC	h	3-1	*Van Wolfswinkel 2 (1p), Mertens*
22/8	Willem II	h	3-0	*Van Wolfswinkel 2 (1p), Mertens*
29/8	Twente	a	0-4	
12/9	Groningen	a	0-1	
19/9	VVV	h	3-2	*Van Wolfswinkel 2 (1p), Asare*
25/9	AZ	a	0-1	
3/10	Ajax	a	2-1	*Van Wolfswinkel 2 (2p)*
16/10	De Graafschap	h	2-2	*Wuytens, Mulenga*
24/10	Vitesse	a	4-1	*og (Rajković), Mertens, Cornelisse, Mulenga*
27/10	Excelsior	h	2-0	*Mulenga, Van Wolfswinkel*
31/10	Den Haag	a	0-1	
7/11	PSV	h	1-2	*Demouge*
21/11	NEC	h	4-0	*Van Wolfswinkel (p), Duplan, Neşu, Demouge*
24/11	Roda	a	1-1	*Duplan*
28/11	Heracles	a	1-2	*Cornelisse*
5/12	Heerenveen	h	2-1	*Mertens, Wuytens*
11/12	NAC	a	1-3	*Silberbauer*

2011

19/1	VVV	a	2-1	*Demouge, Yildirim*
23/1	Ajax	h	3-0	*Duplan 2, Vorstermans*
1/2	De Graafschap	a	0-0	
6/2	Twente	h	1-1	*De Kogel*
12/2	Willem II	a	3-3	*Mertens 2, Vorstermans*
18/2	Heracles	h	1-1	*Van Wolfswinkel*
27/2	NEC	a	1-1	*Van Wolfswinkel*
6/3	Roda	h	1-1	*De Kogel*
11/3	Groningen	h	1-0	*Demouge*
20/3	PSV	a	0-1	
3/4	Den Haag	h	2-3	*Duplan, Strootman*
10/4	Feyenoord	h	0-4	
15/4	Heerenveen	a	0-3	
24/4	Vitesse	h	4-2	*og (Yasuda), Mertens, Strootman, Demouge*
1/5	Excelsior	a	1-3	*Demouge*
15/5	AZ	h	5-1	*Mertens 3, Van Wolfswinkel 2*

No	Name	Nat	DoB	Pos	Aps	(s)	Gls
42	Zakaria AMRANI		29/3/91	M		(1)	
15	Nana ASARE	GHA	11/7/86	M	17	(1)	1
40	Evert BROUWERS		17/6/90	A		(3)	
48	Davy BULTHUIS		28/6/90	D	1		
2	Tim CORNELISSE		3/4/78	D	32		2
23	Erixon DANSO		22/7/89	A	1	(3)	
12	Frank DEMOUGE		25/6/82	A	12	(8)	6
7	Édouard DUPLAN	FRA	13/5/83	A	29	(1)	5
56	Mike VAN DER HOORN		15/10/92	D		(1)	
41	Anouar KALI		3/6/91	M		(2)	
22	Sander KELLER		18/9/79	D	1	(2)	
47	Leon DE KOGEL		13/11/91	A	2	(10)	2
20	Jacob LENSKY	CAN	16/12/88	D	25	(2)	
7	Loïc LOVAL	FRA	28/9/81	A		(1)	
14	Mark VAN DEN MAAREL		12/8/89	D	3	(2)	
18	Barry MAGUIRE		27/10/89	M	7	(9)	
43	Gévero MARKIET		8/4/91	D		(1)	
11	Dries MERTENS	BEL	6/5/87	M	30	(1)	10
24	Jacob MULENGA	ZAM	12/2/84	A	7	(2)	3
3	Mihai Mircea NEŞU	ROU	19/2/83	D	26	(2)	1
27	Gianluca NIJHOLT		14/2/90	M	5	(12)	
10	Tommy OAR	AUS	10/12/91	A	3	(4)	
30	Adam SAROTA	AUS	28/12/88	M	2	(4)	
17	Alje SCHUT		18/2/81	D	25	(2)	
8	Michael SILBERBAUER	DEN	7/7/81	M	27		1
19	Khalid SINOUH	MAR	2/5/75	G	1		
6	Kevin STROOTMAN		13/2/90	M	14		2
1	Michel VORM		20/10/83	G	33		
25	Ismo VORSTERMANS	BEL	30/3/89	D	9	(1)	2
9	Ricky VAN WOLFSWINKEL		27/1/89	A	26	(3)	15
29	Jan WUYTENS	BEL	9/6/85	D	32		2
44	Attila YILDIRIM		22/11/90	A		(2)	1
26	Michael ZULLO	AUS	11/9/88	M	4	(2)	

VITESSE

Coach – Theo Bos; (22/10/10) Hans van Arum; (15/11/10) Albert Ferrer (ESP)

Founded – 1892

Stadium – Gelredome (26,600)

2010

8/8	Den Haag	h	3-1	*Nilsson 2 (2p), Pluim*
14/8	Ajax	a	2-4	*Pröpper, Van Ginkel*
21/8	Twente	h	0-3	
29/8	Feyenoord	a	0-4	
11/9	Heerenveen	a	1-2	*Pröpper*
18/9	NAC	h	0-0	
26/9	Excelsior	a	2-0	*Stevanovič, Aissati*
1/10	Willem II	h	0-0	
17/10	Roda	a	1-4	*Jenner*
24/10	Utrecht	h	1-4	*Pedersen*
27/10	PSV	h	0-2	
31/10	NEC	a	0-0	
7/11	AZ	h	1-1	*Aissati*
14/11	VVV	a	5-1	*Pluim, Jenner, Pedersen 2, Aissati*
20/11	Heracles	h	2-0	*Pröpper, Stevanovič*
28/11	De Graafschap	a	1-1	*Pluim*
3/12	Groningen	a	1-4	*Pedersen*
12/12	Ajax	h	0-1	
18/12	NAC	a	1-1	*Jenner*

2011

22/1	Willem II	a	0-1	
29/1	Roda	h	5-2	*Matić, Van Ginkel 2, Jordi, Babangida*
6/2	Feyenoord	h	1-1	*Aissati (p)*
12/2	Twente	a	0-1	
20/2	De Graafschap	h	2-0	*Wilfried, Matić*
26/2	Heracles	a	1-6	*Kashia*
5/3	VVV	h	2-0	*Van Ginkel, og (De Regt)*
12/3	Heerenveen	h	1-1	*Martí*
18/3	AZ	a	1-3	*Van Ginkel*
3/4	NEC	h	2-1	*Wilfried, Pedersen*
9/4	Den Haag	a	0-1	
16/4	Groningen	h	2-1	*Wilfried, Kashia*
24/4	Utrecht	a	2-4	*Kashia, Tighadouini*
1/5	PSV	a	1-2	*Jordi*
15/5	Excelsior	h	1-4	*Martí*

No	Name	Nat	DoB	Pos	Aps	(s)	Gls
[illegible]	Ismael AISSATI		16/8/88	M	28	(1)	4
4	Haruna BABANGIDA	NGA	1/10/82	A	5	(2)	1
0	Nacer BARAZITE		27/5/90	A	5	(4)	
22	Alexander BÜTTNER		11/2/89	M	22	(2)	
21	Luca CALDIROLA	ITA	1/2/91	D	8	(3)	
5	Jeroen DROST		21/1/87	D	6	(1)	
25	Gino FELIXDAAL		5/1/90	M	3	(4)	
15	Marco VAN GINKEL		1/12/92	M	16	(10)	5
27	Julian JENNER		28/2/84	A	10	(4)	3
4	JORDI López Felpeto	ESP	28/12/81	M	15		2
18	Guram KASHIA	GEO	4/7/87	D	28		3
16	Laryea KINGSTON	GHA	7/11/80	M	1	(2)	
20	MARTÍ Riverola Bataller	ESP	26/1/91	M	15		2
13	Nemanja MATIĆ	SRB	1/8/88	M	26	(1)	2
8	Rogier MOLHOEK		22/7/81	M		(1)	
9	Lasse NILSSON	SWE	3/1/82	A	11	(2)	2
19	Marcus PEDERSEN	NOR	8/6/90	A	5	(11)	5
30	Hayri PINARCI		10/1/91	M		(2)	
26	Wiljan PLUIM		4/1/89	A	10	(6)	3
24	Davy PRÖPPER		2/9/91	A	23	(6)	3
23	Slobodan RAJKOVIĆ	SRB	3/2/89	D	24		
29	Eloy ROOM		6/2/89	G	33		
40	Roy DE RUITER		19/8/89	A		(1)	
17	Genaro SNIJDERS		29/7/89	A	7	(8)	
4	Civard SPROCKEL		10/5/83	D	10		
10	Dalibor STEVANOVIČ	SVN	27/9/84	M	17	(7)	2
43	Adnane TIGHADOUINI		30/11/92	A		(2)	1
6	Frank VAN DER STRUIJK		28/3/85	D	24	(1)	
1	Piet VELTHUIZEN		3/11/86	G	1		
9	Bony WILFRIED	CIV	10/12/88	A	6	(1)	3
16	Michihiro YASUDA	JPN	20/12/87	D	15		

VVV-VENLO

Coach – Jan van Dijk; (12/1/11) Willy Boessen
Founded – 1903
Stadium – Seacon (7,500)
MAJOR HONOURS: Dutch Cup – (1) 1959.

2010				
7/8	NEC	a	0-1	
14/8	Heracles	h	1-0	*Boymans*
22/8	Den Haag	h	2-3	*Ahahaoui, Boymans*
28/8	NAC	a	0-2	
11/9	Twente	h	1-2	*Paauwe (p)*
19/9	Utrecht	a	2-3	*Boymans 2*
26/9	De Graafschap	h	1-0	*Boymans*
3/10	PSV	a	0-3	
16/10	AZ	h	0-1	
23/10	Heerenveen	a	0-2	
27/10	Feyenoord	a	0-3	
30/10	Groningen	h	3-5	*Tóth, Ahahaoui (p), Uchebo*
5/11	Willem II	a	4-1	*Boymans 2 (1p), Tóth, Diogo Viana*
14/11	Vitesse	h	1-5	*Boymans (p)*
20/11	Excelsior	a	0-1	
28/11	Ajax	h	0-2	
10/12	Heracles	a	2-2	*Boymans, Uchebo*
14/12	Roda	h	0-4	
2011				
19/1	Utrecht	h	1-2	*Leemans*
23/1	PSV	h	0-3	
29/1	AZ	a	1-6	*Musa*
5/2	NAC	h	3-0	*Musa, Jorge Chula, Ahahaoui*
12/2	Den Haag	a	0-3	
20/2	Ajax	a	0-1	
25/2	Excelsior	h	1-0	*Cullen*
5/3	Vitesse	a	0-2	
13/3	Twente	a	1-2	*De Regt*
19/3	Willem II	h	0-0	
3/4	Groningen	a	2-3	*Vujičević, Cullen*
9/4	NEC	h	1-4	*Musa (p)*
16/4	Roda	a	2-5	*Timisela, Uchebo*
23/4	Heerenveen	h	2-2	*Boymans 2*
1/5	Feyenoord	h	3-2	*Musa 2, Uchebo*
15/5	De Graafschap	a	0-1	

No	Name	Nat	DoB	Pos	Aps	(s)	Gls
11	Achmed AHAHAOUI		6/2/83	A	22	(4)	3
16	Kevin BEGOIS	BEL	13/5/82	G	15		
9	Ruud BOYMANS		28/4/89	A	28	(2)	11
24	Robert CULLEN	JPN	7/6/85	A	12	(3)	2
24	Soufiane DADDA		18/6/90	A		(1)	
21	DIOGO Filipe Guerreiro VIANA	POR	20/2/90	A	6	(4)	1
44	Youssef EL AKCHAOUI	MAR	18/2/81	D	14		
5	Niels FLEUREN		1/11/86	D	20		
1	Dennis GENTENAAR		30/9/75	G	19		
8	JORGE Miguel Feijoca CHULA	POR	13/2/90	A	11	(13)	1
10	JOSUÉ Filipe Soares Pesqueira	POR	17/9/90	M	11	(2)	
4	Frank VAN KOUWEN		2/7/80	D	8	(2)	
17	Quin KRUIJSEN		27/11/90	M	4	(3)	
6	Ken LEEMANS	BEL	5/1/83	M	25	(4)	1
7	Bryan LINSSEN		8/10/90	M	3	(7)	
23	Ahmed MUSA	NGA	14/10/92	A	21	(2)	5
15	Alex Emenike NKUME	NGA	1/1/90	D	8	(6)	
19	Rachid OFRANY		17/1/87	A		(1)	
26	Funso OJO	BEL	28/8/91	M	2	(6)	
27	Patrick PAAUWE		27/12/75	M	19		1
12	Ferry DE REGT		29/8/88	D	26	(7)	1
2	Michael TIMISELA		5/5/86	D	29	(1)	1
29	Balázs TÓTH	HUN	24/9/81	M	28	(1)	2
14	Michael Okechukwu UCHEBO	NGA	27/9/90	A	9	(13)	4
25	Rick VERBEEK		14/12/88	A	1	(7)	
21	Dario VUJIČEVIĆ	CRO	1/4/90	M	15		1
3	Maya YOSHIDA	JPN	24/8/88	D	18	(2)	

WILLEM II

Coach – Gert Heerkes; (15/4/11) John Feskens
Founded – 1896
Stadium – Willem II (14,700)
MAJOR HONOURS: Dutch League – (3) 1916, 1952, 1955; Dutch Cup – (2) 1944, 1963.

2010				
7/8	Heracles	a	0-3	
15/8	NEC	h	3-5	*Hakola, Demouge, Lasnik (p)*
22/8	Utrecht	a	0-3	
27/8	Groningen	h	0-3	
11/9	Ajax	a	0-2	
18/9	Den Haag	h	2-4	*Rigters, Levchenko*
26/9	NAC	a	1-2	*Landgren*
1/10	Vitesse	a	0-0	
17/10	PSV	h	2-4	*Landgren, og (Bouma)*
24/10	AZ	a	0-3	
27/10	Twente	h	1-3	*Van Zaanen*
31/10	Roda	a	2-2	*Lasnik, Sheotahul*
5/11	VVV	h	1-4	*Rigters*
21/11	Heerenveen	a	0-5	
24/11	De Graafschap	h	0-1	*(first 59 mins played 12/11)*
27/11	Excelsior	h	1-1	*Levchenko*
5/12	Feyenoord	h	1-1	*og (Van Haaren)*
11/12	NEC	a	1-3	*Lasnik (p)*
18/12	Den Haag	a	1-2	*Biemans*
2011				
22/1	Vitesse	h	1-0	*Janga*
29/1	PSV	a	1-2	*Biemans*
6/2	Groningen	a	1-7	*Lasnik (p)*
12/2	Utrecht	h	3-3	*Van der Heijden, Hakola, Rigters*
19/2	Excelsior	a	0-4	
26/2	Heerenveen	h	4-3	*Biemans, Swinkels, Van der Heijden, Rigters*
4/3	De Graafschap	a	1-2	*Hakola*
13/3	Ajax	h	1-3	*Janga*
19/3	VVV	a	0-0	
3/4	Roda	h	4-5	*Lasnik 2 (1p), Biemans, Rigters*
9/4	Heracles	h	2-6	*Lasnik (p), Halilovič*
17/4	Feyenoord	a	1-6	*Lasnik*
23/4	AZ	h	2-1	*Lasnik, Levchenko*
1/5	Twente	a	0-4	
15/5	NAC	h	0-1	

No	Name	Nat	DoB	Pos	Aps	(s)	Gls
3	Bart BIEMANS	BEL	14/3/88	D	26	(1)	4
9	Frank DEMOUGE		25/6/82	A	3		1
2	Giovanni GRAVENBEEK		11/5/88	M	15	(4)	
7	Juha Pekka HAKOLA	FIN	27/10/87	A	16	(1)	3
25	Denis HALILOVIČ	SVN	2/3/86	D	15	(1)	1
17	Jan-Arie VAN DER HEIJDEN		3/3/88	M	32		2
22	Lars HUTTEN		18/3/90	A	3	(16)	
18	Ricardo IPPEL		31/8/90	M	12	(3)	
32	Rangelo JANGA		16/4/92	A	9	(9)	2
20	Dragan JELIČ	SVN	27/2/86	A	3	(2)	
51	Vladan KUJOVIĆ	SRB	23/3/78	G	8		
5	Veli LAMPI	FIN	20/3/84	D	27	(1)	
24	Andreas LANDGREN	SWE	17/3/89	M	12	(1)	2
23	Andreas LASNIK	AUT	9/11/83	M	32	(1)	9
8	Yevhen LEVCHENKO	UKR	2/1/78	M	14	(5)	3
15	Josimar LIMA	CPV	2/8/89	D		(2)	
12	Junior LIVRAMENTO		12/12/87	M	1	(5)	
1	Niki MÄENPÄÄ	FIN	23/1/85	G	12		
6	Marlon PEREIRA		26/3/87	M	34		
12	Gerrit PRESSEL	GER	19/6/90	D	4	(2)	
10	Maceo RIGTERS		22/1/84	A	22	(6)	5
19	Gerson SHEOTAHUL		19/4/87	A	6	(8)	1
9	David STŘIHAVKA	CZE	4/3/83	A	5	(6)	
4	Arjan SWINKELS		15/10/84	D	29		1
21	Davino VERHULST	BEL	25/11/87	G	14		
16	Niek VOSSEBELT		8/8/91	M	8	(10)	
20	Jasper WAALKENS		13/2/89	M		(2)	
11	Rowin VAN ZAANEN		18/9/84	A	12	(7)	1

TOP GOALSCORERS 2010/11

23	Björn VLEMINCKX (NEC)
21	Dmitriy BULYKIN (Den Haag)
20	Mads JUNKER (Roda)
16	Tim MATAVŽ (Groningen)
	Balázs DZSUDZSÁK (PSV)
15	Kolbeinn SIGTHÓRSSON (AZ)
	Luc CASTAIGNOS (Feyenoord)
	EVERTON (Heracles)
	Ola TOIVONEN (PSV)
	Ricky VAN WOLFSWINKEL (Utrecht)

UEFA EUROPA LEAGUE PLAY-OFFS

FIRST ROUND

(19/5/10 & 22/5/10)
Den Haag 4 *(Immers 3, Kubík 14, Bulykin 23, Vicento 41)*, Roda 2 *(Skoubo 27, Meulens 78)*
Roda 1 *(Skoubo 14)*, Den Haag 2 *(Piqué 31, Verhoek 79)*
(Den Haag 6-3)

Heracles 3 *(Armenteros 6, 56, Douglas 15)*, Groningen 2 *(Ivens 17, Bacuna 57)*
Groningen 2 *(Andersson 29, Oluwafemi 47)*, Heracles 1 *(Plet 87)*
(4-4; Groningen on away goals)

SECOND ROUND

(26/5/10 & 29/5/10)
Den Haag 5 *(Toornstra 21, 53, 72, Immers 68, Leeuwin 84)*, Groningen 1 *(Ivens 64)*
Groningen 5 *(Matavž 24, 88p, Van Dijk 50, 58, Bacuna 56)*, Den Haag 1 *(Immers 37) (aet)*
(6-6; Den Haag 4-3 on pens)

PROMOTED CLUB

RKC WAALWIJK

Coach – Ruud Brood
Founded – 1940
Stadium – Mandemakers (7,500)

SECOND LEVEL FINAL TABLE 2010/11

		Pld	W	D	L	F	A	Pts
1	RKC Waalwijk (*4)	34	22	7	5	85	40	73
2	FC Zwolle (*1)	34	20	10	4	69	27	69
3	Helmond Sport	34	17	8	9	61	43	59
4	BV Veendam	34	15	12	7	54	44	53
5	SC Cambuur Leeuwarden	34	15	9	10	64	52	51
6	FC Volendam (*2)	34	14	9	11	56	50	51
7	Go Ahead Eagles	34	13	11	10	58	43	50
8	FC Den Bosch	34	11	14	9	56	47	47
9	Sparta Rotterdam	34	12	7	15	71	65	43
10	MVV Maastricht (*3)	34	14	8	12	44	50	42
11	FC Dordrecht	34	12	9	13	52	56	41
12	FC Eindhoven	34	10	10	14	41	49	40
13	FC Emmen	34	8	11	15	48	64	35
14	Telstar	34	8	10	16	43	54	34
15	AGOVV Apeldoorn	34	11	7	16	54	77	31
16	RBC Roosendaal	34	7	8	19	38	66	26
17	Fortuna Sittard	34	7	7	20	42	70	26
18	Almere City FC	34	8	7	19	45	84	25

NB (*) period champions; AGOVV Apeldoorn - 9 pts deducted; MVV Maastricht - 8 pts deducted; Almere City FC - 6 pts deducted; BV Veendam & FC Dordrecht - 4 pts deducted; SC Cambuur Leeuwarden & RBC Roosendaal - 3 pts deducted; Fortuna Sittard - 2 pts deducted; FC Zwolle - 1 pt deducted.

PROMOTION/RELEGATION PLAY-OFFS

FIRST ROUND

(10/5/10 & 13/5/10)

Den Bosch 1, Go Ahead Eagles 0
Go Ahead Eagles 1, Den Bosch 2
(Den Bosch 3-1)

MVV 2, Volendam 3
Volendam 2, MVV 0
(Volendam 5-2)

SECOND ROUND

(19/5/10 & 22/5/10)

Cambuur 2, Zwolle 1
Zwolle 2, Cambuur 1 *(aet)*
(3-3; Zwolle 7-6 on pens)

Den Bosch 3, Excelsior 3
Excelsior 3, Den Bosch 1
(Excelsior 6-4)

Veendam 3, Helmond Sport 3
Helmond Sport 1, Veendam 0
(Helmond Sport 4-3)

Volendam 1, VVV 2
VVV 2, Volendam 0
(VVV 4-1)

THIRD ROUND

(26/5/10 & 29/5/10)

Helmond Sport 1, Excelsior 5
Excelsior 4, Helmond Sport 2
(Excelsior 9-3)

Zwolle 1, VVV 2
VVV 2, Zwolle 2
(VVV 4-3)

DOMESTIC CUP 2010/11

KNVB BEKER

THIRD ROUND

(21/9/10)
Emmen 1, Heerenveen 3
Excelsior 31 0, Den Haag 2
Flevo Boys 0, Vitesse 6
Genemuiden 2, ACV 0
Hollandia 1, Volendam 2
HSC 21 0, Go Ahead Eagles 2
Noordwijk 3, Voorschoten 97 1
RKC 4, Almere City 1
SDC Putten 1, DOVO 1 *(aet; 4-3 on pens)*
Spakenburg 0, RBC 0 *(aet; 5-3 on pens)*
Sparta Nijkerk 2, Kozakken Boys 1
Telstar 3, Fortuna Sittard 1
Veendam 2, Helmond Sport 1 *(aet)*
Zwolle 2, Willem II 2 *(aet; 5-4 on pens)*

(22/9/10)
Ajax 5, MVV 0
ARC 0, Heracles 3
Capelle 1, Twente 4
De Treffers 5, Katwijk 1
Den Bosch 2, AZ 3
EVV 3, Eindhoven 5
Feyenoord 1, Roda 1 *(aet; 3-4 on pens)*
Gemert 0, AGOVV 4 *(aet)*
Graafschap 1, Utrecht 1 *(aet; 4-5 on pens)*
Groene Ster 2, Dijkse Boys 2 *(aet; 1-4 on pens)*
Haaglandia 1, Groningen 4 *(aet)*
PSV 3, Sparta 0
VVSB 0, Cambuur 2
WKE 0, Excelsior 3

(23/9/10)
Achilles 29 2, Oss 0
Dordrecht 4, NEC 3
NAC 3, VVV 1

(29/9/10)
Rijnsburgse Boys 4, Deurne 2 *(aet)*

FOURTH ROUND

(9/11/10)
Cambuur 1, RKC 4
Dordrecht 1, Volendam 2
Heerenveen 0, NAC 2
SDC Putten 0, Telstar 2
Sparta Nijkerk 2, Excelsior 1
Zwolle 1, Twente 1 *(aet; 3-5 on pens)*

(10/11/10)
AGOVV 0, Utrecht 2
AZ 3, Eindhoven 0
De Treffers 0, Noordwijk 1
Dijkse Boys 1, Genemuiden 9
Go Ahead Eagles 0, Roda 2
PSV 3, Spakenburg 0
Vitesse 3, Rijnsburgse Boys 0

(11/11/10)
Achilles 29 5, Heracles 3
Ajax 3, Veendam 0
Groningen 1, Den Haag 1 *(aet; 5-4 on pens)*

FIFTH ROUND

(21/12/10)
Twente 5, Vitesse 0

(22/12/10)
Roda 1, PSV 3
Utrecht 1, Volendam 0

(23/12/10)
Ajax 1, AZ 0

(18/1/11)
Achilles 29 2, RKC 2 *(aet; 1-3 on pens)*
Genemuiden 2, Groningen 3
Sparta Nijkerk 3, Noordwijk 3 *(aet; 3-5 on pens)*
Telstar 0, NAC 1

QUARTER-FINALS

(25/1/11)
RKC 6 *(De Groot 8, Van Hout 14, 20, 24, Boerrigter 39, 65)*, Noordwijk 0

(26/1/11)
Twente 1 *(Janssen 70p)*, PSV 1 *(Koevermans 90)* *(aet; 7-6 on pens)*
Utrecht 3 *(Wuytens 12, Mertens 31p, Asare 53)*, Groningen 2 *(Matavž 18, Granqvist 48p)*

(27/1/11)
Ajax 4 *(De Jong 18, Sulejmani 35, 83, Anita 82)*, NAC 1 *(Idabdelhay 8)*

SEMI-FINALS

(2/3/11)
Twente 1 *(Janko 77)*, Utrecht 0

(3/3/11)
Ajax 5 *(Ebecilio 13, El Hamdaoui 33, De Jong 55, 85, De Zeeuw 58)*, RKC 1 *(Blind 27og)*

FINAL

(8/5/11)
De Kuip, Rotterdam
FC TWENTE 3 *(Brama 45, Janssen 56, Janko 117)*
AFC AJAX 2 *(De Zeeuw 19, Ebecilio 40)*
(aet)
Referee – *Blom*
TWENTE – *Boschker, Tiendalli, Wisgerhof (Bengtsson 100), Douglas, Buysse, Brama, Landzaat, Janssen, Ruiz, De Jong (Janko 106), Chadli (Bajrami 91).*
AJAX – *Vermeer, Van der Wiel (Cvitanich 91), Alderweireld, Vertonghen, Boilesen (Blind 73), De Zeeuw (Enoh 66), Eriksen, Anita, Sulejmani, De Jong, Ebecilio.*

CLUB COMMUNICATION 2011/12

ADO Den Haag
Postbus 32400
NL-2503 AC Den Haag

Tel	+31 70 305 4500
Fax	+31 70 305 4599
Web	adodenhaag.nl
Email	info@adodenhaag.nl
Media Officer	Nathalie Nuiten

AFC Ajax
Postbus 12522, Arena boulevard 29
NL-1100 AM Amsterdam

Tel	+31 20 311 1444
Fax	+31 20 311 1675
Web	ajax.nl
Email	info@ajax.nl
Media Officer	Miel Brinkhuis

AZ Alkmaar
Postbus 1010
NL-1810 KA Alkmaar

Tel	+31 72 547 8000
Fax	+31 72 547 8080
Web	az.nl
Email	info@az.nl
Media Officer	Daan Schippers

SBV Excelsior
Postbus 4369
NL-3006 AJ Rotterdam

Tel	+31 10 404 6041
Fax	+31 10 411 4161
Web	sbvexcelsior.nl
Email	info@sbvexcelsior.nl
Media Officer	Vincent Wernke

Feyenoord
Postbus 9635
NL-3007 AP Rotterdam

Tel	+31 10 292 6808
Fax	+31 10 482 4843
Web	feyenoord.nl
Email	info@feyenoord.nl
Media Officer	Gido Vader

De Graafschap
Lijsterbeslaan 101 a, PO Box 249
NL-7000 AE Doetinchem

Tel	+31 314 368 450
Fax	+31 314 368 451
Web	degraafschap.nl
Email	info@degraafschap.nl
Media Officer	Marc Teloh

FC Groningen
Postbus 1399
NL-9701 BJ Groningen

Tel	+31 50 587 8787
Fax	+31 50 312 5194
Web	fcgroningen.nl
Email	info@fcgroningen.nl
Media Officer	Richard Van Elsacker

sc Heerenveen
PO Box 513
NL-8440 AM Heerenveen

Tel	+31 513 612 100
Fax	+31 513 615 061
Web	sc-heerenveen.nl
Email	info@sc-heerenveen.nl
Media Officer	Erica Kooyenga

Heracles Almelo
Stadionlaan 1, PO Box 157
Polman Stadium, NL-7600 AD Almelo

Tel	+31 546 817 070
Fax	+31 546 811 184
Web	heracles.nl
Email	info@heracles.nl
Media Officer	Edwin van Lenthe

NAC Breda
PO Box 3356, Stadionstraat 23, Rat Verlegh Stadium, NL-4800 DJ Breda

Tel	+31 76 521 4500
Fax	+31 76 521 1975
Web	nac.nl
Email	info@nac.nl
Media Officer	Michele Eland

NEC Nijmegen
PO Box 6562
NL-6503 GB Nijmegen

Tel	+31 24 359 0360
Fax	+31 24 356 7475
Web	nec-nijmegen.nl
Email	info@nec-nijmegen.nl
Media Officer	Marij Peters

PSV Eindhoven
Postbus 886
NL-5600 AW Eindhoven

Tel	+31 40 250 5505
Fax	+31 40 250 5639
Web	psv.nl
Email	info@psv.nl
Media Officer	Pedro Salazar-Hewitt

RKC Waalwijk
PO Box 4, Akkerlaan 2, Mandemakers stadium, NL-5140 AA Waalwijk

Tel	+31 416 334 356
Fax	+31 416 342 310
Web	rkcwaalwijk.nl
Email	info@rkcwaalwijk.nl
Media Officer	Martin Versteeg

Roda JC
Postbus 1156
NL-6460 BD Kerkrade

Tel	+31 45 631 7000
Fax	+31 45 631 7100
Web	rodajc.nl
Email	info@rodajc.nl
Media Officer	Ger Senden

FC Twente
Postbus 564
NL-7500 AN Enschede

Tel	+31 53 852 5525
Fax	+31 53 852 5555
Web	fctwente.nl
Email	administratie@fctwente.nl
Media Officer	Robert Berenschot

FC Utrecht
Postbus 85159
NL-3508 AD Utrecht

Tel	+31 30 888 5500
Fax	+31 30 888 5559
Web	fcutrecht.nl
Email	info@fcutrecht.nl
Media Officer	Harry van Dam

Vitesse
PO Box 366, Batavierenweg 25, GelreDome Stadion, NL-6800 AJ Arnhem

Tel	+31 26 880 7888
Fax	+31 26 880 7309
Web	vitesse.nl
Email	info@vitesse.nl
Media Officer	Ester Bal

VVV-Venlo
Postbus 947
NL-5900 AX Venlo

Tel	+31 77 351 5806
Fax	+31 77 351 0270
Web	vvv-venlo.nl
Email	info@vvv-venlo.nl
Media Officer	Ellen Berden

NORTHERN IRELAND

Irlande du Nord I Nordirland

Irish Football Association (IFA)

COMMUNICATION

Address	20 Windsor Avenue GB-Belfast BT9 6EG	**President**	Jim Shaw
Tel	+44 2890 669 458	**Chief Executive**	Patrick Nelson
Fax	+44 2890 667 620	**Media Officer**	Sueann Harrison
E-mail	info@irishfa.com	**Year of Formation**	1880
Website	irishfa.com	**National Stadium**	Windsor Park, Belfast (12,950)

DOMESTIC COMPETITION SUMMARY 2010/11

PREMIERSHIP FINAL TABLE

			Home					Away					Total						
		Pld	W	D	L	F	A	W	D	L	F	A	W	D	L	F	A	Pts	Comp
1	Linfield FC	38	14	4	1	39	9	12	3	4	41	20	26	7	5	80	29	85	UCL
2	Crusaders FC	38	13	2	4	43	26	10	3	6	35	33	23	5	10	78	59	74	UEL
3	Glentoran FC	38	9	5	5	28	17	11	1	7	35	24	20	6	12	63	41	66	UEL
4	Cliftonville FC	38	10	2	7	38	31	7	5	7	22	25	17	7	14	60	56	58	UEL
5	Portadown FC	38	9	3	7	26	24	6	2	11	23	34	15	5	18	49	58	50	
6	Lisburn Distillery FC	38	6	3	9	25	39	8	3	9	25	27	14	6	18	50	66	48	
7	Coleraine FC	38	10	2	9	33	31	7	3	7	18	19	17	5	16	51	50	56	
8	Dungannon Swifts FC	38	7	4	7	22	23	7	5	8	28	30	14	9	15	50	53	51	
9	Ballymena United FC	38	5	6	8	21	31	7	7	5	27	25	12	13	13	48	56	49	
10	Glenavon FC	38	8	2	9	25	24	4	7	8	35	35	12	9	17	60	59	45	
11	Donegal Celtic FC	38	3	6	9	27	41	5	2	13	28	48	8	8	22	55	89	32	
12	Newry City FC	38	5	5	10	24	34	1	3	14	13	31	6	8	24	37	65	26	*Relegated*

NB League split into top and bottom halves after 33 games, with each team playing a further five matches exclusively against clubs from its half of the table.

Top Scorer Peter Thompson (Linfield), 23 goals

Promoted Club Carrick Rangers FC

Cup Final Linfield FC 2, Crusaders FC 1

Historic 50th league title for Linfield

In the year of their 125th anniversary, Linfield FC captured the Irish League title for a record 50th time. That landmark triumph was accompanied by the club's 41st victory in the Irish Cup as the Blues claimed their fifth domestic double in six seasons, enabling manager David Jeffrey to increase his personal trophy collection to 28 during his 14-year tenure at the club.

Linfield striker Peter Thompson enjoyed another prolific season in front of goal for the domestic double winners

Celebrations abounded at Windsor Park, but back in August, when Linfield picked up one point from their opening two Premiership encounters, there were genuine fears that the jubilee would fall flat. Indeed, it was mid-October before Jeffrey's men overtook arch-rivals Glentoran FC and climbed to the top of the table. Once there, they were never shifted, and although Crusaders FC, under manager Stephen Baxter, made a determined run at them with ten consecutive victories, Linfield ended that sequence with a crucial 1-0 win at Seaview on 1 April to halt the North Belfast side's challenge. With victories in their last eight games Linfield finished up 11 points clear of the Crues, with Glentoran and Cliftonville FC completing a European clean sweep for the capital by taking third and fourth places, respectively.

Top man Thompson

Linfield and Crusaders met again in the Irish Cup final. Declan Caddell put the Crues ahead shortly after half-time, but the Blues responded with late goals from their top two scorers in the league – Golden Boot winner Peter Thompson and Mark McAllister – to turn the match around. Thompson's goal – his 33rd of the season – was his sixth in five cup finals and helped to maintain his remarkable record of never having been on the losing side for Linfield in the competition.

Although absent from the cup final, Linfield legend Noel Bailie won his tenth league title with the club he joined in 1988 and decided to hang up his boots, having played a record 1013 games for the South Belfast outfit. Another player to announce his retirement was Bailie's ex-Linfield team-mate Glenn Ferguson, who finally called it quits to end a 24-year career that spawned a staggering 563 goals. Ferguson even bowed out with a trophy, helping Tommy Wright's Lisburn Distillery FC to victory in the League Cup, which they claimed with a 2-1 win over Portadown FC to record their first trophy success in 26 years.

It was another forgettable season for Nigel Worthington's Northern Ireland. A good start to the UEFA EURO 2012 qualifying campaign – with a 1-0 win in Slovenia followed by a 0-0 draw at home to Italy – was checked by a draw in the Faroe Islands and a defeat in Serbia, and after receiving three drubbings in the new Nations Cup, the team ended the season in the midst of a rotten run of one win in 19 matches.

National Team

International Tournament Appearances – FIFA World Cup - (3) 1958 (qtr-finals), 1982 (2nd phase), 1986.

Top Five All-time Caps – Pat Jennings (119); Mal Donaghy (91); Sammy McIlroy (88); Maik Taylor (87); Keith Gillespie & David Healy (86)

Top Five All-time Goals – David Healy (35); Colin Clarke & Billy Gillespie (13); Gerry Armstrong, Joe Bambrick, Ian Dowie & Jimmy Quinn (12)

NATIONAL TEAM RESULTS 2010/11

11/8/10	Montenegro	A	Podgorica	0-2	
3/9/10	Slovenia (ECQ)	A	Maribor	1-0	*Evans C. (70)*
8/10/10	Italy (ECQ)	H	Belfast	0-0	
12/10/10	Faroe Islands (ECQ)	A	Toftir	1-1	*Lafferty (76)*
17/11/10	Morocco	H	Belfast	1-1	*Patterson (86p)*
9/2/11	Scotland	N	Dublin (IRL)	0-3	
25/3/11	Serbia (ECQ)	A	Belgrade	1-2	*McAuley (40)*
29/3/11	Slovenia (ECQ)	H	Belfast	0-0	
24/5/11	Republic of Ireland	A	Dublin	0-5	
27/5/11	Wales	N	Dublin (IRL)	0-2	

NATIONAL TEAM APPEARANCES 2010/11

Coach – Nigel WORTHINGTON	**4/11/61**		**Mne**	**SVN**	**ITA**	**FRO**	**Mar**	**Sco**	**SRB**	**SVN**	**Irl**	**Wal**	**Caps**	**Goals**
Maik TAYLOR	4/9/71	Birmingham (ENG)	G	G	G	G							87	-
Andrew LITTLE	12/5/89	Rangers (SCO)	D										6	-
Ryan McGIVERN	8/1/90	Man. City (ENG) /Walsall (ENG)	D68				D62						13	-
Stephen CRAIGAN	29/10/76	Motherwell (SCO)	D	D	D	D		D66		D			54	-
Jonny EVANS	3/1/88	Man. United (ENG)	D		D	D	D		D86	D			26	1
Chris BAIRD	25/2/82	Fulham (ENG)	M46	M	M	M		D	M	M			51	-
Martin PATERSON	10/5/87	Burnley (ENG)	M46										12	-
Steven DAVIS	1/1/85	Rangers (SCO)	M	M	M	M		M58			M76		46	2
Sammy CLINGAN	13/1/84	Coventry (ENG)	M64						M	M	M		28	-
Chris BRUNT	14/12/84	West Brom (ENG)	M46	M89	M71	M	A46		A	A			33	1
Kyle LAFFERTY	16/9/87	Rangers (SCO)	A58	s67	s66	A			A46				29	8
Grant McCANN	15/4/80	Peterborough (ENG)	s46	M67	M80			M46		M72			33	4
Corry EVANS	30/7/90	Man. United (ENG) /Hull (ENG)	s46	s67	s80	s83		M	M	M91			11	1
Warren FEENEY	17/1/81	Oldham (ENG)	s46	A	A	A50			s78	A82	A73	A73	42	5
Johnny GORMAN	26/10/92	Wolves (ENG)	s58	s89			M		M78		M55	M	8	-
Oliver NORWOOD	12/4/91	Man. United (ENG)	s64					s58			s46	M	4	-
David HEALY	5/8/79	Sunderland (ENG) /Rangers (SCO)	s68	A67	A66	s50		s46	s46				86	35
Gareth McAULEY	5/12/79	Ipswich (ENG)		D	D	D		D	D	D	D	D	30	2
Aaron HUGHES	8/11/79	Fulham (ENG)		D	D	D	D46		D				76	-
Craig CATHCART	6/2/89	Blackpool (ENG)		D					D	D	D	D63	5	-
Niall McGINN	20/7/87	Celtic (SCO)			s71	M83	M69	M72			s73	A80	13	-
Jonathan TUFFEY	20/1/87	Inverness (SCO)					G46	G				G	8	-
Lee HODSON	2/10/91	Watford (ENG)					D	s46			D	D	4	-
Adam BARTON	7/1/91	Preston (ENG)					M						1	-
Patrick McCOURT	16/12/83	Celtic (SCO)					M46	M	s86	s82			7	-
Rory PATTERSON	16/7/84	Plymouth (ENG)					A	A					5	1
Alan BLAYNEY	9/10/91	Linfield					s46				G		5	-
Josh McQUOID	15/12/89	Bournemouth (ENG) /Millwall (ENG)					s46			s72	A46		3	-
Rory McARDLE	1/5/87	Aberdeen (SCO)					s46	D46					4	-
Michael O'CONNOR	6/10/87	Scunthorpe (ENG)					s46						10	-
Colin COATES	26/10/85	Crusaders					s62				s55	D	6	-
Josh MAGENNIS	15/8/90	Aberdeen (SCO)					s69						3	-
Adam THOMPSON	28/9/92	Watford (ENG)						s66			D 53*		2	-
Liam BOYCE	8/4/91	Werder (GER)						s72		s91	s73	s73	4	-
Lee CAMP	22/8/84	Nottingham Forest (ENG)							G	G			2	-
Joshua CARSON	3/6/93	Ipswich (ENG)									M73	M	2	-
Robert GARRETT	5/5/88	Linfield									s76	M76	5	-
Stuart DALLAS	19/4/91	Crusaders										s63	1	-
Carl WINCHESTER	12/4/93	Oldham (ENG)										s76	1	-
Jordan OWENS	9/7/89	Crusaders										s80	1	-

CLUB-BY-CLUB

BALLYMENA UNITED FC

Manager – Roy Walker
Founded – 1928
Stadium – The Showgrounds (4,390)
MAJOR HONOURS: Irish Cup – (6) 1929, 1940, 1958, 1981, 1984, 1989.

2010

7/8	Linfield	a	0-0	
14/8	Donegal Celtic	h	0-4	
21/8	Portadown	a	3-1	*Surgenor, Hanley, McCutcheon*
27/8	Glenavon	a	2-0	*McCutcheon, Gibson*
31/8	Crusaders	a	1-2	*McCutcheon*
4/9	Cliftonville	h	1-1	*McCutcheon*
11/9	Newry	h	1-0	*Carson*
21/9	Glentoran	a	2-1	*Murray, Gibson*
25/9	Coleraine	a	0-1	
2/10	Dungannon	h	1-1	*Murray*
5/10	Lisburn	h	0-1	
9/10	Donegal Celtic	a	3-2	*Hanley, Murray, Gibson*
16/10	Portadown	h	3-1	*Gibson, Hanley, McCutcheon*
30/10	Linfield	h	3-3	*Gibson (p), Surgenor 2*
6/11	Glenavon	h	3-3	*McCutcheon 2, Watson*
9/11	Lisburn	a	1-1	*Surgenor*
13/11	Cliftonville	a	0-5	
19/11	Newry	a	4-0	*McCutcheon, Smith M., Murray, Hanley*
27/11	Crusaders	h	1-1	*Berry*
11/12	Dungannon	a	2-1	*McCutcheon 2*

2011

1/1	Glenavon	a	1-3	*McCutcheon*
4/1	Portadown	h	3-1	*Smith A., Murray 2*
29/1	Linfield	a	0-0	
5/2	Cliftonville	a	2-2	*Murray, Smith M.*
8/2	Coleraine	h	0-1	
14/2	Glentoran	h	0-2	
19/2	Coleraine	h	1-1	*Haveron*
26/2	Donegal Celtic	h	0-3	
1/3	Crusaders	h	0-3	
5/3	Lisburn	a	1-0	*McCutcheon*
19/3	Glentoran	h	2-3	*Surgenor, McCafferty*
22/3	Dungannon	a	0-1	
26/3	Newry	a	1-1	*Boyd A.*
1/4	Coleraine	a	1-1	*Smith M.*
16/4	Donegal Celtic	a	3-3	*Boyd A., Murray, McCutcheon*
23/4	Newry	h	1-0	*Berry*
26/4	Dungannon	h	0-2	
30/4	Glenavon	h	1-0	*McCutcheon*

No	Name	Nat	DoB	Pos	Aps	(s)	Gls
7	Ryan BERRY		5/9/88	M	10	(4)	2
21	Aaron BOYD		12/2/91	A	4	(4)	2
22	Matthew BOYD		30/8/89	M		(2)	
1	Ryan BROWN		27/11/80	G	23		
20	Rory CARSON		31/12/90	M	9	(4)	1
3	Lee COLLIGAN		11/2/89	D	22	(9)	
12	Denver GAGE		3/5/87	D	27	(2)	
	Richard GIBSON		11/1/85	A	13	(6)	5
	Nathan HANLEY		18/7/90	M	17		4
4	Gary HAVERON		6/3/81	M	22	(10)	1
	Neil LOWRY		9/8/93	A		(1)	
16	Paul McAREAVEY		3/12/80	M	1	(2)	
14	Neil McCAFFERTY		19/7/84	M	15		1
	Lee McCAUGHERN		16/4/91	M	1		
10	Gary McCUTCHEON	SCO	8/10/78	A	38		14
11	Maurice McDOWELL		24/4/85	A	3	(11)	
	James McLAUGHLIN		6/3/90	A		(1)	
15	Eamon MURRAY		11/5/88	M	30	(3)	8
18	Dwayne NELSON		5/9/84	G	15		
	Orman OKUNAIYA		16/4/86	M		(1)	
	David REID		3/5/94	D		(1)	
9	Andy SMITH		25/9/80	A	11	(6)	1
2	Michael SMITH		4/9/88	D	37		3
19	Michael J. SMITH		1/7/92	M	1	(2)	
6	Aaron STEWART		3/12/89	D	30	(1)	
13	Mark SURGENOR		19/12/85	D	29	(3)	5
8	Gavin TAGGART		15/11/84	M	22	(5)	
5	Albert WATSON		8/9/85	D	37		1
17	George YOUNG		23/11/89	M	1	(7)	

CLIFTONVILLE FC

Manager – Eddie Patterson; (2/4/11) (Tommy Breslin)
Founded – 1879
Stadium – Solitude (2,552)
MAJOR HONOURS: Irish League – (3) 1906 (shared), 1910, 1998; Irish Cup – (8) 1883, 1888, 1897, 1900, 1901, 1907, 1909, 1979.

2010

14/8	Newry	a	1-0	*Scannell C.*
20/8	Dungannon	h	2-0	*McMullan 2*
27/8	Crusaders	a	3-1	*Boyce, Scannell C., McMullan (p)*
31/8	Glentoran	a	0-2	
4/9	Ballymena	a	1-1	*Hutton*
11/9	Linfield	a	0-0	
21/9	Coleraine	h	0-2	
25/9	Lisburn	a	1-1	*Lynch*
2/10	Donegal Celtic	h	4-2	*McMullan (p), Garrett, Scannell C., Donnelly*
5/10	Glenavon	a	2-1	*McMullan (p), Caldwell*
9/10	Newry	h	2-1	*Donnelly, Garrett*
16/10	Glentoran	h	2-1	*Donnelly, Caldwell*
30/10	Portadown	h	0-1	
6/11	Coleraine	a	1-3	*Garrett*
9/11	Glenavon	h	0-2	
13/11	Ballymena	h	5-0	*Scannell R., Scannell C. 3, McMullan*
20/11	Lisburn	h	1-3	*Scannell R.*
27/11	Dungannon	a	1-0	*Garrett*
10/12	Linfield	h	3-1	*O'Connor, Caldwell (p), Connolly (p)*
27/12	Crusaders	h	2-1	*og (Coates), Holland M.*

2011

1/1	Coleraine	a	2-3	*Caldwell, Scannell C.*
4/1	Lisburn	h	3-2	*Scannell R. 2, Holland M.*
11/1	Donegal Celtic	a	1-1	*Donnelly*
22/1	Linfield	h	2-4	*Scannell C., Garrett*
31/1	Glenavon	a	2-0	*McMullan, og (Shannon)*
5/2	Ballymena	h	2-2	*Caldwell, Fleming*
8/2	Portadown	a	1-2	Scannell C.
12/2	Newry	a	2-0	*Kane, Holland M.*
19/2	Dungannon	h	3-2	*og (Fitzpatrick), Scannell C., McMullan (p)*
26/2	Glentoran	a	0-0	
12/3	Portadown	h	1-3	*Donnelly*
19/3	Crusaders	a	0-5	
26/3	Glentoran	h	1-2	*Donnelly*
1/4	Donegal Celtic	h	2-2	*McMullan, Burns*
16/4	Portadown	a	1-0	*McMullan (p)*
23/4	Linfield	a	0-1	
26/4	Crusaders	h	3-0	*O'Connor, Seydak, Garrett*
30/4	Lisburn	a	3-4	*Seydak 2, Donnelly*

No	Name	Nat	DoB	Pos	Aps	(s)	Gls
19	Jason BANNON		7/9/89	D	3	(1)	
	Liam BOYCE		8/4/91	A	3		1
26	Kevin BRADLEY		29/4/92	D	1		
20	Conal BURNS		31/1/90	M	3	(9)	1
14	Ciaran CALDWELL		10/10/89	D	17	(3)	5
17	Ryan CATNEY		17/2/87	M	9		
1	John CONNOLLY	IRL	1/2/77	G	30		1
6	Ciaran DONAGHY		26/3/82	D	22	(1)	
22	Rory DONNELLY		18/2/89	A	8	(22)	7
13	Jack DUFFIN		3/2/92	G	8		
2	Liam FLEMING		2/7/81	D	25	(5)	1
10	Stephen GARRETT		13/4/87	A	37	(1)	6
5	Barry HOLLAND		10/5/84	D	19		
7	Mark HOLLAND		20/7/78	M	16	(3)	3
4	Peter HUTTON		2/3/73	D	23		1
16	Barry JOHNSTON		28/10/80	M	19	(5)	
23	Martin JONES		16/1/88	A	6	(7)	
24	Tony KANE		28/8/87	D	8		1
21	Jody LYNCH		23/7/89	M	5	(7)	1
8	George McMULLAN		4/8/81	M	30	(2)	10
25	Dermot McVEIGH		24/7/90	D	19	(2)	
18	Kieran O'CONNOR		29/8/81	M	27	(4)	2
28	Kevin O'NEILL		19/10/91	M		(2)	
	Mark PATTERSON		9/10/89	D		(1)	
9	Chris SCANNELL		7/9/77	A	35	(2)	10
3	Ronan SCANNELL		11/5/79	D	20	(4)	4

No	Name	Nat	DoB	Pos	Aps	(s)	Gls
	Eamon SEYDAK		25/12/86	D	18	(2)	3
	Aaron SMYTH		25/5/87	D	6	(2)	
	Darren STUART		31/3/92	A		(1)	
	Emmett TEMPLETON		29/10/92	D	1		

COLERAINE FC

Manager – David Platt; (5/2/11) Oran Kearney

Founded – 1927

Stadium – The Showgrounds (3,960)

MAJOR HONOURS: Irish League – (1) 1974; Irish Cup – (5) 1965, 1972, 1975, 1977, 2003.

010				
8	Glenavon	h	0-2	
4/8	Glentoran	a	0-2	
1/8	Crusaders	h	0-3	
7/8	Linfield	a	0-1	
1/8	Lisburn	h	0-1	
9	Portadown	a	0-2	
1/9	Donegal Celtic	h	4-0	*Ogilby 2, Brown, Carson*
1/9	Cliftonville	a	2-0	*Scullion, Lowry*
5/9	Ballymena	h	1-0	*Scullion*
/10	Newry	h	2-0	*McVey, Boyce*
/10	Dungannon	a	0-3	
/10	Linfield	h	0-2	
6/10	Glenavon	a	2-1	*Knight 2*
0/10	Crusaders	a	0-2	
/11	Cliftonville	h	3-1	*Knight 2, Carson*
/11	Glentoran	h	1-2	*McVey*
3/11	Lisburn	a	3-0	*Ogilby, Boyce 2*
0/11	Donegal Celtic	a	1-2	*Harkin*
7/11	Portadown	h	1-3	*Boyce*
011				
/1	Cliftonville	h	3-2	*Boyce, Ogilby, Lowry*
/1	Glentoran	h	3-1	*McVey, Black, Knight*
8/1	Newry	a	2-2	*Scullion, Knight*
9/1	Dungannon	a	0-1	
/2	Dungannon	h	0-3	
/2	Lisburn	h	1-2	*Scullion*
3/2	Ballymena	a	1-0	*McVey (p)*
14/2	Portadown	h	1-1	*Carson*
19/2	Ballymena	a	1-1	*Mukendi*
21/2	Donegal Celtic	a	1-1	*Mukendi*
26/2	Newry	h	3-1	*Lowry, Mukendi, Knight*
12/3	Linfield	a	1-0	*Hegarty*
19/3	Glenavon	a	2-1	*Knight, Scullion*
26/3	Crusaders	h	1-3	*Boyce*
1/4	Ballymena	h	1-1	*Mukendi*
16/4	Glenavon	h	3-1	*Ogilby, Knight 2*
23/4	Dungannon	h	2-1	*Knight 2*
26/4	Donegal Celtic	h	3-1	*Knight, Harkness (p), Tommons*
30/4	Newry	a	2-0	*Harkness, Knight*

No	Name	Nat	DoB	Pos	Aps	(s)	Gls
2	Howard BEVERLAND		30/3/90	D	31	(1)	
8	Aaron BLACK		19/12/83	M	17	(2)	1
7	Darren BOYCE		25/1/86	M	25	(6)	6
21	Paul BROWN		20/1/80	A	10	(3)	1
12	Aaron CANNING		7/3/92	D	34		
11	Stephen CARSON		6/10/80	M	31	(3)	3
30	Gavin CULLEN		21/11/80	G	6		
25	Ryan DOHERTY		28/4/92	A	2	(3)	
19	Chris DONNELL		1/1/86	A		(2)	
22	Stephen DOOLEY		19/10/91	M	1		
17	Gareth HARKIN		19/12/87	M	13	(4)	1
3	Johnny HARKNESS		18/11/85	D	19	(5)	2
	David HEALY		17/5/94	A		(2)	
4	Michael HEGARTY		9/12/83	M	31	(1)	1
9	Leon KNIGHT	ENG	16/9/82	A	23		14
18	Stephen LOWRY		14/10/86	M	24	(6)	3
20	Laurence McCORMICK		23/8/86	G	3		
26	Daibhibd McIVOR		9/9/92	M	5	(6)	
15	Paddy McLAUGHLIN		10/10/79	D	2	(2)	
5	Kyle McVEY		7/7/86	D	23	(2)	4
23	Stuart MILLAR		5/12/91	M		(1)	
	Craig MOORE		28/12/91	M		(1)	
	Sammy MORROW		3/3/85	A	2		
6	Mark MUKENDI	IRL	25/6/87	D	10	(7)	4
1	David O'HARE		2/3/72	G	29		
24	David OGILBY		2/6/84	D	27	(2)	5
10	David SCULLION		27/4/84	A	22	(5)	5
16	Gareth TOMMONS		18/5/89	M	17	(9)	1
14	John WATT		20/3/86	M	11	(9)	
	Paul WELLS		29/8/92	G		(1)	

CRUSADERS FC

Manager – Stephen Baxter

Founded – 1898

Stadium – Seaview (3,330)

MAJOR HONOURS: Irish League – (4) 1973, 1976, 1995, 1997; Irish Cup (3) 1967, 1968, 2009.

2010				
7/8	Donegal Celtic	a	3-1	*Halliday, Owens 2*
14/8	Lisburn	h	1-2	*Donnelly*
21/8	Coleraine	a	3-0	*Dallas 2, Donnelly*
27/8	Cliftonville	h	1-3	*Arthurs*
31/8	Ballymena	h	2-1	*Coates, Owens*
11/9	Glenavon	h	5-4	*Owens 2, Morrow, Bell, Dallas*
21/9	Dungannon	h	1-1	*Halliday*
25/9	Portadown	a	2-0	*Halliday, Dallas*
2/10	Glentoran	h	1-0	*Halliday*
5/10	Newry	a	1-1	*Owens*
9/10	Lisburn	a	4-2	*Dallas 2, Halliday, Owens*
15/10	Donegal Celtic	h	4-5	*Donnelly 3, Dallas*
18/10	Linfield	a	1-8	*Owens*
30/10	Coleraine	h	2-0	*Halliday 2*
6/11	Glentoran	a	1-3	*Dallas*
9/11	Dungannon	a	3-2	*Owens, Donnelly, Coates*
13/11	Linfield	h	2-1	*Dallas, Morrow*
20/11	Glenavon	a	1-2	*Dallas*
27/11	Ballymena	a	1-1	*Owens*
11/12	Portadown	h	3-1	*Rainey, Donnelly, Morrow*
27/12	Cliftonville	a	1-2	*Morrow*
2011				
1/1	Dungannon	h	2-2	*Morrow 2 (1p)*
4/1	Linfield	a	1-3	*Halliday*
10/1	Glenavon	h	1-0	*Halliday*
25/1	Newry	h	2-1	*Magee, Halliday (p)*
29/1	Donegal Celtic	h	2-1	*Owens, Cassidy*
5/2	Newry	a	3-2	*Owens, Dallas, Coates (p)*
21/2	Glentoran	h	2-1	*Coates, Owens*
26/2	Portadown	a	1-0	*Dallas*
1/3	Ballymena	a	3-0	*Owens, Coates (p), Morrow*
12/3	Lisburn	a	1-0	*Owens*
19/3	Cliftonville	h	5-0	*Owens 2, Dallas 2, Watson*
26/3	Coleraine	a	3-1	*Coates, Caddell 2*
1/4	Linfield	h	0-1	
16/4	Lisburn	h	4-1	*McKeown, Halliday, Dallas, Owens*
23/4	Portadown	h	3-1	*Caddell, Halliday (p), Owens*
26/4	Cliftonville	a	0-3	
30/4	Glentoran	a	2-2	*Morrow, Owens*

No	Name	Nat	DoB	Pos	Aps	(s)	Gls
16	Ross ARTHURS		13/10/89	M		(13)	1
4	David BELL		13/5/85	D	9		1
15	Declan CADDELL		13/4/88	M	15	(10)	3
24	Darren CASSIDY		6/7/83	M	2	(9)	1
6	Colin COATES		26/10/85	D	32		6
8	Stuart DALLAS		19/4/91	M	35		15
	Eamon DOHERTY		4/1/74	M	1	(2)	
11	Martin DONNELLY		28/8/88	M	25	(2)	7
14	Willie FAULKNER		18/1/90	M		(3)	
17	David GIBSON		15/2/90	D	4	(3)	
9	Michael HALLIDAY		28/5/79	A	25	(10)	12
21	Aaron HOGG		14/1/88	G	5		
1	Chris KEENAN		11/7/87	G	29		
19	Jonathan MAGEE		27/9/88	D	11	(1)	1
5	David MAGOWAN		4/10/83	D	34		
3	Stephen McBRIDE		6/4/83	D	26	(1)	
7	Ryan McCANN		15/9/82	M	6	(1)	
2	Gareth McKEOWN		14/7/83	D	31		1
21	David McMASTER		29/12/88	M	11	(9)	
12	Chris MORROW		20/9/85	M	35		8
25	Niall MURPHY		14/9/91	G	4		
20	Jordan OWENS		9/7/89	A	29	(3)	20

10	David RAINEY	6/4/76	A	16	(11)	1
23	Vincent SWEENEY	12/3/81	A	3	(6)	
22	Aidan WATSON	16/8/86	M	28	(2)	1
	Ian WEST	1/10/91	D	2		

DONEGAL CELTIC FC

Manager – Marty Tabb; (10/9/10) Paddy Kelly

Founded - 1970

Stadium – Suffolk Road (3,000)

2010				
7/8	Crusaders	h	1-3	*McNamee*
14/8	Ballymena	a	4-0	*Cleary, McAlorum, McVeigh P. 2 (1p)*
21/8	Glenavon	a	1-3	*McNamee*
28/8	Glentoran	h	0-3	
31/8	Portadown	h	4-4	*McVeigh P. 3, McCann*
4/9	Newry	a	1-2	*McVeigh P.*
11/9	Coleraine	a	0-4	
21/9	Lisburn	h	2-1	*McVeigh A., McVeigh P.*
25/9	Dungannon	a	0-0	
2/10	Cliftonville	a	2-4	*McVeigh P. 2 (1p)*
5/10	Linfield	h	1-3	*Gargan*
9/10	Ballymena	h	2-3	*McNamee, Gargan*
15/10	Crusaders	a	5-4	*Henderson 2, McVeigh P. 2 (1p), Dickson*
31/10	Newry	h	0-3	
6/11	Dungannon	h	3-4	*McAllister, Gargan, McVeigh P.*
9/11	Linfield	a	2-6	*Gargan, O'Hara*
13/11	Portadown	a	0-3	
20/11	Coleraine	h	2-1	*Gargan, Henderson*
11/12	Glentoran	a	0-1	
14/12	Glenavon	h	1-4	*McVeigh P. (p)*
31/12	Linfield	h	2-0	*McNamee, Henderson*
2011				
4/1	Dungannon	a	1-3	*Henderson*
11/1	Cliftonville	h	1-1	*McNamee*
18/1	Lisburn	a	3-1	*Henderson 2, McVeigh P. (p)*
29/1	Crusaders	a	1-2	*Henderson*
5/2	Portadown	h	0-2	
19/2	Lisburn	a	1-3	*McVeigh P.*
21/2	Coleraine	h	1-1	*Henderson*
26/2	Ballymena	a	3-0	*McAllister, McNamee, McVeigh P. (p)*
1/3	Glentoran	a	0-4	
12/3	Glenavon	h	3-3	*Henderson, Dickson, Glenholmes*
19/3	Newry	h	0-0	
1/4	Cliftonville	a	2-2	*McVeigh P., McAllister*
8/4	Newry	a	1-0	*Henderson*
16/4	Ballymena	h	3-3	*Henderson 2, McVeigh P. (p)*
23/4	Glenavon	a	0-3	
26/4	Coleraine	a	1-3	*McVeigh P.*
30/4	Dungannon	h	1-2	*og (McCaffrey)*

Name	Nat	DoB	Pos	Aps	(s)	Gls
Niall ATKINSON		4/9/90	M	2	(7)	
Liam BRADLEY		21/9/81	M	24		
Stephen BRENNAN		21/12/83	D	9	(1)	
Declan BROWN		21/12/83	G	27		
Gavin BURNS		8/3/88	D		(1)	
Paul CARVILL		20/8/85	D	10	(4)	
Andrew CLEARY		6/4/86	D	17	(2)	1
Marty CUNNINGHAM		25/8/92	D		(1)	
Ian CURRAN		23/9/88	D	6	(3)	
Mark DICKSON		12/12/81	A	16	(15)	2
Chris FAY		21/8/88	A	1	(5)	
James FERRIN		23/9/89	A		(1)	
Ciaran GARGAN		9/2/86	M	28	(5)	5
Conor GLENHOLMES		11/4/90	D	7	(11)	1
Daniel HANNA		29/12/88	M	12	(3)	
Stephen HARBINSON		15/8/85	G	5		
Ryan HENDERSON		26/10/84	A	23	(6)	13
Thomas LAMBE		19/12/90	D	10	(1)	
Eamon McALLISTER		19/11/87	A	28	(7)	3
Stephen McALORUM		11/061986	M	31		1
Patrick McCAFFREY		4/1/90	M		(1)	
Tomas McCANN		16/7/87	M	2	(6)	1
Sean McGREEVEY		4/5/73	G	5		
Jim McMENAMIN		15/8/83	D	7	(3)	
Darren McNAMEE		7/10/85	M	32	(2)	6
Aiden McVEIGH		24/6/83	A	6	(4)	1
Gerard McVEIGH		21/3/89	G	1		
Paul McVEIGH		11/3/77	A	35	(1)	19
Ciaran MUIR		11/2/87	D	14	(4)	
Declan O'HARA		4/2/83	D	33	(2)	1
Barry SPENCE		25/3/86	D	14	(1)	
Liam WATSON		11/8/82	D	13		

DUNGANNON SWIFTS FC

Manager – Dixie Robinson

Founded – 1949

Stadium – Stangmore Park (2,154)

2010				
7/8	Newry	a	0-3	
14/8	Linfield	h	2-1	*Ward, McCaffrey*
20/8	Cliftonville	a	0-2	
27/8	Portadown	h	0-1	
31/8	Glenavon	a	1-2	*Adamson*
4/9	Lisburn	h	2-2	*Adamson, og (McShane)*
11/9	Glentoran	h	1-3	*og (Ward)*
21/9	Crusaders	a	1-1	*McIlmoyle*
25/9	Donegal Celtic	h	0-0	
02/10	Ballymena	a	1-1	*Ward*
5/10	Coleraine	h	3-0	*Adamson 3*
9/10	Portadown	a	2-2	*McIlmoyle, O'Neill R.*
16/10	Lisburn	a	1-4	*og (Simpson)*
30/10	Glenavon	h	2-1	*Ward 2*
6/11	Donegal Celtic	a	4-3	*og (Carvill), McCaffrey, Adamson 2*
9/11	Crusaders	h	2-3	*Lavery P., Adamson*
13/11	Glentoran	a	2-0	*McCaffrey, Adamson*
20/11	Linfield	a	0-1	
27/11	Cliftonville	h	0-1	
11/12	Ballymena	h	1-2	*Henderson*
2011				
1/1	Crusaders	a	2-2	*McCluskey, McCaffrey*
4/1	Donegal Celtic	h	3-1	*Ward, Lavery P. 2*
29/1	Coleraine	h	1-0	*Adamson*
1/2	Coleraine	a	3-0	*Adamson, McCaffrey, Ward (p)*
5/2	Linfield	h	0-4	
8/2	Glentoran	a	0-0	
19/2	Cliftonville	a	2-3	*Ward, Funston*
21/2	Newry	h	0-0	
26/2	Lisburn	h	1-2	*Ward*
1/3	Newry	a	1-0	*Lavery P.*
19/3	Portadown	a	1-2	*O'Neill R.*
22/3	Ballymena	h	1-0	*Ward*
26/3	Glenavon	h	2-2	*McCaffrey, Ward (p)*
31/3	Glenavon	a	2-1	*McIlmoyle, og (Jennings)*
16/4	Newry	h	1-0	*og (McCann P.)*
23/4	Coleraine	a	1-2	*McCaffrey*
26/4	Ballymena	a	2-0	*Donnelly, Lavery P.*
30/4	Donegal Celtic	a	2-1	*Ward, McIlmoyle*

Name	Nat	DoB	Pos	Aps	(s)	Gls
Timmy ADAMSON		5/1/83	A	25	(2)	11
Shane CONEY		2/11/78	A	2	(3)	
Philip DONNELLY		20/4/92	M	1	(2)	1
Alain EMERSON		13/8/79	M	6	(6)	
Andy FERGUSON		22/2/89	D	2	(1)	
Terry FITZPATRICK		23/3/82	M	28	(7)	
Aidan FORKER		6/4/92	M	2	(3)	
Conor FORKER		10/4/82	A	2	(9)	
Michael FUNSTON	IRL	15/5/85	M	13	(2)	1
John Paul GALLAGHER		28/7/82	D	3		
Niall HENDERSON		7/2/88	M	23	(5)	1
Patrick J. LAVERY		3/5/89	M	8	(13)	5
Stefan LAVERY		20/7/93	A	1	(9)	
Fergal McALISKEY		29/6/89	D	4	(2)	
Dermot McCAFFREY		29/3/86	D	36		7
Marc McCANN		6/8/80	M	2	(2)	
Craig McCLEAN		6/7/85	D	28	(2)	
Ryan McCLUSKEY		2/6/81	M	28	(2)	1
Ryan McILMOYLE		12/12/84	M	24	(7)	4
Michael McKERR		23/2/90	D	5	(1)	
Adam McMINN		15/1/84	D	8	(4)	
Johnny MONTGOMERY		6/4/74	D	19	(3)	
Shane MULGREW		4/8/88	D	6	(1)	

van MULLAN		11/11/88	D	17	(3)	
arren MURPHY		23/1/75	D	6	(6)	
van O'NEILL		19/1/90	D	24	(1)	2
ean O'NEILL		11/4/88	G	38		
hnny TOPLEY		12/7/80	M	21	(5)	
chael WARD		17/4/84	A	36		11

GLENAVON FC

Manager – Marty Quinn
Founded – 1889
Stadium – Mourneview Park (4,160)
MAJOR HONOURS: Irish League – (3) 1952, 1957, 1960; Irish Cup – (5) 1957, 1959, 1961, 1992, 1997.

010				
/8	Coleraine	a	2-0	*Miskimmin 2*
3/8	Portadown	h	1-0	*Shannon*
/8	Donegal Celtic	h	3-1	*Grant 2, Molloy*
7/8	Ballymena	h	0-2	
1/8	Dungannon	h	2-1	*Grant 2*
/9	Glentoran	h	0-1	
/9	Crusaders	a	4-5	*Molloy 3 (1p), Costello*
1/9	Linfield	h	0-1	
4/9	Newry	a	1-2	*Miskimmin*
/10	Lisburn	a	2-2	*McDonagh 2*
/10	Cliftonville	h	1-2	*Molloy*
/10	Glentoran	a	1-4	*Miskimmin*
6/10	Coleraine	h	1-2	*Haughey*
0/10	Dungannon	a	1-2	*Hamilton*
/11	Ballymena	a	3-3	*Hamilton 2, Neill*
/11	Cliftonville	a	2-0	*Grant, Hamilton*
2/11	Newry	h	2-1	*Molloy, Hamilton*
0/11	Crusaders	h	2-1	*Hamilton, Costello*
1/12	Lisburn	h	1-1	*King*
4/12	Donegal Celtic	a	4-1	*Miskimmin, Molloy, Hamilton (p), Walsh*
7/12	Portadown	a	2-2	*Haughey, Hamilton*
2011				
/1	Ballymena	h	3-1	*Molloy, Grant 2*
/1	Newry	h	2-1	*Walsh, Hamilton*
0/1	Crusaders	a	0-1	
25/1	Linfield	a	0-1	
31/1	Cliftonville	h	0-2	
5/2	Glentoran	a	2-2	*Molloy, Miskimmin (p)*
3/2	Lisburn	h	0-1	
19/2	Portadown	a	1-1	*Haughey*
26/2	Linfield	h	2-2	*Harpur, McDonagh*
12/3	Donegal Celtic	a	3-3	*McDonagh, Miskimmin, Hamilton*
19/3	Coleraine	h	1-2	*Hamilton*
26/3	Dungannon	a	2-2	*Molloy, Hamilton (p)*
31/3	Dungannon	h	1-2	*Harpur*
16/4	Coleraine	a	1-3	*Hamilton*
23/4	Donegal Celtic	h	3-0	*Grant, og (O'Hara), Lavery*
26/4	Newry	a	4-0	*Lavery 2, O'Carroll, Miskimmin*
30/4	Ballymena	a	0-1	

No	Name	Nat	DoB	Pos	Aps	(s)	Gls
17	James COSTELLO		9/6/86	A	6	(21)	2
9	Tony GRANT	IRL	20/8/76	A	26	(8)	8
80	Gary HAMILTON		6/10/80	A	24	(1)	13
15	Adrian HARPER	IRL	4/5/85	M	15	(6)	
7	Ryan HARPUR		1/12/88	M	19	(7)	2
16	Mark HAUGHEY		23/1/91	D	26	(1)	3
	Pat JENNINGS	ENG	24/9/79	G	5		
	Barry JOHNSTON		28/10/80	M	1	(3)	
11	Stuart KING		20/3/81	M	19	(3)	1
22	Chris LAVERY		20/1/91	M	4	(5)	3
4	Jay MAGEE		4/5/88	D	36		
6	Will McDONAGH	IRL	14/3/83	M	20	(1)	4
12	Mark MISKIMMIN		11/6/88	A	20	(15)	8
10	Trevor MOLLOY	IRL	14/4/77	A	32	(2)	10
3	Kyle NEILL		3/3/78	D	34		1
14	Diarmuid O'CARROLL		16/3/87	A	6	(5)	1
1	Andrew PLUMMER	ENG	13/10/89	G	33		
2	Brendan SHANNON		27/9/88	D	37		1
23	Sammy STEWART		25/11/90	M	11	(7)	
18	Mark TURKINGTON		20/3/84	D	23	(1)	
8	Cono WALSH		11/3/83	M	21	(6)	2

GLENTORAN FC

Manager – Scott Young
Founded – 1882
Stadium – The Oval (9,400)
MAJOR HONOURS: Irish League – (23) 1894, 1897, 1905, 1912, 1913, 1921, 1925, 1931, 1951, 1953, 1964, 1967, 1968, 1970, 1972, 1977, 1981, 1988, 1992, 1999, 2003, 2005, 2009; Irish Cup – (20) 1914, 1917, 1921, 1932, 1933, 1935, 1951, 1966, 1973, 1983, 1985, 1986, 1987, 1988, 1990, 1996, 1998, 2000, 2001, 2004.

2010				
7/8	Lisburn	a	6-1	*Fordyce 5 (1p), Martyn*
14/8	Coleraine	h	2-0	*Fordyce, Waterworth*
21/8	Newry	a	0-0	
28/8	Donegal Celtic	a	3-0	*Gawley, Fordyce, Burrows*
31/8	Cliftonville	h	2-0	*Gawley, Fordyce*
4/9	Glenavon	a	1-0	*Martyn*
11/9	Dungannon	a	3-1	*Nixon, Burrows, Fordyce*
21/9	Ballymena	h	1-2	*Gardiner*
27/9	Linfield	h	0-0	
2/10	Crusaders	a	0-1	
5/10	Portadown	h	1-0	*Burrows*
9/10	Glenavon	h	4-1	*Burrows 2, Waterworth, Black*
16/10	Cliftonville	a	1-2	*Burrows*
30/10	Lisburn	h	1-3	*Burrows*
6/11	Crusaders	h	3-1	*Burrows, Nixon, Steele*
9/11	Coleraine	a	2-1	*Clarke, Black*
13/11	Dungannon	h	0-2	
20/11	Portadown	a	1-0	*Burrows*
27/11	Newry	h	2-0	*Waterworth, Steele*
11/12	Donegal Celtic	h	1-0	*Burrows*
2011				
1/1	Portadown	h	0-1	
4/1	Coleraine	a	1-3	*Steele*
18/1	Linfield	a	1-2	*Nixon*
29/1	Lisburn	a	2-0	*Fordyce, Gibson*
5/2	Glenavon	h	2-2	*Clarke, Howland*
8/2	Dungannon	h	0-0	
14/2	Ballymena	a	2-0	*Clarke, Howland*
21/2	Crusaders	a	1-2	*Fordyce*
26/2	Cliftonville	h	0-0	
1/3	Donegal Celtic	h	4-0	*Waterworth, Fordyce 2, Burrows*
12/3	Newry	a	4-3	*Burrows 3 (1p), Fordyce*
19/3	Ballymena	a	3-2	*Waterworth 2, Steele*
26/3	Cliftonville	a	2-1	*Fordyce, Burrows*
16/4	Linfield	h	1-2	*Fordyce*
19/4	Linfield	a	2-3	*Nixon, Fordyce (p)*
23/4	Lisburn	h	2-1	*Waterworth, Steele*
26/4	Portadown	a	0-2	
30/4	Crusaders	h	2-2	*Waterworth, Clarke*

No	Name	Nat	DoB	Pos	Aps	(s)	Gls
3	Johnny BLACK		26/2/88	D	16	(7)	2
	Daniel BURNS		17/8/91	M	1	(1)	
12	Matty BURROWS		15/10/85	A	18	(15)	15
22	Jimmy CALLACHER		11/6/91	M	15	(9)	
20	Kyle CHERRY		13/5/93	A		(1)	
4	Richard CLARKE		28/11/85	M	33	(4)	4
	Michael DORAN		6/1/91	A	1	(3)	
16	Daryl FORDYCE		2/1/87	M	35	(2)	17
	Grant GARDINER		13/9/88	M	11	(6)	1
11	Neal GAWLEY		20/2/86	M	23	(10)	2
13	Richard GIBSON		11/1/85	A	4	(1)	1
21	Andrew HALL		19/9/89	M	2	(2)	
24	Jason HILL		24/2/82	D	30	(2)	
26	David HOWLAND		17/9/86	M	20		2
5	Paul LEEMAN		21/1/78	D	23		
8	Ciaran MARTYN	IRL	25/3/80	M	8		2
17	Shane McCABE		21/12/81	M	3		
25	Jamie McGOVERN		29/5/89	M	33	(1)	
1	Elliott MORRIS		4/5/81	G	32		
23	Martin MURRAY		18/8/93	A		(1)	
2	Colin NIXON		8/9/78	D	35		4
26	Jim O'HANLON		14/3/93	M		(1)	
14	Peter STEELE		3/8/90	A	5	(18)	5
18	James TAYLOR		12/5/84	G	6		
15	Johnny TAYLOR		30/6/84	D	8	(4)	
7	Sean WARD		12/4/84	D	24	(1)	
9	Andrew WATERWORTH		11/4/86	A	32	(3)	8

LINFIED FC

Manager – David Jeffrey
Founded – 1886
Stadium – Windsor Park (12,950)
MAJOR HONOURS: Irish League – (50) 1891, 1892, 1893, 1895, 1898, 1902, 1904, 1907, 1908, 1909, 1911, 1914, 1922, 1923, 1930, 1932, 1934, 1935, 1949, 1950, 1954, 1955, 1956, 1959, 1961, 1962, 1966, 1969, 1971, 1975, 1978, 1979, 1980, 1982, 1983, 1984, 1985, 1986, 1987, 1989, 1993, 1994, 2000, 2001, 2004, 2006, 2007, 2008, 2010, 2011;
Irish Cup – (41) 1891, 1892, 1893, 1895, 1898, 1899, 1902, 1904, 1912, 1913, 1915, 1916, 1919, 1922, 1923, 1930, 1931, 1934, 1936, 1939, 1942, 1945, 1946, 1948, 1950, 1953, 1960, 1962, 1963, 1970, 1978, 1980, 1982, 1994, 1995, 2002, 2006, 2007, 2008, 2010, 2011.

2010				
7/8	Ballymena	h	0-0	
14/8	Dungannon	a	1-2	*Munster*
21/8	Lisburn	h	1-0	*Carvill*
27/8	Coleraine	h	1-0	*Munster*
31/8	Newry	a	2-1	*og (Hazley), Allen*
11/9	Cliftonville	h	0-0	
21/9	Glenavon	a	1-0	*McAllister*
27/9	Glentoran	a	0-0	
2/10	Portadown	h	4-0	*Allen 2, Thompson 2*
5/10	Donegal Celtic	a	3-1	*Thompson 2, Garrett*
9/10	Coleraine	a	2-0	*McAllister, Thompson*
15/10	Newry	h	4-0	*Thompson 2, Casement, Burns A.*
18/10	Crusaders	h	8-1	*McAllister 2, Ervin, Allen 2, Thompson, Burns A., Mulgrew*
30/10	Ballymena	a	3-3	*McAllister, og (Nelson), Thompson*
5/11	Portadown	a	2-1	*Garrett, Thompson*
9/11	Donegal Celtic	h	6-2	*Thompson 2, Allen 2, Garrett, McAllister*
13/11	Crusaders	a	1-2	*Garrett*
20/11	Dungannon	h	1-0	*Thompson*
27/11	Lisburn	a	4-0	*Lowry, Thompson 2, Garrett*
10/12	Cliftonville	a	1-3	*Burns A.*
31/12	Donegal Celtic	a	0-2	
2011				
4/1	Crusaders	h	3-1	*McAllister, Thompson 2*
18/1	Glentoran	h	2-1	*Thompson, McAllister*
22/1	Cliftonville	a	4-2	*Thompson 2, Lowry, Kane*
25/1	Glenavon	h	1-0	*Gault*
29/1	Ballymena	h	0-0	
5/2	Dungannon	a	4-0	*Hanley, Mulgrew, Gault, Allen*
19/2	Newry	h	1-1	*Lowry*
26/2	Glenavon	a	2-2	*og (Turkington), McAllister*
12/3	Coleraine	h	0-1	
19/3	Lisburn	h	2-0	*Murphy, Thompson*
22/3	Portadown	a	4-0	*Gault, Murphy, McAllister 2*
1/4	Crusaders	a	1-0	*Garrett*
16/4	Glentoran	a	2-1	*Munster, Carvill*
19/4	Glentoran	h	3-2	*Lowry 2, Casement*
23/4	Cliftonville	h	1-0	*Thompson*
26/4	Lisburn	a	4-0	*Carvill 2, Thompson (p), McAllister*
30/4	Portadown	h	1-0	*Allen*

No	Name	Nat	DoB	Pos	Aps	(s)	Gls
18	Stuart ADDIS		5/7/79	G	1		
17	Curtis ALLEN		22/2/88	A	18	(5)	9
3	David ARMSTRONG		23/1/87	D	15		
11	Noel BAILIE		23/2/71	D	6	(3)	
1	Alan BLAYNEY		9/10/81	G	37		
	Aaron BOYD		12/2/91	A		(1)	
14	Aaron BURNS		29/5/92	D	18	(5)	3
12	Billy Joe BURNS		24/4/89	D	11	(8)	
10	Michael CARVILL		3/4/88	A	6	(14)	4
28	Chris CASEMENT		12/1/88	D	25	(1)	2
7	Damien CURRAN		17/10/81	M	22	(4)	
2	Stephen DOUGLAS		27/9/77	D	10	(1)	
21	Jim ERVIN		5/6/85	D	29	(1)	1
20	Robert GARRETT		5/5/88	M	33	(2)	6
4	Michael GAULT		15/4/83	M	28	(1)	3
15	Nathan HANLEY		18/7/90	M	4	(2)	1
26	Marcus KANE		8/12/91	M	4	(3)	1
6	Kris LINDSAY		5/2/84	D	1		
8	Philip LOWRY		15/7/89	M	21	(11)	5
25	Mark McALLISTER		26/4/88	A	26	(2)	12
24	Brian McCAUL		6/8/90	M	2	(1)	
22	Jamie MULGREW		5/6/86	M	24	(8)	2
23	Paul MUNSTER		9/2/82	A	10	(17)	3
5	William MURPHY		29/1/74	D	20	(2)	2
16	Aidan O'KANE		24/11/79	D	5	(1)	
9	Peter THOMPSON		2/5/84	A	34		23
34	Jamie TOMELTY		16/9/83	M	8	(8)	

LISBURN DISTILLERY FC

Manager – Tommy Wright
Founded – 1879
Stadium – New Grosvenor (2,220)
MAJOR HONOURS: Irish League – (6) 1896, 1899, 1901, 1903, 1906 (shared), 1963;
Irish Cup – (12) 1884, 1885, 1886, 1889, 1894, 1896, 1903, 1905, 1910, 1925, 1956, 1971.

2010				
7/8	Glentoran	h	1-6	*Davidson*
14/8	Crusaders	a	2-1	*Cushley, Browne*
21/8	Linfield	a	0-1	
28/8	Newry	h	2-1	*Hunter, Liggett*
31/8	Coleraine	a	1-0	*Ferguson*
4/9	Dungannon	a	2-2	*Thompson G., Patton*
11/9	Portadown	h	2-0	*Ferguson, Browne (p)*
21/9	Donegal Celtic	a	1-2	*Ferguson*
25/9	Cliftonville	h	1-1	*Coyle*
2/10	Glenavon	h	2-2	*Browne (p), Liggett*
5/10	Ballymena	a	1-0	*Thompson G.*
9/10	Crusaders	h	2-4	*Ferguson, Simpson*
16/10	Dungannon	h	4-1	*Browne 2, Cushley, Davidson*
30/10	Glentoran	a	3-1	*Browne 2, Liggett*
5/11	Newry	a	1-1	*Ferguson*
9/11	Ballymena	h	1-1	*Ferguson*
13/11	Coleraine	h	0-3	
20/11	Cliftonville	a	3-1	*Thompson G., Browne, Ferguson*
27/11	Linfield	h	0-4	
11/12	Glenavon	a	1-1	*Ferguson*
31/12	Newry	a	1-2	*Thompson G.*
2011				
4/1	Cliftonville	a	2-3	*Cushley, Cooling*
18/1	Donegal Celtic	h	1-3	*Liggett*
25/1	Portadown	a	0-1	
29/1	Glentoran	h	0-2	
4/2	Coleraine	a	2-1	*Simpson, Ferguson*
8/2	Glenavon	a	1-0	*Cushley*
19/2	Donegal Celtic	h	3-1	*Cushley, Browne, Patton*
26/2	Dungannon	a	2-1	*Patton, Browne*
5/3	Ballymena	h	0-1	
12/3	Crusaders	h	0-1	
19/3	Linfield	a	0-2	
26/3	Portadown	h	2-1	*Liggett 2*
16/4	Crusaders	a	1-4	*Hughes*
19/4	Portadown	a	0-1	
23/4	Glentoran	a	1-2	*Ferguson*
26/4	Linfield	h	0-4	
30/4	Cliftonville	h	4-3	*Liggett 2, Browne, Davidson*

No	Name	Nat	DoB	Pos	Aps	(s)	Gls
27	Eoin BOYLE		4/1/91	A		(2)	
13	Billy BRENNAN	IRL	6/3/85	G	12		
10	Gary BROWNE		17/1/83	D	32	(3)	11
31	Aaron CALLAGHAN		1/7/86	M	15		
17	Philip CARSON		6/1/88	M	2	(1)	
11	Mark COOLING		27/2/89	M	22	(8)	1
14	Darren COYLE		28/4/92	M		(7)	1
4	John CURRAN		17/5/82	D	9	(1)	
19	David CUSHLEY		22/7/89	A	14	(16)	5
16	Scott DAVIDSON		27/9/91	M	22	(10)	3
26	Andy DEVLIN		12/10/91	D	11	(4)	
9	Glenn FERGUSON		10/7/69	A	29	(7)	10
20	Jordan FORSYTHE		11/2/91	M	3	(11)	

Name	Nat	DoB	Pos	Aps	(s)	Gls
Jordan HUGHES		27/1/91	M	1	(3)	1
Andy HUNTER		19/1/81	D	25	(1)	1
Andy KILMARTIN		18/1/83	M	34	(1)	
Gary LIGGETT		28/9/87	A	21	(12)	8
Philip MATTHEWS		26/3/74	G	21		
Peter McCANN		18/1/81	D	1		
Chris McCLUSKEY		20/7/89	G	5		
Pat McSHANE		28/11/74	D	29	(1)	
Bradley MORTON		22/12/92	M		(1)	
Paul MUIR		18/10/75	D	20		
Mark PATTON		21/6/89	M	24	(7)	3
Philip SIMPSON		21/10/86	D	31		2
George STEWART		19/6/90	M		(2)	
Gary THOMPSON		26/5/90	M	23	(4)	4
Stuart THOMPSON		9/7/85	D	5		
Aaron TRAYNOR		24/7/90	M	7	(1)	

NEWRY CITY FC

Manager – Gerry Flynn; (2/3/11) Pat McGibbon
Founded – 1923
Stadium – The Showgrounds (2,822)

010				
/8	Dungannon	h	3-0	*Rowe (p), Graham, Downey*
4/8	Cliftonville	h	0-1	
1/8	Glentoran	h	0-0	
8/8	Lisburn	a	1-2	*Convery*
1/8	Linfield	h	1-2	*Murphy*
/9	Donegal Celtic	h	2-1	*Graham 2*
1/9	Ballymena	a	0-1	
1/9	Portadown	a	2-4	*Davidson 2 (1p)*
4/9	Glenavon	h	2-1	*Graham, Murray*
/10	Coleraine	a	0-2	
/10	Crusaders	h	1-1	*Murray*
/10	Cliftonville	a	1-2	*Rowe (p)*
5/10	Linfield	a	0-4	
1/10	Donegal Celtic	a	3-0	*Hazley, Graham 2*
/11	Lisburn	h	1-1	*Convery*
/11	Portadown	h	4-2	*Davidson 3, Murray*
2/11	Glenavon	a	1-2	*Davidson*
9/11	Ballymena	h	0-4	
27/11	Glentoran	a	0-2	
31/12	Lisburn	h	2-1	*Teggart, Graham*
2011				
4/1	Glenavon	a	1-2	*Davidson*
18/1	Coleraine	h	2-2	*Keenan, McDonnell*
25/1	Crusaders	a	1-2	*Keenan*
29/1	Portadown	a	1-2	*Murray*
5/2	Crusaders	h	2-3	*Graham, Davidson*
12/2	Cliftonville	h	0-2	
19/2	Linfield	a	1-1	*Murray*
21/2	Dungannon	a	0-0	
26/2	Coleraine	a	1-3	*Alderdice*
1/3	Dungannon	h	0-1	
12/3	Glentoran	h	3-4	*McCallion, McCann P. 2*
19/3	Donegal Celtic	a	0-0	
26/3	Ballymena	h	1-1	*McCann M.*
8/4	Donegal Celtic	h	0-1	
16/4	Dungannon	a	0-1	
23/4	Ballymena	a	0-1	
26/4	Glenavon	h	0-4	
30/4	Coleraine	h	0-2	

Name	Nat	DoB	Pos	Aps	(s)	Gls
Neil ALDERDICE		30/11/84	D	7		1
David ANDERSON		26/11/91	M	1		
Neil BARR		30/7/91	D		(1)	
Ross BLACK		10/5/88	D	33	(1)	
Andy COLEMAN		13/6/85	G	25		
John CONVERY		1/4/80	D	35		2
Alan DAVIDSON		19/3/88	M	26	(2)	8
Ruairi DEVLIN		2/5/90	A		(11)	
Conor DOWNEY		12/3/82	D	13	(7)	1
Jamie DUFFY	USA	20/11/83	A	2	(2)	
Cullen FEENEY		17/8/80	D	8	(2)	
Steven FERGUSON		25/2/83	M	12	(2)	
Andy GRAHAM		9/12/88	A	30	(8)	8
Conor HAGAN		31/3/82	D	24	(2)	
Jemar HALL		4/8/93	A		(1)	
Marty HAVERN		25/2/87	M	4	(13)	
Matthew HAZLEY		30/12/87	M	21	(5)	1
Paul KEENAN		3/12/84	A	6	(10)	2
Darren KING		16/10/85	M	22	(1)	
Tommy McCALLION		18/1/77	M	16		1
Marc McCANN		6/8/80	M	9		1
Peter McCANN		18/1/81	D	7	(1)	2
Andy McCOY		16/3/89	D		(1)	
Gavin McDONNELL	IRL	16/6/78	D	28	(1)	1
Stefan McKEVITT		27/6/87	D		(1)	
Nathan MORLEY-HILLEN		25/6/90	G	13		
Darren MUNSTER		24/2/79	D	24	(1)	
Francis MURPHY		28/6/79	M	19	(2)	1
Darren MURRAY		24/10/91	A	17	(14)	5
Gerard ROWE	IRL	3/8/84	A	13		2
Neil TEGGART		16/9/84	A	3	(6)	1

PORTADOWN FC

Coach – Ronnie McFall
Founded – 1924
Stadium – Shamrock Park (15,800)
MAJOR HONOURS: Irish League – (4) 1990, 1991, 1996, 2002; Irish Cup – (3) 1991, 1999, 2005.

2010				
13/8	Glenavon	a	0-1	
21/8	Ballymena	h	1-3	*Mouncey*
27/8	Dungannon	a	1-0	*Braniff*
31/8	Donegal Celtic	a	4-4	*Boyle 2, Braniff 2*
4/9	Coleraine	h	2-0	*og (Brown), Braniff*
11/9	Lisburn	a	0-2	
21/9	Newry	h	4-2	*Lecky 3, McCafferty*
25/9	Crusaders	h	0-2	
2/10	Linfield	a	0-4	
5/10	Glentoran	a	0-1	
9/10	Dungannon	h	2-2	*Teggart, Kelly*
16/10	Ballymena	a	1-3	*Boyle*
30/10	Cliftonville	a	1-0	*Lecky*
5/11	Linfield	h	1-2	*Braniff*
8/11	Newry	a	2-4	*Braniff, Clarke*
13/11	Donegal Celtic	h	3-0	*Braniff 2, Boyle*
20/11	Glentoran	h	0-1	
27/11	Coleraine	a	3-1	*Boyle, Mackle, Clarke*
11/12	Crusaders	a	1-3	*Boyle*
27/12	Glenavon	h	2-2	*Boyle 2*
2011				
1/1	Glentoran	a	1-0	*Lecky*
4/1	Ballymena	a	1-3	*Tipton (p)*
25/1	Lisburn	h	1-0	*Tipton*
29/1	Newry	h	2-1	*Mackle 2*
5/2	Donegal Celtic	a	2-0	*Tipton, O'Hara*
8/2	Cliftonville	h	2-1	*Cawley, Braniff*
14/2	Coleraine	a	1-1	*Tipton*
19/2	Glenavon	h	1-1	*Tipton*
26/2	Crusaders	h	0-1	
12/3	Cliftonville	a	3-1	*Tipton, og (Hutton), Braniff*
19/3	Dungannon	h	2-1	*Baker, Gartland*
22/3	Linfield	h	0-4	
26/3	Lisburn	a	1-2	*Braniff*
16/4	Cliftonville	h	0-1	
19/4	Lisburn	h	1-0	*Lecky*
23/4	Crusaders	a	1-3	*Lecky*
26/4	Glentoran	h	2-0	*Lecky, Teggart*
30/4	Linfield	a	0-1	

No	Name	Nat	DoB	Pos	Aps	(s)	Gls
13	Neil ARMSTRONG		18/12/75	G	8		
14	Jordan BAKER		18/4/89	A	14	(7)	1
7	Wesley BOYLE		30/3/79	M	30	(4)	8
10	Kevin BRANIFF		4/3/83	A	28		11
6	Gary BREEN	IRL	17/3/89	D	11		
16	Alan CAWLEY	IRL	3/1/82	M	2	(5)	1
8	Richard CLARKE		29/5/79	M	22	(7)	2

23	Philip CRAIG		25/4/85	D	11	(1)	
19	Brain GARTLAND	IRL	4/11/86	D	14		1
15	Aaron HAIRE		27/11/90	A	1	(5)	
21	Aaron HOGG		14/1/88	G	1		
	Darren KELLY		30/6/79	D	15	(3)	1
18	Richard LECKY		13/5/84	M	14	(19)	8
2	Sean MACKLE	SCO	10/4/88	D	20	(6)	3
17	Shane McCABE		21/12/81	M	25	(3)	
	Neil McCAFFERTY		19/7/84	M	13	(5)	1
	David McCULLOUGH		24/4/87	M	1		
	Shane McKINNEY		8/4/94	D		(1)	
	Henry McSTAY	IRL	6/3/85	D	11	(3)	
1	David MISKELLY		3/9/79	G	29		
11	Tim MOUNCEY		27/4/82	M	24	(1)	1
4	Keith O'HARA		3/2/81	D	32	(1)	1
24	Matthew PAGET		14/9/90	D		(2)	
5	Chris RAMSEY		24/5/90	D	29	(2)	
3	Ross REDMAN		23/11/89	D	35		
12	Alan TEGGART		24/11/86	M	12	(10)	2
9	Matthew TIPTON	WAL	30/4/90	A	16		6

TOP GOALSCORERS 2010/11

23	Peter THOMPSON (Linfield)
20	Jordan OWENS (Crusaders)
19	Paul McVEIGH (Donegal Celtic)
17	Daryl FORDYCE (Glentoran)
15	Stuart DALLAS (Crusaders) Matty BURROWS (Glentoran)
14	Gary McCUTCHEON (Ballymena) Leon KNIGHT (Coleraine)
13	Ryan HENDERSON (Donegal Celtic) Gary HAMILTON (Glenavon)

PROMOTED CLUB

CARRICK RANGERS FC

Coach – Stephen Small

Founded - 1939

Stadium – Taylor's Avenue (6,000)

MAJOR HONOURS: Irish Cup – (1) 1976.

SECOND LEVEL FINAL TABLE 2010/11

		Pld	W	D	L	F	A	Pts
1	Carrick Rangers FC	26	18	4	4	57	27	58
2	Limavady United FC	26	15	6	5	53	27	51
3	Dergview FC	26	15	3	8	51	32	48
4	Bangor FC	26	11	8	7	45	38	41
5	Ballinamallard United FC	26	11	6	9	45	38	39
6	Harland & Wolff Welders FC	26	11	6	9	45	38	39
7	Ards FC	26	9	7	10	37	42	34
8	Institute FC	26	10	4	12	28	43	34
9	Larne FC	26	8	6	12	38	41	30
10	Loughgall FC	26	8	6	12	37	48	30
11	Banbridge Town FC	26	7	7	12	31	39	28
12	Glebe Rangers FC	26	7	7	12	36	46	28
13	Ballymoney United FC	26	5	8	13	31	48	23
14	Ballyclare Comrades FC	26	5	6	15	28	55	21

DOMESTIC CUP 2010/11

IRISH CUP

FIFTH ROUND

(15/1/11)
Albert Foundry 0, Nortel 2
Annagh United 2, Glenavon 6
Ballinamallard 3, Larne 1
Ballymena 1, Glentoran 1
Carrick 3, Shankill United 3
Crusaders 3, Newry 2
Dundela 1, Lisburn 4
Dungannon 5, Ballymoney 1
Dunmurry Recreation 2, Kilmore Recreation 2
Linfield 5, Institute 1
Loughgall 3, Sports & Leisure 1
Portadown 4, Donegal Celtic 3
Queen's University 1, Crumlin United 0
Warrenpoint Town 1, Cliftonville 1

(25/1/11)
Ards 2, Harland & Wolff Welders 2
Limavady United 1, Coleraine 2

Replays

(25/1/11)
Cliftonville 0, Warrenpoint Town 0 *(aet; 1-3 on pens)*
Glentoran 3, Ballymena 2 *(aet)*
Kilmore Recreation 0, Dunmurry Recreation 5

(26/1/11)
Carrick 6, Shankill United 1

(1/2/11)
Ards 0, Harland & Wolff Welders 1 *(aet)*

SIXTH ROUND

(12/2/11)
Carrick 1, Coleraine 3
Crusaders 2, Nortel 1
Dungannon 4, Warrenpoint Town 2
Glenavon 2, Queen's University 0
Glentoran 3, Loughgall 1
Harland & Wolff Welders 1, Portadown 1
Linfield 1, Dunmurry Recreation 1
Lisburn 2, Ballinamallard 2

Replays

(21/2/11)
Ballinamallard 4, Lisburn 2
Linfield 3, Dunmurry Recreation 0
Portadown 1, Harland & Wolff Welders 0

QUARTER-FINALS

(5/3/11)
Ballinamallard 0, Crusaders 5 *(Morrow 9, Coates 20, Dallas 33, McBride 55, Owens 62)*

Dungannon 0, Linfield 2 *(Thompson 41, 79p)*

Glentoran 1 *(Waterworth 29p)*, Coleraine 1 *(Mukendi 86)*

Portadown 3 *(Mouncey 10, Boyle 61, Lecky 90)*, Glenavon 3 *(Hamilton 25p, Neill 48, Grant 90)*

Replays

(14/3/11)
Coleraine 3 *(Carson 56, Mukendi 90, Lowry 110p)*, Glentoran 3 *(Waterworth 16, 90, Nixon 112) (aet; 2-3 on pens)*

Glenavon 0, Portadown 3 *(Baker 22, 60, Tipton 58)*

SEMI-FINALS

(9/4/11)
Crusaders 3 *(Halliday 46, Caddell 68, Owens 85)*, Portadown 1 *(Clarke 4)*

Linfield 2 *(Tomelty 32, Thompson 56)*, Glentoran 0

FINAL

(7/5/11)
Windsor Park, Belfast
LINFIELD FC 2 *(Thompson 78, McAllister 87)*
CRUSADERS FC 1 *(Caddell 54)*
Referee – *Courtney*
LINFIELD – *Blayney, Ervin (Tomelty 75), Douglas, Casement, Curran, Lowry (Mulgrew 63), Gault, Garrett, Carvill, Thompson, McAllister.*
CRUSADERS – *Keenan, McKeown, Magowan, Coates, McBride, Morrow (McMaster 86), Caddell, Dallas, Watson, Halliday (Rainey 80), Owens.*

CLUB COMMUNICATION 2011/12

Ballymena United FC

The Showgrounds, Warden Street
GB-Ballymena BT43 7DR

Tel +44 2825 652 049
Fax +44 2825 652 049
Web ballymenaunitedfc.com
Email ballymenaunited@live.co.uk
Media Officer Don Stirling

Carrick Rangers FC

Taylor's Avenue
GB-Carrickfergus BT38 7HF

Tel
Fax
Web carrickrangers.co.uk
Email
Media Officer Noel Patterson

Cliftonville FC

Solitude, Cliftonville Street
GB-Belfast BT14 6LP

Tel +44 2890 748 635
Fax +44 7053 635 438
Web cliftonvillefc.net
Email secretary@cliftonvilefc.net
Media Officer David Begley

Coleraine FC

The Showgrounds, Ballycastle Road
GB-Coleraine BT52 2DY

Tel +44 2827 667 452
Fax +44 2870 002 074
Web colerainefc.com
Email secretary@colerainefc.com
Media Officer Steven Crawford

Crusaders FC

Seaview, St. Vincent Street
GB-Belfast BT15 3QG

Tel +44 2890 370 777
Fax +44 2890 771 049
Web crusadersfc.com
Email ncrues@aol.com
Media Officer Alistair Montgomery

Donegal Celtic FC

32 Suffolk Road
GB-Belfast BT11 9PE

Tel +44 2890 629 810
Fax +44 2890 612 022
Web
Email dchgreen@googlemail.com
Media Officer Alex McGreevy

Dungannon Swifts FC

Stangmore Park, Co. Tyrone
GB-Dugannon BT71 6PP

Tel +44 2887 723 257
Fax +44 2887 725 309
Web dungannonswiftsfc.co.uk
Email info@dungannonswiftsfc.co.uk
Media Officer Sarah Winslow

Glenavon FC

Mourneview Park, Mourneview Avenue
GB-Lurgan BT66 8EW

Tel +44 2838 322 472
Fax +44 2838 327 694
Web glenavonfc.com
Email glenavonfootballclub@utvinternet.com
Media Officer Philip Hawthorne

Glentoran FC

Parkgate Drive
GB-Belfast BT4 1EW

Tel +44 2890 456 137
Fax +44 2890 732 956
Web glentoran.com
Email secretary@glentoran.com
Media Officer Russell Lever

Linfield FC

Windsor Park, Donegall Avenue
GB-Belfast BT12 6LW

Tel +44 2890 244 198
Fax +44 2890 242 761
Web linfieldfc.com
Email office@linfieldfc.com
Media Officer Andrew Conn

Lisburn Distillery FC

New Grosvenor Stadium, 57 Ballyskeagh Road, GB-Lisburn BT27 5TE

Tel +44 2890 301 148
Fax +44 2890 672 154
Web lisburn-distillery.net
Email ash_ldfc@hotmail.com
Media Officer Colin Hopkins

Portadown FC

Shamrock Park, Brownstown Road
GB-Portadown BT62 3PZ

Tel +44 2838 332 726
Fax +44 2838 332 726
Web portadownfc.co.uk
Email secretary@portadownfc.co.uk
Media Officer Trevor Clydesdale

NORWAY

Norvège I Norwegen

Norges Fotballforbund (NFF)

COMMUNICATION

Address	Serviceboks 1, Ullevaal stadion, NO-0840 Oslo	**President**	Yngve Hallén
		General Secretary	Paul Glomsaker
		Media Officer	Svein Graff
Tel	+47 210 29300		
Fax	+47 210 29301	**Year of Formation**	1902
E-mail	nff@fotball.no	**National Stadium**	Ullevaal, Oslo (25,572)
Website	fotball.no		

DOMESTIC COMPETITION SUMMARY 2010

TIPPELIGAEN FINAL TABLE

			Home					Away					Total						
		Pld	**W**	**D**	**L**	**F**	**A**	**W**	**D**	**L**	**F**	**A**	**W**	**D**	**L**	**F**	**A**	**Pts**	**Comp**
1	Rosenborg BK	30	10	5	0	34	12	9	6	0	24	12	19	11	0	58	24	68	UCL
2	Vålerenga Fotball	30	13	2	0	47	11	6	2	7	22	25	19	4	7	69	36	61	UEL
3	Tromsø IL	30	10	2	3	19	9	4	6	5	17	21	14	8	8	36	30	50	UEL
4	Aalesunds FK	30	9	4	2	29	15	5	1	9	17	22	14	5	11	46	37	47	UEL
5	Odd Grenland	30	8	4	3	26	15	4	6	5	22	26	12	10	8	48	41	46	
6	FK Haugesund	30	9	5	1	34	13	3	4	8	17	26	12	9	9	51	39	45	
7	Strømsgodset IF	30	10	2	3	32	24	3	2	10	19	35	13	4	13	51	59	43	UEL
8	IK Start	30	8	5	2	34	21	3	4	8	23	39	11	9	10	57	60	42	
9	Viking FK	30	8	4	3	32	16	2	7	6	16	25	10	11	9	48	41	41	
10	Lillestrøm SK	30	7	6	2	31	18	2	7	6	20	26	9	13	8	51	44	40	
11	Molde FK	30	7	4	4	23	19	3	6	6	19	26	10	10	10	42	45	40	
12	Stabæk Fotball	30	7	2	6	24	22	4	4	7	22	25	11	6	13	46	47	39	
13	SK Brann	30	5	7	3	29	23	3	3	9	19	27	8	10	12	48	50	34	
14	Hønefoss BK	30	5	4	6	16	21	2	2	11	12	41	7	6	17	28	62	27	*Relegated*
15	Kongsvinger IL	30	2	6	7	16	23	2	2	11	11	35	4	8	18	27	58	20	*Relegated*
16	Sandefjord Fotball	30	2	3	10	17	26	0	3	12	8	32	2	6	22	25	58	12	*Relegated*

Top Scorer Baye Djiby Fall (Molde), 16 goals

Promoted Clubs Sogndal IL Fotball
Sarpsborg 08 FF
Fredrikstad FK

Cup Final Strømsgodset IF 2, Follo FK 0

Invincible Rosenborg make history

For the second successive year Norway's Tippeligaen was dominated by record champions Rosenborg BK. The Trondheim club shrugged off the inconvenience of a mid-season change of coach to become the first team ever to win the Norwegian top division undefeated.

Indeed, but for a last-gasp 3-2 defeat by IK Start in October 2009, Rosenborg would have gone two straight seasons unbeaten. It was a show of strength that suggested the club had returned to their glory days of 1992-2004 when they won 13 consecutive league titles. That Nils Arne Eggen, the coach who had overseen most of that halcyon period, should be back to help Rosenborg return to their position of supremacy was fitting – if not quite part of the club's masterplan.

Groundwork laid

Eggen was summoned from retirement in June to serve as caretaker following Erik Hamrén's departure, three months ahead of schedule, to take charge of the Swedish national team. Hamrén, the club's title-winning coach in 2009, laid the groundwork for a successful title defence, but although Rosenborg were on course when he left, they had won only seven of their 13 matches and endured four goalless draws. Furthermore, they trailed Tromsø IL by three points.

No sooner had Eggen assumed command than Rosenborg were back on top of the table, a thumping 4-0 win over Kongsvinger IL enabling them to leapfrog Tromsø. They would remain in situ for the rest of the season, fortifying their position from one week to the next. As Tromsø faded, Vålerenga Fotball became their closest rivals, but when the Oslo outfit arrived in Trondheim in early October, they required a win to keep the title race alive. After being reduced early on to ten men, they never stood a chance, and Rosenborg coasted to a 3-1 win that put them eight points clear with four games to go. Three weeks later, with a 1-0 win over Tromsø in Trondheim, Rosenborg's 22nd championship crown was secure.

It was the 14th Tippeligaen title for Eggen (his 13th as a coach) and the 16th for the club's veteran midfielder Roar Strand, who, at 40, finally decided to hang up his boots – 22 years after making his Rosenborg debut and with an all-time record of 436 appearances in Norway's top flight.

Player of the year

Strand figured only intermittently in 2010, but he was not really needed. His domain – the centre of midfield – was superbly marshalled by Ghanaian international Anthony Annan, who was voted Tippeligaen player of the year before leaving for FC Schalke 04. Other key players who moved abroad at the season's end were ex-Tottenham Hotspur FC striker Steffen Iversen, who top-scored with 14 goals and returned to London to join Crystal Palace FC, and centre-back Vadim Demidov, recruited by Real Sociedad de Fútbol. Although Hamrén left in mid-campaign, four of his fellow Swedes continued to serve Rosenborg well – goalkeeper Daniel Örlund, defender Mikael Lustig, captain Mikael Dorsin and 13-goal striker Rade Prica. The revelation of Rosenborg's season was Markus Henriksen, son of assistant coach Trond Henriksen,

Anthony Annan – a rock in the Rosenborg midfield

who established himself as a regular at 17 and contributed seven goals.

Vålerenga finished 11 points clear as runners-up. With coach Martin Andresen having stood down from playing duties, the club from the capital were always attractive to watch, scoring 69 goals, more than two thirds of that number coming at the Ullevaal stadium, where they were irrepressible. Disappointing away form and the departure in August of the Tippeligaen's leading scorer at the time, 15-goal Mohammed Abdellaoue, combined to dilute their title challenge, but it was a memorable season nonetheless, with former English Premier League players Lars Hirschfeld and Luton Shelton among their standout performers.

Tromsø third

Although Tromsø's season petered out, they did well to retain third place and qualify for Europe. Unlike Vålerenga, Per-Mathias Høgmo's team struggled for goals, registering just 36, a tally bettered by every team bar the three that were relegated – Sandefjord Fotball, Kongsvinger IL and Hønefoss BK. The latter went down after a play-off thrashing by Fredrikstad FK, who thus regained top-flight membership after a year away. Sogndal IL Fotball won the second division and were accompanied up by part-timers and top-flight novices Sarpsborg 08 FF.

The Norwegian Cup was won, for the fifth time, by Strømsgodset IF, but it was the team they defeated in the final that hogged the headlines. Second-tier minnows Follo FK - average home attendance 480 – had already caused a stir by reaching the semi-finals, but once there they took their giant-killing to new heights by defeating the mighty Rosenborg 3-2 after extra time. Although Follo went on to lose the final 2-0 – and their second-division status after declining to apply for a new licence – the distinction of being the only Norwegian club to defeat Rosenborg in 2010 was one to treasure.

Rosenborg did lose rather frequently in Europe, however. Although they overcame Swedish champions AIK Solna in UEFA Champions League qualifying, they went out in the play-offs to another Scandinavian side, FC København. One win and five defeats in the UEFA Europa League was a rather bitter pill to swallow – not just for Rosenborg but for Norwegian football in general following the early exits of the country's other three European representatives – but at least the national team, led once again by Egil 'Drillo' Olsen, restored some pride with a strong start to the UEFA EURO 2012 qualifying campaign.

With victories in their opening three matches – 2-1 successes in Iceland and Cyprus sandwiching a famous 1-0 triumph over Portugal in Oslo – Norway took early control of their group, and although they were later joined at the top of the table by both Denmark and Portugal after drawing 1-1 at home to the former and losing 1-0 to the latter in Lisbon, the prospect of a first major tournament appearance in 12 years remained, particularly with newcomers such as Abdellaoue, Erik Huseklepp and Henning Hauger blending in well with experienced veterans like John Arne Riise, Morten Gamst Pedersen and inspirational captain Brede Hangeland.

National Team

International Tournament Appearances –
FIFA World Cup - (3) 1938, 1994, 1998 (2nd round)
UEFA European Championship - (1) 2000.

Top Five All-time Caps – Thorbjørn Svenssen (103); Henning Berg (100); Erik Thorstvedt (97); John Arne Riise (96); John Carew (88)

Top Five All-time Goals – Jørgen Juve (33); Einar Gundersen (26); Harald Hennum (25); John Carew, Tore André Flo & Ole Gunnar Solskjær (23)

NATIONAL TEAM RESULTS 2010/11

11/8/10	France	H	Oslo	2-1	*Huseklepp (51, 71)*
3/9/10	Iceland (ECQ)	A	Reykjavik	2-1	*Hangeland (58), Abdellaoue (75)*
7/9/10	Portugal (ECQ)	H	Oslo	1-0	*Huseklepp (21)*
8/10/10	Cyprus (ECQ)	A	Larnaca	2-1	*Riise J.A. (2), Carew (42)*
12/10/10	Croatia	A	Zagreb	1-2	*Abdellaoue (21)*
17/11/10	Republic of Ireland	A	Dublin	2-1	*Gamst Pedersen (34), Huseklepp (86)*
9/2/11	Poland	N	Faro (POR)	0-1	
26/3/11	Denmark (ECQ)	H	Oslo	1-1	*Huseklepp (81)*
4/6/11	Portugal (ECQ)	A	Lisbon	0-1	
7/6/11	Lithuania	H	Oslo	1-0	*Gamst Pedersen (84)*

NATIONAL TEAM APPEARANCES 2010/11

Coach – Egil OLSEN	22/4/42		Fra	ISL	POR	CYP	Cro	Irl	Pol	DEN	POR	Ltu	Caps	Goals
Jon KNUDSEN	20/11/74	Stabæk	G	G	G	G		G46	G				20	-
Tom HØGLI	20/2/74	Tromsø	D	D	D	D		D			D	s59	19	-
Kjetil WÆHLER	16/3/76	AaB (DEN)	D46	D	D28	D	s64	D	D59	D		D	24	1
Brede HANGELAND	20/6/81	Fulham (ENG)	D	D	D	D	D64	D	D	D	D	D	70	1
John Arne RIISE	24/9/80	Roma (ITA)	D	D		D	D	D	D	D	D	D81	96	13
Erik HUSEKLEPP	5/9/84	Brann	M	M76	M	M80	s59	M90						
		/Bari (ITA)							M77	M89	M75	A	21	6
Bjørn Helge RIISE	21/6/83	Fulham (ENG)	M87	M57	M	M74		s46	s46		M	M59	31	1
		/Sheffield United (ENG)								M				
Henning HAUGER	17/7/85	Stabæk	M90	M	M	M	s46	M	M46	M	M	M46	21	-
Christian GRINDHEIM	17/7/83	Heerenveen (NED)	M62	M	M86	M	s46	M55	M	M	M83		43	2
Morten GAMST PEDERSEN	8/9/81	Blackburn (ENG)	M	M	M	M	M	M	M87	M	M	M	68	15
Mohammed ABDELLAOUE	23/10/85	Vålerenga	A46											
		/Hannover (GER)		A88	s38	s83	A59		s59	A	s60	A46	14	2
Vadim DEMIDOV	10/10/86	Rosenborg	s46		s28		D							
		/Real Sociedad (ESP)							s59		D		8	-
Espen RUUD	26/2/84	OB (DEN)	s46	s76	D	s80	D		D	D78		D	10	-
Jan Gunnar SOLLI	19/4/81	Brann	s62	s88									40	1
Per Ciljan SKJELBRED	16/6/87	Rosenborg	s87										16	-
Ruben YTTERGÅRD JENSSEN	4/5/88	Tromsø	s90		s86		M46	s55	s46			M46	7	-
Steffen IVERSEN	10/11/76	Rosenborg		s57										
		/Crystal Palace (ENG)								s89			79	21
John CAREW	5/9/79	Aston Villa (ENG)			A38	A83	s64							
		/Stoke (ENG)							A59					
		/unattached									A60		88	23
Petter VAAGAN MOEN	5/2/84	Brann				s74	M85	M78						
		/QPR (ENG)							s87				9	1
Rune Almenning JARSTEIN	29/9/84	Viking					G			G	G	G	12	-
Daniel Omoya BRAATEN	25/5/82	Toulouse (FRA)					M64			s78	s75	s46	30	2
Markus HENRIKSEN	25/7/92	Rosenborg					M46				s83		2	-
Knut Olav RINDARØY	17/7/85	Deportivo (ESP)					s85						2	-
Thorstein HELSTAD	28/4/77	Le Mans (FRA)						A46					38	10
Espen Bugge PETTERSEN	10/5/80	Molde						s46					2	-
Kristofer HÆSTAD	9/12/83	Vålerenga						s78					28	1
Morten MOLDSKRED	13/6/80	Rosenborg						s90	s77				9	1
Alexander TETTEY	4/4/86	Rennes (FRA)							M46				7	-
Simen BRENNE	17/3/81	Odd Grenland										s46	8	1
Håvard NORDTVEIT	21/6/90	Mönchengladbach (GER)										s46	1	-
Jonathan PARR	21/10/88	Aalesund										s81	2	-

CLUB-BY-CLUB

AALESUNDS FK

Coach – Kjetil Rekdal
Founded – 1914
Stadium – Color Line (10,778)
MAJOR HONOURS: Norwegian Cup - (1) 2009.

2010

14/3	Lillestrøm	h	3-0	*Arnefjord, Aarøy, Diego Silva*
21/3	Hønefoss	a	2-0	*Phillips 2*
28/3	Stabæk	h	2-2	*Aarøy, Sylling Olsen*
5/4	Kongsvinger	a	2-1	*Aarøy 2*
11/4	Viking	h	3-1	*Aarøy 2, Herrera (p)*
14/4	Haugesund	a	1-2	*Roberts*
19/4	Rosenborg	h	1-1	*Carlsen*
25/4	Sandefjord	a	1-0	*Diego Silva*
3/5	Start	h	2-0	*Herrera, Mathisen*
6/5	Molde	a	1-2	*Sylling Olsen*
9/5	Odd Grenland	h	2-3	*Mathisen 2*
16/5	Vålerenga	a	0-3	
24/5	Strømsgodset	h	3-1	*og (Riddez), Mathisen, Aarøy*
6/6	Brann	a	1-2	*Diego Silva*
4/7	Tromsø	a	1-0	*Phillips*
10/7	Molde	h	0-0	
18/7	Start	a	0-1	
24/7	Vålerenga	h	1-0	*Mathisen*
1/8	Strømsgodset	a	1-3	*Larsen*
8/8	Tromsø	h	2-0	*Aarøy 2*
22/8	Lillestrøm	a	0-1	
29/8	Hønefoss	h	1-3	*Sylling Olsen*
12/9	Odd Grenland	a	1-2	*og (Fevang)*
19/9	Kongsvinger	h	2-0	*Mathisen, Larsen*
26/9	Haugesund	h	2-1	*Fredriksen, Aarøy*
3/10	Stabæk	a	1-2	*Mathisen*
17/10	Sandefjord	h	2-2	*Arneng, Arnefjord*
24/10	Viking	a	3-1	*Aarøy 2, Barrantes*
31/10	Brann	h	3-1	*Mathisen 2 (1p), Herrera (p)*
7/11	Rosenborg	a	2-2	*Barrantes, Sylling Olsen*

No	Name	Nat	DoB	Pos	Aps	(s)	Gls
8	Tor Hogne AARØY		20/3/77	A	28	(2)	12
15	Daniel ARNEFJORD	SWE	21/3/79	D	27		2
10	Johan ARNENG	SWE	14/6/79	M	24	(1)	1
31	Michael BARRANTES Rojas	CRC	4/10/83	M	4	(3)	2
22	Fredrik CARLSEN		1/12/89	M	23		1
25	DIEGO SILVA	BRA	26/5/80	A	2	(9)	3
20	Didrik FLØTRE		31/12/91	A		(2)	
7	Trond FREDRIKSEN		21/5/77	M	4	(10)	1
25	Lars FUHRE		29/9/89	A	4	(4)	
11	Pablo HERRERA Barrantes	CRC	14/2/87	A	11	(8)	3
16	Enar JÄÄGER	EST	18/11/84	D	23	(3)	
5	Ville JALASTO	FIN	19/4/86	D	26	(1)	
19	Peter Orry LARSEN		25/2/89	M	20	(6)	2
13	Anders LINDEGAARD	DEN	13/4/84	G	30		
21	Alexander MATHISEN		14/11/86	A	17	(5)	9
14	Jonathan PARR		21/10/88	D	25		
17	Demar PHILLIPS	JAM	23/9/83	A	16	(1)	3
9	Glenn ROBERTS		26/6/88	A	2	(6)	1
2	Amund SKIRI		25/2/78	M	17	(2)	
18	Khari STEPHENSON	JAM	18/1/81	A	1	(5)	
6	Magnus SYLLING OLSEN		2/7/83	A	14	(10)	4
4	Jonatan TOLLÅS Nation		1/7/90	D	12	(5)	
27	Dan Peter ULVESTAD		4/4/89	D		(1)	
23	Fredrik ULVESTAD		19/5/92	M		(1)	

SK BRANN

Coach – Steinar Nilsen; (22/5/10) (Rune Skarsfjord); (9/6/10) Rune Skarsfjord
Founded – 1908
Stadium – Brann (17,317)
MAJOR HONOURS: Norwegian League - (3) 1962, 1963, 2007; Norwegian Cup - (6) 1923, 1925, 1972, 1976, 1982, 2004.

2010

13/3	Haugesund	h	0-0	
21/3	Viking	a	0-4	
29/3	Sandefjord	h	3-2	*Mjelde, Guastavino 2*
5/4	Molde	a	2-3	*Vaagan Moen, Huseklepp*
11/4	Start	h	3-4	*Guastavino, Mjelde, Bakke*
14/4	Rosenborg	a	0-3	
18/4	Vålerenga	h	1-1	*Huseklepp*
25/4	Strømsgodset	h	4-0	*Vaagan Moen 2, Guastavino*
2/5	Odd Grenland	a	0-0	
5/5	Tromsø	h	0-1	
9/5	Stabæk	a	1-2	*Vaagan Moen*
16/5	Lillestrøm	h	1-1	*Vaagan Moen*
24/5	Hønefoss	a	0-2	
6/6	Aalesund	h	2-1	*Sævarsson, Vaagan Moen*
4/7	Kongsvinger	a	3-0	*Solli, Bakke, Vaagan Moen*
10/7	Haugesund	a	1-1	*Mjelde*
18/7	Stabæk	h	2-2	*Solli, Huseklepp*
25/7	Sandefjord	a	4-1	*Bakke, Vaagan Moen, Guastavino, Huseklepp*
1/8	Molde	h	1-1	*Huseklepp*
8/8	Start	a	1-3	*Huseklepp (p)*
21/8	Strømsgodset	a	1-1	*Guastavino*
30/8	Viking	h	3-3	*Bakke, Vaagan Moen, og (Bertelsen)*
11/9	Tromsø	a	3-0	*Bakke, Guastavino, Vaagan Moen*
19/9	Rosenborg	h	2-3	*Sævarsson, Vaagan Moen*
26/9	Vålerenga	a	0-1	
2/10	Hønefoss	h	3-2	*Vaagan Moen, Mjelde, Huseklepp*
17/10	Lillestrøm	a	2-3	*Vaagan Moen, Huseklepp*
25/10	Kongsvinger	h	3-1	*Vaagan Moen, Huseklepp 2*
31/10	Aalesund	a	1-3	*Guastavino*
7/11	Odd Grenland	h	1-1	*Amankwah*

No	Name	Nat	DoB	Pos	Aps	(s)	Gls
25	Yaw Ihle AMANKWAH		7/7/88	D	17	(3)	1
5	Rodolph AUSTIN	JAM	1/6/85	M	25		
17	Eirik BAKKE		13/9/77	A	26		5
18	Ólafur Örn BJARNASON	ISL	15/5/75	D	9	(2)	
18	DIEGO Henrique Pachega de Souza	BRA	20/4/92	M		(1)	
8	Gylfi EINARSSON	ISL	27/10/78	M	1	(4)	
7	Hassan EL FAKIRI		18/4/77	D	24	(1)	
15	Diego GUASTAVINO	URU	26/7/84	A	17	(5)	9
4	Cato GUNTVEIT		6/8/75	D	9	(6)	
19	Cato HANSEN		26/5/88	A	1	(16)	
16	Bjarte HAUGSDAL		9/3/90	M	1	(5)	
26	Bjørnar HOLMVIK		2/6/85	D	13	(1)	
13	Erik HUSEKLEPP		5/9/84	A	30		10
14	Tijan JAITEH	GAM	31/12/88	M	7	(10)	
20	Jacinto Júnior Conceição Cabral "JUNINHO"	BRA	10/3/92	A		(5)	
3	Christian KALVENES		8/3/77	D	9		
21	Zsolt KORCSMÁR	HUN	9/1/89	D	10		
6	Erik MJELDE		6/3/84	M	28	(2)	4
10	David NIELSEN	DEN	1/12/76	A	1	(9)	
12	Håkon André OPDAL		11/6/82	G	30		
9	Jan Gunnar SOLLI		19/4/81	M	19	(3)	2
2	Birkir Már SÆVARSSON	ISL	11/11/84	D	27		2
11	Petter VAAGAN MOEN		5/2/84	M	26	(1)	14

FK HAUGESUND

Coach – Jostein Grindhaug
Founded – 1993
Stadium – Haugesund (5,200)

010				
3/3	Brann	a	0-0	
1/3	Strømsgodset	h	2-2	*Sørum, Nilsen*
8/3	Odd Grenland	a	1-4	*Sørum*
/4	Hønefoss	h	5-1	*Andreassen, Nygaard, Sørum, Đurđić, Steinsland*
1/4	Tromsø	a	0-2	
4/4	Aalesund	h	2-1	*og (Aarøy), Pelu*
8/4	Lillestrøm	a	1-1	*Pozniak*
5/4	Kongsvinger	h	3-0	*Sørensen, Sørum, Steinsland*
/5	Stabæk	a	0-0	
/5	Viking	a	0-1	
/5	Rosenborg	h	0-0	
6/5	Molde	a	1-2	*Đurđić*
4/5	Sandefjord	h	2-0	*Mæland (p), Andreassen*
/6	Vålerenga	a	2-5	*Mæland (p), Sørensen*
/7	Start	h	4-2	*Sørensen, Sørum 2, Mæland (p)*
0/7	Brann	h	1-1	*Mæland*
8/7	Strømsgodset	a	1-2	*Ørsal*
5/7	Viking	h	4-0	*Andreassen 2, Sørensen, Đurđić*
/8	Rosenborg	a	3-4	*Đurđić, Tronseth, Nilsen*
3/8	Vålerenga	h	2-0	*Đurđić (p), Sørum*
22/8	Kongsvinger	a	1-0	*Steinsland*
28/8	Tromsø	h	0-0	
12/9	Hønefoss	a	2-0	*Sørum 2*
20/9	Lillestrøm	h	3-3	*Đurđić 2, Tronseth*
26/9	Aalesund	a	1-2	*Đurđić*
3/10	Odd Grenland	h	3-0	*Steinsland, Andreassen, Sørum*
17/10	Stabæk	h	2-1	*Andreassen, Sørum*
24/10	Sandefjord	a	1-0	*Đurđić (p)*
31/10	Molde	h	1-2	*Đurđić (p)*
7/11	Start	a	3-3	*Đurđić 2, Sørensen*

No	Name	Nat	DoB	Pos	Aps	(s)	Gls
11	Tor Arne ANDREASSEN		16/3/83	M	26	(1)	6
16	Ugonna ANYORA	NGA	29/4/91	M		(2)	
7	Martin CHRISTENSEN	DEN	23/12/87	M	6	(8)	
44	Nikola ĐURĐIĆ	SRB	1/4/86	A	23	(4)	12
22	Sten Ove EIKE		8/10/81	A		(14)	
3	Rok ELSNER	SVN	25/1/86	D	4	(1)	
1	Per Morten KRISTIANSEN		14/7/81	G	29		
13	Eirik MÆLAND		15/2/89	M	16	(5)	4
2	Joakim Våge NILSEN		24/4/91	D	28		2
5	Trygve NYGAARD		19/8/75	M	28		1
15	Allan OLESEN	DEN	20/5/82	D	5	(4)	
9	John PELU	SWE	2/2/82	A	8	(10)	1
4	Chris POZNIAK	CAN	10/1/81	D	28		1
20	Juska SAVOLAINEN	FIN	1/9/83	M	2	(12)	
18	Vegard SKJERVE		22/5/88	D	28		
14	Jarle STEINSLAND		7/10/80	M	14	(9)	4
8	Jacob SØRENSEN	DEN	12/2/83	A	27		5
6	Thomas SØRUM		17/11/82	A	28		11
25	Are TRONSETH		3/9/81	D	28		2
17	Dag Roar ØRSAL		20/7/80	A	1	(5)	1
12	Lars ØVERNES		28/2/89	G	1		

HØNEFOSS BK

Coach – Ole Bjørn Sundgot; (18/4/10) (Tom Gulbrandsen); (29/6/10) Tom Gulbrandsen & Reidar Vågnes
Founded – 1895
Stadium – AKA Arena (4,400)

2010				
14/3	Tromsø	a	0-2	
21/3	Aalesund	h	0-2	
28/3	Lillestrøm	a	0-6	
5/4	Haugesund	a	1-5	*Saaliti*
11/4	Kongsvinger	h	1-2	*Bangura*
17/4	Viking	h	0-1	
21/4	Stabæk	a	1-0	*Angan*
25/4	Start	a	0-2	
2/5	Molde	h	1-1	*Obiefule*
5/5	Vålerenga	a	0-0	
9/5	Sandefjord	h	1-0	*Lafton F.*
16/5	Rosenborg	a	0-3	
24/5	Brann	h	2-0	*og (Opdal), og (Holmvik)*
6/6	Odd Grenland	a	0-1	
4/7	Strømsgodset	h	1-1	*Angan*
10/7	Tromsø	h	2-2	*Steffensen 2*
18/7	Viking	a	0-4	
26/7	Lillestrøm	h	3-2	*Obiefule (p), Angan, Steffensen*
1/8	Odd Grenland	h	2-1	*Bangura, Konate*
8/8	Kongsvinger	a	3-3	*Dmitrijev, Angan, Steffensen*
22/8	Stabæk	h	0-4	
29/8	Aalesund	a	3-1	*Jensen, Byfuglien, Lafton L.*
12/9	Haugesund	h	0-2	
19/9	Molde	a	0-1	
27/9	Start	h	0-0	
2/10	Brann	a	2-3	*Lafton L. (p), Olsen L.*
17/10	Rosenborg	h	0-2	
24/10	Strømsgodset	a	1-4	*Jensen*
31/10	Vålerenga	h	3-1	*og (Strandberg), Angan 2 (1p)*
7/11	Sandefjord	a	1-6	*og (Nystuen)*

No	Name	Nat	DoB	Pos	Aps	(s)	Gls
20	Davy Claude ANGAN	CIV	20/9/87	A	25	(3)	6
10	Umaru BANGURA	SLE	7/10/87	M	27	(2)	2
27	Kevin BEUGRE	CIV	23/8/92	A		(1)	
18	Rune BOLSETH		4/7/80	M	13	(2)	
7	Kjetil BYFUGLIEN		23/5/77	D	15	(4)	1
26	Steve CLARK	USA	14/4/86	G	4		
4	Abdou DARBOE	GAM	22/12/90	A	1	(4)	
19	Aleksandr DMITRIJEV	EST	18/2/82	M	19	(3)	1
5	Erik HAGEN		20/7/75	D	17		
23	Alexander HASSUM		2/1/92	D	4	(2)	
16	Tor Øyvind HOVDA		24/9/89	D	15	(7)	
24	Kenneth Di Vita JENSEN		22/7/90	A	9	(10)	2
99	Madiou KONATE	SEN	12/1/82	A	14	(5)	1
2	Frode LAFTON		3/3/76	D	30		1
9	Lars LAFTON		1/3/80	A	3	(8)	2
15	Håkon LANGDALEN		6/4/92	M		(2)	
25	Paul OBIEFULE	NGA	15/5/86	M	18	(3)	2
11	Benny OLSEN		18/2/76	D	5	(5)	
17	Leo OLSEN		25/9/81	M	10	(6)	1
21	Kamal SAALITI		2/8/79	A	14	(8)	1
6	Kristján Örn SIGURDSSON	ISL	7/10/80	D	26	(1)	
1	Thomas SOLVOLL		22/11/80	G	26	(1)	
14	Lennart STEFFENSEN		12/7/77	M	23	(3)	4
28	Christian TRAORÉ	DEN	18/4/82	D	12	(1)	

KONGSVINGER IL

Coach – Trond Amundsen; (12/4/10) (Øyvind Eide, Stein Arve Lohne & Vidar Riseth); (27/4/10) Tony Gustavsson (SWE)
Founded – 1892
Stadium – Gjemselund (4,800)

2010				
14/3	Strømsgodset	a	0-2	
21/3	Odd Grenland	h	1-2	*Frejd*
28/3	Tromsø	a	0-1	
5/4	Aalesund	h	1-2	*Güven*
11/4	Hønefoss	a	2-1	*Johannesen, Güven*
14/4	Lillestrøm	h	0-0	
18/4	Stabæk	a	2-4	*Güven, Johannesen*
25/4	Haugesund	a	0-3	
2/5	Viking	h	1-1	*Johannesen (p)*
5/5	Sandefjord	a	1-0	*Niang*
8/5	Vålerenga	h	1-2	*Torp*
16/5	Start	a	0-3	

24/5	Molde	h	3-1	*Johannesen, Torp, Güven*
6/6	Rosenborg	a	0-4	
4/7	Brann	h	0-3	
11/7	Strømsgodset	h	0-2	
17/7	Vålerenga	a	2-5	*Johannesen (p), Güven*
25/7	Tromsø	h	1-1	*Niang*
31/7	Lillestrøm	a	2-2	*Güven, Johannesen*
8/8	Hønefoss	h	3-3	*Risholt R., Risholt K., Niang*
22/8	Haugesund	h	0-1	
29/8	Odd Grenland	a	0-0	
12/9	Sandefjord	h	1-0	*Sellin*
19/9	Aalesund	a	0-2	
26/9	Stabæk	h	1-2	*og (Skjønsberg)*
3/10	Molde	a	0-2	
17/10	Start	h	3-3	*Holmen, Gerson, Niang*
25/10	Brann	a	1-3	*Risholt K.*
31/10	Rosenborg	h	0-0	
7/11	Viking	a	1-3	*Güven*

No	Name	Nat	DoB	Pos	Aps	(s)	Gls
25	Olav DALEN		6/3/85	G	7		
4	Edier FREJD	SWE	10/12/79	D	26	(2)	1
5	Bobbie FRIBERG DA CRUZ	SWE	16/2/82	D	29		
22	Lars Christian Krogh GERSON	LUX	5/2/90	M	12	(9)	1
8	Adem GÜVEN		11/10/85	A	25	(5)	7
6	Ørjan Berg HANSEN		29/4/84	M	20	(3)	
7	Kim Kristian HOLMEN		14/7/82	A	13	(15)	1
15	Yngvar HÅKONSEN		29/1/78	D	22	(1)	
11	Olav Tuelo JOHANNESEN		23/2/84	A	22	(4)	6
57	Tobias Holmen JOHANSEN		29/8/90	G	3		
9	Martin LINNES		20/9/91	D	11	(4)	
1	Thomas MYHRE		16/10/73	G	20		
12	Mame Cheikh NIANG	SEN	30/3/84	A	15	(12)	4
10	Vidar RISETH		21/4/72	D	14		
24	Kai RISHOLT		10/4/79	A	11	(17)	2
20	Roger RISHOLT		10/4/79	M	15	(2)	1
14	Kai Olav RYEN		10/9/78	D	1	(1)	
17	Kjell Rune SELLIN		1/6/89	A	7	(3)	1
2	Henry Joseph SHINDIKA	TAN	3/11/85	D	22	(1)	
16	Magne STURØD		19/10/79	M	8	(3)	
21	Carl-Erik TORP		17/9/84	M	27	(2)	2

LILLESTRØM SK

Coach – Henning Berg

Founded – 1917

Stadium – Åråsen (12,000)

MAJOR HONOURS: Norwegian League - (5) 1959, 1976, 1977, 1986, 1989; Norwegian Cup - (5) 1977, 1978, 1981, 1985, 2007.

2010				
14/3	Aalesund	a	0-3	
21/3	Tromsø	h	2-0	*Sundgot, Ujah*
28/3	Hønefoss	h	6-0	*Kippe 2, Ujah, Pedersen, Elyounoussi, Sundgot*
5/4	Viking	a	0-0	
10/4	Stabæk	h	0-0	
14/4	Kongsvinger	a	0-0	
18/4	Haugesund	h	1-1	*Nsaliwa (p)*
25/4	Rosenborg	a	0-0	
2/5	Sandefjord	h	4-0	*Pedersen, Sigurdarson, Elyounoussi, Occean*
6/5	Start	a	3-2	*Sundgot 2, Sigurdarson*
9/5	Strømsgodset	h	3-1	*Pedersen, Igiebor, Sigurdarson*
16/5	Brann	a	1-1	*Igiebor*
25/5	Odd Grenland	h	2-2	*Elyounoussi, Mouelhi (p)*
6/6	Molde	a	3-3	*Kippe, Elyounoussi, Ujah*
4/7	Vålerenga	h	1-4	*Ujah*
10/7	Rosenborg	h	1-2	*Ujah*
19/7	Tromsø	a	0-0	
26/7	Hønefoss	a	2-3	*Kippe, Ujah*
31/7	Kongsvinger	h	2-2	*Sigurdarson, Ujah*
9/8	Odd Grenland	a	1-2	*Sundgot*
22/8	Aalesund	h	1-0	*Eziyodawe*
29/8	Stabæk	a	1-2	*Ujah*
12/9	Start	h	3-2	*Kippe, Mouelhi, Ujah*
20/9	Haugesund	a	3-3	*Sundgot, Mouelhi, Kippe*
25/9	Molde	h	1-1	*Ujah*
3/10	Sandefjord	a	1-0	*Bolly*
17/10	Brann	h	3-2	*Søgård, Ujah, Kippe*
23/10	Vålerenga	a	1-2	*Essediri*
31/10	Viking	h	1-1	*Sundgot*
7/11	Strømsgodset	a	4-5	*Omoijuanfo, Ujah 3 (1p)*

No	Name	Nat	DoB	Pos	Aps	(s)	Gls
23	Pål Steffen ANDRESEN		19/5/82	D		(1)	
26	Mathis BOLLY		14/11/90	M	6	(2)	1
4	Mads DAHM		21/10/88	D	6	(1)	
17	Tarik ELYOUNOUSSI		23/2/88	A	14		4
3	Lars-Kristian ERIKSEN		28/6/83	D	22	(4)	
21	Karim ESSEDIRI	TUN	29/7/79	D	29		1
14	Edwin EZIYODAWE	NGA	9/5/88	A	9	(9)	1
28	Lunan Ruben GABRIELSEN		10/3/92	D	1	(2)	
19	Fredri GULBRANDSEN		10/9/92	M		(5)	
29	André HANSEN		17/12/89	G	1		
10	Emanuell Nosakhare IGIEBOR	NGA	9/11/90	M	26	(2)	2
15	Marius JOHNSEN		28/8/81	D		(1)	
13	Frode KIPPE		17/1/78	D	30		7
11	Erling KNUDTZON		15/12/88	M	18	(5)	
12	Stefán Logi MAGNÚSSON	ISL	5/9/80	G	29		
25	Khaled MOUELHI	TUN	13/2/81	M	14	(6)	3
5	Tamandani NSALIWA	CAN	28/1/82	M	2	(4)	1
30	Olivier OCCEAN	CAN	23/10/81	A		(3)	1
16	Ohi OMOIJUANFO		30/11/93	A	1		1
2	Steinar PEDERSEN		6/6/75	D	30		3
20	Stian RINGSTAD		29/8/91	D	1	(2)	
5	Tom SADEH		23/4/91	D	1	(2)	
8	Björn Bergmann SIGURDARSON	ISL	26/2/91	A	18		4
18	Arild SUNDGOT		17/4/78	A	20	(7)	7
7	Espen SØGÅRD		10/10/79	M	29		1
22	Kristoffer TOKSTAD		5/7/91	M	2	(1)	
9	Anthony UJAH	NGA	20/11/90	A	21	(3)	14

MOLDE FK

Coach – Kjell Jonevret (SWE); (30/8/10) Uwe Rösler (GER)

Founded – 1911

Stadium – Aker (11,167)

MAJOR HONOURS: Norwegian Cup - (2) 1994, 2005.

2010				
14/3	Rosenborg	h	1-2	*Runström*
21/3	Sandefjord	a	1-3	*Hoseth*
27/3	Start	a	1-1	*Holm*
5/4	Brann	h	3-2	*Berg Hestad, Hoseth, Moström*
12/4	Vålerenga	a	1-2	*Fall*
15/4	Strømsgodset	h	3-2	*Moström 2, Hoseth (p)*
18/4	Odd Grenland	a	1-1	*Steen*
26/4	Tromsø	h	2-3	*Fall, Hoseth*
2/5	Hønefoss	a	1-1	*Berg Hestad*
6/5	Aalesund	h	2-1	*Hoseth (p), Fall*
10/5	Viking	a	1-4	*Skjølsvik*
16/5	Haugesund	h	2-1	*Fall, og (Skjerve)*
24/5	Kongsvinger	a	1-3	*Fall*
6/6	Lillestrøm	h	3-3	*Fall 2, Skjølsvik*
5/7	Stabæk	a	3-4	*Berg Hestad, Skjølsvik, Fall*
10/7	Aalesund	a	0-0	
18/7	Sandefjord	h	0-0	
25/7	Start	h	1-2	*Hoseth (p)*
1/8	Brann	a	1-1	*Thioune*
8/8	Viking	h	2-2	*Fall 2*
22/8	Rosenborg	a	1-3	*Hoseth*
29/8	Vålerenga	h	0-1	
13/9	Strømsgodset	a	3-1	*Holm, Thioune, Fall*

9/9	Hønefoss	h	1-0	*Fall*
5/9	Lillestrøm	a	1-1	*Fall*
/10	Kongsvinger	h	2-0	*Fall, Diouf*
8/10	Tromsø	a	1-0	*Hoseth*
4/10	Odd Grenland	h	0-0	
1/10	Haugesund	a	2-1	*Hoseth, Fall*
/11	Stabæk	h	1-0	*Fall (p)*

o	Name	Nat	DoB	Pos	Aps	(s)	Gls
2	Ben AMOS	ENG	10/4/90	G	8		
	Marcus ANDREASSON	SWE	13/7/78	D	20	(4)	
	Daniel BERG HESTAD		30/7/75	M	24	(2)	3
7	Daniel CHIMA Chukwu	NGA	4/4/91	A		(4)	
1	Pape Paté DIOUF	SEN	4/4/86	A	11	(2)	1
9	Baye Djiby FALL	SEN	20/4/85	A	28		16
4	Vegard FORREN		16/2/88	D	28		
	Øyvind GJERDE		18/3/77	D	2	(4)	
	Thomas HOLM		19/2/81	M	26	(1)	2
0	Magne HOSETH		13/10/80	M	24	(1)	9
7	Emil JOHANSSON	SWE	11/8/86	D	21	(3)	
22	Jan Kjell LARSEN		24/6/83	G	7		
	Knut Dørum LILLEBAKK		27/4/78	G	3		
27	Simon MARKENG		9/9/92	A		(2)	
9	Mattias MOSTRÖM	SWE	25/2/83	A	24	(4)	3
2	Kristoffer PAULSEN VATSHAUG		3/6/81	D	18		
12	Espen Bugge PETTERSEN		10/5/80	G	12		
23	Knut Olav RINDARØY		17/7/85	D	15		
29	Björn RUNSTRÖM	SWE	1/3/84	A	7	(10)	1
18	Magne SIMONSEN		13/7/88	D	15	(9)	
15	Aksel Berget SKJØLSVIK		15/5/87	M	10	(16)	3
32	Magnus STAMNESTRØ		18/4/92	M		(3)	
14	Christian STEEN		2/7/77	D	10	(4)	1
21	Kristian STRANDHAGEN		26/7/89	M		(2)	
8	El Hadji Makhtar THIOUNE	SEN	5/8/84	M	17	(1)	2

ODD GRENLAND

Coach – Dag-Eilev Fagermo

Founded – 1894

Stadium – Skagerak Arena (13,500)

MAJOR HONOURS: Norwegian Cup - (12) 1903, 1904, 1905, 1906, 1913, 1915, 1919, 1922, 1924, 1926, 1931, 2000.

2010				
14/3	Stabæk	h	2-3	*Myklebust, Fevang*
21/3	Kongsvinger	a	2-1	*Myklebust, Hagen*
28/3	Haugesund	h	4-1	*Akabueze 2, Brenne, Kovács*
5/4	Sandefjord	a	1-1	*Brenne*
11/4	Rosenborg	h	1-3	*Kovács*
14/4	Start	a	1-1	*Myklebust*
18/4	Molde	h	1-1	*Kovács*
25/4	Vålerenga	a	1-6	*Børven*
2/5	Brann	h	0-0	
5/5	Strømsgodset	a	4-0	*Gulsvik, Fevang, Storbæk, Brenne*
9/5	Aalesund	a	3-2	*Brenne, Fevang, Børven*
16/5	Tromsø	h	1-1	*Fevang*
25/5	Lillestrøm	a	2-2	*Kovács, Fevang (p)*
6/6	Hønefoss	h	1-0	*Samuelsen*
4/7	Viking	a	1-3	*Hagen*
12/7	Vålerenga	h	1-2	*Akabueze*
18/7	Rosenborg	a	1-1	*og (Stadsgaard)*
25/7	Strømsgodset	h	2-0	*Storbæk, Berge*
1/8	Hønefoss	a	1-2	*Kovács*
9/8	Lillestrøm	h	2-1	*Akabueze 2*
22/8	Tromsø	a	1-3	*Kovács*
29/8	Kongsvinger	h	0-0	
12/9	Aalesund	h	2-1	*Fevang (p), Børven*
19/9	Stabæk	a	3-0	*Brenne 2, Børven*
26/9	Sandefjord	h	5-0	*Børven 4 (1p), Berge*
3/10	Haugesund	a	0-3	
17/10	Viking	h	2-1	*Akabueze 2*
24/10	Molde	a	0-0	
31/10	Start	h	2-1	*Akabueze, Rambekk*
7/11	Brann	a	1-1	*Akabueze*

No	Name	Nat	DoB	Pos	Aps	(s)	Gls
26	Chukwuma AKABUEZE	NGA	6/5/89	A	29		9
9	Mattias ANDERSSON	SWE	7/10/81	A	4		
1	Árni Gautur ARASON	ISL	7/5/75	G	24		
14	Fredrik Semb BERGE		6/2/90	D	16	(4)	2
6	Simen BRENNE		17/3/81	M	27	(1)	6
22	Torgeir BØRVEN		3/12/91	A	8	(13)	8
4	Morten FEVANG		6/3/75	D	29		6
23	Fredrik GULSVIK		29/8/89	A	3	(5)	1
21	Steffen HAGEN		8/3/86	D	30		2
5	Torjus HANSÉN		29/10/73	D	20	(4)	
17	Emil JONASSEN		17/2/93	D		(1)	
9	Péter KOVÁCS	HUN	7/2/78	A	22		6
19	Snorre KROGSGÅRD		25/5/91	A		(2)	
10	Magnus LEKVEN		13/1/88	M	28	(1)	
30	Andreas LIE		31/8/87	G	6		
13	Magnus MYKLEBUST		8/7/85	A	15	(6)	3
3	Anders RAMBEKK		17/8/76	D	25	(5)	1
8	Jone SAMUELSEN		6/7/84	M	25	(3)	1
2	Håvard STORBÆK		25/5/86	A	13	(16)	2
11	Morten SUNDLI		31/3/90	M		(8)	
7	Tommy SVINDAL LARSEN		11/8/73	M	6	(9)	

ROSENBORG BK

Coach – Erik Hamrén (SWE); (1/6/10) Nils Arne Eggen

Founded - 1917

Stadium - Lerkendal (21,166)

MAJOR HONOURS: Norwegian League - (22) 1967, 1969, 1971, 1985, 1988, 1990, 1992, 1993, 1994, 1995, 1996, 1997, 1998, 1999, 2000, 2001, 2002, 2003, 2004, 2006, 2009, 2010; Norwegian Cup - (9) 1960, 1964, 1971, 1988, 1990, 1992, 1995, 1999, 2003.

2010				
14/3	Molde	a	2-1	*Prica, Lustig*
22/3	Start	h	3-3	*Iversen, Olsen 2*
28/3	Vålerenga	a	0-0	
5/4	Strømsgodset	h	3-0	*Olsen, Iversen 2*
11/4	Odd Grenland	a	3-1	*Henriksen 2, Prica*
14/4	Brann	h	3-0	*Iversen, Sellin 2*
19/4	Aalesund	a	1-1	*Prica*
25/4	Lillestrøm	h	0-0	
2/5	Tromsø	a	0-0	
5/5	Stabæk	h	2-0	*Prica 2*
9/5	Haugesund	a	0-0	
16/5	Hønefoss	h	3-0	*Dorsin, Lustig, Iversen*
24/5	Viking	a	2-1	*Lustig, Iversen (p)*
6/6	Kongsvinger	h	4-0	*Winsnes, Iversen (p), Skjelbred, Prica*
3/7	Sandefjord	h	1-0	*Strand*
10/7	Lillestrøm	a	2-1	*Lustig, Dorsin*
18/7	Odd Grenland	h	1-1	*Iversen (p)*
25/7	Stabæk	a	2-1	*Olsen, Moldskred*
1/8	Haugesund	h	4-3	*Iversen 3, og (Skjerve)*
7/8	Sandefjord	a	3-1	*Prica (p), Henriksen, Moldskred*
22/8	Molde	h	3-1	*Strand, Dorsin, Iversen*
29/8	Start	a	3-2	*Prica 2, Henriksen*
12/9	Viking	h	1-1	*Jamtfall*
19/9	Brann	a	3-2	*Henriksen 2, Iversen (p)*
26/9	Strømsgodset	a	1-1	*Strand*
3/10	Vålerenga	h	3-1	*Iversen (p), Moldskred, Henriksen*
17/10	Hønefoss	a	2-0	*Prica 2*
24/10	Tromsø	h	1-0	*Prica*
31/10	Kongsvinger	a	0-0	
7/11	Aalesund	h	2-2	*Dorsin, Prica*

No	Name	Nat	DoB	Pos	Aps	(s)	Gls
4	Anthony ANNAN	GHA	21/7/86	M	26		
21	Mushaga BAKENGA		8/8/92	A		(5)	
5	Mattias BJÄRSMYR	SWE	3/1/86	D	6	(1)	
11	Vadim DEMIDOV		10/10/86	D	26		
3	Mikael DORSIN	SWE	6/10/81	D	30		4
28	Pål André HELLAND		4/1/90	M		(1)	
19	Markus HENRIKSEN		25/7/92	M	26	(2)	7
14	Steffen IVERSEN		10/11/76	A	24	(6)	14
9	Michael Kleppe JAMTFALL		24/3/87	A	3	(2)	1
18	Alejandro LAGO	URU	28/6/79	D	6	(1)	
2	Mikael LUSTIG	SWE	13/12/86	D	29		4
10	Morten MOLDSKRED		13/6/80	A	16	(4)	3
7	Trond OLSEN		5/2/84	A	7	(17)	4
1	Daniel ÖRLUND	SWE	23/6/80	G	30		
30	Rade PRICA	SWE	30/6/80	A	21	(2)	13
27	Bakary Bouba SARÉ	CIV	5/5/90	M	2	(1)	
17	Kjell Rune SELLIN		1/6/89	A	2	(5)	2
15	Per Ciljan SKJELBRED		16/6/87	M	27	(2)	1
13	Kris STADSGAARD	DEN	1/8/85	D	20		
6	Roar STRAND		2/2/70	M	4	(9)	3
20	Abdou Razack TRAORÉ	CIV	28/12/88	M	2	(6)	
16	Simen WANGBERG		6/5/91	D	3		
8	Fredrik WINSNES		28/12/75	M	19	(7)	1
23	Gjermund ÅSEN		22/5/91	M	1	(3)	

SANDEFJORD FOTBALL

Coach – Patrick Walker (IRL)

Founded – 1998

Stadium – Komplett.no Arena (9,000)

2010				
14/3	Start	a	0-2	
21/3	Molde	h	3-1	*Šarić 2, Ertsås*
29/3	Brann	a	2-3	*Demba Bindia, Ertsås*
5/4	Odd Grenland	h	1-1	*Lamøy*
11/4	Strømsgodset	a	2-4	*Nystuen, Mane*
15/4	Vålerenga	h	0-1	
21/4	Tromsø	a	1-2	*Dimitriadis*
25/4	Aalesund	h	0-1	
2/5	Lillestrøm	a	0-4	
5/5	Kongsvinger	h	0-1	
9/5	Hønefoss	a	0-1	
16/5	Viking	h	0-0	
24/5	Haugesund	a	0-2	
6/6	Stabæk	h	1-1	*Zanetti*
3/7	Rosenborg	a	0-1	
10/7	Start	h	1-2	*Mane*
18/7	Molde	a	0-0	
25/7	Brann	h	1-4	*Hansen*
1/8	Viking	a	0-0	
7/8	Rosenborg	h	1-3	*Røyrane*
23/8	Vålerenga	a	0-3	
29/8	Strømsgodset	h	0-3	
12/9	Kongsvinger	a	0-1	
19/9	Tromsø	h	3-5	*Lamøy, Gulsvik, Gabrielsen*
26/9	Odd Grenland	a	0-5	
3/10	Lillestrøm	h	0-1	
17/10	Aalesund	a	2-2	*Lamøy, Gabrielsen*
24/10	Haugesund	h	0-1	
31/10	Stabæk	a	1-2	*Dimitriadis*
7/11	Hønefoss	h	6-1	*Mane 3, Lamøy, Dimitriadis 2*

No	Name	Nat	DoB	Pos	Aps	(s)	Gls
4	Victor DEMBA BINDIA	SEN	6/8/89	D	25	(4)	1
7	Panajotis DIMITRIADIS	SWE	12/8/86	M	29		4
18	Vamouti DIOMANDE	CIV	20/1/91	M	15	(7)	
10	Rune ERTSÅS		24/5/87	A	13	(3)	2
2	Alexander GABRIELSEN		18/11/85	D	21	(2)	2
10	Fredrik GULSVIK		29/8/89	A	8	(1)	1
23	Henrik GUSTAVSEN		8/4/92	M	5	(10)	
6	Rune HANSEN	DEN	4/6/85	D	18	(6)	1
1	Joacim Lund HEIER		27/1/86	G	12		
16	Samuel ISAKSEN		14/4/82	D	3	(1)	
3	Martin JENSEN	DEN	27/7/78	D	21		
19	Eirik André LAMØY		4/11/84	M	19	(5)	4
14	Malick MANE	SEN	14/10/88	A	19	(7)	5
20	MARCIANO José do Nascimento	BRA	12/7/80	M	11	(3)	
8	Espen NYSTUEN		19/12/81	D	29		1
12	Espen Bugge PETTERSEN		10/5/80	G	18		
21	Admir RAŠČIĆ	BIH	16/9/81	A	4	(7)	
13	Ørjan RØYRANE		10/7/88	M	6	(11)	1
9	Samir ŠARIĆ	BIH	27/5/84	A	6	(7)	2
15	Ebrima SOHNA	GAM	8/3/88	M	24	(3)	
25	Martin TORP		3/3/92	M	5	(8)	
17	Olav ZANETTI		29/4/76	D	19	(1)	1

STABÆK FOTBALL

Coach – Jan Jönsson (SWE)

Founded – 1912

Stadium – Telenor Arena (15,600)

MAJOR HONOURS: Norwegian League – (1) 2008; Norwegian Cup - (1) 1998.

2010				
14/3	Odd Grenland	a	3-2	*Nannskog, Andersson, Hoff*
20/3	Vålerenga	h	1-1	*Andersson*
28/3	Aalesund	a	2-2	*Diskerud, Farnerud*
5/4	Tromsø	h	0-1	
10/4	Lillestrøm	a	0-0	
18/4	Kongsvinger	h	4-2	*Andersson, Nannskog 2, Hoff*
21/4	Hønefoss	h	0-1	
24/4	Viking	a	0-2	
2/5	Haugesund	h	0-0	
5/5	Rosenborg	a	0-2	
9/5	Brann	h	2-1	*Hoff, Eiríksson*
16/5	Strømsgodset	a	3-1	*Andersson 2, Hoff*
24/5	Start	h	3-0	*Nannskog 2, Høiland*
6/6	Sandefjord	a	1-1	*Diskerud*
5/7	Molde	h	4-3	*Gunnarsson 3 (2p), Hoff*
10/7	Viking	h	2-3	*Tømmernes 2*
18/7	Brann	a	2-2	*Diskerud, Gunnarsson*
25/7	Rosenborg	h	1-2	*Gunnarsson*
1/8	Tromsø	a	0-3	
8/8	Strømsgodset	h	1-2	*Tømmernes*
22/8	Hønefoss	a	4-0	*Høiland, Gunnarsson 2, Helle*
29/8	Lillestrøm	h	2-1	*Farnerud, Diskerud*
12/9	Vålerenga	a	2-3	*Farnerud, Diogo*
19/9	Odd Grenland	h	0-3	
26/9	Kongsvinger	a	2-1	*Andersson, Gunnarsson*
3/10	Aalesund	h	2-1	*Gunnarsson, Hedenstad*
17/10	Haugesund	a	1-2	*Pálmason*
24/10	Start	a	2-3	*Andersson, Helle*
31/10	Sandefjord	h	2-1	*Gunnarsson, Hammer*
7/11	Molde	a	0-1	

No	Name	Nat	DoB	Pos	Aps	(s)	Gls
19	Johan ANDERSSON	SWE	22/8/83	A	18		7
22	Iven AUSTBØ		22/2/85	G	1	(1)	
14	DIOGO da Costa Oliveira	BRA	14/1/88	A	6	(13)	1
21	Mikkel DISKERUD	USA	2/10/90	M	29	(1)	4
2	Bjarni Ólafur EIRÍKSSON	ISL	28/3/82	D	29		1
17	Pontus FARNERUD	SWE	4/6/80	M	20		3
16	Tor Marius GROMSTAD		8/7/89	D	6	(2)	
10	Veigar Páll GUNNARSSON	ISL	21/3/80	A	23	(1)	10
5	Jørgen HAMMER		2/4/91	D	4	(3)	1
7	Henning HAUGER		17/7/85	M	30		
23	Vegar Eggen HEDENSTAD		26/6/91	D	27		1
18	Marius HELLE		11/8/83	A	4	(3)	2
8	Espen HOFF		20/11/81	A	15	(3)	5
18	Bernt HULSKER		9/9/77	A	2	(9)	
3	Jon Inge HØILAND		20/9/77	D	26	(1)	2
1	Jon KNUDSEN		20/11/74	G	29		
11	Daniel NANNSKOG	SWE	22/5/74	A	11		5
5	Kristian Flittie ONSTAD		9/5/84	D	8	(2)	

3	Pálmi Rafn PÁLMASON	ISL	9/11/84	M	8	(13)	1
4	Jørgen SKJELVIK		5/7/91	M	5	(13)	
5	Morten Morisbak SKJØNSBERG		12/2/83	D	16	(3)	
	Tom STENVOLL		27/3/78	D	4	(4)	
9	Jan Banan TØMMERNES		26/1/87	A	9	(12)	3

IK START

Coach – Knut Tørum

Founded – 1905

Stadium – Sør Arena (14,563)

MAJOR HONOURS: Norwegian League – (2) 1978, 1980.

2010				
14/3	Sandefjord	h	2-0	*og (Hansen), Kleiven*
22/3	Rosenborg	a	3-3	*Kleiven, Børufsen, Årst*
27/3	Molde	h	1-1	*Bolaños*
5/4	Vålerenga	h	5-3	*Bolaños, Kleiven 2, Årst 2*
11/4	Brann	a	4-3	*Årst 2, Bolaños, Kleiven*
14/4	Odd Grenland	h	1-1	*Børufsen*
18/4	Strømsgodset	a	1-3	*Kleiven*
25/4	Hønefoss	h	2-0	*Freeman, og (Obiefule)*
3/5	Aalesund	a	0-2	
6/5	Lillestrøm	h	2-3	*Mathisen, Stokkelien*
9/5	Tromsø	a	0-1	
16/5	Kongsvinger	h	3-0	*Børufsen 2, Årst*
24/5	Stabæk	a	0-3	
7/6	Viking	h	1-1	*Årst*
4/7	Haugesund	a	2-4	*Børufsen, Fevang*
10/7	Sandefjord	a	2-1	*Goodson, Vikstøl*
18/7	Aalesund	h	1-0	*Goodson*
25/7	Molde	a	2-1	*Stokkelien, Børufsen*
2/8	Vålerenga	a	1-8	*Owello*
8/8	Brann	h	3-1	*Stokkelien (p), Bolaños 2*
22/8	Viking	a	2-2	*Stokkelien, Børufsen*
29/8	Rosenborg	h	2-3	*Bolaños, Hoff*
12/9	Lillestrøm	a	2-3	*Vikstøl, Børufsen*
19/9	Strømsgodset	h	4-2	*Årst 3, Goodson*
27/9	Hønefoss	a	0-0	
3/10	Tromsø	h	1-1	*Vikstøl*
17/10	Kongsvinger	a	3-3	*Kleiven, Årst, Stokkelien*
24/10	Stabæk	h	3-2	*Pepa, Knudsen, Mathisen*
31/10	Odd Grenland	a	1-2	*Årst*
7/11	Haugesund	h	3-3	*Hoff, Børufsen, Hulsker*

No	Name	Nat	DoB	Pos	Aps	(s)	Gls
9	Christian BOLAÑOS	CRC	17/5/84	M	20		6
20	Bård BORGERSEN		20/5/72	D	10		
14	Espen BØRUFSEN		4/3/88	A	26	(1)	9
11	Geir Ludvig FEVANG		17/11/80	A	14	(1)	1
16	Christian FOLLERÅS		3/10/91	D		(1)	
2	Hunter FREEMAN	USA	8/1/85	D	24		1
4	Clarence GOODSON	USA	17/5/82	D	26		3
15	Petter Bruer HANSSEN		8/1/86	M	12	(4)	
19	Knut Henry HARALDSEN		14/12/76	D	2		
8	Espen HOFF		20/11/81	A	11		2
16	Bernt HULSKER		9/9/77	A		(7)	1
27	Morten HÆSTAD		11/3/87	M		(8)	
24	Kenneth HØIE		11/9/79	G	30		
30	Christer KLEIVEN		9/4/88	A	25		7
29	Espen KNUDSEN		5/3/91	D	2	(4)	1
26	Jesper MATHISEN		17/3/87	D	11	(8)	2
3	Branislav MILIČEVIĆ	SRB	23/7/83	D	4	(3)	
5	Oladapo OLUFEMI	NGA	5/11/88	M	3	(15)	
10	Solomon James OWELLO	NGA	25/12/88	M	25	(1)	1
22	Avni PEPA		14/11/88	D	16	(3)	1
18	Mads STOKKELIEN		15/3/90	A	14	(14)	5
7	Fredrik STRØMSTAD		20/1/82	M	5	(1)	
28	Rolf Daniel VIKSTØL		22/2/89	D	26		3
8	Jonas WERNER		27/2/92	M		(1)	
25	Ole Martin ÅRST		19/7/74	A	24	(1)	12

STRØMSGODSET IF

Coach – Ronny Deila

Founded – 1907

Stadium – Marienlyst (8,500)

MAJOR HONOURS: Norwegian League – (1) 1970; Norwegian Cup – (5) 1969, 1970, 1973, 1991, 2010.

2010				
14/3	Kongsvinger	h	2-0	*Pedersen, Nordkvelle*
21/3	Haugesund	a	2-2	*Berget, Storflor*
28/3	Viking	h	2-1	*Berget, og (Steenslid)*
5/4	Rosenborg	a	0-3	
11/4	Sandefjord	h	4-2	*Pedersen 2, Sætra, Berget*
15/4	Molde	a	2-3	*Berget, Pedersen*
18/4	Start	h	3-1	*Andersen, Nordkvelle, Kamara*
25/4	Brann	a	0-4	
1/5	Vålerenga	h	1-0	*Pedersen*
5/5	Odd Grenland	h	0-4	
9/5	Lillestrøm	a	1-3	*og (Eriksen)*
16/5	Stabæk	h	1-3	*Pedersen*
24/5	Aalesund	a	1-3	*Sankoh*
5/6	Tromsø	h	2-1	*Storflor, Andersen*
4/7	Hønefoss	a	1-1	*Keita*
11/7	Kongsvinger	a	2-0	*Rnkovic 2*
18/7	Haugesund	h	2-1	*Andersen, Pedersen*
25/7	Odd Grenland	a	0-2	
1/8	Aalesund	h	3-1	*Storflor, Vilsvik (p), Sætra*
8/8	Stabæk	a	2-1	*Sætra, Keita*
21/8	Brann	h	1-1	*Nordkvelle*
29/8	Sandefjord	a	3-0	*Aunan, Nordkvelle, Kamara*
13/9	Molde	h	1-3	*Keita*
19/9	Start	a	2-4	*Kamara 2*
26/9	Rosenborg	h	1-1	*Kamara*
4/10	Viking	a	1-3	*Storflor*
16/10	Vålerenga	a	1-4	*Storflor*
24/10	Hønefoss	h	4-1	*Jóhannsson, Johansen 2, Kamara*
31/10	Tromsø	a	1-2	*Storflor*
7/11	Lillestrøm	h	5-4	*Berget 2, Kamara, Vilsvik (p), Rnkovic*

No	Name	Nat	DoB	Pos	Aps	(s)	Gls
6	Alexander AAS		14/9/78	D	12		
20	Mohammed ABU	GHA	14/11/91	M	5	(3)	
7	Komlan AMEWOU	TOG	15/12/83	M	6	(8)	
2	Glenn ANDERSEN		5/4/80	D	29		3
5	Krister AUNAN		25/12/87	D	15	(5)	1
10	Jo Inge BERGET		11/9/90	A	13	(5)	6
22	André HANSSEN		31/1/81	M	20	(5)	
21	Gardar JÓHANNSSON	ISL	1/4/80	A	4	(2)	1
13	Jim JOHANSEN		6/2/87	A	4	(14)	2
11	Ola KAMARA		15/10/89	A	14	(11)	7
23	Muhamed KEITA		2/9/90	A	20	(2)	3
12	Adam LARSEN		12/12/87	G	29		
16	Akeem LATIFU	NGA	16/11/89	A		(2)	
24	Kim André MADSEN		12/3/89	D	11		
17	Jason MORRISON	JAM	7/6/84	M	8	(2)	
14	Fredrik NORDKVELLE		13/9/85	M	22	(2)	4
19	Marcus PEDERSEN		8/6/90	A	16		7
25	Joel RIDDEZ	SWE	21/5/80	D	24		
28	Petar RNKOVIC		28/11/78	A	4	(7)	3
18	Mads RYGHSETER		17/8/91	A		(3)	
27	Alfred SANKOH	SLE	22/10/88	M	18	(7)	1
9	Øyvind STORFLOR		18/12/79	A	24		6
1	Lars STUBHAUG		18/4/90	G	1	(1)	
3	Lars SÆTRA		24/7/91	D	10	(8)	3
26	Lars Christopher VILSVIK		18/10/88	D	21	(1)	2

TROMSØ IL

Coach – Per-Mathias Høgmo

Founded – 1920

Stadium – Alfheim (10,000)

MAJOR HONOURS: Norwegian Cup - (2) 1986, 1996.

2010				
14/3	Hønefoss	h	2-0	*Knarvik, Rushfeldt*
21/3	Lillestrøm	a	0-2	
28/3	Kongsvinger	h	1-0	*Rushfeldt*
5/4	Stabæk	a	1-0	*Koppinen*
11/4	Haugesund	h	2-0	*Johansen, Rushfeldt*
14/4	Viking	a	1-1	*Mourad*
21/4	Sandefjord	h	2-1	*Ahamed, Drage*
26/4	Molde	a	3-2	*Mourad 2, Björck*
2/5	Rosenborg	h	0-0	
5/5	Brann	a	1-0	*Rushfeldt*
9/5	Start	h	1-0	*Yndestad*
16/5	Odd Grenland	a	1-1	*Ahamed*
24/5	Vålerenga	h	2-1	*Rushfeldt, Haugen*
5/6	Strømsgodset	a	1-2	*Rushfeldt (p)*
4/7	Aalesund	h	0-1	
10/7	Hønefoss	a	2-2	*Ahamed, Koppinen*
19/7	Lillestrøm	h	0-0	
25/7	Kongsvinger	a	1-1	*og (Friberg da Cruz)*
1/8	Stabæk	h	3-0	*Mourad 2 (1p), Johansen*
8/8	Aalesund	a	0-2	
22/8	Odd Grenland	h	3-1	*Kayke 2, Mourad*
28/8	Haugesund	a	0-0	
11/9	Brann	h	0-3	
19/9	Sandefjord	a	5-3	*Johansen, Kayke 3, Mourad*
26/9	Viking	h	1-0	*Mourad (p)*
3/10	Start	a	1-1	*Johansen*
18/10	Molde	h	0-1	
24/10	Rosenborg	a	0-1	
31/10	Strømsgodset	h	2-1	*Rushfeldt 2*
7/11	Vålerenga	a	0-3	

No	Name	Nat	DoB	Pos	Aps	(s)	Gls
20	Mohammed AHAMED Jama		5/8/85	A	16	(11)	3
27	Lars Henrik ANDREASSEN		14/5/91	M		(1)	
23	Stevan BATES	SRB	29/11/81	D	1		
3	Fredrik BJÖRCK	SWE	22/10/79	D	28		1
19	Vegard BRAATEN		30/6/87	A	1	(4)	
22	Caliou CISS	SEN	15/9/89	D	5	(8)	
4	Mignane DIOUF	SEN	2/1/89	A		(1)	
21	Thomas DRAGE		20/2/92	M	3	(13)	1
6	Helge HAUGEN		15/2/82	M	10	(13)	1
26	Tom HØGLI		20/2/74	D	30		
17	Remi JOHANSEN		4/9/90	M	29		4
2	Sérigne Modou KARA Mbodji	SEN	11/11/89	D	22	(1)	
30	KAYKE Moreno de Andrade Rodrigues	BRA	1/4/88	A	8	(2)	5
18	Tommy KNARVIK		1/11/79	M	17	(5)	1
7	Miika KOPPINEN	FIN	5/7/78	D	27		2
5	Kevin LARSEN		10/5/86	D	1	(2)	
9	George MOURAD	SWE	18/9/82	A	20	(5)	8
4	Jade Bronson NORTH	AUS	7/1/82	D	6		
12	Sead RAMOVIĆ	BIH	14/3/79	G	8		
8	Mads REGINIUSSEN		2/1/88	M	1	(10)	
10	Sigurd RUSHFELDT		11/12/72	A	18	(2)	8
1	Marcus SAHLMAN	SWE	2/1/85	G	22	(2)	
24	Dominique TABOGA	AUT	6/11/82	D		(1)	
16	Hans Åge YNDESTAD		24/7/80	D	27	(1)	1
11	Ruben YTTERGÅRD JENSSEN		4/5/88	M	30		

VIKING FK

Coach – Åge Hareide

Founded – 1899

Stadium – Viking (16,300)

MAJOR HONOURS: Norwegian League - (8) 1958, 1972, 1973, 1974, 1975, 1979, 1982, 1991; Norwegian Cup - (5) 1953, 1959, 1979, 1989, 2001.

2010				
15/3	Vålerenga	a	0-2	
21/3	Brann	h	4-0	*Ingelsten, Nisja, Ødegaard, Bjarnason*
28/3	Strømsgodset	a	1-2	*Ingelsten*
5/4	Lillestrøm	h	0-0	
11/4	Aalesund	a	1-3	*Ingelsten*
14/4	Tromsø	h	1-1	*Gíslason*
17/4	Hønefoss	a	1-0	*Ingelsten (p)*
24/4	Stabæk	h	2-0	*Nisja, Danielsen*
2/5	Kongsvinger	a	1-1	*Bjarnason*
5/5	Haugesund	h	1-0	*Bjarnason*
10/5	Molde	h	4-1	*Ingelsten, Sigurdsson, Bjarnason, Skogseid*
16/5	Sandefjord	a	0-0	
24/5	Rosenborg	h	1-2	*Ingelsten*
7/6	Start	a	1-1	*Skogseid*
4/7	Odd Grenland	h	3-1	*Fillo 3 (1p)*
10/7	Stabæk	a	3-2	*Høiland 2, Nisja*
18/7	Hønefoss	h	4-0	*Ødegaard, Steenslid, Ingelsten 2*
25/7	Haugesund	a	0-4	
1/8	Sandefjord	h	0-0	
8/8	Molde	a	2-2	*Nevland, Danielsen*
22/8	Start	h	2-2	*og (Goodson), Nevland*
30/8	Brann	a	3-3	*Høiland, Danielsen (p), Nevland*
12/9	Rosenborg	a	1-1	*Bjarnason*
18/9	Vålerenga	h	3-4	*Nevland, Danielsen, Bjarnason*
26/9	Tromsø	a	0-1	
4/10	Strømsgodset	h	3-1	*Fillo 2, Nevland*
17/10	Odd Grenland	a	1-2	*Sigurdsson*
24/10	Aalesund	h	1-3	*Nevland*
31/10	Lillestrøm	a	1-1	*Berisha*
7/11	Kongsvinger	h	3-1	*Bjarnason 2, Danielsen*

No	Name	Nat	DoB	Pos	Aps	(s)	Gls
23	Ole Marius AASEN		30/11/91	A	2	(3)	
18	Andreas Ulland ANDERSEN		6/5/89	M	7	(2)	
11	Joakim Rune AUSTNES		20/2/83	A	1	(4)	
22	Valon BERISHA		7/2/93	M	4	(8)	1
2	Trond Erik BERTELSEN		5/6/84	D	24	(5)	
21	Birkir BJARNASON	ISL	27/5/88	M	24	(1)	8
14	André DANIELSEN		20/1/85	M	29		5
16	Martin FILLO	CZE	7/2/86	A	13	(2)	5
5	Stefán GÍSLASON	ISL	15/3/80	M	9	(3)	1
28	Jørgen HORN		7/6/87	D	7	(1)	
19	Tommy HØILAND		11/4/89	A	6	(14)	3
9	Patrik INGELSTEN	SWE	25/1/82	A	20	(1)	8
1	Rune Almenning JARSTEIN		29/9/84	G	26		
17	Toni KALLIO	FIN	9/8/78	D		(1)	
12	Artur KOTENKO	EST	20/8/81	G		(1)	
13	Christian LANDU LANDU		25/1/92	D	3	(9)	
26	Yann-Erik de LANLAY		14/5/92	M		(2)	
15	Erik NEVLAND		10/11/77	A	12		6
8	Vidar NISJA		21/8/86	A	28	(1)	3
20	Indridi SIGURDSSON	ISL	12/10/81	D	29		2
6	Håkon SKOGSEID		14/1/88	D	29		2
7	Tomasz SOKOLOWSKI		25/6/85	M	16	(2)	
3	Børre STEENSLID		25/6/85	D	22	(1)	1
10	Alexander ØDEGAARD		13/9/80	A	15	(10)	2
24	Arild ØSTBØ		19/4/91	G	4	(1)	

VÅLERENGA FOTBALL

Coach – Martin Andresen
Founded – 1913
Stadium – Ullevaal (25,572)
MAJOR HONOURS: Norwegian League - (5) 1965, 1981, 1983, 1984, 2005; Norwegian Cup - (4) 1980, 1997, 2002, 2008.

2010

5/3	Viking	h	2-0	*Abdellaoue Moh. 2*
20/3	Stabæk	a	1-1	*og (Skjønsberg)*
28/3	Rosenborg	h	0-0	
5/4	Start	a	3-5	*Abdellaoue Moh., Strandberg, Abdellaoue Mos.*
12/4	Molde	h	2-1	*Fellah, Berre*
15/4	Sandefjord	a	1-0	*Fellah*
18/4	Brann	a	1-1	*Abdellaoue Moh.*
25/4	Odd Grenland	h	6-1	*Madsen, Hæstad 2, Abdellaoue Moh., Singh, Zajić*
1/5	Strømsgodset	a	0-1	
5/5	Hønefoss	h	0-0	
8/5	Kongsvinger	a	2-1	*Shelton, Sæternes*
16/5	Aalesund	h	3-0	*Berre, Abdellaoue Moh., Santos*
24/5	Tromsø	a	1-2	*Sæternes*
6/6	Haugesund	h	5-2	*Abdellaoue Moh., Fellah, Berre, Santos, Muri*
4/7	Lillestrøm	a	4-1	*Abdellaoue Moh. 2, Shelton 2*
12/7	Odd Grenland	a	2-1	*Abdellaoue Moh. 2*
17/7	Kongsvinger	h	5-2	*Berre, og (Myhre), Singh, Abdellaoue Moh., Shelton*
24/7	Aalesund	a	0-1	
2/8	Start	h	8-1	*Sæternes 2, Zajić, Muri, Abdellaoue Moh. 3, Singh (p)*
8/8	Haugesund	a	0-2	
23/8	Sandefjord	h	3-0	*Shelton 2, Abdellaoue Mos.*
29/8	Molde	a	1-0	*og (Andreasson)*
12/9	Stabæk	h	3-2	*Berre, Zajić, Abdellaoue Mos.*
18/9	Viking	a	4-3	*Singh, Shelton, Fellah, Berre*
26/9	Brann	h	1-0	*Shelton*
3/10	Rosenborg	a	1-3	*Zajić*
16/10	Strømsgodset	h	4-1	*Shelton 2, Sæternes, Singh (p)*
23/10	Lillestrøm	h	2-1	*Shelton, Sæternes*
31/10	Hønefoss	a	1-3	*Abdellaoue Mos.*
7/11	Tromsø	h	3-0	*Shelton, Abdellaoue Mos., Sæternes*

No	Name	Nat	DoB	Pos	Aps	(s)	Gls
25	Mohammed ABDELLAOUE		23/10/85	A	19	(1)	15
20	Mostafa ABDELLAOUE		1/8/88	A	4	(14)	5
5	Shåresh AHMADI		1/5/94	A		(1)	
11	Morten BERRE		10/8/75	A	30		6
31	Kristian BRIX		12/6/90	D	2	(3)	
17	Mohammed FELLAH		24/5/89	M	27	(2)	4
27	Adnan HAIDAR		3/8/89	M		(4)	
1	Lars HIRSCHFELD	CAN	17/10/78	G	30		
23	Kristofer HÆSTAD		9/12/83	M	26	(1)	2
7	Victor JOHANSEN		16/6/94	D		(1)	
19	Dawda LEIGH		27/6/86	A	1	(5)	
22	Birger MADSEN		23/4/82	D	3	(3)	1
4	André MURI		22/4/81	D	30		2
13	Håvard NIELSEN		15/7/93	A		(1)	
3	Andreas NORDVIK		18/3/87	D	26		
33	Amin NOURI		10/1/90	D	8	(11)	
13	Fegor OGUDE	NGA	29/7/87	M	1	(5)	
6	Freddy dos SANTOS		2/10/76	D	25		2
21	Luton SHELTON	JAM	11/11/85	A	25	(3)	12
28	Harmeet SINGH		12/11/90	M	30		5
10	Lars Iver STRAND		7/5/83	A		(2)	
24	Stefan STRANDBERG		25/7/90	D	26	(2)	1
14	Bengt SÆTERNES		1/1/75	A	3	(22)	7
26	Bojan ZAJIĆ	SRB	17/6/80	M	14	(6)	4

TOP GOALSCORERS 2010

16	Baye Djiby FALL (Molde)
15	Mohammed ABDELLAOUE (Vålerenga)
14	Petter VAAGAN MOEN (Brann) Anthony UJAH (Lillestrøm) Steffen IVERSEN (Rosenborg)
13	Rade PRICA (Rosenborg)
12	Tor Hogne AARØY (Aalesund) Nikola ĐURĐIĆ (Haugesund) Ole Martin ÅRST (Start) Luton SHELTON (Vålerenga)

PROMOTED CLUBS

SOGNDAL IL FOTBALL

Coach – Harald Aabrekk
Founded – 1926
Stadium – Fosshaugane Campus (4,000)

SARPSBORG 08 FF

Coach – Roar Johansen
Founded – 2000
Stadium – Sarpsborg (4,930)

FREDRIKSTAD FK

Coach – Tom Freddy Aune
Founded – 1903
Stadium – Fredrikstad (12,560)
MAJOR HONOURS: Norwegian League - (9) 1938, 1939, 1949, 1951, 1952, 1954, 1957, 1960, 1961; Norwegian Cup - (11) 1932, 1935, 1936, 1938, 1940, 1950, 1957, 1961, 1966, 1984, 2006.

SECOND LEVEL FINAL TABLE 2010

		Pld	W	D	L	F	A	Pts
1	Sogndal IL Fotball	28	17	5	6	51	28	56
2	Sarpsborg 08 FF	28	16	6	6	54	36	54
3	Fredrikstad FK	28	14	8	6	53	37	50
4	Løv-Ham Fotball	28	13	4	11	46	38	43
5	Ranheim IL Fotball	28	12	7	9	37	38	43
6	FK Bodø/Glimt	28	12	6	10	41	28	42
7	Strømmen IF	28	12	4	12	43	42	40
8	Alta IF	28	10	6	12	41	51	36
9	Bryne FK	28	10	5	13	57	52	35
10	Mjøndalen IF	28	10	5	13	41	49	35
11	Nybergsund IL-Trysil	28	9	8	11	38	47	35
12	Follo FK	28	8	8	12	35	43	32
13	Sandnes Ulf	28	8	7	13	33	40	31
14	Tromsdalen UIL	28	8	4	16	33	50	28
15	Moss FK	28	7	5	16	32	56	26
16	FK Lyn Oslo	0	0	0	0	0	0	0

NB Follo FK did not apply for licence to 2011 season and were relegated; Sandnes Ulf remain at second level; FK Lyn Oslo withdrew after round 11. All their matches annulled.

PROMOTION/RELEGATION PLAY-OFFS

(12/11/10)
Fredrikstad 2, Løv-Ham 0

(14/11/10)
Hønefoss 2, Ranheim 1 *(aet)*

(21/11/10 & 25/11/10)
Hønefoss 1, Fredrikstad 4
Fredrikstad 4, Hønefoss 0
(Fredrikstad 8-1)

DOMESTIC CUP 2010

NORGESMESTERSKAPET

FIRST ROUND

(12/5/10)
Brumunddal 5, Oslo City 2
Fjøra 1, Førde 6
Fløya 2, Senja 0
Fyllingen 0, Os Turn 0 *(aet; 4-2 on pens)*
Grorud 1, Eidsvold Turn 2
Hana 2, Sandnes Ulf 7
Kjelsås 4, Fram Larvik 2
Kongsberg 1, Strømmen 6
Kopervik 1, Vard Haugesund 2
Lillehammer 3, Manglerud Star 2
Mo 1, Steinkjer 2
Nardo 0, Frigg 0 *(aet; 5-4 on pens)*
Nest-Sotra 2, Åsane 1
Orkla 1, Byåsen 5
Randaberg 2, Ålgård 1
Skarbøvik 1, Hødd 0
Skeid 1, Lørenskog 0
Stavanger 3, Vidar 0
Strindheim 6, Kolstad 2
Stålkameratene 2, Harstad 1
Tollnes 0, Notodden 6
Træff 0, Kristiansund 1
Vadmyra 1, Fana 4
Varegg 0, Stord 1
Verdal 0, Levanger 3
Årdal 0, Sogndal 4

(13/5/10)
Arna-Bjørnar 0, Brann 2
Birkebeineren 0, Mjøndalen 3
Brodd 0, Viking 2
Drøbak/Frogn 1, Sarpsborg 08 3
Flisa 1, Nybergsund 1 *(aet; 2-4 on pens)*
Frøyland 1, Bryne 2
Gjøvik 1, Raufoss 3
Hammerfest 0, Alta 3
Hasle-Løren 0, Sandefjord 1
Hauerseter 0, Lillestrøm 5
Herkules 2, Odd Grenland 3
Hovding 0, Løv-Ham 4
Høland 1, Stabæk 12
Innstranden 2, Bodø/Glimt 5
Ishavsbyen 0, Tromsdalen 5
Jerv 0, Start 3
Jevnaker 0, Hønefoss 7
KFUM Oslo 1, Ørn Horten 0 *(aet)*
Klepp 0, Haugesund 4
Kolbotn 0, Follo 5
Korsvoll 1, Moss 4
Malvik 2, Ranheim 5
Mandalskameratene 1, Vindbjart 0
Modum 1, Strømsgodset 5
Oldenborg 0, Kongsvinger 1
Oppsal 1, Vålerenga 11
Ottestad 0, HamKam 6
Pors Grenland 1, Bærum 2
Sagene 0, Lyn 3
Sortland 0, Tromsø 6
Sprint/Jeløy 1, Asker 3 *(aet)*
Stjørdals-Blink 0, Rosenborg 4
Surnadal 1, Molde 3
Trauma 1, Fløy 3
Trosvik 0, Fredrikstad 6
Tønsberg 5, Ullensaker/Kisa 2
Volda 0, Aalesund 1
Voss 1, Valdres 4

SECOND ROUND

(19/5/10)
Alta 3, Nardo 1
Asker 1, Sarpsborg 08 2
Brumunddal 1, Lillestrøm 6
Bryne 5, Stavanger 1
Byåsen 0, Tromsø 2
Bærum 0, Stabæk 2
Eidsvold Turn 0, Strømmen 4
Fana 0, Lyn 3
Fløy 1, Odd Grenland 2
Fyllingen 1, Brann 0
Førde 2, Sogndal 3
HamKam 0, Nybergsund 0 *(aet; 10-11 on pens)*
Kjelsås 2, Sandefjord 3
Kristiansund 1, Ranheim 2 *(aet)*
Lillehammer 2, Kongsvinger 5
Mandalskameratene 1, Start 2
Moss 3, KFUM Oslo 1
Nest-Sotra 1, Løv-Ham 4
Notodden 0, Mjøndalen 1
Randaberg 2, Viking 4
Raufoss 0, Strømsgodset 1
Sandnes Ulf 1, Stord 0
Skarbøvik 2, Aalesund 3
Steinkjer 1, Rosenborg 4
Strindheim 2, Molde 4
Stålkameratene 0, Bodø/Glimt 4
Tromsdalen 5, Fløya 1
Tønsberg 3, Vålerenga 2
Valdres 3, Hønefoss 3 *(aet; 4-5 on pens)*
Vard Haugesund 1, Haugesund 2

(20/5/10)
Levanger 2, Follo 3
Skeid 2, Fredrikstad 4

THIRD ROUND

(9/6/10)
Bodø/Glimt 1, Ranheim 2 *(aet)*
Follo 4, Lillestrøm 2
Haugesund 6, Bryne 1
Kongsvinger 2, Nybergsund 1 *(aet)*
Lyn 2, Strømsgodset 4
Løv-Ham 2, Aalesund 1
Molde 1, Sogndal 3
Odd Grenland 6, Mjøndalen 2
Sandefjord 4, Moss 2
Stabæk 3, Tønsberg 3 *(aet; 3-4 on pens)*
Strømmen 2, Fredrikstad 5
Tromsdalen 0, Tromsø 2 *(aet)*

(10/6/10)
Fyllingen 1, Viking 4
Start 2, Sandnes Ulf 0

(30/6/10)
Rosenborg 3, Alta 1
Sarpsborg 08 2, Hønefoss 2 *(aet; 3-5 on pens)*

FOURTH ROUND

(7/7/10)
Fredrikstad 0, Start 1
Hønefoss 1, Odd Grenland 5
Sandefjord 1, Rosenborg 4
Sogndal 3, Løv-Ham 1
Strømsgodset 3, Haugesund 0
Tromsø 0, Ranheim 2
Tønsberg 0, Follo 2
Viking 2, Kongsvinger 0

QUARTER-FINALS

(14/8/10)
Ranheim 1 *(Aas 4)*, Strømsgodset 2 *(Keita 44, Nordkvelle 72)*
Rosenborg 4 *(Iversen 27p, Lustig 46, Annan 49, Olsen 51)*, Start 3 *(Hoff 5, Årst 9, 53)*

(15/8/10)
Follo 3 *(Skogmo 70, Markegård 75, 90)*, Sogndal 1 *(Olsen 15)*
Odd Grenland 2 *(Bertelsen 22og, Kovács 57)*, Viking 1 *(Ingelsten 28)*

SEMI-FINALS

(22/9/10)
Follo 3 *(Dahl Hagen 41, Markegård 75, Clausen 114)*, Rosenborg 2 *(Henriksen 5, Iversen 62) (aet)*
Strømsgodset 2 *(Morrison 100, Kamara 119)*, Odd Grenland 0 *(aet)*

FINAL

(14/11/10)
Ullevaal stadion, Oslo
STRØMSGODSET IF 2 *(Kamara 30, Andersen 42)*
FOLLO FK 0
Referee – *Hagen*
STRØMSGODSET – *Larsen, Vilsvik, Aas, Andersen, Riddez, Storflor (Jóhannsson 86), Hanssen (Sankoh 71), Morrison, Nordkvelle, Berget (Rnkovic 78), Kamara.*
FOLLO – *Hansen, Skogmo, Skagestad, Petersen, Dahl Hagen, Shipshani (Karoliussen 70), Grini, Jahnsen (Clausen 90), Ruud Tveter, Markegård, Maruti (Bwamy 89).*

CLUB COMMUNICATION 2011

Aalesunds FK
PO Box 193, Sentrum, Color Line Stadion
NO-6008 Ålesund

Tel +47 70 107 780
Fax +47 70 107 781
Web aafk.no
Email kontor@aafk.no
Media Officer Frank Lunde

SK Brann
Kniksens plass 1, Postboks 8 Minde
NO-5821 Bergen

Tel +47 55 598 500
Fax +47 55 598 525
Web brann.no
Email post@brann.no
Media Officer Gorm Nattlandsmyr

Fredrikstad FK
Postboks 300, KG Meldahlsvei 9,
1671 Kraakeroy, NO-1601 Fredrikstad

Tel +47 69 301720
Fax +47 69 301721
Web fredrikstadfk.no
Email info@fredrikstadfk.no
Media Officer Thomas Torjusen

FK Haugesund
Postboks 406
NO-5501 Haugesund

Tel +47 52 808 980
Fax +47 52 808 901
Web fkh.no
Email post@fkh.no
Media Officer Svein Hegland

Lillestrøm SK
C.J. Hansensvei 3B, Åråsen Stadion
NO-2007 Kjeller

Tel +47 63 805 660
Fax +47 63 805 670
Web lsk.no
Email lsk@lsk.no
Media Officer Ole Kristian Bakkene

Molde FK
Julsundveien 14
NO-6412 Molde

Tel +47 71 202 500
Fax +47 71 202 501
Web moldefk.no
Email mfk@moldefk.no
Media Officer Per Lianes

Odd Grenland
Postboks 5, Falkum
NO-3705 Skien

Tel +47 35 900 150
Fax of the club +47 35 900 159
Web oddgrenland.no
Email info@oddgrenland.no
Media Officer Bjørn Hogstad

Rosenborg BK
Lerkendal Stadion
NO-7492 Trondheim

Tel +47 73 822 100
Fax +47 73 944 070
Web rbk.no
Email info@rbk.no
Media Officer Nils Heldal

Sarpsborg 08 FF
Boks 129,
NO-1701 Sarpsborg

Tel +47 69 151 975
Fax
Web sarpsborg08.no
Email post@sarpsborg08.no
Media Officer Ann Cathrin Juul

Sogndal IL Fotball
PO Box 164, Fosshaugane
NO-6851 Sogndal

Tel +47 57 629 050
Fax +47 57 629 030
Web sogndalfotball.no
Email sil@angrip.no
Media Officer Torgeir Skålid

Stabæk Fotball
PO Box 178, Wideroeveien 1, 1360
Fornebu, NO-1326 Lysaker

Tel +47 94 800 400
Fax +47 67 599 602
Web stabak.no
Email admin@stabak.no
Media Officer Lars J. Mæhlum

IK Start
Stadionveien 21, Postboks 1533 Valhalla
NO-4688 Kristiansand

Tel +47 38 106 666
Fax +47 38 097 535
Web ikstart.no
Email admin@ikstart.no
Media Officer Roy Emanuelsen

Strømsgodset IF
Pb. 4055 Gulskogen, Øvre Eikervei 25
NO-3005 Drammen

Tel +47 32 265 770
Fax +47 32 830 175
Web godset.no
Email godset@godset.no
Media Officer Helge Helgesen

Tromsø IL
Postboks 5, Stadionveien 3/5
NO-9251 Tromsø

Tel +47 97 173 000
Fax +47 77 602 601
Web til.no
Email post@til.no
Media Officer Eirik Haldorsen

Viking FK
Viking Stadion, Jåttåvågen 11 A
NO-4020 Stavanger

Tel +47 51 329 700
Fax +47 51 329 701
Web viking-fk.no
Email viking@viking-fk.no
Media Officer Eirik Arntsen

Vålerenga Fotball
Vallhall Fotballhall, Innspurten, 16
NO-0663 Oslo

Tel +47 23 247 800
Fax +47 23 247 801
Web vif-fotball.no
Email post@vif.no
Media Officer Lasse Vangstein

POLAND

Pologne I Polen

Polski Związek Piłki Nożnej (PZPN)

COMMUNICATION

Address Bitwy Warszawskiej 1920 r.7 PL-02 366 Warszawa

Tel +48 22 551 2300

Fax +48 22 551 2240

E-mail pzpn@pzpn.pl

Website pzpn.pl

President Grzegorz Lato

General Secretary Zdzisław Kręcina

Media Officer Agnieszka Olejkowska

Year of Formation 1919

DOMESTIC COMPETITION SUMMARY 2010/11

EKSTRAKLASA FINAL TABLE

			Home					Away					Total						
		Pld	W	D	L	F	A	W	D	L	F	A	W	D	L	F	A	Pts	Comp
1	Wisła Kraków	30	11	2	2	27	11	6	3	6	17	18	17	5	8	44	29	56	UCL
2	WKS Śląsk Wrocław	30	7	5	3	27	13	6	5	4	19	21	13	10	7	46	34	49	UEL
3	Legia Warszawa	30	10	1	4	27	16	5	3	7	18	22	15	4	11	45	38	49	UEL
4	Jagiellonia Białystok	30	11	2	2	29	11	3	4	8	9	21	14	6	10	38	32	48	UEL
5	KKS Lech Poznań	30	10	4	1	27	6	3	2	10	10	17	13	6	11	37	23	45	
6	Górnik Zabrze	30	9	4	2	24	10	4	2	9	12	30	13	6	11	36	40	45	
7	KSP Polonia Warszawa	30	7	3	5	22	12	5	5	5	19	14	12	8	10	41	26	44	
8	KS Lechia Gdańsk	30	8	3	4	20	12	4	4	7	17	24	12	7	11	37	36	43	
9	RTS Widzew Łódź	30	7	6	2	26	12	4	4	7	15	22	11	10	9	41	34	43	
10	GKS Bełchatów	30	9	4	2	18	10	1	6	8	13	23	10	10	10	31	33	40	
11	Zagłębie Lubin	30	7	4	4	14	12	3	5	7	17	26	10	9	11	31	38	39	
12	Ruch Chorzów	30	6	5	4	14	12	4	3	8	15	20	10	8	12	29	32	38	
13	Korona Kielce	30	5	5	5	20	22	5	2	8	14	26	10	7	13	34	48	37	
14	MKS Cracovia Kraków	30	7	2	6	30	21	1	3	11	7	26	8	5	17	37	47	29	
15	Arka Gdynia	30	6	5	4	19	19	0	5	10	3	24	6	10	14	22	43	28	*Relegated*
16	KS Polonia Bytom	30	4	5	6	17	18	2	4	9	12	27	6	9	15	29	45	27	*Relegated*

Top Scorer Tomasz Frankowski (Jagiellonia), 14 goals

Promoted Clubs ŁKS Łódź
TS Podbeskidzie Bielsko-Biała

Cup Final Legia Warszawa 1, KKS Lech Poznań 1 (aet; 5-4 on pens)

Wisła Kraków reclaim Ekstraklasa crown

In a season that saw Poland intensify preparations, both on and off the pitch, for UEFA EURO 2012, domestic football took something of a back seat. It was not a vintage Ekstraklasa championship, which Wisła Kraków won despite a modest campaign in which they scored infrequently and lost eight times. Furthermore, the Polish Cup final, in which Legia Warszawa defeated outgoing champions KKS Lech Poznań on penalties, was marred by post-match crowd disturbances that prompted a government inquest.

Wisła were commandeered to their third league title in four seasons by Dutchman Robert Maaskant, who joined in August after the club had been humiliatingly knocked out of the UEFA Europa League by Qarabağ FK of Azerbaijan – a result that ended the five-month tenure of coach Henryk Kasperczak. Having surrendered the title to Lech in extremis the previous season, Wisła, champions in 2007/08 and 2008/09, were keen to reassert their authority. It took Maaskant and his cosmopolitan squad a while to get their act together, but a strong finish to the autumn enabled them to stalk surprise halfway leaders Jagiellonia Białystok, and in the spring they moved up a couple of gears, took 17 points from their next seven games, including a 2-0 home win over Jagiellonia, and were never subsequently challenged.

Derby decider

Having lost the 2009/10 title in a local derby against MKS Cracovia Kraków, it was fitting that Wisła should clinch their 13th title – one shy of the national record – against the same opposition, a 17th-minute goal from Israeli import Maor Meliksson bringing a 1-0 win in front of 17,500 spectators that wrapped up proceedings with three matches remaining. Although Wisła lost two of their last three fixtures, they still ended up with a seven-point victory margin.

The title win was very much a team effort, with the overseas brigade, comprising one representative each from 17 different nations, making a notable contribution. The star of the show was Slovenian international midfielder Andraž Kirm, also the side's top scorer, with nine goals, while winter signings Meliksson, Sergei Pareiko – an Estonian international goalkeeper – and Tsvetan Genkov – a Bulgarian international striker – were all influential in the spring title surge. The most prominent Poles were captain Radosław Sobolewski and capricious young winger Patryk Małecki, while Paweł Brożek, the Ekstraklasa's top marksman in each of Wisła's last two title wins, scored six goals before departing with twin brother Piotr to Trabzonspor AŞ in January.

To a degree, Wisła's run to the title was upstaged by the extraordinary recovery of WKS Śląsk Wrocław, who, after replacing coach Ryszard Tarasiewicz with Orest Lenczyk in late September following five successive defeats, climbed from the relegation zone to the runners-up spot, losing only twice in 23 outings under the 68-year-old veteran to record their highest league placing in 30 years and return to Europe for the first time since 1987. Śląsk secured second place on the final day with their biggest win of the season, 5-0 at home to Arka Gdynia, who were thus relegated alongside KS Polonia Bytom, also heavily beaten, 4-0 at Legia.

Dutch coach Robert Maaskant steered Wisła Kraków to the Polish title at the first attempt

Three of Śląsk's goals against Arka were scored by Argentinian striker Cristián Díaz. It was only the fourth hat-trick of an Ekstraklasa campaign that suffered throughout from a shortage of goals. With that 5-0 win Śląsk became the league's top-scoring team with just 46 in 30 games, while the award for top individual marksman was collected – for the fourth time – by 36-year-old Tomasz Frankowski with a relatively meagre tally of 14 for his hometown club Jagiellonia.

Cup winners in 2009/10, and consequently European debutants in 2010/11, Jagiellonia made a quick return to continental competition by finishing higher than ever before in fourth – despite their decline in the spring. Third place was taken by Legia, who blew hot and cold under the youthful Maciej Skorża (the former double title-winning coach of Wisła) but ended a three-year spell without silverware by lifting the Polish Cup for a record 14th time, overcoming Lech on penalties at the end of a tight, tempestuous encounter in Bydgoszcz, Poland's 'speedway capital', where sparks of a different kind flew as the two sets of fans clashed violently with each other and the local police after the game.

European exploits

Lech were unable to recover sufficient ground in the league after their cup final setback to qualify for Europe. They had done the nation proud with their UEFA Europa League exploits earlier in the season, drawing twice with Juventus and beating Manchester City FC 3-1 in their impressive new EURO-ready stadium before narrowly going out to SC Braga. Their bid to reach the UEFA Champions League group stage, however, had ended in early August with elimination by AC Sparta Praha, and when the team lost four successive league games in mid-autumn, title-winning boss Jacek Zieliński was sacked and replaced by Spaniard José María Bakero, who only a few weeks earlier had been harshly dismissed from early pacesetters KSP Polonia Warszawa.

Lech Poznań defender Ivan Đurđević applauds the fans after his team's UEFA Europa League victory over Manchester City

Lech missed the goals of Robert Lewandowski, who went on to bigger things in Germany with Borussia Dortmund, but his replacement, Latvian international Artjoms Rudņevs, proved a big hit early on with an amazing hat-trick against Juve in Turin. He followed it up by scoring 11 goals in the league plus a couple of crucial strikes in the cup semi-final against TS Podbeskidzie Bielsko-Biała, who would earn promotion to the Ekstraklasa with second division champions ŁKS Łódź.

Mierzejewski emerges

Lewandowski reinforced his standing as Poland's great hope for UEFA EURO 2012 by scoring four international goals in 2010/11 to take his cumulative tally into double figures. His Dortmund team-mates Łukasz Piszczek and Jakub Błaszczykowski also transported their fine Bundesliga form into the international arena, and there was high promise too from skilful 24-year-old midfield schemer Adrian Mierzejewski, who, after claiming the 2010/11 Ekstraklasa player of the year award, left Polonia Warszawa for Trabzonspor. His first international goal came in a memorable 2-1 win over Argentina in June – with his prospective club colleague Paweł Brożek scoring the winner – but as that was immediately followed by a 1-0 defeat to France, it left Franciszek Smuda's team with an even end-of-season balance sheet – 12 months before the big EURO kick-off – of four wins, five draws and four defeats.

National Team

International Tournament Appearances – FIFA World Cup - (7) 1938, 1974 (3rd), 1978 (2nd phase), 1982 (3rd), 1986 (2nd round), 2002, 2006. UEFA European Championship – (1) 2008.

Top Five All-time Caps – Michał Żewłakow (102); Grzegorz Lato (100); Kazimierz Deyna (97); Jacek Bąk & Jacek Krzynówek (96)

Top Five All-time Goals – Włodzimierz Lubański (48); Grzegorz Lato (45); Kazimierz Deyna (41); Ernest Pol (39); Andrzej Szarmach (32)

NATIONAL TEAM RESULTS 2010/11

11/8/10	Cameroon	H	Szczecin	0-3	
4/9/10	Ukraine	H	Lodz	1-1	*Jeleń (42)*
7/9/10	Australia	H	Krakow	1-2	*Lewandowski (18)*
9/10/10	United States	A	Chicago	2-2	*Matuszczyk (30), Błaszczykowski (73)*
12/10/10	Ecuador	N	Montreal (CAN)	2-2	*Smolarek (61), Obraniak (70)*
17/11/10	Ivory Coast	H	Poznan	3-1	*Lewandowski (19, 80), Obraniak (66)*
10/12/10	Bosnia & Herzegovina	N	Antalya (TUR)	2-2	*Brożek (7, 52)*
6/2/11	Moldova	N	Vila Real (POR)	1-0	*Plizga (15)*
9/2/11	Norway	N	Faro (POR)	1-0	*Lewandowski (19)*
25/3/11	Lithuania	A	Kaunas	0-2	
29/3/11	Greece	A	Piraeus	0-0	
5/6/11	Argentina	H	Warsaw	2-1	*Mierzejewski A. (26), Brożek (67)*
9/6/11	France	H	Warsaw	0-1	

NATIONAL TEAM APPEARANCES 2010/11

Coach – Franciszek SMUDA 22/6/48			Cmr	Ukr	Aus	Usa	Ecu	Civ	Bih	Mda	Nor	Ltu	Gre	Arg	Fra	Caps	Goals
Łukasz FABIAŃSKI	18/4/85	Arsenal (ENG)	G46					G								17	-
Grzegorz WOJTKOWIAK	26/1/84	Lech	D38	D	D			D	D	D				D	D	13	-
Michał ŻEWŁAKOW	22/4/76	Ankaragücü (TUR)	D	D	D	D	D						D63			102	3
Kamil GLIK	3/2/88	Palermo (ITA) /Bari (ITA)	D				D				D	D				9	1
Maciej SADLOK	29/6/89	Ruch /Polonia Warszawa	D					D	D78			D	D			14	-
Jakub BŁASZCZYKOWSKI	14/12/85	Dortmund (GER)	M	M84	M	M		M			M	M85	M	M	M87	41	4
Dariusz DUDKA	9/12/83	Auxerre (FRA)	M72								D	M85	M	M	M	53	2
Rafał MURAWSKI	9/10/81	Rubin (RUS) /Lech	M58	M	M	M	M	M			M89	M46	s46	M76	M	34	1
Ludovic OBRANIAK	10/11/84	Lille (FRA)	M78			M	M	M89			M79	M69	M83		M88	16	4
Paweł BROŻEK	21/4/83	Wisła Kraków /Trabzonspor (TUR)	A46					s72	A63					s56	s87	25	6
Robert LEWANDOWSKI	21/8/88	Dortmund (GER)	A	s64	A	A	A88	A85			A	A74	A83	A90	A	34	10
Marcin KOWALCZYK	9/4/85	Dinamo Moskva (RUS)	s38													7	-
Maciej RYBUS	19/8/89	Legia	s46	s84					M46							12	1
Przemysław TYTOŃ	4/1/87	Roda (NED)	s46		G		G									4	-
Adrian MIERZEJEWSKI	6/11/86	Polonia Warszawa	s58			M71	M82	M72	M			M46	M46	M81	M79	12	1
Adam MATUSZCZYK	14/2/89	Köln (GER)	s72	s46		M		M90			M90			s76	s79	10	1
Sławomir PESZKO	19/2/85	Lech /Köln (GER)	s78	M	M75							s46	M77			18	1
Artur BORUC	20/2/80	Fiorentina (ITA)		G		G										46	-
Łukasz PISZCZEK	3/6/85	Dortmund (GER)		D	D	D	D61	D			D	D	D	D	D	18	-
Sebastian BOENISCH	1/2/87	Werder (GER)		D	D											2	-
Tomasz BANDROWSKI	18/9/84	Lech		M46												7	-
Maciej IWAŃSKI	7/5/81	Legia		M64	s83											10	2
Ireneusz JELEŃ	9/4/81	Auxerre (FRA)		A87	A83						A64					28	5
Euzebiusz SMOLAREK	9/1/81	Polonia Warszawa		s87	s70		M68	s89								47	20
Dariusz PIETRASIAK	12/2/80	Polonia Warszawa			M70	D										2	-
Kamil GROSICKI	8/6/88	Jagiellonia /Sivasspor (TUR)			s75		s68		A		s64	s46	s77	M56		10	-
Łukasz MIERZEJEWSKI	31/8/82	Cracovia				D	D									5	-
Andrzej NIEDZIELAN	27/2/79	Korona				s71	s88									19	5

NATIONAL TEAM APPEARANCES 2010/11 (contd.)

			Cmr	Ukr	Aus	Usa	Ecu	Civ	Bih	Mda	Nor	Ltu	Gre	Arg	Fra	Caps	Goals
Hubert WOŁĄKIEWICZ	21/10/85	Lechia Gdansk /Lech					M	s90	D62	D						4	-
Artur JĘDRZEJCZYK	4/11/87	Legia					s61									1	-
Radosław MAJEWSKI	15/12/86	Nottingham Forest (ENG)					s82									8	-
Tomasz JODŁOWIEC	8/9/85	Polonia Warszawa						D	D			s85	s63	D	D	18	-
Ariel BORYSIUK	29/7/91	Legia						s85	M63	M78						3	-
Grzegorz SANDOMIERSKI	5/9/89	Jagiellonia							G	G			G			3	-
Marcin KIKUT	25/6/83	Lech							M46	D						2	-
Szymon PAWŁOWSKI	4/11/86	Zagłębie Lubin							s46	M		s85			s88	8	-
Dawid PLIZGA	17/11/85	Zagłębie Lubin							s46	M						2	1
Piotr CELEBAN	25/6/85	Śląsk Wrocław							s62	D						4	-
Marcin ROBAK	29/11/82	Widzew							s63							4	1
Cezary WILK	12/2/86	Wisła Kraków							s63	s78						2	-
Tomasz KUPISZ	2/1/90	Jagiellonia							s78							1	-
Janusz GOL	11/11/85	Bełchatów								M	s90					4	-
Michał KUCHARCZYK	20/3/91	Legia								A46		s74	s83	s81		4	-
Dawid NOWAK	30/11/84	Bełchatów								A						8	-
Jakub RZEŹNICZAK	26/10/86	Legia								s46						7	-
Wojciech SZCZĘSNY	18/4/90	Arsenal (ENG)									G			G	G	4	-
Arkadiusz GŁOWACKI	13/3/79	Trabzonspor (TUR)									D	D	D			24	-
ROGER Guerreiro	25/5/82	AEK (GRE)									s79	s69	s83			25	4
Grzegorz KRYCHOWIAK	29/1/90	Reims (FRA)									s89					2	-
Sebastian MAŁKOWSKI	2/3/87	Lechia Gdansk										G				1	-
Jakub WAWRZYNIAK	7/7/83	Legia												D	D	18	-
Mateusz KLICH	13/6/90	Cracovia												s90		1	-

CLUB-BY-CLUB

ARKA GDYNIA

Coach – Dariusz Pasieka; (23/3/11) František Straka (CZE)

Founded – 1929

Stadium – Narodowy Stadion Rugby (3,000); Stadion Miejski (15,139)

MAJOR HONOURS: Polish Cup – (1) 1979.

2010				
8/8	Wisła	a	0-1	
14/8	Lech	a	0-0	
21/8	Górnik	h	2-0	*Burkhardt (p), Labukas*
28/8	Zagłębie	a	0-1	
11/9	Widzew	h	1-1	*Szmatiuk*
19/9	Jagiellonia	h	1-0	*Labukas*
25/9	Cracovia	a	0-2	
2/10	Polonia Warszawa	h	0-0	
17/10	Lechia	a	0-1	
23/10	Bełchatów	h	1-0	*Ivanovski*
30/10	Ruch	a	0-0	
6/11	Korona	h	2-1	*Labukas, Zawistowski*
13/11	Polonia Bytom	a	0-2	
19/11	Legia	a	0-3	
27/11	Śląsk Wrocław	h	2-2	Labukas 2 (1p)
2011				
25/2	Wisła	h	0-1	
5/3	Lech	h	0-3	
11/3	Górnik	a	2-2	*Noll 2*
18/3	Zagłębie	h	1-1	*Glavina*
2/4	Widzew	a	0-0	
10/4	Jagiellonia	a	0-1	
17/4	Cracovia	h	3-0	*og (Kaczmarek), Labukas, Ivanovski*
23/4	Polonia Warszawa	a	0-4	
1/5	Lechia	h	2-2	*Noll, Labukas*
8/5	Bełchatów	a	1-1	*Ivanovski*
11/5	Ruch	h	0-2	
14/5	Korona	a	0-1	
21/5	Polonia Bytom	h	2-1	*Szmatiuk, Labukas*
25/5	Legia	h	2-5	*Szmatiuk 2*
29/5	Śląsk Wrocław	a	0-5	

No	Name	Nat	DoB	Pos	Aps	(s)	Gls
29	Robert BEDNAREK		23/2/79	D	6	(1)	
19	Miroslav BOŽOK	SVK	19/10/84	M	26		
22	Marciano BRUMA	NED	7/3/84	D	25		
10	Marcin BUDZIŃSKI		6/7/90	M	14	(2)	
25	Filip BURKHARDT		23/3/87	M	10	(8)	1
31	Paweł CZOSKA		31/8/90	M	2	(8)	
18	GIOVANNI Vemba-Duarte	ANG	21/1/91	A	5	(7)	
36	Denis GLAVINA	CRO	3/3/86	M	20		1
27	Mirko IVANOVSKI	MKD	31/10/89	A	18	(9)	3
24	Douglas JÚNIOR ROSS Santillana	PER	19/2/86	A	2	(2)	
11	Tadas LABUKAS	LTU	10/1/84	A	24	(5)	8
1	MARCELO MORETTO de Souza	BRA	10/5/78	G	14		
21	Joseph Désiré MAWAYE	CMR	14/5/86	A	9	(11)	
20	Emil NOLL	COD	21/11/78	D	29		3
8	Michał PŁOTKA		11/6/88	D	18	(2)	
13	Piotr ROBAKOWSKI		1/5/90	D	1	(1)	

	Ante ROŽIĆ	AUS	8/3/86	D	21	(1)	
7	Mateusz SIEBERT		4/4/89	D	4	(1)	
6	Rafał SIEMASZKO		11/9/86	A	4	(8)	
5	Ervin SKELA	ALB	17/11/76	M	3	(2)	
3	Maciej SZMATIUK		9/5/80	D	27		4
7	Wojciech WILCZYŃSKI		18/3/90	D	9	(10)	
3	Norbert WITKOWSKI		5/8/81	G	15		
	Paweł ZAWISTOWSKI		4/6/84	M	21	(4)	1
9	Hieronim ZOCH		30/9/90	G	1		
28	Krystian ŻOŁNIEREWICZ		21/4/93	D	2	(2)	

GKS BEŁCHATÓW

Coach – Maciej Bartoszek

Founded – 1977

Stadium – GKS (5,238)

2010				
6/8	Polonia Bytom	h	2-0	*Fonfara, Kuświk*
14/8	Jagiellonia	a	1-3	*Żewłakow*
21/8	Ruch	h	3-2	*Żewłakow, Wróbel, Kuświk*
27/8	Legia	a	2-0	*Żewłakow 2*
11/9	Lechia	h	1-0	*Gol*
18/9	Górnik	a	0-1	
26/9	Wisła	h	1-1	*Małkowski*
3/10	Lech	h	1-0	*Popek*
16/10	Korona	a	1-3	*Małkowski*
23/10	Arka	a	0-1	
29/10	Widzew	h	1-0	*Drzymont*
6/11	Śląsk Wrocław	h	0-1	
14/11	Zagłębie	a	1-1	*Małkowski*
21/11	Polonia Warszawa	h	3-2	*Nowak 3 (1p)*
26/11	Cracovia	a	2-3	*Bocian, Nowak*
2011				
26/2	Polonia Bytom	a	1-1	*Nowak*
5/3	Jagiellonia	h	0-0	
12/3	Ruch	a	1-2	*Małkowski*
20/3	Legia	h	2-0	*Żewłakow, Małkowski*
1/4	Lechia	a	0-0	
8/4	Górnik	h	1-1	*Żewłakow*
15/4	Wisła	a	1-3	*Lačić*
23/4	Lech	a	0-0	
30/4	Korona	h	1-0	*og (Tataj)*
8/5	Arka	h	1-1	*Nowak*
11/5	Widzew	a	1-1	*Nowak*
14/5	Śląsk Wrocław	a	2-4	*Żewłakow, Nowak*
20/5	Zagłębie	h	0-2	
25/5	Polonia Warszawa	a	0-0	
29/5	Cracovia	h	1-0	*Kuświk*

No	Name	Nat	DoB	Pos	Aps	(s)	Gls
3	Grzegorz BARAN		23/12/82	M	23	(1)	
45	Bartłomiej BARTOSIAK		26/2/91	M		(2)	
51	Łukasz BOCIAN		29/5/88	M	6	(6)	1
53	Łukasz BUDZIŁEK		19/3/91	G	1	(1)	
20	Paweł BUZAŁA		27/12/85	A		(4)	
10	Mateusz CETNARSKI		6/7/88	M	15	(5)	
28	Marcin DRZYMONT		16/9/81	D	27		1
22	Grzegorz FONFARA		8/6/83	D	19	(4)	1
5	Janusz GOL		11/11/85	M	14		1
84	Wojciech JARMUŻ		5/1/84	D	4		
11	Pavel KOMOLOV	RUS	10/3/89	M	4	(6)	
17	Grzegorz KUŚWIK		23/5/87	A	5	(16)	3
14	Mate LAČIĆ	CRO	12/9/80	D	29		1
8	Maciej MAŁKOWSKI		19/3/85	M	28	(1)	5
99	MARCUS VINÍCIUS da Silva de Oliveira	BRA	29/3/84	A	9	(11)	
19	Maciej MYSIAK		4/2/84	D	9		
9	Dawid NOWAK		30/11/84	A	16	(10)	8
4	Jacek POPEK		20/8/78	D	20	(1)	1
19	Kamil POŹNIAK		11/12/89	M	10	(4)	
12	Łukasz SAPELA		21/9/82	G	29		
6	Szymon SAWALA		25/9/82	M	9	(1)	
27	Zlatko TANEVSKI	MKD	3/8/83	D	16		
7	Jeremiah WHITE	USA	3/4/82	M		(3)	
23	Tomasz WRÓBEL		10/7/82	M	18	(4)	1
55	Łukasz WROŃSKI		13/1/94	M		(1)	
29	Mariusz ZAWODZIŃSKI		11/2/89	M		(2)	
21	Marcin ŻEWŁAKOW		22/4/76	A	19	(5)	7

MKS CRACOVIA KRAKÓW

Coach – Rafał Ulatowski; (28/10/10) (Marcin Sadko); (31/10/10) Yuriy Shatalov (UKR)

Founded – 1906

Stadium – Hutnik Kraków (5,500); Marszałek Piłsudski (15,016)

MAJOR HONOURS: Polish League – (5) 1921, 1930, 1932, 1937, 1948.

2010				
13/8	Śląsk Wrocław	h	2-3	*og (Fojut), Polczak*
16/8	Legia	a	1-2	*Ślusarski (p)*
22/8	Lech	a	0-5	
27/8	Korona	a	0-1	
11/9	Górnik	h	2-3	*Matusiak 2*
17/9	Lechia	a	0-1	
25/9	Arka	h	2-0	*og (Witkowski), Ślusarski*
2/10	Zagłębie	a	0-0	
17/10	Ruch	h	2-3	*Dudzic, Mierzejewski*
23/10	Polonia Warszawa	a	0-3	
30/10	Polonia Bytom	h	0-1	
5/11	Wisła	h	0-1	
12/11	Widzew	a	2-2	*Ślusarski, Dudzic*
20/11	Jagiellonia	a	2-4	*Ntibazonkiza 2*
26/11	Bełchatów	h	3-2	*Dudzic, Krzywicki, Pawlusiński*
2011				
25/2	Legia	h	3-3	*Jarabica, Suvorov (p), Ntibazonkiza*
4/3	Śląsk Wrocław	a	0-0	
13/3	Lech	h	1-0	*Klich*
19/3	Korona	h	3-0	*Klich, Višņakovs, Ntibazonkiza*
3/4	Górnik	a	0-1	
9/4	Lechia	h	3-0	*Trivunović, Klich, Višņakovs*
17/4	Arka	a	0-3	
21/4	Zagłębie	h	2-2	*Kosanović, Suvorov*
1/5	Ruch	a	0-1	
7/5	Polonia Warszawa	h	3-1	*Trivunović, Suvorov, Višņakovs*
10/5	Polonia Bytom	a	2-1	*Ntibazonkiza, Suvorov (p)*
15/5	Wisła	a	0-1	
21/5	Widzew	h	1-2	*Szeliga*
25/5	Jagiellonia	h	3-0	*Klich, Suvorov, Struna*
29/5	Bełchatów	a	0-1	

No	Name	Nat	DoB	Pos	Aps	(s)	Gls
18	Mateusz BARTCZAK		15/8/79	M	9	(1)	
15	Vladimir BOLJEVIĆ	MNE	17/1/88	M	4	(8)	
33	Marcin CABAJ		23/5/80	G	12		
37	Bartłomiej DUDZIC		18/8/88	A	15	(12)	3
7	Piotr GIZA		28/2/80	M	3	(2)	
77	Michał GOLIŃSKI		17/3/81	M		(1)	
23	Krzysztof JANUS		25/3/86	M	12		
4	Marián JARABICA	SVK	27/4/89	D	13	(1)	1
83	Wojciech KACZMAREK		29/3/83	G	15		
66	Mateusz KLICH		13/6/90	M	24	(3)	4
3	Miloš KOSANOVIĆ	SRB	28/5/90	D	15	(1)	1
20	Marcin KRZYWICKI		29/11/86	A		(12)	1
10	Wojciech ŁUCZAK		28/7/89	M	2	(2)	
33	Pavol MASARYK	SVK	11/2/80	A	1	(5)	
7	Radosław MATUSIAK		1/1/82	A	7	(3)	2
35	Łukasz MERDA		4/5/80	G	3		
24	Łukasz MIERZEJEWSKI		31/8/82	D	11	(1)	1
18	Tomasz MOSKAŁA		5/4/77	A	2		
32	Łukasz NAWOTCZYŃSKI		30/5/82	D	4		
17	Saïdi NTIBAZONKIZA	BDI	1/5/87	M	27		5
9	Dariusz PAWLUSIŃSKI		24/11/77	M	3	(6)	1
16	Piotr POLCZAK		25/8/86	D	14		1
11	Bojan PUZIGAĆA	BIH	10/5/85	D	1	(1)	
6	Arkadiusz RADOMSKI		27/6/77	M	23		
14	Mariusz SACHA		19/7/87	A	7	(2)	
15	Paweł SASIN		2/10/83	M	5	(1)	
25	Andraž STRUNA	SVN	23/4/89	D	8	(2)	1
8	Hesdey SUART	NED	20/1/86	D	16	(3)	

No	Name	Nat	DoB	Pos	Aps	(s)	Gls
19	Alexandru SUVOROV	MDA	2/2/87	M	15	(8)	5
21	Sławomir SZELIGA		17/7/82	D	24	(1)	1
13	Bartosz ŚLUSARSKI		11/12/81	A	12	(1)	3
26	Vule TRIVUNOVIĆ	BIH	13/3/83	D	11		2
9	Aleksejs VIŠŅAKOVS	LVA	3/2/84	M	8	(6)	3
5	Marek WASILUK		3/6/87	D	4	(1)	

GÓRNIK ZABRZE

Coach – Adam Nawałka

Founded – 1948

Stadium – Ernesta Pohla (10,000)

MAJOR HONOURS: Polish League – (14) 1957, 1959, 1961, 1963, 1964, 1965, 1966, 1967, 1971, 1972, 1985, 1986, 1987, 1988; Polish Cup – (6) 1965, 1968, 1969, 1970, 1971, 1972.

2010				
6/8	Polonia Warszawa	h	0-2	
14/8	Zagłębie	a	2-1	*Zahorski, Świątek*
21/8	Arka	a	0-2	
29/8	Ruch	h	1-0	*Magiera*
11/9	Cracovia	a	3-2	*Gierczak, Zahorski, Bonin*
18/9	Bełchatów	h	1-0	*Zahorski*
25/9	Lechia	a	1-5	*Wodecki*
2/10	Jagiellonia	h	0-1	
17/10	Wisła	h	1-0	*Kwiek*
24/10	Lech	h	2-0	*Wodecki 2*
31/10	Legia	a	1-2	*Sikorski*
6/11	Polonia Bytom	h	1-1	*Jonczyk*
13/11	Śląsk Wrocław	a	0-4	
19/11	Korona	h	2-1	*Zahorski, Sikorski*
27/11	Widzew	a	0-4	
2011				
27/2	Polonia Warszawa	a	0-0	
5/3	Zagłębie	h	5-1	*Kwiek, Gašparík 2, Sikorski, Jež*
11/3	Arka	h	2-2	*Banaś, Wodecki*
18/3	Ruch	a	0-3	
3/4	Cracovia	h	1-0	*Sikorski*
8/4	Bełchatów	a	1-1	*Bonin*
15/4	Lechia	h	0-0	
20/4	Jagiellonia	a	0-2	
30/4	Wisła	a	2-0	*Gašparík, Sikorski*
7/5	Lech	a	0-2	
10/5	Legia	h	1-1	*Sikorski*
13/5	Polonia Bytom	a	2-1	*Jež 2*
20/5	Śląsk Wrocław	h	3-1	*og (Socha), og (Pawelec), Bonin*
25/5	Korona	a	0-1	
29/5	Widzew	h	4-0	*Jež 2, Bemben 2*

No	Name	Nat	DoB	Pos	Aps	(s)	Gls
27	Vladimír BALÁT	SVK	1/2/87	M	1	(2)	
25	Adam BANAŚ		25/12/82	D	24		1
24	Michael BEMBEN	GER	28/1/76	D	23	(1)	2
7	Maciej BĘBENEK		22/9/84	M		(7)	
5	Grzegorz BONIN		2/12/83	M	23		3
14	Tomasz CHAŁAS		20/7/88	A		(4)	
26	Adam DANCH		15/12/87	M	16	(5)	
88	Michal GAŠPARÍK	SVK	19/12/81	M	8	(2)	3
8	Piotr GIERCZAK		2/5/76	M	7	(1)	1
81	Róbert JEŽ	SVK	10/7/81	M	10	(4)	5
9	Michał JONCZYK		11/3/92	A	1	(3)	1
3	Mariusz JOP		3/8/78	D	21	(2)	
6	Aleksander KWIEK		13/1/83	M	23		2
21	Mariusz MAGIERA		25/8/84	D	30		1
13	Maciej MAŃKA		30/6/89	M		(2)	
16	Adam MARCINIAK		28/9/88	D	19	(2)	
30	Gabriel NOWAK		26/7/86	M	1	(10)	
82	Sebastian NOWAK		13/1/82	G	7		
2	Michał PAZDAN		21/9/87	D	11	(6)	
23	Rafał PIETRZAK		30/1/92	M	1	(4)	
19	Mariusz PRZYBYLSKI		19/1/82	M	18	(5)	
10	Daniel SIKORSKI	AUT	2/11/87	A	20	(6)	6
15	Szymon SOBCZAK		7/12/92	A		(4)	
1	Adam STACHOWIAK		18/12/86	G	23		
86	Adrian ŚWIĄTEK		22/7/86	A	3	(6)	1

No	Name	Nat	DoB	Pos	Aps	(s)	Gls
11	Marcin WODECKI		14/1/88	A	17	(5)	4
14	Mateusz ZACHARA		27/3/90	A		(1)	
22	Tomasz ZAHORSKI		22/11/84	A	23	(6)	4

JAGIELLONIA BIAŁYSTOK

Coach – Michał Probierz

Founded – 1932

Stadium – Stadion Miejski (6,000)

MAJOR HONOURS: Polish Cup – (1) 2010.

2010				
8/8	Śląsk Wrocław	a	0-0	
14/8	Bełchatów	h	3-1	*Frankowski 2 (1p), Makuszewski*
22/8	Lechia	a	2-1	*Kupisz, Skerla*
29/8	Lech	h	2-0	*Frankowski, Grosicki*
10/9	Wisła	h	2-1	*Grosicki, Frankowski (p)*
19/9	Arka	a	0-1	
26/9	Zagłębie	h	2-0	*Grosicki, Kupisz*
2/10	Górnik	a	1-0	*Skerla*
16/10	Polonia Bytom	h	3-0	*Frankowski 2, Kijanskas*
23/10	Widzew	a	1-4	*Frankowski*
29/10	Polonia Warszawa	h	1-0	*Frankowski*
6/11	Legia	a	0-2	
14/11	Korona	a	1-1	*Grosicki*
20/11	Cracovia	h	4-2	*Grosicki 2, Kupisz, Burkhardt*
28/11	Ruch	a	0-0	
2011				
5/3	Bełchatów	a	0-0	
8/3	Śląsk Wrocław	h	1-1	*Frankowski (p)*
12/3	Lechia	h	1-2	*Lato*
19/3	Lech	a	0-2	
3/4	Wisła	a	0-2	
10/4	Arka	h	1-0	*Burkhardt*
16/4	Zagłębie	a	2-0	*Kijanskas (p), Seratlić*
20/4	Górnik	h	2-0	*Frankowski, Hermes*
30/4	Polonia Bytom	a	2-3	*Seratlić, Skerla*
7/5	Widzew	h	1-3	*Frankowski*
10/5	Polonia Warszawa	a	0-2	
13/5	Legia	h	0-0	
21/5	Korona	h	4-0	*Frankowski 2, Kupisz 2*
25/5	Cracovia	a	0-3	
29/5	Ruch	h	2-1	*Frankowski, og (Grodzicki)*

No	Name	Nat	DoB	Pos	Aps	(s)	Gls
25	Robert ARZUMANYAN	ARM	24/7/85	D	8		
23	Marcin BURKHARDT		25/9/83	M	18	(9)	2
7	Franck ESSOMBA	CMR	9/2/87	M	1	(14)	
21	Tomasz FRANKOWSKI		16/8/74	A	23	(6)	14
2	Mariusz GOGOL		28/7/91	D		(1)	
10	Kamil GROSICKI		8/6/88	A	11	(4)	6
22	Rafał GRZYB		16/1/83	M	24	(2)	
11	HERMES Neves Soares	BRA	19/9/74	M	27	(1)	1
3	Mladen KAŠĆELAN	MNE	13/2/83	M	14	(8)	
24	Tadas KIJANSKAS	LTU	6/9/85	D	14	(2)	2
8	Tomasz KUPISZ		2/1/90	M	29	(1)	5
13	Jarosław LATO		17/6/77	M	23	(6)	1
4	Igor LEWCZUK		30/5/85	D	1		
20	Maciej MAKUSZEWSKI		29/9/89	M	7	(12)	1
26	Ndabenkulu NCUBE	ZIM	2/8/88	M		(1)	
17	Alexis Patricio NORAMBUENA Ruz	CHI	31/3/84	D	25	(2)	
18	Bartłomiej PAWŁOWSKI		13/11/92	A	1	(6)	
6	Luka PEJOVIĆ	MNE	31/7/85	D	10	(1)	
28	Adam RADECKI		18/3/94	D		(1)	
12	Grzegorz SANDOMIERSKI		5/9/89	G	29		
31	Ermin SERATLIĆ	MNE	21/8/90	M	8	(4)	2
14	El Mehdi SIDQY	MAR	6/1/84	D	1		
5	Andrius SKERLA	LTU	29/4/77	D	30		3
1	Jakub SŁOWIK		31/8/91	G	1		
99	Vuk SOTIROVIĆ	SRB	13/7/82	A	3	(1)	
4	Micha STEĆ		6/10/91	A		(2)	
15	THIAGO RANGEL Cionek	BRA	21/4/86	D	21		
9	Przemysław TRYTKO		26/8/87	A	1	(5)	

KORONA KIELCE

Coach – Marcin Sasal; (12/5/11) Włodzimierz Gąsior

Founded – 1973

Stadium – Stadion Miejski Arena Kielc (15,550)

010

/8	Zagłębie	h	1-1	*Niedzielan*
5/8	Widzew	h	1-2	*Niedzielan*
1/8	Polonia Bytom	a	1-0	*Niedzielan*
7/8	Cracovia	h	1-0	*Niedzielan*
2/9	Polonia Warszawa	a	3-1	*og (Brzyski), Niedzielan 2*
7/9	Wisła	a	2-2	*Vuković, Niedzielan*
4/9	Śląsk Wrocław	h	2-1	*og (Wołczek), Markiewicz*
/10	Ruch	a	1-0	*Niedzielan*
6/10	Bełchatów	h	3-1	*og (Tanevski), Tataj, Andradina (p)*
2/10	Legia	h	1-4	*Staňo*
0/10	Lechia	a	1-0	*Korzym*
/11	Arka	a	1-2	*Andradina*
4/11	Jagiellonia	h	1-1	*Vuković*
19/11	Górnik	a	1-2	*Staňo*
27/11	Lech	h	0-0	

2011

26/2	Zagłębie	a	1-1	*Niedzielan*
5/3	Widzew	a	1-3	*Andradina*
12/3	Polonia Bytom	h	3-3	*Niedzielan, Puri, Korzym*
19/3	Cracovia	a	0-3	
2/4	Polonia Warszawa	h	1-3	*Staňo*
10/4	Wisła	h	2-2	*Korzym, og (Wilk)*
17/4	Śląsk Wrocław	a	1-0	*Staňo*
23/4	Ruch	h	0-1	
30/4	Bełchatów	a	0-1	
6/5	Legia	a	1-3	*Lech*
11/5	Lechia	h	2-3	*Jovanović, Niedzielan*
14/5	Arka	h	1-0	*Sobolewski*
21/5	Jagiellonia	a	0-4	
25/5	Górnik	h	1-0	*Niedzielan (p)*
29/5	Lech	a	0-4	

No	Name	Nat	DoB	Pos	Aps	(s)	Gls
16	Edi Carlo Dias Marçal "ANDRADINA"	BRA	13/9/74	A	26	(3)	3
30	Jakub BĄK		28/5/93	A	2	(2)	
1	Radosław CIERZNIAK		24/4/83	G	3	(1)	
27	DIRCEU Inácio da Silva Júnior	BRA	29/1/89	D	2	(5)	
11	Krzysztof GAJTKOWSKI		26/9/80	A	1	(2)	
6	Paweł GOLAŃSKI		12/10/82	D	18	(1)	
4	HERNÂNI José da Rosa	BRA	3/2/84	D	26		
11	Dawid JANCZYK		23/9/87	A	2	(4)	
7	Lukáš JANIČ	SVK	30/12/86	M		(2)	
8	Vlastimir JOVANOVIĆ	BIH	3/4/85	M	24	(3)	1
18	Paweł KACZMAREK		1/7/85	M	2	(3)	
20	Maciej KORZYM		2/5/88	A	21	(5)	3
3	Kamil KUZERA		11/3/83	D	8	(5)	
22	Grzegorz LECH		10/1/83	M	12	(2)	1
18	Tomasz LISOWSKI		4/4/85	D	11	(1)	
34	Piotr MALARCZYK		1/8/91	D	7	(4)	
21	Łukasz MALISZEWSKI		27/4/85	M	2	(3)	
33	Zbigniew MAŁKOWSKI		19/1/78	G	24	(1)	
15	Jacek MARKIEWICZ		18/4/76	D	17	(7)	1
10	Nikola MIJAILOVIĆ	SRB	15/2/82	D	11		
23	Andrzej NIEDZIELAN		27/2/79	A	23	(2)	12
28	Tomasz NOWAK		30/10/85	M	1	(7)	
2	Andrzej PAPROCKI		9/10/92	A	1	(1)	
80	Krzysztof PILARZ		9/11/80	G	1		
7	Sander PURI	EST	7/5/88	M	3	(5)	1
29	Paweł SOBOLEWSKI		20/6/79	M	25	(3)	1
17	Pavol STAŇO	SVK	29/9/77	D	29		4
13	Grzegorz SZAMOTULSKI		13/5/76	G	2		
31	Maciej TATAJ		9/1/80	A	4	(14)	1
5	Aleksandar VUKOVIĆ	SRB	25/8/79	M	22	(1)	2

KKS LECH POZNAŃ

Coach – Jacek Zieliński; (3/11/10) José María Bakero (ESP)

Founded – 1922

Stadium – Stadion Miejski (41,344)

MAJOR HONOURS: Polish League – (6) 1983, 1984, 1990, 1992, 1993, 2010; Polish Cup – (5) 1982, 1984, 1988, 2004, 2009.

2010

7/8	Widzew	a	1-1	*Rudņevs*
14/8	Arka	h	0-0	
22/8	Cracovia	h	5-0	*og (Jarabica), Peszko, Rudņevs 2 (1p), Wilk*
29/8	Jagiellonia	a	0-2	
11/9	Śląsk Wrocław	a	2-1	*Peszko, Rudņevs*
24/9	Legia	a	1-2	*Krivets*
3/10	Bełchatów	a	0-1	
16/10	Zagłębie	h	0-1	
24/10	Górnik	a	0-2	
31/10	Wisła	h	4-1	*Injac, Krivets, Štilić (p), Możdżeń*
7/11	Ruch	a	0-1	
10/11	Polonia Warszawa	h	2-2	*Rudņevs, Wilk*
13/11	Lechia	h	2-0	*Peszko, Rudņevs*
20/11	Polonia Bytom	h	1-0	*Rudņevs*
27/11	Korona	a	0-0	

2011

27/2	Widzew	h	1-0	*Wilk*
5/3	Arka	a	3-0	*Ślusarski, Rudņevs, Mikołajczak*
13/3	Cracovia	a	0-1	
19/3	Jagiellonia	h	2-0	*Štilić 2*
1/4	Śląsk Wrocław	h	2-2	*Krivets, Ubiparip*
8/4	Polonia Warszawa	a	0-1	
16/4	Legia	h	1-0	*Rudņevs*
23/4	Bełchatów	h	0-0	
29/4	Zagłębie	a	0-1	
7/5	Górnik	h	2-0	*Rudņevs, Štilić*
11/5	Wisła	a	0-1	
14/5	Ruch	h	1-0	*Kiełb*
22/5	Lechia	a	1-2	*Ślusarski*
25/5	Polonia Bytom	a	2-1	*Wilk, Štilić*
29/5	Korona	h	4-0	*Štilić, Đurđević, Rudņevs, Wilk*

No	Name	Nat	DoB	Pos	Aps	(s)	Gls
5	Manuel Santos ARBOLEDA Sánchez	COL	2/8/79	D	23		
6	Tomasz BANDROWSKI		18/9/84	M	4		
19	Bartosz BOSACKI		20/12/75	D	20	(2)	
30	Jasmin BURIĆ	BIH	18/2/87	G	11		
15	Kamil DRYGAS		7/9/91	M	3	(1)	
3	Ivan ĐURĐEVIĆ	SRB	5/2/77	D	15	(3)	1
2	Seweryn GANCARCZYK		22/11/81	D	7	(2)	
25	Luis Alfonso HENRÍQUEZ Ledezma	PAN	23/11/81	D	24	(2)	
21	Dimitrije INJAC	SRB	12/8/80	M	25	(3)	1
8	Jacek KIEŁB		10/1/88	M	10	(9)	1
23	Marcin KIKUT		25/6/83	D	18	(1)	
27	Krzysztof KOTOROWSKI		12/9/76	G	19		
10	Sergei KRIVETS	BLR	8/6/86	M	18	(7)	3
26	Tomasz MIKOŁAJCZAK		11/12/87	A	2	(6)	1
32	Mateusz MOŻDŻEŃ		14/3/91	M	4	(9)	1
11	Rafał MURAWSKI		9/10/81	M	12	(2)	
17	Sławomir PESZKO		19/2/85	M	14	(1)	3
16	Artjoms RUDŅEVS	LVA	13/1/88	A	21	(6)	11
18	Bartosz ŚLUSARSKI		11/12/81	A	7	(3)	2
14	Semir ŠTILIĆ	BIH	8/10/87	M	25	(3)	6
20	Joël Omari TSHIBAMBA	COD	22/9/88	A	3	(8)	
28	Vojo UBIPARIP	SRB	10/5/88	A	5	(4)	1
18	Artur WICHNIAREK		28/2/77	A	1	(6)	
7	Jakub WILK		11/7/85	M	15	(7)	5
22	Grzegorz WOJTKOWIAK		26/1/84	D	16		
20	Hubert WOŁĄKIEWICZ		21/10/85	D	8	(3)	
13	Ján ZÁPOTOKA	SVK	23/3/88	M		(1)	

KS LECHIA GDAŃSK

Coach – Tomasz Kafarski
Founded – 1945
Stadium – GOSiR (11,811)
MAJOR HONOURS: Polish Cup – (1) 1983.

2010				
8/8	Ruch	h	0-0	
14/8	Polonia Bytom	a	1-1	*Buzała*
22/8	Jagiellonia	h	1-2	*Nowak*
28/8	Śląsk Wrocław	h	2-0	*Wiśniewski, Buzała*
11/9	Bełchatów	a	0-1	
17/9	Cracovia	h	1-0	*Buval*
25/9	Górnik	h	5-1	*Traoré 2, Bajić, Buzała, Sazankov*
2/10	Legia	a	3-0	*Buval, Wołąkiewicz, Nowak*
17/10	Arka	h	1-0	*Wiśniewski*
23/10	Wisła	a	2-5	*Bąk, Dawidowski*
30/10	Korona	h	0-1	
7/11	Polonia Warszawa	a	2-1	*Traoré 2 (1p)*
13/11	Lech	a	0-2	
20/11	Widzew	h	3-1	*Lukjanovs, Buzała, Wiśniewski*
27/11	Zagłębie	a	1-3	*Traoré (p)*
2011				
26/2	Ruch	a	0-0	
6/3	Polonia Bytom	h	2-0	*Traoré 2 (1p)*
12/3	Jagiellonia	a	2-1	*og (Sandomierski), Traoré*
19/3	Śląsk Wrocław	a	1-2	*Vučko*
1/4	Bełchatów	h	0-0	
9/4	Cracovia	a	0-3	
15/4	Górnik	a	0-0	
23/4	Legia	h	2-1	*Traoré, Lukjanovs*
1/5	Arka	a	2-2	*Nowak, Vučko*
8/5	Wisła	h	0-3	
11/5	Korona	a	3-2	*og (Staňo), Surma, Nowak*
14/5	Polonia Warszawa	h	0-0	
22/5	Lech	h	2-1	*Traoré 2 (1p)*
25/5	Widzew	a	0-1	
29/5	Zagłębie	h	1-2	*Traoré*

No	Name	Nat	DoB	Pos	Aps	(s)	Gls
3	Vytautas ANDRIUŠKEVIČIUS	LTU	8/10/90	D	16	(1)	
23	Marko BAJIĆ	SRB	28/9/85	M	13	(7)	1
5	Krzysztof BĄK		22/6/82	D	28	(1)	1
18	Bédi BUVAL	FRA	16/6/86	A	18	(5)	2
20	Paweł BUZAŁA		27/12/85	A	12	(2)	4
10	Tomasz DAWIDOWSKI		4/2/78	A	5	(13)	1
26	Luiz Carlos Santos "DELEU"	BRA	1/3/84	D	25	(3)	
20	Levon HAYRAPETYAN	ARM	17/4/89	D	6	(4)	
2	Rafał JANICKI		5/7/92	D	3		
29	Marcin KACZMAREK		3/12/79	M	2	(5)	
1	Paweł KAPSA		24/7/82	G	19		
4	Sergejs KOŽANS	LVA	18/2/86	D	10		
11	Ivans LUKJANOVS	LVA	24/1/87	A	26	(3)	2
33	Sebastian MAŁKOWSKI		2/3/87	G	11		
22	Paweł NOWAK		27/1/79	M	28	(1)	4
17	Marcin PIETROWSKI		1/3/88	M	12	(11)	
16	Jakub POPIELARZ		16/3/90	M	2	(2)	
25	Kamil POŹNIAK		11/12/89	M	4	(8)	
9	Aleksandr SAZANKOV	BLR	18/3/84	A	1	(8)	1
8	Łukasz SURMA		28/6/77	M	30		1
6	Damian SZUPRYTOWSKI		25/6/89	M	1	(1)	
7	Abdou Razack TRAORÉ	CIV	28/12/88	M	26	(1)	12
6	Luka VUČKO	CRO	11/4/84	D	15		2
14	Piotr WIŚNIEWSKI		11/8/82	M	4	(7)	3
21	Hubert WOŁĄKIEWICZ		21/10/85	D	11		1
15	Jakub ZEJGLIC		18/5/90	A	1	(3)	
25	Marek ZIEŃCZUK		24/9/78	M	1	(2)	

LEGIA WARSZAWA

Coach – Maciej Skorża
Founded – 1916
Stadium – Stadion Wojska Polskiego im. Marszałka Józefa Piłsudskiego (23,257)
MAJOR HONOURS: Polish League – (8) 1955, 1956, 1969, 1970, 1994, 1995, 2002, 2006;
Polish Cup – (14) 1955, 1956, 1964, 1966, 1973, 1980, 1981, 1989, 1990, 1994, 1995, 1997, 2008, 2011.

2010				
13/8	Polonia Warszawa	a	0-3	
16/8	Cracovia	h	2-1	*Komorowski, Iwański*
20/8	Śląsk Wrocław	a	1-0	*Rybus*
27/8	Bełchatów	h	0-2	
12/9	Ruch	a	0-1	
18/9	Zagłębie	a	1-2	*Vrdoljak (p)*
24/9	Lech	h	2-1	*Kucharczyk, Bruno Mezenga*
2/10	Lechia	h	0-3	
15/10	Widzew	a	1-0	*Vrdoljak*
22/10	Korona	a	4-1	*Kucharczyk, Vrdoljak (p), Iwański, Radović*
31/10	Górnik	h	2-1	*Radović, Bruno Mezenga*
6/11	Jagiellonia	h	2-0	*og (Skerla), Rzeźniczak*
12/11	Wisła	a	0-4	
19/11	Arka	h	3-0	*Vrdoljak (p), Bruno Mezenga, Kiełbowicz*
26/11	Polonia Bytom	a	1-0	*Radović*
2011				
25/2	Cracovia	a	3-3	*Kucharczyk, Hubník, Wawrzyniak*
6/3	Polonia Warszawa	h	1-0	*og (Sadlok)*
11/3	Śląsk Wrocław	h	1-2	*Borysiuk*
20/3	Bełchatów	a	0-2	
2/4	Ruch	h	2-3	*Rybus, Radović*
9/4	Zagłębie	h	2-2	*Vrdoljak (p), Hubník*
16/4	Lech	a	0-1	
23/4	Lechia	a	1-2	*og (Bąk)*
29/4	Widzew	h	1-0	*Cabral*
6/5	Korona	h	3-1	*Cabral, Radović 2*
10/5	Górnik	a	1-1	*Wawrzyniak*
13/5	Jagiellonia	a	0-0	
21/5	Wisła	h	2-0	*Cabral (p), Szałachowski*
25/5	Arka	a	5-2	*Manú, Radović, Kucharczyk 2, Borysiuk*
29/5	Polonia Bytom	h	4-0	*og (Radzewicz), Szałachowski, Radović 2*

No	Name	Nat	DoB	Pos	Aps	(s)	Gls
1	Marijan ANTOLOVIĆ	CRO	7/5/89	G	8		
16	Ariel BORYSIUK		29/7/91	M	24	(2)	2
80	BRUNO Ferreira Mombra Rosa "MEZENGA"	BRA	8/8/88	A	3	(10)	3
27	Alejandro Ariel CABRAL	ARG	11/9/87	M	10	(12)	3
82	Takesure CHINYAMA	ZIM	30/9/82	A	7	(4)	
4	Dickson CHOTO	ZIM	19/3/81	D	11		
7	Piotr GIZA		28/2/80	M		(1)	
5	Janusz GOL		11/11/85	M	7	(2)	
7	Michal HUBNÍK	CZE	1/6/83	A	8	(3)	2
15	IÑAKI ASTIZ Ventura	ESP	5/11/83	D	17		
8	Maciej IWAŃSKI		7/5/81	M	6	(5)	2
2	Artur JĘDRZEJCZYK		4/11/87	D	9	(5)	
13	Dejan KELHAR	SVN	5/4/84	D	2		
11	Tomasz KIEŁBOWICZ		21/2/76	D	13	(1)	1
23	Srđa KNEŽEVIĆ	SRB	15/4/85	D	3	(1)	
17	Marcin KOMOROWSKI		17/4/84	D	23	(1)	1
18	Michał KUCHARCZYK		20/3/91	A	21	(6)	5
55	Kostyantyn MAKHNOVSKIY	UKR	1/1/89	G	6		
9	Emanuel de Jesus Bonfim Evaristo "MANÚ"	POR	28/8/82	M	27		1
77	Felix OGBUKE	NGA	18/9/85	M		(7)	
32	Miroslav RADOVIĆ	SRB	16/1/84	M	23	(5)	9
31	Maciej RYBUS		19/8/89	M	12	(8)	2
25	Jakub RZEŹNICZAK		26/10/86	D	22		1

4	Wojciech SKABA		9/4/84	G	16		
)	Sebastian SZAŁACHOWSKI		21/1/84	M	5	(8)	2
	Ivica VRDOLJAK	CRO	19/9/83	M	26		5
4	Jakub WAWRZYNIAK		7/7/83	D	18	(2)	2
3	Rafał WOLSKI		10/11/92	M		(4)	
3	Michał ŻYRO		20/9/92	D	3	(3)	

KS POLONIA BYTOM

Coach –Yuriy Shatalov (UKR); (30/10/10) Jan Urban; (13/12/10) Robert Góralczyk; (24/5/11) Dariusz Fornalak

Founded – 1945

Stadium – Stadion im. Edwarda Szymkowiaka (6,000)

MAJOR HONOURS: Polish League – (2) 1954, 1962.

2010				
/8	Bełchatów	a	0-2	
4/8	Lechia	h	1-1	*Sawala*
1/8	Korona	h	0-1	
8/8	Wisła	a	1-2	*Matawu*
0/9	Zagłębie	h	2-0	*Sawala, Ujek*
8/9	Ruch	h	1-0	*Jarecki*
5/9	Polonia Warszawa	a	2-2	*Ujek, Hanek*
/10	Widzew	h	2-2	*Barčík, Jarecki*
6/10	Jagiellonia	a	0-3	
2/10	Śląsk Wrocław	h	0-0	
0/10	Cracovia	a	1-0	*Jarecki*
/11	Górnik	a	1-1	*og (Magiera)*
3/11	Arka	h	2-0	*Ujek, og (Bruma)*
20/11	Lech	a	0-1	
26/11	Legia	h	0-1	
2011				
26/2	Bełchatów	h	1-1	*Tymiński*
6/3	Lechia	a	0-2	
12/3	Korona	a	3-3	*Trytko, og (Hernâni), Radzewicz*
20/3	Wisła	h	2-2	*Radzewicz, Jarecki*
2/4	Zagłębie	a	0-2	
9/4	Ruch	a	2-0	*Telichowski, Podstawek*
16/4	Polonia Warszawa	h	0-2	
23/4	Widzew	a	1-3	*Telichowski*
30/4	Jagiellonia	h	3-2	*Barčík, Vaščák, Jarecki*
7/5	Śląsk Wrocław	a	0-0	
10/5	Cracovia	h	1-2	*Żytko (p)*
13/5	Górnik	h	1-2	*Żytko (p)*
21/5	Arka	a	1-2	*Drozdowicz*
25/5	Lech	h	1-2	*Radzewicz*
29/5	Legia	a	0-4	

No	Name	Nat	DoB	Pos	Aps	(s)	Gls
7	Miroslav BARČÍK	SVK	26/5/78	M	22	(3)	2
19	Marek BAŽÍK	SVK	9/2/76	M	3	(10)	
33	Maciej BYKOWSKI		22/2/77	A	5	(4)	
5	Adrian CHOMIUK		23/6/88	D	13	(2)	
11	Emil DROZDOWICZ		5/7/86	A	2	(1)	1
15	Marcin DZIEWULSKI		24/10/82	M	5		
15	Jacek FALKOWSKI		10/10/84	M	2	(2)	
30	Szymon GĄSIŃSKI		8/7/83	G	11		
27	Michal HANEK	SVK	18/9/80	D	28		1
8	Peter HRICKO	SVK	25/7/81	D	20		
16	Dariusz JARECKI		23/3/81	M	18	(6)	5
1	Marcin JUSZCZYK		23/1/85	G	15		
87	Seweryn KIEŁPIN		18/12/87	G	4		
2	Lukáš KILLAR	CZE	5/8/81	D	9		
13	David KOBYLÍK	CZE	27/6/81	M	21	(4)	
28	Krzysztof KRÓL		6/2/87	D	6	(1)	
9	Clement MATAWU	ZIM	29/11/82	M	7	(1)	1
17	Łukasz MATUSIAK		7/5/85	M	2	(1)	
26	Tomasz MIKOŁAJCZAK		11/12/87	A	1	(3)	
11	Vladimir MILENKOVIĆ	SRB	22/6/82	A	1	(2)	
22	Arkadiusz MYSONA		11/5/81	D	10		
10	Grzegorz PODSTAWEK		25/6/79	A	6	(11)	1
20	Marcin RADZEWICZ		30/6/80	M	22	(7)	3
21	Szymon SAWALA		25/9/82	M	15		2
23	Błażej TELICHOWSKI		6/6/84	D	16	(3)	2
26	Przemysław TRYTKO		26/8/87	A	4	(2)	1
4	Łukasz TYMIŃSKI		8/11/90	M	15	(3)	1

25	Mariusz UJEK		6/12/77	A	8		3
18	Blažej VAŠČÁK	SVK	21/11/83	M	8	(11)	1
14	Robert WOJSYK		11/9/90	A	4	(6)	
3	Mateusz ŻYTKO		27/11/82	D	27	(1)	2

KSP POLONIA WARSZAWA

Coach – José María Bakero (ESP); (13/9/10) Paweł Janas; (6/1/11) Theo Bos (NED); (14/3/11) Piotr Stokowiec; (23/3/11) Jacek Zieliński

Founded – 1911

Stadium – Stadion Polonii (6,800)

MAJOR HONOURS: Polish League – (2) 1946, 2000; Polish Cup – (2) 1952, 2001.

2010				
6/8	Górnik	a	2-0	*Sobiech, Mierzejewski*
13/8	Legia	h	3-0	*Bruno, Smolarek, Mierzejewski*
20/8	Zagłębie	h	2-1	*Sobiech, Smolarek*
28/8	Widzew	a	0-0	
12/9	Korona	h	1-3	*Bruno*
25/9	Polonia Bytom	h	2-2	*Sobiech, Gancarczyk*
2/10	Arka	a	0-0	
16/10	Śląsk Wrocław	a	2-2	*Pietrasiak, Bruno*
23/10	Cracovia	h	3-0	*Tralka, Sobiech, Gołębiewski*
29/10	Jagiellonia	a	0-1	
7/11	Lechia	h	1-2	*Mierzejewski*
10/11	Lech	a	2-2	*Mierzejewski (p), Bruno*
13/11	Ruch	h	3-1	*Sobiech 2, Smolarek*
21/11	Bełchatów	a	2-3	*Gołębiewski 2*
28/11	Wisła	h	0-1	
2011				
27/2	Górnik	h	0-0	
6/3	Legia	a	0-1	
13/3	Zagłębie	a	0-1	
19/3	Widzew	h	0-1	
2/4	Korona	a	3-1	*Sobiech, Mierzejewski, Smolarek (p)*
8/4	Lech	h	1-0	*Sobiech*
16/4	Polonia Bytom	a	2-0	*Piątek, Gołębiewski*
23/4	Arka	h	4-0	*Trałka, Mierzejewski 2 (1p), Piątek*
30/4	Śląsk Wrocław	h	0-1	
7/5	Cracovia	a	1-3	*Smolarek*
10/5	Jagiellonia	h	2-0	*Bruno, Sobiech*
14/5	Lechia	a	0-0	
22/5	Ruch	a	3-0	*Brzyski, Smolarek, Bruno*
25/5	Bełchatów	h	0-0	
29/5	Wisła	a	2-0	*Smolarek, Trałka*

No	Name	Nat	DoB	Pos	Aps	(s)	Gls
44	Miloš ADAMOVIĆ	SRB	19/6/88	M	1	(2)	
16	ANDREU Guerao Mayoral	ESP	17/6/83	M	19	(3)	
32	BRUNO Coutinho Martins	BRA	21/6/86	M	26	(1)	6
22	Tomasz BRZYSKI		10/1/82	D	22	(3)	1
5	Đorđe ČOTRA	SRB	13/9/84	D	4	(1)	
5	Piotr DZIEWICKI		26/6/79	D	3		
7	Janusz GANCARCZYK		19/6/84	M	7	(12)	1
1	Michał GLIWA		8/4/88	G	8		
19	Daniel GOŁĘBIEWSKI		15/7/87	A	5	(22)	4
6	Tomasz JODŁOWIEC		8/9/85	D	21		
13	Adam KOKOSZKA		6/10/86	D	10	(1)	
8	MARCELO Fazzio SARVAS	BRA	16/10/81	M	2	(2)	
10	Adrian MIERZEJEWSKI		6/11/86	M	27		7
2	Radek MYNÁŘ	CZE	22/11/74	D	9	(3)	
28	Łukasz PIĄTEK		21/9/85	M	16	(7)	2
3	Dariusz PIETRASIAK		12/2/80	D	16	(2)	1
81	Sebastian PRZYROWSKI		30/11/81	G	22		
20	Patryk RACHWAŁ		27/1/81	M	7	(5)	
21	Maciej SADLOK		29/6/89	D	10		
13	Łukasz SKRZYŃSKI		31/1/78	D	7		
9	Euzebiusz SMOLAREK		9/1/81	A	18	(5)	7
90	Artur SOBIECH		12/6/90	A	22	(1)	9
11	Marek SOKOŁOWSKI		11/3/78	M	3		
17	Łukasz TEODORCZYK		3/6/91	A	1	(5)	
24	Jakub TOSIK		21/5/87	D	18	(5)	
18	Łukasz TRAŁKA		11/5/84	M	25	(1)	3
23	Paweł WSZOŁEK		30/4/92	A	1	(6)	

RUCH CHORZÓW

Coach – Waldemar Fornalik
Founded – 1920
Stadium – Stadion Ruchu (10,000)
MAJOR HONOURS: Polish League – (14) 1933, 1934, 1935, 1936, 1938, 1951, 1952, 1953, 1960, 1968, 1974, 1975, 1979, 1989; Polish Cup – (3) 1951, 1974, 1996.

2010			
8/8	Lechia	a 0-0	
15/8	Wisła	h 2-0	*Nykiel, Straka*
21/8	Bełchatów	a 2-3	*Olszar, Jankowski*
29/8	Górnik	a 0-1	
12/9	Legia	h 1-0	*Grzyb*
18/9	Polonia Bytom	a 0-1	
25/9	Widzew	h 1-1	*Piech*
3/10	Korona	h 0-1	
17/10	Cracovia	a 3-2	*Sadlok, Jankowski, Janoszka*
24/10	Zagłębie	a 0-0	
30/10	Arka	h 0-0	
7/11	Lech	h 1-0	*Janoszka*
13/11	Polonia Warszawa	a 1-3	*Jankowski*
20/11	Śląsk Wrocław	a 1-2	*Komac*
28/11	Jagiellonia	h 0-0	
2011			
26/2	Lechia	h 0-0	
4/3	Wisła	a 1-3	*Grzyb*
12/3	Bełchatów	h 2-1	*Jankowski, Grzyb*
18/3	Górnik	h 3-0	*Zieńczuk, Piech, Malinowski*
2/4	Legia	a 3-2	*Piech 3*
9/4	Polonia Bytom	h 0-2	
16/4	Widzew	a 0-0	
23/4	Korona	a 1-0	*Jankowski*
1/5	Cracovia	h 1-0	*Komac*
6/5	Zagłębie	h 2-2	*Grzyb, Jankowski*
11/5	Arka	a 2-0	*Janoszka, Jankowski*
14/5	Lech	a 0-1	
22/5	Polonia Warszawa	h 0-3	
25/5	Śląsk Wrocław	h 1-2	*Janoszka*
29/5	Jagiellonia	a 1-2	*Jankowski*

No	Name	Nat	DoB	Pos	Aps	(s)	Gls
99	Paweł ABBOTT		5/5/82	A		(7)	
24	Grzegorz BRONOWICKI		4/8/80	D	8		
11	Łukasz DERBICH		23/10/83	D	2		
4	Željko ĐOKIĆ	BIH	10/5/82	D	13		
15	Rafał GRODZICKI		28/10/83	D	27		
6	Wojciech GRZYB		21/12/74	M	28		4
29	Ariel JAKUBOWSKI		7/9/77	D	6	(1)	
7	Maciej JANKOWSKI		4/1/90	A	22	(6)	8
14	Łukasz JANOSZKA		18/3/87	A	16	(11)	4
22	Andrej KOMAC	SVN	4/12/79	M	15	(6)	2
31	Paweł LISOWSKI		8/10/91	M	9	(10)	
23	Marcin MALINOWSKI		6/11/75	M	24	(2)	1
8	Krzysztof NYKIEL		8/8/82	D	15	(3)	1
10	Sebastian OLSZAR		16/12/81	A	8	(9)	1
30	Matko PERDIJIĆ	CRO	26/5/82	G	21		
33	Michal PEŠKOVIČ	SVK	8/2/82	G	2		
18	Arkadiusz PIECH		7/6/85	A	11	(15)	5
80	Krzysztof PILARZ		9/11/80	G	7		
17	Michał PULKOWSKI		1/1/79	M	12	(5)	
21	Maciej SADLOK		29/6/89	D	14		1
2	Piotr STAWARCZYK		29/9/83	D	23	(1)	
28	Gábor STRAKA	SVK	18/12/81	M	16		1
20	Marek SZYNDROWSKI		30/10/80	D	13		
26	Damian ŚWIERBLEWSKI		17/1/84	M		(4)	
9	Marcin ZAJĄC		19/5/75	M	7	(6)	
5	Marek ZIEŃCZUK		24/9/78	M	11	(3)	1

WKS ŚLĄSK WROCŁAW

Coach – Ryszard Tarasiewicz; (22/9/10) (Paweł Barylski); (27/9/10) Orest Lenczyk
Founded – 1947
Stadium – Stadion Piłkarski (8,346)
MAJOR HONOURS: Polish League – (1) 1977; Polish Cup – (2) 1976, 1987.

2010			
8/8	Jagiellonia	h 0-0	
13/8	Cracovia	a 3-2	*Sotirović, Díaz 2*
20/8	Legia	h 0-1	
28/8	Lechia	a 0-2	
11/9	Lech	h 1-2	*Díaz (p)*
18/9	Widzew	a 2-5	*Ćwielong, Sobota*
24/9	Korona	a 1-2	*Gikiewicz*
1/10	Wisła	a 0-0	
16/10	Polonia Warszawa	h 2-2	*og (Piątek), Kaźmierczak*
22/10	Polonia Bytom	a 0-0	
30/10	Zagłębie	h 3-1	*Kaźmierczak, Sotirović, Jezierski*
6/11	Bełchatów	a 1-0	*Sotirović*
13/11	Górnik	h 4-0	*Kaźmierczak, Sotirović, Celeban 2*
20/11	Ruch	h 2-1	*og (Grzyb), Celeban*
27/11	Arka	a 2-2	*Kaźmierczak 2 (1p)*
2011			
4/3	Cracovia	h 0-0	
8/3	Jagiellonia	a 1-1	*Kaźmierczak*
11/3	Legia	a 2-1	*Kaźmierczak, Mila*
19/3	Lechia	h 2-1	*Kaźmierczak, Ćwielong*
1/4	Lech	a 2-2	*Mila (p), Sztylka*
9/4	Widzew	h 2-2	*Madej, Mila (p)*
17/4	Korona	h 0-1	
21/4	Wisła	h 2-0	*og (Sobolewski), Gikiewicz*
30/4	Polonia Warszawa	a 1-0	*Sobota*
7/5	Polonia Bytom	h 0-0	
10/5	Zagłębie	a 1-0	*Celeban*
14/5	Bełchatów	h 4-2	*Mila (p), Szewczuk, Díaz 2*
20/5	Górnik	a 1-3	*Elsner*
25/5	Ruch	a 2-1	*Ćwielong, Elsner*
29/5	Arka	h 5-0	*Díaz 3, Sztylka, Kelemen (p)*

No	Name	Nat	DoB	Pos	Aps	(s)	Gls
3	Piotr CELEBAN		25/6/85	D	30		4
20	Piotr ĆWIELONG		23/4/86	A	21	(5)	3
21	Cristián Omar DÍAZ	ARG	3/11/86	A	12	(6)	8
7	Sebastian DUDEK		19/1/80	M		(3)	
29	Rok ELSNER	SVN	25/1/86	D	7		2
23	Jarosław FOJUT		17/10/87	D	23		
9	Marek GANCARCZYK		19/2/83	M	10	(10)	
27	Łukasz GIKIEWICZ		26/10/87	A	9	(11)	2
16	Remigiusz JEZIERSKI		19/1/76	A	2	(9)	1
1	Wojciech KACZMAREK		29/3/83	G	1		
26	Przemysław KAŹMIERCZAK		5/5/82	M	23		8
25	Marián KELEMEN	SVK	7/12/79	G	29		1
22	Antoni ŁUKASIEWICZ		26/6/83	D	7	(2)	
8	Łukasz MADEJ		14/4/82	M	6	(13)	1
11	Sebastian MILA		10/7/82	M	28		4
17	Mariusz PAWELEC		14/4/86	D	14	(1)	
5	Waldemar SOBOTA		19/5/87	M	17	(12)	2
24	Tadeusz SOCHA		15/2/88	D	21	(1)	
10	Vuk SOTIROVIĆ	SRB	13/7/82	A	13		4
4	Amir SPAHIĆ	BIH	13/9/83	D	23		
6	Tomasz SZEWCZUK		3/12/78	A	5	(6)	1
19	Dariusz SZTYLKA		2/5/78	M	16	(3)	2
14	Ljubiša VUKELJA	SRB	22/7/83	A		(1)	
2	Krzysztof WOŁCZEK		17/4/79	D	13	(2)	

RTS WIDZEW ŁÓDŹ

Coach – Andrzej Kretek; (15/11/10) Czesław Michniewicz
Founded – 1922
Stadium – Widzew (10,500)
MAJOR HONOURS: Polish League – (4) 1981, 1982, 1996, 1997; Polish Cup – (1) 1985.

2010

8	Lech	h	1-1	*Šernas*
5/8	Korona	a	2-1	*Šernas 2*
1/8	Wisła	h	0-1	
3/8	Polonia Warszawa	h	0-0	
1/9	Arka	a	1-1	*Šernas*
3/9	Śląsk Wrocław	h	5-2	*Robak 3 (1p), Šernas 2*
5/9	Ruch	a	1-1	*Grzelczak*
10	Polonia Bytom	a	2-2	*Bruno Pinheiro, Grzelczak*
5/10	Legia	h	0-1	
3/10	Jagiellonia	h	4-1	*Robak 2, Panka, Grzelczak*
9/10	Bełchatów	a	0-1	
11	Zagłębie	a	0-1	
2/11	Cracovia	h	2-2	*Broź, Budka*
0/11	Lechia	a	1-3	*Kuklis*
7/11	Górnik	h	4-0	*Šernas (p), Robak 2, Đurić*

2011

7/2	Lech	a	0-1	
/3	Korona	h	3-1	*Dzalamidze, Ukah, Budka*
2/3	Wisła	a	0-2	
9/3	Polonia Warszawa	a	1-0	*Budka*
/4	Arka	h	0-0	
/4	Śląsk Wrocław	a	2-2	*Madera, Dzalamidze*
6/4	Ruch	h	0-0	
3/4	Polonia Bytom	h	3-1	*Nakoulma (p), og (Juszczyk), Oziębała*
9/4	Legia	a	0-1	
7/5	Jagiellonia	a	3-1	*Grzelczak, Šernas 2 (1p)*
1/5	Bełchatów	h	1-1	*Grzelczak*
15/5	Zagłębie	h	2-1	*Ostrowski, Šernas*
21/5	Cracovia	a	2-1	*Grzelczak 2*
25/5	Lechia	h	1-0	*Grzelczak*
29/5	Górnik	a	0-4	

No	Name	Nat	DoB	Pos	Aps	(s)	Gls
77	Souheïl BEN RADHIA	TUN	26/8/85	D	11	(1)	
5	Jarosław BIENIUK		4/6/79	D	11	(1)	
28	Łukasz BROŹ		17/12/85	D	29		1
3	BRUNO Filipe Tavares PINHEIRO	POR	21/8/87	D	13	(1)	1
16	Adrian BUDKA		26/1/80	M	21	(3)	3
33	Carlos Eduardo de Souza Tomé "DUDU PARAÍBA"	BRA	11/3/85	D	29		
30	Velibor ĐURIĆ	BIH	5/5/82	M	8	(5)	1
17	Nika DZALAMIDZE	GEO	6/1/92	A	9	(5)	2
7	Paul GRISCHOK	GER	26/2/86	M	9	(4)	
8	Rafał GRZELAK		24/6/82	M	1	(6)	
26	Piotr GRZELCZAK		2/3/88	A	15	(11)	8
24	Łukasz GRZESZCZYK		29/7/87	M		(2)	
23	Bartosz KANIECKI		11/7/88	G	9	(1)	
25	Piotr KUKLIS		14/1/86	M	4	(2)	1
17	Tomasz LISOWSKI		4/4/85	D	7	(4)	
19	Sebastian MADERA		30/5/85	D	12		1
13	Maciej MIELCARZ		15/10/80	G	21		
40	Piotr MROZIŃSKI		24/8/92	M	1		
22	Prejuce NAKOULMA	BFA	21/4/87	A	3	(5)	1
14	Krzysztof OSTROWSKI		3/5/82	M	7	(6)	1
20	Przemysław OZIĘBAŁA		24/8/86	A	6	(5)	1
18	Mindaugas PANKA	LTU	1/5/84	M	24	(1)	1
35	Damian RADOWICZ		20/12/89	M	1	(4)	
37	Sebastian RADZIO		2/4/91	M		(3)	
10	Riku RISKI	FIN	16/8/89	M	5	(4)	
11	Marcin ROBAK		29/11/82	A	10		7
9	Darvydas ŠERNAS	LTU	22/7/84	A	25	(5)	10
2	Wojciech SZYMANEK		1/3/82	D	24	(1)	
4	Ugochukwu UKAH	NGA	18/1/84	D	12		1
38	Sebastian ZALEPA		7/2/90	D	2		
11	Jurijs ŽIGAJEVS	LVA	14/11/85	M	1	(2)	

WISŁA KRAKÓW

Coach – Tomasz Kulawik; (22/8/10) Robert Maaskant (NED)
Founded – 1906
Stadium – Hutnik Kraków (5,500); Stadion Miejski im. Henryka Reymana (23,953)
MAJOR HONOURS: Polish League – (13) 1927, 1928, 1949, 1950, 1978, 1999, 2001, 2003, 2004, 2005, 2008, 2009, 2011; Polish Cup – (4) 1926, 1967, 2002, 2003.

2010

8/8	Arka	h	1-0	*Małecki*
15/8	Ruch	a	0-2	
21/8	Widzew	a	1-0	*Paljić*
28/8	Polonia Bytom	h	2-1	*Małecki, Żurawski*
10/9	Jagiellonia	a	1-2	*Brożek Pa.*
17/9	Korona	h	2-2	*Brożek Pa., Wilk*
26/9	Bełchatów	a	1-1	*Boguski (p)*
1/10	Śląsk Wrocław	h	0-0	
17/10	Górnik	a	0-1	
23/10	Lechia	h	5-2	*Małecki, Sobolewski, Brożek Pa. (p), Kirm 2*
31/10	Lech	a	1-4	*Brożek Pa.*
5/11	Cracovia	a	1-0	*Boukhari*
12/11	Legia	h	4-0	*Brożek Pa. 2 (1p), Małecki, Wilk*
21/11	Zagłębie	h	1-0	*Kirm*
28/11	Polonia Warszawa	a	1-0	*og (Pietrasiak)*

2011

25/2	Arka	a	1-0	*Małecki*
4/3	Ruch	h	3-1	*Kirm, Jirsák, Meliksson*
12/3	Widzew	h	2-0	*Małecki, Kirm*
20/3	Polonia Bytom	a	2-2	*Kirm, Małecki (p)*
3/4	Jagiellonia	h	2-0	*Kirm, Genkov*
10/4	Korona	a	2-2	*Genkov 2*
15/4	Bełchatów	h	3-1	*Meliksson, Genkov, Wilk*
21/4	Śląsk Wrocław	a	0-2	
30/4	Górnik	h	0-2	
8/5	Lechia	a	3-0	*Genkov, Kirm, Sivakov*
11/5	Lech	h	1-0	*Genkov*
15/5	Cracovia	h	1-0	*Meliksson*
21/5	Legia	a	0-2	
25/5	Zagłębie	a	3-0	*Kirm, Meliksson (p), Ríos*
29/5	Polonia Warszawa	h	0-2	

No	Name	Nat	DoB	Pos	Aps	(s)	Gls
9	Rafał BOGUSKI		9/6/84	A	1	(7)	1
74	Nourdin BOUKHARI	MAR	30/6/80	M	6	(3)	1
15	Serge BRANCO	CMR	11/10/80	D	2	(2)	
23	Paweł BROŻEK		21/4/83	A	12	(1)	6
8	Piotr BROŻEK		21/4/83	D	3	(4)	
45	Daniel BRUD		20/5/89	M		(2)	
6	Gordan BUNOZA	BIH	5/2/88	D	14		
30	Łukasz BURLIGA		10/5/88	D	2	(1)	
4	Osman Danilo CHÁVEZ Güity	HON	29/7/84	D	21		
22	Erik ČIKOŠ	SVK	31/7/88	D	27		
25	CLÉBER Guedes de Lima	BRA	29/4/74	D	8		
15	Júnior Enrique DÍAZ Campbell	CRC	12/9/83	M	4		
10	Łukasz GARGUŁA		25/2/81	M	7	(7)	
18	Tsvetan GENKOV	BUL	8/2/84	A	12	(1)	6
2	Kew JALIENS	NED	15/9/78	D	12		
16	Tomáš JIRSÁK	CZE	29/6/84	M	13	(6)	1
1	Milan JOVANIĆ	SRB	31/7/85	G	2		
17	Andraž KIRM	SVN	6/9/84	M	22	(3)	9
24	Mateusz KOWALSKI		30/9/86	D	4		
12	Filip KURTO		14/6/91	G	1	(1)	
11	Wojciech ŁOBODZIŃSKI		20/10/82	M		(6)	
19	Patryk MAŁECKI		1/8/88	M	25	(3)	7
5	Maor MELIKSSON	ISR	30/10/84	M	15		4
13	Dragan PALJIĆ	GER	8/4/83	D	27	(1)	1
25	Segei PAREIKO	EST	31/1/77	G	14		
81	Mariusz PAWEŁEK		17/3/81	G	13		
35	Kamil RADO		20/9/90	M	2		
21	Andrés Lorenzo RÍOS	ARG	8/1/89	A	6	(11)	1
8	Mikhail SIVAKOV	BLR	16/1/88	M	7	(7)	1
44	Damian SKOŁORZYŃSKI		12/2/91	D		(1)	
7	Radosław SOBOLEWSKI		13/12/76	M	26		1
28	Cezary WILK		12/2/86	M	13	(9)	3
79	Maciej ŻURAWSKI		12/9/76	A	9	(12)	1

ZAGŁĘBIE LUBIN

Coach – Marek Bajor; (7/3/11) (Marcin Broniszewski); (10/3/11) Jan Urban
Founded – 1945
Stadium – Dialog Arena (16,100)
MAJOR HONOURS: Polish League – (2) 1991, 2007.

2010				
7/8	Korona	a	1-1	*Bartczak M.*
14/8	Górnik	h	1-2	*Wilczek*
20/8	Polonia Warszawa	a	1-2	*Bartczak M.*
28/8	Arka	h	1-0	*Woźniak*
10/9	Polonia Bytom	a	0-2	
18/9	Legia	h	2-1	*Plizga, Kędziora*
26/9	Jagiellonia	a	0-2	
2/10	Cracovia	h	0-0	
16/10	Lech	a	1-0	*Bartczak M.*
24/10	Ruch	h	0-0	
30/10	Śląsk Wrocław	a	1-3	*Kocot*
5/11	Widzew	h	1-0	*Plizga*
14/11	Bełchatów	h	1-1	*Bartczak M.*
21/11	Wisła	a	0-1	
27/11	Lechia	h	3-1	*Bartczak M., Kędziora, Pawłowski*
2011				
26/2	Korona	h	1-1	*Stasiak*
5/3	Górnik	a	1-5	*Pawłowski*
13/3	Polonia Warszawa	h	1-0	*Stasiak*
18/3	Arka	a	1-1	*Traoré*
2/4	Polonia Bytom	h	2-0	*Pawłowski 2*
9/4	Legia	a	2-2	*Abwo, og (Iñaki Astiz)*
16/4	Jagiellonia	h	0-2	
21/4	Cracovia	a	2-2	*Traoré, Plizga*
29/4	Lech	h	1-0	*Traoré*
6/5	Ruch	a	2-2	*Traoré, Wilczek*
10/5	Śląsk Wrocław	h	0-1	
15/5	Widzew	a	1-2	*Pawłowski*
20/5	Bełchatów	a	2-0	*Plizga (p), og (Fonfara)*
25/5	Wisła	h	0-3	
29/5	Lechia	a	2-1	*Woźniak, Hanzel*

No	Name	Nat	DoB	Pos	Aps	(s)	Gls
20	David ABWO	NGA	10/5/86	M	14	(1)	1
19	Grzegorz BARTCZAK		21/6/85	D	8		
8	Mateusz BARTCZAK		15/8/79	M	15		5
6	Mateusz BARTKÓW		23/5/91	D		(1)	
24	Adrian BŁĄD		16/4/91	M	4	(5)	
90	Patryk BRYŁA		4/3/90	M		(2)	
14	Damian DĄBROWSKI		27/8/92	M	16		
31	Dušan ĐOKIĆ	SRB	20/2/80	A	3	(3)	
85	Martins EKWUEME	NGA	2/10/85	M	7	(6)	
5	FERNANDO Alberto Morais DINIS	POR	25/7/82	D	7	(2)	
86	Dominykas GALKEVIČIUS	LTU	16/10/86	M		(1)	
25	Łukasz HANZEL		16/9/86	M	22	(3)	1
3	Csaba HORVÁTH	SVK	2/5/82	D	27		
50	Bojan ISAILOVIĆ	SRB	25/3/80	G	27		
27	Wojciech KĘDZIORA		20/12/80	A	5	(8)	2
15	Przemysław KOCOT		31/1/86	D	19	(1)	1
33	Costa NHAMOINESU	ZIM	6/1/86	D	11		
22	Amer OSMANAGIĆ	BIH	7/5/89	M	8	(9)	
23	Szymon PAWŁOWSKI		4/11/86	M	18	(1)	5
7	Dawid PLIZGA		17/11/85	M	23		4
30	Aleksander PTAK		4/11/77	G	3		
8	Deniss RAKELS	LVA	20/8/92	A	1	(3)	
17	Adrian RAKOWSKI		7/10/90	M	1	(3)	
13	Sergio Mauricio REINA Piedrahita	COL	26/1/85	D	18	(1)	
21	Bartosz RYMANIAK		13/11/89	D	21	(1)	
4	Michał STASIAK		12/3/81	D	12		2
99	Mauhamadou TRAORÉ	SEN	16/4/82	A	20	(5)	4
88	Kamil WILCZEK		14/1/88	M	10	(6)	2
11	Arkadiusz WOŹNIAK		1/6/90	A	10	(10)	2

TOP GOALSCORERS 2010/11

14	Tomasz FRANKOWSKI (Jagiellonia)
12	Andrzej NIEDZIELAN (Korona)
	Abdou Razack TRAORÉ (Lechia)
11	Artjoms RUDŅEVS (Lech)
10	Darvydas ŠERNAS (Widzew)
9	Miroslav RADOVIĆ (Legia)
	Artur SOBIECH (Polonia Warszawa)
	Andraž KIRM (Wisła)
8	Tadas LABUKAS (Arka)
	Dawid NOWAK (Bełchatów)
	Maciej JANKOWSKI (Ruch)
	Cristián Omar DÍAZ (Śląsk Wrocław)
	Przemysław KAŹMIERCZAK (Śląsk Wrocław)
	Piotr GRZELCZAK (Widzew)

PROMOTED CLUBS

ŁKS ŁÓDŹ

Coach – Andrzej Pyrdoł
Founded - 1908
Stadium – Stadion ŁKS (7,000)
MAJOR HONOURS: Polish League – (2) 1958, 1998; Polish Cup – (1) 1957.

TS PODBESKIDZIE BIELSKO-BIAŁA

Coach – Robert Kasperczyk
Founded – 1995
Stadium – Miejski (4,500)

SECOND LEVEL FINAL TABLE 2010/11

		Pld	W	D	L	F	A	Pts
1	ŁKS Łódź	34	20	11	3	59	34	71
2	TS Podbeskidzie Bielsko-Biała	34	20	9	5	53	23	69
3	MKS Flota Świnoujście	34	19	9	6	58	34	66
4	MKS Sandecja Nowy Sącz	34	15	11	8	52	34	56
5	GKS Piast Gliwice	34	13	13	8	45	31	52
6	MKS Pogoń Szczecin	34	14	9	11	55	42	51
7	KS Warta Poznań	34	14	8	12	44	43	50
8	GKS Bogdanka Łęczna	34	14	8	12	44	39	50
9	KS Ruch Radzionków	34	13	7	14	34	32	46
10	KS Górnik Polkowice	34	12	6	16	31	39	42
11	GKS Katowice	34	10	11	13	47	57	41
12	KS Kolejarz Stróże	34	10	8	16	30	43	38
13	MKS Dolcan Ząbki	34	10	7	17	33	39	37
14	LKS Termalica Bruk-Bet Nieciecza	34	10	7	17	40	53	37
15	MKS Kluczbork	34	8	12	14	36	44	36
16	KSZO Ostrowiec Świętokrzyski	34	9	9	16	32	43	36
17	MKS Odra Wodzisław Śląski	34	9	5	20	29	58	32
18	GKP Gorzów Wielkopolski	34	7	8	19	28	62	29

NB GKP Gorzów Wielkopolski withdrew after round 28 – their remaining matches were awarded as 0-3 defeats.

DOMESTIC CUP 2010/11

PUCHAR POLSKI

FIRST ROUND

(24/8/10)
Jarota Jarocin 1, Flota Świnoujście 1 *(aet; 4-5 on pens)*
Miedź Legnica 1, GKS Gorzów Wielkopolski 2
MKS Kutno 0, KSZO Ostrowiec Świętokrzyski 3
Świt Nowy Dwór Mazowiecki 1, MKS Kluczbork 0

(25/8/10)
Concordia Piotrków Trybunalski 2, Stal Stalowa Wola 1
GKS Tychy 1, Sandecja Nowy Sącz 0
OKS 1945 Olsztyn 2, Warta Poznań 1 *(aet)*
Olimpia Elbląg 1, ŁKS Łódź 2 *(aet)*
Ruch Zdzieszowice 1, GKS Katowice 0
Stal Sanok 0, Dolcan Ząbki 3
Start Otwock 2, Podbeskidzie Bielsko-Biała 2 *(aet; 5-6 on pens)*
Unia Swarzędz 0, Pogoń Szczecin 4
Wigry Suwałki 2, Bogdanka Łęczna 1
Wisła Płock 1, Górnik Zabrze 3
Zawisza Bydgoszcz 0, Widzew Łódź 3

SECOND ROUND

(21/9/10)
Concordia Piotrków Trybunalski 0, GKS Bełchatów 1
Dolcan Ząbki 0, Wisła Kraków 1
GKP Gorzów Wielkopolski 0, Cracovia Kraków 1
GKS Tychy 0, Lech Poznań 1
Górnik Zabrze 0, Lechia Gdańsk 2
ŁKS Łódź 3, Polonia Bytom 0
Pogoń Szczecin 0, Legia Warszawa 1
Świt Nowy Dwór Mazowiecki 0, Śląsk Wrocław 1
Wigry Suwałki 0, Korona Kielce 2
Znicz Pruszków 0, Polonia Warszawa 1

(22/9/10)
Flota Świnoujście 0, Jagiellonia Białystok 1
KSZO Ostrowiec Świętokrzyski 2, Arka Gdynia 1 *(aet)*
OKS 1945 Olsztyn 2, Odra Wodzisław 0
Podbeskidzie Bielsko-Biała 2, Piast Gliwice 0
Ruch Zdzieszowice 1, Ruch Chorzów 3
Widzew Łódź 1, Zagłębie Lubin 0 *(aet)*

1/8 FINALS

(26/10/10)
Korona Kielce 0, Jagiellonia Białystok 1
KSZO Ostrowiec Świetokrzyski 0, Polonia Warszawa 2 *(aet)*
ŁKS Łódź 0, Lechia Gdańsk 0 *(aet; 1-3 on pens)*
Podbeskidzie Bielsko-Biała 2, GKS Bełchatów 0
Śląsk Wrocław 1, Legia Warszawa 2
Wisła Kraków 1, Widzew Łódź 0

(27/10/10)
Cracovia Kraków 1, Lech Poznań 4
OKS 1945 Olsztyn 0, Ruch Chorzów 0 *(aet; 0-3 on pens)*

QUARTER-FINALS

(20/2/11 & 2/3/11)
Lech Poznań 0, Polonia Warszawa 1 *(Arboleda 54og)*
Polonia Warszawa 1 *(Kokoszka 34)*, Lech Poznań 2 *(Bosacki 4p, Ślusarski 23)*
(2-2; Lech Poznań on away goals)

(1/3/11 & 15/3/11)
Ruch Chorzów 1 *(Piech 15)*, Legia Warszawa 1 *(Komorowski 54p)*
Legia Warszawa 2 *(Vrdoljak 45, 59)*, Ruch Chorzów 0
(Legia Warszawa 3-1)

(1/3/11 & 16/3/11)
Wisła Kraków 0, Podbeskidzie Bielsko-Biała 1 *(Malinowski 88)*
Podbeskidzie Bielsko-Biała 2 *(Cieśliński 59, Górkiewicz 75)*, Wisła Kraków 2 *(Demjan 25og, Genkov 53)*
(Podbeskidzie Bielsko-Biała 3-2)

(2/3/11 & 16/3/11)
Lechia Gdańsk 0, Jagiellonia Białystok 0
Jagiellonia Białystok 1 *(Skerla 37)*, Lechia Gdańsk 1 *(Lukjanovs 25)*
(1-1; Lechia Gdańsk on away goal)

SEMI-FINALS

(5/4/11 & 19/4/11)
Lech Poznań 1 *(Ślusarski 58)*, Podbeskidzie Bielsko-Biała 1 *(Cieśliński 90)*
Podbeskidzie Bielsko-Biała 2 *(Chmiel 25, Malinowski 58)*, Lech Poznań 3 *(Štilić 73, Rudņevs 75, 90)*
(Lech Poznań 4-3)

(6/4/11 & 20/4/11)
Lechia Gdańsk 0, Legia Warszawa 1 *(Kucharczyk 88)*
Legia Warszawa 4 *(Pietrowski 24og, Vrdoljak 63, Bąk 77og, Kucharczyk 79)*, Lechia Gdańsk 0
(Legia Warszawa 5-0)

FINAL

(3/5/11)
Stadion Miejski im. Zdzisława Krzyszkowiaka, Bydgoszcz
LEGIA WARSZAWA 1 *(Manú 66)*
KKS LECH POZNAŃ 1 *(Injac 29)*
(aet; 5-4 on pens)
Referee – *Gil*
LEGIA – *Skaba, Rzeźniczak, Choto (Cabral 76), Iñaki Astiz (Komorowski 46), Wawrzyniak, Manú, Borysiuk, Vrdoljak, Radović, Rybus (Kucharczyk 59), Hubník.*
LECH – *Kotorowski, Wojtkowiak, Bosacki, Wołąkiewicz, Henríquez, Krivets (Mikołajczak 103), Injac (Štilić 69), Đurđević, Murawski, Wilk (Kiełb 75), Rudņevs.*

CLUB COMMUNICATION 2011/12

GKS Bełchatów

ul. Sportowa 3
PO-97-400 Bełchatów

Tel +48 44 635 0355
Fax +48 44 635 0791
Web gksbelchatow.com
Email gks@gksbelchatow.com
Media Officer Michal Antczak

MKS Cracovia Kraków

Wielicka 101
PO-30-552 Kraków

Tel +48 12 29 29 100
Fax +48 12 655 18 82
Web cracovia.pl
Email klub@cracovia.pl
Media Officer Przemysław Urbański

Górnik Zabrze

Roosevelta 81
PO-41-800 Zabrze

Tel +48 32 271 4926
Fax +48 32 271 0530
Web gornikzabrze.pl
Email gornikzabrze@gornikzabrze.pl
Media Officer Stanislaw Oslizlo

Jagiellonia Białystok

ul. Legionowa 28
PO-15-281 Białystok

Tel +48 85 665 2100
Fax +48 85 665 2104
Web jagiellonia.pl
Email klub@jagiellonia.pl
Media Officer Agnieszka Syczewska

Korona Kielce

ul. Ściegiennego 8
PO-25-033 Kielce

Tel +48 41 340 3403
Fax +48 41 340 3415
Web korona-kielce.pl
Email korona.sa@korona-kielce.pl
Media Officer Paweł Janczyk

KKS Lech Poznań

ul. Bułgarska 17
PO-60-320 Poznań

Tel +48 61 886 3000
Fax +48 61 886 3010
Web lechpoznan.pl
Email lech@lechpoznan.pl
Media Officer Joanna Dzios

KS Lechia Gdańsk

ul Szklana Huta 7
PO-80-529 Gdańsk

Tel + 48 58 345 2187
Fax + 48 58 345 2187
Web lechia.pl
Email biuro@lechia.pl
Media Officer Blazej Slowikowski

Legia Warszawa

Ul. Lazienkowska 3
PO-00-449 Warszawa

Tel +48 22 318 20 00
Fax +48 22 318 20 01
Web legia.com
Email info@legia.pl
Media Officer Michał Kocieba

ŁKS Łódź

Al. Unii Lubelskiej 2
PO-94-020 Łódź

Tel +48 42 686 19 87
Fax +48 42 686 19 87
Web lkslodz.pl
Email biuro@lkslodz.pl
Media Officer Jarosław Paradowski

TS Podbeskidzie Bielsko-Biała

ul. Rychlińskiego 21
PO-43-300 Bielsko-Biała

Tel +48 33 498 3988
Fax +48 33 497 5278
Web ts.podbeskidzie.pl
Email biuro@ts.podbeskidzie.pl
Media Officer Jarosław Zięba

KSP Polonia Warszawa

Ul. Konwiktorska 6
PO-00-206 Warszawa

Tel +48 22 771 7804
Fax +48 22 771 7941
Web ksppolonia.pl
Email biuro@ksppolonia.pl
Media Officer Jakub Krupa

Ruch Chorzów

Ul. Cicha 6
PO-41-506 Chorzów

Tel +48 32 24 17 554
Fax +48 32 346 35 35
Web ruchchorzow.com.pl
Email ruch@ruchchorzow.com.p
Media Officer Donata Chruściel

WKS Śląsk Wrocław

ul. Oporowska 62
PO-53-434 Wrocław

Tel +48 71 722 3936
Fax +48 71 722 3947
Web slaskwroclaw.pl
Email biuro@slaskwroclaw.pl
Media Officer Michał Mazur

RTS Widzew Łódź

Al. Pilsudskiego 138
PO-92-230 Łódź

Tel +48 42 676 5260
Fax +48 42 676 5262
Web widzew.pl
Email secretariat@widzew.pl
Media Officer Michał Kulesza

Wisła Kraków

Ul. Reymonta 22
PO-30-059 Kraków

Tel +48 12 630 7600
Fax +48 12 630 7691
Web wisla.krakow.pl
Email sekretariat@wisla.krakow.pl
Media Officer Adrian Ochalik

Zagłębie Lubin

Marii Sklodowskiej-Curie 98
PO-59-301 Lubin

Tel +48 76 746 96 00
Fax +48 76 746 96 01
Web zaglebie-lubin.pl
Email sekretariat@zaglebie.kghm.pl
Media Officer Wacław Wachnik

PORTUGAL

Portugal I Portugal

Federação Portuguesa de Futebol (FPF)

COMMUNICATION

Address Rua Alexandre
Herculano 58
Apartado 24013
PT-1250-012 Lisboa

Tel +351 21 325 2700
Fax +351 21 325 2780

E-mail info@fpf.pt
Website fpf.pt

President Gilberto Madaíl
General Secretary Ângelo Brou
Media Officer Onofre Costa

Year of Formation 1914

National Stadium Estádio Nacional, Lisbon (37,000)

DOMESTIC COMPETITION SUMMARY 2010/11

LIGA FINAL TABLE

			Home					Away					Total						
		Pld	W	D	L	F	A	W	D	L	F	A	W	D	L	F	A	Pts	Comp
1	FC Porto	30	14	1	0	43	11	13	2	0	30	5	27	3	0	73	16	84	UCL
2	SL Benfica	30	11	2	2	36	14	9	1	5	25	17	20	3	7	61	31	63	UCL
3	Sporting Clube de Portugal	30	6	5	4	18	16	7	4	4	23	15	13	9	8	41	31	48	UEL
4	SC Braga	30	9	2	4	28	15	4	5	6	17	18	13	7	10	45	33	46	UEL
5	Vitória SC	30	7	6	2	16	10	5	1	9	20	27	12	7	11	36	37	43	UEL
6	CD Nacional	30	7	4	4	14	12	4	5	6	14	19	11	9	10	28	31	42	UEL
7	FC Paços de Ferreira	30	6	5	4	20	23	4	6	5	15	19	10	11	9	35	42	41	
8	Rio Ave FC	30	6	4	5	17	13	4	4	7	18	20	10	8	12	35	33	38	
9	CS Marítimo	30	5	4	6	14	14	4	4	7	19	18	9	8	13	33	32	35	
10	UD Leiria	30	6	1	8	12	20	3	7	5	13	18	9	8	13	25	38	35	
11	SC Olhanense	30	4	8	3	16	17	3	5	7	8	17	7	13	10	24	34	34	
12	Vitória FC	30	5	5	5	18	22	3	5	7	11	20	8	10	12	29	42	34	
13	SC Beira-Mar	30	5	5	5	17	17	2	7	6	15	19	7	12	11	32	36	33	
14	A. Académica de Coimbra	30	4	6	5	16	17	3	3	9	16	31	7	9	14	32	48	30	
15	Portimonense SC	30	4	3	8	18	24	2	4	9	11	25	6	7	17	29	49	25	*Relegated*
16	A. Naval 1° Maio	30	2	5	8	12	24	3	3	9	14	27	5	8	17	26	51	23	*Relegated*

Top Scorer Hulk (Porto), 23 goals

Promoted Club Gil Vicente FC
CD Feirense

Cup Final FC Porto 6, Vitória SC 2

Villas-Boas lifts Porto to new heights

A season in which Portugal boasted three of the four UEFA Europa League semi-finalists, and both finalists, was an especially memorable one for fans and followers of the winners, FC Porto, who also captured the domestic double, smashing their way undefeated to a 25th Liga title and completing a magnificent treble with a 6-2 win over Vitória SC in the final of the Portuguese Cup.

The principal author of Porto's remarkable success story was their inexperienced coach, 33-year-old André Villas-Boas. Newly acquired from A. Académica da Coimbra, the former assistant to José Mourinho made such an impact in Portugal and beyond that by the end of the season he was being branded as the 'New Special One' and 'Mourinho Mark II'. Indeed, his reputation had soared to such lofty heights that Porto could not afford to keep him, Chelsea FC willingly forking out the €15m necessary to activate the release clause in his contract and transport him from the Estádio do Dragão to Stamford Bridge, where he had previously worked during Mourinho's spell as manager from 2004-07.

Porto players bask in the glory of their UEFA Europa League triumph

The ascent of Villas-Boas was aided by a remarkable effort from his Porto team. Absent from the UEFA Champions League for the first time in eight years, the Dragons used the opportunity not only to blow away the opposition on the domestic front but also to re-establish their international credentials in the UEFA Europa League. From the very start of the campaign, when they defeated defending champions SL Benfica 2-0 to lift the Portuguese Super Cup, to the very end, when they won two major finals in four days, Porto were an irrepressible force.

Invincible champions

If victory in the UEFA Europa League – sealed with a 1-0 victory over SC Braga in Dublin – was the most prestigious and widely publicised of Porto's four trophy successes under Villas-Boas, their recapture of the domestic Liga title was surely the most emphatic. Wins in each of their opening six matches set them off on a procession towards the title that was never remotely threatened. In fact, the only significant challenge presented to them was whether they could go through the entire 30-match campaign without losing. There had been no undefeated Portuguese champion since Benfica took the 1972/73 title, but Porto, assisted by a 16-match winning streak from December to early May, joined the history-makers with a 2-0 win against CS Marítimo in Madeira on the final day, leaving them with 27 victories, three draws and a record-breaking victory margin of 21 points.

The title had been secured several weeks earlier, on the first weekend of April, when Porto won 2-1

Porto's Brazilian striker Hulk topped the Portuguese Liga scoring charts with 23 goals

at closest – but very distant – pursuers Benfica. That completed a memorable double over the Lisbon giants, the first encounter having resulted in a resounding 5-0 triumph in November. That was - and would be - Porto's biggest win of the season, but it was just one of many master-class performances from Villas-Boas's men. Another saw them recover from a 2-0 home defeat to Benfica in the first leg of the Portuguese Cup semi-final with a brilliant 3-1 win at the Estádio da Luz.

Defence-destroying Hulk

In Europe, Porto were equally formidable. They scored 44 goals in their 17 ties, ramming five past FC Spartak Moskva (twice) and Villarreal CF at the business end of the competition. Colombian centre forward Radamel Falcao set a new individual goalscoring record for the UEFA Europa League/UEFA Cup by finding the net 17 times (plus once in the play-off round), a tally he concluded in appropriate fashion with the only goal of the final. There were also eight goals in Europe for Falcao's attacking accomplice Hulk, but the gifted Brazilian left-footer was even more of a pest to domestic defences, topping the Liga charts with 23 goals (seven more than joint-runner-up Falcao) and adding 13 assists. He also struck four times in the Portuguese Cup, including once in the final.

Falcao and Hulk were the undisputed star turns of Villas-Boas's winning machine, but others also impressed. João Moutinho lifted his standing to a new level following his summer move from Sporting Clube de Portugal as he established himself as Porto's playmaker-in-chief. There were gaps to fill following the pre-season sale of the club's two talismen, centre back Bruno Alves (to FC Zenit St Petersburg) and Raul Meireles (to Liverpool FC), but neither player was missed as Rolando brilliantly marshalled the defence and Freddy Guarín emerged as a highly effective and industrious goalscoring midfielder. Portuguese international Silvestre Varela also commanded attention with his effervescent wing play and plentiful supply of assists and goals.

So all-encompassing was Porto's dominance that the only crumb of comfort they left to the opposition was in the Taça da Liga – the secondary Portuguese domestic knockout competition – where they fielded an understrength team and were eliminated in the group stage. Benfica went on to win the competition for the third successive year, with their Spanish midfielder Javi García scoring the winning goals in both the semi-final, against Sporting, and the final, won 2-1 against FC Paços de Ferreira.

Bad start for Benfica

That trophy was small beer, however, for a club that had enjoyed such an excellent first season under coach Jorge Jesus in 2009/10. Their title defence was over almost as soon it began, three defeats in their opening four games – the club's worst ever start to a domestic championship – putting them nine points in arrears of Porto by mid-September. With several key players from the previous season either sold or underperforming – Portuguese international Fábio Coentrão being a notable exception – there was disappointment, too, in the UEFA Champions League as the Eagles lost all three away fixtures without scoring and only just scraped into the UEFA Europa League. Quarter-finalists in 2009/10, they went one stage further after disposing of PSV Eindhoven, but with a final appearance against Porto in Dublin there for the taking, they lost the semi-final on away goals to Braga.

Although overshadowed by Porto's treble triumph, Braga's run to the UEFA Europa League final was a remarkable story in its own right. Like Benfica, their European campaign began in the UEFA Champions League but, unlike the Lisbon club, they had to negotiate two qualifying rounds before acceding to the group stage. They did that successfully, thanks to impressive victories over Celtic FC and Sevilla FC, but after looking out of their depth in their opening two group games, losing 6-0 at Arsenal FC and 3-0 at home to FC Shakhtar Donetsk, Domingos Paciência's side burst back into life, winning their next three matches, reaching the UEFA Europa League and repeatedly overcoming the odds to see off Liverpool FC, FC Dynamo Kyiv and, ultimately, Benfica before battling their way to a narrow defeat against Porto in Dublin. Short of exceptional individuals, Braga were all about the values of teamwork and collective endeavour. Their defence was consistently magnificent, keeping clean sheets in eight of their nine home games and all four, decisively, in the UEFA Europa League.

Hot property

Braga boss Domingos, a former Porto and Portugal striker, was hot property after his team's European exploits and left the club to become the new coach at Sporting. The Lisbon Lions were frustratingly tame and toothless in 2010/11 – firstly under Paulo Sérgio; then, from late February onwards, under José Couceiro. Veteran striker Liedson returned to his native Brazil in January, and although Rui Patrício performed well in goal and André Santos made a decent fist of filling João Moutinho's boots, the team as a whole performed poorly, with results to match. It was only with a last-day win over Braga that they leapfrogged into third place, but with a 15-point deficit on runners-up Benfica, and a vast 36-point gap distancing them from the champions, it was a season to forget for Sporting.

National Team

International Tournament Appearances – FIFA World Cup - (5) 1966 (3rd), 1986, 2002, 2006 (4th), 2010 (2nd round).
UEFA European Championship – (5) 1984 (semi-finals), 1996 (qtr-finals), 2000 (semi-finals), 2004 (runners-up), 2008 (qtr-finals).

Top Five All-time Caps – Luís Figo (127); Fernando Couto (110); Rui Costa (94); Pedro Resendes "Pauleta" (88); Simão Sabrosa (85)

Top Five All-time Goals – Pedro Resendes "Pauleta" (47); Eusébio Ferreira Silva (41); Luís Figo (32); Nuno Gomes (29); Cristiano Ronaldo & Rui Costa (26)

There was better news for ex-Sporting coach Paulo Bento, who enjoyed an encouraging first season in charge of the Portuguese national team. He was appointed in September 2010 to replace Carlos Queiroz, who, although officially still in charge, was actually suspended by the Portuguese anti-doping authority from taking his seat on the bench for Portugal's opening two UEFA EURO 2012 qualifiers – a 4-4 draw at home to Cyprus followed by an even more damaging 1-0 defeat in Norway.

The new man kicked off positively with back-to-back 3-1 wins against Denmark and Iceland – in which superstar Cristiano Ronaldo made an impressive return from injury – before leading the team to an astonishing 4-0 win over world champions Spain in a Lisbon friendly. Hélder Postiga, a double scorer against Spain, registered an even more precious goal the following June to give Portugal three more qualifying points in a 1-0 home win over Norway that took them level at the top of the Group H table alongside their vanquished opponents and Denmark. Although the momentum was with Paulo Bento's side, qualification remained in the balance, with Portugal's hopes of clinching a fifth successive UEFA European Championship finals berth set to be determined by the outcome of their final group fixture on 11 October in Copenhagen.

NATIONAL TEAM RESULTS 2010/11

3/9/10	Cyprus (ECQ)	H	Guimaraes	4-4	*Hugo Almeida (8), Raul Meireles (29), Danny (50), Manuel Fernandes (60)*
7/9/10	Norway (ECQ)	A	Oslo	0-1	
8/10/10	Denmark (ECQ)	H	Porto	3-1	*Nani (29, 30), Cristiano Ronaldo (85)*
12/10/10	Iceland (ECQ)	A	Reykjavik	3-1	*Cristiano Ronaldo (3), Raul Meireles (27), Hélder Postiga (72)*
17/11/10	Spain	H	Lisbon	4-0	*Carlos Martins (45), Hélder Postiga (49, 68), Hugo Almeida (90+3)*
9/2/11	Argentina	N	Geneva (SUI)	1-2	*Cristiano Ronaldo (21)*
26/3/11	Chile	H	Leiria	1-1	*Varela (16)*
29/3/11	Finland	H	Aveiro	2-0	*Rúben Micael (10, 71)*
4/6/11	Norway (ECQ)	H	Lisbon	1-0	*Hélder Postiga (53)*

NATIONAL TEAM APPEARANCES 2010/11

Coach – (AGOSTINHO Oliveira) /(20/9/10) PAULO BENTO	5/2/47 / 20/6/69		CYP	NOR	DEN	ISL	Esp	Arg	Chi	Fin	NOR	Caps	Goals
EDUARDO Carvalho	19/9/82	Genoa (ITA)	G	G	G	G	G46	G46		G	G	27	-
MIGUEL Monteiro	4/1/80	Valencia (ESP)	D									59	1
BRUNO ALVES	27/11/81	Zenit (RUS)	D	D			D	D		D	D	41	5
RICARDO CARVALHO	18/5/78	Real Madrid (ESP)	D	D	D	D	D46		D46	s78		74	4
FÁBIO COENTRÃO	11/3/88	Benfica	D		D	D		D	D	D61	D	15	-
RAUL MEIRELES	17/3/83	Liverpool (ENG)	M	M	M	M	M	M79	M	M61	M	47	8
MANUEL FERNANDES	5/2/86	Valencia (ESP)	M79	M			s63					8	2
"DANNY" Miguel Alves Gomes	7/8/83	Zenit (RUS)	M61	s72		s87	s46	s60	s84	A		21	3
Luís Cunha "NANI"	17/11/86	Man. United (ENG)	A	A	A88	A87	A88	A60	A84	s69	A86	45	9
RICARDO QUARESMA	26/9/83	Beşiktaş (TUR)	A	A84				s61	s60	A69		30	3
HUGO ALMEIDA	23/5/84	Werder (GER) /Beşiktaş (TUR)	A84	A	A69	A65	s76	A60	s81	A		36	12
LIEDSON Muniz	17/12/77	Sporting	s61	s84								15	4
JOÃO MOUTINHO	8/9/86	Porto	s79		M	M	M	M	M	s46	M	34	1
YANNICK DJALÓ	5/5/86	Sporting	s84									1	-
MIGUEL VELOSO	11/5/86	Genoa (ITA)		D				s79				16	1
SÍLVIO Ferreira	28/9/87	Braga		D					s40	s61	s73	4	-
TIAGO Mendes	2/5/81	Atlético (ESP)		M72	s75	s77						58	3
Képler Ferreira "PEPE"	26/2/83	Real Madrid (ESP)			D	D	s46		s46	D78	D	33	2
JOÃO PEREIRA	25/2/84	Sporting			D	D	D	D	D40		D73	6	-
CARLOS MARTINS	29/4/82	Benfica			M75	M77	M63	M85	M71	M46	M69	12	2
CRISTIANO RONALDO	5/2/85	Real Madrid (ESP)			A	A	A46	A61			A	81	26
HÉLDER POSTIGA	2/8/82	Sporting			s69	s65	A76	s60	A81		A	40	15
Silvestre VARELA	2/2/85	Porto			s88				A60		s86	4	1
José BOSINGWA	24/8/82	Chelsea (ENG)					D					24	-
RUI PATRÍCIO	15/2/88	Sporting					s46	s46	G			3	-
PAULO MACHADO	31/3/86	Toulouse (FRA)					s88	s85	s71	s61		4	-
ROLANDO Fonseca	31/8/85	Porto						D	D			10	-
NÉLSON Marcos	10/6/83	Osasuna (ESP)								D		2	-
RÚBEN MICAEL	19/8/86	Porto								M75	s69	2	2
ANDRÉ SANTOS	20/3/89	Sporting								s75		1	-

CLUB-BY-CLUB

A. ACADÉMICA DE COIMBRA

Coach – Jorge Costa; (19/12/10) José Guilherme; (20/1/11) Ulisses Morais

Founded – 1876

Stadium – Cidade de Coimbra (30,075)

MAJOR HONOURS: Portuguese Cup – (1) 1939.

2010				
15/8	Benfica	a	2-1	*Miguel Fidalgo, Laionel*
20/8	Olhanense	h	1-1	*Diogo Gomes*
29/8	Beira-Mar	a	1-2	*Modou Sougou*
12/9	Naval	h	3-0	*Modou Sougou (p), Miguel Fidalgo, Berger*
19/9	Rio Ave	a	2-2	*Diogo Valente, Modou Sougou*
25/9	Guimarães	h	3-1	*Diogo Melo, Modou Sougou, Laionel*
1/10	Leiria	a	1-2	*Miguel Fidalgo*
23/10	Nacional	h	2-1	*Miguel Fidalgo, Berger*
30/10	Porto	h	0-1	
6/11	Portimonense	a	2-2	*Miguel Fidalgo, Hugo Morais*
13/11	Sporting	h	1-2	*Miguel Fidalgo*
26/11	Setúbal	a	1-0	*Diogo Valente*
8/12	Marítimo	h	1-5	*Miguel Fidalgo*
17/12	Braga	a	0-5	
2011				
9/1	Paços Ferreira	h	0-0	
16/1	Benfica	h	0-1	
22/1	Olhanense	a	1-2	*Adrien Silva*
6/2	Beira-Mar	h	3-3	*Diogo Melo, Modou Sougou, Addy*
13/2	Naval	a	1-3	*Modou Sougou (p)*
20/2	Rio Ave	h	0-1	
25/2	Guimarães	a	2-0	*Éder, Laionel*
4/3	Leiria	h	0-0	
13/3	Nacional	a	1-1	*Laionel*
20/3	Porto	a	1-3	*Addy*
2/4	Portimonense	h	1-0	*Laionel*
9/4	Sporting	a	0-2	
15/4	Setúbal	h	1-1	*Miguel Fidalgo*
1/5	Marítimo	a	0-1	
8/5	Braga	h	0-0	
15/5	Paços Ferreira	a	1-5	*Éder*

No	Name	Nat	DoB	Pos	Aps	(s)	Gls
60	David Nii ADDY	GHA	21/2/90	D	13	(1)	2
28	ADRIEN Sebastien Perruchet SILVA		15/3/89	M	5	(1)	1
2	Euripedes Daniel Adão AMOREIRINHA		5/8/84	D	4	(2)	
5	Markus BERGER	AUT	21/1/85	D	27		2
7	Amaury Armindo BISCHOFF		31/3/87	M	5	(4)	
9	Enrique Javier CARRREÑO Salvago	ESP	27/11/86	A	1	(4)	
85	DIOGO Soares GOMES	BRA	12/9/85	M	8	(2)	1
50	DIOGO Jefferson Mendes MELO	BRA	18/4/84	M	25	(3)	2
23	DIOGO Jorge Moreno VALENTE		23/9/84	M	28	(1)	2
21	ÉDERzito António Macedo Lopes	GNB	22/12/87	A	9	(12)	2
13	Paulo Rafael GRILO Neves		19/8/91	M		(5)	
55	HÉLDER José Vaz CABRAL		7/5/84	D	17	(1)	
7	HUGO Eduardo Santos MORAIS		12/2/78	A	23		1
88	Adeval Ignácio Pereira JÚNIOR "PARAÍBA"	BRA	1/1/88	A		(13)	
11	LAIONEL Silva Ramalho	BRA	27/4/86	A	4	(22)	5
4	LUIZ Fernando NUNES Duarte	BRA	4/12/80	D	12	(2)	
14	Nuno MIGUEL FIDALGO dos Santos		19/3/82	A	20	(3)	8
18	Papa Amodou "MODOU" SOUGOU	SEN	18/12/84	A	27	(1)	6
66	NUNO Miguel Prata COELHO		23/11/87	M	18		
15	Rui ORLANDO Ribeiro Santos Neto		24/10/79	D	13		
19	Pedro Miguel da Silva Rocha "PEDRINHO"		6/3/85	D	20		
30	PEDRO Miguel de Brandão COSTA		21/11/81	D	10	(1)	
1	Romuald Desire PEISER	FRA	3/8/79	G	30		
91	Ibrahim SISSOKO	CIV	29/11/91	M	1	(8)	
8	Pape Habib SOW	SEN	2/12/85	M	10	(4)	

SC BEIRA-MAR

Coach – Leonardo Jardim; (2/3/11) Rui Bento

Founded – 1922

Stadium – Municipal de Aveiro (31,100)

MAJOR HONOURS: Portuguese Cup – (1) 1999.

2010				
15/8	Leiria	h	0-0	
20/8	Porto	a	0-3	
29/8	Académica	h	2-1	*Wilson Eduardo, Mahamat*
13/9	Setúbal	a	0-0	
18/9	Marítimo	h	1-1	*Rui Sampaio*
26/9	Portimonense	a	0-1	
4/10	Sporting	h	1-1	*Renan*
23/10	Paços Ferreira	a	1-1	*Leandro Tatu*
31/10	Naval	h	3-1	*Artur, Leandro Tatu, Wilson Eduardo*
7/11	Braga	a	3-2	*Leandro Tatu, Ronny 2*
14/11	Olhanense	a	1-1	*Renan*
28/11	Benfica	h	1-3	*Rui Varela*
5/12	Rio Ave	a	1-1	*Leandro Tatu*
18/12	Guimarães	h	3-2	*Leandro Tatu, Wilson Eduardo 2*
2011				
9/1	Nacional	a	0-0	
16/1	Leiria	a	3-0	*Ronny, Artur, Wang*
22/1	Porto	h	0-1	
6/2	Académica	a	3-3	*Mahamat, Artur, Leandro Tatu*
14/2	Setúbal	h	0-0	
20/2	Marítimo	a	0-1	
27/2	Portimonense	h	0-1	
6/3	Sporting	a	0-1	
11/3	Paços Ferreira	h	3-1	*Leandro Tatu, Mahamat, Renan*
20/3	Naval	a	2-2	*Leandro Tatu, Artur*
2/4	Braga	h	1-2	*Leandro Tatu*
10/4	Olhanense	h	1-0	*Wilson Eduardo*
17/4	Benfica	a	1-2	*Yartey*
1/5	Rio Ave	h	1-1	*Yohan*
8/5	Guimarães	a	0-1	
15/5	Nacional	h	0-2	

No	Name	Nat	DoB	Pos	Aps	(s)	Gls
22	ALEXsandro Carvalho Lopes "MARANHÃO"	BRA	30/4/85	M		(5)	
23	ANDRÉ Filipe Farias MARQUES		1/8/87	D	13	(1)	
7	ARTUR Filipe Bernardes Moreira		18/2/84	A	26		4
2	DANILO Tavares Oliveira		13/8/79	D	2		
9	ÉLIO Bruno Teixeira Martins		26/3/85	D	5	(4)	
5	HUGO Miguel Fernandes Vieira		11/8/76	D	27		
26	HUGO Filipe Pereira SEIXAS		19/4/91	A		(3)	
14	JAIME Daniel Melão Simões		11/6/89	D	3	(2)	
29	JOÃO LUIZ Ramires Vieira	BRA	20/12/85	M	21	(3)	
25	António Eduardo Pereira Santos "KANU"	BRA	3/5/84	D	15		
30	LEANDRO Ângelo Martins "TATU"	BRA	26/4/82	A	21	(6)	9
20	Djamal Abdoulaye MAHAMAT Bindi	LBY	26/4/83	M	27		3
18	PEDRO António Coelho MOREIRA		23/10/83	D	28		
28	RENAN Fernandes Garcia	BRA	19/6/86	M	28	(2)	3
11	RICARDO Nuno Oliveira ROCHA		18/11/82	D	1	(3)	
27	RONNY Carlos Silva	BRA	25/2/83	A	14	(4)	3
6	RÚBEN Alexandre Rocha LIMA		3/10/89	D	1	(5)	
24	RUI Manuel Castanheira RÊGO		5/7/80	G	30		
13	Fernando RUI Valadas SAMPAIO		29/5/87	M	28	(2)	1
15	RUI Manuel Costa VARELA		9/8/83	M	6	(4)	1
10	SÉRGIO Miguel Relvas OLIVEIRA		2/6/91	M	1	(5)	
24	Luis Fernando Gonçalves Fernandes TINOCO		17/10/86	D		(1)	
11	WANG Gang	CHN	17/2/89	A		(14)	1
8	WILSON Bruno Naval EDUARDO		8/7/90	A	13	(14)	5
32	Ishmael YARTEY	GHA	11/1/90	A	4	(6)	1
4	YOHAN Tavares		2/3/88	D	16	(5)	1

SL BENFICA

Coach – Jorge Jesus

Founded – 1904

Stadium – Luz (65,647)

MAJOR HONOURS: European Champion Clubs' Cup – (2) 1961, 1962; Portuguese League – (32) 1936, 1937, 1938, 1942, 1943, 1945, 1950, 1955, 1957, 1960, 1961, 1963, 1964, 1965, 1967, 1968, 1969, 1971, 1972, 1973, 1975, 1976, 1977, 1981, 1983, 1984, 1987, 1989, 1991, 1994, 2005, 2010;
Portuguese Cup – (27) 1930, 1931, 1935, 1940, 1943, 1944, 1949, 1951, 1952, 1953, 1955, 1957, 1959, 1962, 1964, 1969, 1970, 1972, 1980, 1981, 1983, 1985, 1986, 1987, 1993, 1996, 2004.

2010				
15/8	Académica	h	1-2	*Jara*
21/8	Nacional	a	1-2	*Carlos Martins*
28/8	Setúbal	h	3-0	*Cardozo, Luisão, Aimar*
10/9	Guimarães	a	1-2	*Saviola*
19/9	Sporting	h	2-0	*Cardozo 2*
25/9	Marítimo	a	1-0	*Fábio Coentrão*
3/10	Braga	h	1-0	*Carlos Martins*
24/10	Portimonense	a	1-0	*Javi García*
31/10	Paços Ferreira	h	2-0	*Aimar, Alan Kardec*
7/11	Porto	a	0-5	

4/11	Naval	h	4-0	*Alan Kardec, Gaitán 2, Nuno Gomes*
8/11	Beira-Mar	a	3-1	*Cardozo 2, Saviola*
/12	Olhanense	h	2-0	*Cardozo, Saviola*
8/12	Rio Ave	h	5-2	*Aimar, Saviola 2, Salvio 2*

011

/1	Leiria	a	3-0	*Saviola, Gaitán, Cardozo*
6/1	Académica	a	1-0	*Saviola*
2/1	Nacional	h	4-2	*Gaitán, Sidnei, Cardozo, Jara*
/2	Setúbal	a	2-0	*Gaitán, Jara*
3/2	Guimarães	h	3-0	*Sidnei, Aimar, Carlos Martins*
0/2	Sporting	a	2-0	*Salvio, Gaitán*
7/2	Marítimo	h	2-1	*Salvio, Fábio Coentrão*
/3	Braga	a	1-2	*Saviola*
3/3	Portimonense	h	1-1	*Nuno Gomes*
21/3	Paços Ferreira	a	5-1	*Cardozo (p), Aimar, Gaitán, Nuno Gomes 2*
3/4	Porto	h	1-2	*Saviola (p)*
0/4	Naval	a	1-2	*Alan Kardec*
17/4	Beira-Mar	h	2-1	*Sidnei, Jara*
1/5	Olhanense	a	1-1	*Jara*
3/5	Rio Ave	a	2-1	*Cardozo 2*
15/5	Leiria	h	3-3	*Cardozo, Javi García, Jara*

No	Name	Nat	DoB	Pos	Aps	(s)	Gls
10	Pablo César AIMAR	ARG	3/11/79	M	21	(2)	5
2	AÍRTON Ribeiro Santos	BRA	21/2/90	M	7	(8)	
31	ALAN KARDEC Souza Pereira Júnior	BRA	12/1/89	A	9	(3)	3
7	Óscar René CARDOZO	PAR	20/5/83	A	20	(2)	12
17	CARLOS Jorge Neto MARTINS		29/4/82	M	14	(11)	3
24	Lionel Jules CAROLE	FRA	12/4/91	D	6		
25	Paulo CÉSAR Silva PEIXOTO		12/5/80	M	9	(7)	
23	DAVID LUIZ Moreira Marinho	BRA	22/4/87	D	16		
18	FÁBIO Alexandre da Silva COENTRÃO		11/3/88	M	23		2
24	FELIPE MENEZES Jácomo	BRA	20/1/88	M	4	(3)	
28	José Luis FERNÁNDEZ	ARG	26/8/87	A	1	(1)	
20	Osvaldo Nicolás Fabián GAITÁN	ARG	23/2/88	A	23	(3)	7
11	Franco Daniel JARA	ARG	15/7/88	A	9	(17)	6
33	JARDEL Nivaldo Vieira	BRA	29/3/86	D	5	(3)	
6	Francisco JAVIe GARCÍA Fernández	ESP	8/2/87	M	24		2
13	JÚLIO CÉSAR Jacobi	BRA	2/9/86	G	4		
22	LUÍS FILIPE Angelo Rodrigues Fernandes		14/6/79	D	3		
4	Anderson Luís da Silva "LUISÃO"	BRA	12/2/81	D	23		1
14	Victorio MAXImiliano PEREIRA Páez	URU	8/6/84	D	23	(3)	
1	José Filipe Silva MOREIRA		20/3/82	G	2		
21	NUNO Miguel Soares Ribeiro GOMES		5/7/76	A		(6)	4
12	ROBERTO Jiménez Gago	ESP	10/2/86	G	24	(1)	
15	RODERICK Jefferson Gonçalves Miranda		30/3/91	D	4	(1)	
5	RUBEN Filipe Marques AMORIM		27/1/85	M	6	(6)	
8	Eduardo António SALVIO	ARG	13/7/90	A	12	(7)	4
30	Javier Pedro SAVIOLA	ARG	11/12/81	A	24		9
27	SIDNEI Rechel da Silva Júnior	BRA	23/6/89	D	14	(2)	3
19	WELDON Santos de Andrade	BRA	6/8/80	A		(4)	

SC BRAGA

Coach – Domingos Paciência

Founded – 1921

Stadium – Municipal de Braga (30,286)

MAJOR HONOURS: Portuguese Cup – (1) 1966.

2010

13/8	Portimonense	h	3-1	*Matheus, Paulo César, Leandro Salino*
21/8	Setúbal	a	0-0	
29/8	Marítimo	h	1-0	*Sílvio*
11/9	Porto	a	2-3	*Luís Aguiar, Lima*
19/9	Paços Ferreira	a	2-2	*Moisés, Luís Aguiar*
24/9	Naval	h	3-1	*Mossoró, og (Orestes), Paulo César*
3/10	Benfica	a	0-1	
23/10	Olhanense	h	3-1	*Mossoró, Lima 2*
30/10	Rio Ave	a	0-2	
7/11	Beira-Mar	h	2-3	*Meyong (p), Lima*
13/11	Guimarães	a	1-2	*Alan*
28/11	Nacional	h	2-0	*Lima, Paulo César*
4/12	Leiria	a	1-3	*Matheus*
17/12	Académica	h	5-0	*Paulo César, Paulão, Keita, Meyong, Hugo Viana*

2011

8/1	Sporting	a	1-2	*Paulo César*
14/1	Portimonense	a	3-0	*Hélder Barbosa, Lima, Alan*
22/1	Setúbal	h	2-2	*Hélder Barbosa, Guilherme*
5/2	Marítimo	a	2-1	*Hélder Barbosa, Custódio*
13/2	Porto	h	0-2	
20/2	Paços Ferreira	h	1-2	*Ukra*
28/2	Naval	a	0-0	
6/3	Benfica	h	2-1	*Hugo Viana, Mossoró*
21/3	Rio Ave	h	1-0	*Hugo Viana*
27/3	Olhanense	a	2-0	*Alan 2 (1p)*
2/4	Beira-Mar	a	2-1	*og (Jaime), Meyong*
11/4	Guimarães	h	3-1	*Paulão, Ukra, Alan*
18/4	Nacional	a	1-1	*Heldér Barbosa*
1/5	Leiria	h	0-0	
8/5	Académica	a	0-0	
15/5	Sporting	h	0-1	

No	Name	Nat	DoB	Pos	Aps	(s)	Gls
30	ALAN Osório da Costa Silva	BRA	19/9/79	A	23	(4)	5
23	ANDRÉS David MADRID	ARG	29/7/81	M	1	(4)	
48	ANÍBAL Araújo CAPELA		8/5/91	D	1		
1	ARTUR Guilherme Gusmão Moraes	BRA	25/1/81	G	18		
27	CUSTÓDIO Miguel Dias Castro		24/5/83	M	10	(3)	1
20	Uwa Elderson ECHIÉJILÉ	NGA	20/1/88	D	20		
85	ELTON Rodrigues Brandão	BRA	1/8/85	A	2	(4)	
40	Luiz FELIPE Ventura Santos	BRA	22/2/84	G	12		
40	GUILHERME Costa Marques	BRA	21/5/91	D	1	(4)	1
10	HELDER Jorge Leal Rodrigues BARBOSA		25/5/87	M	7	(10)	4
45	HUGO Miguel Ferreira VIANA		15/1/83	M	17	(6)	3
4	Claudiano Bezerra Silva "KÁKÁ"	BRA	16/5/81	D	11	(1)	
11	Ladji KEITA	SEN	29/4/83	A	4		1
25	LEANDRO SALINO Carmo	BRA	22/4/85	M	12	(7)	1
16	LEOnardo FORTUNATO Santos	BRA	14/3/83	M	2		
18	Rodrigo José LIMA Santos	BRA	11/8/83	A	25	(3)	6
10	LUÍS Bernardo AGUIAR Burgos	URU	17/11/85	M	9	(3)	2
99	MATHEUS Leite do Nascimento	BRA	15/1/83	A	9	(4)	2
19	Albert MEYONG Zé	CMR	19/10/80	A	2	(13)	3
15	MIGUEL Ângelo Moita GARCIA		4/2/83	D	16	(2)	
5	MOISÉS Moura Pinheiro	BRA	25/7/79	D	13		1
8	José Márcio Costa "MOSSORÓ"	BRA	4/7/83	A	12	(9)	3
3	Paulo Afonso Santos Júnior "PAULÃO"	BRA	6/8/82	D	17	(2)	2
9	PAULO CÉSAR Rocha Rosa	BRA	5/1/80	A	15	(6)	5
2	Alberto Junior RODRÍGUEZ Valdelomar	PER	31/3/84	D	17	(1)	
28	SÍLVIO Manuel Azevedo Ferreira Sá Pereira		28/9/87	D	20		1
7	André Filipe Alves Monteiro "UKRA"		16/3/88	A	12		2
88	Vanderson Válter de Almeida "VANDINHO"	BRA	15/2/78	M	21	(2)	
6	VINÍCIUS Oliveira Franco	BRA	16/5/86	D	1	(2)	

CS MARÍTIMO

Coach – Mitchell van der Gaag (NED); (15/9/10) Pedro Martins
Founded – 1910
Stadium – Barreiros (8,922)
MAJOR HONOURS: Portuguese Cup – (1) 1926.

2010				
14/8	Setúbal	h	0-1	
22/8	Sporting	a	0-1	
29/8	Braga	a	0-1	
12/9	Paços Ferreira	h	1-1	*Kléber*
18/9	Beira-Mar	a	1-1	*Baba Diawara*
25/9	Benfica	h	0-1	
3/10	Rio Ave	a	0-0	
24/10	Naval	h	1-0	*Roberge*
31/10	Olhanense	a	1-1	*Kléber*
7/11	Leiria	h	1-1	*Kléber*
12/11	Nacional	a	0-0	
27/11	Guimarães	h	2-0	*Kléber (p), Baba Diawara*
8/12	Académica	a	5-1	*Tchô (p), Baba Diawara, Marquinho 2, Kanu*
19/12	Portimonense	h	1-1	*Tchô (p)*
2011				
8/1	Porto	a	1-4	*Baba Diawara*
16/1	Setúbal	a	4-2	*Sidnei, Baba Diawara 2, João Guilherme*
24/1	Sporting	h	0-3	
5/2	Braga	h	1-2	*Baba Diawara*
13/2	Paços Ferreira	a	0-1	
20/2	Beira-Mar	h	1-0	*Baba Diawara*
27/2	Benfica	a	1-2	*Djalma*
6/3	Rio Ave	h	0-1	
13/3	Naval	a	3-0	*Kléber, Djalma, Baba Diawara*
20/3	Olhanense	h	4-0	*Baba Diawara, Benachour 2, Djalma*
1/4	Leiria	a	3-1	*Kléber 2, Djalma*
8/4	Nacional	h	1-1	*Djalma*
16/4	Guimarães	a	0-2	
1/5	Académica	h	1-0	*Baba Diawara*
8/5	Portimonense	a	0-1	
15/5	Porto	h	0-2	

No	Name	Nat	DoB	Pos	Aps	(s)	Gls
20	ADILSON Tibes Granemann	BRA	1/1/82	A	1		
2	ALONSO Ferreira de Matos	BRA	11/8/80	D	17	(5)	
35	Papa BABAcar DIAWARA	SEN	5/1/88	A	29		11
81	Salim BENACHOUR	FRA	8/9/81	M	9	(2)	2
21	Nuno Miguel Pereira Souza "BRIGUEL"		8/3/79	D	12		
16	Abdelmalek CHERRAD	ALG	14/1/81	A	1	(4)	
30	DANILO Leandro DIAS	BRA	6/11/85	A	12	(9)	
17	DJALMA Braume Manuel Abel Campos	ANG	30/5/87	A	23	(4)	5
33	Dylan Ludovic DUVENTRU Huret	FRA	3/1/89	A		(1)	
28	Arnaldo Edi Lopes Silva "EDINHO"		7/7/82	A	2	(7)	
40	EDIVÂNDIO Sequeira Reis	CPV	1/1/91	A		(2)	
31	Philipe FIDELIS dos Santos	BRA	14/6/89	M		(4)	
26	HELDON Augusto Almeida Ramos	CPV	1/1/88	A	3	(12)	
43	IGOR Rossi Branco	BRA	10/3/89	D	1		
44	JOÃO GUILHERME Leme Amorin	BRA	21/4/86	M	10	(4)	1
11	Elias de Oliveira Rosa "KANU"	BRA	8/2/83	A	2	(5)	1
22	KLÉBER Laube Pinheiro	BRA	2/5/90	A	15	(3)	7
27	LUCIANO AMARAL Silva Alves	BRA	20/10/82	D	21	(1)	
18	LUÍS Miguel OLIM Andrade		22/8/81	D		(1)	
99	Vangelis MANTZIOS	GRE	22/4/83	A	1		
49	Sérgio Romeo MARAKIS		11/11/91	M		(1)	
1	MARCELO Boeck	BRA	28/11/84	G	30		
39	Marco Aurélio Lubel "MARQUINHO"	BRA	8/7/86	A	9	(3)	2
25	RAFAEL MIRANDA Conceição	BRA	11/8/84	M	27	(2)	
6	RICARDO Filipe Santos ESTEVES		18/9/79	D	17	(3)	
16	Valentin Sébastien ROBERGE	FRA	9/6/87	D	23	(2)	1
26	ROBERTO de SOUSA Resende	BRA	18/1/85	M	18	(3)	
6	ROBSON Severino da Silva	BRA	10/7/83	D	26		
54	SIDNEI dos Santos Reis Mariano	CPV	21/4/86	M	12	(3)	1
23	Valdecir Souza Júnior "TCHÔ"	BRA	21/4/87	A	9	(9)	2

CD NACIONAL

Coach – Predrag Jokanović (SRB); (13/3/11) Ivo Vieira
Founded – 1910
Stadium – Madeira (5,132)

2010				
15/8	Rio Ave	a	1-0	*Felipe Lopes*
21/8	Benfica	h	2-1	*Luís Alberto, Orlando Sá*
28/8	Guimarães	h	1-3	*Bruno Amaro*
12/9	Leiria	a	1-2	*Juninho*
20/9	Porto	h	0-2	
26/9	Sporting	a	1-1	*Danielson*
3/10	Portimonense	h	3-1	*Claudemir 2 (1p), Edgar Costa*
23/10	Académica	a	1-2	*Danielson*
31/10	Setúbal	h	1-0	*Orlando Sá*
6/11	Paços Ferreira	a	1-0	*Mateus*
12/11	Marítimo	h	0-0	
28/11	Braga	a	0-2	
7/12	Naval	h	2-1	*Claudemir (p), Nuno Pinto*
19/12	Olhanense	a	0-0	
2011				
9/1	Beira-Mar	h	0-0	
16/1	Rio Ave	h	1-0	*Diego Barcellos*
22/1	Benfica	a	2-4	*Luís Alberto, Mihelič*
26/1	Porto	a	0-3	
6/2	Guimarães	a	0-0	
12/2	Leiria	h	0-1	
27/2	Sporting	h	1-0	*Mateus*
7/3	Portimonense	a	1-1	*Školnik*
13/3	Académica	h	1-1	*Orlando Sá*
20/3	Setúbal	a	1-2	*Anselmo*
3/4	Paços Ferreira	h	1-0	*Edgar Costa*
8/4	Marítimo	a	1-1	*Diego Barcelos*
18/4	Braga	h	1-1	*Luís Alberto*
1/5	Naval	a	2-1	*Diego Barcelos, Claudemir (p)*
8/5	Olhanense	h	0-1	
15/5	Beira-Mar	a	2-0	*Diego Barcelos, Edgar Costa*

No	Name	Nat	DoB	Pos	Aps	(s)	Gls
18	ANSELMO Gonçalves Cardoso		6/1/84	A	5	(11)	1
14	Darko BODUL	CRO	11/1/89	M	1	(3)	
13	BRUNO AMARO Sousa Barros		17/2/83	M	18	(7)	1
22	CLAUDEMIR Ferreira Silva	BRA	17/8/84	D	20	(1)	4
33	DANIELSON Ferreira Trindade	BRA	9/1/81	D	30		2
19	DIEGO Lima BARCELOS	BRA	5/4/85	A	23	(1)	4
17	José EDGAR Andrade COSTA		14/4/87	A	17	(8)	3
3	FELIPE Aliste LOPES	BRA	7/8/87	D	30		1
23	JOÃO Miguel Coimbra AURÉLIO		17/8/88	A	8	(11)	
83	Júnior César Arcanjo "JUNINHO"	BRA	11/1/83	M	1	(3)	1
8	LUÍS ALBERTO Silva dos Santos	BRA	17/11/83	M	25		3
11	MÁRCIO André Encarnação MADEIRA		19/8/85	M		(4)	
31	MATEUS Galiano da Costa	ANG	19/6/84	A	17	(6)	2
7	Rene MIHELIČ	SVN	5/7/88	M	9	(5)	1

No	Name	Nat	DoB	Pos	Aps	(s)	Gls
5	NUNO Miguel Sousa PINTO		6/8/86	D	15	(1)	1
	ORLANDO Carlos Braga SÁ		26/5/88	A	11	(5)	3
	Bruno Alexandre dos Santos PATACAS		30/11/77	D	10	(2)	
0	Nejc PEČNIK	SVN	3/1/86	M	4	(5)	
9	PEDRO Henrique OLDONI Nascimento	BRA	26/9/85	A	1		
	RAFAEL Wibhi BRACALLI	BRA	5/5/81	G	30		
6	RICARDO Miguel Coelho FERNANDES		29/9/91	M		(1)	
	Dejan ŠKOLNIK	SVN	1/1/89	M	25	(1)	1
	Danijel STOJANOVIĆ	CRO	18/8/84	D	7	(1)	
7	THIAGO GENTIL	BRA	8/4/80	M	8	(2)	
5	Ivan TODOROVIĆ	SRB	29/7/83	M	11	(5)	
4	Žarko TOMAŠEVIĆ	MNE	22/2/90	D	4	(5)	

A. NAVAL 1° MAIO

Coach – Victor Zvunka (FRA); (26/9/10) (Fernando Mira); (10/10/10) Rogério Gonçalves; (23/12/10) Carlos Mozer (BRA)

Founded – 1893

Stadium – Municipal José Bento Pessoa (9,116)

2010				
14/8	Porto	h	0-1	
22/8	Portimonense	a	1-0	*Godemèche*
30/8	Sporting	h	1-3	*João Pedro*
12/9	Académica	a	0-3	
19/9	Setúbal	h	0-0	
24/9	Braga	a	1-3	*Fábio Júnior*
3/10	Paços Ferreira	h	1-2	*João Pedro*
24/10	Marítimo	a	0-1	
31/10	Beira-Mar	a	1-3	*Bolívia*
7/11	Olhanense	h	1-1	*Bolívia*
14/11	Benfica	a	0-4	
28/11	Rio Ave	h	0-1	
7/12	Nacional	a	1-2	*Camora*
19/12	Leiria	h	0-3	
2011				
9/1	Guimarães	a	2-1	*Fábio Júnior, Marinho*
16/1	Porto	a	1-3	*Gomis (p)*
22/1	Portimonense	h	1-1	*Previtali*
4/2	Sporting	a	3-3	*Fábio Júnior (p), Michel Simplício, Godemèche*
13/2	Académica	h	3-1	*Gomis (p), Michel Simplício, Giuliano Amaral*
20/2	Setúbal	a	1-1	*Fábio Júnior*
28/2	Braga	h	0-0	
7/3	Paços Ferreira	a	0-0	
13/3	Marítimo	h	0-3	
20/3	Beira-Mar	h	2-2	*Manuel Curto 2 (2p)*
3/4	Olhanense	a	3-1	*Bruno Moraes 2, Bolívia*
10/4	Benfica	h	2-1	*Bruno Moraes, Marinho*
17/4	Rio Ave	a	0-1	
1/5	Nacional	h	1-2	*Bolívia*
8/5	Leiria	a	0-1	
15/5	Guimarães	h	0-3	

No	Name	Nat	DoB	Pos	Aps	(s)	Gls
11	Edvaldo Rojas Hermoza "BOLÍVIA"	BRA	17/11/85	A	27	(2)	4
24	BRUNO Miguel Silva Jorge		14/8/84	G	1		
99	BRUNO Santos MORAES	BRA	7/7/84	A	3	(6)	3
45	Mário Jorge Malico Paulino "CAMORA"		10/11/86	M	23	(4)	1
7	Carlos Pereira Rodrigues "CARLITOS"		5/12/81	D	27		
6	DANIEL Lopes CRUZ	BRA	1/6/82	D	12		
10	DAVIDE Alexandre Pinto Dias		12/4/83	M		(1)	
28	FÁBIO JÚNIOR dos Santos	BRA	6/10/82	A	18	(5)	4
30	GIULIANO Dias AMARAL	BRA	8/9/80	M	4	(9)	1
25	Nicolas GODEMÈCHE	FRA	22/6/84	M	24		2
16	Manuel Augusto Pinho GODINHO		1/8/85	M	2	(4)	
26	Kevin GOMIS	FRA	20/1/89	M	17	(4)	2
15	Alexandre HAUW	FRA	22/1/82	M	10	(3)	
37	HUGO Miguel Alves MACHADO		4/7/82	M	10	(6)	
20	JOÃO PEDRO Guerra Cunha		13/5/83	M	11	(15)	2
13	JOÃO Daniel Mendes REAL		13/5/83	D	17	(2)	
62	JONATHAS Ricardo Souza Costa	BRA	10/4/85	D	3		
1	JORGE Carlos Santos Moreira BAPTISTA		2/4/77	G	2		
31	JOSÉ MÁRIO Pinto dos Santos		16/7/89	D		(1)	
3	Ulick LUPÈDE	FRA	6/1/84	D	4		
5	MANUEL José Luz CURTO		9/7/86	M	16	(2)	2
77	Mário Rui Correia Tomás "MARINHO"		26/4/83	A	21	(5)	2
9	MICHEL SIMPLÍCIO Rossetto	BRA	26/3/86	A	14	(8)	2
4	ORESTES Junior Alves	BRA	24/3/81	D	13	(1)	
19	Robin Gabriel Gerard PREVITALI	FRA	5/6/87	A	6	(5)	1
91	ROGÉRIO Santos Conceição	BRA	20/9/84	D	16	(2)	
17	Romain Jules SALIN	FRA	29/7/84	G	27		
23	TIAGO Miguel Luís ROSA		6/3/86	D	2		

SC OLHANENSE

Coach – Daúto Faquirá

Founded – 1912

Stadium – José Arcanjo (11,622)

2010				
16/8	Guimarães	h	0-0	
20/8	Académica	a	1-1	*Yontcha (p)*
29/8	Leiria	h	1-0	*Nuno Piloto*
11/9	Sporting	a	0-0	
17/9	Portimonense	h	2-0	*Paulo Sérgio, Djalmir (p)*
25/9	Porto	a	0-2	
2/10	Setúbal	h	3-1	*Maurício, João Gonçalves, Jardel*
23/10	Braga	a	1-3	*Maurício*
31/10	Marítimo	h	1-1	*Yontcha (p)*
7/11	Naval	a	1-1	*Cadu*
14/11	Beira-Mar	h	1-1	*Adilson*
27/11	Paços Ferreira	a	0-1	
3/12	Benfica	a	0-2	
19/12	Nacional	h	0-0	
2011				
9/1	Rio Ave	a	1-0	*Maurício*
15/1	Guimarães	a	0-1	
22/1	Académica	h	2-1	*Nuno Piloto, Rui Duarte*
6/2	Leiria	a	2-0	*Carlos Fernandes, Paulo Sérgio*
13/2	Sporting	h	2-2	*Ismaily, og (Daniel Carriço)*
19/2	Portimonense	a	1-1	*Djalmir (p)*
27/2	Porto	h	0-3	
6/3	Setúbal	a	0-0	
20/3	Marítimo	a	0-4	
27/3	Braga	h	0-2	
3/4	Naval	h	1-3	*Djalmir*
10/4	Beira-Mar	a	0-1	
16/4	Paços Ferreira	h	0-0	
1/5	Benfica	h	1-1	*Djalmir*
8/5	Nacional	a	1-0	*Toy*
15/5	Rio Ave	h	2-2	*Yontcha, Dady*

T

No	Name	Nat	DoB	Pos	Aps	(s)	Gls
17	ADILSON Tibes Granemann	BRA	1/1/82	A	6	(7)	1
4	ANDRÉ MICAEL Pereira		4/2/89	D	4	(1)	
2	ANSELMO França Almeida	BRA	10/6/81	D	4	(2)	
1	BRUNO Miguel Ribeiro VERÍSSIMO		7/4/76	G	6	(1)	
14	Carlos Eduardo Castro Silva "CADU"	BRA	23/4/82	D	9	(10)	1
13	CARLOS Miguel Brandão FERNANDES		5/5/78	D	23		1
21	Esteban Andrés CARVAJAL Tapia	CHI	17/11/88	A		(2)	

No	Name	Nat	DoB	Pos	Aps	(s)	Gls
20	Eduardo Fernando Pereira Gomes "DADY"	CPV	13/8/91	A	5	(3)	1
27	DELSON Ferreira	BRA	26/7/80	M	7	(2)	
11	DJALMIR Vieira de Andrade	BRA	22/3/76	A	9	(12)	4
65	FERNANDO José Ribeiro ALEXANDRE		2/8/85	M	25	(1)	
7	ISMAILY Santos Gonçalves	BRA	11/1/90	D	13	(5)	1
3	JARDEL Nivaldo Vieira	BRA	29/3/86	D	16		1
18	JOÃO Pedro Espírito Santo GONÇALVES		18/1/88	M	22		1
19	JORGE Miguel Dias GONÇALVES		31/10/83	A	26	(3)	
10	Luís Marcelo Morais Reis "LULINHA"	BRA	10/4/90	A	2	(11)	
5	MAURÍCIO Fernandes	BRA	5/7/76	D	26	(1)	3
30	Adson Andre Sitoe "MEXER"	MOZ	8/9/88	D	13	(2)	
31	Marcelo MORETTO Souza	BRA	10/5/78	G	13		
6	NUNO Miguel Torres PILOTO		19/3/82	M	19	(1)	2
23	PAULO SÉRGIO Moreira Gonçalves		24/1/84	A	23	(1)	2
45	PAVEL Pinho Vieira	GUI	15/2/92	M		(1)	
51	RICARDO Jorge Cecília BATISTA		19/11/86	G	11		
16	RUI PedroViegas Silva Gomes DUARTE		16/9/78	M	14	(9)	1
27	Cristian Fernando SUÁREZ Figueroa	CHI	6/2/87	D	6	(2)	
35	William Kwabena TIERO	GHA	3/12/80	M	2	(2)	
9	Vítor Manuel Andrade Gomes Costa "TOY"	CPV	15/6/77	A	5	(11)	1
6	VINÍCIUS Oliveira Franco	BRA	16/5/86	M	12		
99	Jean Paul YONTCHA	CMR	14/5/83	A	9	(10)	3

FC PAÇOS DE FERREIRA

Coach – Rui Vitória

Founded – 1950

Stadium – Mata Real (5,172)

2010				
14/8	Sporting	h	1-0	*Rondón*
22/8	Leiria	a	0-0	
29/8	Portimonense	h	2-2	*Jorginho, Pizzi*
12/9	Marítimo	a	1-1	*Nelson Oliveira*
19/9	Braga	h	2-2	*Baiano, Cohene*
27/9	Setúbal	a	0-1	
3/10	Naval	a	2-1	*Rondón, Nelson Oliveira*
23/10	Beira-Mar	h	1-1	*Baiano*
29/10	Benfica	a	0-2	
6/11	Nacional	h	0-1	
14/11	Rio Ave	a	1-3	*Rondón*
27/11	Olhanense	h	1-0	*André Leão*
4/12	Guimarães	a	1-1	*Nelson Oliveira*
19/12	Porto	h	0-3	
2011				
9/1	Académica	a	0-0	
15/1	Sporting	a	3-2	*Samuel, Manuel José (p), Pizzi*
22/1	Leiria	h	1-1	*Pizzi*
6/2	Portimonense	a	1-0	*Nelson Oliveira*
13/2	Marítimo	h	1-0	*Rondón*
20/2	Braga	a	2-1	*Manuel José, og (Sílvio)*
27/2	Setúbal	h	2-0	*Rondón, Filipe Anunciação*
7/3	Naval	h	0-0	
11/3	Beira-Mar	a	1-3	*Rondón*
21/3	Benfica	h	1-5	*og (Carole)*
3/4	Nacional	a	0-1	
10/4	Rio Ave	h	1-6	*Rondón*
16/4	Olhanense	a	0-0	
1/5	Guimarães	h	2-1	*Leonel Olímpio (p), Caetano*
8/5	Porto	a	3-3	*Pizzi 3*
15/5	Académica	h	5-1	*Rondón 2, Ozéia, og (Diogo Valente), Pizzi*

No	Name	Nat	DoB	Pos	Aps	(s)	Gls
70	Álvaro Ricardo Faustino Gomes "ALVARINHO"		3/9/90	M		(1)	
21	Pádraig AMOND	IRL	15/4/88	A		(17)	
50	ANDRÉ Filipe Ribeiro LEÃO		20/5/85	M	23	(2)	1
15	Wanderson de Souza Carneiro "BAIANO"	BRA	23/2/87	D	28		2
30	BRUNO Flávio DI PAULA	BRA	5/2/89	M	7	(3)	
13	Miguel Angelo Marques Granja "BURA"		17/12/88	D	10	(3)	
11	Rui Miguel Teixeira CAETANO		20/4/91	A	7	(8)	1
1	CÁSSIO Abuquerque dos Anjos	BRA	12/8/80	G	29		
84	Júlio Manuel Pires COELHO		18/7/84	G	1		
5	Javier António COHENE Mereles	PAR	3/5/87	M	22	(1)	1
10	DAVID Martins SIMÃO		15/5/90	M	19	(6)	
96	FILIPE Alexandre Dias ANUNCIAÇÃO		27/5/79	D	11	(4)	1
14	Jorge Manuel Amador Galufo "JORGINHO"		29/5/78	D	13		1
16	LEONEL OLÍMPIO	BRA	7/7/82	M	28		1
21	LUCAS Espindola Silva	BRA	6/5/90	A		(2)	
81	MANUEL JOSÉ Azevedo Vieira		4/2/81	A	27		2
7	MAYKON Daniel Elias Araújo	BRA	20/4/84	D	18	(3)	
24	NELSON Miguel Castro OLIVEIRA		8/8/91	A	10	(13)	4
45	António Filipe NORINHO Carvalho		14/4/85	G		(1)	
17	NUNO Filipe Oliveira SANTOS		19/6/80	A	4	(10)	
2	OZÉIA de Paula Maciel	BRA	2/1/82	D	13		1
6	José PAULO SOUSA Silva		13/5/75	M	1		
20	PEDRO Miguel Barbosa QUEIRÓS		8/8/84	D	2	(2)	
31	Luís Miguel Afonso Fernandes "PIZZI"		6/10/89	A	22	(5)	7
20	ROMEU Freitas Torres		7/9/86	M		(1)	
19	Mario Junior RONDÓN Fernández	VEN	26/3/86	A	24	(3)	9
4	SAMUEL Elias Carmo Soares	BRA	7/3/88	D	11		1

PORTIMONENSE SC

Coach – Luís Carvalha "Litos"; (29/12/10) Carlos Azenha

Founded – 1914

Stadium – Municipal (5,047)

2010				
13/8	Braga	a	1-3	*Elias*
22/8	Naval	h	0-1	
29/8	Paços Ferreira	a	2-2	*Ivanildo, André Pinto*
12/9	Rio Ave	h	3-1	*Kadi, Pedro Moreira, Candeias*
17/9	Olhanense	a	0-2	
26/9	Beira-Mar	h	1-0	*Peña*
3/10	Nacional	a	1-3	*Jumisse*
24/10	Benfica	h	0-1	
1/11	Guimarães	a	0-2	
6/11	Académica	h	2-2	*Renatinho, Nilson*
14/11	Porto	a	0-2	
29/11	Leiria	h	1-2	*Lito*
5/12	Sporting	h	1-3	*Pires*
19/12	Marítimo	a	1-1	*og (Rafael Miranda)*
2010				
7/1	Setúbal	h	3-4	*Lito, Pires, Ricardo Pessoa (p)*
14/1	Braga	h	0-3	
22/1	Naval	a	1-1	*Ivanildo*
6/2	Paços Ferreira	h	0-1	
13/2	Rio Ave	a	0-2	
19/2	Olhanense	h	1-1	*Lito*
27/2	Beira-Mar	a	1-0	*Ricardo Pessoa (p)*
7/3	Nacional	h	1-1	*Pedro Moreira*
13/3	Benfica	a	1-1	*Ricardo Pessoa (p)*
18/3	Guimarães	h	2-1	*André Pinto, Pires*

2/4	Académica	a	0-1	
10/4	Porto	h	2-3	*Rúben, Mourad*
17/4	Leiria	a	1-0	*Pedro Silva (I)*
1/5	Sporting	a	1-2	*Pires*
8/5	Marítimo	h	1-0	*Ivanildo*
15/5	Setúbal	a	1-3	*Pedro Silva (I)*

No	Name	Nat	DoB	Pos	Aps	(s)	Gls
3	ANDRÉ PINTO Almeida		5/10/89	D	26		2
28	ANDRÉ Filipe Monteiro VILAS BOAS		4/6/83	M	3	(1)	
10	ARAGONEY Silva Santos	BRA	7/3/87	M	1	(2)	
22	Daniel João Santos CANDEIAS		25/2/88	A	27	(1)	1
4	João Paulo DI FÁBIO	BRA	10/2/79	D	14	(1)	
18	DONG Fangzhuo	CHN	23/1/85	A		(3)	
8	ELIAS Alves Silva	BRA	4/9/81	M	21	(3)	1
70	HÉLDER Fernando Ferreira CASTRO		24/1/86	M	6	(4)	
9	IVANILDO Soares Cassama	GNB	9/1/86	A	14	(5)	3
2	JOÃO PAULO Santos Oliveira Gomes	BRA	25/2/89	D	3		
7	Eduardo Tomás Luís JUMISSE	MOZ	6/6/84	M	13	(1)	1
21	Matome Calvin KADI	RSA	12/12/87	A	16	(6)	1
11	Cláudio Zélito Fonseca Fernandes Aguiar "LITO"	CPV	3/2/75	A	15	(7)	3
82	George MOURAD	SYR	18/9/82	A	1	(4)	1
16	NILSON António Veiga Barros	CPV	5/8/87	M	11	(1)	1
99	PATRICK Leonardo Carneiro Silva	BRA	23/8/90	A	2	(6)	
66	PEDRO Joaquim Fortunato MOITA		14/12/79	M		(1)	
15	PEDRO Manuel Silva MOREIRA		15/3/89	M	9	(12)	2
19	PEDRO Alves SILVA (I)	BRA	25/4/84	D	21		2
24	PEDRO Manuel Freitas SILVA (II)		18/2/74	G	2		
30	Helder Justino PELEMBE	MOZ	20/9/87	A	3	(8)	
23	Louis Angelo PEÑA	VEN	25/12/89	A	2	(3)	1
20	Jorge Costa PIRES		4/4/81	A	11	(10)	4
77	Renato Carlos Martins Júnior "RENATINHO"	BRA	14/5/87	A	4	(1)	1
29	RICARDO Santos NASCIMENTO	BRA	7/2/87	D	13		
5	RICARDO Jorge Rodrigues PESSOA		5/2/82	D	29		3
26	RÚBEN Miguel Santos Fernandes		6/5/86	D	19	(1)	1
25	William SOARES Silva	BRA	30/12/88	M	15	(6)	
1	Hugo VENTURA Ferreira Moura Guedes		19/1/88	G	28		
13	Alhassan WAKASO	GHA	7/1/82	D	1	(3)	

FC PORTO

Coach – André Villas-Boas

Founded – 1893

Stadium – Dragão (50,476)

MAJOR HONOURS: European Champion Clubs' Cup/UEFA Champions League – (2) 1987, 2004; UEFA Cup – (1) 2003; UEFA Europa League – (1) 2011; UEFA Super Cup – (1) 1987; World Club Cup – (2) 1987, 2004; Portuguese League – (25) 1935, 1939, 1940, 1956, 1959, 1978, 1979, 1985, 1986, 1988, 1990, 1992, 1993, 1995, 1996, 1997, 1998, 1999, 2003, 2004, 2006, 2007, 2008, 2009, 2011; Portuguese Cup – (20) 1922, 1925, 1932, 1937, 1956, 1958, 1968, 1977, 1984, 1988, 1991, 1994, 1998, 2000, 2001, 2003, 2006, 2009, 2010, 2011.

2010				
14/8	Naval	a	1-0	*Hulk (p)*
22/8	Beira-Mar	h	3-0	*Falcao 2, Belluschi*
29/8	Rio Ave	a	2-0	*Hulk 2*
11/9	Braga	h	3-2	*Varela 2, Hulk*
20/9	Nacional	a	2-0	*og (João Aurélio), Varela*
25/9	Olhanense	h	2-0	*Otamendi, Hulk*
4/10	Guimarães	a	1-1	*Hulk*
25/10	Leiria	h	5-1	*Hulk 2, Varela, Falcao 2*
30/10	Académica	a	1-0	*Varela*
7/11	Benfica	h	5-0	*Varela, Falcao 2, Hulk 2 (1p)*
14/11	Portimonense	h	2-0	*Walter, Hulk (p)*
27/11	Sporting	a	1-1	*Falcao*
6/12	Setúbal	h	1-0	*Hulk*
19/12	Paços Ferreira	a	3-0	*Otamendi, Hulk (p), Walter*
2011				
8/1	Marítimo	h	4-1	*Guarín 2, Hulk, Rodríguez J.*
16/1	Naval	h	3-1	*Falcao, Hulk 2*
22/1	Beira-Mar	a	1-0	*Hulk (p)*
26/1	Nacional	h	3-0	*Hulk 2, Rodríguez J.*
6/2	Rio Ave	h	1-0	*Varela*
13/2	Braga	a	2-0	*Otamendi 2*
27/2	Olhanense	a	3-0	*Belluschi, Falcao 2*
5/3	Guimarães	h	2-0	*Falcao, Rodríguez C.*
14/3	Leiria	a	2-0	*Guarín, Hulk (p)*
20/3	Académica	h	3-1	*Guarín, Maicon, Varela*
3/4	Benfica	a	2-1	*Guarín, Hulk (p)*
10/4	Portimonense	a	3-2	*Hulk, Falcao, Maicon*
17/4	Sporting	h	3-2	*Falcao 2, Walter*
1/5	Setúbal	a	4-0	*og (Valdomiro), Otamendi, Walter, Varela*
8/5	Paços Ferreira	h	3-3	*Falcao 2, Hulk*
15/5	Marítimo	a	2-0	*Varela, Walter*

No	Name	Nat	DoB	Pos	Aps	(s)	Gls
15	ÁLVARO Daniel PEREIRA Barragán	URU	28/1/85	D	21		
7	Fernando Daniel BELLUSCHI	ARG	10/9/83	M	23	(3)	2
24	António Alberto Bastos Pimparel "BETO"		1/5/82	G	5	(1)	
26	André CASTRO Pereira		2/4/88	M		(1)	
15	EMÍDIO RAFAEL Augusto Silva		24/1/86	D	5		
9	Radamel FALCAO García Zárate	COL	10/2/86	A	22		16
25	FERNANDO Francisco Reges	BRA	25/7/87	M	18	(3)	
13	Jorge Ciro FUCILE Perdomo	URU	19/11/84	D	11	(5)	
6	Freddy Alejandro GUARÍN Vásquez	COL	30/6/86	M	12	(10)	5
1	HÉLTON da Silva Arruda	BRA	18/5/78	G	25		
12	Givanildo Vieira de Souza "HULK"	BRA	25/7/86	A	26		23
8	JOÃO Filipe Iria Santos MOUTINHO		8/9/86	M	26	(1)	
31	Paweł KIESZEK	POL	16/4/84	G		(1)	
4	MAICON Pereira Roque	BRA	14/9/88	D	18	(3)	2
11	MARIANO Nicolás GONZÁLEZ	ARG	5/5/81	A	1	(9)	
30	Nicolás Hernan OTAMENDI	ARG	12/2/88	D	13	(2)	5
10	Cristian Gabriel RODRÍGUEZ Barroti	URU	30/9/85	A	1	(12)	1
19	James David RODRÍGUEZ Rubio	COL	12/7/91	A	10	(5)	2
14	ROLANDO Jorge Pires da Fonseca		31/8/85	D	29		
28	RÚBEN MICAEL Freitas da Ressurreição		19/8/86	M	8	(11)	
21	Ionuţ Cristian SĂPUNARU	ROU	5/4/84	D	18	(1)	
16	Henrique SERENO Fonseca		18/5/85	D	5	(2)	
23	Josef SOUZA Dias	BRA	11/2/89	M	4	(8)	
27	André Filipe Alves Monteiro "UKRA"		16/3/88	A	1	(1)	
17	Silvestre Manuel Gonçalves VARELA		2/2/85	A	25	(1)	10
18	WALTER Henrique da Silva	BRA	22/7/89	A	3	(10)	5

RIO AVE FC

Coach – Carlos Brito
Founded – 1939
Stadium – Rio Ave (12,815)

2010			
15/8	Nacional	h 0-1	
23/8	Guimarães	a 0-0	
29/8	Porto	h 0-2	
12/9	Portimonense	a 1-3	*Yazalde*
19/9	Académica	h 2-2	*João Tomás 2*
26/9	Leiria	a 0-1	
3/10	Marítimo	h 0-0	
24/10	Sporting	a 0-1	
30/10	Braga	h 2-0	*Zé Gomes, João Tomás*
5/11	Setúbal	a 3-3	*Yazalde, João Tomás 2*
14/11	Paços Ferreira	h 3-1	*João Tomás 2, Braga*
28/11	Naval	a 1-0	*Bruno Gama*
5/12	Beira-Mar	h 1-1	*Yazalde*
18/12	Benfica	a 2-5	*João Tomás 2 (1p)*
2011			
9/1	Olhanense	h 0-1	
16/1	Nacional	a 0-1	
22/1	Guimarães	h 2-3	*João Tomás 2*
6/2	Porto	a 0-1	
13/2	Portimonense	h 2-0	*João Tomás, Yazalde*
20/2	Académica	a 1-0	*Bruno Gama*
27/2	Leiria	h 1-0	*João Tomás*
6/3	Marítimo	a 1-0	*Braga*
12/3	Sporting	h 0-0	
21/3	Braga	a 0-1	
3/4	Setúbal	h 2-0	*Yazalde, Saúlo*
10/4	Paços Ferreira	a 6-1	*João Tomás 2 (1p), Braga, Saúlo 2, Tarantini*
17/4	Naval	h 1-0	*Milhazes*
1/5	Beira-Mar	a 1-1	*Tarantini*
8/5	Benfica	h 1-2	*Braga*
15/5	Olhanense	a 2-2	*Yazalde, João Tomás*

No	Name	Nat	DoB	Pos	Aps	(s)	Gls
22	ANDRÉ Filipe Aguiar DIAS		18/4/92	D		(1)	
11	Bruno Manuel Araújo BRAGA		17/6/83	A	11	(10)	4
14	BRUNO Manuel Rodrigues Silva "CHINA"		5/8/82	M	14		
7	BRUNO Alexandre Vilela GAMA		15/11/87	A	27	(2)	2
26	CÍCERO Casimiro Sanches Semedo	GNB	8/5/86	A	1	(12)	
33	EDER Monteiro Fernandes	BRA	21/9/83	D	8	(1)	
81	FÁBIO Alexandre Duarte FELÍCIO		2/5/82	M	3	(4)	
2	José GASPAR da Silva Azevedo		1/6/75	D	26		
5	JEFERSON Miguel da Silva	BRA	15/1/86	D	19		
9	JOÃO Henrique Pataco TOMÁS		27/5/75	A	29		16
6	JÚLIO Regufe ALVES		29/6/91	M	3	(6)	
89	José LIONN Barbosa Lucena	BRA	29/1/89	D	7		
24	MÁRIO Jorge Quintas FELGUEIRAS		12/12/86	G	7	(1)	
13	João Pedro Moreira MENDES		22/3/88	A	1	(8)	
25	Carlos Alberto Moreira MILHAZES		17/3/81	D	9	(1)	1
37	PAULO Jorge Silva SANTOS		11/12/72	G	23		
3	RICARDO Alberto Medeiro CHAVES		27/10/77	M	13	(1)	
17	SAÚLO Rodrigues Santos		18/2/82	A	8	(11)	3
19	SIDNEI Sciola Moraes	BRA	2/11/86	A		(9)	
8	Ricardo José Vaz Monteiro "TARANTINI"		7/10/83	M	26	(2)	2
15	TIAGO Miguel Baía PINTO		1/2/88	D	19	(3)	
1	Pedro José Silva TRIGUEIRA		4/1/88	G		(1)	
10	VÍTOR Hugo GOMES da Silva		25/12/87	M	9	(9)	
30	WIRES José de Souza	BRA	30/12/82	M	24	(1)	
88	YAZALDE Pinto Gomes		10/9/88	A	24	(4)	6
18	José "ZÉ" Manuel GOMES da Silva		24/9/76	D	19	(1)	1

SPORTING CLUBE DE PORTUGAL

Coach – Paulo Sérgio; (26/2/11) José Couceiro
Founded – 1906
Stadium – José Alvalade (50,466)
MAJOR HONOURS: UEFA Cup Winners' Cup – (1) 1964; Portuguese League – (18) 1941, 1944, 1947, 1948, 1949, 1951, 1952, 1953, 1954, 1958, 1962, 1966, 1970, 1974, 1980, 1982, 2000, 2002; Portuguese Cup – (19) 1923, 1934, 1936, 1938, 1941, 1945, 1946, 1948, 1954, 1963, 1971, 1973, 1974, 1978, 1982, 1995, 2002, 2007, 2008.

2010			
14/8	Paços Ferreira	a 0-1	
22/8	Marítimo	h 1-0	*Matías Fernández (p)*
30/8	Naval	a 3-1	*Liedson, Matías Fernández (p), Yannick Djaló*
11/9	Olhanense	h 0-0	
19/9	Benfica	a 0-2	
26/9	Nacional	h 1-1	*Carlos Saleiro*
4/10	Beira-Mar	a 1-1	*João Pereira*
24/10	Rio Ave	h 1-0	*Abel*
31/10	Leiria	a 2-1	*Valdés 2*
8/11	Guimarães	h 2-3	*Hélder Postiga, Vukčević*
13/11	Académica	a 2-1	*Valdés (p), Vukčević*
27/11	Porto	h 1-1	*Valdés*
5/12	Portimonense	a 3-1	*Hélder Postiga, Maniche, André Santos*
20/12	Setúbal	a 3-0	*Yannick Djaló 2, Abel*
2011			
8/1	Braga	h 2-1	*Diogo Salomão, Valdés*
15/1	Paços Ferreira	h 2-3	*Liedson, Diogo Salomão*
24/1	Marítimo	a 3-0	*Zapater 2, Liedson*
6/2	Naval	h 3-3	*Liedson 2, Hélder Postiga (p)*
13/2	Olhanense	a 2-2	*Hélder Postiga 2*
20/2	Benfica	h 0-2	
27/2	Nacional	a 0-1	
6/3	Beira-Mar	h 1-0	*Matías Fernández (p)*
12/3	Rio Ave	a 0-0	
19/3	Leiria	h 0-0	
3/4	Guimarães	a 1-1	*Matías Fernández (p)*
10/4	Académica	h 2-0	*Yannick Djaló 2*
17/4	Porto	a 2-3	*André Santos, Matías Fernández*
1/5	Portimonense	h 2-1	*Hélder Postiga, João Pereira*
8/5	Setúbal	h 0-1	
15/5	Braga	a 1-0	*Yannick Djaló*

No	Name	Nat	DoB	Pos	Aps	(s)	Gls
78	ABEL Fernando Moreira Ferreira		22/12/78	D	10	(2)	2
4	ANDERSON Corrêa POLGA	BRA	9/2/79	D	19	(1)	
26	ANDRÉ Filipe Bernardes SANTOS		20/3/89	M	26		2
9	CARLOS Miguel Mondim SALEIRO		25/2/86	A		(27)	1
41	CÉDRIC Ricardo Alves Soares		31/8/91	D	2		
80	CRISTIANO Moraes Oliveira	BRA	28/9/83	A	1	(3)	
3	DANIEL Filipe Martins CARRIÇO		4/8/88	D	24		
33	DIOGO Ferreira SALOMÃO		14/9/88	A	5	(7)	2
5	EVALDO Santos Fabiano	BRA	18/3/82	D	29		
18	Leandro Damián Marcelo GRIMI	ARG	2/9/85	D	1	(1)	
23	HÉLDER Manuel Marques POSTIGA		2/8/82	A	23	(2)	6
7	Marat IZMAILOV	RUS	21/9/82	A	2	(1)	
21	JOÃO Pedro da Silva PEREIRA		25/2/84	D	23	(1)	2
31	LIEDSON da Silva Muniz		17/12/77	A	14		5

3	Nuno Ricardo Oliveira Ribeiro "MANICHE"		11/11/77	M	14	(3)	1
14	MATÍAS Ariel Fernández FERNÁNDEZ	CHI	15/5/86	M	16	(5)	5
44	NUNO André Silva COELHO		7/1/86	D	7	(2)	
2	PEDRO Miguel da Silva MENDES		26/2/79	M	6	(1)	
1	RUI Pedro dos Santos PATRÍCIO		15/2/88	G	30		
2	Marco Natanel TORSIGLIERI	ARG	12/1/88	D	13	(3)	
15	Jaime Andrés VALDÉS Zapata	CHI	11/1/81	A	17	(7)	5
10	Simon VUKČEVIĆ	MNE	29/1/86	A	15	(9)	2
20	YANNICK dos Santos DJALÓ		5/5/86	A	17	(4)	6
49	WILLIAM Silva CARVALHO		7/4/92	M		(1)	
21	Albert ZAPATER Arjol	ESP	13/6/85	M	16	(6)	2

UD LEIRIA

Coach – Pedro Caixinha

Founded – 1966

Stadium – Dr Magalhães Pessoa (23,850)

2010				
15/8	Beira-Mar	a	0-0	
22/8	Paços Ferreira	h	0-0	
29/8	Olhanense	a	0-1	
12/9	Nacional	h	2-1	*Marcos Paulo, N'Gal*
18/9	Guimarães	a	0-1	
26/9	Rio Ave	h	1-0	*Carlão (p)*
1/10	Académica	h	2-1	*Carlão, Zhang*
25/10	Porto	a	1-5	*Carlão (p)*
31/10	Sporting	h	1-2	*Carlão*
7/11	Marítimo	a	1-1	*Carlão*
14/11	Setúbal	h	1-0	*N'Gal*
29/11	Portimonense	a	2-1	*Zé António, Carlão*
4/12	Braga	h	3-1	*Carlão 2 (1p), Silas (p)*
19/12	Naval	a	3-0	*Carlão (p), Zhang, Diogo Amado*
2011				
9/1	Benfica	h	0-3	
16/1	Beira-Mar	h	0-3	
22/1	Paços Ferreira	a	1-1	*Vinícius*
6/2	Olhanense	h	0-2	
12/2	Nacional	a	1-0	*Fabrício*
18/2	Guimarães	h	0-1	
27/2	Rio Ave	a	0-1	
4/3	Académica	a	0-0	
14/3	Porto	h	0-2	
19/3	Sporting	a	0-0	
1/4	Marítimo	h	1-3	*João Silva*
10/4	Setúbal	a	1-4	*Fabrício*
17/4	Portimonense	h	0-1	
1/5	Braga	a	0-0	
8/5	Naval	h	1-0	*João Silva*
15/5	Benfica	a	3-3	*João Silva 2, Leandro Lima*

No	Name	Nat	DoB	Pos	Aps	(s)	Gls
28	Rúben Luís Maurício BRÍGIDO		23/6/91	M	6	(19)	
13	BRUNO MIGUEL Moreira de Sousa		24/9/82	D	9	(2)	
29	Lucas Deus Santos "CÁCÁ"	BRA	9/10/82	M	5	(7)	
83	Carlos Alexandre Souza Silva "CARLÃO"	BRA	1/8/86	A	13	(1)	9
94	CARLOS DANIEL Cevada Teixeira		11/7/94	A		(1)	
90	Bruno Alexandre Caetano CEPEDA Costa		19/1/90	M		(1)	
3	DIEGO Goldim GAÚCHO	BRA	15/11/81	D	5	(1)	
6	DIOGO Carlos Correia AMADO		21/1/90	M	11	(4)	1
24	Anđelko ĐURIČIĆ	SRB	21/11/80	G	1		
18	FABRÍCIO Santos Simões	BRA	26/12/84	A	10	(2)	2
85	Eduardo GOTTARDI	BRA	18/10/85	G	26		
25	HUGO André Viriato dos Santos GOMES		11/10/79	D	15	(1)	
16	Manuel Rolando ITURRA Urrutia	CHI	23/6/84	M	10	(1)	
19	JOÃO Pedro Pereira SILVA		21/5/90	A	7	(5)	4
70	George LEANDRO Abreu LIMA	BRA	9/11/85	M	13	(9)	1
20	MARCO Paulo da Silva SOARES	CPV	16/6/84	M	4	(4)	
21	MARCOS PAULO Gelmini Gomes	BRA	13/7/88	M	25	(1)	1
91	Michael Simões Domingues "MIKA"		8/3/91	G	3		
27	Serge Charles N'GAL	CMR	13/1/86	M	14	(3)	2
26	Saïdou Mady PANANDÉTIGUIRI	BFA	22/3/84	M	12	(4)	
4	Ricardo da Costa PATEIRO		31/5/80	M	21	(3)	
80	PATRICK Fabionn Lopes	BRA	20/8/80	D	24	(1)	
7	PAULO SÉRGIO Ferreira Gomes	BRA	21/7/81	M	16	(1)	
9	RODRIGO Silva	BRA	15/6/83	A	3	(4)	
11	Jorge Manuel Rebelo Fernandes "SILAS"		1/9/76	M	12	(1)	1
30	Mamadou TALL	BFA	4/12/82	D	5	(1)	
5	Paulo VINÍCIUS de Souza Nascimento	BRA	12/8/84	D	21	(2)	1
14	Vjatšeslav ZAHOVAIKO	EST	29/12/81	A	2	(5)	
77	José "ZÉ" ANTÓNIO Santos Silva		14/3/77	D	29		1
99	ZHANG Chengdong	CHN	9/2/89	A	8	(6)	2

VITÓRIA FC (SETÚBAL)

Coach – Manuel Fernandes

Founded – 1910

Stadium – Bonfim (18,694)

MAJOR HONOURS: Portuguese Cup – (3) 1965, 1967, 2005.

2010				
14/8	Marítimo	a	1-0	*Jaílson*
21/8	Braga	h	0-0	
28/8	Benfica	a	0-3	
13/9	Beira-Mar	h	0-0	
19/9	Naval	a	0-0	
27/9	Paços Ferreira	h	1-0	*Cláudio Pitbull*
2/10	Olhanense	a	1-3	*Ricardo Silva*
23/10	Guimarães	h	2-1	*Hugo Leal, Anderson do Ó*
31/10	Nacional	a	0-1	
5/11	Rio Ave	h	3-3	*Jaílson, Valdomiro, Neca*
14/11	Leiria	a	0-1	
26/11	Académica	h	0-1	
6/12	Porto	a	0-1	
20/12	Sporting	h	0-3	
2011				
7/1	Portimonense	a	4-3	*Cláudio Pitbull 2 (1p), Ney, Henrique*
16/1	Marítimo	h	2-4	*Cláudio Pitbull 2*
22/1	Braga	a	2-2	*Djikiné, Cláudio Pitbull*
6/2	Benfica	h	0-2	
14/2	Beira-Mar	a	0-0	
20/2	Naval	h	1-1	*Neca*
27/2	Paços Ferreira	a	0-2	
6/3	Olhanense	h	0-0	
12/3	Guimarães	a	1-1	*William*
20/3	Nacional	h	2-1	*Neca, Jaílson*
3/4	Rio Ave	a	0-2	
10/4	Leiria	h	4-1	*William, Neca, Cláudio Pitbull, José Pedro*
15/4	Académica	a	1-1	*Cláudio Pitbull*
1/5	Porto	h	0-4	
8/5	Sporting	a	1-0	*Jaílson*
15/5	Portimonense	h	3-1	*Neca (p), Cláudio Pitbull, Michel*

No	Name	Nat	DoB	Pos	Aps	(s)	Gls
6	ANDERSON Oliveira Almeida DO Ó	BRA	14/12/80	D	18		1
41	Ivan Fiel Silva "BRASÃO"	BRA	1/1/82	A	5	(3)	
87	CLÁUDIO Mejolaro "PITBULL"	BRA	8/1/82	A	25	(1)	9
2	Aurélien Marcel COLLIN	FRA	8/3/86	D	12	(2)	
25	DIEGO Silva Costa	BRA	11/5/79	G	30		
14	Mamadou DJIKINÉ	MLI	16/5/87	D	2	(1)	1
7	Bruno Vieira GALLO Freitas	BRA	7/5/88	M	6	(3)	
91	HENRIQUE Jesus Bernardo	BRA	19/1/87	A	9	(12)	1
20	HUGO Miguel Ribeiro LEAL		21/5/80	M	23	(1)	1
9	JAÍLSON Alexandre Santos	BRA	16/6/81	A	8	(12)	4
11	JOSÉ PEDRO Alves Salazar		18/10/78	M	10	(5)	1
1	Ricardo Filipe Rodrigues MATOS		15/2/79	G		(1)	
22	Jean MICHEL Sousa Bertasso	BRA	6/3/85	D	6	(5)	1
5	José Miguel Organista Aguiar "MIGUELITO"		4/2/81	D	29		
79	João Alexandre Duarte Ferreira Fernandes "NECA"		31/12/79	M	22	(3)	5
68	Uédson NEY dos Santos	BRA	23/2/81	D	23		1
8	Paulo Roberto Costa REGULA		12/3/89	M		(4)	
3	RICARDO Emídio Ramalho SILVA		26/9/75	D	26		1
77	Jefferson Gomes Oliveira "SASSÁ"	BRA	26/1/88	A	7	(12)	
19	Adama François SENE	SEN	30/11/89	D	7	(4)	
8	Weliander SILVA Nascimento	BRA	6/8/84	M	22		
66	Bernardo David Mendes Salgueiro Campos TENGARRINHA		17/2/89	M	3	(4)	
4	VALDOMIRO Duarte Macedo	BRA	6/2/79	D	19	(1)	1
17	José Carlos Gonçalves Rodrigues "ZECA"		31/8/88	M	13	(13)	
27	WILLIAM Arthur Conceição Santos	BRA	27/7/82	A	5	(4)	2

VITÓRIA SC (GUIMARÃES)

Coach – Manuel Machado

Founded – 1922

Stadium – D. Afonso Henriques (30,146)

2010				
16/8	Olhanense	a	0-0	
23/8	Rio Ave	h	0-0	
28/8	Nacional	a	3-1	*Toscano 3 (1p)*
10/9	Benfica	h	2-1	*Edgar, Rui Miguel*
18/9	Leiria	h	1-0	*Maranhão*
25/9	Académica	a	1-3	*Edgar*
4/10	Porto	h	1-1	*Faouzi*
23/10	Setúbal	a	1-2	*Edgar*
1/11	Portimonense	h	2-0	*Edgar, Maranhão*
8/11	Sporting	a	3-2	*Tiago Targino 2, Bruno Teles*
13/11	Braga	h	2-1	*Maranhão, og (Miguel Garcia)*
27/11	Marítimo	a	0-2	
4/12	Paços Ferreira	h	1-1	*Edgar*
18/12	Beira-Mar	a	2-3	*Edgar, Pereirinha*
2010				
9/1	Naval	h	1-2	*João Alves*
15/1	Olhanense	h	1-0	*João Ribeiro*
22/1	Rio Ave	a	3-2	*Edgar 2 (1p), Douglas*
6/2	Nacional	h	0-0	
13/2	Benfica	a	0-3	
20/2	Leiria	a	1-0	*João Alves*
25/2	Académica	h	0-2	
5/3	Porto	a	0-2	
12/3	Setúbal	h	1-1	*Rui Miguel*
18/3	Portimonense	a	1-2	*Tiago Targino*
3/4	Sporting	h	1-1	*João Paulo*
11/4	Braga	a	1-3	*Edgar (p)*
16/4	Marítimo	h	2-0	*Rui Miguel, Renan Silva*
1/5	Paços Ferreira	a	1-2	*Faouzi*
8/5	Beira-Mar	h	1-0	*Toscano*
15/5	Naval	a	3-0	*Jorge Ribeiro 2, Edgar*

No	Name	Nat	DoB	Pos	Aps	(s)	Gls
79	Domingos ALEXandre Martins Costa		6/9/79	D	28		
33	ANDERSON Santana Santos	BRA	24/4/86	D	4		
99	BRUNO Martins TELES		1/5/86	D	26		1
28	CLÉBER Monteiro Oliveira	BRA	23/5/80	D	23	(1)	
30	Rafael CRIVELLARO	BRA	18/2/89	M	1	(1)	
27	CUSTÓDIO Miguel Dias Castro		24/5/83	M		(2)	
9	DOUGLAS de Oliveira	BRA	30/1/86	A	4	(3)	1
29	EDGAR Bruno Silva	BRA	3/1/87	A	23	(7)	10
21	EDSON Feliciano SITTA	BRA	17/6/83	M	13	(2)	
20	Abdelghani FAOUZI	MAR	22/2/85	A	7	(9)	2
26	FLÁVIO Miguel Magalhães de Sousa MEIRELES		3/10/76	M	3	(5)	
2	Leandro FREIRE Araújo	BRA	21/8/89	D	9	(3)	
80	JOÃO Artur Rocha ALVES		18/8/80	M	19	(3)	2
40	JOÃO PAULO Andrade		6/6/81	D	22		1
42	JOÃO PEDRO Geraldino Santos Galvão		19/3/82	A	2	(4)	
25	JOÃO Rocha RIBEIRO		13/8/87	M	22	(4)	1
14	JORGE Miguel Oliveira RIBEIRO		9/11/81	D	10	(4)	2
77	Rogério Alves Nunes "MARANHÃO"	BRA	29/1/85	A	3	(7)	3
44	Mahamadou N'DIAYE	MLI	21/7/90	D	9	81	
1	NILSON Corrêa Júnior	BRA	26/12/75	G	30		
23	Bruno Alexandre Marques PEREIRINHA		2/3/88	D	4	(6)	1
70	Tiago RAFAEL Freitas Costa		27/1/91	A	1	(2)	
11	RENAN Teixeira SILVA	BRA	29/3/85	M	12		1
19	RICARDO Jorge Ferreira SILVA	CPV	19/8/80	D	17		
17	RUI MIGUEL Melo Rodrigues		15/11/83	M	8	(13)	3
8	TIAGO João TARGINO da Silva		6/6/86	A	7	(6)	3
99	António Manuel Fernandes Mendes "TÓ MANÉ"		23/10/92	A		(1)	
55	Anthony Da Silva "TONY"		20/12/80	D	1		
90	Marcelo Aparecido TOSCANO	BRA	12/5/85	A	21	(4)	4
4	VALDOMIRO Duarte Macedo	BRA	6/12/79	D	1		
12	WILLIAM Artur Conceição antos	BRA	27/7/82	A		(3)	

TOP GOALSCORERS 2010/11

23	HULK (Porto)
16	Radamel FALCAO (Porto)
	JOÃO TOMÁS (Rio Ave)
12	Óscar CARDOZO (Benfica)
11	BABA DIAWARA (Marítimo)
10	Silvestre VARELA (Porto)
	EDGAR (Guimarães)
9	LEANDRO TATU (Beira-Mar)
	Javier SAVIOLA (Benfica)
	Mario RONDÓN (Paços Ferreira)
	CARLÃO (Leiria)
	CLÁUDIO PITBULL (Setúbal)

PROMOTED CLUBS

GIL VICENTE FC
Coach – Paulo Alves
Founded – 1924
Stadium – Cidade de Barcelos (12,080)

CD FEIRENSE
Coach – Joaquim Machado Gonçalves "Quim Machado"
Founded – 1918
Stadium – Marcolino Castro (3,300)

SECOND LEVEL FINAL TABLE 2010/11

		Pld	W	D	L	F	A	Pts
1	Gil Vicente FC	30	15	10	5	55	38	55
2	CD Feirense	30	17	4	9	41	31	55
3	CD Trofense	30	15	9	6	41	27	54
4	UD Oliveirense	30	12	9	9	36	35	45
5	FC Arouca	30	11	10	9	47	41	43
6	Leixões SC	30	10	12	8	35	27	42
7	Moreirense FC	30	10	10	10	36	41	40
8	CD Aves	30	10	10	10	35	31	40
9	CD Santa Clara	30	10	8	12	26	29	38
10	GD Estoril Praia	30	9	11	10	36	31	38
11	SC Freamunde	30	8	13	9	37	39	37
12	FC Penafiel	30	9	9	12	37	44	36
13	CF Os Belenenses	30	8	11	11	33	36	35
14	SC Covilhã	30	9	5	16	32	48	32
15	Varzim SC	30	6	13	11	38	47	31
16	CD Fátima	30	5	8	17	29	49	23

DOMESTIC CUP 2010/11

TAÇA DE PORTUGAL

THIRD ROUND

(10/10/10)
1° Dezembro 1, Braga 2
(16/10/10)
Benfica 5, Arouca 1
Estoril 1, Sporting 2
Gil Vicente 1, Setúbal 1 *(aet; 2-4 on pens)*
Leiria 1, União Madeira 2 *(aet)*
Porto 4, Limianos 1
Rio Ave 4, Vendas Novas 1
(17/10/10)
Anadia 1, Feirense 2
Atlético 3, Macedo de Cavaleiros 1
Bombarralense 2, Louletano 1 *(result void; both clubs eliminated)*
Carregado 0, Fátima 0 *(aet; 3-2 on pens)*
Cesarense 1, Académica 2 *(aet)*
Guimarães 4, Malveira 0
Juventude Évora 1, Santa Clara 0
Lagoa 0, Torreense 0 *(aet; 4-5 on pens)*
Leixões 3, Mafra 2
Merelinense 2, Farense 1
Mirandela 1, Beira-Mar 1 *(aet; 2-4 on pens)*
Mondinense 2, Coimbrões 1 *(aet)*
Nacional 4, Padroense 2
Naval 1° Maio 0, Marítimo 2
Operário 0, Moreirense 2
Paços Ferreira 3, São João de Ver 1
Pinhalnovense 3, Fafe 0
Portimonense 2, Cinfães 0
Ribeirão 2, Belenenses 0
Santa Maria 1, Penalva Castelo 0 *(aet)*
Sertanense 0, Olhanense 0 *(aet; 1-4 on pens)*
Sporting Espinho 4, Pontassolense 1
Tirsense 5, Sampedrense 1
Tourizense 2, Aliados Lordelo 1 *(aet)*
(23/12/10)
Varzim 0, Gondomar 0 *(aet; 4-2 on pens)*

FOURTH ROUND

(21/11/10)
Atlético 2, Tourizense 2 *(aet; 6-5 on pens)*
Beira-Mar 0, Académica 2
Juventude Évora 3, Santa Maria 0
Maritímo 1, Setúbal 2
Merelinense 2, Carregado 0
Mondinense 1, Torreense 2 *(aet)*
Moreirense 0, Porto 1
Olhanense 1, Nacional 0
Pinhalnovense 2, Tirsense 0
Portimonense 1, Guimarães 2
Rio Ave 3, Feirense 0
Sporting 1, Paços Ferreira 0
Sporting Espinho 1, Leixões 2
(12/12/10)
Benfica 2, Braga 0
(5/1/11)
Varzim 4, Ribeirão 3 *(aet)*
Bye – União Madeira

FIFTH ROUND

(11/12/10)
Porto 4, Juventude Évora 0
Setúbal 2, Sporting 1
(12/12/10)
Guimarães 2, Torreense 0
Leixões 1, Pinhalnovense 1 *(aet; 4-5 on pens)*
Rio Ave 4, Atlético 1
(12/1/11)
Académica 3, União Madeira 1
Benfica 5, Olhanense 0
Varzim 1, Merelinense 2

QUARTER-FINALS

(12/1/11)
Porto 2 *(Hulk 78, 90)*, Pinhalnovense 0
(26/1/11)
Rio Ave 0, Benfica 2 *(Cardozo 44, 87p)*
(27/1/11)
Merelinense 0, *Guimarães 2 (Edgar 30, Cléber 45)*
(28/1/11)
Académica 3 *(Éder 39, Modou Sougou 44, Bischoff 86p)*, Setúbal 2 *(Brasão 16, Collin 88)*

SEMI-FINALS

(2/2/11 & 20/4/11)
Porto 0, Benfica 2 *(Fábio Coentrão 6, Javi García 25)*
Benfica 1 *(Cardozo 80p)*, Porto 3 *(João Moutinho 64, Hulk 73, Falcao 75)*
(3-3; Porto on away goals)
(3/2/11 & 27/3/11)
Guimarães 1 *(Faouzi 80)*, Académica 0
Académica 0, Guimarães 0
(Guimarães 1-0)

FINAL

(22/5/11)
Estádio Nacional, Lisbon
FC PORTO 6 *(Rodríguez J. 3, 45+2, 73, Varela 22, Rolando 35, Hulk 42)*
VITÓRIA SC 2 *(Álvaro Pereira 20og, Edgar 23)*
Referee – *João Ferreira*
PORTO – *Beto, Săpunaru, Rolando, Maicon, Álvaro Pereira, Belluschi (Souza 62), Fernando (Guarín 46), João Moutinho, Varela (Mariano González 76), Hulk, Rodríguez J.*
GUIMARÃES – *Nilson, Alex, Freire, João Paulo, Anderson, Renan Silva (João Alves 46), Cléber (Toscano 56), Rui Miguel, Tiago Targino (Jorge Ribeiro 56), Edgar, Faouzi.*

CLUB COMMUNICATION 2011/12

A. Académica de Coimbra

Academia Dolce Vita, Estrada Nacional 111-1
Campos do Bolão, PT-3025-300 Coimbra

Tel +351 239 793 890
Fax +351 239 793 892
Web academica-oaf.pt
Email geral@academica-oaf.pt
Media Officer Filipe Dinis

SC Beira-Mar

Estádio Municipal de Aveiro
Apartado 3105, PT-3804-508 Aveiro

Tel +351 234 910 100
Fax +351 234 910 101
Web beiramar.pt
Email secretaria@beiramar.pt
Media Officer

SL Benfica

Avda. Gen.Norton de Matos 1500
Estádio do SL Benfica, Apartado 4100
PT-1501-805 Lisboa

Tel +351 21 721 9555
Fax +351 21 721 9551
Web slbenfica.pt
Email sec.geral@slbenfica.pt
Media Officer Ricardo Maia

SC Braga

Estádio Municipal de Braga, Apartado 12
PT-4700-087 Braga

Tel +351 253 206 860
Fax +351 253 612 929
Web scbraga.pt
Email mail@scbraga.pt
Media Officer Marco Carvalho

CD Feirense

Av.ª 25 de Abril nº 14, Apartado 27
PT-4524-909 Santa Maria da Feira

Tel +351 256 362 472
Fax +351 256 372 230
Web cdfeirense.pt
Email secretaria@cdfeirense.pt
Media Officer José Pina

Gil Vicente FC

Rua D. Diogo Pinheiro 25, Apartado 197
PT-4750-282 Barcelos

Tel +351 253 811 523
Fax +351 253 823 102
Web gilvicentefc.pt
Email geral@gilvicentefc.pt
Media Officer Francisco Baptista Pereira

CS Marítimo

Complexo Desportivo-Futebol, Rua campo do Marítimo, Santo António
PT-9020-073 Funchal

Tel +351 291 708 300
Fax +351 291 708 310
Web csmaritimo.pt
Email csmaritimo@netmadeira.com
Media Officer Duarte Azevedo

CD Nacional

Rua do Esmeraldo 46
PT-9060 Funchal

Tel +351 291 227 324
Fax +351 291 225 590
Web cdnacional.pt
Email geral@cdnacional.pt
Media Officer Satornino Sousa

SC Olhanense

Estádio José Arcanjo, Apartado 104
PT-8700 Olhão

Tel +351 289 702 632
Fax +351 289 702 632
Web scolhanense.com
Email geral@scolhanense.com
Media Officer

FC Paços de Ferreira

Rua do Estádio, Apartado 26
PT-4594-909 Paços de Ferreira

Tel +351 255 965 230
Fax +351 255 866 149
Web fcpf.pt
Email geral@fcpf.pt
Media Officer Luís Barros

FC Porto

Estádio do Dragão, Via F.C. Porto, Entrada Poente, piso 3, PT-4350-415 Porto

Tel +351 22 507 0500
Fax +351 22 507 0550
Web fcporto.pt
Email geral@portosad.pt
Media Officer Rui Cequeira

Rio Ave FC

Praça da República 35, Apartado 42
PT-4481-909 Vila do Conde

Tel +351 252 640 590
Fax +351 252 640 599
Web rioave-fc.pt
Email rioave@mail.telepac.pt
Media Officer Afonso Carvalho

Sporting Clube de Portugal

Rua Prof. Fernando da Fonseca
Apartado 42099, PT-1601-801 Lisboa

Tel +351 21 751 6205
Fax +351 21 751 6285
Web sporting.pt
Email sporting@sportmultimedia.pt
Media Officer Irene Palma

UD Leiria

Estádio Dr. Magalhães Pessoa
Apartado 3074, PT-2400 Leiria

Tel +351 244 831 779
Fax +351 244 827 987
Web uniaodeleiria.pt
Email geral@uniaodeleiria.pt
Media Officer Rodolfo Vaz

Vitória FC

Estádio do Bonfim, Apartado 132
PT-2901-882 Setúbal

Tel +351 265 544 270
Fax +351 265 536 513
Web vfc.pt
Email sad@vfc.pt
Media Officer Marco Santos

Vitória SC

Complexo Desportivo Dr. António Pimenta Machado, Apartado 505
PT-4802-914 Guimarães

Tel +351 253 432 570
Fax +351 253 432 573
Web vitoriasc.pt
Email geral@vitoriasc.pt
Media Officer Duarte Magalhães

REPUBLIC OF IRELAND

Irlande I Irland

Cumann Peile na héireann/ Football Association of Ireland (FAI)

COMMUNICATION

Address	National Sports Campus Abbotstown IE-Dublin 15	**Chairman** **Chief Executive** **Media Officer**	Paddy McCaul John Delaney Peter Sherrard
Tel **Fax**	+353 1 8999500 +353 1 8999501	**Year of Formation**	1921
E-mail **Website**	info@fai.ie fai.ie	**National Stadium**	Dublin Arena, Dublin (50,000)

DOMESTIC COMPETITION SUMMARY 2010

LEAGUE OF IRELAND PREMIER DIVISION FINAL TABLE

			Home					Away					Total						
		Pld	W	D	L	F	A	W	D	L	F	A	W	D	L	F	A	Pts	Comp
1	Shamrock Rovers FC	36	11	4	3	31	12	8	6	4	26	22	19	10	7	57	34	67	UCL
2	Bohemian FC	36	9	7	2	23	10	10	3	5	27	19	19	10	7	50	29	67	UEL
3	Sligo Rovers FC	36	11	4	3	37	16	6	8	4	24	20	17	12	7	61	36	63	UEL
4	Sporting Fingal FC	36	7	7	4	31	23	9	7	2	29	15	16	14	6	60	38	62	
5	Saint Patrick's Athletic FC	36	10	3	5	27	14	6	6	6	28	19	16	9	11	55	33	57	UEL
6	Dundalk FC	36	7	4	7	26	24	7	2	9	20	26	14	6	16	46	50	48	
7	University College Dublin AFC	36	7	3	8	22	21	4	5	9	25	33	11	8	17	47	54	41	
8	Galway United FC	36	4	8	6	23	27	5	3	10	15	32	9	11	16	38	59	38	
9	Bray Wanderers AFC	36	3	5	10	20	39	3	4	11	15	33	6	9	21	35	72	27	
10	Drogheda United FC	36	2	4	12	15	38	2	5	11	15	36	4	9	23	30	74	21	

NB Sporting Fingal FC withdrew from the 2011 Premier Division, enabling Drogheda United FC to avoid relegation.

Top Scorer Gary Twigg (Shamrock Rovers), 20 goals

Promoted Club Derry City FC

Cup Final Sligo Rovers FC 0, Shamrock Rovers FC 0 (aet; 2-0 on pens)

Shamrock Rovers return to the top

The battle for the 2010 League of Ireland title turned into an encore of the 2009 two-horse race between Dublin rivals Shamrock Rovers FC and Bohemian FC. The difference was in the outcome, with Rovers prevailing by the narrowest of margins to take their first championship title in 16 years and thereby deny Bohemians – and manager Pat Fenlon – a historic hat-trick.

Rovers, coached by former Northern Ireland international Michael O'Neill, looked unstoppable as they turned for home with a seven-point cushion. But a 17-match unbeaten run was abruptly halted in mid-September by a 5-1 defeat away to their bogey side Dundalk FC – where they had last lost in early May – and that prompted a crisis in confidence which led to three straight defeats in early October, the second of them against a Bohemians side struggling for form themselves.

Nervous end

When the Hoops missed a penalty and conceded two late goals to lose 2-1 at home to Sporting Fingal FC the following week, Bohs took over at the top with two games remaining. But Bohemians had their own bête noire in Galway United FC, and their west of Ireland blues continued when they lost 3-2 at Terryland Park, a defeat compounded by Rovers' 2-0 victory at home to lowly Drogheda United FC. On the final day Rovers knew that a win at struggling Bray Wanderers AFC would clinch the title, with a draw sufficing as long as Bohemians failed to beat Dundalk by five goals. In the event Bohs won 3-1, while a nervous Rovers scraped a 2-2 draw to take their 16th title on goal difference

The goals of Scottish striker Gary Twigg, who had followed manager O'Neill to Rovers from Brechin City FC, were of crucial importance. His tally of 20, though four fewer than in 2009, enabled him to retain the Premier Division Golden Boot. Rovers' success was a hard-earned reward for a club that had laboured for over 20 years without a permanent home. Having slipped into administration and relegation in 2005, the community-owned club rose from the depths to re-establish themselves in their splendid, council-owned stadium in the south-west Dublin satellite town of Tallaght.

The faltering conclusion to the campaign of both champions and runners-up meant that the fast-finishing Sligo Rovers FC and Sporting Fingal eventually closed the gap at the top to four and five points, respectively. Both sides deserved their places in the 2011/12 UEFA Europa League, although Fingal were to fold before the start of the 2011 season, enabling fifth-placed Saint Patrick's Athletic FC to inherit their European berth. Another consequence of Fingal's demise was Drogheda's escape from relegation. The 2007 champions had looked doomed after a disastrous season compounded by the use of five managers. Bray were the unlikely beneficiaries of Drogheda's woes. Having prepared for life in the First Division in 2010 before the last-minute collapse of Cork City FC propelled them back into the top flight, they struggled all season until club legend Pat Devlin took over the managerial reins and inspired a remarkable late revival. Wanderers had just enough in reserve to squeeze through the play-offs and secure another season in the Premier Division.

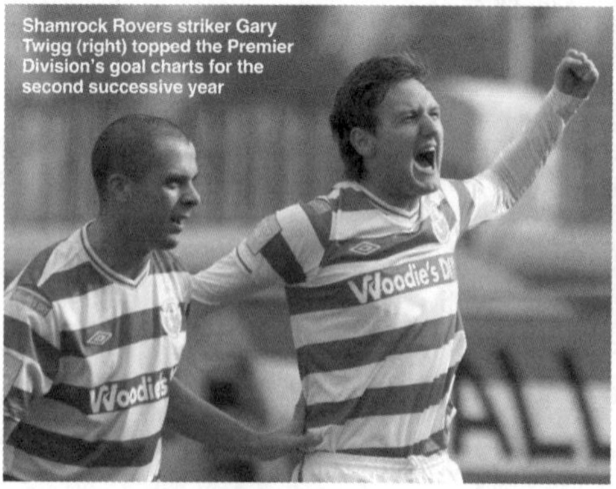

Shamrock Rovers striker Gary Twigg (right) topped the Premier Division's goal charts for the second successive year

National Team

International Tournament Appearances – FIFA World Cup - (3) 1990 (qtr-finals), 1994 (2nd round), 2002 (2nd round).
UEFA European Championship – (1) 1988.

Top Five All-time Caps – Shay Given (113); Kevin Kilbane (110); Robbie Keane (108); Stephen Staunton (102); Niall Quinn (91)

Top Five All-time Goals – Robbie Keane (51); Niall Quinn (21); Frank Stapleton (20); John Aldridge, Tony Cascarino & Don Givens (19)

In the First Division, Derry City FC, who had been demoted in 2009 for financial irregularities, made an immediate return to the top flight. Gritty Monaghan United FC had threatened to push them all the way but they slipped to third before raising themselves once again in the play-offs, where only a penalty shoot-out defeat to Bray denied them promotion. It was tough on the Ulster club, whose impressive campaign had also seen them reach the League Cup final and FAI Cup semi-final.

The FAI Cup final between Shamrock Rovers and Sligo – the first club match at the newly constructed Dublin Arena – attracted a crowd of 36,101, the fixture's highest attendance in over 30 years. Although there were plenty of spectators, there were no goals, and the contest went to penalties, where Sligo goalkeeper Ciarán Kelly emerged as the hero, saving all four of Shamrock Rovers' shoot-out spot-kicks to complete an unlikely double for Sligo, who had earlier won the League Cup. It was a fitting reward for the club's English manager Paul Cook, whose stylish team, inspired by star midfielder Richie Ryan, won many admirers.

Performances in Europe were mixed. Bohemians were distraught to crash out of the UEFA Champions League against The New Saints FC, while Irish highlights in the UEFA Europa League were provided by Shamrock Rovers, whose reward for defeating Bnei Yehuda Tel-Aviv FC in steamy Israel was a plum tie against Juventus. Rovers competed well in both legs, but Juve's class saw them through 3-0 on aggregate.

Record-breaker Keane

The Republic of Ireland's UEFA EURO 2012 qualifying campaign began with solid wins in Armenia and – in their new home - against Andorra, but a spirited comeback at home to Russia could not paper over the cracks of an otherwise poor performance, which brought a damaging 3-2 defeat, and further points were dropped in a 1-1 draw away to Slovakia in which Robbie Keane missed three good chances, including a penalty. The Ireland skipper would make amends, however, with three goals in the next two qualifiers – home and away wins over the Former Yugoslav Republic of Macedonia, which served to revive Ireland's qualifying hopes. His goal in Dublin meant that he had scored for his country 14 years running - a world record – and his two goals in Skopje took his cumulative tally past the 50-mark.

Keane scored eight international goals in all during the season – four times as many as he managed in club football. Three of them helped Ireland to victory in the inaugural Nations Cup, which they hosted in Dublin, cruising to three comfortable wins over Wales, Northern Ireland and Scotland. Disappointingly low attendances, however, put the future of the competition in doubt.

NATIONAL TEAM RESULTS 2010/11

11/8/10	Argentina	H	Dublin	0-1	
3/9/10	Armenia (ECQ)	A	Yerevan	1-0	*Fahey (76)*
7/9/10	Andorra (ECQ)	H	Dublin	3-1	*Kilbane (15), Doyle (41), Keane (54)*
8/10/10	Russia (ECQ)	H	Dublin	2-3	*Keane (72p), Long (78)*
12/10/10	Slovakia (ECQ)	A	Zilina	1-1	*St Ledger (16)*
17/11/10	Norway	H	Dublin	1-2	*Long (5p)*
8/2/11	Wales	H	Dublin	3-0	*Gibson (60), Duff (67), Fahey (82)*
26/3/11	FYROM (ECQ)	H	Dublin	2-1	*McGeady (2), Keane (21)*
29/3/11	Uruguay	H	Dublin	2-3	*Long (15), Fahey (47p)*
24/5/11	Northern Ireland	H	Dublin	5-0	*Ward (24), Keane (27, 53p), Cathcart (44og), Cox (79)*
29/5/11	Scotland	H	Dublin	1-0	*Keane (23)*
4/6/11	FYROM (ECQ)	A	Skopje	2-0	*Keane (8, 37)*
7/6/11	Italy	N	Liege (BEL)	2-0	*Andrews (36), Cox (90)*

REPUBLIC OF IRELAND

NATIONAL TEAM APPEARANCES 2010/11

Coach – Giovanni TRAPATTONI (ITA) 17/3/39			Arg	ARM	AND	RUS	SVK	Nor	Wal	MKD	Uru	Nir	Sco	MKD	Ita	Caps	Goals
Shay GIVEN	20/4/76	Man. City (ENG)	G	G	G	G	G	G	G			G72	G	G		113	-
Paul McSHANE	6/1/86	Hull (ENG)	D									D	D		D	26	-
Richard DUNNE	21/9/79	Aston Villa (ENG)	D	D	D	D	D		D	D						65	7
John O'SHEA	30/4/81	Man. United (ENG)	D	D	D75	D	D	D	D85					D		70	1
Kevin KILBANE	1/2/77	Hull (ENG)	D56	D	D	D	D							D		110	8
		/Huddersfield (ENG)								D							
Keith FAHEY	15/1/83	Birmingham (ENG)	M77	s68		s71	M71	M	s58	s77	M65		M			11	3
Keith ANDREWS	13/9/80	Blackburn (ENG)	M67									M	M	M	M	20	2
Paul GREEN	10/4/83	Derby (ENG)	M	M	M	M	M42		s76		M					9	1
Damien DUFF	2/3/79	Fulham (ENG)	M					M74	M71	M						87	8
Cillian SHERIDAN	23/2/89	Celtic (SCO)	A56													3	-
Robbie KEANE	8/7/80	Tottenham (ENG)	A	A85	A	A	A					A62	A83	A		108	51
		/West Ham (ENG)								A87							
Greg CUNNINGHAM	31/1/91	Man. City (ENG)	s56														
		/Leicester (ENG)						D								3	-
Andy KEOGH	16/5/86	Wolves (ENG)	s56									s62			A75	21	1
		/Cardiff (WAL)		s85	s82		s71										
		/Bristol City (ENG)							s71		M85						
Darron GIBSON	25/10/87	Man. United (ENG)	s67		s61	s66	s42		M81	M77	s65					16	1
Keith TREACY	13/9/88	Preston (ENG)	s77								s65	M	s83		s75	5	-
Sean ST LEDGER	28/12/84	Preston (ENG)		D	D	D	D		D						D	18	2
Glenn WHELAN	13/1/84	Stoke (ENG)		M	M61	M66	M	M	M76	M				M	s60	29	2
Liam LAWRENCE	14/12/81	Portsmouth (ENG)		M	M	M62		M46			M79	s55	M62			15	2
Aiden McGEADY	4/4/86	Spartak Moskva (RUS)		M68	M	M	M	s46		M	s79			M		40	1
Kevin DOYLE	18/9/83	Wolves (ENG)		A	A82	A71		A46	A46	A20						41	9
Stephen KELLY	6/9/83	Fulham (ENG)			s75			D			D	D	D	D	s83	25	-
Shane LONG	22/1/87	Reading (ENG)				s62	A	A	s46	s20	A			s65	A60	21	6
Darren O'DEA	4/2/87	Ipswich (ENG)						D67	s85	D	D						
		/Celtic (SCO)											D66	D	D83	9	-
Jonathan WALTERS	20/9/83	Stoke (ENG)						s46	A							2	-
Kevin FOLEY	1/11/84	Wolves (ENG)						s67		D	D	M70	s66		M60	8	-
Stephen HUNT	1/8/81	Wolves (ENG)						s74				s70	M	M	M	30	1
Ciaran CLARK	26/9/89	Aston Villa (ENG)							D		D75					2	-
Séamus COLEMAN	11/10/88	Everton (ENG)							M58			M55	s62		M	4	-
Marc WILSON	17/8/87	Stoke (ENG)							s81							1	-
Keiren WESTWOOD	23/10/84	Coventry (ENG)								G	G					7	-
James McCARTHY	12/11/90	Wigan (ENG)								s87	A65					3	-
Damien DELANEY	20/7/81	Ipswich (ENG)									s75	D			s90	5	-
Anthony STOKES	25/7/88	Celtic (SCO)									s85					4	-
Stephen WARD	20/8/85	Wolves (ENG)										D	D		D90	3	1
Simon COX	28/4/87	West Brom (ENG)										A	A	A65	s60	4	2
David FORDE	20/12/79	Millwall (ENG)										s72			G	2	-

CLUB-BY-CLUB

BOHEMIAN FC

Manager – Pat Fenlon
Founded – 1890
Stadium – Dalymount Park (6,000)
MAJOR HONOURS: League of Ireland – (11) 1924, 1928, 1930, 1934, 1936, 1975, 1978, 2001, 2003 (spring), 2008, 2009; Irish Cup – (1) 1908; FAI Cup – (7) 1928, 1935, 1970, 1976, 1992, 2001, 2008.

2010				
/3	Fingal	h	1-0	*Brennan (p)*
6/3	UCD	a	2-1	*Byrne, Cretaro*
9/3	Drogheda	a	4-2	*Byrne 2, McGlynn, Madden*
26/3	Sligo	h	0-0	
/4	St Patrick's	h	1-1	*Byrne*
/4	Shamrock Rovers	a	0-1	
6/4	Galway	h	2-3	*Cretaro, Byrne*
23/4	Dundalk	a	0-1	
26/4	Fingal	a	2-0	*Keegan, McGlynn*
30/4	UCD	h	0-0	
3/5	Drogheda	h	1-0	*Higgins*
8/5	Sligo	a	2-1	*Byrne, Quigley*
21/5	St Patrick's	a	1-3	*Byrne*
29/5	Shamrock Rovers	h	0-0	
1/6	Bray	a	2-0	*og (Doyle D.), Brennan*
8/6	Galway	a	2-2	*Madden 2*
25/6	Dundalk	h	3-0	*Madden, Higgins, McGlynn*
2/7	Fingal	h	1-1	*Madden*
5/7	UCD	a	2-0	*Madden 2 (1p)*
16/7	Sligo	h	2-0	*Keegan, Oman*
23/7	Bray	a	3-0	*Madden 2, Brennan*
30/7	St Patrick's	h	1-1	*Heary*
8/8	Shamrock Rovers	a	0-3	
13/8	Galway	h	0-2	
17/8	Bray	h	2-0	*Cretaro 2*
20/8	Dundalk	a	2-1	*Quigley, Keegan*
23/8	Drogheda	a	1-0	*McGlynn*
3/9	Fingal	a	0-0	
10/9	UCD	h	3-1	*Byrne, McGlynn, Quigley*
13/9	Drogheda	h	2-0	*Brennan, Byrne*
21/9	Sligo	a	1-1	*Quigley*
1/10	Bray	h	0-0	
5/10	Shamrock Rovers	h	1-0	*Byrne*
9/10	St Patrick's	a	1-0	*Cretaro*
22/10	Galway	a	2-3	*Keegan, Byrne (p)*
29/10	Dundalk	h	3-1	*Madden, Greene, Byrne (p)*

Name	Nat	DoB	Pos	Aps	(s)	Gls
Killian BRENNAN		31/1/84	M	23	(6)	4
Gary BURKE		27/3/91	M	1	(1)	
Jason BYRNE		23/2/78	A	24	(6)	12
Rafael CRETARO		15/10/81	M	16	(9)	5
Glenn CRONIN		14/9/81	M	28	(4)	
Lee DIXON		1/5/91	M		(1)	
Steven GRAY		19/10/81	D	4		
Aaron GREENE		2/1/90	A	5	(13)	1
Owen HEARY		4/10/76	D	26	(1)	1
Ruairí HIGGINS		11/10/89	M	11	(11)	2
Paul KEEGAN		5/7/84	M	32	(1)	4
Patrick MADDEN		4/3/90	A	18	(15)	10
Gareth McGLYNN		29/10/82	M	27	(2)	5
Jason McGUINNESS		8/8/82	D	13	(1)	
Anto MURPHY		1/8/82	M	4	(5)	
Barry MURPHY		8/6/85	G	22	(1)	
Chris O'CONNOR	AUS	7/5/85	G	14	(1)	
Ken OMAN		29/7/82	D	26		1
Conor POWELL		26/8/87	D	26	(1)	
Mark QUIGLEY		27/10/85	A	24	(10)	4
Mark ROSSITER		27/5/83	D	18	(2)	
Brian SHELLEY		15/11/81	M	34		

BRAY WANDERERS AFC

Manager – Eddie Gormley; (9/8/10) Pat Devlin
Founded – 1942
Stadium – Carlisle Grounds (3,000)
MAJOR HONOURS: FAI Cup – (2) 1990, 1999.

2010				
5/3	Dundalk	h	0-1	
12/3	Galway	a	1-2	*Knight*
19/3	Fingal	h	1-3	*O'Neill S.*
26/3	UCD	a	0-1	
5/4	Drogheda	a	0-0	
9/4	Sligo	h	2-3	*og (Brush), Kelly J. (p)*
20/4	St Patrick's	h	0-4	
23/4	Shamrock Rovers	a	0-1	
26/4	Dundalk	a	3-2	*Kelly J. 2 (1p), Doyle R.*
30/4	Galway	h	0-2	
4/5	Fingal	a	0-1	
7/5	UCD	h	0-6	
21/5	Drogheda	h	2-2	*Kelly J., O'Neill S.*
29/5	Sligo	a	1-5	*Mulroy*
1/6	Bohemians	h	0-2	
8/6	St Patrick's	a	0-3	
25/6	Shamrock Rovers	h	0-0	
5/7	Galway	a	2-2	*O'Neill S., Doyle R.*
9/7	Fingal	h	0-3	
16/7	UCD	a	0-4	
23/7	Bohemians	h	0-3	
30/7	Drogheda	a	2-0	*Mulroy, Kelly J.*
6/8	Sligo	h	1-3	*Kelly J.*
13/8	St Patrick's	h	3-2	*O'Neill S., Kelly J. 2*
17/8	Bohemians	a	0-2	
20/8	Shamrock Rovers	a	1-4	*Dempsey*
3/9	Dundalk	a	2-0	*Shaw, Kelly J.*
10/9	Galway	h	4-0	*Kelly J. 2 (1p), Shaw, Zambra*
13/9	Fingal	a	2-2	*Kelly J. 2*
20/9	Dundalk	h	2-0	*Prendergast, O'Neill S.*
24/9	UCD	h	2-2	*Doyle D. 2*
1/10	Bohemians	a	0-0	
5/10	Sligo	a	1-2	*Dempsey*
10/10	Drogheda	h	1-1	*O'Neill S. (p)*
22/10	St Patrick's	a	0-2	
29/10	Shamrock Rovers	h	2-2	*Kelly J., Shaw*

Name	Nat	DoB	Pos	Aps	(s)	Gls
Richie BAKER		17/4/80	M	7	(3)	
Stephen BRENNAN		26/3/83	D	7	(4)	
Nicky BYRNE		11/3/89	D	2	(5)	
Gary DEMPSEY		15/1/81	M	14		2
Daire DOYLE		18/10/80	M	25	(1)	2
Robbie DOYLE		22/4/82	A	14	(6)	2
Andrei GEORGESCU	ROU	12/3/83	A		(3)	
Matt GREGG	ENG	30/11/78	G	15		
Sean HOUSTON		29/10/89	M	10	(1)	
Brian KANE		6/7/90	G	21		
James KAVANAGH		12/1/93	M	14	(5)	
Graham KELLY		31/10/91	M	3	(1)	
Jake KELLY		18/6/90	A	24	(4)	14
Philip KNIGHT		18/9/90	D	2	(1)	1
Dane MASSEY		17/4/88	D	24	(7)	
Adam MITCHELL		23/6/80	D	10	(2)	
John MULROY		27/12/87	A	17	(8)	2
Mark O'BRIEN		13/5/84	M	1	(3)	
Adam O'CONNOR		20/7/90	M		(4)	
Danny O'CONNOR		28/9/80	M	16		
Shane O'CONNOR		19/6/90	D	28	(1)	
David O'NEILL		17/8/90	M	2	(3)	
Shane O'NEILL		9/1/89	A	25	(4)	6
Derek PRENDERGAST		17/10/84	D	18		1
Pablo RODRÍGUEZ Aracil	ESP	20/7/85	A	2	(4)	
Gary SHAW		10/5/92	A	3	(4)	3
Chris SHIELDS		27/12/90	D	26	(5)	

No	Name	Nat	DoB	Pos	Aps	(s)	Gls
	Colm TRESSON		29/6/71	D	13	(5)	
	Ian TUOHY		18/6/90	D	5	(5)	
	David TYRRELL		6/5/85	M	7	(2)	
	Dylan VICKERS		18/11/90	M	2	(1)	
	Dave WEBSTER		8/9/89	D	22	(3)	
	Dean ZAMBRA		30/7/88	M	17	(3)	1

DROGHEDA UNITED FC

Manager – Alan Mathews; (17/5/10) (Darius Kierans); (30/6/10) Paul Lumsden; (3/7/10) (Darius Kierans); (13/7/10) Brian Donnelly; (21/9/10) (Darius Kierans); (27/9/10) Bobby Browne

Founded – 1919

Stadium – United Park (2,500)

MAJOR HONOURS: League of Ireland – (1) 2007; FAI Cup – (1) 2005.

2010

5/3	UCD	h	0-3	
14/3	Dundalk	a	2-2	*Fitzpatrick, Kendrick (p)*
19/3	Bohemians	h	2-4	*Crowley, Kendrick (p)*
26/3	Fingal	a	1-4	*Martin*
2/4	Sligo	h	2-2	*Duffy, Daly*
5/4	Bray	h	0-0	
9/4	St Patrick's	a	1-0	*Osbourne*
16/4	Shamrock Rovers	h	0-2	
23/4	Galway	a	1-3	*Treacy*
26/4	UCD	a	0-2	
30/4	Dundalk	h	1-3	*og (Burns)*
3/5	Bohemians	a	0-1	
7/5	Fingal	h	1-1	*O'Connor*
15/5	Sligo	a	0-6	
21/5	Bray	a	2-2	*McGill B., Kendrick (p)*
29/5	St Patrick's	h	2-1	*Crowley, Flood*
8/6	Shamrock Rovers	a	1-1	*Flood*
25/6	Galway	h	0-1	
2/7	UCD	h	1-0	*McNally*
5/7	Dundalk	a	1-2	*Flood*
19/7	Fingal	a	2-1	*McMahon, McNally*
23/7	Sligo	h	2-3	*Fitzpatrick, McEnteggart*
30/7	Bray	h	0-2	
6/8	St Patrick's	a	0-2	
13/8	Shamrock Rovers	h	0-2	
20/8	Galway	a	1-2	*Fitzpatrick (p)*
23/8	Bohemians	h	0-1	
3/9	UCD	a	1-1	*Fitzpatrick (p)*
10/9	Dundalk	h	1-3	*Meenan*
13/9	Bohemians	a	0-2	
24/9	Fingal	h	0-4	
2/10	Sligo	a	1-2	*McGill E.*
5/10	St Patrick's	h	0-3	
10/10	Bray	a	1-1	*Haro*
22/10	Shamrock Rovers	a	0-2	
29/10	Galway	h	3-3	*McGill B., McMahon, McNamara*

No	Name	Nat	DoB	Pos	Aps	(s)	Gls
4	Damien BRENNAN		30/8/80	D	2	(2)	
19	Ryan BRENNAN		11/11/91	M	19	(10)	
10	Paul CROWLEY		13/8/80	M	27	(1)	2
16	Michael DALY		18/10/89	M	31	(2)	1
8	Jamie DUFFY		20/11/83	M	6	(10)	1
23	Robert DUGGAN		1/4/87	G	13		
18	Glenn FITZPATRICK		26/1/81	A	23	(2)	4
11	John FLOOD		16/1/84	A	24	(6)	3
	Yael HARO Chavane	ESP	15/12/88	D	10		1
15	Jamie HARRIS	WAL	28/6/79	D	17	(3)	
4	Ciarán HOEY		10/8/91	D	1		
3	Joe KENDRICK		26/6/83	D	17		3
	Christopher KERR		18/6/91	M		(3)	
20	Derek KIERANS		9/7/91	D		(2)	
17	Brian KING		8/1/87	M	13		
9	Robbie MARTIN		27/7/82	A	4	(1)	1
	Paul MATONDO	COD	20/12/86	M		(3)	
	Ronan McENTEGGART		2/2/91	M	4	(5)	1
7	Brendan McGILL		22/3/81	M	17		2
6	Eric McGILL		16/10/87	M	22	(2)	1
14	Peter McMAHON		20/4/89	M	12	(3)	2
5	Alan McNALLY		15/9/82	D	35		2
13	Darragh McNAMARA		16/6/90	A	5	(6)	1
9	Darren MEENAN		16/11/86	M	12	(3)	1
23	Paul MURPHY		28/3/83	G	10		
3	Stephen MURPHY		6/1/89	M	1		
14	Garreth O'CONNOR		10/11/78	M	14	(2)	1
12	Eoghan OSBOURNE		25/3/92	D	14	(5)	1
17	Kevin ROSS		16/7/91	M	3	(2)	
8	Conor SINNOTT		19/1/86	M	5	(3)	
1	Paul SKINNER		3/2/89	G	13		
21	Colm SMYTH		20/8/91	A	3	(6)	
2	Corie TREACY		11/1/89	D	19		1
	William WOODS		5/7/91	A		(1)	

DUNDALK FC

Manager – Ian Foster (ENG)

Founded – 1903

Stadium – Oriel Park (4,000)

MAJOR HONOURS: League of Ireland – (9) 1933, 1963, 1967, 1976, 1979, 1982, 1988, 1991, 1995; FAI Cup – (9) 1942, 1949, 1952, 1958, 1977, 1979, 1981, 1988, 2002 (spring).

2010

5/3	Bray	a	1-0	*Breen G.*
14/3	Drogheda	h	2-2	*Fenn (p), Kuduzović*
21/3	Shamrock Rovers	a	2-0	*Fenn, Maher*
26/3	St Patrick's	h	0-0	
5/4	Sligo	a	2-2	*Gaynor, McGuigan*
9/4	UCD	h	3-0	*Melligan, Breen G., Kuduzović*
16/4	Fingal	a	1-2	*Melligan*
19/4	Galway	a	1-0	*Gaynor*
23/4	Bohemians	h	1-0	*Hatswell*
26/4	Bray	h	2-3	*Burns, Breen J.*
30/4	Drogheda	a	3-1	*Breen G. 2, Gaynor*
3/5	Shamrock Rovers	h	2-1	*Fenn, Melligan*
7/5	St Patrick's	a	0-1	
14/5	Galway	h	0-0	
21/5	Sligo	h	1-0	*Kuduzović*
29/5	UCD	a	1-3	*Kuduzović*
8/6	Fingal	h	1-2	*Kuduzović*
25/6	Bohemians	a	0-3	
5/7	Drogheda	h	2-1	*McDonnell, Mulvenna*
11/7	Shamrock Rovers	a	0-4	
18/7	St Patrick's	h	0-3	
25/7	Galway	a	1-1	*Fenn*
31/7	Sligo	a	0-1	
6/8	UCD	h	1-1	*Tipton*
13/8	Fingal	a	0-1	
20/8	Bohemians	h	1-2	*Tipton (p)*
3/9	Bray	h	0-2	
10/9	Drogheda	a	3-1	*Gaynor, Tipton, Kuduzović*
13/9	Shamrock Rovers	h	5-1	*Miller, Kuduzović, Tipton 3*
20/9	Bray	a	0-2	
24/9	St Patrick's	a	2-1	*Tipton, Gaynor*
1/10	Galway	h	3-0	*Kuduzović 3*
9/10	Sligo	h	2-4	*Gaynor 2*
15/10	UCD	a	2-0	*Kuduzović, Breen J.*
22/10	Fingal	h	0-2	
29/10	Bohemians	a	1-3	*Kuduzović*

No	Name	Nat	DoB	Pos	Aps	(s)	Gls
14	Dean BENNETT	ENG	13/12/77	M	13		
5	Garry BREEN		17/3/89	D	27		4
19	John BREEN		25/2/91	A	2	(13)	2
6	Liam BURNS	NIR	30/10/78	D	25	(1)	1
8	Alan CAWLEY		3/1/82	M	6	(4)	
1	Peter CHERRIE	SCO	1/10/83	G	33		
10	Neale FENN		18/1/77	A	21	(1)	4
11	Ross GAYNOR		9/9/87	A	31	(2)	7
22	Matt GREGG	ENG	30/11/78	G	3		
3	Wayne HATSWELL	ENG	8/2/75	D	34		1
21	Daniel KEARNS		26/8/91	M	12		
2	Shaun KELLY		15/10/89	D	28	(2)	
9	Fahrudin KUDUZOVIĆ	BIH	10/10/84	M	35		12
20	Steven LENNON	SCO	20/1/88	A	3	(7)	
12	Simon MADDEN		1/5/88	D	15		

	Stephen MAHER		3/3/88	M	25	(5)	1
	Stephen McDONNELL		20/3/92	M	5	(4)	1
3	Michael McGOWAN	NIR	22/2/85	M	3	(4)	
5	Ciarán McGUIGAN	NIR	8/12/89	D	6	(14)	1
	John Joseph "JJ" MELLIGAN		11/2/82	M	15		3
	Tom MILLER	ENG	29/6/90	M	32	(1)	1
7	Tiarnán MULVENNA		10/12/88	M	2	(6)	1
3	Nathan MURPHY		1/11/92	A	6	(2)	
2	Michael SYNNOTT		20/1/87	D	1	(3)	
)	Matthew TIPTON	WAL	29/6/80	A	13	(1)	7

GALWAY UNITED FC

Manager – Sean Connor (NIR)

Founded – 1937

Stadium – Terryland Park (5,000)

MAJOR HONOURS: FAI Cup – (1) 1991.

010				
/3	St Patrick's	a	0-2	
2/3	Bray	h	2-1	*Sheppard K., O'Brien*
0/3	Sligo	a	0-1	
6/3	Shamrock Rovers	h	0-1	
/4	UCD	a	0-0	
/4	Fingal	h	2-2	*Sheppard K., Flood*
6/4	Bohemians	a	3-2	*Sheppard K. 2, O'Donnell (p)*
9/4	Dundalk	h	0-1	
3/4	Drogheda	h	3-1	*Flood 2, Meynell*
26/4	St Patrick's	h	0-2	
0/4	Bray	a	2-0	*Flood, Sheppard K.*
/5	Sligo	h	0-0	
/5	Shamrock Rovers	a	0-2	
14/5	Dundalk	a	0-0	
21/5	UCD	h	2-2	*Flood, O'Donnell (p)*
29/5	Fingal	a	0-2	
/6	Bohemians	h	2-2	*O'Donnell (p), King*
25/6	Drogheda	a	1-0	*O'Donnell*
2/7	St Patrick's	a	2-4	*Flood, Curran*
5/7	Bray	h	2-2	*Curran, Flood*
9/7	Sligo	a	0-3	
18/7	Shamrock Rovers	h	0-1	
25/7	Dundalk	h	1-1	*Walsh*
30/7	UCD	a	1-0	*Sheppard K.*
6/8	Fingal	h	0-1	
13/8	Bohemians	a	2-0	*O'Donnell, O'Brien*
20/8	Drogheda	h	2-1	*O'Donnell 2 (2p)*
3/9	St Patrick's	h	1-1	*Reilly*
10/9	Bray	a	0-4	
13/9	Sligo	h	2-2	*Curran, Sheppard K.*
24/9	Shamrock Rovers	a	0-3	
1/10	Dundalk	a	0-3	
9/10	UCD	h	1-4	*O'Donnell (p)*
15/10	Fingal	a	1-3	*Walsh*
22/10	Bohemians	h	3-2	*O'Brien (p), Molloy 2*
29/10	Drogheda	a	3-3	*O'Brien, Sheppard K., Gartlan*

No	Name	Nat	DoB	Pos	Aps	(s)	Gls
19	Gerard CHEEVERS		4/10/90	M	1	(3)	
2	Séamus CONNEELY		9/7/88	D	31		
3	James CREANEY	SCO	19/10/88	D	11	(7)	
16	Gary CURRAN		22/9/87	M	27	(3)	3
9	Darragh DUGGAN		10/6/93	A		(1)	
18	Anto FLOOD		31/12/84	A	16		7
6	Ciaran FOLEY		29/7/81	M	22	(1)	
	Rory GARTLAN		6/6/92	D		(1)	1
	Daire GERAGHTY		7/11/88	G	5		
4	Thomas HEARY		14/2/79	D	9	(5)	
21	Jonathan KEANE		16/12/87	M	2	(6)	
12	Neal KEANE		13/4/83	A	1	(1)	
	Gary KELLY		1/7/91	M	1	(1)	
	Shane KEOGH		1/9/93	M		(2)	
17	Thomas KING		30/6/89	D	10	(16)	1
5	Jamie MacKENZIE	SCO	8/5/86	D	33		
15	Cian McBRIEN		19/6/89	M	7	(4)	
14	Rhys MEYNELL	ENG	17/8/88	D	30		1
14	Rhys MEYNELL (same player)	ENG	17/8/88	G	1		
9	Jason MOLLOY		22/9/88	A	10	(8)	2
11	Derek O'BRIEN		14/11/79	M	23	(4)	4
8	Stephen O'DONNELL		15/1/86	M	24	(2)	8
12	Evan PRESTON-KELLY		24/11/90	D	2	(3)	
4	Philip REILLY		28/3/86	D	7	(1)	1
1	Barry RYAN		29/8/78	G	29		
7	Bobby RYAN		1/5/79	M	19	(1)	
	Emmett SHAW		2/2/90	M		(1)	
7	David SHEPPARD		14/9/89	M	1	(3)	
10	Karl SHEPPARD		14/2/91	A	33		8
20	Paul SINNOTT		24/7/86	D	27	(2)	
17	Stephen WALSH		29/8/90	D	13	(2)	2
26	Conor WINN		26/2/92	G	1		

SAINT PATRICK'S ATHLETIC FC

Manager – Pete Mahon

Founded – 1929

Stadium – Richmond Park (5,000)

MAJOR HONOURS: League of Ireland – (7) 1952, 1955, 1956, 1990, 1996, 1998, 1999; FAI Cup – (2) 1959, 1961.

2010				
5/3	Galway	h	2-0	*Guy, Williams*
16/3	Shamrock Rovers	a	2-0	*Bermingham, Faherty*
19/3	UCD	h	3-0	*Faherty, Guy 2*
26/3	Dundalk	a	0-0	
2/4	Fingal	h	0-0	
6/4	Bohemians	a	1-1	*Faherty*
9/4	Drogheda	h	0-1	
20/4	Bray	a	4-0	*Byrne P., Kenna, Guthrie, Coughlan*
23/4	Sligo	h	1-0	*McAllister*
26/4	Galway	a	2-0	*Byrne P., Byrne S.*
30/4	Shamrock Rovers	h	1-2	*Williams*
3/5	UCD	a	0-1	
7/5	Dundalk	h	1-0	*Byrne P.*
21/5	Bohemians	h	3-1	*Doyle, Byrne P., Byrne S.*
29/5	Drogheda	a	1-2	*Faherty*
8/6	Bray	h	3-0	*Faherty 2, Sinnott*
26/6	Sligo	a	0-0	
2/7	Galway	h	4-2	*Doyle 3, Faherty*
5/7	Shamrock Rovers	a	1-2	*Doyle*
9/7	UCD	h	2-1	*Guthrie 2*
18/7	Dundalk	a	3-0	*Mulcahy 2, Kenna*
25/7	Fingal	h	1-1	*Mulcahy*
30/7	Bohemians	a	1-1	*Mulcahy*
6/8	Drogheda	h	2-0	*McAllister, Doyle*
13/8	Bray	a	2-3	*North 2*
20/8	Sligo	h	0-0	
23/8	Fingal	a	3-2	*Faherty, McAllister, Doyle*
3/9	Galway	a	1-1	*Guy*
10/9	Shamrock Rovers	h	1-3	*Guy*
13/9	UCD	a	2-3	*North, Stewart*
24/9	Dundalk	h	1-2	*Lynch*
2/10	Fingal	a	2-2	*Mulcahy, North*
5/10	Drogheda	a	3-0	*Guy, North, O'Connor*
9/10	Bohemians	h	0-1	
22/10	Bray	h	2-0	*North 2*
29/10	Sligo	a	0-1	

No	Name	Nat	DoB	Pos	Aps	(s)	Gls
20	Chris BENNION	SCO	30/8/80	G	1		
3	Ian BERMINGHAM		8/1/89	D	24	(1)	1
11	Paul BYRNE		19/5/86	A	14	(11)	4
8	Stuart BYRNE		4/11/76	M	28	(3)	2
14	Brian CASH		24/11/82	M	10	(16)	
16	Thomas CAWLEY		21/9/91	A		(1)	
15	Gareth COUGHLAN		2/5/90	M	5	(4)	1
25	Derek DOYLE		30/4/86	A	20	(4)	7
10	Vinny FAHERTY		13/6/87	A	26	(7)	8
5	Shane GUTHRIE		11/12/84	D	28		3
21	Ryan GUY	USA	5/9/85	M	30	(2)	6
19	Noel HAVERTY		24/2/89	D	7		
4	Conor KENNA		21/8/84	D	36		2
6	Damien LYNCH		31/7/79	D	21	(3)	1
7	David McALLISTER		29/12/88	M	26	(6)	3
17	Dave MULCAHY		28/1/78	M	30	(3)	5

9	Danny NORTH	ENG	7/9/87	A	11	(7)	7
23	Jamie O'BRIEN		8/6/90	M	1	(7)	
18	Garreth O'CONNOR		10/11/78	M	9	(5)	1
2	Derek PENDER		2/10/84	D	25	(2)	
1	Gary ROGERS		25/9/81	G	35		
18	Conor SINNOTT		19/1/86	D	2	(4)	1
	Sean STEWART		4/2/92	M	1	(6)	1
9	Alex WILLIAMS	SCO	15/1/83	A	6	(8)	2

SHAMROCK ROVERS FC

Manager – Michael O'Neill (NIR)

Founded – 1901

Stadium – Tallaght Stadium (6,500)

MAJOR HONOURS: League of Ireland – (16) 1923, 1925, 1927, 1932, 1938, 1939, 1954, 1957, 1959, 1964, 1984, 1985, 1986, 1987, 1994, 2010; FAI Cup – (24) 1925, 1929, 1930, 1931, 1932, 1933, 1936, 1940, 1944, 1945, 1948, 1955, 1956, 1962, 1964, 1965, 1966, 1967, 1968, 1969, 1978, 1985, 1986, 1987.

2010				
6/3	Sligo	a	1-1	*Chambers (p)*
16/3	St Patrick's	h	0-2	
21/3	Dundalk	h	0-2	
26/3	Galway	a	1-0	*Sullivan*
2/4	UCD	h	0-0	
5/4	Fingal	a	1-1	*Chambers (p)*
9/4	Bohemians	h	1-0	*Dennehy*
16/4	Drogheda	a	2-0	*Bayly, Twigg*
23/4	Bray	h	1-0	*Twigg*
26/4	Sligo	h	1-1	*Twigg*
30/4	St Patrick's	a	2-1	*Stewart 2*
3/5	Dundalk	a	1-2	*Twigg*
7/5	Galway	h	2-0	*Rice, Murray*
14/5	UCD	a	2-1	*Chambers, Twigg*
21/5	Fingal	h	1-1	*Chambers*
29/5	Bohemians	a	0-0	
8/6	Drogheda	h	1-1	*Bayly*
25/6	Bray	a	0-0	
2/7	Sligo	a	2-1	*og (Keane), Turner*
5/7	St Patrick's	h	2-1	*Stewart 2*
11/7	Dundalk	h	4-0	*Chambers 2, og (Maher), Twigg*
18/7	Galway	a	1-0	*Twigg*
1/8	Fingal	a	3-3	*Sives, Twigg, Rice*
8/8	Bohemians	h	3-0	*Murray, Twigg, Dennehy*
13/8	Drogheda	a	2-0	*Twigg, Dennehy*
20/8	Bray	h	4-1	*og (Houston), Rice, Twigg 2*
23/8	UCD	h	4-1	*Bradley, Dennehy, Twigg, Murray*
3/9	Sligo	h	1-0	*Dennehy*
10/9	St Patrick's	a	3-1	*Twigg, Stewart, Dennehy*
13/9	Dundalk	a	1-5	*Twigg*
24/9	Galway	h	3-0	*Twigg 2, Sives*
1/10	UCD	a	2-3	*Twigg, Turner (p)*
5/10	Bohemians	a	0-1	
9/10	Fingal	h	1-2	*Stewart*
22/10	Drogheda	h	2-0	*Stewart, Twigg*
29/10	Bray	a	2-2	*Twigg, Stewart*

No	Name	Nat	DoB	Pos	Aps	(s)	Gls
10	Dessie BAKER		25/8/77	M	4	(11)	
14	Graham BARRETT		6/10/81	A	5	(6)	
25	Robert BAYLY		22/2/88	M	18	(8)	2
7	Stephen BRADLEY		19/11/84	M	13	(3)	1
11	Ollie CAHILL		29/9/75	M	7	(5)	
8	James CHAMBERS		14/2/87	M	26	(5)	6
22	Don COWEN		16/11/89	A		(3)	
20	Billy DENNEHY		17/2/87	M	27	(7)	6
11	Neale FENN		18/1/77	A	5	(4)	
13	Pat FLYNN		13/1/85	D	18	(3)	
15	Patrick KAVANAGH		29/12/85	M	19	(3)	
1	Alan MANNUS	NIR	19/5/82	G	36		
19	Danny MURPHY		4/12/82	D	23	(3)	
24	Dan MURRAY	ENG	16/5/82	D	28		3
17	Sean O'CONNOR		21/10/83	M	6	(12)	
5	Aidan PRICE		8/12/81	D	26	(1)	
6	Stephen RICE		6/10/84	M	22	(11)	3
4	Craig SIVES	SCO	9/4/86	D	24	(1)	2
3	Enda STEVENS		9/7/90	D	17	(1)	
23	Thomas STEWART	NIR	12/11/86	A	25	(7)	8
2	Pat SULLIVAN		30/10/82	D	2		1
18	Chris TURNER	NIR	3/1/87	M	19	(6)	2
9	Gary TWIGG	SCO	19/3/84	A	26	(3)	20

SLIGO ROVERS FC

Manager – Paul Cook (ENG)

Founded – 1928

Stadium – The Showgrounds (5,500)

MAJOR HONOURS: League of Ireland – (2) 1937, 1977; FAI Cup – (3) 1983, 1994, 2010.

2010				
6/3	Shamrock Rovers	h	1-1	*Doyle*
12/3	Fingal	a	1-1	*Amond*
20/3	Galway	h	1-0	*Doyle*
26/3	Bohemians	a	0-0	
2/4	Drogheda	a	2-2	*Amond, McCabe*
5/4	Dundalk	h	2-2	*McCabe, Almeida*
9/4	Bray	a	3-2	*O'Grady, Amond, Marshall*
23/4	St Patrick's	a	0-1	
26/4	Shamrock Rovers	a	1-1	*Amond*
1/5	Fingal	h	0-1	
4/5	Galway	a	0-0	
8/5	Bohemians	h	1-2	*Blinkhorn*
15/5	Drogheda	h	6-0	*Ryan, Peers, Amond 3, Dillo*
21/5	Dundalk	a	0-1	
29/5	Bray	h	5-1	*Amond 2, Doyle, Russell, Nd*
8/6	UCD	a	2-0	*Amond, Peers*
26/6	St Patrick's	h	0-0	
2/7	Shamrock Rovers	h	1-2	*Doyle*
5/7	Fingal	a	1-1	*Doyle*
9/7	Galway	h	3-0	*Ndo, Dillon, Amond*
13/7	UCD	h	2-1	*Amond 2*
16/7	Bohemians	a	0-2	
23/7	Drogheda	a	3-2	*Peers, Amond 2*
31/7	Dundalk	h	1-0	*McCabe*
6/8	Bray	a	3-1	*Amond, Blinkhorn, Boco*
14/8	UCD	h	4-0	*O'Grady, Amond, Blinkhorn, Foran*
20/8	St Patrick's	a	0-0	
3/9	Shamrock Rovers	a	0-1	
10/9	Fingal	h	4-3	*Peers, Boco 2, Doyle*
13/9	Galway	a	2-2	*Ryan, Russell*
21/9	Bohemians	h	1-1	*Russell*
2/10	Drogheda	h	2-1	*Keane (p), McCabe*
5/10	Bray	h	2-1	*Blinkhorn, Keane (p)*
9/10	Dundalk	a	4-2	*Blinkhorn, Ryan, Keane (p), Ndo*
22/10	UCD	a	2-1	*Blinkhorn, Boco*
29/10	St Patrick's	h	1-0	*Keane (p)*

Name	Nat	DoB	Pos	Aps	(s)	Gls
Mauro ALMEIDA	POR	29/1/82	D	4	(2)	1
Pádraig AMOND		23/4/88	A	25	(2)	17
Matthew BLINKHORN	ENG	2/3/85	A	18	(8)	6
Romuald BOCO	BEN	8/7/85	A	9	(1)	4
Richard BRUSH	ENG	26/11/84	G	23		
Iarfhlaith DAVOREN		12/5/86	D	28		
John DILLON	ENG	2/8/88	M	16	(12)	2
Mark DONINGER	ENG	19/10/89	M	4	(8)	
Eoin DOYLE		12/3/88	A	25	(10)	6
Derek FORAN		9/10/89	D	7	(5)	1
John GIBSON	SCO	31/1/89	G	6		
Alan KEANE		23/9/84	D	34		4
Ciarán KELLY		14/3/80	G	7	(2)	
Jim LAUCHLAN	SCO	2/2/77	D	16		
Dean MARSHALL		15/3/90	M		(4)	1
Gary McCABE		1/8/88	M	24	(9)	4
Jason McCARTNEY		6/9/86	A	1	(2)	
Lee McEVILLY	NIR	15/4/82	A		(2)	
Mark McGOLDRICK		27/11/91	A		(3)	
Joseph NDO	CMR	28/4/76	M	29		3
Conor O'GRADY		27/5/80	M	10	(15)	2
Gavin PEERS		10/11/85	D	31		4

ohn RUSSELL		18/5/85	M	19	(1)	3
chie RYAN		6/1/85	M	33		3
anny VENTRE	ENG	23/1/86	D	22	(5)	
aul WHELAN		29/6/87	D	5	(2)	

SPORTING FINGAL FC

Manager – Liam Buckley
Founded – 2007
Stadium – Morton Stadium (4,000)
MAJOR HONOURS: FAI Cup – (1) 2009.

010				
/3	Bohemians	a	0-1	
2/3	Sligo	h	1-1	*O'Neill*
9/3	Bray	a	3-1	*Zayed, O'Neill 2*
6/3	Drogheda	h	4-1	*Zayed, Finn, og (Harris), O'Neill*
/4	St Patrick's	a	0-0	
/4	Shamrock Rovers	h	1-1	*Byrne*
/4	Galway	a	2-2	*Zayed, O'Neill*
6/4	Dundalk	h	2-1	*og (Hatswell), Kirby (p)*
22/4	UCD	a	0-0	
26/4	Bohemians	h	0-2	
/5	Sligo	a	1-0	*Finn*
/5	Bray	h	1-0	*McFaul*
/5	Drogheda	a	1-1	*Finn*
21/5	Shamrock Rovers	a	1-1	*Crowe*
29/5	Galway	h	2-0	*Finn, Zayed*
8/6	Dundalk	a	2-1	*Williams, Finn*
25/6	UCD	h	1-2	*Zayed*
2/7	Bohemians	a	1-1	*O'Brien*
5/7	Sligo	h	1-1	*Byrne*
9/7	Bray	a	3-0	*Crowe, Kirby 2*
19/7	Drogheda	h	1-2	*Zayed*
25/7	St Patrick's	a	1-1	*Byrne*
1/8	Shamrock Rovers	h	3-3	*Zayed, O'Neill, Finn*
6/8	Galway	a	1-0	*Byrne*
13/8	Dundalk	h	1-0	*Williams*
20/8	UCD	a	2-1	*Byrne, Browne*
23/8	St Patrick's	h	2-3	*Williams, Byrne*
3/9	Bohemians	h	0-0	
10/9	Sligo	a	3-4	*O'Neill, Browne, Williams*
13/9	Bray	h	2-2	*Kirby, Zayed*
24/9	Drogheda	a	4-0	*Byrne, Hawkins, O'Neill, Kirby (p)*
2/10	St Patrick's	h	2-2	*Crowe, Finn*
9/10	Shamrock Rovers	a	2-1	*O'Neill, Crowe*
15/10	Galway	h	3-1	*Kirby, Hawkins, Fitzgerald*
22/10	Dundalk	a	2-0	*Williams, Finn*
29/10	UCD	h	4-1	*Crowe 2, O'Neill 2*

Name	Nat	DoB	Pos	Aps	(s)	Gls
Shane BARRETT		23/11/81	A		(2)	
Kenny BROWNE		7/8/86	D	30		2
Conan BYRNE		10/7/85	M	36		7
Ollie CAHILL		29/9/75	M	7	(6)	
Brendan CLARKE		17/10/85	G	17		
Glen CROWE		25/12/77	A	16	(17)	6
Kevin DAWSON		30/6/90	M	4	(7)	
Ronan FINN		21/12/87	M	34		8
Lorcan FITZGERALD		3/1/89	D	24		1
John FROST		20/5/80	D	7		
Brian GANNON		11/4/85	D	5	(4)	
Colin HAWKINS		17/8/77	D	9		2
Colm JAMES		16/6/83	M	5	(6)	
Alan KIRBY		8/9/77	M	24	(6)	6
Shaun MAHER		10/6/78	D	19		
Shane McFAUL		23/5/86	M	25	(1)	1
Ger O'BRIEN		2/7/84	D	29	(1)	1
Gary O'NEILL		30/1/82	A	25	(3)	11
Stephen PAISLEY		28/7/83	D	6	(1)	
Darren QUIGLEY		10/6/86	G	19		
Keith QUINN		22/9/88	M	5	(15)	
Shaun WILLIAMS		19/10/86	M	31	(1)	5
Eamon ZAYED	LBY	4/10/83	A	19	(6)	8

UNIVERSITY COLLEGE DUBLIN AFC

Manager – Martin Russell
Founded – 1895
Stadium – Belfield Bowl (2,500)
MAJOR HONOURS: FAI Cup – (1) 1984.

2010				
5/3	Drogheda	a	3-0	*Kilduff 2, Bolger*
16/3	Bohemians	h	1-2	*Bolger (p)*
19/3	St Patrick's	a	0-3	
26/3	Bray	h	1-0	*Kilduff*
2/4	Shamrock Rovers	a	0-0	
5/4	Galway	h	0-0	
9/4	Dundalk	a	0-3	
22/4	Fingal	h	0-0	
26/4	Drogheda	h	2-0	*Bolger (p), Kilduff*
30/4	Bohemians	a	0-0	
3/5	St Patrick's	h	1-0	*McMillan D.*
7/5	Bray	a	6-0	*McMillan D. 2, Bolger 2, og (Kane), McMillan E.*
14/5	Shamrock Rovers	h	1-2	*Corry*
21/5	Galway	a	2-2	*McMillan D., Mulhall*
29/5	Dundalk	h	3-1	*McMillan D., Kilduff, Corry*
8/6	Sligo	h	0-2	
25/6	Fingal	a	2-1	*Boyle, McMillan E.*
2/7	Drogheda	a	0-1	
5/7	Bohemians	h	0-2	
9/7	St Patrick's	a	1-2	*Mulhall*
13/7	Sligo	a	1-2	*Kilduff*
16/7	Bray	h	4-0	*Kilduff 3, Bolger*
30/7	Galway	h	0-1	
6/8	Dundalk	a	1-1	*Mulhall*
14/8	Sligo	a	0-4	
20/8	Fingal	h	1-2	*Kilduff*
23/8	Shamrock Rovers	a	1-4	*Kilduff*
3/9	Drogheda	h	1-1	*Kilduff*
10/9	Bohemians	a	1-3	*Corry*
13/9	St Patrick's	h	3-2	*McMillan D., Kilduff, Bolger (p)*
24/9	Bray	a	2-2	*McMillan D. 2*
1/10	Shamrock Rovers	h	3-2	*Kilduff, Shortall, Ward*
9/10	Galway	a	4-1	*Ward 3, Corry*
15/10	Dundalk	h	0-2	
22/10	Sligo	h	1-2	*Kilduff*
29/10	Fingal	a	1-4	*Leahy*

Name	Nat	DoB	Pos	Aps	(s)	Gls
Gerard BARRON		3/6/89	G	7		
Greg BOLGER		9/9/88	M	28	(1)	7
Andrew BOYLE		7/3/91	D	25		1
Billy BRENNAN		6/3/85	G	29		
Paul CORRY		3/2/91	M	23	(6)	4
Robert CREEVY		24/8/89	M	13	(13)	
Danny FALLON		9/3/90	M	1		
Shane FITZGERALD		12/1/87	M	1	(2)	
Sean HARDING		17/9/88	D	11	(4)	
Sean HOUSTON		29/10/89	M		(1)	
Michael KELLY		14/1/89	D	3		
Ciaran KILDUFF		29/9/88	A	34	(1)	15
Michael LEAHY		30/4/89	D	9	(4)	1
Gareth MATTHEWS		13/2/90	D	1	(3)	
Peter McMAHON		20/4/89	M	8	(2)	
David McMILLAN		14/12/88	A	20	(3)	8
Evan McMILLAN		20/11/86	D	35		2
Karl MOORE		9/11/88	M	6	(4)	
Chris MULHALL		9/11/88	M	26	(4)	3
Ciaran NANGLE		23/3/90	D	25	(2)	
David O'CONNOR		24/8/91	D	1		
Paul O'CONOR		10/8/87	M	14	(2)	
Stephen ROCHE		5/7/86	M	5	(6)	
Graham RUSK		13/12/89	A	15	(9)	
Sean RUSSELL		10/12/93	D	2		
Brian SHORTALL		28/5/85	D	25	(2)	1
Keith WARD		12/10/90	M	15	(11)	4
Dwayne WILSON		14/6/87	M	14	(8)	

TOP GOALSCORERS 2010

20 Gary TWIGG (Shamrock Rovers)
17 Pádraig AMOND (Sligo)
15 Ciaran KILDUFF (UCD)
14 Jake KELLY (Bray)
12 Jason BYRNE (Bohemians)
Fahrudin KUDUZOVIĆ (Dundalk)
11 Gary O'NEILL (Fingal)
10 Patrick MADDEN (Bohemians)
8 Stephen O'DONNELL (Galway)
Karl SHEPPARD (Galway)
Vinny FAHERTY (St Patrick's)
Thomas STEWART (Shamrock Rovers)
Ronan FINN (Fingal)
Eamon ZAYED (Fingal)
David McMILLAN (UCD)

PROMOTED CLUB

DERRY CITY FC

Manager – Stephen Kenny
Founded - 1928
Stadium – The Brandywell (7,700)
MAJOR HONOURS: Irish League – (1) 1965; League of Ireland – (2) 1989, 1997; Irish Cup – (3) 1949, 1954, 1964; FAI Cup – (4) 1989, 1995, 2002 (autumn), 2006.

SECOND LEVEL FINAL TABLE 2010

		Pld	W	D	L	F	A	Pts
1	Derry City FC	33	20	9	4	65	24	69
2	Waterford United FC	33	20	6	7	59	27	66
3	Monaghan United FC	33	18	8	7	59	29	62
4	Shelbourne FC	33	18	7	8	57	31	61
5	Limerick FC	33	17	6	10	55	35	57
6	Cork City FORAS Co-Op	33	15	7	11	39	31	52
7	Wexford Youths FC	33	13	6	14	44	52	45
8	Finn Harps FC	33	10	10	13	37	43	40
9	Longford Town FC	33	9	8	16	39	53	35
10	Athlone Town FC	33	6	13	14	35	50	31
11	Mervue United FC	33	5	4	24	34	84	19
12	Salthill Devon FC	33	2	6	25	24	88	12

PROMOTION/RELEGATION PLAY-OFFS

(2/11/10)
Galway 1, Bray 0
Waterford 1, Monaghan 3

(5/11/10 & 8/11/10)
Monaghan 0, Bray 0
Bray 1, Monaghan 1 *(aet)*
(1-1; Bray 7-6 on pens)

DOMESTIC CUP 2010

FAI CUP

THIRD ROUND

(4/6/10)
Cork 1, Bluebell United 1
Derry 1, Bray 1
Drogheda 1, UCD 2
Dublin Bus 0, Shelbourne 2
Dundalk 0, St Patrick's 1
Fingal 1, Mervue 1
Finn Harps 3, Crumlin United 0
Galway 5, Malahide United 0
Limerick 3, Tolka Rovers 1
Longford 1, Waterford 0
Shamrock Rovers 5, Wexford 1
Sligo 1, Athlone 0

(5/6/10)
Belgrove 2, Avondale United 1
Tullamore Town 1, Salthill 3

(6/6/10)
Carlow 1, Monaghan 1
Glenville 1, Bohemians 7

Replays

(8/6/10)
Bluebell United 0, Cork 1

(28/6/10)
Bray 3, Derry 2

(29/6/10)
Monaghan 2, Carlow 1

(10/8/10)
Mervue 0, Fingal 4

FOURTH ROUND

(27/8/10)
Bohemians 1, Shelbourne 0
Cork 0, Monaghan 1
Fingal 2, Limerick 2
Finn Harps 0, Sligo 1
Galway 1, Salthill 1
Longford 1, Shamrock Rovers 2
St Patrick's 2, Belgrove 0
UCD 2, Bray 3

Replays

(30/8/10)
Limerick 0, Fingal 0 *(aet; 3-4 on pens)*
Salthill 1, Galway 3

QUARTER-FINALS

(17/9/10)
Bohemians 3 *(Quigley 21, Cretaro 53, Greene 79)*, Bray 0
Shamrock Rovers 6 *(Stewart 12, Meynell 23og, Chambers 33, 65, Conneely 67og, Baker 78)*, Galway 0

(18/9/10)
St Patrick's 3 *(Guy 22, Lynch 52, Faherty 86)*, Fingal 1 *(Williams 53)*
Sligo 3 *(Keane 25p, Boco 47, McGoldrick 90)*, Monaghan 0

SEMI-FINALS

(15/10/10)
Bohemians 0, Sligo 1 *(Peers 75)*

(17/10/10)
Shamrock Rovers 2 *(Turner 16, Twigg 64)*, St Patrick's 2 *(McAllister 29, Kavanagh 90og)*

Replay

(19/10/10)
St Patrick's 0, Shamrock Rovers 1 *(Turner 70)*

FINAL

(17/11/10)
Aviva Stadium, Dublin
SLIGO ROVERS FC 0
SHAMROCK ROVERS FC 0
(aet; 2-0 on pens)
Referee – *Connolly*
SLIGO – *Kelly, Keane, Peers, Lauchlan, Davoren, Boco, Ndo, Ventre (O'Grady 117), McCabe, Russell, Doyle.*
SHAMROCK ROVERS – *Mannus, Rice, Flynn, Sives, Stevens, Chambers (Baker 69; Price 113), Turner, Bradley, Dennehy, Stewart (Kavanagh 102), Twigg.*
Sent off: *Bradley 110*

CLUB COMMUNICATION 2011

ohemian FC
alymount Park, Phibsborough
-Dublin 7

l	+353 1 868 0923
ax	+353 1 868 6460
eb	bohemians.ie
mail	lynn@bohemians.ie
edia Officer	Brian Trench

ray Wanderers AFC
arlisle Grounds
-Bray

l	+353 1 282 8214
ax	+353 1 282 8684
eb	braywanderers.ie
mail	carlislegrounds@eircom.net
edia Officer	Vincent Kirwan

erry City FC
he Brandywell Stadium, 200 Lone Moor
oad, GB-Derry BT48 9LB, Northern Ireland

el	+44 2871 373 111
ax	+44 2871 373 263
Veb	derrycityfc.net
mail	derrycityfc@football.fai.ie
ledia Officer	Sean Barrett

Drogheda United FC
Hunky Dory's Park, Windmill Road
IE-Drogheda, Co. Louth

Tel	+353 41 983 0190
Fax	+353 41 983 0195
Web	droghedaunited.ie
Email	info@droghedaunited.ie
Media Officer	Roisin Phillips

Dundalk FC
Oriel Park, Carrick Road
IE-Dundalk, Co. Louth

Tel	+353 42 93 353 98
Fax	+353 42 93 300 03
Web	dundalkfc.com
Email	dlkfc@eircom.net
Media Officer	Colm Crosson

Galway United FC
Terryland Park, Dyke Road
IE-Galway

Tel	+353 91 767 336
Fax	+353 91 767 356
Web	
Email	info@galwayunitedfc.ie
Media Officer	Vincent O'Connor

Saint Patrick's Athletic FC
Richmond Park, 125 Emmet Road
Inchicore, IE-Dublin 8

Tel	+353 1 454 6332
Fax	+353 1 454 6211
Web	stpatsfc.com
Email	info@stpatsfc.com
Media Officer	Gemma Fitzgerald

Shamrock Rovers FC
Tallaght Stadium, Whitestown Way
Tallaght, IE-Dublin 24

Tel	+353 1 460 5948
Fax	+353 1 460 4875
Web	shamrockrovers.ie
Email	info@shamrockrovers.ie
Media Officer	Martina Genockey

Sligo Rovers FC
PO Box 275
IE-Sligo

Tel	353 71 913 0455
Fax	353 71 915 3745
Web	sligorovers.com
Email	sligoroversfc@eircom.net
Media Officer	Rory Houston

University College Dublin AFC
Sports Centre, UCD, Belfield
IE-Dublin 4

Tel	+353 1 716 2142
Fax	+353 1 269 8099
Web	ucdsoccer.com
Email	diarmuid.mcnally@ucd.ie
Media Officer	Gordon O'Callghan

ROMANIA

Roumanie I Rumänien

Federaţia Română de Fotbal (FRF)

COMMUNICATION

Address Casa Fotbalului
Str. Serg. Serbanica
Vasile 12
RO-022186 Bucureşti

Tel +40 21 325 0678
Fax +40 21 325 0679

E-mail frf@frf.ro
Website frf.ro

President Mircea Sandu
General Secretary Adalbert Kassai
Media Officer Paul-Daniel Zaharia

Year of Formation 1909

National Stadium Naţional – Lia Manoliu Bucharest (55,000)

DOMESTIC COMPETITION SUMMARY 2010/11

LIGA I FINAL TABLE

			Home					Away					Total						
		Pld	W	D	L	F	A	W	D	L	F	A	W	D	L	F	A	Pts	Comp
1	FC Oţelul Galaţi	34	12	5	0	29	12	9	2	6	17	13	21	7	6	46	25	70	UCL
2	FC Timişoara	34	11	6	0	37	17	6	9	2	26	21	17	15	2	63	38	66	
3	FC Vaslui	34	12	4	1	34	14	6	7	4	17	14	18	11	5	51	28	65	UCL
4	FC Rapid Bucureşti	34	10	6	1	28	7	6	5	6	15	15	16	11	7	43	22	59	UEL
5	FC Steaua Bucureşti	34	9	4	4	28	16	7	5	5	16	11	16	9	9	44	27	57	UEL
6	FC Dinamo Bucureşti	34	9	4	4	40	28	7	4	6	28	24	16	8	10	68	52	56	UEL
7	CS Gaz Metan Mediaş	34	8	7	2	22	12	6	6	5	19	20	14	13	7	41	32	55	UEL
8	FC Universitatea Cluj	34	7	6	4	28	21	6	2	9	20	33	13	8	13	48	54	47	
9	FC Astra Ploieşti	34	7	6	4	18	12	3	9	5	18	18	10	15	9	36	30	45	
10	CFR 1907 Cluj	34	8	4	5	26	17	3	8	6	24	28	11	12	11	50	45	45	
11	FCM Târgu Mureş	34	9	1	7	21	20	3	8	6	13	21	12	9	13	34	41	45	
12	FC Braşov	34	6	8	3	20	18	4	5	8	14	22	10	13	11	34	40	43	
13	CS Pandurii Târgu Jiu	34	8	5	4	22	15	1	5	11	14	31	9	10	15	36	46	37	
14	ACF Gloria 1922 Bistriţa	34	6	8	3	20	18	2	3	12	14	31	8	11	15	34	49	35	
15	FC Universitatea Craiova	34	4	5	8	16	18	3	4	10	19	30	7	9	18	35	48	30	*Relegated*
16	FC Victoria Brăneşti	34	4	6	7	19	22	1	4	12	16	39	5	10	19	35	61	25	*Relegated*
17	FC Unirea Urziceni	34	6	4	7	15	21	0	3	14	8	42	6	7	21	23	63	25	*Relegated*
18	FC Sportul Studenţesc Bucureşti	34	6	1	10	26	22	1	1	15	12	36	7	2	25	38	58	23	

NB FC Timişoara & ACF Gloria 1922 Bistriţa did not receive licence for 2011/12 Liga I. FC Sportul Studenţesc Bucureşti subsequently remained at top level as the only relegated team with valid licence for 2011/12 Liga I.

Top Scorer Ianis Zicu (Timişoara), 18 goals

Promoted Clubs FC Ceahlăul Piatra Neamţ
CS Concordia Chiajna
FC Petrolul Ploieşti
CS Mioveni
CSU Voinţa Sibiu

Cup Final FC Steaua Bucureşti 2, FC Dinamo Bucureşti 1

Munteanu leads Oţelul to first title

With Dorinel Munteanu, the country's most-capped international, as their inspirational coach, FC Oţelul Galaţi won the 2010/11 Romanian championship. It was the first major honour in the 47-year history of the club from the steel town on the Moldovan border, and it came in a Liga I season disfigured and distorted by financial crises, licensing issues and club withdrawals.

Even before the 2010/11 campaign began there was a change to the Liga I line-up, with FC Internaţional Curtea de Argeş withdrawing and ceding their place to relegated CS Pandurii Târgu Jiu. Serious money problems also beset 2008/09 champions FC Unirea Urziceni, who, following the club's failure to return to the UEFA Champions League group stage, had to slash their budget and release all their best players – most of them to FC Steaua Bucureşti. Although Unirea beat Steaua shortly after the mass exodus, they were never competitive and finished 17th, having used more than 50 players.

Licensing confusion

FC Sportul Studenţesc Bucureşti were the only team to finish below Unirea but oddly, unlike Unirea and the other two teams in the relegation zone, FC Universitatea Craiova and FC Victoria Brăneşti, they did not surrender their Liga I place. This was because, despite financial difficulties of their own, they managed to secure a licence to compete in the top flight in 2011/12. The league's licensing commission was forced to work overtime in the early summer, and while Unirea and Victoria were resigned to going down, three existing top-flight clubs had their applications declined – Universitatea Craiova, 14th-placed ACF Gloria 1922 Bistriţa and, most tellingly, league runners-up FC Timişoara. With one of the promoted teams, FC Bihor Oradea, also failing to fulfil the licensing criteria, an additional play-off was required in early July to determine the last of the five teams that

Dorinel Munteanu – the coach of Romanian champions Oţelul

would go up, CSU Voinţa Sibiu eventually joining FC Ceahlăul Piatra Neamţ, CS Concordia Chaijna, FC Petrolul Ploieşti and CS Mioveni.

Given this administrative chaos, it was perhaps appropriate that Oţelul's Liga I triumph was confirmed off the field – namely, by a decision from the Court of Arbitration for Sport to uphold their walkover win over Pandurii in February. The verdict was delivered on 18 May – three days after Oţelul had won 2-1 at home to Timişoara, a result that gave them a four-point advantage over their rivals with a game to play.

Oţelul's title triumph came out of the blue, but it did highlight the merits of persevering with one coach rather than the constant chopping and changing that was in vogue at most Liga I clubs. Appointed in the summer of 2009, Munteanu had taken Oţelul to eighth place in his first full season, and the fruits of his labour were harvested in his second. The club made a good start and built on that momentum, holding a five-point lead at Christmas and, thanks to victories in their last five matches, keeping Timişoara and FC Vaslui at arm's length through to the finish.

Munteanu's men were efficient rather than entertaining. Fifteen of their 21 victories were by the odd goal, including all of the last five. The team scored only 46 goals, and no individual reached double figures. Their stand-out players were those with defensive responsibilities, such as midfield anchorman Adrian Sălăgean and highly promising young full back Cornel Râpă, both of whom received international call-ups.

Timişoara pushed Oţelul all the way. Indeed, despite a change of coach, with Cosmin Contra resigning in December to make way for Dušan Uhrin Jr, they remained unbeaten for 26 matches before going down 3-2 at FC Rapid Bucureşti in mid-April. The defeat at Oţelul was only their second of the campaign, but it was their inability to convert draws into victories that proved decisive. Finishing second should have brought a UEFA Champions League qualifying place, but the club's licensing problems enforced their exclusion from Europe, which enabled Vaslui, third for the second successive season, to claim the prize instead. Vaslui went extremely well under experienced coach Viorel Hizo, who was brought in after a troubled start to the campaign under former Real Madrid CF coach Juan Ramón López Caro. Although refused permission to buy new players in January, Vaslui lost just once in the spring to finish well clear of the three Bucharest clubs directly below them.

Steaua defeat Dinamo

Steaua, despite endless coaching changes, ended the season with a trophy – their first for five years – after defeating FC Dinamo Bucureşti 2-1 in the Romanian Cup final. It was the arch-rivals' first

Romanian international Ianis Zicu of Timişoara headed the Liga I goal charts

National Team

International Tournament Appearances – FIFA World Cup - (7) 1930, 1934, 1938, 1970, 1990 (2nd round), 1994 (qtr-finals), 1998 (2nd round). UEFA European Championship - (4) 1984, 1996, 2000 (qtr-finals), 2008.

Top Five All-time Caps – Dorinel Munteanu (134); Gheorghe Hagi (124); Gheorghe Popescu (115); László Bölöni (102); Dan Petrescu (95)

Top Five All-time Goals – Gheorghe Hagi (35); Adrian Mutu (32); Iuliu Bodola (30); Viorel Moldovan (25); László Bölöni (23)

meeting in the fixture since 1990 and Steaua's first victory in the competition since 1999. The match was decided 2-1 in Steaua's favour by a bizarre own goal early in the second half from Dinamo defender Ştefan Bărboianu.

Both Steaua and Dinamo had competed in the 2010/11 UEFA Europa League, with Steaua the only one of five Romanian participants to reach the group stage. They would have progressed further still but for costly late goals conceded in both matches against SSC Napoli. CFR 1907 Cluj, granted automatic access to the UEFA Champions League group stage, won their opening game but could only muster one more point, at home to AS Roma, by which stage their fate was sealed. The 2009/10 double winners sacked coach Andrea Mandorlini after a bad start to the domestic campaign, from which they never fully recovered, ending up out of the European picture in tenth place.

Lucescu quits

Romanian interest in UEFA EURO 2012 looked to be over after Răzvan Lucescu's team took just two points from four games and then fell behind at home to Luxembourg. But a couple of goals from Adrian Mutu and another from Liga I top scorer Ianis Zicu (Timişoara) gave Romania their first win, and when that was followed in June by a 3-0 victory over Bosnia & Herzegovina – achieved without captain Cristian Chivu, who had just announced his international retirement – qualification was back on the agenda. Then, however, Lucescu made the shock announcement that he was standing down to return to his former job at Rapid Bucureşti. The post was offered to Romanian football legend Gheorghe Hagi, but he passed it up and it was taken instead, for the third time, by Victor Piţurcă, the man who preceded Lucescu in the role and led the team at UEFA EURO 2008.

NATIONAL TEAM RESULTS 2010/11

11/8/10	Turkey	A	Istanbul	0-2	
3/9/10	Albania (ECQ)	H	Piatra Neamt	1-1	*Stancu (80)*
7/9/10	Belarus (ECQ)	A	Minsk	0-0	
9/10/10	France (ECQ)	A	Saint-Denis	0-2	
17/11/10	Italy	N	Klagenfurt (AUT)	1-1	*Marica (34)*
8/2/11	Ukraine	N	Paralimni (CYP)	2-2	*Alexa (34, 44) (2-4 on pens)*
9/2/11	Cyprus	A	Paralimni	1-1	*Torje (56) (5-4 on pens)*
26/3/11	Bosnia & Herzegovina (ECQ)	A	Zenica	1-2	*Marica (29)*
29/3/11	Luxembourg (ECQ)	H	Piatra Neamt	3-1	*Mutu (24, 68), Zicu (78)*
3/6/11	Bosnia & Herzegovina (ECQ)	H	Bucharest	3-0	*Mutu (37), Marica (41, 55)*
8/6/11	Brazil	A	Sao Paulo	0-1	
11/6/11	Paraguay	A	Asuncion	0-2	

NATIONAL TEAM APPEARANCES 2010/11

Coach – Râzvan LUCESCU /(4/6/11) (Ştefan IOVAN)	**17/2/69 23/8/60**		**Tur**	**ALB**	**BLR**	**FRA**	**Ita**	**Ukr**	**Cyp**	**BIH**	**LUX**	**BIH**	**Bra**	**Par**	**Caps**	**Goals**
Bogdan Ionuţ LOBONŢ	18/1/78	Roma (ITA)	G	G											78	-
Ovidiu Liviu DĂNĂNAE	26/8/85	Univ Craiova	D												4	-
Gabriel Sebastian TAMAŞ	9/11/83	West Brom (ENG)	D	D	D	D	D		D	D	D65	D			55	3
Cristian Eugen CHIVU	26/10/80	Inter (ITA)	D61		D	D	D15								75	3
Răzvan Dincă RAŢ	26/5/81	Shakhtar (UKR)	D	D	D	D	D	D	s68	D	D	D			75	1
Răzvan COCIŞ	19/2/83	Al Nassr (KSA)	M	M77	s46	M87										
		/Karpaty (UKR)								s70					40	2
Mirel Matei RĂDOI	22/3/81	Al Hilal (KSA)	M	D	M	M									67	2
George FLORESCU	21/5/84	Alania (RUS)	M	M	M	M	M		M	M76					9	1
Ciprian Ioan DEAC	16/2/86	CFR Cluj	M77													
		/Schalke (GER)		M	M83	s46	M90	M		M85					11	-
Marius Ioan BILAŞCO	13/7/81	Unirea Urziceni	A51													
		/Steaua			A										5	-
Daniel George NICULAE	6/10/82	Monaco (FRA)	A88	A64	s73	A63									35	8
Ciprian Andrei MARICA	2/10/85	Stuttgart (GER)	s51	A	s83	s63	A		A	A	A	A87	A72		49	16
George Daniel GALAMAZ	5/4/81	Unirea Urziceni	s61												3	-
Bănel NICOLIŢĂ	7/1/85	Steaua	s77 /90												30	1
Bogdan Sorin STANCU	28/6/87	Steaua	s88	s64	A73	A	A									
		/Galatasaray (TUR)							A68		M46				7	1
Cristian TÂNASE	18/2/87	Steaua	s90				s58					s63	s46	M73	12	1
Cosmin Marius CONTRA	15/12/75	unattached		D56											73	7
Andrei Gabriel TORJE	22/11/89	Dinamo Bucureşti		M	M46		M58		M	M70	s46	M	M	M84	9	1
Gabriel MUREŞAN	13/2/82	CFR Cluj		s56				M79			M	M	M80	M61	8	-
Nicolae Ovidiu HEREA	26/3/85	Rapid Bucureşti		s77											1	-
Costin Fane PANTILIMON	1/2/87	Timişoara			G	G	G46	G		G			s67	G	13	-
Vasile MAFTEI	1/1/81	Unirea Urziceni			D											
		/CFR Cluj						D							12	1
Ionuţ Cristian SĂPUNARU	5/4/84	Porto (POR)				D					D	D			9	-
Ianis Alin ZICU	23/10/83	Timişoara				M46		s57	M85	s85	M		s72	A46	12	1
Mihai ROMAN	16/11/84	Rapid Bucureşti				s87		M58							9	-
Cornel Emilian RÂPĂ	16/1/90	Oţelul					D		D	D			D	D	5	-
Adrian ROPOTAN	8/5/86	Dinamo Moskva (RUS)					M80		M	s76	M				5	-
Dorin Nicolae GOIAN	12/12/80	Palermo (ITA)					s15			D	s65				37	5
Ciprian Anton TĂTĂRUŞANU	9/2/86	Steaua					s46		G		G	G	G67		5	-
Dan ALEXA	28/10/79	Timişoara					s80	M		M			s80	s61	6	2
Silviu ILIE	27/6/88	Oţelul					s90	s58	s68						3	-
Florin GARDOŞ	29/10/88	Steaua						D			D		D	D	4	-
Paul PAPP	11/11/89	Vaslui						D				D	D	D46	4	-
Gheorghe BUCUR	8/4/80	Kuban (RUS)						A57	s85						21	4
Sabrin SBURLEA	12/5/89	Rapid Bucureşti						A68							1	-

NATIONAL TEAM APPEARANCES 2010/11 (contd.)

			Tur	ALB	BLR	FRA	Ita	Ukr	Cyp	BIH	LUX	BIH	Bra	Par	Caps	Goals
Liviu Adrian GANEA	23/2/88	Dinamo Bucureşti						s68							1	-
Iulian Cătălin APOSTOL	3/12/80	Unirea Urziceni						s79							7	1
Dragoş GRIGORE	7/9/86	Dinamo Bucureşti							D						1	-
Adrian Ioan SĂLĂGEAN	9/4/83	Oţelul							D68						1	-
Adrian MUTU	8/1/79	Fiorentina (ITA)								A	A84	A83			70	32
Marius Silviu ALEXE	22/2/90	Dinamo Bucureşti									s84	s87	s53	A	4	-
Alexandru Viorel BOURCEANU	24/4/85	Timişoara										M	M66	s46	4	-
Lucian Iulian SÂNMĂRTEAN	13/3/80	Vaslui										M63	M53	s46	6	-
Romeo Constantin SURDU	12/1/84	Steaua										s83	A46	s73	6	-
Iasmin LATOVLEVICI	11/5/86	Steaua											D	D	2	-
Gabriel Nicu GIURGIU	3/9/82	Oţelul											s66	M46	2	-
Cristian Daniel OROS	15/8/84	Braşov												s46	1	-
Liviu ANTAL	2/6/89	Oţelul												s84	1	-

CLUB-BY-CLUB

FC ASTRA PLOIEŞTI

Coach – Mihai Stoichiţă; (6/9/10) Tibor Selymes

Founded – 1937

Stadium – Astra (7,000)

2010				
25/7	Dinamo	h	1-2	*Lukacs*
31/7	Gloria Bistriţa	a	1-1	*Rohat*
8/8	Gaz Metan	h	0-2	
13/8	CFR Cluj	a	2-2	*Pătraşcu, Fatai*
21/8	Univ Craiova	h	2-2	*Popara, Rohat*
30/8	Victoria	a	1-1	*Seto*
12/9	Timişoara	h	1-1	*Fatai*
20/9	Steaua	a	1-1	*Măţel*
26/9	Sportul Studenţesc	a	1-0	*Fatai*
1/10	Pandurii	h	2-0	*Pătraşcu, Fatai*
15/10	Rapid	a	0-3	
23/10	Târgu Mureş	h	0-0	
1/11	Univ Cluj	a	0-1	
6/11	Braşov	h	3-0	*Paulinho (p), Seto, Fatai*
12/11	Vaslui	a	0-0	
22/11	Unirea	h	1-0	*Mihalcea*
27/11	Oţelul	a	1-2	*Tigoianu*
4/12	Dinamo	a	2-2	*Seto, Opršal*
2011				
28/2	Gloria Bistriţa	h	1-0	*Opršal*
6/3	Gaz Metan	a	0-0	
14/3	CFR Cluj	h	1-1	*Strătilă*
20/3	Univ Craiova	a	1-1	*Măţel*
1/4	Victoria	h	2-0	*og (Oprea), Măţel*
6/4	Timişoara	a	2-2	*Miranda, N'Doye (p)*
10/4	Steaua	h	1-0	*Mihalache*
13/4	Sportul Studenţesc	h	1-0	*Fatai*
16/4	Pandurii	a	0-1	
22/4	Rapid	h	0-0	
27/4	Târgu Mureş	a	0-1	
1/5	Univ Cluj	h	1-2	*Strătilă*
4/5	Braşov	a	3-0	*N'Doye, Tigoianu 2*
9/5	Vaslui	h	1-1	*Fatai*
13/5	Unirea	a	3-0	*Rusu, Stan, Măţel*
21/5	Oţelul	h	0-1	

No	Name	Nat	DoB	Pos	Aps	(s)	Gls
11	Atanas BORNOSUZOV	BUL	5/10/79	M	3	(6)	
9	Constantin Valentin BUDESCU		19/2/89	A	4	(2)	
25	Eugen Florin CRĂCIUN		22/3/86	D	5	(2)	
10	Marius CROITORU		2/10/80	M	4	(4)	
23	Viorel DINU		18/9/78	M	5	(2)	
12	Pierre Romain Owono EBÉDE	CMR	9/2/80	G	6		
21	Kehinde Abdul FATAI	NGA	7/9/90	A	21	(5)	7
16	Marian FLOREA		11/6/82	M	6	(6)	
25	Cătălin Alexandru GHEORGHE		12/12/79	D		(1)	
6	Lucian GOIAN		10/2/83	D	23		
1	Cătălin GRIGORE		6/10/77	G	21		
13	Iranilton Sousa Moraes JÚNIOR "MARANHÃO"	BRA	22/7/86	M	14		
25	Raymond LUKACS		30/5/88	A	4	(4)	1
2	Alexandru MĂŢEL		17/10/89	D	26	(2)	4
4	Marius Ovidiu MIHALACHE		14/12/84	D	32	(1)	1
15	Adrian Dumitru MIHALCEA		24/5/76	A	2	(6)	1
23	Osvaldo Noé MIRANDA	ARG	24/6/84	A	23	(1)	1
82	Bogdan Ionuţ MIRON		2/1/82	G	7		
29	Ousmane N'DOYE	SEN	21/3/78	M	11		2
24	Salif NOGO	BFA	31/12/86	D	7		
15	Daniel OCHIA		8/7/81	M		(1)	
3	Radek OPRŠAL	CZE	9/5/78	D	14	(7)	2
7	Paulo Dinarte Gouveia Pestana "PAULINHO"	POR	30/1/85	M	11	(7)	1
14	Florin PĂTRAŞCU		12/4/86	D	10	(2)	2
7	Pavle POPARA	SRB	20/5/87	M	4	(2)	1
5	Gheorghe ROHAT		23/1/75	D	6	(2)	2
17	Bogdan RUSU		9/4/90	A	1	(5)	1
17	Valentin SANDU		28/2/83	D	4		
8	Takayuki SETO	JPN	5/2/86	M	33		3
20	Alexandru Constantin STAN		1/2/89	M	7	(12)	1
18	Sorin Daniel STRĂTILĂ		20/10/86	M	29	(2)	2
19	Ben TEEKLOH	LBR	6/12/83	M	6	(3)	
11	Marius Paul TIGOIANU		29/9/89	M	15	(7)	3
10	Claudiu Ionuţ TUDOR		29/4/85	A	4	(4)	
16	Alexandru ŢIGĂNAŞU		12/6/90	A	5	(2)	
9	Daniel Petru VĂDRARIU		25/6/90	A	1	(1)	
23	WILLIAM Douglas de Amorim	BRA	15/12/91	M		(1)	

FC BRAŞOV

Coach – Daniel Isăilă;
(18/12/10) António Conceição "Toni" (POR)

Founded – 1937

Stadium – Silviu Ploeşteanu (12,670)

2010				
26/7	Târgu Mureş	a	1-0	*Badea*
1/8	Univ Cluj	h	3-1	*Ilyeş, Ionescu, Chipciu*
7/8	Steaua	h	1-1	*Ilyeş*

14/8	Vaslui	a	1-2	*Ionescu*
23/8	Unirea	h	1-1	*Hadnagy*
29/8	Oţelul	a	0-1	
12/9	Dinamo	h	2-2	*Chipciu, Dedu*
20/9	Gloria Bistriţa	a	0-0	
27/9	Gaz Metan	h	0-0	
3/10	CFR Cluj	a	0-4	
18/10	Univ Craiova	h	0-3	
22/10	Victoria	a	1-1	*Cristescu*
31/10	Timişoara	h	0-0	
6/11	Astra	a	0-3	
13/11	Sportul Studenţesc	h	2-0	*Majerník, Ilyeş (p)*
19/11	Pandurii	a	1-2	*Ilyeş*
27/11	Rapid	h	2-0	*Rusu, Chipciu*
3/12	Târgu Mureş	h	1-1	*Ilyeş*
2011				
27/2	Univ Cluj	a	1-1	*Ilyeş (p)*
6/3	Steaua	a	3-0	*Cristescu, Filipe Teixeira, Oros*
14/3	Vaslui	h	1-1	*og (Kuciak)*
21/3	Unirea	a	1-1	*Cristescu*
1/4	Oţelul	h	1-0	*Ilyeş*
6/4	Dinamo	a	1-2	*Nuno Viveiros*
9/4	Gloria Bistriţa	h	0-1	
13/4	Gaz Metan	a	0-0	
17/4	CFR Cluj	h	2-2	*Ilyeş, Distéfano (p)*
24/4	Univ Craiova	a	2-1	*Rusu, Distéfano*
27/4	Victoria	h	1-0	*Hadnagy*
30/4	Timişoara	a	0-2	
4/5	Astra	h	0-3	
8/5	Sportul Studenţesc	a	2-1	*Josías, Mateiu*
15/5	Pandurii	h	3-2	*Ilyeş (p), Josías, Majerník*
21/5	Rapid	a	0-1	

No	Name	Nat	DoB	Pos	Aps	(s)	Gls
23	Valentin BADEA		23/10/82	A	3	(8)	1
14	Valentin BĂDOI		16/12/75	M	5	(6)	
4	Daniel Ilie BĂLAŞA		6/8/81	D	3	(1)	
7	Alexandru CHIPCIU		18/5/89	M	28	(3)	3
3	Emanuel CREŢULESCU		17/6/92	M		(1)	
18	Marian CRISTESCU		17/3/85	M	29	(1)	3
17	Cătălin DEDU		16/5/87	A	9	(5)	1
22	Lamine DIARRASSOUBA	CIV	25/11/86	A	5	(1)	
4	DIEGO Godim "GAÚCHO"	BRA	15/11/81	D	9		
14	David Andrés DISTÉFANO	ARG	10/7/87	M	3	(8)	2
55	Laurenţiu Alexandru DUMITRU		24/5/83	D		(1)	
80	FILIPE de Andrade TEIXEIRA	POR	2/10/80	M	11	(1)	1
9	Attila HADNAGY		8/9/80	A	14	(9)	2
49	Cristian HĂISAN		3/3/81	G	3	(1)	
10	Robert ILYEŞ		4/2/74	M	32	(1)	9
12	Cristian Mihai IONESCU		1/3/78	D	27	(1)	2
23	JOSÍAS Paulo Cardoso Júnior	BRA	7/11/81	M	3	(6)	2
13	Gabriel KAJCSA		7/7/74	G	6	(1)	
6	Peter MAJERNÍK	SVK	31/12/78	D	16	(4)	2
1	Alexandru MARC		16/1/83	G	9		
11	Dejan MARTINOVIĆ	CRO	19/7/83	M	11	(6)	
8	Alexandru MATEIU		10/12/89	M	2	(2)	1
32	Mihai Adrian MINCĂ		8/10/84	G	16		
27	Cosmin NĂSTĂSIE		22/6/83	M	3	(10)	
16	NUNO Filipe Vasconcelos VIVEIROS	POR	22/6/83	M	17	(8)	1
15	Cristian Daniel OROS		15/8/84	D	28		1
21	Adrian RUSU		28/7/84	D	23	(3)	2
5	Florin STÂNGĂ		22/6/78	M	3	(2)	
25	Juan Andrés TOLOZA	CHI	4/5/85	M	15		
20	Ionuţ Cosmin VOICU		2/8/84	D	22	(1)	
26	José WILLIAMS da Silva Mendonça	BRA	5/8/83	M	19	(5)	

CFR 1907 CLUJ

Coach – Andrea Mandorlini (ITA); (13/9/10) Sorin Cârţu; (24/11/10) Alin Minteuan

Founded – 1907

Stadium – Dr Constantin Rădulescu (23,200)

MAJOR HONOURS: Romanian League – (2) 2008, 2010; Romanian Cup (3) 2008, 2009, 2010.

2010				
24/7	Univ Craiova	a	0-0	
2/8	Victoria	h	2-0	*Mureşan, Culio*
8/8	Timişoara	a	2-3	*Bjelanović, Koné E.*
13/8	Astra	h	2-2	*Traoré, Bud*
20/8	Sportul Studenţesc	a	0-3	
28/8	Pandurii	h	2-1	*Koné E., Hugo Alcântara*
10/9	Rapid	a	0-2	
19/9	Târgu Mureş	h	1-2	*Dică*
24/9	Univ Cluj	a	1-1	*Traoré*
3/10	Braşov	h	4-0	*Rafael Bastos, Cadú, Traoré, De Zerbi*
15/10	Vaslui	a	3-5	*De Zerbi, Rafael Bastos, Dică*
24/10	Unirea	h	3-0	*Traoré, De Zerbi 2*
30/10	Oţelul	a	1-1	*Peralta*
7/11	Dinamo	h	1-0	*Bjelanović*
15/11	Gloria Bistriţa	a	3-0	*Traoré 2, Bjelanović*
19/11	Gaz Metan	h	1-1	*De Zerbi*
28/11	Steaua	a	2-2	*Culio, Peralta*
3/12	Univ Craiova	h	2-1	*Traoré, Kivuvu*
2011				
27/2	Victoria	a	1-1	*Mureşan*
5/3	Timişoara	h	1-2	*Cadú (p)*
14/3	Astra	a	1-1	*Batin*
20/3	Sportul Studenţesc	h	2-0	*Rafael Bastos, Mureşan*
3/4	Pandurii	a	1-2	*Rafael Bastos*
7/4	Rapid	h	0-1	
11/4	Târgu Mureş	a	0-0	
14/4	Univ Cluj	h	1-1	*Koné E.*
17/4	Braşov	a	2-2	*Koné E., Rada*
23/4	Vaslui	h	1-0	*Cadú (p)*
27/4	Unirea	a	3-1	*Nicoară, Koné E., Batin*
2/5	Oţelul	h	0-1	
6/5	Dinamo	a	2-1	*Batin, Hora*
9/5	Gloria Bistriţa	h	2-2	*Bud, Mureşan*
13/5	Gaz Metan	a	2-3	*Rada, Hora*
21/5	Steaua	h	1-3	*Buş*

No	Name	Nat	DoB	Pos	Aps	(s)	Gls
30	ANSELMO Ramon Alves Erculano	BRA	23/6/88	A		(2)	
29	Paul BATIN		29/6/87	A	2	(12)	3
32	Saša BJELANOVIĆ	CRO	11/6/79	A	8	(5)	3
85	Cristian BUD		26/6/85	A	7	(14)	2
25	Sergiu Florin BUŞ		2/11/92	A	8	(4)	1
20	Ricardo Manuel Ferreira de Sousa "CADÚ"	POR	21/12/81	D	29		3
19	Emmanuel Juan CULIO	ARG	30/8/84	M	18		2
30	DANIel Ricardo da Silva Soares	POR	30/1/82	M	3	(2)	
10	Roberto DE ZERBI	ITA	6/6/79	M	6	(2)	5
10	Ciprian Ioan DEAC		16/2/86	M	4		
7	Emil Cosmin DICĂ		17/7/82	M	15	(1)	2
66	EDIMAR Curitiba Fraga	BRA	21/5/86	D	11	(1)	
22	Ioan Adrian HORA		21/8/88	M	13	(11)	2
15	HUGO da Silva ALCÂNTARA	BRA	28/7/79	D	8	(3)	1
9	Pantelis KAPETANOS	GRE	8/6/83	A	1	(1)	
8	Dominique KIVUVU	ANG	16/9/87	M	14	(7)	1
28	Emmanuel KONÉ	CIV	31/12/86	M	16	(5)	5
5	Yssouf KONÉ	BFA	19/2/82	A	3		
23	LÉOnardo Henrique VELOSO	BRA	29/5/87	D	5	(5)	
17	Vasile MAFTEI		1/1/81	D	3		
32	Mihai Adrian MINCĂ		8/10/84	G	7	(1)	
6	Gabriel MUREŞAN		13/2/82	D	16		4

No	Name	Nat	DoB	Pos	Aps	(s)	Gls
21	Sergiu NEGRUŢ		1/4/93	M		(1)	
11	Viorel NICOARĂ		27/9/87	M	11	(3)	1
1	NUNO CLARO Simões Coimbra	POR	7/1/77	G	22		
55	NUNO Miguel Pereira DIOGO	POR	13/6/81	D	11	(1)	
4	Cristian Călin PANIN		9/6/78	D	24	(1)	
18	Sixto Raimundo PERALTA Salso	ARG	16/4/69	M	19	(5)	2
13	Felice PICCOLO	ITA	27/8/83	D	13	(1)	
24	Ionuţ RADA		6/7/82	D	21	(1)	2
16	RAFAEL BASTOS	BRA	1/1/85	A	17	(6)	4
5	Bakary Bouba SARÉ	CIV	5/5/90	M	7	(3)	
99	Ferdinando SFORZINI	ITA	4/12/84	A	1	(2)	
44	Eduard Cornel STĂNCIOIU		3/3/81	G	5		
11	TOMÁS COSTA	ARG	30/1/85	M	6		
2	Anthony da Silva "TONY"	POR	20/12/80	D	9		
9	Lacina TRAORÉ	CIV	20/5/85	A	11	(2)	7

FC DINAMO BUCUREŞTI

Coach – Ioan Andone

Founded – 1948

Stadium – Dinamo (15,300)

MAJOR HONOURS: Romanian League – (18) 1955, 1962, 1963, 1964, 1965, 1971, 1973, 1975, 1977, 1982, 1983, 1984, 1990, 1992, 2000, 2002, 2004, 2007;
Romanian Cup – (12) 1959, 1964, 1968, 1982, 1984, 1986, 1990, 2000, 2001, 2003, 2004, 2005.

2010				
25/7	Astra	a	2-1	*N'Doye, Cristea Ad.*
1/8	Sportul Studenţesc	h	5-3	*Garat, N'Doye (p), Torje, Ganea, Cristea Ad.*
8/8	Pandurii	a	2-2	*Cristea An., Niculae*
15/8	Rapid	h	3-2	*Ganea 2, Torje*
21/8	Târgu Mureş	a	6-2	*og (Topić), N'Doye, Ganea, Niculae, Munteanu C., Cristea An. (p)*
27/8	Univ Cluj	h	3-4	*Cristea Ad., Torje, N'Doye*
12/9	Braşov	a	2-2	*Cristea Ad. (p), N'Doye*
19/9	Vaslui	h	1-2	*Ganea*
27/9	Unirea	a	0-1	
1/10	Oţelul	h	1-2	*Munteanu C.*
17/10	Steaua	h	2-1	*Cristea Ad. (p), Niculae (p)*
22/10	Gloria Bistriţa	a	2-0	*Dănciulescu, Cristea An.*
29/10	Gaz Metan	h	3-2	*Alexe, Cristea An. (p), Scarlatache*
7/11	CFR Cluj	a	0-1	
14/11	Univ Craiova	h	2-2	*Cristea Ad (p), Torje*
22/11	Victoria	a	4-2	*Dănciulescu, Koné, Óscar Rubio, Alexe*
27/11	Timişoara	h	0-0	
4/12	Astra	h	2-2	*Munteanu C. (p), Cristea Ad.*
2011				
26/2	Sportul Studenţesc	a	1-0	*Munteanu C.*
4/3	Pandurii	h	2-2	*Alexe, Torje*
12/3	Rapid	a	0-0	
20/3	Târgu Mureş	h	4-1	*Ganea, Torje 2, Dănciulescu*
1/4	Univ Cluj	a	1-2	*Dănciulescu*
6/4	Braşov	h	2-1	*Alexe, Ganea*
9/4	Vaslui	a	0-2	
12/4	Unirea	h	3-1	*Mehmedović, Dănciulescu (p), Bakaj*
16/4	Oţelul	a	3-3	*Munteanu C., Ţucudean, Grigore*
25/4	Steaua	a	1-0	*Torje*
28/4	Gloria Bistriţa	h	3-0	*Ganea, Bakaj, Torje*
2/5	Gaz Metan	a	1-2	*Alexe*
6/5	CFR Cluj	h	1-2	*Dănciulescu (p)*
9/5	Univ Craiova	a	2-0	*Koné, Bakaj*
16/5	Victoria	h	3-1	*Bakaj, Koné, Dănciulescu*
21/5	Timişoara	a	1-4	*Ţucudean*

No	Name	Nat	DoB	Pos	Aps	(s)	Gls
10	Marius Silviu ALEXE		22/2/90	A	22	(3)	5
20	Elis BAKAJ	ALB	25/6/87	M	8	(8)	4
31	Elías Iván BAZZI	ARG	23/5/81	D	4		
34	Cristian Emanuel BĂLGRĂDEAN		21/3/88	G	10		
18	Ştefan Nicolae BĂRBOIANU		24/1/88	D	9		
16	Valeriu Ionuţ BORDEANU		2/2/77	D	13	(4)	
17	Eugen CRĂCIUN		22/3/86	D		(1)	
20	Adrian CRISTEA		30/11/83	M	15	(2)	7
17	Andrei CRISTEA		15/5/84	A	7	(4)	4
1	George CURCĂ		8/5/81	G	4		
15	Ionel Daniel DĂNCIULESCU		6/12/76	A	15	(14)	7
2	Zie DIABATÉ	CIV	2/3/89	D	16		
36	Emilian Ioan DOLHA		3/11/79	G	14		
19	Liviu Adrian GANEA		23/2/88	A	24	(7)	8
30	Juan Pablo GARAT	ARG	19/4/83	D	8	(2)	1
24	Marius Valerică GĂMAN		25/2/89	D	6		
18	Lucian GOIAN		10/2/83	D	2		
21	Dragoş GRIGORE		7/9/86	D	20		1
16	HÉLDER Maurico da Silva Ferreira	BRA	13/4/88	D	1	(1)	
27	Sergiu HOMEI		6/7/87	D	2		
5	Djakaridja KONÉ	CIV	22/6/86	M	22	(4)	3
26	Andrei Silviu MĂRGĂRITESCU		1/1/80	M	13	(4)	
29	Ersin MEHMEDOVIĆ	SRB	10/5/81	D	1	(3)	1
4	Cosmin Iosif MOŢI		3/12/84	D	28		
7	Cătălin Constantin MUNTEANU		26/1/79	M	21	(8)	5
30	Vlad MUNTEANU		16/1/81	A	1	(3)	
29	Ousmane N'DOYE	SEN	21/3/78	M	10	(3)	5
12	Kristijan NAUMOVSKI	MKD	17/9/88	G	6	(1)	
9	Marius Constantin NICULAE		16/5/81	A	8	(8)	3
3	ÓSCAR RUBIO Fauria	ESP	14/5/84	D	19		1
8	Aurelian Bogdan PĂTRAŞCU		7/5/79	D	5	(5)	
14	Georgian PĂUN		24/10/85	A	2	(2)	
3	Cristian Corneliu PULHAC		17/8/84	D	2		
6	Laurenţiu RUS		7/5/85	D		(1)	
25	Manuel Adrian SCARLATACHE		5/12/86	D	6	(2)	1
33	Raphael STĂNESCU		27/6/93	M		(2)	
22	Andrei Gabriel TORJE		22/11/89	M	27	(2)	9
9	George ŢUCUDEAN		30/4/91	A	3	(7)	2

CS GAZ METAN MEDIAŞ

Coach – Cristian Pustai

Founded – 1945

Stadium – Municipal, Sibiu (14,200) & Gaz Metan (5,000)

2010				
26/7	Victoria	a	3-2	*Eric 2, Zaharia*
1/8	Timişoara	h	2-2	*Eric 2 (1p)*
8/8	Astra	a	2-0	*Eric 2 (1p)*
15/8	Sportul Studenţesc	h	3-0	*Marković, Munteanu, Eric*
21/8	Pandurii	a	0-0	
27/8	Rapid	h	0-1	
12/9	Târgu Mureş	a	0-1	
17/9	Univ Cluj	h	3-1	*Eric, Munteanu, Kubala*
27/9	Braşov	a	0-0	
3/10	Vaslui	h	0-0	
15/10	Unirea	a	1-0	*Todea*
23/10	Oţelul	h	0-2	
29/10	Dinamo	a	2-3	*Liţu, Trtovac*
5/11	Gloria Bistriţa	h	2-1	*Pârvulescu, Khubutia*
14/11	Steaua	a	1-0	*Eric*
19/11	CFR Cluj	a	1-1	*og (Edimar)*
29/11	Univ Craiova	h	1-0	*Liţu*
3/12	Victoria	h	2-2	*Aganović 2*
2011				
26/2	Timişoara	a	1-3	*Dudiţă*
6/3	Astra	h	0-0	
13/3	Sportul Studenţesc	a	1-0	*Eric (p)*
18/3	Pandurii	h	2-0	*Eric, Zaharia*
3/4	Rapid	a	1-2	*Todea*
6/4	Târgu Mureş	h	0-0	
9/4	Univ Cluj	a	2-2	*Eric, Roman*
13/4	Braşov	h	0-0	
18/4	Vaslui	a	0-3	

4/4	Unirea	h	2-0	*Munteanu, Liţu*
8/4	Oţelul	a	2-2	*Bawab, Eric*
/5	Dinamo	h	2-1	*Bawab, Pârvulescu*
/5	Gloria Bistriţa	a	0-0	
/5	Steaua	h	0-0	
3/5	CFR Cluj	h	3-2	*Eric 2, Pârvulescu*
1/5	Univ Craiova	a	2-1	*Liţu, Pârvulescu*

No	Name	Nat	DoB	Pos	Aps	(s)	Gls
	Admir AGANOVIĆ	BIH	25/8/86	A	9	(4)	2
8	Thaer Fayed BAWAB	JOR	1/3/85	A	11	(3)	2
	Andrei Dan BOZEŞAN		12/2/88	M	4	(14)	
0	Florin BRATU		2/1/80	A	4	(1)	
30	Miloš BUCHTA	CZE	19/7/80	G	1		
	Ionuţ Arghir BUZEAN		18/9/82	D	10	(5)	
1	Cristian Lucian CIGAN		15/7/87	A		(1)	
7	Doru DUDIŢĂ		7/9/77	M	8	(8)	1
7	ERIC de Oliveira Pereira	BRA	5/12/85	M	30	(1)	15
5	Ovidiu Ştefan HOBAN		27/12/82	M	31		
3	Akak KHUBUTIA	GEO	17/3/86	D	31		1
	Michal KUBALA	SVK	12/6/80	M	14	(3)	1
9	Florin Daniel LAZĂR		15/1/80	D	28		
	Alin Constantin LIŢU		22/10/86	A	6	(15)	4
25	Žarko MARKOVIĆ	SRB	28/1/87	D	16		1
30	Romulus Daniel MICLEA		5/4/80	M	2	(11)	
5	Alexandru MUNTEANU		1/1/88	M	24	(5)	3
88	Paul PÂRVULESCU		11/8/88	M	27	(2)	4
12	Răzvan PLEŞCA		25/11/82	G	31		
18	Jaroslav PREKOP	SVK	8/8/79	M		(1)	
14	RAÚL Martin del Campo	ESP	27/7/82	A	1	(3)	
30	Dan Mihai ROMAN		23/12/85	A	3	(9)	1
10	Cristian Radu SILVĂŞAN		25/2/82	A	3	(3)	
21	Cristian TODEA		18/10/78	M	29		2
3	Jasmin TRTOVAC	SRB	27/12/86	D	23	(4)	1
82	Cosmin Andrei VÂTCĂ		7/3/81	G	2		
29	Ivan VUKADINOVIĆ	SRB	21/8/84	D	8		
16	Radu Neculai ZAHARIA		25/1/89	D	18	(7)	2

ACF GLORIA 1922 BISTRIŢA

Coach – Laurenţiu Reghecampf; (25/10/10) Nicolae Manea

Founded – 1922

Stadium – Gloria (12,000)

MAJOR HONOURS: Romanian Cup – (1) 1994.

2010				
24/7	Timişoara	a	2-2	*Mureşan, Coroian (p)*
31/7	Astra	h	1-1	*Predescu*
9/8	Sportul Studenţesc	a	2-4	*Predescu, Júnior Moraes*
13/8	Pandurii	h	3-0	*Mureşan, Predescu, Júnior Moraes*
20/8	Rapid	a	0-2	
30/8	Târgu Mureş	h	3-1	*Băjenaru, Júnior Moraes, Szukała*
10/9	Univ Cluj	a	1-2	*Júnior Moraes*
20/9	Braşov	h	0-0	
25/9	Vaslui	a	0-1	
2/10	Unirea	h	0-0	
17/10	Oţelul	a	1-2	*Júnior Moraes (p)*
22/10	Dinamo	h	0-2	
31/10	Steaua	h	1-0	*Júnior Moraes (p)*
5/11	Gaz Metan	a	1-2	*Szukała*
15/11	CFR Cluj	h	0-3	
20/11	Univ Craiova	a	2-1	*Júnior Moraes 2*
29/11	Victoria	h	1-0	*Băjenaru*
4/12	Timişoara	h	3-3	*Velcovici, Keita 2*
2011				
28/2	Astra	a	0-1	
5/3	Sportul Studenţesc	h	1-0	*Cavalli*
11/3	Pandurii	a	0-0	
18/3	Rapid	h	3-2	*Cavalli 2, Băjenaru (p)*
2/4	Târgu Mureş	a	0-2	
5/4	Univ Cluj	h	2-4	*Cafasso 2*
9/4	Braşov	a	1-0	*D'Agostino*
12/4	Vaslui	h	1-1	*Băjenaru (p)*
15/4	Unirea	a	1-2	*Bâlbă*
24/4	Oţelul	h	0-0	
28/4	Dinamo	a	0-3	
1/5	Steaua	a	1-3	*Bâlbă*
5/5	Gaz Metan	h	0-0	
9/5	CFR Cluj	a	2-2	*Nalaţi, Tudose*
16/5	Univ Craiova	h	1-1	*Curtuiuş*
21/5	Victoria	a	0-2	

No	Name	Nat	DoB	Pos	Aps	(s)	Gls
14	Sebastian Zoltan ACHIM		2/6/86	D	22		
22	Septimiu Călin ALBUŢ		23/5/81	G	33		
29	Paul Viorel ANTON		10/5/91	M	19	(1)	
28	Thaer Fayed BAWAB	JOR	1/3/85	A		(7)	
30	Liviu BĂJENARU		6/5/83	M	26	(4)	4
77	Ionuţ Mihai BÂLBĂ		1/11/81	A	3	(2)	2
9	BRUNO dos Santos MORAES	BRA	7/7/84	A	8	(4)	
18	Fernando CAFASSO	ARG	9/2/83	M	8		2
9	Simone CAVALLI	ITA	10/1/79	A	9		3
6	Riccardo CORALLO	ITA	31/3/80	D	11		
7	Cristian Ambrozie COROIAN		14/3/73	A	3	(6)	1
20	Ionuţ Alexandru COSTACHE		19/12/83	D	1	(4)	
19	Marius Aurelian CURTUIUŞ		13/8/89	M	4		1
8	Antonino D'AGOSTINO	ITA	8/10/78	M	1	(3)	1
24	Gigel ENE		4/9/82	M	3	(2)	
18	Cosmin Vali FRĂSINESCU		10/2/85	D	12		
19	Sorin Adrian IODI		12/6/76	D		(1)	
26	Ilie IORDACHE		23/3/85	M	3	(6)	
12	Ionuţ IRIMIA		17/5/79	G	1		
10	Aluísio Chaves Ribeiro JÚNIOR MORAES	BRA	4/4/87	A	15		8
21	Souleymane KEITA	SEN	4/11/87	M	16	(4)	2
23	Alexandru MANDEA		27/3/89	M	4	(5)	
16	Radu Leon MĂRGINEAN		3/1/83	M	18	(6)	
20	MIGUEL Tavares Veiga de Pina	POR	26/2/81	A	3	(1)	
6	Andrei Iosif MUREŞAN		1/8/85	M	16	(1)	2
15	Adrian NALAŢI		21/5/83	M	10	(8)	1
4	Valentin Vasile NĂSTASE		4/10/74	D	15	(3)	
28	Victor PASENCIUC		20/3/88	A		(3)	
9	Alin Dumitru PĂDURARIU		15/7/92	M		(1)	
2	Ciprian Cătălin PETRE		10/12/80	M	20	(8)	
25	Cornel Alexandru PREDESCU		21/12/87	M	11	(6)	3
17	Robert Elian SĂCEANU		22/6/83	D	7	(4)	
27	Łukasz SZUKAŁA	POL	26/5/84	D	28		2
3	Alexandru TUDOSE		3/4/87	D	17	(4)	1
5	Gabriel Cristian VELCOVICI		2/10/84	D	25	(2)	1
11	YGOR Tadeu de Souza	BRA	27/7/86	A	2	(3)	

FC OŢELUL GALAŢI

Coach – Dorinel Munteanu

Founded – 1964

Stadium – Oţelul (13,500)

MAJOR HONOURS: Romanian League – (1) 2011.

2010				
23/7	Sportul Studenţesc	a	1-0	*Iorga*
30/7	Pandurii	h	2-0	*Pena, Sârghi*
6/8	Rapid	a	0-0	
16/8	Târgu Mureş	h	1-0	*Antal*
22/8	Univ Cluj	a	1-2	*Borbély*
29/8	Braşov	h	1-0	*Costin*
13/9	Vaslui	a	0-4	
18/9	Unirea	h	4-1	*Viglianti 2, Giurgiu 2*
26/9	Steaua	h	1-0	*Sârghi*
1/10	Dinamo	a	2-1	*Sălăgean, Ilie*
17/10	Gloria Bistriţa	h	2-1	*Antal, Viglianti (p)*
23/10	Gaz Metan	a	2-0	*Paraschiv 2*
30/10	CFR Cluj	h	1-1	*Iorga*
5/11	Univ Craiova	a	1-0	*Ilie*
12/11	Victoria	h	1-1	*Pena*
21/11	Timişoara	a	0-2	
27/11	Astra	h	2-1	*Antal (p), Pena*
5/12	Sportul Studenţesc	h	1-0	*Pena*

2011

25/2	Pandurii	a	3-0	*(w/o)*
5/3	Rapid	h	1-0	*Pena*
12/3	Târgu Mureş	a	0-1	
19/3	Univ Cluj	h	3-0	*Paraschiv, Giurgiu, Râpă*
1/4	Braşov	a	0-1	
6/4	Vaslui	h	0-0	
9/4	Unirea	a	3-0	*Ibeh, Iorga, Punoševac*
13/4	Steaua	a	0-1	
16/4	Dinamo	h	3-3	*Antal, Giurgiu, Pena*
24/4	Gloria Bistriţa	a	0-0	
28/4	Gaz Metan	h	2-2	*Antal (p), Pena*
2/5	CFR Cluj	a	1-0	*Antal*
5/5	Univ Craiova	h	2-1	*Paraschiv 2*
9/5	Victoria	a	2-1	*Buş, Paraschiv*
15/5	Timişoara	h	2-1	*Antal, Pena*
21/5	Astra	a	1-0	*Punoševac*

No	Name	Nat	DoB	Pos	Aps	(s)	Gls
8	Liviu ANTAL		2/6/89	M	19	(9)	7
32	Laszlo Csaba BORBÉLY		5/7/80	A	2	(6)	1
1	Cristian BRĂNEŢ		14/7/77	G	1		
9	Laurenţiu BUŞ		27/8/87	M	4	(5)	1
20	Samoel COJOC		8/7/89	D	1	(6)	
18	Sergiu Ioan Viorel COSTIN		21/11/78	D	31		1
19	Robert ELEK		13/6/88	A		(2)	
24	Ioan FILIP		20/5/89	M	9	(2)	
29	Gabriel Nicu GIURGIU		3/9/82	M	28		4
12	Branko GRAHOVAC	MNE	8/7/83	G	32		
15	Jackie Ike IBEH	NGA	16/4/86	M	6	(3)	1
14	Silviu ILIE		27/6/88	M	25	(4)	2
7	Laurenţiu Cătălin IORGA		17/3/88	M	15	(13)	3
26	Ionuţ NEAGU		26/10/89	M	26		
11	Răzvan Iulian OCHIROŞII		13/3/89	M	7	(8)	
10	Gabriel Ioan PARASCHIV		27/3/78	M	24	(2)	6
27	Marius George PENA		2/5/85	A	14	(14)	8
30	Milan PERENDIJA	SRB	5/1/86	D	21	(2)	
5	Laurenţiu PETEAN		5/5/88	D		(6)	
19	Bratislav PUNOŠEVAC	SRB	9/7/87	A	3	(7)	2
3	Cornel Emilian RÂPĂ		16/1/90	D	33		1
23	Adrian Ioan SĂLĂGEAN		9/4/83	M	29		1
16	Cristian SÂRGHI		22/2/87	D	14	(2)	2
37	Gabriel Alejandro VIGLIANTI	ARG	12/6/79	M	19	(6)	3

CS PANDURII TÂRGU JIU

Coach – Ionuţ Badea; (2/10/10) Petre Grigoraş

Founded – 1974

Stadium – Tudor Vladimirescu (10,000) & Municipal, Drobeta-Turnu Severin (20,054)

2010

23/7	Unirea	h	0-0	
30/7	Oţelul	a	0-2	
8/8	Dinamo	h	2-2	*Brata, Orac (p)*
13/8	Gloria Bistriţa	a	0-3	
21/8	Gaz Metan	h	0-0	
28/8	CFR Cluj	a	1-2	*Voiculeţ*
13/9	Univ Craiova	h	3-1	*Orac, Apostu 2*
17/9	Victoria	a	0-2	
26/9	Timişoara	h	0-1	
1/10	Astra	a	0-2	
16/10	Sportul Studenţesc	h	1-0	*Iordache I.*
25/10	Steaua	a	0-2	
1/11	Rapid	a	1-1	*Voiculeţ*
6/11	Târgu Mureş	h	4-1	*Voiculeţ, Băcilă, Pintilii 2*
13/11	Univ Cluj	a	1-1	*Štromajer*
19/11	Braşov	h	2-1	*Pintilii, Apostu*
26/11	Vaslui	a	1-3	*Voiculeţ*
6/12	Unirea	a	1-1	*Štromajer*

2011

25/2	Oţelul	h	0-3	*(w/o)*
4/3	Dinamo	a	2-2	*Apostu, Voiculeţ (p)*
11/3	Gloria Bistriţa	h	0-0	
18/3	Gaz Metan	a	0-2	
3/4	CFR Cluj	h	2-1	*Lemnaru, Vranješ*
7/4	Univ Craiova	a	2-0	*Štromajer, Lemnaru*
10/4	Victoria	h	4-2	*Vranješ, Nistor, Štromajer, Băcilă*
13/4	Timişoara	a	2-2	*Vranješ, Lemnaru*
16/4	Astra	h	1-0	*Voiculeţ*
22/4	Sportul Studenţesc	a	1-2	*Vranješ*
28/4	Steaua	h	1-1	*Štromajer*
1/5	Rapid	h	0-1	
4/5	Târgu Mureş	a	0-1	
8/5	Univ Cluj	h	2-0	*Rada, Brata*
15/5	Braşov	a	2-3	*Vranješ (p), Štromajer*
21/5	Vaslui	h	0-1	

No	Name	Nat	DoB	Pos	Aps	(s)	Gls
18	Andrei ANTOHI		16/12/88	A	2	(1)	
9	Radu Bogdan APOSTU		20/4/82	A	11	(9)	4
19	Alexandru AVRAMESCU		3/6/91	M		(7)	
7	Cosmin Nicolae BĂCILĂ		10/9/83	M	25	(1)	2
17	Ciprian BRATA		24/3/91	M	7	(13)	2
6	Carlos Alexandre CARDOSO	BRA	11/9/84	D	12	(3)	
4	Alin Nicu CHIBULCUTEAN		20/11/78	D	1		
21	Vlad CHIRICHEŞ		14/11/89	D	23	(1)	
11	Alexandru CIUCUR		1/3/90	M		(1)	
29	Constantin GRECU		8/6/88	D	26	(2)	
10	Florin HIDIŞAN		24/6/82	M	4	(5)	
23	Adrian Dragoş IORDACHE		13/11/81	A	4	(6)	
30	Ilie IORDACHE		23/3/85	M	9	(4)	1
22	David LAZĂR		8/8/91	G	4		
27	Valentin Ionuţ LEMNARU		24/6/84	A	12		3
26	Ajdin MAKSUMIĆ	BIH	24/7/85	D	2		
2	Gabriel MATEI		26/2/90	D	25	(1)	
28	Nasser MENASSEL	FRA	6/1/83	M	8	(1)	
80	João Pedro MINGOTE Ribeiro	POR	6/8/80	G	17		
24	George Alexandru NEAGU		24/4/85	D		(1)	
16	Dan NISTOR		5/6/88	M	19	(7)	1
8	Daniel ORAC		6/4/85	M	12	(3)	2
5	Doru Mihai PINTILII		9/11/84	D	29		3
25	Marian PLEAŞCĂ		6/2/90	M	7	(4)	
12	Marius POPA		31/7/78	G	12		
8	Florin POPETE		27/12/77	D	2	(10)	
23	Ionuţ RADA		16/3/90	D	5	(2)	1
20	Jaka ŠTROMAJER	SVN	27/7/83	A	19	(7)	6
26	Ionuţ TĂTARU		5/10/89	D	1		
3	Ousmane VIERA	CIV	21/12/86	M	27	(1)	
14	Claudiu Dorian VOICULEŢ		8/8/85	M	21	(3)	6
15	Albert VOINEA		6/12/92	A		(2)	
27	Stojan VRANJEŠ	BIH	22/6/88	M	16	(1)	5
19	Vojislav VRANJKOVIĆ	SRB	1/1/83	M	1	(2)	

FC RAPID BUCUREŞTI

Coach – Marius Şumudică; (28/4/11) (Marian Rada)

Founded – 1923

Stadium – Valentin Stănescu (19,100)

MAJOR HONOURS: Romanian League – (3) 1967, 1999, 2003; Romanian Cup – (13) 1935, 1937, 1938, 1939, 1940, 1941, 1942, 1972, 1975, 1998, 2002, 2006, 2007.

2010

23/7	Vaslui	h	2-0	*Herea, Césinha*
31/7	Unirea	a	0-0	
6/8	Oţelul	h	0-0	
15/8	Dinamo	a	2-3	*Herea 2*
20/8	Gloria Bistriţa	h	2-0	*Herea 2 (1p)*
27/8	Gaz Metan	a	1-0	*Herea (p)*
10/9	CFR Cluj	h	2-0	*Cássio 2*
17/9	Univ Craiova	a	1-1	*Constantin (p)*
26/9	Victoria	h	7-1	*Cássio 2, Césinha, Roman, Constantin (p), Frunză, Lazăr*
2/10	Timişoara	a	1-2	*Césinha*

15/10	Astra	h	3-0	*Cássio 2, Juliano Spadacio*
24/10	Sportul Studenţesc	a	2-0	*Marcos António, Herea (p)*
1/11	Pandurii	h	1-1	*Cássio*
3/11	Steaua	h	0-0	
14/11	Târgu Mureş	a	0-1	
19/11	Univ Cluj	h	3-0	*Roman, Herea, Sburlea*
27/11	Braşov	a	0-2	
5/12	Vaslui	a	1-1	*Herea*
2011				
25/2	Unirea	h	1-0	*Sburlea*
5/3	Oţelul	a	0-1	
12/3	Dinamo	h	0-0	
18/3	Gloria Bistriţa	a	2-3	*Roman, Herea*
3/4	Gaz Metan	h	2-1	*Gláuber, og (Zaharia)*
7/4	CFR Cluj	a	1-0	*Juliano Spadacio*
11/4	Univ Craiova	h	0-0	
14/4	Victoria	a	0-0	
17/4	Timişoara	h	3-2	*Božović, Roman, Pancu*
22/4	Astra	a	0-0	
26/4	Sportul Studenţesc	h	0-1	
1/5	Pandurii	a	1-0	*Pancu*
4/5	Steaua	a	1-0	*Pancu*
7/5	Târgu Mureş	h	1-1	*Grigore*
14/5	Univ Cluj	a	2-1	*Herea, Frunză*
21/5	Braşov	h	1-0	*Sburlea*

No	Name	Nat	DoB	Pos	Aps	(s)	Gls
33	Mircea Alexandru BORNESCU		3/5/80	G	20		
19	Vladimir BOŽOVIĆ	MNE	13/11/81	D	27	(1)	1
81	CÂNDIDO Alves Moreira da COSTA	POR	30/4/81	D	7	(5)	
99	CÁSSIO Vargas Barbosa	BRA	25/11/83	A	16	(5)	7
7	Carlos César dos Santos "CÉSINHA"	BRA	12/3/80	A	16	(5)	3
16	Andrei CIOLACU		9/9/92	A		(1)	
1	Dănuţ Dumitru COMAN		28/3/79	G	13		
23	Marius Marcel CONSTANTIN		25/10/84	D	17		2
26	Alexandru DOBROIU		23/2/88	A		(1)	
6	EZEQUIAS Roosevelt Tavares de Melo	BRA	28/1/81	D	14	(7)	
11	Sorin FRUNZĂ		29/3/78	M	12	(12)	2
27	GLÁUBER Leandro Honorato Berti	BRA	5/8/83	D	18	(6)	1
8	Nicolae GRIGORE		19/7/83	M	19	(3)	1
20	Ştefan Costel GRIGORIE		31/1/82	M	7	(13)	
25	GUSTAVO Nacarato Veronesi	BRA	7/5/82	M		(2)	
10	Nicolae Ovidiu HEREA		26/3/85	M	26	(5)	11
6	Alexandru IONIŢĂ		14/12/94	M		(1)	
30	JULIANO Gonçalves SPADACIO	BRA	16/11/80	M	26	(1)	2
15	Costin LAZĂR		24/4/81	M	21	(2)	1
4	MARCOS ANTÓNIO Elias Santos	BRA	25/5/83	D	32		1
13	OLBERDAM de Oliveira Serra	BRA	6/2/85	M	6	(6)	
77	Daniel Gabriel PANCU		17/8/77	A	5	(5)	3
9	Lucian Dorin RĂDUŢĂ		16/8/88	A	2	(3)	
14	Mihai ROMAN		16/10/84	M	27	(2)	4
2	RUI Sandro de Carvalho DUARTE	POR	11/10/80	D	24	(1)	
21	Sabrin SBURLEA		12/5/89	A	13	(10)	3
89	Cătălin George STRATON		9/10/89	G	1	(1)	
5	Pavel VIDANOV	BUL	1/8/88	D	5	(1)	

FC SPORTUL STUDENŢESC BUCUREŞTI

Coach – Tibor Selymes; (10/9/10) Dinu Viorel Moldovan; (1/11/10) Florin Tene; (10/1/11) Gabriel Popescu; (13/3/11) (Florin Tene); (15/3/11) Gheorghe Mulţescu

Founded – 1916

Stadium – Sportul Studenţesc (11,500)

2010				
23/7	Oţelul	h	0-1	
1/8	Dinamo	a	3-5	*Curelea, Bălan, Varga*
9/8	Gloria Bistriţa	h	4-2	*Curelea 2, Bălan, Varga*
15/8	Gaz Metan	a	0-3	
20/8	CFR Cluj	h	3-0	*Bălan 2, Pătraşcu*
28/8	Univ Craiova	a	0-1	
11/9	Victoria	h	2-2	*Bălan, Varga (p)*
18/9	Timişoara	a	1-2	*Patriche*
26/9	Astra	h	0-1	
3/10	Steaua	a	2-4	*Varga 2 (1p)*
16/10	Pandurii	a	0-1	
24/10	Rapid	h	0-2	
30/10	Târgu Mureş	a	1-4	*Pătraşcu*
7/11	Univ Cluj	h	2-0	*Bălan, Varga (p)*
13/11	Braşov	a	0-2	
21/11	Vaslui	h	0-1	
26/11	Unirea	a	1-2	*Bălan*
5/12	Oţelul	a	0-1	
2011				
26/2	Dinamo	h	0-1	
5/3	Gloria Bistriţa	a	0-1	
13/3	Gaz Metan	h	0-1	
20/3	CFR Cluj	a	0-2	
2/4	Univ Craiova	h	3-0	*Ferfelea, Curelea, Bălan (p)*
5/4	Victoria	a	1-1	*Ferfelea*
10/4	Timişoara	h	2-3	*Ferfelea, Bălan*
13/4	Astra	a	0-1	
16/4	Steaua	h	1-2	*Irimia*
22/4	Pandurii	h	2-1	*Bălan 2*
26/4	Rapid	a	1-0	*Bălan*
30/4	Târgu Mureş	h	1-2	*Curelea*
5/5	Univ Cluj	a	0-2	
8/5	Braşov	h	1-2	*Irimia*
15/5	Vaslui	a	2-4	*Maxim (p), Curelea*
21/5	Unirea	h	5-1	*Curelea 3, Ferfelea 2*

No	Name	Nat	DoB	Pos	Aps	(s)	Gls
28	Tiberiu Gabriel BĂLAN		17/2/81	M	25		12
2	Marian Dean BEŢA		11/5/91	D	4		
4	Lucian Cristian CAZAN		25/12/89	D	8	(3)	
31	Lucian CHEŢAN		25/5/86	M	3	(7)	
18	Octavian CHIHAIA		18/3/81	A		(8)	
3	Codruţ CIORANU		10/1/91	D		(1)	
15	Raul CIUPE		24/11/83	D	14	(4)	
19	Florentin CRUCERU		25/3/81	M	12	(7)	
9	Costln CURELEA		11/7/84	A	33		9
25	Leonard DOBRE		16/6/92	A	4	(6)	
29	Răzvan Ştefănel FARMACHE		1/11/78	D	18	(4)	
10	Viorel FERFELEA		26/4/85	M	30	(3)	5
11	Costin GHEORGHE		8/1/89	M	2	(8)	
13	Sebastian GHINGA		12/2/87	D	20		
30	Cristian IRIMIA		7/7/81	M	22	(3)	2
5	Daniel Cristian LUNG		2/3/87	D	17	(2)	
16	Andrei LUNGU		29/1/89	M	6	(3)	
23	Florin Sandu MAXIM		2/3/81	D	25	(1)	1
8	Marius NAE		9/2/81	A	5	(8)	
4	Valentin NEGRU		4/9/82	M	5	(2)	
12	Vladimir George NICULESCU		26/9/87	G	16		
24	Nichita Răzvan PATRICHE		29/4/86	D	28	(1)	1
7	Bogdan PĂTRAŞCU		7/5/79	D	12	(1)	2
1	Andrei Sorin POPESCU		20/2/85	G	7		
22	Marius POSTOLACHE		11/2/84	M	9	(10)	
27	Alin Robert RAŢIU		14/9/82	D	19	(2)	
26	Liviu RUSU		16/4/81	D	1	(2)	
14	Ionuţ TÂRNĂCOP		22/4/87	D	1	(3)	
17	Andrei Cristian TRUŢĂ		3/5/91	A		(3)	
20	Dacian Şerban VARGA		15/10/84	M	15		6
21	Nicola VASILE		15/12/84	M	2	(5)	
33	Adrian VICIU		14/1/91	G	11	(2)	

FC STEAUA BUCUREŞTI

Coach – Victor Piţurcă; (7/8/10) (Eugen Neagoe); (10/8/10) Ilie Dumitrescu; (21/9/10) (Eduard Iordănescu); (26/9/10) Marius Lăcătuş; (8/3/11) Sorin Cârţu; (5/5/11) (Gabriel Caramarin)

Founded – 1947

Stadium – Steaua (27,000)

MAJOR HONOURS: European Champion Clubs' Cup – (1) 1986; UEFA Super Cup – (1) 1986; Romanian League – (23) 1951, 1952, 1953, 1956, 1960, 1961, 1968, 1976, 1978, 1985, 1986, 1987, 1988, 1989, 1993, 1994, 1995, 1996, 1997, 1998, 2001, 2005, 2006; Romanian Cup – (22) 1949, 1950, 1951, 1952, 1955, 1962, 1966, 1967, 1969, 1970, 1971, 1976, 1979, 1985, 1987, 1988, 1989, 1992, 1996, 1997, 1999, 2011.

2010				
25/7	Univ Cluj	a	2-1	*Stoica, Stancu*
31/7	Univ Craiova	h	2-1	*Stancu, Surdu*
7/8	Braşov	a	1-1	*Nicoliţă*
16/8	Victoria	h	2-1	*Stancu 2 (1p)*
22/8	Vaslui	a	3-0	*Surdu 2, Stancu*
29/8	Timişoara	h	1-1	*Păcurar*
11/9	Unirea	a	0-1	
20/9	Astra	h	1-1	*Kapetanos*
26/9	Oţelul	a	0-1	
3/10	Sportul Studenţesc	h	4-2	*Stancu 2, og (Pătraşcu), Bilaşco*
17/10	Dinamo	a	1-2	*Stancu*
25/10	Pandurii	h	2-0	*Stancu 2*
31/10	Gloria Bistriţa	a	0-1	
8/11	Rapid	a	0-0	
14/11	Gaz Metan	h	0-1	
20/11	Târgu Mureş	a	1-0	*Bilaşco*
28/11	CFR Cluj	h	2-2	*Stancu 2 (1p)*
6/12	Univ Cluj	h	3-0	*Martinović, Bilaşco, Stancu*
2010				
27/2	Univ Craiova	a	1-0	*Bilaşco*
6/3	Braşov	h	0-3	
11/3	Victoria	a	1-0	*Surdu*
19/3	Vaslui	h	1-1	*Nicoliţă*
2/4	Timişoara	a	0-0	
5/4	Unirea	h	5-0	*Nicoliţă, Geraldo Alves 2, Dică (p), Burdujan*
10/4	Astra	a	0-1	
13/4	Oţelul	h	1-0	*Maicon*
16/4	Sportul Studenţesc	a	2-1	*Maicon 2*
25/4	Dinamo	h	0-1	
28/4	Pandurii	a	1-1	*Tănase*
1/5	Gloria Bistriţa	h	3-1	*Onofraş, Dică 2*
4/5	Rapid	h	0-1	
8/5	Gaz Metan	a	0-0	
16/5	Târgu Mureş	h	1-0	*Dică (p)*
21/5	CFR Cluj	a	3-1	*Surdu, Nicoliţă, Bilaşco*

No	Name	Nat	DoB	Pos	Aps	(s)	Gls
4	Octavian ABRUDAN		16/3/84	D	6	(1)	
20	Stanislav ANGELOV	BUL	12/4/78	M	3		
32	Iulian Cătălin APOSTOL		3/12/80	M	3	(2)	
26	Eric Cosmin BICFALVI		5/2/88	M	14	(5)	
17	Marius Ioan BILAŞCO		13/7/81	A	19	(6)	5
5	Pablo Daniel BRANDÁN	ARG	5/3/83	D	22	(4)	
9	Lucian BURDUJAN		18/2/84	A	1	(4)	1
20	Nicolae Constantin DICĂ		9/5/80	A	9	(2)	4
29	ÉDER José Oliveira BONFIM	BRA	3/4/81	D	19		
3	Ifeanyi EMEGHARA	NGA	24/3/84	D	11		
22	George Daniel GALAMAZ		5/4/81	D	11		
6	Florin GARDOŞ		29/10/88	D	20	(3)	
23	GERALDO Washington Regufe ALVES	POR	8/11/80	D	27		2
4	Valentin ILIEV	BUL	11/8/80	D	4		
9	Pantelis KAPETANOS	GRE	8/6/83	A	4	(8)	1
14	Iasmin LATOVLEVICI		11/5/86	D	24	(3)	
99	MAICON Pereira de Oliveira	BRA	8/5/88	A	3	(3)	3
27	Laurenţiu Nicolae MARINESCU		25/8/84	M	9	(7)	
18	Novak MARTINOVIĆ	SRB	31/1/85	D	8	(1)	1
91	Cosmin Gabriel MATEI		30/9/91	M		(5)	
16	Bănel NICOLIŢĂ		7/1/85	M	26	(1)	4
11	Marius Daniel ONOFRAŞ		17/8/80	A	5	(8)	1
11	Alexandru PĂCURAR		20/1/82	M	3	(3)	1
8	Mihai Cosmin RĂDUŢ		18/3/90	M	14	(6)	
21	RICARDO Gomes VILANA	BRA	18/7/81	M	11	(5)	
1	Răzvan Marian STANCA		18/1/80	G	1		
28	Bogdan Sorin STANCU		28/6/87	A	18		13
5	Dorel STOICA		15/12/78	M	5		1
24	Romeo Constantin SURDU		12/1/84	A	12	(9)	5
7	János József SZEKELY		13/5/83	M	4	(7)	
10	Cristian TĂNASE		18/2/87	M	25	(2)	1
12	Ciprian Anton TĂTĂRUŞANU		9/2/86	G	33	(1)	

FCM TÂRGU MUREŞ

Coach – Adrian Falub; (11/9/10) Ioan Ovidiu Sabău

Founded – 2008

Stadium – Trans-Sil (7,000)

2010				
26/7	Braşov	h	0-1	
30/7	Vaslui	a	1-1	*Roman*
7/8	Unirea	h	1-0	*Matei*
16/8	Oţelul	a	0-1	
21/8	Dinamo	h	2-6	*Dan, Vancea*
30/8	Gloria Bistriţa	a	1-3	*Matei*
12/9	Gaz Metan	h	1-0	*Dan*
19/9	CFR Cluj	a	2-1	*Munteanu, Stere*
27/9	Univ Craiova	h	1-4	*Dan (p)*
4/10	Victoria	a	0-0	
16/10	Timişoara	h	2-3	*Stere, Munteanu*
23/10	Astra	a	0-0	
30/10	Sportul Studenţesc	h	4-1	*Tâmăvean, Vasilache, Cordoş, Stere (p)*
6/11	Pandurii	a	1-4	*Munteanu*
14/11	Rapid	h	1-0	*Sosa*
20/11	Steaua	h	0-1	
28/11	Univ Cluj	a	1-1	*Vagner*
3/12	Braşov	a	1-1	*og (Ilyeş)*
2011				
28/2	Vaslui	h	0-2	
4/3	Unirea	a	1-0	*Iencsi*
12/3	Oţelul	h	1-0	*Ruiz*
20/3	Dinamo	a	1-4	*og (Ganea)*
2/4	Gloria Bistriţa	h	2-0	*Didy 2*
6/4	Gaz Metan	a	0-0	
11/4	CFR Cluj	h	0-0	
14/4	Univ Craiova	a	1-2	*Răduţă*
17/4	Victoria	h	4-0	*Rus, Didy, Ruiz, og (Bar)*
23/4	Timişoara	a	0-0	
27/4	Astra	h	1-0	*Vasilache*
30/4	Sportul Studenţesc	a	2-1	*Dan, Astafei*
4/5	Pandurii	h	1-0	*Astafei*
7/5	Rapid	a	1-1	*Dan*
16/5	Steaua	a	0-1	
21/5	Univ Cluj	h	0-2	

No	Name	Nat	DoB	Pos	Aps	(s)	Gls
21	Victor ASTAFEI		6/7/87	A	22	(3)	2
90	Issa BA	SEN	7/10/81	M	19	(1)	
22	Dragoş BALAURU		11/11/89	G	12		
3	Marius BĂLĂU		12/6/80	D	6	(1)	
18	Alin Nelu BIŢIŞ		2/5/81	M	3	(6)	
33	BRUNO João Nandinga FERNANDES	GNB	6/11/78	D	20		
1	Alessandro CAPARCO	ITA	7/9/83	G	5		
10	CARLOS Agustín CASQUERO Ruiz	ESP	14/9/81	M	5	(1)	
3	Lucian CAZAN		25/12/89	D	2		

4	Andrei CORDOŞ		6/6/88	D	13	(4)	1
19	Florin Cristian DAN		1/4/79	M	28	(1)	5
12	Remus Cristian DĂNĂLACHE		14/1/84	G	7		
29	Cleidimar Magalhães Silva "DIDY"	BRA	10/9/82	A	16	(6)	3
90	Mario DONADONI	ITA	19/11/79	D	1	(1)	
28	EDUardo ESPADA Gallardo	ESP	8/3/81	A	1	(3)	
17	Mihai Adrian IENCSI		15/3/75	D	14		1
27	Luigi LAVECCHIA	ITA	25/8/81	D		(1)	
23	Dan Marian MATEI		25/6/81	D	11	(3)	2
6	Flavius Lucian MOLDOVAN		27/7/76	D	5		
28	Cristian Lucian MUNTEANU		17/10/80	D	14	(5)	3
5	Mihai Marian ONICAŞ		27/1/90	M	6	(5)	
11	George Sorin PETCUŢ		16/9/86	M		(5)	
20	Cristian Daniel POP		6/2/81	D	6	(2)	
88	Laurenţiu Florin POPETE		27/12/77	D	3		
5	Lucian RĂDUŢĂ		16/8/88	A	5	(5)	1
17	Dan Mihai ROMAN		22/12/85	M	7	(5)	1
9	Diego Alejandro RUIZ	ARG	19/12/80	A	2	(9)	2
15	Laurenţiu RUS		7/5/85	D	16		1
16	Sebastian SFÂRLEA		26/7/81	M	1		
6	Cristian Fabián SOSA	URU	20/10/85	D	4		1
7	Florin Cornel STÂNGĂ		22/6/78	M	5	(9)	
14	Mihai STERE		30/12/75	M	13	(3)	3
24	Lorand SZILAGYI		25/2/87	D	14		
30	Mihai Doru ŞTEŢCA		7/3/81	G	10	(1)	
11	Călin TÂRNĂVEAN		3/1/84	A	3		1
32	Borislav TOPIĆ	BIH	22/5/84	D	16		
25	Alexandru Ion VAGNER		19/8/89	M	18	(5)	1
9	Cosmin VANCEA		24/12/84	A	6	(4)	1
26	Ciprian VASILACHE		14/9/83	M	21	(2)	2
8	Rareş VÂRTIC		18/9/85	M	4	(5)	
13	Rade VELJOVIĆ	SRB	9/8/86	A	1	(2)	
80	Dorel ZAHARIA		21/2/78	A	9	(3)	

FC TIMIŞOARA

Coach – Vladimir Petrović (SRB); (15/9/10) Cosmin Contra; (14/12/10) Dušan Uhrin Jr (SVK)

Founded – 2002

Stadium – Dan Păltinişanu (32,019)

2010				
24/7	Gloria Bistriţa	h	2-2	*Goga, Magera*
1/8	Gaz Metan	a	2-2	*Magera, Axente*
8/8	CFR Cluj	h	3-2	*Curtean 2, Axente*
15/8	Univ Craiova	a	1-1	*Zicu*
22/8	Victoria	h	2-1	*Magera, Zicu*
29/8	Steaua	a	1-1	*Contra*
12/9	Astra	a	1-1	*Hélder*
18/9	Sportul Studenţesc	h	2-1	*Scutaru 2*
26/9	Pandurii	a	1-0	*Axente*
2/10	Rapid	h	2-1	*Zicu 2*
16/10	Târgu Mureş	a	3-2	*Zicu 2, Chiacu*
22/10	Univ Cluj	h	2-2	*Axente, Zicu*
31/10	Braşov	a	0-0	
6/11	Vaslui	h	2-1	*Zicu (p), Goga*
13/11	Unirea	a	1-1	*Popovici*
21/11	Oţelul	h	2-0	*Čišovský, Nikolić*
27/11	Dinamo	a	0-0	
4/12	Gloria Bistriţa	a	3-3	*Luchin, Zicu, Axente*
2011				
26/2	Gaz Metan	h	3-1	*Goga, Zicu 2*
5/3	CFR Cluj	a	2-1	*Zicu (p), Ricketts*
13/3	Univ Craiova	h	4-0	*Zicu, Magera 2, Goga*
18/3	Victoria	a	2-0	*Zicu (p), Goga*
2/4	Steaua	h	0-0	
6/4	Astra	h	2-2	*Zicu (p), Zăgrean*
10/4	Sportul Studenţesc	a	3-2	*Zăgrean 2, Goga*
13/4	Pandurii	h	2-2	*Magera, Zicu*
17/4	Rapid	a	2-3	*Zicu, Alexa*
23/4	Târgu Mureş	h	0-0	
27/4	Univ Cluj	a	2-1	*Alexa, Ignjatijević*
30/4	Braşov	h	2-0	*Bourceanu, Goga*
5/5	Vaslui	a	1-1	*Goga*
9/5	Unirea	h	3-1	*Magera, Čišovský, Zăgrean*
15/5	Oţelul	a	1-2	*Zicu*
21/5	Dinamo	h	4-1	*Luchin, Nikolić 2, Ignjatijević*

No	Name	Nat	DoB	Pos	Aps	(s)	Gls
5	Dan ALEXA		28/10/79	M	28		2
9	Mircea Ionuţ AXENTE		14/3/87	A	21	(6)	5
55	Alexandru Viorel BOURCEANU		24/4/85	M	22	(3)	1
25	Ovidiu Nicuşor BURCĂ		16/3/80	D	20		
15	Hristu CHIACU		6/9/86	M	1	(5)	1
28	Marián ČIŠOVSKÝ	SVK	2/11/79	D	22	(1)	2
22	Cosmin Marius CONTRA		15/12/75	D	1	(8)	1
7	Alexandru Paul CURTEAN		27/3/87	M	14	(3)	2
2	ÉDER José Oliveira BONFIM	BRA	3/4/81	D	1		
24	Sorin GHIONEA		11/5/79	D	15		
21	Dorin Ioan GOGA		2/7/84	A	25	(4)	8
20	HÉLDER Maurico da Silva Ferreira	BRA	13/4/88	D	22		1
6	Nikola IGNJATIJEVIĆ	SRB	12/12/83	D	8	(3)	2
4	Srdjan LUCHIN		4/3/86	D	25	(2)	2
17	Lukáš MAGERA	CZE	17/1/83	A	20	(9)	7
11	Gueye MANSOUR	SEN	30/12/85	A		(1)	
22	Ionuţ MATEI		2/7/84	M		(1)	
14	Ioan MERA		5/1/87	D	4	(2)	
19	Stefan NIKOLIĆ	MNE	18/5/90	A	5	(13)	3
29	Constantin Fane PANTILIMON		1/2/87	G	27	(1)	
7	Artur PATRAS	MDA	10/1/88	M	1	(2)	
31	Adrian Florin POPARADU		13/10/87	M	2	(3)	
20	Adrian Alexandru POPOVICI		6/9/88	A		(2)	1
30	Carlos RAFAEL ROCHA Ferreira	BRA	14/3/89	D	1	(3)	
87	Tosaint RICKETTS	CAN	6/8/87	A	4	(5)	1
13	Cristian Dorel SCUTARU		13/4/87	D	13	(1)	2
8	László SEPSI		7/6/86	D	27	(1)	
99	Pedro Manuel TABORDA Moreira	POR	22/6/78	G	7	(1)	
10	Iulian TAMEŞ		6/12/78	M	13	(5)	
15	Andrei ZĂGREAN		16/10/86	A	3	(5)	4
27	Ianis Alin ZICU		23/10/83	M	22	(8)	18

FC UNIREA URZICENI

Coach – Roni Levi (ISR); (25/8/10) (Eugen Nae); (7/9/10) Octavian Grigore; (18/2/11) Marian Pană

Founded – 1954

Stadium – Tineretului (8,000)

MAJOR HONOURS: Romanian League – (1) 2009.

2010				
23/7	Pandurii	a	0-0	
31/7	Rapid	h	0-0	
7/8	Târgu Mureş	a	0-1	
14/8	Univ Cluj	h	0-1	
23/8	Braşov	a	1-1	*Bilaşco*
29/8	FC Vaslui	h	2-1	*Maftei, Bordeanu (p)*
11/9	Steaua	h	1-0	*Semedo*
18/9	Oţelul	a	1-4	*Todoran (p)*
27/9	Dinamo	h	1-0	*Rusescu (p)*
2/10	Gloria Bistriţa	a	0-0	
15/10	Gaz Metan	h	0-1	
24/10	CFR Cluj	a	0-3	
1/11	Univ Craiova	h	1-2	*Todoran*
8/11	Victoria	a	1-4	*Semedo*
13/11	Timişoara	h	1-1	*Todoran*
22/11	Astra	a	0-1	
26/11	Sportul Studenţesc	h	2-1	*Maftei, Semedo*
6/12	Pandurii	h	1-1	*og (Chiricheş)*

2011

25/2	Rapid	a	0-1	
4/3	Târgu Mureş	h	0-1	
12/3	Univ Cluj	a	2-4	*Mihalcea 2*
21/3	Braşov	h	1-1	*Apostol*
1/4	Vaslui	a	0-2	
5/4	Steaua	a	0-5	
9/4	Oţelul	h	0-3	
12/4	Dinamo	a	1-3	*Mihalcea*
15/4	Gloria Bistriţa	h	2-1	*Patras, Rusescu*
24/4	Gaz Metan	a	0-2	
27/4	CFR Cluj	h	1-3	*og (Peralta)*
1/5	Univ Craiova	a	0-3	
4/5	Victoria	h	2-1	*Patras, Rusescu*
9/5	Timişoara	a	1-3	*og (Čišovský)*
13/5	Astra	h	0-3	
21/5	Sportul Studenţesc	a	1-5	*Tobă*

No	Name	Nat	DoB	Pos	Aps	(s)	Gls
32	Iulian Cătălin APOSTOL		3/12/78	M	9	(2)	1
1	Giedrius ARLAUSKIS	LTU	1/12/87	G	3		
1	Cristian Emanuel BĂLGRĂDEAN		21/3/88	G	3	(1)	
9	Marius Cornel BÂTFOI		29/5/90	A	1	(2)	
7	Marius Ioan BILAŞCO		13/7/81	A	5		1
18	George BLAY	GHA	7/8/80	D	9	(2)	
23	Valeriu Ionuţ BORDEANU		2/2/77	D	3	(1)	1
19	Pablo Daniel BRANDÁN	ARG	5/3/83	D	6		
15	George Valentin BUŞCĂ		2/2/85	D	10		
77	Cornel CERNEA		22/4/76	G	12		
1	George CURCĂ		8/5/81	G	13		
9	Maurice Junior DALÉ	FRA	12/7/85	A	1	(1)	
23	Lucian Ionuţ FILIP		25/9/90	D	1	(3)	
30	Sorin FRUNZĂ		29/3/78	M	5	(1)	
6	George Daniel GALAMAZ		5/4/81	D	6		
30	Petre GOGE		29/9/91	D	7	(2)	
77	Cătălin GRIGORE		6/10/77	G	3		
27	Victor Sergiu HOMEI		6/7/87	D	3		
5	Marius IONIŢĂ		12/2/91	D	4	(4)	
11	Arman KARAMYAN	ARM	14/11/79	A	2	(3)	
10	Artavazd KARAMYAN	ARM	14/11/79	M	3		
5	Valeriu LUPU		24/1/91	D	9	(8)	
24	Vasile MAFTEI		1/1/81	D	15		2
12	Felix MANCIU		26/2/92	G		(1)	
30	Georgian MARCU		27/11/88	M	4	(5)	
36	Petre MARIN		8/9/73	D	4		
20	Laurenţiu Nicolae MARINESCU		25/8/84	M	3	(1)	
21	Florentin MATEI		15/4/93	M	1	(4)	
4	Ersin MEHMEDOVIĆ	SRB	10/5/81	D	13		
24	Ioan MERA		5/1/87	D	11	(1)	
90	Adrian Dumitru MIHALCEA		24/5/76	A	10	(5)	3
2	Bogdan MUSTAŢĂ		28/7/90	D	3	(1)	
8	Nicolae MUŞAT		4/12/86	D	12		
6	Apostol MUZAC		6/7/87	M	21	(3)	
25	Adrian Constantin NEAGA		4/6/79	A	1	(5)	
8	Epaminonda NICU		17/12/79	D	25		
25	Mihai Marian ONICAŞ		27/1/90	M	6	(2)	
11	Marius Daniel ONOFRAŞ		17/8/80	A	5	(1)	
8	Sorin Ion PARASCHIV		17/6/81	M	2		
11	Alexandru PĂDUREŢU		17/9/86	M		(2)	
10	Răzvan PĂDUREŢU		19/6/81	M	18		
28	Artur PATRAS	MDA	10/1/88	M	8		2
14	Raul Andrei RUSESCU		9/7/88	A	24	(5)	3
22	Sergiu SCĂRLĂTESCU		26/10/88	M	7	(5)	
22	António Paulo Sanches SEMEDO	POR	1/6/79	M	14		3
31	Adrian SENIN		27/8/79	M	6	(3)	
3	Fabian Vasile TEUŞAN		31/10/88	D	6	(1)	
9	Georgian TOBĂ		23/5/89	M	10	(2)	1
15	Dinu Marius TODORAN		8/9/78	M	14	(1)	3
20	Alin TOŞCA		14/3/92	D	11	(8)	
17	Paul ŢENE		27/3/91	M	2	(3)	
7	Robert Theodor VĂDUVA		5/9/92	A		(4)	

FC UNIVERSITATEA CLUJ

Coach – Marian Pană; (8/11/10) (Claudiu Niculescu); (19/11/10) Ionuţ Badea

Founded – 1919

Stadium – Cetate, Alba Iulia (18,000) & Gaz Metan, Medias (5,000)

MAJOR HONOURS: Romanian Cup – (1) 1965.

2010

25/7	Steaua	h	1-2	*Niculescu (p)*
1/8	Braşov	a	1-3	*Niculescu*
6/8	Vaslui	h	1-1	*Čvirik*
14/8	Unirea	a	1-0	*Lemnaru*
22/8	Oţelul	h	2-1	*Mendy, Boştină (p)*
27/8	Dinamo	a	4-3	*Niculescu 2, Lemnaru, Delgado*
10/9	Gloria Bistriţa	h	2-1	*Niculescu, Baldé*
17/9	Gaz Metan	a	1-3	*Čvirik*
24/9	CFR Cluj	h	1-1	*Niculescu*
1/10	Univ Craiova	a	0-3	
18/10	Victoria	h	2-3	*Machado 2*
22/10	Timişoara	a	2-2	*Szilágyi, Machado*
1/11	Astra	h	1-0	*Boştină (p)*
7/11	Sportul Studenţesc	a	0-2	
13/11	Pandurii	h	1-1	*Boştină*
19/11	Rapid	a	0-3	
28/11	Târgu Mureş	h	1-1	*Niculescu*
6/12	Steaua	a	0-3	

2011

27/2	Braşov	h	1-1	*Delgado (p)*
7/3	Vaslui	a	0-2	
12/3	Unirea	h	4-2	*Niculescu, Machado, Cristea, Voican*
19/3	Oţelul	a	0-3	
1/4	Dinamo	h	2-1	*Niculescu, Menassel*
5/4	Gloria Bistriţa	a	4-2	*Cristea 2, Pelé, Nwakaeme*
9/4	Gaz Metan	h	2-2	*Niculescu 2*
14/4	CFR Cluj	a	1-1	*Cojocnean*
18/4	Univ Craiova	h	3-0	*Cojocnean 2, Morar*
23/4	Victoria	a	2-0	*Cojocnean, Machado*
27/4	Timişoara	h	1-2	*Niculescu*
1/5	Astra	a	2-1	*Niculescu, Păcurar*
5/5	Sportul Studenţesc	h	2-0	*Voican, Boştină*
8/5	Pandurii	a	0-2	
14/5	Rapid	h	1-2	*Păcurar (p)*
21/5	Târgu Mureş	a	2-0	*Păcurar, Machado*

No	Name	Nat	DoB	Pos	Aps	(s)	Gls
6	Octavian ABRUDAN		16/3/84	D	14		
10	Noé ACOSTA Rivera	ESP	10/12/83	M	2	(7)	
16	Nicola ASCOLI	ITA	11/9/79	D	4	(1)	
24	Habib-Jean BALDÉ	GUI	8/2/85	M	17	(3)	1
14	Elías Iván BAZZI	ARG	23/5/81	D	9	(1)	
20	Zoran BELOŠEVIĆ	SRB	20/6/83	D	3	(1)	
33	Ionuţ BOŞNEAG		15/2/82	G	2		
22	Gabriel BOŞTINĂ		22/5/77	M	28		4
2	Bogdan Constantin BUHUŞ		30/10/79	D	14	(5)	
26	Boban CENIĆ	SRB	13/11/81	D		(1)	
20	Sebastian COJOCNEAN		11/7/89	M	11	(2)	4
30	Adrian CRISTEA		30/11/83	M	12	(1)	3
23	Rareş CUCUI		30/10/93	D	1		
23	Peter ČVIRIK	SVK	13/6/79	D	10	(1)	2
16	Roberto Alfonso DELGADO	ESP	7/5/89	M	20	(8)	2
28	Vasile GHEORGHE		9/9/85	M	16	(5)	
12	Sebastian HUŢAN		26/10/83	G	10		
6	Adrian IONESCU		13/7/85	M	2	(3)	
13	Silviu IZVORANU		3/12/82	D	8	(2)	
27	Valentin LEMNARU		24/6/84	A	11	(4)	2
11	Gabriel Teixeira MACHADO	BRA	2/9/89	A	20	(5)	6
1	Florin MATACHE		3/8/82	G	10		
8	Nasser MENASSEL	FRA	6/1/83	M	12	(1)	1
3	Gaston MENDY	SEN	22/11/85	D	18	(3)	1
27	Vlad MORAR		1/8/93	M		(1)	1
25	Daniel George MUNTEANU		6/6/78	D	15	(3)	
9	Claudiu Iulian NICULESCU		23/6/76	A	23	(3)	13
26	Anthony NWAKAEME Nuatuzor	NGA	4/4/83	A	2	(7)	1

0	Alexandru PĂCURAR		20/1/82	M	14	(6)	3
[illegible]	Steven Robert PELÉ	FRA	28/8/81	D	12		1
14	Adrian PIŢ		16/7/83	M	4	(5)	
12	Marius Viorel POPA		31/7/78	G	12		
3	REINALDO José Zacarias da Silva	BRA	25/5/84	M	5	(3)	
4	Zsolt Lóránt SZILÁGYI		29/6/81	D	6	(1)	1
29	Georgian TOBĂ		23/5/89	M	1	(4)	
18	Bogdan Alexandru UNGURUŞAN		20/2/83	D	23	(3)	
17	Andrei VOICAN		14/1/91	A	3	(9)	2

FC UNIVERSITATEA CRAIOVA

Coach – Aurel Ţicleanu; (26/8/10) Victor Piţurcă; (14/1/11) Nicolò Napoli (ITA); (5/4/11) Laurenţiu Reghecampf; (28/4/11) Aurel Ţicleanu; (7/5/11) Gheorghe Biţă

Founded – 1948

Stadium – Ion Oblemenco (25,250)

MAJOR HONOURS: Romanian League – (4) 1974, 1980, 1981, 1991; Romanian Cup – (6) 1977, 1978, 1981, 1983, 1991, 1993.

2010				
24/7	CFR Cluj	h	0-0	
31/7	Steaua	a	1-2	*Iliev*
6/8	Victoria	a	0-1	
15/8	Timişoara	h	1-1	*Piţurcă*
21/8	Astra	a	2-2	*Piţurcă, Ciucă*
28/8	Sportul Studenţesc	h	1-0	*Stoianof*
13/9	Pandurii	a	1-3	*Iliev*
17/9	Rapid	h	1-1	*Wobay*
27/9	Târgu Mureş	a	4-1	*Găman, Costea M. (p), Prepeliţă, Wobay*
1/10	Univ Cluj	h	3-0	*Dina, Iliev, Wobay*
18/10	Braşov	a	3-0	*og (Oros), Dina, Stoica*
23/10	Vaslui	h	0-1	
1/11	Unirea	a	2-1	*Gargorov (p), Dina*
5/11	Oţelul	h	0-1	
14/11	Dinamo	a	2-2	*Piţurcă 2*
20/11	Gloria Bistriţa	h	1-2	*Ciucă*
29/11	Gaz Metan	a	0-1	
3/12	CFR Cluj	a	1-2	*Stoica*
2011				
27/2	Steaua	h	0-1	
7/3	Victoria	h	1-1	*Costea M.*
13/3	Timişoara	a	0-4	
20/3	Astra	h	1-1	*Subotic*
2/4	Sportul Studenţesc	a	0-3	
7/4	Pandurii	h	0-2	
11/4	Rapid	a	0-0	
14/4	Târgu Mureş	h	2-1	*Costea F., Subotic*
18/4	Univ Cluj	a	0-3	
24/4	Braşov	h	1-2	*Stoianof*
27/4	Vaslui	a	1-2	*Subotic*
1/5	Unirea	h	3-0	*Subotic, Stoica, Firţulescu*
5/5	Oţelul	a	1-2	*Subotic*
9/5	Dinamo	h	0-2	
16/5	Gloria Bistriţa	a	1-1	*Stoica*
21/5	Gaz Metan	h	1-2	*Costea M.*

No	Name	Nat	DoB	Pos	Aps	(s)	Gls
2	Ştefan Nicolae BĂRBOIANU		24/1/88	D	13	(1)	
27	Vlad BUJOR		3/2/89	A		(4)	
86	Florian BULEICĂ		12/9/91	D	3	(5)	
5	Sorin Marian BUŞU		8/7/89	D	10		
6	Mădălin Marius CIUCĂ		4/11/82	D	15	(3)	2
10	Florin Constantin COSTEA		16/5/85	A	7	(6)	1
9	Mihai Alexandru COSTEA		29/5/88	A	21	(6)	3
3	DAVID Júnior LOPES	BRA	19/7/82	D	13	(2)	
18	Ovidiu Liviu DĂNĂNAE		26/8/85	D	31		
13	Spase DILEVSKI	AUS	13/5/85	M	11	(2)	
20	Mihai DINA		15/3/85	M	16	(4)	3
25	Dragoş Petruţ FIRŢULESCU		15/5/89	M	6	(12)	1
23	Emil GARGOROV	BUL	15/2/81	M	9	(4)	1
7	Marius Valerică GĂMAN		25/2/89	D	17		1
28	Cosmin GÂNGIOVEANU		4/9/89	M	7	(15)	
7	Costinel GUGU		20/5/92	D	9		
4	Valentin ILIEV	BUL	11/8/80	D	10		3
11	Walter Alberto LÓPEZ	URU	15/10/85	D	4		
21	Silviu LUNG Jr.		4/6/89	G	23		
88	Jackie NICOLAE		5/1/91	M	6	(1)	
8	Marius Alexandru OLOGU		16/7/89	M	10	(4)	
27	Alexandru Victorio PIŢURCĂ		28/10/83	A	12	(2)	4
30	Andrei PREPELIŢĂ		8/12/85	M	28		1
92	Mihai ROMAN		31/5/92	A	2	(4)	
1	Răzvan Marian STANCA		18/1/80	G	11		
19	Ovidiu STOIANOF		28/6/85	A	7	(15)	2
5	Dorel STOICA		15/12/78	D	28		4
20	Danijel SUBOTIC	SUI	31/1/89	A	15	(1)	5
77	Olivian SURUGIU		23/5/90	M		(3)	
13	WENDEL Raul Gonçalves Gomes	BRA	25/5/84	D	2	(1)	
77	Julius Gibrilla WOBAY	SLE	17/5/84	A	14	(1)	3
4	Marc André ZORO	CIV	27/12/83	D	14		

FC VASLUI

Coach – Juan Ramón López Caro (ESP); (8/10/10) Viorel Hizo

Founded – 2001

Stadium – Municipal (15,000)

2010				
23/7	Rapid	a	0-2	
30/7	Târgu Mureş	h	1-1	*Gladstone*
6/8	Univ Cluj	a	1-1	*Wesley*
14/8	Braşov	h	2-1	*Papp, Pouga*
22/8	Steaua	h	0-3	
29/8	Unirea	a	1-2	*Wesley (p)*
13/9	Oţelul	h	4-0	*Adaílton 2, Wesley, Pouga*
19/9	Dinamo	a	2-1	*og (Bordeanu), Wesley*
25/9	Gloria Bistriţa	h	1-0	*Adaílton*
3/10	Gaz Metan	a	0-0	
15/10	CFR Cluj	h	5-3	*Sânmărtean, Adaílton 2, Burdujan 2*
23/10	Univ Craiova	a	1-0	*Bello*
29/10	Victoria	h	1-0	*Cânu*
6/11	Timişoara	a	1-2	*Papp*
12/11	Astra	h	0-0	
21/11	Sportul Studenţesc	a	1-0	*Bello*
26/11	Pandurii	h	3-1	*Wesley, Bello, Costin*
5/12	Rapid	h	1-1	*Costin*
2011				
28/2	Târgu Mureş	a	2-0	*Wesley 2*
7/3	Univ Cluj	h	2-0	*Papp, Adaílton*
14/3	Braşov	a	1-1	*Wesley*
19/3	Steaua	a	1-1	*Adaílton*
1/4	Unirea	h	2-0	*Sânmărtean, Adaílton*
6/4	Oţelul	a	0-0	
9/4	Dinamo	h	2-0	*Wesley, Cânu*
12/4	Gloria Bistriţa	a	1-1	*Temwanjera*
18/4	Gaz Metan	h	3-0	*Wesley (p), Adaílton, Bello*
23/4	CFR Cluj	a	0-1	
27/4	Univ Craiova	h	2-1	*og (Stoica), Wesley*
30/4	Victoria	a	3-1	*Wesley, Cânu, Adaílton*
5/5	Timişoara	h	1-1	*og (Alexa)*
9/5	Astra	a	1-1	*Temwanjera*
15/5	Sportul Studenţesc	h	4-2	*Bălace, Pouga, Adaílton, Wesley*
21/5	Pandurii	a	1-0	*Cânu*

No	Name	Nat	DoB	Pos	Aps	(s)	Gls
14	ADAÍLTON Martins Bolzan	BRA	24/1/77	A	27	(2)	11
15	Richard Aticah ANNANG	GHA	30/4/91	D	5		
17	Silviu BĂLACE		13/11/78	D	11	(5)	1
25	Yero BELLO	NGA	11/12/87	A	17	(10)	4
21	Rodolfo BODIPO Díaz	EQG	25/10/77	A	2	(1)	
9	Lucian BURDUJAN		18/2/84	A	6	(2)	2
2	Alejandro CAMPANO Hernando	ESP	29/12/78	M	10	(6)	
28	Gabriel CÂNU		18/1/81	D	23		4
1	Vytautas ČERNIAUSKAS	LTU	12/3/89	G	4		
30	Raul Răzvan COSTIN		29/1/85	D	19	(8)	2

No	Name	Nat	DoB	Pos	Aps	(s)	Gls
6	DAVID RIVAS Rodríguez	ESP	2/12/78	D	9	(3)	
26	Pavol FARKAŠ	SVK	27/3/85	D	8	(2)	
4	Stanislav GENCHEV	BUL	20/3/81	M	26	(1)	
10	Willian GERLEM de Jesus Almeida	BRA	7/8/84	M	4	(1)	
31	Adrian Ion GHEORGHIU		30/11/81	M	8	(10)	
85	GLADSTONE Pereira della Valentina	BRA	29/1/85	D	4		1
27	HUGO Duarte de Sousa "LUZ"	POR	24/2/82	D	8		
69	Dušan KUCIAK	SVK	21/5/85	G	30		
20	Zhivko MILANOV	BUL	15/7/84	D	30		
11	Nemanja MILISAVLJEVIĆ	SRB	1/11/84	M	12	(15)	
7	Răzvan NEAGU		25/5/87	A		(2)	
8	Daniel Gabriel PANCU		17/8/77	A		(5)	
3	Paul PAPP		11/11/89	D	32		3
23	Miloš PAVLOVIĆ	SRB	27/11/83	M	9	(1)	
9	Christian POUGA	CMR	19/6/86	A	7	(14)	3
18	Lucian Iulian SÂNMĂRTEAN		13/3/80	M	27	(2)	2
19	Mike TEMWANJERA	ZIM	21/5/82	A	3	(4)	2
80	WESLEY Lopes da Silva	BRA	10/11/80	A	30	(2)	13
5	Denis ZMEU	MDA	8/5/85	M	3	(1)	

FC VICTORIA BRĂNEŞTI

Coach – Ilie Stan; (25/4/11) Ciprian Urican

Founded – 1968

Stadium – Gloria, Buzau (17,000) & Concordia, Chiajna (3,500)

2010				
26/7	Gaz Metan	h	2-3	*Olariu, Oprea*
2/8	CFR Cluj	a	0-2	
6/8	Univ Craiova	h	1-0	*Simion*
16/8	Steaua	a	1-2	*Olariu (p)*
22/8	Timişoara	a	1-2	*Negru*
30/8	Astra	h	1-1	*Olariu*
11/9	Sportul Studenţesc	a	2-2	*Olariu (p), Popa*
17/9	Pandurii	h	2-0	*Marincău, Simion*
26/9	Rapid	a	1-7	*Simion*
4/10	Târgu Mureş	h	0-0	
18/10	Univ Cluj	a	3-2	*Oprea, Olariu, Nicoară*
22/10	Braşov	h	1-1	*Olariu*
29/10	Vaslui	a	0-1	
8/11	Unirea	h	4-1	*Olariu 2 (2p), Simion, Coman*
12/11	Oţelul	a	1-1	*Avram*
22/11	Dinamo	h	2-4	*Maghici, Simion*
29/11	Gloria Bistriţa	a	0-1	
3/12	Gaz Metan	a	2-2	*Novac, Popa*
2011				
27/2	CFR Cluj	h	1-1	*Coman*
7/3	Univ Craiova	a	1-1	*Coman*
11/3	Steaua	h	0-1	
18/3	Timişoara	h	0-2	
1/4	Astra	a	0-2	
5/4	Sportul Studenţesc	h	1-1	*Oprea*
10/4	Pandurii	a	2-4	*Oprea, Olariu*
14/4	Rapid	h	0-0	
17/4	Târgu Mureş	a	0-4	
23/4	Univ Cluj	h	0-2	
27/4	Braşov	a	0-1	
30/4	Vaslui	h	1-3	*Popa*
4/5	Unirea	a	1-2	*Avram*
9/5	Oţelul	h	1-2	*Zuluf*
16/5	Dinamo	a	1-3	*Ispir*
21/5	Gloria Bistriţa	h	2-0	*Oprea, Zuluf*

No	Name	Nat	DoB	Pos	Aps	(s)	Gls
30	Răzvan AVRAM		12/10/86	M	19	(5)	2
5	Sergiu BAR		19/3/80	D	33		
1	Alin BORDEANU		8/8/80	G	7		
19	Alexandru BUHUŞI		31/5/90	M		(2)	
4	George CĂLINŢARU		26/2/89	M	1	(6)	
22	Cornel CERNEA		22/4/76	G	6		
21	Augustin CHIRIŢĂ		10/10/75	M	2		
9	Cornel Ion COMAN		13/7/81	A	12	(8)	3
15	Alexandru IACOB		14/4/89	M	14	(2)	
23	Stelian ISAC		19/9/81	D	3	(1)	
20	Sorin ISPIR		26/7/88	M	13	(5)	1
3	József LÖRINCZ		13/4/85	D	8	(1)	
2	Casian Augustin MAGHICI		5/5/84	D	26	(1)	1
24	Raul Paul MARINCĂU		27/4/81	D	21	(1)	1
26	Valentin NEGRU		4/9/82	M	3	(6)	1
4	Viorel NICOARĂ		27/9/87	M	16	(1)	1
16	Eduard NICOLA		23/5/83	D	27	(1)	
25	Daniel NOVAC		26/9/87	M	13	(9)	1
17	Vasile OLARIU		22/7/87	M	27		9
10	Bogdan OPREA		29/9/82	A	27	(4)	5
34	Florentin PETRE		15/1/76	M	4	(6)	
8	Dorin POPA		29/11/88	D	25	(4)	3
26	Andrei POVERLOVICI		17/10/85	D	5	(1)	
29	Ciprian PRODAN		28/4/79	A	4	(5)	
22	George Daniel SAVU		20/3/83	G	1		
11	Valentin SIMION		6/10/86	A	16	(7)	5
28	Daniel STAN		4/1/92	M		(2)	
27	Cristian STOICESCU		19/3/80	G	20	(1)	
28	Bogdan Adrian STRĂUŢ		28/4/86	D	9	(3)	
7	Dinu Marius TODORAN		8/9/78	M	8	(2)	
13	Andrei VASILESCU		13/6/86	A		(3)	
6	Valentin VELICU		21/10/85	D	2		
19	Nicolae ZULUF		3/4/88	M	2	(13)	2

TOP GOALSCORERS 2010/11

18	Ianis ZICU (Timişoara)
15	ERIC (Gaz Metan)
13	Bogdan STANCU (Steaua)
	Claudiu NICULESCU (Univ Cluj)
	WESLEY (Vaslui)
12	Tiberiu BĂLAN (Sportul Studenţesc)
11	Ovidiu HEREA (Rapid)
	ADAÍLTON (Vaslui)
10	Adrian CRISTEA (Dinamo/Univ Cluj)
9	Robert ILYEŞ (Braşov)
	Gabriel TORJE (Dinamo)
	Costin CURELEA (Sportul Studenţesc)
	Vasile OLARIU (Victoria)

PROMOTED CLUBS

FC CEAHLĂUL PIATRA NEAMŢ

Coach – Marin Barbu; (2/2/11) Constantin Enache

Founded – 1919

Stadium – Ceahlăul (18,000)

CS CONCORDIA CHIAJNA

Coach – Laurenţiu Diniţă; (1/9/10) Bogdan Argeş Vintilă; (24/10/10) Costel Orac; (5/5/11) Cristian Niţă

Founded – 1957

Stadium – Concordia (3,500)

FC PETROLUL PLOIEŞTI

Coach – Valeriu Răchită

Founded – 1952

Stadium – Conpet (1,300)

MAJOR HONOURS: Romanian League – (3) 1958, 1959, 1966; Romanian Cup – (2) 1963, 1995.

CS MIOVENI

Coach – Cristian Negru; (23/10/10) Ionuţ Popa

Founded – 2000

Stadium – Mioveni (10,000)

CSU VOINŢA SIBIU

Coach – Alexandru Pelici

Founded – 2007

Stadium – Municipal (14,200)

SECOND LEVEL FINAL TABLES 2010/11

SERIA I		Pld	W	D	L	F	A	Pts
1	FC Ceahlăul Piatra Neamţ	30	20	7	3	65	23	67
2	CS Concordia Chiajna	30	17	10	3	48	27	61
3	AFC Săgeata Năvodari	30	18	4	8	50	27	58
4	FC Delta Tulcea	30	17	4	9	50	37	55
5	FCM Dunărea Galaţi	30	13	9	8	44	26	48
6	CS Otopeni	30	14	4	12	35	38	46
7	FC Botoşani	30	12	6	12	48	46	42
8	FC Viitorul Constanţa	30	10	11	9	37	37	41
9	FC Astra II Giurgiu	30	11	8	11	42	44	41
10	FC Gloria Buzău	30	9	11	10	33	34	38
11	FC Snagov	30	11	4	15	36	52	37
12	FC Dinamo II Bucureşti	30	9	7	14	30	44	34
13	FC Farul Constanţa	30	8	6	16	27	45	30
14	FC Steaua II Bucureşti	30	7	6	17	29	48	27
15	CF Brăila	30	5	6	19	28	47	21
16	CS Juventus Bucureşti	30	4	7	19	26	53	19

SERIA II		Pld	W	D	L	F	A	Pts
1	FC Petrolul Ploieşti	28	18	5	5	46	22	59
2	FC Bihor Oradea	28	17	7	4	43	20	58
3	CS Mioveni	28	17	6	5	43	19	57
4	CSU Voinţa Sibiu	28	14	8	6	36	17	50
5	CS ALRO Slatina	28	14	6	8	46	26	48
6	ACSMU Politehnica Iaşi	28	14	5	9	41	30	47
7	CSM Râmnicu Vâlcea	28	11	3	14	35	39	36
8	FCM UTA Arad	28	13	8	7	48	36	35
9	FC Arieşul Turda	28	8	9	11	26	31	33
10	CS Gaz Metan CFR Craiova	28	8	7	13	36	39	31
11	FC Unirea Alba Iulia	28	8	6	14	22	35	30
12	FC Argeş Piteşti	28	8	5	15	27	40	29
13	CS Mureşul Deva	28	7	5	16	31	48	26
14	CS ACU Arad	28	6	7	15	18	36	25
15	FC Silvania Şimleul Silvaniei	28	3	1	24	9	69	10

NB FC Bihor Oradea did not receive licence for Liga I; CS Mioveni promoted instead. CS Minerul Lupeni withdrew after round 6 – all their matches annulled; FC Silvania Şimleul Silvaniei withdrew after round 15 – their remaining matches were awarded as 0-3 defeat; FCM UTA Arad – 12 pts deducted.

PROMOTION PLAY-OFF

NB As a result of licensing issues for 2011/12 Liga I an additional play-off was required to determine one additional promotion place.

(2/7/11 & 6/7/11)
Săgeata 0, Voinţa 0
Voinţa 2, Săgeata 0
(Voinţa 2-0)

DOMESTIC CUP 2010/11

CUPA ROMÂNIEI

FIRST ROUND

(21/9/10)
ACU Arad 0, CFR Cluj 1 *(aet)*
Rapid Bucureşti 5, Petrolul Ploieşti 0
Univ Cluj 1, Victoria Brăneşti 0
Univ Craiova 5, Minerul Lupeni 0
Voinţa Sibiu 3, Gaz Metan Mediaş 1 *(aet)*

(22/9/10)
ALRO Slatina 0, Vaslui 0 *(aet; 4-3 on pens)*
Dinamo Bucureşti 2, Ceahlăul 0
Gloria Bistriţa 3, Astra II Giurgiu 0
Juventus Bucureşti 1, Timişoara 3
Pandurii 3, Viitorul Constanţa 2
Silvania Şimleul Silvaniei 0, Târgu Mureş 1
Sportul Studenţesc 3, Otopeni 1
Unirea Urziceni 1, Delta Tulcea 0

(23/9/10)
Astra Ploieşti 2, Oţelul 1
Chimia Brazi 0, Braşov 1
Gaz Metan CFR Craiova 0, Steaua 1

SECOND ROUND

(26/10/10)
Braşov 2, Univ Cluj 1
Dinamo Bucureşti 3, ALRO Slatina 1
Timişoara 1, Voinţa Sibiu 1 *(aet; 4-3 on pens)*

(27/10/10)
CFR Cluj 2, Târgu Mureş 0
Gloria Bistriţa 1, Unirea Urziceni 0
Steaua 1, Sportul Studenţesc 1 *(aet; 3-1 on pens)*

(28/10/10)
Astra Ploieşti 0, Rapid Bucureşti 2 *(aet)*
Pandurii 0, Univ Craiova 2

QUARTER-FINALS

(10/11/10)
Braşov 1 *(Cristescu 90)*, Timişoara 0
Dinamo Bucureşti 1 *(Munteanu C. 67)*, Univ Craiova 1 *(Dina 31)* *(aet; 3-1 on pens)*

(11/11/10)
CFR Cluj 0, Gloria Bistriţa 1 *(Júnior Moraes 73p)*
Rapid Bucureşti 0, Steaua 1 *(Surdu 49)*

SEMI-FINALS

(20/4/11 & 12/5/11)
Gloria Bistriţa 0, Dinamo Bucureşti 2 *(Dănciulescu 53, Alexe 87)*
Dinamo Bucureşti 5 *(Munteanu V. 10, Dănciulescu 27p, 61, Ţucudean 54, 90)*, Gloria Bistriţa 1 *(Păduraru 45)*
(Dinamo Bucureşti 7-1)

(21/4/11 & 11/5/11)
Steaua 0, Braşov 0
Braşov 1 *(Ilyeş 41p)*, Steaua 1 *(Dică 86)*
(1-1; Steaua on away goal)

FINAL

(25/5/11)
Stadionul Tineretului, Brasov
FC STEAUA BUCUREŞTI 2 *(Dică 24, Bărboianu 51og)*
FC DINAMO BUCUREŞTI 1 *(Torje 33)*
Referee – *Avram*
STEAUA – *Tătăruşanu, Emeghara, Galamaz, Gardoş, Latovlevici, Brandán, Nicoliţă, Tănase (Iliev 90), Surdu, Bilaşco (Szekely 75), Dică (Bicfalvi 62).*
DINAMO BUCUREŞTI – *Bălgrădean, Bărboianu, Moţi, Grigore, Bordeanu, Mărgăritescu (Ţucudean 87), Koné (Bakaj 72), Torje, Munteanu C., Alexe, Dănciulescu (Ganea 67).*

CLUB COMMUNICATION 2011/12

FC Astra Ploieşti

Str. Sondelor 19A
RO-100272 Ploieşti

Tel +40 244 510 050
Fax +40 244 510 050
Web fcastraploiesti.ro
Email fc.astraploiesti@yahoo.com
Media Officer Geo Raetchi

FC Braşov

Str. Poienelor nr. 5
RO-500419 Braşov

Tel +40 268 325 454
Fax +40 268 325 454
Web fcbrasov.ro
Email fcbrasov2007@yahoo.com
Media Officer Adrian Marica

FC Ceahlăul Piatra Neamţ

Str. Eroilor 18
RO-610053 Piatra Neamţ

Tel +40 233 212 702
Fax +40 233 216 613
Web fcceahlaul.ro
Email ceahlaul@decebal.ro
Media Officer Gelu Cracana

CFR 1907 Cluj

Str. Romulus Vuia no. 23
RO-400214 Cluj-Napoca

Tel +40 264 598 831
Fax +40 264 598 842
Web cfr1907.ro
Email club@cfr1907.ro
Media Officer Tudor Pop

CS Concordia Chiajna

Str. Drumul Garii 1-3
RO-77040 Comuna Chiajna, jud. Ilfov

Tel +40 214 361 536
Fax +40 214 361 536
Web csconcordia.com
Email office@csconcordia.ro
Media Officer Florin Petrescu

FC Dinamo Bucureşti

Sos. Ştefan cel Mare 7-9, Sector 2
RO-020121 Bucureşti

Tel +40 21 210 6974
Fax +40 21 211 3072
Web fcdinamo.ro
Email secretariat@fcdinamo.ro
Media Officer Ionel Culina

CS Gaz Metan Mediaş

Str. Regele Ferdinand I nr.12
RO-551002 Mediaş

Tel +40 69 844 623
Fax +40 26 983 3123
Web gaz-metan-medias.ro
Email clubsportivgazmetan@yahoo.com
Media Officer Alex Pintea

CS Mioveni

Bd. Dacia, Bl. G1, parter
RO-115400 Mioveni jud. Argeş

Tel +40 248 291 007
Fax +40 248 291 007
Web csmioveni.ro
Email office@csmioveni.ro
Media Officer Răzvan Tunaru

FC Oţelul Galaţi

Str. Regiment 11 Siret 2A
RO-800322 Galaţi

Tel +40 236 499 009
Fax +40 236 499 009
Web otelul-galati.ro
Email club_otelul@yahoo.com
Media Officer Danuţ Lungu

CS Pandurii Târgu Jiu

Str. Victoriei nr.22
RO-210234 Târgu Jiu jud. Gorj

Tel +40 253 223 588
Fax +40 253 223 588
Web pandurii-tg-jiu.ro
Email pandurii@pandurii-tg-jiu.ro
Media Officer Monalisa Popescu

FC Petrolul Ploieşti

str. Stadionului nr. 26
RO-100173 Ploieşti

Tel +40 244 517 594
Fax +40 244 517 594
Web fcpetrolul.ro
Email office@fcpetrolul.ro
Media Officer Ionuţ Pana

FC Rapid Bucureşti

Bdul Poligrafiei 1C, 1st floor, Room 21,
Sector 1, RO-013704 Bucureşti

Tel +40 21 668 7555
Fax +40 21 668 7588
Web fcrapid.ro
Email rapid@fcrapid.ro
Media Officer Cristian Costache

FC Sportul Studenţesc Bucureşti

Str. Mihail Moxa nr 3-5, sector 1
RO-10962 Bucureşti

Tel +40 212 125 059
Fax +40 212 12 061
Web fcsportulstudentesc.ro
Email office@fcsportulstudentesc.ro
Media Officer Florin Alboiu

FC Steaua Bucureşti

Bulevardul Ghencea nr 45, Sector 6
RO-061692 Bucureşti

Tel +40 21 411 4656
Fax +40 21 410 2182
Web steauafc.com
Email office@steauafc.com
Media Officer Răzvan Rotaru

FCM Târgu Mureş

Str. Bega no.2
RO-540390 Târgu Mureş

Tel +40 265 250 731
Fax +40 265 250 731
Web fcm-tirgumures.ro
Email office@fcm-tirgumures.ro
Media Officer Vlad Podar

FC Universitatea Cluj

Str. Buna Ziua nr. 34-36
RO-400495 Cluj-Napoca

Tel +40 264 594 038
Fax +40 264 459 039
Web universitateacluj.ro
Email contact@universitateacluj.ro
Media Officer Flaviu Popa

FC Vaslui

Str. Decebal nr.16
RO-730227 Vaslui

Tel +40 335 409 552
Fax +40 235 316 097
Web vasluifc.ro
Email sportingclubvaslui@yahoo.com
Media Officer Alex Guzganu

CSU Voinţa Sibiu

Str. Poet Vasile Carlova 28
RO-Sibiu

Tel +40 269 233 669
Fax +40 269 223 669
Web csu-vointa-sibiu.ro
Email csuvointa@gmail.com
Media Officer Marius Lungu

RUSSIA

Russie I Russland

The Football Union of Russia

COMMUNICATION

Address	Ulitsa Narodnaya 7 RU-115172 Moskva	**President**	Sergei Fursenko
Tel	+7 495 9261300	**Chief Executive**	Andrei Balashov
Fax	+7 495 9261305	**Media Officer**	Irina Baranova
E-mail	info@rfs.ru	**Year of Formation**	1912
Website	rfs.ru	**National Stadium**	Luzhniki, Moscow (78,360)

DOMESTIC COMPETITION SUMMARY 2010/11

PREMIER-LIGA FINAL TABLE

			Home					Away					Total						
		Pld	W	D	L	F	A	W	D	L	F	A	W	D	L	F	A	Pts	Comp
1	FC Zenit St Petersburg	30	10	4	1	31	8	10	4	1	30	13	20	8	2	61	21	68	UCL
2	PFC CSKA Moskva	30	9	4	2	27	13	9	4	2	24	9	18	8	4	51	22	62	UCL
3	FC Rubin Kazan	30	9	5	1	22	7	6	8	1	15	9	15	13	2	37	16	58	UCL
4	FC Spartak Moskva	30	9	3	3	27	15	4	7	4	16	18	13	10	7	43	33	49	UEL
5	FC Lokomotiv Moskva	30	9	2	4	22	14	4	7	4	12	15	13	9	8	34	29	48	UEL
6	PFC Spartak Nalchik	30	9	3	3	27	19	3	5	7	13	18	12	8	10	40	37	44	
7	FC Dinamo Moskva	30	7	6	2	26	14	2	7	6	12	17	9	13	8	38	31	40	
8	FC Tom Tomsk	30	6	6	3	19	19	4	1	10	16	24	10	7	13	35	43	37	
9	FC Rostov	30	6	2	7	12	16	4	2	9	15	28	10	4	16	27	44	34	
10	FC Saturn Moskovskaya Oblast	30	4	7	4	15	15	4	3	8	12	23	8	10	12	27	38	34	
11	FC Anzhi Makhachkala	30	5	4	6	13	13	4	2	9	16	26	9	6	15	29	39	33	
12	FC Terek Grozny	30	6	7	2	16	11	2	2	11	12	23	8	9	13	28	34	33	
13	FC Krylya Sovetov Samara	30	5	4	6	15	15	2	6	7	13	25	7	10	13	28	40	31	
14	FC Amkar Perm	30	8	1	6	16	13	0	5	10	8	22	8	6	16	24	35	30	
15	FC Alania Vladikavkaz	30	5	7	3	18	16	2	2	11	7	25	7	9	14	25	41	30	UEL / *Relegated*
16	FC Sibir Novosibirsk	30	3	4	8	19	28	1	4	10	15	30	4	8	18	34	58	20	*Relegated*

NB FC Saturn Moskovskaya Oblast withdrew from 2011 Premier-Liga.

Top Scorer	Welliton (Spartak Moskva), 19 goals
Promoted Clubs	FC Kuban Krasnodar FC Volga Nizhniy Novgorod FC Krasnodar
Cup Final	PFC CSKA Moskva 2, FC Alania Vladikavkaz 1

Spalletti lifts Zenit to new heights

2010 was a year that Russian football followers will never forget. It ended with the nation being granted hosting rights for the 2018 FIFA World Cup – a decision that will change the footballing landscape and infrastructure in the country for decades to come. It was also the last year in which the Russian Premier-Liga was staged from spring to autumn, with a new-look year-straddling championship set to begin in 2012/13 after a lengthy two-tiered transitionary season from March 2011 through to May 2012.

It was a very special year too for FC Zenit St Petersburg, who won the Russian domestic double for the first time, supplementing their mid-season cup win with a magisterial romp to the Premier-Liga title. Led by ex-AS Roma coach Luciano Spalletti, the generously-funded former UEFA Cup winners blazed a trail to the title that proved too hot for both defending champions FC Rubin Kazan and the usual cluster of challengers from Moscow. The club's second championship in four seasons was secured a fortnight before its conclusion with a 5-0 battering of FC Rostov in Zenit's Petrovskiy Stadium home. Despite the freezing, mid-November temperatures, Spalletti joined in the locals' traditional celebrations by removing his shirt and baring his chest – and shaven head – to the elements.

Luciano Spalletti led Zenit to a domestic double in his first year as coach

Record-breaking run

After a 2009 season in which almost every foreign coach in the Premier-Liga struggled to make an impact, Zenit's acquisition of the effervescent Italian might have been seen as a gamble, but all reservations were cast aside as Spalletti stitched together a tidy run of results that soon developed into a record-breaking sequence of 23 league games unbeaten. With the cup win thrown in, Zenit were proving an invincible force in their homeland, which made their shock elimination from the UEFA Champions League in the August play-offs by French club AJ Auxerre all the more unfathomable and difficult to bear. Zenit's reaction to their brutal 2-0 defeat at the Stade Abbé-Deschamps (they had won the first leg 1-0) was to win every one of their six UEFA Europa League group games – the only one of the 48 teams to do so – before departing the competition in the spring after a narrow last-16 defeat to FC Twente.

So there would be no European conquest to follow the domestic crown – as Zenit had managed under Dick Advocaat in 2007/08 – but Spalletti certainly ranked as highly in the hearts and minds of the Zenit faithful as his Dutch predecessor. His team had not just been the most productive in the Premier-Liga but also the most attractive, scoring ten goals more than the team that finished runners-up, six points behind them, PFC CSKA Moskva.

CSKA Moskva striker Seydou Doumbia scored twice to take his team to victory in the 2011 Russian Cup final

Although CSKA delayed Zenit's title celebrations by four days when they brilliantly defeated them 3-1 at the Petrovskiy, a late change of leadership would have been a travesty. After all, Zenit lost only one other game – at FC Spartak Moskva in late October – and were victorious in 20 of their 30 matches. In Portuguese No10 Danny, who scored ten goals, they possessed the league's most skilful and dynamic individual, and there was a highly successful return to the club for striker Aleksandr Kerzhakov, who, having been sold to Sevilla FC before the club's 2007/08 feats, made the most of his second opportunity by scoring 13 goals.

Zenit's purchase power was reflected in the summer transfer market when they recruited World Cup defenders Bruno Alves and Aleksandar Luković as well as denuding titleholders Rubin of two key players – veteran Russian international midfielder Sergei Semak and ace marksman Aleksandr Bukharov. Not to be outdone, CSKA also waded into the mid-term market to bring in Ivory Coast striker Seydou Doumbia and Serbian winger Zoran Tošić and re-engage from Brazil their former long-serving centre forward Vágner Love.

Good buys

If anything, CSKA's buys proved more astute than Zenit's as the 2009/10 UEFA Champions League quarter-finalists ended the campaign with a 12-match unbeaten run that assured them of second place and a return to Europe's elite club competition in 2011/12. Like Zenit, they had to get their European kicks from the UEFA Europa League in 2010/11, and, like Zenit again, they breezed through the group stage – only a Matchday 6 draw at AC Sparta Praha denied them a clean sweep of victories – before falling in the round of 16 to eventual winners FC Porto.

CSKA were to claim yet another Russian Cup in 2011 – their fifth in seven years – when they overcame FC Alania Vladikavkaz 2-1 in the final thanks to a brace of goals from the ever-improving Doumbia. As Alania were a second-division team at the time, having been relegated from the top flight in 2010, their participation was a surprise, but the true miracle of their presence in Yaroslavl was that they had come through to face CSKA without scoring a single goal en route. Three of their four ties had been won on penalties after goalless draws, while their quarter-final was awarded to them as a forfeit because their prospective opponents, FC Saturn Moskovskaya Oblast, had gone out of business during the winter.

Saturn's demise meant that with Alania and 2010 Russian Cup runners-up FC Sibir Novosibirsk automatically relegated, three promotion places were available for the new, elongated 2011/12 Premier-Liga. FC Kuban Krasnodar, coached by former Romania star Dan Petrescu, made a quick return alongside FC Volga Nizhniy Novgorod, but the third place went not to third-placed FC Nizhniy Novgorod, nor to fourth-placed FC KamAZ Naberezhnye Chelny, but to fifth-placed FC Krasnodar, who, unlike the two teams above them, were happy to accept the free gift that came their way.

Rock-solid Rubin

If the third promotion place proved to be something of a hot potato, there was no relinquishing the third UEFA Champions League spot, which was claimed, with room to spare, by Kurban Berdyev's Rubin. There would be no title hat-trick for the team from Tatarstan, but third place was no mean achievement given that they lost two key players to Zenit and had terrible trouble putting the ball in the net. They scored only 37 goals in their 30 games, but it was their rock-solid defence, breached just 16 times, and an ability to avoid defeat – like Zenit, they lost only twice – that led them to such a lofty position. They even held FC Barcelona at home in the UEFA Champions League, but could not repeat their remarkable Camp Nou triumph of a year earlier and, as in 2009/10, finished third in their group to cross over into the UEFA Europa League. Like Zenit, but a round earlier, they were ousted by reigning Dutch champions Twente.

FC Spartak Moskva also began their European campaign in the group stage of the UEFA Champions League, but the 2009 Premier-Liga runners-up - who despite the prolific Welliton in attack finished a disappointing and distant fourth in 2010 - failed to build on a fine start and followed Rubin into the UEFA Europa League. There, with coach Valeriy Karpin pulling the strings, they despatched the prospective champions of Switzerland (FC Basel 1893) and the Netherlands (AFC Ajax) before feeling the full force of Porto in the quarter-finals and losing 10-3 on aggregate.

Spartak were the last of a powerful Russian battalion to exit Europe. The first to fall, alongside Sibir, were FC Lokomotiv Moskva, whose penalty shoot-out defeat by Swiss second-tier outfit FC Lausanne-Sport was arguably the shock of the play-off round. The Railwaymen did, however, manage to recover their composure and go unbeaten through the last three months of the Premier-Liga campaign to take fifth place and re-qualify for Europe, but in December they lost their venerable coach Yuriy Semin to FC Dynamo Kyiv for the second time in three years.

National Team

International Honours* – UEFA European Football Championship - (1) 1960.

International Tournament Appearances* – FIFA World Cup - (9) 1958 (qtr-finals), 1962 (qtr-finals), 1966 (4th), 1970 (qtr-finals), 1982 (2nd phase), 1986 (2nd round), 1990, 1994, 2002. UEFA European Championship - (9) 1960 (Winners), 1964 (runners-up), 1968 (4th), 1972 (runners-up), 1988 (runners-up), 1992, 1996, 2004, 2008 (semi-finals).

Top Five All-time Caps (including USSR/CIS) – Viktor Onopko (113); Oleh Blokhin (112); Rinat Dasaev (91); Albert Shesternyov (90); Anatoliy Demyanenko (80)

Top Five All-time Goals (including USSR/CIS) – Oleh Blokhin (42); Oleh Protasov (29); Vladimir Beschastnykh & Valentin Ivanov (26), Eduard Streltsov (25)

(before 1992 as USSR; 1992 as CIS)*

Work in progress

Although assured of competing at the 2018 World Cup, Russia still had plenty of work to do in their bid to reach the finals of UEFA EURO 2012 as they ended the 2010/11 season level on points with the Republic of Ireland and Slovakia in Group B. Having failed to qualify for the 2010 World Cup, under Guus Hiddink, the onus was on the team to make amends under another Dutchman, Advocaat, but while a 3-2 win in Dublin offered an indication of Russia's class and pedigree, the home defeat by Slovakia that preceded it provided fresh evidence of the team's frustrating inability to translate their superiority on to the scoresheet, a further example of which came six months later when they were held to a goalless draw in Armenia.

NATIONAL TEAM RESULTS 2010/11

11/8/10	Bulgaria	H	St Petersburg	1-0	*Shirokov (6)*
3/9/10	Andorra (ECQ)	A	Andorra la Vella	2-0	*Pogrebnyak (14, 64p)*
7/9/10	Slovakia (ECQ)	H	Moscow	0-1	
8/10//0	Republic of Ireland (ECQ)	A	Dublin	3-2	*Kerzhakov (11), Dzagoev (29), Shirokov (50)*
12/10/10	FYROM (ECQ)	A	Skopje	1-0	*Kerzhakov (8)*
17/11/10	Belgium	H	Voronezh	0-2	
9/2/11	Iran	N	Abu Dhabi (UAE)	0-1	
26/3/11	Armenia (ECQ)	A	Yerevan	0-0	
29/3/11	Qatar	A	Doha	1-1	*Pavlyuchenko (34)*
4/6/11	Armenia (ECQ)	H	St Petersburg	3-1	*Pavlyuchenko (26, 59, 73p)*
7/6/11	Cameroon	N	Salzburg (AUT)	0-0	

NATIONAL TEAM APPEARANCES 2010/11

oach – Dick ADVOCAAT (NED) 27/9/47			Bul	AND	SVK	IRL	MKD	Bel	Irn	ARM	Qat	ARM	Cmr	Caps	Goals
or AKINFEEV	8/4/86	CSKA Moskva	G	G	G	G	G	G	G	G		G		49	-
leksandr ANYUKOV	28/9/82	Zenit	D46	D	D	D	D		s46		D	D75		57	1
ergei IGNASHEVICH	14/7/79	CSKA Moskva	D	D	D81	D	D	D63	D	D	D46	D		66	4
asiliy BEREZUTSKIY	20/6/82	CSKA Moskva	D	D	D	D	D	D46	D	D	D	D	D46	54	2
uriy ZHIRKOV	20/8/83	Chelsea (ENG)	D46		D	D	D	D		D	D46	D	s56	43	-
oman SHIROKOV	6/7/81	Zenit	M	M	M	M	M	M		M	M46			13	2
mitriy TORBINSKIY	28/4/84	Lokomotiv Moskva	M70						M46		s46	M	s76	24	2
gor SEMSHOV	6/4/78	Dinamo Moskva	M	M	M61	s68		s63	s69		s46	M69	s46	52	2
onstantin ZYRYANOV	5/10/77	Zenit	M	M	M	M68	M	M63	M	M	M46	M82		41	7
ndrey ARSHAVIN	29/5/81	Arsenal (ENG)	A80	A	A	A	A81	A	A	A90	A46	A		61	16
avel POGREBNYAK	8/11/83	Stuttgart (GER)	A46	A85	A71	s80	s79	A		s78	s46		A	27	7
Denis KOLODIN	11/1/82	Dinamo Moskva	s46											23	-
Diniyar BILYALETDINOV	27/2/85	Everton (ENG)	s46	M	s81			M73	s46	s90	s46		M76	41	5
Roman PAVLYUCHENKO	15/12/81	Tottenham (ENG)	s46	s85	s71				s46		A	A		40	19
Alan DZAGOEV	17/6/90	CSKA Moskva	s70	s60	M	M85	M61	M		M		s82	M	14	1
Dmitriy SYCHEV	26/10/83	Lokomotiv Moskva	s80											47	15
Vladimir BYSTROV	31/1/84	Zenit		M60	s61		s81		M46					35	4
Igor DENISOV	17/5/84	Zenit				M	M		M	M	M46	M		18	-
Aleksandr KERZHAKOV	27/11/82	Zenit				A80	A79		A69	A78				54	17
Aleksei BEREZUTSKIY	20/6/82	CSKA Moskva				s85	s61		D46		s46		D	39	-
Roman SHISHKIN	27/1/87	Lokomotiv Moskva						D	D46	D			D	5	-
Viktor VASIN	6/10/88	Spartak Nalchik						s46						1	-
Pavel MAMAYEV	17/9/88	CSKA Moskva						s63	s46					2	-
Aleksandr BUKHAROV	12/3/85	Zenit						s73						2	-
Sergei RYZHIKOV	19/9/80	Rubin									G46			1	-
Aleksei IONOV	18/2/89	Zenit									A46			1	-
Denis GLUSHAKOV	28/1/87	Lokomotiv Moskva									s46	s69	M	3	-
Yevgeniy MAKEEV	24/7/89	Spartak Moskva									s46			1	-
Vyacheslav MALAFEEV	4/3/79	Zenit									s46		G	18	-
Renat YANBAYEV	7/4/84	Lokomotiv Moskva										s75	D	11	-
Aleksandr RYAZANTSEV	5/9/86	Rubin											M56	1	-
Aleksandr SHESHUKOV	15/4/83	Spartak Moskva											M46	1	-
Taras BURLAK	22/2/90	Lokomotiv Moskva											s46	1	-

CLUB-BY-CLUB

FC ALANIA VLADIKAVKAZ

Coach – Vladimir Shevchuk
Founded – 1921
Stadium – Spartak (32,464)
MAJOR HONOURS: Russian League – (1) 1995.

2010

14/3	Saturn	h	1-1	*Kirillov*
19/3	Spartak Nalchik	a	1-2	*Bazayev J. (p)*
26/3	Amkar	h	0-0	
3/4	Anzhi	a	0-2	
11/4	CSKA	h	1-3	*Kuznetsov*
17/4	Sibir	h	2-1	*Kirillov, Marenich*
25/4	Rostov	a	1-0	*Stoyanov*
2/5	Rubin	h	1-1	*Stoyanov*
5/5	Krylya Sovetov	a	0-1	
10/5	Spartak Moskva	h	5-2	*Marenich, Gabulov 2, Khubulov, Oganyan*
15/5	Dinamo	a	0-2	
9/7	Zenit	h	1-3	*Ivanov*
18/7	Lokomotiv	a	0-3	
24/7	Tom	h	2-1	*Marenich, Gnanou*
31/7	Terek	a	0-2	
8/8	Spartak Nalchik	h	1-0	*Nizamutdinov*
15/8	Amkar	a	0-1	
22/8	Anzhi	h	0-0	
29/8	CSKA	a	1-2	*Florescu (p)*
11/9	Sibir	a	2-1	*Gnanou, Babatunde*
18/9	Rostov	h	0-0	
25/9	Rubin	a	0-1	
2/10	Krylya Sovetov	h	2-3	*Marenich, Bikmoev*
15/10	Spartak Moskva	a	0-3	
23/10	Dinamo	h	0-0	
31/10	Zenit	a	0-3	
7/11	Lokomotiv	h	0-0	
13/11	Tom	a	1-1	*Gabulov*
20/11	Terek	h	2-1	*Bikmoev, Gabulov*
28/11	Saturn	a	1-1	*Ivanov*

No	Name	Nat	DoB	Pos	Aps	(s)	Gls
99	Aleksandr ALKHAZOV		27/5/84	A		(2)	
30	Babajide Collins BABATUNDE	NGA	2/12/88	A	7	(3)	1
27	Georgiy BAZAYEV		26/8/78	M	4	(1)	
18	Jambulat BAZAYEV		18/8/79	M	6	(1)	1
29	Shota BIBILOV		6/8/90	M		(1)	
75	Marat BIKMOEV	UZB	1/1/86	M	7	(6)	2
43	David BUGULOV		14/7/92	D	4		
26	Simeon BULGARU	MDA	26/5/85	D	8		
97	Atsamaz BURAYEV		5/2/90	A		(1)	
19	Vitaliy CHOCHIYEV		17/12/79	M	3	(2)	
11	Serghey DADU	MDA	23/1/81	A		(4)	
20	Akès da Costa GOORE	CIV	31/12/84	D	26		
22	George FLORESCU	ROU	21/5/84	M	20		1
42	Georgiy GABULOV		4/9/88	M	24	(2)	4
2	Ibrahim GNANOU	BFA	8/11/86	D	24	(1)	2
52	Georgiy GOGICHAYEV		16/1/91	A	4	(4)	
34	Nariman GUSALOV		22/5/90	D	1		
25	Ivan IVANOV	BUL	25/2/88	D	23	(1)	2
6	Sani Haruna KAITA	NGA	2/5/86	M	6		
41	Mikhail KERZHAKOV		28/1/87	G	14	(2)	
16	Dmitriy KHOMICH		4/10/84	G	16		
9	Arsen KHUBULOV		13/12/90	M		(7)	1
42	Yuri KIRILLOV		19/1/90	M	15	(8)	2
79	Serhiy KUZNETSOV	UKR	31/8/82	A	7	(3)	1
24	Abdul Gafar MAMAH	TOG	24/8/85	D	11	(2)	
14	Aleksandr MARENICH		29/4/89	A	18	(8)	4
15	Aslan MASHUKOV		4/11/84	M	15		
31	Eldar NIZAMUTDINOV		31/5/81	M	19	(4)	1
7	Karen OGANYAN		25/6/82	A	1	(9)	1
4	Boris ROTENBERG	FIN	19/5/86	D	13	(3)	
73	Ivan STOYANOV	BUL	24/8/83	M	21	(3)	2
90	Aleksandr TIKHONOVETSKIY		11/4/79	A	3	(3)	
17	Taras TSARIKAYEV		17/6/89	A	3	(4)	
95	Dioh Clarence WILLIAMS	LBR	8/1/84	A	1		
32	José Luís Francisco ZUELA dos Santos	ANG	3/8/83	D	6		

FC AMKAR PERM

Coach – Rashid Rakhimov
Founded – 1993
Stadium – Zvezda (20,000)

2010

12/3	CSKA	a	0-1	
20/3	Anzhi	h	1-0	*Cherenchikov*
26/3	Alania	a	0-0	
3/4	Sibir	h	3-1	*Peev 2, Volkov*
11/4	Rostov	a	1-2	*Sokolov*
17/4	Rubin	h	0-1	
26/4	Krylya Sovetov	a	1-1	*Novaković*
2/5	Spartak Moskva	h	0-2	
5/5	Dinamo	a	1-1	*Grishin*
10/5	Zenit	h	0-2	
15/5	Lokomotiv	a	0-2	
10/7	Tom	h	2-1	*Kolomeitsev, Kushev*
18/7	Terek	a	0-1	
25/7	Saturn	h	0-1	
30/7	Spartak Nalchik	a	1-2	*Sirakov*
7/8	Anzhi	a	0-1	
15/8	Alania	h	1-0	*Volkov*
22/8	Sibir	a	0-1	
28/8	Rostov	h	1-0	*Peev*
11/9	Rubin	a	0-3	
18/9	Krylya Sovetov	h	2-1	*Ristic, og (Savin)*
24/9	Spartak Moskva	a	2-2	*Novaković, Cherenchikov*
2/10	Dinamo	h	0-1	
16/10	Zenit	a	0-2	
24/10	Lokomotiv	h	1-2	*Topchu*
31/10	Tom	a	0-1	
6/11	Terek	h	2-0	*Novaković, Ristic*
12/11	Saturn	a	2-2	*Ristic, Peev*
20/11	Spartak Nalchik	h	3-1	*Ristic, Topchu, Belorukov*
28/11	CSKA	h	0-0	

No	Name	Nat	DoB	Pos	Aps	(s)	Gls
21	Dmitriy BELORUKOV		24/3/83	D	24		1
18	Nikita BURMISTROV		6/7/89	A	6	(2)	
23	Ivan CHERENCHIKOV		25/8/84	D	19		2
6	Denys DEDECHKO	UKR	2/7/87	M	5		
4	Vitaliy FEDORIV	UKR	21/10/87	D	12	(1)	
15	Miklós GAÁL	HUN	13/5/81	D	12	(2)	
32	Vadim GAGLOYEV		18/1/89	M		(3)	
5	Vitaliy GRISHIN		9/9/80	M	19	(5)	1
25	JEAN CARLOS Sales Bemvindo	BRA	17/3/84	A		(3)	
28	Vyacheslav KALASHNIKOV		12/5/85	D	3	(3)	
33	Josip KNEŽEVIĆ	CRO	3/10/88	M	9	(4)	
19	Aleksandr KOLOMEITSEV		21/2/89	M	19		1
29	Martin KUSHEV	BUL	25/8/73	A	15	(8)	1
27	Mikhail MAKAGONOV		6/2/89	D	1		
9	Seiichiro MAKI	JPN	7/8/80	A	4	(5)	
42	Sergei NARUBIN		5/12/81	G	16		
13	Mitar NOVAKOVIĆ	MNE	27/9/81	M	29		3
7	Georgi Ivanov PEEV	BUL	11/3/79	M	23		4
70	Noka PILIYEV		21/3/91	M	4	(1)	
11	Aleksei POMERKO		3/5/90	M	3	(3)	
24	Aleksei POPOV	KAZ	7/7/78	D	22	(3)	
99	Stevica RISTIC	MKD	23/5/82	M	10		4
63	Damir SADIKOV		12/7/91	A	1	(3)	

No	Name	Nat	DoB	Pos	Aps	(s)	Gls
9	Andrei SEKRETOV		13/12/89	M		(5)	
4	Zahari SIRAKOV	BUL	8/10/77	D	22		1
7	Dmitriy SOKOLOV		1/3/88	M	6	(2)	1
0	Andrei TOPCHU		17/4/80	M	12	(8)	2
	Igor USMINSKIY		23/4/77	G	14		
1	Victor Irineu Medeiros de Souza "VITO"	BRA	3/4/89	A	2	(4)	
	Sergei VOLKOV		27/9/80	A	18	(2)	2
3	Luka ŽINKO	SVN	23/3/83	M		(3)	

FC ANZHI MAKHACHKALA

Coach – Omari Tetradze; (18/3/10) (Arsen Akayev); (18/4/10) Gadzhi Gadzhiev

Founded – 1991

Stadium – Dinamo (16,863)

2010				
3/3	Spartak Nalchik	h	0-0	
0/3	Amkar	a	0-1	
6/3	CSKA	h	1-2	*Streltsov*
/4	Alania	h	2-0	*Holenda, Streltsov (p)*
1/4	Sibir	a	4-2	*Tsorayev 2, Holenda 2*
9/4	Rostov	h	1-2	*Tsorayev*
5/4	Rubin	a	0-0	
0/4	Krylya Sovetov	h	0-0	
/5	Spartak Moskva	a	0-3	
11/5	Dinamo	h	1-1	*Mamayev*
/7	Zenit	a	1-2	*Tagirbekov*
10/7	Lokomotiv	a	1-2	*Tagirbekov*
18/7	Tom	a	4-1	*Agalarov, Josan (p), Gadzhibekov, Tsorayev*
25/7	Terek	h	1-0	*Tsorayev*
30/7	Saturn	a	0-1	
7/8	Amkar	h	1-0	*Josan (p)*
15/8	CSKA	a	0-4	
22/8	Alania	a	0-0	
30/8	Sibir	h	1-0	*Tsorayev (p)*
12/9	Rostov	a	0-1	
19/9	Rubin	h	0-1	
27/9	Krylya Sovetov	a	0-3	
3/10	Spartak Moskva	h	0-1	
17/10	Dinamo	a	0-4	
24/10	Zenit	h	3-3	*Holenda, Josan, Bakayev*
31/10	Lokomotiv	h	0-1	
6/11	Tom	h	1-0	*Strelkov*
13/11	Terek	a	3-1	*Holenda, Josan, Tsorayev*
20/11	Saturn	h	1-2	*Tsorayev (p)*
28/11	Spartak Nalchik	a	3-1	*Streltsov, Kukharchuk 2*

No	Name	Nat	DoB	Pos	Aps	(s)	Gls
1	Ilia ABAYEV		2/8/81	G	16		
7	Kamil AGALAROV		11/6/88	M	27		1
19	Zurabi ARZIANI	GEO	19/10/87	M	5	(5)	
20	Mikhail BAKAYEV		5/8/87	M	28	(1)	1
32	Revazi BARABADZE	GEO	4/10/88	A	1	(1)	
23	Shamil BURZIYEV		1/4/85	M		(7)	
63	Ali GADZHIBEKOV		6/8/89	D	19		1
17	Jan HOLENDA	CZE	22/8/85	A	16	(3)	5
26	Giorgi ILURIDZE	GEO	20/2/92	A	1	(4)	
14	Dmitriy IVANOV		14/2/87	M	10	(4)	
15	Nicolae JOSAN	MDA	18/9/83	M	18	(4)	4
5	Ali Ibrahim KÉBÉ Baye	SEN	24/12/78	M	23	(1)	
77	Otar KHIZANEISHVILI	GEO	26/9/81	D	6	(2)	
10	Gocha KHOJAVA	GEO	16/3/85	M	4	(5)	
3	Oskars KĻAVA	LVA	8/8/83	D	7	(4)	
18	Ilia KUKHARCHUK		2/8/90	A	3	(9)	2
2	David KVIRKVELIA	GEO	27/6/80	D	13		
89	Akhmad MAGOMEDOV		10/8/89	D		(3)	
70	Eldar MAMAYEV		14/6/85	M	1	(8)	1
96	Sharif MUKHAMMAD		21/3/90	M		(2)	
31	Mitar PEKOVIĆ	SRB	28/9/81	D	19		
29	Nukri REVISHVILI	GEO	2/3/87	G	14		
28	Igor STRELKOV		21/3/82	A	10	(3)	1
8	Andrei STRELTSOV		18/3/84	M	12	(6)	3
4	Mahir ŞÜKÜROV	AZE	12/12/82	D	20		
13	Rasim TAGIRBEKOV		4/5/84	D	28		2
86	Todor TIMONOV	BUL	3/9/86	M	1	(10)	
6	David TSORAYEV		7/5/83	M	28		8

PFC CSKA MOSKVA

Coach – Leonid Slutskiy

Founded – 1911

Stadium – Luzhniki (78,360); Arena Khimki (18,000)

MAJOR HONOURS: UEFA Cup – (1) 2005;
USSR League – (7) 1946, 1947, 1948, 1950, 1951, 1970, 1991;
Russian League – (3) 2003, 2005, 2006;
USSR Cup – (5) 1945, 1948, 1951, 1955, 1991;
Russian Cup – (6) 2002, 2005, 2006, 2008, 2009, 2011.

2010				
12/3	Amkar	h	1-0	*Honda*
21/3	Dinamo	h	0-0	
26/3	Anzhi	a	2-1	*Honda, Necid*
11/4	Alania	a	3-1	*Guilherme, Krasić, Dzagoev (p)*
17/4	Lokomotiv	h	1-1	*Guilherme*
24/4	Sibir	a	4-1	*Ignashevich, Guilherme, Necid, Dzagoev*
28/4	Zenit	h	0-2	
2/5	Tom	h	3-1	*Krasić, Guilherme 2*
6/5	Rostov	a	0-1	
10/5	Terek	h	4-1	*Odiah, Mark González, Dzagoev 2*
14/5	Rubin	a	1-0	*Mark González*
10/7	Saturn	h	1-1	*Dzagoev*
19/7	Krylya Sovetov	a	1-0	*Dzagoev (p)*
25/7	Spartak Nalchik	h	1-2	*Necid*
1/8	Spartak Moskva	a	2-1	*Ignashevich, Vágner Love*
15/8	Anzhi	h	4-0	*Oliseh 2, Vágner Love, Tošić*
29/8	Alania	h	2-1	*Doumbia, Tošić*
12/9	Lokomotiv	a	0-1	
20/9	Sibir	h	1-0	*Oliseh*
26/9	Tom	a	3-0	*Vágner Love, Doumbia, Necid*
3/10	Rostov	h	2-0	*Vágner Love 2 (1p)*
17/10	Terek	a	3-0	*Doumbia, Vágner Love, Honda*
24/10	Rubin	h	0-0	
27/10	Dinamo	a	0-0	
31/10	Saturn	a	1-1	*Necid*
7/11	Krylya Sovetov	h	4-3	*Berezutskiy A., Necid 2, Tošić*
10/11	Zenit	a	3-1	*Vágner Love, Mark González, Doumbia*
14/11	Spartak Nalchik	a	1-1	*Vágner Love (p)*
20/11	Spartak Moskva	h	3-1	*Honda, Doumbia, Vágner Love*
28/11	Amkar	a	0-0	

No	Name	Nat	DoB	Pos	Aps	(s)	Gls
35	Igor AKINFEEV		8/4/86	G	28		
22	Yevgeniy ALDONIN		22/1/80	M	6	(8)	
6	Aleksei BEREZUTSKIY		20/6/82	D	24		1
24	Vasiliy BEREZUTSKIY		20/6/82	D	21		
1	Sergei CHEPCHUGOV		15/7/85	G	2		
8	Seydou DOUMBIA	CIV	31/12/87	A	11		5
10	Alan DZAGOEV		17/6/90	M	19	(5)	6
20	GUILHERME Milhomem Gusmão GUILHERME	BRA	22/10/88	A	9	(3)	5
7	Keisuke HONDA	JPN	13/6/86	M	23	(5)	4
4	Sergei IGNASHEVICH		14/7/79	D	28		2
17	Miloš KRASIĆ	SRB	1/11/84	M	9	(5)	2
11	Pavel MAMAYEV		17/9/88	M	18	(9)	
13	MARK Dennis GONZÁLEZ MARK GONZÁLEZ	CHI	10/7/84	M	12	(9)	3
14	Kirill NABABKIN		8/9/86	D	12	(1)	
89	Tomáš NECID	CZE	13/8/89	A	12	(12)	7
15	Chidi ODIAH	NGA	17/12/83	D	9	(2)	1
26	Sekou OLISEH	NGA	5/6/90	A	13	(3)	3
25	Elvir RAHIMIĆ	BIH	4/4/76	M	3	(8)	
42	Georgiy SCHENNIKOV		27/4/91	D	24	(1)	

2	Deividas ŠEMBERAS	LTU	2/8/78	D	21	(5)	
21	Zoran TOŠIĆ	SRB	28/4/87	M	11	(4)	3
9	VÁGNER Silva de Sousa "LOVE"	BRA	11/6/84	A	15		9

FC DINAMO MOSKVA

Coach – Andrei Kobelev; (27/4/10) Miodrag Božović (MNE)

Founded – 1923

Stadium – Arena Khimki (18,000)

MAJOR HONOURS: USSR League – (11) 1936 (spring), 1937, 1940, 1945, 1949, 1954, 1955, 1957, 1959, 1963, 1976 (spring); USSR Cup – (6) 1937, 1953, 1967, 1970, 1977, 1984; Russian Cup – (1) 1995.

2010				
14/3	Spartak Moskva	a	1-0	*Semshov*
21/3	CSKA	a	0-0	
27/3	Zenit	h	1-2	*Kombarov D. (p)*
4/4	Lokomotiv	a	2-3	*Voronin, Kombarov D. (p)*
10/4	Tom	h	0-0	
18/4	Terek	a	1-1	*Kombarov D.*
24/4	Saturn	h	1-0	*Epureanu*
1/5	Spartak Nalchik	a	0-1	
5/5	Amkar	h	1-1	*Voronin*
11/5	Anzhi	a	1-1	*Semshov*
15/5	Alania	h	2-0	*Kombarov K. 2*
9/7	Sibir	a	2-2	*Kombarov D., Fernández*
17/7	Rostov	h	3-2	*Kolodin, Voronin, Granat*
24/7	Rubin	a	0-2	
31/7	Krylya Sovetov	h	1-1	*Semshov*
14/8	Zenit	a	1-1	*Kurányi*
22/8	Lokomotiv	h	3-0	*Kurányi 2, Česnauskis*
29/8	Tom	a	0-1	
12/9	Terek	h	3-1	*Kurányi, Samedov, Semshov*
18/9	Saturn	a	2-3	*Kurányi, Dujmović*
26/9	Spartak Nalchik	h	0-3	
2/10	Amkar	a	1-0	*Kurányi*
17/10	Anzhi	h	4-0	*Kurányi (p), Fernández, Česnauskis, Voronin (p)*
23/10	Alania	a	0-0	
27/10	CSKA	h	0-0	
30/10	Sibir	h	4-1	*Kurányi, Fernández, Samedov, Semshov*
6/11	Rostov	a	1-1	*Samedov*
13/11	Rubin	h	2-2	*Epureanu, Kurányi*
20/11	Krylya Sovetov	a	0-1	
28/11	Spartak Moskva	h	1-1	*Khokhlov*

No	Name	Nat	DoB	Pos	Aps	(s)	Gls
88	Edgaras ČESNAUSKIS	LTU	5/2/84	M	14	(8)	2
18	Tomislav DUJMOVIĆ	CRO	26/2/81	M	12	(1)	1
15	Alexandru EPUREANU	MDA	27/9/86	D	23		2
6	Leandro Sebastián FERNÁNDEZ	ARG	30/1/83	D	20		3
30	Vladimir GABULOV		19/10/83	G	21		
13	Vladimir GRANAT		22/5/87	D	19	(3)	1
26	Martin JAKUBKO	SVK	26/2/80	A		(10)	
8	Dmitriy KHOKHLOV		22/12/75	M	13	(7)	1
99	Aleksandr KOKORIN		19/3/91	A	9	(14)	
25	Denis KOLODIN		11/1/82	D	14	(1)	1
9	Dmitriy KOMBAROV		22/1/87	M	12	(4)	4
7	Kirill KOMBAROV		22/1/87	M	8	(3)	2
4	Marcin KOWALCZYK	POL	9/4/85	D	4	(4)	
22	Kevin KURÁNYI	GER	2/3/82	A	16		9
77	Irakli LOGUA		29/7/91	D		(1)	
32	Marko LOMIĆ	SRB	13/9/83	D	10	(1)	
13	Aleksei REBKO		23/4/86	M	9	(10)	
20	Adrian ROPOTAN	ROU	8/5/86	M	14	(6)	
19	Aleksandr SAMEDOV		19/7/84	M	27		3
21	Igor SEMSHOV		6/4/78	M	27	(2)	5
1	Anton SHUNIN		27/1/87	G	9		
11	Fyodor SMOLOV		9/2/90	A		(2)	
23	Luke WILKSHIRE	AUS	2/10/81	D	26		
10	Andriy VORONIN	UKR	21/7/79	A	23	(2)	4

FC KRYLYA SOVETOV SAMARA

Coach – Yuriy Gazzayev; (27/7/10) Aleksandr Tarkhanov

Founded – 1942

Stadium – Metallurg (32,990)

2010				
13/3	Zenit	h	0-1	
20/3	Lokomotiv	a	0-3	
27/3	Tom	h	2-3	*og (Ivanov), og (Gultyaev)*
4/4	Terek	a	0-2	
10/4	Saturn	h	2-1	*Bober, Đorđević*
18/4	Spartak Nalchik	a	0-1	
26/4	Amkar	h	1-1	*Adjindjal*
30/4	Anzhi	a	0-0	
5/5	Alania	h	1-0	*Strelkov*
10/5	Sibir	a	1-4	*Tkachyov*
14/5	Rostov	h	1-2	*Alkhazov*
9/7	Rubin	a	0-3	
19/7	CSKA	h	0-1	
25/7	Spartak Moskva	h	0-0	
31/7	Dinamo	a	1-1	*og (Kolodin)*
7/8	Lokomotiv	h	0-0	
14/8	Tom	a	1-1	*Savin*
21/8	Terek	h	1-3	*Leílton*
28/8	Saturn	a	1-1	*Taranov*
12/9	Spartak Nalchik	h	2-0	*Đorđević, Yakovlev*
18/9	Amkar	a	1-2	*Savin*
27/9	Anzhi	h	3-0	*Samsonov, Ivanov, Savin (p)*
2/10	Alania	a	3-2	*Samsonov, Tsallagov, Yakovlev*
17/10	Sibir	h	1-1	*Yakovlev*
24/10	Rostov	a	2-1	*Đorđević, Yakovlev*
29/10	Rubin	h	0-2	
7/11	CSKA	a	3-4	*Ivanov, Leílton (p), Tkachyov*
14/11	Spartak Moskva	a	0-0	
20/11	Dinamo	h	1-0	*Savin*
28/11	Zenit	a	0-0	

No	Name	Nat	DoB	Pos	Aps	(s)	Gls
21	Ruslan ADJINDJAL		22/6/74	M	16		1
18	Aleksandr ALKHAZOV		27/5/84	A	1	(7)	1
63	Aleksandr BELOZYOROV		27/10/81	D	15	(1)	
7	Anton BOBER		28/9/82	M	16	(8)	1
44	Aleksandr BUDANOV		27/4/91	M	2		
29	Sergei BUDYLIN		31/10/79	D	19		
79	Nenad ĐORĐEVIĆ	SRB	7/8/79	D	23	(1)	3
33	Goran DRMIĆ	BIH	1/1/90	D	10		
88	Juan Carlos ESCOBAR	COL	30/10/82	M		(3)	
8	Daniil GRIDNEV		2/2/86	M	10	(6)	
99	Oleg IVANOV		4/8/86	M	14	(1)	2
80	Dragan JELIČ	SVN	27/2/86	A	2	(4)	
2	Vladimir KHOZIN		3/7/89	M	2		
56	Aleksandr KHRAMOV		4/2/89	D		(1)	
5	Aleksei KONTSEDALOV		24/7/90	D	2		
43	Dmitriy KOSTYAYEV		13/12/89	M	1	(1)	
23	Denis KOVBA	BLR	6/9/79	M	4		
27	Sergei KUZNETSOV		7/5/86	M	15		
3	LEÍLTON Silva dos Santos	BRA	7/3/82	D	14	(3)	2
31	Eduardo Eugenio LOBOS Landaeta	CHI	30/7/81	G	25		
10	Branimir PETROVIĆ	SRB	26/6/82	M	10	(1)	
13	Roman POLOVOV		9/2/90	D		(1)	
39	Aleksei POPOV		8/7/90	A		(1)	
25	Artur RYLOV		12/4/89	M		(2)	
20	Aleksandr SALUGIN		23/10/88	A	1	(3)	
6	Oleg SAMSONOV		7/9/87	M	17	(3)	2
9	Yevgeniy SAVIN		19/4/84	A	23	(5)	4
53	Anton SOSNIN		27/1/90	M	10	(1)	
17	Aleksandr STAVPETS		4/7/89	A	3	(4)	
11	Igor STRELKOV		21/3/82	A	5	(3)	1
4	Ivan TARANOV		22/6/86	D	24	(2)	1
77	Sergei TKACHYOV		19/5/89	M	12	(4)	2
46	Ibragim TSALLAGOV		12/12/90	M	20	(3)	1
16	Mykola TSYGAN	UKR	9/8/84	G	3		

No	Name	Nat	DoB	Pos	Aps	(s)	Gls
	Farkhod VASIEV	TJK	14/4/90	D	1	(2)	
	Pavel YAKOVLEV		7/4/91	A	8	(4)	4
	David YURCHENKO		27/3/86	G	2		

FC LOKOMOTIV MOSKVA

Coach – Yuriy Semin

Founded – 1923

Stadium – Lokomotiv (28,800)

MAJOR HONOURS: Russian League – (2) 2002, 2004; USSR Cup – (2) 1936, 1957; Russian Cup – (5) 1996, 1997, 2000, 2001, 2007.

010

4/3	Rubin	a	0-2	
0/3	Krylya Sovetov	h	3-0	*Aliyev 2 (1p), Sychev (p)*
8/3	Spartak Moskva	a	1-2	*Aliyev*
/4	Dinamo	h	3-2	*Aliyev 2, Tarasov*
1/4	Zenit	a	0-1	
7/4	CSKA	a	1-1	*Kuzmin*
4/4	Tom	h	2-1	*Glushakov, Aliyev*
/5	Terek	a	0-0	
/5	Saturn	h	0-1	
1/5	Spartak Nalchik	a	1-1	*Dujmović*
5/5	Amkar	h	2-0	*Aliyev, Maicon*
0/7	Anzhi	h	2-1	*Dujmović, Aliyev*
8/7	Alania	h	3-0	*Aliyev, Sychev 2*
4/7	Sibir	a	2-2	*Aliyev 2*
/8	Rostov	h	0-1	
/8	Krylya Sovetov	a	0-0	
5/8	Spartak Moskva	h	2-3	*Aliyev, Sychev*
21/8	Dinamo	a	0-3	
29/8	Zenit	h	0-3	
12/9	CSKA	h	1-0	*Maicon*
19/9	Tom	a	1-1	*Gatagov*
26/9	Terek	h	2-1	*Aliyev (p), Maicon*
3/10	Saturn	a	1-0	*Loskov*
17/10	Spartak Nalchik	h	1-0	*Sychev*
24/10	Amkar	a	2-1	*Aliyev (p), Rodolfo*
31/10	Anzhi	a	1-0	*Sychev*
7/11	Alania	a	0-0	
14/11	Sibir	h	1-1	*Sychev*
20/11	Rostov	a	2-1	*Sychev, Rodolfo*
28/11	Rubin	h	0-0	

No	Name	Nat	DoB	Pos	Aps	(s)	Gls
88	Olexandr ALIYEV	UKR	3/2/85	M	25		14
30	Malkhaz ASATIANI	GEO	4/8/81	D	19	(3)	
23	Marko BAŠA	MNE	29/12/82	D	22		
99	Taras BURLAK		22/2/90	D	1	(2)	
16	CHARLES Fernando Basílio da Silva	BRA	14/2/85	M	3	(1)	
15	Haminu DRAMANI	GHA	1/4/86	M	1	(1)	
5	Tomislav DUJMOVIĆ	CRO	26/2/81	M	12	(1)	2
28	Ján ĎURICA	SVK	10/12/81	D	9	(1)	
81	Alan GATAGOV		21/1/91	M	5	(13)	1
1	GUILHERME Alvim Marinato	BRA	12/12/85	G	30		
8	Denis GLUSHAKOV		28/1/87	M	21	(7)	1
20	Branko ILIČ	SVN	6/2/83	D	1		
44	Ruslan KAMBOLOV		1/1/90	D	1		
3	Oleg KUZMIN		9/5/83	D	10		1
10	Dmitriy LOSKOV		12/2/74	M	11	(2)	1
90	MAICON Marques Bitencourt	BRA	18/2/90	A	15	(3)	3
9	Peter ODEMWINGIE	NGA	15/7/81	A	8	(2)	
27	Magomed OZDOYEV		5/11/92	M		(3)	
4	RODOLFO Dantas Bispo	BRA	23/10/82	D	10	(6)	2
17	Dmitriy SENNIKOV		24/6/76	D	1		
36	Makhmadnaim SHARIFI		3/6/92	D	1		
49	Roman SHISHKIN		27/1/87	D	15		
14	Igor SMOLNIKOV		8/8/88	D	6	(8)	
7	Dmitriy TARASOV		18/3/87	M	21	(5)	1
21	Dmitriy TORBINSKIY		28/4/84	M	13	(4)	
19	Dramane TRAORÉ	MLI	17/6/82	A	6	(11)	
11	Dmitriy SYCHEV		26/10/83	A	27		8
13	WÁGNER Ferreira dos Santos	BRA	29/1/85	M	7	(7)	
55	Renat YANBAYEV		7/4/84	M	29		

FC ROSTOV

Coach – Oleh Protasov (UKR)

Founded – 1930

Stadium – Olimp 2 (15,840)

2010

13/3	Tom	h	0-2	
20/3	Terek	a	1-1	*Ahmetović*
28/3	Saturn	h	1-0	*Pavlenko*
3/4	Spartak Nalchik	a	2-5	*Ahmetović, Adamov (p)*
11/4	Amkar	h	2-1	*Ahmetović, Anđelković*
19/4	Anzhi	a	2-1	*Adamov, Kalachev*
25/4	Alania	h	0-1	
2/5	Sibir	a	0-2	
6/5	CSKA	h	1-0	*Ahmetović*
10/5	Rubin	h	0-2	
14/5	Krylya Sovetov	a	2-1	*Adamov 2*
9/7	Spartak Moskva	h	1-0	*Kulchiy*
17/7	Dinamo	a	2-3	*Adamov, Lebedenko*
24/7	Zenit	h	1-3	*Lebedenko (p)*
1/6	Lokomotiv	a	1-0	*Valikaev*
6/8	Terek	h	1-0	*Pavlenko*
14/8	Saturn	a	2-0	*Adamov, Lebedenko*
20/8	Spartak Nalchik	h	1-1	*Adamov (p)*
28/8	Amkar	a	0-1	
12/9	Anzhi	h	1-0	*Kalachev*
18/9	Alania	a	0-0	
26/9	Sibir	h	0-1	
3/10	CSKA	a	0-2	
16/10	Rubin	a	1-2	*Pavlenko*
24/10	Krylya Sovetov	h	1-2	*Adamov*
30/10	Spartak Moskva	a	1-2	*Hagush*
6/11	Dinamo	h	1-1	*Yankov*
14/11	Zenit	a	0-5	
20/11	Lokomotiv	h	1-2	*Blatnjak*
28/11	Tom	a	1-3	*Yankov*

No	Name	Nat	DoB	Pos	Aps	(s)	Gls
9	Roman ADAMOV		21/6/82	A	24		8
19	Mersudin AHMETOVIĆ	BIH	19/2/85	A	5	(23)	4
10	Dmitriy AKIMOV		14/9/80	A	5	(6)	
1	Anton AMELCHENKO	BLR	27/3/85	G	23		
3	Dušan ANĐELKOVIĆ	SRB	15/6/82	D	26		1
81	Dragan BLATNJAK	BIH	1/8/81	M	12	(11)	1
5	Aleksandr CHERKES		2/9/76	D	15		
84	Alexandru GATCAN	MDA	27/3/84	M	24		
24	Sorin GHIONEA	ROU	11/5/79	D	18		
8	Gia GRIGALAVA	GEO	5/8/89	D	8	(1)	
14	Anri HAGUSH		23/9/86	D	16	(4)	1
21	HONG Yong-jo	PRK	22/5/82	A		(1)	
77	Stanislav IVANOV	MDA	7/10/80	M	6	(3)	
2	Timofei KALACHEV	BLR	1/5/81	M	16	(1)	2
38	Anri KHAGBA		7/1/92	D		(1)	
7	Aleksandr KULCHIY	BLR	1/11/73	M	25		1
11	Igor LEBEDENKO		27/5/83	A	29	(1)	3
6	Roman LENGYEL	CZE	3/11/78	D	1	(1)	
87	Yevgeniy LUTSENKO		25/2/87	A	2	(3)	
4	Isaac OKORONKWO	NGA	1/5/78	D	22		
25	Aleksandr PAVLENKO		20/1/85	M	18	(6)	3
34	Andriy PROSHIN	UKR	19/2/85	D	1	(2)	
22	Dejan RADIĆ	SRB	8/7/80	G	7		
15	Aleksei SUGAK		27/2/90	A		(2)	
33	Sergei TUMASYAN		31/1/90	M		(2)	
20	Artur VALIKAEV		8/1/88	D	5	(2)	1
23	Chavdar YANKOV	BUL	29/3/84	M	8	(3)	2
26	Ivan ŽIVANOVIĆ	SRB	10/12/81	D	14	(1)	

FC RUBIN KAZAN

Coach – Kurban Berdyev
Founded – 1936
Stadium – Central (30,133)
MAJOR HONOURS: Russian League – (2) 2008, 2009.

2010				
14/3	Lokomotiv	h	2-0	*Gorbanets, Bukharov*
22/3	Tom	a	1-0	*Bukharov*
28/3	Terek	h	0-0	
4/4	Saturn	a	0-0	
12/4	Spartak Nalchik	h	1-1	*Noboa*
17/4	Amkar	a	1-0	*Natcho*
25/4	Anzhi	h	0-0	
2/5	Alania	a	1-1	*Kasaev*
6/5	Sibir	h	1-0	*Noboa*
10/5	Rostov	a	2-0	*Semak, Bukharov*
14/5	CSKA	h	0-1	
9/7	Krylya Sovetov	h	3-0	*Kasaev, Bukharov, Ryazantsev (p)*
17/7	Spartak Moskva	a	1-0	*Noboa*
24/7	Dinamo	h	2-0	*Kasaev 2*
31/7	Zenit	a	0-2	
8/8	Tom	h	2-1	*Ryazantsev, Orekhov*
15/8	Terek	a	1-1	*Noboa*
22/8	Saturn	h	2-0	*Noboa (p), Medvedev*
28/8	Spartak Nalchik	a	1-1	*Kasaev*
11/9	Amkar	h	3-0	*Carlos Eduardo 2, Martins (p)*
19/9	Anzhi	a	1-0	*Gökdeniz*
25/9	Alania	h	1-0	*Bocchetti*
3/10	Sibir	a	2-2	*Noboa (p), Bocchetti*
16/10	Rostov	h	2-1	*Natcho, Martins*
24/10	CSKA	a	0-0	
29/10	Krylya Sovetov	a	2-0	*Kornilenko 2*
8/11	Spartak Moskva	h	1-1	*Kornilenko*
13/11	Dinamo	a	2-2	*Noboa 2*
20/11	Zenit	h	2-2	*César Navas, Medvedev*
28/11	Lokomotiv	a	0-0	

No	Name	Nat	DoB	Pos	Aps	(s)	Gls
3	Cristian Daniel ANSALDI	ARG	20/9/86	D	19	(1)	
21	Alexandru ANTONIUC	MDA	23/5/89	A		(1)	
44	Giedrius ARLAUSKIS	LTU	1/12/87	G	2		
23	Yevgeniy BALYAIKIN		19/5/88	M	4	(9)	
4	Salvatore BOCCHETTI	ITA	30/11/86	D	6	(1)	2
11	Aleksandr BUKHAROV		12/3/85	A	11	(1)	4
5	Pyotr BYSTROV		15/7/79	M	7	(11)	
87	CARLOS EDUARDO Marques	BRA	18/7/87	M	6		2
4	CÉSAR González NAVAS	ESP	14/2/80	D	29		1
10	FATİH Tekke	TUR	9/9/77	A	2	(3)	
49	Vagiz GALIULIN	UZB	10/10/87	M	7		
61	GÖKDENİZ Karadeniz	TUR	11/1/80	M	11	(6)	1
32	Andrei GORBANETS		24/8/85	M	7	(10)	1
99	HASAN Kabze	TUR	26/5/82	A	2	(3)	
33	JORDI Figueras Montel	ESP	16/5/87	D	7	(1)	
19	Vitaliy KALESHIN		3/10/80	D	14	(1)	
14	Alan KASAEV		8/4/86	M	27	(1)	5
88	Sergei KORNILENKO	BLR	14/6/83	A	5	(3)	3
2	Oleg KUZMIN		9/5/83	D	12	(1)	
28	Obafemi MARTINS	NGA	28/10/84	A	9	(3)	2
26	Aleksei MEDVEDEV		5/1/77	A	6	(7)	2
15	Rafał MURAWSKI	POL	9/10/81	M	20	(3)	
20	Bakhodir NASIMOV	UZB	2/5/87	A	1	(1)	
66	Bibras NATCHO	ISR	18/2/88	M	10	(4)	2
16	Cristian Fernando NOBOA	ECU	8/4/85	M	26	(1)	8
22	Aleksandr OREKHOV		29/11/83	D	19		1
97	Igor PORTNYAGIN		7/1/89	A		(4)	
8	Aleksandr RYAZANTSEV		5/9/86	M	9	(4)	2
77	Sergei RYZHIKOV		19/9/80	G	28		
9	Lasha SALUKVADZE	GEO	21/12/81	D	9	(1)	
7	Sergei SEMAK		27/2/76	M	8		1
76	Roman SHARONOV		8/9/76	D	2		
6	MacBeth SIBAYA	RSA	25/11/77	M	5	(2)	

FC SATURN MOSKOVSKAYA OBLAST

Coach – Andrei Gordeev
Founded – 1946
Stadium – Saturn (16,726)

2010				
14/3	Alania	a	1-1	*Ivanov*
20/3	Sibir	h	1-1	*Ivanov*
28/3	Rostov	a	0-1	
4/4	Rubin	h	0-0	
10/4	Krylya Sovetov	a	1-2	*Nemov*
18/4	Spartak Moskva	h	0-0	
24/4	Dinamo	a	0-1	
2/5	Zenit	h	0-1	
5/5	Lokomotiv	a	1-0	*Kirichenko*
11/5	Tom	h	1-2	*Kirichenko*
14/5	Terek	a	0-2	
10/7	CSKA	a	1-1	*Kirichenko*
19/7	Spartak Nalchik	h	3-1	*Kirichenko 2 (1p), Sapeta*
25/7	Amkar	a	1-0	*Boyarintsev*
30/7	Anzhi	h	1-0	*Sapeta*
8/8	Sibir	a	1-0	*Nemov*
14/8	Rostov	h	0-2	
22/8	Rubin	a	0-2	
28/8	Krylya Sovetov	h	1-1	*Yevseyev*
11/9	Spartak Moskva	a	1-2	*Kirichenko*
18/9	Dinamo	h	3-2	*Nemov 2, Kirichenko*
25/9	Zenit	a	1-6	*Kirichenko*
3/10	Lokomotiv	h	0-1	
16/10	Tom	a	2-2	*Karyaka, Topić*
23/10	Terek	h	1-0	*Sapeta*
31/10	CSKA	h	1-1	*Ivanov*
5/11	Spartak Nalchik	a	0-2	
12/11	Amkar	h	2-2	*Topić, Karyaka*
20/11	Anzhi	a	2-1	*Makhmudov, Topić*
28/11	Alania	h	1-1	*Zelão*

No	Name	Nat	DoB	Pos	Aps	(s)	Gls
24	Benoît Christian ANGBWA	CMR	1/1/82	D	23	(1)	
11	Denis BOYARINTSEV		6/2/78	M	9	(7)	1
64	Sergei BRYZGALOV		15/11/92	D	1		
33	Vitali CHILYUSHKIN		21/1/90	G	3	(1)	
6	Dmitriy GRACHYOV		6/10/83	D	15	(2)	
19	Denis HALILOVIČ	SVN	2/3/86	D	2		
5	Aleksei IGONIN		18/3/76	D	21		
88	Aleksei IVANOV		1/9/81	M	29		3
20	Martin JAKUBKO	SVK	26/2/80	A	6	(6)	
21	Andrei KARYAKA		1/4/78	M	25	(1)	2
1	Antonín KINSKÝ	CZE	31/5/75	G	20		
14	Dmitriy KIRICHENKO		17/1/77	A	21	(7)	8
25	Kamil KOPÚNEK	SVK	18/5/84	M	3	(4)	
29	Leonid KOVEL	BLR	29/7/86	A		(4)	
13	Dmitriy KUDRYASHOV		13/5/83	M		(1)	
46	Viktor KUZMICHOV		19/3/92	M	2	(1)	
28	Vladimir KUZMICHOV		28/7/79	M	2	(5)	
10	Dmitriy LOSKOV		12/2/74	M	4	(2)	
67	Emin MAKHMUDOV		27/4/92	D	16	(5)	1
15	Ruslan NAKHUSHEV		5/9/84	D	21	(1)	
7	Pyotr NEMOV		18/10/83	M	24	(2)	4
2	Dmytro PARFENOV	UKR	11/9/74	D	13		
77	Artyom REBROV		4/3/84	G	7		
41	Aleksandr SAPETA		28/6/89	M	17	(7)	3
56	Vladimir SOBOLEV		30/7/91	M		(2)	
8	Marko TOPIĆ	BIH	1/1/76	A	3	(6)	3
4	Roman VOROBIYOV		24/3/84	M	5	(9)	
16	Vadim YEVSEYEV		8/1/76	D	17	(3)	1
26	Luiz Ricardo da Silva "ZELÃO"	BRA	12/11/84	D	21	(1)	1
69	Dmitriy ZINOVICH		19/5/89	D		(1)	

FC SIBIR NOVOSIBIRSK

Coach – Igor Kriushenko (BLR)
Founded – 1936
Stadium – Spartak (13,400)

10

4/3	Terek	h	0-2	
7/3	Saturn	a	1-1	*Medvedev*
6/3	Spartak Nalchik	h	0-2	
4	Amkar	a	1-3	*Molosh*
1/4	Anzhi	h	2-4	*Medvedev, Astafiev*
7/4	Alania	a	1-2	*Čížek*
4/4	CSKA	h	1-4	*Čížek*
/5	Rostov	h	2-0	*Medvedev, Nagibin*
5	Rubin	a	0-1	
0/5	Krylya Sovetov	h	4-1	*Čížek, Medvedev, Klimavičius, Astafiev*
/7	Dinamo	h	2-2	*Shevchenko, Nagibin*
7/7	Zenit	a	0-2	
1/7	Spartak Moskva	a	3-5	*Antipenko, Čížek, Astafiev*
5/7	Lokomotiv	h	2-2	*Medvedev, Molosh*
/8	Tom	a	2-3	*Medvedev, Shevchenko*
/8	Saturn	h	0-1	
4/8	Spartak Nalchik	a	2-4	*Shevchenko, Molosh*
22/8	Amkar	h	1-0	*Shevchenko*
30/8	Anzhi	a	0-1	
1/9	Alania	h	1-2	*Zinoviev*
20/9	CSKA	a	0-1	
26/9	Rostov	a	1-0	*Grzelak*
3/10	Rubin	h	2-2	*Joseph-Reinette, Belyayev*
17/10	Krylya Sovetov	a	1-1	*Oyewole*
23/10	Spartak Moskva	h	0-0	
30/10	Dinamo	a	1-4	*Grzelak*
7/11	Zenit	h	2-5	*Nagibin, Grzelak*
14/11	Lokomotiv	a	1-1	*Molosh*
20/11	Tom	h	0-1	
28/11	Terek	a	1-1	*Čížek*

No	Name	Nat	DoB	Pos	Aps	(s)	Gls
9	Aleksandr ANTIPENKO		27/5/82	A	10	(8)	1
27	Aleksei ARAVIN		9/7/86	M	19	(4)	
88	Maksim ASTAFIEV		8/12/82	M	18	(6)	3
95	Roman BELYAYEV		14/2/88	A		(7)	1
10	Gennadiy BLIZNYUK	BLR	30/7/80	A	5		
17	Denis BUKHRYAKOV		28/4/81	D	11		
28	Roger CAÑAS Henao	COL	27/3/90	M	9	(5)	
11	Tomáš ČÍŽEK	CZE	27/11/78	M	19	(5)	5
14	Aleksandr DEGTYARYOV		7/9/83	M	8	(10)	
22	Yegor FILIPENKO	BLR	10/4/88	D	15	(3)	
49	Vagiz GALIULIN	UZB	10/10/87	M	9	(2)	
12	Bartłomiej GRZELAK	POL	9/8/81	A	8		3
70	Martin HORÁK	CZE	16/9/80	D	1		
6	Steeve JOSEPH-REINETTE	FRA	2/12/83	M	13		1
24	Arūnas KLIMAVIČIUS	LTU	5/10/82	D	7	(4)	1
30	Wojciech KOWALEWSKI	POL	11/5/77	G	14		
8	Aleksandr MAKARENKO		4/2/86	D	9	(2)	
13	Aleksei MEDVEDEV		5/1/77	A	15		6
3	Dmitriy MOLOSH	BLR	10/12/81	D	22		4
15	Ivan NAGIBIN		21/3/86	M	15	(9)	3
2	Adessoye OYEWOLE		18/9/82	D	6	(1)	1
7	Mantas SAVĖNAS	LTU	27/8/82	M		(1)	
99	Igor SHEVCHENKO		2/2/85	A	14	(5)	4
20	Aleksandr SHULENIN		31/10/79	M	10	(2)	
91	Aleksandr SHUMOV		8/3/91	M		(1)	
1	Aleksei SOLOSIN		11/8/87	G	10	(2)	
25	Velice SUMULIKOSKI	MKD	24/4/81	M	13		
21	Nikola VALENTIĆ	SRB	6/8/83	D	10	(2)	
40	Petr VAŠEK	CZE	9/4/79	G	6		
54	Aleksei VASILYEV		28/10/87	M	2	(7)	
4	Tomáš VYCHODIL	CZE	7/10/75	D	23		
52	Yevgeniy ZINOVIEV		15/6/81	M	8	(3)	1
23	Leonid ZUYEV		12/1/91	M	1		

FC SPARTAK MOSKVA

Coach – Valeriy Karpin
Founded – 1922
Stadium – Luzhniki (78,360)

MAJOR HONOURS: USSR League – (12) 1936 (autumn), 1938, 1939, 1952, 1953, 1956, 1958, 1962, 1969, 1979, 1987, 1989; Russian League – (9) 1992, 1993, 1994, 1996, 1997, 1998, 1999, 2000, 2001; USSR Cup – (10) 1938, 1939, 1946, 1947, 1950, 1958, 1963, 1965, 1971, 1992; Russian Cup – (3) 1994, 1998, 2003.

2010

14/3	Dinamo	h	0-1	
21/3	Zenit	a	1-1	*Welliton*
28/3	Lokomotiv	h	2-1	*Suchý, Ari*
4/4	Tom	a	2-2	*Welliton, Ibson*
10/4	Terek	h	2-1	*og (Ferreira), Welliton*
18/4	Saturn	a	0-0	
25/4	Spartak Nalchik	h	0-0	
2/5	Amkar	a	2-0	*Ari, Welliton*
6/5	Anzhi	h	3-0	*Welliton 2, Alex*
10/5	Alania	a	2-5	*Welliton, og (Florescu)*
9/7	Rostov	a	0-1	
17/7	Rubin	h	0-1	
21/7	Sibir	h	5-3	*Ari 2, Ananidze 2, Jiránek*
25/7	Krylya Sovetov	a	0-0	
1/8	CSKA	h	1-2	*og (Berezutskiy V.)*
15/8	Lokomotiv	a	3-2	*Welliton 3*
21/8	Tom	h	4-2	*Welliton 3, Alex*
28/8	Terek	a	0-2	
11/9	Saturn	h	2-1	*Welliton 2*
20/9	Spartak Nalchik	a	2-0	*Ari 2*
24/9	Amkar	h	2-2	*Welliton, McGeady*
3/10	Anzhi	a	1-0	*Sheshukov*
15/10	Alania	h	3-0	*Ari, Alex, og (Ivanov)*
23/10	Sibir	a	0-0	
27/10	Zenit	h	1-0	*Kombarov (p)*
30/10	Rostov	h	2-1	*Welliton, McGeady (p)*
8/11	Rubin	a	1-1	*Welliton*
14/11	Krylya Sovetov	h	0-0	
20/11	CSKA	a	1-3	*Ibson*
28/11	Dinamo	a	1-1	*Welliton*

No	Name	Nat	DoB	Pos	Aps	(s)	Gls
12	ALEXandre Raphael Meschini	BRA	25/3/82	M	21	(1)	3
27	Zhano ANANIDZE	GEO	10/10/92	A	12	(11)	2
9	ARIclenes da Silva Ferreira	BRA	11/12/85	A	18	(6)	7
21	Nikita BAZHENOV		1/2/85	A	4	(8)	
56	Aleksandr BELENOV		13/9/86	G	1		
8	Nikola DRINČIĆ	MNE	7/9/84	M	2	(2)	
31	Andriy DYKAN	UKR	16/7/77	G	12		
1	Soslan DZHANAEV		13/3/87	G	12		
24	Artyom DZYUBA		22/8/88	A		(2)	
29	Pavel GOLYSHEV		7/7/87	M		(1)	
7	IBSON Barreto Gonçalves da Silva	BRA	7/11/83	M	27	(1)	2
18	Andrei IVANOV		8/10/88	D	11	(1)	
25	Martin JIRÁNEK	CZE	25/5/79	D	10		1
26	Anton KHODYREV		26/1/92	M	2	(1)	
23	Igor KIREYEV		17/2/92	M		(1)	
99	Dmitriy KOMBAROV		22/1/87	M	13	(1)	1
49	Aleksandr KOZLOV		19/3/93	A		(12)	
13	Fyodor KUDRYASHOV		5/4/87	D	8	(1)	
2	Cristian Óscar MAIDANA	ARG	24/1/87	M	4	(6)	
16	Yevgeniy MAKEEV		24/7/89	M	19	(3)	
64	Aiden McGEADY	IRL	4/4/86	M	11		2
48	Filip OZOBIĆ	CRO	8/4/91	M		(1)	
19	Nicolás Martín PAREJA	ARG	19/1/84	D	10	(1)	
15	Sergei PARSHIVLYUK		18/3/89	D	21		
30	Sergei PESYAKOV		16/12/88	G	5		
6	Renat SABITOV		13/6/85	M	11	(7)	

10	Ivan SAENKO		17/10/83	A	8	(2)	
5	Aleksandr SHESHUKOV		15/4/83	D	22	(1)	1
3	Martin STRANZL	AUT	16/6/80	D	14	(1)	
17	Marek SUCHÝ	CZE	29/3/88	D	25		1
11	WELLITON Soares de Morais	BRA	22/10/86	A	24	(1)	19
14	Pavel YAKOVLEV		7/4/91	A	1	(5)	
20	Aleksandr ZOTOV		27/8/90	M	2	(2)	

PFC SPARTAK NALCHIK

Coach – Yuriy Krasnozhan

Founded – 1935

Stadium – Spartak (14,200)

2010				
13/3	Anzhi	a	0-0	
19/3	Alania	h	2-1	*Shchanitsyn, Gogua*
27/3	Sibir	a	2-0	*Dyadyun 2*
3/4	Rostov	h	5-2	*Siradze, Leandro (p), Amisulashvili (p), Dyadyun 2*
12/4	Rubin	a	1-1	*Rusič*
18/4	Krylya Sovetov	h	1-0	*Kisenkov*
25/4	Spartak Moskva	a	0-0	
1/5	Dinamo	h	1-0	*Malyarov*
6/5	Zenit	a	1-3	*Malyarov*
11/5	Lokomotiv	h	1-1	*Leandro*
15/5	Tom	a	0-1	
8/7	Terek	h	2-1	*Kontsedalov, Leandro (p)*
19/7	Saturn	a	1-3	*Bikmoev*
25/7	CSKA	a	2-1	*Siradze, Gogua*
30/7	Amkar	h	2-1	*Kontsedalov, Leandro*
8/8	Alania	a	0-1	
14/8	Sibir	h	4-2	*Dyadyun, Leandro 2 (2p), Gogua*
20/8	Rostov	a	1-1	*Kontsedalov*
28/8	Rubin	h	1-1	*Jovanović*
12/9	Krylya Sovetov	a	0-2	
20/9	Spartak Moskva	h	0-2	
26/9	Dinamo	a	3-0	*Dyadyun 3*
3/10	Zenit	h	2-3	*Golić, Vasin*
17/10	Lokomotiv	a	0-1	
23/10	Tom	h	2-1	*Dyadyun, Siradze*
31/10	Terek	a	1-1	*Dyadyun*
5/11	Saturn	h	2-0	*Kontsedalov (p), Goshokov*
14/11	CSKA	h	1-1	*Goshokov*
20/11	Amkar	a	1-3	*Golić*
28/11	Anzhi	h	1-3	*Mitrishev*

No	Name	Nat	DoB	Pos	Aps	(s)	Gls
19	Roman AMIRKHANOV		13/5/89	D	1		
5	Aleksandre AMISULASHVILI	GEO	20/8/82	D	11		1
9	Marat BIKMOEV	UZB	1/1/86	A	3	(9)	1
20	Miodrag DŽUDOVIĆ	MNE	6/9/79	D	28		
22	Vladimir DYADYUN		12/7/88	M	28		10
99	Aslan DYSHEKOV		15/1/87	M	3	(2)	
14	Patrick ETSHINI Kindenge	CGO	26/2/89	A	1	(4)	
17	Valentin FILATOV		19/3/82	D	12		
30	Otto FREDRIKSON	FIN	30/11/81	G	22		
33	Kazbek GETERIYEV	KAZ	30/6/85	M	23	(1)	
7	Gogita GOGUA	GEO	4/10/83	M	21	(5)	3
28	Jovan GOLIĆ	SRB	18/9/86	M	9	(6)	2
44	Arsen GOSHOKOV		5/6/91	A	6	(10)	2
29	Milan JOVANOVIĆ	MNE	21/7/83	D	13		1
2	Vladislav KHATANZHENKOV		2/5/84	D	2	(2)	
88	Aleksandr KHOKHLOV		30/9/88	M	1		
18	Vladimir KISENKOV		8/10/81	D	16		1
73	Aleksandrs KOĻINKO	LVA	18/6/75	G	8		
14	Roman KONTSEDALOV		11/5/86	M	24		4
31	LEANDRO da Silva	BRA	26/7/85	D	24	(2)	6
10	Nikita MALYAROV		23/10/89	M	8	(9)	2
51	Magomed MITRISHEV		10/9/92	A		(1)	1
39	Zaurbek PLIYEV		27/9/91	M	3	(1)	
60	RICARDO JESUS da Silva	BRA	16/5/85	A	2	(4)	
15	Dejan RUSIČ	SVN	5/12/82	A	1	(6)	1
43	Artur RYLOV		12/4/89	M	1	(6)	
13	Aleksandr SHCHANITSYN		2/12/84	M	10	(6)	1
8	David SIRADZE	GEO	21/10/81	A	19	(7)	3
3	Viktor VASIN		6/10/88	D	18	(2)	1
38	Andrei VASYANOVICH		13/6/88	D	12	(1)	

FC TEREK GROZNY

Coach – Anatoliy Baidachnyi

Founded – 1946

Stadium – Sultan Bilimhanov (10,300)

MAJOR HONOURS: Russian Cup – (1) 2004.

2010				
14/3	Sibir	a	2-0	*Asildarov, Kobenko*
20/3	Rostov	h	1-1	*Asildarov*
28/3	Rubin	a	0-0	
4/4	Krylya Sovetov	h	2-0	*Bracamonte 2*
10/4	Spartak Moskva	a	1-2	*Asildarov*
18/4	Dinamo	h	1-1	*Lahiyalov (p)*
25/4	Zenit	a	0-0	
1/5	Lokomotiv	h	0-0	
6/5	Tom	a	1-2	*Asildarov*
10/5	CSKA	a	1-4	*Georgiev*
14/5	Saturn	h	2-0	*Maurício, Bracamonte*
8/7	Spartak Nalchik	a	1-2	*Gvazava*
18/7	Amkar	h	1-0	*Asildarov*
25/7	Anzhi	a	0-1	
31/7	Alania	h	2-0	*Maurício, Utsiev*
6/8	Rostov	a	0-1	
15/8	Rubin	h	1-1	*Bracamonte*
21/8	Krylya Sovetov	a	3-1	*Maurício, Lahiyalov, Asildarov*
28/8	Spartak Moskva	h	2-0	*Asildarov, Utsiev*
12/9	Dinamo	a	1-3	*Lahiyalov*
20/9	Zenit	h	0-0	
26/9	Lokomotiv	a	1-2	*Maurício*
2/10	Tom	h	1-0	*Asildarov*
17/10	CSKA Moskva	h	0-3	
23/10	Saturn	a	0-1	
31/10	Spartak Nalchik	h	1-1	*og (Vasyanovich)*
6/11	Amkar	a	0-2	
13/11	Anzhi	h	1-3	*Sadaev*
20/11	Alania	a	1-2	*Ediev*
28/11	Sibir	h	1-1	*Asildarov*

No	Name	Nat	DoB	Pos	Aps	(s)	Gls
71	Juan Carlos ARCE Justiniano	BOL	10/4/85	M	16	(4)	
11	Shamil ASILDAROV		18/5/83	A	28	(1)	9
19	Héctor Andrés BRACAMONTE	ARG	16/2/78	A	21	(7)	4
18	Timur DJABRAILOV		5/8/73	D		(1)	
31	Andriy DYKAN	UKR	16/7/77	G	18		
1	Soslan DZHANAEV		13/3/87	G	3		
33	Ismail EDIEV		16/2/88	D	8	(1)	1
9	Guy Stéphane ESSAME	CMR	25/11/84	M	16	(4)	
5	António FERREIRA de Oliveira Júnior	BRA	24/8/84	D	25	(1)	
7	Blagoy GEORGIEV	BUL	21/12/81	M	17	(2)	1
22	Levan GVAZAVA	GEO	8/7/80	M	8	(11)	1
4	Zeev HAIMOVICH	ISR	4/4/83	D	8		
12	Yaroslav HODZYUR	UKR	6/3/85	G	9		
17	Adlan KATSAEV		20/2/88	M	8	(10)	
20	Andrei KOBENKO		25/7/82	M	14	(6)	1
10	Shamil LAHIYALOV		28/10/79	M	23	(1)	3
8	MAURÍCIO José da Silveira Júnior	BRA	21/10/88	M	25	(3)	4
2	Sergei OMELYANCHUK	BLR	8/8/80	D	24	(2)	
28	RODRIGO Bonifácio da Rocha "TIUÍ"	BRA	4/12/85	A		(8)	
70	Zayr SADAEV		6/11/89	A	3	(12)	1
40	Rizvan UTSIEV		7/2/88	D	24	(1)	2
3	Dmitriy YATCHENKO		25/8/86	A	30		
14	Herve Xavier ZENGUE	CMR	22/1/84	D	2	(3)	

FC TOM TOMSK

Coach – Valeriy Nepomniachi

Founded – 1957

Stadium – Trud (15,000)

010				
3/3	Rostov	a	2-0	*Kornilenko 2*
2/3	Rubin	h	0-1	
7/3	Krylya Sovetov	a	3-2	*Michkov (p), Kovalchuk, Jokić*
/4	Spartak Moskva	h	2-2	*Kornilenko (p), Klimov*
0/4	Dinamo	a	0-0	
7/4	Zenit	h	0-0	
24/4	Lokomotiv	a	1-2	*Kornilenko*
/5	CSKA	a	1-3	*Kharitonov*
/5	Terek	h	2-1	*Kornilenko (p), Dzyuba*
11/5	Saturn	a	2-1	*Gultyaev, Kornilenko*
15/5	Spartak Nalchik	h	1-0	*Kornilenko (p)*
10/7	Amkar	a	1-2	*Kornilenko (p)*
18/7	Anzhi	h	1-4	*Dzyuba*
24/7	Alania	a	1-2	*Kornilenko (p)*
2/8	Sibir	h	3-2	*Dzyuba 2, Smirnov*
8/8	Rubin	a	1-2	*Dzyuba*
14/8	Krylya Sovetov	h	1-1	*Djioev*
21/8	Spartak Moskva	a	2-4	*Kornilenko 2 (1p)*
29/8	Dinamo	h	1-0	*Dzyuba (p)*
11/9	Zenit	a	0-2	
19/9	Lokomotiv	h	1-1	*og (Yanbayev)*
26/9	CSKA	h	0-3	
2/10	Terek	a	0-1	
16/10	Saturn	h	2-2	*Dzyuba 2*
23/10	Spartak Nalchik	a	1-2	*Starikov*
31/10	Amkar	h	1-0	*Kharitonov*
6/11	Anzhi	a	0-1	
13/11	Alania	h	1-1	*Dzyuba (p)*
20/11	Sibir	a	1-0	*Dzyuba (p)*
28/11	Rostov	h	3-1	*Kharitonov 2, Kovalchuk*

No	Name	Nat	DoB	Pos	Aps	(s)	Gls
9	Serghey COVALCIUC	MDA	20/1/82	M	20	(3)	
23	Georgiy DJIOEV		13/6/86	D	16	(4)	1
20	Artyom DZYUBA		22/8/88	A	22	(2)	10
13	Iliya GULTYAEV		5/9/88	D	24	(2)	1
17	Andrei IVANOV		8/10/88	D	11	(2)	
37	Đorđe JOKIĆ	SRB	20/1/81	D	25		1
83	Aleksandr KHARITONOV		4/4/83	M	22	(2)	4
18	Vladislav KHATANZHENKOV		2/5/84	D	4	(4)	
55	KIM Nam-il	KOR	14/3/77	M	24		
8	Denis KISILYOV		2/7/77	A		(2)	
3	Valeriy KLIMOV		31/1/74	M	24	(3)	1
14	Sergei KORNILENKO	BLR	14/6/83	A	12	(3)	11
11	Kyrylo KOVALCHUK	UKR	11/6/86	M	4	(11)	2
36	Fyodor KUDRYASHOV		5/4/87	D	9	(1)	
33	Daisuke MATSUI	JPN	11/5/81	M	3	(4)	
10	Goran MAZNOV	MKD	22/4/81	A	8	(9)	
6	Dmitriy MICHKOV		22/2/80	M	29	(1)	1
81	Norbert NÉMETH	HUN	5/5/81	M		(1)	
25	Sergei PAREIKO	EST	31/1/77	G	26		
21	Nikola PETKOVIĆ	SRB	28/3/86	D	7		
12	Aleksei POLYAKOV		28/2/74	G	4		
19	Aleksandr PRUDNIKOV		26/2/89	A		(6)	
5	Sergei SKOBLYAKOV		2/1/77	M	13	(7)	
9	Dmitriy N. SMIRNOV		9/11/80	D	16	(5)	1
87	Yevgeniy STARIKOV		17/11/88	A	6	(3)	1
26	Viktor STROYEV		16/1/87	D	1	(7)	
75	Viktor SVEZHOV		17/5/91	M		(1)	

FC ZENIT ST PETERSBURG

Coach – Luciano Spalletti (ITA)

Founded – 1925

Stadium – Petrovskiy (22,025)

MAJOR HONOURS: UEFA Cup – (1) 2008; UEFA Super Cup – (1) 2008; USSR League – (1) 1984; Russian League – (2) 2007, 2010; USSR Cup – (1) 1944; Russian Cup – (2) 1999, 2010.

2010				
13/3	Krylya Sovetov	a	1-0	*Danny*
21/3	Spartak Moskva	h	1-1	*Lombaerts*
27/3	Dinamo	a	2-1	*Danny, Bystrov*
11/4	Lokomotiv	h	1-0	*Bystrov*
17/4	Tom	a	0-0	
25/4	Terek	h	0-0	
28/4	CSKA	a	2-0	*Križanac, Kerzhakov*
2/5	Saturn	a	1-0	*Lombaerts*
6/5	Spartak Nalchik	h	3-1	*Bystrov, Shirokov (p), Danny*
10/5	Amkar	a	2-0	*Kanunnikov, Danny*
4/7	Anzhi	h	2-1	*Zyryanov, Bystrov*
9/7	Alania	a	3-1	*Shirokov (p), Bystrov, Lazović*
17/7	Sibir	h	2-0	*Lombaerts, Shirokov*
24/7	Rostov	a	3-1	*Kerzhakov, Danny, Fayzulin*
31/7	Rubin	h	2-0	*Kerzhakov 2*
14/8	Dinamo	h	1-1	*Lazović*
29/8	Lokomotiv	a	3-0	*Danny, Bukharov, Shirokov*
11/9	Tom	h	2-0	*og (Petković), Bukharov*
20/9	Terek	a	0-0	
25/9	Saturn	h	6-1	*Kerzhakov 3, Danny (p), Lazović, Rosina*
3/10	Spartak Nalchik	a	3-2	*Kerzhakov 2, Shirokov*
16/10	Amkar	h	2-0	*Kerzhakov, Shirokov (p)*
24/10	Anzhi	a	3-3	*Danny 2, Zyryanov*
27/10	Spartak Moskva	a	0-1	
31/10	Alania	h	3-0	*Lazović, Kerzhakov 2*
7/11	Sibir	a	5-2	*Bystrov, og (Joseph-Reinette), Danny, Semak, Anyukov*
10/11	CSKA	h	1-3	*Rosina*
14/11	Rostov	h	5-0	*Lazović (p), Semak, Kerzhakov, Bukharov 2*
20/11	Rubin	a	2-2	*Fayzulin, Huszti*
28/11	Krylya Sovetov	h	0-0	

No	Name	Nat	DoB	Pos	Aps	(s)	Gls
2	Aleksandr ANYUKOV		28/9/82	D	26	(1)	1
22	Dmitriy BORODIN		8/10/77	G	1		
3	BRUNO Eduardo Regufe ALVES	POR	27/11/81	D	14		
9	Aleksandr BUKHAROV		12/3/85	A	4	(6)	4
34	Vladimir BYSTROV		31/1/84	M	22	(3)	6
10	Daniel Miguel Alves Gomes "DANNY"	POR	7/8/83	M	27		10
27	Igor DENISOV		17/5/84	M	24		
20	Viktor FAYZULIN		22/4/86	M	3	(10)	2
5	FERNANDO José da Silva Freitas MEIRA	POR	5/6/78	D	7	(4)	
14	Tomáš HUBOČAN	SVK	17/9/85	D	23		
23	Szabolcs HUSZTI	HUN	18/4/83	M	3	(10)	1
57	Aleksei IONOV		18/2/89	M	2	(9)	
99	Maksim KANUNNIKOV		14/7/91	A		(12)	1
11	Aleksandr KERZHAKOV		27/11/82	A	26	(2)	13
4	Ivica KRIŽANAC	CRO	13/4/79	D	13	(1)	1
8	Danko LAZOVIĆ	SRB	17/5/83	A	14	(6)	5
6	Nicolas LOMBAERTS	BEL	20/3/85	D	26		3
24	Aleksandar LUKOVIĆ	SRB	23/10/82	D	10	(1)	
28	Michael LUMB	DEN	9/1/88	D	1	(1)	
16	Vyacheslav MALAFEEV		4/3/79	G	21		
17	Alessandro ROSINA	ITA	31/1/84	M	5	(10)	2
25	Sergei SEMAK		27/2/76	M	10	(2)	2
15	Roman SHIROKOV		6/7/81	M	17	(4)	6
30	Yuriy ZHEVNOV	BLR	17/4/81	G	8		
18	Konstantin ZYRYANOV		5/10/77	M	23	(5)	2

TOP GOALSCORERS 2010

19 WELLITON (Spartak Moskva)

14 Olexandr ALIYEV (Lokomotiv)
Sergei KORNILENKO (Tom/Rubin)

13 Aleksandr KERZHAKOV (Zenit)

10 Vladimir DYADYUN (Spartak Nalchik)
Artyom DZYUBA (Tom)
DANNY (Zenit)

9 VÁGNER LOVE (CSKA)
Kevin KURÁNYI (Dinamo)
Shamil ASILDAROV (Terek)

PROMOTED CLUBS

FC KUBAN KRASNODAR
Coach – Dan Petrescu (ROU)
Founded – 1928
Stadium – Kuban (31,654)

FC VOLGA NIZHNIY NOVGOROD
Coach – Aleksandr Pobegalov; (8/5/10) Omari Tetradze
Founded – 1963
Stadium – Lokomotiv (17,856)

FC KRASNODAR
Coach – Sergei Tashuyev
Founded – 2007
Stadium – Kuban (31,654)

SECOND LEVEL FINAL TABLE 2010

		Pld	W	D	L	F	A	Pts
1	FC Kuban Krasnodar	38	24	8	6	51	20	80
2	FC Volga Nizhniy Novgorod	38	19	14	5	62	25	71
3	FC Nizhniy Novgorod	38	21	7	10	60	41	70
4	FC KamAZ Naberezhnye Chelny	38	19	9	10	55	43	66
5	FC Krasnodar	38	17	10	11	60	44	61
6	FC Mordovia Saransk	38	16	10	12	53	40	58
7	FC Ural Yekaterinburg	38	14	16	8	38	28	58
8	FC Zhemchuzhina Sochi	38	16	9	13	45	44	57
9	FC Volgar-GazProm Astrakhan	38	16	9	13	45	48	57
10	FC Shinnik Yaroslavl	38	14	13	11	43	31	55
11	FC SKA-Energia Khabarovsk	38	15	8	15	37	39	53
12	FC Luch-Energia Vladivostok	38	13	13	12	42	42	52
13	FC Khimki	38	11	17	10	39	38	50
14	FC Dinamo Bryansk	38	11	11	16	53	54	44
15	FC Baltika Kaliningrad	38	11	10	17	38	47	43
16	FC Dinamo St Petersburg	38	9	10	19	32	53	37
17	FC Rotor Volgograd	38	9	7	22	27	64	34
18	FC Salyut-Energia Belgorod	38	7	13	18	30	47	34
19	FC Irtysh Omsk	38	6	10	22	26	52	28
20	FC Avangard Kursk	38	7	6	25	31	67	27

NB FC Krasnodar promoted as FC Saturn Moskovskaya Oblast withdrew from 2011 Premier-Liga; FC Nizhniy Novgorod and FC KamAZ Naberezhnye Chelny declined promotion.

DOMESTIC CUP 2010/11

KUBOK ROSSII

1/16 FINALS

(13/7/10)
Avangard Kursk 2, Sibir 5 *(aet)*
Dinamo St Petersburg 1, Zenit 3
KamAZ Naberezhnye Chelny 0, Alania 0 *(aet; 2-4 on pens)*
Luch-Energia 4, Terek 0
Metallurg Lipetsk 0, Spartak Moskva 1
Mordovia Saransk 1, Dinamo Moskva 2
Salyut-Energia Belgorod 0, Rostov 4
Shinnik 2, Krylya Sovetov 1
Volga Nizhniy Novgorod 5, Spartak Nalchik 0
Volgar-GazProm Astrakhan 1, Rubin 0

(14/7/10)
Chernomorets Novorossiisk 0, Amkar 1
Gornyak Uchaly 1, Lokomotiv Moskva 0
Krasnodar 2, Tom 1 *(aet)*
Pskov-747 1, Anzhi 2
Sakhalin Yuzhno-Sakhalinsk 1, Saturn 1 *(aet; 3-4 on pens)*
Torpedo Moskva 0, CSKA Moskva 2

1/8 FINALS

(22/9/10)
Alania 0, Gornyak Uchaly 0 *(aet; 5-4 on pens)*
Dinamo Moskva 4, Volga Nizhniy Novgorod 1
Rostov 2, Volgar-GazProm Astrakhan 0
Saturn 2, Luch-Energia 1

(28/2/11)
CSKA Moskva 1, Shinnik 0

(1/3/11)
Anzhi 2, Zenit 3

(3/3/11)
Sibir 0, Spartak Moskva 2

(6/3/11)
Amkar 0, Krasnodar 1 *(aet)*

QUARTER-FINALS

(20/4/11)
Alania 3, Saturn 0 (w/o)
Dinamo Moskva 1 *(Sapeta 41)*, Rostov 2 *(Grigoryev 22, Blatnjak 90)*
Spartak Moskva 2 *(Rojo 69, Welliton 72)*, Krasnodar 1 *(Gogniev 84)*
Zenit 0, CSKA Moskva 2 *(Doumbia 40, Ignashevich 57p)*

SEMI-FINALS

(11/5/11)
Rostov 0, Alania 0 *(aet; 5-6 on pens)*
Spartak Moskva 3 *(Kombarov D. 45, Ari 61, Ibson 76)*, CSKA Moskva 3 *(Necid 42, Doumbia 72, Vágner Love 82) (aet; 4-5 on pens)*

FINAL

(22/5/11)
Shinnik, Yaroslavl
PFC CSKA MOSKVA 2 *(Doumbia 13, 69)*
FC ALANIA VLADIKAVKAZ 1 *(Danilo Neco 23)*
Referee – *Bezborodov*
CSKA MOSKVA – *Akinfeev, Nababkin, Ignashevich, Berezutskiy V., Berezutskiy A., Dzagoev (Honda 65), Mamayev (Necid 89), Tošić (Šemberas 83), Aldonin, Doumbia, Vágner Love.*
ALANIA – *Khomich, Gnanou, Bulgaru, Grigoryev, Grachyov, Gigolayev (Gogichayev 71), Bazayev J. (Burayev 46), Goore (Tsarikayev 75), Dudiev, Bikmoev, Danilo Neco.*

CLUB COMMUNICATION 2011

C Amkar Perm

ibysheva str. 95
J-614010 Perm

l	+7 342 244 0281
ax	+7 342 244 0281
eb	fc-amkar.org
nail	fc-amkar@amkar.ru
edia Officer	Viktoria Ivanova

C Anzhi Makhachkala

agestan, Mahachkala, Dahadaeva st., 23
U-367025 Makhachkala

el	+7 872 2678520
ax	+7 872 2682008
/eb	fc-anji.ru
mail	info@fc-anji.ru
edia Officer	Aleksandr Udaltsov

FC CSKA Moskva

eningradsky Prospekt 39, land 39, bld. 1
U-125167 Moskva

el	+7 495 612 0780
ax	+7 495 613 2809
Neb	pfc-cska.com
Email	refer@pfc-cska.com
Media Officer	Sergei Aksenov

FC Dinamo Moskva

Leningradsky Prospekt 36, bld. 21
RU-125167 Moskva

Tel	+7 495 612 7172
Fax	+7 495 613 1612
Web	fcdynamo.ru
Email	office@fc.dynamo.su
Media Officer	Konstantin Alekseev

FC Krasnodar

Moscovskaya st. 59/1
RU-350072 Krasnodar

Tel	+7 861 279 7209
Fax	+7 861 279 7209
Web	fckrasnodar.ru
Email	ratkina@fckrasnodar.ru
Media Officer	Denis Danilchenko

FC Krylya Sovetov Samara

Shushenskaya str. 50-A
RU-443011 Samara

Tel	+7 846 335 5441
Fax	+7 846 221 9840
Web	kc-camapa.ru
Email	fc@ks-samara.com
Media Officer	Maxim Shestnov

FC Kuban Krasnodar

Polevoy proezd 11/1
RU-350051 Krasnodar

Tel	+7 861 211 5075
Fax	+7 861 211 5077
Web	fckuban.ru
Email	office@fckuban.ru
Media Officer	Vacheslav Ivanov

FC Lokomotiv Moskva

Bolshaya Cherkizovskaya Str 125, bld. 1
RU-107553 Moskva

Tel	+7 495 500 3101
Fax	+7 495 500 3070
Web	fclm.ru
Email	info@fclm.ru
Media Officer	Stanislav Pahomov

FC Rostov

pr. Sholohova 31 E
RU-344029 Rostov-na-Donu

Tel	+7 863 251 7865
Fax	+7 863 251 95 39
Web	fc-rostov.ru
Email	fcrostov@aaanet.ru
Media Officer	Maksim Ponomarev

FC Rubin Kazan

Kopylova St. 2
RU-420036 Kazan

Tel	+7 843 571 1724
Fax	+7 843 533 0108
Web	rubin-kazan.ru
Email	info@rubin-kazan.ru
Media Officer	Maksim Lopukhov

FC Spartak Moskva

Krasnopresnenskaya Naberezhnaya 10,
bld. 4, RU-123100 Moskva

Tel	+7 495 646 1926
Fax	+7 495 646 1926
Web	spartak.com
Email	sport@spartak.com
Media Officer	Leonid Trahtenberg

PFC Spartak Nalchik

KBR, Nalchik, Shogentsukova St. 13
RU-360051 Nalchik

Tel	+7 8662 47 3520
Fax	+8 8662 47 3520
Web	spartak-nalchik.ru
Email	info@spartak-nalchik.ru
Media Officer	Albert Bekov

FC Terek Grozny

Chechenskaya rep., Krasnyh Frontovikov
st. 3, RU-364051 Grozny

Tel	+7 8793 724 507
Fax	+7 8793 725 407
Web	fc-terek.ru
Email	terek2005@mail.ru
Media Officer	Kazbek Hadzhiev

FC Tom Tomsk

Belinskogo st 11/1
RU-639029 Tomsk

Tel	+7 3822 532 623
Fax	+7 3822 532 623
Web	fctomtomsk.ru
Email	fctom-office@mail.ru
Media Officer	Oleg Igrushkin

FC Volga Nizhniy Novgorod

Balaklavsky pereulok 1 Г
RU-603010 Nizhniy Novgorod

Tel	+7 831 245 12 18
Fax	+7 831 245 43 05
Web	fcvolgann.ru
Email	info@fcvolgann.ru
Media Officer	Sergei Kozunov

FC Zenit St Petersburg

Paradnaya st. 1, Voznesensky pr.
57/127 liter A, ac.4-H
RU-191014 St Petersburg

Tel	+7 812 244 8888
Fax	+7 812 244 8888
Web	fc-zenit.ru
Email	office@fc-zenit.ru
Media Officer	Yevgeniy Gusev

SAN MARINO

Saint-Marin I San Marino

Federazione Sammarinese Giuoco Calcio (FSGC)

COMMUNICATION

Address	Strada di Montecchio 17 SM-47890 San Marino	**President**	Giorgio Crescentini
Tel	+378 0549 990 515	**General Secretary**	Luciano Casadei
Fax	+378 0549 992 348	**Media Officer**	Elisa Felici
E-mail	fsgc@omniway.sm	**Year of Formation**	1931
Website	fsgc.sm	**National Stadium**	Stadio Olimpico, Serravalle (5,115)

DOMESTIC COMPETITION SUMMARY 2010/11

CAMPIONATO SAMMARINESE FINAL TABLES

FIRST PHASE

	Group A	Pld	W	D	L	F	A	Pts	Comp
1	S.S. Pennarossa	20	13	3	4	31	15	42	
2	SP La Fiorita	20	10	6	4	44	28	36	
3	S.S. Cosmos	20	11	3	6	22	22	36	
4	AC Juvenes-Dogana	20	8	5	7	37	31	29	UEL
5	SC Faetano	20	7	3	10	30	33	24	
6	S.S. Fiorentino	20	5	4	11	22	37	19	
7	SP Cailungo	20	2	4	14	17	40	10	

	Group B	Pld	W	D	L	F	A	Pts	Comp
1	SP Tre Fiori	21	11	6	4	41	26	39	UCL
2	SP Libertas	21	10	7	4	26	13	37	
3	SP Tre Penne	21	10	6	5	32	19	36	UEL
4	S.S. Murata	21	9	8	4	34	19	35	
5	S.S. Virtus	21	8	6	7	32	32	30	
6	S.S. San Giovanni	21	9	2	10	29	34	29	
7	S.S. Folgore/Falciano	21	3	4	14	21	44	13	
8	Domagnano FC	21	0	9	12	17	42	9	

CHAMPIONSHIP PLAY-OFFS

Final SP Tre Fiori 1, SP Tre Penne 0

Top Scorer Alessandro Giunta (Tre Fiori), 13 goals (including play-offs)

Cup Final AC Juvenes-Dogana 4, S.S. Virtus 1

Three in a row for Tre Fiori

SP Tre Fiori completed a hat-trick of Campionato Sammarinese titles, defeating SP Tre Penne in the play-off final for the second successive year. Striker Alessandro Giunta, the club's top scorer during the regular season, grabbed the title-clinching goal midway through the first half, but there was a sting in the tail to the team's post-match celebrations when coach Floriano Sperindio announced that he was leaving the club with immediate effect.

Tre Fiori's hopes of a second successive domestic double had been crushed when they were beaten on penalties in the quarter-final of the Coppa Titano by S.S. Pennarossa, but Sperindio's men avenged that defeat with a 2-1 extra-time victory when the two first-phase group winners met in their first tie of the championship play-offs.

Cup joy for Juvenes-Dogana

The Coppa Titano was regained by 2008/09 winners AC Juvenes-Dogana, who made light work in the final of another team that failed to make the championship play-offs, S.S. Virtus, defeating them 4-1 in Serravalle to secure both the trophy and a UEFA Europa League place. Tre Penne's league runners-up spot earned them a return to the same European competition in which they had come within a goal of eliminating HŠK Zrinjski of Bosnia & Herzegovina the previous summer. Tre Fiori's UEFA Champions League adventure ended in the first qualifying round with a 7-1 aggregate defeat by Montenegrin champions FK Rudar Pljevlja.

Alessandro Giunta scored Tre Fiori's winning goal in the championship play-off final

The UEFA EURO 2012 qualifying campaign brought no joy for Giampaolo Mazza's national side as they lost their first seven qualifiers without scoring a goal. Their best performance came at home to Finland in June, when they conceded just once to a team that had put eight goals past them in Helsinki. Despite that result, the team's overworked goalkeeper Aldo Simoncini earned a mid-season move to Italian top-flight side AC Cesena – although by the end of the season he was still awaiting his Serie A debut.

National Team

Top Five All-time Caps – Damiano Vannucci (61); Simone Bacciocchi (53); Andy Selva (52); Mirco Gennari (48); Paolo Montagna (45)

Top Five All-time Goals – Andy Selva (8)
NB No other player has scored more than one goal.

NATIONAL TEAM RESULTS 2010/11

3/9/10	Netherlands (ECQ)	H	Serravalle	0-5
7/9/10	Sweden (ECQ)	A	Malmo	0-6
8/10/10	Hungary (ECQ)	A	Budapest	0-8
12/10/10	Moldova (ECQ)	H	Serravalle	0-2
17/11/10	Finland (ECQ)	A	Helsinki	0-8
9/2/11	Liechtenstein	H	Serravalle	0-1
3/6/11	Finland (ECQ)	H	Serravalle	0-1
7/6/11	Hungary (ECQ)	H	Serravalle	0-3

SAN MARINO

NATIONAL TEAM APPEARANCES 2010/11

Coach – Giampaolo MAZZA (ITA)	26/2/56		NED	SWE	HUN	MDA	FIN	Lie	FIN	HUN	Caps	Goal
Aldo SIMONCINI	30/8/86	Bellaria Igea (ITA) /Cesena (ITA)	G	G	G	G	G	G	G	G	23	-
Carlo VALENTINI	15/3/82	Murata/Sammaurese (ITA)	D	s79	D 92*						38	-
Fabio VITAIOLI	5/4/84	Murata/Sammaurese (ITA)	D	D	D	D	D72	D65	D88	D46	19	-
Davide SIMONCINI	30/8/86	Libertas/Santa Giustina (ITA)	D61	D		D		D65	D		21	-
Alessandro DELLA VALLE	8/6/82	Sanvitese (ITA)	D	D	D		D	D	D	D	35	-
Damiano VANNUCCI	30/7/77	Juvenes-Dogana	D	D	D	D	s72	D 3*	D	D	61	-
Maicol BERRETTI	1/5/89	Pennarossa/Verucchio (ITA) /Formigine (ITA)	M	s56	M	s60	M67	M	s77	s64	18	-
Manuel MARANI	7/6/84	Murata/Riccione (ITA)	M76	M56	M	M	s79	M75	M	M64	28	1
Pier Filippo MAZZA	20/8/88	Sant'Ermete (ITA)	M	M		M		M84	M77	M	6	-
Matteo VITAIOLI	27/10/89	Fiorentino/San Marino (ITA)	M82	M	M77	M	M	M	M81	M	17	-
Andy SELVA	23/5/76	Verona (ITA)	A	A			A		A	A	52	8
Simone BACCIOCCHI	22/1/77	Juvenes-Dogana	s61	D79	D52	D		s65	s88	s79	53	-
Alex GASPERONI	30/6/84	Tre Penne	s76	s72							18	1
Nicola CIACCI	7/7/82	Pennarossa	s82			s67		s75			17	1
Nicola CHIARUZZI	25/12/87	Tre Penne		M72							1	-
Fabio BOLLINI	19/9/83	La Fiorita			M84	M67		M46	M	M79	9	-
Paolo MONTAGNA	28/5/76	Cosmos			A	A81	M79	A46	s81		45	-
Nicola ALBANI	15/4/81	Murata			s52		D				39	1
Matteo BUGLI	10/3/83	Murata/Cosmos /Novasecchiano (ITA)			s77		D	s84			20	-
Michele CERVELLINI	14/4/88	Juvenes-Dogana			s84	D60	D	s65	D	D	8	-
Matteo COPPINI	5/5/89	Pol. Campitello (ITA)				s81	M	s46			3	-
Alex DELLA VALLE	13/6/90	Faetano/Real Rimini (ITA) /Cattolica (ITA)					s67			s46	2	-
Andrea MORONI	10/10/85	Faetano/Verucchio (ITA)						s46			1	-
Giacomo BENEDETTINI	7/10/82	Tre Fiori								D	3	-

NB Amateur players can represent more than one club at the same time.

CHAMPIONSHIP PLAY-OFFS

FIRST ROUND

(3/5/11)
Libertas 0, Cosmos 2 *(Montagna 25, Lazzarini 71)*

(4/5/11)
La Fiorita 3 *(Bollini F. 50, Parma 56, Monac 65)*, Tre Penne 1 *(Cibelli 9)*

SECOND ROUND

(7/5/11)
Cosmos 4 *(Lazzarini 2, Montagna 10, 19p, Fucili 25)*, La Fiorita 2 *(Parma 12, Bollini F. 29)*
Libertas 1 *(Mazzoli 38)*, Tre Penne 4 *(Cibelli 10, 12, Valli 34, Simoncini 84)*
(Libertas eliminated)

THIRD ROUND

(11/5/11)
Pennarossa 1 *(Andreini 34og)*, Tre Fiori 2 *(Buonocore 52, Macerata 110) (aet)*

(12/5/11)
Tre Penne 2 *(Di Giuli 40, Olivieri 52)*, La Fiorita 0
(La Fiorita eliminated)

FOURTH ROUND

(16/5/11)
Tre Penne 3 *(Valli 71, Cibelli 84, Pignieri 90+4)*, Pennarossa 1 *(Berretti 90)*
(Pennarossa eliminated)

(17/5/11)
Tre Fiori 2 *(Menin 72, Aruta 90+1p)*, Cosmos 0

SEMI-FINAL

(21/5/11)
Tre Penne 2 *(Molinari 25og, Di Giuli 115)*, Cosmos 1 *(Montagna 35p) (aet)*
(Cosmos eliminated)

FINAL

(26/5/11)
Stadio Olimpico, Serravalle
SP TRE FIORI 1 *(Giunta 21)*
SP TRE PENNE 0
Referee – *Rossi*
TRE FIORI – *Micheletti, Canarezza (Vendemini 90), Ballanti, Lisi, Macerata, Benedettini, Andreini, Vannoni, Menin (Macina 68), Tarini (Aruta 50), Giunta.*
TRE PENNE – *Valentini, Zavoli, Nanni, Lisi (Simoncini 53), Franchini, Valentini, Olivieri (Chiaruzzi 53), Rossi, Pignieri, Di Giuli (Bonini 65), Cibelli.*

TOP GOALSCORERS 2010/11

(excluding Play-offs)

12	Roberto GATTI (Murata) Alessandro GIUNTA (Tre Fiori) José Adolfo HIRSCH (Virtus)
11	Francesco VIROLI (Faetano) Marco UGOLINI (San Giovanni)
10	Marco FANTINI (Juvenes-Dogana) Daniele PIGNIERI (Tre Penne)
9	Simon PARMA (La Fiorita) Sossio ARUTA (Tre Fiori) Elton SHABANI (Virtus)

DOMESTIC CUP 2010/11

COPPA TITANO

FIRST PHASE

(Played in Groups)

GROUP A

(11/9/10)
Cailungo 0, Libertas 1
Virtus 2, Pennarossa 1

(22/9/10)
Pennarossa 0, Folgore/Falciano 0
Virtus 2, Cailungo 2

(10/11/10)
Folgore/Falciano 1, Virtus 2
Pennarossa 4, Libertas 2

(1/12/10)
Libertas 2, Virtus 2

(15/1/11)
Libertas 1, Folgore/Falciano 2

(16/1/11)
Cailungo 2, Pennarossa 1

(26/1/11)
Libertas 1, Cailungo 1
Pennarossa 3, Virtus 5

(29/1/11)
Cailungo 0, Virtus 1

(30/1/11)
Folgore/Falciano 0, Pennarossa 1

(2/2/11)
Folgore/Falciano 1, Cailungo 0

(16/3/11)
Libertas 1, Pennarossa 2
Virtus 3, Folgore/Falciano 0

(23/3/11)
Cailungo 1, Folgore/Falciano 3
Virtus 0, Libertas 0

(30/3/11)
Folgore/Falciano 3, Libertas 0
Pennarossa 2, Cailungo 0

Final Standings
1 Virtus 18 pts; 2 Pennarossa 13 pts; 3 Folgore/Falciano 13 pts *(qualified)*; 4 Libertas 6 pts; 5 Cailungo 5 pts *(eliminated)*

GROUP B

(12/9/10)
Cosmos 1, La Fiorita 3
Faetano 1, Tre Fiori 1

(22/9/10)
Cosmos 1, Domagnano 1
La Fiorita 3, Faetano 2

(10/11/10)
La Fiorita 0, Domagnano 2
Tre Fiori 1, Cosmos 1

(1/12/10)
Domagnano 0, Faetano 1
Tre Fiori 2, La Fiorita 2

(16/1/11)
Domagnano 0, Tre Fiori 1
Faetano 0, Cosmos 0

(25/1/11)
La Fiorita 1, Cosmos 2
Tre Fiori 1, Faetano 0

(29/1/11)
Faetano 4, La Fiorita 3

(30/1/11)
Domagnano 0, Cosmos 1

(16/3/11)
Cosmos 0, Tre Fiori 2
Domagnano 3, La Fiorita 3

(23/3/11)
Faetano 1, Domagnano 3
La Fiorita 1, Tre Fiori 1

(30/3/11)
Cosmos 2, Faetano 0
Tre Fiori 0, Domagnano 5

Final Standings
1 Tre Fiori 13 pts; 2 Cosmos 12 pts; 3 Domagnano 11 pts *(qualified)*;
4 La Fiorita 9 pts; 5 Faetano 8 pts *(eliminated)*

GROUP C

(11/9/10)
San Giovanni 2, Juvenes-Dogana 4

(12/9/10)
Fiorentino 1, Tre Penne 2

(22/9/10)
Fiorentino 1, Murata 2
Tre Penne 5, San Giovanni 1

(10/11/10)
Juvenes-Dogana 3, Fiorentino 0
Tre Penne 1, Murata 1

(1/12/10)
Juvenes-Dogana 2, Tre Penne 2
Murata 2, San Giovanni 2

(15/1/11)
Murata 1, Juvenes-Dogana 3
San Giovanni 0, Fiorentino 1

(25/1/11)
Juvenes-Dogana 4, San Giovanni 2

(26/1/11)
Tre Penne 2, Fiorentino 2

(29/1/11)
San Giovanni 1, Tre Penne 0

(30/1/11)
Murata 1, Fiorentino 1

(16/3/11)
Fiorentino 2, Juvenes-Dogana 1
Murata 1, Tre Penne 1

(23/3/11)
San Giovanni 1, Murata 3
Tre Penne 1, Juvenes-Dogana 1

(30/3/11)
Fiorentino 2, San Giovanni 1
Juvenes-Dogana 0, Murata 2

Final Standings
1 Juvenes-Dogana 14 pts; 2 Murata 13 pts *(qualified)*;
3 Tre Penne 11 pts; 4 Fiorentino 11 pts; 5 San Giovanni 4 pts *(eliminated)*

QUARTER-FINALS

(21/4/11)
Cosmos 0, Murata 5 *(De Sousa 10, 38, Gatti 30, Cardini 53, Casadei 83)*

Juvenes-Dogana 3 *(Santini 25, 88, Ceci 90+3)*, Folgore/Falciano 1 *(Zaboul 90+1)*

Tre Fiori 1 *(Giunta 76)*, Pennarossa 1 *(Grigore 13) (aet; 4-6 on pens)*

Virtus 1 *(Shabani 92)*, Domagnano 0 *(aet)*

SEMI-FINALS

(26/4/11)
Juvenes-Dogana 1 *(Baldini 81)*, Pennarossa 0

Virtus 2 *(Hirsch 60, Rossitto 70)*, Murata 1 *(De Sousa 80)*

FINAL

(30/4/11)
Stadio Olimpico, Serravalle
AC JUVENES-DOGANA 4 *(Ceci 17, Santini 30, Hirsch 65og, Colombini 83)*
S.S. VIRTUS 1 *(Hirsch 64)*
Referee – *Podeschi*
JUVENES-DOGANA – *Gobbi, Casadei, Cavalli (Colombini 75), Dominici, Baldini, Bacciocchi, Ceci (Selva 70), Cervellini, Santini, Caminati (Fantini 89), Vannucci.*
VIRTUS – *Ramazzotti, Dominici (Semprini 46), Bianchi, Zavoli, Giacobbi (Bucci 67), Greco, Rossitto, Bracci (Francioni 51), Maurizi, Hirsch, Montanari.*

CLUB COMMUNICATION 2011/12

SP Cailungo
Strada Cà dei Lunghi 132
SM-47893 Borgo Maggiore

Tel +378 0549 903 322
Fax
Web
Email cailungo@fsgc.info
Media Officer

SP Cosmos
Via E. Balducci, 39
SM-47899 Serravalle

Tel
Fax
Web
E-mail cosmos@fsgc.info
Media Officer

Domagnano FC
Via G. Carducci 11
SM-47895 Domagnano

Tel +378 0549 906 864
Fax +378 0549 906 864
Web
Email domagnano@fsgc.info
Media Officer Elisa Felici

SC Faetano
Piazza del Massaro 2
SM-47896 Faetano

Tel
Fax
Web faetanocalcio.sm
Email faetano@fsgc.info
Media Officer

S.S. Fiorentino
Via La Rena 19
SM-47897 Fiorentino

Tel +378 0549 878 208
Fax
Web
Email fiorentino@fsgc.info
Media Officer

S.S. Folgore/Falciano
Strada La Zanetta, 10
SM-47891 Falciano

Tel +378 0549 908 088
Fax
Web folgorecalcio.com
Email folgore@fsgc.info
Media Officer

AC Juvenes-Dogana
Via E. Balducci, 36
SM-47899 Serravalle

Tel 00378 549 900 689
Fax 00378 549 905 156
Web acjuvenesdogana.sm
Email juvenes@fsgc.info
Media Officer

SP La Fiorita
Via del Dragone 17
SM-47898 MOntegiardino

Tel
Fax +378 0549 996728
Web lafiorita.sm
Email lafiorita@fsgc.info
Media Officer Alan Gasperoni

SP Libertas
Via 28 Luglio 1/B
SM-47893 Borgo Maggiore

Tel +378 0549 906475
Fax
Web polisportivalibertas.com
Email info@polisportivalibertas.com
Media Officer Elisa Felici

S.S. Murata
Via del Serrone 100
SM-47890 Murata

Tel +378 0549 992 311
Fax
Web
Email murata@fsgc.info
Media Officer Elisa Felici

S.S. Pennarossa
Piazza Salvatore Conti, 13
SM-47894 Chiesanuova

Tel
Fax +36 334 27 99 696
Web pennarossa.com
Email pennarossa@fsgc.info
Media Officer Elisa Felici

S.S. San Giovanni
Strada Di San Gianno
SM-47893 Borgo Maggiore

Tel
Fax
Web
Email
Media Officer

SP Tre Fiori
Via 21 Settembre, 93
SM-47897 Fiorentino

Tel +378 0549 878 026
Fax +378 0549 878 026
Web
Email astercasali@omniway.sm
Media Officer

SP Tre Penne
Strada Cardio 80
SM-47891 Dogana

Tel +378 0549 906 699
Fax +378 0549 903 758
Web trepenne.sm
Email trepenne@omniway.sm
Media Officer

S.S. Virtus
Piazza Castello Montecerreto 2
SM-47892 Acquaviva

Tel +378 0549 999 168
Fax
Web
Email vitus@fsgc.info
Media Officer

SCOTLAND

Écosse I Schottland

Scottish Football Association (SFA)

COMMUNICATION

Address	Hampden Park GB-Glasgow G42 9AY	**President**	Campbell Ogilvie
Tel	+44 141 616 6000	**General Secretary**	Stewart Regan
Fax	+44 141 616 6001	**Media Officer**	Darryl Broadfoot
E-mail	info@scottishfa.co.uk	**Year of Formation**	1873
Website	scottishfa.co.uk	**National Stadium**	Hampden Park, Glasgow (52,054)

DOMESTIC COMPETITION SUMMARY 2010/11

SCOTTISH PREMIER LEAGUE FINAL TABLE

			Home					Away					Total						
		Pld	W	D	L	F	A	W	D	L	F	A	W	D	L	F	A	Pts	Comp
1	Rangers FC	38	14	2	3	43	14	16	1	2	45	15	30	3	5	88	29	93	UCL
2	Celtic FC	38	15	3	1	51	11	14	2	3	34	11	29	5	4	85	22	92	UEL
3	Heart of Midlothian FC	38	9	5	5	27	21	9	4	6	26	24	18	9	11	53	45	63	UEL
4	Dundee United FC	38	13	1	5	34	22	4	9	6	21	28	17	10	11	55	50	61	UEL
5	Kilmarnock FC	38	6	4	9	26	31	7	6	6	27	24	13	10	15	53	55	49	
6	Motherwell FC	38	8	3	8	24	24	5	4	10	16	36	13	7	18	40	60	46	
7	Inverness Caledonian Thistle FC	38	7	4	8	25	24	7	7	5	27	20	14	11	13	52	44	53	
8	Saint Johnstone FC	38	6	5	8	10	19	5	6	8	13	24	11	11	16	23	43	44	
9	Aberdeen FC	38	6	2	11	22	21	5	3	11	17	38	11	5	22	39	59	38	
10	Hibernian FC	38	5	6	8	21	29	5	1	13	18	32	10	7	21	39	61	37	
11	Saint Mirren FC	38	4	6	9	20	27	4	3	12	13	30	8	9	21	33	57	33	
12	Hamilton Academical FC	38	1	8	10	12	26	4	3	12	12	33	5	11	22	24	59	26	*Relegated*

NB League split into top and bottom halves after 33 games, with each team playing a further five matches exclusively against clubs from its half of the table.

Top Scorer	Kenny Miller (Rangers), 21 goals
Promoted Club	Dunfermline Athletic FC
Cup Final	Celtic FC 3, Motherwell FC 0
League Cup Final	Rangers FC 2, Celtic FC 1 (aet)

Rangers give Smith the perfect parting gift

A 2010/11 season riddled with scandal and controversy ended in familiar fashion as Rangers FC edged Old Firm rivals Celtic FC to become champions of Scotland for a record 54th time. A nine-month tug-o'-war for the title went to the final day, on which Rangers easily overcame Kilmarnock FC 5-1 to provide their manager Walter Smith with his tenth Scottish Premier League triumph – a fitting farewell gift for the distinguished 63-year-old as he left the Ibrox club after a highly successful second spell in charge.

As usual, the tussle for the title was a private two-team affair. Celtic, in their first full season under former Northern Ireland international Neil Lennon, ran Rangers close, and indeed had the better of the four league encounters, winning two and drawing one, but a late missed penalty by Greek striker Georgios Samaras in the last of those Old Firm clashes, a 0-0 draw at Ibrox, proved very costly – as did a 3-2 defeat away to newly promoted Inverness Caledonian Thistle FC in a rearranged fixture carried over from the first phase of the championship (before the 33-match 'split'). That setback in the Scottish Highlands to a team managed by ex-Rangers stalwart Terry Butcher put the Ibrox club back in charge, and they did not let Celtic off the hook, beating Heart of Midlothian FC and Dundee United FC with relative ease at home before a flurry of brilliantly executed early goals at Kilmarnock ensured that any last-day nerves were exclusively of the pre-match variety.

Rangers manager Walter Smith (left) and his assistant Ally McCoist salute the fans after the club's SPL title win

Cups shared

Rangers ended the campaign on 93 points, six more than they had accumulated in taking the 2009/10 title, and they needed every one of them because Celtic were just one point behind with a superior goal difference. That third-placed Hearts finished a full 30 points in arrears of the champions re-emphasised the Old Firm's dominance – as did the Glasgow clubs' sharing of the spoils in the two domestic knockout competitions, with Rangers retaining the League Cup by defeating Celtic 2-1 after extra time in the final and the Bhoys finding consolation in a record 35th Scottish Cup triumph, which they sealed with a 3-0 victory at Hampden over Motherwell FC after they had earlier eliminated Rangers in a fifth-round replay.

With a record seven Old Firm clashes taking place over the season, and the title race so keenly contested, the tension between the two clubs was ever-present. Unfortunately, it got out of hand on several occasions, and Celtic's abrasive boss Lennon became a central figure in two wholly regrettable episodes that brought shame on the Scottish game. The first scandal occurred in late November when excessive criticism of referees led to the match officials going on strike and replacements having to be drafted in from overseas in order to fulfil the SPL fixture programme. No sooner had that crisis been overcome than the outspoken Lennon grabbed the attention again when he became the target of a vicious hate campaign. Two parcel bombs addressed to him were mercifully intercepted, but despite being placed under bodyguard

National Team

International Tournament Appearances –
FIFA World Cup – (8) 1954, 1958, 1974, 1978, 1982, 1986, 1990, 1998.
UEFA European Championship – (2) 1992, 1996.

Top Five All-time Caps – Kenny Dalglish (102); Jim Leighton (91); Alex McLeish (77); Paul McStay (76); Tommy Boyd (72)

Top Five All-time Goals – Kenny Dalglish & Denis Law (30); Hughie Gallacher (24); Lawrie Reilly (22), Ally McCoist (19)

protection he was physically assaulted from behind by a spectator while standing on the touchline during a late-season match at Hearts.

Lesser men than Lennon would have put their personal safety first and called it quits, but he chose to stay on and help Celtic regroup for 2011/12. His new counterpart at Ibrox would be Ally McCoist, a former prolific goalscorer for Rangers and Smith's protégé and right-hand man. McCoist was a high-profile figure already in 2010/11, especially during Rangers' run in Europe, which started in the group stage of the UEFA Champions League and ended in the last 16 of the UEFA Europa League. Rangers actually won only one of their ten European games – one fewer than Celtic managed in being bumped out of both European competitions at the first attempt, their age-old travel sickness rearing its ugly head again in heavy defeats away to SC Braga and FC Utrecht.

Because of Scotland's diminishing returns in Europe – with Dundee United, Hibernian FC and Motherwell all joining the Bhoys on the summer scrapheap in 2010 - Celtic's runners-up spot in the 2010/11 SPL was only worth a UEFA Europa League spot, while Rangers were obliged to pre-qualify for the UEFA Champions League. That slide down the UEFA coefficient tables is unlikely to be arrested as long as financial constraints restrict Scottish clubs' ability to attract top-class talent, but there were a few impressive new arrivals to the SPL in 2010/11, with adventurous Honduran left back Emilio Izaguirre proving to be the pick of a cosmopolitan crop of signings at Celtic, and Croatian striker Nikica Jelavić shrugging off the dual handicap of serious injury and European ineligibility to make a profound mark at Rangers – especially after top scorer Kenny Miller left in January to join Turkish club Bursaspor, the team against whom Rangers had claimed that sole European win, 1-0 at Ibrox in the group stage of the UEFA Champions League.

Miller takes armband

Despite playing for only half a season Miller would end up as the SPL's leading marksman, on 21 goals, edging out Celtic's bargain-buy English striker Gary Hooper by one and Scotland's Young Player of the Year, Dundee United's David Goodwillie, by four. Miller was also handed the captaincy of the Scottish national team in the spring, a responsibility he carried proudly into the new Nations Cup tournament, in which Scotland finished second after beating Northern Ireland and Wales but losing the decider 1-0 to hosts the Republic of Ireland.

With no UEFA EURO 2012 qualifying fixtures scheduled for the second half of the season, manager Craig Levein had almost a year in which to contemplate a poor start to the campaign that had brought just one victory in four games – and that a face-saving, last-gasp home win over Liechtenstein. Still, with the emergence of Rangers duo Allan McGregor and Steven Naismith, plus the impressive development of playmaker Charlie Adam in England, where other youngsters are also maturing, there are at least some chinks of light coming into view at the end of a tunnel from which the Tartan Army has not ventured en masse since the 1998 FIFA World Cup in France.

NATIONAL TEAM RESULTS 2010/11

11/8/10	Sweden	A	Solna	0-3	
3/9/10	Lithuania (ECQ)	A	Kaunas	0-0	
7/9/10	Liechtenstein (ECQ)	H	Glasgow	2-1	*Miller (63), McManus (90+7)*
8/10/10	Czech Republic (ECQ)	A	Prague	0-1	
12/10/10	Spain (ECQ)	H	Glasgow	2-3	*Naismith (58), Piqué (66og)*
16/11/10	Faroe Islands	H	Aberdeen	3-0	*Wilson D. (24), Commons (31), Mackie (45)*
9/2/11	Northern Ireland	N	Dublin (IRL)	3-0	*Miller (19), McArthur (32), Commons (51)*
27/3/11	Brazil	N	London (ENG)	0-2	
25/5/11	Wales	N	Dublin (IRL)	3-1	*Morrison (55), Miller (64), Berra (70)*
29/5/11	Republic of Ireland	A	Dublin	0-1	

SCOTLAND

NATIONAL TEAM APPEARANCES 2010/11

Coach – Craig LEVEIN	22/10/64		Swe	LTU	LIE	CZE	ESP	Fro	Nir	Bra	Wal	Irl	Caps	Goals
Allan McGREGOR	31/1/82	Rangers	G	G	G	G	G		G	G	G	G	13	-
Kirk BROADFOOT	8/8/84	Rangers	D74										4	1
Garry KENNETH	21/6/87	Dundee United	D					s60					2	-
Christophe BERRA	31/1/85	Wolves (ENG)	D	s90					D	D73	D	D	13	1
Lee WALLACE	1/8/87	Hearts	D		D54								5	-
Barry ROBSON	7/11/78	Middlesbrough (ENG)	M78	M69	s54	s84					s74	M75	14	-
Darren FLETCHER	1/2/84	Man. United (ENG)	M	M	M	M	M	M68					53	4
Kevin THOMSON	14/10/84	Middlesbrough (ENG)	M54										3	-
Charlie ADAM	10/12/85	Blackpool (ENG)	M64				s46	M55	M58	M78	M88	M63	11	-
James McFADDEN	14/4/83	Birmingham (ENG)	M	s69	M46								48	15
Steven FLETCHER	26/3/87	Wolves (ENG)	A64										8	1
Scott ROBERTSON	7/4/85	Dundee United	s54										2	-
Kris BOYD	18/8/83	Middlesbrough (ENG)	s64		A66								18	7
James MORRISON	25/5/86	West Brom (ENG)	s64	s75	s46	M84	M88		M79	M90	M74		13	1
Steven WHITTAKER	16/6/84	Rangers	s74	D90		D	D 89*			M64	D81	D	12	-
Chris IWELUMO	1/8/78	Burnley (ENG)	s78			s76							4	-
Alan HUTTON	30/11/84	Tottenham (ENG)		D	D	D			D	D			20	-
David WEIR	10/5/70	Rangers		D	D	D	D						69	1
Stephen McMANUS	10/9/82	Middlesbrough (ENG)		D	D	D	D						26	2
Lee McCULLOCH	14/5/78	Rangers		M	M		M46						18	1
Scott BROWN	25/6/85	Celtic		M75	M					M	M	M	25	2
Steven NAISMITH	14/9/86	Rangers		M	s66	M	M		M58		M	M	10	1
Kenny MILLER	23/12/79	Rangers /Bursaspor (TUR)		A	A	s76	A		A87	A87	A	A	55	14
Gary CALDWELL	12/4/82	Wigan (ENG)				M76				D	D84		40	2
Graham DORRANS	5/5/87	West Brom (ENG)				M	M80						5	-
Jamie MACKIE	22/9/85	QPR (ENG)				M76	s80	A					3	1
Phil BARDSLEY	28/6/85	Sunderland (ENG)					D	D71	D58		s81	D	5	-
Shaun MALONEY	24/1/83	Celtic					s88	M					19	1
Craig GORDON	31/12/82	Sunderland (ENG)						G68					40	-
Steven CALDWELL	12/9/80	Wigan (ENG)						D	D				12	-
Danny WILSON	27/12/91	Liverpool (ENG)						D60	s87	s73			3	1
Stephen CRAINEY	22/6/81	Blackpool (ENG)						D		D	D81		9	-
Kris COMMONS	30/8/83	Derby (ENG) /Celtic						M76	M72	s64			9	2
Barry BANNAN	1/12/89	Aston Villa (ENG) /Leeds (ENG)						M	s58	s56	s73	s63	5	-
James McARTHUR	7/10/87	Wigan (ENG)						s55	M	M56	s88		4	1
Cameron BELL	18/9/86	Kilmarnock						s68					1	-
Craig BRYSON	6/11/86	Kilmarnock						s68					1	-
Steven SAUNDERS	23/2/91	Motherwell						s71					1	-
David GOODWILLIE	28/3/89	Dundee United						s76					1	-
Robert SNODGRASS	7/9/87	Leeds (ENG)							s58	s78			2	-
Mark WILSON	5/6/84	Celtic							s58				1	-
Craig CONWAY	2/5/85	Dundee United							s72				2	-
Chris MAGUIRE	16/1/89	Aberdeen							s79			s75	2	-
Craig MACKAIL-SMITH	25/2/84	Peterborough (ENG)								s87			1	-
Don COWIE	15/2/83	Watford (ENG)								s90			3	-
Ross McCORMACK	18/8/86	Leeds (ENG)									M73	s85	7	1
Russell MARTIN	4/1/86	Norwich (ENG)									s81		1	-
Grant HANLEY	20/11/91	Blackburn (ENG)									s84	D	2	-
James FORREST	7/7/91	Celtic										M85	1	-

CLUB-BY-CLUB

ABERDEEN FC

Manager – Mark McGhee; (3/12/10) (Neil Cooper); (10/12/10) Craig Brown
Founded – 1903
Stadium – Pittodrie (22,199)
MAJOR HONOURS: UEFA Cup Winners' Cup – (1) 1983; UEFA Super Cup – (1) 1983; Scottish League – (4) 1955, 1980, 1984, 1985; Scottish Cup – (7) 1947, 1970, 1982, 1983, 1984, 1986, 1990; Scottish League Cup – (5) 1956, 1977, 1986, 1990, 1996.

2010				
14/8	Hamilton	h	4-0	*Hartley 3 (3p), Diamond*
21/8	St Johnstone	a	1-0	*Mackie*
28/8	Kilmarnock	h	0-1	
11/9	Dundee United	a	1-3	*Vernon*
18/9	Motherwell	a	1-1	*Vernon*
26/9	Rangers	h	2-3	*Vernon, Maguire*
2/10	Inverness	a	0-2	
16/10	Hearts	h	0-1	
23/10	Hibernian	h	4-2	*Maguire, og (Bamba), Vernon, Hartley (p)*
30/10	St Mirren	a	1-2	*McArdle*
6/11	Celtic	a	0-9	
9/11	Inverness	h	1-2	*Velička*
13/11	Rangers	a	0-2	
20/11	St Johnstone	h	0-1	
27/11	Kilmarnock	a	0-2	
11/12	Hearts	a	0-5	
26/12	Hibernian	a	2-1	*Folly, Vernon*
29/12	Hamilton	a	1-0	*Vernon*
2011				
1/1	Dundee United	h	1-1	*Maguire*
15/1	St Mirren	h	2-0	*Vernon 2*
22/1	Celtic	a	0-1	
26/1	Inverness	a	2-0	*Jack, Blackman*
1/2	Celtic	h	0-3	
15/2	Motherwell	h	1-2	*Aluko*
19/2	Kilmarnock	h	5-0	*Vernon, Aluko, Maguire (p), McArdle, Magennis*
22/2	Hamilton	h	1-0	*Maguire (p)*
26/2	Hearts	h	0-0	
2/3	St Johnstone	a	0-0	
7/3	Dundee United	a	1-3	*Magennis*
2/4	Motherwell	a	1-2	*Vujadinović*
6/4	St Mirren	a	2-3	*og (Murray), Milsom*
9/4	Hibernian	h	0-1	
13/4	Rangers	h	0-1	
25/4	Hamilton	a	1-1	*Blackman*
30/4	Inverness	h	1-0	*Pawlett*
7/5	St Johnstone	h	0-2	
10/5	St Mirren	h	0-1	
14/5	Hibernian	a	3-1	*Magennis, Maguire 2*

No	Name	Nat	DoB	Pos	Aps	(s)	Gls
11	Sone ALUKO	NGA	19/2/89	A	27	(1)	2
25	Myles ANDERSON	ENG	9/1/90	D		(1)	
24	Nick BLACKMAN	ENG	11/11/89	A	10	(5)	2
6	Andrew CONSIDINE		1/4/87	D	26	(1)	
5	Zander DIAMOND		3/12/85	D	32		1
4	Yoann FOLLY	TOG	6/6/85	M	18		1
3	Richard FOSTER		31/7/85	M		(1)	
43	Ryan FRASER		24/2/94	M		(2)	
17	Fraser FYVIE		27/3/93	M	1	(4)	
52	Jack GRIMMER		25/1/94	M	1	(1)	
35	Hallur HANSSON	FRO	8/7/92	M		(1)	
8	Paul HARTLEY		19/10/76	M	23	(1)	4
21	Mark HOWARD	ENG	21/9/86	G	8	(1)	
16	Jerel IFIL	ENG	27/6/82	D	13	(4)	
22	Ryan JACK		27/2/92	M	26	(4)	1
33	Dean JARVIS	NIR	1/6/92	D		(1)	
1	Jamie LANGFIELD		22/12/79	G	30	(1)	
31	Nicky LOW		6/1/92	M		(1)	
10	Darren MACKIE		1/5/82	A	7	(4)	1
20	Josh MAGENNIS	NIR	15/8/90	A	10	(19)	3
7	Chris MAGUIRE		16/1/89	A	35		7
2	Rory McARDLE	NIR	1/5/87	D	27	(1)	2
3	David McNAMEE		10/10/80	D	9	(1)	
23	Mitchel MEGGINSON		27/7/92	A	1	(5)	
27	Robert MILSOM	ENG	2/1/87	M	18		1
19	Michael PATON		25/3/89	A	4	(6)	
15	Peter PAWLETT		18/6/91	M	6	(7)	1
42	Clark ROBERTSON		5/9/93	D	7	(6)	
37	Joe SHAUGHNESSY	IRL	6/7/92	D	1		
16	Steven SMITH		30/4/85	D	15	(1)	
18	Andrius VELIČKA	LTU	5/4/79	A	1	(5)	1
9	Scott VERNON	ENG	13/12/83	A	29	(4)	9
13	Nikola VUJADINOVIĆ	MNE	31/7/86	D	13	(5)	1
14	Derek YOUNG		27/5/80	M	20	(9)	

CELTIC FC

Manager – Neil Lennon (NIR)
Founded – 1888
Stadium – Celtic Park (60,832)
MAJOR HONOURS: European Champion Clubs' Cup – (1) 1967; Scottish League – (42) 1893, 1894, 1896, 1898, 1905, 1906, 1907, 1908, 1909, 1910, 1914, 1915, 1916, 1917, 1919, 1922, 1926, 1936, 1938, 1954, 1966, 1967, 1968, 1969, 1970, 1971, 1972, 1973, 1974, 1977, 1979, 1981, 1982, 1986, 1988, 1998, 2001, 2002, 2004, 2006, 2007, 2008; Scottish Cup – (35) 1892, 1899, 1900, 1904, 1907, 1908, 1911, 1912, 1914, 1923, 1925, 1927, 1931, 1933, 1937, 1951, 1954, 1965, 1967, 1969, 1971, 1972, 1974, 1975, 1977, 1980, 1985, 1988, 1989, 1995, 2001, 2004, 2005, 2007, 2011; Scottish League Cup – (14) 1957, 1958, 1966, 1967, 1968, 1969, 1970, 1975, 1983, 1998, 2000, 2001, 2006, 2009.

2010				
14/8	Inverness	a	1-0	*McCourt*
22/8	St Mirren	h	4-0	*Ledley, Maloney, Forrest, Ki*
29/8	Motherwell	a	1-0	*Murphy (p)*
11/9	Hearts	h	3-0	*Forrest, Maloney, McCourt*
19/9	Kilmarnock	a	2-1	*Murphy (p), Stokes*
25/9	Hibernian	h	2-1	*Brown, Loovens*
2/10	Hamilton	h	3-1	*Maloney 2, Hooper*
17/10	Dundee United	a	2-1	*Hooper 2*
24/10	Rangers	h	1-3	*Hooper*
30/10	St Johnstone	a	3-0	*McGinn 2, Izaguirre*
6/11	Aberdeen	h	9-0	*Stokes 3 (2p), Hooper 3, og (Magennis), Ledley, McCourt (p)*
10/11	Hearts	a	0-2	
14/11	St Mirren	a	1-0	*Hooper*
20/11	Dundee United	h	1-1	*Hooper*
27/11	Inverness	h	2-2	*Ki, McCourt*
21/12	Kilmarnock	h	1-1	*Rogne*
26/12	St Johnstone	h	2-0	*Cha, Ki*
29/12	Motherwell	h	1-0	*McCourt*
2011				
2/1	Rangers	a	2-0	*Samaras 2 (1p)*
12/1	Hamilton	a	1-1	*Stokes (p)*
15/1	Hibernian	a	3-0	*Hooper, Stokes 2 (1p)*
22/1	Aberdeen	h	1-0	*Stokes*
26/1	Hearts	h	4-0	*Forrest, Stokes 2, McCourt*
1/2	Aberdeen	a	3-0	*Hooper, Wilson, Stokes*
13/2	Dundee United	a	3-1	*Stokes, Wilson, Majstorovic*
20/2	Rangers	h	3-0	*Hooper 2, Commons*
27/2	Motherwell	a	0-2	
5/3	Hamilton	h	2-0	*Commons 2*
6/4	Hibernian	h	3-1	*Stokes, Hooper 2 (1p)*
9/4	St Mirren	h	1-0	*Commons*
12/4	St Johnstone	a	1-0	*Kayal*
20/4	Kilmarnock	a	4-0	*Commons 2, Hooper, Stokes*
24/4	Rangers	a	0-0	
1/5	Dundee United	h	4-1	*Hooper, Kayal, Commons, Murphy*
4/5	Inverness	a	2-3	*Commons 2 (1p)*
8/5	Kilmarnock	a	2-0	*Brown, Commons*
11/5	Hearts	a	3-0	*Hooper 2, Commons*
15/5	Motherwell	h	4-0	*Hooper, Samaras, Maloney, McCourt*

No	Name	Nat	DoB	Pos	Aps	(s)	Gls
8	Scott BROWN		25/6/83	M	26	(2)	2
11	CHA Du-ri	KOR	25/7/80	D	14	(2)	1
15	Kris COMMONS		30/8/83	M	11	(3)	11
17	Marc CROSAS Luque	ESP	9/1/88	M		(1)	
49	James FORREST		7/7/91	A	15	(4)	3
26	Fraser FORSTER	ENG	17/3/88	G	36		
10	Marc-Antoine FORTUNÉ	FRA	2/7/81	A	2		
6	Jos HOOIVELD	NED	22/4/83	D	4	(1)	
88	Gary HOOPER	ENG	26/1/88	A	26		20
3	Emilio IZAGUIRRE	HON	10/5/86	D	33		1
4	Efraín JUÁREZ	MEX	22/2/88	M	5	(8)	
77	Olivier KAPO	FRA	27/8/80	A	1	(1)	
33	Biram KAYAL	ISR	2/5/88	M	18	(3)	2
18	KI Sung-yong	KOR	24/1/89	M	18	(8)	3
16	Joe LEDLEY	WAL	23/1/87	M	26	(3)	2
7	Fredrik LJUNGBERG	SWE	16/4/77	M	1	(6)	
22	Glenn LOOVENS	NED	22/10/83	D	13		1
5	Daniel MAJSTOROVIC	SWE	5/4/77	D	32		1
13	Shaun MALONEY		24/1/83	A	15	(6)	5
20	Patrick McCOURT	NIR	16/12/83	M	8	(17)	7
14	Niall McGINN	NIR	20/7/87	M	6	(5)	2
21	Charles MULGREW		6/3/86	D	20	(3)	
27	Daryl MURPHY	IRL	15/3/83	A	9	(9)	3
25	Thomas ROGNE	NOR	29/6/90	D	14	(2)	1
9	Georgios SAMARAS	GRE	21/2/85	A	16	(6)	3
10	Anthony STOKES	IRL	25/7/88	A	22	(7)	14
45	Lewis TOSHNEY		26/4/92	D		(1)	
31	Richard TOWELL	IRL	17/7/91	M		(1)	
12	Mark WILSON		5/6/84	D	25		2
24	Łukasz ZAŁUSKA	POL	16/6/82	G	2	(1)	

DUNDEE UNITED FC

Manager – Peter Houston

Founded – 1909

Stadium – Tannadice Park (14,209)

MAJOR HONOURS: Scottish League – (1) 1983;
Scottish Cup – (2) 1994, 2010;
Scottish League Cup – (2) 1980, 1981.

2010				
14/8	St Mirren	a	1-1	*Daly*
22/8	Inverness	h	0-4	
29/8	Hearts	a	1-1	*Gomis*
11/9	Aberdeen	h	3-1	*Daly, og (Howard), Goodwillie (p)*
18/9	Rangers	a	0-4	
25/9	St Johnstone	h	1-0	*Goodwillie*
2/10	Kilmarnock	a	2-1	*Goodwillie, Daly*
17/10	Celtic	h	1-2	*Goodwillie*
23/10	Motherwell	a	1-2	*Goodwillie (p)*
30/10	Hibernian	h	1-0	*Goodwillie*
6/11	Hamilton	a	1-0	*Goodwillie*
10/11	St Mirren	h	1-2	*Buaben*
13/11	Kilmarnock	h	1-1	*Russell*
20/11	Celtic	a	1-1	*Dillon*
29/12	Hibernian	a	2-2	*Goodwillie 2*
2011				
1/1	Aberdeen	a	1-1	*Goodwillie*
12/1	Motherwell	h	2-0	*Russell, Goodwillie*
22/1	Kilmarnock	a	1-1	*Kenneth*
26/1	St Mirren	a	1-1	*Robertson D.*
30/1	Hibernian	h	3-0	*Daly, Conway, Russell*
13/2	Celtic	h	1-3	*Goodwillie*
19/2	Hearts	a	1-2	*Douglas*
22/2	St Johnstone	a	0-0	
26/2	Hamilton	a	1-1	*Shala*
1/3	Inverness	a	2-0	*Buaben, Robertson D.*
7/3	Aberdeen	h	3-1	*Douglas, Conway, Swanson*
10/3	Hamilton	h	2-1	*Goodwillie, Daly*
16/3	Hearts	h	2-0	*Russell 2*
19/3	Inverness	h	1-0	*Swanson*
2/4	Rangers	a	3-2	*Robertson D., Russell, Goodwillie*
6/4	Motherwell	a	1-2	*Russell*
9/4	St Johnstone	h	2-0	*Russell, Robertson D.*
19/4	Rangers	h	0-4	
23/4	Kilmarnock	h	4-2	*Severin, Goodwillie 2, Conway*
1/5	Celtic	a	1-4	*Russell*
7/5	Motherwell	h	4-0	*Daly 3, Watson*
10/5	Rangers	a	0-2	
15/5	Hearts	h	2-1	*Daly, Goodwillie*

No	Name	Nat	DoB	Pos	Aps	(s)	Gls
25	Stuart ARMSTRONG		30/3/92	M	2	(9)	
15	Prince BUABEN	GHA	23/4/88	D	29	(6)	2
10	Danny CADAMARTERI	ENG	12/10/79	A	2	(8)	
6	Craig CONWAY		2/5/85	M	21	(2)	3
9	Jonathan DALY	IRL	2/5/85	A	18	(11)	9
2	Sean DILLON	IRL	30/7/83	D	34		1
3	Pau DIXON		22/11/86	D	28	(2)	
5	Darren DODS		7/6/75	D	3		
17	Barry DOUGLAS		4/9/89	D	19	(4)	2
30	Ryan DOW		7/6/91	A		(1)	
16	Morgaro "Jimmy" GOMIS	SEN	14/7/85	M	32	(2)	1
25	David GOODWILLIE		28/3/89	A	37	(1)	17
18	Gary KENNETH		21/6/87	D	26	(2)	1
19	Mihael KOVACEVIC	SUI	6/3/88	D	2		
7	Jennison MYRIE-WILLIAMS	ENG	17/5/88	M		(1)	
1	Dušan PERNIŠ	SVK	28/11/84	G	38		
12	David ROBERTSON		23/9/86	M	22	(8)	4
8	Scott ROBERTSON		7/4/85	M	29	(5)	
27	Jonathan RUSSELL		8/4/90	A	21	(9)	9
4	Scott SEVERIN		15/2/79	D	14	(1)	1
20	Andis SHALA	GER	15/11/88	A	1	(9)	1
14	Daniel SWANSON		28/12/86	M	9	(12)	2
21	Timothy VAN DER MEULEN	NED	2/3/90	D	4	(3)	
23	Keith WATSON		14/11/89	D	27	(2)	1

HAMILTON ACADEMICAL FC

Coach – Billy Reid

Founded – 1874

Stadium – New Douglas Park (6,078)

2010				
14/8	Aberdeen	a	0-4	
21/8	Hearts	h	0-4	
28/8	Inverness	a	1-0	*Imrie*
11/9	Rangers	h	1-2	*og (Bougherra)*
18/9	Hibernian	a	1-1	*Marco Paixão*
25/9	Kilmarnock	h	2-2	*Flávio Paixão, Hasselbaink*
2/10	Celtic	a	1-3	*McLaughlin*
16/10	St Mirren	a	2-2	*Routledge, Imrie*
23/10	St Johnstone	h	1-2	*Mensing (p)*
30/10	Motherwell	a	1-0	*Hasselbaink*
6/11	Dundee United	h	0-1	
10/11	Kilmarnock	a	0-3	
13/11	Inverness	h	1-3	*Imrie*
20/11	Hearts	a	0-2	
27/11	St Mirren	h	0-0	
29/12	Aberdeen	h	0-1	
2011				
1/1	Motherwell	h	0-0	
12/1	Celtic	h	1-1	*Mensing*
15/1	Rangers	a	0-4	
22/1	Inverness	a	1-1	*Antoine-Curier (p)*
29/1	Kilmarnock	h	1-1	*Antoine-Curier*
1/2	St Johnstone	a	0-2	
12/2	Hearts	h	0-2	
19/2	Motherwell	a	0-1	
22/2	Aberdeen	a	0-1	
26/2	Dundee United	h	1-1	*Antoine-Curier (p)*
1/3	Hibernian	h	1-2	*Flávio Paixão*
5/3	Celtic	a	0-2	
10/3	Dundee United	a	1-2	*Flávio Paixão*
19/3	St Johnstone	h	0-0	
2/4	St Mirren	a	1-3	*Buchanan*
10/4	Rangers	h	0-1	

17/4	Hibernian	a	2-1	*Chambers, og (Miller)*
25/4	Aberdeen	h	1-1	*Imrie*
2/5	St Mirren	a	1-0	*Antoine-Curier*
7/5	Hibernian	h	1-0	*Hasselbaink*
10/5	St Johnstone	a	0-1	
14/5	Inverness	h	1-2	*Mensing*

No	Name	Nat	DoB	Pos	Aps	(s)	Gls
99	Mickaël ANTOINE-CURIER	FRA	5/3/83	A	10	(3)	4
12	David BUCHANAN	NIR	6/5/86	D	27	(1)	1
4	Martin CANNING		3/12/81	D	23		
13	Mark CARRINGTON	ENG	4/5/87	M	6	(6)	
9	Damián CASALINUOVO	ARG	6/6/87	A	6	(13)	
1	Tomáš ČERNÝ	CZE	10/4/85	G	37		
16	James CHAMBERS	IRL	14/2/87	M	6	(3)	1
17	Alister CRAWFORD		30/7/91	M	9	(5)	
32	Michael DEVLIN		3/10/93	M	1		
25	David ELEBERT	IRL	21/3/86	D	16	(3)	
36	Thomas ELLIOTT	ENG	9/11/89	A	1	(6)	
18	FLÁVIO Emanuel Lopes PAIXÃO	POR	19/9/84	A	26	(4)	3
24	Grant GILLESPIE		2/7/91	D	8	(9)	
2	James GOODWIN	IRL	20/11/81	D	14		
34	Ziggy GORDON		1/1/94	D	2		
5	Andrew GRAHAM		22/9/83	D	10	(5)	
30	Nigel HASSELBAINK	NED	21/11/90	A	21	(6)	3
28	David HOPKIRK		17/1/93	A	2	(3)	
7	Douglas IMRIE		3/8/83	M	35		4
33	Lee KILDAY		4/2/92	D	4	(1)	
20	Jordan KIRKPATRICK		6/3/92	M	2	(3)	
15	Derek LYLE		13/2/81	A	1	(3)	
21	MARCO Filipe Lopes PAIXÃO	POR	19/9/84	A	9	(9)	1
11	James McALISTER		2/11/85	M	15	(4)	
8	Gary McDONALD		10/4/82	M	22	(3)	
6	Mark McLAUGHLIN		2/12/75	D	21		1
38	Brian McQUEEN		1/1/91	M	1		
27	Simon MENSING	ENG	27/6/82	M	30		3
9	Kieran MILLAR		14/10/93	A		(1)	
19	Sean MURDOCH		31/7/86	G	1		
10	Alexander NEIL		9/6/81	M	8	(2)	
	Jack ROSS		5/6/76	D	2		
22	Jonathan ROUTLEDGE	ENG	23/11/89	M	22	(2)	1
3	Gavin SKELTON	ENG	27/3/81	M	14	(2)	
16	Joël THOMAS	FRA	30/6/87	A	1	(2)	
15	Aaron WILDIG	WAL	26/1/90	M	2	(1)	
14	Kyle WILKIE		20/2/91	M	3	(3)	

HEART OF MIDLOTHIAN FC

Manager – Jim Jefferies

Founded – 1874

Stadium – Tynecastle Stadium (17,420)

MAJOR HONOURS: Scottish League – (4) 1895, 1897, 1958, 1960; Scottish Cup – (7) 1891, 1896, 1901, 1906, 1956, 1998, 2006; Scottish League Cup – (4) 1955, 1959, 1960, 1963.

2010

14/8	St Johnstone	h	1-1	*Elliott C.*
21/8	Hamilton	a	4-0	*Elliott C. 2, Templeton, Kyle (p)*
29/8	Dundee United	h	1-1	*Templeton*
11/9	Celtic	a	0-3	
18/9	Inverness	a	3-1	*og (Innes), Stevenson, Elliott C.*
25/9	Motherwell	h	0-2	
2/10	Rangers	h	1-2	*Skácel*
16/10	Aberdeen	a	1-0	*Kyle*
23/10	St Mirren	h	3-0	*Skácel 3*
31/10	Kilmarnock	h	0-3	
7/11	Hibernian	a	2-0	*Templeton, Elliott S.*
10/11	Celtic	h	2-0	*Black, Templeton*
13/11	St Johnstone	a	2-0	*Kyle (p), Stevenson*
20/11	Hamilton	h	2-0	*Skácel, Templeton*
11/12	Aberdeen	h	5-0	*Templeton, Skácel 2, Elliott S., Novikovas*
14/12	Motherwell	a	2-1	*og (Reynolds), Kyle (p)*
18/12	Inverness	h	1-1	*Kyle (p)*
29/12	St Mirren	a	2-0	*Templeton, Kyle (p)*
2011				
1/1	Hibernian	h	1-0	*Kyle*
18/1	Kilmarnock	a	2-1	*Elliott S. 2*
22/1	Rangers	h	1-0	*Stevenson*
26/1	Celtic	a	0-4	
29/1	St Johnstone	h	1-0	*Skácel*
2/2	Rangers	a	0-1	
12/2	Hamilton	a	2-0	*Elliott S. 2*
19/2	Dundee United	h	2-1	*Skácel, Žaliūkas*
26/2	Aberdeen	a	0-0	
5/3	Kilmarnock	h	0-2	
16/3	Dundee United	a	0-2	
19/3	St Mirren	h	3-2	*Skácel 2, Stevenson*
3/4	Hibernian	a	2-2	*Stevenson, Elliott S.*
9/4	Motherwell	h	0-0	
16/4	Inverness	a	1-1	*Elliott S.*
23/4	Motherwell	h	3-3	*Thomson C. (p), Skácel, Stevenson*
30/4	Kilmarnock	a	2-2	*Skácel, Stevenson*
7/5	Rangers	a	0-4	
11/5	Celtic	h	0-3	
15/5	Dundee United	a	1-2	*Glen*

No	Name	Nat	DoB	Pos	Aps	(s)	Gls
5	Darren BARR		17/3/85	D	11	(2)	
8	Ian BLACK		14/3/85	M	29	(3)	1
21	Ismaël BOUZID	ALG	21/7/83	D	31	(1)	
11	Andrew DRIVER	ENG	12/11/87	M	4	(10)	
14	Calum ELLIOTT		30/3/87	A	11	(8)	4
10	Stephen ELLIOTT	IRL	6/1/84	A	21	(9)	8
23	Gary GLEN		12/3/90	A	2	(9)	1
4	Eggert Gunnthor JÓNSSON	ISL	18/8/88	D	29		
25	Marián KELLO	SVK	5/9/82	G	31		
9	Kevin KYLE		7/6/81	A	16	(3)	7
30	Jamie MACDONALD		17/4/86	G	7		
17	Ryan McGOWAN	AUS	15/8/89	D	3	(5)	
31	Adrian MROWIEC	POL	1/12/83	M	26	(4)	
18	Arvydas NOVIKOVAS	LTU	18/12/90	M	1	(5)	1
13	David OBUA	UGA	10/4/84	M	7	(6)	
27	Scott ROBINSON		12/3/92	A	1	(3)	
6	RUBÉN PALAZUELOS García	ESP	11/4/83	M	31	(2)	
19	Rudolf SKÁCEL	CZE	17/7/79	M	27	(2)	13
22	Gordon SMITH		14/2/91	A		(1)	
16	Ryan STEVENSON		1/1/83	M	18	(13)	7
7	Jesús Manuel "SUSO" SANTANA Abréu	ESP	2/3/85	M	16	(3)	
12	David TEMPLETON		7/1/89	M	27	(5)	7
24	Craig THOMSON		17/4/91	D	20	(7)	1
20	Jason THOMSON		26/7/87	D	3	(3)	
3	Lee WALLACE		1/8/87	D	9		
15	Andrew WEBSTER		23/4/82	D	9		
26	Marius ŽALIŪKAS	LTU	10/11/83	D	28		1

HIBERNIAN FC

Manager – John Hughes; (18/10/10) Colin Calderwood

Founded – 1875

Stadium – Easter Road (20,421)

MAJOR HONOURS: Scottish League – (4) 1903, 1948, 1951, 1952; Scottish Cup – (2) 1887, 1902; Scottish League Cup – (3) 1973, 1992, 2007.

2010

15/8	Motherwell	a	3-2	*Stokes, Hanlon, Miller*
22/8	Rangers	h	0-3	
29/8	St Mirren	a	0-1	
11/9	Inverness	h	1-1	*Riordan*
18/9	Hamilton	h	1-1	*Riordan*
25/9	Celtic	a	1-2	*Riordan*
2/10	St Johnstone	a	0-2	
16/10	Kilmarnock	h	2-1	*Hogg 2*

23/10	Aberdeen	a	2-4	*Nish, Bamba*
30/10	Dundee United	a	0-1	
7/11	Hearts	h	0-2	
10/11	Rangers	a	3-0	*Miller, Rankin, Dickoh*
13/11	Motherwell	h	2-1	*Riordan 2*
20/11	Inverness	a	2-4	*Riordan, Miller (p)*
27/11	St Johnstone	h	0-0	
18/12	Kilmarnock	a	1-2	*Riordan*
26/12	Aberdeen	h	1-2	*Riordan*
29/12	Dundee United	h	2-2	*Bamba, Hanlon*
2011				
1/1	Hearts	a	0-1	
15/1	Celtic	h	0-3	
22/1	Motherwell	a	0-2	
26/1	Rangers	h	0-2	
30/1	Dundee United	a	0-3	
2/2	St Mirren	h	2-0	*Riordan, Wotherspoon*
12/2	Kilmarnock	h	2-1	*Sodje, Pálsson (p)*
20/2	St Mirren	a	1-0	*Dickoh*
26/2	Inverness	h	2-0	*Booth, Stevenson*
1/3	Hamilton	a	2-1	*Sodje, Riordan*
5/3	St Johnstone	a	1-1	*Wotherspoon*
3/4	Hearts	h	2-2	*Miller (p), Vaz Té*
6/4	Celtic	a	1-3	*Miller (p)*
9/4	Aberdeen	a	1-0	*Sodje*
17/4	Hamilton	h	1-2	*Sodje*
24/4	St Mirren	h	1-1	*Sodje*
30/4	St Johnstone	h	1-2	*Sodje*
7/5	Hamilton	a	0-1	
11/5	Inverness	a	0-2	
14/5	Aberdeen	h	1-3	*Riordan*

No	Name	Nat	DoB	Pos	Aps	(s)	Gls
8	Souleymane BAMBA	CIV	13/1/85	D	16		2
28	Callum BOOTH		30/5/91	D	17		1
31	Mark BROWN		28/2/81	G	26		
29	Kurtis BYRNE	IRL	9/4/90	A		(3)	
8	Edwin DE GRAAF	NED	30/4/80	M	16	(2)	
14	Francis DICKOH	GHA	13/12/82	D	27	(1)	2
41	Jakub DIVIŠ	CZE	27/7/86	G	3		
19	Darryl DUFFY		16/4/84	A	2	(5)	
22	Daniel GALBRAITH		19/8/90	M	8	(14)	
3	Jonathan GROUNDS	ENG	2/2/88	D	13		
39	Daniel HANDLING		6/2/94	M		(1)	
20	Paul HANLON		20/1/90	D	30	(3)	2
2	Michael HART		10/2/80	D	16	(2)	
4	Christopher HOGG	ENG	21/3/85	D	6	(1)	2
27	Lewis HORNER	ENG	1/2/92	M		(1)	
17	Kevin McBRIDE		14/6/81	M	10	(1)	
33	Liam MILLER	IRL	13/2/81	M	30	(3)	5
6	Ian MURRAY		20/3/81	M	14	(6)	
9	Colin NISH		3/7/81	A	11	(9)	1
91	Gudlaugur Victor PÁLSSON	ISL	30/4/91	M	15	(1)	1
11	John RANKIN		27/6/83	M	14	(3)	1
10	Derek RIORDAN		16/1/83	A	28	(5)	11
44	Martin SCOTT		15/2/86	M	8	(3)	
21	Graeme SMITH		8/6/83	G	3	(1)	
18	Akpo SODJE	ENG	31/1/80	A	13	(2)	6
1	Graham STACK	IRL	26/9/81	G	6		
25	David STEPHENS	WAL	18/10/91	D	6	(4)	
16	Lewis STEVENSON		5/1/88	M	11	(8)	1
18	Anthony STOKES	IRL	25/7/88	A	3		1
30	Scott TAGGART		27/12/91	D	2	(1)	
15	Steven THICOT	FRA	14/2/87	D	4	(3)	
26	Matthew THORNHILL	ENG	11/10/88	M	5	(3)	
34	Richard TOWELL	IRL	17/7/91	D	15	(1)	
23	Valdas TRAKYS	LTU	20/3/79	A	4	(5)	
8	Ricardo Jorge VAZ TÉ	POR	1/10/86	A	7	(3)	1
24	David WOTHERSPOON		29/12/91	M	26	(9)	2
7	Meroaune ZEMMAMA	MAR	7/10/83	M	3	(1)	

INVERNESS CALEDONIAN THISTLE FC

Manager – Terry Butcher (ENG)

Founded – 1994

Stadium – Caledonian Stadium (7,819)

2010				
14/8	Celtic	h	0-1	
22/8	Dundee United	a	4-0	*McCann, Rooney 2 (1p), Duncan*
28/8	Hamilton	h	0-1	
11/9	Hibernian	a	1-1	*Rooney (p)*
18/9	Hearts	h	1-3	*Odhiambo*
25/9	St Mirren	a	2-1	*Odhiambo 2*
2/10	Aberdeen	h	2-0	*Hayes, Rooney*
16/10	St Johnstone	h	1-1	*Hayes*
23/10	Kilmarnock	a	2-1	*Rooney (p), Hayes*
30/10	Rangers	a	1-1	*Odhiambo*
6/11	Motherwell	h	1-2	*Duff*
9/11	Aberdeen	a	2-1	*Rooney (p), Munro*
13/11	Hamilton	a	3-1	*Rooney 2, Hayes*
20/11	Hibernian	h	4-2	*Foran, Rooney 3 (1p)*
27/11	Celtic	a	2-2	*Foran, Munro*
11/12	Rangers	h	1-1	*Hayes*
18/12	Hearts	a	1-1	*Munro*
26/12	St Mirren	h	1-2	*Cox*
29/12	Kilmarnock	h	1-3	*Foran*
2011				
2/1	St Johnstone	a	0-1	
15/1	Motherwell	a	0-0	
18/1	Rangers	a	0-1	
22/1	Hamilton	h	1-1	*Dani Sánchez*
26/1	Aberdeen	h	0-2	
12/2	St Mirren	a	3-3	*Rooney 2, Doran*
19/2	St Johnstone	h	2-0	*Tokely, Duncan*
26/2	Hibernian	a	0-2	
1/3	Dundee United	h	0-2	
5/3	Motherwell	h	3-0	*Sutherland, Foran, MacDonald*
19/3	Dundee United	a	0-1	
9/4	Kilmarnock	a	1-1	*Hayes*
16/4	Hearts	h	1-1	*Doran*
25/4	St Johnstone	a	3-0	*Innes, Doran, Foran*
30/4	Aberdeen	a	0-1	
4/5	Celtic	h	3-2	*og (Mulgrew), Munro, Sutherland*
7/5	St Mirren	h	1-0	*Rooney*
11/5	Hibernian	h	2-0	*Rooney, Ross*
14/5	Hamilton	a	2-1	*Foran, Rooney*

No	Name	Nat	DoB	Pos	Aps	(s)	Gls
18	Gil BLUMENSHTEIN	ISR	21/5/90	M	1	(4)	
6	Lee COX	ENG	2/12/90	M	25	(2)	1
23	DANIel SÁNCHEZ Andrades	ESP	10/11/84	A	3	(6)	1
26	Aaron DORAN	IRL	13/5/91	A	11	(3)	3
4	Stuart DUFF		23/1/82	D	34		1
8	Russell DUNCAN		15/9/80	M	20	(4)	2
1	Ryan ESSON		19/3/80	G	35		
9	Richard FORAN	IRL	16/6/80	A	30	(2)	6
24	Kenny GILLET	FRA	3/1/86	D	12	(1)	
5	Stuart GOLABEK		5/11/74	D		(2)	
11	Jonathan HAYES	IRL	9/7/87	M	23	(1)	6
28	Christopher HOGG		12/3/85	D	10		
15	Christopher INNES		13/7/76	D	10	(3)	1
27	Alexander MacDONALD		14/4/90	A	2	(8)	1
16	Roy McBAIN		7/11/84	M		(2)	
25	Kevin McCANN		11/9/87	D	8		1
17	Gavin MORRISON		3/1/90	M	3	(7)	
14	Grant MUNRO		15/9/80	D	34	(1)	4
7	Eric ODHIAMBO	TAN	12/5/89	A	18	(13)	4
39	Liam POLWORTH		12/10/94	M		(1)	
2	David PROCTOR		4/5/84	D	7	(3)	
10	Adam ROONEY	IRL	21/4/88	A	37	(1)	15
19	Nicholas ROSS		11/11/91	M	30	(4)	1
21	Graeme SHINNIE		4/8/91	D	19		
20	Shane SUTHERLAND		23/10/90	A	9	(20)	2
3	Ross TOKELY		8/3/79	D	34	(1)	1
12	Jonathan TUFFEY	NIR	20/1/87	G	3		

KILMARNOCK FC

Manager – Mixu Paatelainen (FIN); (1/4/11) (Kenny Shiels)
Founded – 1869
Stadium – Rugby Park (18,128)
MAJOR HONOURS: Scottish League – (1) 1965; Scottish Cup – (3) 1920, 1929, 1997.

2010				
14/8	Rangers	a	1-2	*Hamill*
22/8	Motherwell	h	0-1	
28/8	Aberdeen	a	1-0	*Hamill*
11/9	St Mirren	h	2-1	*Dayton, Eremenko*
19/9	Celtic	h	1-2	*Sammon*
25/9	Hamilton	a	2-2	*Hamill, Sammon*
2/10	Dundee United	h	1-2	*Sammon*
16/10	Hibernian	a	1-2	*David Silva*
23/10	Inverness	h	1-2	*Rui Miguel*
31/10	Hearts	a	3-0	*Wright, Sammon, Eremenko*
6/11	St Johnstone	a	3-0	*og (Duberry), Sammon, Kelly*
10/11	Hamilton	h	3-0	*Gordon, Sammon 2*
13/11	Dundee United	a	1-1	*Sammon*
20/11	Rangers	h	2-3	*Sammon 2*
27/11	Aberdeen	h	2-0	*Sammon, Hamill (p)*
18/12	Hibernian	h	2-1	*Kelly 2*
21/12	Celtic	a	1-1	*Sammon*
29/12	Inverness	a	3-1	*Bryson, Kelly, Hamill*
2011				
3/1	St Mirren	a	2-0	*Kelly, Bryson*
15/1	St Johnstone	h	1-1	*Sammon*
18/1	Hearts	h	1-2	*Rui Miguel*
22/1	Dundee United	h	1-1	*Sammon*
29/1	Hamilton	a	1-1	*Sammon*
2/2	Motherwell	a	1-0	*David Silva*
12/2	Hibernian	a	1-2	*Hamill (p)*
19/2	Aberdeen	a	0-5	
26/2	St Mirren	h	2-0	*Gros, Eremenko*
5/3	Hearts	a	2-0	*David Silva, Eremenko*
13/3	Rangers	a	1-2	*Hamill (p)*
19/3	Motherwell	h	3-1	*Pascali, Hamill (p), Kelly*
2/4	St Johnstone	a	0-0	
9/4	Inverness	h	1-1	*Kelly*
20/4	Celtic	h	0-4	
23/4	Dundee United	a	2-4	*David Silva, Pascali*
30/4	Hearts	h	2-2	*Fowler, Agard*
8/5	Celtic	h	0-2	
11/5	Motherwell	a	1-1	*Aubameyang*
15/5	Rangers	h	1-5	*Dayton*

No	Name	Nat	DoB	Pos	Aps	(s)	Gls
17	Kieran AGARD	ENG	10/10/89	A	3	(5)	1
87	William Fils AUBAMEYANG	GAB	16/2/87	M	4	(2)	1
13	Cameron BELL		18/9/86	G	31		
15	Billy BERNTSSON	SWE	6/1/84	D		(4)	
7	Craig BRYSON		6/11/86	M	33		2
2	Timothy CLANCY	IRL	8/6/84	D	19	(2)	
14	DAVID Mendes da SILVA	POR	11/10/86	M	17	(12)	4
23	James DAYTON	ENG	12/12/88	M	7	(3)	2
20	Alexei EREMENKO Jr	FIN	24/3/83	M	31		4
34	Gary FISHER		6/6/92	D		(3)	
19	Harry FORRESTER	ENG	2/1/91	A	3	(4)	
4	James FOWLER		26/10/80	D	21	(5)	1
16	Benjamin GORDON	ENG	2/3/91	D	18		1
28	William GROS	FRA	31/3/92	A	8	(3)	1
8	Jamie HAMILL		29/7/86	M	31	(1)	8
3	Garry HAY		9/7/77	D	17	(5)	
11	Danny INVINCIBILE	AUS	31/3/79	M	3	(4)	
53	Anssi JAAKKOLA	FIN	13/3/87	G	7	(1)	
22	Liam KELLY		10/2/90	M	30	(2)	7
38	Rory McKENZIE		7/10/93	A		(1)	
19	Ryan O'LEARY		24/8/87	D	3		
29	Manuel PASCALI	ITA	9/9/81	A	34	(1)	2
26	Alex PURSEHOUSE	ENG	6/5/92	D		(1)	
9	RUI MIGUEL Marinho Reis	POR	30/1/84	A	8	(12)	2
18	Conor SAMMON	IRL	6/11/86	A	19	(4)	15
6	Mahamadou SISSOKO	FRA	8/8/88	D	26	(1)	
10	Mehdi TAOUIL	MAR	20/5/83	M	18	(6)	
5	Frazer WRIGHT		23/12/79	D	27		1

MOTHERWELL FC

Manager – Craig Brown; (10/12/10) (Gordon Young); (30/12/10) Stuart McCall
Founded – 1886
Stadium – Fir Park (13,742)
MAJOR HONOURS: Scottish League – (1) 1932; Scottish Cup – (2) 1952, 1991; Scottish League Cup – (1) 1951.

2010				
15/8	Hibernian	h	2-3	*Sutton, Murphy (p)*
22/8	Kilmarnock	a	1-0	*Blackman*
29/8	Celtic	h	0-1	
11/9	St Johnstone	a	2-0	*Blackman, og (Rutkiewicz)*
18/9	Aberdeen	h	1-1	*Murphy*
25/9	Hearts	a	2-0	*Blackman, Sutton*
2/10	St Mirren	h	3-1	*Humphrey, Hateley (p), Murphy*
16/10	Rangers	a	1-4	*Blackman*
23/10	Dundee United	h	2-1	*og (Severin), og (Dillon)*
30/10	Hamilton	h	0-1	
6/11	Inverness	a	2-1	*Gow, Blackman*
10/11	St Johnstone	h	4-0	*Blackman 3, Sutton*
13/11	Hibernian	a	1-2	*Blackman (p)*
20/11	St Mirren	a	1-1	*Blackman*
14/12	Hearts	h	1-2	*Lasley*
26/12	Rangers	h	1-4	*Sutton*
29/12	Celtic	a	0-1	
2011				
1/1	Hamilton	a	0-0	
12/1	Dundee United	a	0-2	
15/1	Inverness	h	0-0	
22/1	Hibernian	h	2-0	*Murphy, Saunders*
26/1	St Johnstone	a	0-1	
2/2	Kilmarnock	h	0-1	
12/2	Rangers	a	0-6	
15/2	Aberdeen	a	2-1	*Jeffers, Murphy*
19/2	Hamilton	h	1-0	*Sutton (p)*
23/2	St Mirren	h	0-1	
27/2	Celtic	h	2-0	*Sutton 2 (1p)*
5/3	Inverness	a	0-3	
19/3	Kilmarnock	a	1-3	*Sutton*
2/4	Aberdeen	h	2-1	*Humphrey, Hutchinson*
6/4	Dundee United	h	2-1	*Murphy, Humphrey*
9/4	Hearts	a	0-0	
23/4	Hearts	a	3-3	*Sutton 2, Hateley*
30/4	Rangers	h	0-5	
7/5	Dundee United	a	0-4	
11/5	Kilmarnock	h	1-1	*Jones*
15/5	Celtic	a	0-4	

No	Name	Nat	DoB	Pos	Aps	(s)	Gls
22	Nick BLACKMAN	ENG	11/11/89	A	15	(3)	10
42	Stewart CARSWELL		9/9/93	M	3	(1)	
31	Angelis CHARALAMBOUS	CYP	31/5/89	D		(1)	
5	Stephen CRAIGAN	NIR	29/10/76	D	32	(3)	
23	ESTEBAN Casagolda Collazo	ESP	5/1/87	A	3	(9)	
17	Marc FITZPATRICK		11/5/86	D	3	(2)	
18	Ross FORBES		3/3/89	M	11	(12)	
24	Alan GOW		9/10/82	A	9	(6)	1
4	Gavin GUNNING	IRL	26/1/91	D	12	(2)	
3	Steven HAMMELL		18/2/82	D	26	(5)	
6	Thomas HATELEY	ENG	12/9/89	M	36	(2)	2
12	Lee HOLLIS		12/3/86	G	1		
7	Christopher HUMPHREY		19/9/87	M	33	(3)	3
19	Shaun HUTCHINSON	ENG	23/11/90	D	18	(1)	1
24	Francis JEFFERS	ENG	25/1/81	A	8	(2)	1
8	Steven JENNINGS	ENG	28/10/84	M	30		
17	Steven JONES	NIR	25/10/76	M	10	(2)	1
14	Keith LASLEY		21/9/79	M	26		1
16	Robert McHUGH		16/7/91	A		(11)	
27	Steven MEECHAN		30/3/91	M		(2)	
9	Jamie MURPHY		28/8/89	A	31	(4)	6
20	Jonathan PAGE	ENG	8/2/90	D	3	(6)	
32	Jamie POLLOCK		20/2/92	M		(3)	
10	Darren RANDOLPH	IRL	12/5/87	G	37		
4	Mark REYNOLDS		7/5/87	D	19		

4	Maurice ROSS		3/2/81	D	5	(1)	
2	Steven SAUNDERS		23/2/91	D	22	(3)	1
33	Gary SMITH		28/5/91	A		(1)	
11	John SUTTON	ENG	26/12/83	A	25	(10)	10

RANGERS FC

Manager – Walter Smith

Founded – 1873

Stadium – Ibrox Stadium (51,082)

MAJOR HONOURS: UEFA Cup Winners' Cup – (1) 1972;
Scottish League – (54) 1891 (joint), 1899, 1900, 1901, 1902, 1911, 1912, 1913, 1918, 1920, 1921, 1923, 1924, 1925, 1927, 1928, 1929, 1930, 1931, 1933, 1934, 1935, 1937, 1939, 1947, 1949, 1950, 1953, 1956, 1957, 1959, 1961, 1963, 1964, 1975, 1976, 1978, 1987, 1989, 1990, 1991, 1992, 1993, 1994, 1995, 1996, 1997, 1999, 2000, 2003, 2005, 2009, 2010, 2011;
Scottish Cup – (33) 1894, 1897, 1898, 1903, 1928, 1930, 1932, 1934, 1935, 1936, 1948, 1949, 1950, 1953, 1960, 1962, 1963, 1964, 1966, 1973, 1976, 1978, 1979, 1981, 1992, 1993, 1996, 1999, 2000, 2002, 2003, 2008, 2009;
Scottish League Cup – (27) 1947, 1949, 1961, 1962, 1964, 1965, 1971, 1976, 1978, 1979, 1982, 1984, 1985, 1987, 1988, 1989, 1991, 1993, 1994, 1997, 1999, 2002, 2003, 2005, 2008, 2010, 2011.

2010				
14/8	Kilmarnock	h	2-1	*Miller, Naismith*
22/8	Hibernian	a	3-0	*Miller 3*
28/8	St Johnstone	h	2-1	*Papac, Miller*
11/9	Hamilton	a	2-1	*Jelavić, Miller*
18/9	Dundee United	h	4-0	*og (Dillon), Miller 2, Naismith*
26/9	Aberdeen	a	3-2	*Miller 2 (1p), Jelavić*
2/10	Hearts	a	2-1	*Lafferty, Naismith*
16/10	Motherwell	h	4-1	*Naismith, Davis, Miller, Weiss*
24/10	Celtic	a	3-1	*og (Loovens), Miller 2 (1p)*
30/10	Inverness	h	1-1	*Edu*
7/11	St Mirren	a	3-1	*og (McAusland), Naismith, Miller*
10/11	Hibernian	h	0-3	
13/11	Aberdeen	h	2-0	*Miller, Weiss*
20/11	Kilmarnock	a	3-2	*Miller 3 (2p)*
11/12	Inverness	a	1-1	*Miller*
26/12	Motherwell	a	4-1	*Miller 2, og (Saunders), Weiss*
2011				
2/1	Celtic	h	0-2	
15/1	Hamilton	h	4-0	*Weiss 2, Whittaker (p), Edu*
18/1	Inverness	h	1-0	*Davis*
22/1	Hearts	a	0-1	
26/1	Hibernian	a	2-0	*Bougherra, Jelavić*
2/2	Hearts	h	1-0	*Lafferty*
12/2	Motherwell	h	6-0	*Naismith, Jelavić 3, og (Hutchinson), Healy*
20/2	Celtic	a	0-3	
27/2	St Johnstone	h	4-0	*Jelavić 2, Lafferty, Papac*
6/3	St Mirren	a	1-0	*Bartley*
13/3	Kilmarnock	h	2-1	*Diouf, og (Clancy)*
2/4	Dundee United	h	2-3	*Jelavić, Naismith*
5/4	St Johnstone	a	2-0	*Lafferty, Naismith*
10/4	Hamilton	a	1-0	*Jelavić*
13/4	Aberdeen	a	1-0	*Jelavić*
16/4	St Mirren	h	2-1	*Papac, Whittaker (p)*
19/4	Dundee United	a	4-0	*Whittaker 2 (2p), Jelavić, Lafferty*
24/4	Celtic	h	0-0	
30/4	Motherwell	a	5-0	*Lafferty, Davis, Jelavić, Naismith 2*
7/5	Hearts	h	4-0	*Jelavić, Lafferty, Davis, og (Stevenson)*
10/5	Dundee United	h	2-0	*Jelavić, Lafferty*
15/5	Kilmarnock	a	5-1	*Lafferty 3, Naismith, Jelavić*

No	Name	Nat	DoB	Pos	Aps	(s)	Gls
25	Neil ALEXANDER		10/3/78	G	1		
21	Kyle BARTLEY	ENG	22/5/91	D	5		1
19	James BEATTIE	ENG	27/2/78	A	5	(2)	
24	Madjid BOUGHERRA	ALG	7/10/82	D	31		1
4	Kirk BROADFOOT		8/8/84	D	5	(3)	
8	Steven DAVIS	NIR	1/1/85	M	37		4
17	El Hadji DIOUF	SEN	15/1/81	A	6	(9)	1
7	Maurice EDU	USA	18/4/86	M	27	(6)	2
10	John FLECK		24/8/91	M	3	(10)	
12	Richard FOSTER		31/7/85	D	11	(4)	
15	David HEALY	NIR	5/8/79	A	2	(6)	1
41	Kyle HUTTON		5/2/91	M	1	(6)	
18	Nikica JELAVIĆ	CRO	27/8/85	A	20	(8)	16
28	Salim KERKAR	FRA	4/8/87	M		(1)	
11	Kyle LAFFERTY	NIR	16/9/87	A	23	(8)	11
34	Rory LOY		19/3/88	A		(1)	
6	Lee McCULLOCH		14/5/78	D	17	(4)	
10	Allan McGREGOR		31/1/82	G	37		
9	Kenny MILLER		23/12/79	A	17	(1)	21
14	Steven NAISMITH		14/9/86	A	28	(3)	11
40	Jamie NESS		2/3/91	M	8	(3)	
5	Saša PAPAC	BIH	7/2/80	D	34		3
22	Andrew WEBSTER		23/4/82	D	1		
3	David WEIR		10/5/70	D	37		
20	Vladimír WEISS	SVK	30/11/89	M	17	(6)	5
16	Steven WHITTAKER		16/6/84	D	36		4
39	Gregg WYLDE		23/3/91	M	9	(6)	

SAINT JOHNSTONE FC

Coach – Derek McInnes

Founded – 1894

Stadium – McDiarmid Park (10,673)

2010				
14/8	Hearts	a	1-1	*Parkin*
21/8	Aberdeen	h	0-1	
28/8	Rangers	a	1-2	*Grainger*
11/9	Motherwell	h	0-2	
18/9	St Mirren	h	2-1	*Jackson, Parkin*
25/9	Dundee United	a	0-1	
2/10	Hibernian	h	2-0	*Craig, Haber*
16/10	Inverness	a	1-1	*Samuel*
23/10	Hamilton	a	2-1	*Parkin, Grainger*
30/10	Celtic	h	0-3	
6/11	Kilmarnock	h	0-3	
10/11	Motherwell	a	0-4	
13/11	Hearts	h	0-2	
20/11	Aberdeen	a	1-0	*og (Diamond)*
27/11	Hibernian	a	0-0	
11/12	St Mirren	a	2-1	*Parkin, Craig*
26/12	Celtic	a	0-2	
2011				
2/1	Inverness	h	1-0	*Samuel*
15/1	Kilmarnock	h	1-1	*Taylor*
22/1	St Mirren	h	0-0	
26/1	Motherwell	h	1-0	*Craig (p)*
29/1	Hearts	a	0-1	
1/2	Hamilton	h	2-0	*May 2*
19/2	Inverness	a	0-2	
22/2	Dundee United	h	0-0	
27/2	Rangers	a	0-4	
2/3	Aberdeen	h	0-0	
5/3	Hibernian	h	1-1	*og (Towell)*
19/3	Hamilton	a	0-0	
2/4	Kilmarnock	h	0-0	
5/4	Rangers	h	0-2	
9/4	Dundee United	a	0-2	
12/4	Celtic	h	0-1	
25/4	Inverness	h	0-3	
30/4	Hibernian	a	2-1	*Craig, Moon*
7/5	Aberdeen	a	2-0	*og (Smith), Adams*
10/5	Hamilton	h	1-0	*Craig (p)*
14/5	St Mirren	a	0-0	

No	Name	Nat	DoB	Pos	Aps	(s)	Gls
24	Jamie ADAMS		26/8/87	M	9	(2)	1
12	Steven ANDERSON		19/12/85	D	24	(1)	
37	Liam CADDIS		20/9/93	M	1	(2)	
10	Liam CRAIG		27/12/86	M	29	(5)	5
20	Murray DAVIDSON		7/3/88	M	33	(1)	
18	Scott DOBIE		10/10/78	A	1	(3)	
6	Michael DUBERRY	ENG	14/10/75	D	32	(1)	
10	Peter ENCKELMAN	FIN	10/3/77	G	29		

19	Graham GARTLAND	IRL	13/7/83	D	4	(3)	
3	Daniel GRAINGER	ENG	28/7/87	D	31	(2)	2
27	Marcus HABER	CAN	11/1/89	A	5	(6)	1
22	Danny INVINCIBILE	AUS	31/3/79	M	8	(2)	
23	Andy JACKSON	IRL	9/1/88	A	10	(7)	1
16	Peter MACDONALD		17/11/80	A	14	(10)	
2	David MACKAY		2/5/80	D	32		
32	Steven MAY		2/11/92	A	8	(11)	2
19	Alan MAYBURY	IRL	8/8/78	D	23	(7)	
7	Christopher MILLAR		30/3/83	M	29	(1)	
22	Steven MILNE		5/5/80	A	1	(1)	
14	Kevin MOON		8/6/87	M	4	(2)	1
4	Jody MORRIS	ENG	22/12/78	M	23		
25	Jennison MYRIE-WILLIAMS	ENG	17/6/88	M	4	(2)	
8	Arvydas NOVIKOVAS	LTU	18/12/90	M	1	(2)	
9	Samuel PARKIN	ENG	14/3/81	A	17	(4)	4
26	Stephen REYNOLDS		11/6/92	A		(5)	
28	Jordan ROBERTSON	ENG	12/2/88	A	2	(4)	
5	Kevin RUTKIEWICZ		10/5/80	D	4	(6)	
21	Collin SAMUEL	TRI	27/8/81	A	20	(8)	2
15	Graeme SMITH		3/10/82	G	9		
11	Cleveland TAYLOR	JAM	9/9/83	M	11	(10)	1

SAINT MIRREN FC

Manager – Danny Lennon (NIR)

Founded – 1877

Stadium – St Mirren Park (8,023)

MAJOR HONOURS: Scottish Cup – (3) 1926, 1959, 1987.

2010				
14/8	Dundee United	h	1-1	*Lynch*
22/8	Celtic	a	0-4	
29/8	Hibernian	h	1-0	*Dargo*
11/9	Kilmarnock	a	1-2	*Thomson*
18/9	St Johnstone	a	1-2	*Lynch*
25/9	Inverness	h	1-2	*McGowan*
2/10	Motherwell	a	1-3	*Wardlaw*
16/10	Hamilton	h	2-2	*Higdon 2*
23/10	Hearts	a	0-3	
30/10	Aberdeen	h	2-1	*McAusland, Travner*
7/11	Rangers	h	1-3	*Higdon (p)*
10/11	Dundee United	a	2-1	*Higdon 2*
14/11	Celtic	h	0-1	
20/11	Motherwell	h	1-1	*Wardlaw*
27/11	Hamilton	a	0-0	
11/12	St Johnstone	h	1-2	*Higdon*
26/12	Inverness	a	2-1	*Thomson 2*
29/12	Hearts	h	0-2	
2011				
3/1	Kilmarnock	h	0-2	
15/1	Aberdeen	a	0-2	
22/1	St Johnstone	a	0-0	
26/1	Dundee United	h	1-1	*McGregor*
2/2	Hibernian	a	0-2	
12/2	Inverness	h	3-3	*Higdon (p), Thomson, McGregor*
20/2	Hibernian	h	0-1	
23/2	Motherwell	a	1-0	*Higdon*
26/2	Kilmarnock	a	0-2	
6/3	Rangers	h	0-1	
19/3	Hearts	a	2-3	*Higdon 2*
2/4	Hamilton	h	3-1	*Higdon 3 (1p)*
6/4	Aberdeen	h	3-2	*Higdon, Dargo, Thomson*
9/4	Celtic	a	0-1	
16/4	Rangers	a	1-2	*McGregor*
24/4	Hibernian	a	1-1	*Dargo (p)*
2/5	Hamilton	h	0-1	
7/5	Inverness	a	0-1	
10/5	Aberdeen	a	1-0	*Wardlaw*
14/5	St Johnstone	h	0-0	

No	Name	Nat	DoB	Pos	Aps	(s)	Gls
3	David BARRON		10/9/87	M	4	(5)	
4	Garry BRADY		7/9/76	M	3	(2)	
27	Patrick CREGG	IRL	21/2/86	M	18	(4)	
9	Craig DARGO		1/3/78	A	14	(8)	3
1	Paul GALLACHER		16/8/79	G	27		
11	James GOODWIN	IRL	20/11/81	M	16	(1)	
21	Nicholas HEGARTY	ENG	25/6/86	M	2	(1)	
10	Michael HIGDON	ENG	3/9/83	A	26	(2)	14
40	Mark LAMONT		15/3/90	M		(1)	
25	Ally LOVE		22/8/91	D		(1)	
20	Sean LYNCH		31/1/87	M	8	(6)	2
5	Lee MAIR		9/12/80	D	22	(2)	
17	Marc McAUSLAND		13/9/88	D	24	(1)	1
22	Jamie McCLUSKEY		6/11/87	M		(3)	
19	Paul McGOWAN		7/10/87	A	33		1
14	Darren McGREGOR		7/8/85	D	36		3
45	Kenneth McLEAN		8/1/92	M	10	(9)	
29	Mark McLENNAN		28/4/91	M		(1)	
15	Paul McQUADE		17/5/87	A		(5)	
33	Aaron MOOY	AUS	15/9/90	M	7	(6)	
7	Hugh MURRAY		8/1/79	M	21	(3)	
6	John-Paul POTTER		15/12/79	D	32	(2)	
47	Graham RAMAGE		28/8/92	M		(1)	
11	Steven ROBB		8/3/82	M	3		
12	Craig SAMSON		1/4/84	G	11		
8	Steven THOMSON		23/1/78	M	25	(2)	5
16	Jure TRAVNER	SVN	28/9/85	D	35	(2)	1
2	David VAN ZANTEN	IRL	8/5/82	D	25	(3)	
18	Grareth WARDLAW		7/4/79	A	16	(7)	3

TOP GOALSCORERS 2010/11

21	Kenny MILLER (Rangers)
20	Gary HOOPER (Celtic)
17	David GOODWILLIE (Dundee United)
16	Nikica JELAVIĆ (Rangers)
15	Anthony STOKES (Hibernian/Celtic) Adam ROONEY (Inverness) Conor SAMMON (Kilmarnock)
14	Michael HIGDON (St Mirren)
13	Rudolf SKÁCEL (Hearts)
12	Nick BLACKMAN (Motherwell/Aberdeen)

PROMOTED CLUB

DUNFERMLINE ATHLETIC FC

Coach – Jim McIntyre

Founded – 1885

Stadium – East End Park (11,380)

MAJOR HONOURS: Scottish Cup - (2) 1961, 1968.

SECOND LEVEL FINAL TABLE 2010/11

		Pld	W	D	L	F	A	Pts
1	Dunfermline Athletic FC	36	20	10	6	66	31	70
2	Raith Rovers FC	36	17	9	10	47	35	60
3	Falkirk FC	36	17	7	12	57	41	58
4	Queen of the South FC	36	14	7	15	54	53	49
5	Partick Thistle FC	36	12	11	13	44	39	47
6	Dundee FC	36	19	12	5	54	34	44
7	Greenock Morton FC	36	11	10	15	39	43	43
8	Ross County FC	36	9	14	13	30	34	41
9	Cowdenbeath FC	36	9	8	19	41	72	35
10	Stirling Albion FC	36	4	8	24	32	82	20

NB Dundee FC – 25 pts deducted.

DOMESTIC CUPS 2010/11

SCOTTISH CUP

FOURTH ROUND

(8/1/11)
Aberdeen 6, East Fife 0
Dundee United 0, Ross County 0
Hamilton 2, Alloa 0
Hibernian 0, Ayr United 0
Inverness 2, Elgin City 0
Montrose 2, Dunfermline 2
St Mirren 0, Peterhead 0

(9/1/11)
Berwick Rangers 0, Celtic 2
Dundee 0, Motherwell 4

(10/1/11)
Rangers 3, Kilmarnock 0

(11/1/11)
Falkirk 2, Partick Thistle 2
Hearts 0, St Johnstone 1
Queen of the South 1, Brechin City 2

(18/1/11)
Greenock Morton 2, Airdrie United 2
Stenhousemuir 0, Stranraer 0

(19/1/11)
East Stirlingshire 1, Buckie Thistle 0

Replays

(18/1/11)
Ayr United 1, Hibernian 0
Peterhead 1, St Mirren 6
Dunfermline 5, Montrose 3
Patrick Thistle 1, Falkirk 0
Ross County 0, Dundee United 0 *(aet; 3-4 on pens)*

(25/1/11)
Airdrie United 2, Greenock Morton 5
Stranraer 4, Stenhousemuir 3

FIFTH ROUND

(5/2/11)
Ayr United 1, St Mirren 2
Buckie Thistle 0, Brechin City 2
Hamilton 1, Dundee United 3
Inverness 5, Greenock Morton 1
Stranraer 0, Motherwell 2

(6/2/11)
Aberdeen 1, Dunfermline 0
Rangers 2, Celtic 2

(9/2/11)
St Johnstone 2, Partick Thistle 0

Replay

(2/3/11)
Celtic 1, Rangers 0

QUARTER-FINALS

(12/3/11)
Brechin City 2 *(McAllister 42p, 78)*, St Johnstone 2 *(Millar 48, Invincibile 62)*
St Mirren 1 *(McGowan 77)*, Aberdeen 1 *(McArdle 90)*

(13/3/11)
Dundee United 2 *(Goodwillie 40, Daly 73)*, Motherwell 2 *(Sutton 2, 72)*

(16/3/11)
Inverness 1 *(Rooney 44p)*, Celtic 2 *(Ledley 45, 68)*

Replays

(16/3/11)
Aberdeen 2 *(Maguire 4, Vernon 44)*, St Mirren 1 *(Vujadinović 87og)*

(22/3/11)
St Johnstone 1 *(Samuel 37)*, Brechin City 0

(30/3/11)
Motherwell 3 *(Murphy 8, Humphrey 36, Jeffers 63)*, Dundee United 0

SEMI-FINALS

(16/4/11)
Motherwell 3 *(Craigan 5, Murphy 14, Sutton 39)*, St Johnstone 0

(17/4/11)
Aberdeen 0, Celtic 4 *(Mulgrew 49, Ledley 57, Commons 63p, Maloney 84)*

FINAL

(21/5/11)
Hampden Park, Glasgow
CELTIC FC 3 *(Ki 32, Craigan 75og, Mulgrew 87)*
MOTHERWELL FC 0
Referee – *Murray*
CELTIC – *Forster, Wilson, Majstorovic, Loovens, Izaguirre, Commons (Forrest 81), Brown, Ki, Mulgrew, Hooper (McCourt 89), Samaras (Stokes 68).*
MOTHERWELL – *Randolph, Hammell (Jeffers 72), Craigan, Hutchinson, Gunning, Hateley, Jennings, Lasley, Humphrey, Sutton, Murphy (Jones 80).*

LEAGUE CUP

QUARTER-FINALS

(26/10/10)
Aberdeen 2 *(Hartley 64, 90p)*, Falkirk 1 *(Khalis 33)*
Motherwell 1 *(Gow 86)*, Dundee United 0

(27/10/10)
Kilmarnock 0, Rangers 2 *(Little 25, Naismith 61)*
St Johnstone 2 *(Parkin 31, Davidson 54)*, Celtic 3 *(Stokes 8, 13, McGinn 12)*

SEMI-FINALS

(29/1/11)
Aberdeen 1 *(Vernon 61)*, Celtic 4 *(Commons 6, Mulgrew 10, Rogne 21, Stokes 34p)*

(30/1/11)
Rangers 2 *(Edu 20, Naismith 75)*, Motherwell 1 *(Lasley 66)*

FINAL

(20/3/11)
Hampden Park, Glasgow
RANGERS FC 2 *(Davis 24, Jelavić 98)*
CELTIC FC 1 *(Ledley 31)*
(aet)
Referee – *Thomson*
RANGERS – *Alexander, Whittaker, Weir, Bougherra (Hutton 82), Papac, Naismith, Edu, Davis, Wylde, Jelavić (Diouf 116), Lafferty (Weiss 90).*
CELTIC – *Forster, Wilson, Rogne (Loovens 73), Mulgrew, Izaguirre, Brown (Ki 65), Kayal, Ledley, Commons (McCourt 103), Hooper, Samaras.*
Sent off: *Izaguirre (120)*

CLUB COMMUNICATION 2011/12

Aberdeen FC

Pittodrie Street, Pittodrie Stadium
GB-Aberdeen AB24 5QH

Tel +44 1224 650 400
Fax +44 1224 650 469
Web afc.co.uk
Email davidj@afc.co.uk
Media Officer Dave Macdermid

Celtic FC

Celtic Park
GB-Glasgow G40 3RE

Tel +44 141 551 4298
Fax +44 141 554 8845
Web celticfc.net
Email dscoular@celticfc.co.uk
Media Officer Iain Jamieson

Dundee United FC

Tannadice Park, Tannadice Street
GB-Dundee DD3 7JW

Tel +44 1382 833 166
Fax +44 1382 889 398
Web dundeeunitedfc.co.uk
Email admin@dundeeunitedfc.co.uk
Media Officer Joseph Rice

Dunfermline Athletic FC

East End Park, Halbeath Road
GB-Dunfermline KY12 7RB

Tel +44 1383 745 964
Fax +44 1383 723 468
Web dafc.co.uk
Email shirley@dafc.co.uk
Media Officer Karen Brown

Heart of Midlothian FC

Tynecastle Stadium, Gorgie Road
GB-Edinburgh EH11 2NL

Tel +44 131 200 7245
Fax +44 131 200 7247
Web heartsfc.co.uk
Email hearts@homplc.co.uk
Media Officer Clare Cowan

Hibernian FC

Easter Road Stadium, 12 Albion Place
GB-Edinburgh EH7 5QG

Tel +44 131 661 2159
Fax +44 131 659 6488
Web hibernianfc.co.uk
Email club@hibernianfc.co.uk
Media Officer Andrew Sleight

Inverness Caledonian Thistle FC

Tulloch Caledonian Stadium
East Longman, GB-Inverness IV1 1FF

Tel +44 1463 222 880
Fax +44 1463 715 816
Web ictfc.co.uk
Email jim.falconer@ictfc.co.uk
Media Officer Bill McAllister

Kilmarnock FC

Rugby Park, Rugby Road
GB-Kilmarnock KA1 2DP

Tel +44 1563 545 300
Fax +44 1563 545 303
Web kilmarnockfc.co.uk
Email kirstencallaghan@kilmarnockfc.co.uk
Media Officer Kirsten Callaghan

Motherwell FC

Fir Park Street, Fir Park Stadium
GB-Motherwell ML1 2QN

Tel +44 1698 333 333
Fax +44 1698 338 001
Web motherwellfc.co.uk
Email mfc@motherwellfc.co.uk
Media Officer Alan Burrows

Rangers FC

150 Edmiston Drive, Ibrox Stadium
GB-Glasgow G51 2XD

Tel +44 141 580 8647
Fax +44 141 419 0600
Web rangers.co.uk
Email amanda.millar@rangers.co.uk
Media Officer Carol Patton

Saint Johnstone FC

McDiarmid Park, Crieff Road
GB-Perth PH1 2SJ

Tel +44 1738 459 090
Fax +44 1738 625 771
Web perthstjohnstonefc.co.uk
Email enquiries@perthsaintsfc.co.uk
Media Officer Paul Smith

Saint Mirren FC

St Mirren Park, 75 Greenhill Road
GB-Paisley PA3 1RU

Tel +44 141 889 2558
Fax +44 141 848 6444
Web saintmirren.net
Email info@saintmirren.net
Media Officer Brian Caldwell

SERBIA
Serbie I Serbien

Fudbalski savez Srbije (FSS)

COMMUNICATION

Address Terazije 35, CP 263
RS-11000 Beograd
Tel +381 11 323 4253
Fax +381 11 323 3433
E-mail office@fss.rs
Website fss.org.rs

President Tomislav Karadžić
General Secretary Zoran Laković
Media Officer Aleksandar Bošković

Year of Formation 1919

National Stadium FK Crvena zvezda, Belgrade (51,328)

DOMESTIC COMPETITION SUMMARY 2010/11

SUPERLIGA FINAL TABLE

			Home					Away					Total						
		Pld	W	D	L	F	A	W	D	L	F	A	W	D	L	F	A	Pts	Comp
1	FK Partizan	30	13	1	1	42	9	11	3	1	33	12	24	4	2	75	21	76	UCL
2	FK Crvena zvezda	30	12	2	1	34	11	10	2	3	18	7	22	4	4	52	18	70	UEL
3	FK Vojvodina	30	11	3	1	28	7	9	4	2	16	7	20	7	3	44	14	67	UEL
4	FK Rad	30	9	4	2	26	9	5	6	4	12	12	14	10	6	38	21	52	UEL
5	FK Spartak Zlatibor voda	30	7	3	5	25	18	4	7	4	9	9	11	10	9	34	27	43	
6	FK Sloboda Point Sevojno	30	7	4	4	17	11	5	3	7	17	24	12	7	11	34	35	43	
7	OFK Beograd	30	9	2	4	17	9	3	4	8	10	17	12	6	12	27	26	42	
8	FK Javor	30	6	7	2	11	7	4	4	7	10	17	10	11	9	21	24	41	
9	FK Borac Čačak	30	5	7	3	13	10	3	5	7	9	21	8	12	10	22	31	36	
10	FK Smederevo	30	5	8	2	11	9	3	3	9	13	22	8	11	11	24	31	35	
11	FK BSK Borča	30	6	4	5	14	12	2	5	8	9	25	8	9	13	23	37	33	
12	FK Jagodina	30	4	4	7	12	14	4	4	7	14	19	8	8	14	26	33	32	
13	FK Hajduk Kula	30	6	2	7	16	17	1	6	8	9	20	7	8	15	25	37	29	
14	FK Metalac	30	5	4	6	14	16	3	1	11	7	22	8	5	17	21	38	29	
15	FK Inđija	30	5	4	6	16	16	2	1	12	13	31	7	5	18	29	47	26	*Relegated*
16	FK Čukarički	30	0	2	13	7	27	0	3	12	3	38	0	5	25	10	65	5	*Relegated*

Top Scorer Andrija Kaluđerović (Crvena zvezda) & Ivica Iliev (Partizan), 13 goals

Promoted Clubs FK Radnički 1923
FK Novi Pazar

Cup Final FK Partizan 2, FK Vojvodina 1 (match abandoned; awarded 3-0)

Peerless Partizan break new ground

FK Partizan made history in 2010/11 by becoming the first Serbian/Yugoslav team to win four national league titles in a row. It was a successful season on all fronts for the Belgrade club as they reached the group stage of the UEFA Champions League and also won the Serbian Cup – the latter albeit in controversial circumstances when their opponents in the final, FK Vojvodina, walked off the field in protest, forcing the match to be abandoned.

The first part of the double to be secured was the cup, awarded to Partizan as a 3-0 forfeit after the Vojvodina players had trooped off the field in the 81st minute, never to return, following a number of major refereeing decisions that they believed had erroneously gone against them, including the penalty with which Partizan went 2-1 up. Vojvodina, who had enjoyed a superb season under their new coach Zoran Milinković, beating Partizan home and away in the SuperLiga and challenging hard on both domestic fronts, were eager to win the national cup for the first time in their 97-year history, but ultimately their desperation to succeed got the better of them, the walk-off not only handing the trophy to Partizan but also resulting in six-month bans for Milinković, club president Ratko Buturović and veteran midfielder Nikola Lazetić.

Pivotal day

Vojvodina would end up third in the SuperLiga, nine points adrift of Partizan and three points behind runners-up FK Crvena zvezda. Partizan, under their impressive young coach Aleksandar Stanojević, controlled proceedings for most of the season, but the two defeats to Vojvodina – the only ones they incurred all season – prevented them from breaking away, and when they hosted Crvena zvezda on 23 April, the two Belgrade giants were level on points, with Vojvodina close behind. It proved to be a pivotal day in the title race, because as Vojvodina lost 1-0 at OFK Beograd, Partizan completed the double over Crvena zvezda with a 1-0 win, the goal coming from Ghanaian striker Prince Tagoe, a mid-season loan signing from German club TSG 1899 Hoffenheim brought in to replace Brazilian hit man Cléo, who had left in January to play in China.

If veteran skipper Mladen Krstajić – in his swansong campaign – and up-and-coming midfielder Radosav Petrović were Partizan's most influential players over the whole season, Cléo had certainly been the standout performer during the first half, scoring eight goals in the SuperLiga and another ten in Europe, including three in the UEFA Champions League play-off against RSC Anderlecht that Stanojević's men won on penalties to qualify for the group stage for only the second time. The Brazilian was the sole Partizan player to score in the group stage, home and away against Arsenal FC, as Serbia's finest lost all six matches. Although a whitewash was not part of Partizan's plans, participation among Europe's 32-team elite was a source of satisfaction in itself, so criticism of Stanojević and his players was minimal. They

Mladen Krstajić ended his playing career by captaining Partizan to a Serbian domestic double

certainly outshone Serbia's other three European representatives, Crvena zvezda included, who all perished in the third qualifying round of the UEFA Europa League.

Prosinečki appointed

Crvena zvezda were unable to celebrate the 20th anniversary of their European Champion Clubs' Cup triumph with anything substantial, although they did mark the occasion by appointing one of the stars of that legendary 1991 team, Robert Prosinečki, as their new coach. Recruited to replace Aleksandar Kristić in December, when Crvena zvezda were trailing Partizan by five points, Prosinečki made an excellent start, steering the team to eight successive league victories. But, like his predecessor, he was found wanting against Partizan, the all-important league defeat in April coming after Crvena zvezda had lost 2-1 on aggregate to their rivals in the semi-finals of the Serbian Cup. Although Prosinečki's men beat Vojvodina 2-0 in Novi Sad on the final day to take the runners-up spot, with striker Andrija Kaluđerović scoring his 13th goal of the season to join Partizan veteran Ivica Iliev as the SuperLiga's top scorer, 2010/11 was another season in which 'Red Star' failed to dazzle.

Kaluđerović had scored 17 league goals for FK Rad in 2009/10, but his cross-town transfer to Crvena zvezda was impressively absorbed by the lesser known Belgrade club, who, under the astute guidance of coach Marko Nikolić, surprisingly finished fourth in the SuperLiga to secure European football for the first time in 22 years. It was a different story for another club from the capital, FK Čukarički, who failed to win a game and finished bottom with five measly points, going down with FK Inđija.

National Team

International Tournament Appearances* –
FIFA World Cup – (11) 1930 (semi-finals), 1950, 1954 (qtr-finals), 1958 (qtr-finals), 1962 (4th), 1974 (2nd phase), 1982, 1990 (qtr-finals), 1998 (2nd round), 2006, 2010.
UEFA European Championship – (5) 1960 (runners-up), 1968 (runners-up), 1976 (4th), 1984, 2000 (qtr-finals).

Top Five All-time Caps – (including Yugoslavia and Serbia & Montenegro)
Savo Milošević (102); Dejan Stanković (98); Dragan Džajić (85); Dragan Stojković (84); Predrag Mijatović (73)

Top Five All-time Goals – (including Yugoslavia and Serbia & Montenegro)
Stjepan Bobek (38); Milan Galić & Savo Milošević (37); Blagoje Marjanović (36); Rajko Mitić (32)

(before 2006 as Yugoslavia; 2006 as Serbia & Montenegro)*

Following a first-round elimination from the 2010 FIFA World Cup, the Serbian national team endured more disappointment in the UEFA EURO 2012 qualifiers. World Cup coach Radomir Antić was suspended for the start of the campaign then jettisoned after his assistant Rešad Kunovac oversaw a 1-1 home draw with Slovenia. Things were to get worse, however, under new coach Vladimir Petrović (ex-Serbia Under-21s and Crvena zvezda) when Serbia were sensationally beaten 3-1 at home by Estonia then surrendered three further points four days later when their match against Italy in Genoa had to be abandoned after just six minutes because of violence and vandalism from the visiting Serbian fans. A 3-0 forfeit was supplemented by a one-match home spectator ban, and although Serbia won that eerie encounter in Belgrade, 2-1 against Northern Ireland, a subsequent 1-1 draw in Tallinn left the team with an uphill battle to qualify for the play-offs.

NATIONAL TEAM RESULTS 2010/11

11/8/10	Greece	H	Belgrade	0-1	
3/9/10	Faroe Islands (ECQ)	A	Torshavn	3-0	*Lazović (14), Stanković (18), Žigić (90+1)*
7/9/10	Slovenia (ECQ)	H	Belgrade	1-1	*Žigić (86)*
8/10/10	Estonia (ECQ)	H	Belgrade	1-3	*Žigić (60)*
12/10/10	Italy (ECQ)	A	Genoa	0-3	*(w/o; original match abandoned after 6 mins)*
17/11/10	Bulgaria	A	Sofia	1-0	*Žigić (80)*
9/2/11	Israel	A	Tel-Aviv	2-0	*Tošić (23), Trivunović (76)*
25/3/11	Northern Ireland (ECQ)	H	Belgrade	2-1	*Pantelić (65), Tošić (74)*
29/3/11	Estonia (ECQ)	A	Tallinn	1-1	*Pantelić (38)*
3/6/11	South Korea	A	Seoul	1-2	*Petrović (87)*
7/6/11	Australia	A	Melbourne	0-0	

NATIONAL TEAM APPEARANCES 2010/11

Coach – (Rešad KUNOVAC) (15/9/10) Vladimir PETROVIĆ	24/8/53 1/7/55		Gre	FRO	SVN	EST	ITA	Bul	Isr	NIR	EST	Kor	Aus	Caps	Goals
Anđelko ĐURIČIĆ	21/11/80	Leiria (POR)	G	G	G									4	-
Branislav IVANOVIĆ	22/4/84	Chelsea (ENG)	D			D	D	D	D66	D	D			41	4
Nemanja VIDIĆ	21/10/81	Man. United (ENG)	D	D	D	D		D65			D			54	2
Neven SUBOTIĆ	10/12/88	Dortmund (GER)	D	D	D		D	D	D	D		D83	s65	24	1
Ivan OBRADOVIĆ	25/7/88	Zaragoza (ESP)	D46	D46					s77			s46	D	18	1
Radosav PETROVIĆ	8/3/89	Partizan	M57	s58				M46	M46	s86	M	M	M	18	1
Zdravko KUZMANOVIĆ	22/9/87	Stuttgart (GER)	M	M	M	M79	M		s46			M67	M65	38	4
Miloš KRASIĆ	1/11/84	CSKA Moskva (RUS) /Juventus (ITA)	M46	M	s46	M	M		M46	M86				41	3
Nenad MILIJAŠ	30/4/83	Wolves (ENG)	M46					M65	M46	M46	M			23	4
Milan JOVANOVIĆ	18/4/81	Liverpool (ENG)	M65	M	M64	M46				s46	M74			35	10
Nikola ŽIGIĆ	25/9/80	Birmingham (ENG)	A74	A	A	A		s46 90*			s74			54	20
Aleksandar KOLAROV	10/11/85	Man. City (ENG)	s46					D	D77	D	D	D46		21	-
Miloš NINKOVIĆ	25/12/84	Dynamo Kyiv (UKR)	s46	s83	s64	s46				s46	M14			17	-
Zoran TOŠIĆ	28/4/87	CSKA Moskva (RUS)	s46		M46	s46	M	M	M	M	M	M	M90	32	6
Gojko KAČAR	26/1/87	Hamburg (GER)	s57		s71	M46	M							22	-
Dragan MRĐA	23/1/84	Vojvodina /Sion (SUI)	s65				A	A46	A66					10	2
Marko PANTELIĆ	15/9/78	unattached /Olympiacos (GRE)	s74						s66	A	A			38	9
Antonio RUKAVINA	26/1/84	1860 München (GER)		D	D									22	-
Dejan STANKOVIĆ	11/9/78	Inter (ITA)		M58	M71	M	M			M		M77	M83	98	15
Danko LAZOVIĆ	17/5/83	Zenit (RUS)		A83	A	s79								43	11
Aleksandar LUKOVIĆ	23/10/82	Zenit (RUS)		s46	D	D	D							26	-
Vladimir STOJKOVIĆ	28/7/83	Partizan				G								37	-
Marko LOMIĆ	13/9/83	Dinamo Moskva (RUS)				D								2	-
Željko BRKIĆ	9/7/86	Vojvodina					G			G	G			5	-
Slobodan RAJKOVIĆ	3/2/89	Vitesse (NED)					D	s65				s83	D65	6	-
Bojan JORGAČEVIĆ	12/2/82	Gent (BEL)						G	G					2	-
Marko MIRIĆ	26/3/87	Spartak Zlatibor voda						M75				M46	s90	3	-
Adem LJAJIĆ	29/9/91	Fiorentina (ITA)						M86	M	M46			M65	4	-
Ivan RADOVANOVIĆ	29/8/88	Bologna (ITA)						s46						1	-
Veseljko TRIVUNOVIĆ	13/1/80	OFK Beograd						s65	s46		s14	s67	s65	5	1
Miralem SULEJMANI	5/12/88	Ajax (NED)						s75						7	-
Pavle NINKOV	20/4/85	Crvena zvezda						s86						4	-
Milan BIŠEVAC	31/8/83	Valenciennes (FRA)							D	D	D	D	s75	8	-
Dimitrije INJAC	12/8/80	Lech (POL)							s46					1	-
Nenad TOMOVIĆ	30/8/87	Lecce (ITA)							s66			D	D75	5	-
Bojan ŠARANOV	22/9/87	OFK Beograd										G		1	-
Ranko DESPOTOVIĆ	21/1/83	Girona (ESP)										A76	s65	4	-
Jovan DAMJANOVIĆ	4/10/82	Borac Čačak										s46	A	2	-
Brana ILIĆ	16/2/85	Vojvodina										s76		1	-
Dušan PETRONIJEVIĆ	9/11/83	Borac Čačak										s77		1	-
Damir KAHRIMAN	19/11/84	Tavriya (UKR)											G	2	-
Milan VILOTIĆ	21/10/86	Crvena zvezda											D	1	-
Branislav JOVANOVIĆ	21/9/85	Rad											s83	1	-

NB The Serbian FA (FSS) awarded caps for the abandoned match against Italy.

CLUB-BY-CLUB

FK BORAC ČAČAK

Coach – Nenad Milovanović; (16/12/10) Slavko Petrović
Founded – 1926
Stadium – Kraj Morave (5,200)

2010				
14/8	Javor	h	1-1	*Knežević*
21/8	Čukarički	a	1-0	*Washington*
28/8	Metalac	h	1-0	*og (Pavlović Pe.)*
11/9	Sloboda	a	0-0	
19/9	Partizan	h	0-2	
26/9	Hajduk	a	1-1	*Dmitrović (p)*
2/10	OFK Beograd	h	1-1	*Washington*
17/10	Rad	a	1-3	*Ignjatović*
23/10	Inđija	h	0-0	
30/10	Spartak	h	0-0	
6/11	Vojvodina	a	0-4	
13/11	Smederevo	h	0-1	
21/11	Crvena zvezda	a	0-2	
27/11	Jagodina	h	1-1	*Prtenjak*
4/12	BSK Borča	a	0-2	
2011				
5/3	Javor	a	1-1	*Kostić (p)*
9/3	Čukarički	h	3-0	*Stojmirović, Prtenjak, Damjanović*
12/3	Metalac	a	0-0	
19/3	Sloboda	h	1-0	*Damjanović*
2/4	Partizan	a	0-2	
9/4	Hajduk	h	1-0	*Damjanović*
16/4	OFK Beograd	a	1-2	*Damjanović*
20/4	Rad	h	0-0	
23/4	Inđija	a	0-2	
30/4	Spartak	a	2-1	*Petronijević, Damjanović*
7/5	Vojvodina	h	1-1	*Damjanović*
15/5	Smederevo	a	1-0	*Knežević*
21/5	Crvena zvezda	h	2-0	*Knežević, Kostić (p)*
25/5	Jagodina	a	1-1	*Višnjić*
29/5	BSK Borča	h	1-3	*Kostić (p)*

No	Name	Nat	DoB	Pos	Aps	(s)	Gls
13	Zoran ANTIĆ		7/2/75	D	8		
3	Nikola BORANIJAŠEVIĆ		19/5/92	D		(1)	
8	Jovan DAMJANOVIĆ		4/10/82	A	12		6
6	Boban DMITROVIĆ		2/4/72	D	14		1
2	Dušan DUNJIĆ		29/3/87	D	5	(2)	
27	Nebojša GAVRIĆ		27/8/91	M	1		
4	Aleksandar IGNJATOVIĆ		11/4/88	D	17	(4)	1
7	Slaviša JEREMIĆ		15/2/83	M	6	(2)	
18	Radenko KAMBEROVIĆ		13/2/83	D	9	(8)	
77	Filip KNEŽEVIĆ		8/11/91	M	25	(4)	3
11	Zoran KOSTIĆ		14/11/82	M	27		3
88	Marko KRASIĆ		1/12/85	M	11	(1)	
14	Slavko MARIĆ		7/3/84	D	13	(6)	
10	Dušan MARTINOVIĆ		22/12/87	M	3	(2)	
17	Mario MASLAĆ		9/9/90	D	23	(1)	
23	Bogdan MILIČIĆ		6/1/89	M	18	(1)	
28	Nikola MILOJEVIĆ		16/4/81	G	29		
25	Filip MLADENOVIĆ		15/8/91	D	18		
24	Slađan NIKODIJEVIĆ		1/5/90	A	6	(11)	
31	Dušan PETRONIJEVIĆ		9/11/83	M	12		1
1	Filip PIJEVAC		2/5/90	G	1		
21	Nebojša PRTENJAK		10/5/83	M	15	(6)	2
15	Semir SADOVIĆ		14/4/91	M		(1)	
22	Stefan SPIROVSKI	MKD	23/9/90	M	6	(11)	
3	Boban STOJANOVIĆ		27/2/79	A	7	(6)	
8	Miloš STOJČEV		19/1/87	M	4	(3)	
7	Aleksandar STOJMIROVIĆ		11/12/82	A	12	(1)	1
26	Miloš TOMAŠEVIĆ		30/4/90	M	3	(3)	
5	Nenad VIŠNJIĆ		25/4/83	D	1	(3)	1
9	WASHINGTON Roberto Mariano da Silva	BRA	19/6/85	A	6	(6)	2
20	WILLIAM Rocha Alves	BRA	7/5/86	D	18		

FK BSK BORČA

Coach – Srđan Vasiljević; (23/9/10) Milenko Kiković
Founded – 1937
Stadium – Omladinski stadion (13,900)

2010				
14/8	Spartak	a	1-1	*Alivodić*
21/8	Vojvodina	h	0-2	
28/8	Smederevo	a	1-1	*Stojanović*
12/9	Crvena zvezda	h	1-3	*Knežević*
18/9	Jagodina	a	0-2	
25/9	Inđija	a	0-0	
2/10	Javor	h	1-0	*Kajević*
16/10	Čukarički	a	0-0	
23/10	Metalac	h	1-0	*Babić*
30/10	Sloboda	a	1-2	*Vukadinović*
7/11	Partizan	h	0-3	
14/11	Hajduk	a	1-0	*Đukić (p)*
20/11	OFK Beograd	h	1-1	*Krstić*
28/11	Rad	a	0-5	
4/12	Borac	h	2-0	*Babić, Krstić*
2011				
5/3	Spartak	h	0-0	
9/3	Vojvodina	a	1-2	*Kajević*
12/3	Smederevo	h	0-0	
20/3	Crvena zvezda	a	1-4	*Babić*
3/4	Jagodina	h	1-0	*Kajević*
9/4	Inđija	h	4-0	*Alivodić 3, Bošković*
16/4	Javor	a	0-0	
20/4	Čukarički	h	3-1	*Jovanović, Bošković, Vignjević*
23/4	Metalac	a	0-2	
30/4	Sloboda	h	0-1	
6/5	Partizan	a	0-4	
15/5	Hajduk	h	0-0	
21/5	OFK Beograd	a	0-1	
25/5	Rad	h	0-1	
29/5	Borac	a	3-1	*Babić, Jovanović, Damnjanović*

No	Name	Nat	DoB	Pos	Aps	(s)	Gls
9	Enver ALIVODIĆ		27/12/84	A	28		4
23	Dražen ANĐUŠIĆ	MNE	25/1/93	M		(1)	
1	Tomislav ARČABA	AUS	12/12/83	G	1		
20	Dejan BABIĆ		20/4/89	M	26	(2)	4
24	Marko BOŠKOVIĆ		15/4/82	D	17	(6)	2
25	Nikola CESAREVIĆ		3/10/82	M	21	(1)	
29	Ivan DAMNJANOVIĆ		6/1/90	A	1	(7)	1
1	Nemanja DŽODŽO		12/12/86	G	3		
22	Aleksandar ĐUKIĆ		30/11/80	A	12		1
19	Bojan GRDINIĆ	MNE	13/2/90	D		(1)	
34	Milan JOVANOVIĆ		31/7/91	M	9	(2)	2
14	Asmir KAJEVIĆ	MNE	15/2/90	M	25	(1)	3
5	Zoran KNEŽEVIĆ		15/8/86	M	12		1
11	Ljubo KOVAČEVIĆ		8/9/78	G	26		
5	Miloš KRSTIĆ		19/11/88	D	4	(2)	
18	Vladimir KRSTIĆ		28/6/87	M	18	(7)	2
28	Vojkan MILJKOVIĆ		4/6/91	M	12	(1)	
13	Branislav MILOŠEVIĆ		13/5/88	D	26	(1)	
7	Nebojša PEJIĆ	BIH	5/1/88	M	2	(15)	
2	Dušan PLAVŠIĆ		25/5/92	A		(2)	
6	Aleksandar RADUNOVIĆ		9/5/80	D	25		
8	Miloš RELJIĆ		12/6/89	A	7	(6)	
15	Stefan SAVIĆ	MNE	8/1/91	D	2	(1)	
21	Mile SAVKOVIĆ		11/3/92	M		(1)	
12	Stefan STOJANOVIĆ		12/1/88	D	2	(7)	1
15	Bojan UŠUMOVIĆ	BIH	24/6/88	M	1	(2)	
3	Nikola VASILJEVIĆ	BIH	19/12/83	D	4		
17	Milan VIGNJEVIĆ		30/3/89	M	7	(16)	1
28	Ivan VUKADINOVIĆ		21/8/84	D	13		1
4	Dragan ŽARKOVIĆ		16/4/86	D	26	(2)	

FK CRVENA ZVEZDA

Coach – Aleksandar Kristić;
(15/12/10) Robert Prosinečki (CRO)
Founded – 1945
Stadium – FK Crvena zvezda (51,328)

MAJOR HONOURS: European Champion Clubs' Cup – (1) 1991; World Club Cup – (1) 1991; Yugoslav/Serbian League – (25) 1951, 1953, 1956, 1957, 1959, 1960, 1964, 1968, 1969, 1970, 1973, 1977, 1980, 1981, 1984, 1988, 1990, 1991, 1992, 1995, 2000, 2001, 2004, 2006, 2007; Yugoslav/Serbian Cup – (23) 1948, 1949, 1950, 1958, 1959, 1964, 1968, 1970, 1971, 1982, 1985, 1990, 1993, 1995, 1996, 1997, 1999, 2000, 2002, 2004, 2006, 2007, 2010.

2010				
14/8	Smederevo	a	0-0	
22/8	Inđija	a	1-0	*Trifunović*
29/8	Jagodina	h	2-1	*Kaluđerović, Cadú*
12/9	BSK Borča	a	3-1	*Trifunović 2, Vešović*
18/9	Javor	h	1-0	*Kaluđerović*
26/9	Čukarički	a	1-0	*Milovanović*
3/10	Metalac	h	2-0	*Kaluđerović, Cadú*
17/10	Sloboda	a	3-0	*Trifunović, Sávio, Kaluđerović*
23/10	Partizan	h	0-1	
31/10	Hajduk	a	0-2	
6/11	OFK Beograd	h	1-0	*Trifunović*
14/11	Rad	a	1-0	*Trifunović*
21/11	Borac	h	2-0	*Cadú, Milovanović*
28/11	Spartak	a	2-1	*Koroman, Kaluđerović*
4/12	Vojvodina	h	2-2	*Kaluđerović, Reljić*
2011				
5/3	Smederevo	h	1-0	*Cadú (p)*
9/3	Inđija	h	3-1	*Ninkov, Koroman, Vešović*
12/3	Jagodina	a	2-0	*Jevtić, Evandro*
20/3	BSK Borča	h	4-1	*Evandro 2, Borja, Kaluđerović*
2/4	Javor	a	2-0	*Jevtić, Kaluđerović*
10/4	Čukarički	h	4-0	*Perović 2, Evandro (p), Borja*
16/4	Metalac	a	1-0	*Mikić*
20/4	Sloboda	h	5-1	*Ćosić, Lazović, Kaluđerović, Borja, Evandro*
23/4	Partizan	a	0-1	
1/5	Hajduk	h	3-1	*Milovanović, Reljić, Kaluđerović*
7/5	OFK Beograd	a	0-0	
15/5	Rad	h	2-1	*Cadú, Kaluđerović*
21/5	Borac	a	0-2	
25/5	Spartak	h	2-2	*Kaluđerović, Tošić*
29/5	Vojvodina	a	2-0	*Lazović, Kaluđerović*

No	Name	Nat	DoB	Pos	Aps	(s)	Gls
13	Lee ADDY	GHA	7/7/90	D	17	(2)	
26	Mohammed AWAL ISSAH	GHA	4/4/86	M	24	(2)	
1	Boban BAJKOVIĆ	MNE	15/3/85	G	9		
32	Vladimir BOGDANOVIĆ		5/10/86	M	1	(4)	
19	Cristian Martínez BORJA	COL	1/1/88	A	13	(1)	3
20	Carlos Eduardo de Fiori Mendes "CADÚ"	BRA	31/8/86	M	24	(2)	5
5	Uroš ĆOSIĆ		24/10/92	D	8		1
18	Slavoljub ĐORĐEVIĆ		15/2/81	D	7		
10	EVANDRO Goebel	BRA	23/8/86	A	8	(1)	5
6	Nikola IGNJATIJEVIĆ		12/12/83	D	4	(2)	
7	Milan JEREMIĆ		22/9/88	M	1		
21	Aleksandar JEVTIĆ		30/3/85	A	11	(11)	2
99	Andrija KALUĐEROVIĆ		5/7/87	A	26	(2)	13
9	Ognjen KOROMAN		19/9/78	M	13	(10)	2
8	Darko LAZOVIĆ		15/9/90	M	11	(5)	2
25	Danijel MIHAJLOVIĆ		2/6/85	D	2	(1)	
27	Srđan MIJAILOVIĆ		10/11/93	M	6	(7)	
14	Nikola MIKIĆ		13/9/85	D	15	(1)	1
88	Dejan MILOVANOVIĆ		21/1/84	M	13	(5)	3
24	Pavle NINKOV		20/4/85	D	22	(1)	1
23	Slavko PEROVIĆ		9/6/89	A	3	(9)	2
16	Stevan RELJIĆ	MNE	31/3/86	D	10		2
2	SÁVIO Oliveira do Valle	BRA	1/11/84	M	4	(5)	1
55	Slavoljub SRNIĆ		12/1/92	M		(1)	
22	Saša STAMENKOVIĆ		5/1/85	G	21		
3	Duško TOŠIĆ		19/1/85	D	24	(1)	1
11	Miloš TRIFUNOVIĆ		15/10/84	A	10	(5)	6
29	Marko VEŠOVIĆ	MNE	28/8/91	M	13	(11)	2
15	Milan VILOTIĆ		21/10/86	D	10		

FK ČUKARIČKI

Coach – Aleksandar Jović; (7/11/10) Vladimir Romčević; (11/1/11) Dragan Lacmanović
Founded – 1926
Stadium – FK Čukarički Stankom (3,120)

2010				
15/8	Rad	a	0-4	
21/8	Borac	h	0-1	
28/8	Spartak	a	0-2	
11/9	Vojvodina	h	0-2	
18/9	Smederevo	a	0-2	
26/9	Crvena zvezda	h	0-1	
2/10	Jagodina	a	1-1	*Rašković*
16/10	BSK Borča	h	0-0	
23/10	Javor	a	0-2	
30/10	Inđija	a	0-0	
6/11	Metalac	h	1-2	*Višnjić (p)*
13/11	Sloboda	a	0-4	
20/11	Partizan	h	2-4	*Cakić 2*
27/11	Hajduk	a	1-1	*Cakić*
4/12	OFK Beograd	h	0-2	
2011				
5/3	Rad	h	0-3	
9/3	Borac	a	0-3	
12/3	Spartak	h	0-2	
19/3	Vojvodina	a	0-3	
2/4	Smederevo	h	0-1	
10/4	Crvena zvezda	a	0-4	
16/4	Jagodina	h	1-3	*Kovačević*
20/4	BSK Borča	a	1-3	*Morariju*
23/4	Javor	h	0-1	
30/4	Inđija	h	1-2	*Petronijević*
8/5	Metalac	a	0-1	
15/5	Sloboda	h	1-2	*Morariju*
21/5	Partizan	a	0-4	
25/5	Hajduk	h	1-1	*Popović (p)*
29/5	OFK Beograd	a	0-4	

No	Name	Nat	DoB	Pos	Aps	(s)	Gls
29	Aleksandar ANDREJEVIĆ		28/3/92	M	1		
28	Igor ANIČIĆ		7/11/89	A	9	(3)	
18	Marko BASARA		29/7/84	M	1		
9	Bojan BRAJKOVIĆ		5/4/83	A	4	(3)	
20	Mihajlo CAKIĆ		27/5/90	M	11		3
13	Nikola DRAGIĆEVIĆ		23/6/88	D	18	(1)	
50	Nikola ĐOKIĆ		31/5/92	G	6		
30	Igor FILIPOVIĆ		17/4/92	D	1		
17	Nemanja ILIĆ		15/2/88	D		(2)	
11	Saša JANAĆKOVIĆ		13/8/88	D	5	(3)	
24	Vladimir JEVĐENIJEVIĆ		19/1/86	D	9	(4)	
28	Nenad KISO	BIH	30/4/89	M	14	(1)	
18	Stefan KOČANOVIĆ		31/3/90	A		(1)	
16	Danko KOVAČEVIĆ	MNE	10/7/91	M	8	(5)	1
25	Saša KRAJNOVIĆ		15/8/89	M	2	(4)	
33	Nikola KRČMAREVIĆ		18/12/91	M	22	(1)	
4	Milan KUZMANOVIĆ		5/4/86	D	6	(9)	
8	Dejan MARIĆ		21/8/85	A	11	(2)	
8	Dragan MILOVANOVIĆ		3/1/86	A	3	(5)	
14	Danijel MORARIJU		1/1/91	M	16	(4)	2
35	Igor NEDELJKOVIĆ		24/9/91	A	3	(4)	
20	Miroslav PETRONIJEVIĆ		6/12/87	M	11	(1)	1
10	Aleksandar PETROVIĆ		22/3/83	M	17	(1)	
19	Božidar PETROVIĆ		24/7/90	D	8	(2)	
3	Ivan POPOVIĆ		3/11/79	D	21		1

1	Saša RADIVOJEVIĆ		10/4/79	G	7		
15	Đorđe RADOJEVIĆ		29/7/91	A	2	(7)	
9	Milanko RAŠKOVIĆ		13/3/81	A	11		1
7	Vladimir RIBIĆ		28/3/81	A	3	(3)	
23	Nikola RNIĆ		11/1/84	M	8	(1)	
32	Nemanja SĆEKIĆ	MNE	17/12/91	G	17		
34	Petar SPASIĆ		18/1/92	A	1	(8)	
6	Vladimir STANOJEVIĆ		1/5/90	D	9	(7)	
17	Filip STOJANOVIĆ		21/1/88	M	1	(1)	
11	Aleksandar STOJMIROVIĆ		11/12/82	A	14		
21	Predrag TANASKOVIĆ		13/5/89	A		(1)	
12	Aleksandar TRNINIĆ		27/3/87	D	9		
27	Stefan UDOVIČIĆ	BIH	20/9/91	A	1	(5)	
5	Nenad VIŠNJIĆ		25/4/83	D	12		1
2	Marko VUKOVIĆ		19/9/83	M	1		
5	Aleksandar ŽIVANOVIĆ		8/4/87	D	15		
5	Gojko ŽIŽIĆ	MNE	27/1/89	D	12	(1)	

FK HAJDUK KULA

Coach – (Ranko Delić); (1/8/10) Zdenko Glumac (CRO); (23/9/10) Dragoljub Bekvalac

Founded – 1925

Stadium – SPC Hajduk (11,710)

2010

15/8	Sloboda	h	1-2	*Kasalica*
29/8	Inđija	h	1-3	*Komazec*
4/9	Partizan	a	0-2	
12/9	OFK Beograd	h	1-2	*Petrović*
19/9	Rad	a	0-1	
26/9	Borac	h	1-1	*Radanović*
2/10	Spartak	a	0-1	
17/10	Vojvodina	h	0-1	
23/10	Smederevo	a	1-1	*Komazec*
31/10	Crvena zvezda	h	2-0	*Kovačević V., Petrović*
6/11	Jagodina	a	0-3	
14/11	BSK Borča	h	0-1	
20/11	Javor	a	0-0	
27/11	Čukarički	h	1-1	*Komazec*
4/12	Metalac	a	1-1	*Komazec*

2011

5/3	Sloboda	a	2-2	*Đukić, Pauljević*
9/3	Partizan	h	0-4	
16/3	Inđija	a	2-1	*Komazec (p), Živanović M.*
19/3	OFK Beograd	a	0-1	
3/4	Rad	h	0-1	
9/4	Borac	a	0-1	
16/4	Spartak	h	1-0	*Živanović M.*
20/4	Vojvodina	a	1-2	*Bošković*
23/4	Smederevo	h	2-0	*Jovanović, Đukić*
1/5	Crvena zvezda	a	1-3	*Jovanović*
8/5	Jagodina	h	1-0	*Kasalica*
15/5	BSK Borča	a	0-0	
21/5	Javor	h	2-0	*Živanović M. 2 (1p)*
25/5	Čukarički	a	1-1	*Đukić*
29/5	Metalac	h	3-1	*Živanović M., Đukić, Komazec*

No	Name	Nat	DoB	Pos	Aps	(s)	Gls
27	Gavro BAGIĆ	CRO	2/5/85	A		(1)	
8	Nikola BOGIĆ		30/6/81	M	22		
23	Nemanja BOŠKOVIĆ		8/5/90	M	10	(4)	1
1	Bojan BRAČ		28/2/89	G	27		
29	Aleksandar ĆOVIN		23/11/88	A	2	(2)	
14	Aleksandar ĐUKIĆ		30/11/80	A	11		4
4	Vuk ĐURIĆ	MNE	30/9/88	D	1	(2)	
3	Darko FEJSA		27/8/87	D	20	(1)	
7	Aleksandar JOVANOVIĆ	BIH	26/10/84	M	25	(2)	2
17	Filip KASALICA	MNE	17/12/88	A	14	(10)	2
10	Dejan KEKEZOVIĆ		16/6/82	M	1		
9	Saša KIŠ		7/4/89	A	10	(6)	
11	Nikola KOMAZEC		15/11/87	A	7	(20)	6
26	Miloš KOVAČEVIĆ		31/3/91	M	10	(2)	
21	Vladimir KOVAČEVIĆ		11/11/92	D	13	(3)	1
10	Igor KOZOŠ		4/8/74	D		(3)	
20	Blažo LALEVIĆ	MNE	11/5/84	M	3	(1)	
47	Slobodan LALIĆ		18/2/92	D	2	(1)	
22	Novica MAKSIMOVIĆ		4/4/88	M	18	(3)	
12	Angel MANOLOV	BUL	30/12/81	G	3		
29	Ivan MARAŠ	MNE	12/11/91	A		(1)	
18	Rodoljub MARJANOVIĆ		27/1/88	A	6	(2)	
27	Miloš MIŠIĆ	CRO	29/8/89	A		(3)	
6	Đorđe MRĐANIN		26/2/81	D	11		
6	Petar MUDREŠA		1/1/85	D	9	(1)	
19	Ognjen MUDRINSKI		15/11/91	A		(2)	
14	Slobodan NOVAKOVIĆ		15/10/86	M	7	(2)	
24	Vladimir PANJKOVIĆ		30/12/87	A	4		
19	Branko PAULJEVIĆ		1/5/87	A	26	(2)	1
10	Dejan PERIĆ		16/4/79	M		(4)	
13	Aleksandar PETROVIĆ		1/2/85	M	19	(5)	2
4	Siniša RADANOVIĆ		23/11/79	D	13		1
15	Emran RAMADANI		29/1/92	M		(1)	
5	Damir TOPČAGIĆ		8/4/90	D	1	(1)	
46	Boris VARGA		15/6/93	M	1		
5	Aleksandar ŽIVANOVIĆ		8/4/87	D	12		
28	Miloš ŽIVANOVIĆ		24/7/88	A	22	(3)	5

FK INĐIJA

Coach – Momčilo Raičević; (19/11/10) Saša Nikolić; (23/12/10) Zoran Janković; (15/4/11) Simo Krunić (BIH)

Founded – 1933

Stadium – FK Inđija (4,500)

2010

14/8	Partizan	a	1-2	*Ljubinković*
22/8	Crvena zvezda	h	0-1	
29/8	Hajduk	a	3-1	*Davidov, Isidorović, Bubalo*
11/9	Jagodina	h	2-0	*Bubalo, Batioja*
18/9	OFK Beograd	a	1-2	*Kostić*
25/9	BSK Borča	h	0-0	
3/10	Rad	a	0-2	
16/10	Javor	h	1-1	*Bubalo*
23/10	Borac	a	0-0	
30/10	Čukarički	h	0-0	
6/11	Spartak	a	2-5	*Čovilo 2*
13/11	Metalac	h	1-0	*Kodžo*
20/11	Vojvodina	a	0-2	
27/11	Sloboda	h	1-3	*Vučetić (p)*
4/12	Smederevo	a	1-2	Kostić

2011

5/3	Partizan	h	1-3	*Davidov*
9/3	Crvena zvezda	a	1-3	*Jakšić*
16/3	Hajduk	h	1-2	*Vučetić (p)*
19/3	Jagodina	a	0-2	
2/4	OFK Beograd	h	1-2	*Isidorović*
9/4	BSK Borča	a	0-4	
16/4	Rad	h	1-1	*Jovanović*
20/4	Javor	a	1-2	*Vučetić*
23/4	Borac	h	2-0	*Kostić, Isidorović*
30/4	Čukarički	a	2-1	*Jovanović, Dubajić*
10/5	Spartak	h	2-1	*Isidorović, og (Čovilo)*
15/5	Metalac	a	1-2	*Isidorović*
21/5	Vojvodina	h	1-2	*Isidorović*
25/5	Sloboda	a	0-1	
29/5	Smederevo	h	2-0	*Vučetić, Bubalo*

No	Name	Nat	DoB	Pos	Aps	(s)	Gls
11	Marko ANĐELKOVIĆ		12/10/84	M	1	(2)	
21	Đorđe ANTONIĆ		6/4/91	A		(4)	
9	Guido Gabriel BARREYRO	ARG	21/6/88	A		(2)	
71	Augusto Quintero BATIOJA	ECU	4/5/90	A	7	(8)	1
29	Vojislav BLAGOJEVIĆ		2/2/92	A		(1)	
17	Milan BUBALO		8/5/90	A	26	(1)	4
26	Miroslav ČOVILO	BIH	6/5/86	M	14		2
12	Milan DAVIDOV		1/6/79	M	23	(3)	2

0	Srđan DIMITROV		28/7/92	M	6	(9)	
	Bojan DUBAJIĆ		1/9/90	A	4	(7)	1
	Aleksandar DUBLJEVIĆ	MNE	9/3/85	D	14		
3	Nenad ĐUROVIĆ	MNE	17/1/86	D	5	(3)	
9	Darko ISIDOROVIĆ		17/4/87	A	19	(6)	6
4	Marko JAKŠIĆ		6/3/87	D	19		1
8	Marko JANJUZ		4/1/94	D		(1)	
	Zoran JANKOVIĆ		8/2/74	M	5	(2)	
	Milan JOKSIMOVIĆ		9/2/90	D	19	(1)	
	Borislav JOVANOVIĆ		16/8/86	D	12	(1)	2
10	Predrag KODŽO		30/1/73	M	2	(7)	1
18	Branimir KOSTIĆ		23/9/88	M	25		3
22	Darko LEMAJIĆ		20/8/93	A	2	(2)	
21	Zoran LJUBINKOVIĆ		4/7/82	D	9	(1)	1
4	Boris MILIČIĆ		4/4/79	M	1	(1)	
77	Asmir MISINI		29/9/85	M		(4)	
3	Aleksandar NAGLIĆ		14/1/84	A	5	(3)	
26	Bojan NEZIRI		26/2/82	D	4		
27	Borko NOVAKOVIĆ		24/4/81	D	27	(1)	
24	Dragoslav POLEKSIĆ	MNE	24/4/70	G	28		
3	Slobodan SLOVIĆ		9/2/75	M	5		
6	Jovan TANASIJEVIĆ	MNE	20/1/78	D	5		
25	Saša TOMANOVIĆ		20/9/89	M	4	(2)	
23	Branislav VEJNOVIĆ		20/5/88	M	2		
20	Marko VUČETIĆ		24/6/86	M	19	(6)	4
33	Vladimir VUJASINOVIĆ		3/7/92	G	2		
15	Dragomir VUKOBRATOVIĆ		12/5/88	M	15	(2)	
13	Nenad ŽIVANOVIĆ		20/7/80	D	1		

FK JAGODINA

Coach – Mladen Dodić; (27/10/10) Miljojko Gošić; (2/4/11) Jovica Škoro

Founded – 1918

Stadium – Pod Đurđevim brdom (15,000)

2010				
15/8	Vojvodina	a	0-0	
21/8	Smederevo	h	1-0	*Beljić*
29/8	Crvena zvezda	a	1-2	*Đenić*
11/9	Inđija	a	0-2	
18/9	BSK Borča	h	2-0	*Bojović 2 (1p)*
25/9	Javor	a	0-0	
2/10	Čukarički	h	1-1	*Beljić*
16/10	Metalac	a	2-1	*Ilić, Đenić*
23/10	Sloboda	h	0-1	
30/10	Partizan	a	0-3	
6/11	Hajduk	h	3-0	*Živković B. 2, Beljić*
13/11	OFK Beograd	a	1-0	*Đilas*
21/11	Rad	h	1-1	*Đilas (p)*
27/11	Borac	a	1-1	*Simić*
5/12	Spartak	h	0-1	
2011				
5/3	Vojvodina	h	1-2	*Đenić*
9/3	Smederevo	a	0-0	
12/3	Crvena zvezda	h	0-2	
19/3	Inđija	h	2-0	*Vušljanin, Dragićević*
3/4	BSK Borča	a	0-1	
9/4	Javor	h	0-1	
16/4	Čukarički	a	3-1	*Đilas 2, Novković*
20/4	Metalac	h	0-2	
23/4	Sloboda	a	0-2	
1/5	Partizan	h	0-2	
8/5	Hajduk	a	0-1	
15/5	OFK Beograd	h	0-0	
21/5	Rad	a	4-2	*Dragićević, Bojović, Novković, Stojanović*
25/5	Borac	h	1-1	*Đilas*
29/5	Spartak	a	2-3	*Tomić, Đilas*

No	Name	Nat	DoB	Pos	Aps	(s)	Gls
17	Bojan BELJIĆ		8/5/85	A	23	(3)	3
10	Milan BOJOVIĆ		13/4/87	A	17	(3)	3
11	Igor BONDŽULIĆ		5/10/80	G	16		
2	Luka ĆANČAREVIĆ		17/6/84	D	8	(2)	
25	Ivan DRAGIĆEVIĆ		21/10/81	D	6	(2)	2
13	Duško DUKIĆ		21/6/86	D	4		
24	Dejan ĐENIĆ		2/6/86	A	11	(8)	3
19	Vladimir ĐILAS		3/3/83	A	18	(7)	6
4	Marko ĐORĐEVIĆ		22/5/83	D	8	(1)	
14	Predrag ĐORĐEVIĆ		30/6/90	A	4	(10)	
29	Aleksandar FILIPOVIĆ		20/12/94	D		(2)	
26	Vladimir ILIĆ	MNE	23/3/82	D	23		1
21	Milutin IVANOVIĆ		30/10/90	A	5	(7)	
1	Budimir JANOŠEVIĆ		21/10/89	G	2		
22	Ivan JOVANOVIĆ		21/10/89	G		(2)	
6	Saša MARJANOVIĆ		13/11/87	M	6		
25	Danijel MIHAJLOVIĆ		2/6/85	D	2		
27	Marko MUGOŠA	MNE	4/4/84	M	10	(1)	
23	Nenad NASTIĆ		8/5/81	D	9		
4	Saša NIKODIJEVIĆ		16/7/87	M	2	(3)	
8	Srđan NOVKOVIĆ		29/3/82	M	17	(7)	2
9	Perica OGNJENOVIĆ		24/2/77	A	13	(5)	
20	Marko POPOVIČ	SVN	25/8/82	D	6		
15	Josip PROJIĆ		23/8/87	D	12		
3	Radoš PROTIĆ		31/10/87	D	19	(1)	
28	Mateo RADOVANOVIĆ		17/6/91	G	1		
25	Marko SIMIĆ		16/6/87	D	12		1
18	Miloš STOJANOVIĆ		25/12/84	A	8	(4)	1
30	Dragan STOJKOV	MKD	23/2/88	D	6	(5)	
22	Aleksandar STOJKOVIĆ		15/8/90	M	3	(1)	
12	Marko ŠIMIĆ	CRO	8/9/85	G	11		
30	Nenad ŠLJIVIĆ		8/6/85	M	14		
5	Vukašin TOMIĆ		8/4/87	D	5	(1)	1
6	Aleksandar VASILJEVIĆ		19/6/82	D	10	(1)	
7	Irfan VUŠLJANIN		7/1/86	M	13	(2)	1
29	Bojan ŽIVKOVIĆ		10/11/81	M	6	(5)	2
28	Miloš G. ŽIVKOVIĆ		1/12/84	D		(3)	
8	Miloš V. ŽIVKOVIĆ		24/5/84	M		(2)	

FK JAVOR

Coach – Radovan Ćurčić; (28/9/10) Zoran Njeguš

Founded – 1912

Stadium – Kraj Moravice (5,000)

2010				
14/8	Borac	a	1-1	*Eliomar*
22/8	Spartak	h	0-0	
28/8	Vojvodina	a	0-2	
11/9	Smederevo	h	0-0	
18/9	Crvena zvezda	a	0-1	
25/9	Jagodina	h	0-0	
2/10	BSK Borča	a	0-1	
16/10	Inđija	a	1-1	*Odita*
23/10	Čukarički	h	2-0	*Rendulić, Momčilović*
30/10	Metalac	a	3-1	*Milovanović, Eliomar, Momčilović*
6/11	Sloboda	h	1-0	*Rendulić*
13/11	Partizan	a	1-4	*Gogić*
20/11	Hajduk	h	0-0	
28/11	OFK Beograd	a	1-0	*Stanisavljević*
4/12	Rad	h	2-1	*Odita, Stojaković*
2011				
5/3	Borac	h	1-1	*Rendulić*
9/3	Spartak	a	0-0	
12/3	Vojvodina	h	0-1	
19/3	Smederevo	a	1-2	*Hadžibulić*
2/4	Crvena zvezda	h	0-2	
9/4	Jagodina	a	1-0	*Milovanović*
16/4	BSK Borča	h	0-0	
20/4	Inđija	h	2-1	*Rendulić (p), Hadžibulić*
23/4	Čukarički	a	1-0	*Hadžibulić*
30/4	Metalac	h	1-0	*Hadžibulić*
7/5	Sloboda	a	0-2	
15/5	Partizan	h	1-1	*Hadžibulić*
21/5	Hajduk	a	0-2	
25/5	OFK Beograd	h	1-0	*Rendulić*
29/5	Rad	a	0-0	

SERBIA

No	Name	Nat	DoB	Pos	Aps	(s)	Gls
25	Željko ĐOKIĆ		10/5/82	D	9	(3)	
13	Goran DRAGOVIĆ		20/10/81	D	20	(4)	
10	ELIOMAR Correia Silva	BRA	16/3/88	M	28	(1)	2
23	Petar GLINTIĆ		9/6/92	G	1	(1)	
5	Goran GOGIĆ		24/4/86	M	13	(1)	1
14	Sead HADŽIBULIĆ		30/1/83	A	14	(1)	5
3	Ivan JOSOVIĆ		27/12/89	D	6	(3)	
1	Damir KAHRIMAN		19/11/84	G	15		
18	Aleksandar LEPOSAVIĆ		3/11/87	A		(4)	
8	Goran LUKOVIĆ		17/5/78	M	11	(3)	
19	Bojan MALIŠIĆ		14/1/85	D	14	(1)	
4	Boris MILIČIĆ		4/4/79	M	1		
22	Marko MILINKOVIĆ		4/5/92	D	10	(4)	
18	Miloš MILIVOJEVIĆ		17/11/86	A	2	(5)	
21	Marko MILOVANOVIĆ		12/8/82	D	29		2
17	Marko MOMČILOVIĆ		11/6/87	M	29		2
14	Obiorah Emanuel ODITA	NGA	14/5/83	A	15		2
16	Emeka Hypolite OGEUGBU	NGA	14/2/90	M		(3)	
11	Ifeanyi ONYILO	NGA	31/10/90	A	4	(12)	
5	Branko OSTOJIĆ		3/1/84	M	13	(1)	
29	Nenad PANIĆ		12/11/84	M	6	(8)	
24	Filip PETROV	MKD	23/2/89	A	1	(7)	
7	Zoran RENDULIĆ		22/5/84	D	24		5
12	Srđan SOLDATOVIĆ		10/1/74	G	3	(1)	
4	Filip STANISAVLJEVIĆ		20/5/87	M	28		1
9	Marko STEVANOVIĆ		26/7/83	A	1	(7)	
15	Igor STOJAKOVIĆ		27/5/80	M	22	(3)	1
27	Nemanja SUPIĆ	BIH	12/1/82	G	11		

FK METALAC

Coach – Zvonko Živković; (28/10/10) Miodrag Radanović; (14/4/11) Nenad Milovanović

Founded – 1961

Stadium – Čika Dača, Kragujevac (19,242)

2010				
14/8	OFK Beograd	a	0-1	
21/8	Rad	h	0-0	
28/8	Borac	a	0-1	
11/9	Spartak	h	0-1	
18/9	Vojvodina	a	1-1	*Otašević*
25/9	Smederevo	h	0-3	
3/10	Crvena zvezda	a	0-2	
16/10	Jagodina	h	1-2	*Betoligar*
23/10	BSK Borča	a	0-1	
30/10	Javor	h	1-3	*Krasić*
6/11	Čukarički	a	2-1	*Adamović, Otašević*
13/11	Inđija	a	0-1	
20/11	Sloboda	h	3-2	*Betoligar 2, Simović*
28/11	Partizan	a	0-5	
4/12	Hajduk	h	1-1	*Simović*
2011				
5/3	OFK Beograd	h	2-0	*Gojak, Naglić*
9/3	Rad	a	0-2	
12/3	Borac	h	0-0	
19/3	Spartak	a	0-2	
2/4	Vojvodina	h	0-1	
9/4	Smederevo	a	0-1	
16/4	Crvena zvezda	h	0-1	
20/4	Jagodina	a	2-0	*Stanojlović, Simović*
23/4	BSK Borča	h	2-0	*Simović, Adamović*
30/4	Javor	a	0-1	
8/5	Čukarički	h	1-0	*Betoligar*
15/5	Inđija	h	2-1	*Pavlović Pr., Betoligar*
21/5	Sloboda	a	1-0	*Adamović*
25/5	Partizan	h	1-1	*Betoligar*
29/5	Hajduk	a	1-3	*Pavlović Pr.*

No	Name	Nat	DoB	Pos	Aps	(s)	Gls
7	Nenad ADAMOVIĆ		12/1/89	M	28	(1)	3
13	Zoran ANTIĆ		7/2/75	D	4	(3)	
16	Branislav BAJIĆ		5/5/77	D	18	(1)	
14	Misdongard BETOLIGAR	CHA	26/9/85	A	28		6
1	Dejan BOGUNOVIĆ		13/5/81	G	27		
10	Rajko BREŽANČIĆ		21/8/89	D	6	(1)	
30	Nikola ĆIRKOVIĆ		11/5/92	M	1	(2)	
6	Bojan GOJAK		28/8/79	M	13	(1)	1
18	Abel HAMMOND	GHA	6/1/85	M		(4)	
18	Aleksandar IVANOVIĆ		20/11/88	M		(1)	
9	Filip KLJAJIĆ		16/8/90	G	3		
8	Marko KRASIĆ		1/12/85	M	12	(1)	1
20	Vladimir KRNJINAC		20/3/83	M	20	(3)	
4	Nikola LUKIĆ		14/5/90	M	20	(5)	
25	Svetislav MILIĆ		17/6/90	M	1	(1)	
8	Aleksandar NAGLIĆ		14/1/84	A		(3)	1
3	Ljubo NENADIĆ		29/4/86	D	22	(3)	
15	Miloš NIKOLIĆ		22/2/89	M	6	(3)	
5	Vladimir OTAŠEVIĆ		8/6/86	D	29		2
17	Ivan PAUNOVIĆ		17/6/86	M	3	(1)	
2	Petar PAVLOVIĆ		3/3/87	D	26	(1)	
10	Predrag PAVLOVIĆ		16/6/86	A	11	(2)	2
13	Darko RAKOČEVIĆ		13/9/81	D	5	(6)	
23	Vladimir SAVIĆEVIĆ		12/5/86	A	4	(9)	
11	Srđan SIMOVIĆ		17/6/85	M	21	(4)	4
19	Nebojša STANOJLOVIĆ		2/4/89	M	7	(15)	1
21	Nemanja STOŠKOVIĆ		21/2/90	M	2	(2)	
24	Milan SVOJIĆ		9/10/85	A	11	(6)	
15	Miloš ŽIVKOVIĆ		1/12/84	D	2	(2)	
22	Bojan ZORANOVIĆ		12/4/90	A		(1)	

OFK BEOGRAD

Coach – Dejan Đurđević

Founded – 1911

Stadium – Omladinski stadion (13,900)

MAJOR HONOURS: Yugoslav League – (5) 1931, 1933, 1935, 1936, 1939;
Yugoslav Cup – (4) 1953, 1955, 1962, 1966.

2010				
14/8	Metalac	h	1-0	*Kecojević*
21/8	Sloboda	a	0-1	
29/8	Partizan	h	0-2	
12/9	Hajduk	a	2-1	*Radivojević 2*
18/9	Inđija	h	2-1	*Kecojević, Sinđić*
26/9	Rad	h	0-1	
2/10	Borac	a	1-1	*Trivunović (p)*
16/10	Spartak	h	2-0	*Kecojević, Trivunović*
24/10	Vojvodina	a	0-0	
30/10	Smederevo	h	2-2	*Rodić, Milić N.*
6/11	Crvena zvezda	a	0-1	
13/11	Jagodina	h	0-1	
20/11	BSK Borča	a	1-1	*Simić*
28/11	Javor	h	0-1	
4/12	Čukarički	a	2-0	*Žeravica 2*
2011				
5/3	Metalac	a	0-2	
9/3	Sloboda	h	1-0	*Trivunović (p)*
12/3	Partizan	a	1-2	*Rodić*
19/3	Hajduk	h	1-0	*Simić*
2/4	Inđija	a	2-1	*Milić N., Batioja*
10/4	Rad	a	0-2	
16/4	Borac	h	2-1	*Milić N., Trivunović (p)*
20/4	Spartak	a	1-3	*Krstić*
23/4	Vojvodina	h	1-0	*Batioja*
30/4	Smederevo	a	0-1	
7/5	Crvena zvezda	h	0-0	
15/5	Jagodina	a	0-0	
21/5	BSK Borča	h	1-0	*Brkić*
25/5	Javor	a	0-1	
29/5	Čukarički	h	4-0	*og (Vuković), Aleksić, Popović M. 2*

No	Name	Nat	DoB	Pos	Aps	(s)	Gls
20	Bojan ALEKSIĆ		12/4/91	A	1	(9)	1
14	Augusto Quintero BATIOJA	ECU	4/5/90	A	7	(6)	2
7	Goran BRKIĆ		28/4/91	M	2	(5)	1
24	Aleksandar ĐORIĆ		18/9/93	M		(1)	
28	Miloš FILIPOVIĆ		9/5/90	M	1	(11)	
9	Nenad INJAC		4/9/85	A	4	(8)	

6	Igor JELIĆ		28/12/89	M	5	(2)	
	Ivan KECOJEVIĆ	MNE	10/4/88	D	27		3
9	Miloš KRSTIĆ		7/3/87	M	16	(8)	1
[illegible]	Aleksandar MARKOVIĆ		13/3/91	M	23	(2)	
	Stevan MARKOVIĆ	MNE	31/1/88	D	7	(3)	
1	Nikola MATEK		5/10/90	G	1		
4	Luka MERDOVIĆ	MNE	14/3/89	A	2	(1)	
	Aleksandar MIJATOVIĆ		20/9/82	D	2	(2)	
	Novica MILENOVIĆ		14/1/89	D	9		
5	Marko MILIĆ		6/11/87	D	2		
9	Nemanja MILIĆ		25/5/90	A	21	(2)	3
1	Luka MILUNOVIĆ		21/12/91	A		(1)	
	Miloš MRVALJEVIĆ	MNE	13/2/89	D		(1)	
1	Danilo NIKOLIĆ		29/7/83	D	18		
3	Marko PAVLOVSKI		7/2/94	M		(1)	
2	Marko PETKOVIĆ		3/9/92	D	15	(2)	
7	Filip PJEVIĆ		29/5/91	D	1		
5	Petar PLANIĆ		16/3/89	D	16		
7	Igor POPOVIĆ		10/8/83	D	6	(2)	
32	Mladen POPOVIĆ		29/8/88	A	4	(5)	2
36	Jovan RADIVOJEVIĆ		19/10/82	M	14	(3)	2
18	Milan RODIĆ		2/4/91	D	18	(2)	2
22	Nikola SIMIĆ		30/7/81	M	19	(6)	2
3	Uroš SINĐIĆ		19/1/86	M	11	(2)	1
1	Bojan ŠARANOV		22/9/87	G	27		
3	Tamás TAKÁCS	HUN	20/2/91	A	1		
27	Đorđe TOPALOVIĆ		11/1/79	G	2		
10	Veseljko TRIVUNOVIĆ		13/1/80	M	28		4
13	Miloš ŽERAVICA		22/7/88	M	20	(4)	2

FK PARTIZAN

Coach – Aleksandar Stanojević

Founded – 1945

Stadium – FK Partizan (30,900)

MAJOR HONOURS: Yugoslav/Serbian League – (23) 1947, 1949, 1961, 1962, 1963, 1965, 1976, 1978, 1983, 1986, 1987, 1993, 1994, 1996, 1997, 1999, 2002, 2003, 2005, 2008, 2009, 2010, 2011; Yugoslav/Serbian Cup – (12) 1947, 1952, 1954, 1957, 1989, 1992, 1994, 1998, 2001, 2008, 2009, 2011.

2010				
14/8	Inđija	h	2-1	*Cléo, Petrović*
29/8	OFK Beograd	a	2-0	*Iliev, Tomić*
4/9	Hajduk	h	2-0	*Cléo, Šćepović*
11/9	Rad	h	3-0	*Boya 2, Petrović*
19/9	Borac	a	2-0	*Cléo, Bogunović*
24/9	Spartak	h	0-0	
3/10	Vojvodina	a	0-2	
15/10	Smederevo	h	5-3	*Iliev, Šćepović 2, Boya, Petrović*
23/10	Crvena zvezda	a	1-0	*Moreira*
30/10	Jagodina	h	3-0	*Moreira, Iliev, Petrović (p)*
7/11	BSK Borča	a	3-0	*Šćepović, Petrović, Moreira*
13/11	Javor	h	4-1	*Iliev, Babović, Cléo, Petrović*
20/11	Čukarički	a	4-2	*Iliev, Babović, Moreira, Cléo*
28/11	Metalac	h	5-0	*Babović 2, Cléo, Iliev 2*
4/12	Sloboda	h	5-2	*Cléo 2, Petrović, Babović, Iliev*
2011				
5/3	Inđija	a	3-1	*Tagoe 2, Iliev*
9/3	Hajduk	a	4-0	*Tagoe, Tomić, Petrović (p), Šćepović*
12/3	OFK Beograd	h	2-1	*Tagoe, Smiljanić*
20/3	Rad	a	2-2	*Tomić, Iliev*
2/4	Borac	h	2-0	*Ilić S., Lazevski*
10/4	Spartak	a	2-1	*Petrović (p), Tomić*
16/4	Vojvodina	h	0-1	
20/4	Smederevo	a	4-1	*Tagoe, Babović, Iliev, Vukić*
23/4	Crvena zvezda	h	1-0	*Tagoe*
1/5	Jagodina	a	2-0	*Krstajić, Tagoe*
6/5	BSK Borča	h	4-0	*Savić, Vukić 2, Iliev*
15/5	Javor	a	1-1	*Babović*
21/5	Čukarički	h	4-0	*Miljković, Tagoe, Šćepović, Iliev (p)*
25/5	Metalac	a	1-1	*Babović*
29/5	Sloboda	a	2-1	*Tagoe, Miljković*

No	Name	Nat	DoB	Pos	Aps	(s)	Gls
40	Dominic ADIYIAH	GHA	29/11/89	A	3	(3)	
25	Stefan BABOVIĆ		7/1/87	M	19	(3)	8
19	Miloš BOGUNOVIĆ		10/6/85	A	1	(5)	1
11	Pierre BOYA	CMR	16/1/84	A	2	(5)	3
14	Darko BRAŠANAC		12/2/92	M	1	(3)	
9	Cléverson Gabriel Córdova "CLÉO"	BRA	9/8/85	A	13	(1)	8
23	Aleksandar DAVIDOV		7/10/83	M	7	(6)	
5	Ljubomir FEJSA		14/8/88	M		(2)	
33	Radiša ILIĆ		20/9/77	G	3		
22	Saša ILIĆ		30/12/77	M	24	(1)	1
77	Ivica ILIEV		27/10/79	A	22	(5)	13
13	Marko JOVANOVIĆ		26/3/88	D	13	(5)	
4	Mohamed "Medo" KAMARA	SLE	16/11/87	M	9	(9)	
27	Joseph Nestroy KIZITO	UGA	27/7/82	D	14		
20	Mladen KRSTAJIĆ		4/3/74	D	21		1
18	Aleksandar LAZEVSKI	MKD	21/1/88	D	13		1
50	Lazar MARKOVIĆ		2/3/94	M		(1)	
2	Aleksandar MILJKOVIĆ		26/2/90	D	22		2
10	Almani Samori da Silva MOREIRA	POR	16/6/78	M	8		4
8	Radosav PETROVIĆ		8/3/89	M	17	(8)	9
15	Stefan SAVIĆ	MNE	8/1/91	D	19	(1)	1
99	Milan SMILJANIĆ		19/11/86	M	11	(7)	1
6	Vojislav STANKOVIĆ		22/9/87	D	7	(1)	
3	Ivan STEVANOVIĆ		24/6/83	D	8		
88	Vladimir STOJKOVIĆ		28/7/83	G	26		
31	Marko ŠĆEPOVIĆ		23/5/91	A	6	(13)	6
28	Prince TAGOE	GHA	9/11/86	A	14	(1)	9
7	Nemanja TOMIĆ		21/1/88	M	16	(7)	4
80	Zvonimir VUKIĆ		19/7/79	M	10	(3)	3
12	Živko ŽIVKOVIĆ		14/4/89	G	1		

FK RAD

Coach – Marko Nikolić; (24/05/11) (Milan Bosanac)

Founded – 1958

Stadium – FK Rad (6,000)

2010				
15/8	Čukarički	h	4-0	*Kojić, Luka, Dimitrijević, Andrić*
21/8	Metalac	a	0-0	
28/8	Sloboda	h	0-0	
11/9	Partizan	a	0-3	
19/9	Hajduk	h	1-0	*Dimitrijević*
26/9	OFK Beograd	a	1-0	*Luka*
3/10	Inđija	h	2-0	*Dimitrijević, Stanojević*
17/10	Borac	h	3-1	*Dimitrijević (p), Jovančić, Luka*
24/10	Spartak	a	2-1	*Dimitrijević, Kojić*
31/10	Vojvodina	h	1-0	*Andrić*
7/11	Smederevo	a	0-0	
14/11	Crvena zvezda	h	0-1	
21/11	Jagodina	a	1-1	*Koković (p)*
28/11	BSK Borča	h	5-0	*Čotra 2, Jovančić 2, Jovanović*
4/12	Javor	a	1-2	*Jovanović*
2011				
5/3	Čukarički	a	3-0	*Luka 2, Jovančić*
9/3	Metalac	h	2-0	*Stanojević, Jovanović*
12/3	Sloboda	a	0-0	
20/3	Partizan	h	2-2	*Pajović, Leković*
3/4	Hajduk	a	1-0	*Jovančić*
10/4	OFK Beograd	h	2-0	*Luka, Stanojević (p)*
16/4	Inđija	a	1-1	*Stanojević*
20/4	Borac	a	0-0	
23/4	Spartak	h	1-1	*Jovančić*
30/4	Vojvodina	a	0-2	
8/5	Smederevo	h	1-0	*Ranđelović*
15/5	Crvena zvezda	a	1-2	*Jovančić*
21/5	Jagodina	h	2-4	*Jovančić, og (Dragićević)*
25/5	BSK Borča	a	1-0	*Kojić*
29/5	Javor	h	0-0	

No	Name	Nat	DoB	Pos	Aps	(s)	Gls
22	Nemanja ANDRIĆ		13/6/87	M	25	(3)	2
26	Milan BORJAN	CAN	23/10/87	G	23		
24	Lazar ĆIRKOVIĆ		22/8/92	D		(2)	
3	Đorđe ČOTRA		13/9/84	D	2	(2)	2
1	Branislav DANILOVIĆ		24/6/88	G	7	(1)	

No	Name	Nat	DoB	Pos	Aps	(s)	Gls
10	Uroš DELIĆ		10/8/87	M	2	(5)	
7	Miloš DIMITRIJEVIĆ		16/2/84	M	13	(1)	5
23	Vladimir JOVANČIĆ		31/5/87	A	23	(3)	8
8	Branislav JOVANOVIĆ		21/9/85	M	18	(1)	3
27	Nemanja KOJIĆ		3/2/90	A	9	(18)	3
5	Radomir KOKOVIĆ		6/1/84	D	17		1
14	Aleksandar KOSORIĆ	BIH	30/1/87	D	10		
30	Nikola LEKOVIĆ		19/12/89	D	27		1
20	Predrag LUKA		11/5/88	M	26		6
29	Filip MALBAŠIĆ		18/11/92	M	1	(3)	
19	Luka MILIVOJEVIĆ		7/4/91	M	16	(10)	
25	Milan MITROVIĆ		2/7/88	D	18	(1)	
9	Andrej MRKELA		9/4/92	M	2	(3)	
3	Nemanja OBRADOVIĆ		29/5/89	D		(10)	
15	Tomislav PAJOVIĆ		15/3/86	D	25		1
2	Aleksandar PANTIĆ		11/4/92	D	5		
7	Andrija PAVLOVIĆ		13/1/93	M		(1)	
11	Milan PRŠO		29/6/90	A	3	(6)	
6	Marko RANĐELOVIĆ		16/8/84	D	17		1
21	Nikola RASPOPOVIĆ		18/10/89	M	5	(2)	
16	Ivan ROGAČ		30/11/91	D		(1)	
28	Marko STANOJEVIĆ		22/6/88	M	20	(9)	4
17	Nikola STOJILJKOVIĆ		17/8/92	A		(4)	
4	Aleksandar TODOROVSKI	MKD	26/2/84	D	15		
18	Stefan TRIPKOVIĆ		21/9/94	A		(1)	
31	Saša VARGA		19/8/93	A		(1)	
13	Uroš VITAS		6/7/92	A	1		

FK SLOBODA POINT SEVOJNO

Coach – Ljubiša Stamenković

Founded – 1925

Stadium – Mladost, Lučani (8,000)

2010				
15/8	Hajduk	a	2-1	*Arsenijević, Pavićević (p)*
21/8	OFK Beograd	h	1-0	*Pavićević*
28/8	Rad	a	0-0	
11/9	Borac	h	0-0	
19/9	Spartak	a	2-2	*Ademović, Pavićević*
26/9	Vojvodina	h	0-0	
2/10	Smederevo	a	0-0	
17/10	Crvena zvezda	h	0-3	
23/10	Jagodina	a	1-0	*Arsenijević*
30/10	BSK Borča	h	2-1	*Lazić, Ademović*
6/11	Javor	a	0-1	
13/11	Čukarički	h	4-0	*Arsenijević 3, Ljubinković*
20/11	Metalac	a	2-3	*Ljubinković, Lazić*
27/11	Inđija	a	3-1	*Arsenijević 2, Ljubinković*
4/12	Partizan	a	2-5	*Stevančević, Ademović*
2011				
5/3	Hajduk	h	2-2	*Maksimović, og (Lalić)*
9/3	OFK Beograd	a	0-1	
12/3	Rad	h	0-0	
19/3	Borac	a	0-1	
2/4	Spartak	h	0-1	
9/4	Vojvodina	a	1-3	*Šunjevarić*
16/4	Smederevo	h	2-1	*og (Lukić), Ademović*
20/4	Crvena zvezda	a	1-5	*Lazić*
23/4	Jagodina	h	2-0	*Ademović, Bossman*
30/4	BSK Borča	a	1-0	*Vasilić*
7/5	Javor	h	2-0	*Lazić 2*
15/5	Čukarički	a	2-1	*Ademović, Pavićević*
21/5	Metalac	h	0-1	
25/5	Inđija	h	1-0	*Kovačević (p)*
29/5	Partizan	h	1-2	*Pejović*

No	Name	Nat	DoB	Pos	Aps	(s)	Gls
23	Edim ADEMOVIĆ		2/10/87	A	16	(8)	6
19	Nemanja ARSENIJEVIĆ		29/3/86	A	15		7
3	Francis Jojo BOSSMAN	GHA	24/6/84	M	15	(3)	1
25	Darko BOŽOVIĆ	MNE	9/8/78	G	13		
4	Radoš BULATOVIĆ		5/6/84	D	26		
8	Njegoš GOLOČEVAC		21/8/83	M	11	(6)	
30	Petar JOVANOVIĆ		12/7/82	D	13		
44	Maroš KLIMPL	SVK	4/7/80	D	12		
20	Savo KOVAČEVIĆ		15/8/88	A	4	(7)	1
18	Predrag LAZIĆ		15/1/82	M	28		5
20	Marko LJUBINKOVIĆ		7/12/81	M	4		3
31	Nikola MAKSIMOVIĆ		25/11/91	D	18	(2)	1
15	Dušan MIHAJLOVIĆ		30/6/85	M	6	(4)	
1	Milorad NIKOLIĆ		6/2/84	G	16		
44	Rade NOVKOVIĆ		25/6/80	D	2		
9	Marko PAVIĆEVIĆ		3/9/86	A	25		4
13	Aleksandar PEJOVIĆ		28/12/90	M	1	(11)	1
55	Aleksandar PETROVIĆ		8/2/85	D	1		
17	Ivan PETROVIĆ		17/7/86	M		(5)	
17	Bogdan PLANIĆ		19/1/92	D		(1)	
33	Tomáš POLÁČEK	CZE	29/8/80	A	5	(5)	
5	Dragan RADOSAVLJEVIĆ		24/10/82	D	26		
19	Ricardo Silva de Almeida "RICARDINHO"	BRA	2/6/89	M	1	(2)	
11	Igor STANISAVLJEVIĆ		3/8/78	D	15	(1)	
14	Đuro STEVANČEVIĆ		25/6/83	M	11	(8)	1
12	Bojan ŠEJIĆ		14/7/83	G	1		
7	Radan ŠUNJEVARIĆ		10/2/83	M	29		1
6	Gjorgji TANUŠEV	MKD	7/1/91	M	1	(6)	
16	TIAGO GALVÃO da Silva	BRA	24/8/89	A	1	(10)	
2	Jovica VASILIĆ		8/7/90	D	10		1
22	Vladimir VUJOVIĆ		20/12/85	A	4	(3)	
10	Vladimir VUKAJLOVIĆ		25/8/83	M		(3)	

FK SMEDEREVO

Coach – Dragan Đorđević

Founded – 1924

Stadium – FK Smederevo (17,200)

MAJOR HONOURS: Yugoslav Cup – (1) 2003.

2010				
14/8	Crvena zvezda	h	0-0	
21/8	Jagodina	a	0-1	
28/8	BSK Borča	h	1-1	*Ranković S.*
11/9	Javor	a	0-0	
18/9	Čukarički	h	2-0	*Živković D., Ćeran*
25/9	Metalac	a	3-0	*Ćeran, Živković D., Marinković*
2/10	Sloboda	h	0-0	
15/10	Partizan	a	3-5	*Ranković S. 2, Ćeran*
23/10	Hajduk	h	1-1	*Marinković (p)*
30/10	OFK Beograd	a	2-2	*Ćeran, Marinković*
7/11	Rad	h	0-0	
13/11	Borac	a	1-0	*Stanić*
20/11	Spartak	h	0-0	
27/11	Vojvodina	a	1-4	*Marinković*
4/12	Inđija	h	2-1	*Ranković S., Milosavljević I.*
2011				
5/3	Crvena zvezda	a	0-1	
9/3	Jagodina	h	0-0	
12/3	BSK Borča	a	0-0	
19/3	Javor	h	2-1	*Živković D., Ognjanović*
2/4	Čukarički	a	1-0	*Živković D.*
9/4	Metalac	h	1-0	*Stojanović*
16/4	Sloboda	a	1-2	*Ćeran (p)*
20/4	Partizan	h	1-4	*Ćeran*
23/4	Hajduk	a	0-2	
30/4	OFK Beograd	h	1-0	*Stojanović*
8/5	Rad	a	0-1	
15/5	Borac	h	0-1	
21/5	Spartak	a	1-2	*Bojatović*
25/5	Vojvodina	h	0-0	
29/5	Inđija	a	0-2	

No	Name	Nat	DoB	Pos	Aps	(s)	Gls
19	Branislav ATANACKOVIĆ		5/8/83	D	23		
11	Vojislav BOJATOVIĆ		26/8/82	A	9	(12)	1
15	Dušan BRKOVIĆ		20/1/89	D	29		
7	Dragan ĆERAN		6/10/87	A	28		6
32	Igor GRKAJAC		26/4/87	A		(5)	
20	Predrag JERINIĆ		5/12/88	M	18	(4)	
6	Miloš KARIŠIK		7/10/88	D	3	(2)	
44	Stevan KOVAČEVIĆ		9/1/88	M	13	(2)	
30	Nikola LEKIĆ		28/8/90	M		(4)	

5	Mladen LIČINA		14/3/91	M		(1)	
	Slavko LUKIĆ		14/3/89	D	13		
0	Nenad MARINKOVIĆ		28/9/88	A	15		4
	Ivan MILOSAVLJEVIĆ		14/2/83	D	18	(1)	1
4	Marko MILOSAVLJEVIĆ		20/12/87	M	17	(9)	
4	Igor MIOVIĆ		31/3/86	D	6	(1)	
7	Marko NIKOLIĆ		28/9/89	A		(3)	
[illegible]	Dejan OGNJANOVIĆ	MNE	21/6/78	D	22		1
9	Vladimir PERALOVIĆ		10/10/91	M		(1)	
[illegible]	Miloš RADOSAVLJEVIĆ		20/5/88	M	3	(11)	
2	Dejan RANKOVIĆ		25/7/76	G	28		
[illegible]	Saša RANKOVIĆ		21/9/79	A	14	(1)	4
7	Branislav STANIĆ		30/7/88	M	16	(8)	1
3	Marko STANOJEVIĆ		17/2/91	D	1		
8	Slaviša STOJANOVIĆ		27/1/89	M	8	(14)	2
6	Zoran TODOROV	MKD	31/10/82	M	16	(3)	
1	Ivan VILARET		31/3/86	A		(1)	
3	Dejan ŽIVKOVIĆ		28/4/82	M	28		4
[illegible]	Mladen ŽIVKOVIĆ		26/8/89	G	2	(1)	

FK SPARTAK ZLATIBOR VODA

Coach – Dragan Miranović; (25/11/10) Ilija Dobrić; (17/12/10) Ljubomir Ristovski

Founded – 1921

Stadium – Gradski (25,000)

2010				
14/8	BSK Borča	h	1-1	*Torbica*
22/8	Javor	a	0-0	
28/8	Čukarički	h	2-0	*Ubiparip, Bratić*
11/9	Metalac	a	1-0	*Mirić*
19/9	Sloboda	h	2-2	*Torbica (p), Ubiparip*
24/9	Partizan	a	0-0	
2/10	Hajduk	h	1-0	*Ubiparip*
16/10	OFK Beograd	a	0-2	
24/10	Rad	h	1-2	*Mirić*
30/10	Borac	a	0-0	
6/11	Inđija	h	5-2	*Ubiparip 2, Nikolić 2, Mirić*
14/11	Vojvodina	h	0-1	
20/11	Smederevo	a	0-0	
28/11	Crvena zvezda	h	1-2	*Torbica (p)*
5/12	Jagodina	a	1-0	*Ubiparip*
2011				
5/3	BSK Borča	a	0-0	
9/3	Javor	h	0-0	
12/3	Čukarički	a	2-0	*Puškarić, Torbica (p)*
19/3	Metalac	h	2-0	*Simović, Torbica*
2/4	Sloboda	a	1-0	*Torbica (p)*
10/4	Partizan	h	1-2	*Mirić*
16/4	Hajduk	a	0-1	
20/4	OFK Beograd	h	3-1	*Torbica (p), Adamović, Nosković*
23/4	Rad	a	1-1	*Vujaklija*
30/4	Borac	h	1-2	*Vujaklija*
10/5	Inđija	a	1-2	*Bratić*
15/5	Vojvodina	a	0-1	
21/5	Smederevo	h	2-1	*Torbica (p), Antonić*
25/5	Crvena zvezda	a	2-2	*Nosković 2*
29/5	Jagodina	h	3-2	*Nikolić, Nosković, Vujaklija*

No	Name	Nat	DoB	Pos	Aps	(s)	Gls
7	Marko ADAMOVIĆ		11/3/91	M	13	(7)	1
12	Branimir ALEKSIĆ		24/12/90	G	29		
17	Goran ANTONIĆ		3/11/90	D	29		1
10	Aleksandar AVRIĆ		6/3/88	M	4	(12)	
19	Miloš BOKIĆ		30/10/91	D		(2)	
22	Darko BOŠKOVIĆ	MNE	16/9/87	M		(3)	
6	Vidak BRATIĆ		20/10/76	M	28		2
16	CHENG Mouyi	CHN	24/2/85	M	1	(2)	
18	Nemanja CRNOGLAVAC		13/1/90	D	1		
14	Miroslav ČOVILO	BIH	6/5/86	M	1	(6)	
28	Marko JONDIĆ		11/8/93	M		(1)	
26	Darko KARADŽIĆ	MNE	17/4/89	M		(4)	
25	Goran LABUS		28/4/85	G	1		
24	Nebojša MEZEI		15/2/91	D	2	(2)	
5	Nikola MILANKOVIĆ		23/4/86	M	16	(6)	
21	Marko MIRIĆ		26/3/87	A	25	(2)	4
22	Igor MIŠAN		5/5/90	M	2		
15	Nemanja NIKOLIĆ	MNE	1/1/88	M	14	(8)	3
11	Aleksandar NOSKOVIĆ		12/12/88	A	4	(18)	4
20	Darko PUŠKARIĆ		13/7/85	D	14	(3)	1
4	Slobodan SIMOVIĆ		22/5/89	M	29		1
2	Siniša STEVANOVIĆ		12/1/89	D	23	(1)	
3	Dragan ŠARAC		27/9/75	D	28	(1)	
8	Vladimir TORBICA		20/9/80	A	28		8
14	Vojo UBIPARIP		10/5/88	A	14		6
13	Vladimir VESELINOV		25/5/84	M	11	(5)	
23	Lazar VESELINOVIĆ		4/8/86	A	1	(2)	
9	Srđan VUJAKLIJA		21/3/88	A	12	(2)	3

FK VOJVODINA

Coach – Zoran Milinković

Founded – 1914

Stadium – Karađorđe (15,754)

MAJOR HONOURS: Yugoslav League – (2) 1966, 1989.

2010				
15/8	Jagodina	h	0-0	
21/8	BSK Borča	a	2-0	*Antwi, Katai*
28/8	Javor	h	2-0	*Merebashvili 2*
11/9	Čukarički	a	2-0	*Oumarou, Stevanović*
18/9	Metalac	h	1-1	*Oumarou*
26/9	Sloboda	a	0-0	
3/10	Partizan	h	2-0	*Gjurovski (p), Merebashvili*
17/10	Hajduk	a	1-0	*Bilbija*
24/10	OFK Beograd	h	0-0	
31/10	Rad	a	0-1	
6/11	Borac	h	4-0	*Merebashvili (p), Oumarou (p), Ilić, Mitošević*
14/11	Spartak	a	1-0	*Oumarou*
20/11	Inđija	h	2-0	*Lazetić, Ilić*
27/11	Smederevo	h	4-1	*Merebashvili 2, Ilić, Tumbasević*
4/12	Crvena zvezda	a	2-2	*Antwi, Oumarou*
2011				
5/3	Jagodina	a	2-1	*Merebashvili (p), Ilić*
9/3	BSK Borča	h	2-1	*Oumarou, Katai*
12/3	Javor	a	1-0	*Ilić*
19/3	Čukarički	h	3-0	*Oumarou 2, Tumbasević*
2/4	Metalac	a	1-0	*Ilić*
9/4	Sloboda	h	3-1	*Lazetić, Katai, Trajković*
16/4	Partizan	a	1-0	*Oumarou*
20/4	Hajduk	h	2-1	*Stevanović 2*
23/4	OFK Beograd	a	0-1	
30/4	Rad	h	2-0	*Stevanović, Antwi*
7/5	Borac	a	1-1	*Novaković M.*
15/5	Spartak	h	1-0	*Oumarou*
21/5	Inđija	a	2-1	*Medojević, Oumarou (p)*
25/5	Smederevo	a	0-0	
29/5	Crvena zvezda	h	0-2	

No	Name	Nat	DoB	Pos	Aps	(s)	Gls
28	Nnaemeca AJURU	NGA	28/9/86	M	5	(1)	
18	Yaw ANTWI	GHA	15/6/85	A	7	(9)	3
21	Nemanja BILBIJA	BIH	2/11/90	A	3	(15)	1
1	Željko BRKIĆ		9/7/86	G	28		
10	Mario GJUROVSKI	MKD	11/12/85	M	7	(2)	1
9	Brana ILIĆ		16/2/85	A	21	(1)	6
24	Dejan KARAN		13/8/88	D	9	(1)	
27	Aleksandar KATAI		6/2/91	A	8	(15)	3
4	Nebojša KOSOVIĆ	MNE	24/2/95	M		(2)	
11	Nikola LAZETIĆ		9/2/78	M	19		2
3	Slobodan MEDOJEVIĆ		20/10/90	M	28		1
17	Giorgi MEREBASHVILI	GEO	15/8/86	M	21	(4)	7
20	Milovan MILOVIĆ		24/10/80	D	6		
13	Vuk MITOŠEVIĆ		12/2/91	M	12	(7)	1
5	Daniel MOJSOV	MKD	25/12/87	D	21		
19	Ognjen MUDRINSKI		15/11/91	A		(1)	
23	Dušan NESTOROVIĆ		26/6/86	D	3		
15	Milko NOVAKOVIĆ	MNE	21/1/88	D	3		1

10	Slobodan NOVAKOVIĆ		15/10/86	M	1	(4)	
14	Aboubakar OUMAROU	CMR	4/1/87	A	27		11
32	Filip PAJOVIĆ		30/7/93	G	2		
31	Vladan PAVLOVIĆ		24/2/84	D	22		
25	Vladimir SILAĐI		8/6/94	M		(1)	
4	Goran SMILJANIĆ		31/1/90	M	6	(1)	
16	Miroslav STEVANOVIĆ	BIH	12/2/91	M	8	(16)	4
6	Branislav TRAJKOVIĆ		29/8/89	D	18		1
8	Janko TUMBASEVIĆ	MNE	14/1/85	M	18	(8)	2
22	Miroslav VULIĆEVIĆ		29/5/85	D	27		

TOP GOALSCORERS 2010/11

13	Andrija KALUĐEROVIĆ (Crvena zvezda)
	Ivica ILIEV (Partizan)
11	Aboubakar OUMAROU (Vojvodina)
9	Radosav PETROVIĆ (Partizan)
	Prince TAGOE (Partizan)
8	Stefan BABOVIĆ (Partizan)
	CLÉO (Partizan)
	Vladimir JOVANČIĆ (Rad)
	Vladimir TORBICA (Spartak)
7	Nemanja ARSENIJEVIĆ (Sloboda)
	Giorgi MEREBASHVILI (Vojvodina)

PROMOTED CLUBS

FK RADNIČKI 1923

Coach – Vlado Čapljić
Founded – 1923
Stadium – Čika Dača (19,242)

FK NOVI PAZAR

Coach – Saša Štrbac; (10/9/10) Jovica Škoro; (1/1/11) Mladen Dodić
Founded – 1928
Stadium – Gradski stadion – Abdulah Gegić "Duce" (6,500)

SECOND LEVEL FINAL TABLE 2010/11

		Pld	W	D	L	F	A	Pts
1	FK BASK	34	24	5	5	54	21	77
2	FK Radnički 1923	34	22	8	4	61	22	74
3	FK Novi Pazar	34	21	8	5	46	20	71
4	FK Banat	34	15	11	8	41	31	56
5	FK Sinđelić	34	15	8	11	41	34	53
6	FK Napredak	34	13	10	11	35	32	49
7	FK Radnički Sombor	34	13	10	11	30	29	49
8	FK Proleter Novi Sad	34	12	9	13	46	40	45
9	FK Mladost Lučani	34	11	12	11	29	32	45
10	FK Mladi radnik	34	12	7	15	38	49	43
11	RFK Novi Sad	34	11	9	14	37	42	42
12	FK Bežanija	34	11	7	16	28	28	40
13	FK Teleoptik	34	9	12	13	35	44	39
14	FK Srem Sremska Mitrovica	34	8	12	14	30	43	36
15	FK Kolubara	34	9	9	16	33	43	33
16	FK Zemun	34	8	9	17	34	40	33
17	FK Big Bull Radnički	34	7	5	22	26	50	26
18	FK Dinamo Vranje	34	7	5	22	23	65	26

NB FK BASK declined promotion and sold their Superliga 2011/12 place to FK Novi Pazar; FK Kolubara – 3 pts deducted.

DOMESTIC CUP 2010/11

KUP SRBIJE

FIRST ROUND

(22/9/10)
Borac Čačak 2, Inđija 0
BSK Borča 1, Srem Sremska Mitrovica 1 *(2-4 on pens)*
Donji Srem 0, Rad 2
Hajduk Kula 0, Kolubara 0 *(4-5 on pens)*
Jagodina 4, Bežanija 0
Metalac 1, Novi Sad 1 *(4-2 on pens)*
Mladi radnik 1, Sloboda Sevojno 3
Mokra gora 0, Smederevo 0 *(8-9 on pens)*
Proleter Novi Sad 1, Napredak 0
Sinđelić 2, Čukarički 0
Sloga Kraljevo 0, Crvena zvezda 2
Sloga Petrovac 0, Vojvodina 2
Srem Jakovo 2, Javor 2 *(5-4 on pens)*
Teleoptik 2, OFK Beograd 1

(28/9/10)
Spartak Zlatibor voda 2, Novi Pazar 1

(6/10/10)
Mladost Apatin 0, Partizan 6

SECOND ROUND

(27/10/10)
Crvena zvezda 4, Borac Čačak 0
Kolubara 1, Spartak Zlatibor voda 2
Partizan 3, Proleter Novi Sad 0
Sinđelić 0, Rad 0 *(5-3 on pens)*
Sloboda Sevojno 2, Metalac 1
Smederevo 0, Teleoptik 0 *(3-4 on pens)*
Srem Jakovo 2, Vojvodina 2 *(4-5 on pens)*
Srem Sremska Mitrovica 0, Jagodina 2

QUARTER-FINALS

(10/11/10)
Crvena zvezda 2 *(Kaluđerović 48, 89)*, Teleoptik 1 *(Antelj 22)*
Sinđelić 0, Partizan 4 *(Šćepović 18, 89, Ilić S. 49, Moreira 72)*
Sloboda Sevojno 3 *(Arsenijević 12, Goločevac 43, Šunjevarić 45)*, Spartak Zlatibor voda 2 *(Ubiparip 27, Nosković 49)*
Vojvodina 1 *(Oumarou 89)*, Jagodina 0

SEMI-FINALS

(16/3/11 & 6/4/11)
Partizan 2 *(Tagoe 4, 48)*, Crvena zvezda 0
Crvena zvezda 1 *(Kaluđerović 72)*, Partizan 0
(Partizan 2-1)

Sloboda Sevojno 1 *(Kovačević 20)*, Vojvodina 2 *(Oumarou 26, Mojsov 76)*
Vojvodina 1 *(Katai 7)*, Sloboda Sevojno 0
(Vojvodina 3-1)

FINAL

(11/5/11)
Stadion FK Crvena zvezda, Belgrade
FK PARTIZAN 2 *(Tagoe 17, Vukić 72p)*
FK VOJVODINA 1 *(Mojsov 63)*
(Abandoned after 81 mins; awarded 3-0)
Referee – *Veselinović*
PARTIZAN – *Stojković, Miljković, Savić, Krstajić, Jovanović, Babović, Smiljanić (Petrović 82), Kamara, Tomić (Ilić S. 73), Tagoe, Iliev (Vukić 62).*
VOJVODINA – *Brkić, Vulićević, Mojsov, Trajković, Pavlović, Medojević, Tumbasević, Stevanović (Merebashvili 60), Lazetić (Katai 74), Ilić, Oumarou.*

CLUB COMMUNICATION 2011/12

FK Borac Čačak

Gradski bedem br 6, PO Box 5
RS-32000 Čačak

Tel +381 32 222 481
Fax +381 32 225 458
Web boracfk.com
Email fk.borac@open.telekom.rs
Media Officer Dejan Kolarević

FK BSK Borča

JNA 1a, Borca
RS-11211 Borča

Tel +381 11 3329 780
Fax +381 11 3329 781
Web bskborca.org
Email bskborca@open.telekom.rs
Media Officer Sanja Gvoić

FK Crvena zvezda

Ljutice Bogdana 1a
RS-11000 Beograd

Tel +381 11 3672 060
Fax +381 11 3672 070
Web crvenazvezdafk.com
Email office@crvenazvezdafk.com
Media Officer Marko Nikolovski

FK Hajduk Kula

ul. Svetozara Markovića 8
RS-25230 Kula

Tel +381 25 723 569
Fax +381 25 723 045
Web fkhajduk.org.rs
Email fkhajdukkula@open.telekom.rs
Media Officer Đorđo Bojanić

FK Jagodina

Gradski stadion bb
RS-35000 Jagodina

Tel +381 35 252 404
Fax +381 35 252 303
Web fkjagodina.org.rs
Email fkjagodina@open.telekom.rs
Media Officer Ljubiša Vujić

FK Javor

13 Septembar bb
RS-32250 Ivanjica

Tel +381 32 664 478
Fax +381 32 664 464
Web fkjavor.com
Email javor1912@gmail.com
Media Officer Beba Bojović

FK Metalac

Despotovačka bb
RS-32300 Gornji Milanovac

Tel +381 32 716 808
Fax +381 32 716 808
Web fkmetalac.rs
Email fkmetalac@gmail.com
Media Officer Zvonko Jevremović

FK Novi Pazar

Oslobodjenje br. 82
RS-36300 Novi Pazar

Tel +381 20 315 275
Fax +381 20 315 275
Web fknovipazar.com
Email fknovipazar@yahoo.com
Media Officer Karisik Fehim

OFK Beograd

Mije Kovacevica 10a
RS-11000 Beograd

Tel +381 11 3291 514
Fax +381 11 2762 364
Web ofkbeograd.co.rs
Email irina@ofkbeograd.co.rs
Media Officer Miodrag Fiser

FK Partizan

Humska 1
RS-11000 Beograd

Tel +381 11 3693 815
Fax +381 11 3693 812
Web partizan.rs
Email football@partizan.rs
Media Officer Marko Vjetrović

FK Rad

Crnotravska bb
RS-11000 Beograd

Tel +381 11 3671 267
Fax +381 11 3672 110
Web fcrad.co.rs
Email fcradbgd@gmail.com
Media Officer Vladimir Savić

FK Radnički 1923

Kralja Milana IV 21
RS-34000 Kragujevac

Tel +381 34 353 540
Fax +381 34 353 530
Web fkradnicki.com
Email office@fkradnicki.com
Media Officer Milena Živković

FK Sloboda Point Sevojno

Omladinska bb
RS-31000 Užice

Tel +381 31 510 260
Fax +381 31 510 260
Web fkslobodapointsevojno.rs
Email office@fkslobodapointsevojno.rs
Media Officer Vladimir Pavlović

FK Smederevo

Goranska 12
RS-11300 Smederevo

Tel +381 26 223 030
Fax +381 26 224 509
Web fksmederevo.com
Email kontakt@fksmederevo.com
Media Officer Milan Kočić

FK Spartak Zlatibor voda

Park Rajhl Ferenca br. 10
RS-24000 Subotica

Tel +381 24 553 818
Fax +381 24 553 818
Web fkspartakzlatiborvoda.com
Email fkspartakzlatiborvoda@gmail.com
Media Officer Mina Banjac

FK Vojvodina

Novosadski Put 114
RS-21000 Novi Sad

Tel +381 21 820 490
Fax +381 21 820 490
Web fkvojvodina.rs
Email office@fcvojvodina.co.rs
Media Officer Sanja Trivić

SLOVAKIA

Slovaquie I Slowakei

Slovenský futbalový zväz (SFZ)

COMMUNICATION

Address Trnavská 100/II
SK-821 01 Bratislava
Tel +421 2 4820 6000
Fax +421 2 4820 6099
E-mail office@futbalsfz.sk
Website futbalsfz.sk

President Ján Kováčik
General Secretary Jozef Kliment
Media Officer Juraj Čurný

Year of Formation 1938

DOMESTIC COMPETITION SUMMARY 2010/11

1. LIIGA FINAL TABLE

			Home					Away					Total						
		Pld	W	D	L	F	A	W	D	L	F	A	W	D	L	F	A	Pts	Comp
1	ŠK Slovan Bratislava	33	13	3	1	39	7	7	5	4	24	15	20	8	5	63	22	68	UCL
2	FK Senica	33	10	4	3	30	13	8	3	5	24	17	18	7	8	54	30	61	UEL
3	MŠK Žilina	33	8	7	2	25	15	6	5	5	22	13	14	12	7	47	28	54	UEL
4	FC Spartak Trnava	33	8	6	2	23	9	5	4	8	17	21	13	10	10	40	30	49	UEL
5	Dukla Banská Bystrica	33	10	4	3	25	11	3	5	8	14	21	13	9	11	39	32	48	
6	FC ViOn Zlaté Moravce	33	9	3	4	24	16	3	7	7	11	15	12	10	11	35	31	46	
7	MFK Ružomberok	33	6	8	3	14	10	4	3	9	9	23	10	11	12	23	33	41	
8	FC Nitra	33	6	4	7	14	22	5	3	8	16	29	11	7	15	30	51	40	
9	DAC 1904 Dunajská Streda	33	7	4	5	18	18	2	5	10	6	21	9	9	15	24	39	36	
10	MFK Košice	33	7	2	7	18	19	1	7	9	10	25	8	9	16	28	44	33	
11	1. FC Tatran Prešov	33	6	5	5	17	18	3	1	13	13	31	9	6	18	30	49	33	
12	MFK Dubnica	33	6	4	6	12	19	1	6	10	11	28	7	10	16	23	47	31	*Relegated*

Top Scorer Filip Šebo (Slovan), 22 goals

Promoted Club FK AS Trencín

Cup Final ŠK Slovan Bratislava 3, MŠK Žilina 3 (aet; 5-4 on pens)

Slovan triumph in season of two halves

An astonishing fightback during the second half of the season saw ŠK Slovan Bratislava reclaim the Slovakian 1. Liga title they had surrendered the previous season to MŠK Žilina. Twelve points and four places behind the defending champions at the winter break, Slovan pulled off a minor miracle in the spring, winning 14 of their 15 fixtures to capture a record sixth Slovakian title and complete a third domestic double.

The two figures at the heart of Slovan's remarkable renaissance were Slovakian international striker Filip Šebo, who returned to his homeland after a five-year absence in mid-September, and coach Karel Jarolím, who arrived a month later as the replacement for Jozef Jankech. It took the two men time to settle in, but by the start of the spring campaign both were primed and ready for battle. Jarolím, a successful coach across the border with SK Slavia Praha, proved his worth as Slovan began to play with increasing confidence. Šebo, meanwhile, struck a rich vein of goalscoring form that would stay with him through to the end of the campaign, plundering 17 goals in 14 matches from early March to late May.

Czech coach Karel Jarolím steered Slovan to the Slovakian 1. Liga title

With 43 points from a possible 45 in the spring – only MFK Dubnica, who would end up relegated, denied them a clean sweep of victories - Slovan finished the season with a seven-point victory margin over FK Senica, who, skilfully led by Stanislav Griga, rolled home in second place. Senica, who had earned their top-flight status in 2009 by amalgamating with AŠK Inter Bratislava, were almost as strong as Slovan at the spring resumption, posting eight successive clean sheets. That defensive solidity, allied to the explosive form of Czech striker Ondřej Smetana (second to Šebo in the top scorer charts), enabled them to top the table for a while, but although Slovan overtook them, they held on to second place thanks to the spring meltdown of winter champions Žilina.

Žilina pride

Pavel Hapal's team were the pride of Slovakia in August when they beat AC Sparta Praha twice in the UEFA Champions League play-offs to reach the group stage for the first time. That they then lost all six games to Chelsea FC, Olympique de Marseille and FC Spartak Moskva was no great surprise. The only problem was that the lengthy European campaign, which comprised 12 matches in total, eventually sapped Žilina's energy reserves, leaving them powerless in the spring to reproduce the fine domestic form that had put them six points clear at the 1. Liga summit in November.

Furthermore, Žilina sold three key players during the winter – defender Mário Pečalka, playmaker Róbert Jež, and ten-goal top scorer Tomáš Oravec. Unable to win any of their seven away fixtures in the spring, their frustrations boiled over in the big match at home to Slovan on 1 April when, with the score at 0-0 and tension on the field at fever pitch following the sending-off of Žilina striker Mamadou Ceesay, a home fan physically assaulted, and injured, one of the linesmen, forcing the game to be abandoned. Although 89 of the 90 minutes had elapsed, the result was annulled and the match awarded 3-0 to Slovan. It proved to be a major turning point in the season, with Slovan's 'victory' enabling them to close the gap at the top to four points.

A few weeks later Slovan and Žilina met again, in the Slovakian Cup final. It was another closely contested encounter, but this time there were goals, and plenty of them, as two strikes from Šebo, the second of them seven minutes from the end of extra time, appeared to have given Slovan a 3-2 win, only for Žilina defender Patrik Mráz to score a dramatic equaliser in the 121st minute. The ensuing penalty shoot-out was symptomatic of the two teams' fortunes at the time, with Slovan prevailing 5-4 to successfully defend the trophy and leave Žilina still seeking their first victory in the competition.

Prized scalp

Having knocked Italy out of the 2010 FIFA World Cup, the Slovakian national team claimed another prized scalp when they beat Russia 1-0 in Moscow in the second match of their UEFA EURO 2012 qualifying campaign. With Miroslav Stoch's winning goal coming just four days after Filip Hološko's added-time strike had brought an opening 1-0 win at home to the Former Yugoslav Republic of Macedonia, Vladimír Weiss's team could scarcely have made a better start. But a defeat in Armenia and a home draw with the Republic of Ireland, in which skipper Miroslav Karhan became the first Slovakian footballer to reach 100 international caps, killed some of the joy, and although Andorra were subsequently beaten twice, Slovakia could only win both games 1-0. The end-of-season Group B standings, in which Slovakia shared top place with Ireland and Russia, left all possibilities open ahead of their final four fixtures.

National Team

International Tournament Appearances – FIFA World Cup – (1) 2010 (2nd round).

Top Five All-time Caps – Miroslav Karhan (103); Róbert Vittek (78); Szilárd Németh (58); Stanislav Varga (54); Radoslav Zabavník (53)

Top Five All-time Goals – Róbert Vittek (23); Szilárd Németh (22); Miroslav Karhan & Marek Mintál (14); Peter Dubovský (12)

NATIONAL TEAM RESULTS 2010/11

11/8/10	Croatia	H	Bratislava	1-1	*Stoch (50)*
3/9/10	FYROM (ECQ)	H	Bratislava	1-0	*Hološko (90+1)*
7/9/10	Russia (ECQ)	A	Moscow	1-0	*Stoch (27)*
8/10/10	Armenia (ECQ)	A	Yerevan	1-3	*Weiss (37)*
12/10/10	Republic of Ireland (ECQ)	H	Zilina	1-1	*Ďurica (36)*
17/11/10	Bosnia & Herzegovina	H	Bratislava	2-3	*Šebo (3), Grajciar (63)*
9/2/11	Luxembourg	A	Luxembourg	1-2	*Jendrišek (55)*
26/3/11	Andorra (ECQ)	A	Andorra la Vella	1-0	*Šebo (21)*
29/3/11	Denmark	H	Trnava	1-2	*Hološko (32)*
4/6/11	Andorra (ECQ)	H	Bratislava	1-0	*Karhan (63)*

NATIONAL TEAM APPEARANCES 2010/11

Coach – Vladimír WEISS	**22/9/64**		**Cro**	**MKD**	**RUS**	**ARM**	**IRL**	**Bih**	**Lux**	**AND**	**Den**	**AND**	**Caps**	**Goals**
Ján MUCHA	5/12/82	Everton (ENG)	G	G	G	G	G	G83	G77	G			27	-
Peter PEKARÍK	30/10/86	Wolfsburg (GER)	D	D90		D		D79	D68	D	D		31	1
Martin ŠKRTEĽ	15/12/84	Liverpool (ENG)	D	D	D	D				D	D		49	5
Kornel SALÁTA	24/1/85	Slovan Bratislava /Rostov (RUS)	D	D76	D	D	D	D		s90	D46	s83	14	-
Tomáš HUBOČAN	17/9/85	Zenit (RUS)	D	D	D		D		D40			D	11	-
Juraj KUCKA	26/2/87	Sparta Praha (CZE) /Genoa (ITA)	M46	s76	M58	s57	M		M64			M46	16	-
Vladimír WEISS	30/11/89	Man. City (ENG) /Rangers (SCO)	M68	M61		M	M70	M61	M64				18	1
Miroslav STOCH	19/10/89	Fenerbahçe (TUR)	M	M	M92	M57	s70	M61	s64	M90			24	3
Miroslav KARHAN	21/6/76	Mainz (GER)	M84		M73	M	M	M	M			D	103	14

NATIONAL TEAM APPEARANCES 2010/11 (contd.)

			Cro	MKD	RUS	ARM	IRL	Bih	Lux	AND	Den	AND	Caps	Goals
Filip HOLOŠKO	17/1/84	Beşiktaş (TUR) /İstanbul BB (TUR)	A46	A	A	s57	s70	s61		s87	A80	A74	49	7
Stanislav ŠESTÁK	16/12/82	Ankaragücü (TUR)	A68			A	M70	M46	s40			s46	42	11
Kamil KOPÚNEK	18/5/84	Spartak Trnava /Saturn (RUS) /Bari (ITA)	s46			M57		s79			M77		15	2
Marek HAMŠÍK	27/7/87	Napoli (ITA)	s46	M	M	M	M	s46	M	M	M	M	46	8
Erik JENDRIŠEK	26/10/86	Schalke (GER) /Freiburg (GER)	s68	s61	s58		A84	M	M	M87	M60		26	3
Róbert VITTEK	1/4/82	Ankaragücü (TUR)	s68 /72							A78	s60	A	78	23
Marek ČECH	26/1/83	West Brom (ENG)	s72								M	D83	44	5
Radoslav ZABAVNÍK	16/9/80	Mainz (GER)	s84		D	D81	D	s61	s64				53	1
Zdeno ŠTRBA	9/6/76	Xanthi (GRE)		M	M								26	-
Marek SAPARA	31/7/82	Ankaragücü (TUR)		M	s73			M46					29	2
Jakub SYLVESTR	2/2/89	Dinamo Zagreb (CRO)		s90									1	-
Mário PEČALKA	28/12/80	Žilina /H. Tel-Aviv (ISR)			s92				D				3	-
Filip ŠEBO	24/2/84	Slovan Bratislava				s81		A		A	s46	A	13	7
Ján ĎURICA	10/12/81	Lokomotiv Moskva (RUS)					D	D	D	D	s46	D	49	2
Tomáš ORAVEC	3/7/80	Žilina					s84						9	3
Peter GRAJCIAR	17/9/83	Konyaspor (TUR)						s46					2	1
Dušan PERNIŠ	28/11/84	Dundee United (SCO)						s83					3	-
Adam NEMEC	2/9/85	Kaiserslautern (GER)							A				2	-
František KUBÍK	14/3/89	Den Haag (NED)							s68				1	-
Marián KELLO	5/9/82	Hearts (SCO)							s77		G	G	3	-
Filip LUKŠÍK	3/2/85	Senica								D	D46		2	-
Tomáš KÓŇA	1/3/84	Senica								M	s80		2	-
Juraj PIROSKA	27/2/87	Senica								s78	A		2	-
Marek KAŠČÁK	22/5/82	Spartak Trnava									s77		1	-
Róbert JEŽ	10/7/81	Górnik Zabrze (POL)										M	5	2
Igor ŽOFČÁK	10/4/83	Slovan Bratislava										s74	13	-

CLUB-BY-CLUB

DAC 1904 DUNAJSKÁ STREDA

Coach – Mikuláš Radványi
Founded – 1904
Stadium – DAC (16,410)
MAJOR HONOURS: Czechoslovakian Cup – (1) 1987.

2010

18/7	Banská Bystrica	a	0-2	
24/7	Nitra	h	0-1	
9/7	Ružomberok	a	0-2	
7/8	Senica	h	2-3	*Harsányi (p), Yavarzadeh*
14/8	Trnava	a	1-1	*Matúš*
21/8	Tatran	h	2-1	*Konečný, Harsányi*
28/8	Dubnica	a	1-2	*Hílek*
11/9	Zlaté Moravce	a	1-1	*Harsányi*
18/9	Košice	h	1-0	*Filo*
24/9	Žilina	a	0-0	
2/10	Slovan	h	2-1	*Hrabač, Gašparík*
16/10	Banská Bystrica	h	0-0	
23/10	Nitra	a	1-0	*Filo*
30/10	Ružomberok	h	3-0	*Struhár, Helísek, Harsányi*
6/11	Senica	a	1-1	*Hrabač*
12/11	Trnava	h	1-0	*Gašparík*
20/11	Tatran	a	0-1	
27/11	Dubnica	h	0-0	

2011

26/2	Zlaté Moravce	h	2-1	*Tomčák, Filo*
5/3	Košice	a	0-1	
11/3	Žilina	h	2-2	*Tomčák 2*
15/3	Slovan	a	0-1	
19/3	Banská Bystrica	a	0-2	
2/4	Nitra	h	1-2	*Melinho*
8/4	Ružomberok	a	0-1	
15/4	Senica	h	0-3	
23/4	Trnava	a	0-3	
30/4	Tatran	h	2-1	*Helísek, Struhár*
4/5	Dubnica	a	1-0	*Matúš*
11/5	Zlaté Moravce	a	0-3	
14/5	Košice	h	0-0	
21/5	Žilina	a	0-0	
25/5	Slovan	h	0-3	

No	Name	Nat	DoB	Pos	Aps	(s)	Gls
17	Martin Diolong ABENA	CMR	14/6/86	A		(1)	
18	Jean Paul BOYA	CMR	23/9/84	M	25	(1)	
24	Arpád CSONKA		14/8/91	A		(2)	

10	Josip ČORIĆ	CRO	9/11/88	M	3	(1)	
2	Pavol ĎURICA		17/5/83	M	17	(8)	
25	Michal FILO		28/2/84	A	11	(6)	3
10	Michal GAŠPARÍK		19/12/81	M	18		2
20	Ilami HALIMI	MKD	8/11/75	M	10	(13)	
12	Zoltán HARSÁNYI		1/6/87	A	15		4
21	Ismail Ahmed HASSAN	DJI	23/5/87	M	8	(5)	
19	David HELÍSEK	CZE	4/9/82	M	31	(2)	2
5	Jaroslav HÍLEK		6/6/78	M	32		1
14	Igor HRABAČ		10/5/83	D	29		2
	Jan KADLEC	CZE	19/7/89	A		(7)	
1	Daniel KISS		14/4/84	G	7		
23	Roman KONEČNÝ		25/7/83	D	23	(3)	1
32	Pavol KOVÁČ		12/8/74	G	10		
7	Tomáš LÉNÁRTH		7/6/90	M	8	(9)	
3	Ján MARCIN		7/9/85	D	2	(2)	
11	Lukáš MATÚŠ	CZE	6/10/80	A	19	(8)	2
12	Rogério Pereira Tarcisio "MELINHO"	BRA	26/3/80	M	2	(4)	1
22	Martin NAHODIL	CZE	15/3/86	G	2		
8	Zsolt NÉMETH		1/2/90	D	4	(1)	
4	Staniša NIKOLIĆ	BIH	28/11/80	D		(1)	
28	Guillaume NKENDO	CMR	6/6/86	A	8	(10)	
32	Ján NOVOTA		29/11/83	G	14	(1)	
6	Igor OBERT		14/7/82	D	28	(1)	
21	Markus SEELAUS	AUT	16/2/87	M		(1)	
13	Peter STRUHÁR		17/1/84	D	18	(1)	2
30	Ondřej SZABÓ	CZE	23/2/79	M	1	(1)	
9	Marián TOMČÁK		13/7/80	A	15		3
9	Behshad YAVARZADEH	IRN	7/1/83	A	3	(3)	1

MFK DUBNICA

Coach – Peter Gergely

Founded – 1926

Stadium – Dubnica (5,450)

2010				
17/7	Nitra	a	2-3	*Ižvolt, Tubonemi*
24/7	Ružomberok	h	1-0	*Gorelka*
31/7	Senica	a	0-1	
7/8	Trnava	h	0-4	
14/8	Tatran	a	1-1	*Klabník*
21/8	Zlaté Moravce	a	1-2	*Ižvolt*
28/8	Dunajská Streda	h	2-1	*Gorelka, Ižvolt (p)*
11/9	Košice	a	0-1	
18/9	Žilina	h	2-5	*Grabež, Bruško (p)*
26/9	Slovan	a	1-6	*Porázik*
1/10	Banská Bystrica	h	1-0	*Grabež*
16/10	Nitra	h	1-1	*Gorelka*
23/10	Ružomberok	a	1-0	*Nosek*
30/10	Senica	h	0-1	
6/11	Trnava	a	0-4	
13/11	Tatran	h	0-1	
20/11	Zlaté Moravce	h	0-4	
27/11	Dunajská Streda	a	0-0	
2011				
26/2	Košice	h	0-0	
5/3	Žilina	a	0-0	
12/3	Slovan	h	1-1	*Polách*
15/3	Banská Bystrica	a	0-1	
19/3	Nitra	a	1-1	*Polách*
2/4	Ružomberok	h	0-0	
9/4	Senica	a	0-0	
16/4	Trnava	h	1-0	*Kuzma*
23/4	Tatran	a	1-2	*Ľupták*
30/4	Zlaté Moravce	a	1-2	*Kuzma*
4/5	Dunajská Streda	h	0-1	
11/5	Košice	a	1-1	*Augustíni*
14/5	Žilina	h	1-0	*Šulek*
21/5	Slovan	a	1-3	*Vavrík*
25/5	Banská Bystrica	h	2-0	*Ižvolt, Kuzma*

No	Name	Nat	DoB	Pos	Aps	(s)	Gls
7	Oliver AUGUSTÍNI		12/6/90	M	9	(18)	1
1	Pavol BAJZA		4/9/91	G	18		
3	Lukáš BEŇO		7/1/89	D	30		
12	Marek BOŽOŇ		17/4/90	D	2		
22	Tomáš BRUŠKO		21/2/83	M	30	(1)	1
2	Miroslav DUGA		29/1/89	D	5	(7)	
22	Matej GORELKA		3/4/89	M	16	(8)	3
10	Srđan GRABEŽ	SRB	9/3/90	M	16	(13)	2
16	Matej IŽVOLT		5/6/86	D	32		4
20	Martin KLABNÍK		22/11/91	D	15		1
21	Kristián KOLČÁK		30/1/90	D	9	(2)	
31	Dušan KOLMOKOV		17/5/85	G		(1)	
33	Pavol KOVÁČ		12/8/74	G	15		
18	Marek KUZMA		22/6/88	M	12	(1)	3
14	Erik ĽUPTÁK		7/6/90	M		(6)	1
19	Juraj MASARÍK		1/3/90	M		(2)	
23	Martin NOSEK		26/1/87	D	30		1
21	Tomáš POLÁCH	CZE	16/1/77	M	14	(1)	2
9	Andrej PORÁZIK		27/6/77	A	21	(3)	1
8	Miloš RIEČIČIAR		10/2/90	M	6		
11	Peter ŠULEK		21/9/88	M	29		1
25	Jan TROUSIL	CZE	9/4/76	D	15		
13	Hector TUBONEMI	NGA	5/9/88	A		(11)	1
15	Ľubomír ULRICH		1/2/89	A		(5)	
4	Ján VARGA		21/7/90	A	1	(2)	
5	Juraj VAVRÍK		9/2/91	M	30	(2)	1
13	Ján ZÁPOTOKA		23/3/88	M	7	(5)	
15	Tomáš ZÁPOTOKA		4/2/87	M	1	(5)	
8	Michal ŽIVČIC		8/6/92	M		(1)	

DUKLA BANSKÁ BYSTRICA

Coach – Karol Marko; (8/11/10) Štefan Zatko

Founded – 1965

Stadium – Na Štiavničkách (9,881)

MAJOR HONOURS: Slovakian Cup – (1) 2005.

2010				
18/7	Dunajská Streda	h	2-0	*Adámik, Pich*
25/7	Košice	a	1-1	*Pich*
31/7	Žilina	h	1-2	*Pich*
8/8	Slovan	a	0-2	
14/8	Zlaté Moravce	h	0-0	
21/8	Nitra	h	2-0	*Pich 2*
28/8	Ružomberok	a	0-1	
11/9	Senica	h	1-0	*Seye*
18/9	Trnava	a	1-1	*Hlinka*
26/9	Tatran	h	3-0	*Hučko, Vajda 2*
1/10	Dubnica	a	0-1	
16/10	Dunajská Streda	a	0-0	
23/10	Košice	h	4-1	*Uškovič, Hesek, Pich, Gajdoš*
29/10	Žilina	a	3-3	*Hesek 2, Uškovič*
5/11	Slovan	h	0-0	
13/11	Zlaté Moravce	a	2-0	*Hučko, Pich*
20/11	Nitra	a	2-0	*Pleva, Brašeň*
27/11	Ružomberok	h	1-0	*Hesek*
2011				
26/2	Senica	a	0-3	
5/3	Trnava	h	1-2	*Hesek (p)*
12/3	Tatran	a	1-2	*og (Vyskočil)*
15/3	Dubnica	h	1-0	*Brašeň*
19/3	Dunajská Streda	h	2-0	*Jakubko, Hesek*
2/4	Košice	a	1-2	*Jakubko*
9/4	Žilina	h	0-0	
16/4	Slovan	a	1-3	*Johancsik*
23/4	Zlaté Moravce	h	1-1	*Jakubko*
30/4	Nitra	h	0-1	
4/5	Ružomberok	a	0-0	
11/5	Senica	h	3-2	*Turňa, Pečovský, Slančík*
14/5	Trnava	a	2-0	*Uškovič, Pančík*
21/5	Tatran	h	3-2	*Hučko, Uškovič, Brašeň*
25/5	Dubnica	a	0-2	

o	Name	Nat	DoB	Pos	Aps	(s)	Gls
	Jozef ADÁMIK		10/4/85	D	20		1
3	Peter BOROŠ		17/2/80	G	23		
1	Jakub BRAŠEŇ		2/5/89	M	25	(5)	3
6	Ľuboš CHMELÍK		1/5/89	D		(1)	
	Ján ĎURČO		25/2/88	G	1	(2)	
3	Peter ĎURICA		3/5/86	M	2		
6	Michal ĎURIŠ		1/6/88	A	4	(1)	
3	Michal FAŠKO		24/8/94	M		(2)	
7	Vratislav GAJDOŠ		13/1/86	M	12	(4)	1
7	Andrej HESEK		12/6/81	A	13	(6)	6
3	Marek HLINKA		4/10/90	D	20	(3)	1
	Tomáš HUČKO		3/10/85	M	29	(2)	3
0	Martin JAKUBKO		26/2/80	A	9	(2)	3
	Patrik JOHANCSIK		9/5/90	A	7	(3)	1
8	Ľuboš KUPČÍK		3/3/89	D	10	(3)	
6	Lukáš LAKSÍK		21/1/90	A		(5)	
4	Michal PANČÍK		18/8/82	M	24	(6)	1
2	Viktor PEČOVSKÝ		24/5/83	M	27	(2)	1
	Róbert PICH		12/11/88	A	16	(2)	7
31	Branislav PINDROCH		30/10/91	G	9		
3	Dalibor PLEVA		2/4/84	D	19		1
4	Martin POLJOVKA		9/1/75	D	20		
11	Jakub POVAŽANEC		11/1/91	M	9	(10)	
18	Jaroslav PREKOP		8/8/79	M	6	(3)	
24	Jozef REJDOVJAN		18/3/91	M		(1)	
34	Saša SAVIĆ	SRB	5/2/84	D	17	(3)	
10	Mouhamadou SEYE	SEN	10/10/88	A	7	(3)	1
22	Fabian SLANČÍK		22/9/91	A	4	(4)	1
19	Matúš TURŇA		11/5/86	D	10	(4)	1
9	Dušan UŠKOVIČ		9/4/85	A	7	(13)	4
27	Patrik VAJDA		20/3/89	D	13	(2)	2

MFK KOŠICE

Coach – Žarko Đurović (SRB); (28/9/10) Štefan Tarkovič

Founded – 2005

Stadium – Lokomotivy v Čermeli (10,787)

MAJOR HONOURS: Slovakian Cup – (1) 2009.

2010				
18/7	Slovan	a	0-2	
24/7	Banská Bystrica	h	1-1	*Pačinda*
31/7	Nitra	a	1-1	*Škutka*
7/8	Ružomberok	h	0-1	
14/8	Senica	a	0-1	
21/8	Trnava	h	0-2	
28/8	Tatran	a	1-1	*Đoković*
11/9	Dubnica	h	1-0	*Jurčo*
18/9	Dunajská Streda	a	0-1	
26/9	Zlaté Moravce	a	1-4	*Viazanko*
2/10	Žilina	h	0-4	
16/10	Slovan	h	1-2	*Milinković (p)*
23/10	Banská Bystrica	a	1-4	*Jurčo*
30/10	Nitra	h	3-0	*Karaš, Škutka, Milinković*
6/11	Ružomberok	a	2-2	*Škutka, Đoković*
13/11	Senica	h	2-1	*Đoković, Viazanko*
20/11	Trnava	a	0-0	
26/11	Tatran	h	4-0	*Milinković 3, Matić*
2011				
26/2	Dubnica	a	0-0	
5/3	Dunajská Streda	h	1-0	*Dobias*
12/3	Zlaté Moravce	h	0-1	
15/3	Žilina	a	0-2	
19/3	Slovan	a	0-4	
2/4	Banská Bystrica	h	2-1	*Matić, Kuzma*
9/4	Nitra	a	0-1	
16/4	Ružomberok	h	0-2	
22/4	Senica	a	1-1	*Juhar*
27/4	Trnava	h	1-3	*Juhar*
4/5	Tatran	a	3-0	*Kuzma, Matić (p), Viazanko*
11/5	Dubnica	h	1-1	*Juhar (p)*
14/5	Dunajská Streda	a	0-0	
21/5	Zlaté Moravce	a	0-1	
25/5	Žilina	h	1-0	*Diaby*

No	Name	Nat	DoB	Pos	Aps	(s)	Gls
25	Jozef BRUDŇÁK		8/11/87	G	1		
13	Róbert CICMAN		3/9/84	D	29	(2)	
19	Matúš ČONKA		15/10/90	D	28		
23	Bojan ČUKIĆ	SRB	5/2/88	M	2	(2)	
27	Karim DIABY Coulibaly	FRA	23/12/89	A	3	(6)	1
34	Matúš DIGOŇ		18/11/88	A		(3)	
8	Timon DOBIAS		28/7/89	M	22	(5)	1
20	Lukáš DŽOGAN		1/7/87	D		(2)	
4	Ivan ĐOKOVIĆ	SRB	20/12/82	D	24	(2)	3
5	Peter GÁL-ANDREZLY		3/5/90	M	1	(7)	
22	Toto Sena GOVOU	FRA	23/12/89	M		(1)	
41	Patrik HOJSTRIČ		15/3/91	M		(1)	
40	Juraj HOVANČÍK		22/11/90	M	5		
12	Floris ISOLA	FRA	31/10/91	M	4	(2)	
11	Martin JUHAR		9/3/88	D	19	(4)	3
22	Pavol JURČO		12/2/86	A	13		2
24	Kamil KARAŠ		1/3/91	M	9	(8)	1
16	Peter KAVKA		20/11/90	M	9	(1)	
9	Jaroslav KOLBAS		10/1/85	D	26		
2	Vladimír KRAŽEL		28/9/91	D	1		
18	Tomáš KUBÍK		18/3/92	A	2	(3)	
7	Kamil KUZMA		8/3/88	M	17	(1)	2
55	Uroš MATIĆ	SRB	23/5/90	M	17	(6)	3
99	Marko MILINKOVIĆ	SRB	16/4/88	M	11		5
17	Erik PAČINDA		9/5/89	A	6	(14)	1
30	Miloje PREKOVIĆ	SRB	7/6/91	G	1		
21	Roland REPISKÝ		30/5/90	G	1		
6	Jozef SKVAŠÍK		8/9/91	M		(5)	
10	Vladan SPASOJEVIĆ	SRB	11/10/80	A	6	(1)	
29	Peter ŠINGLÁR		24/7/79	D	24		
26	Dávid ŠKUTKA		25/5/88	A	26	(1)	3
1	Darko TOFILOSKI	MKD	13/1/86	G	30		
15	Mikuláš TÓTH		15/3/88	D	4	(1)	
23	Róbert UJČÍK		19/9/89	A	1	(5)	
14	Miroslav VIAZANKO		27/10/81	M	21	(9)	3

FC NITRA

Coach – Ivan Galád; (22/11/10) Ivan Vrabec; (13/3/11) Cyril Stachura

Founded – 1919

Stadium – Pod Zoborom (11,384)

2010				
17/7	Dubnica	h	3-2	*Rák (p), Sloboda, Kolár*
24/7	Dunajská Streda	a	1-0	*Rák*
31/7	Košice	h	1-1	*Rák (p)*
7/8	Žilina	a	1-5	*Šimončič*
14/8	Slovan	h	1-0	*Rák*
21/8	Banská Bystrica	a	0-2	
28/8	Zlaté Moravce	h	1-1	*og (Majerník)*
11/9	Ružomberok	h	1-2	*Rák (p)*
17/9	Senica	a	0-2	
24/9	Trnava	h	1-0	*Leško*
2/10	Tatran	a	2-1	*Sloboda, Mikuš*
16/10	Dubnica	a	1-1	*Hodúr (p)*
23/10	Dunajská Streda	h	0-1	
30/10	Košice	a	0-3	
6/11	Žilina	h	0-2	
13/11	Slovan	a	0-0	
20/11	Banská Bystrica	h	0-2	
27/11	Zlaté Moravce	a	2-1	*Mikuš, Hodúr*
2011				
26/2	Ružomberok	a	0-1	
4/3	Senica	h	0-5	
12/3	Trnava	a	1-4	*Kolár*
15/3	Tatran	h	1-0	*Rák*
19/3	Dubnica	h	1-1	*Rák*
2/4	Dunajská Streda	a	2-1	*Kolár, Mikuš*
9/4	Košice	h	1-0	*Kolár*
16/4	Žilina	a	0-2	
23/4	Slovan	h	0-1	
30/4	Banská Bystrica	a	1-0	*Ivančík*

4/5	Zlaté Moravce	h	0-0	
11/5	Ružomberok	h	0-2	
14/5	Senica	a	2-3	*Kolmokov, Rák (p)*
21/5	Trnava	h	3-2	*Rák (p), Mikuš, Schulmeister*
25/5	Tatran	a	3-3	*Mikuš 2, Ivančík*

No	Name	Nat	DoB	Pos	Aps	(s)	Gls
5	Michal ÁČ		17/5/85	D	18		
11	Slavomír BALIŠ		26/9/85	M	2	(3)	
4	Martin BOSZORÁD		13/11/90	D		(2)	
1	Martin CHUDÝ		23/4/89	G	4		
17	Marek GAJDOŠÍK		16/8/90	M		(5)	
18	Róbert GLENDA		6/3/86	D	11	(9)	
6	Ján HARBUĽÁK		15/11/88	D	15	(1)	
10	Ivan HODÚR		7/10/79	M	22		2
31	Lukáš HROŠŠO		19/4/87	G	28		
15	Andrej IVANČÍK		25/5/90	M	5	(3)	2
16	Petr KASPŘÁK	CZE	17/1/84	D	19	(2)	
29	Filip KINČEK		24/8/91	M		(1)	
7	Ľuboš KOLÁR		1/9/89	M	18	(4)	4
2	Marián KOLMOKOV		23/3/91	D	16	(3)	1
22	Matej KOPECKÝ		9/6/90	G	1		
12	Marek KOŠÚT		26/9/88	A	3	(5)	
26	Igor KOTORA		13/7/89	D	19	(3)	
25	Matej KRÁL		28/12/90	M	10	(7)	
23	Ján LEŠKO		6/7/86	D	13	(3)	1
9	Matúš MIKUŠ		8/7/91	A	22	(6)	6
24	Matúš PAUKNER		20/6/91	A		(4)	
77	Róbert RÁK		15/1/78	A	24	(4)	9
5	Patrik SAILER		28/6/89	D		(2)	
20	Vojtěch SCHULMEISTER	CZE	9/9/83	M	6	(5)	1
21	Roman SLOBODA		14/1/87	A	13	(14)	2
14	Miloš ŠIMONČIČ		27/5/87	M	25	(6)	1
12	Róbert ŠKROVÁŇ		30/9/90	M		(2)	
8	Lukáš ŠTETINA		28/7/91	D	18		
3	Martin TÓTH		23/10/86	D	30		
20	Róbert VALENTA		10/1/90	A	13	(4)	
11	Lukáš ZELENICKÝ		10/4/90	D	8		

MFK RUŽOMBEROK

Coach – Ladislav Jurkemik; (10/10/10) Goran Milojević (SRB); (25/3/11) Ladislav Jurkemik

Founded – 1906

Stadium – Mestský štadión (4,817)

MAJOR HONOURS: Slovakian League – (1) 2006; Slovakian Cup – (1) 2006.

2010				
17/7	Tatran	h	1-0	*Kroupa*
24/7	Dubnica	a	0-1	
31/7	Dunajská Streda	h	2-0	*Kroupa 2*
7/8	Košice	a	1-0	*Ďubek (p)*
13/8	Žilina	h	1-1	*Hoferica*
22/8	Slovan	a	0-3	
28/8	Banská Bystrica	h	1-0	*Pekár*
11/9	Nitra	a	2-1	*Kroupa, Ďubek*
18/9	Zlaté Moravce	h	1-1	*Kroupa*
26/9	Senica	h	1-2	*Maslo J.*
2/10	Trnava	a	0-2	
16/10	Tatran	a	1-1	*Ďubek*
23/10	Dubnica	h	0-1	
30/10	Dunajská Streda	a	0-3	
6/11	Košice	h	2-2	*Maslo J., Maslo P.*
13/11	Žilina	a	1-3	*Chovanec J.*
20/11	Slovan	h	0-0	
27/11	Banská Bystrica	a	0-1	
2011				
26/2	Nitra	h	1-0	*Chovanec T.*
5/3	Zlaté Moravce	a	0-3	
12/3	Senica	a	0-4	
15/3	Trnava	h	0-0	
19/3	Tatran	h	0-1	
2/4	Dubnica	a	0-0	
8/4	Dunajská Streda	h	1-0	*Ďubek (p)*
16/4	Košice	a	2-0	*Blažić, Hoferica*
23/4	Žilina	h	0-0	
30/4	Slovan	a	0-1	
4/5	Banská Bystrica	h	0-0	
11/5	Nitra	a	2-0	*Blažić 2*
14/5	Zlaté Moravce	h	0-0	
21/5	Senica	h	3-2	*Hoferica 2, Maslo J.*
25/5	Trnava	a	0-0	

No	Name	Nat	DoB	Pos	Aps	(s)	Gls
5	Lukáš BIELÁK		14/12/86	M	17	(8)	
25	Marko BLAŽIĆ	SRB	2/8/85	M	10	(1)	3
15	Ján CHOVANEC		22/3/84	M	25	(1)	1
24	Tomáš CHOVANEC		21/11/87	A	4	(5)	1
26	Tomáš ĎUBEK		22/1/87	M	31		4
2	Michal GALLO		2/6/88	D	20	(2)	
6	Lukáš GREŠŠAK		23/1/89	M	7		
11	Peter HOFERICA		28/6/83	M	15	(8)	4
33	Libor HRDLIČKA		2/1/86	G	23		
20	Marko JAKŠIĆ	SRB	10/8/83	A	8	(2)	
25	Daniel JURČ		7/3/83	D	4	(2)	
4	Jaroslav KOSTELNÝ		19/4/85	D	27		
23	Ivan KOTORA		27/6/91	M	11	(8)	
8	Vladimír KOVÁČ		29/4/91	D	4	(4)	
16	Karel KROUPA	CZE	27/4/80	A	18		5
12	Andrej LOVÁS		28/5/91	A	3	(8)	
3	Ján MASLO		5/2/86	D	27		3
17	Peter MASLO		2/2/87	D	29		1
27	Martin NAGY		5/9/90	M		(1)	
24	Lukáš ONDREK		11/1/93	A		(2)	
19	Štefan PEKÁR		3/12/88	A	5	(11)	1
1	Pavol PENKSA		7/11/85	G	10	(1)	
22	Pavol PILÁR		27/7/86	A	11	(11)	
9	Marko RADIĆ	BIH	1/10/85	D	8	(5)	
7	Tomáš SEDLÁK		3/2/83	M	5	(3)	
22	Ardit SHAQIRI	MKD	4/5/85	M		(2)	
14	Milomir SIVČEVIĆ	SRB	1/1/79	D	27	(2)	
10	Anton SLOBODA		10/7/87	M	13	(1)	
20	Tomáš VLČEK		7/7/83	M	1		

FK SENICA

Coach – Stanislav Griga

Founded – 1921

Stadium – Mestský štadión (4,165)

2010				
17/7	Trnava	a	0-3	
24/7	Tatran	a	1-0	*Diviš*
31/7	Dubnica	h	1-0	*Pillár*
7/8	Dunajská Streda	a	3-2	*Diviš, Kóňa, Strnad*
14/8	Košice	h	1-0	*Smetana*
21/8	Žilina	a	0-0	
29/8	Slovan	h	3-2	*Kóňa, Smetana 2 (1p)*
11/9	Banská Bystrica	a	0-1	
17/9	Nitra	h	2-0	*Lukšík (p), Piroska*
26/9	Ružomberok	a	2-1	*Diviš, Lukšík*
2/10	Zlaté Moravce	h	0-1	
16/10	Trnava	h	1-2	*Smetana*
23/10	Tatran	h	1-1	*Piroska (p)*
30/10	Dubnica	a	1-0	*Smetana*
6/11	Dunajská Streda	h	1-1	*Diviš*
13/11	Košice	a	1-2	*Diviš*
19/11	Žilina	h	2-1	*Diviš, Smetana*
27/11	Slovan	a	2-2	*Diviš, Smetana*
2011				
26/2	Banská Bystrica	h	3-0	*Piroska, Diviš, Smetana (p)*
4/3	Nitra	a	5-0	*Piroska 3 (1p), Pillár, Smetana*
12/3	Ružomberok	h	4-0	*Smetana 2, Kóňa, Hošek*
15/3	Zlaté Moravce	a	0-0	
18/3	Trnava	h	4-0	*Smetana (p), Strnad, Lukšík, Hošek*

4	Tatran	a	1-0	*Piroska*
4	Dubnica	h	0-0	
5/4	Dunajská Streda	a	3-0	*Smetana 2, og (Konečný)*
2/4	Košice	h	1-1	*Smetana*
9/4	Žilina	a	1-0	*Kóňa*
5	Slovan	h	1-2	*Diviš*
1/5	Banská Bystrica	a	2-3	*Smetana (p), og (Poljovka)*
4/5	Nitra	h	3-2	*Poliaček, Smetana 2*
1/5	Ružomberok	a	2-3	*Pillár, Hošek*
5/5	Zlaté Moravce	h	2-0	*Pillár, Diviš*

lo	Name	Nat	DoB	Pos	Aps	(s)	Gls
	Ivan BELÁK		23/1/78	M	4	(4)	
6	Petr BOLEK	CZE	13/6/84	G	33		
0	Luís Fernando Furtado de Oliveira "BOLINHA"	BRA	29/11/90	M	1	(4)	
4	Jaroslav DIVIŠ	CZE	9/7/86	M	32		10
	Martin ĎURICA		11/7/81	M	11	(7)	
1	Petr FALDYNA	CZE	11/7/76	A	6	(7)	
	Vratislav GAJDOŠ		13/1/86	M	2	(9)	
	Ján GAJDOŠÍK		12/10/78	D	26		
6	Nicolás Ezequiel GOROSITO	ARG	17/8/88	D	15		
1	Petr HOŠEK	CZE	12/4/89	A	1	(12)	3
6	Miloš JUHÁSZ		3/10/84	M	1	(6)	
0	David Leonel Faleiro "KAKÁ"	BRA	12/1/91	M		(1)	
4	Martin KOMÁREK	CZE	14/10/84	D	7	(3)	
3	Tomáš KÓŇA		1/3/84	M	32		4
23	Juraj KRIŽKO		20/9/85	M	8	(2)	
13	Filip LUKŠÍK		3/2/85	D	33		3
5	Samir MERZIĆ	BIH	29/6/84	D	17		
7	Peter PETRÁN		18/4/81	D	3	(1)	
17	Róbert PILLÁR		27/5/91	D	30	(1)	4
33	Juraj PIROSKA		27/2/87	A	29	(1)	7
5	Miroslav POLIAČEK		13/7/83	M	3	(6)	1
19	Ondřej SMETANA	CZE	4/9/82	A	26	(3)	18
10	Onome SODJE	NGA	17/7/88	A		(1)	
2	Tomáš STRNAD	CZE	8/12/80	M	24	(1)	2
20	Róbert SZEGEDI		26/5/85	M	4	(5)	
12	Stef WIJLAARS	NED	19/1/98	M	15	(2)	

ŠK SLOVAN BRATISLAVA

Coach – Jozef Jankech; (13/10/10) Karel Jarolím (CZE)

Founded – 1919

Stadium – Pasienky (13,295)

MAJOR HONOURS: UEFA Cup Winners´Cup – (1) 1969;
Czechoslovakian League – (8), 1949, 1950, 1951, 1955, 1970, 1974, 1975, 1992;
Slovakian League – (10), 1940, 1941, 1942, 1944, 1994, 1995, 1996, 1999, 2009, 2011;
Czechoslovakian Cup – (5) 1962, 1963, 1968, 1974, 1982;
Slovakian Cup – (5) 1994, 1997, 1999, 2010, 2011.

2010				
18/7	Košice	h	2-0	*Slovák, Ivana*
24/7	Žilina	a	2-2	*Bagayoko, Božić*
1/8	Zlaté Moravce	h	3-0	*Grendel 2, Kiss*
8/8	Banská Bystrica	h	2-0	*Kiss (p), Grendel*
14/8	Nitra	a	0-1	
22/8	Ružomberok	h	3-0	*Kiss, Guédé, Sylvestr*
29/8	Senica	a	2-3	*Guédé, Slovák*
12/9	Trnava	h	1-1	*Kiss*
18/9	Tatran	a	1-2	*Kiss*
26/9	Dubnica	h	6-1	*Kiss, Halenár 2, Dobrotka, Šebo 2*
2/10	Dunajská Streda	a	1-2	*Halenár (p)*
16/10	Košice	a	2-1	*Dobrotka, Šebo*
23/10	Žilina	h	0-1	
30/10	Zlaté Moravce	a	1-1	*Šebo*
5/11	Banská Bystrica	a	0-0	
13/11	Nitra	h	0-0	
20/11	Ružomberok	a	0-0	
27/11	Senica	h	2-2	*Šebo, Saláta*

2011				
25/2	Trnava	a	3-1	*Milinković, Žofčák, Guédé*
5/3	Tatran	h	4-0	*Žofčák (p), Kordić, Šebo 2*
12/3	Dubnica	a	1-1	*Šebo*
15/3	Dunajská Streda	h	1-0	*Milinković*
19/3	Košice	h	4-0	*Šebo 2, Milinković (p), Kordić*
1/4	Žilina	a	3-0	*(w/o; abandoned after 89 mins at 0-0)*
9/4	Zlaté Moravce	h	1-0	*Šebo*
16/4	Banská Bystrica	h	3-1	*Šebo 2, Guédé*
23/4	Nitra	a	1-0	*Dobrotka*
30/4	Ružomberok	h	1-0	*Šebo*
4/5	Senica	a	2-1	*Božić, Šebo*
17/5	Trnava	h	3-0	*Šebo 3*
14/5	Tatran	a	2-0	*Žofčák (p), Božić*
21/5	Dubnica	h	3-1	*Guédé, Šebo 2*
25/5	Dunajská Streda	a	3-0	*Grendel, Šebo 2*

No	Name	Nat	DoB	Pos	Aps	(s)	Gls
18	Mamadou BAGAYOKO	CIV	31/12/89	D	25	(1)	1
1	Peter BARTALSKÝ		27/1/78	G	1		
11	Mario BOŽIĆ	BIH	25/5/82	M	15	(8)	3
14	Michal BREZNANÍK		16/12/85	M	3	(1)	
6	Martin DOBROTKA		22/1/85	D	26	(1)	3
29	Radek DOSOUDIL	CZE	20/6/83	D	22		
8	Erik GRENDEL		13/10/88	M	23	(7)	4
19	Karim GUÉDÉ	TOG	7/1/85	M	28	(2)	5
28	Marián HAD		16/9/82	D	5	(2)	
9	Juraj HALENÁR		28/6/83	A	6	(6)	3
5	Tomáš HRDLIČKA	CZE	17/2/82	D	14		
13	Milan IVANA		26/11/83	M	13	(6)	1
24	Peter JÁNOŠÍK		2/1/88	D	10	(6)	
15	Filip KISS		13/10/90	M	18	(12)	6
23	Kristián KOLČÁK		30/1/90	D	9	(1)	
20	Krešimir KORDIĆ	BIH	3/9/81	A	7	(8)	2
4	Jan KRÁLIK	CZE	7/3/87	M	3	(3)	
7	Marek KUZMA		22/6/88	M	6	(6)	
7	Marko MILINKOVIĆ	SRB	16/4/88	M	12		3
25	Lukáš PAUSCHEK		9/12/92	D	10	(2)	
5	Andrej PEČNIK	SVN	27/9/81	M	3		
30	Matúš PUTNOCKÝ		1/11/84	G	32		
2	Kornel SALÁTA		24/1/85	D	17	(1)	1
10	Samuel SLOVÁK		17/10/75	M	2	(3)	2
17	Jakub SYLVESTR		2/2/89	A	4	(1)	1
14	Ákos SZÁRKA		24/11/90	A	2	(4)	
33	Filip ŠEBO		24/2/84	A	22	(1)	22
21	Peter ŠTEPANOVSKÝ		12/1/88	M	3	(15)	
12	Boris TURČÁK		21/2/93	M	1	(1)	
16	Igor ŽOFČÁK		10/4/83	M	21		3

FC SPARTAK TRNAVA

Coach – Dušan Radolský; (21/3/11) Peter Zelenský

Founded – 1923

Stadium – Antona Malatinského (18,448)

MAJOR HONOURS: Czechoslovakian League – (5) 1968, 1969, 1971, 1972, 1973;
Czechoslovakian Cup – (4) 1967, 1971, 1975, 1986;
Slovakian Cup – (1) 1998.

2010				
17/7	Senica	h	3-0	*Bernáth 2, Procházka*
24/7	Zlaté Moravce	a	0-2	
31/7	Tatran	h	1-0	*Bernáth*
7/8	Dubnica	a	4-0	*Bernáth 3, Procházka (p)*
14/8	Dunajská Streda	h	1-1	*Machovec*
21/8	Košice	a	2-0	*Koné, Bernáth*
28/8	Žilina	h	0-0	
12/9	Slovan	a	1-1	*Wellington*
18/9	Banská Bystrica	h	1-1	*Koné (p)*
25/9	Nitra	a	0-1	
2/10	Ružomberok	h	2-0	*Koné, Machovec*
16/10	Senica	a	2-1	*Gross, Bicák*
23/10	Zlaté Moravce	h	0-0	

30/10	Tatran	a	0-0	
6/11	Dubnica	h	4-0	*Gross 3, Diallo*
12/11	Dunajská Streda	a	0-1	
20/11	Košice	h	0-0	
28/11	Žilina	a	1-1	*Koné (p)*
2011				
25/2	Slovan	h	1-3	*Tomaček*
5/3	Banská Bystrica	a	2-1	*Tomaček, Higor (p)*
12/3	Nitra	h	4-1	*Tomaček, Koné 2, Kaprálik*
15/3	Ružomberok	a	0-0	
18/3	Senica	a	0-4	
2/4	Zlaté Moravce	a	0-1	
9/4	Tatran	h	2-1	*Bicák, Koné*
16/4	Dubnica	a	0-1	
23/4	Dunajská Streda	h	3-0	*Procházka, Koné, Mikovič*
27/4	Košice	a	3-1	*Tomaček, Koné, Petráš*
4/5	Žilina	h	1-0	*Koné*
17/5	Slovan	a	0-3	
14/5	Banská Bystrica	h	0-2	
21/5	Nitra	a	2-3	*Gogolák, Kaščák (p)*
25/5	Ružomberok	h	0-0	

No	Name	Nat	DoB	Pos	Aps	(s)	Gls
18	Denis BALIŠ		6/4/92	M		(1)	
3	Patrik BANOVIČ		13/11/91	D	2	(1)	
15	Ľuboš BERNÁTH		3/9/85	A	19	(3)	7
27	Mário BICÁK		21/10/79	M	23	(2)	2
19	Radoslav CIPRYS		24/6/87	A	6	(2)	
23	Ján ČARNOTA		8/6/85	M	13	(6)	
17	Patrik ČARNOTA		10/10/86	D	25	(5)	
8	Josip ČORIĆ	CRO	9/11/88	M	5	(6)	
26	Boubacar DIALLO	GUI	25/12/85	D	22	(2)	1
21	Jakub DOHNÁLEK	CZE	12/1/88	D	3	(1)	
9	Ľubomír GOGOLÁK		24/2/90	A	3	(1)	1
20	Patrik GROSS	CZE	6/5/78	D	32		4
11	Martin GULDAN		9/9/90	A	1	(4)	
18	Ľuboš HANZEL		7/5/87	D	3	(4)	
12	HIGOR de Sales Coimbra	BRA	7/8/87	D	11	(8)	1
2	Zdenko KAPRÁLIK		28/8/85	D	8	(2)	1
29	Marek KAŠČÁK		22/5/82	M	26		1
4	Matúš KLENKOVIČ		2/6/90	D		(1)	
25	Koro Issa Ahmed KONÉ	CIV	5/7/89	A	25		10
28	Lukáš KOVÁČ		21/6/87	M	3	(6)	
16	Jaroslav MACHOVEC		5/9/86	M	26	(1)	2
2	Nikola MELNJAK	CRO	6/9/81	M	2		
10	Tomáš MIKINIČ		22/11/92	M	2	(6)	
7	Martin MIKOVIČ		12/9/90	M	3	(8)	1
19	Peter MRÁZ		4/5/85	D	10	(3)	
32	Ján PETRÁŠ		18/2/86	M	3	(5)	1
6	Roman PROCHÁZKA		14/3/89	M	29	(1)	3
22	Martin RAŠKA	CZE	31/1/77	G	33		
24	Erik SABO		22/11/91	M	3	(1)	
9	Ladislav TOMAČEK		26/9/82	A	9		4
5	WELLINGTON Cândido da Silva Júnior	BRA	20/6/89	A	13	(8)	1

1. FC TATRAN PREŠOV

Coach – Roman Pivarník; (23/8/10) Ladislav Pecko
Founded – 1898
Stadium – Tatran (5,410)

2010				
17/7	Ružomberok	a	0-1	
24/7	Senica	h	0-1	
31/7	Trnava	a	0-1	
7/8	Zlaté Moravce	a	0-1	
14/8	Dubnica	h	1-1	*Piter-Bučko*
21/8	Dunajská Streda	a	1-2	*Belejík*
28/8	Košice	h	1-1	*Josl*
11/9	Žilina	a	1-2	*Piter-Bučko*
18/9	Slovan	h	2-1	*Papaj, og (Saláta)*
26/9	Banská Bystrica	a	0-3	
2/10	Nitra	h	1-2	*Belejík*
16/10	Ružomberok	h	1-1	*Papaj*
23/10	Senica	a	1-1	*Meszároš (p)*
30/10	Trnava	h	0-0	
6/11	Zlaté Moravce	h	1-0	*Belejík*
13/11	Dubnica	a	1-0	*Farbák*
20/11	Dunajská Streda	h	1-0	*Vršajević*
26/11	Košice	a	0-4	
2011				
26/2	Žilina	h	2-0	*Krajník, Macko (p)*
5/3	Slovan	a	0-4	
12/3	Banská Bystrica	h	2-1	*Bernardo 2*
15/3	Nitra	a	0-1	
19/3	Ružomberok	a	1-0	*Čep*
2/4	Senica	h	0-1	
9/4	Trnava	a	1-2	*Meszároš*
16/4	Zlaté Moravce	a	3-2	*og (Žilák), Katona, Meszároš*
23/4	Dubnica	h	2-1	*Bernardo, Čep*
30/4	Dunajská Streda	a	1-2	*Farbák*
4/5	Košice	h	0-3	
11/5	Žilina	a	1-2	*Meszároš*
14/5	Slovan	h	0-2	
21/5	Banská Bystrica	a	2-3	*Žůrek 2*
25/5	Nitra	h	3-3	*Bernardo 2, Žůrek*

No	Name	Nat	DoB	Pos	Aps	(s)	Gls
16	Marián ADAM		20/9/81	M		(1)	
27	Pavol BALÁŽ		1/4/84	M	5	(3)	
21	Martin BARAN		3/1/88	M	18	(3)	
32	Peter BAŠISTA		6/4/85	D	19		
14	Ivan BELÁK		23/1/78	M	1	(3)	
16	Ľuboš BELEJÍK		23/9/85	A	13	(4)	3
19	Jhonatan Mariano BERNARDO	BRA	7/11/88	A	8	(6)	5
12	Zoltán BOGNÁR		9/2/88	A	4	(2)	
7	Pavol CICMAN		24/1/85	A	5	(1)	
3	David ČEP	CZE	4/10/80	D	12		2
23	Jakub DIVIŠ	CZE	27/12/86	G	18		
10	Jozef DOLNÝ		13/5/92	M		(2)	
18	Marián FARBÁK		10/2/83	D	22	(2)	2
29	Dávid GUBA		29/6/91	A	1	(6)	
51	Jakub HEIDENREICH	CZE	27/4/89	D	7	(1)	
28	Tomáš JOSL	CZE	12/11/84	D	19		1
34	Michal KAMENČÍK		2/1/93	M		(1)	
11	Peter KATONA		12/4/88	M	14	(13)	1
26	Slavomír KICA		13/10/84	D	5	(3)	
5	Michal KRAJNÍK		5/4/88	D	15	(1)	1
19	Dávid LEŠKO		4/6/88	D	5	(3)	
6	Viliam MACKO		22/10/81	M	15	(9)	1
17	Ľubomír MESZÁROŠ		23/3/79	A	19	(2)	4
24	Ján PAPAJ		16/6/79	M	30	(1)	2
4	Matúš PEKÁR		16/3/84	M		(3)	
66	Boris PEŠKOVIČ		30/6/76	G	4		
18	Peter PETRÁŠ		7/5/79	D	25		
2	Michal PITER-BUČKO		28/10/85	D	22	(1)	2
30	Jakub PLÁNIČKA	CZE	25/12/84	G	11	(1)	
20	Martin PRIBULA		29/11/85	M	3	(7)	
8	Ján ŠAFRANKO		15/8/75	M	1		
35	Roland ŠTEVKO		8/4/83	A	1	(2)	
9	Avdija VRŠAJEVIĆ	BIH	6/3/86	M	23	(5)	1
22	Martin VYSKOČIL	CZE	15/9/82	M	10	(4)	
17	Artem YEVLANOV	UKR	18/5/84	M		(1)	
77	Libor ŽŮREK	CZE	2/11/79	A	8	(5)	3

FC VION ZLATÉ MORAVCE

Coach – Juraj Jarábek
Founded – 1995
Stadium – Štadión ViOn (5,000)
MAJOR HONOURS: Slovakian Cup – (1) 2007.

2010				
17/7	Žilina	a	1-2	*Kuračka*
24/7	Trnava	h	2-0	*Orávik 2*
1/8	Slovan	a	0-3	

/8	Tatran	h	1-0	*Náther*
4/8	Banská Bystrica	a	0-0	
1/8	Dubnica	h	2-1	*Pavlovič (p), Candrák*
8/8	Nitra	a	1-1	*Kuračka*
1/9	Dunajská Streda	h	1-1	*Kuračka (p)*
8/9	Ružomberok	a	1-1	*Náther*
6/9	Košice	h	4-1	*Chren, Tomko 2, Kuračka*
/10	Senica	a	1-0	*Stojanović*
5/10	Žilina	h	0-4	
3/10	Trnava	a	0-0	
0/10	Slovan	h	1-1	*Náther*
/11	Tatran	a	0-1	
3/11	Banská Bystrica	h	0-2	
0/11	Dubnica	a	4-0	*Pavelka 2, Tomášek, Pavlovič*
27/11	Nitra	h	1-2	*Kuračka*
2011				
26/2	Dunajská Streda	a	1-2	*og (Obert)*
5/3	Ružomberok	h	3-0	*Babic, Janečka, Pavlovič*
12/3	Košice	a	1-0	*Kuračka*
15/3	Senica	h	0-0	
19/3	Žilina	a	0-1	
2/4	Trnava	h	1-0	*Candrák*
9/4	Slovan	a	0-1	
16/4	Tatran	h	2-3	*Hruška, Brčák*
23/4	Banská Bystrica	a	1-1	*Candrák*
30/4	Dubnica	h	2-1	*Orávik, Babic*
4/5	Nitra	a	0-0	
11/5	Dunajská Streda	h	3-0	*Majerník, Pavelka 2*
14/5	Ružomberok	a	0-0	
21/5	Košice	h	1-0	*Brčák*
25/5	Senica	a	0-2	

No	Name	Nat	DoB	Pos	Aps	(s)	Gls
7	Martin BABIC		27/7/82	M	31		2
15	Matúš BÔŽIK		31/7/91	M		(1)	
16	Andrej BRČÁK		17/8/84	M	6	(9)	2
9	Adrian CANDRÁK		18/12/82	A	30	(3)	3
12	Martin CHREN		2/1/84	D	29		1
23	Peter FARKAŠ		11/11/82	D	3	(4)	
6	Ján HOZL		13/2/84	M	1	(7)	
4	Martin HRUŠKA	CZE	11/5/81	M	14		1
17	Marek JANEČKA		9/6/83	D	29	(1)	1
22	Martin KUCIAK		15/3/82	G	33		
13	Peter KURAČKA		13/7/78	M	28		6
3	Juraj KURÁŇ		11/8/88	M		(6)	
19	Pavol MAJERNÍK		31/12/78	D	32		1
11	Matej NÁTHER		23/7/85	M	12	(3)	3
8	Martin ONDREJKA		8/1/83	M	2	(11)	
14	Peter ORÁVIK		18/12/88	M	15	(9)	3
20	Karol PAVELKA		31/7/83	A	17	(4)	4
5	Patrik PAVLENDA		3/5/82	D	25		
2	Milan PAVLOVIČ		22/11/80	D	17	(3)	3
18	Miloš STOJANOVIĆ	SRB	25/12/84	M	14	(1)	1
10	Juraj TOMÁŠEK		6/7/88	M	6	(16)	1
21	Róbert TOMKO		16/12/79	A	11	(6)	2
18	Adam ŽILÁK		7/12/91	M	8	(7)	

MŠK ŽILINA

Coach – Pavel Hapal (CZE)

Founded – 1908

Stadium – Pod Dubňom (11,181)

MAJOR HONOURS: Slovakian League – (5) 2002, 2003, 2004, 2007, 2010.

2010				
17/7	Zlaté Moravce	h	2-1	*Majtán, Oravec*
24/7	Slovan	h	2-2	*Oravec, Lietava*
31/7	Banská Bystrica	a	2-1	*Zošák, Ceesay*
7/8	Nitra	h	5-1	*Zošák (p), Babatunde 2, Šourek, Fotyik*
13/8	Ružomberok	a	1-1	*Majtán*
21/8	Senica	h	0-0	
28/8	Trnava	a	0-0	
11/9	Tatran	h	2-1	*Jež, Vladavić (p)*
18/9	Dubnica	a	5-2	*Jež, Majtán 2, Vittor, Oravec*
24/9	Dunajská Streda	h	0-0	
2/10	Košice	a	4-0	*Ceesay, Majtán, Vladavić, Pečalka*
15/10	Zlaté Moravce	a	4-0	*Majtán 3, Zošák*
23/10	Slovan	a	1-0	*Majtán*
29/10	Banská Bystrica	h	3-3	*Oravec 3*
6/11	Nitra	a	2-0	*Oravec, Jež*
13/11	Ružomberok	h	3-1	*og (Kostelný), Vladavić, Oravec*
19/11	Senica	a	1-2	*Oravec*
28/11	Trnava	h	1-1	*Oravec*
2011				
26/2	Tatran	a	0-2	
5/3	Dubnica	h	0-0	
11/3	Dunajská Streda	a	2-2	*Lietava, og (Hílek)*
15/3	Košice	h	2-0	*Zjuzins, Lietava*
19/3	Zlaté Moravce	h	1-0	*Babatunde*
1/4	Slovan	h	0-3	*(w/o; abandoned after 89 mins at 0-0)*
9/4	Banská Bystrica	a	0-0	
16/4	Nitra	h	2-0	*Majtán, Gergel*
23/4	Ružomberok	a	0-0	
29/4	Senica	h	0-1	
4/5	Trnava	a	0-1	
11/5	Tatran	h	2-1	*Pich, Angelovič*
14/5	Dubnica	a	0-1	
21/5	Dunajská Streda	h	0-0	
25/5	Košice	a	0-1	

No	Name	Nat	DoB	Pos	Aps	(s)	Gls
2	Stanislav ANGELOVIČ		26/3/82	D	23	(4)	1
28	Bello BABATUNDE	BEN	6/10/89	M	20	(2)	3
11	Wim BOKILA	NED	28/9/87	M		(1)	
17	Mamadou CEESAY	GAM	24/12/88	A	14	(13)	2
24	Juraj CHUPÁČ		17/3/88	D	1	(1)	
30	Martin DÚBRAVKA		15/1/89	G	24		
19	Dominik FOTYIK		16/9/90	M	2	(10)	1
42	Roman GERGEL		22/2/88	M	18	(3)	1
5	Ľubomír GULDAN		30/1/83	D	25		
12	Róbert JEŽ		10/7/81	M	15		3
22	Martin KRNÁČ		30/1/85	G	9		
7	Vladimír LEITNER		28/6/74	D	10	(2)	
39	Ivan LIETAVA		20/7/83	A	11	(4)	3
45	Ernest MABOUKA	CMR	16/6/88	D	9	(1)	
10	Tomáš MAJTÁN		30/3/87	A	23	(7)	10
6	Patrik MRÁZ		1/2/87	D	19	(2)	
29	Prince OFORI	GHA	6/10/88	D	2	(1)	
14	Tomáš ORAVEC		3/7/80	A	11	(3)	10
3	Mário PEČALKA		28/12/80	D	11		1
15	Jozef PIAČEK		20/6/83	D	16	(1)	
17	Róbert PICH		12/11/88	A	10	(1)	1
20	Pavol POLIAČEK		2/4/88	M	10	(7)	
9	Emil RILKE	CZE	19/11/83	M	7	(6)	
4	Patrik ŠIMKO		5/7/91	D	1	(2)	
24	Rudolf ŠKROBÁK		14/4/89	M		(1)	
20	Michal ŠKVARKA		19/8/92	M	2	(8)	
23	Ondřej ŠOUREK	CZE	26/4/83	D	24	(1)	1
66	Zdeno ŠTRBA		9/6/76	M	9		
37	Sergio Javier VITTOR	ARG	9/7/89	M	4	(1)	1
44	Admir VLADAVIĆ	BIH	29/6/82	M	10		3
11	Marin VYSKOČIL	CZE	15/9/82	M	2	(6)	
14	Artūrs ZJUZINS	LVA	18/6/91	M	2	(3)	1
27	Štefan ZOŠÁK		3/4/84	M	19	(3)	3
4	Adam ŽILÁK		7/12/91	M		(1)	

TOP GOALSCORERS 2010/11

22 Filip ŠEBO (Slovan)

18 Ondřej SMETANA (Senica)

10 Jaroslav DIVIŠ (Senica)
Koro KONÉ (Trnava)
Tomáš MAJTÁN (Žilina)
Tomáš ORAVEC (Žilina)

9 Róbert RÁK (Nitra)

8 Róbert PICH (Banská Bystrica/Žilina)
Marko MILINKOVIĆ (Košice/Slovan)

7 Juraj PIROSKA (Senica)
Ľuboš BERNÁTH (Trnava)

PROMOTED CLUB

FK AS TRENCÍN

Coach – Adrián Guľa
Founded – 1992
Stadium – Štadión Trenčín (4,200)

SECOND LEVEL FINAL TABLE 2010/11

		Pld	W	D	L	F	A	Pts
1	FK AS Trencín	33	22	6	5	77	30	72
2	FC Rimavská Sobota	33	16	6	11	41	35	54
3	MFK Petržalka	33	13	12	8	55	36	51
4	MFK Zemplín Michalovce	33	15	6	12	51	48	51
5	SFM Senec	33	13	9	11	39	39	48
6	MFK Tatran Litpovský Mikuláš	33	14	6	13	43	44	48
7	FK Bodva Moldava	33	13	8	12	46	40	47
8	MFK Dolný Kubín	33	13	7	13	45	38	46
9	FK LAFC Lučenec	33	11	8	14	41	48	41
10	MFK Ružomberok B	33	10	8	15	37	44	38
11	FK Slovan Duslo Šaľa	33	9	6	18	24	44	33
12	FK Púchov	33	6	4	23	24	77	22

DOMESTIC CUP 2010/11

SLOVENSKÝ POHÁR

SECOND ROUND

(21/9/10)
Kremnička 0, Dubnica 3
Myjava 3, Senica 1
Petržalka 2, Dunajská Streda 1
Pezinok 0, Senec 3
Poprad 0, Banská Bystrica 1
Šaľa 0, Nitra 1
Šamorín 2, Zlaté Moravce 5
Vranov 0, Žilina 5

(22/9/10)
Humenné 1, Liptovský Mikuláš 2
Jaslovské Bohunice 0, Trencín 5
Lipany 1, Tatran 1 *(4-3 on pens)*
Michalovce 0, Ružomberok 0 *(3-4 on pens)*
Podbrezová 2, Dolný Kubín 0
Slovan Bratislava 6, Púchov 0
Spišská Nová Ves 3, MFK Košice 0

(28/9/10)
Nemšová 0, Spartak Trnava 2

THIRD ROUND

(19/10/10)
Lipany 0, Ružomberok 1
Liptovský Mikuláš 0, Banská Bystrica 0 *(4-2 on pens)*
Myjava 1, Dubnica 0
Podbrezová 0, Nitra 1
Spišká Nová Ves 0, Spartak Trnava 5
Trencín 1, Slovan Bratislava 1 *(2-3 on pens)*
Zlaté Moravce 2, Petržalka 1

(26/10/10)
Senec 1, Žilina 3

QUARTER-FINALS

(2/11/10 & 23/11/10)
Myjava 0, Slovan Bratislava 1 *(Kordić 12)*
Slovan Bratislava 2 *(Kordić 14, Králik 87)*, Myjava 0
(Slovan Bratislava 3-0)

Nitra 1 *(Rák 83)*, Zlaté Moravce 0
Zlaté Moravce 2 *(Kuračka 59, Pavlovič 88)*, Nitra 0
(Zlaté Moravce 2-1)

Ružomberok 0, Spartak Trnava 3 *(Čarnota J. 17, Koné 57, Higor 87)*
Spartak Trnava 3 *(Gross 59, Higor 66, Bernáth 70)*, Ružomberok 0
(Spartak Trnava 6-0)

(10/11/10 & 1/12/10)
Liptovský Mikuláš 0, Žilina 1 *(Kaplán 4og)*
Žilina 3 *(Poliaček 20, Jež 45, Majtán 46)*, Liptovský Mikuláš 0
(Žilina 4-0)

SEMI-FINALS

(5/4/11 & 19/4/11)
Slovan Bratislava 2 *(Koné 41og, Milinković 7)*, Spartak Trnava 2 *(Koné 28, Machovec 39)*
Spartak Trnava 2 *(Tomaček 69, 90)*, Slovan Bratislava 3 *(Grendel 12, Guédé 27, Dobrotka 33)*
(Slovan Bratislava 5-4)

Žilina 3 *(Ceesay 29, 50, Majtán 69p)*, Zlaté Moravce 0
Zlaté Moravce 1 *(Janečka 11)*, Žilina 0
(Žilina 3-1)

FINAL

(8/5/11)
Na Štiavničkách, Banska Bystrica
ŠK SLOVAN BRATISLAVA 3 *(Guldan 7og, Šebo 76, 113)*
MŠK ŽILINA 3 *(Zošák 15, Lietava 40, Mráz 120+1)*
(aet; 5-4 on pens)
Referee – *Královec*
SLOVAN BRATISLAVA – *Putnocký, Pauschek, Dosoudil, Dobrotka, Hrdlička, Božić (Szárka 73), Milinković (Bagayoko 60), Guédé, Žofčák, Šebo, Kordić (Grendel 46).*
ŽILINA – *Dúbravka, Mabouka, Piaček, Šourek, Leitner (Pich 107), Babatunde, Guldan, Zošák (Gergel 84), Majtán (Mráz 63), Lietava, Ceesay.*

CLUB COMMUNICATION 2011/12

DAC 1904 Dunajská Streda

Športová 4744
SK-929 01 Dunajská Streda

Tel +421 31 552 5306
Fax +421 31 552 5301
Web fkdac1904.eu
Email futbaldac@gmail.com
Media Officer Attila Karaffa

Dukla Banská Bystrica

Hutná 3
SK-974 04 Banská Bystrica

Tel +421 22 085 5500
Fax +421 22 085 5501
Web fkdukla.sk
Email fkdukla@fkdukla.sk
Media Officer Zuzana Očenášová

MFK Košice

Trieda SNP 48/A
SK-040 11 Košice

Tel +421 55 3211 351
Fax +421 55 3211 351
Web mfkkosice.sk
Email sekretariat@mfkkosice.sk
Media Officer Eugen Magda

FC Nitra

Jesenského 4
SK-949 01 Nitra

Tel +421 37 651 3480
Fax +421 37 741 4958
Web fcnitra.sk
Email fcnitra@fcnitra.sk
Media Officer Matej Ivan

MFK Ružomberok

Žilinská cesta 21
SK-034 01 Ružomberok

Tel +421 44 4322 506
Fax +421 44 4323 589
Web mfkruzomberok.sk
Email sekretariat@mfkruzomberok.sk
Media Officer Michal Mertinyák

FK Senica

Sadová 639/22
SK-905 01 Senica

Tel +421 34 651 5303
Fax +421 34 651 5303
Web fksenica.sk
Email fksenica@fksenica.sk
Media Officer Marek Svátek

ŠK Slovan Bratislava

Viktora Tegelhoffa 4
SK-831 04 Bratislava

Tel +421 2 446 36 363
Fax +421 2 446 36 365
Web skslovan.com
Email info@slovanfutbal.com
Media Officer Tomáš Cho

FC Spartak Trnava

Koniarekova 19
SK-917 21 Trnava

Tel +421 33 5503 804
Fax +421 33 5503 806
Web fcspartakas.eu
Email sekretariat@fcspartakas.eu
Media Officer

1. FC Tatran Prešov

Čapajevova 47
SK-080 01 Prešov

Tel +421 51 7481 838
Fax +421 51 7481 843
Web 1fctatran.sk
Email 1fctatran@stonline.sk
Media Officer Ivan Kriššák

FK AS Trencín

Mládežnícka 2313
SK-911 01 Trenčín

Tel +421 32 2902 001
Fax +421 32 7441 137
Web astrencin.sk
Email astrencin@astrencin.sk
Media Officer Martin Galajda

FC ViOn Zlaté Moravce

Továrenská 64
SK-953 01 Zlaté Moravce

Tel +421 37 6403 333
Fax +421 37 6403 337
Web fcvion.sk
Email fcvion@fcvion.sk
Media Officer Michal Červený

MŠK Žilina

Športová 9
SK-010 01 Žilina

Tel +421 41 5622 280
Fax +421 41 5626 9 55
Web mskzilina.sk
Email mskzilina@mskzilina.sk
Media Officer Roman Grešo

SLOVENIA

Slovénie | Slowenien

Nogometna zveza Slovenije (NZS)

COMMUNICATION

Address	Cerinova 4 PP 3986 SI-1001 Ljubljana	**President**	Aleksander Čeferin
Tel	+386 1 530 0400	**General Secretary**	Aleš Zavrl
Fax	+386 1 530 0410	**Media Officer**	Matjaž Krajnik
E-mail	nzs@nzs.si	**Year of Formation**	1920
Website	nzs.si	**National Stadium**	Ljudski vrt, Maribor (12,432)

DOMESTIC COMPETITION SUMMARY 2010/11

PRVA LIGA FINAL TABLE

			Home					Away					Total						
		Pld	**W**	**D**	**L**	**F**	**A**	**W**	**D**	**L**	**F**	**A**	**W**	**D**	**L**	**F**	**A**	**Pts**	**Comp**
1	NK Maribor	36	11	5	2	35	13	10	7	1	30	12	21	12	3	65	25	75	UCL
2	NK Domžale	36	13	2	3	35	14	7	5	6	22	21	20	7	9	57	35	67	UEL
3	FC Koper	36	12	3	3	39	20	5	6	7	18	23	17	9	10	57	43	60	UEL
4	NK Olimpija Ljubljana	36	8	4	6	25	14	7	6	5	34	29	15	10	11	59	43	55	UEL
5	ND Gorica	36	7	7	4	24	28	6	2	10	18	25	13	9	14	42	53	48	
6	NK Rudar Velenje	36	7	4	7	26	19	5	6	7	32	31	12	10	14	58	50	46	
7	ND Triglav	36	7	5	6	24	27	3	4	11	14	32	10	9	17	38	59	39	
8	NK Celje	36	8	4	6	27	23	1	6	11	14	32	9	10	17	41	55	37	
9	NK Nafta	36	5	5	8	27	32	5	2	11	20	35	10	7	19	47	67	37	
10	NK Primorje	36	5	6	7	23	29	3	1	14	17	45	8	7	21	40	74	31	*Relegated*

NB NK Nafta avoided promotion/relegation play-off as second level runners-up NK IB Ljubljana declined to participate.

Top Scorer Marcos Tavares (Maribor), 16 goals

Promoted Club ND Mura 05

Cup Final NK Domžale 4, NK Maribor 3

Milanič's Maribor reclaim their crown

NK Maribor captured the Slovenian title for the second time in three years – and ninth in all – but they were unable to secure their first domestic double since 1998/99 when NK Domžale, runners-up in the league, defeated them 4-3 in an engrossing Slovenian Cup final.

Maribor were led to the Prva Liga title by the same coach who had overseen their 2008/09 triumph, ex-Slovenian international defender Darko Milanič. Disappointed to finish second, behind FC Koper, in 2009/10, they began the new campaign in determined fashion, winning five of their opening six games and remaining unbeaten in their first 20, by which stage, in early March, they were out of sight at the top of the table with an 11-point lead. Three defeats in five games brought their title charge to a temporary halt, but they picked up the pace again in April and, despite a run of four successive draws in May, were able to seal the title one round from the end with a 2-1 win away to NK Primorje that also confirmed their hosts' relegation.

Domžale's revenge

Although Maribor were struggling for form at the finish, they beat Domžale 2-0 at home on the last day to extend their final margin of victory to eight points. The more important meeting with Domžale had taken place four days earlier, however, when the two clubs came face to face for the second year running in the final of the Slovenian Cup. Maribor had prevailed 3-2 in 2010 thanks to a last-gasp extra-time winner, and there was drama and incident aplenty once more as underdogs Domžale gained their revenge with a thrilling 4-3 triumph that gave the club the trophy for the first time. Ex-Maribor striker Damir Pekič was Domžale's match-winning hero, the second of his two goals, 12 minutes from time, knocking the stuffing out of the just-crowned champions who had looked firm favourites to win following the sending-off of Domžale midfielder Dalibor Teinović a couple of minutes earlier.

Brazilian marksman Marcos Tavares (left) inspired Maribor to their ninth Slovenian championship title

Maribor's season might have ended in disappointment, but it had started with a succession of highs, not just in the Prva Liga but also in Europe, where they convincingly eliminated Videoton FC of Hungary and Hibernian FC of Scotland from the qualifying rounds of the UEFA Europa League before succumbing valiantly to the Italians of US Città di Palermo in the play-offs. Maribor won all three home legs, and it was a superb performance – and goal – in the 3-2 victory over Palermo by young midfielder Josip Iličič that earned him an immediate transfer to the Sicilian club, where he would go on to enjoy a fine debut season in Serie A. With Iličič gone, Maribor's star player was Brazilian striker and newly appointed club captain Marcos Tavares, who, on top of his four goals in Europe, added 16 in the domestic league to become the Prva Liga's leading marksman – three ahead of Domžale's Pekič and the previous season's winner, 35-year-old Milan Osterc, then of ND Gorica, now of Koper.

Despite the best efforts of the former Slovenia striker, Koper never threatened a repeat of their 2009/10 title success. Championship-winning coach Nedžad Okčič was sacked in the early autumn after a miserable run, only to be reinstated six months later. He ended the season carrying the team into a respectable third place, which earned them qualification for the UEFA Europa League alongside Domžale and NK Olimpija Ljubljana, who took fourth spot for the second successive season.

Promotion declined

Although Primorje, as the bottom club, were automatically relegated, ninth-placed NK Nafta were spared the ordeal of a promotion/relegation play-off after second division runners-up NK IB Ljubljana withdrew, citing financial constraints. It was a similar story for second division champions NK Aluminij, whose hard-earned automatic promotion was also declined. In order to maintain a ten-team top flight, fourth-placed ND Mura 05 received a special invitation to make up the Prva Liga numbers in 2011/12.

With one of the most settled international teams in Europe, Slovenia made decent, if discreet, progress in their UEFA EURO 2012 qualifying group. They started badly with a home defeat to Northern Ireland but took seven points from their next three games and by the summer sat second behind runaway leaders Italy with every chance of reaching the play-offs. The most prominent newcomer to Matjaž Kek's team was Iličič, who featured in all ten internationals, while Tim Matavž, who had a fine season in the Netherlands with FC Groningen, raised his profile with four goals in two games against the Faroe Islands, the first three, in Ljubljana, making him, at 21, the youngest player to score a hat-trick for Slovenia.

National Team

International Tournament Appearances – FIFA World Cup – (2) 2002, 2010. UEFA European Championship - (1) 2000.

Top Five All-time Caps – Zlatko Zahovič (80); Milenko Ačimovič & Aleš Čeh (74); Džoni Novak (71); Marinko Galič (66)

Top Five All-time Goals – Zlatko Zahovič (35); Milivoje Novakovič (19); Sašo Udovič (16); Ermin Šiljak (14); Milenko Ačimovič (13)

NATIONAL TEAM RESULTS 2010/11

11/8/10	Australia	H	Ljubljana	2-0	*Dedič (78), Ljubijankič (90)*
3/9/10	Northern Ireland (ECQ)	H	Maribor	0-1	
7/9/10	Serbia (ECQ)	A	Belgrade	1-1	*Novakovič (63)*
8/10/10	Faroe Islands (ECQ)	H	Ljubljana	5-1	*Matavž (25, 36, 65), Novakovič (72p), Dedič (84)*
12/10/10	Estonia (ECQ)	A	Tallinn	1-0	*Sidorenkov (67og)*
17/11/10	Georgia	H	Koper	1-2	*Cesar (51)*
9/2/11	Albania	A	Tirana	2-1	*Novakovič (24), Dedič (90p)*
25/3/11	Italy (ECQ)	H	Ljubljana	0-1	
29/3/11	Northern Ireland (ECQ)	A	Belfast	0-0	
3/6/11	Faroe Islands (ECQ)	A	Toftir	2-0	*Matavž (29), Baldvinsson (47og)*

NATIONAL TEAM APPEARANCES 2010/11

Coach - Matjaž KEK	**9/9/61**		Aus	NIR	SRB	FRO	EST	Geo	Alb	ITA	NIR	FRO	Caps	Goals
Samir HANDANOVIČ	14/7/84	Udinese (ITA)	G	G	G	G	G	G53		G	G	G	51	-
Mišo BREČKO	1/5/84	Köln (GER)	D	D	D	D	D	D	D	D70	D	D	44	-
Boštjan CESAR	9/7/82	Chievo (ITA)	D	D	D	D	D	D	D	D		D	55	4
Matej MAVRIČ	29/1/79	Kapfenberg (AUT)	D	D	D						D	s47	37	1
Bojan JOKIČ	17/5/86	Chievo (ITA)	D80	D	D	D	D	D71	D	D	D	D	47	1
Robert KOREN	20/9/80	unattached /Hull (ENG)	M	M	M	M	M	M46		M	M	M	58	5
Andraž KIRM	6/9/84	Wisła Kraków (POL)	M86	M74	M89	s51	s67	M81	M87	M	M	s76	39	3
Aleksandar RADOSAVLJEVIČ	25/4/79	unattached /Den Haag (NED)	M	M	M	M59	M	s46	M	M			26	1
Valter BIRSA	7/8/86	Auxerre (FRA)	M68	M	M78	M51	M91	M46	M59	M74	M	M47	47	3
Milivoje NOVAKOVIČ	18/5/79	Köln (GER)	A75	A74	A	A73	A	A	A68	A	A84	A55	51	19
Tim MATAVŽ	13/1/89	Groningen (NED)	A46	s88		A	A53	s46	A46			A76	9	4
Zlatko DEDIČ	5/10/84	Bochum (GER)	s46	s74	A77	s73	s53	A46	s46	A56	s84		36	6

NATIONAL TEAM APPEARANCES 2010/11(contd.)

			Aus	NIR	SRB	FRO	EST	Geo	Alb	ITA	NIR	FRO	Caps	Goals
Josip ILIČIĆ	29/1/88	Maribor /Palermo (ITA)	s68	s74	s78	M	M67	s46	s59	s74	M29	M	10	-
Zlatan LJUBIJANKIČ	15/12/83	Gent (BEL)	s75	A88	s77		s91	s81	s68	s56	s29	s55	29	6
Branko ILIĆ	6/2/83	Lokomotiv Moskva (RUS)	s80					s71					39	-
Dare VRŠIČ	26/9/84	unattached	s86										6	2
Dalibor STEVANOVIČ	27/9/84	Vitesse (NED)			s89								16	1
Marko ŠULER	9/3/83	Gent (BEL)				D	D	D	D	D	D	D 25*	27	2
Armin BAČINOVIČ	24/10/89	Palermo (ITA)				s59		M	M66		M90	M	6	-
Jasmin HANDANOVIČ	28/1/78	Empoli (ITA)						s53	G				5	-
Goran ŠUKALO	24/8/81	Duisburg (GER)							s66		s90		34	2
Siniša ANĐELKOVIČ	13/2/86	Palermo (ITA)							s87	s70			2	-

CLUB-BY-CLUB

NK CELJE

Coach – Milan Đuričić (CRO); (18/9/10) Damjan Romih; (16/10/10) Stane Bevc

Founded – 1919

Stadium – Petrol Arena (13,400)

MAJOR HONOURS: Slovenian Cup – (1) 2005.

2010				
17/7	Domžale	h	0-1	
24/7	Triglav	a	1-1	*Močič*
31/7	Rudar	h	5-1	*Zajc, Mujakovič (p), Bezjak, Rep 2*
7/8	Gorica	a	3-3	*Rep 2, Purišič*
14/8	Olimpija	h	1-1	*Bezjak*
22/8	Maribor	a	0-2	
28/8	Nafta	h	2-4	*Štraus (p), Bezjak*
11/9	Koper	h	2-1	*Cadikovski, Klebčar*
22/9	Domžale	a	0-1	
25/9	Triglav	h	1-1	*Zajc*
2/10	Rudar	a	2-3	*Bezjak, Cadikovski*
10/10	Primorje	a	0-2	
16/10	Gorica	h	1-0	*Cadikovski*
23/10	Olimpija	a	0-1	
30/10	Maribor	h	0-4	
6/11	Nafta	a	2-2	*Klebčar, Cadikovski*
13/11	Koper	a	3-7	*Močič, Gobec, Medved*
20/11	Primorje	h	3-0	*Močivnik, Beršnjak (p), Zajc*
2011				
20/2	Domžale	h	0-0	
27/2	Triglav	a	0-0	
5/3	Rudar	h	1-0	*og (Cadikovski)*
12/3	Gorica	a	1-1	*Akakpo*
16/3	Olimpija	h	1-3	*Bezjak*
19/3	Maribor	a	0-2	
1/4	Nafta	h	3-0	*Pavlovič (p), Zajc, Krajcer*
6/4	Koper	h	0-3	
9/4	Primorje	a	1-0	*Krajcer*
15/4	Domžale	a	0-2	
22/4	Triglav	h	2-0	*Beršnjak 2*
30/4	Rudar	a	0-1	
3/5	Gorica	h	3-1	*Bezjak 2, Pavlovič (p)*
7/5	Olimpija	a	1-3	*Firer*
10/5	Maribor	h	0-0	
14/5	Nafta	a	0-0	
21/5	Koper	a	0-1	
29/5	Primorje	h	2-3	*Močivnik, Firer*

No	Name	Nat	DoB	Pos	Aps	(s)	Gls
3	Serge AKAKPO	TOG	15/7/87	M	14		1
14	Goran ALENC		16/1/87	D	1	(4)	
6	Milan ANDŽELKOVIČ		1/9/81	D	6		
4	Tomaž AVGUŠTIN		28/1/92	M	1	(1)	
13	Saša BAKARIČ		18/3/87	D	16	(7)	
70	Dominik BERŠNJAK		15/7/81	D	18	(1)	3
9	Roman BEZJAK		21/2/89	A	30	(2)	7
3	David BEZOVNIK		2/7/92	D	2	(2)	
7	Danijel BREZIČ		15/2/76	M	31	(1)	
11	Dragan CADIKOVSKI	MKD	13/1/82	A	9	(1)	4
82	Mirsad FAZLIČ		9/3/92	D		(1)	
26	Ivan FIRER		19/11/84	M	12	(3)	2
23	Tadej GABER		22/1/92	M		(1)	
25	Sebastjan GOBEC		6/12/79	M	29		1
3	Dragutin GOLUB	CRO	29/8/79	M	2	(1)	
21	Aleš KAČIČNIK		28/9/73	D	10	(5)	
15	Bekim KAPIČ		2/1/79	M	12	(2)	
18	Maximiliano KLEBČAR	ARG	20/2/87	A	2	(5)	2
4	Simon KLUN		23/12/89	M	11	(1)	
33	Marko KRAJCER		3/7/85	M	13	(2)	2
8	Anže KRALJIČ		25/9/90	M		(1)	
88	Klemen MEDVED		10/11/88	M	25	(1)	1
23	Boris MIJATOVIČ		7/2/88	D	11		
28	Mario MOČIČ		4/5/89	M	12	(3)	2
17	Iztok MOČIVNIK		22/1/92	M	5	(6)	2
20	Amel MUJAKOVIČ		4/5/82	M	12	(2)	1
1	Amel MUJČINOVIČ		20/11/73	G	36		
5	Dejan PANTOVIČ		16/7/90	A	1		
20	Zoran PAVLOVIČ		27/6/76	M	16		2
10	Denis POPOVIČ		15/10/89	M	11	(11)	
19	Dejan PURIŠIČ		16/7/83	A	1	(6)	1
19	Miroslav RADULOVIČ		6/9/84	A	8		
16	Almir RAHMANOVIČ		25/3/86	M		(1)	
55	Rajko REP		20/6/90	M	3	(4)	4
99	Rok ŠTRAUS		3/3/87	M	15	(10)	1
2	Benjamin VERBIČ		27/11/93	M		(1)	
30	Tadej VIDMAJER		10/3/92	D	3	(2)	
9	Gorazd ZAJC		28/12/87	A	18	(9)	4

NK DOMŽALE

Coach – Darko Birjukov (BIH)

Founded – 1921

Stadium – Športni park (3,212)

MAJOR HONOURS: Slovenian League – (2) 2007, 2008; Slovenian Cup – (1) 2011.

2010				
17/7	Celje	a	1-0	*Smukavec*
24/7	Koper	h	2-0	*Pekič, Horvat*
31/7	Primorje	a	0-0	
7/8	Nafta	a	2-3	*Pekič, Smukavec*
14/8	Triglav	h	3-0	*Teinović, Smukavec, Drevenšek*
21/8	Rudar	a	1-0	*Apatič*
28/8	Gorica	h	1-0	*Pekič*
10/9	Olimpija	a	1-0	*Drevenšek*
22/9	Celje	h	1-0	*Juninho*
25/9	Koper	a	0-2	
2/10	Primorje	h	4-1	*Brezovački, Zatkovič 2, Pekič*
9/10	Maribor	h	0-1	
16/10	Nafta	h	1-1	*Horvat*
24/10	Triglav	a	3-1	*Horvat, Zatkovič 2*
31/10	Rudar	h	2-3	*Simunovic, Kosmač*
6/11	Gorica	a	3-0	*Knezović, Drevenšek, Horvat*
14/11	Olimpija	h	2-1	*Pekič, Drevenšek*
20/11	Maribor	a	1-1	*Apatič*
2011				
20/2	Celje	a	0-0	
26/2	Koper	h	1-2	*Knezović*
6/3	Primorje	a	0-0	
12/3	Nafta	a	3-2	*Juninho 2, Vuk*
16/3	Triglav	h	3-1	*Pekič 2, Knezović*
19/3	Rudar	a	1-3	*Pekič*
1/4	Gorica	h	2-0	*og (Buzeti), Juninho*
5/4	Olimpija	a	0-0	
9/4	Maribor	h	2-2	*Juninho, Pekič (p)*
15/4	Celje	h	2-0	*Zatkovič, Teinović*
23/4	Koper	a	1-3	*Zatkovič*
30/4	Primorje	h	1-0	*Smukavec*
4/5	Nafta	h	3-2	*Pekič 2, Juninho*
8/5	Triglav	a	4-2	*Simunovic, Drevenšek, Pekič, Zec*
11/5	Rudar	h	2-0	*Zatkovič, Juninho*
14/5	Gorica	a	1-2	*Pekič (p)*
21/5	Olimpija	h	3-0	*Smukavec, Vuk, Apatič*
29/5	Maribor	a	0-2	

No	Name	Nat	DoB	Pos	Aps	(s)	Gls
87	Tadej APATIČ		7/7/87	D	30	(1)	3
9	Florent AZIRI		3/9/88	A	5	(4)	
8	Blaž BREZOVAČKI		29/4/87	D	20	(1)	1
22	Darko BRLJAK		23/12/84	G	26		
6	Nik CIMPRIČ		15/8/91	M		(4)	
4	Lamin DIALLO		31/8/91	D	1	(1)	
24	Gaber DOBROVOLJC		27/1/93	D	1		
20	Marko DREVENŠEK		10/9/87	M	32	(4)	5
32	Luka ELSNER		2/8/82	D	21	(1)	
5	Rok HANŽIČ		6/4/81	D	12	(1)	
21	Lucas Mario HORVAT	ARG	13/10/85	M	13	(3)	4
25	Wilson Aparecido Xavier Júnior "JUNINHO"	BRA	15/3/84	M	28	(2)	7
13	Ivan KNEZOVIĆ	CRO	15/9/82	D	29	(3)	3
19	Nace KOSMAČ		6/9/86	A	2	(9)	1
17	Marko KOVJENIČ		2/2/93	M	1	(1)	
18	Saša KOVJENIČ		12/2/90	M		(1)	
14	Amer KRCIČ		23/5/89	M	7	(5)	
26	Emir LJUBIJANKIČ		5/5/92	A		(2)	
10	Damir PEKIČ		15/1/79	A	31	(1)	13
26	Matic SEFEROVIČ		22/12/86	M	8	(4)	
28	Mato SIMUNOVIC	AUT	27/9/85	A	21	(2)	2
23	Jernej SMUKAVEC		6/8/91	A	6	(21)	5
7	Dalibor TEINOVIĆ	BIH	22/3/77	M	32	(1)	2
3	Darko TOPIČ		3/3/85	M	11	(5)	
41	Nejc VIDMAR		31/3/89	G	10		
4	Jovan VIDOVIČ		6/1/89	M	13	(3)	
15	Sebastjan VUK		15/9/89	D	3	(2)	2
11	Mitja ZATKOVIČ		7/6/83	M	20	(6)	7
2	Darko ZEC		21/2/89	D	13	(3)	1
77	Sead ZILIĆ	BIH	17/9/82	A		(5)	

ND GORICA

Coach – Danijel Peršič; (4/5/11) Miran Srebrnič

Founded – 1947

Stadium – Športni Park (5,000)

MAJOR HONOURS: Slovenian League – (4) 1996, 2004, 2005, 2006; Slovenian Cup – (2) 2001, 2002.

2010				
18/7	Nafta	h	1-0	*Komel*
25/7	Olimpija	h	2-2	*Velikonja 2 (1p)*
1/8	Maribor	a	1-3	*Mevlja M.*
7/8	Celje	h	3-3	*og (Andželkovič), Arčon, Velikonja (p)*
14/8	Koper	a	0-1	
21/8	Primorje	h	3-2	*Širok, Demirović, Arčon*
28/8	Domžale	a	0-1	
11/9	Triglav	h	2-1	*og (Stjepanovič), Jogan K.*
18/9	Rudar	a	2-1	*Kršič, Jogan K.*
22/9	Nafta	a	0-3	
25/9	Olimpija	a	0-0	
2/10	Maribor	h	0-2	
16/10	Celje	a	0-1	
23/10	Koper	h	2-2	*Demirović, Jogan K.*
31/10	Primorje	a	2-0	*Jogan K., Balažič*
6/11	Domžale	h	0-3	
14/11	Triglav	a	0-2	
20/11	Rudar	h	1-1	*Velikonja*
27/11	Nafta	h	1-0	*Mevlja M.*
2011				
26/2	Olimpija	h	1-3	*Arčon*
5/3	Maribor	a	2-1	*Rakuščček,Franklin*
12/3	Celje	h	1-1	*Plut*
16/3	Koper	a	2-2	*Plut, Franklin*
19/3	Primorje	h	4-1	*Galešić 2, Franklin, Plut*
1/4	Domžale	a	0-2	
5/4	Triglav	h	1-0	*Galešić*
9/4	Rudar	a	1-0	*Arčon*
16/4	Nafta	a	4-1	*Plut 3, Arčon*
22/4	Olimpija	a	0-1	
30/4	Maribor	h	0-6	
3/5	Celje	a	1-3	*Plut*
7/5	Koper	h	0-0	
11/5	Primorje	a	3-2	*Mevlja M., Demirović (p), Galešić*
14/5	Domžale	h	2-1	*Galešić, Franklin*
21/5	Triglav	a	0-1	
29/5	Rudar	h	0-0	

No	Name	Nat	DoB	Pos	Aps	(s)	Gls
18	Sandi ARČON		6/1/91	D	21	(13)	5
9	Gregor BALAŽIČ		12/2/88	M	16		1
11	Rok BUZETI		10/2/88	A	12	(3)	
24	Enes DEMIROVIĆ	BIH	13/6/72	M	17	(5)	3
9	FRANKLIN William Vicente	BRA	12/6/89	M	14		4
3	Goran GALEŠIĆ	BIH	11/3/89	M	22	(2)	5
35	Miha GREGORIČ		22/8/89	M	7	(4)	
27	Alen JOGAN		24/8/85	M	16		
32	Kris JOGAN		14/9/91	A	14	(13)	4
19	Sebastjan KOMEL		18/2/86	M	14	(1)	1
10	Admir KRŠIČ		7/11/82	M	28	(2)	1
14	Jasmin KURTIČ		10/1/89	M	15		
15	Dino MARTINOVIČ		20/7/90	A	1	(8)	
17	Miha MEVLJA		12/6/90	M	30	(4)	3
16	Nejc MEVLJA		12/6/90	D	21	(4)	

26	Boris MIJATOVIČ		7/2/88	D	3	(1)	
25	Welle N'DIAYE	SEN	5/4/90	M	1		
14	Vito PLUT		8/7/88	A	16		7
21	Nejc PRAPROTNIK		17/1/93	M		(4)	
31	Danijel RAKUŠČEK		10/6/86	M	14	(5)	1
22	Anže RUPNIK		6/4/87	G	4	(1)	
12	Vasja SIMČIČ		1/7/83	G	32		
20	Dalibor STOJANOVIČ		4/4/89	M	2	(4)	
23	Matija ŠIROK		31/5/91	D	21	(5)	1
11	Etien VELIKONJA		26/12/88	A	18		4
7	Amedej VETRIH		16/9/90	M		(1)	
29	Nemanja VIDIĆ	SRB	6/8/89	M	2	(5)	
8	Luka VOLARIČ		13/1/91	M	4	(4)	
6	Aris ZARIFOVIČ		2/6/88	D	28	(1)	
28	Dejan ŽIGON		30/3/89	A	3	(8)	

FC KOPER

Coach – Nedžad Okčič; (2/10/10) Primož Gliha; (20/4/11) Nedžad Okčić

Founded – 1955

Stadium – Bonifika (10,000)

MAJOR HONOURS: Slovenian League – (1) 2010; Slovenian Cup – (2) 2006, 2007.

2010				
16/7	Primorje	h	4-1	*Brulc 2, Marčeta, Karič*
24/7	Domžale	a	0-2	
31/7	Triglav	h	1-1	*Handanagič*
7/8	Rudar	a	1-2	*Karič*
14/8	Gorica	h	1-0	*Hasič (p)*
22/8	Olimpija	a	2-1	*Osterc, Hasič (p)*
29/8	Maribor	h	0-1	
11/9	Celje	a	1-2	*Hasič (p)*
18/9	Nafta	h	0-3	
22/9	Primorje	a	1-3	*Handanagič*
25/9	Domžale	h	2-0	*og (Brezovački), Jelenič*
3/10	Triglav	a	0-0	
16/10	Rudar	h	2-1	*Osterc, Marčeta*
23/10	Gorica	a	2-2	*Osterc 2*
30/10	Olimpija	h	2-0	*Guberac, Osterc*
6/11	Maribor	a	0-2	
13/11	Celje	h	7-3	*Brulc, Osterc 4 (1p), Tomić, Jelenič*
20/11	Nafta	a	2-0	*Marčeta, Pavlin L.*
27/11	Primorje	h	2-1	*Hasič (p), Brulc*
2011				
26/2	Domžale	a	2-1	*Grižonič, Osterc*
5/3	Triglav	h	0-1	
12/3	Rudar	a	1-0	*Osterc*
16/3	Gorica	h	2-2	*Marčeta, Marijanovič*
19/3	Olimpija	a	0-4	
2/4	Maribor	h	3-0	*Struna Al., Hasič (p), Vassiljev*
6/4	Celje	a	3-0	*Osterc, Marijanovič, Struna Al.*
9/4	Nafta	h	4-1	*Stančič 2, Vassiljev, Karič*
16/4	Primorje	a	1-1	*Đukić*
23/4	Domžale	h	3-1	*Brulc, Vassiljev, Stančič*
30/4	Triglav	a	0-0	
4/5	Rudar	h	3-3	*Bubanja 2, Hasič (p)*
7/5	Gorica	a	0-0	
11/5	Olimpija	h	2-1	*Hadžič 2*
14/5	Maribor	a	1-1	*Bubanja*
21/5	Celje	h	1-0	*Osterc*
29/5	Nafta	a	1-2	*Guberac (p)*

No	Name	Nat	DoB	Pos	Aps	(s)	Gls
18	Danijel BEŠIČ		31/7/90	A		(2)	
5	Milan BLAŽIČ		8/5/93	D	10	(1)	
21	Saša BOŽIČIČ		8/5/83	M	2	(1)	
25	Mitja BRULC		7/12/79	A	21	(6)	5
32	Davor BUBANJA		26/9/87	A	23	(3)	3
9	David BUNDERLA		31/7/87	A	4	(9)	
28	Bojan ĐUKIĆ	CRO	6/11/86	M	13	(1)	1
23	Željko FILIPOVIČ		3/10/88	D	1	(3)	
19	Marko GRIŽONIČ		1/12/82	M	18	(3)	1
7	Ivica GUBERAC		5/7/88	M	22	(4)	2
27	Damir HADŽIČ		1/10/84	D	15	(7)	2
6	Enes HANDANAGIČ		15/9/79	D	33	(1)	2
1	Ermin HASIČ		19/9/75	G	30		6
13	Matic HOJNIK		17/6/92	D		(1)	
29	Enej JELENIČ		11/12/92	M	7	(5)	2
10	Amer JUKAN		28/11/78	M	6	(1)	
20	Amir KARIČ		31/12/73	M	16	(3)	3
8	Nebojša KOVAČEVIČ		8/9/77	M	23	(4)	
3	Adis LIZALOVIČ		19/3/92	M		(1)	
22	Danijel MARČETA		4/1/89	M	19	(5)	4
3	Milidrag MARIČ		9/11/83	D	6		
33	Dejan MARIJANOVIČ		2/1/87	A	10	(6)	2
21	Igor NENEZIČ		23/3/84	G	4		
9	Igor NOVAKOVIĆ	CRO	24/5/79	M	1	(6)	
35	Milan OSTERC		4/7/75	A	25		13
29	Matej PALČIČ		21/6/93	M		(2)	
14	Luka PAVLIN		16/10/88	M	1	(6)	1
11	Miran PAVLIN		8/10/71	M	2		
5	Kristijan POLOVANEC	CRO	10/10/79	D	14		
21	Ivan SESAR	CRO	29/8/89	M	3		
26	Dino STANČIČ		25/1/92	M	5	(10)	3
17	Aljaž STRUNA		4/8/90	M	19	(5)	2
24	Andraž STRUNA		23/4/89	D	14	(3)	
30	Admir SUHONJIČ		23/3/81	G	2	(1)	
18	Leo ŠTULAC		26/9/94	M		(4)	
30	Filip TIMOV	MKD	22/5/92	A		(2)	
20	Ante TOMIĆ	CRO	23/5/83	M	11		1
16	Konstantin VASSILJEV	EST	16/8/84	M	16		3
15	Marko VUKELIČ		19/1/92	M		(1)	

NK MARIBOR

Coach – Darko Milanič

Founded – 1960

Stadium – Ljudski vrt (12,432)

MAJOR HONOURS: Slovenian League – (9) 1997, 1998, 1999, 2000, 2001, 2002, 2003, 2009, 2011; Slovenian Cup – (6) 1992, 1994, 1997, 1999, 2004, 2010.

2010				
18/7	Triglav	h	5-0	*Plut 3, Pavličić, Mertelj*
25/7	Rudar	a	0-0	
1/8	Gorica	h	3-1	*Cvijanovič 2, Džinič*
14/8	Nafta	h	3-1	*Marcos Tavares 3*
22/8	Celje	h	2-0	*Iličič, Berič*
29/8	Koper	a	1-0	*Berič*
11/9	Primorje	h	1-1	*Volaš*
22/9	Triglav	a	2-2	*Volaš 2 (1p)*
25/9	Rudar	h	3-1	*Pavličić, Rep 2*
29/9	Olimpija	a	1-0	*Berič*
2/10	Gorica	a	2-0	*Marcos Tavares, Cvijanovič*
9/10	Domžale	a	1-0	*Volaš*
16/10	Olimpija	h	0-0	
23/10	Nafta	a	2-0	*Marcos Tavares 2*
30/10	Celje	a	4-0	*Volaš 3, Marcos Tavares*
6/11	Koper	h	2-0	*Marcos Tavares, Cvijanovič*
14/11	Primorje	a	0-0	
20/11	Domžale	h	1-1	*Berič*
27/11	Triglav	h	3-1	*Marcos Tavares, Milec 2*
2011				
26/2	Rudar	a	4-2	*Marcos Tavares, Mezga 2 (1p), Velikonja*
5/3	Gorica	h	1-2	*Berič*
12/3	Olimpija	a	0-0	
16/3	Nafta	h	0-1	
19/3	Celje	h	2-0	*Milec, Marcos Tavares*
2/4	Koper	a	0-3	
5/4	Primorje	h	2-0	*Mezga 2*

9/4	Domžale	a	2-2	*og (Knezović), Marcos Tavares*
17/4	Triglav	a	2-1	*Mezga, Berič*
23/4	Rudar	h	2-1	*Velikonja, Viler*
30/4	Gorica	a	6-0	*Marcos Tavares 3, Cvijanovič, Velikonja, Mezga*
4/5	Olimpija	h	2-2	*Velikonja, Berič*
7/5	Nafta	a	1-1	*Rajčevič*
10/5	Celje	a	0-0	
14/5	Koper	h	1-1	*Velikonja*
21/5	Primorje	a	2-1	*Marcos Tavares, Berič*
29/5	Domžale	h	2-0	*Velikonja, Ploj*

No	Name	Nat	DoB	Pos	Aps	(s)	Gls
66	Siniša ANĐELKOVIČ		13/2/86	D	17	(1)	
21	Armin BAČINOVIČ		24/10/89	M	3		
32	Robert BERIČ		17/6/91	A	13	(17)	8
39	David BUNDERLA		31/7/87	A		(3)	
20	Goran CVIJANOVIČ		9/9/86	M	32	(2)	5
2	Matic ČRNIČ		12/6/92	D	1	(2)	
29	Timotej DODLEK		23/11/89	M	20	(9)	
3	Elvedin DŽINIČ		25/8/85	D	9	(2)	1
5	Željko FILIPOVIČ		3/10/88	D	8	(7)	
8	João GABRIEL da Silva	BRA	4/7/84	M	5	(2)	
27	Josip ILIČIČ		29/1/88	M	3	(2)	1
11	Dragan JELIČ		27/2/86	A	3	(2)	
15	Luka KRAJNC		19/9/94	M	1		
36	Aleš MAJER		2/8/89	D	25	(1)	
9	MARCOS Magno Morales TAVARES	BRA	30/3/84	A	31	(2)	16
7	Aleš MEJAČ		18/3/83	D	10	(2)	
70	Aleš MERTELJ		22/3/87	M	20		1
8	Dejan MEZGA	CRO	16/7/85	M	19	(2)	6
6	Martin MILEC		20/9/91	M	3	(5)	3
10	Tomislav PAVLIČIĆ	CRO	6/12/83	M	8	(7)	2
27	Alen PLOJ		30/6/92	A		(2)	1
14	Vito PLUT		8/7/88	A	10	(7)	3
22	Nejc POTOKAR		2/12/88	M	12	(1)	
12	Marko PRIDIGAR		18/5/85	G	13		
13	Matej RADAN		13/5/90	G	23	(1)	
26	ALeksander RAJČEVIČ		27/11/86	D	28	(1)	1
55	Rajko REP		20/6/90	M	14	(12)	2
23	Mitja REŠEK		15/1/91	M	1	(2)	
25	Semir SPAHIČ		26/1/91	D		(1)	
11	Etien VELIKONJA		26/12/88	A	15	(1)	6
4	Jovan VIDOVIČ		6/1/89	D	6	(1)	
28	Mitja VILER		1/9/86	M	32	(2)	1
30	Dalibor VOLAŠ		27/2/87	A	11	(4)	7

NK NAFTA

Coach – Damir Rob; (18/4/11) Stanko Preradovič

Founded – 1903

Stadium – Lendava (5,000)

2010				
18/7	Gorica	a	0-1	
24/7	Primorje	h	2-1	*Vassiljev (p), Benko*
2/8	Olimpija	a	1-0	*Vinko*
7/8	Domžale	h	3-2	*Vinko, Vassiljev (p), Buzeti*
14/8	Maribor	a	1-3	*Benko*
21/8	Triglav	h	2-1	*Benko, Vinko*
28/8	Celje	a	4-2	*Benko, Filipovič, Vinko, Kokol*
10/9	Rudar	h	3-3	*Benko 2, Bečiri*
18/9	Koper	a	3-0	*Vassiljev, Benko 2*
22/9	Gorica	h	3-0	*Vaš, Benko, Pavel*
26/9	Primorje	a	2-4	*Dvorančič, Benko*
2/10	Olimpija	h	2-3	*og (Kašnik), Bečiri*
16/10	Domžale	a	1-1	*Benko*
23/10	Maribor	h	0-2	
31/10	Triglav	a	0-2	
6/11	Celje	h	2-2	*Gerenčer, Caban*
13/11	Rudar	a	0-0	
20/11	Koper	h	0-2	
27/11	Gorica	a	0-1	
2011				
26/2	Primorje	h	1-2	*Vinko*
5/3	Olimpija	a	0-2	
12/3	Domžale	h	2-3	*Vinko, Jovanovič*
16/3	Maribor	a	1-0	*Oluić*
19/3	Triglav	h	1-1	*Jovanovič*
1/4	Celje	a	0-3	
5/4	Rudar	h	1-2	*Vinko*
9/4	Koper	a	1-4	*Vinko*
16/4	Gorica	h	1-4	*Matjašec*
23/4	Primorje	a	4-1	*Vinko, Levačič, Tomažič Šeruga, Lesjak*
30/4	Olimpija	h	1-2	*Vinko*
4/5	Domžale	a	2-3	*Lesjak 2 (1p)*
7/5	Maribor	h	1-1	*Levačič*
11/5	Triglav	a	0-4	
14/5	Celje	h	0-0	
21/5	Rudar	a	0-4	
29/5	Koper	h	2-1	*Pavel, Lesjak (p)*

No	Name	Nat	DoB	Pos	Aps	(s)	Gls
1	Aleš AJLEC		27/6/88	G	10	(1)	
6	Marko BALAŽIC		31/7/84	D	15	(4)	
20	Erdžan BEČIRI		24/8/85	M	16		2
8	Jože BENKO		22/3/80	A	17	(1)	11
24	Rok BUZETI		10/2/88	M	19		1
23	Stjepan CABAN	CRO	23/2/80	D	19		1
30	Aleš ČEH		22/7/80	M	18		
11	Slaviša DVORANČIČ		22/1/79	A	9	(16)	1
15	Ivan FILIPOVIČ		9/8/87	D	7	(3)	1
18	Peter GERENČER		28/4/85	M		(7)	1
5	Leon HORVAT		24/8/86	M		(2)	
10	Agim IBRAIMI	MKD	29/8/88	A	16	(1)	
88	Said IDRIZI		26/4/90	A	4	(3)	
21	Rade JOVANOVIČ		8/1/91	D	5	(10)	2
66	Nemanja JOZIČ		28/5/84	G	8		
9	Miha KOKOL		23/11/89	A		(6)	1
11	Dejan KOMLJENOVIČ		11/7/84	A	2		
14	Miha KOROŠEC		11/8/91	M	8	(3)	
5	Igor LAZIČ		30/10/79	D	11	(1)	
4	Zoran LESJAK	CRO	1/2/88	D	32		4
16	Saša LEVAČIČ		26/2/88	M	16	(3)	2
17	Matic MARUŠKO		30/11/90	M	9	(5)	
3	Bojan MATJAŠEC		16/4/84	D	31		1
22	Tomaž MURKO		7/2/79	G	18		
19	Nikola OLUIĆ	CRO	1/4/91	A	1	(3)	1
7	Simon PAVEL		20/3/92	A	8	(8)	2
20	Luka PRAŠNIKAR		11/6/87	A	4	(7)	
26	Patrik RADUHA		9/2/90	M	2	(4)	
9	David TOMAŽIČ ŠERUGA		30/4/86	M	15	(1)	1
14	Konstantin VASSILJEV	EST	16/8/84	M	19		3
25	Arpad VAŠ		31/7/89	M	30		1
22	Vedran VINKO		22/2/90	A	25	(1)	10
27	Patrik VOROS		16/10/90	M	2	(12)	

NK OLIMPIJA LJUBLJANA

Coach – Safet Hadžič; (28/8/10) Andrej Kračman; (11/9/10) Dušan Kosič

Founded – 2005

Stadium – Stožice (16,038)

2010				
18/7	Rudar	h	1-3	*Lovrečič*
25/7	Gorica	a	2-2	*Rakovič 2*
2/8	Nafta	h	0-1	
14/8	Celje	a	1-1	*og (Mijatovič)*
22/8	Koper	h	1-2	*Bešič*
29/8	Primorje	a	1-5	*Rujovič*
10/9	Domžale	h	0-1	
19/9	Triglav	a	5-0	*Bešič, Šokota, Salkič, Zeljkovič, Rujovič*

22/9	Rudar	a	1-1	*Salkič*
25/9	Gorica	h	0-0	
29/9	Maribor	h	0-1	
2/10	Nafta	a	3-2	*Zeljkovič (p), Rakovič, Smiljanič*
16/10	Maribor	a	0-0	
23/10	Celje	h	1-0	*Cimerotič (p)*
30/10	Koper	a	0-2	
6/11	Primorje	h	3-0	*Škerjanc, Gabriel, Jovič*
14/11	Domžale	a	1-2	*Salkič*
20/11	Triglav	h	1-0	*Bešič*
2011				
22/2	Rudar	h	2-2	*Škerjanc, Radujko*
26/2	Gorica	a	3-1	*Šokota 2, Radujko*
5/3	Nafta	h	2-0	*Šokota, Bešič*
12/3	Maribor	h	0-0	
16/3	Celje	a	3-1	*Šokota 2 (1p), Lovrečič*
19/3	Koper	h	4-0	*Vršič 2, Škerjanc, Lovrečič*
2/4	Primorje	a	2-2	*Jovič, Vršič*
5/4	Domžale	h	0-0	
10/4	Triglav	a	4-1	*Vršič, Šokota, Lovrečič, Škerjanc*
16/4	Rudar	a	3-1	*Lovrečič, Bešič, og (Cipot)*
22/4	Gorica	h	1-0	*Škerjanc*
30/4	Nafta	a	2-1	*Škerjanc 2*
4/5	Maribor	a	2-2	*Škerjanc, Jovič*
7/5	Celje	h	3-1	*Rujovič, Jovič, Omladič*
11/5	Koper	a	1-2	*Bešič*
14/5	Primorje	h	5-0	*Bešič 2, Vršič, Lovrečič, Zeljkovič*
21/5	Domžale	a	0-3	
29/5	Triglav	h	1-3	*Vršič (p)*

No	Name	Nat	DoB	Pos	Aps	(s)	Gls
13	Milan ANĐELKOVIČ		1/9/81	D	17	(3)	
15	Adnan BEŠIČ		28/3/91	A	15	(15)	8
16	Damir BOTONJIČ		14/9/81	G	29		
32	Blaž BOŽIČ		23/10/90	M	14	(4)	
14	Sebastjan CIMEROTIČ		14/9/74	A	5	(1)	1
21	Miroslav CVIJANOVIČ		14/5/85	D	13	(5)	
8	João GABRIEL da Silva GABRIEL	BRA	4/7/84	M	5		1
5	Boban JOVIČ		25/6/91	D	29	(1)	4
4	David KAŠNIK		16/1/87	D	23	(1)	
3	Mitja KOVAČEVIČ		12/4/91	D	2	(4)	
1	Kristian LIPOVAC		3/12/89	G	7		
25	Anej LOVREČIČ		10/5/87	M	22	(7)	6
17	Nik OMLADIČ		21/8/89	M	12	(3)	1
24	Damjan OŠLAJ		25/8/76	D	5		
20	Luka PRAŠNIKAR		11/6/87	A		(6)	
85	Dalibor RADUJKO		17/6/85	M	17		2
11	Ermin RAKOVIČ		7/9/77	A	7	(3)	3
8	Saša RANIČ		7/11/81	M	3	(2)	
10	Enes RUJOVIČ		29/5/89	M	16	(13)	3
33	Erik SALKIČ		10/4/87	D	34		3
18	Stefan SMILJANIČ		10/7/91	A	6	(13)	1
31	Sreten SRETENOVIĆ	SRB	12/1/85	D	13	(1)	
7	Petar STOJANOVIČ		8/3/90	M	3	(15)	
9	Davor ŠKERJANC		7/1/86	M	33	(1)	8
29	Tomislav ŠOKOTA	CRO	8/4/77	A	18	(1)	7
22	Dare VRŠIČ		26/9/84	A	16		6
6	Alen VUČKIČ		1/2/90	D	11	(3)	
30	Zoran ZELJKOVIČ		9/5/80	M	21	(2)	3

NK PRIMORJE

Coach –Vjekoslav Lokica (CRO); (14/8/10) Milan Petrovič; (29/4/11) Sandi Valentinčič

Founded – 1924

Stadium – Šiška (6,000)

2010				
16/7	Koper	a	1-4	*Kremenovič*
24/7	Nafta	a	1-2	*Jukan*
31/7	Domžale	h	0-0	
8/8	Triglav	a	2-3	*Đukić, Marijanovič*
15/8	Rudar	h	1-1	*og (Korun)*
21/8	Gorica	a	2-3	*Marijanovič (p), Ihbeisheh*
29/8	Olimpija	h	5-1	*Živec Si., Čoralič, Kremenovič, Ihbeisheh, Živec Sa.*
11/9	Maribor	a	1-1	*Lo Duca*
22/9	Koper	h	3-1	*Lo Duca, Kremenovič 2*
26/9	Nafta	h	4-2	*Marijanovič, Kremenovič, Čoralič, Tomić*
2/10	Domžale	a	1-4	*Kremenovič*
10/10	Celje	h	2-0	*Huskič, Živec Si.*
23/10	Rudar	a	1-3	*Tomić*
27/10	Triglav	h	0-3	
31/10	Gorica	h	0-2	
6/11	Olimpija	a	0-3	
14/11	Maribor	h	0-0	
20/11	Celje	a	0-3	
27/11	Koper	a	1-2	*Kremenovič*
2011				
26/2	Nafta	a	2-1	*Ihbeisheh, Jukan (p)*
6/3	Domžale	h	0-0	
13/3	Triglav	a	0-2	
16/3	Rudar	h	0-6	
19/3	Gorica	a	1-4	*Vidmar*
2/4	Olimpija	h	2-2	*Ihbeisheh, Čuturilo*
5/4	Maribor	a	0-2	
9/4	Celje	h	0-1	
16/4	Koper	h	1-1	*Živec Si.*
23/4	Nafta	h	1-4	*Jukan*
30/4	Domžale	a	0-1	
4/5	Triglav	h	1-0	*Božičić*
7/5	Rudar	a	1-0	*Živec Sa.*
11/5	Gorica	h	2-3	*Ihbeisheh 2*
14/5	Olimpija	a	0-5	
21/5	Maribor	h	1-2	*Kolman N.*
29/5	Celje	a	3-2	*Božič 2, Lo Duca*

No	Name	Nat	DoB	Pos	Aps	(s)	Gls
17	Mark BOŽIČ		10/10/88	M	9	(4)	2
21	Saša BOŽIČIČ		8/5/83	M	12	(3)	1
22	Domen BOŽJAK		14/6/89	G	19		
5	Alen ČORALIČ		8/9/85	D	15	(1)	2
20	Neven ČUTURILO	CRO	13/5/85	M	19	(3)	1
25	Danijel DEŽMAR		31/3/88	M	7	(1)	
29	Bojan ĐUKIĆ	CRO	6/11/86	D	6		1
9	Ivan GRAF	CRO	17/6/87	M	15	(1)	
23	Etien HUSKIČ		11/3/88	A	9	(3)	1
11	Jaka IHBEISHEH		29/6/86	M	30	(1)	6
3	Denis JAZBAR		18/8/91	D		(2)	
10	Amer JUKAN		28/11/78	M	18	(2)	3
7	Nejc KOLMAN		26/2/89	A	10	(4)	1
5	Saša KOLMAN		1/5/84	D	1	(1)	
7	Darko KREMENOVIČ		5/6/81	A	12	(2)	7
21	Saša LALOVIČ		11/12/85	M	2	(6)	
18	Tim LO DUCA		17/12/85	A	14	(10)	3
24	Gregor MARC		9/3/90	M		(2)	
99	Milidrag MARIČ		9/11/83	D	15	(1)	
16	Dejan MARIJANOVIČ		2/1/87	A	14	(3)	3
2	Enes MEHANOVIČ		29/5/92	D	1	(1)	
27	Francisco MEROLA	SUI	24/5/86	M		(1)	
28	Sanel MULAHMETOVIČ		30/8/91	A		(1)	
14	Sašo OGRIČ		20/9/88	M	19	(7)	
4	Vladimir OSTOJIČ		27/11/81	D	32		
1	Dawid PIETRZKIEWICZ	POL	9/2/88	G	10		
1	Admir SUHONJIČ		23/5/81	G	7		
30	David SVIBEN		30/9/89	D		(1)	
13	Luka ŠKRBINA		13/8/85	D	21	(1)	
24	Matej ŠUTIČ		5/8/90	M		(3)	
6	Almir TANJIČ		16/1/79	D	14	(1)	
8	Željko TOMIĆ	CRO	21/12/85	M	10	(7)	2
19	Nejc VIDMAR		19/5/85	M	7	(12)	1
15	Saša Aleksander ŽIVEC		2/4/91	M	28	(3)	2
26	Simon ŽIVEC		10/1/81	M	20		3

NK RUDAR VELENJE

Coach – Bojan Prašnikar; (15/3/11) Robert Pevnik
Founded – 1948
Stadium – Ob Jezeru (7,000)
MAJOR HONOURS: Slovenian Cup – (1) 1998.

2010				
18/7	Olimpija	a	3-1	*Bratanovič 2, Tolimir*
25/7	Maribor	h	0-0	
31/7	Celje	a	1-5	*Kronaveter*
7/8	Koper	h	2-1	*Đermanovič 2*
15/8	Primorje	a	1-1	*Tolimir*
21/8	Domžale	h	0-1	
29/8	Triglav	a	0-1	
10/9	Nafta	a	3-3	*Korun, Tolimir, Trifkovič*
18/9	Gorica	h	1-2	*Korun*
22/9	Olimpija	h	1-1	*Đermanovič*
25/9	Maribor	a	1-3	*Đermanovič*
2/10	Celje	h	3-2	*Trifkovič, Dedič, Mešić*
16/10	Koper	a	1-2	*Korun*
23/10	Primorje	h	3-1	*Roj, Trifkovič, Đermanovič*
31/10	Domžale	a	3-2	*Đermanovič, Trifkovič, Tolimir*
6/11	Triglav	h	5-0	*Mešić 3, Đermanovič 2*
13/11	Nafta	h	0-0	
20/11	Gorica	a	1-1	*og (Jogan K.)*
2011				
22/2	Olimpija	a	2-2	*Mešić, Grbič*
26/2	Maribor	h	2-4	*Mujakovič Am., Cadikovski*
5/3	Celje	a	0-1	
12/3	Koper	h	0-1	
16/3	Primorje	a	6-0	*Trifkovič 2, Tolimir, Bratanovič, Rotman, Cipot*
19/3	Domžale	h	3-1	*Bratanovič, Tolimir, Cadikovski*
2/4	Triglav	a	4-1	*Bratanovič, Cadikovski 2 (1p), Rotman*
5/4	Nafta	a	2-1	*Cadikovski, Bratanovič*
9/4	Gorica	h	0-1	
16/4	Olimpija	h	1-3	*Mujakovič Am.*
23/4	Maribor	a	1-2	*Rotman*
30/4	Celje	h	1-0	*Rotman*
4/5	Koper	a	3-3	*Kelenc, Bratanovič, Korun*
7/5	Primorje	h	0-1	
11/5	Domžale	a	0-2	
14/5	Triglav	h	0-0	
21/5	Nafta	h	4-0	*Bratanovič, Grbič, Rotman, Kelenc*
29/5	Gorica	a	0-0	

No	Name	Nat	DoB	Pos	Aps	(s)	Gls
16	Sebastjan BERKO		20/6/84	M	18	(3)	
21	Elvis BRATANOVIČ		21/8/92	M	16	(10)	8
11	Dragan CADIKOVSKI	MKD	13/1/82	A	15	(1)	5
6	Fabijan CIPOT		25/8/76	D	28	(1)	1
27	Rusmin DEDIČ		11/9/82	D	18		1
14	Dejan ĐERMANOVIČ		17/6/88	A	18		8
10	Denis GRBIČ		15/3/86	M	9	(12)	2
1	Safet JAHIČ		25/1/87	G	16		
25	Boštjan JELEČEVIČ		16/3/85	D	21	(2)	
3	Aleš JESENIČNIK		28/6/84	D	32		
18	Doris KELENC		8/2/86	M	6	(12)	2
23	Denis KLINAR		21/2/92	M		(3)	
4	Marko KOLSI	FIN	20/1/85	M	6		
7	Uroš KORUN		25/5/87	A	21	(7)	4
18	Rok KRONAVETER		7/12/86	M	3		1
9	Mirza MEŠIĆ	BIH	28/6/80	A	12	(17)	5
29	František METELKA	CZE	8/4/80	D	7	(8)	
19	Almedin MUHAREMOVIČ		22/4/92	M		(1)	
20	Alem MUJAKOVIČ		6/4/78	M	6	(1)	
2	Amel MUJAKOVIČ		4/5/82	M	16		2
5	Nenad NOVAKOVIĆ	BIH	23/3/86	M	26		
15	RENATO de Morães	BRA	16/8/80	M	1	(1)	
17	Rok ROJ		8/10/86	M	16	(8)	1
15	Rajko ROTMAN		19/3/89	M	13	(2)	5
26	Boban SAVIĆ	SRB	3/4/79	G	20		
22	Nikola TOLIMIR		1/4/89	M	25	(9)	6
13	Marian TOMČAK	SVK	13/7/80	M	1	(3)	
8	Damjan TRIFKOVIČ		22/7/87	M	26	(5)	6

ND TRIGLAV

Coach – Siniša Brkič
Founded – 2000
Stadium – Stanko Mlakar (5,000)

2010				
18/7	Maribor	a	0-5	
24/7	Celje	h	1-1	*Krcič*
31/7	Koper	a	1-1	*Burgar*
8/8	Primorje	h	3-2	*Špelič 2 (1p), Krcič*
14/8	Domžale	a	0-3	
21/8	Nafta	a	1-2	*Stjepanovič*
29/8	Rudar	h	1-0	*Jelar*
11/9	Gorica	a	1-2	*Krcič*
19/9	Olimpija	h	0-5	
22/9	Maribor	h	2-2	*Burgar, Stjepanovič*
25/9	Celje	a	1-1	*og (Kapič)*
3/10	Koper	h	0-0	
24/10	Domžale	h	1-3	*Dolžan*
27/10	Primorje	a	3-0	*Jelar, Burgar, Stjepanovič*
31/10	Nafta	h	2-0	*Burgar, Sever*
6/11	Rudar	a	0-5	
14/11	Gorica	h	2-0	*Burgar 2 (1p)*
20/11	Olimpija	a	0-1	
27/11	Maribor	a	1-3	*Burgar*
2011				
27/2	Celje	h	0-0	
5/3	Koper	a	1-0	*Redžič*
13/3	Primorje	h	2-0	*Burgar, Stjepanovič*
16/3	Domžale	a	1-3	*Burgar*
19/3	Nafta	a	1-1	*Jelar*
2/4	Rudar	h	1-4	*og (Jelečevič)*
5/4	Gorica	a	0-1	
10/4	Olimpija	h	1-4	*Ovčina*
17/4	Maribor	h	1-2	*Jelar*
22/4	Celje	a	0-2	
30/4	Koper	h	0-0	
4/5	Primorje	a	0-1	
7/5	Domžale	h	2-4	*Sever, Dolžan*
11/5	Nafta	h	4-0	*Redžič 2, Stojnič, Pirc*
14/5	Rudar	a	0-0	
21/5	Gorica	h	1-0	*Redžič*
29/5	Olimpija	a	3-1	*Redžič 2, og (Botonjič)*

No	Name	Nat	DoB	Pos	Aps	(s)	Gls
9	Rok BRAJIČ		13/1/85	A	23	(3)	
8	Dejan BURGAR		10/5/86	A	29	(4)	9
13	Dejan DIMITROV		26/8/90	D	2	(5)	
11	Rok DOLŽAN		21/9/85	M	33	(2)	2
1	Miha GRACAR		28/8/87	G	21		
16	Anže JELAR		18/8/91	M	24	(9)	4
18	David JERKOVIČ		3/5/90	D	4	(3)	
3	Dragan JURIČ		11/8/91	D	1	(1)	
13	Domen KOŠNIK		19/9/90	M		(1)	
10	Alen KRCIČ		19/11/88	A	22	(2)	3
26	Boštjan KREFT		23/2/81	D	2	(1)	
27	Damir MARIJAN		3/6/90	M	7	(10)	
19	Robert NAJDENOV		26/10/81	D	28	(2)	
7	Mihael NOVAK		24/3/87	A		(3)	
29	Dragan OVČINA		13/5/82	M	26	(6)	1
28	Žan PELKO		28/9/90	G	15	(1)	
21	Matej PIRC		18/5/91	M	1	(9)	1
23	Jalen POKORN		7/6/79	D	26		
22	Nejc POTOKAR		2/12/88	D	19		
14	Ajdin REDŽIČ		5/12/89	M	11	(4)	6
9	Gregor ROMIČ		4/8/92	A		(6)	
17	Matic SEVER		4/1/90	A	13	(8)	2
2	Uroš SMOLEJ		14/10/85	D	28	(2)	
20	Danijel STANAREVIČ		31/1/91	M	4	(6)	
6	Bernard STJEPANOVIČ		22/12/88	M	24	(2)	4
24	Petar STOJNIČ		29/9/81	D	16		1
14	Josip ŠPELIČ		22/10/83	A	10	(5)	2
5	Janez ZAVRL		25/12/82	M	7		
4	Edvin ZOLIČ		6/11/88	M		(1)	

TOP GOALSCORERS 2010/11

16 MARCOS TAVARES (Maribor)

13 Damir PEKIČ (Domžale)
Milan OSTERC (Koper)

11 Jože BENKO (Nafta)

10 Eiten VELIKONJA (Gorica/Maribor)
Vito PLUT (Maribor/Gorica)
Vedran VINKO (Nafta)

9 Dragan CADIKOVSKI (Celje/Rudar)
Dejan BURGAR (Triglav)

8 Robert BERIČ (Maribor)
Adnan BEŠIČ (Olimpija)
Davor ŠKERJANC (Olimpija)
Elvis BRATANOVIČ (Rudar)
Dejan ĐERMANOVIČ (Rudar)

PROMOTED CLUB

ND MURA 05

Coach – Stanislav Maučec
Founded – 2005
Stadium – Fazanerija (5,400)

SECOND LEVEL FINAL TABLE 2010/11

		Pld	W	D	L	F	A	Pts
1	NK Aluminij	27	13	9	5	54	22	48
2	NK IB Ljubljana	27	13	8	6	38	25	47
3	ND Dravinja	27	11	10	6	31	23	43
4	ND Mura 05	27	12	5	10	42	37	41
5	NK Drava	27	11	6	10	38	41	39
6	NK Roltek Dob	27	11	5	11	43	44	38
7	NK Bela Krajina	27	9	10	8	38	39	37
8	NK Krško	27	8	7	12	24	35	31
9	NK Šenčur	27	4	10	13	37	52	22
10	NK Šmartno 1928	27	6	4	17	31	58	22

NB NK Aluminij declined promotion; NK IB Ljubljana declined participation in promotion/relegation play-off; ND Mura 05 promoted instead via invitation.

DOMESTIC CUP 2010/11

POKAL NZS

FIRST ROUND

(24/8/10)
Malečnik 1, Domžale 4

(25/8/10)
Bistrica 2, Aluminij 4 *(aet)*
Brda 2, Nafta 4
Dogoše 0, Primorje 4
Drava 2, Dob 4
Dravinja 1, Šenčur 0
Hotiza 0, IB Ljubljana 4
Krka 2, Ankaran 5
Krško 1, Celje 2
Postojna 0, Triglav 3
Tromejnik 1, Rudar Velenje 3 *(aet)*
Zavrč 4, Mura 3

Byes – Gorica, Koper, Maribor, Olimpija

SECOND ROUND

(14/9/10)
Olimpija 2, Celje 0

(15/9/10)
Aluminij 0, Gorica 2
Ankaran 1, Domžale 6
Dob 1, Maribor 1 *(aet; 5-6 on pens)*
Dravinja 0, Koper 1 *(aet)*
Triglav 2, Rudar Velenje 1
Zavrč 0, Nafta 3

(29/9/10)
IB Ljubljana 3, Primorje 2 *(aet)*

QUARTER-FINALS

(20/10/10 & 27/10/10)
Domžale 0, Olimpija 2 *(Rujovič 51, Stojanovič 90)*
Olimpija 0, Domžale 4 *(Zatkovič 12, Pekič 47, Simunovic 59, Apatič 90+4p)*
(Domžale 4-2)

IB Ljubljana 4 *(Majcen 35, Valenčič 79, 83, Podlogar 86)*, Gorica 2 *(Velikonja 13p, 60)*
Gorica 0, IB Ljubljana 0
(IB Ljubljana 4-2)

Nafta 1 *(Pavel 56)*, Maribor 1 *(Volaš 65)*
Maribor 4 *(Marcos Tavares 9, Dodlek 38, Volaš 52p, Mertelj 70)*, Nafta 0
(Maribor 5-1)

(20/10/10 & 3/11/10)
Triglav 1 *(Burgar 31p)*, Koper 0
Koper 3 *(Osterc 15, Smolej 53og, Bubanja 78)*, Triglav 0
(Koper 3-1)

SEMI-FINALS

(20/4/11 & 26/4/11)
IB Ljubljana 0, Domžale 0
Domžale 2 *(Juninho 57, Smukavec 81)*, IB Ljubljana 0
(Domžale 2-0)
Koper 1 (Osterc 10), Maribor 1 *(Mezga 90p)*
Maribor 1 *(Velikonja 56)*, Koper 0
(Maribor 2-1)

FINAL

(25/5/11)
Stožice, Ljubljana
NK DOMŽALE 4 *(Juninho 22, Pekič 38, 78, Simunovic 51)*
NK MARIBOR 3 *(Filipovič 15, Berič 55, Mezga 63p)*
Referee – *Skomina*
DOMŽALE – *Vidmar, Elsner, Knezović, Zec (Topič 70), Apatič, Teinović, Drevenšek, Zatkovič (Hanžič 89), Simunovic, Pekič (Smukavec 81), Juninho.*
Sent off: *Teinović (76).*
MARIBOR – *Radan, Vidovič, Filipovič, Rajčevič, Majer (Velikonja 83), Mezga, Cvijanovič (Črnič 82), Rešek, Viler, Berič, Marcos Tavares.*

CLUB COMMUNICATION 2011/12

NK Celje

Opekarniška cesta 15 a
SI-3000 Celje

Tel	+386 3 428 1860
Fax	+386 3 428 1880
Web	nkcelje.si
Email	info@nk-celje.si
Media Officer	Dejan Obrez

NK Domžale

Kopališka 4
SI-1230 Domžale

Tel	+386 17 226 550
Fax	+386 17 210 373
Web	nkdomzale.si
Email	info@nkdomzale.si
Media Officer	Grega Krmavnar

ND Gorica

Bazoviška ulica 4
SI-5000 Nova Gorica

Tel	+386 5 333 4086
Fax	+386 5 333 4087
Web	nd-gorica.com
Email	nd.gorica@siol.net
Media Officer	Peter Maraz

FC Koper

Ljubljanska cesta 2
SI-6000 Koper

Tel	+386 56 313 101
Fax	+386 56 313 101
Web	fckoper.si
Email	info@fckoper.si
Media Officer	Sandi Jerman

NK Maribor

Mladinska Ulica 29
SI-2000 Maribor

Tel	+386 2 228 4700
Fax	+386 2 228 4701
Web	nkmaribor.com
Email	info@nkmaribor.com
Media Officer	Željko Latin

ND Mura 05

Kopališka ulica 45
SI-9001 Murska Sobota

Tel	+386 2 534 1766
Fax	+386 2 534 1767
Web	mura05.si
Email	mura05@gmail.com
Media Officer	Simon Horvat

NK Nafta

Kolodvorska 7, PP.46
SI-9220 Lendava

Tel	+386 2 5788 753
Fax	+386 2 5788 753
Web	nknafta.si
Email	nkafta@siol.net
Media Officer	Igor Magdič

NK Olimpija Ljubljana

Dvorakova 3, Ljubljana
SI-1000 Ljubljana

Tel	+386 1 431 0144
Fax	+386 1 566 1240
Web	nkolimpija.si
Email	info@nkolimpija.si
Media Officer	Tine Zupan

NK Rudar Velenje

Cesta na Jezero 7
SI-3320 Velenje

Tel	+386 3 891 9013
Fax	+386 3 891 9014
Web	nkrudar.com
Email	nk.rudar.velenje@t-2.net
Media Officer	Adem Biščič

ND Triglav

Partizanska 37
SI-4000 Kranj

Tel	+386 4 238 0050
Fax	+386 4 238 0051
Web	nktriglav.com
Email	nk.triglav@siol.net
Media Officer	Miran Subič

SPAIN

Espagne I Spanien

Real Federación Española de Fútbol (RFEF)

COMMUNICATION

Address Ramón y Cajal s/n
Apartado postal 385
ES-28230 Las Rozas
(Madrid)

Tel +34 91 495 9800
Fax +34 91 495 9801

E-mail rfef@rfef.es
Website rfef.es

President Ángel María Villar Llona
General Secretary Jorge Juan Pérez Arias
Media Officer Antonio Bustillo Abella

Year of Formation 1909

DOMESTIC COMPETITION SUMMARY 2010/11

LIGA FINAL TABLE

			Home					Away					Total						
		Pld	W	D	L	F	A	W	D	L	F	A	W	D	L	F	A	Pts	Comp
1	FC Barcelona	38	16	2	1	46	10	14	4	1	49	11	30	6	2	95	21	96	UCL
2	Real Madrid CF	38	16	1	2	61	12	13	4	2	41	21	29	5	4	102	33	92	UCL
3	Valencia CF	38	10	5	4	34	21	11	3	5	30	23	21	8	9	64	44	71	UCL
4	Villarreal CF	38	13	3	3	33	14	5	5	9	21	30	18	8	12	54	44	62	UCL
5	Sevilla FC	38	10	4	5	35	27	7	3	9	27	34	17	7	14	62	61	58	UEL
6	Athletic Club	38	12	1	6	32	20	6	3	10	27	35	18	4	16	59	55	58	UEL
7	Club Atlético de Madrid	38	10	3	6	35	20	7	4	8	27	33	17	7	14	62	53	58	UEL
8	RCD Espanyol	38	11	2	6	33	22	4	2	13	13	33	15	4	19	46	55	49	
9	CA Osasuna	38	10	6	3	28	14	3	2	14	17	32	13	8	17	45	46	47	
10	Real Sporting de Gijón	38	9	6	4	23	16	2	8	9	12	26	11	14	13	35	42	47	
11	Málaga CF	38	7	3	9	29	29	6	4	9	25	39	13	7	18	54	68	46	
12	Real Racing Club	38	8	6	5	25	21	4	4	11	16	35	12	10	16	41	56	46	
13	Real Zaragoza	38	9	3	7	26	27	3	6	10	14	26	12	9	17	40	53	45	
14	Levante UD	38	9	4	6	25	20	3	5	11	16	32	12	9	17	41	52	45	
15	Real Sociedad de Fútbol	38	11	2	6	27	21	3	1	15	22	45	14	3	21	49	66	45	
16	Getafe CF	38	9	3	7	33	26	3	5	11	16	34	12	8	18	49	60	44	
17	RCD Mallorca	38	9	4	6	25	19	3	4	12	16	37	12	8	18	41	56	44	
18	RC Deportivo La Coruña	38	8	6	5	22	19	2	7	10	9	28	10	13	15	31	47	43	*Relegated*
19	Hércules CF	38	7	5	7	27	27	2	3	14	9	33	9	8	21	36	60	35	*Relegated*
20	UD Almería	38	3	10	6	23	35	3	2	14	13	35	6	12	20	36	70	30	*Relegated*

Top Scorer Cristiano Ronaldo (Real Madrid), 40 goals

Promoted Clubs Real Betis Balompié
Rayo Vallecano de Madrid
Granada CF

Cup Final Real Madrid CF 1, FC Barcelona 0 (aet)

Brilliant Barça set new standards

After conquering the world in South Africa, Spain's status as the No1 power in the game showed no signs of flagging in 2010/11. A perfect run of results by Vicente del Bosque's world champions in their UEFA EURO 2012 qualifying group was supplemented by a victory for the next generation of Spanish superstars at the UEFA European Under-21 Championship in Denmark. Above all, though, the nation's newly-earned reputation for footballing excellence was epitomised by Josep Guardiola's FC Barcelona, who, inspired by the great Lionel Messi, enthralled neutrals and partisans alike with a fabulous double triumph in the Spanish championship and the UEFA Champions League.

Barcelona were denied a repeat of their historic 2008/09 treble only by an extra-time defeat in the final of the Copa del Rey to José Mourinho's Real Madrid CF. The whole season was shaped by the head-to-head meetings between the bitter arch-rivals from the capital and Catalonia. In all there were five Gran Clásicos – two in La Liga, one in the Spanish Cup final, and another two in the semi-final of the UEFA Champions League. Four of them took place within 17 highly eventful days in the spring, and although Madrid ended a three-year wait for a major trophy by winning the domestic cup, the two bigger prizes were both claimed by Barça, who went on to become champions of Europe for the fourth time with a majestic 3-1 win over Manchester United FC in the final at Wembley.

Magical Messi

With seven members of the World Cup-winning team to call on, including new signing David Villa, Spain's top scorer in South Africa, it was little wonder that Barcelona hit the heights again. The man who made the difference, though, was Messi. It was almost inconceivable that he could surpass what he had achieved in the previous two seasons, but he did, scoring 53 goals in all competitions and also claiming 24 assists. He illuminated every game in which he played – 55 in total over the season, the last of them at Wembley, where he bestrode the most important match of the year with his remarkable talent, repeatedly mesmerising the United defence and also scoring his side's second goal.

Messi claimed the UEFA Champions League top-scorer prize for the third successive season. The most spectacular of his 12 goals was his second in the first leg of the semi-final, at the Estádio Santiago Bernabéu – a scintillating solo effort that gave Barcelona a 2-0 advantage over Madrid to take into the return at Camp Nou. Messi's brilliance could not, alas, gloss over what had been an unpleasant and ugly encounter, with both teams guilty of gamesmanship and violent play and a red card for Madrid's midfield enforcer Pepe, with the score at 0-0, effectively swinging the tie in favour of the Catalans. Things calmed down for the return leg, which the suspended Mourinho watched from his hotel room, and a 1-1 draw carried Barcelona safely through to the final.

Lionel Messi lifts the UEFA Champions League trophy after Barcelona's 3-1 win over Manchester United at Wembley

Another 1-1 draw, in the first of the four springtime showdowns two and a half weeks earlier in Madrid, had effectively sealed Barça's third successive Liga triumph. Guardiola's team went into the game with an eight-point lead and an unbeaten record in the league stretching back to early September. Sensing perhaps that the title was already beyond his team's reach, Mourinho sought to strangle Barça's fluent midfield by opting for a strategy of containment. The best he could manage was a share of the spoils as Cristiano Ronaldo's late penalty cancelled out an earlier spot-kick from Messi, but there was some residual benefit from his plan when, four days later, Madrid deservedly won the Copa del Rey final in Valencia, Ronaldo's thumping header at the end of the first period of extra time deciding the outcome of a contest that the men in white had dominated in the early stages.

The real glory, though, belonged to Barcelona, and if there was any doubt that Guardiola had got the better of Mourinho, the clock only needed to be rewound to the first Clásico of the season in November, when Barça blitzed their rivals 5-0 in what was widely acknowledged as one of the finest exhibitions of attacking football ever seen. Barça had warmed up by thrashing Almería CF 8-0, and although Madrid went into the game undefeated under Mourinho and with a one-point lead at the top of the table, Guardiola's team of many talents simply blew them away, goals from Xavi, Pedro, David Villa (2) and Jeffren – though, for once, not Messi – embellishing a magnificent collective demonstration of pace, technique and industry.

Record-breaking run

That win was the seventh in a Liga record sequence of 16 which ensured that Barça, having dislodged Madrid from top spot, would remain there for the rest of the campaign. Having suffered a shock 2-0 defeat by Hércules CF in their opening home fixture, Barça did not lose again in any competition until Real Betis Balompié beat them 3-1 in the second leg of their Copa del Rey quarter-final in January, but as Barça had won the first leg 5-0, it barely mattered. Their next defeat came at Arsenal FC, 2-1 in the UEFA Champions League, but again Barça prevailed overall, rectifying matters with a 3-1 win at Camp Nou. When Barça did eventually lose a bona fide 90-minute contest, 2-1 away to Real Sociedad de Fútbol on the last day of April, again the defeat was largely inconsequential as 11 days later, with a 1-1 draw in Valencia at Levante UD, they wrapped up the Liga title.

Cristiano Ronaldo set a new Liga record by scoring 40 goals for Real Madrid

By the end of term Barcelona had won 30 matches, including more away from home – 14 – than any other team in Liga history. Although they fell three points and three goals short of their 2009/10 tallies – with 96 and 95, respectively – their defensive figures improved, with just 21 goals conceded (compared with 24). The bare statistics could not, however, relate the grand style in which Barcelona played. The majestic Messi apart, Xavi and Andrés Iniesta were their usual ultra-reliable selves in midfield, always raising their game for the big occasion. Although captain Carles Puyol missed much of the season through injury, he was immense when he played. Goalkeeper Víctor Valdés, centre-back Gerard Piqué and midfield anchorman Sergio Busquets also maintained a high and consistent standard, while Pedro and Villa aided Messi up front, scoring 31 goals between them – albeit the same number as the No10 managed on his own.

Ronaldo's Pichichi

One prize that escaped Messi was the prestigious Pichichi award for La Liga's leading marksman. He had been neck-and-neck with Madrid's Cristiano

Ronaldo for most of the season, but the Portuguese international soared clear at the finish, scoring 11 goals in the last four matches to lever his final tally to 40 – a record figure for the Primera División, overtaking the previous mark of 38 set by Athletic Club's Telmo Zarra in 1950/51 and matched by Madrid's Hugo Sánchez in 1989/90. His efforts also enabled Madrid to break the 100-goal barrier for the second successive season.

Although Ronaldo was not always at his riveting best against Barcelona, his goal output was phenomenal. Like Messi, he managed 53 in all competitions, and his efforts were especially important following the back injury sustained by first-choice centre-forward Gonzalo Higuaín that sidelined the Argentinian international for the best part of five months. Frenchman Karim Benzema also helped out, emerging from the shadows with 15 goals in the league and six more in the UEFA Champions League, including two against his former club Olympique Lyonais that enabled Madrid to end their six-year hoodoo of being eliminated in the first knockout round. It was another central striker, mid-season loan acquisition Emmanuel Adebayor, who did most to take the team through the next round with two goals at home to Tottenham Hotspur FC.

Split verdict

All of Madrid's major new signings acquitted themselves well, from Ricardo Carvalho in central defence to wing wizard Ángel Di María and the young German midfield duo of Sami Khedira and Mesut Özil. Goalkeeper Iker Casillas and midfield orchestrator Xabi Alonso also starred, while Marcelo surprised even Mourinho with his rapid development at left-back. The post-season verdict among Madrid fans on the 'Special One' himself appeared to be split. Although he had not captured the two most important trophies and at times promoted a safety-first approach to winning matches that ran contrary to the club's philosophy and traditions, his celebrated talents as a motivator and strategist – not to mention media manipulator and agent provocateur – were plain for all to see. All appeared to be in agreement, though, that he deserved another shot at Barcelona in 2011/12.

The domination of the Primera División by the Big Two was illustrated by the 21-point gap that separated second and third place. Valencia CF did well to finish as the best of the rest for the second successive year. Having lost David Silva (to Manchester City FC) as well as David Villa, they were expected to suffer the consequences, but youngster Juan Mata relished the extra responsibility and, with new strikers Roberto Soldado and Aritz Aduriz settling in fast, Valencia accumulated points with impressive regularity. They failed to collect any from Barcelona and Real Madrid, but they were not alone in that respect. In fact, the major disappointment for Unai Emery's side was their failure to join Barça and Madrid in the quarter-finals of the UEFA Champions League, a 4-2 aggregate loss to FC Schalke 04 unexpectedly eliminating them in the first knockout round.

Valencia's east-coast neighbours Villarreal CF also had a fine season under their relatively unknown coach Juan Carlos Garrido, reaching the semi-finals of the UEFA Europa League while also climbing three places in La Liga to finish fourth. They won all eight European matches at El Madrigal, eliminating SSC Napoli, Bayer 04 Leverkusen and FC Twente before succumbing to FC Porto with a second-half collapse in Portugal. With Italian international Giuseppe Rossi consistently troubling defences and midfielders Borja Valero and Santi Cazorla offering valuable support, Villarreal were able to survive a stuttering finish and still take fourth place with room to spare.

A trio of clubs – Sevilla FC, Athletic and Club Atlético de Madrid – all finished level on points to claim 2011/12 UEFA Europa League berths. Sevilla sacked their 2009/10 Copa del Rey-winning coach Antonio Álvarez following their failure to beat SC Braga in the UEFA Champions League play-offs,

National Team

International Honours –
FIFA World Cup – (1) 2010.
UEFA European Championship – (2) 1964, 2008.

International Tournament Appearances –
FIFA World Cup – (13) 1934, 1950 (4th), 1962, 1966, 1978, 1982 (2nd phase), 1986 (qtr-finals), 1990 (2nd round), 1994 (qtr-finals), 1998, 2002 (qtr-finals), 2006 (2nd round), 2010 (Winners).
UEFA European Championship – (8) 1964 (Winners), 1980, 1984 (runners-up), 1988, 1996 (qtr-finals), 2000 (qtr-finals), 2004, 2008 (Winners).

Top Five All-time Caps – Andoni Zubizarreta (126); Iker Casillas (121); Raúl González (102); Xavi Hernández (101); Carles Puyol (94)

Top Five All-time Goals – David Villa (47); Raúl González (44); Fernando Ruiz Hierro (29); Fernando Morientes & Fernando Torres (27)

NATIONAL TEAM RESULTS 2010/11

11/8/10	Mexico	A	Mexico City	1-1	*David Silva (90+1)*
3/9/10	Liechtenstein (ECQ)	A	Vaduz	4-0	*Fernando Torres (18, 54), David Villa (26), David Silva (62)*
7/9/10	Argentina	A	Buenos Aires	1-4	*Llorente (84)*
8/10/10	Lithuania (ECQ)	H	Salamanca	3-1	*Llorente (47, 56), David Silva (79)*
12/10/10	Scotland (ECQ)	A	Glasgow	3-2	*David Villa (44p), Iniesta (55), Llorente (79)*
17/11/10	Portugal	A	Lisbon	0-4	
9/2/11	Colombia	H	Madrid	1-0	*David Silva (86)*
25/3/11	Czech Republic (ECQ)	H	Granada	2-1	*David Villa (69, 72p)*
29/3/11	Lithuania (ECQ)	A	Kaunas	3-1	*Xavi (19), Kijanskas (70og), Mata (83)*
4/6/11	United States	A	Boston	4-0	*Santi Cazorla (27, 41), Negredo (32), Fernando Torres (73)*
7/6/11	Venezuela	A	Puerto La Cruz	3-0	*David Villa (5), Pedro (29), Xabi Alonso (45)*

NATIONAL TEAM APPEARANCES 2010/11

Coach – Vicente DEL BOSQUE	**23/12/50**		**Mex**	**LIE**	**Arg**	**LTU**	**SCO**	**Por**	**Col**	**CZE**	**LTU**	**Usa**	**Ven**	**Caps**	**Goals**
Iker CASILLAS	20/5/81	Real Madrid	G46	G		G	G	G	G	G	G	s76	s89	121	-
Álvaro ARBELOA	17/1/83	Real Madrid	D		D	s82		s73	s56	D	D	D	D62	25	-
Carlos MARCHENA	31/7/79	Villarreal	D65	D	D		s90	s46		s86			D	69	2
Carles PUYOL	13/4/78	Barcelona	D46			D	D	D73						94	3
Ignacio MONREAL	26/2/86	Osasuna	D		D									4	-
BRUNO Soriano	12/6/84	Villarreal	M72									s46		2	-
SANTI CAZORLA	13/12/84	Villarreal	M		s46	M	M70	s58	s56	s58	M67	M	s46	34	4
Cesc FÀBREGAS	4/5/87	Arsenal (ENG)	M46	s46	M56			s46						58	6
Juan Manuel MATA	28/4/88	Valencia	M46								s67			11	4
Sergio BUSQUETS	16/7/88	Barcelona	M61	M	M	M	M90	M	M	M		M46	M	30	-
Fernando LLORENTE	26/2/85	Athletic	A46		s46	A77	s76	s58	s81		A		A62	16	7
VÍCTOR VALDÉS	14/1/82	Barcelona	s46		s46								G89	4	-
SERGIO RAMOS	30/3/86	Real Madrid	s46	D		D82	D	D	D	D	s90	D65		76	5
XABI ALONSO	25/11/81	Real Madrid	s46	M	M71		M	M58	M76	M46	M	M	M46	86	10
JESÚS NAVAS	21/11/85	Sevilla	s46		s46				s68	M86				13	1
DAVID SILVA	8/1/86	Man. City (ENG)	s46	s57	M46	M	M76	M	s76		s54	M65	s46	48	11
XAVI Hernández	25/1/80	Barcelona	s61	M46	s56			M46	M56	M	M			101	10
Gerard PIQUÉ	2/2/87	Barcelona	s65	D	D	D	D	D46	D	D	D90	D		33	4
PEDRO Rodríguez	28/7/87	Barcelona	s72	s65	s71				M81				A	13	2
Joan CAPDEVILA	3/2/78	Villarreal		D		D	D	D	D56	D58		s65	s62	60	4
Andrés INIESTA	11/5/84	Barcelona		M65	M46	M	M	M58	M68	M		s46	M46	58	8
DAVID VILLA	3/12/81	Barcelona		A	A46	A76	A	A46	A56	A	A54	A46	A46	75	47
FERNANDO TORRES	20/3/84	Liverpool (ENG) /Chelsea (ENG)		A57				s46	s56	s46		s46	s62	86	27
José Manuel REINA	31/8/82	Liverpool (ENG)			G46							G76		22	-
PABLO HERNÁNDEZ	11/4/85	Valencia				s76	s70							4	1
Aritz ADURIZ	11/2/81	Valencia				s77								1	-
Raúl ALBIOL	4/9/85	Real Madrid							D		D	D	D	27	-
Andoni IRAOLA	22/6/82	Athletic									D		D	6	-
JAVI MARTÍNEZ	2/9/88	Athletic									M			4	-
Álvaro NEGREDO	20/8/85	Sevilla										A46		5	3
BORJA VALERO	12/1/85	Villarreal										s65		1	-
MANU DEL MORAL	25/2/84	Getafe											s46	1	-

and although they subsequently came through a tough UEFA Europa League group, their European involvement ended in February at Porto. Their domestic form was patchy – despite 20 goals from the excellent Álvaro Negredo – and at the end of the season their new coach, Gregorio Manzano, became their old one as he moved north to replace Quique Sánchez Flores at Atlético, while Marcelino headed south from Real Racing Club to take charge at the Estádio Ramón Sánchez Pizjuán.

Atlético defeated Inter 2-0 in Monaco to win the UEFA Super Cup but their defence of the UEFA Europa League ended unexpectedly early following two defeats by Greek underdogs Aris Thessaloniki FC. 2010 FIFA World Cup Golden Ball winner Diego Forlán had a season to forget, but fortunately his strike partner Sergio 'Kun' Agüero remained in fine fettle, especially in the closing weeks when he struck ten of his 20 goals to help Atlético overtake RCD Espanyol and join their near-namesakes from the Basque country in the European qualifying frame. Like Sevilla and Atlético, Athletic possessed a potent centre-forward, Spanish international Fernando Llorente striking 18 times to fire the Bilbao club into the top six.

Depor down

Every club from ninth place down had to contend with the threat of relegation, and although Almería and Hércules were eventually detached from the pack, as many as six teams risked joining them in the Segunda División at the start of the final round. Ultimately, there would be no escape for RC Deportivo La Coruña, whose 2-0 defeat at home to Valencia condemned them to the drop after an unbroken 20-year run in the top flight, during which they had won the Spanish title and two domestic cups and enjoyed regular excursions in the UEFA Champions League, reaching the semi-finals in 2003/04. Even a historic late equalising goal by Daniel Aranzubia at Almería – the first in open play by a goalkeeper in Liga history – could not save the team they once called 'Super Depor' from the dreaded drop. Promotion to the Primera División was claimed by Betis, Rayo Vallecano de Madrid and, after a couple of nerve-racking play-off ties, Granada CF.

The Spanish national team ended their World Cup-winning year with a 4-0 pummelling by Portugal. They had also been taken apart by Argentina a

Thiago (left) and Daniel Parejo celebrate Spain's success at the UEFA European Under-21 Championship

couple of months earlier, losing 4-1 in Buenos Aires, but in the matches that mattered Del Bosque's men were not found wanting. Victories over Liechtenstein, Lithuania (twice), Scotland and the Czech Republic – in which David Villa became Spain's all-time top goalscorer – all but ensured their presence in Poland/Ukraine to defend their UEFA European Championship title. An end-of-season tour to the Americas brought handsome victories over the United States and Venezuela, the latter enabling Del Bosque to claim his 37th win as Spain coach – more than any of his predecessors – in only his 44th game in charge.

Although only a handful of newcomers were introduced to play alongside the World Cup-winning regulars in 2010/11, the European triumph of Luis Milla's U21 side suggested that Spain's current run of success is not about to end any time soon. Mata, playmaker Thiago, goalkeeper David de Gea, captain Javi Martínez and tournament top scorer Adrián López were among several young Spaniards who caught the eye in Denmark, and even if UEFA EURO 2012 comes too soon for most of Milla's men, several of them could find themselves boarding the plane to Brazil for the World Cup defence in 2014.

CLUB-BY-CLUB

UD ALMERÍA

Coach – Juan Manuel Lillo; (21/11/10) José Luis Oltra; (5/4/11) Roberto Olabe

Founded – 1989

Stadium – Juegos Mediterráneos (22,000)

2010				
29/8	Osasuna	a	0-0	
13/9	Real Sociedad	h	2-2	*Piatti, Ulloa*
18/9	Espanyol	a	0-1	
22/9	Levante	h	0-1	
26/9	Deportivo	a	2-0	*Uche 2*
3/10	Málaga	h	1-1	*Uche*
17/10	Racing	a	0-1	
24/10	Hércules	h	1-1	*Ulloa*
31/10	Atlético	a	1-1	*Piatti*
7/11	Sporting	h	1-1	*Corona*
13/11	Athletic	a	0-1	
20/11	Barcelona	h	0-8	
28/11	Valencia	a	1-2	*Ulloa*
5/12	Zaragoza	h	1-1	*Piatti*
11/12	Sevilla	a	3-1	*Vargas, Piatti 2*
19/12	Getafe	h	2-3	*Uche, Ulloa*
2011				
3/1	Villarreal	a	0-2	
9/1	Mallorca	a	1-4	*Crusat*
16/1	Real Madrid	h	1-1	*Ulloa*
23/1	Osasuna	h	3-2	*Carlos García, Ulloa, Jakobsen*
29/1	Real Sociedad	a	0-2	
5/2	Espanyol	h	3-2	*Marcelo Silva, Uche, Bernardello*
13/2	Levante	a	0-1	
20/2	Deportivo	h	1-1	*Piatti*
28/2	Málaga	a	1-3	*Feghouli*
3/3	Racing	h	1-1	*Crusat*
6/3	Hércules	a	2-1	*Feghouli, M'Bami*
12/3	Atlético	h	2-2	*Crusat, Goitom*
20/3	Sporting	a	0-1	
4/4	Athletic	h	1-3	*Piatti*
9/4	Barcelona	a	1-3	*Corona*
16/4	Valencia	h	0-3	
25/4	Zaragoza	a	0-1	
1/5	Sevilla	h	0-1	
7/5	Getafe	a	0-2	
11/5	Villarreal	h	0-0	
15/5	Mallorca	h	3-1	*Uche, Juanma Ortiz, Piatti*
21/5	Real Madrid	a	1-8	*Uche*

No	Name	Nat	DoB	Pos	Aps	(s)	Gls
18	Wilmar Santiago ACASIETE Ariadela	PER	22/11/77	D	17	(3)	
25	Hernán Darío BERNARDELLO	ARG	3/8/86	M	33		1
21	CARLOS GARCÍA Badías		29/4/84	D	33		1
15	Miguel Ángel García Pérez Roldán "CORONA"		12/2/81	M	21	(9)	2
8	Albert CRUSAT Domene		13/5/82	A	30	(4)	3
1	DIEGO ALVES Carreira	BRA	24/6/85	G	33		
13	ESTEBAN Andrés Suárez		27/6/75	G	5		
7	Sofiane FEGHOULI	FRA	26/12/89	M	4	(5)	2
23	Henok GOITOM	SWE	16/9/84	A	8	(18)	1
2	Michael JAKOBSEN	DEN	2/1/86	D	14	(2)	1
10	JOSÉ ORTIZ Bernal		4/8/77	M		(16)	
24	Juan Jesús Gutiérrez Robles "JUANITO"		17/2/80	M	5	(4)	
17	Juan Manuel "JUANMA" ORTIZ Palazón		1/3/82	M	24	(2)	1
40	Manuel Castellano Castro "LILLO"		27/3/89	D	1	(1)	
14	Antonio LUNA Rodríguez		17/3/91	D	13		
3	MARCELO Andrés SILVA Fernández	URU	21/3/89	D	21		1
19	Modeste M'BAMI	CMR	9/10/82	M	28	(2)	1
16	MÍCHEL Macedo Rocha Machado	BRA	15/2/90	D	30	(1)	
7	Miguel Ángel NIETO de la Calle		12/1/86	M		(1)	
4	Hernán Darío PELLERANO	ARG	4/6/84	D	7	(1)	
11	Pablo Daniel PIATTI	ARG	31/3/89	A	34	(1)	8
14	Baltasar RIGO Cifre		26/6/85	M	1		
5	Kalu UCHE	NGA	15/11/82	A	26	(6)	7
20	José Leonardo ULLOA	ARG	26/7/86	A	16	(18)	6
9	Diego Hernán VALERI	ARG	1/5/86	M	2	(7)	
22	Fabián Andrés VARGAS	COL	17/4/80	M	12	(8)	1

ATHLETIC CLUB

Coach – Joaquín Caparrós

Founded – 1898

Stadium – San Mamés (40,000)

MAJOR HONOURS: Spanish League – (8) 1930, 1931, 1934, 1936, 1943, 1956, 1983, 1984;

Spanish Cup – (23) 1903, 1904, 1910, 1911, 1914, 1915, 1916, 1921, 1923, 1930, 1931, 1932, 1933, 1943, 1944, 1945, 1950, 1955, 1956, 1958, 1969, 1973, 1984.

2010				
28/8	Hércules	a	1-0	*Llorente*
11/9	Atlético	h	1-2	*Llorente*
18/9	Sporting	a	2-2	*Gurpegui, Llorente*
21/9	Mallorca	h	3-0	*David López, San José (p), Íñigo Pérez*
25/9	Barcelona	h	1-3	*Gabilondo*
2/10	Valencia	a	1-2	*Gabilondo*
17/10	Zaragoza	h	2-1	*Iraola, Llorente*
24/10	Sevilla	a	3-4	*Llorente 2, Gabilondo*
31/10	Getafe	h	3-0	*Iraola, San José (p), Gabilondo*
7/11	Villarreal	a	1-4	*Llorente*
13/11	Almería	h	1-0	*Llorente*
20/11	Real Madrid	a	1-5	*Llorente*
28/11	Osasuna	h	1-0	*Gurpegui*
5/12	Real Sociedad	a	0-2	
12/12	Espanyol	h	2-1	*Llorente, David López*
18/12	Levante	a	2-1	*Gabilondo, Javi Martínez*
2011				
2/1	Deportivo	h	1-2	*Llorente*
8/1	Málaga	a	1-1	*Javi Martínez*
15/1	Racing	h	2-1	*Javi Martínez, Muniain*
24/1	Hércules	h	3-0	*Javi Martínez, Llorente, Muniain*
30/1	Atlético	a	2-0	*Toquero 2*
5/2	Sporting	h	3-0	*David López (p), Toquero, Llorente*
14/2	Mallorca	a	0-1	
20/2	Barcelona	a	1-2	*Iraola (p)*
27/2	Valencia	h	1-2	*Llorente*
2/3	Zaragoza	a	1-2	*Llorente*
6/3	Sevilla	h	2-0	*og (Fazio), Iraola (p)*
14/3	Getafe	a	2-2	*og (Manu del Moral), Vera*
20/3	Villarreal	h	0-1	
4/4	Almería	a	3-1	*Muniain, Toquero, Orbaiz*
9/4	Real Madrid	h	0-3	
17/4	Osasuna	a	2-1	*Llorente, Muniain*
23/4	Real Sociedad	h	2-1	*Muniain, Toquero*
2/5	Espanyol	a	1-2	*Susaeta*
7/5	Levante	h	3-2	*Toquero, David López (p), Llorente*
10/5	Deportivo	a	1-2	*Toquero*
15/5	Málaga	h	1-1	*David López (p)*
21/5	Racing	a	2-1	*David López, Llorente*

No	Name	Nat	DoB	Pos	Aps	(s)	Gls
20	AITOR OCIO Carrión		28/11/76	D	3	(1)	
5	Fernando AMOREBIETA Mardaras		29/3/85	D	16	(1)	
29	Jon AURTENECHE Brode		3/1/92	D	9	(1)	
19	Mikel BALENZIAGA Oruesagasti		29/2/88	D	1		
22	Xabier CASTILLO Aranburu		20/3/86	D	10	(1)	

7	DAVID LÓPEZ Moreno		10/9/82	M	17	(11)	6
10	Óscar DE MARCOS Arana		14/4/89	M	3	(10)	
23	Iñigo DÍAZ DE CERIO Conejero		15/5/84	D		(2)	
32	Borja EKIZA Imaz		6/3/88	D	21		
11	Igor GABILONDO del Campo		10/2/79	M	10	(19)	5
18	Carlos GURPEGUI Nausía		19/8/80	M	28	(3)	2
28	IBAI GÓMEZ Pérez		11/11/89	A		(3)	
26	IGOR MARTÍNEZ Caseras		19/7/89	M	5	(3)	
17	ÍÑIGO PÉREZ Soto		18/1/88	M		(3)	1
21	ION VÉLEZ Martínez		17/2/85	A		(5)	
1	Gorka IRAIZOZ Moreno		6/3/81	G	37		
15	Andoni IRAOLA Sagarna		22/6/82	D	37		4
8	Ander ITURRASPE Derteano		8/3/89	M	5	(12)	
24	JAVIer MARTÍNEZ Aginaga		2/9/88	M	35		4
3	KOIKILI Lertxundi Del Campo		23/12/80	D	16		
9	Fernando LLORENTE Torres		26/2/85	A	37	(1)	18
27	Iker MUNIAIN Goñi		19/12/92	M	30	(5)	5
16	Pablo ORBAIZ Lesaca		6/2/79	M	18	(8)	1
13	RAÚL Fernández-Cavada Mateos		13/3/88	G	1		
6	Mikel SAN JOSÉ Domínguez		30/5/89	D	30	(1)	2
14	Markel SUSAETA Lasjurain		14/12/87	M	15	(13)	1
2	Gaizka TOQUERO Pinedo		9/8/84	M	26	(4)	7
4	USTARITZ Aldekoaotalora Astarloa		16/2/83	D	8	(2)	
33	Urko VERA Mateos		12/5/87	A		(5)	1

CLUB ATLÉTICO DE MADRID

Coach – Enrique "Quique" Sánchez Flores

Founded – 1903

Stadium – Vicente Calderón (54,851)

MAJOR HONOURS: UEFA Cup Winners' Cup – (1) 1962; UEFA Europa League – (1) 2010; UEFA Super Cup – (1) 2010; World Club Cup – (1) 1974; Spanish League – (9) 1940, 1941, 1950, 1951, 1966, 1970, 1973, 1977, 1996; Spanish Cup – (9) 1960, 1961, 1965, 1972, 1976, 1985, 1991, 1992, 1996.

2010				
30/8	Sporting	h	4-0	*Jurado, Forlán 2, Simão*
11/9	Athletic	a	2-1	*Forlán, Tiago*
19/9	Barcelona	h	1-2	*Raúl García*
22/9	Valencia	a	1-1	*Simão*
26/9	Zaragoza	h	1-0	*Diego Costa*
3/10	Sevilla	a	1-3	*Diego Costa*
16/10	Getafe	h	2-0	*og (Codina), Diego Costa*
24/10	Villarreal	a	0-2	
31/10	Almería	h	1-1	*Agüero*
7/11	Real Madrid	a	0-2	
13/11	Osasuna	h	3-0	*Forlán 2, Agüero*
21/11	Real Sociedad	a	4-2	*Forlán, Agüero 2, Simão (p)*
27/11	Espanyol	h	2-3	*Tiago, Agüero*
4/12	Levante	a	0-2	
11/12	Deportivo	h	2-0	*Agüero 2*
19/12	Málaga	a	3-0	*Tiago 2, Álvaro Domínguez*
2011				
3/1	Racing	h	0-0	
10/1	Hércules	a	1-4	*Reyes*
17/1	Mallorca	h	3-0	*Valera, Forlán, Reyes*
23/1	Sporting	a	0-1	
30/1	Athletic	h	0-2	
5/2	Barcelona	a	0-3	
12/2	Valencia	h	1-2	*Reyes*
19/2	Zaragoza	a	1-0	*Agüero*
26/2	Sevilla	h	2-2	*Koke, Reyes*
2/3	Getafe	a	1-1	*Elías*
5/3	Villarreal	h	3-1	*Reyes, Agüero, Forlán*
12/3	Almería	a	2-2	*Agüero 2*
19/3	Real Madrid	h	1-2	*Agüero*
3/4	Osasuna	a	3-2	*Diego Costa 3*
10/4	Real Sociedad	h	3-0	*Filipe Luís, Mario Suárez, Agüero*
17/4	Espanyol	a	2-2	*Koke, Agüero*
24/4	Levante	h	4-1	*Elías, Agüero 2 (1p), og (Munúa)*
30/4	Deportivo	a	1-0	*Agüero*
7/5	Málaga	h	0-3	
10/5	Racing	a	1-2	*Mario Suárez*
15/5	Hércules	h	2-1	*Álvaro Domínguez, Reyes*
21/5	Mallorca	a	4-3	*Agüero 3, Juanfran*

No	Name	Nat	DoB	Pos	Aps	(s)	Gls
10	Sergio Leonel "Kun" AGÜERO	ARG	2/6/88	A	31	(1)	20
18	ÁLVARO DOMÍNGUEZ Soto		15/5/89	D	17	(2)	2
3	ANTONIO LÓPEZ Guerrero		13/9/81	D	15	(2)	
13	David DE GEA Quintana		7/11/90	G	38		
22	DIEGO da Silva COSTA	BRA	7/10/88	A	13	(15)	6
9	ELÍAS Mendes Trindade	BRA	16/5/85	M	10	(5)	2
14	FILIPE LUIS Kasmirski	BRA	9/8/85	D	23	(4)	1
7	Diego Martín FORLÁN Corazo	URU	19/5/79	A	23	(9)	8
11	FRANcisco MÉRIDA Pérez		4/3/90	M	6	(11)	
15	Diego Roberto GODÍN Leal	URU	16/2/86	D	25		
20	Juan Francisco Torres Belén "JUANFRAN"		9/1/85	M	5	(10)	1
9	José Manuel JURADO Marín		29/6/86	M	1		1
32	Jorge Resurrección Merodio "KOKE"		8/1/92	M	8	(9)	2
4	MARIO SUÁREZ Mata		24/2/87	M	18	(9)	2
51	Alberto NOGUERA Ripoll		24/9/89	M		(2)	
12	PAULO ASSUNÇAO da Silva	BRA	25/1/80	M	17	(7)	
21	Luis Amaranto PEREA Mosquera	COL	30/1/79	D	28		
43	Jorge PULIDO Mayoral		8/4/91	D	2		
8	RAÚL GARCÍA Escudero		11/7/86	M	18	(11)	1
19	José Antonio REYES Calderón		1/9/83	M	34		6
20	SIMÃO Pedro Fonseca Sabrosa	POR	31/10/79	M	15	(1)	3
5	TIAGO Cardoso Mendes	POR	2/5/81	M	28	(3)	4
17	Tomáš UJFALUŠI	CZE	24/3/78	D	32		
2	Juan VALERA Espín		21/12/84	D	11	(4)	1

FC BARCELONA

Coach – Josep Guardiola

Founded – 1899

Stadium – Camp Nou (98,772)

MAJOR HONOURS: European Champion Clubs' Cup/UEFA Champions League – (4) 1992, 2006, 2009, 2011; UEFA Cup Winners' Cup – (4) 1979, 1982, 1989, 1997; Inter Cities Fairs Cup – (3) 1958, 1960, 1966; UEFA Super Cup – (3) 1992, 1997, 2009; FIFA Club World Cup – (1) 2009; Spanish League – (21) 1929, 1945, 1948, 1949, 1952, 1953, 1959, 1960, 1974, 1985, 1991, 1992, 1993, 1994, 1998, 1999, 2005, 2006, 2009, 2010, 2011; Spanish Cup – (25) 1910, 1912, 1913, 1920, 1922, 1925, 1926, 1928, 1942, 1951, 1952, 1953, 1957, 1959, 1963, 1968, 1971, 1978, 1981, 1983, 1988, 1990, 1997, 1998, 2009.

2010				
29/8	Racing	a	3-0	*Messi, Iniesta, David Villa*
11/9	Hércules	h	0-2	
19/9	Atlético	a	2-1	*Messi, Piqué*
22/9	Sporting	h	1-0	*David Villa*
25/9	Athletic	a	3-1	*Keita, Xavi, Busquets*
3/10	Mallorca	h	1-1	*Messi*
16/10	Valencia	h	2-1	*Iniesta, Puyol*
23/10	Zaragoza	a	2-0	*Messi 2*
30/10	Sevilla	h	5-0	*Messi 2, David Villa 2, Dani Alves*
7/11	Getafe	a	3-1	*Messi, David Villa, Pedro*
13/11	Villarreal	h	3-1	*David Villa, Messi 2*
20/11	Almería	a	8-0	*Messi 3, Iniesta, og (Acasiete), Pedro, Bojan 2*
29/11	Real Madrid	h	5-0	*Xavi, Pedro, David Villa 2, Jeffren*
4/12	Osasuna	a	3-0	*Pedro, Messi 2 (1p)*
12/12	Real Sociedad	h	5-0	*David Villa, Iniesta, Messi 2, Bojan*
18/12	Espanyol	a	5-1	*Pedro 2, Xavi, David Villa 2*

2011

2/1	Levante	h	2-1	*Pedro 2*
8/1	Deportivo	a	4-0	*David Villa, Messi, Iniesta, Pedro*
16/1	Málaga	h	4-1	*Iniesta, David Villa 2, Pedro*
22/1	Racing	h	3-0	*Pedro, Messi (p), Iniesta*
29/1	Hércules	a	3-0	*Pedro, Messi 2*
5/2	Atlético	h	3-0	*Messi 3*
12/2	Sporting	a	1-1	*David Villa*
20/2	Athletic	h	2-1	*David Villa, Messi*
26/2	Mallorca	a	3-0	*Messi, David Villa, Pedro*
2/3	Valencia	a	1-0	*Messi*
5/3	Zaragoza	h	1-0	*Keita*
13/3	Sevilla	a	1-1	*Bojan*
19/3	Getafe	h	2-1	*Dani Alves, Bojan*
2/4	Villarreal	a	1-0	*Piqué*
9/4	Almería	h	3-1	*Messi 2 (1p), Thiago*
16/4	Real Madrid	a	1-1	*Messi (p)*
23/4	Osasuna	h	2-0	*David Villa, Messi*
30/4	Real Sociedad	a	1-2	*Thiago*
8/5	Espanyol	h	2-0	*Iniesta, Piqué*
11/5	Levante	a	1-1	*Keita*
15/5	Deportivo	h	0-0	
21/5	Málaga	a	3-1	*Bojan (p), Afellay, Bartra*

No	Name	Nat	DoB	Pos	Aps	(s)	Gls
22	Éric ABIDAL	FRA	11/9/79	D	23	(3)	
21	ADRIANO Correia Claro	BRA	26/10/84	D	11	(4)	
20	Ibrahim AFELLAY	NED	2/4/86	M	7	(9)	1
32	Marc BARTRA Aregall		15/1/91	D	2		1
9	BOJAN Krkić Pérez		28/8/90	A	9	(18)	6
16	Sergio BUSQUETS Burgos		16/7/88	M	25	(3)	1
2	DANIel ALVES da Silva	BRA	6/5/83	D	31	(4)	2
7	DAVID VILLA Sánchez		3/12/81	A	32	(2)	18
26	Andreu FONTÀS Prat		14/11/89	D	5	(1)	
8	Andrés INIESTA Luján		11/5/84	M	32	(2)	8
11	JEFFREN Suárez Bermúdez		20/1/88	M	4	(4)	1
34	JONATHAN dos Santos Ramírez	MEX	26/4/90	M	1	(1)	
15	Seydou KEITA	MLI	16/1/80	M	15	(20)	3
14	Javier Alejandro MASCHERANO	ARG	8/6/84	M	18	(9)	
19	MAXWELL Scherer Cabeleiro Andrade	BRA	27/8/81	D	19	(6)	
10	Lionel Andrés MESSI	ARG	24/6/87	A	31	(2)	31
18	Gabriel Alejandro MILITO	ARG	7/9/80	D	8	(2)	
40	Martín MONTOYA Torralbo		14/4/91	D	1	(1)	
27	Manuel Agudo Durán"NOLITO"		15/10/86	A		(2)	
17	PEDRO Eliezer Rodríguez Ledesma		28/7/87	A	24	(9)	13
13	José Manuel PINTO Colorado		8/11/75	G	6		
3	Gerard PIQUÉ Bernabeu		2/2/87	D	29	(2)	3
5	Carles PUYOL Saforcada		13/4/78	D	17		1
37	Oriol ROMEU Vidal		24/9/91	M		(1)	
28	SERGI ROBERTO Carnicer		7/2/92	A	1		
30	THIAGO Alcántara do Nascimento		11/4/91	M	6	(6)	2
1	VÍCTOR VALDÉS Arribas		14/1/82	G	32		
6	XAVIer Hernández Creus		25/1/80	M	29	(2)	3

RC DEPORTIVO LA CORUÑA

Coach – Miguel Ángel Lotina

Founded – 1906

Stadium – Riazor (34,600)

MAJOR HONOURS: Spanish League – (1) 2000; Spanish Cup – (2) 1995, 2002.

2010

29/8	Zaragoza	h	0-0	
12/9	Sevilla	a	0-0	
20/9	Getafe	h	2-2	*Guardado 2 (2p)*
23/9	Villarreal	a	0-1	
26/9	Almería	h	0-2	
3/10	Real Madrid	a	1-6	*Juan Rodríguez*
17/10	Osasuna	h	0-0	
25/10	Real Sociedad	a	0-3	
31/10	Espanyol	h	3-0	*Adrián López, Lopo, Colotto*
7/11	Levante	a	2-1	*Riki, Aythami*
14/11	Mallorca	a	0-0	
21/11	Málaga	h	3-0	*Adrián López (p), Colotto, Pablo Álvarez*
28/11	Racing	a	0-1	
6/12	Hércules	h	1-0	*Lassad*
11/12	Atlético	a	0-2	
18/12	Sporting	h	1-1	*Aythami*

2011

2/1	Athletic	a	2-1	*Adrián López 2 (1p)*
8/1	Barcelona	h	0-4	
16/1	Valencia	a	0-2	
23/1	Zaragoza	a	0-1	
29/1	Sevilla	h	3-3	*Lassad 2, Laure*
5/2	Getafe	a	1-4	*Riki (p)*
13/2	Villarreal	h	1-0	*Lopo*
20/2	Almería	a	1-1	*Aranzubia*
26/2	Real Madrid	h	0-0	
2/3	Osasuna	a	0-0	
7/3	Real Sociedad	h	2-1	*Riki, Adrián López*
13/3	Espanyol	a	0-2	
20/3	Levante	h	0-1	
3/4	Mallorca	h	2-1	*Xisco, Lassad*
10/4	Málaga	a	0-0	
17/4	Racing	h	2-0	*Lassad, Xisco*
24/4	Hércules	a	0-1	
30/4	Atlético	h	0-1	
7/5	Sporting	a	2-2	*Adrián López 2*
10/5	Athletic	h	2-1	*og (Gurpegui), og (Castillo)*
15/5	Barcelona	a	0-0	
21/5	Valencia	h	0-2	

No	Name	Nat	DoB	Pos	Aps	(s)	Gls
10	ADRIÁN LÓPEZ Álvarez		8/1/88	A	31	(5)	7
16	ANTONIO TOMÁS González		19/1/85	M	20	(1)	
1	Daniel ARANZUBIA Aguado		18/9/79	G	32		1
23	AYTHAMI Artiles Oliva		2/4/86	D	17	(2)	2
19	Diego Daniel COLOTTO	ARG	10/3/81	D	36		2
20	Yves Hadley DESMARETS	FRA	17/9/79	M	9	(3)	
34	DIONIsio Villalba Rojano		21/12/89	A	1	(3)	
18	José Andrés GUARDADO Hernández	MEX	28/9/86	M	18	(2)	2
28	JUAN DOMÍNGUEZ Lamas		8/1/90	M	9	(11)	
22	JUAN Antonio RODRÍGUEZ Villamuela		1/4/82	M	29	(2)	1
6	Juliano Roberto Antonello "JUCA"	BRA	19/11/79	M	1	(7)	
8	LASSAD Hassen Nouioui	TUN	8/7/85	A	16	(17)	5
15	LAURE Sanabria Ruiz		22/3/85	D	21	(1)	1
7	Alberto LOPO García		5/5/80	D	33		2
13	MANUel Fernández Muñiz		9/3/86	G	6		
2	MANUEL PABLO García Díaz		25/1/76	D	30		
9	Miguel Ángel Herrero Javaloyas "MÍCHEL"		29/7/88	M	7	(1)	
3	Claudio Marcelo MOREL Rodríguez	PAR	2/2/78	D	14	(1)	
14	PABLO ÁLVAREZ Núñez		14/5/80	M	3	(14)	1
11	Iván Sánchez Rico Soto "RIKI"		11/8/80	A	8	(11)	3
24	Knut Olav RINDARØY	NOR	17/7/85	D	3	(1)	
27	David ROCHELA Calvo		19/2/90	D	2		
4	RUBÉN Salvador PÉREZ del Mármol		26/4/89	M	31	(1)	
24	José Gustavo SAND	ARG	17/7/80	A	2	(3)	
12	SAÚL Fernández García		9/4/85	M	8	(5)	
33	Diego SEOANE Pérez		26/4/88	D	8	(3)	
17	Jonathan Matías URRETAviscaya da Luz	URU	19/3/90	M	5	(1)	
21	Juan Carlos VALERÓN Santana		17/6/75	M	9	(12)	
17	Francisco "XISCO" Jiménez Tejada		26/6/86	A	5	(4)	2
5	José "ZÉ" Eduardo Rosa Vale CASTRO	POR	13/1/83	D	4	(2)	

RCD ESPANYOL

Coach – Mauricio Pochettino (ARG)
Founded – 1900
Stadium – Cornellá-El Prat (40,500)
MAJOR HONOURS: Spanish Cup – (4) 1929, 1940, 2000, 2006.

2010				
29/8	Getafe	h	3-1	*Osvaldo 2, Dátolo*
12/9	Villarreal	a	0-4	
18/9	Almería	h	1-0	*Callejón*
21/9	Real Madrid	a	0-3	
26/9	Osasuna	h	1-0	*Álvaro Vázquez*
2/10	Real Sociedad	a	0-1	
17/10	Mallorca	a	1-0	*Luis García (p)*
24/10	Levante	h	2-1	*Dátolo, Callejón*
31/10	Deportivo	a	0-3	
6/11	Málaga	h	1-0	*Javi Márquez*
14/11	Racing	a	0-0	
21/11	Hércules	h	3-0	*Verdú, Osvaldo (p), Luis García (p)*
27/11	Atlético	a	3-2	*Luis García (p), Verdú, Osvaldo*
5/12	Sporting	h	1-0	*Luis García*
12/12	Athletic	a	1-2	*Osvaldo*
18/12	Barcelona	h	1-5	*Osvaldo*
2011				
2/1	Valencia	a	1-2	*og (Ricardo Costa)*
9/1	Zaragoza	h	4-0	*Osvaldo, Luis García (p), Álvaro Vázquez, Sergio García*
15/1	Sevilla	a	2-1	*Callejón 2*
23/1	Getafe	a	3-1	*Luis García, Callejón, Sergio García*
30/1	Villarreal	h	0-1	
5/2	Almería	a	2-3	*Verdú, Álvaro Vázquez*
13/2	Real Madrid	h	0-1	
20/2	Osasuna	a	0-4	
26/2	Real Sociedad	h	4-1	*Álvaro Vázquez, Sergio García, Callejón, Javi Márquez*
1/3	Mallorca	h	1-2	*Álvaro Vázquez*
6/3	Levante	a	0-1	
13/3	Deportivo	h	2-0	*Iván Alonso, Verdú*
20/3	Málaga	a	0-2	
3/4	Racing	h	1-2	*Osvaldo (p)*
10/4	Hércules	a	0-0	
17/4	Atlético	h	2-2	*Osvaldo 2*
24/4	Sporting	a	0-1	
2/5	Athletic	h	2-1	*Osvaldo, Iván Alonso*
8/5	Barcelona	a	0-2	
11/5	Valencia	h	2-2	*Osvaldo, Galán*
15/5	Zaragoza	a	0-1	
21/5	Sevilla	h	2-3	*Osvaldo, Verdú*

No	Name	Nat	DoB	Pos	Aps	(s)	Gls
28	ÁLVARO VÁZQUEZ García		27/4/91	A	8	(22)	5
7	José Raúl BAENA Urdiales		2/3/89	M	13	(2)	
8	José María CALLEJÓN Bueno		11/2/87	M	36	(1)	6
2	Francisco Javier CHICA Torres		17/5/85	D	28	(1)	
20	Ferran COROMINAS Telechea		5/1/83	A		(1)	
25	CRISITAN Darío ÁLVAREZ	ARG	13/11/85	G	5		
23	Jesús Alberto DÁTOLO	ARG	19/5/84	M	3	(11)	2
3	DAVID GARCÍA de la Cruz		16/1/81	D	16	(1)	
33	DAVID LÓPEZ Silva		9/10/89	M		(3)	
9	Iván DE LA PEÑA López		6/5/76	M		(2)	
5	DÍDAC Vila Roselló		9/6/89	D	12	(1)	
22	Aldo Pedro DUSCHER	ARG	22/3/79	M	14	(5)	
37	ERIC LÓPEZ Royo		1/4/93	A		(2)	
18	Juan Daniel FORLÍN	ARG	10/1/88	D	21		
14	Ernesto GALÁN Iñigo		17/6/86	D	21	(1)	1
40	ISAÍAS Sánchez Cortés		9/2/87	M		(4)	
24	IVÁN Daniel ALONSO Vallejo	URU	10/4/79	A	10	(10)	2
16	JAVIer LÓPEZ Rodríguez		21/1/86	M	18	(7)	
4	JAVIer MÁRQUEZ Moreno		11/5/86	D	26	(3)	2
27	JORDI AMAT Mas		21/3/92	D	23	(3)	
1	Idriss Carlos KAMENI	CMR	18/2/84	G	33		
10	LUIS GARCÍA Fernández		6/2/81	M	36	(1)	6
29	Manuel Antonio MOLINA Valero		20/11/91	M	1	(6)	
17	Pablo Daniel OSVALDO	ITA	12/1/86	A	22	(2)	13
32	RAÚL RODRÍGUEZ Navarro		22/9/87	D	8	(2)	
35	RUI Pedro da Rocha FONTE	POR	23/4/90	A		(11)	
19	SERGIO GARCÍA de la Fuente		9/6/83	A	13	(8)	3
39	THIEVY Guivane Bifouma Koulossa	FRA	13/5/92	A		(2)	
11	Joan VERDÚ Fernández		5/5/83	M	36	(1)	5
34	VÍCTOR ÁLVAREZ Delgado		14/3/93	D		(1)	
6	VÍCTOR RUIZ Torre		25/1/89	D	15		

GETAFE CF

Coach – José Miguel González "Míchel"
Founded – 1983
Stadium – Coliseum Alfonso Pérez (17,000)

2010				
29/8	Espanyol	a	1-3	*og (Galán)*
12/9	Levante	h	4-1	*Gavilán 2, Adrián Colunga, Arizmendi*
20/9	Deportivo	a	2-2	*og (Colotto), Arizmendi*
23/9	Málaga	h	0-2	
26/9	Racing	a	1-0	*Víctor Sánchez*
3/10	Hércules	h	3-0	*Parejo, Manu del Moral, Miku*
16/10	Atlético	a	0-2	
24/10	Sporting	h	3-0	*Boateng, Adrián Colunga (p), Marcano*
31/10	Athletic	a	0-3	
7/11	Barcelona	h	1-3	*Manu del Moral (p)*
14/11	Valencia	a	0-2	
22/11	Zaragoza	h	1-1	*Adrián Colunga (p)*
27/11	Sevilla	a	3-1	*Manu del Moral (p), Miku, Pedro Ríos*
5/12	Mallorca	h	3-0	*Pedro Ríos 2, Parejo*
11/12	Villarreal	h	1-0	*Albín*
19/12	Almería	a	3-2	*Manu del Moral, Miku, Boateng*
2011				
3/1	Real Madrid	h	2-3	*Parejo, Albín*
9/1	Osasuna	a	0-0	
15/1	Real Sociedad	h	0-4	
23/1	Espanyol	h	1-3	*Miku*
29/1	Levante	a	0-2	
5/2	Deportivo	h	4-1	*Adrián Colunga 2, Miku, Pedro Ríos*
13/2	Málaga	a	2-2	*Miku, Adrián Colunga*
20/2	Racing	h	0-1	
27/2	Hércules	a	0-0	
2/3	Atlético	h	1-1	*Manu del Moral*
6/3	Sporting	a	0-2	
14/3	Athletic	h	2-2	*Manu del Moral 2*
19/3	Barcelona	a	1-2	*Manu del Moral*
2/4	Valencia	h	2-4	*Manu del Moral, Adrián Sardinero*
11/4	Zaragoza	a	1-2	*Casquero*
16/4	Sevilla	h	1-0	*Miku*
24/4	Mallorca	a	0-2	
1/5	Villarreal	a	1-2	*Pedro Ríos*
7/5	Almería	h	2-0	*Adrián Colunga, Pedro Ríos*
10/5	Real Madrid	a	0-4	
15/5	Osasuna	h	2-0	*og (Miguel Flaño), Pedro Ríos*
21/5	Real Sociedad	a	1-1	*Cata Díaz*

No	Name	Nat	DoB	Pos	Aps	(s)	Gls
9	ADRIÁN COLUNGA Pérez		17/11/84	A	22	(7)	7
27	ADRIÁN SARDINERO Corpa		13/10/90	A	4	(7)	1
10	Juan Ángel ALBÍN Leites	URU	17/7/86	A	4	(14)	2
19	Ángel Javier ARIZMENDI de Lucas		3/3/84	A	7	(12)	2
18	Derek Owusu BOATENG	GHA	2/5/83	M	30	(2)	2
6	BORJA Fernández Fernández		14/1/81	M	4	(9)	
22	Francisco Javier CASQUERO Paredes		11/3/76	M	15	(12)	1
2	Daniel Alberto "CATA" DÍAZ	ARG	13/3/79	D	35		1
13	Jordi CODINA Rodríguez		27/4/82	G	22	(1)	
8	Jaime GAVILÁN Martínez		12/5/85	M	15	(3)	2
3	José Manuel Jiménez Ortiz "MANÉ"		21/12/81	D	30	(1)	
14	MANUel DEL MORAL Fernández		25/2/84	M	28	(2)	9
20	Iván MARCANO Sierra		23/6/87	D	26	(3)	1
5	Pedro MARIO Álvarez Abrante		2/2/82	D	3		
7	Nicolás Ladislao Fedor Flores "MIKU"	VEN	19/8/85	A	24	(7)	7
21	Pedro MOSQUERA Parada		21/4/88	M	4	(10)	
11	Daniel PAREJO Muñoz		16/4/89	M	28	(8)	3

No	Name	Nat	DoB	Pos	Aps	(s)	Gls
6	PEDRO RÍOS Maestre		12/12/81	M	27	(4)	7
0	Pablo César PINTOS	URU	1/7/87	D	4	(2)	
5	RAFAel LÓPEZ Gómez		9/4/85	D	17	(2)	
4	Miguel TORRES Gómez		28/1/86	D	32		
	Óscar Alfredo USTARI	ARG	3/7/86	G	16		
4	VÍCTOR SÁNCHEZ Mata		20/1/87	M	21	(8)	1

HÉRCULES CF

Coach – Esteban Vigo; (21/2/11) Miroslav Đukić (SRB)

Founded – 1922

Stadium – José Rico Pérez (29,584)

2010				
28/8	Athletic	h	0-1	
11/9	Barcelona	a	2-0	*Valdez 2*
19/9	Valencia	h	1-2	*Trezeguet (p)*
22/9	Zaragoza	a	0-0	
26/9	Sevilla	h	2-0	*Trezeguet 2 (1p)*
3/10	Getafe	a	0-3	
18/10	Villarreal	h	2-2	*Valdez, Trezeguet*
24/10	Almería	a	1-1	*Valdez*
30/10	Real Madrid	h	1-3	*Trezeguet*
7/11	Osasuna	a	0-3	
14/11	Real Sociedad	h	2-1	*Trezeguet, Drenthe*
21/11	Espanyol	a	0-3	
28/11	Levante	h	3-1	*Valdez 2, Trezeguet*
6/12	Deportivo	a	0-1	
12/12	Málaga	h	4-1	*Trezeguet, Drenthe (p), Abraham Paz, Kiko Femenía*
20/12	Racing	a	0-0	
2011				
3/1	Mallorca	a	0-3	
10/1	Atlético	h	4-1	*Tote, Valdez, Thomert, Trezeguet*
15/1	Sporting	a	0-2	
24/1	Athletic	a	0-3	
29/1	Barcelona	h	0-3	
6/2	Valencia	a	0-2	
13/2	Zaragoza	h	2-1	*Farinós, Trezeguet*
20/2	Sevilla	a	0-1	
27/2	Getafe	h	0-0	
2/3	Villarreal	a	0-1	
6/3	Almería	h	1-2	*Abraham Paz*
12/3	Real Madrid	a	0-2	
20/3	Osasuna	h	0-4	
3/4	Real Sociedad	a	3-1	*Portillo, Drenthe 2*
10/4	Espanyol	h	0-0	
17/4	Levante	a	1-2	*Trezeguet*
24/4	Deportivo	h	1-0	*Tiago Gomes*
1/5	Málaga	a	1-3	*Valdez*
7/5	Racing	h	2-3	*Sendoa, Tiago Gomes*
11/5	Mallorca	h	2-2	*Sendoa 2*
15/5	Atlético	a	1-2	*Trezeguet*
21/5	Sporting	h	0-0	

No	Name	Nat	DoB	Pos	Aps	(s)	Gls
14	ABEL Enrique AGUILAR Tapias	COL	6/1/85	M	33	(1)	
5	ABRAHAM PAZ Cruz		29/6/79	D	29		2
1	Juan Jesús CALATAYUD Sánchez		21/12/79	G	34		
21	David CORTÉS Caballero		29/8/79	D	34		
6	CRISTIAN Hidalgo González		21/9/83	M	2	(17)	
12	Royston DRENTHE	NED	8/4/87	M	15	(2)	4
8	Francisco Javier FARINÓS Zapata		29/3/78	M	11	(1)	1
18	Matías Lionel FRITZLER	ARG	23/8/86	M	22	(4)	
3	Juan Ramón Cabrero Obrer "JUANRA"		24/4/80	D	13	(1)	
15	Francisco "KIKO" FEMENÍA Far		2/2/91	M	21	(13)	1
29	LUIS CARLOS Martín Asensio		16/12/90	A		(1)	
23	Noé PAMAROT	FRA	14/4/79	D	28	(1)	
16	Francisco PEÑA Romero		25/7/78	D	28		
9	Javier García PORTILLO		30/3/82	A	11	(15)	1
12	Cristian Corneliu PULHAC	ROU	17/8/84	D	9		
7	Francisco Joaquín Pérez RUFETE		20/11/76	M	3	(11)	
4	Mohamed Adama SARR	SEN	23/12/83	D	2		
11	SENDOA Aguirre Basterrechea		31/12/75	M	7	(16)	3
19	SERGIO RODRÍGUEZ García		17/8/84	D	10	(3)	
22	Olivier THOMERT	FRA	28/3/80	A	12	(6)	1
24	TIAGO Filipe Figueiras GOMES	POR	18/8/85	A	25	(3)	2
10	Jorge López Marco "TOTE"		23/11/78	A	15	(6)	1
17	David TREZEGUET	FRA	15/10/77	A	28	(3)	12
13	UNAI ALBA Pagadizabal		19/2/78	G	1	(1)	
20	Nelson Haedo VALDEZ	PAR	28/11/83	A	22	(3)	8
25	Piet VELTHUIZEN	NED	3/11/86	G	3		

LEVANTE UD

Coach – Luis García Plaza

Founded – 1939

Stadium – Ciutat de València (25,354)

2010				
28/8	Sevilla	h	1-4	*Rubén Suárez (p)*
12/9	Getafe	a	1-4	*Rafa Jordá*
19/9	Villarreal	h	1-2	*Caicedo*
22/9	Almería	a	1-0	*Sergio*
25/9	Real Madrid	h	0-0	
3/10	Osasuna	a	1-1	*Sergio*
17/10	Real Sociedad	h	2-1	*Del Horno, Caicedo*
24/10	Espanyol	a	1-2	*Stuani*
1/11	Mallorca	a	1-2	*Stuani*
7/11	Deportivo	h	1-2	*Juanlu*
14/11	Málaga	a	0-1	
21/11	Racing	h	3-1	*Caicedo 2, Stuani*
28/11	Hércules	a	1-3	*Rubén Suárez*
4/12	Atlético	h	2-0	*Nano, Caicedo*
12/12	Sporting	a	1-1	*Caicedo*
18/12	Athletic	h	1-2	*Caicedo*
2011				
2/1	Barcelona	a	1-2	*Stuani*
9/1	Valencia	h	0-1	
15/1	Zaragoza	a	0-1	
22/1	Sevilla	a	1-4	*Xisco Muñoz*
29/1	Getafe	h	2-0	*Valdo, Caicedo*
5/2	Villarreal	a	1-0	*Valdo*
13/2	Almería	h	1-0	*Caicedo*
19/2	Real Madrid	a	0-2	
27/2	Osasuna	h	2-1	*Ballesteros, Caicedo*
2/3	Real Sociedad	a	1-1	*Del Horno*
6/3	Espanyol	h	1-0	*Caicedo*
13/3	Mallorca	h	1-1	*Juanlu*
20/3	Deportivo	a	1-0	*Rubén Suárez*
3/4	Málaga	h	3-1	*Stuani 2, Rubén Suárez*
10/4	Racing	a	1-1	*Rafa Jordá*
17/4	Hércules	h	2-1	*Rubén Suárez, Juanlu*
24/4	Atlético	a	1-4	*Caicedo (p)*
1/5	Sporting	h	0-0	
7/5	Athletic	a	2-3	*Stuani, Nano*
11/5	Barcelona	h	1-1	*Caicedo*
15/5	Valencia	a	0-0	
21/5	Zaragoza	h	1-2	*Stuani*

No	Name	Nat	DoB	Pos	Aps	(s)	Gls
18	Sergio Martínez BALLESTEROS		4/9/75	D	35		1
25	Felipe Salvador CAICEDO Corozo	ECU	5/9/88	A	22	(5)	13
2	David CERRAjería Rubio		4/6/83	D	7	(2)	
15	Asier DEL HORNO Cosgaya		19/1/81	D	21	(1)	2
8	GORKA LARREA García		7/4/84	M	2	(4)	
4	HÉCTOR RODAS Ramírez		7/3/88	D	5		
10	Vicente IBORRA De la Fuente		16/1/88	M	14	(2)	
17	JAVIer Rodríguez VENTA		13/12/75	D	33		
12	Juan Francisco García García "JUANFRAN"		15/7/76	D	22	(1)	
20	Juan Luis Gómez López "JUANLU"		18/5/80	M	28	(2)	3

No	Name	Nat	DoB	Pos	Aps	(s)	Gls
27	Adrián LOIS Sixto		12/2/89	M		(1)	
31	Sergio Abad Beyxer "MONO"		1/3/89	M		(1)	
24	Jefferson Antonio MONTERO Vite	ECU	1/9/89	A	4	(7)	
13	Gustavo Adolfo MUNÚA Vera	URU	27/1/78	G	20		
24	Ignacio "NACHO" María GONZÁLEZ Gatti	URU	14/5/82	M	2	(1)	
3	Victoriano Rivas Álvaro "NANO"		7/7/80	D	28	(4)	2
6	Miguel PALLARDÓ González		5/9/86	M	21	(6)	
9	RAFAel JORDÁ Ruiz de Assin		1/1/84	A	7	(10)	2
1	Manuel REINA Rodríguez		1/4/85	G	18		
5	Miguel ROBUSTÉ Colomer		20/5/85	D	4	(3)	
21	RUBÉN SUÁREZ Estrada		19/2/79	A	18	(9)	5
16	SERGIO González Soriano		10/11/76	M	9	(5)	2
22	Christian Ricardo STUANI Curbelo	URU	12/1/86	A	11	(19)	8
23	Valmiro Lopes Rocha "VALDO"		23/4/81	M	25	(4)	2
11	WELLINGTON Alves da Silva	BRA	6/1/93	A		(2)	
14	XAVIER TORRES Buigues		21/11/86	M	34	(1)	
19	Francisco "XISCO" Javier MUÑOZ Llompart		9/5/80	M	16	(10)	1
7	Francisco "XISCO" Sebastián NADAL Martorell		27/6/86	A	12	(13)	

MÁLAGA CF

Coach – Jesualdo Ferreira (POR); (2/11/10) (Rafael Francisco Gil Sánchez); (7/11/10) Manuel Pellegrini (CHI)

Founded – 1994

Stadium – La Rosaleda (28,963)

2010				
28/8	Valencia	h	1-3	*Sebas Fernández*
12/9	Zaragoza	a	5-3	*Fernando 2, Juanmi 2, Owusu-Abeyie*
19/9	Sevilla	h	1-2	*Rondón*
23/9	Getafe	a	2-0	*Rondón, Apoño (p)*
27/9	Villarreal	h	2-3	*Eliseu, Rondón*
3/10	Almería	a	1-1	*Owusu-Abeyie*
16/10	Real Madrid	h	1-4	*Stadsgaard*
24/10	Osasuna	a	0-3	
31/10	Real Sociedad	h	1-2	*Juanmi*
6/11	Espanyol	a	0-1	
14/11	Levante	h	1-0	*Eliseu*
21/11	Deportivo	a	0-3	
28/11	Mallorca	a	0-2	
5/12	Racing	h	4-1	*Eliseu, Recio, Rondón 2*
12/12	Hércules	a	1-4	*Sebas Fernández*
19/12	Atlético	h	0-3	
2011				
2/1	Sporting	a	2-1	*Weligton, Apoño (p)*
8/1	Athletic	h	1-1	*Demichelis*
16/1	Barcelona	a	1-4	*Duda*
22/1	Valencia	a	3-4	*Rondón 2, Júlio Baptista*
29/1	Zaragoza	h	1-2	*Duda*
6/2	Sevilla	a	0-0	
13/2	Getafe	h	2-2	*Júlio Baptista (p), Rondón*
20/2	Villarreal	a	1-1	*Sebas Fernández*
28/2	Almería	h	3-1	*Maresca, Rondón, Juanmi*
3/3	Real Madrid	a	0-7	
6/3	Osasuna	h	0-1	
13/3	Real Sociedad	a	2-0	*Duda, Rondón*
20/3	Espanyol	h	2-0	*Rondón 2*
3/4	Levante	a	1-3	*Sebas Fernández*
10/4	Deportivo	h	0-0	
16/4	Mallorca	h	3-0	*Sebas Fernández, Júlio Baptista 2*
24/4	Racing	a	2-1	*Júlio Baptista, Sebas Fernández*
1/5	Hércules	h	3-1	*Júlio Baptsita 2, Rondón*
7/5	Atlético	a	3-0	*Rondón, Júlio Baptista, Maresca*
10/5	Sporting	h	2-0	*Júlio Baptista, Eliseu*
15/5	Athletic	a	1-1	*Recio*
21/5	Barcelona	h	1-3	*Sebas Fernández*

No	Name	Nat	DoB	Pos	Aps	(s)	Gls
10	Antonio Galdeano Benítez "APOÑO"		13/2/84	M	26	(1)	2
1	Francesc ARNAU Grabalosa		23/5/75	G	7	(2)	
13	Sergio ASENJO Andrés		28/6/89	G	5		
7	Nabil BAHA	MAR	12/8/81	A	4	(1)	
13	Wilfredo Daniel CABALLERO	ARG	28/9/81	G	15		
37	Sergio CALAtayud Lebrón		2/3/90	M		(1)	
24	Ignacio CAMACHO Barnola		4/5/90	M	12	(3)	
5	Martín DEMICHELIS	ARG	20/12/80	D	18		1
17	Sergio Paulo Barbosa Valente "DUDA"	POR	27/6/80	M	20		3
9	Arnaldo Edi Lopes da Silva "EDINHO"	POR	7/7/82	M	1	(7)	
16	EDUardo RAMOS Gómez		17/2/92	M	1	(4)	
18	ELISEU Pereira dos Santos	POR	1/10/83	M	34	(1)	4
8	FERNANDO Miguel Fernández Escribano		2/6/79	M	12	(9)	2
13	Rodrigo José GALATTO	BRA	10/4/83	G	4		
14	HÉLDER Miguel do ROSARIO	POR	9/3/80	D	3		
6	IVÁN GONZÁLEZ López		15/2/88	D	4	(2)	
2	JESÚS GÁMEZ Duarte		10/4/85	D	30		
24	Juan Jesús Gutiérrez Robles "JUANITO"		17/2/80	M	5	(1)	
26	Juan Miguel Jiménez López "JUANMI"		20/5/93	A	6	(11)	4
6	JÚLIO César BAPTISTA	BRA	1/10/81	A	11		9
5	Alberto LUQUE Martos		11/3/78	M		(3)	
20	Manuel Gaspar Haro "MANOLO"		3/2/81	D	7	(2)	
4	MANUel TORRES Caturla		14/8/89	D	5	(2)	
16	Enzo MARESCA	ITA	10/2/80	M	9	(11)	2
19	Patrick MTILIGA	DEN	28/1/81	D	17	(2)	
21	Quincy OWUSU-ABEYIE	GHA	15/4/86	A	15	(10)	2
27	Francisco PORTILLO Soler		13/6/90	A	7	(10)	
45	José Luis García del Pozo "RECIO"		11/1/91	M	18	(5)	2
23	José Salomón RONDÓN Giménez	VEN	16/9/89	A	28	(2)	14
25	RUBÉN MARTÍNEZ Andrade		22/6/84	G	7		
22	SANDRO Laurindo da SILVA	BRA	29/4/84	M	12	(12)	
11	SEBAStián Bruno FERNÁNDEZ Miglierina	URU	23/5/85	A	21	(9)	7
12	Kris STADSGAARD	DEN	1/8/85	D	23	(2)	1
3	WELIGTON Robson Pena de Oliveira	BRA	26/8/79	D	31		1

RCD MALLORCA

Coach – Michael Laudrup (DEN)

Founded – 1916

Stadium – Iberostar Estadio (23,142)

MAJOR HONOURS: Spanish Cup – (1) 2003.

2010				
29/8	Real Madrid	h	0-0	
12/9	Sporting	a	0-2	
18/9	Osasuna	h	2-0	*Castro (p), De Guzmán*
21/9	Athletic	a	0-3	
26/9	Real Sociedad	h	2-0	*Cavenaghi 2*
3/10	Barcelona	a	1-1	*Nsue*
17/10	Espanyol	h	0-1	
23/10	Valencia	a	2-1	*Castro 2 (1p)*
1/11	Levante	h	2-1	*Pereira, Webó*
7/11	Zaragoza	a	2-3	*Webó, Pereira*
14/11	Deportivo	h	0-0	
21/11	Sevilla	a	2-1	*Pereira, Webó*
28/11	Málaga	h	2-0	*Webó, Castro*
5/12	Getafe	a	0-3	
12/12	Racing	h	0-1	
18/12	Villarreal	a	1-3	*De Guzmán*
2011				
3/1	Hércules	h	3-0	*Nsue, Víctor, Pereira*
9/1	Almería	h	4-1	*Ramis, Víctor, Nsue, Pereira*
17/1	Atlético	a	0-3	
23/1	Real Madrid	a	0-1	
29/1	Sporting	h	0-4	
5/2	Osasuna	a	1-1	*Castro*
14/2	Athletic	h	1-0	*Webó*
21/2	Real Sociedad	a	0-1	
26/2	Barcelona	h	0-3	

'3	Espanyol	a	2-1	*Webó, Nsue*
'3	Valencia	h	1-2	*Ramis (p)*
3/3	Levante	a	1-1	*Ramis*
9/3	Zaragoza	h	1-0	*De Guzmán*
4	Deportivo	a	1-2	*Webó*
'4	Sevilla	h	2-2	*Ienaga, De Guzmán*
6/4	Málaga	a	0-3	
4/4	Getafe	h	2-0	*Nunes, Ienaga*
/5	Racing	a	0-2	
/5	Villarreal	h	0-0	
1/5	Hércules	a	2-2	*Víctor, Webó*
5/5	Almería	a	1-3	*Webó*
:1/5	Atlético	h	3-4	*De Guzmán (p), Webó 2*

No	Name	Nat	DoB	Pos	Aps	(s)	Gls
13	Dudu AWAT	ISR	17/10/77	G	35		
7	AYOZE Díaz Díaz		25/5/82	D	19		
1	Gonzalo CASTRO Irazábal	URU	14/9/84	M	25	(8)	5
10	Fernando CAVENAGHI	ARG	21/9/83	A	7	(4)	2
22	Pablo CENDRÓS López		1/4/87	D	29	(2)	
23	Enrique CORRALES Martín		1/3/82	M	1	(1)	
20	Jonathan DE GUZMÁN	NED	13/9/87	M	33		5
14	Akihiro IENAGA	JPN	13/6/86	M	3	(11)	2
3	JOÃO VÍCTOR de Albuquerque Bruno	BRA	7/11/88	M	21	(11)	
29	KEVIN García Martínez		8/9/89	D	18	(1)	
1	Germán Darío LUX	ARG	7/6/82	G	3	(1)	
19	José Luis MARTÍ Soler		28/4/75	M	33	(1)	
21	MARTÍ CRESPÍ Pascual		15/6/87	D	3	(2)	
8	Emilio NSUE López		30/9/89	A	34	(4)	4
16	José Carlos de Araújo NUNES	POR	7/3/77	D	34		1
7	Michael PEREIRA	FRA	8/12/87	A	24	(11)	5
4	Iván Andrés RAMIS Barrios		25/10/84	D	33		3
2	Edson Ramos Silva "RATINHO"	BRA	31/5/86	D	7		
5	RUBÉN GONZÁLEZ Rocha		29/1/82	D	7	(5)	
26	SERGI Enrich Ametller		26/2/90	D	1	(4)	
27	SERGIO TEJERA Rodríguez		28/5/90	A	10	(6)	
28	TOMÁS PINA Isla		14/10/87	M	1	(8)	
18	VÍCTOR Casadesús Castaño		28/2/85	A	9	(10)	3
9	Pierre Achille WEBÓ Kouamo	CMR	20/1/82	A	28	(6)	11

CA OSASUNA

Coach – José Antonio Camacho; (15/2/11) José Luis Mendilíbar

Founded – 1920

Stadium – Reyno de Navarra (19,800)

2010				
29/8	Almería	h	0-0	
11/9	Real Madrid	a	0-1	
18/9	Mallorca	a	0-2	
21/9	Real Sociedad	h	3-1	*Pandiani, Camuñas, Aranda*
26/9	Espanyol	a	0-1	
3/10	Levante	h	1-1	*Pandiani*
17/10	Deportivo	a	0-0	
24/10	Málaga	h	3-0	*Nekounam (p), Shojaei, Aranda*
31/10	Racing	a	1-4	*Nekounam (p)*
7/11	Hércules	h	3-0	*Monreal, Lolo, Vadócz*
13/11	Atlético	a	0-3	
21/11	Sporting	h	1-0	*Shojaei*
28/11	Athletic	a	0-1	
4/12	Barcelona	h	0-3	
13/12	Valencia	a	3-3	*Juanfran, Miguel Flaño, Aranda*
19/12	Zaragoza	h	0-0	
2011				
2/1	Sevilla	a	0-1	
9/1	Getafe	h	0-0	
15/1	Villarreal	a	2-4	*Vadócz, Calleja*
23/1	Almería	a	2-3	*Aranda, Lekić*
30/1	Real Madrid	h	1-0	*Camuñas*
5/2	Mallorca	h	1-1	*Miguel Flaño*
13/2	Real Sociedad	a	0-1	
20/2	Espanyol	h	4-0	*Nekounam 2 (1p), Lolo, Soriano*
27/2	Levante	a	1-2	*Pandiani*
2/3	Deportivo	h	0-0	
6/3	Málaga	a	1-0	*Sergio*
13/3	Racing	h	3-1	*Kike Sola, Nekounam (p), Soriano*
20/3	Hércules	a	4-0	*Camuñas, Nelson, Vadócz, Kike Sola*
3/4	Atlético	h	2-3	*Kike Sola, Nekounam (p)*
10/4	Sporting	a	0-1	
17/4	Athletic	h	1-2	*Kike Sola*
23/4	Barcelona	a	0-2	
1/5	Valencia	h	1-0	*Álvaro Cejudo*
8/5	Zaragoza	a	3-1	*Camuñas, Sergio, Kike Sola*
11/5	Sevilla	h	3-2	*Kike Sola 2, Lekić*
15/5	Getafe	a	0-2	
21/5	Villarreal	h	1-0	*Álvaro Cejudo*

No	Name	Nat	DoB	Pos	Aps	(s)	Gls
16	ÁLVARO CEJUDO Carmona		29/1/84	M	13		2
28	Javier Fernández ANNUNZIATA		31/8/87	M		(1)	
7	Carlos Reina ARANDA		27/7/80	A	15	(5)	4
19	Javier CALLEJA Revilla		12/5/78	M	4	(14)	1
17	Javier CAMUÑAS Gallego		17/7/80	M	30	(1)	4
12	Ferran COROMINAS Telechea		5/1/83	A	4	(2)	
24	DAMIÀ Abella Pérez		15/4/82	D	22	(5)	
14	José Romero Urtasun "JOSETXO"		25/2/77	D	6	(3)	
12	Juan Francisco Torres Belén "JUANFRAN"		9/1/85	M	18		1
18	Enrique "KIKE" SOLA Clemente		25/2/86	A	12	(4)	7
9	Dejan LEKIĆ	SRB	7/6/85	A	5	(22)	2
5	Manuel Ortiz Toribio "LOLO"		22/8/84	M	23	(4)	2
4	MIGUEL FLAÑO Bezunartea		19/8/84	D	28	(2)	2
3	Ignacio MONREAL Eraso		26/2/86	D	31		1
6	Javad NEKOUNAM	IRN	7/9/80	M	26		6
2	NELSON Augusto Tomar Marcos	POR	10/6/83	D	25	(4)	1
15	OIER Sanjurjo Mata		25/5/86	D	2	(1)	
11	Walter Gerardo PANDIANI Urquiza	URU	27/4/76	A	13	(8)	3
10	Francisco PUÑAL Martínez		6/9/75	M	32	(1)	
1	RICARDO López Felipe		30/12/71	G	38		
22	Roberto López Esquiroz "RÚPER"		4/6/87	M		(4)	
23	SERGIO Fernández González		23/5/77	D	22		2
8	Masoud Soleimani SHOJAEI	IRN	9/6/84	M	14	(4)	2
20	Fernando SORIANO Marcos		24/9/79	M	23	(7)	2
30	David TIMOR Copoví		17/1/89	M		(1)	
21	Krisztián VADÓCZ	HUN	30/5/85	M	12	(19)	3

REAL RACING CLUB

Coach – Miguel Ángel Portugal; (8/2/11) Marcelino García Toral

Founded – 1913

Stadium – El Sardinero (22,222)

2010				
29/8	Barcelona	h	0-3	
11/9	Valencia	a	0-1	
19/9	Zaragoza	h	2-0	*Henrique, Ariel*
23/9	Sevilla	a	1-1	*Pinillos*
26/9	Getafe	h	0-1	
3/10	Villarreal	a	0-2	
17/10	Almería	h	1-0	*Munitis*
23/10	Real Madrid	a	1-6	*Rosenberg*
31/10	Osasuna	h	4-1	*Bakircioglü, Rosenberg 2, Torrejón*
6/11	Real Sociedad	a	0-1	
14/11	Espanyol	h	0-0	
21/11	Levante	a	1-3	*Lacen*
28/11	Deportivo	h	1-0	*Rosenberg*
5/12	Málaga	a	1-4	*Rosenberg*
12/12	Mallorca	a	1-0	*Serrano*
20/12	Hércules	h	0-0	
2011				
3/1	Atlético	a	0-0	
9/1	Sporting	h	1-1	*og (Arnolin)*
15/1	Athletic	a	1-2	*Iván Bolado*
22/1	Barcelona	a	0-3	

31/1	Valencia	h	1-1	*Ariel*
5/2	Zaragoza	a	1-1	*Christian Fernández*
12/2	Sevilla	h	3-2	*Christian Fernández, og (Rakitić), Arana*
20/2	Getafe	a	1-0	*Pinillos (p)*
27/2	Villarreal	h	2-2	*Ariel, Giovani*
3/3	Almería	a	1-1	*Colsa*
6/3	Real Madrid	h	1-3	*Bakircioglü*
13/3	Osasuna	a	1-3	*Rosenberg*
20/3	Real Sociedad	h	2-1	*Bakircioglü, Giovani*
3/4	Espanyol	a	2-1	*Colsa, Giovani*
10/4	Levante	h	1-1	*og (Nano)*
17/4	Deportivo	a	0-2	
24/4	Málaga	h	1-2	*Rosenberg*
1/5	Mallorca	h	2-0	*Rosenberg, Bakircioglü*
7/5	Hércules	a	3-2	*Giovani 2, Henrique*
10/5	Atlético	h	2-1	*Bakircioglü, Rosenberg*
15/5	Sporting	a	1-2	*Christian Fernández*
21/5	Athletic	h	1-2	*Bakircioglü*

No	Name	Nat	DoB	Pos	Aps	(s)	Gls
23	ADRIÁN González Morales		25/5/88	M	16	(7)	
33	ÁLVARO González Soberón		8/1/90	D	3		
17	Manuel Jesús ARANA Rodríguez		3/12/84	M	5	(9)	1
22	ARIEL Geraldo Nahuelpán Ostén	ARG	15/10/87	A	15	(15)	3
16	Kennedy BAKIRCIOGLÜ	SWE	2/11/80	A	30	(2)	6
3	CHRISTIAN FERNÁNDEZ Salas		15/10/85	D	13	(5)	3
6	Domingo CISMA González		9/2/82	D	27	(5)	
8	Gonzalo COLSA Albendea		2/4/79	M	30	(1)	2
21	Papa Kouli DIOP	SEN	19/3/86	M	13	(6)	
18	EDUardo BEDIA Peláez		23/3/89	M		(6)	
15	FRANCISco Jesús Pérez Malia		17/12/81	D	20	(4)	
17	GIOVANI dos Santos Ramírez	MEX	11/5/89	M	9	(7)	5
2	HENRIQUE Adriano Buss	BRA	14/10/86	D	35		2
9	IVÁN BOLADO Palacios		3/7/89	A	7	(12)	1
5	Mehdi LACEN	ALG	15/5/84	M	24	(9)	1
30	Julián LUQUE Conde		27/3/92	A	1	(6)	
25	MARIO Fernández Cuesta		30/4/88	G	1		
10	Pedro Manuel MUNITIS Álvarez		19/6/75	M	33	(3)	1
25	OSMAR Barba Ibáñez		8/6/88	D	2	(2)	
14	Pablo PINILLOS Caro		9/7/74	D	19	(1)	2
24	Waldo Alonso PONCE Carrizo	CHI	4/12/82	D	2		
28	RAMÓN ARCAS Cárdenas		25/1/91	M	1		
12	Markus ROSENBERG	SWE	27/9/82	A	29	(4)	9
11	Óscar SERRANO Rodríguez		30/9/81	M		(4)	1
32	Luis Alberto Díez Ocerín "TATO"		9/7/92	D	1	(1)	
7	Mohamed TCHITÉ	COD	31/1/84	A	1		
13	Antonio Rodríguez Martínez "TOÑO"		17/12/79	G	37		
19	Marc TORREJÓN Moya		18/2/86	D	36		1
20	Alexandros TZIOLIS	GRE	13/2/85	M	8	(2)	

REAL MADRID CF

Coach – José Mourinho (POR)

Founded – 1902

Stadium – Santiago Bernabeu (80,354)

MAJOR HONOURS: European Champion Clubs' Cup/UEFA Champions League – (9) 1956, 1957, 1958, 1959, 1960, 1966, 1998, 2000, 2002;
UEFA Cup – (2) 1985, 1986; UEFA Super Cup – (1) 2002;
World Club Cup – (3) 1960, 1998, 2002;
Spanish League – (31) 1932, 1933, 1954, 1955, 1957, 1958, 1961, 1962, 1963, 1964, 1965, 1967, 1968, 1969, 1972, 1975, 1976, 1978, 1979, 1980, 1986, 1987, 1988, 1989, 1990, 1995, 1997, 2001, 2003, 2007, 2008;
Spanish Cup – (18) 1905, 1906, 1907, 1908, 1917, 1934, 1936, 1946, 1947, 1962, 1970, 1974, 1975, 1980, 1982, 1989, 1993, 2011.

2010				
29/8	Mallorca	a	0-0	
11/9	Osasuna	h	1-0	*Ricardo Carvalho*
18/9	Real Sociedad	a	2-1	*Di María, Pepe*
21/9	Espanyol	h	3-0	*Cristiano Ronaldo (p), Higuaín, Benzema*
25/9	Levante	a	0-0	
3/10	Deportivo	h	6-1	*Cristiano Ronaldo 2, Özil, Di María, Higuaín, og (Zé Castro)*
16/10	Málaga	a	4-1	*Higuaín 2, Cristiano Ronaldo 2 (1p)*
23/10	Racing	h	6-1	*Higuaín, Cristiano Ronaldo 4 (1p), Özil*
30/10	Hércules	a	3-1	*Di María, Cristiano Ronaldo 2*
7/11	Atlético	h	2-0	*Ricardo Carvalho, Özil*
14/11	Sporting	a	1-0	*Higuaín*
20/11	Athletic	h	5-1	*Higuaín, Cristiano Ronaldo 3 (1p), Sergio Ramos (p)*
29/11	Barcelona	a	0-5	
4/12	Valencia	h	2-0	*Cristiano Ronaldo 2*
12/12	Zaragoza	a	3-1	*Özil, Cristiano Ronaldo, Di María*
19/12	Sevilla	h	1-0	*Di María*
2011				
3/1	Getafe	a	3-2	*Cristiano Ronaldo 2 (1p), Özil*
9/1	Villarreal	h	4-2	*Cristiano Ronaldo 3, Kaká*
16/1	Almería	a	1-1	*Granero*
23/1	Mallorca	h	1-0	*Benzema*
30/1	Osasuna	a	0-1	
6/2	Real Sociedad	h	4-1	*Kaká, Cristiano Ronaldo 2, Adebayor*
13/2	Espanyol	a	1-0	*Marcelo*
19/2	Levante	h	2-0	*Benzema, Ricardo Carvalho*
26/2	Deportivo	a	0-0	
3/3	Málaga	h	7-0	*Benzema 2, Di María, Marcelo, Cristiano Ronaldo 3 (1p)*
6/3	Racing	a	3-1	*Adebayor, Benzema 2*
12/3	Hércules	h	2-0	*Benzema 2*
19/3	Atlético	a	2-1	*Benzema, Özil*
2/4	Sporting	h	0-1	
9/4	Athletic	a	3-0	*Kaká 2 (2p), Cristiano Ronaldo*
16/4	Barcelona	h	1-1	*Cristiano Ronaldo (p)*
23/4	Valencia	a	6-3	*Benzema, Higuaín 3, Kaká 2*
30/4	Zaragoza	h	2-3	*Sergio Ramos, Benzema*
7/5	Sevilla	a	6-2	*Sergio Ramos, Cristiano Ronaldo 4, Kaká*
10/5	Getafe	h	4-0	*Cristiano Ronaldo 3 (1p), Benzema*
15/5	Villarreal	a	3-1	*Marcelo, Cristiano Ronaldo 2*
21/5	Almería	h	8-1	*Cristiano Ronaldo 2, Adebayor 3, Benzema 2, Joselu*

No	Name	Nat	DoB	Pos	Aps	(s)	Gls
13	Antonio ADÁN Garrido		13/5/87	G	2	(1)	
6	Emmanuel ADEBAYOR	TOG	26/2/84	A	6	(8)	5
18	Raúl ALBIOL Tortajada		4/9/85	D	13	(7)	
30	Alejandro Fernández Iglesias "ÁLEX"		15/10/92	M		(1)	
17	Álvaro ARBELOA Coca		17/1/83	D	20	(6)	
9	Karim BENZEMA	FRA	19/12/87	A	20	(13)	15
16	Sergio CANALES Madrazo		16/2/91	M	3	(7)	
1	Iker CASILLAS Fernández		20/5/81	G	35		
7	CRISTIANO RONALDO dos Santos Aveiro	POR	5/2/85	A	32	(2)	40
22	Ángel Fabián DI MARÍA	ARG	14/2/88	A	29	(6)	6
10	Lassana DIARRA	FRA	10/3/85	M	19	(7)	
6	Mahamadou DIARRA	MLI	18/5/81	M		(3)	
25	Jerzy DUDEK	POL	23/3/73	G	1		
5	Fernando Rubén GAGO	ARG	10/4/86	M	1	(3)	
19	Ezequiel Marcelo GARAY	ARG	10/10/86	D	4	(1)	
11	Esteban GRANERO Molina		2/7/87	M	8	(11)	1
20	Gonzalo Gerardo HIGUAÍN	ARG	10/12/87	A	16	(1)	10
28	JESÚS FERNÁNDEZ Collado		11/6/88	G		(1)	
39	José Luis Sanmartín Mato "JOSELU"		27/3/90	A		(1)	1
26	JUAN CARLOS Pérez López		30/3/90	A		(1)	
8	Ricardo Izecson dos Santos Leite "KAKÁ"	BRA	22/4/82	M	11	(3)	7
24	Sami KHEDIRA	GER	4/4/87	M	20	(5)	
12	MARCELO Vieira da Silva Júnior	BRA	12/5/88	D	31	(1)	3
40	Tomás MEJÍAS Osorio		30/1/89	G		(1)	

9	Álvaro Borja MORATA Martín		23/10/92	A		(1)	
5	José Ignacio "NACHO" Fernández Iglesias		18/1/90	M	2		
9	Mesut ÖZIL	GER	15/10/88	M	30	(6)	6
1	PEDRO LEÓN Sánchez Gil		24/11/86	M		(6)	
	Képler Laveran Lima Ferreira "PEPE"	POR	26/2/83	D	25	(1)	1
	RICARDO Alberto Silveira de CARVALHO	POR	18/5/78	D	31	(2)	3
	SERGIO RAMOS García		30/3/86	D	30	(1)	3
4	XABIer ALONSO Olano		25/11/81	M	29	(5)	

REAL SOCIEDAD DE FÚTBOL

Coach – Martín Lasarte (URU)

Founded – 1909

Stadium – Anoeta (32,000)

MAJOR HONOURS: Spanish League – (2) 1981, 1982;
Spanish Cup – (2) 1909, 1987.

2010				
29/8	Villarreal	h	1-0	*Xabi Prieto*
13/9	Almería	a	2-2	*Tamudo, Sutil*
18/9	Real Madrid	h	1-2	*Tamudo*
21/9	Osasuna	a	1-3	*Tamudo*
26/9	Mallorca	a	0-2	
2/10	Espanyol	h	1-0	*og (Forlín)*
17/10	Levante	a	1-2	*Sarpong*
25/10	Deportivo	h	3-0	*Llorente, Griezmann, Agirretxe*
31/10	Málaga	a	2-1	*Griezmann, Llorente*
6/11	Racing	h	1-0	*Llorente*
14/11	Hércules	a	1-2	*Griezmann*
21/11	Atlético	h	2-4	*og (Ujfaluši), Diego Rivas*
28/11	Sporting	a	3-1	*Xabi Prieto, Zurutuza, Aranburu*
5/12	Athletic	h	2-0	*Xabi Prieto (p), og (San José)*
12/12	Barcelona	a	0-5	
18/12	Valencia	h	1-2	*Xabi Prieto (p)*
2011				
3/1	Zaragoza	a	1-2	*Xabi Prieto*
8/1	Sevilla	h	2-3	*Diego Rivas, Llorente*
15/1	Getafe	a	4-0	*Xabi Prieto (p), Griezmann, Aranburu 2*
23/1	Villarreal	a	1-2	*Aranburu*
29/1	Almería	h	2-0	*Ansotegi, Tamudo*
6/2	Real Madrid	a	1-4	*og (Arbeloa)*
13/2	Osasuna	h	1-0	*Tamudo*
21/2	Mallorca	h	1-0	*Tamudo*
26/2	Espanyol	a	1-4	*Estrada*
2/3	Levante	h	1-1	*Zurutuza*
7/3	Deportivo	a	1-2	*Agirretxe*
13/3	Málaga	h	0-2	
20/3	Racing	a	1-2	*Griezmann*
3/4	Hércules	h	1-3	*Ifrán*
10/4	Atlético	a	0-3	
17/4	Sporting	h	2-1	*Griezmann 2*
23/4	Athletic	a	1-2	*og (Javi Martínez)*
30/4	Barcelona	h	2-1	*Ifrán, Xabi Prieto (p)*
7/5	Valencia	a	0-3	
11/5	Zaragoza	h	2-1	*Tamudo, Aranburu*
15/5	Sevilla	a	1-3	*Agirretxe*
21/5	Getafe	h	1-1	*Sutil*

No	Name	Nat	DoB	Pos	Aps	(s)	Gls
9	Imanol AGIRRETXE Arruti		24/2/87	A	1	(10)	3
15	Ion ANSOTEGI Gorostola		13/7/82	D	32		1
11	Mikel ARANBURU Eizagirre		18/2/79	M	27	(5)	5
1	Claudio Andrés BRAVO Muñoz	CHI	13/4/83	G	38		
2	CARLOS MARTÍNEZ Díez		9/4/86	D	25		
24	Alberto DE LA BELLA Madueño		2/12/85	D	28	(2)	
16	Vadim DEMIDOV	NOR	10/10/86	D	12	(1)	
19	DIEGO RIVAS Gutiérrez		27/4/80	M	31	(1)	2
4	Gorka ELUSTONDO Urkola		18/3/87	M	13	(5)	
22	Daniel ESTRADA Agirrezabalaga		3/1/87	M	18	(1)	1
7	Antoine GRIEZMANN	FRA	21/3/91	A	34	(3)	7
21	Diego IFRÁN Sala	URU	8/6/87	A	3	(7)	2
26	Asier ILLARRAMENDI Andonegui		8/3/90	M	2	(1)	
6	Mikel LABAKA Zuriarrain		10/8/80	D	9	(5)	
8	Joseba LLORENTE Echarri		24/11/79	A	15	(3)	4
5	MARKEL BERGARA Larrañaga		5/5/85	M	9	(10)	
3	MIKEL GONZÁLEZ Martínez		24/9/85	D	30	(2)	
14	Jeffrey SARPONG	NED	3/8/88	M	1	(15)	1
23	Francisco SUTIL Tirado		21/12/84	M	4	(13)	2
23	Raúl TAMUDO Montero		19/10/77	A	20	(11)	7
18	Borja VIGUERA Manzanares		26/3/87	A		(5)	
10	XABIer PRIETO Argarate		29/8/83	M	36	(1)	7
17	David ZURUTUZA Veillet	FRA	19/7/86	M	30	(6)	2

SEVILLA FC

Coach – Antonio Álvarez; (27/9/10) Gregorio Manzano

Founded – 1905

Stadium – Ramón Sánchez Pizjuán (45,500)

MAJOR HONOURS: UEFA Cup – (2) 2006, 2007;
UEFA Super Cup – (1) 2006;
Spanish League – (1) 1946;
Spanish Cup – (5) 1935, 1939, 1948, 2007, 2010.

2010				
28/8	Levante	a	4-1	*Konko 2, Negredo (p), Renato*
12/9	Deportivo	h	0-0	
19/9	Málaga	a	2-1	*Alfaro, Cáceres*
23/9	Racing	h	1-1	*Negredo (p)*
26/9	Hércules	a	0-2	
3/10	Atlético	h	3-1	*Negredo, Perotti, Kanouté*
17/10	Sporting	a	0-2	
24/10	Athletic	h	4-3	*Luís Fabiano 2, Kanouté 2 (2p)*
30/10	Barcelona	a	0-5	
8/11	Valencia	h	2-0	*Negredo, Alfaro*
14/11	Zaragoza	a	2-1	*Luís Fabiano, Negredo*
21/11	Mallorca	h	1-2	*Luís Fabiano*
27/11	Getafe	h	1-3	*Kanouté*
5/12	Villarreal	a	0-1	
11/12	Almería	h	1-3	*Kanouté*
19/12	Real Madrid	a	0-1	
2011				
2/1	Osasuna	h	1-0	*Kanouté*
8/1	Real Sociedad	a	3-2	*Kanouté 2, Luís Fabiano*
15/1	Espanyol	h	1-2	*Negredo*
22/1	Levante	h	4-1	*Luís Fabiano 3 (1p), Escudé*
29/1	Deportivo	a	3-3	*Negredo 2, Escudé*
6/2	Málaga	h	0-0	
12/2	Racing	a	2-3	*Fazio, Luís Fabiano (p)*
20/2	Hércules	h	1-0	*Rakitić*
26/2	Atlético	a	2-2	*Negredo, Rakitić*
1/3	Sporting	h	3-0	*Luís Fabiano (p), Perotti, Negredo*
6/3	Athletic	a	0-2	
13/3	Barcelona	h	1-1	*Jesús Navas*
20/3	Valencia	a	1-0	*Rakitić*
3/4	Zaragoza	h	3-1	*Perotti, Kanouté (p), Negredo (p)*
9/4	Mallorca	a	2-2	*Negredo (p), Rakitić*
16/4	Getafe	a	0-1	
24/4	Villarreal	h	3-2	*Rakitić, Negredo, Romaric*
1/5	Almería	a	1-0	*Renato*
7/5	Real Madrid	h	2-6	*Negredo 2*
11/5	Osasuna	a	2-3	*Negredo 2*
15/5	Real Sociedad	h	3-1	*Kanouté 2, Negredo*
21/5	Espanyol	a	3-2	*Negredo 2, Kanouté*

No	Name	Nat	DoB	Pos	Aps	(s)	Gls
21	Lautaro Germán ACOSTA	ARG	14/3/88	M	2	(8)	
23	ALEXIS Ruano Delgado		4/8/85	D	21		
15	Alejandro ALFARO Ligero		23/11/86	M	8	(12)	2
4	José Martín CÁCERES Silva	URU	7/4/87	D	24	(1)	1
19	Luca CIGARINI	ITA	20/6/86	M	5	(1)	
20	Mouhamadou DABO	FRA	28/11/86	D	21	(3)	
16	DIEGO Ángel CAPEL Trinidad		16/2/88	A	17	(10)	
3	Ivica DRAGUTINOVIĆ	SRB	13/11/75	D		(2)	
14	Julien ESCUDÉ	FRA	17/8/79	D	27	(1)	2
34	Bernardo José ESPINOSA Zúñiga	COL	11/7/89	D	1		

No	Name	Nat	DoB	Pos	Aps	(s)	Gls
2	Federico Julián FAZIO	ARG	17/3/87	D	17	(2)	1
5	FERNANDO NAVARRO Corbacho		25/6/82	D	30		
25	Tiberio GUARENTE	ITA	1/11/85	M	3	(4)	
13	JAVIer VARAS Herrera		10/9/82	G	19	(2)	
7	JESÚS NAVAS González		21/11/85	M	15		1
30	JOSÉ CARLOS Fernández Vázquez		17/7/87	M	2	(4)	
12	Frédéric KANOUTÉ	MLI	2/9/77	A	19	(9)	12
22	Arouna KONÉ	CIV	11/11/83	A		(1)	
24	Abdoulay KONKO	FRA	9/3/84	D	9	(2)	2
26	LUIS ALBERTO Romero Alconchel		28/9/92	M	1	(1)	
10	LUÍS FABIANO Clemente	BRA	8/11/80	A	16	(5)	10
27	Antonio LUNA Rodríguez		17/3/91	D	2		
24	Gary Alexis MEDEL Soto	CHI	3/8/87	M	15		
18	Álvaro NEGREDO Sánchez		20/8/85	M	29	(9)	20
1	Andrés PALOP Cervera		22/10/73	G	19		
9	Diego PEROTTI	ARG	26/7/88	A	27	(4)	3
25	Ivan RAKITIĆ	CRO	10/3/88	M	13		5
11	RENATO Dirnei Florencio Santos	BRA	15/5/79	M	12	(12)	2
31	RODRIgo Ríos Lozano		6/6/90	A	2	(3)	
6	Christian Koffi Ndri "ROMARIC"	CIV	4/6/83	M	19	(7)	1
17	SERGIO SÁNCHEZ Ortega		3/4/86	D	6	(1)	
8	Didier ZOKORA	CIV	14/12/80	M	17	(6)	

REAL SPORTING DE GIJÓN

Coach – Manuel Preciado

Founded – 1905

Stadium – El Molinón (24,000)

2010				
30/8	Atlético	a	0-4	
12/9	Mallorca	h	2-0	*Botía, Diego Castro (p)*
18/9	Athletic	h	2-2	*De las Cuevas, Sangoy*
22/9	Barcelona	a	0-1	
25/9	Valencia	h	0-2	
2/10	Zaragoza	a	2-2	*og (Obradović), Diego Castro (p)*
17/10	Sevilla	h	2-0	*Sangoy, Diego Castro*
24/10	Getafe	a	0-3	
31/10	Villarreal	h	1-1	*Diego Castro (p)*
7/11	Almería	a	1-1	*Nacho Novo*
14/11	Real Madrid	h	0-1	
21/11	Osasuna	a	0-1	
28/11	Real Sociedad	h	1-3	*Arnolin*
5/12	Espanyol	a	0-1	
12/12	Levante	h	1-1	*Eguren*
18/12	Deportivo	a	1-1	*Diego Castro*
2011				
2/1	Málaga	h	1-2	*Diego Castro (p)*
9/1	Racing	a	1-1	*Diego Castro*
15/1	Hércules	h	2-0	*Barral, Nacho Cases*
23/1	Atlético	h	1-0	*Barral*
29/1	Mallorca	a	4-0	*Diego Castro, og (Kevin), André Castro, Nacho Novo*
5/2	Athletic	a	0-3	
12/2	Barcelona	h	1-1	*Barral*
19/2	Valencia	a	0-0	
26/2	Zaragoza	h	0-0	
1/3	Sevilla	a	0-3	
6/3	Getafe	h	2-0	*De las Cuevas, André Castro*
13/3	Villarreal	a	1-1	*Diego Castro (p)*
20/3	Almería	h	1-0	*De las Cuevas*
2/4	Real Madrid	a	1-0	*De las Cuevas*
10/4	Osasuna	h	1-0	*Barral*
17/4	Real Sociedad	a	1-2	*De las Cuevas*
24/4	Espanyol	h	1-0	*Nacho Novo*
1/5	Levante	a	0-0	
7/5	Deportivo	h	2-2	*Ayoze (p), Barral (p)*
10/5	Málaga	a	0-2	
15/5	Racing	h	2-1	*De las Cuevas, Nacho Novo*
21/5	Hércules	a	0-0	

No	Name	Nat	DoB	Pos	Aps	(s)	Gls
16	ANDRÉ CASTRO Pereira	POR	2/4/88	M	11	(5)	2
12	Grégory ARNOLIN	FRA	10/11/80	D	23		1
7	AYOZE García Pérez		22/11/85	D	6	(7)	1
23	David BARRAL Torres		10/5/83	A	24	(10)	5
9	Mate BILIĆ	CRO	23/10/80	A	3	(15)	
2	Alberto Tomás BOTÍA Rabasco		27/1/89	D	27	(1)	1
15	Roberto CANELLA Suárez		7/2/88	D	15	(2)	
6	CARMELO González Jiménez		9/7/83	M	9	(9)	
13	Iván CUÉLLAR Sacristán		27/5/84	G	13		
20	Miguel Angel DE LAS CUEVAS Barberá		19/6/86	M	30	(7)	6
17	DIEGO CASTRO Jiménez		2/7/82	A	26	(2)	9
19	Sebastián EGUREN Ledesma	URU	8/1/81	M	27	(3)	1
14	IVÁN HERNÁNDEZ Soto		27/2/80	D	24	(1)	
25	JAVIer POVES Gómez		28/9/86	D		(1)	
4	JORGE García Torre		13/1/84	D	2	(3)	
3	JOSÉ ÁNGEL Valdés Díaz		5/9/89	M	23	(3)	
1	JUAN PABLO Colinas Ferreras		2/9/78	G	24	(1)	
21	Marcos LANDEIRA Álvarez		2/5/87	A		(1)	
11	Alberto LORA Ramos		25/3/87	D	35	(1)	
18	LUIS MORÁN Sánchez		26/7/87	M	6	(9)	
24	Sergio MATABUENA Delgado		12/2/79	M	3	(1)	
30	Guillermo MÉNDEZ Pereiro		31/1/92	D		(1)	
28	Juan MUÑIZ Gallego		14/3/92	M		(1)	
31	Ignacio "NACHO" CASES Mora		22/12/87	M	17	(1)	1
10	Ignacio "NACHO" Javier Gómez NOVO		26/3/79	A	15	(15)	4
16	Cristian PORTILLA Rodríguez		28/8/88	M		(1)	
27	RAÚL Domínguez Carral		1/11/86	G	1		
5	Alberto RIVERA Pizarro		18/2/78	M	30		
8	Gastón Maximiliano SANGOY	ARG	5/10/84	A	14	(5)	2
22	Rafael SASTRE Reus		22/10/78	D	7	(1)	
26	SERGIO ÁLVAREZ Díaz		23/1/92	M	3	(5)	

VALENCIA CF

Coach – Unai Emery

Founded – 1919

Stadium – Mestalla (52,000)

MAJOR HONOURS: UEFA Cup Winners' Cup – (1) 1980; UEFA Cup – (1) 2004; Inter Cities Fairs Cup – (2) 1962, 1963; UEFA Super Cup – (2) 1980, 2004; Spanish League – (6) 1942, 1944, 1947, 1971, 2002, 2004; Spanish Cup – (7) 1941, 1949, 1954, 1967, 1979, 1999, 2008.

2010				
28/8	Málaga	a	3-1	*Aduriz, Joaquín 2*
11/9	Racing	h	1-0	*Maduro*
19/9	Hércules	a	2-1	*Mata, Pablo Hernández*
22/9	Atlético	h	1-1	*Aduriz*
25/9	Sporting	a	2-0	*Mehmet, Soldado*
2/10	Athletic	h	2-1	*Aduriz, Vicente*
16/10	Barcelona	a	1-2	*Pablo Hernández*
23/10	Mallorca	h	1-2	*Soldado (p)*
30/10	Zaragoza	h	1-1	*og (Lanzaro)*
8/11	Sevilla	a	0-2	
14/11	Getafe	h	2-0	*Tino Costa, David Navarro*
20/11	Villarreal	a	1-1	*og (Gonzalo)*
28/11	Almería	h	2-1	*Soldado 2*
4/12	Real Madrid	a	0-2	
13/12	Osasuna	h	3-3	*Soldado, Stankevičius, Aduriz*
18/12	Real Sociedad	a	2-1	*Tino Costa, Aduriz*
2011				
2/1	Espanyol	h	2-1	*Aduriz, Mata*
9/1	Levante	a	1-0	*Mata*
16/1	Deportivo	h	2-0	*Mathieu, Pablo Hernández*
22/1	Málaga	h	4-3	*Mata (p), Soldado, Éver Banega, Aduriz*
31/1	Racing	a	1-1	*Tino Costa*
6/2	Hércules	h	2-0	*Aduriz, Tino Costa*
12/2	Atlético	a	2-1	*Joaquín 2*
19/2	Sporting	h	0-0	

7/2	Athletic	a	2-1	*Mata, Jonas*
3	Barcelona	h	0-1	
3	Mallorca	a	2-1	*Pablo Hernández 2*
2/3	Zaragoza	a	0-4	
0/3	Sevilla	h	0-1	
/4	Getafe	a	4-2	*Soldado 4*
0/4	Villarreal	h	5-0	*Soldado 2, Mata 2, Éver Banega*
6/4	Almería	a	3-0	*Soldado, Stankevičius, Jordi Alba*
3/4	Real Madrid	h	3-6	*Soldado, Jonas, Jordi Alba*
/5	Osasuna	a	0-1	
/5	Real Sociedad	h	3-0	*Soldado 2, Jonas*
1/5	Espanyol	a	2-2	*Soldado, Mata*
5/5	Levante	h	0-0	
21/5	Deportivo	a	2-0	*Aduriz, Soldado*

No	Name	Nat	DoB	Pos	Aps	(s)	Gls
1	Aritz ADURIZ Zubeldia		11/2/81	A	20	(9)	9
6	David ALBELDA Aliques		1/9/77	M	12	(4)	
2	BRUNO Saltor Grau		1/10/80	D	17	(2)	
1	CÉSAR SÁNCHEZ Domínguez		2/9/71	G	15		
4	DAVID NAVARRO Pedrós		25/5/80	D	16	(1)	1
15	Ángel DEALBERT Ibáñez		1/1/83	D	10	(4)	
3	Alejandro Damián DOMÍNGUEZ	ARG	10/6/81	M	3	(6)	
21	ÉVER Maximiliano BANEGA	ARG	29/6/88	M	19	(9)	2
12	Sofiane FEGHOULI	FRA	26/12/89	M		(3)	
13	Vicente GUAITA Panadero		18/2/87	G	19	(2)	
26	Francisco Alarcón Suárez "ISCO"		21/4/92	A		(4)	
7	JOAQUÍN Sánchez Rodríguez		21/7/81	A	24	(6)	4
18	JONAS Gonçalves Oliveira	BRA	1/4/84	A	8	(5)	3
28	JORGE ALBA Ramos		21/3/89	A	14	(13)	2
3	Hedwiges MADURO	NED	13/2/85	M	17	(1)	1
18	MANUEL Henrique Tavares FERNANDES	POR	5/2/86	M	5	(2)	
10	Juan Manuel MATA García		28/4/88	M	31	(2)	8
22	Jérémy MATHIEU	FRA	29/10/83	D	27	(2)	1
5	MEHMET Topal	TUR	3/3/86	M	21	(2)	1
23	Luís MIGUEL Brito García Monteiro	POR	4/1/80	D	20	(4)	
25	Miguel Ánge MOYÁ Rumbo		2/4/84	G	4		
19	PABLO HERNÁNDEZ Domínguez		11/4/85	M	20	(7)	5
20	RICARDO Miguel Moreira da COSTA	POR	16/5/81	D	29		
9	Roberto SOLDADO Rillo		27/5/85	A	26	(8)	18
17	Marius STANKEVIČIUS	LTU	15/7/81	D	19	(2)	2
24	Alberto Facundo "TINO" COSTA	ARG	9/1/85	M	17	(7)	4
14	VICENTE Rodríguez Guillén		16/7/81	M	5	(9)	1

VILLARREAL CF

Coach – Juan Carlos Garrido

Founded – 1923

Stadium – El Madrigal (25,400)

2010				
29/8	Real Sociedad	a	0-1	
12/9	Espanyol	h	4-0	*Rossi 2 (1p), Borja Valero, Nilmar*
19/9	Levante	a	2-1	*Nilmar 2*
23/9	Deportivo	h	1-0	*Nilmar*
27/9	Málaga	a	3-2	*Santi Cazorla 2, Rossi*
3/10	Racing	h	2-0	*Nilmar, Rossi*
18/10	Hércules	a	2-2	*Capdevila, Borja Valero*
24/10	Atlético	h	2-0	*Cani, Rossi*
31/10	Sporting	a	1-1	*Rossi (p)*
7/11	Athletic	h	4-1	*Nilmar, Santi Cazorla, Rossi, Montero*
13/11	Barcelona	a	1-3	*Nilmar*
20/11	Valencia	h	1-1	*Rossi*
27/11	Zaragoza	a	3-0	*Senna, Santi Cazorla, Nilmar*
5/12	Sevilla	h	1-0	*Nilmar*
11/12	Getafe	a	0-1	
18/12	Mallorca	h	3-1	*Santi Cazorla, Rossi (p), Nilmar*
2011				
3/1	Almería	h	2-0	*Catalá, Borja Valero*
9/1	Real Madrid	a	2-4	*Cani, Marco Ruben*
15/1	Osasuna	h	4-2	*Marco Ruben, Cani, Capdevila, Gonzalo*
23/1	Real Sociedad	h	2-1	*Rossi 2*
30/1	Espanyol	a	1-0	*Rossi*
5/2	Levante	h	0-1	
13/2	Deportivo	a	0-1	
20/2	Málaga	h	1-1	*Marco Ruben*
27/2	Racing	a	2-2	*Marco Ruben, Nilmar*
2/3	Hércules	h	1-0	*Rossi*
5/3	Atlético	a	1-3	*Rossi*
13/3	Sporting	h	1-1	*Rossi*
20/3	Athletic	a	1-0	*Marco Ruben*
2/4	Barcelona	h	0-1	
10/4	Valencia	a	0-5	
18/4	Zaragoza	h	1-0	*Rossi (p)*
24/4	Sevilla	a	2-3	*Marchena, Rossi*
1/5	Getafe	h	2-1	*Cani, Rossi*
8/5	Mallorca	a	0-0	
11/5	Almería	a	0-0	
15/5	Real Madrid	h	1-3	*Cani*
21/5	Osasuna	a	0-1	

No	Name	Nat	DoB	Pos	Aps	(s)	Gls
12	Jozy ALTIDORE	USA	6/11/89	A		(3)	
6	ÁNGEL Domingo López Ruano		10/3/81	D	18		
20	BORJA VALERO Iglesias		12/1/85	M	34	(1)	3
21	BRUNO Soriano Llido		12/6/84	M	36	(1)	
10	Rubén Gracia Calmache "CANI"		3/8/81	M	25	(9)	5
11	Joan CAPDEVILA Méndez		3/2/78	D	30	(1)	2
29	CARLOS TOMÁS Ferrer		18/5/88	D	1		
15	José Manuel CATALÁ Mazuecos		1/1/85	D	10	(6)	1
24	Cicero João de Cézare "CICINHO"	BRA	24/6/80	D		(6)	
18	CRISTÓBAL Márquez Crespo		21/4/84	M	1	(1)	
13	DIEGO LÓPEZ Rodríguez		3/11/81	G	38		
2	GONZALO Javier Rodríguez	ARG	10/4/84	D	20	(3)	1
3	JOAN ORIOL Gracia		5/11/86	D	1	(5)	
26	Francisco José Olivas Alba "KIKO"		21/8/88	D	2	(2)	
5	Carlos MARCHENA López		31/7/79	D	27	(1)	1
9	MARCO Gastón RUBEN Rodríguez	ARG	26/10/86	A	12	(18)	5
32	MARCOS GULLÓN Ferrera		20/2/89	M	1		
27	MARIO Gaspar Pérez Martínez		24/11/90	D	20	(2)	
17	Javier Magro MATILLA		16/8/88	M	3	(8)	
23	Jefferson Antonio MONTERO Vite	ECU	1/9/89	A		(9)	1
43	Wakaso MUBARAK	GHA	25/7/90	M	1	(10)	
4	Mateo Pablo MUSACCHIO	ARG	26/8/90	D	27	(4)	
31	Ignacio "NACHO" INSA Bohigues		9/6/89	M		(1)	
42	Nicki Bille NIELSEN	DEN	7/2/88	A		(1)	
7	NILMAR Honorato da Silva	BRA	14/7/84	A	27	(4)	11
22	Giuseppe ROSSI	ITA	1/2/87	A	35	(1)	18
8	SANTIago CAZORLA González		13/12/84	M	34	(3)	5
19	Marcos Antonio SENNA da Silva		17/7/76	M	15	(5)	1

REAL ZARAGOZA

Coach – José Aurelio Gay; (18/11/10) Javier Aguirre (MEX)

Founded – 1932

Stadium – La Romareda (34,596)

MAJOR HONOURS: UEFA Cup Winners' Cup – (1) 1995;
Inter Cities Fairs Cup – (1) 1964;
Spanish Cup – (6) 1964, 1966, 1986, 1994, 2001, 2004.

2010				
29/8	Deportivo	a	0-0	
12/9	Málaga	h	3-5	*Edmílson, Marco Pérez, Sinama-Pongolle*
19/9	Racing	a	0-2	
22/9	Hércules	h	0-0	
26/9	Atlético	a	0-1	
2/10	Sporting	h	2-2	*Sinama-Pongolle 2*
17/10	Athletic	a	1-2	*Braulio*
23/10	Barcelona	h	0-2	
30/10	Valencia	a	1-1	*Lanzaro*

7/11	Mallorca	h	3-2	*Lafita, Bertolo, Gabi (p)*
14/11	Sevilla	h	1-2	*Bertolo*
22/11	Getafe	a	1-1	*Bertolo*
27/11	Villarreal	h	0-3	
5/12	Almería	a	1-1	*Gabi (p)*
12/12	Real Madrid	h	1-3	*Gabi (p)*
19/12	Osasuna	a	0-0	
2011				
3/1	Real Sociedad	h	2-1	*Sinama-Pongolle, Braulio*
9/1	Espanyol	a	0-4	
15/1	Levante	h	1-0	*Gabi*
23/1	Deportivo	h	1-0	*Boutahar*
29/1	Málaga	a	2-1	*Bertolo, Sinama-Pongolle*
5/2	Racing	h	1-1	*Boutahar*
13/2	Hércules	a	1-2	*Braulio*
19/2	Atlético	h	0-1	
26/2	Sporting	a	0-0	
2/3	Athletic	h	2-1	*Jarošík, Uche*
5/3	Barcelona	a	0-1	
12/3	Valencia	h	4-0	*Jarošík, Ander Herrera, Gabi 2 (2p)*
19/3	Mallorca	a	0-1	
3/4	Sevilla	a	1-3	*Jarošík*
11/4	Getafe	h	2-1	*Ponzio, Bertolo*
18/4	Villarreal	a	0-1	
25/4	Almería	h	1-0	*og (Diego Alves)*
30/4	Real Madrid	a	3-2	*Lafita 2, Gabi (p)*
8/5	Osasuna	h	1-3	*Lafita*
11/5	Real Sociedad	a	1-2	*Gabi*
15/5	Espanyol	h	1-0	*Ponzio*
21/5	Levante	a	2-1	*Gabi 2*

No	Name	Nat	DoB	Pos	Aps	(s)	Gls
8	ANDER HERRERA Aguera		14/8/89	M	30	(3)	1
10	Nicolás Santiago BERTOLO	ARG	2/1/86	M	25	(11)	5
20	Saïd BOUTAHAR	NED	12/8/82	M	12	(9)	2
16	BRAULIO Nóbrega Rodríguez		18/9/85	A	12	(15)	3
4	Matteo CONTINI	ITA	16/4/80	D	24		
19	Paulo DA SILVA	PAR	1/2/80	D	10	(3)	
2	Carlos Andrés DIOGO Enseñat	URU	18/7/83	D	33		
1	Antonio DOBLAS Santana		5/8/80	G	17	(1)	
5	EDMÍLSON José Gomes Moraes	BRA	10/7/76	M	8	(4)	1
14	Gabriel Fernández Arenas "GABI"		10/7/83	M	36		10
21	Jiří JAROŠÍK	CZE	27/10/77	M	36		3
7	JORGE LÓPEZ Montaña		19/9/78	M	12	(15)	
29	KEVIN LACRUZ Coscolín		13/2/92	M	2	(1)	
17	Ángel LAFITA Castillo		7/8/84	M	22	(8)	4
6	Maurizio LANZARO	ITA	14/3/82	D	17		1
25	LEOnardo Neoren FRANCO	ARG	20/5/77	G	21	(2)	
18	MARCO Jhonnier PÉREZ Murillo	COL	18/9/90	A	3	(13)	1
15	Guirane NDAW	SEN	24/4/84	M	3	(6)	
24	Ivan OBRADOVIĆ	SRB	25/7/88	A	19	(1)	
3	Javier PAREDES Arango		5/7/82	M	16	(3)	
22	Ádám PINTÉR	HUN	12/6/88	D	4	(5)	
23	Leonardo Daniel PONZIO	ARG	29/1/82	M	30	(2)	2
11	Florent SINAMA-PONGOLLE	FRA	20/10/84	A	15	(9)	5
9	Ikechukwu UCHE	NGA	5/1/84	A	11	(3)	1

TOP GOALSCORERS 2010/11

40	CRISTIANO RONALDO (Real Madrid)
31	Lionel MESSI (Barcelona)
20	Sergio AGÜERO (Atlético) Álvaro NEGREDO (Sevilla)
18	Fernando LLORENTE (Athletic) DAVID VILLA (Barcelona) Roberto SOLDADO (Valencia) Giuseppe ROSSI (Villarreal)
15	Karim BENZEMA (Real Madrid)
14	Salomón RONDÓN (Málaga)

PROMOTED CLUBS

REAL BETIS BALOMPIÉ

Coach – José Mel
Founded – 1907
Stadium – Benito Villamarín (52,745)
MAJOR HONOURS: Spanish League – (1) 1935; Spanish Cup – (2) 1977, 2005

RAYO VALLECANO DE MADRID

Coach – José Ramón Sandoval
Founded – 1924
Stadium – Teresa Rivero (15,500)

GRANADA CF

Coach – Fabriciano González "Fabri"
Founded – 1931
Stadium – Nuevo Los Cármenes (16,212)

SECOND LEVEL FINAL TABLE 2010/11

		Pld	W	D	L	F	A	Pts
1	Real Betis Balompié	42	25	8	9	85	44	83
2	Rayo Vallecano de Madrid	42	23	10	9	73	48	79
3	FC Barcelona B	42	20	11	11	85	62	71
4	Elche CF	42	18	15	9	55	42	69
5	Granada CF	42	18	14	10	71	47	68
6	RC Celta de Vigo	42	17	16	9	62	43	67
7	Real Valladolid CF	42	19	9	14	65	51	66
8	Xerez CD	42	17	9	16	60	64	60
9	AD Alcorcón	42	17	7	18	57	52	58
10	CD Numancia	42	17	6	19	65	63	57
11	Girona FC	42	15	12	15	58	56	57
12	RC Recreativo de Huelva	42	12	20	10	44	37	56
13	FC Cartagena	42	16	8	18	48	63	56
14	SD Huesca	42	13	16	13	39	45	55
15	UD Las Palmas	42	13	15	14	56	71	54
16	Córdoba CF	42	13	13	16	58	63	52
17	Villarreal CF B	42	15	6	21	43	63	51
18	Club Gimnàstic de Tarragona	42	12	13	17	37	45	49
19	UD Salamanca	42	13	7	22	46	68	46
20	CD Tenerife	42	9	11	22	42	66	38
21	SD Ponferradina	42	5	19	18	36	63	34
22	Albacete Balompié	42	7	11	24	35	64	32

NB FC Barcelona B ineligible for promotion; Real Valladolid CF entered promotion play-offs instead.

PROMOTION PLAY-OFFS

(8/6/11 & 11/6/11)
Celta 1, Granada 0
Granada 1, Celta 0 (aet)
(1-1; Granada 5-4 on pens)

(9/6/11 & 12/6/11)
Valladolid 1, Elche 0
Elche 3, Valladolid 1
(Elche 3-2)

(15/6/11 & 18/6/11)
Granada 0, Elche 0
Elche 1, Granada 1
(1-1; Granada on away goal)

DOMESTIC CUP 2010/11

COPA DEL REY

FOURTH ROUND

(26/10/10 & 10/11/10)
Ceuta v Barcelona 0-2; 1-5 *(1-7)*
Murcia v Real Madrid 0-0; 1-5 *(1-5)*

(27/10/10 & 9/11/10)
Córdoba v Racing 2-0; 1-3 *(aet) (3-3; Córdoba on away goal)*
Valladolid v Espanyol 0-2; 1-1 *(1-3)*

(27/10/10 & 10/11/10)
Betis v Zaragoza 0-1; 2-1 *(2-2; Betis on away goals)*
Ejido v Villarreal 1-1; 0-2 *(1-3)*
Real Unión v Sevilla 0-4; 1-6 *(1-10)*
Universidad Las Palmas v Atlético 0-5; 1-1 *(1-6)*
Xerez v Levante 2-3; 2-1 *(4-4; Levante on away goals)*

(27/10/10 & 11/11/10)
Hércules v Málaga 0-0; 2-3 *(2-3)*
Logroñés v Valencia 0-3; 1-4 *(1-7)*
Mallorca v Sporting Gijón 3-1; 2-2 *(5-3)*
Portugalete v Getafe 1-1; 0-0 *(1-1; Getafe on away goal)*

(28/10/10 & 10/11/10)
Alcorcón v Athletic 0-1; 0-2 *(0-3)*
Osasuna v Deportivo 1-1; 1-2 *(2-3)*
Real Sociedad v Almería 2-3; 1-2 *(3-5)*

FIFTH ROUND

(21/12/10 & 5/1/11)
Barcelona v Athletic 0-0; 1-1 *(1-1; Barcelona on away goal)*
Córdoba v Deportivo 1-1; 1-3 *(aet) (2-4)*

(21/12/10 & 6/1/11)
Valencia v Villarreal 0-0; 2-4 *(2-4)*

(22/12/10 & 5/1/11)
Sevilla v Málaga 5-3; 3-0 *(8-3)*

(22/12/10 & 6/1/11)
Almería v Mallorca 4-3; 4-3 *(8-6)*
Atlético v Espanyol 1-0; 1-1 *(2-1)*
Betis v Getafe 1-2; 3-1 *(4-3)*
Real Madrid v Levante 8-0; 0-2 *(8-2)*

QUARTER-FINALS

(12/1/11 & 18/1/11)
Villarreal 3 *(Cani 23, Rossi 28, Marco Ruben 55)*, Sevilla 3 *(Negredo 38, 59, Alexis 88)*
Sevilla 3 *(Renato 6, Kanouté 47, Alexis 49)*, Villarreal 0 *(Sevilla 6-3)*

(12/1/11 & 19/1/11)
Barcelona 5 *(Messi 44, 62, 73, Pedro 76, Keita 83)*, Betis 0
Betis 3 *(Molina 2, 7, Arzu 45)*, Barcelona 1 *(Messi 37)*
(Barcelona 6-3)

(13/1/11 & 19/1/11)
Almería 1 *(Rindarøy 34og)*, Deportivo 0
Deportivo 2 *(Pablo Álvarez 43p, Adrián López 51)*, Almería 3 *(Corona 19, Crusat 20, Goitom 55p)*
(Almería 4-2)

(13/1/11 & 20/1/11)
Real Madrid 3 *(Sergio Ramos 14, Cristiano Ronaldo 61, Özil 90)*, Atlético 1 *(Forlán 7)*
Atlético 0, Real Madrid 1 *(Cristiano Ronaldo 22)*
(Real Madrid 4-1)

SEMI-FINALS

(26/1/11 & 2/2/11)
Sevilla 0, Real Madrid 1 *(Benzema 17)*
Real Madrid 2 *(Özil 81, Adebayor 90+2)*, Sevilla 0
(Real Madrid 3-0)

Barcelona 5 *(Messi 9, 16, David Villa 11, Pedro 30, Keita 88)*, Almería 0
Almería 0, Barcelona 3 *(Adriano 34, Thiago 55, Afellay 65)*
(Barcelona 8-0)

FINAL

(20/4/11)
Mestalla, Valencia
REAL MADRID CF 1 *(Cristiano Ronaldo 103)*
FC BARCELONA 0
(aet)
Referee – *Undiano Mallenco*
REAL MADRID – *Casillas, Arbeloa, Sergio Ramos, Ricardo Carvalho (Garay 119), Marcelo, Pepe, Xabi Alonso, Khedira (Granero 104), Özil (Adebayor 70), Cristiano Ronaldo, Di María.*
Sent off: *Di María (120).*
BARCELONA – *Pinto, Dani Alves, Piqué, Mascherano, Adriano (Maxwell 118), Xavi, Busquets (Keita 108), Iniesta, Pedro, Messi, David Villa (Afellay 105).*

CLUB COMMUNICATION 2011/12

Athletic Club

Alameda Mazarredo 23
ES-48009 Bilbao

Tel +34 94 424 0877
Fax +34 94 423 3324
Web athletic-club.net
Email prensa@athletic-club.net
Media Officer Patxi Xabier Fernández

Club Atlético de Madrid

Paseo Virgen del Puerto 67, Puerta 5
ES-28005 Madrid

Tel +34 91 366 4707
Fax +34 91 364 1448
Web clubatleticodemadrid.com
Email comunicacion@clubatleticodemadrid.com
Media Officer Enrique Ramón

FC Barcelona

Avda. Arístides Maillol s/n
ES-08028 Barcelona

Tel +34 93 496 3600
Fax +34 93 411 2219
Web fcbarcelona.cat
Email oab@fcbarcelona.cat
Media Officer José Miguel (Chemi) Teres

Real Betis Balompié

Avda. de Heliópolis s/n
ES-41012 Sevilla

Tel +34 902 191 907
Fax +34 954 614 774
Web realbetisbalompie.es
Email lourdes@realbetisbalompie.es
Media Officer Julio Jiménez Heras

RCD Espanyol

Avinguda del Baix Lobregat, 100
ES-08940 Cornellá de Llobregat (Barcelona)

Tel +34 932 927 700
Fax +34 934 254 552
Web rcdespanyol.com
Email info@rcdespanyol.com
Media Officer Rafael Ramos Escudero

Getafe CF

Avda. Teresa de Calcuta s/n
ES-28903 Getafe (Madrid)

Tel +34 91 6959 771
Fax +34 91 6811 212
Web getafecf.com
Email fsantos@getafecf.com
Media Officer Luz Monzón

Granada CF

Recogidas, 35
ES-18005 Granada

Tel +34 958 253 300
Fax +34 958 253 304
Web granadacf.es
Email marketing@granadacf.es
Media Officer Javier Fernández Rufete

Levante UD

Calle San Vicente de Paúl, 44
ES-46019 Valencia

Tel +34 96 337 9530
Fax +34 96 337 9531
Web levanteud.com
Email admon@levanteud.es
Media Officer Alberto Gil Irún

Málaga CF

Paseo de Martíricos s/n
ES-29011 Málaga

Tel +34 952 104 488
Fax +34 952 613 737
Web malagacf.es
Email m.urda@malagacf.es
Media Officer Víctor Jesús Varela Ruiz

RCD Mallorca

Camí dels Reis s/n, Estadio Son Moix
ES-07011 Palma de Mallorca

Tel +34 971 221 221
Fax +34 971 452 351
Web rcdmallorca.es
Email prensa@rcdmallorca.es
Media Officer

CA Osasuna

C/ Sadar s/n, Estadio Reyno de Navarra
ES-31006 Pamplona

Tel +34 948 152 636
Fax +34 948 151 655
Web osasuna.es
Email osasuna@osasuna.es
Media Officer Guillermo Pérez Azcona

Rayo Vallecano de Madrid

Avda. Payaso Fofó s/n
ES-28018 Madrid

Tel +34 91 478 2253
Fax +34 91 477 1754
Web rayovallecano.es
Email infoweb@rayovallecano.es
Media Officer Fernando López Gilarranz

Real Racing Club

Real Racing Club s/n
ES-39005 Santander

Tel +34 942 282 828
Fax +34 942 281 428
Web realracingclub.es
Email oficinas@realracingclub.es
Media Officer Alberto Aparicio Barba

Real Madrid CF

Avda. Concha Espina 1
ES-28036 Madrid

Tel +34 91 3984 300
Fax +34 91 3984 391
Web realmadrid.com
Email international@realmadrid.es
Media Officer Marta Santisteban López

Real Sociedad de Fútbol

Anoeta Pasealekua 1
ES-20014 San Sebastian

Tel +34 943 462 833
Fax +34 943 458 941
Web realsociedad.com
Email realsoc@realsociedad.com
Media Officer Andoni Iraola

Sevilla FC

C/Sevilla F.C., s/n, Estadio Ramón Sánchez-Pizjuán, ES-41005 Sevilla

Tel +34 902 510 011
Fax +34 954 536 061
Web sevillafc.es
Email sevillafc@sevillafc.es
Media Officer Jesús Gómez Jiménez

Real Sporting de Gijón

Camino de Mareo a Granda,
645 Mareo de Abajo
ES-33390 Gijón (Asturias)

Tel +34 98 516 7677
Fax +34 98 516 7632
Web realsporting.com
Email efmareo@realsporting.com
Media Officer José Luis Rubiera

Valencia CF

Plaza Valencia Club de Fútbol, 2
ES-46010 Valencia

Tel +34 902 011 919
Fax +34 96 337 2335
Web valenciacf.com
Email jbruixola@valenciacf.es
Media Officer Alejandro Navarro

Villarreal CF

Camino Miralcamp s/n
ES-12540 Villarreal

Tel +34 964 500 250
Fax +34 964 500 167
Web villarrealcf.es
Email futbolbase@villarrealcf.es
Media Officer Hernán Sanz

Real Zaragoza

Pabellón Multiusos, C/ Eduardo Ibarra 6
ES-50009 Zaragoza

Tel +34 976 567 777
Fax +34 976 568 863
Web realzaragoza.com
Email real@realzaragoza.com
Media Officer Rubén Ramos

SWEDEN

Suède | Schweden

Svenska Fotbollförbundet (SvFF)

COMMUNICATION

Address Råsundastadion
PO Box 1216
SE-171 23 Solna

Tel +46 8 7350900
Fax +46 8 7350901

E-mail svff@svenskfotboll.se
Website svenskfotboll.se

President Lars-Åke Lagrell
General Secretary Mikael Santoft
Media Officer Jonas Nystedt

Year of Formation 1904

National Stadium Råsundastadion, Solna (Stockholm) (36,608)

DOMESTIC COMPETITION SUMMARY 2010

ALLSVENSKAN FINAL TABLE

			Home					Away					Total						
		Pld	W	D	L	F	A	W	D	L	F	A	W	D	L	F	A	Pts	Comp
1	Malmö FF	30	13	1	1	27	7	8	3	4	32	17	21	4	5	59	24	67	UCL
2	Helsingborgs IF	30	12	2	1	27	11	8	3	4	22	15	20	5	5	49	26	65	UEL
3	Örebro SK	30	11	1	3	24	10	5	3	7	16	20	16	4	10	40	30	52	UEL
4	IF Elfsborg	30	10	4	1	37	13	2	7	6	18	27	12	11	7	55	40	47	UEL
5	Trelleborgs FF	30	9	3	3	22	16	4	2	9	17	26	13	5	12	39	42	44	
6	Mjällby AIF	30	7	6	2	21	10	4	4	7	15	19	11	10	9	36	29	43	
7	IFK Göteborg	30	6	6	3	25	12	4	4	7	17	17	10	10	10	42	29	40	
8	BK Häcken	30	6	3	6	20	22	5	4	6	20	20	11	7	12	40	42	40	UEL
9	Kalmar FF	30	6	3	6	22	22	4	7	4	14	16	10	10	10	36	38	40	
10	Djurgårdens IF	30	7	4	4	19	17	4	3	8	16	25	11	7	12	35	42	40	
11	AIK Solna	30	7	2	6	19	13	3	3	9	10	23	10	5	15	29	36	35	
12	Halmstads BK	30	7	2	6	22	17	3	3	9	9	25	10	5	15	31	42	35	
13	GAIS Göteborg	30	4	7	4	15	16	4	1	10	9	19	8	8	14	24	35	32	
14	Gefle IF	30	4	5	6	18	23	3	3	9	15	23	7	8	15	33	46	29	
15	Åtvidabergs FF	30	4	6	5	18	19	3	2	10	14	32	7	8	15	32	51	29	*Relegated*
16	IF Brommapojkarna	30	5	2	8	13	23	1	5	9	7	25	6	7	17	20	48	25	*Relegated*

Top Scorer Alexander Gerndt (Gefle/Helsingborg), 20 goals

Promoted Clubs Syrianska FC
IFK Norrköping

Cup Final Helsingborgs IF 1, Hammarby Fotboll 0

Centenary celebrations for Malmö

Sweden's Allsvenskan has become one of Europe's most openly contested national championships, and in 2010 another new plotline developed as the two teams that had contested the title the previous season – AIK Solna and IFK Göteborg – slipped from the spotlight, leaving the stage set for another captivating two-way tussle, between southern rivals Malmö FF and Helsingborgs IF.

Seventh and eighth, respectively, in 2009, the two clubs were not expected to challenge so strongly, let alone have the title race all to themselves, but that is how the season panned out as the more fancied contenders, such as AIK, Göteborg and pre-season favourites IF Elfsborg, all failed to deliver. In the case of AIK, champions and cup winners in 2009, the fall from grace was spectacular. After a miserable start – the worst by a titleholder since the Allsvenskan began in 1927 - and the departure of title-winning coach Mikael Stahre to Greek side Panionios GSS, they spent the bulk of the campaign hovering precariously close to the relegation zone and were ultimately relieved to finish as high as 11th. As for 2009 runners-up Göteborg, they dropped to seventh place after a season blighted by maddening inconsistency.

Whirlwind start

Helsingborg, newly coached by Conny Karlsson, who joined from Assyriska Föreningen, got off to a whirlwind start, winning ten of their opening 13 games and drawing the others. A virtually unbreachable defence was their chief asset, but as time went by they began to leak goals more frequently, and although they added considerably to their strike power with the mid-season acquisition of Gefle IF goal-grabber Alexander Gerndt, they soon found themselves with company at the top of the table after Malmö, coached by former Helsingborg favourite Roland Nilsson, put together a blistering summer surge of six successive wins – all without conceding a goal.

Roland Nilsson – Malmö's Swedish title-winning coach

On 15 September the two title contenders met at Malmö's glistening new Swedbank Stadion level on points. Helsingborg had won the earlier head-to-head, 2-1 in April, but this time it was the Sky Blues who took the spoils, registering their tenth home win on the trot, 2-0, to go three points clear at the top. Five days later the two teams were neck and neck again as Malmö lost to Djurgårdens IF, and as the season entered its final day, on 7 November, the only factor separating the two teams was Malmö's significantly superior goal difference.

Malmö knew that a home win against Mjällby AIF would secure the title and crown the year of the club's centenary in fitting style. Nothing, however, was guaranteed. Not only had Mjällby exceeded all expectations in their first Allsvenskan campaign for 25 years, pushing even for a European place; they had also proved to be a particularly savage bête noire for Malmö, beating them 4-2 in the league in

May and 4-1 in the Swedish Cup in July. But on their day of days Malmö did not let their supporters down. Midfielder Jiloan Hamad, on his last day as a teenager, settled the nerves with a sharp 17th-minute volley before another youngster, Agon Mehmeti, doubled the advantage on the cusp of half-time with his 11th goal of the season. From that moment on Malmö freewheeled to victory and, with Helsingborg being held 0-0 at home to Kalmar FF, the Allsvenskan title – the 16th in the club's history – was duly theirs.

Sweet victory

For coach Nilsson the triumph was especially sweet. Low on achievement in his first two seasons at the club, his position was anything but secure at the start of the campaign. By the end of it, however, he was being fêted not just by Malmö fans but by football followers across the country who remembered him with great fondness from his playing days as a long-serving right-back for the Swedish national team. At the source of his success was the ability to manage and motivate a group of young players from diverse cultural backgrounds and mould them into a team that was not just hard to beat but also delivered adventurous, entertaining football.

The end-of-season balance sheet showed Malmö with the league's best attack and best defence, and although few individuals stood out from the collective, special mention was due to ten-goal striker Daniel Larsson for his all-round versatility and to the revelation of the season, 19-year-old midfield schemer Ivo Pekalski. It was also a year to remember for long-serving skipper Daniel Andersson. One of only two survivors from Malmö's previous title win in 2004 – Cameroonian left back Joseph Elanga was the other – he relinquished his familiar midfield role and reinvented himself as a classy central defender, starting all 30 matches and scoring five goals.

Second best in the Allsvenskan, Helsingborg eased their pain by winning the other major domestic trophy, the Svenska Cupen, with a 1-0 victory over second-tier Hammarby Fotball, who had knocked out four Allsvenskan sides en route to the final in their home stadium. Helsingborg's fourth victory in the competition was secured with an 80th-minute goal from 20-year-old striker Rasmus Jönsson. The youngster had been upstaged in the Helsingborg attack during the second half of the season as new signing Gerndt racked up the goals – including 11 in six home games – to take the Allsvenskan Golden Boot by a one-goal margin from another up-and-coming young Swedish striker, 22-year-old Denni Avdic of Elfsborg.

Gerndt honoured

While Gerndt was elected as the official Allsvenskan player of the year, Avdic left Elfsborg for SV Werder Bremen. Although the 2010 season had been productive for Avdic from an individual perspective, it was one of underachievement and inconsistency for his team, who finished fourth, 20 points behind the champions. Above Elfsborg in third were outsiders Örebro SK, who, with Finnish coach Sixten Boström at the helm, achieved their highest final placing for 16 years. Their reward was a place in the UEFA Europa League alongside Helsingborg, Elfsborg and – courtesy of the Respect Fair Play rankings – eighth-placed BK Häcken.

With no Swedish team having reached the group stage of the UEFA Champions League since Helsingborg in 2000/01, the international stature of the Swedish club game is in urgent need of a boost. Once again there was collective disappointment for Allsvenskan's five-strong European task force in 2010/11, with AIK falling to Rosenborg BK in the third qualifying round of the UEFA Champions League and subsequently to PFC Levski Sofia in the UEFA Europa League play-offs, where Elfsborg also perished for the

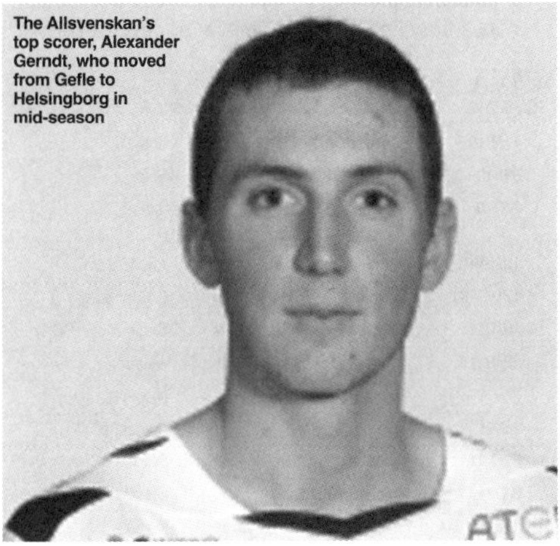

The Allsvenskan's top scorer, Alexander Gerndt, who moved from Gefle to Helsingborg in mid-season

second successive season at the hands of Italian opposition, SSC Napoli emulating the feat of S.S. Lazio 12 months earlier. The only ties won by the Swedish ensemble were against opponents from Luxembourg, Moldova, the Former Yugoslav Republic of Macedonia and the Faroe Islands.

Fortunately the end-of-season report for the Swedish national side was much more encouraging. Reinvigorated by new head coach Erik Hamrén after the team's failure to qualify even for the play-offs of the 2010 FIFA World Cup, Sweden pocketed 15 points from a possible 18 on the road to UEFA EURO 2012. The only downside was that such a handsome tally was insufficient to take top spot in their qualifying group, a position held by World Cup runners-up the Netherlands. It was the Oranje who inflicted on Sweden their only defeat – 4-1 in Amsterdam – but with the return fixture still to come, all was still to play for. Indeed, Hamrén's team stood well placed to claim the automatic qualifying place reserved for the best runners-up – assuming they could successfully negotiate trips to Hungary, San Marino and Finland before they hosted the Dutch.

Goals galore

With 20 goals scored in their first six qualifiers, Sweden could not be accused of short-changing their public. Nine of those came in June, when a 4-1 victory in Moldova was swiftly followed by a memorable 5-0 rout of Finland in the Råsundastadion. The star of the show that early-summer evening was Zlatan Ibrahimović, who, short of fitness, came off the bench to score three goals in less than half an hour. Twelve months earlier the superstar striker had indicated that he might retire from international football, but fortunately for Swedish fans he elected to carry on, and after scoring just four minutes into his comeback game – a friendly against Scotland – and striking twice against San Marino in his home town of Malmo, the 2010 Swedish Footballer of the Year capped an impressive return to national colours with that quick-fire hat-trick against the Finns.

An Italian champion with AC Milan 'Ibra' was not the only domestic title winner in the Sweden squad. Mikael Lustig set the ball rolling by helping Rosenborg to the 2010 Norwegian title before Oscar Wendt and Johan Wiland claimed Danish championship medals with FC København, Emir Bajrami triumphed in Switzerland with FC Basel 1893 and Olof Mellberg came up trumps with Olympiacos FC in Greece. Mellberg increased his number of international caps to 107 in the UEFA EURO 2012 qualifier against Finland but that was still some way behind Anders Svensson, who, in making his 116th international appearance, joined Roland Nilsson as Sweden's most-capped outfield player.

National Team

International Tournament Appearances – FIFA World Cup – (11) 1934 (2nd round), 1938 (4th), 1950 (3rd), 1958 (runners-up), 1970, 1974 (2nd phase), 1978, 1990, 1994 (3rd), 2002 (2nd round), 2006 (2nd round).
UEFA European Championship – (4) 1992 (semi-finals), 2000, 2004 (qtr-finals), 2008.

Top Five All-time Caps – Thomas Ravelli (143); Roland Nilsson & Anders Svensson (116); Björn Nordqvist (115); Niclas Alexandersson (109)

Top Five All-time Goals – Sven Rydell (49); Gunnar Nordahl (43); Henrik Larsson (37); Gunnar Gren (32); Kennet Andersson (31)

NATIONAL TEAM RESULTS 2010/11

11/8/10	Scotland	H	Solna	3-0	*Ibrahimović (4), Bajrami (39), Toivonen (56)*
3/9/10	Hungary (ECQ)	H	Solna	2-0	*Wernbloom (51, 73)*
7/9/10	San Marino (ECQ)	H	Malmo	6-0	*Ibrahimović (7, 77), Simoncini D. (11og), Simoncini A. (26og), Granqvist (51), Berg (90+2)*
12/10/10	Netherlands (ECQ)	A	Amsterdam	1-4	*Granqvist (69)*
17/11/10	Germany	H	Gothenburg	0-0	
19/1/11	Botswana	N	Cape Town (RSA)	2-1	*Gerndt (31), Svensson (74)*
22/1/11	South Africa	A	Nelspruit	1-1	*Hysén (30)*
8/2/11	Cyprus	A	Nicosia	2-0	*Hysén (26), Berg (45+1)*
9/2/11	Ukraine	N	Nicosia (CYP)	1-1	*Elmander (7) (4-5 on pens)*
29/3/11	Moldova (ECQ)	H	Solna	2-1	*Lustig (30), Larsson S. (81)*
3/6/11	Moldova (ECQ)	A	Chisinau	4-1	*Toivonen (11), Elmander (30, 58), Gerndt (88)*
7/6/11	Finland (ECQ)	H	Solna	5-0	*Källström (11), Ibrahimović (31, 35, 53), Bajrami (83)*

NATIONAL TEAM APPEARANCES 2010/11

Coach – Erik HAMRÉN	27/6/57		Sco	HUN	SMR	NED	Ger	Bot	Rsa	Cyp	Ukr	MDA	MDA	FIN	Caps	Goals
Andreas ISAKSSON	3/10/81	PSV (NED)	G	G46		G	G				G	G	G	G	84	-
Mikael LUSTIG	13/12/86	Rosenborg (NOR)	D46	D	D	D	D68				D	D	D	D	16	1
Olof MELLBERG	3/9/77	Olympiacos (GRE)	D	D	D 33*						s46		D	D	107	7
Daniel MAJSTOROVIC	5/4/77	Celtic (SCO)	D	D	D	D	D				D46		D	D	42	2
Behrang SAFARI	9/2/85	Basel (SUI)	D	D	D	D46	s68				D78				21	-
Anders SVENSSON	17/7/76	Elfsborg	M73	M33		M	M	M	M		M78		M	M	116	18
Pontus WERNBLOOM	25/6/86	AZ (NED)	M46	M	M69	M54	M75			M89		M65	s69	s81	16	2
Johan ELMANDER	27/5/81	Bolton (ENG)	M78	M49	s69	M					M60	M89	A76	A81	55	16
Ola TOIVONEN	3/7/86	PSV (NED)	M	M	M46	M79	A68			M78			M69	M25	15	3
Emir BAJRAMI	7/3/88	Twente (NED)	M64	M	M						s60	M73	s41	M	10	2
Zlatan IBRAHIMOVIĆ	3/10/81	Barcelona (ESP) /Milan (ITA)	A59	A	A82	A					A46	A		s25	69	28
Kim KÄLLSTRÖM	24/8/82	Lyon (FRA)	s46	s33	M	s54	M88				M	M	M	M	82	14
Sebastian LARSSON	6/6/85	Birmingham (ENG)	s46	s49	M	M	M				M	M	M	M89	31	1
Tobias HYSÉN	9/3/82	Göteborg	s59					M	M63	M			M41		16	2
Christian WILHELMSSON	8/12/79	Al Hilal (KSA)	s64				M				M			s89	66	5
Oscar WENDT	24/10/85	København (DEN)	s73			s46	D			D		D	D	D	16	-
Marcus BERG	17/8/86	PSV (NED)	s78		s82	s79	s68			A89					19	5
Johan WILAND	24/1/81	København (DEN)		s46	G					G					6	-
Andreas GRANQVIST	16/4/85	Groningen (NED)			s46	D	D				D	D			11	2
Rasmus ELM	17/3/88	AZ (NED)					s75			M		s65			15	1
Alexander GERNDT	14/7/86	Helsingborg					s88	A82	s63	s66		s89	s76		6	2
Pär HANSSON	22/6/86	Helsingborg						G							1	-
Adam JOHANSSON	21/2/83	Göteborg						D		D					9	-
Niklas BACKMAN	13/11/88	AIK						D	s58						2	-
Michael ALMEBÄCK	4/4/88	Örebro						D	D58	D					4	-
Pierre BENGTSSON	12/4/88	Nordsjælland (DEN) /København (DEN)						D	s73	s89					3	-
Sebastian ERIKSSON	31/1/89	Göteborg						M	s73	s89	s78				5	-
Guillermo MOLINS	26/9/88	Malmö						M72	M63						4	-
Rasmus JÖNSSON	27/1/90	Helsingborg						M72	s63						2	-
Jiloan HAMAD	6/11/90	Malmö						s72	M						2	-
Daniel LARSSON	25/1/87	Malmö						s72	A						5	-
Nordin GERZIC	9/11/83	Örebro						s82	M73						2	-
Viktor NORING	3/2/91	Trelleborg							G46						1	-
Emil SALOMONSSON	28/4/89	Halmstad							D						1	-
Marcus NILSSON	26/2/88	Helsingborg							D						1	-
Emil JOHANSSON	11/8/86	Molde (NOR)							D73						2	-
Kristoffer NORDFELDT	23/6/89	Brommapojkarna							s46						1	-
Jonas OLSSON	10/3/83	West Brom (ENG)								D					2	-
Martin OLSSON	17/5/88	Blackburn (ENG)								M66		s73			3	2
Jimmy DURMAZ	22/3/89	Malmö								s78					1	-
Viktor ELM	13/11/85	Heerenveen (NED)									s46				10	-
Fredrik STENMAN	2/6/83	Groningen (NED)									s78				3	-
Mikael ANTONSSON	31/5/81	København (DEN)										D			4	-

CLUB-BY-CLUB

AIK SOLNA

Coach – Mikael Stahre; (26/4/10) Björn Wesström; (23/6/10) Alex Miller (SCO)

Founded – 1891

Stadium – Råsundastadion (36,608)

MAJOR HONOURS: Swedish League – (11) 1900, 1901, 1911, 1914, 1916, 1923, 1932, 1937, 1992, 1998, 2009; Swedish Cup – (8) 1949, 1950, 1976, 1985, 1996, 1997, 1999, 2009.

2010

14/3	Mjällby	h	0-0	
20/3	Brommapojkarna	a	0-0	
29/3	GAIS	a	1-3	*Atta*
5/4	Örebro	h	0-1	
11/4	Gefle	a	0-1	
14/4	Halmstad	h	0-1	
19/4	Kalmar	a	3-0	*Burgič 2, Johnson*
24/4	Häcken	h	1-1	*Johnson*
29/4	Helsingborg	a	0-1	
2/5	Djurgården	h	1-2	*og (Toivio)*
6/5	Göteborg	a	0-4	
9/5	Trelleborg	h	1-0	*Antônio Flávio*
12/5	Elfsborg	a	0-4	
17/5	Åtvidaberg	h	4-1	*Burgič 3 (1p), Walker*
17/7	Malmö	h	2-0	*Pavey (p), Antônio Flávio*
24/7	Malmö	a	0-1	
31/7	Mjällby	a	0-0	
8/8	Brommapojkarna	h	2-1	*Bangura 2*
14/8	GAIS	h	1-0	*Pavey (p)*
23/8	Örebro	a	0-1	
29/8	Göteborg	h	1-2	*Bangura*
11/9	Trelleborg	a	1-4	*Lundberg*
22/9	Kalmar	h	0-1	
18/9	Häcken	a	1-0	*Lundberg*
27/9	Helsingborg	h	2-3	*Bangura, og (Nilsson)*
3/10	Djurgården	a	1-2	*Pavey (p)*
16/10	Gefle	h	2-0	*Ljubojević, Bangura*
25/10	Halmstad	a	2-1	*Lundberg, Pavey (p)*
31/10	Elfsborg	h	2-0	*Bangura, Lundberg*
7/11	Åtvidaberg	a	1-1	*Ljubojević*

No	Name	Nat	DoB	Pos	Aps	(s)	Gls
11	ANTÔNIO FLÁVIO Aires dos Santos	BRA	5/1/87	A	25	(2)	2
6	Walid ATTA		28/8/86	D	13		1
2	Niklas BACKMAN		13/11/88	D	22	(2)	
20	Mohamed BANGURA	SLE	27/7/89	A	12	(1)	6
9	Miran BURGIČ	SVN	25/9/84	A	8	(4)	5
21	Admir CATOVIC		5/9/87	M	4	(6)	
20	CLÉCIO Nascimento Santos	BRA	31/5/88	A	1	(2)	
7	Helgi Valur DANÍELSSON	ISL	13/7/81	M	14	(1)	
7	Bojan DJORDJIC		6/2/82	M	12		
33	Sebastian EGUREN	URU	8/1/81	M	7		
26	Pontus ENGBLOM		11/11/91	A	8	(9)	
23	Christoffer ERIKSSON		25/5/90	D	4	(2)	
24	Daniel GUSTAFSSON		29/8/90	M		(7)	
17	Saihou JAGNE		10/10/86	A		(4)	
4	Nils-Eric JOHANSSON		13/1/80	D	26		
30	Dulee JOHNSON	LBR	7/11/84	M	18	(2)	2
3	Per KARLSSON		2/1/86	D	21		
10	Martin KAYONGO-MUTUMBA		15/6/85	M	13		
9	Goran LJUBOJEVIĆ	CRO	4/5/83	A	7	(4)	2
16	Martin LORENTZSON		21/7/84	D	11	(3)	
28	Viktor LUNDBERG		4/3/91	M	12	(10)	4
12	Toni MAANOJA	FIN	12/9/86	G	14		
18	Niklas MARIPUU		2/3/92	D		(2)	
5	Jorge ORTÍZ	ARG	20/6/84	M	7		
14	Kenny PAVEY	ENG	23/8/79	M	24	(1)	4
13	Kenny STAMATOPOULOS	CAN	28/8/79	G	4		
8	Daniel TJERNSTRÖM		19/2/74	M	15	(5)	
27	Ivan TURINA	CRO	3/10/81	G	12		
15	Kevin WALKER		3/8/89	M	2	(2)	1
5	Robert ÅHMAN PERSSON		26/3/87	M	13		
29	Gabrel ÖZKAN		23/5/86	M	1	(6)	

IF BROMMAPOJKARNA

Coach – Kim Bergstrand; (7/10/10) Robert Björknesjö

Founded – 1942

Stadium – Grimsta IP (8,000)

2010

14/3	Helsingborg	a	0-1	
20/3	AIK	h	0-0	
31/3	Djurgården	a	0-0	
6/4	GAIS	h	1-0	*Runnemo*
11/4	Göteborg	a	1-1	*Chhadeh*
15/4	Örebro	h	0-1	
19/4	Trelleborg	a	1-0	*Guterstam*
25/4	Gefle	h	2-1	*Piñones-Arce, Guidetti*
29/4	Elfsborg	a	0-1	
2/5	Halmstad	h	1-0	*og (Žvirgždauskas)*
5/5	Åtvidaberg	a	1-4	*Runnemo*
10/5	Kalmar	h	2-3	*Korkmaz, Albornoz Ma.*
15/5	Häcken	h	2-1	*Guidetti, Guterstam*
24/5	Malmö	a	1-2	*Guidetti*
17/7	Mjällby	a	0-0	
24/7	Mjällby	h	1-0	*Chhadeh*
2/8	Helsingborg	h	1-3	*Stefanidis*
8/8	AIK	a	1-2	*Piñones-Arce*
18/8	Djurgården	h	0-1	
23/8	GAIS	a	1-1	*Ayranci*
28/8	Åtvidaberg	h	0-2	
13/9	Kalmar	a	0-3	
16/9	Trelleborg	h	0-3	
19/9	Gefle	a	0-2	
26/9	Elfsborg	h	2-2	*Ayranci, Segerström (p)*
3/10	Halmstad	a	0-2	
17/10	Göteborg	h	1-2	*Guterstam*
25/10	Örebro	a	1-1	*Runnemo*
1/11	Malmö	h	0-4	
7/11	Häcken	a	0-5	

No	Name	Nat	DoB	Pos	Aps	(s)	Gls
4	Mauricio ALBORNOZ		10/3/88	M	10	(9)	1
18	Miiko ALBORNOZ		30/11/90	M	17	(1)	
16	Pär ASP		14/8/82	D	25	(1)	
26	Sinan AYRANCI		9/7/90	A	8	(2)	2
14	Nabil BAHOUI		5/2/91	A	1	(5)	
23	Dalil BENYAHIA	ALG	21/4/90	M	19	(6)	
30	Yasaar BILADAMA		10/4/91	A		(1)	
13	Tim BJÖRKSTRÖM		8/1/91	D	26		
9	Imad CHHADEH	SYR	12/10/79	M	20	(1)	2
21	Andreas ERIKSSON		3/11/81	M	18	(3)	
25	John GUIDETTI		15/4/92	M	7	(1)	3
11	Olof GUTERSTAM		4/1/83	A	21	(7)	3
3	Mikkel JENSEN	DEN	6/1/77	M	8	(2)	
6	Ferhat KORKMAZ		14/9/81	D	12		1
1	Benny LEKSTRÖM		19/2/81	G	5	(1)	
15	André MÖLLERSTAM		14/5/91	D	1		
19	Serge-Junior NGOUALI		23/1/92	M	4	(8)	
20	Kristoffer NORDFELDT		23/6/89	G	25		
5	Kim ODELIUS		20/6/85	D	13	(2)	
7	Gabriel PETROVIC		25/5/84	M	24	(2)	

10	Pablo PIÑONES-ARCE	27/8/81	M	12	(9)	2
3	Joakim RUNNEMO	10/3/88	A	15	(14)	3
2	Pontus SEGERSTRÖM	17/2/81	D	26	(1)	1
12	Babis STEFANIDIS	8/3/81	M	13	(6)	1

DJURGÅRDENS IF

Coach – Lennart Wass & Carlos Banda

Founded – 1891

Stadium – Stockholms stadion (14,417)

MAJOR HONOURS: Swedish League – (11) 1912, 1915, 1917, 1920, 1955, 1959, 1964, 1966, 2002, 2003, 2005; Swedish Cup – (4) 1990, 2002, 2004, 2005.

2010

14/3	Häcken	a	1-2	*Igboananike*
21/3	Helsingborg	h	0-1	
31/3	Brommapojkarna	h	0-0	
6/4	Göteborg	a	1-1	*Hellquist*
12/4	Trelleborg	h	3-0	*Oremo, Ekong, Touma*
15/4	Elfsborg	a	1-3	*Oremo (p)*
20/4	Åtvidaberg	h	2-1	*og (Alberis), og (Karlsson P.)*
26/4	Malmö	a	1-2	*Hämäläinen*
29/4	Mjällby	h	1-0	*Igboananike*
2/5	AIK	a	2-1	*Perovuo, Oremo*
6/5	GAIS	h	1-1	*Hämäläinen*
9/5	Örebro	a	0-1	
15/5	Halmstad	a	0-2	
22/5	Gefle	h	1-1	*Youssef*
18/7	Kalmar	h	0-2	
25/7	Kalmar	a	1-0	*Hellquist*
31/7	Häcken	h	0-3	
5/8	Helsingborg	a	3-3	*Igboananike, Jonson, Touma*
18/8	Brommapojkarna	a	1-0	*Rajalakso*
22/8	Göteborg	h	2-0	*Hellquist, Igboananike*
27/8	GAIS	a	1-0	*Touma*
12/9	Örebro	h	2-1	*Touma, Toivio*
15/9	Åtvidaberg	a	1-2	*Jonson*
20/9	Malmö	h	1-0	*Igboananike*
27/9	Mjällby	a	0-3	
3/10	AIK	h	2-1	*Igboananike, Touma*
17/10	Trelleborg	a	1-3	*Youssef*
24/10	Elfsborg	h	4-4	*Igboananike 2, Ekong, Gustafsson*
31/10	Gefle	a	2-2	*Youssef, Igboananike*
7/11	Halmstad	h	0-2	

No	Name	Nat	DoB	Pos	Aps	(s)	Gls
34	Joakim ALRIKSSON		18/8/92	M		(1)	
3	Yosif AYUBA		30/11/90	D	4		
26	André CALISIR		13/6/90	D	2	(4)	
14	Kebba CEESAY	GAM	14/11/87	D	26	(1)	
8	Prince Ikpe EKONG	NGA	5/10/78	M	17	(5)	2
5	Petter GUSTAFSSON		1/1/85	D	16	(1)	1
4	Patrik HAGINGE		2/4/85	D	9	(3)	
22	Philip HELLQUIST		21/5/91	M	19	(5)	3
16	Kasper HÄMÄLÄINEN	FIN	8/8/86	M	30		2
7	Kennedy IGBOANANIKE	NGA	26/2/89	A	16	(11)	9
12	Mattias JONSON		16/1/74	A	9	(5)	2
29	Danilo KUZMANOVIĆ	SRB	4/1/92	D	1		
6	Jani LYYSKI	FIN	16/3/83	D	17	(3)	
19	Hrvoje MILIĆ	CRO	10/5/89	M	8	(2)	
9	Johan OREMO		24/10/86	A	14	(9)	3
21	Joel PEROVUO	FIN	11/8/85	M	13	(10)	1
25	Sebastian RAJALAKSO		23/9/88	M	12	(8)	1
33	Luis Antonio RODRÍGUEZ	ARG	4/3/85	D	11		
11	Daniel SJÖLUND	FIN	22/4/83	M	12	(2)	
2	Joona TOIVIO		10/3/88	D	28	(1)	1
17	Sharbel TOUMA		25/3/79	M	20	(6)	5
15	Pa Dembo TOURAY	GAM	31/3/81	G	23		
35	Tommi VAIHO		13/9/88	G	7	(2)	
10	Christer YOUSSEF		1/12/87	A	16	(5)	3

IF ELFSBORG

Coach – Magnus Haglund

Founded – 1904

Stadium – Borås Arena (16,894)

MAJOR HONOURS: Swedish League – (5) 1936, 1939, 1940, 1961, 2006; Swedish Cup – (2) 2001, 2003.

2010

15/3	Gefle	a	0-0	
22/3	Halmstad	h	6-0	*Larsson 2, Keene 2, Berglund, Avdic*
27/3	Kalmar	a	2-2	*Mobaeck, Nordmark*
6/4	Häcken	h	0-0	
11/4	Helsingborg	a	1-2	*Avdic*
15/4	Djurgården	h	3-1	*Avdic 2, Ericsson*
18/4	Göteborg	a	1-5	*Ericsson*
25/4	Trelleborg	h	4-1	*Avdic 2, Bajrami, Larsson*
29/4	Brommapojkarna	h	1-0	*Larsson*
2/5	Åtvidaberg	a	1-1	*Avdic*
5/5	Malmö	h	2-2	*Avdic 2*
9/5	Mjällby	a	0-2	
12/5	AIK	h	4-0	*Avdic 2 (1p), Ericsson, Jawo*
16/5	GAIS	a	2-0	*Bajrami, Avdic*
18/7	Örebro	h	3-3	*Ericsson, Avdic, Ishizaki*
26/7	Örebro	a	0-3	
1/8	Gefle	h	1-0	*Ishizaki*
8/8	Halmstad	a	3-1	*Avdic 2, Ishizaki*
14/8	Kalmar	h	4-1	*Florén, Larsson, Avdic, Keene*
22/8	Häcken	a	1-1	*Avdic*
29/8	Malmö	a	0-1	
11/9	Mjällby	h	2-0	*Ericsson (p), Nordmark*
19/9	Trelleborg	a	1-1	*Avdic*
22/9	Göteborg	h	1-1	*Jönsson*
26/9	Brommapojkarna	a	2-2	*Jönsson, Hult*
3/10	Åtvidaberg	h	4-1	*Ishizaki 2, Larsson, Keene*
18/10	Helsingborg	h	1-3	*Florén*
24/10	Djurgården	a	4-4	*og (Ekong), Ishizaki, Jawo, Avdic*
31/10	AIK	a	0-2	
7/11	GAIS	h	1-0	*Andersson*

No	Name	Nat	DoB	Pos	Aps	(s)	Gls
5	Martin ANDERSSON		16/1/81	D	11		1
9	Denni AVDIC		15/9/88	A	25	(4)	19
20	Emir BAJRAMI		7/3/88	M	13		2
18	Fredrik BERGLUND		21/3/79	A		(10)	1
99	Jesper CHRISTIANSEN	DEN	24/4/78	G	7		
1	Ante COVIC	AUS	13/6/75	G	16	(1)	
10	Martin ERICSSON		4/9/80	M	18	(3)	5
2	Mathias FLORÉN		11/8/76	M	28		2
29	Oscar HILJEMARK		28/6/92	M	4		
23	Niklas HULT		13/2/90	M	3	(6)	1
24	Stefan ISHIZAKI		15/5/82	M	10	(3)	6
12	Amadou JAWO		26/9/84	A	10	(10)	2
6	Jon JÖNSSON		8/7/83	D	15		2
4	Johan KARLSSON		6/4/75	D	20	(2)	
17	James KEENE	ENG	26/12/85	A	14	(11)	4
20	Andreas KLARSTRÖM		23/12/77	M	12		
25	Elmin KURBEGOVIC		3/6/87	M		(1)	
32	Anton LANS		17/4/91	D	2		
21	Johan LARSSON		5/5/90	M	23	(6)	6
15	Teddy LUCIC		15/4/73	D	11	(1)	
11	Daniel MOBAECK		22/5/80	D	27		1
16	Daniel NORDMARK		4/1/88	M	12	(13)	2
26	Amadiya RENNIE	LBR	17/3/90	M	1	(1)	
8	Anders SVENSSON		17/7/76	M	27		
13	Anders WIKSTRÖM		14/12/81	D	14	(4)	
30	Joakim WULFF		24/1/81	G	7	(1)	

GAIS GÖTEBORG

Coach – Alexander Axén

Founded – 1894

Stadium – Nya Gamla Ullevi (19,000)

MAJOR HONOURS: Swedish League – (4) 1919, 1922, 1931, 1954; Swedish Cup – (1) 1942.

2010				
15/3	Malmö	h	0-0	
21/3	Mjällby	a	0-3	
29/3	AIK	h	3-1	*Johansson 2, Andersson*
6/4	Brommapojkarna	a	0-1	
12/4	Örebro	a	2-0	*Wanderson, Khalili*
15/4	Gefle	h	2-1	*Lundgren, Wanderson*
18/4	Halmstad	a	0-3	
25/4	Kalmar	h	2-2	*og (Wastå), Wanderson*
28/4	Häcken	a	2-0	*Hédinsson 2*
3/5	Helsingborg	h	0-0	
6/5	Djurgården	a	1-1	*Wanderson*
10/5	Göteborg	h	0-0	
16/5	Elfsborg	h	0-2	
22/5	Trelleborg	a	0-2	
18/7	Åtvidaberg	h	0-0	
24/7	Åtvidaberg	a	1-0	*Khalili*
1/8	Malmö	a	0-1	
7/8	Mjällby	h	3-2	*Celik 2, Andersson (p)*
14/8	AIK	a	0-1	
23/8	Brommapojkarna	h	1-1	*Hédinsson*
27/8	Djurgården	h	0-1	
13/9	Göteborg	a	1-2	*Andersson*
18/9	Kalmar	a	1-3	*Celik*
22/9	Halmstad	h	1-1	*Andersson*
29/9	Häcken	h	2-1	*og (Wahlström), Hédinsson*
2/10	Helsingborg	a	1-0	*Romarinho*
20/10	Örebro	h	0-1	
24/10	Gefle	a	0-1	
30/10	Trelleborg	h	1-3	*Lindberg*
7/11	Elfsborg	a	0-1	

No	Name	Nat	DoB	Pos	Aps	(s)	Gls
22	Björn ANDERSSON		12/6/82	A	24	(1)	4
13	Calum ANGUS	ENG	15/4/86	D	2	(1)	
6	Reuben AYARNA	GHA	22/10/85	M	17	(1)	
27	Mervan CELIK		26/5/90	M	22	(5)	3
2	Richard EKUNDE	COD	4/8/82	D	20	(2)	
10	Jesper FLORÉN		11/9/90	M	10	(4)	
20	Kenneth GUSTAFSSON		15/9/83	D	25		
23	Eyjólfur HÉDINSSON	ISL	1/1/85	M	26	(1)	4
1	Dime JANKULOVSKI		18/9/77	G	29		
21	Joel JOHANSSON		16/1/86	A	15	(8)	2
4	Hallgrímur JÓNASSON	ISL	4/5/86	D	25	(1)	
18	Aram KHALILI	NOR	28/7/89	A	4	(16)	2
14	Jonas LINDBERG		24/3/89	M	9	(4)	1
7	Jonas LUNDÉN		27/12/80	D	13	(3)	
15	Fredrik LUNDGREN		26/10/79	M	19		1
11	Tommy LYCÉN		5/10/81	M	15	(8)	
17	Johan MÅRTENSSON		1/4/89	M	26		
25	Niklas OLSSON		18/11/92	M			
19	Kyle PATTERSON	ENG	6/1/86	M		(9)	
24	Johan PETTERSSON		12/6/82	M	1	(4)	
29	Romário Pereira Sipião "ROMARINHO"	BRA	15/4/86	M	8	(9)	1
28	Johan RUNDQVIST		5/3/91	D	1	(4)	
32	Henri SILLANPÄÄ	FIN	4/6/79	G	1		
26	Jimmy TAMANDI		12/5/80	D	3		
25	Francisco WANDERSON do Carmo Carneiro	BRA	26/5/90	A	15		4

GEFLE IF

Coach – Per Olsson & Urban Hammar

Founded – 1882

Stadium – Strömvallen (7,200)

2010				
15/3	Elfsborg	h	0-0	
22/3	Åtvidaberg	a	1-0	*Gerndt*
28/3	Malmö	h	1-3	*Gerndt*
5/4	Mjällby	a	3-1	*Lantto, Gerndt 2*
11/4	AIK	h	1-0	*Gerndt*
15/4	GAIS	a	1-2	*Berg*
19/4	Örebro	h	1-3	*Gerndt (p)*
25/4	Brommapojkarna	a	1-2	*Orlov*
28/4	Halmstad	a	0-1	
2/5	Kalmar	h	0-0	
5/5	Häcken	a	2-0	*Gerndt, Berg*
10/5	Helsingborg	h	1-3	*Gerndt*
16/5	Göteborg	h	0-0	
22/5	Djurgården	a	1-1	*Orlov*
18/7	Trelleborg	a	1-2	*Lantto*
25/7	Trelleborg	h	1-3	*Orlov*
1/8	Elfsborg	a	0-1	
8/8	Åtvidaberg	h	4-2	*Lantto, Orlov, Öhagen, Kapčević*
15/8	Malmö	a	0-2	
21/8	Mjällby	h	3-3	*Lantto, Orlov 2*
29/8	Häcken	h	0-2	
11/9	Helsingborg	a	1-3	*Chibsah*
19/9	Brommapojkarna	h	2-0	*Berggren, Lantto*
22/9	Örebro	a	1-3	*Berggren (p)*
27/9	Halmstad	h	1-2	*Chibsah*
3/10	Kalmar	a	1-1	*Kapčević*
16/10	AIK	a	0-2	
24/10	GAIS	h	1-0	*Orlov*
31/10	Djurgården	h	2-2	*Orlov, og (Ekong)*
7/11	Göteborg	a	2-2	*Orlov, Kapčević*

No	Name	Nat	DoB	Pos	Aps	(s)	Gls
23	Jonatan BERG		9/5/85	M	10		2
13	Hans BERGGREN		18/2/73	A	8	(6)	2
12	Daniel BERNHARDSSON		31/1/78	D	30		
24	Yussif CHIBSAH	GHA	30/12/83	M	28		2
15	Mikael DAHLBERG		6/3/85	A	27	(1)	
18	James FREMPONG		11/1/89	M	11	(4)	
16	Alexander GERNDT		14/7/86	A	14		8
6	Øyvind GRAM	NOR	11/10/85	M	1	(4)	
19	Marcus HANSSON		12/2/90	M	23	(4)	
1	Mattias HUGOSSON		24/1/74	G	30		
5	Omar JAWO	GAM	8/11/81	D	19	(2)	
16	Dragan KAPČEVIĆ	BIH	10/11/85	A	3	(7)	3
17	Jonas LANTTO		22/5/87	A	29		5
21	Eric LARSSON		15/7/91	D		(2)	
2	Olof MÅRD		31/1/89	D	7	(1)	
14	Bernhard NYSTRÖM		8/5/85	M	2	(9)	
10	Jakob ORLOV		15/3/86	A	19	(7)	9
14	Jens PORTIN	FIN	13/12/84	D	17	(4)	
4	Sebastian SENATORE		17/12/85	D	17		
7	Haruna Moshi SHABANI	TAN	21/5/87	M	2	(3)	
3	Daniel THEORIN		4/8/83	D	25		
28	Erik TÖRNROS		11/6/93	A		(2)	
20	Daniel WESTLIN		24/1/80	A		(7)	
11	Hjalmar ÖHAGEN		17/5/85	M	8	(9)	1

IFK GÖTEBORG

Coach – Stefan Rehn

Founded – 1904

Stadium – Nya Gamla Ullevi (19,000)

MAJOR HONOURS: UEFA Cup – (2) 1982, 1987; Swedish League – (18) 1908, 1910, 1918, 1935, 1942, 1958, 1969, 1982, 1983, 1984, 1987, 1990, 1991, 1993, 1994, 1995, 1996, 2007; Swedish Cup – (5) 1979, 1982, 1983, 1991, 2008.

2010				
13/3	Kalmar	a	3-0	*Hysén 2, Jónsson*
22/3	Häcken	h	0-1	
29/3	Helsingborg	a	0-2	
6/4	Djurgården	h	1-1	*Johansson J.*
11/4	Brommapojkarna	h	1-1	*Ericsson*
15/4	Trelleborg	a	1-2	*Olsson*
18/4	Elfsborg	h	5-1	*Eriksson, Jónsson, Johansson J. 2, Söder*
24/4	Åtvidaberg	a	1-2	*Söder*
29/4	Malmö	h	0-2	
3/5	Mjällby	a	0-0	
6/5	AIK	h	4-0	*Olsson 2, Söder, Bjarnason*
10/5	GAIS	a	0-0	
13/5	Örebro	h	0-0	
16/5	Gefle	a	0-0	
17/7	Halmstad	h	3-0	*Hysén, Svensson G., Sigurdsson*
25/7	Halmstad	a	0-1	
1/8	Kalmar	h	3-1	*Hysén 2, Stiller*
8/8	Häcken	a	5-1	*Selakovic 3, Stiller, Bjarnason*
15/8	Helsingborg	h	0-0	
22/8	Djurgården	a	0-2	
29/8	AIK	a	2-1	*Bjarnason, Bärkroth*
13/9	GAIS	h	2-1	*Stiller, Hysén*
19/9	Åtvidaberg	h	3-0	*Johansson J., Bjarnason, Hysén*
22/9	Elfsborg	a	1-1	*Hysén*
26/9	Malmö	a	1-2	*Hysén*
3/10	Mjällby	h	0-0	
17/10	Brommapojkarna	a	2-1	*Selakovic, Atashkadeh*
25/10	Trelleborg	h	1-2	*Hysén*
1/11	Örebro	a	1-2	*Selakovic*
7/11	Gefle	h	2-2	*Johansson A., Sana*

No	Name	Nat	DoB	Pos	Aps	(s)	Gls
31	Niklas ANDERSÉN		5/8/92	D	1		
26	William ATASHKADEH		12/4/92	A		(5)	1
28	Theódór Elmar BJARNASON	ISL	4/3/87	A	21	(1)	4
21	Niklas BÄRKROTH		19/1/92	A	6	(10)	1
3	Nicklas CARLSSON		13/11/79	D	10	(2)	
1	Kim CHRISTENSEN	DEN	16/7/79	G	14		
25	Erik DAHLIN		28/4/89	G	1	(2)	
18	Pär ERICSSON		21/7/88	A	8	(5)	1
23	Sebastian ERIKSSON		31/1/89	D	23	(3)	1
20	Alexander FALTSETAS		4/7/87	M	3	(16)	
7	Tobias HYSÉN		9/3/82	M	22		10
30	Lawal ISMAIL		5/9/91	A		(2)	
6	Adam JOHANSSON		21/2/83	D	26	(1)	1
15	Jakob JOHANSSON		21/6/90	M	23	(3)	4
14	Hjálmar JÓNSSON	ISL	29/7/80	D	22	(3)	2
16	Erik LUND		6/11/88	D	21	(1)	
8	Thomas OLSSON		15/2/76	M	16	(8)	3
17	Fredrik RISP		15/12/80	D	3		
22	Tobias SANA		11/7/89	M	6	(5)	1
12	Markus SANDBERG		7/11/90	G	15		
9	Stefan SELAKOVIC		9/1/77	A	26	(2)	5
10	Ragnar SIGURDSSON	ISL	19/6/86	M	28		1
19	Hannes STILLER		3/7/78	A	7	(4)	3
13	Gustav SVENSSON		9/2/87	M	15	(3)	1
2	Karl SVENSSON		21/3/84	D	4	(1)	
11	Robin SÖDER		1/4/91	A	9	(4)	3
5	Tuomo Mikael TURUNEN	FIN	30/8/87	D		(1)	

HALMSTADS BK

Coach – Lars Jacobsson

Founded – 1914

Stadium – Örjans Vall (15,500)

MAJOR HONOURS: Swedish League – (4) 1976, 1979, 1997, 2000; Swedish Cup – (1) 1995.

2010				
14/3	Trelleborg	h	0-0	
22/3	Elfsborg	a	0-6	
28/3	Åtvidaberg	h	4-0	*Raskaj, Salomonsson, Prent, Lundberg*
6/4	Malmö	a	1-1	*Görlitz*
11/4	Mjällby	h	1-2	*Sise*
14/4	AIK	a	1-0	*Sævarsson*
18/4	GAIS	h	3-0	*Anselmo (p), Olsson, Kujovic*
25/4	Örebro	a	0-3	
28/4	Gefle	h	1-0	*Anselmo*
2/5	Brommapojkarna	a	0-1	
5/5	Kalmar	a	0-1	
9/5	Häcken	h	1-2	*Lundberg*
15/5	Djurgården	h	2-0	*Anselmo 2*
22/5	Helsingborg	a	1-2	*Jönsson*
17/7	Göteborg	a	0-3	
25/7	Göteborg	h	1-0	*Rosén*
2/8	Trelleborg	a	0-1	
8/8	Elfsborg	h	1-3	*Kujovic*
16/8	Åtvidaberg	a	1-1	*Sævarsson*
23/8	Malmö	h	0-2	
29/8	Kalmar	h	2-1	*Olsson 2*
10/9	Häcken	a	0-2	
19/9	Örebro	h	1-1	*Olsson*
22/9	GAIS	a	1-1	*Jönsson*
27/9	Gefle	a	2-1	*Sise 2*
3/10	Brommapojkarna	h	2-0	*Sise, Sævarsson*
17/10	Mjällby	a	0-2	
25/10	AIK	h	1-2	*Anselmo*
31/10	Helsingborg	h	2-4	*Anselmo 2 (1p)*
7/11	Djurgården	a	2-0	*Görlitz, Sise*

No	Name	Nat	DoB	Pos	Aps	(s)	Gls
14	ANSELMO Tadeu Silva do Nascimento	BRA	24/10/80	A	13	(9)	7
22	Marcus ANTONSSON		8/5/91	A		(1)	
23	Guri BAQAJ		12/9/90	A		(5)	
5	Markus GUSTAFSON		12/8/87	D		(1)	
7	Michael GÖRLITZ	GER	8/3/87	M	27	(3)	2
2	Per JOHANSSON		6/5/78	D	5	(6)	
1	Karl-Johan JOHNSSON		28/1/90	G	7	(2)	
16	Christian JÄRDLER		3/6/82	D	15		
4	Tommy JÖNSSON		4/3/76	D	18	(1)	2
9	Emir KUJOVIC		22/6/88	A	11	(10)	2
23	Viktor LJUNG		19/4/91	A		(1)	
3	Johnny LUNDBERG		15/4/82	D	21	(2)	2
25	Richard MAGYAR		3/5/91	D	3		
20	Robin MALMKVIST		13/11/87	G	23	(1)	
24	Ryan MILLER	USA	14/12/84	D	26		
18	Marcus OLSSON		17/5/88	M	24	(6)	4
11	Alexander PRENT	NED	25/5/83	M	2	(14)	1
10	Anel RASKAJ	ALB	19/8/89	M	25	(1)	1
6	Mikael ROSÉN		15/8/74	D	25	(1)	1
8	Jónas Gudni SÆVARSSON	ISL	28/11/83	M	13	(3)	3
19	Emil SALOMONSSON		28/4/89	M	29	(1)	1
15	Joe SISE		12/12/89	A	18	(4)	5
25	Michael THOMAS	USA	8/3/88	M	2	(3)	

13	Kristoffer THYDELL		17/3/93	M	5	(2)	
17	Joakim WRELE		7/1/91	M		(1)	
12	Tomas ŽVIRGŽDAUSKAS	LTU	18/3/75	D	18		

HELSINGBORGS IF

Coach – Conny Karlsson

Founded – 1907

Stadium – Olympia (17,200)

MAJOR HONOURS: Swedish League – (4) 1933, 1934, 1941, 1999; Swedish Cup – (4) 1941, 1998, 2006, 2010.

2010				
14/3	Brommapojkarna	h	1-0	*Lindström*
21/3	Djurgården	a	1-0	*Jönsson*
29/3	Göteborg	h	2-0	*Lindström, Nilsson*
5/4	Trelleborg	a	0-0	
11/4	Elfsborg	h	2-1	*Gashi, Holgersson*
14/4	Åtvidaberg	a	3-0	*Andersson 2, Sundin*
20/4	Malmö	h	2-1	*Gashi, Nilsson*
26/4	Mjällby	a	1-0	*Sundin*
29/4	AIK	h	1-0	*Lindström*
3/5	GAIS	a	0-0	
6/5	Örebro	h	2-1	*Andersson, Jönsson*
10/5	Gefle	a	3-1	*Mahlangu, Ekstrand, Lantz (p)*
16/5	Kalmar	a	0-1	
22/5	Halmstad	h	2-1	*Gashi 2*
22/7	Häcken	a	1-2	*Andersson*
26/7	Häcken	h	3-1	*Sundin 2, Holgersson*
2/8	Brommapojkarna	a	3-1	*Jönsson, Andersson, Gashi*
5/8	Djurgården	h	3-3	*Gerndt 3*
15/8	Göteborg	a	0-0	
25/8	Trelleborg	h	1-0	*Gerndt*
28/8	Örebro	a	0-3	
11/9	Gefle	h	3-1	*Gerndt 3*
15/9	Malmö	a	0-2	
20/9	Mjällby	h	2-1	*Gerndt 2 (1p)*
27/9	AIK	a	3-2	*Sundin, Jönsson, Andersson*
2/10	GAIS	h	0-1	
18/10	Elfsborg	a	3-1	*Mahlangu, Sundin 2*
24/10	Åtvidaberg	h	3-0	*Gerndt 2, Sundin*
31/10	Halmstad	a	4-2	*Jönsson 2, Mahlangu, Gerndt (p)*
7/11	Kalmar	h	0-0	

No	Name	Nat	DoB	Pos	Aps	(s)	Gls
21	Christoffer ANDERSSON		22/10/78	M	30		6
33	Samuel AZIZ		5/7/91	M		(1)	
4	Marcus BERGHOLTZ		15/12/89	M		(6)	
1	Oscar BERGLUND		13/4/84	G		(1)	
13	Rachid BOUAOUZAN	NED	20/2/84	M	5	(6)	
14	Erik EDMAN		11/11/78	D	29		
27	Johan EISWOHLD		21/6/90	M		(3)	
26	Joel EKSTRAND		4/2/89	D	23		1
8	Ardian GASHI	NOR	20/6/81	M	24	(3)	5
18	Alexander GERNDT		14/7/86	A	11	(4)	12
30	Pär HANSSON		22/6/86	G	30		
15	Markus HOLGERSSON		12/4/85	D	28		2
19	Rasmus JÖNSSON		27/1/90	A	30		6
20	Abdul KHALILI		7/6/92	M		(2)	
10	Marcus LANTZ		23/10/75	M	27		1
7	Mattias LINDSTRÖM		18/4/80	M	25	(3)	3
29	Fredrik LIVERSTAM		4/3/88	D		(2)	
6	May MAHLANGU	RSA	1/1/89	M	10	(9)	3
16	René MAKONDELE	COD	20/4/82	M	3	(4)	
24	Marcus NILSSON		26/2/88	D	28		2
5	Hannu PATRONEN	FIN	23/5/84	D	4	(7)	
11	RAFAEL PORCELLIS de Oliveira	BRA	19/1/87	A		(6)	
9	Erik SUNDIN		1/3/79	M	20	(6)	8
23	Erik WAHLSTEDT		16/4/76	D	3	(4)	

BK HÄCKEN

Coach – Peter Gerhardsson

Founded – 1940

Stadium – Rambergsvallen (8,480)

2010				
14/3	Djurgården	h	2-1	*Paulinho, Östberg*
22/3	Göteborg	a	1-0	*Vinícius Lopes*
30/3	Trelleborg	h	4-2	*Bjurström, Chibuike, Paulinho, Karlsson*
6/4	Elfsborg	a	0-0	
10/4	Åtvidaberg	h	0-0	
14/4	Malmö	a	1-3	*Paulinho*
19/4	Mjällby	h	0-1	
24/4	AIK	a	1-1	*Chatto*
28/4	GAIS	h	0-2	
2/5	Örebro	a	0-2	
5/5	Gefle	h	0-2	
9/5	Halmstad	a	2-1	*Henriksson 2*
15/5	Brommapojkarna	a	1-2	*Ranégie*
22/5	Kalmar	h	1-1	*Henriksson (p)*
22/7	Helsingborg	h	2-1	*Ranégie, Paulinho*
26/7	Helsingborg	a	1-3	*Östberg*
31/7	Djurgården	a	3-0	*Henriksson, Ranégie, Paulinho*
8/8	Göteborg	h	1-5	*Henriksson*
16/8	Trelleborg	a	2-3	*Ranégie 2*
22/8	Elfsborg	h	1-1	*Henriksson*
29/8	Gefle	a	2-0	*Ranégie 2*
10/9	Halmstad	h	2-0	*Karlsson, Makondele*
15/9	Mjällby	a	2-2	*Ranégie 2*
19/9	AIK	h	0-1	
29/9	GAIS	a	1-2	*Paulinho (p)*
3/10	Örebro	h	2-1	*Henriksson, Paulinho*
17/10	Åtvidaberg	a	0-0	
27/10	Malmö	h	0-4	
31/10	Kalmar	a	3-1	*og (Öhman), Ranégie 2*
7/11	Brommapojkarna	h	5-0	*Chibuike 2, og (Jensen), Ranégie, Paulinho (p)*

No	Name	Nat	DoB	Pos	Aps	(s)	Gls
15	Kari ARKIVUO	FIN	23/6/83	M	5		
7	Jonas BJURSTRÖM		24/3/79	M	16	(1)	1
20	Dominic CHATTO	NGA	12/7/85	M	26		1
25	John CHIBUIKE	NGA	10/10/88	M	21	(5)	3
22	Daniel FORSELL		4/1/82	D	17	(6)	
17	Erik FRIBERG		10/2/86	M	19	(8)	
6	David FRÖLUND		4/6/79	D	13	(1)	
21	Jonas HENRIKSSON		24/3/79	M	30		7
16	Marcus JARLEGREN		16/9/83	D	4		
8	Josef KARLSSON		13/7/82	M	11	(7)	2
9	KAYKE Moreno de Andrade Rodrigues	BRA	1/4/88	A		(4)	
4	Mohammed Ali KHAN		21/1/86	D	8	(4)	
1	Christoffer KÄLLQVIST		26/8/83	G	28		
2	Johan LIND		8/2/74	D	17	(1)	
33	René MAKONDELE	COD	20/4/82	M	10	(2)	1
26	Damir MEHIC		18/4/87	G	2		
14	Peter NYSTRÖM		27/8/84	M		(2)	
10	Paulo José de Oliveira "PAULINHO"	BRA	9/4/86	A	15	(9)	8
13	Mathias RANÉGIE		14/6/84	A	27	(3)	12
27	Tom SÖDERBERG		25/8/87	D	8	(3)	
11	VINÍCIUS Silva LOPES Souto	BRA	29/1/88	A	3	(18)	1
5	Emil WAHLSTRÖM		2/3/87	D	25		
18	Abdul Majeed WARIS	GHA	19/9/81	M	1	(9)	
3	Mattias ÖSTBERG		24/8/77	D	24	(1)	2

KALMAR FF

Coach – Nanne Bergstrand

Founded – 1910

Stadium – Fredriksskans IP (8,973)

MAJOR HONOURS: Swedish League – (1) 2008; Swedish Cup – (3) 1981, 1987, 2007.

2010				
13/3	Göteborg	h	0-3	
21/3	Trelleborg	a	1-1	*Ricardo Santos*
27/3	Elfsborg	h	2-2	*Ricardo Santos 2*
6/4	Åtvidaberg	a	0-0	
11/4	Malmö	h	2-3	*Dauda, Eriksson*
15/4	Mjällby	a	0-0	
19/4	AIK	h	0-3	
25/4	GAIS	a	2-2	*Eriksson, Marcel Sacramento*
28/4	Örebro	h	4-1	*Daniel Mendes, Ricardo Santos 2, Rydström (p)*
2/5	Gefle	a	0-0	
5/5	Halmstad	h	1-0	*Dauda*
10/5	Brommapojkarna	a	3-2	*Ricardo Santos 2, Åhlander*
16/5	Helsingborg	h	1-0	*Daniel Mendes*
22/5	Häcken	a	1-1	*Daniel Sobralense*
18/7	Djurgården	a	2-0	*Dauda, Daniel Mendes*
25/7	Djurgården	h	0-1	
1/8	Göteborg	a	1-3	*Douglas*
8/8	Trelleborg	h	2-1	*Ricardo Santos, Daniel Mendes*
14/8	Elfsborg	a	1-4	*Ricardo Santos*
22/8	Åtvidaberg	h	1-2	*Daniel Sobralense*
29/8	Halmstad	a	1-2	*Daniel Mendes*
13/9	Brommapojkarna	h	3-0	*Daniel Mendes, Israelsson, Rydström (p)*
18/9	GAIS	h	3-1	*Dauda 2, Israelsson*
22/9	AIK	a	1-0	*Daniel Mendes*
28/9	Örebro	a	0-1	
3/10	Gefle	h	1-1	*Daniel Mendes*
18/10	Malmö	a	1-0	*Daniel Mendes*
24/10	Mjällby	h	1-1	*Ricardo Santos*
31/10	Häcken	h	1-3	*Bertilsson*
7/11	Helsingborg	a	0-0	

No	Name	Nat	DoB	Pos	Aps	(s)	Gls
6	Paulus ARAJUURI	FIN	15/6/88	D	12	(1)	
7	Jimmie AUGUSTSSON		13/4/81	M	6		
45	Zlatan AZINOVIC		31/1/88	G	1		
99	Etrit BERISHA	ALB	10/3/89	G	14		
18	Johan BERTILSSON		15/2/88	M	6	(7)	1
5	Tobias CARLSSON		25/2/75	D	22	(2)	
17	DANIEL Freira MENDES	BRA	18/1/81	A	19	(6)	9
12	DANIEL Lopes da Silva "SOBRALENSE"	BRA	10/2/82	M	23		2
11	Abiola DAUDA	NGA	3/2/88	A	16	(13)	5
10	DOUGLAS da Silva Vieira	BRA	12/11/87	M	1	(10)	1
25	Tobias ERIKSSON		19/3/85	M	18		2
20	Erik ISRAELSSON		25/2/89	M	21		2
21	JAEL Ferreira Vieira	BRA	30/10/88	A		(2)	
23	Mattias JOHANSSON		16/2/92	D	11	(2)	
27	Joakim KARLSSON		4/2/89	M		(2)	
3	Joachim LANTZ		10/5/77	D	11	(3)	
9	Stefan LARSSON		21/1/83	D	30		
4	Marcus LINDBERG		31/8/80	D	7	(3)	
28	MARCEL Silva SACRAMENTO	BRA	24/1/87	A	3	(11)	1
26	Emin NOURI		22/7/85	D	24		
19	RICARDO Henrique da Silva dos SANTOS	BRA	13/2/87	A	25	(4)	10
8	Henrik RYDSTRÖM		16/2/76	M	29		2
77	Johann SMITH	USA	25/4/87	A		(2)	
10	Daryl SMYLIE	ENG	10/9/85	M	4	(6)	
34	Måns SÖDERQVIST		8/2/93	A		(1)	
1	Petter WASTÅ		2/2/76	G	15		
14	Stefan ÅHLANDER		25/4/83	D	11	(5)	1
2	Ludvig ÖHMAN		10/10/91	D	1		

MALMÖ FF

Coach – Roland Nilsson

Founded – 1910

Stadium – Swedbank Stadion (24,000)

MAJOR HONOURS: Swedish League – (16) 1944, 1949, 1950, 1951, 1953, 1965, 1967, 1970, 1971, 1974, 1975, 1977, 1986, 1988, 2004, 2010; Swedish Cup – (14) 1944, 1946, 1947, 1951, 1953, 1967, 1973, 1974, 1975, 1977, 1980, 1984, 1986, 1989.

2010				
15/3	GAIS	a	0-0	
23/3	Örebro	h	3-0	*Mehmeti 2, Molins*
28/3	Gefle	a	3-1	*Åhman Persson 2, Andersson*
6/4	Halmstad	h	1-1	*Åhman Persson*
11/4	Kalmar	a	3-2	*Ofere, Wílton Figueiredo, Halsti*
14/4	Häcken	h	3-1	*Ofere, Andersson, Molins*
20/4	Helsingborg	a	1-2	*Wílton Figueiredo (p)*
26/4	Djurgården	h	2-1	*Larsson 2*
29/4	Göteborg	a	2-0	*Larsson, Molins*
2/5	Trelleborg	h	2-0	*Durmaz, Molins*
5/5	Elfsborg	a	2-2	*Durmaz, Wílton Figueiredo*
8/5	Åtvidaberg	h	3-1	*Mehmeti, Molins, Wílton Figueiredo*
15/5	Mjällby	a	2-4	*Larsson, Jansson*
24/5	Brommapojkarna	h	2-1	*Nilsson 2*
17/7	AIK	a	0-2	
24/7	AIK	h	1-0	*Mehmeti*
1/8	GAIS	h	1-0	*Pekalski*
7/8	Örebro	a	3-0	*Hamad, Mehmeti, Larsson (p)*
15/8	Gefle	h	2-0	*Larsson, Mehmeti*
23/8	Halmstad	a	2-0	*Mehmeti 2*
29/8	Elfsborg	h	1-0	*Andersson*
11/9	Åtvidaberg	a	3-3	*Mehmeti, Larsson, Yago*
15/9	Helsingborg	h	2-0	*Rexhepi, Wílton Figueiredo*
20/9	Djurgården	a	0-1	
26/9	Göteborg	h	2-1	*Andersson, Larsson*
3/10	Trelleborg	a	3-0	*Hamad, Larsson (p), Molins*
18/10	Kalmar	h	0-1	
27/10	Häcken	a	4-0	*Larsson, Molins, Yago 2*
1/11	Brommapojkarna	a	4-0	*Aubynn, Mehmeti, Rexhepi, Andersson (p)*
7/11	Mjällby	h	2-0	*Hamad, Mehmeti*

No	Name	Nat	DoB	Pos	Aps	(s)	Gls
8	Daniel ANDERSSON		28/8/77	D	30		5
36	Muamet ASANOVSKI		14/7/91	M		(1)	
11	Jeffrey AUBYNN		12/5/77	M	10	(10)	1
27	Johan DAHLIN		8/9/86	G	29		
21	Jimmy DURMAZ		22/3/89	D	15	(12)	2
4	Joseph ELANGA	CMR	2/5/79	D	4	(6)	
30	Dejan GARACA		21/7/91	G	1	(1)	
6	Markus HALSTI	FIN	19/3/84	D	6	(1)	1
26	Jiloan HAMAD		6/11/90	M	15	(12)	3
15	Pontus JANSSON		13/2/91	A	14	(3)	1
10	Rick KRUYS	NED	5/9/85	M	2	(2)	
7	Daniel LARSSON		25/1/87	A	29		10
24	Agon MEHMETI		20/11/89	M	23	(1)	11
14	Guillermo MOLINS		26/9/88	M	23	(5)	7
5	Miljan MUTAVDŽIĆ	SRB	3/2/86	D	1	(11)	
28	Alexander NILSSON		23/10/92	A	1	(2)	2
18	Edward OFERE	NGA	28/3/86	A	4	(3)	2
17	Ivo PEKALSKI		3/11/90	M	20	(4)	1

44	Dardan REXHEPI		16/1/92	A	1	(9)	2
20	Ricardo Ferreira da Silva "RICARDINHO"	BRA	9/9/84	D	22		
29	Jasmin SUDIC		24/11/90	D	6		
2	Ulrich VINZENTS	DEN	11/4/76	D	29		
9	WÍLTON Aguiar FIGUEIREDO	BRA	17/3/82	A	27		5
16	YAGO Fernández Prieto	POR	5/1/88	D	10		3
3	Robert ÅHMAN PERSSON		26/3/87	M	8	(1)	3

MJÄLLBY AIF

Coach – Peter Swärdh

Founded – 1939

Stadium – Strandvallen (7,000)

2010

14/3	AIK	a	0-0	
21/3	GAIS	h	3-0	*Ekenberg 3 (1p)*
29/3	Örebro	a	2-0	*Ekenberg, El Kabir*
5/4	Gefle	h	1-3	*Ekenberg*
11/4	Halmstad	a	2-1	*Nicklasson, Löfquist*
15/4	Kalmar	h	0-0	
19/4	Häcken	a	1-0	*El Kabir*
26/4	Helsingborg	h	0-1	
29/4	Djurgården	a	0-1	
3/5	Göteborg	h	0-0	
6/5	Trelleborg	a	1-2	*Löfquist*
9/5	Elfsborg	h	2-0	*Grahn, Löfquist*
15/5	Malmö	h	4-2	*El Kabir 2, Löfquist, Nicklasson*
22/5	Åtvidaberg	a	2-1	*Ekenberg, El Kabir*
17/7	Brommapojkarna	h	0-0	
24/7	Brommapojkarna	a	0-1	
31/7	AIK	h	0-0	
7/8	GAIS	a	2-3	*Ekenberg, Robledo*
16/8	Örebro	h	1-0	*Ekenberg*
21/8	Gefle	a	3-3	*El Kabir 2, Robledo*
29/8	Trelleborg	h	1-1	*Grahn*
11/9	Elfsborg	a	0-2	
15/9	Häcken	h	2-2	*Löfquist, Asper*
20/9	Helsingborg	a	1-2	*Rosengren*
27/9	Djurgården	h	3-0	*El Kabir, Gitselov 2*
3/10	Göteborg	a	0-0	
17/10	Halmstad	h	2-0	*El Kabir, Löfquist*
24/10	Kalmar	a	1-1	*El Kabir*
1/11	Åtvidaberg	h	2-1	*Berner, Ekenberg*
7/11	Malmö	a	0-2	

No	Name	Nat	DoB	Pos	Aps	(s)	Gls
1	Mattias ASPER		20/3/74	G	30		1
11	Adam BERNER		25/1/87	A	1	(10)	1
15	Robin CEDERBERG		25/2/83	D	25	(1)	
10	Marcus EKENBERG		16/6/80	A	27	(1)	9
88	Moestafa EL KABIR	NED	5/10/88	A	23	(1)	10
9	Peter GITSELOV		18/7/83	M	7	(11)	2
22	Tobias GRAHN		5/3/80	M	25	(1)	2
4	Daniel IVANOVSKI	MKD	27/6/83	D	3	(3)	
5	William LEANDERSSON		9/1/84	D	15	(1)	
12	David LÖFQUIST		6/8/86	M	20	(9)	6
14	Daniel NICKLASSON		23/4/81	M	12	(8)	2
17	Christopher NILSSON		12/3/90	M		(1)	
13	Daniel NILSSON		21/9/82	M	25	(1)	
8	Patrick OSIAKO	KEN	15/11/86	M	26	(1)	
33	Juan ROBLEDO	CHI	21/8/79	D	22	(1)	2
6	Patrik ROSENGREN		25/7/71	D	26		1
23	Emanuel SVENSSON		20/2/89	M	1	(14)	
7	Johan SVENSSON		22/1/81	M	14	(12)	
21	Kim THÖRNBERG		14/6/87	A		(1)	
2	Jesper WESTERBERG		1/2/86	D	28		

TRELLEBORGS FF

Coach – Tom Prahl

Founded – 1926

Stadium – Vångavallen (10,000)

2010

14/3	Halmstad	a	0-0	
21/3	Kalmar	h	1-1	*Jensen*
30/3	Häcken	a	2-4	*Drugge (p), Wihlborg*
5/4	Helsingborg	h	0-0	
12/4	Djurgården	a	0-3	
15/4	Göteborg	h	2-1	*Drugge, Adelstam*
19/4	Brommapojkarna	h	0-1	
25/4	Elfsborg	a	1-4	*Sjöhage*
29/4	Åtvidaberg	h	0-3	
2/5	Malmö	a	0-2	
6/5	Mjällby	h	2-1	*Asp, Adelstam*
9/5	AIK	a	0-1	
17/5	Örebro	a	0-2	
22/5	GAIS	h	2-0	*Asp, Adelstam*
18/7	Gefle	h	2-1	*Drugge, Jensen*
25/7	Gefle	a	3-1	*Adelstam, Drugge, Abelsson*
2/8	Halmstad	h	1-0	*Adelstam*
8/8	Kalmar	a	1-2	*Drugge*
19/8	Häcken	h	3-2	*Andersson, Haynes, Wihlborg*
25/8	Helsingborg	a	0-1	
29/8	Mjällby	a	1-1	*Haynes*
11/9	AIK	h	4-1	*Drugge, Jensen 2, Haynes*
16/9	Brommapojkarna	a	3-0	*Koroma, Pode, Nilsson Joa.*
19/9	Elfsborg	h	1-1	*Haynes*
28/9	Åtvidaberg	a	1-3	*Drugge*
3/10	Malmö	h	0-3	
17/10	Djurgården	h	3-1	*Jensen 2, Pode*
25/10	Göteborg	a	2-1	*Nilsson Joa., Pode*
30/10	GAIS	a	3-1	*Haynes 2, Andersson*
7/11	Örebro	h	1-0	*Sjöhage*

No	Name	Nat	DoB	Pos	Aps	(s)	Gls
4	Peter ABELSSON		14/7/77	D	18		1
27	Mattias ADELSTAM		7/3/82	A	25	(4)	5
21	Magnus ANDERSSON		27/4/81	M	27	(2)	2
26	Jonathan ASP		6/5/90	M	20	(4)	2
11	Andreas DRUGGE		20/1/83	A	29		7
20	Yousef FAKHRO		3/5/83	D	9	(7)	
23	Max FUXBERG		23/7/85	D	4		
8	Kristian HAYNES		20/12/80	M	26	(1)	6
25	Robin JAKOBSSON		28/3/90	A		(4)	
13	Fredrik JENSEN		13/6/85	A	18	(1)	6
6	Zoran JOVANOVIC		25/9/86	M	1		
35	Ibrahim KOROMA	SLE	8/7/84	D	9	(2)	1
3	Dennis MELANDER		19/1/83	D	21		
14	Philip MILENKOVIC		11/11/88	D		(4)	
7	Joakim NILSSON		16/5/85	M	14	(8)	2
5	Johan NILSSON Guiomar		15/3/85	D	7	(3)	
31	Viktor NORING		3/2/91	G	22		
1	Fredrik PERSSON		20/2/83	G	8		
17	Thommie PERSSON		4/8/84	D	21	(5)	
10	Marcus PODE		27/3/86	A	17	(2)	3
18	Fisnik SHALA		16/1/89	A	1	(5)	
12	Joakim SJÖHAGE		27/9/86	A	4	(12)	2
19	Viktor SVENSSON		6/3/90	M	5	(7)	
15	Tuomo Mikael TURUNEN	FIN	30/8/87	D	15		
23	Carl Fredrik WACHTMEISTER		23/6/89	G		(1)	
2	Andreas WIHLBORG		18/1/87	M	9	(7)	2

ÅTVIDABERGS FF

Coach – Daniel Wiklund; (31/3/10) Andreas Thomsson

Founded – 1907

Stadium – Kopparvallen (8,000)

MAJOR HONOURS: Swedish League – (2) 1972, 1973; Swedish Cup – (2) 1970, 1971.

2010				
15/3	Örebro	a	0-2	
22/3	Gefle	h	0-1	
28/3	Halmstad	a	0-4	
6/4	Kalmar	h	0-0	
10/4	Häcken	a	0-0	
14/4	Helsingborg	h	0-3	
20/4	Djurgården	a	1-2	*Radetinac*
24/4	Göteborg	h	2-1	*Eboagwu, Arvidsson*
29/4	Trelleborg	a	3-0	*Prodell, Bergström, Eboagwu*
2/5	Elfsborg	h	1-1	*Radetinac*
5/5	Brommapojkarna	h	4-1	*Bergström, Arvidsson, Roiha, Suljic*
8/5	Malmö	a	1-3	*Eboagwu*
17/5	AIK	a	1-4	*Roiha*
22/5	Mjällby	h	1-2	*og (Rosengren)*
18/7	GAIS	a	0-0	
24/7	GAIS	h	0-1	
2/8	Örebro	h	0-2	
8/8	Gefle	a	2-4	*Suljic, Möller*
16/8	Halmstad	h	1-1	*Roiha*
22/8	Kalmar	a	2-1	*Moberg, Möller*
28/8	Brommapojkarna	a	2-0	*Möller, Roiha*
11/9	Malmö	h	3-3	*Arvidsson (p), Möller, Roiha*
15/9	Djurgården	h	2-1	*Roberts, Möller*
19/9	Göteborg	a	0-3	
28/9	Trelleborg	h	3-1	*Roiha, Möller, Arvidsson*
3/10	Elfsborg	a	1-4	*Radetinac*
17/10	Häcken	h	0-0	
24/10	Helsingborg	a	0-3	
1/11	Mjällby	a	1-2	*Roiha*
7/11	AIK	h	1-1	*Prodell*

No	Name	Nat	DoB	Pos	Aps	(s)	Gls
4	ALBERIS Sérgio Ângelo da Silva	BRA	2/12/84	D	23	(1)	
18	Jesper ARVIDSSON		1/1/85	D	27	(1)	4
7	Kristian BERGSTRÖM		8/1/74	M	29		2
12	BRUNO Manoel MARINHO	BRA	5/7/84	M	18	(1)	
6	Dejan DOSLIC		24/1/90	M	1	(6)	
25	Etuwe Prince EBOAGWU	NGA	7/6/86	M	10	(7)	3
1	Henrik GUSTAVSSON		21/10/76	G	30		
5	Daniel HALLINGSTRÖM		10/2/81	D	28		
15	Emil HERGE		15/1/90	M	1	(2)	
9	Christoffer KARLSSON		27/1/88	M	18	(5)	
10	Pontus KARLSSON		19/8/83	M	6	(6)	
3	Erik MOBERG		5/7/86	D	29		1
17	Oscar MÖLLER		15/4/87	A	19	(8)	6
14	Johan NIKLASSON		17/1/85	D	6	(3)	
8	Viktor PRODELL		29/2/88	A	12	(14)	2
11	Haris RADETINAC		28/10/85	M	30		3
24	Glenn ROBERTS	NOR	26/6/88	A	5	(8)	1
22	Paulus ROIHA	FIN	3/8/80	A	17	(11)	7
2	Steinar STRØMNES	NOR	19/5/87	D	8	(3)	
19	Amir SULJIC		9/2/89	M	12	(8)	2
16	Daniel SWÄRD		22/2/90	A		(1)	
23	Anton TINNERHOLM		26/2/91	D	1	(1)	

ÖREBRO SK

Coach – Sixten Boström (FIN)

Founded – 1908

Stadium – Behrn Arena (14,500)

2010				
15/3	Åtvidaberg	h	2-0	*Astvald, Olsen*
23/3	Malmö	a	0-3	
29/3	Mjällby	h	0-2	
5/4	AIK	a	1-0	*Olsen*
12/4	GAIS	h	0-2	
15/4	Brommapojkarna	a	1-0	*Bedoya*
19/4	Gefle	a	3-1	*Wowoah, Porokara, Wirtanen*
25/4	Halmstad	h	3-0	*Kihlberg, Olsen, Paulinho Guará*
28/4	Kalmar	a	1-4	*Astvald*
2/5	Häcken	h	2-0	*Kihlberg, Paulinho Guará*
6/5	Helsingborg	a	1-2	*Paulinho Guará*
9/5	Djurgården	h	1-0	*og (Ceesay)*
13/5	Göteborg	a	0-0	
17/5	Trelleborg	h	2-0	*Porokara, Wowoah*
18/7	Elfsborg	a	3-3	*Anttonen, Porokara, Ajdarevic*
26/7	Elfsborg	h	3-0	*Ajdarevic 2, Wowoah*
2/8	Åtvidaberg	a	2-0	*Gerzic, Paulinho Guará*
7/8	Malmö	h	0-3	
16/8	Mjällby	a	0-1	
23/8	AIK	h	1-0	*Gerzic*
28/8	Helsingborg	h	3-0	*Wikström, Kihlberg, Astvald*
12/9	Djurgården	a	1-2	*Wikström*
19/9	Halmstad	a	1-1	*Johansson*
22/9	Gefle	h	3-1	*Paulinho Guará, Gerzic 2*
28/9	Kalmar	h	1-0	*Bedoya*
3/10	Häcken	a	1-2	*Anttonen*
20/10	GAIS	a	1-0	*og (Lycén)*
25/10	Brommapojkarna	h	1-1	*Ajdarevic (p)*
1/11	Göteborg	h	2-1	*Ajdarevic, Gerzic*
7/11	Trelleborg	a	0-1	

No	Name	Nat	DoB	Pos	Aps	(s)	Gls
12	Denis ABDULAHI	FIN	22/5/90	M		(4)	
2	Astrit AJDAREVIC		17/4/90	M	3	(9)	5
19	Michael ALMEBÄCK		4/4/88	D	28		
82	John ALVBÅGE		10/8/82	G	30		
9	Patrik ANTTONEN		6/3/80	D	25	(1)	2
18	Markus ASTVALD		3/9/90	M	30		3
15	Eric BASSOMBENG	CMR	2/11/83	M	1	(8)	
17	Alejandro BEDOYA	USA	29/4/87	M	26		2
31	Anthony FLOOD	IRL	31/12/84	A		(3)	
25	Nordin GERZIC		9/11/83	M	26		5
5	Per JOHANSSON		6/4/89	D	5	(8)	1
7	Markus KIHLBERG		25/10/73	M	24	(4)	3
14	Simon LEONIDSSON		17/1/92	A		(1)	
21	Erik NILSSON		30/7/89	M	1	(10)	
8	Fredrik NORDBACK	FIN	20/3/79	M	7	(4)	
23	Simon NURME		24/10/82	G		(1)	
6	Kim OLSEN	DEN	2/11/79	A	13		3
29	Paulo Roberto Chamon de Castilho "PAULINHO GUARÁ"	BRA	29/8/79	A	21	(6)	5
33	Roni POROKARA	FIN	12/12/83	M	25	(1)	3
10	Robin STAAF		26/9/86	A		(10)	
4	Magnus WIKSTRÖM		7/12/77	D	30		2
11	Tommy WIRTANEN	FIN	19/1/83	M	5	(4)	1
20	Samuel WOWOAH		17/6/76	D	28		3
3	Bertin Samuel ZÉ NDILE	CMR	17/12/88	D	2	(4)	

TOP GOALSCORERS 2010

20 Alexander GERNDT (Gefle/Helsingborg)

19 Denni AVDIC (Elfsborg)

12 Mathias RANÉGIE (Häcken)

11 Agon MEHMETI (Malmö)

10 Tobias HYSÉN (Göteborg)
RICARDO SANTOS (Kalmar)
Daniel LARSSON (Malmö)
Moestafa EL KABIR (Mjällby)

9 Kennedy IGBOANANIKE (Djurgården)
Jakob ORLOV (Gefle)
DANIEL MENDES (Kalmar)
Markus EKENBERG (Mjällby)

PROMOTED CLUBS

SYRIANSKA FC

Coach – Özkan Melkemichel
Founded – 1977
Stadium – Södertälje Fotbollsarena (6,400)

IFK NORRKÖPING

Coach – Göran Bergort
Founded – 1897
Stadium – Nya Parken (17,234)
MAJOR HONOURS: Swedish League – (12) 1943, 1945, 1946, 1947, 1948, 1952, 1956, 1957, 1960, 1962, 1963, 1989; Swedish Cup – (6) 1943, 1945, 1969, 1988, 1991, 1994.

SECOND LEVEL FINAL TABLE 2010

		Pld	W	D	L	F	A	Pts
1	Syrianska FC	30	16	8	6	46	27	56
2	IFK Norrköping	30	17	5	8	51	33	56
3	GIF Sundsvall	30	13	12	5	56	39	51
4	Assyriska FF	30	13	7	10	48	42	46
5	Landskrona BoIS	30	13	6	11	40	39	45
6	Ljungskile SK	30	11	11	8	47	35	44
7	Falkenbergs FF	30	11	11	8	46	34	44
8	Hammarby Fotboll	30	12	7	11	45	40	43
9	Örgryte IS	30	9	15	6	43	35	42
10	Degerfors IF	30	12	6	12	43	45	42
11	IK Brage	30	11	8	11	36	38	41
12	Ängelholms FF	30	9	10	11	39	39	37
13	Jönköping Södra IF	30	9	9	12	40	47	36
14	Östers IF	30	8	5	17	30	54	29
15	FC Trollhättan	30	5	8	17	32	66	23
16	Väsby United	30	4	6	20	31	60	18

PROMOTION/RELEGATION PLAY-OFFS

(10/11/10)
Sundsvall 0, Gefle 1
(14/11/10)
Gefle 2, Sundsvall 0
(Gefle 3-0)

DOMESTIC CUP 2010

SVENSKA CUPEN

THIRD ROUND

(18/5/10)
Limhamn Bunkeflo 0, Mjällby 1
Ljungskile 2, Djurgården 0
Syrianska 0, Malmö 1 *(aet)*
Ängelholm 1, Halmstad 0
(19/5/10)
Degerfors 0, Elfsborg 2
Falkenberg 0, Brommapojkarna 2
Hammarby TFF 1, Helsingborg 3
Jönköping Södra 2, Åtvidaberg 1 *(aet)*
Trollhättan 0, Kalmar 3
Väsby 0, Göteborg 2
Östersund 0, Häcken 5
(25/5/10)
Norrköping 0, Örebro 2 *(aet)*
Sundsvall 1, GAIS 2 *(aet)*
Örgryte 0, Gefle 1
Öster 1, AIK 3 *(aet)*
(3/6/10)
Hammarby 3, Trelleborg 1

FOURTH ROUND

(27/6/10)
Göteborg 3, Kalmar 4 *(aet)*
Ljungskile 0, Gefle 1
(1/7/10)
Hammarby 3, Elfsborg 1
(2/7/10)
Jönköping Södra 0, Örebro 2
(4/7/10)
GAIS 0, Brommapojkarna 0 *(aet; 3-4 on pens)*
Mjällby 4, Malmö 1
(5/7/10)
Helsingborg 2, Häcken 1
Ängelholm 1, AIK 2 *(aet)*

QUARTER-FINALS

(9/7/10)
AIK 1 *(Ljubojević 33)*, Helsingborg 1 *(Lindström 44) (aet; 3-4 on pens)*
(10/7/10)
Örebro 0, Mjällby 3 *(Nicklasson 9, El Kabir 89, Gitselov 90)*
(11/7/10)
Kalmar 3 *(Ricardo Santos 31, Rydström 105p, Bertilsson 109)*, Gefle 1 *(Lantto 15) (aet)*
(21/7/10)
Hammarby 2 *(Castro-Tello 23p, Hallenius 45)*, Brommapojkarna 2 *(Segerström 13, 81) (aet; 5-4 on pens)*

SEMI-FINALS

(27/10/10)
Hammarby 2 *(Törnstrand 25, Castro-Tello 42)*, Kalmar 2 *(Daniel Sobralense 76, Israelsson 83) (aet; 4-3 on pens)*
(28/10/10)
Helsingborg 2 (Sundin 63, Holgersson 78), Mjällby 0

FINAL

(13/11/10)
Söderstadion, Stockholm
HELSINGBORGS IF 1 *(Jönsson 80)*
HAMMARBY FOTBOLL 0
Referee – *Stålhammar*
HELSINGBORG – *Hansson, Edman, Ekstrand, Nilsson, Andersson (Wahlstedt 46), Bouaouzan (Gashi 46), Lantz, Mahlangu, Jönsson (Patronen 89), Gerndt, Sundin.*
HAMMARBY – *Hopf, Johansson, Törnstrand (Gerrbrand 46), Monteiro, Malke, Furuseth (Gustafsson 75), Traoré, Dahl, Sema, Castro-Tello, Forsberg (Helg 80).*

CLUB COMMUNICATION 2011

AIK Solna
PO Box 1257
SE-171 24 Solna

Tel +46 8 735 9650
Fax +46 8 735 9679
Web aikfotboll.se
Email info@aik.se
Media Officer Stefan Mellerborg

Djurgårdens IF
Klocktornet Lidingövägen 1
SE-114 33 Stockholm

Tel +46 8 5451 5800
Fax +46 8 5451 5801
Web dif.se
Email dif.fotboll@dif.se
Media Officer Jonas Riedel

IF Elfsborg
Ålgårdsvägen 32
SE-50630 Borås

Tel +46 33 139 191
Fax +46 33 129 191
Web elfsborg.se
Email info@elfsborg.se
Media Officer Göran Lohne

GAIS Göteborg
Gamla Boråsvägen
SE-41276 Göteborg

Tel +46 31 403 690
Fax +46 31 406 685
Web gais.se
Email kansli@gais.se
Media Officer Anders Björklund

Gefle IF
PO Box 857
SE-801 31 Gävle

Tel +46 26 652 233
Fax +46 26 610 240
Web gefleiffotboll.se
Email fotboll@gefleif.se
Media Officer Eva von Schéele-Frid

IFK Göteborg
Kamratgårdsvägen 50
SE-41655 Göteborg

Tel +46 31 703 7300
Fax +46 31 404 121
Web ifkgoteborg.se
Email info@ifkgoteborg.se
Media Officer Anna Landberg

Halmstads BK
PO Box 223
SE-30106 Halmstad

Tel +46 35 171 880
Fax +46 35 103 436
Web hbk.se
Email info@hbk.se
Media Officer Mattias Skoog

Helsingborgs IF
PO Box 2074
SE-25002 Helsingborg

Tel +46 42 377 000
Fax +46 42 377 027
Web hif.se
Email info@hif.se
Media Officer Frederik Ericsson

BK Häcken
Entreprenadvägen 6, Box 22051
SE-400 72 Göteborg

Tel +46 31 506 790
Fax +46 31 506 799
Web bkhacken.se
Email kansli@bkhacken.se
Media Officer Marcus Jodin

Kalmar FF
Trångsundsvägen 40
SE-393 56 Kalmar

Tel +46 48 044 4430
Fax +46 48 088 720
Web kalmarff.se
Email kalmarff@kalmarff.se
Media Officer Anders Bengtsson

Malmö FF
PO Box 19067
SE-20073 Malmö

Tel +46 40 326 600
Fax +46 40 326 601
Web mff.se
Email info@mff.se
Media Officer Patrik Jandelin

Mjällby AIF
Campingvägen 44
SE-294 95 Sölvesborg

Tel +46 45 652 939
Fax +46 45 656 239
Web maif.se
Email info@maif.se
Media Officer Jens Wahlström

IFK Norrköping
Ektorpsgatan 1
SE-60237 Norrköping

Tel +46 11 215 500
Fax +46 11 215 515
Web ifknorrkoping.se
Email ifk@ifknorrkoping.se
Media Officer Eva Åberg

Syrianska FC
PO Box 222
SE-15123 Södertälje

Tel 46 85 503 4184
Fax 46 85 038 7939
Web syrianskafc.com
Email info@syrianskafc.com
Media Officer Cecilia Somi

Trelleborgs FF
Östervångsvägen Vångavallen
SE-231 55 Trelleborg

Tel +46 41 057 780
Fax +46 41 013 125
Web trelleborgsff.se
Email info@tff.m.se
Media Officer Håkan Lundkvist

Örebro SK
Rudbecksgatan 52 G
SE-702 23 Örebro

Tel +46 19 167 300
Fax +46 19 167 319
Web oskfotboll.se
Email fotboll@oskfotboll.se
Media Officer Michael Karlberg

SWITZERLAND
Suisse I Schweiz

Schweizerischer Fussballverband/ Association Suisse de Football (SFV/ASF)

COMMUNICATION

Address Worbstrasse 48
Postfach
CH-3000 Bern 15
Tel +41 31 950 8111
Fax +41 31 950 8181

E-mail sfv.asf@football.ch
Website football.ch

President Peter Gilliéron
General Secretary Alex Miescher
Media Officer Marco von Ah

Year of Formation 1895

DOMESTIC COMPETITION SUMMARY 2010/11

SUPER LEAGUE FINAL TABLE

			Home					Away					Total						
		Pld	W	D	L	F	A	W	D	L	F	A	W	D	L	F	A	Pts	Comp
1	FC Basel 1893	36	13	3	2	43	20	8	7	3	33	24	21	10	5	76	44	73	UCL
2	FC Zürich	36	11	6	1	37	17	10	3	5	37	27	21	9	6	74	44	72	UCL
3	BSC Young Boys	36	8	8	2	35	23	7	4	7	30	27	15	12	9	65	50	57	UEL
4	FC Sion	36	9	4	5	25	16	6	5	7	22	20	15	9	12	47	36	54	UEL
5	FC Thun	36	5	8	5	26	23	6	8	4	22	20	11	16	9	48	43	49	UEL
6	FC Luzern	36	8	5	5	32	25	5	4	9	30	32	13	9	14	62	57	48	
7	Grasshopper-Club	36	7	4	7	26	28	3	7	8	19	26	10	11	15	45	54	41	
8	Neuchâtel Xamax FC	36	4	3	11	23	35	4	5	9	21	32	8	8	20	44	67	32	
9	AC Bellinzona	36	4	6	8	21	34	3	5	10	21	41	7	11	18	42	75	32	*Relegated*
10	FC St Gallen	36	3	4	11	15	33	5	3	10	19	34	8	7	21	34	67	31	*Relegated*

Top Scorer Alexander Frei (Basel), 27 goals

Promoted Clubs FC Lausanne-Sport
Servette FC

Cup Final FC Sion 2, Neuchâtel Xamax FC 0

Champions Basel break the mould

FC Basel 1893 broke new ground in 2010/11, successfully defending the Swiss title in a season during which they also participated in the group stage of the UEFA Champions League. Their previous two visits to the elite round of Europe's flagship club competition, in 2002/03 and 2008/09, had been accompanied by disappointment on the domestic front, but it was third time lucky in 2010/11 as they resisted the extra pressure of top-grade European exposure to retain their Super League crown by a one-point margin from FC Zürich.

Led again by Thorsten Fink, the German coach who had steered the club to the domestic double in his debut season, Basel were deeply involved in the title race throughout but, despite a brilliant start to the spring campaign when they reeled off eight consecutive victories, they could never quite shake Zürich off their tail. Although victorious in each of their first three head-to-head encounters, they went into the fourth, at the Letzigrund on 11 May, in second place on goal difference. The match ended 2-2, with Basel's evergreen striker Alexander Frei twice giving the defending champions priceless equalisers, and four days later the value to Basel of that draw was confirmed when they thrashed FC Thun 5-1 at the St Jakob-Park while Zürich went down 3-1 in their derby against Grasshopper-Club.

Last-day triumph

Now, with two games left, it was Basel's title to lose. They could only scramble a 0-0 draw at struggling FC St Gallen the following week while Zürich returned to form with a handsome 5-0 win at FC Luzern – the team that had led the Super League at halfway before plummeting like a stone in the spring. Fortunately, Basel's final fixture was at home to the same opposition, and their one-point advantage was protected with a comfortable 3-0 win, the result never looking in doubt once Frei had opened the scoring in the sixth minute. Zürich also won, 1-0 at home to Thun, but Urs Fischer's gallant side would have to be content with a runners-up spot and a place in the third qualifying round of the 2011/12 UEFA Champions League.

Basel's reward, as champions, was direct qualification for the UEFA Champions League group stage. In 2010/11 they had been obliged to negotiate two qualifying rounds before entering the main event – which they did in style, against Debreceni VSC and FC Sheriff. They were not expected to go any further after drawing FC Bayern München and AS Roma, but a shock 3-1 win in Rome and a 1-0 home success over CFR 1907 Cluj allowed them to pass over into the UEFA Europa League, where they were narrowly edged out in the round of 32 by FC Spartak Moskva.

Although 31-year-old Frei was unquestionably Basel's top dog, his final Super League goal tally of 27 winning him the Golden Boot by a distance, Basel were a productive blend of young and old, with bullish 19-year-old playmaker Xherdan Shaqiri a shooting star of immense promise and elegant 18-year-old midfielder Granit Xhaka, another Swiss youth international of Kosovan origin, also making a strong impression in the latter stages of the campaign. The experience of Marco Streller and

Alexander Frei spearheaded Basel's Super League triumph with 27 goals

Benjamin Huggel was also important, and there were strong contributions too from Argentinian duo Franco Costanzo (in goal) and David Abraham (in defence).

Zürich were less star-studded than Basel, which made the strength and stamina of their title challenge all the more commendable. Under new boss Fischer they were both gutsy and adventurous, with another Swiss young gun Admir Mehmedi repeatedly catching the eye. Zürich finished 15 points ahead of the previous season's runners-up, BSC Young Boys, whose third place was not enough to save coach Vladimir Petković from the sack. The Berne club had an eventful season in Europe, eliminating Fenerbahçe SK from the UEFA Champions League, then taking a 3-0 lead at home to Tottenham Hotspur FC in the play-offs before eventually dropping into the UEFA Europa League, where they won all four matches in the Stade de Suisse en route to a narrow round-of-32 elimination by Russian champions FC Zenit St Petersburg. At home, though, Young Boys never properly recovered from a hesitant start, and a bad run in April cost Petković his job.

Basel's Xherdan Shaqiri – a superstar in the making

National Team

International Tournament Appearances –
FIFA World Cup – (9) 1934, 1938 (qtr-finals), 1950, 1954 (qtr-finals), 1962, 1966, 1994 (2nd round), 2006 (2nd round), 2010.
UEFA European Championship – (3) 1996, 2004, 2008.

Top Five All-time Caps – Heinz Hermann (118); Alain Geiger (112); Stéphane Chapuisat (103); Johann Vogel (94), Hakan Yakin (87)

Top Five All-time Goals – Alexander Frei (42), Xam Abegglen III & Kubilay Türkyilmaz (34), André Abegglen II & Jacky Fatton (29)

Fourth place was filled by FC Sion, who also won the final of the Swiss Cup – for the 12th time in as many appearances. That astonishing run of success in the fixture never looked in peril after goals from French striker Giovanni Sio and Hungarian international defender Vilmos Vanczák put Laurent Roussey's team 2-0 up inside the first six minutes against Neuchâtel Xamax FC in Basel. Four days before the final, Xamax had saved themselves from relegation thanks to a 0-0 draw against Sion in the league, but there would be no favours at the St Jakob-Park, where recently installed Xamax coach Bernand Challandes tasted defeat against the club that had sacked him only three months earlier.

Thun surprise

Challandes, who led Zürich to the Swiss title in 2008/09, did not stay long at his hometown club, however, preferring to accept an offer from Thun, who, a year after promotion, had just qualified for Europe by finishing fifth in the Super League under ex-Swiss international defender Murat Yakin. Thun were the season's surprise package, proving extremely tough to beat, but Yakin did not hang around to see the club move into their new Thun Süd Stadium in 2011/12. He moved instead to Luzern, whose coach Rolf Fringer had been unable to survive the club's horrendous spring decline, when they dropped from first place to sixth and out of the European frame.

A tight three-way battle at the bottom resulted in automatic relegation for Switzerland's oldest club, FC St Gallen, who, after almost folding earlier in the campaign, dropped down to the Challenge League with a last-day defeat at Young Boys. AC Bellinzona finished ninth again but, unlike the previous year, lost their play-off, 3-2 on aggregate to Servette FC, who thus restored top-flight football to Geneva six years after the club had been declared bankrupt.

NATIONAL TEAM RESULTS 2010/11

11/8/10	Austria	A	Klagenfurt	1-0	*Costanzo (73)*
3/9/10	Australia	H	St Gallen	0-0	
7/9/10	England (ECQ)	H	Basel	1-3	*Shaqiri (71)*
8/10/10	Montenegro (ECQ)	A	Podgorica	0-1	
12/10/10	Wales (ECQ)	H	Basel	4-1	*Stocker (8, 89), Streller (21), Inler (82p)*
17/11/10	Ukraine	H	Geneva	2-2	*Frei (39, 61)*
9/2/11	Malta	A	Ta' Qali	0-0	
26/3/11	Bulgaria (ECQ)	A	Sofia	0-0	
4/6/11	England (ECQ)	A	Wembley	2-2	*Barnetta (32, 35)*

NATIONAL TEAM APPEARANCES 2010/11

Coach – Ottmar HITZFELD (GER)	**12/1/49**		**Aut**	**Aus**	**ENG**	**MNE**	**WAL**	**Ukr**	**Mlt**	**BUL**	**ENG**	**Caps**	**Goals**
Diego BENAGLIO	8/9/83	Wolfsburg (GER)	G		G		G8		G		G	35	-
Stephan LICHTSTEINER	16/1/84	Lazio (ITA)	D	D46	D 65*		D	D71	D	D	D	39	-
François AFFOLTER	13/3/91	Young Boys	D	D				D	s31			4	-
Stéphane GRICHTING	30/3/79	Auxerre (FRA)	D46	D46	D	D	D		D31	D		45	1
Reto ZIEGLER	16/1/86	Sampdoria (ITA)	D	s70	D	D	D	D	D	D	D	24	1
Xherdan SHAQIRI	10/10/91	Basel	M58	s46	s46	M67		s46	s62		M	11	1
Gökhan INLER	27/6/84	Udinese (ITA)	M	M46	M	M	M	M46	M73	M	M	48	4
Pirmin SCHWEGLER	9/3/87	Eintracht (GER)	M81	s46	M83	M	M91	M66	M41			11	-
Valentin STOCKER	12/4/89	Basel	M75			M76	M	M84	M62	M67		9	3
Hakan YAKIN	22/2/77	Luzern	A71			s76		A	A46			87	20
Eren DERDIYOK	12/6/88	Leverkusen (GER)	A71	A46	A	s67	s79		M	s67	A75	32	2
Mario EGGIMANN	24/1/81	Hannover (GER)	s46									10	-
Marco PADALINO	8/12/83	Sampdoria (ITA)	s58									9	1
Nassim BEN KHALIFA	13/1/92	Wolfsburg (GER)	s71					s76				2	-
Moreno COSTANZO	20/2/88	Young Boys	s71	s67	s83			s66				4	1
Albert BUNJAKU	29/11/83	Nürnberg (GER)	s75	M								6	-
Gelson FERNANDES	2/9/86	St-Étienne (FRA) /Chievo (ITA)	s81	D			s91	s46	s73	s17		33	2
Marco WÖLFLI	22/8/82	Young Boys		G		G	s8	G		G		10	-
David DEGEN	15/2/83	Young Boys		M70	M64			s84	s80			14	-
Xavier MARGAIRAZ	7/1/84	Zürich		M	M46							18	1
Alexander FREI	15/7/79	Basel		A67	A	A	A79	A76	A80	A		84	42
Steve VON BERGEN	10/6/83	Cesena (ITA)		s46	D	D	D	s71	D	D		21	-
Scott SUTTER	13/5/86	Young Boys		s46		D						2	-
Marco STRELLER	18/6/81	Basel			s64	A67	A		s46	A77		37	12
Tranquillo BARNETTA	22/5/85	Leverkusen (GER)				s67	M	M46			M90	59	8
Johan DJOUROU	18/1/87	Arsenal (ENG)						D			D	26	1
Blerim DZEMAILI	12/4/86	Parma (ITA)							s41	M	s59	13	-
Valon BEHRAMI	19/4/85	Fiorentina (ITA)								M17	M59	30	2
Mario GAVRANOVIC	24/11/89	Schalke (GER)								s77		1	-
Philippe SENDEROS	14/2/85	Fulham (ENG)									D	42	5
Granit XHAKA	27/9/92	Basel									M	1	-
Admir MEHMEDI	16/3/91	Zürich									s75	1	-
Innocent EMEGHARA	27/5/89	Grasshoppers									s90	1	-

SWITZERLAND

Another phoenix rose from the flames as FC Lausanne-Sport won the Challenge League to return to the top division after nine years away. In addition to promotion, the lakeside club enjoyed a bonus run in the UEFA Europa League, reaching the group stage after sensationally overcoming FC Lokomotiv Moskva on penalties.

Poor start

Switzerland's bid to reach a fifth successive major international tournament got off to a terrible start when Ottmar Hitzfeld's team, still nursing their FIFA World Cup wounds, lost their opening two qualifiers, at home to England and away to Montenegro. An uplifting 4-1 victory over Wales in Basel came next, but despite holding both Bulgaria and England to worthy away draws in the spring, five points from five matches left them requiring a maximum haul from their last three fixtures to have any hope of reaching the play-offs.

The goalless draw in Sofia proved to be the last match in the illustrious international career of Switzerland's record scorer Frei, who, in tandem with his Basel team-mate Streller, reacted to some harsh media criticism by announcing his immediate retirement from the team. With 42 goals in 84 matches, he will be a hard act to follow, but with the likes of Shaqiri, Xhaka, Mehmedi, Innocent Emeghara and goalkeeper Yann Sommer all making a profound impression at the 2011 UEFA European Under-21 Championship in Denmark, where Pierluigi Tami's Swiss team finished runners-up to Spain, there is every chance that Switzerland's senior side will be challenging strongly at FIFA World Cups and UEFA European Championships over the next decade and beyond. Indeed, Hitzfeld effectively turned a new page for the team in his selection for the June qualifier at Wembley, where the oldest player on view was 27-year-old goalkeeper Diego Benaglio and the average age of a starting XI that included Shaqiri and Xhafa was just 24 years and eight months.

CLUB-BY-CLUB

FC BASEL 1893

Coach – Thorsten Fink (GER)

Founded – 1893

Stadium – St Jakob-Park (38,500)

MAJOR HONOURS: Swiss League – (14) 1953, 1967, 1969, 1970, 1972, 1973, 1977, 1980, 2002, 2004, 2005, 2008, 2010, 2011; Swiss Cup – (10) 1933, 1947, 1963, 1967, 1975, 2002, 2003, 2007, 2008, 2010.

2010				
20/7	Zürich	h	3-2	*Frei 2, Zoua*
24/7	Sion	a	2-1	*Frei, Abraham*
1/8	St Gallen	h	3-0	*Frei, Yapi Yapo, Almerares*
7/8	Bellinzona	a	0-1	
14/8	Luzern	h	1-4	*Tembo*
21/8	Thun	a	1-1	*Schürpf*
28/8	Xamax	h	4-1	*Streller, Frei 3 (1p)*
12/9	Young Boys	a	2-2	*Frei, Chipperfield*
22/9	Grasshoppers	h	2-2	*Abraham, Streller*
25/9	Zürich	a	4-1	*Inkoom, Streller 2, Stocker*
3/10	Sion	h	1-1	*Stocker*
24/10	St Gallen	a	3-1	*Streller 3*
30/10	Bellinzona	h	3-1	*Chipperfield 2, Almerares*
7/11	Luzern	a	1-1	*Almerares*
13/11	Thun	h	1-3	*Chipperfield*
28/11	Xamax	a	2-1	*Almerares, Stocker*
4/12	Young Boys	h	3-1	*Frei 2, Shaqiri*
12/12	Grasshoppers	a	1-2	*Streller*
2011				
6/2	Thun	a	3-2	*Stocker, Abraham, Frei*
12/2	St Gallen	h	3-0	*Huggel, Frei, Abraham*
20/2	Sion	h	1-0	*Shaqiri*
27/2	Luzern	a	1-0	*Frei*
6/3	Zürich	h	3-1	*Zoua, Frei 2*
13/3	Bellinzona	a	4-0	*Shaqiri, Zoua, Stocker 2*
20/3	Grasshoppers	a	2-1	*Streller, Frei*
2/4	Xamax	h	1-0	*Frei*
10/4	Young Boys	a	3-3	*Frei, Streller, Tembo (p)*
17/4	Grasshoppers	h	2-2	*Frei, Abraham*
20/4	Xamax	a	2-2	*Stocker, Frei*
23/4	Young Boys	h	2-1	*Chipperfield, Frei*
1/5	Sion	a	0-3	
8/5	Bellinzona	h	2-0	*Huggel, Frei*
11/5	Zürich	a	2-2	*Frei 2*
15/5	Thun	h	5-1	*Huggel, Frei 2 (1p), Xhaka G., Shaqiri*
22/5	St Gallen	a	0-0	
25/5	Luzern	h	3-0	*Frei, Shaqiri, Zoua*

No	Name	Nat	DoB	Pos	Aps	(s)	Gls
19	David Ángel ABRAHAM	ARG	15/7/86	D	27	(1)	5
15	Federico ALMERARES	ARG	2/5/85	A	3	(11)	4
35	Matthias BARON	GER	17/8/88	A		(4)	
24	Adilson Tavares Varela "CABRAL"		22/10/88	M	10	(11)	
4	ÇAĞDAŞ Atan	TUR	29/2/80	D	10		
11	Scott CHIPPERFIELD	AUS	30/12/75	A	6	(15)	5
23	Massimo COLOMBA		24/8/77	G		(1)	
1	Franco COSTANZO	ARG	5/9/80	G	32		
6	Aleksandar DRAGOVIC	AUT	6/3/91	D	16		
28	Beg FERATI		10/11/86	D	15	(1)	
13	Alexander FREI		15/7/79	A	33	(2)	27
8	Benjamin HUGGEL		7/7/77	M	23	(3)	3
22	Samuel INKOOM	GHA	22/8/89	D	15	(1)	1
21	Genséric KUSUNGA		12/3/88	D	4	(3)	
20	Behrang SAFARI	SWE	9/2/85	D	28		
7	Pascal SCHÜRPF		15/7/89	M	1	(4)	1
17	Xherdan SHAQIRI		10/10/91	M	26	(3)	5
18	Yann SOMMER		17/12/88	G	4		
27	Markus STEINHÖFER	GER	7/3/86	D	18		
14	Valentin STOCKER		12/4/89	M	25	(1)	7
9	Marco STRELLER		18/6/81	A	27		10
30	Fwayo TEMBO	ZAM	2/5/89	M	15	(10)	2
26	Daniel UNAL		18/1/90	M	1	(3)	
33	Sandro WIESER	LIE	3/2/93	M		(2)	
34	Granit XHAKA		27/9/92	M	11	(9)	1
16	Taulant XHAKA		28/3/91	D		(5)	
10	Gilles Donald YAPI YAPO	CIV	30/1/82	M	30	(1)	1
32	Reto ZANNI		9/2/80	D	4	(1)	
31	Jacques ZOUA Daogari	CMR	6/9/91	A	12	(10)	4

AC BELLINZONA

Coach – Roberto Morinini; (21/3/11) Carlo Tebi (ITA)
Founded – 1904
Stadium – Stadio Comunale (6,000)
MAJOR HONOURS: Swiss League – (1) 1948.

2010				
18/7	Sion	h	0-2	
25/7	St Gallen	a	2-3	*Lustrinelli (p), Diarra*
31/7	Young Boys	h	2-1	*Feltscher, Lustrinelli*
7/8	Basel	h	1-0	*Lustrinelli*
15/8	Zürich	a	2-2	*og (Koch P.), Diarra*
22/8	Xamax	a	2-1	*Diarra, Raso*
29/8	Grasshoppers	h	1-1	*Mihajlović*
12/9	Luzern	a	2-6	*Lustrinelli 2*
23/9	Thun	h	2-2	*Feltscher, Sermeter*
26/9	Sion	a	1-1	*Sermeter*
1/10	St Gallen	h	1-3	*Edusei*
24/10	Young Boys	a	1-1	*Mattila*
30/10	Basel	a	1-3	*Feltscher*
6/11	Zürich	h	1-2	*Lustrinelli*
13/11	Xamax	h	3-3	*Lustrinelli, Diarra, Feltscher*
27/11	Grasshoppers	a	3-2	*Ciarrocchi, og (Paulo Menezes), Sermeter*
5/12	Luzern	h	0-3	
11/12	Thun	a	0-0	
2011				
5/2	Young Boys	h	1-5	*Conti*
12/2	Sion	a	0-1	
20/2	Luzern	h	2-0	*Lustrinelli, Mihoubi*
26/2	Zürich	a	0-5	
6/3	Xamax	a	2-1	*Lustrinelli, Mihajlović*
13/3	Basel	h	0-4	
19/3	St Gallen	a	0-1	
2/4	Grasshoppers	a	2-2	*Thiesson, Lustrinelli*
9/4	Thun	h	1-1	*Lustrinelli*
16/4	Young Boys	a	0-4	
19/4	Sion	h	2-2	*Lustrinelli, Konan*
23/4	Luzern	a	2-3	*Lustrinelli, Konan*
1/5	Zürich	h	0-1	
8/5	Basel	a	0-2	
11/5	St Gallen	h	1-3	*Lustrinelli*
14/5	Xamax	h	1-1	*Conti*
22/5	Thun	a	1-3	*og (Bättig)*
25/5	Grasshoppers	h	2-0	*Feltscher 2*

No	Name	Nat	DoB	Pos	Aps	(s)	Gls
15	Branko BANKOVIC		11/4/92	A	2	(4)	
29	Mamadou Djamil CAMARA	SEN	15/10/90	A		(2)	
32	Alessandro CIARROCCHI		3/1/88	A	10	(10)	1
10	Andrea CONTI	ITA	23/8/77	M	8	(8)	2
2	Aimo DIANA	ITA	2/1/78	D	16		
24	Drissa DIARRA	MLI	7/7/85	M	32	(2)	4
23	Mark EDUSEI	GHA	29/9/76	M	30	(2)	1
21	Frank FELTSCHER		17/5/88	M	29	(5)	6
1	Matteo GRITTI	ITA	11/6/80	G	30		
11	Axel Cédric KONAN	CIV	25/1/83	A	13	(3)	2
25	Iacopo LA ROCCA	ITA	17/2/84	D	12		
26	Ildefonso LIMA Solà	AND	10/12/79	D	9	(10)	
16	Mauro LUSTRINELLI		26/2/76	A	28	(2)	14
5	Alessandro MANGIARRATTI		15/9/78	D	19	(6)	
17	Sakari Mikael MATTILA	FIN	14/7/89	M	16	(9)	1
14	Dragan MIHAJLOVIĆ	BIH	22/8/91	M	15	(11)	2
3	Hemza MIHOUBI	ALG	13/1/86	M	15	(4)	1
27	Pavel PERGL	CZE	14/11/77	D	24		
7	Angelo RASO	ITA	20/7/81	D	17	(3)	1
22	Manuel Garrido RIVERA		16/3/78	M	2	(2)	
8	Gürkan SERMETER		14/2/74	M	9	(15)	3
4	Henry SIQUEIRA-BARRAS		15/1/85	D	17	(1)	
13	Ville Olavi TAULO	FIN	14/8/85	M	1	(2)	
6	Jérôme THIESSON		6/8/87	D	33		1
20	Adewale Dauda WAHAB	NGA	4/10/84	M	3	(6)	
30	Carlo ZOTTI	ITA	3/9/82	G	6	(1)	

GRASSHOPPER-CLUB

Coach – Ciriaco Sforza
Founded – 1886
Stadium – Letzigrund (26,000)
MAJOR HONOURS: Swiss League – (27) 1898, 1900, 1901, 1905, 1921, 1927, 1928, 1931, 1937, 1939, 1942, 1943, 1945, 1952, 1956, 1971, 1978, 1982, 1983, 1984, 1990, 1991, 1995, 1996, 1998, 2001, 2003; Swiss Cup – (18) 1926, 1927, 1932, 1934, 1937, 1938, 1940, 1941, 1942, 1943, 1946, 1952, 1956, 1983, 1988, 1989, 1990, 1994.

2010				
17/7	Xamax	h	1-1	*Rennella*
25/7	Zürich	a	0-2	
1/8	Thun	a	2-2	*Smiljanic 2 (2p)*
8/8	Young Boys	h	1-2	*Rennella*
15/8	St Gallen	a	2-1	*Salatic, Toko*
22/8	Luzern	h	0-3	
29/8	Bellinzona	a	1-1	*og (Mangiarratti)*
22/9	Basel	a	2-2	*Paulo Menezes, Emeghara*
27/9	Xamax	a	1-1	*Emeghara*
3/10	Zürich	h	1-2	*Freuler*
24/10	Thun	h	0-0	
31/10	Young Boys	a	0-1	
7/11	St Gallen	h	2-0	*Abrashi, Zuber*
10/11	Sion	h	0-4	
14/11	Luzern	a	2-3	*Zuber, Hajrovic*
27/11	Bellinzona	h	2-3	*Paulo Menezes, Pavlovic*
5/12	Sion	a	0-2	
12/12	Basel	h	2-1	*Emeghara 2*
2011				
6/2	St Gallen	a	4-1	*Frick, Emeghara 2, Smiljanic (p)*
13/2	Thun	h	0-0	
19/2	Xamax	a	0-0	
26/2	Sion	a	0-2	
5/3	Young Boys	h	3-2	*Rennella 2, Hajrovic*
12/3	Luzern	a	0-1	
20/3	Basel	h	1-2	*Toko*
2/4	Bellinzona	h	2-2	*Rennella, Callà*
10/4	Zürich	a	0-1	
17/4	Basel	a	2-2	*Pavlovic, Callà*
20/4	St Gallen	h	1-3	*Callà*
25/4	Thun	a	1-0	*Emeghara*
30/4	Luzern	h	2-1	*Smiljanic (p), Zuber*
7/5	Xamax	h	3-1	*Hajrovic, Zuber, Adili*
10/5	Young Boys	a	2-2	*Rennella, Emeghara*
15/5	Zürich	h	3-1	*Rennella 2, Hajrovic (p)*
22/5	Sion	h	2-0	*Hajrovic, Emeghara*
25/5	Bellinzona	a	0-2	

No	Name	Nat	DoB	Pos	Aps	(s)	Gls
8	Amir ABRASHI		27/3/90	M	22	(5)	1
25	Endogan ADILI		3/8/94	M	1	(14)	1
19	Vullnet BASHA		11/7/90	M	2	(3)	
27	Ivan BENITO		27/8/76	G	10	(1)	
27	Roman BÜRKI		14/11/90	G	11		
15	Ricardo CABANAS		17/1/79	M	3	(1)	
10	Davide CALLÀ		6/10/84	M	9	(1)	3
5	Josip COLINA		8/11/80	D	17	(9)	
24	Dušan CVETINOVIĆ	SRB	24/12/88	D	5	(2)	
7	Innocent EMEGHARA		27/5/89	A	26	(7)	9
30	Remo FREULER		15/4/92	M	2	(3)	1
34	Mario FRICK	LIE	7/9/74	A	7	(1)	1
21	Milan GAJIĆ	SRB	17/11/86	M	6	(1)	
19	Mirco GRAF		1/6/88	A	2	(5)	
14	Izet HAJROVIC		4/8/91	M	10	(11)	5
22	Gianluca HOSSMANN		25/3/91	D	1		
1	Swen KÖNIG		3/9/85	G	15		
9	Steven LANG		3/9/87	M	17	(5)	
16	Emir LENJANI		5/8/89	M	1	(5)	
3	PAULO MENEZES	BRA	14/7/82	D	31	(1)	2
28	Dusan PAVLOVIC		22/4/88	D	23	(4)	2

20	Vincenzo RENNELLA	ITA	8/10/88	A	13	(7)	8
11	Alessandro RIEDLE	GER	14/8/91	A		(8)	
13	Enzo Daniel RUIZ Eizaga	URU	31/8/88	D	3	(3)	
17	Veroljub SALATIC		14/11/85	M	31		1
35	SILAS dos Santos Brindeiro	BRA	14/7/87	A	2	(1)	
21	Boris SMILJANIC		28/9/76	D	18	(1)	4
28	Nzuzi Bundebele TOKO	COD	20/11/90	M	27	(2)	2
4	Guillermo Juan VALLORI Grimalt	ESP	25/6/82	D	35		
16	Andrés Javier VÁSQUEZ	SWE	16/7/87	M		(1)	
2	Kay VOSER		4/1/87	D	13		
31	Steven ZUBER		17/8/91	M	33	(1)	4

FC LUZERN

Coach – Rolf Fringer; (2/5/11) (Christian Brand (GER))
Founded – 1901
Stadium – Gersag, Emmenbrucke (8,100)
MAJOR HONOURS: Swiss League – (1) 1989;
Swiss Cup – (2) 1960, 1992.

2010				
18/7	St Gallen	h	4-0	*Yakin, Gygax 2, Ferreira*
24/7	Young Boys	a	1-1	*Ianu*
1/8	Xamax	h	4-2	*Ferreira, Ianu 2, og (Dampha)*
8/8	Sion	h	2-3	*Ferreira, Yakin*
14/8	Basel	a	4-1	*Gygax, Yakin 2 (1p), Pacar*
22/8	Grasshoppers	a	3-0	*Ferreira, Yakin, Paiva*
29/8	Thun	h	1-1	*Puljić*
12/9	Bellinzona	h	6-2	*Paiva 2, Ferreira, Yakin, Puljić, Pacar*
25/9	St Gallen	a	2-1	*Ferreira, Paiva*
3/10	Young Boys	h	2-0	*Zverotić, Pacar*
23/10	Xamax	a	1-2	*Paiva*
27/10	Zürich	a	2-2	*Paiva, Gygax*
30/10	Sion	a	1-4	*Yakin*
7/11	Basel	h	1-1	*Ferreira*
14/11	Grasshoppers	h	3-2	*Gygax, Paiva, Kibebe*
27/11	Thun	a	1-1	*Yakin (p)*
5/12	Bellinzona	a	3-0	*Yakin, Gygax, Lustenberger*
11/12	Zürich	h	1-1	*Puljić*
2011				
5/2	Zürich	a	0-2	
13/2	Xamax	h	2-1	*Lambert, Siegrist*
20/2	Bellinzona	a	0-2	
27/2	Basel	h	0-1	
6/3	Thun	a	3-3	*Puljić, Renggli (p), Gygax*
12/3	Grasshoppers	h	1-0	*Yakin*
20/3	Young Boys	a	1-3	*Siegrist*
3/4	St Gallen	h	1-1	*Gygax*
9/4	Sion	h	0-1	
17/4	Xamax	a	1-2	*Renggli*
20/4	Thun	h	0-1	
23/4	Bellinzona	h	3-2	*Puljić, Ferreira, og (Gritti)*
30/4	Grasshoppers	a	1-2	*og (Bürki)*
7/5	Young Boys	h	1-1	*Lustenberger*
10/5	Sion	a	2-3	*Siegrist, Ferreira*
14/5	St Gallen	a	4-0	*Siegrist, Yakin 2, Ianu*
22/5	Zürich	h	0-5	
25/5	Basel	a	0-3	

No	Name	Nat	DoB	Pos	Aps	(s)	Gls
28	Sava Miladinovic BENTO	POR	2/1/91	M	3	(4)	
33	Mario BÜHLER		5/1/92	D	2		
2	Daniel FANGER		11/8/88	D	8	(5)	
21	Nélson FERREIRA	POR	26/5/82	M	35		9
11	Daniel GYGAX		28/8/81	M	34	(1)	8
16	Cristian Florin IANU	ROU	16/10/83	A	10	(10)	4
4	Benjamin KIBEBE	SWE	13/8/81	D	8	(3)	1
20	Benedikt KOLLER		5/3/90	M		(1)	
29	Hekuran KRYEZIU		12/2/93	M	1		
22	Burim KUKELI	ALB	16/1/84	M	24	(4)	
13	Christophe LAMBERT		23/2/87	D	13	(4)	1
3	Babatunde Adekunle LUKMON	NGA	10/10/84	D	3	(2)	
7	Claudio LUSTENBERGER		6/1/87	D	26		2
31	Calderon MAVEMBO		28/7/90	A		(2)	
15	Janko PACAR		18/8/90	A	4	(25)	3
14	João Pedro de Lemos PAIVA	POR	8/2/83	A	9	(7)	7
8	Thomas PRAGER	AUT	13/9/85	M		(18)	
6	Tomislav PULJIĆ	CRO	21/3/83	D	32		5
5	Michel RENGGLI		19/3/80	M	35		2
25	Nico SIEGRIST		9/6/91	A	15	(3)	4
26	Dejan SORGIĆ	SRB	15/9/89	A		(1)	
27	Marijan URTIĆ	CRO	16/1/91	D	4	(1)	
17	Dušan VESKOVAĆ	SRB	16/3/86	D	27		
24	Alain WISS		21/8/90	M	14	(8)	
30	Gabriel WÜTHRICH		28/8/81	G	1		
10	Hakan YAKIN		22/2/77	M	32		12
1	David ZIBUNG		10/1/84	G	35		
19	Elsad ZVEROTIĆ	MNE	31/10/86	D	21	(6)	1

NEUCHÂTEL XAMAX FC

Coach – Jean-Michel Aeby; (27/8/10) (Radu Nunweiler); (2/9/10) Didier Ollé-Nicolle (FRA); (12/5/11) Bernard Challandes
Founded – 1970
Stadium – La Maladière (11,977)
MAJOR HONOURS: Swiss League – (2) 1987, 1988.

2010				
17/7	Grasshoppers	a	1-1	*Kuljic*
25/7	Thun	h	2-3	*Varela (p), Gohou*
1/8	Luzern	a	2-4	*Gelabert, Gohou*
7/8	Zürich	h	3-4	*Nuzzolo, Page 2*
14/8	Young Boys	a	1-0	*Wüthrich*
22/8	Bellinzona	h	1-2	*Niasse*
28/8	Basel	a	1-4	*Gohou*
12/9	St Gallen	h	0-1	
23/9	Sion	a	2-1	*Kuljic, Wüthrich*
27/9	Grasshoppers	h	1-1	*Geiger*
2/10	Thun	a	2-1	*Gohou, Niasse*
23/10	Luzern	h	2-1	*Gohou, Ismail*
30/10	Zürich	a	1-3	*Gohou*
7/11	Young Boys	h	2-4	*Besle, Page*
13/11	Bellinzona	a	3-3	*Tréand, Ismail, Nuzzolo*
28/11	Basel	h	1-2	*Nuzzolo*
4/12	St Gallen	a	2-0	*Ismail, Mveng*
12/12	Sion	h	0-3	
2011				
6/2	Sion	h	1-0	*Nuzzolo*
13/2	Luzern	a	1-2	*Keller*
19/2	Grasshoppers	h	0-0	
27/2	Young Boys	a	2-3	*Almerares, Page*
6/3	Bellinzona	h	1-2	*Almerares*
13/3	Thun	a	0-1	
19/3	Zürich	h	1-2	*Gelabert*
2/4	Basel	a	0-1	
10/4	St Gallen	a	1-1	*Nuzzolo (p)*
17/4	Luzern	h	2-1	*Almerares 2*
20/4	Basel	h	2-2	*Niasse, Nuzzolo*
28/4	Zürich	a	0-3	
1/5	St Gallen	h	2-1	*Niasse, Tréand*
7/5	Grasshoppers	a	1-3	*Keller*
11/5	Thun	h	1-4	*Keller*
14/5	Bellinzona	a	1-1	*Gohou*
22/5	Young Boys	h	1-2	*Nuzzolo*
25/5	Sion	a	0-0	

No	Name	Nat	DoB	Pos	Aps	(s)	Gls
10	Federico ALMERARES	ARG	2/5/85	A	14	(2)	4
1	Jean-François BEDENIK	FRA	20/11/78	G	17		

4	Stéphane BESLE	FRA	23/1/84	D	33		1
3	Gilles Augustin BINYA	CMR	29/8/84	M	27	(3)	
6	Abdou Rahman DAMPHA	GAM	27/12/91	M	9	(8)	
8	Mickaël FACCHINETTI		15/2/91	D	15	(7)	
23	FAUSTO Jorge Dias Lourenço	POR	19/1/87	A	1	(8)	
30	Luca FERRO	ITA	28/8/78	G	19		
10	Shkelzen GASHI		15/7/88	M		(1)	
33	Bastien GEIGER		26/2/85	D	16	(2)	1
20	Marcos Agustín GELABERT	ARG	16/9/81	M	17	(1)	2
9	Gérard Bi Goua GOHOU	CIV	29/12/88	A	17	(13)	7
15	Abdullah Omar ISMAIL	BHR	1/1/87	D	21	(6)	3
17	Sander KELLER	NED	18/9/79	D	15	(1)	3
27	Sanel KULJIC	AUT	10/10/77	A	5	(7)	2
34	Freddy MVENG	CMR	29/5/92	M	21	(5)	1
13	Ibrahima NIASSE Baye	SEN	18/4/88	M	28	(3)	4
14	Raphael NUZZOLO		5/7/83	M	31	(1)	7
24	Frédéric PAGE		28/12/78	D	34	(1)	4
5	Martinho Martins Mukana "PAÍTO"	MOZ	5/7/82	D	28	(1)	
11	Geoffrey TRÉAND	FRA	16/1/86	M	13	(14)	2
7	Carlos VARELA	ESP	15/9/77	M	4		1
22	Sébastien WÜTHRICH		29/5/90	M	11	(13)	2

FC SION

Coach – Bernard Challandes; (23/2/11) Laurent Roussey (FRA)

Founded – 1909

Stadium – Tourbillon (16,500)

MAJOR HONOURS: Swiss League – (2) 1992, 1997; Swiss Cup – (12) 1965, 1974, 1980, 1982, 1986, 1991, 1995, 1996, 1997, 2006, 2009, 2011.

2010				
18/7	Bellinzona	a	2-0	*Bühler, Prijovic*
24/7	Basel	h	1-2	*Dingsdag (p)*
31/7	Zürich	a	1-1	*Ogăraru*
8/8	Luzern	a	3-2	*Sio, Obradović 2*
15/8	Thun	h	1-1	*Zambrella*
21/8	St Gallen	a	1-1	*Sio*
29/8	Young Boys	h	2-0	*Obradović, Sio*
23/9	Xamax	h	1-2	*Vanczák*
26/9	Bellinzona	h	1-1	*Mrđa*
3/10	Basel	a	1-1	*Bühler*
23/10	Zürich	h	1-1	*Vanczák*
30/10	Luzern	h	4-1	*Vanczák, Sio, Ogăraru, Sauthier*
6/11	Thun	a	0-1	
10/11	Grasshoppers	a	4-0	*Adaílton, Mrđa 2 (1p), Obradović*
14/11	St Gallen	h	0-2	
28/11	Young Boys	a	1-2	*Rodrigo*
5/12	Grasshoppers	h	2-0	*Sio, Mrđa*
12/12	Xamax	a	3-0	*Vanczák, Mrđa (p), Sio*
2011				
6/2	Xamax	a	0-1	
12/2	Bellinzona	h	1-0	*Mrđa*
20/2	Basel	a	0-1	
26/2	Grasshoppers	h	2-0	*Mrđa (p), Yoda*
5/3	St Gallen	h	2-0	*Prijovic, Mrđa*
12/3	Zürich	a	0-2	
20/3	Thun	h	1-0	*Prijovic*
3/4	Young Boys	h	0-2	
9/4	Luzern	a	1-0	*Vanczák*
16/4	Zürich	h	0-2	
19/4	Bellinzona	a	2-2	*Zambrella, Sio*
23/4	St Gallen	a	1-0	*Prijovic*
1/5	Basel	h	3-0	*Prijovic 2, Sio*
7/5	Thun	a	1-3	*Domínguez*
10/5	Luzern	h	3-2	*Adaílton, Domínguez (p), Sio*
15/5	Young Boys	a	1-1	*Sio*
22/5	Grasshoppers	a	0-2	
25/5	Xamax	h	0-0	

No	Name	Nat	DoB	Pos	Aps	(s)	Gls
33	ADAÍLTON José dos Santos Filho	BRA	16/4/83	D	27	(3)	2
17	Saidu Alade ADESHINA	NGA	4/4/83	A		(1)	
17	Florian BERISHA		18/1/90	M		(2)	
31	Arnaud BÜHLER		17/1/85	D	35		2
14	Loïc CHATTON		26/2/91	A	3	(11)	
16	Didier CRETTENAND		24/2/86	M	1		
5	Michael Christiaan DINGSDAG	NED	18/10/82	D	33	(1)	1
23	Álvaro José DOMÍNGUEZ	COL	10/6/81	M	15	(8)	2
3	Jonas ELMER		28/2/88	D	8	(12)	
4	Enes FERMINO		29/5/87	M		(1)	
18	Kevin FICKENTSCHER		6/7/88	G	3	(1)	
7	Nicolas MARIN	FRA	29/8/80	M	8	(9)	
34	Christ MBONDI	CMR	2/2/92	A	1		
29	Yancoub MÉÏTÉ	CIV	10/2/90	M	1		
19	Dragan MRĐA	SRB	23/1/84	A	17	(1)	8
22	Goran OBRADOVIĆ	SRB	1/3/76	M	31	(2)	4
6	Gheorghe Cristian OGĂRARU	ROU	3/2/80	D	27	(1)	2
9	Aleksandar PRIJOVIC		21/4/90	A	14	(11)	6
8	RODRIGO Lacerda Ramos Ferruzem	BRA	6/10/80	M	26	(4)	1
32	Anthony SAUTHIER		5/2/91	M	14	(14)	1
26	Sereso "SEREY" Geoffroy Gonzaroua DIE	CIV	7/11/84	M	8	(5)	
13	Giovanni SIO	FRA	31/3/89	A	26	(4)	10
20	Vilmos VANCZÁK	HUN	20/6/83	D	32	(1)	5
1	Andris VAŅINS	LVA	30/4/80	G	33		
21	Abdoul Karim YODA		25/10/88	M	12	(8)	1
10	Fabrizio ZAMBRELLA		1/3/86	M	21	(6)	2

FC ST GALLEN

Coach – Uli Forte; (1/3/11) (Giorgio Contini & Roger Zürcher); (8/3/11) Jeff Saibene (LUX)

Founded – 1879

Stadium – AFG Arena (19,694)

MAJOR HONOURS: Swiss League – (2) 1904, 2000; Swiss Cup – (1) 1969.

2010				
18/7	Luzern	a	0-4	
25/7	Bellinzona	h	3-2	*Frei 2 (1p), Muntwiler*
1/8	Basel	a	0-3	
8/8	Thun	a	0-3	
15/8	Grasshoppers	h	1-2	*Schenkel*
21/8	Sion	h	1-1	*Abegglen*
28/8	Zürich	a	1-3	*Frei*
12/9	Xamax	a	1-0	*Lang*
22/9	Young Boys	h	1-2	*Muntwiler*
25/9	Luzern	h	1-2	*Bakens*
1/10	Bellinzona	a	3-1	*Frick, og (Raso), Calabro*
24/10	Basel	h	1-3	*Frei*
31/10	Thun	h	2-1	*Schenkel 2*
7/11	Grasshoppers	a	0-2	
14/11	Sion	a	2-0	*Calabro, Frei*
28/11	Zürich	h	0-3	
4/12	Xamax	h	0-2	
12/12	Young Boys	a	1-1	*Frei*
2011				
6/2	Grasshoppers	h	1-4	*Lavrič*
12/2	Basel	a	0-3	
19/2	Zürich	a	1-3	*Jagne*
27/2	Thun	h	0-1	
5/3	Sion	a	0-2	
13/3	Young Boys	h	0-2	
19/3	Bellinzona	h	1-0	*Nushi*
3/4	Luzern	a	1-1	*Gonçalves*
10/4	Xamax	h	1-1	*Hämmerli*

17/4	Thun	a	0-0	
20/4	Grasshoppers	a	3-1	*Abegglen, Scarione, Frei*
23/4	Sion	h	0-1	
1/5	Xamax	a	1-2	*Regazzoni*
8/5	Zürich	h	2-2	*Owona, Muntwiler*
11/5	Bellinzona	a	3-1	*Owona, Scarione (p), Regazzoni*
14/5	Luzern	h	0-4	
22/5	Basel	h	0-0	
25/5	Young Boys	a	2-4	*Lang, Nushi*

No	Name	Nat	DoB	Pos	Aps	(s)	Gls
26	Nico ABEGGLEN		16/2/90	A	11	(15)	2
4	Tim BAKENS	NED	2/11/82	D	16	(1)	1
8	Daniel BEICHLER	AUT	13/10/88	M	3	(4)	
11	Sandro Renato CALABRO	NED	11/4/83	A	6	(9)	2
28	Daniel DUNST	AUT	12/4/84	D	9	(2)	
3	FERNANDO César de Souza	BRA	12/9/80	D	16		
14	Fabian FREI		8/1/89	M	32	(2)	7
10	Mario FRICK	LIE	7/9/74	A	11	(3)	1
16	José Julio GONÇALVES	POR	17/9/85	D	17		1
24	Marco HÄMMERLI		7/5/85	D	15	(5)	1
19	Daniel IMHOF	CAN	22/11/77	M	26	(2)	
9	Pa Modou JAGNE	GAM	26/12/89	M	5	(12)	1
8	Thomas KNÖPFEL		9/11/83	M		(1)	
6	Michael LANG		8/2/91	D	28	(3)	2
29	Klemen LAVRIČ	SVN	12/6/81	A	8	(5)	1
23	Sven LEHMANN		18/12/91	A		(1)	
1	Daniel LOPAR		19/4/85	G	10		
21	Ivan MARTIĆ	CRO	2/10/90	D	10	(2)	
15	Philipp MUNTWILER		25/2/87	M	33		3
7	Kristian NUSHI	ALB	21/7/82	M	15	(13)	2
20	Brice OWONA	CMR	4/3/89	A	11	(2)	2
32	Alberto REGAZZONI		4/5/83	A	14	(2)	2
10	Ezequiel Ósca SCARIONE	ARG	14/7/85	M	14	(1)	2
5	Lukas SCHENKEL		1/4/84	D	35		3
13	Manuel SUTTER	AUT	8/3/91	A	2	(11)	
22	TUNAHAN Çiçek	TUR	12/5/92	M		(4)	
30	Germano VAILATI		30/8/80	G	26		
25	Adrian WINTER		8/7/86	M	23	(5)	

FC THUN

Coach – Murat Yakin

Founded – 1898

Stadium – Lachen (9,540)

2010

17/7	Young Boys	h	1-1	*Proschwitz*
25/7	Xamax	a	3-2	*Morello, Hediger, Proschwitz*
1/8	Grasshoppers	h	2-2	*Scarione, Glarner*
8/8	St Gallen	h	3-0	*Proschwitz, Glarner, og (Bakens)*
15/8	Sion	a	1-1	*Scarione*
21/8	Basel	h	1-1	*Rama*
29/8	Luzern	a	1-1	*Proschwitz*
11/9	Zürich	h	1-3	*Klose*
23/9	Bellinzona	a	2-2	*Matić, Scarione*
26/9	Young Boys	a	2-2	*Glarner, Proschwitz*
2/10	Xamax	h	1-2	*Matić*
24/10	Grasshoppers	a	0-0	
31/10	St Gallen	a	1-2	*Morello*
6/11	Sion	h	1-0	*Scarione (p)*
13/11	Basel	a	3-1	*Scarione (p), Proschwitz, Taljevic*
27/11	Luzern	h	1-1	*Scarione*
5/12	Zürich	a	0-0	
11/12	Bellinzona	h	0-0	

2011

6/2	Basel	h	2-3	*Scarione, Lezcano*
13/2	Grasshoppers	a	0-0	
20/2	Young Boys	h	1-1	*Taljevic*
27/2	St Gallen	a	1-0	*Matić*
6/3	Luzern	h	3-3	*Klose, Proschwitz, Taljevic*
13/3	Xamax	h	1-0	*Proschwitz*
20/3	Sion	a	0-1	
3/4	Zürich	h	2-3	*Neumayr, Klose*
9/4	Bellinzona	a	1-1	*Matić (p)*
17/4	St Gallen	h	0-0	
20/4	Luzern	a	1-0	*Lüthi*
25/4	Grasshoppers	h	0-1	
30/4	Young Boys	a	1-0	*Lezcano*
7/5	Sion	h	3-1	*Lezcano (p), Andrist, Rama*
11/5	Xamax	a	4-1	*Rama, Taljevic, Andrist, Salamand*
15/5	Basel	a	1-5	*Andrist*
22/5	Bellinzona	h	3-1	*Sanogo, Neumayr, Taljevic*
25/5	Zürich	a	0-1	

No	Name	Nat	DoB	Pos	Aps	(s)	Gls
7	Stephan ANDRIST		12/12/87	M	8	(13)	3
6	Roland BÄTTIG		28/7/79	M	33	(1)	
1	David DA COSTA		19/4/86	G	35		
8	Muhamed DEMIRI	MKD	20/11/85	M	31	(1)	
35	Dragan DJUKIC		15/7/87	G	1		
5	Ervin GASHI		27/8/90	D		(1)	
31	Stefan GLARNER		21/11/87	M	20	(9)	3
17	Dennis HEDIGER		22/9/86	M	19		1
15	Timm KLOSE		9/5/88	D	29	(1)	3
21	Dario LEZCANO Mendoza	PAR	30/6/90	A	14	(3)	3
33	Benjamin LÜTHI		30/11/88	D	31		1
24	Stipe MATIĆ	CRO	6/2/79	D	33		4
20	Giuseppe MORELLO	ITA	12/10/85	A	7	(8)	2
23	Markus NEUMAYR	GER	26/3/86	M	8	(5)	2
11	Nick PROSCHWITZ	GER	28/11/86	A	25	(6)	8
9	Milaim RAMA		29/2/76	A	2	(12)	3
26	Thomas REINMANN		9/4/83	D	10	(8)	
32	Mathieu SALAMAND	FRA	17/4/91	M		(1)	1
13	Sékou SANOGO Júnior	CIV	5/5/89	M	8	(6)	1
10	Ezequiel Óscar SCARIONE	ARG	14/7/85	M	18		7
14	Nicolas SCHINDELHOLZ		12/2/88	D	14	(2)	
27	Enrico SCHIRINZI	ITA	14/11/84	D	9	(1)	
19	Marc SCHNEIDER		23/7/80	D	18	(4)	
4	Michael SIEGFRIED		18/2/88	D		(3)	
30	Ifet TALJEVIC	GER	12/6/80	M	10	(4)	5
12	Mirson VOLINA		8/1/90	M		(1)	
28	Andreas WITTWER		5/10/90	D	13	(13)	

BSC YOUNG BOYS

Coach – Vladimir Petković; (8/5/11) (Erminio Piserchia)

Founded – 1898

Stadium – Stade de Suisse (32,000)

MAJOR HONOURS: Swiss League – (11) 1903, 1909, 1910, 1911, 1920, 1929, 1957, 1958, 1959, 1960, 1986; Swiss Cup – (6) 1930, 1945, 1953, 1958, 1977, 1987.

2010

17/7	Thun	a	1-1	*Bienvenu*
24/7	Luzern	h	1-1	*Dudar*
31/7	Bellinzona	a	1-2	*Mayuka*
8/8	Grasshoppers	a	2-1	*Bienvenu, Costanzo*
14/8	Xamax	h	0-1	
22/8	Zürich	h	1-0	*Degen*
29/8	Sion	a	0-2	
12/9	Basel	h	2-2	*Jemal, Degen*
22/9	St Gallen	a	2-1	*Mayuka 2*
26/9	Thun	h	2-2	*Costanzo 2*
3/10	Luzern	a	0-2	
24/10	Bellinzona	h	1-1	*Lulić*
31/10	Grasshoppers	h	1-0	*Bienvenu*
7/11	Xamax	a	4-2	*Jemal, Costanzo (p), Degen, Schneuwly C.*
14/11	Zürich	a	2-2	*Mayuka, Bienvenu*
28/11	Sion	h	2-1	*Lulić, Schneuwly M.*
4/12	Basel	a	1-3	*Doubai*
12/12	St Gallen	h	1-1	*Nef*

2011

5/2	Bellinzona	a	5-1	*Bienvenu 2, Lulić, Mayuka, og (Thiesson)*
13/2	Zürich	h	4-2	*og (Jorge Teixeira), Farnerud 2, Raimondi*
20/2	Thun	a	1-1	*Jemal*
27/2	Xamax	h	3-2	*Bienvenu 2, Mayuka*
5/3	Grasshoppers	a	2-3	*Bienvenu, Lulić*
13/3	St Gallen	a	2-0	*Bienvenu, Mayuka*
20/3	Luzern	h	3-1	*Nef 2, Farnerud*
3/4	Sion	a	2-0	*Costanzo, Mayuka*
10/4	Basel	h	3-3	*Bienvenu, Lulić, Raimondi (p)*
16/4	Bellinzona	h	4-0	*Jemal, Farnerud 2, Mayuka*
19/4	Zürich	a	1-2	*Lulić*
23/4	Basel	a	1-2	*Bienvenu*
30/4	Thun	h	0-1	
7/5	Luzern	a	1-1	*Costanzo*
10/5	Grasshoppers	h	2-2	*Bienvenu, Jemal*
15/5	Sion	h	1-1	*Schneuwly M.*
22/5	Xamax	a	2-1	*Schneuwly C., Bienvenu*
25/5	St Gallen	h	4-2	*Bienvenu 2, Costanzo, Degen*

No	Name	Nat	DoB	Pos	Aps	(s)	Gls
20	François AFFOLTER		13/3/91	D	33		
15	Henri BIENVENU Ntsama	CMR	5/7/88	A	28	(6)	16
35	Roman BÜRKI		14/11/90	G	1	(1)	
10	Moreno COSTANZO		20/2/88	M	25	(6)	7
13	Adriano DE PIERRO		11/1/91	D		(2)	
21	David DEGEN		15/2/83	M	30	(2)	4
30	Kouadio Pascal DOUBAI	CIV	22/5/92	M		(1)	
11	Thierry DOUBAI	CIV	1/7/88	M	32	(2)	1
5	Emiliano Ariel DUDAR	ITA	12/8/81	D	17		1
8	Alexander FARNERUD	SWE	1/5/84	M	15	(2)	5
22	Xavier HOCHSTRASSER		1/7/88	M	9	(3)	
25	Ammar JEMAL	TUN	20/4/87	D	22	(4)	5
6	Hassan LINGANI	CIV	30/12/87	D		(2)	
19	Senad LULIĆ	BIH	18/1/86	M	27	(4)	6
24	Emmanuel MAYUKA	ZAM	21/11/90	A	11	(16)	9
4	Alain NEF		6/2/82	D	26	(1)	3
16	Mario RAIMONDI		10/7/80	M	14	(14)	2
23	Alberto REGAZZONI		4/5/83	A	4	(8)	
14	Christian SCHNEUWLY		7/2/88	M	6	(12)	2
9	Marco SCHNEUWLY		27/3/85	A	4	(12)	2
29	Albert SPAHIU		3/8/90	A		(1)	
17	Christoph SPYCHER		30/3/78	D	26		
7	Scott SUTTER		13/5/86	M	30	(2)	
26	Matteo TOSETTI		15/2/92	M	1	(5)	
1	Marco WÖLFLI		22/8/82	G	35		

FC ZÜRICH

Coach – Urs Fischer

Founded – 1896

Stadium – Letzigrund (26,000)

MAJOR HONOURS: Swiss League – (12) 1902, 1924, 1963, 1966, 1968, 1974, 1975, 1976, 1981, 2006, 2007, 2009; Swiss Cup – (7) 1966, 1970, 1972, 1973, 1976, 2000, 2005.

2010

20/7	Basel	a	2-3	*Jorge Teixeira, Djuric*
25/7	Grasshoppers	h	2-0	*Jorge Teixeira, Kukuruzović*
31/7	Sion	h	1-1	*Jorge Teixeira*
7/8	Xamax	a	4-3	*Alphonse 2, og (Dampha), Schönbächler*
15/8	Bellinzona	h	2-2	*og (Mangiarratti), Zouaghi*
22/8	Young Boys	a	0-1	
28/8	St Gallen	h	3-1	*Djuric, Nikci, Mehmedi*
11/9	Thun	a	3-1	*Mehmedi, Margairaz (p), Chermiti*
25/9	Basel	h	1-4	*Margairaz*
3/10	Grasshoppers	a	2-1	*Alphonse, Djuric*
23/10	Sion	a	1-1	*Chermiti*
27/10	Luzern	h	2-2	*Zouaghi, Alphonse*
30/10	Xamax	h	3-1	*Alphonse, Chermiti, Mehmedi*
6/11	Bellinzona	a	2-1	*Chermiti 2*
14/11	Young Boys	h	2-2	*Alphonse, Schönbächler*
28/11	St Gallen	a	3-0	*Mehmedi 2, Nikci*
5/12	Thun	h	0-0	
11/12	Luzern	a	1-1	*Alphonse*

2011

5/2	Luzern	h	2-0	*Aegerter, Schönbächler*
13/2	Young Boys	a	2-4	*Aegerter, Hassli (p)*
19/2	St Gallen	h	3-1	*Margairaz, Mehmedi, Hassli*
26/2	Bellinzona	h	5-0	*Hassli 2 (1p), Schönbächler, Chermiti, Djuric*
6/3	Basel	a	1-3	*Chermiti*
12/3	Sion	h	2-0	*Chermiti, Margairaz (p)*
19/3	Xamax	a	2-1	*Jorge Teixeira, Béda*
3/4	Thun	a	3-2	*Chermiti, Magnin, Nikci*
10/4	Grasshoppers	h	1-0	*Zouaghi*
16/4	Sion	a	2-0	*Nikci, Alphonse*
19/4	Young Boys	h	2-1	*og (Nef), Mehmedi*
28/4	Xamax	h	3-0	*Rodriguez, Stahel, Schönbächler*
1/5	Bellinzona	a	1-0	*Mehmedi*
8/5	St Gallen	a	2-2	*Nikci, Djuric*
11/5	Basel	h	2-2	*Djuric, Nikci*
15/5	Grasshoppers	a	1-3	*Alphonse*
22/5	Luzern	a	5-0	*Nikci, Margairaz (p), Mehmedi 2, Djuric*
25/5	Thun	h	1-0	*Alphonse*

No	Name	Nat	DoB	Pos	Aps	(s)	Gls
7	Silvan AEGERTER		5/5/80	M	31		2
12	Alexandre ALPHONSE	FRA	17/6/82	A	20	(6)	10
21	Heinz BARMETTLER		21/7/87	D	3		
28	Mathieu BÉDA	FRA	28/7/81	D	15		1
15	Oliver BUFF		3/8/92	M	5	(4)	
9	Amine CHERMITI	TUN	26/12/87	A	15	(2)	9
17	Yassine CHIKHAOUI	TUN	22/9/86	M	1	(4)	
31	Dugagjin DEDAJ	ALB	15/9/89	D	1		
14	Dusan Predrag DJURIC	SWE	16/9/84	M	33		7
31	Josip DRMIC		8/8/92	A	2	(5)	
20	Milan GAJIĆ	SRB	17/11/86	M	2	(3)	
32	Andrea GUATELLI	ITA	5/5/84	G	23		
29	Éric HASSLI	FRA	3/5/81	A	10	(6)	4
2	JORGE Filipe Avelino TEIXEIRA	POR	27/8/86	D	26		4
16	Philippe KOCH		8/2/91	D	26	(1)	
4	Raphael KOCH		20/1/90	D	6	(5)	
8	Stjepan KUKURUZOVIĆ	CRO	7/6/89	M	8	(19)	1
1	Johnny LEONI		30/6/84	G	13		
23	Ludovic MAGNIN		20/4/79	D	24	(1)	1
5	Xavier MARGAIRAZ		7/1/84	M	25	(2)	5
25	Admir MEHMEDI		16/3/91	A	21	(12)	10
11	Adrian NIKCI		10/11/89	M	8	(19)	7
19	Alain ROCHAT		1/2/83	D	11		
3	Ricardo RODRIGUEZ		25/8/92	D	11	(2)	1
27	Marco SCHÖNBÄCHLER		11/1/90	M	27	(2)	5
13	Florian STAHEL		10/3/85	D	10	(2)	1
6	Chake ZOUAGHI	TUN	10/1/85	M	19	(10)	3

TOP GOALSCORERS 2010/11

27	Alexander FREI (Basel)
16	Henri BIENVENU (Young Boys)
14	Mauro LUSTRINELLI (Bellinzona)
12	Hakan YAKIN (Luzern)
10	Marco STRELLER (Basel) Giovanni SIO (Sion) Alexandre ALPHONSE (Zürich) Admir MEHMEDI (Zürich)
9	Innocent EMEGHARA (Grasshoppers) Nélson FERREIRA (Luzern) Ezequiel SCARIONE (Thun/St Gallen) Emmanuel MAYUKA (Young Boys) Amine CHERMITI (Zürich)

PROMOTED CLUBS

FC LAUSANNE-SPORT

Coach – Martin Rueda
Founded – 1896
Stadium – Olympique de la Pontaise (15,850)
MAJOR HONOURS: Swiss League – (7) 1913, 1932, 1935, 1936, 1944, 1951, 1965;
Swiss Cup – (9) 1935, 1939, 1944, 1950, 1962, 1964, 1981, 1998, 1999.

SERVETTE FC

Coach – João Alves (POR)
Founded – 1890
Stadium – Stade de Genève (30,084)
MAJOR HONOURS: Swiss League – (17) 1907, 1918, 1922, 1925, 1926, 1930, 1933, 1934, 1940, 1946, 1950, 1961, 1962, 1979, 1985, 1994, 1999;
Swiss Cup – (7) 1928, 1949, 1971, 1978, 1979, 1984, 2001.

SECOND LEVEL FINAL TABLE 2010/11

		Pld	W	D	L	F	A	Pts
1	FC Lausanne-Sport	30	20	5	5	67	28	65
2	Servette FC	30	19	5	6	75	27	62
3	FC Lugano	30	20	2	8	57	35	62
4	FC Vaduz	30	19	3	8	59	41	60
5	FC Wil 1900	30	14	4	12	45	42	46
6	FC Stade Nyonnais	30	13	7	10	48	51	46
7	FC Chiasso	30	12	5	13	34	38	41
8	SR Delémont	30	12	4	14	47	60	40
9	FC Biel/Bienne	30	11	6	13	57	57	39
10	FC Wohlen	30	9	10	11	45	44	37
11	FC Aarau	30	9	9	12	39	51	36
12	SC Kriens	30	9	6	15	26	50	33
13	FC Winterthur	30	8	8	14	42	51	32
14	FC Locarno	30	8	7	15	40	52	31
15	FC Schaffhausen	30	7	5	18	36	53	26
16	Yverdon-Sport FC	30	6	2	22	27	64	20

PROMOTION/RELEGATION PLAY-OFFS

(28/5/11 & 31/5/11)
Bellinzona 1, Servette 0
Servette 3, Bellinzona 1
(Servette 3-2)

DOMESTIC CUP 2010/11

SCHWEIZER CUP/COUPE DE SUISSE

FIRST ROUND

(18/9/10)
Bavois 1, Aarau 3
Binningen 0, Baulmes 2
Black Stars Basel 5, Brühl St Gallen 0
Buochs 2, Delémont 1 *(aet)*
Chênois 1, Chiasso 3
Collex-Bossy 5, Champvent 1
Collombey-Muraz 4, Courtételle 0
Eschenbach 1, Wohlen 3 *(aet)*
Flawil 1, St Gallen 5 *(aet)*
Le Mont LS 1, Kriens 5
Liestal 2, Schaffhausen 5
Losone 0, Biel/Bienne 3
Malley LS 3, Grand-Lancy 2 *(aet)*
Meyrin 1, Locarno 3
Montreux 1, Grenchen 2
Racing Club Zürich 1, Yverdon 7
Schötz 0, Zürich 6
Seefeld Zürich 1, Bellinzona 3
Spiez 0, Young Boys 7
Subingen 0, Gumefens/Sorens 1
Taverne 0, Sion 4
Uznach 1, Xamax 3
Wettswil-Bonstetten 0, Servette 2

(19/9/10)
Béroche-Gorgier 0, Grasshoppers 9
Cham 0, Thun 4
Entfelden 0, Luzern 3
Freienbach 2, Winterthur 3 *(aet)*
Ibach 0, Lugano 2
Mendrisio-Stabio 0, Basel 5
Perly-Certoux 0, Nyon 1
Tuggen 2, Wil 1

(22/9/10)
Langenthal 2, Lausanne 5

SECOND ROUND

(15/10/10)
Yverdon 0, Basel 2

(16/10/10)
Black Stars Basel 0, Lugano 3
Buochs 0, Thun 3
Chiasso 0, Xamax 0 *(aet; 3-4 on pens)*
Collex-Bossy 0, Sion 5
Collombey-Muraz 2, Young Boys 5
Lausanne 0, Bellinzona 2
Malley LS 0, Biel/Bienne 3
Tuggen 4, Grenchen 0
Wohlen 5, Winterthur 1

(17/10/10)
Aarau 2, Kriens 3
Baulmes 2, Servette 5
Gumefens/Sorens 0, Grasshoppers 12
Locarno 0, Zürich 3
Nyon 1, Luzern 2
Schaffhausen 2, St Gallen 6

THIRD ROUND

(20/11/10)
Tuggen 0, Zürich 4
Servette 1, Basel 1 *(aet; 3-4 on pens)*
St Gallen 0, Thun 1

(21/11/10)
Lugano 2, Sion 3 *(aet)*
Biel/Bienne 2, Luzern 2 *(aet; 5-3 on pens)*
Wohlen 1, Grasshoppers 2
Xamax 1, Bellinzona 0
Kriens 1, Young Boys 2

QUARTER-FINALS

(2/3/11)
Grasshoppers 1 *(Abrashi 56)*, Sion 2 *(Mrđa 19, Obradović 88)*
Thun 1 *(Klose 120)*, Xamax 1 *(Tréand 105) (aet; 0-3 on pens)*

Young Boys 3 *(Farnerud 54, Bienvenu 56, Mayuka 82)*, Zürich 4 *(Schönbächler 5, Margairaz 41, 116, Chermiti 49) (aet)*

(3/3/11)
Biel/Bienne 3 *(Egli 53, Morello 80, Etoundi 84)*, Basel 1 *(Kehrli 43og)*

SEMI-FINALS

(25/4/11)
Zürich 1 *(Jorge Teixeira 26)*, Xamax 1 *(Tréand 66) (aet; 6-7 on pens)*

(28/4/11)
Sion 2 *(Sio 62, Vanczák 85)*, Biel/Bienne 1 *(Kehrli 48)*

FINAL

(29/5/11)
St Jakob-Park, Basel
FC SION 2 *(Sio 2, Vanczák 6)*
NEUCHÂTEL XAMAX FC 0
Referee – *Laperrière*
SION – *Vanins, Vanczák, Adaílton, Dingsdag, Crettenand, Obradović (Rodrigo 87), Zambrella, Serey Die, Bühler (Elmer 67), Prijovic (Domínguez 52), Sio.*
XAMAX – *Bedenik, Mveng, Besle, Gelabert (Ismail 62), Facchinetti, Page, Binya, Nuzzolo, Wüthrich (Tréand 46), Niasse, Gohou (Fausto 46).*

CLUB COMMUNICATION 2011/12

FC Basel 1893

Birsstrasse 320 A, Postfach
CH-4020 Basel

Tel	+41 61 375 1010
Fax	+41 61 375 1011
Web	fcb.ch
Email	info@fcb.ch
Media Officer	Josef Zindel

Grasshopper-Club

Dielsdorferstrasse 165, Postfach 377
CH-8155 Niederhasli

Tel	+41 44 447 4646
Fax	+41 44 447 4690
Web	gcz.ch
Email	info@gcz.ch
Media Officer	Eugen Desiderato

FC Lausanne-Sport

Case postale 175
CH-1018 Lausanne 18

Tel	+41 21 804 1070
Fax	+41 21 804 1071
Web	lausanne-sport.ch
Email	info@lausanne-sport.ch
Media Officer	Aurélie Fontanellaz

FC Luzern

Horwerstrasse 34, Postfach 2718
CH-6002 Luzern

Tel	+41 848 317 000
Fax	+41 41 317 0999
Web	fcl.ch
Email	office@fcl.ch
Media Officer	Stefan Bucher

Neuchâtel Xamax FC

Case postale 2749
CH-2001 Neuchâtel

Tel	+41 32 725 4428
Fax	+41 32 724 2128
Web	xamax.ch
Email	secretariats@xamax.ch
Media Officer	Marc Imwinkelried

Servette FC

Case postale 431
CH-1219 Châtelaine

Tel	+41 22 340 5474
Fax	+41 22 340 5473
Web	servettefc.ch
Email	secretariat@servettefc.ch
Media Officer	Didier Rieder

FC Sion

Olympique des Alpes SA
CH-1921 Martigny-Croix

Tel	+41 27 747 1313
Fax	+41 27 747 1314
Web	fc-sion.ch
Email	info@fc-sion.ch
Media Officer	Nicolas Pillet

FC Thun

Stadion Lachen, Postfach 4249
CH-3604 Thun

Tel	+41 33 225 1898
Fax	+41 33 225 1899
Web	fcthun.ch
Email	sekretariat@fcthun.ch
Media Officer	Reto Bloesch

BSC Young Boys

Papiermühlestrasse 77, Postfach 61
CH-3000 Bern 22

Tel	+41 31 344 8000
Fax	+41 31 344 8089
Web	bscyb.ch
Email	info@bscyb.ch
Media Officer	Albert Staudenmann

FC Zürich

Postfach 3375
CH-8021 Zürich

Tel	+41 43 521 1212
Fax	+41 43 521 1213
Web	fcz.ch
Email	fcz@fcz.ch
Media Officer	Giovanni Marti

TURKEY

Turquie I Türkei

Türkiye Futbol Federasyonu (TFF)

COMMUNICATION

Address Istinye Mahallesi
Darüşşafaka Caddesi
No. 45 Kat 2
Sarıyer
TR-34330 İstanbul

Tel +90 212 362 2222
Fax +90 212 323 4968

E-mail intdept@tff.org
Website tff.org

President Mehmet Ali Aydınlar
General Secretary (acting) Lufti Arıboğan
Media Officer Türker Tozar

Year of Formation 1923

DOMESTIC COMPETITION SUMMARY 2010/11

SÜPER LİG FINAL TABLE

			Home					Away					Total						
		Pld	W	D	L	F	A	W	D	L	F	A	W	D	L	F	A	Pts	Comp
1	Fenerbahçe SK	34	14	3	0	41	8	12	1	4	43	26	26	4	4	84	34	82	UCL
2	Trabzonspor AŞ	34	12	4	1	34	12	13	3	1	35	11	25	7	2	69	23	82	UCL
3	Bursaspor	34	9	4	4	22	20	8	6	3	28	9	17	10	7	50	29	61	UEL
4	Gaziantepspor	34	10	5	2	26	16	7	3	7	18	17	17	8	9	44	33	59	UEL
5	Beşiktaş JK	34	8	5	4	35	24	7	4	6	18	12	15	9	10	53	36	54	UEL
6	Kayserispor	34	9	4	4	25	17	5	5	7	21	27	14	9	11	46	44	51	
7	Eskişehirspor	34	8	5	4	18	12	4	6	7	23	28	12	11	11	41	40	47	
8	Galatasaray AŞ	34	8	2	7	22	21	6	2	9	19	25	14	4	16	41	46	46	
9	Kardemir Karabükspor	34	9	2	6	28	24	3	6	8	18	29	12	8	14	46	53	44	
10	Manisaspor	34	7	1	9	24	27	6	3	8	25	25	13	4	17	49	52	43	
11	Antalyaspor	34	5	7	5	22	22	5	5	7	19	26	10	12	12	41	48	42	
12	İstanbul BB SK	34	7	3	7	18	21	5	3	9	22	24	12	6	16	40	45	42	
13	MKE Ankaragücü	34	6	5	6	30	32	4	6	7	22	30	10	11	13	52	62	41	
14	Gençlerbirliği SK	34	6	3	8	24	28	4	7	6	19	23	10	10	14	43	51	40	
15	Sivasspor	34	6	7	4	26	24	2	4	11	17	33	8	11	15	43	57	35	
16	Bucaspor	34	6	4	7	23	26	0	4	13	14	39	6	8	20	37	65	26	*Relegated*
17	Konyaspor	34	2	9	6	13	21	2	3	12	15	28	4	12	18	28	49	24	*Relegated*
18	Kasımpaşa SK	34	3	3	11	15	37	2	5	10	16	34	5	8	21	31	71	23	*Relegated*

Top Scorer Alex (Fenerbahçe), 28 goals

Promoted Clubs Mersin İdman Yurdu
Samsunspor
Orduspor

Cup Final Beşiktaş JK 2, İstanbul BB SK 2 (aet; 4-3 on pens)

Fenerbahçe title celebrations cut short

A discreet season for Turkish football in the international arena, with none of the big Istanbul clubs competing in the group stage of the UEFA Champions League, was offset by a dramatic domestic campaign in which Fenerbahçe snatched the Süper Lig title away from Tranzonspor AŞ by the slenderest of margins – thanks to a superior head-to-head record – only to have their triumph plunged into doubt by post-season allegations of match-fixing.

As Fenerbahçe club president Aziz Yıldırım was arrested and taken into custody in early July, a giant shadow was cast over what, to all intents and purposes, had been an epic, record-breaking 18th Turkish championship title for the Istanbul club. Nine points adrift of Trabzonspor at the halfway stage of the season, Fener blitzed their way back into contention, winning 16 of their final 17 matches and drawing the other. Their most important win came early on in that sequence when they defeated Trabzonspor 2-0 at the Şükrü Saracoğlu Stadium in late January. It was a predictably fiery encounter, with three red cards, but the outcome allowed Fener not only to close the gap between the teams to four points but also to claim a head-to-head advantage (on goal difference) following their 3-2 defeat in Trabzon back in August.

Last-day drama

With the Black Sea club also stacking up the points during the run-in, winning 12 and drawing three of their last 15 fixtures, the destiny of the title all came down to that head-to-head statistic. Level on points throughout the month of May, with each of the two contenders refusing to buckle, Fenerbahçe travelled to their final fixture, away at lowly Sivasspor, knowing that a 26th win of the season would guarantee that historic title, putting them one ahead of bitter rivals Galatasaray AŞ in the all-time roll of honour. The pressure was on, especially as the team had gifted the title to Bursaspor in similar circumstances 12 months earlier with a draw against – of all teams – Trabzonspor. But, after putting their fans through the mill yet again, Fenerbahçe eked out a dramatic 4-3 win, rendering Trabzonspor's comfortable 4-0 victory at Kardemir Karabükspor inconsequential.

Fenerbahçe were led to victory by former striker Aykut Kocaman. Reassigned from his 2009/10 role as director of football to the position of head coach following the departure of Christoph Daum, he appeared to be on very shaky ground early on when Fener were dumped out of both the UEFA Champions League and the UEFA Europa League before the group stage. Just two wins in their first five league games and, subsequently, a humiliating early exit in the Turkish Cup were a further test of Aziz Yıldırım's patience, but then came the remarkable resurgence after the turn of the year and suddenly Aykut's position was not just safe, but he was on course to make history as the first man to win the Turkish title for Fenerbahçe as both player and coach.

Fenerbahçe captain Alex led by example in the Istanbul club's Turkish title triumph

National Team

International Tournament Appearances – FIFA World Cup – (2) 1954, 2002 (3rd). UEFA European Championship – (3) 1996, 2000 (qtr-finals), 2008 (semi-finals).

Top Five All-time Caps – Rüştü Reçber (119); Hakan Şükür (112); Bülent Korkmaz (102); Tugay Kerimoğlu (94); Alpay Özalan (90)

Top Five All-time Goals – Hakan Şükür (51); Tuncay Şanlı (22); Lefter Küçükandonyadis (21); Cemil Turan, Metin Oktay & Nihat Kahveci (19)

Aykut would certainly not have succeeded without the extraordinary efforts of his Brazilian captain Alex. The gifted 33-year-old playmaker, a Fener stalwart since 2004, enjoyed his best ever campaign, rifling in 28 goals – the highest individual tally in the Süper Lig – and providing assists for another 14. With direct involvement in exactly half of the club's goal output, Alex was a shoo-in for the Süper Lig player of the year award, but there were several other influential figures in the title-winning team, such as new African recruits Mamadou Niang and Joseph Yobo, Uruguayan FIFA World Cup captain Diego Lugano and the Turkish international trio of Emre Belözoğlu, Gökhan Gonül and Volkan Demirel.

Trabzonspor stars

Trabzonspor also had their star performers, notably up front where ex-Fener striker Burak Yılmaz scored 19 goals and was joined on double figures by attacking accomplices Umut Bulut and Jajá. Their chief inspiration, however, was coach Şenol Güneş, a veritable club legend who, as a former goalkeeper, was active in all six of the club's previous Turkish title wins, from 1976-84. Having steered the Black Sea club to victory in the 2009/10 Turkish Cup shortly after embarking on his fourth spell as coach, the man who also led Turkey to the semi-finals of the 2002 World Cup was so close to achieving his proudest feat. To win 25 matches, lose just two and still end up second-best in the title race was scarcely credible, but at least the runners-up spot carried with it the consolation of a UEFA Champions League qualifying berth.

Burak Yılmaz scored 19 goals for Süper Lig runners-up Trabzonspor

Trabzonspor had started the season by beating Bursaspor 3-0 to win the Turkish Super Cup, but it was the defending champions who actually led the Süper Lig for much of the autumn – while simultaneously competing in the UEFA Champions League. Curiously, it was only after their European exit – they managed just one point and two goals in the company of Manchester United FC, Valencia CF and Rangers FC - that the wheels came off their title challenge. Second at the winter break, Ertuğrul Sağlam's side ended up just one position lower in the final standings but the gap that separated them from the top two had expanded to a cavernous 21 points.

Gaziantepsor, fired in the spring by the goals of boy wonder Cenk Tosun, took fourth place and also reached the semi-finals of the Turkish Cup, where they were ousted by a Beşiktaş JK side that went on to win the trophy, defeating İstanbul BB SK on penalties in the final after a 2-2 draw. It was the club's fourth cup win in six years and made up for a sorry season in the league, which, accompanied by a shattering 8-1 aggregate defeat to FC Dynamo Kyiv in the UEFA Europa League, led to the departure of German coach Bernd

NATIONAL TEAM RESULTS 2010/11

11/8/10	Romania	H	Istanbul	2-0	*Emre (82p), Arda (86)*
3/9/10	Kazakhstan (ECQ)	A	Astana	3-0	*Arda (24), Hamit (26), Nihat (76)*
7/9/10	Belgium (ECQ)	H	Istanbul	3-2	*Hamit (48), Semih (66), Arda (78)*
8/10/10	Germany (ECQ)	A	Berlin	0-3	
12/10/10	Azerbaijan (ECQ)	A	Baku	0-1	
17/11/10	Netherlands	A	Amsterdam	0-1	
9/2/11	South Korea	H	Trabzon	0-0	
29/3/11	Austria (ECQ)	H	Istanbul	2-0	*Arda (28), Gökhan (77)*
3/6/11	Belgium (ECQ)	A	Brussels	1-1	*Burak (22)*

NATIONAL TEAM APPEARANCES 2010/11

Coach – Guus HIDDINK (NED)	8/11/46		Rou	KAZ	BEL	GER	AZE	Ned	Kor	AUT	BEL	Caps	Goals
VOLKAN Demirel	27/10/81	Fenerbahçe	G			G	G	G	G	G	G	50	-
GÖKHAN Gönül	4/1/85	Fenerbahçe	D		s73	D	D	D	s46	D		24	1
SERVET Çetin	17/3/81	Galatasaray	D	D	D	D	D	D	D	D	D	56	3
HAKAN Balta	23/3/83	Galatasaray	D	D			D			D		28	1
İSMAİL Köybaşı	10/7/89	Beşiktaş	D		D			D	D			7	-
MEHMET AURÉLIO	15/12/77	Betis (ESP) /Beşiktaş	M69	M89	M	M24						36	2
HAMİT Altıntop	8/12/82	Bayern (GER)	M69	M	M	M	M	M83	M59	M		64	6
ARDA Turan	30/1/87	Galatasaray	M89	M	M					M89	M85	44	11
EMRE Belözoğlu	7/9/80	Fenerbahçe	M	M	M	M	M		M 60*		M	76	7
NURİ Şahin	5/9/88	Dortmund (GER)	A46			M78		M		M		26	1
MEVLÜT Erdinç	25/2/87	PSG (FRA)	A46									13	1
KAZIM Kazım	26/8/86	Fenerbahçe /Galatasaray	s46	s89				s62	s46		A	30	-
TUNCAY Şanlı	16/1/82	Stoke (ENG)	s46	A80	A82	s24	A62					80	22
SELÇUK Şahin	31/1/81	Fenerbahçe	s69		s82						M	21	-
SERCAN Yıldırım	5/4/90	Bursaspor	s69			s78	s62					10	2
NİHAT Kahveci	23/11/79	Beşiktaş	s89	A82			s46					69	19
ONUR Kıvrak	1/1/88	Trabzonspor		G	G							3	-
SABRİ Sarıoğlu	26/7/84	Galatasaray		D	D73	D		M76	M79		D	38	1
ÖMER Erdoğan	3/5/77	Bursaspor		D	D	D						3	-
HALİL Altıntop	8/12/82	Eintracht (GER)		s80		A63	s82					37	8
SELÇUK İnan	10/2/85	Trabzonspor		s82	M46		M82	M89	M	M	M78	12	-
SEMİH Şentürk	29/4/83	Fenerbahçe			s46	s63	A			s72	s85	27	8
ÖZER Hurmacı	20/11/86	Fenerbahçe				M	M46					2	-
İBRAHİM Toraman	20/11/81	Beşiktaş					D					30	1
SERDAR Kesimal	24/1/89	Kayserispor						D	D	D	D	4	-
UMUT Bulut	15/3/83	Trabzonspor						A62	A46			3	-
BURAK Yılmaz	15/7/85	Trabzonspor						A62	s59	A72	A76	8	1
MEHMET Ekici	25/3/90	Nürnberg (GER)						s62	A59	M63	s76	4	-
ENGİN Baytar	11/7/83	Trabzonspor						s76				1	-
YEKTA Kurtuluş	11/12/85	Kasımpaşa						s83				1	-
YİĞİT İncedemir	9/3/85	Manisaspor						s89	s79			2	-
SERKAN Balcı	22/8/83	Trabzonspor							D46			23	-
TUNAY Torun	21/4/90	Hamburg (GER)							s59			1	-
MEHMET Topuz	7/9/83	Fenerbahçe								s63		17	-
MEHMET Topal	3/3/86	Valencia (ESP)								s89	s78	18	-
ÇAĞLAR Birinci	2/10/85	Galatasaray									D	4	-

Schuster. It was his assistant – and former Beşiktaş player – Tayfur Havutçu who oversaw the cup triumph.

Galatasaray gloom

Galatasaray endured a disastrous season on all fronts, going out of Europe in August, losing more games than they won in the league, finish an embarrassing eighth to miss out on European qualification, and severely damaging the reputations of two big-name coaches, Frank Rijkaard and Gheorghe Hagi, in the process. By the end of a season in which the only highlight was the unveiling of a magnificent new stadium they, like Fener and Beşiktaş, were turning to one of their own for comfort, reappointing ex-Turkey boss Fatih Terim for a third spell in charge.

A foreigner did remain in charge of the Turkish national team, however, as Dutchman Guus Hiddink, reportedly targeted for a return to Chelsea FC before the London club turned their advances elsewhere, committed himself to seeing out his contract and attempting to take Turkey to the finals of UEFA EURO 2012. The road to Poland/Ukraine began smoothly with wins over Kazakhstan and Belgium but encountered a double hold-up the following month when a predictable defeat in Berlin (0-3) was followed by a humiliating one in Baku (0-1). Midfield maestro Arda Turan, who had scored in the opening two games, was tellingly absent for the two losses against Germany and Azerbaijan, but he returned to score another valuable goal as Turkey overcame Austria in Istanbul. Potentially even more important was the equaliser scored by Trabzonspor striker Burak to give Turkey a 1-1 draw in Brussels. With four games remaining, three of them at home, Hiddink's men were well placed to finish in second place behind Germany and take their chances in the play-offs.

CLUB-BY-CLUB

MKE ANKARAGÜCÜ

Coach – Ümit Özat; (28/2/11) Mesut Bakkal

Founded – 1910

Stadium – 19 Mayıs (19,209)

MAJOR HONOURS: Turkish Cup – (2) 1972, 1981.

2010				
15/8	Trabzonspor	h	0-2	
22/8	Manisaspor	a	3-0	*Šesták, Özgür, Güven*
27/8	Kayserispor	h	1-1	*Mehmet Çakır*
11/9	Beşiktaş	a	0-4	
18/9	Kasımpaşa	h	3-0	*Metin, Sapara, og (Luiz Henrique)*
25/9	Gençlerbirliği	a	0-1	
2/10	Konyaspor	h	4-1	*Metin, Rajnoch, Özgür, Šesták*
17/10	Galatasaray	a	4-2	*Metin, Özgür, Šesták, Turgut Doğan*
24/10	Bursaspor	h	1-5	*Šesták*
30/10	Eskişehirspor	a	0-0	
6/11	Gaziantepspor	h	0-2	
13/11	Bucaspor	a	0-0	
21/11	İstanbul BB	h	2-2	*Aydın, Turgut Doğan*
28/11	Karabükspor	a	1-5	*Sapara*
4/12	Sivasspor	h	1-1	*Klukowski*
12/12	Fenerbahçe	h	2-1	*Šesták 2*
18/12	Antalyaspor	a	2-2	*Żewłakow, Sapara*
2011				
22/1	Trabzonspor	a	1-1	*Gabrić*
30/1	Manisaspor	h	1-3	*Metin*
5/2	Kayserispor	a	1-2	*Murat*
13/2	Beşiktaş	h	1-0	*Serdar*
19/2	Kasımpaşa	a	1-2	*Fatih (p)*
26/2	Gençlerbirliği	h	2-4	*Metin, og (Orhan)*
5/3	Konyaspor	a	2-0	*Gabrić 2*
13/3	Galatasaray	h	3-2	*Šesták 3*
21/3	Bursaspor	a	0-0	
2/4	Eskişehirspor	h	2-2	*Fatih, Serdar*
10/4	Gaziantepspor	a	2-3	*Rajnoch, Özgür*
16/4	Bucaspor	h	5-3	*Murat 2, Vittek (p), Metin, Özgür*
24/4	İstanbul BB	a	4-1	*Ümit, Turgut Doğan, Fatih, Gabrić*
2/5	Karabükspor	h	0-0	
8/5	Sivasspor	a	1-1	*Šesták*
15/5	Fenerbahçe	a	0-6	
21/5	Antalyaspor	h	2-3	*Rajnoch, Bednář*

No	Name	Nat	DoB	Pos	Aps	(s)	Gls
66	ADEM Koçak		1/9/83	M	25	(3)	
25	AYDIN Toscalı		14/8/80	D	20	(1)	1
22	BAYRAM Olgun		26/4/90	G	2		
89	Roman BEDNÁŘ	CZE	26/3/83	A	2	(6)	1
23	BİLAL Gülden		1/5/93	M		(1)	
35	BORA Körk		9/6/80	G	3		
61	ERGİN Keleş		1/1/87	A	1	(1)	
33	FATİH Tekke		9/9/77	A	7	(2)	3
99	Drago GABRIĆ	CRO	27/9/86	M	18	(5)	4
19	GÜVEN Varol		2/6/81	M	20	(1)	1
50	HÜRRİYET Güçer		25/10/81	M	4	(2)	
6	KAĞAN Söylemezgiller		4/3/88	M	15	(3)	
5	Michael KLUKOWSKI	CAN	27/5/81	D	20		1
8	MEHMET Çakır		4/1/84	A	2	(5)	1
16	MEHMET Çoğum		5/2/83	M	2	(3)	
10	METİN Akan		28/5/83	A	13	(11)	6
21	Roguy MÉYÉ	GAB	7/10/86	A	3	(5)	
4	MUHAMMET HANİFİ Yoldaş		20/4/83	D	4		
18	MURAT Duruer		15/1/88	M	20	(3)	3
71	ORHAN Evci		9/3/91	M		(1)	
41	ÖZDEN Öngün		10/9/78	G	16	(1)	
60	ÖZGÜR Çek		3/1/91	M	12	(14)	5
17	Jan RAJNOCH	CZE	30/9/81	M	31	(1)	3
27	Marek SAPARA	SVK	31/7/82	M	24		3
1	Štefan SENECKÝ	SVK	6/1/80	G	13		
81	SERDAR Özkan		1/1/87	M	7		2
9	Stanislav ŠESTÁK	SVK	16/12/82	A	20	(3)	10
7	TURGUT DOĞAN Şahin		2/2/88	A	8	(14)	3
3	UĞUR Uçar		5/4/87	D	24	(1)	
20	UMUT Sözen		27/1/90	M	1	(5)	
80	ÜMİT Kurt		2/5/91	D	1		1
11	Róbert VITTEK	SVK	1/4/82	A	9	(3)	1
15	Theo Lewis WEEKS	LBR	19/1/90	M	8	(4)	
14	Michał ŻEWŁAKOW	POL	22/4/76	D	19		1

ANTALYASPOR

Coach – Mehmet Özdilek
Founded – 1966
Stadium – Mardan (7,428)

2010

15/8	Fenerbahçe	a	0-4	
21/8	Sivasspor	h	1-1	*Tita*
30/8	Trabzonspor	h	0-0	
11/9	Manisaspor	a	2-1	*Necati 2*
18/9	Kayserispor	h	2-1	*Djiehoua, Sedat*
25/9	Beşiktaş	a	1-2	*Tita*
3/10	Kasımpaşa	h	3-1	*Tita 2, Kerem*
17/10	Gençlerbirliği	a	3-2	*Kerem, Tita 2*
23/10	Konyaspor	h	1-0	*Kerem*
30/10	Galatasaray	a	1-2	*Musa*
6/11	Bursaspor	h	2-2	*Uğur, Kerem*
13/11	Eskişehirspor	a	0-0	
21/11	Gaziantepspor	h	0-1	
28/11	Bucaspor	a	0-1	
5/12	İstanbul BB	h	1-0	*og (Tum)*
11/12	Karabükspor	a	0-2	
18/12	Ankaragücü	h	2-2	*Necati 2 (1p)*

2011

22/1	Fenerbahçe	h	0-1	
29/1	Sivasspor	a	1-1	*Tita*
6/2	Trabzonspor	a	0-0	
13/2	Manisaspor	h	1-4	*Zitouni*
20/2	Kayserispor	a	0-2	
28/2	Beşiktaş	h	0-2	
6/3	Kasımpaşa	a	3-2	*İbrahim, Mehmet, Tita*
13/3	Gençlerbirliği	h	0-0	
19/3	Konyaspor	a	0-0	
4/4	Galatasaray	h	3-0	*Erkan, Necati 2 (1p)*
8/4	Bursaspor	a	3-2	*Uğur 2, Necati*
17/4	Eskişehirspor	h	2-2	*Zitouni, Necati (p)*
24/4	Gaziantepspor	a	1-2	*Kenan*
30/4	Bucaspor	h	3-3	*Necati 2 (2p), Veysel*
7/5	İstanbul BB	a	1-1	*Tita*
13/5	Karabükspor	h	1-2	*Necati*
21/5	Ankaragücü	a	3-2	*Tita, Necati 2 (1p)*

No	Name	Nat	DoB	Pos	Aps	(s)	Gls
57	ALİ Turan		6/9/83	D	16		
24	DENİZ Barış		2/7/77	D	30		
29	Serge DJIEHOUA	CIV	25/9/81	A	9	(12)	1
6	ERKAN Sekman		17/4/84	D	30		1
58	ERTUĞRUL Arslan		26/1/80	M	4	(10)	
19	HÜSEYİN Atalay		27/10/91	M	1	(4)	
4	İBRAHİM Dağaşan		15/6/84	M	15	(1)	1
39	İLKEM Özkaynak		1/5/82	D	7	(5)	
99	KENAN Özer		16/8/87	A	3	(15)	1
5	KEREM Şeras		1/1/84	M	26	(4)	4
61	MEHMET Yılmaz		22/5/79	A	12	(2)	1
7	MUSA Nizam		8/9/90	M	2		1
33	Sammy N'DJOCK	CMR	25/2/90	G	7		
10	NECATİ Ateş		3/1/80	A	28		13
1	ÖMER Çatkıç		15/10/74	G	25		
18	POLAT Keser		4/12/85	G	2		
12	Grégory PROMENT	FRA	10/12/78	M	5	(3)	
27	Ivan RADELJIĆ	BIH	14/9/80	D	21	(2)	
15	SEDAT Ağçay		22/9/81	M	22	(7)	1
86	Sidney Cristiano dos Santos "TITA"	BRA	20/7/81	A	32	(1)	10
35	TUNA Üzümcü		6/8/82	D	2		
8	UĞUR İnceman		25/5/81	M	28		3
50	VEYSEL Cihan		4/2/76	A	7	(15)	1
28	YENAL Tuncer		28/4/85	D	28	(1)	
11	Ali ZITOUNI	TUN	11/1/81	A	12	(14)	2

BEŞİKTAŞ JK

Coach – Bernd Schuster (GER); (15/3/11) Tayfur Havutçu
Founded – 1903
Stadium – İnönü (32,086)
MAJOR HONOURS: Turkish League – (13) 1957, 1958, 1960, 1966, 1967, 1982, 1986, 1990, 1991, 1992, 1995, 2003, 2009; Turkish Cup – (9) 1975, 1989, 1990, 1994, 1998, 2006, 2007, 2009, 2011.

2010

14/8	Bucaspor	a	1-0	*Bobô*
21/8	İstanbul BB	h	0-2	
29/8	Karabükspor	a	4-1	*Mert Nobre 2, Guti (p), Ricardo Quaresma*
11/9	Ankaragücü	h	4-0	*Bobô 2, İbrahim Toraman, Mert Nobre*
19/9	Fenerbahçe	a	1-1	*Guti (p)*
25/9	Antalyaspor	h	2-1	*Bobô 2*
3/10	Trabzonspor	a	0-1	
16/10	Manisaspor	h	2-3	*Bobô, Ernst*
25/10	Kayserispor	a	0-1	
31/10	Sivasspor	h	2-1	*Bobô, Necip*
8/11	Kasımpaşa	h	1-1	*İsmail*
14/11	Gençlerbirliği	a	2-0	*Guti (p), Hilbert*
20/11	Konyaspor	h	2-2	*og (Kéré), Hološko*
28/11	Galatasaray	a	2-1	*Guti (p), Mert Nobre*
5/12	Bursaspor	h	1-0	*Hološko*
10/12	Eskişehirspor	a	0-2	
19/12	Gaziantepspor	h	1-1	*Ali*

2011

21/1	Bucaspor	h	5-1	*Mert Nobre 2, Guti 2 (1p), Simão*
30/1	İstanbul BB	a	1-2	*Simão*
5/2	Karabükspor	h	1-1	*og (Deumi)*
13/2	Ankaragücü	a	0-1	
20/2	Fenerbahçe	h	2-4	*Ekrem, İbrahim Toraman*
28/2	Antalyaspor	a	2-0	*Ekrem, Guti*
6/3	Trabzonspor	h	1-2	*Bobô*
11/3	Manisaspor	a	0-0	
19/3	Kayserispor	h	4-2	*Hugo Almeida 2, Ernst, Ricardo Quaresma*
2/4	Sivasspor	a	0-1	
11/4	Kasımpaşa	a	1-0	*Hugo Almeida*
15/4	Gençlerbirliği	h	2-2	*Simão, İbrahim Toraman*
25/4	Konyaspor	a	1-1	*Ricardo Quaresma (p)*
30/4	Galatasaray	h	2-0	*Mehmet Aurélio, Simão*
7/5	Bursaspor	a	3-0	*(w/o)*
16/5	Eskişehirspor	h	3-1	*Manuel Fernandes, Hugo Almeida, Simão (p)*
21/5	Gaziantepspor	a	0-0	

No	Name	Nat	DoB	Pos	Aps	(s)	Gls
37	ALİ Kuçik		17/6/91	A	3	(1)	1
93	ATINÇ Nukan		20/7/93	D	2		
13	Deivson Rogério da Silva "BOBÔ"	BRA	9/6/85	A	13	(8)	8
99	CENK Gönen		21/2/88	G	14	(1)	
2	CUMALİ Bişi		15/6/93	M		(1)	
10	Matías Emilio DELGADO	ARG	15/12/82	M	1	(1)	
66	DOĞUKAN Pala		10/7/92	D	1		
17	EKREM Dağ	AUT	5/12/80	D	16		2
44	ERHAN Güven		15/5/82	D	4	(4)	
28	Fabian ERNST	GER	30/5/79	M	23	(5)	2
22	ERSAN Gülüm		17/5/87	D	10		
33	FATİH Tekke		9/9/77	A		(2)	
27	Matteo FERRARI	ITA	5/12/79	D	7		
5	Michael FINK	GER	1/2/82	M	3	(2)	
14	José María GUTIérrez Hernández	ESP	31/10/76	M	20	(2)	7
21	HAKAN Arıkan		17/8/82	G	8		
9	Roberto HILBERT	GER	16/10/84	M	20	(5)	1
21	Filip HOLOŠKO	SVK	17/1/84	A	9	(5)	2
34	HUGO Miguel Pereira de ALMEIDA	POR	23/5/84	A	9	(3)	4
20	İBRAHİM Toraman		20/11/81	D	29		3

No	Name	Nat	DoB	Pos	Aps	(s)	Gls
19	İBRAHİM Üzülmez		10/3/74	D	14	(1)	
3	İSMAİL Köybaşı		10/7/89	D	17	(2)	1
4	MANUEL Henrique Tavares FERNANDES	POR	5/2/86	M	9	(5)	1
55	Marco "MEHMET" AURÉLIO Brito dos Pazeres		15/12/77	M	18	(5)	1
11	Márcio "MERT" Ferreira NOBRE	BRA	6/11/80	A	14	(7)	6
54	MERTCAN Demirer		14/3/93	D		(1)	
18	NECİP Uysal		24/1/91	M	18	(6)	1
8	NİHAT Kahveci		23/11/79	A	7	(4)	
26	ONUR Bayramoğlu		4/1/90	M	2	(5)	
7	RICARDO Andrade QUARESMA Bernardo	POR	26/9/83	M	18	(3)	3
77	RIDVAN Şimşek		17/1/91	D	2	(1)	
15	RODRIGO Barbosa TABATA	BRA	19/11/80	M	9	(5)	
1	RÜŞTÜ Reçber		10/5/73	G	11		
31	SIMÃO Pedro Fonseca Sabrosa	POR	31/10/79	M	15		5
6	Tomáš SIVOK	CZE	15/9/83	D	11		
57	VOLKAN Ekici		23/3/91	M		(1)	
29	YUSUF Şimşek		20/7/75	M		(1)	
30	Tomáš ZÁPOTOČNÝ	CZE	13/9/80	D	6	(1)	

BUCASPOR

Coach – Bülent Uygun; (7/10/10) Samet Aybaba; (14/4/11) Sait Karafırtınalar

Founded – 1928

Stadium – Yeni Buca (6,231)

2010				
14/8	Beşiktaş	h	0-1	
23/8	Kasımpaşa	a	0-0	
28/8	Gençlerbirliği	h	3-1	*Orhan, Koray, Manucho*
11/9	Konyaspor	a	1-1	*Orhan*
18/9	Galatasaray	h	0-1	
24/9	Bursaspor	a	0-1	
1/10	Eskişehirspor	h	0-0	
16/10	Gaziantepspor	a	0-2	
22/10	Sivasspor	a	1-1	*Erkan*
31/10	İstanbul BB	h	0-2	
6/11	Karabükspor	a	0-3	
13/11	Ankaragücü	h	0-0	
22/11	Fenerbahçe	a	2-5	*Manucho, Musa*
28/11	Antalyaspor	h	1-0	*Orhan*
3/12	Trabzonspor	a	0-2	
11/12	Manisaspor	h	1-1	*og (Kahê)*
18/12	Kayserispor	a	0-2	
2011				
21/1	Beşiktaş	a	1-5	*Musa*
29/1	Kasımpaşa	h	4-0	*Musa 2, Leandrão, Erkan*
6/2	Gençlerbirliği	a	0-1	
12/2	Konyaspor	h	3-2	*Musa, Leko 2 (1p)*
19/2	Galatasaray	a	0-1	
25/2	Bursaspor	h	0-2	
6/3	Eskişehirspor	a	0-1	
13/3	Gaziantepspor	h	2-1	*Ragıp, Ali Kuçik*
20/3	Sivasspor	h	0-4	
3/4	İstanbul BB	a	1-2	*Abdülkadir*
9/4	Karabükspor	h	2-1	*Jibrine, Ali Kuçik*
16/4	Ankaragücü	a	3-5	*Jibrine, Erkan, Ediz*
24/4	Fenerbahçe	h	3-5	*Musa, Abdülkadir 2*
30/4	Antalyaspor	a	3-3	*Mendy, Musa, Abdülkadir*
8/5	Trabzonspor	h	1-2	*Abdülkadir*
14/5	Manisaspor	a	2-4	*Mendy, Musa*
21/5	Kayserispor	h	3-3	*Mendy, Abdülkadir, Mehmet İncebacak*

No	Name	Nat	DoB	Pos	Aps	(s)	Gls
42	ABDÜLKADİR Özgen		8/9/86	A	5	(2)	6
59	AHMET Çörekçi		1/2/92	A	15	(3)	
20	ALİ Güneş		23/11/78	D	1	(2)	
80	ALİ Kuçik		17/6/91	A	10	(2)	2
16	ATİLLA Özmen		11/5/88	G	8		
25	André Roberto Soares da Silva "BETO"	BRA	2/10/81	A	8	(1)	
13	CARLOS Alberto Fernandes	ANG	8/12/79	G	14		
55	CENK İşler		25/2/74	A	1	(8)	
22	CİVAR Çetin		1/1/92	M	1	(4)	
30	Eduardo Fernando Pereira Gomes "DADY"	CPV	13/8/81	A		(5)	
9	Mohamed DAHMANE	ALG	9/4/82	A	2	(4)	
3	EDİZ Bahtiyaroğlu		2/1/86	D	11	(5)	1
54	EMRE Aktaş		23/9/86	A	2	(6)	
21	ERKAN Taşkıran		22/4/85	A	24	(2)	3
45	ERMAN Güraçar		24/8/74	D	5	(2)	
92	HABİB Uzun		6/5/92	A		(1)	
8	İBRAHİM Dağaşan		15/6/84	M	13	(2)	
19	Tawrick JIBRINE	GHA	14/1/91	M	8		2
4	KORAY Çölgeçen		28/5/85	D	19		1
68	José Leandro Gomes "LEANDRÃO"	BRA	5/1/84	D	7		1
23	Jerko LEKO	CRO	9/4/80	M	27	(3)	2
1	Pavel LONDAK	EST	14/5/80	G	8		
9	Mateus Alberto Contreiras Gonçalves "MANUCHO"	ANG	7/3/83	A	12		2
91	MEHMET İncebacak		9/2/91	M	1	(3)	1
27	MEHMET Polat		8/6/78	D		(2)	
11	Victor MENDY	SEN	22/12/81	A	25	(5)	3
93	MERT Özcanlar		5/2/93	M		(1)	
5	Landry MULEMO	BEL	17/9/86	D	19	(2)	
7	MUSA Aydın		1/11/80	M	28	(3)	8
77	ONUR Tuncer		19/2/84	M	16	(2)	
6	ORHAN Ak		29/9/79	D	17		3
46	ÖMER Kahveci		15/2/92	G	4		
61	RAGIP Başdağ		9/6/78	M	24	(4)	1
34	SAMET Bülbül		13/3/91	M	2	(3)	
10	SERCAN Kaya		15/3/88	M	13	(11)	
87	SERKAN Yanık		2/4/87	D	12	(3)	
17	SERVER Yılmaz		15/6/92	D		(1)	
2	Stjepan TOMAS	CRO	6/3/76	D	8	(1)	
43	VELİ Kızılkaya		1/2/85	D	2		
35	ZAFER Çevik		20/1/84	M	2	(7)	

BURSASPOR

Coach – Ertuğrul Sağlam

Founded – 1963

Stadium – Atatürk (25,213)

MAJOR HONOURS: Turkish League – (1) 2010; Turkish Cup – (1) 1986.

2010				
16/8	Konyaspor	h	1-0	*Sercan*
22/8	Galatasaray	a	2-0	*Ergić 2*
28/8	Sivasspor	a	2-0	*Volkan, Ali*
10/9	Eskişehirspor	h	2-1	*Núñez, Sercan*
20/9	Gaziantepspor	a	3-0	*(w/o; match abandoned after 62 mins at 1-0 Ömer)*
4/9	Bucaspor	h	1-0	*Hüseyin*
3/10	İstanbul BB	a	0-0	
15/10	Karabükspor	h	2-2	*Turgay 2*
24/10	Ankaragücü	a	5-1	*İbrahim, Turgay, Ömer, Ergić, Sercan*
29/10	Fenerbahçe	h	1-1	*Ergić*
6/11	Antalyaspor	a	2-2	*Ali, Ozan İpek*
13/11	Trabzonspor	h	0-2	
20/11	Manisaspor	a	2-0	*Turgay, Batalla*
29/11	Kayserispor	h	2-0	*Insúa, Sercan*
5/12	Beşiktaş	a	0-1	
13/12	Kasımpaşa	h	2-1	*Turgay, og (Tolga)*
18/12	Gençlerbirliği	a	5-1	*Sercan 2, Ozan İpek, Turgay, Núñez*
2011				
23/1	Konyaspor	a	0-0	
29/1	Galatasaray	h	2-0	*Miller, Gökçek Vederson*

'2	Sivasspor	h	2-1	*og (Hayrettin), Miller*
3/2	Eskişehirspor	a	1-1	*Ergić*
9/2	Gaziantepspor	h	1-4	*og (Nounkeu)*
5/2	Bucaspor	a	2-0	*Batalla, Miller*
/3	İstanbul BB	h	1-1	*Batalla*
2/3	Karabükspor	a	1-1	*Miller*
1/3	Ankaragücü	h	0-0	
/4	Fenerbahçe	a	0-0	
/4	Antalyaspor	h	2-3	*Altidore, Miller*
7/4	Trabzonspor	a	0-1	
3/4	Manisaspor	h	2-1	*Sercan, Ömer*
/5	Kayserispor	a	0-1	
'/5	Beşiktaş	h	0-3	*(w/o)*
5/5	Kasımpaşa	a	3-0	*İbrahim, Turgay, Ozan Has*
1/5	Gençlerbirliği	h	1-0	*Volkan*

No	Name	Nat	DoB	Pos	Aps	(s)	Gls
'2	AHMET Arı		13/1/89	A		(1)	
21	ALİ Tandoğan		25/12/77	D	23		2
12	Jozy ALTIDORE	USA	6/11/89	A	6	(6)	1
17	Pablo BATALLA	ARG	16/1/84	M	25	(7)	3
25	Ivan ERGIĆ	SRB	21/1/81	M	19	(8)	5
3	Wederson Luiz da Silva Medeiros "GÖKÇEK VEDERSON"		22/7/81	D	27	(1)	1
5	HÜSEYİN Çimşir		26/5/79	M	12	(4)	1
7	Federico INSÚA	ARG	3/1/80	M	9	(8)	1
27	Dimitar IVANKOV	BUL	30/10/75	G	28		
38	İBRAHİM Öztürk		21/6/81	D	21		2
35	İSMAİL HAKTAN Odabaşı		7/8/91	M	2	(1)	
11	Giani Stelian KIRIŢĂ	ROU	3/3/77	M	4	(2)	
18	Kenny MILLER	SCO	23/12/79	A	14	(1)	5
23	MUSTAFA Keçeli		15/9/78	D	16	(1)	
29	Leonel NÚÑEZ	ARG	13/10/84	A	4	(9)	2
6	OZAN Has		18/2/85	M	10	(9)	1
20	OZAN İpek		10/10/86	M	28	(2)	2
4	ÖMER Erdoğan		3/5/77	D	23	(2)	3
58	RAMAZAN Sal		27/6/85	D		(1)	
9	SERCAN Yıldırım		5/4/90	A	11	(11)	7
2	SERDAR Aziz		23/10/90	D	13	(2)	
19	Héctor Damián STEINERT	ARG	25/2/86	M	1	(2)	
55	Milan STEPANOV	SRB	2/4/83	D	9	(1)	
13	Gustav SVENSSON	SWE	7/2/87	M	16		
22	TURGAY Bahadır		15/1/84	A	17	(7)	7
10	VOLKAN Şen		7/7/87	M	20	(7)	2
1	YAVUZ Özkan		19/5/85	G	5	(2)	

ESKİŞEHİRSPOR

Coach – Rıza Çalımbay; (6/10/10) Bülent Uygun

Founded – 1965

Stadium – Atatürk (13,520)

MAJOR HONOURS: Turkish Cup – (1) 1971.

2010

14/8	Gençlerbirliği	h	0-0	
20/8	Konyaspor	a	1-2	*Pelé*
29/8	Galatasaray	h	1-3	*Vučko*
10/9	Bursaspor	a	1-2	*Sezer*
18/9	Sivasspor	a	1-1	*Adem*
25/9	Gaziantepspor	h	0-1	
1/10	Bucaspor	a	0-0	
16/10	İstanbul BB	h	1-0	*Batuhan*
22/10	Karabükspor	a	2-1	*Sezgin, Batuhan*
30/10	Ankaragücü	h	0-0	
6/11	Fenerbahçe	a	2-4	*Sezer, Serdar*
13/11	Antalyaspor	h	0-0	
21/11	Trabzonspor	a	0-0	
26/11	Manisaspor	h	2-1	*Burhan, Batuhan*
6/12	Kayserispor	a	2-2	*Diego Ângelo, Burhan*
10/12	Beşiktaş	h	2-0	*Veysel, Sezer*
19/12	Kasımpaşa	a	2-0	*Batuhan, Ümit*

2011

22/1	Gençlerbirliği	a	1-0	*Burhan*
31/1	Konyaspor	h	1-0	*Sezer*
6/2	Galatasaray	a	2-4	*Burhan, Ümit*
13/2	Bursaspor	h	1-1	*Sezer (p)*
18/2	Sivasspor	h	2-1	*Serdar, Pelé*
26/2	Gaziantepspor	a	1-2	*Ümit*
6/3	Bucaspor	h	1-0	*Ümit*
12/3	İstanbul BB	a	2-0	*Burhan, Sezer (p)*
20/3	Karabükspor	h	1-0	*og (Deumi)*
2/4	Ankaragücü	a	2-2	*Burhan, Batuhan*
9/4	Fenerbahçe	h	1-3	*Batuhan*
17/4	Antalyaspor	a	2-2	*Batuhan, Sezer*
22/4	Trabzonspor	h	0-0	
1/5	Manisaspor	a	1-3	*Sezer*
6/5	Kayserispor	h	1-2	*Serdar*
16/5	Beşiktaş	a	1-3	*Erkan*
22/5	Kasımpaşa	h	4-0	*Serdar 3, Diego Ângelo*

No	Name	Nat	DoB	Pos	Aps	(s)	Gls
58	ADEM Sarı		9/5/85	A	5	(5)	1
6	ALPER Potuk		8/4/91	M	20	(4)	
29	ATİLLA Koca		16/7/80	G	5	(1)	
26	BATUHAN Karadeniz		24/4/91	A	17	(8)	7
21	BURHAN Eşer		1/1/85	M	19	(5)	6
55	BÜLENT Ertuğrul		17/9/78	M	17	(6)	
11	BÜLENT Kocabey		8/6/84	M	1	(1)	
3	DIEGO ÂNGELO de Oliveira	BRA	17/2/86	D	17	(3)	2
20	DOĞA Kaya		30/6/84	M	18	(9)	
77	ERKAN Zengin		5/8/85	M	24	(7)	1
19	Agim IBRAIMI	MKD	29/8/88	M		(1)	
1	Vanja IVEŠA	CRO	21/7/77	G	29		
22	Jaycee JOHN Okwunwanne	BHR	8/10/85	A	6	(3)	
51	KORAY Arslan		1/10/83	D	16	(2)	
95	MİKAİL Albayrak		6/4/92	M		(3)	
13	Safet NADAREVIĆ	BIH	30/8/80	D	28	(2)	
94	NURİ FATİH Aydın		1/1/95	M		(2)	
8	Vítor Hugo Gomes Passos "PELÉ"	POR	14/8/87	M	20	(6)	2
41	Räşad F. SADIQOV	AZE	16/6/82	D	5		
15	SERDAR Özbayraktar		22/11/81	A	12	(11)	6
10	SEZER Öztürk		3/11/85	M	26	(3)	8
5	SEZGİN Coşkun		23/8/84	D	28	(1)	1
14	Rodrigo Álvaro Valenzuela TELLO	CHI	14/10/79	M	9	(7)	
99	ÜMİT Karan		1/10/76	A	8	(9)	4
88	VEYSEL Sarı		25/7/88	D	10	(3)	1
7	VOLKAN Yaman		27/8/82	D	30		
27	Luka VUČKO	CRO	11/4/84	D	4		1

FENERBAHÇE SK

Coach – Aykut Kocaman

Founded – 1907

Stadium – Şükrü Saracoğlu (53,586)

MAJOR HONOURS: Turkish League – (18) 1959, 1961, 1964, 1965, 1968, 1970, 1974, 1975, 1978, 1983, 1985, 1989, 1996, 2001, 2004, 2005, 2007, 2011;
Turkish Cup – (4) 1968, 1974, 1979, 1983.

2010

15/8	Antalyaspor	h	4-0	*Semih 2, Alex, Gökhan Gönül*
23/8	Trabzonspor	a	2-3	*Lugano, Mehmet*
29/8	Manisaspor	h	4-2	*Alex, Lugano, Niang 2*
11/9	Kayserispor	a	0-2	
19/9	Beşiktaş	h	1-1	*Niang*
27/9	Kasımpaşa	a	6-2	*Alex 2 (1p), Emre, Niang 3*
2/10	Gençlerbirliği	h	3-0	*Niang, og (Aykut), André Santos*
18/10	Konyaspor	a	4-1	*Emre 2, Semih, Stoch*
24/10	Galatasaray	h	0-0	
29/10	Bursaspor	a	1-1	*Semih*
6/11	Eskişehirspor	h	4-2	*Alex (p), Semih 2, Gökhan Gönül*

13/11	Gaziantepspor	a	1-2	*Alex*
22/11	Bucaspor	h	5-2	*Alex 3, Niang, Semih*
27/11	İstanbul BB	a	1-0	*Alex*
5/12	Karabükspor	h	2-1	*Lugano, Alex*
12/12	Ankaragücü	a	1-2	*Niang*
18/12	Sivasspor	h	1-0	*Alex*
2011				
22/1	Antalyaspor	a	1-0	*Gökhan Gönül*
30/1	Trabzonspor	h	2-0	*Lugano, Niang*
5/2	Manisaspor	a	3-1	*Alex (p), Niang, Dia*
14/2	Kayserispor	h	2-0	*Niang, Lugano*
20/2	Beşiktaş	a	4-2	*og (Necip), Alex 3 (1p)*
26/2	Kasımpaşa	h	2-0	*Alex, Dia*
7/3	Gençlerbirliği	a	4-2	*Lugano, Alex (p), Niang, André Santos*
13/3	Konyaspor	h	2-0	*Niang, Semih*
18/3	Galatasaray	a	2-1	*Semih, Alex*
3/4	Bursaspor	h	0-0	
9/4	Eskişehirspor	a	3-1	*Caner, Niang, Semih*
16/4	Gaziantepspor	h	1-0	*André Santos*
24/4	Bucaspor	a	5-3	*Emre, Alex 2 (1p), Güiza, André Santos*
1/5	İstanbul BB	h	2-0	*Stoch, Alex*
8/5	Karabükspor	a	1-0	*Lugano*
15/5	Ankaragücü	h	6-0	*Alex 5 (3p), Bekir*
22/5	Sivasspor	a	4-3	*André Santos, Selçuk, Alex, Yobo*

No	Name	Nat	DoB	Pos	Aps	(s)	Gls
10	ALEXsandro de Souza	BRA	14/9/77	A	32	(1)	28
27	ANDRÉ Clarindo dos SANTOS	BRA	8/3/83	D	22	(3)	5
4	BEKİR İrtegün		20/4/84	D	7	(7)	1
88	CANER Erkin		4/10/88	D	15	(7)	1
16	CRISTIAN Mark Junio Nascimento Oliveira Baroni	BRA	25/6/83	M	20	(8)	
92	Issiar DIA	SEN	8/6/87	M	12	(13)	2
5	EMRE Belözoğlu		7/9/80	M	27		4
58	FÁBIO Alves da Silva "BILICA"	BRA	14/1/79	D	6	(2)	
14	GÖKAY İravul		18/10/92	M	3	(8)	
77	GÖKHAN Gönül		4/1/85	D	30		3
39	GÖKHAN Ünal		23/7/82	A		(3)	
9	Daniel GÜIZA	ESP	17/8/80	A		(3)	1
6	İLHAN Eker		1/1/83	D		(1)	
8	KAZIM Kazım		26/8/86	M	1	(4)	
2	Diego LUGANO	URU	2/11/80	D	28		7
38	MEHMET Topuz		7/9/83	M	34		1
34	MERT Günok		1/3/89	G	2	(1)	
7	Mamadou NIANG	SEN	13/10/79	A	28	(1)	15
17	OKAN Alkan		1/10/92	D	2		
20	ÖZER Hurmacı		20/11/86	M	6	(8)	
21	SELÇUK Şahin		31/1/81	M	12	(6)	1
23	SEMİH Şentürk		29/4/83	A	10	(15)	10
11	Miroslav STOCH	SVK	19/10/89	M	16	(7)	2
1	VOLKAN Demirel		27/10/81	G	32		
3	Joseph YOBO	NGA	6/9/80	D	29	(1)	1

GALATASARAY AŞ

Coach – Frank Rijkaard (NED); (22/10/10) Gheorghe Hagi (ROU); (25/3/11) Bülent Ünder

Founded – 1905

Stadium – Ali Sami Yen (23,785); Türk Telecom Arena (52,695)

MAJOR HONOURS: UEFA Cup – (1) 2000;
UEFA Super Cup – (1) 2000;
Turkish League – (17) 1962, 1963, 1969, 1971, 1972, 1973, 1987, 1988, 1993, 1994, 1997, 1998, 1999, 2000, 2002, 2006, 2008;
Turkish Cup – (14) 1963, 1964, 1965, 1966, 1973, 1976, 1982, 1985, 1991, 1993, 1996, 1999, 2000, 2005.

2010				
14/8	Sivasspor	a	1-2	*Mustafa*
22/8	Bursaspor	h	0-2	
29/8	Eskişehirspor	a	3-1	*Baroš, og (Volkan), Servet*
13/9	Gaziantepspor	h	1-0	*Kewell (p)*
18/9	Bucaspor	a	1-0	*Ayhan*
26/9	İstanbul BB	h	3-1	*Baroš 3 (1p)*
1/10	Karabükspor	a	1-2	*Barış*
17/10	Ankaragücü	h	2-4	*Baroš 2*
24/10	Fenerbahçe	a	0-0	
30/10	Antalyaspor	h	2-1	*Servet, Pino*
7/11	Trabzonspor	a	0-2	
14/11	Manisaspor	h	0-2	
21/11	Kayserispor	a	0-0	
28/11	Beşiktaş	h	1-2	*Kewell*
4/12	Kasımpaşa	a	3-0	*Kewell, Pino, Hakan*
11/12	Gençlerbirliği	h	0-2	
19/12	Konyaspor	a	1-0	*Anıl*
2011				
23/1	Sivasspor	h	1-0	*Servet*
29/1	Bursaspor	a	0-2	
6/2	Eskişehirspor	h	4-2	*Cana, Stancu, Kewell, Baroš*
12/2	Gaziantepspor	a	0-1	
19/2	Bucaspor	h	1-0	*Culio*
26/2	İstanbul BB	a	1-3	*Baroš*
5/3	Karabükspor	h	0-0	
13/3	Ankaragücü	a	2-3	*Aydın, Pino*
18/3	Fenerbahçe	h	1-2	*Kazım*
4/4	Antalyaspor	a	0-3	
10/4	Trabzonspor	h	0-1	
18/4	Manisaspor	a	3-2	*Arda 2, Culio*
23/4	Kayserispor	h	1-1	*Gökhan*
30/4	Beşiktaş	a	0-2	
9/5	Kasımpaşa	h	3-1	*Stancu, Baroš (p), Servet*
14/5	Gençlerbirliği	a	3-2	*Kewell, Culio, Kazım*
20/5	Konyaspor	h	2-0	*Kazım, Culio*

No	Name	Nat	DoB	Pos	Aps	(s)	Gls
4	ALİ Turan		6/9/83	D	8	(2)	
66	ANIL Dilaver		20/11/90	A	2		1
10	ARDA Turan		30/1/87	M	8	(4)	2
7	AYDIN Yılmaz		29/1/88	M	7	(12)	1
18	AYHAN Akman		23/2/77	M	24	(2)	1
1	AYKUT Erçetin		14/9/82	G	5	(1)	
8	BARIŞ Özbek		14/9/86	M	9	(9)	1
15	Milan BAROŠ	CZE	28/10/81	A	11	(5)	9
19	Lorik CANA	ALB	27/7/83	M	20	(4)	1
40	CEM Sultan		27/2/91	A		(1)	
27	Emmanuel Juan CULIO	ARG	30/8/83	M	15		4
3	ÇAĞLAR Birinci		2/10/85	D	7	(3)	
9	ELANO Ralph Blumer	BRA	14/6/81	M	6	(1)	
52	EMRE Çolak		20/5/91	M	6	(7)	
5	GÖKHAN Zan		7/9/81	D	13	(2)	1
22	HAKAN Balta		23/3/83	D	18	(2)	1
6	Emiliano Adrián INSÚA	ARG	7/1/89	D	12	(4)	
80	KAZIM Kazım		26/8/86	M	13		3
99	Harry KEWELL	AUS	22/9/78	A	16	(4)	5
11	MEHMET Batdal		24/2/86	A		(6)	
21	Zvjezdan MISIMOVIĆ	BIH	5/6/82	M	8	(1)	
35	MUSA Çağıran		17/11/92	M		(1)	
16	MUSTAFA Sarp		5/11/80	M	13	(8)	1
2	Lucas NEILL	AUS	9/3/78	D	24	(1)	
20	Juan Pablo PINO	COL	30/3/87	A	14	(5)	3
55	SABRİ Sarıoğlu		26/7/84	M	21	(2)	
77	SERDAR Özkan		1/1/87	M	1	(1)	
23	SERKAN Kurtuluş		1/1/90	D	12	(2)	
76	SERVET Çetin		17/3/81	D	31		4
28	Bogdan Sorin STANCU	ROU	28/6/87	A	12	(2)	2
86	UFUK Ceylan		23/6/86	G	19		
25	YEKTA Kurtuluş		11/12/85	M	9	(4)	
87	Robinson ZAPATA Montaño	COL	30/9/78	G	10		

GAZİANTEPSPOR

Coach – Tolunay Kafkas
Founded – 1969
Stadium – Kamil Ocak (16,981)

010				
4/8	Kasımpaşa	h	0-0	
2/8	Gençlerbirliği	a	0-0	
7/8	Konyaspor	h	2-2	*Mehmet, Júlio César (p)*
3/9	Galatasaray	a	0-1	
0/9	Bursaspor	h	0-3	*(w/o; match abandoned after 62 mins at 0-1)*
5/9	Eskişehirspor	a	1-0	*Serdar*
/10	Sivasspor	a	1-1	*Júlio César*
6/10	Bucaspor	h	2-0	*Sosa (p), Popov*
3/10	İstanbul BB	a	0-1	
0/10	Karabükspor	h	0-0	
/11	Ankaragücü	a	2-0	*Olcan, Ivan*
3/11	Fenerbahçe	h	2-1	*Serdar, Olcan*
1/11	Antalyaspor	a	1-0	*Serdar*
7/11	Trabzonspor	h	1-3	*Emre*
/12	Manisaspor	a	0-2	
2/12	Kayserispor	h	2-0	*Júlio César, Ahmet*
9/12	Beşiktaş	a	1-1	*Olcan*
2011				
23/1	Kasımpaşa	a	1-0	*Sosa*
30/1	Gençlerbirliği	h	1-1	*Olcan*
5/2	Konyaspor	a	2-0	*og (Hakan), Olcan*
12/2	Galatasaray	h	1-0	*Sosa*
19/2	Bursaspor	a	4-1	*Wágner, Yalçın, Cenk 2*
26/2	Eskişehirspor	h	2-1	*Cenk 2*
5/3	Sivasspor	h	3-1	*Wágner, Popov, Cenk*
13/3	Bucaspor	a	1-2	*Cenk*
19/3	İstanbul BB	h	4-1	*Hürriyet, Olcan 3*
2/4	Karabükspor	a	2-3	*Ivan, Olcan*
10/4	Ankaragücü	h	3-2	*Olcan, Cenk 2*
16/4	Fenerbahçe	a	0-1	
24/4	Antalyaspor	h	2-1	*Cenk 2*
1/5	Trabzonspor	a	0-3	
7/5	Manisaspor	h	1-0	*Olcan*
15/5	Kayserispor	a	2-1	*Olcan, Murat*
21/5	Beşiktaş	h	0-0	

No	Name	Nat	DoB	Pos	Aps	(s)	Gls
7	AHMET Arı		13/1/89	M	2	(4)	1
17	ALPER Akçam		1/9/87	A		(3)	
9	André Roberto Soares da Silva "BETO"	BRA	2/10/81	A	2	(6)	
23	CENK Tosun		7/6/91	A	14		10
3	ELYASA Süme		13/8/83	D	24	(2)	
4	EMRE Güngör		1/8/84	D	25	(1)	1
34	ERAY Birniçan		20/7/88	G	2		
19	ERMAN Özgür		13/4/77	M	1		
20	GÖKHAN Öztürk		22/3/90	M		(2)	
50	HÜRRİYET Güçer		25/10/81	M	11		1
21	İBRAHİM FERDİ Coşkun		20/4/87	M		(2)	
6	IVAN Saraiva de Souza	BRA	18/1/82	D	31		2
11	Jorge Luíz Pereira da Silva "JORGINHO"	BRA	6/5/77	M	7	(7)	
99	JÚLIO CÉSAR da Silva e Souza	BRA	26/2/80	A	9	(9)	3
1	Žydrūnas KARČEMARSKAS	LTU	24/5/83	G	31		
22	MAHMUT Bezgin		1/3/86	G	1		
10	MEHMET Yılmaz		22/5/79	A	7	(1)	1
15	MUHAMMET Demir		10/1/92	A		(2)	
5	MURAT Ceylan		2/3/88	M	24	(4)	1
13	Dany NOUNKEU	CMR	11/4/86	D	18		
29	OLCAN Adın		30/9/85	M	27	(6)	12
61	ORHAN Gülle		15/1/92	M	10	(12)	
71	Ivelin POPOV	BUL	26/10/87	A	26	(2)	2
16	SERDAR Kurtuluş		23/7/87	D	21		3
18	Ismael SOSA	ARG	18/1/87	A	21	(8)	3
14	ŞENOL Can		3/4/83	D	10	(7)	
25	WÁGNER Ferreira Dos Santos	BRA	29/1/85	M	15	(2)	2
2	YALÇIN Ayhan		1/5/82	D	22	(5)	1
8	Cristian Rodrigo ZURITA	ARG	24/7/79	M	13	(13)	

GENÇLERBİRLİĞİ SK

Coach – Thomas Doll (GER); (21/10/10) Ralf Zumdick (GER); (25/4/11) Mustafa Kaplan
Founded – 1923
Stadium – 19 Mayıs (19,209)
MAJOR HONOURS: Turkish Cup – (2) 1987, 2001.

2010				
14/8	Eskişehirspor	a	0-0	
22/8	Gaziantepspor	h	0-0	
28/8	Bucaspor	a	1-3	*Oktay*
13/9	İstanbul BB	h	2-1	*Mehmet (p), Orhan*
19/9	Karabükspor	a	0-3	
25/9	Ankaragücü	h	1-0	*Smeltz (p)*
2/10	Fenerbahçe	a	0-3	
17/10	Antalyaspor	h	2-3	*Mehmet (p), Zec*
23/10	Trabzonspor	a	1-3	*Serkan*
31/10	Manisaspor	h	2-0	*Serkan, Zec*
5/11	Kayserispor	a	1-1	*Zec*
14/11	Beşiktaş	h	0-2	
20/11	Kasımpaşa	a	1-1	*Cem Can*
27/11	Sivasspor	h	1-1	*Soner*
5/12	Konyaspor	a	1-2	*Kulušić*
11/12	Galatasaray	a	2-0	*Hurşut, Orhan*
18/12	Bursaspor	h	1-5	*Soner*
2011				
22/1	Eskişehirspor	h	0-1	
30/1	Gaziantepspor	a	1-1	*Yasin*
6/2	Bucaspor	h	1-0	*Oktay*
12/2	İstanbul BB	a	1-0	*Mustafa*
19/2	Karabükspor	h	2-3	*Mununga, og (Deumi)*
26/2	Ankaragücü	a	4-2	*Oktay, Mustafa, Serkan, Orhan*
7/3	Fenerbahçe	h	2-4	*Orhan, Hurşut*
13/3	Antalyaspor	a	0-0	
20/3	Trabzonspor	h	1-2	*Cem Can*
3/4	Manisaspor	a	3-0	*Jedinak, Serkan, Mustafa*
10/4	Kayserispor	h	4-1	*Mustafa, Zec, Jedinak, Aykut*
15/4	Beşiktaş	a	2-2	*Jedinak, Mustafa*
24/4	Kasımpaşa	h	1-1	*Oktay*
29/4	Sivasspor	a	1-1	*Oktay*
8/5	Konyaspor	h	2-1	*Yasin, Oktay*
14/5	Galatasaray	h	2-3	*Emre Aygün 2*
21/5	Bursaspor	a	0-1	

No	Name	Nat	DoB	Pos	Aps	(s)	Gls
3	ALPARSLAN Erdem		11/12/88	D		(10)	
4	AYKUT Demir		22/10/88	D	25		1
12	Randall AZOFEIFA	CRC	30/12/84	M	11	(3)	
19	Bekim BALA	ALB	11/1/91	A		(1)	
61	BİLAL Çubukçu		16/5/87	M	1	(1)	
2	BURAK Özsaraç		7/6/79	D	12		
27	CEM Atan		30/6/85	M		(1)	
40	CEM Can		1/4/81	M	32		2
5	Debatik CURRI	ALB	28/12/83	D	6		
30	EMRE Aygün		1/6/85	M	2	(3)	2
55	EMRE Balak		11/8/88	D	3	(1)	
77	ERDAL Kılıçaslan		23/8/84	A		(3)	
8	Labinot HARBUZI	SWE	4/4/86	M	11	(3	
17	HURŞUT Meriç		31/7/83	M	21	(7)	2
14	Mile JEDINAK	AUS	3/8/84	M	19	(2)	3
6	Ante KULUŠIĆ	CRO	6/6/86	D	14	(1)	1
26	MAHMUT Boz		16/4/91	D	15	(3)	
21	Franck MAWUENA	TOG	21/11/92	M		(2)	
9	Billy MEHMET	IRL	3/1/84	A	8	(6)	2

No	Name	Nat	DoB	Pos	Aps	(s)	Gls
28	MEHMET Akgün		6/8/86	D	11	(7)	
88	Joachim MUNUNGA	BEL	30/6/88	M	6	(1)	1
69	MURAT Kalkan		20/5/86	D	26		
11	MUSTAFA Pektemek		11/8/88	A	6	(4)	5
13	OKTAY Delibalta		27/10/85	M	23	(6)	6
67	ORHAN Şam		1/6/86	D	24		4
58	ÖZKAN Karabulut		16/1/91	G	7	(1)	
22	RAMAZAN Köse		12/5/88	G	2	(2)	
1	SERDAR Kulbilge		7/7/80	G	25		
7	SERKAN Çalık		15/3/86	A	25	(3)	4
99	Shane SMELTZ	NZL	29/9/81	A	5	(1)	1
20	SONER Aydoğdu		5/1/91	M	4	(6)	2
16	Patiyo TAMBWE	COD	7/1/84	A	4	(6)	
41	YASİN Öztekin		19/3/87	M	6	(11)	2
10	Ermin ZEC	BIH	6/6/88	M	20	(4)	4

İSTANBUL BB SK

Coach – Abdullah Avcı

Founded – 1990

Stadium – Atatürk Olimpiyat (76,092)

2010				
16/8	Kayserispor	h	0-2	
21/8	Beşiktaş	a	2-0	*İskender, İbrahim Akın*
28/8	Kasımpaşa	h	3-1	*İskender, İbrahim Akın, Tum*
13/9	Gençlerbirliği	a	1-2	*Gökhan Süzen*
19/9	Konyaspor	h	1-0	*Tum*
26/9	Galatasaray	a	1-3	*Tum*
3/10	Bursaspor	h	0-0	
16/10	Eskişehirspor	a	0-1	
23/10	Gaziantepspor	h	1-0	*Tevfik*
31/10	Bucaspor	a	2-0	*İbrahim Akın, Tevfik*
7/11	Sivasspor	a	4-0	*Holmén, Tum, İbrahim Akın 2*
14/11	Karabükspor	h	2-1	*Tum 2*
21/11	Ankaragücü	a	2-2	*İbrahim Akın, Tum*
27/11	Fenerbahçe	h	0-1	
5/12	Antalyaspor	a	0-1	
12/12	Trabzonspor	h	1-3	*Tum*
19/12	Manisaspor	a	0-1	
2011				
24/1	Kayserispor	a	2-3	*Holmén, Gökhan Ünal*
30/1	Beşiktaş	h	2-1	*Vinícius, İskender*
5/2	Kasımpaşa	a	3-1	*Holmén, Gökhan Ünal, Ali*
12/2	Gençlerbirliği	h	0-1	
20/2	Konyaspor	a	0-0	
26/2	Galatasaray	h	3-1	*Holmén, İbrahim Akın 2 (1p)*
6/3	Bursaspor	a	1-1	*Efe*
12/3	Eskişehirspor	h	0-2	
19/3	Gaziantepspor	a	1-4	*Hološko*
3/4	Bucaspor	h	2-1	*og (Orhan), Hološko*
10/4	Sivasspor	h	1-2	*Hološko*
16/4	Karabükspor	a	2-0	*Hološko, Tum*
24/4	Ankaragücü	h	1-4	*Metin*
1/5	Fenerbahçe	a	0-2	
7/5	Antalyaspor	h	1-1	*Hološko*
15/5	Trabzonspor	a	1-3	*Holmén*
20/5	Manisaspor	h	0-0	

No	Name	Nat	DoB	Pos	Aps	(s)	Gls
4	ABDÜLKADİR Kayalı		30/1/91	M	4	(3)	
10	ALİ Güzeldal		10/4/86	M	6	(12)	1
14	BEHRAM Zülaloğlu		30/8/82	G	2		
2	CAN Arat		21/1/84	D	16	(2)	
20	CİHAN Haspolatlı		4/1/80	M	23	(4)	
6	EFE İnanç		24/3/80	M	9	(11)	1
17	EKREM Ekşioğlu		16/1/78	D	28		
66	ERGÜN Berisha		24/6/88	M	1		
9	GÖKHAN Kaba		24/11/83	A		(2)	
81	GÖKHAN Süzen		12/7/87	D	22	(8)	1
99	GÖKHAN Ünal		23/7/82	A	7	(4)	2
1	Kenan HASAGİĆ	BIH	1/2/80	G	19		
89	HASAN ALİ Durtuluk		1/1/89	A		(5)	
23	Samuel HOLMÉN	SWE	28/6/84	M	28	(1)	5
37	Filip HOLOŠKO	SVK	17/1/84	A	9	(1)	5
11	İBRAHİM Akın		4/1/84	A	27	(3)	8
94	İBRAHİM Yılmaz		6/2/94	A	2	(3)	
12	İSKENDER Alın		28/2/84	A	11	(14)	3
28	Marcin KUŚ	POL	2/9/81	D	14	(1)	
21	MAHMUT Tekdemir		20/1/88	D	27		
44	Marcos Roberto da Silva Barbosa "MARQUINHOS"	BRA	21/10/82	D	2		
16	MEHMET Yılmaz		26/3/88	D	2		
3	METİN Depe		10/1/81	D	18	(1)	1
61	OĞUZHAN Bahadır		24/12/79	G	13		
53	RIZVAN Şahin		30/10/81	D	13	(1)	
84	SERHAT Akyüz		10/8/84	D	16	(2)	
7	SERHAT Gülpınar		1/1/79	M	1	(2)	
88	TEVFİK Köse		12/7/88	A	20	(9)	2
18	Hervé TUM	CMR	15/2/79	A	17	(7)	9
29	Marcus Cesário VINÍCIUS	BRA	22/3/86	D	4		1
8	ZEKİ Korkmaz		1/9/88	M	13	(5)	

KARDEMİR KARABÜKSPOR

Coach –Yücel İldiz

Founded – 1969

Stadium – Necmettin Şeyhoğlu (7,593)

2010				
15/8	Manisaspor	h	2-1	*Emenike, Angelov*
20/8	Kayserispor	a	0-1	
29/8	Beşiktaş	h	1-4	*Emenike*
13/9	Kasımpaşa	a	2-1	*Cernat, Ferdi*
19/9	Gençlerbirliği	h	3-0	*Emenike 2, Hakan Özmert*
26/9	Konyaspor	a	2-2	*Cernat, Hakan Özmert*
1/10	Galatasaray	h	2-1	*Cernat (p), Hakan Özmert*
15/10	Bursaspor	a	2-2	*Cernat 2 (1p)*
22/10	Eskişehirspor	h	1-2	*Emenike*
30/10	Gaziantepspor	a	0-0	
6/11	Bucaspor	h	3-0	*Emenike 3*
14/11	İstanbul BB	a	1-2	*Šerić*
20/11	Sivasspor	a	1-5	*Şenol*
28/11	Ankaragücü	h	5-1	*Emenike 2, İlhan, Birol 2*
5/12	Fenerbahçe	a	1-2	*Emenike*
11/12	Antalyaspor	h	2-0	*Deumi, Emenike*
17/12	Trabzonspor	a	0-3	
2011				
22/1	Manisaspor	a	2-4	*Hakan Söyler, Birol (p)*
29/1	Kayserispor	h	0-0	
5/2	Beşiktaş	a	1-1	*Emenike*
13/2	Kasımpaşa	h	1-3	*Bülent Kocabey*
19/2	Gençlerbirliği	a	3-2	*İlhan 2 (1p), Muhammet*
27/2	Konyaspor	h	2-1	*Cernat (p), Ragued*
5/3	Galatasaray	a	0-0	
12/3	Bursaspor	h	1-1	*İlhan*
20/3	Eskişehirspor	a	0-1	
2/4	Gaziantepspor	h	3-2	*Yasin, Angelov, İlhan*
9/4	Bucaspor	a	1-2	*Cernat (p)*
16/4	İstanbul BB	h	0-2	
23/4	Sivasspor	h	2-1	*Emenike, Birol*
2/5	Ankaragücü	a	0-0	
8/5	Fenerbahçe	h	0-1	
13/5	Antalyaspor	a	2-1	*Coelho 2*
22/5	Trabzonspor	h	0-4	

No	Name	Nat	DoB	Pos	Aps	(s)	Gls
99	Emil ANGELOV	BUL	17/7/80	A	9	(12)	2
58	AYDIN Karabulut		25/1/88	M		(3)	
5	BİROL Hikmet		24/3/82	M	22	(10)	4
16	BÜLENT Bal		5/8/77	D	9	(4)	
77	BÜLENT Kocabey		8/6/84	M	5	(8)	1
10	Florin Lucian CERNAT	ROU	10/3/80	M	20	(2)	7
18	Dyego Rocha COELHO	BRA	22/3/83	D	6	(4)	2

2	Armand DEUMI	CMR	12/3/79	D	33		1
8	Emmanuel EMENIKE	NGA	10/5/87	A	22	(1)	14
2	ENGİN Aktürk		7/8/83	D	1	(3)	
31	FATİH Ceylan		25/11/80	M	3		
	FATİH Öztürk		14/6/83	G	1		
9	FERDİ Elmas		13/2/85	A	3	(8)	1
3	HAKAN Özmert		3/6/85	M	19	(12)	3
58	HAKAN Söyler		6/4/83	M	29	(1)	1
23	İLHAN Parlak		18/1/87	A	25	(5)	5
11	KERİM Zengin		13/4/85	M	25	(1)	
6	MEHMET Çoğum		5/2/83	M	3	(4)	
35	MERTER Yüce		18/2/85	M		(5)	
41	MUHAMMET Özdin		10/9/78	D	19	(1)	1
60	MUHAMMET HANİFİ Yoldaş		20/4/83	D	4	(1)	
26	MURAT Selvi		10/7/82	D	3		
82	Hocine RAGUED	TUN	11/2/83	M	11	(2)	1
20	Ante ŠERIĆ	CRO	15/1/79	D	32		1
7	ŞENOL Akın		20/12/84	M	11	(7)	1
19	Vjekoslav TOMIĆ	CRO	19/7/83	G	33		
34	Mariel Everton Cosmo Da Silva "TOZO"	BRA	15/8/80	M	13	(1)	
17	YASİN Avcı		10/4/83	A	13	(7)	1

KASIMPAŞA SK

Coach – Yılmaz Vural; (27/12/10) Fuat Çapa

Founded – 1921

Stadium – Recep Tayip Erdoğan (9,576)

2010				
14/8	Gaziantepspor	a	0-0	
23/8	Bucaspor	h	0-0	
28/8	İstanbul BB	a	1-3	*Luiz Henrique*
13/9	Karabükspor	h	1-2	*Tjikuzu*
18/9	Ankaragücü	a	0-3	
27/9	Fenerbahçe	h	2-6	*Şahin, Ersen*
3/10	Antalyaspor	a	1-3	*Ersen*
17/10	Trabzonspor	h	0-7	
24/10	Manisaspor	a	1-2	*Varela*
31/10	Kayserispor	h	1-2	*Ersen*
8/11	Beşiktaş	a	1-1	*Ersen*
14/11	Sivasspor	h	2-0	*Yekta, Varela*
20/11	Gençlerbirliği	h	1-1	*Dimitrov*
27/11	Konyaspor	a	2-2	*Özgür, Varela*
4/12	Galatasaray	h	0-3	
13/12	Bursaspor	a	1-2	*Yekta*
19/12	Eskişehirspor	h	0-2	
2011				
23/1	Gaziantepspor	h	0-1	
29/1	Bucaspor	a	0-4	
5/2	İstanbul BB	h	1-3	*Ersen*
13/2	Karabükspor	a	3-1	*Gökhan, Halil, Hüseyin*
19/2	Ankaragücü	h	2-1	*Robledo, Halil*
26/2	Fenerbahçe	a	0-2	
6/3	Antalyaspor	h	2-3	*Halil, Robledo*
12/3	Trabzonspor	a	0-1	
19/3	Manisaspor	h	1-0	*Varela*
3/4	Kayserispor	a	3-1	*Ersen 2, Şahin*
11/4	Beşiktaş	h	0-1	
17/4	Sivasspor	a	1-1	*Gökhan*
24/4	Gençlerbirliği	a	1-1	*Halil*
30/4	Konyaspor	h	2-2	*Halil, Ersen*
9/5	Galatasaray	a	1-3	*Dimitrov*
15/5	Bursaspor	h	0-3	
22/5	Eskişehirspor	a	0-4	

No	Name	Nat	DoB	Pos	Aps	(s)	Gls
12	Michael Ikem ANWULI	NGA	19/3/92	M	1		
22	BARIŞ Başdaş		17/1/90	A	12	(1)	
90	Gustave BEBBE	CMR	22/6/82	M	3	(5)	
11	Nikolay DIMITROV	BUL	15/10/87	A	16	(7)	2
4	ERDİ Öner		4/7/86	D	16	(4)	
15	ERGÜN Teber		1/9/85	D	20	(4)	
9	ERSEN Martin		23/5/79	A	23	(2)	8
25	ERTAÇ Özbir		25/10/89	G	1		
41	FIRAT Kocaoğlu		5/2/88	G	11		
24	GÖKHAN Güleç		25/9/85	A	10	(10)	2
14	HALİL Çolak		29/1/88	A	15	(3)	5
31	HÜSEYİN Kala		5/5/87	M	16	(5)	1
52	İSA Kaykun		5/6/88	A		(2)	
99	Azar KARADAS	NOR	9/8/81	A	6	(9)	
2	Christian KELLER	DEN	17/8/80	D	27	(1)	
87	KORHAN Öztürk		28/6/81	M	11	(10)	
13	LUIZ HENRIQUE de Souza Santos	BRA	23/9/82	D	28		1
28	MERTHAN Açıl		15/2/82	M	9	(2)	
1	MURAT Şahin		4/2/76	G	9		
20	OĞULCAN Engin		30/8/90	M	1	(1)	
88	ONUR Aydın		13/1/88	A	2	(2)	
23	ÖZGÜR Öçal		5/10/81	D	10	(4)	1
33	Juan Orlando ROBLEDO	CHI	21/8/79	D	16		2
5	SANCAK Kaplan		25/5/82	D	17	(5)	
8	Georgi SARMOV	BUL	7/9/85	M	13	(3)	
17	Aboul Rahim SEBAH	GHA	27/12/91	D	3	(2)	
10	ŞAHİN Aygüneş		1/10/90	A	16	(6)	2
92	TANER Yıldız		23/12/92	M		(2)	
6	Razundara TJIKUZU	NAM	6/12/79	M	15	(4)	1
68	TOLGA Özgen		28/2/80	G	13		
7	Fernando VARELA Ramos	ESP	1/9/79	M	17	(4)	4
35	YEKTA Kurtuluş		11/12/85	M	17		2

KAYSERİSPOR

Coach – Shota Arveladze (GEO)

Founded – 1966

Stadium – Kadir Has Şehir (40,458)

MAJOR HONOURS: Turkish Cup – (1) 2008.

2010				
16/8	İstanbul BB	a	2-0	*Cángele, Santana*
20/8	Karabükspor	h	1-0	*Cángele*
27/8	Ankaragücü	a	1-1	*Serdar*
11/9	Fenerbahçe	h	2-0	*Santana, Furkan*
18/9	Antalyaspor	a	1-2	*Zalayeta*
26/9	Trabzonspor	h	0-0	
2/10	Manisaspor	a	2-0	*Ömer, André Moritz (p)*
17/10	Sivasspor	h	4-1	*Serdar, Amisulashvili, og (Diallo), Zalayeta*
25/10	Beşiktaş	h	1-0	*Furkan*
31/10	Kasımpaşa	a	2-1	*Zalayeta, Amisulashvili*
5/11	Gençlerbirliği	h	1-1	*Mehmet Eren*
12/11	Konyaspor	a	1-0	*Zalayeta*
21/11	Galatasaray	h	0-0	
29/11	Bursaspor	a	0-2	
6/12	Eskişehirspor	h	2-2	*Ömer, Ali*
12/12	Gaziantepspor	a	0-2	
18/12	Bucaspor	h	2-0	*Ömer 2*
2011				
24/1	İstanbul BB	h	3-2	*og (Ekrem), Amrabat, Mehmet Eren*
29/1	Karabükspor	a	0-0	
5/2	Ankaragücü	h	2-1	*Kujovic, Zalayeta*
14/2	Fenerbahçe	a	0-2	
20/2	Antalyaspor	h	2-0	*Kujovic 2*
27/2	Trabzonspor	a	3-3	*Abdullah 2, Kujovic*
4/3	Manisaspor	h	1-2	*Zalayeta*
13/3	Sivasspor	a	0-1	
19/3	Beşiktaş	a	2-4	*Zalayeta, Selim (p)*
3/4	Kasımpaşa	h	1-3	*Selim*
10/4	Gençlerbirliği	a	1-4	*Ali*
17/4	Konyaspor	h	1-3	*Ömer*
23/4	Galatasaray	a	1-1	*Abdullah*
1/5	Bursaspor	h	1-0	*Santana*
6/5	Eskişehirspor	a	2-1	*Ömer 2*
15/5	Gaziantepspor	h	1-2	*Önder*
21/5	Bucaspor	a	3-3	*Mehmet Eren, Santana, André Moritz*

No	Name	Nat	DoB	Pos	Aps	(s)	Gls
8	ABDULLAH Durak		1/4/87	M	21	(9)	3
18	ABDÜLKADİR Özgen		8/9/86	A	4	(5)	
17	ALİ Bilgin		17/12/81	M	8	(7)	2
5	Aleksandre AMISULASHVILI	GEO	20/8/82	D	21		2
40	Nordin AMRABAT	MAR	31/3/87	M	13	(1)	1
19	ANDRÉ Francisco MORITZ	BRA	6/8/86	M	16	(5)	2
27	BURAK Bükel		13/3/92	A		(1)	
10	Franco Darío CÁNGELE	ARG	16/7/84	A	4	(1)	2
2	EREN Güngör		2/4/88	D	1		
23	FURKAN Özçal		3/9/90	M	7	(12)	2
12	GÖKHAN Değirmenci		21/3/89	G	7		
16	Souleymanou HAMIDOU	CMR	22/11/73	G	24		
15	HAMZA Çakır		30/9/85	D	17	(2)	
3	HASAN ALİ Kaldırım		9/12/89	D	33		
37	Emir KUJOVIC	SWE	22/6/88	A	7	(5)	4
11	MEHMET EREN Boyraz		11/10/81	M	24	(6)	3
22	ÖMER Şişmanoğlu		1/8/89	A	13	(12)	7
35	ÖNDER Turacı		14/7/81	D	26		1
14	Jonathan SANTANA Ghere	PAR	19/10/81	M	17	(3)	4
20	SAVAŞ Yılmaz		1/1/90	M	7	(8)	
6	SELİM Teber		7/3/81	M	32		2
21	SEMİH Aydilek		16/1/89	A	4	(6)	
4	SERDAR Kesimal		24/1/89	D	29		2
39	TOLGA Yıldız		29/3/90	D		(1)	
7	James TROISI	AUS	3/7/88	A	12	(2)	
34	VOLKAN Babacan		11/8/88	G	3	(1)	
9	Marcelo ZALAYETA	URU	5/12/78	A	12	(2)	7
38	Karim ZIANI	ALG	17/8/82	M	12	(1)	

KONYASPOR

Coach – Ziya Doğan; (15/2/11) Yılmaz Vural

Founded – 1981

Stadium – Atatürk (22,459)

2010				
16/8	Bursaspor	a	0-1	
20/8	Eskişehirspor	h	2-1	*Lietava, Adnan*
27/8	Gaziantepspor	a	2-2	*Montaño, Emre Toraman*
11/9	Bucaspor	h	1-1	*Hakan*
19/9	İstanbul BB	a	0-1	
26/9	Karabükspor	h	2-2	*Lietava, Grajciar*
2/10	Ankaragücü	a	1-4	*Grajciar (p)*
18/10	Fenerbahçe	h	1-4	*Grajciar*
23/10	Antalyaspor	a	0-1	
1/11	Trabzonspor	h	1-2	*Erdinç*
7/11	Manisaspor	a	1-0	*Ali Dere*
12/11	Kayserispor	h	0-1	
20/11	Beşiktaş	a	2-2	*Grajciar 2*
27/11	Kasımpaşa	h	2-2	*Tazemeta, Serkan*
5/12	Gençlerbirliği	h	2-1	*Erdinç, Kéré*
12/12	Sivasspor	a	0-1	
19/12	Galatasaray	h	0-1	
2011				
23/1	Bursaspor	h	0-0	
31/1	Eskişehirspor	a	0-1	
6/2	Gaziantepspor	h	0-2	
12/2	Bucaspor	a	2-3	*Robak, og (Leandrão)*
20/2	İstanbul BB	h	0-0	
27/2	Karabükspor	a	1-2	*Zayatte*
5/3	Ankaragücü	h	0-2	
13/3	Fenerbahçe	a	0-2	
19/3	Antalyaspor	h	0-0	
2/4	Trabzonspor	a	0-1	
9/4	Manisaspor	h	0-0	
17/4	Kayserispor	a	3-1	*Robak, Grajciar, Ali Dere*
25/4	Beşiktaş	h	1-1	*Robak*
30/4	Kasımpaşa	a	2-2	*Mehmet Sedef, Robak*
8/5	Gençlerbirliği	a	1-2	*Musa*
14/5	Sivasspor	h	1-1	*Grajciar*
20/5	Galatasaray	a	0-2	

No	Name	Nat	DoB	Pos	Aps	(s)	Gls
55	ADNAN Güngör		20/9/80	D	27	(2)	1
3	Bassim Abbas AL OGAILI	IRQ	1/7/82	D	17		
42	ALİ Dere		29/9/92	M	10	(10)	2
91	ALİ Kireş		24/1/91	M		(1)	
18	Ibrahima BANGOURA	GUI	8/12/82	M	1	(7)	
23	BARBAROS Barut		26/1/83	M	5		
15	BURAK Karaduman		23/2/85	M	2		
88	Bořek DOČKAL	CZE	30/9/88	M	8	(1)	
34	EMRAH Eren		13/11/78	D	2		
5	EMRE Toraman		5/1/79	M	13	(1)	1
28	EMRE Yüksektepe		29/9/91	M	3	(2)	
7	ERDAL Kılıçaslan		23/8/84	A	4	(6)	
4	ERDİNÇ Yavuz		4/10/78	D	18	(1)	2
58	ERTUĞRUL Arslan		26/1/80	M	13	(1)	
12	ESER Yağmur		29/5/83	A	1	(5)	
70	GÖKHAN Emreciksin		10/9/84	M	11	(2)	
99	GÖKHAN Tokgöz		22/4/79	G	12		
27	Peter GRAJCIAR	SVK	17/9/83	M	22	(6)	7
38	HAKAN Aslantaş		26/8/85	M	30	(2)	1
25	İBRAHİM Ege		3/2/83	M	2	(2)	
44	Mahamoudou KÉRÉ	BFA	2/1/82	D	25	(2)	1
13	Martin KLEIN	CZE	2/7/84	D	2	(2)	
39	Ivan LIETAVA	SVK	20/7/83	A	6	(3)	2
77	MEHMET Batdal		24/2/86	A	1	(2)	
17	MEHMET Sedef		5/8/87	M	14	(1)	1
33	Álvaro MEJÍA Pérez	ESP	18/1/82	D	9	(1)	
11	Johnnier MONTAÑO	COL	14/1/83	M	11	(7)	1
21	MURAT Tosun		26/2/84	M	3	(2)	
35	MUSA Çağıran		17/11/92	M	13	(1)	1
1	ORKUN Usak		5/11/80	G	5		
81	Mariusz PAWEŁEK	POL	17/3/81	G	17		
8	RAMAZAN Kahya		16/9/84	M	2	(3)	
22	Marcin ROBAK	POL	29/11/82	A	16		4
30	Muamer SALIBAŠIĆ	BIH	3/12/84	M		(1)	
71	SERBAY Yağız		19/8/91	M		(1)	
14	SERKAN Şahin		15/2/88	D	10	(5)	1
24	Kanfory SYLLA	GUI	7/7/80	D	1		
9	Thierry TAZEMETA	EQG	13/10/82	A	10	(8)	1
20	VELİ Acar		30/8/81	M	14	(5)	
6	Kamil ZAYATTE	GUI	7/3/85	D	14		1

MANİSASPOR

Coach – Hakan Kutlu; (13/9/10) Hikmet Karaman

Founded – 1965

Stadium – 19 Mayıs (14,965)

2010				
15/8	Karabükspor	a	1-2	*Kahê*
22/8	Ankaragücü	h	0-3	
29/8	Fenerbahçe	a	2-4	*Promise, Simpson*
11/9	Antalyaspor	h	1-2	*Eren*
17/9	Trabzonspor	a	3-1	*Makukula 2, Simpson*
26/9	Sivasspor	h	3-0	*Simpson 3*
2/10	Kayserispor	h	0-2	
16/10	Beşiktaş	a	3-2	*Promise, Dixon, Yiğit Gökoğlan*
24/10	Kasımpaşa	h	2-1	*Makukula, Simpson*
31/10	Gençlerbirliği	a	0-2	
7/11	Konyaspor	h	0-1	
14/11	Galatasaray	a	2-0	*Makukula, Simpson (p)*
20/11	Bursaspor	h	0-2	
26/11	Eskişehirspor	a	1-2	*Mehmet*
4/12	Gaziantepspor	h	2-0	*og (Emre), Kahê*
11/12	Bucaspor	a	1-1	*Simpson*
19/12	İstanbul BB	h	1-0	*Kahê*
2011				
22/1	Karabükspor	h	4-2	*Simpson, Kahê, Yiğit Gökoğlan, Yiğit İncedemir*
30/1	Ankaragücü	a	3-1	*Kahê, Mehmet 2*
5/2	Fenerbahçe	h	1-3	*Kahê*

13/2	Antalyaspor	a	4-1	*Hüseyin, Promise, Simpson, Dixon*
21/2	Trabzonspor	h	1-2	*Dixon*
27/2	Sivasspor	a	2-4	*Simpson, Hüseyin*
4/3	Kayserispor	a	2-1	*Iwański, Kahê*
11/3	Beşiktaş	h	0-0	
19/3	Kasımpaşa	a	0-1	
3/4	Gençlerbirliği	h	0-3	
9/4	Konyaspor	a	0-0	
18/4	Galatasaray	h	2-3	*Dixon, Kahê*
23/4	Bursaspor	a	1-2	*Mehmet*
1/5	Eskişehirspor	h	3-1	*Kahê 2, Murat*
7/5	Gaziantepspor	a	0-1	
14/5	Bucaspor	h	4-2	*Yiğit Gökoğlan, Makukula, Murat, Simpson*
20/5	İstanbul BB	a	0-0	

No	Name	Nat	DoB	Pos	Aps	(s)	Gls
88	BEKİR Yılmaz		6/3/88	M	9	(8)	
3	BURAK Özsaraç		7/6/79	D	5	(1)	
83	BÜLENT Cevahir		13/2/92	M	2		
20	Nicolae Constantin DICĂ	ROU	9/5/80	M	1	(4)	
55	Jimmy DIXON	LBR	10/10/81	D	31		4
34	EREN Aydın		16/1/82	D	21	(2)	1
85	FERHAT Çökmüş		14/2/85	M	20	(3)	
6	GABRIEL de Paulo Limeira	BRA	20/8/83	D	1		
7	GÖKHAN Emreciksin		10/9/84	M	5	(3)	
54	HÜSEYİN Tok		9/9/88	D	12	(1)	2
16	Maciej IWAŃSKI	POL	7/5/81	M	6	(3)	1
19	İLHAN Özek		1/1/88	M	2	(4)	
1	İLKER Avcıbay		1/10/78	G	33		
15	Oumar KALABANE	GUI	8/4/81	D	18		
11	Carlos Eduardo de Souza Floresta "KAHÊ"	BRA	28/8/82	A	16	(14)	10
99	Ariza MAKUKULA	POR	4/3/81	A	15	(13)	5
26	Mateus Alberto Contreiras Gonçalves "MANUCHO"	ANG	7/3/83	A	3	(6)	
8	MEHMET Güven		30/7/87	M	27	(3)	4
29	Jacques MOMHA	CMR	7/8/82	D	3	(1)	
33	MURAT Erdoğan		1/8/76	M	24	(3)	2
5	NİZAMETTİN Çalışkan		20/3/87	M	5		
67	ONUR Karakabak		8/4/92	M		(1)	
41	ÖMER AYSAN Barış		23/7/82	D	20	(1)	
10	Isaac PROMISE	NGA	2/12/87	A	25	(5)	3
14	RECEP Biler		8/5/81	G	1	(1)	
39	SEMAVİ Özgür		6/2/82	M	2	(4)	
9	Joshua SIMPSON	CAN	15/3/83	A	30	(2)	12
45	YİĞİT Gökoğlan		5/6/89	M	10	(18)	3
4	YİĞİT İncedemir		9/3/85	M	27		1

SİVASSPOR

Coach – Mesut Bakkal; (24/10/10) Rıza Çalımbay

Founded – 1967

Stadium – 4 Eylül (14,998)

2010

14/8	Galatasaray	h	2-1	*Zita, Cihan*
21/8	Antalyaspor	a	1-1	*Sedat Bayrak*
28/8	Bursaspor	h	0-2	
13/9	Trabzonspor	a	1-6	*Cihan*
18/9	Eskişehirspor	h	1-1	*Ceyhun*
26/9	Manisaspor	a	0-3	
3/10	Gaziantepspor	h	1-1	*Mehmet Yıldız*
17/10	Kayserispor	a	1-4	*Zita*
22/10	Bucaspor	h	1-1	*Ceyhun*
31/10	Beşiktaş	a	1-2	*Pedriel*
7/11	İstanbul BB	h	0-4	
14/11	Kasımpaşa	a	0-2	
20/11	Karabükspor	h	5-1	*Cihan, Mehmet Yıldız (p), Pedriel 3*
27/11	Gençlerbirliği	a	1-1	Pedriel
4/12	Ankaragücü	a	1-1	*Erman*
12/12	Konyaspor	h	1-0	*Erman*
18/12	Fenerbahçe	a	0-1	

2011

23/1	Galatasaray	a	0-1	
29/1	Antalyaspor	h	1-1	*Erman*
4/2	Bursaspor	a	1-2	*Grosicki*
12/2	Trabzonspor	h	2-3	*Grosicki, Kamanan*
18/2	Eskişehirspor	a	1-2	*og (Diego Ângelo)*
27/2	Manisaspor	h	4-2	*Grosicki 3 (1p), Eneramo*
5/3	Gaziantepspor	a	1-3	*Erman*
13/3	Kayserispor	h	1-0	*Pedriel*
20/3	Bucaspor	a	4-0	*Eneramo, Grosicki, Erman, Cihan*
2/4	Beşiktaş	h	1-0	*Cihan*
10/4	İstanbul BB	a	2-1	*Pedriel, Erman*
17/4	Kasımpaşa	h	1-1	*Erman*
23/4	Karabükspor	a	1-2	*Eneramo*
29/4	Gençlerbirliği	h	1-1	*Navrátil*
8/5	Ankaragücü	h	1-1	*Sedat Bayrak*
14/5	Konyaspor	a	1-1	*og (Zayatte)*
22/5	Fenerbahçe	h	3-4	*Navrátil, Erman 2*

No	Name	Nat	DoB	Pos	Aps	(s)	Gls
61	ABDURRAHMAN Dereli		15/2/81	D	11	(1)	
35	AKIN Vardar		2/4/78	G	5		
74	ALİŞAN Şeker		4/7/86	G	3		
10	CEYHUN Eriş		15/5/77	M	9	(6)	2
18	CİHAN Yılmaz		15/6/83	M	18	(9)	5
25	Mamadou DIALLO	GUI	2/12/84	D	11	(1)	
14	Michael ENERAMO	NGA	20/11/85	A	13	(2)	3
11	ERMAN Kılıç		20/9/83	M	22	(8)	9
88	FERHAT Bıkmaz		6/7/88	D	3		
22	Kamil GROSICKI	POL	8/6/88	A	16	(1)	6
58	HAYRETTİN Yerlikaya		13/8/81	D	16	(3)	
4	Deniss IVANOVS	LVA	11/1/84	D	13	(3)	
99	İBRAHİM Şahin		1/3/84	A	1	(7)	
8	KADİR Bekmezci		5/7/85	M	31		
90	KAĞAN Konuk		1/1/90	M	1		
38	Yannick KAMANAN	FRA	5/10/81	A	4	(5)	1
77	Ľuboš KAMENÁR	SVK	17/6/87	G	1		
86	Souleymane KEÏTA	MLI	24/11/86	M	5	(6)	
1	KORCAN Çelikay		31/12/87	G	15		
7	MEHMET Nas		20/11/79	M	26	(4)	
9	MEHMET Yıldız		14/9/81	A	23	(8)	2
5	MURAT Sözgelmez		21/8/85	D	3	(3)	
21	Jakub NAVRÁTIL	CZE	1/2/84	D	17		2
30	Ricardo PEDRIEL Suárez	BOL	19/1/87	A	16	(9)	7
98	Tomáš RADA	CZE	28/9/83	D	8	(7)	
12	Sead RAMOVIĆ	BIH	14/3/79	G	10		
17	Alioum SAIDOU	CMR	19/2/78	M	3	(1)	
33	SANDRO da Silva Mendonça	BRA	1/10/83	M	1	(5)	
6	SEDAT Bayrak		10/4/81	D	23		2
20	SEDAT Yeşilkaya		10/6/80	M	1	(5)	
67	UĞUR Kavuk		11/9/79	D	21	(4)	
13	Bruno Mbanangoyé ZITA	GAB	15/7/80	M	7	(1)	2
3	ZİYA Erdal		5/1/88	D	17	(2)	

TRABZONSPOR AŞ

Coach – Şenol Güneş

Founded – 1967

Stadium – Hüseyin Avni Aker (22,749)

MAJOR HONOURS: Turkish League – (6) 1976, 1977, 1979, 1980, 1981, 1984; Turkish Cup – (8) 1977, 1978, 1984, 1992, 1995, 2003, 2004, 2010.

2010

15/8	Ankaragücü	a	2-0	*Gutiérrez 2*
23/8	Fenerbahçe	h	3-2	*og (Mehmet), Yattara, Głowacki*
30/8	Antalyaspor	a	0-0	
13/9	Sivasspor	h	6-1	*Yattara 2, Selçuk, Gutiérrez 2, Burak*
17/9	Manisaspor	h	1-3	*Selçuk*
26/9	Kayserispor	a	0-0	
3/10	Beşiktaş	h	1-0	*Mustafa*

17/10	Kasımpaşa	a	7-0	*Alanzinho, Burak 2, Umut 2, Jajá 2*
23/10	Gençlerbirliği	h	3-1	*Burak, Jajá, Umut*
1/11	Konyaspor	a	2-1	*Umut, Egemen*
7/11	Galatasaray	h	2-0	*Umut 2*
13/11	Bursaspor	a	2-0	*Jajá 2*
21/11	Eskişehirspor	h	0-0	
27/11	Gaziantepspor	a	3-1	*Burak 2 (1p), Jajá*
3/12	Bucaspor	h	2-0	*Umut, Colman (p)*
12/12	İstanbul BB	a	3-1	*Burak 2 (1p), Umut*
17/12	Karabükspor	h	3-0	*og (Engin), Engin, Burak*
2011				
22/1	Ankaragücü	h	1-1	*Jajá*
30/1	Fenerbahçe	a	0-2	
6/2	Antalyaspor	h	0-0	
12/2	Sivasspor	a	3-2	*Jajá, Burak 2*
21/2	Manisaspor	a	2-1	*Umut, Alanzinho*
27/2	Kayserispor	h	3-3	*Jajá, Burak, Głowacki*
6/3	Beşiktaş	a	2-1	*Ceyhun, Burak*
12/3	Kasımpaşa	h	1-0	*Jajá*
20/3	Gençlerbirliği	a	2-1	*Giray, Alanzinho*
2/4	Konyaspor	h	1-0	*Umut*
10/4	Galatasaray	a	1-0	*Burak*
17/4	Bursaspor	h	1-0	*Burak*
22/4	Eskişehirspor	a	0-0	
1/5	Gaziantepspor	h	3-0	*Burak 2, Brożek Pa.*
8/5	Bucaspor	a	2-1	*Burak, Umut*
15/5	İstanbul BB	h	3-1	*Brożek Pa., Burak, Jajá*
22/5	Karabükspor	a	4-0	*Egemen, Jajá, Umut 2*

No	Name	Nat	DoB	Pos	Aps	(s)	Gls
25	Alan Carlos Gomes da Costa "ALANZINHO"	BRA	22/2/83	M	15	(14)	3
21	BARIŞ Ataş		1/2/87	M	1	(16)	
32	Paweł BROŻEK	POL	21/4/83	A	5	(7)	2
14	Piotr BROŻEK	POL	21/4/83	M	7		
17	BURAK Yılmaz		15/7/85	A	27	(3)	19
3	Hrvoje ČALE	CRO	4/3/85	D	22	(1)	
6	CEYHUN Gülselam		25/12/87	M	8	(17)	1
20	Gustavo COLMAN	ARG	19/4/85	M	31		1
16	EGEMEN Korkmaz		3/11/82	D	25		2
5	ENGİN Baytar		11/7/83	M	10	(8)	1
66	FERHAT Öztorun		8/5/87	D	3	(5)	
23	GİRAY Kaçar		15/3/85	D	25	(3)	1
4	Arkadiusz GŁOWACKI	POL	13/3/79	D	13	(2)	2
9	Teófilo GUTIÉRREZ	COL	17/5/85	A	6		4
50	Jakson Avelino Coelho "JAJÁ"	BRA	28/2/86	A	27	(2)	12
88	MEHMET Çakır		4/1/84	M		(2)	
22	MUSTAFA Yumlu		25/9/87	D	10	(3)	1
35	ONUR Kıvrak		1/1/88	G	25		
8	SELÇUK İnan		10/2/85	M	33		2
30	SERKAN Balcı		22/8/83	D	31		
26	SEZER Badur		20/6/84	M		(2)	
18	TAYFUN Cora		5/12/83	D	2	(1)	
29	TOLGA Zengin		10/10/83	G	9		
10	UMUT Bulut		15/3/83	A	30	(3)	13
61	Ibrahima YATTARA	GUI	3/6/80	A	9	(12)	3

TOP GOALSCORERS 2010/11

28	ALEX (Fenerbahçe)
19	BURAK Yılmaz (Trabzonspor)
15	Mamadou NIANG (Fenerbahçe)
14	Emmanuel EMENIKE (Karabükspor)
13	NECATİ Ateş (Antalyaspor)
	UMUT Bulut (Trabzonspor)
12	OLCAN Adın (Gaziantepspor)
	Joshua SIMPSON (Manisaspor)
	JAJÁ (Trabzonspor)
10	Stanislav ŠESTÁK (Ankaragücü)
	TITA (Antalyaspor)
	SEMİH Şentürk (Fenerbahçe)
	CENK Tosun (Gaziantepspor)
	KAHÊ (Manisaspor)

PROMOTED CLUBS

MERSIN İDMAN YURDU

Coach – Yüksel Yeşilova; (20/10/10) Nurullah Sağlam
Founded – 1925
Stadium – Tevfik Sırrı Gür (10,128)

SAMSUNSPOR

Coach – Hüseyin Kalpar
Founded – 1965
Stadium – 19 Mayıs (12,720)

ORDUSPOR

Coach – Uğur Tütüneker; (22/3/11) Metin Diyadin
Founded – 1967
Stadium – 19 Eylül (11,024)

SECOND LEVEL FINAL TABLES 2010/11

		Pld	W	D	L	F	A	Pts
1	Mersin İdman Yurdu	32	17	7	8	39	29	58
2	Samsunspor	32	16	10	6	45	20	58
3	Gaziantep BBK	32	16	9	7	43	26	57
4	Rizespor	32	15	9	8	36	24	54
5	Orduspor	32	14	12	6	47	29	54
6	Tavşanli Linyitspor	32	13	12	7	32	28	51
7	Boluspor	32	14	7	11	47	31	49
8	Kayseri Erciyesspor	32	11	15	6	40	29	48
9	Denizlispor	32	11	11	10	40	31	44
10	Karşiyaka SK	32	10	11	11	26	34	41
11	Giresunspor	32	11	5	16	27	32	38
12	Adanaspor	32	8	13	11	41	42	37
13	Kartalspor	32	7	13	12	21	29	34
14	Akhisar Belediyespor	32	8	9	15	27	39	33
15	Güngören Belediyespor	32	7	12	13	19	42	33
16	Altay SK	32	7	10	15	27	43	31
17	Diyarbakirspor	32	1	7	24	10	59	7

NB Diyarbakirspor – 3 pts deducted; Ankaraspor withdrew before season.

PROMOTION PLAY-OFFS

(23/5/11 & 26/5/11)
Orduspor 4, Rizespor 0
Rizespor 3, Orduspor 3
(Orduspor 7-3)

Tavşanlı Linyitspor 1, Gaziantep BBK 2
Gaziantep BBK 0, Tavşanlı Linyitspor 1
(2-2; Gaziantep BBK on away goals)

(29/5/11)
Orduspor 1, Gaziantep BBK 0

DOMESTIC CUP 2010/11

TÜRKİYE KUPASI

THIRD ROUND

(26/10/10)
Beypazarı Şekerspor 1, Karabükspor 1 *(aet; 7-6 on pens)*
Gençlerbirliği 4, Akçaabat Sebatspor 1

(27/10/10)
Ankaragücü 3, Tokatspor 1
Eskişehirspor 1, Denizlispor 2
Gaziantep BBK 2, Samsunspor 0
Gaziantepspor 4, Türk Telekom 0
İstanbul BB 1, Dardanelspor 0
Kayseri Erciyesspor 1, Konya Torku Şekerspor 3
Kırıkhanspor 0, Bandırmaspor 0 *(aet; 4-3 on pens)*
Konyaspor 0, Bucaspor 1
Menemen Belediyespor 1, Kasımpaşa 4
Orduspor 1, Antalyaspor 2 *(aet)*
Sivasspor 1, Manisaspor 2
Yeni Malatyaspor 2, Hacettepe 0 *(aet)*

(28/10/10)
Beşiktaş 3, Mersin İdman Yurdu 0 *(aet)*
Karşıyaka 3, Kayserispor 2 *(aet)*

Byes – Bursaspor, Fenerbahçe, Galatasaray, Trabzonspor

GROUP STAGE

Group A

(9/11/10)
Antalyaspor 1, Gaziantepspor 3

(10/11/10)
Galatasaray 3, Denizlispor 1

(22/12/10)
Beypazarı Şekerspor 1, Antalyaspor 1
Gaziantepspor 1, Galatasaray 1

(11/1/11)
Galatasaray 3, Beypazarı Şekerspor 1

(12/1/11)
Denizlispor 0, Gaziantepspor 1

(16/1/11)
Beypazarı Şekerspor 2, Denizlispor 1

(18/1/11)
Antalyaspor 0, Galatasaray 0

(26/1/11)
Denizlispor 2, Antalyaspor 2
Gaziantepspor 2, Beypazarı Şekerspor 0

Final Standings
1 Gaziantepspor 10 pts;
2 Galatasaray 8 pts *(qualified)*;
3 Beypazarı Şekerspor 4 pts;
4 Antalyaspor 3 pts; 5 Denizlispor 1 pts *(eliminated)*

Group B

(10/11/10)
Konya Torku Şekerspor 2, Manisaspor 1

(11/11/10)
Gaziantep BBK 1, Beşiktaş 0

(21/12/10)
Trabzonspor 2, Gaziantep BBK 2

(22/12/10)
Beşiktaş 3, Konya Torku Şekerspor 2

(11/1/11)
Konya Torku Şekerspor 1, Trabzonspor 3

(12/1/11)
Manisaspor 2, Beşiktaş 3

(16/1/11)
Gaziantep BBK 2, Konya Torku Şekerspor 2
Trabzonspor 3, Manisaspor 1

(26/1/11)
Beşiktaş 2, Trabzonspor 1
Manisaspor 1, Gaziantep BBK 2

Final Standings
1 Beşiktaş 9 pts; 2 Gaziantep BBK 8 pts *(qualified)*;
3 Trabzonspor 7 pts; 4 Konya Torku Şekerspor 4 pts; 5 Manisaspor 0 pts *(eliminated)*

Group C

(9/11/10)
Ankaragücü 4, Fenerbahçe 2
Bucaspor 2, Yeni Malatyaspor 1

(21/12/10)
Fenerbahçe 2, Bucaspor 3

(22/12/10)
Gençlerbirliği 1, Ankaragücü 1

(12/1/11)
Bucaspor 1, Gençlerbirliği 2

(13/1/11)
Yeni Malatyaspor 2, Fenerbahçe 1

(16/1/11)
Gençlerbirliği 2, Yeni Malatyaspor 0

(17/1/11)
Ankaragücü 1, Bucaspor 1

(27/1/11)
Fenerbahçe 2, Gençlerbirliği 1
Yeni Malatyaspor 0, Ankaragücü 0

Final Standings
1 Gençlerbirliği 7 pts; 2 Bucaspor 7 pts *(qualified)*;
3 Ankaragücü 6 pts; 4 Yeni Malatyaspor 4 pts; 5 Fenerbahçe 3 pts *(eliminated)*

Group D

(10/11/10)
Bursaspor 1, Kırıkhanspor 1

(11/11/10)
İstanbul BB 1, Kasımpaşa 3

(21/12/10)
Karşıyaka 0, Bursaspor 2

(22/12/10)
Kırıkhanspor 0, İstanbul BB 1

(11/1/11)
İstanbul BB 1, Karşıyaka 0
Kasımpaşa 2, Kırıkhanspor 0

(15/1/11)
Bursaspor 0, İstanbul BB 1
Karşıyaka 0, Kasımpaşa 1

(26/1/11)
Kasımpaşa 3, Bursaspor 1
Kırıkhanspor 2, Karşıyaka 5

Final Standings
1 Kasımpaşa 12 pts; 2. İstanbul BB 9 pts *(qualified)*;
3 Bursaspor 4 pts; 4 Karşıyaka 3 pts; 5 Kırıkhanspor 1 pts *(eliminated)*

QUARTER-FINALS

(2/2/11 & 3/3/11)
Beşiktaş 5 *(Bobô 22, 50p, Manuel Fernandes 31, 47, Ricardo Quaresma 61)*, Gaziantep BBK 0
Gaziantep BBK 0, *Beşiktaş 3 (Mert Nobre 11, Hilbert 75, Hugo Almeida 89)*
(Beşiktaş 8-0)

İstanbul BB 0, Kasımpaşa 0
Kasımpaşa 1 *(Varela 119p)*, İstanbul BB 1 *(Holmén 110) (aet)*
(1-1; İstanbul BB on away goal)

(3/2/11 & 2/3/11)
Gaziantepspor 3 *(Cenk 16, 78, Elyasa 67)*, Galatasaray 2 *(Kazım 38, Stancu 63)*
Galatasaray 0, Gaziantepspor 0
(Gaziantepspor 3-2)

Gençlerbirliği 2 *(Zec 72, Koray 75og)*, Bucaspor 0
Bucaspor 1 *(Ali Kuçik 13)*, Gençlerbirliği 2 *(Zec 44, Jedinak 62)*
(Gençlerbirliği 4-1)

SEMI-FINALS

(6/4/11 & 20/4/11)
Beşiktaş 3 *(Simão 65, 86, Hugo Almeida 74)*, Gaziantepspor 0
Gaziantepspor 2 *(Olcan 4, 67)*, Beşiktaş 2 *(Simão 32p, Hugo Almeida 48)*
(Beşiktaş 5-2)

(7/4/11 & 21/4/11)
İstanbul BB 1 *(Hološko 61p)*, Gençlerbirliği 1 *(Mustafa 20)*
Gençlerbirliği 0, İstanbul BB 3 *(İbrahim Akın 10, 21, Tum 25)*
(İstanbul BB 4-1)

FINAL

(11/5/11)
Kadir Has Stadyumu, Kayseri
BEŞİKTAŞ JK 2 *(Ricardo Quaresma 33, Sivok 78)*
İSTANBUL BB SK 2 *(İbrahim Akın 53p, Gökhan Ünal 68)*
(aet; 4-3 on pens)
Referee – *Yunus Yıldırım*
BEŞİKTAŞ – *Rüştü, Ekrem, Sivok, Mehmet Aurélio, İsmail, Manuel Fernandes, Necip, Guti (Hilbert 105), Simão, Ricardo Quaresma, Bobô (Hugo Almeida 55).*
İSTANBUL BB – *Hasagić, Rızvan, Can, Metin, Ekrem, Cihan, Mahmut, Holmén, İbrahim Akın (Gökhan Süzen 83), İskender (Tevfik 104), Tum (Gökhan Ünal 55).*

CLUB COMMUNICATION 2011/12

MKE Ankaragücü
Tandoğan Tesisleri , GMK Bulvarı 06570
Gazi Mah., TR-06560 Ankara

Tel +90 312 231 5078
Fax +90 312 231 2772
Web ankaragucu.org.tr
Email info@ankaragucu.org.tr
Media Officer Erhan Doğan

Antalyaspor
M. Mahallesi Fuar Alani, Karsisi 100, Hasan Subaşı Spor Tesisleri, TR-07030 Antalya

Tel +90 242 237 0881
Fax +90 242 237 4951
Web antalyaspor.com.tr
Email info@antalyaspor.com.tr
Media Officer Ahmet Balci

Beşiktaş JK
Süleyman Seba Cad, No.48 BJK Plaza
B-Blok Giriş Kat, Akaretler-Beşiktaş
TR-34357 İstanbul

Tel +90 212 310 1000
Fax +90 212 258 8194
Web bjk.com.tr
Email info@bjk.com.tr
Media Officer Kürsad Kaplan

Bursaspor
Özlüce Tesisleri Izmir Yolu 4.km, Ertuğrul Mah. Özlüce / Nilüfer, TR-16120 Bursa

Tel +90 224 413 6300
Fax +90 224 413 6306
Web bursaspor.org.tr
Email bursaspor@bursaspor.org.tr
Media Officer Mehmet Gerçeksi

Eskişehirspor
Vali Hanefi Demirkol Tesisleri, Esentepe Mah. Çevre Yolu, Polis Evi Yanı
TR-26100 Eskişehir

Tel +90 222 322 9890
Fax +90 222 323 0617
Web eskisehirspor.org.tr
Email bilgi@eskisehirspor.org
Media Officer Mehmet Öztürk

Fenerbahçe SK
Bagdat Str. Fenerbahçe Sükrü Saraçoğlu Stadyumu, Kadiköy, TR-34724 Istanbul

Tel +90 216 542 1907
Fax +90 216 542 1960
Web fenerbahce.org
Email tacar@fenerbahce.org
Media Officer Orkun Yazgan / Övgü Doğan

Galatasaray AŞ
Metin Oktay Tesisleri Harman Sok.
Florya / İstanbul, TR-34153 İstanbul

Tel +90 212 663 0090
Fax +90 212 574 0424
Web galatasaray.org
Email info@galatasaray.org
Media Officer Hasan Tankaya

Gaziantepspor
Celal Doğan Tesisleri Gaziantep
Dülük Ormanları Karşısı, Baba Mevkii
TR-27700 Gaziantep

Tel +90 342 322 2000
Fax +90 342 322 2069
Web gaziantepspor.org.tr
Email info@gaziantepspor.org.tr
Media Officer Mehmet Salih Kizil

Gençlerbirliği SK
Çiftlik Cad. No 30, Beştepe, 19 Mayis Stadi, TR-06510 Ankara

Tel +90 312 215 3000
Fax +90 312 221 2125
Web genclerbirligi.org.tr
Email genclerbirligi@genclerbirligi.org.tr
Media Officer Altan Altun

İstanbul BB SK
İBB Cebeci Spor Kompleksi, Atatürk Bulvarı No: 56 Sultangazi
TR-34270 İstanbul

Tel +90 212 475 0101
Fax +90 212 475 0111
Web ibbspor.com
Email info@istanbulbbsk.org
Media Officer İlkay Sağir

Kardemir Karabükspor
Metin Türker Tesisleri Çamlık Mevkii
Yenişehir, TR-78200 Karabük

Tel +90 370 413 2260
Fax +90 372 412 5422
Web kardemirkarabukspor.org.tr
Email kkarabukspor@hotmail.com
Media Officer Mustafa Çelik

Kayserispor
Erkilet Bulvarı Kadir Has Tesisleri No:327
Kocasinan, TR-38080 Kayseri

Tel +90 352 351 27 27
Fax +90 352 351 2219
Web kayserispor.org.tr
Email kayserispor@kayserispor.org.tr
Media Officer Sevil Turkmen

Manisaspor
Ahmet Bedevi Mah., Halil Erdoğan Cad.
No: 34, Izmir Alsancak stadium
TR-45020 Manisa

Tel +90 236 231 4505
Fax +90 236 237 4558
Web manisaspor.org.tr
Email bilgi@manisaspor.org.tr
Media Officer Selami Delan

Mersin İdman Yurdu
Hamidiye Mah. İsmet İnönü Bulvarı
Sevim Çalışkan Apartmanı 3/3
TR-33100 Mersin

Tel +90 324 238 0332
Fax +90 324 238 0341
Web mersinidmanyurdu.com.tr
Email mersin_idmanyurdu@windowslive.com
Media Officer Rıfkı Çinar

Orduspor
Vali Kemal Yazıcıoğlu Orduspor Tesisleri, Durugöl Mah, TR-52200 Ordu

Tel +90 452 234 7864
Fax +90 452 234 6515
Web orduspor.org.tr
Email info@orduspor.org.tr
Media Officer Murat Gürsoy

Samsunspor
Nuri Aşan Tesisleri Doğupark
TR-55550 Samsun

Tel +90 362 238 3696
Fax +90 362 238 3788
Web samsunspor.org.tr
Email info@samsunspor.org.tr
Media Officer Kazım Gürol Yilmaz

Sivasspor
Gultepe Mah., Cevreyolu Sivasspor Tes
"4 Eylül" stadium, TR-58030 Sivas

Tel +90 346 226 4180
Fax +90 346 226 2458
Web sivasspor.org.tr
Email sivasspor1967@windowslive.com
Media Officer Uğur Akkuş

Trabzonspor AŞ
Mehmet Ali Yilmaz Tesisleri Üniversite Mah.
Ahmet Suat Özyazıcı Cad. No:35
TR-61000 Trabzon

Tel +90 462 325 0967
Fax +90 462 325 5515
Web trabzonspor.org.tr
Email info@trabzonspor.org.tr
Media Officer Altuğ Atalay

UKRAINE

Ukraine I Ukraine

Federatsiya Futbola Ukrainy (FFU)

COMMUNICATION

Address	Provulok Laboratorniy 7-A PO Box 55 UA-01133 Kyiv	**President**	Grigoriy Surkis
Tel	+380 44 521 0518	**General Secretary**	Olexandr Bandurko
Fax	+380 44 521 0550	**Media Officer**	Serhiy Vasilyev
E-mail	info@ffu.org.ua	**Year of Formation**	1991
Website	ffu.org.ua	**National Stadium**	NSK Olimpiyskyi, Kyiv (65,400)

DOMESTIC COMPETITION SUMMARY 2010/11

PREMIER-LIHA FINAL TABLE

			Home					Away					Total						
		Pld	W	D	L	F	A	W	D	L	F	A	W	D	L	F	A	Pts	Comp
1	FC Shakhtar Donetsk	30	13	1	1	31	4	10	2	3	22	12	23	3	4	53	16	72	UCL
2	FC Dynamo Kyiv	30	12	2	1	36	7	8	3	4	24	17	20	5	5	60	24	65	UCL
3	FC Metalist Kharkiv	30	8	2	5	35	21	10	4	1	23	5	18	6	6	58	26	60	UEL
4	FC Dnipro Dnipropetrovsk	30	8	4	3	22	10	8	5	2	24	10	16	9	5	46	20	57	UEL
5	FC Karpaty Lviv	30	11	2	2	25	12	2	7	6	16	22	13	9	8	41	34	48	UEL
6	FC Vorskla Poltava	30	5	5	5	17	13	5	4	6	20	19	10	9	11	37	32	39	UEL
7	SC Tavriya Simferopol	30	6	5	4	20	15	4	4	7	24	31	10	9	11	44	46	39	
8	FC Metalurh Donetsk	30	6	2	7	19	25	5	3	7	17	20	11	5	14	36	45	38	
9	FC Arsenal Kyiv	30	5	3	7	16	19	5	4	6	20	19	10	7	13	36	38	37	
10	FC Obolon Kyiv	30	5	6	4	15	14	4	1	10	11	24	9	7	14	26	38	34	
11	FC Volyn Lutsk	30	4	4	7	12	22	5	3	7	15	27	9	7	14	27	49	34	
12	FC Zorya Luhansk	30	4	4	7	17	22	3	5	7	11	18	7	9	14	28	40	30	
13	FC Kryvbas Kryvyi Rih	30	4	5	6	12	20	2	6	7	15	25	6	11	13	27	45	29	
14	FC Illychivets Mariupil	30	4	6	5	28	34	3	2	10	17	33	7	8	15	45	67	29	
15	PFC Sevastopol	30	6	3	6	16	15	1	3	11	10	33	7	6	17	26	48	27	*Relegated*
16	FC Metalurh Zaporizhya	30	4	4	7	13	21	2	2	11	5	19	6	6	18	18	40	24	*Relegated*

Top Scorer Yevhen Seleznev (Dnipro), 17 goals

Promoted Clubs PFC Olexandriya
FC Chornomorets Odesa

Cup Final FC Shakhtar Donetsk 2, FC Dynamo Kyiv 0

Season of cheer for Shakhtar

FC Shakhtar Donetsk marked their 75th anniversary in grand style with the most successful season in their history. In addition to retaining the Ukrainian Premier-Liha title and lifting the Ukrainian Cup, they also went further than ever before in the UEFA Champions League, reaching the quarter-finals, where they were ousted by eventual winners FC Barcelona.

FC Dynamo Kyiv also reached a European quarter-final, in the UEFA Europa League, but they were upstaged in all of the major competitions by Shakhtar and, for the first time in the 20-year staging of independent Ukrainian football, had to endure the agony of going two successive seasons without a trophy. Their misery was made complete in the last game of the season when Shakhtar defeated them 2-0 in the final of the Ukrainian Cup to complete their third domestic double.

Winning run

The championship race was effectively done and dusted by November. With 19 of the 30 matchdays scheduled before the mid-season break, it was important to make a decisive move during the autumn, and Shakhtar did just that, reeling off ten successive victories. That run included a 2-0 home win over Dynamo plus away successes at title outsiders FC Metalist Kharkiv and FC Dnipro Dnipropetrovsk, enabling the Pitmen to pack away their tools for the three-month winter shutdown with a virtually unassailable 12-point lead.

The fifth Premier-Liha title in the eight-year reign of Shakhtar's Romanian coach Mircea Lucescu was duly secured with two games to spare thanks to a 2-0 win at home to city rivals FC Metalurh Donetsk on the first Saturday in May. The perfect scenario for Shakhtar and their fans would have been to clinch the championship on the first Sunday of the month, six days earlier, in the lair of the arch-enemy, but Dynamo spoiled the Orange and Black party by producing their best performance of the season to win 3-0. Although it had no bearing on the title race, the victory did at least help to safeguard Dynamo's second place and ensure their return to the UEFA Champions League. A repeat win over Shakhtar in the cup final at the end of the month would have been even sweeter, but Lucescu's men took the trophy for the seventh time thanks to second-half strikes from Croatian international Eduardo, who was later sent off, and the team's ten-goal top scorer in the league, Luiz Adriano.

Darijo Srna skippered Shakhtar to the Ukrainian double and the UEFA Champions League quarter-finals

Those two strikers were both prominent in Shakhtar's run to the last eight of the UEFA Champions League, scoring four goals apiece, with Eduardo, predominantly a substitute, bagging one in each of the group games against the club that had sold him in the summer, Arsenal FC. Despite a sobering 5-1 defeat by the Gunners in London, Shakhtar went on to top the group, winning their other five games, including 3-0 at SC Braga, where no other visiting team scored all season in Europe. Despite entering the first knockout round out of season, Shakhtar produced another impressive away win, 3-2 at AS Roma, Luiz Adriano's fourth goal of the campaign being preceded by two other first-half strikes from his fellow Brazilians Jádson and Douglas Costa. It was another of Shakhtar's large Brazilian clan, winger Willian, who secured the club's first UEFA Champions League quarter-final with two spectacular goals in the return leg, won 3-0 in front of a full house in the majestic Donbass Arena.

It was Shakhtar's misfortune to be drawn away to Barcelona in the last eight, and they were simply outclassed by the Catalans, losing 6-1 on aggregate, with just defender Yaroslav Rakytskiy's consolation goal at Camp Nou to show for their efforts. The young central defender enjoyed an outstanding season and was one of four Shakhtar players to start all ten European games, the others being Luiz Adriano, Willian and goalkeeper Andriy Pyatov, who was voted 2010 Ukrainian footballer of the year. Stalwart skipper Darijo Srna was another who delivered the goods on a regular basis while Jádson and Douglas Costa consistently spiced up Shakhtar's play with their skill and invention.

Dynamo progress

Shakhtar were not the only Ukrainian team to leave their mark on European competition in 2010/11. Dynamo were disappointed to drop into the UEFA Europa League after losing narrowly to AFC Ajax in the UEFA Champions League play-offs, but they made impressive progress in the secondary competition. Although a 2-0 defeat away to FC Sheriff led to the resignation of coach Valeriy Gazzayev, his replacement, former full back Oleh Luzhniy, steered the team to the top of the group with three successive victories. At Christmas, Luzhny made way for returning Russian coach Yuriy Semin, who had previously been in charge from December 2007 to May 2009, and he led the team to a thumping victory over Beşiktaş JK before Manchester City FC were memorably eliminated in the round of 16. Going well in the Premier-Liha at the time, and with Ukrainian internationals Andriy Yarmolenko and Oleh Gusev in top form, Dynamo were fully expected to see off Braga in the quarter-finals. But a red card for talisman Andriy Shevchenko in the first leg proved fatal and they went out on away goals after a second-leg stalemate in northern Portugal.

Oleh Blokhin was reappointed to lead the Ukrainian national team to UEFA EURO 2012

Of Ukraine's four original UEFA Europa League entrants SC Tavriya Simferopol and Dnipro were ousted in the play-offs but Metalist and FC Karpaty Lviv reached the group stage, the latter memorably knocking out Galatasaray AŞ with an added-time equaliser in Lviv. Karpaty found the going too tough after that, but Metalist won their opening group game 5-0 away at Hungarian champions Debreceni VSC and moved through to the knockout phase, where they, like Tavriya before them, were hit for six by Bayer 04 Leverkusen.

There would be a return to the UEFA Europa League in 2011/12 for Metalist, Dnipro and Karpaty, who finished third, fourth and fifth, respectively, in the Premier-Liha for the second year in a row. Metalist, in fact, made it five third places in succession. With long-serving Myron Markevych having stood down from his role as Ukrainian national team coach in August 2010 to return to full-time duties at the club, Metalist might have been expected to challenge Dynamo harder for second spot, but inconsistent performances and an inability to beat the big two (they took just one point from the four games against Shakhtar and Dynamo – in contrast to little FC Obolon Kyiv, who plundered ten) left them five points shy of the runners-up spot. The gap would have been larger had Dynamo not inexplicably lost their last league game, 3-2 away to FC Illychivets Marupil, surrendering a 2-0 half-time lead and thereby allowing their opponents to come back and claim the win they needed to avoid relegation and send PFC Sevastopol down, with FC Metalurh Zaporizhya, instead.

Sevastopol lost their final-day showdown in the Crimea, 1-0 against near neighbours Tavriya, but the result was not good enough to take the Simferopol side, cup winners in 2009/10, back into Europe. Instead it was FC Vorskla Poltava who seized sixth place thanks to a late equalising goal from Albanian striker Ahmed Januzi that placed them level on points with Tavriya but above them on the head-to-head rule – on away goals.

Dnipro supplied the Premier-Liha's leading marksman in 17-goal Ukrainian international striker Yevhen Seleznev, but the appointment of high-profile Spaniard Juande Ramos in early October and a large outlay on winter transfers suggested that they, too, might push harder for the second UEFA Champions League place. While mid-season signings Samuel Inkoom and Ivan Strinić looked the part at the back, the two Brazilians, Matheus (from Braga) and 20-year-old Giuliano (from Copa Libertadores winners SC Internacional), failed to live up to expectations.

A more concerted challenge is anticipated from the big-spending Dnipropetrovsk club in 2011/12 – a season that will end with Ukraine in the European footballing spotlight as the co-host nation of UEFA EURO 2012. The cities of Kyiv, Donetsk, Lviv and Kharkiv will all be dressed up for the occasion, and there will be high hopes that the Ukrainian national team, largely comprising Premier-Liha players, will do the country proud and at least reach the quarter-finals.

National Team

International Tournament Appearances – FIFA World Cup – (1) 2006 (qtr-finals).

Top Five All-time Caps – Anatoliy Tymoshchuk (106); Andriy Shevchenko (101); Olexandr Shovkovskiy (89); Serhiy Rebrov (75); Andriy Gusin (71)

Top Five All-time Goals – Andriy Shevchenko (45); Serhiy Rebrov (15); Serhiy Nazarenko (11); Andriy Gusin & Andriy Vorobei (9)

Blokhin back

Although there was little evidence during the 2010/11 season to suggest that Ukraine will pose a major problem for Europe's top teams, expectations rose in the spring when it was announced that national icon Oleh Blokhin, the only man to have coached Ukraine at a previous major tournament, the 2006 FIFA World Cup, would be leading the team towards and into their first UEFA European Championship. The highlights from his predecessor Yuriy Kalitvintsev's eight-month, eight-match reign were a win at home to Chile, a couple of penalty shoot-out victories in Cyprus and 100th caps for Shevchenko and Anatoliy Tymoshcuk; less impressive were 2-0 defeats to Brazil and Italy. Although Blokhin started with a win, 2-0 against Uzbekistan in Kyiv, he was given an indication of the size of the task awaiting him when, five days later, his team surrendered a lead against France in Donetsk and conceded three goals in the last few minutes to lose 4-1.

NATIONAL TEAM RESULTS 2010/11

11/8/10	Netherlands	H	Donetsk	1-1	*Aliyev (74)*
4/9/10	Poland	A	Łódź	1-1	*Seleznev (90+1)*
7/9/10	Chile	H	Kyiv	2-1	*Rakytskiy (36), Aliyev (65)*
8/10/10	Canada	H	Kyiv	2-2	*Milevskiy (59), Tymoshchuk (80)*
11/10/10	Brazil	N	Derby (ENG)	0-2	
17/11/10	Switzerland	A	Geneva	2-2	*Aliyev (48), Konoplyanka (75)*
8/2/11	Romania	N	Paralimni (CYP)	2-2	*Rakytskiy (23), Milevskiy (31) (4-2 on pens)*
9/2/11	Sweden	N	Nicosia (CYP)	1-1	*Dević (20p) (5-4 on pens)*
29/3/11	Italy	H	Kyiv	0-2	
1/6/11	Uzbekistan	H	Kyiv	2-0	*Tymoshchuk (54), Voronin (60)*
6/6/11	France	H	Donetsk	1-4	*Tymoshchuk (53)*

NATIONAL TEAM APPEARANCES 2010/11

Coach – Myron MARKEVYCH **/(25/8/10) (Yuriy KALITVINTSEV)** **/(21/4/11) Oleh BLOKHIN**	**1/2/51** **5/5/68** **5/11/52**		**Ned**	**Pol**	**Chi**	**Can**	**Bra**	**Sui**	**Rou**	**Swe**	**Ita**	**Uzb**	**Fra**	**Caps**	**Goals**
Andriy PYATOV	28/6/84	Shakhtar	G	G		G		G	G90				G	24	-
Artem FEDETSKIY	26/4/85	Karpaty	D77	D		D	D	D		D	D	D		11	-
Dmytro CHYHRYNSKIY	7/11/86	Shakhtar	D					D	D					27	-
Yaroslav RAKYTSKIY	3/8/89	Shakhtar	D		D			D	D		D			10	3
Olexandr ROMANCHUK	21/10/84	Metalist	D	D85	D74	D	D			D				8	-
Anatoliy TYMOSHCHUK	30/3/79	Bayern (GER)	M	M	M	s46	M	M	M	s71	D	M84	M	106	4
Ruslan ROTAN	29/10/81	Dnipro	M35			M46	M		s62	M	M76	s46	M	51	6
Olexandr ALIYEV	3/2/85	Lokomotiv Moskva (RUS) /Dynamo Kyiv	M	M53	s52	s46	M	M	M68	s64	M53			20	6
Yevhen KONOPLYANKA	29/9/89	Dnipro	M		M71			M87	M69	s46				8	2
Andriy SHEVCHENKO	29/9/76	Dynamo Kyiv	A57	A59	A71	A90						A46		101	45
Andriy VORONIN	21/7/79	Dinamo Moskva (RUS)	A46	s46		A46						s46	A59	66	7
Vasyl KOBIN	24/5/85	Shakhtar	s35										D	11	-
Artem MILEVSKIY	12/1/85	Dynamo Kyiv	s46			s46	A62	s46	A			M46	s59	36	6
Yevhen SELEZNEV	20/7/85	Dnipro	s57	s59	s81	A46	s62				A	s55	s69	23	5
Denys OLIYNYK	16/6/87	Metalist	s77 /90			s46		s74		M73	s76	M46		9	-
Yevhen CHEBERYACHKO	19/6/83	Dnipro	s90											1	-
Taras MYKHALYK	28/10/83	Dynamo Kyiv		D	D			M65		D				22	-
Yevhen KHACHERIDI	28/7/87	Dynamo Kyiv		D								D	s32	7	-
Oleh KRASNOPEROV	25/7/80	Vorskla		M65	s71									3	-
Oleh GUSEV	25/4/83	Dynamo Kyiv		M46	M	s46	M46		D		M	M70	M73	65	7
Marko DEVIĆ	27/10/83	Metalist		A46	A81			A46	A46	A46	s53	A55	A69	12	1
Denys KULAKOV	1/5/86	Vorskla		s46		M46								2	-
Volodymyr POLYOVIY	28/7/85	Metalurh Zaporizhya		s53	s74		D73							5	-
Ihor KHUDOBYAK	20/2/85	Karpaty		s65	M52	s90	s46						s73	6	-
Denys KOZHANOV	13/6/87	Karpaty		s85	s71							s46	s61	4	-
Andriy DYKAN	16/7/77	Spartak Moskva (RUS)			G		G					G		4	-
Vitaliy MANDZYUK	24/1/86	Dnipro			D	D	D	D						17	-
Olexandr KUCHER	22/10/82	Shakhtar				D	D			D		D	D32	24	1
Olexiy HAI	6/11/82	Shakhtar				M46	s73							24	1
Andriy YARMOLENKO	23/10/89	Dynamo Kyiv						M74	s69	M64	M			11	2
Taras STEPANENKO	8/8/89	Shakhtar						s65	M62	M71	M			4	-
Mykola MOROZYUK	17/1/88	Metalurh Donetsk						s87	s46	s73				3	-
Vitaliy FEDORIV	21/10/87	Amkar (RUS)							D					2	-
Artem KRAVETS	3/6/89	Dynamo Kyiv							s68	A				2	-
Olexandr SHOVKOVSKIY	2/1/75	Dynamo Kyiv							s90	G	G			89	-
Ihor OSHCHYPKO	25/10/85	Karpaty									D			3	-
Vyacheslav SHEVCHUK	13/5/79	Shakhtar										D	D	18	-
Serhiy NAZARENKO	16/2/80	Dnipro										s70	M61	43	11
Serhiy KRAVCHENKO	24/4/83	Dnipro										s84		9	1
Mykola ISHCHENKO	9/3/83	Shakhtar											D	1	-

CLUB-BY-CLUB

FC ARSENAL KYIV

Coach – Yuriy Bakalov

Founded – 2001

Stadium – NTB im. Viktor Bannikov (1,678); Kolos, Boryspil (5,654)

2010				
9/7	Metalurh Zaporizhya	h	1-0	*Bartulović*
18/7	Zorya	a	2-0	*Khomyn, Shatskikh (p)*
24/7	Sevastopol	h	0-1	
30/7	Shakhtar	h	1-3	*Symonenko*
8/8	Karpaty	a	1-2	*Shatskikh (p)*
15/8	Volyn	h	1-1	*Shatskikh*
21/8	Illychivets	a	2-2	*Bartulović, og (Samusiovas)*
28/8	Obolon	h	1-0	*Shatskikh*
11/9	Tavriya	a	1-0	*Mazilu*
19/9	Metalist	h	0-1	
26/9	Dynamo	a	2-3	*Shatskikh, Starhorodskiy*
2/10	Metalurh Donetsk	h	3-1	*Starhorodskiy, Shatskikh, Mikoliūnas*
17/10	Vorskla	a	1-0	*Gusev*
23/10	Dnipro	h	1-2	*Bogdanov*
31/10	Kryvbas	a	1-1	*Zakarlyuka (p)*
6/11	Metalurh Zaporizhya	a	1-2	*Starhorodskiy*
14/11	Zorya	h	1-1	*Matyukhin*
19/11	Sevastopol	a	2-0	*Samodin, Shatskikh*
28/11	Shakhtar	a	0-4	
2011				
6/3	Karpaty	h	2-2	*Mazilu, Gusev*
12/3	Volyn	a	0-0	
20/3	Illychivets	h	3-1	*Shatskikh, Mazilu 2*
2/4	Obolon	a	1-1	*Arzhanov*
9/4	Tavriya	h	1-2	*Mazilu*
16/4	Metalist	a	1-2	*Mazilu*
23/4	Dynamo	h	0-3	
30/4	Metalurh Donetsk	a	5-1	*Shatskikh (p), Mazilu, Bogdanov, Arzhanov, Samodin*
7/5	Vorskla	h	0-1	
15/5	Dnipro	a	0-1	
21/5	Kryvbas	h	1-0	*Kovpak*

No	Name	Nat	DoB	Pos	Aps	(s)	Gls
27	Volodymyr ARZHANOV		29/11/85	M	10	(1)	2
30	Mladen BARTULOVIĆ	CRO	5/10/86	M	10	(4)	2
17	Andriy BOGDANOV		21/1/90	M	23	(2)	2
18	Aleksandr DANILOV	BLR	10/9/80	M	5	(1)	
8	Rolan GUSEV	RUS	17/9/77	M	18	(5)	2
35	Olexandr HRYTSAI		30/9/77	M	26		
33	Andriy KHOMYN		2/1/82	D	6	(9)	1
19	Aleksandre KOBAKHIDZE	GEO	11/2/87	A	1	(1)	
90	Olexandr KOVPAK		2/2/83	A	2	(7)	1
10	Yehor LUGACHEV		24/12/88	M	1	(2)	
88	Vytautas LUKŠA	LTU	14/8/84	M		(1)	
3	Serhiy MATYUKHIN		21/3/80	D	20		1
7	Ionuţ Costinel MAZILU	ROU	9/2/82	A	21	(3)	7
50	Ika MEPORIA		26/1/89	M		(1)	
13	Saulius MIKOLIŪNAS	LTU	2/5/84	M	3	(14)	1
23	Serhiy POHORILIY		28/7/86	G	17	(1)	
28	Volodymyr POLYOVIY		28/7/85	M	10		
1	Vitaliy REVA		19/11/74	G	13		
20	Sergei SAMODIN	RUS	14/2/85	A	9	(10)	2
15	Maksim SHATSKIKH	UZB	30/8/78	A	28		9
5	Bohdan SHERSHUN		14/5/81	D	25	(1)	
6	Florin Costin ŞOAVĂ	ROU	24/7/78	D	14	(4)	
11	Artem STARHORODSKIY		17/1/82	M	12	(9)	3
4	Serhiy SYMONENKO		12/6/81	M	18	(1)	1
99	Andrei YESHCHENKO	RUS	9/2/84	D	30		
9	Serhiy ZAKARLYUKA		17/8/76	M	8	(1)	1
77	Yaroslav ZAKHAREVYCH		24/9/89	M		(1)	

FC DNIPRO DNIPROPETROVSK

Coach – Volodymyr Bessonov; (18/9/10) (Vadym Tyshchenko); (2/10/10) Juande Ramos (ESP)

Founded – 1918

Stadium – Dnipro-Arena (31,003)

MAJOR HONOURS: USSR League – (2) 1983, 1988; USSR Cup – (1) 1989.

2010				
10/7	Karpaty	h	1-0	*Cheberyachko*
18/7	Volyn	h	2-0	*Seleznev, Homenyuk*
24/7	Illychivets	a	5-1	*Konoplyanka, Seleznev 3, Ferreyra*
1/8	Obolon	h	3-0	*Seleznev, Kalynychenko, Homenyuk*
8/8	Tavriya	a	1-0	*Rotan*
14/8	Metalist	h	0-1	
22/8	Dynamo	a	0-0	
30/8	Metalurh Donetsk	h	1-2	*Konoplyanka*
12/9	Vorskla	a	2-0	*Konoplyanka, Nazarenko (p)*
18/9	Sevastopol	a	1-2	*Seleznev*
26/9	Kryvbas	h	1-1	*Seleznev*
1/10	Metalurh Zaporizhya	a	3-0	*Mandzyuk, Homenyuk, Kravchenko*
17/10	Zorya	h	1-1	*Homenyuk*
23/10	Arsenal	a	2-1	*Seleznev 2*
30/10	Shakhtar	h	0-1	
7/11	Karpaty	a	0-0	
14/11	Volyn	a	1-1	*Konoplyanka*
21/11	Illychivets	h	2-0	*Seleznev 2*
28/11	Obolon	a	1-0	*Seleznev*
2011				
6/3	Tavriya	h	2-2	*Seleznev, Strinić*
13/3	Metalist	a	2-2	*Konoplyanka 2*
20/3	Dynamo	h	1-0	*Strinić*
2/4	Metalurh Donetsk	a	2-3	*Nazarenko 2 (1p)*
9/4	Vorskla	h	2-0	*Seleznev 2*
17/4	Sevastopol	h	2-2	*Nazarenko 2 (1p)*
23/4	Kryvbas	a	3-0	*Shakhov, Seleznev 2*
30/4	Metalurh Zaporizhya	h	3-0	*Hladkiy 2, Rusol*
7/5	Zorya	a	1-0	*Shakhov*
15/5	Arsenal	h	1-0	*Nazarenko*
21/5	Shakhtar	a	0-0	

No	Name	Nat	DoB	Pos	Aps	(s)	Gls
21	ALCIDES Eduardo Mendes de Araújo Alves	BRA	13/3/85	D	1	(1)	
36	Ruslan BABENKO		8/7/92	M		(4)	
14	Yevhen CHEBERYACHKO		19/6/83	D	26		1
19	Vitaliy DENISOV	UZB	23/2/87	D	23		
23	Valeriy FEDORCHUK		5/10/88	M	3	(6)	
18	Osmar Daniel FERREYRA	ARG	9/1/83	M	8	(9)	1
8	GIULIANO Victor de Paula	BRA	31/5/90	M	10	(1)	
22	Olexandr HLADKIY		24/8/87	A	9	(10)	2
25	Mario HOLEK	CZE	28/10/86	M	9		
9	Volodymyr HOMENYUK		19/7/85	A	9	(5)	4
2	Samuel INKOOM	GHA	1/6/89	D	9	(2)	
26	Maxym KALYNYCHENKO		26/1/79	M	4	(8)	1
32	Anton KANIBOLOTSKIY		16/5/88	G	10		
42	Yevhen KONOPLYANKA		29/9/89	A	25		6
4	Serhiy KRAVCHENKO		24/4/83	M	24	(3)	1
27	Jan LAŠTŮVKA	CZE	7/7/82	G	20		
88	Dmytro LIOPA		23/11/88	M	1	(14)	
3	Ucha LOBJANIDZE	GEO	23/2/87	D	14	(3)	
5	Vitaliy MANDZYUK		24/1/86	D	23	(1)	1
99	MATHEUS Leite Nascimento	BRA	15/1/83	A	2	(1)	
28	Serhiy NAZARENKO		16/2/80	M	17	(8)	6
24	Pavlo PASHAYEV		4/1/88	D		(2)	
6	Nelson Enrique RIVAS López	COL	25/3/83	D	1		
29	Ruslan ROTAN		29/10/81	M	21		1
16	Andriy RUSOL		16/1/83	D	20		1
11	Yevhen SELEZNEV		20/7/85	A	24		17
30	Yevhen SHAKHOV		30/11/90	M	11	(8)	2
17	Ivan STRINIĆ	CRO	17/7/87	D	6		2

FC DYNAMO KYIV

Coach – Valeriy Gazzayev (RUS); (1/10/10) (Oleh Luzhniy)); (24/12/10) Yuriy Semin (RUS)

Founded – 1927

Stadium – Dynamo im. Valeriy Lobanovskiy (16,873)

MAJOR HONOURS: UEFA Cup Winners' Cup – (2) 1975, 1986; UEFA Super Cup – (1) 1975; USSR League – (13) 1961, 1966, 1967, 1968, 1971, 1974, 1975, 1977, 1980, 1981, 1985, 1986, 1990; Ukrainian League – (13) 1993, 1994, 1995, 1996, 1997, 1998, 1999, 2000, 2001, 2003, 2004, 2007, 2009; USSR Cup – (9) 1954, 1964, 1966, 1974, 1978, 1982, 1985, 1987, 1990; Ukrainian Cup – (9) 1993, 1996, 1998, 1999, 2000, 2003, 2005, 2006, 2007.

2010

9/7	Obolon	a	2-2	*Shevchenko, Yarmolenko*
17/7	Tavriya	h	2-1	*Eremenko, Shevchenko (p)*
23/7	Metalist	a	2-1	*Shevchenko (p), Harmash*
31/7	Sevastopol	a	3-0	*Yarmolenko, Mykhalyk, Shevchenko*
8/8	Metalurh Donetsk	h	1-0	*Shevchenko*
14/8	Vorskla	a	1-3	*Leandro Almeida*
22/8	Dnipro	h	0-0	
29/8	Kryvbas	a	1-0	*Yarmolenko*
11/9	Metalurh Zaporizhya	h	2-0	*Ninković, Milevskiy (p)*
19/9	Zorya	a	2-1	*Shevchenko, Vukojević*
26/9	Arsenal	h	3-2	*Gusev, Milevskiy, Yarmolenko*
3/10	Shakhtar	a	0-2	
16/10	Karpaty	h	1-0	*Leandro Almeida*
24/10	Volyn	a	2-1	*Yarmolenko 2*
31/10	Illychivets	h	9-0	*Yarmolenko, Gusev, Milevskiy 4, og (Savin), Guilherme, Danilo Silva*
7/11	Obolon	h	0-2	
14/11	Tavriya	a	1-1	*Milevskiy*
21/11	Metalist	h	1-1	*Gusev*
27/11	Sevastopol	h	2-0	*Eremenko, Vukojević*

2011

5/3	Metalurh Donetsk	a	2-0	*Popov, Yarmolenko*
13/3	Vorskla	h	2-0	*Kravets, Yarmolenko*
20/3	Dnipro	a	0-1	
2/4	Kryvbas	h	3-0	*Yarmolenko, Eremenko, Gusev*
10/4	Metalurh Zaporizhya	a	1-1	*Shevchenko*
18/4	Zorya	h	2-0	*Gusev, Leandro Almeida*
23/4	Arsenal	a	3-0	*Yarmolenko, Shevchenko, Gusev*
1/5	Shakhtar	h	3-0	*Gusev 2 (1p), Shevchenko*
7/5	Karpaty	a	2-1	*Gusev, Vukojević*
15/5	Volyn	h	5-1	*Milevskiy 2, Kravets 2, Aliyev*
21/5	Illychivets	a	2-3	*Aliyev, Shevchenko*

No	Name	Nat	DoB	Pos	Aps	(s)	Gls
8	Olexandr ALIYEV		3/2/85	M	3	(3)	2
11	ANDRÉ Felipe Ribeiro de Souza	BRA	27/9/90	A	1	(2)	
18	Facundo Daniel BERTOGLIO	ARG	30/6/90	M	3	(1)	
3	Ebert William Amâncio "BETÃO"	BRA	11/11/83	D	19	(5)	
71	Denys BOIKO		29/1/88	G	8		
2	DANILO Aparecido da SILVA	BRA	24/11/86	D	22	(3)	1
30	Badr EL KADDOURI	MAR	31/1/81	D	12	(4)	
23	Roman EREMENKO	FIN	19/3/87	M	24	(2)	3
4	Tiberiu GHIOANE	ROU	18/6/81	M		(3)	
77	GUILHERME Milhomem Gusmão	BRA	22/10/88	A	2	(3)	1
20	Oleh GUSEV		25/4/83	M	19	(4)	9
19	Denys HARMASH		19/4/90	M	12	(8)	1
45	Vladyslav KALITVINTSEV		4/1/93	M		(1)	
34	Yevhen KHACHERIDI		28/7/87	D	15	(1)	
36	Maxym KOVAL		9/12/92	G	12		
22	Artem KRAVETS		3/6/89	A	4	(7)	3
44	LEANDRO ALMEIDA da Silva	BRA	14/3/87	D	13	(5)	3
21	Gérson Alencar Lima Júnior "MAGRÃO"	BRA	13/6/85	M	6		
10	Artem MILEVSKIY		12/1/85	A	20	(6)	9
17	Taras MYKHALYK		28/10/83	M	16	(2)	1
26	Andriy NESMACHNIY		28/2/79	D	2	(1)	
36	Miloš NINKOVIĆ	SRB	25/12/84	M	7	(6)	1
6	Goran POPOV	MKD	2/10/84	M	15		1
7	Andriy SHEVCHENKO		29/9/76	A	16	(2)	10
1	Olexandr SHOVKOVSKIY		2/1/75	G	10		
5	Ognjen VUKOJEVIĆ	CRO	20/12/83	M	28	(1)	3
9	Andriy YARMOLENKO		23/10/89	A	22	(4)	11
37	Ayila YUSSUF	NGA	4/11/84	M	12	(1)	
49	Roman ZOZULYA		17/11/89	M	7	(5)	

FC ILLYCHIVETS MARIUPIL

Coach – Illya Blyznyuk; (1/11/10) (Olexandr Volkov); (28/11/10) Valeriy Yaremchenko

Founded – 2003

Stadium – Illychivets (12,460)

2010

9/7	Metalurh Donetsk	h	1-1	*Tyshchenko*
17/7	Vorskla	a	3-1	*Antonov, Pukanych, Yaroshenko*
24/7	Dnipro	h	1-5	*Antonov*
31/7	Kryvbas	a	0-1	
6/8	Metalurh Zaporizhya	h	0-0	
13/8	Zorya	a	2-2	*Yaroshenko, og (Kovalev)*
21/8	Arsenal	h	2-2	*Kozoriz, Antonov*
29/8	Shakhtar	a	0-1	
12/9	Karpaty	h	2-3	*Kozoriz, Antonov*
17/9	Volyn	a	1-3	*Tyshchenko*
25/9	Sevastopol	h	4-2	*Yaroshenko, Pukanych, Yatsenko, Antonov*
2/10	Obolon	h	1-0	*Pukanych*
15/10	Tavriya	a	2-2	*Putivtsev, Tyshchenko*
24/10	Metalist	h	1-4	*Yaroshenko*
31/10	Dynamo	a	0-9	
7/11	Metalurh Donetsk	a	3-0	*Pukanych, Yaroshenko 2 (2p)*
13/11	Vorskla	h	2-6	*Antonov, Kravchenko*
21/11	Dnipro	a	0-2	
26/11	Kryvbas	h	1-1	*Tyshchenko*

2011

4/3	Metalurh Zaporizhya	a	4-0	*Antonov 2, Putivtsev, Kryvosheyenko*
13/3	Zorya	h	2-2	*Pukanych 2*
20/3	Arsenal	a	1-3	*Nevmyvaka*
1/4	Shakhtar	h	1-3	*Budkivskiy*
10/4	Karpaty	a	1-3	*Yaroshenko*
16/4	Volyn	h	2-2	*Yaroshenko, Pukanych*
24/4	Sevastopol	a	0-1	
30/4	Obolon	a	0-2	
8/5	Tavriya	h	5-1	*Kryvosheyenko, Yaroshenko, Tyshchenko, Antonov 2*
15/5	Metalist	a	0-3	
21/5	Dynamo	h	3-2	*Yaroshenko, Pukanych, Tyshchenko*

No	Name	Nat	DoB	Pos	Aps	(s)	Gls
69	Olexiy ANTONOV		8/5/86	A	22	(1)	10
23	Ihor BAZHAN		2/12/81	G	3	(1)	
92	Pylyp BUDKIVSKIY		10/3/92	A	6	(1)	1
8	Ihor CHAIKOVSIY		7/10/91	M	9		
24	Ihor CHUCHMAN		15/2/85	D	13	(1)	
17	Vitaliy FEDOTOV		16/7/91	M	1	(7)	
55	Giorgi GABEDAVA	GEO	3/10/89	A		(4)	
6	Dmytro GRECHISHKIN		22/9/91	M	7	(1)	
45	Yehor KARTUSHOV		5/1/91	M	3	(5)	
46	Anton KICHA		1/5/90	M		(1)	
56	Ivan KOZORIZ		14/9/79	M	12	(4)	2
7	Kostyantyn KRAVCHENKO		24/9/86	M	3	(2)	1
11	Ivan KRYVOSHEYENKO		11/5/84	A	27	(2)	2
4	Vadym MELNYK		16/5/80	D	5	(11)	
2	Stanislav MYKYTSEI		7/9/89	D	3		
25	Vladyslav NASIBULIN		6/7/89	M	2	(11)	
3	Dmytro NEVMYVAKA		19/3/84	D	11		1
80	Tornike OKRIASHVILI	GEO	12/2/92	M	5	(5)	
5	Adrian PUKANYCH		22/6/83	M	26		8
77	Artem PUTIVTSEV		29/8/88	D	21	(3)	2
1	Vsevolod ROMANENKO		24/3/77	G	18		
3	Mantas SAMUSIOVAS	LTU	8/9/78	D	3	(5)	
14	Artem SAVIN		20/1/81	D	22		
33	Bohdan SHUST		4/3/86	G	9		

No	Name	Nat	DoB	Pos	Aps	(s)	Gls
20	Artur SIRYK		17/2/89	A		(2)	
19	Ihor TYSHCHENKO		11/5/89	M	27	(1)	6
9	Kostyantyn YAROSHENKO		12/9/86	M	28	(1)	10
51	Olexandr YATSENKO		24/2/85	D	16		1
21	Serhiy YAVORSKIY		5/7/89	M	23	(4)	
70	Vladlen YURCHENKO		22/1/94	A		(3)	
22	Artur ZAPADNYA		4/6/90	M	5	(3)	

FC KARPATY LVIV

Coach – Oleg Kononov (BLR)
Founded – 1963
Stadium – Ukraina (27,925)
MAJOR HONOURS: USSR Cup – (1) 1969.

2010				
10/7	Dnipro	a	0-1	
18/7	Kryvbas	a	0-0	
25/7	Metalurh Zaporizhya	h	1-0	*Fedetskiy*
1/8	Zorya	a	2-2	*Tkachuk (p), Hudyma*
8/8	Arsenal	h	2-1	*Kozhanov, Batista*
15/8	Shakhtar	a	0-1	
22/8	Sevastopol	h	2-1	*Kopolovets, Holodyuk*
30/8	Volyn	h	1-0	*Zenjov*
12/9	Illychivets	a	3-2	*Holodyuk, Zenjov, Kozhanov*
19/9	Obolon	h	3-0	*Kuznetsov 2, Khudobyak*
26/9	Tavriya	a	1-3	*Zenjov*
3/10	Metalist	h	0-1	
16/10	Dynamo	a	0-1	
24/10	Metalurh Donetsk	h	2-1	*Kozhanov, Godwin*
30/10	Vorskla	a	1-1	*Kuznetsov*
7/11	Dnipro	h	0-0	
14/11	Kryvbas	h	2-1	*Holodyuk, Khudobyak*
21/11	Metalurh Zaporizhya	a	0-0	
27/11	Zorya	h	4-2	*Khudobyak, Kuznetsov 2, Checher*
2011				
6/3	Arsenal	a	2-2	*Balažič, Milošević*
13/3	Shakhtar	h	1-0	*Cociş*
19/3	Sevastopol	a	1-3	*Cociş*
3/4	Volyn	a	3-0	*Kozhanov 2, Khudobyak*
10/4	Illychivets	h	3-1	*Khudobyak, Tkachuk (p), Holodyuk*
15/4	Obolon	a	1-1	*Zenjov*
23/4	Tavriya	h	1-0	*Fedetskiy*
30/4	Metalist	a	1-1	*Batista*
7/5	Dynamo	h	1-2	*Kopolovets*
15/5	Metalurh Donetsk	a	1-4	*Khudobyak*
21/5	Vorskla	h	2-2	*Kozhanov 2*

No	Name	Nat	DoB	Pos	Aps	(s)	Gls
21	Gregor BALAŽIČ	SVN	12/2/88	M	5		1
30	Borys BARANETS		22/7/86	M	3	(2)	
28	Hryhoriy BARANETS		22/7/86	M	4	(5)	
80	Wiliam Rocha BATISTA	BRA	27/7/80	A	10	(7)	2
64	Volodymyr BIDLOVSKIY		31/5/88	A		(1)	
32	Martin BOGATINOV	MKD	26/4/86	G	8		
57	BORJA GÓMEZ Pérez	ESP	14/5/88	D	7		
70	Vyacheslav CHECHER		15/12/80	D	7	(2)	1
81	Răzvan Vasile COCIŞ	ROU	19/2/83	A	11		2
89	DANILO Fernando AVELAR	BRA	9/6/89	M	16	(2)	
44	Artem FEDETSKIY		26/4/85	D	23		2
7	Samson GODWIN	NGA	11/11/83	M	22	(3)	1
10	Aleksandre GURULI	GEO	9/11/85	A	7	(11)	
99	Yuriy HABOVDA		6/5/89	A		(4)	
41	Stepan HIRSKIY		8/5/91	D		(1)	
17	Oleh HOLODYUK		2/1/88	M	16	(2)	4
36	Volodymyr HUDYMA		20/7/90	A	2	(4)	1
16	Ihor Yaroslavovych KHUDOBYAK		20/2/85	M	26		6
18	Mykhailo KOPOLOVETS		29/1/84	M	6	(18)	2
9	Denys KOZHANOV		13/6/87	A	26	(1)	7
79	Serhiy KUZNETSOV		31/8/82	A	10	(3)	5
29	LUCAS Pérez Martínez	ESP	10/9/88	A	4	(4)	
19	Yaroslav MARTYNYUK		20/2/89	M		(2)	
4	Ivan MILOŠEVIĆ	SRB	3/11/84	D	23		1
88	Genison Piacentini de Quadra "NENU"	BRA	14/10/88	M	1		
8	Ihor OSHCHYPKO		25/10/85	D	10		
15	Taras PETRIVSKIY		3/2/84	D	11	(5)	
1	Vitaliy RUDENKO		26/1/81	G	7		
34	Andriy SAHAIDAK		2/1/89	D	1		
33	Yevhen TARASENKO		3/3/83	D	3	(1)	
90	THIAGO Alberto Constância	BRA	21/12/84	M	1	(1)	
37	Ihor TISTYK		27/5/89	D		(1)	
25	Andriy TKACHUK		18/11/87	M	20	(3)	2
22	Andriy TLUMAK		7/3/79	G	15		
5	Nemanja TUBIĆ	SRB	8/4/84	A	14		
11	Sergei ZENJOV	EST	20/4/89	A	11	(7)	4

FC KRYVBAS KRYVYI RIH

Coach – Yuriy Maximov
Founded – 1959
Stadium – Metalurh (29,734)

2010				
10/7	Shakhtar	a	0-2	
18/7	Karpaty	h	0-0	
23/7	Volyn	a	0-0	
31/7	Illychivets	h	1-0	*Maximov*
7/8	Obolon	a	1-1	*Maximov*
14/8	Tavriya	h	1-4	*Kutsenko (p)*
22/8	Metalist	a	4-3	*Ivashchenko 2 (1p), Voronkov 2*
29/8	Dynamo	h	0-1	
11/9	Metalurh Donetsk	a	2-2	*Khomchenovskiy, Maximov*
18/9	Vorskla	h	1-0	*Kostyshyn*
26/9	Dnipro	a	1-1	*Ivashchenko*
3/10	Sevastopol	a	2-2	*Voronkov 2*
17/10	Metalurh Zaporizhya	h	0-0	
23/10	Zorya	a	0-1	
31/10	Arsenal	h	1-1	*Borovyk*
6/11	Shakhtar	h	0-2	
14/11	Karpaty	a	1-2	*Voronkov*
20/11	Volyn	h	2-4	*Ivashchenko (p), Maximov*
26/11	Illychivets	a	1-1	*Maximov*
2011				
5/3	Obolon	h	2-2	*Ivashchenko 2*
12/3	Tavriya	a	1-2	*Ivashchenko (p)*
19/3	Metalist	h	0-0	
2/4	Dynamo	a	0-3	
10/4	Metalurh Donetsk	h	1-0	*Voronkov*
16/4	Vorskla	a	0-3	
23/4	Dnipro	h	0-3	
1/5	Sevastopol	h	3-1	*Valeyev, Matič, Bartulović*
6/5	Metalurh Zaporizhya	a	2-1	*Jeslínek 2*
15/5	Zorya	h	0-2	
21/5	Arsenal	a	0-1	

No	Name	Nat	DoB	Pos	Aps	(s)	Gls
12	Denys ANDRIYENKO		12/4/80	D	10	(1)	
17	Michel BABATUNDE	NGA	24/12/92	M		(10)	
11	Mladen BARTULOVIĆ	CRO	5/10/86	M	4	(3)	1
23	Yevhen BOROVYK		2/3/85	G	23		1
33	Serhiy DANYLOVSKIY		20/8/81	M	8	(2)	
32	Rostyslav DYAKIV		17/8/90	A	1	(2)	
37	Valeriy FEDORCHUK		5/10/88	M	10		
17	Beka GOTSIRIDZE	GEO	17/8/88	M	1	(4)	
77	Olexandr IVASHCHENKO		19/2/85	A	24	(2)	7
9	Jiří JESLÍNEK	CZE	30/9/87	M	7	(4)	2
20	Jaba KANKAVA	GEO	18/3/86	D	7	(1)	
9	Vitaliy KAVERIN		4/9/90	A	1	(5)	
27	Anatoliy KITSUTA		22/12/85	M	20	(1)	
37	Dmytro KHOMCHENOVSKIY		16/4/90	M	8	(2)	1
19	Aleksandre KOBAKHIDZE	GEO	11/2/87	M		(1)	
10	Ruslan KOSTYSHYN		8/1/77	M	18	(4)	1
22	Valeriy KUTSENKO		2/11/86	M	11	(8)	1
44	Vitaliy LYSYTSKIY		16/4/82	M	25	(1)	
28	Darijan MATIČ	SVN	28/5/83	M	8		1
30	Olexandr MAXIMOV		13/2/85	M	24		5
11	Serhiy MOTUZ		6/7/82	A	1	(7)	
5	Kyrylo PETROV		22/6/90	M	11	(8)	
7	Serhiy ROZHOK		25/4/85	M	15	(5)	
3	Vyacheslav SERDYUK		28/1/85	D	16	(5)	
55	Artem SHTANKO		6/9/80	G	7		
50	Serhiy SHUMILIN		21/2/90	A		(1)	
88	Rinar VALEYEV		22/8/87	M	21	(4)	1

No	Name	Nat	DoB	Pos	Aps	(s)	Gls
14	Denys VASILIYEV		8/5/87	D	17	(3)	
8	Andrei VORONKOV	BLR	8/2/89	A	19	(2)	6
25	Olexandr ZHDANOV		27/5/84	D	13	(3)	

FC METALIST KHARKIV

Coach – Myron Markevych

Founded – 1925

Stadium – OSK Metalist (41,307)

MAJOR HONOURS: USSR Cup – (1) 1988.

2010				
10/7	Tavriya	a	1-0	*Oliynyk*
17/7	Sevastopol	a	0-0	
23/7	Dynamo	h	1-2	*Fininho*
1/8	Metalurh Donetsk	a	3-0	*Dević (p), Cleiton 2*
7/8	Vorskla	h	2-3	*Vorobei, Dević (p)*
14/8	Dnipro	a	1-0	*Fininho*
22/8	Kryvbas	h	3-4	*Vorobei, Dević 2*
29/8	Metalurh Zaporizhya	a	2-0	*Dević, Cleiton*
12/9	Zorya	h	3-0	*Valyayev, Vorobei, Cleiton*
19/9	Arsenal	a	1-0	*Taison*
25/9	Shakhtar	h	1-2	*Taison*
3/10	Karpaty	a	1-0	*Oliynyk*
16/10	Volyn	h	3-1	*Dević 2, Vorobei*
24/10	Illychivets	a	4-1	*Oliynyk 3, Taison*
30/10	Obolon	h	2-1	*Oliynyk, Edmar*
7/11	Tavriya	h	2-3	*Taison, Oliynyk*
13/11	Sevastopol	h	4-0	*Dević 2 (1p), Gueye, Fininho*
21/11	Dynamo	a	1-1	*Dević (p)*
27/11	Metalurh Donetsk	h	3-1	*Taison, Oliynyk, Pshenychnykh*
2011				
5/3	Vorskla	a	0-0	
13/3	Dnipro	h	2-2	*Cleiton 2*
19/3	Kryvbas	a	0-0	
3/4	Metalurh Zaporizhya	h	3-0	*Taison 2, Shelayev*
8/4	Zorya	a	2-0	*Dević, Villagra*
16/4	Arsenal	h	2-1	*Oliynyk 2*
23/4	Shakhtar	a	1-2	*Dević*
30/4	Karpaty	h	1-1	*Dević*
8/5	Volyn	a	4-1	*Cristaldo 3, Taison*
15/5	Illychivets	h	3-0	*Oliynyk 2, Dević*
21/5	Obolon	a	2-0	*Cristaldo 2*

No	Name	Nat	DoB	Pos	Aps	(s)	Gls
19	Serhiy BARYLKO		5/1/87	M		(3)	
4	Andriy BEREZOVCHUK		16/4/81	D	11		
37	Vitalie BORDIAN	MDA	11/8/84	D	4	(10)	
10	CLEITON Ribeiro Xavier	BRA	23/3/83	M	26		6
21	Jonathan Ezequiel CRISTALDO	ARG	5/3/89	A	4	(5)	5
27	Serhiy DAVYDOV		16/12/84	A	1	(2)	
33	Marko DEVIĆ		27/10/83	M	19	(5)	14
81	Vladimir DIŠLJENKOVIĆ	SRB	2/7/81	G	18		
8	EDMAR Golovski de Lacerda Aparecida	BRA	16/6/80	M	26	(1)	1
15	Vinícius Aparecido Pereira de Santana Campos "FININHO"	BRA	3/11/83	A	20	(1)	3
29	Olexandr GORYAINOV		29/6/75	G	5		
30	Papa GUEYE	SEN	7/6/84	D	19	(1)	1
50	Jackson Avelino Coelho "JAJÁ"	BRA	28/2/86	A	2		
42	Sani Haruna KAITA	NGA	2/5/86	M		(6)	
22	Milan OBRADOVIĆ	SRB	3/8/77	D	26		
11	Denys OLIYNYK		16/6/87	M	21	(6)	12
17	Serhiy PSHENYCHNYKH		19/11/81	D	7	(7)	1
2	Olexandr ROMANCHUK		21/10/84	D	20	(1)	
87	Vyacheslav SHARPAR		2/6/87	M	3	(4)	
5	Oleh SHELAYEV		5/11/76	M	13	(10)	1
20	Maxym STARTSEV		20/1/80	G	7	(1)	
80	Lukáš ŠTETINA	SVK	28/7/91	D	2		
77	TAISON Barcellos Freda	BRA	13/1/88	A	21		8
71	Sergei TKACHEV	RUS	19/5/89	M	3	(4)	
18	Aleksandar TRIŠOVIĆ	SRB	25/11/83	M		(1)	
7	Serhiy VALYAYEV		16/9/78	M	23	(2)	1
3	Cristian Carlos VILLAGRA	ARG	27/12/85	D	23		1
9	Andriy VOROBEI		29/11/78	A	6	(14)	4
1	Dmytro ZHDANKOV		18/11/84	G		(1)	

FC METALURH DONETSK

Coach – Nikolay Kostov (BUL); (12/11/10) (Volodymyr Pyatenko); (12/1/11) Andrei Gordeyev (RUS); (3/5/11) (Volodymyr Pyatenko)

Founded – 1996

Stadium – Metalurh (5,094)

2010				
9/7	Illychivets	a	1-1	*Mguni*
16/7	Obolon	h	3-0	*Godin, Morozyuk, Mkhitaryan (p)*
24/7	Tavriya	a	1-2	*Mkhitaryan*
1/8	Metalist	h	0-3	
8/8	Dynamo	a	0-1	
15/8	Sevastopol	a	1-0	*Tănasă*
21/8	Vorskla	h	2-0	*Adeleye, Mkhitaryan*
30/8	Dnipro	a	2-1	*Tănasă, Mguni*
11/9	Kryvbas	h	2-2	*Cleyton, Mguni*
17/9	Metalurh Zaporizhya	a	2-1	*Pryima, Lazić*
26/9	Zorya	h	1-1	*Lazić*
2/10	Arsenal	a	1-3	*China*
15/10	Shakhtar	h	0-2	
24/10	Karpaty	a	1-2	*Volovyk*
31/10	Volyn	h	0-2	
7/11	Illychivets	h	0-3	
12/11	Obolon	a	1-1	*Mguni*
21/11	Tavriya	h	2-1	*Zé Soares, Tănasă*
27/11	Metalist	a	1-3	*Zé Soares*
2011				
5/3	Dynamo	h	0-2	
12/3	Sevastopol	h	1-0	*Godin*
18/3	Vorskla	a	1-1	*Adeleye*
2/4	Dnipro	h	3-2	*Ivanko, Adeleye, Holaido*
10/4	Kryvbas	a	0-1	
17/4	Metalurh Zaporizhya	h	0-1	
24/4	Zorya	a	2-0	*Ricardo Fernandes 2 (1p)*
30/4	Arsenal	h	1-5	*Ricardo Fernandes*
7/5	Shakhtar	a	0-2	
15/5	Karpaty	h	4-1	*Lazić 2, Ricardo Fernandes, Checher*
21/5	Volyn	a	3-1	*Adi, Tănasă, og (Hodovaniy)*

No	Name	Nat	DoB	Pos	Aps	(s)	Gls
5	Ayodele ADELEYE	NGA	25/12/88	D	26		3
22	Fanendo ADI	NGA	10/10/90	A	7	(2)	1
12	Olexandr BANDURA		30/5/86	G	11		
4	Vyacheslav CHECHER		15/12/80	D	12		1
27	João Pedro Santos Gonçalves "CHINA"	POR	15/4/82	D	19	(2)	1
83	Alexandre Henri Marco CLEYTON Silva	BRA	8/3/83	M	7	(2)	1
11	Artak DASHYAN	ARM	20/11/89	M	5	(4)	
18	Velizar DIMITROV	BUL	13/4/79	M	11	(1)	
8	FILIPE de Andrade TEIXEIRA	POR	2/10/80	M	1	(6)	
30	Mario GJUROVSKI	MKD	11/12/85	M		(6)	
27	Olexiy GODIN		2/2/83	M	13	(3)	2
84	Denys HOLAIDO		3/6/84	M	2	(5)	1
43	Pavlo HRYSHCHENKO		6/7/90	M		(1)	
46	Vitaliy IVANKO		9/4/92	A	4	(14)	1
3	Ihor KOROTETSKIY		13/9/87	D	1	(3)	
9	Đorđe LAZIĆ	SRB	18/6/83	M	28	(1)	4
28	MÁRIO SÉRGIO Leal Nogueira	POR	28/7/81	D	27		
7	Musawengosi MGUNI	ZIM	5/4/83	A	6	(6)	4
99	Oleh MISHCHENKO		10/10/89	M		(1)	
22	Henrikh MKHITARYAN	ARM	21/1/89	A	8		3
6	Karlen MKRTCHYAN	ARM	25/11/88	M	5	(1)	
77	Mykola MOROZYUK		17/1/88	M	18	(8)	1
1	Dmytro NEPOGODOV		17/2/88	G	14		
36	Mykyta POLYULYAKH		15/3/93	M		(1)	
44	Vasyl PRYIMA		10/6/91	D	20	(2)	1
10	RICARDO Ribeiro FERNANDES	POR	21/4/78	M	9		4
50	Anton SAVIN		7/2/90	M		(1)	
88	Serhiy SHYSHCHENKO		13/1/76	A			
15	Ciprian Ion TĂNASĂ	ROU	2/2/81	A	15	(10)	4
13	Serhiy TKACHENKO		10/2/79	M		(1)	
14	Olexandr VOLOVYK		28/10/85	D	30		1
31	Dmytro VOROBYOV		27/8/77	G	5		
10	Chavdar YANKOV	BUL	29/3/84	D	2	(2)	
17	José "ZÉ" SOARES da Silva Filho	BRA	27/7/83	M	24	(1)	2

FC METALURH ZAPORIZHYA

Coach – Oleh Lutkov;
(3/5/11) Serhiy Zaitsev & Hryhoriy Negiryov
Founded – 1935
Stadium – Slavutych-Arena (11,756)

2010

9/7	Arsenal	a	0-1	
18/7	Shakhtar	h	1-1	*Alozi*
25/7	Karpaty	a	0-1	
31/7	Volyn	h	0-1	
6/8	Illychivets	a	0-0	
14/8	Obolon	h	1-2	*Anderson Ribeiro*
22/8	Tavriya	a	0-2	
29/8	Metalist	h	0-2	
11/9	Dynamo	a	0-2	
17/9	Metalurh Donetsk	h	1-2	*Tatanashvili*
26/9	Vorskla	a	1-2	*Arzhanov*
1/10	Dnipro	h	0-3	
17/10	Kryvbas	a	0-0	
23/10	Sevastopol	a	0-1	
30/10	Zorya	h	1-0	*Arzhanov*
6/11	Arsenal	h	2-1	*Pisotskiy, Fábio*
13/11	Shakhtar	a	1-2	*Pisotskiy*
21/11	Karpaty	h	0-0	
28/11	Volyn	a	0-1	

2011

4/3	Illychivets	h	0-4	
11/3	Obolon	a	0-1	
20/3	Tavriya	h	2-2	*Fabiano, Pisotskiy*
3/4	Metalist	a	0-3	
10/4	Dynamo	h	1-1	*Tsurikov*
17/4	Metalurh Donetsk	a	1-0	*Pisotskiy*
22/4	Vorskla	h	2-0	*og (Peskov), Júnior*
30/4	Dnipro	a	0-3	
6/5	Kryvbas	h	1-2	*Skepskiy*
15/5	Sevastopol	h	1-0	*Nesterov*
21/5	Zorya	a	2-0	*Skepskiy, Júnior*

No	Name	Nat	DoB	Pos	Aps	(s)	Gls
16	Michael Chidi ALOZI	NGA	16/10/86	A	6	(6)	1
9	ANDERSON RIBEIRO Mende	BRA	2/7/81	M	3	(4)	1
99	Mohamed Larbi AROURI	TUN	13/5/83	D	12		
17	Volodymyr ARZHANOV		29/11/85	M	16		2
24	Dmytro BEZOTOSNIY		15/11/83	G	22		
19	Vasile CARAUS	MDA	6/8/88	M	1		
38	FABIANO de Lima Campos Maria	BRA	24/11/85	M	7	(1)	1
15	FÁBIO Emanuel Moreira Silva	CPV	3/4/85	M	6	(7)	1
7	Paweł HAJDUCZEK	POL	17/5/82	M	7	(6)	
26	Yuriy HLUSHKO		5/2/91	A	1	(1)	
18	JEFERSON Douglas dos Santos Batista	BRA	13/2/89	M		(2)	
12	Luiz Antônio de Godoy Alves JÚNIOR	BRA	20/9/78	A	18	(1)	2
10	Mindaugas KALONAS	LTU	28/2/84	A	7	(1)	
30	Artur KASKOV		18/11/91	A	4	(7)	
11	Mohamed Achraf KHALFAOUI	TUN	24/10/80	M	10	(1)	
1	Maxym KOVAL		9/12/92	G	3		
20	Yan KOVALEVSKIY		26/6/93	A		(1)	
2	MATHEUS Henrique do Carmo Lopes	BRA	8/3/85	D	10		
6	Olexiy MOISEYENKO		25/10/91	A		(1)	
21	Andriy NESTEROV		2/7/90	D	6	(3)	1
3	Dmytro NEVMYVAKA		19/3/84	D	19		
39	Yevhen OPANASENKO		25/8/90	M	25		
31	Yevhen PISOTSKIY		22/4/87	M	20	(1)	4
14	Volodymyr POLYOVIY		28/7/85	M	17		
16	Sead RAMOVIĆ	BIH	14/3/79	G	2		
1	Vitaliy RUDENKO		26/1/81	G	3		
32	Serhiy RUDYKA		14/6/88	M	6	(2)	
14	Denys SKEPSKIY		5/7/87	M	2	(2)	2
4	Ivan SPYCHKA		18/1/91	M		(1)	
34	Serhiy SYDORCHUK		2/5/91	M	6	(14)	
18	Dimitri TATANASHVILI	GEO	19/10/83	A	8	(2)	1
23	Adolf Kamgeng TEIKU	CMR	23/6/90	D	26		
9	Igor TIGIRLAS	MDA	24/2/84	A	3	(4)	
20	Yan TIGOREV	BLR	10/3/84	D	17		
22	Andriy TSURIKOV		5/10/92	M	9	(4)	1
5	Vitaliy VERNYDUB		17/10/87	D	17	(4)	
8	Dmytro YEREMENKO		20/6/90	M	11	(8)	
28	Yevhen ZADOYA		5/1/91	M		(1)	

FC OBOLON KYIV

Coach – Serhiy Kovalets
Founded – 1992
Stadium – Obolon ARENA (5,100)

2010

9/7	Dynamo	h	2-2	*Mandzyuk 2*
16/7	Metalurh Donetsk	a	0-3	
25/7	Vorskla	h	0-1	
1/8	Dnipro	a	0-3	
7/8	Kryvbas	h	1-1	*Kotenko*
14/8	Metalurh Zaporizhya	a	2-1	*Mandzyuk, Kucherenko (p)*
20/8	Zorya	h	1-0	*Panas*
28/8	Arsenal	a	0-1	
10/9	Shakhtar	h	1-0	*Khudzik*
19/9	Karpaty	a	0-3	
26/9	Volyn	h	0-1	
2/10	Illychivets	a	0-1	
16/10	Sevastopol	h	2-2	*Mandzyuk, Khudzik*
22/10	Tavriya	h	2-1	*Kucherenko (p), Khudzik*
30/10	Metalist	a	1-2	*Miroshnychenko*
7/11	Dynamo	a	2-0	*Khudzik, Sybiryakov*
12/11	Metalurh Donetsk	h	1-1	*Kucherenko (p)*
21/11	Vorskla	a	1-0	*Kutas*
28/11	Dnipro	h	0-1	

2011

5/3	Kryvbas	a	2-2	*Mandzyuk, Panas*
11/3	Metalurh Zaporizhya	h	1-0	*Baranets H.*
19/3	Zorya	a	0-1	
2/4	Arsenal	h	1-1	*Baranets B.*
9/4	Shakhtar	a	1-0	*Kucherenko*
15/4	Karpaty	h	1-1	*Lozynskiy*
22/4	Volyn	a	0-1	
30/4	Illychivets	h	2-0	*Plastun, Mandzyuk*
7/5	Sevastopol	a	1-3	*Panas*
15/5	Tavriya	a	1-3	*Lupashko*
21/5	Metalist	h	0-2	

No	Name	Nat	DoB	Pos	Aps	(s)	Gls
19	Borys BARANETS		22/7/86	M	7	(4)	1
6	Hryhoriy BARANETS		22/7/86	M	4	(4)	1
22	Ihor BEREZOVSKIY		24/8/90	G	4	(1)	
17	Olexandr BONDARENKO		28/7/89	A	4	(14)	
9	Ihor ILKIV		13/3/05	D	5	(1)	
23	Oleh KARAMUSHKA		30/4/84	D	3	(4)	
27	Pavlo KHUDZIK		29/4/85	M	25	(1)	4
24	Ivan KOTENKO		28/4/85	M	11	(4)	1
10	Serhiy KUCHERENKO		7/1/84	M	13	(8)	4
77	Pavlo KUTAS		3/9/82	D	25	(1)	1
29	Oleh LEONIDOV		16/8/85	D	2		
7	Yevhen LOZYNSKIY		7/2/82	D	27		1
15	Vladyslav LUPASHKO		4/12/86	M	26	(2)	1
5	Olexandr MANDZYUK		10/1/83	A	28	(1)	6
25	Oleh MAZURENKO		8/11/77	M	5	(3)	
78	Artem MIROSHNYCHENKO		9/11/78	M		(4)	1
12	Oleh OSTAPENKO		27/10/77	G	4		
11	Vadym PANAS		23/5/85	M	19	(8)	3
32	Ihor PLASTUN		20/8/90	M	28		1
2	Yuriy PUTRASH		29/1/90	D	4	(2)	
1	Olexandr RYBKA		10/4/87	G	22		
4	Vadym SAPAI		7/2/84	D	26	(2)	
21	Anton SHEVCHUK		8/2/90	A	1	(6)	
14	Valentyn SLYUSAR		15/9/77	M	18	(1)	
8	Serhiy SYBIRYAKOV		1/1/82	M	19	(7)	1
18	Olexandr TOLSTYAK		4/2/90	M		(2)	
99	Yevhen ZARICHNYUK		3/2/89	M		(1)	

PFC SEVASTOPOL

Coach – Serhiy Shevchenko; (11/9/10) (Oleh Leshchynskiy); (21/12/10) Angel Chervenkov (BUL)

Founded – 2002

Stadium – SK Sevastopol (6,000); Lokomotyv, Simferopol (19,978)

2010

9/7	Zorya	a	0-0	
17/7	Metalist	h	0-0	
24/7	Arsenal	a	1-0	*Khudobyak*
31/7	Dynamo	h	0-3	
7/8	Shakhtar	a	0-5	
15/8	Metalurh Donetsk	h	0-1	
22/8	Karpaty	a	1-2	*Ferenchak*
27/8	Vorskla	h	0-0	
10/9	Volyn	a	0-1	
18/9	Dnipro	h	2-1	*Zborovskiy 2*
25/9	Illychivets	a	2-4	*Lewandowski (p), Kiva*
3/10	Kryvbas	h	2-2	*Lewandowski, Zborovskiy*
16/10	Obolon	a	2-2	*Aghahowa,og (Plastun)*
23/10	Metalurh Zaporizhya	h	1-0	*Bredun*
31/10	Tavriya	a	1-2	*Lewandowski*
6/11	Zorya	h	0-1	
13/11	Metalist	a	0-4	
19/11	Arsenal	h	0-2	
27/11	Dynamo	a	0-2	

2011

3/3	Shakhtar	h	0-1	
12/3	Metalurh Donetsk	a	0-1	
19/3	Karpaty	h	3-1	*Zhabokrytskiy, Skoba, Ferenchak*
3/4	Vorskla	a	0-4	
9/4	Volyn	h	4-1	*Zhabokrytskiy, Lewandowski 2 (1p), Ibraimi*
17/4	Dnipro	a	2-2	*Salhi, Ferenchak*
24/4	Illychivets	h	1-0	*Skoba*
1/5	Kryvbas	a	1-3	*Lewandowski*
8/5	Obolon	h	3-1	*Ibraimi 2, Kiva*
15/5	Metalurh Zaporizhya	a	0-1	
21/5	Tavriya	h	0-1	

No	Name	Nat	DoB	Pos	Aps	(s)	Gls
55	Julius AGHAHOWA	NGA	12/2/82	A	10		1
30	Vadim BOLOHAN	MDA	15/8/86	D	23		
6	Yevhen BREDUN		10/9/82	M	16	(1)	1
22	Oleh DOPILKA		12/3/86	D	11		
4	Igor DULJAJ	SRB	29/10/79	D	19	(4)	
18	Serhiy FERENCHAK		27/4/84	M	27	(1)	3
19	Dmytro GOLOLOBOV		1/1/85	D	1		
77	Mate GVINIANIDZE	GEO	10/12/86	D	10		
20	Besart IBRAIMI	MKD	17/12/86	A	5	(6)	3
23	Ihor Orestovych KHUDOBYAK		5/4/87	A	1	(5)	1
9	Andriy KIVA		21/11/89	M	9	(13)	2
7	Artem KULTYSHEV		28/3/84	M	8	(6)	
17	Mariusz LEWANDOWSKI	POL	18/5/79	D	25		6
9	Maxym LISOVIY		21/5/85	M	1	(1)	
72	Ihor LYTOVKA		5/6/88	G	1	(1)	
33	Maryan MARUSHCHAK		10/5/79	G	3		
7	Alexander Stoychev MLADENOV	BUL	25/6/82	D	1	(2)	
99	Serhiy NUDNIY		6/10/80	M	2	(3)	
88	Genison Piacentini de Quadra "NENU"	BRA	14/10/88	M	8	(3)	
21	Vladyslav PISKUN		28/12/84	D	7		
2	Yuriy PLESHAKOV		29/8/88	A	4	(5)	
13	Oleh POLISHCHUK		17/4/91	D	10	(1)	
11	Toafik SALHI	TUN	21/8/79	M	13	(6)	1
3	Oleh SHANDRUK		30/1/83	D	16	(5)	
14	Andriy SHEVCHUK		12/8/85	A	11	(8)	
5	Olexandr SHEVELYUKHIN		27/8/82	D	21	(1)	
88	Ihor SKOBA		21/5/82	M	8	(2)	2
1	Olexandr SOKORENKO		23/2/76	G	15		
15	Andriy STEPANOV		11/6/78	D	5	(3)	
16	Sergei VEREMKO	BLR	16/10/82	G	11		
8	Roman VOINAROVSKIY		5/1/80	M	2	(2)	
24	Serhiy VORONIN		24/3/87	D	3	(2)	
25	Andriy ZBOROVSKIY		25/2/86	M	11	(3)	3
10	Olexandr ZHABOKRYTSKIY		29/1/81	M	12	(4)	2

FC SHAKHTAR DONETSK

Coach – Mircea Lucescu (ROU)

Founded – 1936

Stadium – Donbass Arena (50,149)

MAJOR HONOURS: UEFA Cup – (1) 2009;
Ukrainian League – (6) 2002, 2005, 2006, 2008, 2010, 2011;
USSR Cup – (4) 1961, 1962, 1980, 1983;
Ukrainian Cup – (7) 1995, 1997, 2001, 2002, 2004, 2008, 2011.

2010

10/7	Kryvbas	h	2-0	*Rakytskiy, Willian*
18/7	Metalurh Zaporizhya	a	1-1	*Fernandinho*
25/7	Zorya	h	1-0	*Chyhrynskiy*
30/7	Arsenal	a	3-1	*Douglas Costa 2, Luiz Adriano*
7/8	Sevastopol	h	5-0	*Fernandinho, Eduardo, Luiz Adriano, Douglas Costa, Marcelo Moreno*
15/8	Karpaty	h	1-0	*Willian*
21/8	Volyn	a	1-0	*Eduardo*
29/8	Illychivets	h	1-0	*Willian*
10/9	Obolon	a	0-1	
19/9	Tavriya	h	4-1	*Srna, Luiz Adriano, Jádson, Mkhitaryan*
25/9	Metalist	a	2-1	*Eduardo, Mkhitaryan*
3/10	Dynamo	h	2-0	*Luiz Adriano, Alex Teixeira*
15/10	Metalurh Donetsk	a	2-0	*Chyhrynskiy, Alex Teixeira*
23/10	Vorskla	h	1-0	*Alex Teixeira*
30/10	Dnipro	a	1-0	*Luiz Adriano*
6/11	Kryvbas	a	2-0	*Eduardo, Jádson*
13/11	Metalurh Zaporizhya	h	2-1	*Luiz Adriano (p), Marcelo Moreno*
20/11	Zorya	a	3-1	*Vitsenets, Marcelo Moreno, Luiz Adriano*
28/11	Arsenal	h	4-0	*Jádson (p), Marcelo Moreno, Eduardo, Douglas Costa (p)*

2011

3/3	Sevastopol	a	1-0	*Luiz Adriano*
13/3	Karpaty	a	0-1	
20/3	Volyn	h	4-0	*Jádson (p), Mkhitaryan, Alex Teixeira, Marcelo Moreno*
1/4	Illychivets	a	3-1	*Srna, Luiz Adriano, Douglas Costa*
9/4	Obolon	h	0-1	
17/4	Tavriya	a	2-1	*Jádson (p), Fernandinho*
23/4	Metalist	h	2-1	*Alex Teixeira, Eduardo*
1/5	Dynamo	a	0-3	
7/5	Metalurh Donetsk	h	2-0	*Luiz Adriano, Srna*
14/5	Vorskla	a	1-1	*Vitsenets*
21/5	Dnipro	h	0-0	

No	Name	Nat	DoB	Pos	Aps	(s)	Gls
17	Julius AGHAHOWA	NGA	12/2/82	A		(1)	
29	ALEX TEIXEIRA Santos	BRA	6/1/90	M	9	(17)	5
37	BRUNO Renan Trombelli	BRA	19/4/91	M		(1)	
36	Olexandr CHIZHOV		10/8/86	D	6		
27	Dmytro CHYHRYNSKIY		7/11/86	D	16		2
20	DOUGLAS COSTA de Souza	BRA	14/9/90	M	19	(8)	5
11	EDUARDO Alves da Silva	CRO	25/2/83	A	14	(8)	6
7	Fernando Luís Roza "FERNANDINHO"	BRA	4/5/85	M	14	(1)	3
19	Olexiy HAI		6/11/82	M	9	(2)	
21	Olexandr HLADKIY		24/8/87	A	2	(3)	
3	Tomáš HÜBSCHMAN	CZE	4/9/81	M	11	(3)	
32	Mykola ISHCHENKO		9/3/83	D	8	(2)	
8	JÁDSON Rodrigues da Silva	BRA	5/10/83	M	19	(5)	5
12	Rustam KHUDZHAMOV		5/10/82	G	1		
14	Vasyl KOBIN		24/5/85	M	9		
23	Kostyantyn KRAVCHENKO		24/9/86	M		(2)	
38	Serhiy KRIVTSOV		15/3/91	D	2		
5	Olexandr KUCHER		22/10/82	D	8	(2)	
9	LUIZ ADRIANO de Souza da Silva	BRA	12/4/87	A	13	(8)	10
99	MARCELO MORENO Martins	BOL	18/6/87	A	10	(8)	5
22	Henrikh MKHITARYAN	ARM	21/1/89	A	12	(5)	3
30	Andriy PYATOV		28/6/84	G	29		
44	Yaroslav RAKYTSKIY		3/8/89	D	21		1
26	Răzvan Dincă RAŢ	ROU	26/5/81	D	15	(2)	
13	Vyacheslav SHEVCHUK		13/5/79	D	10		

33	Darijo SRNA	CRO	1/5/82	M	26	(1)	3
15	Taras STEPANENKO		8/8/89	D	14	(1)	
90	Vitaliy VITSENETS		3/8/90	M	5	(9)	2
10	WILLIAN Borges da Silva	BRA	9/8/88	M	28		3

SC TAVRIYA SIMFEROPOL

Coach – Serhiy Puchkov; (22/9/10) Valeriy Petrov; (8/5/11) (Olexandr Shudryk)

Founded – 1958

Stadium – Lokomotyv (19,978)

MAJOR HONOURS: Ukrainian League – (1) 1992; Ukrainian Cup – (1) 2010.

2010				
10/7	Metalist	h	0-1	
17/7	Dynamo	a	1-2	*Idahor*
24/7	Metalurh Donetsk	h	2-1	*Kovpak, Idahor*
30/7	Vorskla	a	0-0	
8/8	Dnipro	h	0-1	
14/8	Kryvbas	a	4-1	*Kovpak 3, Monakhov*
22/8	Metalurh Zaporizhya	h	2-0	*Holaido, Platon*
29/8	Zorya	a	3-5	*Platon, Idahor 2*
11/9	Arsenal	h	0-1	
19/9	Shakhtar	a	1-4	*Kovpak*
26/9	Karpaty	h	3-1	*Kornev, Idahor 2*
2/10	Volyn	a	2-2	*Idahor 2*
15/10	Illychivets	h	2-2	*Korobka 2*
22/10	Obolon	a	1-2	*Idahor*
31/10	Sevastopol	h	2-1	*Kornev, og (Shandruk)*
7/11	Metalist	a	3-2	*Shinder, Kornev, Donets*
14/11	Dynamo	h	1-1	*Platon*
21/11	Metalurh Donetsk	a	1-2	*Platon*
27/11	Vorskla	h	2-2	*Feshchuk, Idahor*
2011				
6/3	Dnipro	a	2-2	*Platon, Feshchuk*
12/3	Kryvbas	h	2-1	*Shinder 2*
20/3	Metalurh Zaporizhya	a	2-2	*Kablash, Idahor (p)*
2/4	Zorya	h	0-0	
9/4	Arsenal	a	2-1	*Prychynenko 2*
17/4	Shakhtar	h	1-2	*Humenyuk*
23/4	Karpaty	a	0-1	
29/4	Volyn	h	0-0	
8/5	Illychivets	a	1-5	*Idahor*
15/5	Obolon	h	3-1	*Feshchuk 2, Platon*
21/5	Sevastopol	a	1-0	*Idahor*

No	Name	Nat	DoB	Pos	Aps	(s)	Gls
23	Sendley Sidney BITO	ANT	20/7/83	A	1	(1)	
27	Ayodeji Adeniy BROWN	NGA	12/9/88	D	1		
37	Kyrylo DAVYDOV		6/11/88	M		(1)	
4	Andriy DONETS		3/1/81	D	12	(2)	1
28	Maxym FESHCHUK		25/11/85	A	10	(11)	4
19	Illya GALYUZA		16/11/79	M	19	(3)	
20	Vasyl GIGIADZE	GEO	3/6/77	A	8	(14)	
7	Ivan GRAF	CRO	17/6/87	M	7	(1)	
27	Denys HOLAIDO		3/6/84	M	13	(1)	1
30	Oleh HUMENYUK		3/5/83	D	16	(2)	1
10	Lucky Isi IDAHOR	NGA	30/8/80	A	28	(2)	13
6	Saša JURIČIĆ	CRO	1/8/79	D	19	(1)	
29	Olexandr KABLASH		5/9/89	M		(5)	1
1	Damir KAHRIMAN	SRB	19/11/84	G	9	(1)	
17	Nikolai KASHEVSKIY	BLR	5/10/80	M	2		
1	Vasiliy KHOMUTOVSKIY	BLR	30/8/78	G	6	(1)	
8	Andriy KORNEV		1/11/78	M	27		3
14	Volodymyr KOROBKA		22/7/89	D		(13)	2
9	Olexandr KOVPAK		2/2/83	A	12	(2)	5
38	Olexiy KURILOV		24/4/88	D	2		
2	LEANDRO Messias dos Santos	BRA	29/12/83	D	11	(2)	
22	Željko LJUBENOVIĆ	SRB	9/7/81	M	29		
15	Yevhen LUTSENKO		10/11/80	M	2		
5	Slobodan MARKOVIĆ	SRB	9/11/78	D	23	(4)	
18	Ivan MATYAZH		15/2/88	M	2	(3)	
11	Anton MONAKHOV		31/1/82	D	22		1
7	Anton MUKHOVIKOV		20/6/84	M	1	(2)	
24	Ruslan PLATON		12/1/82	A	13	(4)	6
69	Rollan POGORELTSEV		16/7/90	D	2		
21	Vitaliy POSTRANSKIY		2/8/77	G	7		
9	Stanislav PRYCHYNENKO		26/6/91	M	3	(2)	2
17	Anton SHINDER		13/6/87	M	13	(8)	3
1	Maxym STARTSEV		20/1/80	G	1		
12	Dmytro STOIKO		3/2/75	G	7		
23	Matija ŠPIČIĆ	CRO	24/2/88	M	2	(1)	

FC VOLYN LUTSK

Coach – Vitaliy Kvartsyaniy

Founded – 1960

Stadium – Avanhard (10,792)

2010				
10/7	Vorskla	h	0-4	
18/7	Dnipro	a	0-2	
23/7	Kryvbas	h	0-0	
31/7	Metalurh Zaporizhya	a	1-0	*Pavlov*
7/8	Zorya	h	0-1	
15/8	Arsenal	a	1-1	*Pichkur*
21/8	Shakhtar	h	0-1	
30/8	Karpaty	a	0-1	
10/9	Sevastopol	h	1-0	*Maicon*
17/9	Illychivets	h	3-1	*Paraschiv, Maicon, Stević*
26/9	Obolon	a	1-0	*Vashchuk (p)*
2/10	Tavriya	h	2-2	*Butko, Hoshkoderya*
16/10	Metalist	a	1-3	*Pavlov*
24/10	Dynamo	h	1-2	*Skoba*
31/10	Metalurh Donetsk	a	2-0	*Pishchur (p), Paraschiv*
5/11	Vorskla	a	1-0	*Pishchur (p)*
14/11	Dnipro	h	1-1	*Pichkur*
20/11	Kryvbas	a	4-2	*Skoba, Pishchur 2 (1p), Butko*
28/11	Metalurh Zaporizhya	h	1-0	*Pishchur*
2011				
5/3	Zorya	a	0-3	
12/3	Arsenal	h	0-0	
20/3	Shakhtar	a	0-4	
3/4	Karpaty	h	0-3	
9/4	Sevastopol	a	1-4	*Pishchur (p)*
16/4	Illychivets	a	2-2	*Pishchur, Butko*
22/4	Obolon	h	1-0	*Stević*
29/4	Tavriya	a	0-0	
8/5	Metalist	h	1-4	*Pryndeta*
15/5	Dynamo	a	1-5	*Herasymyuk*
21/5	Metalurh Donetsk	h	1-3	*Pishchur*

No	Name	Nat	DoB	Pos	Aps	(s)	Gls
26	Olexiy BABYR		15/3/90	A	3	(6)	
77	Cornel BUTA	ROU	1/11/77	D	13	(3)	
6	Artem BUTENIN		3/10/89	D		(1)	
37	Bohdan BUTKO		13/1/91	M	26	(1)	3
9	Oleh HERASYMYUK		25/9/86	M	13	(5)	1
36	Roman HODOVANIY		4/10/90	M	8		
7	Vitaliy HOSHKODERYA		8/1/88	M	14	(6)	1
29	Andriy HRINCHENKO		23/1/86	D	17		
22	Silviu IZVORANU	ROU	12/3/82	M	9		
28	Roman KARASYUK		27/3/91	M		(1)	
4	Bohdan KARKOVSKIY		29/1/88	D	11		
7	Serhiy KOSTYUK		5/3/86	M		(1)	
37	Volodymyr KOVALYUK		3/3/72	D		(1)	
38	LEOnardo Aleixa da COSTA	BRA	15/4/84	A	1	(2)	
7	Maxym LISOVIY		21/5/85	M	1		
10	Volodymyr LYSENKO		20/4/88	A	3	(4)	
20	MAICON Pereira de Oliveira	BRA	8/5/88	A	14	(1)	2
15	Roman MAXYMYUK		14/6/74	D	7	(9)	
24	Viktor MELNYK		11/8/80	M	1		
1	Issa NDOYE	SEN	12/12/85	G	12		
16	Adrian Constantin NEAGA	ROU	4/6/79	A	3	(1)	
42	Vitaliy NEDILKO		21/8/82	G	18		
41	Harrison OMOKO	NGA	12/12/81	D	10		
34	Sorin Ioan PARASCHIV	ROU	17/6/81	M	6	(5)	2
17	Yevhen PAVLOV		12/3/91	A	13	(7)	2
25	Yevhen PICHKUR		30/8/79	M	12	(15)	2
25	Olexandr PISHCHUR		26/1/81	A	17		8
18	Vitaliy PRYNDETA		2/2/93	M	2	(1)	1
31	Stevan RAČIĆ	SRB	17/1/84	A	4		
5	RAMON LOPES de Freitas	BRA	7/8/89	M	3	(4)	

2	Dmytro SEMOCHKO		25/1/79	D	1		
55	Oleh SHANDRUK		30/1/83	D	1		
20	Vyacheslav SHARPAR		2/6/87	D	15		
3	Serhiy SIMININ		9/10/87	M	13	(3)	
70	Ihor SKOBA		21/5/82	M	9	(1)	2
35	Saša STEVIĆ	SRB	31/5/81	M	21	(1)	2
14	Vladyslav VASHCHUK		2/1/75	D	21	(3)	1
8	Oleh ZHENYUKH		22/3/87	M	2	(3)	
73	Dmytro ZOZULYA		9/6/88	D	6		

FC VORSKLA POLTAVA

Coach – Mykola Pavlov

Founded – 1984

Stadium – Vorskla im. Olexiy Butovskiy (24,795)

MAJOR HONOURS: Ukrainian Cup – (1) 2009.

2010

10/7	Volyn	a	4-0	*Sachko 2, Januzi, Yesin*
17/7	Illychivets	h	1-3	*Sachko*
25/7	Obolon	a	1-0	*Sachko*
30/7	Tavriya	h	0-0	
7/8	Metalist	a	3-2	*Krasnoperov, Selin, Markoski*
14/8	Dynamo	h	3-1	*Sachko, Krasnoperov, Bezus (p)*
21/8	Metalurh Donetsk	a	0-2	
27/8	Sevastopol	a	0-0	
12/9	Dnipro	h	0-2	
18/9	Kryvbas	a	0-1	
26/9	Metalurh Zaporizhya	h	2-1	*Dallku, Bezus*
2/10	Zorya	a	1-1	*Bezus*
17/10	Arsenal	h	0-1	
23/10	Shakhtar	a	0-1	
30/10	Karpaty	h	1-1	*Januzi*
5/11	Volyn	h	0-1	
13/11	Illychivets	a	6-2	*Sachko 3, Markoski, Yesin, Selin*
21/11	Obolon	h	0-1	
27/11	Tavriya	a	2-2	*Chesnakov, Januzi*

2011

5/3	Metalist	h	0-0	
13/3	Dynamo	a	0-2	
18/3	Metalurh Donetsk	h	1-1	*Januzi*
3/4	Sevastopol	h	4-0	*Januzi 2, Kulakov, Sachko*
9/4	Dnipro	a	0-2	
16/4	Kryvbas	h	3-0	*og (Kitsuta), Bezus, Osipenko*
22/4	Metalurh Zaporizhya	a	0-2	
1/5	Zorya	h	1-0	*Sachko*
7/5	Arsenal	a	1-0	*Bezus*
14/5	Shakhtar	h	1-1	*Januzi*
21/5	Karpaty	a	2-2	*Osipenko, Januzi*

No	Name	Nat	DoB	Pos	Aps	(s)	Gls
24	Oleh BARANNYK		20/3/92	A		(1)	
9	Roman BEZUS		26/9/90	M	18	(8)	5
48	Volodymyr CHESNAKOV		12/2/88	D	20	(2)	1
18	Olexiy CHICHIKOV		30/9/87	A		(5)	
4	Armend DALLKU	ALB	16/6/83	D	29		1
1	Serhiy DOLHANSKIY		15/9/74	G	23		
19	Artem GROMOV		14/1/90	M	13	(12)	
27	Ahmed JANUZI	ALB	8/7/88	A	15	(6)	8
27	Maksim KARPOVICH	BLR	27/2/86	M	1	(2)	
5	Oleh KRASNOPEROV		25/7/80	M	29		2
8	Denys KULAKOV		1/5/86	M	30		1
78	Olexiy KURILOV		24/4/88	D	4		
35	Pavlo LESHKO		8/11/87	D	6		
7	Jovan MARKOSKI	SRB	23/6/80	M	29		2
2	Olexandr MATVEYEV		11/2/89	D	1		
25	Hennadiy MEDVEDEV		7/2/75	D	9	(1)	
77	Andriy OBEREMKO		18/3/84	M		(4)	
14	Alexandru ONICA	MDA	29/7/84	M		(4)	
14	Dmitriy OSIPENKO	BLR	12/12/82	A	11		2
13	Yevhen PESKOV		22/9/81	D	12	(4)	
55	Olexandr RYKUN		6/5/78	M	2	(1)	
17	Vasyl SACHKO		3/5/75	A	17	(8)	10
33	Yevhen SELIN		9/5/88	D	29		2
34	Yevhen TKACHUK		27/6/91	D		(1)	
22	Ihor TYMCHENKO		16/1/86	A		(1)	
12	Serhiy VELYCHKO		9/8/76	G	7		
3	Serhiy VOVKODAV		2/7/88	D	5		
37	Hryhoriy YARMASH		4/1/85	D	11	(2)	
70	Dmytro YESIN		15/4/80	M	9	(12)	2

FC ZORYA LUHANSK

Coach – Anatoliy Chantsev

Founded – 1923

Stadium – Avanhard (22,288); Olimpiyskiy, Donetsk (26,100); Stal, Alchevsk (9,200)

MAJOR HONOURS: USSR League – (1) 1972.

2010

9/7	Sevastopol	h	0-0	
18/7	Arsenal	h	0-2	
25/7	Shakhtar	a	0-1	
1/8	Karpaty	h	2-2	*Vitsenets, Sylyuk*
7/8	Volyn	a	1-0	*Kasiyan*
13/8	Illychivets	h	2-2	*Yezerskiy 2*
20/8	Obolon	a	0-1	
29/8	Tavriya	h	5-3	*Lazarovych 2, Vitsenets, Polyanskiy, Kamenyuka*
12/9	Metalist	a	0-3	
19/9	Dynamo	h	1-2	*Biliy*
26/9	Metalurh Donetsk	a	1-1	*Sylyuk*
2/10	Vorskla	h	1-1	*Fomin*
17/10	Dnipro	a	1-1	*Lazarovych*
23/10	Kryvbas	h	1-0	*Yezerskiy*
30/10	Metalurh Zaporizhya	a	0-1	
6/11	Sevastopol	a	1-0	*Fomin*
14/11	Arsenal	a	1-1	*Lazarovych*
20/11	Shakhtar	h	1-3	*Xhihani*
27/11	Karpaty	a	2-4	*Sylyuk, og (Tubić)*

2011

5/3	Volyn	h	3-0	*Lazarovych, Biliy, Kasiyan*
13/3	Illychivets	a	2-2	*Biliy, Polyanskiy*
19/3	Obolon	h	1-0	*Fomin*
2/4	Tavriya	a	0-0	
8/4	Metalist	h	0-2	
18/4	Dynamo	a	0-2	
24/4	Metalurh Donetsk	h	0-2	
1/5	Vorskla	a	0-1	
7/5	Dnipro	h	0-1	
15/5	Kryvbas	a	2-0	*Polyanskiy, Khomchenovskiy*
21/5	Metalurh Zaporizhya	h	0-2	

No	Name	Nat	DoB	Pos	Aps	(s)	Gls
20	Daniel ADDO	GHA	3/8/89	D	4		
33	Maxym BILIY		27/4/89	A	28	(1)	3
5	Mihajlo CAKIĆ	SRB	31/7/84	D	1	(3)	
10	Ihor CHAIKOVSKIY		7/10/91	M	14		
19	Ruslan FOMIN		2/3/86	A	11	(3)	3
6	Mykyta KAMENYUKA		3/6/85	M	30		1
91	Yehor KARTUSHOV		5/1/91	A	5	(7)	
9	Olexandr KASIYAN		27/1/89	A	11	(10)	2
37	Dmytro KHOMCHENOVSKIY		16/4/90	M	4	(4)	1
4	Maxym KOVALEV		20/3/89	M	20	(5)	
48	Mykyta KYSLIY		2/3/91	A		(1)	
27	Taras LAZAROVYCH		22/4/82	A	28	(2)	5
10	Jaba LIPARTIA	GEO	16/11/87	A	11		
39	Franck Olivier MADOU	CIV	15/9/87	A	2	(7)	
1	Yuriy MARTYSHCHUK		22/4/86	G	7	(1)	
22	Vadym MILKO		22/8/86	M	1	(9)	
2	Stanislav MYKYTSEI		7/9/89	D	12	(1)	
3	Olexiy POLYANSKIY		12/4/86	M	29		3
7	Artem SEMENENKO		2/9/88	M	7	(5)	
11	Serhiy SHEVCHUK		18/6/85	D	5	(8)	
99	Ihor SHUKHOVTSEV		13/7/71	G	16		
35	Bohdan SHUST		4/3/86	G	7		
44	Serhiy SYLYUK		5/6/85	A	17	(4)	3
10	Lukáš TESÁK	SVK	8/3/85	D	18	(3)	
23	Vitaliy VITSENETS		3/8/90	M	6	(1)	2
14	Parid XHIHANI	ALB	18/7/83	M	1	(2)	1
16	Hryhoriy YARMASH		4/1/85	M	4	(1)	
15	Roman YEMELYANOV	RUS	8/5/92	M	12	(2)	
5	Volodymyr YEZERSKIY		15/11/76	D	19	(1)	3

TOP GOALSCORERS 2010/11

17 Yevhen SELEZNEV (Dnipro)

14 Marko DEVIĆ (Metalist)

13 Lucky IDAHOR (Tavriya)

12 Denys OLIYNYK (Metalist)

11 Andriy YARMOLENKO (Dynamo)

10 Andriy SHEVCHENKO (Dynamo)
Olexiy ANTONOV (Illichyvets)
Kostyantyn YAROSHENKO (Illichyvets)
LUIZ ADRIANO (Shakhtar)
Vasyl SACHKO (Vorskla)

PROMOTED CLUBS

PFC OLEXANDRIYA

Coach – Volodymyr Sharan
Founded – 1991
Stadium – KSK Nika (7,000)

FC CHORNOMORETS ODESA

Coach – Ihor Nakonechniy; (16/11/10) Roman Hryhorchuk
Founded – 1958
Stadium – Chornomorets (20,836)
MAJOR HONOURS: Ukrainian Cup - (2) 1992, 1994.

SECOND LEVEL FINAL TABLE 2010/11

		Pld	W	D	L	F	A	Pts
1	PFC Olexandriya	34	21	6	7	55	25	69
2	FC Chornomorets Odesa	34	18	11	5	53	26	65
3	FC Stal Alchevsk	34	18	8	8	55	31	62
4	FC Krymteplytsya Molodizhne	34	18	7	9	43	30	61
5	FC Lviv	34	17	8	9	52	28	59
6	FC Zakarpattya Uzhhorod	34	16	8	10	51	40	56
7	FC Bukovyna Chernivtsiy	34	17	5	12	48	45	56
8	FC Dynamo-2 Kyiv	34	15	7	12	39	35	52
9	FC Arsenal Bila Tserkva	34	15	6	13	42	43	51
10	PFC Nyva Vinnytsya	34	14	8	12	44	42	50
11	FC Tytan Armyansk	34	13	5	16	32	42	44
12	FC Zirka Kirovohrad	34	12	7	15	43	44	43
13	FC Dnister Ovidiopol	34	10	12	12	39	42	42
14	FC Naftovyk-Ukrnafta Okhtyrka	34	10	11	13	40	44	41
15	FC Helios Kharkiv	34	10	10	14	31	44	40
16	FC Enerhetyk Burshtyn	34	10	6	18	29	49	36
17	FC Prykarpattya Ivano-Frankivsk	34	5	1	28	27	82	16
18	FC Feniks-Illychivets Kalinino	34	3	2	29	17	48	8

NB FC Feniks-Illychivets Kalinino withdrew after round 20 – their remaining matches were awarded as goalless defeats; FC Feniks-Illychivets Kalinino – 3 pts deducted.

DOMESTIC CUP 2010/11

KUBOK UKRAÏNY

THIRD ROUND

(21/9/10)
Karpaty Yaremche 4, Volyn Lutsk 5

(22/9/10)
Chornomorets Odesa 1, Vorskla Poltava 2 *(aet)*
Dnipro Dnipropetrovsk 4, Tavriya Simferopol 1
Hirnyk-Sport Komsomolsk 0, Karpaty Lviv 5
Krymteplytsya Molodizhne 0, Dynamo Kyiv 1
Kremin Kremenchuk 1, Shakhtar Sverdlovsk 0
Metalist Kharkiv 1, Arsenal Kyiv 2
Metalurh Zaporizhya 1, Illychivets Mariupil 0
PFC Olexandriya 0, Metalurh Donetsk 0 *(aet; 5-3 on pens)*
FC Poltava 2, Obolon Kyiv 1 *(aet)*
Prykarpattya Ivano-Frankivsk 0, Zorya Luhansk 1
Shakhtar Donetsk 6, Kryvbas Kryvyi Rih 0
Stal Alchevsk 3, Arsenal Bila Tserkva 1
Stal Dniprodzerzhynsk 1, Feniks-Illichivets Kalinino 1 *(aet; 5-6 on pens)*
Tytan Armyansk 0, PFC Sevastopol 3
Yednist Plysky 0, Naftovyk-Ukrnafta Okhtyrka 1

FOURTH ROUND

(27/10/10)
Feniks-Illychivets Kalinino 1, Metalurh Zaporizhya 2
Karpaty Lviv 3, Vorskla Poltava 0
Kremin Kremenchuk 0, Dnipro Dnipropetrovsk 3
Naftovyk-Ukrnafta Okhtyrka 0, Zorya Luhansk 1
PFC Olexandriya 1, Arsenal Kyiv 2
FC Poltava 0, Shakhtar Donetsk 2
PFC Sevastopol 1, Dynamo Kyiv 2
Stal Alchevsk 1, Volyn Lutsk 0

QUARTER-FINALS

(10/11/10)
Karpaty Lviv 0, Arsenal Kyiv 2 *(Samodin 7, Gusev 82)*
Shakhtar Donetsk 1 *(Teiku 14og)*, Metalurh Zaporizhya 0
Stal Alchevsk 2 *(Shevchenko 44, Loktionov 90+2)*, Dynamo Kyiv 3 *(Milevskiy 49, 60, Odintsov 54og)*
Zorya Luhansk 1 *(Polyanskiy 36)*, Dnipro Dnipropetrovsk 1 *(Hladkiy 75) (aet; 4-5 on pens)*

SEMI-FINALS

(11/5/11)
Dynamo Kyiv 2 *(Yarmolenko 10, Shevchenko 51)*, Arsenal Kyiv 0
Shakhtar Donetsk 2 *(Willian 15, Alex Teixeira 25)*, Dnipro Dnipropetrovsk 1 *(Hübschman 63og)*

FINAL

(25/5/11)
Yuvileyniy stadium, Sumy
FC SHAKHTAR DONETSK 2 *(Eduardo 64, Luiz Adriano 87)*
FC DYNAMO KYIV 0
Referee – *Shvetsov*
SHAKHTAR – *Pyatov, Srna, Rakytskiy, Shevchuk, Kucher, Hübschman, Willian (Alex Teixeira 78), Jádson (Mkhitaryan 80), Fernandinho, Eduardo, Luiz Adriano (Douglas Costa 90+5).*
Sent off: *Eduardo (75)*
DYNAMO KYIV – *Shovkovskiy, Danilo Silva (Betão 57), Khacheridi, Popov, Gusev, Yussuf, Vukojević, Yarmolenko, Eremenko (Aliyev 69), Milevskiy, Shevchenko.*
Sent off: *Betão (85)*

CLUB COMMUNICATION 2011/12

FC Arsenal Kyiv
14/1 Mechnikova str., NSK Olimpiyskiy
UA-01133 Kyiv

Tel	+380 44 246 4505
Fax	+380 44 246 4505
Web	fcarsenal.com.ua
Email	office@fcarsenal.com.ua
Media Officer	Volodymyr Katsman

FC Chornomorets Odesa
Gagarin Avenue 12A, Chornomorets stadium, UA-65039 Odesa

Tel	+380 48 719 8608
Fax	+380 48 719 8606
Web	chernomorets.odessa.ua
Email	fc@chernomorets.odessa.ua
Media Officer	Serguei Martynov

FC Dnipro Dnipropetrovsk
Pionerskiy lane, 12
UA-49000 Dnipropetrovsk

Tel	+380 562 34 29 89
Fax	+380 562 34 29 90
Web	fcdnipro.ua
Email	fcdnipro@a-teleport.com
Media Officer	Dmitryi Pelin

FC Dynamo Kyiv
M. Grushevskogo Street 3
UA-01001 Kyiv

Tel	+380 44 597 0008
Fax	+380 44 278 4135
Web	fcdynamo.kiev.ua
Email	alina@goal.com.ua
Media Officer	Aleksey Semenenko

FC Illychivets Mariupil
45-A Evpatoriyska Street, Illychivets stadium, UA-87515 Mariupil

Tel	+380 629 474 443
Fax	+380 629 534 486
Web	fcilich.com
Email	fcmm@fcilyich.com.ua
Media Officer	Dmytro Ostronos

FC Karpaty Lviv
1 B. Yanusha Str., Ukrayina stadium
UA-79000 Lviv

Tel	+380 32 298 8410
Fax	+380 32 297 6663
Web	fckarpaty.lviv.ua
Email	net@fckarpaty.lviv.ua
Media Officer	Youry Nazarkevytch

FC Kryvbas Kryvyi Rih
Metalurhiv av. 5, Metalurh stadium
UA-50006 Kryvyi Rih

Tel	+380 564 047 000
Fax	+380 564 047 000
Web	fckryvbas.com.ua
Email	fck@ukrpost.ua
Media Officer	Grygory Turenko

FC Metalist Kharkiv
Plekhanovskaya Street, 65, Metalist
UA-61001 Kharkiv

Tel	+380 57 763 2309
Fax	+380 57 737 2374
Web	metalist.ua
Email	info@metallist.kharkov.ua
Media Officer	Maksym Sukachov

FC Metalurh Donetsk
Kuybyshev Street 25a
UA-83062 Donetsk

Tel	+380 62 385 0488
Fax	+380 62 385 0486
Web	metallurg.donetsk.ua
Email	postmaster@metallurg.donetsk.ua
Media Officer	Aleksey Klykov

FC Obolon Kyiv
8 Pivnichna Str., NSC Olimpiyskiy stadium
UA-04214 Kyiv

Tel	+380 44 411 3910
Fax	+380 44 411 2051
Web	fc.obolon.ua
Email	fcobolon@kiev.obolon.ua
Media Officer	Vitaliy Mylnychuk

PFC Olexandriya
Stroiteley ave. 39
UA-28000 Olexandriya

Tel	+380 5235 90 909
Fax	+380 5235 90 909
Web	pfcalexandria.com.ua
Email	pfc-alexandria@rambler.ru
Media Officer	Bilanyuk Yuriy

FC Shakhtar Donetsk
Artema Street 86A
UA-83050 Donetsk

Tel	+380 623 870 102
Fax	+380 623 870 104
Web	shakhtar.com
Email	feedback@shakhtar.com
Media Officer	Ruslan Marmazov

SC Tavriya Simferopol
Pushkina Street 46, Lokomotyv stadium
UA-95011 Simferopol

Tel	+380 652 548 501
Fax	+380 652 255 383
Web	sctavriya.com
Email	sc@sctavriya.com
Media Officer	Borys Levin

SC Volyn Lutsk
7-A, Peremogy Av., Avangard satdium
UA-43005 Lutsk

Tel	+380 332 240 557
Fax	+380 332 405 57
Web	fcvolyn.com
Email	fvolyn@lt.uktel.net
Media Officer	Anton Zelep

FC Vorskla Poltava
Nezalezhnosti Sq.16, Poltava City
Vorskla stadium, UA-36000 Poltava

Tel	+380 53 222 1670
Fax	+380 53 222 4833
Web	vorskla.com.ua
Email	fc_vorskla@poltava.ukrtel.net
Media Officer	Artyom Lobanov

FC Zorya Luhansk
Oboronnaya str., 4 V
UA-91011 Luhansk

Tel	+380 642 536 345
Fax	+380 642 536 345
Web	zarya-lugansk.com
Email	fc@zarya-lugansk.com
Media Officer	Andrey Kolot

WALES

Pays de Galles I Wales

Cymdeithas Bêl-droed Cymru / Football Association of Wales (FAW)

COMMUNICATION

Address 11/12 Neptune Court, Vanguard Way, GB-Cardiff CF24 5PJ

Tel +44 29 2043 5830

Fax +44 29 2049 6953

E-mail info@faw.org.uk

Website faw.org.uk

President Phil Pritchard

General Secretary Jonathan Ford

Media Officer Ceri Stennett

Year of Formation 1876

National Stadium Millennium Stadium, Cardiff (72,500)

DOMESTIC COMPETITION SUMMARY 2010/11

WELSH PREMIER LEAGUE FINAL TABLE

SECOND PHASE

Championship Pool		Pld	Home W	Home D	Home L	Home F	Home A	Away W	Away D	Away L	Away F	Away A	Total W	Total D	Total L	Total F	Total A	Pts	Comp
1	Bangor City FC	32	12	1	3	51	21	10	3	3	29	23	22	4	6	80	44	70	UCL
2	The New Saints FC	32	13	2	1	57	15	7	6	3	30	19	20	8	4	87	34	68	UEL
3	Neath FC	32	7	6	3	27	18	9	4	3	35	23	16	10	6	62	41	58	UEL
4	Llanelli AFC	32	8	3	5	32	25	7	5	4	26	16	15	8	9	58	41	53	UEL
5	Prestatyn Town FC	32	6	7	3	22	14	4	3	9	22	32	10	10	12	44	46	40	
6	Port Talbot Town FC	32	4	5	7	18	19	4	7	5	19	29	8	12	12	37	48	36	

Relegation Pool		Pld	Home W	Home D	Home L	Home F	Home A	Away W	Away D	Away L	Away F	Away A	Total W	Total D	Total L	Total F	Total A	Pts	Comp
7	Aberystwyth Town FC	32	6	5	5	21	23	5	4	7	21	31	11	9	12	42	54	42	
8	Airbus UK Broughton FC	32	5	6	5	33	26	6	2	8	20	26	11	8	13	53	52	41	
9	Newtown AFC	32	4	7	5	18	21	4	4	8	22	34	8	11	13	40	55	35	
10	Carmarthen Town AFC	32	5	2	9	22	30	5	3	8	17	34	10	5	17	39	64	35	
11	Bala Town FC	32	6	1	9	24	25	4	2	10	17	32	10	3	19	41	57	33	
12	Haverfordwest County AFC	32	3	1	12	17	34	2	3	11	13	43	5	4	23	30	77	19	*Relegated*

NB League split into top and bottom halves after First Phase of 22 games, with each team playing a further ten matches (home and away) exclusively against clubs from its half of the table.

Top Scorer Rhys Griffiths (Llanelli), 25 goals

Promoted Club Afan Lido FC

Cup Final Llanelli AFC 4, Bangor City FC 1

Bangor take title in last-day showdown

A new, streamlined Welsh Premier League, reduced from 18 participants to 12 and split into two phases, delivered the climax its planners can only have dreamed of when the championship was decided on the final day in a head-to-head clash between the two title contenders.

For much of the season the title race appeared to be a non-event as cup specialists Bangor City FC, without a league crown since 1995, tore out of the traps and won their first 15 matches. It was a phenomenal start, but even when the team shed their first points, with a 1-1 draw at Airbus UK Broughton FC just before Christmas, their 15-point advantage over defending champions and closest pursuers The New Saints FC looked unbreachable.

Form slide

Come the New Year, however, and Bangor's form suddenly began to evaporate. The sale of their leading marksman, goal-a-game Jamie Reed, to York City FC stalled their momentum and in a grim streak during March and early April that coincided with the start of the championship's second phase they hit the wall completely, taking just two points from six games, the last of them a horrendous 5-2 home defeat by Llanelli AFC. Six points ahead of TNS going into the second phase, Bangor now found themselves four points behind with just three games to go.

Craig Garside scored Bangor's title-clinching winner against TNS on the final day of the season

TNS, on a 22-match unbeaten run, were now firm favourites to land a sixth Premier League title, but another remarkable twist to the title race was just around the corner. Undefeated in 40 home matches, TNS hosted Neath FC on Good Friday seeking to consolidate their advantage, but the visitors grabbed a sensational 3-2 win. With Bangor then ending their winless run at Port Talbot Town FC the following day, the title was once again up for grabs. Both challengers claimed victories on Easter Monday, Bangor at Neath (2-1) and TNS at home to Llanelli (3-1), which left the perfect scenario for the final day – a showdown at Bangor's Farrar Road ground in which the home side needed a win and the visitors only a point.

Garside pounces

It was a tense, keenly contested encounter, but Bangor, backed by a capacity crowd of almost 2,000, eventually won the game – and the title – when midfielder Craig Garside, who had scored both goals in the win at Neath, pounced midway through the second half. City's first title in 16 years also earned them qualification for the UEFA Champions League for the first time.

That was not the end of the season for either side. Just two days later TNS travelled down the Welsh coast to meet Llanelli in the League Cup final in Aberystwyth, where they bounced back with a dramatic 4-3 extra-time win. Six days later Llanelli were in action again, in the final of the Welsh Cup, staged in their home town at the local rugby stadium, Parc-y-Scarlets. Bangor were seeking to win the trophy for a fourth successive year – all of them under manager Nev Powell – but their 22-match unbeaten run in the competition came to grief against a hyper-motivated Llanelli side, who romped home 4-1 to deny their opponents the double and lift the Welsh Cup for the first time.

Unsurprisingly, two of Llanelli's goals were scored by resident marksman Rhys Griffiths, who, with 25 in 28 league appearances, scooped the Golden Boot for a remarkable sixth successive season. The 31-year-old part-timer, a fireman by trade, was also voted player of the season. Less predictable was the qualification of Neath for the UEFA Europa League, the Eagles earning a passport to Europe for the first time after winning the new end-of-season play-offs. Five teams were involved, with Andy Dyer's side making the most of home advantage to claim the prize with successive victories over Aberystwyth Town FC (2-1) and Prestatyn Town FC (3-2).

There were even bigger celebrations just down the road from Neath a few days later when Swansea City AFC defeated Reading FC at Wembley Stadium to become the first Welsh club to win promotion to the English Premier League. Their play-off victory was all the sweeter for the fact that their great rivals Cardiff City FC had lost to Reading in the semi-finals.

Speed appointed

Swansea's success provided Welsh football with a timely boost at the end of a season in which the national team went through three managers and failed to collect a point from their opening four UEFA EURO 2012 qualifiers. John Toshack stood down after an opening loss in Montenegro, to be replaced temporarily by Under-21 boss Brian Flynn, who oversaw further defeats against Bulgaria and Switzerland. The job was then handed on a permanent basis to Gary Speed, a novice in management but a former Welsh international midfielder of some pedigree.

The size of Speed's task was made apparent when Wales lost their first three matches under his command, including the big EURO qualifier in the Millennium Stadium at home to England, but a win did finally arrive in Wales' last game of the Nations Cup tournament in Dublin when goals from Aaron Ramsey – fast-tracked to the captaincy at the age of 20 – and Robert Earnshaw brought a 2-0 victory over Northern Ireland. For each of his first four matches Speed was denied the services of Welsh football's great hope for the future – Tottenham Hotspur FC wing wizard Gareth Bale, who, thanks largely to a magnificent debut season in the UEFA Champions League, was voted Player of the Year by his fellow professionals in England.

National Team

International Tournament Appearances – FIFA World Cup – (1) 1958 (qtr-finals).

Top Five All-time Caps – Neville Southall (92); Gary Speed (85); Dean Saunders (75); Peter Nicholas & Ian Rush (73)

Top Five All-time Goals – Ian Rush (28); Ivor Allchurch & Trevor Ford (23); Dean Saunders (22); Craig Bellamy (18)

Gary Speed – the new manager of Wales

NATIONAL TEAM RESULTS 2010/11

11/8/10	Luxembourg	H	Llanelli	5-1	*Cotterill (34), Ledley (47p), King (55), Williams (78), Bellamy (82)*
3/9/10	Montenegro (ECQ)	A	Podgorica	0-1	
8/10/10	Bulgaria (ECQ)	H	Cardiff	0-1	
12/10/10	Switzerland (ECQ)	A	Basel	1-4	*Bale (13)*
8/02/11	Republic of Ireland	A	Dublin	0-3	
26/3/11	England (ECQ)	H	Cardiff	0-2	
25/5/11	Scotland	N	Dublin (IRL)	1-3	*Earnshaw (36)*
27/5/11	Northern Ireland	N	Dublin (IRL)	2-0	*Ramsey (35), Earnshaw (68)*

NATIONAL TEAM APPEARANCES 2010/11

			Lux	MNE	BUL	SUI	Irl	ENG	Sco	Nir	Caps	Goals
Coach – John TOSHACK	**22/3/49**											
/(13/9/10) (Brian FLYNN)	**12/10/55**											
/(14/12/10) Gary SPEED	**8/9/69**											
Wayne HENNESSEY	24/1/87	Wolves (ENG)	G46	G	G	G	G	G		G74	32	-
Chris GUNTER	21/7/89	Nottingham Forest (ENG)	D	D	D 93*		s46	D	s46	D	29	-
Craig MORGAN	18/6/85	Preston (ENG)	D	s75					D		23	-
Ashley WILLIAMS	23/8/84	Swansea	D85	D	D	D		D			25	1
Sam RICKETTS	11/10/81	Bolton (ENG)	D	D	D		D82				42	-
Brian STOCK	24/12/81	Doncaster (ENG)	M46								3	-
Steve MORISON	29/8/83	Millwall (ENG)	M	A78	A82	s77		A65	s72	A80	7	-
Joe LEDLEY	23/1/87	Celtic (SCO)	M	M	M59		s60	M			37	3
David COTTERILL	4/12/87	Swansea	M82						s60	M	19	1
Craig BELLAMY	13/7/79	Man. City (ENG) /Cardiff	A	M				M		A61	62	18
Robert EARNSHAW	6/4/81	Nottingham Forest (ENG)	A46	s68			A79		A	s61	54	16
Boaz MYHILL	9/11/82	West Brom (ENG)	s46						G		10	-
Andy KING	29/10/88	Leicester (ENG)	s46		s59	M	M	M65	M61		9	1
David VAUGHAN	18/2/83	Blackpool (ENG)	s46	M	M	M89	M60	s65	s72	M	25	1
Andrew CROFTS	29/5/84	Norwich (ENG)	s82			M	M	M			17	-
Neal EARDLEY	6/11/88	Blackpool (ENG)	s85				D46		D61		16	-
James COLLINS	23/8/83	Aston Villa (ENG)		D75	D	D	D	D			39	2
David EDWARDS	3/2/86	Wolves (ENG)		M68	M69	M77					22	3
Gareth BALE	16/7/89	Tottenham (ENG)		M	M	M					27	3
Simon CHURCH	12/12/88	Reading (ENG)		s78	s69	A	A				12	1
Danny COLLINS	6/8/80	Stoke (ENG)			D	D	D	D		D	12	-
Hal ROBSON-KANU	21/5/89	Reading (ENG)			s82		M67				3	-
Darcy BLAKE	13/12/88	Cardiff				D54			D		2	-
Christian RIBEIRO	14/12/89	Bristol City (ENG)				s54					2	-
Shaun MacDONALD	17/6/88	Swansea				s89					1	-
Freddy EASTWOOD	29/10/83	Coventry (ENG)					s67				11	4
Jermaine EASTER	15/1/82	Crystal Palace (ENG)					s79		A		10	-
Lewin NYATANGA	18/8/88	Bristol City (ENG)					s82				34	-
Aaron RAMSEY	26/12/90	Arsenal (ENG)						M	s61	M89	14	3
Ched EVANS	28/12/88	Sheffield United (ENG)						s65			13	1
Neil TAYLOR	7/2/89	Swansea							D46	D72	3	-
Owain TUDUR-JONES	15/10/84	Norwich (ENG)							M72	s61	6	-
Andy DORMAN	1/5/82	Crystal Palace (ENG)							M60	s89	3	-
Sam VOKES	21/10/89	Wolves (ENG)							M72	s80	18	2
Adam MATTHEWS	13/1/92	Cardiff							s61	s72	2	-
Danny GABBIDON	8/8/79	West Ham (ENG)								D	44	-
Jack COLLISON	2/10/88	West Ham (ENG)								M61	8	-
Lewis PRICE	19/7/84	Crystal Palace (ENG)								s74	8	-

CLUB-BY-CLUB

ABERYSTWYTH TOWN FC

Manager – Alan Morgan
Founded – 1884
Stadium – Park Avenue (3,000)
MAJOR HONOURS: Welsh Cup – (1) 1900.

2010

14/8	Carmarthen	a	3-2	*Edwards, Marriott, Evans*
20/8	Newtown	h	2-2	*Evans (p), Sherbon*
28/8	Airbus	a	1-3	*Thomas*
4/9	Prestatyn	h	1-0	*McCarten*
10/9	Port Talbot	a	1-1	*Murtagh*
18/9	Neath	h	1-1	*Sherbon*
26/9	Bangor	a	1-2	*Edwards*
2/10	Bala	h	2-1	*Codling, Evans (p)*
10/10	TNS	a	0-5	
15/10	Llanelli	a	3-2	*Williams, Evans (p), Codling*
22/10	Carmarthen	h	2-2	*Edwards, Codling*
31/10	Newtown	a	0-0	
20/11	Prestatyn	a	0-4	
26/11	Port Talbot	h	2-2	*Codling 2*
11/12	Bangor	h	1-3	*Evans*

2011

1/1	Haverfordwest	h	0-2	
8/1	TNS	h	0-2	
11/1	Airbus	h	2-1	*Evans 2*
15/1	Llanelli	h	0-2	
21/1	Bala	a	3-2	*Stott 2, Evans*
30/1	Neath	a	1-1	*Evans (p)*
12/2	Haverfordwest	a	0-0	
18/2	Bala	h	1-2	*Stott*
4/3	Airbus	a	3-5	*Codling 2, Edwards*
11/3	Haverfordwest	h	2-1	*Evans 2 (1p)*
18/3	Newtown	h	2-2	*Evans (p), Stott*
25/3	Carmarthen	a	1-0	*Codling*
1/4	Bala	a	1-2	*Stott*
10/4	Airbus	h	2-0	*McCarten, Morgan B.*
15/4	Haverfordwest	a	3-1	*Finselbach 2, Stott*
23/4	Newtown	a	0-1	
30/4	Carmarthen	h	1-0	*Davies*

Name	Nat	DoB	Pos	Aps	(s)	Gls
Steve CANN		20/1/88	G	32		
Lewis CODLING	ENG	1/11/90	A	27	(2)	8
Cledan DAVIES		10/3/90	M	2	(5)	1
Steffan EDWARDS		10/10/89	M	17	(13)	4
Ricky EVANS		29/4/76	M	30	(1)	12
Anthony FINSELBACH		5/1/91	M	15	(9)	2
Michael HOWARD	ENG	2/12/78	M	29	(1)	
Gareth HUGHES		8/1/81	D	21		
Sion JAMES		3/2/80	D	21	(5)	
Ryan MARRIOTT	ENG	18/11/88	A	4	(4)	1
James McCARTEN	ENG	8/11/90	D	29	(3)	2
Bari MORGAN		13/8/80	M	18	(3)	1
Richard MORGAN		14/2/78	M		(1)	
Conall MURTAGH	NIR	29/6/85	M	20	(5)	1
Adam PEPPER	ENG	2/12/91	A	17	(6)	
Luke POWELL	ENG	2/11/90	A	1	(5)	
Luke SHERBON	ENG	6/6/86	M	15		2
Ashley STOTT	ENG	14/6/88	M	13	(1)	6
Aneurin THOMAS		27/1/73	D	16	(8)	1
Craig WILLIAMS		21/12/87	D	25	(3)	1

AIRBUS UK BROUGHTON FC

Manager – Craig Harrison (ENG); (25/3/11) Darren Ryan
Founded – 1946
Stadium – The Airfield (3,000)

2010

15/8	Llanelli	h	1-2	*Desormeaux*
21/8	Carmarthen	a	4-1	*Edwards (p), Desormeaux, Moran 2*
28/8	Aberystwyth	h	3-1	*Moran (p), Owen, Allen*
4/9	Port Talbot	h	2-0	*Moran (p), Owen*
10/9	Bangor	a	1-5	*Rushton*
17/9	TNS	h	2-2	*og (Evans), Allen (p)*
25/9	Haverfordwest	a	0-4	
10/10	Prestatyn	a	1-1	*McManus*
17/10	Neath	h	2-2	*Moran (p), Cook*
20/10	Newtown	h	1-1	*Moran*
24/10	Llanelli	a	1-1	*Rushton*
30/10	Carmarthen	h	2-4	*Rushton, Moran*
20/11	Port Talbot	a	0-2	
4/12	TNS	a	0-2	
11/12	Haverfordwest	h	4-0	*Rushton, McManus, Moran (p), Rowlands*
14/12	Bangor	h	1-1	*Moran*

2011

2/1	Bala	a	2-1	*Owen, Feliciello*
7/1	Prestatyn	h	3-4	*Hope, Moran, Sheridan*
11/1	Aberystwyth	a	1-2	*Moran*
15/1	Neath	a	0-1	
29/1	Newtown	a	3-2	*Sheridan, McCready, McManus*
5/2	Bala	h	1-2	*McCready*
19/2	Carmarthen	a	2-1	*Edwards, Cadwallader*
4/3	Aberystwyth	h	5-3	*Desormeaux, og (Evans), Sheridan 2, Nash*
11/3	Bala	a	3-0	*og (Kelly), Sheridan, Allen*
20/3	Haverfordwest	h	5-0	*Sheridan 3, Clarke, Hope*
25/3	Newtown	a	0-1	
2/4	Carmarthen	h	0-0	
10/4	Aberystwyth	a	0-2	
15/4	Bala	h	1-1	*Sheridan*
23/4	Haverfordwest	a	2-0	*Sheridan, McManus*
30/4	Newtown	h	0-3	

Name	Nat	DoB	Pos	Aps	(s)	Gls
Jack ABRAHAM	ENG	2/10/90	M	5		
Mark ALLEN	ENG	2/9/76	D	28	(3)	3
Niki-Lee BULMER	ENG	6/9/91	G	10		
Gavin CADWALLADER		18/4/86	D	13		1
Danny CALVERT	ENG	19/4/91	D		(1)	
Phil CLARKE	ENG	20/10/88	D	21	(2)	1
Leon CLOWES		27/2/92	D	19	(2)	
Matthew COOK		7/9/85	M	12	(5)	1
James DAVIES	ENG	27/10/93	D	1		
Danny DESORMEAUX	ENG	15/5/84	M	29	(1)	3
Richie DORMAN	ENG	14/6/88	M	14	(6)	
Ryan EDWARDS		22/6/88	D	27		2
Giovanni FELICIELLO	ENG	21/11/89	D	10	(5)	1
Asa HAMILTON		21/1/92	M		(6)	
Callum HAWTHORNE	ENG	18/9/89	G	5		
Eddie HOPE	ENG	3/9/86	M	16		2
John LEAH	ENG	3/8/78	M	4	(2)	
Craig MAYERS	ENG	22/11/86	A		(1)	
Tom McCREADY	ENG	7/6/91	A	5		2
Paul McMANUS	ENG	22/4/90	A	15	(10)	4
Andy MORAN	ENG	7/10/79	A	18	(4)	11
Rhys NASH		8/3/93	M	1	(7)	1
Carl OWEN		9/4/80	A	13	(1)	3
Josh PARRY		1/12/88	M	1	(1)	
Rhys ROBERTS		17/7/85	D	1		
Kristian ROGERS		2/6/73	G	17		
Tom ROWLANDS		28/10/85	A	1	(2)	1
Nick RUSHTON		3/2/92	A	18	(11)	4
Ian SHERIDAN	ENG	12/3/89	A	14	(1)	10
Jamie SMITH	ENG	17/9/74	M		(2)	
Simon SMITH	ENG	5/7/90	M	2	(5)	
Ashley WILLIAMS	ENG	8/10/87	M	15	(1)	
Matty WOODWARD	ENG	14/6/83	D	17	(3)	

BALA TOWN FC

Manager – Colin Caton
Founded – 1880
Stadium – Maes Tegid (2,000)

2010				
15/8	Port Talbot	a	0-2	
21/8	Bangor	h	2-3	*Mason, Fisher N.*
29/8	TNS	a	1-2	*Jones*
5/9	Haverfordwest	h	0-1	
11/9	Newtown	a	1-1	*MacAuley*
17/9	Prestatyn	h	2-1	*MacAuley, Irving*
26/9	Neath	a	1-3	*Mason*
2/10	Aberystwyth	a	1-2	*Mason*
9/10	Llanelli	h	1-0	*Mason*
16/10	Carmarthen	a	1-4	*Jones*
24/10	Port Talbot	h	0-0	
29/10	Bangor	a	0-3	
12/11	TNS	h	3-4	*Kelly, MacAuley 2 (1p)*
20/11	Haverfordwest	a	1-0	*Mason*
12/12	Neath	h	0-2	
2011				
2/1	Airbus	h	1-2	*MacAuley (p)*
5/1	Newtown	h	4-1	*MacAuley (p), Mason, Jones 2*
8/1	Llanelli	a	1-3	*Jefferies*
11/1	Prestatyn	a	0-2	
21/1	Aberystwyth	h	2-3	*Williams, Jones*
25/1	Carmarthen	h	1-2	*Mason*
5/2	Airbus	a	2-1	*Hayes, Mason*
18/2	Aberystwyth	a	2-1	*Jones, Mason*
4/3	Newtown	h	0-2	
11/3	Airbus	h	0-3	
19/3	Carmarthen	a	1-3	*Jefferies*
27/3	Haverfordwest	a	3-2	*Mason, Hayes 2*
1/4	Aberystwyth	h	2-1	*Connolly 2*
9/4	Newtown	a	1-2	*Mason (p)*
15/4	Airbus	a	1-1	*Connolly*
24/4	Carmarthen	h	4-0	*Kelly, Hayes 2, Marriott*
30/4	Haverfordwest	h	2-0	*Jones, Connolly (p)*

Name	Nat	DoB	Pos	Aps	(s)	Gls
Leon BIMPSON	ENG	16/6/77	G	13		
Marc CONNOLLY	ENG	2/7/84	D	10		4
Gethin EDWARDS		14/1/84	D		(1)	
Paul ENNIS	ENG	1/2/90	M	12	(2)	
Robert EVANS		24/1/89	M	4	(9)	
Neil FISHER	ENG	8/7/83	A	3	(2)	1
Steven FISHER	ENG	19/6/73	D	7		
Mike HAYES	ENG	21/11/87	A	17		5
John IRVING	ENG	17/9/88	D	31		1
Ross JEFFERIES		5/8/79	A	23	(3)	2
Danny JELLICOE		27/9/76	D	20		
Mark JONES		15/8/84	M	31		7
Shaun KELLY	ENG	11/12/88	D	24	(1)	2
Steve LEWIS	ENG	10/11/87	A	2	(1)	
Gethin LLOYD		14/11/83	M	16	(1)	
Josh MacAULAY	ENG	2/3/91	A	16	(9)	6
Ryan MARRIOTT	ENG	18/11/88	A	7	(6)	1
Chris MASON	ENG	28/11/90	A	26	(3)	11
Terry McCORMICK	ENG	25/8/83	G	15		
Steve MORRISON	ENG	10/9/88	A	12	(10)	
Mark POWELL	ENG	8/5/75	M	20	(3)	
Owain ROBERTS		23/6/79	M	7		
Michael THOMPSON	ENG	5/1/84	M	9	(2)	
Craig VERNON	ENG	7/2/89	G	4		
Danny WILLIAMS		12/7/79	M	23	(3)	1
Jason WOOD		10/7/86	M		(1)	

BANGOR CITY FC

Manager – Nev Powell
Founded – 1876
Stadium – Farrar Road (1670)
MAJOR HONOURS: Welsh League – (3) 1994, 1995, 2011; Welsh Cup – (8) 1889, 1896, 1962, 1998, 2000, 2008, 2009, 2010.

2010				
14/8	Neath	h	2-1	*Morley (p), Jebb*
21/8	Bala	a	3-2	*Morley (p), Garside, Bull*
28/8	Llanelli	h	2-0	*Morley (p), Reed*
4/9	Carmarthen	a	1-0	*Morley (p)*
10/9	Airbus	h	5-1	*Reed 3, Bull, Davies*
18/9	Port Talbot	a	2-1	*Jebb, Reed*
26/9	Aberystwyth	h	2-1	*Jones C., Davies*
2/10	TNS	h	4-3	*Bull, Brewerton, Reed, Davies*
9/10	Haverfordwest	a	2-1	*Bull 2*
16/10	Newtown	h	5-2	*Bull 2, Morley (p), Ward, Brewerton*
23/10	Neath	a	2-1	*Davies, Reed*
29/10	Bala	h	3-0	*Reed 2, Ward*
20/11	Carmarthen	h	5-0	*Bull 3, Morley (p), Edwards*
4/12	Port Talbot	h	8-1	*Reed 5, Garside, Hoy 2*
11/12	Aberystwyth	a	3-1	*Davies, Reed 2*
14/12	Airbus	a	1-1	*Bull*
29/12	Prestatyn	h	2-1	*Jones C., Morley (p)*
2011				
2/1	Prestatyn	a	2-4	*Reed 2*
5/1	Llanelli	a	0-2	
8/1	Haverfordwest	h	6-0	*Jones C., Davies 2, Morley, Bull, Hoy*
15/1	Newtown	a	1-0	*Garside*
18/1	TNS	a	2-2	*Bull, Morley (p)*
20/2	Prestatyn	a	2-1	*Morley 2*
5/3	Neath	h	1-2	*Davies*
12/3	Llanelli	a	2-2	*Davies, Garside*
19/3	TNS	a	2-3	*Jones C. 2*
25/3	Port Talbot	h	2-2	*Bull, Moss*
1/4	Prestatyn	h	1-2	*Jones C.*
16/4	Llanelli	h	2-5	*Edwards, Davies*
23/4	Port Talbot	a	2-1	*Bull 2*
25/4	Neath	a	2-1	*Garside 2*
30/4	TNS	h	1-0	*Garside*

Name	Nat	DoB	Pos	Aps	(s)	Gls
James BREWERTON		17/11/79	D	25		2
Alan BULL	ENG	25/11/87	A	32		16
Les DAVIES		29/10/84	A	25	(7)	10
Sion EDWARDS		1/8/87	M	5	(23)	2
Craig GARSIDE	ENG	11/1/85	M	21	(6)	7
Peter HOY	ENG	16/5/82	D	28		3
Eddie JEBB	ENG	31/12/81	M	4	(25)	2
Michael JOHNSTON		16/12/87	D	32		
Chris JONES		9/10/85	M	28	(1)	6
Danial JONES		27/8/93	G	1		
Michael JUKES	ENG	11/7/92	M		(5)	
Marc LIMBERT		3/10/73	M		(1)	
David MORLEY	ENG	25/9/77	D	31		11
Darren MOSS		24/5/81	D	8		1
Chris OLDFIELD	ENG	14/1/91	G	3		
Jamie REED		13/8/87	A	17	(1)	18
Chris ROBERTS		14/8/85	D	30		
Paul SMITH		6/12/77	G	28		
Marc SMYTH	ENG	9/1/85	M	1	(8)	
Nicky WARD		30/11/87	M	29	(1)	2
Clive WILLIAMS		1/1/91	D	4	(13)	

CARMARTHEN TOWN AFC

Manager – Tomi Morgan
Founded – 1896
Stadium – Richmond Park (3,000)
MAJOR HONOURS: Welsh Cup – (1) 2007.

2010				
14/8	Aberystwyth	h	2-3	*Bevan, Frater*
21/8	Airbus	h	1-4	*Hicks*
27/8	Port Talbot	a	2-1	*Hicks (p), Passmore*
4/9	Bangor	h	0-1	
11/9	TNS	a	0-7	
17/9	Haverfordwest	h	2-2	*Harrhy, Evans A.*
25/9	Newtown	a	1-0	*Harrhy*
2/10	Prestatyn	h	2-1	*Walters (p), Griffiths Dal.*
10/10	Neath	a	1-2	*Walters*
16/10	Bala	h	4-1	*Hicks, Harrhy 2, Walters*

22/10	Aberystwyth	a	2-2	*Harrhy, Walters*
30/10	Airbus	a	4-2	*Howard 2, Griffiths Dar., Griffiths Dal.*
12/11	Port Talbot	h	1-3	*Griffiths Dar.*
20/11	Bangor	a	0-5	
11/12	Newtown	h	1-1	*Hicks*
29/12	Haverfordwest	a	2-3	*Walters, Hicks*
2011				
1/1	Llanelli	h	1-3	*Thomas C.*
7/1	Neath	h	0-3	
12/1	TNS	h	1-3	*Harrhy*
18/1	Prestatyn	a	0-0	
25/1	Bala	a	2-1	*Harrhy, Bevan*
12/2	Llanelli	a	1-4	*Harrhy*
19/2	Airbus	h	1-2	*Walters*
4/3	Haverfordwest	a	1-2	*Sheehan*
12/3	Newtown	a	1-0	*Hicks*
19/3	Bala	h	3-1	*Hicks 3 (1p)*
25/3	Aberystwyth	h	0-1	
2/4	Airbus	a	0-0	
8/4	Haverfordwest	h	1-0	*Harrhy*
16/4	Newtown	h	2-1	*Hicks, Palmer*
24/4	Bala	a	0-4	
30/4	Aberystwyth	a	0-1	

Name	Nat	DoB	Pos	Aps	(s)	Gls
Oliver ARDOLINO		19/4/92	A		(4)	
Gary BANSOR	ENG	25/10/88	D	11	(5)	
Lee BEVAN		10/7/87	D	18	(2)	2
Deryn BRACE		15/3/75	D	3		
Bobby BRIERS		29/9/88	D	2	(5)	
Calvin DAVIES		14/5/83	A		(5)	
Mattie DAVIES		8/1/76	A		(1)	
Shane EARP		6/3/89	G	1		
Andy EVANS		1/4/78	A	5	(7)	1
Stephen EVANS		25/9/80	M	20		
Antonio FACCIUTO		27/2/91	D		(1)	
Craig FRATER		8/12/90	A	2	(5)	1
Dale GRIFFITHS		2/11/85	D	25	(3)	2
Darren GRIFFITHS		5/9/87	A	12	(7)	2
Liam HANCOCK		13/11/85	M	4		
Taylor HARDING		16/11/92	A		(5)	
Nick HARRHY		14/9/82	M	27	(1)	9
Tim HICKS		5/4/83	A	25	(1)	10
Kieron HOWARD		17/1/91	M	26	(2)	2
Richard HUGHES		11/12/86	D	15		
Kristian JAMES		5/2/82	D	1		
Owain JAMES		15/10/91	A		(1)	
Lee JENKINS		28/6/79	M	15	(1)	
Mike LEWIS		4/4/89	G	31		
Nicky PALMER		11/6/81	D	14		1
Geraint PASSMORE		18/2/86	M	18	(2)	1
Lee PHILLIPS		18/3/79	D	17		
Stephen POCKETT		11/2/84	M	9		
Daniel SHEEHAN		22/12/90	M	7	(4)	1
Alex THOMAS		7/5/92	A		(1)	
Corey THOMAS		30/11/89	D	15	(8)	1
Sacha WALTERS		20/6/84	M	27	(1)	6
Steffan WILLIAMS		8/6/92	M	2	(9)	

HAVERFORDWEST COUNTY AFC

Manager – Derek Brazil (IRL); (25/11/10) Gavin Chesterfield; (28/2/11) Derek Brazil (IRL)

Founded – 1899

Stadium – New Bridge Meadow (3,000)

2010				
14/8	Newtown	h	0-1	
21/8	Prestatyn	a	0-1	
27/8	Neath	h	0-3	
5/9	Bala	a	1-0	*O'Sullivan*
17/9	Carmarthen	a	2-2	*Thomas D., Thomas N.A.*
25/9	Airbus	h	4-0	*Thomas N A., Christopher, Collins, O'Sullivan*
28/9	Llanelli	h	0-4	
1/10	Port Talbot	a	0-3	
9/10	Bangor	h	1-2	*Hudgell*
16/10	TNS	a	1-6	*Christopher*
23/10	Newtown	a	1-1	*Thomas N.A.*
30/10	Prestatyn	h	2-3	*Hudgell, O'Sullivan (p)*
12/11	Neath	a	0-4	
20/11	Bala	h	0-1	
11/12	Airbus	a	0-4	
29/12	Carmarthen	h	3-2	*Christopher, Thomas D. 2*
2011				
1/1	Aberystwyth	a	2-0	*Christopher 2*
8/1	Bangor	a	0-6	
11/1	Llanelli	a	1-2	*Elliott*
15/1	TNS	h	1-4	*Christopher*
25/1	Port Talbot	h	0-1	
12/2	Aberystwyth	h	0-0	
19/2	Newtown	a	4-4	*Christopher 2, Hudgell, Dixon*
4/3	Carmarthen	h	2-1	*Christopher 2*
11/3	Aberystwyth	a	1-2	*Christopher*
20/3	Airbus	a	0-5	
27/3	Bala	h	2-3	*Christopher 2*
2/4	Newtown	h	1-4	*O'Sullivan (p)*
8/4	Carmarthen	a	0-1	
15/4	Aberystwyth	h	1-3	*Thomas N.A.*
23/4	Airbus	h	0-2	
30/4	Bala	a	0-2	

Name	Nat	DoB	Pos	Aps	(s)	Gls
Harry ALLEN		22/4/88	M		(1)	
Vincent ATUEYI	NGA	20/7/92	A	1	(2)	
Jamie BRADFORD		14/9/83	M	9	(8)	
Jack CHRISTOPHER		18/5/87	A	27	(1)	13
Matty COLLINS		31/3/86	M	15		1
Jaymes DIXON		5/2/88	A	1	(3)	1
Mark DODDS		29/5/80	D	30		
Gareth ELLIOTT		8/6/83	D	17		1
Nathan EVANS		21/6/92	M	1	(2)	
Richard EVANS		19/6/83	M	27	(2)	
Terry EVANS		1/8/76	D	9	(2)	
Craig GEORGE		30/7/90	M	1	(2)	
Kyle GRAVES	ENG	1/4/89	D	27		
Kristian GRIFFITHS		24/1/87	D	7	(7)	
Lee HUDGELL		2/11/83	M	16	(5)	3
Kirk HUGGINS		4/6/85	D	5	(1)	
Lee IDZI		8/2/88	G	20		
Lee JARMAN		16/12/77	D	19	(3)	
James MANSON		13/12/89	G	2		
Rob MORGANS		5/10/92	M		(2)	
Chris O'SULLIVAN		16/2/82	M	25	(5)	4
Dyfan PIERCE		20/12/80	D	2	(5)	
Mike PREDDY		4/11/80	M		(1)	
Tom RAMASUT		30/8/77	M	20	(6)	
David REES		29/5/84	D	2		
Christian ROBERTS		22/10/79	M	3	(4)	
Duncan ROBERTS	ENG	24/6/79	G	1		
Luke ROBINSON		12/5/91	A	2	(1)	
Danny THOMAS		13/5/85	A	24	(6)	3
Neil THOMAS		2/6/73	G	9		
Neil A. THOMAS		22/2/82	M	26		4
Ricky WATTS		7/11/91	M	4	(1)	
Steffan WILLIAMS		8/6/92	M		(12)	

LLANELLI AFC

Manager – Andy Legg

Founded – 1892

Stadium – Stebonheath Park (3,000)

MAJOR HONOURS: Welsh League – (1) 2008; Welsh Cup – (1) 2011.

2010				
15/8	Airbus	a	2-1	*Griffiths 2*
20/8	Port Talbot	h	0-3	

28/8	Bangor	a	0-2	
4/9	TNS	h	2-1	*Griffiths, Warlow*
19/9	Newtown	h	2-1	*Thomas W., Griffiths*
25/9	Prestatyn	a	1-1	*Griffiths*
28/9	Haverfordwest	a	4-0	*Griffiths 3, Warlow*
1/10	Neath	h	1-4	*Llewellyn*
9/10	Bala	a	0-1	
15/10	Aberystwyth	h	2-3	*Griffiths 2*
24/10	Airbus	h	1-1	*Griffiths*
30/10	Port Talbot	a	1-1	*og (De Vulgt)*
2011				
1/1	Carmarthen	a	3-1	*Follows 2, Moses*
5/1	Bangor	h	2-0	*Griffiths (p), Llewellyn*
8/1	Bala	h	3-1	*Llewellyn, Thomas W., Moses*
11/1	Haverfordwest	h	2-1	*Moses, Williams*
15/1	Aberystwyth	a	2-0	*Thomas W., Williams*
18/1	Neath	a	1-1	*Venables*
26/1	Newtown	a	0-0	
1/2	Prestatyn	h	2-2	*Griffiths (p), Williams*
8/2	TNS	a	0-2	
12/2	Carmarthen	h	4-1	*Griffiths 3, Williams*
20/2	Neath	a	4-0	*Griffiths 2, Bowen, Williams*
12/3	Bangor	h	2-2	*Orme, Griffiths*
18/3	Port Talbot	a	0-0	
25/3	Prestatyn	a	2-1	*Venables, Griffiths*
29/3	TNS	h	0-2	
1/4	Neath	h	4-0	*Williams 2, Jones S., Bowen*
16/4	Bangor	a	5-2	*Moses, Thomas C., Bowen, Griffiths 2*
22/4	Prestatyn	h	3-0	*Griffiths, Moses, Follows*
25/4	TNS	a	1-3	*Griffiths*
30/4	Port Talbot	h	2-3	*Griffiths, Orme*

No	Name	Nat	DoB	Pos	Aps	(s)	Gls
18	Ryan BATLEY	ENG	17/11/91	D	4	(2)	
7	Jason BOWEN		24/8/72	M	22	(4)	3
8	Antonio CORBISIERO	ENG	17/11/84	M	29	(2)	
23	Jordan DAVIES		5/7/90	D	2	(3)	
25	Ashley EVANS		18/7/89	M	12	(1)	
27	Scott EVANS		6/1/89	M	7	(2)	
14	Jordan FOLLOWS		23/3/90	A	10	(15)	3
3	Martyn GILES		10/4/83	D	12	(1)	
9	Rhys GRIFFITHS		1/3/80	A	28		25
10	Chris HOLLOWAY		5/2/80	M	16	(1)	
20	Stephen JENKINS		16/7/72	D	3	(1)	
17	Declan JOHN		14/5/91	M		(1)	
28	Lewis JONES		1/5/92	M		(1)	
15	Ross JONES		17/2/90	M	2	(3)	
5	Stuart JONES		14/3/84	D	22		1
21	Andy LEGG		28/7/66	D	9	(9)	
11	Chris LLEWELLYN		28/8/79	A	13	(1)	3
1	Ashley MORRIS		31/3/84	G	24		
12	Craig MOSES		12/4/88	A	13	(4)	5
24	Adam ORME		24/10/91	M	4	(16)	2
19	Craig RICHARDS		25/1/91	G	8		
2	Chris THOMAS		16/1/83	D	31		1
6	Wyn THOMAS		11/1/79	D	25	(1)	3
4	Chris VENABLES		23/7/85	M	26		2
22	Owain WARLOW		25/10/87	M	16	(2)	2
16	Craig WILLIAMS		28/1/83	M	14		7

NEATH FC

Manager – Andy Dyer

Founded – 2005

Stadium – The Gnoll (10,000)

2010				
14/8	Bangor	a	1-2	*Hancock*
27/8	Haverfordwest	a	3-0	*O'Leary, Trundle 2*
5/9	Newtown	h	5-0	*Cochlin, O'Leary, Hughes, Trundle, Bond*
11/9	Prestatyn	a	1-1	*Jones*
18/9	Aberystwyth	a	1-1	*Jones*
26/9	Bala	h	3-1	*O'Leary, Trundle (p), Jones*
1/10	Llanelli	a	4-1	*Trundle 3, Fowler*
10/10	Carmarthen	h	2-1	*Fowler, Thomas*
17/10	Airbus	a	2-2	*Hill, Bond*
23/10	Bangor	h	1-2	*Jones (p)*
31/10	TNS	a	1-3	*Hughes*
12/11	Haverfordwest	h	4-0	*Hughes, Cooper, Fowler, Hill*
20/11	Newtown	a	6-3	*Bond 3, Hughes, Jones, Cooper*
24/11	TNS	h	1-1	*Trundle (p)*
12/12	Bala	a	2-0	*Jones, Fowler*
2011				
2/1	Port Talbot	a	3-1	*Bond, Trundle 2*
7/1	Carmarthen	a	3-0	*Cochlin, Trundle 2*
15/1	Airbus	h	1-0	*Bond*
18/1	Llanelli	h	1-1	*Trundle*
23/1	Prestatyn	h	2-1	*Hill 2*
30/1	Aberystwyth	h	1-1	*Trundle*
8/2	Port Talbot	h	2-1	*Cochlin, Hill*
20/2	Llanelli	h	0-4	
5/3	Bangor	a	2-1	*O'Leary, Trundle*
13/3	Port Talbot	h	0-0	
19/3	Prestatyn	a	1-1	*Hill*
25/3	TNS	h	2-2	*Trundle 2 (1p)*
1/4	Llanelli	a	0-4	
16/4	Port Talbot	a	2-1	*Fowler, Hughes*
22/4	TNS	a	3-2	*Fowler, Rees, Hughes*
25/4	Bangor	h	1-2	*Trundle*
30/4	Prestatyn	h	1-1	*Hughes*

Name	Nat	DoB	Pos	Aps	(s)	Gls
Chad BOND		20/4/87	A	24	(8)	7
James BURGIN	ENG	6/9/89	D	14		
Paul COCHLIN		23/8/83	D	22	(1)	3
Matty COLLINS		31/3/86	M	8	(2)	
Kevin COOPER	ENG	8/2/75	M	19	(5)	2
Luke CUMMINGS		25/10/91	D	5	(7)	
Michael DAVEY		7/3/93	M		(1)	
Liam DAVY		28/7/93	M		(1)	
Ashley EVANS		18/7/89	M	7	(8)	
Andrew FAIRBAIRN		20/9/83	D	9	(1)	
Paul FOWLER		8/2/85	M	30	(1)	6
Liam HANCOCK		29/7/82	D	18		1
Andy HILL		18/10/78	A	13	(15)	6
Ian HILLIER		26/12/79	D	25	(1)	
Craig HUGHES		18/12/78	A	10	(9)	7
Lee IDZI		8/2/88	G	8		
Chris JONES		14/2/90	A	30	(1)	6
Laurie MARSH		14/4/93	M		(1)	
Craig MORRIS		27/7/81	G	21		
Kristian O'LEARY		30/8/77	M	32		4
Stephen POCKETT		11/2/84	M	8	(6)	
Matthew REES		2/9/82	D	13	(1)	1
Liam THOMAS		6/11/91	M	4	(10)	1
Lee TRUNDLE	ENG	10/10/76	A	29		18
Wyn WALTERS		28/2/84	G	3		

NEWTOWN AFC

Manager – Andy Cale (ENG)

Founded – 1896

Stadium – GF Grigg Latham Park (6,000)

MAJOR HONOURS: Welsh Cup – (2) 1879, 1895.

2010				
14/8	Haverfordwest	a	1-0	*Whitfield*
20/8	Aberystwyth	a	2-2	*Cadwallader, Sutton*
28/8	Prestatyn	h	1-0	*Keddle*
5/9	Neath	a	0-5	
11/9	Bala	h	1-1	*Whitfield*
19/9	Llanelli	a	1-2	*Whitfield (p)*
25/9	Carmarthen	h	0-1	
9/10	Port Talbot	h	0-0	
16/10	Bangor	a	2-5	*Keddle, Whitfield*
20/10	Airbus	a	1-1	*McKenna*
23/10	Haverfordwest	h	1-1	*Davies*

31/10	Aberystwyth	h	0-0	
12/11	Prestatyn	a	1-2	*Lloyd-Williams*
20/11	Neath	h	3-6	*Partridge 2, Hartland*
11/12	Carmarthen	a	1-1	*Whitfield*
2011				
1/1	TNS	a	0-4	
5/1	Bala	a	1-4	*Keddle*
8/1	Port Talbot	a	0-3	
15/1	Bangor	h	0-1	
26/1	Llanelli	h	0-0	
29/1	Airbus	h	2-3	*Hartshorn, Millington*
12/2	TNS	h	2-2	*Highdale, Jones St.*
19/2	Haverfordwest	h	4-4	*Millington 2, Cook, Jones St.*
4/3	Bala	a	2-0	*Millington, Bailey*
12/3	Carmarthen	h	0-1	
18/3	Aberystwyth	a	2-2	*Jones St. 2*
25/3	Airbus	h	1-0	*Bailey*
2/4	Haverfordwest	a	4-1	*Millington 3, Cook*
9/4	Bala	h	2-1	*Whitfield (p), og (Jefferies)*
16/4	Carmarthen	a	1-2	*Bailey*
23/4	Aberystwyth	h	1-0	*Millington*
30/4	Airbus	a	3-0	*Jones St. 3*

Name	Nat	DoB	Pos	Aps	(s)	Gls
Sam BAILEY	ENG	28/3/86	D	11	(1)	3
Dylan BLAIN		10/11/82	M	27	(4)	
Jamie BREEZE		10/1/92	M	11	(10)	
Gavin CADWALLADER		18/4/86	D	12	(1)	1
Matthew COOK	ENG	7/9/85	M	13		2
Craig DAVIES		21/12/88	A	2	(5)	1
Joshua EVANS		24/8/92	D	2	(8)	
Wayne EVANS		25/8/71	M		(1)	
Zac EVANS		3/5/91	M	3	(4)	
Andrew FROST		8/7/79	A		(1)	
Chris HARTLAND		20/6/90	A	8	(5)	1
Lee HARTSHORN		12/3/87	A	31	(1)	1
Sean HIGHDALE	ENG	4/3/91	D	2	(1)	1
Craig HUTCHINSON	ENG	28/1/73	M	1	(1)	
Michael JACKSON	ENG	14/12/79	D	20		
Robbie JAMES		20/12/88	D	1	(1)	
Rhys JONES		28/8/93	M		(1)	
Sean JONES	ENG	16/6/90	D	4	(6)	
Steve JONES	ENG	25/4/86	A	13		7
Paul KEDDLE		18/11/83	D	31		3
Marc LLOYD-WILLIAMS		8/2/73	A	4	(1)	1
John McKENNA	ENG	15/5/90	M	13		1
Robbie MILLINGTON	ENG	4/6/92	M	10	(4)	8
Gareth PARTRIDGE		26/9/91	A	6	(9)	2
Jamie PRICE		22/7/88	A	4	(10)	
Dave ROBERTS		10/12/88	G	29		
Tom ROWLANDS		28/10/85	M	1	(1)	
Shane SUTTON		31/1/89	D	31		1
David SWANICK	ENG	16/9/79	D	9	(1)	
Craig WHITFIELD	ENG	16/8/89	D	18	(8)	6
Lee WILLIAMS	ENG	9/4/68	G	3		
Adam WORTON	ENG	10/4/87	M	32		

PORT TALBOT TOWN FC

Manager – Mark Jones

Founded – 1901

Stadium – GenQuip Stadium (3,000)

2010				
15/8	Bala	h	2-0	*Brooks, og (Irving)*
20/8	Llanelli	a	3-0	*McCreesh, Bowen L., Cotterrall*
27/8	Carmarthen	h	1-2	*Rose (p)*
4/9	Airbus	a	0-2	
10/9	Aberystwyth	h	1-1	*Bowen L. (p)*
18/9	Bangor	h	1-2	*John*
25/9	TNS	a	1-6	*Bowen L.*
1/10	Haverfordwest	h	3-0	*Bowen L., Rose (p), McCreesh*
9/10	Newtown	a	0-0	
17/10	Prestatyn	h	0-3	
24/10	Bala	a	0-0	
30/10	Llanelli	h	1-1	*Bowen L.*
12/11	Carmarthen	a	3-1	*Rees, Rose (p), McCreesh*
20/11	Airbus	h	2-0	*McCreesh, Rose*
26/11	Aberystwyth	a	2-2	*Rose, Bowen L.*
4/12	Bangor	a	1-8	*Grist*
11/12	TNS	h	0-2	
2011				
2/1	Neath	h	1-3	*Bowen L.*
8/1	Newtown	h	3-0	*Grist, John, Fahiya*
15/1	Prestatyn	a	1-1	*Thompson*
25/1	Haverfordwest	a	1-0	*Bowen L.*
8/2	Neath	a	1-2	*Brooks*
19/2	TNS	a	1-1	*og (Harrison)*
13/3	Neath	a	0-0	
18/3	Llanelli	h	0-0	
25/3	Bangor	a	2-2	*Bowen L., Grist*
2/4	TNS	h	0-0	
9/4	Prestatyn	a	0-2	
16/4	Neath	h	1-2	*Bowen L.*
23/4	Bangor	h	1-2	*Bowen L.*
25/4	Prestatyn	h	1-1	*Grist*
30/4	Llanelli	a	3-2	*Bowen L. (p), Surman 2*

Name	Nat	DoB	Pos	Aps	(s)	Gls
Gary BANSOR	ENG	25/10/88	D		(1)	
Luke BOWEN		7/3/88	A	32		12
Oliver BOWEN		2/9/93	A		(1)	
Dave BROOKS		19/5/89	M	15	(6)	2
David BURNETT		28/1/90	G	4		
David CORNELL		28/3/91	G	13		
Nathan COTTERRALL		15/12/76	M	9	(17)	1
Leigh DE VULGT		10/3/81	D	15	(8)	
Jordan EDWARDS		6/10/93	M		(3)	
Kye EDWARDS		1/11/91	D	22	(1)	
Drew FAHIYA		17/4/88	A	9	(10)	1
Lloyd GRIST		13/11/85	M	30		4
Nicky HOLLAND		24/4/89	M	18	(5)	
Lee JOHN		4/9/84	M	31	(1)	2
Craig JONES		28/3/87	M	7	(10)	
Lee KENDALL		8/1/81	G	15		
Josh KNIGHT		16/11/90	M		(1)	
Karl LEWIS		27/6/81	M	1	(3)	
Liam McCREESH		9/9/85	M	26	(1)	4
Gareth PHILLIPS		19/8/79	M	26	(3)	
Matthew REES		2/9/82	D	16		1
Martin ROSE	ENG	29/2/84	A	16	(1)	5
Lee SURMAN		3/4/86	D	26	(1)	2
Casey THOMAS		14/11/90	A	9		
Matthew THOMPSON	ENG	29/5/88	M	12	(11)	1

PRESTATYN TOWN FC

Manager – Neil Gibson; (29/3/11) Lee Jones

Founded – 1910

Stadium – Bastion Road (3,000)

2010				
13/8	TNS	a	2-5	*Hunt 2*
21/8	Haverfordwest	h	1-0	*Hunt*
28/8	Newtown	a	0-1	
4/9	Aberystwyth	a	0-1	
11/9	Neath	h	1-1	*Hunt*
17/9	Bala	a	1-2	*Hunt (p)*
25/9	Llanelli	h	1-1	*O'Neill*
2/10	Carmarthen	a	1-2	*O'Neill*
10/10	Airbus	h	1-1	*Rogers*
17/10	Port Talbot	a	3-0	*Hunt 2, Davies*
22/10	TNS	h	0-0	
30/10	Haverfordwest	a	3-2	*Hunt 2 (1p), Hayes*
12/11	Newtown	h	2-1	*Hayes, Stephens*
20/11	Aberystwyth	h	4-0	*Parker 2, Rogers 2*
29/12	Bangor	a	1-2	*Rogers*

2011

2/1	Bangor	h	4-2	*Hunt, Stephens, Rogers 2*
7/1	Airbus	a	4-3	*O'Neill, Hunt, Parker, Stephens*
11/1	Bala	h	2-0	*Fisher-Cooke 2*
15/1	Port Talbot	h	1-1	*Fisher-Cooke*
18/1	Carmarthen	h	0-0	
23/1	Neath	a	1-2	*Stephens (p)*
1/2	Llanelli	a	2-2	*og (Corbisiero), Wilson*
20/2	Bangor	h	1-2	*Hunt*
11/3	TNS	a	0-4	
19/3	Neath	h	1-1	*Hunt (p)*
25/3	Llanelli	h	1-2	*Stephens*
1/4	Bangor	a	2-1	*Rogers, O'Neill*
9/4	Port Talbot	h	2-0	*Hunt 2*
15/4	TNS	h	0-2	
22/4	Llanelli	a	0-3	
25/4	Port Talbot	a	1-1	*Hunt (p)*
30/4	Neath	a	1-1	*Stephens*

Name	Nat	DoB	Pos	Aps	(s)	Gls
Ryan DAVIDSON		12/4/92	M		(1)	
Chris DAVIES		21/10/90	M	18	(3)	1
Kai EDWARDS		20/1/91	D	26		
Dan EVANS		1/3/87	M	8	(11)	
Jon FISHER-COOKE		13/5/82	A	8	(13)	3
Adam FRANCE		18/8/87	D	7	(3)	
Neil GIBSON		11/10/79	M	23	(3)	
Ian GRIFFITHS		2/1/85	A	4	(8)	
Steve HARRIS	NIR	5/2/86	M	1	(6)	
David HAYES		15/1/82	D	27		2
Jon HILL-DUNT		13/5/86	G	27		
Steve HOULT		17/1/81	A	3		
Lee HUNT	ENG	5/6/82	A	24		16
Russ JONES		31/5/82	D	3		
Jack LEWIS		18/5/88	D	31		
Karl MURRAY		24/9/90	M		(3)	
Paul O'NEILL		17/6/82	D	25		4
Rhys OWEN		10/6/93	M		(1)	
Michael PARKER		31/10/87	M	29	(2)	3
Jack ROBERTS		2/12/86	M	1	(1)	
Steve ROGERS	ENG	16/12/78	A	28	(3)	7
Ross STEPHENS		28/5/85	M	26	(3)	6
Simon WILLIAMS		28/6/91	G	5		
Gareth WILSON		23/5/78	M	28		1

THE NEW SAINTS FC

Coach – Mike Davies

Founded – 1959

Stadium – The Venue (3,000)

MAJOR HONOURS: Welsh League – (5) 2000, 2005, 2006, 2007, 2010; Welsh Cup – (2) 1996, 2005.

2010

13/8	Prestatyn	h	5-2	*Sharp 3 (1p), Jones, Holmes D.*
29/8	Bala	h	2-1	*Sharp, Darlington*
4/9	Llanelli	a	1-2	*Darlington*
11/9	Carmarthen	h	7-0	*Williams, Darlington 2, og (Griffiths Dal.), Ruscoe 2, Berkeley*
17/9	Airbus	a	2-2	*Williams, Partridge*
25/9	Port Talbot	h	6-1	*Partridge, Holmes D., Jones, Ruscoe (p), Williams, Hogan*
2/10	Bangor	a	3-4	*Evans, Darlington, Jones*
10/10	Aberystwyth	h	5-0	*Darlington, Partridge 3, Berkeley*
16/10	Haverfordwest	h	6-1	*Berkeley, Partridge, Williams 2, Sharp, Seargeant*
22/10	Prestatyn	a	0-0	
31/10	Neath	h	3-1	*Williams, Darlington, Partridge*
12/11	Bala	a	4-3	*Williams 3, Sharp*
24/11	Neath	a	1-1	*Williams*
4/12	Airbus	h	2-0	*Baker, Jones*
11/12	Port Talbot	a	2-0	*Sharp, Partridge*

2011

1/1	Newtown	h	4-0	*Darlington 4 (1p)*
8/1	Aberystwyth	a	2-0	*Partridge 2*
12/1	Carmarthen	a	3-1	*og (Pockett), Berkeley, Ruscoe (p)*
15/1	Haverfordwest	a	4-1	*Jones, Williams 2, Sharp*
18/1	Bangor	h	2-2	*Partridge, Edwards*
8/2	Llanelli	h	2-0	*Williams 2 (1p)*
12/2	Newtown	a	2-2	*Williams, Edwards*
19/2	Port Talbot	h	1-1	*Baker*
11/3	Prestatyn	h	4-0	*Darlington 2, Williams (p), Seargeant*
19/3	Bangor	h	3-2	*Williams, Edwards, Jones*
25/3	Neath	a	2-2	*Sharp, Ruscoe*
29/3	Llanelli	a	2-0	*og (Thomas C.), Jones*
2/4	Port Talbot	a	0-0	
15/4	Prestatyn	a	2-0	*Holmes D., Sharp*
22/4	Neath	h	2-3	*Williams, Seargeant*
25/4	Llanelli	h	3-1	*Sharp 2, Williams (p)*
30/4	Bangor	a	0-1	

No	Name	Nat	DoB	Pos	Aps	(s)	Gls
4	Phil BAKER	ENG	4/11/82	D	21		2
99	Matthew BERKELEY	ENG	3/8/87	A	8	(12)	4
20	Alex DARLINGTON		26/12/88	A	12	(10)	13
23	Aeron EDWARDS		16/2/88	A	23	(1)	3
5	Steve EVANS		26/2/79	D	8		1
29	Marcus GIGLIO	ENG	1/9/92	A		(1)	
1	Paul HARRISON	ENG	18/12/84	G	32		
8	Barry HOGAN	ENG	15/12/83	M	14	(6)	1
2	Danny HOLMES	ENG	6/1/89	D	26		3
6	Tommy HOLMES	ENG	1/9/79	D	24		
14	Craig JONES		20/3/87	M	30	(1)	7
3	Chris MARRIOTT		24/9/89	D	16		
17	John McKENNA	ENG	15/5/90	D	5	(2)	
27	Richie PARTRIDGE	IRL	12/9/80	M	26		11
16	Connell RAWLINSON		22/9/91	D	8	(6)	
7	Scott RUSCOE		15/12/77	M	31		5
12	Christian SEARGEANT	ENG	13/9/86	M	21	(11)	3
9	Chris SHARP	ENG	19/6/86	A	17	(7)	12
11	Matthew WILLIAMS		5/11/82	A	25	(3)	19
18	Jamie WOOD	CAY	21/9/78	A	5	(14)	

TOP GOALSCORERS 2010/11

25	Rhys GRIFFITHS (Llanelli)
19	Matthew WILLIAMS (TNS)
18	Jamie REED (Bangor) Lee TRUNDLE (Neath)
16	Alan BULL (Bangor) Lee HUNT (Prestatyn)
13	Jack CHRISTOPHER (Haverfordwest) Alex DARLINGTON (TNS)
12	Ricky EVANS (Aberystwyth) Luke BOWEN (Port Talbot) Chris SHARP (TNS)

UEFA EUROPA LEAGUE PLAY-OFFS

FIRST ROUND

(10/5/11)
Aberystwyth 2 *(Stott 58, McCarten 87)*, Airbus UK 1 *(Sheridan 21p)*

SEMI-FINALS

(15/5/11)
Neath 2 *(Hughes 32, Fowler 34)*, Aberystwyth 1 *(McCarten 90)*
Prestatyn 2 *(Hunt 84p, Hayes 88)*, Port Talbot 1 *(Surman 29)*

FINAL

(21/5/11)
Neath 3 *(Bond 1, Hill 55, 84)*, Prestatyn 2 *(Hunt 24, Fisher-Cooke 90+2)*

PROMOTED CLUB

AFAN LIDO FC

Coach – Kim Bowley
Founded – 1967
Stadium – Marston Stadium (1,700)

SECOND LEVEL FINAL TABLES 2010/11

NORTH		Pld	W	D	L	F	A	Pts
1	Connah's Quay FC	30	23	2	5	89	33	71
2	Rhyl FC	30	19	5	6	73	32	62
3	Cefn Druids AFC	30	18	6	6	60	29	60
4	Rhos Aelwyd FC	30	15	6	9	68	64	51
5	Caersws FC	30	15	5	10	59	49	50
6	Llandudno FC	30	13	10	7	50	35	49
7	Flint Town United FC	30	13	7	10	64	55	46
8	CPD Porthmadog	30	14	4	12	59	53	46
9	Buckley Town FC	30	13	6	11	46	48	45
10	Llangefni Town FC	30	11	4	15	67	64	37
11	CPD Penrhyncoch	30	9	10	11	49	56	37
12	Ruthin Town FC	30	11	4	15	39	58	37
13	Guilsfield FC	30	8	6	16	43	56	30
14	Rhydymwyn FC	30	4	6	20	27	82	18
15	Rhayader Town FC	30	4	3	23	34	76	15
16	Welshpool Town FC	30	5	6	19	39	76	0

NB Welshpool Town FC – 21pts deducted; no promotion as neither Connah's Quay FC nor Rhyl FC obtained a domestic licence.

SOUTH		Pld	W	D	L	F	A	Pts
1	Bryntirion Athletic FC	30	23	1	6	76	27	70
2	Afan Lido FC	30	20	5	5	63	28	65
3	Cambrian & Clydach Vale	30	17	6	7	68	37	57
4	Pontardawe Town FC	30	15	6	9	54	44	51
5	Caerau (Ely) AFC	30	15	4	11	66	52	49
6	Bridgend Town AFC	30	14	5	11	60	47	47
7	West End FC	30	13	6	11	57	47	45
8	Cardiff Corinthians FC	30	12	4	14	58	52	40
9	Taffs Well AFC	30	12	3	15	47	57	39
10	Aberaman Athletic FC	30	12	3	15	58	74	39
11	Goytre United FC	30	10	8	12	47	53	38
12	Cwmbran Celtic FC	30	10	7	13	45	50	37
13	Barry Town FC	30	9	8	13	39	55	35
14	Caldicot Town FC	30	8	3	19	37	48	27
15	Garden Village AFC	30	6	7	17	41	75	25
16	Penrhiwceiber Rangers FC	30	4	4	22	27	97	16

NB Only Afan Lido FC promoted as Bryntirion Athletic FC did not apply for a domestic licence.

DOMESTIC CUP 2010/11

WELSH CUP

THIRD ROUND

(5/11/10)
Airbus 2, TNS 3

(6/11/10)
Aberaman 0, Cefn Druids 4
Bangor 2, Bryntirion 1
Bow Street 2, UWIC 2 *(aet; 5-6 on pens)*
Caersws 4, Llanidloes 2 *(aet)*
Cambrian & Clydach Vale 2, Prestatyn 3
Connah's Quay 5, Porth 3 *(aet)*
Corus Steel 0, Cardiff Grange 2
Goytre United 2, Carmarthen 3
Guilsfield 1, Rhos Aelwyd 2
Gwalchmai 1, Port Talbot 4
Haverfordwest 3, Holyhead 2 *(aet)*
Neath 1, Rhyl 1 *(aet; 6-7 on pens)*
Newtown 1, Bridgend 2
Porthmadog 0, Bala 1

(13/11/10)
Llanelli 1, Aberystwyth 0 *(aet)*

FOURTH ROUND

(29/1/11)
Cardiff Grange 1, Bridgend 0
Carmarthen 2, Connah's Quay 3 *(aet)*
UWIC 4, Bala 1

(5/2/11)
Bangor 5, Haverfordwest 3
Cefn Druids 1, Llanelli 4
Port Talbot 3, Caersws 0
Rhos Aelwyd 1, Prestatyn 6
Rhyl 1, TNS 2

QUARTER-FINALS

(26/2/11)
Connah's Quay 4 *(O'Toole 2, Scheuber 5, Thurston 9, Collins 87)*, UWIC 0
Port Talbot 0, Bangor 3 *(Moss 49, Morley 75p, Bull 78)*
TNS 2 (Williams 105, Darlington 113), Cardiff Grange 0 *(aet)*

(5/3/11)
Llanelli 1 (Legg 17), Prestatyn 0

SEMI-FINALS

(9/4/11)
Bangor 1 *(Jones C. 83)*, Connah's Quay 0
Llanelli 1 *(Venables 84)*, TNS 0

FINAL

(8/5/11)
Parc-y-Scarlets, Llanelli
LLANELLI AFC 4 *(Griffiths 15, 60, Moses 20, Venables 64)*
BANGOR CITY FC 1 *(Bull 51)*
Referee – *Petch*
LLANELLI – *Morris, Thomas C., Jones S., Venables, Thomas W., Bowen (Follows 74), Corbisiero, Holloway, Evans A., Moses, Griffiths.*
BANGOR – *Smith, Hoy, Roberts, Morley, Moss, Johnston, Jones C. (Edwards 75), Williams (Smyth 62), Ward, Davies, Bull (Jebb 75).*

CLUB COMMUNICATION 2011/12

Aberystwyth Town FC
Park Avenue
GB-Aberystwyth SY23 1PG

Tel	+44 1970 617 939
Fax	+44 1970 617 939
Web	atfc.org.uk
Email	webteam@atfc.org.uk
Media Officer	Thomas Crockett

Afan Lido FC
56 Abbeyville Avenue
GB-Port Talbot S12 6PE

Tel	
Fax	
Web	afanlidofc.com
Email	afanlido67@btconnect.com
Media Officer	

Airbus UK Broughton FC
The Airfield, Airbus UK FC, Chester Road
GB-Broughton

Tel	+44 1244 522 253
Fax	+44 1244 528 317
Web	airbusfc.com
Email	mayhems@meadow008.fsnet.co.uk
Media Officer	Phil Bailey

Bala Town FC
38 Yr Hafan
GB-Bala Gwynedd LL23 7AU

Tel	+44 1678 521 823
Fax	+44 1678 521 823
Web	balatownfc.co.uk
Email	ruth.crump@aykroyds.co.uk
Media Officer	Gavin Billington

Bangor City FC
The Stadium, Farrar Road
GB-Bangor LL57 3HY

Tel	+44 1248 355 852
Fax	+44 1492 355 852
Web	bangorcityfc.com
Email	info@bangorcityfc.com
Media Officer	Huw Pritchard

Carmarthen Town AFC
Richmond Park, Heol y Prior
GB-Carmarthen SA31 1LR

Tel	+44 1267 222 851
Fax	+44 1267 222 851
Web	carmarthentownafc.net
Email	admin@carmarthentownafc.net
Media Officer	Vince James

Llanelli AFC
Stebonheath Park, Penallt Road
GB-Llanelli SA15 1EY

Tel	+44 1554 758 018
Fax	+44 1554 758 018
Web	llanelliafc.org
Email	nigel@llanelliafc.org
Media Officer	Nigel Richards

Neath FC
15 Bosworth Road, Skewen
GB-Neath SA10 6BU

Tel	+44 7814 475 493
Fax	+44 1792 321 364
Web	neathfc.com
Email	amelding@fsmail.net
Media Officer	Tony Melding

Newtown AFC
Mid Wales Leisure Latham Park
Park Lane, GB-Newtown SY16 1EN

Tel	+44 1686 623 120
Fax	+44 1686 623 120
Web	newtownafc.co.uk
Email	office@newtownafc.co.uk
Media Officer	Barry Gardiner

Port Talbot Town FC
The GenQuip Stadium, Victoria Road
GB-Port Talbot SA12 6AD

Tel	+44 1639 882 465
Fax	+44 1639 886 991
Web	porttalbottown.co.uk
Email	mark@porttalbottown.co.uk
Media Officer	Matthew Burgess

Prestatyn Town FC
3 Sea Road, Prestatyn
GB-Denbighshire LL197NN

Tel	+44 1745 856 226
Fax	+44 1745 856 226
Web	ptfconline.co.uk
Email	tbutterworth2001@hotmail.com
Media Officer	Mark Jones

The New Saints FC
The Venue at Park Hall, Burma Road
GB-Oswestry SY11 4AS

Tel	+44 1691 684 840
Fax	+44 1691 659 553
Web	saints-alive.co.uk
Email	ian.tnsfc@gmail.com
Media Officer	Andrew Lincoln

GRAPHIC GUIDE

UEFA COMPETITION PARTICIPANTS 2011/12

This section contains national federation crests, international kits, club badges for the participants of UEFA competitions* and maps for all 53 UEFA member associations.

*subject to UEFA's club licensing regulations.

Key to country pages

◯	UEFA Champions League	©	champions
◯	UEFA Europa League	*	domestic Cup winners
◯	Clubs in top division	[fp]	Fair Play qualifiers
◯	Promoted Clubs		
●	Relegated or Excluded/Withdrawn Clubs		

UEFA MEMBER ASSOCIATIONS

Graphic Guide Index

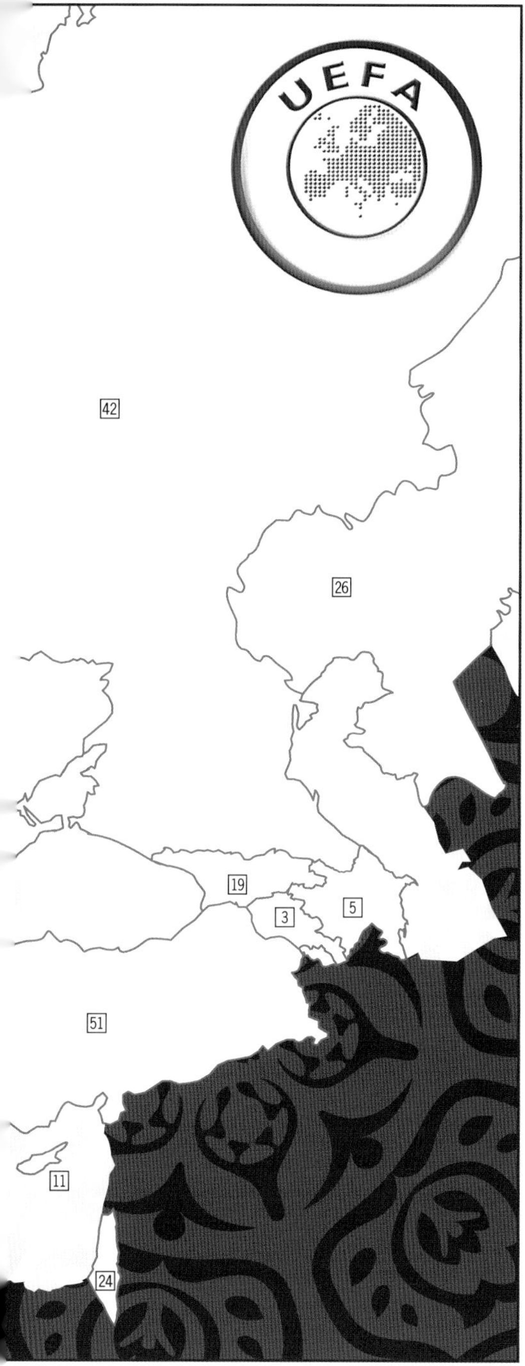

ALBANIA

Albanie | Albanien

HOME INTERNATIONAL KIT

AWAY INTERNATIONAL KIT

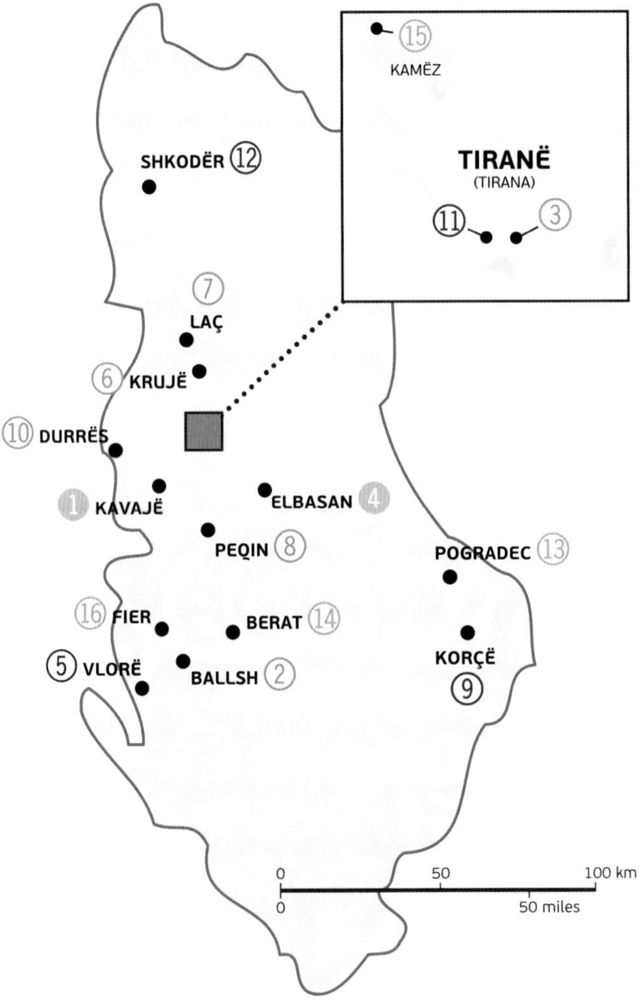

TOP DIVISION CLUBS

1. **KS Besa**
no website
2. **KS Bylis**
no website
3. **FK Dinamo Tirana**
dinamo.al
4. **KF Elbasani**
kfelbasani.com
5. **KS Flamurtari**
skflamurtari.com — UEFA EUROPA LEAGUE
6. **KS Kastrioti**
no website
7. **KF Laçi**
no website
8. **KS Shkumbini**
ksshkumbini.com
9. **KS Skënderbeu** ©
skenderbeukorce.webs.com — UEFA CHAMPIONS LEAGUE
10. **KS Teuta**
kfteuta.com
11. **KF Tirana** *
sktirana.com — UEFA EUROPA LEAGUE
12. **KF Vllaznia**
vllaznia.eu — UEFA EUROPA LEAGUE

PROMOTED CLUBS

13. **KS Pogradeci**
no website
14. **FK Tomori**
fktomori.com
15. **KS Kamza**
no website
16. **KF Apolonia**
kfapoloniafier.wordpress.com

ANDORRA

Andorre | Andorra

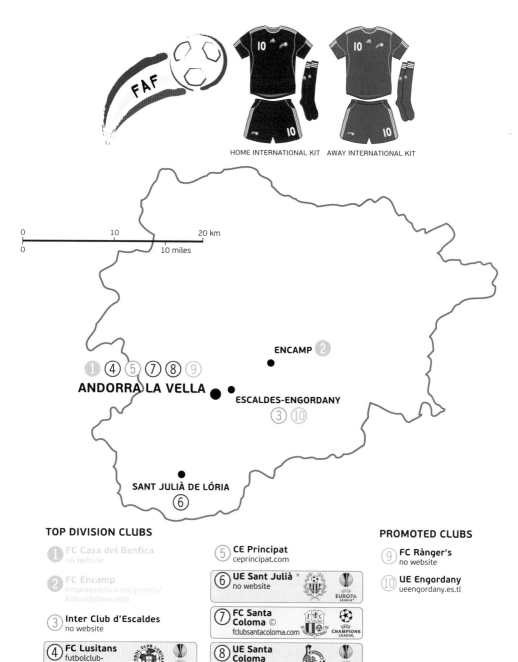

HOME INTERNATIONAL KIT   AWAY INTERNATIONAL KIT

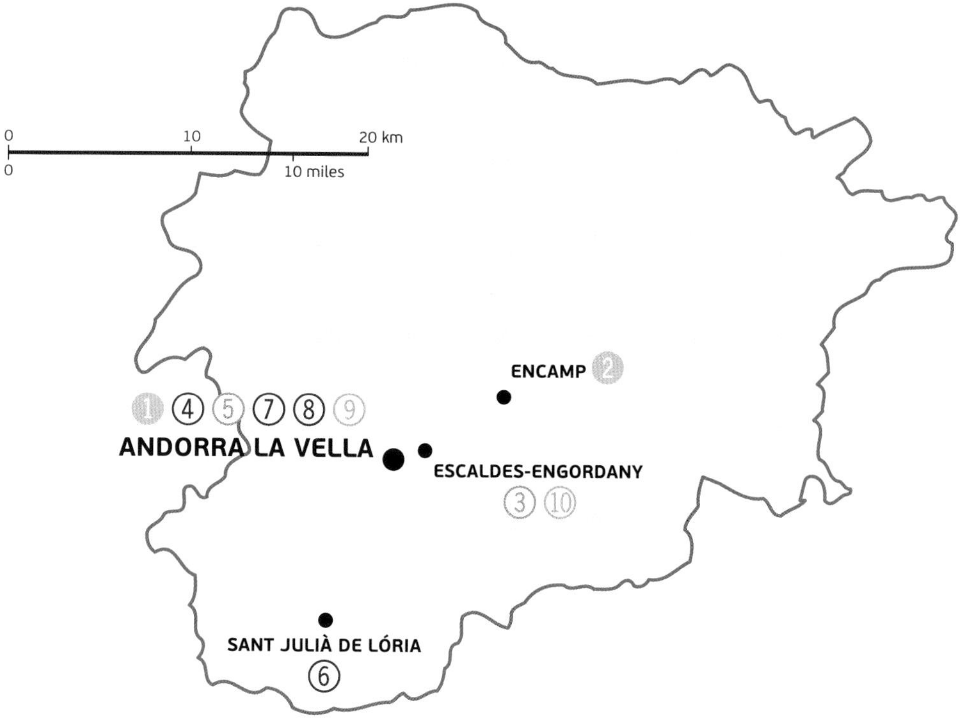

TOP DIVISION CLUBS

1 **FC Casa del Benfica**
no website

2 **FC Encamp**
empresaactiva.net/proves/futbolclubencamp

3 **Inter Club d'Escaldes**
no website

4 **FC Lusitans**
futbolclub-lusitanos.com

5 **CE Principat**
ceprincipat.com

6 **UE Sant Julià** *
no website

7 **FC Santa Coloma** ©
fclubsantacoloma.com

8 **UE Santa Coloma**
uesantacoloma.com

PROMOTED CLUBS

9 **FC Rànger's**
no website

10 **UE Engordany**
ueengordany.es.tl

ARMENIA

Arménie | Armenien

HOME INTERNATIONAL KIT   AWAY INTERNATIONAL KIT

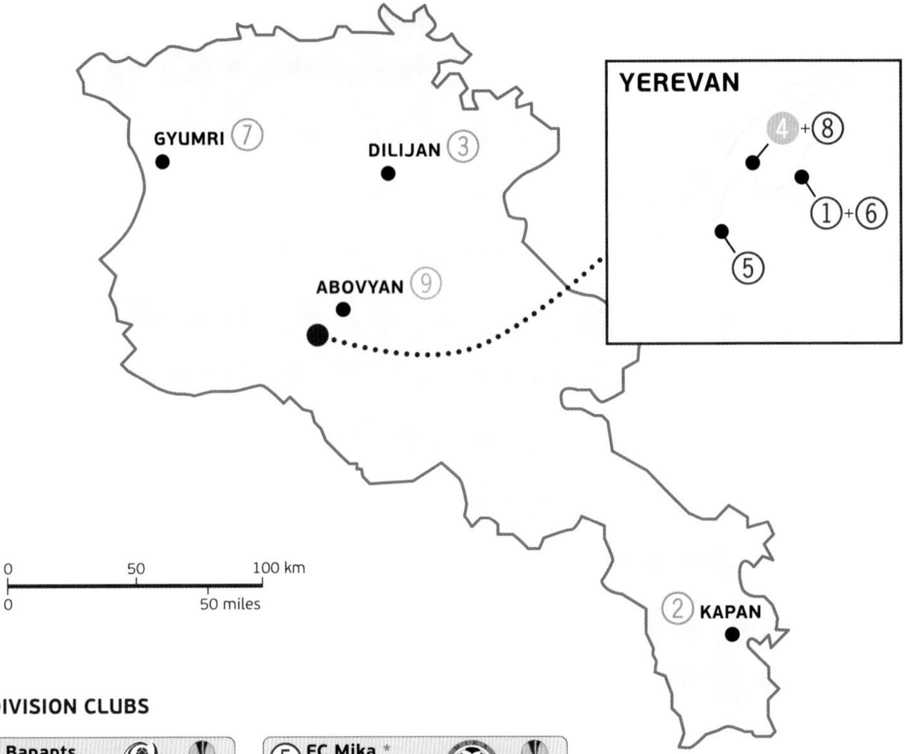

TOP DIVISION CLUBS

1 **FC Banants**
fcbanants.com

2 **FC Gandzasar**
no website

3 **FC Impuls**
fcimpulse.com

4 **FC Kilikia**
no website

5 **FC Mika** *
fcmika.am

6 **FC Pyunik** ©
fcpyunik.am

7 **FC Shirak**
fcshirak.am

8 **Ulisses FC**
fculisses.am

PROMOTED CLUB

9 **FC Ararat**
fcararat.com

AUSTRIA

Autriche | Österreich

HOME INTERNATIONAL KIT AWAY INTERNATIONAL KIT

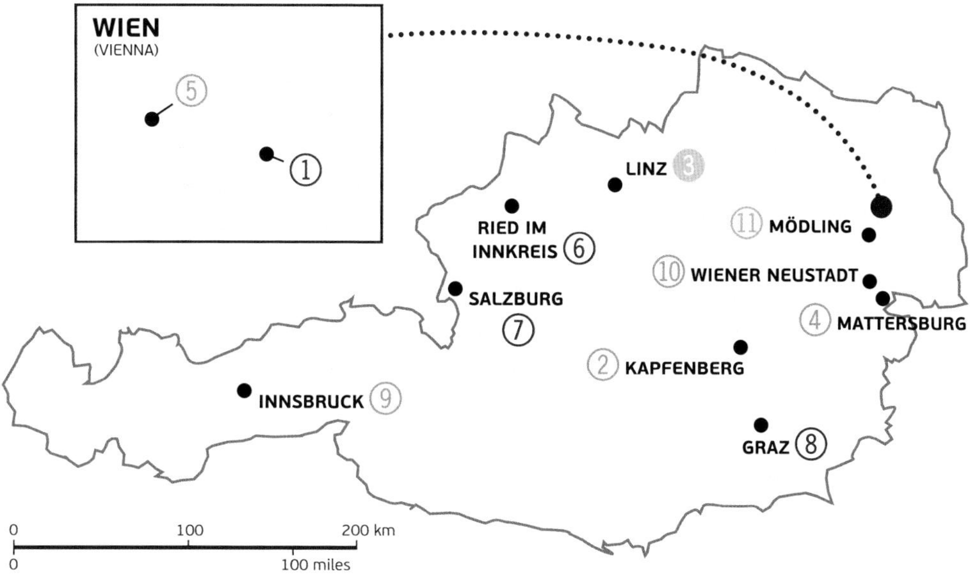

TOP DIVISION CLUBS

1 **FK Austria Wien** ★★
fk-austria.at

2 **Kapfenberger SV**
ksv-fussball.at

3 **LASK Linz**
lask.at

4 **SV Mattersburg**
svm.at

5 **SK Rapid Wien**
skrapid.at

6 **SV Ried** *
svried.at

7 **FC Salzburg**
redbulls.com

8 **SK Sturm Graz** ©
sksturm.at

9 **FC Wacker Innsbruck**
fc-wacker-innsbruck.at

10 **SC Wiener Neustadt**
scwn.at

PROMOTED CLUB

11 **FC Admira/Wacker Mödling**
trenkwalder-admira.com

AZERBAIJAN

Azerbaïjan | Aserbeidschan

HOME INTERNATIONAL KIT AWAY INTERNATIONAL KIT

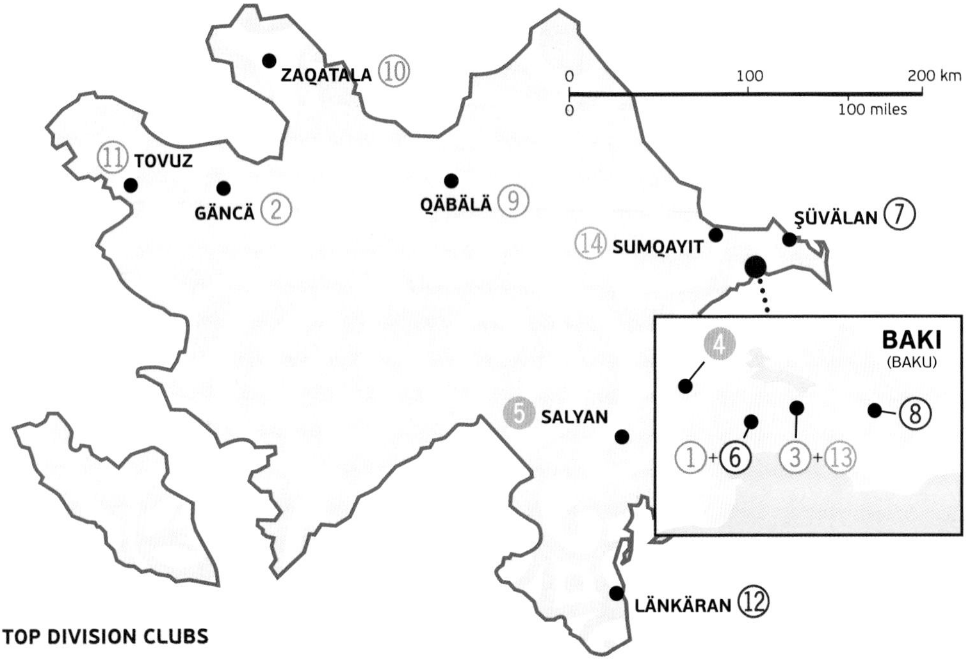

TOP DIVISION CLUBS

(1) **Bakı FK**
fcbaku.com

(2) **Gäncä PFK**
gancapfk.az

NB Gäncä PFK changed name to Käpäz PFK for 2011/12 season.

(3) **İnter Bakı PİK**
inter.az

(4) **MOİK Bakı PFK**
no website

(5) **Muğan Salyan FK**
muganfc.az

(6) **Neftçi PFK** ©
neftchifc.com

(7) **Olimpik-Şüvälan PFK**
azalpfc.az

(8) **Qarabağ FK**
qarabagh.com

(9) **Qäbälä FK**
gabalafc.az

(10) **Simurq Zaqatala PFK**
simurqpfk.com

(11) **Turan PFK**
turanpfc.com

(12) **Xäzär Länkäran FK** *
lankaranfc.com

PROMOTED CLUBS

(13) **Rävan Bakı FK**
no website

(14) **Sumqayıt Şähär PFK**
no website

BELARUS

Belarus | Belarus

HOME INTERNATIONAL KIT AWAY INTERNATIONAL KIT

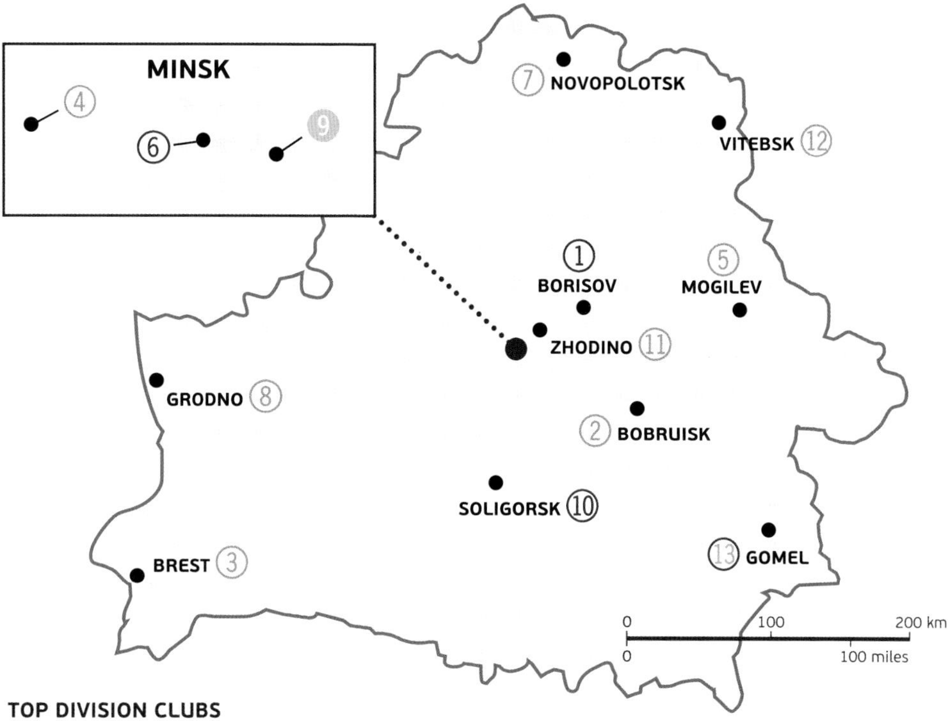

TOP DIVISION CLUBS

1. **FC BATE Borisov** ©
   fcbate.by
2. **FC Belshina Bobruisk**
   fcbelshina.by
3. **FC Dinamo Brest**
   dynamo.brest.by
4. **FC Dinamo Minsk**
   dynamo-minsk.by
5. **FC Dnepr Mogilev**
   fcdnepr.by
6. **FC Minsk**
   fcminsk.by
7. **FC Naftan Novopolotsk**
   fcnaftan.com
8. **FC Neman Grodno**
   fcneman.by
9. **FC Partizan Minsk**
   mtz-ripo.by
10. **FC Shakhtyor Soligorsk**
    fcshakhter.by
11. **FC Torpedo Zhodino**
    tarpeda.zhodzina.info
12. **FC Vitebsk**
    fc.vitebsk.by

PROMOTED CLUB

13. **FC Gomel** *
    fcgomel.by

BELGIUM

Belgique | Belgien

HOME INTERNATIONAL KIT AWAY INTERNATIONAL KIT

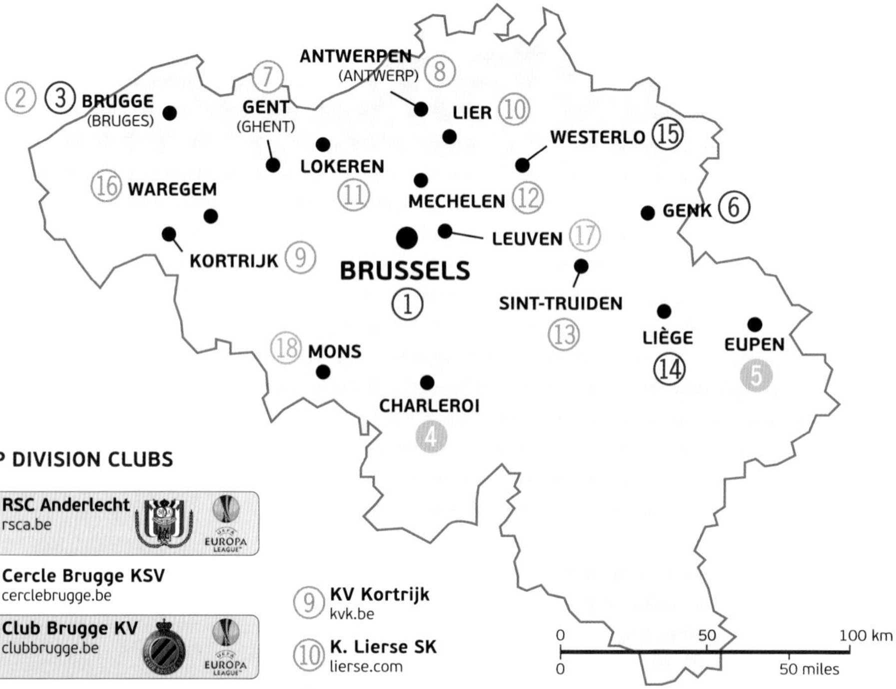

TOP DIVISION CLUBS

1. **RSC Anderlecht** rsca.be — EUROPA LEAGUE
2. **Cercle Brugge KSV** cerclebrugge.be
3. **Club Brugge KV** clubbrugge.be — EUROPA LEAGUE
4. **R. Charleroi SC** sporting-charleroi.be
5. **KAS Eupen** as-eupen.be
6. **KRC Genk** © krcgenk.be — CHAMPIONS LEAGUE
7. **KAA Gent** kaagent.be
8. **KFC Germinal Beerschot Antwerpen** beerschot.be

NB KFC Germinal Beerschot Antwerpen changed name to K. Beerschot AC for 2011/12 season.

9. **KV Kortrijk** kvk.be
10. **K. Lierse SK** lierse.com
11. **KSC Lokeren OV** sporting.be
12. **KV Mechelen** kvmechelen.be
13. **K. Sint-Truidense VV** stvv.com
14. **R. Standard de Liège** * standard.be — CHAMPIONS LEAGUE
15. **KVC Westerlo** kvcwesterlo.be — EUROPA LEAGUE
16. **SV Zulte Waregem** svzw.be

PROMOTED CLUBS

17. **Oud-Heverlee Leuven** ohl.be
18. **RAEC Mons** raec-mons.be

BOSNIA & HERZEGOVINA

Bosnie-Herzégovine | Bosnien-Herzegowina

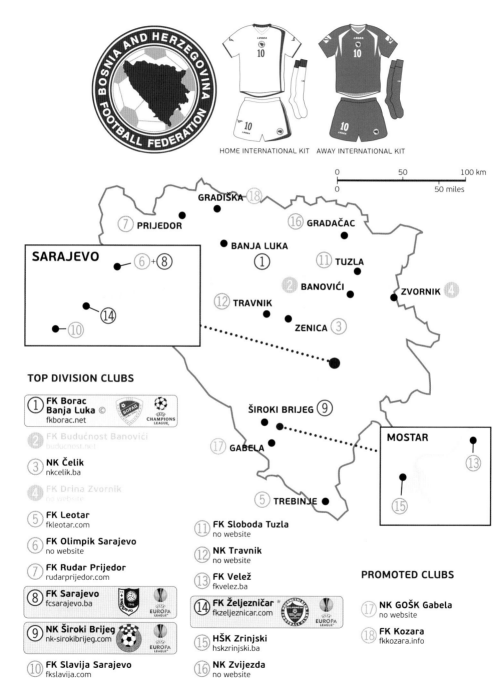

HOME INTERNATIONAL KIT AWAY INTERNATIONAL KIT

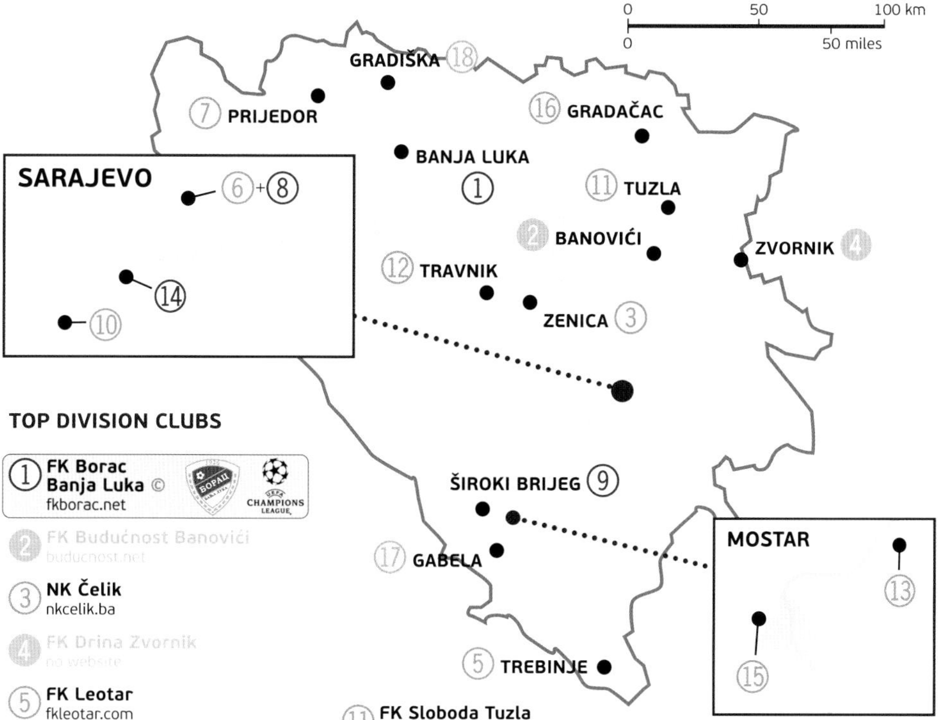

TOP DIVISION CLUBS

1. **FK Borac Banja Luka** © fkborac.net
2. **FK Budućnost Banovići** buducnost.net
3. **NK Čelik** nkcelik.ba
4. **FK Drina Zvornik** no website
5. **FK Leotar** fkleotar.com
6. **FK Olimpik Sarajevo** no website
7. **FK Rudar Prijedor** rudarprijedor.com
8. **FK Sarajevo** fcsarajevo.ba
9. **NK Široki Brijeg** nk-sirokibrijeg.com
10. **FK Slavija Sarajevo** fkslavija.com
11. **FK Sloboda Tuzla** no website
12. **NK Travnik** no website
13. **FK Velež** fkvelez.ba
14. **FK Željezničar** * fkzeljeznicar.com
15. **HŠK Zrinjski** hskzrinjski.ba
16. **NK Zvijezda** no website

PROMOTED CLUBS

17. **NK GOŠK Gabela** no website
18. **FK Kozara** fkkozara.info

BULGARIA

Bulgarie | Bulgarien

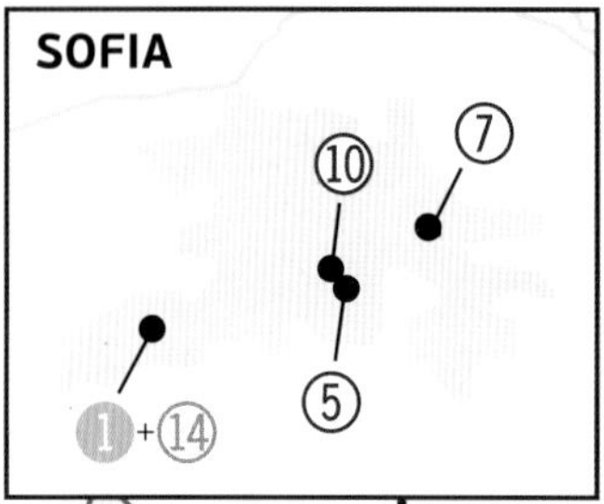

HOME INTERNATIONAL KIT   AWAY INTERNATIONAL KIT

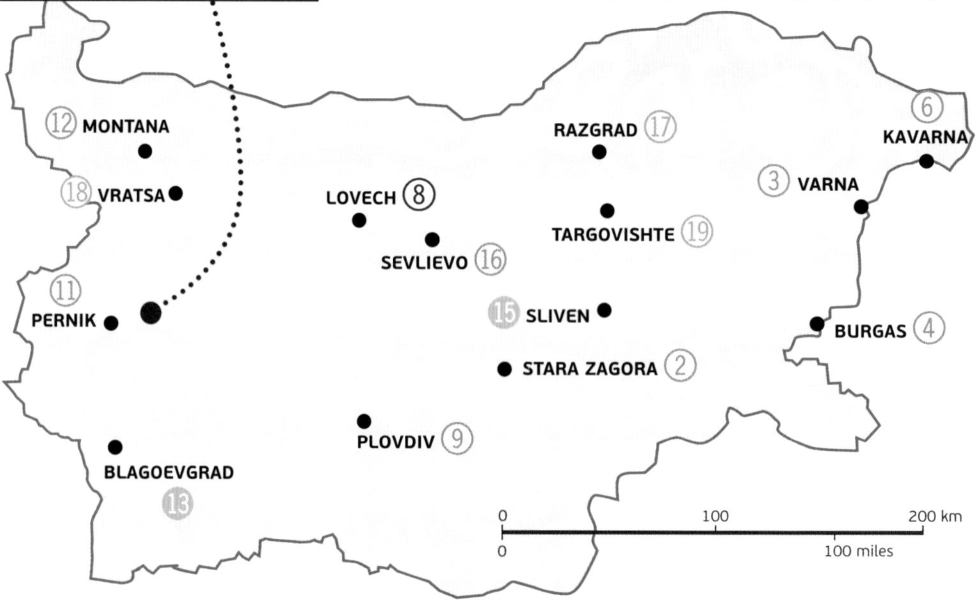

TOP DIVISION CLUBS

1. **PFC Akademik Sofia** akademik-sofia.com
2. **PFC Beroe Stara Zagora** beroe.eu
3. **PFC Cherno More Varna** chernomorepfc.bg
4. **PSFC Chernomorets Burgas** chernomoretz.bg
5. **PFC CSKA Sofia** * cska.bg
6. **PFC Kaliakra Kavarna** fckaliakra.com
7. **PFC Levski Sofia** levski.bg
8. **PFC Litex Lovech** © pfclitex.com
9. **PFC Lokomotiv Plovdiv 1936** lokomotivpd.com
10. **PFC Lokomotiv Sofia** lokomotivsofia.bg
11. **PFC Minior Pernik** minyor.com
12. **PFC Montana 1921** no website
13. **PFC Pirin Blagoevgrad** pirinfc.com
14. **PFC Slavia Sofia** pfcslavia.com
15. **OFC Sliven 2000** sliven-fc.com
16. **PFC Vidima-Rakovski Sevlievo** vidimarakovski.bg

PROMOTED CLUBS

17. **PFC Ludogorets Razgrad** ludogorets.com
18. **OFC Botev Vratsa** botevvratza.com
19. **PFC Svetkavitsa Targovishte** no website

CROATIA

Croatie | Kroatien

TOP DIVISION CLUBS

1 **HNK Cibalia**
hnk-cibalia.hr

2 **GNK Dinamo Zagreb** ©*
nk-dinamo.hr
CHAMPIONS LEAGUE

3 **HNK Hajduk Split**
hajduk.hr
EUROPA LEAGUE

4 **NK Hrvatski dragovoljac Zagreb**
nk-hrvatskidragovoljac.hr

5 **NK Inter Zaprešić**
inter.hr

6 **NK Istra**
nkistra1961.hr

7 **NK Karlovac**
nk-karlovac.hr

8 **NK Lokomotiva Zagreb**
nklokomotiva.hr

9 **NK Osijek**
nk-osijek.hr

10 **HNK Rijeka**
nk-rijeka.hr

11 **HNK Šibenik**
hnk-sibenik.hr

12 **NK Slaven Koprivnica**
nk-slaven-belupo.hr

13 **RNK Split**
rnksplit.hr
EUROPA LEAGUE

14 **NK Varaždin**
no website
EUROPA LEAGUE

15 **NK Zadar**
nkzadar.hr

16 **NK Zagreb**
nkzagreb.hr

PROMOTED CLUB

17 **NK Lučko**
nk-lucko.hr

HOME INTERNATIONAL KIT

AWAY INTERNATIONAL KIT

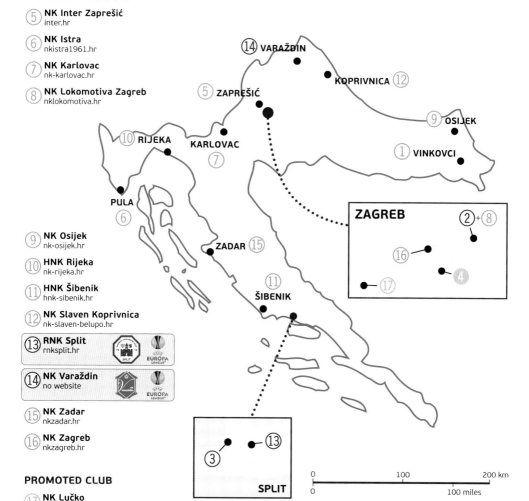

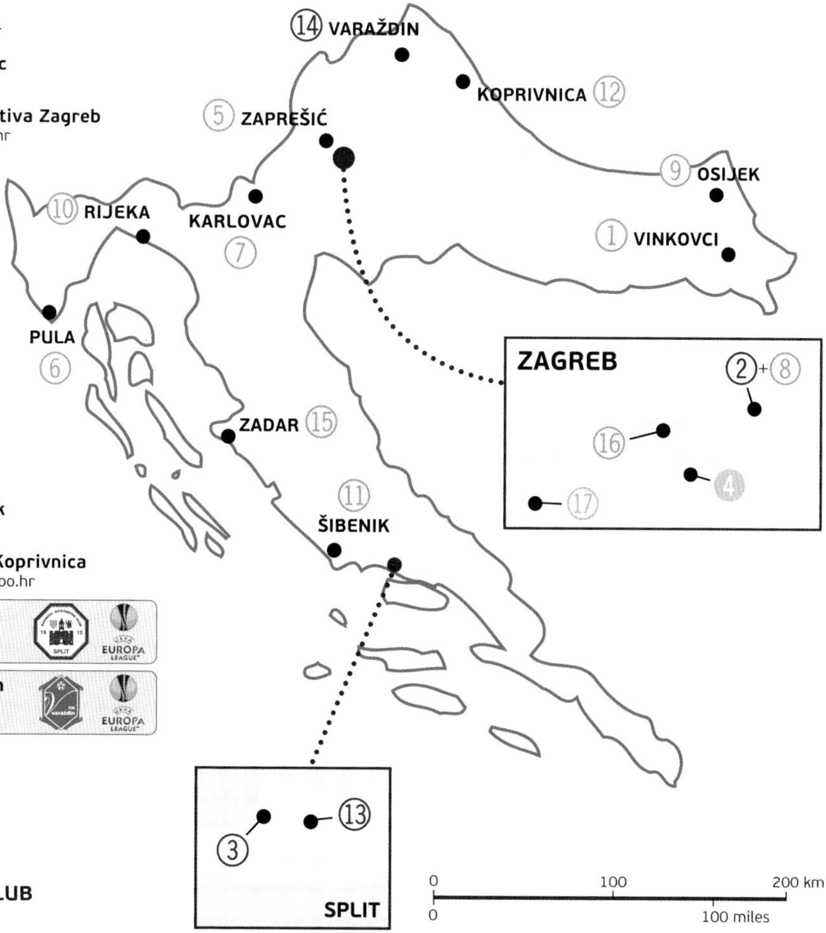

CYPRUS

Chypre | Zypern

TOP DIVISION CLUBS

1 **AEK Larnaca FC**
aek.com.cy

2 **AEL Limassol FC**
aelfc.com

3 **AEP Paphos FC**
pafosfc.com

4 **Alki Larnaca FC**
alkifc.com.cy

5 **Anorthosis Famagusta FC**
anorthosisfc.com

6 **APOEL FC** ©
apoelfc.com.cy

7 **Apollon Limassol FC**
apollon.com.cy

8 **APOP/Kinyras Peyias FC**
apopkinyrasfc.com

9 **Doxa Katokopia FC**
doxakatokopiasfc.com

10 **Enosis Neon Paralimni FC**
enpfc.com

11 **Ermis Aradippou FC**
ermisaradippoufc.com

12 **Ethnikos Achnas FC**
no website

13 **Olympiakos Nicosia FC**
olympiakos.com.cy

14 **AC Omonia** *
omonoia.com.cy

PROMOTED CLUBS

15 **Aris Limassol FC**
aris-fc.com

16 **Nea Salamis FC**
neasalamis.com.cy

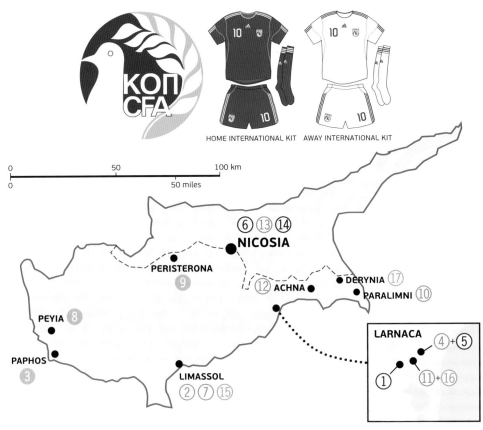

17 **Anagennisi Derynia FC**
anagennisis1920.net

CZECH REPUBLIC

République Tchèque | Tschechische Republik

HOME INTERNATIONAL KIT AWAY INTERNATIONAL KIT

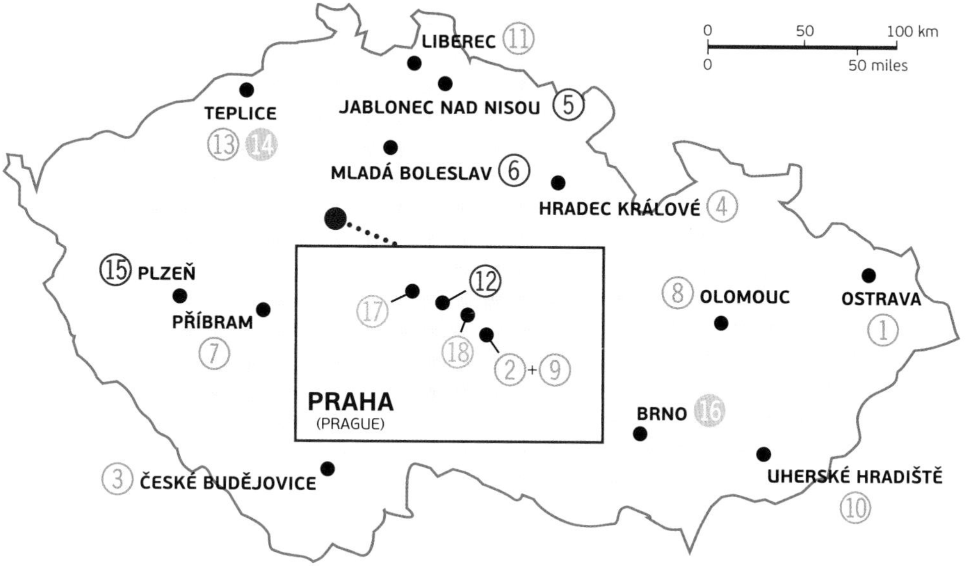

TOP DIVISION CLUBS

1. **FC Baník Ostrava** fcb.cz
2. **Bohemians 1905** bohemians.cz
3. **SK Dynamo České Budějovice** dynamocb.cz
4. **FC Hradec Králové** fchk.cz
5. **FK Jablonec** fkjablonec.cz (UEFA Europa League)
6. **FK Mladá Boleslav** * fkmb.cz (UEFA Europa League)
7. **1. FK Příbram** fkpribram.cz
8. **SK Sigma Olomouc** sigmafotbal.cz
9. **SK Slavia Praha** slavia.cz
10. **1. FC Slovácko** fcslovacko.cz
11. **FC Slovan Liberec** fcslovanliberec.cz
12. **AC Sparta Praha** sparta.cz (UEFA Europa League)
13. **FK Teplice** fkteplice.cz
14. **FK Ústí nad Labem** fkusti.cz
15. **FC Viktoria Plzeň** © fcviktoria.cz (UEFA Champions League)
16. **FC Zbrojovka Brno** fczbrno.cz

PROMOTED CLUBS

17. **FK Dukla Praha** fkdukla.cz
18. **FK Viktoria Žižkov** fkvz.cz

DENMARK

Danemark | Dänemark

HOME INTERNATIONAL KIT AWAY INTERNATIONAL KIT

TOP DIVISION CLUBS

1. **Aalborg BK** aabsport.dk
2. **Brøndby IF** brondby.com
3. Esbjerg fB efb.dk
4. **AC Horsens** achorsens.dk
5. **FC København ©** fck.dk
6. **Lyngby BK** lyngby-boldklub.dk
7. **FC Midtjylland** fcm.dk
8. **FC Nordsjælland** * fcn.dk
9. **Odense BK** ob.dk
10. Randers FC randersfc.dk
11. **Silkeborg IF** silkeborgif.com
12. **SønderjyskE** soenderjyske.dk

PROMOTED CLUBS

13. **AGF Århus** agffodbold.dk
14. **HB Køge** hb.dk

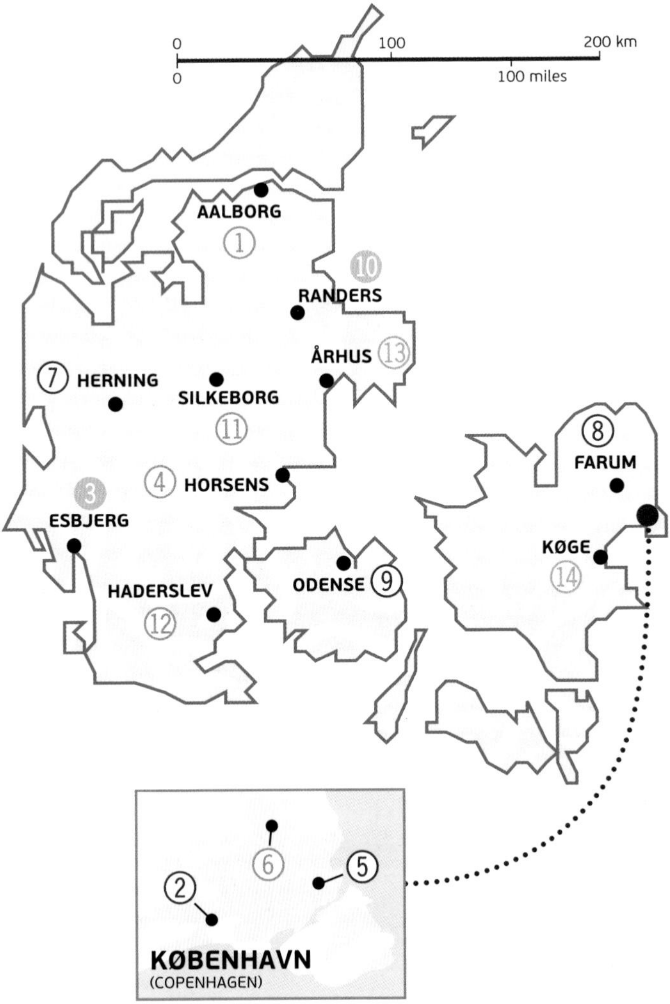

ENGLAND

Angleterre | England

HOME INTERNATIONAL KIT   AWAY INTERNATIONAL KIT

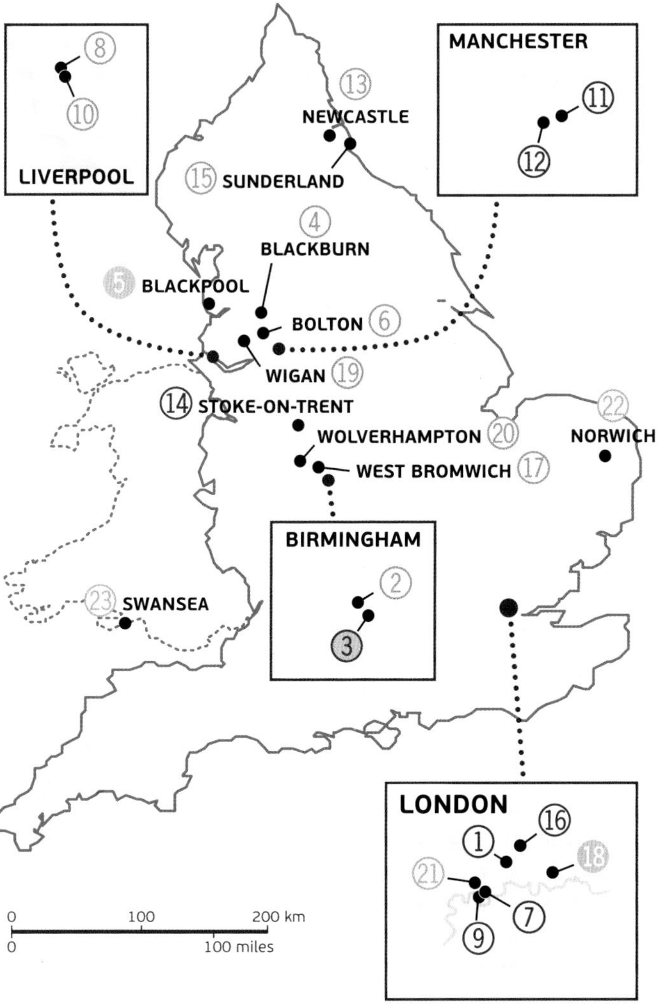

TOP DIVISION CLUBS

1. **Arsenal FC** arsenal.com — CHAMPIONS LEAGUE
2. **Aston Villa FC** avfc.co.uk
3. **Birmingham City FC** bcfc.com — EUROPA LEAGUE
4. **Blackburn Rovers FC** rovers.co.uk
5. **Blackpool FC** blackpoolfc.co.uk
6. **Bolton Wanderers FC** bwfc.co.uk
7. **Chelsea FC** chelseafc.com — CHAMPIONS LEAGUE
8. **Everton FC** evertonfc.com
9. **Fulham FC** [fp] fulhamfc.com — EUROPA LEAGUE
10. **Liverpool FC** liverpoolfc.tv
11. **Manchester City FC** * mcfc.co.uk — CHAMPIONS LEAGUE
12. **Manchester United FC** © manutd.com — CHAMPIONS LEAGUE
13. **Newcastle United FC** nufc.co.uk
14. **Stoke City FC** stokecityfc.com — EUROPA LEAGUE
15. **Sunderland AFC** safc.com
16. **Tottenham Hotspur FC** tottenhamhotspur.com — EUROPA LEAGUE
17. **West Bromwich Albion FC** wba.co.uk
18. **West Ham United FC** whufc.com
19. **Wigan Athletic FC** wiganlatics.co.uk
20. **Wolverhampton Wanderers FC** wolves.co.uk

PROMOTED CLUBS

21. **Queens Park Rangers FC** qpr.co.uk
22. **Norwich City FC** canaries.co.uk
23. **Swansea City AFC** swanseacity.net

ESTONIA
Estonie | Estland

HOME INTERNATIONAL KIT AWAY INTERNATIONAL KIT

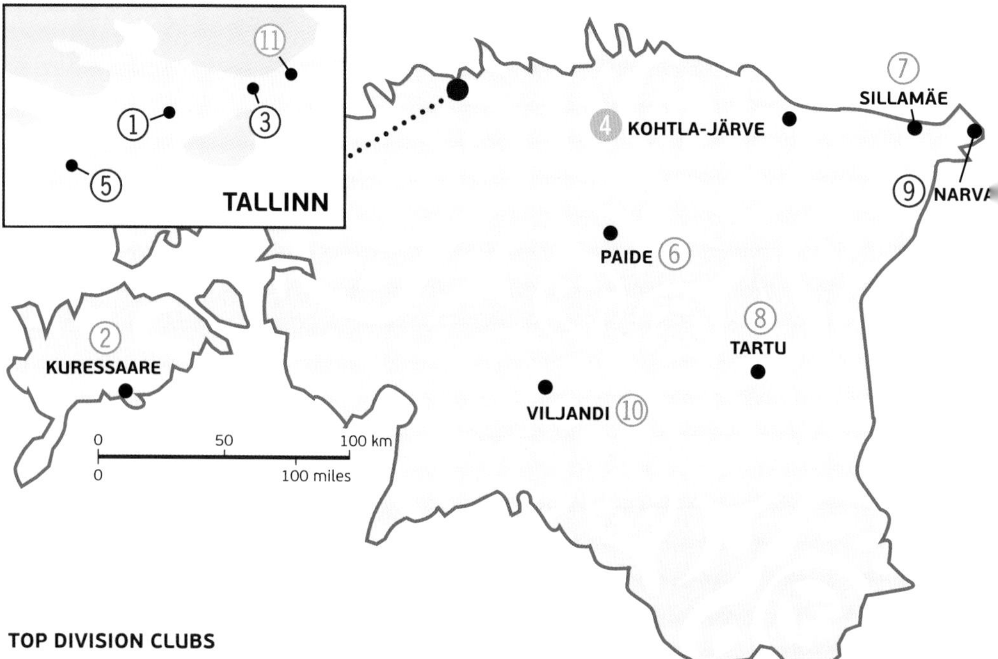

TOP DIVISION CLUBS

1. **FC Flora Tallinn** © *
fcflora.ee

2. **FC Kuressaare**
fckuressaare.ee

3. **FC Levadia Tallinn**
fclevadia.ee

4. **FC Lootus Kohtla-Järve**
fclootus.ee

5. **JK Nõmme Kalju**
jkkalju.ee

6. **Paide Linnameeskond**
linnameeskond.com

7. **JK Sillamäe Kalev**
fcsillamae.ee

8. **JK Tammeka Tartu**
jktammeka.ee

9. **JK Trans Narva**
fctrans.ee

10. **JK Tulevik Viljandi**
jktulevik.ee

NB JK Tulevik Viljandi changed name to FC Viljandi for 2011 season.

PROMOTED CLUB

11. **FC Ajax Lasnamäe**
fcajax.ee

FAROE ISLANDS

Îles Féroé | Färöer-Inseln

HOME INTERNATIONAL KIT AWAY INTERNATIONAL KIT

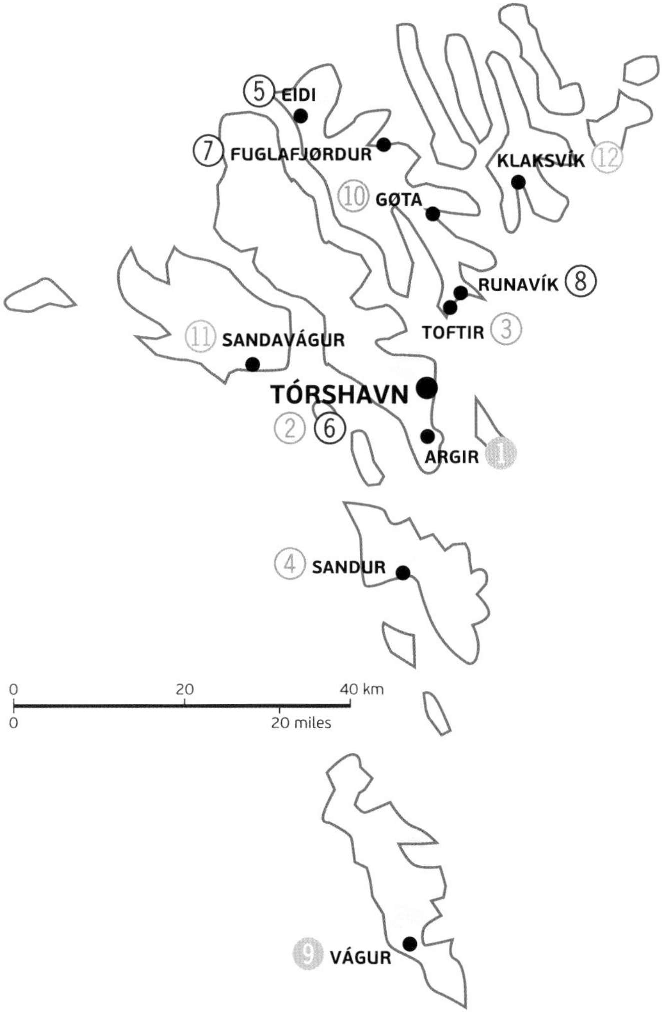

TOP DIVISION CLUBS

1 **AB Argir**
ab.fo

2 **B36 Tórshavn**
b36.fo

3 **B68 Toftir**
b68.fo

4 **B71 Sandoy**
b71-sandoy.com

5 **EB/Streymur** *
eb-streymur.fo

6 **HB Tórshavn** ©
hb.fo

7 **ÍF Fuglafjørdur**
if.fo

8 **NSÍ Runavík**
nsi.fo

9 **FC Suduroy**
fcsuduroy.com

10 **Víkingur**
vikingur.fo

PROMOTED CLUBS

11 **07 Vestur**
07vestur.fo

12 **KÍ Klaksvík**
ki.fo

FINLAND

Finlande | Finnland

HOME INTERNATIONAL KIT AWAY INTERNATIONAL KIT

TOP DIVISION CLUBS

1. **HJK Helsinki** © — hjk.fi — UEFA Champions League
2. **FC Honka Espoo** — fchonka.fi — UEFA Europa League
3. **FC Inter Turku** — fcinter.com
4. **FF Jaro** — ffjaro.fi
5. **JJK Jyväskylä** — fcjjk.com
6. **KuPS Kuopio** — kups.fi — UEFA Europa League
7. **FC Lahti** — fclahti.fi
8. **IFK Mariehamn** — ifkmariehamn.com/fotboll
9. **Myllykosken Pallo-47** — mypa.fi
10. **AC Oulu** — acoulu.fi
11. **Tampere United** — tampereunited.com
12. **TPS Turku** * — fctps.fi — UEFA Europa League
13. **Valkeakosken Haka** — fchaka.fi
14. **VPS Vaasa** — vepsu.fi

PROMOTED CLUB

15. **RoPS Rovaniemi** — rops.fi

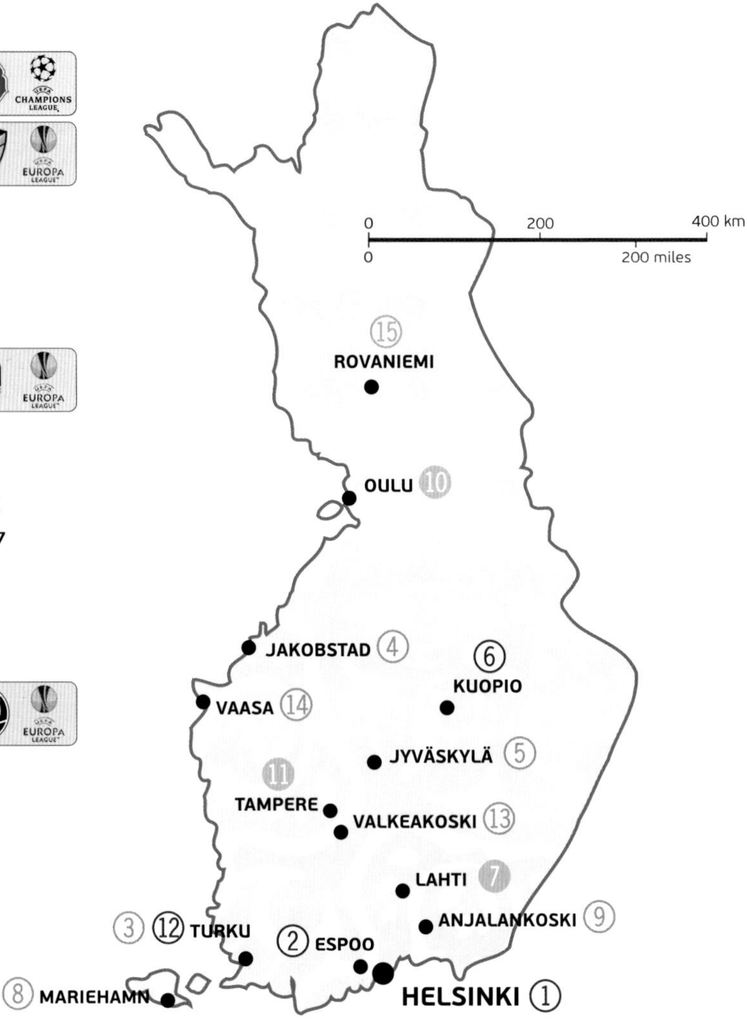

FRANCE

France | Frankreich

HOME INTERNATIONAL KIT AWAY INTERNATIONAL KIT

TOP DIVISION CLUBS

1 AC Arles-Avignon
acarlesavignon.fr

2 **AJ Auxerre**
aja.fr

3 **FC Girondins de Bordeaux**
girondins.com

4 **Stade Brestois 29**
sb29.com

5 **SM Caen**
smcaen.fr

6 RC Lens
rclens.fr

7 **LOSC Lille Métropole** ©*
losc.fr

8 **FC Lorient**
fclweb.fr

9 **Olympique Lyonnais**
olweb.fr

10 **Olympique de Marseille**
om.net

11 AS Monaco FC
asm-fc.com

12 **Montpellier Hérault SC**
mhscfoot.com

13 **AS Nancy-Lorraine**
asnl.net

14 **OGC Nice**
ogcnice.com

15 **Paris Saint-Germain FC**
psg.fr

16 **Stade Rennais FC**
staderennais.com

17 **AS Saint-Étienne**
asse.fr

18 **FC Sochaux-Montbéliard**
fcsochaux.fr

19 **Toulouse FC**
tfc.info

20 **Valenciennes FC**
va-fc.com

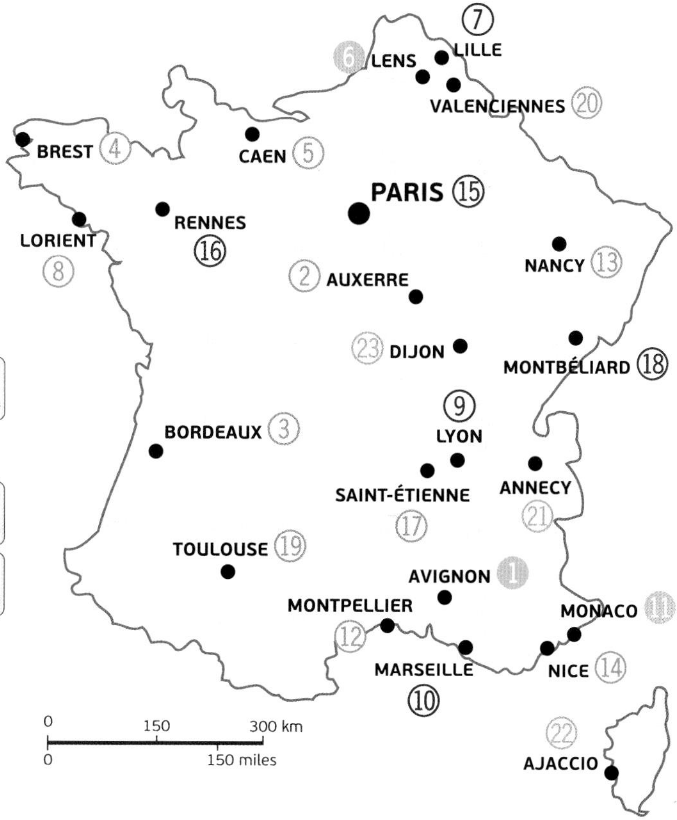

PROMOTED CLUBS

21 **Évian Thonon Gaillard FC**
etgfc.com

22 **AC Ajaccio**
ac-ajaccio.com

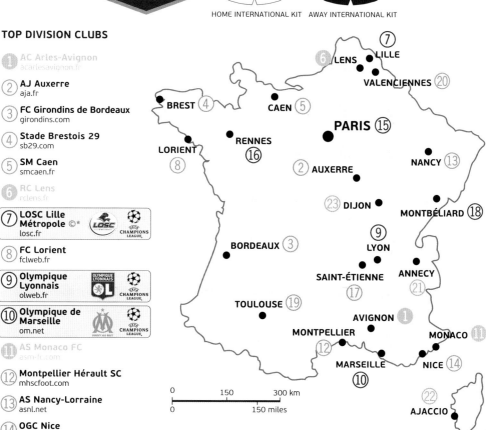

23 **Dijon FCO**
dfco.fr

GEORGIA

Géorgie | Georgien

HOME INTERNATIONAL KIT AWAY INTERNATIONAL KIT

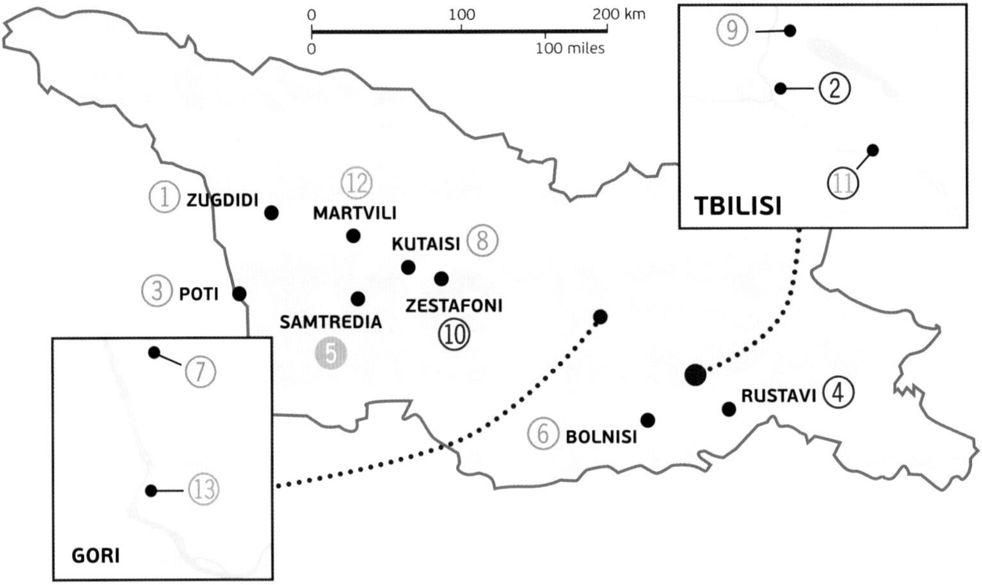

TOP DIVISION CLUBS

1. **FC Baia Zugdidi**
no website

2. **FC Dinamo Tbilisi**
fcdinamo.ge

3. **FC Kolkheti Poti**
no website

4. **FC Olimpi Rustavi**
fcml.ge

NB FC Olimpi Rustavi changed name to FC Metalurgi Rustavi for 2011/12 season.

5. **FC Samtredia**
no website

6. **FC Sioni Bolnisi**
no website

7. **FC Spartaki Tskhinvali**
no website

8. **FC Torpedo Kutaisi**
fctorpedo.ge

9. **FC WIT Georgia**
witgeorgia.ge

10. **FC Zestafoni** ©
fczestafoni.ge

PROMOTED CLUBS

11. **FC Gagra** *
fcgagra.ge

12. **FC Merani Martvili**
no website

13. **FC Dila Gori**
no website

GERMANY

Allemagne | Deutschland

HOME INTERNATIONAL KIT AWAY INTERNATIONAL KIT

TOP DIVISION CLUBS

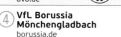

1. **Bayer 04 Leverkusen**
   bayer04.de
2. **FC Bayern München**
   fcbayern.telekom.de
3. **Borussia Dortmund** ©
   bvb.de
4. **VfL Borussia Mönchengladbach**
   borussia.de
5. Eintracht Frankfurt
   eintracht.de
6. **SC Freiburg**
   scfreiburg.com
7. **Hamburger SV**
   hsv.de
8. **Hannover 96**
   hannover96.de
9. **TSG 1899 Hoffenheim**
   achtzehn99.de
10. **1. FC Kaiserslautern**
    fck.de
11. **1. FC Köln**
    fc-koeln.de
12. **1. FSV Mainz 05**
    mainz05.de
13. **1. FC Nürnberg**
    fcn.de
14. **FC Schalke 04** *
    schalke04.de
15. FC St Pauli
    fcstpauli.com
16. **VfB Stuttgart**
    vfb.de
17. **SV Werder Bremen**
    werder.de
18. **VfL Wolfsburg**
    vfl-wolfsburg.de

PROMOTED CLUBS

19. **Hertha BSC Berlin**
    herthabsc.de
20. **FC Augsburg**
    fcaugsburg.de

GREECE

Grèce | Griechenland

TOP DIVISION CLUBS

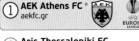

1. **AEK Athens FC** * aekfc.gr — UEFA Europa League
2. **Aris Thessaloniki FC** arisfc.gr
3. **Asteras Tripolis FC** asterastripolis.gr
4. **Atromitos FC** atromitosfc.gr
5. **Ergotelis FC** ergotelis.gr
6. **Iraklis FC** iraklis-fc.gr
7. **Kavala FC** kavalafc.gr
8. **Kerkyra FC** aokerkyra.com.gr
9. **Larissa FC** ael1964.gr
10. **Olympiacos FC** © olympiacos.org — UEFA Champions League
11. **Olympiacos Volou FC** paeolympiakosvoloufc.gr — UEFA Europa League
12. **Panathinaikos FC** pao.gr — UEFA Champions League
13. **Panionios GSS** pgss.gr
14. **Panserraikos FC** panserraikos.eu
15. **PAOK FC** paokfc.gr — UEFA Europa League
16. **Xanthi FC** skodaxanthifc.gr

PROMOTED CLUBS

17. **Panaitolikos GFS** panaitolikos.gr
18. **PAS Giannina FC** pasgiannina.gr
19. **OFI Crete FC** ofi.gr

HOME INTERNATIONAL KIT AWAY INTERNATIONAL KIT

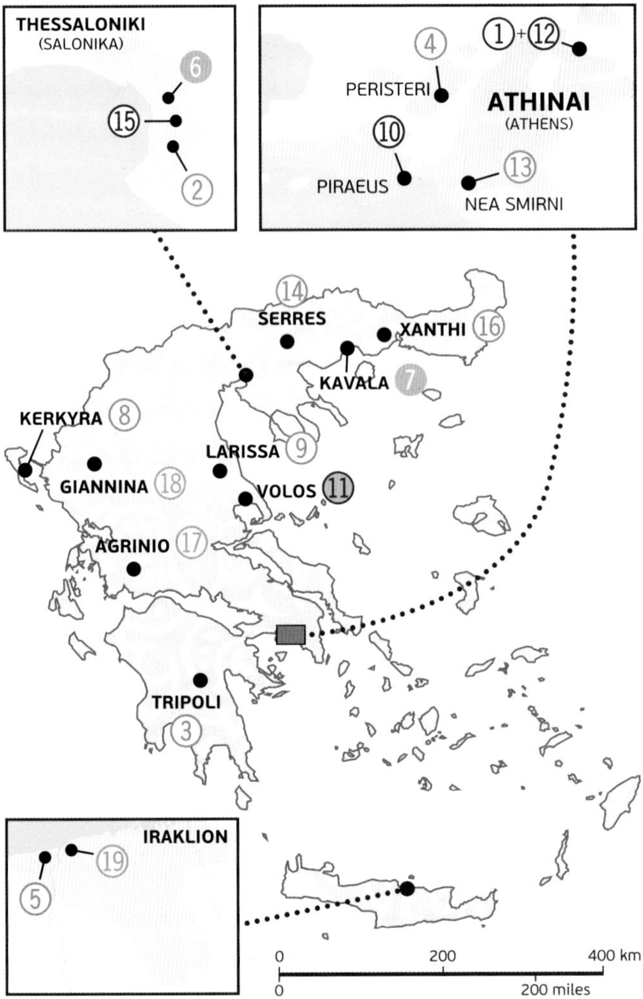

HUNGARY

Hongrie | Ungarn

HOME INTERNATIONAL KIT AWAY INTERNATIONAL KIT

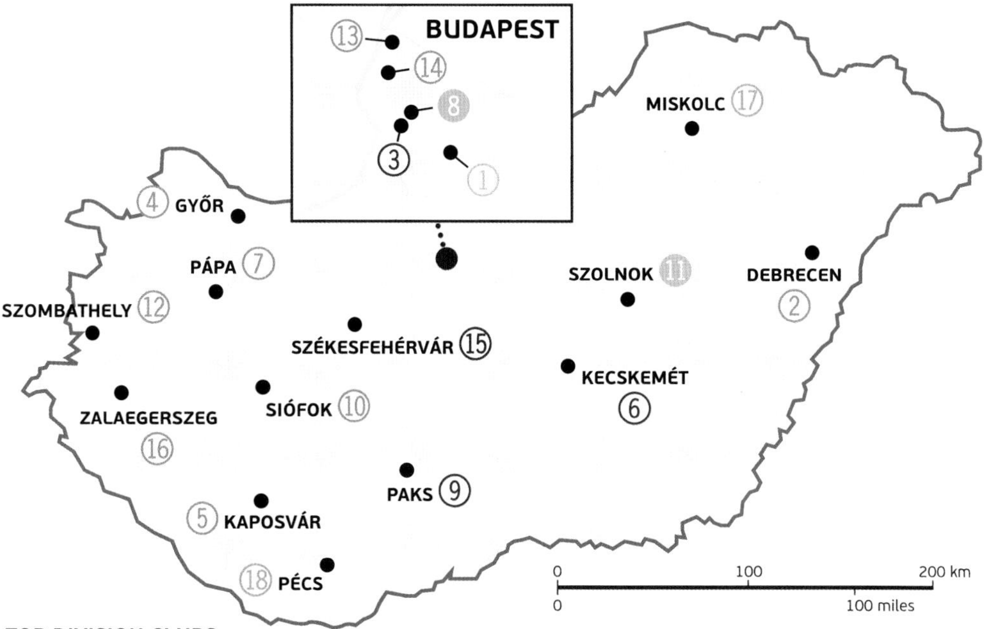

TOP DIVISION CLUBS

1 **Budapest Honvéd FC**
honvedfc.hu

2 **Debreceni VSC**
dvsc.hu

3 **Ferencvárosi TC**
ftc.hu

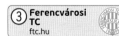

4 **Győri ETO FC**
eto.hu

5 **Kaposvári Rákóczi FC**
rakoczifc.hu

6 **Kecskeméti TE** *
kecskemetite.hu

7 **Lombard-Pápa TFC**
lombardfcpapa.hu

8 **MTK Budapest**
mtkhungaria.hu

9 **Paksi SE**
paksise.hu

10 **BFC Siófok**
bfc-siofok.hu

11 **Szolnoki MÁV FC**
szolnokimavfc.hu

12 **Szombathelyi Haladás**
haladas.hu

13 **Újpest FC**
ujpestfc.hu

14 **Vasas SC**
vasassc.hu

15 **Videoton FC** ©
vidi.hu

16 **Zalaegerszegi TE**
ztefc.hu

PROMOTED CLUBS

17 **Diósgyőri VTK**
dvtk.eu

18 **Pécsi MFC**
pmfc.hu

ICELAND

Islande | Island

HOME INTERNATIONAL KIT   AWAY INTERNATIONAL KIT

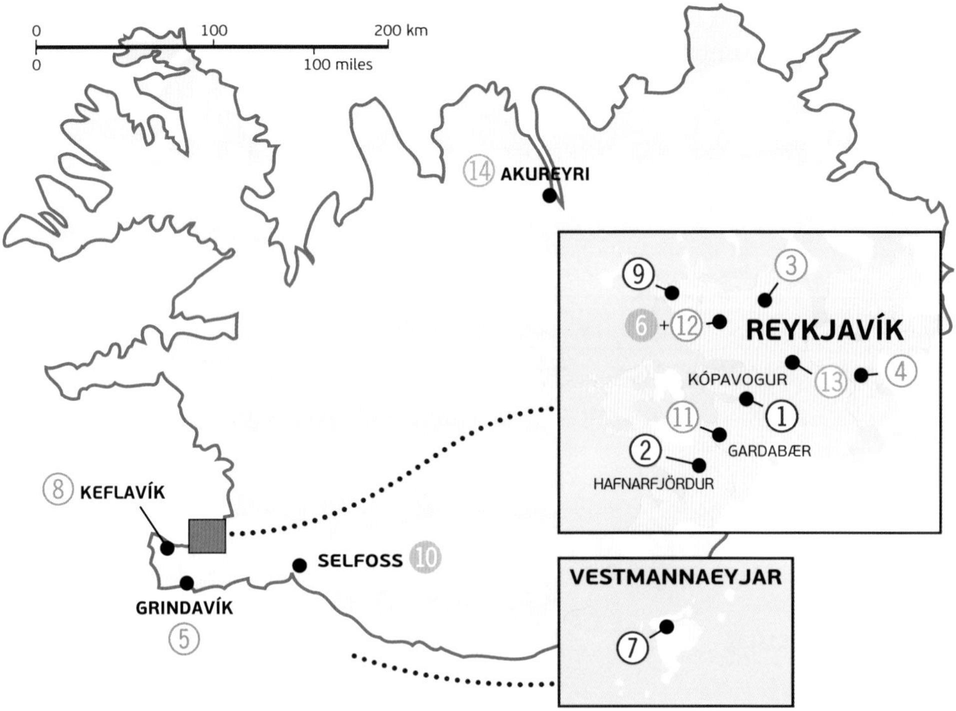

TOP DIVISION CLUBS

1 **Breidablik** ©
breidablik.is

2 **FH Hafnarfjördur***
fh.is

3 **Fram Reykjavík**
fram.is

4 **Fylkir**
fylkir.com

5 **Grindavík**
umfg.is

6 **Haukar**
haukar.is

7 **ÍBV Vestmannaeyjar**
ibvsport.is

8 **Keflavík**
keflavik.is

9 **KR Reykjavík**
kr.is

10 **Selfoss**
umfs.is

11 **Stjarnan**
stjarnan.is

12 **Valur Reykjavík**
valur.is

PROMOTED CLUBS

13 **Víkingur Reykjavík**
vikingur.is

14 **Thór Akureyri**
thorsport.is

ISRAEL

Israël | Israel

HOME INTERNATIONAL KIT AWAY INTERNATIONAL KIT

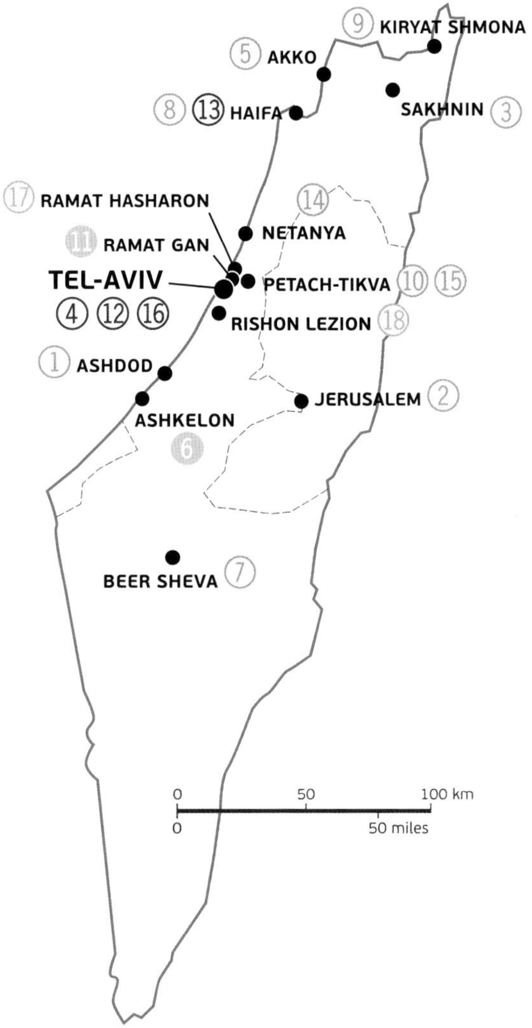

TOP DIVISION CLUBS

1 **FC Ashdod**
fcashdod.com

2 **Beitar Jerusalem FC**
beitarfc.co.il

3 **Bnei Sakhnin FC**
no website

4 **Bnei Yehuda Tel-Aviv FC**
bneiyehuda.com
EUROPA LEAGUE

5 **Hapoel Akko FC**
no website

6 **Hapoel Ashkelon FC**
no website

7 **Hapoel Beer Sheva FC**
hapoelb7.co.il

8 **Hapoel Haifa FC**
hapoel-haifa.org.il

9 **Hapoel Kiryat Shmona FC**
iturank8.co.il

10 **Hapoel Petach-Tikva FC**
no website

11 **Hapoel Ramat Gan FC**
hapoelrg-fc.co.il

12 **Hapoel Tel-Aviv FC** *
hapoelta-fc.co.il
EUROPA LEAGUE

13 **Maccabi Haifa FC** ©
maccabi-haifafc.walla.co.il
CHAMPIONS LEAGUE

14 **Maccabi Netanya FC**
fcmn.co.il

15 **Maccabi Petach-Tikva FC**
m-pt.co.il

16 **Maccabi Tel-Aviv FC**
maccabi-tlv.co.il
EUROPA LEAGUE

PROMOTED CLUBS

17 **Hapoel Ironi Nir Ramat HaSharon FC**
rhfc.co.il

18 **Hapoel Ironi Rishon-LeZion FC**
rishonia.co.il

ITALY

Italie | Italien

HOME INTERNATIONAL KIT

AWAY INTERNATIONAL KIT

TOP DIVISION CLUBS

1 **AS Bari**
asbari.it

2 **Bologna FC**
bolognafc.it

3 **Brescia Calcio**
bresciaonline.it

4 **Cagliari Calcio**
cagliaricalcio.net

5 **Calcio Catania**
calciocatania.it

6 **AC Cesena**
cesenacalcio.it

7 **AC Chievo Verona**
chievoverona.tv

8 **ACF Fiorentina**
violachannel.tv

9 **Genoa CFC**
genoacfc.it

10 **FC Internazionale Milano** *
inter.it
CHAMPIONS LEAGUE

11 **Juventus**
juventus.com

12 **S.S. Lazio**
sslazio.it
EUROPA LEAGUE

13 **US Lecce**
uslecce.it

14 **AC Milan** ©
acmilan.com
CHAMPIONS LEAGUE

15 **SSC Napoli**
sscnapoli.it
CHAMPIONS LEAGUE

16 **US Città di Palermo**
ilpalermocalcio.it
EUROPA LEAGUE

17 **Parma FC**
fcparma.com

18 **AS Roma**
asroma.it
EUROPA LEAGUE

19 **UC Sampdoria**
sampdoria.it

20 **Udinese Calcio**
udinese.it
CHAMPIONS LEAGUE

PROMOTED CLUBS

21 **Atalanta BC**
atalanta.it

22 **AC Siena**
acsiena.it

23 **Novara Calcio**
novaracalcio.com

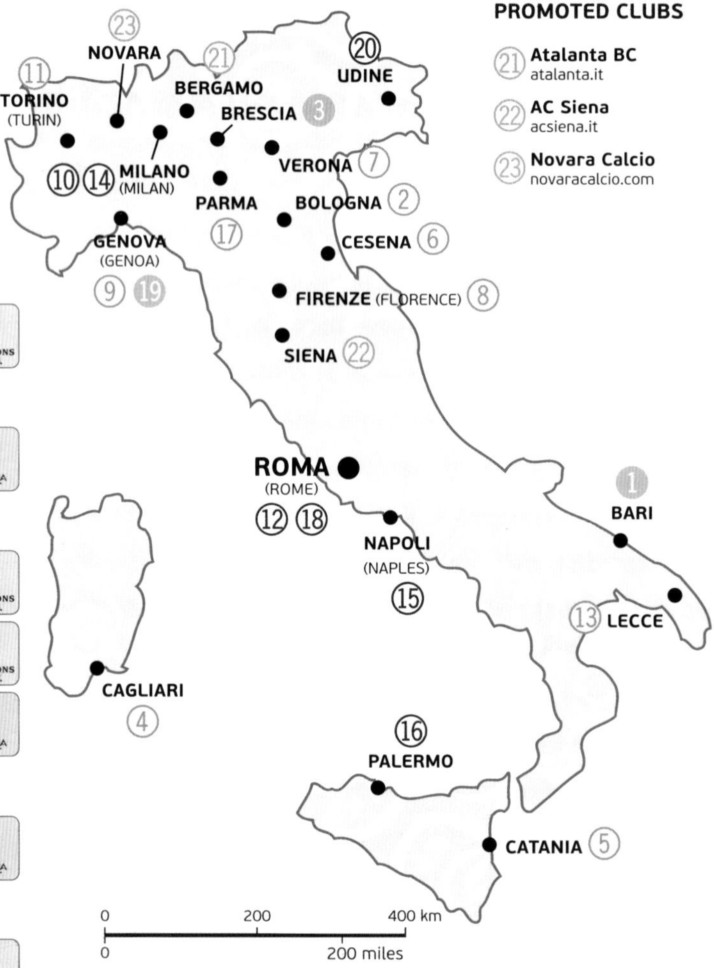

KAZAKHSTAN

Kazakhstan | Kasachstan

HOME INTERNATIONAL KIT   AWAY INTERNATIONAL KIT

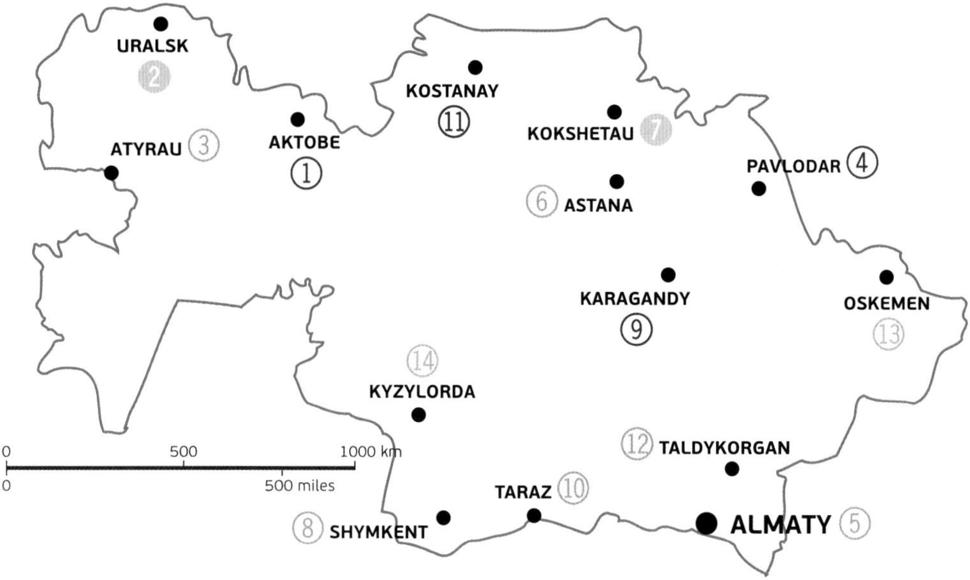

TOP DIVISION CLUBS

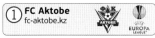

1. **FC Aktobe** fc-aktobe.kz
2. **FC Akzhaiyk Uralsk** akzhaik.info
3. **FC Atyrau** rfcatyrau.kz
4. **FC Irtysh Pavlodar** fcirtysh.kz
5. **FC Kairat Almaty** fckairat.kz
6. **FC Lokomotiv Astana** * fca.kz

NB FC Lokomotiv Astana changed name to FC Astana for 2011 season.

7. **FC Okzhetpes Kokshetau** okzhetpes.kz
8. **FC Ordabasy Shymkent** fcordabasy.kz
9. **FC Shakhter Karagandy** shahter.kz
10. **FC Taraz** fctaraz.kz
11. **FC Tobol Kostanay** © fc-tobol.kz
12. **FC Zhetysu Taldykorgan** fc-zhetisu.kz

PROMOTED CLUBS

13. **FC Vostok Oskemen** fc-vostok.kz
14. **FC Kaysar Kyzylorda** fc-kaysar.kz

LATVIA

Lettonie | Lettland

HOME INTERNATIONAL KIT AWAY INTERNATIONAL KIT

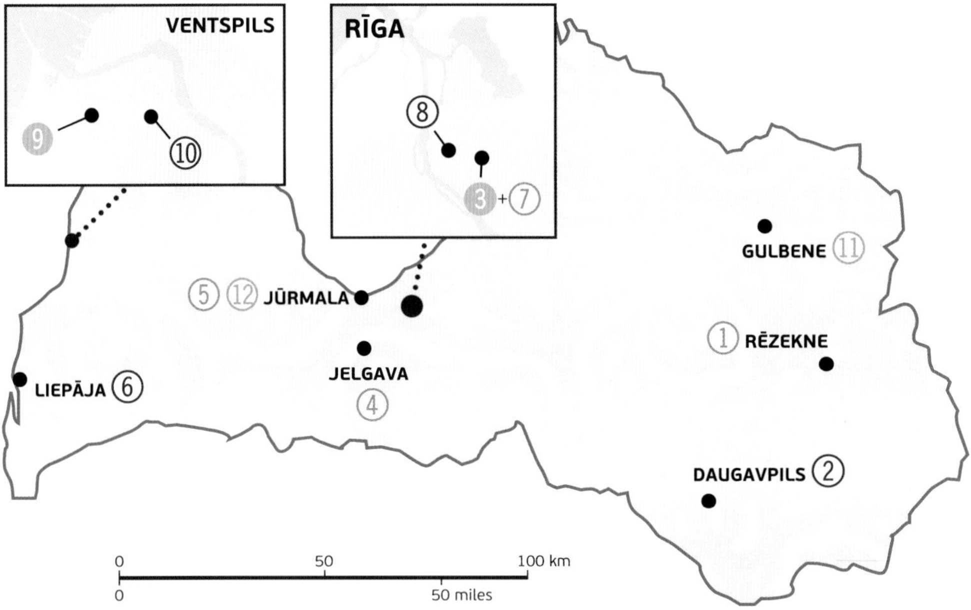

TOP DIVISION CLUBS

1. **SK Blāzma Rēzekne**
   no website
2. **FC Daugava Daugavpils**
   fcdaugava.lv
3. FK Jaunība Rīga
   fcj.lv
4. **FK Jelgava**
   fkjelgava.lv
5. **FK Jūrmala-VV**
   fcjurmala.lv
6. **SK Liepājas Metalurgs**
   skliepajasmetalurgs.lv
7. **JFK Olimps/RFS**
   no website
8. **Skonto FC** ©
   skontofc.lv
9. FC Tranzit
   no website
10. **FK Ventspils** *
    fkventspils.lv

PROMOTED CLUBS

11. **FB Gulbene 2005**
    no website
12. **FC Jūrmala**
    jurmalafc.lv

LIECHTENSTEIN

Llechtenstein | Liechtenstein

HOME INTERNATIONAL KIT AWAY INTERNATIONAL KIT

1. **FC Balzers**
   fcbalzers.li
2. **USV Eschen/Mauren**
   usv.li
3. **FC Ruggell**
   fcruggell.li
4. **FC Schaan**
   fcschaan.li
5. **FC Triesen**
   fctriesen.li
6. **FC Triesenberg**
   fctriesenberg.li
7. **FC Vaduz** *
   fcvaduz.li

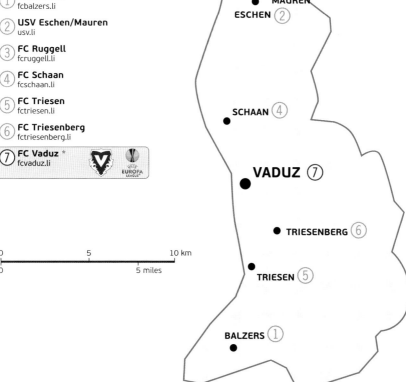

0 5 10 km
0 5 miles

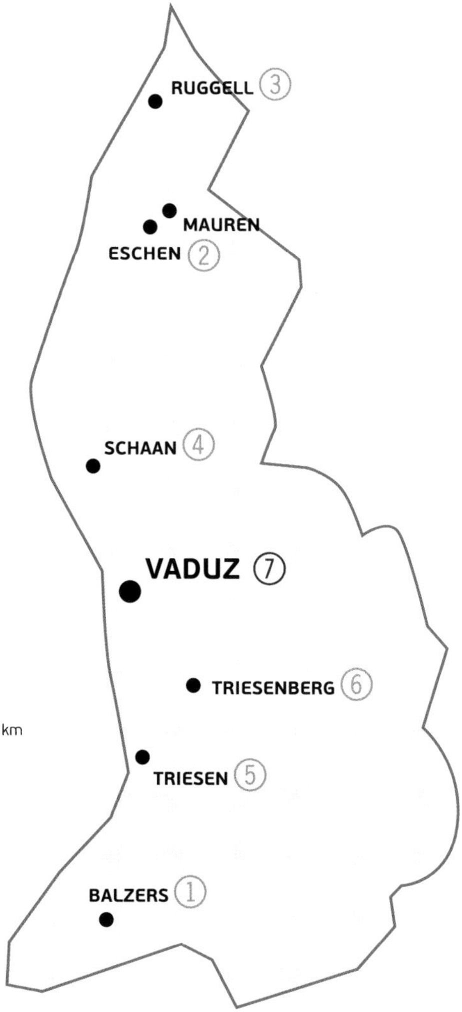

LITHUANIA

Lituanie | Litauen

HOME INTERNATIONAL KIT AWAY INTERNATIONAL KIT

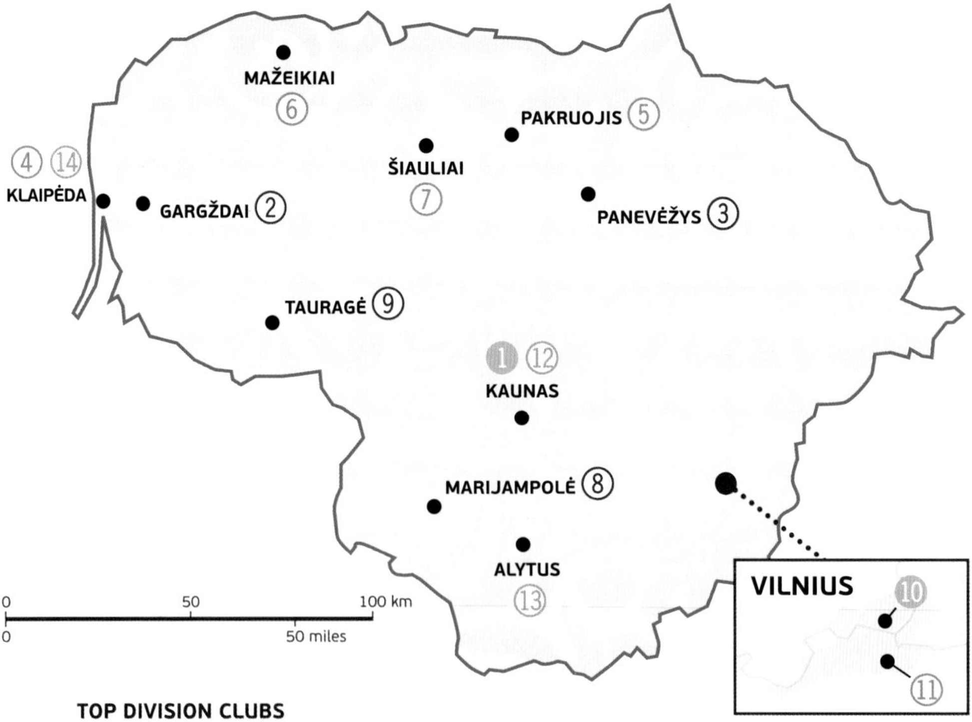

TOP DIVISION CLUBS

1 **FK Atletas**
no website

2 **FK Banga**
fkbanga.lt

3 **FK Ekranas** © *
fkekranas.lt

4 **FK Klaipėda**
klaipeda-fc.lt

5 **FK Kruoja**
fkkruoja.lt

6 **FK Mažeikiai**
fkmazeikiai.lt

7 **FC Šiauliai**
fcsiauliai.lt

8 **FK Sūduva**
fksuduva.lt

9 **FK Tauras**
fktauras.lt

10 **FK Vėtra**
fkvetra.lt

11 **VMFD Žalgiris**
zalgiris-vilnius.lt

PROMOTED CLUBS

12 **FBK Kaunas**
fbk.lt

13 **FK Dainava**
fkdainava.lt

14 **FK Atlantas**
atlantas.lt

LUXEMBOURG

Luxembourg | Luxemburg

HOME INTERNATIONAL KIT AWAY INTERNATIONAL KIT

TOP DIVISION CLUBS

1. **FC Differdange 03** * — fcd03.lu
2. **F91 Dudelange** © — f91.lu
3. FC Etzella Ettelbruck — fc-etzella.lu
4. **CS Fola Esch** — csfola.lu
5. **CS Grevenmacher** — csg.lu
6. **FC RM Hamm Benfica** — rmhb.lu
7. Jeunesse Canach — fccanach.lu
8. **AS Jeunesse Esch** — jeunesse-esch.lu
9. **UN Käerjéng 97** — un-kaerjeng.lu
10. **CS Pétange** — cspetange.lu
11. **FC Progrès Niedercorn** — progres.lu
12. **Racing FC Union Lëtzebuerg** — racing-fc.lu
13. **FC Swift Hesper** — swifthesper.lu
14. FC Wiltz 71 — fcwiltz.lu

PROMOTED CLUBS

15. **FC Union 05 Kayl/Tétange** — union05.lu
16. **US Rumelange** — usrumelange.lu
17. **US Hostert** — ushostert.lu

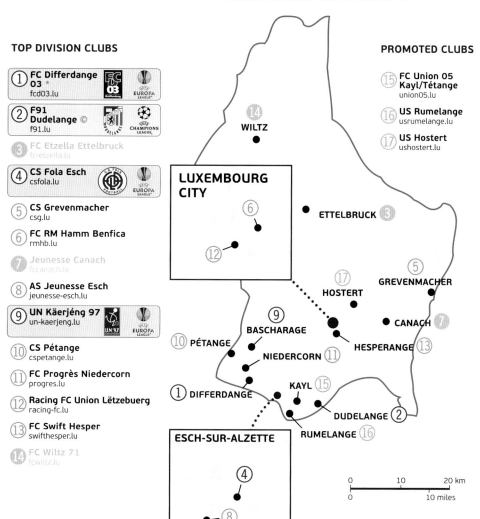

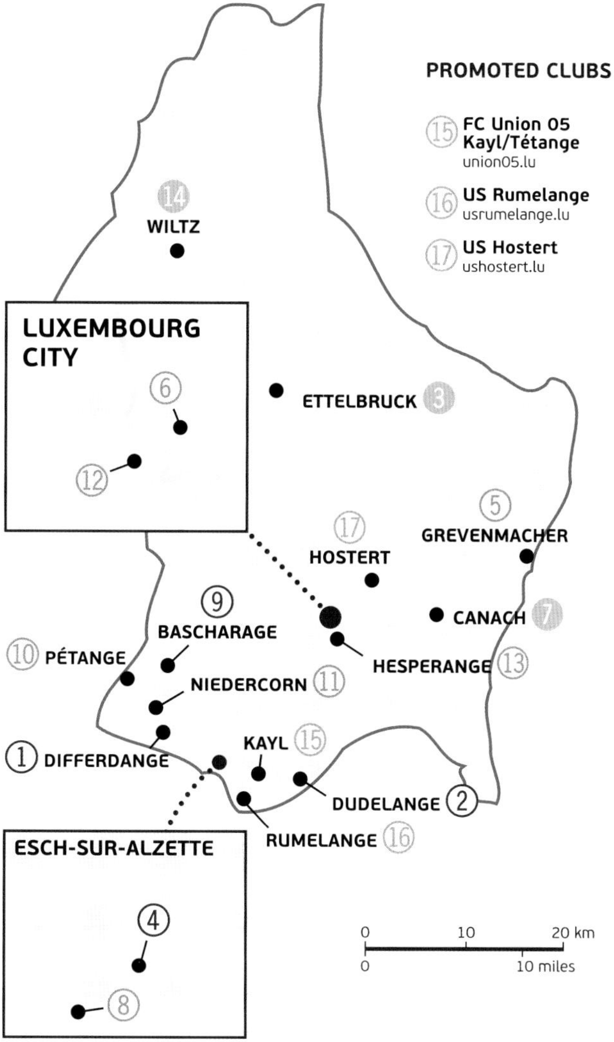

FORMER YUGOSLAV REPUBLIC OF MACEDONIA

ARY de Macédoine | EJR Mazedonien

HOME INTERNATIONAL KIT

AWAY INTERNATIONAL KIT

TOP DIVISION CLUBS

1. **FK Bregalnica Stip**
   bregalnicastip.tk
2. **FK Metalurg Skopje** *
   fcmetalurg.com.mk
   EUROPA LEAGUE
3. **FK Napredok**
   no website
4. **FK Pelister**
   fkpelister.com.mk
5. **FK Rabotnicki**
   rabotnicki.com
   EUROPA LEAGUE
6. **FK Renova**
   renova.com.mk
   EUROPA LEAGUE
7. **FK Shkëndija 79** ©
   no website
   CHAMPIONS LEAGUE
8. **FK Sileks**
   no website
9. **FK Skopje**
   no website
10. **FK Teteks**
    no website
11. **FK Turnovo**
    fkhorizontturnovo.mk
12. **FK Vardar**
    no website

PROMOTED CLUBS

13. **FK 11 Oktomvri**
    fk11oktomvri.com
14. **FK Ohrid 2004**
    fkohrid.weebly.com

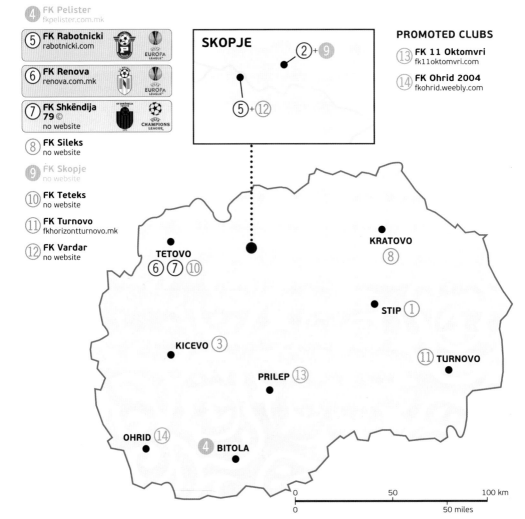

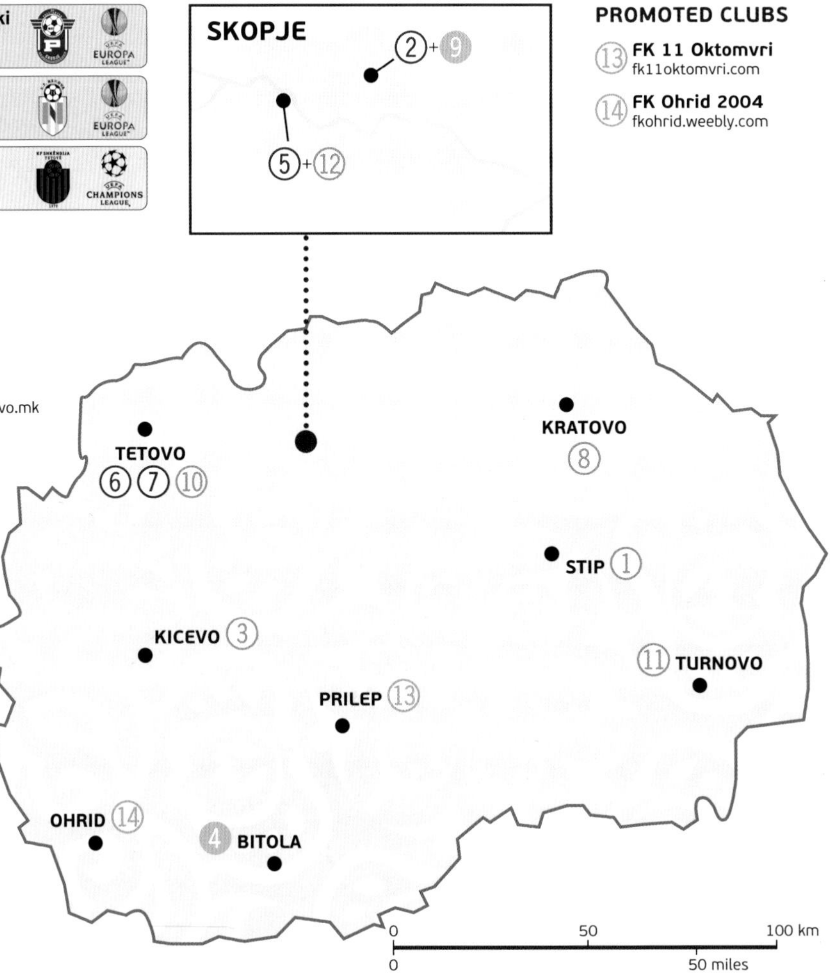

MALTA

Malte | Malta

HOME INTERNATIONAL KIT   AWAY INTERNATIONAL KIT

TOP DIVISION CLUBS

1. **Birkirkara FC** birkirkarafc.com
2. **Floriana FC** * florianafc.com
3. **Hamrun Spartans FC** hamrunspartansfc.com
4. **Hibernians FC** hiberniansfc.org
5. **Marsaxlokk FC** no website
6. **Qormi FC** qormifc.com
7. **Sliema Wanderers FC** sliemawfc.org
8. **Tarxien Rainbows FC** no website
9. **Valletta FC** © vallettafc.net
10. **Vittoriosa Stars FC** vittoriosastars.com

PROMOTED CLUBS

11. **Balzan Youths FC** balzanyouthsfc.net
12. **Mqabba FC** mqabbafc.com
13. **Mosta FC** mostafootballclub.com

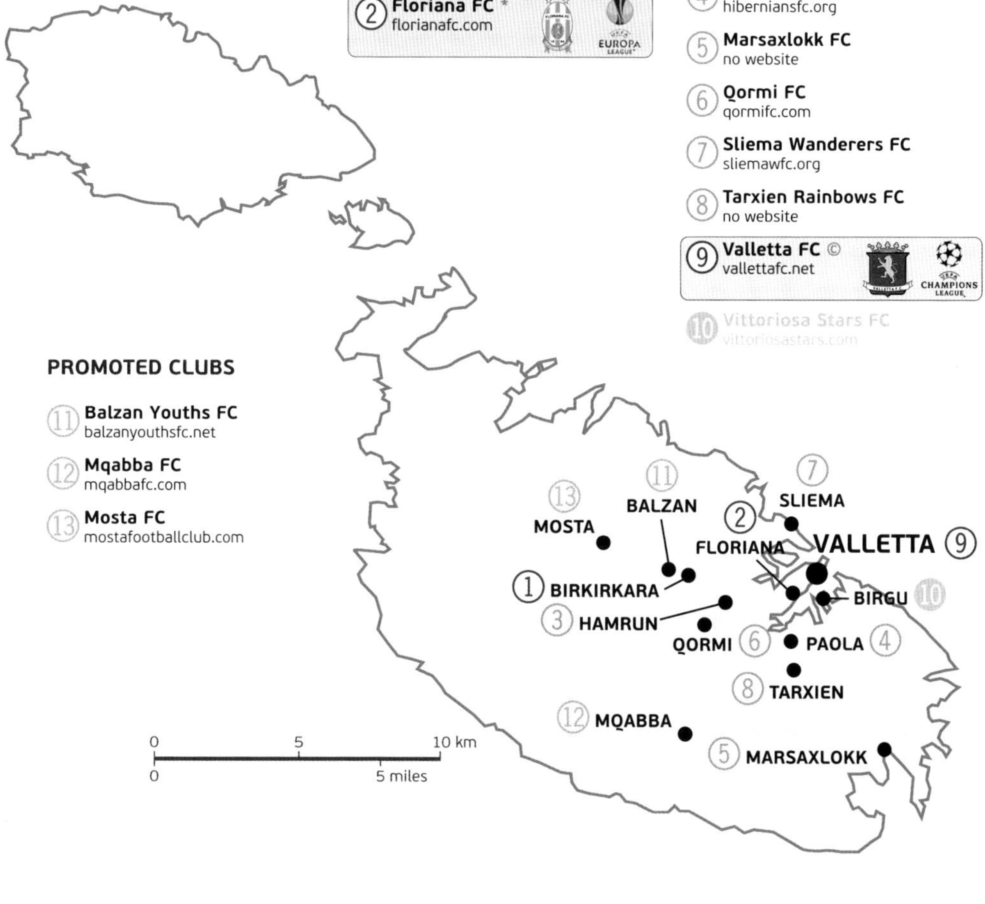

MOLDOVA

Moldavie | Moldawien

HOME INTERNATIONAL KIT AWAY INTERNATIONAL KIT

TOP DIVISION CLUBS

1. **FC Academia UTM Chisinau**
   academia.md
2. **FC Costuleni**
   fccostuleni.md
3. **FC Dacia Chisinau** ©
   fcdacia.md
4. **FC Dinamo Bender**
   dynamo-bendery.narod.ru
5. **CF Gagauziya Comrat**
   no website
6. **FC Iskra-Stal** *
   iskra-stal.com
7. **FC Milsami**
   milsami.md

NB FC Milsami merged with FC Ursidos to become FC Milsami-Ursidos for 2011/12 season.

8. **FC Nistru Otaci**
   fc-nistru.dnestr.net
9. **FC Olimpia Balti**
   fcolimpia.md
10. **FC Rapid Ghidighici**
    fcrapid.md

NB FC Rapid Ghidighici changed name to CSCA-Rapid Chisinau for 2011/12 season.

11. **FC Sfintul Gheorghe Suruceni**
    sgsfc.md
12. **FC Sheriff**
    fc-sheriff.com
13. **FC Tiraspol**
    fc-tiraspol.com
14. **FC Zimbru Chisinau**
    zimbru.md

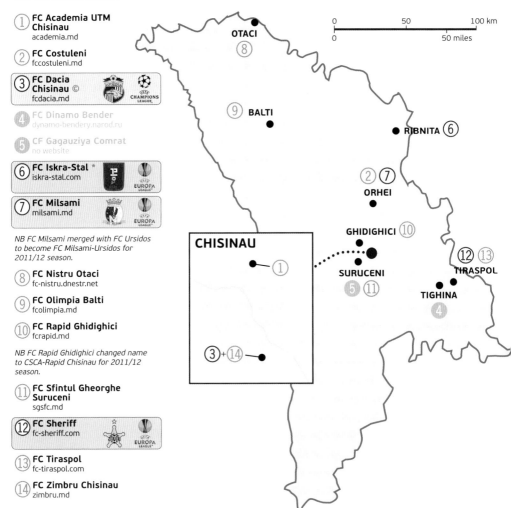

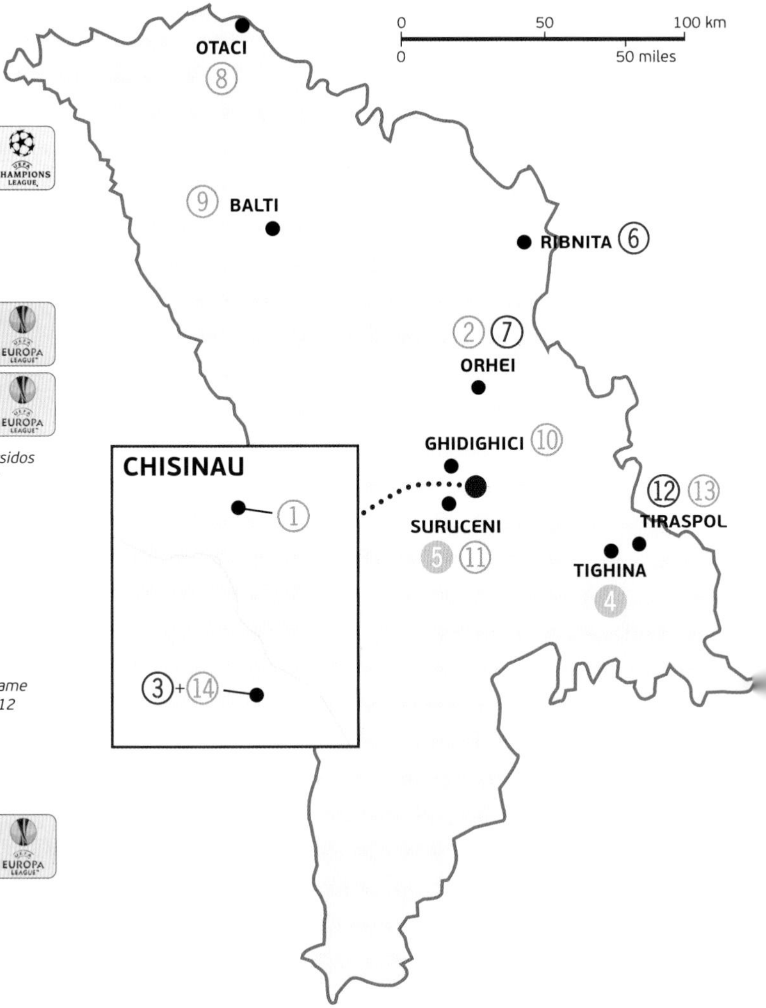

MONTENEGRO

Monténégro | Montenegro

HOME INTERNATIONAL KIT AWAY INTERNATIONAL KIT

TOP DIVISION CLUBS

1 **OFK Bar**
no website

2 **FK Budućnost Podgorica**
fkbuducnost.co.me

3 **FK Dečić**
fkdecictuzi.com

4 **FK Grbalj**
no website

5 **FK Lovćen**
fklovcen.co.me

6 **FK Mladost Podgorica**
no website

7 **FK Mogren** ©
fkmogren.com

8 **FK Mornar**
no website

9 **OFK Petrovac**
ofkpetrovac.com

10 **FK Rudar Pljevlja** *
fcrudarpljevlja.com

11 **FK Sutjeska**
no website

12 **FK Zeta**
no website

PROMOTED CLUBS

13 **FK Bokelj**
no website

14 **FK Berane**
no website

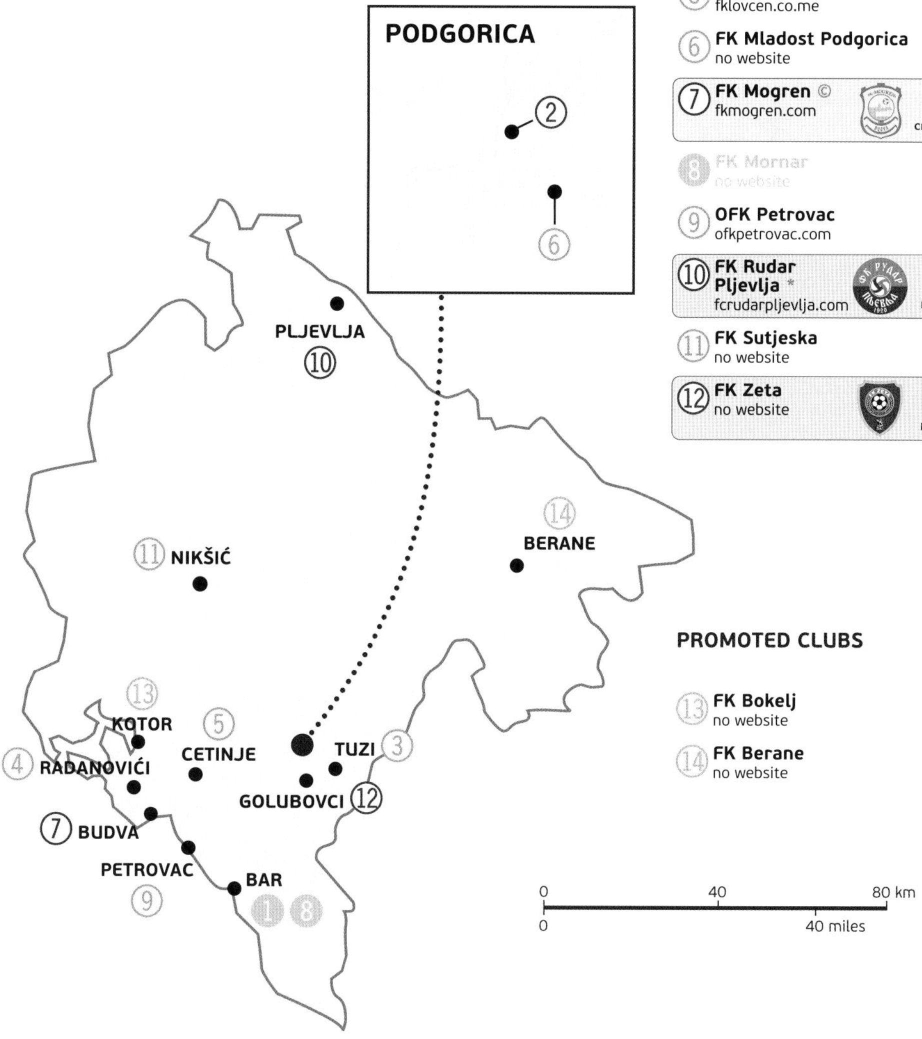

NETHERLANDS

Pays-Bas | Niederlande

TOP DIVISION CLUBS

1. **ADO Den Haag** adodenhaag.nl — UEFA Europa League
2. **AFC Ajax** © ajax.nl — UEFA Champions League
3. **AZ Alkmaar** az.nl — UEFA Europa League
4. **SBV Excelsior** sbvexcelsior.nl
5. **Feyenoord** feyenoord.nl
6. **De Graafschap** degraafschap.nl
7. **FC Groningen** fcgroningen.nl
8. **sc Heerenveen** sc-heerenveen.nl
9. **Heracles Almelo** heracles.nl
10. **NAC Breda** nac.nl
11. **NEC Nijmegen** nec-nijmegen.nl
12. **PSV Eindhoven** psv.nl — UEFA Europa League
13. **Roda JC** rodajc.nl
14. **FC Twente** * fctwente.nl — UEFA Champions League
15. **FC Utrecht** fcutrecht.nl
16. **Vitesse** vitesse.nl
17. **VVV-Venlo** vvv-venlo.nl
18. **Willem II** willem-ii.nl

PROMOTED CLUB

19. **RKC Waalwijk** rkcwaalwijk.nl

KNVB

HOME INTERNATIONAL KIT AWAY INTERNATIONAL KIT

NORTHERN IRELAND

Irlande du Nord | Nordirland

HOME INTERNATIONAL KIT AWAY INTERNATIONAL KIT

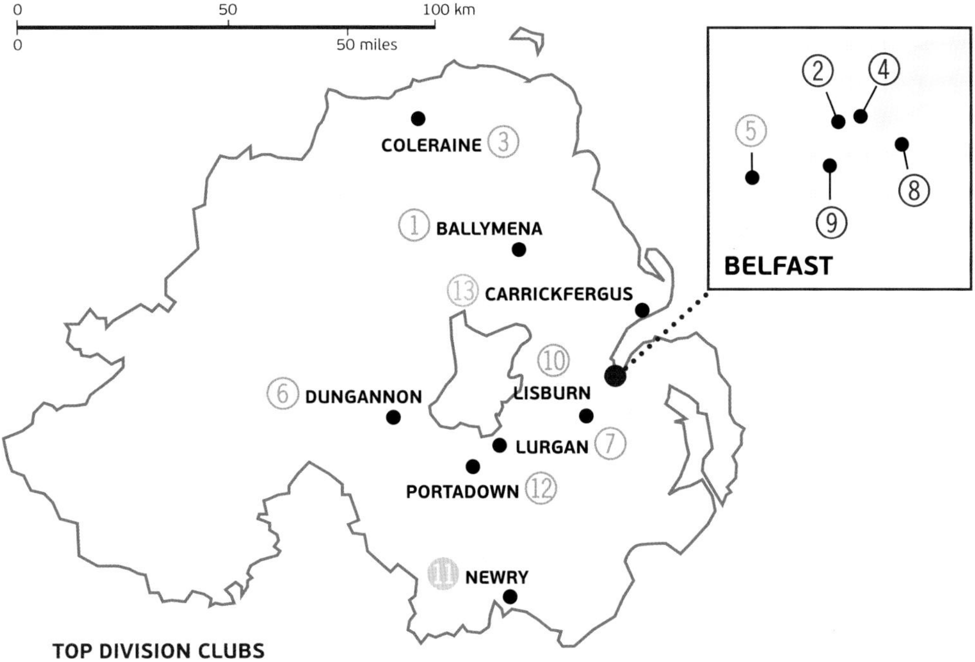

TOP DIVISION CLUBS

1. **Ballymena United FC** ballymenaunitedfc.com
2. **Cliftonville FC** cliftonvillefc.net — UEFA EUROPA LEAGUE
3. **Coleraine FC** colerainefc.com
4. **Crusaders FC** crusadersfc.com — UEFA EUROPA LEAGUE
5. **Donegal Celtic FC** no website
6. **Dungannon Swifts FC** dungannonswiftsfc.co.uk
7. **Glenavon FC** glenavonfc.com
8. **Glentoran FC** glentoran.com — UEFA EUROPA LEAGUE
9. **Linfield FC** © * linfieldfc.com — UEFA CHAMPIONS LEAGUE
10. **Lisburn Distillery FC** lisburn-distillery.net
11. **Newry City FC** newrycityfc.com
12. **Portadown FC** portadownfc.co.uk

PROMOTED CLUB

13. **Carrick Rangers FC** carrickrangers.co.uk

NORWAY

Norvège | Norwegen

HOME INTERNATIONAL KIT AWAY INTERNATIONAL KIT

TOP DIVISION CLUBS

1. **Aalesunds FK** [fp] aafk.no — UEFA EUROPA LEAGUE
2. **SK Brann** brann.no
3. **FK Haugesund** fkh.no
4. **Hønefoss BK** honefossbk.no
5. **Kongsvinger IL** kil.no
6. **Lillestrøm SK** lsk.no
7. **Molde FK** moldefk.no
8. **Odd Grenland** oddgrenland.no
9. **Rosenborg BK** © rbk.no — UEFA CHAMPIONS LEAGUE
10. **Sandefjord Fotball** sandefjordfotball.no
11. **Stabæk Fotball** stabak.no
12. **IK Start** ikstart.no
13. **Strømsgodset IF** * godset.no — UEFA EUROPA LEAGUE
14. **Tromsø IL** til.no — UEFA EUROPA LEAGUE
15. **Viking FK** viking-fk.no
16. **Vålerenga Fotball** vif-fotball.no — UEFA EUROPA LEAGUE

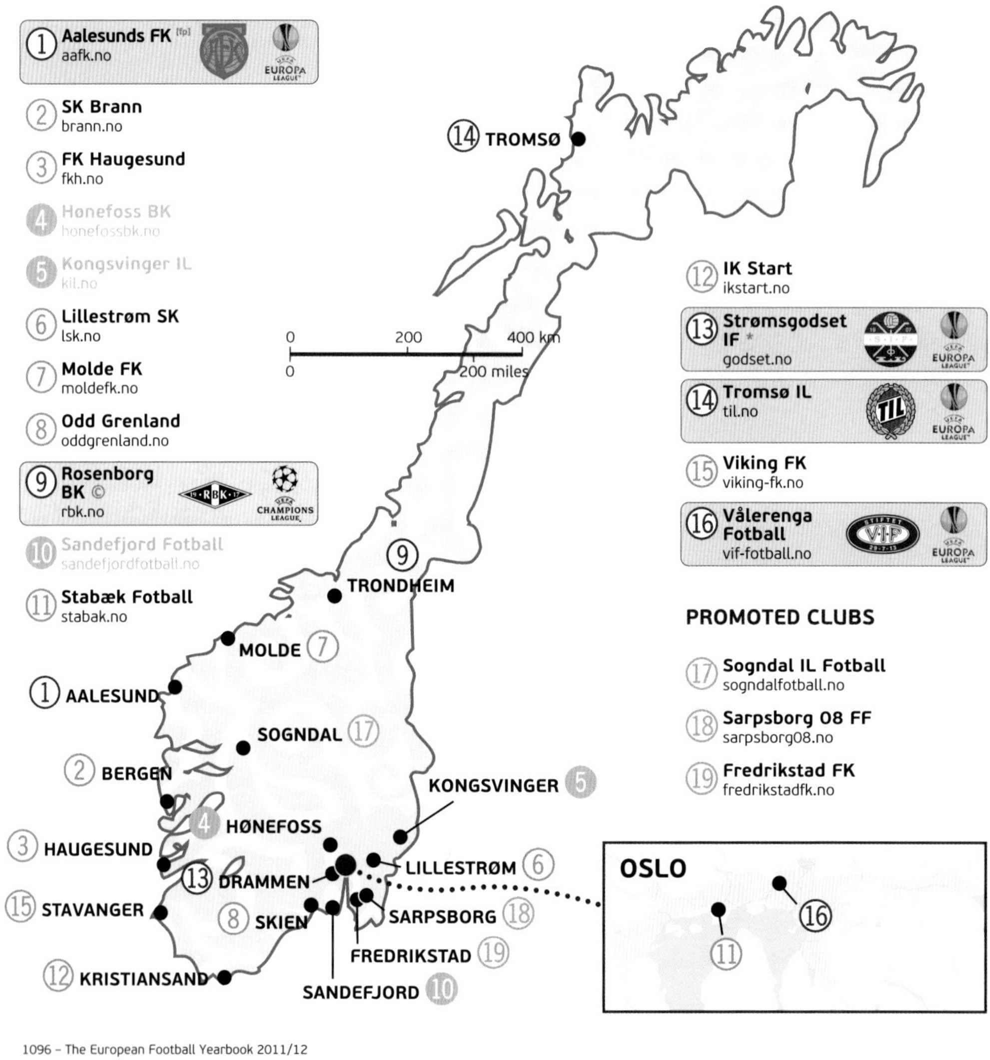

PROMOTED CLUBS

17. **Sogndal IL Fotball** sogndalfotball.no
18. **Sarpsborg 08 FF** sarpsborg08.no
19. **Fredrikstad FK** fredrikstadfk.no

POLAND

Pologne | Polen

PZPN

HOME INTERNATIONAL KIT AWAY INTERNATIONAL KIT

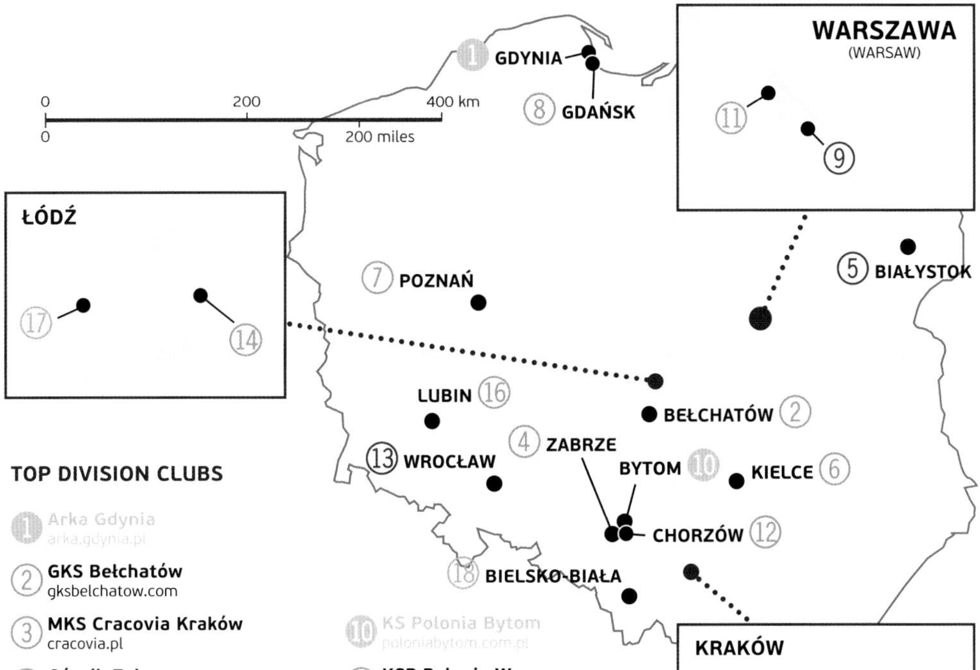

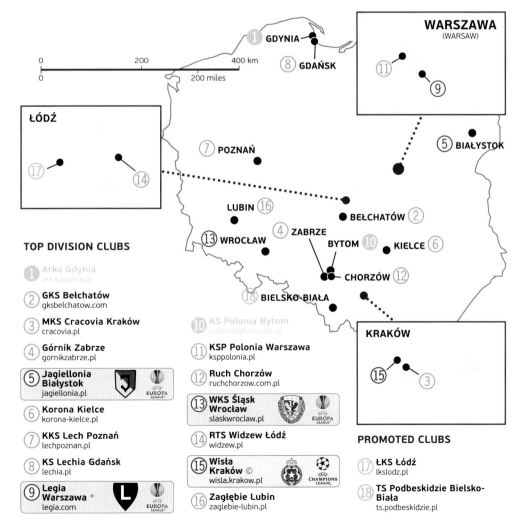

TOP DIVISION CLUBS

1 Arka Gdynia
arka.gdynia.pl

2 GKS Bełchatów
gksbelchatow.com

3 MKS Cracovia Kraków
cracovia.pl

4 Górnik Zabrze
gornikzabrze.pl

5 Jagiellonia Białystok
jagiellonia.pl

6 Korona Kielce
korona-kielce.pl

7 KKS Lech Poznań
lechpoznan.pl

8 KS Lechia Gdańsk
lechia.pl

9 Legia Warszawa *
legia.com

10 KS Polonia Bytom
poloniabytom.com.pl

11 KSP Polonia Warszawa
ksppolonia.pl

12 Ruch Chorzów
ruchchorzow.com.pl

13 WKS Śląsk Wrocław
slaskwroclaw.pl

14 RTS Widzew Łódź
widzew.pl

15 Wisła Kraków ©
wisla.krakow.pl

16 Zagłębie Lubin
zaglebie-lubin.pl

PROMOTED CLUBS

17 ŁKS Łódź
lkslodz.pl

18 TS Podbeskidzie Bielsko-Biała
ts.podbeskidzie.pl

PORTUGAL

Portugal | Portugal

TOP DIVISION CLUBS

1. **A. Académica de Coimbra**
academica-oaf.pt
2. **SC Beira-Mar**
beiramar.pt
3. **SL Benfica**
slbenfica.pt
UEFA CHAMPIONS LEAGUE
4. **SC Braga**
scbraga.pt
UEFA EUROPA LEAGUE
5. **CS Marítimo**
csmaritimo.pt
6. **CD Nacional**
cdnacional.pt
UEFA EUROPA LEAGUE
7. **A. Naval 1° Maio**
naval1demaio.com
8. **SC Olhanense**
scolhanense.com
9. **FC Paços de Ferreira**
fcpf.pt
10. **Portimonense SC**
portimonensesc.pt
11. **FC Porto** ©*
fcporto.pt
UEFA CHAMPIONS LEAGUE
12. **Rio Ave FC**
rioave-fc.pt
13. **Sporting Clube de Portugal**
sporting.pt
UEFA EUROPA LEAGUE
14. **UD Leiria**
uniaodeleiria.pt
15. **Vitória FC**
vfc.pt
16. **Vitória SC**
vitoriasc.pt
UEFA EUROPA LEAGUE

HOME INTERNATIONAL KIT AWAY INTERNATIONAL KIT

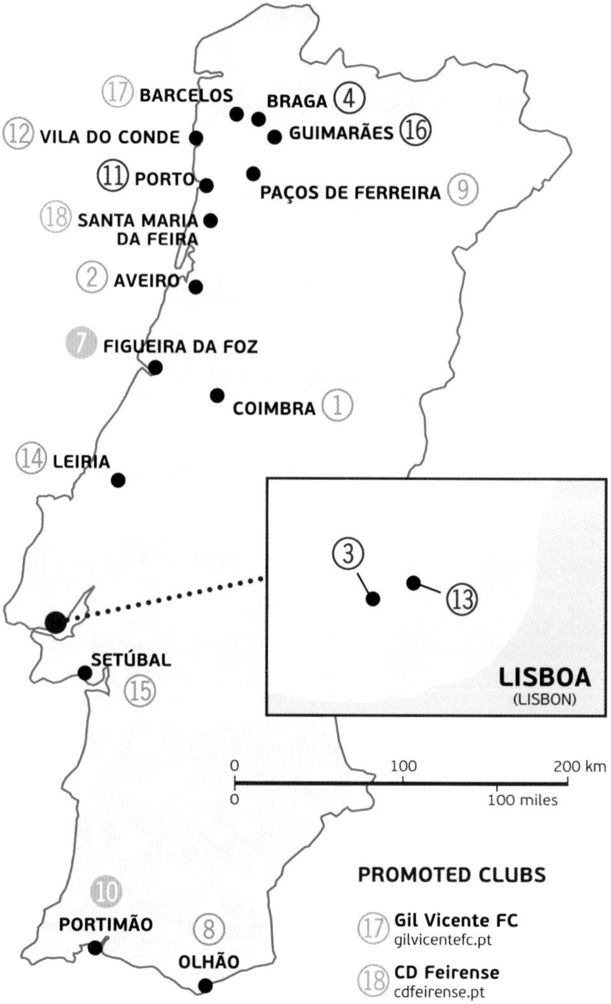

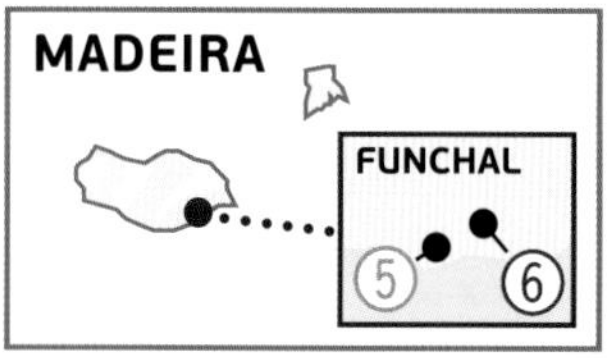

PROMOTED CLUBS

17. **Gil Vicente FC**
gilvicentefc.pt
18. **CD Feirense**
cdfeirense.pt

REPUBLIC OF IRELAND

Irlande | Irland

HOME INTERNATIONAL KIT AWAY INTERNATIONAL KIT

TOP DIVISION CLUBS

1. **Bohemian FC** bohemians.ie
2. **Bray Wanderers AFC** braywanderers.ie
3. **Drogheda United FC** droghedaunited.ie
4. **Dundalk FC** dundalkfc.com
5. **Galway United FC** no website
6. **Saint Patrick's Athletic FC** stpatsfc.com
7. **Shamrock Rovers FC** © shamrockrovers.ie
8. **Sligo Rovers FC** * sligorovers.com
9. **Sporting Fingal FC** sportingfingal.ie
10. **University College Dublin AFC** ucdsoccer.com

PROMOTED CLUB

11. **Derry City FC** derrycityfc.net

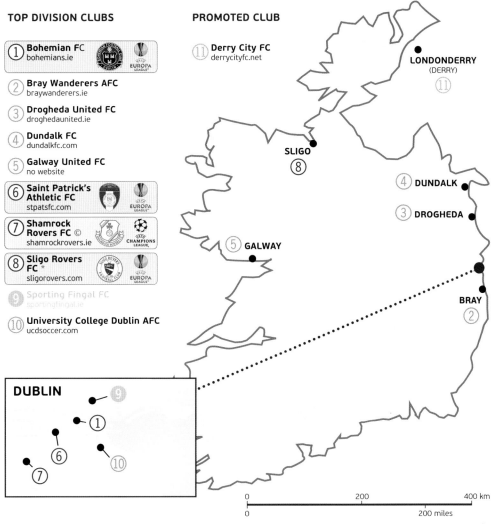

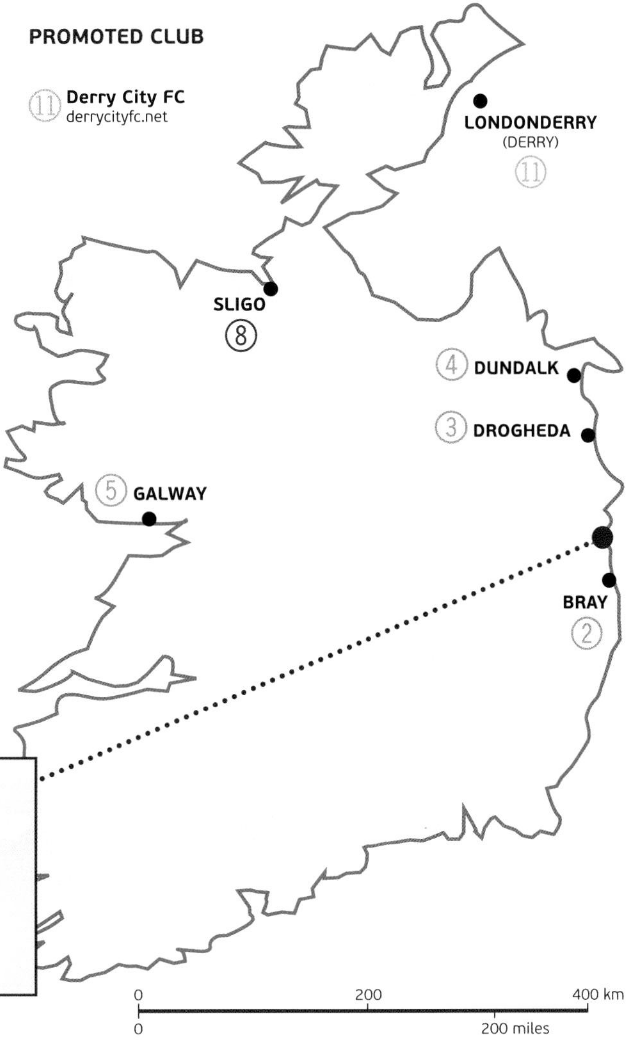

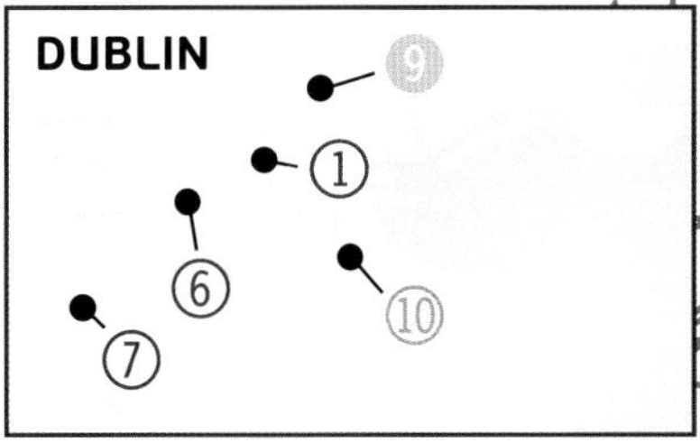

ROMANIA

Roumanie | Rumänien

TOP DIVISION CLUBS

1 **FC Astra Ploieşti**
fcastraploiesti.ro

2 **FC Braşov**
fcbrasov.ro

3 **CFR 1907 Cluj**
cfr1907.ro

4 **FC Dinamo Bucureşti**
fcdinamo.ro

5 **CS Gaz Metan Mediaş**
gaz-metan-medias.ro

6 **ACF Gloria 1922 Bistriţa**
cfgloria.ro

HOME INTERNATIONAL KIT AWAY INTERNATIONAL KIT

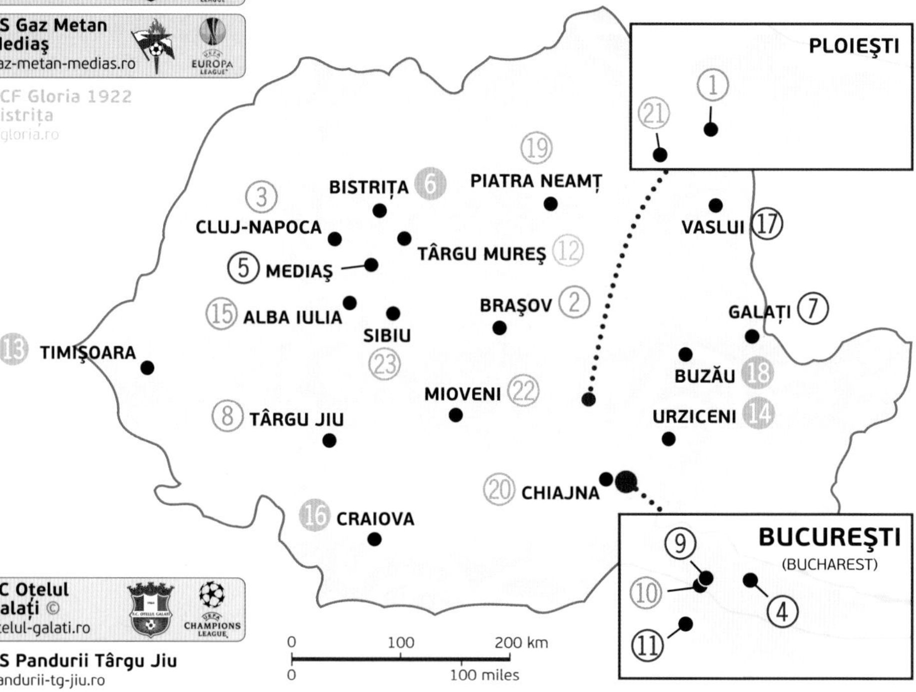

7 **FC Oţelul Galaţi ©**
otelul-galati.ro

8 **CS Pandurii Târgu Jiu**
pandurii-tg-jiu.ro

9 **FC Rapid Bucureşti**
fcrapid.ro

10 **FC Sportul Studenţesc Bucureşti**
fcsportulstudentesc.ro

11 **FC Steaua Bucureşti** *
steauafc.com

12 **FCM Târgu Mureş**
fcm-tirgumures.ro

13 **FC Timişoara**
politimisoara.com

14 **FC Unirea Urziceni**
fcunirea.ro

15 **FC Universitatea Cluj**
universitateacluj.ro

16 **FC Universitatea Craiova**
fcuniversitatea.ro

17 **FC Vaslui**
vasluifc.ro

18 **FC Victoria Brăneşti**
victoriafc.ro

PROMOTED CLUBS

19 **FC Ceahlăul Piatra Neamţ**
fcceahlaul.ro

20 **CS Concordia Chiajna**
csconcordia.com

21 **FC Petrolul Ploieşti**
fcpetrolul.ro

22 **CS Mioveni**
csmioveni.ro

23 **CSU Voinţa Sibiu**
csu-vointa-sibiu.ro

RUSSIA

Russie | Russland

HOME INTERNATIONAL KIT   AWAY INTERNATIONAL KIT

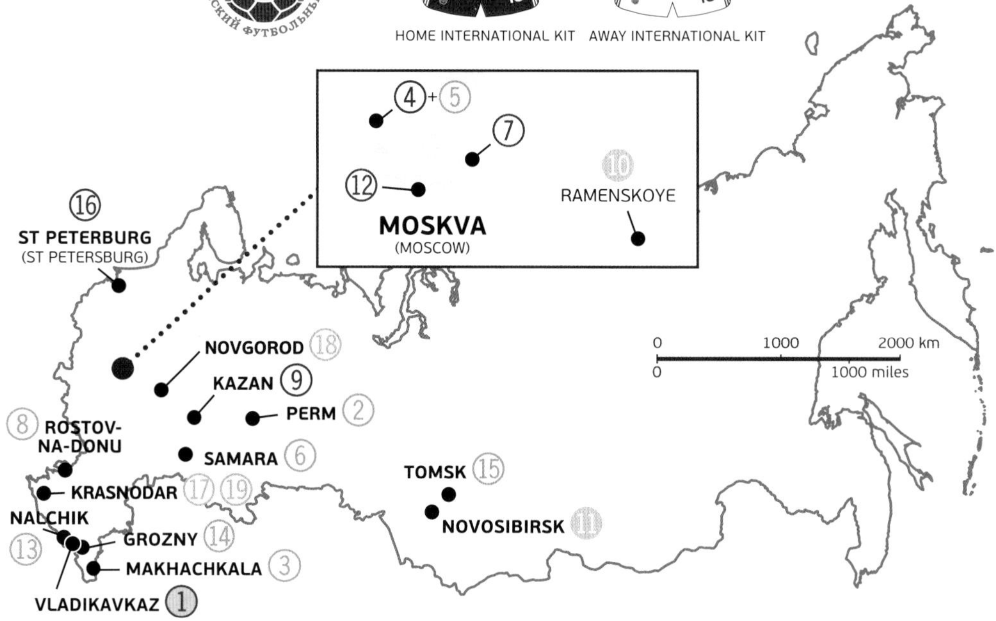

TOP DIVISION CLUBS

1 **FC Alania Vladikavkaz** fc-alania.ru

2 **FC Amkar Perm** fc-amkar.org

3 **FC Anzhi Makhachkala** fc-anji.ru

4 **PFC CSKA Moskva** * pfc-cska.com

5 **FC Dinamo Moskva** fcdynamo.ru

6 **FC Krylya Sovetov Samara** fkc-camapa.ru

7 **FC Lokomotiv Moskva** fclm.ru

8 **FC Rostov** fc-rostov.ru

9 **FC Rubin Kazan** rubin-kazan.ru

10 **FC Saturn Moskovskaya Oblast** saturn-fc.ru

11 **FC Sibir Novosibirsk** fc-sibir.ru

12 **FC Spartak Moskva** spartak.com

13 **PFC Spartak Nalchik** spartak-nalchik.ru

14 **FC Terek Grozny** fc-terek.ru

15 **FC Tom Tomsk** fctomtomsk.ru

16 **FC Zenit St Petersburg** © fc-zenit.ru

PROMOTED CLUBS

17 **FC Kuban Krasnodar** fckuban.ru

18 **FC Volga Nizhniy Novgorod** fcvolgann.ru

19 **FC Krasnodar** fckrasnodar.ru

SAN MARINO

Saint-Marin | San Marino

HOME INTERNATIONAL KIT AWAY INTERNATIONAL KIT

TOP DIVISION CLUBS

1. **SP Cailungo**
no website
2. **S.S. Cosmos**
no website
3. **Domagnano FC**
no website
4. **SC Faetano**
faetanocalcio.sm
5. **S.S. Fiorentino**
no website
6. **S.S. Folgore/Falciano**
folgorecalcio.com
7. **AC Juvenes-Dogana** *
acjuvenesdogana.sm
8. **SP La Fiorita**
lafiorita.sm
9. **SP Libertas**
polisportivalibertas.com
10. **S.S. Murata**
no website
11. **S.S. Pennarossa**
pennarossa.com
12. **S.S. San Giovanni**
no website
13. **SP Tre Fiori** ©
no website
14. **SP Tre Penne**
trepenne.sm
15. **S.S. Virtus**
no website

SCOTLAND

Écosse | Schottland

HOME INTERNATIONAL KIT   AWAY INTERNATIONAL KIT

TOP DIVISION CLUBS

1. **Aberdeen FC**
   afc.co.uk
2. **Celtic FC** *
   celticfc.net
   EUROPA LEAGUE
3. **Dundee United FC**
   dundeeunitedfc.co.uk
   EUROPA LEAGUE
4. Hamilton Academical FC
   acciesfc.co.uk
5. **Heart of Midlothian FC**
   heartsfc.co.uk
   EUROPA LEAGUE
6. **Hibernian FC**
   hibernianfc.co.uk
7. **Inverness Caledonian Thistle FC**
   ictfc.co.uk
8. **Kilmarnock FC**
   kilmarnockfc.co.uk
9. **Motherwell FC**
   motherwellfc.co.uk
10. **Rangers FC** ©
    rangers.co.uk
    CHAMPIONS LEAGUE
11. **Saint Johnstone FC**
    perthstjohnstonefc.co.uk
12. **Saint Mirren FC**
    saintmirren.net

PROMOTED CLUB

13. **Dunfermline Athletic FC**
    dafc.co.uk

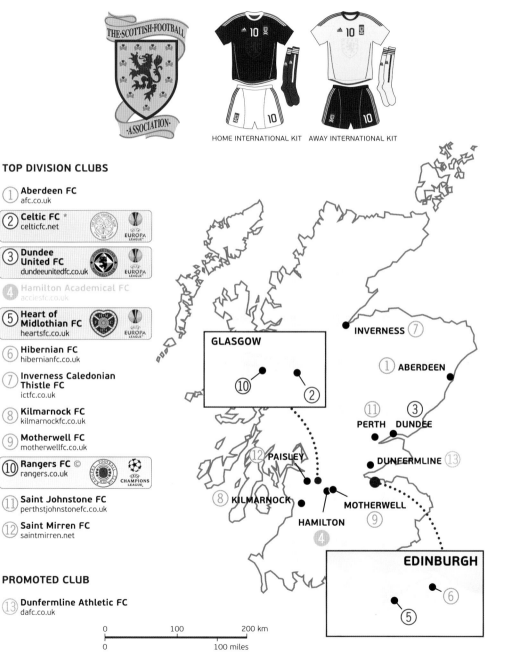

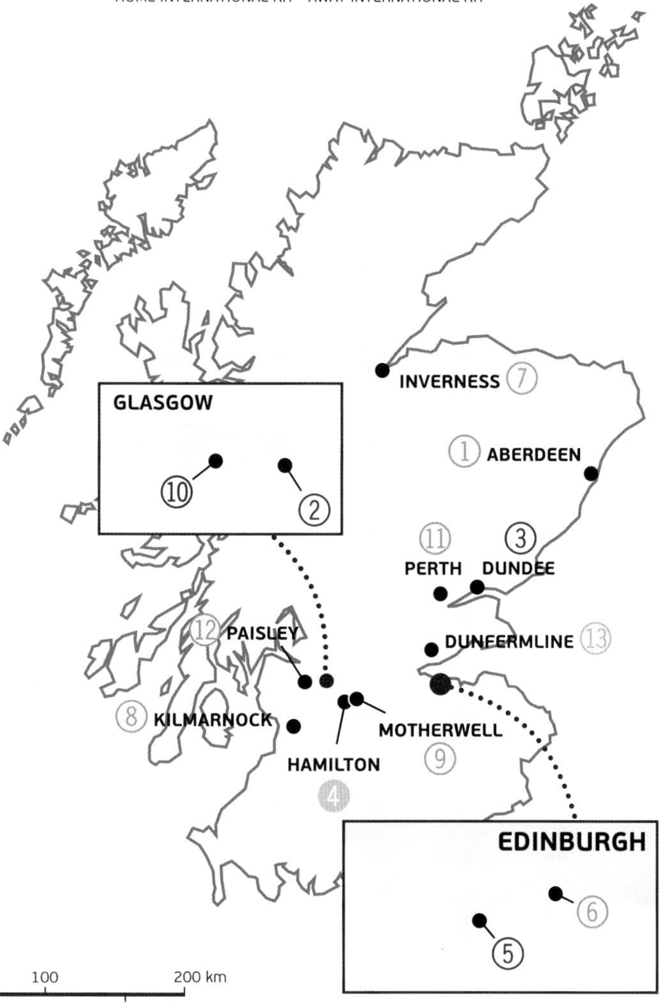

0 100 200 km
0 100 miles

SERBIA

Serbie | Serbien

TOP DIVISION CLUBS

1. **FK Borac Čačak**
   boracfk.com
2. **FK BSK Borča**
   bskborca.org
3. **FK Crvena zvezda**
   crvenazvezdafk.com
   UEFA EUROPA LEAGUE
4. **FK Čukarički**
   cukarickistankom.com
5. **FK Hajduk Kula**
   fkhajduk.org.rs
6. **FK Inđija**
   fkindjija.com
7. **FK Jagodina**
   fkjagodina.org.rs
8. **FK Javor**
   fkjavor.com
9. **FK Metalac**
   fkmetalac.rs
10. **OFK Beograd**
    ofkbeograd.co.rs
11. **FK Partizan** ©*
    partizan.rs
    UEFA CHAMPIONS LEAGUE
12. **FK Rad**
    fcrad.co.yu
    UEFA EUROPA LEAGUE
13. **FK Sloboda Point Sevojno**
    fkslobodapointsevojno.rs
14. **FK Smederevo**
    fksmederevo.com
15. **FK Spartak Zlatibor voda**
    fkspartakzlatiborvoda.com
16. **FK Vojvodina**
    fkvojvodina.rs
    UEFA EUROPA LEAGUE

HOME INTERNATIONAL KIT AWAY INTERNATIONAL KIT

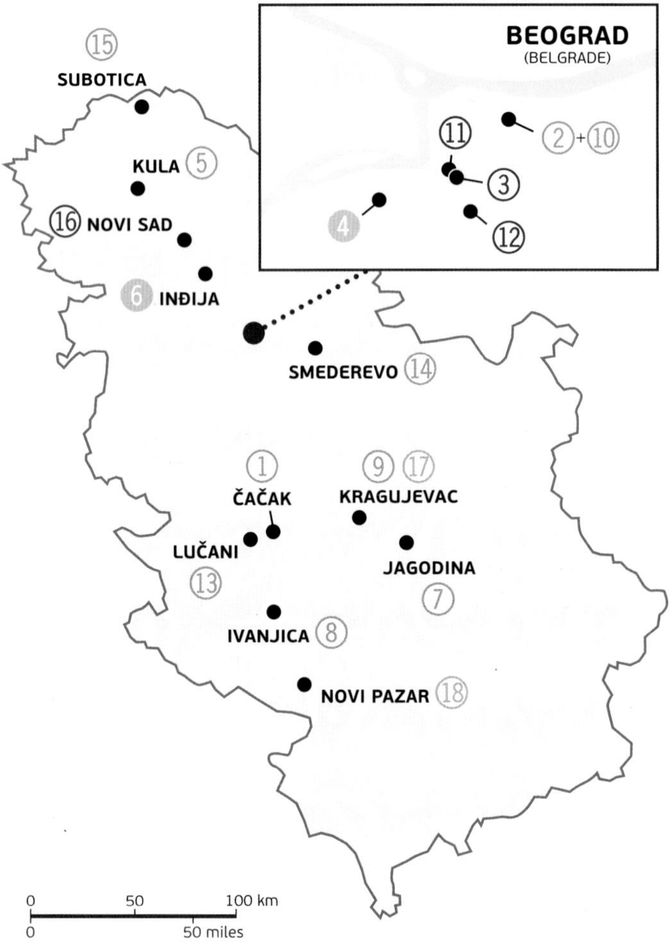

PROMOTED CLUBS

17. **FK Radnički 1923**
    fkradnicki.com
18. **FK Novi Pazar**
    fknovipazar.com

SLOVAKIA

Slovaquie | Slowakei

HOME INTERNATIONAL KIT AWAY INTERNATIONAL KIT

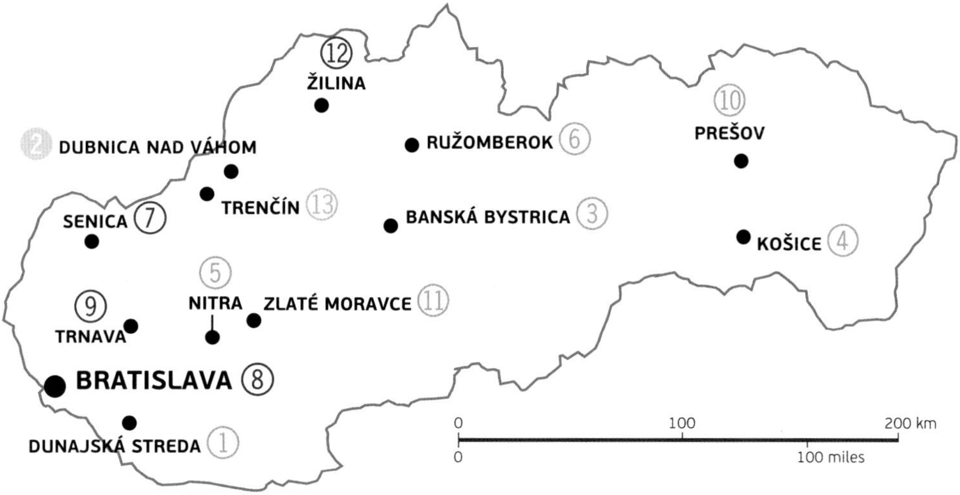

TOP DIVISION CLUBS

1. **DAC 1904 Dunajská Streda**
fkdac1904.eu

2. **MFK Dubnica**
fkdubnica.sk

3. **Dukla Banská Bystrica**
fkdukla.sk

4. **MFK Košice**
mfkkosice.sk

5. **FC Nitra**
fcnitra.sk

6. **MFK Ružomberok**
mfkruzomberok.sk

7. **FK Senica**
fksenica.sk
EUROPA LEAGUE

8. **ŠK Slovan Bratislava** ©*
skslovan.com
CHAMPIONS LEAGUE

9. **FC Spartak Trnava**
fcspartakas.eu
EUROPA LEAGUE

10. **1. FC Tatran Prešov**
1fctatran.sk

11. **FC ViOn Zlaté Moravce**
fcvion.sk

12. **MŠK Žilina**
mskzilina.sk
EUROPA LEAGUE

PROMOTED CLUB

13. **FK AS Trencín**
astrencin.sk

SLOVENIA
Slovénie | Slowenien

HOME INTERNATIONAL KIT

AWAY INTERNATIONAL KIT

TOP DIVISION CLUBS

1 **NK Celje**
nkcelje.si

2 **NK Domžale** *
nkdomzale.si

3 **ND Gorica**
nd-gorica.com

4 **FC Koper**
fckoper.si

5 **NK Maribor** ©
nkmaribor.com

6 **NK Nafta**
nknafta.si

7 **NK Olimpija Ljubljana**
nkolimpija.si

8 **NK Primorje**
primorje-nklub.si

9 **NK Rudar Velenje**
nkrudar.com

10 **ND Triglav**
nktriglav.com

PROMOTED CLUB

11 **ND Mura 05**
mura05.si

SPAIN
Espagne | Spanien

TOP DIVISION CLUBS

1. **UD Almería** udalmeriasad.com
2. **Athletic Club** athletic-club.net — UEFA EUROPA LEAGUE
3. **Club Atlético de Madrid** clubatleticodemadrid.com — UEFA EUROPA LEAGUE
4. **FC Barcelona** © fcbarcelona.cat — UEFA CHAMPIONS LEAGUE
5. **RC Deportivo La Coruña** canaldeportivo.com
6. **RCD Espanyol** rcdespanyol.com
7. **Getafe CF** getafecf.com
8. **Hércules CF** herculescf.es
9. **Levante UD** levanteud.com
10. **Málaga CF** malagacf.es
11. **RCD Mallorca** rcdmallorca.es
12. **CA Osasuna** osasuna.es
13. **Real Racing Club** realracingclub.es
14. **Real Madrid CF** * realmadrid.com — UEFA CHAMPIONS LEAGUE
15. **Real Sociedad de Fútbol** realsociedad.com
16. **Sevilla FC** sevillafc.es — UEFA EUROPA LEAGUE
17. **Real Sporting de Gijón** realsporting.com
18. **Valencia CF** valenciacf.com — UEFA CHAMPIONS LEAGUE
19. **Villarreal CF** villarrealcf.es — UEFA CHAMPIONS LEAGUE
20. **Real Zaragoza** realzaragoza.com

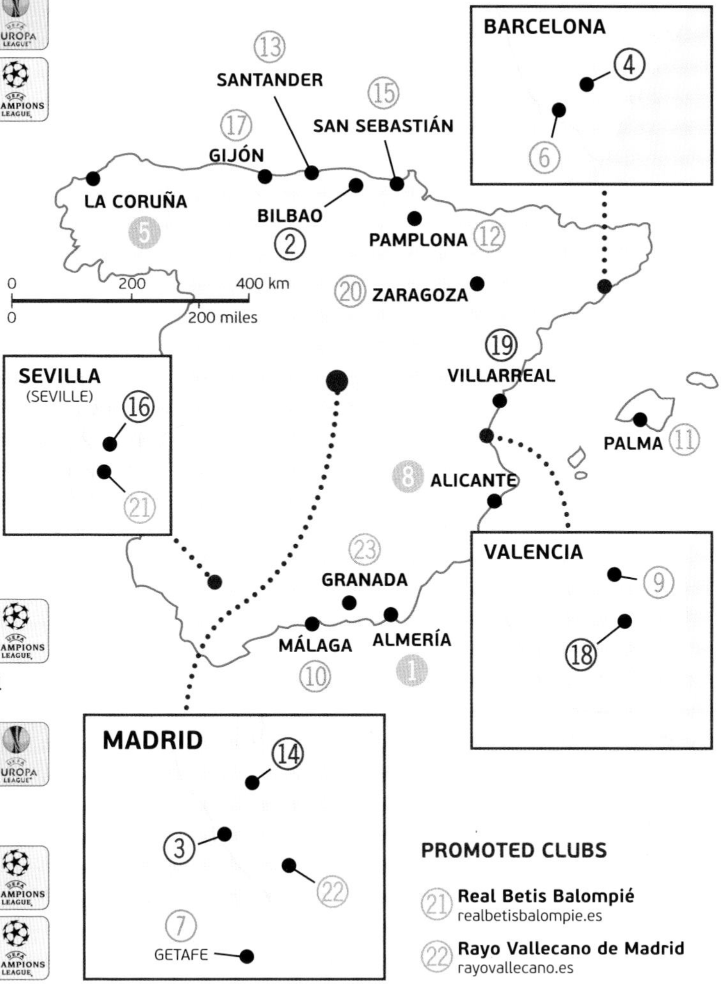

PROMOTED CLUBS

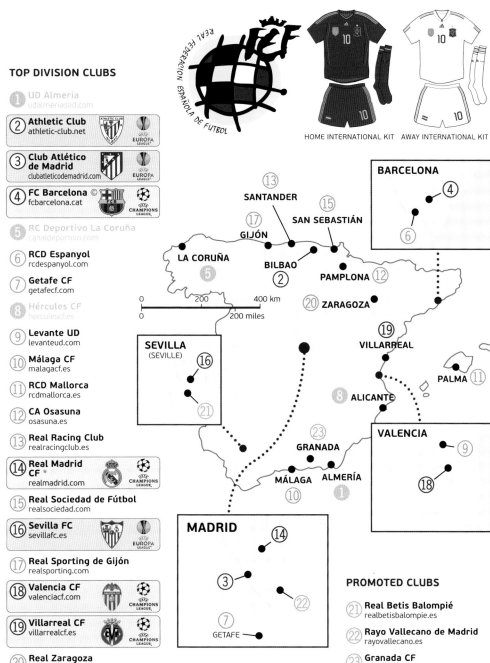

21. **Real Betis Balompié** realbetisbalompie.es
22. **Rayo Vallecano de Madrid** rayovallecano.es
23. **Granada CF** granadacf.es

SWEDEN

Suède | Schweden

HOME INTERNATIONAL KIT AWAY INTERNATIONAL KIT

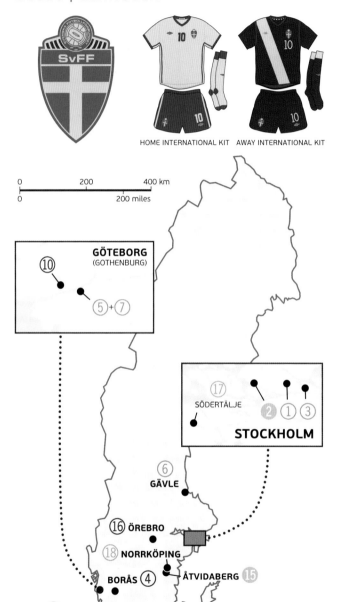

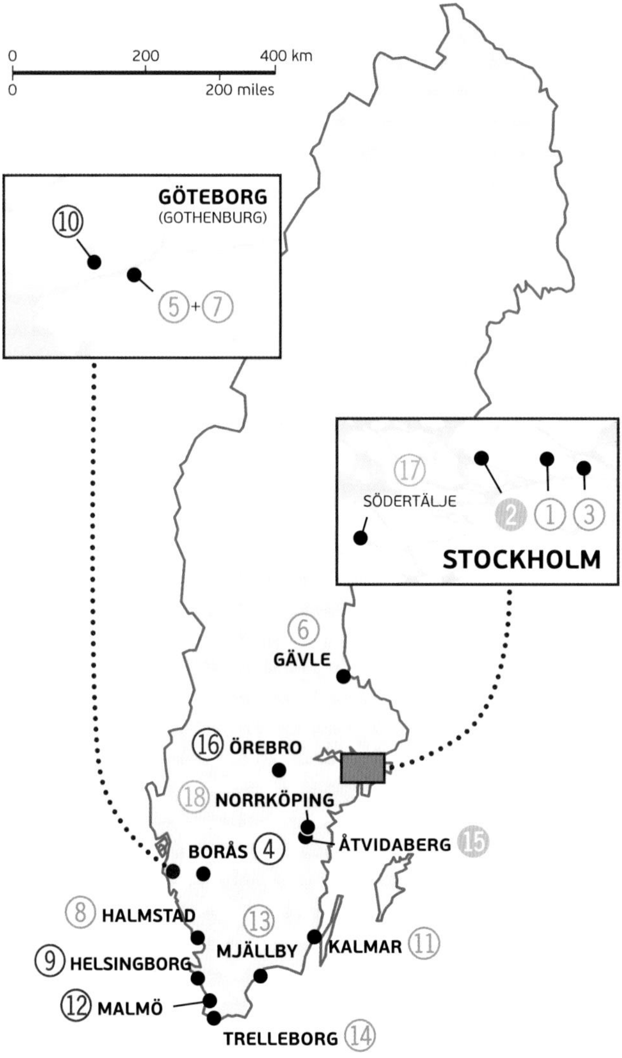

TOP DIVISION CLUBS

1. **AIK Solna**
   aikfotboll.se
2. **IF Brommapojkarna**
   brommapojkarna.se
3. **Djurgårdens IF**
   dif.se
4. **IF Elfsborg**
   elfsborg.se — UEFA EUROPA LEAGUE
5. **GAIS Göteborg**
   gais.se
6. **Gefle IF**
   gefleiffotboll.se
7. **IFK Göteborg**
   ifkgoteborg.se
8. **Halmstads BK**
   hbk.se
9. **Helsingborgs IF** *
   hif.se — UEFA EUROPA LEAGUE
10. **BK Häcken** (fp)
    bkhacken.se — BK HÄCKEN — UEFA EUROPA LEAGUE
11. **Kalmar FF**
    kalmarff.se
12. **Malmö FF** ©
    mff.se — UEFA CHAMPIONS LEAGUE
13. **Mjällby AIF**
    maif.se
14. **Trelleborgs FF**
    trelleborgsff.se
15. **Åtvidabergs FF**
    atvidabergsff.se
16. **Örebro SK**
    oskfotboll.se — UEFA EUROPA LEAGUE

PROMOTED CLUBS

17. **Syrianska FC**
    syrianskafc.com
18. **IFK Norrköping**
    ifknorrkoping.se

SWITZERLAND

Suisse | Schweiz

HOME INTERNATIONAL KIT

AWAY INTERNATIONAL KIT

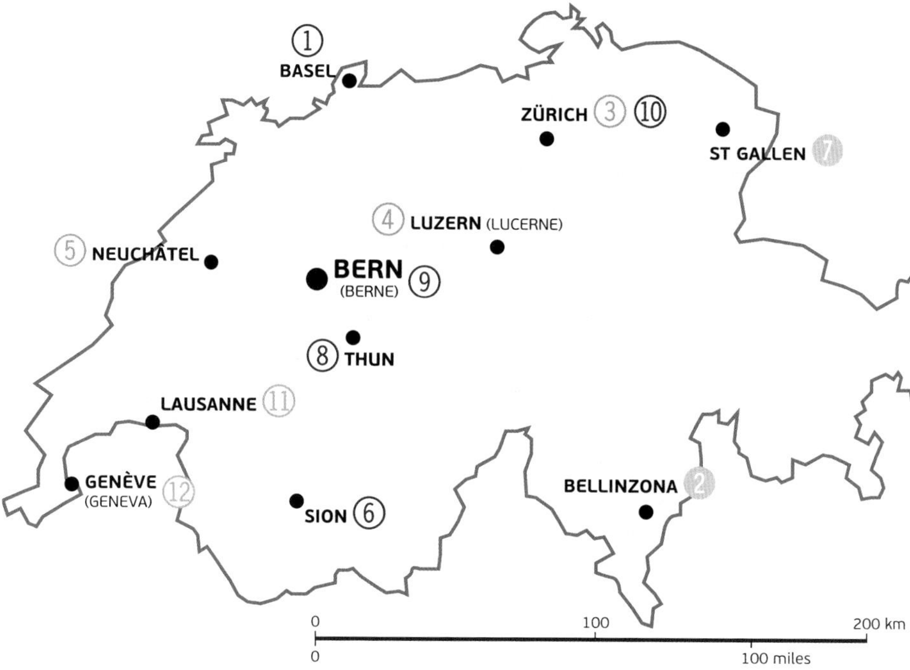

TOP DIVISION CLUBS

① **FC Basel 1893** ©
fcb.ch

② AC Bellinzona
acbellinzona.ch

③ **Grasshopper-Club**
gcz.ch

④ **FC Luzern**
fcl.ch

⑤ **Neuchâtel Xamax FC**
xamax.ch

⑥ **FC Sion** *
fc-sion.ch

⑦ FC St Gallen
fcsg.ch

⑧ **FC Thun**
fcthun.ch

⑨ **BSC Young Boys**
bscyb.ch

⑩ **FC Zürich**
fcz.ch

PROMOTED CLUBS

⑪ **FC Lausanne-Sport**
lausanne-sport.ch

⑫ **Servette FC**
servettefc.ch

TURKEY

Turquie | Türkei

HOME INTERNATIONAL KIT AWAY INTERNATIONAL KIT

PROMOTED CLUBS

(19) **Mersin İdman Yurdu**
mersinismanyurdu.com.tr

(20) **Samsunspor**
samsunspor.org.tr

(21) **Orduspor**
orduspor.org.tr

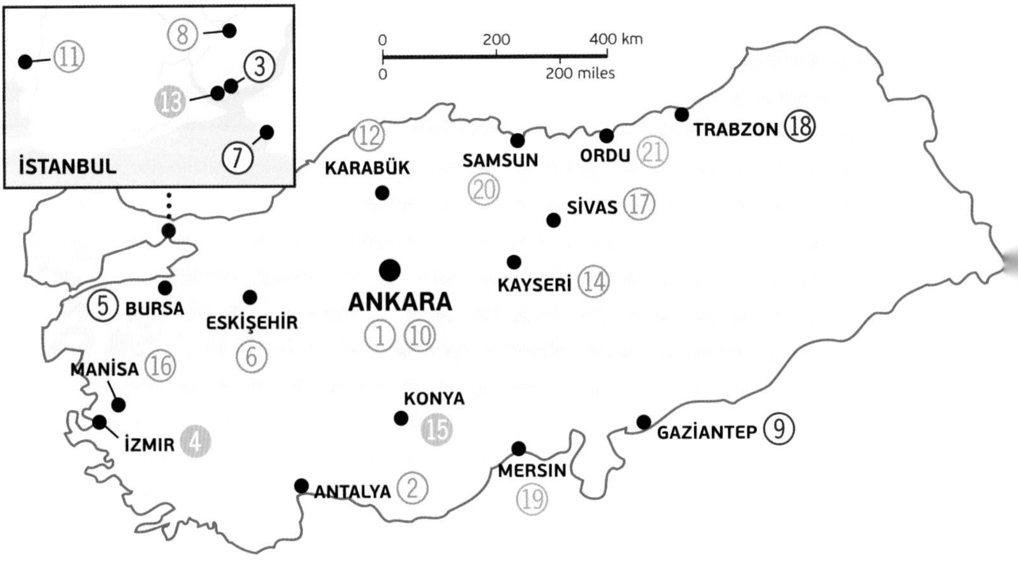

TOP DIVISION CLUBS

(1) **MKE Ankaragücü**
ankaragucu.org.tr

(2) **Antalyaspor**
antalyaspor.com.tr

(3) **Beşiktaş JK** *
bjk.com.tr

(4) Bucaspor
no website

(5) **Bursaspor**
bursaspor.org.tr

(6) **Eskişehirspor**
eskisehirspor.org.tr

(7) **Fenerbahçe SK** ©
fenerbahce.org

(8) **Galatasaray AŞ**
galatasaray.org

(9) **Gaziantepspor**
gaziantepspor.org.tr

(10) **Gençlerbirliği SK**
genclerbirligi.org.tr

(11) **İstanbul BB SK**
ibbspor.com

(12) **Kardemir Karabükspor**
kardemirkarabukspor.org.tr

(13) Kasımpaşa SK
kasimpasaspor.org.tr

(14) **Kayserispor**
kayserispor.org.tr

(15) Konyaspor
konyaspor.org.tr

(16) **Manisaspor**
manisaspor.org.tr

(17) **Sivasspor**
sivasspor.org.tr

(18) **Trabzonspor AŞ**
trabzonspor.org.tr

UKRAINE

Ukraine | Ukraine

TOP DIVISION CLUBS

(1) **FC Arsenal Kyiv**
fcarsenal.com.ua

(2) **FC Dnipro Dnipropetrovsk**
fcdnipro.ua
UEFA EUROPA LEAGUE

(3) **FC Dynamo Kyiv**
fcdynamo.kiev.ua
UEFA CHAMPIONS LEAGUE

(4) **FC Illychivets Mariupil**
fcilich.com

HOME INTERNATIONAL KIT AWAY INTERNATIONAL KIT

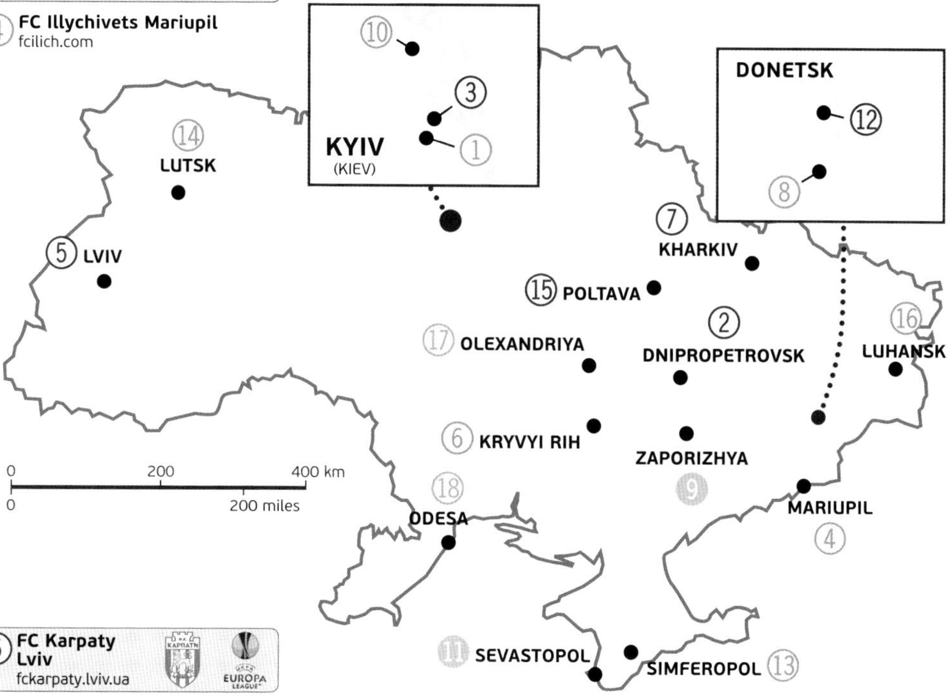

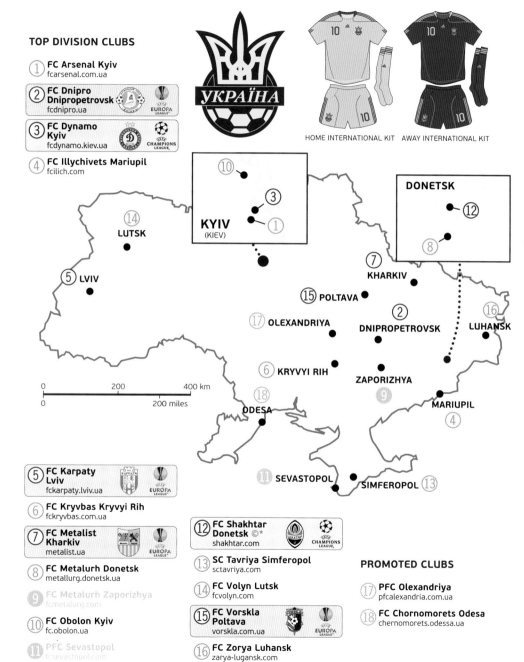

(5) **FC Karpaty Lviv**
fckarpaty.lviv.ua
UEFA EUROPA LEAGUE

(6) **FC Kryvbas Kryvyi Rih**
fckryvbas.com.ua

(7) **FC Metalist Kharkiv**
metalist.ua
UEFA EUROPA LEAGUE

(8) **FC Metalurh Donetsk**
metallurg.donetsk.ua

(9) **FC Metalurh Zaporizhya**
fcmetalurg.com

(10) **FC Obolon Kyiv**
fc.obolon.ua

(11) **PFC Sevastopol**
fcsevastopol.com

(12) **FC Shakhtar Donetsk** ©*
shakhtar.com
UEFA CHAMPIONS LEAGUE

(13) **SC Tavriya Simferopol**
sctavriya.com

(14) **FC Volyn Lutsk**
fcvolyn.com

(15) **FC Vorskla Poltava**
vorskla.com.ua
UEFA EUROPA LEAGUE

(16) **FC Zorya Luhansk**
zarya-lugansk.com

PROMOTED CLUBS

(17) **PFC Olexandriya**
pfcalexandria.com.ua

(18) **FC Chornomorets Odesa**
chernomorets.odessa.ua

WALES

Pays de Galles | Wales

TOP DIVISION CLUBS

1. **Aberystwyth Town FC**
   atfc.org.uk
2. **Airbus UK Broughton FC**
   airbusfc.com
3. **Bala Town FC**
   balatownfc.co.uk
4. **Bangor City FC** ©
   bangorcityfc.com
5. **Carmarthen Town AFC**
   carmarthentownafc.net
6. **Haverfordwest County AFC**
   haverfordwestcounty.co.uk
7. **Llanelli AFC** *
   llanelliafc.org
8. **Neath FC**
   neathfc.com
9. **Newtown AFC**
   newtownafc.co.uk
10. **Port Talbot Town FC**
    porttalbottown.co.uk
11. **Prestatyn Town FC**
    ptfconline.co.uk
12. **The New Saints FC**
    saints-alive.co.uk

PROMOTED CLUB

13. **Afan Lido FC**
    afanlidofc.com

GORAU CHWARAE CYD CHWARAE

HOME INTERNATIONAL KIT AWAY INTERNATIONAL KIT

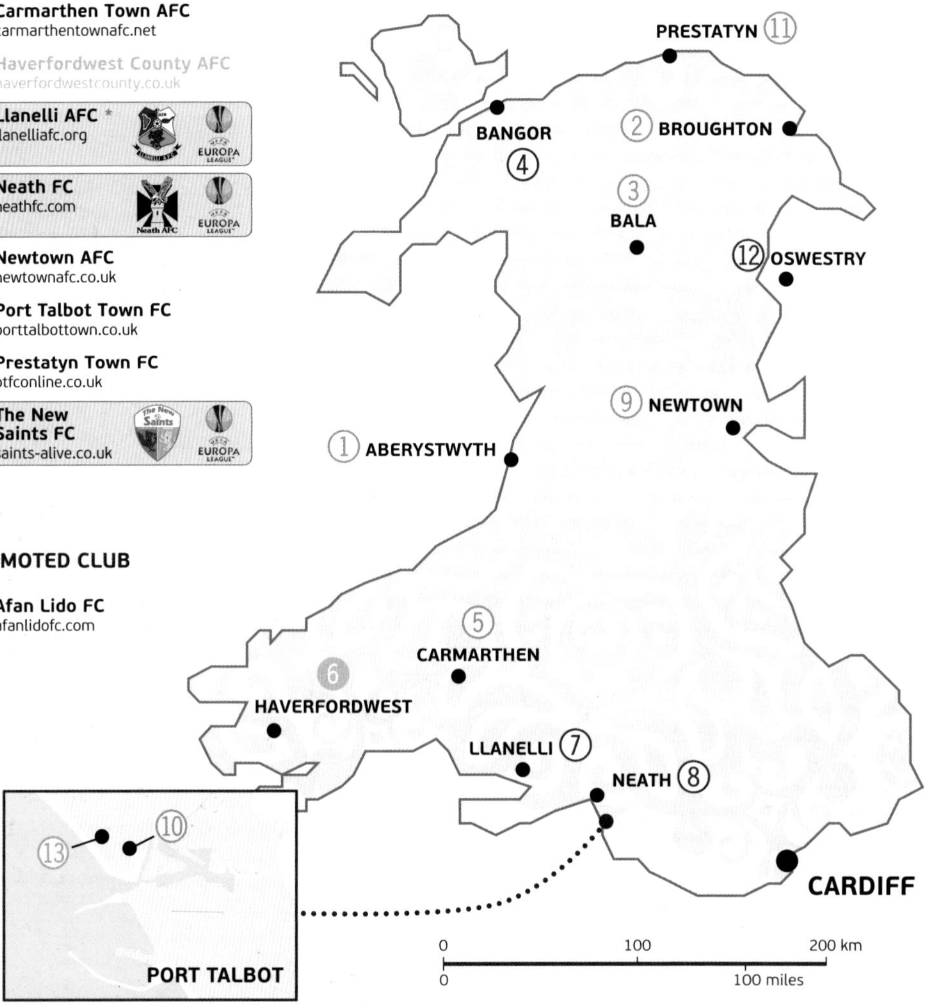

RESPECT

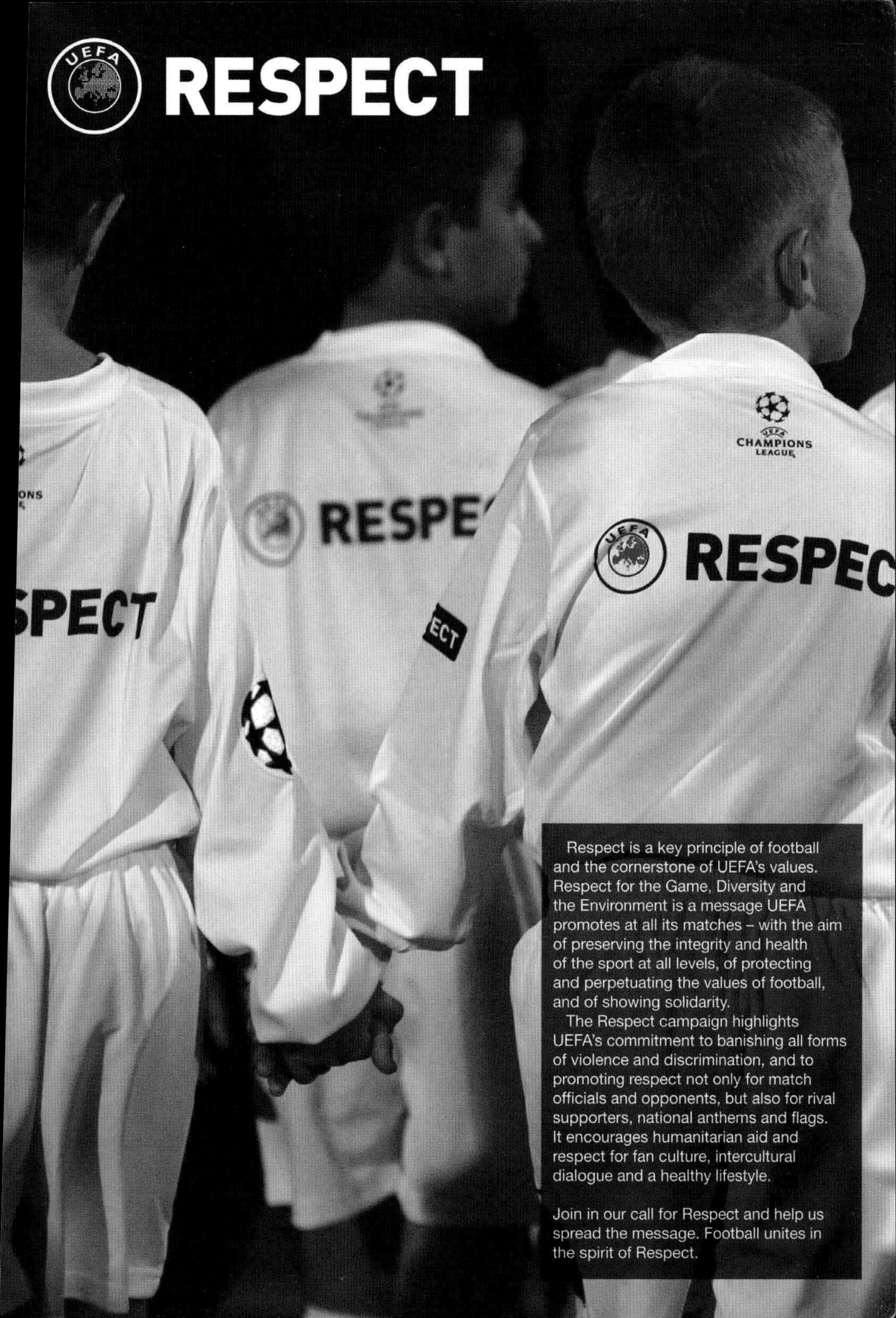

Respect is a key principle of football and the cornerstone of UEFA's values. Respect for the Game, Diversity and the Environment is a message UEFA promotes at all its matches – with the aim of preserving the integrity and health of the sport at all levels, of protecting and perpetuating the values of football, and of showing solidarity.

The Respect campaign highlights UEFA's commitment to banishing all forms of violence and discrimination, and to promoting respect not only for match officials and opponents, but also for rival supporters, national anthems and flags. It encourages humanitarian aid and respect for fan culture, intercultural dialogue and a healthy lifestyle.

Join in our call for Respect and help us spread the message. Football unites in the spirit of Respect.

UEFA

Route de Genève 46
Case postale
CH-1260 Nyon 2
Switzerland

Tel: +41 (0) 848 00 2727
Fax: +41 (0) 848 01 2727
Web: UEFA.com

Media Desk
Tel: +41 (0) 848 04 2727

Founded: 15 June 1954

Affiliated national associations: 53

Number of clubs: 176,715

Number of players: 20,434,998

Number of female players: 1,893,136

Number of referees: 286,853

(all figures are approximate)

UEFA EXECUTIVE COMMITTEE

President
Michel Platini (France)

Vice-Presidents
Şenes Erzik (Turkey)
Geoffrey Thompson (England)
Ángel María Villar Llona (Spain)
Marios N. Lefkaritis (Cyprus)
Giancarlo Abete (Italy)

Members
Sergei Fursenko (Russia)
Peter Gilliéron (Switzerland)
Allan Hansen (Denmark)
František Laurinec (Slovakia)
Avraham Luzon (Israel)
Borislav Mihaylov (Bulgaria)
Mircea Sandu (Romania)
Grigoriy Surkis (Ukraine)
Michael van Praag (Netherlands)
Theo Zwanziger (Germany)

Honorary President
Lennart Johansson (Sweden)

General Secretary
Gianni Infantino

UEFA Events Calendar 2011/12

NATIONAL TEAM

UEFA EURO 2012

2, 3 & 6/9/2011	Qualifying round matches
7, 8 & 11/10/2011	Qualifying round matches
13/10/2011	Play-off draw (Krakow, Poland)
11-12/11/2011	Qualifying play-offs, first leg
15/11/2011	Qualifying play-offs, second leg
2/12/2011	Final tournament draw (Kyiv, Ukraine)
29/2/2012	100 days to kick-off
8-9/3/2012	Finalists workshop (Warsaw, Poland)
8/6-1/7/2012	Final tournament (Poland & Ukraine)
8/6/2012	Opening match (Warsaw, Poland)
1/7/2012	Final (Kyiv, Ukraine)

2013 UEFA EUROPEAN UNDER-21 CHAMPIONSHIP

1-6/9/2011	Qualifying round matches
6-11/10/2011	Qualifying round matches
10-15/11/2011	Qualifying round matches
29/2/2012	Qualifying round matches
31/5-6/6/2012	Qualifying round matches
8-13/6/2012	Qualifying round matches
14-15/8/2012	Qualifying round matches
6, 7 & 10/9/2012	Qualifying round matches

CLUB

2011/12 UEFA CHAMPIONS LEAGUE

25/8/2011	Group stage draw (Monaco)
13-14/9/2011	Group stage, Matchday 1
27-28/9/2011	Group stage, Matchday 2
18-19/10/2011	Group stage, Matchday 3
1-2/11/2011	Group stage, Matchday 4
22-23/11/2011	Group stage, Matchday 5

UEFA Events Calendar 2011/12

CHAMPIONS LEAGUE

6-7/12/2011	Group stage, Matchday 6
16/12/2011	Round of 16 draw (Nyon, Switzerland)
14-15/2/2012	Round of 16, first leg
21-22/2/2012	Round of 16, first leg
6-7/3/2012	Round of 16, second leg
13-14/3/2012	Round of 16, second leg
16/3/2012	Quarter-finals, Semi-finals and Final draw (Nyon, Switzerland)
27-28/3/2012	Quarter-finals, first leg
3-4/4/2012	Quarter-finals, second leg
17-18/4/2012	Semi-finals, first leg
24-25/4/2012	Semi-finals, second leg
19/5/2012	Final (Munich, Germany)

2011/12 UEFA EUROPA LEAGUE

26/8/2011	Group stage draw (Monaco)
15/9/2011	Group stage, Matchday 1
29/9/2011	Group stage, Matchday 2
20/10/2011	Group stage, Matchday 3
3/11/2011	Group stage, Matchday 4
30/11-1/12/2011	Group stage, Matchday 5
14-15/12/2011	Group stage, Matchday 6
16/12/2011	Round of 32 and Round of 16 draw (Nyon, Switzerland)
16/2/2012	Round of 32, first leg
23/2/2012	Round of 32, second leg
8/3/2012	Round of 16, first leg
15/3/2012	Round of 16, second leg
16/3/2012	Quarter-finals, Semi-finals and Final draw (Nyon, Switzerland)
29/3/2012	Quarter-finals, first leg
5/4/2012	Quarter-finals, second leg
19/4/2012	Semi-finals, first leg
26/4/2012	Semi-finals, second leg
9/5/2012	Final (Bucharest, Romania)

2011 UEFA SUPER CUP

26/8/2011	Final (Monaco)

2011 FIFA CLUB WORLD CUP

8-18/12/2011	Final tournament (Japan)

YOUTH & AMATEUR

2011/12 UEFA EUROPEAN UNDER-19 CHAMPIONSHIP

21/9-15/11/2011	Qualifying round matches
29/11/2011	Elite round draw (Nyon, Switzerland)
1/3-3/6/2012	Elite round matches
6/6/2012	Final tournament draw (Estonia, venue tbd)
3-15/7/2012	Final tournament (Estonia)

2012/13 UEFA EUROPEAN UNDER-19 CHAMPIONSHIP

29/11/2011	Qualifying round draw (Nyon, Switzerland)

2011/12 UEFA EUROPEAN UNDER-17 CHAMPIONSHIP

1/9-15/11/2011	Qualifying round matches
29/11/2011	Elite round draw (Nyon, Switzerland)
1/3-31/3/2012	Elite round matches
4/4/2012	Final tournament draw (Slovenia,venue tbd)
4-16/5/2012	Final tournament (Slovenia)

2012/13 UEFA EUROPEAN UNDER-17 CHAMPIONSHIP

29/11/2011	Qualifying round draw (Nyon, Switzerland)

WOMEN'S

2011/12 UEFA WOMEN'S CHAMPIONS LEAGUE

11-16/8/2011	Qualifying round matches
23/8/2011	Round of 32 & 16 draw (Nyon, Switzerland)
28-29/9/2011	Round of 32, first leg
5-6/10/2011	Round of 32, second leg
2-3/11/2011	Round of 16, first leg
9-10/11/2011	Round of 16, second leg
17/11/2011	Quarter-finals, Semi-finals and Final draw (Nyon, Switzerland)
14-15/3/2012	Quarter-finals, first leg
21-22/3/2012	Quarter-finals, second leg
14-15/4/2012	Semi-finals, first leg
21-22/4/2012	Semi-finals, second leg
17/5/2012	Final (Munich, Germany)

UEFA Events Calendar 2011/12

2013 UEFA EUROPEAN WOMEN'S CHAMPIONSHIP

17-18 & 21-22/9/2011	Qualifying round matches
22-23 & 26-27/10/2011	Qualifying round matches
19-20 & 23-24/11/2011	Qualifying round matches
15-16/2/2012	Qualifying round matches
31/3-1/4/2012	Qualifying round matches
4-5/4/2012	Qualifying round matches
16-17/6 & 20-21/6/2012	Qualifying round matches
15-16 & 19/9/2012	Qualifying round matches
tbd	Play-off round draw (venue, tbd)
20-21 & 24-25/10/2012	Play-off matches
July 2013	Final tournament (Sweden)

2011/12 UEFA EUROPEAN WOMEN'S UNDER-19 CHAMPIONSHIP

11-16/9/2011	First qualifying round matches
15/11/2011	Second qualifying round draw (Nyon, Switzerland)
31/3-5/4/2012	Second qualifying round matches
tbd	Final tournament draw (Turkey, venue tbd)
2-14/7/2012	Final tournament (Turkey)

2012/13 UEFA EUROPEAN WOMEN'S UNDER-19 CHAMPIONSHIP

15/11/2011	First qualifying round draw (Nyon, Switzerland)

2011/12 UEFA EUROPEAN WOMEN'S UNDER-17 CHAMPIONSHIP

1/8-31/10/2011	First qualifying round matches
15/11/2011	Second qualifying round draw (Nyon, Switzerland)
1/3-15/4/2012	Second qualifying round matches
26-29/6/2012	Final tournament (Nyon, Switzerland)

2012/13 UEFA EUROPEAN WOMEN'S UNDER-17 CHAMPIONSHIP

15/11/2011	First qualifying round draw (Nyon, Switzerland)